musicHound

Soundtracks

musicHound

Soundtracks

The
Essential
Album
Guide

to Film,
Television and
Stage Music

Edited by
Didier C. Deutsch

Forewords by
Lukas Kendall   Julia Michels

VISIBLE
INK
PRESS

DETROIT • SAN FRANCISCO • LONDON • BOSTON • WOODDRIDGE, CT

musicHound® *Soundtracks*
The
Essential
Album
Guide to Film, Television, and Stage Music

Copyright © 2000 Visible Ink Press®

A Cunning Canine Production®

Published by Visible Ink Press
a division of Gale Group, Inc.
27500 Drake Rd.
Farmington Hills, MI 48331-3535

Library of Congress Cataloging-in-Publication Data

MusicHound Soundtracks: the essential album guide / edited by Didier C. Deutsch
        cm.
    Includes bibliographical references and indexes.
    ISBN 1-57859-101-5 (softcover)

    1. Musicals—Discography. 2. Musical films—Discography.
    3. Motion picture music—Discography.   4. Television music—Discography.
    ML156.9.M87   1999
    016.7821'40266—dc2199-42807
                                 CIP

musicHound *Contents*

list of sidebars vii
the purist point of view
   (by lukas kendall) ix
the new age of soundtracks—behind
   the scenes (by julia michels) xiii
introduction (by didier c. deutsch) . . .xvii
musicHound owner's manual xix
credits xxi
acknowledgments xxv

a–z guide to soundtracks / **1**

composers / **661**

compilation albums / **741**

books, magazines, and newsletters / **745**

web sites / **747**

record labels / **749**

five-bone album index / **753**

composer index / **757**

conductor index / **773**

lyricist index / **783**

series index / **787**

musicHound *Sidebars*

10 Essential Scores

John Barry 665
Elmer Bernstein 77
Georges Delerue 327
Danny Elfman 505
Jerry Goldsmith 579
Bernard Herrmann 631
James Horner 693
Mark Isham 175
Maurice Jarre 193
Henry Mancini 463
Ennio Morricone 375
Alfred Newman 649
Nino Rota 517
Miklos Rozsa 717
Max Steiner 221
John Williams 165

They Know the Score

Luis Bacalov 167
John Barry 239, 387, 545

John Beal 697
Elmer Bernstein 431
Alf Clausen 69
Bill Conti 255
Ry Cooder 289
Michael Danna 421
Danny Elfman 25, 509, 669
Neal Hefti 589
Mark Isham 497, 607
Maurice Jarre 447, 619, 713
Michael Kamen 219, 367, 525, 681
Rachel Portman 135
Lalo Schifrin 271
John Scott 339, 475
Eckart Seeber 57
Eric Serra 641
David Shire 39
Alan Silvestri 103, 309
Mark Snow 91, 727
John Williams 405, 563
Hans Zimmer 3, 205, 349, 733

The Purist Point of View

by lukas kendall **ix**

Walking around my apartment last weekend, I suddenly marveled at the state of technology. Forget about the fax machine, stereo system, cable TV, and Internet-capable computer. I have running hot water on demand, a dishwasher, food refrigeration, gas stove, all sorts of lights. Sure, things break; but most of the time they work perfectly. A hundred years ago, I wouldn't have had all this stuff and life would have been far rougher, to say nothing of how the guy unthawed in *Iceman* (good score by Bruce Smeaton) lived. Easier living is the 20th century's gift to us. I am happy I don't have to kill my food or cart in my own fresh water. I appreciate the convenience. We all retain the energy and anxiety that allowed us to survive in the old days, artificially pumped up by safe, vicarious pursuits like television watching. The "entertainment industry" should more accurately be called the "leisure industry." "Entertainment" makes it sound active; "leisure" is more cynical, but appropriate. By the way, I'm not pining for the good old days of starving to death. I respect my forefathers by being as lazy as they hoped I could be.

All of this is to explain why you are reading a big fat book about movie soundtracks, but also to frame the developments of that particular industry, which has become more significant in the last 10 years. Somehow, somewhere, film music was elevated from throw-away, utilitarian fodder into an art form worthy of big fat books. It's truly bizarre, because most of this music was not intended for private listening, but was to be heard only with the images it helped to define. By definition it should only be so interesting.

It begins with the movies and their music. I still laugh out loud when I hear great passages by my favorite composers: Herrmann, Goldsmith, Barry, Williams, Morricone, Bernstein, Jarre,

Schifrin. All of the great film composers have their unique thumb prints, and when the movie calls for it, they can let go with a signature "ta-da!" splash of color, sound, and melody. For Herrmann, it's when one of the bad guys falls off Mount Rushmore in *North by Northwest*; for Williams, the moment occurs when Superman takes off in pursuit of nuclear rockets. In *Dirty Harry,* Scorpio (the killer) puts on his gloves and wiggles his fingers and Schifrin's score bubbles forth with rock percussion and dissonant sustains. In David Lean's masterpiece, Lawrence of Arabia has ventured into the desert to bring back one of his followers. As he emerges against all odds, Jarre's melody surges (we hear it around 800 times in the movie, and each time the passage is stirring), conspiring with Freddie Young's cinematography to create an indelible moment. It's these movie moments, unreal moments, that the music seals. The music makes one-dimensional figures on celluloid come alive—symbolic and specific at the same time. People latch onto these moments where image and sound transcend the limitations of the cinema. Like all great art, they provide gasoline for the imagination, but also snapshots of the sublime. Real people make these marriages of music and image come to life, and for the soundtrack aficionado, these creators become the heroes, rather than the fictional protagonists depicted on screen.

And thus, from its earliest days, people have fallen in love with and have wanted to capture the sounds of cinema whenever possible. They have become . . . Soundtrack Collectors. Many people discover soundtracks as kids, and so fantasy/adventure films have often provided the initiation into the genre—from *King Kong* to *Planet of the Apes* to *Jurassic Park*. These thunderous orchestral scores are the signposts of the hobby. The problem was, people couldn't always acquire them. Until recently, soundtrack releases were few and far between, put out by large companies almost by accident. The first organizations of fandom happened in the 1970s, when the late Charles Gerhardt and George Korngold produced a series of Classic Film Scores albums on RCA Victor (Elmer Bernstein did the same soon thereafter). Fanzines soon developed around the appreciation of soundtrack composers and the buying, selling, trading, and finding of the soundtrack LPs thus far in existence. In 1977, John Williams's extremely popular score for *Star Wars* provided a shot in the arm, as symphonic film scores (replaced in the '60s and '70s by rock scores and smaller ensemble works) came back in vogue.

With the advent of the CD, the high life came. For one thing, recordings could finally sound decent. Smaller companies that had been specializing in vinyl reissues (Varèse Sarabande, Fifth Continent) made the jump to digital and were joined by more labels catering to film score aficionados (Intrada, Silva Screen). Slowly, an impressive catalog of great film music became available on CD, with classic works being released alongside new ones created by a younger generation of composers. Film music was beginning to be recognized as a legitimate art form worthy of respect and preservation.

Around this time, at age 16, I started a small newsletter for fun. Creating a fan club about soundtracks seemed to fill a niche that, in the U.S. at least, had thus far gone ignored. Had I waited even three or four years, I would have organized my "Soundtrack Club" as a Web site or bulletin board, and not as print newsletter, which is expensive and more difficult to do. Web sites did not exist in 1990, making my choice easier. Now, plowing into a new century, easy access to film music information is a reality. The work I began has been taken up by a new generation of aficionados. Today, there are dozens of Web sites devoted to film music, thousands of recordings, and some mighty good books, too. Look at what you are holding! Today, virtually every new score has a CD release, obscure anecdotes are known to thousands, and great (and not-so-great) scores from the past are being restored (both in their original recordings and new ones).

This last point deserves elaboration. When a score from the past is released for the first time, sometimes it's the original recording made for the film. Or a new recording is made because the original no longer exists or perhaps the record company was feeling adventurous. This is remarkable, because in the old days the consumer could be burned by purchasing what appeared to be an LP of a beloved work but was instead a cheap, pop-oriented mutation designed to cash in on the easy-listening market (*True Grit* comes to mind). Today, record labels actually commission orchestras to perform film scores with the reverence of classical music or, more remarkable still, with the cinematic ambiance of film music. Rerecording a classic score is still a hard thing to get right, but many have gotten close, and in the process, original manuscripts have been dusted off and restored.

If anything, a marketplace saturation is taking place from all the archival activity. My experience with film music has been a great case study in pack mentality, and to paraphrase from *The Simpsons,* this is the kind of thing that gives the word "mob" a bad name. Frankly, I think it might be difficult, even with the thoughtful reviews and ratings, for a newcomer to read through this book and be able to differentiate between classic and average works. Soundtracks represent a lexicon and catalog that takes time to learn. This is probably a good place to segue (film music speak for "took two short pieces and stuck them together to hide how trivial they are") to the burning issue of soundtrack collectors vs. popular culture.

Despite how cool it is, most people do not care about film music. Popular music is mostly simple stuff with words and elements that are very easy to understand. I think soundtrack collectors are at heart outcasts who fall in love with movies and movie music as a way of feeding their egos (identifying with heroic characters and music) and finding societal acceptance. I should know, because I'm this way. There's something wonderfully self-confirming in rejecting the pop culture of the world that has rejected you, and latching on to fantastic characters and their theme music. Then you spend the rest of your life reconciling your fantasy and factual worlds, and feverishly collecting CDs of all the old music you loved while you punch the clock and raise the kids.

The nemesis throughout the history of soundtrack collecting has been the intrusion of popular music into our beloved film music. First there were title songs in the 1950s; then the intrusion of jazz and rock elements; pop scores like *The Graduate,* followed by *Saturday Night Fever, Top Gun, Dirty Dancing,* and so forth; and finally, today's aesthetically vacant world where a movie is made into a marketing tool for a collection of irrelevant songs. These new CD releases are problematic for this book because they are so utterly dissimilar from film scores; they have little to do with the actual movies and are instead collections of songs that are barely heard on screen—perhaps in the end credits, in the background on a car radio, or, at best, in a montage. They reach a totally different, albeit much larger, audience, but reviewing them is like talking about the products

Michael Jordan endorses (i.e. there's a Madonna song on such-and-such a soundtrack), rather than his actual play on the basketball court. Of course, occasionally these songtracks do work, creating that same sense of cinematic transcendence the best film music has to offer.

In fact, between these pop albums, the sorry state of movies, and the horrendous state of movie music in creative terms, I have never felt more alienated from my former refuge from reality. The ironic thing is that I've come to adore most of the pop-oriented film music of the past, and song-based soundtracks like *Superfly* are among my all-time favorites. In fact, pop music from any era in the past usually cracks me up because it exposes how arbitrary and superficial commercial ventures are, and how plain-as-day the culture industry works. So, as you read this, film music is in a state of heated overdrive, with aficionados furiously gobbling up additional scores and data, and the mainstream media co-opting our private sphere of fun for terrible movies. I deal with this stuff every day, which is why I might sound like I'm flying off the tracks.

But, now that you're at the end of this mad rant, realize that the reason all of this exists is because of those great works by movie composers who, through talent, blind luck, intuition, and probably ignorance, created the magical film scores for the ages. And boy, is it frustrating not to be able to play the actual music for you right now. But whether it is John Barry on *James Bond,* Erich Wolfgang Korngold on *Robin Hood,* Jerry Goldsmith on *Star Trek,* or any other composer and seminal work, their scores continue to create a unique landscape different from anything else in the musical vocabulary. Your favorite moment of movie/music interaction can bring repeated bliss as it lights up the imagination, once again fusing image and sound in a very special poetry. I hope you can use this book to help discover those works.

Lukas Kendall is the editor and publisher of Film Score Monthly, *the leading journal of film music news and reviews (www. filmscoremonthly.com). He has also produced several albums of film music released through his magazine, and contributed liner notes to many more, among them the* Star Wars Trilogy *and* Raiders of the Lost Ark.

Putting It Together

When Didier asked me to write a foreword to *MusicHound Soundtracks,* I immediately said yes. No problem, I thought—as the former soundtrack director at Capitol Records, I can write a few words about how a soundtrack is put together. Now that I am actually sitting down to write, I'm struck by all the things that have to coincide for a soundtrack to materialize from an idea into an actual product you can play on your stereo. I will give you a brief overview of how a soundtrack is created from the point of view of the record label. I'll discuss who the players are, take you through the creative process, the deal-making process, pre-production and mastering, and marketing. Then I'll give a brief editorial on what I think makes a good soundtrack.

The Players

"So," people would say to me, "you put songs in movies?" I wish it were that easy and I could've taken all the credit. But it takes many people and many a collaborative effort to conceptualize and create a soundtrack for a film. There is the record label, of course (that was my area), the music division of the studio that is releasing the film, the director, one or more producers, and the independent music supervisor hired by the film company to be a liaison between all parties. Although everyone works toward the same goal of building a great soundtrack with huge sales potential, each party has its own agenda. Taking all of that into consideration, it is mind blowing that it somehow comes together in the end. But when it does, there is no greater satisfaction.

The Creative Process

My favorite part! Listening to music, listening to music, listening to music. Music would come to me from many sources.

Publishers and record labels sent me songs from bands with upcoming records. Where I'd go to look for music depended on what type/genre of music the film called for. For the purposes of this foreword, my references will be toward creating a contemporary pop soundtrack. The desire on the marketing end for a contemporary pop soundtrack is to have many new songs that are not otherwise available. If the consumers can't buy it on another record, they have to buy the soundtrack! It doesn't always work this way, however. Many established artists are not interested in creating a new song for a soundtrack when they already have a record in the marketplace. They would rather have their fans buy the existing record than a soundtrack, sometimes on a competing label, with just one of their songs. A more recent trend is for an artist's label to release a single from their current record and allow the same song to be a soundtrack single on another label. Although it used to be frowned upon by bands and managers, this type of "piggy back" marketing is now being viewed as a technique that can increase a band's exposure. With so many artists chasing so few radio spots, this practice is becoming more the norm. Having said that, the person putting together the soundtrack still wants to approach artists to create songs specifically for the film. Many times, artists that are between records are very receptive to this idea. Take the case in which the Goo Goo Dolls wrote "Iris" for *City of Angels.* Not only did that break the band, but it also set up the success of their next record. Not all songs succeed like that, but it is what we all hope for!

One advantage of working for a record label is being able to use a soundtrack to expose or break "baby bands." A baby band is a new band or artist recently signed that doesn't have a record in the marketplace yet. With no songs on the radio, chances are many consumers are not aware of the new act. One of my favorite calls to make was to a manager of a new act recently signed to a major label to say, "Guess what? You're going to be on *Never Been Kissed.*" Quite often, flowers will follow.

Another way a song can end up on a soundtrack compilation is if it's created specifically for the movie. This can happen when artists or bands write their own song or when we would find a great unreleased song from a publisher and hire a band or artist to cover it. Although the latter song is not technically "created" for the movie, in essence it is. Where the Goo Goo Dolls wrote "Iris" specifically for *City of Angels,* the Grammy-winning and Academy Award–nominated "I Will Always Love You" from *The Bodyguard* was an old Dolly Parton song that Whitney Houston so eloquently made famous. The soundtrack for *The Bodyguard* sold millions of records based on that song alone.

When the time comes for a band or artist to go into the studio to record a new song, a producer needs to be hired. A good producer can be the key to turning a decent demo into a hit recording. While at Capitol, I was fortunate to work on the double platinum–selling (two million copies) soundtrack to *Hope Floats*. The smartest thing we did by far was hire Grammy-winning producer Don Was as both music supervisor and record producer. Because Don produced many songs for the record and the film, the soundtrack has a common musical thread running throughout that gives it a Texas flavor. Listening to the *Hope Floats* soundtrack is akin to reliving the experience of watching the film. That, in my opinion, is the ultimate goal. After a song is produced, hopefully by a hit producer, it gets mixed, then mastered, and is then ready to be cut into the film and put on the soundtrack.

So many planets have to align before a song is actually "locked" into a picture. All the players I mentioned earlier—director, producer(s), music supervisor, studio, and record label—have to agree, and the song has to work in the scene. Ultimately, everyone tries to protect the integrity of the film, because if the music doesn't work in the movie, no one will buy the soundtrack. Usually the director has the final say, but he or she will occasionally give in if others plead a good case.

While many soundtracks now have songs from a variety of labels, I have learned that the first single from the soundtrack needs to be a song from an artist signed to the label that releases the soundtrack album. Ultimately, you cannot rely on any label to get behind, believe in, and work a song at radio as well as your own label. Without citing examples, I'll simply say that this has been one of the hardest lessons I have learned.

The Deal Making

Now, I'm sure I don't have to tell you that no music comes to a soundtrack for free. Every song has to be "licensed" or "cleared" for use in the film and on the soundtrack. While this could entail an entire essay by itself, I do want to touch on the process briefly.

Two licenses have to be obtained and fees paid for each song: the master use (the actual recording of the song) and the synchronization use (the publishing of the song). A master-use license is issued from the record label, the company that owns the recording; the synch-use license is issued from the publisher, the company that owns the publishing rights. Both types of license must be obtained for the film and again for the soundtrack. An outside clearance person or the music supervisor are the individuals that actually execute this grueling task. I would get involved only when the license pertained to Capitol artists and even then it was under the guidance and expertise of our business affairs department. Licensing is a complicated, time-consuming, and ongoing process, and it will sometimes sway the decision as to whether or not a song goes into a film.

Pre-Production and Mastering

Another aspect of my job was to oversee the pre-production and mastering of the actual recording. Capitol Records has a product planning department that is responsible for readying the soundtrack for manufacturing. It was my responsibility to provide all the information and resources needed to do so. The final track listing is the most important piece of this information. Once that is finalized, the Product Planning department can start to obtain the label copy (song title credits) and the art department can start to create the packaging.

While the packaging was being created and the label copy was being collected, I would also overseeing a process called mastering. Mastering is the process by which all the music gets put on one final source. This was actually my favorite part because it was the first time I got to hear all the music in sequence as a complete listening experience. Each song gets recorded onto a mastering software program. This program compresses the music and sets all the levels so the listener can enjoy the soundtrack at one continuous level. The final product created from mastering then ships to the plant for manufacturing. From that point, thousands of discs are pressed to go into the final packaging and jewel cases. Once the mastered product and the art separations are shipped to the plant, it was out of my hands, and I usually breathed a sigh of relief.

Marketing and Promotion

A great soundtrack does not translate into great record sales unless the consumer is aware of the product. A label's marketing, promotion, sales, and publicity departments work together to create an overall marketing plan.

The main focus of the marketing department is to facilitate soundtrack awareness that will help to sell records. Capitol and the film studio's marketing departments work in conjunction toward this goal. Usually the first priority is making a video to submit to cable music networks like MTV and VH1—huge markets for generating record awareness. Capitol's in-house video department and the film studio collaborate on this project. Film footage is often used in the video to aid the consumer in associating the song with the movie. This is especially important if the soundtrack single is also on a competing label's release. We want the buyer to purchase the soundtrack rather than the other record.

Early on, both marketing departments desperately try to get music from the soundtrack used in the trailer that runs in theaters a few weeks before the movie opens. This may seem like an open and shut case, but it often isn't. The reason is that trailer houses are separate from the film studios and therefore hard to influence. When this campaign is successful, it is a real coup because audiences begin to associate the film with the soundtrack music—an uphill battle the label always fights and occasionally wins.

Marketing also creates the television and radio spots that advertise the soundtrack. This is an opportunity to highlight the label's acts by using them in the spots. At the end of the theater trailer and television spot, a short list of artists featured on the soundtrack will appear. This dead card, as it is called, is another marketing opportunity to associate the music with the film and hopefully translate it into soundtrack sales.

The promotion department's main goal is to get songs played on the radio. Promotion's involvement starts early in the creative process when the soundtrack singles are being determined. The advice of the promotion department is important in speculating which songs will receive active radio play. If a Capitol act is the first single from the soundtrack, then obviously Capitol promotion will be working the track at radio. If there are singles from the soundtrack on competing labels, both Capitol and the respective label should be working the track simultaneously. This department also determines at which radio format

(alternative, AAA, modern AC, top 40) the single may break. Once that is determined, it is up to them to make it happen!

The sales department develops and executes the plan for product placement. It determines which retail outlets (Warehouse, Tower, Best Buy) are optimally suited to stock and sell the soundtrack. The desire is to have the record as highly visible in the retail stores as possible. A creative merchandising plan is often the key to steering the consumer toward purchasing this Capitol soundtrack as opposed to another. Due to heavy competition and the saturated soundtrack market, this must be carefully planned. The sales department is also responsible for taking periodic inventory and keeping product in the marketplace. Without a creative sales department, the soundtrack could get lost among the masses.

The goal of the publicity department is to generate as much long-lead press as possible. By long lead I mean far in advance of the movie opening. Magazines, newspapers, and television are usually the target. Along with the video for the single, many times an electronic press kit (EPK) is created to send out to help promote the film and its soundtrack. The EPK could include interviews with the actors, interviews with the band or artist that contributed to the soundtrack, and behind-the-scenes insight into the making of the film and/or video. This is another great way to alert the press and other media and hopefully start generating some excitement.

What Makes a Good Soundtrack

In my opinion, a good soundtrack should revive the emotions you felt when you watched the film. If you've ever tried to watch a film without music, you know that it is an emotionless mix of bits of dialogue pieced together. Music can help the director accomplish what many times cannot be done with dialogue, editing, or other filmmaking devices. Music is the catalyst that brings it all together. A good example of this, in addition to *Hope Floats*, is the soundtrack to *Good Will Hunting*. The director chose one artist, Elliot Smith, to be the voice of his film. Elliot's songs are woven throughout the film in such a way that the audience cannot help but feel the emotions of the characters. We put the soundtrack together in a similar fashion so the listener can have the same experience just by playing the songs.

Last, but not least, it certainly helps to have great songs!

Julia Michels was formerly the Director of Soundtracks at Capitol Records. She has since moved on to bigger and better things in the music industry.

In recent years the film music landscape has changed considerably, something that a visit to your local record store will easily confirm: bins upon bins in the best appointed stores reveal the existence of hundreds of titles, all related to recent or vintage films. Some may be song compilations, others new instrumental scores, others still reissues and/or re-creations of classic vintage scores. To some degree, this is a bonanza for fans and collectors eager to expand their collection, yet it also proves quite frustrating inasmuch as the abundance of titles might go counter to a limited spending budget. Hence the question, what to buy, what not to buy?

MusicHound Soundtracks offers to help you sift through the viable titles and, pardon the word, the garbage! In preparing the book, we have tried to give an objective opinion about the many soundtrack and cast albums available, sometimes suggesting titles that are worth having in one's collection, at other times loudly deploring the paucity of artistic values to be found in what pass in some circles as "soundtrack" albums.

In every instance, we have been motivated by our deep, abiding love of music—the primary consideration in listening to and appreciating any CD that is available in the marketplace. Occasionally, we might have vented our frustrations, or strongly expressed likes and dislikes that may not correspond with those of the readers. Objectivity in assessing what is good or bad music varies considerably from one listener to another, and the reader will understand that our opinions may not always reflect what others may think about the CDs reviewed in this volume.

Nonetheless, we hope we have put together a compendium of assessments that will enable the hardcore fan to simply decide what to add to his collection, and help the neophyte to build a fascinating collection, offering a broad range of styles and different approaches to what is, after all, a very subjective form of expression.

So how do you use *MusicHound Soundtracks*? Here's what you'll find in the entries, and what we intend to accomplish with each point:

Following the title are many important pieces of information. First is a source icon indicating whether the recording is from a film, television show, or stage production. Following that are a number of different items, including the CD release year, the label, the film production studio, and the release year for the film, television show, or stage production. Lastly in this section, you'll find the bone rating. Now, you ask, what's with these bones? It's not hard to figure out—*ꕷꕷꕷꕷ* is nirvana, a **woof!** is dog food.

The **album notes** section contains the credits for each particular recording. This may include composer, conductor, lyricist, orchestra, cast members, performers, and other pertinent credits. (Note: Not all recordings will have this section.)

Following this will be the review—the meat of the entry. Here you'll read entertaining and expert advice on the soundtracks listed in this volume.

We should also remind you that *MusicHound Soundtracks* is a *buyer's* guide. Therefore, for the most part we only discuss CDs that are currently in print and available in the United States.

As with any opinions, all of what you're about to read is subjective and personal. MusicHound has a bit of junkyard dog in it, too; it likes to start fights. We hope it does, too. Ultimately, we think the Hound will point you in the right direction, and if you buy the *ꕷꕷꕷꕷ* and *ꕷꕷꕷ* choices, you'll have an album collection to howl about. But if you've got a bone to pick, the Hound wants to hear about it—and promises not to bite (but maybe bark a little bit). If you think we're wagging our tails in the wrong direction or lifting our leg at something that doesn't deserve it, let us know. If you think something has been capriciously excluded—or charitably included—tell us. Your comments and suggestions will serve the greater MusicHound audience and future projects, so don't be shy.

Editor

Didier C. Deutsch is a Grammy Award–nominated record producer who has expressed a lifelong interest in film music and Broadway musicals, and has written about both for various publications such as *Record World, After Dark, Essence, Soundtrack!, Musicals,* and *Show Music.* He eventually began producing film music and Broadway show compilations and reissues for such labels as Sony, RCA Victor, Rhino, and Arista. Among his most notable achievements, Deutsch has produced CD boxed sets for artists such as Johnny Mathis, Tony Bennett, and Frank Sinatra (which was nominated for a Grammy in 1994).

Series Editor

Gary Graff is an award-winning music journalist and series editor of the MusicHound album guide series. A native of Pittsburgh, Pennsylvania, his work is published regularly by Reuters, *Guitar World,* the *San Francisco Chronicle,* the *Cleveland Plain Dealer,* Michigan's *Oakland Press,* Launch Radio Networks, *Country Song Roundup,* the *Pittsburgh Post-Gazette,* CDnow, *Schwann Spectrum,* and other publications. A regular contributor to the Web sites Mr. Showbiz/ Wall of Sound, JAMtv, and Electric Village, his weekly "Rock 'n' Roll Insider" report airs on Detroit rock station WRIF-FM (101.1). He also appears on public television station WTVS' *Backstage Pass* program and is a board member of the North American Music Critics Association and co-producer of the annual Detroit Music Awards. The co-editor of *MusicHound Rock, MusicHound Country,* and *MusicHound R&B,* Gary lives in the Detroit suburbs with his wife, daughter, and two stepsons.

Managing Editor

Jeff Hermann is an editor at Visible Ink Press. Recently engaged, he plans to live out his days in harmony and prosperity with his wife-to-be.

Associate Managing Editors

Dean Dauphinais is an obsessive-compulsive senior editor at Visible Ink Press and the managing editor of several MusicHound titles. He doesn't see movies, but he does listen to music—and even owns a few soundtracks. *Black Orpheus,* with music by Antonio Carlos Jobim, is among his favorites.

Judy Galens is a senior editor with Visible Ink Press and managing editor of several MusicHound titles. She lives in domestic bliss (most of the time) with her husband and their son, Graham, in the Detroit area.

Copy Editors

Barbara Cohen is a copyediting and indexing whiz, and has had a hand in a number of Visible Ink titles. She also lectures and writes on indexing and the training of indexers.

Christina Fuoco, the former music writer for the *Observer & Eccentric* newspapers in Livonia, Michigan, is now the senior content producer for Detroit.CitySearch.Com. She's addicted to working on MusicHound books and also freelances for Allstar, Michigan's *Flint Journal,* and CDnow.

Pamela Shelton is a freelance writer and copy editor living in Connecticut. She used to write a bluegrass column for *Country in the City News.*

Devra Sladics is currently a writer with the National Proposal Group at KPMG and freelances in her spare time. She spent seven years as an editor with the Gale Group, working four of those years for Visible Ink Press, editing titles such as *Video-Hound's Soundtracks* and *VideoHound's World Cinema.* She lives in Chicago.

Publisher
Martin Connors

MusicHound Staff
Michelle Banks, Christa Brelin, Jim Craddock, Justin Karr, Diane Maniaci, Brad Morgan, Matt Nowinski, Carol Schwartz, Christine Tomassini

Proofreading
Lynne Konstantin, Pam Shelton, Devra Sladics

Resource Section Compilation
Steve Knopper

Art Direction
Tracey Rowens, Michelle DiMercurio, Cindy Baldwin

Graphic Services
Randy Bassett, Leatha Etheridge-Sims, Mary Grimes, Pam Reed, Barbara Yarrow

Permissions
Edna Hedblad, Maria Franklin

Production
Mary Beth Trimper, Dorothy Maki, Evi Seoud, Wendy Blurton, Rita Wimberley

Technology Wizards
Wayne Fong, Jeffrey Muhr

Typesetting Virtuoso
Marco Di Vita of the Graphix Group

Marketing & Promotion
PJ Butland, Marilou Carlin, Kim Marich, Betsy Rovegno, Lauri Taylor

MusicHound Development
Julia Furtaw

Contributors
Bob Belden, a multiple Grammy Award recipient, is a multi-talented musician/composer/producer/writer/recording artist, whose own albums have been released on various labels, including Blue Note Records. His interest in film music is but one of his hobbies.

Jeff Bond owes his knowledge of film music to years of watching television reruns and movies in the '60s and '70s, when he could often be found holding the microphone of his cassette recorder up to the speaker of his TV set to record the themes from *Star Trek, The Undersea World of Jacques Cousteau,* and *The Man from U.N.C.L.E.* In 1992 he began writing reviews for *Film Score Monthly* and has been regularly featured in that magazine ever since. He has also contributed regular features and reviews to *SciFi Universe* magazine, and has written articles on music from the *Star Trek* television series and feature films for *Star Trek Communicator* magazine. He and his wife, Brook, currently reside in Los Angeles.

Andy Dursin has profiled film composers and filmmakers for *Film Score Monthly, Home Movies,* and *Movie Collector* magazines, where he has also written extensively about films, soundtrack albums, and laserdisks. A graduate of Boston College, Andy is a proud native Rhode Islander, whom you'll find at the beach if he's not at the local movie theater.

Gary Graff is MusicHound series editor (see above).

Chuck Granata, record producer, is an authority on Frank Sinatra; Chuck's work can be seen on a variety of CD titles released by Sony, Capitol, and Reprise. He is also very knowledgeable about and a fan of Broadway and film music, and often writes about both.

David Hirsch, an avid soundtrack collector, learned to appreciate film music when, before video tape, the only way to relive one's favorite film or TV show was through its soundtrack album. Formerly an associate editor of *Starlog* magazine, David has co-authored eight books, including the *Space: 1999 Official Alpha Moonbase Technical Manual* and *TV Episode Guides, Vols. 1 & 2.* A former music columnist for both *Starlog* and *Soundtrack!* magazines, he has also written liner notes for, consulted on, or produced over 50 soundtrack albums including *Supergirl, Flight of the Navigator,* and *Star Trek: Volume 2.*

Lukas Kendall is the editor and publisher of *Film Score Monthly.* He has also produced several albums of film music released through his magazine, and contributed liner notes to many more, among them the *Star Wars Trilogy* and *Raiders of the Lost Ark.*

Marc Kirkeby, a former editor at *Rolling Stone,* writes frequently about music, theater, and film. His essays have appeared in the *New Yorker,* the *Village Voice,* and *American Film.*

Beth Krakower is the founder and President of CineMedia Promotions, the only full-service publicity, radio, and Web promotions firm specializing in the needs of film and Broadway music. Beth is also the editor of the *CineRadio* chart, published monthly in *Film Music* magazine, and is the chapter manager of Film Music Network in New York. A 10-year music industry veteran with an extensive background in numerous genres, Beth became immersed in the soundtrack world while she was director of promotions (radio and Web) at Milan Records.

Randall D. Larson is the former editor and publisher of *CinemaScore: The Film Music Journal,* and a long-time contributing editor to *Soundtrack!* A frequent film music writer for *Cinefantastique,* Larson is also the author of *Musique Fantastique: A Survey of Film Music in the Fantastic Cinema* (Scarecrow, 1984) and *Music for the House of Hammer* (Scarecrow, 1986).

Paul Andrew MacLean contributes reviews and interviews to *Film Score Monthly, Soundtrack!,* and *Music from the Movies,* and also serves as film reviewer for *Renaissance* magazine.

David Poole reviews soundtracks for CDnow, writes a monthly column on film music in the Angelika and Ritz Filmbills (www.ritzfilmbill.com), and recently authored the liner notes to *Crash* and *Beavis and Butthead Do America.* His writing on other genres of music has appeared in *Detour, Art Forum, Time Out New York, Cover,* and *MusicHound World.*

Max O. Preeo, an ardent fan of the show business scene, is the editor of the glossy magazine *Show Music,* which he created some 15 years ago. The magazine, one of the most popular publications in the field, focuses primarily on the American musical theatre and the many recordings it has spawned around the world, and has emerged as the authoritative voice in this specific musical genre. In addition, Max has written extensive liner notes for various cast album reissues and personality recordings released by Sony, MCA, and other labels

Amy Rosen, whose interest in film music steered her from her native Atlanta to Hollywood, is an up-and-coming music supervisor. She was music coordinator on *Titanic, The Mod Squad, The Opposite of Sex, Trees Lounge, The Thirteenth Floor,* and many other motion pictures. She will debut as music supervisor with the upcoming film, *SFO,* starring Timothy Hutton and Maria Grazia Cucinotta. She is also a published writer, most recently providing liner notes for the Rhino records movie music compilation, *Love Scene,* which she also co-compiled.

Daniel Schweiger, like so many film score enthusiasts of his generation, hasn't been the same since he put *Logan's Run* on his record turntable in 1976. Now Daniel is the soundtrack editor of *Venice Magazine,* an arts publication based in Los Angeles. His composer interviews, articles, and reviews have also appeared in *Film Score Monthly, Music from the Movies, Soundtrack!,* and *Fangoria.* He has contributed liner notes to such soundtracks as *Elmer Gantry, Capricorn One/Outland, Escape from L.A.,* and *Star Trek: Insurrection.* Professionally, Daniel has put together temporary soundtracks for dozens of films, including *Anastasia, Teaching Miss Tingle,* and *Mighty Joe Young.* Daniel can be seen seen in a co-starring role as "himself" in the movie *Free Enterprise.*

Jerry Thomas, a collector and fan of Broadway and screen musicals, writes frequently about both, and has also contributed to liner notes for a number of Broadway cast album and film soundtrack releases.

musicHound *Acknowledgments*

I would like to express my gratitude to all the wonderful writers and critics who have contributed to this book: Jeff Bond, Andy Dursin, Gary Graff, Chuck Granata, David Hirsch, Marc Kirkeby, Randall Larson, Paul Andrew MacLean, and Jerry Thomas, whose reviews appeared in the first edition; and Bob Belden, Beth Krakower, David Poole, Max O. Preeo, Amy Rosen, and Dan Schweiger, who added their voices to this second edition. Thanks to Visible Ink's Jeff Hermann for his editorship and to Devra Sladics for her work on the first edition of this book and guidance on the second. Special thanks are due to Lukas Kendall, Daniel Schweiger, Robert Hoshowsky, Paul Andrew MacLean, Andy Dursin, Will Shivers, Matthias Büdinger, Doug Adams, Paul M. Riordan, and everyone at *Film Score Monthly* for supplying us with the great sidebars.

I also would like to extend my thanks to all the individuals at the various labels who have generously suggested titles to be covered, and have made sure we received the CDs reviewed in this book. And particularly: Julie D'Angelo at Rhino; Jeff Jones, Steve Berkowitz, Adam Block, John Jackson, and Patti Matheny at Legacy; Warren Wernick, Peter Cho, Colin Cigarran, and Michelle Errante at Sony Classical; Andy McKaie and Dana Smart at MCA/Universal; Gary Pacheco at Arista; Hugh Fordin at DRG; Ian Gilchrist at Rykodisc; Toby Pienek at Milan; Yusuf Gandhi and James Fitzpatrick at Silva; Douglass Fake at Intrada; Eric Zarlenga at Varèse Sarabande; Tom Null at Citadel; Gregg Geller at Warner Bros./Reprise; David Landau at Beyond; Randy Gerston at Compass III; Julia Michels, formerly at Capitol; Gene Norman at Crescendo; Charles D'Atri at Hollywood; and Brad Pressman at Sonic Images.

Thanks also to Ron Saja at Footlight, Craig Spaulding at Screen Archives Entertainment, and Wendy and the staff at Soundtrack Album Retailers. Most of the albums reviewed in this book can be obtained through these specialized mail and retail outlets (see the list at the bottom of this page for more information).

A very special thanks and a note of admiration to Lois Carruth, too. Last, but not least, I would like to thank my two West Coast friends, Lukas Kendall at *Film Score Monthly*, who has supported my efforts since the beginning and has contributed both reviews and introductions to the first and second editions of the book; and Ford A. Thaxton, who has always been an ardent supporter, and has offered many valuable suggestions. Lukas and Ford have totally different characters and dislike each other intensely, but both are motivated by the same love of film music, that passion that binds all of us together and compels us all to be members of a very exclusive club. Welcome to the club!

Didier C. Deutsch

Specialty Shops and Dealers

Many of the albums listed in *MusicHound Soundtracks* can be found at record stores across the country, or can be ordered from the following specialized shops and dealers.

Dress Circle
57/59 Monmouth St.
Upper St. Martin's Ln.
London WC2H 9DG
England
0 (171) 240-2227
Fax: 0 (171) 379-8540
E-mail: online@dresscircle.co.uk

Footlight Records
113 East 12th St.
New York, NY 10003
(212) 533-1572
Fax: (212) 673-1496
E-mail: Footlight@aol.com

Screen Archives Entertainment
PO Box 5636
Washington, DC 20016-1236
(202) 364-4333
Fax: (202) 364-4343

Soundtrack Album Retailers
PO Box 487
New Holland, PA 17557-0487
(717) 656-0121

A

A ciascuno il suo/Una questione d'onore

1996, GDM Music/Italy, from the films *A ciascuno il suo (We Still Kill the Old Way)*, Lopert, 1966, and *Una questione d'onore (A Matter of Honor)*, Lopert, 1965 ♪♪♪♪

album notes: A ciascuno il suo: Music: Luis Bacalov; **Conductor:** Bruno Nicolai; **Una questione d'onore: Music:** Luis Bacalov; **Conductor:** Bruno Nicolai.

Two films set in Sicily, where petty crimes and matters of honor have always been at the core of everyday life, the first dealing with it on a serious note, while the second takes a much lighter approach. Though neither film was a great success, both gave composer Luis Bacalov an opportunity to create atmospheric scores that not only helped the action on screen, but also provide a most enjoyable listening experience. *A ciascuno il suo,* released in this country as *We Still Kill the Old Way,* was a tale of revenge Sicilian-style, which translated into a realistic score from Bacalov, in which a somber theme, played on the cello, cast an appropriately ominous aura. Injecting a different mood was a samba-like motif, which recurred in counterpoint to the main theme, and gave levity to the score, and a bluesy jazz selection. Reflecting a greater awareness of the exotic Italian sonorities, *Una questione d'onore,* a comedy starring Ugo Tognazzi, featured lighter moods, with many ingratiating themes ("Serenata," "La festa," "Una banda per un assassinio") emerging from this previously unreleased score. This recording may be difficult to find. Check with a used CD store, mail-order company, or a dealer specializing in rare, out-of-print, or import recordings.

Didier C. Deutsch

Absolute Power

1997, Varèse Sarabande Records, from the film *Absolute Power,* Castle Rock Entertainment, 1997 ♪♪♥

album notes: Music: Lennie Niehaus; **Conductor:** Lennie Niehaus.

The dour, oppressive themes developed by Lennie Niehaus for this contemporary political drama are frequently too derivative and too unmelodic to satisfy a casual listener. The story is about a retired detective investigating a covered-up murder possibly involving the president of the United States. Meandering musical lines, occasionally punctuated by synthesized pulses, may work very well on the screen behind the action, but do not make much of an impact when isolated from their primary function. Exceptions include a jazz-tinged "Christy's Dance," and the lovely, melodic "Kate's Theme," played in concertante style with the "End Credits."

Didier C. Deutsch

The Abyss

1989, Varèse Sarabande Records, from the film *The Abyss,* 20th Century Fox, 1989 ♪♪♪

album notes: Music: Alan Silvestri; **Conductor:** Alan Silvestri.

This score for director James Cameron's underwater epic is as eclectic as the film itself. Composer Alan Silvestri deftly mixes three distinct styles, each to represent the film's three protagonists. Standard scoring techniques, in particular the composer's own trademarked bombastic horn punches, are used to represent the human element of the film. As the protagonists penetrate deeper into the undersea trench, a New Age-style electronic theme is used to express the overall mystery that builds throughout the film. Finally, a choir personifies the delicate translucent alien life form hiding below. As the film builds to its climax, all three motifs merge into one chorus, a hymn for an uncertain future. The music tells us there's still a mystery, but perhaps a better world will come of it all.

David Hirsch

The Accidental Tourist

1989, Warner Bros. Records, from the film *The Accidental Tourist,* Warner Bros., 1989 ♫♫♫♫
album notes: Music: John Williams; **Conductor:** John Williams.

For this contemporary story of a man's slow emotional rebirth following the breakup of a long-term relationship, John Williams wrote an unabashedly romantic and gorgeously understated score, in which the piano, the oboe, and the clarinet play an important solo role to create the appropriate reflective moods. The recurring main theme binds the various cues together, in a display of thoughtful music that holds its own on a purely listening basis. The faster-paced "A Second Chance" contrasts happily with the more sullen expression in the other tracks, and exudes a warm, glorious feeling.

Didier C. Deutsch

Ace Ventura: When Nature Calls

1995, MCA Records, from the film *Ace Ventura: When Nature Calls,* Warner Bros., 1995 ♫♫♫♫

It's hard to come up with a soundtrack that adequately conveys the energy Jim Carrey brings to the screen. This one does in spots–on the Goo Goo Dolls' fiery cover of INXS' "Don't Change," on the Presidents of the United States of America's "Boll Weevil," and on Reverend Horton Heat's "Watusi Rodeo." Sting teams up with Pato Banton for a fluid rendition of the Police's "Spirits in the Material World," while White Zombie's "Blur the Technicolor" is appropriately frenetic. The breakthrough from this album was almost Mr. Mirainga, whose "Burnin' Rubber" was a minor radio hit, but the band never came through on its own.

Gary Graff

Aces: Iron Eagle III

1991, Intrada Records, from the film *Aces: Iron Eagle III,* Carolco Pictures, 1991 ♫♫♫♫
album notes: Music: Harry Manfredini; **Conductor:** Harry Manfredini.

Harry Manfredini has come up with a heroic score built around a trio of themes for this aerial adventure film. The dominant motif is the "Aces Theme," an old-fashioned militaristic march that carries the heroism of the vintage fighter pilots throughout the score. A secondary theme, associated with the heroine, is played by French horns and strings counterpointed by piping trumpets and winds; the counterpointed measures lend a forceful drive to the slow-moving theme. The third major motif is that of the Nazi drug lord–a fast-paced polyrhythmic riff for percussion and electric bass counterpointed against marimba and flute that captures the cold, relentless violence of the villain. Manfredini has concocted a cohesive score that works well in the film and on the CD, although the orchestra occasionally sounds a little thin. The 50-minute disc is nicely sequenced and packaged, including detailed notes by the composer who describes each cue and his use of the various themes.

Randall D. Larson

Across 110th Street

1998, Rykodisc, from the film *Across 110th Street,* MGM-UA 1972 ♫♫
album notes: Music: J. J. Johnson.

A relatively dated score that features wah-wah guitars, a large brass section, and cliché bass lines. Typical of the blaxploitation soundtracks, there is not much synchronization with the picture, just loosely structured vamps. "Harlem Love Theme" is very colorful and is the closest thing to good writing on this soundtrack. The Bobby Womack tracks have nothing to do with jazz, a fact that holds true for most of this soundtrack. Not so good, and a waste of J. J. Johnson's talent.

Bob Belden

Across the Sea of Time

1995, Epic Soundtrax, from the film *Across the Sea of Time,* Columbia Pictures, 1995 ♫♫♫♫
album notes: Music: John Barry; **Orchestra:** The English Chamber Orchestra; **Conductor:** John Barry.

The American experience (or more pointedly the New York experience) elicited this unusual score from composer John Barry for a documentary made in cooperation with Sony New Technologies to promote the IMAX system. Typical of Barry's scores of late, it is a lyrical effort, marked by long lovely melodic lines in which the music effortlessly soars and captures the imagination. The catchy recurring main theme "The Wonder of America" binds together the various selections, often in a dialogue between a solitary reed and the string section. An occasional pulsating tune ("The Subway Ride," or the blues-tinged "Times Square and Broadway") adds an extra dimension to the score, and keeps reminding the listener that John Barry, who was a master at it, used to write more frequently in that vein earlier in his career.

Didier C. Deutsch

The Act

1988, DRG Records, from the Broadway musical *The Act,* 1978 ♪♪♪♪

album notes: Music: John Kander; **Lyrics:** Fred Ebb; **Book:** George Furth; **Musical Direction:** Stanley Lebowsky; **Cast:** Liza Minnelli, Roger Minami, Gayle Crofoot.

Liza Minnelli had one of her most engaging stage parts in this little show, written for her by John Kander and Fred Ebb, in which she portrayed a singer trying her act and honing it before a Broadway opening. In full possession (at the time) of her vocal means, Minnelli gave a superbly shaded performance that was dutifully captured in this exciting cast album. While the songs themselves may not have had the impact of others written by Kander and Ebb, Liza's powerful delivery of "City Lights" has justifiably made it a mini-standard.

Didier C. Deutsch

Act of Piracy/The Great White

1991, Prometheus Records/Belgium, from the films *Act of Piracy,* and *The Great White,* Laurelwood Productions, 1991 ♪♪♪

album notes: Music: Morton Stevens; **Conductor:** Ken Thorne.

Pleasant enough music is mostly notable as Morton Stevens's last score before his untimely passing in 1988. Conducted by Ken Thorne, this is a more melodic work than the average action film score (the main title theme is particularly indelible) and the influence of Jerry Goldsmith is certainly evident. Stevens worked with Goldsmith for many years, both as an orchestrator and co-composer (he did the final two installments of the mini-series *Masada,* and the finale fight cue for *Outland*). Since much of his music has gone unreleased, one can forgive the desire to include the flatter sounding recording of *The Great White,* a 1982 *Jaws* wannabe also included on this CD. Oddly, track titles on the package are laid out in LP fashion with numbering restarting at "1" after track "13."

David Hirsch

The Addams Family

1965, RCA Records, from the television series *The Addams Family,* 1964-65 ♪♪♪

album notes: Music: Vic Mizzy; **Conductor:** Vic Mizzy.

Vic Mizzy's theme music from "The Addams Family" is one of the most instantly recognizable pieces of music to originate from a film or television program, so it goes without saying that if you like the theme song, you're bound to get a rise out of this infectious soundtrack album, initially issued in 1965 by RCA. Mizzy's music often has a toe-tapping beat, a quirky tone that's

---

frequently brought down to Earth by the composer's distinctive melodies. That quality is totally in evidence here, with clear digital remastering punching up the typically '60s production sheen courtesy of original producer Joe Reisman. A new interview with Mizzy is included in the booklet notes, along with the previously unreleased, opening TV edit of the main theme. The short running time might have been augmented by adding cues from some of Mizzy's excellent unreleased film scores *(The Ghost and Mr. Chicken, The Spirit Is Willing),* though that will have to wait for another day.

Andy Dursin

The Addams Family

1991, Capitol Records, from the film *The Addams Family,* Paramount Pictures, 1991 ♪♪♪

album notes: Music: Marc Shaiman; **Conductor:** Hummie Mann.

This broadly comedic score by Marc Shaiman is partly inspired by Vic Mizzy's oddball music for the 1960s TV series and Danny Elfman's "Beetlejuice," but owes much to the classic 1930s Universal horror films which both movie and underscore occasionally parody. Surprisingly romantic in places, the ample orchestral endeavor exhibits a delightful lunatic charm. Several tunes by Duke Ellington and Eddie Cantor are interpolated into the score, which includes the song "Mamushka," co-written by Shaiman with legendary Broadway lyricists Betty Comden and Adolph Green.

David Hirsch

Addams Family Values

1993, Varèse Sarabande Records, from the film *Addams Family Values*, Paramount Pictures, 1993 🎬🎬🎬

album notes: Music: Marc Shaiman; **Conductor:** Artie Kane.

With the same flamboyant style with which he scored the original *Addams Family* feature, Marc Shaiman brings a similar mix of *Beetlejuice* and *Frankenstein* to the podium and lets it fly in all directions. The score is rampantly farcical—quotations from various sources abound—to keep up with the film's hysterical visuals. From riotous bombast to compelling violin virtuosities and moody tangos, everything from Stravinsky to Hans Salter to Astor Piazzola is fair brew in Shaiman's musical stew. With plenty of borrowings from Vic Mizzy's original *Addams Family* TV theme, the score is firmly tongue-in-cheek, but is held together by a straight-faced main theme for the Addams family, which stands powerful and proud, albeit encrusted with a few moldering skeletons in the closet. The orchestral movement on the CD is interrupted by a couple of songs (one of which wasn't used in the film) which are better off programmed out, but the sequel score is a likable mix of musical mayhem. Not quite as fresh or as dynamic as the original score, but likable enough.

Randall D. Larson

Addicted to Love

1997, TVT Records, from the film *Addicted to Love*, Warner Bros., 1997 🎬🎬🎬🎬

album notes: Music: Rachel Portman; **Conductor:** David Snell.

The folks at TVT can be forgiven for overloading this soundtrack album with selections that apparently were not even in the film (but who can complain when those selections include the classic "Walk Away Renee," Serge Gainsbourg and Jane Birkin whispering the sensuous "Je T'aime, Moi Non Plus," and Stéphane Grappelli fiddling his way through "Autumn Leaves"). They also had the good sense of presenting a dozen cues composed by Rachel Portman for the romantic comedy starring Matthew Broderick and Meg Ryan. Portman, one of the best new film composers, reveals a quirky, whimsical style that's very engaging. She displays an uncanny feel for catchy, melodic material that has an unusual quality to it, and finds a

life of its own outside of its primary function. The jaunty theme and variations that find their way in the various cues, occasionally interrupted by more romantic moments ("Sam and Maggie Make Love," "Painting the Wall") make this soundtrack album a real joy to listen to. Don't miss it!

Didier C. Deutsch

Addio Zio Tom

1994, RCA/Japan, from the film *Addio Zio Tom (Goodbye Uncle Tom)*, Euro International, 1971 🎬🎬🎬🎬

album notes: Music: Riz Ortolani; **Conductor:** Riz Ortolani.

The unintentionally funny song, "Oh My Love," performed by Katyna Ranieri (the lyrics sound translated and unnatural) is not a harbinger of what this pleasant soundtrack album contains. Always deeply entertaining, this story about two children, a white girl and a black boy, coming of age in Africa during the slave trade days, enticed Ortolani to create a music that relied on its unusual instrumentations (a harpsichord and chimes in most tracks) to attract the listener. Despite some of the grimmer aspects of its narrative, Ortolani's music remains bouncy and enjoyable, conforming with the view of the two children who are at the center of the action. An album that's quite delightful. This title may be out of print or just plain hard to find. Mail-order companies, used CD shops, or dealers of rare or import recordings will be your best bet.

Didier C. Deutsch

The Adventures of Baron Munchausen

1988, Warner Bros. Records, from the film *The Adventures of Baron Munchausen*, Columbia Pictures, 1988 🎬🎬🎬🎬

album notes: Music: Michael Kamen; **Orchestras:** The Graunke Orchestra of Munich and The National Philharmonic Orchestra of London; **Conductor:** Michael Kamen.

Terry Gilliam's epic film of the legendary European liar is blessed with a lavish and innovative orchestral score by Michael Kamen. The opportunity is here to cover just about every kind of mood from dire peril to pompous farce, and Kamen handles it all with an amazing dexterity. From the adventurous flight of "The Balloon" suite, to the choral requiem "What Will Become of the Baron," and finally to the balmy songs for "The Sultan" suite (co-written with ex-"Monty Python" member Eric Idle), the score transcends each diverse level as if they truly belonged together. Kamen even manages to musically capture comedian Robin Williams's inspired zaniness in "On the Moon," a deft mix of orchestral instruments, electronics, and natural sounds.

David Hirsch

The Adventures of Huck Finn

1993, Varèse Sarabande Records, from the film *The Adventures of Huck Finn,* Walt Disney Films, 1993 ♪♪♪♪

album notes: Music: Bill Conti; Conductor: Bill Conti.

Bill Conti wrote an uplifting, jubilant score for this 1993 Disney adaptation of Mark Twain's classic novel. While the film took some liberties with Twain's text, Conti's score perfectly captures the innocence of childhood with a lyrical soundtrack dominated by strong melodic, often boisterous themes. Not surprisingly, this down-home score has been used as underscore on countless televised sports programs since, most notably the Kentucky Derby. Since *Rocky,* Conti has often had the rotten luck of writing music for either bad movies or films that never had soundtrack albums. *Huck Finn* is not only one of the best albums to originate from the composer since his success with that 1976 Sylvester Stallone milestone, but is also one of his more enjoyable efforts to date.

Andy Dursin

The Adventures of Pinocchio

1996, London Records, from the animated feature *The Adventures of Pinocchio,* New Line Cinema, 1996 ♪♪♪♪

album notes: Music: Rachel Portman.

Rachel Portman's lovely score for this retelling of the Pinocchio story is almost dwarfed by the pseudo operatic selections created by Lee Holdridge, Brian May, David Goldsmith, and album producer Spencer Proffer, among others, which are heard at the beginning of the set, and shamelessly call the listener's attention to them. At times recalling the manic style in Danny Elfman's music, Portman's score is wonderfully imaginative, diversified, and eclectic, moving effortlessly from wild displays of fiery orchestral outbursts to evocative chamber-like expressions, sometimes all within the same cue, as in "Lorenzini." In fact, it's almost a shame the CD didn't give her music more playing time. Unfortunately, the only tracks that don't fit within the context here are the vocals by Stevie Wonder, who also contributed some exquisite instrumentals in "Kiss Lonely Goodbye" and "Pinocchio's Evolution." His style of singing does not match the "period" moods established in the other numbers, and the derivative "What We Are Made Of," performed by Brian May and Sissel, which also sounds too contemporary.

Didier C. Deutsch

The Adventures of Priscilla, Queen of the Desert

1994, Mother Records, from the film *The Adventures of Priscilla, Queen of the Desert,* Gramercy Pictures, 1994 ♪♪♪♪

The misadventures of three transvestites on a car trip across Australia became the occasion for this soundtrack album in which some of disco's greatest hits have been compiled in a festive, joyous display. Oddly enough, the lone track that seems utterly out of place in this unbridled dance party is Lena Horne's rendition of the classic "A Fine Romance," which sounds, er . . . too polite! But don't let that misstep keep you away from this delightful album, honey: you'll love it.

Didier C. Deutsch

The Adventures of Robin Hood

1983, Varèse Sarabande Records, from the film *The Adventures of Robin Hood,* Warner Bros., 1938 ♪♪♪♪♪

album notes: Music: Erich Wolfgang Korngold; Orchestra: The Utah Symphony Orchestra; Conductor: Varujan Kojian.

Over the years there have been tantalizing snippets of Korngold's thrilling score for *The Adventures of Robin Hood* in various compilations, but none as complete or as exciting as this brilliant recording produced by George Korngold, son of the composer. Here is all the pageantry, color, and gorgeous melodies from the original, faithfully reproduced in spacious stereo, in a recording that has long been a trendsetter in its field, and is an essential title in any collection.

Excerpts from the score can also be found in *Music by Erich Wolfgang Korngold,* conducted by Lionel Newman, a recording initially released by Warner Bros. in the early '60s, and for many years a much sought-after collector's item; and in *Captain Blood: Classic Film Scores for Errol Flynn,* and *The Sea Hawk: Classic Film Scores of Erich Wolfgang Korngold,* both conducted by Charles Gerhardt.

see also: The Sea Hawk, Anthony Adverse

Didier C. Deutsch

The Adventures of Robinson Crusoe

1997, Silva Screen (U.K.) from the television series, *The Adventures Of Robin Crusoe,* ♪♪♪♪

album notes: Music: Robert Mellin, Gian-Piero Reverberi.

The adventures of Robinson Crusoe, as depicted by Daniel Defoe in his 1721 novel, have inspired many filmmakers who have thrived on the tale's universal themes of ingenuity, friendship, and survival in an alien environment. The 1964–1965 13-part se-

The Adventures of Robin Hood **(The Kobal Collection)**

ries, with a score by Robert Mellin and Gian-Piero Reverberi, is unusual in that it parallels Crusoe's current existence in the wild with flashbacks about his earlier life: his youth in York, his unhappy apprenticeship to a lawyer, his running off to sea, and his capture by and escape from slave traders, all elements found in Defoe's novel but seldom exploited to such an extent beforehand. As a result, the score reflects the greater diversity in the storyline, and in the midst of cues describing Crusoe's precarious existence on the (actually not so) deserted island, can afford to portray other aspects of his life ("Crusoe's Youth Remembered," "Away From Home," "Flashback: Escapades in York," etc.). The music, mostly steeped into the 1960s-style of light pop, makes an occasional detour toward more descriptive, romantic accents, usually to contrast Crusoe's current situation with reminiscences of his earlier life. It's a strange combination, particularly for a story allegedly set in the 18th century, but it's fun to listen to, which is ultimately the goal set by this oddball CD.

This expanded release, with nine extra tracks, including a seven-minute suite reprising some of the same themes, neither adds nor detracts from the impression made by the original CD.

It seems sonics have been tampered with ever so slightly and evidence greater clarity.

Didier C. Deutsch

The Adventures of the Great Mouse Detective

1992, Varèse Sarabande Records, from the animated feature *The Adventures of the Great Mouse Detective*, The Walt Disney Company, 1992 𝄞𝄞𝄞𝄞𝄞

album notes: Music: Henry Mancini; **Conductor:** Henry Mancini.

There often is a cartoon-like quality to Henry Mancini's most inspired musical scores, and it evidently all came together in this delightful series of cues for an animated feature distributed by the Disney company. The villain here, a nasty rat, is none other than Vincent Price, doing a sensational job in two songs (including the revealing "The World's Greatest Criminal," delivered with the right amount of sneers and nasty posturing), and that Mancini's music is constantly amusing and thoroughly entertaining. For added pleasure, Melissa Manchester contributes "Let Me Be Good to You," which she wrote for the occasion. Delicious through and through.

Didier C. Deutsch

An Affair to Remember

1993, Epic Soundtrax; from the film *An Affair to Remember*, 20th Century Fox, 1957 ♫♫♫

album notes: Music: Hugo Friedhofer; **Orchestra:**The 20th Century Fox Orchestra; **Choir:** The 20th Century Fox Chorus; **Conductor:** Lionel Newman.

This stylish 1957 soap opera starring Cary Grant, as an eligible bachelor engaged to a socialite, and Deborah Kerr, as the painter he meets during a trans-Atlantic voyage and with whom he falls in love only to lose track of her after she has a car accident, is best remembered today for the fact that it played an important role in *Sleepless in Seattle*. The score, composed by Hugo Friedhofer, imaginatively played its role behind the scenes, but stands out on its own as a pleasant listening experience. Several vocals by Marni Nixon and Vic Damone's rendition of the title tune add an extra touch of their own to the enjoyment. The only drawback here is the EQ that gives the recording a slightly unpleasant nasal sound.

see also: Sleepless in Seattle

Didier C. Deutsch

Affliction

1998, Citadel, from the film *Affliction*, Lions Gate 1998 ♫♫♫

album notes: Music: Michael Brook.

Composer Michael Brook's moody, ambient score for *Affliction*, which earned Nick Nolte an Oscar nomination, takes the listener deep into the emotions of love and loss expressed throughout the film. The music stands well enough alone in an atmosphere of murky depths and subterranean inner thoughts. Relying on low tones and long, sweeping melodies, *Affliction* succeeds in creating sonic distance. It is a well-executed score, with only a few minor distractions, but it's a bit too long and a bit too dark. Brook's prior collaborations with Brian Eno and Bryan Ferry bear influence in the diverse sound distortions heard throughout the score.

Beth Krakower

After Dark My Sweet

1990, Varèse Sarabande Records, from the film *After Dark My Sweet*, Avenue Pictures, 1990 ♫♫♫

album notes: Music: Maurice Jarre; **Performers:** Michael Boddicker, Ralph Grierson, Michael Fisher.

Written just prior to his popular score for *Ghost*, *After Dark My Sweet* is one of the last completely electronic scores Maurice Jarre composed. An excellent film noir about a vagrant ex-prize-fighter seduced by an older woman into a kidnapping scheme, the film benefits greatly from its moody, atmospheric score. A mournful solo EVI opens the album with a lonely theme for the protagonist. A pleasant, airy love theme also figures into the score, set most memorably in track four, with clever electronic percussion writing. The album also features music that was not included in the film and is among Jarre's most engaging electronic work. Some of the suspense cues are perhaps a bit programmatic-sounding on disc and dominate the last half of the album. *After Dark My Sweet* nevertheless holds some of Jarre's most inviting melodic invention, ranging from pleasant nostalgia to chilling terror.

Paul Andrew MacLean

After the Fox

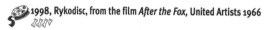
1998, Rykodisc, from the film *After the Fox*, United Artists 1966 ♫♫♫

album notes: Music: Burt Bacharach.

Unfortunately, Burt Bacharach didn't write many soundtracks, which means we have to make do with those that are available. *After the Fox,* an innocuous comedy set in Italy, elicited a score that was pleasantly sunny and conventional, in a 1960s kind of way. No need to go into too many details about this madcap adventure in which a sly con artist (Peter Sellers) poses as a celebrated Italian filmmaker, the better to steal genuine gold bullion. Victor Mature co-starred as a hefty actor on the way out, whose presence in the "film" added credibility to the plot conceived by the foxy Sellers. Not a great score by any stretch of the imagination, but one that invites repeated listening and always leaves a pleasant glow. The bits of dialogue neither add nor detract from the overall impression, although they do not make the soundtrack, which runs at a scant 33 minutes, any longer.

Didier C. Deutsch

Afterglow

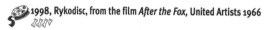
1998, Columbia Records, from the film *Afterglow*, Sony Pictures Classics 1998 ♫♫♫

album notes: Music: Mark Isham; **Featured Musicians:** Charles Lloyd, saxophone; Gary Burton, vibes; Mark Isham, trumpet, flumpet; Sid Page, violin; Geri Allen, piano; Billy Higgins, drums; Jeff Littleton, bass.

A modern score that expresses the beauty of the romantic side of jazz. Mark Isham has always favored the harmonically darker side of jazz. These fuller jazz harmonies give the music a warm and mysterious feeling. Isham also has a tone that's part Miles Davis, part Freddie Hubbard. "After the Glow Is Gone" is pure, straight-ahead jazz. "Veses . . ." accents the tender tone of Charles Lloyd. "A Life Suspended" evokes Miles Davis and Kenny Wheeler. "The Frenzy" is Coltrane-inspired, with Lloyd reaching for the heavens. "Afterglow" is a beautiful ballad that could have come from the pen of Herbie Hancock, with Lloyd providing just the right mood to the song. All in all, a beautiful score that captures just the right amount of jazz and film music.

Bob Belden

The Age of Innocence

1993, Epic Soundtrax/Sony Music, from the film *The Age of Innocence*, Columbia Pictures, 1993 🎬🎬🎬🎬
album notes: Music: Elmer Bernstein; **Conductor:** Elmer Bernstein.

This is a surprisingly different effort from Elmer Bernstein, an unexpectedly delightful symphonic waltz that captures the flavor of director Martin Scorsese's period romance where a man had to marry the right kind of woman, not his true love, the one with a past. The album is marvelously sequenced, playing like a rich melodic concert. You can close your eyes and allow the music to effortlessly transport you back a century. Although it will probably never rank with *The Magnificent Seven* as a pillar of his career, this score is nonetheless one of the finest works by Bernstein. Several classical pieces, excerpted in the film, lead off the album, preceding the main theme which serves as the album's overture.

David Hirsch

Agnes of God

1992, Varèse Sarabande Records, from the film *Agnes of God*, Columbia Pictures, 1985 🎬🎬🎬🎬
album notes: Music: Georges Delerue; **Orchestra:** The Toronto Symphony Orchestra; **Conductor:** Georges Delerue.

A dramatic film with a religious background provided Georges Delerue with the opportunity to write a deeply moving score in which his natural flair for long romantic lines effectively combined with the mystical moods suggested by the locale, an isolated convent where a naive nun, Agnes, apparently gave birth to a baby whom she subsequently murdered, a mystery investigated by a psychiatrist (Jane Fonda) assigned to the case. Throughout, the moods are quietly evoked in a captivating series of cues (unfortunately untitled) that subtly underscore the more poignant moments in the story and also make for an intelligent, if at times eerie, audio experience.

Didier C. Deutsch

The Agony and the Ecstasy

1998, Varèse-Sarabande, from the film *The Agony and the Ecstasy*, 20th Century Fox 1965 🎬🎬🎬🎬
album notes: Music: Alex North; **Conductor:** Jerry Goldsmith.

A recent entry in the Varèse-Sarabande catalogue, this re-recording of Alex North's sumptuous score for the 1965 epic about Michelangelo, Pope Julius II, and the painting of the Sistine Chapel ceiling in Rome comes with all the right credentials: none other than Jerry Goldsmith conducts the well-trained Royal Scottish National Orchestra, with Robert Townson producing. While it misses some cues found in the original soundtrack album available at one time on Cloud Nine (coupled with George Antheil's *The Pride and the Passion*), this recording substitutes other selections and eventually towers above its predecessor, if only because of the sheer quality of the end product. When a score is that deserving, and when it elicits this kind of treatment in the hands of such professionals, the only thing one can do is savor the results.

Didier C. Deutsch

The Agony and the Ecstasy/
The Pride and the Passion

1991, Cloud Nine Records, from the films *The Agony and the Ecstasy*, 20th Century Fox, 1965, and *The Pride and the Passion*, United Artists, 1957 🎬🎬🎬
album notes: The Agony and the Ecstasy: Music: Alex North; **Conductor:** Alex North; **The Pride and the Passion: Music:** George Antheil; **Conductor:** Ernest Gold.

While best remembered as one of Frank Sinatra's colossal film flops, *The Pride and the Passion* merits attention primarily because of Sinatra's pairing with his celebrated co-stars, Cary Grant and Sophia Loren. Despite the fairly thin story line, composer George Antheil's score survives as a thoughtful work of art, and magnificent staging aside, the film's single appealing quality.

Antheil effectively captures the spirit of the Spanish setting, beginning with a bold, rhythmic "Main Title" that is rooted in the elements of Latin American music, particularly the bolero. What follows is an array of romantic and dramatic themes, based on authentic Hispanic motifs, and Iberian folk music. The CD issue utilizes the original 1957 Capitol Records masters, and other than a bit of analog tape hiss, the monophonic sound is enjoyable.

The Agony and the Ecstasy tells the story of the intense artistic and personal conflict between artist Michaelangelo and Pope Julius II, after the Papal command for the artist to paint the ceiling of the Sistine Chapel. Utilizing both modern and ancient instrumental voicings, composer Alex North stunningly paints a portrait that is at once majestic, religious, and reflective of the tension of the relationship between the artist, his work, and the Pope.

With the original masters culled from the film's soundstage recordings, the stereo recording displays its age, and could use a dose of modern sonic restoration. Nonetheless, this is a splendid score, and a most enjoyable recording.

Charles L. Granata

Aida

1999, Rocket/Island Records, from the Disney stage production *Aida*, 1999 🎵🎵🎵

album notes: Songs: Elton John, Tim Rice.

Somewhere out there, Verdi is spinning in his grave. That's because pop star Elton John and lyricist and former Andrew Lloyd Weber–partner Tim Rice—the duo that distinguished themselves with Walt Disney's Oscar-winning music for *The Lion King*—have appropriated the plot of Verdi's opera *Aida* and made it their own pop extravaganza with this all-star recording (and subsequent stage adaptation) that takes it from classic to contemporary. This new *Aida* has a few splendid moments, including the crunchy soul of Lenny Kravitz's "Like Father like Son," Sting's reggae romp through "Another Pyramid" (co-produced by Sly Dunbar and Robbie Shakespeare), Boyz II Men's deftly harmonized "Not Me," the nice teaming of Tina Turner and Angelique Kidjo for "Easy as Life," and James Taylor's silky warm "How I Know You." John himself is a dueting fool throughout the album, although the one that really clicks is "The Messenger," which he sings with 1960s thrush Lulu. This won't make us forget Verdi's *Aida,* but if it makes a few pop fans curious to hear the original, it will justify its existence.

Gary Graff

Ain't Misbehavin'

1987, RCA Victor, from the Broadway production *Ain't Misbehavin',* 1978 🎵🎵🎵🎵

album notes: Music: Thomas "Fats" Waller; **Lyrics:** Andy Razaf, Lester A. Santly, Clarence Williams, Richard Maltby Jr., Murray Horwitz, Billy Rose, J.C. Johnson, George Marion Jr., Ed Kirkeby; **Cast:** Nell Carter, Andre De Shields, Armelia McQueen, Ken Page, Charlaine Woodard.

The songs of Thomas "Fats" Waller received the Broadway treatment in a great revue that not only created a stir at the time it opened on May 9, 1978, but paved the way for other similar shows, including *Sophisticated Ladies* and *Eubie.* With just five fantastically gifted performers on stage (Nell Carter, Armelia McQueen, Charlaine Woodard, Ken Page, and Andre De Shields), a solid band led by Luther Henderson, and a wealth of wonderful numbers, the show became the most talked-about

hit on Broadway that season, won several Tony Awards, including the one for Best Musical, and enjoyed an unprecedented run of 1,604 performances.

Didier C. Deutsch

Air America

1990, MCA Records, from the film *Air America,* Carolco Pictures, 1990 🎵🎵🎵🎵

A bright, intelligent pop collection, this compilation represents the soundtrack for the film based on Christopher Robbins's 1979 book, about two pilots flying the CIA's "dope airline," the agency's privately owned Air America, which was used to deal in drugs in order to finance the war effort in Southeast Asia. The songs, representative of the era, contain several interesting selections, and unlike some compilations that become quite redundant when they are tagged as "soundtrack" albums, this one makes sense and is quite enjoyable.

Didier C. Deutsch

Air Bud

1997, Hollywood Records, from the film *Air Bud,* Walt Disney 1997 🎵

album notes: Music: Brahm Wenger.

Air Bud is an entertaining children's movie about a lonely kid who befriends a stray dog with Jordan-like basketball playing abilities. There is, on the other hand, nothing entertaining about Brahm Wenger's unmemorable score for the film, or the songs by Jimmy Z and Gilbert O'Sullivan.

Beth Krakower

Air Force One

1997, Varèse-Sarabande, from the film *Air Force One,* Columbia Pictures, 1997 🎵🎵🎵🎵

album notes: Music: Jerry Goldsmith; **Conductor:** Jerry Goldsmith.

A fast-paced, gripping thriller about a steadfast U.S. president kidnapped by Russian neo-nationalists and faced with an impossible dilemma—give in to the terrorists' demands or sacrifice his country's interests and the lives of his wife and daughter—*Air Force One* gave Jerry Goldsmith an opportunity to write a scorching score, in which martial accents dominate. At the center of the score (and this CD), "The Hijacking" is a taut cue that quickly builds to a climax, and pretty much sums up the general tone of this exciting release.

Didier C. Deutsch

Air Power/Holocaust

1990, Koch Int'l, from the CBS-TV documentary series *Air Power*, 1956, and the NBC-TV miniseries *Holocaust*, 1978 ♫♫♫

album notes: Music: Norman Dello Joio, Morton Gould; **Conductor:** David Amos.

Two major modern-day classical composers, Norman Dello Joio and Morton Gould, find themselves "coupled" in this release, which offers selections from their respective scores to two highly publicized television documentary series. *Air Power,* made in 1956 by CBS News, was a comprehensive, 26-part production about the history of aviation, from mankind's early attempts to its ultimate use as a weapon of war. Dello Joio later on assembled the various cues into an orchestral suite in three parts, "Frolics of the Early Days" (tracks 2–4 in the present recording), a rollicking account; "Mission in the Sky" (tracks 5–8), a descriptive bombing raid over Germany; and "War Scenes" (tracks 9–14), detailing various related World War II episodes.

Presented by NBC in 1978, *Holocaust* was a dramatic miniseries that focused on the attempts by the Nazis to annihilate a Jewish family during the war. Morton Gould devised his score around several themes that focused on various historical incidents ("Crystal Night," "Babi Yar"), or that depicted the series' characters ("Berta and Joseph's Theme," a tune for piano and orchestra). Performance by the Krakow Philharmonic Orchestra, conducted by David Amos, is polished and attractive, although the recording level seems at times unusually low.

Didier C. Deutsch

Airport

1993, Varèse Sarabande Records, from the film *Airport,* Universal Pictures, 1970 ♫♫♫♫

album notes: Music: Alfred Newman; **Conductor:** Alfred Newman.

Alfred Newman received a posthumous Oscar nomination for this score, in which he deftly created a set of contemporary cues to evoke the passion and drama on board a jet taken over by a terrorist who wants the plane to land at an airport during a snow blizzard. To say that they don't write scores like this anymore is an understatement. Melodic to a fault, and thoroughly attractive, the various cues stand out on their own, making this CD as enjoyable a listening experience as it is a memento of the film itself. The popular "Love Theme" ranks high among the best selections here, along with tracks like "Inez' Theme," "Ada Quonsett Stowaway," "Triangle!," or the action-packed "Emergency Landing!"

Didier C. Deutsch

Aladdin

1992, Walt Disney Records, from the animated feature *Aladdin,* Walt Disney, 1992 ♫♫♫♫

album notes: Music: Alan Menken; **Lyrics:** Howard Ashman, Tim Rice.

Following the success of the *Little Mermaid* and *Beauty and the Beast,* Alan Menken and Howard Ashman turned their talents to creating an animated musical based on the 1001-night tale of Aladdin. A large measure of the film's success was due to Robin Williams's inspired performance as the voice of the Genie (which was drawn after Williams's mimicries). The score itself was true to the formula already set by the previous two films, with a standard share of romantic numbers for Ali and Jasmine (vocals by Brad Kane and Lea Salonga), some exciting instrumentals, a couple of humorous moments for the Genie, and a hit song ("A Whole New World"), which won an Academy Award that year.

Didier C. Deutsch

The Alamo

1995, Sony Legacy, from the film *The Alamo,* Batjac/MGM, 1960 ♫♫♫♫

album notes: Music: Dimitri Tiomkin; **Conductor:** Dimitri Tiomkin.

Christopher Palmer, in his book *The Composer in Hollywood,* cites *The Alamo* as "the best of the great Tiomkin westerns." Few would dispute this, despite the fact that some might argue in favor of some of the composer's other classic film scores, including *High Noon, Gunfight at O.K. Corral, The Guns of Navarone* and *Rio Bravo.*

Opinions aside, one thing is certain: *The Alamo* is an absolute treasure! Bursting with color and drama, Tiomkin's score contributes mightily to the successful realization of the story, as envisioned by producer, director, and star John Wayne. All of the excitement that sparked the magic of the film and its music are vividly preserved in this newly remastered edition, which restores eight musical cues that were left off the original Columbia soundtrack LP.

Charles L. Granata

Albino Alligator

1997, 4AD Records, from the film *Albino Alligator,* Miramax Pictures, 1997 ♫♫♫

album notes: Music: Michael Brook.

Newcomer Michael Brook fashioned a satisfying moody score for this story, set in New Orleans, about a trio of misfits involved in a robbery, who seek refuge in an old bar below street level with no windows and no backdoor exit, where they are soon trapped by police and federal agents (the title of the film apparently refers to a pool-playing ruse in which a player misses a shot on purpose in order to better defeat his opponent later). The jazz, in turns jazzy and disquieting, is particularly effective at enhancing the claustrophobic atmosphere that permeates much of the film, an impression further reinforced in the gloomy rendition of the Harold Arlen–Ted Koehler song, "Ill Wind."

Didier C. Deutsch

Alexander the Great/Barabbas

🎬 1996, DRG Records, from the films *Alexander the Great,* United Artists, 1956, and *Barabbas,* Columbia Pictures, 1962 ♪♪♪

album notes: Music: Mario Nascimbene; **Conductor:** Mario Nascimbene.

Following the success of his score for *The Barefoot Contessa* (q.v.), Mario Nascimbene wrote the music for *Alexander the Great,* a big screen epic starring Richard Burton as the famed conqueror and military genius. In it, he essentially developed two sets of cues, one played by a large brass ensemble to evoke Alexander's armies on the move, the other using acoustic Oriental instruments for the more intimate scenes. Both play off each other in this recording to create a vivid musical tapestry befitting the subject matter.

Equally original and impressive is the composer's score for *Barabbas,* a retelling of the Crucifixion, starring Anthony Quinn as the thief and murderer whose life was traded for Jesus Christ. Using a sound-mixing console to create a wide range of unusual sonorities, Nascimbene wrote a score that is evocative and strangely attractive. The only drawback here is the overall sound quality of the recording, very dry in both scores, with some notable distortion and poor editing in *Alexander,* and a generally muffled tone in *Barabbas,* made all the more striking in these digital transfers.

Didier C. Deutsch

Alfie

🎬 1997, MCA Records, from the film *Alfie,* Paramount Pictures, 1966 ♪♪♪♪♪

album notes: Music: Sonny Rollins; **Conductor:** Oliver Nelson; **Featured Musicians:** Sonny Rollins, Oliver Nelson, Bob Ashton, tenor sax; Jimmy Cleveland, J.J. Johnson, trombone; Phil Woods, alto sax; Danny Bank, baritone sax; Kenny Burrell, guitar; Roger Kellaway, piano; Walter Booker, bass; Frankie Dunlop, drums.

Everybody, it seems, remembers the song "What's it all about, Alfie?," warbled by Dionne Warwick, so this soundtrack album, which does not even include it, may come as a refreshing surprise. Actually, the song itself, by Burt Bacharach and Hal David, never made it into the final version of the film. However, the jazzy score, written and performed by Sonny Rollins, is an essential element that contributes enormously to the success of this modern-day story of a charming, if somewhat glib and at

times cynical Cockney romeo, whose sole pursuit in life is to bed down any woman crossing his path. The album, long a favorite among jazz collectors, finds the tenor saxophonist at the top of his creativity, surrounded by many familiar jazz aces, including J.J. Johnson, Phil Woods, Kenny Burrell, Roger Kellaway, and arranger Oliver Nelson. The long selections enable everyone to "stretch" and make some excellent music in the process.

Didier C. Deutsch

Alfredo Alfredo

🎬 1993, CAM Records/Italy, from the film *Alfredo Alfredo (Alfredo I Love You),* Cineriz, 1972 ♪♪♪

album notes: Music: Carlo Rustichelli; **Conductor:** Carlo Rustichelli.

This sly romantic comedy, directed by Pietro Germi (his last film), starred Dustin Hoffman as a shy bank employee, married to a jealous and possessive woman, who thinks he's discovered true love at last when he meets the lovely Caroline. When divorce becomes legal in Italy, Alfredo leaves his wife, and marries Caroline . . . who turns out to be just as jealous and possessive. Setting this societal tale to music, Carlo Rustichelli wrote a series of cues that reflect the main character's romantic leanings, his dreams and his desires, as well as the comedic situations in which he invariably finds himself. It's an enjoyable score that lacks some unity, and consists of themes that are often much too short to make a solid impression. This recording may be difficult to find. Check with a used CD store, mail-order company, or a dealer specializing in rare, out-of-print, or import recordings.

Didier C. Deutsch

Alice in Wonderland

🎬 1998, Disney, from the film *Alice in Wonderland,* Disney 1951 ♪♪♪

album notes: Music: Oliver Wallace; **Songs:** Bob Hilliard, Sammy Fain; **Conductor:** Oliver Wallace.

If anyone doubted that the Disney illustrators must have been on acid, *Alice in Wonderland* might provide positive proof: nowhere, it seems, was their imagination more unbridled and their creativity more strange than in this brilliant cartoon retelling of the old Lewis Carroll story. Fortunately (or unfortunately?), this soundtrack album barely tells the tale: it contains all the great songs from the film, bits of dialogue, instrumental bridges, and everything one might expect to find in a Disney soundtrack album, but it is quite straightforward. And enjoyable, too! Although, while listening to it, one misses the bright colors, wild patterns, and crazy concepts that made the film so unique.

Didier C. Deutsch

Alice's Restaurant

1998, Rykodisc, from the film *Alice's Restaurant,* United Artists 1968 ♪♪♪♪

album notes: Music: Garry Sherman; Songs: Arlo Guthrie.

This movie is based on the "talking blues" song by folk artist Arlo Guthrie about the true story of how one Thanksgiving he tried to bring some garbage that had accumulated at a restaurant owned by his friends, Alice and Ray, to a dump. The dump was closed for the holiday, which forced Arlo to dump the garbage off the side of the road, leading to a huge investigation and Arlo's arrest, thereafter preventing him from being drafted. Director Arthur Penn heard the song, decided to film it with Arlo Guthrie brilliantly cast as Arlo Guthrie, Officer Obie as Officer Obie, the blind judge as the blind judge, and Alice and Ray, played by Pat Quinn and James Broderick, as extras; and for this Penn received an Oscar nomination in 1969. The first time on CD, this release contains 11 bonus tracks, thus proving you can get all the music from the movie that you want at Alice's Restaurant.

Didier C. Deutsch

Alien

1988, Silva Screen, from the film *Alien,* 20th Century Fox, 1979 ♪♪♪♪

album notes: Music: Jerry Goldsmith; Conductor: Jerry Goldsmith.

Jerry Goldsmith not only set the tone for the series with his dark melodies, but he once again developed a style that would be often mimicked throughout the genre. Brooding, sometimes romantically melodic, the score for the first film is peppered with various shrill and innovative percussion effects that set the heart racing. The monster, vaguely seen through most of the film, is represented both on- and off-screen through Goldsmith's music. What is most surprising about the soundtrack album is that it reflects the composer's original intent for the film, the final score having been alerted with "tracked" cues by director Ridley Scott who used Howard Hanson's Symphony #2 "Romantic" as the finale and end title, and cues from Goldsmith's own score to *Freud.*

David Hirsch

Alien Nation

1990, GNP Crescendo, from the television series *Alien Nation,* 20th Century Fox TV, 1989-90 ♪♪♪♪♪

album notes: Music: Steve Dorff, Larry Herbstritt, David Kurtz.

One of the most intriguing aspects of this series is its remarkably creative and melodic score, a rarity in a medium that tends to demand subtle and oft-times indiscernible work. Scoring du-ties for the series were divided between composers Steve Dorff, Larry Herbstritt, and David Kurtz, with producer Ken Johnson providing the alien language lyrics for the vocals. The principal characters are members of a civilization of aliens, marooned in central Los Angeles. The composers sought to create a unique musical signature for their society by combining Caribbean and African rhythms with a progression of weird vocal and electronic effects. The album features a variety of intriguing alien "pop" tunes ("Tenctonlian (sic) Mode Groove," "Slag Pop"), but the most stimulating are the religious ceremonial chants. "Howdy Pod," a prayer for childbirth, is one of the most memorable ones with an *a cappella* vocal that segues into a gentle, synthesized theme. A superior score because of its unique and delightful mix of vocals with electronic and acoustical instruments.

David Hirsch

Alien Resurrection

1998, RCA Victor, from the film *Alien Resurrection,* 20th Century-Fox 1998 ♪♪♪♪

album notes: Music: John Frizzell; Conductor: Artie Kane.

John Frizzell's eerie "Main Title," a straightforward big orchestral theme mixed with sudden ominous, dissonant accords that presages that something's afoot, is a great opener for this soundtrack to the fourth entry in the *Alien* series, again starring Sigourney Weaver. There is little need to go into this space-based sci-fi horror story: essentially, with some slight modifications, it's the same plot that's being successfully exploited, although director Jean-Pierre Jeunet (of *Delicatessen* and *The City of Lost Children* fame) brings a fresh vision to this tale and manages to keep the franchise interesting and surprising. The distorted chords and strange effects in Frizzell's score also keep the suspense going ("Post-Op," "Face Huggers," "What's Inside Purvis") and create a strange sensation of their own. Two long cues, "They Swim . . ." and "The Battle of the Newborn," enable the composer to expand on his orchestral concepts, with rewarding results. It's a bit formulaic, but it is still effective.

Didier C. Deutsch

Alien 3

1992, MCA Records, from the film *Alien 3,* 20th Century Fox, 1992 ♪♪♪♪

album notes: Music: Elliot Goldenthal; Conductor: Jonathan Sheffer.

For the third film in the series, Elliot Goldenthal created an intricately orchestrated symphony that is overwhelmingly sad, sometimes frightening but not without beauty, and curiously closer in tone to another Goldsmith score, *The Omen,* particularly in its use of a boy soprano soloist on "Agnus Dei." This motif not only reflects the religious zeal of the prison inmates, but also prefaces Ripley's own pseudo-crucifixion at the end of the film. Goldenthal is most effective when he represents the spider-like Face Hugger with rattling sounds, in the track "Bait and Chase," in which he breaks from his usual style in an innovative technique that shocks the listener. This is also the case in the attempted rape of Ripley ("Wreckage and Rape"), in which a violent flurry of percussion and screaming vocal effect is used to reflect the vileness of the attack. This score is far superior to the film.

David Hirsch

Aliens

1986, Varèse Sarabande Records, from the film *Aliens*, 20th Century Fox, 1986 ♪♪♪

album notes: Music: James Horner; **Orchestra:** The London Symphony Orchestra; **Conductor:** James Horner.

Although James Horner created a military motif and a bolder sound to represent director James Cameron's tale of U.S. Space Marines versus an entire horde of creatures, the basis of his score, particularly the plodding "creeping" figure, is derived from Goldsmith's work. Where Horner deviates the most is on bold action cues such as "Going After Newt" or "Resolution" (a cue tracked into the finale of *Die Hard* and countless film trailers). Standard percussion effects are used to establish tension while electronics represent the aliens. Aram Khachaturian's adagio from his "Gayne Ballet Suite" is incorporated into the main and closing titles, the first of several adaptations of this piece. In all, it is an average effort for Horner, not without its moments.

David Hirsch

Alive

1993, Hollywood Records, from the film *Alive*, Touchstone Pictures, 1993 ♪♪♪♪

album notes: Music: James Newton Howard; **Conductor:** Marty Paich.

A gruesome tale of survival in the subfreezing Andes following a plane crash (resulting in cannibalism, no less!), *Alive*, based on a true story, received an atmospheric score from James Newton Howard, who wrote appropriately sullen (one might be tempted to say frigid) cues reflective of the intense action and its desolate locale. The evocation of other situations ("Home"), enhanced by the current situation of the survivors, is hinted at in an attractive fashion, but the *piece de resistance,* so to speak, is the five-minute "Eating," in which the composer turns the ultimate act of survival into . . . an almost palatable morsel. The film's topic might not have been to everyone's taste, but this score should.

Didier C. Deutsch

All Dogs Go to Heaven

1989, Curb Records, from the animated feature *All Dogs Go to Heaven,* United Artists, 1989 ♪♪♪♪

album notes: Music: Ralph Burns; **Songs:** Al Kasha, Joel Hirschhorn, Michael Lloyd, Charles Strouse, T.J. Kuenster.

The incredible success of the Disney animated features was bound to compel other animators to try and tap the same market of youngsters and their captive parents, while providing songwriters with another opportunity to create catchy songs to beef up the inevitable soundtrack albums. Created by Don Bluth, the two *All Dogs Go to Heaven* movies rank among the best efforts in the genre, though the two CDs that accompany them differ wildly in impact and appeal. This original soundtrack, with a lively score by Ralph Burns and diversified songs by Charles Strouse (of *Bye Bye Birdie* and *Annie* fame), Al Kasha, and Joel Hirschhorn, has a definite Caribbean flair (check out the infectious calypso instrumental, "Mardi Gras," or the colorful "What's Mine Is Yours"). It is a melodic, bouncy affair, superbly pulled off by some of the performers who lent their talents—Burt Reynolds, Dom DeLuise, Melba Moore, Irene Cara, and Freddie Jackson, among them.

Didier C. Deutsch

All Dogs Go to Heaven 2

1996, Angel Records, from the animated feature *All Dogs Go to Heaven 2,* MGM, 1996 ♪♪♪

album notes: Music: Mark Watters; **Songs:** Barry Mann, Cynthia Weil.

This sequel to *All Dogs Go to Heaven* has catchy songs by Barry Mann and Cynthia Weil, and a portentous score by Mark Watters that dwarfs the simplicity of Ralph Burns's contribution to the original. Sheena Easton heads the cast of singers who perform the songs here, including Jesse Corti and Jim Cummings, and Broadway veteran George Hearn teams up with Ernest Borgnine for a devastating "It Feels So Good to Be Bad," the CD's highlight. But somehow the element of fun that made the first album so enjoyable seems to be sorely missing here.

Didier C. Deutsch

All I Want for Christmas

1991, Curb Records, from the film *All I Want for Christmas,* Paramount 1991 ♪♪♪

album notes: Music: Bruce Broughton; **Conductor:** Bruce Broughton.

Christmas-time comedies usually prompt composers to come up with some of their glitziest material (i.e., John Williams and *Home Alone*): the season (and the subject) does not suggest somber thoughts, and as a result many scores are brightly inventive and melodically enjoyable. Case in point is this set of cues by Bruce Broughton for the 1991 *All I Want for Christmas,* which does not qualify as Oscar material, but is congenially entertaining and listenable. This charming entry, about two kids who want to bring their estranged parents back together for Christmas, is strictly lightweight, something that finds an echo in the score itself. Adding to the overall moods are several pop songs, in which "All I Want," by Stephen Bishop, "Stagger Lee," by Lloyd Price, and "Yakety Yak," by the Coasters easily stand out.

see also: Home Alone, Jingle All the Way, Christmas in Connecticut

Didier C. Deutsch

All over Me

1998, TVT Records, from the film *All over Me,* FineLine 1998 ♪

album notes: Music: Miki Navazio; **Featured Musicians:** Mike Navazio, guitars; Erik Friedlander, cello; Drew Gress, bass; Grisha Alexieu, drums, percussion.

If what passes at times as "music" or "songs" were only mildly interesting, or interestingly performed, one might excuse the appalling fact that much of today's songs are totally devoid of quality. Such is the case with this contemporary soundtrack album that contains songs performed by screechers (rather than belters or crooners), some of whom, like the vocalist from Babes in Toyland, can't even carry a tune. The high recording level of course doesn't help, as it tends to emphasize the total lack of melody in most of these selections. One refreshing exception is the Ozark Mountain Daredevils' "Jackie Blue," which evidences a strong melody, some good lyrics, and a catchy performance. Wish all the tracks were that good.

Didier C. Deutsch

All the Brothers Were Valiant

1991, Prometheus Records/Belgium, from the film *All the Brothers Were Valiant,* MGM, 1953 ♪♪♪♪

album notes: Music: Miklos Rozsa; **Orchestra:** The MGM Studio Orchestra; **Conductor:** Miklos Rozsa.

A seafaring adventure film starring Robert Taylor, Stewart Granger, and Ann Blyth, *All the Brothers Were Valiant* received a commanding, rousing Miklos Rozsa score, which ended up in shambles in the final version of the film. This recording restores it the way the composer created it, and it is a fitting companion to the many titles on CD under his name. For this story of two brothers with contrasting characters aboard a New England whaler, their love for the same woman, and their search for an elusive treasure, Rozsa wrote a series of cues that capture the drama and action in this colorful production. Sonically, the recording could have used a little reverb, but the

stereo imaging and the close micing belie the age of the original session tapes.

Didier C. Deutsch

Almost an Angel

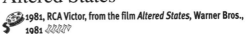

1990, Varèse Sarabande Records, from the film *Almost an Angel,* Paramount Pictures, 1990 ♪♪♪♪

album notes: Music: Maurice Jarre; **Conductor:** Maurice Jarre.

Spearheaded by the song "Some Wings," attractively performed by Vanessa Williams, the score for this romantic fantasy unfolds in atypical fashion, with exquisite melodies lining this story of a con man and electronics expert who has a revelation following an accident and dedicates the rest of his life doing some good around himself. The mixture of bold orchestral chords, synth counterpoints, heavenly choir and organ obbligato (for the out-of-body experience by the con man who "dreams" he meets with God) provides a diversified texture that enhances the appeal of this concoction, presented without a break, as a continuous suite. The 10-minute-plus "Let There Be Light" brings all these elements into sharp focus for a last musical exploration that reveals the fluidity in Jarre's style and his knack for striking melodic concepts.

Didier C. Deutsch

Altered States

1981, RCA Victor, from the film *Altered States,* Warner Bros., 1981 ♪♪♪♪

album notes: Music: John Corigliano; **Conductor:** Christopher Keene.

Looking back from the jaundiced perspective of the '90s it's hard to believe that a single year, 1981, could produce three scores as memorable as John Williams's *Raiders of the Lost Ark,* Alex North's *Dragonslayer,* and *Altered States,* concert hall composer John Corigliano's mind-blowing score for director Ken Russell's trippy sci-fi tale of one man's exploration of racial memory and its terrible consequences. Corigliano wrote a primarily acoustic work that is powerful, frightening, disorienting, and as mind-expanding as the peyote that William Hurt's obsessed anthropologist ingests in order to facilitate his archetypal, hallucinogenic sense memories in the film. The composer produced wild, colorful passages to underscore the film's spectacular hallucination sequences and coiling, rumbling low string and brass clusters to illustrate Dick Smith's remarkable makeup transformations as Hurt's body is physically altered by his experiences. There are also stunning evocations of primitivism as Hurt experiences memories of ancient rituals and is himself transformed into a loping man-beast late in the film. Corigliano is just as adept at characterizing the film's dramatic and psychological elements: There's a deeply disturbing distor-

Tom Hulce in Amadeus. **(The Kobal Collection)**

tion of a religious chorale associated with Hurt's father in the film, as well as a rich and moving love theme that resolves this score's incredibly agitated final passage. It's a wild, virtuoso effort that won't be to everyone's taste, but a must for anyone interested in late 20th-century composition.

Jeff Bond

Always

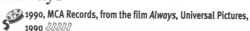 1990, MCA Records, from the film *Always,* Universal Pictures, 1990 ♪♪♪♪

album notes: Music: John Williams; Conductor: John Williams.

Although the main characters in the film fight forest fires from the air, this is really an intimate story of three people. Pete, a pilot who has been killed, has unfinished business keeping him earthbound and he must guide his love, Dorinda, and old friend Hap through the pain. Despite the fact that Steven Spielberg's camera work captures the scope of the wide American vistas, this John Williams score is remarkably restrained, delicate, as if it all existed on glass. Even the action cue "The Rescue Opera-

tion" is overwhelmed with a gentleness that contrasts with the action. An appropriately dreamy New Age-style cue "Pete in Heaven," is used in a scene set in a fire ravaged forest where Pete talks to an angel. The album features 47 minutes of instrumental music with five country/western tunes heard in the bar hangout, and two versions of the film's apropos signature song, "Smoke Gets in Your Eyes."

David Hirsch

Amadeus

1984, Fantasy Records, from the film *Amadeus,* Orion Pictures, 1984 ♪♪♪♪♪

album notes: **Music:** Wolfgang-Amadeus Mozart; **Orchestra:** The Academy of St. Martin-in-the-Fields; **Conductor:** Neville Marriner.

From beginning to end, this album is a real treat! One of the most outstanding elements in this outrageous film is the use of music. As a result, each track brings to mind a specific dramatic moment in the film in which it is heard. Of course, there is more music on this album than in the film because only fragments were utilized at key moments by the director. However, the longer excerpts give the listener the joy of hearing more of this wonderful music. The performances are all excellent and fully up to the standards expected by the classical crowd. While the selections include many familiar works, there are also enough unfamiliar or unusual excerpts to interest and challenge even the most reticent connoisseur. For those who are knowledgeable about Mozart and classical music, and for those who aren't but are interested, this album is a must.

Jerry J. Thomas

Amarcord

1991, CAM Records, from the film *Amarcord,* Warner Bros., 1973

album notes: Music: Nino Rota; **Conductor:** Carlo Savina.

Nino Rota's vibrant musical cues are forever linked to the best films made by Federico Fellini, but this "recollection" from the director's youth evidently inspired the composer to write a score that teems with bouncy, zestful selections. Whether illustrating some of the wild denizens in Fellini's memories (a saucy hairdresser, a crazy man called Giudizio, the fascists who take over the town), or the myriad incidents that provided fodder in their everyday lives and contributed to the film's disjointed narrative, Rota's score is beautifully illustrative and melodically striking. Released on the Italian CAM label (distributed in this country), it is well worth hunting down even if you have never seen the film.

Didier C. Deutsch

Amazing Grace and Chuck

1987, Varèse Sarabande Records, from the film *Amazing Grace and Chuck,* Tri-Star Pictures, 1987

album notes: Music: Elmer Bernstein; **Conductor:** Elmer Bernstein; **Featured Musicians:** Klaus Koenig, oboe; Cynthia Millar, Ondes Martenot.

The anti-nuclear message in the film, about a Little League pitcher, Chuck, whose refusal to play after he is shown a missile under the field where he is practicing and eventually provokes the near cancellation of the baseball season when the pro athletes join in his protest, may be hokey, but it prompted Elmer Bernstein to write a delightful score, oozing with emotion and lyricism. Contrasting the innocence and simple-life pleasures of Chuck, expressed by the oboe, the ominous tone of the low strings and the Ondes Martenot and the composer's signature syncopations signal the threat posed by the "other side," those who endanger civilization with their nuclear arsenal. The conflict between the two, and the more personal relationship that develops between the kid and Amazing Grace Smith, star of the Boston Celtics and Chuck's first supporter, eventually lead to the rousing "Final Victory," a track that resolves everything, at least where the film is concerned. It's a brilliant score you shouldn't miss.

Didier C. Deutsch

American Buffalo/Threesome

1996, Varèse Sarabande Records, from the films *American Buffalo,* Samuel Goldwyn, 1996, and *Threesome,* TriStar Pictures, 1994

album notes: Music: Thomas Newman.

Two scores by the vastly talented Thomas Newman, the first for a claustrophobic character study based on David Mamet's play about an attempted robbery which never happens; the second for a smart coming-of-age comedy with all the trappings the genre itself invokes. The contrasting moods in both films are fully explored, with *American Buffalo* conjuring up several tracks that are dominated by heavy percussive effects, and booming bass guitar lines, reflective of the confined, one-set environment in which the mostly psychological action takes place. On a purely audio basis, it has its moments, but it is not the kind of music one might want to listen to on a bad day. Conversely, *Threesome* features some light and airy cues, pleasant to the ear and quite attractive, with repetitive lines building up in layers to create a melodic texture.

Didier C. Deutsch

American Graffiti

1973, MCA Records, from the film *American Graffiti,* Universal Pictures, 1983

The first, and by far the best, rock 'n' roll compilation you're likely to find anywhere, this soundtrack album to this film by George Lucas sums up everything that was and still is so exciting about the early years of pop-rock music. Even if Elvis is sorely missing from this double CD of oldies/goodies, there is enough here to satisfy the most demanding customer, including all the glorious hits you might ever want to hear from these exciting years when rock songs didn't last more than two minutes, performed by the stars who made them famous, Bill Haley & The Comets, Buddy Holly, The Beach Boys, Chuck Berry, The Platters, Fats Domino, The Big Bopper, and on and on. An eye-popping, ear-blasting collection that'll keep you bopping for days on end.

Didier C. Deutsch

American History X

1998, Angel Records, from the New Line Cinema film *American History X,* 1998

album notes: Music: Anne Dudley; **Conductor:** Anne Dudley.

Gene Kelly and Leslie Caron in An American in Paris. **(The Kobal Collection)**

The last thing one would expect from a movie about neo-Nazi skinheads in southern California is a full-blown orchestral score. But that's the beauty of it. This movie is not a fun one; it's very disturbing, as we see on-screen flashbacks about how a normal kid can easily be corrupted into a life of hate, crime, and redemption, and how he now must prevent his brother from doing the same thing. Faced with this kind of story, composer Anne Dudley created a masterpiece, presented here pretty much as it was heard in the film, with none of the accompanying hardcore hate music. Particularly evocative are the cues for the flashback scenes, and (without giving too much of the story away) the final death scene.

Didier C. Deutsch

An American in Paris

1996, Rhino Records, from the screen musical *An American in Paris*, MGM, 1951 🎬🎬🎬🎬

album notes: Music: George Gershwin; **Lyrics:** Ira Gershwin; **Orchestra:** The MGM Studio Orchestra; **Choir:** The MGM Studio Orchestra;

Conductor: Johnny Green; **Cast:** Gene Kelly, Leslie Caron, Oscar Levant, Georges Guetary.

When George Gershwin wrote his masterful tone poem *An American in Paris,* he based it upon his experiences in that great city, where he resided for a time in the late '20s. As in his other works, Gershwin composed the piece in a way that encouraged personal visualization on the part of the listener. Apparently, Gershwin's composition left a great impression on famed MGM producer Arthur Freed. Freed deftly created a film plot that used the orchestral suite as the vehicle for a ballet within the picture, and enlisted the services of dancing star Gene Kelly: two moves that practically guaranteed the film's success. Rounding out the musical lot were nearly two dozen George and Ira Gershwin songs that, at the time, were already certifiable standards.

What emerges from this expertly restored edition of the original film soundtrack is just how solid Freed's concept, and his execution of the musical portion of the film, really were. It is a delight to hear not only the title composition (cleverly arranged by the venerable Saul Chaplin), but all of the familiar Gershwin tunes that have become so tightly woven into the fabric of American popular music: "Embraceable You," "But Not For Me," "Love Walked In," "I've Got a Crush on You," "Love Is Here to Stay" . . . the list goes on and on!

As with each of the Rhino restorations of the soundtracks from the MGM film library, this two-CD set is replete with historically important "bonus" material, culled from the original session recordings, including alternate and outtakes, and extended versions of songs. Insightful liner notes, and a wonderful interview of Saul Chaplin by Michael Feinstein provide the listener with a complete understanding of the importance of the film, and its music.

Charles L. Granata

The American President

1995, MCA Records, from the film *The American President,* Castle Rock Entertainment, 1995 🎬🎬🎬
album notes: Music: Marc Shaiman.

It's a tribute to composer Marc Shaiman that his music for *The American President* is every bit as romantic, sweeping, and yes, even perhaps as sappy as you would imagine this score to be, yet it's nevertheless memorable and works well—both as an album and as an underscore to Rob Reiner's formulaic film. Shaiman, who's had the fortune (or misfortune, in the case of the director's more recent movies) to score all of Reiner's films since *Misery,* utilizes his usual orchestral approach for *The American President,* which is ideal since the film requires a specific, straightforward musical statement, namely an uplifting, "feel-good" score to back up the on-screen romance of Michael Douglas and Annette Bening. And, just as he did on *City Slickers,* Shaiman has risen to the occasion by creating a pleasant, distinguished score that once again highlights his penchant for composing distinct, well-developed themes, the likes of which should bring listeners, particularly those who enjoy sugary scores with heavy dramatic passages, back for more on repeat listenings.

Andy Dursin

An American Tail

1986, MCA Records, from the animated feature *An American Tail,* Universal Pictures, 1986 🎬🎬🎬🎬🎬
album notes: Music: James Horner; **Orchestra:** The London Symphony Orchestra; **Conductor:** James Horner.

James Horner struck a particularly rich vein with this score for Steven Spielberg's animated features about a cute little Russian mouse, Fievel, seeking personal safety and a chance to live in peace away from the Cossack cats, and finding instead adventure and emotion galore in New York City. The instrumental cues, both action and romantic, emphasize Horner's particular gift for melodic material, with the songs adding an extra shade to his

creativity. Highlights include the rollicking "There Are No Cats in America," performed by Nehemiah Persoff, John Guarnieri, and Warren Hays, which gives Horner an opportunity to deal successfully with various ethnic styles; "A Duo," shared by Dom DeLuise and Phillip Glasser (the voice of Fievel); and the exhilarating "Flying Away and End Credits," which neatly sums up the pains and joys of the film's charming hero and his friends.

Didier C. Deutsch

An American Tail: Fievel Goes West

1991, MCA Records, from the animated feature *An American Tail: Fievel Goes West,* Universal Pictures, 1991 🎬🎬🎬🎬🎬
album notes: Music: James Horner; **Conductor:** James Horner.

In this very imaginative sequel, which is mostly instrumental, Horner's musical brogue goes wild with western type cues ("Headin' Out West," "Green River/Trek Through the Desert," "Building a New Town," "The Shoot-Out") that deftly recall some of the best scores in the genre while retaining a winning edge of originality.

Didier C. Deutsch

An American Werewolf in Paris

1997, Hollywood Records, from the Hollywood film *An American Werewolf in Paris,* 1997 🎬🎬
album notes: Music: Wilbert Hirsch.

If you can believe the premise of this horror film, Tom Everett Scott plays an American tourist who falls for a Parisian werewolf. Fortunately, this soundtrack compilation features some interesting alternative and rap artists including Better than Ezra, Cake, and Phunk Junkeez, although not all of the songs appear in the movie. Bush's lead track, "Mouth," is the highlight. Also included on the CD is one track from the score by Wilbert Hirsch, "Theme from 'An American Werewolf in Paris'," which sounds like "Phantom of the Opera."

Beth Krakower

Amistad

1998, DreamWorks Records, from the DreamWorks film *Amistad,* 1998 🎬🎬
album notes: Music: John Williams; **Conductor:** John Williams; **Featured Soloists:** Tim Morrison, trumpet; Jim Thatcher, French horn; Jim Walker, flute; Pamela Dillard, mezzo soprano.

John Williams isn't usually known for writing subtle scores. But his music for this film, his 15th collaboration with director

Steven Spielberg, is so subtle, it often borders on being merely boring. The general tedium is only relieved by "Dry Your Tears, Afrika," a wonderful vocal track based on Bernard Dodie's poem of the same name, which opens and ends the CD.

Beth Krakower

Amore piombo e furore

1996, Prometheus Records/Belgium, from the film *Amore piombo e furore (China 9, Liberty 37), 1978* 🎬🎬🎬🎬

album notes: Music: Pino Donaggio; **Conductor:** Natale Massara.

A Spanish-Italian-American co-production that had the unusual merit of having Sam Peckinpah portray a newspaper reporter, *China 9, Liberty 37* (the title refers to a sign at a crossroad indicating the distance to the nearest towns) was a fast and furious spaghetti western. One of the best in the genre, it dealt with a notorious gunfighter hired by a railroad tycoon to kill a recalcitrant farmer who literally stands in the way of his tracks, with the gunfighter siding with his intended victim. Even though he was dealing with a western, Pino Donaggio wrote a haunting score that sounds subdued and quiet for the most part, with the harmonica playing a major role ("The Range," "Love Theme"), while south-of-the-border accents provide the required exoticism ("Al confine messicano," "Mexican Song"). It proves to be a very attractive effort. This title may be out of print or just plain hard to find. Mail-order companies, used CD shops, or dealers of rare or import recordings will be your best bet.

Didier C. Deutsch

Anaconda

1997, edel America Records, from the film *Anaconda*, Columbia Pictures, 1997 🎬🎬🎬

album notes: Music: Randy Edelman; **Conductor:** Randy Edelman.

Randy Edelman was supposed to write a score at least partially integrating Brazilian jungle music for this sleeper hit, but what ended up in the finished product sounded an awful lot like the typical Edelman soundtrack—that distinct combination of synthesizers and orchestra with a strong percussive sound. In Louis Llosa's film, Edelman's music is all over the action, often undermining the suspense and tension of the situations at hand. As a soundtrack album, the score is much easier to digest, with the composer's penchant for composing easily accessible melodic ideas on full display. Given Edelman's musical capabilities, *Anaconda,* then, is not the great, interesting ethnic score it might have been, but it's still a step up from the traditionally cliched horror soundtrack.

Andy Dursin

Anastasia

1993, Varèse Sarabande Records, from the film *Anastasia,* 20th Century Fox, 1956 🎬🎬🎬🎬🎬

album notes: Music: Alfred Newman; **Orchestra:** The 20th Century Fox Studio Orchestra; **Conductor:** Alfred Newman.

1997, Atlantic Records, from the 20th Century-Fox animated film *Anastasia,* 1997 🎬🎬🎬

album notes: Music: Stephen Flaherty; **Lyrics:** Lynn Ahrens; **Score:** David Newman; **Conductor:** David Newman; **Cast:** Jonathan Dokuchitz, Kelsey Grammer, Liz Callaway, Jim Cummings, Bernadette Peters, Angela Lansbury, Lacey Charbert.

Typical of Alfred Newman, the music for this passionate 1956 film drama about a destitute woman who may be the sole heir to the Romanoff throne and fortune, spearheaded by the familiar main theme, teems with broadly romantic and expansive themes. The various European settings of the action suggested to the composer a series of colorful images that evoke these locales ("Paris," "Russian Easter," "The Tivoli"); but it is in the underscoring to some of the film's more powerful scenes that Newman let his lyricism take over, delivering cues that match in intensity Anna's search for her own identity and recognition from those around her ("Who Am I," "The Meeting," "Recognition"). Adding a different color to the Oscar-nominated score, some brilliant setpieces ("Valse," "Anastasia Waltz," "Marche de Bataille") reveal yet another side to Newman's creativity and composing genius. As a bonus, a previously unreleased track finds the composer playing the main theme on the piano.

Taking a page of recent history and turning it into an animated feature, Don Bluth and Gary Goldman posited that the fall of Imperial Russia in 1916 was entirely due to the deeds of Rasputin, a sinister sorcerer. This simplistic abbreviation allowed them to cast Czar Nicholas's beautiful daughter, Anastasia, as a romantic figure who manages to escape the evil doings of the mad monk, and eventually becomes the lovely Anya. The long-defunct Rasputin, now living in a faraway purgatory, pursues the poor girl with his curse all the way to Paris, where she hopes to be recognized by the Dowager Empress Marie, the only other escapee from the massacre. Add to this unlikely concoction some jarringly cute animal characters, and voilà, you have a musical that should appeal to kids of all ages.

There is only one problem: this trivialization makes as much sense as a retelling of the American Civil War as seen by some birds witnessing it from a nearby tree and trying to comprehend what's wrong with those crazy humans. The formula score by Lynn Ahrens and Stephen Flaherty (responsible for the Broadway hit *Ragtime*) is strictly by-the-numbers, with songs that are hardly memorable or impressive. Considering that vocals are handled by such Broadway luminaries as Bernadette Peters, Angela Lansbury, and Liz Callaway, it all seems a bit of a waste.

Didier C. Deutsch

Anastasia: The Mystery of Anna

1986, Southern Cross Records, from the TV film, *Anastasia: The Mystery of Anna*, Telecom Entertainment, 1986 ✍✍✍✍

album notes: Music: Laurence Rosenthal; **Orchestra:** The Munich Philharmonic Orchestra; **Conductor:** Laurence Rosenthal.

Anastasia: The Mystery of Anna, shown in 1986, with Amy Irving in the title role and a cast that included Olivia de Havilland, Elke Sommer, Claire Bloom, Omar Sharif, and Rex Harrison, essentially covers the same grounds as the 1956 film of the same name starring Ingrid Bergman and Yul Brynner. But to composer Laurence Rosenthal, the story suggested a totally different approach than the one taken in the film by Alfred Newman. As Rosenthal describes it in his notes, his score is essentially three scores instead of one, each reflecting the locales in which the story unfolds, their specific atmosphere and their distinct cultural milieu. Initially stately and elegant, like the waltz from Tchaikosvky's "Eugene Onegin," from which it borrows its exulted tone, the score turns melancholic as the Tsar and his family are forced to go into exile, a mood reinforced by the "implacable drums and pathetic wisps of woodwind."

The second part of the score depicting Anna's life in Berlin in the 1920s, echoes the atonality that prevailed at the time in imitation of the music written in Vienna. The third influence in the score, underlying Anna's recovery and her romance with a young German aristocrat, finds its accents in the jazz-age music that was beginning to make inroads. The music, in all its diversity, manages to retain a cohesive flavor, and makes an entertaining statement.

Didier C. Deutsch

Anatomy of a Murder

1987, Rykodisc, from the film *Anatomy of a Murder*, 1959 ✍✍✍✍✍

album notes: Music: Edward Kennedy "Duke" Ellington; **Orchestra:** The Duke Ellington Orchestra; **Conductor:** Duke Ellington; **Featured Soloists:** Clark Terry, Cat Anderson, Shorty Baker, Ray Nance, trumpet; Paul Gonsalves, Jimmy Hamilton, Russell Procope, Johnny Hodges, Harry Carney, saxophone.

During his lifetime, Duke Ellington wrote for almost every possible medium, including the stage and the screen. Even though his forays in the latter were somewhat limited, he left two outstanding film scores, *Paris Blues,* which has yet to be reissued

on compact disc, and *Anatomy of a Murder,* written for a film directed by Otto Preminger. A gripping murder mystery, involving an Army officer, his wife, and the tenacious lawyer who defends them, the film called for a score with contemporary overtones that would give the action a solid musical support, and achieve a life of its own. Ellington delivered just the right thing—set-pieces that add a necessary dramatic flair to the action, but that can also provide great listening pleasure. With many long-time members of his band taking solo turns, the soundtrack album is a great, festive Ellington party, sometimes gently low-keyed, sometimes brilliantly effervescent.

Didier C. Deutsch

1999, Legacy Records, from the film *Anatomy of a Murder*, 1959 ✍✍✍✍

album notes: Music: Edward Kennedy "Duke" Ellington.

A case in point that jazz can sometime work both for the picture and against it. Ellington's music is so personal that the individuality of his style often transcends the action on the screen. "Main Title" is a great use of the sleazy side of jazz, the strip joint atmosphere that is often associated with the music itself. "Firsthand" is typically swinging Ellington. "Low Key Lightly" has an exquisite Ellington solo piano intro. "Happy Anatomy" (from the score) is a bright swinger with a bouncing solo by Clark Terry. "Almost Cried" is an example of the sublime side of Ellington. The quiet mood is held throughout, and the band performs beautifully. "Happy Anatomy–P.I. Five" is a New Orleans–based romp that features a quintet. "Haupe" is a sexy vehicle for Johnny Hodges. "Upper and Outest" ends the original soundtrack with a bravura performance by Cat Anderson. There are 13 additional tracks on the recently released Columbia CD, including chatter from the studio.

Bob Belden

And the Band Played On

1993, Varèse Sarabande Records, from the film *And the Band Played On*, HBO Pictures, 1993 ✍✍✍✍

album notes: Music: Carter Burwell; **Conductor:** Carter Burwell.

This is a dark and brooding effort by Carter Burwell which deftly captures the pathos of the incipient advance of one of the most terrible diseases of our time. The film recounts the story of how early detection and investigation into AIDS is hindered not only by a clash of egos within the medical community, but a serious lack of general concern (especially since the affliction was initially thought to be restricted only to homosexuals). Burwell's music, perhaps one of his most inspired mainstream efforts, best personifies the advance of the disorder with slow string and woeful brass motifs, connecting with discomforting clarity the image of souls slowly wasting away from the effects. He counterpoints with a demented waltz motif, played by plucking the string instruments, representing scientists as they dance around each other. Surely anyone who has grieved for the loss of a loved one can connect with the bleak atmosphere Burwell conjures up.

David Hirsch

Andre

 1994, Milan Records, from the film *Andre,* Paramount Pictures, 1994 🎬🎬🎬

album notes: Music: Bruce Rowland; **Orchestra:** The Victorian Philharmonic Orchestra; **Conductor:** Bruce Rowland.

For this *Free Willy* clone, about the friendship between a young girl and a seal, Bruce Rowland plays the sentimental chords with cues that tug at all the right heart strings. But this highly charged score is also chockful of delightful little moments that make it much more important and interesting than it would appear to be in the first place. At its most inspired, string instruments (harp, guitar) and wind instruments combine to create an amalgam of vivid little vignettes that are endearing and quite attractive. At other times, a lovely piano melody is strikingly set off by a lute or a harp to evoke images that may work very well within the context of the screen action but that also have a magic of their own as music. Many of the tracks, however, could have taken a longer exposition, and while several manage to grab one's attention, only the six minute-plus "The Storm" succeeds in creating a strong momentum.

Didier C. Deutsch

Angel

1993, Intrada Records, from the film *Angel,* New World Pictures, 1993 🎬🎬

album notes: Music: Craig Safan; **Conductor:** Craig Safan.

This modest little score by Craig Safan is, regretfully, very much like the film in that it really should have been more fun than it turned out to be. Despite some pleasant themes ("Angel," "Yo-Yo Man"), the bulk of the score comes across as a surprisingly uninspired effort when compared to his other work, like the sensational *The Last Starfighter,* for example. The orchestra is dressed with some tired, standard electronic overlays that inspire very little as musical entertainment. This film score most likely suffers because Safan admittedly was only given a week in which to compose it—a ridiculously short period of time. *Angel* is certainly not a poor album, but Safan deserves to be judged by other works that better reflect his talents.

David Hirsch

Angels in the Outfield

1994, Hollywood Records, from the film *Angels in the Outfield,* Walt Disney Pictures, 1994 🎬🎬🎬🎬

album notes: Music: Randy Edelman; **Conductor:** Randy Edelman.

The opening of this score recalls the stately grace of Edelman's magnificent score for *Gettysburg,* recorded the previous year; at least until a pop beat is added. The beat gives the score a catchy, up-tempo feel, associated with the contemporary milieu and the kids around whom the story revolves, while the initial theme returns to capture the mysterious glory of the angelic sportsmen who offer invisible aid to a failing baseball team. Between the two styles of music is an engaging score. It's mostly lighthearted and breezy, but with enough passion to make it genuinely moving in spots. Edelman's theme for the angels becomes just as much a theme for the boy who can see them, whose story becomes the focus of the picture.

Randall Larson

Another baseball fantasy with angelic overtones, *Angels in the Outfield* must have particularly inspired Edelman. His score is wonderfully whimsical ("Al Pops Up"), exhilaratingly melodic ("Magical Moments"), and just plain beautiful. The themes, lightly sketched but attractive, convey the moods in the film, from the despair felt by the players whose team has not won in many moons in "Torn Apart" to the sudden arrival of saviours from above in "Rock and Roll Angels," and on to the final inning. It helps, of course, that this is a Disney film, and that the players get some encouragement from two kids who truly believe in their eventual victory, but Edelman knows how to write melodic material that sticks in the ear and demonstrates it effortlessly in this totally engaging score.

Didier C. Deutsch

Angie

1994, Varèse Sarabande Records, from the film *Angie,* Hollywood Pictures, 1994 🎬🎬

album notes: Music: Jerry Goldsmith; **Conductor:** Jerry Goldsmith.

Jerry Goldsmith's status as a legendary film composer just about guarantees that any film he scores will have a soundtrack album released. Case in point: This slight effort for the Geena Davis "dramedy" *Angie,* which Goldsmith scored with a low-key, subtly pop-influenced approach that's like a very subdued version of some of his tender dramatic scores of the '60s like *Patch of Blue* and *The Trouble with Angels.* Unfortunately audience intolerance for the kind of rhythmic and orchestrational development Goldsmith brought to his '60s scores makes *Angie* so subtle you'll barely notice you're listening to it. It's pleasant but rarely interesting, with one traveling cue that's similar to chase material from Goldsmith's *Basic Instinct* and a piece of classical source music that eats up a large chunk of this album's brief running time.

Jeff Bond

Angus

1995, Reprise Records, from the New Line Cinema film *Angus*, 1995 ♪♪♪♪

Punk rock is the music for outcasts, so it's appropriate that the soundtrack for this film about an overweight kid with low self-esteem who gets picked on by the bullies would be comprised of the punk rock of its time. Hence, Angus plays to the angsty sounds of Green Day ("J.A.R.""), Ash ("Jack Names the Planets," "Kung Fu'"), Love Spit Love ("Am I Wrong"), Smoking Popes ("Mrs. You and Me"), and the gay trio Pansy Division ("Deep Water"). All these groups rage with a bit of a wink, though; they certainly take their audience—epitomized in "Angus"—seriously, but they also understand the temporal nature of the human condition, which gives this soundtrack an agreeable, resolute buoyancy.

Gary Graff

Animal House

1978, MCA Records, from the film *National Lampoon's Animal House*, Universal Pictures, 1978 ♪♪

album notes: Music: Elmer Bernstein; **Conductor:** Elmer Bernstein.

At a time when most Hollywood composers were looking for an instrumental gig anywhere, this film and its soundtrack album gave veteran Elmer Bernstein a reputation as the best man in town to score comedies in the *Saturday Night Live* vein. Unfortunately the album shortchanges the composer, sadly represented by only a couple of tracks, the "Faber College Theme" used at the top of the set and again as the closing number, and the "Intro" strangely positioned somewhere in the middle. However, that theme captures the zany moods of the film starring John Belushi better than the many vocal selections assembled here, with the possible exception of Belushi singing "Louie, Louie," which also qualifies as a genuine film track.

Didier C. Deutsch

Annie

1977, Columbia Records, from the Broadway production *Annie*, 1977 ♪♪♪♪

album notes: Music: Charles Strouse; **Lyrics:** Martin Charnin; **Musical Direction:** Peter Howard; **Cast:** Andrea McArdle, Reid Shelton, Sandy Faison, Robert Fitch, Dorothy Loudon, Raymond Thorne.

1987, Columbia Records, from the screen version *Annie*, Columbia Pictures, 1982 ♪♪♪

album notes: Music: Charles Strouse; **Lyrics:** Martin Charnin; **Cast:** Aileen Quinn, Albert Finney, Ann Reinking, Carol Burnett, Bernadette Peters, Tim Curry, Geoffrey Holder Edward Herrmann.

The sun did come out on Broadway when big-voiced moppet Andrea McArdle stepped on the stage as Little Orphan Annie, and belted the show-stopping "Tomorrow," her triumphant claim to fame. The show, based on the celebrated comic strip, opened on April 21, 1977, won seven Tony Awards (including for its score and for Best Musical), and had an enduring run of 2,377 performances, though the popularity of this one-hit wonder was probably overrated, as a recent revival on Broadway sadly confirmed. Co-starring Reid Shelton as Daddy Warbucks, and Dorothy Loudon (another Tony winner) in an over-the-top performance as the nefarious Miss Hannigan, the musical had its ingratiating moments, wonderfully captured in the original cast album. In 1982, it was transferred to the screen in a splashy version that starred Carol Burnett (delightfully delirious as Miss Hannigan), Albert Finney as Daddy Warbucks, the cute Aileen Quinn as Annie, and Tim Curry, Bernadette Peters, Geoffrey Holder, and Ann Reinking. Despite all the talent that went into its production, the musical looked like an anomaly on the screen and showed signs of decrepitude.

Didier C. Deutsch

1998, Sony Classical/Legacy, from the Broadway musical *Annie*, 1977 ♪♪♪

album notes: Music: Charles Strouse; **Lyrics:** Martin Charnin; **Conductor:** Peter Howard; **Cast:** Andrea McArdle, Reid Shelton, Sandy Faison, Robert Fitch, Dorothy Loudon.

The wildly popular story of a little orphan girl, Annie, gets the reissue treatment here with some interesting additional material. This release features composer Charles Strouse and lyricist Martin Charnin performing their first draft of the show for a backer's auditions in 1972. It's interesting to hear how they originally envisioned the play. However, the sound quality is not very good on these tracks, and the material really doesn't add much to the original recording. It's almost like reading O. Henry and then looking at his napkin notes.

Beth Krakower

Annie Get Your Gun

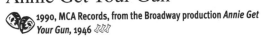

1990, MCA Records, from the Broadway production *Annie Get Your Gun*, 1946 ♪♪♪

album notes: Music: Irving Berlin; **Lyrics:** Irving Berlin; **Conductor:** Jay Blackton; **Cast:** Ethel Merman, Ray Middleton.

1988, RCA Victor, from the Broadway revival *Annie Get Your Gun*, 1966 ♪♪♪♪♪

album notes: Music: Irving Berlin; **Lyrics:** Irving Berlin; **Conductor:** Franz Allers; **Cast:** Ethel Merman, Bruce Yarnell, Jerry Orbach, Benay Venuta.

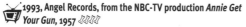

1993, Angel Records, from the NBC-TV production *Annie Get Your Gun*, **1957** ♫♫♫♫

album notes: Music: Irving Berlin; **Lyrics:** Irving Berlin; **Conductor:** Louis Adrian; **Cast:** Mary Martin, John Raitt.

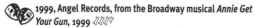

1999, Angel Records, from the Broadway musical *Annie Get Your Gun*, **1999** ♫♫♫♪

album notes: Book: Peter Stone; **Music:** Irving Berlin; **Lyrics:** Irving Berlin; **Musical Direction:** John McDaniel; **Cast:** Bernadette Peters, Tom Wopat, Ron Holgate, Valerie Wright, Andrew Palermo, Ronn Carroll.

The life story of Wild West sharpshooter Annie Oakley became the central idea for a lively, exuberant musical starring Ethel Merman, for whom the show was written. Irving Berlin, who had initially declined to create the score for a "book" show, eventually agreed to undertake it and wrote an incredible amount of popular songs, many of which have since become standards—"They Say It's Wonderful," "You Can't Get a Man With a Gun," "Doin' What Comes Natur'lly," "I Got the Sun in the Morning," "Anything You Can Do," and the all-time anthem to the entertainment industry, "There's No Business Like Show Business." In the somewhat simplified plot devised by Herbert and Dorothy Fields, Colonel Buffalo Bill discovers Annie Oakley, and makes her part of his famous Wild West Show, in which she shares billing with Frank Butler. Soon, Annie discovers that "You Can't Get a Man With a Gun," though in the end love prevails over the rivalry between the two. *Annie Get Your Gun* opened on May 16, 1946, and had an extended run of 1,147 performances; in 1950, it was made into a rip-roaring movie, starring Betty Hutton and Howard Keel.

Of the recordings listed here, the first is the 1946 original cast album, starring Merman and Ray Middleton. Though no longer up to standard sonics, it is a valuable document, with la Merman at the top of her vocal powers. Twenty years later, the actress returned to the role in a much-touted revival, presented by producer Richard Rodgers at the then new Music Theater of Lincoln Center in New York, in which Bruce Yarnell was cast as Frank Butler. The cast album recording, on RCA, stands out as the best representation of the score, in vivid stereo sound, with a new song, "An Old Fashioned Wedding," written for this occasion by Irving Berlin.

The recording on Angel features Mary Martin and John Raitt in a 1957 NBC-TV spectacular, reprising the roles they had played 10 years earlier in the original road company of the show, and in a San Francisco Civic Light Opera revival a few months prior to the telecast. Though in mono, it is an excellent alternate presentation of the score. At this writing, the soundtrack to the film has not yet been reissued on compact disc, though songs from the score, performed by Judy Garland, who was scheduled to star in the film before she withdrew from it, can be heard on a Rhino compilation.

Warning: any resemblance between the 1999 cast album and previous incarnations of Irving Berlin's seminal masterpiece is purely coincidental. But that applies, too, to the current revival of the musical which, in order to make it more relevant to today's audience and (presumably) more politically correct has been entirely revamped to disastrous results. To wit—the songs have been reshuffled to accommodate a change in settings (the musical now takes place as a show-within-a-show in Buffalo Bill's touring Western circus), and some judged offensive (like the good-natured spoof, "I'm an Indian, too") have been dropped.

What remains is an empty shell of a show, with Bernadette Peters valiantly trying to keep things together and Tom Wopat pretending to enact the handsome Frank Butler. Fortunately, listening to the cast album, superbly recorded it must be said, you will be spared the limp direction, the over-aggressive choreography (like the young men rolling on the floor while Wopat sings "My Defenses Are Down"), Peters's silly back-of-the-woods spoken accent, and the cheesy decors.

In the recording, Peters shines like the real trouper she is, although she cannot erase the memory of Ethel Merman, for whom the show and the songs were written; Wopat displays a comfortable light baritone; and the others in the cast come across with the appropriate gusto, even though the tempi in most of the songs would have gained at being brisker. All told, not a bad recording, but not the overall success it should have been had the entire production been better.

Didier C. Deutsch

Another Dawn

1996, Marco Polo, from the film *Another Dawn*, **Warner Bros., 1937** ♫♫♫♫

album notes: Music: Erich Wolfgang Korngold; **Orchestra:** The Moscow Symphony Orchestra; **Conductor:** William T. Stromberg.

Known more for his "swashbuckler" scores, Erich Wolfgang Korngold shows his tender side on this CD, yet another Errol Flynn film, the 1937 soap opera *Another Dawn*. There's plenty of action, to be sure, but the film was intended to be a romantic endeavor for its two stars. Efforts by the producers to save the poorly plotted film resulted in some heavy editing of Korngold's score, but John Morgan has wisely chosen to go back and lovingly reconstruct what Korngold originally wrote, including the initial finale, changed when an alternate ending was used so that Flynn's character would survive. Another unusual selection, the "Ballet/Fantasy" from *Escape Me Never*, leads off the album.

David Hirsch

Another Day in Paradise

1998, V2 Records, from the Trimark film *Another Day in Paradise,* 1998 🎵🎵🎵

A compelling, gritty little drama, starring Melanie Griffith in an unusual role as an unglamorous misfit, a heroin addict in a midwestern community, *Another Day in Paradise,* set in the 1970s, gains much of its atmosphere and realism from the soundtrack, which features several blues numbers, some from that period, others of more recent vintage, performed by Otis Redding, Bobby Womack, Allen Toussaint, Sam Moore, and Clarence Carter, who appears in the film as a nightclub singer. The CD appropriately evokes the film with its collection of tracks, which also include songs by Bob Dylan.

Didier C. Deutsch

Another 48 Hrs.

1990, Scotti Bros., from the film *Another 48 Hrs.,* Paramount Pictures, 1990 🎵
album notes: Music: James Horner.

Listeners may want to dispense with the vocal selections that are totally interchangeable (In addition to getting strictly one-dimensional performances by Curio, "Give It All You Got," "I Just Can't Let It End" and "I've Got My Eye on You" evidence the same one-two rhythmic beat and trite lyrics) and concentrate instead on the four instrumental cues composed and conducted by James Horner, but chances are you will also be disappointed. Writing in a contemporary vein, the composer relies on synth accents to play off a wailing clarinet that at times evokes Kenny G, with pulse-pounding effects to suggest that this is an action film. It may be quite effective behind the scenes, but taken on its own musical terms, it is ultimately less than endearing.

Didier C. Deutsch

Anthony Adverse

1991, Varèse Sarabande Records, from the film *Anthony Adverse,* Warner Bros., 1936 🎵🎵🎵🎵
album notes: Music: Erich Wolfgang Korngold; **Orchestra:** The Berlin Radio Symphony Orchestra; **Conductor:** John Scott.

In comparison to his most flamboyant efforts (*The Adventures of Robin Hood* and *Sea Hawk,* for instance), the music Korngold wrote for this screen adaptation of the Harvey Allen bestseller sounds more pleasant than epic. But his lyricism is present everywhere in these seven long suites that regroup together all the principal themes and settings heard in the film as shorter cues. Though the script provided plenty of action scenes and unexpected developments in this romantic tale set during the

Napoleonic era, the composer seemed to have been primarily attracted to the challenge presented by the varying moods in the main characters, and set out to write what is essentially an operatic score without the words. As a result, the leitmotifs that recur throughout may not have the immediacy and vibrancy of pure action cues, but the thematic material unfolds in breathtaking fashion to create a score that has great impact and strength. Possibly also as a result, The Berlin Radio Symphony Orchestra, conducted by John Scott, does not display the flashy style exhibited by the Utah Symphony in both *Robin Hood* and *Sea Hawk* for the same label. The production values, though, are still first-rate.

Didier C. Deutsch

Antony and Cleopatra

1992, JOS Records, from the film *Antony and Cleopatra,* Rank Films, 1972 🎵🎵🎵🎵
album notes: Music: John Scott; **Orchestra:** The Berlin Radio Symphony Orchestra; The Berlin Radio Symphony Choir; **Conductor:** John Scott.

This 1972 filmed adaptation of Shakespeare's play (not to be confused with another 1963 extravaganza with a somewhat similar title) was directed by and starred Charlton Heston in one of his most felicitous screen portrayals as Antony, opposite Hildegard Neil as Cleopatra. Deftly using the medium's wide possibilities, Heston opened up the stage play and beefed it up with often impressive panoramic battle scenes shot on location in Spain. Matching his vision almost frame for frame, John Scott provides a score that shares its best moments between sweeping romantic themes ("Undying Love," "One Last Night of Love") and throbbing action cues ("Battle of Actium"). The Berlin Radio Symphony Orchestra, conducted by the composer, plays it with all the fire and passion necessary, making this CD a highly desirable addition to any collection, though, like the hard-to-get film, you probably will have to do some digging to find it.

Didier C. Deutsch

Antz

1998, Angel Records, from the Dreamworks film *Antz,* 1998 🎵🎵🎵

album notes: Music: Harry Gregson-Williams, John Powell; **Conductor:** Gavin Greenaway; **Featured Soloists:** Jonathan Snowden, flute; Phil Todd, saxophone; Brian Gulland, crumhorns; Oren Marshall, elephant and antelope horns; Skaila Kanga, harp; Frank Ricotti, bass marimba; Chris Lawrence, bass; Louis Jardin, percussion; Ian Thomas, drums; Ryeland Allison, Bob Daspit, percussion loops; Nicole Tibbles, Janet Mooney, Kenny Andrews, Marcos D'Cruze, Michael Dmitri, vocals.

Antz features a bouncy, jazzy score by composers John Powell and Harry Gregson-Williams, who wrote a very entertaining set of cues to this animated movie about a utopian society and the worker ant (Z, voiced by Woody Allen) who strives to be an individual in it. There are many cute moments in this delightful film, but two highlights include Z and Princess Bala (voiced by Sharon Stone), heiress to the ant throne, dancing à la *Pulp Fiction* to the accents of "Guantanamera," and the soldier ants going to war singing "The Antz Go Marching One by One! Hurrah, Hurrah!," both of which are included here. Often fresh and spontaneous, the music of *Antz* will be enjoyed by kids of all ages.

see also: A Bug's Life

Didier C. Deutsch

Anyone Can Whistle

 1988, Columbia Records, from the Broadway production *Anyone Can Whistle*, 1964 ♪♪♪♪

album notes: Music: Stephen Sondheim; **Lyrics:** Stephen Sondheim; **Vocal Arrangements and Musical Direction:** Herbert Greene; **Cast:** Angela Lansbury , Lee Remick, Harry Guardino, Gabriel Dell.

A brilliant (and brilliantly flawed) musical by Stephen Sondheim, *Anyone Can Whistle* is one of those fabulous flops the history of the American Musical Theatre occasionally spawns. A sardonic study of political corruption in a small town, the show details the efforts by the city management to capitalize on a fake miraculous spring to revive the town's flagging economy. The plans are derailed when patients from a local mental hospital escape and begin mingling with the tourists, much to the horror and dismay of the town council. Starring Angela Lansbury, Harry Guardino, and Lee Remick, three film stars with little or no previous Broadway experience, the show was roundly lambasted and closed after only nine performances. It was, however, recorded by Goddard Lieberson, head of A&R at Columbia Records, who, with incredible foresight, saw in it something quite unique. Posterity proved him right: today, *Anyone Can Whistle* is often mentioned as a precursor to the great shows (*Company, Follies, Sweeney Todd*) Sondheim wrote a decade later, a work way ahead of its time in which one can find in embryo the themes the composer developed subsequently, including man's isolation in the modern world, and the fact that "no one's always what they seem to be."

Beth Krakower

Anything Goes

 1962, Epic Records, from the off-Broadway revival *Anything Goes*, 1962 ♪♪♪♪

album notes: Music: Cole Porter; **Lyrics:** Cole Porter; **Conductor:** Julian Stein; Cast: Eileen Rodgers, Hal Linden, Barbara Lang, Kenneth Mars.

They Know the Score

Danny Elfman

I was raised on film. My musical experience is all via film, it's not from classical music. I think that's one of the things that has always put me in kind of an odd niche. It's that all of my understanding of orchestral music is via film, not via classical music like it's supposed to be. To me it's the same, it doesn't make any difference. I've never understood why it's any different to be inspired by Bernard Herrmann as opposed to Wagner or whomever. They're both composers and they're both geniuses. And what difference does it make whether it's Shostakovich or Franz Waxman?

Courtesy of **Film Score Monthly**

1988, RCA Victor; from the Broadway revival *Anything Goes*, 1988 ♪♪♪♪♪

album notes: Music: Cole Porter; **Lyrics:** Cole Porter; **Conductor:** Edward Strauss; **Cast:** Patti LuPone, Howard McGillin, Kathleen Mahony-Bennett, Anthony Heald.

One of Cole Porter's wittiest shows, and a hoot and a holler, *Anything Goes* introduces Broadway audiences to nightclub performer Reno Sweeney, her friend Billy Crocker, in love with socialite Hope Harcourt, and Public Enemy #13 Moonface Martin, all of them passengers on a cruise ship where, as the title whimsically points out, everything and anything goes (actually a reference to the problems initially encountered when putting together the musical, about a shipwreck, in the face of several disasters, including the unrelated sinking of the "S.S. Morro"). Ethel Merman, William Gaxton, and Victor Moore starred in the goofball original, for which Porter had written some of his most memorable tunes, including "All Through the Night," "Blow, Gabriel, Blow," "You're the Top," and the title tune. It opened November 21, 1934, for 420 performances, the fourth longest running production of the decade, and was made into a screen musical two years later with Bing Crosby, Ethel Merman, and Charlie Ruggles in the principal roles. In 1956, Crosby starred

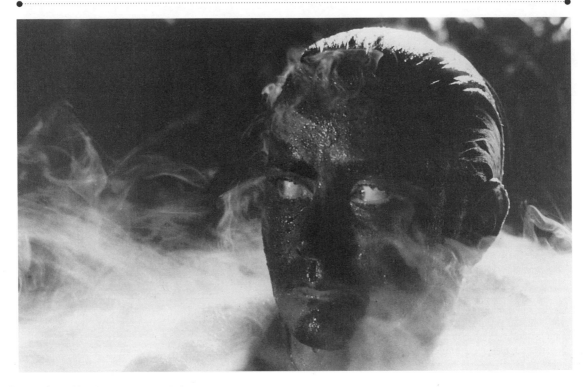

Apocalypse Now **(The Kobal Collection)**

with Donald O'Connor, Mitzi Gaynor, and Zizi Jeanmaire, in another film version which only retained the title of the original, and a couple of songs by Porter. In a somewhat pared down revival, *Anything Goes* returned to off Broadway in 1962, with Hal Linden, Eileen Rodgers, and Mickey Deems, with the cast album recording on Epic, documenting this enjoyable but uneven production. Then, in 1987, it was again revived in a sensational new production, starring Patti LuPone as Reno Sweeney, which opened at Lincoln Center's Vivian Beaumont Theatre, on October 13, 1987, for a long run of 804 performances. That production yielded the original cast album on RCA, which includes several interpolations and is the best representation of the score available by far.

Didier C. Deutsch

Apocalypse Now

1979, Elektra Records, from the film *Apocalypse Now*, United Artists, 1979 🎬🎬

album notes: Music: Carmine Coppola, Francis Coppola.

This is really a two-disc, abridged, audio presentation of the film that mixes music and dialogue. When it was first released in 1979, it may have been something unique, but today it has become something of a relic. After all, since you can now buy the film on video for less money and with better sound, why not just watch it? The set pretty much covers all the best sequences and features The Doors' title track. As with most albums of this kind, the dialogue is mixed much lower than the music, creating a jarring parade of sound levels.

David Hirsch

Apollo 13

1995, MCA Records, from the film *Apollo 13*, Universal Pictures, 1995 🎬🎬🎬

album notes: Music: James Horner.

One of James Horner's most effective works is marred by a hodgepodge album presentation that, for all intents and purposes, is nothing more than an audio dramatization of the film. Eight pop songs of the period, dialogue sequences and sound effects weave in and out of the score. One might as well just watch the film on home video for all the enjoyment it gives. The fact that portions of the music are obviously lifted verbatim from Horner's own score for *Sneakers* doesn't help either. You may add a rating point if none of this matters. The soundtrack album is also available in a Dolby Surround 24k gold CD with additional dialogue.

David Hirsch

The Apostle

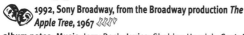 1998, Rising Tide Records, from the October film *The Apostle*, 1998 🎬🎬🎬

Robert Duvall plays a Texas preacher who attacks his wife's lover, then leaves his congregation to seek salvation when he starts up another church. While David Mansfield's score remains unpublished, this compilation of gospel traditionals and gospel-influenced country music is an outstanding introduction to both new talent and classic performers such as Johnny Cash, Emmylou Harris, and the Carter Family. *The Apostle*'s theme of redemption makes for some powerful songs, and these complement an outstanding and provocative performance by Duvall.

David Poole

The Apple Tree

🎲🎲 1992, Sony Broadway, from the Broadway production *The Apple Tree*, 1967 🎬🎬🎬🎬

album notes: Music: Jerry Bock; **Lyrics:** Sheldon Harnick; **Cast:** Barbara Harris, Alan Alda, Larry Blyden.

An innovative three one-act musical production, starring Alan Alda, Larry Blyden, and Barbara Harris, *The Apple Tree* was the creation of Jerry Bock and Sheldon Harnick, following their hugely successful *Fiddler on the Roof*. The production took its name from the first work, based on Mark Twain's amusing "The Diary of Adam and Eve," and also included Frank R. Stockton's "The Lady and the Tiger," and Jules Feiffer's "Passionella." Though hardly on the same level as its glorious predecessor, *The Apple Tree* was warmly received by critics when it opened on October 18, 1966, and enjoyed a run of 463 performances. It won a Tony for Barbara Harris's hilarious performance in the third play as a chimney sweeper who dreams of becoming a mooooovie star.

Beth Krakower

Apt Pupil

🎬 1998, RCA Victor, from the Phoenix Pictures film *Apt Pupil*, 1998 🎬🎬🎬🎬

album notes: Music: John Ottman; **Conductor:** Larry Groupe.

The story of a former Nazi war criminal being unmasked by a small-town high school student, *Apt Pupil* elicited an ominous, at times eerie score from John Ottman, who displayed a great deal of versatility in his choice of themes. As director Bryan Singer notes, in a terse but to-the-point statement/love letter to his composer, "I needed you to summon your demons and create a dark and chilling musical journey. . . . With it you have brought a truly disturbing hint of tragic history, ethnic irony, and the evil that lurks beneath the roots of those green fields and deer-filled pastures." All that, and then some.

Didier C. Deutsch

Arabesque

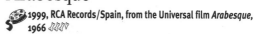 1999, RCA Records/Spain, from the Universal film *Arabesque*, 1966 🎬🎬

album notes: Music: Henry Mancini; **Conductor:** Henry Mancini; **Featured Soloists:** Jack Sheldon, Manny Klein, trumpets; Dick Nash, trombone; Vince De Rosa, French horn; Ted Nash, alto sax; Ethmer Roten, flute; Arnold Koblenz, oboe; Bob Bain, mandola; Jimmy Rowles, piano; Shelly Manne, drums.

Gregory Peck and Sophia Loren were top-billed in this drama, in which he played an American professor at Oxford and she a sultry siren of Arab extraction, both irremediably enmeshed in a tale of foreign intrigue that involved different Middle East terrorist groups. Loaded with chases, attempted murders, and vaguely disguised threats to keep the suspense heightened, the film also benefited from a score by Henry Mancini. Not one of his best efforts, it is still a vibrant series of cues, enhanced by the contributions of jazz/studio musicians with impeccable reputations. The vaguely suggestive Arabic accents in some of the selections are a bit hokum, but the pleasantly swaying "Something for Sophia" shows the deft hand of a master of melody.

Didier C. Deutsch

Arabian Knight

🎬 1995, Milan Records, from the animated feature *Arabian Knight*, Miramax Films, 1995 🎬🎬🎬

album notes: Music: Robert Folk; **Orchestra:** The London Symphony Orchestra; **Conductor:** Robert Folk; **Songs:** Norman Gimbel, Robert Folk.

Not to be confused with Disney's *Aladdin*, Robert Folk's large orchestral music for *Arabian Knight* makes for an exciting soundtrack album with a style that is reminiscent of a typical James Horner fantasy score (think *Willow* or *Krull*). The film, originally titled *The Thief and the Cobbler* and released on video under that name, was an ambitious effort from Oscar-winning animator Richard Williams that sat on the shelf for nearly two decades before it was taken out of his hands and completed by other filmmakers. Some of the new elements added to the director's original vision include songs written by Folk and lyricist Norman Gimbel in a pseudo-Alan Menken style, but what should be of interest to most listeners ought to be the score, which is derivative but entertaining, marked by lush themes performed to perfection by the London Symphony Orchestra. It has fun toiling around in the vein of Erich Wolfgang Korngold and John Williams, and sounds just as much of a homage to those sources as the Aladdin-"inspired" songs appear modeled right after their superior Disney counterparts.

Andy Dursin

Arachnophobia

1990, Hollywood Records, from the movie *Arachnophobia,* Hollywood Pictures, 1990. ♪♪♪

album notes: Music: Trevor Jones; **Conductor:** Shirley Walker.

A quirky combination of often goofy songs and a fun score by Trevor Jones comprise this soundtrack album for one of 1990s surprise box-office hits. With the album's running time split virtually halfway between Jones's music and the pop songs, there ought to be something here for every listener. Sara Hickman's catchy "Blue Eyes Are Sensitive to the Light" and Jimmy Buffett's silly "Don't Bug Me" are indicative of the tongue-in-cheek tone of the songs, which also include forgettable rock tracks by Brent Hutchins, The Party, Pleasure Thieves, and The Poorboys, along with an alternate version of Russell Hitchcock's ballad "Swear to Your Heart" called "Caught in Your Web." Jones's music fares better, with a terrific main title theme supporting itself quite well through a number of theme and variations. Purists may object to the inclusion of dialogue on some tracks (a hard-to-find German import of the soundtrack features more score, less songs, and no dialogue by comparison), but given the tone of this album, they seem to fit right in.

Andy Dursin

Arlington Road

1998, Will Records, from the Screen Gems film *Arlington Road,* 1998 ♪♪♪

album notes: Music: Angelo Badalamenti.

A powerful suspense drama that recalls the intricately devised plots of Alfred Hitchcock, *Arlington Road* is a compelling film about a college professor who finds himself unwillingly drawn into a dangerous psychological cat-and-mouse game with an over-friendly next door neighbor, who may not be what he appears to be in the first place. Add to this elements of suspicion about government involvement, terrorist activities, and two strongly defined characters, and you have the basis for a clever thriller, filled with twists and turns that enhance the impending sense of doom. While not too terribly musical on its own terms,

Angelo Badalamenti's taut score provides a chilling counterpoint to the action, stressing its darker aspects and occasionally enlivening it. Most of the music is synthesized, with heavy chord poundings that accentuate the hidden sense of danger that permeates the film, with only a mournful reminiscence ("Lament for Leah," "Leah's Theme," named after the professor's wife, killed in an earlier terrorist attack) to offset the drama in the score.

Didier C. Deutsch

Armageddon

1998, Columbia/Sony Music Soundtrax, from the Touchstone film *Armageddon,* 1998 ♪♪♪

album notes: Music: Trevor Rabin; **Conductor:** Gordon Goodwin; **Featured Musicians:** Lou Molina, drums; Hugh Marsh, violin.

When a huge asteroid hurtling through space threatens the planet, a team of renegade astronauts, led by Bruce Willis, attempts to blow out the rock before it creates havoc on Earth. The plot, also the premise for *Deep Impact* (q.v.) released a few months earlier, sounds like a sure-fire thriller, but execution sometimes leaves a lot to be desired, particularly when the action becomes clobbered by an inane secondary plot, a love story between a younger astronaut, Ben Affleck, and Willis's daughter, played by Liv Tyler (both are heard in "Animal Crackers" on the song compilation CD). Punctuating every instant in the action are loud songs by Aerosmith (who had a hit with "I Don't Want to Miss a Thing," the best moment in the lot), Jon Bon Jovi, ZZ Top, Journey, and other top-flight groups and individuals, whose contributions are heard in bits and pieces in the film but in their entirety in a song compilation album; and an equally noisy and slightly unimaginative score by Trevor Rabin, whose idea of illustrating musically the screen action is to try to match the sound level of the many special effects in Dolby Stereo. It works for a while in the film, but not as a soundtrack album.

Didier C. Deutsch

Army of Darkness

1992, Varèse-Sarabande Records, from the Universal film *Army of Darkness,* 1992 ♪♪♪♪

album notes: Music: Jo Lo Duca; **Conductor:** Tim Simonec; **Choral Conductor:** Dennis J. Tini.

Joseph Lo Duca blazed the swashbuckling style of his latter work on the *Hercules* and *Xena* TV series with this highly enjoyable horror-adventure score. While De Luca's music for the first two *Evil Dead* movies were in a far more terrifying vein, the series took an uneven leap into *Conan the Barbarian* territory with its third outing. Lo Duca's music is far more successful at capturing the sword-and-sorcery approach than the film itself, his thunderous symphonic music bringing images of Errol Flynn to mind, as opposed to bloodthirsty zombies on screen. *Army of Darkness* is one of those rare soundtracks that's a great listen on its own, particularly due to the melody and humor that Lo Duca brings to his action music. To date, *Army of Darkness* is the only major Hollywood film that the composer has scored, and it's too bad he has chosen to keep his talents mostly confined to the television screen. Danny Elfman also contributes a theme with "March of the Dead," a fun, typically "Elfmanesque" piece that's more ghoulish than anything else on the album.

Dan Schweiger

Around the World in 80 Days

1989, MCA Records, from the film *Around the World in 80 Days*, Universal Pictures, 1956 🎬🎬🎬🎬

album notes: Music: Victor Young; **Orchestra:** The Universal-International Orchestra; **Conductor:** Victor Young.

At a time when big screen all-star super-productions were still something relatively new, Michael Todd's treatment of Jules Verne's *Around the World in 80 Days* was as big as they came. Wasting little time for character studies, it relied on a breathless pace to recount in three hours the many adventures of round-the-world travelers Phineas Fogg (David Niven) and his astute manservant Passepartout (Cantinflas), from their English homebase to such exotic locales as Spain, India, Japan, and America. Along the way, they encounter and match wits with a literal who's who of 1950s filmdom, including John Carradine, Frank Sinatra, Marlene Dietrich, George Raft, Red Skelton, Charles Boyer, Noel Coward, Buster Keaton, Peter Lorre, Cesar Romero, and, as a lovely Indian princess they rescue from a funeral pyre, Shirley MacLaine.

Superbly filmed using the Todd-AO Process, the film also benefited from a sensational Academy Award-winning score composed by Victor Young, spearheaded by the evocative "Main Title," a tune that has since become a particular favorite. While the soundtrack album only contains about 45 minutes from that score, the selections cover enough to provide a fair sampling of Young's contribution, including such memorable cues as "Passepartout," the jaunty "Paris Arrival," the Spanish-flavored "Invitation to a Bull Fight" and "Entrance of the Bull March," the exotic "India Country Side" and "The Pagoda of Pillagi," and the western-inspired "Prairie Sail Car." On a purely technical basis, the CD was evidently mastered using the original 1958 two-track stereo tapes, and its overall sound quality no longer meets the stringent requirements of the digital era. The recording evidences a somewhat brittle sound, some distortion, and a lot of noticeable hiss on the tracks. This is one

clear instance when an important score deserves to be completely redone from the multi-track session tapes.

Didier C. Deutsch

1989, Cinedisc Records, from the NBC-TV mini-series *Around the World in 80 Days*, 1989 🎬🎬🎬

Music: Billy Goldenberg; **Conductor:** Billy Goldenberg.

While Billy Goldenberg is best known for his work on Broadway, he revisited the small screen in 1988 with this enjoyable score for the NBC mini-series version of Jules Verne's classic novel, starring Pierce Brosnan, Eric Idle, and Peter Ustinov. Goldenberg's music is always listenable and the energetic main theme is particularly infectious; the rest of his score is likewise buoyant, well performed under the composer's direction in Ireland. Trivia buffs take note: This was a relatively early soundtrack release in the CD format, manufactured by Cinedisc in a full digital recording, with a deceptively long running time because Goldenberg's "Main Theme" is included four times on the album, each time in the same version!

Andy Dursin

The Arrival

1996, Silva Screen, from the film *The Arrival,* Orion Pictures, 1996 🎬🎬🎬

album notes: Music: Arthur Kempel; **Orchestra:** The Northwest Sinfonia; **Conductor:** Arthur Kempel.

Atypical sci-fi action score makes good use of synthesized effects to create an air of unease as radio astronomer Charlie Sheen investigates alien infestation. To further suggest the gulf between the invaders' covert operation and humanity's ignorance, composer Arthur Kempel paints each world with distinct musical colors, juxtaposing the idyllic "New Age" sounds of Sheen's lackadaisical life against the back street percussion of a hostile south of the border town.

David Hirsch

Arthur 2

1988, A&M Records, from the film *Arthur 2: On the Rocks,* Warner Bros, Pictures, 1988 🎬🎬

album notes: Music: Burt Bacharach.

You know how the saying goes: If you liked the original, you'll love the sequel. Well, not in this case! While the soundtrack of the first *Arthur* still awaits a first release on compact disc, this sorry hodgepodge only hints at the elements that made the original so enjoyable. The pop selections, while relatively pleasant, seem more manufactured than in the first album, and even Burt Bacharach's themes ("The Best of Times," and "Love Theme") do not have the freshness that characterized his earlier contributions. The film, too, was not on the same comedic level as the original, so that might also explain why its soundtrack sounds less inspired.

Didier C. Deutsch

Article 99

1992, Varèse Sarabande Records, from the film *Article 99*, Orion Pictures, 1992 ♫♫♫

album notes: Music: Danny Elfman; **Conductor:** Shirley Walker.

Danny Elfman nearly buries his traditional, dark-tinged self in an uplifting, noble musical score for an earnest but fatally flawed comedy-drama about Veterans' Administration hospital abuses by the U.S. government. Elfman's score is atypical for the composer in a number of ways, from the lack of dark, dissonant sections of music to the stable, soaring main theme, which represents the heart of the score. It's interesting to see how the composer, along with his usual collaborators (orchestrator Steve Bartek and conductor Shirley Walker), treats the music for this well-intentioned movie. The tone is inspiring, it's nice to listen to, but it all tends to evaporate right after you hear it, a fact further compounded by the scant running time and notable lack of thematic development (the love theme, for example, barely runs a minute). Best recommended for Elfman completists.

Andy Dursin

As Good as It Gets

1998, Columbia, from the Tri-Star film *As Good as It Gets,* 1998 ♫♫♫

album notes: Music: Hans Zimmer; **Conductor:** Harry Gregson-Williams, Lucas Richmond; **Featured Musicians:** Mike Lang, piano; James Kanter, clarinet; Ralph Morrison, violin; Brian Dembrow, viola; Steve Erdody, Armen Ksajikian, cello; Nico Abondolo, bass; James Walker, flute; Philip Ayling, oboe; David Riddles, Ronald Sannelli, bassoon; Katie Kirkpatrick, harp.

From *The Prince of Egypt* to *The Thin Red Line,* Hans Zimmer is one of the busiest, most prolific composers around. *As Good as It Gets* is a lovely score, but regretfully, only five of its sometimes whimsical, sometimes wistful cues are represented on the soundtrack album. The rest of the album consists of songs from the film, mainly middle of the road selections by the likes of Nat King Cole, Shawn Colvin, and Art Garfunkel. The movie, on the other hand, is far from middle of the road and takes a fresh, insightful look at the complexities of mental illness and the breaking down of walls between two lonely, idiosyncratic people. But the soundtrack is probably best appreciated by true Zimmer die-hards only.

Amy Rosen

Ascenseur pour l'échafaud

1959, Philips/France ♫♫♫♫♫

album notes: Music: Miles Davis; **Featured Musicians:** Charlie Parker, alto sax; John Coltrane. tenor sax; Bill Evans, piano; Kenny Clarke, drums; Barney Wilen, tenor sax.

Miles Davis's seminal score for the Louis Malle film *Ascenseur pour l'échafaud* can be found in this CD in the Compact Jazz series, along with other selections not from the film.

An experimental approach to film "scoring" using the then-current (1957) hard-bop style. The director, Louis Malle, had Miles Davis improvise to the picture. The fast and edgy approach of Davis makes an effective backdrop to the French New Wave style that Malle helped create. This is real jazz, played for the moment, like most good jazz is. The dialog between drummer Kenny Clarke and Davis pushes the music to an intensity that matches the tension created by the movie storyline, which borders on a study of paranoia. The opening track, "Générique," is a brooding, minor-key piece that has all of the elements of pure Davis; a funky mid-tempo that he can sing over. "Sur l'autoroute . . ." features a muted Davis playing at full speed. "Diner au motel" is a fast blues. Davis had incredible "time," which means he plays consistently within the parameters of jazz's static "beat." Tenor sax player Barney Wilen and pianist Rene Urtreger play with passion, and add greatly to the mood of the music. Some themes are repeated ("Générique"), giving unification to the music. It is rare when pure jazz works with a picture. This soundtrack straddles both the concept of the film and the musical style of Miles Davis in a beautiful way. The real plus is that this music stands alone as a straight recording. Modern jazz at its best.

Bob Belden

The Associate

1997, Super Tracks, from the film *The Associate,* Hollywood Pictures, 1997 ♫♫♫♫

album notes: Music: Christopher Tyng; **Orchestra:** The Seattle Symphony Orchestra; **Choir:** Tri-City Singers Gospel Choir; **Conductor:** Christopher Tyng.

Freshman Christopher Tyng just flies in the face of modern (i.e. nondescript) film scoring to create a delightfully bright and energetic score for this Whoopi Goldberg comedy in which she plays a financial analyst facing the legendary glass ceiling. Blatantly comedic, Tyng's music is primary like that for an animated film, highlighting (a.k.a. "Mickey Mousing") each moment. Although it's nothing original, Tyng's use of gospel singers, doing everything from excerpts from "Joy to the World" to scats, keeps the energy level constantly up. You'll never know, however, where the music is going to go next, into a pleasant theme or a flurry of brass. This features superb performances by the Seattle Symphony Orchestra and the Tri-City Singers Gospel Choir.

David Hirsch

The Astronomers

1991, Intrada Records, from the KCET-TV series *The Astronomers*, 1991 ♫♫♫

album notes: Music: J.A.C. Redford; **Featured Musicians:** Stu Goldberg, synthesizers; George Doering, guitars; Ray Kelly, cello; Jon Clarke, woodwinds; Joel Peskin, saxophones.

J.A.C. Redford's score for this 1991 PBS documentary is a pleasant enough soundtrack from Intrada Records, with a nice diversity of tracks making for a smooth listening experience. Redford's score is grounded primarily in an expansive melody ("The Astronomers") that recurs throughout the album. It also includes cues that are by turns magical, mystical, dissonant and even disturbing, reflecting all of the various elements that comprise our universe—from the warmth of our own sun to the puzzling phenomena of black holes outside our solar system. Virtually the entire score is performed on synthesizers (with only some tracks featuring a small acoustic ensemble), but to the composer's credit, the score remains as imaginative aurally as the galactic visions it underscores.

Andy Dursin

The A-Team

1990, Silva Screen Records, from the TV series *The A-Team*, 1983-84 ♫♫♫

album notes: Music: Mike Post, Pete Carpenter; **Conductor:** Daniel Caine.

A faithful recreation of the themes composed for the 1983–87 series by Mike Post and Pete Carpenter with their team of co-composers (three are credited here). Principally, the album is made up of the splashy action and second unit transitional cues, the music often played as hands are seen building some odd vehicle or weapon from assorted bits and pieces. The show wasn't known for moments of tense interpersonal drama; cars crashed and things just blew up, so many of the music cues were variations of the main theme. The album features a Mexican flavored motif ("Bandits!") and several other location establishing themes ("The A-Team in New York City"), but all too often there's little variety to be found. The main theme is excessively repeated. No fault goes to Derek Wadsworth, who did a fine job adapting the music for the album from the original scores. He also conducts the orchestra under the pseudonym of Daniel Caine.

David Hirsch

At First Sight

1998, Milan Records, from the MGM film *At First Sight*, 1998 ♫♫♫♫

album notes: Music: Mark Isham; **Conductor:** Ken Kugler.

An unusual low-key drama about a blind young man (Val Kilmer) who recovers his sight, *At First Sight* found in Mark Isham a composer with a great feel for attractive musical textures that combine to create a colorful, inventive tapestry. The cues, a mixture of romantic themes and dramatic moments, come across as a wistful collection that gave the film some of its moods, while adding their own comments on the action, and stand out on their own in this evocative soundtrack album. Vocal selections by Louis Armstrong, Ella Fitzgerald, and Gigi Worth (replacing Diana Krall who sang the theme song, "Love Is Where You Are" in the film but, surprisingly, not on the CD, even though she is included in another selection) round out the tracks.

Didier C. Deutsch

At Play in the Fields of the Lord

1992, Fantasy Records, from the film *At Play in the Fields of the Lord*, 1992 ♫♫♫

album notes: Music: Zbigniew Preisner; **Orchestra:** The Polish Radio Grand Symphony Orchestra; **Conductor:** Antoni Wit.

Three composers were used to incorporate indigenous tribal music into Zbigniew Preisner's orchestral score. This mixing of diverse styles works brilliantly on film and probably would have on the CD, unfortunately, the album fails to allow the haunting underscore to fully develop the mood it tries so very hard to create. While the score cues move effortlessly between the sustained harmonics of its orchestral themes and the powerful rhythms of the Niaruna tribe, the haphazard placement of several "Jukebox" recordings completely sabotage what could have been a mystical musical journey.

David Hirsch

Atlantic City

1981, DRG Records, from the film *Atlantic City*, Paramount Pictures, 1981 ♫♫♫

album notes: Music: Michel Legrand; **Conductor:** Michel Legrand.

Burt Lancaster portrayed a small-time mafioso in this film by Louis Malle, set in the New Jersey gambling mecca, for which Michel Legrand provided a gritty, diversified score far removed from his most recognizable screen contributions. At its liveliest and most genuinely interesting, the score offers jazz selections ("Piano Blackjack," "Road Map for a Free Jazz Group," "Trio

Jazz") in which the composer plays the piano, surrounded by an assortment of uncredited sidemen (including, probably, Ron Carter on bass). On the other side of the scale, a strident "Bellini Rock" proves a real turn-off, while the meandering "No Gambling Allowed" and "Slot Machine Baby" are not sufficiently developed to really attract. Somewhere in-between, Robert Goulet is remarkably bland but okay in the Paul Anka song, "Atlantic City, My Old Friend," making this album a little bit of undefined everything for everybody.

Didier C. Deutsch

August

1995, Debonair Records/U.K., from the Granada film *August,* 1995 ✍✍✍✍

album notes: Music: Anthony Hopkins.

Anthony Hopkins, usually better known as a remarkable actor (*Silence of the Lambs*), reveals another facet of his many talents with this soundtrack album for a film based on Chekov's *Uncle Vanya,* in which he starred and for which he wrote the engaging music. Reflecting the languor of a Welsh summer and the beauty of the countryside, as well as the feelings of the "boring minor characters" who inhabit the film, Hopkins created an elegiac series of attractive cues, quite evocative and strikingly musical. John Williams doesn't need to worry about his future, but if you have the patience to hunt for this CD, released in England but available here through the usual mail-order specialists, you won't regret it.

Didier C. Deutsch

Austin Powers

1997, Hollywood Records, from the film *Austin Powers,* New Line Cinema, 1997 ✍✍✍✍

album notes: Music: George S. Clinton.

The soundtrack to this amiable send-up of the spy thrillers of the 1960s will no doubt bring a smile to anyone listening to it. The film, about a nerd who imagines he is the world's greatest spy, is rife with references to that benign period when our man Flint was cool as a cucumber and even smarter and when the funniest flick of its kind was another spoof, *Casino Royale.* There is more than a passing reference to that last film, as a matter of fact, with Susanna Hoffs singing "The Book of Love" (too bad they couldn't get the actual recording by Dusty Springfield!), and composer Burt Bacharach (who scored it), contributing a new version of "What the World Needs Now" to this mildly zany album. There are also other genuinely engaging tracks, including Sergio Mendes's "Mas Que Nada," and Quincy Jones's "Soul Bossa Nova," but the palm must go to George S. Clinton's whimsical "Shag-adelic" medley, filled with

amusing quotes from the James Bond and other spy films of the period. It's not a great album, but quite delightful.

Didier C. Deutsch

Austin Powers: The Spy Who Shagged Me

1999, Maverick Records, from the New Line Cinema film *Austin Powers: The Spy Who Shagged Me, 1999* ✍✍✍✍

The secret agent who made the world safe for shagging and calling women bay-a-by carts a pretty impressive musical mission on the reprise to his 1997 smash hit. And this time, creator Mike Myers—who plays Austin and arch-enemy "Dr. Evil"— lends his own vocal tones to a dry, clipped version of "Just the Two of Us." But mostly, *The Spy Who Shagged Me* draws its strength from tastefully chosen and executed covers, including Lenny Kravitz's hard-hitting take of the Guess Who's "American Woman," R.E.M.'s lope through Tommy James & the Shondells' "Draggin' the Line," and Stone Temple Pilot frontman Scott Weiland's trip through the Zombie's "Time of the Season." Burt Bacharach and Elvis Costello cast a dignified spirit on the former's "I'll Never Fall in Love Again," while Madonna's "Beautiful Stranger" is a nice piece of '60s Brit pop retro—until, of course, the Who's "My Generation" blows it and practically everything else off the disc.

Gary Graff

Avalon

1990, Reprise Records, from the film *Avalon,* Tri-Star Pictures, 1990 ✍✍✍✍

album notes: Music: Randy Newman; **Featured Musicians:** Stuart Canin, violin; Michael Lang, piano; Malcolm McNab, trumpet; Randy Newman, piano.

This delightful score by Randy Newman is tinged with melancholy. Director Barry Levinson's critically acclaimed story tells of the loss of faith felt by an immigrant as he watches his family grow up not with the values of his homeland, but those of America. Newman's music takes us along through the years of hopes and shattered dreams in a moving symphony.

David Hirsch

The Avengers

1998, Compass III Records, from the Warner Bros. film *The Avengers,* 1998 ✍✍

album notes: Music: Joel McNeely; **Conductor:** Joel McNeely; **Featured Musicians:** Judd Miller, synthesizer and EVI; Ron Aston, electronic percussion.

1998, Atlantic Records, from the Warner Bros. film *The Avengers*, 1998 ♫♫

There are several trends in the '90s that keep popping up. One is to make a motion picture based on an old TV show. Another is to release two soundtrack albums: a song album with "music from and inspired by" the film and a score album. Thus we have two different albums for a film that didn't quite make it. Call it an unrequited embarrassment of riches. *The Avengers* seemed like it should have been a hit. A glossy slick production, it starred Ralph Fiennes, in his first high-profile role since *The English Patient*, as Jon Steed and the curvaceous Uma Thurman portraying Emma Peel. But the movie did not fare well, due in part to the total lack of screen chemistry between the two main characters.

The song-driven album, on Atlantic, consists mostly of alternative tracks from artists such as Annie Lennox, Dishwalla, and The Verve Pipe. At best, it is a ho-hum compilation. The Compass III recording contains the score composed by Joel McNeely, who did a pretty good job, bringing along some bits of music that are reminiscent of the Bond films and using bars from "The Flight of the Bumble Bee" to create "The Flight of the Mechanical Bees," a stand-out track.

Beth Krakower

Awakenings

1991, Reprise Records, from the film *Awakenings*, Columbia Pictures, 1991 ♫♫♫♫

album notes: Music: Randy Newman; **Featured Musicians:** Dan Higgins, soprano sax; Ralph Grierson, piano; Louise Ditullio, flute.

This moving Randy Newman score captures very well the parallels in the two existences that are at the core of this film—a shy doctor who avoids dealing with his own life, and that of a former comatose patient, awakened to find he has to deal with being a middle-aged adult. Though it starts off on a very poignant note, as the two men learn from each other how to cope with their lives, the score evolves to become brighter and more optimistic. The album also includes the song "Time of the Season" by The Zombies.

David Hirsch

An Awfully Big Adventure

1995, Filmtracks, from the Fine Line film *An Awfully Big Adventure*, 1995 ♫♫♫♫

album notes: Music: Richard Hartley; **Conductor:** Richard Hartley.

Hugh Grant had another winning screen role in this dry tale of a small theatrical repertory company, its ruthless director, Meredith Potter, and the ingenue, Stella, who falls in love with him. Belying the darker aspects of the film, in which Potter and the star of the company, the dashing P. L. O'Hara, battle over

Stella's love and affection while rehearsing a production of *Peter Pan*, Richard Hartley's score is very low-key, with a recurring romantic theme as its attractive anchor. Occasionally, a brighter moment is evoked ever so briefly ("Let's Hang the Cloth"), but the overall tone is wistful, making this a lovely, unusual score with a lot to offer.

Didier C. Deutsch

B

Babe

1995, Varèse Sarabande Records, from the film *Babe*, Universal Pictures, 1995 ♫♫♫

album notes: Music: Nigel Westlake; **Orchestra:** The Victorian Philharmonic Orchestra; **Conductors:** David Stanhope, Carl Vine.

Delightful concept album that mixes music and dialogue from the hit fantasy film about a farm populated by talking animals. Though live-action, composer Nigel Westlake chose well to paint this film with a broad cartoon-like score. While most soundtrack purists find the notion detestable, the dialogue sound bites are well interpolated here with the film's underscore, which is based primarily on various classical and contemporary compositions. Most notable is the adaption of Saint-Saens's *Symphony No. 3* which, with lyrics by Johnathon Hodge, became the signature tune for the film's singing mice trio. The result is just plain fun and a good way to introduce the classics to young children.

David Hirsch

The Babe

1991, MCA Records, from the film *The Babe*, Universal, 1991 ♫♫♫♫

album notes: Music: Elmer Bernstein; **Conductor:** Elmer Bernstein.

The Babe, of course, was Babe Ruth, whose picturesque life story is the basis for this screen biography starring John Goodman. An important part of the film's flair is due to Elmer Bernstein's broad score, whose more rambunctious cues echo the exuberant lifestyle of one of baseball's most colorful folk heroes. Obviously sharing director Arthur Hiller's evident fondness for the character, Bernstein wrote one of his most rewarding middle-of-the-road efforts here, drawing his inspiration from the period (the 1920s and '30s), the locales where the action unfolds, and the natural vitality in the sport itself. Among the many remarkable highlights, "Kids Ride," the inventive "Proposal," "Claire and the Dream," and "Helen Leaves" strike

James Cromwell in Babe. **(The Kobal Collection)**

a more felicitous note, but the whole score is unusually lively and enjoyable.

Didier C. Deutsch

Babe: Pig in the City

1998, Geffen Records, from the Universal film *Babe: Pig in the City*, 1998 ♪♪♪♪

album notes: Music: Edward Shearmur; **Conductor:** Edward Shearmur.

It was bound to happen: the success of the little comedy *Babe* spawned a sequel, *Babe: Pig in the City,* equally imaginative and endearing. How that translated into a soundtrack in which a speeded-up version of Edith Piaf's anthem, "Je ne regrette rien," can be found next to "That's Amore," by Dean Martin, "Chattanooga Choo Choo," by Glen Miller and his orchestra, or a Cat Chorus of "Three Blind Mice," is another matter altogether. The fact is, this soundtrack album, despite its diversified sounds (from pop tunes to tongue-in-pig-cheek themes by Ed Shearmur) is a hoot (excuse me, a squeal!) from beginning to end.

Didier C. Deutsch

Babes in Arms

1990, New World Records, from the studio cast recording *Babes in Arms*, 1990 ♪♪♪♪♪

album notes: Music: Richard Rodgers; **Lyrics:** Lorenz Hart; **Orchestra:** The New Jersey Symphony Orchestra; **Conductor:** Evans Haile; **Cast:** Gregg Edelman, Judy Blazer, Jason Graae, Donna Kane, Judy Kaye, Adam Grupper.

In a classic let's-put-a-barnyard-show-together, a group of teenagers, all of them children of vaudevillian performers, decide to stage a revue in order to avoid being sent to work school, in this whimsical musical by Richard Rodgers and Lorenz Hart. It opened on April 14, 1937, and yielded such standards as "Where or When," "I Wish I Were in Love Again," "My Funny Valentine," "Johnny One-Note," and "The Lady Is a Tramp." The studio cast album listed above, the only one currently available in the catalogue, beautifully captures the spirited moods of the musical, and brings them forth in an excellent recording that enhances the impish, youthful exuberance of the score.

Didier C. Deutsch

The Baby-Sitters Club

1995, Sony Wonder, from the film *The Baby-Sitters Club*, Columbia Pictures, 1995 ♪♪♪

An endearing, charmingly offbeat big screen take on the familiar book and cable series by Ann M. Martin, *The Baby-Sitters Club* is the occasion for a group of seven young girls to create a pool so that someone would always be available should a sitter be otherwise engaged (usually with a boyfriend). Modest and somewhat untheatrical, the film boasts a soundtrack consisting of nicely scrubbed pop songs without a single offensive lyric (which may explain, in a way, why it was issued on Sony Wonder, Sony's kiddie label). The performances are also appropriately harmless.

Didier C. Deutsch

Baby the Rain Must Fall/The Caretakers

1991, Mainstream Records, from the films *Baby the Rain Must Fall*, Columbia Pictures, 1965; and *The Caretakers*, United Artists, 1963. ♪♪♪

album notes: Music: Elmer Bernstein.

Two early Elmer Bernstein scores, unfortunately marred by poor mastering and heavy reverb which hearkens back to the 1960s. Starring Steve McQueen as a rockabilly singer who takes a walk on the wild side, *Baby the Rain Must Fall* elicited a rock-based score from Bernstein, with folk vocals by The We Three Trio that also reflect the film's time period. Shorty Rogers's explosive arrangements are a big plus.

Robert Stack and Joan Crawford share billing in *The Caretakers,* a shallow drama set in a West Coast mental institution. Belying the serious subject matter, Bernstein's score turns out to be for the most part a bouncy, jazzy affair, with only two tracks ("The Cage" and "Electrotherapy") making direct references to the film's background. Sonically, the CD sounds very hissy, with distortion on some of the tracks, and particularly noticeable hum in *The Caretakers.*

Didier C. Deutsch

Babylon 5

1998, Sonic Images, from the Warner Bros. television series *Babylon 5*, 1997, 1998 ♪♪

album notes: Music: Christopher Franke.

The music of *Babylon 5,* an audio journey that captures the soul of the series, has received two different kinds of releases on CD. Two albums, *Darkness Ascending* and *The Face of the Enemy,* represent continuous suites from various shows, with new compositions. The other releases (of which there are many) document the music heard on individual episodes, containing all the cues heard on each show, presented in sequential order. Each has an approximate playing time of 30 minutes, and each features at least an extended cue, as heard in the actual episode it documents.

It's not often that a TV show, or a film for that matter, receives the lavish musical attention elicited by this series, and the multiplicity of titles seems to suggest that Sonic Images is intent on releasing every note of music written for it. The problem here is that composer Christopher Franke is not too terribly talented. Sure, he creates the right out-of-this-world riffs, the required crescendos, and the appropriate percolating rhythms. But after a few minutes of listening to these albums one gets the distinct impression that Franke is, at best, a gifted composer with a limited imagination—his music is serviceable and formulaic, but hardly memorable. Compare, if you will, what he writes with the scores of people like John Williams, Jerry Goldsmith, Joel McNeely, or Jay Chattaway: there is an out-of-this world of difference. The different CD designs, though, are cute.

Didier C. Deutsch

Back to School

See: Pee-Wee's Big Adventure/Back to School

Back to the Future

1985, MCA Records, from the film *Back to the Future,* Universal Pictures, 1985 ♪♪♪♪

album notes: Music: Alan Silvestri; **Orchestra:** The Outatime Orchestra; **Conductor:** Alan Silvestri.

The time travel paradox format of the *Back to the Future* trilogy has allowed series composer Alan Silvestri to rework his themes in several ways. The first album is nothing more than a song compilation, though all the songs actually are heard in the film, especially during the big dance sequence. The theme is included as well as a nine-minute suite of the finale credited as the "Back to the Future Overture."

David Hirsch

Back to the Future, Part II

1989, MCA Records, from the film *Back to the Future, Part II,* Universal Pictures, 1989 ♪♪♪

album notes: Music: Alan Silvestri; **Conductor:** Alan Silvestri.

Back to the Future, Part II is all underscore, but because of the darker aspects of the film, Silvestri does tend to paint a gloomy picture by stretching things out a bit. The themes crawl along before they are resolved, and while the need exists to make the danger more severe, the comedic aspect of the series is only sporadically present.

David Hirsch

Back to the Future, Part III

1990, Varèse Sarabande Records, from the film *Back to the Future, Part III*, Universal Pictures, 1990 ♫♫♫♫

album notes: Music: Alan Silvestri; **Conductor:** Alan Silvestri.

For the third installment in the series, Silvestri backtracks even further away from the naivete of the 1950s to adopt a whimsical tone for this child-like, innocent adventure and romance of the old, wild west. He even successfully spoofs the genre by interpolating classic (if not clichéd) western motifs like the harmonica. He also develops a delightfully romantic new theme presented here for Doc Brown's love interest, Clara, the schoolmarm. Some film series tend to abandon the overuse of thematic material to keep things from getting boring (i.e. the James Bond films), but the need was never so vital to keep audiences clued in as in this trilogy's vast plate of reoccurring time travel gags.

David Hirsch

Back to Titanic

See: Titanic

Backbeat

1994, Virgin Records, from the PolyGram/Gramercy film *Backbeat*, 1994 ♫♫

album notes: Featured Musicians: Greg Dulli, Dave Pirner, lead vocals; Don Fleming, Thurston Moore, guitar, vocals; Dave Grohl, drums; Mike Mills, bass, vocals.

A film that purports to portray the early Beatles, *BackBeat* also gives some youthful imitators an opportunity to cover non-Beatles rock'n'roll songs, including "Long Tall Sally," "Twist and Shout," "Please Mr. Postman," "Rock'n'Roll Music," and "Good Golly Miss Molly." The performances are generally quite acceptable, but with so many greater renditions available, the purpose of this CD, even as a soundtrack album, seems insignificant.

Didier C. Deutsch

Backdraft

1991, Milan Records, from the film *Backdraft*, Universal Pictures, 1991 ♫♫♫♫

album notes: Music: Hans Zimmer

A memorable and powerful score by Hans Zimmer, *Backdraft* represents one of the composer's earliest but most successful cinematic endeavors, one which continues to be used in count-less movie trailers and television spots. With his trademark collection of heavy percussion, pounding synthesizers, and blaring orchestra, Zimmer uses strong melodic themes to underscore Ron Howard's entertaining firefighting melodrama. It fits this particular film like a glove; from the bombastic and triumphant opening fanfare to its dissonant sections with chorus, *Backdraft* is a larger-than-life dramatic score that makes for an ideal listening experience, and certainly remains one of Zimmer's most satisfying efforts to date. The album also contains a pair of good songs by Bruce Hornsby & the Range, one of which ("Set Me in Motion") was written specifically for the movie.

Andy Dursin

The Bad and the Beautiful

1996, Rhino Records, from the film *The Bad and the Beautiful*, MGM, 1952 ♫♫♫♫

album notes: Music: David Raksin; **Orchestra:** The MGM Studio Orchestra; **Conductor:** David Raksin.

It is always preferable to listen to a recording of a piece of music that has been orchestrated and conducted by the composer himself, because theoretically, the listener is guaranteed that every musical texture, dynamic, and nuance that the composer had in mind when creating the music will survive through their own, personal interpretation for the recording. Such is the case with Rhino's comprehensive release of David Raksin's score for *The Bad and the Beautiful,* which is a long-awaited, eagerly anticipated CD issue.

In creating this complete soundtrack recording, the producer has included 44 musical cues (some far greater in length than those edited for the final cut of the film), and three supplemental versions of the main and end titles, which were revised by the composer for the edited film. Such completeness and the inclusion of the bonus tracks allows film music buffs and historians alike to analyze the creative process and understand exactly how the scoring and editing process works. In this case, this enjoyable task is made even easier, because of the wonderfully personal recollections of Raksin himself, who has penned a concise history of the film and his music for the accompanying 28-page booklet. While the original stereo master recordings were destroyed in the 1960s, 1/4 mono tape copies survived and are the primary source for this release, which has very pleasing sonic characteristics.

Charles L. Granata

Bad Girls

1994, Fox Records, from the film *Bad Girls*, 20th Century Fox, 1994 ♫♫♫

album notes: Music: Jerry Goldsmith; **Conductor:** Jerry Goldsmith.

Although the film itself was wretched, Jerry Goldsmith wrote a rousing action score for this all-female western that's one of the composers best works of the '90s. After a pastoral opening of keyboard and guitar, the score takes off with some break-neck cues for chases, a bank robbery, and an ambush, as well as a good-natured, bucolic "Jail Break," all done in the composer's indelible western style of the '60s and '70s. It's percussive and highly inventive rhythmically, with a big, broad John Wayne–style brass theme blasting over many of the action highlights; the "Ambush" cue is a particularly exciting and sustained piece featuring a thrilling brass fugue.

Jeff Bond

Bad Moon

1996, Silva America, from the film *Bad Moon*, Morgan Creek Production, 1996 🎬🎬🎬

album notes: Music: Daniel Licht; **Orchestra:** The Northwest Sinfonia; **Conductor:** Pete Anthony.

Still too young to be jaded, composer Daniel Licht seems to have ignored the quality of this film and put his best foot forward. He shows real potential by pulling off this surprisingly well-composed and entertaining orchestral score. It manages to inject a surprising amount of emotional drama into a strictly cliched "Lassie vs. The Werewolf" horror film that really didn't deserve this much effort. He's definitely a promising talent.

David Hirsch

Ballad of a Gunfighter

1998, Citadel Records, from the Plaster City film *Ballad of a Gunfighter*, 1998 🎬🎬

album notes: Music: Jim Fox.

Jim Fox sounds like he has listened to a lot of western soundtracks, particularly those written by Ennio Morricone and Francesco de Masi, and figured out that he could compose that kind of music. Except that, while he pulls all the familiar stops (harmonica wailing, guitar strumming, etc.), he lacks one essential ingredient in the mix: musical invention. As a result, *Ballad of a Gunfighter*, a score I wanted to like before I even began to play it, ends up being a monotonous collection of selections (I hesitate to even call them "tunes") that seem in search of a movie. That it was almost entirely created on electronic instruments changes little, despite director Christopher Coppola's evident enthusiasm for his composer (also his former music teacher at the University of Redlands). Here and there, one can catch glimpses of melodies that might have made the whole difference ("The Road to Disaster," "The Games," "End Credits"), but these moments are too few and far between.

Didier C. Deutsch

The Ballad of Little Jo

1993, Intrada Records, from the film *The Ballad of Little Jo*, Fine Line Features, 1993 🎬🎬🎬

album notes: Music: David Mansfield.

Some films (and some soundtracks) are like rare wines—they need to be tasted to be fully appreciated, but the rewards are enormous. Such is the case with this delightful score by David Mansfield, who also created the music for the revisionist western *Heaven's Gate*. The film's setting, the post-Civil War American West, inspired the composer to write a series of charmingly expressive cues that find their roots in the traditional music of the frontier. The film, which starred Bo Hopkins, Ian McKellen, and Carrie Snodgress, was not a tremendous success and quickly disappeared. Its soundtrack album is well worth hunting for.

Didier C. Deutsch

Ballroom

1992, Sony Broadway, from the Broadway production, *Ballroom* 1979 🎬🎬🎬

album notes: Music: Billy Goldenberg; **Lyrics:** Alan and Marilyn Bergman; **Conductor:** Don Jennings; **Cast:** Dorothy Loudon, Vincent Gardenia, Lynn Roberts, Bernie Knee.

In what is essentially a two-character show, Dorothy Loudon and Vincent Gardenia starred in *Ballroom*, a big dance musical based on the television musical drama, "Queen of the Stardust Ballroom." The drama had aired four years earlier with Maureen Stapleton and Charles Durning, respectively, as a widow and a middle-age married man who meet on the dance floor and have an affair. Brilliantly staged by Michael Bennett, and a showcase for his unique talent as a choreographer, the musical (with a score by Billy Goldenberg, and Alan and Marilyn Bergman) introduced the show-stopping "Fifty Percent," sung by Loudon at the peak of her talent, and presented several big band–styled numbers performed by Lynn Roberts and Bernie Knee. Though it only enjoyed a short run of 116 performances, following its December 14, 1978, opening, it yielded a cast album which is perhaps the best thing it had to offer.

Beth Krakower

Balto

1995, MCA Records, from the animated feature *Balto*, Universal Pictures, 1995 🎬🎬🎬🎬

album notes: Music: James Horner; **Orchestra:** The London Symphony Orchestra; **Conductor:** James Horner.

Balto is another animated feature from Steven Spielberg's Amblin Entertainment, sporting another winning score by James Horner. Who could complain about it! Avoiding the obvious cute approach the medium might have suggested, the composer decided instead to write a set of epic cues to accompany this inspiring story of a stray half-dog, half-wolf on a rescue mission to a remote Alaskan outpost filled with sick kids. In the course of the action, Balto gets to win the heart of an attractive female, Jenna, whose owner, Rosy, is one of the sick children, and shares some light-hearted moments in the company of his friends, Boris, a Russian goose, and Muk and Luk, two polar bears. Most of Horner's cues are often more exciting than the action would seem to require, but the bombast is offset by a couple of introspective selections, like "Rosy Goes to the Doctor," that give the whole score greater scope and impact.

Didier C. Deutsch

Bambi

 1998, Disney Records, from the Disney film *Bambi,* 1947 𝄞𝄞𝄞𝄞𝄞

album notes: Music: Frank Churchill, Larry Morey, Ed Plumb; **Conductor:** Alexander Steinert.

Of all the early major Disney cartoon features, *Bambi* may well be the most perfect in conception and execution. Though infrequently mentioned among the studio's greatest achievements, this story of the graceful little fawn who grows up to become Prince of the Forest, is an endearing tale, filled with striking imagery, gorgeous designs, and music that matches in beauty the various elements of the film. This restored edition brings out all the cues in Frank Churchill's eloquent score, which delineates the story in bold, colorful strokes, with Larry Morey contributing simple but effective lyrics to the songs performed by the anonymous studio chorus. The whole thing is grandly evocative, quite entertaining, and right on target. A joy from beginning to end.

Didier C. Deutsch

Bandolero!

1990, Cinema Show/edel Records, from the film *Bandolero!* 20th Century Fox, 1968 𝄞𝄞𝄞𝄞

album notes: Music: Jerry Goldsmith; **Orchestra:** The 20th Century Fox Orchestra; **Conductor:** Lionel Newman.

Jerry Goldsmith's picaresque score for this 1968 Jimmy Stewart western features a classically direct, folksy title theme that's whistled over shots of Stewart riding the range. The rest of the score offers a fascinating contrast between the traditional elements of the title music and the kind of hard-edged, experimental writing Goldsmith produced for his legendary *Planet of the Apes* score released the same year. There are several exciting action cues marked by powerful staccato rhythms and striking use of a grinding bass harmonica, as well as a moody love

theme for marimba. It's an unusual score very much recommended to fans of Goldsmith's '60s style, its comic elements working almost as a satire of the standard western sound.

Jeff Bond

The Band Wagon

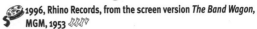 1996, Rhino Records, from the screen version *The Band Wagon,* MGM, 1953 𝄞𝄞𝄞

album notes: Music: Arthur Schwartz; **Lyrics:** Howard Dietz; **Orchestra:** The MGM Studio Orchestra; **Conductor:** Adolph Deutsch; **Cast:** Fred Astaire, Cyd Charisse, Oscar Levant, Nanette Fabray, Jack Buchanan, James Mitchell.

Another in a long line of producer Arthur Freed's films built around specific composers' song catalogs, *The Band Wagon* centers on the music of Arthur Schwartz and the lyrics of Howard Dietz. Starring Fred Astaire and Cyd Charisse, it includes many of the pair's most celebrated collaborations, including "By Myself," "That's Entertainment," "Dancing in the Dark," "You and the Night and the Music," and "I Guess I'll Have to Change My Plan."

The Band Wagon proved to be one of MGM's last brilliant successes, and this newly restored "complete" edition, produced under the auspices of George Feltenstein and Bradley Flanagan, is an important addition to the ever-growing library of MGM film recordings being preserved by Rhino Records.

Unfortunately, the sonic quality of this particular release is not up to Rhino's usual standard for the MGM line, primarily due to the way that the film company transferred the original stereo tracks. According to Feltenstein, while most of the original 1953 sessions were recorded in stereo on 3-track magnetic tape, the only surviving reels are the monophonic, 1/4" mixdowns done in the 1960s, which were the masters used for this release. The outstanding music makes it easy to overlook the abundance of tape hiss, however. As is customary with these issues, Rhino has dipped into the vault and included a specially produced mix of "The Girl Hunt Ballet," and two demo recordings by associate producer Roger Edens.

Charles L. Granata

Bandwagon

1997, RCA/BMG, from the Lakeshore Entertainment film *Bandwagon,* 1997 𝄞𝄞𝄞

album notes: Music: Greg Kendall.

Bandwagon, which was originally shown at the Sundance Film Festival, is a charming movie about Circus Monkey, a fictitious unsigned band from North Carolina, searching for the illusive recording contract. The band's members are quirky, one's a pothead, one's a bad boy, one's a want-to-be womanizer, and the singer only writes songs about his "girlfriend" Ann. Since the movie looked at the underground scene in the Southeast, most of the bands on the album were unsigned at the time of its release. Tackle Box and Incinerator both contributed two songs each to the album, and they are the best of the lot. But don't dismiss the incredibly catchy, alternapop songs by "Circus Monkey," which were composed by Greg Kendall, an ex-member of the Connells. In fact, if you are a fan of alternative bands like the Connells or Barenaked Ladies, you owe it to yourself to check out this CD.

Beth Krakower

B.A.P.s

1997, Milan Records, from the film *B.A.P.s,* New Line Cinema, 1997 ♫♫♫

album notes: Music: Stanley Clarke; **Conductor:** William Kidd.

Once you get past those seven mediocre rap and pop music tunes intended to appeal to the kids, you'll be pleasantly surprised to find an impressively well-written orchestral score. Hidden at the end, Stanley Clarke's music is filled with a lot of emotion, supported by a charming main theme. It's quite a contrast from the tone set by the album's first half and certainly more practical entertainment. That may not be enough of a reason, for Clarke's music only amounts to about seventeen minutes on this album. That translates to spending $1 per minute on it. Considering this score was written for a mediocre comedy film, who would go out of their way to purchase this album? Perhaps only Stanley Clarke fans, for few others might feel the investment worthwhile.

David Hirsch

Barabbas

See: Alexander the Great

Baraka

1992, Milan Records, from the film *Baraka,* Samuel Goldwyn, 1992 ♫♫♫

album notes: Music: Michael Stearns.

Quoting the liner notes, "Baraka is an ancient Sufi word [. . .] simply translated as a blessing, or the breath or essence of life from which the evolutionary process unfolds." Taking a cue from this concept, director Ron Fricke took his cameras to such diverse locations as Brazil, Nepal, Cambodia, Kuwait, India, Tanzania, and Iran to create a "non-verbal" film that tells the story of our planet's evolution, man's diversity, and the impact we have had on the environment. To illustrate musically this "journey of rediscovery that plunges into nature, history, the

human spirit, and finally into the realm of the infinite," the soundtrack gathers together performances recorded around the world, with composer Michael Stearns contributing the instrumental cues that link these selections into a seamless entity. Call this the ultimate world music soundtrack.

Didier C. Deutsch

The Barbarians

1990, Intrada Records, from the film *The Barbarians,* Cannon International, 1987 ♫♫

album notes: Music: Pino Donaggio; **Orchestra:** The Unione Musicisti di Roma; **Conductor:** Natale Massara.

This big score by Pino Donaggio with spectacular ambient sound is a blend of heavily pulsating synth sounds framed by the orchestral support provided by Rome's Unione Musicisti, one of Italy's grandest film orchestras. The film, a pseudo epic starring two beefy musclemen, David and Peter Paul, is more cartoonish in approach than *Conan* or *Xena,* and, for that matter, so is Donaggio's music. However, in the midst of the pounding "action" cues, the composer reveals a tender side with lovely melodic tunes like "Encounter Twins and Canary," or "Kadar in Harem," which soften the music and make it sound more attractive than it really is. One serious drawback in the gorgeously layered sound is the fact that some cues don't seem to be totally realized and end up in a quick fade without actually making much of an impact. "Ruby Dawn," a vocal tune with an anachronistic Eurobeat, closes the set.

Didier C. Deutsch

The Barefoot Contessa/The Quiet American/Room at the Top

1996, DRG Records, from the films *The Barefoot Contessa,* United Artists, 1954; *The Quiet American,* Warner Bros., 1958; and *Room at the Top,* Continental Film Distribution, 1959 🎬🎬🎬

album notes: Music: Mario Nascimbene; **Orchestrations:** Mario Nascimbene.

Italian film composer Mario Nascimbene made quite an impression with his score for *The Barefoot Contessa,* which gave Ava Gardner one of her most sensual screen roles as a cabaret dancer whose rise to international fame and subsequent marriage to an Italian count ends after he murders her in a jealous fit. Writing in a remarkably subdued and melodic vein, Nascimbene delivered a series of eloquent cues that set off the film's most important scenes.

As a result of the film's success, the composer was asked to work on such illustrious projects as *Alexander the Great* and David O. Selznick's *A Farewell to Arms* (q.v.), before scoring *The Quiet American,* a pre-Vietnam War old-fashioned thriller set in Saigon, starring Audie Murphy, for which he used a blend of ethnic instruments to give his music the right tonal color.

For the British working-class drama, *Room at the Top,* created a year after *The Quiet American,* Nascimbene again devised a score that set off the screen action and enhanced it with a series of musical cues that drew much of their dramatic strength from the judicious use of brass instruments over the orchestral texture. All three scores, presented here in a recording supervised by the composer, show their age, with the CD containing many technical flaws (image shifting, hiss, distortion, bad editing) that do little to enhance their presentation.

Didier C. Deutsch

Barnum

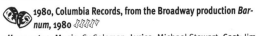

1980, Columbia Records, from the Broadway production *Barnum,* 1980 🎬🎬🎬🎬

album notes: Music: Cy Coleman; **Lyrics:** Michael Stewart. **Cast:** Jim Dale, Glen Close.

The life of Phineas Taylor (P.T.) Barnum provided Cy Coleman, Michael Stewart and Mark Bramble with the gem of an idea for a brassy Broadway show. Agilely portrayed by Jim Dale, with Glenn Close playing Barnum's long-suffering wife, Chairy, the musical was not, by any stretch of the imagination, a circus tent attraction, but an honest-to-goodness production, with big numbers solidly integrated within the development of a book that retraced Barnum's phenomenal career as a showman. Wittily staged by Joe Layton, it offers stylized side glances at circus life, and concentrates instead on Barnum's humble beginnings, his first successes, his romantic involvement with Jenny Lind, the Swedish Nightingale, and his eventual teaming with James A. Bailey in creating the Greatest Show on Earth. Bright, extraordinarily lively and exciting, the score yielded many hits, including "The Colors of My Life," "Come Follow the Band," and "Join the Circus," all delivered with the right amount of dash and personal glee by the energetic Jim Dale (who won a Tony for his performance), as heard in the original cast album. The show opened on Broadway on April 30, 1980, and had a run of 854 performances.

Didier C. Deutsch

Barocco

1992, CAM Records/Italy, from the film *Barocco,* 1976 🎬🎬🎬🎬

album notes: Music: Philippe Sarde; **Conductor:** Hubert Rostaing and Carlo Savina.

A sophisticated thriller, directed by André Techine and starring Gérard Depardieu and Isabelle Adjani, *Barocco* is particularly interesting in that it was initially supposed to be scored by Ennio Morricone, who was eventually replaced by Philippe Sarde. The film, about a woman who meets and falls in love with the killer of her former lover, was particularly effective in Techine's attempts at shedding the usual tenets of the genre, by expanding the scope and timing of the action itself, which gave his film an artificial and ultimately fascinating look. Sarde's music details the story with sometimes unusual results (a carnival atmosphere pervades "Modern Times"), with the composer's trademark low string effects giving an ominous, dark tone to most of the selections. An exception is a Latin-influenced "The Radical One," with a jazz riff. The film also yielded a vocal track, "On se voit se voir," performed by Marie-France Garcia, which became a hit in Europe, and has been heard on countless film music anthologies. As is often the case with albums released by CAM, total playing time comes to 20:30, which is quite short for the price. This recording may be difficult to find. Check with a used CD store, mail-order company, or a dealer specializing in rare, out-of-print, or import recordings.

Didier C. Deutsch

Baron Blood

See: Black Sunday/Baron Blood

Barton Fink

See: Fargo/Barton Fink

BASEketball

1998, Mojo Records, from the Universal film *BASEketball*, 1998 ♫♫♫

Any album that has a Dickies track is on pretty good footing, and the soundtrack for *BASEketball*—the comedy vehicle for *South Park* creators Trey Parker and Matt Stone—has even more than the seminal punk-parody band's version of "Nobody but Me" to recommend it. Touching all the requisite modern rock bases, *BASEketball* tips off with ska-punk outfit Reel Big Fish's take on the a-ha hit "Take on Me," which leads into the dramatic, sarcastic bombast of Nerf Herder's "Don't Hate Me"; two songs in, and we're already sweeping wide. The album has a definite Caribbean flavor thanks to Cherry Poppin' Daddies' cover of Harry Belafonte's "Jump in Line" and the electro-reggae of Louchie Lou an & Michie One's "The Honeymoon Is Over," but it also touches on authentic modern pop (Deep Blue Something's "Tonight"), old school new wave (Soul Asylum's "I Will Still Be Laughing"), soulful bop (the Ernies' "Motivate"), and more ska in the form of Goldfinger's "Hopeless" and Smash Mouth's proven cover of War's "Why Can't We Be Friends." Although not quite a home run, *BASEketball* is definitely a solid three-pointer.

Gary Graff

Basic Instinct

1992, Varèse Sarabande Records, from the film *Basic Instinct*, Tri-Star Pictures, 1992 ♫♫♫
album notes: Music: Jerry Goldsmith.

Goldsmith's most recent Oscar-nominated score for director Paul Verhoven's erotic thriller has become a staple of movie previews with its insinuating, atmospheric title music and hammering, ostinato-driven chase cues. Goldsmith achieves some evocative "sex music" with an undulating string figure and a minor mode woodwind melody that functions as a moody siren song beckoning Michael Douglas's detective character to his ruin; his scoring of the movie's graphic sex scenes employs a moaning wind instrument effect similar to his use of the medieval serpent in *Alien*. The pulsating car chase cues "Night Life" and "Roxy Loses" are vintage Goldsmith action pieces that the composer honed to perfection here and in Verhoven's earlier *Total Recall*. The brooding low-key piano theme that

emerges out of the center of the score sometimes recalls John Barry's work on *Body Heat*, but Goldsmith carves out his own territory here for a consistently involving album.

Jeff Bond

Basket Case 2/Frankenhooker

1990, Silva Screen/U.K., from the Shapiro Glickenhaus films *Basket Case 2*, 1990, and *Frankenhooker*, 1990 ♫♫♫
album notes: Music: Joe Renzetti.

Sex and gore may have seemed to mix uneasily in *Basket Case 2* and *Frankenhooker*, but the end result was a cheery tongue-in-cheek delight that, in both cases, poked fun at the cult horror film genre and never quite took itself seriously. Starring jazz singer Annie Ross as a demented Granny, the first, a sequel to the 1982 film, involved a collection of freakish characters, all living in the Staten Island home of a "crusader for the rights of unique individuals," until all hell breaks loose; as for *Frankenhooker*, in a variation of the old Frankenstein legend, it found another mad scientist reconstructing his girlfriend (turned to minced meat in a freak lawnmower accident) with the bodies of dead prostitutes. Both films got synthesized scores by Joe Renzetti, a composer "crazed enough to write the perfect musical accompaniment for two little mutants having sex," in director Frank Henenlotter's apt description. Nothing earthshaking, but if you like this type of music, you might as well indulge yourself for a second or two.

Didier C. Deutsch

The Basketball Diaries

1995, Island Records, from the New Line Cinema film *The Basketball Diaries*, 1995 ♫♫
album notes: Music: Graeme Revell, Jim Carroll.

Leonardo di Caprio had an early starring role in this minor effort, primarily distinguished by the fact that its soundtrack included performances by familiar rock groups such as Pearl Jam, the Doors, the Cult, and Soundgarden, among others. Jim Carroll, on whose novel the film was based, also composed some of the numbers and/or appeared with some of the performers, most notably with Graeme Revell, whose score got somewhat lost in the process.

Didier C. Deutsch

Bat 21

1988, Varèse Sarabande Records, from the film *Bat 21*, Tri-Star Pictures, 1988 ♫♫♫♫
album notes: Music: Christopher Young.

Batman **(The Kobal Collection)**

Early mainstream breakout score for Christopher Young that is driven by the intensity of his passion to create unusual sound clusters. In fact, Young set a whole new standard that was repeatedly copied thereafter for scoring Vietnam-era war films. By utilizing Far Eastern instruments, like the shakuhachi, for solo performances, as opposed to relegating them for mere effects, this formula effectively brings an intense anxiety to the film's isolated jungle settings. A simple, but highly charged, emotional theme (something Young is reluctant to admit he does exceptionally well) counterpoints the action cues. This theme represents the growing bond between the downed officer and his would-be rescuer, circling above.

David Hirsch

Batman

1966, PolyGram/Casablanca Records, from the television series *Batman,* 20th Century Fox TV, 1966 ♪
album notes: Music: Nelson Riddle.

It would be tempting to recommend this CD. After all, it is the soundtrack to one of the early 1960s most popular television shows, with music by the great Nelson Riddle and featuring the voices of cast members Adam West (Batman), Burt Ward (Robin), Burgess Meredith (The Penguin), George Sanders (Mr. Freeze), Anne Baxter (The Great Zelda), and Frank Gorshin (The Riddler). In other words, there's nothing but the best. But the CD offers less than 25 minutes of actual playing, which at the price of laser light these days, is a bit offensive. So unless you have just inherited a fortune and have money to burn, skip it!

Didier C. Deutsch

Batman

1989, Warner Bros. Records, from the film *Batman,* Warner Bros., 1989 ♪♪♪♪
album notes: Music: Danny Elfman; **Conductor:** Shirley Walker.

1989, Warner Bros. Records, from the movie *Batman,* Warner Bros., 1989 ♪♪♪
album notes: Music: Prince.

Danny Elfman's music for the first two *Batman* films proves a splendid complement to director Tim Burton's vision of the world of Gotham City. Much of the flavor harkens back to the film-noir genre of the 1940s, set in large, dark metropolitan vistas where evil grows and the good must fight back in any way possible. Costumed superheroes are only believable if the worlds they inhabit are realistic, and in the first one, Elfman used his lush palette to develop this nightmarish vision. He musically portrayed the constant struggle of good versus evil and beauty against ugliness by twisting an alluring lullaby into something uncomfortable, thus representing the duality of Batman/Bruce Wayne and the Joker's twisted psyche.

Prince's contributions to the first film, a series of percolating vocal and instrumental numbers, are exactly what you might expect from the artist-with-the-most-complicated-identifying-logo-in-the-whole-history-of-the-music-industry (why didn't he call himself the Artist-With-No-Name, instead?). This is certainly not meant as a put-down, but your overall acceptance of the set will hinge entirely on how you feel about Prince himself, whose brilliance and creativity is not always to everyone's taste.

David Hirsch and Didier C. Deutsch

Batman and Robin

1997, Warner Bros. Records, from the film *Batman And Robin*, Warner Bros. Pictures, 1997 &&&&
album notes: Music: Elliot Goldenthal.

The jukebox approach of *Batman Forever* worked so well that there was no question what approach would be taken for the fourth edition of the caped crusader's series. Like its predecessor, this aims squarely at pop radio, bringing together top artists from the modern rock and R&B worlds. Smashing Pumpkins bookend the set with the same song performed two different ways—"The End is the Beginning is the End" and "The Beginning is the End is the Beginning." R. Kelly's gospel-tinged "Gotham City" is gentle ear candy, while Me'shell Ndegeocello offers a clever re-invention of the classic "Poison Ivy."

Gary Graff

Batman Forever

1995, Atlantic Records, from the film *Batman Forever,* Warner Bros., 1995 &&&
album notes: Music: Elliot Goldenthal; **Conductor:** Jonathan Shaeffer.

1995, Atlantic Records, from the film *Batman Forever,* Warner Bros., 1995 &&
With *Batman Forever,* came a new look as director Joel Schumacher abandoned Burton's ghostly lighting for the bright colors of the Sunday comics. Elliot Goldenthal, already having

scored *Alien* and *Demolition Man* with his unique orchestrations, was set to reveal a whole new music voice for the world of the Caped Crusader. Once again, the film's schizophrenia is reflected in the music's ever changing style. Though suited perfectly for the screen action, Goldenthal's score is less enjoyable on CD. Very few themes ever complete themselves before they become overwhelmed with something newer and busier. Even the new theme for Batman (really just a fanfare) never reaches a satisfying climax. The listener is sadly left wanting. Points do go to the most clever cues titles ever, though.

The pop compilation for this film brings together various performers, in selections that have a much more limited appeal than did the selections for the first *Batman*. In the film, these songs were mercifully heard as snippets in the background and did not interfere with the action, but brought upfront in the CD, they reveal their apparent lack of creativity, and do not stand well under close scrutiny.

David Hirsch and Didier C. Deutsch

Batman: Mask of the Phantasm

1993, Reprise Records, from the animated feature *Batman: Mask of the Phantasm,* Warner Bros., 1993 &&&&
album notes: Music: Shirley Walker.

Shirley Walker, who developed quite a following through her work on some of Hans Zimmer's most intelligent soundtracks, began striking out on her own, notably with this score, written for an animated feature based on the Batman comic strip, which evidences her solid qualities as a film composer. In contrast to the bombastic action cues one might expect to find in a film of this kind, "First Love" reveals a romantic side that's most endearing, with chimes mingling around a melodic line to create an attractive cue. "A Plea For Help" evolves around another lovely melody, played on the organ with orchestral backing, and limned by the soft accompaniment of a choir (a recurring device in Walker's score). An obligatory vocal by Tia Carrere, however, proves jarring amid all the great orchestral sounds devised by the composer, while it fails to add anything to the recording itself.

Didier C. Deutsch

Batman Returns

1992, Warner Bros. Records, from the film *Batman Returns,* Warner Bros., 1992 &&&&
album notes: Music: Danny Elfman; **Conductor:** Jonathan Sheffer.

For the second film *Batman Returns,* Elfman centered his score around the two new villains, the Penguin and Catwoman. Since the former is initially represented on screen only by his deformed hands, Elfman musically painted the Penguin with a darker version of his *Edward Scissorhands* score, with sweeping strings and chorus. Less subtle, perhaps, are the screeching string passages used as Catwoman goes on the prowl. Although *Batman* set the standard for the series, it is with the second film that Elfman really created his most entertaining and intriguing work.

David Hirsch

*batteries not included

🎞 1987, MCA Records, from the film *batteries not included*, Universal Pictures, 1987 🎬🎬🎬🎬

album notes: Music: James Horner; **Conductor:** James Horner.

The "Main Title," a great big band number, sets the tone for this attractive soundtrack album. Horner's score, for this "space"-related story about alien visitors presented under the aegis of Steven Spielberg, is a deft mixture of ominous-sounding instrumental chords and thoroughly enjoyable 1940s dance numbers. Two exhilarating selections stand out in the mix, "Hamburger Rhumba" and "Cafe Swing," both of which evoke specific corresponding scenes in the film.

Creating a different, though equally attractive aura of their own, the long cues marked "Night Visitors," "Time Square and Farewell," "Arson," and "A New Family/End Credits" enable the composer to fully develop his musical ideas and present them in ways that emphasize the intricacies and the solidity in the writing.

Didier C. Deutsch

Battle of Neretva

🎞 1987, Southern Cross Records, from the film *Battle of Neretva*, American International Pictures, 1970 🎬🎬🎬🎬🎬

album notes: Music: Bernard Herrmann; **Orchestra:** The London Philharmonic Orchestra; **Conductor:** Bernard Herrmann.

Even though it boasts an international cast that includes Yul Brynner, Curt Jurgens, Franco Nero, Hardy Kruger, Silva Koscina, and Orson Welles, portraying an unlikely royalist senator, the epic *Battle of Neretva,* made in 1971, is not particularly remembered, nor is, for that matter, Bernard Herrmann's score mentioned among his best known achievements. One of the many decisive battles fought during World War II, Neretva was the scene of an intense, brutal confrontation between Tito's ragged, small partisan army and Hitler's well-appointed Panzer divisions. Though he had only scored one war film before that, *The Naked and the Dead,* in 1958, Herrmann proved his skills in this score, drawing descriptive motifs from Ukrainian folk-type melodies, brass figures, and string ostinato to portray the scene of the action and the unequal forces at play. Characteris-

tically flavorful, it is an unusual score, with strongly evocative themes, which deserves to be discovered, though the recording itself would gain at sounding a bit warmer than it does.

Didier C. Deutsch

Beaches

🎞 1988, Atlantic Records, from the film *Beaches,* Touchstone Pictures, 1988 🎬🎬🎬🎬

This is nothing more than a clever Bette Midler showcase, with solid renditions of songs she wrote ("Otto Titsling," "Oh Industry"), some standards ("Under the Boardwalk"), some unusual choices ("Baby Mine," from the Disney film *Dumbo,* and Cole Porter's "I've Still Got My Health"), the whole thing capped by a short instrumental theme penned by Georges Delerue. It may be strictly for fans, but don't deny yourself the enjoyments of which there are quite a few!

Didier C. Deutsch

Bean

🎞 1997, Mercury Records, from the PolyGram/Working Title film *Bean,* 1997 🎬🎬🎬

Like much of British comedy, Rowan Atkinson's rubber-faced, dry-witted Mr. Bean is an acquired taste, and the companion soundtrack to his first big-screen adventure appropriately follows suit, with a selection of Britpop from acts that never quite translated their homeland superstardom to the United States. Among this group are Boyzone ("Picture of You"), Wet Wet Wet ("Yesterday"), Louise ("Running Back for More"), and 10CC ("Art for Art's Sake"), although an exception is expatriate Katrina and the Waves' "Walking on Sunshine," which eventually became a worldwide hit and, subsequently, a popular commercial jingle. The set also features Howard Goodall's "Bean Theme (Mad Piano)" and a cover of Stealer's Wheel's "Stuck in the Middle with You" by ex-Bangle Susanna Hoffs, plus Iron Maiden singer Bruce Dickinson's whomping "Elected."

Gary Graff

The Bear

🎞 1989, Ariola/France, from the film *The Bear (L'ours), 1989* 🎬🎬🎬🎬

album notes: Music: Philippe Sarde; **Orchestra:** The London Symphony Orchestra; **Conductor:** Carlo Savina.

This affecting, often breathtaking story of a little orphan bear having to fend for itself in a hostile environment, directed by Jean-Jacques Annaud (who also made *Quest For Fire*), enabled Philippe Sarde to write a profuse score, almost uninterrupted (the absence of dialogue helping tremendously). More an impressionistic tone poem than a score, Sarde's music proves to be very catchy and rewarding, particularly in the gorgeous orchestrations written by Bill Byers and Alexander Courage. The suites contain unindexed cues that follow the misadventures of the cub, precariously perched on a fallen tree atop a river, following a grunting adult bear, or trying to escape hunters. It's a lovely score, filled with pleasant musical surprises. This title may be out of print or just plain hard to find. Mail-order companies, used CD shops, or dealers of rare or import recordings will be your best bet.

Didier C. Deutsch

The Beast

 1988, A&M Records, from the film *The Beast,* Columbia Pictures, 1988 ♪♪♪

album notes: Music: Mark Isham.

A powerful war drama set in 1981, based on *Nanawatai,* a play by William Mastrosimone, *The Beast* recounts a fictional incident during the Russian occupation of Afghanistan, about a tank, the "beast" of the title, and its occupants, who are trapped in a valley following the destruction of a village. There is a confrontational situation elicited between the Russian soldiers and their commander, a fanatic not above killing his own men, and the Afghan partisans. But while Mark Isham's atmospheric synth score might have well served the tense screen action, it proves less than compelling on its own terms, with electronic lines and an occasional horn sound colliding with percussive effects in the two stretched-out tracks that recombine the cues composed for the occasion.

Didier C. Deutsch

The Beast

1996, Varèse-Sarabande Records, from the MTE film *The Beast,* 1996 ♪♪♪

album notes: Music: Don Davis.

Just when you thought it was safe to go back into your local movie theater came this stark reminder that audiences may always be in serious danger. In a repeat of the plot from *Jaws,* also based on a novel by Peter Benchley, this one involved yet another deep sea predator, a giant squid, coming too close to shore for the safety of swimmers unaware of the potential deleterious results. But unlike its successful predecessor, *The Beast* had a score by Don Davis, who is an eloquent composer but is not John Williams. As a result, while perfectly suited for the film, the music sounds like it was written by the numbers, with ominous strains signaling the approach of the monster and sudden crescendi informing of the unforeseen attacks on

humans. It's all quite effective, but certainly not as subliminally powerful as Williams's music for *Jaws.*

Didier C. Deutsch

Beastmaster 2: Through the Portal of Time

1991, Intrada Records, from the film *Beastmaster 2: Through the Portal of Time,* New Line Cinema, 1991 ♪♪♪♪

album notes: Music: Robert Folk; **Orchestra:** Berlin Radio Concert Orchestra.

Robert Folk succeeded Lee Holdridge for this sequel to the epic *The Beastmaster,* featuring another sword-wielding muscled Adonis whose peculiar talent is that he can communicate with animals and travel through time. As he explains in his notes to the album, Folk seized upon the opportunity *Beastmaster 2: Through the Portal of Time* offered him to write a score firmly rooted in the epic genre, yet laid out in contemporary terms because portions of the story take place in modern-day San Francisco. In every respect, he fulfilled his obligation, creating a set of musical cues that evoke the primitive world from which the hero comes, and the modern setting in which he suddenly finds himself.

But beyond the mere logistics that were imposed on him by the storyline, Folk wrote an outstanding score, beautifully delineated and lyrically expressive, that must count among the best efforts in the genre. Cue after cue, the music, superbly performed by the Berlin Radio Concert Orchestra, unveils its many layers of gorgeous sounds and satisfying melodies to create a musical programming that stands out on its own merits. There are many highlights in the set, but for starters you may want to try "Dar the Hero," "Through the Portal," "The Great Escape," and "Key to the Heart." Now, about that unbelievable story about a muscleman from the past who . . .

Didier C. Deutsch

Beaumarchais l'insolent

1996, Erato Records/France, from the film *Beaumarchais l'insolent (Insolent Beaumarchais),* 1996 ♪♪♪♪♪

album notes: Music: Jean-Claude Petit; **Orchestra:** The London Studio Orchestra; **Conductor:** Jean-Claude Petit.

Although probably only known in this country for his *The Barber of Seville,* Pierre Augustin Caron de Beaumarchais, one of the most celebrated playwrights of the 18th century, was also a secret agent who often went on special missions at the behest of King Louis XV of France. This little-known side of his activities inspired Sacha Guitry (the Gallic equivalent of Noel Coward) to write a play that went unpublished for decades, until Edouard Molinaro discovered it and decided to turn it into a film, with Fabrice Luchini portraying the "Insolent Beaumarchais." Jean-Claude Petit wrote a typically two-sided score, utilizing delicate harmonies evocative of the nonchalant 18th century, and swashbuckling accents more representative of the fast-paced screen action. At times grandly exciting, at times strikingly attractive, this is a classic example of the kind of work the composer can conjure up with apparently great ease. This recording may be difficult to find. Check with a used CD store, mail-order company, or a dealer specializing in rare, out-of-print, or import recordings.

Didier C. Deutsch

The Beautician and the Beast

1997, Milan Records, from the film *The Beautician and the Beast*, Paramount Pictures, 1997 ♫♫♫♡

album notes: Music: Cliff Eidelman; **Orchestra:** The London Metropolitan Orchestra; **Conductor:** Cliff Eidelman.

This album boasts a charmingly old-fashioned romantic score by Cliff Eidelman, which certainly adds some big screen feel to *The Nanny* Fran Drescher's uninspired feature film variation on her TV persona. Much of Eidelman's score is appropriately built on a waltz motif, an attempt to create an atmosphere similar to the one established in Hollywood films of the 1940s, the ones with European locales. Romance is certainly an emotion that Eidelman writes from the heart. Includes the standard "L'Internationale," sung with a full chorus.

David Hirsch

Beautiful Thing

1998, MCA Records, from the Sony film *Beautiful Thing*, 1998 ♫♫♫♫

album notes: Music: John Altman.

A low-budget adaptation of a 1994 London stage hit written by Jonathan Harvey, *Beautiful Thing* transcends its openly gay theme to offer an infectious and frequently funny comedy about a working-class British boy who flees his dysfunctional family, and discovers homosexuality and love all at once in the arms of a long-time neighboring kid. The often buoyant moods of the film are brilliantly set off with the use of several songs performed by Cass Elliott and the Mamas and the Papas, including some of their golden hits, such as "California Dreamin'," "Monday, Monday," and "Creeque Alley." John Altman's effective score is reduced here to an eight-minute medley built around a very evocative theme and played almost *sotto voce* to great effect.

see also: Kiss Me, Guido, The Incredible True Adventure of Two Girls in Love

Didier C. Deutsch

Beauty and the Beast

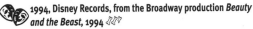 1991, Walt Disney Records, from the animated feature *Beauty and the Beast,* Walt Disney Pictures, 1991 ♫♫♫♫

album notes: Music: Alan Menken; **Lyrics:** Howard Ashman; **Cast:** Robby Benson, Jesse Corti, Angela Lansbury, Paige O'Hara, Jerry Orbach, David Ogden Stiers, Richard White.

1994, Disney Records, from the Broadway production *Beauty and the Beast,* 1994 ♫♫♫♡

album notes: Music: Alan Menken; **Lyrics:** Howard Ashman, Tim Rice; **Cast:** Susan Egan, Terrence Mann, Kenny Raskin, Burke Moses, Tom Bosley, Heath Lamberts, Gary Beach, Beth Fowler.

The venerable classic 1757 tale by Mme. Leprince de Beaumont, about a beautiful maiden and the horrible beast who becomes her guardian in exchange for her father's life, had been a wonderful magical source for the creativity of French filmmaker Jean Cocteau. It proved equally reliable when Disney decided to adapt it for an animated musical feature released in 1991. Deftly combining standard animation and computer imagery, the studio craftsmen created a work that is technically polished and sophisticated, yet completely delightful as only the Disney films can be. Adding to the impact of the film and its soundtrack, well-known performers lent their vocal talents to the film, including Angela Lansbury as the homebody Mrs. Potts; Robby Benson, as the Beast, who turns out to be a Prince under an evil spell; Paige O'Hara, whose crystalline voice gives Beauty incredible life on the screen; and Jerry Orbach who, as Lumiere, the candelabra-holding genial host at the Beast's castle, adds a welcome touch of show biz chutzpah. Also particularly welcome is the score by Alan Menken and Howard Tashman, which features some excellent numbers, including "Beauty and the Beast," sensitively rendered by Angela Lansbury, and reprised by Celine Dion and Peabo Bryson in a pop version heard over the end credits; the humorous "Gaston," bellowed by Richard White as the insufferable "lover" of Beauty, and Jesse Corti, as Lefou, Gaston's all-'round yes man and friend; and "Be Our Guest," in which Angela Lansbury, Jerry Orbach, and the other household characters at the Beast's castle celebrate the arrival of Beauty.

Much of the magic and enchantment found in the film had dissipated by the time a live version of the musical opened on Broadway on April 18, 1994. Where the animated feature is clever and whimsical, the stage version is heavy-handed and caricatural. New songs added to the original score only confirm this impression, with the all-too-human characters on stage having a difficult time trying to keep up with the animated screen counterparts, and not succeeding too well. As a result, the cast album, featuring Terrence Mann as the Beast, Susan

Egan as Belle, and Burke Moses as Gaston may be of interest to those who have seen the show, still running on Broadway, but if you haven't seen the show or aren't sure which version to get, stick with the original soundtrack from the film.

Didier C. Deutsch

Beavis and Butt-Head Do America

🎬 1996, Milan Records, from the animated feature *Beavis and Butt-Head Do America*, 1996 ♫♫♫

album notes: Music: John Frizzell; **Orchestra:** The London Metropolitan Orchestra; **Conductor:** Allan Wilson.

John Frizzell's unbelievably large-scale orchestral score sounds nothing like what you'd expect for the feature film spin-off of this MTV animated series. The composer wisely chose to play against type by not writing a comedic score, and somehow it works remarkably well. Pieces like "Beavis the Sperm" are so honestly sincere in their intent that they just can't fail in making the film even funnier by taking it all so seriously. We're sure the real words in "Judgorian Chant" say nothing good, but who can tell?

David Hirsch

Becoming Colette

🎬 1998, JOS Records, from the film *Becoming Colette*, 1991 ♫♫♫♫♫

album notes: Music: John Scott; **Conductor:** John Scott.

The always elegant John Scott delivered another winner with this score to a film describing the coming-of-age of an innocent schoolgirl at the turn of the century who eventually became the great French writer Colette. Still a provincial, awkward girl, young Gabrielle Colette attracts the attention of roué publisher Henry Gauthier-Villars, known as Willy, who marries her and introduces her into Belle Epoque Parisian society. Soon after, he convinces his mistress, Polaire, to seduce her, marking the young girl's introduction to a libertine world in which drugs and sexuality *à trois* seem as ordinary as living and breathing. When his wife begins to show signs of becoming a great writer, Willy publishes her novels under his own name, until she rebels and realizes at long last that she can live without him. Adding to the impact of the film, Scott wrote an exciting set of cues that comment on the action while enhancing each scene. Taken on its own musical merits, the score easily stands out as a gorgeous piece of music that has a strong identity of its own and evokes a time period that was rich and feisty.

Didier C. Deutsch

Bed & Breakfast

🎬 1992, Varèse Sarabande Records, from the film *Bed & Breakfast*, Hemdale Films, 1992 ♫♫♫♫

album notes: Music: David Shire; **Orchestra:** The Irish Film Orchestra; **Conductor:** David Shire.

Bed and Breakfast is a 1991 film nobody saw, beautifully photographed on the Maine coast, about a charming rogue (Roger Moore) who comes to stay with a household of women from three generations. One of them is a violinist, which inspires a large portion of David Shire's gem of a score, a lost piece of melodic *joie de vivre* put out on Varèse Sarabande's short-lived composer-vanity label (i.e. a few albums Varèse released, but not through their regular distributor). Shire comes from a background of Broadway and film (he did such '70s masterpieces as *The Taking of Pelham One Two Three, The Conversation* and *All the President's Men*) and the two genres merge for a score that features several completely realized pieces, but is dramatically understated and flowing throughout. Solo lines dominate, brimming with melody, making the score like another character in the film–at times dancing, reflecting, singing, or speaking a soft lullaby. The size of the orchestra would almost seem too much for the story, but with his chamber/minimalist-like arpeggios Shire makes it honest, gentle and poignant. It's not as large as the Maine coast, or as small as an individual, but rather as big as life by the sea can make you feel.

Lukas Kendall

Bed of Roses

🎬 1996, Milan Records, from the film *Bed of Roses,* New Line Cinema, 1996 ♫♫♫

album notes: Music: Michael Convertino; **Conductor:** Artie Kane.

Michael Convertino is one of those composers who writes distinct and consistently fine music for films, but always seems to get overlooked. *Bed of Roses,* the watchable but almost fatally low-key romance with Christian Slater and Mary Stuart Masterson, features a Convertino score that provides a musical atmosphere that's melodic and earthy, characterized by an almost new-age feel that provides ambiance at the same time it works to accentuate the relationship of the two characters. Convertino's music often lacks numerous "themes" in the traditional sense, but rather contains recurring motives that come and go within the musical "space" that the composer creates in his scores. The result here is an emotional but tranquil effort that is different enough from traditional film scores to grab your attention, and good enough to keep you listening intently.

Andy Dursin

Beethoven

🎬 1991, MCA Records, from the film *Beethoven,* Universal Pictures, 1991 ♪♪♪

album notes: Music: Randy Edelman.

Were it not for the jaunty main theme, you might think that Randy Edelman's grander-than-life music for *Beethoven* had been composed for an epic. Actually, it may be one of the score's greatest flaws. While quite attractive and ultimately fun to listen to, it is much too lush to convince anyone that the film was nothing more than a minor comedy. In fact, in cue after cue, it sounds as if Edelman had been trying to outclass Danny Elfman or James Horner. This said, there are many delightful moments amid the bombast for one to enjoy on a pleasant Sunday afternoon, or any other day for that matter.

Didier C. Deutsch

Beethoven's 2nd

🎬 1993, Columbia Records, from the film *Beethoven's 2nd,* Universal Pictures, 1993 ♪♪♪

album notes: Music: Randy Edelman.

Since it worked so well the first time, Edelman encored for the sequel, in which his cues sound equally lovely and overly orchestrated. Now let's be realistic—the film may be called *Beethoven's 2nd,* but it really has nothing to do with Ludwig van, and a little restraint might have worked just as well.

Didier C. Deutsch

Beetlejuice

🎬 1988, Geffen Records, from the film *Beetlejuice,* Warner Bros., 1988 ♪♪♪♪

album notes: Music: Danny Elfman; **Conductor:** William Ross.

This delightfully manic Danny Elfman score actually proves that carnival-style music can be used to make a bona fide film score! Bright and bouncy, it crosses effortlessly between the equally bizarre world of the undead and a country home possessed by the ghosts of its former owners. With the dark and twisted textures of director Tim Burton's production design, the score turns it all into a twisted live action cartoon. Heavy influences are drawn from Harry Belafonte's Caribbean songs, two of which are featured on the album, for some very bizarre musical numbers.

David Hirsch

Before and After

🎬 1996, Hollywood Records, from the film *Before and After,* Hollywood Pictures, 1996 ♪♪♪♪

album notes: Music: Howard Shore; **Orchestra:** The London Philharmonic Orchestra; **Conductor:** Howard Shore.

A criminal case with romantic undertones, starring Meryl Streep and Liam Neeson, *Before and After* elicited a dramatic score from Howard Shore, who demonstrates his skills at writing attractive themes, despite the film's deliberately slow and ominous tone. The relentless somber moods might not be to everyone's liking, but the music is quite striking with the recording by the London Philharmonic Orchestra extracting all the flavor in a very effective reading.

Didier C. Deutsch

The Belle of New York

🎬 1991, Sony Music Special Products, from the screen musical *The Belle of New York,* MGM, 1952 ♪♪♪♪

album notes: Music: Harry Warren; **Lyrics:** Johnny Mercer; **Orchestra:** The MGM Studio Orchestra; **Choir:** The MGM Studio Chorus; **Conductor:** Adolph Deutsch; **Cast:** Fred Astaire, Vera-Ellen, Alice Pearce.

Based on a musical created in 1897, but sporting a brand new score by Harry Warren and Johnny Mercer, *The Belle of New York* is a classic Arthur Freed production, starring Fred Astaire as a dissolute playboy who finds redemption in the arms of an unlikely Salvation Army-type officer, in what is a sly bow in the direction of *Guys and Dolls,* still a running hit on Broadway at the time. Naturally bright and breezy, the screen musical was the occasion for several song-and-dance numbers, among which the most memorable and successful include a long sequence shot before various backdrops borrowed from the Currier and Ives lithographs; "Baby Doll," which became a standard; and "I Wanna Be a Dancin' Man," which Astaire turned into an exuberant signature song.

Didier C. Deutsch

Bells Are Ringing

🎬 1989, Columbia Records, from the Broadway production *Bells Are Ringing,* 1956 ♪♪♪♪♪

album notes: Music: Jule Styne; **Lyrics:** Betty Comden, Adolph Green; **Cast:** Judy Holliday, Sydney Chaplin, Jean Stapleton, Eddie Lawrence, Eddie Heim, Peter Gennaro.

🎬 1989, Capitol Records, from the screen musical *Bells Are Ringing,* MGM, 1960 ♪♪♪♪

album notes: Music: Jule Styne; **Lyrics:** Betty Comden, Adolph Green; **Orchestra:** The MGM Studio Orchestra; **Choir:** The MGM Studio Chorus; **Conductor:** Andre Previn; **Cast:** Judy Holliday, Dean Martin, Jean Stapleton, Eddie Foy Jr.

An "original book" musical (as opposed to an adaptation), *Bells Are Ringing,* which opened on November 29, 1956, for a run of 924 performances, was the brainchild of Betty Comden, Adolph Green, and composer Jule Styne, who fashioned a breezy, often hilarious show for their star, Judy Holliday. The show, about a lonely operator at an answering phone service who meddles in the lives of her customers

Michael Keaton in Beetlejuice. **(The Kobal Collection)**

and gets involved with a playwright with a temporary creative block, is peopled by a collection of colorful characters (actors, socialites, bookies, policemen, and subway riders), and is the occasion for a festival of bright, cheery tunes. Among those, the score introduced the jaunty "Just in Time," and one of Broadway's great show-stopping hits, the mournful "The Party's Over." The cast album, Columbia's first in stereo, ranks among the top recordings ever released by the label.

Holliday reprised her Tony Award-winning performance, and Dean Martin replaced Sydney Chaplin as the playwright, when *Bells Are Ringing* went Hollywood in 1960 for a big screen treatment that remained somewhat faithful to the original. Even though its score is seriously downsized, it includes a couple of new numbers, including "Do It Yourself," performed by Martin, and "Better Than a Dream," a duet shared by the two stars, and yielded a soundtrack album that has some bright moments, even though it is a poor substitute to the original.

Didier C. Deutsch

Beloved

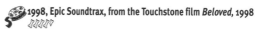 **1998, Epic Soundtrax, from the Touchstone film *Beloved*, 1998**
♪♪♪♪

album notes: Music: Rachel Portman.

Slavery and the physical and emotional scars it left on scores of innocent people found a disturbing resonance in *Beloved*, a period drama based on Toni Morrison's Pulitzer Prize-winning novel, that deals with the grim psychological legacies of slavery. Starring Oprah Winfrey, it tells the story of a middle-aged mother of two, a former slave now living in Cincinnati in the days following the Civil War, who is haunted not only by violent and sickening memories of rape and murder, but, literally, by her dead child, Beloved, who has been killed in gruesome circumstances. Paralleling this often convoluted story, the superbly evocative score by Rachel Portman adds its own expression to the moods of the film, with cues that enhance the deliberately slow-moving action ("That's Ohio," "Cincinnati Streets," "Winter Thaw") and hold the listener rapt. African-sounding songs, performed by Oumou Sangare, the African Children's

Choir, and La Troupe Makandal, interspersed in the score, give an extra ethnic color to some of the selections heard in this CD.

Didier C. Deutsch

Ben Franklin in Paris

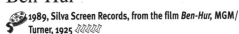
1993, Angel Records, from the Broadway production, *Ben Franklin in Paris*, 1964 🎵🎵

album notes: Music: Mark Sandrich Jr.; **Lyrics:** Sidney Michaels; **Cast:** Robert Preston, Ulla Sallert, Susan Watson.

The primary interest in this cast album resides in Robert Preston's portrayal of Benjamin Franklin, his first role on Broadway since *The Music Man*. Saddled with an impossible book recounting Franklin's visit to Versailles and the court of French King Louis XVI, and his alleged involvement with Comtesse Diane de Vobrillac, Preston also had to struggle with a score that lacked fire and imagination, and a costar with whom he shared little stage chemistry. Despite the beguiling presence of Susan Watson, fresh as a daisy in a secondary role, and a minor hit in the song "Half the Battle," spiritedly delivered by Preston and cohorts, the show floundered and mercifully closed after 215 performances.

Didier C. Deutsch

Ben-Hur

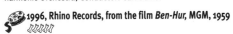
1989, Silva Screen Records, from the film *Ben-Hur*, MGM/ Turner, 1925 🎵🎵🎵🎵

album notes: Music: Carl Davis; **Orchestra:** The Royal Liverpool Philharmonic Orchestra; **Conductor:** Carl Davis.

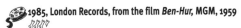
1996, Rhino Records, from the film *Ben-Hur*, MGM, 1959 🎵🎵🎵🎵🎵

album notes: Music: Miklos Rozsa; **Orchestra:** The MGM Studio Orchestra; **Choir:** The MGM Studio Chorus; **Conductor:** Miklos Rozsa.

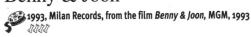
1985, London Records, from the film *Ben-Hur*, MGM, 1959 🎵🎵🎵🎵

album notes: Music: Miklos Rozsa; **Orchestra:** The National Philharmonic Orchestra; The National Philharmonic Chorus; **Conductor:** Miklos Rozsa.

Anyone familiar with Miklos Rozsa's massive score for the 1959 *Ben-Hur* will be doubly interested in listening to Carl Davis's soundtrack. First because Carl Davis was differently inspired than Rozsa by the basic storyline, second because Davis writing a new score for the silent film of 1925 was not under the same constraints and limitations imposed to Rozsa, and may have been more at liberty to let his imagination run free.

The basic concepts of religious reverence and epic outbursts are very much in evidence in his score, as they were

in Rozsa's, and his treatment of "The Chariot Race," for instance, has nothing to envy the music for the 1959 version. If anything Davis's thunderous "Gathering of the Chariots," with its heavy reliance on drums, contrasts with Rozsa's clarion-clear trumpet calls. But while Davis's overall approach may sound more traditionally symphonic in a Wagnerian sense, the end result is a score that is equally stirring. Playing by the Royal Liverpool is consistently solid and exciting.

A hugely popular soundtrack, the music from the 1959 version of *Ben-Hur* was initially released on one LP by MGM Records to coincide with the film's first run. The success of that album soon prompted the label to issue a second volume on the subsidiary label, Leo Records, though that album was deleted soon after.

With the advent of CDs, *Ben-Hur* was then reissued several times, but the Rhino set finally presents the colossal score in all its grandeur, with each cue properly sequenced, plus many outtakes and selections that were initially composed but discarded before the final cut.

Though Rozsa created many outstanding scores during his long and prolific career as a film composer, *Ben-Hur* must be considered his crowning achievement. The two-CD set does it full justice. For those less inclined to purchase the Rhino set, the National Philharmonic Orchestra and Chorus, under the direction of the composer, give a sumptuous reading of highlights from the score, in what might be a recording of choice.

Didier C. Deutsch

Benny & Joon

1993, Milan Records, from the film *Benny & Joon*, MGM, 1993 🎵🎵🎵🎵

album notes: Music: Rachel Portman; **Conductor:** J.A.C. Redford.

In recent years, women composers have succeeded in making themselves heard in a field that had essentially been a man's world. High on that list of relative newcomers is Rachel Portman, who made quite an impression with this quirky score for a film starring Johnny Depp, in which the influence of Danny Elfman is occasionally apparent. Writing for a handful of solo instruments within the larger framework provided by the orchestra, Portman developed a series of attractive cues anchored by the main theme, with the clarinet and the flute playing an essential role in the mix ("Balloon," "In the Park," "Love Theme").

Didier C. Deutsch

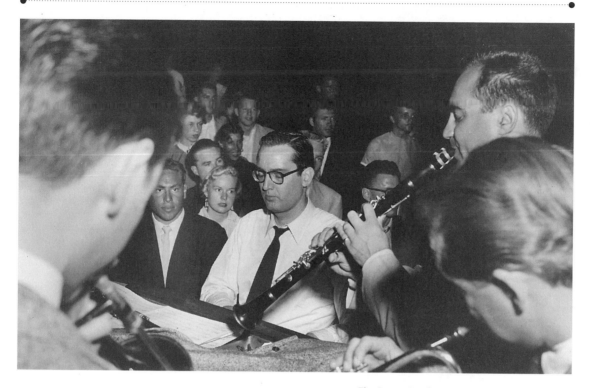

The Benny Goodman Story **(The Kobal Collection)**

The Benny Goodman Story

1972, MCA Records, from the film *The Benny Goodman Story*,
Universal Pictures, 1955, 🎬🎬🎬🎬🎬

album notes: Featured Musicians: Benny Goodman and His Orchestra, The Benny Goodman Quartet, The Benny Goodman Trio.

Even if the story of the legendary Benny Goodman is highly romanticized in the film *The Benny Goodman Story* and hardly reflected the reality of his life, one thing that is truly authentic in the film is the music, performed by the great man himself, and many of the sidemen who had made the journey to fame with him back in the '30s, including Harry James, Gene Krupa, Lionel Hampton, Teddy Wilson, and Martha Tilton, among many others. The selections heard in this soundtrack album are actual recreations of the band's most famous hits, including Goodman's signature songs, "Let's Dance," "One O'Clock Jump," and "Stompin' at the Savoy," as well as "Moonglow," "Avalon," "And the Angels Sing," "Don't Be That Way," and the always thrilling "Sing Sing Sing" with its "Christopher Columbus" interpolation, which was one of the highlights at the celebrated Carnegie Hall concert in 1938. If you like jazz, and if you like big

bands, and even if you hate the saccharine film, you owe it to yourself to have this album.

Didier C. Deutsch

Besieged

1999, Milan Records, from the Fine Line film *Besieged*, 1999
🎬🎬🎬

album notes: Music: Alessio Vlad; **Featured Soloist:** Stefano Arnaldi.

The story of a young African woman, Shandurai, who leaves her homeland, after her husband is imprisoned as a political foe of the totalitarian regime, and ends up in Rome where she becomes the live-in maid of Jason Kinsky, an eccentric English musician, *Besieged* is an unusual, forcefully compelling drama that draws much of its impact from Thandie Newton's portrayal as Shandurai, and the soundtrack which consists of a mix of African pop songs and classical works for the piano. As Shandurai tries to free herself from her past and the servile condition in which events have forced her, Kinsky discovers passion next to her and a creative force that eventually frees him from a self-imposed solitary existence. These dramatic elements are translated in the soundtrack, in which Kinsky's "masterpiece-in-progress," "Ostinato," begins to include fragments of African melodies. The contrast between the African songs (including a collaboration between Ali Farka Toure and Ry Cooder) and the classical works heard on the soundtrack makes this one of the most original and unlikely albums to come out of a contemporary film.

Didier C. Deutsch

Best Foot Forward

1988, DRG Records, from the off-Broadway revival *Best Foot Forward,* 1963 ♫♫♫

album notes: **Music:** Hugh Martin, Ralph Blane; **Lyrics:** Hugh Martin, Ralph Blane; **Cast:** Paula Wayne, Liza Minnelli, Karin Wolfe, Glenn Walken, Christopher Walken.

The 1963 revival of *Best Foot Forward,* the self-proclaimed "bright musical comedy hit," is best remembered today for the fact that it introduced Liza Minnelli in her first stage role. Initially produced on Broadway in 1941, where it enjoyed a run of 326 performances, *Best Foot Forward* had been a lightweight but delightful vehicle for a group of talented newcomers, including June Allyson and Nancy Walker. They were cast as prep school students at Winsocki, Pennsylvania, upset when a Hollywood starlet (Rosemary Lane) steals the spotlight and their boyfriends when she appears as a publicity stunt at the school's annual prom. The show, directed by George Abbott, also launched the careers of Hugh Martin and Ralph Blane. In 1943, it was brought to the screen by Arthur Freed, with Lucille Ball, William Gaxton and Gloria de Haven joining Allyson and Walker, the only holdovers from the original stage production.

Presented at the Stage 73 Theatre on April 2, 1963, the revival starred Paula Wayne, Christopher Walken, and Karin Wolfe, and kept the original score in which Martin and Blane had interpolated two new songs, including "You Are For Loving," performed as a second act solo by Liza Minnelli. It had a run of 224 performances. Though an obvious piece of fluff, the recording reveals a score that is fairly uncomplicated and easy on the ear, with some recognizable numbers. It will mostly appeal to completists.

Didier C. Deutsch

The Best Little Whorehouse in Texas

1988, MCA Records, from the screen musical *The Best Little Whorehouse in Texas,* Universal Pictures, 1982 ♫♫♫

album notes: **Music:** Carol Hall; **Lyrics:** Carol Hall.

Like rock, country music has seldom made a successful foray on Broadway, though a particularly effective exception was *The Best Little Whorehouse in Texas,* which opened in 1978. Created by Carol Hall, the musical deals with the Chicken Ranch, a legendary Texas emporium and the only authorized brothel in the country, and efforts by some self-appointed protectors of morality to close the place, even though (or perhaps because) its customers include several influential politicians and important citizens. Deliberately lewd and raunchy, the show was a hit on Broadway and enjoyed a lengthy run of 1,584 performances.

In 1982 it was turned into a screen musical, starring Dolly Parton (who contributed a couple of songs to the score) as Miss Mona, the house owner, and Burt Reynolds as the local sheriff and Mona's former lover. The recording presents what remains of Carol Hall's profuse score, which is very little, but it includes the show-stopper "The Sidestep," in which Charles Durning, a politician and customer at the Chicken Ranch, gives his own version of the tactful art of diplomacy, and "Hard Candy Christmas," a novel Yule anthem. In 1994, the show spawned a sequel in *The Best Little Whorehouse Goes Public,* staged by Tommy Tune, which flopped, though it yielded a cast album on the Varèse Sarabande label.

Didier C. Deutsch

The Best of Shaft

1999, Hip-O Records, from the MGM films *Shaft,* 1971, and *Shaft in Africa,* 1973 ♫♫♫

album notes: **Music:** Isaac Hayes, Johnny Pate.

Eons ago, in the days when black exploitation films were the rage, none seemed more popular than the *Shaft* series, in which Richard Roundtree portrayed the black private eye. One of the reasons for the films' success, particularly the first, could have been the now-famous theme written and performed by Isaac Hayes. It was powerful, it was energetic, it was sophisticated, everything Shaft seemed to have going for him.

There were three films in the series, *Shaft,* in 1971, scored by Isaac Hayes; *Shaft's Big Score,* a year later, scored by Gordon Parks; and *Shaft In Africa,* in 1973, scored by Johnny Pate. Sadly, only the first and the third are represented in this compilation, which leaves a significant item in the trilogy absent. Still, that leaves plenty of music accounted for, including, of course, Isaac Hayes's themes, excerpts from the score by Johnny Pate, and the hit song, "Are You Man Enough?," performed by The Four Tops.

Didier C. Deutsch

The Best Years of Our Lives

1988, Preamble Records, from the film *The Best Years of Our Lives,* Samuel Goldwyn Productions, 1946 🎬🎬🎬🎬🎬

album notes: Music: Hugo Friedhofer; **Orchestra:** The London Philharmonic Orchestra; **Conductor:** Franco Collura.

This classic Academy Award winning score by Hugo Friedhofer was created to illustrate the lives of three veterans coming back to their hometown at the end of World War II, and the problems they encounter trying to adjust to the changes that have occurred within themselves and around them. Beautifully lyrical, but eschewing a maudlin sentimentality that could have seemed unnecessary in less experienced hands, Friedhofer wrote a score that confronted and underlined the powerful, emotionally charged story in which the full range of human feelings found an expression, from wrenching torment to liberating love, from tears to laughter. The recording, one of the earliest reconstructions of a classic film score, does full justice to the many beauties contained in the music, with the London Philharmonic Orchestra, conducted by Franco Collura, giving a top-notch performance, further enhanced by the superlative ambient sound.

Didier C. Deutsch

Betrayed

1988, Varèse Sarabande Records, from the film *Betrayed,* United Artists, 1988 🎬🎬🎬🎬

album notes: Music: Bill Conti; **Conductor:** Bill Conti.

Bill Conti fashioned a very engaging, country-styled score for this political thriller, set in the Midwest, about an attractive undercover FBI operative (Debra Winger), who infiltrates a radical group suspected of having murdered a controversial radio talk show host. With a predominance of motifs for guitar and harmonica, the flavorful cues set the scene of the action and give specific moments in it a vibrant musical support ("The Way," "Riding to Work," "Another Way," "Rock Country"), making this an album that's quite pleasant to listen to.

Didier C. Deutsch

Betty Blue

1986, Virgin Records, from the film *Betty Blue,* Alive Films, 1986 🎬🎬🎬🎬

album notes: Music: Gabriel Yared.

For this gritty drama by *Diva* director Jean-Jacques Beineix, Gabriel Yared wrote a convincing score that blends elements of romance and pathos. The story of two youngsters, steady Zorg and batty Betty, on a free-wheeling romp in the country, the film is noticeably distinguished by Beineix's colorful approach

to filmmaking, and by Beatrice Dalle's sensual portrayal as Betty. Yared's music captures the poetic focus that contrasted and enhanced the character's slow descent into madness.

Didier C. Deutsch

The Beverly Hillbillies

1996, Columbia/Legacy Records, from the CBS-TV series *The Beverly Hillbillies,* 1962 🎬🎬

album notes: Featured Artists: Buddy Ebsen, Irene Ryan, Max Baer, Donna Douglas, Nancy Kulp, Raymond Bailey.

1993, Fox Records, from the film *The Beverly Hillbillies,* 20th Century Fox, 1993 🎬🎬🎬🎬

Propelled by Earl and Scruggs's familiar "Ballad of Jed Clampett" ("Oil, that is, black gold!"), this collection of songs and skits from the popular television comedy can only be taken on its own terms—it's amusing for a while, but never really profound or compelling. If you were a fan of the series, you won't have any problem enjoying this ditty. Otherwise, you might end up wondering what the fuss was all about. One way or the other, you'll find the CD is fun while it lasts.

The big-screen remake of the television series yielded an exuberant soundtrack album, graced by the presence of a great lineup of country performers, including Dolly Parton, The Oak Ridge Boys, Ricky Van Shelton, The Texas Tornadoes, and Lorrie Morgan who does a great rendition of "Crying Time." There is really very little to say about a compilation such as this. The songs are good natured and pleasant and very enjoyable, and your reaction to the album will largely depend on how you feel about the artists and their stylings. For the record, though, it should be noted that Jerry Scoggins does a cover version of "The Ballad of Jed Clampett." They probably should have used the original!

Didier C. Deutsch

Beverly Hills Cop

1984, MCA Records, from the film *Beverly Hills Cop,* Paramount Pictures, 1984 🎬🎬🎬🎬

album notes: Music: Harold Faltermeyer.

One of the more popular song compilation albums still in print years after the release of the film, it owes much of its success to an excellent selection of artists. Many of the songs are prominently featured in the film, particularly some fine work by Patti LaBelle ("New Attitude," "Stir It Up"), Glen Frey ("The Heat Is On"), and The Pointer Sisters ("Neutron Dance"). The album also features "Gratitude," a vocal performance by Danny Elfman who would breakout the following year with *Pee Wee's Big Adventure.* A few other songs that were not used in the movie still capture the energy and mood of this fast-paced

Beverly Hills Cop (The Kobal Collection)

Eddie Murphy comedy/adventure vehicle. Of course there's also the original version of Harold Faltermeyer's "Axel F" theme, the only piece that could possibly be considered underscore since it was used so often throughout the film.

David Hirsch

Beverly Hills Cop III

1994, MCA Records, from the film *Beverly Hills Cop III*, Paramount Pictures, 1994 🎬🎬

Like the film series, the "Beverly Hills Cop" musical franchise ran out of steam by its third time out. One can never speak ill of a Supremes classic like "Come See About Me," and there are reasonably good selections from Tony! Toni! Tone! ("Leavin'"), and Terence Trent D'Arby ("Right Thing, Wrong Way"). But there's certainly nothing as memorable as any of the hits from the original "Beverly Hills Cop" soundtrack.

Gary Graff

Beverly Hills 90210

1992, Giant/Reprise Records, from the television series *Beverly Hills 90210*, 1992 🎬

The caliber of talent involved in this compilation is enough to create more than a passing interest. Where else would you find people like Paula Abdul, Vanessa Williams, Shanice, Jody Watley, Michael McDonald, Chaka Khan, and Color Me Badd on the same album? The problem, however, is that the genres in which each expresses themselves don't mix very well. After you jump, without much rhyme nor reason, from ballads to rockers to electronic pop, you feel as if you're on overdrive, and you need some relief that not even John Davis's theme can provide. The beats sound the same, the performances bleed into each other, and the overall effect is trite and disappointingly dry. The show may be hip, but the CD ain't.

Didier C. Deutsch

Beverly Hills Ninja

1997, EMI Records, from the film *Beverly Hills Ninja*, TriStar Pictures, 1997 🎬🎬🎬

album notes: Music: George S. Clinton.

Introduced by a funny bit of dialogue, "You're a Ninja? . . ." that sets the scene for the album, this compilation presents several songs that are part of the soundtrack for this frequently hilarious film about a karate expert who became a Ninja when it would seem he should have been a sumo wrestler instead. But don't let the silliness of the premise drive you crazy—watching the film will suffice. Or try this album, informed by several other moments of nonsense from the soundtrack ("My identity

must remain mysterious . . . " "You're the big, fat Ninja, aren't you?" "Close to the temple, not inside . . ."), and featuring some songs guaranteed to entertain you, even if they don't always delight you, like "Tsugihagi Boogie Woogie," "Tarzan Boy," "Turning Japanese," and Lene Lovich's perversely humorous rendition of "I Think We're Alone Now (Japanese Version)."

Didier C. Deutsch

Beyond Rangoon

1994, Milan/BMG, from the Castle Rock/Columbia film *Beyond Rangoon*, 1994 🎬🎬🎬🎬

album notes: Music: Hans Zimmer; Conductor: Nick Glennie-Smith; Featured Musicians: Richard Harvey, ethnic pipes.

A tough, chilling film, *Beyond Rangoon* concerns a young American (Patricia Arquette) on vacation in the Far East. In Burma, she does everything she's told not to, her passport gets stolen, and she witnesses things she's not supposed to see. She befriends a local guide and they end up on the run trying to escape government officials who want to prevent her from telling about the atrocities she's seen. Composer Hans Zimmer uses ethnic flutes to spice up his score, giving it an airy quality that belies the tension in the story and blends quite nicely with the cinematography in the film.

Beth Krakower

Beyond the Law

See: Day of Anger/Beyond the Law

The Big Chill/ The Big Chill: More Songs from the Original Soundtrack

The Big Chill; 1983, Motown Records, from the film *The Big Chill*, Columbia Pictures, 1983 🎬🎬🎬🎬

The Big Chill: More Songs from the Original Soundtrack; 1998, Motown Records, from the Columbia film *The Big Chill*, 1983 🎬🎬🎬🎬

A solid collection of golden oldies that marked a generation and actually rekindled the fortunes of Motown Records when they were used in the soundtrack of this film. Nothing but the best here, and each song chockful of fond memories. Okay, the album is kind of short with 10 tracks adding up to 31 minutes of playing time, but for once you still might want to pick up a copy and listen to it, just for the fun of it. The second volume adds several titles not heard in the original soundtrack album, most notably "When a Man Loves a Woman" by Percy Sledge, "Dancing in the Street" by Martha Reeves & the Vandellas, "What's Going On" by Marvin Gaye, and "In the Midnight Hour" by the

Rascals. As the Four Tops proffer in one of their most successful hits of the era, "It's the Same Old Song," but by the same token, it's always pleasant to hear it again, particularly in a collection such as this.

Didier C. Deutsch

The Big Country

1988/1995, Silva America, from the film *The Big Country*, United Artists, 1958 ♪♪♪♪♪

album notes: Music: Jerome Moross; **Orchestra:** The Philharmonia Orchestra; **Conductor:** Tony Bremner.

One of the great western scores, the music for *The Big Country* was, for many years, available only on a United Artists mono or rechanneled stereo LP of dubious sonic quality. The score deserved a reevaluation, and this superior recording fills the gap. With The Philharmonia, conducted by Tony Bremner, giving an outstanding performance, Jerome Moross's music emerges full force as the extraordinary effort it always was. Everything in this recording works to emphasize the positive aspects of the score, including the splendid, wide-open sonics, as well as the packaging, with an informative booklet providing behind-the-score glances that will delight any fan of film music.

Didier C. Deutsch

Big Daddy

1999, C2/American, from the Columbia Pictures film, *Big Daddy*, 1999 ♪♪♪

This soundtrack to a surprise hit film of the summer of 1999 is a hodgepodge of good songs (by Sheryl Crow, Melanie C, Shawn Mullins, Yvonne Elliman, and other heavy duty performers), and somewhat dispensable selections (by Limp Bizkit, Wise Guys, and The Pharcycle), occasionally interrupted by bits of dialogue from the soundtrack that sound repetitious and superfluous after repeated listening. It may have worked within the context of the film, when songs became a subliminal element in the visuals, but with a few exceptions here it proves much less attractive.

Didier C. Deutsch

The Big Easy

1987, Antilles Records, from the film *The Big Easy*, Columbia Pictures, 1987 ♪♪♪♪

The New Orleans setting of this offbeat police drama suggests a score that would make use of the specific sounds heard in that city, with The Dixie Cups, Professor Longhair, Buckwheat Zydeco, and Aaron Neville & The Neville Brothers among the local artists represented. Dennis Quaid, who plays an extrovert

homicidal detective hot after Ellen Barkin, a transfer from another city, the moment she shows up in his office, also wrote and performs a number, "Closer to You," which does not seem so out of place in the context. The soundtrack is a flavorful, frequently exhilarating album.

Didier C. Deutsch

The Big Hit

1998, TVT Records, from the TriStar film *The Big Hit*, 1998 ♪♪♪♪

album notes: Music: Graeme Revell.

An action film by any other name, *The Big Hit* mixed the high-level energy of a stunt-loaded thriller and the low-grade humor of a comedy. While the stunts, amazingly staged, evoked the best work in kung fu fare, the comedy elements fell a bit too lame to make much of a dent, the one good joke being that the leader of a group of villains has a soft heart and hides, beneath his killer instincts, a strong desire to be liked. Directed by Hong Kong maven Che-Kirk Wong, *The Big Hit* constantly aimed for below-the-belt chuckles and partially succeeded. Also faring decently is its soundtrack, in which a couple of tracks make a good impression, among them a take-off on the Shadows' "Apache," performed by Sugarhill Gang taking the title of the song literally; an amusing Latino-Russian cocktail titled "Voto Latino" by Molotov; and an equally funny "I'm the Man" by Buck-O-Nine. Also quite interesting in their own right are "Magic Carpet Ride," a curiously enjoyable instrumental by Mighty Club Katz, and "The Fun Lovin' Criminal," a bouncy rap number by Fun Lovin' Criminals. Graeme Revell's "Big Hit Theme" caps the recording with a lively vamp that seems to go nowhere, but does it in humorous fashion.

Didier C. Deutsch

Big Jake

See: The Shootist

Big Night

1996, TVT Records, from the Rysher Entertainment film *Big Night*, 1996 ♪♪♪♪

album notes: Music: Gary DeMichele.

Big Night is the story of two Italian immigrant brothers in the 1950s who open a restaurant in a big northeastern American city. As a result, the soundtrack contains various Italian and American-Italian songs, and as would be expected Louis Prima is featured prominently on the album, as is Italian singer Claudio Villa. Also featured are five instrumental tracks by composer Gary DeMichele, whose score ranges from Italian-style folk to waltz, to jazz. If you listen closely to "Dinner," you almost can hear the sound of clanking dishes. Itsa lotta fun.

Beth Krakower

Big River

1985, MCA Records, from the Broadway production *Big River*, 1985. ♪♪♪♪

album notes: Music: Roger Miller; **Lyrics:** Roger Miller; **Cast:** Daniel Jenkins, Ron Richardson, Bob Gunton, Rene Auberjonois.

"King of the Road" songwriter Roger Miller enjoyed a long, 1,005-performance run with the multiple Tony Award-winning musical *Big River,* a clever adaptation of the Mark Twain stories about Huck Finn and the runaway slave Jim, as they travel on a raft down the Mississippi, from St. Petersburg, Missouri, to Hillsboro, Arkansas. With Heidi Landesman providing the evocative settings that gave the show its local folk colors, *Big River* was a powerful hit that survives to this day through its flavorful cast recording album.

Didier C. Deutsch

The Big Squeeze

1998, Citadel Records, from the First Look film *The Big Squeeze,* 1998 ♪♪♪♪

album notes: Music: Mark Mothersbaugh.

When bartender Tanya discovers her born-again husband about to donate a secret fortune to a Spanish mission, she hires con-man Benny to obtain the stash for herself. Tanya is pursued by her smitten co-worker Jesse, who in turn is tailed by his jealous girlfriend Cece. These love-crossed characters stumble over each other in pursuit of riches during this rapid paced, and sadly neglected, farce. Devo frontman Mark Mothersbaugh's jazzy score matches the film's pep with up-tempo Latin cocktail music, zippy tam-tams, and cheesy Hammond organ. The zany percussion and synthesized pops and swirls propel the chase scenes and characters' near misses. Cesar Rosas, singer of Los Lobos, lends his strong tenor and production skills to Latin interpretations of '60s love songs. The Iguanas back him up with snappy trombone, vintage reverbed guitar, and La Bamba-style rhythms. *The Big Squeeze* plays well as a party album, Mothersbaugh's canny pop skills and witty borrowings from acid jazz and Esquivel make for a fun addition to anyone's collection.

David Poole

Big Time

1988, Island Records, from the film *Big Time,* Island Visual Arts, 1988 ♪♪

album notes. Music. Tom Waits.

They Know the Score

Eckart Seeber

I believe the differences between Europe and North America with respect to the role of music in film or TV stem from the difference in status that the composer enjoys in the two environments. In Europe, I believe, the composer enjoys a more respected status as a specialist/artist. A European producer would feel more uncomfortable to dictate to the composer what he or she should do musically than his or her American counterpart. In many cases composers have gone through fairly extensive formal training and may hold university degrees. I think this would intimidate a European filmmaker more than his or her American counterpart. I also think that the European filmmaking tradition is more of a collaboration where filmmaker and composer contribute to a film project independently in some way.

In the States it seems more often than not that the filmmaker hires the composer to deliver a product on the basis of some fairly specific instructions. It seems that in a lot of cases the producer/director is not necessarily interested in how creative you can be but he or she is interested in you filling certain specifications. That in itself, however, does not preclude creativity. In fact, limitations and certain parameters may require quite a lot of creativity in order for you to still be original. More often than not, American film productions are produced within very tight timelines, which does not leave a lot of room open for experimentation. The film requires a certain sound, a certain score to accentuate the filmmaker's vision. This is what is needed and that is why the producer hires a certain composer to deliver that product.

Courtesy of **Film Score Monthly**

An account of live performances by Tom Waits and his band, recorded in Los Angeles, San Francisco, Dublin, Stockholm, and Berlin, this album is largely a showcase for the songwriter and presents songs with which his fans will identify. As is frequently the case in films such as this, the scope and impact are limited, with Waits's raucous vocals unlikely to attract anyone other than hardcore followers.

Didier C. Deutsch

Big Top Pee-Wee

1988, Arista Records, from the film *Big Top Pee-Wee,* Paramount Pictures, 1988 🎬🎬🎬
album notes: Music: Danny Elfman; **Conductor:** William Ross.

This 1988 follow-up to the 1985 cult classic *Pee-Wee's Big Adventure* didn't bring Tim Burton back behind the camera, but did, at least, reunite Danny Elfman with its daffy protagonist, who here gets involved with a traveling carnival. This setting affords Elfman the opportunity at writing some irresistibly goofy circus music and fanfares, interspersed with more charming, Rota-esque Pee-Wee motifs, newly composed for this sequel (the result of the picture being produced by another studio). There's even a song Pee-Wee croons in his best Sinatra style ("The Girl on the Flying Trapeze"), along with a duet between Pee-Wee and his farm animal sidekicks. The result is an enthusiastic score filled with all the quirky instrumentations associated with Elfman's most offbeat works; dialogue is incorporated in several of the tracks, but they do less to detract from the music than they do to cement the charm of the material. One of Elfman's early scores, the Arista album is now hard-to-find but worth the effort to seek out.

Andy Dursin

Billy Bathgate

1991, Milan Records, from the film *Billy Bathgate,* Touchstone Pictures, 1991 🎬🎬🎬
album notes: Music: Mark Isham; **Conductors:** J.A.C. Redford, Enrico DiCecco.

This is an excessively somber orchestral score by Mark Isham. I actually appreciated the welcome breaks afforded by the selection of period music, pieces such as Cole Porter's "I Get a Kick Out of You." These songs are the only bright spots in a composition that captures the ill-fated life of a young man who joins up with gangster Dutch Schultz (Dustin Hoffman). Isham's work interacts very well with songs, flowing easily and providing some stable emotional support to the film. However, by "A Chase at the Races," it all becomes extremely dark and ominous. Actress Rachel York's vocal version of "Bye Bye Blackbird" is included on the album, as is "Oyfn Pripetshok (On the Heath)," a children's choir theme used for the *Schindler's List* trailers.

David Hirsch

Bird

1988, Columbia Records, from the Warner Bros. film *Bird,* 1988 🎬🎬🎬
album notes: Featured Musicians: Charlie Parker, Charles McPherson, alto sax; Monty Alexander, Barry Harris, Walter Davis Jr., piano; Ray Brown, Chuck Berghofer, Ron Carter, bass; John Guerin, drums; Jon Faddis, Red Rodney, trumpet; Charlie Shoemake, vibes.

A case in point demonstrating the problem of jazz music that is played and recorded in a style much too modern for the picture. Charlie Parker and the musicians he collaborated with played hard, very hard (substitute intense, driving pulse for hard). These musicians had an arrogance created by the world they lived in. The music not only was played intensely, the recorded sound was intense (a period sound due to the low-fi nature of early jazz recordings). Because of that, the real problem with *Bird* is its modern sound. The synchronization is remarkable on the screen. Hats off to the producer for including Parker's incredible solo on "Lester Leaps In," "Cool Blues," and "This Time the Dream's on Me." But some of the solos from the 1988 pool of musicians show how stylistically they have evolved since 1953. This evolution has a strange effect on hearing this soundtrack: ideas that the 1988 musicians play came from a later time when be-bop was becoming refined. This is the distraction of modern jazz in a period jazz film.

Bob Belden

The Birdcage

1996, edel America Records, from the film *The Birdcage,* United Artists, 1996. woof!

This is a clear example of Hollywood at its most commercially crass. Take a funny foreign movie, *La Cage Aux Folles* (a.k.a. *Birds of a Feather),* and remake it with an American cast, but make sure to revamp it so that it sounds as if it had originated here. Where the original had a marvelous, whimsical score by Ennio Morricone, replace it now with nondescript songs from various sources (including, God forgive them!, a couple of numbers written by Stephen Sondheim, Broadway's emeritus composer/lyricist and wunderkind, performed in screeching style by the film's stars). Put together a "soundtrack" album, and the poor suckers who saw the film will shell out their $16 gladly to get it. Sorry, but the album truly doesn't deserve it.

Didier C. Deutsch

Birds and Planes

See: The Shooting Party/Birds and Planes

The Bitter Suite: A Musical Odyssey

See: Xena: Warrior Princess

Black Beauty

1994, Giant Records, from the Warner Bros. film *Black Beauty*, 1994 🎬🎬🎬🎬

album notes: Music: Danny Elfman; **Conductor:** J. A. C. Redford.

In one of his early efforts, composer Danny Elfman delivered a gorgeous, subtly understated score for this beautiful story, about a black stallion and its various owners. At times elegiac ("Mommy"), at other times florid and strikingly breathtaking ("Frolic"), the cues follow the narrative closely but provide a listening experience that is never less than totally rewarding, and demonstrate Elfman's uncanny sense of musicality and melodic construction. Because the label is no longer active, this CD might be somewhat difficult to find, but don't give up—it's a real gem!

Didier C. Deutsch

The Black Cauldron

1985, Varèse Sarabande Records, from the animated feature *The Black Cauldron*, Walt Disney Pictures, 1985 🎬🎬🎬🎬

album notes: Music: Elmer Bernstein; **Orchestra:** The Utah Symphony Orchestra; **Conductor:** Elmer Bernstein.

Based on Lloyd Alexander's sword-and-sorcery "Chronicles of Prydain," *The Black Cauldron* may have seemed too serious and adult an animated feature to entice its target audience of tykes, despite the fact that it involved a stock assortment of daring youngsters and their cuddly animal characters in their fight-to-save-the-world against a group of evil monsters. But it prompted composer Elmer Bernstein to write one of his most interesting scores, a subtle brew of epic and romance, well-designed to play under the screen action and give it more impact while making for an enjoyable listening experience when appreciated on its own terms. The Utah Symphony, conducted by the composer, delivers the goods in this spacious-sounding CD, with the right gusto and usual flourishes.

Didier C. Deutsch

Black Dog

1998, Decca Records, from the Universal film *Black Dog*, 1998 🎬🎬🎬

A truckin' movie needs some truckin' tunes—other than C. W. McCall's "Convoy," that is. *Black Dog* is loaded with appropri-

ate Nashville road songs, including Rhett Akins's cover of Eddie Rabbitt's "Drivin' My Life Away," Lee Ann Womack's spirited (and suggestive) "A Man with 18 Wheels," Big House's "Road Man" . . . and the list goes on. But there's a good deal of solid stuff here, from Steve Earle's "Nowhere Road" to Chris Knight's "The Hammer Going Down" to Patty Loveless's "On Down the Line." The thematic unity of these 11 tracks nicely ties together the myriad voices that sing them.

Gary Graff

Black Orpheus

1989, Verve Records, from the film *Black Orpheus*, 1960 🎬🎬🎬🎬

album notes: Music: Luis Bonfa, Antonio Carlos Jobim.

Two of Brazil's most important composers, Antonio Carlos Jobim and Luis Bonfa, teamed to create the explosive musical score for this colorful retelling of the Orpheus legend set in Rio during the Carnival. The film was the Grand Prize Winner at the Cannes Film Festival in 1959. The song "Manha de Carnaval" (Morning of the Carnival), performed by Breno Mello, the film's Orfeo to Marpessa Dawn's Eurydice, is an early expression of the bossa nova movement that swept this country in the mid-1960s.

Didier C. Deutsch

Black Rain

1989, Virgin Movie Music, from the film *Black Rain*, Paramount Pictures, 1989 🎬🎬

album notes: Music: Hans Zimmer.

Hans Zimmer's volatile percussive mix of orchestral and synthesized performances is a perfect mate for Ridley Scott's breakneck-paced action film. The composer keeps the instrumentation at the high end, avoiding bass instruments, and interpolates familiar Far Eastern motifs to create an ethnic flavor for the Japanese locale of the story. Unfortunately, without Scott's visuals, the music loses a lot of the dramatic power it has in the film. The result is a surprising, but disappointingly ordinary synth score. The 20 minutes presented here as the "Black Rain Suite" is a forerunner to the assembled concert style presentations Zimmer would adopt on later albums like *Crimson Tide*. Among the six songs that lead off the CD is "Laserman," a composition by fellow film composer Ryuichi Sakamoto.

David Hirsch

Black Robe

1991, Varèse Sarabande Records, from the film *Black Robe*, Alliance Communications/Samuel Goldwyn, 1991 🎬🎬🎬

album notes: Music: Georges Delerue; **Orchestra:** The String Plus; The Sydney Philharmonia Choir; **Conductor:** Georges Delerue.

In one of his last efforts shortly before his death, Georges Delerue wrote a highly emotionally charged score for Bruce Beresford's epic adventure of a young, idealistic Jesuit priest who embarks on a perilous journey through the rugged 17th-century Canadian wilderness to convert the Huron Indians. Both story and locale provided the composer with the essential ingredients he needed. The deep mysticism of the film's hero, the romantic aspects of his quest, the culture clash between his own upbringing and the lifestyle of the Indians he seeks to convert, and the majestic beauty of the Canadian wilderness all found their way into his musical expression. As a result, his score is intensely reflective and deeply exciting, an attractive mixture that reflects both aspects of the screen action.

Didier C. Deutsch

Black Sunday/Baron Blood

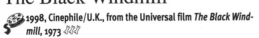

1992, Bay Cities Records, from the films *Black Sunday*, 1960; and *Baron Blood*, 1972 ♫♫♫

album notes: Music: Les Baxter; Conductor: Les Baxter.

Black Sunday and *Baron Blood* are two horror films scored by Les Baxter, better known today as a kitschy band arranger-conductor and pop orchestrator. Made in 1960 in Italy, *Black Sunday* was a stylish adaptation of a ghost story by Gogol, starring Barbara Steele in a dual role as a charming innocent and as her sexually irresistible ancestor who returns from the undead to haunt her. Baxter's score, uncommonly dark, with bizarre effects and instrumentations, seemed the perfect complement to the film, and though in mono sound in this recording (in which the cues are presented together in one long suite) it is still profoundly affecting and scary.

Another Italian-made film, *Baron Blood,* released in 1972, dealt with the impoverished owner of an estate in Europe whose evil ancestor, in an all-too familiar twist, returns from the undead to haunt him. Once again, Baxter provided a perfectly spooky score, even more chilling and pervasive than the one for *Black Sunday,* in which light, airy melodies contrast and inform the more malevolent accents in the music. And he did it all without any synthesizer! Makes you wonder . . .

Didier C. Deutsch

The Black Windmill

1998, Cinephile/U.K., from the Universal film *The Black Windmill*, 1973 ♫♫♫

album notes: Music: Roy Budd.

Part of a series of soundtracks written by Roy Budd and released recently by Cinephile in England, *The Black Windmill* was composed for a 1973 thriller, based on Clive Egleton's

"Seven Days to a Killing," in which Michael Caine portrayed a spy whose son has been kidnapped by another agent. Characteristic of Budd's approach to film scoring, the cues sound like straightforward accounts of the scenes for which they were created, with intensely dark and moody cues, some built around a three-note motif ("Drabble Calling") to give them an almost hypnotic effect. But the diversity in the composer's writing can be found in his extensive use of varied sonorities, from florid jazz riffs to ominous orchestral chords that occasionally contrast with the simplicity of a few notes on a lonely piano. On a pure musical level, it has its moments, but it is not the kind of soundtrack album one might play frequently.

see also: Diamonds, Paper Tiger, Fear Is the Key, Sinbad and the Eye of the Tiger

Didier C. Deutsch

Blacula

1998, Razor & Tie, from the American International film *Blacula*, 1972 ♫♫♫♫

album notes: Music: Gene Page; Conductor: Gene Page.

Some of the most creative film music from the 1970s was composed for the blaxploitation genre. *Blacula* ranks up there with *Shaft* and *Superfly* as the most recognizable titles from that genre. Gene Page composed a masterpiece for this film about a Black Prince bitten by a vampire who hunts on the streets of LA. Page combined the sounds of a traditional orchestra with more unusual instruments like African water drums, a harpsichord, an Arp, and guitars with a variety of effects. He also used eight crystal glasses, filled with different amounts of water, which were vibrated to create eerie sounds. This soundtrack contains five songs as well, two composed by Page and performed by the 21st Century Ltd., and three performed by the Hues Corporation.

Beth Krakower

Blade

1998, TVT Records, from the New Line Cinema film *Blade*, 1998 ♫♫

This is one of those "Music from and Inspired by . . ." collections, which generally means the label didn't have quite enough faith in the music that's actually in the movie so it recruited some big names to record additional tracks that will generate a little more heat in the consumer realm. Nothing was hotter than hip-hop during 1998, and to its credit, *Blade* favors imagination over commercial potency. The albums' dual themes—Mystikal's "The Edge of the Blade" and KRS-One's "Blade"—are nicely written and strongly delivered, while DJ Krush's "Dig This Vibe" will have you doing just that. But a dis-

Harrison Ford in Blade Runner. **(The Kobal Collection)**

appointingly uneventful "showdown" between Mantronik and EPMD on "Strictly Business" and some second- and third-tier acts such as Wolfpak and Majesty take a slice out of *Blade*'s overall focus.

Gary Graff

 **1998, Varèse-Sarabande Records, from the New Line Cinema film *Blade*, 1998** 🎬🎬🎬

album notes: Music: Mark Isham.

The score album, composed by Mark Isham, is rife with ominous-sounding cues that serve the film itself well but may at first deter the casual listener. While the moods remain somber throughout, an occasional theme weaves its way into the darker aspects of the score, lightening it, and making it suddenly more attractive than it appeared at first. But the primary purpose of the cues heard here is to suggest the moods of this complex modern-day vampire saga, and in this respect they are basically limited.

Didier C. Deutsch

Blade Runner

🎬 **1982, Warner Bros. Records, from the film *Blade Runner*, Warner Bros., 1982** 🎬🎬🎬

album notes: Music: Vangelis; **Orchestra:** The New American Orchestra; **Conductor:** Jack Elliott.

🎬 **1994, Atlantic Records; from the film *Blade Runner*, Warner Bros., 1982** 🎬🎬🎬🎬

album notes: Music: Vangelis.

Because Vangelis's original score had long been unavailable (despite mention of a soundtrack release in the film's on-screen credits), a re-recorded version done by the New American Orchestra was produced shortly after the release of the film. Vangelis's score is almost completely electronic and the well-intentioned attempts (some arranged by Patrick Williams) to recreate the music orchestrally fail miserably. But the jazzier tracks (notably "Memories of Green" and "Bladerunner Blues") actually benefit from the elimination of some of the bleating electronic textures employed by Vangelis in the film.

Vangelis finally released his original score in 1995, but it too is a compromise for those interested in hearing the unadulterated score. Vangelis interpolates dialogue and sound effects, as well as a few rather more pop-flavored compositions ostensibly composed for but not used in the final cut of the film. Some of these are actually enjoyable listening ("Rachel's Song" for example, is hauntingly beautiful), but are markedly different from the primarily atmospheric, dreamy textures Vangelis created for the rest of the film's music. Most of the high points are here, however, including the rapturous scoring of an early Spinner car flight, the wailing, quasi-oriental "Legends of Future Past," Vangelis's touching, saxophone-solo love music and his hammering, cheesy disco-era end titles. Fans of New Age "space" music will find this album fits right into their collection.

Jeff Bond

Blankman

1994, Epic Soundtrax, from the Columbia film *Blankman*, 1994 ♪♪♪

album notes: Music: Miles Goodman.

Comedian Damon Wayans created a smart vehicle for himself with this amiable spoof of film (and comic book) superheroes, informed in this recording with the lively "Super Hero," written by Prince-before-he-changed-his-name, and performed with great enthusiasm by the New Power Generation. In the film, Wayans portrays a self-appointed amateur sleuth and klutz who is so broke he fights crime in his underwear. Although he has no superpowers, no money, and no name, he makes the most of his bargain-basement budget, and can even turn an orthopedic shoe into a lethal boomerang. The contemporary soundtrack calls upon various pop songs to accompany the action, some pretty much straightforward, like "Could It Be I'm Falling in Love," performed by II D Extreme; others, like "Anyone Can Be a Hero," by Lalah Hathaway, or "Talk of the Town," by K-Dee, with their tongue firmly in cheek.

Didier C. Deutsch

Blast from the Past

1999, Capitol Records, from the New Line Cinema film *Blast from the Past*, 1999 ♪♪♪♪

This has to be the weirdest collection of tracks ever compiled on a single soundtrack album. The funny part about it is that it works wonderfully, and it's quite exhilarating. But the performers come from varied backgrounds, and their musical expression reflects this diversity. There is the idiosyncrasy of Block with the curiously wacky "Rhinoceros," the big band salute by Cherry Poppin' Daddies in the tongue-in-cheek "So Long Toots," the heavy metal approach of Dishwalla with "Pretty Ba-

bies," and, for a blast from another past, the crooning of Perry Como ("He's Mr. Excitement, you know!") on "It's a Good Day." The film itself, a time-warp comedy that involves a couple locked for 35 years in a shelter 50 feet underground as a result of a "nuclear" attack (at least that's what they think), only to find themselves transported in a brave new world in which they feel totally alienated, explains the many differences in musical directions. But the compilation is, well . . . a blast!

Didier C. Deutsch

Bleeding Hearts

1998, Laserlight Records, from the City film *Bleeding Hearts*, 1998 ♪

album notes: Music: Stanley Clarke.

An attractive, light score by Stanley Clarke for a film directed by Gregory Hines that made little impact at the box office. But, with the exception of a hint of Miles Davis's "All Blues" on "In Another Way" and the aptly titled "Jazz Tune," this is not a jazz soundtrack. Most of the selections are mood cues, showing off Stanley Clarke's orchestration. But there is no real jazz here.

Bob Belden

Blind Date

1987, Rhino Records, from the film *Blind Date*, Tri-Star Pictures, 1987 ♪

album notes: Music: Henry Mancini; **Conductor:** Henry Mancini.

Another sorry example of a favorite composer undone by the commercial considerations that often preside over the creation of a film soundtrack and its related album. The unfortunate victim in this instance is Henry Mancini, only represented here by two cues he created for this otherwise hilarious Blake Edwards romp about a serious-minded financial analyst on a date with a dizzy girl who can't hold her champagne, and the mayhem that ensues at a function after she's had two glasses. Billy Vera and The Beaters and the other performers here are doing what they have been asked to do, but their vocal contributions mean very little while Mancini's cues only whet one's desire to hear more of his music for this film.

Didier C. Deutsch

Blink

1994, Milan Records, from the film *Blink,* New Line Cinema, 1994 ♪♪

album notes: Music: Brad Fiedel; **Featured Musicians:** Ross Levinson, electric violin; Doug Norwine, saxophones.

Known more for his industrial strength synthesized scores for *The Terminator* films, Brad Fiedel created a serene, and somewhat enjoyable low-key score, thanks in part to the use of piano solos to represent the central character, the visually impaired Emma. Her sight only recently restored, but not quite perfect, she may or may not have witnessed a murder. For that aspect of the film, Fiedel relied on his old musical bag of tricks. The alternative Irish/American band, The Drovers, appears as itself in the film (Emma is purported to be its roadie) and it is featured in four songs on the soundtrack.

David Hirsch

Bliss

1997, Varèse Sarabande Records, from the film *Bliss*, Triumph Films, 1997 🎬🎬🎬

album notes: Music: Jan A.P. Kaczmarek; **Orchestra:** The Sinfonia Varsovia; **Conductor:** Krzesimir Debski; **Featured Musicians:** Pawel Losakiewicz, Krzesimir Debski, violin; Andrzej Jagodzinski, piano; Jacek Urbaniak, recorder; **Featured Vocalist:** Marta Boberska, soprano.

If the movie itself, about a young couple and their sexual problems, was not so banal and only worthy of a quick fadeout at the box office, this soundtrack might possibly attract more people than it will, and it should. Lushly romantic, with attractive melodies to sustain one's attention, it has at least some redeeming values. But don't let the track titles throw you off course. While they apply to the narrative and follow poor Joseph and Maria on their path to marital bliss, they are simply meant here as an indication of the intent actually pursued by the composer to conform with the storyline. You won't need them to enjoy the album.

Didier C. Deutsch

Blood & Wine

1997, Angel Records, from the film *Blood & Wine*, 1997 🎬🎬🎬

album notes: Music: Michal Lorenc; **Conductors:** Tadeusz Karolak and Zdislaw Szostak; **Featured Soloists:** Mariusz Puchlowski, Bogdan Kupisiewicz, Jacek Ostaszewski, flutes; Jose Torres, percussion; Bob Rafelson, lastra.

Jack Nicholson starred in this unusual drama, involving a robbery and unsavory characters trying to exact revenge, that was scored by Michael Lorenc, a Polish composer. Reflecting the moods of the film, the cues are darkly hued with long, ominous strains suggesting similar moments in the action. Even a cue marked "Action" or "Jason's Revenge," for instance, elicited a subdued theme with only a brief crescendo here and there to signal the stridency of the moment. Playing by the National Philharmonic Orchestra of Warsaw is lush and on the button, but don't play this CD if you need to uplift your mood.

Didier C. Deutsch

The Blood of Heroes

1989, Intrada Records, from the film *The Blood of Heroes,* New Line Cinema, 1989 🎬🎬🎬

album notes: Music: Todd Boekelheide; **Conductor:** Mark Adler.

Not a score that will be appreciated by every ear, but nonetheless a fascinatingly creative work to experience, Todd Boekelheide abandons most conventional forms of musical composition to portray the barbaric world of a decaying future. He does this, not only by interpolating usual instruments into his orchestra, but by sampling sounds created by throwing odd pieces of junk around his basement! Every so often, he breaks away with some standard fare, like the harmonic solo on "Watching, Waiting," or the offbeat "Party, Party, Party," which sounds more like it would at home in the bar on "The Drew Carey Show." Played frequently in 12/8 time, a rhythm favored in African music, Boekelheide's score is both powerful and refreshingly original.

David Hirsch

Blood Simple

See: Raising Arizona/Blood Simple

Blow-Up

1998, Rhino, from the MGM film *Blow Up*, 1970 🎬🎬🎬

album notes: Music: Herbie Hancock; **Featured Musicians:** Herbie Hancock, piano; Freddie Hubbard, Joe Newman, trumpets; Phil Woods, alto sax; Joe Henderson, tenor sax; Paul Griffin, organ; Jim Hall, guitar; Ron Carter, bass; Jack DeJohnette, drums.

Herbie Hancock's first foray into film music was for director Michelangelo Antonioni's study of illusion, *Blow-Up.* Set against the backdrop of London's "swinging '60s," Hancock's warm and romantic music plays against this edgy "pop" setting. The main title, "Main Theme/Blow Up" and "Jane's Theme" are now a part of jazz's canon of compositions, being rediscovered by young musicians in the early '90s. The original LP contained only one non-Hancock song ("Stroll on"), performed by the Yardbyrds. The CD version here has added too many pop songs that were used (or not used) and that defined the sound of the times, but this collection collides with Hancock's original music and takes away from the beauty and sophistication of his score. Although Hancock's music does not necessarily work against the picture, the mood of the performances transcends the remoteness of Antonioni's abstract film concept. The musicians on Hancock's music are the best in jazz: Freddie Hubbard, Joe Henderson, Ron Carter, Jack DeJohnette, Phil Woods, and Jim Hall. Only "The Kiss" and "Jane's Theme" would be considered complete jazz performances, and they are superb in bringing out the romantic mood that defines part of Hancock's style. The rest of the Hancock cues are too short to feel like jazz performances.

Bob Belden

Blown Away

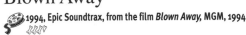1994, Epic Soundtrax, from the film *Blown Away*, MGM, 1994

album notes: Music: Alan Silvestri; **Conductor:** Alan Silvestri.

A modest but pleasant listen that mixes big names with fresh talent. It's hard to go too wrong when there are *two* Aretha Franklin cuts to listen to, and U2's "With or Without You" sounds good in most any contest. Meanwhile, the hipness impaired will be well-educated by sampling songs by the Sundays, the Jayhawks, and Big Head Todd and the Monsters.

Gary Graff

Blue Chips

1994, MCA Records, from the film *Blue Chips*, Paramount Pictures, 1994

A sports film without Queen's "We Will Rock You"—now *there's* a concept. Bookended by versions of Joe Williams's "Baby, Please Don't Go"—one by John Mellencamp, the other by Them—*Blue Chips* mixes oldies with score pieces by Chic's Nile Rodgers. Having fairly obscure stuff like John Lee Hooker doing "Money (That's What I Want)" and Slim Harpo's "Shake Your Hips" puts *Blue Chips* in the bonus. And at least there's no rapping from hoops sensation and film co-star Shaquille O'Neal.

Gary Graff

Blue Hawaii

1996, RCA Records, from the movie *Blue Hawaii*, Paramount Pictures, 1961

Released in 1961, *Blue Hawaii* is, by most accounts, the most successful film in which Elvis starred. In it, he portrayed an islander, more interested in being a tourist guide than in supervising his family's pineapple business, much to the chagrin of his mother, played by Angela Lansbury. Besides its attractive locations, the film provided Elvis with a strong array of songs, among which the title tune (initially written in 1937 by Leo Robin and Ralph Rainger for Bing Crosby in *Waikiki Wedding*) particularly stands out, as does "Can't Help Falling in Love," which became a multi-million seller.

Didier C. Deutsch

Blue in the Face

1995, Luaka Bop/Warner Bros. Records, from the film *Blue in the Face*, Miramax Films, 1995

David Byrne's somewhat iconoclastic approach is evident all over this soundtrack album in which Danny Hoch, assuming various personalities, introduces some of the selections, performed by a motley group of recording stars, from Soul Coughing to Astor Piazzolla, from Paula Cole to Lou Reed, from Selena (and David Byrne) to Vijaya Anand (and David Byrne). Some good, exotic tracks, too, with La Casa's "Mi Barrio," Spearhead and Zap Mama's "To My Ba-bay!," and John Lurie National Orchestra's "Let's Get Ready to Rhumba," among the best. Spicy hot and tasty!

Didier C. Deutsch

The Blue Lagoon

1987, Southern Cross Records, from the film *The Blue Lagoon*, Columbia Pictures, 1980

album notes: Music: Basil Poledouris; **Orchestra:** The Australian Symphony Orchestra; **Conductor:** Basil Poledouris.

Many viewers have tried to forget this tepid 1980 remake about a boy and a girl stranded on a desert isle, allowing only the images of Brooke Shields, Nestor Almendros's sumptuous cinematography, and the lovely music by Basil Poledouris to linger in their memories. Poledouris, coming off his fine score for John Milius's *Big Wednesday* (which remains sadly unavailable), scored the movie with a lyrical passage for a piano solo that gradually integrates the full orchestra, setting the stage for an evocative collection of romantic cues that never feels overtly saccharine in its most melodramatic moments. A contrasting music-box motif evokes the innocence of the stranded teens without pounding you over the head with its importance to the narrative, and this relatively low-key approach fills the entire score. The Australian Symphony Orchestra's performance is competent and the soundtrack remains one of Poledouris's most interesting scores for its subject matter, which is as far removed from his work on the Milius and Paul Verhoeven films as one could imagine.

Andy Dursin

The Blue Max

1995, Legacy Records/Sony Music, from the film *The Blue Max*, 20th Century Fox, 1966

album notes: Music: Jerry Goldsmith; **Conductor:** Jerry Goldsmith.

While Jerry Goldsmith's dramatic score for the World War I epic *The Blue Max* has been reissued several times, this Columbia/Legacy CD issue offers its most complete presentation to date.

Assembled from the original elements (including nine reels of previously lost music, located in a vault at the Fox Studios), this gorgeous restoration effectively captures the occasionally dark, yet always strong spirit of the film's plot, the aerial confrontation of two skilled pilots, on opposite sides of the conflict, and Goldsmith's poignant musical themes. While it is generally considered one of the composer's lesser known works, it is highly recommended as one of his finest, as this outstanding reissue definitely demonstrates.

Charles L. Granata

Blue Velvet

🎞 1986, Varèse Sarabande Records, from the film *Blue Velvet,* Dino De Laurentiis Entertainment, 1986 ♫♫♫

album notes: Music: Angelo Badalamenti; **Orchestra:** The Film Symphony of Prague; **Conductor:** Angelo Badalamenti.

Angelo Badalamenti's score for David Lynch's stylish mystery thriller is darkly romantic. His melodies are pretty but somber, a beautiful gown worn by a corpse. The omnipresent darkness and deviation that is the film's undercurrent is reflected in Badalamenti's musical style. His main theme, violins playing against violins in almost kaleidoscopic spirals, creates a somewhat Hitchcockian mood of hidden menace. Another theme, heard vocally as well as in two instrumentals, is a sorrowful love song, resolutely unhappy—is also appropriate to the film's depiction of romance gone askew. There's only about 20 minutes of score on the CD, the balance filled out by moody songs, source music, even a strange sound effects suite.

Randall Larson

The Blues Brothers

🎞 1980, WEA/Atlantic, from the film *The Blues Brothers,* Universal 1980 ♫♫♫♫

You've gotta give John Belushi and Dan Aykroyd credit; the "Saturday Night Live" vets played Jake and Elwood Blues—their suited, shaded, and fedoraed musical alter egos—for great comic schtick, but they also tried to make the music work. From the get-go, the duo enlisted ace players such as guitarists Steve Cropper and Matt "Guitar" Murphy and bassist Donald "Duck" Dunn, who played on a chunk of the R&B classics they were covering. They raised the bar another notch with the first "Blues Brothers" film, enlisting heroes such as James Brown, Aretha Franklin, Ray Charles and Cab Calloway into the proceedings. Despite raggedly uproarious versions of the Spencer Davis Group's "Gimme Some Lovin'" and the seminal "Sweet Home Chicago," Jake and Elwood cheerfully pale before their guests here—particularly Franklin, who turns in a rendition of "Think" that puts an extra jewel in her Queen of Soul

crown. Brown's turn on "The Old Landmark," backed by the Rev. James Cleveland Choir, puts a rare spotlight on his church roots, while Cab Calloway shows that it's hard to do a bad version of "Minnie the Moocher." Belushi and Aykrod, meanwhile, hold their own with Charles on "Shake a Tail Feather." There are more thorough treatments of the Blues Brothers' recording career available, but the presence of these legends gives the act a bit more perspective and underlies the sincerity of the actors' love for the music.

Gary Graff

Blues Brothers 2000

🎞 1998, Universal Records, from the Universal film *Blues Brothers 2000,* 1997 ♫♫♫♫

album notes: Music: Paul Shaffer.

In what is a warmed-up attempt at cashing in on a formula that had its moment of success, Dan Aykroyd enlisted the help of John Goodman to cook up this sequel to the 1980 *Blues Brothers,* again directed by John Landis. The problem is Goodman is not John Belushi, who was an inspired presence in the original film, and Dan Aykroyd, who played magnificently against his old foil, seems a bit breathless in this sequel. Putting this album in a different perspective, however, some heavy-duty people turned up to perform on the soundtrack, including B. B. King, Gary U.S. Bonds, Eric Clapton, Bo Diddley, Jon Faddis, Jack DeJohnette, Isaac Hayes, Dr. John, Billy Preston, Lou Rawls, Koko Taylor, Grover Washington Jr., and Steve Winwood, among others, all performing under the *nom de stage* the Louisiana Gator Boys, whose "How Blue Can You Get" and "New Orleans" are two highlights here; also, Aretha Franklin, Eddie Floyd, Wilson Pickett, Taj Mahal, and Sam Moore (of Sam and Dave), all heard to best effect in various other tracks. Aykroyd, Goodman, and the Blues Brothers Band, led by Paul Shaffer, provide the rest of the entertainment, which, it must be said, is on a high level of quality.

Didier C. Deutsch

Bodies, Rest & Motion

🎞 1993, Big Screen Records, from the film *Bodies, Rest & Motion,* Fine Line Features, 1993 ♫♫♫♫

album notes: Music: Michael Convertino.

Set in the Arizona desert, this odd tale of youngsters who meet, make love, and go on their merry way elicited from Michael Convertino a New Age score permeated with Native American sounds and chanting. Strangely atmospheric and unusual, it is greatly evocative and quite attractive, though it probably gains at being heard in connection with the screen action. Some selections like "To the August House" or "It's a Big Planet" are particularly pretty.

Didier C. Deutsch

Body Bags

1993, Varèse Sarabande Records, from the film *Body Bags,* Showtime, 1993 ♪

album notes: Music: John Carpenter, Jim Lang.

Listening to this soundtrack album, one almost feels tempted to say, like Shakespeare, that it is "much ado about nothing." John Carpenter, who has occasionally shown bits of brilliance in his scores, seems to have taken the easy way out here. The musical ideas are trite, the expression vapid, the execution uninspired. Here and there, one can hear flashes of interesting ideas trying to develop ("Long Beautiful Hair," "I Can See"), but generally speaking the score is one long, unsubstantial exercise.

Didier C. Deutsch

Body Heat

1989, SCSE Records, from the film *Body Heat,* The Ladd Company, 1981 ♪♪♪♪

album notes: Music: John Barry.

The quintessential John Barry mystery score. You can just feel all the sweat of a hot and humid summer night in South Florida. The principal theme, played by an alto sax, has since been covered on many jazz albums and has often been copied in other films. Barry's score is surprisingly limited thematically and very often repetitious. It's nothing unusual for this composer, whose music is still dramatically powerful. It captures not just the sexual tension between lovers William Hurt and Kathleen Turner ("Kill for Pussy"), but the anxiety of their plot to murder Turner's husband. The buildup to the explosion of the house ("Better Get Him") is a real nail biter, one of Barry's most suspenseful moments. The album includes John Williams's music for the Ladd Company logo and detailed notes by Royal S. Brown. It is rumored to have been mastered from an audio cassette, which may account for the minor tape hiss and some high end audio breakup that can be heard, but none of that has kept this score from becoming a highly prized album. Originally released as a limited edition, first as a 45 rpm vinyl 12" disc in 1983, and then on CD six years later, *Body Heat* became a top collectible fetching upward of $150 for either format.

David Hirsch

Body of Evidence

1993, Milan Records, from the movie *Body of Evidence,* Dino de Laurentiis/MGM Pictures, 1993 ♪♪♪

album notes: Music: Graeme Revell.

The actual, very real merits of *Body of Evidence,* a crime drama of a different kind, may have been obscured by the fact that it stars Madonna as a sex-starved woman, accused of having inflicted too much of a good thing on her now-defunct husband, and willing to demonstrate *in situ* to the district attorney what it is she did. Among the elements that are somewhat ignored in the process is Graeme Revell's contemporary score, a mix of synth effects and orchestral lines that seem to be there more for atmosphere than for musical support, though a couple of strong selections (notably "The Passion Theme," performed by Warren Hill, and "The Handcuffs") are particularly memorable.

Didier C. Deutsch

Body Parts

1991, Varèse Sarabande Records, from the film *Body Parts,* Paramount Pictures, 1991 ♪♪♪

album notes: Music: Loek Dikker; **Orchestra:** The Munich Symphony Orchestra; **Conductor:** Allan Wilson.

Ever heard a "singing saw" before? If not, then here's your chance—Loek Dikker's soundtrack for this modestly entertaining 1991 horror movie with Jeff Fahey and Kim Delaney features, yes, a singing saw that creates an appropriately eerie sound. Director Eric Red clearly wanted a large orchestral score for his "dangers of body transplants" thriller, and the composer has responded with a low-key, almost subtle (at times) music score that has some rather odd sounding string arrangements to nicely complement the singing saw. The tone is dissonant and rather unembracing, but hey, it's a horror movie out of the Dr. Frankenstein school, so why carp? Body Parts is a better movie, and music score, than many of its genre peers.

Andy Dursin

The Bodyguard

1992, Arista Records; from the film *The Bodyguard,* Warner Bros., 1992 ♪♪♪♪

Whitney Houston's film debut made musical history. Her broad, melodramatic rendition of Dolly Parton's "I Will Always Love You" set a record for consecutive weeks at # 1 on the Billboard charts (14) before being upended by Boyz II Men. This is actually half a Houston album, but she certainly made the most of it, putting two more singles ("I Have Nothing" and "I'm Every Woman") into the Top 5, though her best performances comes on the gospel showcase "Jesus Loves Me." The album was also good news for British rocker Nick Lowe. Curtis Stigers covered his "Peace, Love, and Undertstanding," snaring Lowe a well-deserved $1 million royalty check.

Gary Graff

Whitney Houston in The Bodyguard. **(The Kobal Collection)**

Bolero

1984, Prometheus Records/Belgium, from the film *Bolero,* Cannon Films, 1984 ♫♫♫

album notes: Music: Peter Bernstein; **Orchestra:** The Rome Studio Symphony Orchestra; **Conductor:** Elmer Bernstein.

Evidently, Peter Bernstein has learned his music lessons well, and the score he wrote for *Bolero,* Bo Derek's unending search for the man who will ravish her and make her a woman, is greatly satisfying. Happily mixing genres (as in tauromachy and Spanish dancing for the cleverly titled "Bullero"), Bernstein's cues denote a sure hand and an even surer ear for attractive film music. It helps, of course, that Papa Elmer is at the helm conducting the Rome Studio Symphony, and that he contributed a couple of selections, but the bulk of the score is Peter's and many of his compositions ("The Sleepless Night," "Ride on the Beach," "Foreplay/The Sheik") are appropriately descriptive. In the midst of the heavily scented evocations, he also threw in some fiery moments, including a languorous "Bolero Bolero," a throbbing "Tango for Rudy," and an impassioned "Gypsy Dance."

Didier C. Deutsch

The Bonfire of the Vanities

1991, Atlantic Records, from the film *The Bonfire of the Vanities,* Warner Bros., 1991 ♫♫♫

album notes: Music: Dave Grusin; **Conductor:** Dave Grusin.

This standard jazz fusion fare from Dave Grusin sounds more like any one of his own GRP albums than a film score. While his bouncy music suggests that he seemed to find the film funnier than most audiences and critics did, on CD it makes a pleasant diversion. The music maintains its attitude all the way through, apparently never taking things too seriously. Inexplicably, Grusin's name appears nowhere on the cover of this Atlantic Records' release, except in the small print on the movie credit block. It's odd considering his popularity as a jazz artist.

David Hirsch

Boogie Nights

1998, Capitol Records, from the New Line Cinema film *Boogie Nights,* 1998 ♫♫♫♫

Centering on the porn industry in the '70s, this is a movie about lost souls who find each other and become the family support that each never had. The music, split over two CDs, including tracks not used in the movie, range from disco to rock to soul, with these two song compilations capturing the feel and spirit of the era. The interesting thing about both albums is that neither really uses the A-level hits one would expect. In fact, the most recognizable tracks on the first CD include "Best of My Love" (The Emotions), "Spill the Wine" (War with Eric Burton), and "Brand New Key" (Melanie), while the second features "Boogie Shoes" (KC and the Sunshine Band), "Mama Told Me Not to Come" (Three Dog Night), and "Fooled Around and Fell in Love" (Elvin Bishop). Oddly placed on each CD is a song from the '80s, "Sister Christian" (Night Ranger) and "Jesse's Girl" (Rick Springfield), which somewhat alters the overall feel. But in this case who cares! It's nice to see a movie based in the '70s that refrains from using Donna Summer or Gloria Gaynor and actually utilizes a lesser-known KC and the Sunshine Band track!

Beth Krakower

Book of Love

1990, Atlantic Records, from the New Line Cinema film *Book of Love*, 1990 ♪♪♪♡

A warm look at a writer's early, teenage years, when he was smitten by a young girl his age, this pleasant romantic comedy spawned a soundtrack that has been in the catalogue for some time, but still deserves to be discovered (you may find it at specialized shops, although it's unlikely your Virgin or Tower stores still carries it). Consisting of a dozen golden oldies, the album starts off with a great reading of the song that gave the film its title, in a powerful rendition by Ben E. King and Bo Diddley, set to sparkling arrangements by Stanley Clarke, with Doug Lazy putting it in a more contemporary mold. From then on, the sailing is nothing but enjoyable with classics like "The Great Pretender" by the Platters, "Little Darlin'" by the Diamonds, "Rip It Up" by Little Richard, "Sincerely" by the Moonglows, and "Why Do Fools Fall in Love" by the Teenagers and Frankie Lymon. Nothing new under the sun, really, but always fun to listen to in any circumstance.

see also: Why Do Fools Fall in Love

Didier C. Deutsch

Bopha!

1993, Big Screen Records, from the film *Bopha!* Paramount Pictures, 1993 ♪♪

album notes: Music: James Horner.

James Horner abandoned much of the compositional techniques for which he's become known to take a fresh approach for this film. Perhaps the score owes much of its inspiration to the African motifs that are incorporated, particularly the Zulu tribal marches which are interpolated with electronic effects. This medley yields a tense and dark otherworldly effect that is most likely effective as a film score. However, what it gains for creativity, it lacks in pure entertainment value making this one of Horner's less interesting albums.

David Hirsch

Born on the Fourth of July

1989, MCA Records, from the film *Born on the Fourth of July*, Universal Pictures, 1989 ♪♪♪♪♪

album notes: Music: John Williams; **Conductor:** John Williams.

An outstanding score by John Williams is the centerpiece of the soundtrack album for Oliver Stone's cluttered 1989 biopic of Vietnam vet Ron Kovic. Williams's score is so masterful in conveying all the dramatic requirements of Kovic's decades-spanning story that you forget his music actually takes up less than half of the album's running time, the remainder of which contains Edie Brickell & New Bohemians' "A Hard Rain's a Gonna Fall" along with a number of period songs strictly generic in their selection (Don McLean's "American Pie," Van Morrison's "Brown Eyed Girl," Henry Mancini's "Moon River," etc.). But Williams's score, featuring a downbeat trumpet fanfare performed by Tim Morrison, is one of his most powerful and potent efforts, offering both moments of tragedy and uplift, culminating in a knockout finale. It's just one more jewel in Williams's crown, and certainly one of the best film scores to come out of the last half of the 1980s.

Andy Dursin

Born to Be Wild

1995, Milan Records, from the film *Born to Be Wild*, Warner Bros., 1995 ♪♪♪

album notes: Music: Mark Snow; **Conductor:** Mark Snow.

Known primarily these days for his brilliant non-thematic work on the *X-Files* TV series, Mark Snow gets to strut his melodic stuff here for one of the several *Free Willy* knock-offs produced around the time, with a domesticated gorilla replacing the seagoing beastie. Backed with a full symphonic orchestra, Snow has created a bright score, featuring some charming, albeit sugar-coated themes ("Goodbye") with several tracks interpolated with African-inspired rhythms ("Plucked from the Jungle"). Artist Lebo M, who also worked with Jerry Goldsmith on *Congo*, co-composed the song "Back to the Species" with

Snow and performs on the album. The rock group Green Jelly also brings Steppenwolf's "Born to Be Wild" into the '90s.

David Hirsch

The Borrowers

1998, Mojo Records, from the PolyGram film *The Borrowers*, 1998 &&&&

album notes: Music: Harry Gregson-Williams; **Additional Music:** Steve Jablonsky, Gavin Greenaway; **Conductor:** Harry Gregson-Williams.

A charming fantasy for kids of all ages, *The Borrowers* is a happy mixture of British eccentric attitudes and great special effects. Based on the novels of Mary Norton, the story involves the little folks who live under the floorboards in a cozy British house, the "borrowers" of the title, so-called because of their habit of "borrowing" things from the house's tenants. Faced with possible extinction when a greedy lawyer, Ocious P. Potter, wants to raze the house, after the death of the old lady who owned it, the Borrowers—Pod and Homily, and their children Arrietty and Peagreen—eventually manage to save themselves and the house after they venture in the "outside world," barely one step ahead of the lawyer, and secure the old lady's last will that promises that the house won't be destroyed. Putting the proper musical illustration to this fancy tale, Harry Gregson-Williams wrote a score that keeps the action in perspective in a brazen display of energetic and colorful cues.

Didier C. Deutsch

Borsalino/Borsalino & Co.

1998, Milan/France, from the films *Borsalino*, Paramount, 1970, and *Borsalino and Co.*, Paramount, 1974 &&&&

album notes: Music: Claude Bolling; **Conductor:** Claude Bolling.

Placing things into perspective, Marseilles in the 1920s and '30s was not unlike Chicago at the same time: a bustling city where crime was rampant and gangs usually challenged each other for the control of the city's businesses, legit and otherwise. This was the backdrop for the two films by Jacques Deray, *Borsalino* and *Borsalino and Co.* (so named for the felt hats that seemed to be part of the gang members' "uniforms"), which starred Alain Delon and Jean-Paul Belmondo. Bolling, often mentioned as the French Mancini, scored both films with a great deal of feel for the period, and wrote a great number of cues that are both catchy and evocative, with the score for the first film rating higher than the one for the sequel. The selections are presented in a jumbled way that doesn't follow the screen action, but this may have been done intentionally to emphasize certain aspects of the music. At any rate, it doesn't distract from one's enjoyment. This title

They Know the Score

Alf Clausen

From our very first meeting, [Matt Groening] said to me, 'We don't look upon [*The Simpsons*] as a cartoon, we look upon it as a drama where the characters are drawn,' and that always stuck with me. He said, 'As long as you treat your musical approach in that manner I don't think you'll go wrong with us,' and it's really served me well because, as you know, most animated shows come from a history of Looney Tunes and Bugs Bunny and Elmer Fudd where there's a lot of catching of various action scenes. They really don't like me to do that with *The Simpsons*. They like me to score the emotion of it and it has really turned out to a be an interesting way to approach an animated show. It's very different than, I think, just about every other animated show that's around. Once in a while I'll look at a scene and try to figure out what I'm going to do with a cue, and when in doubt it's always, score the emotion and never Mickey Mouse anything. Go for the emotion first and the action second. It's been interesting. I did a seminar at the Berklee college on *The Simpsons* and I mentioned that one of the first things I figured out about doing this show was, forget intros. There's no time to set up a mood because with this particular series it's, bam!, the mood is right there. You have to state the mood very quickly and wrap it up very quickly and move on.

***Courtesy of* Film Score Monthly**

may be out of print or just plain hard to find. Mail-order companies, used CD shops, or dealers of rare or import recordings will be your best bet.

see also: Claude Bolling in Composers

Didier C. Deutsch

The Bourne Identity

1988, Intrada Records, from the film The Bourne Identity, Warner Bros., 1988 🎬🎬🎬🎬

album notes: Music: Laurence Rosenthal; **Orchestra:** The Film Symphony of Prague; **Conductor:** Laurence Rosenthal.

A political thriller, starring Richard Chamberlain as an amnesiac who finds himself involved in a crime, *The Bourne Identity* benefits from its many European locales and colorful characters, as well as the more mysterious aspects of its screen action, all of which suggest a splendidly evocative score to composer Laurence Rosenthal. As a result, the overall musical fabric is beautifully diversified, most often solidly grounded in orchestral themes that have great impact and melodic content, but with occasional strange electronic sounds that delineate more specifically the psychological aspects of the story. At times attractive, at times disquieting, it's a great score with some excellent moments in it.

Didier C. Deutsch

The Boxer

1997, MCA Records, from the Universal film The Boxer, 1997 🎬🎬🎬

album notes: Music: Gavin Friday, Maurice Selzer; **Conductor:** Fiachra Trench; **Featured Artists:** Gary Ashley, Maurice Seezer, vocals, keyboards, electronics, guitar, bass, rhythms, accordion, piano; Andrew Phillpott, drums, programming, keyboards, guitar, bass, electronics; Renaud Pion, wind instruments.

This unorthodox score, a strange mixture of electronics, pulsating rockers, orchestral lines, acoustic numbers, sprinkled with bits of dialogue, was created for an unusual little film starring Daniel Day-Lewis as a former boxer, who has spent 14 years in jail because of his IRA activities, leaving him withdrawn and somewhat uncommunicative. Back in his neighborhood, he tries to renew an awkward relationship with his former girlfriend, and decides to resume his career, first by rebuilding the old gym that has been destroyed in a wave of violence. Despite changes in the political landscape, and a warming trend between Catholics, Protestants, and the British occupants, old hatreds subsist that might jeopardize the boxer's plans. The score composed by Gavin Friday and Maurice Seezer, hitherto unknown, puts the accents on some of these elements in a very evocative fashion, with cues that emphasize the melancholy moods that pervade the film. Unorthodox but satisfying.

Didier C. Deutsch

The Boy Friend

1989, RCA Victor, from the off-Broadway production The Boy Friend, 1954 🎬🎬🎬

album notes: Music: Sandy Wilson; **Lyrics:** Sandy Wilson; **Cast:** Millicent Martin, Julie Andrews, Ann Wakefield, Stella Claire, Dilys Lay, Paulette Girard, Bob Scheerer, Ruth Altman, Eric Berry, John Hewer, Geoffrey Hibbert.

A lighthearted send-up of the simple musicals of the 1920s, *The Boy Friend,* written by Sandy Wilson, was initially created in London in 1953 as an after-hour entertainment at an intimate private theatre club. Set on the Riviera in 1926, its skimpy storyline deals with a young English heiress at Madame Dubonnet's finishing school, and the young delivery boy (actually a peer in disguise) with whom she falls in love. On September 30, 1954, *The Boy Friend* opened at the Royale Theater under the aegis of producers Cy Feuer and Ernest Martin where it played a total of 485 performances. In its cast was a fresh 19-year-old, Julie Andrews, whose next stop on Broadway two years later would be in the huge hit *My Fair Lady.* The show was revived off-Broadway in 1958, for a run that lasted 763 performances, and again on Broadway in 1970 for 119 performances, with Sandy Duncan and Judy Carne in the cast. The 1954 cast album listed above, while in mono, presents Andrews and cohorts in the first production, in what turns out to be a delightful recording of Sandy Wilson's whimsical score.

Didier C. Deutsch

Boy on a Dolphin

1992, MCA Records/Japan, from the film Boy on a Dolphin, 20th Century-Fox, 1957 🎬🎬🎬

album notes: Music: Hugo Friedhofer; **Lyrics:** Paul Francis Webster, Takis Morakis; **Orchestra:** The 20th Century Fox Orchestra; **Choir:** The 20th Century Fox Chorus; **Conductor:** Lionel Newman.

Alan Ladd and Sophia Loren, looking for an antique Greek sculpture buried at the bottom of the Aegean Sea, discovered more than they bargained for in this pleasantly innocuous film shot on location and sporting a serenely evocative Academy Award-nominated score by Hugo Friedhofer. Using the basic components at his disposal—a romantic love story, an exotic setting, and a rich musical culture—the composer created a stylishly impressionistic series of cues, effectively mixing into them elements of Mediterranean folk music to give them the right tonal colors. Mary Kaye delivers the nostalgic title tune, while Marni Nixon vocalizes on a couple of tracks. The CD, issued in Japan only, can be found in this country at specialty stores.

Didier C. Deutsch

The Boy Who Could Fly

1986, Varèse Sarabande Records, from the film The Boy Who Could Fly, Lorimar Motion Pictures, 1986 🎬🎬🎬🎬

album notes: Music: Bruce Broughton.

This gentle, monothematic score by Bruce Broughton tells of the blooming friendship between a young girl who moves next door to an autistic boy. Millie has a younger brother who has been tormented by the local bullies and dreams simply of just getting safely around the block. The mysterious Eric, however, believes he can really fly and before long, Millie begins to suspect it might be true. By altering his one theme, Broughton was able to create a symphonic poem for the three youngsters that grows from its light, innocent beginning ("Main Title") to a full-flourished orchestral movement that tells that real life can be even more amazing than one's fantasies ("In the Air").

David Hirsch

The Boys from Syracuse

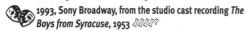 **1993, Sony Broadway, from the studio cast recording** *The Boys from Syracuse*, **1953** 🎬🎬🎬🎬🎬

album notes: Music: Richard Rodgers; **Lyrics:** Lorenz Hart; **Conductor:** Lehman Engel; **Cast:** Portia Nelson, Jack Cassidy, Bibi Osterwald, Holly Harris, Stanley Prager, Bob Shaver.

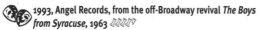 **1993, Angel Records, from the off-Broadway revival** *The Boys from Syracuse*, **1963** 🎬🎬🎬🎬

album notes: Music: Richard Rodgers; **Lyrics:** Lorenz Hart; **Cast:** Ellen Hanley, Stuart Damon, Clifford David, Karen Morrow, Cathryn Damon, Julienne Marie, Danny Carroll, Rudy Tronto, Gary Oakes.

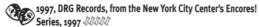 **1997, DRG Records, from the New York City Center's Encores! Series, 1997** 🎬🎬🎬🎬

album notes: Music: Richard Rodgers; **Lyrics:** Lorenz Hart; **Conductor:** Rob Fisher; **Cast:** Tom Aldredge, Sarah Uriarte Berry, Mario Cantone, Davis Gaines, Malcolm Gets, Debbie Gravitte, Julie Halston, Rebecca Luker, Michael McGrath.

"If it's good enough for Shakespeare, it's good enough for us." With these words to the wise, on November 23, 1938, Rodgers and Hart introduced their latest musical, *The Boys from Syracuse*. A wild romp through classic antiquity, the musical is based on the Bard's *Comedy of Errors,* itself borrowed from Plautus's *Menaechmi,* and is about two sets of twins separated at birth, one pair living in Ephesus, in Asia Minor, the other in Syracuse. When the boys from Syracuse, named Antipholus and Dromio, arrive in Ephesus, they are immediately mistaken for their Ephesus twins, also named Antipholus and Dromio. In the end, of course, all's well that ends well, with the reunited twins and their respective spouses and mates ready to enjoy life together.

With its irreverent book by George Abbott and a score brimming with many great tunes ("Falling in Love with Love," "This Can't Be Love"), *The Boys from Syracuse* enjoyed a run of 235 performances. In 1940, it was transferred to the screen in a film version that starred Allan Jones and Martha Raye. On April 15, 1963, it was successfully revived off-Broadway for a 25th anniversary production which had a run of 500 performances. That production is documented in the Angel recording listed above, with Stuart Damon, Cathryn

Damon, Clifford David, and Karen Morrow in its cast. It is a lively, spirited recording that echoes the impish moods in this amusing musical.

Though a mono recording, the 1953 studio cast recording, starring Jack Cassidy, Portia Nelson, and Bibi Osterwald is of interest because it features a fuller orchestra than the 1963 revival, the original orchestrations, and a vibrant cast that evidently enjoys singing the songs by Rodgers and Hart. As an alternative option, you can't go wrong.

The Boys from Syracuse recently received a splendid, all-too-brief concert presentation as part of the City Center's Encore! series, from which the 1997 recording was made. If you don't know your classics and can't make out your Antipholuses from your Dromios, no need to try and explain it to you. What needs to be said, however, is that the score elicited superlative performances from Rebecca Luker, David Gaines, Sarah Uriarte Berry, Debbie Gravitte, Michael McGrath, and the other principals in the cast. Superbly recorded, this is a *Boys from Syracuse* for the ages.

Didier C. Deutsch

Boys on the Side

🎬 **1995, Arista Records, from the film** *Boys on the Side*, **Warner Bros., 1995** 🎬🎬🎬🎬

Whoopi Goldberg, Mary-Louise Parker, and Drew Barrymore star in this comedy romp as a trio of cross-country travelers heading for San Diego and much more than they had bargained for when they started off. Making the trip a great deal more enjoyable are the songs heard on the soundtrack, performed by some of the top female singers today, including Bonnie Raitt, Melissa Etheridge, Sheryl Crow, Stevie Nicks, Annie Lennox, and Whoopi herself. The album brings the performers and their songs center stage for what amounts to a sensational all-star showcase. When pop compilation soundtracks are that good, one only has to listen and enjoy.

Didier C. Deutsch

The Brady Bunch Movie

🎬 **1995, Milan Records, from the film** *The Brady Bunch Movie*, **Paramount Pictures, 1995** 🎬🎬

album notes: Featured Artists: Mudd Pagoda, Generation Why, The Original Brady Bunch Kids.

Stop laughing! Not only did they make the movie—it was a hit! The same can't be said for the companion album, though, whose only chart hits are prior smashes by Venus ("Shocking Blue") and RuPaul ("Supermodel [You Better Work]"). For kitsch lovers, this set includes the original Brady cast's "It's a Sunshine

Day" as well as cute Monkee Davy Jones serenading Marcia with "Girl." And, of course, there's the Brady Bunch theme, which you can hear at least three times a day on cable TV.

Gary Graff

Brainstorm

1983, Varèse Sarabande Records, from the film *Brainstorm*, MGM/UA, 1983 ♪♪♪♪

album notes: **Music:** James Horner; **Orchestra:** The London Symphony Orchestra, **Choirs:** The Ambrosian Singers, The Boys Choir of New College, Oxford; **Conductor:** James Horner.

This is a strikingly powerful early effort in James Horner's career, one of the scores that made a lot of people sit up and take notice of his ability to convey the emotions reflected on-screen. As a team of scientists seek to perfect a virtual reality device that records from and plays back images directly to the brain, Horner conceived symphonic battle between the light and the dark, with a screeching army of voices to speak for the unknown. The seven tracks form individual movements of a concerto, bouncing from the fear of death with heavy-handled percussion effects ("Lillian's Heart Attack") to the wonder of a living man's peak at heaven with the use of a mixed boys and adult choir ("Final Playback"). Horner uses a passionate, classically inspired love theme ("Michael's Gift to Karen") when researcher Christopher Walken attempts to rekindle the lost passion with his estranged wife by showing her a VR recording of how he really perceives her. This is an immensely entertaining effort, despite the fact that several themes have since been reused on other Horner scores. "Race for Time," for example, was recycled into *Clear and Present Danger* for virtually the same sequence! This early digital recording has a superb dynamic range.

David Hirsch

Brancaleone alle Crociate

See: L'Armata Brancaleone/Brancaleone alle Crociate

Brassed Off!

1997, RCA Victor Records, from the film *Brassed Off!*, Miramax Films, 1997 ♪♪♪♪

album notes: **Music:** Trevor Jones; **Conductor:** Trevor Jones.

This roaring, brassy album, with incidental music by Trevor Jones, is so ingratiating it's almost too good to miss. The film, about a fictional Yorkshire mining town (slyly named Grimley, in reference to Grimethorpe) faced with the closure of its pit, and threatening to retaliate with the disbanding of its champion brass band, called for a soundtrack that features brass numbers. Among the selections heard in the film and on this CD, several (Rodrigo's "Concerto de Aranjuez," Alford's "Colonel

Bogey," and Elgar's "Pomp and Circumstance," among them) will be well known, even if the arrangements for brass give them a new luster. Other lesser known tunes provide pleasant discoveries. In the mix, Trevor Jones's touching, haunting cues seem swallowed, but are equally enjoyable and on the button.

Didier C. Deutsch

The Brave One

1990, MCA/Japan, from the RKO film *The Brave One*, 1956 ♪♪♪♪

album notes: **Music:** Victor Young; **Conductor:** Victor Young.

Be prepared to pay a mint for this CD, only available as an import from Japan when it can be found at specialized shops. But it's well worth it. A much underrated effort by composer Victor Young, the cues aptly describe the screen action in which a little Mexican peon befriends a bull (Gitano) and eventually must go to Mexico to beg the Presidente to save his pet, now fighting for its life in an arena, through an *indulto* (reprieve). It's all very touching, and quite convincing. Young's music brings out the south-of-the-border flavor in the film, with a dash of sentimentality that's most becoming. Not a well-known score or recording, but a definite winner.

Didier C. Deutsch

Braveheart/Braveheart: More Musicfrom the Original Soundtrack

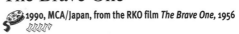Braveheart; 1995, London Records, from the film *Braveheart*, Paramount Pictures, 1995 ♪♪♪♪

album notes: **Music:** James Horner; **Orchestra:** The London Symphony Orchestra; **Conductor:** James Horner.

In Mel Gibson's marvelous historical drama, the character of William Wallace is that of a man who rises from despair and loss to lead a nation in gaining their independence, becoming a larger-than-life, mythic figure along the way. In James Horner's equally brilliant film score, the composer captures the intimacy of Wallace with his allies and loved ones, just as he adeptly echoes the stirring, impassioned cries for freedom that Wallace represents. For all of its 70-plus minutes, then, Horner's *Braveheart* takes you on a rich sonic journey with changing emotions and varied dramatic situations, and virtually all of it works—the battle music is propulsive and dynamic, the main theme moving, tragic, and triumphant all at the same time, while the ethnic instrumentation works perfectly with the London Symphony Orchestra in building a lyrical musical landscape that's undoubtedly one of Horner's most complex and satisfying works yet.

Andy Dursin

Braveheart: More Music from the Original Soundtrack; 998, London Records, from the Paramount film *Braveheart*, 1995 ♫♫♫

album notes: Music: James Horner; **Conductor:** James Horner; **Featured Soloists:** Tony Hinnegan, kena, whistle; James Horner, keyboards; Mike Taylor, Bodhran pipes; Ian Underwood, synth programming.

This second volume of music from the Middle Ages saga starring Mel Gibson is a bit like trying to get more golden eggs from the proverbial goose. It worked the first time, it's not as successful the second time around. Blending excerpts from the film's dialogue with pseudo ethnic and traditional songs, and additional selections from James Horner's superlative score, this is an effective soundtrack album that doesn't always measure up to the first volume. Mel Gibson is quite forceful in the tracks in which he is featured ("Sons of Scotland" is a great reminder of the film's powerful effect), but it all sounds a bit like warmed-up leftovers.

Didier C. Deutsch

Brazil

1992, Milan Records, from the film *Brazil*, Universal Pictures, 1992 ♫♫♫♫

album notes: Music: Michael Kamen; **Orchestra:** The National Philharmonic Orchestra of London; **Conductor:** Michael Kamen.

Michael Kamen's music provides a superb backdrop to Terry Gilliam's multi-faceted drama of dreams and disillusionment in the near future. Central to the score is the 1930 Ary Borroso tune "Brazil," which refers both to the character of revolutionary Jill Brazil, and to a place better than the dismal bureaucratic world in which Sam Lowry exists. The Borroso tune runs throughout, but Kamen's own romantic theme, a sweeping, soaring Korngoldesque melody, captures all of Lowry's hopeful longing and accompanies his visions of heroism and love. Scattered amongst these two cornerstone motifs is a great variety of music, from comic "Central Services" pseudo-TV advertisements (seen in the film on video monitors), to pop tunes used as background fillers, and plenty of adventurous symphonic cues.

Randall D. Larson

Breakfast at Tiffany's

1990, RCA Records, from the film *Breakfast at Tiffany's*, Paramount Pictures, 1961 ♫♫

album notes: Music: Henry Mancini; **Conductor:** Henry Mancini.

Someone with some clout at BMG, the controlling agent for RCA Victor Records, should take the bull by the horns, make the executive decision to begin a thoughtful, realistic assessment of their immense, historically vital catalog, and create CD reissues that reflect the importance of the music. Is anybody out there listening? A perfect case to argue this point is the label's so-called budget series that contains many of RCA Victor's legendary albums, including Henry Mancini's pivotal soundtracks for the television series *Peter Gunn,* and films such as *The Pink Panther* and *Breakfast at Tiffany's.* The last one is an important film, and next to the two other aforementioned Mancini works, the composer's most celebrated effort, including the most gorgeous version of "Moon River" ever. It is sad that the powers-that-be at RCA don't believe the soundtrack is deserving of better treatment. This low-end, early CD issue will have to do for now, with no liner notes or historical information, no extra musical selections or up-to-date digital restoration. It's a shame! (The rating doesn't reflect the quality of the music, but its shabby presentation).

Charles L. Granata

Breaking the Waves

1996, Hollywood Records, from the film *Breaking the Waves*, October Films, 1996 ♫♫♫

There is something perversely endearing about an album that brings together selections by T-Rex ("Hot Love"), Deep Purple ("Child in Time"), Leonard Cohen (the classic "Suzanne"), Procol Harum ("A Whiter Shade of Pale"), Elton John ("Goodbye Yellow Brick Road"), and . . . Johann-Sebastian Bach (the "Siciliana" movement from the Sonata BWV 1031)! How these relate to the film written and directed by Lars von Trier is quite another question, but the fact is the disparities in the musical programming actually work very nicely.

Didier C. Deutsch

Breakout

1999, Prometheus/Belgium, from the Columbia film *Breakout*, 1975 ♫♫♫♫

album notes: Music: Jerry Goldsmith; **Conductor:** Jerry Goldsmith.

Charles Bronson starred as a grizzled, carefree pilot in this action movie, in which he was hired by Jill Ireland to rescue her husband, Robert Duvall, an engineer held in a Mexican prison after he was framed by his father-in-law, played by John Huston. While the film itself was hardly a success (all the principals played as if they had other, more important things in mind), it elicited a tough, gritty score from Jerry Goldsmith, who used the Mexican background to introduce in his music such elements as a xylophone, guitars, and castanets to evoke the locale with a dark bolero theme. As befits a film in which a love interest also develops, the composer created a secondary romantic theme that added some lighter touches to what is otherwise an oppressive action film score. In the Goldsmith canon, this may not be a major score, but it is an important one. Try it for a change!

Didier C. Deutsch

Audrey Hepburn in Breakfast at Tiffany's. **(The Kobal Collection)**

The Bride of Frankenstein

1993, Silva Screen, from the film *The Bride of Frankenstein,* **Universal Pictures, 1935** 🎬🎬🎬🎬

album notes: Music: Franz Waxman; **Orchestra:**The Westminster Philharmonic Orchestra; **Conductor:** Kenneth Alwyn.

Franz Waxman's monumental score for the 1935 *The Bride of Frankenstein* was one of the earliest fully developed film scores in a day when most films had very sparse musical accompaniment. With its blend of romantic motifs and a variety of inventive horrific passages—the most notable being the "Creation" music, wherein the composer musically depicted the chilling noises of the laboratory equipment to create an impressionistic and unique musical sequence—it was a milestone in film music. This recreation of the score is superbly performed and very nicely packaged, including a 20-page booklet which analyzes the music one cue at a time. The CD is also notable for including, for the first time, a six-minute suite from Waxman's *The Invisible Ray,* another very early and very good Universal horror score.

Randall D. Larson

Bride of the Re-Animator

See: The Re-Animator/Bride of the Re-Animator

The Bridge on the River Kwai

1995, Legacy Records/Sony Music Entertainment, from the film *The Bridge on the River Kwai,* **Columbia Pictures, 1957** 🎬🎬

album notes: Music: Malcolm Arnold; **Orchestra:** The Royal Philharmonic Orchestra; **Conductor:** Malcolm Arnold.

When Columbia Records released the soundtrack to *The Bridge on the River Kwai* in late 1957, no one anticipated the immense popularity it would enjoy. While the score by British classical composer Malcolm Arnold would go on to win an Academy Award, the Columbia soundtrack LP would remain a "hit" in its own right, despite some technical flaws that affected its sonics. Probably the greatest boost for the evocative, dramatic score was the waxing of the film's most memorable themes, "The River Kwai March" and "Colonel Bogey March" by Mitch Miller. Issued as a single and included on the soundtrack LP, this million-selling hit drew heaps of attention to the film, and its captivating music. Freshly restored from the original mono session tapes, the CD offers pitch/speed corrected masters (a problem inherent in the original LP issues), and while not quite perfect, markedly improved sound. As a bonus, three newly discovered session tracks are included.

Charles L. Granata

The Bridges of Madison County

1995, Malpaso Records, from the film *The Bridges of Madison County*, Warner Bros. Pictures, 1995 ♪♪♡

album notes: Music: Lennie Niehaus, Clint Eastwood; **Conductor:** Lennie Niehaus.

The movie might have been slow and monotonous, but at least the soundtrack album is a bit easier to take, being comprised of Lennie Niehaus instrumentals and a selection of jazz standards. Included are several tracks each from Dinah Washington, including "I'll Close My Eyes" and "Blue Gardenia," and Johnny Hartman's "For All We Know" and "It Was Almost Like a Song," in addition to songs from Barbara Lewis and Irene Kral. Niehaus's score is represented on the album by two cuts—a brief opening cut and a full rendition of the theme "Doe Eyes," composed by Niehaus and Clint Eastwood, heard in the end credits of the picture and on the end of the album. Like Eastwood's theme for *Unforgiven*, "Doe Eyes" is a lovely, lyrical tune that is minimally performed at first (here by solo piano) before being developed gradually into a full-fledged orchestral arrangement. It all makes for pleasant listening, though still recommended most strongly for fans of the film.

Andy Dursin

Brigadoon

1988, RCA Victor, from the Broadway production *Brigadoon*, 1947 ♪♪♪♪♪

album notes: Music: Frederick Loewe; **Lyrics:** Alan Jay Lerner; **Cast:** David Brooks, Marion Bell, Pamela Britton, Virginia Bosler, Delbert Anderson, Hayes Gordon, Earl Redding, Lee Sullivan.

1996, Rhino Records, from the screen version *Brigadoon*, MGM, 1954 ♪♪♪

album notes: Music: Frederick Loewe; **Lyrics:** Alan Jay Lerner; **Orchestra:** The MGM Studio Orchestra, The MGM Studio Chorus; **Conductor:** Johnny Green; **Cast:** Gene Kelly, Van Johnson, Cyd Charisse, Elaine Stewart.

1992, Angel Records, from the studio cast recording *Brigadoon*, 1992 ♪♪♪♪♪

album notes: Music: Frederick Loewe; **Lyrics:** Alan Jay Lerner; **Cast:** Brent Barrett, Rebecca Luker, Judy Kaye, Jackie Morrison, Ian Caley, Leo Andrew, Donald Maxwell, John Mark Ainsley, Frank Middlemass, Gregory Jbara, Susannah Fellows, Mark W. Smith.

A musical about a Scottish village which reappears for one day every hundred years and the two American travelers that stumble upon it seems a fairly unlikely proposition for a hit Broadway show. However, Alan Jay Lerner and Frederick Loewe succeeded admirably. While the score is near perfection, it does vacillate a bit between traditional musical comedy and the new style of musical play. Regardless, the tunes and lyrics are easily hummed and remain in the memory long after the album ends. In the 1947 original cast album, Marion Bell is lovely as Fiona, the Highland lass who falls in love with the American Tommy, ardently sung by David Bell. Lee Sullivan is a winning Charlie Dalrymple and Pamela Britton enthusiastically sings only one of Meg Brockie's two numbers. This release gets the highest rating in spite of too many cuts and rather ordinary monaural sound.

While the 1954 film has beautiful settings and costumes and well-seasoned performers, it doesn't measure up to the original Broadway production. Unfortunately, the same can be said for the soundtrack. The orchestrations are beautifully done, the singing is more than acceptable and the sound is in stereo, but the score is cut to shreds and several wonderful songs are not included, although a few outtakes and much dance music previously unavailable are. Gene Kelly, Carol Richards, and Van Johnson do their best, but there is a certain blandness that affected many of the era's big MGM musicals taken from the Broadway theater.

For its most recent incarnation, the 1992 studio cast, John McGlinn did a wonderful job recreating a theatrical atmosphere within the sterile confines of the recording studio. In fact, the recording is so spectacular, you can almost feel the mist of the Scottish Highlands drift out from your speakers. Arguably, there are no better performers in the Broadway theater today than the ones chosen for this recording. Rebecca Luker is a lovely, charming Fiona MacLaren, with Brent Barrett a strong, yet sensitive Tommy Albright. Judy Kaye portrays Meg Brockie as a lusty Highland wench and John Mark Ainsley as Charlie Dalrymple sings his songs from the heart. The Ambrosian Chorus and the London Sinfonietta play as if the music were in their blood, which is a very high compliment from this corner. Don't miss this extraordinary recording in terrific, modern stereo digital sound.

Jerry J. Thomas

Bright Angel

1991, Intrada Records, from the film *Bright Angel*, Hemdale Film Corporation, 1991 ♪♪♪♪

album notes: Music: Christopher Young.

Christopher Young masterfully captured the emotional disposition of this Middle American character play about a troubled teenage boy as he travels cross-country with an equally distressed young girl. His main themes are a collection of anxious, bluegrass-style tunes, all lacking in any tranquility and over-burdened with brooding anguish. The real creativity, however, comes with cues like "Wasteland White Light," a jumble of dissonant melodies that reflect the confusion in the lives of the young protagonists. Real life endings aren't always happy, and Young accomplished what he set out to do for the film—instill a real sense that there would ever be one for these two.

David Hirsch

Bring in 'Da Noise, Bring in 'Da Funk

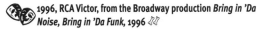 1996, RCA Victor, from the Broadway production *Bring in 'Da Noise, Bring in 'Da Funk*, 1996 ♫♫

album notes: Music: Daryl Waters, Zane Mark, Ann Duquesnay; **Lyrics:** Reg E. Gaines; **Featured Musicians:** Zane Mark, keyboards, Lafayette Harris Jr., keyboards; Zane Paul, saxophone/clarinet/flute; David Rogers, trumpet/flugelhorn/kazoo; Vince Henry, guitar/harmonica/banjo; Luico Hopper, bass; Leroy Clouden, drums/percussion; **Cast:** Savion Glover, Ann Duquesnay, Jeffrey Wright, Vincent Bingham, Duke Hill, Jimmy Tate, Baakari Wilder, Jared Crawford, Raymond King.

Some shows are an effective blend of songs and dances, combined with a solid dramatic texture that gives the whole package an uncompromising theatrical flair. Usually, these shows translate very well to the recording medium, even though a large part of their theatricality is no longer part of the mix. Others just don't fare so well. Such is the case with *Bring in 'Da Noise, Bring in 'Da Funk,* a dramatic retelling of the struggle of African Americans from the days of slavery to the Civil Rights movement, as seen though a show which is essentially a songfest of tap dancing and percussion. On stage, the concept is quite effective, largely because of the drive and energy demonstrated by Savion Glover and the dancers in his company. In fact, "Industrialization," a scene which explores the industrial revolution only in terms of tap and percussion, proves an explosive show-stopper. However, the concept proves much less effective on record, simply because it is primarily visual. For this medium, many numbers have mercifully been abbreviated, with the focus shifted to Ann Duquesnay's inspiring but eventually limited songs. The cast album (if that's what it is) cannot even convey the fire and excitement displayed on stage, much less the intensity evident in most of the performances.

Didier C. Deutsch

Broken Arrow

1995, Milan Records, from the film *Broken Arrow,* 20th Century Fox, 1995 ♫♫♫

album notes: Music: Hans Zimmer; **Conductors:** Bruce Fowler, Don Harper.

Hans Zimmer's score for *Broken Arrow* makes the most out of its musical palette. A few faint melodies trickle throughout, but the music's main attribute is its ambient texture. Typical of the composer's approach, the 10:47 "Nuke" carries on this resolute disposition with a dispassionate female choir, intoning slowly over eerie shards of electronic sound, broken for a momentary segue into a rhythmic action melody. The cue develops into a cyclone of ambient sound whirling around a relentless rhythm of percussiveness that builds in speed and force through its culmination with choir and high-end synths. Another, "Greed," carries the form into further regions, creating a compelling rhythm of slow-moving synth tones over fast-moving percussive taps—and of course altering the shape, size, and speed of the rhythm throughout the cue. Zimmer's orchestration swirls in layers, waves of sound overlapping each other, each wave conveying with it another new sound on a storm-tossed musical tide. It's to Zimmer's credit that the CD's hour's-worth of music is consistently varied, fresh, and audibly interesting, not always the case with action scores.

Randall D. Larson

A Bronx Tale

1993, Epic Soundtrax, from the film *A Bronx Tale,* Tribeca/Savoy Pictures, 1993 ♫♫♫♫

The diversified collection of pop vocals heard in this album reflects the choices made by executive producer Robert De Niro to serve as the soundtrack to this film which bears his creative imprint. The story of a young boy torn between his streetwise, working class father, played by De Niro, and a charismatic neighborhood crime boss (Chazz Palminteri), whom the boy worships, *A Bronx Tale* finds a natural musical mine in the songs that dominated the radio air waves in the 1960s, the period of the film. The mix of doo-wop songs and classic rock tunes is strongly evocative of the era, extending as it does from golden oldies by Dion and the Belmonts, The Cleftones, and The Moon Glows, to hits by Dean Martin, Della Reese, Aaron Neville, The Moody Blues, and Jimi Hendrix. A trip down Memory Lane if ever there was one.

Didier C. Deutsch

Brother's Keeper

1993, Angel Records, from the documentary *Brother's Keeper,* American Playhouse Theatrical Films, 1993 ♫♫♫♫

album notes: Music: Jay Ungar, Molly Mason; **Featured Musicians:** Jay Ungar, violin, viola, mandolin, guitar; Molly Mason, guitar, bass; Guy "Fooch" Fischetti, pedal steel guitar; Peter O'Brien, drums.

For this award-winning documentary about four New York State dairy farming brothers whose lives are shattered when one is accused of murder, Jay Ungar and Molly Mason wrote a score that draws its inspiration from its strong rural American roots. Eloquent in its simplicity, it makes no concessions to current trends, and succeeds in being both profoundly compelling and unusually attractive.

Didier C. Deutsch

Bubbling Brown Sugar

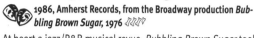 **1986, Amherst Records, from the Broadway production** *Bubbling Brown Sugar*, **1976** 🎵🎵🎵

At heart a jazz/R&B musical revue, *Bubbling Brown Sugar* took some 40 musical numbers by some of the brightest songwriters of the 1930s, and aimed to bring back an era that was particularly rich and evocative, melodically and theatrically speaking. With a cast that included stage stars Josephine Premice and Avon Long (best remembered from the original *Porgy And Bess),* expert tap dancer Joseph Attles, and nightclub performer Vivian Reed, the revue presented its cast in various songs. Many of them were familiar numbers like "Stompin' at the Savoy," "Take the 'A' Train," "Sophisticated Lady," "Honeysuckle Rose," "I Got It Bad (And That Ain't Good)," "God Bless the Child," and "It Don't Mean a Thing," that are still available in their original versions. Propelled by its star-power and its song roster, the musical enjoyed an excellent run of 768 performances following its Broadway premiere on March 2, 1976.

Didier C. Deutsch

The Buccaneer

🎬 **1988, Varèse Sarabande Records, from the film** *The Buccaneer,* **Paramount Pictures, 1958** 🎵🎵🎵🎵

album notes: Music: Elmer Bernstein; **Conductor:** Elmer Bernstein.

One of the last great swashbucklers, *The Buccaneer* starred Yul Brynner as buccaneer Jean Lafitte, and Charlton Heston as Andrew Jackson, who wins the 1812 Battle of New Orleans against the British, only after he strikes a deal with Lafitte who provides him with much-needed men and guns. Not always historically accurate, but rife with action scenes, the colorful production, supervised by Cecil B. De Mille and directed by Anthony Quinn, received a brilliant score created by Elmer Bernstein. In a vibrant display of all the tones at his disposal on his musical palette, the composer wrote a series of cues that cover the gamut of emotions in the action, from the derring-do of the high seas adventures to the romantic interludes between Lafitte and his tempestuous mistress (portrayed by Claire Bloom), from the courtly living in the Jackson ranks to the ultimate devastating battle that sealed the fate of the British forces. The 1958 recording, in aggressive stereo, is in need of good mastering.

Didier C. Deutsch

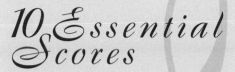

10 Essential Scores
by Elmer Bernstein

The Man with the Golden Arm
The Grifters
Rambling Rose
Baby the Rain Must Fall
To Kill a Mockingbird
The Great Escape
The Magnificent Seven
The Ten Commandments
Devil in a Blue Dress
Hawaii

The Buccaneers

📺 **1995, Mercury Records, from the BBC-TV miniseries** *The Buccaneers*, **1995** 🎵🎵🎵🎵

album notes: Music: Colin Towns; **Conductor:** Colin Towns; **Featured Soloists:** Olive Simpson, soprano; Rolf Wilson, violin; Andrea Hess, cello.

Colin Towns, whose striking score for the television series *Cadfael* was such a delightful discovery, wrote the music for this 1995 BBC dramatization of Edith Wharton's last novel. The story of four spirited and attractive American girls—Virginia and Nan St. George, Conchita Closson, and Lizzy Elmsworth—and their diverse lives in 1870s' London and New York societies, *The Buccaneers* enabled the composer to create a score that teemed with great themes and reflected the four girls' youthful exuberance, their eventual mismatched marriages, the loss of their ambitions, and their shattered dreams. On the whole, the music is gorgeously attractive, with melodic material that transcends the television series' initial intent, and stands on its own melodic terms for a wonderful listening experience. Some selections ("Birth of an Heir," "Waltz of a Lost Room," "Love Theme") are beautifully descriptive and eloquently attractive.

Didier C. Deutsch

Buddy

1997, Varèse-Sarabande, from the Columbia film *Buddy,* 1997 ♪♪♪

album notes: Music: Elmer Bernstein; **Conductor:** Elmer Bernstein.

At times appropriately romantic, at times jaunty and humorously descriptive, Elmer Bernstein's score for *Buddy* stressed the many assets of this amiable comedy about a '20s Brooklyn socialite and the baby gorilla who becomes her "buddy." The beast in the gorilla suddenly wakes up when it is taken to the 1933 World's Fair in Chicago and develops a case of back-to-ancestral-habit-itis ("Disaster"), which results in its being sent to a zoo and a more suitable habitat ("New Life"). Typical of the composer in his serviceable score are syncopated rhythms that might recall some of his western scores, although surprisingly (given the time period of the storyline) he failed to rely on the jazz elements he used to such great effects in other films. In this context, it might have seemed like the natural way to go.

Didier C. Deutsch

A Bug's Life

1998, Walt Disney Records, from the Walt Disney film *A Bug's Life,* 1998 ♪♪♪♪

album notes: Music: Randy Newman.

There's no one better than Randy Newman to score a Disney animated feature. He always comes up with one catchy tune, which he sings with that ever-recognizable style, and which he then develops into some great over-the-top cartoony music. *A Bug's Life,* for which he received an Oscar nomination, is no exception. From the jazzy "The Flik Machine" and "The City" to the old-time western-sounding "Flik Leaves" and "Dot's Rescue," the tracks all seem to blend seamlessly into one another, creating the effect of one long suite, with various movements. The score as a whole is an exhilarating audio experience.

Beth Krakower

Bugsy

1991, Epic Soundtrax, from the film *Bugsy,* Tri-Star Pictures, 1991 ♪♪♪♪

album notes: Music: Ennio Morricone; **Orchestra:** Unione musicisti di Roma; **Conductor:** Ennio Morricone.

A frequently compelling romantic drama about the man who "created" Las Vegas, *Bugsy* found in Ennio Morricone a composer with a special understanding for psychological studies mixed with gangster overtones. Based on the true, grander-than-life story of Bugsy Siegel, a childhood friend of George Raft and Meyer Lansky, the film retraces his arrival in Hollywood, his involvement with a charming but empty-headed would-be actress, his friendship with Lucky Luciano, his high society connections, and his ignominious death by the hands of his former friends and protectors. With typical flair, Morricone details various salient moments in the action, outlining them with themes that are ingeniously sketched and interestingly written. While the overall tone of the cues is in the slow mode characteristic of his writing style for the thriller genre, the score contains some signature effects, like a pesky buzzing over an ominous string line ("Humiliated"), or a lovely theme for oboe against a full orchestral texture ("Act of Faith"). Augmenting the score and providing a different mood, four standards by Johnny Mercer, Peggy Lee, and Jo Stafford situate the action and its musical accompaniment squarely into its 1940s time period.

Didier C. Deutsch

Bugsy Malone

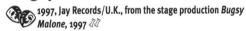

1997, Jay Records/U.K., from the stage production *Bugsy Malone,* 1997 ♪♪

album notes: Music: Paul Williams; **Lyrics:** Paul Williams; **Libretto:** Alan Parker; **Musical Direction:** John Pearson; **Cast:** Janee Bennett, Malinda Parris, Sheridan Smith, Stuart Piper, Hannah Spearritt, Shean Williams, Alex Lee, Paul Lowe, Matt Fraser, Michael Sturges, Leanne Connelly, Chris Dyer, Nana Kumi.

The idea of having kids play *Guys and Dolls* characters has its charms, but it tends to become tedious, particularly in a musical where the performers' voices have obviously not reached full maturity. In the non-musical film of the same name, the overall effect was much more amusing and convincing. Here, the kids sound like kids, and particularly when they are called upon to impersonate well-known characters like Tallulah Bankhead. Paul Williams's songs are cute, but do not make a lasting impression.

Didier C. Deutsch

Bull Durham

1988, Capitol Records, from the film *Bull Durham,* Orion Pictures, 1988 ♪♪♪◊

A hodgepodge, sure enough, but it's a good hodgepodge. A double, if not quite a home run. John Fogerty's "Centerfield" is appropriate. George Thorogood's "Bad to the Bone" seems a bit heavy duty for a film about minor league baseball, but juke joint stuff like the Fabulous Thunderbirds' "Can't Tear It Up Enuff," and Los Lobos' "I Got Loaded" fits the bill perfectly. Dr. John is the real all-star here, though, working out on three songs, including duets with Stevie Ray Vaughan and Bonnie Raitt. A cracker jack collection, fer sure.

Gary Graff

Bulletproof

1996, Varèse Sarabande Records, from the film *Bulletproof*, Universal, 1996 ♪♪♪

album notes: Music: Elmer Bernstein; Conductor: Elmer Bernstein.

It seems kind of odd that Elmer Bernstein would come back to a genre he obviously abandoned a decade earlier. There is a lot to be said of the fun in listening to any score reminiscent of his many comedy/adventure scores and, in fact, portions of "Flying" frequently quote a motif he used in *Ghostbusters*. Overall, though, this score seems to be somewhat nondescript, with no real character. It leaves you feeling as if you walked into the second act of something, perhaps an episode of a 1960s TV cop show. Maybe Adam Sandler's antics just don't motivate Bernstein, or maybe he's truly tired of this genre.

David Hirsch

Bullets over Broadway

1994, Sony Classical, from the Miramax film *Bullets over Broadway*, 1994 ♪♪♪♪

Woody Allen has a special knack for writing comedies that are clever little studies of various Manhattan cultural or ethnic groups, and for peppering his films with the right musical excerpts, usually relying on standards of the 1930s and early '40s. The story of a would-be Broadway writer in the 1930s, and the eccentric stage divas, assorted nuts, and mobsters he must deal with, *Bullets over Broadway* was no exception, and used selections performed by the likes of Al Jolson, Bix Beiderbecke, Irving Aaronson & His Commanders, Duke Ellington, and Red Nichols, to evoke the proper period atmosphere, with Dick Hyman and the Three Deuces Musicians—a motley group consisting of well-known studio musicians such as Phil Bodner, Derek Smith, and Sid Cooper—adding their own versions of sounds from the era. Perhaps not everyone's cup of tea, but a great soundtrack album nonetheless.

Didier C. Deutsch

Bulworth

Bulworth; 1998, Interscope, from the 20th Century-Fox film *Bulworth*, 1998 ♪♪♪♪

The greatest disappointment of this album is that film star Warren Beatty's raps aren't given the showcase they deserve, just for their sheer comic audacity. Nevertheless, *Bulworth* gives us a strong survey of the hip-hop world, with some interesting collaborations that bring together Dr. Dre and LL Cool J ("Zoom"), the Fugees' Pras Michel, Ol' Dirty Bastard and Mya ("Ghetto Superstar (That Is What You Are)"), Cannibus and Senegal's Youssou N'Dour ("How Come"), Mack 10 and Ice Cube ("Maniac in

the Braniac"), and the power-lunch gathering of Method Man, KRS-One, Prodigy, and KAM on "Bulworth (They Talk about It While We Live It)." Also be sure to check out "Lunatics in the Grass," a solo track by Cypress Hill's B Real, and "The Chase" from RZA of the Wu Tang Clan.

Gary Graff

Bulworth; 1998, RCA Victor, from the 20th Century-Fox film, *Bulworth*, 1998 ♪♪♪♪

album notes: Music: Ennio Morricone; Conductor: Ennio Morricone; Vocals: Amii Stewart and Edda Dell'Orso.

Presented in two long, uninterrupted suites, Ennio Morricone's instrumental score is particularly noteworthy for its emotionally reflective moods, expressed through greatly evocative melodic lines, and for the vocal support of Amii Stewart and Edda Dell'Orso, who are both showcased in the first part. It is a powerful musical statement, made all the more eloquent given the fact that the music has ample time to establish its identity and make its impact.

Didier C. Deutsch

The Burning Shore

1991, Mercury Records, from the TV film *The Burning Shore*, Titanus Films, 1991 ♪♪♪♪

album notes: Music: Michel Legrand; Orchestra: The Leningrad Symphony Orchestra: Conductor: Michel Legrand.

Composer Michel Legrand, whose bend for lovely thematic music is one of his most endearing traits, created another exquisite score for this adventure film made for television, based on the eponymous novel by Wilbur Smith. The cues, in turns grandiose and romantic, are for the most part very catchy and melodic, weaving a robust musical tapestry that has many charms. Occasionally, a drumbeat suggests the African background against which the story itself unfolds, with the cues describing the action in bold, colorful terms. The performance by the Leningrad Symphony Orchestra is quite enthusiastic.

Didier C. Deutsch

Buster

1988, Atlantic Records, from the film *Buster*, Vestron Pictures, 1988 ♪♪♪♪

album notes: Music: Anne Dudley; Orchestra:The London Film Orchestra; Conductor: Anne Dudley.

Phil Collins stars as the title happy-go-lucky small-time thief, who hits the big time when he robs a trainload of used banknotes with the help of a gang led by a friend. On the run from the law, he moves to Mexico, only to find out that once the money is gone life in the sun is not as rosy as he had anticipated. Punctuating this bittersweet comedy are several classic rock tracks by Gerry & The Pacemakers, Dusty Springfield,

Sonny and Cher, and The Hollies, among others, as well as a couple of new original songs by Collins. Tying in all these elements together is the incidental music, composed by Anne Dudley, in one of her early efforts, and already demonstrating some of the qualities that have made her a top scorer in more recent years. A bright, breezy album that's quite enjoyable.

Didier C. Deutsch

Butch Cassidy and the Sundance Kid

1987, A&M Records, from the film *Butch Cassidy and the Sundance Kid*, 20th Century Fox, 1969 𝄞𝄞𝄞𝄞

album notes: Music: Burt Bacharach; **Lyrics:** Hal David; **Conductor:** Burt Bacharach.

Burt Bacharach wrote one of his most endearing scores for this amusing western loosely based on the exploits of the so-called Hole-in-the-Wall band of outlaws, led by the quick-witted Butch Cassidy and his quiet cohort, the Sundance Kid (portrayed by Paul Newman and Robert Redford, respectively). While their screen exploits, glossier no doubt than the pair's real-life petty crimes, and the two stars' obvious chemistry helped make the film a tremendous box-office hit. That success was also due in large part to Bacharach's whimsical and jaunty score, in which the song "Raindrops Keep Fallin' on My Head" played an important role. The recording's only drawback is that its playing time is so short (less than 28 minutes). When the going is that good and that enjoyable, you wish it would last a bit longer.

Didier C. Deutsch

Butterfly

1991, Prometheus Records/Belgium, from the movie *Butterfly*, Par-Par Productions, 1991 𝄞𝄞𝄞

album notes: Music: Ennio Morricone; **Conductor:** Ennio Morricone.

This is a somewhat pedestrian romantic score, and quite an unexpected effort from Ennio Morricone. Perhaps he couldn't keep a straight face while watching this Pia Zadora vanity effort financed by her ex-husband, in which she plays a young waif claiming to be miner Stacy Keach's long-lost daughter, and then seduces him! Morricone plays everything with a very minimalist approach and that does keep with the film's claustrophobic nature, but it doesn't make for a too thoroughly entertaining listen. The CD is twice as long as the original LP release and features 11 tracks (approximately 21 minutes) previously unreleased. Surprisingly, these are some of Morricone's more interesting cues. Zadora performs the song "It's Wrong for Me to Love You," proving she's a far better singer than actress.

David Hirsch

Bye Bye Birdie

1989, Columbia Records, from the Broadway production, *Bye Bye Birdie*, 1960 𝄞𝄞𝄞𝄞

album notes: Music: Charles Strouse; **Lyrics:** Lee Adams; **Cast:** Dick Van Dyke, Chita Rivera, Karin Wolfe, Marissa Mason, Sharon Lerit, Louise Quick, Lada Edmund, Jessica Albright, Susan Watson, Paul Lynde, Dick Gautier.

1988, RCA Records, from the screen version, *Bye Bye Birdie*, Columbia Pictures, 1963 𝄞𝄞

album notes: Music: Charles Strouse; **Lyrics:** Lee Adams; **Orchestra:** The Columbia Studio Orchestra; **Conductor:** Johnny Green; **Cast:** Dick Van Dyke, Janet Leigh, Ann-Margret, Paul Lynde, Jesse Pearson, Maureen Stapleton, Bobby Rydell, Ed Sullivan.

Taking a cue from Elvis Presley's much publicized induction in the Army, composer Charles Strouse and lyricist Lee Adams, making their Broadway bow, wrote a joyously exhilarating musical which poked amiable fun at its famous model. The first of the great pop-rock musicals, the show was in truth an old-fashioned affair that relied on the trials and tribulations of Albert Peterson, a former English teacher turned music publisher and manager of Conrad Birdie (the show's Elvis alter ego), and his long-suffering girlfriend and secretary, Rose. The device used here is the hope that with Conrad being drafted, Albert might have more time to spend with Rose and make her dream of getting married a reality.

On a broader scale, the show also takes sharp aim at life in a small American town (where Conrad is going to make his last public appearance in a well-orchestrated disappearing act), and at the generational misunderstanding between Conrad's teenage fans, all smitten by the nascent rock 'n' roll craze, and their uncomprehending parents.

The musical became a springboard for many of its creators, including choreographer Gower Champion, and stars Dick Van Dyke and Chita Rivera. Several songs soon emerged from the score, including the unqualified hit, "Put on a Happy Face."

In its transfer to the big screen, the show retained most of its winning elements, substituting Janet Leigh for Rivera, and adding Ann-Margret for box-office appeal. The recording, however, leaves a lot to be desired, with some distortion on the vocals and overall strident sonics that make it less than an acceptable representation in this digital age.

Didier C. Deutsch

Bye Bye, Love

1995, Giant Records, from the film *Bye Bye, Love*, 20th Century Fox, 1995 𝄞𝄞𝄞

album notes: Music: J.A.C. Redford; **Conductor:** J.A.C. Redford.

Okay, let's get this straight. The Everly Brothers *don't* perform their classic rendition of the title track. That one's done by the

Liza Minelli in the film version of Cabaret. **(The Kobal Collection)**

Proclaimers. But the Everlys turn up twice, singing "So Sad (To Watch Good Love Go Bad)" and joining the Beach Boys on an harmony-drenched version of "Don't Worry Baby." Jackson Browne and Eagles bassist Timothy B. Schmit are also duet partners ("Let It Be Me"), while Ben Taylor—son of James Taylor and Carly Simon—contributes "I Will." But so-so performances and already available songs make this a tepid collection.

Gary Graff

Cabaret

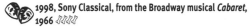 **1998, Sony Classical, from the Broadway musical** *Cabaret,* **1966** ♪♪♪♪

album notes: Music: John Kander; **Lyrics:** Fred Ebb; **Book:** Joe Masteroff; **Musical Direction:** Harold Hastings; **Cast:** Joel Grey, Bert Convy, Edward Winter, Lotte Lenya, Jack Gilford, Jill Haworth.

1989, MCA Records, from the Allied Artists film *Cabaret,* **1972** ♪♪♪♪♪

album notes: Music: John Kander; **Lyrics:** Fred Ebb; **Musical Direction:** Ralph Burns; **Cast:** Liza Minnelli, Marisa Berenson, Fritz Wepper, Michael York, Joel Grey.

In a stunning way, *Cabaret* captures a story set in the late 1920s, when storm clouds were beginning to gather over Germany and subsequently over all of Europe. Joel Grey was terrific as the sleazy Master of Ceremonies of the Kit Kat Klub with its slimy, decadent atmosphere of a Berlin that was going mad. Whatever performance she gave on stage, Jill Haworth, as Sally Bowles, created a strong character that comes charmingly across on the original cast album. Her delivery contains the perfect combination of humor and raucousness needed for the part. Saddled with a nondescript part, Bert Convy made the most of his numbers. Lotte Lenya, who personified these very Berlin years with just a shred of voice, was wonderful as Fraulein Schneider, whether expressing delight, tenderness, or bitterness. Jack Gilford, a noted comedian, showed another side of his talent as the very sweet and vulnerable Herr Schultz, who, in spite of the madness around him, just wants to marry

Fraulein Schneider. This new reissue of the original cast album, properly remixed, sounds a great deal better than its previous incarnation and has been fitted with some genuinely great bonus tracks: songs written (and performed) by Kander and Ebb for the show before it came to Broadway, songs which were subsequently deleted. It is a fascinating glimpse into the creative process of the team, with both exhibiting a lot of show-biz chutzpah in their performances.

The film, which was a completely re-thought version of the show, was one of the last hit musical films based on a Broadway musical. Every performer in it is perfect, from the stars to the extras behind them, which is very evident on the recording. Arguably, Liza Minnelli, who won an Oscar for her portrayal as Sally Bowles, gave the greatest performance of her career in this film. Joel Grey, recreating and refining his stunning stage portrayal as the Master of Ceremonies in an Oscar-winning performance, was, if possible, even more sleazy and decadent on film than he was on stage. Both take up most of the soundtrack, together and separately. The plot songs from the stage were cut for the film and a few new songs were added. The punch-in-the-gut quality comes across very well on the album, but be warned that the packaging has no cast list and is very, very stingy with much-needed information. However, the stereo sound is fine and adds to the impact of this truly enjoyable recording.

Jerry J. Thomas

 1998, RCA Victor Records, from the Broadway revival *Cabaret*, 1998 ♪♪♪♪

album notes: Music: John Kander; **Lyrics:** Fred Ebb; **Musical Direction:** Patrick Vaccariello; **Cast:** Alan Cumming, Natasha Richardson, John Benjamin Hickey, Mary Louise Wilson, Denis O'Hare, Ron Rifkin.

A smash on Broadway all over again, *Cabaret* is now miles away from the show that made its initial bow in 1966. Besides being presented in a nightclub surrounding, truer to the story itself, it has become raunchier and seedier, thanks in large part to Alan Cumming's portrayal as the lecherous, sexually ambivalent emcee, portrayed in the original by Joel Grey. Natasha Richardson, who reprised the role created in the original by Jill Haworth, reveals in grimmer details the desultory life Sally Bowles leads in Berlin. But Mary Louise Wilson cannot erase the impression initially made by Lotte Lenya in the original, which also benefits from the bonus tracks in which Kander and Ebb perform songs that were eventually discarded from the show. Still, a quick comparison between the two recordings underscores the tremendous transformation the show has undergone in 30 years, and even if the RCA cast album is a definite must-have in any respected collection, the original with its definite Broadway flair also belongs.

Didier C. Deutsch

Cabin in the Sky

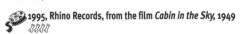 1993, Angel Records, from the off-Broadway revival *Cabin in the Sky*, 1963 ♪♪♪♪

album notes: Music: Vernon Duke; **Lyrics:** John Latouche; **Conductor:** Sy Oliver; **Cast:** Helen Ferguson, Rosetta LeNoire, Tony Middleton, Sam Laws, Harold Pierson.

1995, Rhino Records, from the film *Cabin in the Sky*, 1949 ♪♪♪♪

album notes: Music: Vernon Duke; **Lyrics:** John Latouche; **Orchestra:** The MGM Studio Orchestra; **Conductor:** Georgie Stoll; **Cast:** Butterfly McQueen, Ethel Waters, Eddie "Rochester" Anderson, Rex Ingram, Lena Horne.

A black musical fable about the eternal struggle between Good and Evil and a rather unsteady sinner named Little Joe Jackson, *Cabin in the Sky* opened on Broadway on Oct. 25, 1940, and immediately became the hottest show in town. With a great score by Vernon Duke and John Latouche, in which a big hit was "Taking a Chance on Love," and a cast that included Ethel Waters, Todd Duncan, Dooley Wilson, Rex Ingram, and Katherine Dunham, the show recounted how Little Joe, seriously wounded in a street brawl, was given a reprieve of six months by the Lawd's General to prove himself or be forever cast in Hell, where Lucifer Jr. gleefully waited for him. In a twist that recalled several other shows with similar storylines (*Liliom, The Green Pastures,* and even *Damn Yankees,* many seasons later), Lucifer Jr. tried to trip Little Joe with the help of a sultry siren named Georgia Brown, but to little avail.

Ethel Waters, as Petunia, Little Joe's trusting wife, and Rex Ingram, as Lucifer Jr., were also the stars of the 1943 film version, which was directed by Vincente Minnelli for MGM. The film's cast also included Eddie "Rochester" Anderson, playing Little Joe, Lena Horne as Georgia Brown, Louis Armstrong, and Duke Ellington and his orchestra. Unlike the stage musical, the film concluded on a different note, with Little Joe waking up at the end to realize it was all a bad dream. Also undergoing modifications was the score, in which only three songs from the original were retained, supplemented with several numbers written by Harold Arlen and E.Y. Harburg, including "Happiness Is a Thing Called Joe," and "Life's Full of Consequences." The film yielded a sensational soundtrack album, recently given the superlative Rhino treatment.

The original stage show was revived in 1964, with Rosetta LeNoire starring as Petunia, in an off-Broadway production that had a limited run of 47 performances. The Angel cast album chronicles that revival and is of interest as the only recording of the production as it was originally presented.

Didier C. Deutsch

Cadfael

1996, Angel Records, from the UK Television production *Cadfael*, 1996–97 🎵🎵🎵🎵🎵

album notes: Music: Colin Towns; **Conductor:** Colin Towns; **Gregorian Chants:** The Clerkes of St. Albans Abbey; **Gregorian Chants director:** Barry Rose.

One of the best murder mystery series to be seen on television these days involves, of all people, a monk, Brother Cadfael (Derek Jacobi), playing detective in the Middle Ages. Handsomely photographed in natural settings, with crisply written stories, the series also boasts a spell—binding score which mixes Gregorian chants with pseudo—Gothic musical cues, composed by Colin Towers. The overall effect is both austere and richly evocative, as this compelling soundtrack album so effectively demonstrates. Culling from various episodes in the series, the CD offers an overview of the musical textures, with many glorious moments to be enjoyed. It may not convert you, but if you are not a viewer it might compel you to look at some episodes and find out for yourself why this medieval monk might soon become as popular as Poirot or Miss Marple on television.

Didier C. Deutsch

Cahill, United States Marshall

See: The Shootist

Cal

1984, Vertigo/PolyGram, from the film *Cal,* 1984 🎵🎵🎵🎵🎵

album notes: Music: Mark Knopfler; **Featured Musicians:** Mark Knopfler, guitars; Paul Brady, mandolin; tin whistle; Liam O'Flynn, Uillean pipes; Guy Fletcher, keyboards; John Illsley, bass; Terry Williams, drums.

The nice thing about Mark Knopfler is that when he writes film scores they tend to be gracefully attractive, sometimes sentimental, but usually very expressive. For *Cal,* a romantic drama with political overtones set in Ireland, he fashioned a wonderful score in which the Uillean pipes and tin whistle help create the proper atmosphere, while the guitars, mandolin, and keyboards state the various melodies with great restraint and much feeling. Two long cues ("Father and Son" and "The Long Road") are particularly representative of the score itself, with gorgeous melodies that capture the tender moods in the story and bring them forward in a compelling display that transcends the medium for which they were originally designed.

Didier C. Deutsch

Calendar Girl

1993, Columbia Records, from the Columbia film *Calendar Girl,* 1993 🎵

album notes: Music: Hans Zimmer.

A film that desperately wants to be contemporary, even reworking the Frankie Lymon's chestnut "Why Do Fools Fall in Love" into a rap song, while remaining true to its early 1960s roots, this lame story of three suburban friends who drive their convertible to California in the vain hope of meeting Marilyn Monroe falls short on every level. Even the presence in the soundtrack (and the album) of performers such as Aaron Neville, the Everly Brothers, Chubby Checker, and Neil Sedaka fails to elicit the anticipated excitement. Hans Zimmer's only selection, augmented by a great guitar vamp by Pete Haycock, seems totally lost.

Didier C. Deutsch

California Suite

1980, CBS Records, from the film *California Suite,* Columbia Pictures, 1978 🎵🎵🎵🎵

album notes: Music: Claude Bolling; **Featured Musicians:** Hubert Laws, flute; Claude Bolling, piano; Chuck Damonico, bass; Shelly Manne, drums; Bud Shank, flute/soprano sax; Tommy Tedesco, guitar; Ralph Grierson.

This bouncy, easy-going, jazzy soundtrack did much to establish the popularity of Claude Bolling in America, and provided a pleasantly innocuous musical setting to the screen comedy, based on a stage play by Neil Simon. The catchy themes, developed by the composer at the piano with master flutist Hubert Laws, presage Bolling's future pop-classical collaborations with Jean-Pierre Rampal, Yo-Yo Ma, Pinchas Zukerman, and other great soloists.

Didier C. Deutsch

Call Me Madam

1995, DRG Records, from the New York City Center concert presentation *Call Me Madam,* 1995 🎵🎵🎵🎵

album notes: Music: Irving Berlin; **Lyrics:** Irving Berlin; **Orchestra:** The Coffee Club Orchestra; **Conductor:** Rob Fisher; **Cast:** Tyne Daly, Walter Charles, Melissa Errico, MacIntyre Dixon, Christopher Durang, Ken Page.

Ethel Merman, the actress with the mostes', portrayed a reasonable facsimile of Perle Mesta, the hostess with the mostes' (who had recently been appointed American ambassador to Luxembourg by president Harry Truman), in *Call Me Madam,* an engaging musical by Irving Berlin, which opened on October 12, 1950. The show, a breezy satire dealing with an abrasively direct and definitely not diplomatic woman named ambassador to a tiny duchy (the action is set, according to the program notes, "in two mythical countries, Lichtenburg and the United States"), pokes

gentle fun at American-style politics abroad, with Berlin delivering a serviceable and frequently enjoyable score. In 1953, the show reached the big screen, with Merman reprising the role, and George Sanders and Donald O'Connor in the cast.

This recording, starring Tyne Daly, originated at New York City Center's Encore! series, and, in the absence of original cast and soundtrack album recordings, provides a clear vision of the score, which included the popular hits "It's a Lovely Day Today" and "You're Just in Love." As is usually the case with this concert series, the performances are spirited and quite enjoyable.

Didier C. Deutsch

Camelot

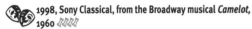 **1998, Sony Classical, from the Broadway musical *Camelot*, 1960** 🎧🎧🎧🎧

album notes: Music: Frederick Loewe; **Lyrics:** Alan Jay Lerner; **Book:** Alan Jay Lerner, based on "The Once and Future King" by T. H. White; **Musical Direction:** Franz Allers; **Cast:** Richard Burton, Julie Andrews, Robert Goulet.

This is clearly the best part of *Camelot:* Richard Burton, Julie Andrews, Robert Goulet, the great score, the legend of Camelot, without the three-plus-hour production. Thankfully, Sony finally re-sequenced the tracks of the original cast recording, so that unlike previous releases, this version remains true to the sequence of songs in the show. For instance, whereas previous versions combined "Overture" with "I Wonder What the King Is Doing Tonight," they are now separated by the instrumental "March (Parade)." Similarly, "C'est Moi" and "The Lusty Month of May" have been flip-flopped, while "Before I Gaze at You Again" comes after "How to Handle a Woman," itself followed by "If Ever I Would Leave You." It takes some doing to get used to, particularly if you are familiar with the original album sequencing, but it eventually works quite nicely. Highly recommended.

Beth Krakower

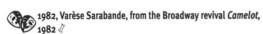 **1982, Varèse Sarabande, from the Broadway revival *Camelot*, 1982** 🎧

album notes: Music: Frederick Loewe; **Lyrics:** Alan Jay Lerner; **Musical Direction:** Gerry Allison; **Cast:** Richard Harris, Fiona Fullerton, Robert Meadmore, Michael Howe, Roger Nott, David Bexon, Claire Moore.

While the recording of the London revival (on Varèse Sarabande) is wrong where the album of the 1960 Broadway cast is right, there are a few virtues to be found in it. More of the score has been included on this CD than on the original, and it is fairly well played by the orchestra, if somewhat out of tune here and there. The brilliance of the writing by Lerner and Loewe comes through with top honors. Unfortunately, the performances, with the possible exception of Robert Meadmore, a passionate yet sensitive Lancelot, are mediocre at best. Whatever the quality of his performance on stage, and though he

tries hard, Richard Harris is just not good as Arthur on this album. He was much more effective in the film and on its soundtrack. Fiona Fullerton gives a small, whiney performance as Guenevere. The rest of the cast is acceptable. However, as there is no Arthur and Guenevere worth the listen, then there is no point in listening. This album is only for completists.

Didier C. Deutsch

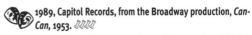 **1967, Warner Bros. Records, from the Warner Bros. Pictures film *Camelot*, 1967** 🎧🎧🎧

album notes: Music: Frederick Loewe; **Lyrics:** Alan Jay Lerner; **Musical Direction:** Alfred Newman; **Cast:** Richard Harris, Vanessa Redgrave, Franco Nero, David Hemmings, Lionel Jeffries, Laurence Naismith.

While visual elements of the film were so stunning that the music and lyrics tended to get lost, on the soundtrack recording, the images don't mean anything and one can focus on the musical performances. Unfortunately, Richard Harris as King Arthur, Vanessa Redgrave as Queen Guenevere, and Franco Nero (dubbed by Gene Merlino) as Lancelot do not measure up to the original cast in any way. With the exception of Merlino, the actors are non-singers and can be rather difficult to listen to, especially if one is familiar with the Broadway cast album. That said, there are also things to enjoy here. While her tempos and style of singing are quite different, Redgrave is an excellent Guenevere. Harris's Arthur is also very strong and likable, and the singing of Merlino comes across almost as powerful as the original. My choice will always be the original Broadway cast album as the best and most complete version of this truly magical score. However, the soundtrack album has its own particular joys and is well worth the time spent listening to it.

Jerry J. Thomas

Can-Can

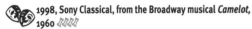 **1989, Capitol Records, from the Broadway production, *Can-Can*, 1953.** 🎧🎧🎧🎧

album notes: Music: Cole Porter; **Lyrics:** Cole Porter; **Cast:** Lilo, Peter Cookson, Hans Conried, Gwen Verdon.

Cole Porter's particular fondness for things French found one of its best expressions in *Can Can,* a lullaby to turn-of-the-century Paris, when the "naughty" new dance at the Moulin-Rouge attracted huge crowds of society revelers . . . and the police, eager to close the place for these lewd exhibitions. In the show, the clash between Judge Forestier, a bastion of morality, and La Môme Pistache, owner of Bal du Paradis, a night club where the dissolute dance is performed nightly, eventually leads to a compromise when the Judge falls for La Môme, and becomes one of the Can-Can's most ardent defenders. Starring Lilo as Pistache and Peter Cookson as Forestier, the show also introduced Gwen Verdon, whose memorable Tony Award-winning

Can-Can *composer, Cole Porter.* (Archive Photos, Inc.)

turn in the seductive "Garden of Eden" ballet led to a starring role two years later in *Damn Yankees*. The score, one of Porter's most elegantly achieved, included at least two great songs, "C'est magnifique" and "I Love Paris." *Can Can,* which opened on May 7, 1953, had a run of 892 performances.

Didier C. Deutsch

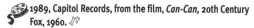 1989, Capitol Records, from the film, *Can-Can,* 20th Century Fox, 1960. 🎧🎧

album notes: Music: Cole Porter; **Lyrics:** Cole Porter; **Orchestra:** The 20th Century Fox Orchestra; **Conductor:** Nelson Riddle; **Cast:** Shirley MacLaine, Louis Jourdan, Frank Sinatra, Maurice Chevalier.

What a shame that one of the most endearing of all of Frank Sinatra's film soundtracks has never enjoyed a proper presentation, one befitting the charming Cole Porter score, and its very special performances. Such is the case with *Can-Can,* originally released in 1960 as an LP on Capitol Records. At the time, little attention was paid to either the technical quality of the recording, or the actual sequencing of the songs. Unfortunately, little has changed with the transfer of the LP to compact

disc. As in the LP, the "Entr'acte" opens the disc, while the "Main Title" appears in the middle of the program.

Sonically, the recording is dull, and the quality of the sound varies from track to track. Particularly distressing is the muffled, distorted sound on one of Sinatra's finest songs, "It's All Right With Me." Others, like the Sinatra-Maurice Chevalier duet on "I Love Paris," sound plain flat and one-dimensional. Overall, the equalization is poor, and the original transfer engineers liberally used reverb to conceal a myriad of defects. These unforgivable technical problems aside, the Frank Sinatra, Maurice Chevalier, and Shirley MacLaine performances of some of Porter's finest songs are essential and deserve attention for their artistic value.

Charles L. Granata

Candide

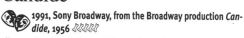 1991, Sony Broadway, from the Broadway production *Candide,* 1956 🎧🎧🎧🎧🎧

album notes: Music: Leonard Bernstein; **Lyrics:** Richard Wilbur; **Additional Lyrics:** John Latouche, Dorothy Parker; **Cast:** Max Adrian, Barbara Cook, Robert Rounseville, Irra Petina.

1985, New World Records, from the New York City Opera revival *Candide,* **1985** 𝄞𝄞𝄞𝄾

album notes: Music: Leonard Bernstein; **Lyrics:** Richard Wilbur; **Additional Lyrics:** John Latouche, Stephen Sondheim; **Cast:** John Lankston, Erie Mills, David Eisler, Joyce Castle.

1997, RCA Victor, from the Broadway revival *Candide,* **1997** 𝄞𝄞𝄞𝄞

album notes: Music: Leonard Bernstein; **Lyrics:** Richard Wilbur.

Some Broadway shows undergo extensive rewrites before their opening, and occasionally even after they have received their official premiere. But few have been as extensively altered and modified than *Candide,* which initially opened on Broadway on Dec. 1, 1956, only to close 76 performances later, and has since been revived (and revised) several times, both winningly and unsatisfactorily.

The first version, written by Lillian Helman, remained faithful to Voltaire's tale of the two innocent lovers, Candide and Cunegonde, who go through the most incredible misadventures before they can live together, wiser and presumably happier. However, it couldn't reconcile the various elements in the narrative with the tale's often idiosyncratic tone set by Voltaire in his satirical comments that all that happens happens for a good reason "in the best of all possible worlds," the truism uttered by Doctor Pangloss, Candide, and Cunegonde's beloved teacher. Sometimes too heavy-handed, sometimes awkward, Helman's book failed to match the light, humorous tones in Leonard Bernstein's brilliant score, which so effectively echoed the irony in Voltaire's novella. Despite its failure on Broadway, the show became a cult favorite, thanks largely to its cast album, which remained a constant best-seller in the Columbia catalogue, with Barbara Cook radiant as Cunegonde, and Robert Rounseville handsomely fetching as Candide.

Finally, in 1973, producer-director Harold Prince decided to try and revisit the show. Helman's book was discarded, and Hugh Wheeler was brought in to write a new, more theatrical version, with Stephen Sondheim contributing some new lyrics to Bernstein's songs. The revised show, pruned down and more effective, opened on Broadway on March 10, 1974, to ecstatic reviews, and enjoyed a run of 740 performances. A cast album, released at the time by Columbia Records, has never been reissued on compact disc, but with a few additional revisions reflecting Prince's more operatic approach to a new staging for the New York City Opera, the New World recording listed above gives an idea of the extensive work that went into the score.

More recently, on April 29, 1997, *Candide* returned to Broadway in a sparkling new edition, again produced and directed by Prince, with more revisions brought to it, and a sensational cast headed by Jim Dale as Pangloss, Harolyn Blackwell as Cunegonde, Jason Daniely as Candide, and Andrea Martin as

The Old Lady. The cast album on RCA Victor provides a fresh alternative to the other two listed above. In the final analysis, however, the 1956 recording is probably the one that will endure, if only because it was one of the original show's most satisfactory ingredients, and is not weighted down by the book as was the case with the production itself.

Didier C. Deutsch

Can't Hardly Wait

1998, Elektra Records, from the Columbia film *Can't Hardly Wait,* **1998** 𝄞𝄞𝄞𝄾

The movie's about a group of new high school graduates celebrating their convocation, so the soundtrack should reflect what they'd be partying to at their gathering. And it does—for the most part. Late '90s teens certainly like to mix up their modern rock and hip-hop, and this batch o' tunes represents both via Third Eye Blind ("Graduate"), Smash Mouth ("Can't Get Enough of You Baby"), Blink 182 ("Dammit"), Busta Rhymes ("Fire It Up"), and a hip-hop sisters triumvirate of Missy "Misdemeanor" Elliot, Lil' Kim, and Mocha on "Hit 'Em wit da Hee." The inclusion of older bands such as Guns 'n' Roses ("Paradise City") and the Replacements ("Can't Hardly Wait") seems odd but not awful, and Parliament- Funkadelic's "Flash Light" makes you feel like there is hope for the youth of America. It's also nice to hear something from the under-appreciated Dog's Eye View, whose "Umbrella" will be a pleasant discovery for many listeners.

Gary Graff

Cape Fear

1991, MCA Records, from the film *Cape Fear,* **Universal Pictures, 1991** 𝄞𝄞𝄞𝄞

album notes: Music: Bernard Herrmann; **Conductor:** Elmer Bernstein.

The original soundtrack recording from Martin Scorsese's 1991 remake of the 1962 classic, *Cape Fear* is the perfect vehicle for the collaboration of two of the most celebrated modern-day film composers—Bernard Herrmann and Elmer Bernstein. Working from the late Herrmann's original score, Bernstein has deftly adapted and re-orchestrated the original's eerie, chilling theme music, and in doing so, has filled a (hitherto) noticeable void in the Herrmann catalog. Notes director Scorsese, "[Herrmann's] music is noted for its unique instrumentation, and the manner in which it underlines the psychology of the characters, often creating a trance-like state." In this instance, Herrmann's exquisite use of the orchestra (mostly strings, but including other elements as well) imbues just the right essence of terrifying fear and drama—reminiscent of, yet different in texture and orchestral voicing, from his work for the great Hitchcock film thrillers. With this newly revised score, Bernstein has hit the mark dead-on, bringing us a first-rate, high-fidelity documentation of one of Herrmann's most important compositions.

Charles L. Granata

Capricorn One

See: Outland/Capricorn One

Car Wash

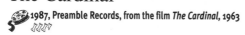 1996/1988, MCA Records, from the film *Car Wash,* Universal Pictures, 1976 𝄞𝄞𝄞

album notes: Music: Norman Whitfield; **Conductor:** Paul Riser; **Featured Performers:** Rose Royce, The Pointer Sisters, Richard Pryor.

In a rare synergy between pop music and the movies, the songs are an important element to the dramatic/comedic action in *Car Wash,* a film which took place, as its title indicates, in a downtown Los Angeles gas station where a loud speaker continually blares the latest hits. The songs, created by Norman Whitfield and performed for the most part by Rose Royce, are woven into the screen action which involved such colorful characters as Franklyn Ajaye, George Carlin, Irwin Corey, Ivan Dixon, and, as a fancy preacher, Richard Pryor, followed by his retinue of attractive females, The Pointer Sisters. The soundtrack album offers all the original songs heard in the film (there were quite a few others that probably were not licensed to the label), while a shorter version, the "Best of Rose Royce," features only the tracks recorded by that group.

Didier C. Deutsch

The Cardinal

1987, Preamble Records, from the film *The Cardinal,* 1963 𝄞𝄞𝄞

album notes: Music: Jerome Moross; **Conductor:** Jerome Moross

Composer Jerome Moross's rich Americana style is unmistakable, whether it's in the service of a western like *The Big Country,* a medieval epic like *The War Lord,* or a soaper like Otto Preminger's *The Cardinal.* In this last effort, Moross's opening theme, set against the bells of a cathedral, is a warm, sentimental brass-and-string anthem alternating against a wavering brass figure that winds majestically heavenward and forms the graceful spine of much of the later material. There's a rather mocking waltz setting for "Vienna" and a dance-like melody that's an ingenious take on the opening phrase of the Shaker melody Aaron Copland adapted for his *Appalachian Spring* ballet. Even in this sometimes-glitzy setting Moross's melodic progressions are sublime, and although this score doesn't match the power of

some of his better-known works, it makes a welcome addition to the Moross canon.

Jeff Bond

The Caretakers

See: Baby the Rain Must Fall/The Caretakers

Carlito's Way

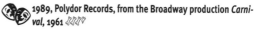 1993, Varèse Sarabande, from the film *Carlito's Way,* 1993 𝄞𝄞𝄞

album notes: Music: Patrick Doyle; **Conductor:** William Kraft.

A disco-era gangster film gives us, well, plenty of disco. And once you've had *Saturday Night Fever,* everything else seems superfluous. *Carlito's Way* has a few of the genre's greatest hits–K.C. & the Sunshine Band's "That's the Way I Like It," LaBelle's "Lady Marmalade," and the Hues Corporation's "Rock the Boat." And Carlos Santana is probably alarmed at how comfortably his "Oye Como Va" fits into the proceedings. But Billy Preston's "You Are So Beautiful" doesn't hold a candle to Joe Cocker's.

Gary Graff

Carnival

1989, Polydor Records, from the Broadway production *Carnival,* 1961 𝄞𝄞𝄞

album notes: Music: Bob Merrill; **Lyrics:** Bob Merrill; **Cast:** Anna-Maria Alberghetti, Jerry Orbach, James Mitchell, Kaye Ballard, Pierre Olaf.

MGM's lovely fable, *Lili,* about the little orphan girl who joins a carnival and befriends the puppets who saved her life when she was considering suicide became the basis for a new Broadway musical, *Carnival.* The musical had a book by Michael Stewart and a score by Bob Merrill, and opened on April 13, 1961, for a run of 719 performances. While missing some of the charm and lilt of the film, a pervasive song to match the memorable "Hi-Lili, Hi-Lo," and the ingratiating waif-like presence of Leslie Caron, the stage show had a fetching attitude of its own that was most engaging, a lovely hit in the song "Love Makes the World Go 'Round," and Tony Award-winner Anna-Maria Alberghetti as Lili. In it, Jerry Orbach portrayed Paul, the crippled puppeteer whose crankiness contrasted with the warmth he displayed in his puppets behind the scrim. The musical also featured James Mitchell as Marco the Magician, the flashy circus entertainer with whom Lili falls in love, not knowing he is already married to Kaye Ballard. The cast album, one of the first to be reissued on compact disc, provides a pleasant memento of the relatively nondescript score, with various bonus tracks that may be of minor interest to musical theatre fans.

Didier C. Deutsch

Carousel

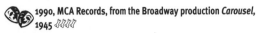
1990, MCA Records, from the Broadway production *Carousel,* **1945** ♪♪♪

album notes: Music: Richard Rodgers; **Lyrics:** Oscar Hammerstein II; **Cast:** John Raitt, Jan Clayton, Jean Darling, Christine Johnson, Eric Mattson.

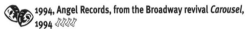
1990, Capitol Records, from the film *Carousel,* **20th Century Fox, 1956** ♪♪♪

album notes: Music: Richard Rodgers; **Lyrics:** Oscar Hammerstein II; **Orchestra:** The 20th Century Fox Orchestra; **Conductor:** Alfred Newman; **Cast:** Gordon MacRae, Shirley Jones, Barbara Ruick, Claramae Turner, Robert Rounseville, Cameron Mitchell.

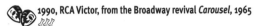
1990, RCA Victor, from the Broadway revival *Carousel,* **1965** ♪♪♪

album notes: Music: Richard Rodgers; **Lyrics:** Oscar Hammerstein II; **Cast:** John Raitt, Eileen Christy, Susan Watson, Katherine Hilgenberg, Reid Shelton, Jerry Orbach.

1994, Angel Records, from the Broadway revival *Carousel,* **1994** ♪♪♪♪

album notes: Music: Richard Rodgers; **Lyrics:** Oscar Hammerstein II; **Cast:** Michael Hayden, Sally Murphy, Audra Ann McDonald, Shirley Verrett.

The second Rodgers and Hammerstein musical has, in half a century, aged as well as any of their work, and the CD listener can hear it in a variety of forms. The original cast album, on MCA, presents an edited and rearranged version of the score (in monaural, of course) performed by selected cast members. John Raitt, the template for the Broadway leading man of the era, is a fine, larger-than-life Billy Bigelow, and Jan Clayton makes a feisty Julie Jordan. The supporting roles are all also first-rate. The standards—"If I Loved You," "June Is Bustin' Out All Over," "You'll Never Walk Alone"—stand up against their countless cover versions.

Rodgers and Hammerstein's unfairly "sentimental" reputation stems mostly from the movies, not the Broadway shows, and the film version of *Carousel*—which softened and lightened the original—was one of the chief culprits. But Alfred Newman's musical direction and Ken Darby's vocal arrangements put a fresh spin on the soundtrack—less operatic, especially, than the various Broadway recordings; Gordon MacRae (replacing Frank Sinatra, who quit) "acted" his songs in a compelling way; and Shirley Jones is this listener's favorite Julie. Capitol's CD puts back a couple of songs cut from the movie, and because the film recording was multi-track, the sound is a sort of before-its-time stereo.

Twenty years on, John Raitt returned to play Billy in one of the first of the grand-scale Broadway revivals at the (then new!) Lincoln Center. RCA took the opportunity to release a stereo version of the score with Eileen Christy, Susan Watson, Katherine Hilgenberg, and Jerry Orbach in supporting roles. Raitt's

Billy no longer sounds desperate enough to kill himself, but the singing holds up. The recording also includes a couple of reprises omitted from the earlier recording.

Fast forward another three decades, and Lincoln Center again presented a *Carousel,* this one a hugely successful British import remarkably staged by Nicholas Hytner. Minus the memorable set and choreography, this loses a bit of its impact, but nonetheless makes a worthy addition to the recorded legacy. Michael Hayden plays Billy as younger and less formidable than Raitt or MacRae, but if anything this makes the character more believable. Among the supporting roles, Audra Ann McDonald's Carrie stands out. The Angel recording offers more of the score than any of its precursors, including the music for the ballet in Act Two. The booklet provides pages of color photography from the show, and an instructive essay by Ethan Mordden.

Marc Kirkeby

Carrie

1997, Rykodisc, from the United Artists film *Carrie,* **1976** ♪♪♪

album notes: Music: Pino Donaggio; **Conductor:** Pino Donaggio.

This was the first of several collaborations between composer Pino Donaggio and director Brian De Palma. In this adaptation of a Stephen King novel about a naive girl with telekinetic abilities, Donaggio managed to capture the innocence of the girl as she self-destructs. In one of the film's most memorable scenes, poor Carrie is attacked by schoolmates on the greatest night of her life and, forced to the breaking point, goes home to get attacked by her fanatical mother. Aside from the two dated songs, both of which appear in the movie, the score is at times reminiscent of Bernard Herrmann's work for Alfred Hitchcock, which makes sense since De Palma has often acknowledged his debt to the director of *Psycho.* Dialogue elements on this CD are nicely used.

Didier C. Deutsch

Carried Away

1996, Intrada Records, from the film *Carried Away,* **Fine Line Features, 1996** ♪♪♪

album notes: Music: Bruce Broughton; **Conductor:** Bruce Broughton.

An acclaimed "small" picture from director Bruno Rubeo, *Carried Away* boasts an intimate score by Bruce Broughton. Performed by a small ensemble orchestra that's ideally suited for this character-driven drama starring Dennis Hopper and the director's wife, Amy Irving, the score is grounded in a theme for solo piano that reflects the inner emotions of the film's characters. The orchestra is used sparingly, thereby reducing overly melodramatic moments. The cumulative effect is that of an extremely subdued but amiable and poignant work nicely illustrating the composer's quieter side, though anyone expecting *Silverado* or even *The Boy Who Could Fly* will most likely be disappointed.

Andy Dursin

Carrington

 1995, Argo Records, from the film *Carrington,* Gramercy Pictures, 1995 ♪♪♪♪

album notes: Music: Michael Nyman; **Featured Musicians:** The Michael Nyman Band: Michael Nyman, piano; Beverly Davison, Ann Morfee, Claire Thompson, Nicholas Ward, Boguslow Kosteki, Harriet Davies, violin; Catherine Musker, Bruce White, Philip D'Arcy, Jim Sleigh, viola; Anthony Hinnigan, Justin Pearson, Tony Lewis, cello; Martin Elliott, bass guitar; David Roach, soprano/alto sax; Jamie Talbot, alto/tenor sax; Richard Clews, horn.

Christopher Hampton's biographical drama about the relationship between painter Dora Carrington and writer Lytton Strachey sports a beautiful score by Michael Nyman that blends the sort of formalized chamber orchestra approach you might expect from this sort of period movie with the composer's own minimalist leanings. The repeated phrases, primarily played by strings, manage to evoke all sorts of things: the uncontainable energy of sex, the creative drive as expressed through Carrington's paintings, and especially Carrington's obsessive feelings for Strachey, which eventually lead to her suicide after Strachey's death (a sequence effectively treated with a lengthy and morose Schubert adagio). There's a Coplandesque, syncopated cue for a carriage ride, and Nyman's thematic material for the love relationship between the two artists is gorgeous. On the whole this is one of the composer's most accessible and effective works for film.

Jeff Bond

Casablanca

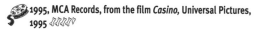 1997, Rhino, from the Warner Bros. film *Casablanca,* 1942 ♪♪♪

album notes: Music: Max Steiner; **Conductor:** Max Steiner.

What can you say about a long overdue first-ever soundtrack from such a timeless classic like *Casablanca*? I would like to say hallelujah, but I fear that I am a bit spoiled. It's tough to judge the first release of a 50-year-old soundtrack by the same standards as a new release. A good number of the tracks on this CD come straight from the film, and include dialogue that overpowers the background music. It makes for a nice souvenir of famous lines like Humphrey Bogart's "Of all of the gin joints in all the towns," "Here's looking at you, kid," and Sam (Dooley Wilson) being asked to "play it again." However if you are expecting perfect quality, rich-sounding music on the CD, you

may be a bit disappointed. With the overpowering dialogue, at times this comes off more like a Cliff's Notes version of the movie. In fact, the best moments on the CD are the supplemental tracks at the end, which include three vocals by Dooley Wilson, and three medleys— "Shine/It Had to Be You," "Ilsa Returns/As Time Goes By," and "Laszlo/As Time Goes By"—and none of the obtrusive dialogue. Still Max Steiner's composition, which carefully intertwines the melody from "As Time Goes By" into the score, is a masterpiece.

Beth Krakower

Casino

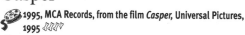 1995, MCA Records, from the film *Casino,* Universal Pictures, 1995 ♪♪♪♪♪

The Band's Robbie Robertson produced this gem, a collection of bluesy '60s and '70s rock spiced by a few left turns—Dean Martin's "You're Nobody Till Somebody Loves You," for instance, or "Flight of the Bumble Bee." The rest of the set blends Britain (the Rolling Stones, the Moody Blues, Jeff Beck, Eric Burdon), Memphis (B.B. King, the Staple Singers, Otis Redding) and New York (Lou Reed) into a hot stew of consistently good tunes.

Gary Graff

Casino Royale

1990, Varèse Sarabande, from the film *Casino Royale,* Columbia Pictures, 1967 ♪♪♪♪

album notes: Music: Burt Bacharach; **Lyrics:** Hal David; **Conductor:** Burt Bacharach.

As soundtracks go, this is really a piece of fluff, but at the time it was created, it beautifully captured the lightweight zany atmosphere of the late 1960s, and of the film itself, an amusing spoof of the James Bond spy thrillers. Some selections ("The Look of Love," and "Casino Royale") have since become hits in their own right, and it is a renewed pleasure to find them again here. The instrumental cues, while not as well known, pretty much define the best comedic aspects of the film, and make for a very entertaining listening experience.

Didier C. Deutsch

Casper

1995, MCA Records, from the film *Casper,* Universal Pictures, 1995 ♪♪♪

album notes: Music: James Horner; **Conductor:** James Horner.

Considering this is a film geared toward young children, James Horner had the unenviable task of reminding the audience that Casper is the ghost of a dead child. To be sure, there are funny

elements to the story, but the pathos of Casper's unearthly existence is an essential plot point. A gentle lullaby for orchestra and chorus perfectly captures the soul of the friendly ghost, despite the all too obvious comparisons to Danny Elfman's *Beetlejuice* on the comedy bits. That said, this is a marvelously pleasant listen, marred only by Little Richard's screeching rendition of the old cartoon theme, better adapted by Horner for the main title (though it is regrettably absent from the CD).

David Hirsch

Casper, A Spirited Beginning

1997, EMI-Capitol Records, from the Saban/20th Century-Fox film *Casper, A Spirited Beginning*, 1997 🎵🎵🎵

Propelled by a spirited version of the theme from the old television show, performed by K.C. and the Sunshine Band, this CD takes off in grand style and manages to sustain its moods throughout, thanks notably to the presence of Bobby McFerrin (whose "Don't Worry Be Happy" is by far the best song in the lot), Oingo Boingo ("No One Lives Forever," another winner), and the Backstreet Boys ("I Want to Be with You"). But the release of this album raises a question—for whom is it intended? Kids who have forcibly dragged their parents to see it? Unlikely. Their parents? They probably have most of these tracks somewhere else. So, the question remains. . . .

Didier C. Deutsch

The Cassandra Crossing

1990, RCA/BMG Ariola (Italy), from the film *The Cassandra Crossing*, 1977 🎵🎵🎵

album notes: Music: Jerry Goldsmith; **Orchestra:** The Symphonic Orchestra Unione Musicisti di Roma; **Conductor:** Jerry Goldsmith.

Goldsmith's music to this peculiar disaster/conspiracy thriller is a watershed '70s action score with a distinctly European sound set up in its moody, romantic title theme (later adapted into a song, "It's All a Game"). The agitated string writing of action cues like "Break In" and "I Can't Go" bring to mind Goldsmith's work on *Logan's Run*, but the score's set piece, "Helicopter Rescue" is in a class by itself. It's a spectacular cue built around some wildly unpredictable, jazz-influenced rhythms that you could probably dance to if you were double-jointed. Almost as good is the propulsive "The Climber," with its more literal use of locomotive-like rhythms and sounds from the orchestra. Other cues emphasize harpsichord and bongos, a melancholy woodwind theme and a reverberating metallic sound to underscore scenes of the Cassandra Crossing itself, a gigantic, rickety metal bridge. This Italian release adds another song, "I'm Still on My Way" warbled by actress Ann Turkel, but

the star is Goldsmith's score, despite a less-than-stellar orchestral performance.

Jeff Bond

Castle Freak

1995, Intrada Records, from the film *Castle Freak*, Full Moon Entertainment, 1995 🎵🎵

album notes: Music: Richard Band; **Conductor:** Richard Band.

Richard Band has always managed to squeeze every last dollar out of his meager scoring budgets to yield the maximum effect. By combining his home studio battery of state-of-the-art synthesizers with as many acoustic players as he can afford (in this case a battery of strings for the theme for the title freak), he can avoid many of the shapeless, and mindless, sound clusters that have become standard fare for the horror film genre. Typical of much of Band's other genre work, this score is no less effective.

David Hirsch

Casualties of War

1989, Columbia Records, from the film *Casualties of War*, Columbia Pictures, 1989 🎵🎵🎵🎵

album notes: Music: Ennio Morricone; **Orchestra:** Unione Musicisti di Roma; **Chorus:** Unione Musicisti di Roma; **Conductor:** Ennio Morricone; **Featured Soloist:** Trencito De Los Andes, Pan flutes.

This grim portrayal of war and the terrible toll it takes on soldiers and civilians alike elicited a moving score from Morricone, in which the haunting Pan flute creates a nostalgic aura. Brian DePalma's film, the story of four American GIs who rape and kill a Vietnamese woman, became the basis for a broad indictment of this country's role in Vietnam in the 1960s. It prompted Morricone to write a profoundly reflective score, in which the horrors of war and the sorrow brought by the crime itself are subtly intermingled. The nine minute-plus title track, a dirge-like elegy for chorus and orchestra, punctuated by the Pan flute, sets the tone for the entire album, with its long melodic lines suggestive of an eerie civilized world where such "casualties" can happen. The other selections pretty much follow the thread of the story, from the woman's abduction, her rape, and her death over the objections of one of the men, a "cherry" private played by Michael J. Fox. Recalling in some ways his music for *The Mission* (q.v.), Morricone's score is a powerful statement, all at once disturbing and compellingly attractive.

Didier C. Deutsch

Cat People

1982, MCA Records, from the film *Cat People*, RKO-Universal Picture, 1982 🎵🎵🎵

album notes: Music: Giorgio Moroder.

This stylish remake of the 1942 thriller, which takes as its premise that a race of cat people, resulting from the ancient mating of women with big cats, roams the Earth and, under certain conditions, reverts to the predators' killer instinct before turning human again, may be best remembered today for the fact that Nastassia Kinski, who stars in it, is such a lovely cat woman. Giving the film an extra aura of mystery and fright, Giorgio Moroder's electronic/instrumental score has its ominous moments, and generally speaking holds its own. At times melodic, but most often exploring sound effects that are more effective on the screen, the album is a mixed bag. David Bowie's hypnotic performance of the main theme, "Putting Out Fire," is a definite plus.

Didier C. Deutsch

Cats

1983, Geffen Records, from the Broadway production *Cats,* 1983 ♫♫♫♫

album notes: Music: Andrew Lloyd Webber; **Lyrics:** T.S. Eliot; **Cast:** Betty Buckley, Ken Page, Christine Langner, Wendy Edmead, Terrence Mann, Cynthia Onrubia.

Who would have thought that T.S. Eliot's "Old Possum's Book of Practical Cats" would one day provide the dramatic texture for a musical, and a successful one at that? Yet, *Cats,* which opened in New York on Oct. 7, 1982, has not only enjoyed more than the proverbial nine lives it was supposed to have, but has now become the longest running show on Broadway, leaving behind such blockbusters as *A Chorus Line, Les Miserables, Phantom of the Opera, 42nd Street, Grease,* and *Fiddler on the Roof.* Much of the success of the show, of course, falls squarely on Andrew Lloyd Webber's score, an amalgam of rock 'n' pop songs and big theatrical numbers that work effectively on stage and off. Listening to the cast album, one is constantly reminded how delightful the songs are, and how perfectly the melodies complement and enhance Eliot's words. Simple, unaffected, wonderfully direct and effective, Webber's score is far different from the pompous works he has created since, so much so that *Cats* may be considered his most inspired creation. In truth, he just hit the right note with this one, and it shows.

Didier C. Deutsch

Cats Don't Dance

1997, Mercury Records, from the Warner Bros. animated film *Cats Don't Dance,* 1997 ♫♫♫♫
album notes: Music: Steve Goldstein; **Songs:** Randy Newman.

The need to create features that effectively compete in a marketplace almost exclusively dominated by Disney has prompted many wannabe animators to go after this seemingly

lucrative market (what with merchandising being what it is these days, think of the tremendous gains made when you have a hit), with some resolutely mixed results. One of the potentially best was this amusing ditty, about a small-town cat who wants to go to Hollywood and become a success, which boasted some terrific big band songs by Randy Newman, including a sensational "Animal Jam," alone worth the price of the CD. Performed by some excellent singers—Scott Bakula, always a great talent, and Lindsay Ridgeway, a youngster with a powerful voice and assured talent to go with it, among others—the first part of this recording is just remarkable. The score itself, while not always on the same level of overall quality, also kicks high in several places, making this one of the better such film soundtracks available.

Didier C. Deutsch

Catwalk

1994, Atlantic Records, from the MTV television series *Catwalk,* 1994 ♫♫♫♫

A collection of urban contemporary songs specifically composed to illustrate this series. Some solid rocking numbers, some flavorful ballads, all of which creates a strong impression. Several songs actually do stand out in the lot, most specifically "Something to Cry About," "Reckless," and "Love Is a Dream," which are quite good. This is a good CD which aches to be discovered and enjoyed.

Didier C. Deutsch

CB4

🎬 1993, MCA Records, from the Universal film *CB4*, 1992 **woof!**

The premise of this smart little comedy seemed lively enough—two "gangsta rappers" rap their way out of jail and into politics—but after listening to the same beat repeated over the 13 tracks in this album, even the most lenient listener might go nuts. It's not that rap is a bad form of expression, whether taken literally or as a spoof, it simply is not musical enough to sustain repeated playing. In small doses, it might do, but not on a massive diet. And, frankly, the day when groups like Public Enemy, the Beastie Boys, or Backstreet discover the power of melody behind their explicit lyrics, they might make more converts to their brand of . . . talent.

Didier C. Deutsch

Celebrity

🎬 1998, Milan Records, from the Miramax film *Celebrity*, 1998
🎵🎵🎵

Another sharply observed entry from Woody Allen, *Celebrity* was set in the glamorous worlds of filmmaking, book publishing, fashion, and television and took a poignant look at the ways in which love could be lost and found after a 15-minute brush in the limelight. As is usual in Allen's films, the soundtrack was peppered with musical standards, some of which found their way into this delicious album. The predominance of piano tracks singles out the album, with excellent transcriptions of such oldies as "Fascination" by Liberace, "I Got Rhythm" by Teddy Wilson, "Cocktails for Two" by Carmen Cavallaro, "Will You Still Be Mine" and "Lullaby of Birdland" by Erroll Garner, and "Soon" by Ray Cohen. While it's always a pleasure to hear music of a high caliber, one might quibble here with the fact that the album has a short total playing time of less than 35 minutes.

Didier C. Deutsch

The Cemetery Club

🎬 1993, Varèse Sarabande, from the film *The Cemetery Club*, Touchstone Pictures, 1993 🎵🎵🎵
album notes: Music: Elmer Bernstein; **Conductor:** Elmer Bernstein; **Featured Soloist:** Cynthia Millar, piano.

Ignoring the sadder aspects of the story, Elmer Bernstein concentrated on the feel-good side of this sly, bittersweet comedy about three widows, whose bereavement brings them together, and who band to face the outside world with more serenity before launching themselves again on the dating scene. While the score has its moments of melancholy, most of the moods projected in the cues are lovely expressions of romanticism that are quite endearing, when not outright charming, with a recurring motif for "Esther, Doris and Lucille" tying everything together, and reaching a climax in a spirited little waltz ("The Club"). Three pop selections are welcome additions and complement the feelings expressed in the score.

Didier C. Deutsch

C'era una volta

🎬 1997, Screen Trax/Italy, from the film *C'era una volta (More Than A Miracle)*, MGM, 1967 🎵🎵🎵
album notes: Music: Piero Piccioni; **Conductor:** Piero Piccioni and Bruno Nicolai; **Featured Musician:** Severino Gazzelloni, flute.

Set in a mythical epoch which could be the 16th century, this whimsical fairy tale starred Omar Sharif as a Prince Charming in search of a bride, and Sophia Loren, looking more resplendent than ever, portraying the peasant girl who gets to marry him after many mishaps. Were it not for Loren, a real looker in this one, the film would not amount to much. But that didn't prevent Piero Piccioni from writing a score that is richly textured, and is dominated by two themes, one for the Prince, the other for the love story itself, a lilting romantic tune played by the strings or a flute. Piccioni's knack for conjuring up various moods is also exemplified in the raucously funny "Le chef"; the polyphonic "Volo nel cielo" and "Volo alto," written for a flying monk (don't even ask!) who plays an important part in bringing the Prince and his peasant girl together; and the brass accents of "Torneo," which, combined with the percussion instruments, signal the start of a colorful joust. This recording may be difficult to find. Check with a used CD store, mail-order company, or a dealer specializing in rare, out-of-print, or import recordings.

Didier C. Deutsch

César et Rosalie

🎬 1991, CAM Records/Italy, from the film *César et Rosalie*, Orion Classics, 1973 🎵🎵🎵
album notes: Music: Philippe Sarde; **Conductor:** Hubert Rostaing.

Starring Yves Montand and Romy Schneider in the title roles, *César et Rosalie*, directed by Claude Sautet, focused on the difficult relationship between a woman, her current companion, César, a scraps dealer, and David, a former lover. She rejects the prospect of a "ménage à trois," eventually leaving her unsteady life and the two men, who have become friends. Echoing the moments of tenderness in the film, along with the self-doubt of its central character, and the initial rivalry between the two men, Sarde's music brought its own vibrancy to it, with the inevitability in the story informed by an effective staccato over a pounding main theme. Interestingly, in the midst of the somewhat traditional music, a cue marked "Free Jazz" throws a curved ball, and sends the score into a totally unexpected direction. Note that the recording has a total playing time of slightly over 22 minutes. This title may be out of print or just plain hard to find. Mail-order companies, used CD shops, or dealers of rare or import recordings will be your best bet.

Didier C. Deutsch

Chain Reaction

🎬1996, Varèse Sarabande, from the film *Chain Reaction*, 20th Century Fox Film, 1996 ♫♫♫

album notes: Music: Jerry Goldsmith; **Conductor:** Jerry Goldsmith.

Regretfully, this is simply an uninspired assemblage of cues from Jerry Goldsmith's score that repeatedly teases you with the prospect that it's going to go somewhere, but never quite manages to make the effort. The same three-note motif (the main theme?) is aimlessly repeated. Hopelessly dull and unentertaining overall, it's only with the final cue, "Out of the Hole" that any true sign of the master is revealed, but by then it's just too late for you to care.

Jeff Bond

Goldsmith's score for one of the more idiotic action films of the '90s marked a return to the heavy, elaborate orchestral stylings of late '70s/early '80s efforts like *Outland* and *The Swarm* in several large-scale action cues, notably the five minute "Ice Chase" and the percussive "Closed Door". The staccato, heavily rhythmic action material stands rather uncomfortably alongside less textured (and less interesting) quasi-romantic cues like "Open Minds" and "Out of the Hole" that are more in keeping with Goldsmith's current, subdued style, while the chase cues hint at the glories of the past. The score also features a wailing electric guitar as a motif for paunchy hero Keanu Reeves, an effect that rarely achieves organic unison with the modernistic film score sound of the rest of the music.

David Hirsch

The Chairman

See: Ransom/The Chairman

The Chamber

🎬1996, Varèse Sarabande, from the film *The Chamber*, Universal Pictures, 1996 ♫♫

album notes: Music: Carter Burwell; **Conductor:** Carter Burwell.

This is a fairly straightforward Carter Burwell effort that is well-composed and orchestrated, but just never quite seems to stick in your mind. It is surprisingly unmemorable for such an established composer, probably because Burwell seems to do his best work for the quirky films created by the Coen Brothers, like *Raising Arizona* and *The Hudsucker Proxy*.

David Hirsch

Change of Habit

See: Live a Little, Love a Little/Charro!/The Trouble With Girls/Change of Habit

Chaplin

🎬1992, Epic Soundtrax, from the film *Chaplin,* Tri-Star Pictures, 1992 ♫♫

album notes: Music: John Barry; **Orchestra:** The English Chamber Orchestra; **Conductor:** John Barry.

While the music from *Chaplin* is fine accompaniment to the film, it doesn't stand quite as well on its own as a general "listening" CD. Composer John Barry has created a quietly beautiful score, but without the visuals, it often sounds heavy and plodding—perhaps because it lacks any real, melodic "theme." While it has a number of interesting moments ("Salt Lake City Episode" and "The Roll Dance" among them), fans of the film will probably enjoy it more than casual listeners. A vocal version of Chaplin's own composition, "Smile," performed by Robert Downey Jr., is included. The sonics are, as expected, excellent.

Charles L. Granata

Charade

🎬1988, RCA Records, from the film *Charade,* Universal Pictures, 1963 ♫♫♫♫

album notes: Music: Henry Mancini; **Conductor:** Henry Mancini.

A romantic comedy thriller set in France, *Charade* received the right musical touch from maestro Mancini, whose amiable and diverting score seems a perfect companion to the screen action. The story involves Audrey Hepburn, a widow in distress pursued by a trio of thugs trying to recover the money her late husband may have swindled from them, and Cary Grant, as the dashing knight in suit and tie who comes to her rescue. Like many Mancini scores, the tone in the cues is lightweight and attractive, with the pleasantly catchy title tune, with lyrics by Johnny Mercer, adding a melodically memorable element to the proceedings. One drawback, however, characteristic of RCA at that time, is that the recording is aggressively close-miked and dry, resulting in a brittle, unflattering sound, with a significant amount of hiss at the top.

Didier C. Deutsch

Chariots of Fire

1981, Polydor Records, from the film *Chariots of Fire,* 20th Century Fox, 1981 ♪♪♪♪

album notes: Music: Vangelis.

A daring effort by director Hugh Hudson that could have backfired as brilliantly as it paid off. Imagine the idea of completely scoring a film about two runners at the 1924 Olympics with electronics, composed by a musician known for making the music up as he watches the film instead of writing it in advance. The concept seems like something destined for failure, but under the brilliant instincts of Vangelis, the music created garnered both a best-selling soundtrack album and a 1981 Academy Award for Best Original Score. An early music video, showing slow-motion runners moving in time to the theme, made the music synonymous with the sport in the public's mind. The 21-minute "Chariots of Fire" track is most likely a suite of the original underscore cues, while the five initial tracks appear to be fleshed out cover versions of the primary themes.

David Hirsch

A Charlie Brown Christmas

1986, Fantasy Records, from the CBS–TV Television Special, *A Charlie Brown Christmas,* 1986 ♪♪♪♪

album notes: Music: Vince Guaraldi; **Lyrics:** Mendelson; **Featured Musicians:** The Vince Guaraldi Trio.

However crass the American celebration of Christmas—however stale the notion of pop Christmas music—this little soundtrack from a little TV special continues to improve with the passing years. The late Vince Guaraldi not only created a perfect environment for the animated *Peanuts* characters, he made what must now be considered a modern jazz classic, in an era when such things have almost ceased to be. Half originals, half piano—trio arrangements of familiar Christmas songs, the CD captures the blend of sadness, nostalgia and beauty that characterize—for many of us—a season that's seldom been altogether jolly.

Marc Kirkeby

Charro!

See: Live a Little, Love a Little/Charro!/The Trouble With Girls/Change of Habit

The Chase

1989, Varèse Sarabande, from the film *The Chase,* Columbia Pictures, 1966 ♪♪♪♪

album notes: Music: John Barry; **Conductor:** John Barry.

John Barry wrote a taut score for this pulse-pounding story of an escaped convict (Robert Redford) who returns to his hometown, a small Texas community, to try and clear himself from what might have been a false charge, only to be hunted down by the town's high-minded citizens. The film, a study of a close-knit society where alcoholism, adultery, and fanatical evangelism are the prevailing ills, prompted Barry to write a score in which the dominant note is a pervading sense of drama about to erupt at any moment. The ominous tone in most of the tracks is temporarily relieved by an occasional blues number, in what is essentially a richly expressive and rewarding score.

Didier C. Deutsch

Chasers

1994, Morgan Creek Records, from the Morgan Creek/Warner Bros. film *Chasers,* 1994 ♪♪♪

Dwight Yoakam and Pete Anderson wrote a bouncy series of songs for this silly little film about two Navy officers who are assigned to escort a maximum security prisoner to a naval base in Charleston, only to discover that the prisoner is a shapely blonde with only one goal in mind: escape a jail sentence by going AWOL. While the film had little to recommend it, except perhaps for Erika Eleniak, this soundtrack album should please anyone interested in a guzzle of beer, a bevy of beautiful babes, and great country tunes to go along with them, with good performances by Dwight Yoakam ("Doin' What I Did," and "Guitars, Cadillacs"), Buck Owens ("Cryin' Time"), Tommy Conwell & the Young Rumblers ("Rock with You"), Ralph Stanley ("Train 45"), and Bob Donough & Victoria Duffy ("Right on My Way Home"), among many others.

Didier C. Deutsch

Che!

1999, Aleph Records, from the 20th Century-Fox film *Che!,* 1969 ♪♪♪

album notes: Music: Lalo Schifrin; **Conductor:** Lalo Schifrin; **Featured Musician:** Juanjo Dominguez, guitar.

Lalo Schifrin seems intent on reissuing on his own label, Aleph Records, all the scores he wrote that are no longer available and/or that may have reverted back to him. Case in point, this rare soundtrack written for a 1969 film about the famous Cuban revolutionary and intimate friend of Fidel Castro, respectively played by Omar Sharif and Jack Palance. Eschewing the obvious political aspects of a film such as this, told in flashbacks by "real" people who have allegedly known Che, Schifrin chose to concentrate instead on the Latin-American elements that would give his music a definite original edge. Admittedly, no one is better equipped than he is to do that, and his score reveals a keen love and appreciation of the kind of music heard in Cuba, Argentina, and the Andes, which pervade it. The album, which contains several previously unreleased tracks, is remarkable for its diversity and overall appeal, with poignant guitar solos by Juanjo Dominguez.

Didier C. Deutsch

Cherry, Harry & Raquel

1997, Laserlight, from the Panamint film *Cherry, Harry & Raquel*, 1969 ♫♫

album notes: Music: William Loose.

This pleasant, if innocuous score by William Loose is everything one might expect to hear behind a Russ Meyer film, where buxomy babes and simulated sex action prevail over intellectual messages or, for that matter, great musical content. If you play this album without actually listening to it, you still might enjoy it. But if you're looking for Beethoven's Ninth Symphony or Bob Dylan's "Knockin' on Heaven's Door," better get the real thing.

see also: Vixen, The Devil in Miss Jones

Didier C. Deutsch

Cheyenne Autumn

1987, Label X, from the film *Cheyenne Autumn*, Warner Bros. Pictures, 1964 ♫♫♫♫

album notes: Music: Alex North; **Conductor:** Alex North.

Alex North produced this rich, thoughtful western score at the tail end of his epic period (shortly after composing *Spartacus* and *Cleopatra),* and *Cheyenne Autumn* works as a kind of warmer response to those occasionally brutal works, shot through with Americana and the ceremonial dignity of the Native American people with whom John Ford's film concerned itself. The score mixes sharp-edged martial fanfares with somber, reflective passages marking the hardship of the Cheyenne tribe struggling to maintain its identity as it is relegated to reservation life in the late 1800s. There are deeply percussive battle cues, a melancholy Americana love theme, even a Samuel Barber-like satirical use of the "Camptown Races" melody for a revisionist sequence involving Wyatt Earp (Jimmy Stewart). Ford evidently hated this score, but it's by far the best music ever associated with one of his features, and no film composer ever captured the emotion of anguish better than North.

Jeff Bond

Chicago

1996, Arista Records, from the Broadway production *Chicago*, 1975 ♫♫♫♫

album notes: Music: John Kander; **Lyrics:** Fred Ebb; **Cast:** Gwen Verdon, Chita Rivera, Jerry Orbach, Mary McCurty, M. O'Haughey.

 1996, RCA Victor, from the Broadway revival *Chicago*, 1996 ♫♫

album notes: Music: John Kander; **Lyrics:** Fred Ebb; **Cast:** Ann Reinking, Bebe Neuwirth, James Naughton, Marcia Lewis, D. Sabella, Joel Grey.

Subtitled "A Musical Vaudeville," this groundbreaking musical received, the first time around, an original cast recording that enshrined a score filled with such dramatic truth as to make it nearly indispensable to anyone who values the musical theater. While Gwen Verdon as Roxie Hart, and Chita Rivera as Velma Kelly, reveal a certain vocal roughness, they surely give the performances of their career, as two "merry murderesses of the Cook County Jail." Jerry Orbach, as the silver-tongued shyster Billy Flynn, and Mary McCarty as Matron Mama Morton, show just the right combination of sleaze and greed. Barney Martin and M.(ichael) O'Haughey are terrific as the unwary innocents caught in a web of deceit, lust, cynicism, and venality. The rest of the small cast is superb, as is the orchestra. Everything seems just about perfect, including the remastered sound. Fred Ebb's lyrics and John Kander's music capture the spirit of the 1920s as well as the flavor of the 1970s in such a timeless manner that it sounds as if the score had been written yesterday.

Brought back to Broadway 20 years later, the splendid score of this incredible musical is given a better recording than the production deserves. More of the score and book is included here than on the 1975 recording and the sound of this recent digital recording is slightly better. But the cynicism of the original is no longer tempered with subtlety. Every joke and situation is related in the most coarse and obvious manner, with Bebe Neuwirth, James Naughton, and the orchestra the standouts in the new cast album. The real problem is Ann Reinking as Roxy Hart. She hits each moment with the impact of a sledgehammer, thereby losing the admittedly few tender and vulnerable moments Roxy was allowed. These moments are important to our understanding of the character and what drives her very callous acts throughout the show. As it is, there is nothing scintillating about this sinner.

Jerry J. Thomas

Chicago Hope

1997, Sonic Images, from the television series *Chicago Hope*, 20th Century-Fox, 1997 ♫♫♫♫

album notes: Music: Jeff Rona; **Featured Musicians:** Mark Isham, Craig Hara, trumpets; Peter Maunu, guitars; Bob Shepard, soprano sax; Marni Huffum, Leslie Reed, oboe/English horn; David Low, John Walz, Martin Tillman, cellos; Jeff Rona, keyboards/flutes/whistles; P. J. Hanke, piano solo.

The popular television drama spawned this CD featuring the music of Jeff Rona and the artistry of several distinguished players, among them Mark Isham, Peter Maunu, Bob Shepard, P. J. Hanke, and Rona. Writing for television is an art that some composers have down pat, and despite the limitations of the genre they succeed in creating music that's quite acceptable on its own terms and enjoyable. Rona belongs in that category: his music may be serviceable, but there are moments when it attracts the listener's attention with themes that are interesting or unusual instrumentations that make it more vibrant than the genre usually calls for. Several selections stand out in this album, and while they may reflect the action specific to certain episodes, they also make for attractive listening in a different environment. An album that's well worth getting and getting into.

Didier C. Deutsch

Children of a Lesser God

1986, GNP Crescendo, from the film *Children of a Lesser God*, Paramount Pictures, 1986 ♪♪♪♪

album notes: Music: Michael Convertino; **Conductor:** Shirley Walker.

This early new age-style score by Michael Convertino is hauntingly romantic and, with its simple, catchy main theme, is one of the key reasons for the film's success. Played primarily by string instruments and a synclavier, the score captures the unblemished innocence of a young, introverted deaf woman (Marlee Matlin in her Academy Award-winning performance) brought out of self-imposed isolation by teacher William Hurt. Originally released as an LP, the inclusion of the song "Boomerang" on track nine devastates the score's dreamy pacing. Packaging, a holdover from the LP version as well, fails to list any track numbers (but does have the bizarre legends "Side One" and "Side Two").

David Hirsch

Children of the Corn II

1992, Bay Cities Records, from the film *Children of the Corn II*, Fifth Avenue Entertainment, 1992 ♪♪♪

album notes: Music: Daniel Licht; **Conductor:** Tim Simonec.

This early effort by Daniel Licht (*Bad Moon*) shows he was always able to rise above this type of trash. Licht does manage to squeeze quite a lot energy out of his meager budget, even finding a way to combine a modest-sized choir with his orchestra. The voices chant out pseudo-American Indian verses to represent "He Who Walks Between the Rows," the evil spirit that has possessed the young. "Nosebleed" is the cue that perhaps best represents the composer's intent for the dark nature of the children. He also manages to inject some pleasant alternative direction with the romantic start to "A Combine and a House," while imbuing some genuine oddness with the use of some Far Eastern motifs. Licht endows this film, the second

chapter in a laughingly bad trilogy adapted from a single Stephen King short story, with some credence of seriousness. He deserves better opportunities than these.

David Hirsch

Children of the Night

1990, Bay Cities Records, from the film *Children of the Night*, Fangoria Films, 1990 ♪♪♪

album notes: Music: Daniel Licht; **Conductor:** Tim Simonec.

Though written for a horror film, this melodic score shows Daniel Licht in a very positive light, with themes that are for the most part attractive and catchy, and seem to belie the darker aspects of the story itself. The score opens on a series of cues that presage the arrival of a vampire in the small middle-American town where the action takes place, and where various light incidents are the occasion for spirited musical moments that are quite engaging. But as the action progresses, the moods evolve into a darker, more percussive mode, though without losing their melodic content, and become increasingly more ominous and darker. Using the full forces of the orchestra, Licht then unleashes the final strokes with themes that signal the end of the nightmare. It's all very effective and enjoyably easy on the ear.

Didier C. Deutsch

China 9, Liberty 37

See: Amore piombo e furore

Chinatown

1995, Varèse Sarabande, from the film *Chinatown*, Paramount Pictures, 1974 ♪♪♪♪

album notes: Music: Jerry Goldsmith; **Featured Artist:** Uan Rasey, trumpet; **Conductor:** Jerry Goldsmith.

This moody and incredibly atmospheric work was a replacement score written and recorded by Goldsmith in an astonishing 11 days. The richly nostalgic solo trumpet theme is justly famous and lends tremendous emotional weight to cues like "Jake and Evelyn" and "The Wrong Clue," while the rest of the score creates a memorably dark feeling almost entirely with piano, from hand-stopped low end notes to an almost tide-like effect created by brushing the piano strings themselves. There's also a brutally violent staccato piano solo and some disturbing, atonal avant garde string effects that stretch the tension and masterfully hint at the terrible psychological wounds hidden within the characters of Roman Polanski's brilliant gumshoe film. This long-overdue release from Varèse boasts superb sound that immerses the listener in the score's percussive sonic world, and its few pieces of period source music blend seamlessly with Goldsmith's music. This is a must-have.

Jeff Bond

Chinese Box

1998, Metro Blue/Capitol Records, from the Trimark film *Chinese Box*, 1998 ♫♫♫♪

album notes: Music: Graeme Revell; **Conductor:** Graeme Revell; **Featured Musicians:** Richard Thompson, piano; Dadawa, lead vocals.

This romantic melodrama, starring Jeremy Irons as a British journalist living in Hong Kong on the eve of the handover to China, didn't make much of an impression at the box office or on video when it was released a year or so ago. Despite solid credentials and a love affair that involved the journalist and a Chinese bar owner, the film, which aimed to document the end of the British colonial era and the impending switch to Chinese rule, lacked a strong focus and looked more like a claustrophobic documentary than a feature film. It was, however, enlivened by Graeme Revell's florid score, which mixed in vocal Chinese to get its local color. Evoking at times the scores of Ennio Morricone, Revell's music breathed great life into the film itself, artistically taking it onto another level altogether.

It is unfortunate that the label decided to reduce his contributions to only four tracks, all variations on the "Chinese Box Theme," with vocalizations by Dadawa, opting instead to overload the album with vocal selections by Screamin' Jay Hawkins, Lori Lava-Coates, Club 69, Marlene Dietrich, and Ruben Blades which, while complementing the film's soundtrack, seemed less important than the instrumental music itself. This set aside, the soundtrack album, which also features performances by Bobby Chen, Johnny Chen, and a hilariously dated version of "Rose, Rose I Love You" by the Paramount Jazz Band, is delectable.

Didier C. Deutsch

Chitty Chitty Bang Bang

1997, Rykodisc, from the United Artists film *Chitty Chitty Bang Bang*, 1967 ♫♫♫♪

album notes: Music: Richard M., Sherman, Robert B. Sherman; **Lyrics:** Richard M. Sherman, Robert B. Sherman; **Conductor:** Irwin Kostal; **Cast:** Dick Van Dyke, Sally Ann Howes.

A truly scrumptious soundtrack to a wonderful film. Dick Van Dyke portrays an inventor who purchases a used car from a junk lot. He renovates the car and takes his two children and new friend, Truly Scrumptious (played by Sally Ann Howes, doing her best Julie Andrews impersonation) on a picnic near the seashore. The four end up in the car, surrounded by water, and under attack by the Baron Bomhurst, evil ruler of Vulgaria.

To everyone's amazement, a life preserver appears under the car and sails the four safely ashore . . . in Vulgaria! They end up having a wild adventure in a land where children are not allowed. The songs on the original release of this soundtrack were not sequenced according to their appearance in the film. For this reissue, however, Rykodisc has gone back and rearranged the tracks to match the order in which they are heard in the movie. Some fun dialogue was added and this enhanced CD also contains the original trailer.

Didier C. Deutsch

A Chorus Line

1998, Sony Classical, from the Broadway musical *A Chorus Line*, 1976 ♫♫♫♫

album notes: Music: Marvin Hamlisch; **Lyrics:** Edward Kleban; **Book:** James Kirkwood and Nicholas Dante; **Cast:** Scott Allen, Renee Baughman, Carole (Kelly) Bishop, Pamela Blair, Wayne Cilento, Chuck Cissel, Clive Clerk, Kay Cole, Ronald Dennis, Donna Drake, Brandt Edwards, Patricia Garland, Carolyn Kirsch, Ron Kuhlman, Nancy Lane, Baayork Lee, Priscilla Lopez, Robert LuPone, Cameron Mason, Donna McKechnie, Don Percassi, Michael Serrecchia, Michael Stuart, Thomas J. Walsh, Sammy Williams, Crissy Wilzak.

1985, Casablanca Records, from the Embassy Films/PolyGram Pictures film *A Chorus Line*, 1985 woof!

album notes: Music: Marvin Hamlisch; **Lyrics:** Edward Kleban; **Conductor:** Ralph Burns; **Cast:** Michael Blevins, Yamil Borges, Jan Gan Boyd, Sharon Brown, Gregg Burge, Michael Douglas, Cameron English, Tony Field, Nicole Fosse, Vicki Frederick, Janet Jones, Michelle Johnston, Audrey Landers, Pam Klinger, Terrence Mann, Charles McGowan, Alyson Reed, Justin Ross, Blane Savage, Matt West.

Essentially a work in progress, *A Chorus Line*, a musical without a book, gave a voice and a face to the gypsies, the often unheralded boys and girls whose thankless task it is to set off and enhance the performance of a musical's headliner. Thrown in the spotlight for the first time, they were allowed to confront their own demons, reveal the sacrifices they had to make just to be in a show, confess the problems and difficulties they so often encountered in their pursuit of an elusive instant in the limelight, before returning as surely into the obscurity and anonymity which is their usual lot. Devised by Michael Bennett, with the collaboration of the various actors and actresses involved in the show itself, *A Chorus Line* recounted the grueling audition all the gypsies have to go through when they answer a casting call, this time for an unnamed big Broadway musical in which the star (probably a well-known female performer) is "the one." If at times it sounds a bit confessional and revelatory of secrets buried deep within each member of the cast, it is only because the musical itself eventually was a celebration of the talent they all bring to a show.

The score, with music by Marvin Hamlisch and lyrics by Ed Kleban, was unusually sympathetic to members of the cast, and it provided solo turns where all could express their aspirations and anguish and mesmerize the audience with their individual talents. A multi–Tony Award winner (for Best Musical, Best Score, Best Direction, and Best Book, among many others), *A Chorus Line* enjoyed incredible life on Broadway, breaking all records with its run of 6,137 performances, only subsequently surpassed by *Cats*. The cast album recording, since 1976 a popular title in the Columbia catalogue, has just been remixed and mastered, giving it an overall vibrancy and sheen that makes it sound better than it ever did. This expanded edition, newly remixed and remastered, brings all the positive elements in the recording to the fore, with the greater sonics adding to a livelier sense of the individual performances.

Sadly, the same cannot be said about the film, a travesty of the genre if there ever was one and a total disservice to the gypsies it aimed to celebrate. When Fred Astaire began to dance on the screen in his now legendary films with Ginger Rogers for RKO, he made sure that the dances would show him and his partner from head to toe, unlike what had been done before when dancers in action would often be framed down to the waist. The film version of *A Chorus Line* framed the musical and its performers down to the waist, losing so many great aspects from the show in this sorry transfer to the screen that it emerged as a very pale image of the original, loud, brash, and totally misguided. The same faults apply to the soundtrack album, which, when compared to the original recording, is a total disaster. The performers who struggled through this mishmash deserved better.

Beth Krakower

Christmas in Connecticut/Love at Stake

🎬 1992, Cinerama Records, from the Turner film *Christmas in Connecticut*, 1992, and the Hemdale film *Love at Stake*, 1987 ♪♪♪
album notes: Music: Charles Fox; **Conductor:** Charles Fox.

Movies with a Christmas theme are a dime a dozen, so it's little wonder that this lame remake of the 1945 hit, about a nationally known TV cook and homemaker who is single and can't even prepare a meal, didn't make much of a dent. For the record, it was directed by Arnold Schwarzenegger (?), and starred Dyan Cannon, Kris Kristofferson, Richard Roundtree, and Tony Curtis. So much for specifics. The score was written by Charles Fox, whose tunes for this mild comedy are pleasant, but not earth-shaking. Nor are, for that matter, the cues he composed for *Love at Stake,* a spoof about the Puritans, set in 1692 in Salem, Massachusetts, which are also strictly on the pleasantly listenable side.

Didier C. Deutsch

Christopher Columbus: The Discovery

🎬 1992, Varèse Sarabande, from the film *Christopher Columbus: The Discovery,* Warner Bros. Pictures, 1992 ♪♪♪♪
album notes: Music: Cliff Eidelman; **Orchestra:** The Seattle Symphony Orchestra; **Conductor:** Cliff Eidelman.

Once in a while you come across music written for a bad movie that is far better than it has any right to be, and even surpasses the picture itself in terms of its popularity. That's certainly the case with *Christopher Columbus: The Discovery,* the first of two big-budget 1992 flops depicting the discovery of the New World. This film, produced by Alexander Salkind, features a grand, old-fashioned orchestral score by Cliff Eidelman, who seized the opportunity to write music in the great swashbuckling tradition of Korngold and latter-day composers like John Williams. It's stirring, robust, and downright glorious in its best portions, illustrating young Eidelman's adept handling of both chorus and orchestra, and resulting in what is really a sensational album. The movie might be a dud, but just as Vangelis wrote a great score for the equally disastrous Ridley Scott bomb *1492,* Eidelman has come up with a terrific stand-alone work that has already outlasted the unintentionally funny inadequacies of its source.

see also: 1492: Conquest of Paradise

Andy Dursin

Cinderella

🎬 1996, Walt Disney Records, from the Walt Disney Pictures animated feature *Cinderella,* 1948 ♪♪♪♪
album notes: Music: Mack David, Jerry Livingston, Al Hoffman; **Lyrics:** Mack David, Jerry Livingston, Al Hoffman; **Music:** Oliver Wallace, Paul J. Smith; **Cast:** Ilene Woods, William Phipps, Eleanor Audley, Rhoda Williams, Lucille Bliss, Verna Felton.

📺 1999, Sony Classical/Legacy Records, from the CBS-TV special *Cinderella,* 1957 ♪♪♪
album notes: Music: Richard Rodgers; **Lyrics:** Oscar Hammerstein II; **Conductor:** Alfredo Antonini; **Cast:** Julie Andrews, Jon Cypher, Howard Lindsay, Dorothy Stickney, Kaye Ballard, Alice Ghostley, Edith Adams.

📺 1993, Columbia Records, from the CBS-TV production *Cinderella,* 1964 ♪♪♪
album notes: Music: Richard Rodgers; **Lyrics:** Oscar Hammerstein II; **Musical Direction:** John Green; **Cast:** Lesley Ann Warren, Stuart Damon, Walter Pidgeon, Ginger Rogers, Jo Van Fleet, Pat Carroll, Barbara Ruick, Celeste Holm, Don Heitgerd.

Another wonderful animated transmogrification of a classic fairy tale, *Cinderella,* released on March 4, 1950, was Walt Disney's return to a genre that had proved quite successful for the studio, following several less distinguished "compilations" of mini-cartoons, a challenge the studio faced head-on

Cinema Paradiso **(The Kobal Collection)**

with extraordinary vitality. Adding a new twist to the worn-out tale of the poor orphan girl mistreated by her stepmother and stepsisters, who discovers an 11th-hour romance with a Prince Charming thanks to her fairy godmother, the film introduced several animal characters who provided comic relief and a dose of enjoyment even the Charles Perrault original had never envisioned. Most particularly, the feature was graced by a sensational score in which songs like "Bibbidi Bobbidi Boo," an Academy Award winner, "So This Is Love," and "A Dream Is a Wish Your Heart Makes" soon emerged as standards. The newly mastered CD, with a lot of extra, previously unavailable material, is a lively reminder that the Disney scores were frequently great sources of entertainment in their own right.

Charles Perrault's popular fairy tale became an attractive television special when Richard Rodgers and Oscar Hammerstein set it to music in 1957, in a production that starred Julie Andrews, fresh from her own success as Eliza Dolittle in *My Fair Lady*. While hardly comparable to their stage works, *Cinderella* nonetheless proved particularly en-

dearing, with the pair working their own magic in tunes like "In My Own Little Corner," in which Cinderella laments her unglamorous existence and dreams for better tomorrows, and "Ten Minutes Ago," a glorious waltz in which Cinderella and the Prince discover that their hearts beat to the same 3/4 time. The addition of four bonus tracks to this new, expanded edition provides a different perspective: the tracks were part of a demo record that was sent to radio stations and deejays ahead of the broadcast airing, which featured Julie Andrews singing two of the songs she performed in the telecast and Richard Rodgers at the piano leading a studio orchestra in two instrumental selections. Overall sound quality has been dramatically improved, making this a welcome reissue and one that probably will stand out for years to come.

In 1964 Rodgers returned to the work for a new production, also televised by CBS, which introduced Lesley Ann Warren as Cinderella and was quite enjoyable, although not as exciting as the original.

Beth Krakower

Cinema Paradiso

1990, DRG Records, from the film *Cinema Paradiso*, 1989
𝄞𝄞𝄞𝄞𝄞

album notes: Music: Ennio Morricone; **Orchestra:** Orchestra Unione Musicisti di Roma; **Conductor:** Ennio Morricone; **Featured Soloists:** Franco Tamponi, violin; Baldo Maestri, saxophone, clarinet; Marianne Eckstein, flute; Enrico Pierannunzi, Alberto Pomeranz, piano; Francesco Romano, guitar.

Ennio Morricone struck a particularly emotional chord in this Academy Award–winning score for the film of Giuseppe Tornatore, permeated with a deep sense of melancholy and nostalgia. Heard behind the screen action, the score subtly underlines the feelings of a successful filmmaker who goes back to his little hometown only to be confronted by the ghosts of his past, and particularly the memory of an old projectionist who became his first mentor and sparked his interest in the movies. But beyond being a mere recollection of a youngster slowly coming of age, the film is a paean to a time when the cinema was something special and unique in the lives of everyone, and when going to the movies meant an unforgettable magic adventure in a land that only existed on celluloid. In his score, Morricone was able to capture the deep emotional moods evoked by the film, and turned in one of the most eloquent soundtracks of his long and distinguished career.

Didier C. Deutsch

Circle of Friends

1995, Warner Bros. Records, from the film *Circle of Friends*, Savoy Pictures, 1995 𝄞𝄞𝄞

album notes: Music: Michael Kamen; **Orchestra:** The London Metropolitan Orchestra; **Conductor:** Michael Kamen.

Soundtrack listeners tend to dislike dialogue mixed in with their music, and with *Circle of Friends,* you can see why—the dialogue disrupts any momentum that Michael Kamen's score attempts to build up during the course of its abbreviated running time. What you end up with, then, are very brief, mostly unexceptional snippets of music interspersed with dialogue that will only appeal to die-hard fans of the movie. This comes in spite of the fact that Kamen's music is pleasant enough (with the Chieftains onboard, it comes off as an agreeable distant cousin to *Far and Away),* and the Shane McGowan–Maire Brennan duet, "You're the One," written by Kamen and McGowan, is actually quite good, even with a pair of vocalists whose styles are seemingly at odds with each other. But what more can you say about an under-30-minute album where dialogue is seemingly used to pad the running time?

Andy Dursin

Citizen Kane

1991, Preamble Records, from the film *Citizen Kane,* RKO Radio Pictures, 1941 𝄞𝄞𝄞𝄞𝄞

album notes: Music: Bernard Herrmann; **Orchestra:** The Australian Philharmonic Orchestra; **Conductor:** Tony Bremner.

This sensational recreation of Bernard Herrmann's music for Orson Welles's *Citizen Kane* must rank among the most successful attempts at bringing into the digital era a score from the early days of Hollywood. Herrmann recorded at various times some cues from his score. Others, notably Charles Gerhardt in his *Classic Film Scores* series, have made sure to include excerpts from the momentous score, but this recording is its only complete representation, with Tony Bremner conducting the Australian Philharmonic Orchestra in a flawless performance. A trend-setter in every way *Citizen Kane* is probably the most famous film ever made in Hollywood, an icon of movie-making which launched the screen careers of many of its creators, including writer/director Welles, and co-star Joseph Cotten.

For Herrmann, by his own admission, it was a dream come true. Unlike the prevailing practice that gives a composer two to three weeks to write his music once the film is shot, he began scoring it almost from the first day of shooting. His cues not only reflect the unfolding screen action, but become part of it when Welles decided to match some scenes to the music Herrmann had written. The cues presented here follow the drama about press tycoon Charles Kane, from his youth to his two marriages and the last word ("Rosebud") he whispers on his deathbed. At times deeply introspective, at times vibrant and descriptive, the score immediately established Herrmann as a vigorous, somewhat iconoclastic composer who worked by his own rules, a reputation he nurtured throughout the rest of his career. Like some books in a personal library, some recordings are essential in any basic collection. *Citizen Kane* is one of them.

Didier C. Deutsch

Citizen X

1995, Varèse Sarabande, from the television movie *Citizen X,* HBO Pictures, 1995 𝄞𝄞𝄞𝄞

album notes: Music: Randy Edelman; **Conductor:** Randy Edelman.

A television movie, starring Stephen Rea and Donald Sutherland based on the novel *The Killer Department* by Robert Cullen, *Citizen X* prompted Randy Edelman to write a broad, symphonic score, lush and attractive, often dark and brooding, with many catchy themes evolving from the overall texture. Some cues, like "Leaving the Station" or "The Strain Begins to Show," are actually quite compelling, making this more than a mere routine effort. CD alert: Music on each track starts a couple of seconds before indexing does, so if you're looking for the start of a specific cue you will have to backtrack to the end of the previous one.

Didier C. Deutsch

City Hall

1996, Varèse Sarabande, from the film *City Hall*, Castle Rock Films, 1996 ♪♪♪

album notes: Music: Jerry Goldsmith; **Conductor:** Jerry Goldsmith.

Jerry Goldsmith brought some echoes of *On the Waterfront* to this story of New York political intrigue, one of the few intelligent dramas scored by the composer in the '90s. There's a relentless pulse of timpani moving through virtually every cue of this score that functions as a kind of heartbeat for the Big Apple, moving from the gritty romanticism of the opening blues theme through hammering, violent street crime encounters, and finally surging under the film's subtle dramatic underscoring, which ranges from a swaggering blues theme for a political "kingpin" to more lyrical, introspective moments filling out the back end of the album. There's a real regression from the percussive, agitated first half of the CD to the more measured tones on which it ends, but the rumble of low percussion makes for an unusually cohesive listening experience.

Jeff Bond

City of Angels

1990, Columbia Records, from the Broadway production *City of Angels*, 1989 ♪♪♪♪

album notes: Music: Cy Coleman; **Lyrics:** David Zippel; **Cast:** James Naughton, Gregg Edelman, Kay McClelland, Randy Graff, Rene Auberjonois, Dee Hoty, Rachel York, Shawn Elliott.

1993, RCA Victor, from the London production *City of Angels*, 1993 ♪♪♪♪

album notes: Music: Cy Coleman; **Lyrics:** David Zippel; **Cast:** Roger Allam, Martin Smith, Fiona Hendley, Haydn Gwynne, Henry Goodman.

Broadway maverick composer Cy Coleman had a winning show in *City of Angels,* a whimsical spoof of the 1940s' film noir genre, further made exhilarating by its offbeat approach about a Hollywood scriptwriter with a poor record with women, and his alter ego, a gumshoe with a successful track record. With a book by Larry Gelbart, and lyrics by David Zippel, the show opposed the two men, Stine, whose existence happened in a black and white decor, and Stone, who enjoyed the glitz and color of Hollywood films, in another nifty touch that added zest to the stage proceedings. Along for the musical ride were Stine's long-suffering wife, Gabby, and Stone's secretary, Oolie, as well as a bevy of other attractive characters, some sharing Stine's real-life existence, some stemming from Stone's invented background. The score invented by Coleman matched the various moods in the story, with a zest directly borrowed from the big band sound of

the 1940s, and songs that were all extremely enjoyable on stage and off, as can be experienced in the original cast album. *City of Angels* opened on Dec. 11, 1989, and enjoyed a run of 878 performances. Among its awards, it won the Tonys for best musical, book, and score. The London cast album, on RCA Victor, is basically similar to the Broadway cast album, though it seems to lack the crackling energy in evidence in its predecessor.

Didier C. Deutsch

City of Angels

1998, Reprise Records, from the Warner Bros. film *City of Angels*, 1998 ♪♪♪♪

album notes: Music: Gabriel Yared.

Simply one of the best soundtrack albums of the late nineties, *City of Angels* features songs that were masterfully placed in the movie, perfectly complementing the story of an angel who falls in love with a mortal and ultimately sacrifices his immortality to be with her. It's rare indeed for a soundtrack to serve as a true souvenir of a movie, but listening to this soundtrack does truly evoke the stirring emotion of *City of Angels.* Even though there are very few previously unreleased tracks on the album, and a bit more of Gabriel Yared's gorgeous orchestral score would have been desirable, this soundtrack album receives the highest of ratings for its distinction of being the real deal, a bona fide soundtrack.

Amy Rosen

City of Joy

1992, Epic Soundtrax, from the film *City of Joy,* TriStar Pictures, 1992 ♪♪♪♪

album notes: Music: Ennio Morricone; **Orchestra:** The Unione musicisti di Roma; **Conductor:** Ennio Morricone; **Featured Musicians:** Laura Pontecorvo, recorder; Paolo Zampini, flutes; Stefano Novelli, piccolo clarinet; Felice and Raffaele Clemente, Pan pipes; Amedeo Tommasi, Gianluca Podio, synthesizers; **Orchestra:** The London Studio Orchestra; **Choir:** The Stephen Hills Singers; **Conductor:** Ennio Morricone; **Featured Musicians:** Mike Taylor, Indian flute; Levine Andrade, viola; Sirish Manji, tabla; Manti Aswin, tampura; Chandra Ramesh, sitar; Erwin Keiles, scinai; Glen Keiles, Richard Blackford, synthesizers.

In a style not unlike the one that served him so well for *The Mission,* Ennio Morricone conceived for *City of Joy* a score that exudes vibrancy and excitement, with an impressive array of musicians and vocalists lending their help. The film, about an American doctor in Calcutta and the struggle he wages against local thugs trying to control the slums, motivated Morricone to write a deeply emotive and lyrical score, in which the Indian instruments often play a dominant role. It is a very stylized, attractive effort with many qualitative themes that paint vivid, colorful pictures.

Didier C. Deutsch

City Slickers

🎬 1991, Varèse Sarabande, from the film *City Slickers*, Castle Rock Entertainment, 1991 ♫♫♫♫

album notes: Music: Marc Shaiman; **Conductor:** Hummie Mann, Mark McKenzie.

With *City Slickers*, and its sequel *The Legend of Curly's Gold*, Marc Shaiman wrote a music that takes its inspiration in the western genre, while gently poking fun at it, in much the same way Elmer Bernstein devised his score for *The Hallelujah Trail*, which *City Slickers* sometimes evokes. The rambunctious, rollicking adventures of three urban cowboy wannabes on a two-week vacation at a dude ranch, driving cattle across the west under the guidance of a surly cowboy named Curly (Jack Palance), the first film became a festive occasion to oppose two totally different lifestyles, with many humorous situations evolving from the confrontation. Shaiman's score, taking a cue from the script, keeps its musical tongue firmly in cheek and makes several amusing turns that will delight fans of film music as well as first listeners. A performance of the classic song "Young At Heart," by Jimmy Durante, seems oddly out of place in the context.

Didier C. Deutsch

City Slickers II: The Legend of Curly's Gold

🎬 1994, Chaos Records, from the film *City Slickers II: The Legend of Curly's Gold*, 1994 ♫♫♫♫

album notes: Music: Marc Shaiman; **Conductor:** Artie Kane.

The Legend of Curly's Gold finds the three city slickers (Billy Crystal, Daniel Stern, and Bruno Kirby) back in the west, looking for a treasure their late trail boss might have hidden somewhere. Helping along in the search is Curly's brother (also played by Palance). The film may tread over familiar grounds, but once again the moods are kept lightweight and entertaining, with Shaiman's score, much more expansive in this longer-playing recording, revisiting his previous effort, and adding several new themes for another enjoyable musical romp.

Didier C. Deutsch

The Civil War

🎬 1999, Atlantic Records, from the Broadway musical *The Civil War*, 1999 ♫♫♫♫

album notes: Music: Frank Wildhorn; **Lyrics:** Frank Wildhorn, Gregory Boyd, Jack Murphy; **Conductor:** Kim Scharnberg.

The newest musical by Frank Wildhorn to reach Broadway, *The Civil War* is a show that purports to survey four years of devastating fratricidal struggles and destruction in songs that seem to have little connection with the subject matter. This two-CD set, recorded prior to the Broadway premiere by an all-star cast, presents most of the songs heard on stage, in studio performances by Patti LaBelle, Dr. John and Dr. Maya Angelou, Hootie and the Blowfish, and Bebe Winans, to only name a few. There is no denying the fact that Wildhorn has a knack for writing songs in a pop vein that are quite enjoyable and attractive. Such is the case here: the recording counts, at least a dozen songs that are real standouts as pop songs, and that could be the envy of many modern day songwriters; easy on the ear and sporting catchy musical lines, they are for the most part very exciting to hear. But how they stand as songs for a Broadway musical show is another matter altogether. Whereas Wildhorn's previous efforts (*Jekyll & Hyde, The Scarlet Pimpernel*) remained truer to the spirit of the Broadway musical formula, the songs from *The Civil War* no longer make any such attempt: while the show is definitely set in its own time frame, the songs are firmly rooted in the contemporary mold, which may seem a bit jarring to some. Meanwhile, this two-CD set, not coincidentally recorded in Nashville, the hub of country music, will acquaint you with Wildhorn's latest creations, in glossy versions that transcend what the show is all about.

Didier C. Deutsch

The Civil War

📺 1990, Elektra Records, from the PBS–TV series *The Civil War*, 1990 ♫♫♫♫

album notes: Music Research and Coordination: Jesse Carr; **Featured Artists:** The Old Bethpage Brass Band, Dr. Kirby Jolly, director; **Performers:** The Abyssinian Baptist Church Sanctuary Choir, Dr. Jewel T. Thompson, director; The New American Brass Band, Robert Sheldon, director.

An effective selection of traditional period music, authentically recreated to underscore Ken Burns's monumental documentary on the "War Between the States." No original underscore is featured here as the selected cues do a fine job capturing the era. Each track has its own unique presentation, "The Battle Cry of Freedom" is played by solo piano while "We Are Climbing Jacob's Ladder" is sung a cappella, "Angel Band" is performed by a duo of acoustic guitar players and "Dixie" marches to an old fashioned brass band. The album stands well on its own as an artifact to a bygone era, mixing many well known songs with the more esoteric, which do well to educate what was once considered the popular music of it day.

David Hirsch

The Clan of the Cave Bear

🎬 1986, Varèse Sarabande, from the film *The Clan of the Cave Bear*, Warner Bros., 1986 ♫♫♫

album notes: Music: Alan Silvestri.

Like Raquel Welch before her, Daryl Hannah is an eye-popping prehistoric siren in *The Clan of the Cave Bear,* but very little else in this unimaginative adaptation of Jean Auel's novel matched her physical charms or the rugged beauty of the Canadian scenery. One exception however is Alan Silvestri's compelling score, a deft blend of orchestral and synthesized sounds, some devised to resemble the grunts that passed for language at that remote time, others to evoke moods and feelings in a society with minimal forms of expression. Not every track works in the context, and while some ("Ayla Alone") are particularly effective, others ("The Glacier Trek") sound repetitive and dry. But one might excuse the flaws in this score, as the overall impression it leaves is positive.

Didier C. Deutsch

Clash of the Titans

1997, P.E.G., from the MGM film *Clash of the Titans,* 1981 ♪♪♪♪♪

album notes: Music: Laurence Rosenthal; Conductor: Laurence Rosenthal.

This was one of those scores fans were clamoring for long before it was released on CD. Laurence Rosenthal wrote a wonderful orchestral score, complete with one of the most infectious themes ever composed for the screen. In this fantasy film, Harry Hamlin portrayed Perseus, the son of Zeus (Laurence Olivier). Perseus follows his destiny, which leads him to fall in love with a princess who's supposed to marry the son of Hera. Perseus tames Pegasus, fights the Kraken and Medusa, and is aided by his golden owl sidekick, Bubo. Rosenthal's score is absolutely brilliant, capturing the feel of the epic elements, the more lighthearted moments, and the tender moods of the love story as well. He reintroduces themes well throughout both the film and the recording, creating the effect of a continuum — with a clear beginning, middle, and end. A note about the packaging of the CD: there is an error in the track numbers in the artwork. Although it's not the expanded CD fans had hoped it to be, it's still a great score.

Beth Krakower

Class Action

1991, Varèse Sarabande, from the film *Class Action,* 20th Century Fox, 1991 ♪♪♪♪
album notes: Music: James Horner.

A taut courtroom drama opposing a veteran lawyer against his own daughter in a class action suit, *Class Action* was an ideal vehicle for Gene Hackman and Mary Elizabeth Mastrantonio, both stimulatingly effective in a face-to-face confrontation that pulled no punches but wound up sounding realistic and emo-

They Know the Score

Alan Silvestri

There was a real interesting level of responsibility I started to feel about [*Forrest Gump*]. I felt that [director] Bob [Zemeckis], and the actors, Tom Hanks and Gary Sinise and everybody, Arty Schmidt the editor, and Joanna [Johnson, costume designer], and everybody . . . we've made a lot of movies together, and every one seemed to just take this leap. I felt like the last runner on a relay team, and the first four runners all broke the world's record. And here's this guy running up to you with the baton in his hand saying, 'Here Al, you're up! Go!' I felt this really interesting kind of responsibility because of the effort they had made, and not a small amount of fear as a result of it. It was interesting to feel that level of commitment in myself. The music came out terribly easy, but living with the pressure was different.

***Courtesy of* Film Score Monthly**

tionally charged. In a very uncharacteristic, low-key style, James Horner wrote a series of cues that subtly underlined the action while avoiding to call too much attention to them. Taken on their own musical merits, however, they emerge as attractive pieces of music, beautifully realized and captivating. A piano solo performance of the old chestnut "The More I See You," by Ralph Grierson, adds the right poetic touch to the score itself.

Didier C. Deutsch

Clear and Present Danger

1994, Milan Records, from the film *Clear and Present Danger,* Paramount Pictures, 1994 ♪♪♪
album notes: Music: James Horner; Conductor: James Horner.

Except for the occasional use of South American flutes to suggest the Colombian scenes, *Clear and Present Danger* is rooted in dramatic Americana. Opening with a heraldic trumpet fanfare, a graceful melody for strings over low brass tones creates an elegant, dignified feel. The feeling doesn't last long, though, as most of the score consists of suspense and action motifs. There are plenty of rhythmic, surging cues for brass and percussion, some vaguely pretty but more often furtive violin melodies, dissimulated by dark, brooding string chords, plenty of suspenseful woodwinds and percussion figures, and some neat textural synth-percussion effects. Horner develops the score's minor two-note motif from minimalist winds and drums to a fever pitch of frenzied swirling strings, pounding drums, eerily rising brasses, and scattering piano notes. It's a good score, its listenability, reduced somewhat due to an overabundance of the action/suspense motifs, but on the whole it is effectively presented and well orchestrated.

Randall D. Larson

Clerks

1994, Chaos/Columbia Records, from the film *Clerks,* Miramax Films, 1994 🎬🎬🎬

Life in a convenience store, and the odd assortment of people it seems to attract on a regular basis, *Clerks,* an independent black-and-white film that made a splash at the Sundance Festival, has its moments of humor and pathos, but amounts to little else than a splash-dash effort of unconnected scenes, all aiming to chronicle the problems faced on his first day by a new clerk, Dante. Punctuating the action, and giving it an extra dimension, is the soundtrack, a collection of grunge songs by such groups as Girls Against Boys, Alice In Chains, Supernova, Love Among Freaks, and others. Bits of dialogue (some actually quite funny) are interspersed from time to time, the better to situate the songs in the development of the action.

Didier C. Deutsch

The Client

1994, Elektra Records, from the film *The Client,* Warner Bros., 1994 🎬🎬🎬

album notes: Music: Howard Shore; **Conductor:** Howard Shore; **Featured Musicians:** Steve Jordan, Danny Kotchmar, Michael Lang, Rim May, Simon Franglen.

A fairly intense dramatic score by Howard Shore for the 1994 adaptation of John Grisham's best-seller. The album is extremely dark in its overall tone, taking seriously the concept of its central figure, a child whose life is in jeopardy from the Mob. In the use of a "Southern Twang" motif to reinforce the setting ("Reggie's Theme"), the apprehension is extremely prevalent, and even at the end, when the good guys win, Shore doesn't let us off too easily.

David Hirsch

Cliffhanger

1993, Scotti Bros., from the film *Cliffhanger,* Tri-Star Pictures, 1993 🎬🎬

album notes: Music: Trevor Jones; **Orchestra:** The London Philharmonic Orchestra; **Conductor:** David Snell.

This Trevor Jones score opens well with the unabashedly romantic "Cliffhanger Theme." Never before has dangling over a sheer drop seemed so adventurous. At that moment, you really think you're about to hear a sweeping score. Wrong. From that point on, everything slows down to a crawl and whatever momentum the main theme has generated is quickly lost. The album plods through the next five tracks before showing some signs of life on "Tolerated Help." Most of the album's gusto seems to have been saved for the final five or six tracks, particularly the seven and a half minute "End Credits."

David Hirsch

Clockers

1995, Columbia Records, from the film *Clockers,* Universal Pictures, 1995 🎬🎬🎬

album notes: Music: Terence Blanchard; **Featured Musicians:** Terence Blanchard, trumpet; Edward Simon, piano; Troy Davis, percussion; **Conductor:** Terence Blanchard.

Terence Blanchard's music to this Spike Lee "joint" is the last thing you'd expect for a gritty urban crime procedural—a heartfelt, richly emotional orchestral score that's almost suggestive of Aaron Copland in its opening moments of plaintive woodwind playing. Relentlessly downbeat, with a steady, deliberate rhythmic tread that suggests the inevitability of the film's tragic storyline, the score has some of the same emotional directness and sense of anguish that made Howard Shore's *Silence of the Lambs* so effective. There are some very low key suggestions of a blues sensibility at work in the score, but for most of this album Blanchard just works away at an ebbing, regretful melody with his small group of strings, piano, and woodwinds.

Jeff Bond

1995, MCA Records, from the film *Clockers,* Universal Pictures, 1995 🎬🎬🎬

Bringing a different, streetwise sensibility to the film by Spike Lee, this collection of songs illuminate this tale of an inner-city kid, involved in a crime to which his brother confesses. Marc Dorsey's "People in Search of a Life" serves as an effective introduction to the lineup of songs, with its implied references to the story itself, with Chaka Khan's "Love Me Still," Seal's "Bird of Freedom," and Des'ree's "Silent Hero" among the highlights. "Return of the Crooklyn Dodgers" provides a bridge to another Spike Lee film, and the reggae-like "Bad Boy No Go a Jail," by

Close Encounters of the Third Kind **(Archive Photos, Inc.)**

Mega Banton, is also flavorful, but the other tracks do not provide the same levels of enjoyment.

Didier C. Deutsch

A Clockwork Orange

1972, Warner Bros. Records, from the film *A Clockwork Orange,* Warner Bros., 1971 ♫♫♫♡
album notes: Music: Wendy Carlos, Rachel Elkind.

Composer and early synthesizer player Wendy Carlos (working under the pseudonym Walter Carlos, deemed more acceptable in some music quarters at the time) contributed atmospheric electronic variations to classical selections, plus her own compositions for this extraordinary study by Stanley Kubrick of violence and depravation in British youth. Even though synthesizers have long since become an integral part of many horror films, this chilling score remains one of the most powerfully expressive of its kind and plainly justifies its Academy Award nomination.

Didier C. Deutsch

Close Encounters of the Third Kind

1998, Arista Records, from the Columbia Pictures film *Close Encounters of the Third Kind,* 1977 ♫♫♫♫
album notes: Music: John Williams; **Conductor:** John Williams.

John Williams did the impossible task of topping his score to *Star Wars* with his gorgeous soundtrack for the other classic sci-fi film of the 1970s. If Williams's swashbuckling music for *Star Wars* inspired a young generation's dream of becoming saviors of the universe, then his score for *Close Encounters* captured a more mature wish for the human race. It was on this side of possibility: making contact with an alien race and calling them friends. Indeed, music is the key to this, and the five-note theme in *Close Encounters* might be the most famous motif in film score history—unless you count the four-note theme that the composer wrote for *Jaws,* his previous collaboration with director Steven Spielberg.

Williams's majestic orchestrations for *Close Encounters* represent film music at the magical height of its ability to move audiences. His tender, innocent melodies touch the soul and imagination with any number of simple, yet extraordinarily beautiful themes. His use of a chorus also enhances the god-like quality of the aliens, while his contrasting use of impressionistic and often terrifying music plays the uncertainty of their intentions. Arista's newly expanded release has nearly all of the score, and it has never sounded more powerful. It's too bad that this long-awaited CD couldn't have included one of the score's best touches, an end credit version that used "When You Wish Upon a Star" for the mothership's take-off. But no matter. Listening to Williams's classic score remains a blissful score for the ages.

Dan Schweiger

The Clowns

🎬 1991, CAM Records/Italy, from the film *The Clowns*, Levitt-Pickman, 1970 ♪♪♪
album notes: Music: Nino Rota; **Conductor:** Carlo Savina.

An audio documentary, more so than a score *per se*, Nino Rota's music for Federico Fellini's *The Clowns* combines bits of dialogue, sound effects, crowd reactions and animal farts, with themes the composer borrowed from some of his previous scores, and music heard in circuses around the world. Knowing Fellini's love for the circus (*La Strada* certainly was an early indication of his feelings), it made sense that the director would eventually make a film about the people who espouse that itinerant way of life, and *The Clowns*, a semi-documentary among circus clowns, was as much a description of their existence as it was a vibrant homage to them. Rota matched his musical vision with that of the director, but in this instance discretely let his music play a secondary, though complementary role to the visual portrait Fellini was painting. This makes this CD more unusual than a conventional soundtrack album, but certainly as worthy. This recording may be difficult to find. Check with a used CD store, mail-order company, or a dealer specializing in rare, out-of-print, or import recordings.

Didier C. Deutsch

Clubland

🎬 1999, Capitol Records, from the Legacy film *Clubland*, 1999 ♪♪

There's a disturbingly anonymous feel to the dance music that populates this set, one that's not unlike a novice walking into a club and not being able to get beyond the undistinguished sameness of the individual songs or artists. Zebrahead stands out with "Check," while John Oszaja's "Bi-Sexual Chick" has both humor and sexy energy. Save for the winking wit of Block's album-closing "I Used to Manage PM Dawn," the rest of *Clubland* lurches from one aspiring dance artist to the next, never quite getting into a compelling groove.

Gary Graff

Clueless

🎬 1998, Capitol Records, from the Paramount film *Clueless*, 1998 ♪♪♪

Like, what type of music would you expect on the soundtrack of the *Valley Girl* of the '90s? Classical? As if! This song-driven compilation features a who's who of hit alternative artists, including the Beastie Boys (Ad-Rock is such a Baldwin), Jill Sobule, and a great acoustic version of their hit "The Ghost in You" by Counting Crows. The movie, a teenage treatment of Jane Austen's *Emma*, delightful and right to the point, brought back knee socks, miniskirts, and "Kids in America" (covered by the Muffs). The soundtrack album, very representative of the feel of the movie, is fun if you are a fan of alternative music.

Beth Krakower

Cobb

🎬 1994, Sony Classical, from the film *Cobb*, Warner Bros., 1994 ♪♪♪♪
album notes: Music: Elliot Goldenthal; **Conductor:** Jonathan Sheffer; **Featured Musicians:** Phil Smith, trumpet; Billy Drewes, saxophone; Bill Mays, piano; John Beal, bass; Jamie Haddad, drums; Elliot Goldenthal, vocals, piano rags.

Powerful orchestral score by Elliot Goldenthal that weaves Gospel and classical music to create an edgy Americana motif worthy of one of baseball's most volatile figures. The overall mood is oppressive and dark, completely overwhelming, much like Ty Cobb himself. This even holds true for the somewhat romantic "Cooperstown Aria," which never quite seems to climb into the light. Interestingly, the cue "The Beast Within" was tracked in from Goldenthal's own *Alien* score and included on this album, so it's easy to draw parallels between the two scores about the nature of the beast. The composer performs some of the vocals and the piano rags on the album.

David Hirsch

Cocktail

🎬 1988, Elektra Records, from the film *Cocktail*, Touchstone Pictures, 1988 ♪♪♪♪

Cocktail, a *Saturday Night Fever* in a bar, is marked by an exhilarating performance from Tom Cruise, as a handsome young man, fresh from the Army, who takes New York and the hip crowd by storm as an eclectic bartender in a chic, well-appointed room. Contributing a contemporary flavor to the film is its clever assortment of pop songs, featuring performances by frontline artists such as The Beach Boys, John Cougar Mellencamp, Ry Cooder, The Fabulous Thunderbirds, and Starship. On its own terms, the album proves a powerful reminder of the screen action, as well as a pleasantly programmed compilation. Bobby McFerrin's cheery "Don't Worry, Be Happy" is a highlight.

Didier C. Deutsch

Cocoon

1985, Polydor, from the film *Cocoon*, 20th Century Fox, 1985 ♪♪♪♪

album notes: Music: James Horner; **Conductor:** James Horner.

In some of his early scores, James Horner often indulged his love for the big bands. In both *Cocoon* and *Cocoon: The Return,* he included some tracks ("The Boys Are Out," in the former, "Taking Bernie to the Beach" and "Basketball Swing," in the latter) that reflect his fondness for the genre and his particular talent at writing exciting cues in that vein. By far, those are the most engaging moments in both this and the sequel's score. The rest of the time, the music, sometimes grandiloquent, sometimes understated, is confined to reflecting the moods of some senior citizens in a Florida retirement home who become young again after they discover a miraculous spring. A pop vocal by Michael Sembello ("Gravity") proves totally unnecessary and, in fact, breaks the overall unity of the score.

see also: *batteries not included

Didier C. Deutsch

Cocoon: The Return

1988, Varèse Sarabande, from the film *Cocoon: The Return,* 20th Century Fox, 1988 ♪♪♪♪

album notes: Music: James Horner; **Conductor:** James Horner.

Horner again suceeds with the score to this sequel. Both films, in combining the Peter Pan syndrome with pseudo-galactical fantasies, succeeded in tapping into humanity's age-old dream of remaining forever young and healthy. Except for the exuberant numbers, Horner's scores echoed these feelings with great restraint and subtle understatement, achieving in the process a cohesive musical presentation which, in these recordings, comes across quite effectively.

Didier C. Deutsch

Cold Heaven

See: Trusting Beatrice/Cold Heaven

The Collector

1991, Mainstream Records, from the film *The Collector,* Columbia Pictures, 1965 ♪♪♪♪

album notes: Music: Maurice Jarre; **Conductor:** Maurice Jarre,

Leave it to Maurice Jarre to take a chilling film of abduction, and score it 180-degrees different from the psychological thrillers of Hitchcock and Herrmann only a few years earlier. *The Collector* is a 1966 picture directed by the legendary William Wyler, starring Terence Stamp as a nut who kidnaps his true love, an art student played by Samantha Eggar. The bulk of the film is the struggle between captor and captive, but Jarre's score is practically upbeat, featuring a pleasant, if a bit hyperactive waltz that is disturbing due to its sheer obliviousness towards the on-screen action. It's like this little fantasy running through the abductor's head, a serene and infectious tune laced with harpsichord, as if it was "playing house" throughout, or scoring the idyllic setting in a rural English home. The score is nicely listenable on its own, a ballet of sweetness amidst a gripping, tragic tale of an "I'll *make* her love me" wacko gone unchecked.

Lukas Kendall

Color of Night

1994, Mercury Records, from the Hollywood film *Color of Night,* 1994 ♪♪♪♪

album notes: Music: Dominic Frontiere; **Featured Musician:** Jonathan Dane, trumpet.

A thriller about a psychologist who decides to investigate the murder of another therapist, when he suspects that the killer might have been a member of the victim's group therapy, *Color of Night* received a very attractive synthesizer score from composer Dominic Frontiere. The cues (among them, "Color Blind," "Rose's Theme," with an evocative muted trumpet line played by Jonathan Dane, "Etude for Murder," and the title tune) are elaborately constructed, with solid melodic hooks that are catchy and memorable. A couple of vocal tracks featuring Lauren Christy and Lowen & Navarro provide a different sound, but fit neatly within the overall musical concept.

Didier C. Deutsch

The Color Purple

1986 Warner Bros. Records, from the Warner Bros. film *The Color Purple,* 1985 ♪♪♪♪

album notes: Music: Quincy Jones.

It's hardly surprising this soundtrack album sounds so good, given the caliber of the players involved in its production—close to 200 musicians and vocalists, including such heavy-duty studio aces as Ralph Grierson, Greg Phillinganes, and Michael Boddicker on keyboards; Paulinho da Costa and Harvey Mason on percussion; Snooky Young and Oscar Brashear on trumpet; George Bohanon on trombone; Hubert Laws on flute; Jerome Richardson on saxophone, Paul Jackson on guitars; Ernie Watts on recorder; the list is endless. But when Quincy Jones calls you in, you answer, knowing it will be for something quite exceptional.

Exceptional, indeed, is the key word here. This soundtrack for the film directed by Steven Spielberg, spread over two CDs, is just plain gorgeous: the melodies are strong and ear-catching, the music is rich and diversified, and even if it didn't evoke the film itself, it would stand out as one of the great scores written for the screen. More than 14 years after it was recorded, it still sounds fresh and exciting. If you really care about film music, you owe it to yourself to own this recording.

Didier C. Deutsch

Coma

🎬🎵1990, Bay Cities Records, from the film *Coma*, MGM, 1978 ♪♪♪

album notes: Music: Jerry Goldsmith; **Conductor:** Jerry Goldsmith.

A superior thriller score that blends the Goldsmith trademarks of staccato piano playing and unnerving string effects with an eerie, dangling metallic clang that foreshadows the film's set piece of a roomful of comatose living organ donors hanging from the ceiling. Michael Crichton's film had no music at all until it was halfway over, so without a piece of title music the album is a jumble of non-chronological cues and some regrettable source pieces from the disco era. But the score's highlights are well worth searching for, from the Bartok-influenced creepiness and fluttering, unsettling piano runs of "The Jefferson Institute" to the clanking, malevolent "O.R. 8" and the climactic, heart-pounding piano chase, "A Lucky Patient," this is a textbook example of Goldsmith's command of the genre.

Jeff Bond

The Comancheros/True Grit

🎬🎵1985, Varèse Sarabande, from the films *The Comancheros*, 20th Century Fox, 1961, and *True Grit*, Paramount Pictures, 1969 ♪♪♪♪♪

album notes: Music: Elmer Bernstien; **Orchestra:** The Utah Symphony Orchestra; **Conductor:** Elmer Bernstein; **Featured Soloists:** Edmund Cord, trumpet; Leonard Braus, violin.

Through their many contributions in the genre, some composers defined the western score and gave its most recognizable musical expressions (one would almost be tempted to say "cliches"), but none as eloquently and exhilaratingly as Elmer Bernstein. Whether writing for a serious film (*The Magnificent Seven*, of course, but also *The Comancheros* or *True Grit*, both represented here), or spoofing himself (as he did so effectively in *The Hallelujah Trail*), Bernstein never lost sight of what made his western movie music so characteristic. It always was, in a

nutshell, as it should always sound—bold, spacious, and spectacular. Between the pulse-racing motifs suggesting the wide-open spaces, or the Mexican-tinged accents descriptive of south of the border action, his music is always thrilling, colorful, exciting. These two scores are fine examples of his approach to the genre, and both evidence the very qualities that make his music so uniquely lively. This is the first time *The Comancheros* is available in an album, and while there is an original soundtrack album to *True Grit* (q.v.), this re-recording is far superior to it sonically and introduces several cues not found elsewhere. The Utah Symphony, conducted by the composer, plays these scores with the right amount of dynamism and gusto.

see also: The Shootist

Didier C. Deutsch

Come See the Paradise

🎬🎵1990, Varèse Sarabande, from the film *Come See the Paradise*, 20th Century Fox, 1990 ♪♪♪

album notes: Music: Randy Edelman; **Conductor:** Randy Edelman.

This charming, emotionally moving score by Randy Edelman suffers greatly on CD from poor sequencing. Period songs, most sung in Japanese (and one with record surface noise!), frequently break in between the cues. They were probably inserted in this fashion because the actual underscore cues take up very little total time. The music, a blend of electronics and acoustics, would have probably flowed better had the underscore been edited into a suite. Alex and Jake Parker wrote three tracks. Edelman's dramatically charged "Fire in a Brooklyn Theatre" is used frequently in film trailers.

David Hirsch

The Commitments/The Commitments, Vol. 2

🎬🎵1991/1992, MCA Records, from the film *The Commitments*, 20th Century Fox, 1991 ♪♪♪♪

album notes: Featured Musicians: Conor Brady, guitar; Fran Beehan, drums; Paul Bushnell, bass; Ronan Dooney, trumpet; Eamann Flynn, keyboards; Carl Geraghty, tenor/baritone sax; Felim Gormley, alto sax; Alex Acuna, percussion; Mitchell Froome, keyboards; Dean Parks, guitar.

Not the original, but an incredible simulation. This ensemble of Irish musicians is charming in the movie and they play these old rhythm 'n' blues favorites with convincing spirit, and the best vocalists—Maria Doyle and Andrew Strong—often make the Commitments sound even better than a top-shelf bar band. Seven of the songs on "Vol. 2" weren't performed in the film, but it really doesn't matter; like *The Big Chill*, this is feel-good stuff that doubles as terrific party music.

Gary Graff

Company

1997, Sony/Legacy, from the Broadway production *Company*, 1970 🎵🎵🎵🎵🎵

album notes: Music: Stephen Sondheim; **Lyrics:** Stephen Sondheim; **Cast:** Dean Jones, Barbara Barrie, Charles Kinbrough, Merle Louise, John Cunningham, Teri Ralston, George Coe, Beth Elaine Stritch, Charles Braswell, Donna McKechnie, Susan Browning

1996, Angel Records, from the Broadway revival *Company*, 1995 🎵🎵🎵🎵

album notes: Music: Stephen Sondheim; **Lyrics:** Stephen Sondheim; **Cast:** Boyd Gaines, Kate Burton, Robert Westenberg, Patricia Ben Peterson, Jonathan Dokuchitz, Debra Monk.

A seminal work, *Company* opened on April 26, 1970, and was the first in a streak of productions written by Stephen Sondheim and directed by Harold Prince that revolutionized the Broadway musical throughout the decade. Unlike the shows that were created at the time, many of which still relied on the tried-and-true formula that had prevailed until then, the new musical by Sondheim, finally hitting his stride, took a sobering, uncompromising look at contemporary life in a brilliant, unstructured display that had theatrical flair and personality. With the 35th birthday of Robert, the central character and link between the vignettes that made up the book by George Furth, providing the anchor for most of the action, *Company* was a critical study of married life in a big city, with its various couples revealed in their less-than-happy existence, often portrayed as neurotic individuals, fighting, smoking pot, boozing, and desperately clinging to each other, all the while wishing their lives would be different. The score yielded at least one showstopper in "The Ladies Who Lunch," delivered in drunken stupor by Elaine Stritch, but also brimmed with many great musical moments that come strikingly alive in the newly remixed and mastered CD reissue. It includes two bonus tracks performed by Larry Kert, who replaced Dean Jones on Broadway and went on to star in the London production. The winner of seven Tony Awards (including best musical, book, music, lyrics, and direction), *Company* had a run of 706 performances.

The 1995 revival, headed by Boyd Gaines, took a slightly diffident new approach by hinting at Robert's possible underlying homosexuality, and by also offering the suggestion of his involvement in an interracial relationship. The cast, however talented they may have been, could not compete with the incandescent original.

Didier C. Deutsch

Company Business

1991, Intrada Records, from the film *Company Business*, MGM, 1991 🎵🎵

album notes: Music: Michael Kamen; **Conductor:** Michael Kamen.

This is one of those soundtracks which reminds the listener that film music, while it sometimes makes for a listenable recording, is nevertheless not written with that purpose in mind. Michael Kamen is of course an immensely gifted composer, but the programmatic requirements of this spy thriller, for whatever reason, needed music that does not work on a record album. The first track, "Journey to Alexanderplatz" is a surging suspense cue, nicely orchestrated (by Kamen himself). However, removed from the film, it simply meanders on disc (that this track is also 11 minutes long does not increase its allure). The second track, "Faisal's Escape" is similarly meandering, but more subdued and even less interesting (and this track lasts 15 minutes). The only listenable cue is "Cafe Jatte," a jazzy pastiche/source cue for saxophone, piano, and rhythm section, which unfortunately segues into more meandering suspense music after three minutes. The sax theme returns however in the closing track, "The Island." The score for *Company Business* is not bad. It is just programmatic to the extent that there is no shape, architecture or melody for the listener to grab hold of. As such, listening to this CD is ultimately a maddening experience.

Paul Andrew MacLean

Con Air

1997, Hollywood Records, from the film *Con Air*, Touchstone Pictures, 1997 🎵

album notes: Music: Mark Mancina, Trevor Rabin; **Conductor:** Gordon Goodwin, Nick Glennie-Smith; **Featured Musician:** Lou Molino III, drums.

An action-driven score, it took not one but two composers to come up with this electronic-cum-orchestra mishmash which probably makes a lot of appropriate noises in connection with the various scenes on screen, but elicits a yawn otherwise. Making a prominent place for the drumming of Lou Molino III, who carries the majority of the tunes, the selections unfold one after the other, sounding exactly alike, with soft moments leading to big surges that mean very little, at least in musical terms. In the mush, one track, "Trisha," actually comes out for a hot minute as being genuinely attractive.

Didier C. Deutsch

Conan

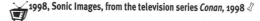 **1998, Sonic Images, from the television series *Conan*, 1998** 🎵

album notes: Music: Charles Fox; **Conductor:** Charles Fox.

Like the muscular no-name actor who strikes an imposing posture à la Arnold Schwarzenegger on the cover of this CD but can't erase the memory of the beefy Mr. S in the two films in which he starred, Charles Fox, who composed the music for the TV series, cannot compare with Basil Poledouris who scored the films. If you have any doubt about it, listen to the cue titled "Atlantean Sword" in *Conan the Barbarian,* and then to "The Sword of Atlantis" in this CD. The difference is like night and day! Poledouris's themes were written in a style that recalled the swashbucklers of old, something that completely eludes Charles Fox. In contrast, his cues, heavy on the synthesizer, with a preponderance of percussive effects to give them more importance, sound solemn, uninviting, and totally superfluous. Even the use of disembodied voices to punctuate some riffs seems a total waste of time, as the voices do little to elevate the cues from the morass in which they appear. Terry Reid (bless him!) provides two vocals of the same song, "In Love and War," that seem to belong to another recording. Go back to "The Anvil of Crom," instead.

Didier C. Deutsch

Conan the Barbarian

1989, Varèse Sarabande, from the film *Conan the Barbarian,* Universal Pictures, 1982 ♪♪♪♪♪

album notes: Music: Basil Poledouris; **Text:** Basil Poledouris; **Text Translation:** Beth Lawson, Teresa Cortey; **Orchestra and Choir:** Orchestra and Chorus of Santa Cecila and the Radio Symphony of Rome; **Conductor:** Basil Poledouris.

Basil Poledouris's music for the two Conan movies, a poetic tribute to the romantic notions of Robert E. Howard's pulp fiction tales set in a bloody, uncivilized age, established him as a premier composer for epic action films. During the opening 20 minutes of the first film, director John Milius kept dialogue to a minimum, using Poledouris's music to literally tell the story of Conan's early life (tracks one through four on the CD). All of the cues are not epic, however, and some, like "Wifeing," provide a counterpoint to the bombast with remarkable gentleness. Various choral verses, drawn from Latin and Gregorian chants, are also interpolated to great effect to reflect the religious fervor of villain Thulsa Doom's dreaded Snake Cult.

David Hirsch

Conan the Destroyer

1989, Varèse Sarabande, from the film *Conan the Destroyer,* Universal Pictures, 1984 ♪♪♪

album notes: Music: Basil Poledouris; **Orchestra:** The Unione Musicisti di Roma Orchestra; **Conductor:** Basil Poledouris.

In comparison to the first score, the music for the second film pales because of the paltry budget that was set aside for the creation of its score. Saddled with an orchestra that was just a shadow of the powerhouse he had on the first film, Poledouris wrote a score that works best in its softer moments, the action

cues suffering from a notable lack of percussion. Still, this album has a lot of fine music to offer (i.e. "The Horn of Dagoth"), but it simply cannot compete with its predecessor's intensity.

David Hirsch

Coneheads

1993, Warner Bros. Records, from the film *Coneheads,* Paramount Pictures, 1993 ♪♪♪

This one's aimed hard at the modern rock market, with new offerings from the Red Hot Chili Peppers ("Soul to Squeeze," a hit) and R.E.M. ("It's a Free World Baby," a dud). Remakes are the order of the day on the rest of the album, including hilarious takes on "Fight the Power" by Barenaked Ladies and a show-stopping duet on "No More Tears (Enough is Enough)" by k.d. lang and Erasure's Andy Bell. The latter is as much fun as a potent cone ring.

Gary Graff

The Conformist/A Man's Tragedy

1995, DRG Records, from the film *The Conformist,* 1971, and *A Man's Tragedy,* 1981 ♪♪♪

album notes: Music: Georges Delerue, Ennio Morricone; **Conductor:** Georges Delerue, Ennio Morricone.

One of the most brilliant directors of his generation, Bernardo Bertolucci attempted to establish in his films a parallel between the psychological and personal concerns of his characters, and the broader political and social backdrop which framed their stories in a curious and fascinating amalgam of ideas that would have pleased Karl Marx and Sigmund Freud. This was never more pointed than in two of the films that firmly established his reputation—*The Conformist* and *A Man's Tragedy.* Set in the years before and during World War II, the former, starring French actor Jean-Louis Trintignant, involved a member of the Italian Fascist secret service on a mission to Paris to kill one of his former teachers, a virulent critic of Mussolini; the latter detailed the personal tragedy faced by the owner of a cheese factory, played by Ugo Tognazzi, whose son has been kidnapped and is being held for ransom. In both cases, Georges Delerue and Ennio Morricone devised scores that have withstood the test of time, the first by writing a series of impressionistic cues that act as a subtle counterpoint to the screen action, the second by characteristically composing variations on a central theme in which the accordion figured prominently. While this montage of two widely different scores on the same CD may seem odd at first, they provide a vivid memento of two films that were equally important in the Bertolucci *oeu-*

Arnold Schwarzenegger in Conan the Barbarian. (The Kobal Collection)

vre, while helping to accentuate the director's own appreciation of music and the role it played in his films.

Didier C. Deutsch

Congo

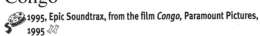

1995, Epic Soundtrax, from the film *Congo,* Paramount Pictures, 1995 🎬🎬

album notes: Music: Jerry Goldsmith; **Conductor:** Jerry Goldsmith.

Give Jerry Goldsmith a creative challenge and he can usually create something better than any film as silly as this ever deserved. The score's strength comes from "Spirit of Africa," a beautiful theme song co-written by Goldsmith with singer/songwriter Lebo M, that's sung first in an African dialect, then later in English. This is the high point of the album and, unfortunately, the film doesn't inspire much else. Goldsmith interjects various African rhythms throughout, but uses his standard electronic jiggery-pokery to spice up the rather ordinary action cues. Adding to the irritation, the correct order of the CD tracks can only be found on the disc itself, not on the packaging!

David Hirsch

Consenting Adults

1992, Milan/BMG, from the Hollywood film *Consenting Adults,* 1992 🎬🎬

album notes: Music: Michael Small; **Conductor:** Michael Small.

Life in the suburbs gets a new twist in this suspense film that also involves such pastime activities as wife-swapping leading to murder and an innocent man being accused of it. Adding an eerie tone to these screen high-jinks, Michael Small developed a score that sounds at times ominous and bleak. Two vocals by Q. Rose strike a different note, but the overall moods of this score album are particularly somber. Definitely not the kind of album you want to listen to when you already have the blahs.

Didier C. Deutsch

Conspiracy Theory

1997, TVT Records, from the Warner Bros film *Conspiracy Theory,* 1997 🎬🎬🎬

album notes: Music: Carter Burwell; **Conductor:** Carter Burwell.

Mel Gibson portrayed a paranoid character convinced that the greater powers-that-be are out to conspire against the general public in this mildly amusing but severely unfocused thriller that never quite knew what kind of film it was supposed to be. Punctuating the wacky action with verve and imagination, the score by Carter Burwell made the various scenes a great deal

more lively than they would have been. The cues contained here give a measure of what the score managed to do, with some excellent moments, like "Turning into a Jerry," notably standing out.

Didier C. Deutsch

Contact

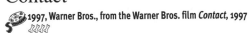

1997, Warner Bros., from the Warner Bros. film *Contact,* 1997 🎬🎬🎬🎬

album notes: Music: Alan Silvestri; **Conductor:** Alan Silvestri.

After their Oscar-nominated work on *Forrest Gump,* the composer-director team of Alan Silvestri and Robert Zemekis continued their move into dramatic territory with this New Age updating of *Close Encounters.* In his novel *Contact,* the late Carl Sagan used the search for alien life as a metaphoric voyage for his astronomer heroine (played in the film by Jodie Foster) to get in touch with her inner child. Silvestri's music reflects this dramatic center, the tender quality of his *Gump* score reprising itself here. Silvestri's score displays a sense of wonder, while also revealing the psychological wounds that drive Foster to touch the stars. While the main themes of *Contact* are a bit repetitive during the course of this CD, Silvestri thankfully keeps the emotions subtle, his lush music going for the heart instead of the handkerchiefs. The score's science fiction qualities come out in its synthesizers, their unique sound ranging between the eerie and the profound. Particularly good is the music leading up to Foster's launch into the unknown, a tense countdown of electronic percussion and orchestral swells. Overall, Silvestri's work on this film represents another major leap for the composer into the dimension of "adult" music, one at which he's quite adept.

Dan Schweiger

Cookie

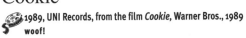

1989, UNI Records, from the film *Cookie,* Warner Bros., 1989 woof!

album notes: Music: Thomas Newman.

Unless you listen attentively or you read the fine print on the label copy, you probably wouldn't guess that Thomas Newman wrote the score for this dispensable comedy about a mafia boss, back home after some years spent behind bars, and the independent teenage daughter with whom he must now contend. The people lending their talents to this soundtrack album probably deserve better; so did Newman, represented here by the "Cookie Theme"; so do you.

Didier C. Deutsch

Cookie's Fortune

1999, Windham Hill Records, from the October film *Cookie's Fortune*, 1999 🎬🎬🎬🎬

album notes: Music: David A. Stewart; **Featured Musicians:** David A. Stewart, guitars, dubro, bass; Steve McLaughlin, programming, vocal sampling; Pat Seymour, harmonium; Kenny Dickenson, harmonium; Reece Gilmore, drums, programming; Caroline Dale, cello; Candy Dulfer, saxophone.

Weaving together musical performances with dialogue samples from this Robert Altman film, former Eurythmic Dave Stewart creates a textured sonic collage that's as peaceful and flowing as the bayou waters depicted in the movie. Stewart's chief foil is saxophonist Candy Dulfer, with whom he worked on the 1992 theme for the Dutch film *Lily Was Here,* which was an international hit. Here they catch fire on pieces such as "Cookie" and the impressionistic "Camilla's Prayer," with Dulfer honking soulfully over the twangy ambiance of Stewart's guitar and dobro. U2's Bono slips some subtle background vocals into the warped blues of "A Good Man," while his bandmate the Edge intertwines his biting guitar licks with Dulfer's sax on "Patrol Car Blues." And actress Ruby Wilson's "I'm Comin' Home" is a late-night juke joint classic, so dusty and moody it should only be played during the final five minutes before sunrise.

Gary Graff

Cool Hand Luke

1996, MCA Records/Japan, from the film *Cool Hand Luke*, Warner Bros., 1967 🎬🎬🎬🎬

album notes: Music: Lalo Schifrin; **Conductor:** Lalo Schifrin.

In one of his better screen roles, Paul Newman portrays in *Cool Hand Luke* a convicted felon doing time on a chain gang in a Southern prison, a loner ("What we have here is a failure to communicate") whose only salvation comes when he is gunned down by prison guards after he tries to escape. As memorable as Newman's tour de force portrayal is Lalo Schifrin's biting Academy Award–nominated score, in which the use of various solo instruments (notably the harmonica and the banjo) adds a distinctive Southern rural touch. Schifrin's signature staccato orchestral outbursts permeate some of the most powerful moments in the score (particularly the "Tar Sequence," which New Yorkers should recognize as the theme used by a local news station, and "The Chase"), while the tense moods are occasionally relieved by lighter tracks like "Egg-Beating Contest" or the lilting "Ballad of Cool Hand Luke." This CD, released in Japan only, can be found in specialty stores.

Didier C. Deutsch

Cool World

1992, Varèse Sarabande, from the film *Cool World,* Paramount Pictures, 1992 🎬🎬🎬🎬

album notes: Music: Mark Isham; **Orchestra:** The Munich Symphony Orchestra; **Conductor:** Allan Wilson; **Featured Musicians:** Terry Bozzio, drums; Nigel Hitchcock, saxophone; Dave Hartley, piano; Greg Knowles, percussion; Claus Reishatallen, trumpet; Mark Isham, trumpet; Rick Keller, saxophone; Roy Babbington, double bass; Felici Civitareale, lead trumpet.

This is one of those instances where the soundtrack is far more interesting than the film for which it was composed. Mark Isham here gets the chance at writing a score that's right up his alley—an eclectic mixture of swinging big band, jazz, techno, and orchestral passages that zips right along for nearly the entire duration of the album. A small jazz ensemble, including Isham on the trumpet, leads the way through the score's liveliest passages, like "The Cool World Stomp," while the composer also includes a lush love theme for saxophone and orchestra to go along with the fast-tempo of the majority of the score. Simply put, there is something here to please both traditional soundtrack listeners and fans of Isham's solo albums, even though many tracks were either buried under sound effects or entirely taken out of the movie itself (and are designated as such here). Regardless, this is an energetic, often dynamic effort that functions perfectly as an album.

Andy Dursin

1992, Warner Bros. Records, from the Paramount film *Cool World,* 1992 🎬🎬🎬

Cool World was such a . . . well, cool film, mixing as it did realistic animation with live action, that anything that evokes it is bound to be welcome. To wit, this compilation album that features a lot of great songs, some heard only in bits and pieces in the film, others merely "inspired" by it, a device that may be reprehensible in many cases, but that passes muster here. The Ralph Bashki animated feature, which starred Kim Basinger as a lusty cartoon *femme fatale* even Tex Avery wouldn't have disowned, was by no means intended for kids, so this soundtrack album, loaded with hard rocking numbers, will please all young adults who identified with the film in the first place. And how can you go wrong when the selections include performances by David Bowie, Thompson Twins, the Cult, and Brian Eno, among the best moments?

Didier C. Deutsch

Copycat

1995, Milan Records, from the film *Copycat,* Warner Bros., 1995 🎬🎬🎬🎬

album notes: Music: Christopher Young; **Conductor:** Thomas Milano; **Featured Soloist:** Gary Nesteruk, piano.

Playing against the film's storyline, Chris Young's symphonic score paints a dark psychological portrait of the serial murderer who copies infamous crimes of past serial killers. Offsetting this evil poignancy is Young's deliciously frightening suspense and terror music. In one outstanding cue after another, he keeps reminding us that the terror is still there, even if off screen. "Pastoral Horror" is a prime example of the music's duality, alternately horrifying and elegant, yet thoroughly captivating. "Lay Me Down," which concludes the score with a graceful dynamic, has slowly swaying violins over a writhing sea of rustling strings in a powerful resolve to the music that's gone before. The cue—melodic yet ambient, compelling yet frightening—is penetrating, and recalls previous horrors while acknowledging the price of survival.

Randall D. Larson

Corrina, Corrina

1994, RCA Records, from the film *Corrina, Corrina,* New Line Cinema, 1994 ♪♪♪♪

album notes: Music: Thomas Newman

An interracial love affair between a black housekeeper and her white employer, father of a motherless little girl, is the interesting premise of this enjoyable comedy, which yielded this equally delightful soundtrack compilation. The 1950s setting of the film pretty much dictated what the music would be, with songs from the period performed by Sarah Vaughan, Dinah Washington, Billie Holiday, and Louis Armstrong and Oscar Peterson forming the core of this compilation. New songs, also in the style of the era, complement the soundtrack album, with the title tune, a jaunty little tune, making a particularly favorable impression in Big Joe Turner's rendition. Thomas Newman's single incidental music cue, "Home Movies," would suggest that he wrote more in this vein, though it never made it to the album.

Didier C. Deutsch

The Cotton Club

1984, Geffen Records, from the film *The Cotton Club,* Orion Picture, 1984 ♪♪♪♪

album notes: Music: John Barry; **Music Re-creation:** Bob Wilber; **Conductor:** John Barry; **Featured Musicians:** Dave Brown, Marky Markowitz, Randy Sandke, Lew Soloff, trumpet; Bob Wilber, Lawrence Feldman, Joe Temperley, Frank Wess, Chuck Wilson, reeds; Dan Barrett, Joel Helleny, Britt Woodman, trombone; John Goldsby, bass; Mike Peters, guitar, banjo; Chuck Riggs, drums; Mark Shane, piano.

Music by Duke Ellington, and acceptable facsimiles by John Barry, make up this rousing soundtrack to a gangster movie set in Harlem in the 1930s. The big band recreations, in full digital sound, are tremendously exciting, and played to the hilt by a group of seasoned musicians for whom this kind of music no longer has any secret. An occasional vocal sparks the proceedings, with film star Gregory Hines contributing an excellent version of the classic "Copper Colored Gal." The cues by John Barry fit nicely within this program of standards, and add an element of originality to the soundtrack.

Didier C. Deutsch

Courage Under Fire

1996, Angel Records, from the film *Courage Under Fire,* 20th Century Fox, 1996 ♪♪♪

album notes: Music: James Horner; **Conductor:** James Horner.

When you're presented with track titles like "Hymn" and "The Elegy" on a soundtrack album for a film that isn't a biblical drama, you can't help but wonder if somebody isn't taking things a little too seriously. James Horner's *Courage Under Fire* score has a tendency to drown the listener in its good intentions, canonizing the fictional character Meg Ryan plays in the film, when the point of the narrative is that Ryan's character is all too human, neither superhero, coward or saint. The score is most convincing when it deals with the adrenaline-charged rhythms of the battlefield, from an ascending two-note motif in low brass (similar to an effect often employed by composer Jerry Goldsmith in scores like *Capricorn One*) to some fierce orchestral heroics that presage some of the exciting effects Horner achieved in his *Apollo 13* score. The above-mentioned "Hymn" and "Elegy" offer some moving, lyrical melodies that function quite beautifully on their own but pad out the album's lengthy denouement unmercifully.

Jeff Bond

The Court Jester

See: Hans Christian Andersen/The Court Jester

Cousin Bette

1998, RCA Victor, from the Fox Searchlight film *Cousin Bette,* 1998 ♪♪♪♪

album notes: Music: Simon Boswell; **Conductor:** Terry Davies.

A big screen adaptation of Balzac's novel, *Cousin Bette* starred Jessica Lange as the poor relative of an aristocratic family, who seeks to avenge the injustices she has been forced to endure from her arrogant relatives. Set in Paris in 1846, at the time when political life was in turmoil, the period drama enabled Elisabeth Shue, as a music hall star, to perform several spirited songs, which are the highlights of this soundtrack album. The lush score written by Simon Boswell for the film is replete with attractive themes, some adapted from Pierre de Beranger, which sound appropriately authentic and in period. All these elements combine to make this album a particularly successful one.

Didier C. Deutsch

Cousins

1989, Warner Bros. Records, from the film *Cousins*, Paramount Pictures, 1989 ♪♪♪♪

album notes: Music: Angelo Badalamenti; **Featured Musicians:** Mike Lang, piano; Kirk Whalum, saxophone; **Conductor:** Angelo Badalamenti, Nick Perrito

There's something about the often avant-garde musical sensibilities of Angelo Badalamenti that lend itself easily to the creepy dreamscapes of David Lynch, but people tend to forget that the composer has penned some other, equally successful film scores for genres that are as far removed from *Twin Peaks* as you could imagine. *Cousins* is the enjoyable 1989 remake of the French farce *Cousin, Cousine,* and it contains a romantic score by Badalamenti that can be best described as infectious—the elegant piano solo which comprises the love theme, the daffy chase music that sounds like it's out of some Henry Mancini score from the '60s, and the lyrical "Cousins Waltz" all help to make this an easy-going, charming score, illustrating that Badalamenti can work quite well outside of atmospheric mood pieces and horror shows, if he's ever given the chance.

Andy Dursin

The Cowboy Way

1994, Epic Soundtrax, from the Universal film *The Cowboy Way,* 1994 ♪♪♪♪

A modern western involving two rodeo stars on their way to New York from New Mexico to avenge the death of a friend, *The Cowboy Way* was made more ingratiating thanks to its percolating soundtrack, in which great rocking numbers were performed by groups like Bon Jovi, Cracker, the Gibson/Miller Band, the Allman Brothers Band, and individuals such as Emmylou Harris, Jeff Beck and Paul Rodgers (doing a mean rendition of the Leiber and Stoller chestnut, "On Broadway"), and George Thorogood. En Vogue's "Free Your Mind," however, seems out of place in the context. But don't let that deter you from listening to this album, if you haven't yet done so.

Didier C. Deutsch

The Cowboys

1994, Varèse Sarabande, from the film *The Cowboys,* Warner Bros., 1974 ♪♪♪♪♪

album notes: Music: John Williams; **Orchestra:** The Warner Bros. Studio Orchestra; **Conductor:** John Williams.

It took 20 years for this soundtrack to get a commercial release, but it was well worth the wait. John Williams, who has often expressed himself in the adventure and epic genres, only wrote occasionally in the western idiom (unless you consider all the *Indiana Jones* films to be westerns of a different kind) but one happy exception was the score he wrote for *The Cowboys.* Starring John Wayne as an aging, leather-tough trail master who takes along with him a band of inexperienced youngsters to drive a herd of cattle across 400 miles of the West's most treacherous territory after his regular hands desert him, the film elicited from the composer a rambunctious, Americana-flavored music, which at times evokes *The Reivers,* also directed by Mark Rydell, but most often creates its own poetic imagery. For several years, the only selection from the score that was available was the brilliant overture Williams recorded with The Boston Pops. Much shorter, and with different instrumentations, it is found here as the "Main Title," with the other tracks pretty much following the storyline from "Learning the Ropes," to "The Drive," which finds the young cowboys delivering the herd after successfully completing their journey. In an awkward bit of sequencing, however, an alternate version of the "Main Title" and the "Overture" have been inserted in the middle of the program, while both the "Entr'acte" and "End Credits," which are available on the laser disc, are missing.

Didier C. Deutsch

The Craft

1996, Columbia Records, from the film *The Craft,* Columbia Pictures, 1996 ♪♪♪♪

album notes: Music: Graeme Revell.

A supernatural thriller about four high school girls who discover their inner power through witchcraft, *The Craft* yielded this song compilation album which features an eclectic mix of cutting-edge bands and artists introducing new songs or doing covers of songs created by others, like The Beatles' "Tomorrow Never Knows," The Cars' "Dangerous Type," The Smiths' "How Soon Is Now," Peter Gabriel's "I Have The Touch," and Harry Nilsson's "Jump into the Fire." This witches' brew works most of the time, with "All This and Nothing" by Sponge, "Witches Song" by Juliana Hatfield, and "Under the Water" by Jewel, among the tunes best remembered from the film, in which they make a perfect counterpoint to the screen action. Both Elastica and Spacehog present previously unreleased material ("Spastica" and "The Horror," respectively), with Graeme Revell contributing "Bells, Books and Candles," from his original score.

Didier C. Deutsch

1996, Varèse Sarabande, from the film *The Craft,* Columbia Pictures, 1996 ♪♪♪

album notes: Music: Graeme Revell.

Graeme Revell has conjured up another inventive fantasy film score. Very similar to *The Crow* in its approach, he combines various opposing musical styles once again to create an unsettling mood. Indian chants are principally used ("The Magic Store") to separate "normal" reality from the supernatural world into which four young girls will cross once they begin dabbling in witchcraft. As the girls start using their powers, Revell mates the chanting with a rock track to signify these are '90s "Bitches of Eastwick."

David Hirsch

Crash

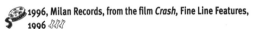 1996, Milan Records, from the film *Crash,* Fine Line Features, 1996 ♫♫♫

album notes: Music: Howard Shore; **Electronic Music Preparation:** Simon Franglen; **Conductor:** Howard Shore; **Featured Musicians:** Robert Piltch, Mike Francis, Edward Quinlan, James Tait, Rick Whitelaw, Tony Zory, electronic guitars; Erica Goodman, Marie Boisvert, Janice Lindskoog, harps; Joseph Orlowski, Melvin Berman, Douglas Stewart, woodwinds; Robin Engelman, Brian Leonard, percussion.

Crash, David Cronenberg's latest examination of sexual aberration, features an unusual score, performed by a small group consisting of six electric guitars, three harps, three woodwinds and two percussionists, with the unusual ensemble creating a uniquely effective miasmic ambiance that emphasizes the contemporary sensuality of the picture. Created by Cronenberg's long-time collaborator Howard Shore, its highly modernistic, somewhat decadently erogenous accents are very suitable to the obsessive, carnal darkness of the filmmaker's cinematic vision. There are no real melodies, but the guitars and harps that double one another succeed in evoking an almost unbearable claustrophobic sensitivity. Remixing and resynthesizing the tracks also added to this chaotic ambiance. Though the overall discordant sound suffers somewhat on its own, Shore's inventiveness translates into an interesting and sensually charged score.

Randall D. Larson

Crazy for You

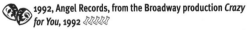 1992, Angel Records, from the Broadway production *Crazy for You,* 1992 ♫♫♫♫

album notes: Music: George Gershwin; **Lyrics:** Ira Gershwin; **Musical Direction:** Paul Gemignani; **Cast:** Harry Groener, Jodi Benson, Beth Leavel, Stacey Logan, Stephen Temperley.

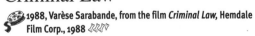 1993, RCA Victor, from the London production *Crazy for You,* 1993 ♫♫♫♫

album notes: Music: George Gershwin; **Lyrics:** Ira Gershwin; **Musical Direction:** Jae Alexander; **Cast:** Kirby Ward, Ruthie Hanshall, Vanessa Leigh-Hicks, Helen Way.

The Gershwins' 1930 hit *Girl Crazy* got a new lease on life as *Crazy for You,* a heavily revamped and modernized version which took Broadway by storm on February 19, 1992, and racked up 1,622 performances, a great deal more than the 272 accumulated by the original. The new book, by Ken Ludwig, made few concessions to current trends, and in fact harkened back to the days of yore when inconsequential storylines merely served as a way to introduce new songs by the brilliant tunesmiths of the day. However, what mattered here was the score featuring many familiar numbers by the Gershwins, including "Shall We Dance," "Embraceable You," "Someone to Watch Over Me," and "They Can't Take That Away from Me," all cleverly threaded into the thin plot, and delivered with the right amount of gusto and fun by the spirited cast. The London cast album is an apt alternative to the Broadway cast, with equally ingratiating performances.

Didier C. Deutsch

Crimes of the Heart

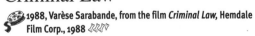 1986, Varèse Sarabande, from the film *Crimes of the Heart,* Dino De Laurentiis Entertainment, 1986 ♫♫♫♫♫

album notes: Music: Georges Delerue; **Conductor:** Georges Delerue; **Featured Soloists:** Roy Willox, alto sax; Ronnie Price, keyboards.

Based on Beth Henley's 1980 eponymous stage play, *Crimes of the Heart* became a wonderful screen vehicle for Jessica Lange, Diane Keaton and Sissy Spacek, portraying three sisters who get back together momentarily in their North Carolina home and reflect about their past, the world around them and their relationship with one another, in a riveting display of superb acting and gripping melodramatic comedy. Enhancing the many moods of the film and giving the action an extra boost of its own, Georges Delerue wrote a strongly appealing score, in which the main motif, a soulful saxophone romance leading to an exuberant waltz, developed in "Crimes of the Heart," sets the tone. Drawing upon his many resources as a master melodist, he detailed the sisters and other characters with whom they interrelate in individual cues that are among the choicest moments in this beautiful score, and imaginatively described in striking musical terms some of the action's most important scenes.

Didier C. Deutsch

Criminal Law

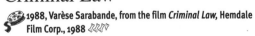 1988, Varèse Sarabande, from the film *Criminal Law,* Hemdale Film Corp., 1988 ♫♫♫♪

album notes: Music: Jerry Goldsmith; **Conductor:** Jerry Goldsmith.

This second all-electronic score by Jerry Goldsmith, after the abrasive *Runaway,* is far more textural, moving from a fluttering, echoed pan flute effect to a delicately lyrical piano theme (the only acoustic sounds in the score) and some throbbing, ostinato-driven suspense cues for Martin Campbell's entry in the briefly-popular "lawyers-in-distress" film cycle of the late '80s. Unlike the obvious electronic sounds of *Runaway, Criminal Law* is often indistinguishable from acoustically created music and it's an extremely listenable (albeit brief) album, although essentially ambient in nature. Like Goldsmith's earlier work on films like *Freud* and his *Twilight Zone* television scores, *Criminal Law* doesn't so much grab you by the throat as slowly hypnotize you.

Jeff Bond

Crimson Tide

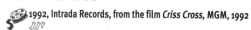 1995, Hollywood Records, from the film *Crimson Tide*, Hollywood Pictures, 1995 🎬🎬

album notes: Music: Hans Zimmer; **Conductor:** Nick Glennie-Smith; **Choir:** The London Choir; **Conductor:** Harry Gregson-Williams; **Featured Musician:** Malcolm McNab, trumpet.

This album of Hans Zimmer's score was heavily edited into five suites to create a lavish 67-minute symphonic presentation. Unfortunately, the downside of this overlong album (one track, "Alabama," is almost 24 minutes long!) is that the music spends too much time languishing on low-key "tension" music. The score is filled with seemingly wild electronic effects, and one can't help but grow tired of it all very quickly. As a result, there's quite often the feeling that you've heard the same passage before. Worse still, every so often Zimmer quotes a string passage that he used earlier in *Backdraft*. Perhaps this flurry of action music serves just to keep you awake.

David Hirsch

Criss Cross

1992, Intrada Records, from the film *Criss Cross*, MGM, 1992 🎬🎬🎬

album notes: Music: Trevor Jones; **Conductor:** Guy Dagul; **Featured Musicians:** Trevor Jones, Guy Dagul, Roger King, synthesizers; Andy Sheppard, saxophone; Mike Moran, synthesizer programmer; Gerry Leonard, electric guitar.

Trevor Jones's monothematic score for this quiet relationship drama is suitably small and poignant. Drawn around an acoustic guitar melody embellished by massed strings, the music lends a voice to the inner hearts of the working mother and teenage son whose broken relationship becomes the focus of the story. Aside from the guitar theme, Jones provides a variety of ambient material to support activities, while the guitar theme always speaks for the heart. As pretty as the main theme is, it's rather simple and as a result it grows rather repetitious. The synth motifs are effective but don't make for entirely enjoyable listening. *Criss Cross* is a pretty score but in the end it may be too reliant upon its one melodic theme to sustain the entire score. It is likeable but not a big repeat player.

Randall D. Larson

Critters

1993, Intrada Records, from the film *Critters*, New Line Cinema, 1993 🎬🎬🎬

album notes: Music: David Newman; **Conductor:** David Newman.

A minor, long-forgotten classic horror film, *Critters* gave David Newman an unusual opportunity to write a score which effectively blends electronics and a full orchestra in a slow build-up that forcefully reaches a climax and dissipates until the unavoidable sequel. In an unusual display of craftsmanship, Newman only uses the electronics at the very start of the "Main Title," during the pre-title segment set in outer space (where the critters of the title are growing and multiplying before they invade Earth). As soon as the action switches to the farm where most of the action next takes place, the orchestra takes over. From then on, most of the cues rely on the orchestra and individual solo instruments, adding layers of frightful sounds that paint the horror pictured in the film as the voracious man-eating critters wreak havoc in middle America.

Only once the critters have been destroyed does the music relax and end on a peaceful note. At the same time, in another compositional *tour de force*, Newman has devised many soft-sounding, elegiac cues that belie and contrast the tension in the film. It is a clever device that forces the listener's attention, while it effectively conveys the power of the drama unfolding on the screen. Taken as a listening experience, the score offers many inspiring moments, though ultimately it probably will appeal mostly to those who have seen the film and have enjoyed it thoroughly.

Didier C. Deutsch

Crooklyn/Crooklyn: Volume II

Crooklyn; 1994, MCA Records, from the film *Crooklyn*, Universal Pictures, 1994 🎬🎬🎬

Shamelessly old school, this soundtrack reaches back for vintage Jackson 5 ("ABC"), Sly & the Family Stone ("Everyday People"), JB's ("Pass the Peas"), Staple Singers ("Respect Yourself"), Chambers Brothers ("Time Has Come Today") and too many more to mention. The Crooklyn Dodgers' hip-hopping "Crooklyn," however, pales before such vaunted company.

Gary Graff

Crooklyn: Volume II; 1994, MCA Records, from the film *Crooklyn*, Universal Pictures, 1994 🎬🎬🎬

Continuing along the same lines as volume one, this second anthology of wonderful 1960s black pop tunes delivers the

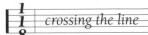

goods, with tunes by The Stylistics, Stevie Wonder, The Jackson Five, Smokey Robinson, Isaac Hayes, Johnny Nash, and several others. Uncomplicated, direct, enjoyable, it may be a throwback to happier (?) times, but it's also something that you can put on your CD player, and play many times over, just for the fun of it.

Didier C. Deutsch

Crossing the Line

🎬 1991, Varèse Sarabande, from the film *Crossing the Line*, Miramax Films, 1991 🎵🎵🎵

album notes: Music: Ennio Morricone; **Orchestra:** The Unione musicisti di Roma; **Conductor:** Ennio Morricone.

Ennio Morricone's darkly hued score for orchestra and chorus powerfully underlines the drama and the tension in this film set in Scotland about a miner, a man of ideals, down on his luck and in search of his own self. Many of the cues in the score are on the down side, with moody expressions reflecting both the rural environment in which the action unfolds and the feelings of the film's main character, played by Liam Neeson. Following his slow ascent to personal salvation, the music builds up to a climax that sums up his experience and points the way to a gradual acceptance of the fate he's inherited. In the profusely descriptive score, some cues emerge for their lyricism, notably "Road Training 2," or "The Wasteland," in which the main theme, played by a saxophone against a floating string line, is inexplicably marred by a sudden glitch in the recording.

Didier C. Deutsch

Crossroads

🎬 1986, Warner Bros. Records, from the film *Crossroads*, Warner Bros., 1986 🎵🎵🎵

album notes: Music: Ry Cooder; **Featured Musicians:** Ry Cooder, Otis Taylor, guitar; Jim Keltner, John Price, drums; Jim Dickinson, Van Dyke Parks, William Smith, piano, organ; Alan Pasqua, synthesizer; Nathan East, Jorge Calderon, Richard Holmes, bass, Sonny Terry, Frank Frost, John Logan, harmonica; George Bohannon, baritone horn; Walt Sereth, saxophone; Miguel Cruz, percussion.

Rooted in the music of the South, this excellent soundtrack album will mostly appeal to anyone interested in the blues, but it should also find a broader audience among those who have enjoyed this saga of a young Juilliard scholar who embarks on a tour of the Mississippi Delta, allegedly to discover Robert Johnson's "unknown 30th song." Deftly performing the works of local songwriters, including Johnson's title tune, as well as his own compositions, Cooder and cohorts deliver a potent brew of foot-stompers and gut-wrenchers, both vocal and instrumental, that are difficult to resist, let alone ignore.

Didier C. Deutsch

The Crow

🎬 1994, Varèse Sarabande, from the film *The Crow*, Miramax/ Dimension Pictures, 1994 🎵🎵🎵

album notes: Music: Graeme Revell; **Conductor:** Tim Simonec; **Featured Musicians:** Djivan Gasparyan, Armenian duduk; Kazu Matsui, shakuhachi; Oscar Brashear, trumpet; M.B. Gordy, percussion; Karl Verheyen, Philip Tallman, guitars; Graeme Revell, keyboards; Bobbie Page, Darlene Koldenhoven, Chris Snyder, voices.

Gritty urban score that successfully mixes diverse elements of jazz and rock music with European, eastern, and island elements. Electric guitars unconventionally share the spotlight with an Armenian duduk and a Japanese shakuhachi. There's even two remarkably tender love themes, a complete contrast from everything else, one for the back-from-the-dead rock musician who seeks vengeance on the punks who murdered both him and his fiancee, and one for the child who loved them both. Dark, deeply moving, at times disturbing, but boldly creative.

David Hirsch

🎬 1994, Atlantic Records, from the Miramax film *The Crow*, 1994 🎵🎵🎵

The Crow pairs an ultra-hip comic book with a collection of ultra-hip modern rockers for a sampler of the genre that's compelling, even if none of the individual tracks are particularly memorable. Most of the 14 selections either evoke the film's dark eeriness—such as the Cure's "Burne"—or underscore its aggressive action sequences, scoring murder and mayhem to the sounds of Helmet's "Milktoast," Pantera's "The Badge," Rollins Band's "Ghostriders," or "After the Flesh" by My Life with the Thrill Kill Kult. Big names such as Stone Temple Pilots, Nine Inch Nails, and Rage Against the Machine seem brought aboard more for commercial clout than for their respective songs, but the album does display a certain amount of hubris by closing with Jane Siberry's soaringly hopeful "It Can't Rain All the Time."

Gary Graff

The Crow: City of Angels

🎬 1996, Miramax Records; from the film *The Crow: City of Angels*, Miramax/Dimension Films, 1996 🎵🎵🎵

Following a predecessor that hit No. 1 is an unenviable task—especially since *The Crow* also established a foothold for modern (a.k.a. alternative) rock in Hollwyood. *City of Angels* didn't hit the same heights, but it's nearly as good, with Hole's steroid-fueled version of Fleetwood Mac's "Gold Dust Woman," White Zombie's "I'm Your Boogieman" and an inspired duet by Linda Perry and Jefferson Airplane/Starship matron Grace Slick on "Knock Me Out." Tricky and The Gravediggaz team up on the head-bobbing

"Tonite is a Special Nite," and Iggy Pop's "I Wanna Be Your Dog" is a welcome inclusion on any rock collection.

Gary Graff

 **1996, Miramax/Hollywood Records, from the film** *The Crow: City of Angels,* **Miramax/ Dimension Pictures, 1996** ♪♪♪♪

album notes: Music: Graeme Revell; **Conductor:** Tim Simonec; **Featured Musicians:** Masakazu Yoshizawa, shakuhachi; M.B. Gordy, drums, percussion; Karl Verheyen, guitars.

Graeme Revell's score for this sequel is decidedly darker than his work for the original, if that's even possible. It's a true mark of talent that he can form something fresh from what was simply a poor retread of the original film. Once again, Revell combines an eclectic mix of instrumentation and vocals, from the almost ordinary chant "Santa Muerte" to the gloomy and twisted "Temple of Pain." The original theme from *The Crow* is quoted on several tracks and Revell co-wrote the song "Believe in Angels" with singer Heather Nova.

David Hirsch

The Crucible

 **1996, RCA Victor, from the film** *The Crucible,* **20th Century Fox, 1996** ♪♪♪♪

album notes: Music: George Fenton; **Conductor:** George Fenton.

This depressing tale about sexual hysteria and religious persecution in 17th-century Salem, Mass., translated itself into a striking score for George Fenton, who wrote a series of cues well-designed to subliminally enhance the screen action. Based on Arthur Miller's wrenching play, a thinly disguised indictment written at the height of the McCarthy witch hunt of the 1950s, the film depicted the religious repression that follows accusations by some sexually exacerbated Puritan girls that a local farmer is an agent of the Devil. The main motifs devised by Fenton to underscore the story strictly evoke the drama in a very subdued way, more threatening than any violent outburst. Occasionally, a simple melody suggests the innocence of the victims ("Elizabeth Accused"), but much of the music is bathed in the undefined ominous moods that permeate it. A heady score it may be, but a magnificent one nonetheless.

Didier C. Deutsch

Cry Freedom

 **1987, MCA Records, from the film** *Cry Freedom,* **Universal Pictures, 1987** ♪♪♪♪

album notes: Music: George Fenton, Jonas Gwangwa; **Conductor:** George Fenton; **Featured Musicians:** Torera, Mbira; Thebe Lipere, Berembau, percussion; *"Shebeen" Band:* Lucky Ranku, guitar; Ernest Mothle, bass; Fats Mogoboya, congas; Churchill Jolobe, drums; Mervin Africa, piano; Dudu Pukwana, Teddy Osei, Bheki Mseleku, saxophone; David De Fries, trumpet.

For Richard Attenborough's moving depiction of apartheid as experienced by newspaperman Donald Woods and South African activist Stephen Biko, George Fenton has delved deeply into African musical traditions to create a score which is rich in rhythm, song and soft melody. Its combination of orchestral and vocal music, African and European, sorrowful and triumphant, gives it a unique quality. There are four primary themes, two African and two European in style. The first half of the film tells Biko's story, and the music consequently is predominantly African. After his death, the film focuses on Woods's efforts to publicize Biko's martyrdom, and the European music dominates amid faint echoes of the African sounds.

The closing song, "Cry Freedom" (sung by Fenton and Gwangwa, backed by a large choir), reflects the pain and suffering of what Biko and too many others have gone through in the cause of freedom; yet the music remains filled with pride, hope, and confidence. Despite the suffering, it suggests that the cause is not lost.

Randall D. Larson

Cry of the Banshee

See: The Edgar Allan Poe Suite/Cry of the Banshee/Horror Express

Cry the Beloved Country

 **1995, Epic Soundtrax, from the film** *Cry the Beloved Country,* **Miramax, 1995** ♪♪♪♪

album notes: Music: John Barry; **Conductor:** John Barry.

Alan Paton's distinctive novel about the murder of a white man in South Africa and the relationship that evolves between the dead man's father and a black minister, whose son is the murderer, was initially filmed in 1951 in a stirring version that starred Sidney Poitier (it was also the basis for the Broadway musical, *Lost in the Stars,* q.v.). This remake, starring James Earl Jones and Richard Harris, released in 1995, was a glossy, taut recreation that failed to capitalize on the evil of apartheid to place the relationship of both men into sharper focus. Also seemingly ill-fitting was John Barry's score, too pretty for its own good, at least in the context, and given to grandiose flurries that contrasted with the stark realism of the story itself.

However, judged on its own musical merits, it stands out as another masterpiece from the composer, a work that may be much better when it is not closely associated with the film for which it was originally conceived. A master of the genre, Barry tends to write scores that are unusually florid, with deeply moving themes in a grand romantic style. The cues here are superb and suggestively set off by the traditional songs that are

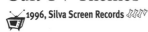
included. An extra welcome bonus is Ladysmith Black Mambazo's exciting take on "Amazing Grace."

Didier C. Deutsch

Cult TV Themes

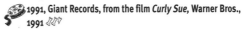

1996, Silva Screen Records 🎵🎵🎵

album notes: Choir: The Royal Philharmonic Concert Orchestra; **Conductor:** Mike Townend; **Orchestra:** The Daniel Caine Orchestra; **Conductor:** Daniel Caine.

With a full title like *Mission: Impossible & Cult TV Themes of The Atomic Age and Beyond,* this compilation CD has carte blanche to contain just about anything. In addition to Lalo Schifrin's unforgettable *Mission: Impossible* theme music, and with titles like Earl Hagen's bluesy modern noir theme for *Mike Hammer* and Quincy Jones's *Ironside* theme with its distinctive, alarm—like opening, the definition of "cult" gets stretched quite a bit. But regardless of whether shows like *Kojak* and *Barnaby Jones* deserve to be describe as cult programs, their theme music is memorable and exciting, and this newly recorded mix does a better job than most of recreating the tempos and arrangements of these tight little compositions. Included are Henry Mancini's gritty, rocking *Peter Gunn* music and his sneaky theme for *The Pink Panther,* Morton Stevens's hard—driving surfer music for *Hawaii 5–0,* Fred Steiner's bluesy, evocative *Perry Mason* theme, Ron Grainer's propulsive music for The Prisoner, as well as Billy Goldenberg's oddly sweeping *Kojak* theme and Jerry Goldsmith's low—key but catchy *Barnaby Jones.* The arrangements and performances are mostly dead—on, but some of the pieces suffer from the extended treatments which add some ill—advised improvisational sections to pan the cues out to more than two minutes.

Jeff Bond

The Cure

1995, GRP Records, from the film *The Cure,* Universal Pictures, 1995 🎵🎵🎵

album notes: Music: Dave Grusin; **Featured Musicians:** Dean Parks, George Doering, guitars; Jimmy Johnson, electric bass; Harvey Mason, drums; Mike Fisher, percussion; Jim Walker, recorder, penny-whistle, alto flute; Tommy Morgan, hamonica, blues harp; Dave Grusin, piano; Ralph Grierson, orchestral piano; **Conductor:** Dave Grusin.

A lyrical, touching score by Dave Grusin accompanied this 1995 drama of two young boys learning to cope with terminal illness. Much like his score for *On Golden Pond* and equally reminiscent of *The Heart Is a Lonely Hunter,* Grusin utilizes his roots in orchestral film scoring and jazz recording in combining both poignant, emotional cues and strong, bouncy country/R&B tracks, giving the film an atmospheric, rural musical accompa-

niment. As with many Grusin albums (and soundtracks), most of the selections here are performed by the composer on piano with solid backing from fellow jazz artists, including Jim Walker, Dean Parks, George Doering, and Jimmy Johnson. If you enjoy Grusin's jazz albums and want a taste of his film scoring, *The Cure* works as a perfect introductory album, just as it comes highly recommended for listeners already accustomed to his fine work for movies and television.

Andy Dursin

Curly Sue

1991, Giant Records, from the film *Curly Sue,* Warner Bros., 1991 🎵🎵

album notes: Music: Georges Delerue; **Conductor:** Georges Delerue.

John Hughes has worked with virtually every major composer in Hollywood, talents ranging from John Williams, Michael Kamen, Alan Silvestri, Bruce Broughton, Jerry Goldsmith, and Maurice Jarre, and his 1991 comedy *Curly Sue,* sported an adequate score by the late Georges Delerue. The music is lyrical with long, flowing melodic lines, the trademark of Delerue, who came from a background in France where he scored numerous films for Francois Truffaut and other esteemed directors. This score is forgettable, genteel, and harmless, working to convey a fairy tale quality in Hughes's film, though, like a lot of Delerue's Hollywood work from this time, doesn't quite have the freshness or spontaneity of some of his earlier works. The album also includes several source music tracks, along with a catchy Ringo Starr ballad, "You Never Know," written by Steve Dorff.

Andy Dursin

Cyrano de Bergerac

1990, DRG Records, from the film *Cyrano de Bergerac,* Orion Classics, 1990 🎵🎵🎵🎵

album notes: Music: Jean-Claude Petit; **Conductor:** Jean-Claude Petit; **Featured Musician:** Thierry Caens, trumpet.

A seemingly faithful adaptation of Edmond Rostand's novel about that long-nosed fellow who was a poet and dreamer, and one hell of a spade, *Cyrano de Bergerac* starred Gerard Depardieu in one of his better screen performances. To score this 17th century swashbuckler, Jean-Claude Petit devised a happy mixture in which period instruments (a harpsichord, a street organ, a lute) and colorful orchestral tones give his score a rare depth and extraordinary versatility. The themes, attractively sketched, outline crucial moments in the action, with rambunctious outbursts ("The Duel," "Cyrano") commenting on the grander-than-life personality of the central character, romantic ballads ("The Letters," "Cyrano's Declaration") pinpointing his repressed sorrow over love unrequited, and liturgical chants outlining the quasi-religious tone of some scenes ("The Spaniards' Mass," "Song of the Nuns"). It's a richly textured, emphatic score that is musically quite impressive. This title may be out of print or just plain hard to find. Mail-order companies, used CD shops, or dealers of rare or import recordings will be your best bet.

Didier C. Deutsch

 **D**

Da

See: My Left Foot/Da

Daddy Nostalgie

1990, CBS/France, from the film *Daddy Nostalgie*, UGC, 1990 𝄞𝄞𝄞𝄞

album notes: Music: Antoine Duhamel; **Featured Musicians:** Philip Catherine, guitar; Jean-Charles Capon, cello; Ron Carter, bass; Jimmy Rowles, piano; Louis Sclavis, clarinet; Jacques DiDonato, clarinet.

Bertrand Tavernier, who directed the memorable *'Round Midnight,* a tribute to American jazzmen living in France after World War II, commissioned a terrific jazz score from composer Antoine Duhamel to illustrate this bittersweet story about an estranged father and daughter reuniting after many years on the Riviera, shortly before his untimely death. Reflecting the subtly shaded moods of the film, the score consisted for the most of softer numbers, played by Philip Catherine on guitar, Jimmy Rowles at the piano, and Ron Carter on bass, among the musicians heard on this soundtrack. Adding a nostalgic note of its own, the score also included the standard "These Foolish Things," heard here in three different versions, including a vocal duet between Jane Birkin, who starred in the film, and Jimmy Rowles. This recording may be difficult to find. Check with a used CD store, mail-order company, or a dealer specializing in rare, out-of-print, or import recordings.

Didier C. Deutsch

Damage

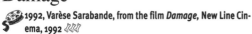1992, Varèse Sarabande, from the film *Damage,* New Line Cinema, 1992 𝄞𝄞𝄞

album notes: Music: Zbigniew Preisner; **Orchestra:** The Symphonic Orchestra of Warsaw; **Conductor:** Wojciech Michniewski; **Featured Soloists:** Lapinski Zdzislaw, cello; Konrad Mastylo, piano; the Tomasz Stonko Jazz Group.

Zbigniew Preisner follows British politician Jeremy Irons down the road to ruin in an affair with his son's girlfriend, Juliette

Binoche. One might expect a score of hot sexual tension, a la *Body Heat,* but Preisner mainly uses a classical air to express the stuffiness of the English family and make the affair seem that much more "dirty." Even the occasional use of a jazz motif (particularly on "The Last Time") only further acts to degrade the conduct of Irons and Binoche.

David Hirsch

Dames at Sea

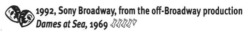1992, Sony Broadway, from the off-Broadway production *Dames at Sea,* 1969 𝄞𝄞𝄞𝄞

album notes: Music: Jim Wise; **Lyrics:** George Haimsohn, Robin Miller; **Musical Direction:** Richard J. Leonard; **Cast:** Tamara Long, Sally Stark, Steve Elmore, Bernadette Peters.

A frequently funny, delightful send-up of the Hollywood musicals of the 1930s, *Dames at Sea* took as its plot a storyline not unlike the one developed for the film *42nd Street,* in which a new chorine gets to replace the star of a Broadway-bound musical when the latter can't go on (in this case because she gets seasick when the show, kicked out of its theatre, opens on board a ship anchored in the harbor). Bernadette Peters made a splash in this production, her first major show, as the new kid on the block, with Tamara Long as the displaced star. The score, while not always as musically memorable as the Harry Warren–Al Dubin works it spoofed, came up with some hilariously campy tunes of its own, like "Choo-Choo Honeymoon," "Singapore Sue," and "The Echo Waltz."

Didier C. Deutsch

Damien: Omen II

1988, Silva Screen, from the film *Damien: Omen II,* 20th Century Fox, 1978 𝄞𝄞𝄞𝄞

album notes: Music: Jerry Goldsmith; **Conductor:** Lionel Newman; **Choral Director:** John McCarthy.

Jerry Goldsmith adapted much of his music for the original *Omen* thriller for this sequel, expanding his orchestrations for a rich, lush-sounding album. The opening title music features a driving, epic-style rendition of his "Ave Satani" music from *The Omen,* while other cues emphasize heavy, driving rhythms to create the effect of a kind of "machine of evil" that cranks up as devil boy Damien's satanic cohorts deal death and destruction to all who oppose him. Most of the cues explode with spectacular violence, and Goldsmith and his choir leader conjure up some unnerving vocal effects as choir members hiss, growl, and wail their way through the composer's "black mass." Goldsmith serves up some spectral, spine-chilling moments of tonal beauty along with the mayhem in cues like "Sleepless Night."

see also: The Final Conflict/The Omen

Jeff Bond

Damn Yankees

1988, RCA Victor, from the Broadway production *Damn Yankees*, 1955 🎵🎵🎵🎵

album notes: Music: Richard Adler, **Lyrics:** Jerry Ross; **Musical Direction:** Hal Hastings; **Cast:** Gwen Verdon, Stephen Douglass, Ray Walston, Robert Shafer, Shannon Bolin.

1989, RCA Victor, from the film *Damn Yankees*, Warner Bros. Pictures, 1958 🎵🎵🎵🎵

album notes: Music: Richard Adler, **Lyrics:** Jerry Ross; **Orchestra:** The Warner Bros. Studio Orchestra; **Choir:** The Warner Bros. Studio Chorus; **Conductor:** Ray Heindorf; **Cast:** Gwen Verdon, Tab Hunter, Ray Walston, Robert Shafer, Shannon Bolin.

1994, Mercury Records, from the Broadway revival *Damn Yankees*, 1994 🎵🎵🎵🎵

album notes: Music: Richard Adler, **Lyrics:** Jerry Ross; **Musical Direction:** David Chase; **Cast:** Bebe Neuwirth, Jarrod Emick, Victor Garber, Dennis Kelly, Linda Stephens.

The old Faustian legend about the man who sells his soul to the Devil in order to regain youth and good looks received a clever updating in this whimsical musical, which took the tale and squarely set it against the background of America's favorite pastime, baseball. As reconceived by Douglas Wallop and George Abbott, *Damn Yankees,* based on Mr. Wallop's novel "The Year the Yankees Lost the Pennant," transplanted Faust into middle-America and gave him the name Joe Boyd. After he makes a pact with the Devil, a businessman more prosaically named Mr. Applegate, Boyd becomes "Shoeless" Joe Hardy, a hard-hitter, who takes the Washington Senators, his favorite team (and perpetual losers), all the way to the finals of the American League game, where they face those "damn Yankees." But this being a musical, set in America, there is a happy ending to the story. In spite of Mr. Applegate, and his assistant, the sultry Lola, Joe Hardy invokes the "escape clause" he and the Devil had agreed on initially. At the last minute, just before curtain time, returns to his loving wife as Joe Boyd, serene in the knowledge that it was he who helped the Senators win the pennant.

A multiple Tony Award-winner (including for Best Musical) in 1956, *Damn Yankees* ran for 1,019 performances (a rarity at the time), and made a star of Gwen Verdon, playing Lola, whose siren song, "Whatever Lola Wants," became a huge popular hit. Virtually intact, and with only one major cast change (Tab Hunter replacing Stephen Douglass as Joe Hardy), the show was transferred to the screen in 1958, in a splashy screen transfer that retained all the flavor and guile of the original.

After extensive revisions, in 1994 it was revived on Broadway, with Bebe Neuwirth as Lola and Victor Garber as Mr. Applegate, where it enjoyed a successful run, before going on the road, with Jerry Lewis, billed above the title, taking over as the Devil.

Of the three recordings available, the first Broadway cast offers the original stars (Gwen Verdon, Stephen Douglass, and Ray Walston as Mr. Applegate) in a spirited rendition that has all the freshness and excitement usually experienced when a show first hits Broadway. Its only drawback (if that's the word!) is that it is in mono sound. Stereo didn't become an industry standard until later that year.

The soundtrack album, available for the first time in stereo in this CD version, is almost identical to the Broadway cast album, but offers, in addition to the cast change noted above, and Ray Heindorf's flavorful orchestrations, longer versions of some of the songs, as well as better polished performances overall.

The 1994 Broadway cast album, with its abundance of new selections and dynamic renditions of the songs by Bebe Neuwirth, Victor Garber, and the other members of the cast, is as good a recording as can be gotten. It has the vibrancy, the fun, and the excitement one usually expects in that kind of production, and its sound quality is up to the latest standards.

Didier C. Deutsch

Dance with Me

1998, Epic/Sony Music Soundtrax, from the Columbia film *Dance with Me*, 1998 🎵🎵🎵🎵

Like the film that it represents, the soundtrack album to *Dance with Me* is a sexy affair, bouncy and infectious, and loaded with great dance tunes with a Latin beat performed by some of the best artists of the moment—including Sergio Mendes, Gloria Estefan, Jon Secada, Ruben Blades, and the two stars from the film, Vanessa L. Williams and Chayanne. The story of a young Cuban who goes to Houston to meet his father, arriving just in time to enter the World Open Dance only a month away, which he wins when he teams with another dancer, portrayed by Vanessa L. Williams, the film was a skimpy argument for some torrid dance numbers that constituted much of the show, with the fluid direction helping tremendously, and the songs setting off the necessary sparks. This is one soundtrack album that evokes great memories about a good flick, and that's great listening to the rest of the time.

Didier C. Deutsch

Dances with Wolves

1990, Epic Records/CBS Records, from the film *Dances with Wolves*, Orion Pictures, 1990 🎵🎵🎵🎵

album notes: Music: John Barry; **Conductor:** John Barry.

Rarely do cinematic beauty and musical splendor marry as sympathetically as in Kevin Costner's epic tale, *Dances with*

Wolves. John Barry's Academy Award-winning score is simply breathtaking, hauntingly majestic, and melancholy in an almost imperceptible way. The themes have unique melodic qualities–the Main Title ("Looks Like a Suicide") is stark and foreboding; "The John Dunbar Theme" and "Journey to Fort Sedgewick" deceptively simple, yet rich with complex harmonies that resonate grandly with the exquisite orchestrations of Greig McRitchie. Each selection is, in its own right, a musical gem. The recordings, made at Columbia Studios in Los Angeles, are superb. The strings shimmer, the horns and woodwinds shine, and the percussion rumbles with heart-stopping, earth-shaking depth.

Charles L. Granata

Dancing at Lughnasa

1998, Sony Classical, from the Sony Pictures Classics film *Dancing at Lughnassa*, 1998 ♪♪♪

album notes: Music: Bill Whelan; **Conductor:** Prionnsias O'Duinn; **Featured Musicians:** Nollaig Casey, fiddle; Martin O'Coonor, accordion; Davy Spillane, pipes, low whistle; Martin Murray, banjo; Sean D. Halpenny, bodhran; Bill Whelan, drums, percussion; Dolores Keane, vocals.

Dancing at Lughnasa (pronounced Loo-nissa) stars Meryl Streep as one of the five Mundy sisters scraping by on a farm in 1930s Ireland. The turning point in the movie comes as they fix their primitive radio and impulsively dance a reel to the title track. The fast tempo is maintained by percussionist and composer Bill Whelan, who has had great success with the traditional Irish clog dancing of *Riverdance.* When Whelan lets loose on drums, as with the title track and "The Lughnasa Fires," the music works best, benefiting from Davy Spillane on pipes and the lightning fast fiddle of Nollaig Casey. The orchestral sections lack the pizzazz of Whelan's energetic dance music, yet provide pleasant string music with a Celtic flavor and variations on the sentimental theme tune.

David Poole

Dangerous Beauty

1998, Restless Records, from the Warner Bros. film *Dangerous Beauty*, 1998 ♪♪♪

album notes: Music: George Fenton; **Conductor:** George Fenton.

A romantic love story set in the sixteenth-century Venetian court, *Dangerous Beauty* involved a feisty, independent young woman, anxious to rise above her current station on the fringes of the highest social circles, and the young nobleman she would like to marry in spite of both his and her parents' objections. Punctuating the many incidents in this sparkingly reconstructed saga in which somber episodes contrasted with moments of levity, George Fenton wrote a score that owed little to

Vivaldi and much to his own ingenious way with music. That is to say that the many cues found in this album are quite attractive, although they fail to inform on the time period of the movie itself. Even though an occasional rondo tries to convey the fact that this is a historical picture ("Warming to the Idea"), the dominant key here is the romantic aspects of the story, which Fenton illustrates with great sweeping themes that are beautifully designed.

Didier C. Deutsch

Dangerous Liaisons

1989, Virgin Movie Music, from the film *Dangerous Liaisons*, Warner Bros., 1989 ♪♪♪♪♪

album notes: Music: George Fenton; **Conductors:** George Fenton, David Woodcock (Baroque Orchestra); **Orchestra:** Baroque Orchestra; **Featured Musicians:** Maurice Cochrane, harpsichords, fortepiano, baroque organ; Elizabeth Wallfisch, Alison Bury, solo violins.

Happily mixing original cues with works by some of the best Baroque composers, George Fenton's music for *Dangerous Liaisons* is a rare treat, a score that brims with great taste and intelligence, and a delightful audio experience from beginning to end. If you really like film music and don't mind being a bit adventurous, don't let the above description deter you. Classical music, when well adapted to the needs of screen action, can be as effective as any score you are likely to hear. One of our most sophisticated composers, Fenton knows and understands the qualities that make classical selections so perfectly suited to a specific screen action. Even when he adapts the works by other composers or he writes his own music, he succeeds in creating cues that sound true to the period, yet have an edge of modernity that is appropriate to the cinematic medium itself. Typically, his score for *Dangerous Liaisons* shows great elegance and appeal. In the film, it perfectly matched the tone of the action; on its own, it makes for an attractive recording which will provide many hours of listening pleasure.

Didier C. Deutsch

Dangerous Minds

1995, MCA Records, from the film *Dangerous Minds*, Hollywood Pictures, 1995 ♪♪♪

This was a career launcher for rapper Coolio. It vaulted his "Gangsta's Paradise" to No. 1 on the Billboard charts, which in turn carried the album to No. 1 as well, with sales in excess of four million copies. No other song on the album is as successful, but it remains a decent sampler of mid-'90s urban styles, including the teenybop of Immature's "Feel the Funk," and the potent street swagger of selections by Rappin' 4-Tay, DeVante, and Aaron Hall.

Gary Graff

Michelle Pfeiffer and John Malkovich in Dangerous Liaisons. **(The Kobal Collection)**

Dante's Peak

1997, Varèse Sarabande, from the film *Dante's Peak,* Universal
Pictures, 1997 ♪♪♪♪

album notes: Music: John Frizzell; **Conductor:** Artie Kane.

Built around an effectively apocalyptic James Newton Howard
theme, John Frizzell's score overflows with hyper-dramatic action. Frizzell orchestrates this energetic material effectively and
creates plenty of sonic suspense through a cohesive orchestral
dissonance. Heavy on brass and percussion, the score is sufficiently cataclysmic, though it seems at its best when grounded
solidly upon the Howard theme. Frizzell does incorporate his
own love theme in "On the Porch," accompanying a tender dialog between Pierce Brosnan and Linda Hamilton, then recapitu-
lates it as a triumphant finale in "The Rescue." But it's
Howard's ominous horn theme that's linked to the malevolent
mountain; all other musical material remains subordinate to
the volcanic fury of the mountain's music. It's this material that
will, ultimately, remain the most memorable on the CD. At

30:27 minutes, though, it's quite a short one, and the fury of
much of the music makes it go by all that much quickly.

Randall D. Larson

Dark City

1998, TVT Records, from the film *Dark City,* 1998 ♪♪♪

album notes: Music: Trevor Jones; **Conductor:** Geoff Alexander; **Featured Musicians:** Phil Todd, Ewi; Gareth Cousins, synthesizers.

Directed by Alex Proyas, who also did *The Crow,* this sci-fi/fan-
tasy film noir takes an eerie look at a group of vampire-like
Strangers from another world who are able to change time and
reality to fit their own purpose (they call it "tuning"), and who
have invaded the Earth in search of an answer to their mortal-
ity. One way to achieve this is to rob humans of their memory,
with one victim being a man who finds himself accused of several murders he knows he couldn't have committed. Giving an
extra-mysterious edge to the strange screen proceedings is
Trevor Jones's score, which often sounds ominous, moving

through vales and hills around disembodied vocals. It serves its purpose behind the action, making it even more frightening. The moods throughout remain pretty much sullen, with only the selection titled "You Have the Power" demonstrating a great deal of energy. This soundtrack album also contains several vocals, including two evergreens by Anita Kelsey, "Sway" and "The Night Has a Thousand Eyes." Echo & the Bunnymen and Gary Numan are also heard in songs that are not in the film, but could have been.

Didier C. Deutsch

The Dark Half

1993, Varèse Sarabande, from the film *The Dark Half,* Orion Pictures, 1993. ⅃⅃

album notes: Music: Christopher Young; **Orchestra:** The Munich Symphony Orchestra; **Conductor:** Allan Wilson.

Despite a pleasantly melodic opening, the underscore for this film doesn't quite yield an entertaining CD. Then again, Christopher Young's primary goal is always to support the film, not make records. If the filmmakers' ultimate intent was that they needed a dreary, sullen score, then he certainly succeeded in delivering the goods. Once down in its pit of despair, it rarely rises up. One has to wonder, however, if Young was simply prohibited from devising another one of his creative orchestrations for fear that it might outshine the film, which was critically lambasted and disowned by Stephen King, and which could have used all the help it could get. If so, then Young's talent was certainly wasted.

David Hirsch

Dark Shadows: The 30th Anniversary Collection

1996, Varèse Sarabande, from the television series *Dark Shadows,* 1966–1970 ⅃⅃⅃⅃

album notes: Music: Robert Cobert; **Lyrics:** Charles Randolph Green; **Conductor:** Robert Cobert.

A sleek, elegant vampire show, "Dark Shadows" dominated television nights for three years, starting off as a conventional melodrama with spooky elements, but soon finding its own voice with the arrival of Barnabas Collins. One reason for the success of the show can be attributed to the score devised by Robert Cobert, who purposely ignored the trappings of the genre and developed an orchestral music that is totally indigenous to the show and gives it its unmistakable cachet.

Marking the 30th anniversary of the show, which premiered on June 27, 1966, this clever compilation not only samples many of the cues written by Cobert, but also adds unusual recordings, like "Barnabas Theme," performed by The First Theremin

Era, a psychedelic group. Fans of the series will no doubt love this great compilation; others will have to discover for themselves what kept an entire nation riveted to the television for so many thrilling evenings.

Didier C. Deutsch

Darkman

1990, MCA Records, from the film *Darkman,* Universal Pictures, 1990 ⅃⅃⅃

album notes: Music: Danny Elfman; **Conductor:** Shirley Walker.

Danny Elfman wrote a lot of "dark" scores during the late 1980s—*Batman, Beetlejuice,* and *Nightbreed* among them—but *Darkman* may just be the most representative score of the composer's work from this period. The music is popular enough to be copied in subsequent genre films in addition to being used in numerous movie trailers, so listeners may be familiar with the score even if they don't instantly know where the music comes from. With his trademark frantic, jumpy, unstable strings, an ominous, foreboding tone, and colorful orchestrations (courtesy of collaborator Steve Bartek), Elfman has written a score that's always interesting to listen to, very much in the style of *Batman* and his other efforts around this time, though its intense tone may wear some listeners down in album format.

Andy Dursin

Darling Lili

1999, RCA Records/Spain, from the Paramount film *Darling Lili,* 1970 ⅃⅃⅃⅃

album notes: Music: Henry Mancini; **Lyrics:** Johnny Mercer; **Conductor:** Henry Mancini.

Julie Andrews played a winsome and unlikely spy in the life of World War I flying ace Rock Hudson in this flawed big screen musical drama, in which she performed a number of songs written for her by Henry Mancini and Johnny Mercer. In a sometimes lavish production that included flavorful musical moments and aerial dogfights, mixed in with suspense and adventure, and the usually assured directing hand of Blake Edwards, the only distracting note was the fact that the film never quite knew whether it was a period drama or a romantic comedy, going back and forth between the two. The score, by Mancini and Mercer, contains some delicious moments ("I'll Give You Three Guesses," "Whistling away the Dark," "Smile away Each Rainy Day," performed in sunny fashion by Andrews), and instrumental cues that are typically melodic and catchy. Not an outstanding effort, but a memorable one with enough positive elements to win over the most difficult curmudgeon.

Didier C. Deutsch

Darling of the Day

1998, RCA Victor, from the Broadway musical *Darling of the Day*, 1968 ♪

album notes: Music: Jule Styne; **Lyrics:** E. Y. Harburg; **Cast:** Vincent Price, Patricia Routledge, Brenda Forbes, Peter Woodthorpe, Teddy Green.

Before she became known to television audiences as the irrepressible Hyacinth Buckett in the British series *Keeping up Appearances,* Patricia Routledge came to Broadway on a couple of occasions, one being this musical version of Arnold Bennett's *Buried Alive,* in which she shared top billing with Vincent Price, of all people. To be charitable about it, the show was a bomb! Sad to say, but both Jule Styne (music) and E. Y. Harburg (lyrics) had known better days in their respective careers, and their score barely ignited the tedium of the action; and with the possible exception of a song called "Not on Your Nellie," the star had very little to do to keep audiences amused. Routledge eventually returned to Broadway in a comedy in which a highlight found her on stage with an invisible dog on a leash that kept wanting to bite her. People are still talking about it . . .

Didier C. Deutsch

Das Boot

1998, Atlantic Records, from the TriStar film *Das Boot,* 1981 ♪♪♪♪♪

album notes: Music: Klaus Doldinger.

A searing account of life aboard a German U-boat during World War II, *Das Boot* (*The Boat*) was an unforgettable seafaring drama, in which the tension was heightened by the knowledge that the submarine and the sailors would probably not survive to the end of the conflict. This long-awaited, expanded edition of the Klaus Doldinger's score, raw and uncompromising, includes the musical tracks as they were heard in the film itself, with the re-recordings found in the original soundtrack album added here as bonus tracks. It's a sensational score that gets better with each repeated listening.

Didier C. Deutsch

Dave

1993, Big Screen Records, from the film *Dave,* Warner Bros., 1993 ♪♪♪♪♪

album notes: Music: James Newton Howard; **Conductor:** Marty Paich.

James Newton Howard's score for this romantic comedy is a delightful series of cues that are well adapted to the screen action but also exude strong musical characteristics that make this soundtrack album a particularly enjoyable one to listen to. At times elegiac ("The Picnic"), at times amusingly delineated ("She Hates Me"), it overflows with attractive ideas, compactly expressed yet totally convincing and strongly suggestive. In a rare display of Newton Howard's best qualities as a film composer, *Dave* is a real charming effort.

Didier C. Deutsch

Dawn of the Dead

1979, Varèse Sarabande, from the film *Dawn of the Dead,* United Film Distribution, 1979 ♪♪♪

album notes: Music: Goblin; **Featured Musicians:** Massimo Morante, guitars, bass, mandolin; Claudio Simonetti, keyboards, synthesizers, organ, violin; Fabio Pignatelli, guitar, bass; Agostino Marangolo, piano, percussion; Maurizio Guarini, synthesizer, violin.

For George Romero's visceral horror show, the Italian group Goblin was brought in by executive producer Dario Argento, who had worked with them before and insisted they replace many of the library cues originally patched together by Romero. Goblin provides an effective counterpart to Romero's vivid scenes of flesh-eating zombies invading an abandoned shopping mall, eager for the surviving humans trapped inside. Their music is desolate and brutal, but often satirical, and built around pulsating rock rhythms and textures, both electric and acoustic. Dominated by guitar and drums, the music leads the assault of the zombies, evoking a claustrophobic mood of impending and inescapable terror. It worked very well in the film, but it's less interesting on CD where it tends to drone away rather aimlessly. Unless you're into the throbbing zombie beat, the CD may not be a frequent flyer on your home stereo.

Randall D. Larson

Day of Anger/Beyond the Law

1991, RCA/Italy, from the film *Day Of Anger,* Corona/Divina, 1967; and from the film *Beyond the Law,* Roxy, 1968 ♪♪♪♪

album notes: Music: Riz Ortolani; **Conductor:** Riz Ortolani.

Lee Van Cleef played Mr. Taciturn again in this couple of spaghetti westerns made in 1967 and 1968, and flamboyantly scored by Riz Ortolani. *Day of Anger,* directed by Tonino Valerii (best known for the classic *My Name Is Nobody*) dealt with a hardened gunfighter and the young man he takes under his protection to teach him the tricks of his trade, before a final showdown finds them on opposite sides of the street. In a slight reversal of his screen persona, Van Cleef portrayed a good guy in *Beyond the Law,* long enough that is to rob a silver convoy. In both instances, Riz Ortolani wrote scores that went beyond the obvious spaghetti western sounds to have a personality of their own. In the first one, frequently too strident for its own good, "The Days of Anger" amusingly features the familiar sound of spurs of the walking gunfighter, but the score itself is basically a collection of loud themes that involve the usual contingent of big band arrangements, electric guitar pizzicatos, and trumpet solos that defined the genre. Much more successful is *Beyond the Law,* more quiet and melodic, with softer arrangements for guitar, harmonica and muted trumpets over subtle string lines and percussion effects proving quite effective, if at times a bit too traditional. The sound quality in this one is also warmer, making it more enjoyable as a result. This title may be out of print or just plain hard to find. Mail-order companies, used CD shops, or dealers of rare or import recordings will be your best bet.

Didier C. Deutsch

The Day of the Dolphin

1991, SLC Records/Japan, from the Avco Embassy film *The Day of the Dolphin,* 1974 🎬🎬🎬🎬
album notes: Music: Georges Delerue; **Conductor:** Georges Delerue.

Georges Delerue contributed an important, glorious score to this misguided story about a marine scientist, played by George C. Scott, who is convinced he can verbally communicate with dolphins, only to see his efforts thwarted by government agents more interested in having the mammals used for more lethal purposes. Although only released in Japan on the SLC label, this is a splendid effort by the French composer, at the peak of his form, well worth being looked into and acquired by anyone interested in film music of the highest order.

Didier C. Deutsch

The Day the Earth Stood Still

1993, Fox Records, from the film *The Day the Earth Stood Still,* 20th Century Fox, 1951 🎬🎬🎬
album notes: Music: Bernard Herrmann; **Orchestra:** The 20th Century Fox Orchestra; **Conductor:** Bernard Herrmann, Lionel Newman, Alfred Newman; **Featured Artist:** Sam Hoffman, theremin

Herrmann's music for the 1951 Robert Wise film about a wise extraterrestrial ambassador's visit to Earth is the quintessential '50s sci-fi score, most often remembered for its wailing, eerie theremin effects. The score was unavailable apart from some brief re-recorded suites prior to this 1993 release, which assembles the entire original score, including a few moments not used in the film. The portentous title music gives way to Herrmann's nervous "Radar" cue of low piano and vibraphone, but the highlight of the album involves the arrival of the alien Klaatu (Michael Rennie) and his immense robot Gort, characterized by Herrmann with an unforgettable series of crushing, ascending brass chords and hair-raising theremin glissandos as the robot lays waste to a phalanx of soldiers in Washington, D.C. No fan of Herrmann or science fiction film scores should be without this classic release.

Jeff Bond

The Day the Fish Came Out

1992, Sakkaris Records/Greece, from the film *The Day the Fish Came Out,* 20th Century Fox, 1967 🎬🎬🎬
album notes: Music: Mikis Theodorakis.

Despite impeccable credentials (it was directed by Michael Cacoyannis, who had previously made the hugely successful *Zorba the Greek,* and it starred Tom Courtenay and Candice Bergen as a pair of lovers vacationing in the Mediterranean), the film was a turkey. A light comedy that relied on a silly story about two atom bombs lost in the Greek islands, the plot poked fun at homosexuals and used sado-masochist jokes to elicit some laughter. When everything else failed, Mikis Theodorakis provided a tune or two that helped make the action a little more bearable. Taken on its own terms, the soundtrack is still enjoyable, with Greek harmonies that reflect the locale, and themes that are for the most part relatively listenable. This CD, however, seems to have been transferred directly from an LP, with apparent surface noise and crackles, and uneven levels. This recording may be difficult to find. Check with a used CD store, mail-order company, or a dealer specializing in rare, out-of-print, or import recordings.

Didier C. Deutsch

Daylight

1996, Universal Records, from the film *Daylight,* Universal Pictures, 1996 🎬🎬🎬
album notes: Music: Randy Edelman; **Conductor:** Randy Edelman

An unusual, relatively subtle action score from Randy Edelman, *Daylight* coasts right along with some exciting action cues that fortunately never overwhelm the claustrophobic suspense of Sylvester Stallone's entertaining disaster movie. Edelman utilizes his standard bag of tricks here (synths combined with full orchestra), but the percussive beat of many of his scores is notably missing, and it results in a solid outing that ought to appeal to action fans and aficionados of the composer. The album also includes "Wherever There is Love," a power ballad performed by Bruce Roberts and Donna Summer, which—thanks to its catchy chorus and typically lush David Foster production sheen—is one of the more enjoyable songs to come out of a disaster movie since, well, "The Morning After" from *The Poseidon Adventure,* anyway.

Andy Dursin

Days of Thunder

1990, DGC Records, from the film *Days of Thunder,* Paramount Pictures, 1990 🎬🎬🎬

Ever since *Risky Business,* Tom Cruise star vehicles have been good for high-profile soundtracks. And this one doesn't disappoint, with a jukebox chock full o' biggies—Elton John, Tina

Turner, Chicago, Cher. Hard rockers Guns 'N Roses stuck their previously unavailable cover of Bob Dylan's "Knockin' on Heaven's Door" here to lure the rock crowd, and ambitious listeners could find some real gems, like Terry Reid's version of "Gimme Some Lovin'" and Maria McKee's "Show Me Heaven" amidst a load of lukewarm castaways from the more established names.

Gary Graff

The Dead/Journey Into Fear

1987, Varèse Sarabande, from the film *The Dead*, Vestron Pictures, 1987; and *Journey Into Fear*, Stirling Gold, 1975 ♪♪♪♪

album notes: Music: Alex North; **The Dead: Featured Musicians:** Ann Stockton, Irish harp; Paul Shure, Bonnie Douglas, Sheldon Sanov, Arnold Belnick, Bruce Dukov, Israel Baker, violin; Milton Thomas, David Schwartz, viola; Frederick Seykora, Dennis Karmazyn, cello; Milton Kastenbaum, bass; Sheridon Stokes, flute; Tom Boyd, oboe; Dominick Fera, clarinet; John Berkman, keyboard; **Journey Into Fear: Orchestrations:** Richard E. Bronskill; **Orchestra:** The Graunke Symphony Orchestra; **Conductor:** Alex North.

Belying its apparently downbeat subject, a dramatic screen rendition of the Joyce story set at the turn of the century, the score for *The Dead,* a film directed by John Huston, is an attractive series of little musical miniatures for chamber orchestra and solo instruments, among them the flute, the oboe and the clarinet. Introduced by the "Main Title," a piece for solo harp, it segues into a collection of themes that underline the screen action, notably about Gretta, married to Gabriel, who, on the occasion of a family reunion at their aunts' home in Dublin, reveals to her husband that she loved another when she was younger.

In contrast to the romantic simplicity and loveliness of *The Dead, Journey Into Fear,* a contemporary murder mystery, elicited a score that sometimes verges on the atonal, with bursts of orchestral violence to portray the "aggressiveness inherent in this propulsive story," as the composer himself described it. Occasionally, a melodic interlude ("Loneliness," "Troubled Romance") provides some relief to the musical tension, but the title of the film appropriately describes the overall tones of the score, played with great energy by the Graunke Symphony Orchestra.

Didier C. Deutsch

Dead Again

1991, Varèse Sarabande, from the film *Dead Again,* Paramount Pictures, 1991 ♪♪♪

album notes: Music: Patrick Doyle; **Conductor:** William Kraft.

The second collaboration between director-actor Kenneth Branagh and composer Patrick Doyle results in a bombastic, often over-the-top but nevertheless enjoyable score similar to the composer's most pulsating works (think *Mary Shelley's Frankenstein*). To fit the Hitchcock-esque tone of Branagh's entertaining *film noir,* Doyle ventures into some elegiac string territory worthy of Bernard Herrmann, while still retaining his own voice through the propulsive action music accompanying the film's opening titles or the poignant love theme, with echoes of tragedy, that brings the picture to a close. Minor quibble: Some of the music is written in strict accordance to the action on-screen, meaning some tracks don't translate well to album form, though the brief running time at least means that the music never wears out its welcome. A worthy effort into the Branagh-Doyle series, though it is far from the best—or the worst—score to result from their collaborative relationship.

Andy Dursin

Dead Man Walking

1995, Columbia Records, from the film *Dead Man Walking,* Gramercy Pictures, 1995 ♪♪♪

album notes: Music: David Robbins, Eddie Vedder, Nusrat Fateh Ali Khan, Ry Cooder, V.M. Bhatt; **Featured Musicians:** Ry Cooder, David Robbins, David Spinozza, guitar; Frank Centeno, bass guitar; Brian Dobbs, Joel Diamond, organ; Joachim Cooder, dumbek; David Ratajczak, drums; Mino Cinelu, percussion; John Vartan, tambour; Joel Diamond, organ; **Featured Vocalists:** The Dusing Singers.

A complex psychological film, set in New Orleans, *Dead Man Walking* told the unique story of a nun and a convicted killer awaiting execution, and the unusual emotional ties that eventually bind their existences. Adding a pertinent fold to the absorbing drama, the soundtrack relied on the powerful combination of contemporary songs and rare instrumental cues written by a wide range of composers. A cornucopia of top frontline performers provide the enjoyment in the first album which brings together the talents of Bruce Springsteen, Johnny Cash, Suzanne Vega, Lyle Lovett, Mary Chapin Carpenter, Tom Waits, and Patti Smith, to name a few. Unless you have seen the film (and even if you have), it is sometimes difficult to assess how each song fits within the dramatic texture of the screen action, but taken on its own musical merits this compilation album is certainly better than most.

In a total genre departure, the second album presents various selections, many of them in the Pakistani Sufi idiom, a devotional style rich with tradition, used to express the transcendental moods that permeate some of the scenes in the film. By combining those with the songs of a gospel choir, film composer David Robbins was able to create a highly unusual, strikingly powerful soundtrack that does not seek any compromise and will probably regrettably attract only a limited audience.

Sean Penn and Susan Sarandon in Dead Man Walking. **(The Kobal Collection)**

But if you like the first album, try to find the second for a broader, richer musical experience.

Didier C. Deutsch

A solid set that has great merits. Oh, and there is the main theme by Danny Elfman . . .

Didier C. Deutsch

Dead Presidents

1995, Capitol Records, from the Hollywood film *Dead Presidents,* 1995 ♫♫♫♫

album notes: Music: Danny Elfman; **Conductor:** Danny Elfman.

It may be a bit redundant to signal that Danny Elfman wrote the score to this film as his contribution is sadly reduced here to one theme. This contemporary urban drama, about a Bronx youth who goes to Vietnam and returns home to see his life go down the drain, is musically limned with a hard-edged soundtrack that teems with popular R&B songs, many of them heard sporadically throughout the film but found here in their full version. And what a collection: Sly and the Family Stone, Isaac Hayes, the Spinners, James Brown, Harold Melvin and the Blue Notes, Curtis Mayfield, the O'Jays, Aretha Franklin, and not necessarily performing their greatest hits.

Dead Solid Perfect

1990, Silva Screen Records, from the film *Dead Solid Perfect,* HBO Pictures, 1989 ♫♫♫♫

album notes: Music: Tangerine Dream.

Unlike most Tangerine Dream albums, this score for a light-hearted pre-*Tin Cup* look at the world of professional golf was assembled not from the full-length themes composed by the group, but from the cues edited down to create the film underscore. Until I was asked to assist engineer Alan Howarth and producer Ford A. Thaxton in creating a listenable album, I had not fully appreciate the group's ability to capture the nature of a film. I soon found we could assemble the wealth of short pieces into one big coherent symphonic suite. Having been most familiar with the film, and its quirky ambience, I discovered much to my amazement that Tangerine Dream's musical instincts were pretty much on target. I could hear pro-golfer Randy Quaid struggling with both his personal and professional life, with the music effectively capturing both the tension of the tournaments and Quaid's more lighthearted off-the-green antics ("A Whore in One").

David Hirsch

The Dead Zone

1994, Milan Records, from the film *Dead Zone*, Paramount Pictures, 1983 ♪♪♪

album notes: Music: Michael Kamen; **Orchestra:** The National Philharmonic Orchestra of London; **Conductor:** Michael Kamen; **Featured Soloist:** Sid Sax, violin; **Album Producer:** Michael Kamen.

This long overdue release of Michael Kamen's score to director David Cronenberg's successful adaption of the Stephen King story will be welcomed by all fans of the composer. Dreamy in pacing, subdued in nature, Kamen centers it all around Johnny, a man who has awakened from a coma to find he now has "second sight." It's not a gift, but a curse and Johnny, no matter how good his deed, will not be rewarded with happiness. He foreshadows the inevitable conclusion by drawing out as much pathos as he can muster, and even the theme "Lost Love" reeks with agony. As Johnny descends ineluctably into madness, Kamen makes sure we know that.

David Hirsch

Deadfall

1997, Retrograde Records, from the film *Deadfall*, 20th Century Fox, 1968 ♪♪♪

album notes: Music: John Barry; **Orchestra:** The London Philharmonic Orchestra; **Conductor:** John Barry; **Featured Soloist:** Renata Tarrago, guitar.

For many years, this soundtrack album (released on LP by 20th Century Fox Records, at a time when such a label existed) was every collector's prized possession or most-wanted title. There is, of course, a very simple reason for that. Written by John Barry for a thriller directed by Bryan Forbes, it featured among its choicest moments a sensational romance for guitar and orchestra which is considered one of the composer's most complete, most comprehensive creations, as well as one of his most attractive. Superbly performed by Renata Tarrago, it is the centerpiece of this new CD release, and impresses once again as a work of striking beauty and imagination (it is heard during one of the film's crucial sequences, a robbery that takes place during a concert, and lasts precisely as long as the performance of the piece itself). Characteristic of Barry's highly charged style, it is a work of striking originality, with strong romantic leanings, played for all its worth. The rest of the score, announced by Shirley Bassey's vocal on the song "My Love Has Two Faces," is an amalgam of flavorful cues that de-

lineate specific moments in the action, with this CD edition adding two previously unreleased tracks, both featuring the main song title in an alternate instrumental, and in a male vocal version.

Didier C. Deutsch

The Deadly Affair

See: The Pawnbroker

Deadly Care

1992, Silva America Records, from the film *Deadly Care*, Universal Pictures, 1987 ♪♪♪

album notes: Music: Tangerine Dream.

This score is one of Christopher Franke's last collaborations with the group Tangerine Dream before he left in 1987 to launch his own career as a film composer. It is a dark representation of a nurse's descent into drug and alcohol abuse, told with somber melodies and minimal orchestrations. It is an interesting change of pace for the group, known more for somewhat brighter harmonies (though not as bleak as *The Keep)*. The CD was assembled from the group's original studio recordings as opposed to the edited down versions adapted for use as the underscore.

David Hirsch

Dear World

1992, Sony Broadway, from the Broadway production *Dear World*, 1969 ♪♪♪

album notes: Music: Jerry Herman; **Lyrics:** Jerry Herman; **Musical Direction:** Donald Pippin; **Cast:** Angela Lansbury, Jane Connell, Carmen Mathews, Milo O'Shea, Pamela Hall, Kurt Peterson, Joe Masiell

Jean Giraudoux's play *The Madwoman of Chaillot* was the source for this flawed musical by Jerry Herman, which opened on Feb. 6, 1969, for a meager run of 132 performances. Starring Angela Lansbury, Jane Connell, Carmen Mathews, and Milo O'Shea, as sure-footed a cast as any, the musical failed to duplicate the success of *Mame* three years earlier largely because its characters were not as endearing, and audiences did not connect with this story about three holdovers from another era trying to fight big business in their desire to save the Paris environment. Though the title song was repeated as frequently in the score as "Hello, Dolly!" and "Mame" were in their respective shows, it too failed to make an impact.

Didier C. Deutsch

Death Becomes Her

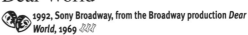

1992, Varèse Sarabande, from the film *Death Becomes Her*, Universal Pictures, 1992 ♪♪

album notes: Music: Alan Silvestri; **Conductor:** Alan Silvestri; **Featured Soloist:** Stuart Canin, violin.

If you took the most frantic, frenzied string sections of *Who Framed Roger Rabbit?* and *Back to the Future,* then wrote an entire score around them without composing a substantial theme to tie it all together, what you'd come up with would undoubtedly resemble *Death Becomes Her.* An often engaging, macabre fantasy from Robert Zemeckis (made after the *Future* sequels and prior to *Forrest Gump)* that never quite hits the bull's-eye, this rather tedious score from his long-time collaborator Alan Silvestri frequently grates on the listener for almost the length of its entire album, offering little variation or musical surprises outside of its dark, dissonant nature and thumping percussion section. It's an atmosphere score to be certain, working just fine as musical wallpaper in the movie, but it doesn't function at all outside of the film context it was intended to accompany. Recommended only for Silvestri completists.

Andy Dursin

Death Wish

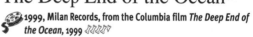1998, SMSP, from the Paramount film *Death Wish,* 1974 🎬🎬🎬

album notes: Music: Herbie Hancock.

Hancock third film score (after *Blow-Up* and *The Spook that Sat by the Door)* was for Michael Winner's revenge thriller *Death Wish.* Here Hancock fully realizes his film music talents and incorporates his compositional style into the demands of the picture and the basic Hollywood philosophy of more is better. The music is laden with strings and woodwinds. "Death Wish Main Title" is a funk groove typical of the Hancock Sextet from the early seventies. "Joanna's Theme" leans toward easy listening. "Suite Revenge" is a well-developed composition (the main title bass line incorporated into the background) that exposes the moods and colors of Hancock's music; it also features Hancock's acoustic piano playing, and he shows that his ears are wide open. "Party People" is performed by the Headhunters, and in the fashion of the times, the track reaches a magical climax, especially during Bennie Maupin's solo. The energy on the track demonstrates a rare-for-film-music level of intensity. The band is truly "going for it." Most of the other selections are mood cues created to lay well against the picture, but aren't performed as jazz vehicles.

Bob Belden

The Deceivers

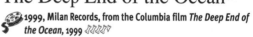1988, RCA Victor, from the film *The Deceivers,* Merchant Ivory Productions, 1988 🎬🎬🎬🎬

album notes: Music: John Scott; **Orchestra:** The Graunke Symphony Orchestra; **Conductor:** John Scott.

John Scott, another highly literate composer, provided the attractive score for this Merchant Ivory production, starring Pierce Brosnan, set in India at the turn of the century. Though the instrumentations occasionally call for an "ethnic" drum or rhythm, sometimes mixed with the more traditional orchestral figures, much of the music is written in broad, colorful epic and romantic tones that have little to do with the setting but that describe in bold terms the dramatic action on the screen.

Many cues are particularly attractive in the overall mix, but some stand out noticeably, among them the descriptive "Purge," a stately lovely "Deceivers Waltz," a jaunty "Madya Quadrille," and the bold "Defeat of the Deceivers." Performance by the Graunke Symphony Orchestra is right on target, though sonics are somewhat unfocused due to distant miking which flatters individual solo instruments but results in less definition when the full orchestra is heard.

Didier C. Deutsch

The Deep End of the Ocean

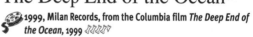1999, Milan Records, from the Columbia film *The Deep End of the Ocean,* 1999 🎬🎬🎬🎬

album notes: Music: Elmer Bernstein; **Conductor:** Elmer Bernstein.

Based on the popular novel by Jacquelyn Mitchard, *The Deep End of the Ocean* is an engrossing drama about a family completely devastated by the sudden disappearance of their 3-year-old son and the pervasive effects of his return nine years later. Adding a sensitive overlay to the story, Elmer Bernstein's score is a very evocative effort, unfortunately given short shrift here in this abusively short CD. Echoing the moods in the drama, the themes are very subdued and low-key, tinged with regrets and sorrow, and, like the film itself, which ends on a question mark for all concerned (with the boy now torn between his biological and his adopted families), the score may give the impression of being unresolved. It is only an impression, as Bernstein, a superb craftsman, certainly knows how to write music that makes a profound effect on the listener. His score for *The Deep End of the Ocean* may also be one of his finest achievements.

Didier C. Deutsch

Deep Impact

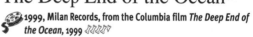1998, Sony Classical, from the Dreamworks film *Deep Impact,* 1998 🎬🎬🎬

album notes: Music: James Horner; **Conductor:** James Horner.

Deep Impact and *Armageddon* were the two meteor-on-the-loose films of 1998, and it's a measure of James Horner's score that *Impact* is by far the better one. Instead of adrenalin overkill, Horner delivers a smoothly humane score, one that's more concerned with human feeling than with disaster score clichés. That's not saying that the composer has reinvented the emotional style that he's used so well in *Titanic* and *Glory.* But it's just as effective here, a lush orchestra, heavenly chorus, and patriotic brass conveying the grave situation at hand for planet Earth, particularly for the American continent. Horner's style is both intimate and epic, with one moving theme sweeping in after another. While most of *Deep Impact* has the moving somberness of a memorial speech, Horner still delivers a terrific action cue with brass and strings beating a relentlessly suspenseful countdown to an atomic blast. *Deep Impact* reliably delivers the kind of symphonic fireworks that have become Horner's trademark in the land of Hollywood myth-making.

Dan Schweiger

Deep in the Heart (of Texas)

1998, Shanachie Records, from the film *Deep in the Heart (of Texas),* 1998 &&&&

Some great country stars perform on this soundtrack to a small, independently made film that may have eluded even the hardcore fans who might have enjoyed seeing it. Set in and around Austin, the amiable comedy drama started as a stage play, *In the West,* consisting of monologues delivered by an oddball assortment of individuals. The same concept was kept but expanded for the screen, something that might have proved ultimately detrimental as the focus of the film seemed too thin and diluted to have much of an effect, dramatic or otherwise. But the soundtrack offered several big-name artists an opportunity to perform on it, including Willie Nelson, Waylon Jennings, Marcia Ball, and Wayne Hancock, among others. The selections are quite enjoyable, and include Jennings and Jesse Coulter sharing a deeply felt duet, "Deep in the West," Lavelle White doing a stirring "Voodoo Man," Willie Nelson and Kimmie Rhodes trading vocals on "Just One Love," Lou Ann Barton wailing through "Stop These Teardrops," and Walter Hyatt, to whom this CD is dedicated, in two numbers, "This Time Lucille" and "Last Call," among other highlights. Missing here, however, probably for contractual reasons, is Lyle Lovett's "That's Right (You're Not from Texas)," which brought the film to a sturdy conclusion.

Didier C. Deutsch

Deep Rising

1998, Hollywood Records, from the Hollywood film *Deep Rising,* 1998 &&&

album notes: Music: Jerry Goldsmith; **Conductor:** Jerry Goldsmith.

Jerry Goldsmith must have had a great deal of fun scoring this film, while not spending too much time doing it: his themes are somewhat predictable, yet they are engagingly provocative, and one gets the impression that the soundtrack actually must have been much better than the film for which it was created. A story high on special effects and low on substance, *Deep Rising* was an old-fashioned whodunit in a new skin, involving Treat Williams and Famke Janssen somewhere in the South China Sea trying to get rid of a giant monster that has attacked and devastated a luxury liner on its maiden voyage. Nothing in the cue listing indicates how the music fits within the concept on the screen, but the brassy effects and sudden orchestral spurts show the sure hand of a master at the peak of his craft. It's not a great score, but it still is a lot of fun.

Didier C. Deutsch

The Deer Hunter

1989, Capitol Records, from the film *The Deer Hunter,* Universal Pictures, 1979 &&

album notes: Music: Stanley Myers; **Conductor:** Stanley Myers; **Featured Artist:** John Williams, guitar.

A stirring, sprawling saga, *The Deer Hunter* is an epic film in every sense of the word. Laced with literary allusions, it follows a group of friends from a small town in Pennsylvania whose coming-of-age includes a Russian orthodox marriage, a hunt, and a stint in Vietnam, where they are captured by the Vietcong and forced to submit to a game of Russian roulette. While symbols and references abound in the film directed by Michael Cimino, a contributing element to its success is its soundtrack, which incorporates Stanley Myers's informed music, traditional songs, and sound effects. This short (24 minutes) CD can hardly be said to effectively represent the film, but it contains Myers's lovely "Cavatina," performed by guitarist John Williams. Certainly, a film of this importance (it won five Oscars, including Best Picture and Best Direction) would justify a soundtrack album more representative than this.

Didier C. Deutsch

Def-Con 4

1990, Intrada Records, from the film *Def-Con 4: Defense Condition 4,* New World Pictures, 1990 &&&&

album notes: Music: Christopher Young; **Conductor:** Paul Francis Witt; **Featured Musicians:** John Fitzgerald, metallic sound sculptures, drums; Ara Tokatlian, South American woodwinds; Gary Nesteruk, piano; Larry Giannecchini, electric guitar; Mike Nelson, sax; Gregg Nestor, classical guitar; Karl Vincent, bass; David McKelvy, harmonica.

This excellent overview anthology of Christopher Young's early career starts off with 14 selections from his score to the 1985 post-apocalypse film *Def-Con 4,* notable because this was where he first created what he refers to as "Metallic Sound Sculptures." This tact is allowed to flourish even further on "Thantos," a track from the score for *Torment,* which, despite its electronic sounding demeanor, is strictly an acoustic creation. For fans of his more tonal work, Young has nicely contrasted these with selections from *Avenging Angel,* featuring a fine mix of broadly comical music and street jazz, and *The Telephone.* For the latter, he composed some excellent jazz tunes, but these cues were abandoned by the filmmakers in favor of previously tracked material. Some of the music from *Def-Con 4,* particularly "Armageddon," was tracked into the U.S. version of *Godzilla 1985.*

David Hirsch

Demolition Man

1993, A&M Records, from the Warner Bros. film *Demolition Man,* 1993 ⌀

album notes: Songs: Sting.

1993, Varèse-Sarabande Records, from the Warner Bros. film *Demolition Man,* 1993 ⌀⌀⌀

album notes: Music: Elliott Goldenthal; **Conductor:** Jonathan Sheffer.

Don't get misled by the fact that everything on the A&M album's cover seems to indicate that it is a soundtrack album: only the title tune is "featured" in the film. The other selections come from a live concert in Italy and have no relation to the Sylvester Stallone/Wesley Snipes sci-fi action drama. Unless you are a rabid Sting fan who must have everything bearing his name, you can forget this CD.

Conversely, you might want to listen to the soundtrack album, with music by Elliot Goldenthal. While the cues sound at times a bit routine—with big brassy effects contrasting with darker quieter moments—they are for the most part highly enjoyable, and certainly more representative of the film itself, implausibly set in a near future, in which the two protagonists eventually wake up after having been cryogenically frozen for a spell. Since this futuristic world is rather strait-laced sexually, much of the fun is derived from the violent action that opposes Sly and an incredibly blond Snipes, with the composer just having fun underscoring the action, with all the tenets of the genre thrown in for good measure, but not without a touch of impish malice ("Obligatory Car Chase," "Silver Screen Kiss").

Didier C. Deutsch

Dennis the Menace

1993, Big Screen Records, from the film *Dennis the Menace,* Warner Bros., 1993 ⌀⌀⌀

album notes: Music: Jerry Goldsmith; **Conductor:** Jerry Goldsmith; **Featured Musicians:** Jim Self, tuba; Tommy Morgan, harmonica

Jerry Goldsmith's entry in the *Home Alone* sweepstakes captures the spirit of its adorable tike star a bit too well. It's brimming with energy and good feeling, but also awfully annoying. The title theme is positively exuberant, charging along with the title character in a manner enjoyably reminiscent of the composer's propulsive theme to *The Great Train Robbery,* but most of the remainder of the album descends into Mickey Mousing hell as Goldsmith is forced to score the film's numerous pratfalls and kindergarten-level sight gags. Everything comes together for the obligatory heart-tugging finale, but by then you might be tempted to leave this CD with the sitter.

Jeff Bond

The Dentist/The Dentist 2

1998, Citadel Records, from the Trimark films *The Dentist,* 1996, and *The Dentist 2,* 1998 ⌀⌀⌀

album notes: Music: Alan Howarth.

Just when you though it was safe to go and see your orthodontist. . . . As befits its subject matter, the two scores by Alan Howarth (combined here in one seamless presentation) are pretty much offered *tongue in cheek.* There is a subtly *gnawing* desperation in some of the tracks, with others evidencing a much stronger *bite* to them. But all things being equal, you just might want to sink your . . . *teeth* into this one!

Didier C. Deutsch

Desert Blue

1999, Razor & Tie, from the film *Desert Blue,* 1999 ⌀⌀⌀

Directed by Morgan J. Freeman, this offbeat comedy takes place in Baxter, California, a town with a population of 89, known mostly for being the home of the "World's Biggest Ice Cream Cone" and a soda pop factory. During the visit of a traveling professor and his TV actress daughter, Skye (Kate Hudson), a truck full of the soda's secret ingredient crashes, spilling the ingredient and quarantining the town. Cynical city-girl Skye learns to appreciate the simple things in life with the help of newfound friends. Featuring an all-star Gen X cast, which also includes Christina Ricci, Casey Affleck, Sara Gilbert, and Brenden Sexton III as Blue, the movie boasts an understated soundtrack with songs by Janis Ian, Rocket from the Crypt, OP8 featuring Lisa Germano, Ben Lee, and unsigned band Rilo Kiley. Also featured on the soundtrack is the first duet from Nina Persson (the Cardigans) and Nathan Larson (Shudder to Think).

Beth Krakower

Desperado

1995, Epic Soundtrax, from the film *Desperado*, Columbia Pictures, 1995 ♫♫♫

album notes: Music: Los Lobos; **Songs:** Los Lobos

If you had picked up this soundtrack, you might not have been surprised when Antonio Banderas landed the Che role in "Evita"—although his warble-along with Los Lobos on "Cancion Del Mariachi (Morena De Mi Corazon)" hardly establishes his singing prowess. The rest of the album flaunts a cooly consistent Latin flavor, though it seems more restrained than it should be. Carlos Santana plays some beautiful solos on "Bella," and Link Wray & His Ray Men get a welcome resurrection on "Jack the Ripper."

Gary Graff

Desperate Measures

1998, Velvel Records, from the Mandalay Entertainment film *Desperate Measures*, 1998 ♫♫

album notes: Music: Trevor Jones; **Conductor:** Geoff Alexander.

Trevor Jones wrote a by-the-number score for this minor thriller starring Michael Keaton as a psychopath killer on the loose, wreaking havoc in a hospital and in a prison next door, after a good cop, looking for a bone marrow transplant candidate for his ailing son, zeroes in on him. Presumably the creepy synthesizer sounds are supposed to evoke the claustrophobic ambiance of the film, but they merely confirm the fact that Jones, a gifted composer, has been pigeonholed of late in a genre that doesn't allow him to progress or create something more interesting. As music-to-listen-to, *Desperate Measures* unfortunately comes across as a real letdown.

Didier C. Deutsch

Desperately Seeking Susan

See: Making Mr. Right/Desperately Seeking Susan

Destination Moon

1994, Citadel Records, from the film *Destination Moon*, Eagle-Lion Films, 1950 ♫♫♫♫

album notes: Music: Leith Stevens; **Orchestra:** The Vienna Concert Orchestra; **Conductor:** Heinz Sandauer.

A trend-setter and pioneering effort in space exploration, *Destination Moon* may seem laughable today, particularly in view of the tremendous technical advances made by the movies since it was produced almost half a century ago. But in its time, it was a tremendous cinematographic achievement that owed a large part of its success to George Pal's extraordinary special effects, and to Leith Stevens's bold score, a perfect musical illustration of the engrossing screen adventure. Presented in five sections, including two long cues, the score essentially follows the film's action, with "In Outer Space" attempting to describe in sheer musical terms the effects of weightlessness, and with the "Finale" erupting in joyous accents as the daring space explorers make their trip back to Earth. The score may be closer in spirit to the musical techniques used at the time than the selections that eventually made it into the much more advanced *2001: A Space Odyssey* (q.v.). But it is very effective in capturing the moods of this early odyssey, at a time when going to the moon was still a dream, and stands out well as a pure piece of film music.

Didier C. Deutsch

Devil in a Blue Dress

1995, Columbia Records, from the film *Devil in a Blue Dress*, TriStar Pictures, 1995 ♫♫♫

album notes: Music: Elmer Bernstein; **Conductor:** Elmer Bernstein.

Anyone buying this soundtrack album on the assumption that the music was composed by Elmer Bernstein may be confronted with a serious case of mistaken identity. Bernstein indeed wrote the score for this film, a murder mystery set in Los Angeles in the days following World War II that mixes races and politics, but his contribution is only represented here by three selections, including the film's "Theme" and "End Credits." In this case, however, the rest of the music is solidly rooted into some of the period's classic recordings, with rare and exciting sides by T-Bone Walker, Jimmy Witherspoon, Duke Ellington, Thelonious Monk, and Memphis Slim, among others, that define better than any other the rich background of the film itself. Contrasting with these mono recordings, Bernstein's cues may sound oddly out of place, but since they are relatively short and come completely at the end the effect is not too jarring. Also, it must be said that, though stylistically different, they are quite attractive, whetting one's appetite for a more comprehensive "score" album.

Didier C. Deutsch

The Devil in Miss Jones

1998, Oglio Records, from the film *The Devil in Miss Jones*, 1972 ♫♫♫

album notes: Music: Alden Shuman; **Conductor:** Peter DeAngelis, Ron Straigis.

The first pornographic feature to achieve widespread notoriety, *The Devil in Miss Jones* might also have been the first to have a soundtrack album, courtesy of Alden Shuman, whose atmospheric score owes little to the grand masters of the genre, although it occasionally has its own charms. Even if the music fails to conjure up erotic pictures, it holds its own. But mastering has left the music sounding shrill and at times unpleasant.

Didier C. Deutsch

Devil's Advocate

1997, TVT Records, from the Warner Bros. film *Devil's Advocate*, 1997 🎬🎬

album notes: Music: James Newton Howard; **Conductor:** Artie Kane; **Featured Musician:** Keegan DeLancie; **Choral Conductor:** Paul Salamunovich.

In the middle of this score, heavily loaded with big orchestral strains, out-of-this-world choruses, three-note riffs, and synthesizer effects, all appropriate for a film dealing simultaneously with lawyers and the Faust legend, composer James Newton Howard breaks into a great little jazzy tune, "Lovemaking," which places everything else into a different perspective. The track alone would be worth the price of this soundtrack album. The score itself is a standard orchestral effort, in which the supernatural moments are informed by the chords of an organ playing behind a wordless chorus over ominous instrumental lines. It's classic, except for the fact that the big cues are also devoid of melodic hooks. It creates a deep, unsettling sense of the mysterious, but as an audio experience it is not very enjoyable or even appealing. Bits of dialogue, by Al Pacino and Keanu Reeves, bookend this release, with Virgil Fox performing Bach's "Air on the G String" sounding totally alien in the middle of this mush.

Didier C. Deutsch

The Devil's Own

1997, Beyond Music, from the film *The Devil's Own*, Columbia Pictures, 1997 🎬🎬🎬🎬🎬

album notes: Music: James Horner; **Conductor:** James Horner; **Featured Musicians:** Sara Clancy, Tony Hinnigan, Tommy Hayes, Randy Kerber, Eric Rigler, Ian Underwood.

The Gaelic folk song "There Are Flowers Growing Upon the Hill," which bookends this album and contrasts its most searing moments, seems a perfect complement to this engrossing story of a member of the IRA who avoids arrest and prosecution by going into hiding in America and moving into the house of a New York Irish cop. Between the action cues that detail his flight from justice and involvement in additional revolutionary activities from his American base and the more lyrical accents that underscore the Irish soul of the story, James Horner's music, unusually low key and emotionally affecting, unfolds with great majesty and power. Some cues ("The New World," or "Secrets Untold," with its distant evocation of Ralph Vaughan Williams) are particularly attractive and denote a new level of maturity in the composer. Similarly, cues like "Launching the

Boat" draw their strength from the deft use of Irish-inspired melodies and instruments (notably the Uilleann flute and hornpipe) that confer them greater intensity and poetry. It all adds up to a very attractive and enjoyable soundtrack album.

Didier C. Deutsch

Diabolique

1996, edel America Records, from the film *Diabolique*, 1996 🎬🎬🎬

album notes: Music: Randy Edelman; **Conductor:** Randy Edelman; **Featured Soloist:** Randy Edelman, piano.

Though lacking some of the suspense in Henri-Georges Clouzot's 1955 thriller upon which this remake was based, *Diabolique* offers its share of throat-tightening moments in this exploration of the murder of an authoritarian schoolmaster in the hands of his sickly wife and strong-headed mistress, played by Isabelle Adjani and Sharon Stone respectively. Informing the chiller and some of its most visually frightful moments, Randy Edelman's score at times evokes Bernard Herrmann's urgently feverish music for some of Alfred Hitchcock's best dramas. Most often, however, there is little tension in the cues and none of the hallucinatory effects that would have taken the score to a higher level of effective illustration, as if the composer had

been afraid to be too extrovert. "A Stimulating Bath," "Empty Pool," and "Darkened Hallway," however, are appropriately somber and ominous sounding.

Didier C. Deutsch

Diamonds

1998, Cinephile/U.K., from the film *Diamonds,* Auco Embassy, 1975 ⅃⅃⅃⅃

album notes: Music: Roy Budd.

Richard Roundtree, Robert Shaw, and Shelley Winters were the main protagonists in this 1975 caper, in which a British aristocrat becomes a jewel thief the better to break into the high-security Tel Avid Diamond Repository built by his own brother. While the topic itself may have seemed a bit flimsy, it inspired Roy Budd to write a score heavily rooted in a contemporary mold. Mixing elements of Jewish folk tradition with jazz riffs and sounds usually associated with the "blaxploitation" movies (Roundtree's presence in the cast might have suggested these shades of *Shaft* for his own score), Budd also created a sensuous main theme that opens the CD and sets the tone for much of what follows. In the mix, he also included all sorts of unusual instruments—tablas, drums, wah-wah guitars, saxophones, harpsichords, cymbaloms, electronic keyboards—which combined with the orchestra to create attractive and exotic moods. Some selections easily stand out in the album, like "Diamond Fortress," with its Bob James-y brassy calls, reminiscent of early Grover Washington recordings, or the jazz samba "I Think I'm Being Followed," in which Duncan Lamont's fluent sax becomes a major feature. Bringing a different dimension to the score, the Three Degrees perform three vocals that further enhance the proceedings.

see also: The Black Windmill, Fear Is the Key, Paper Tiger, Sinbad and the Eye of the Tiger, Get Carter

Didier C. Deutsch

Diamonds are Forever

1995, Capitol-EMI Music, from the film *Diamonds are Forever,* United Artists, 1971 ⅃⅃⅃⅃

album notes: Music: John Barry; Conductor: John Barry.

John Barry was at the peak of his creativity when he scored the James Bond films. Though he derisively characterized his contributions to the screen exploits of Agent 007 as "million-dollar Mickey Mouse music," the fact is that no one else (and there have been others) managed to match the sense of fun and sheer merriment Barry brought to his scores. Fans of Bond and Barry (the two names have become almost inseparable) often

argue over which of Barry's scores stand out among those he wrote, but *Diamonds are Forever* is often mentioned as one of the best, which doesn't mean that this recorded representation is necessarily as good as it should be. As a matter of fact, among the Bond score recordings, this is probably the one that most closely resembles a near-miss: The best cues in the film have been left out of the soundtrack album, and those that have been included sound in dire need of a good remixing and mastering. Still, there are some memorable moments in the album, notably the quirky "Moon Buggy Ride," with its fun extrapolations on xylophone and flute; "Tiffany Case," a seductive kitschy lounge cue; the jazzy "Q's Trick," with its enjoyable big band riff; and of course Shirley Bassey's rendition of the title tune, which was perhaps not as pungent as "Goldfinger," but again nothing could have possibly matched that song and Bassey's treatment of it.

Didier C. Deutsch

Dick Tracy/Madonna: I'm Breathless

Dick Tracy (score); 1990, Sire Records, from the film *Dick Tracy,* Warner Bros., 1990 ⅃⅃⅃

album notes: Music: Danny Elfman; Conductor: Shirley Walker.

It only seemed natural that after *Batman,* Danny Elfman would become the top composer of the comic strip hero, a position he quickly tired of. In his music for *Dick Tracy,* however, the novelty had not yet worn out, and his whimsical approach is less rooted in the dark detective film-noir, and more in the gangster epics of Elliot Ness and *The Untouchables,* and the music of Gershwin. Making it even more seductive, there's some nice "Big Band" influences to portray bad girl torch singer Breathless Mahoney, and an innocent love theme for Tracy's girl, Tess Trueheart.

David Hirsch

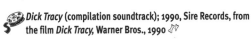

Dick Tracy (compilation soundtrack); 1990, Sire Records, from the film *Dick Tracy,* Warner Bros., 1990 ⅃⅃

Madonna: I'm Breathless; 1990, Sire Records, from the film *Dick Tracy,* Warner Bros., 1990 ⅃⅃⅃

If Andy Paley, whose name is all over the first album as producer, writer or co-writer of most of the songs, and occasional artist/performer, were slightly more talented, this *Dick Tracy* CD could actually be enjoyable. But the pop songs he wrote for the occasion border on the banal, and only the performances by an all-star cast (which includes k.d. lang, Jerry Lee Lewis, Darlene Love, Patti Austin, Al Jarreau, August Darnell, Ice-T, and LaVern Baker, among its most recognizable names) make this album more interesting than it actually is. Also, notably missing from that collection are the songs written by Stephen Sondheim and performed by Madonna as Breathless Mahoney, which can be found on the second CD. In this case, the combination of the gifted songwriter and the talented performer proves explosive and turns the album into a totally delirious burst of enjoyment. Madonna demonstrates another side of her creativity by cowriting some of the other songs on the album, which are not at all bad.

Didier C. Deutsch

Die Hard 2: Die Harder

1990, Varèse Sarabande, from the film *Die Hard 2: Die Harder*, 20th Century Fox, 1990 ♪♪

album notes: Music: Michael Kamen; **Orchestra:** The Los Angeles Motion Picture All-Stars Orchestra; **Conductor:** Michael Kamen; **Featured Soloists:** Mel Colins, saxophone; Derick Collins, clarinet; Sid Sax, violin.

This lackluster follow-up to the original film score (still unreleased at press time) fails to capture the energy Michael Kamen established with his first effort.

David Hirsch

Die Hard with a Vengeance

1995, RCA Victor, from the film *Die Hard with a Vengeance*, 20th Century Fox, 1995 ♪

album notes: Music: Michael Kamen; **Orchestra:** The Symphony Seattle; *Conducted:* Michael Kamen.

Like *Die Hard 2*, this album wanders aimlessly, "Mickey Mousing" the action with nary a memorable theme present. This all may be partly due to poor sequencing, since the score was unfinished when the CD was pressed to meet its release date (which also explains the lack of track titles on the packaging). Pop songs and classical cues were added on the latter to fill time.

David Hirsch

Diggstown

1992, Varèse Sarabande, from the film *Diggstown*, MGM, 1992 ♪

album notes: Music: James Newton Howard; **Conductor:** James Newton Howard; **Featured Musicians:** Marc Bonilla, guitars; John Robinson, drums; Neil Stubenhaus, bass guitar; Tommy Morgan, harmonica; Michael Finnigan, Hammond organ; Bob Zimmitti, percussion.

The lack of musical focus in this score may be its most characteristic aspect. Literally speaking, the music is all over the place, not knowing whether to call it rock, soundtrack, folk, or quits. For the most part, the cues tend to be dominated by electric guitar riffs over long synth lines that go nowhere, and an obligatory booming drum beat. Unfortunately, it sounds very dry, not very

inspired and in bad need of a central thematic idea. Even semi-interesting concepts like "Tank," with its blues ending, are not sufficiently developed to catch one's interest. James Newton Howard has done much better things before and since.

Didier C. Deutsch

Diner

1982, Elektra/Asylum Records, from the film *Diner*, MGM, 1982 ♪♪♪♪♪

Great movie, great soundtrack–in fact, maybe the best collection of '50s music in any movie this side of *American Graffiti*. It doesn't have everybody (no Chuck Berry, for instance), but the names that are here—Elvis Presley, Jerry Lee Lewis, Fats Domino, Jimmy Reed, Dion & the Belmonts, Jack Scott, and more—are all hall-of-fame choices. ·

Gary Graff

Dingo

1991, Warner Bros. Records, from the film *Dingo*, Greycat Films, 1991 ♪♪♪♪♪

album notes: Music: Miles Davis, Michel Legrand; **Featured Musicians:** Miles Davis, Chuck Findley, Nolan Smith, Ray Brown, George Graham, Oscar Brashear, trumpet; Kei Akagi, Alan Oldfield, Michel Legrand, piano; Mark Rivett, guitar; John Bigham, Ricky Wellman, Harvey Mason, Alphonse Mouzon, drums, percussion; Benny Rietveld, "Foley," Abe Laboriel, bass; Kenny Garrett.

Early in their respective careers, Miles Davis and French composer Michel Legrand worked together on a trend-setting jazz album, so this soundtrack may, in a sense, be considered a reunion of sorts. The score, for a film made in Australia, is mostly noteworthy for Legrand's sometimes explosive cues ("Concert on the Runway," "Letter as Hero," "Paris Walking II," "The Jam Session"), and for Davis's unmistakable style. Chuck Findley, who takes the spotlight on several tracks, brings to the proceedings a different flair, with both trumpeters receiving solid support from an impressive array of seasoned performers, including Abe Laboriel on bass, Harvey Mason and Alphonse Mouzon on drums, and Legrand himself on piano. An occasional bit of dialogue places some of the tracks into the film's context.

Didier C. Deutsch

The Dinosaurs

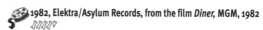 1993, Narada Cinema, from the PBS television series *The Dinosaurs*, 1993 ♪♪♪♪

album notes: Music: Peter Melnick; **Featured Musicians:** Peter Melnick, piano, synthesizers, acoustic slide guitar; George Doering, electric and nylon–string guitar; Bryce Martin, didjeridu, the screaming pipe; John Yoakum, saxophones, oboe, English horn, clarinet, flutes,

David Stone, bass; Brad Dutz, percussion; Charles Judge, keyboards and synthesizer.

Suddenly, dinosaurs are popping up all over the place, in the movies where *Jurassic Park* and *The Lost World* present their own version of the terrifying world of 140 million years ago and on television where various series attempt to recreate that Neanderthal time when huge monsters roamed the earth. One such series, *The Dinosaurs!* seen on PBS, took a professorial approach to its subject, and investigated the scientific aspects of the question, as well as its most speculative elements.

Augmenting the presentation is Peter Melnick's score, a deft mixture of acoustic and electronic instruments. Since no music existed at the time, one must assume that Melnick's, contemporary as it may sound, is as valid as anything else, at least where the series is concerned. Taken at face value, it is a pleasant blend of New Age–sounding cues, that has the enormous merit of sounding quite pleasant out of its own environment. For someone who has not seen the four–part series, it is difficult to comprehend what a cue like "From Maastricht to Paris" might be doing in the middle of a program dedicated to dinosaurs, but the music eloquently speaks for itself, so who cares?

Didier C. Deutsch

Dirty Dancing /Dirty Dancing (More Dirty Dancing)

 *Dirty Dancing*; 1987 RCA Records, from the Vestron film *Dirty Dancing*, 1987 ♪♪♪♪

 *Dirty Dancing: More Dirty Dancing*; 1988, RCA Records, from the Vestron film *Dirty Dancing*, 1987 ♪♪♪♪

album notes: Music: John Morris.

Dirty Dancing is a wonderful coming-of-age story of a Jewish girl whose family goes to the Catskills for the summer of 1963. There she meets a dance instructor from the wrong side of the tracks, played by Patrick Swayze. When his dance partner can't dance, she takes over and they fall in love. The success of the film spawned two soundtrack albums. The first combines classic '60s tunes like "Stay," "Be My Baby," and "Love Is Strange" with new songs written for the movie, including "(I've Had) The Time of My Life," which became a hit for Bill Medley and Jennifer Warnes, and "Hungry Eyes," also a hit for Eric Carmen.

More Dirty Dancing contains two instrumental versions of "(I've Had) The Time of My Life," more great '60s songs, "Kellerman's Anthem" performed in the movie, and several of the tracks that were danced to in the movie but never made it to the first soundtrack. The recently reissued version of *Dirty Dancing* in-

cludes special packaging and, you guessed it, the movie version of "(I've Had) The Time of My Life." Four versions of the same song in two CDs seems a bit excessive.

Beth Krakower

The Disappearance of Garcia Lorca

 1997, Intrada Records, from the Triumph film *The Disappearance of Garcia Lorca*, 1997 ♪♪♪♪

album notes: Music: Mark McKenzie; **Conductor:** Mark McKenzie; **Featured Musician:** Manolo Seguira, flamenco singing.

Federico Garcia Lorca (1898–1936) was a celebrated Spanish poet and playwright, who inspired this film, based on the books of Ian Gibson, directed by Marcos Zurinaga. The film, in turn, inspired this wonderful instrumental score, written by Mark McKenzie, who acknowledges in a brief commentary that he set out to reflect in his music the "pathos, romance, passion, and drama" that were the essence of Lorca's poetry. With an occasional assist from Manolo Seguira, a flamenco singer whose contribution essentially supports the concept of death so frequently invoked by the poet, the music occasionally suggests vivid images of a sunburnt Spain, but mostly the psychological and emotional feelings of the film's central character, in themes that are eloquent in their expression, such as "Ricardo's Theme," "A Thunderstorm Is Brewing," "Blood of a Poet," or the admirably titled "The Crumbling Sound of Daisies." Capping the whole score is an orchestral suite that enables the composer to develop some of his themes into a more cohesive, more elaborate format. It provides a fitting finale to this excellent album.

Didier C. Deutsch

Disclosure

 1995, Virgin Movie Music, from the film *Disclosure*, Warner Bros., 1995 ♪♪♪♪

album notes: Music: Ennio Morricone; **Orchestra:** Orchestra Unione Musicisti di Roma; **Conductor:** Ennio Morricone.

The lovely "Serene Family" that introduces this score soon gives way to more ominous sounds, as if to indicate that not everything is quite right in this complex story of a computer analyst whose new boss turns out to be an old flame and who finds himself accused of sexual harassment when he refuses to rekindle their love affair. With his usual crafty sense of drama and tension, Morricone conjures up the best and worst in the screen action, with cues that subtly underscore it while creating an aura of their own that is difficult to dismiss. Most fascinating in this set of musical images are the three similarly themed "Passacaglias," in which the composer uses all the orchestral resources at his disposal to create cues that are particularly evocative.

Dirty Dancing **(The Kobal Collection)**

Didier C. Deutsch

The Distinguished Gentleman

1992, Varèse Sarabande, from the film *The Distinguished Gentleman*, Hollywood Pictures, 1992 ♫♫♫

album notes: Music: Randy Edelman; **Conductor:** Randy Edelman.

An exuberant calypso, "Where the Money Is," sets the extravagant tone to this colorful comedy starring Eddie Murphy as a small-time con man from Miami who is transported into the world of politics after he is mistaken for a deceased congressman. Contrasting the happy tones of this telling tune, Randy Edelman created a series of grander-than-life cues to depict the general atmosphere that pervades the new surroundings in which the con man and his associates, suddenly find themselves. It is an amusing juxtaposition that gives the score its greatest strength, and turns it into a joyous musical affair. In the process, the composer reveals a quirky mind in tunes like the pleasantly lilting "Lucrative Luncheon," and a flair for the grandiloquent in selections like "The Distinguished Gentleman March" or "Taking Sides on the Issue." It would be significantly

more exciting, however, had the cues been further developed than they are (many of them hover between a minute and a minute-and-a-half of playing time, not enough to truly make a lasting impression).

Didier C. Deutsch

Disturbing Behavior

1998, Sonic Images, from the MGM film *Disturbing Behavior*, 1998 ♫♫

album notes: Music: Mark Snow.

There is no denying the fact that Mark Snow knows how to use synthesizer riffs to write music that is effective in creating weird, unsettling moods. He proves it all over again in this score for a film that didn't deserve all the attention. Set in a quiet little town in Middle America, the quaint storyline, a loose adaptation of the 1975 *Stepford Wives*, opposes the forces of good and evil, personified here by a new kid in town and the "freak" who sides with him, and a bunch of "perfect" high school students who may be part of a sinister conspiracy caused by the school's psychiatrist. Mark Snow informs the plot with ominous-sounding synth chords that want to sound threatening, although they only achieve a numbing effect, not unlike the gloomy moods suggested by his music for the TV series *The X-Files.* Occasionally, a quiet little chime startles a bit, but this is strictly a score by the numbers.

Didier C. Deutsch

Diva

1986, Rykodisc/DRG Records, from the film *Diva,* Galaxie Films & Greenwich Film Productions, 1981 🎬🎬🎬

album notes: Music: Vladimir Cosma; **Orchestra:** The London Symphony Orchestra; **Conductor:** Vladimir Cosma; **Featured Soloists:** Hubert Varron, cello; Raymond Allesandri, piano; Vladimir Cosma, piano; **Featured Artist:** Wilhelmenia Wiggins Fernandez.

Vladimir Cosma, one of France's most popular film composers but a relative unknown in this country, delivered one of his best scores for this film, directed by Jean-Jacques Beineix, about the young admirer of a celebrated soprano, and a recording he made of one of her performances, which bootleggers want to acquire. The film did much to popularize Alfredo Catalini's aria from the obscure opera "La Wally," but it also attracted attention to Cosma for the wonderful qualities in his score, particularly the evocative "Sentimental Walk," heard in a scene in which the soprano and her young fan are seen walking in the rain in the desolated Jardin des Tuileries in Paris. Unlike some of Cosma's more quirky efforts, however, the other selections here are less defined and not as powerfully imaginative.

Didier C. Deutsch

Divine Madness

1980, Atlantic Records, from the film *Divine Madness,* Warner Bros., 1980 🎬🎬🎬🎬

This recording of standards and new tunes performed by the exhilarating Bette Midler will no doubt appeal to all her fans, if they don't already own the CD. Others will react to it according to their own tolerance for the tongue-in-cheek style of the star, and her often outrageous stage antics. Recorded during a concert performance, the selections have the spontaneity and energetic drive that usually characterize the singer's free-wheeling approach when she finds herself in front of an audience totally attuned to her. Sonically, the recording is not all that it should be, with the large hall blurring some of the sound qualities, particularly in the big up-tempo numbers, but don't let that deter you from enjoying it.

Didier C. Deutsch

Django

1995, King Records/Japan, from the film *Django,* 1966 🎬🎬🎬

album notes: Music: Luis Bacalov; **Conductor:** Luis Bacalov.

A film by Sergio Corbucci, and perhaps one of the best spaghetti westerns he directed, *Django* starred Franco Nero as a former Yankee soldier, dragging along with him a coffin, who settles in a little Texas border town and finds himself caught in the crossfire between a ruthless Mexican general and a rebel gang leader. Bacalov studiously avoided the Morricone-like accents, and tried to develop his own style, in which the bass guitar plays an essential role in evoking the tension in the action, as well as its Mexican locale, evoked in the attractive "Waltz of Juana Yimena." But the dominant discordant effects underline the unusual aspects of this thrilling score, with "Vamonos Muchachos," frequently heard in compilations, striking a more familiar note. This title may be out of print or just plain hard to find. Mail-order companies, used CD shops, or dealers of rare or import recordings will be your best bet.

see also: Quien sabe?, Sugar Colt

Didier C. Deutsch

Do I Hear a Waltz?

1992, Sony Broadway, from the Broadway production *Do I Hear A Waltz?* 1965 🎬🎬🎬

album notes: Music: Richard Rodgers; **Lyrics:** Stephen Sondheim; **Musical Direction:** Frederick Dvonch; **Cast:** Elizabeth Allen, Sergio Franchi, Carol Bruce, Madeleine Sherwood, Julienne Marie, Stuart Damon.

Based on Arthur Laurents's *Time of the Cuckoo,* which had already served as the basis for the film *Summertime,* starring Katharine Hepburn and Rossano Brazzi, *Do I Hear a Waltz?* had all the earmarks of a great musical. With a score by Richard Rodgers, his first since *No Strings,* and lyrics by Broadway wunderkind Stephen Sondheim, a protégé of the late Oscar Hammerstein, it was already touted as the next Tony Award winner and a rightful successor to some of the best works bearing Rodgers's name. By the time it finally opened on Broadway, on March 18, 1965, however, things had soured considerably, and despite some positive reviews and glowing comments about the score, it failed to attract an audience and closed after 220 performances. Surprisingly, it was the combination Rodgers-Sondheim that failed to ignite: The composer, a traditionalist at heart, evidently didn't take too kindly some of the lyrics his younger collaborator proposed; conversely, Sondheim, forced to comply with the criteria of a "Rodgers musical," was unable to display some of the wit and sardonic edge he had previously exhibited in his own works, like *A Funny Thing*

Happened on the Way to the Forum, and more specifically *Anyone Can Whistle.*

By the time the show reached Broadway, this story of an American spinster visiting Venice and falling in love with a married Italian man had become so edulcorated that it had lost much of its bite and had become quite ordinary, if not actually tepid. Further compounding the problems the show encountered during its tryout period was the evident lack of stage chemistry between Elizabeth Allen as the spinster and Sergio Franchi obviously ill-at-ease as her Latin lover. Still the cast album recording reveals many attractive moments in the score, particularly the lilting title tune, which is Leona's way to find out that she's in love, and the diaphanous "Moon in My Window," in which Leona and two other women dream about love everlasting while looking at the bright Venetian moon.

Beth Krakower

Do It A Cappella

1990, Elektra Records, from the PBS–TV Great Performances special *Spike & Co.: Do It A Cappella,* 1990 ✍✍✍✍

album notes: Featured Artists: True Image, The Mint Juleps, Rockapella, The Persuasions, Ladysmith Black Mambazo, Take 6.

Director Spike Lee will surely be remembered for many achievements, but this glorious made—for—public–TV salute to a cappella singing groups should not be overlooked. He didn't direct it, merely played host, but it wouldn't have happened without him. Filmed mainly at an ancient movie palace in Brooklyn, N.Y., the performances range from the Persuasions' post—doo–wop, to Rockapella's greaser cabaret, to Take 6's neo–jazz–gospel, and include a show–stopping set by South Africa's Ladysmith Black Mambazo. The video laser disc includes nearly half an hour of extra music.

Marc Kirkeby

Do Re Mi

1994, RCA Victor, from the Broadway production *Do Re Mi,* 1961 ✍✍✍✍

album notes: Music: Jule Styne; **Lyrics:** Betty Comden & Adolph Green; **Musical Direction:** Lehman Engel; **Cast:** Phil Silvers, Nancy Walker, John Reardon, Nancy Dussault, David Burns.

Television and film comedian Phil Silvers starred as an unflinching wheeler-dealer in this delirious musical with a score by Jule Styne, Betty Comden, and Adolph Green. In the book written by Garson Kanin, Silvers portrayed a would-be music tycoon, convinced he can make a big deal if he muscles his way into the then-nascent jukebox business with the help of three of his cronies. While he hardly succeeds, he manages to launch the career of a singer, played by Nancy Dussault. Another

beloved clown, Nancy Walker, portrayed Silvers's long-suffering wife, with both ensuring that the show, which opened Dec. 26, 1960, would have a long run of 400 performances. Also contributing to the success of the musical was the strong score, in which "Make Some Happy" soon emerged as a show-stopping number, as did "It's Legitimate," with Silvers, and his three mobster friends (David Burns, George Mathews, and George Givot), evoking the success they're bound to find as music entrepreneurs.

Didier C. Deutsch

Do the Right Thing

1989, Columbia Records, from the Filmworks film *Do The Right Thing,* 1988 ✍✍✍

album notes: Music: Bill Lee; **Conductor:** Bill Lee; **Featured Musicians:** Branford Marsalis, tenor/soprano sax; Donald Harrison, alto sax; Terence Blanchard, Marlon Jordan, trumpet; Robert Hurst, bass; Jeff "Tain" Watts, drums; Kenny Barron, James Williams, piano.

There's something immensely attractive about Spike Lee's films, and particularly his early efforts where he didn't try to be too preachy, yet made films that had a universal appeal, while keeping firmly to their black roots. Such a film was *Do the Right Thing,* which, while taking a comedic tone, made sharply pointed comments about life in New York's Bed-Stuy, a hotbed of violence that eventually engulfed the 'hood after it was ignited by a controversial pizzeria owned by white folks. True to form, the soundtrack for this one, composed by Bill Lee, featured some solid jazz playing, courtesy of Branford Marsalis and Donald Harrison, ably supported by Terence Blanchard, Marlon Jordan, Robert Hurst, Jeff Watts, Kenny Barron, and James Williams. The only reproach one might have about this album is that most of the tracks are much too short. With the exception of a couple of selections clocking in at more than four minutes ("Mookie," "Father to Son," and "Wake Up Finale"), the other tracks all come under two minutes, which, in a medium like jazz, is saying that there is no music at all. In fact, these tunes sound as if they were incomplete or unfinished. Too bad: with those players, it could have been a terrific CD.

Didier C. Deutsch

D.O.A.

1988, Varèse-Sarabande, from the Touchstone film *D.O.A.,* 1988 ✍✍✍✍

album notes: Music: Chaz Jankel.

The pop-orchestral style was the film scoring rage of the late 1980s, a dated, but funky blend of synth rhythms and strings that was practiced by every composer from Harold Faltermeyer to Jerry Goldsmith. But one composer who got lost in the shuffle was Chaz Jankel, whose score to *D.O.A.* might stand as the niftiest entry in the bunch. While there isn't much to remember in this lame remake about a poisoned man trying to track down his killer, Jankel's score conjures a memorable atmosphere of dread, sadness, and suspense with a number of cool themes. Jankel certainly has a unique vision of a film noir score, his orchestra dancing through rock guitars, creepy synth samples, and exotic cymbalom. The whole score seems on the verge of breaking into a pop song, which it nearly does in its memorable "Love Scene." This ultra-rare Varèse CD is worth hunting down to hear Jankel's unique and catchy sound. After *D.O.A.*, he went on to score *Making Mr. Right, The Rachel Papers,* and *K2*, and then dropped out of film scoring sight. I can only hope that Chaz Jankel's innovative sound doesn't remain "D.O.A."

Dan Schweiger

Doc Hollywood

1991, Varèse Sarabande, from the film *Doc Hollywood*, Warner Bros., 1991 ♪♪♪♪

album notes: Music: Carter Burwell; **Conductor:** Sonny Kompanek.

Ths delightfully off-base score by Carter Burwell does well contrasting the high-powered dreams of a big city doctor (Michael J. Fox) sentenced to perform community service in a small Southern town. The use of zydeco music, previously established in the *Northern Exposure* TV series, adds the right amount of absurdity, especially in a hilarious sequence called "Pee Zydeco" (see the movie to find out). However, it's Burwell's moving variations on a romantic, ambient vocal theme, particularly "Voices Across the Lake," that really stick in the mind.

David Hirsch

Doctor Dolittle

1997, Philips Records, from the film *Doctor Dolittle*, 20th Century Fox, 1967 ♪♪♪

album notes: Music: Leslie Bricusse; **Lyrics:** Leslie Bricusse; **Orchestra:** The 20th Century Fox Orchestra; **Conductor:** Lionel Newman; **Cast:** Rex Harrison, Samantha Eggar, Anthony Newley.

1998, Atlantic Records, from the 20th Century-Fox film *Doctor Dolittle*, 1998 woof!

A big, sprawling musical, *Doctor Dolittle* aimed to be another *Mary Poppins*, though it lacked that film's undeniable charm and memorable songs. Based on Hugh Lofting's original stories about a 19th Century veterinarian who has learned to talk to the animals (in everything from "Alligatorese" to "Zebran"), it starred Rex Harrison as the benign Doctor, along with Anthony Newley, Samantha Eggar, and a large, colorful cast. Sadly, the songs by Leslie Bricusse fail to capture the whimsy of the stories. While they are enjoyable in their own right, they never quite achieved the anticipated popularity, though "Talk to the Animals" received an Academy Award in 1967 for "Best Original Song." The CD reissue, marking the 30th anniversary of the film's release, simply replicates the original LP, and is noticeable for the fact that it is particularly hissy in some passages.

The new version, with Eddie Murphy portraying the good doctor who talks to the animals, may appall people who were groomed on the earlier film starring Rex Harrison in the titular role. Equally appalling is the use, in this update, of "contemporary" songs that lack total melodic appeal. It's amazing what may pass today as song material—"noise" that has little music in it, lyrics that are frighteningly trite and inane, and a beat that seems to be the same no matter what the so-called songs might be about. Yet we seem to accept this form of expression as being "cool" and "real." And why would anyone redo "Lady Marmalade," not a great track to begin with but one that had some spunk, if it is to do it in a way that sounds so miserable? In the midst of all this morass, Dawn Robinson and Jody Watley try very hard to survive, and somewhat succeed. But 69 Boyz sum it up best: **woof! woof!**

Didier C. Deutsch

Doctor Faustus

See: Francis of Assisi/Doctor Faustus

Dr. Giggles

1992, Intrada Records, from the film *Dr. Giggles*, Largo Entertainment/Universal Pictures, 1992 ♪♪♪

album notes: Music: Brian May; **Orchestra:** Brian May.

Brian May scored the first two *Mad Max* films for director George Miller, and even though the film brought great success to Miller and star Mel Gibson, the Australian May never quite broke into the Hollywood studio system, despite having a great deal of talent that never seemed to realize its full potential on this side of the Atlantic. One of May's rare late excursions into U.S. films came when he scored *Dr. Giggles*, Manny Coto's tired horror-parody with *L.A. Law* star Larry Drake. With a full-blooded orchestra behind him, May wrote a decent score for a movie that didn't deserve as much, marked by a motif for the title protagonist that's dark and menacing, but more like an old-time Universal horror movie than Danny Elfman. The music is well done but offers few surprises, so genre addicts might want to check it out, though others are advised to head elsewhere.

Andy Dursin

Dr. Jekyll and Ms. Hyde

1995, Intrada Records, from the film *Dr. Jekyll and Ms. Hyde,* Savoy Pictures, 1995 ♪♪♪♪

album notes: Music: Mark McKenzie; **Conductor:** Randy Thornton; **Featured Vocalist:** Patricia Swanson, soprano.

A spin off the old chestnut horror story about Dr. Jekyll and his nefarious alter ego Mr. Hyde (in this case a feminine incarnation for added fun), *Dr. Jekyll and Ms. Hyde* gave Mark McKenzie an opportunity to write an expansive, lyrical score, in which broad swathes of musical humor add an unexpected and welcome touch. The recurring main theme, a deft confrontation of two musical elements (one for each of the main character's dual personalities), amusingly pervades the score, in which an occasional Gothic accent is brought by the cliched contribution of an organ. Throughout, in keeping with the film's tongue-in-cheek approach to its subject, McKenzie displays his thorough musical flair, with some delightful moments ("Off to Work," "A Little Surprise," "Helen Deflates") emerging as a result. Even the inclusion of the "Habanera," from Bizet's opera *Carmen,* does not seem so out of place in the overall outrageous score.

Didier C. Deutsch

Dr. No

1995, EMI Records, from the film *Dr. No,* United Artists, 1962 ♪♪

album notes: Music: Monty Norman; **Conductor:** Monty Norman.

Forget the credits, this album automatically raises the question who did actually write the famous "James Bond Theme?" Is it Monty Norman, whose only other screen credits include the obscure *House of Fright* and *Dickens of London?* Or is it, as he all along contended, John Barry, whose impeccable credentials include, in addition to a dozen other James Bond scores, a flurry of Academy Award–nominated and winning contributions? Whatever the case, this soundtrack to the first James Bond film teems with some good moments, mostly those relating to the exotic Caribbean locale of the action, like "Kingston Calypso," "Jump-Up," "Under the Mango Tree," and some painfully dispensable ones, like "Audio Bongo," for instance, which offers very little, musically speaking, or the dated "Twisting With James." This, however, is not the only problem with this generally charmless album. The fact that the tracks are improperly sequenced notwithstanding, this is probably the worst-sounding CD you are likely to find, with a lot of hiss on the tracks, some distortion, and a shrillness that makes the best tracks difficult to listen to. Chalk this one up as yet another soundtrack album that needs to be properly EQ'd before it is deemed acceptable by digital standards.

Didier C. Deutsch

Doctor Who

See: Evolution: The Music from Dr. Who

Doctor Who: The Curse of Fenric

1991, Silva Screen Records, from the BBC–TV series *Doctor Who,* 1971–1990 ♪♪♪

album notes: Music: Mark Ayres; **Arrangements:** Mark Ayres; **Music Performed by:** Mark Ayres.

This synthesized score was written and performed by Mark Ayers for one of the final stories for long–running BBC–TV series. Of all the *Doctor Who* scores, this is perhaps one of the more well–developed, in particular its striking themes for the alien presence that pervades a World War II British Naval Camp and the adjacent town. Despite the notoriously short transitional cues that all the composers were often faced with writing, Ayers has developed a work here that on the whole builds nicely toward its climax. This was his second of three *Doctor Who* scores, both *Ghost Light* and *The Greatest Show in the Galaxy* have also been released and this album features additional music he composed for the expanded home video release. The version of the classic *Doctor Who* theme (composed by Ron Grainer) is not the version featured in the final show.

David Hirsch

Doctor Zhivago

1995, Rhino Records, from the film *Doctor Zhivago,* MGM, 1965 ♪♪♪♪♪

album notes: Music: Maurice Jarre; **Orchestra:** The MGM Studio Orchestra; **Conductor:** Maurice Jarre.

This new reissue of Maurice Jarre's score for *Dr. Zhivago* is another brilliant example of what can be accomplished with vision, diligence, and creative fortitude. For that's what the Rhino editions of the MGM classic soundtracks are all about–dedication. If you love *Dr. Zhivago,* this disc is for you. Every snippet of Jarre's music for the tremendously successful film can be found here, in its original, unedited form. Of course, "Lara's Theme" (the leitmotif for the entire film) is included, and as a bonus, the producers have added three alternate versions that were made as impromptú "tension breakers" at the original scoring sessions. It's a treat to hear this group of veteran Hollywood musicians interpret the theme as a jazz, rock, and swing tune. There are also a number of out-takes and the accompanying booklet contains commentary by Jarre, and in-depth examinations of the story and score. The sound, as is often the case with these Rhino reissues, is excellent.

Charles L. Granata

Doctor Zhivago *composer Maurice Jarre.* (Archive Photos, Inc.)

Dolores Claiborne

1995, Varèse Sarabande, from the film *Dolores Claiborne*, Columbia Pictures, 1995 &&&&

album notes: Music: Danny Elfman; Conductor: Richard Stone.

This is a superb, poetic score from Danny Elfman, who here downplays his brooding "dark" tone (from *Batman*, *Nightbreed*, et. al.) in favor of equally somber but more restrained cues that reflect the distinct personalities of the two female protagonists at the heart of Stephen King's novel, outstandingly adapted here for the screen by Taylor Hackford. Elfman's string-laden score is effective throughout, whether it frantically underscores the revelation of the title character's dark secret, or the growing bond between the hardened Dolores Claiborne and her troubled journalist daughter. Elfman teamed with his usual film-music collaborators here (including Steve Bartek, who receives no credit on the album for some strange reason), and the result is one of his best. Alas, Varèse's album runs a scant 30 minutes, and would have benefited from some additional cues that could have fleshed out the album to a more satisfying length.

Andy Dursin

Dominick & Eugene

1988, Varèse Sarabande, from the film *Dominick & Eugene*, Orion Pictures, 1988 &&&

album notes: Music: Trevor Jones; Conductor: Trevor Jones.

This film about the relationship of two brothers, one of them retarded, furnished Trevor Jones with one of the few "people" stories in a list of credits which otherwise encompasses mostly thrillers or epics. Jones has always had a particular gift for memorable and engaging themes and does not disappoint here. The main theme is a beautiful lament for small orchestra and solo guitar, performed by an uncredited John Williams. Much as in Jones's *Last of the Mohicans* however, this is a case of a wonderful theme stretched a little too thin. Lovely as it is, this theme appears several times with little variation and by the fourth appearance becomes rather redundant. The other cues are mostly synthesized "atmosphere" or suspense cues, which, while effective in the film, are not really very listenable. Still, the main theme remains wonderful, and this alone makes this CD worth owning.

Paul Andrew MacLean

Don Juan DeMarco

1995, A&M Records, from the film *Don Juan DeMarco*, New Line Cinema, 1995 &&&&&

album notes: Music: Michael Kamen; Orchestra: The London Metropolitan Orchestra; Conductor: Michael Kamen; Featured Musicians: Julian Bream, Paul Kamen, Paco de Lucia, Juan Martin, John Themis, Chucko Merchan, Orlando Rincon, Sol de Mexico, Anna Maria Velez, guitar; Christopher Warren-Green, violin; Caroline Dale, cello; Luis Jardim, percussion.

You may dispense with Bryan Adams's "Have You Ever Really Loved a Woman?" which sounds hopelessly wrong for this modern retelling of Lord Byron's *Don Juan*. The film finds Johnny Depp as the latest incarnation of the fabled great lover, now apparently distraught over the loss of the one woman he actually loved, and Marlon Brando the psychiatrist who gives him new hopes and to whom Don Juan tells about his more than 1,000 conquests. The great strength of this album is Michael Kamen's gorgeous Mexican-flavored score, complete with guitar calls, castanets, and the full array of south of the border colorful tonalities one hopes to find (but seldom does) in a music of this kind. The composer's own rendition of the title song, with Spanish vocals by Jose Hernandez and Nydia, is everything Bryan Adams's version is not, and one of the pleasurable highlights in the album. Other tracks that attract and make a lasting impression include the delicate "Dona Julia," the habanera-like "Arabia," and "Dona Ana," another beautiful selection.

Didier C. Deutsch

Donnie Brasco

1997, Hollywood Records, from the film *Donnie Brasco*, Mandalay Entertainment, 1997 &&&

album notes: Music: Patrick Doyle.

The true soundtrack to this true-life mob infiltration film is gunfire, but that doesn't play well on a CD. Instead, this is a hodgepodge of mostly danceable songs from the era of the Donnie Brasco investigation, with a few well-worn hits—Electric Light Orchestra's "Don't Bring Me Down," Blondie's "Heart of Glass," the Trammps' *Saturday Night Fever* hit "Disco Inferno"—and some less familiar fare, such as the Miracles' "Love Machine, Pt. 1," the Pointer Sisters' "Happiness," and Herbie Hancock's "Just Around the Corner." Ultimately, this is the kind of random collection you're better off *fahgeddin'* about.

Gary Graff

1996, Varèse Sarabande, from the film *Donnie Brasco*, Mandalay Entertainment, 1996 &&&

album notes: Music: Patrick Doyle; Conductor: David Snell.

Despite a first-class cast that included Al Pacino, Johnny Depp, and James Russo, this contemporary drama about friendship and betrayal in a big city didn't rate very high at the box office. Patrick Doyle, usually inspired by the films he scores, contributed a very low-key effort, in which even the Latin America rhythms heard in some tracks ("Mickey Mantle Arrives") seem almost too subdued.

Didier C. Deutsch

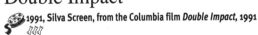
Don't Be a Menace to South Central While Drinking Your Juice in the Hood

🎬 **1996, Island Records, from the film** *Don't Be a Menace to South Central While Drinking Your Juice in the Hood,* **Miramax Films, 1996** ♪♪

A good assemblage of contemporary R&B talent, mostly of the hip-hop variety, keeps all of its best songs bottled up here. Joe's "All the Things (Your Man Won't Do)" is a worthy hit, but the other top names—R. Kelly, Jodeci, Doug E. Fresh, and Lost Boyz—come in with mediocre fare that may add some flavor to the film but doesn't make for much of a listening experience.

Gary Graff

Double Dragon

🎬 **1994, Milan Records, from the film** *Double Dragon,* **Universal Pictures, 1994** ♪

album notes: Music: Jay Ferguson.

Everybody has been through this scenario before: you walk into a record store's cut-out bin hoping to find a buried treasure for a cheap price. After thumbing through hundreds of titles, all you can find are some Vanilla Ice albums and several copies of *Double Dragon,* the lousy soundtrack to the 1994 adaptation of the popular video game that came and went from theaters in a matter of days. Jay Ferguson composed the primarily electronic score, which is surrounded by bubble gum tracks by the likes of Crystal Waters, Stevie B., and rapper Coolio, who performs "I Remember." To put it mildly, the music to *Mortal Kombat* is a bit more effective.

Andy Dursin

Double Impact

🎬 **1991, Silva Screen, from the Columbia film** *Double Impact,* **1991** ♪♪♪

album notes: Music: Arthur Kempel.

An action thriller starring Jean-Claude Van Damme and . . . Jean-Claude Van Damme (hence the double impact of the title), this film, made in Hong Kong, California, and other exotic places, brought together two brothers, separated at birth, to uncover and destroy the men responsible for their parents' death. Arthur Kempel must have felt the vibes: he wrote a score that percolates and pulsates, with standard riffs that echo the screen action, rhythms that suggest some violent scenes, crescendos that reflect the twin Van Dammes at the peak of their martial art showiness. Moments of quiet are few ("I Miss You"), as what matters here is the pulse and energy one ex-

pects from this type of film and score. It's all pretty much predictable, and it has an edge of familiarity that makes it quite acceptable on its own terms. It's not great music, but you can listen to it for a while and not be turned off after two bars.

Didier C. Deutsch

Down in the Delta

🎬 **1998, Virgin Records, from the Miramax film** *Down in the Delta,* **1998** ♪♪♪♪

album notes: Music: Stanley Clarke.

Maya Angelou wrote a compelling story about members of a dysfunctional inner-city family on a personal recovery when they spend a summer vacation with relatives in the Mississippi Delta. This return to the her roots enables the central character, an unemployed single mother, to take stock of what her life has become, and slowly rebuild her family, consisting of two young children and her mother. Punctuating the screen action, and giving it its proper emphasis, Stanley Clarke devised an effective black urban contemporary score, unfortunately represented here by only one selection. The other tracks, however, present a collection of superlative songs performed by the cream of African-American entertainers, including Janet Jackson, Stevie Wonder, Me'Shell N'Degeocello, Chaka Khan, Keb' Mo, Luther Vandross, Ashford and Simpson, and Sweet Honey in the Rock, to single out a few. It's a splendid collection that is consistently attractive and evocative of the film's best moments.

Didier C. Deutsch

Dracula

🎬 **1990, Varèse Sarabande, from the film** *Dracula,* **Universal Pictures, 1979** ♪♪♪♪

album notes: Music: John Williams; **Orchestra:** The London Symphony Orchestra; **Conductor:** John Williams.

John Williams's *Dracula* music is highly romantic, emphasizing, as did John Badman's filmic style in this 1979 variation, the exotic sensuality of the vampire. Opening with a swelling, fully symphonic love theme, the music grasps us into its harmonic power much the way Count Dracula seduces the hapless heroine in his own hypnotic power. Eschewing the throbbing, pulse-pounding, gut-wrenching dissonances of previous *Dracula* scores, Williams invests into the film a sense of poignancy and lyricism that embodies the power, passion, and horror of the Dracula figure, while at the same time lending a noble sympathy to his adversaries.

Randall D. Larson

🎬 **1992, Columbia, from the Columbia film** *Dracula,* **1992** ♪♪♪♪

album notes: Music: Woljiec Kilar; **Conductor:** Anton Coppola.

Wojciech Kilar created a perfectly chilling score for this umpteenth screen incarnation of Bram Stoker's *Dracula,* starring Gary Oldman, Anthony Hopkins, Keanu Reeves, and Winona Ryder as the lady-in-distress. Starting with a long selection ("The Beginning"), ominously featuring a low-key call of strings, the score builds to an eventual crescendo as the Prince of Darkness makes his appearance, and is being incessantly pursued (a march played in the low registers gives a dramatic dimension to such cues as "Vampire Hunters" and "The Hunt Builds," with drums increasing the impression of sustained danger), while a suggestive, diaphanous theme with oboe and harp playing in counterpoint ("Love Remembered") puts a different, almost erotic perspective to the proceedings. The final track, again a long one, reprises the "Vampire Hunters" march and signals the probable end of the ghoul (although knowing how imaginative filmmakers tend to be, one never knows for sure . . .). In fact, the only selection in this instrumental CD that doesn't seem to work is the perfunctory "Love Song for a Vampire," performed by Annie Lennox, which mercifully wasn't titled "Dracula, I Love You."

Didier C. Deutsch

Dragon: The Bruce Lee Story

1993, MCA Records, from the film *Dragon: The Bruce Lee Story,* Universal Pictures, 1993 ♪♪♪♪

album notes: Music: Randy Edelman; **Conductor:** Randy Edelman.

Dragon: The Bruce Lee Story inspired Randy Edelman to write a florid score in which the throbbing action cues (with dominant synth effects) mix with more reflective selections (played by the orchestra) intended to underscore the scenes in which Lee is seen not as an indomitable screen hero and karate expert but as the vulnerable human being he was off screen. These last cues ("Lee Hoi Chuen's Love," "Bruce and Linda," "Sailing on the South China Sea") are by far the most revealing, as they enable the composer to show his sentimental side and come up with melodies that are quite attractive. A splendid anthem, "The Dragon's Heartbeat," first played on the piano and reprised by the full orchestra that eventually dissolves into a pulsating rocker, sums up the general moods projected by the score. A blues ("First Date," with its faint echo of "Moonglow and Theme from Picnic") and an exotic number ("The Hong Kong Cha Cha") round up the selections.

see also: Game of Death

Didier C. Deutsch

Dragonheart

1996, MCA Records, from the film *Dragonheart,* Universal Pictures, 1996 ♪♪♪♪♪

album notes: Music: Randy Edelman; **Conductor:** Randy Edelman.

The delightful epic fantasy score by Randy Edelman exploits the whimsical notion of a dragon slayer teaming with the last dragon to scam villagers of "protection money." At the core of the score is the bond that forms between two former mortal enemies who now must depend on each other to survive in a world that has outgrown them. Although he touches briefly on instrumentation appropriate for the era, Edelman scored the picture more as a contemporary "buddy" adventure that could be set in any era. In so doing, he breathed a dignified life into the mythical creature.

David Hirsch

Dragonslayer

1990, SCSE Records, from the film *Dragonslayer,* Paramount Pictures, 1981 ♪♪♪♪

album notes: Music: Alex North; **Conductor:** Alex North.

Alex North's final entry in the epic genre is this stunningly complex, modernistic masterwork for Hal Barwood's fascinatingly cynical tale of a dragon, sorcery, and medieval corruption. I can't imagine anything more portentous than North's title music, a crushing blast of low horns, grinding, dissonant string chords and nervous piccolo exclamations, leading into a cowed, mournful low string melody for the medieval villagers struggling under the threat of the dragon Vermithrax Pejorative. North wrote a glistening series of piccolo and celeste effects for the death and resurrection of a sorcerer, two scenes that bookend the film's action. There are disturbing, percussive passages for the dragon attacks, a religious chorale for the death of an arrogant monk, a brutal, lengthy battle cue for the hero's first confrontation with the monster, a subdued love theme, and a remarkable introduction to the film's final showdown between sorcerer and dragon, full of spine-tingling sense-of-wonder orchestrations. North adapted music from his rejected score to Stanley Kubrick's *2001* for several sequences and the overall tone and approach of both scores is quite similar. The music for the final battle with the dragon (an unusually lyrical approach to the action) went unused in the film along with a couple of other cues, but the album presents the score as composed by North. Highly recommended to fans of this composer, but North's hard-edged, tonally uncentered style may be tough to digest for the uninitiated.

Jeff Bond

Dramma della gelosia

1995, EMI General Music/SLC/Japan, from the film *Dramma della gelosia (Drama Of Jealousy),* 1970 ♪♪♪♪

album notes: Music: Armando Trovaioli; **Conductor:** Armando Trovaioli; **Featured Musicians:** I Cantori Moderni, conducted by Alessandro Alessandroni

Marcello Mastroianni and Monica Vitti starred in this delicious comedy, in which the light, amusing tones were enhanced by Armando Trovaioli's attractively melodic score. Both stars were also surprisingly effective in the two vocal duets, "I Saw A Shadow On Your Face" and "Do Not Forsake Me," which they shared on screen and on this album (talking through the songs, in Italian, of course, though they were obviously dubbed in the most demanding moments). Trovaioli's cues provide for consistently pleasant listening, with this recording, released by SLC in Japan, highly recommended. This recording may be difficult to find. Check with a used CD store, mail-order company, or a dealer specializing in rare, out-of-print, or import recordings.

Didier C. Deutsch

Drat! The Cat!

1997, Varèse-Sarabande, from the Broadway musical *Drat! The Cat!*, 1965 🎵🎵🎵🎵

album notes: Music: Milton Schafer; **Book:** Ira Levin; **Lyrics:** Ira Levin; **Conductor:** Todd Ellison; **Cast:** Jason Graae, Susan Egan, Elaine Stritch, Jonathan Freeman, Judy Kaye.

Leslie Ann Warren and Elliott Gould starred on Broadway in this musical that had a run of eight performances in 1965. The story of a cat burglar operating in New York City's high society in the 1890s, the score by Milton Schafer and Ira Levin, who also wrote the book, was a lively affair that lingered on thanks to a couple of songs that became minor hits, including "He Touched Me," which was recorded at the time by Barbra Streisand. But hopes of seeing the show revived or at best recorded seemed farfetched. Until the folks at Varèse-Sarabande decided to put together a cast album. The results, as one might suspect, are much more convincing than the souvenir left by the 1965 production.

This scintillating studio recording features a superlative cast, including Jason Graae as Bob Purefoy, a policeman whose father is the city's Chief of Detectives; Susan Egan, as Alice Van Guilder, the attractive socialite who doubles as the Cat; Judy Kaye, Jonathan Freeman, and Elaine Stritch, among other notables. After these many years, this recording of *Drat! The Cat!* demonstrates that the show itself might have been completely misjudged by its contemporaries.

Didier C. Deutsch

The Draughtsman's Contract

1993, DRG Records, from the film *The Draughtsman's Contract*, 1993 🎵🎵

album notes: Music: Michael Nyman; **Featured Musicians:** The Michael Nyman Band: Michael Nyman, harpsichord, piano; Alexander Balanescu, Elizabeth Perry, violin; Malcolm Bennett, bass guitar; Andrew Findon, John Harle, Ian Mitchell, Keith Thompson, saxophones, clarinets; Stave Saunders, bass trombone, euphonium; Barry Guy, double bass.

Michael Nyman's music may not be to everyone's liking, but it won't leave you indifferent. And whether you respond to it favorably or not will depend in large part on how you react to his minimalist approach to film scoring. The music, performed here by a small chamber ensemble, played an important role in this odd story about an architect working for a British lady who trades his landscaping designs for her favors. But taken on its own merits, it tends to sound dry and unattaching after a while. And when it takes, as in the last track, endless variations on the same theme, it may turn off even the most lenient listener. Not helping either is the grating sound quality of the recording.

Didier C. Deutsch

Dream Lover

1994, Koch Screen, from the film *Dream Lover*, Gramercy Pictures, 1994 🎵🎵🎵🎵

album notes: Music: Christopher Young; **Conductor:** Pete Anthony; **Synthesizers and Percussions:** Mark Zimoski.

Tubular bells over an attractive orchestral melody supported by ethereal vocalists, a quirky waltz performed by a carousel organ, and an exuberant ragtime are some of the many delights that await the listener in this soundtrack signed by Christopher Young for an erotic drama about a young architect and the emotionally unbalanced sexy woman who becomes his wife. The broad range and wide diversity of the musical cues, which also include a pseudo-oriental composition and a Parisian-styled waltz, combine to create a score that is both challenging and consistently satisfying.

Didier C. Deutsch

Dreamgirls

1982, Geffen Records, from the Broadway production *Dreamgirls*, 1982 🎵🎵🎵

album notes: Music: Henry Krieger; **Lyrics:** Tom Eyen; **Musical Direction:** Yolanda Segovia; **Cast:** Deborah Burrell, Vanessa Bell, Tenita Jordan, Brenda Pressley, Sheryl Lee Ralp, Loretta Devine, Jennifer Holliday, Vondie Curtis-Hall, Obba, Cleavant Derricks.

Following the success of *A Chorus Line*, Michael Bennett returned to the world of show business and backstage struggles in *Dreamgirls*, which opened Dec. 20, 1981. The plot follows a trio of black female singers who eventually hit the big time, but only after one of them (considered too heavy and therefore less marketable) is replaced by a more glamorous singer. Not only did the show make a star of Jennifer Holliday (the one who was dumped), its sleek, hard-driving look also ensured its enormous success. In fact, it ran for 1,522 performances. With the exception of "And I Am Telling You I'm Not Going," the plaintive lament of Effie (the character played by Holliday) after she has been told that she is no longer a member of the Dreams, a trio

Anthony Higgins in The Draughtsman's Contract. **(The Kobal Collection)**

loosely shaped after the Supremes, the action-driven score by Henry Krieger and Tom Eyen sounds much less memorable and exciting in the original cast recording than it did in the theatre. With its careful dose of theatrical, by-the-numbers rhythm-and-blues songs, it is enjoyable to a point, but only hits a high in the occasional glitzy moments when the Dreams actually perform together ("Dreamgirls," "One Night Only"). The rest of the time, it is merely routine and without much zest.

Didier C. Deutsch

Dressed to Kill

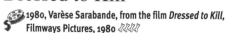 1980, Varèse Sarabande, from the film *Dressed to Kill*, Filmways Pictures, 1980 ♪♪♪♪

album notes: Music: Pino Donaggio; **Conductor:** Natale Massara.

Brian de Palma took more than a single cue from suspense master Alfred Hitchcock when he directed this stylish essay about an attractive woman with a particularly sexy disposition, who meets with a rather nasty killer in an elevator, and the high-class prostitute who finds herself accused of the murder.

And while Pino Donaggio is not Bernard Herrmann, his score for the film was the perfect musical complement to De Palma's erotic visions ("The Shower," "The Erotic Story," "The Cab"). Even if "Death in the Elevator" lacks the subtle, terrifying impact of Herrmann's famous shower scene in *Psycho*, Donaggio's elegant and classy musical cues set this score aside and qualify it as a real winner.

Didier C. Deutsch

Driftwood

 1997, Oceandeep Soundtracks, from the Goldcrest Films International film *Driftwood*, 1997 ♪♪♪♪

album notes: Music: John Cameron; **Conductor:** John Cameron; **Featured Musicians:** Liam O'Flynn, Uilleann pipes; Tony Roberts, penny whistle.

Set in the wilds of the Irish coastline, *Driftwood* introduced two equally lonely people: a reclusive artist and a man without a past. When a woodcarver, living alone, finds an unconscious man on the shore with a fractured leg, obviously the victim of a sea disaster, she brings him to her shack and nurses him back to health. But as the man, who has lost his memory, tries to finds his past, his benefactor begins to show signs that loneliness has finally gotten the best of her, and despite the passion that binds them ever so briefly, the end can only be disastrous. Musically underscoring the tragic events that develop on the screen, John Cameron's music, appropriately ominous and suggestive, makes ample use of the atmospheric Uileann pipes to suggest the romantic bleakness of the Irish locale and the emotional remoteness of the characters. The score itself builds up around a central yearning theme as the story evolves, only to disintegrate as the relationship between the two characters reaches a climax, to end up with the theme repeated by the lonely pipes. It's quite evocative, with several high points that enhance the music's effectiveness, and turn this score into an interesting audio experience.

Didier C. Deutsch

Driving Miss Daisy

1989, Varèse Sarabande, from the film *Driving Miss Daisy*, Warner Bros. Pictures, 1989 ♪♪♪♪♪
album notes: Music: Hans Zimmer.

The soundtrack to this Academy Award–winning film is an odd lot. First you have pop standards, Louis Armstrong doing the tango "Kiss of Fire," and Eartha Kitt singing her signature Yule song, "Santa Baby." On the other side of the spectrum, there is a long excerpt from Antonin Dvorak's "Song to the Moon," performed by the soprano Gabriela Benachova with the Czech Philharmonic. Somewhere in between are four cues from the score composed by Hans Zimmer, an effervescent synthesizer music that helps evoke this affectionate story about an elderly Southern lady and the black chauffeur who has been in her employ for years, and the warm relationship that has settled between them. Surprisingly, the combination of all these elements works wonders, with the album eliciting a positive response despite its disparate components.

Didier C. Deutsch

Drop Zone

1994, Varèse Sarabande, from the film *Drop Zone*, Paramount Pictures, 1994 ♪♪♪♪
album notes: Music: Hans Zimmer, Nick Glennie-Smith, Ryeland Allison; **Featured Vocalists:** Rose Stone, Randelle K. Stainback.

With this energetic mix of rockin' synthesizers and orchestra, Hans Zimmer triumphs with this highly charged score for the John Badham–directed Wesley Snipes action film. There's never a dull moment. The music shifts effortlessly from the movie's thrilling guitar-driven skydiving cues ("Hi Jack") to the more poignant emotional sequences ("Terry Dropped Out"). Kudos especially to Zimmer's wonderful and humorously well-titled "Too Many Notes—Not Enough Rests," the bane of any action movie composer's existence. One of Zimmer's best works for this genre.

David Hirsch

D3: The Mighty Ducks

1996, Hollywood Records, from the film *D3: The Mighty Ducks*, Walt Disney Pictures, 1996 ♪♪
album notes: Music: J.A.C. Redford; **Conductor:** J.A.C. Redford.

The weakest of the "Ducks" films actually has one of the series' more interesting soundtracks, though it's nothing particularly special. Barenaked Ladies' "Grade 9" is a good showcase of the Canadian band's wit, while Dr. John's "Ac-cent-tchu-ate the Positive" and Southside Johnny's "Shake 'em Down" are classy inclusions. Most of the set belongs to J.A.C. Redford's score, that is better off in the penalty box than on your CD player.

Gary Graff

Due South, Vol. 2

1998, Unforscene Music, from the Alliance/BBC television series *Due South* ♪♪♪
album notes: Music: Jay Semko, Jack Lenz.

This collection of songs was heard in the television series starring Paul Gross and Callum Keith Rennie, made in Canada, that was seen in some border territories although it never made an impact on the U.S. mainland. Two instrumental tracks from the original score, "Mountie on the Bounty" and "Western End of the Trail," are suggestive of the action, involving a Canadian mountie and his civilian alter ego, but the meat of the album consists of vocal selections by Sarah McLachlan ("Song for a Winter's Night"), Dutch Robinson ("Slave to Your Love"), Michelle Wright ("Nobody's Girl"), and Tara MacLean ("Holy Tears"). The rest is easily dispensable.

Didier C. Deutsch

The Dukes of Hazzard

1982, Scotti Bros. Records, from the Warner Bros. television series *The Dukes of Hazzard*, 1981 ♪♪♪

Another compilation of songs heard in or inspired by the television series *The Dukes of Hazzard,* this one with a squarely country and western accent. Johnny Cash, the Hazzard County Boys, Doug Kershaw, and cast regulars Tom Wopat, James Best, Sorrell Booke, and Catherine Bach are among the stars who perform here, either singing or providing bits of dialogue that link the songs together. It's good-natured stuff, entertaining and lively ("Flash"), even if it is not too cerebral.

Didier C. Deutsch

Dumbo

1998, Disney, from the Disney film *Dumbo*, 1941 ♫♫♫♫

album notes: Music: Frank Churchill, Oliver Wallace; **Lyrics:** Ned Washington; **Conductor:** Oliver Wallace.

Another entry in the Disney catalogue of animated feature soundtrack reissues, this one about the cute elephant with oversized ears who suddenly discovers (after a night of libation) that he can fly. Considering the fact that it was made close to 60 years ago, it is remarkable how the black lingo used by the Crows (who discover Dumbo asleep up a tree and perform the song "When I See an Elephant Fly") resembles today's inner city urban language. The Disney animators also had another field day with the psychedelic "Pink Elephants on Parade," a definite highlight in the film and on this CD. Sound mastering has been done with evident TLC, and the restoration shows the improvements that can be achieved nowadays with historical material. As is now familiar with this series of reissues, the CD includes the songs, instrumental bridges, and underscoring in a nifty, complete presentation.

Didier C. Deutsch

Dune

1998, PEG Records, from the Universal film *Dune*, 1984 ♫♫♫♫

album notes: Music: Toto.

Director David Lynch is known for his bizarre stylistic choices, maybe none more audacious than hiring the rock group Toto to score a science fiction epic. Lynch's gamble paid off handsomely with *Dune,* the only soundtrack written by the group behind such '80s pop hits as "Africa." It still stands as one of the wholly original soundtracks done for the genre—a fusion of symphonic music, flutes, metallic percussion, electric guitars, and weird synthesizers, a score caught somewhere between Wagner and a rock opera. There's little trace of *Star Wars* in Toto's music, which concentrates on the mystical elements of the adaptation of Frank Herbert's novel. *Dune* is full of imposing sounds, from the main orchestral-electronic theme that roars over the sand dunes to the choral finale that brings rain to the wasteland. Toto's music is never more lovely or haunting than when it plays the tribal society that lives beneath the sand, flutes and odd synth samples becoming ethnic music for another world. This new edition of *Dune* has been issued as a promotional soundtrack, collecting all of Toto's music. Hearing the many unused cues for the film makes Toto's accomplishment even more impressive, their impressionistic music a superb match for David Lynch's visuals. About the only piece missing here is Brian Eno's "Prophecy" theme, so hold onto your old *Dune* soundtrack.

Dan Schweiger

Dying Young

1991, Arista Records, from the film *Dying Young*, 20th Century Fox, 1991 ♫♫♫♫♫

album notes: Music: James Newton Howard; **Conductor:** Marty Paich; **Featured Musicians:** Kenny G, Michael Lang, piano; Dean Parks, guitar; Jeffrey Porcaro, drums; Michael Fisher, percussion; Neil Stubbenhaus, bass; Gayle Levant, harp.

For once, Kenny G's detractors will have to admit that his contribution to this film score actually enhances it. Playing in the romantic style that has insured his enormous success, *Dying Young,* a soap opera if there ever was one, provides the instrumentalist with the right emotional moods to express his own romanticism in a way that's extremely attractive and welcome. Much of the credit must also go to James Newton Howard, obviously inspired by this maudlin story of a doomed love affair, for which he wrote a lush series of cues, in which the dominant note is also strongly evocative of the film's main theme. The old standard, "All the Way," performed as a vocal by Jeffrey Osborne and as an instrumental by King Curtis, contributes an inspired note to this standout soundtrack album.

Didier C. Deutsch

The Eagle Has Landed

1999, Aleph Records, from the ITC film *The Eagle Has Landed*, 1977 ♫♫♫♫

album notes: Music: Lalo Schifrin; **Conductor:** Lalo Schifrin.

A rather fancy story about an alleged plan by the German High Command to kidnap Winston Churchill, *The Eagle Has Landed* was an exciting World War II drama that was considerably heightened by Lalo Schifrin's excellent score. A previous issue, in which some cues were coupled with the composer's music for Richard Lester's *The Four Musketeers,* is now superseded by this complete score on Schifrin's own label. Following the screen action step by step—in which a Nazi colonel under orders from Himmler himself smuggles a group of English-speaking German soldiers and a rebel Irishman to dispose of the Prime Minister, when he is scheduled to take a rest in a small country village— the cues inform and detail it with orchestral flourishes that are quite convincing. But eschewing the more obvious accents suggested by the genre itself, Schifrin chose to write a series of cues built around a simple two-note motif that recurs throughout, builds up, and finally develops into a full-fledged military march only as the finale of the film. As a result of this device, the score is surprisingly controlled and effective. This expanded format is a valuable addition for anyone who is a fan of his music in general, or of film music in particular.

Didier C. Deutsch

Earthquake

1990, Varèse Sarabande, from the film *Earthquake*, Universal Pictures, 1974 🎬🎬🎬

album notes: Music: John Williams; **Conductor:** John Williams.

Before he became the uncontested champion of big orchestral scores with *Star Wars* in 1977, John Williams carved himself a special niche as the composer best qualified to write the music for the many disaster films which flourished in the early 1970s, including *Jaws, The Towering Inferno,* and *The Poseidon Adventure.* Add to those the score he created for *Earthquake,* the film that saw Los Angeles disappear long before it was toast in *Volcano* . . . (or was it *Dante's Peak?*). In this particularly remarkable effort, Williams wrote a broad range of cues, from a tender love scene to a chase to the actual disaster. In addition, there are many other moments to enjoy in his diversified music, from a bluesy "City Theme," to a lightly jazzy "Something for Rosa," to a lusty "Love Theme." A word of warning: the last two tracks are low-rumbling recordings of an earthquake that will rattle and destroy your speakers if you play the CD too loud.

Didier C. Deutsch

Easter Parade

1995, Rhino Records, from the film *Easter Parade*, MGM, 1948 🎬🎬🎬🎬🎬

album notes: Music: Irving Berlin; **Lyrics:** Irving Berlin; **Orchestra:** The MGM Studio Orchestra; **Choir:** The MGM Studio Chorus; **Conductor:** Johnny Green, Georgie Stoll; **Cast:** Fred Astaire, Judy Garland, Peter Lawford, Ann Miller, Jules Munshin.

A great musical, splashed all over the screen in brilliant colors, *Easter Parade* had a lot going for it: A pleasant story about a hoofer trying to find a new dance partner and discovering love in the process, an inspired pair of co-stars in Fred Astaire and Judy Garland, and a sprightly score by Irving Berlin. The title tune, originally written in 1933 for the Broadway show *As Thousands Cheer,* became the occasion for a festive musical number. While the storyline seemed at best serviceable, it provided many pegs for various big production numbers that continue to delight and dazzle to this day–"A Fella With an Umbrella," shared by Garland and Peter Lawford; "Shakin' the Blues Away," performed in typical frantic manner by Ann Miller; "Steppin' Out With My Baby," which

gave Fred Astaire an opportunity to dance in slow-mo in a remarkably inventive moment; "A Couple Of Swells," in which Astaire and Garland echoed an earlier duet, "Be a Clown," between Garland and Gene Kelly in *The Pirate;* and an exhilarating, long "Vaudeville Montage," built around several songs by Irving Berlin ("I Love a Piano," "Snookey Okums," "Ragtime Violin," and "When the Midnight Choo-Choo Leaves for Alabam'"). The soundtrack recording on Rhino, newly mastered and augmented with several instrumental bridges, outtakes, and other incrementa, brings out all the juicy moments from the film, and then some.

Didier C. Deutsch

Easy Come, Easy Go

1995, RCA Records, from the film *Easy Come, Easy Go*, Paramount Pictures, 1967 🎬🎬🎬

In *Easy Come, Easy Go* Elvis portrayed another happy-go-lucky character: a frogman who discovers a treasure chest inside a sunken ship, which he traces back to a pert young woman played by Dodie Marshall. In between various action scenes, he found time to sing several non-descript numbers, none of which made it to the charts.

Didier C. Deutsch

Eat Drink Man Woman

1994, Varèse Sarabande, from the film *Eat Drink Man Woman*, Samuel Goldwyn, 1994 🎬🎬🎬

album notes: Music: Mader; **Featured Musicians:** Wu Man, pipa, ruan; Wang Tien Jou, erhu; Cao Ying Ying, sanxian; Sarah Plant, flute; Steve Elson, saxophone, clarinet; Hector Martignon, piano; Thomas Ulrich, cello; Mario Rodriguez, bass; Armando Sanchez, percussion; Louis F. Bouzo, percussion; Joe Gonzales, percussion; Mader, marimba, keyboard; Dina Emerson, vocals.

Absolutely nothing like what you'd expect for a film about a collision of generations in a Chinese/American household. Composer Mader has created a brilliant montage of musical styles that complement each other in a refreshing way few scores do. The album moves with a surprising ease between an authentic Chinese motif to a contemporary film cue and finally to mambo! Mader, in an act of sheer gall, composed a blues piece, "The Daughter's Heart 1," that suddenly shifts into a passage played by Chinese instruments! This is a true melting pot of world music and a delightful change of pace.

David Hirsch

Ed Wood

🎞 1994, Hollywood Records, from the film *Ed Wood*, Touchstone
Pictures, 1994 ♪♪♪

album notes: Music: Howard Shore; **Orchestra:** The London Philharmonic Orchestra; **Conductor:** Howard Shore; **Featured Musicians:** Lydia Kavina, theremin; Cynthia Millar, Ondes Martenot.

Dedicated to the memory of Henry Mancini, Howard Shore's fine score for *Ed Wood* brims with nostalgia. Shore perfectly captures the sonic nuances of low-budget 1950s sci-fi/monster film music, including the use of the icons of science fiction instruments, the theremin and the Ondes Martenot. His music lends an appropriate backdrop to the film's production scenes—recreations of such classic bargain-basement sci-fi as *Bride of the Monsters* and *Plan 9 From Outer Space,* the stereotypical 1950s horror music—and also quotes from Tchaikovsky's "Swan Lake" and the main title music from the original *Dracula* and *Mummy* films. In contrast a number of beat-generation jazz cues provide a contemporary mid-'50s sound, suitably thin and carrying their own sense of nostalgia and slight weirdness. More than an exercise in nostalgia, though, it's a finely crafted composition that works effectively as film music while also conveying a sort of homage to these corny, yet beloved film music clichés.

                                                        Randall D. Larson

Eddie

🎞 1996, Island/Hollywood, from the Hollywood film *Eddie,* 1996
♪

Whoopi Goldberg walked through this picture as if she were totally out of her element as the coach of a national basketball team, on drugs, or both. She might have just been bored to distraction, and listening to this "soundtrack" album, a compilation of rap songs without much focus, one cannot entirely blame her. In the middle of so much beat and vamp and no melody, "Say It Again" by Nneka, and "Tell Me" by Dru Hill almost come up as pleasant surprises. Almost.

                                                        Didier C. Deutsch

The Eddy Duchin Story

🎞 1990, MCA Records, from the film *The Eddy Duchin Story,* Columbia Pictures, 1956 ♪♪♪

album notes: Orchestra: The Columbia Picture Studio Orchestra; **Conductor:** Morris Stoloff; **Featured Musician:** Carmen Cavallaro, piano.

The life story of sweet band pianist and conductor Eddie Duchin, portrayed by Tyrone Power, provides for a remarkably effective musical film in which the highlights are the many standards from the 1920s and 1930s that Duchin performed to the great delight of high society people. Carmen Cavallaro,

himself an accomplished pianist, plays these selections on the soundtrack and in this album which is consistently enjoyable, even when all that's required is background music.

                                                        Didier C. Deutsch

The Edgar Allan Poe Suite/ Cry of the Banshee/Horror Express

📺 1996, Citadel Records; from the television special *An Evening with Edgar Allan Poe,* 1970, and the American-International films *Cry of the Banshee,* 1970, and *Horror Express,* 1972 ♪♪♪♪

album notes: Music: Les Baxter, John Cacavas; **Conductor:** Les Baxter, John Cacavas.

Besides being an amazing orchestrator, band leader, and recording artist (connoisseurs have long sought some of his most advanced albums, recently reissued on CD by Capitol, such as *Ritual of the Savage* and *Tamboo*), Les Baxter was a film composer of considerable talent who scored many films in a 20-year span, including such horror classics as *Black Sunday, Master of the World, Baron Blood,* and *The Dunwich Horror.*

When American-International, which had released many of these films, decided to host an evening dedicated to the works of Edgar Allan Poe, starring Vincent Price, Les Baxter was brought in to provide the score. He created a suite in four parts, inspired by some of the scores he had composed for the full-length features, which was then recorded as *The Edgar Allan Poe Suite.* And despite budget limitations, he was able to deliver what amounted to an impressive score, in which he used a small group of string players and percussionists and judiciously chosen electronic touches to add a special flavor to the ensemble. That same year, he scored another full-length feature for American-International, *Cry of the Banshee,* again starring Vincent Price as a sadistic judge in eighteenth-century England bent on getting rid of all forms of witchcraft in his district. Baxter wrote a score that was appropriately melodic in the right places, and chilling when the action required it.

Totally different in concept and writing is John Cacavas's music for *Horror Express,* a black comedy made in 1972, with Christopher Lee, Telly Savalas, and Peter Cushing in the cast. As Cushing described the plot, it all had to do with "mad Russian monks, Cossack ruffians and the atom bomb, pretty damsels, hordes of sinister detectives and Russian and Chinese police . . . all played by Spaniards, of course." While the music is dark and somber in the appropriate moments, Cacavas is not as inventive as Baxter, and the juxtaposition of his score with Baxter's works against him.

                                                        Didier C. Deutsch

The Edge

🎬 1997, RCA Victor, from the 20th Century-Fox film *The Edge*, 1997 ♪♪♪♪

album notes: Music: Jerry Goldsmith; **Conductor:** Jerry Goldsmith; **Featured Musicians:** Mike Lang, piano; Chuck Domanico, bass; Steve Schaeffer, drums.

A psychological thriller in which the action develops against spectacular scenery, *The Edge* pits an older man, a billionaire on a trip to the wilds of Alaska with his glamorous wife for a fashion photo shoot, and the younger, self-assured photographer with whom he finds himself stranded after their plane crashes on a remote location. Surviving the lack of food and appropriate clothing, as well as encounters with predatory wild bears, the experience puts the men to the test—with the photographer losing his cool while the billionaire proves most resourceful and astute—and bringing to the fore the rivalry that might exist between them, since the former might have been dallying with the latter's wife. The dynamics of the film are properly explored and emphasized in Jerry Goldsmith's score, which enhances the physical action but barely touches upon the psychological aspects of the story. A thorough blend of orchestral chords and synthesizer effects, it is notably effective in such tracks as "Deadfall," where the addition of percussive instruments and heavy pounding rhythms provides the basis for a solid evocation of the screen drama.

Didier C. Deutsch

Edge of Seventeen

🎬 1999, Razor & Tie Records, from the Strand film *Edge of Seventeen*, 1999 ♪♪♪♪

John Hughes perfected a formula for teen angst/love stories in the 1980s. The formula was easy: hire a pretty actor with puppy-dog eyes to play a teen looking for love, add an exceptionally pretty actor to portray the one loved from afar, show us how the two find love together, throw in a new wave soundtrack, and voilà! instant teen movie. *Edge of Seventeen* takes this formula and adds a twist: the characters are gay. It's the summer of 1984, and Eric Hunter (Chris Stafford) develops a crush for his co-worker Rod (Anderson Gabrych). The soundtrack features unmistakable 1980s gems, but not the ones that appear on all of the other 1990s movies about the 1980s. It's highly danceable, featuring both new-wave favorites and '80s dance-club standards. Also featured on the soundtrack is actress Lea DeLaria's rendition of Irving Berlin's "Blue Skies," which she performs in the film.

Beth Krakower

Ed's Next Move

🎬 1996, Milan Records, from the Orion film *Ed's Next Move*, 1996 ♪♪♪♪

album notes: Music: Benny Golson; **Featured Musicians:** Jimmy Owens, Lew Soloff, Virgil Jones, Marvin Stamm, trumpets; Steve Turre, Jim Pugh, Dave Taylor, trombones; Steve Wilson, Jerome Richardson, alto sax; Bobby La Vell, Don Braden, tenor sax; Kenny Rogers, baritone sax; Mark Elf, guitar; Bill Mays, piano; Dwayne Burno, bass; Joe Farnsworth, drums.

Ed's Next Move is a whimsical movie about a sweet Midwesterner trying to survive after relocating to New York City. Our hero, coincidentally named Ed, falls for a hardened New Yorker, played by *Homicide: Life on the Street*'s Callie Thorne. Her character plays in a folk band, portrayed on screen by real-life folk band Ed's Redeeming Qualities, aptly described by the writer/director in the liner notes as "uniquely oblique." Benny Golson composed the often-lighthearted jazz score and assembled a big band consisting of some of New York's top jazz talent to perform it. Its use perfectly maps Ed's many adventures while in New York. The other bands heard on the album all are regulars in the New York City club scene. In a rare combination in soundtrack albums today, the score and the songs blend seamlessly.

Beth Krakower

EdTV

🎬 1999, Reprise Records, from the Universal film *EdTV*, 1999 ♪

album notes: Music: Randy Edelman.

Another overly ambitious soundtrack album, trying to please too many different segments of the audience and falling flat, flat, flat. The movie's Ed is an ordinary Joe whose life takes a chaotic turn when he agrees to have his life televised. *Ed*'s soundtrack is also chaotic, to say the least. On the plus side: Cornershop, Ozomatli, and some okay oldies. On the negative side: Bon Jovi, Meredith Brooks . . . and some okay oldies. There's such a thing as eclectic, but this is just an uneven mess. As of press time, the album had failed to crack the *Billboard* Top 200 Albums. If a soundtrack album could go straight to video, this one would surely have done it.

Amy Rosen

The Education of Little Tree

🎬 1998, Sony Classical, from the Paramount film *The Education of Little Tree*, 1998 ♪♪♪♪

album notes: Music: Mark Isham; **Conductor:** Ken Kluger; **Featured Musicians:** Sid Page, Norm Hughes, violin; David Speltz, Martin Tillman, cello; Jon Clark, flutes; Dan Greco, hammered dulcimer; Geoff Levin, dulcimer and banjo; Dean Parks, autoharp.

Mark Isham beautifully captured the sensitive moods of this exquisite little film, set in the 1930s, about the childhood of an eight-year-old Cherokee orphan, Little Tree, who is raised by his grandparents in the knowledge and appreciation of his Indian ancestry, until he goes to a school where his new teachers try to erase everything he has learned about his family traditions. Primarily relying on the low strings and some folk instruments to create the proper atmosphere, with the dulcimer also lending its delicate voice, Isham developed themes that convey the dichotomy between the Indian and the white cultures. It's a gorgeous, often electrifying score that's all the more eloquent that it is subdued and emotionally charged.

Didier C. Deutsch

Edward Scissorhands

1990, MCA Records, from the film *Edward Scissorhands*, 20th Century-Fox, 1990 ♫♫♫♫

album notes: Music: Danny Elfman; **Conductor:** Shirley Walker.

The always inventive Danny Elfman surpassed himself when he wrote this brilliant score for Tim Burton's strange and poetic fantasy about a youth whose hands are scissors, and who, because of it, discovers himself a unique talent as a landscape artist. The childlike qualities in the main character, the creation of a mad scientist who dies before he has a chance to finish his work, as well as the fable-like aspects of the screenplay inspired Elfman to write cues in which the main accents evoke a wonderland where anything and everything can happen, and often does. "Storytime," in fact, sets the right musical atmosphere from the start, with the other selections detailing the strange and wonderful tale of Edward, and the problems he encounters when he attempts to enter the real world. Throughout the soft-hued score, an evanescent chorus and tinkling bells add an imaginative lilt to the cues. In this creative canvas, the only discordant note is Tom Jones's abrasive performance of "With These Hands," mercifully heard at the end, which breaks the moods established by the score.

Didier C. Deutsch

The Egyptian

1990, Varèse Sarabande, from the film *The Egyptian*, 20th Century-Fox, 1954 ♫♫♫♫

album notes: Music: Alfred Newman; Bernard Herrmann; **Orchestra:** The Hollywood Symphony Orchestra and Chorus; **Conductor:** Alfred Newman; **Featured Musician:** Doreen Tryden.

In a collaborative effort almost unique in the annals of film music, two of Hollywood's greatest composers, Alfred Newman and Bernard Herrmann, wrote the glorious score for this offbeat epic drama, set 33 centuries ago, about a monotheist

Pharaoh, and the physician (the "Egyptian" of the title) he befriends, a humanist with a unique vision about his own role on earth. Actually, the two composers didn't work together as each took a certain number of scenes and wrote his cues independently, but the general texture of the score belies its varied origins, and its overall excellence testifies to the professionalism of both composers who viewed the film itself as a limitless forum for musical expression. In his comprehensive liner notes, Kevin Mulhall details which tracks were composed by Herrmann and which by Newman, as well as the unusual situation that brought the two men to write this score. The recording, while appropriately spacious and grandiose, is in mono. Presumably the multi-tracks still exist at 20th Century-Fox and the day when we might hear a full stereophonic version of this great score may not be far away. In the meantime, this CD is the next best thing.

Didier C. Deutsch

The Eiger Sanction

1990, Varèse Sarabande, from the film *The Eiger Sanction*, Universal Pictures, 1975 ♫♫♫♫

album notes: Music: John Williams; **Conductor:** John Williams.

This suspense film starring Clint Eastwood, as a former secret agent and avid mountain climber who comes out of retirement to handle a delicate assignment, elicited another flavorful pre-*Star Wars* score from John Williams. Characteristic of the composer's style at the time, the main theme from the film is a jazzy tune that swings lightly over a melodic orchestral line, and is reprised twice in stylistically different versions. The other cues detail the action in terms that embody it and at the same time provide an appealling musical program. The sound quality in this CD is not as good as it should be, with a semi-monochromatic sound and an EQ that generally lacks brightness.

Didier C. Deutsch

8½

1991, CAM Records/Italy, from the film *8½ (Otto e mezzo)*, Cineriz, 1963 ♫♫♫♫

album notes: Music: Nino Rota; **Conductor:** Carlo Savina.

One of the great Fellini films and a classic in its own right, *8½* was as much a fantasy as it was an introspective look into the mind of the famed director. In the film, Marcello Mastroianni (Fellini's screen alter ego), a famous director with a creativity block, relaxing in a spa, abandons himself to memories from his past that eventually lead to visions ensconced in strange fancies and fantasy worlds. Creating a bridge between the reality and the fiction, Nino Rota wrote a theme, "La passerella di Otto e mezzo," which bathes his score and gives it an anchor on which to get solidly attached. Particularly enticing in this wildly imaginative set of cues are "The Illusionist," "Childhood Memories," and "The Harem," all of which correspond to revealing facets in Fellini's mind. This title may be out of print or just plain hard to find. Mail-order companies, used CD shops, or dealers of rare or import recordings will be your best bet.

Didier C. Deutsch

8 Heads in a Duffel Bag

1997, Varèse Sarabande Records, from the film *8 Heads in a Duffel Bag*, Orion Pictures, 1997 **woof!**

album notes: Music: Andrew Gross; **Orchestra:** The Northwest Sinfonia; **Conductor:** Andrew Gross.

Granted, action in comedies must be swift, and so it derives must be the music that underscores it. But this is ridiculous. Out of 25 tracks in this soundtrack album, fully 10 are under one minute of playing time, and another 11 are under two minutes. Talk about swiftness! The cues by Andrew Gross, a newcomer on the scene, don't even have the time to make any kind of impact.

Didier C. Deutsch

Eight Millimeter

1998, Compass III, from the Columbia film *Eight Millimeter*, 1998 🎬🎬🎬

album notes: Music: Mychael Danna.

A departure from Mychael Danna's moody, ambient music for the films of fellow Canadian Atom Egoyan, *Eight Millimeter,* Danna's first Hollywood thriller, follows Nicolas Cage, P.I. and family man, into the seedy underworld of snuff movies as envisioned by the macabre imagination that brought us *Seven*. The score builds and maintains a tension throughout, characterizing the criminal subculture with oud playing and Arabic rhythms. Danna's seamless integration of traditional Moroccan scales and instrumentation with contemporary orchestral music benefits from his extensive research—Danna consulted with Moroccan musicologists to ensure a satisfactory degree of authenticity. It is a shame that Joel Schumacher's generic film did not meet the high standard of Danna's thoughtful and complex music.

Didier C. Deutsch

8 Seconds

1994, MCA Records, from the film *8 Seconds*, New Line Cinema, 1994 🎬🎬🎬

album notes: Music: Bill Conti.

Some soundtrack compilations have an engaging quality that seems to come through even as you read the credits. Such is the case with this collection of country tracks, featuring some well-

known and respected artists from this side of the border, which is as pleasant and entertaining as can be and which help illustrate the saga of a young and avid bronco rider, whose goal in life is to stay on the eight seconds it takes to qualify at the rodeo. Nothing fancy, just some good clean fun, and a feeling that sometimes soundtrack albums can be as uncomplicated and enjoyable as, well . . . riding a wild beast? In all this country charm, Bill Conti's "Lane's Theme" almost sounds like an odd intruder.

Dider C. Deutsch

El Cid

1996, Koch Int'l, from the film *El Cid*, MGM, 1961 🎬🎬🎬🎬

album notes: Music: Miklos Rozsa; **Orchestra:** The New Zealand Symphony Orchestra; **Conductor:** James Sedares; **Featured Musicians:** Tamra Saylor Fine, organ; The New Zealand Youth Choir; Karen Grylis, director.

1991, Sony Music Special Products, from the film *El Cid*, MGM, 1961 🎬🎬🎬🎬

album notes: Music: Miklos Rozsa; **Orchestra:** The Graunke Symphony Orchestra of Munich; **Conductor:** Miklos Rozsa.

The superlative Koch recording, a superb recreation of the score with several previously unrecorded cues, is the current best representation of the epic music Rozsa wrote for the Samuel Bronston extravaganza, recounting the medieval tale of the Spanish hero (Charlton Heston at his dashing best) and how he defeated several centuries of dominance by the Moors. The handsome package (the booklet features profuse liner notes, including an introduction by Martin Scorsese, and many pictures from the production) is a magnificent complement to the music, delivered with the right amount of zest and enthusiasm by the New Zealand Symphony in sonics that are detailed and spacious, if at times a trifle fuzzy.

The Sony set is the actual soundtrack recording, with the composer conducting the Graunke Symphony in a spirited performance, made even more exciting thanks to the brilliant sound quality of the CD. However, while this album contains a few tracks that are not on the Koch album ("Thirteen Knights," "The Twins") it also misses quite a few others. Hopefully, Rhino, current holder of the rights to this MGM soundtrack, will eventually reissue it in a complete format.

Didier C. Deutsch

Election

1999, Sire Records, from the Paramount film *Election*, 1999 🎬🎬🎬

Very rarely would such a mixed bag of musical sounds provide such a decent overall listening experience. From the country sounds of Mandy Barnett and Jolene to the soulful crooning of

Lionel Richie on the classic Commodores song "Three Times a Lady" to the French pop of chanteuse April March, this is one truly eclectic compilation. The "Election" of the film's title refers to a high school presidential race and the story follows a teacher's unusual obsession with one of the candidates. There's no sense of unity to the album, yet the choices are generally interesting enough that the album doesn't bore you and is worth a second and third listen. Score fans will be also pleased to find a cue from the original motion picture score by Rolfe Kent.

Amy Rosen

The Electric Horseman

1987, Columbia Records, from the film *The Electric Horseman,* Columbia Pictures, 1979 ♪♪♪♪

album notes: Music: Dave Grusin; **Conductor:** Dave Grusin.

Grusin wrote the score, but Willie Nelson (with five songs on this album and a costarring role in the film) gets all the credit. Actually, who should complain when the songs include "My Heroes Have Always Been Cowboys" and "Mammas Don't Let Your Babies Grow Up to Be Cowboys," two of Nelson's most popular hits. As for Dave Grusin, writing in an idiom that is closer to his own roots, he does well for himself with cues that are attractively designed and strongly evocative of the specific atmosphere of the film, a romantic comedy starring Robert Redford as an ex-rodeo champion seeking a richer and more rewarding life, and Jane Fonda as the TV reporter who comes to share his views. "Electro-Phantasma," a bouncy, jazzy tune, and "Disco Magic," Grusin's concession to the omnipresent fad at the time, are quite enjoyable. "Love Theme," in a more subtle vein, proves equally fetching.

Didier C. Deutsch

The Elephant Man

1994, Milan Records, from the film *The Elephant Man,* Paramount Pictures, 1980 ♪♪♪♪

album notes: Music: John Morris; **Orchestra:** The National Philharmonic Orchestra; **Conductor:** John Morris.

A gruesome story about a man's deformity and the strange fascination he exerted on his contemporaries in Victorian England, *The Elephant Man* inspired John Morris to write a generally somber score, well in keeping with the nature of the drama. The horror provoked by John Merrick's appearance, his inner thoughts, and his dream about having a more normal existence, are fully explored in cues in which the main theme, a wistful melody initially heard as a delicately attractive waltz, returns as an adagio filled with morose undertones. In contrast, other cues announce in a gritty, almost unbearably harsh way,

the plastic carnival exuberance that marks his exhibition at various fairgrounds, the only way he could make a living. A sardonic "The Nightmare" blends both elements in a grotesque display that is both vivid and frightening. Adding a somewhat unnecessary touch to this score, strong enough to exist on its own terms, is yet another version of Samuel Barber's "Adagio for Strings," performed by the LSO and Andre Previn.

Didier C. Deutsch

Elizabeth

1998, London Records, from the PolyGram film *Elizabeth,* 1998 ♪♪♪♪

album notes: Music: David Hirschfelder; **Conductor:** Philip Pickett.

Composer David Hirschfelder characterizes Queen Elizabeth I from a girlish, love-smitten Princess to a ruthless, white-faced Empress, evoking her struggle and conflict during this transformation. When Elizabeth commands the massacre of all her opponents, the blood bath is accompanied by the period Latin hymn "Domine Secundum Actum Meum," further intensifying her loss of innocence with the angelic sound of a boys choir. Further period flourishes are supplied by an Elizabethan band, contrasting with selections from the regal Mozart's "Requiem" and Elgar's "Enigma Variations." The conflict between Elizabeth's romance and her duty as a military leader are addressed in the love theme, where wistful strings are punctuated by an underlying military drum march that increasingly asserts itself throughout the film. Fans of Hirschfelder's romantic piano work for *Shine* and playful dance music for *Strictly Ballroom* will find *Elizabeth* a much grander, far more serious, and suitably majestic prospect.

David Poole

Elizabeth and Essex

1992, Bay Cities Records, from the film *The Private Lives of Elizabeth and Essex,* Warner Bros., 1939 ♪♪♪♪♪

album notes: Music: Erich-Wolfgang Korngold; **Orchestra:** The Munich Symphony Orchestra; **Conductor:** Carl Davis.

Carl Davis and the Munich Symphony Orchestra conjure up all the drama and passion in Korngold's score for *The Private Lives of Elizabeth and Essex* in a recording marked by its brilliant sonics and the excellence of its performance. Instead of presenting the score as a disjointed series of short cues, the recording regroups the main themes in six long suites that follow the unfolding historical drama starring Errol Flynn as the ambitious Lord Essex, a hero in his own country after he defeated the Spaniards at Cadiz, and Bette Davis as the Queen of England, with whom Essex has an affair before she has him beheaded when she senses his real ambition is to overthrow her and seize power. Much in the line of his other swashbucklers, like *Sea Hawk* or *Captain Blood,* Korngold wrote a score that teems with gorgeous romantic melodies and rambunctious action cues. The whole brew is served with the right dose of pageantry and pathos by the orchestra, wonderfully together behind its conductor.

Didier C. Deutsch

Elizabeth Taylor in London/Four in the Morning

1992, Play It Again/U.K., from the television special *Elizabeth Taylor in London,* 1963; and from the film *Four in the Morning,* 1966 ♪♪♪♪

album notes: Music: John Barry; **Conductor:** Johnny Spence, John Barry.

Written for a television special starring Elizabeth Taylor, *Elizabeth Taylor in London* elicited from Barry a gorgeously romantic score, with many beautiful tracks that have justifiably become favorites among the composer's many fans. Sonics, however, are the problem here, with the early–'60s recording techniques denoting flaws (strident sound, tape hiss) that mar one's total enjoyment, though they could have been corrected for a digital reissue.

The score for *Four in the Morning,* a series of short stories tied together around the thin device of the clock marking time, is, in contrast, much more vibrant and jazzy, though sound quality is again somewhat of a problem.

Didier C. Deutsch

Elmer Gantry

1998, Rykodisc, from the United Artists film *Elmer Gantry,* 1960 ♪♪♪♪

album notes: Music: Andre Previn; **Conductor:** Andre Previn.

Andre Previn received an Oscar nomination for his score to this highly controversial film about a booze-swilling, prostitute-frequenting salesman-turned Revivalist preacher, a role that earned Burt Lancaster an Oscar in 1960. Mirroring the multiple aspects of the main character's personality, his life as a preacher by day and his bad boy shenanigans by night, the music waivers between in-your-face dissonant themes and bold renditions of hymns. This first-time CD release includes five tracks that were not previously available, including a jazz arrangement of "Onward Christian Soldiers," two spirituals, and a version of "On My Way" sung by Burt Lancaster.

Didier C. Deutsch

Emma

1996, Miramax-Hollywood Records, from the film *Emma,* Miramax Pictures, 1996 ♪♪♪♪

album notes: Music: Rachel Portman; **Conductor:** David Snell; **Featured Musicians:** Hugh Webb, harp; Nick Bucknall, clarinet; Linda Coffin, flute.

With its deft use of classical-sounding themes, many of them crafted for a chamber ensemble in which delicate instruments like the harp, clarinet, and flute play a predominant role, this magnificent score must rank among some of the best film music written in 1996. Composed for yet another adaptation of a Jane Austen novel (Hollywood's greatest screenwriter of late), this discriminating score is achingly beautiful, superbly nuanced, and gorgeously melodic. Heard behind the scenes on the screen, it subtly underscores the action, adding its own commentary without overstressing its presence. Isolated from the film, it stands out as a marvelous example of solid music composition, at times joyously expressive, at times compassionately poignant, but always pleasantly listenable, and constantly inventive. In other words, it's everything good film music should always be.

Didier C. Deutsch

Empire of the Sun

1987, Warner Bros. Records, from the film *Empire of the Sun,* Warner Bros., 1987 ♪♪♪♪

album notes: Music: John Williams; **Conductor:** John Williams.

Considered by many one of John Williams's best efforts, this striking score yielded at least two recognizable hits in the composer's canon, if not on the charts, "Cadillac of the Skies" and the anthem "Exsultate Justi." But this brilliantly colorful film by Steven Spielberg, about a young boy caught in World War II China by the Japanese invasion, inspired the composer to write a rich series of cues, highlighted by some unforgettable moments like "Jim's New Life," "Imaginary Air Battle," or the actively exotic "The Streets of Shanghai." Typical of Williams's florid style, the cues overflow with great melodic themes, excitingly expressive and wonderfully stated. One exception, however, is "The Pheasant Hunt," for percussion and ethnic instruments, which might have been very effective on the screen behind the action, but which makes no real musical statement of its own and seems a bit of a waste in the current context.

Didier C. Deutsch

The Empire Strikes Back

1997, RCA Victor Records, from the film *The Empire Strikes Back,* 20th Century-Fox, 1980 ♪♪♪♪

album notes: Music: John Williams; **Orchestrata:** The London Symphony Orchestra; **Conductor:** John Williams.

Gwyneth Paltrow in Emma. (The Kobal Collection)

John Williams reached the culmination of his blockbuster style with this first *Star Wars* sequel, which features a dizzying array of memorable themes as it underscores the dark middle section of George Lucas's space epic trilogy. Williams originally scored almost every moment of *Empire*, and this deluxe 2-CD set presents the entire score for the first time with amazing fidelity and showmanship. Included is a great deal of music Williams wrote for early sections of the film as action ensues on the ice planet of Hoth, and album producer Nick Redman and sequencer Mark Mattesino have ingeniously organized this music to reflect both the familiar movie editing of the music and the score as it might have been, with plenty of music that's never been released in any form. The throbbing early passages involving Luke Skywalker and Han Solo exploring on their two-legged Taun-Tauns and Williams's thrillingly sustained, agitated battle sequences dominate the first third of the album, while his delicate, exquisitely lyrical material for Yoda lends a reflective quality to the score's midsection. The heavy, percussive sounds of Bespin's carbon freeze chamber and a throbbing, dirge-like melody raise the stakes for the film's climactic sequences, with the composer at his swashbuckling best in "The Duel" and whipping up amazing drama and suspense with Luke "Losing a Hand" and barely escaping Darth Vader during the propulsive jump to "Hyperspace." You might be exhausted by the umpteenth take on "Darth Vader's Theme" by the time this is over, but *Empire* remains a magnificent, unforgettable epic score.

see also: Star Wars, Return of the Jedi

Jeff Bond

The End of Violence

1998, Outpost Records, from the MGM film *The End of Violence*, 1998 ♪♪♪♪♪

album notes: Music: Ry Cooder; **Featured Musicians:** Howie B, mixing; Gil Bernal, tenor sax; Joachim Cooder, drums, percussion, programming; Ry Cooder, guitar, piano; Rick Cox, prepared guitar, bass sax, samples; Sunny D, programming, sampling; Mark Hunel-Adrian, guitar; Flaco Jimenez, accordion; Jim Keltner, drums, programming; Tonya Ridgely, flute; William "Smitty" Smith, organ; Jacky Terrasson, piano; James "Blood" Ulmer, guitar; Amir Yaghmai, guitar; Jon Hassell, trumpet solos.

Wim Wenders's minor 1997 film about high-tech crime surveillance in Los Angeles brought forth two vital soundtrack albums. The song collection is an evocative, rich collection of moody, eclectic rock by the likes of Tom Waits, Spain, Roy Orbison, the Eels, DJ Shadow, Los Lobos, and a great new collaboration between U2 and Sinead O'Connor. Only hindered by its annoying use of sound bites from the movie that distract from the music, this is a superb soundtrack album that completely stands on its own as a highly enjoyable listening experience.

Wim Wenders and Ry Cooder are long time collaborators, whose work together on *Paris, Texas* is considered by many a truly classic soundtrack. Here Cooder has assembled a stellar ensemble of musicians to support him. The players include ace session drummer Jim Keltner, the legendary accordion player Flaco Jimenez, jazz legend Jacky Terrasson on piano, and son Joachim Cooder on additional drums, percussion, and programming. The resulting score album is an unusual blend of acoustic and ambient sounds. Like the song compilation, this score album is strongly recommended.

Amy Rosen

The Endless Game

1989, Virgin Records, from the television serial *The Endless Game*, 1989 ♪♪♪♪♪

album notes: Music: Ennio Morricone; **Orchestra:** Unione musicisti di Roma; **Conductor:** Ennio Morricone.

Occasionally, Ennio Morricone has created scores for television shows. In this country, he is best remembered for *Marco Polo,* a score that cries out to be reissued on CD, and in Italy, he has been involved with a long series about the Bible. *The Endless Game,* a cold war thriller, is another series on which he worked, and in which he indulged many of his signature characteristics (a sharp call of monosyllabic strings here, an ominous theme for low strings there). It all sounds comfortably familiar, yet surprisingly new, with some selections like "The Love Game" and "Caroline's Song" (which sounds as if it had been recycled from the score of *Malamondo*) making a stronger impression because of their melodic content. Perhaps more specifically of interest to rabid Morricone fans, but also a nice discovery for those who may not be familiar with it.

Didier C. Deutsch

Endless Love

1981, Mercury Records, from the PolyGram film *Endless Love,* 1981 ♪♪♪

album notes: Music: Jonathan Tunick.

Brooke Shields had a starring role in this film directed by Franco Zeffirelli, in which she portrayed a 15-year-old who has a torrid love affair with a 17-year-old, although you would never tell from the idiotic smile she wears at all times that she understands or appreciates what sex is all about. The soundtrack was an equally torrid affair that involved Lionel Richie and Diana Ross, who took the title song to the top of the charts for a whopping nine weeks. Cliff Richard and Kiss also did their bit on this one (although a platinum hit, "I Was Made for Lovin' You" only reached #11), all of which cast a pall on Jonathan Tunick's dreamy score and relegated it to the end of this release.

Appropriately florid and romantic in the right places, it was evocative, to say the least, but failed to make much of an impression.

Didier C. Deutsch

The Endless Summer II

1994, Reprise Records, from the New Line Cinema film *The Endless Summer II*, 1994 ♫♫♫

album notes: Songs: Gary Hoey.

When it first came out in 1966, *The Endless Summer,* a surfing documentary, boasted some spectacular photography, exotic locations, a wonderful sense of adventure, a tongue-in-cheek commentary, and some great music. That it took close to 30 years to come up with a sequel may be indicative of the reasons why this second outing quickly wore thin, despite many assets that compared favorably with the first film, including photography, locations, etc., etc. More telling, however, was the fact that the music, written and performed by Gary Hoey, sounded one-dimensional after a while and failed to ignite in the way the first soundtrack did. Still, there are a few good numbers to be found here for those so inclined, including "Sweet Water," the Afro-Cuban "La Rosa Negra," the quasi-country "Surfdoggin'," and the dreamy "The Deep." Not a bad collection altogether, but we've heard much better.

Didier C. Deutsch

Enemies, A Love Story

1989, Varèse Sarabande Records, from the film *Enemies, A Love Story,* 20th Century-Fox, 1989 ♫♫♫♫

album notes: Music: Maurice Jarre; **Conductor:** Maurice Jarre; **Featured Musician:** Giora Feidman, clarinet.

Maurice Jarre returned to a seldom explored side of his vast creative talent with this score written for Paul Mazursky's biting satire about a man, a survivor of the Holocaust, living in New York and married to three women, with all the complications this deliciously unusual situation creates. As he already had demonstrated a year before in the director's *Moon Over Parador,* Jarre can easily handle the most spurious aspects of broad comedy, even going as far as spoofing his own style to add extra pep to his concoctions. Here, the situation enabled him to add to the mix some Jewish accents, with Giora Feidman handling the obligatory clarinet solos. Posing ever so slightly to reflect on the individual charms of the three women, as does the hero of the film, the music moves merrily into its own territory, with a "kretchmar" and a rumba among its most enjoyable side trips.

Didier C. Deutsch

Enemy Mine

1985, Varèse Sarabande, from the film *Enemy Mine,* 20th Century-Fox, 1985 ♫♫♫♫

album notes: Music: Maurice Jarre; **Orchestra:** The Studioorchester of Munich; **Conductor:** Maurice Jarre.

This wonderful thematic score by Maurice Jarre is cleverly sequenced like a symphonic suite so that the music evolves from a focus on electronics to acoustics. In fact, early cues in the film are also more electronic and the finale almost all orchestral. This shifting of orchestrational style allowed Jarre to play up the sci-fi aspects of the film against the emotional core of the story. Even with all the film's futuristic trappings, it still all boils down to a basic story of friendship and parental love between two who were once mortal enemies. Chiefly, Jarre uses his electronics to play the alien aspects of the planet locale and the hostility between the lizard-like Draconian marooned with a human fighter pilot. The theme for the mystical Draconian religion is brought into full bloom during the finale, "Before the Drac Holy Council," through the use of an electronically augmented chorus.

David Hirsch

Enemy of the State

1998, Hollywood Records, from the Touchstone film *Enemy of the State,* 1998 ♫♫

album notes: Music: Trevor Rabin, Harry Gregson-Williams; **Conductor:** Gordon Goodwin.

There's a battle raging in action films between sound effects and music, and it's the scores that are losing, with orchestral instruments and melody buried underneath a barrage of gunfire and explosions. Like the mutant survivors of a nuclear holocaust, *Enemy of the State* represents the new breed of action "music," where synths and symphonic instruments blaze away without any sense or purpose, their sound virtually indistinguishable from the bullet hits that they're desperately trying to catch up to. You can only pity the composers who are asked to score the latest MTV action film from the Simpson-Bruckheimer machine (although *Enemy* manages to be better than most), and there's probably no way that Rabin or Williams could play anything that would make sense during the hundred-edits-per-minute spectacle. So they just play everything, really, really fast until you can't remember the music you heard a second ago. The resulting "score" drives the picture all right, but that's all it's really doing. As a listen, the music in *Enemy* is a mess, caught in that dreaded place between sound effects and score, slivers of melody here and there giving a taste of what the music could have been—if it had stopped and made sense.

Dan Schweiger

The English Patient

🎬 1996, Fantasy Records, from the film *The English Patient,* Miramax Films, 1996 🎵🎵🎵

album notes: Music: Gabriel Yared; **Orchestra:** The Academy of St. Martin-in-the-Fields; **Conductor:** Harry Rabinowitz; **Featured Musician:** John Constable, piano; Marta Sebestyen, vocals.

Dismissing the several pop songs included in this album, which neither add nor detract from the music itself and certainly provide a period flavor, portions of this Oscar-winning score by Gabriel Yared may actually have been more effective on the screen than in this soundtrack album. One basic reason is that many of the cues, short as they are, are not sufficiently developed to really attract, and often sound unfinished. There are, of course, some happy exceptions, including a lovely "Kip's Lights," played by a romantic piano against an attractively evanescent orchestral background; "I'll Always Go Back to That Church," with its faint evocation of Italy; "Convento di Sant'Anna," a piano sonata, staid yet poetic in its subtle simplicity; and "Read Me to Sleep," another piece for piano solo that is starkly eloquent. These, and some of the other selections succeed in recreating the atmosphere that permeates this romantic drama about an amnesiac aviator and the Canadian nurse who tends to him in an old monastery in Tuscany, in the last days of World War II.

Didier C. Deutsch

The Englishman Who Went Up a Hill But Came Down a Mountain

🎬 1995, Epic Soundtrax, from the film *The Englishman Who Went Up a Hill But Came Down a Mountain,* Miramax Films, 1995 🎵🎵🎵🎵🎵

album notes: Music: Stephen Endelman; **Conductor:** Stephen Endelman; **Featured Musicians:** Sian James, vocals; Gwalia Male Voice Choir, vocals; Giles Lewin, bagpipe, flute, pennywhistle.

The beautifully exotic score for this film starring Hugh Grant was composed by Stephen Endelman, who is not to be confused with either Cliff Eidelman or Randy Edelman. Not that you will, once you have heard this extraordinary profuse orchestral score, subtly relying on the flute and the pennywhistle to create its own poetic atmosphere. Rooted in the English folk tradition, the themes evolve out of the orchestral texture to reveal the uncanny talent of the composer who succeeds in accenting the stronger aspects of the story, as well as evoking the raw beauty of the countryside in which it takes place. Some cues ("Never Ending Rain," "Lovers on the Mountain," "Magnificent Peak") are particularly striking, but the score as a whole is remarkably attractive.

Didier C. Deutsch

Entrapment

🎬 1999, Restless Records, from the 20th Century-Fox film *Entrapment,* 1999 🎵🎵🎵

album notes: Music: Christopher Young; **Conductor:** Christopher Young.

The millennium, this flicker of an event that will only last a second (the passage from one year to the next) already inspires films, such as this terrific comedy thriller in which an insurance investigator, Catherine Zeta-Jones, teams with a legendary gentleman thief, played by Sean Connery, by posing as a master thief herself, the better to catch him in the act. The mother of all heists they plan together is set to happen . . . on the eve of the millennium, of course! Setting the whole thing to music, Christopher Young wrote a score that blends a symphony orchestra, a piano playing in concertante style, and the standard contingent of synthesized pulses that seem to have become mandatory in this type of film. The themes are interesting for the most part, though not wildly extravagant, on the romantic side when the screen action warrants it, and appropriately percolating when the thieves perform their deeds. The setpiece here is a long selection titled "The Empress Mask" that's somewhat predictable, with almost imperceptible orchestral moments being interrupted by sudden outbursts, leading to quieter expressions again. The riff-active "Millennium Countdown" offers a sharp contrast, but not enough to compel another listening. Frankly, the film was a great deal more fun.

Didier C. Deutsch

Equus

🎬 1998, Rykodisc, from the United Artists film *Equus,* 1977 🎵🎵

album notes: Music: Richard Rodney Bennett; **Conductor:** Angela Morley.

Richard Burton lords it over *Equus* with his rich toned voice. He plays a psychologist attempting to cure a disturbed young boy who blinded a stable full of horses with a stick. Despite the charisma and poise of Burton's spoken voice, the lengthy monologues included here are gratuitous, notably the patient's energetic sex fantasies regarding horses. Bennett's neoclassical score of soothing chamber music serves as counterpoint to the unsettling plot. Bennett's austere quotations of Bach over four brief movements of strings barely register an emotion. The music maintains an even keel throughout the substantial passion and drama of *Equus,* with only occasional glissandi to hint at the equine atrocity. While balancing an intriguing plot, *Equus* dissipates in isolation.

David Poole

ER

1996, Atlantic Records, from the NBC–TV series *ER,* Amblin Entertainment, 1996 🎵🎵

album notes: Music: James Newton Howard, Martin Davich; **Featured Musicians:** Marc Bonilla, Michael Landau, guitars; Larry Williams, tenor sax; Steve Porcaro, synthesizers.

Last season's big hit (and probably next season's, too), *ER* received its score from composers James Newton Howard and Martin Davich, in which the accent is squarely on contemporary stylings, with lots of synthesized riffs, rhythm tracks, and all the musical trappings usually associated with modern television dramas. The truth is that it does sound a bit dry in the long run, with cues that are written to closely match the action on the screen with little consideration given to a possible soundtrack album. What stands out here are the two songs that have been added, but they are hardly sufficient to compel the listener to return frequently to the album.

Didier C. Deutsch

Eraser

1996, Atlantic Records, from the film *Eraser,* Warner Bros., 1996 🎵🎵

album notes: Music: Alan Silvestri; **Conductor:** Alan Silvestri.

A lackluster action film score, especially by Alan Silvestri standards. There's a sense of boredom all around here as the music just plods along. It takes until track 5, "Kruger Escapes," before there's any sign of life. The screeching guitar passages seem more necessary to keep the listener awake than serve any dramatic purpose. The main theme seems to be going somewhere, but exactly where is never clear.

David Hirsch

Escape from L.A.

1996, Milan Records, from the film *Escape from L.A.,* Paramount Pictures, 1996 🎵🎵

album notes: Music: Shirley Walker; John Carpenter; **Conductor:** Shirley Walker; **Featured Musicians:** Nyle Steiner, electronic valve instrument; Jamie Muhoberac, sample synthesist; Mike Watts, keyboard synthesist; Shirley Walker, keyboard synthesist; Mike Fisher, electronic percussion; Tommy Morgan, harmonica; Daniel Greco, hammer dulcimer; John Goux, guitar; Nathan East, bass guitar; John Rosinson, rock drums; Tom Raney, timpani; Greg Goodall, timpani; Robert Zimmitti, Daiko drum; Endre Granat, violin; Jon Clarke, soprano oboe.

Somewhat disappointing follow up to the delightfully minimalist score to *Escape from New York.* Original composer John Carpenter contributed to this effort, most notably the new Morricone-inspired theme for anti-hero Snake Plisskin. The bulk of the work was created by Shirley Walker, who scored Carpenter's also disappointing *Memoirs of an Invisible Man,* and uses contemporary action film orchestral and synthesizer techniques here, without making any attempt to blend her compositional style with Carpenter's (compare her "Fire Fight" with his "Showdown"). What made the first film's score so popular was that it captured Plisskin's dark, brooding personality so well. He was a bad ass with no love for a world that didn't care about him. This time, Walker and Carpenter seem hell bent on spoofing not only the entire genre of post apocalyptic films, but their own as well. They're even making fun of Kurt Russell's less than subtle Clint Eastwood–like performance of Plisskin by clearly defining the connection musically.

David Hirsch

Escape from the Planet of the Apes

See: Planet of the Apes

E.T.: The Extra-Terrestrial

1982, MCA Records, from the film *E.T.: The Extra-Terrestrial,* Universal Pictures, 1982 🎵🎵🎵🎵

1996, MCA Records, from the film *E.T.: The Extra-Terrestrial,* Universal Pictures, 1982 🎵🎵🎵🎵

album notes: Music: John Williams; **Conductor:** John Williams.

Call it the lighter side of *Close Encounters of the Third Kind,* if you will, but having to deal once again with alien visitors under the aegis of film magician Steven Spielberg, John Williams wrote a score that is as exhilarating and florid as his previous score was brooding and somber. Of course, the story itself suggested as much. Instead of government agents trying to make contact with beings from another planet, not knowing what their ultimate intentions might be, this time around the extra-terrestrial, stranded on Earth following a landing accident, is trying to elude government agents intent on capturing him. With the help of a little guy who captures his confidence, E.T. eventually succeeds in going back home, but not before living some rousing, unforgettable moments. Williams's score, exquisitely shaded and warmly effusive, helps give the tale an extra element of verisimilitude, with a cohesive combination of musical themes all designed to enhance the screen action.

When the film was initially released, Williams went to the studio, and rerecorded several of the themes for an album which has been in the MCA catalogue ever since, first as an LP and, since the late 1980s, as a CD. The music, focusing on the lighter cues in the score, has made many converts, with one selection in particular, "Flying," achieving the status of a popular hit.

Recently, without saying much about it, MCA has added to its catalogue a vastly expanded version of the soundtrack that is remarkably different from the previous album. Instead of using the studio rerecording, these are the actual soundtrack cues, which have different tempi, somewhat altered orchestrations, and a greater abundance of the darker cues from the score. More profuse, and certainly truer to the music one can hear in the film itself, this album makes fewer concessions to the popular aspects of the score and gives a broader scope of Williams's actual work, a startling combination of dark and light moments, all coming together in a mesmerizing display of his creative bent. Which of the two should you get? Both, of course, as they seem to complement each other while offering slightly different takes on the same score.

Didier C. Deutsch

Europa Europa

See: Olivier Olivier

Even Cowgirls Get the Blues

1993, Sire Records, from the film *Even Cowgirls Get the Blues,* Fine Line Features, 1993 ♪♪♪♪
album notes: Music: k.d. lang; Ben Mink.

k.d. lang's songs and score (written in collaboration with Ben Mink) enhance this fantasy based on Tom Robbins's 1973 quirky cult novel, in which a virgin hippie girl with abnormally developed thumbs (ideal for hitchhiking) ends up on an Oregon ranch where the cowboys are actually cowgirls. When the dispirited girls take over the ranch and feed some peyote to a flock of cranes, resulting in an ecological disaster, the Army decides to intervene, in a painful echo to some of the political upheavals of the late 1960s. In this bizarre topsy-turvy set-up, the score explores various styles, with some uplifting rockers among its most endearing moments. While one could dispense with the strange-sounding "Much Finer Place," "Virtual Vortex," and "Apogee," (which is mercifully short) that tie some of the selections together, the other tracks (particularly "Lifted By Love," the old-fashioned "In Perfect Dreams," or the exuberant "Don't Be a Lemming Polka") are quite enjoyable.

Didier C. Deutsch

The Evening Star

1996, Angel Records, from the Paramount film *The Evening Star,* 1996 ♪♪
album notes: Music: William Ross.

This 1996 sequel to the beloved classic *Terms of Endearment* was poorly received by both critics and the movie-going public. Curious album buyers will find a pleasant enough score by William Ross that incorporates composer Michael Gore's original themes from *Terms of Endearment.* The musical reference to the first

movie works well in context to the plot of *The Evening Star,* which finds matriarch Aurora Greenway attempting to salvage her tenuous relationships with her late daughter's children, small kids in the first movie, but now troubled teenagers. However, if you already own the original *Terms of Endearment* soundtrack, you probably don't really need this sequel in your collection.

Amy Rosen

Ever After

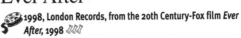 1998, London Records, from the 20th Century-Fox film *Ever After,* 1998 ♪♪♪
album notes: Music: George Fenton; **Conductor:** George Fenton.

The talented George Fenton seems to have a fondness for scoring romantic comedies, as evidenced by his recent work on such films as *You've Got Mail, The Object of My Affection,* and the sleeper hit *Ever After.* The latter score is a lovely orchestral confection, and a very nice fit for this new take on the Cinderella story, with Drew Barrymore (as the Cinderella character) and Anjelica Huston (as the wicked step-mother character) putting a different spin on classic characters. The album also includes a lovely, romantic song by the Scottish band Texas, "Put Your Arms around Me."

Amy Rosen

Everest

1998, ARK 21, from the IMAX film *Everest,* 1998 ♪♪♪♪

album notes: Music: Steve Wood, Daniel May (including the music of George Harrison); **Conductor:** Daniel May; **Featured Musicians:** Richard Hardy, flutes; Techung, voice, piwang, drayan, flute, doungchen; Kurt Rasmussen, percussion; Geetha Bennet, veena, tambura; Michael Hamilton, guitars; Alan Deremo, bass; Frank Cotinola, trap drums; Eric Rigler, Uilleann pipes; Steve Wood, Daniel May, keyboards; the Monks of Gaden-Shartse.

Created for the Sony IMAX 3-D film, the score of *Everest* blends the themes created by Steve Wood and Daniel May with melodies borrowed from some of the songs George Harrison wrote for his solo recordings like "All Things Must Pass," "Give Me Love," and "Life Itself." Written for large orchestra, traditional Tibetan and Indian folk instruments, Buddhist chants, and various sounds obtained from other parts of the world, the score aims to reflect the diversity of Nepal, a country between India and Tibet, where a confluence of several ethnic flows resulted in a diverse cultural background. As instrumental scores go, this one is richly detailed, with great themes evolving from the suggested cues. Since this is a documentary, the music doesn't so much reflect a dramatic action as it does visions of beauty and majestic grandeur ("The Himalaya," "Khumbu Icefall"), occasionally clouded by natural manifestations ("The Blizzard"). Somehow, even "Here Comes the Sun" played by a large symphonic orchestra seems to fit, but the reprise on guitar sounds so much better.

see also: Into Thin Air: Death on Everest

Didier C. Deutsch

Everybody's All American

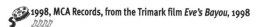 1988, Capitol Records, from the Warner Bros. film *Everybody's All-American*, 1988 ♫♫♫

Based on the book by Frank Deford, *Everybody's All-American* detailed the shattered dreams of a young couple, a former college football star and a cheerleader, as their adult lives belie all the hopes they nursed at one time. Maudlin and manipulative, the film may have been overly sentimental, but it benefited from this soundtrack album, a compilation of tracks by some great performers such as Smiley Lewis, Nat King Cole, Lloyd Price, and Hank Ballard, all of which served as a background to the couple's happy college days. Together, they still manage to overcome the syrupy effect left by "Until Forever," the theme from the film.

Didier C. Deutsch

Everyone Says I Love You

1997, RCA Victor, from the film *Everyone Says I Love You*, Miramax Pictures, 1997 ♫♫

album notes: Music: Dick Hyman; **Orchestra:** The New York Studio Players; **Conductor:** Dick Hyman; **Featured Musicians:** The Helen Miles Singers.

It did make sense, of course, that Woody Allen would eventually attempt to make a film musical, and that he would call upon the services of his favorite composer, Dick Hyman, to create the original score and write the orchestrations for some of the standards heard in it. But like the "tap dancing" in "My Baby Just Cares for Me," this soundtrack album, delightful as it may be, sounds strangely out of step and out of focus. Whether it is the recording itself, oddly without much sonic definition, or the performances that fail to ignite, the result is an album that seems to promise a lot but never quite delivers. The selections include many standards from the 1930s, performed by the stars of the film (including Goldie Hawn, Alan Alda, and Julia Roberts), and some nifty instrumentals with Dick Hyman on piano and Woody Allen himself on clarinet.

Didier C. Deutsch

Eve's Bayou

1998, Sonic Images, from the Trimark film *Eve's Bayou*, 1998 ♫♫♫♫

album notes: Music: Terence Blanchard; **Conductor:** Terence Blanchard; **Featured Musicians:** Edward Simon, piano; Reginald Veal, bass; Troy Davis, drums; Don Vappie, guitar.

10 Essential Scores
by John Williams

Raiders of the Lost Ark
Star Wars
Star Wars: The Phantom Menace
E.T.: The Extra-Terrestrial
Close Encounters of the Third Kind
The Witches of Eastwick
Empire of the Sun
The Accidental Tourist
The Reivers
Schindler's List

1998, MCA Records, from the Trimark film *Eve's Bayou*, 1998 ♫♫♫♫

album notes: Music: Terence Blanchard; **Conductor:** Terence Blanchard; **Featured Musicians:** Don Vappie, guitar; Reginald Veal, bass; Edward Simon, piano; Troy Davis, drums.

A deeply emotional drama set in Louisiana in 1962, *Eve's Bayou* evoked the plays of Tennessee Williams, and came to extraordinary life thanks to a superlative cast, including Diahann Carroll, Samuel L. Jackson, Lynn Whitfield, and a bright newcomer named Jurnee Smollett. Essentially the loss of innocence of a teenager, the story concerned a well-to-do black family, seemingly united around its head, Louis Batiste, a doctor, and his wife, Roz. When their younger daughter, Eve, witnesses an indiscretion on the part of her father, she is shattered by the experience. But, as the film makes clear, she also finds herself manipulated by her older sister and the adults in the family, who dismiss the doctor's adultery and give it a different explanation, all in order to keep face. Adding an eerie note to the story, the director, Kasi Lemmons, also injected elements of Southern Gothic and voodoo rituals that gave the narrative a deeper meaning.

Madonna and Antonio Banderas in the film version of Evita. **(The Kobal Collection)**

Also providing a definite resonance of its own, the soundtrack included various pop songs and a riveting score by Terence Blanchard.

Eve's Bayou: The Collection presents a mixed bag of rock'n'roll, zydeco, and blues songs performed by Bobby "Blue" Bland, Ray Charles, Etta James, Louis Armstrong and Velma Middleton, and Geno Delafosse, and a new song by Erykah Badu, which frames this album. As Kasi Lemmons explains in her notes, each song was chosen for a specific reason, with the amalgam providing a constant undercurrent in it. On a purely audio listening level, they form a cohesive collection.

If the songs reflect the consciousness of the characters in the film, Terence Blanchard's music is the subconscious. A rich, coherent set of cues, it captures the essence of the film, with sonorities that are particularly captivating. A slyly jaunty tune with a great lilt, "Cisely's Take," which features Don Vappie's guitar, gives way to a brooding "Enter Mozelle's House," dark and mysterious. Other highlights include the elegiac "Eve's Paradox," and the reflective "We're Going to Elzora's House." Imaginative and evocative of the action, this is a sensitively

focused score that goes a long way to creating poetic images of its own.

Didier C. Deutsch

Evil under the Sun

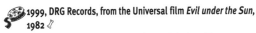 **1999, DRG Records, from the Universal film *Evil under the Sun*, 1982** 🎵

album notes: Music: Cole Porter; **Conductor:** John Lanchberry.

It might have seemed like a great idea to use Cole Porter's music for a film set in the Aegean in the 1930s, about vacationing jet setters and, of all people, the ubiquitous little Belgian detective created by Agatha Christie. It might have seemed like a great idea . . . but it doesn't work, at least not in this soundtrack album. The basic reason is that John Lanchberry's arrangements sound too much like 101 Strings, all gloss and no sparkle. The tunes selected play one into the other without much rhyme or reason, without bridges to tie them in or at least give a semblance of transition (just an abrupt pause will do!), and in some instances it sounds as if the cues on the album were the ones performed for the film, suddenly cutting off (probably) for an important scene. Cole Porter would have been quite unhappy to hear his music treated in this fashion.

Didier C. Deutsch

Evita

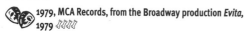 1979, MCA Records, from the Broadway production *Evita*, 1979 ♪♪♪♪

album notes: Music: Andrew Lloyd Webber; **Lyrics:** Tim Rice; **Musical Direction:** Rene Wiegert; **Cast:** Patti LuPone, Mandy Patinkin, Bob Gunton.

1996, Warner Bros. Records, from the film *Evita*, Hollywood Pictures, 1996 ♪♪♪♪

album notes: Music: Andrew Lloyd Webber; **Lyrics:** Tim Rice; **Musical Direction:** John Mauceri, David Caddick, Mike Dixon; **Cast:** Madonna, Antonio Banderas, Jonathan Pryce.

In 1979, Andrew Lloyd Webber and Tim Rice took Broadway by storm with *Evita*, smartly directed by Hal Prince, who certainly deserved to share in the success of the show. A fancy account of the life and times of Eva Peron, wife of the Argentinian dictator and inspiration of her beloved "descamisados," the low-life workers to whom she appealed and who canonized her after her death, *Evita* was also the first sung-through musical to hit Broadway. It was a precursor in many ways of the opera-like works Webber and his followers brought to the stage in subsequent years with varying degrees of success.

With Mandy Patinkin portraying a sympathetic Che Guevarra (who in real life never met Eva Peron), Bob Gunton as Peron, and Patti LuPone crying on cue in her bravura performance of the show's hit tune, "Don't Cry For Me Argentina," *Evita* opened on Broadway on Sept. 25, 1979, to rapturous reviews. It won almost every Tony it could take (for Best Musical, Best Book, Best Score, Best Direction, and for Patti LuPone and Mandy Patinkin, among others), and enjoyed a long run of 1,567 performances. Much of its theatricality dissipates on the original cast album recording, though the undeniable dramatic flair of the score occasionally comes across in great style.

Though the show had to wait more than 15 years to make it to the screen, it was well worth it because it found in Madonna the ideal Evita. An actress with enormous charm and charisma, Madonna evidently studied hard and well to overcome her pop stylings and give her performance a more legit flair. Gorgeously lavish and expressive, the screen version of *Evita* is further enhanced with the presence of Antonio Banderas as Che, and Jonathan Pryce as Peron. The recording, while presenting the same basic flaws in style found in the original, has a more vibrant pop vitality that gives the score greater impact. And Madonna is simply wonderful in a role she was obviously destined to perform.

Didier C. Deutsch

They Know the Score

Luis Bacalov

I was in [*Il Postino*] at the very last moment. They were in contact with other composers before me, I never asked who they were. But at the very last moment I was asked to do the job quickly. Because they had to finish the film before the Venice film festival. I knew that Michael Radford was a difficult man with composers. He had his own ideas. We went on well, he loved the idea to follow the tango. I found the girl in the film a sort of Carmen. So I wrote a Spanish/Latin American score. Michael loved the music. He was worried that the orchestration would make the score too big, but I told him that the score could also be small with a bandoneon. He gave me the free hand in the orchestration.

We never expected that this film would be such a smash hit as it is today. At the end I said that the most incredible thing was that the film was accepted as a very important film. If I had written a much better score for a less important film, I would never had an Oscar. In a way the Oscar was for the Italian film. The Oscar changed my possibilities. The problem now is to say no, instead of yes to offers. To find the good films to go for.

Courtesy of **Film Score Monthly**

Evolution:
The Music from Dr. Who

1997, Prestige Records/U.K., from the BBC television series *Dr. Who*, 1988 ♪♪♪♪

album notes: Music: Keff McCulloch, Ron Grainer, Dominic Glynn; the BBC Radiophonic Workshop.

In England, where it originated, *Dr. Who* has become a cult show of such magnitude that it has spawned several record-

ings, including this album of incidental music composed by Keff McCulloch and Ron Grainer. The episodes to which the selections refer may not mean much in this country, but listeners will certainly identify with and appreciate some of the themes developed for this series, with their heavy reliance on synthesizers, weird spacey effects, and out-of-this-world sounds. The musical concepts are cute, maybe a bit odd at times, but they keep their audience interested and entertained. The BBC Radiophonic Workshop is presumably the same outfit that performs these themes behind the scenes for the series, and if so these musicians are doing an excellent job.

See also: Dr. Who

Didier C. Deutsch

Executive Decision

1996, Varèse Sarabande, from the film *Executive Decision,* Warner Bros., 1996 ♫♫♫
album notes: Music: Jerry Goldsmith; **Conductor:** Jerry Goldsmith.

Jerry Goldsmith's spare, militaristic score for this excellent airborne nail-biter harkens back to the sound of 1970s works like *Twilight's Last Gleaming* and *The Cassandra Crossing,* although the film's claustrophobic setting never really allows much opportunity to open the music up. Most of the score consists of statements of the straightforward military theme that opens the film, and there's at least one hard-charging, pulsating action cue ("All Aboard") that's similar to the composer's driving *Total Recall* title music. Much of the rest of the score consists of some percussive, low-key sneaking-around music as commandos infiltrate a hijacked 747 in midair. A simple, sitar-like electronic motif somewhat jingoistically portrays the Middle Eastern hijackers. The climactic action slugfest is "The Sleeper," with some harsh brass textures and a full-on attack theme as the commandos finally storm the hijackers. It's not exactly *Capricorn One,* but it does mark a welcome return to a grittier orchestral style for the composer.

Jeff Bond

Exit to Eden

1994, Varèse Sarabande Records, from the film *Exit to Eden,* Savoy Pictures, 1994 ♫♫♫
album notes: Music: Patrick Doyle; **Conductor:** David Snell.

A kinky comedy about, of all things, sexual deviations, *Exit to Eden* received an amusingly provocative score from Patrick Doyle, who must have had a field day concocting this one. Driven by a central theme, "Nina," a jaunty little tune that recurs at various points, the score explores many grounds and develops in the process attractive ideas, from a wistful "The Temptation," to a mock anthem ("The Arrival"), to a delightfully well etched selection titled "Get with the Programme." The jazzy

"Sheila in the Mirror" and a ragtime, "Streetscene," add a different and ultimately satisfying touch to the whole thing.

Didier C. Deutsch

Exodus

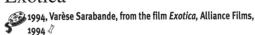1988, RCA Records, from the film *Exodus,* United Artists, 1960 ♫♫♫
album notes: Music: Ernest Gold; **Orchestra:** The Sinfonia of London Orchestra; **Conductor:** Ernest Gold.

The fervently grandiose theme Ernest Gold wrote for this recounting of the events that led to the creation of the State of Israel somehow captures the breadth and scope of the historical facts, but dwarfs in the process his other cues for the film. It must be said that the huge popularity of the theme, which was "covered" by every instrumental group and soloist around the world when it was first created, also turned it into a musical saw that overstayed its welcome. The score received the Oscar in 1960, besting such heavy contenders as Dimitri Tiomkin's *The Alamo,* Elmer Bernstein's *The Magnificent Seven,* and Alex North's *Spartacus,* which probably were more worthy. Certainly, one cannot deny the raw power behind the bombastic cues written by Gold, though the score as a whole seems most effective in its quietest moments ("Karen," "In Jerusalem," "Dawn"). The recording, sloppily remastered, evidences some hiss, a huge amount of reverb, and a rather harsh sound that is not very conducive for repeated listening.

Didier C. Deutsch

Exotica

1994, Varèse Sarabande, from the film *Exotica,* Alliance Films, 1994 ♫
album notes: Music: Mychael Danna; **Featured Musicians:** Amenee Shishakly, clarinet; Ron Korn, flute; Hovhaness Tarpinian, tar; Aruna Narayan Kalle, sarangi; Nabil Saab, oud; Kamel Saab, darabukha; Adel Saab, tambourine; Paul Intson, bass guitar; Rakesh Kumar, vocals; Annie Szamosi, vocals; Garo Tchaliguian, vocals; Harrison Kennedy, vocals.

Winner of the International Critics' Prize at Cannes, this minor essay from Canadian filmmaker Atom Egoyan explores the lower depths of human sentiments in a drama that is set for the most part in a seedy strip joint, and ultimately doesn't prove very interesting. The chilling, depraved atmosphere that pervades the film got a boost from Mychael Danna's score, in which exotic Middle-Eastern instruments add a rather mysterious touch. Still, when it comes to listening to this CD on its own terms, the music sounds rather tepid and fails to attract, in a clear demonstration that not all film scores lend themselves to the soundtrack album treatment.

Didier C. Deutsch

Experiment in Terror

1997, RCA Records/Spain, from the Columbia film *Experiment in Terror*, 1962 ♫♫♫♫

album notes: Music: Henry Mancini; **Conductor:** Henry Mancini.

It's a shame, really, that BMG in this country seems to have totally failed Henry Mancini, who was at one time one of the label's most important artists. Fortunately, the label's affiliates elsewhere are much more conscious of what he and other performers contributed when they were signed to RCA, and so it is with some trepidation that we have seen BMG Music Spain reissue some soundtrack albums by Mancini. This is only one in a series that already includes *The Party, Two for the Road,* and *High Time,* among other titles.

Mancini, who always created scores with an eye on the pop charts, wrote themes that were totally hummable and enjoyable, and always solidly anchored around strong melodies. Directed by Blake Edwards, with whom he had established a long-term artistic partnership, *Experiment in Terror* dealt with a bank teller forced by a psycopath killer to rob the bank for which she worked, and the FBI agent who gets involved with her and helps her foil the threat. Glenn Ford and particularly Lee Remick were given excellent roles in this one, and under Blake's assured direction delivered the goods. So did Mancini, whose score consisted of several selections with a pleasant twist to them, an enchanting old-fashioned tune, "The Good Old Days," and an introspective solo for piano titled "White on White." They don't write them like this anymore.

Didier C. Deutsch

Explorers

1990, Varèse Sarabande, from the film *Explorers,* Paramount Pictures, 1985 ♫♫♫♫

album notes: Music: Jerry Goldsmith; **Conductor:** Jerry Goldsmith.

Jerry Goldsmith's score for this underrated Joe Dante fantasy is perfect, surging with boyish optimism as its pulsing chords and infectiously good-natured melodies underscore the efforts of three socially misfit young boys to construct their own spaceship (with the help of a little alien technology). Although not as audacious as Dante's *Gremlins, Explorers* is more heartfelt, juggling the director's satiric sensibilities (mainly expressed by a bizarre rockabilly theme for some pop culture-obsessed extraterrestrials) with an honest and moving sense of youthful excitement at the wonders of the universe and the thrill of staying up past your bedtime. The cues involving the building and flight of the spacecraft ("Construction," "First Flight," and "No Air") pump as much adrenaline as Goldsmith has ever pumped, particularly as the latter cue launches with a spine-tingling syn-

thesized choir and no-nonsense brass over busily churning strings and woodwinds. Goldsmith developed most of the score from a five-note motif for the alien technology, including a lovely romantic motif for the film's wonderfully optimistic denouement of the boys flying through a dream-like nocturnal cloudscape.

Jeff Bond

Extreme Measures

1996, Varèse Sarabande, from the film *Extreme Measures,* Castle Rock Entertainment, 1996 ♫♫♫♫

album notes: Music: Danny Elfman; **Conductor:** Artie Kane.

This score is both a surprising and refreshing change of pace for Danny Elfman. As the first bars of the "Main Title" play, you'd never guess this is the work of the same man who composed *Batman* or *Beetlejuice.* The film, a murder mystery dealing with the subject of human experimentation by a prominent physician, motivated Elfman to paint on a more mature musical canvas. Although he still uses a chorus of voices similar to those in *Edward Scissorhands,* the effect here is anything but whimsical. They sing a litany for the souls losing their lives in the name of medical progress. The rest of the score is deliciously dark, a concoction of somber motifs filled with a woeful marriage of strings, piano, rolling drums, and a smattering of creative percussion. Elfman has definitely become more proficient as a film composer.

David Hirsch

Extreme Prejudice

1992, Intrada, from the film *Extreme Prejudice,* Tri-Star Films, 1987 ♫♫♫

album notes: Music: Jerry Goldsmith; **Orchestra:** The Hungarian State Opera Orchestra; **Conductor:** Jerry Goldsmith.

This unusual techno-western score is a strange mix of Goldsmith's brassy *Capricorn One*-style atmosphere, some of the electronicized South American feel of *Under Fire,* and a whole lot of drum machines. There are some extended action sequences that are developed in almost lyrical fashion, and the back end of the album boasts a pretty over-the-top synthesized takeoff of Ennio Morricone's familiar spaghetti western motif from *The Good, the Bad and the Ugly.* More effective is an atmospheric, vaguely militaristic solo trumpet effect echoing over the proceedings. This is a transitional score that marks Goldsmith's early foray into electronics, and thus may be less appealing to those weaned on his grittier orchestral efforts of the 1960s and 1970s. Fans of the composers later works might find it more appealing.

Jeff Bond

Eye of the Panther
/Not Since Casanova

1996, Prometheus Records, from the films *Eye of the Panther* and *Not Since Casanova* ♫♫♫

album notes: Music: John Debney; **Conductor:** John Debney.

Two soundtracks could not be more different, yet both reveal facets of a composer who has recently made himself more and more visible in a crowded field. *Eye of the Panther,* Dabney's first full "horror score," was created for a television film about a young woman who turns into a panther at night. It was written for a large chamber orchestra, an unusual style in itself. *Not Since Casanova,* composed for a little-seen independent film, elicited a gentle, romantic score with baroque overtones. In both cases, Dabney asserts himself as an interesting composer, whose talent is undeniable but who has done much better since these early efforts.

Didier C. Deutsch

The Fabulous Baker Boys

1989, GRP Records, from the film *The Fabulous Baker Boys,* 20th Century-Fox, 1989 ♫♫♫

album notes: Music: Dave Grusin; **Conductor:** Dave Grusin; **Featured Musicians:** Ernie Watts, saxophones; Sal Marquez, trumpet; Lee Ritenour, guitar; Brian Bromberg, bass; Harvey Mason, drums; The Duke Ellington Orchestra; Mercer Ellington, conductor; The Benny Goodman Quartet: Benny Goodman, clarinet; Teddy Wilson, piano; Lionel Hampton, vibraphone; Gene Krupa, drums; The Earl Palmer Trio: Karen Hernandez, piano; Ernie McDaniels, bass; Earl Palmer, drums.

Michelle Pfeiffer slinking her way across the top of a grand piano, while warbling a sexy rendition of the old chestnut "Makin' Whoopee," is the image most filmgoers remember from this mildly entertaining romantic comedy. Otherwise, this rather conventional story, about two brothers who hire an attractive vocalist to give more pep to their lackluster lounge act, had its moments of fun but ended up being relatively tame in the end. Echoing the moods in the film, Dave Grusin wrote a score that had its moments, though his contribution fell somewhat short of his usual best. The choice cuts here, as in the film, are the vocals by Pfeiffer, deliciously wanton, and source music by Duke Ellington and Benny Goodman.

Didier C. Deutsch

Faccia a faccia

See: Il mercenario/Faccia a faccia

Face/Off

1997, Hollywood Records, from the film *Face/Off,* Paramount Pictures, 1997 ♫♫♫

album notes: Music: John Powell; **Conductor:** Lucas Richmond; **Featured Musicians:** Michael Fisher, live percussion; Bob Daspit, guitar; Geoff Zanelli, guitar; Craig Hara, trumpet; Martin Tillmann, electric cello; **Featured Performers:** Boston Baroque Orchestra & Chorus.

John Powell, scoring his first major film under the aegis of Hans Zimmer, created an unusual series of cues for this thriller starring John Cage as a crime-driven maniac and John Travolta as an FBI agent trying to nab him. When he finally does, the movie is only halfway through, because Cage's demented brother now threatens to blow up the entire city of Los Angeles, and Travolta, in order to prevent the disaster, takes on Cage's persona, physical as well as psychological, while Cage becomes Travolta. Adding his support to the unusual story, Powell has devised textures that emphasize its various aspects, with heavy emphasis on electronic and live percussion to create a greater sense of urgency. It works terrifically well in the movie, but not, unfortunately, as just film music. Occasionally, when the melodic content in the cues is allowed to develop and be heard, then the soundtrack album becomes lyrical and most effective. Those moments, however, are rare and infrequent.

Didier C. Deutsch

The Faculty

1998, Columbia/Sony Music Soundtrax, from the Miramax film *The Faculty,* 1998 ♫

One could possibly excuse the amateurish rendition of Pink Floyd's "Another Brick in the Wall" if this soundtrack album had other things to offer. But the abominably loud and distorted songs found in this compilation prove for the most part even less engaging, making it a total waste. A few tracks might have redeemed the whole disgraceful project ("School's Out" by Soul Asylum and "Resuscitation" by Sheryl Crow), but forgive me if I don't get excited. The film, incidentally, was about a group of high-school students whose worst suspicions are ultimately confirmed: their teachers are aliens from another planet. They are probably the ones who also produced this CD.

Didier C. Deutsch

Fairy Tale

1997, Atlantic Records, from the Paramount film *Fairy Tale,* 1997

album notes: Music: Zbigniew Preisner; **Conductor:** Jacek Kaspszyk, Zdzislaw Szostak; **Featured Musicians:** Anna Sikorzak-Olek, harp; Janusz Strobel, guitar.

A charming fairy tale (a rarity these days), *Fairy Tale* inspired Zbigniew Preisner to write an equally charming score, in which a sharp call of the high strings suggests a miniature flying fairy who interfaces with the little Alice in Wonderland, the heroine of this "true story." Prominently featuring the harp and guitar to add unusual colorings to his music, Preisner etched a set of cues that are often magically ethereal and diaphanous, as befits the subject matter. It's utterly delightful, subdued, and low key, and all the more convincing as a result. But the kids, for whom this film was obviously meant, won't appreciate or even understand the music. Will their parents?

Didier C. Deutsch

Fake Out

1997, Laserlight Records, from the film *Fake Out,* 1997

album notes: Music: Arthur Rubinstein.

A thriller starring Pia Zadora as a Las Vegas performer involved with a mobster and the cops who want her to "sing" about him, *Fake Out* never really knew if it should be serious or humorous. This is also reflected in Arthur Rubinstein's nondescript synthesizer score, which tries to convey some of the tension in the lightweight drama without making much of an impression. Purely a vanity project for Zadora, not particularly known for her acting talent, it gave her an opportunity to do a couple of songs also included on the CD. If only she could sing. . . .

Didier C. Deutsch

The Falcon and the Snowman

1985, EMI Manhattan, from the film *The Falcon and the Snowman,* Orion Pictures, 1985

album notes: Music: Pat Metheny; Lyle Mays; **Featured Performers:** The Pat Metheny Group.

It is, in a sense, unfortunate that Pat Metheny has not written more frequently for the screen. This fine effort for a real-life Cold War thriller set in the world of computers and drugs, gave him the impetus to create with Lyle Mays a score that is genuinely affecting and exciting. True to their jazz roots, there is plenty of great music, performed by the Pat Metheny Group, in tracks that do not necessarily try to match the screen action, but that constitute the substance for an intelligent, highly enjoyable album. A vocal by David Bowie, "This Is Not America,"

adds an extra dimension, consistent with the tone of the rest of the music.

Didier C. Deutsch

The Fall of the Roman Empire

1989, Varèse Sarabande, from the film *The Fall of the Roman Empire,* PC Films, 1964

1991, Cloud Nine Records, from the film *The Fall of the Roman Empire,* PC Films, 1964

album notes: Music: Dimitri Tiomkin; **Lyrics:** Paul-Francis Webster; **Conductor:** Dimitri Tiomkin.

Dimitri Tiomkin, delving into an area that seemed exclusive to Miklos Rozsa, came up with a sensational epic score for this Samuel Bronston monumental screen extravaganza about the glory that once was Rome. With its spectacular scenes of red-capped legions parading or going to war, its grander-than-life sets, and the majestic sweep of its three-hour story of greed and the abuse of power in ancient Rome, the film needed a score that matched its scope. Tiomkin obliged, writing one of his most memorable efforts. At the time of its release, a somewhat simplified soundtrack album was issued by Columbia Records, consisting of some of the most important cues from the film that had been rearranged for the album. This is the album that was eventually reissued on compact disc by Varèse Sarabande.

The Cloud Nine album, on the other hand, contains the actual film tracks (some unfortunately in mono only) that supplement Tiomkin's rerecording and add to it many cues that had been omitted. Put together, both albums provide a broad picture of the composer's intents, notably revealing that, unlike the scholarly research done for such films as *Quo Vadis* or *Ben-Hur* by Rozsa, who included many reconstructed Roman instruments to give his musical cues the sound of authenticity, Tiomkin was more interested in writing a music that matched the sweep of the screen action, regardless of the period feel (the organ that broadly announces the "Overture," for instance, is a modern creation). Just the same, his score is a splendid effort, one that can sustain repeated playings and provide many hours of listening enjoyment.

Didier C. Deutsch

Falling from Grace

1992, Mercury Records, from the Columbia film *Falling from Grace,* 1992

album notes: Music: Lisa Germano.

A solid family drama, *Falling from Grace* starred John Mellencamp as a country singer who returns home for a spell, only to find himself involved again with an old girlfriend, now married to his brother. The country background provided composer Lisa Germano with an obvious cue for her score, represented here with two selections ("Bud's Theme" and "Little Children"), both of which denote a pleasant use of western strings to create the proper atmosphere. John Mellencamp is also heard on this CD, along with other country luminaries such as Dwight Yoakam and John Prine, as is Janis Ian, in a surprisingly low-key ditty titled "Days like These." It all combines into a most attractive and enjoyable CD, made all the more real with the inclusion of bits of dialogues to set off the musical moments.

Didier C. Deutsch

Falstaff

1993, CAM Records/Italy, from the film *Falstaff (Chimes At Midnight)*, 1966 &&&

album notes: Music: Angelo Francesco Lavagnino; **Conductor:** Pier Luigi Urbini.

Orson Welles draws upon scenes from five of Shakespeare's histories for a character study of the pompous and obese Falstaff (played by Welles), who tragically fails to realize how his Princely friend has no regard for him. Angelo Francesco Lavagnino's score bears many of the Elizabethan flourishes from his other Welles/Shakespeare project, *Othello*, with more of the stately bombast required for Falstaff's historic occasions, as opposed to that Moroccan-tinged tragedy. Lavagnino uses Chinese military music, Roman fanfares, and an epic chorus on "Battaglia e Campo di Morti" to establish the character's grand importance, while Falstaff's more playful side is explored in Elizabethan dances and songs. Lavagnino adds humor, period color, and the necessary grandiosity to this faulty yet masterful film, marred only by a slight hiss in the recording and occasional glitches in the mix, as with the opening flute solo to "Intermezzo Grottesco." This recording may be difficult to find. Check with a used CD store, mail-order company, or a dealer specializing in rare, out-of-print, or import recordings.

David Poole

Fame

1999, DRG Records, from the stage musical *Fame*, 1999 &&&

album notes: Lyrics: Jose Fernandez; **Music:** Steve Margoshes; **Lyrics:** Jacques Levy; **Musical Direction:** Jo Lynn Burks; **Cast:** Gavin Creel, Jose Restrepo, Dwayne Chattman, Natasha Rennalls, Jennifer Gambatese, Carl Tramon, Kim Cea, Regina Le Vert, Dioni Michelle Collins.

First, there was the film; then the television series (see below); and now the Broadway-bound musical. The kids who hope to graduate from the High School of Performing Arts in New York City (an institution that has since been replaced by the High School of Music and Art) have a lot going for them—even if they are unsure about themselves: they are talented, and they know it! And they are dealing with a score that has obviously been crafted with a great amount of care. Steve Margoshes and Jacques Levy (music and lyrics) may not have created another *Chorus Line*, but their songs are engaging, and given the recent popularity of teen-oriented musicals like *Grease* and *Footloose*, their show stands a good chance of having a lucrative existence on Broadway. The high-level energy of some of the numbers will no doubt appeal to younger audiences, while it may leave oldsters deploring the lack of musicals like the ones they used to know eons ago. The generation gap is also felt on Broadway, believe it or not.

As for the story here, spread over four years of hard work and learning at the school, it deals with two students, Nick and Serena, portrayed by Gavin Creel and Jennifer Gambatese, whose relationship is threatened when Serena watches Nick kissing another student, Carmen, played by Natasha Rennalls. But as another playwright once discovered, all's well that ends well, and since this is a musical, the action is sprinkled with a lot of songs, including, in a concession to modern trends, a rap number. Not too terribly original or memorable, but this is not Cole Porter, dude! What it'll do to Broadway once it gets there, no one can tell for sure, but for the time being there are enough good moments in this cast album to make a few converts in the meantime.

Didier C. Deutsch

Fame L.A.

1998, Mercury Records, from the MGM TV series *Fame L.A.*, 1998 &&&

This is not the original television series, shown between 1982 and 1983, that starred Debbie Allen and Janet Jackson, but an L.A. clone starring another bunch of aspiring new actors and actresses with ambitions of striking it big in the entertainment world (the gods of tomorrow are among us). The album gives some of the hopefuls appearing in the series an opportunity to show their wares, and they succeed for the most part in convincing the listeners that they are, indeed, talented and on the brink of being discovered. The star of the show, Heidi Noelle Lenhart, is a singer with a rather breezy voice, who performs four numbers here, but she is outclassed by Molly Rebekka, whose "You Gotta Want It" is a knocker. Other songs that attract include "City of Angels" by Blush, "True Companion" by Brent David Fraser, and "If You've Ever Been in Love" by Az Yet and T. E. Russell, which has inspiring Simon and Garfunkel harmonies to it. They even dragged Irene Cara out of retirement to reprise "Fame," the song she made famous in the film. It all sounds a bit warmed-over, though.

Didier C. Deutsch

The Fan

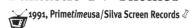1996, TVT Records, from the film *The Fan,* Tristar, 1996

album notes: Music: Hans Zimmer; **Conductor:** Harry Gregson-Williams; **Featured Musicians:** Steve Erdody, cello; Bob Daspit, guitars; Martin Tillman, electric cello.

An unmemorable baseball film starring Robert De Niro and Wesley Snipes, *The Fan* yielded a "soundtrack" album in which undistinguishable selections by Sovory, Mic Geronimo, Honky, and Jeune (some of which actually were not even heard in the film, but are added here in a deceptive ploy to beef up the album) vie for the listener's attention with songs by Terence Trent D'Arby ("Letting Go"), Massive Attack ("Hymn of the Big Wheel"), and a 19- minute-plus instrumental ("Sacrifice"), composed by Hans Zimmer. Not enough to satisfy one's appetite, particularly at today's rates.

Didier C. Deutsch

Fanny

1996, RCA Victor, from the Broadway production *Fanny,* 1954

album notes: Music: Harold Rome; **Lyrics:** Harold Rome; **Musical Direction:** Lehman Engel; **Cast:** Ezio Pinza, Walter Slezak, Florence Henderson, William Tabbert.

Marcel Pagnol's flavorful Mediterranean film trilogy–*Marius, Fanny, Cesar*–became an odd, though interesting musical when Harold Rome presented his take on it with *Fanny,* which opened on November 4, 1954. Collapsing the complex drama from the three films into one production, the show lost some of the insightful details that made the films so uniquely remarkable. It compensated for it, however, with a strongly emotive score, sharply defined characters, and superb performances by Ezio Pinza as Cesar, owner of a cafe in Marseilles; William Tabbert as his only son, Marius, who only dreams of being a sailor; Florence Henderson as Fanny, who loves Marius, and with whom she has a baby; and Tony Award-winner Walter Slezak, as Panisse, a well-to-do local businessman, whom Fanny marries after Marius sails out to sea. The show, the first presented under the aegis of legendary David Merrick, had a run of 888 performances.

Didier C. Deutsch

Fantasia

1990, Disney Records, from the animated feature *Fantasia,* Walt Disney Films, 1940

album notes: Conductor: Leopold Stokowski.

Classical music as the ultimate film score, and for an animated feature no less! But when Leopold Stokowski, ever the pioneer, and Walt Disney teamed to create *Fantasia,* with scenes based on the classical repertoire, this meeting of minds resulted in a breakthrough film that, even today, stands as the most perfect of its kind, even though it met with less than enthusiastic response when it was initially released. The choice of selections, drawing from the compositions most likely to elicit a nod of recognition even from the uninitiated, can hardly be faulted. And even if Stokowski's playing is not to everyone's taste, his flamboyant style comes excitingly through in the most memorable moments from the film, particularly Paul Dukas's *The Sorcerer's Apprentice,* Modeste Mussorgsky's *Night on Bald Mountain,* and everyone's favorite, Amilcare Ponchielli's *Dance of the Hours,* which proved that even hippopotami could make gracile ballerinas. The soundtrack, available here in primitive-sounding stereo, was rerecorded in full digital sound in 1982 with Irwin Kostal conducting the orchestra, but since the new recording attempted to match Stokowski's tempo, it often sounds stilted and unexciting. The original, warts and all, is the one to have.

Didier C. Deutsch

Fantastic TV Themes

1991, Prime*time*usa/Silva Screen Records

album notes: Orchestra: The Royal Philharmonic Orchestra **Conductor:** Daniel Caine.

Obviously, a lot of money went into recording this album, and it shows in the quality of the arrangements, and the often solid performance by the Royal Philharmonic Orchestra. But is the music really worth the effort? Sometimes, the answer has to be yes: Because the themes were written by composers that are among the best in the business (Jerry Goldsmith, Dennis McCarthy, Stu Phillips), and because some of these cannot be found anywhere else. But let's face it, as a rule, TV themes are often trite little things with melodic ideas that are not too terribly substantial and are only interesting when heard within the context of a show, like a recognizable signature one can immediately forget afterward. With some notable exceptions ("Star Trek: The Next Generation," in a performance that sounds thin compared to the original, and not too terribly true to it, either), very little here is of major importance. So, with all due respect, what difference does it make if the selection you hear next is the theme from "V: The Series," "Knight Rider," or "Streethawk"? Ultimately, this is the impression left by this CD which is highly recommended to insomniacs, and otherwise highly forgettable.

Didier C. Deutsch

The Fantastic Voyage

1998, Film Score Monthly Records, from the 20th Century-Fox film *The Fantastic Voyage,* 1966

album notes: Music: Leonard Rosenman; **Conductor:** Leonard Rosenman.

Mickey Mouse in Disney's Fantasia. **(The Kobal Collection)**

There's no way you could call Leonard Rosenman's score "easy listening," or even remotely soothing. That aside, *Fantastic Voyage* remains one of Hollywood's most wildly abstract soundtracks, one so completely divorced from conventional notions of melody and emotional payoffs that it doesn't seem to be part of any known film scoring universe. And that's precisely the goal of Rosenman's brilliantly abstract score, a disorienting sound that captures what it's like for a team of miniaturized explorers to be trapped inside the human body. Rosenman uses instruments in a dissonant, upside-down way, constructing his music out of brassy, high-pitched tonal clusters, which are shrieking more often than not. Subtle themes also manage to cling to these bizarre passages, like tiny bits of melody attached to a dangerous, lumbering collection of atonal music. Rosenman's daring approach accomplishes the movie's goal with tension to spare, a score that conveys a feeling of strange wonder that's always passing you by. But like modern classical music, there's a construction to this insanity. If Igor Stravinsky had written a film score, it might have been *Fantastic Voyage*. Film Score Monthly's label did its usually excellent job packaging this score with remastered sound and insightful liner notes by Jeff Bond.

Dan Schweiger

The Fantasticks

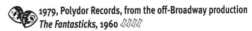 **1979, Polydor Records, from the off-Broadway production**
The Fantasticks, **1960** 🎵🎵🎵🎵

album notes: Music: Harvey Schmidt; **Lyrics:** Tom Jones; **Musical Direction:** Julian Stein; **Cast:** Jerry Orbach, Kenneth Nelson, Rita Gardner, William Larsen, Hugh Thomas.

Close to 40 years and too-many-performances-to-remember later, how do you describe *The Fantasticks,* other than to say it's . . . well, fantastic! A small, off-Broadway musical, loosely based on Edmond Rostand's 1894 play, *Les Romanesques, The Fantasticks* continues to thrive, despite tepid reviews after it opened on May 3, 1960. It has also suffered various disasters, both man-made (newspaper and transportation strikes) and natural (snow blizzards and torrential rainstorms) that all but threatened its precarious run at one time or another. Now comfortably nestled at the 150-seat Sullivan Street Playhouse, in the heart of Greenwich Village, the musical–which launched the careers of Tom Jones and Harvey Schmidt, who wrote it, Jerry Orbach, who first starred in it, and many other thespians–has become a fixture in New York City, an icon that is taken for granted like the Empire State Building or the Statue of Liberty.

At regular intervals, the show's press agent routinely provides the media with the many outstanding figures that speak on behalf of the production: Since its creation, it has known nine presidents (Eisenhower was still at the White House when it first opened), has spawned more than 10,000 productions around the world, and has repaid its investors close to 10,000 percent on their initial cash outlay of $16,500.

A playful variation on the Romeo and Juliet theme of star-crossed lovers who belong to feuding families (though in this case the neighboring fathers are conniving to make believe they are enemies), *The Fantasticks,* lest we forget, introduced one of the musical theater's most evocative songs, "Try to Remember." The song is performed in the show by The Narrator, who also portrays El Gallo, a bandit brought in by the two pater familias to kidnap their Juliet in a well laid out plan so that Romeo will deliver her and fall in love with her.

Didier C. Deutsch

Far and Away

1992, MCA Records, from the film *Far and Away,* Universal Pictures, 1992 🎬🎬🎬

album notes: Music: John Williams; **Conductor:** John Williams; **Featured Musicians:** Paddy Moloney, penny whistle; Jerry O'Sullivan, Uilleann pipes; Tony Hinnigan, pan flutes; Michael Taylor, pan flutes.

For this grand and glorious story of love and life from Ireland to Oklahoma, John Williams has provided a rich, tender, yet often thunderous score drawn from Irish folk styles. The "Main Theme" evokes the plaintive, Irish countryside as much as the boundless Oklahoma plains. It also embodies the proud, resistant spirit of Joseph (Tom Cruise) and of Shannon (Nicole Kidman), as well as eloquently evoking the love the two of them share. It's a grand, sweeping theme that mirrors the intensity of the human spirit depicted in the film. Williams superbly captures both the large scope of the picture as well as the characters' innermost feelings and brings them both to life with this excellent score.

Randall D. Larson

A Far Off Place

1993, Intrada Records, from the film *A Far Off Place,* Walt Disney/Amblin Entertainment, 1993 🎬🎬🎬🎬

album notes: Music: James Horner.

A Walt Disney family adventure set in Africa, about two orphaned teens and their Bushman guide making their way back to civiliza

10 Essential Scores

by Mark Isham

The Moderns
Cool World
A River Runs through It
Romeo Is Bleeding
Mrs. Parker & the Vicious Circle
Afterglow
The Education of Little Tree
October Sky
The Browning Version
The Net

tion, *A Far Off Place* received a broad, symphonic score from James Horner, evidently inspired by the subject matter. The cues overflow with colorful, dynamic accents, sometimes subtly underscored by a variety of exotic-sounding percussive instruments, sometimes framing the contribution of a lonely reed. The lengthy playing time of some of the cues enables them to make more than a passing impression, in effect forcing the listener to become involved and enjoy the music for its own sake. There is a lot to like in this score, which incidentally eschews the facile ethnic effects in favor of a more complex but ultimately more rewarding orchestral approach, with selections like "The Elephants," "Sandstorm," or "Death in the Mine" inviting repeated playing.

Didier C. Deutsch

Faraway, So Close

1994, SBK Records, from the film *Faraway, So Close,* Sony Pictures Classics, 1994 🎬🎬🎬🎬🎬

album notes: Music: Laurent Pettigrand; **Conductor:** Sherry Bertram; **Featured Musicians:** David Darling, cello; Irene Maas, soprano.

Wim Wenders is a filmmaker who uses music to both amplify and to inspire his visuals. This time he weaves Celtic and mostly moody selections into the mix, leaning on artists such as U2, Nick Cave, Simon Bonney, and Laurie Anderson, each of whom contribute two selections. U2's pair—"Stay (Faraway, So Close)" and "The Wanderer" with Johnny Cash—also appear on the group's own *Zooropa* album, but sound fine in this context. First-rate contributions from Lou Reed and House of Love are valuable additions to an exceptional effort.

Gary Graff

A Farewell to Arms /Sons and Lovers

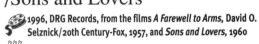 1996, DRG Records, from the films *A Farewell to Arms,* David O. Selznick/20th Century-Fox, 1957, and *Sons and Lovers,* 1960 ♫♫♫

album notes: Music: Mario Nascimbene; **Conductor:** Franco Ferrara, Mario Nascimbene.

If you can live with the degraded sonics in this recording with flutters, distortions, and a harsh, grating sound apparent on most of the tracks, there is a lot to be enjoyed in these two scores from the fertile pen of Italian master Mario Nascimbene. For David O. Selznick's brilliant treatment of the Hemingway novel, starring Rock Hudson and Jennifer Jones as the star-crossed lovers caught on the Italian war front in the last brutal days of World War I, Nascimbene wrote a score that mixes both aspects of the drama—the war effort and the lovers' passion—in cues that teem with romantic themes and heroic echoes. The lovely tune, a waltz, that marks the lovers' first encounter and follows them through their idyll and unhappy ending, has justifiably become a favorite theme among fans of film music, and is heard here in several variations. *Sons and Lovers,* a drama set in the bleak north countryside of England, elicited from Nascimbene a score that contrasts the grim aspects of the story and the environment with cues that sometimes affect a jaunty lilt. Sound quality here is also a problem, with heavy hiss on the tracks, some distortion, and an occasional dropout.

Didier C. Deutsch

Fargo/Barton Fink

1996, TVT Records, from the films *Fargo,* Gramercy Pictures, 1996, and *Barton Fink,* 20th Century-Fox, 1991 ♫♫♫♫

album notes: Music: Carter Burwell; **Featured Musicians:** Paul Peabody, violin; Carter Burwell, piano; **Conductor:** Carter Burwell, Sonny Kompanek, Larry Wilcox.

The nostalgic accents of a fiddle permeate the soundtrack to *Fargo,* a rural crime drama in which a car salesman, over his head in debts, hires two inept ex-cons to kidnap his wife, hoping to extract the ran-

som money from his father-in-law. However, the well-laid plan unravels hopelessly after one of the cons kills a state trooper who had stopped the pair on a minor infraction. While most of the cues Burwell wrote for the film capture the drama-in-the-making, the moods struck are very sullen and grave, and fail to actually communicate the dark humor in the story itself, which made the film so disarmingly funny despite the seriousness of the storyline. *Barton Fink,* also produced by Joel and Ethan Coen, makers of *Fargo,* elicited a score that seems more in keeping with the light, eccentric moods in this story of a Broadway playwright whose success takes him to Hollywood, despite his hatred for the film medium. Soon, however, Fink (played in tortured fashion by John Turturro) has become implicated in a series of murders, and that's only the beginning. . . . The few cues assembled here give an excellent impression of Burwell's surrealist music for the film, with the composer adding his pianistic touch to the proceedings. Enjoyable through and through.

Didier C. Deutsch

Fast, Cheap and Out of Control

1997, Accurate Records, from the Sony Pictures Classics film *Fast, Cheap and Out of Control,* 1997 ♫♫♫♫

album notes: Music: Caleb Sampson.

The four characters who look up from the album's cover (one is smoking a cigar and another is wearing a yellow-red bow tie!) don't give a measure of what the film, a "documentary" by iconoclast extraordinaire Errol Morris, or even the soundtrack by Caleb Sampson, is all about. At times food for thought, at other times totally "fast, cheap and out of control," the film is a series of interviews with ordinary people, which doesn't say anything conclusive about the condition of man and his pursuit of happiness. They're all strange, though, in a humorous way, and the filmmaker stresses gleefully everything that singles out these individuals, in their behavior and in their own minds.

Caleb Simpson, a colleague of Philip Glass, puts all these things into his own perspective, with cues that evoke the pope of minimalism, but have a humorous vision of their own. It's all very entertaining, slightly tongue in cheek, and quite enjoyable.

Didier C. Deutsch

Fast Track to Nowhere

1994, A&M Records, from the Showtime TV series *Rebel Highway,* 1994 ♫♫♫♫

This song-driven soundtrack album to the television series, shown on Showtime, is a solid compilation of hard-edged tracks, performed by a talented group of rockers: Iggy Pop, Los Lobos, the Neville Brothers, Sheryl Crow, Charlie Sexton, the Smithereens—not the kind of line-up you get for a minor thing.

The songs are of a general high caliber, too, which doesn't hurt. Among the many highlights, "Endless Sleep" by Concrete Blonde, "Let the Good Times Roll" by the Neville Brothers, "Evil" by Wild Colonials, and "The Stroll" by the Smithereens stand out; the only one that doesn't really come across here is "Race with the Devil," which is horribly distorted. Otherwise, a rockin' collection!

Didier C. Deutsch

Fatal Attraction

1987, GNP Crescendo Records, from the film *Fatal Attraction*, Paramount Pictures, 1987 ♪

album notes: Music: Maurice Jarre.

Electronic score by Maurice Jarre starts off well enough with its pleasant main theme, but it quickly degrades by track two into a collection of uninteresting effects and several tumults of noise. Much of the electronic instrumentation sounds dated just over 10 years later, making it hard to believe it's not a score for a direct-to-video independent film instead of one of Paramount Pictures' biggest box office hits. Poorly packaged CD uses art from initial LP release and lists only six tracks on the back cover while the player counts off 14!

David Hirsch

Father of the Bride

1991, Varèse Sarabande, from the film *Father of the Bride*, Touchstone Pictures, 1991 ♪♪♪

album notes: Music: Alan Silvestri; Conductor: Alan Silvestri.

Alan Silvestri's sugar-coated score for this 1991 Steve Martin remake of the classic Spencer Tracy film is good fun, thanks to a memorable main theme and a brief collection of tracks that range from introspective and touching to downright jazzy and off the wall. Varèse's album also contains Pachelbel's "Canon" and a cover of "The Way You Look Tonight" by Steve Tyrell, which is also interpolated quite nicely with Silvestri's score as the music comes to a close. Many of the tracks are short and the thematic development of the musical material is, subsequently, fairly limited, but this is a pleasant album as far as it goes, and if you've seen and enjoyed the movie, you'll probably want the soundtrack as well.

Andy Dursin

Father of the Bride, Part II

1995, Hollywood Records, from the film *Father of the Bride, Part II*, Touchstone Pictures, 1995 ♪♪♪♪

album notes: Music: Alan Silvestri.

As uncomplicated as the first score, yet equally melodic and occasionally jazzy, *Father of the Bride, Part II* does not break any new

grounds, but is enjoyable in its own right. Steve Tyrell is back on board for another round of classic standards ("Give Me the Simple Life," "The Way You Look Tonight," "On the Sunny Side of the Street"), with Etta James and Fats Domino also on hand for a couple of tunes, including the always rousing "When the Saints Go Marching In." If any real criticism can be leveled against it, it would have to be about the short playing time of some of the cues (47 seconds for "Annie Returns," not long enough for any theme to make any kind of impression), but the overall balance tips toward the positive. So, play it and have a good time.

Didier C. Deutsch

Fear and Loathing in Las Vegas

1998, Geffen Records, from the Universal film *Fear and Loathing in Las Vegas*, 1998 ♪♪

album notes: Music: Tomoyasu Hotei, Ray Cooper.

If this soundtrack album doesn't give you hallucinogenic dreams, nothing musical will. Where else would you find together on a same CD Big Brother and the Holding Company, Bob Dylan, Perry Como, Debbie Reynolds, Jefferson Airplane, Booker T. & the MGs, and Tom Jones, to name only a few? Laced with the musical meanderings of Tomoyasu Hotei and Ray Cooper, this makes for a very odd soundtrack, probably appropriately reflective of the weird film adaptation of Hunter S. Thompson's 1971 novel by Terry Gilliam. With Johnny Depp playing Raoul Duke, a drugged out L.A. sportswriter on his way to Vegas in the company of his lawyer, the aptly named Dr. Gonzo, the film often feels like a psychedelic nightmare. The tracks in the album are "introduced" by bits of dialogue that relate to the linear non-action in the film, but since most of these selections are available elsewhere, you might simply want to skip what Duke and Dr. Gonzo have to say. Certainly the pop songs and hard-rock anthems don't cohabit very well here.

Didier C. Deutsch

Fear Is the Key

1998, Cinephile/U.K., from the MGM film *Fear Is the Key*, 1972 ♪♪♪♪

album notes: Music: Roy Budd; Conductor: Roy Budd.

Roy Budd's heavily echoed score for *Fear Is the Key*, a 1973 actioner based on Alistair MacLean's novel, speaks volumes about the composer's talent, and the film itself. Set in Louisiana, the story involved an agent going undercover to capture the people responsible for the death of his wife and children, in a heist involving a cargo of priceless gems. The centerpiece of the film (and this CD) is a lengthy car chase that took 10 minutes on the screen and received a spectacular musical treatment from Budd, mixing sound effects with his own or chestral riffs, the better to suggest the intensity in the action. The remainder of the cues is a collection of contemporary themes, several set to a jazz beat.

see also: The Black Windmill, Diamonds, Get Carter, Paper Tiger, Sinbad and the Eye of the Tiger

Didier C. Deutsch

Fearless

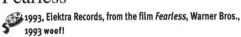1993, Elektra Records, from the film *Fearless,* Warner Bros., 1993 woof!

album notes: Music: Maurice Jarre; **Featured Musicians:** Kronos Quartet; Dumisani Maraire, ngoma, hosho; Dawn Upshaw, soprano.

Multiple Oscar-winning film composer Maurice Jarre is credited with writing the score for this film starring Jeff Bridges. You wouldn't know it from listening to this "soundtrack album," which features two of his cues for a total playing time of four minutes, in addition to long selections from other recordings of modern classical music already available elsewhere on the Elektra label. Unfortunately, this is as misleading as can be, with fans of Jarre and of film music the losers in this dishonest, mindless exploitation.

Didier C. Deutsch

Feast of July

1995, Angel Records, from the film *Feast of July,* Touchstone Pictures, 1995 🎬🎬🎬🎬

album notes: Music: Zbigniew Preisner; **Conductor:** Zdzislaw Szostak.

Characteristic of the Merchant Ivory productions, this slick late 19th-century period drama about a young woman, seduced and abandoned by a married man, and rescued in her hour of need by a kindly couple and their three sons, elicited a flavorful, very restrained score by Zbigniew Preisner, dominated by solo passages for a variety of instruments like the harp, guitar, flute, and piano. While the cues are presented in a haphazard order and do not entirely follow the progression of the screen action, they have also been assembled in four distinctive parts, each part representing a season, a satisfying device that strengthens the overall musical picture and gives it a sharper focus. There are many lovely moments in the score, further enhanced by the addition of three short, folk-themed "Harvest Dances," composed by Rachel Portman. A rich, satisfying score.

Didier C. Deutsch

Fedora

1989, Varèse Sarabande Records, from the film *Fedora,* United Artists, 1979 🎬🎬🎬

album notes: Music: Miklos Rozsa; **Orchestra:** The Graunke Symphony Orchestra; **Conductor:** Miklos Rozsa.

This limited edition CD offers the last score composed by Miklos Rozsa, for a film by Billy Wilder starring William Holden, Marthe Keller, and Henry Fonda, in which the basic themes are the evanescence of youth, the destructive power of beauty, and the romance of a bygone era—the golden days of Hollywood. These moods suggested to the composer a score in which his own romantic leanings and sensitive writing share the scene in a kaleidoscopic display. This is a rare and beautiful example of the composer's creativity, further enhanced with the addition of his guitar suite for *Crisis.*

Didier C. Deutsch

Feds

1988, GNP Crescendo Records, from the film *Feds,* Warner Bros., 1988 🎬🎬🎬

album notes: Music: Randy Edelman.

Randy Edelman, in one of his early efforts, made a good impression with this colorfully inventive score for a low-key comedy about female agents of the FBI, and the havoc they create when they take over a case. The themes, many in an attractive contemporary mold, make little demands on the intellect but are listenable and quite enjoyable in their own right. Some vocal selections alter the focus of the recording at various points, and prove less addictive than the instrumental score.

Didier C. Deutsch

Felicity

1999, Hollywood Records, from the television series *Felicity,* 1998-99 🎬🎬🎬

A bright newcomer on the television landscape, *Felicity,* the story of a young student who goes to New York to follow her dream (the boy on whom she's had a crush for the past four years), and instead finds a situation she had not anticipated, spawned this attractive song album, consisting of performances by veterans Peter Gabriel, Kate Bush, and Aretha Franklin, and rising stars Joe Henry, Heather Nova, Joan Jones, Remy Zero, Morley, Scout, Ivy, and Neil Finn. The soft-rock numbers are unusually evocative and attractive, with "Heart and Shoulder" and "Everyday Down," among those that make an immediate impact. Franklin's tortured rendition of "Bridge over Troubled Water" sounds a bit too dramatic at times for its own good, but Sarah McLachlan's "Good Enough" and Peter Gabriel's "Here Comes the Flood" easily stand out. A pleasant if not exceptional soundtrack album.

Didier C. Deutsch

Fellini's Casanova

See: Il Casanova

Ferngully . . . The Last Rain Forest

1992, MCA Records, from the animated feature *Ferngully . . . The Last Rain Forest*, 20th Century-Fox, 1992 ♪♪♪♪
album notes: Music: Alan Silvestri.

1992, MCA Records, from the animated feature *Ferngully . . . The Last Rain Forest*, 20th Century-Fox, 1992 ♪♪♪♪
album notes: Songs: Thomas Dolby; Jimmy Buffett; Michael Utley; Jimmy Webb; Alan Silvestri; Chris Kenner; Raffi; Bruce Roberts; Elton John.

Characteristic of some recent soundtracks, *Ferngully . . . The Last Rain Forest* (an animated feature with a message—the protection of the rain forests) elicited two different releases, one for the score by Alan Silvestri, the other compiling some of the pop songs heard during the course of the action, sometimes in much abbreviated form. The good news here is that the song album is a first-class compilation, bringing together several frontline performers for some decidedly enjoyable results, including Robin Williams, who does a hilarious "Batty Rap," Johnny Clegg, Tone-Loc, Sheena Easton, and Elton John, particularly effective in the inspirational "Some Other World."

The score album, featuring the music of Alan Silvestri over the varied sounds of a rain forest (birds chirping, a rainfall, thunderstorm), is appropriately atmospheric, with many dynamic elements ("Skylarking," "Crysta's Journey," "The Grotto Song") that enliven it and provide the musical enjoyment. With its careful dosage of big orchestral riffs and effective synthesized sounds, it stands out as a very attractive effort.

Didier C. Deutsch

A Few Good Men

1992, Columbia Records, from the film *A Few Good Men*, Columbia Pictures, 1992 ♪♪♪♡
album notes: Music: Marc Shaiman; **Conductor:** Artie Kane.

A striking murder trial set in a military compound, *A Few Good Men* was a provocative film starring Tom Cruise and Demi Moore charged with the prosecution of two marines accused of killing a cadet, only to discover that a high-ranking officer, played by Jack Nicholson, might have been actually responsible. Contrasting the potent elements in this courtroom drama, Marc Shaiman created a score that is surprisingly melodic and low-key. While some ominous undertones announce the trial itself, and the potential dangers in probing too deeply into the killing, the lovely floating chords used by Shaiman seem to contradict, yet reinforce the moods in the film itself. A performance of "Hound Dog" by Big Mama Thornton, while a part of the soundtrack, seems totally unnecessary to the dramatic development of the score itself.

Didier C. Deutsch

Fiddler on the Roof

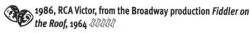

1986, RCA Victor, from the Broadway production *Fiddler on the Roof*, 1964 ♪♪♪♪♪
album notes: Music: Jerry Bock; **Lyrics:** Sheldon Harnick; **Musical Direction:** Milton Greene; **Cast** Zero Mostel, Julia Migenes, Tanya Everett, Joanna Merlin, Maria Karnilova, Austin Pendleton.

1986, Columbia Records, from the London production *Fiddler on the Roof*, 1967 ♪♪♪♪
album notes: Music: Jerry Bock; **Lyrics:** Sheldon Harnick; **Musical Direction:** Gareth Davies, **Cast.** Topol, Linda Gardner, Rosemary Nichols, Caryl Little, Jonathan Lynn.

1971, EMI America, from the film *Fiddler on the Roof*, United Artists, 1971 ♪♪♪
album notes: Music: Jerry Bock; **Lyrics:** Sheldon Harnick; **Musical Direction:** John Williams; **Featured Musician:** Isaac Stern, violin; **Cast:** Topol, Michele Marsh, Neva Small, Rosalind Harris, Norma Crane, Leonard Frey, Paul Mann, Michael Glaser.

Sholom Aleichem's *Tevye and His Daughters* became the basis for one of Broadway's brightest productions of the 1960s, *Fiddler on the Roof*, which opened on Sept. 22, 1964. For a while, it held the record as the longest-running musical with 3,242 performances. A poor milkman in the Russian village of Anatevka, Tevye has five daughters whom he plans to marry off to some of his well-to-do neighbors like the next-door butcher. The girls, however, have different views, and with the tacit support of their mother, the eldest marries a poor tailor, the second sets off for Siberia with a revolutionary student, and the third finds someone who is not even Jewish. By the time the Russian Cossacks come in to destroy the village, forcing the people of Anatevka to move out, Tevye philosophically hangs on to what is left of his family as he prepares to emigrate to America.

In turns profoundly moving and exuberant, *Fiddler on the Roof* owed much of its initial success to Zero Mostel's portrayal as Tevye, one of the legendary characterizations the theatre is often fond of evoking. And indeed, in this all-too-human but grander-than-life role, Mostel was certainly unique. Even though many others essayed the part subsequently, including the Israeli star Topol, who played the role in the London production, the movie version, and in a celebrated Broadway revival, theater-goers who were fortunate enough to see Zero Mostel in the original production still recall his star turn in this show. For those who were not as fortunate, the original cast album on RCA Victor gives a dimension of his portrayal, and still stands out as the best recording available. Topol can be heard in both the London cast recording on Columbia, and the film soundtrack on EMI. The former is an acceptable facsimile that lacks some of the imaginative fire in the original cast recording, and contains at least one less selection ("The Rumor"). The film soundtrack, bigger, glossier, schmaltzier, loses some of the restrained simplicity in the original, and

Fiddler on the Roof **(The Kobal Collection)**

trades it off for the presence of Isaac Stern as the fiddler of the title, lush orchestrations by John Williams (who won an Oscar), and a generally tepid performance by Topol, Molly Picon, Leonard Frey, and the other principals.

Didier C. Deutsch

The Field

🎞 **1991, Varèse Sarabande, from the film *The Field,* Avenue Pictures, 1991** 𝄞𝄞𝄞

album notes: Music: Elmer Bernstein; **Orchestra:** The Irish Film Orchestra; **Conductor:** Elmer Bernstein; **Featured Musician:** Liam O'Flynn, Uilleann pipes.

A film that took as its background the difficult existence of poor Irish farmers in the 1920s and 1930s, *The Field* presented an artistic challenge to composer Elmer Bernstein about what he calls in his notes to this album "the necessity of making a decision about the degree to which the 'language' of the music should contain ethnic elements." To this end, he judiciously chose to use the evocative Uilleann pipes to convey the moods and feelings characteristic to the film's setting, and added to

them subtle electronic effects and the specific sound of the Ondes Martenot, on which he has been increasingly relying in recent years, to delineate the brooding drama about an Irish farmer who obstinately attempts to keep a sterile piece of land from the American developer who wants to buy it. The end result is a generally brooding score occasionally marked by some lovely melodies ("To the Field") and haunting effects ("Auction"), a deft blend that ultimately proves most endearing.

Didier C. Deutsch

Field of Dreams

🎞 **1989, RCA/Novus Records, from the film *Field of Dreams,* Universal Pictures, 1989** 𝄞𝄞𝄞

album notes: Music: James Horner; **Conductor:** James Horner; **Featured Musicians:** Tommy Tedesco; Ian Underwood; Ralph Grierson; Tim May; Steve Schaeffer; Neil Stubenhaus; Jim Thatcher; Mike Taylor; Tony Hennigan.

One of James Horner's most poignant, lyrical and haunting compositions to date, *Field of Dreams* is one of those soundtracks that you'll find in even the libraries of the most casual "pop music" collector. Everybody who hears it just seems to like it. In this score, Horner works his magic through the mystical tones of the film's nostalgic piano beginning and big band section (arranged by Billy May, who worked with Horner a number of times during this period), never overplaying his hand before the film's climax, which culminates in a fugue for the brass section and orchestra that signals the cyclical nature of the film's theme of father and son, of one family generation crossing over into the next. It's a lovely section of music that is alluded to only briefly in the music before, and also one of Horner's best—its usage in numerous televised sports programs and news features since then is clearly a testament to the score's continued popularity with listeners of all musical persuasions.

Andy Dursin

Fierce Creatures

1997, Varèse Sarabande, from the film *Fierce Creatures*, Universal Pictures, 1997 ♪♪♪♪

album notes: Music: Jerry Goldsmith; **Conductor:** Jerry Goldsmith.

For this low-key comedy effort (a sequel to the much more effective and enjoyable *A Fish Called Wanda*), Goldsmith wrote one of his better comedy scores, a blend of amiable, low-key jazz elements and some surprisingly affecting romanticism that thankfully avoids over-emphasizing the comic aspects of the story. There's a bouncy, light quality to many of the cues that's quite infectious, and some surprisingly lyrical moments as Goldsmith underscores some outlandish animal acts. It all adds up to a score that, while not one of Goldsmith's more memorable efforts, still makes for a very enjoyable listening experience on its own.

Jeff Bond

The Fifth Element

1998, Virgin Records, from the Gaumont film *The Fifth Element*, 1998 ♪♪♪♪

album notes: Music: Eric Serra; **Conductor:** Eric Serra.

Like many film composers schooled in Euro-rock, Eric Serra brings a hip-hop sensibility to his scores, a wash of samples, synths, and jazz grooves that distinguishes his scores to such Luc Besson films as *La Femme Nikita, The Big Blue,* and *The Professional*. While this approach proved disastrous for his 007 effort *Goldeneye,* Serra's style was back on track for Besson's *The Fifth Element,* an enjoyable comic riff on *Blade Runner* and *Die Hard*. Serra's electro-funk score might be completely atypical for the genre, but then, so's this film. His music does a good job of capturing an often confused plot, which fuses an ancient mystery with a future where every kind of culture and technology are

mashed together. Serra's kitchen sink approach plays everything from opera to rap, romantic jazz to ghostly synth pads—usually all at once. His music for *The Fifth Element* is terrifically inventive, a science fiction score that you actually can dance to.

Dan Schweiger

55 Days at Peking

1989, Varèse Sarabande, from the film *55 Days at Peking,* Bronston, 1963 ♪♪♪♪♪

album notes: Music: Dimitri Tiomkin; **Orchestra:** The Sinfonia of London; **Conductor:** Dimitri Tiomkin.

A spectacular epic adventure, recounting the 1900 Boxer Rebellion against the major powers established in China at the time (England, France, Germany, and the United States among them), accused of crass commercialism and of exploiting the Chinese, *55 Days at Peking* elicited a vibrant score from Dimitri Tiomkin in which heroic accents and romantic themes vie to draw the listener into their attractive musical web. In typical Tiomkin fashion, the cues that are strongly evocative of the screen action ("Explosion of the Arsenal," "Attack on the French Legation") come off best, with layers upon layers of orchestral riffs building up to a climax. However, the tension in those tracks is pleasantly relieved by some exquisite romantic cues ("Natasha's Waltzes," "Children's Corner") that are equally evocative. Andy Williams's perfunctory rendition of "The Peking Theme" is a dispensable filler. The recording, incidentally, is extremely noisy—a problem that exists on the original tapes, and not exclusively on this CD.

Didier C. Deutsch

54

1998, Tommy Boy, from the Miramax film *54,* 1998 ♪♪♪♪

A disco fan's delight, two CDs were released in conjunction with the release of the film, a loose story about the rise and fall of the famed New York dance club in the 1970s. Both sets contain an orgy of tracks that made the era memorable, with performances by such luminaries as Diana Ross ("The Boss"), Chic ("Dance Dance Dance"), Candi Staton ("Young Hearts Run Free"), Odyssey ("Native New Yorker"), Bonnie Pointer ("Heaven Must Have Sent You"), GQ ("Disco Nights"), Santa Esmeralda ("Please Don't Let Me Be Misunderstood"), Grace Jones ("I Need a Man"), and Blondie ("Heart of Glass").

As is often the case in compilations such as this, there are some glaring omissions (Donna Summer and Paul Jabara, for instance), and odd choices ("Love Hangover" was perhaps more influential than "The Boss"), but both albums play well together and have no problem evoking a pre-AIDS era when everything seemed too simple and enjoyable, as long as the beat was right.

Didier C. Deutsch

Final Analysis

1992, Varèse Sarabande Records, from the film *Final Analysis,* Warner Bros., 1992 ♫♫♫♫
album notes: Music: George Fenton; **Conductor:** George Fenton.

A surprisingly effective old-fashioned thriller, *Final Analysis* brought together Richard Gere, as a San Francisco psychiatrist, and Kim Basinger, as the married sister of one of his patients with whom he has an affair, and who eventually disposes of her husband in order to marry him. The film, which at times evokes such classic thrillers as *The Maltese Falcon* and *Vertigo,* not surprisingly inspired George Fenton to write a vivid score neither Miklos Rozsa nor Bernard Herrmann would have disavowed. Boldly affirmative and muscular for the most part, it follows the narrative with pungent cues that set the tone for much of the screen action, underscoring it or subtly reinforcing it when the need arises. Among its many convincing moments, "The Rain's Stopped," "The Tea Room," "The Bay Marina," and the chilling "The Murder," particularly stand out.

Didier C. Deutsch

The Final Conflict

1990, Varèse Sarabande, from the film *The Final Conflict*, 20th Century-Fox, 1981 ♫♫♫♫♪
album notes: Music: Jerry Goldsmith; **Orchestra:** The National Philharmonic Orchestra, **Conductor:** Lionel Newman.

Jerry Goldsmith wrapped up his *Omen* trilogy with this spectacular work, his equivalent of a biblical epic. Although it continues the Latin chants and evocative choral effects of the first two Omen scores, *The Final Conflict* develops entirely new melodic material, from an imposing horn theme for the adult Damien Thorn (based on a motif from Prokofiev's *Alexander Nevsky*) to a beautiful pastoral melody for the forces of good as they gather to battle Damien's hordes for the fate of mankind. If only the movie had been as spectacular and gripping as the score. The sheer scale of this work easily ranks it as one of the landmarks in Goldsmith's career. Check out the climactic cue, which underscores nothing less than the second coming of Christ! There are also amazingly powerful cues written for a fox hunt and a mystical conjunction of stars. It's the ultimate soundtrack guilty pleasure, a score that evokes the final conflict between good and evil far more convincingly than the film for which it was written.

see also: The Omen, Damien: Omen II

Jeff Bond

The Final Countdown

1980, Casablanca Records/Germany, from the United Artists film *The Final Countdown*, 1980 ♫♫♫
album notes: Music: John Scott; **Conductor:** John Scott.

A terrific sci-fi concept: a nuclear carrier, caught in an electric storm of massive proportions, suddenly finds itself going through a time warp and landing 40 years earlier, with an opportunity to prevent the bombing of Pearl Harbor. With his usual savvy, John Scott delivered a score that takes full advantage of the unusual narrative, enhancing the various moods in the film (an unbelieving 1940s senator demands an explanation from the modern-day U.S. Navy admiral commanding the carrier, who is unable to give him any without seeming to be an idiot in the first place), and stressing the dramatic aspects with lots of gusto, notably in the two storm sequences and in the attack on Pearl Harbor. This album was only released in Germany, but is worth looking for at the usual specialized stores.

Didier C. Deutsch

Finian's Rainbow

1986, Columbia Records, from the Broadway production *Finian's Rainbow,* 1947 ♫♫♫♫
album notes: Music: Burton Lane; **Lyrics:** E.Y. Harburg; **Musical Direction:** Max Meth; **Cast:** Ella Logan, David Wayne, Donald Richards.

1988, RCA Victor, from the Broadway revival *Finian's Rainbow,* 1960 ♫♫♫♪
album notes: Music: Burton Lane; **Lyrics:** E.Y. Harburg; **Musical Direction:** Max Meth; **Cast:** Jeannie Carson, Howard Morris, Biff McGuire, Carol Brice.

A whimsical blend of fantasy and social commentary, *Finian's Rainbow,* which opened on Broadway on Jan. 10, 1947, was the brainchild of playwright-lyricist E.Y. Harburg. Harburg combined together two stories he had tried to develop unsuccessfully, one about a stuffy Southern senator who becomes a black man overnight, the other about a leprechaun whose crock of gold has been stolen and who chases the robber to America. The resulting musical, with a score by Burton Lane, dealt with Finian McLonergan, an Irishman newly arrived with his daughter, Sharon, from his native Ireland, who wants to bury the crock of gold he has stolen near Fort Knox, where it will fructify, unaware of the fact that it has the power to grant three wishes. When they settle in Rainbow Valley, in Missitucky, the place becomes prosperous, attracting the attention of Sen. Billboard Rawkins who wants to expropriate the valley's current denizens, including Finian and several black families. When Sharon inadvertently expresses the wish that Sen. Rawkins should become a black man, things take a turn to the worse, though everything gets straightened out by the last curtain. Following its opening on Broadway, *Finian's Rainbow* had a run of 725 performances. It was successfully revived several times, notably in 1960, and was given a lavish film treatment, directed by Francis Ford Coppola, in 1968, with Fred Astaire cast as Finian (his last dancing role on screen), Petula Clark as Sharon, and Tommy Steele as Og.

The score, with many familiar tunes, yielded the wistful show-stopping "How Are Things In Glocca Morra?" a jazz favorite, "Old Devil Moon;" and the Leprechaun's amusingly distorted reflexion, "When I'm Not Near the Girl I Love," among its better moments. The original cast album, on Columbia, the first for the label, sounds a trifle dated by today's digital standards, but boasts terrific performances by Ella Logan as Sharon, and David Wayne as Og, the Leprechaun.

The 1960 Broadway revival cast, on RCA, has the advantage of being in stereo, with several reprises not found on the Columbia album, but performances are less inspired overall, and lack the immediacy in the original. The soundtrack album, available on a Warner Bros. LP, was never reissued on compact disc.

Didier C. Deutsch

Fiorello!

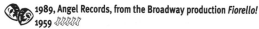 **1989, Angel Records, from the Broadway production** *Fiorello!* **1959** 🎬🎬🎬🎬

album notes: Music: Jerry Bock; **Lyrics:** Sheldon Harnick; **Musical Direction:** Hal Hastings; **Cast:** Tom Bosley, Bob Holiday, Nathaniel Frey, Patricia Wilson, Howard Da Silva, Pat Stanley, Eileen Rodgers.

This Pulitzer Prize-winning musical was the first Broadway hit for composer Jerry Bock and lyricist Sheldon Harnick–who went on to write *Fiddler on the Roof*–and its New York wiseguy blend of history, humor, and wonderful music make it a classic of the genre. The title character, New York City's crusading mayor in the 1930s and '40s, is ably played by Tom Bosley. However, the best songs go to the supporting cast, especially Howard Da Silva as a less-than-idealistic political boss, and Patricia Wilson as the mayor's long-suffering secretary. Up against *The Sound of Music*, the show won or tied for six Tony Awards.

Marc Kirkeby

Fire Down Below

🎬 **1997, Warner Bros. Records, from the Warner Bros. film** *Fire Down Below,* **1997** 🎬🎬🎬🎬

Steven Seagal reveals a previously untapped side of his talent in this soundtrack album, which he exec produced, for which he wrote some songs, and in which he is heard sharing the spotlight with seasoned performers such as Randy Scruggs and Taj Mahal. Will wonders never cease! The film, a standard actioner set in the hills of Kentucky, featured Seagal as an envi-

ronmental protection agent who fights polluters single-handedly . . . and wins, of course, after throwing in some nifty high kicks, his stock in trade. What made the film most enjoyable, in spite of Seagal's mono-expressive screen persona and lack of acting abilities, were the many stunts that sprinkled the action and the bouncy country and western songs on the soundtrack that provided much-needed local color. The songs have been compiled here, and provide a listening program that doesn't have a weak moment.

"Desert Breeze" and "Dark Angel," the two tracks in which Seagal is featured, give him an opportunity to play the guitar, although his contribution is somewhat buried behind those of his cohorts, perhaps as it should be to spare us some embarrassment. Otherwise, this album is great!

Didier C. Deutsch

Firestarter

🎬 **1984, Varèse Sarabande, from the film** *Firestarter,* **Universal Pictures, 1984** 🎬🎬🎬🎬

album notes: Music: Tangerine Dream.

Typical of Tangerine Dream, the score for *Firestarter,* a film about a little girl with pyrokinetic powers, is an amalgam of attractively designed synth figures, laid over a rhythm track, that are fairly evocative. Unlike some of their most adventurous works, however, their music here is accessible, with melodic themes that develop along conventional lines, adding layers upon layers of ideas that prove enjoyable in a purely musical context.

Didier C. Deutsch

The Firm

🎬 **1993, GRP Records, from the film** *The Firm,* **Paramount Pictures, 1993** 🎬🎬🎬🎬

album notes: Music: Dave Grusin; **Conductor:** Dave Grusin.

Dave Grusin wrote one of his most unusual scores for this contemporary drama starring Tom Cruise, with Jimmy Buffett, Lyle Lovett, and Dave Samuels among the performers who also contributed their talent to the soundtrack. While he expresses himself in the jazz style that has been his mainstay for many years, Grusin does so here in unadorned piano solos that are particularly affecting and create a definitely unique atmosphere.

Didier C. Deutsch

First Blood

🎬 **1990, Intrada, from the film** *First Blood,* **Carolco Pictures, 1988** 🎬🎬🎬🎬

album notes: Music: Jerry Goldsmith; **Conductor:** Jerry Goldsmith.

Birthplace of all the main themes for Jerry Goldsmith's mainstream megahit was *Rambo: First Blood Part II,* but with a more human element present than the bombastic superhero-style score of the sequel. There's also a distinct sense of sadness in *First Blood,* personified by the principal theme song, "It's a Long Road." The lyrics are an analogy for the difficulties Vietnam veterans faced while they tried to reassimilate back into society after the war. Although Rambo seeks peace, he is a trained fighter who can explode when pushed too far. Goldsmith's music, likewise, can launch from a pleasant refrain into a flurry of brass. His trademark use of electronic textures serves him well as a means of heightening the tension. The album also includes Dan Hill's vocal version of "It's a Long Road."

see also: Rambo, Rambo III

David Hirsch

First Knight

🎞 1995, Epic Sountrax/Sony Music, from the film *First Knight,* Columbia Pictures, 1995 ♪♪♪♪
album notes: Music: Jerry Goldsmith; **Conductor:** Jerry Goldsmith.

If you can accept Richard Gere as Sir Lancelot you'll be more than willing to take Goldsmith's lush, glitteringly romantic take on the Camelot legend, brimming with large-scale, old-fashioned action cues and fulsome pomp-and-circumstance involving Sean Connery's King Arthur and the glory of Camelot itself. There's a ringing fanfare for Arthur and a Tristam-and-Isolde-style romantic theme that's drenched in hopeless longing. Everything climaxes in a furious choral cue that should bring back fond memories of Goldsmith's *Omen* scores as the forces of good and evil battle for the future of Camelot, and Goldsmith's epic eulogy for the dying Arthur is one of the most moving pieces of music the composer has produced in a long time. Overall *First Knight* stands as a slightly more intelligent take on his earlier approach to the medieval adventure *Lionheart,* and while it may strike some as too traditional in its approach, it will probably be exactly what fans of the composer's recent work are looking for.

Jeff Bond

First Love, Last Rites

🎞 1998, Epic/Sony Music Soundtrax, from the Strand Releasing film *First Love, Last Rites,* 1998 ♪♪♪♪
Natasha Gregson Wagner is the female lead in this charming story of first love. As her love blossoms and eventually sours, she spins 45s that reflect her changing moods. All 15 pop tunes are written and performed by the versatile D.C. art-rock band Shudder to Think, with guest vocalists ranging from Nina Persson of the Cardigans, who sweetly yodels the cowgirl's "Appalachian Lullaby," to Cheap Trick's Robin Zander singing the

Beatle-esque "Automatic Soup." The predominant style is Motown, with contemporary singers recreating the feel of an oldies station from the late Jeff Buckley's Otis Redding-style "I Want Someone Badly," to Liz Phair's suggestive rock tune "Erecting a Movie Star." Unlike Shudder to Think's more aggressive albums and soundtrack projects for *High Art* and the glam rock *Velvet Goldmine, First Love, Last Rites* reveals strong song writing and their most listenable release to date.

David Poole

First Men in the Moon

🎞 1991, Cloud Nine Records, from the film *First Men in the Moon,* Columbia Pictures, 1964 ♪♪♪♪
album notes: Music: Laurie Johnson; **Conductor:** Laurie Johnson.

Though thoroughly outdated by the time it was released in 1964, a few years ahead of Neil Armstrong's first walk on the lunar surface, *First Men in the Moon,* based on H.G. Wells's 1901 novel, is an engrossing space adventure, featuring the wonders of Ray Harryhausen's dynamation skills. The story, slyly brought to the mid-century with the first moon exploration, circa 1964, finding evidence that a previous, unheralded expedition took place at the turn of the century, required a score that would all at once have elements of thrill and romance, something Laurie Johnson provided with accomplished skill. The romantic aspects of the story are detailed in the cues that evoke the turn-of-the-century escapade, with themes that are wonderfully explicit and descriptive. Conversely, for the Moon sequences, the composer devised cues that are more monothematic, using woodwind and brass instruments playing in their nethermost registers, to the exclusion of strings. The combination of both makes for a very unusual, comprehensive score that remains pleasantly attractive when removed from its primary function. Unfortunately, this thin-sounding, mono recording doesn't give a flattering image of the composer's achievements, and proves at times less endearing than it could have been.

Didier C. Deutsch

Fist of the North Star

See: Ticks/Fist of the North Star

The First Wives Club

🎞 1996, Varèse Sarabande Records, from the film *The First Wives Club,* Paramount Pictures, 1996 ♪♪♪♪
album notes: Music: Marc Shaiman; **Conductor:** Artie Kane, Edward Karam.

A stinging social comedy about three married women jilted by their respective husbands who organize a "club" and seek revenge, *The First Wives Club* was scored by Marc Shaiman who developed a series of cues that match the biting tone of the story and display fun touches of their own. First drawing a portrait of the three heroines—Elise (Goldie Hawn), Brenda (Bette Midler), and Annie (Diane Keaton)—Shaiman let the storyline dictate where his music would interfere most effectively, and his cues, as a result, are representative of the unfolding screen action. It is not very difficult to follow the progression as the three abandoned wives agree to create the club, and go into action in order to repay in kind the men who have treated them so badly. All along, Shaiman keeps his score with tongue firmly in cheek with cues that provoke the listener while they recall the film's best scenes. Amusingly entertaining, the music is a total delight.

Didier C. Deutsch

A Fish Called Wanda

1988, Soundscreen, from the film *A Fish Called Wanda*, MGM, 1988 🎬🎬🎬

album notes: Music: John Du Prez; **Conductor:** John Du Prez; **Featured Musicians:** John Williams, guitar; Paul Robinson, drums; Ray Russell, guitar; Luis Jardin, bass, percussion; Kevin Powell, bass; John Du Prez, keyboards.

It matters little if this album is rather oddly sequenced (where else but in a Monty Python album would you find the "End Titles" as the first track?), what counts here is the music. John Du Prez, who has written the scores for several Python films, has created a quirky series of cues, propelled by an omnipresent electronic beat in which guitarist John Williams brings a definitely different flavor. Some tracks ("First Encounter with Otto," "Wanda Meets Archie," "Otto's Jealousy") are meant to underscore specific moments in the film, and as such make less of an impression as pure musical statements. But the longer selections, capped by a long suite, reflect the specific flavor of the zany comedy with the suite essentially reprising the main themes into a long orchestral elaboration. The suite, incidentally, is in effect track 23 (and not 21 as indicated on the backtray information) and lasts 16:55 minutes (not 14:55). Bet you anything that these Python guys were again responsible for that snafu!

Didier C. Deutsch

The Fisher King

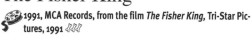1991, MCA Records, from the film *The Fisher King*, Tri-Star Pictures, 1991 🎬🎬🎬

album notes: Music: George Fenton; **Conductor:** George Fenton.

Despite a preponderance of pop songs on this typically song-oriented soundtrack, we are given a good 20 minutes of George Fenton's contemporary mix of classical music and moody jazz to convey the varied personalities housed within Terry Gilliam's

unusual exploration of the thin line between reality and fantasy. The score's standout cue, at almost seven minutes, is the introspective "Red Knight Suite," which offers a contrast to the bristling action cues heard previously. A jazzy trumpet over electric guitar speaks quietly while suggesting a contemporary, urban milieu, while a Morricone-esque harmonica lends an effective counterpoint. The cue moves quickly into the fantastic with the entry of a choir over-driving string and horn figures. The choir supports the film's Grail-like sense of Quest, and the cue builds to a ferocious climax before dissolving, leaving only a stately, classical string motif that heralds a return to normalcy, to sophistication, after our dalliance with fantasy. The assembly of the CD, its first half an attempt to mimic the style of a live radio broadcast with shock-jock introductory patter, may not appeal to those interested only in Fenton's score, but the ability to program the CD allows Fenton's music to be heard without interruption.

Randall D. Larson

A Fistful of Dollars

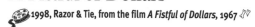1998, Razor & Tie, from the film *A Fistful of Dollars*, 1967 🎬🎬

album notes: Music: Ennio Morricone; **Conductor:** Ennio Morricone.

When you consider the many recordings of the scores Morricone wrote for Sergio Leone's spaghetti westerns that are currently available (some with expanded cues), this reissue of the original RCA LP from 1967 looks a bit redundant. Particularly given the fact that its total playing time is 28:55, which makes the music rather expensive at today's exchange rates. All in all, the music gets a high five-bone rating, but the recording itself gets nothing.

Didier C. Deutsch

500 Nations

📺 1994, Epic Soundtrax Records, from the CBS-TV miniseries *500 Nations*, 1994 🎬🎬🎬

album notes: Music: Peter Buffett; **Featured Musicians:** Peter Buffett, synclavier, keyboards; Chief Hawk Pope, vocals; Douglas Spotted Eagle, flute; David Arkenstone, Jason Klagstad, guitar; Paul Omeinder, cello; Dan Chase, percussion; Gordon Tootoosis, spoken words.

Peter Buffett, you might recall, contributed some pseudo–Native American music to films such as *Dances with Wolves*, and his own recordings has managed to promote the ethnic qualities that exist in most Indian music. Here he does what he knows best, adapting the traditional music of his people to conform with a given topic, and expanding it to make it acceptable to casual listeners perhaps not in tune with this kind of music. Essentially, *500 Nations*, a television miniseries, surveyed the many cultural manifestations of American Indians before the colonials from another world began to decimate them and destroy their culture. The musical illustrations draw from the songs that have survived this form of holocaust and from Buffett's own creations. They provide a vivid background to the portrait of proud people that had a past until that past was almost entirely erased.

see also: The Native Americans

Didier C. Deutsch

Flaming Star/Wild in the Country/Follow That Dream

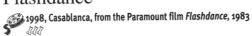 1995, RCA Records, from the films *Flaming Star,* 20th Century Fox, 1960, *Wild in the Country,* 20th Century Fox, 1961, and *Follow That Dream,* United Artists, 1962 🎬🎬🎬

In a rare dramatic role, Elvis portrayed in *Flaming Star* a cowboy in the Old West, the son of a white settler and an Indian mother, whose loyalties are divided after rebel Kiowas kill neighbors of his father. Released in 1960, the film further confirmed Elvis' acting potential, though his vocal talent also received its due in a couple of numbers that included the title tune.

Released a year later, *Wild In The Country* also marked the last time Elvis had a serious role in the movies until his last film. In it, he played another delinquent youth in a poverty-stricken area, who is given a triple choice at redemption, each represented by a different woman (Tuesday Weld, Hope Lange, and Millie Perkins). Both "Lonely Man" and "Wild in the Country," written for the film, became minor hits.

Coupled with the above two soundtracks, the CD offers four songs from the 1962 *Follow That Dream,* in which Elvis played surrogate brother to a brood of adopted orphans in a Dogpatch-like rural setting. Again, the title tune proved a minor charted hit.

Didier C. Deutsch

Flashdance

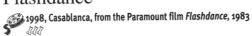 1998, Casablanca, from the Paramount film *Flashdance,* 1983 🎬🎬🎬

album notes: Music: Giorgio Moroder; **Conductor:** Sylvester Levay.

This million-selling album joined the ranks of a whole generation of dance films that spawned a new religion and has continued to spread to this day, even growing beyond the screen to reach the Broadway stage (i.e., *Footloose*). Jennifer Beals, who starred in it as an 18-year-old working in a steel mill in the daytime and transforming herself into a dance marathoner at night, didn't see her career ignite after that film. Others who followed somewhat similar paths included Laura Branigan, who had a

quick binge as a diva before she faded away, Irene Cara who scored high with several hits only to disappear equally fast, and even Giorgio Moroder, who created most of the songs here but was unable to sustain his popularity when the disco era came to an end. They're all present here, along with Michael Sembello, Kim Carnes, Joe Bean Esposito, and dear old Donna Summer, gorgeous relics of an era gone by, but still pretty much in the public eye (and ear) thanks to albums such as this. Truth be told, this soundtrack album is quite exciting, if slightly one-track minded. The songs are not bad at all, enjoyable to a point, and certainly inviting. But where have all the flowers gone . . . ?

Didier C. Deutsch

The Flintstones

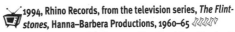 1994, Rhino Records, from the television series, *The Flintstones,* Hanna–Barbera Productions, 1960–65 🎬🎬🎬🎬
album notes: Featured Performers: Alan Reed, Jean Vander Pyl, Mel Blanc, Bea Benaderet.

Cartoon enthusiasts will adore this delightful collection of familiar tunes from the sophisticated animated sit–com, *The Flintstones.* The fun–filled disc includes 23 main and end title themes, soundbites and plot songs from the show's six years of prime time on ABC (1960–1966). Patterned after the ultra successful series *The Honeymooners, The Flintstones* enjoyed guest appearances by some of the entertainment industry's top talent. Featured on this compilation are "Yabba–Dabba–Doo!," sung by songwriter Hoagy Carmichael (the composers's big hit, "Star Dust" also makes an appearance), "Rockenschpeel Jingle," the twistin' "Bedrock Twitch," and Fred's "Hi–Fye" version of "Rockin' Bird." A multitude of title songs ("Meet the Flintstones," "The Man Called Flintstone" among them) round out the light–hearted nature of this package.

Charles L. Granata

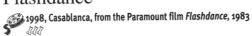 1994, MCA Records, from the film *The Flintstones,* Universal Pictures, 1994 🎬🎬🎬🎬
album notes: Music: David Newman; **Featured Musicians:** B-52s; Was (Not Was); Screaming Blue Messiahs; US3 and Def Jef.

Good concept, good bands and some awfully fun songs. As one might expect, the B-52s—excuse us, the BC-52s—crank up the grins with "Bedrock Twitch" and their version of "(Meet) The Flintstones." Some blasts from the past include Was (Not Was)' "Walk the Dinosaur" and Screaming Blue Messiahs' "I Wanna Be a Flintstone," while "I Showed a Caveman How to Rock" by US3 and Def Jef brings the pre-historic set into the hip-hop age. We're still not sure what Green Jelly's "Anarchy in the U.K." is doing here, but it's just as funny as everthing else. Yabba dabba doo!

Gary Graff

Flower Drum Song *composer and lyricist Richard Rodgers and Oscar Hammerstein.* **(Archive Photos, Inc.)**

Flipper

1996, The Track Factory, from the film *Flipper,* Universal Pictures, 1996

album notes: Music: Joel McNeely; **Orchestra:** The London Symphony Orchestra; **Conductor:** Joel McNeely; **Featured Musicians:** Crosby, Stills and Nash.

If the formula works, why not try it again . . . and again . . . so, after *Willy* and *Andre,* here comes *Flipper,* another docile marine mammal who develops a friendship with a rebellious boy. You get the picture! In this case, though, the film has serious antecedents in the guise of a popular television series in the 1960s and a couple of previous features. It is also the occasion for some attractive underwater and abovewave scenes, and for a pertinent score by Joel McNeely. With the formidable London Symphony Orchestra playing the score for all it's worth, there are some lovely moments to be enjoyed. The "Main Title" (featuring Crosby, Stills and Nash) is a fluid lyrical anthem, faintly evocative of Simon and Garfunkel or The Mamas and The Papas. The other cues are flavorful musical statements with a pervading poetic imagery that are compelling and frequently

attractive, like in "Marv Meets Flipper." The "enhanced CD" also contains various pop vocals by The Beach Boys, Professor Longhair, and Tom Jones (who cares to hear "It's Not Unusual" once more) that can be programmed out.

Didier C. Deutsch

Flora the Red Menace

1992, RCA Victor, from the Broadway production *Flora the Red Menace,* 1965

album notes: Music: John Kander; **Lyrics:** Fred Ebb; **Musical Direction:** Hal Hastings; **Cast:** Liza Minnelli, Bob Dishy, Mary Louise Wilson, Cathryn Damon.

The first musical by John Kander and Fred Ebb (they had previously worked together on Barbra Streisand's hit "My Coloring Book"), *Flora, the Red Menace* also marked the first time Liza Minnelli starred on Broadway, as well as the start of her creative relationship with the songwriting team. The show had its ingratiating moments, although all the parties concerned would eventually know bigger and better successes. Based on Lester Atwell's novel, *Love Is Just Around The Corner, Flora* deals with a young

art student in New York during the Depression years who becomes involved with another student, a Communist, played by Bob Dishy. Received with lukewarm reviews when it opened on May 11, 1965, it copped a Tony for its young star, but closed shortly after, having played only 87 performances. While the score was relatively undistinguished, it offered a couple of good, theatrical moments in "Palomino Pal" and "Dear Love," but today it is hardly memorable. The original cast album reveals why.

Didier C. Deutsch

Flower Drum Song

1993, Sony Broadway, from the Broadway production *Flower Drum Song*, 1958 🎬🎬🎬🎬🎬

album notes: Music: Richard Rodgers; **Lyrics:** Oscar Hammerstein II; **Musical Direction:** Salvatore Dell'Isola; **Cast:** Miyoshi Umeki, Larry Blyden, Juanita Hall, Ed Kenney, Keye Luke, Arabella Hong, Pat Suzuki, Jack Soo.

Sometimes mentioned as one of the least interesting collaborations by Richard Rodgers and Oscar Hammerstein, *Flower Drum Song,* which opened on Dec. 1, 1958, is in need of a thorough reevaluation. While it may not be on the same level as the pair's greatest hits (*Oklahoma!, The King and I, South Pacific,* or *The Sound of Music),* it is nonetheless a lovely, ingratiating musical with a deftly written score. It has many wonderful moments in its story about a shy picture bride from China, who arrives in San Francisco to marry her intended, a nightclub operator more interested in the star of his floor show, only to fall in love with the son of the old-fashioned Chinese man who gives her and her father temporary shelter. Briskly directed by Gene Kelly (in his only directorial venture on Broadway), the show, based on Chin Y. Lee's novel of the same name, took its dramatic turns from the generational conflicts between traditional first-generation Chinese immigrants and their children, more adapted to the mores in their adopted country. The contrast was also brought into sharp focus in the score in which softer Chinese-styled numbers ("A Hundred Million Miracles") contrasted with jazzier American-inspired songs ("I Enjoy Being a Girl," "Grant Avenue").

The musical, which yielded several notable hits ("I Enjoy Being a Girl," "Sunday"), was also the occasion for Oscar Hammerstein to show the extent to which he had mastered his craft as a lyricist in the inventive pantoum "I Am Going to Like It Here." A pantoum is a rare and sophisticated form of poetry that originated in Malaya, in which the second and fourth lines in a stanza are repeated in the first and third lines of the following quatrain, in a cyclical musical movement.

Flower Drum Song enjoyed a long run of 600 performances. It was made into a beautiful film production in 1961 that had the enormous merits of retaining most of the songs in the score, as well as Miyoshi Umeki and Juanita Hall from the Broadway original, while cleverly expanding on the show's best assets, its big musical numbers. Nancy Kwan and Jack Soo also starred. The soundtrack album, available at one time on LP from Decca, was never reissued on compact disc, but the Broadway original cast album is a worthy and necessary addition to any collection.

Beth Krakower

Flubber

1997, Disney Records, from the Walt Disney film *Flubber,* 1997 🎬🎬🎬🎬

album notes: Music: Danny Elfman; **Conductor:** Artie Kane.

Robin Williams had another winning role in this remake of *The Absent-Minded Professor,* in which he portrayed a mathematical genius who has a knack for creating unusual things (like the "flubber," or flying rubber, of the title) and being equally in the fog when it comes to more pedestrian behavior. A green goo with amazing properties and a mind of its own, the strange ectoplasm can bounce, morph itself into anything that crosses its impish imagination, and even dance a wild mambo to the strains of Danny Elfman's quirky music. The soundtrack album evokes many of the most engaging moments in the film, even giving a musical voice to Weebo, the dear professor's other invention, a diminutive robot that has become his constant companion. Typical of Elfman's best efforts, the cues are frequently amusing, inventive, and musically challenging. A song by KC & the Sunshine Band, "Goo a Little Dance," caps the recording in style.

Didier C. Deutsch

The Fly

1986, Varèse Sarabande, from the film *The Fly,* Brooksfilms Ltd., 1986 🎬🎬🎬🎬

album notes: Music: Howard Shore; **Orchestra:** The London Philharmonic Orchestra; **Conductor:** Howard Shore.

Howard Shore's score for this remake of the 1958 classic is a real nail-biting horror score, featuring a poignant three-note main theme with forlorn horns calling out in ever building motifs. What the album lacks, however, is a break from all the tension. Anything that could remotely be called a light moment ("Success with Baboon," "Particle Magazine") simply foreshadows the coming nightmare. One of Shore's more thematic scores for director David Cronenberg may not be considered entertainment by everybody, but it's an excellently written, hauntingly dark piece of work. The CD contains three additional tracks that went unused in the final film.

David Hirsch

Follies

1994, Angel Records, from the Broadway production *Follies*, 1971 🎵🎵🎵

album notes: Music: Stephen Sondheim; **Lyrics:** Stephen Sondheim; **Musical Direction:** Harold Hastings; **Cast:** Michael Bartlett, Dorothy Collins, John McMartin, Gene Nelson, Alexis Smith, Fifi D'Orsay, Ethel Shutta, Yvonne de Carlo.

1990, First Night Records, from the London production *Follies*, 1990 🎵🎵🎵

album notes: Music: Stephen Sondheim; **Lyrics:** Stephen Sondheim; **Musical Direction:** Simon Lowe; **Cast:** Paul Bentley, Julia McKenzie, Daniel Massey, David Healey, Diana Rigg, Maria Charles, Margaret Courtenay, Dolores Gray.

1985, RCA Victor, from the concert performance *Follies*, 1985 Cerito Films, 1974 🎵🎵🎵🎵

album notes: Music: Stephen Sondheim; **Lyrics:** Stephen Sondheim; **Orchestra:** The New York Philharmonic; **Conductor:** Paul Gemignani; **Cast:** Barbara Cook, George Hearn, Mandy Patinkin, Lee Remick, Betty Comden, Adolph Green, Liliane Montevecchi, Elaine Stritch, Phyllis Newman, Carol Burnett.

For some musical-theater devotees, this Stephen Sondheim-James Goldman show about a reunion of Weismann Follies girls is as good as Broadway gets. But the original Broadway production was not a hit. The only major revival to date was in London in 1987. The listener who wants all of *Follies* must invest in the three CD versions listed here.

The Capitol Records original cast album was cut during production from two LPs to one, and except for one song ("One More Kiss"), the deleted material was either discarded or never recorded, so this CD (now on Angel) represents all that survives. Still, the performances are fine throughout, especially that of Alexis Smith, a former Hollywood ingenue who emerged as a Broadway star here.

The London production, on the other hand, was a smash, powered by megawatt performances from Diana Rigg and Julia McKenzie, and established Sondheim's shows as fixtures of the West End. The recording's also first-rate, but here's the catch: With 16 years' hindsight, Sondheim and Goldman rewrote the book, deleted songs and added new ones, and almost completely reworked the "Loveland" fantasy sequence that consumes the show's last half-hour. For this listener, the changes are positive on balance, and matched song-for-song against the Broadway original, this is a better recording, but . . . it's a different show.

If you can only afford one version of *Follies,* however, the RCA set is the one to buy. Culled from two concert performances at New York's Lincoln Center, the recording was conceived and fought for by producer Thomas Z. Shepard, and it endures not just as the only "complete" recording of the original score, but as one of the finest assemblages of musical theater talent ever put on record. Barbara Cook, Lee Remick, Mandy Patinkin, and

George Hearn are the four marvelous principals, but the cameos, by the likes of Elaine Stritch, Carol Burnett, and Phyllis Newman, bring down the house. As far as this listener is concerned, it could go on forever. (Also available, with some hilarious backstage moments, on video.) As a bonus, the 2-CD set also includes the score to *Stavisk,* from 1974.

Marc Kirkeby

1998, TVT Records, from the off-Broadway revival *Follies*, 1998 🎵🎵🎵

album notes: Music: Stephen Sondheim; **Lyrics:** Stephen Sondheim; **Musical Direction:** Jim Coleman, Tom Helm; **Cast:** Kaye Ballard, Michael Gruber, Laurence Guittard, Billy Hartung, Danette Holden, Dee Hoty, Vahan Khanzadian, Donna McKechnie, Ann Miller, Liliane Montevecchi, Natalie Mosco, Phyllis Newman, Meredith Patterson, Tony Roberts, Donald Saddler, Carol Skarimbas, Eddie Bracken.

There have been several recordings of Sondheim's extraordinary musical *Follies,* a scathing look at the disintegration of relationships set against the glamorous backdrop of a Ziegfeld-like production. Beginning with the sadly incomplete original cast album on Capitol, the revamped London cast recording starring Diana Rigg on First Night, and the all-star live version at Lincoln Center on RCA (all of them available on CD), the show has undergone numerous changes and transformations, all of them designed to put more focus on the various characters, all one-time members of the Weismann Follies in years gone by, whose lives are shattered when they meet again for a final farewell to the theater being torn down. Former lovers reminisce about their young enthusiasms, former stars reveal their disappointments about the turns their lives have taken, former rivals tear each other apart again, all of it in a vivid display of passions and bitter memories that never went away.

Evidently revamped again, the show received a new, all-star production at New Jersey's Paper Mill Playhouse that was scheduled to go to Broadway next, but never made it, despite some very positive reviews. This recording is all that remains from that production, and like the other recordings, it invites many comments and criticisms. On the positive side, the cast is absolutely superb, well chosen and graced by the presence of many first-class stars such as Laurence Guittard, Dee Hoty, Ann Miller, Liliane Montevecchi, Kaye Ballard, Phyllis Newman, and Tony Roberts. The recording also offers an insightful look at the many modifications the show received, and features many of the songs that were added or dropped from the production at one time or another.

On the down side, however, the production lacks the imagination and verve found in other recordings, particularly in the Lincoln Center presentation, which still must stand as the best overall for excitement and spontaneity (the live recording providing a stimulating effect that nothing can equal). Some of the performances seem rushed and not fully realized (case in point: Montevecchi, whose singing in the Lincoln Center recording sounded far superior), and the overall sound is dry and unexciting. Still, this is a recording that many fans will want to have, if only because it complements the others already available.

Didier C. Deutsch

Follow That Dream

See: Flaming Star/Wild in the Country/Follow That Dream

Footloose

🎬 **1998, Sony Legacy, from the Paramount film** *Footloose*, **1984** 🎵🎵🎵

The album, one of the quintessential soundtracks of the 1980s, presents the songs that inspired the musical currently on Broadway (see below). For this reissue, Legacy went back to the movie and added three tracks that were omitted from the original soundtrack, as well as a remix of Shalamar's "Dancing in the Sheets." While this makes the new CD more representative of the movie, two of the tracks (Quiet Riot's metallic "Bang Your Head" and the Shalamar remix) seem unnecessary, with the placement of the Quiet Riot track actually detracting from the flow of the dance-oriented soundtrack.

Beth Krakower

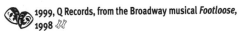 **1999, Q Records, from the Broadway musical** *Footloose*, **1998** 🎵🎵

album notes: Music: Tom Snow; **Lyrics:** Dean Pitchford; **Book:** Dean Pitchford, Walter Bobbie; **Musical Direction:** Doug Katsaros; **Cast:** Stephen Lee Anderson, Dee Hoty, Jeremy Kushnier, Jennifer Laura Thompson, Catherine Cox.

Conversely, anyone who has been nurtured on the soundtrack album may find the Broadway original cast recording leaves a lot to be desired. The familiar songs ("Dancing in the Sheets," "Footloose," "Let's Hear It for the Boy") don't have the same radiance, and in fact sound rather bland in the new context. The beefed-up score doesn't come up to the standards set by the film's soundtrack, and the participants, while pleasant, don't exert the same attraction.

While this story of a Chicago boy—who locks horns with the authority figures in the small town where he and his mother have just moved when he wants to dance—may still have a familiar ring to it, the added importance given the boy's nemesis, the town's preacher, and his soul-searching look like an unnecessary decision to try and enlarge for the stage what is essentially a very tiny plot. The new songs don't help much either. Unless you have seen the show, have loved it, and definitely

want to have an audio keepsake of it, rent the video and play the soundtrack from the film.

Didier C. Deutsch

For Love or Money

🎬 **1992, Big Screen Records, from the film** *For Love or Money*, **Universal-International, 1992** 🎵🎵🎵🎵

album notes: Music: Bruce Broughton; **Conductor:** Bruce Broughton; **Featured Musicians:** "Rev." Dave Boruff, alto sax; Bill Broughton, trombone.

The underscoring for this lightweight comedy starring Michael J. Fox features prominently two solo instruments, an alto sax and a trombone, both of which confer to the music a specific flavor that is at once endearing. If that were not sufficient, however, Broughton's muscular cues revel in exploring musical lines that can be in turn strongly delineated ("Mr. Ireland"), strikingly sentimental ("Doug Goes Home"), bouncy ("Ticket Exchange"), or simply exhilarating ("Done Deal"). An amusing German rendition of "Happy Days are Here Again" adds a different touch to this enjoyable album.

Didier C. Deutsch

For Me and My Girl

🎬 **1996, Rhino Records, from the film** *For Me and My Girl*, **MGM, 1942** 🎵🎵🎵

album notes: Music: George W. Meyer; **Lyrics:** Edgar Leslie, E. Ray Goetz; **Orchestra:** The MGM Studio Orchestra; **Choir:** The MGM Studio Chorus; **Conductor:** Georgie Stoll; **Cast:** Gene Kelly, Judy Garland, George Murphy, Marta Eggerth, Lucille Norman, Richard Quine.

A tuneful Arthur Freed production for MGM, *For Me and My Gal* starred Gene Kelly in his first Hollywood film following the big impression he had made on Broadway in *Pal Joey*, and Judy Garland in her first major film sans her usual partner, Mickey Rooney. Neither Kelly nor Garland would have to complain, as both gave ingratiating performances that showed his screen personality in the best light, and revealed greater depth in her own ability to sing and dance. The lame story of two vaudevillians in the years of World War I, *For Me and My Gal* was the occasion for many breezy musical numbers in which Garland, Kelly, and George Murphy performed songs from the period like "When You Wore A Tulip," "After You've Gone," "Till We Meet Again," and the title tune with style, ease, and a charm that belied the overall corny plot. The recently reissued soundtrack album on Rhino, supplemented with a lot of previously unreleased material, proves irresistible and charmingly dated, with the three principals particularly engaging in these musical moments, individually and together.

Didier C. Deutsch

Kevin Bacon in the film version of Footloose *(The Kobal Collection)*

For the Boys

1991, Atlantic Records, from the film *For the Boys*, 20th Century-Fox, 1991 ♪♪♪♪

The Divine Ms. M. (Bette Midler) struck a particularly felicitous note in this heart-warming story about a singer entertaining the troops over a 50-year period, and her relationship with another performer, James Caan, married to someone else. In her stage shows, Midler's great gift as a vocalist sometimes takes second place to her broad antics, but she is quite fetching in her treatment of the chestnuts that comprise the program in this delightful CD, with sensational charts by veterans Billy May, Ralph Burns, and Marty Paich, among others. A brilliant showcase for this particular side of her talent, Midler shares the spotlight with Caan (whom she easily outshines) on a couple of selections and introduces a previously unrecorded song by Hoagy Carmichael and Paul Francis Webster, as well as a lovely ballad penned by Dave Grusin and Alan and Marilyn Bergman.

Didier C. Deutsch

For Whom the Bell Tolls

1991, Stanyan Records, from the film *For Whom the Bell Tolls*, Warner Bros., 1943 ♪♪♪♪

album notes: Music: Victor Young; Orchestra: The Warner Bros. Studio Orchestra; Conductor: Ray Heindorf.

Victor Young's percussive Oscar-nominated score for this Spanish Civil War drama, based on the novel by Ernest Hemingway, received a loving treatment in a rerecording made in the late 1950s by Ray Heindorf and the Warner Bros. Studio Orchestra. When he wrote it, Young essentially focused on two basic elements, the tragedy of a country and its people split into two warring factions, and the tender feelings that slowly develop between Roberto, an American dynamite expert on the side of the guerrillas, and Maria, an orphan girl. Propelled by a breathtaking "Love Theme," lushly played by the strings, and with the constant support of an acoustic guitar to give the music its flavor, the music unfolds with great passion and strength. The recording itself has the closeness and immediacy usually associated with recordings from the era, with excellent stereo definition. The CD also features a cue from Manos Hadjidakis's score for the 1963 *America, America* and two selections, which are totally out of place in the context, composed by Rod McKuen for the 1978 *The Unknown War*.

Didier C. Deutsch

Forbidden Planet

1989, Small Planet/GNP Crescendo, from the film *Forbidden Planet*, MGM, 1956 ♪♪♪♪♪

album notes: Music: Louis Barron; Bebe Barron.

The Barrons's seminal all-electronic score for this classic 1950s space opera is a true test of the open-mindedness of the listener as this soundtrack stakes out a territory that exists somewhere between music, sound effects, and something altogether indefinable. Created long before the invention of the synthesizer, this "score" was produced by the Barrons by building specially-designed circuits to generate the required sounds and then recording them, but the result is astonishingly organic and atmospheric. Despite the abstract nature of the sounds produced, there are recognizable motifs, such as the percolating theme for Robby the Robot and a frightening "footstep" effect for the movie's invisible Id monster. Some of the cues will set your teeth on edge, particularly the hair-raising "Deceleration," while many create hypnotic, undulating textures that might actually lower your blood pressure. You can argue about whether this is actually music or not, but it's still fascinating listening.

Jeff Bond

Forbidden Zone

1990, Varèse Sarabande Records, from the film *Forbidden Zone*, 1990 ♪♪♪♪

album notes: Music: Danny Elfman; Featured Musicians: Danny Elfman and The Mystic Knights of the Oingo Boingo.

Anyone who has enjoyed Danny Elfman's outstanding contributions to film music over the past six to seven years will have a blast listening (or, as the case may be, discovering for the first time) this delirious score (or "musical schizophrenia," as Elfman himself describes it) for a film made by Richard Elfman that has mercifully left relatively no trace, starring Herve Villechaize and Susan Tyrrell, as rulers of an underground kingdom called the "Sixth Dimension." Many of the composer's quirky musical ideas can be tracked down to this early effort, in which he gets support from The Mystic Knights of the Oingo Boingo, built around period songs (most notably Cab Calloway's "Some of These Days" and "Minnie the Moocher," the last one thoroughly, but enjoyably destroyed by Elfman and Toshiro Baloney). As Danny Elfman writes in his short commentary, the score, which is guaranteed to bring a broad smile to your face, is "a great chance to stretch out and go nuts." He succeeded beyond all expectations!

Didier C. Deutsch

Forever Amber

1998, Varèse-Sarabande, from the 20th Century-Fox film *Forever Amber*, 1947 ♪♪♪

album notes: Music: David Raksin; **Conductor:** Alfred Newman.

Among the most enjoyable trends in recent years, classic scores from the past have been unearthed, appropriately restored by gifted producers who double as film historians, and proposed to avid fans who are sometimes overwhelmed by this sudden abundance of product. Making its first appearance on record, this soundtrack is a joy to behold, even though one's enjoyment may be slightly undermined by the recording's lack of depth in the lower registers, some unsightly halting splices, and an annoying distortion that creeps through many of the tracks.

Based on Kathleen Winsor's 1944 novel of passions and intrigues at the court of King Charles II of England, the period drama focuses on Amber, an ambitious farm girl who flees her Puritan upbringing and sleeps her way to the throne room. Inspired by the music of Henry Purcell and the late Baroque era, Raksin wrote a score that derives its homogeneity from the use of a ground bass, the single anchor for the many melodies developed in the cues. At times subtly evocative, at other times exhilaratingly florid, it ranks among the best efforts from a composer, who, despite the enormous success of his music for *Laura,* continues to be much underrated.

Didier C. Deutsch

Forever Knight

1996, GNP Crescendo, from the television series *Forever Knight*, Tri–Star Television, 1996 ♪♪♪

album notes: Music: Fred Mollin.

This lengthy, comprehensive packaging of music from the USA Network's vampire cop show offers dialogue excerpts from series heavy Nigel Bennett, Fred Mollin's electronic theme and scoring, and several songs done in a kind of Kate Bush/Tori Amos style by Lori Yates. Mollin's title theme is a deliberately monotone, pulsating suspense motif that conjures up the stalking blood thirst of the vampire hero, an effect that echoes throughout most of the scores along with some subtle period effects that underscore blood–slurping detective Nick Knight's memories of his centuries–old life. Mollin is an old hand at this sort of subject matter and he's adept at creating the impression of many more instrumental effects than would seem possible from his keyboards. The mix is effective and highly recommended to fans of the series, although the all–electronic approach (seemingly necessitated more by budget concerns than aesthetics), with its inevitable drum–machine percussion, wears out the ear well before the end of the material is reached.

Jeff Bond

10 Essential Scores
by Maurice Jarre

Doctor Zhivago
Lawrence of Arabia
The Mosquito Coast
Gorillas in the Mist
Is Paris Burning?
A Passage to India
The Damned
The Night of the Generals
Mad Max beyond Thunderdome
The Man Who Would Be King

Forever Young

1992, Big Screen Records, from the film *Forever Young,* Warner Bros., 1992 ♪♪♪

album notes: Music: Jerry Goldsmith; **Conductor:** Jerry Goldsmith; **Featured Musicians:** Mike Lang, piano; Joel Peskin, soprano sax.

Jerry Goldsmith goes for the romance in this glossy but forgettable blend of star-crossed love, Rip Van Winkle, and childhood antics. For chase and flight cues involving Mel Gibson's pilot character Goldsmith brought in some heavy-duty rhythmic orchestral material, similar to some of the pounding, percussive chases in the earlier *Total Recall,* while electronic passages mark suspense in other passages. The centerpiece of the score is a rhapsodic Hollywood-style love theme that Goldsmith developed into its own separate presentation for this album. Unfortunately the theme itself is less effective than some of the less-calculated incidental material that precedes it. That leaves *Forever Young* as a well-crafted and recorded album that just doesn't represent Goldsmith at his most interesting.

Jeff Bond

Forget Paris

1995, Elektra Records, from the film *Forget Paris*, Columbia Pictures, 1995 ♪♪♪♪♪

album notes: Music: Marc Shaiman; **Conductor:** Artie Kane.

The combination of some great songs, great vocal performances, and Marc Shaiman's flavorful jazzy score makes for a particularly strong soundtrack album that has undeniable charm. The film, a romantic comedy starring Billy Crystal and Debra Winger, already had a good flair of its own, but the musical contributions here add significant touches that enhance the screen proceedings. In the context "When You Love Someone," a duet with typical sliding inflections by Anita Baker and James Ingram, may strike as being out of style, but the tracks by Louis Armstrong, Billie Holiday, Louis Prima, and Duke Ellington are wonderful. "April in Paris," played big-band style, and "Come Rain or Come Shine," with David Sanborn blowing a mean sax, also rank among the rewarding selections here, along with the cues by Shaiman, which cover the gamut from a Gallic-flavored "Paris Suite," to several tracks with a pleasant jazz feel ("Craig and Lucy," "To Marriage"), to explosive big band treatments of classic hits ("Nice Work If You Can Get It," "My Melancholy Baby"). A rich and satisfying album.

Didier C. Deutsch

Forrest Gump

1995, Epic Records/Sony Music, from the film *Forrest Gump*, Paramount Pictures, 1995 ♪♪♪♪

1995, Epic Records/Sony Music, from the film *Forrest Gump*, Paramount Pictures, 1995 ♪♪♪♪

album notes: Music: Alan Silvestri; **Conductor:** Alan Silvestri.

The phenomenal success of the 2-CD set illustrates better than most the incredible synergy that exists at times between the movies and the recording industry. One of the most creative compilations of pop songs used in a film, the set includes many of the tunes that marked the period from the late 1950s through the 1970s. Among its highlights are Elvis Presley's "Hound Dog," The Four Tops' "I Can't Help Myself," Aretha Franklin's "Respect," Bob Dylan's "Rainy Day Women #12 & 35," The Mamas and The Papas' "California Dreamin'," Simon & Garfunkel's "Mrs. Robinson," Harry Nilsson's "Everybody's Talkin,'" Willie Nelson's "On the Road Again"—all of the songs that can be found elsewhere but which, combined together, make for a most attractive and enjoyable package.

The score by Alan Silvestri serves as a perfect counterpoint to these classic pop hits, and emphasizes the more romantic aspects of this docu-fable about the slow-witted innocent (played by Tom Hanks) who finds himself unwillingly involved in some of the most remarkable events of the past 30 years.

Didier C. Deutsch

Fort Saganne

1989, Milan Records/France, from the film *Fort Saganne,* 1984 ♪♪♪♪

album notes: Music: Philippe Sarde; **Orchestra:** The London Symphony Orchestra; **Conductor:** Carlo Savina; **Featured Musician:** Xavier Gagnepain, cello.

Set on the eve of World War I in the desolated confines of Northern Africa, *Fort Saganne* presented a harsh picture of the fabled Foreign Legion. Based on a novel by Louis Gardel, the film featured an all-star cast that included Gérard Depardieu as a young officer freshly named at the outpost in the middle of the Sahara Desert, Philippe Noiret as the fort Commander, Catherine Deneuve as his wife who takes a shining to Depardieu, and Sophie Marceau as Madeleine, the young officer's fiancee. The overall romantic tone of the story led Sarde to compose an all-pervading brooding, introspective theme, in which the darker side of the drama is suggested by the cello, while the epic moments in the narrative, expressed by brassy calls of trumpets ("Fantasia," "Nemchou! Allah!"), are contrasted by the fluid lovely tunes that inform the passion that overwhelms these characters. Performance by The London Symphony Orchestra places this score way above the norm. This recording may be difficult to find. Check with a used CD store, mail-order company, or a dealer specializing in rare, out-of-print, or import recordings.

Didier C. Deutsch

Four Days in September

1998, Milan, from the Miramax film *Four Days in September,* 1998 ♪♪♪

album notes: Music: Stewart Copeland; **Featured Musicians:** Judd Miller, Paulinho da Costa, percussion; Klebber Jorge, guitar.

Informed by Tom Jobim's rendition of "The Girl from Ipanema" and Alan Price's instrumental take on "The House of the Rising Sun," this soundtrack album to the film *Four Days in September,* starring Alan Arkin, was composed by Stewart Copeland, best known as the founder of the pop supergroup the Police. Based on a true story, the film is an account of the events that surrounded the kidnapping of the American ambassador to Brazil in 1969. Although the locale might have inspired Copeland to write a Latin-based score, he chose instead to focus on the psychological aspects of the action, and delivered a series of cues that are for the most part subdued and introspective. Sometimes a lonely guitar makes a concession to the south of the border atmosphere ("Adagio Ambassador," "Car Chase"), but even those are few and far between. In its own way, it's effective and appropriately ominous, but heard on its own terms, it tends to be a trifle dry after a while.

Didier C. Deutsch

Four in the Morning

See: Elizabeth Taylor in London

The Four Musketeers/The Eagle Has Landed/Voyage of the Damned

1987, Label X, from the films *The Four Musketeers,* 1975, *The Eagle Has Landed,* 1977, and *Voyage of the Damned,* 1976 ♫♫♫
album notes: Music: Lalo Schifrin; **Conductor:** Lalo Schifrin.

Lalo Schifrin strangely unaffecting score for *The Four Musketeers* is a serious letdown in this sequel to the original film made by Richard Lester, which had been scored by Michel Legrand. But whereas Legrand had approached the first film with great personal empathy for it subject matter, Schifrin's totally detached and by-the-book cues completely miss the flavor of the period and end up sounding as a purely routine job. He fared somewhat better with *The Eagle Has Landed,* a World War II adventure centered around an improbable German plot to kidnap Winston Churchill, in which the cymbalom provides an interesting colorful motif that recurs throughout the score. He also did better with his cues for *The Voyage of the Damned,* a sensitive drama about the plight of Jewish refugees from war-torn Europe on board a ship no country wants to accept. Further marring one's appreciation of these scores, the recording contains various sonic glitches, including poorly focused sound, some analog dropouts, and tape noises that could have been easily eliminated.

see also: The Three Musketeers, The Eagle Has Landed

Didier C. Deutsch

Four Rooms

1995, Elektra, from the Miramax film *Four Rooms,* 1995 ♫♫♫♪

album notes: Featured Musicians: Larry Klimas, tenor sax; Donald Markese, baritone sax/clarinet; Bruce Fowler, trombone; Ralf Rickert, trumpet.

This cheerful, amusingly idiotic soundtrack is the kind of album you might want to play on a grim day, when everything around you is a nightmare. If it doesn't significantly alter your moods, then yours is definitely a lost cause. . . . Consisting of four short films, directed by Allison Anders, Alexandre Rockwell, Robert Rodriguez, and Quentin Tarantino, *Four Rooms* took place in a hotel on New Year's Eve, with Tim Roth as a bewildered bellboy the only link between them. Each of the four segments—"The Missing Ingredient," "The Wrong Man," "The Misbehavers," and "The Man from Hollywood"—receives a distinctive musical accompaniment, usually jocular

and lightweight, in a lounge-music kind of vein (reinforced by the use of two selections featuring the master of the genre, Esquivel), with jazzy or Latin American undertones that are lively and enjoyable. The film was not the anticipated success its creators thought it might be, but this goofy soundtrack album will undoubtedly get repeated playing once you have listened to it.

Didier C. Deutsch

Four Weddings and a Funeral

1994, London Records, from the film *Four Weddings and a Funeral,* Gramercy Pictures, 1994 ♫♫♫♫

album notes: Featured Musicians: Wet Wet Wet; Swing Out Sister; Squeeze; Sting; Elton John.

A cheery collection of British pop, with occasional diversions for wedding reception fare such as Gloria Gaynor's "I Will Survive." The covers are coolest, though—Wet Wet Wet's exuberant "Love is All Around," Swing Out Sister's sumptuous "La La La (Means I Love You)," and Elton John's "Chapel of Love," which is as reckless as he's sounded in years.

Gary Graff

1492: Conquest of Paradise

1992, Atlantic Records, from the film *1492: Conquest of Paradise,* Paramount Pictures, 1992 ♫♫♫♫

album notes: Music: Vangelis; **Featured Musicians:** Bruno Manjares, Spanish guitar, vocals; Pepe Martinez, Spanish guitar, vocals; Francis Darizcuren, mandolin, violin; Didier Malherbe, flutes; Guy Protheroe, vocals; **Orchestra:** The English Chamber Choir; **Conductor:** Guy Protheroe.

Despite the fact that Vangelis uses guitars and mandolins to give his score the necessary Spanish flavor, there is something definitely odd about the sounds of a synthesizer in the context of an epic that takes place in the 15th century. Not that one should necessarily be a stickler for authenticity, but the effect here is somewhat jarring. This said, the score for *1492: Conquest of Paradise* has its share of great musical moments, with sweeping melodies that are appropriately overblown, in keeping with its subject matter. The title tune, a spacey selection with rhythm and choral work, is quite effective. Adding to the impression of a vast musical canvas on display, many of the cues fade into one another, making for a somewhat continuous program of impressive scope and dimension.

see also: Christopher Columbus: The Discovery

Didier C. Deutsch

Four Weddings and a Funeral **(The Kobal Collection)**

42nd Street

 **1980, RCA Victor, from the Broadway production *42nd Street*, 1980** 🎵🎵🎵🎵🎵

album notes: Music: Harry Warren; **Lyrics:** Al Dubin, Johnny Mercer, Mort Dixon; **Musical Direction:** John Lesko; **Cast:** Tammy Grimes, Jerry Orbach, Lee Roy Reams, Wanda Richert.

The 1933 backstage screen musical *42nd Street* became a major stage hit when David Merrick brought it virtually intact to Broadway on Aug. 25, 1980. Retaining the film's basic plot–chorus girl (Wandy Richert) steps up to the spotlight when big star (Tammy Grimes) can't go on and wins the day–as well as many of the songs written by Harry Warren and Al Dubin, plus many others from other films. The show also benefited from the incredible creative energy and choreographic drive Gower Champion (who died hours before the premiere) gave it, in a breathtaking display of ensemble dancing seldom seen on Broadway. With Jerry Orbach portraying Julian Marsh, the hard-driving director of the show-within-a-show, and Lee Roy Reams as Billy Lawlor, Peggy's love interest and eventual dancing partner, the musical, a razzling-dazzling paean to show business,

walked away with the Tony for Best Musical, and enjoyed a long run of 3,486 performances. The original cast album is a brilliant recreation of the musical numbers as they were heard when the show opened.

Didier C. Deutsch

Francis of Assisi/Doctor Faustus

🎵 **1997, DRG Records, from the films *Francis of Assisi*, 20th Century-Fox, 1961; and *Doctor Faustus*, Columbia Pictures, 1968** 🎵🎵🎵

album notes: Music: Mario Nascimbene; **Conductor:** Franco Ferrara; Mario Nascimbene; **Featured Musicians:** Severino Gazzelloni, flute; Lucia Vinardi, soprano; **Orchestra:** Vocal Sextet "Luca Marenzio;" **Conductor:** Piero Cavalli; **Orchestra:** Concentus antiqui; **Conductor:** Carlo Quaranta.

An epic religious drama, *Francis of Assisi* stars Bradford Dillman as the young 13th-century Italian nobleman who swears off a dissolute existence to spend the rest of his life in poverty and contemplation. For this inspirational tale, composer Mario

Nascimbene created a series of cues that mix broad orchestral accents and heavenly choirs in a score that sounds at times dry and cliched, but is occasionally redeemed by some lovely themes ("Chamber Music," "Building the Church," "Clare's Theme"). The mono recording evidences serious tape damage, with flutter, distortion and dropouts on some of the tracks.

Doctor Faustus, starring Richard Burton delivering his lines with the ardor that characterized some of his most theatrical performances, is another variation on the Faust legend in which the good doctor sells his soul to the Devil in exchange for youth and eternal life. Nascimbene's music, heard here in another technically deficient recording with oddly uneven stereo separation, often sounds appropriately ominous, though he did create a lovely theme for Helen that is reprised a couple of times, and also wrote a very attractive series of cues marked "Ballet," "Another Ballet," and "Music at the Court."

Didier C. Deutsch

Frank and Jesse

1994, Intrada Records, from the film *Frank and Jesse,* Trimark Pictures, 1994 💿💿💿💿

album notes: Music: Mark McKenzie; **Conductor:** Mark McKenzie.

In recent times, westerns have fallen into disfavor, and even though there have been attempts at rekindling the genre these have been few and far between. Made in 1994, *Frank and Jesse,* yet another variation on the lives of the famous James brothers, didn't meet with great success at the box office, but it enabled Mark McKenzie, scoring his third feature, to write a bold, impassioned series of cues in which the epic grandeur of the film and its most intimate moments are fully explored. Using a quintet of authentic 19th-century instruments, he created some lovely themes ("Family Moments," "The Peace Ranch") to underscore the close feelings between the siblings, relying on the fuller orchestral textures to depict the moments of action ("Marauding," "Daring Escape," "Northfield Battle"). It may not be *The Magnificent Seven* or *The Alamo,* but the score has a sweep of its own that is ultimately quite engaging.

Didier C. Deutsch

Frankenhooker

See: Basket Case 2/Frankenhooker

Frankenstein

1994, Epic Soundtrax/Sony Music, from the film *Mary Shelley's Frankenstein,* Tri-Star Pictures, 1994 💿💿💿💿

album notes: Music: Patrick Doyle; **Conductor:** David Snell

A chilling, provocative orchestral score, Patrick Doyle's music for *Mary Shelley's Frankenstein* conjures up images of a monster creation let loose in an unsuspecting world, all the more frightening that it is underplayed, as a threat that looms without speaking its name. In bold, colorful strokes, the music paints these visions, first as an idea born in the mind of a deranged scientist, then as a solid plan that eventually yields a real creature, articulate and even more dangerous as a result. A love theme, heard in fragments throughout but eventually fully developed in "The Wedding Night," brings a romantic counterpoint to the subliminal horror. It may be far from the Gothic accents invented by Franz Waxman or Hans Salter in earlier times, but the music created by Doyle is strangely, almost eerily beautiful and elegant, which is part of the fascination it exerts.

Didier C. Deutsch

Frankie & Johnny

1991, Curb Records, from the Paramount film *Frankie & Johnny,* 1991 💿💿💿

album notes: Music: Marvin Hamlisch; **Conductor:** Marvin Hamlisch.

A screen adaptation of Terrence McNally's play *Frankie & Johnny in the Clair de Lune,* this quaint little film starred Al Pacino as an ex-con trying to redeem himself and Michelle Pfeiffer as the waitress at a diner who eventually falls for him. If there was any doubt about the origins of the film, Claude Debussy's "Clair de Lune," performed by Ralph Grierson, is a dead giveaway, but a rather oblique choice in a soundtrack album that consists of contemporary tunes by the Doobie Brothers, Rickie Lee Jones, and the Rhythm. Marvin Hamlisch's instrumental score, represented here by two selections, sounds just like it should—unobtrusive and vaguely familiar.

Didier C. Deutsch

Frankie Starlight

1993, Varèse Sarabande Records, from the film *Frankie Starlight,* Fine Line Features, 1993 💿💿💿💿

album notes: Music: Elmer Bernstein; **Conductor:** Elmer Bernstein; **Featured Musician:** Cynthia Millar, ondes Martenot.

"From My Window," performed by Belinda Pigeon, which recalls some of Sondheim's best moments, effectively introduces this gorgeous soundtrack recording that finds Elmer Bernstein in a very lyrical frame of musical mind. The wistful romantic moods, explored in the main theme, "Moon," are sustained almost throughout the entire score, with gentle extrapolations that are fetching and intelligently expressive. Only occasionally does the score indulge in some more animated releases ("At Play" and "Wild Ride," with its bouncy syncopated rhythms reminiscent of some cues from *The Magnificent Seven),* which provide surprising relief and enjoyment.

Didier C. Deutsch

Frankie's House

1992, Epic Soundtrax, from the Anglia film *Frankie's House,* 1992 ♪♪♡

album notes: Music: Jeff Beck, guitars; Jed Leiber, keyboards.

If it were not for the fact that two respected rockers wrote its soundtrack, *Frankie's House* could be dismissed as a minor cinematographic effort, not worthy of anyone's attention. But you don't brush aside Jeff Beck or Jed Leiber that easily. And, indeed, when the two really get going ("Hi-Heel Sneakers," "Cathouse," "White Mice," "Innocent Victim"), there's some good rockin' to be enjoyed, although in the most reflective moments, Leiber's synthesizer effects and Beck's guitar riffs seem to suggest that their inspiration might have been cut short.

Didier C. Deutsch

Frantic

1988, Elektra Records, from the film *Frantic,* Warner Bros., 1988 ♪♪♪♪♡

album notes: Music: Ennio Morricone; **Conductor:** Ennio Morricone.

Ennio Morricone wrote a particularly effective score for this taut thriller, starring Harrison Ford, about an American doctor unwillingly drawn into a web of political intrigues while attending a convention in Paris. Underscoring the suspense in the film, the cues detail the main character's search for a truth that eludes him, with Morricone's signature rhythmic syncopations subtly conveying the tension that permeates the action. The eerie moods (strangely contrasted in "On the Roofs of Paris" by the lilt of an accordion waltz) build up to a climax that is powerfully stated in a reprise of the main theme. This soundtrack album, enhanced by the forlorn "I'm Gonna Lose You," performed by Simply Red, is both surprising and remarkably enjoyable.

Didier C. Deutsch

Freddie as F.R.O.7.

1992, Great Pyramid/JRS Records, from the Hollywood Road animated feature *Freddie as F.R.O.7.,* 1992 ♪♪♪♡

album notes: Music: David Dundas, Rick Wentworth; **Conductor:** Nick Ingman.

This could be misconstrued as yet another animated feature in search of an identity, but *non, mes amis,* this is different: this one features a French frog with ambitions to be another James Bond. Or like they say in the secret service, *ooh, la la!* The story of how an evil witch transforms a handsome prince into a frog

and how the frog prince uses his superpowers to defeat the old witch and save England's treasures is a cute device that gives a fresh spin to a tired concept (*vive la différence!).* The soundtrack also reflects this approach, with the songs handled by some heavy-duty stars (George Benson, Patti Austin, Grace Jones, the supergroup Asia). Most welcome also is the lengthy suite that, at 23:00, packs a wallop and enables the instrumental score by David Dundas and Rick Wentworth to make a strong, positive impression. Enough here to please the kiddies and their parents.

Didier C. Deutsch

Free Willy

1993, Epic Soundtrax, from the film *Free Willy,* Warner Bros., 1993 ♪♡

album notes: Music: Basil Poledouris; **Conductor:** Basil Poledouris.

This set mixes yawn-inducing instrumental music with yawn-inducing, but far more successful, vocal music. SWV's "Right Here/Human Nature" medley charted higher, but Michael Jackson's emotive "Will You Be There" is the film's theme and its most recognizable track. It could be worse; New Kids on the Block have a song on here, too.

Gary Graff

Free Willy 2

1995, Epic Soundtrax, from the film *Free Willy 2,* Warner Bros., 1995 ♪♪

album notes: Music: Basil Poledouris; **Conductor:** Shirley Walker; Basil Poledouris; **Featured Artist:** Michael Boddicker, synthesizers.

The sappy "Childhood" ("Have you seen my childhood?") crooned by Peter Pan (sorry, Michael Jackson!), introduces this sequel to the story of a child who befriends an orca, with the soundtrack album consisting mostly of similarly youth-oriented pop songs, including two not in the film, that are unlikely to get an R-rating or even an adult warning. In the mush, Basil Poledouris's score is virtually lost with only three selections that add up to 10 minutes of playing time. As usual, his music is flavorful and aggressively romantic, with great orchestral textures, but in this context who cares!

Didier C. Deutsch

Free Willy 3: The Rescue

1997, Varèse-Sarabande, from the Warner Bros. film *Free Willy 3: The Rescue,* 1997 ♪♪♪

album notes: Music: Cliff Eidelman; **Conductor:** Cliff Eidelman; **Featured Musicians:** Francine Poitras, solo voice; Mike Lang, piano.

Of course, you know the old saying: if at once you succeed, try and try again. So here we are with a third installment in the never-ending saga of Willy the whale, who has been freed twice before but still needs the help of his human friend, Jesse. This time, Willy has problems with mean, nasty whalers who ply the grounds where Willy roams. Add to this the necessary ecological message that animals have a mind, if not a soul, and there you have it—another struggle between the forces of good and evil, although in this case the antagonism is toned down, as the whalers are presented as honest people who have done this kind of work for generations and don't see why they should suddenly modify their way of living (and thinking) just because the world around them is changing. Giving a musical echo to all of this is Cliff Eidelman's lush score, which doesn't work so well on the screen, as it tends to overstate its importance, but makes a much better impression on this soundtrack album, where it doesn't distract from the stunning visuals in the film.

Didier C. Deutsch

The French Lieutenant's Woman

1981, DRG Records, from the film *The French Lieutenant's Woman*, Juniper Films, 1981 ♪♪♪♪

album notes: Music: Carl Davis; **Conductor:** Carl Davis; **Featured Musicians:** Erich Gruenber, violin; Kenneth Essex, viola; Keith Harvey, cello; John Lill, piano.

A complex film with a story-within-a-story, this adaptation by Harold Pinter of John Fowles's romantic novel strongly benefitted from Meryl Streep's extraordinary performance as a mysterious woman who befriends a French soldier in 1867 England, only to be ostracized as a result, and as the modern actress who portrays her and who has an affair with the actor (Jeremy Irons) playing an English gentleman attracted to the "French Lieutenant's woman." The screen action, teetering between the contemporary and the period love affairs, received a strong musical support from Carl Davis's effective score, with some of the cues ("Sarah's Walk," "Her Story," "Towards Love") reflecting the romantic surge in the period story, while others ("Location Lunch," "Domestic Scene," "End of Shoot Party") stressed the contemporary aspects of the film in progress.

Didier C. Deutsch

Friday the 13th: The Series

1989, GNP Crescendo; from the television series *Friday the 13th*, Paramount Television, 1989–1990 ♪♪♪♪

album notes: Music: Fred Mollin; **Featured Musicians:** Bert Hermiston, saxophone; Stan Meissner, guitar.

Over the series' three-year run, Fred Mollin somehow managed to turn out a score for each episode almost always by himself. For each, his music had to have an intricate ambience, not that "made up on the spur of the moment" feel so many synthesizers scores often have, and this album reveals several scores

that sound as orchestral as possible. Despite the series' morbid premise involving the recovery of a collection of cursed antiques, it requires a lot of personal character music, instead of the run-of-the-mill horror licks so commonly used in this format. Several of the scores featured as suites (13, naturally) on this album are from episodes where Mollin had to create some of his most inventive musical motifs. One of the best, "Badge of Honor" (naturally involving a cursed police shield) has a hard-hitting *Miami Vice*-style rock flavor augmented with several live sax solos. More classical in nature is "Symphony in B Sharp," while the theme for the children in "The Playhouse" uses a synth chorus. "Eye of Death," a time travel story set during the civil war, uses sampled period instruments. It is an excellent collection of some of Mollin's best work for television.

David Hirsch

Fried Green Tomatoes

1991, MCA Records, from the film *Fried Green Tomatoes*, Universal Pictures, 1991 ♪♪♪♪

1991, MCA Records, from the film *Fried Green Tomatoes*, Universal Pictures, 1991 ♪♪♪♪

album notes: Music: Thomas Newman; **Conductor:** Thomas Newman; **Featured Musicians:** John Beasley, piano; Michael Fisher, percussion; Jeff Elmassian, clarinet; John C. Clarke, double reeds; George Doering, guitars, mandolin.

This affecting story of life in a Southern town, and of an unsolved murder that took place years before, got much of its flavor from Thomas Newman's beautifully stated score and from the many pop songs heard on the soundtrack that both defined the locale and the given time period of the screen action. Thankfully, both are available on individual CDs, with the score detailing some of the most memorable scenes from the film, in cues that have an incredible energy and lyrical expression.

The songs, with performances by a wide range of seasoned performers (Jodeci, Paul Young, Patti LaBelle, Taylor Dayne), capture the essence of the action, and give it a palpable and recognizable frame of reference. Common to both are Marion Williams's spirited numbers which, better than most, provide an appropriate Southern flavor to the albums.

Didier C. Deutsch

Friendly Persuasion

1997, Varèse-Sarabande, from the RKO Radio film *Friendly Persuasion*, 1956 ♪♪

album notes: Music: Dimitri Tiomkin; **Conductor:** Dimitri Tiomkin.

We will have to wait somewhat longer to hear the definitive reissue of Dimitri Tiomkin's magnificent score for the William Wyler's epic saga of pacific Quakers caught in spite of themselves in the turmoil of the Civil War. While this first legal CD reissue rightfully includes Pat Boone's vocal version of the main title (which was heard in the film behind the credits, but was not included in the original LP, due to contractual restrictions), it does nothing to restore the musical cues in their screen order. As a result, the end title is inexplicably thrown in the middle of the recording, with the less than conclusive reprise of the main theme showing up at the very end of the CD. This is all the more infuriating when resequencing the cues would have taken very little time and effort. This one rates an A for the music, but a D for its sloppy presentation.

Didier C. Deutsch

Friends

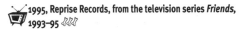 1995, Reprise Records, from the television series *Friends,* 1993–95 ✹✹✹

Despite being bookended by the main title song ("I'll Be There For You" by The Rembrandts, presented in TV and single versions), and the insertion of dialogue after every other song, this compilation has little to do with the popular series. There are a few high-powered artists here, Hootie & the Blowfish ("I Go Blind"), k.d. lang ("Sexuality"), and R.E.M. ("It's a Free World Baby"), performing some excellent songs. Many of these were previously unreleased, though I can't recall any of these songs actually being used on the show. Only a brief medley of Phoebe's songs ("Snowman/Ashes/Dead Mother") appears after track 10. Where's her famous "Smelly Cat," the song everyone remembers? Bonus track alert: The instrumental TV end title follows after a short break on the tail of track 13.

David Hirsch

The Frighteners

1996, MCA Records, from the film *The Frighteners,* Universal Pictures, 1996 ✹✹✹
album notes: Music: Danny Elfman; **Conductor:** Artie Kane.

This score can best be described as *Beetlejuice* gone bad. Portions of Elfman's early work can be heard here in the more humorous use of harpsichord and string arrangements, but because the film wasn't a comedy (though it had been promoted as such), the score was required to be much darker. Unfortunately, the result is that it isn't as fun as *Beetlejuice,* though it's still a cut or two above what anyone else might have done for a similar film. Elfman has a good sense of the absurd, something that is always obvious in much of his other genre work, but this score can boast some genuinely creepy passages, too. The album includes "Don't Fear the Reaper" performed by The Mutton Birds.

David Hirsch

From Dusk Till Dawn

1996, Epic Soundtrax, from the film *From Dusk Till Dawn,* Miramax Films, 1996 ✹✹✹
album notes: Music: Graeme Revell.

If truth be told, you never know what to expect when you listen to a soundtrack album. For example, this compilation put together for a martial arts and vampire film rolled into one, includes headliners like The Blasters, ZZ Top, Stevie Ray Vaughan, and The Mavericks, among others. Not bad, except that the tunes they perform aren't necessarily big hits for them, just run-of-the-mill numbers that have their genuine moments of flash. Throughout, sound bites prove intriguing, if nothing else. And how about a song called "Texas Funeral" performed (spoken ?) by Jon Wayne (no! not the actor, even though many of the tracks here border on the country genre, but check the spelling of the name . . .). It all adds up to a definitely strange but compelling album.

Didier C. Deutsch

From Russia with Love

1995, EMI-America, from the film *From Russia with Love,* United Artists, 1963 ✹✹✹✹
album notes: Music: John Barry; **Lyrics:** Lionel Bart; **Conductor:** John Barry.

Another monster James Bond score signed by John Barry, and probably his most effective effort in the genre. The score, powered by the almost exclusive use of brass and percussion instruments, has an urgency and drive that seldom lessens and wonderfully captures the excitement in the film. A mandatory vocal, performed with great gusto by Matt Monro (a pleasant change from Shirley Bassey's over-the-top performances of "Goldfinger" and "Diamonds are Forever"), adds an extra zing to the album.

Didier C. Deutsch

From the Earth to the Moon

1998, Epic Records, from the HBO Television miniseries *From the Earth to the Moon,* 1998 ✹✹✹✹
album notes: Music: Michael Kamen.

Michael Kamen's epic theme to this TV miniseries about space exploration is but one of the many assets to be enjoyed in this soundtrack album. A collection of great pop tracks, it also offers selections by the Byrds, Donovan, the Who, Lovin' Spoonful, the Archies, Steppenwolf, Wilson Pickett, the Shirelles, and Bobby Darin, all of whom have seldom been found together. The songs are familiar and have long been part of our subconscious, but it's always a pleasure to rediscover them. How they relate to the action is another matter altogether, but when the program is this good, who cares!

Didier C. Deutsch

Frozen Assets

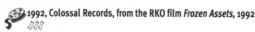1992, Colossal Records, from the RKO film *Frozen Assets,* 1992 ♫♫♫

album notes: Music: Michael Tavera; **Conductor:** Michael Tavera.

Shelley Long starred in this amusing little comedy about a corporate executive who thinks he's hit the jackpot when he is asked to become the president of a bank in Hobart, Oregon, only to find out that the institution in question is a sperm bank. Newcomer Michael Tavera scored this one, developing cues that are enjoyably poppish, and adding his talent to crafting some pop-rock songs that are quietly listenable. And if you want to hear kids singing "The Sperm Count Song" to the tune of "When the Saints Go Marching in," believe it or not it's also here.

Didier C. Deutsch

The Fugitive

1993, Elektra Records, from the film *The Fugitive,* Warner Bros., 1993 ♫♫♫♫

album notes: Music: James Newton Howard; **Conductor:** Marty Paich; **Featured Musicians:** Wayne Shorter, soprano sax; Chuck Domanico, acoustic bass; James Newton Howard, piano.

Harrison Ford, playing another victim of circumstances on the run from justice, has one of his better screen roles in this big screen remake of the eponymous early 1960s television series. Adding a specific flavor of its own to the action, James Newton Howard wrote a series of cues that spell it out while providing an extra dramatic anchor to it. The tension in the drama comes out particularly effectively in the cues marked "Helicopter Chase," "Subway Fight," and "Stairway Chase," in which the taut orchestral textures echo the gripping screen visuals. The more subliminal accents in some of the other selections, notably "Kimble Dyes His Hair" and "Sykes's Apartment," with their faint ominous tones presaging some forthcoming dangers to the hero, are equally effective. The main theme, a delicate duet between a piano and a soprano sax (James Newton Howard and Wayne Shorter), is yet another expressive track.

Didier C. Deutsch

Full Circle:
The Haunting of Julia

1995, Koch Screen, from the Fetter Productions/Classic film *Full Circle,* 1978 ♫♫♫♫

album notes: Music: Colin Towns; **Featured Musicians:** Graham Ashton, trumpet; Phil Todd, baritone sax.

It's amazing how, in the hands of a good composer, a score may become something one might want to listen to several times, and enjoy every time. Written for *The Haunting of Julia,* a film made in 1976, starring Mia Farrow and Keir Dullea, and eventually released as *Full Circle,* Colin Towns's score quietly explores the less mundane aspects of this eerie story about a young woman who has recently lost her infant and moves into a new home apparently haunted by the ghost of a young child. Towns, better known in this country for the music he created for the British series *Cadfael,* wrote themes that are directly simple and unaffected ("Have You Got a Magnificent Problem"), often featuring the single voice of a piano, with an occasional sprinkle of synthesized sounds (sometimes running backwards) to provide an extra dose of eeriness. It's quietly effective, and listenable by the same token. The recording also includes two other non-soundtrack compositions, a concerto for trumpet and string orchestra, and "1930 Cityscape," an atmospheric piece for baritone sax and orchestra that sometimes recalls Morton Gould or Leonard Bernstein.

Didier C. Deutsch

Full Metal Jacket

1987, Warner Bros. Records, from the film *Full Metal Jacket,* Warner Bros., 1987 ♫♫♫

album notes: Music: Abigail Mead.

A somewhat random collection of 1960s classics and instrumental pieces composed for the film. At least the songs— "Surfin' Bird," "I Like It Like That," "These Boots Are Made for Walking"—aren't titles that usually show up in films. The original score is pretty blah, however.

Gary Graff

The Full Monty

1998, RCA Victor, from the Fox Searchlight film *The Full Monty,* 1997 ♫♫♫

album notes: Music: Anne Dudley; **Conductor:** Anne Dudley.

Anne Dudley's excellent score is somewhat wasted in this soundtrack album in which it is only represented by two selections, lost between a collection of super dynamic dance tracks, featuring performances by Hot Chocolate, Tom Jones, Wilson Pickett, Donna Summer, Irene Cara, and Gary Glitter, among others. The story, about working-class men becoming a hot sensation when they join a dance contest and reveal the full monty, was comfortably entertaining and got a serious publicity boost when Prince Charles, not given to such unregal manifestations, actually joined the actors in a demonstration on how to dance. In all its multiple pop aspects, the album is quite enjoyable.

Didier C. Deutsch

Fun in Acapulco

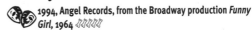

1993, RCA Records from the film *Fun in Acapulco,* Paramount Pictures, 1963 🎬🎬

Exotic locales and Ursula Andress were the main lures in *Fun In Acapulco,* released in 1963, in which Elvis performed "Bossa Nova Baby," the only hit to emerge from the 11 numbers heard in the film. In it, Elvis portrayed a sailor, a trapeze artist, a lifeguard, and, in a spectacular scene, a cliff diver (though he did not perform the stunt himself).

Didier C. Deutsch

The Funeral

1996, Critique Records, from the film *The Funeral,* October Films, 1996 🎬🎬🎬

When a mafia boss is gunned down, his death brings together his brothers, who are determined to find his killer and avenge him. This Prohibition-period crime drama, filmed by Abel Ferrara, received a smart soundtrack album, thanks to the selection of recordings from the era that have been compiled for the occasion. Opening up the proceedings is Carlo Buti's "Il primo amore," which is the only reference to the Italian background of the story. The other tracks include performances by Coleman Hawkins, Bunny Berigan, Benny Goodman, Duke Ellington, Erskine Hawkins, and Artie Shaw, among others. Surprisingly, however, the Billie Holiday song that anchored the film and situated its time period more strongly than any other is noticeably absent from this otherwise flavorful compilation.

Didier C. Deutsch

Funny Face

1996, Verve Records, from the film *Funny Face,* Paramount Pictures, 1956 🎬🎬🎬

album notes: Music: George Gershwin; **Lyrics:** Ira Gershwin; **Orchestra:** The Paramount Studio Orchestra; **Choir:** The Paramount Studio Chorus; **Conductor:** Adolph Deutsch; **Cast:** Fred Astaire, Audrey Hepburn, Kay Thompson.

Utilizing five songs written by the Gershwin brothers for the 1927 stage show of the same name, including the title tune, plus material provided by Roger Edens and Leonard Gershe, on loan from MGM, *Funny Face* was a delightful screen musical that owed much of its charm to the presence of Audrey Hepburn. Hepburn is delicious as a Greenwich Village bookstore operator who is spirited away to Paris by a famous fashion photographer and becomes a top model, though her one objective is to meet the guru of Empathicalism, a new philosophical movement. Strikingly lensed in the French capital, and with the action smoothly integrating its various musical numbers, the *film a clef* (in which Fred Astaire's Avery was a stand-in for

Richard Avedon, who worked on the film as visual consultant, and Michel Auclair's Professor Flostre was a thinly disguised screen image of Jean-Paul Sartre) gave Astaire ample opportunities to show his undiminished talents as a dancer and singer. Astaire spends much of the film either wooing Audrey Hepburn or sharing the spotlight with Kay Thompson, hilariously cast as a no-nonsense top magazine editor. Unfortunately, the CD soundtrack is in mono, and only replicates the original album the way it was initially released in 1957, without any extras.

Didier C. Deutsch

Funny Girl

1994, Angel Records, from the Broadway production *Funny Girl,* 1964 🎬🎬🎬🎬

album notes: Music: Jule Styne; **Lyrics:** Bob Merrill; **Musical Direction:** Milton Rosenstock; **Cast:** Barbra Streisand, Sydney Chaplin, Kay Medford, Jean Stapleton.

1968, Columbia Records, from the film *Funny Girl,* Columbia Pictures, 1964 🎬🎬🎬🎬

album notes: Music: Jule Styne; **Lyrics:** Bob Merrill; **Musical Direction:** Walter Scharf; **Cast:** Barbra Streisand, Omar Sharif, Kay Medford, Mae Questel,.

The story of vaudeville comedian Fanny Brice, her rise to stardom in the Ziegfeld Follies, her emotional involvement with gangster Nick Arnstein, and the eventual break-up of their marriage provided the strong dramatic elements for a musical by Isobel Lennart, with a sensational score by Jule Styne and Bob Merrill. More specifically, it also launched the career of Barbra Streisand, as Fanny Brice, in one of the theatre's legendary portrayals. The show, which opened March 26, 1964, to rave reviews, yielded many hit tunes, all performed by the nascent star, including "Don't Rain On My Parade," "The Music That Makes Me Dance," "I'm The Greatest Star," and "People," which, alone, became a standard for an entire generation. Though it failed to receive a Tony Award (*Hello, Dolly!* was the big winner that year), *Funny Girl* enjoyed a long run of 1,348 performances. Streisand went on to star in the film version, which added to the score two songs associated with Fanny Brice, "I'd Rather Be Blue Over You" and "My Man." Both the original cast and the soundtrack albums are worthy additions to any musical collection. The former features Streisand at the peak of her talent, in a portrayal that has not yet become stilted, with Sydney Chaplin appropriately suave as Nick Arnstein, and Kay Medford and Jean Stapleton in supporting roles.

The soundtrack album, overblown and sounding more elaborate than its stage counterpart, substitutes Omar Sharif as Nick Arnstein, but drops several tunes from the show, adding the two cover songs, as well as "Roller Skate Rag," "The Swan," and "Funny Girl," written specifically for the film. By then, Streisand had become a superstar, and her portrayal, while outstanding, also seemed less fresh and genuine than in the original.

Didier C. Deutsch

Funny Lady

1998, Arista, from the Columbia Pictures film *Funny Lady*, 1975 ♪♪♪♪

album notes: Cast: Barbra Streisand, James Caan, Ben Vereen, Omar Sharif.

Barbra Streisand reprised her Academy Award–winning role of Fanny Brice in this sequel to *Funny Girl*, in which Fanny is divorced from Nicky (Omar Sharif) and sees the Depression threaten her career at the Ziegfield Follies. The film gave her an opportunity to sing standards initially created by Fanny Brice ("Am I Blue," "Great Day," "If I Love Again," and "I Found a Million Dollar Baby," among others) and new songs written by John Kander and Fred Ebb. Although others, notably James Caan and Ben Vereen, were featured in the film and in the soundtrack recording, both showcased la Streisand, who rose to the challenge with her usual confidence and dynamic presence. This CD reissue, remastered and sequenced to follow the action on the screen, also features the single mix of "How Lucky Can You Get," as a bonus track.

Beth Krakower

A Funny Thing Happened on the Way to the Forum

1993, Angel Records, from the Broadway production *A Funny Thing Happened on the Way to the Forum*, 1962 ♪♪♪♪

album notes: Music: Stephen Sondheim; **Lyrics:** Stephen Sondheim; **Musical Direction:** Harold Hastings; **Cast:** Zero Mostel, David Burns, Ruth Kobart, Brian Davies, Jack Gilford, John Carradine, Ronald Holgate.

1996, Angel Records, from the Broadway revival *A Funny Thing Happened on the Way to the Forum*, 1996 ♪♪♪

album notes: Music: Stephen Sondheim; **Lyrics:** Stephen Sondheim; **Musical Direction:** Edward Strauss; **Cast:** Nathan Lane, Lewis J. Stadlen, Mary Testa, Jim Stanek, Mark Linn-Baker, Ernie Sabella, Cris Groenendaal.

Something appealing, nothing appalling, something for, well, almost everyone . . . Stephen Sondheim's first music-and-lyrics Broadway outing endures as well as the jokes in this ancient-Rome-meets-Larry Gelbart farce, a favorite through the years and the show that made Zero Mostel a Broadway star. Mostel "acts" superbly on the original cast album recording, as do co-clowns Jack Gilford, David Burns and John Carradine. Performances of several discarded songs–including the lovely "Love is in the Air"–can be found on various Sondheim CD collections. (Serious collectors–and British listeners–may also want

to seek out EMI/Angel's original London cast recording, also available on CD, starring Frankie Howerd.)

The 1996 revival waited a couple of years for Nathan Lane, and he's fine here, as are fellow jokesters Mark Linn-Baker, Lewis J. Stadlen, and Mary Testa, so why does this technically flawless recording lack the impact of the original? The CD captures valuable bits of dialogue and re-expands several of the songs from the '62 cast album; but here, as in math class, you can't divide by Zero. Unique to this CD is the spoken-and-sung "House of Marcus Lycus," which provides the same strange thrill as hearing someone describe a copy of *Playboy*. The recording producer, Phil Ramone, was also kind enough to restore the essential "Pretty Little Picture," although it was absent from this stage production.

Marc Kirkeby

The Fury

1989, Varèse Sarabande, from the film *The Fury*, 20th Century-Fox, 1978 ♪♪♪♪

album notes: Music: John Williams; **Orchestra:** The London Symphony Orchestra; **Conductor:** John Williams.

The Fury is a dark score, underlining the psychic horror of Brian de Palma's telekinetic terror film with a haunting orchestration. Built around a slow, waltz-like main theme, using the same kind of ascending/descending triads that characterized Bernard Herrmann's score for *Vertigo*, Williams's music develops into a stunning, powerful work, dominated by brass that emphasizes and embellishes de Palma's omnipresent mood of surreal gloom and terrifying apprehension. Interestingly, the CD (like its previous LP incarnation) isn't the original soundtrack but a much-improved rerecording done by Williams and the London Symphony, which includes a four-and-a-half minute epilogue that reconstructs all the score's themes into a thunderous and profound final statement. The CD also includes an additional cue not on the original LP, an alternate version of "Death on the Carousel."

Randall D. Larson

Gaby

1997, LaserLight, from the TriStar film *Gaby*, 1987 ♪♪♪♪

album notes: Music: Maurice Jarre.

Any score by Maurice Jarre is a cause for celebration (well, almost! I can think of at least one score that doesn't fit the de scription), and particularly when it is a score that had not been released previously. Such is the case with *Gaby,* composed in 1987 for a film based on the true story of Gaby Brimmer, who was born with severe cerebral palsy, but overcame the terrible odds against her to becomes a famous writer and poet in Mexico. Starring Liv Ullman, Robert Loggia, and Rachael Leah Levin in the title role, the film inspired Jarre to write a score of enormous musical merit, in which the mix of synthesizers and acoustic instruments creates a nostalgic, wistful atmosphere. The cues detail the screen action and need little explanation, but the themes, which bear the composer's unmistakable signature, add up to a colorful display that is most attractive and enjoyable.

Didier C. Deutsch

The Game

1997, London, from the PolyGram film *The Game,* 1997 ♫♫♫♫

album notes: Music: Howard Shore; **Conductor:** Howard Shore.

A chilling, often unsettling drama, *The Game* involved an investment banker living in San Francisco and the ruleless unusual "entertainment" in which he finds himself drawn after his younger brother gives him the gift of a key to a firm called Consumer Recreation Services. But things are not exactly what they seemed to be, and the banker, used to have things his own way, suddenly finds out that he is no longer in control and that the "game" may actually be deadly. Adding a slowly terrifying edge to the proceedings, Howard Shore's deliberately somber score informs some of the most striking moments in the film and provides a vivid musical description of the disintegration of the banker's well-organized life as well as his callous character. Ultimately, the claustrophobic effects created reflect the film's entire atmosphere in a perfect matching of visuals and underscoring.

Didier C. Deutsch

Game of Death/Night Games

1993, Silva Screen Records, from the films *Game of Death,* 1973, and *Night Games,* Next Decade Entertainment, 1979 ♫♫♫♫♪
album notes: Music: John Barry; **Conductor:** John Barry.

John Barry delivers the punches (make that the chops and the kicks) in the first score for the movie that starred Bruce Lee shortly before his untimely death, and strikes a diffidently erotic note in the second, a sex fantasy directed by Roger Vadim. *Bruce Lee's Game of Death* actually found the composer in great verve, exploring the possibilities of scoring a martial arts film with all the colorful musical resources at his disposal. That he largely succeeded is a credit to his creativity as a film

composer with few peers in the business. The tracks, which sometimes evoke some of Barry's best efforts in the thriller genre in the late 1960s, blend percussive action cues and lovingly detailed romantic expressions in a score that has great strength and vitality. Best are "Garden Fight" and "The Big Motorcycle Fight," among the former, and "Billy's Funeral Dirge" and "Billy and Ann's Love Theme," among the latter. A "Stick Fight" (with sound effects) provides additional fun.

Though *Night Games* is, by all critical accounts, a total disaster and an "insult to adult minds," to quote one reviewer, Barry's music easily soars above the most pedestrian aspects of the film to create an elegant and erotic evocation. Three longer cues ("Descent into Decadence," "Water Sports/The Dominatrix's Waltz," and "Phantom of the Orgasm") are particularly striking with their deft blend of long, melodic lines, occasionally supported by a wordless choir. "The Lesbian Tango," with its slow, exotically syncopated rhythms, is a lot of fun.

see also: Dragon: The Bruce Lee Story

Didier C. Deutsch

Garden of Evil

1998, Marco Polo Records, from the 20th Century-Fox film *Garden of Evil,* 1954 ♫♫♫♫♫
album notes: Music: Bernard Herrmann; **Conductor:** William T. Stromberg.

Since the recent interest in film music reached its paroxysm, collectors and fans have been clamoring for a recording of Bernard Herrmann's adventure score for the 1954 western *Garden of Evil,* which starred Gary Cooper, Susan Hayward, and Richard Widmark. Thanks to film historian John W. Morgan and conductor William T. Stromberg, here it is, magnificently played by the Moscow Symphony Orchestra, in a superlative recording that would have made the composer proud. As Christopher Husted explains in his informative notes, the score for *Garden of Evil* is particularly remarkable in that Herrmann wrote it for a symphony orchestra and nine percussionists. Aware of the advantages offered by stereophony, then in its early stages of development on a grand scale (it had existed since before the 1940s, but had just found its first useful application with the creation of the CinemaScope anamorphic process), Herrmann fully explored its use by carefully planning microphone placements in order to emphasize the effect created by the sudden juxtapositions of mosaic forms that he favored, as well as using reverb to enhance some of the brass chords, resulting in what he described as a "windy sound." All of this is pretty much in evidence in the present recording, which includes all the cues he composed for the film, from the peaceful and serene ("Nocturne," "The Church," "Night Scene") to the active and violent

("The Quarrel," "The Wild Party," "The Chase"). It all results in a highly vibrant score, made even more exciting by the excellent playing Stromberg gets from his musicians. The recording is complemented with a suite from the biographical drama *Prince of Players*, also from 1954.

Didier C. Deutsch

Gattaca

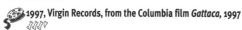 1997, Virgin Records, from the Columbia film *Gattaca*, 1997 ♪♪♪♪

album notes: Music: Michael Nyman; **Conductor:** Michael Nyman.

Gattaca, the elite academy for astronauts, disqualifies a most avid prospect, their janitor Eugene, due to his inferior DNA in this cross between *Good Will Hunting* and the caste system of *Brave New World*. Michael Nyman's score to this stylish sci-fi thriller leaves listeners wondering what took him so long to apply his otherworldly mix of minimal and lushly romantic music to future worlds. In order to fulfill his desire to travel into space, Eugene adopts the identity of the perfect candidate whose theme, a classy piano sonata, contrasts drastically with Eugene's pastoral string music. Eugene's constant state of tension under the most scrutinizing searches is reflected in endlessly repeated musical phrases that never resolve themselves. Gattaca's high fashion, retro cars, and sleek, austere film set are well-matched by Nyman's minimal palette, already honed through his stylized collaborations with director Peter Greenaway. At the sight of a love interest, wistful strings well up, yet throughout the film Eugene's fears, hopes, and desires are tightly contained in a relentless, solemn progression that struggles to stifle a richly romantic underscore. Unfortunately, while *Gattaca* looks great, it lacks substance. Nyman's music added mythic depth to poorly developed characters and stands alone as one of his strongest scores.

David Poole

The General

 1998, Milan Records, from the Sony Pictures Classics film *The General*, 1998 ♪♪♪♪

album notes: Music: Richie Buckley; **Featured Musicians:** Richie Buckley, saxophone; Mick Kinsella, Philip King, harmonica; Dick Buckley, baritone sax; Stephen McDonnell, trumpet, flugel; Michael Buckley, alto flute, tenor sax; Karl Ronan, trombone; Carl Geraghty, baritone sax; Ronan Dooney, trumpet, flugel; Paul McAteer, drums; Bernard Reilly, percussion; Pat Fitzpatrick, Brian Connor, piano/keyboards; Robbie Overson, Arty McGlynn, electric guitar/ acoustic guitar; the Wind Machine, brass section.

Directed by John Boorman (of *Deliverance* and *The Emerald Forest* fame), *The General* detailed the real-life exploits of a legendary freedom fighter, Martin Cahill, who was the mastermind behind a series of daring robberies that stunned Ireland in the

1980s. In a 20-year career that was marked by obsessive secrecy, brutality, and meticulous planning, he stole the equivalent of $60 million, brazenly eluding capture and thumbing his nose at both the police and the IRA, whom he despised—along with the church and the state—as institutional authority figures. In a decision that ran against the norm, Boorman selected Richie Buckley to write a jazz score for his film, with the renowned Irish saxophonist fronting a large band of seasoned performers, providing a music that's compelling and totally enjoyable. Reflecting the most striking moments in the action, the score also assumes a life of its own on this CD, which should delight anyone interested in a smooth jazz sound and catchy tunes.

Didier C. Deutsch

Genocide

🎬 1993, Intrada Records, from the film *Genocide,* MCEG Sterling, 1981 🎬🎬🎬

album notes: Music: Elmer Bernstein; **Orchestra:** The Royal Philharmonic Orchestra; **Conductor:** Elmer Bernstein.

An Academy Award-winner as Best Documentary Feature, *Genocide,* narrated by Elizabeth Taylor and introduced by Simon Wiesenthal, was one more attempt at illustrating and trying to explain the extermination of Jews during World War II. For this moving account, Elmer Bernstein wrote an appropriately somber score, with some cues, like "A Convenient Enemy," "Dachau," and "Slaughter," exploring in musical terms the unexplainable. Even the more exuberant last tracks fail to shake the dark moods that linger long after the music has stopped.

Didier C. Deutsch

Gentlemen Don't Eat Poets

🎬 1997, Pangea Records, from the film *Gentlemen Don't Eat Poets,* Live Entertainment, 1997 🎬🎬🎬🎬

album notes: Music: Anne Dudley; **Conductor:** Anne Dudley; **Featured Musician:** Phil Todd, saxophone.

This clever period piece about a poet, with whom an uppercrust English girl falls in love, and the effects this dalliance has on the family, serves as the departing point for Anne Dudley's stylish score, in which bits of dialogue set up some of the cues, providing the extra dramatic touch that makes them all the more enjoyable. In the middle of all the expansive romantic cues the composer created, a bouncy "Jiving and Jamming" brings a different, albeit welcome, switch in genres that proves surprising and delightful at the same time. A breathy vocal by Sting, who also appears in the film, is quite satisfying in its own right.

Didier C. Deutsch

Gentlemen Prefer Blondes

🎬 1991, Sony Broadway, from the Broadway production *Gentlemen Prefer Blondes,* 1949 🎬🎬🎬🎬

album notes: Music: Jule Styne; **Lyrics:** Leo Robin; **Musical Direction:** Milton Rosenstock; **Cast:** Carol Channing, Yvonne Adair, Jack Mc-Cauley, Eric Brotherson, Rex Evans, Honi Coles, George S. Irving.

Carol Channing, portraying a quintessential 1920s gold-digger, became a star in *Gentlemen Prefer Blondes,* the droll, fictional tale of two dizzy American flappers and their search to nail down the right man, preferably one with a large bank account, based on a short story by Anita Loos. Sporting a brilliant score by Jule Styne and Leo Robin, the musical, which opened on Dec. 8, 1949, had a run of 740 performances, and with many alterations (including the deletion of all but three of the songs from the stage show) became the first starring vehicle for Marilyn Monroe in 1953. In its stage treatment, the song-and-dance extravaganza followed the outline of its original source story, and focused on Lorelei Lee, a "little girl from Little Rock," and her friend from the Follies, Dorothy Shaw, as they embark on a transatlantic trip to Europe, a gift from Lorelei's generous "sugar daddy," a button tycoon. On board the *Ile de France,* both Lorelei and Dorothy meet various suitably accommodating gentlemen, with Lorelei the center of interest for several of them. The show gave Carol Channing the right opportunity to display her flair for comedy in a portrayal that has remained legendary in the annals of the musical theatre. The score, replete with many excellent numbers, yielded the hits "A Little Girl From Little Rock," and "Diamonds Are A Girl's Best Friend."

Beth Krakower

Georgia

🎬 1995, Discovery, from the CIBY 2000 film *Georgia,* 1995 🎬🎬🎬🎬

The revelation on *Georgia* is co-star Mare Winningham, whose seasoning as both a writer and performer came to light in this film about sibling rivalry and co-dependency. Playing the milquetoasty folk-rock star Sadie, Winningham's sweet vocals shine on numbers such as Stephen Foster's "Hard Times," "Mercy," and "If I Wanted," a duet with co-star Jennifer Jason Leigh that Winnigham co-wrote. However, the film is called *Georgia,* and since that's Jason Leigh's character, that's who we mostly get here. Her performance in the film is dynamite—particularly how she so expertly captures Georgia's exuberant but "not ready for prime time" talent on aching renditions of Gladys Knight & the Pips' "Midnight Train to Georgia" and Elvis Costello's "Almost Blue." Unfortunately, taking the vision of her doing this out of the equation doesn't help *Georgia* as a listening experience, so it's left to Winningham and John Doe, as well as to tracks by Van Morrison and Jimmy Witherspoon, to keep this set above water.

Gary Graff

Geronimo

🎬 1993, Columbia, from the film *Geronimo: An American Legend,* Columbia Pictures, 1993 🎬🎬🎬🎬

album notes: Music: Ry Cooder; **Conductor:** George S. Clinton.

Ry Cooder's appropriately authentic score, with the considerable support of Indian music and chants, serves as a colorful backdrop for this account of the life story of the great Apache warrior. With Cooder's usual contingent of sidemen and associates (among them David Lindley, prominently featured on mandolin and bouzouki, and Van Dyke Parks, who provided some of the orchestrations) contributing their talent, the music establishes its own standards and creates in relatively short time the moods that pervade the whole score. The clash between two cultures and two different sets of forces is fully explored in cues in which the Native American music is contrasted with the martial fife and drum accents of the federal armies. A rich and unusual score that requires closer attention than most to endear itself, *Geronimo: An American Legend* may well be one of Cooder's best efforts to date.

Didier C. Deutsch

Get Carter

1998, Cinephile/U.K., from the film *Get Carter*, MGM 1970
♫♫♫♫

album notes: Music: Roy Budd; **Featured Musicians:** Roy Budd, piano; Chris Karan, drums, percussion, tablas; Jeff Cline, double bass, bass guitar; Brian Daly, guitar; Judd Proctor, guitar.

A superlative action thriller starring Michael Caine as a London hood bent on avenging his brother's death, *Get Carter* resulted in a fast-moving film, smartly propelled along by Roy Budd's score, a mix of jazz and contemporary pop, whose main theme, "Carter Takes a Train," set the mood for much of what followed. Setting off the selections in this CD, bits of dialogue that are interspersed throughout place each track in its own dramatic perspective and enable the listener to better appreciate the role the music itself played in the development of the plot, either commenting on it or stressing specific moments in it. The sparse trio format used for some tracks further enhances the direct impact of the music itself, with the unusual addition of a few bars on the harpsichord being both innovative and effectively surprising.

see also: The Black Windmill, Diamonds, Fear Is the Key, Paper Tiger, Sinbad and the Eye of the Tiger

Didier C. Deutsch

Get Smart

1996, Raven/Australia, from the TV series *Get Smart*, 1967–69
woof!

Would you believe a comedy album starring this bumbling idiot of a secret agent, Maxwell Smart? Would you believe, complete with a television laugh track? Would you believe it's not very funny? And what if they had left the audio tracks off and just kept the pictures? And would you believe it comes all the way from Australia? Ah ah! Argh!

Didier C. Deutsch

Get Yourself a College Girl

1992, Sony Music Special Products, from the film *Get Yourself a College Girl*, MGM, 1964 ♫♫♫

Sad to say, but MGM, which for many years had dominated the screen musical genre with productions that set the standards

for the entire industry, found itself releasing films like *Get Yourself a College Girl* in the 1960s, in imitation of works produced (the term is a generous one) by other studios. An inane campus comedy, *Get Yourself . . .* concerned a college student, Mary Ann Mobley (Miss America of 1959), who gets into trouble for writing "sophisticated" songs and spends the ensuing 80 minutes trying to get out of the mess in a film that also stars Nancy Sinatra. One of the film's redeeming values is its soundtrack, sprinkled with "in" songs, performed by an interesting lineup of talent, including The Dave Clark Five, The Animals, Freddie Bell & The Bell Boys, for the bubble-gum trade, and Stan Getz, the Jimmy Smith Trio, and Astrud Gilberto, for their elders. The title tune, delivered in a clear-sounding vocal by Mary Ann Mobley herself, unfortunately sets the intellectual tone for much of the album.

Didier C. Deutsch

Getting Even with Dad

1994, Private Music, from the film *Getting Even with Dad*, MGM, 1994 ♫♫♫

album notes: Music: Miles Goodman; **Conductor:** Miles Goodman.

The many early rock and blues songs heard on the first tracks of this soundtrack album exude a raucous flavor that seems to be missing in Miles Goodman's musical cues. Some of the selections ("The Coin Heist," "The Aquarium," "Getting Closer to Dad") are perhaps more reflective of some of the sentiments expressed in this comedy, about a kid who tries to steer his father, a small-time con artist, in the right direction, but, as is often the case in the genre, music and screen action are sometimes so intimately integrated that once they are separated, the music makes much less sense. But the pop selections are terrific!

Didier C. Deutsch

Gettysburg

1993, Milan Records, from the film *Gettysburg*, New Line Cinema, 1993 ♫♫♫

album notes: Music: Randy Edelman; **Conductor:** Randy Edelman.

Randy Edelman's broad score for this epic Civil War adventure is a vast tribute to the drama and tragedy of the battle that inspired Abraham Lincoln's ageless memorial address. While a couple of traditional cues appear, the score is derived primarily from Edelman's heroic main theme, which gives the score a hugeness befitting the historical battle and its widescreen depiction. Thunderous orchestrations, rendered intimate by acoustic guitar, speak eloquently for the soldiers who fought on both sides. Synths merged with symphs lend the main theme a timeless grace as well as a tone of extreme despondence. Even though the story depicts the savagery of warfare, its primary focus remains the people involved in those battles. The score nobly follows suit. "Battle of Little Round Top," for example, is given a slow, surging undercurrent that runs throughout the scene. Rather then matching the action, Edelman attempts to reflect the feeling of the scene. Even within the dissonance of "The First Battle," with its rousing conflagration of rhythmic strings and synths and rapid strokes of drum and violin, the main theme sounds solid amid the fury of activity—capturing the spirit and heart of those so viciously engaged. And, after the fury is spent, Edelman's theme sounds tender on acoustic guitar, a splendidly intimate paean to the heroes fallen.

Randall D. Larson

Ghost

 1995, Milan Records, from the film *Ghost,* Paramount Pictures, 1990 🎬🎬

album notes: Music: Maurice Jarre; **Conductor:** Maurice Jarre.

Maurice Jarre created a love theme that balances between two emotional extremes, the intense love of a young couple and the sense of sadness felt when Sam (Patrick Swayze) is murdered. The intense bond of the lovers keeps Sam's spirit earthbound until he can find a way to save Molly (Demi Moore) from the same fate. This theme is, however, completely overshadowed by the use of The Righteous Brothers' recording of "Unchained Melody" (composed by Alex North) which, for the film-going public, became *Ghost*'s signature tune. Jarre's instrumental version of "Unchained Melody" is surprisingly busy with studio noise, perhaps because he realized the uphill battle he was saddled with and resented having to record the theme. His own love theme is also played orchestrally to contrast with the flurry of electronic effects that represent the darkness of the "other side." This gloomy mood unfortunately makes up the bulk of the album, so it's disappointing that *Ghost* is not as overly romantic in nature as one would expect. The 1995 reissue of the album contains two additional, but unremarkable, electronic underscore tracks.

David Hirsch

The Ghost and Mrs. Muir

1985, Varèse Sarabande, from the film *The Ghost and Mrs. Muir,* 20th Century-Fox, 1947 🎬🎬🎬🎬

album notes: Music: Bernard Herrmann; **Conductor:** Elmer Bernstein.

In the 1970s, composer Elmer Bernstein created a club for fans of film music, and at their behest began to record significant scores from the past that had not been available or that were in serious danger of totally disappearing. While many of these recordings are still awaiting reissue on compact disc, this rendition of Bernard Herrmann's wonderfully lovely statement for

Joseph L. Mankiewicz's 1947 light fantasy fortunately was released by Varèse Sarabande, and should be sought by anyone with a strong interest in good film music or, more generally speaking, in anything Herrmann ever composed. The most striking character of Herrmann's score is that he avoided any otherwordly effect that might have seemed too obvious. Instead, he concentrated on creating a musical canvas that relied on attractive orchestral textures, sometimes pared down to only a few instruments, at other times using the full contingent of players. Making his music even more accessible, many of the shorter cues have been brought together, making the selections more comprehensive and musically more pungent.

Didier C. Deutsch

The Ghost and the Darkness

1996, Hollywood Records, from the film *The Ghost and the Darkness,* Paramount Pictures, 1996 🎬🎬🎬🎬

album notes: Music: Jerry Goldsmith; **Orchestra:** The National Philharmonic Orchestra of London; **Conductor:** Jerry Goldsmith.

Although Goldsmith's mix of Irish, African, and British Colonial elements in his opening theme is disappointingly literal, the bulk of *The Ghost and the Darkness* makes for one of the composer's best works of the 1990s: a beautiful, flowing score with some amazingly powerful moments, especially when the composer brings in a vivid Hindu chant over his orchestra. Goldsmith's fluid, evocative electronic effects include a repeated breathing effect for the film's man-eating lions, some striking synthesized choral effects, and slashing mixes of vocal effects and animal sounds for the lion attacks. The style of orchestral writing sometimes recalls John Barry in its use of brass, but Goldsmith brings his unmistakable experimentation to the process and the result is probably the composer's most enjoyable album of the the decade.

Jeff Bond

Ghost Story

1990, Varèse Sarabande Records, from the film *Ghost Story,* Universal Picture, 1981 🎬🎬🎬🎬

album notes: Music: Philippe Sarde.

Just about the only memorable element of John Irwin's 1981 supernatural thriller is Phillipe Sarde's deliciously creepy score—a delirious Halloween treat from its opening, spidery double bass chords to the wailing solo soprano "ghost" melody interspersed throughout its cues. There are pounding, percussive chase cues, Grand Guignol-style horror underscoring that includes blasting brass exclamations and pipe organ chords, and a wonderful "danse macabre" ("The House") of scratchy, Stravinsky-esque fiddle, piano, spinet, and celeste. The score leads inevitably from sunny treatments of its gentle love theme down the primrose

Demi Moore and Patrick Swayze in Ghost. (The Kobal Collection)

path to mournful regret and horror, mixing moments of lovely sincerity with a traditional horror movie approach that's so lovably purple you won't know whether to scream or laugh.

Jeff Bond

Ghostbusters II

🎬 1989, MCA Records, from the film *Ghostbusters II*, Columbia Pictures, 1989 ♪♪♪

This sequel set has the distinction of reuniting Bobby Brown and New Edition—on the same album at least. Brown's "On Our Own" is a keeper and is one of the better singles from the summer of 1989, when it resided near the top of the charts. Run-D.M.C.'s "Ghostbusters" is big, hip-hoppin' fun, but the rest is much B-matter by Elton John, Oingo Boingo, and the Eagles' Glenn Frey.

Gary Graff

Ghosts of Mississippi

🎬 1997, Columbia Records, from the film *Ghosts of Mississippi*, Castle Rock Entertainment/Columbia Pictures, 1997 ♪♪♪♪
album notes: Music: Marc Shaiman; **Conductor:** Eddie Karam; Artie Kane.

This account of the life and death of civil rights activist Medgar Evers, and the events spanning 30 years that eventually led to the arrest and conviction of his killer, was powerfully enhanced by Marc Shaiman's appropriately low-key score, in which many of the cues aim to create a quiet rather than a rambunctious atmosphere. Occasionally, a vocal track sets the album on a slightly different course, with B.B. King, Muddy Waters, and the ubiquitous Tony Bennett contributing their talents. Nina Simone's intense performance in "I Wish I Knew How It Would Feel to Be Free," which closes the film and the soundtrack album, is alone worth the price of admission.

Didier C. Deutsch

G.I. Blues

🎬 1988, RCA Records, from the film *G.I. Blues,* Paramount Pictures, 1960 ♪♪♪♪

If Elvis's induction in the Army in 1958 caused many female fans to cry their heart out, it also provided the idea for an engaging film, naturally titled *G.I. Blues,* which was released in 1960. Though he had already appeared in four films, this was Elvis's first screen musical, and the first time he projected a clean-scrubbed image that was different from the rabble-rousers he had portrayed up to that point. Though the soundtrack didn't yield any individual single hit, the album lodged at #1 for five weeks, and stayed on the charts an unprecedented 111 weeks.

Didier C. Deutsch

G.I. Jane

🎬 1998, Hollywood Records, from the Hollywood film *G.I. Jane,* 1997 ♪♪
album notes: Music: Trevor Jones; **Conductor:** Trevor Jones; **Featured Musicians:** Phil Todd, solo EWI; Paul Clarvis, ethnic percussion; Clem Clempson, guitar; Charlie Morgan, drum kit; Belinda Sykes, voice.

Demi Moore becomes the first woman to join the Navy SEALS and sets out to prove to her leering, chortling colleagues that she can be an equal in their ranks. Kinda sends you looking for *Private Benjamin,* no? The soundtrack is no great shakes, either, mostly because it doesn't have a lot to offer. The Pretenders' two tracks, "Goodbye" and "The Homecoming," are welcome inclusions, as is Tarnation's blustery "Two Wrongs Don't Make a Right." But well-worn fare such as Three Dog Night's "Mama Told Me Not to Come" and Bad Company's "Feel like Makin' Love" make this set a bit grayer than it has to be, and the selections from Trevor Jones's score feel like dangling add-ons to an already weak package.

Gary Graff

Giant

🎬 1989, Capitol Records, from the film *Giant,* Warner Bros., 1956 ♪♪♪♪♪
album notes: Music: Dimitri Tiomkin; **Orchestra:** The Warner Bros. Orchestra; **Conductor:** Dimitri Tiomkin; Ray Heindorf.

The sprawling saga in Edna Ferber's novel received a sensational screen treatment in which Rock Hudson, Elizabeth Taylor, and James Dean gave vivid portrayals as the characters whose lives were ultimately dwarfed by the significant social and economical changes that altered the Texan landscape between World War II and the mid-1950s. Contributing significantly to the overall impact of the film was Dimitri Tiomkin's great score, unfortunately abbreviated for its soundtrack album release and available only in mono. Contrasting the gentle idyll between Bick Benedict, the cattle owner, and Leslie, the Maryland girl he marries and brings to Reata, his Texas home lost in the middle of an immense desolated territory ("There's Never Been Anyone Else But You"), Tiomkin created a pungent theme for Jett Rink, the envious handyman who inherits a small piece of land and becomes immensely wealthy when he discovers a huge oil field underneath his plot, first expressing his dreams and aspirations ("Jett Rink Theme"), then his unbearable selfishness and superiority ("Jett Rink, Oil Baron").

On a broader scale, the film also explores the moral and social changes in Texas, from the pervasive influence oil exerted on the society, when the cattle owners gradually lost their power to a disdainful upstart aristocracy, to the greater role racial re-

James Dean in Giant. **(The Kobal Collection)**

lations began to play in this new society, all themes that receive equally strong evocations in Tiomkin's profuse score.

Central to the latter is a memorable fistfight between Bick and a burly diner owner who refuses to serve Bick's stepdaughter because she is Mexican, the entire brawl set to Mitch Miller's thrilling rendition of "The Yellow Rose of Texas," a #1 hit on the charts the year before. The new laserdisc release of the film will contain additional music from that impressive score that will complement, not duplicate, the existing CD.

Didier C. Deutsch

The Giant of Thunder Mountain

1994, Citadel Records, from the film *The Giant of Thunder Mountain*, American Happenings, 1994 ♫♫♫♫

album notes: Music: Lee Holdridge; **Orchestra:** Symphony Orchestra; **Conductor:** Lee Holdridge.

A folk tale that did not make much of an impression at the box office, *The Giant of Thunder Mountain* inspired Lee Holdridge to write an appropriately evocative score, rooted in folk themes

and instrumentations, with some broad orchestral effects to evoke the drama itself. Lovely melodies detail the poetic aspects of the story, while stronger accents underscore moments of action, sometimes, as in "Amy/The Bear," within the same cue. It all adds up to a remarkably effective score, lyrical to a fault and very entertaining for the most part.

Didier C. Deutsch

Gigi

1996, Rhino Records, from the film *Gigi*, MGM, 1958 ♫♫♫♫♫

album notes: Music: Frederick Loewe; **Lyrics:** Alan Jay Lerner; **Orchestra:** The MGM Studio Orchestra, **Choir:** The MGM Studio Choir; **Conductor:** Andre Previn; **Cast:** Leslie Caron, Louis Jourdan, Maurice Chevalier, Hermione Gingold.

1973, RCA Victor Records, from the Broadway production *Gigi*, 1973 ♫♫♫♫

album notes: Music: Frederick Loewe; **Lyrics:** Alan Jay Lerner; **Musical Direction:** Ross Reimeuller; **Cast:** Karin Wolfe, Daniel Massey, Alfred Drake, Agnes Moorehead, Maria Karnilova.

We are truly fortunate to be living in this modern (digital) world. Technology and a new-found appreciation of our Broadway and Hollywood musical heritage has unlocked the archives of recording companies and film studios the world over. The new soundtrack album recording of *Gigi,* on Rhino, is a testament to the treat we all have in store as these archives become more and more available. In addition to the basic songs that have been available over the years in several incarnations, LP, CD, and cassette, we now have available, for our enjoyment, instrumental interludes, reprises, extended versions and even experimental recordings with Leslie Caron's singing voice. As most film buffs are aware, her singing voice was dubbed, in part, by Betty Wand. This classic recording also includes such stars as Maurice Chevalier, Louis Jourdan, and Hermione Gingold. The score of this film again shows the versatile talent of Lerner and Loewe, both of whom can catch a character, a place, and a time like no other song-writing team. While the story of this film is similar to *My Fair Lady,* in a superficial way, the music and lyrics do not sound like the previous musical at all. The new transfers are in the best stereo sound they have ever had and will pour gloriously from your speakers every time you play this album.

In 1973, *Gigi* was turned into a big, lavish Broadway musical which, unfortunately for all involved, ran not quite three months. However, fortunately for us, a recording was made during the run of the show and it is wonderfully alive. Though none of the principals equal their counterparts in the film, they do capture the spirit and the fun of the material beautifully. Karin Wolfe, while not quite an unknown, was perceived as new to the scene and she played Gigi as a charming young girl on the brink of womanhood. Daniel Massey really understood the character of Gaston down to his fingertips and he displays more voice on the recording than his film counterpart. If Alfred Drake wasn't Maurice Chevalier, he was, well . . . Alfred Drake, and he brought a touching self-awareness to the character of Honore. Maria Karnilova and Agnes Moorehead were wonderful as Gigi's two role models. Lerner and Loewe wrote several lovely new songs for the show with "The Contract" being a knockout. The stereo sound on the compact disc is good and it reproduces the many felicities of this score well.

Jerry J. Thomas

Ginger and Fred

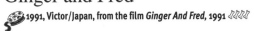 1991, Victor/Japan, from the film *Ginger And Fred,* 1991 🎭🎭🎭🎭

album notes: Music: Nicola Piovani; **Orchestra:** The Orchestra della Unione Musicista di Roma; **Conductor:** Nicola Piovani.

Ginger And Fred should have been a film scored by Nino Rota, except that Rota was no longer around to do it, so Nicola Piovani

wrote the music. He did a fine job, too! This bittersweet story of two former dance partners, portrayed by Giulietta Masina and Marcello Mastroianni (they called themselves Ginger and Fred, after you-know-who), who get back together on the occasion of a television variety show that will be broadcast live on Christmas Eve, provided Fellini with a lightweight, entertaining storyline, the better to cast a critical glance at the superficiality and insignificance of television. In scoring it, Piovani actually wrote a score that recalls Rota, but without the mordant pungency that seemed to make his predecessor the ideal Fellini composer. This said, *Ginger And Fred* is actually quite entertaining, and should particularly attract many listeners for its traditional treatment of various standards associated with the real Ginger and Fred, notably "Cheek to Cheek," "Top Hat," "Let's Face the Music and Dance," and "The Continental." This title may be out of print or just plain hard to find. Mail-order companies, used CD shops, or dealers of rare or import recordings will be your best bet.

Didier C. Deutsch

Girl Crazy

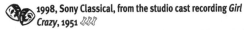 1998, Sony Classical, from the studio cast recording *Girl Crazy,* 1951 🎭🎭🎭

album notes: Music: George Gershwin; **Lyrics:** Ira Gershwin; **Conductor:** Lehman Engel.

The first time the Gershwins' score was recorded, the 1951 *Girl Crazy* was designed to showcase Mary Martin, still appearing in *South Pacific,* by giving her all the hit songs. Because of its '50s orchestrations, this version doesn't sound as authentic as Nonesuch's more recent one (with Lorna Luft) but is nevertheless highly listenable. And with "Bidin' My Time," "Embraceable You," "I Got Rhythm," and "But Not for Me," how could it fail to be enjoyable? Martin is delicious, vocally warm and appealing. She's occasionally spelled by Louise Carlyle (who gets "Sam and Delilah"), Eddie Chappell ("Treat Me Rough"), and various combinations of choruses ("The Lonesome Cowboy," "Bronco Busters," "Barbary Coast"). A different "But Not for Me," recorded by Martin in 1949, is a bonus track.

Max O. Preeo

🎭🎭 1990, Elektra Records, from the studio cast recording *Girl Crazy,* 1990 🎭🎭🎭🎭🎭

album notes: Music: George Gershwin; **Lyrics:** Ira Gershwin; **Musical Direction:** John Mauceri; **Cast:** Lorna Luft, David Carroll, Judy Blazer, Frank Gorshin.

🎬 1996, Rhino Records, from the film *Girl Crazy,* 1943 🎭🎭🎭🎭🎭

album notes: Music: George Gershwin; **Lyrics:** Ira Gershwin; **Chorus:** The MGM Studio Chorus; **Orchestra:** The MGM Studio Orchestra; **Conductor:** Georgie Stoll; **Cast:** Judy Garland, Mickey Rooney, June Allyson, Nancy Walker, Trudy Erwin, Six Hits and a Miss, Tommy Dorsey and His Orchestra.

A radiant little musical with a score by George and Ira Gershwin, *Girl Crazy* made very few pretenses other than amuse and entertain its audiences when it opened on Oct. 14, 1930. Set in Arizona, it dealt with a New York playboy sent to the golden West by his millionaire father to manage a ranch, in the hope that the wastrel will forget his fondness for alcohol and the fair sex in the great open spaces. However, the lad, who arrives in the womanless town of Custerville by taxicab from New York has other ideas, and immediately proceeds to transform the place into a dude ranch, glamorizing it with a girl chorus imported from Broadway. Light as the story might have been, it was the occasion for the wonderful score which contained such gems as "Bidin' My Time," "Embraceable You," "I Got Rhythm," and "But Not For Me," among its better moments. Transferred to the screen in 1943 with its score almost intact and the plot bearing a distant resemblance to the one conceived by Guy Bolton and John McGowan for the original, it became another sprightly vehicle for the popular team of Mickey Rooney and Judy Garland. In true, traditional fashion, they took advantage of the storyline to put on a show, actually a grandiose finale, staged by Busby Berkeley.

The Elektra recording, one of several studio cast recreations of the great Gershwin 1930s musicals, stars Lorna Luft (Judy Garland's daughter), Judy Blazer, and David Carroll in a spirited rendition of the score, beautifully directed by John Mauceri.

While sonically inferior, the Rhino set presents the MGM 1943 film version, starring Judy Garland (a winner in her playful rendition of "Bidin' My Time") and Mickey Rooney, complete with its interpolations (including "Fascinating Rhythm," performed by Rooney at the piano, with Tommy Dorsey and his Orchestra), outtakes, instrumental bridges, and, as is usual for the label, a wealth of written and photographic information that makes this CD the ultimate release for this marvelous soundtrack.

Didier C. Deutsch

Girl Happy/Harum Scarum

1993, RCA Records from the films *Girl Happy*, MGM, 1965, and *Harum Scarum*, MGM, 1965 🎬🎬🎬

Set in Ft. Lauderdale, Florida., *Girl Happy* was the right opportunity for some sun-and-sand fun-and-frolic, with Elvis as a struggling pop singer, surrounded by a bevy of bikini-clad girls, finally opting for Shelley Fabares, who subsequently appeared in two other films with him. The only hit to emerge from the film was "Do The Clam," often cited as one of the worst numbers ever recorded by the King, though the album itself remained on the charts for 31 weeks, peaking at #8.

Loosely inspired by Elvis's own life as a matinee idol, *Harum Scarum* took place in a fantasy Middle East kingdom where the singer has been asked to appear, only to be kidnapped by opponents of the regime. While the action involved a lot of derring-do, it also paused long enough to enable Elvis to sing several numbers, included here.

Didier C. Deutsch

Girl 6

1996, Warner Bros. Records, from the film *Girl 6*, 20th Century-Fox Pictures, 1996 🎬🎬🎬

album notes: Music: Prince.

Prince is the master of this particular Spike Lee joint, whose soundtrack features a collection of his work plus that of long-gone spin-offs such as The Family and Vanity 6. There are a couple of new songs from his New Power Generation ("Count the Days," "Girl 6"), but it's almost unfair to ask them to hold their own alongside proven past favorites such as "Erotic City" and "The Cross."

Gary Graff

Girls! Girls! Girls!/Kid Galahad

1993, RCA Records, from the films *Girls! Girls! Girls!*, Paramount Pictures, 1962, and *Kid Galahad*, United Artists, 1962 🎬🎬🎬

A bright, lively affair, *Girls! Girls! Girls!* seemingly had nothing more on its mind than to entertain Elvis Presley's legions of fans. In it, he appeared as a carefree bachelor: a leisure boat pilot by day who turns into a night club singer at night. With an unusually large number of songs on the soundtrack, the film yielded a strong hit in "Return To Sender," a #2 on the charts.

In Kid Galahad, also released in 1962, Elvis played a boxer, mostly known for his ability to take a lot of punches without flinching. While allegedly a dramatic film (it was a remake of a 1937 drama that starred Humphrey Bogart and Edward G. Robinson), *Kid Galahad* also included several musical numbers, including "This Is Living" and the chartmaking "King Of The Whole Wide World."

Didier C. Deutsch

Giu la testa

1987, Cinevox Records/Italy, from the film *Giu la testa (Duck You Sucker)*, United Artists, 1971 🎬🎬🎬🎬

album notes: Music: Ennio Morricone; Conductor: Ennio Morricone.

By the time he made *Duck You Sucker,* Sergio Leone could no longer take himself or the spaghetti western he had pioneered seriously. As a result, the film was a riot–an improbable adventure, somewhat accidentally set south of the border, which opposed two great hams, Rod Steiger as a Mexican bandito and James Coburn as an Irish revolutionary. Together, they fired up the screen and made for a very funny and exciting team. True to form, Morricone's score matched the visuals scene for scene, with some great cues that gave the film an additional impetus. The recording does not entirely do justice to the Maestro's work, though it has many fun moments. "Mesa verde" and "Dopo l'esplosione" stand out particularly, but the whole album is pure delight from beginning to end. This recording may be difficult to find. Check with a used CD store, mail-order company, or a dealer specializing in rare, out-of-print, or import recordings.

Didier C. Deutsch

Giulietta degli Spiriti

1991, CAM Records/Italy, from the film *Giulietta degli Spiriti (Juliet of the Spirits),* Cineriz, 1965 🎬🎬🎬🎬

album notes: Music: Nino Rota; **Conductor:** Carlo Savina.

Some of the scores Nino Rota wrote for the films of Fellini particularly stand out. *Juliet Of The Spirits* is one of them! Perhaps inspired by the fact that this was Fellini's first color film (with broad swaths of pastels through most of the everyday scenes, and exotic tones illuminating the fantasy scenes), Rota created a score that teems with gorgeous themes, each more inventive than the next. Adding to his inspiration was the topic of the film itself, about a bored housewife, convinced that her husband is unfaithful and obsessed by her own fantasies, who indulges in flights of fancies and creates a world of spirits. Indicative of Rota's approach, tracks like "The Circus Ballerina," "The Nuns' Little Theatre," or "Cupid Has Struck/The Love Mistress" are as essential to the film's enjoyment as the bright, surrealistic scenes Fellini envisioned. An essential recording. This title may be out of print or just plain hard to find. Mail-order companies, used CD shops, or dealers of rare or import recordings will be your best bet.

Didier C. Deutsch

Give My Regards to Broad Street

1984, Columbia Records, from the film *Give My Regards to Broad Street,* 1984 🎬🎬🎬

album notes: Music: Paul McCartney.

To damn with faint praise, the album is better than the movie— by a little. When an artist starts covering his old hits, as Paul McCartney does on this effort, you know that can't be a good thing. And it isn't. The best thing that came out of the *Broad Street* project was a brief working relationship with former 10cc member Eric Stewart, who collaborated with McCartney on some decent new tunes for the film and worked with the ex-Beatle even more fruitfully on the underappreciated "Press to Play" album.

Gary Graff

The Glass Menagerie

1987, MCA Records, from the film *The Glass Menagerie,* Cineplex Odeon Films, 1987 🎬🎬🎬🎬

album notes: Music: Henry Mancini; **Conductor:** Henry Mancini; **Featured Musicians:** Walt Livinsky, soprano sax; Phil Bodner, clarinet/tenor sax; Mel Davis, trumpet; Dave Bargeron, trombone; Grady Tate, drums; Derek Smith, piano; Bucky Pizzarelli, guitar; Brian Torff, bass.

A sensitive adaptation of Tennessee Williams's 1954 stage play, directed by Paul Newman and starring Joanne Woodward (Newman's wife), *The Glass Menagerie* provided Henry Mancini with a rare opportunity to compose an unusually wistful score in which the dark poetic accents evoke strong emotions and unrealized dreams. Central to the score is the theme for Laura, "Blue Roses," the pathetic crippled waif, forever hoping that a gentleman will call for her and whose life is shattered as a result. Also the film's main theme is strongly suggestive "Jonquils" gives the score a solid romantic anchor. In the midst of the dreamy moods suggested by the action, Mancini also created some effective dance numbers that enliven his music, including "The Blues in Three," "The Rumba You Saved for Me," "Slow and Sassy," "Tango Paradiso," and "Paradise Dance Hall Blues," among others, all of which have been placed at the end of the recording in a rather uninspired bit of sequencing.

Didier C. Deutsch

Glengarry Glen Ross

1992, Elektra Records, from the New Line Cinema film *Glengarry Glen Ross,* 1992 🎬🎬🎬🎬

album notes: Music: James Newton Howard; **Featured Musicians:** Wayne Shorter, David "Fathead" Newman, Jeff Clayton, David Sanborn, Bob Shepard, saxophone; Mike Lang, Kenny Barron, Shirley Horn, Jimmy Rowles, Mulgrew Miller, Russ Ferrante, piano; John Patitucci, Ron Carter, Chuck Domanico, Charles Moffit, Anthony Jackson, bass; Jeff Porcaro, Grady Tate, Steve Williams, Jeff Hamilton, Ben Riley, Peter Erskine, Terry Clarke, drums; Lenny Castro, percussion; Larry Bunker, vibes; John Chiodini, guitar; Joe Gisbert, trumpet.

The most common use of jazz music in film is generally as "source music"; in other words, it sounds like it's taken from a recorded performance. Sometimes it works with the picture, but most of the time, it doesn't work. Jazz music is so foreign to the average movie-goer that hearing real jazz in a picture is jarring and distracting. Hard-core jazz is also too static for film. Film changes its mood and color through editing and most jazz is linear. It is only a rare situation that the mood of jazz and the mood of a film blend perfectly. The first three tracks on this CD represent the finest marriage of jazz in film music in recent times. James Newton Howard brings a sense of musical proportion and compositional skill rarely found in underscoring. His jazz voice is Wayne Shorter, and together they capture the gloom and desperation of this picture. Howard has figured out the essence of how jazz fits into the picture. He uses the darker side of Shorter's tone (the ultimate solo voice-choice) and creates a haunting sound, but with the feel of modern jazz. There is a beautiful track with Shirley Horn ("You' Better Go Now"), as well as Little Jimmy Scott's "Street of Dreams," Al Jarreau's "Blue Skies," and quite a few others that were included to fill out the CD, notably by the Bill Holman Big Band and the late Joe Roccisano's big band. But the real story is the artistic collaboration of Howard and Shorter, a partnership that brings a new life to jazz and film.

Bob Belden

The Glenn Miller Story

1985, MCA, from the film *The Glenn Miller Story,* Universal Pictures, 1954 ♪♪♪♪

album notes: Orchestra: The Universal-International Orchestra; **Conductor:** Joseph Gershenson; **Featured Artists:** Louis Armstrong and the All-Stars: Louis Armstrong, trumpet; Trummie Young, trombone; Barney Bigard, clarinet; Billy Kyle, piano; Bud Freeman, tenor sax; Kenny John, drums; Arvell Shaw, bass.

James Stewart is quite believable as Glenn Miller in the otherwise highly romanticized screen biopic based on the life of the big band leader and Air Force pilot. The music, too, plays with great dynamic drive, sounds authentic, with the U-I Studio Orchestra, conducted by Joseph Gershenson, revisiting the hits from the Miller band, including "Moonlight Serenade," "Tuxedo Junction," "In the Mood," and "Pennsylvania 6-5000," among others. But the true highlight in this soundtrack album, as it is in the film, is a scorching version of "Basin Street Blues" by Louis Armstrong and his All-Stars, whose performance is the real thing. No . . . bones about it!

Didier C. Deutsch

Gli ultimi giorni di Pompei

1995, CAM Records/Italy, from the film *Gli ultimi giorni di Pompei (The Last Days of Pompeii),* Warner Bros., 1959 ♪♪♪♪

album notes: Music: Angelo Francesco Lavagnino; **Conductor:** Carlo Savina.

Muscleman Steve Reeves starred in this recounting of *The Last Days of Pompeii,* which owed very little to historical accuracy, and a great deal to the imagination of the screenwriters. The film, however, was interesting in that it was the first feature directed by Sergio Leone, who replaced the original director, Mario Bonnard, when he became ill. In this fanciful recreation, Reeves portrayed a centurion, convinced that the Christians are innocent of all the misdeeds of which they are accused, who is thrown in prison as a result of his beliefs. Needless to say, he manages to escape with the woman he loves, just before the fatal eruption of the Vesuvius destroys everything in its path. Underlining the basic moments in the narrative, Lavagnino wrote a score that sounded a bit too exotic, perhaps in imitation of the Roman spectacles scored by Miklos Rozsa, with chimes and tambourines suggesting the colors and sounds of Ancient Rome. Listening to "Glauco in the Crocodile Pit," however, one can clearly visualize beefy Mr. Reeves struggling with a saurian or two. Effective and fun. This recording may be difficult to find. Check with a used CD store, mail-order company, or a dealer specializing in rare, out-of-print, or import recordings.

Didier C. Deutsch

Glory

1994, Virgin Movie Music, from the film *Glory,* Tri-Star Pictures, 1994 ♪♪♪♪

album notes: Music: James Horner; **Conductor:** James Horner; **Featured** *Artists:* The Boys Choir of Harlem; Dr. Walter J. Turnbull, director.

James Horner's music for this impassioned Civil War drama reveals a powerful depth of feeling and a profound sense of honor for the black soldiers of the 54th Regiment. Horner's poignant theme for the boys' choir and orchestra runs throughout the motif-filled variations and historical music that form the score's musical canvas. His single theme maintains the music's focus on its heroes, the soldiers of the 54th. Though war assaults them on every side and ultimately overcomes them, their glorious theme sounds solemnly and nobly through it all. With superb orchestration and outstanding sound—the low end drums and percussion sound through brilliantly on the CD—the music is grand yet intimate, intensely dramatic yet incredibly poignant. The full choir intones purposefully during the climactic battle scenes, chanting like resolute angels joining the 54th in their final, hopeless charge against Fort Baxter. The score is fully emotive and vastly memorable. The music, as with the film's images, lingers long and is presented in one of Horner's finest compositions.

Randall D. Larson

Go

1999, Work/Sony Music Soundtrax, from the Columbia film *Go,* 1999 ♪♪

Another modern sampler that's headlined by "New," which was the first single from the million-selling ska-poppers No Doubt in two years. It's a good but not defining song, something that can also be said about the *Go* soundtrack as a whole—a disappointment considering the transcendence of director Doug Liman's companion album for *Swingers*. But *Go* has more moments, including Fatboy Slim's "Gangster Tripping," an introduction to the band Len on "Steal My Sunshine," and Lionrock's powerful "Fire Up the Shoesaw." The rest is pedestrian at best or, in the case of Philip Steir's remix of Steppenwolf's "Magic Carpet Ride," hopelessly misguided.

Gary Graff

The Godfather

1988, MCA Records, from the film *The Godfather,* Paramount Pictures, 1972 𝄞𝄞𝄞𝄞

album notes: Music: Nino Rota.

Francis Ford Coppola's impressive treatment of Mario Puzo's novel about the ups and downs of a Mafia family has long been one of the screen's most successful trilogies. Matching colorful characters and narrative intensity with sensational portrayals and effective cinematography, Coppola created a fresco of incredible scope, vitality and beauty, its sympathetic views of some rather shady people notwithstanding. As important to the success of the original 1972 film as all its other ingredients is Nino Rota's exceptional score, which beautifully captures the flavor and the essence of the screen drama, and helps take it to a higher level of importance and recognition. Both the "Main Theme," a mournful waltz heard in various guises at different times throughout the action, and the equally popular "Love Theme," achieved hit status in countless cover versions and vocal/instrumental renditions.

Didier C. Deutsch

The Godfather Part II

1988, MCA Records, from the film *The Godfather Part II,* Paramount Pictures, 1974 𝄞𝄞𝄞𝄞

album notes: Music: Nino Rota, Carmine Coppola; **Conductor:** Carmine Coppola.

Unfortunately, the powerful atmosphere suggested by Rota's original score is considerably diluted by Carmine Coppola's contributions to the second film. The best musical moments belong to Rota who easily outshines Coppola, whose flair for musical underscoring is mediocre at best. Pop vocals provide an extra dimension to the score.

Didier C. Deutsch

The Godfather Part III

1990, Columbia Records, from the film *The Godfather Part III,* Paramount Pictures, 1990 𝄞𝄞𝄞𝄞

album notes: Music: Carmine Coppola, Nino Rota; **Conductor:** Carmine Coppola.

Again, the score to Francis Ford Coppola's third film in the *Godfather* saga can't compare to Rota's original. More pop vocals liven up the score, with Al Martino effectively handling "To Each His Own" in this third volume, but a performance of "Promise Me You'll Remember" by Harry Connick, Jr., is easily dispensable. Overall sound quality in the three albums varies considerably, with a great amount of noticeable distortion.

Didier C. Deutsch

Gods and Monsters

1999, RCA Victor, from the Regent Entertainment film *Gods and Monsters,* 1998 𝄞𝄞𝄞𝄞

album notes: Music: Carter Burwell; **Conductor:** Carter Burwell.

Carter Burwell is no stranger to composing scores for quirky movies. *Gods and Monsters,* which earned Burwell an Oscar nomination, is no exception. The movie is about James Whale, the openly gay producer/director from the 1930s–40s who was responsible for such classics as *The Bride of Frankenstein* and *The Invisible Man.* With this score, Burwell did the unexpected—composing music that is quite delicate at times. This is best exemplified in the waltz that appears in the scene when Whale (portrayed by Ian McKellen) bitterly describes the horror of his European childhood. As director Bill Condon, in the liner notes, correctly summed it up, "In a time when most film scoring is an exercise in redundancy—action sequences hyped by agitated strings, emotional moments underlined by tender tinkling—Carter remains a true iconoclast."

Beth Krakower

Godspell

1971, Arista Records, from the off-Broadway production *Godspell,* 1971 𝄞𝄞𝄞𝄞

album notes: Music: Stephen Schwartz; **Lyrics:** Stephen Schwartz; **Musical Direction:** Stephen Schwartz; **Cast:** Lamar Alford, Peggy Gordon, David Haskell, Joanne Jonas, Robin Lamont.

1973, Arista Records, from the film *Godspell,* Columbia Pictures, 1973 𝄞𝄞𝄞𝄞

album notes: Music: Stephen Schwartz; **Lyrics:** Stephen Schwartz; **Musical Direction:** Stephen Schwartz; **Featured Musicians:** Hugh McCracken, Jesse Cutler, guitar; Chayim Tamar, Shofar; Charles Macey, banjo; Paul Shaffer, piano/organ; Jeffrey Mylett, recorder; Michael Kamen, ARP synthesizer; Corky Hale, harp; **Cast:** Victor Garber, Lynne Thigpen, David Haskell, Robin Lamont.

A modest musical by normal Broadway standards, *Godspell* found its genesis in the Gospel according to St. Matthew, with Stephen Schwartz chronicling the last seven days in the life of Christ, portrayed wearing clown make-up and a T-shirt emblazoned with an "S," to the rhythms of a rock 'n' roll score. Surprisingly, it not only worked very well, it also was quite fetching and entertaining, and not preachy. Initially presented at the off-

Broadway Cherry Lane Theatre, on May 17, 1971, it eventually moved to Broadway on June 22, 1976, for a run of 527 performances. Altogether, it played 2,651 performances in New York alone. In 1973, it also was made into a film musical, which essentially retained all the ingredients from the stage show, merely expanding on them and opening up the stage setting to include outdoors shots against the New York skyline. Both the original cast album and the soundtrack recording are virtually identical, and both are equally enjoyable.

Didier C. Deutsch

Godzilla

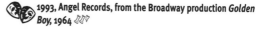 **1998, Epic/Sony Music Soundtrax, from the Tri-Star film *Godzilla*, 1998** ♪♪

album notes: Music: David Arnold

Let's face it: New York doesn't have much luck! It's not so much that in two consecutive seasons it was first thoroughly destroyed by an alien invasion in *Independence Day* and then reduced again to a pile of rubbish by a lumbering lizard on the loose in *Godzilla*. No! It's that in both cases the mayhem and destruction was gleefully orchestrated by David Arnold. Actually, we should be grateful for small favors—a less gifted composer might have done the deeds. . . . Not that we could judge from this album in which Mr. Arnold's ominously suggestive score, with its wandering calls of low brass and percussive effects, has been reduced to two selections (it is available, however, on a "private" release of dubious origins). As is unfortunately the case in these days when the term "soundtrack album" may simply mean a collection of totally unrelated rock songs, this CD compiles together performances by a wide range of artists, some more talented than the others, such as the Wallflowers, Jamiroquai, Rage Against the Machine, Foo Fighters, and Michael Penn. Their various contributions here are occasionally interesting, although one might question what they have to do with the beast that came to hatch in Madison Square Garden, outside of the fact that some have titles like "Deeper Underground," "No Shelter," "Macy Day Parade," or "Out There," which might be construed as a comment on the screen action. But if that's the case, where does a track called "Untitled" fit?

Didier C. Deutsch

Going All the Way

1997, Verve Records, from the Lakeshore/Gramercy film *Going All the Way*, 1997 ♪♪

album notes: Music: tomandandy.

We all probably have different views of what constitutes the best soundtrack for a given period in which we have lived. Ask anyone about the '50s and you're bound to have a wide range of opinions. Case in point: this soundtrack album for a film about two Korean War–era vets coming home to Indianapolis and the stuffy existence both thought they had left behind, peppered with songs from the period. If "A White Sport Coat," the song that put Marty Robbins on the map, is magnificently featured, it is somewhat anachronistic, having charted in 1957, although the film is supposed to take place in 1954.

Other selections, like the Harptones' "A Sunday Kind of Love," Vic Damone's "Why Was I Born?" (from 1949), and Perez Prado's "Skokiaan" are more in period, but these were not the hits that were played at the time, nor were they the hit versions of these songs ("Skokiaan," for instance, was the Four Lads' for anyone who cared).

Considering all the great tracks that lay dormant in the vaults at Mercury, it seems a bit of a waste to have this soundtrack album consisting of songs (many rather obscure, one might add) purporting to represent "an upbeat collection of classic R&B and pop music from the '50s," as a sticker proudly claims on the shrink wrap.

Didier C. Deutsch

Gold Diggers: The Secret of Bear Mountain

1995, Varèse Sarabande Records, from the film *Gold Diggers: The Secret of Bear Mountain*, Universal Pictures, 1995 ♪♪♪♪

album notes: Music: Joel McNeely; **Conductor:** Joel McNeely.

The story of two adventurous young girls, Beth and Jody (played by Christina Ricci and Anna Chlumsky), one the savvy streetwise urbanite, the other the rebellious country pumpkin (and bumpkin), who set out to discover a legendary cache of gold in the wilds of the Pacific Northwest, *Gold Diggers: The Secret of Bear Mountain* elicited a strong, flavorful score from Joel McNeely, whose only major fault is that too often it telegraphed the screen action. On its own, however, it reveals several themes that are quite attractive, including the folk-oriented "Legend of Molly Morgan," laid out in broad, colorful terms. "The Flying Song," performed by Colin Hay in a style that sometimes evokes Phil Collins, is a fine coda to the recording.

Didier C. Deutsch

Golden Boy

1993, Angel Records, from the Broadway production *Golden Boy*, 1964 ♪♪

album notes: Music: Charles Strouse; **Lyrics:** Lee Adams; **Musical Direction:** Elliot Lawrence; **Cast:** Sammy Davis Jr., Paula Wayne, Billy Daniels, Johnny Brown

Despite the presence of Sammy Davis Jr. in the title role, this musical adaptation of Clifford Odets's play was not a great success. Davis, playing an aspiring young boxer who thinks he's made it after he wins a couple of bouts, only to lose a determining championship fight, worked very hard to win support for the show, something that explains his strained voice in this cast album recorded a few weeks after the opening. But the book, a tame version of the play, and particularly the score, by Charles Strouse and Lee Adams (of *Bye Bye Birdie* fame), let the star down. Ultimately, the show had a run of 569 performances, largely due to the star's box office appeal, and the novelty of an interracial relationship between Joe and Lorna (played by Paula Wayne) which challenged Broadway audiences at a time when such things were still being frowned on (see also *No Strings*). The show received Tony nominations for Best Musical, Best Actor, Best Producer, and Best Choreography. Also appearing in the cast were newcomers Louis Gossett and Lola Falana.

Didier C. Deutsch

Golden Gate

1993, Varèse Sarabande, from the film *Golden Gate*, Samuel Goldwyn, 1993 🎬🎬🎬

album notes: Music: Elliot Goldenthal; **Orchestra:** The Pro Arte Orchestra; **Conductor:** Jonathan Sheffer; **Featured Musicians:** Billy Drewes, saxophone; Elliot Goldenthal, keyboards, vocals; Richard Martinez, keyboards; James Haddad, percussion; Steve Gorn, bamboo flute; Matthias Gohl, keyboards; Scott Lee, bass.

Elliot Goldenthal created a fascinating eclectic mix of musical styles that includes jazz, blues, and Chinese motifs for this story of an FBI agent who becomes involved with the Chinese community in San Francisco during the McCarthy witch hunt of the 1950s. The score has a dark, brooding quality that does well to capture the mood of the era. Goldenthal himself performs on "Motel Street Meltdown," a piece reminiscent of the bizarre vocal arrangements featured in the TV series *Twin Peaks*.

David Hirsch

The Golden Voyage of Sinbad

1998, Prometheus Records/Belgium, from the Columbia film *The Golden Voyage of Sinbad*, 1974 🎬🎬🎬🎬

album notes: Music: Miklos Rozsa; **Conductor:** Miklos Rozsa.

In scoring Arabian fantasies, there have been essentially two schools of thought: the Bernard Herrmann kind, in which the accent is squarely put on the weird effects that suggest that the heroes described by the fabled Sheherazade meet all kinds of unusual dangers (the famous "Duel with the Skeletons" in *The 7th Voyage of Sinbad*); and the florid style of Miklos Rozsa, whose lush, exotic touches often recall Rimsky-Korsakov. The contrast is striking.

The first thing that impresses here is the richness of the motifs and the luxuriant colorings of the orchestrations. The themes bear Rozsa's distinctive signature, but not without some unusual sonorities that distinguish them (as in "Arrival of the Homunculus"). Also, there are clearly two influences at play here, as the composer admits in the notes, an Arabic one for the first scenes, and as the action progresses to other shores, an Indian one in which ragas play a dominant role, although in a highly stylized, Hollywood way. The meticulous cue-by-cue description by Doug Raynes emphasizes developments in the score as they match the screen action.

The recording itself is a magnificent display of Rozsa's uniquely colorful style, with the Rome Symphony Orchestra, conducted by the composer, doing a splendid job. The only problem with this welcome reissue is the fact that the sound quality would have gained at being slightly reverbered, with less emphasis on the bottom and a greater definition of the high end, something which a different EQ would have achieved. A minor technical quibble that doesn't take away from the qualities in this recording.

Didier C. Deutsch

Goldeneye

1995, Virgin Movie Music, from the film *Goldeneye*, United Artists, 1995 🎬🎬

album notes: Music: Eric Serra; **Orchestra:** The London Studio Session Orchestra; **Conductor:** John Altman; **Featured Musicians:** Gavyn Wright, violin; George Robertson, viola; Tony Pleeth, cello; Mike Brittain, bass; Andy Findon, flute; Mike Thompson, Frenh horn; Fiona Hibbert, harp.

Whenever someone other than John Barry comes in to score a James Bond movie, you shouldn't hold your breath hoping the results will come close to being a Barry-caliber outing. In fact, the best you can often hope for is that the score won't be an outright dud like Eric Serra's music for *Goldeneye*, Pierce Brosnan's first outing as 007. At times an embarrassing collection of techno/industrial tracks with static orchestral lines, Serra's *Goldeneye* gets off on the wrong foot with what can be best described as "Bond on Bongos" before heading off in other confused directions. His music for the film's tank chase, "A Pleasant Drive in St. Petersburg," included here but thrown out of the film itself, is about as laughable and headache-inducing as the rest of his ill-considered score. The serviceable main theme, performed by Tina Turner and written by U2 members Bono and The Edge, fares much better, but it, too, remains far removed from its more successful predecessors.

Andy Dursin

Goldfinger

1995, EMI-America, from the film *Goldfinger*, United Artists, 1964 🎬🎬🎬🎬

album notes: Music: John Barry; **Lyrics:** Leslie Bricusse; Anthony Newley; **Conductor:** John Barry.

The best, and probably most effective, contribution by John Barry to the James Bond films, *Goldfinger* is the score to which all others have to measure up. With its strong array of thematic material, powerful melodies, suggestive cues and varied instrumentations, the score managed to musically excite as much as the screen action itself. Even Shirley Bassey's over-the-top performance of the title tune, which is badly distorted in the recording itself, contains more energy than any vocal in the other films, including Ms. Bassey's rendition of "Diamonds are Forever" or Tom Jones's vibrant interpretation of "Thunderball." More to the point, Barry's use of electric guitar, brass instruments, and percussive devices to underscore the most stirring moments in the action, defined a style that has been imitated (including by Barry himself) but never equalled in terms of raw vitality. In cue after cue, the composer challenges the listener with muscular musical ideas, electrifying sounds, and pervasive concepts that are sustained throughout the score.

In derisive comments he often made about his contributions to the series, Barry was creating "Mickey Mouse" film music, but it is in fact everything film music should be about—bold, assertive, enthusiastic, a total complement to the screen action, and something one might feel compelled to listen to frequently, just because it provides such pleasure. The CD, incidentally, repeats the flaws in the original LP, and fails to include the four tracks "Golden Girl," "Death of Tilley," "The Laser Beam," and "Pussy Galore's Flying Circus" initially available only in a British pressing, but subsequently released in this country in the 2-CD "30th Anniversary" package (q.v.).

Didier C. Deutsch

Gone Fishin'

1997, Hollywood Records, from the film *Gone Fishin'*, Hollywood Pictures, 1997 🎬🎬🎬🎬

album notes: Music: Randy Edelman; **Conductor:** Randy Edelman.

A strongly colloquial score, with folk undertones, Randy Edelman tapped into a new creative vein for this amiable comedy about two longtime fishing friends who win a grand prize vacation to the Florida Everglades, only to be confronted with all kinds of misfires and adventures they had hardly expected along with their winning. At times humorous, at times wistfully reflective, the overall tone of the score is cleverly rollicking in keeping with the action itself, with the most eventful moments receiving appropriate musical comments that suggestively un-

They Know the Score
Michael Kamen

In the heat of the moment I am very passionate about what I do. I love the music, I love hopefully every note that I write. They are like my children. But when I feel I am under threat, or when I feel not taken seriously enough—God knows, one is never taken seriously enough. But when you are in the middle of doing it. There is a kind of megalomaniac disease about being on the podium conducting an orchestra. And you feel suddenly incredibly important. And it is not very healthy to come home and be asked to take out the garbage. 'You want me to be human?! Who do you think I am? Do you not know who I think I am?'

Courtesy of **Film Score Monthly**

derline them, while making for an entertaining soundtrack album. "Down in the Everglades," by Willie Nelson, and two vocals by The Love Junkies add a welcome touch to the music.

Didier C. Deutsch

Gone to Texas/Hidden in Silence

1997, Prometheus/Belgium, from the films *Gone to Texas* and *Hidden in Silence* 🎬🎬🎬🎬

album notes: Music: Dennis McCarthy; **Conductor:** Dennis McCarthy.

Little information is provided about these two scores, composed by Dennis McCarthy, which is really a shame given the fact that they are actually both quite good, and it would have helped the listener to situate each in its own context.

A 1985 TV movie about the Alamo and Sam Houston's defeat by Santa Ana and his Mexican forces, *Gone to Texas* offers all the ingredients of the genre—staccato and syncopated rhythms, guitars strumming, pounding beats—all to suggest an outdoor saga, with the composer making a sly bow to Dimitri Tiomkin with a quote from "De Guello," which was used to such effect in both *Rio Bravo* and *The Alamo.* Although the orchestral forces are evidently small, the score is lush and exciting and a real joy.

Much more introspective and sedate, *Hidden in Silence,* set during World War II, was a Lifetime Cable movie made in 1994, about a young woman in Nazi Germany who saves 13 Jewish children from being sent to a concentration camp. While comparisons with *Schindler's List* might seem unavoidable, McCarthy consciously approached his subject matter differently than John Williams, and prominently featured the cello to suggest the darkness of the period and its ominous undertones. In the middle of this gloomy, intense score, a lovely treatment of "Silent Night" played by a violin sheds a bright ray of light.

But when you care about the product, and particularly when it is that good, attempts should be made to treat it carefully and with TLC. This release fails the label's ardent followers and the composer's exquisite contributions by being too cavalier about the music.

Didier C. Deutsch

Gone with the Wind

🎞️ **1996, Rhino Records, from the film *Gone with the Wind,*** Selznick International/MGM Pictures, 1939 ✔️✔️✔️✔️✔️

album notes: Music: Max Steiner; **Orchestra:** The Warner Bros. Orchestra; **Conductor:** Max Steiner.

🎞️ **1989, RCA Victor, from the film *Gone with the Wind,*** Selznick International/MGM Pictures, 1939 ✔️✔️✔️✔️✔️

album notes: Music: Max Steiner; **Orchestra:** The National Philharmonic Orchestra; **Conductor:** Charles Gerhardt.

🎞️ **1988, Stanyan Records, from the film *Gone with the Wind,*** Selznick International/MGM Pictures, 1939 ✔️✔️✔️

album notes: Music: Max Steiner; **Orchestra:** The London Sinfonia, **Conductor:** Muir Mathieson.

The lavish 2-CD set from Rhino, replete with profuse liner notes and illustrations, documents one of the all-time great film scores, and includes one of the most celebrated tunes from the movies, "Tara's Theme." It is also the most complete and, true to Rhino's usual standards of excellence, its presentation is nothing short of superb. The variable sonics are the main drawback here, but it's the original music as recorded in 1939, when prevailing techniques were a far cry from today's norms. Despite its technical shortcomings the score largely holds its own, and emerges as a grandiose achievement.

The 1973 RCA Victor rerecording, with the National Philharmonic Orchestra conducted by Charles Gerhardt, while not as comprehensive, boasts superb stereo sound, and playing that is faithful to the spirit of the original.

The only interest in the Stanyan set, conducted by Muir Mathieson, also in stereo, is the fact that it was the first "authentic recording of the complete score authorized by the composer," a claim that is now superseded by the Rhino release. In addition, the bonus selections can only be viewed as unnecessary padding, with some ("America, America" and "The Prime of Miss Jean Brodie") oddly chosen in this context.

Didier C. Deutsch

Good Burger

🎞️ **1997, Capitol Records, from the Paramount film *Good Burger,*** 1997 ✔️✔️

This silly comedy spun off Nickelodeon's silly series *All That* deserves a, well, silly soundtrack—and it gets it. Fun and light-heartedness rule the roost here, from Mint Condition's spirited "That's the Way (It's Goin' Down)" to selections by the Presidents of the United States of America, 1,000 Clowns, and even co-star Kel Mitchell, who joins the group Less than Jake for "We're All Dudes." Spearhead turns in a stylized version of the Police's "Roxanne," while Trulio Disgracias and De La Soul cover George Clinton's appropriate "Do Fries Go with That Shake?"—although Clinton himself shows most of the new schoolers here how it's done on his album-closing collaboration with Digital Underground, "Knee Deep."

Gary Graff

Good Morning, Vietnam

🎞️ **1988, A&M Records, from the film *Good Morning, Vietnam,*** Touchstone Pictures, 1987 ✔️✔️✔️✔️

Credit this album with establishing Louis Armstrong's "What a Wonderful World," deftly deployed over harsh images of warfare, as a cultural standard, a blessing, or a curse depending on how many commercials you've heard it in. Robin Williams's monologues are a joy to have, though the excerpts are often too short. And there's a wealth of tremendous 1960s tunes, some of which—such as the Marvelettes' "Danger Heartbreak Dead Ahead," the Searchers' "Sugar and Spice," and the Vogues, "Five O'Clock World"—are refreshing choices.

Gary Graff

Good News

🎞️ **1991, Sony Music Special Products, from the film *Good News,*** MGM, 1947 ✔️✔️✔️

album notes: Music: Ray Henderson; **Lyrics:** B.G. DeSylva, Lew Brown; **Choir:** The MGM Studio Chorus; **Orchestra:** The MGM Studio Orchestra; **Conductor:** Lennie Hayton; **Cast:** June Allyson, Peter Lawford, Patricia Marshall, Joan McCracken.

A pleasantly mindless campus musical, *Good News* is best remembered today for the fact that it introduced June Allyson and Peter Lawford in their first starring roles. It also boasts a rousing score in which the natural highlights are the standard "The Best Things In Life Are Free," reprised almost ad nauseam throughout the film, "Pass That Peace Pipe," and "The French Lesson," in which Allyson teaches Lawford the rudiments of the language (or was it the other way around?). Bright and zippy, the film offers the wisp of a storyline about football star Lawford, a chronic failure in every other discipline, forced to study with Allyson, who is secretly in love with him, if he wants to graduate. The hint of a romantic conflict is introduced when Lawford falls for an attractive, but ultimately empty-headed co-ed, played by Patricia Marshall, while Mel Torme croons his way through a couple of numbers. All of it is innocuous, fun, and eventually enjoyable, with the whole cast joining in a spirited "Varsity Drag" to bring the screen shenanigans to a pleasant conclusion, just as it can be heard on the recording.

Didier C. Deutsch

The Good Son

1993, Fox Records, from the film *The Good Son*, 20th Century-Fox, 1993 ♪♪♪

album notes: Music: Elmer Bernstein; **Conductor:** Elmer Bernstein; **Featured Musician:** Cynthia Millar, Ondes Martenot.

Elmer Bernstein, a master at evoking a wide range of different moods, came up with one of his most attractive efforts for this film starring Macaulay Culkin, about an orphan boy, and his younger cousin, a psychopath with murderous instincts. Relying on the power of strong, romantic themes, at times gloriously expressed on the piano or Cynthia Millar's oddly atmospheric Ondes Martenot, the music unfolds with often striking beauty, creating an aura that is most fetching. Even the tracks less likely to elicit a positive reaction because of the downbeat moods they evoke ("Killing the Dog," "Skating and Drowning," "Funeral") come out strongly, thanks to the composer's skill at writing particularly exquisite melodies. An unusual, though remarkably sensitive score, only marred by the short playing time of some of the cues.

Didier C. Deutsch

The Good, the Bad and the Ugly

1985, EMI-Manhattan, from the film *The Good, the Bad and the Ugly*, United Artists, 1968 ♪♪♪♪♪

album notes: Music: Ennio Morricone; **Orchestra:** Orchestra Unione Musicisti di Roma; **Conductor:** Ennio Morricone.

10 Essential Scores by Max Steiner

King Kong
Gone with the Wind
Casablanca
The Flame and the Arrow
The Searchers
Treasure of the Sierra Madre
The Charge of the Light Brigade
The Lost Patrol
Virginia City
They Died with Their Boots On

Ennio Morricone had one of his most memorable spaghetti western scores with this film by Sergio Leone, a sprawling saga in which Clint Eastwood, in one of his best film performances, and Eli Wallach, in a delightful portrayal as Eastwood's snarling partner and foe, are the main protagonists. The effective set of cues created by the composer (and included in this sadly incomplete soundtrack album) provides the appropriate musical setting for some of the most relevant scenes in this overblown story about two bounty hunters who become unwilling soldiers of fortune while on their way to finding a hidden cache of gold. Among the tracks that stand out, "March," "The Story of a Soldier," "March without Hope," and "The Ecstasy of Gold" have justifiably become popular among fans of the stunning film. But the whole score, even in its abbreviated presentation, is quite successful at evoking the stirring climate that pervades this engrossing, and grandly over-the-top, western epic.

Didier C. Deutsch

The Good Thief

See: Il ladrone/L'harem

Good Will Hunting

🎬 1998, Capitol Records, from the Miramax film *Good Will Hunting*, 1998 ♪♪♪

album notes: Music: Danny Elfman.

A story of a latent working-class genius afraid to stray from the confines of his Boston neighborhood and utilize his singular gifts, *Good Will Hunting* sports a soundtrack album that is fittingly introspective. Director Gus Van Zant opted to feature Elliott Smith, a little-known Portland, Oregon, troubadour, to serve as the lead character's inner voice. A whopping six songs by Smith are found on the soundtrack album, alongside songs by Al Green, Gerry Rafferty, the Waterboys, two score cues by the ubiquitous Danny Elfman, and more. Smith's big break culminated in his receiving an Academy Award nomination for "Miss Misery" as Best Original Song for a Movie. A smart, well-conceived compilation.

Amy Rosen

Goodbye Lover

🎬 1999, Milan Records, from the Warner Bros. film *Goodbye Lover*, 1999 ♪♪♪♪

album notes: Music: John Ottman; **Conductor:** Larry Groupe

John Ottman delivered a potent score for this wry, delicious thriller that would have tremendously gained had the cues been expanded or reworked for the CD. As it is, some of them are much too short to convey any sense of their potential, which deprives the score as a whole from making a stronger impression (at 00:36, "Peggy's Story" must have been a short one!). What is left, however, reveals music that has its moments of fun, with many attractive cues in which one of the in-jokes is a recurring quote from Rodgers and Hammerstein's *The Sound of Music,* a favorite of the film's main character, in between her various moments of malevolence. Despite the brevity of some of the cues, there is enough here to convince the average listener that Ottman is a composer who has a lot to say and the means with which to say it. Watch and listen.

Didier C. Deutsch

GoodFellas

🎬 1990, Atlantic Records, from the film *GoodFellas,* Warner Bros., 1990 ♪♪♪

album notes: Featured Musicians: Tony Bennett; The Moonglows; The Cadillacs; Aretha Franklin; Bobby Darin; Muddy Waters; Cream; Derek & the Dominos.

A brief 1950s and 1960s set that starts in the ballroom, with Tony Bennett singing "Rags to Riches," moves to the street corner for the doo-wop heaven of The Moonglows, The Cadillacs, and others, then winds its way through girl-group pop before ending up at Muddy Waters's gritty "Mannish Boy" and Cream's

power rock classic "Sunshine of Your Love." Not a bad ride, but it's docked a full bone for including only the piano outro to Derek & the Dominos' "Layla."

Gary Graff

A Goofy Movie

🎬 1995, Walt Disney Records, from the animated feature *A Goofy Movie,* Walt Disney Pictures, 1995 ♪♪♪♪

album notes: Music: Carter Burwell; Don Davis; **Conductor:** Shirley Walker; Don Davis.

The urban contemporary stylings in some of the vocals on this Disney soundtrack album have a flavor that contrasts with the characters originally developed by the master animator, and show how removed from its lily-white image the studio has become in recent years. The fact that the songs probably will not appeal to the film's core audience of underage tykes, or that their elders are unlikely to find anything remotely redeeming in a cartoon about Goofy, leaves open the question about who will eventually be attracted to this album. The question also raises a doubt about the score, created by Carter Burwell, that will have a hard time finding an audience. Smart film-music fans, always eager to discover some of their favorite composers' latest creations, will be a happy exception and will be amply rewarded with a series of short compact cues that are attractively laid out and cohesively creative. Within the limits set by the animated feature, Burwell and Don Davis have invented some nifty musical moments that are effective and enjoyable, with "Bigfoot" and "Runaway Car" particularly noticeable among them.

Didier C. Deutsch

Gorillas in the Mist

🎬 1988, MCA Records, from the film *Gorillas in the Mist,* Warner Bros., 1988 ♪♪♪♪♪

album notes: Music: Maurice Jarre; **Featured Musicians:** Dennis Karmazan, cello; Ron Leonard, cello; The Maurice Jarre Electronic Ensemble: Michael Boddicker, Ralph Grierson, Judd Miller, Michael Fisher, Dan Greco, Rick Marvin, Nyle Steiner, Emil Richards, Alex Acuna.

On various occasions, Maurice Jarre has indulged in creating scores that made a pervasive use of synthesizers, unfortunately not always creatively or interestingly. There have been some happy exceptions, and his score for *Gorillas in the Mist* happens to be one of them. Somehow, the African background for this film about anthropologist Dian Fossey, its exotic sounds, and Jarre's own electronic inventions, supplemented by colorful orchestral textures, seem to blend very well to create a score of great scope and creative importance. Essential to the appreciation of it are two lengthy extrapolations, "African Wonderment," which describes in pure musical terms the landscape and its rich fauna, and "Tenderness and Turmoil," in which Fossey's mind sets find a melodic expression. The other selections are more directly linked to the action, about Fossey's attempts to survey and study the life of gorillas and the primates' response to her presence in their midst. The score received an Oscar nomination and one can easily understand why.

Didier C. Deutsch

Gorky Park

1983, Varèse Sarabande Records, from the film *Gorky Park,* Orion Pictures, 1983 🎬🎬🎬

album notes: Music: James Horner; Conductor: James Horner.

A rather odd East-West crime story about a Russian detective (William Hurt) investigating the murder of three men whose bodies were discovered in Moscow's Gorky Park, and the American sable trader (Lee Marvin) he eventually links with the deed, *Gorky Park* prompted James Horner to write a suitable score, in which the Russian references are swiftly borrowed from Tchaikovsky, enabling him to concentrate on an old-fashioned set of cues that could have been composed for any drama, whatever the setting. With Joanna Pacula adding an extra element to the mix, the score reveals many contrasting moods, all beautifully developed, from the romantic accents in "Irina's Theme" and "Arkady and Irina," to the throbbing riffs in "Chase Through the Park" and "The Sable Shed." While an early effort by Horner, this is also an interesting album well worth looking for.

Didier C. Deutsch

The Governess

1998, Sony Classical, from the Sony Pictures Classics film *The Governess,* 1998 🎬🎬🎬🎬

album notes: Music: Edward Shearmur; Conductor: Edward Shearmur; Featured Musicians: Mark Levy, viola da gamba; Philip Pickett, recorders; Hossam Ramzy, percussion; Pavlo Beznosiuk, rebec, violin; John Themis, lute; Gill Tingay, harp; Sally Heath, piano; Andy Brown, viola; Nick Cooper, Caroline Dearnley, Philip de Groote, cello; Rosemary Furniss, Jonathan Rees, violin; Ofra Haza, vocals.

Minnie Driver plays Rosina, a Jewish girl who poses as a Protestant governess to find a job with a racist Scottish family. Rosina's heritage remains a secret, yet composer Edward Shearmur's music is awash with references to the tonality and instrumentation of Jewish music. Alongside the London Metropolitan Orchestra, Israeli pop star Ofra Haza is heard in a more traditional context, singing a cappella on "Rosina," accompanied by accordion, violin, and harp on "Standchen," and with flute and drums on "Purim Dance." *The Governess* partners Shearmur's knack for emotive piano with Haza's exotic voice for a meditative and uplifting recording. Listeners unimpressed with Shearmur's other period romance, the bland *Wings of a Dove,* should put away their reservations for this excellent album.

David Poole

Grace of My Heart

1996, MCA Records, from the Universal film *Grace of My Heart,* 1996 🎬🎬🎬

The completely charming and unique soundtrack to *Grace of My Heart* is the brainchild of director Allison Anders, who had the inspired concept of pairing up some musical legends with contemporary artists to create music for her story about the career path of a young singer-songwriter in the '60s. Writer pairings included David Baerwald and Lesley "It's My Party" Gore, and Gerry Goffin (of Goffin/King fame) with Los Lobos. This "blind date" artistic process was also responsible for the initial pairing of Burt Bacharach and Elvis Costello, who churned out the stirring "God Give Me Strength," heard sung in the movie by Kristin Vigard, and a version heard in the end titles is sung by Elvis himself. Bacharach and Costello, who have said that they collaborated on their song via phone and fax, enjoyed themselves so much that they went on to subsequently record and release an entire album of collaborations. Other interesting selections here include Shawn Colvin taking on a song by Carole Bayer Sager and Dave Stewart, and R&B girl-group For Real covering Elvis Costello. There's also a lovely Joni Mitchell song that was written specially for the film and recorded by Kristen Vigard. A novel album and a great listen.

Amy Rosen

The Graduate

1987, Columbia Records, from the film *The Graduate,* Embassy Pictures, 1967 🎬🎬🎬

album notes: Music: Dave Grusin; Conductor: Dave Grusin; Songs: Paul Simon, Art Garfunkel.

Not that it set out to be this way, but *The Graduate* should probably be remembered today as the film that, in effect, signalled the start of a 10-year period during which instrumental music almost totally disappeared from the screens. The tremendous success of this album, fueled in large part by the songs written by Simon and Garfunkel, attracted Hollywood producers to the incredible profits that could be generated for them when a soundtrack album went gold and beyond. And the best way to achieve this, it seemed, was to replace instrumental scores by rock songs that could attract a younger, wider audience. As a result, many of the most respected film composers in town suddenly found themselves unemployed. Some, like Bernard Herrmann, Miklos Rozsa, and Dimitri Tiomkin, chose to seek a new career in Europe, where their talents were still admired and widely appreciated. Others, like Elmer Bernstein, "crossed over" and began writing innocuous music scores that could fit neatly between the various songs on the soundtracks, while being unobtrusive and totally unmemorable. It would take John Williams and *Star Wars,* in 1977, to bring back film music to its former

Anne Bancroft and Dustin Hoffman in The Graduate. **(The Kobal Collection)**

glory, and enable a new generation of composers like James Horner, Danny Elfman, and Alan Silvestri, to draw on their predecessors' contributions to the screen and make a name for themselves with broad-scale instrumental scores. Meanwhile, *The Graduate* has its moments, notably its evocative pop songs, and no doubt deserves to be in every collection.

Didier C. Deutsch

Graffiti Bridge

1990, Paisley Park Records, from the film *Graffiti Bridge*, Warner Bros. 1990 ♫♫♫

album notes: Music: Prince; **Featured Musicians:** Morris Day; Sheila E., drums; Boni Soyer, organ; Candy Dulfer, saxophone; Eric Leeds, saxophone; Atlanta Bliss, trumpet; Joseph Fiddler, keyboards.

With the film career of the artist formerly known as Prince now taking a well-deserved vacation, we can acknowledge that the best way to enjoy his movies is to play the soundtrack recordings instead. Case in point: this filmed "sequel" to *Purple Rain* comes within a couple of lively production numbers of being wholly forgettable, and yet the soundtrack CD finds the Prince

"Ur-groove" in the very first track and never lets it go. The result is a party album hot enough to help you forget the money you spent on the movie ticket. Prince regulars Morris Day and The Time pitch in, as do guest vocalists including Mavis Staples and George Clinton.

Marc Kirkeby

Grand Canyon

1991, RCA Records, from the film *Grand Canyon*, 20th Century-Fox, 1991 ♫♫♫♫

album notes: Music: James Newton Howard; **Conductor:** Marty Paloh; **Featured Musicians:** Dean Parks, guitar; Davey Johnstone, guitar; Michael Landau, guitar; Jude Cole, guitars; John Robinson, drums; Michael Fisher, percussion; Gayle Levant, harp; James Newton Howard, piano; Michael Lang, piano; Chuck Domanico, acoustic bass; Michael Boddicker, synth programming; Kirk Whalum, saxophone; Larry Williams, saxophone.

An emotionally moving, superior effort by James Newton Howard that balances the perceptions of life in modern-day Los Angeles, capturing the fears and hopes of those who struggle to survive in the sometimes oppressive, sometimes cold world of the inner city. Although an orchestra is used over the entire score, Howard often primarily utilizes guitars, percussion, and/or synthesizers to keep the scope small and personal. The people are the core of this story, the city only the locale. At times, a chorus passes through, personifying our daydreams of a brighter future. The music deftly alternates through several changes in musical style. Each represents the personal stories of the film's main characters, the privileged upper middle class couple who find themselves growing apart, and those trapped at the bottom in East L.A., struggling to hold onto their dignity and self respect. As their lives converge, each group becomes a source of strength for the other, and Howard melds their themes together, ultimately culminating with the exuberant "Grand Canyon Fanfare," the score's only large-scale orchestral cue. Warren Zevon's song "Searching for a Heart," completely appropriate to the mood, is well placed within the album, breaking the score into two suites.

David Hirsch

Grand Slam

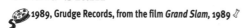 1989, Grudge Records, from the film *Grand Slam*, 1989 🎬

album notes: Music: Bill Conti; **Conductor:** Bill Conti.

Yet another baseball film, in which Bill Conti's contribution is reduced to a scant four cues. In this case, it really doesn't matter, because Conti, a composer whose career started on a high note but who has not sustained the hopes he nurtured at the time, uses his score to develop dry ideas that go nowhere. Driven by an electronic drum that sounds too dry and too robotic, his cues have all the excitement of a wet rag, with the music in search of an attractive melodic hook that never materializes. The rest of the selections consist of very conventional vocals, with Roberta Flack faring the best with her sensitive performance on "Dreams," and Little Richard the worst with his abrasive reading of the line "Ain't nothin' like a grand slam to make you feel like a real man . . ." Forget it!

Didier C. Deutsch

Grease

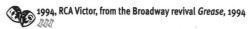 1972, Polydor Records, from the Broadway production *Grease*, 1972 🎵🎵🎵🎵

album notes: Music: Jim Jacobs, Warren Casey; **Lyrics:** Jim Jacobs, Warren Casey; **Musical Direction:** Louis St. Louis; **Cast:** Adrienne Barbeau, Don Billett, Walter Bobbie, Jim Borrelli, Barry Bostwick, Kathi Moss.

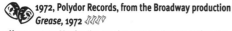 1978, Polydor Records, from the film *Grease*, Paramount Pictures, 1978 🎵🎵🎵🎵

album notes: Music: Jim Jacobs, Warren Casey; **Lyrics:** Jim Jacobs, Warren Casey; **Cast:** Stockard Channing, Edd Byrnes, John Travolta, Olivia Newton-John, Eve Arden, Joan Blondell, Sid Caesar, Alice Ghostley, Dody Goodman, Sha-Na-Na, Frankie Avalon.

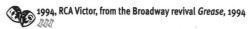 1994, RCA Victor, from the Broadway revival *Grease*, 1994 🎵🎵🎵

album notes: Music: Jim Jacobs, Warren Casey; **Lyrics:** Jim Jacobs, Warren Casey; **Musical Direction:** John McDaniel; **Cast:** Rosie O'Donnell, Brian Bradley, Ricky Paul Goldin, Susan Wood, Marcia Lewis.

A 1950s musical, *Grease* took Broadway pundits off-guard when it premiered on Feb. 14, 1972. With its pungent high-school antics its rivalries between gangs of greasers and Pink Ladies, and its pervasive rhythmic score, the musical offered a devastating, if slightly amusing look at a fictitious high-school group of students in the early days of the rock 'n' roll era. Spirited, direct, somewhat satirical, it was a great deal of fun, and even though it probably grated on the more traditional audiences usually flocking in to catch the latest shows, it enjoyed an unprecedented long run of 3,388 performances, quite an achievement. Of note, it introduced various talented youngsters who eventually went on to bigger and better things, including Barry Bostwick, Adrienne Barbeau (for a long while film-director John Carpenter's egeria), Treat Williams, and John Travolta, who starred in the film version.

The 1978 film version, starring John Travolta and Olivia Newton-John, expanded the concept in the original, and brought in frontline groups and performers to tackle the score, thus making what was essentially a simple stage musical into an all-star rock presentation. Surprisingly, it worked very well, and with the two principals bringing their own vocal and dramatic talents to the roles of Danny, the main greaser, and Sandy, the virtuous newcomer to Rydell High, *Grease* further benefited from the presence in its cast of Frankie Valli, Frankie Avalon, the rock group Sha-Na-Na, and mostly Stockard Channing, hilarious as Betty Rizzo, the leader of the Pink Ladies. The soundtrack album reflected the improvements, and continues to be one of the most enjoyable representations of this musical.

In 1994, the show returned to Broadway in a splashy, plastic presentation, staged by Tommy Tune's protégé Jeff Calhoun, in a production that was all show and little flair. Smartly packaged, however, with various name performers (Rosie O'Donnell, Jasmine Guy, Brooke Shields, Joe Piscopo) starring in it at one time or another, the musical succeeded in building an audience over a period of forty years. RCA Victor released two cast albums that are virtually identical and are only differentiated by the fact that Rosie O'Donnell is in one, and Brooke Shields in the other.

Didier C. Deutsch

The Great Caruso

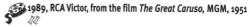 1989, RCA Victor, from the film *The Great Caruso*, MGM, 1951 🎵🎵

album notes: Tracks 1-8: Orchestra: The RCA Victor Orchestra; **Conductor:** Constantine Callinicos; **Tracks 9-20: Conductor:** Paul Baron

John Travolta in the film version of Grease. **(The Kobal Collection)**

At the height of his career, Mario Lanza starred as Enrico Caruso in a highly fictional account of the great singer's life made in Hollywood. In the film, Lanza sang several operatic tunes popularized by Caruso, including the eight selections that were eventually released as the film's "soundtrack" album. Eight years later, he recorded additional songs Caruso had either created or covered in his time, all of them from a more popular source. Film fans will notice that three of these were orchestrated by a young arranger named Ennio Morricone. Otherwise, this set is strictly for devotees.

Didier C. Deutsch

The Great Escape

 1998, Rykodisc, from the United Artists film *The Great Escape*, 1962 ♪♪♪♪

album notes: Music: Elmer Bernstein; **Conductor:** Elmer Bernstein.

This is the third time that this momentous score by Elmer Bernstein is making a digital appearance. In the first edition of this book, Randall D. Larson reviewed it in these terms: "The music is outstanding, built around a variety of themes representing the various characters who people this ultimate World War II POW film. The main theme, a catchy march for wind instruments over trombones and tuba, sustained by a counter melody for violins over militaristic percussion, evokes the concentration camp prisoners, and their spirit of resistance against their captors. A generic cue, 'On the Road,' marked by eerie woodwind tones over gentle harp plucks and quietly rising brass chords, represents the mystery and danger beyond the camp's barbed-wire fences. The final theme for freedom is developed into a grand and glorious melody evoking a sense of quiet victory while retaining a sense of sorrow for those lost and left behind. Brassy punches bridge this and the main theme, which closes out the score. An excellent military score and one of Bernstein's best which is very well preserved on CD."

These comments are still valid and apply just as well to this new release, which has been augmented with three short bits of dialogue ("Give Up," "Big X," and "Meanwhile We Dig"). They add nothing extravagantly new and in fact seem a bit superfluous.

Didier C. Deutsch

Great Expectations

 1998, Atlantic Records, from the 20th Century-Fox film *Great Expectations*, 1998 ♪♪♪♪

album notes: Music: Patrick Doyle; **Conductor:** David Snell; **Featured Musicians:** John Williams, guitar; Cyrus Chestnut, piano; Carey Wilson, whistle; Phil Todd, EWI; James Carter, saxophone; Guy Barker, trumpet; Alvester Garnett, drums.

1998, Atlantic Records, from the 20th Century-Fox film *Great Expectations*, 1998 ♪♪♪♪

A loose adaptation of Charles Dickens's novel, this modern redux will never achieve the classic status of the book, but it yielded two soundtrack albums that are both absolutely wonderful. *Great Expectations: The Album* should be held up as a textbook example of how to create a great song compilation. The CD contains mostly new tracks by both baby bands and more established artists, with a couple of classic cuts thrown in for effect. This soundtrack spawned the hit "Living in Mono" by Mono, "Sunshower" by former Soundgarden vocalist Chris Cornell, and "Today" by Poe. Also on the CD are new tracks by former Stone Temple Pilot vocalist Scott Weiland, Tori Amos, and Duncan Sheik.

Patrick Doyle's beautiful score appears on the second of the two CDs. Doyle uses vocals as an instrument on several tracks, with "Finn," featuring Tori Amos showing up on both CDs (as does Cesaria Evora's version of "Besame Mucho"). She apparently also lends her vocals to a second track on this CD, "Paradiso Perduto," but damned if I can hear her anywhere on that track. Another highlight here is "I Saw No Shadow of Another Parting," performed by Kiri te Kanawa, an aria which Doyle also composed for the film.

Beth Krakower

The Great Muppet Caper

 1995, Jim Henson Records, from the animated feature *The Great Muppet Caper*, Jim Henson Films, 1995 ♪♪♪♪

album notes: Music: Joe Raposo; **Conductor:** Joe Raposo, Marcus Dods; **Cast:** Jim Henson (Kermit The Frog, Dr. Teeth, Rowlf, Swedish Chef, Waldorf); Frank Oz (Fozzie Bear, Miss Piggy, Animal, Sam The Eagle); Jerry Nelson (Floyd, Pops, Robin The Frog); Richard Hunt (Scooter, Sweetums, Statler, Janice, Beaker); Dave Goelz (The Great Gonzo, Zoot, Dr. Bunsen Honeydew); Steve Whitmire (Rizzo The Rat, Lips).

Okay, The Muppets are cute! And Joe Raposo, for many years their musical director, knew better than any other composer how to express in his songs their different personalities and translate the flavor of their antics. But nowhere was this more apparent than in this, their first big screen effort, which saw the whole gang—Kermit, Fozzie, Miss Piggy, Dr. Teeth and the Electric Mayhem—do what they do best, entertain us. Along the way, they performed some entertaining numbers, all found on this sparkling album, most notably "Rainbow Connection," the bouncy "Movin' Right Along," or "I Hope That Somethin' Better Comes Along," Kermit and Rowlf's sad realization that they can't live without a mate. A short (32 minutes) but entertaining album.

Didier C. Deutsch

The Great Outdoors

🎬 **1988, Atlantic Records, from the Universal film *The Great Outdoors,* 1988** ♪

Starring Dan Aykroyd and John Candy, *The Great Outdoors* was a typical comic yarn of a family's pleasant vacation by a lake being disrupted by the arrival of their boorish, unwanted in-laws. What might have seemed like a funny idea turned into a clumsy concept, somewhat unpleasant to watch, and only faintly relieved by the antics of the two stars. Adding insult to injury in this case, several selections in the soundtrack were performed by the Elwood Blues Revue, in a sinister ploy to tap into the success of an earlier movie in which another John (Belushi) made a much better impression.

There may be, on the part of Dan Aykroyd, a desire to provide a forum for a music he earnestly admires, and by conjuring up the Elwood Blues Band at every opportunity he may feel that he accomplishes something worthwhile. However, he may also be ripping off both the black singers who are "featured" on the tracks (Wilson Pickett and Sam Moore, among them), who are much more talented than he is, and the formula he originally created with Belushi, that was funny for a time but is evidently running out of steam. Released in 1988, this album is a sad reminder that some unfunny people with limited talent are much more successful than they truthfully deserve to be.

Didier C. Deutsch

The Great White

See: Act of Piracy/The Great White

The Great White Hype

🎬 **1996, Epic Soundtrax, from the film *The Great White Hype,* 20th Century-Fox, 1996** ♫♫♫

album notes: Featured Musicians: D.J. U-Neek; NYT Owl; Passion; E-40; Bone Thugs-N-Harmony; Lou Rawls; Biz Markie; Insane Clown Posse; Cappadonna; Ghostface Killer; Rza; Camp Lo; Ambersunshower; Jamie Foxx; Dolemite; Premier; Method Man; Marcus Miller.

The dichotomy between the film and the soundtrack album is that one is a spoof of urban, inner-city life and the world of boxing, while the other almost begs to be taken at face value. Combining performances by East Coast and West Coast hip hop artists, the album only begins to echo the film's irreverent style when Lou Rawls and Biz Markie team for a version of "I've Got You Under My Skin" that Cole Porter would never have dreamed of, or when Jamie Foxx shares the spotlight with Dolemite on "Knocked Nekked (From the Waist Down)." But other than those, the tracks on the album don't seem to have the right flair.

Didier C. Deutsch

The Greatest

🎬 **1998, Razor & Tie Records, from the film *The Greatest,* Columbia 1977** ♫♫♫

album notes: Music: Michael Masser.

If anyone should ask who is (was) "the Greatest," there is only one answer, Muhammad Ali, boxer extraordinaire, sensitive poet, and a performer who feels equally at ease in front of the camera as he is in the ring. This filmed biography, made in 1977, before a crippling disease slowed down the Champ, finds Ali in fine fettle, first as a brash young boxer filled with energy and the audacity to challenge everyone, then as a world-class champion whose record became unmatched, but whose personal convictions ran contrary to the conventional mold. Sprinkled throughout the biopic was actual footage of his most famous bouts, with the soundtrack generously providing a musical counterpoint to the screen action. The album itself yielded a couple of hits in "The Greatest Love of All," performed by George Benson, and "Zaire Chant," by Mandrill. Michael Masser's music is appropriately grandstanding and adequately echoes the bombastic tone of the film.

Didier C. Deutsch

The Greatest Story Ever Told

🎬 **1998, Rykodisc, from the United Artists film *The Greatest Story Ever Told,* 1968** ♫♫♫♫

album notes: Music: Alfred Newman; **Conductor:** Alfred Newman.

A picture as colossal as *The Greatest Story Ever Told* deserved a colossal soundtrack. Director George Stevens turned the scoring of this three-hour film over to veteran composer Alfred Newman, who delivered one of his most majestic efforts, pulling out all the stops in a sensational display of his talent. Although he was dealing with a film of great magnitude, he wrote a score that was surprisingly subdued, stressing the "divine" aspects of the story rather than its epic scope. His efforts earned him an Academy Award nomination.

For many years, the only recording collectors and fans could listen to was the re-recording Newman had done for United Artists shortly after the film had been released. Beautifully remastered, it can be found now on the first CD of this unusual three-CD set, released by Rykodisc. But the centerpieces of the set itself are the other two CDs, which contain the original film score as it was heard in the film itself. Listening to both CDs proves really stimulating, like discovering a masterpiece that had been lost. Newman's score ranks among his best achievements, and for once this release does it full justice. If only all soundtrack reissues were handled and preserved in such a way. It is just magnificent, and a fierce statement to all those who claim that film music is a negligible form of expression that should be heard behind a screen but not in the living room. Newman's score ranks among the finest instrumental works ever composed, and has earned its place next to the works of the great classical symphonists.

Didier C. Deutsch

Green Card

1991, Varèse Sarabande Records, from the film *Green Card*, Touchstone Pictures, 1991 🎬🎬🎬🎬

album notes: Music: Hans Zimmer; **Featured Musicians:** Hans Zimmer, synthesizers; Ian Lees, bass.

Hans Zimmer has scored this urban romance as if it were a jungle picture. And appropriately so. Emerging out of an urban-percussion composition by Larry Wright, Zimmer's score for *Green Card* is alternately exotic, toe-tapping, and highly romantic. His opening cue is an evocative blend of voice, synth, and percussion, suggesting the urban jungle and its primitive roots, as multi-layered and compelling as any of Zimmer's thickly-orchestrated compositions. His main theme is a catchy, rhythmic motif for reedy synth and heavy percussion. Synth-woodwind and percussion, including what sounds like synth-steel drum, abound in the instrumentation—an unusual style for a romantic comedy (the musical style is as much director Peter Weir's as it is Zimmer's, according to the composer), but one that adds an engaging quality to the music on film as well as on CD. A romantic piano theme rises above the urban jungle music, signifying the awakening love of the main characters that similarly rises above events in which they are wrapped. Also included on the disc is a Mozart Clarinet Concerto, heard in the film, and a closing pop song.

Randall Larson

Gremlins

1993, Geffen Records, from the film *Gremlins*, Warner Bros., 1984 🎬🎬🎬🎬

album notes: Music: Jerry Goldsmith; **Conductor:** Jerry Goldsmith.

Considering how wonderful Jerry Goldsmith's score for the film is, it seems a real shame that the powers-that-be at Geffen Records chose to include only 15 minutes of his music in this album, on which the playing time is already inordinately short by usual standards. The cues, all four of them, placed at the end of the album, denote the wonderfully whimsical tones adopted by the composer to depict the invasion of an entire city by a colony of furry little things that have an uncanny ability to reproduce once they are exposed to water or any sort of food past the midnight witching hour. "The Gremlin Rag," alone is an outstanding piece of music, delightful and totally enjoyable. While these selections give an idea of the score Goldsmith created for

the film, the album leaves one wanting more. As for the pop selections, they do seem like a lot of padding.

Didier C. Deutsch

Gremlins 2: The New Batch

1990, Varèse Sarabande, from the film *Gremlins 2: The New Batch*, Warner Bros., 1990 🎬🎬🎬

album notes: Music: Jerry Goldsmith; **Conductor:** Jerry Goldsmith.

Goldsmith returned to Gremlins territory for this warm-hearted sequel that jettisoned the horror elements in favor of gentle satire, with his score following director Joe Dante's lead with an eclectic brew of electronic tomfoolery, low-key jazz, and noble-sounding underscoring for the aspirations of the benevolent Donald Trump-like entrepreneur John Glover. The result is some amusing moments and a particularly lovely denouement, but overall this one falls into a group of pretty unmemorable comedy scores Goldsmith produced in the early 1990s.

Jeff Bond

The Grifters

1990, Varèse Sarabande, from the film *The Grifters*, Miramax Pictures, 1990 🎬🎬🎬🎬

album notes: Music: Elmer Bernstein; **Conductor:** Elmer Bernstein.

Including a jaunty little tune that pervades the whole score, *The Grifters* ranks among Elmer Bernstein's top efforts and one of his best scores in recent years. Based on a novel by Jim Thompson about a group of small-time con artists and how everyone in the small group cheats on everyone else, the film is permeated with a blend of mordant humor and brooding darkness that gives the narrative a teasing, elusive quality and stands out as one of the most telling themes developed by the composer. These elements find an echo in the score, essentially written for a small chamber ensemble of woodwinds and brass, with electronic sounds designed by Cynthia Millar. In turns humorously eccentric, darkly original, and solidly anchored around the five-note motif in its main theme, the score comes across as an enticing piece of music, with amusing elements and thoughtful interpolations.

Didier C. Deutsch

Grosse Pointe Blank /Grosse Pointe Blank, Vol. 2

Gross Point Blank; 1997, London Records, from the film *Grosse Pointe Blank*, Hollywood Pictures, 1997 🎬🎬🎬🎬

album notes: Featured Musicians: Violent Femmes, The Clash, The English Beat, David Bowie, Queen, Johnny Nash, Guns 'N' Roses, Faith No More, The Specials, The Jam, Los Fabulosos Cadillacs, Pete Townsend.

A good combination of oldies and new stuff, this soundtrack album serves up a refreshing lineup of great rockers who aren't often found together on the same album. Bookended by two selections by Violent Femmes, the album's best moments include The Clash's "Rudie Can't Fail" and "Armagideon Time," Guns 'N' Roses' cover version of Paul McCartney's "Live and Let Die," and The Jam's take on "Absolute Beginners." David Bowie and Queen's collaboration on "Under Pressure" is always nice to have around, as is Pete Townshend's "Let My Love Open The Door." A pleasant surprise is Los Fabulosos Cadillacs, a rarely heard (at least in this country) Argentinian group whose energetic "El Matador" alone is worth a visit.

Didier C. Deutsch

Grosse Pointe Blank, Vol. 2; 1997, London Records, from the Hollywood film *Grosse Pointe Blank,* 1997 🎞🎞🎞

Another '80s pop compilation by any other name, the second volume from *Grosse Pointe Blank* picks up where its predecessor left off, grabbing more music that would be booming from the tape players and turntables (remember them?) of a tuned-in '80s high schooler. The songs on this set are less obvious than the first, with just a couple of hits—a-ha's "Take on Me," the Dazz Band's "Let It Whip"—and more subversive material from the likes of the Specials ("Rudy, a Message to You," "You're Wondering Now"), the Bauhaus spin-off Tones on Tail ("Go!"), the Pixies ("Monkey Gone to Heaven"), and the Pogues ("Lorca's Novena"). Neither the ultimate nor the definitive collection of this period, *Grosse Pointe Blank* part deux is still a fine, frothy listen.

Gary Graff

Groundhog Day

1993, Epic Soundtrax, from the film *Groundhog Day,* Columbia Pictures, 1993 🎞🎞🎞

album notes: Music: George Fenton; **Conductor:** George Fenton; **Featured Musician:** Dan Higgins, saxophone.

The soundtrack to this zany picture starring Bill Murray is itself deliciously insane, with its blend of a pseudo baroque quartet piece named for the film title next to Sonny and Cher warbling their hit "I Got You, Babe." The story of an egotistical weatherman who keeps living the same day over and over and over, the film's inspired lunacy translated itself into an album that also includes several pop tunes including "Almost Like Being in Love," by Nat King Cole, and "Pennsylvania Polka," played by Frankie Yankovic in another odd pairing. George Fenton contributes some eclectic themes like "Clouds," "Drunks," "The Kidnap and the Quarry," among other, equally welcome moments. Delightfully entertaining is the word.

Didier C. Deutsch

Grumpier Old Men

1995, TVT Records, from the film *Grumpier Old Men,* Warner Bros., 1995 🎞🎞

album notes: Music: Alan Silvestri; **Conductor:** Alan Silvestri.

The constant one-upmanship between two grumpy old friends (Jack Lemmon and Walter Matthau returning to the roles they created in *Grumpy Old Men*) finds its best musical expression in the lively "(I'll Be Glad When You're Dead) You Rascal You," the first selection on the album, performed by Louis Armstrong and Louis Jordan. Unfortunately, the moods in the film are not sustained in this collection of pop tracks, which include Buster Poindexter's derivative rendition of Ray Charles's hit "Hit the Road Jack," Dean Martin's "That's Amore," and Harry Belafonte's exuberant "Jump in the Line (Shake Senora)," already a highlight in the film *Beetlejuice.* Alan Silvestri's score, reduced here to two cues ("What the Heck" and "End Title"), sounds lovely, but who can tell?

Didier C. Deutsch

Guarding Tess

1994, Tristar Music, from the film *Guarding Tess,* Tristar Pictures, 1994 🎞🎞🎞

album notes: Music: Michael Convertino; **Conductor:** Richard Kaufman.

Charming score by Michael Convertino for this comedy film about the war of wills between a former First Lady and her Secret Service bodyguard. As they snipe at each other, the composer hints at their growing bond with a bold arrangement of strings in "Patriots." Conversely, Convertino relies on classical music-inspired arrangements to play up the absurdity of the government's stuffy sense of self importance.

David Hirsch

Gulliver's Travels

1996, RCA Victor, from the television movie *Gulliver's Travels,* RHI Entertainment and Channel Four Television, 1996 🎞🎞🎞

album notes: Music: Trevor Jones; **Conductor:** Geoffrey Alexander.

Trevor Jones's representation on disc has always been hit and miss, his scores often pruned to two or three tracks to make room for pop songs, or worse, spoiled by the inclusion of dialogue. Thus, *Gulliver's Travels* is something of a phenomenon, in that it contains a lengthy representation of exclusively Jones's score. The main theme evokes both an epic sense and a feeling of weariness, expressing the protagonist's endless attempts to return home. "The Emperor's Palace" (perhaps the score's most enjoyable cue) features feisty woodwinds which evoke the arrogance and pettiness of the Lilliputians. A more

Eastern sound figures into "Laputa," with primitive percussion and a darbuka-like synthesizer, while "Battle of the Wasps" chillingly depicts the tiny Gulliver's attempts to ward off a swarm of giant bees.

At a running time of 75:52, the album does become a little static in the last third; the basic thematic material is really not enough to cover the running time and redundancy sets in. Still, there is much allure to the music, and Jones has a particular knack for scoring fantasy that is matched by few others.

Paul Andrew MacLean

Gunmen

1993, MCA Records, from the Dimension film *Gunmen*, 1993 🎬🎬

album notes: Music: John Debney.

Mario Van Peebles, as a DEA agent, and Christopher Lambert, as a smuggler, formed an uneasy alliance to fight a wheelchaired villain and his vicious henchmen over some drug money in this contemporary drama that never quite knew if it should be taken seriously or if it should be a comedy. A wink in the direction of the spaghetti westerns of yore (informed in the song "Bite the Bullet" with a two-note call reminiscent of the Ennio Morricone score for *The Good, the Bad and the Ugly*) doesn't help. Of the songs collected in this album, presumably heard in the film in shortened bits and pieces, "Love and Heritage" by Morgan Heritage, "Stranger in My Life" by Christopher Williams, and "This House" by Cruzados, stand out. "Jungle Chase," by John Debney, is a febrile mix of rapid-fire guitar vamps, flute calls, and percussion that lasts just one minute—not long enough to make much of an impression.

Didier C. Deutsch

Guns for San Sebastian

See: Hang 'Em High

The Guns of Navarone

1989, Varèse Sarabande, from the film *The Guns of Navarone*, Columbia Pictures, 1961 🎬🎬🎬🎬

album notes: Music: Dimitri Tiomkin; **Lyrics:** Paul Francis Webster; **Orchestra:** The Sinfonia of London Orchestra; **Conductor:** Dimitri Tiomkin.

Another blockbuster score by Dimitri Tiomkin, filled with great energy and heroic accents to underline this World War II drama in which Gregory Peck, David Niven, and Anthony Quinn singlehandedly defeat the entire German army when they destroy huge guns on the island of Navarone, off the coast of Greece, guarding the open sea. The "legend," introduced in a prologue narrated by James Robertson Justice, sets the tone and provides the background to the tale itself, musically illustrated by the composer, in a stirring display of his florid style. Three themes evoke the action, a martial one to convey the war effort, another with a Greek flavor to stress the locale, and a third, a lyrical theme, to express the beauty and deep emotional impact of the adventure itself. While the score itself is very attractive and makes for an entertaining listening session, you might want to ignore Mitch Miller and the gang's earnest rendition of the inane title song, in which lyrics try to rhyme such unlikely poetic words as "nitroglycerine" and "saboteurs."

Didier C. Deutsch

Guys and Dolls

1991, MCA Records, from the Broadway production *Guys and Dolls*, 1950 🎬🎬🎬

album notes: Music: Frank Loesser; **Lyrics:** Frank Loesser; **Musical Direction:** Irving Actman; **Cast:** Robert Alda, Vivian Blaine, Sam Levene, Isabel Bigley, Stubby Kaye.

1992, RCA Victor, from the Broadway revival *Guys and Dolls*, 1992 🎬🎬🎬🎬

album notes: Music: Frank Loesser; **Lyrics:** Frank Loesser; **Musical Direction:** Edward Strauss; **Cast:** Peter Gallagher, Josie de Guzman, Nathan Lane, Faith Prince, Walter Bobbie.

1992, Reprise Records, from the studio cast recording, *Guys and Dolls*, 1964 🎬🎬

album notes: Music: Frank Loesser; **Lyrics:** Frank Loesser; **Musical Direction:** Morris Stoloff; **Cast:** Frank Sinatra, Bing Crosby, Dean Martin, Jo Stafford, The McGuire Sisters, Dinah Shore, Debbie Reynolds, Clark Dennis, Allan Sherman, Sammy Davis Jr.

Amid the dazzling array of lights, color, and motion that create the spectacular Gotham-esque atmosphere of the staging for this pivotal musical comedy lies one of the most alluring scores of all time: fun-filled, action-packed and, at the same time, beautifully tender and romantic. And while it's rare for every element of a production to marry and form a perfect union, it is rarer still for nearly *every* song from a show to become a bonafide standard, as is the case with Frank Loesser's magnificent compositions for *Guys and Dolls*.

Fortunately, fans of the theatre can instantly transport themselves back to the glamour and panache of Runyonland, via two superb CD issues: the original 1950 Broadway cast recording, and the unmatched 1992 "new" Broadway cast recording–both highly recommended.

The original 1950 cast recording (starring Robert Alda, Vivian Blaine, and Sam Levene) features all of the familiar hit songs from the original production, and remains a warm, cherished historic document of the charm that made *Guys and Dolls* an immediate critical success. The sonic restorations from the original recording elements (lacquer discs) are quite good, but in general, the monophonic sound lacks the presence that a show with the sizzle of *Guys and Dolls* requires.

However, the 1992 Broadway cast recording, featuring Nathan Lane, Faith Prince, and Peter Gallagher, completely makes up for any of the original's shortcomings. Crackling with intense energy and excitement, Michael Starobin's crisp, tight orchestrations immediately set the stage for some of the most polished, seamless performances in Broadway history–so bright and snappy, it almost makes the original show's tempos and performances seem lackluster! As a bonus, the recording offers two essential dance sequences appearing for the first time on record: "Havana," and "The Crapshooter's Dance."

Regrettably, no officially issued recording exists for the 1955 film version of the show, starring Marlon Brando, Frank Sinatra, and Vivian Blaine. In addition to being a terrific film adaptation, the movie contains several new songs written by Loesser to assist in the show's transition from stage to screen, and the soundtrack is noticeable by its unforgivable absence on the market. Sinatra fans might enjoy the all-star studio recording released by Reprise, enjoyable for the most part except for Debbie Reynolds's misguided performance as Adelaide.

Charles L. Granata

Gypsy

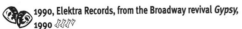 **1999, Sony Classical/Legacy Records, from the Broadway musical *Gypsy*, 1959** 🎜🎜🎜🎜

album notes: Music: Jule Styne; **Lyrics:** Stephen Sondheim; **Conductor:** Milton Rosenstock; **Cast:** Ethel Merman, Jack Klugman, Sandra Church, Lane Bradbury, Jacquelyn Mayro.

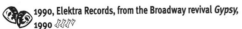 **1990, Elektra Records, from the Broadway revival *Gypsy*, 1990** 🎜🎜🎜🎝

album notes: Music: Jule Styne; **Lyrics:** Stephen Sondheim; **Musical Direction:** Eric Stern; **Cast:** Tyne Daly, Jonathan Hadary, Crista Moore, Tracy Venner, Christen Tassin, Kristen Mahon.

 1993, Atlantic Records, from the television presentation *Gypsy*, 1993 🎜🎜🎜🎝

album notes: Music: Jule Styne; **Lyrics:** Stephen Sondheim; **Musical Direction:** Ken Watson; **Cast:** Bette Midler, Peter Riegert, Cynthia Gibb, Jennifer Beck, Lacey Chabert, Elisabeth Moss, Christine Ebersole.

The old girl from the world of showbiz, Mama Rose proves both indestructible and a fine vehicle for singing female stars. Originally created by Ethel Merman, for whom it was written, the part has been variously handled by Rosalind Russell in the film version (not available on CD), Angela Lansbury, Tyne Daly, and more recently Bette Midler, among many others. The quintessential backstage musical, and for many the best ever written, *Gypsy* related the real-life story of stripper Gypsy Rose Lee and her sister June Haver, and how each was shaped into a star of the first magnitude by their monster of a stage mother. With a fine, solid book by Arthur Laurents and a splendid score by Jule

Styne (music) and Stephen Sondheim (lyrics), the show has endured through repeated revivals, losing none of its freshness and its strength, even though by now its plot and tunes have become remarkably familiar. The three recordings listed here are all superb in their own right, the personality of the actress playing Mama Rose being the main focus.

Tyne Daly, in the 1990 Broadway revival, added her own touch to the role, but without significantly altering it, in a performance that has its moments of excellence.

Bette Midler, in the 1993 television treatment, camps the part a bit, but she is also remarkably true to the spirit of the original in a performance that has been justifiably lauded.

But the original cast album starring Merman, newly remixed and remastered, is a "must buy," not only for fans of the show/cast album but for Sondheim fans, too, because of the included Merman demo records of "Some People" and "Mr. Goldstone/Little Lamb," which has lyrics that were later changed. (And "Little Lamb" comes in the middle of "Mr. Goldstone," not at the end of the number.) A bigger surprise is the included bits and pieces edited from the cast album, many brief orchestral bits that may not really be noticed. But surely everyone will notice Louise's squeals of delight as she dances with Tulsa at the end of "All I Need Is the Girl," which were not there previously, and that there is a somewhat extended "strip sequence" in *Gypsy*'s "Let Me Entertain You." But the most welcome surprise is hearing the complete lyrics of "You Gotta Have a Gimmick" from Tessie's "Dressy Tessie Tura/ Is so much more demurer/ Than all them other ladies because/ You gotta get a gimmick/ If you wanna get applause!" through the three strippers' "Do somethin' special/ Anything that's fresh'll/ Earn you a big fat cigar" round, which was edited for the album all those years ago. It may be a minor addition, but it certainly is a welcome one.

Didier C. Deutsch and Max O. Preeo

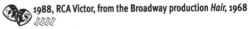

Hair

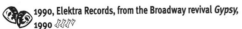 **1988, RCA Victor, from the Broadway production *Hair*, 1968** 🎜🎜🎜🎜

album notes: Music: Galt MacDermot; **Lyrics:** Gerome Ragni, James Rado; **Musical Direction:** Galt MacDermot; **Featured Musicians:** Galt MacDermot, electric piano; Steve Gillette, Alan Fontaine, guitars; Jimmy Lewis, bass; Zane Paul, woodwinds, reeds; Donald Leight; Eddy Williams, trumpets; Warren Chiasson, percussion; Idris Muhammad, drums; **Cast:** James Rado, Gerome Ragni, Ronald Dyson, Steve Curry, Lamont Washington, Lynn Kellogg, Sally Eaton, Melba Moore,

Beverly O' Angelo, Amie Golden, Trent Williams, and Dan Dacus in Hair **(The Kobal Collection)**

Shelley Plimpton, Diane Keaton, Donnie Burks, Lorrie Davis, Leata Galloway, Robert I. Rubinsky.

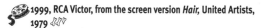 **1999, RCA Victor, from the screen version *Hair*, United Artists, 1979** 🎵🎵🎵

album notes: Music: Galt MacDermot; **Lyrics:** Gerome Ragni, James Rado; **Musical Direction:** Galt MacDermot; **Cast:** John Savage, Treat Williams, Don Dacus, Dorsey Wright, Beverly D'Angelo, Annie Golden, Michael Jeter, Nell Carter, Leata Galloway, Laurie Beechman, Melba Moore, Ronnie Dyson, Twyla Tharp, Charlaine Woodard.

A seminal rock 'n' roll musical, *Hair* opened on April 29, 1968, amid the brouhaha created by several facets of the production. Firstly, conservative Broadway seemed ill-prepared to accept a show advocating the tenets of the flower power generation of the late 1960s. Secondly, the musical was determinedly antimilitarist at a time when the war in Vietnam, though increasingly unpopular, still arose much patriotic fervor. Lastly, a much-publicized "nude" scene went against the accepted, traditionalist norms (the year before, the dancers in *Les Ballets Africains* had been allowed to appear bare-breasted because the revue was an "ethnic" show). The Jerry Falwells of the world notwithstanding, *Hair* became an immediate success, not the

least because it received an unconditional endorsement from Clive Barnes in the *New York Times,* who rhapsodized about its many virtues. A "total experience," the show ushered in a new era on Broadway, though, in retrospect, it appears hopelessly rooted in its own time period and so seriously dated by now that various attempts at reviving it in the late 1970s and early 1980s failed completely.

Propelled by its rhythm-driven score, in which "Aquarius," "Good Morning Starshine," and "Let The Sunshine In" soon became great favorites, and songs which, at the time, enjoyed a *succes de scandale* ("Sodomy," "I Believe In Love," "Hashish," "Colored Spade," "Walking In Space"), the loosely structured show had a run of 1,750 performances, and launched the careers of several performers who appeared in it at one time or another, including Melba Moore, Ronnie Dyson, Diane Keaton, Paul Jabara, Nell Carter, Ben Vereen, Philip Michael Thomas, and Meatloaf.

In 1979, a screen version, directed by Milos Forman, tried to recapture the hippie moods and feelings of the show in an ill-conceived effort that was only mildly successful. Of the two recordings listed, the original cast album is the one to have, though be prepared to experience something of a culture shock when you listen to it today and realize that it is no longer what it was touted to be. Even more of a curiosity, the soundtrack album might be of interest to people who must have every title in their collection.

Beth Krakower

Hallelujah, Baby!

1992, Sony Broadway, from the Broadway production *Hallelujah, Baby!* 1967 🎬🎬🎬

album notes: Music: Jule Styne; **Lyrics:** Betty Comden, Adolph Green; **Musical Direction:** Buster Davis; **Cast:** Leslie Uggams, Robert Hooks, Lillian Hayman, Allen Case, Marilyn Cooper.

Radical chic came to Broadway in 1967 with this look at race relations and show business, but the results were less than what had been anticipated. In trying to be topical, the creators of *Hallelujah, Baby!* (Arthur Laurents, Jule Styne, Betty Comden, and Adolph Green) failed to remember that what mattered in a musical was the music, not so much the message. In trying to portray the life of an entertainer (Leslie Uggams, in a fetching portrayal), her slow ascension to stardom, and her love affairs with a black man (Robert Hooks) and a white man (Allen Case), intertwined through 60 years of race struggles and emancipation, they only succeeded in muddling the stage with a story that was not very convincing (the characters did not age, further confusing the audience), and a score that was not too terribly entertaining. By the time the show won the Tony as Best Musical (by default, it should be mentioned), it already had closed and would have been forgotten were it not for this cast album which actually makes it sound much better than it really was.

Didier C. Deutsch

Halloween

1985, Varèse Sarabande, from the film *Halloween*, Compass International, 1985 🎬🎬🎬🎬🎬

album notes: Music: Alan Howarth; John Carpenter.

While most synthesized horror film scores tend to sound as if they were made up as the performer went along, director John Carpenter uses the limitations of his early synthesizer work to great advantage in *Halloween*. The resulting work is a minimalist creation as relentless as the film's unstoppable killer. Carpenter based his score on three principal themes, the main title with its infectious mix of repetitive piano, rattle, and stomping, the more subtle "creeping" motif, and a desperate, repetitive "stalking" theme. His wise exploitation of the simplicity of the arrangements created both an effective score and entertaining soundtrack album. By avoiding the use of con-

ventional electronic effects, Carpenter's score shows very little dating 20 years later.

David Hirsch

1995, Varèse Sarabande, from the film *Halloween: The Curse of Michael Myers*, Miramax Films, 1995 🎬🎬🎬

album notes: Music: John Carpenter.

Alan Howarth, who worked closely with Carpenter for several years on a variety of scores, took on the *Halloween* series solo in 1988 with the fourth film, *The Return of Michael Myers*. His latest score in the series, 1995's *The Curse of Michael Myers*, still makes good use of the minimalist style established on the first film, but with the use of a battery of state of the art synthesizers, Howarth can now create a score that sounds positively lavish in comparison to Carpenter's. The *Halloween* theme is brought into the 1990s with guitars replacing the piano track and Carpenter's old "creeping" motif returns once again. Howarth puts in a good effort with several interesting moments and some synth passages are so well designed that they sound almost acoustical. It can't, however, equal the first film score simply because of sheer nostalgic value.

David Hirsch

Halloween 2

1981, Varèse Sarabande Records, from the film *Halloween 2: The Nightmare Isn't Over!*, Dino de Laurentiis Corp., 1981 🎬🎬🎬

album notes: Music: John Carpenter; Alan Howarth.

A tired, uninspired sequel to the 1985 original, *Halloween 2* began where the previous film ended, providing Carpenter with a nifty reprise of "Laurie's Theme," with Myers (now identified as The Shape) on the loose, stalking again, and slashing his way through 92 minutes of a tedious horror film. Still, Carpenter's music, complemented by Howarth's contributions, has an edgy, dangerous tone to it ("Still He Kills," "The Shape Stalks Again") that comes across effectively in this minimalist-sounding soundtrack album. The addition of The Chordettes' "Mr. Sandman," at the end, is a refreshing change of pace.

Didier C. Deutsch

Halloween 3:
Season of the Witch

1982, Varèse Sarabande Records, from the film *Halloween 3: Season of the Witch*, 1982

album notes: Music: John Carpenter, Alan Howarth.

Carpenter and Howarth returned to the same grounds once more with *Halloween 3: Season of the Witch*, using the same precision and creativity to come up with a score that's inventive in its own way, even though it increasingly seems to rely on ideas that might have been rejects from the previous two scores. Some tracks emerge, however, as particularly well conceived ("Drive to Santa Mira," "The Rock," and the crushingly exhilarating "Halloween Montage").

Didier C. Deutsch

Halloween 4: The Return of Michael Myers

1988, Varèse Sarabande Records, from the film *Halloween 4: The Return of Michael Myers*, Trancas International Films, 1988 ♫♫♫♪

album notes: Music: Alan Howarth.

Halloween 4: The Return of Michael Myers marked a significant change of pace in the series, with Myers resuming his initial identity, Donald Pleasence returning as Dr. Loomis, and the script consciously ignoring the events that had occurred in the previous two sequels. New also was the fact that Alan Howarth assumed responsibilities as the sole composer, bringing to the score a flair somewhat different from John Carpenter's, better realized, less minimalist, and more melody-driven, despite the abundance of synthesized sounds. Though built around Carpenter's original theme for the series, Howarth's score proves more lush overall, and more listenable than Carpenter's, if only because of the greater variety it exhibits.

Didier C. Deutsch

Halloween 5: The Revenge of Michael Myers

1989, Varèse Sarabande Records, from the film *Halloween 5: The Revenge of Michael Myers*, Galaxy International, 1989 ♫♫♫♪

album notes: Music: Alan Howarth.

The saga of Michael Myers has proven a very fruitful and rewarding franchise for John Carpenter, who initiated it, before leaving to others the fun of completing it (or, as it were, adding to it), and who initially scored it (see above), before turning over this task to Alan Howarth. Though Carpenter's original intentions and not-so-subtle effects eventually were diluted with overuse, one must admit that his successors have skillfully adapted his ideas for maximum results.

The fifth installment in the series, *The Revenge of Michael Myers* found Howarth taking some more distance from the previous efforts, and building his score around a tingling descending little motif introduced as the main theme to "The Revenge," that recurs at intervals in the electronic texture. Darker than *Halloween 4* ("The Shape Also Rises," a combination of distorted grunts, drum beat and low-toned electronic riffs, also heard in "The

Attic," is particularly frightening), but equally effective, the score also marked a progression for Howarth, who introduced some acoustic instruments in the mix. Some pop/rock vocals at the beginning of the album also give a different tone to the recording.

Didier C. Deutsch

Hamlet

1990, Virgin Movie Music, from the film *Hamlet*, Warner Bros., 1990 ♫♫

album notes: Music: Ennio Morricone; **Orchestra:** Orchestra Unione Musicisti di Roma; **Conductor:** Ennio Morricone; **Featured Musicians:** Fausto Anzelmo, viola; Carlo Romano, oboe.

This oddly focused film version of Shakespeare's great play, with Mel Gibson playing the melancholy Dane to Glenn Close's semi-detached Gertrude and Franco Zeffirelli handling the directorial chores, compelled Ennio Morricone to write a dark, often sullen score that may seem apt for a Shakespearean drama but not for a listening experience. While recognizing the inherent power of the music itself, most of the cues, introduced by a strong, brooding orchestral chord, convey the somberness in the action, with an organ occasionally reinforcing the generally gloomy moods. "The Banquet," a lively tune, is the only exception, while "Dance for the Queen," which would suggest a lilt in the action, translates itself into something even more mournful than Ravel's "Pavane for a Dead Princess."

Didier C. Deutsch

Hamlet

1996, Sony Classical, from the film *Hamlet*, Castle Rock/Columbia Pictures, 1996 ♫♫♫

album notes: Music: Patrick Doyle; **Conductor:** Robert Ziegler.

The melancholy Dane gets a perky reworking with this energetic, busy score that settles into more of a chamber mode after its broad orchestral opening. It's percussive, occasionally fiery, coiling along under Kenneth Branaugh's impassioned Hamlet . . . but despite some involving melodies and Doyle's usual dramatic skills this lengthy score never dwells in the memory the way his groundbreaking *Henry V* or even his sumptuous *Much Ado About Nothing* overture still does. This is much more of an incidental score than the through-composed effort of *Henry V*, dependent on the counter-rhythms of dialogue for many of its effects. Only in lengthier cues like "The Ghost" and "Sweets to the sweet—farewell" does Doyle get the opportunity to sustain and build on the melodies he creates, although the brief sword-fight cue ("Part them they are incensed!") offers some agile, taut string writing. The most noticeable misstep is the surprise appearance by Placido

Domingo belting out an opening song, "In Pace," which seems to have little relationship to the score or the film.

Jeff Bond

The Hand that Rocks the Cradle

1993, Hollywood Records, from the film *The Hand that Rocks the Cradle*, Hollywood Pictures, 1993 ♪♪♪♪

album notes: Music: Graeme Revell; **Conductor:** Tim Simonec.

Graeme Revell's oddly compelling score belies the subtly horrifying moods in this thriller, about a babysitter whose increasingly threatening presence brings havoc in the life of a Seattle family. Progressing with the action, the cues take on a darker edge, though without losing their overall melodic appeal ("Marlene's Discovery," "Claire Investigates"), in a skillfull display of beautifully understated musical ideas to create a subliminal effect that subtly underlines the tension in the film itself. Even without the impact of the screen images, the music retains its flavor, and in fact, acquires a sheen that's most revelatory and endearing.

Didier C. Deutsch

A Handful of Dust

1988, DRG Records, from the film *A Handful of Dust*, Stagescreen Productions, 1988 ♪♪♪♪

album notes: Music: George Fenton; **Conductor:** George Fenton; **Featured Musicians:** Mike Taylor, Pan pipes, kenas; Tony Hinnigan, Pan pipes/kenas; Forbes Henderson, charango.

Based on a novel by Evelyn Waugh, *A Handful of Dust* translates into a somewhat slight story about some British aristocrats with little care on their mind other than to live the idle, golden existence to which they feel entitled. As befits this kind of screenplay, the moods were kept light, and even if such unspeakable things as an accidental killing and a divorce spiced it up, it was all jolly good and perfectly swell, an overall feeling which George Fenton's score wrapped with elegant orchestral swirls. The 1930s provided the composer with another definite time period to anchor some of his cues, though the overall tone of his score is kept charmingly low-key and lightly melodic. Listen to the woop-dee-doo tone of "Cafe de Paris," or the equally innocuous "Learning to be Nicer," both of which denote in musical terms an attitude that we have come to accept from the wealthy but slight-headed gentry.

Didier C. Deutsch

The Handmaid's Tale

1990, GNP Crescendo, from the film *The Handmaid's Tale*, Cinecom, 1990 ♪

album notes: Music: Ryuichi Sakamoto.

It is without a doubt a pretty bad idea to amass 27, mostly short, cues into just two overlong 20-minute tracks. The resulting "orchestral suite" approach fails to create any natural sounding flow and yields a rather spotty, unfulfilling mix of musical styles from the Ryuichi Sakamoto score. The lack of indexing especially makes it impossible to follow which of the individual cues listed in mass on the inlay card you are listening to. The album is not without some good points, though they are few and far between. Some of the more poignant moments convey a hint that they might have splendid melodies ("Love in Nick's Room"), but they suffer greatly from some heavy-handed synthesizer work. Generally, there are an awful lot of simplistic musical effects filling up most of the time, from drum tracks to primitive tone build-ups. More often it's vaguely reminiscent of a low-budget horror film score.

David Hirsch

Hang 'Em High/Guns for San Sebastian

1991, Sony Music Special Products, from the films *Hang 'Em High*, United Artists, 1968 and *Guns for San Sebastian*, MGM, 1968 ♪♪♪♪

album notes: *Hang 'Em High:* **Music:** Dominic Frontiere; **Conductor:** Dominic Frontiere; *Guns for San Sebastian:* **Music:** Ennio Morricone; **Conductor:** Ennio Morricone.

Perhaps because *Hang 'Em High* starred Clint Eastwood in a role that recalled his portrayal as the Man-With-No-Name in several spaghetti westerns scored by Ennio Morricone, and *Guns for San Sebastian* had a score by Morricone, it might have seemed like a judicious idea to pair these soundtracks together on one CD. Wrong. Not only are Dominic Frontiere and Morricone miles apart as composers, but the former's derivative contribution, which aims to faintly evoke the latter's, simply doesn't begin to make the sort of impression Morricone's music for Sergio Leone achieved.

If you really are curious to hear a score that Morricone could have written much more eloquently, spend some time with *Hang 'Em High*, then move on to the real thing with *Guns for San Sebastian*, another terrific effort by the master himself. The film, made in Mexico, is a standard story about the legendary mid-18th century rebel Leon Alastray (Anthony Quinn), and his fight against marauding Yaqui Indians, led by Charles Bronson. There is no mistaking the accents or the style in this score, with choral vocals and guitar motifs adding their voice to the relentless orchestral textures created by the composer. Several cues attract particularly here, notably "The Chase," with its percolating riff, the "Love Theme," appropriately lyrical, "Building the Dam," with its evocative guitar lines, and the taut

"The Burning Village," which starts on a percussive orchestral line that dissolves into a romantic guitar theme.

Indicative of the total lack of understanding for the music or general insensitivity that presided over the sequencing of this album, a track from *Kelly's Heroes,* composed by Lalo Schifrin, has been inserted for no apparent reason between *Hang 'Em High* and *The Guns for San Sebastian.* The rating, incidentally, applies only to the Morricone score.

Didier C. Deutsch

The Hanging Garden

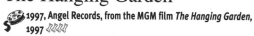1997, Angel Records, from the MGM film *The Hanging Garden,* 1997 ♪♪♪♪

album notes: Music: John Roby.

You shouldn't let Ani DiFranco's frantic "The Million You Never Made" deter you from getting this otherwise lovely soundtrack album to a telefilm made in Canada. With Celtic folk performances illuminating this story of a young Nova Scotia man trying to honor his family traditions without becoming a slave to them, the album teems with original songs that are quite appealing. The highlights here are many, but some arresting moments include "When Spring Comes" by Jane Siberry, singing a duet with herself; "Wash Down" by Meryn Cadell and Mary Margaret O'Hara; "The Tale" by Deb Montgomery; and the gently bouncing "If It Ain't Here" by the Wyrd Sisters. John Roby's gentle "Theme from *The Hanging Garden,*" voiced by Laurel MacDonald, with Roby providing a guitar backing against a simple cello line, makes one wish more of his score had been included on this CD.

Didier C. Deutsch

Hannah and Her Sisters

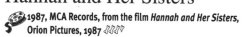1987, MCA Records, from the film *Hannah and Her Sisters,* Orion Pictures, 1987 ♪♪♪♪

In his films, Woody Allen is very careful to use songs or instrumentals that evocatively complement the stories he develops. His taste runs primarily toward the great recordings of the 1940s and early 1950s, with the soundtrack albums compiling these recordings together in a suggestive way. Often, his music director, the excellent Dick Hyman, adds his pianistic touch to the tracks, in a further musical expression that matches the moods of the source material. Both are on display in this album, which includes sides by Harry James ("You Made Me Love You" and "I've Heard That Song Before," both with heavy reverb that totally denatures their original sound) and Count Basie ("Back to the Apple"), a great piano medley by Hyman, as well as standards by Cole Porter and Rodgers and Hart sung by Bobby Short and Derek Smith. Adding a totally different,

and slightly surprising, note is a performance of Bach's "Concerto in F Minor," which has the unfortunate effect of breaking the mood established by the other selections.

Didier C. Deutsch

Hans Christian Andersen/The Court Jester

1994, Varèse Sarabande Records, from the movies *Hans Christian Andersen,* Samuel Goldwyn, 1952, and *The Court Jester,* Paramount Pictures, 1956 ♪♪♪♪

One of the great comic geniuses of his generation, Danny Kaye was equally at ease fooling around or settling down to deliver a sweet ballad when the occasion presented itself. Though his screen persona accented the zany side of his talent, he demonstrated in the remarkable *Hans-Christian Andersen,* a fairy tale account of the great Danish storyteller, that he could also delve into more romantic fares and still charm his public. On this occasion, he was also handsomely serviced by the award-winning score composed by Frank Loesser, in which "Wonderful Copenhagen" still stands out as a highlight. Conversely, *The Court Jester,* probably one of Kaye's funniest movies, is a splendid take-off on the swashbuckler genre, in which he impersonates a would-be knight bent on righting the wrong and saving a beautiful damsel in distress. Spread throughout the action are various musical numbers, including the tongue-twister "Maladjusted Jester," and the lovely lullaby "I'll Take You Dreaming."

Didier C. Deutsch

Hard Bounty

1997, Prometheus/Belgium, from the film *Hard Bounty,* 1997 ♪♪♪

album notes: Music: Enzo Milano.

Retired bounty hunter Martin B. Kanning opens a brothel in the Wild West, only to pick up his guns again when one of his girls is murdered. The whole whorehouse sets off through the Arizona desert to track down the killer in this comedic spaghetti western. *Hard Bounty* pays tribute to the Spanish guitar, mouth organ, and blaring brass of Morricone's spaghetti westerns. The recording is clear, and while the music is derivative, the composer obviously relishes the genre and has a lot of fun exploring the potential for drama, gun fights, and even the hokey saloon music that characterizes the gun-toting prostitutes. The composer remains anonymous, working under the pseudonym Enzo Milano.

David Poole

Hard Core Logo

1998, Velvel Records, from the Rolling Thunder film *Hard Core Logo*, 1998 ✻✻✻

A product of a subculture, Bruce McDonald's *Hard Core Logo* owes some of its screen energy to the heavy metal sounds of the alternative bands Hugh Dillon and Swamp Baby, for whom this album becomes a great showcase, as well as Teenage Head and the Ramones, prominently featured here. Not all the material is first rate, but the self-deprecating humor in "Rock 'n' Roll Is Fat and Ugly," "Blue Tattoo," "China White (Ten Buck F**k)," and "One Foot in the Gutter" gives a specific welcome spin to some old ideas. Chris Spedding's "Wild Wild Women" is another good cut.

Didier C. Deutsch

A Hard Day's Night

1987, EMI Records, from the movie *A Hard Day's Night,* United Artists, 1964 ✻✻✻✻

album notes: Music: John Lennon, Paul McCartney; **Lyrics:** John Lennon, Paul McCartney.

From the first chord of the title song chiming out like Big Ben, the soundtrack recording of the Beatles' first film preserves all the freshness and energy of what still stands as one of the best rock movies ever made. Not preserved—fortunately or not—are producer George Martin's "Swinging London" style big-band orchestrations, a prominent part of the original soundtrack LP in the US. They were dropped from the CD reissue as part of a realignment of the Beatles' early catalogue to conform with the UK releases. The CD features seven songs from the film, plus six others first issued in the US on other Beatles LPs.

see also: Help!

Marc Kirkeby

Hard Rain

1998, Milan, from the Paramount film *Hard Rain,* 1998 ✻✻✻

album notes: Music: Christopher Young; **Conductor:** Pete Anthony; **Featured Musicians:** Jean "Toots" Thielemans, harmonica; Adam Glasser, harmonica.

A thrilling account of a heist defeated by a sudden flood in a small town in the Midwest, *Hard Rain* gave composer Christopher Young a rare opportunity to write a flavorful score for harmonica and orchestra, not your usual stock-in-trade. The results are nothing less than remarkable, particularly since the soloists are none other than Toots Thielemans and Adam Glasser, two artists who have left their mark on contemporary music. Echoing some of the most salient moments in the ac-

tion, which stars Morgan Freeman and Christian Slater as the two hoods who rob an armored truck just as a raging storm of flood-like proportions hits town, the score is frequently breathtaking and important, in the relentless, hard-pounding, taut performance by the London Metropolitan players, in which the brass section has a dominant voice. Both Thielemans and Glasser add their specific colorings to the cues, which have been sequenced differently in the CD to emphasize the vibrancy of each selection.

Didier C. Deutsch

Hard Target

1993, Varèse Sarabande Records, from the film *Hard Target,* Universal Pictures, 1993 ✻✻✻✻

album notes: Music: Graeme Revell; **Conductor:** Tim Simonec; **Featured Musicians:** John Goux, guitar; George Doering, guitar; John Yoakum, saxophone, flute; Jon Clarke, saxophone, flutes; Mike Fisher, percussion; Tom Ranier, keyboards; Mike Lang, keyboards; Rick Marotta, drums.

This is a smart mix, combining the Japanese group Kodo with Graeme Revell's hard-hitting orchestral stylings. It yields an exciting action film score that is quite entertaining on its own. A key part of Revell's work is a delightful blend of musical styles, including some colorful down home bayou strains on cues like "Chance and Carmen" and the poignant "Miles to Go." But it is Kodo's creative percussion work that really kicks the action score into high gear ("Hunting Season Begins").

David Hirsch

The Hard Way

1991, Varèse Sarabande, from the film *The Hard Way,* Universal Pictures, 1991 ✻✻✻✻

album notes: Music: Arthur B. Rubinstein; **Featured Musicians:** Joel Peskin, tenor sax; Warren Luning, trumpet; Rick Baptiste, trumpet; Charlie Loper, trombone; Chuck Domanico, bass; Steve Schaeffer, drums.

This terrific Arthur B. Rubinstein effort starts off with a cue reminiscent of all those jazz scores for the TV cop shows of the 1950s and 1960s ("The Big Apple Juice," "Where Have You Gone, L. Ron?"), but it soon shifts into something with a harder edge. Michael J. Fox plays a spoiled actor who bullies his way into the life of harried New York City police detective James Woods to learn how to act like a real cop. Rubinstein juxtaposes the Hollywood-created world of cops (the jazz themes) with reality by infusing their exploits with more street-wise motifs, a creative fusion of various urban styles (including, for example, Jamaican steel drums). The film songs "Big Girls Don't Cry" and "Run Around Sue" also appear on the album.

David Hirsch

The Harder They Come

1973, Mango Records, from the film *The Harder They Come,* 1972 🎬🎬🎬🎬

album notes: Featured Musicians: Jimmy Cliff; The Maytals; Scotty; The Melodians; The Slickers; Desmond Dekker.

This soundtrack album is mostly interesting for its mix of great reggae songs ("Rivers of Babylon," "Many Rivers to Cross," "Shanty Town"), performed by Jimmy Cliff-whose hit "You Can Get It If You Really Want" is included twice-The Maytals, and other Jamaican stars. The film, shot in the slums of West Kingston, presents an uncompromising look at the raw world of reggae and Jamaican ganja, and is one of the first to portray the power of drugs and music with such unique vision. Today, others have delved largely into this subculture phenomena, but the songs in *The Harder They Come* have lost none of their original impact and still impress in this coherent, powerful compilation.

Didier C. Deutsch

The Harem

See: Il ladrone/L'harem

Harum Scarum

See: Girl Happy/Harum Scarum

Hatari!

1987, RCA Records, from the film *Hatari!,* Paramount Pictures, 1962 🎬🎬🎬

album notes: Music: Henry Mancini; **Conductor:** Henry Mancini.

Even the aggressive stereo separation in this soundtrack recording cannot affect the music written by Henry Mancini, in which the sprightly "Baby Elephant Walk" has emerged as one of the composer's most inspired creations. Like most of his scores, treated in a very lackadaisical way by the label to which he was signed for many years, the playing time is kept relatively short and just slightly over 30 minutes, with only one cue ("The Sounds of Hatari," dramatically steeped into a florid bongo drum line) venturing beyond six minutes. Still, it is another example of how great a melodist Mancini was, with themes that are consistently catchy and entertaining.

Didier C. Deutsch

Haunted Summer

1989, Silva Screen Records, from the film *Haunted Summer,* Cannon Films, 1989 🎬🎬🎬🎬🎬

album notes: Music: Christopher Young,

They Know the Score

John Barry

I remember on *Born Free,* they wanted me to do it in such a rush, and there were certain mistakes made in the orchestra, which Carl Foreman, the producer, in his infinite wisdom, said [fakes New York accent], 'But 'deres goin' to be lions runnin' all over, de'll never notice!' And I said, 'Yeah, but we're going to do an album, Carl.' So I actually brought a lawyer in, and [the lawyer] said, 'But do you agree that John can re-record the whole score for the soundtrack album, that you'd forced him to do this?' And he said, 'Yes, okay, fine.' So he agreed. So the actual soundtrack album of *Born Free* was totally re-recorded, and Carl was right: you don't hear any of the glitches of the soundtrack on the movie, because it was covered by lions . . . and tigers and bears, whatever.

***Courtesy of* Film Score Monthly**

Superb effort by Christopher Young that fabricates its own unique world of idyllic beauty and melancholy through a brilliant orchestration of synthesizers and a small selection of acoustical instruments. "The Night Was Made for Loving" is the centerpiece, presenting the composer at his melodic best in a seven-minute romantic concerto that's gently framed by elegant secondary motifs. Of course, one must remember that this is the story of the summer when Mary Shelley conceived of *Frankenstein,* so there's nightmares forthcoming for Young to gnaw his creative teeth upon. Though the foreboding "Polidori's Potions" breaks up the two suites of "bright" music, it is only a taste of things to come. It is still somewhat melodic for what Young saves for dessert. He turns his muse of the macabre loose on the creation of the 18-minute "Hauntings" suite, an edit of four impressively unsettling cues. It all starts off melodically enough with a classical inspired motif, but soon begins to degrade into a twisted witches' brew of dissonant sounds that crawls up your back. The perfect score for the morally challenged.

David Hirsch

The Haunting of Julia

See: Full Circle (The Haunting of Julia)

Havana

🎬 1990, GRP Records, from the film *Havana*, Universal Pictures, 1990 🎬🎬🎬

album notes: Music: Dave Grusin; **Conductor:** Dave Grusin; **Featured Musicians:** Alex Acuna, drums, percussion; Harvey Mason, drums, percussion; Mike Fisher, drums, percussion; Ephraim Torres, drums, percussion; Abe Laboriel, bass; Brian Bromberg, bass; Clare Fisher, piano; Dave Grusin, piano; Lee Ritenour, guitar; Ramon Stagnaro, guitars; Dave Valentin, flute; Sal Marquez, trumpet; Arturo Sandoval, trumpet; Don Menza, saxophone.

There are very few surprises in this highly competent score by Dave Grusin, whose jazz roots occasionally show up in some selections, both as composer and performer. The themes have a pleasant lilt to them, and conjure up the right kind of atmosphere, within and without their original relationship to the film itself, about an American gambler in Havana in the last days of the Batista regime. The Cuban background is evoked by means of a strumming acoustic guitar, as well as by what could be construed as South-of-the-border rhythms and sonorities ("Cuba Libre," "Santa Clara Suite," "Mambo Lido," "El Conuco"). It's all very pretty, and it essentially fulfills its function.

Didier C. Deutsch

HavPlenty

🎬 1998, Yum Yum Records/550 Music/Sony Music Soundtrax, from the Miramax film *HavPlenty*, 1998 🎬🎬🎬

A hip, young romantic comedy, *HavPlenty* resulted in an engaging album, featuring performances by stars such as Babyface and Tracey Lee, who created the soundtrack to the film, Erykah Badu, and Chico DeBarge, all of whom are heard to great results in this CD. Among the several highlights, "Fire" by Babyface and Des'ree, "I Can't Get You (Out of My Mind)" by Blackstreet, "Any Other Night" by Chico DeBarge, and "Ye Yo" by Erykah Badu, stand out, but there are quite a few other tracks that are well worth listening to here.

Didier C. Deutsch

He Got Game

🎬 1998, Def Jam Records, from the Touchstone film *He Got Game*, 1998 🎬🎬🎬🎬

album notes: Songs: Public Enemy.

🎬 1998, Sony Classical, from the Touchstone film *He Got Game*, 1998 🎬🎬🎬🎬

album notes: Music: Aaron Copland; **Conductor:** Aaron Copland, Leonard Bernstein.

Spike Lee's portrait of high-school basketball star Jesus Shuttleworth benefits from both an album of the late Aaron Copland's classical Americana and a rap album by iconoclasts Public Enemy. In *He Got Game*, Jesus must choose between lucrative offers from the NBA and diligent work at college. By way of social commentary, Public Enemy's Chuck D lambastes the basketball industry in humdingers such as "Politics of the Sneaker Pimps" and "Super Agent." His hefty voice projects with charisma, proving to be scintillating, positively dangerous, and refreshingly relevant. Their single "He Got Game" grabs riffs from Buffalo Springfield's "For What It's Worth," a combination resulting in their most accessible song to date.

Copland adds symphonic majesty after Chuck D's powerful oratory. Lee explains "When I listen to Copland's music, I hear American, and basketball is American." The futile hope inspired by the NBA in the American youth is evoked in the patriotic and optimistic sweep of vast string sections and urgent brass fanfares in "Open Prairie" and movements from "Appalachian Spring" and "Our Town" for an ideal introduction to the oeuvre of this great American composer. First mythologized by Copland, this parable about the American dream is then thoroughly debunked by Chuck D.

David Poole

Heart and Souls

🎬 1993, MCA Records, from the film *Heart and Souls*, Universal Picture, 1993 🎬🎬🎬🎬

album notes: Music: Marc Shaiman; **Conductor:** Artie Kane, J.A.C. Redford.

Marc Shaiman delivered a beautifully lyrical score, built around the Hoagy Carmichael–Frank Loesser standard, also heard in an instrumental version by Dave Koz, which subtly recurs throughout and anchors the music and the film, a delightful comedy starring Robert Downey, Jr., as a young man in whom four victims of a bus accident have reincarnated. While the overtones of the score are deftly romantic, the music takes frequent, short sidesteps into big-band jazz ("Goodbye Thomas," "Souled Out"), the better to offset its more thoughtful moments. Five vocal selections, including "Walk Like a Man," performed by Frankie Valli & the Four Seasons, "What'd I Say," by Ray Charles, and "The Thrill Is Gone," by B.B. King add a different, albeit equally enjoyable flavor to the proceedings.

Didier C. Deutsch

Heart of Midnight

🎬 1992, Silva Screen Records, from the film *Heart of Midnight*, Samuel Goldwyn, 1989 🎬

album notes: Music: Yanni.

If you're expecting the dulcet New Age tones Yanni has become famous for on public TV, forget it. Despite the pleasing "Carol's Theme," this is just another dated synthesized horror score. The sharp electronic effects serve more of a purpose in keeping the listener awake during long passages that sound as if they were made up on the spur of the moment instead of being thought out. This remarkably poor sounding recording is not one of Yanni's better efforts.

David Hirsch

Heartbreak Hotel

1988, RCA Records, from the film *Heartbreak Hotel*, Touchstone Pictures, 1988

album notes: Featured Musicians: *The Zulu Time Band:* Dave Davies, guitars, vocals; Michael Moyer, bass, vocals; Cole Hanson, guitar, vocals; Kevin Pearson, drums; *The T. Graham Brown Band:* Michael Thomas, guitar; Joe McGlohon, saxophone, guitar; Garland, keyboards; Greg Watzel, keyboards; Larry Marrs, bass guitar; Gary Kubal, drums.

You can hear the King sing the title track, then you can hear actors David Keith and Charlie Schlatter take their stab at it. Need we say more? Keith and Schlatter sing far too much here, and while it's nice to have some more tunes from Elvis, as well as Dobie Gray's "Drift Away" and Alice Cooper's "Eighteen," there are far better ways to get them.

Gary Graff

Heartbreaker

1995, Silva America, from the film *Heartbreaker*, Orion Pictures, 1984

album notes: Music: Tangerine Dream: Christopher Franke; Edgar Froese; Johannes Schmoelling.

A bright and bouncy early 1980s Tangerine Dream score from the days of Christopher Franke's association. It holds the attention really well, while capturing all the quirky aspects of the film's story of two lifelong friends and their relationships with women. Where the album works best are on the more gentle cues like "Rain in the City" or "Breathing the Night Away." However, most of the cues, like the aggressive "Twilight Painter," regretfully betray their age with their somewhat dated synthesizer sounds. Add an extra bone if you really do miss the '80s. I don't.

David Hirsch

Heat

1995, Warner Bros. Records, from the film *Heat*, Warner Bros., 1995

album notes: Music: Elliot Goldenthal; **Conductor:** Jonathan Sheffer; Stephen Mercurio; **Featured Artists:** Kronos Quartet, *"Deaf Elk" Guitar Orchestra:* Page Hamilton, Andrew Hawkins, David Reid, Eric Hubel.

Miami Vice showed that director Michael Mann had a flair for marrying arresting music and visuals. But shorn of the latter, the songs on *Heat* seem disparate and random—Kronos Quartet's avant chamber music here, Moby's ambient dance fare there. The collection is notable for "Always Forever Now," a track by the Passengers (aka U2 and Brian Eno), but it's hard to spend time with this as a cohesive listening experience.

Gary Graff

Heathers

1989, Varèse Sarabande Records, from the film *Heathers*, New World Pictures, 1989

album notes: Music: David Newman.

This sharp (and sharply funny) black comedy about a quartet of stuck-up damsels known as the Heathers, so called because it happens to be the first name of three of them, was the occasion for David Newman to write a serious tongue-in-cheek opus, with dark overtones, that smartly complements the moods of the film. Unlike the large orchestral works for which he has become quite famous in film music circles, Newman chose to go the electronic route this time around, and created a synthesized score in which the only occasional acoustic note is injected by an harmonica. Throughout, there are clever, humorous little touches that make the music even more enjoyable, as in "You're Beautiful," "The Dorm," and "Into the Cafeteria."

Didier C. Deutsch

Heavy Metal

1981, Full Moon/Elektra Records, from the animated feature *Heavy Metal*, Columbia Pictures, 1981

album notes: Featured Musicians: Sammy Hagar; Jerry Riggs; Devo; Blue Oyster Cult; Cheap Trick; Don Felder; Donald Fagen; Nazareth; Journey; Grand Funk Railroad; Black Sabbath; Trust; Stevie Nicks.

One of the great animated features of the 1980s, *Heavy Metal* owed little to the genre dominated for so long by Walt Disney. In fact, the raw energy of the various segments in the film, designed by some of the best illustrators of the day, was in sharp contrast with the saccharine images usually created by the House of the Mouse or even, for that matter, with the slyly sarcastic cartoon shorts made by Warner Bros. So was, for that matter, the explosive soundtrack that brought together some of the greatest names in rock 'n' roll—Blue Oyster Cult, Cheap Trick, Devo, Nazareth, Journey, Grand Funk Railroad, and Black Sabbath, among them—names one would not normally associate with a cartoon feature. But the tremendous volatile power of the score and the extraordinary visual images on the screen combined to create a film unlike anything usually seen in movie houses,

The CD returns to the catalogue a long sought-after soundtrack album that deserves to be in every collection. Missing, however, is the instrumental score, composed by Elmer Bernstein, which was available on a separate LP and has never been reissued on compact disc.

Didier C. Deutsch

Hedwig and the Angry Inch

 1999, Atlantic Records, from the off-Broadway musical *Hedwig and the Angry Inch*, 1998 ♪♪♪♪

album notes: Book: John Cameron Mitchell; **Music:** Stephan Trask; **Lyrics:** Stephan Trask; **Cast:** John Cameron Mitchell, Miriam Shor; **Featured Musicians:** Stephen Trask, keyboards, guitar; Chris Weilding, guitar; Scott Bilbrey, bass, acoustic guitar; David McKinley, drums.

The problem with most attempts to blend rock and theater has been pretty elemental—these efforts never really rocked. Until now! The off-Broadway scene-stealer *Hedwig and the Angry Inch* is the spirited, warped tale of an East German boy who suffers a botched sex-change operation and comes to America to experience trailer parks and rock stardom (think *Rocky Horror Show* meets Marlene Dietrich). Written by actor John Cameron Mitchell and musician Stephen Trask, *Hedwig* is unrepentantly outrageous and outlandish, and its energy comes across on this recording of the production's 13 songs. Taken together, they're an homage to '60s Spectorian power pop and its sonic descendants, particularly as David Bowie and Meat Loaf, with aside nods to the Velvet Underground ("The Origin of Love"), Britpop ("The Long Grift"), shuffling country rock ("Sugar Daddy"), and winking, hair-band style metal favored by Trask's own band, Cheater, which is also part of the *Hedwig* troupe. Mitchell proves himself a star as Hedwig, whether he's waxing kitschily sentimental ("The Origin of Love," "Hedwig's Lament"), rocking hard ("Angry Inch," "Tear Me Down"), or soaring to the melodramatic heights of the album-ending epic "Midnight Radio." Enjoyably out there, *Hedwig* is a hoot—every angry inch of it.

Gary Graff

The Helen Morgan Story

1989, RCA Records, from the Warner Bros. film *The Helen Morgan Story*, 1954 ♪♪♪

album notes: Conductor: Ray Heindorf; **Featured Musician:** Gogi Grant, vocals.

One of the great torch singers of the 1920s (she notably starred in *Show Boat,* in which she created the part of Julie), Helen Morgan, played by Ann Blyth, dubbed in the vocal numbers by Gogi Grant, was shortchanged by this routine biopic, which portrayed her as a sad case pushed to drinking by the men in her life (Paul Newman and Richard Carlson). While the film itself was able to capture the roaring atmosphere of the era, it

failed spectacularly in its attempts to make its leading lady a compelling, endearing character. A proficient singer, Gogi Grant tried to give a measure but never quite attained the vocal proficiency of Helen Morgan, although the film (and this soundtrack album) was particularly interesting for its profuse amount of great songs from the period.

Didier C. Deutsch

Hello Again

1987, Cinedisc Records, from the film *Hello Again*, Touchstone Pictures, 1987 ♪♪

album notes: Music: William Goldstein; **Featured Musician:** Dave Boruff, saxophone.

This synthesized comedy score, written and performed by William Goldstein, has an infectious, innocent charm about it. The main theme is bright and bouncy, but its overuse tends to wear out its welcome. Goldstein's arrangements for the most part work well within the limitations of his electronics, and Dave Boruff's occasional sax solos add some welcome life. However, the synthesized instrumentation sounds awfully primitive just 10 years later and, at times, distracts from Goldstein's compositions.

David Hirsch

Hello, Dolly!

1989, RCA Victor, from the Broadway production *Hello, Dolly!*, 1964 ♪♪♪♪♪

album notes: Music: Jerry Herman; **Lyrics:** Jerry Herman; **Musical Direction:** Shepard Coleman; **Cast:** Carol Channing, David Burns, Eileen Brennan, Sondra Lee, Charles Nelson Reilly.

1991, RCA Victor, from the Broadway production *Hello, Dolly!*, 1967 ♪♪♪

album notes: Music: Jerry Herman; **Lyrics:** Jerry Herman; **Musical Direction:** Saul Schechtman; **Cast:** Pearl Bailey, Cab Calloway, Emily Yancy, Chris Calloway.

1994, Philips Records, from the film *Hello, Dolly!*, 20th Century Fox, 1969 ♪♪♪

album notes: Music: Jerry Herman; **Lyrics:** Jerry Herman; **Choir:** The 20th Century Fox Chorus; **Orchestra:** The 20th Century Fox Orchestra; **Conductor:** Lennie Hayton and Lionel Newman; **Cast:** Barbra Streisand, Walter Matthau, Marianne McAndrew, Michael Crawford, Tommy Tune, Louis Armstrong.

Like *Gypsy, Hello, Dolly!* is a splendid vehicle for a grander-than-life performance. Many actresses have tried it, with varying degrees of success, but to the many fans of the musical and its spirited score by Jerry Herman, the best among them remains Carol Channing, who created the part on Broadway. A recent revival in which she returned to the scene of her former triumph proved, if needed, that she was Dolly Gallagher Levy, even if the show itself had become a lame carbon copy of the original.

Pearl Bailey, who was brought in as an odd replacement with an all-black cast to rekindle the show's flagging fortunes at the box office (rumor at the time had it that Liberace had also been considered by producer David Merrick to head an all-male cast), added some of her own idiosyncrasies to a part that already had quite a few them written into it. But the show gave her a rare opportunity to return to Broadway where her absence had been sorely noticed for many years.

Were it not for the presence of Louis Armstrong in the cast, the film version, starring Barbra Streisand, totally miscast in a role written for a much older actress, would be a total disaster. Even then, Armstrong's moment of glory, in the seven-minute long title track, is barely sufficient to recommend this sorry recording, in which future-Phantom Michael Crawford also makes an appearance.

Didier C. Deutsch

Hellraiser: Bloodline

1996, Silva America, from the Dimension film *Hellraiser: Bloodline*, 1996 ♪♪♪

album notes: Music: Daniel Licht; Conductor: Pete Anthony.

A big orchestral score by Daniel Licht gives a surprising voice to this fourth outing in the *Hellraiser* series, which brings back Pinhead from Hell for another round of horrible blood-drenched mishaps. Split between 18th-century France, modern-day New York, and a space station in the 22nd century, the action enables the pincushion to perform his deadly deeds, with Licht gleefully punctuating each and every one of them with appropriate crescendos, flurries, and pounding chords. Bold, brassy, and occasionally accompanied by a wordless chorus, the cues are standard horror film fare, with the large orchestra doing the honors. It's not too terribly scary, nor too terribly inventive, but once you start playing this CD you might want to play it again.

Didier C. Deutsch

Hellraiser III: Hell on Earth

1996, GNP Crescendo, from the film *Hellraiser III: Hell on Earth,* New World Pictures, 1992 ♪♪♪

album notes: Music: Randy Miller.

Although Randy Miller quotes from Chris Young's original *Hellraiser* several times in this third outing, his own main theme is a strong contender to Young's, carrying on the cosmic drama of the former films, while giving this story a musical sensibility of his own. Like the Cenobite torturers of the film, it quickly overcomes the minor musical motifs set before it—such as the heavy and doom-filled theme heard in "Mind Invasion." In "El-

liot's Story," Miller accentuates the interplay between the main theme and the "Mind Invasion" motif, one cue playing softly on the violin, and humanizing the horrific sounds heard earlier. The use of the choir adds drama and power to the score. Low, echoing percussion and slow, shimmering cymbals open the music up to cavernous depths. The main theme sounds strident and omnipresent throughout the score.

Randall D. Larson

Help!

1987, EMI Records, from the movie *Help!,* 1965 ♪♪♪♪

album notes: Music: John Lennon, Paul McCartney, George Harrison; Lyrics: John Lennon, Paul McCartney, George Harrison.

As with *A Hard Day's Night,* the soundtrack CD from the Beatles' second film does away with orchestrations included on the US LP—a shame in this case, because Ken Thorne's witty James Bondish work captured the flavor of the movie in a way that the seven Beatles originals (wonderful though they are) do not. Filling out the CD reissue, once again, are seven other Beatles songs from the original UK LP. For both films, it should be added, the audio tracks on the video laserdisc releases outshine the same music on CD.

see also: A Hard Days Night

Marc Kirkeby

Henry and June

1990, Varèse Sarabande Records, from the film *Henry and June,* Universal Pictures, 1990 ♪♪♪♪♪

Philip Kaufman's brilliant film, *Henry and June,* centered around the erotic life of two Americans living in Paris who became 20th-century literary giants, Henry Miller and Anais Nin. Set in 1931, the film boldly explores their first encounter and their passionate relationship, further pushed to the limits by Miller's enigmatic and hauntingly sensual wife, June. To musically illustrate this first-rate film, Kaufman assembled various recordings that to him symbolized the period, from both its French and its American perspectives, and gave it its unique cachet. With a few exceptions (Bing Crosby's "I Found a Million Dollar Baby," Lucienne Boyer's "Parlez-moi d'amour," and Josephine Baker's "J'ai deux amours," which bookend the soundtrack album), most of the selections are modern recordings of works from the 1930s, which are strongly evocative of the era, yet are sonically modern in concept and interpretation. Like *The Moderns,* also set in Paris in the 1930s, *Henry and June* is a splendid evocation of a period long gone that had a unique flavor to it. The terrific soundtrack album exudes the same irresistible flair.

Didier C. Deutsch

Henry and June **(The Kobal Collection)**

Henry V

 1989, EMI Angel, from the film *Henry V*, 1989 𝄞𝄞𝄞𝄞𝄾

album notes: Music: Patrick Doyle; **Orchestra:** The City of Birmingham Orchestra; **Conductor:** Simon Rattle.

There has rarely been as impressive a film scoring debut as Patrick Doyle's score for Kenneth Branaugh's first-time film directing effort, a gritty and inspiring adaptation of Shakespeare's tale of the British king who overcame incredible odds at the Battle of Agincourt. Opening with a rich, low-string dirge of great, tragic nobility, Doyle's beautiful music accelerates into an exclamation of pure triumph simply to introduce Shakespeare's tale. It's one of the most active underscoring of dialogue in recent memory, pulsing through scenes, erupting in martial fury or in beautiful elegiac lyricism (as in the "Requiem for Falstaff"). Doyle's scoring of Henry's troop-rallying speech before the Agincourt battle is one of the most moving, gorgeous, and inspiring musical cues written for a film in the past couple of decades, and his music for the battle proper is a balletic marvel of percussive, rhythmic drive. The entire score compares quite well with William Walton's legendary effort for the Laurence Olivier *Henry V* of 1944. It's a rare soundtrack album that will appeal to lovers of film scores as well as good music in general.

Jeff Bond

Her Majesty Mrs. Brown

1997, Milan Records, from the film *Her Majesty Mrs. Brown*, Miramax Pictures, 1997 𝄞𝄞𝄞𝄞𝄾

album notes: Music: Stephen Warbeck; **Conductor:** Nick Ingman; **Featured Musicians:** Martin Robertson; Tim Holmes, tarogato; Sarah Horner, whistles; Dermot Crehan, fiddle; Pipe Major Willie Cochrane, bagpipes.

A quaint but apparently true story, *Her Majesty Mrs. Brown* centers on a little known fact about England's Queen Victoria (played by Judi Dench), in the years following the death of her beloved husband, Prince Albert, and the warm friendship that established itself between her and a loyal servant and stableman by the name of John Brown (portrayed by Billy Connolly). Stephen Warbeck wrote a beautifully poignant and emotionally rousing score, developed around a solemn, stately theme for the Queen, and a blend of Celtic melodic fragments (played on a tarogato, a Hungarian wood instrument), for Brown, in an odd, yet compelling musical marriage. Both themes dominate the score, either played singly or intermingled, while other cues explore the landscapes, natural and political, that serve as a backdrop to the unusual relationship between the Queen and her stableman, often in terms that are quietly stated and attractive. Lush and stirring, it is an unusual score that deserves to be heard.

Didier C. Deutsch

Hercules

1997, Disney, from the Disney film *Hercules*, 1997 🎬🎬🎬

album notes: Music: Alan Menken; **Songs:** Alan Menken, David Zippel; **Conductor:** Michael Kosarin.

Tina Turner singing "We Don't Need Another Hero" might have been more appropriate than Michael Bolton's annoying vocals on "Go the Distance," in this CD soundtrack to another Disney animated feature, set to music by Alan Menken and David Zippel. The legendary Greek hero, looking much too good, performs his deeds with great enthusiasm in this film, with the action well served by the zesty score and songs in which the contemporary inflections have little to do with a standard Greek chorus. But the Muses who tell the story and comment on it (Lillias White, Cheryl Freeman, LaChanze, Roz Ryan, and Vanessa Thomas) get to steal the show with powerful moments that stick out ("The Gospel Truth," "Zero to Hero," "A Star Is Born"). The instrumental cues, tacked on at the end in what has become an unfortunate standard practice, sound genuinely exciting and bouncy, although most of them are reduced to their simplest expression, often sounding unfinished and giving the score little opportunity to actually grow on the listener. Only "The Hydra Battle," "Cutting the Thread," and "A True Hero/A Star Is Born" enable Menken's music to really hit the spot, which it does in grand style. But even though it's based on a classic story, one would hardly call this Hercules a Disney classic.

Didier C. Deutsch

Hercules: The Legendary Journeys, Vol. 2

1997, Varèse-Sarabande, from the Universal Television series *Hercules: The Legendary Journeys*, 1997 🎬🎬🎬
album notes: Music: Joseph LoDuca; **Conductor:** Randy Thornton.

This release is a compendium of tracks from various episodes of the series' first three seasons. There's nothing terribly orig-

inal in most of the music composed by Joseph LoDuca, even though he emulates other composers in the fantasy-adventure genre quite well. When he strays from that adventure music mold and explores either the ethnic or emotional aspects of the episodes, his score becomes much more interesting. Unfortunately, these moments are rare and far between.

Beth Krakower

Here We Go 'Round the Mulberry Bush

1998, Rykodisc, from the United Artists film *Here We Go 'Round the Mulberry Bush*, 1968 🎬🎬🎬
album notes: Songs: The Spencer Davis Group, Traffic.

A psychedelic movie about a young man trying to lose his virginity, *Here We Go 'Round the Mulberry Bush* featured a very 1960s British Invasion score consisting of songs by Traffic and the Spencer Davis Group. The title song was a minor hit for Steve Winwood and Traffic. Surprisingly, the songs continue to hold very well, making this soundtrack album a pleasure to listen to, even if it seems at times a bit quaint.

Didier C. Deutsch

Hero

1992, Epic Soundtrax, from the film *Hero*, Columbia Pictures, 1992 🎬🎬🎬
album notes: Music: George Fenton; **Conductor:** George Fenton; **Featured Musicians:** Nat Adderley, Jr., piano, keyboards; Harvey Mason, drums; William "Doc" Powell, guitar; Byron Miller, bass; Paulinho da Costa, percussion; Wayne Linsey, synthesizer programming, keyboards, cymbals.

Comedy scores do not often make for interesting albums (since they tend to be quirky by nature), and *Hero* is no exception. George Fenton is, of course, one of the finest composers of our time (with scores like *Cry Freedom, Dangerous Liaisons,* and *The Fisher King* to his credit, among many others), but this particular score, while dramatically (and comedically) effective, is not really one that comes together to form a cohesive album. The CD opens with Luther Vandross's song, "Heart of a Hero," which is a typically forgettable pop tune. Fenton's ensuing score is a varied amalgam of styles. The main title opens with an arrangement of "Auld Lang Syne," which segues into a Sousa-like march. Much of the music is light pop or programmatic suspense music, but there are a few listenable moments. Track five, "Looking for the Truth," has a nice Americana flavor to it, and is typical of Fenton's more noble side and his gift for writing music of depth that flows effortlessly. *Hero* is certainly a fine score, but one which is better experienced in the film, where it was meant, rather than on disc.

Paul Andrew MacLean

Hero and the Terror

1988, Cinedisc Records, from the film *Hero and the Terror,* Cannon Films, 1988 🎬🎬🎬

album notes: Music: David Michael Frank.

Announced by the relatively tepid "Two Can Be One," warbled in contemporary fashion by Joe Pizzulo and Stephanie Reach, *Hero and the Terror* is a combination of orchestral and synthesizer cues, some attractive, some effective, many of them routine. When he stays within an acoustic or orchestral context, David Michael Frank comes up with some lovely tunes ("Hero's Seduction," "Birthday Wishes," "Angela," "Love and Obsession"), but these are defeated by the obvious, and much less creative approach to the electronic cues that constitute the remainder of the score.

Didier C. Deutsch

The Hi-Lo Country

1999, TVT Records, from the PolyGram/Gramercy film *The Hi-Lo Country,* 1999 🎬🎬🎬

album notes: Music: Carter Burwell; **Conductor:** Carter Burwell; **Featured Musician:** David Torn, guitar.

Patricia Arquette plays the object of two cowboys' affection in *The Hi-Lo Country,* with music split evenly between classic cowboy tunes and a sophisticated orchestral score. Carter Burwell has broken out of his niche as the Coen brothers resident composer, and *The Hi-Lo Country* offers him wide New Mexico vistas to fill with harp, David Torn's Spanish and steel guitar, and glorious trumpet solos that would not be out of place on a spaghetti western. Torn is backed by a full orchestra, and the overall tempo is slow and dignified, counter to the boisterous character played by Woody Harrelson. The cowboy tunes range from a hip collaboration of Beck and Willie Nelson "Drivin' Nails in My Coffin," to the Hank Williams chestnut "Why Don't You Love Me," and for an across-the-border flavor "Que Chulos Ojos" and "O Madre Mia." The Hi-Lo Country Band featuring veterans Don Walser, Leon Rausch, and Marty Stuart adds four more classics to this western love triangle.

David Poole

Hidden in Silence

See: Gone to Texas/Hidden in Silence

Hideaway

1995, TVT Records, from the film *Hideaway,* Tri-Star Pictures, 1995 🎬🎬

album notes: Music: Trevor Jones.

Hideaway appears at first glance no more than just another rock and roll collection, trowelled indiscriminately into the film (and the CD) for commercial purposes. However, the three tracks allotted to Trevor Jones's score (placed at the end of this disc) are highly recommended. At roughly 20 minutes, Jones's score is the kind of full orchestral music that highlighted his early work, in scores like *The Dark Crystal* and *The Last Place on Earth. Hideaway* is a film dealing with mysticism and the afterlife, and Jones's score reflects these fantastical-religious elements with soaring choral music that evokes a spiritual etheria. A brooding statement of the "Dies Irae" opens the final track, "Beyond the Shadow of Death," which culminates in a powerful setting of the main theme, though the heavy rock and roll drums which come-in near the end unfortunately compromise its effect. Overall, *Hideaway* represents some of Trevor Jones's better large-orchestral writing. While the rock songs in this release are a forgettable cacophony, Jones's score is a very good one and ultimately makes for rewarding listening.

Paul Andrew MacLean

High Art

1998, Velvel Records, from the film *High Art,* 1998 🎬🎬🎬🎬

album notes: Music: Shudder to Think.

Another story of two girls in love, *High Art* is a complex character study that involves a naive assistant editor at a fashionable art magazine and a more outwardly sophisticated girl who happens to live in the same building. A chance encounter enables the two to meet, eventually resulting in a passionate love affair. The unhurried score, written by Nathan Larson and Craig Wedren and performed by Shudder to Think, reflects the subtle aspects of this unusual love story, with attractive songs that are softly shaded and lack the abrasive qualities often found in contemporary rock-driven collections.

see also: First Love, Last Rites, The Incredible Adventure of Two Girls in Love

Didier C. Deutsch

High Heels

1992, Antilles Records, from the film *High Heels,* Miramax Films, 1992 🎬🎬🎬

album notes: Music: Ryuichi Sakamoto; **Conductor:** Ryuichi Sakamoto; **Featured Musician:** Basilio Georges, guitar.

This typically flavorful score by Ryuichi Sakamoto was composed for a Spanish film starring Victoria Abril, which partly explains the inclusion of a couple of vocals in that language, as well as several cues with Spanish titles. Though relying on the sounds of a flamenco guitar to provide an occasional exotic color, Sakamoto wrote a score that is not specifically rooted in either the time or place of the action about a young woman who finds out that her new husband once had an affair with her own mother, but is more universal in appeal. A diversified mix, the music is an interesting blend of romantic themes and pop/rock tunes, of synthesizer cues and orchestral sounds, all of which combines to give a definitely unusual style to the album.

Didier C. Deutsch

High Society

1956, Capitol Records, from the film *High Society*, MGM, 1956

album notes: Music: Cole Porter; **Lyrics:** Cole Porter; **Chorus:** The MGM Studio Chorus; **Orchestra:** The MGM Studio Orchestra; **Conductor:** Johnny Green; **Cast:** Bing Crosby, Grace Kelly, Frank Sinatra, Celeste Holm.

One of Cole Porter's very last musical efforts, *High Society* is probably also one of his most memorable works—due in large part to the stellar cast that starred in the film: Frank Sinatra, Grace Kelly, Bing Crosby, Louis Armstrong, and Celeste Holm. Their effervescent performances, and their fine interpretations of some of Porter's wittiest songs have helped rank *High Society* among the classics. Unfortunately, the beauty of the performances, cushioned by the splendid Johnny Green orchestrations, is lost in this soundtrack recording, a sea of sonic murk as are all of Sinatra's Capitol soundtracks.

Poor production values truly detract from enjoyment of the disc. It is difficult to ascertain whether the original film recordings were poorly recorded and inherently sound "brittle" and muffled (doubtful, since new restorations of the MGM soundtracks of the 1940s reveal very pleasing sonics), or if the defects were created later, when the film tracks were transferred by the record company for commercial release. Either way, the situation should have been corrected when the CD was planned for issue. In time, this (and other important soundtracks) will be restored with the attention and care that they deserve. Until then, this unforgivably inferior CD will have to suffice.

Charles L. Granata

1999, DRG Records, from the Broadway musical *High Society*, 1998

album notes: Music: Cole Porter; **Lyrics:** Cole Porter; **Additional Lyrics:** Susan Birkenhead; **Book:** Arthur Kopit; **Musical Direction:** Paul Gemignani; **Cast:** Melissa Errico, Daniel McDonald, Randy Graff, Stephen Bogardus, Anna Kendrick, John McMartin.

The road from Hollywood to Broadway (it only took 42 years) has been detrimental to *High Society,* one of the screen's most interesting original musicals. Created in 1956, with a terrific cast that included Bing Crosby, Frank Sinatra, Grace

Kelly, Celeste Holm, and Louis Armstrong, the film, which was based on the original play *The Philadelphia Story,* by Philip Barry, was a bright affair that ignited the screen as few other films had done that year, spawning a monster hit in the duet "True Love" and reviving the fortunes of Cole Porter, whose most recent stage and screen efforts had been mitigated disasters (actually, it would prove the composer's last work and a fitting swan song to a career that had begun in the 1930s).

Any version, be it on the stage or screen, would have to compare with that film, and in all likelihood would suffer from the comparison. The story of two estranged socialites whose Hampton properties abut and who find that life together still proves irresistible, was an ideal vehicle for Crosby, demure as usual as Dexter, the former husband of Tracy, played by Kelly, splendidly regal in her last screen role, with Sinatra as a conniving journalist, Mike, who wouldn't mind having a fling with the heiress but eventually settles for Liz, the female photographer assigned with him to cover the impending marriage of Tracy with a new suitor.

Possibly because they felt the score was not strong enough for a Broadway transfer, the people involved in this staged production ill-advisedly decided to beef it up with songs borrowed from other Cole Porter scores, including, in one of the most misguided decision, "I Love Paris," which seems oddly out of place here.

Adding insult to injury, they asked Susan Birkenhead to provide additional lyrics, the equivalent of suggesting that Andy Warhol could have added some trees behind the Mona Lisa to enliven the background.

Arthur Kopit didn't tamper too much with the original book and simply attempted to make the various new elements fit with the old ones in a somewhat seamless concoction. Melissa Errico was hired to portray Tracy and brought to the task a haughtiness that seemed befitting, but Daniel McDonald as Dexter sounds bland on this recording, as he appeared on stage, and Stephen Bogardus, in the Sinatra role, almost looked like a dead ringer for the crooner but lacked his distinctive vocal capabilities. John McMartin, as lecherous Uncle Willie, Dexter's strongest ally in the Lord's household, is frequently playing over the top, with the cast often indulging in frantic performances ("Well, Did You Evah?") that are grating at times.

The recording boasts the feel of a standard Broadway show, with William David Brohn's orchestrations typical of the brassy sounds one hears in musicals, but in the final analysis, *High Society* proves a serious letdown.

Didier C. Deutsch

High Spirits

1988, GNP Crescendo, from the film *High Spirits*, TriStar Pictures, 1988 ♫♫♫♪

album notes: Music: George Fenton; **Orchestra:** The Graunke Symphony Orchestra, **Conductor:** George Fenton; **Featured Musicians:** Dermot Crehan, Irish fiddle; Paul Brennan, Uillean pipes; Catherine Bott, vocals.

George Fenton's diverse music for *High Spirits* is as varied as its composer's own repertoire. Varying broadly from mysterious female vocals to farcical symphonics, from riotous electronic/orchestral effects to full-blooded symphonic overtures, the music draws much of its style from Irish folk songs. Yet the score also bristles with the effective moody atmospheres and quaint orchestrations that made Fenton's *A Company of Wolves* so remarkable. The Irish fiddle runs throughout many of the cues, driving the orchestra into a rhythmic frenzy of tunefulness, and Fenton ably intersperses the traditional Irish material with his own adventurous music to create a score that is both exhilarating and dreamlike.

Randall D. Larson

High Time

1998, RCA/Spain, from the 20th Century-Fox film *High Time*, 1960 ♫♫♫♫

album notes: Music: Henry Mancini; **Conductor:** Henry Mancini.

Another Mancini score, released only in Spain, but well worth looking for. Unfortunately, it is simply a transfer of the old RCA album, which means that one of the juiciest moments from the soundtrack, Bing Crosby crooning his way through the delightful Cahn-Van Heusen song, "The Second Time Around," is not included, and is replaced here by an instrumental-with-chorus version that is decidedly more bland in comparison. But Mancini's musical invention was quite high when he wrote this score, and themes abound that are catchy and entertaining.

Didier C. Deutsch

Higher Learning

1994, Epic Soundtrax, from the film *Higher Learning*, Columbia Pictures, 1994 ♫♫♫

album notes: Featured Musicians: Ice Cube; Me'Shell NdegeOcello; Mista Grimm; Raphael Saadiq; Tori Amos; OutKast; Rage Against the Machine; The Brand New Heavies; Liz Phair; Eve's Plumb; Stanley Clarke.

A contemporary drama, set in a modern college campus, *Higher Learning* charts a semester in the lives of a handful of students confronting issues of identity, diversity, sexism, and escalating racial tension, all of which found an echo in the songs chosen to musically illustrate the film. Featuring recordings from the worlds of R&B, hip hop, rap, and alternative music, the diversified soundtrack brought together performers who also appeared in the film like Ice Cube, Eve's Plum, and others whose contributions were part of the behind-the-action musical makeup, notably Tori Amos, Me'shell NdegeOcello, Liz Phair, and Raphael Saadiq from Tony! Toni! Tone!. Adding a different touch to the proceedings, "Deja," composed by Stanley Clarke, rounds up the performances on the album, along with two scenes from the film, "Something to Think About" and "My New Friend," with dialogue written by John Singleton, who directed the film.

Didier C. Deutsch

Highlander: The Original Scores

1995, edel Records, from the films *Highlander*, Republic Pictures, 1985, *Highlander II: The Quickening*, Columbia Pictures, 1990, and *Highlander: The Final Dimension*, Columbia Pictures, 1994 ♫♫♫

album notes: *Highlander:* **Music:** Michael Kamen; **Orchestra:** The National Philharmonic Orchestra; **Conductor:** Michael Kamen; **Featured Musicians:** Bob Murphy, pipes; Ben Murdock, mandora; Alexandra Thompson, vocals; *Highlander II: The Quickening* **Music:** Stewart Copeland; **Orchestra:** The Seattle Symphony Orchestra; **Conductor:** Johnathan Sheffer; **Featured Musicians:** Rusty Anderson, guitars; *Highlander: The Final Dimension* **Music:** J. Peter Robinson; **Orchestra:** The Munich Symphony Orchestra; **Conductor:** J. Peter Robinson.

One of the best fantasy scores of the '80s, Michael Kamen's *Highlander* is represented in a 20-minute suite. A colorful blend of orchestra and synthesizers, with a Gaelic flavor, Kamen's score is adventurous, mythic, and triumphant, and probably the best he's written. There is a rush of enthusiasm here, which sounds like Kamen was having fun writing it (a feeling that does not come across in his later Hollywood blockbuster scores). The effect of opening the album with Kamen's grand original proves anti-climactic however. Neither of the other scores can compare. Stewart Copeland's *Highlander II* is a nonsensical cacophony that mixes coarse synth-rock with orchestra. Jonathan Sheffer's orchestrations are impressive, but working from such ignoble source material he is unable to make it anything special. J. Peter Robinson allots 27 minutes to his music for *Highlander: The Final Dimension*. His music is superior to Copeland's, with a nice romantic theme for MacLeod's 19th-century love affair. However, the meandering "atmosphere" cues, awkward rock and roll passages and bloated climax are disconcerting on disc. Though only 20 minutes, Michael Kamen's *Highlander* is nevertheless magnificent, and the showpiece of the album. It is this score which ultimately makes the CD recommended.

Paul Andrew MacLean

Hilary and Jackie

1998, Sony Classical, from the Film Four/Intermedia/October film *Hilary and Jackie*, 1998 ♪♪♪♪

album notes: Music: Barrington Pheloung; **Conductor:** Barrington Pheloung, Daniel Barenboim (in Elgar's "Concerto for Cello and Orchestra"); **Featured Musicians:** Jacqueline du Pre, cello (in Elgar's "Concerto for Cello and Orchestra"); David Heath, flute; Caroline Dale, cello; Sally Heath, piano.

Emily Watson plays Jacqueline du Pre, the world-class cellist whose profound connection to the music contributed to her mental instability. *Hilary and Jackie* is based on her sister Hilary's true account of du Pre's rise and fall. The centerpiece, du Pre's 1970 performance of fellow Brit Sir Edward Elgar's "Cello Concerto in E Minor" showcases her evident mastery of the cello and deep understanding of Elgar's neglected composition. The concerto was rarely performed, and du Pre made it her own. Just as the "Rach 3" loomed large in *Shine*, the concerto is the main attraction here. Beyond a brief overture by Bach, the remaining 13 minutes feature Barrington Pheloung's cues with Caroline Dale on cello managing to emulate du Pre's style of playing to complement an outstanding, and distinctly English, work of classical music.

David Poole

Hill Street Blues

1990, Silva Screen Records, from the television series *Hill Street Blues*, 1985 ♪♪♪♪

album notes: Music: Mike Post; **Conductor:** Daniel Caine.

The second of two faithfully recreated Mike Post score albums by Derek Wadsworth is by far the better of the pair. Often light on the underscore, this series used music very sparingly. Post often scored the opening or closing montages and occasionally, some of the more highly charged emotional moments. He composed most of the music featured here himself, though Velton Ray Bunch ("Quantum Leap") is credited as co–composer on three of the 15 tracks. The album alternates between the low–key poignant motifs for the character sequences and the more jazzy (or bluesy) riffs that follow the officers as they patrolled "The Hill." Several of Post's shorter themes have also been assembled into a five-minute suite.

David Hirsch

The Hitcher

1991, Silva Screen Records, from the film *The Hitcher*, Cannon Films, 1986 ♪♪♪♪

album notes: Music: Mark Isham; **Featured Musicians:** Kurt Wortman, percussion; Bongo Bob Smith, percussion; Bill Douglass, bass; Mark Isham, electronics/flugelhorn.

Mark Isham's atmospheric score underlines the action in this terror-filled drama, a confrontation between good and evil, about a youth on a cross-country trip and the hitchiker he picks up on a deserted road. Using weird and seemingly disparate extremes, Isham created a flavorful synthesized score that captures the personalities of the characters, as well as the tension in the action. It's all very effective and works well within the limits imposed by the subject matter and its treatment.

Didier C. Deutsch

Hoffa

1993, Fox Records, from the film *Hoffa*, 20th Century-Fox, 1993 ♪♪♪♪

album notes: Music: David Newman; **Conductor:** David Newman.

Director Danny DeVito seeks to tell the story of union organizer Jimmy Hoffa with the larger than life scope afforded to any big screen heroic tale. To establish the appropriate musical accompaniment, DeVito turned to his longtime associate David Newman to create an epic symphonic score that gives Hoffa's battles a major life or death ambience. Cues, such as "RTA Riot & Wake," could have easily been composed for a bloody World War II invasion sequence, rather than a struggle outside an inner city loading dock. Even the small moments, like "Truck Talk," are saturated with Hoffa's noble ambitions for "the cause" and his urgent need to break "big labor" before they break him. Newman's original music for the *Hoffa* advance trailer is also included.

David Hirsch

Hollow Reed

1997, RCA Victor, from the film *Hollow Reed*, Scala Productions, 1997 ♪♪♪

album notes: Music: Anne Dudley; **Conductor:** Anne Dudley; **Featured Musicians:** Michala Petri, recorder; Anne Dudley, piano.

Anne Dudley's score for *Hollow Reed* is generally attractive, with cues that are not always fully realized (many end up too abruptly or trail off without a satisfying conclusion), but develop musical ideas that are essentially compelling. The score, a series of long orchestral lines framing the delicate themes played on a variety of wind instruments, is quite evocative and establishes sustained moods that are striking. The overall effect is one of peace and quietness, which strongly supports the screen action. Judged on its own merits, the score also makes an excellent impression that obliterates its more basic flaws.

Didier C. Deutsch

Holly vs. Hollywood

1998, Intrada, from the Waiting Tables Production film *Holly vs. Hollywood*, 1998 ♫♫♫

album notes: Music: Douglass Fake; **Featured Musicians:** Jim Roth, clarinet; Colleen Lenord, piano; Deborah Steiner Spangler, violin; Todd Boekelheide, marimba.

Under normal circumstances, this album might not have been mentioned or might have been dismissed, given its short playing time. But Douglass Fake, head of Intrada, a label and a store that cater specifically to soundtrack lovers, is a good guy (there are not too many in this business); here, he reveals another side to his love for film music, by actually creating cues that are attractive and compelling. John Williams may not have to fear for his job or lose sleep over this release, but *Holly vs. Hollywood* has its charms, and deserves a listen.

Didier C. Deutsch

Holocaust

See: Air Power/Holocaust

Home Alone

1990, CBS Records, from the film *Home Alone,* 20th Century-Fox, 1990 ♫♫♫

album notes: Music: John Williams; **Lyrics:** Leslie Bricusse; **Conductor:** John Williams.

At a time when most current films seem to eschew the idea of a thoughtful, original score in favor of unremarkable underscoring and commercial-pop style "hook" songs, the soundtrack for *Home Alone* emerges as a warm, fresh and thoroughly appealing disc that lends itself well to repeated playing. John Williams's compositions, both spirited and sensitive, perfectly capture the essence of the Christmas season, with all its wonderment and fun, as viewed through the innocent (well, almost!) eyes of a child, the film's pint-sized star, Macauly Culkin. The lush orchestral score is enriched with a few carefully chosen pop vocal recordings, like The Drifters' classic version of "White Christmas," a searing "Please Come Home for Christmas" sung by rocker Southside Johnny Lyon, and an exquisite rendition of "Have Yourself a Merry Little Christmas" (perhaps the most perfect recording ever) by Mel Torme. Definitely a keeper for Christmas, or any time!

Charles L. Granata

Home Alone 2: Lost in New York

1992, Fox Records, from the film *Home Alone 2: Lost in New York,* 20th Century-Fox, 1992 ♫♫

album notes: Music: John Williams; **Lyrics:** Leslie Bricusse; **Conductor:** John Williams.

Like most film sequels, *Home Alone 2* lacks much of the magic that made the original so endearing, and in many respects, this soundtrack follows suit. What's missing is more of the original John Williams music that enhanced the charm of the original. That said, it is a nice collection of holiday songs, performed by a wide variety of artists, including TLC's rap interpretation of "Sleigh Ride," Alan Jackson performing a country rendition of "A Holly Jolly Christmas," and "My Christmas Tree" sung by the Home Alone Children's Choir. Most interesting are Bette Midler's version of the film's theme, "Somewhere in My Memory," and two Williams compositions, "Merry Christmas, Merry Christmas" and "Christmas Star."

Charles L. Granata

Home Alone 3

1997, Hollywood Records, from the 20th Century-Fox film *Home Alone 3,* 1997 ♫

album notes: Music: Nick Glennie-Smith.

With all due respect, Nick Glennie-Smith, gifted as he may be, is not John Williams, and *Home Alone 3,* a tired sequel, is not the original. All of this to say that the concept of the kid left home for Christmas by his insensitive (and slightly scatter-brained) parents to face alone some crafty burglars who want to break into the premises, and who successfully defeats them thanks to his guile and ingenuity, has overstayed its welcome. And that Glennie-Smith's score doesn't have the appeal and essential qualities found in the one Williams wrote for the first film in the series.

Loaded with percolating rhythms that seem totally inappropriate, synthesized effects, and wild orchestral poundings that are all show and no substance, it simply doesn't work. An occasional lighter touch seems to throw it in a different, more sedate direction, but that's a mere illusion, as the beat returns with a vengeance, the composer being no doubt under the delusive assumption that louder means better. Several pop songs complement the release, some totally unnecessary, such as "My Town" or "All I Wanted Was a Skateboard," others, such as "Let It Snow!" by Dean Martin or "Bad Bad Leroy Brown" by Jim Croce, seemingly out of place.

Didier C. Deutsch

Homeboy

1988, Virgin Records, from the film *Homeboy,* 1988 ♫♫♫♫

album notes: Music: Eric Clapton; Michael Kamen; **Featured Musicians:** Eric Clapton, guitar; Michael Kamen, keyboards; Steve Ferrone, drums; Nathan East, bass.

Eric Clapton's presence (his guitar playing and his writing) dominates the entire album, providing the score for this film—about a washed-out former boxer trying to make a comeback—with much of its drive and energy. While some cues don't work as well as others ("Bridge," for instance, which is much too dry and uninspiring), most of the selections are beautifully reflective of the downbeat, bluesy moods in the film and make a musical statement of their own, with Michael Kamen, Steve Ferrone, and Nathan East providing solid backup to the leader-composer. Occasionally, as in "Training," the rock 'n' roll legend shows his mettle in hard-driving tunes, but these moments are rare and far between and the overall tone of the score is more low-key and subdued. Some vocal numbers not by Clapton add to the flavor of the album.

Didier C. Deutsch

Homeward Bound: The Incredible Journey /Homeward Bound II: Lost in San Francisco

1993, Intrada Records, from the films *Homeward Bound: The Incredible Journey* and *Homeward Bound II: Lost in San Francisco*, Walt Disney Films, 1993, 1995 ♫♫♫♫
album notes: Music: Bruce Broughton; Conductor: Bruce Broughton.

Bruce Broughton captured the striking beauty of the outdoor environment and the frantic pace of the action in his scores for the *Homeward Bound* films, about three animals, two dogs and a cat, first in their incredible journey across the Pacific Northwest, then in a sequel that finds the four-legged stars (voiced by Michael J. Fox, Sally Field, Don Ameche, and Ralph Waite) lost in the San Francisco wild. It may seem a bit of an overkill to have this lush music used in such a context, but the fact remains that Broughton, one of today's top composers, found the proper voice needed to bring these adventures to musical life. In descriptive terms, he managed to write cues that are frequently picturesque and vivid ("The Cougar," in the first film, "Airport Escape," in the sequel) or simply remarkably attractive ("Just over That Next Hill," "Dog on a Date"). The main theme that links both scores (developed as "A Homeward Bound" in the second volume) is a catchy, robust piece of business that recalls some of the best western themes heard on the screen.

Didier C. Deutsch

Honey, I Blew Up the Kid

1992, Intrada Records, from the film *Honey, I Blew Up the Kid*, Walt Disney Pictures, 1992 ♫♫♫
album notes: Music: Bruce Broughton; Conductor: Bruce Broughton.

Broughton's larger-than-life score for the second *Honey...* film is a non-stop comedic score, half cartoon music and half emotive drama. The main theme—associated with Rick Moranis and the colossal results of his experiments—is a jaunty scherzo for saxophone and woodwind that propels the score with the unrelenting force of an animated hurricane. Like Ernest Gold's *It's a Mad, Mad, Mad, Mad World*, Broughton's riotous score throws every piece of its musical pie into the face of its listeners, yet takes time out to soothe them with gentle lyricism when it's called for. Comedy scores often don't hold up well on disc because they either are comprised of tiny, unrelated comic cues or are so full of wall-to-wall Mickey Mouse-isms that they make no sense apart from the visual antics. Broughton's score is a happy exception.

Randall D. Larson

Honeymoon in Vegas

1992, Epic Soundtrax, from the film *Honeymoon in Vegas*, Castle Rock Entertainment, 1992 ♫♫♫
album notes: Featured Musicians: Billy Joel; Ricky Van Shelton; Amy Grant; Travis Tritt; Bryan Ferry; Dwight Yoakam; Trisha Yearwood; Jeff Beck; Vince Gill; John Mellencamp; Willie Nelson; Bono.

An amusing idea (based on the concept that Elvis is alive and well, and performing in Las Vegas) makes for a delightful soundtrack album, with a baker's dozen of the King's hit tunes "covered" by various chartmakers. Not only is this an inspired selection, but anyone who loves Elvis will enjoy discovering these songs performed by others, like Billy Joel, Jeff Beck, Amy Grant, and Willie Nelson, to name a few.

Didier C. Deutsch

Hoodlum

1997, RCA Victor, from the film *Hoodlum*, United Artists, 1997 ♫♫♫♫
album notes: Music: Elmer Bernstein; Conductor: Elmer Bernstein; Featured Musician: Cynthia Miller.

1997, Interscope, from the film *Hoodlum*, United Artists, 1997 ♫♫

Set in the 1930s, this minutely reconstructed thriller about an apocryphal black mobster whose Harlem turf is threatened by the notorious "Dutch" Schultz intent on controlling it, enabled composer Elmer Bernstein to write an excellent, atmospheric score in which a theme morphs into a subtle tango, while another quotes from a Puccini aria, all of it to remarkable effect. The themes, all of them richly detailed and crafted with great care, follow the action and illustrate it with style. A rendering of "Amazing Grace," always a very powerful song, caps this release.

Sarah Jessica Parker and Nicholas Cage in Honeymoon in Vegas. **(The Kobal Collection)**

Conversely, the so-called "song" album, which deceptively advertises itself as being "inspired" by the film, is a cheap rip-off that attempts to capitalize on the film by using its logo and a design similar to the score album. The songs, many of them in a contemporary rap mold, don't even fit the time period of the film, and have as much relation to it as a country and western or a Broadway show album. Some listeners might enjoy listening to these songs, which include a big band version of "Basin Street Blues," performed by L.V. with the Clayton-Hamilton (as in John and Jeff) Jazz Orchestra, and a cool "Lucky Dayz," by Adriana Evans, but don't try and peddle this album as if it were in any way connected with the soundtrack of the film.

Didier C. Deutsch

Hook

1991, Epic Sountrax, from the film *Hook*, Tri-Star Pictures, 1991 ♪♪♪♪♪

album notes: Music: John Williams; **Lyrics:** Leslie Bricusse; **Conductor:** John Williams; **Featured Musician:** Mike Lang, piano.

Williams's frequently over-the-top swashbuckling score almost makes one wish the film, a big-screen treatment of the story of Peter Pan, had been better than this sometimes messy, often spirited movie actually is. The fact is, while the music served its purpose on the screen, it can be best appreciated in this CD in which it makes a different, albeit most enjoyable statement. Williams always excels at creating this type of score, regardless of the merits of the films themselves, and he seldom fails. Here, the score often ends up being quite evocative and exciting, with several cues, like "The Flight to Wonderland," and "The Ultimate War," reaching levels of dynamic enthusiasm that are exhilarating, while others, like "Presenting the Hook," seem to have great fun with the characters and situations they are illustrating. In the process, the composer also takes time to pause and create some lovely melodies, like "Remembering Childhood," for the more reflective moments in the action that add a very good counterpoint to the more active cues. Permeating the whole is the fantasy mood that prevails, making this score one of the composer's most satisfying.

Didier C. Deutsch

Hoosiers

1986, Polydor Records, from the film *Hoosiers*, Orion Pictures, 1986 ♪♪♪♪

album notes: Music: Jerry Goldsmith; **Conductor:** Jerry Goldsmith.

An inspirational film about basketball and the difficult road to final victory of a high school team from a small Indiana town in 1951, *Hoosiers* (aka *Best Shots*) benefited from a rousing *Chariots of Fire*-like score by Jerry Goldsmith. Propelled by a solid synthesizer theme developed over a pounding rhythm, the cues illustrate the various hurdles, professional and personal, the members of the team must overcome under the guidance of their coach, splendidly performed by Gene Hackman. Along the way, Goldsmith finds some striking musical ideas in "The Coach Stays," "Get the Ball," and "The Finals" that more than anything else enhance the sometimes plodding action as it moves to its logical conclusion.

Didier C. Deutsch

Hope Floats

1998, Capitol Records, from the film *Hope Floats*, 20th Century-Fox, 1998 ♪♪♪

The presence of country phenomenon Garth Brooks on a soundtrack to a movie starring perky American sweetheart Sandra Bullock was a potent combination to soundtrack buyers in 1998. *Hope Floats*, a story about how you *can* go home again, has a soundtrack album as homey as its plot about a young woman who relocates back to her hometown when her marriage falls apart. It's an all-American patchwork of roots music, acoustic alternative music, and straight-on country. Except for the unfortunate selection of the tiresome Bryan Adams, this isn't a bad listen, nor is it life altering. But, hey, it does sport the Rolling Stones and Lyle Lovett, so you can always skip through some of the more pedestrian tracks and go straight to Lyle and the Glimmer Twins.

Amy Rosen

1998, RCA Victor, from the film *Hope Floats*, 20th Century-Fox, 1998 ♪♪♪♪

album notes: Music: Dave Grusin; **Featured Musician:** Tom Scott, EWI, saxophone.

Dave Grusin's ethereal, very pretty score is miles away from his fusion jazz albums. A series of dreamy cues, with the piano usually outlining the melody and the strings picking up behind it, this score album exudes a poetic aura that is most fetching. It evokes ponds in the morning mist, vast plains gently caressed by the wind, wild horses perhaps running by a brook, everything that heightens the melancholy felt by Birdee Pruitt, after she found out her husband has been cheating on her with her best friend. The former "Queen of Corn" eventually finds solace in the arms of the handyman who's been loving her all along, and Grusin's cue picks up the tempo for a charmingly uplifting "Getting up Again," which joins a couple of other tracks, like "Snappy Snaps," a swinging tune with a honky-tonk beat, in creating different moods.

Didier C. Deutsch

Horror Express

See: The Edgar Allan Poe Suite/Cry of the Banshee/Horror Express

The Horse Whisperer

1998, Hollywood Records, from the film *The Horse Whisperer,* Touchstone, 1998 🎬🎬🎬🎬

album notes: Music: Thomas Newman; **Featured Musicians:** George Doering, guitars, mandolins; Rick Cox, phrase loops, prepared guitar, bowed bass dulcimer; Sid Page, violin; Michael Fisher, percussion; Steve Tavaglione, George Budd, phrase loops; Steve Kujala, flutes; Erika Duke-Kirkpatrick, Dennis Karmazyn, cello; Jon Clarke, oboe, English horn; Chas Smith, pedal steel guitar; Ralph Grierson, Thomas Newman, piano; Gary Rydstrom, birdsong, wind.

1998, MCA Records, from the film *The Horse Whisperer,* Touchstone, 1998 🎬🎬🎬🎬

This effective story, about a mythical man who has a unique way with horses and helps a young girl recover from a painful past, spawned two different soundtrack albums: a song collection and a score album. Because of its Montana setting and heavily accented western feel, the song album relies on a sturdy collection of country songs, some old cowboy ballads, some new works that "wistfully echo the spirit of the ranching life of the wide open West," in Robert Redford's own words, performed by a wide range of artists, including Dwight Yoakam, Emmylou Harris, Don Edwards, and George Strait, whose evocative rendition of "Red River Valley" is breathtaking.

The score album features music composed for the film by Thomas Newman, who accumulates the sounds from a wide variety of western instruments (guitars, mandolins, violin, steel guitar) to give his cues the right colors and tonalities. The wistful themes reflect the calm and limpidity in an action that is permeated with nostalgic thoughts, whether it is the main protagonist's reminiscences about her past and the loss of her best friend and her favorite horse or, more generally, reflections about the fading of a frontier style that has become out of touch with today's realities. We are far from the familiar instrumental strains heard in *The Magnificent Seven, Giant,* or *Once upon a Time in the West,* to cite only a few. But as westerns go, this score easily stands out on its own merits, even if it evokes a West that is no longer, as opposed to a West that should have been.

Didier C. Deutsch

The Horseman on the Roof

See: Le Hussard sur le toit

Hot Shots!

1991, Varèse Sarabande, from the film *Hot Shots!,* 20th Century-Fox, 1991 🎬🎬🎬

album notes: Music: Sylvester Levay; **Conductor:** Sylvester Levay; **Featured Musician:** Duane Sciacqua, guitars.

The difference between this score and the score for the sequel, *Hot Shots! Part Deux,* is what separates a laborious ef-

fort from a truly imaginative one. Sylvester Levay is quite an acceptable composer whose ideas are, for the most part, interesting, but a trifle hackneyed. Thus, if there was only Levay's score to listen to, it probably would pass muster and be judged quite favorably. As it is, this is clearly the lesser of the two recordings.

Didier C. Deutsch

Hot Shots! Part Deux

1993, Varèse Sarabande, from the film *Hot Shots! Part Deux,* 20th Century-Fox, 1993 🎬🎬🎬🎬

album notes: Music: Basil Poledouris; **Conductor:** Basil Poledouris.

Hot Shots! Part Deux, with its broadly humoristic evocations, stands so far above the original that the music devised by Sylvester Levay doesn't quite make the grade in comparison. Basil Poledouris, on the other hand, brings to the task a flair that is truly unmistakable. This, by the way, is also in keeping with the general tone in both films, with the first an amiable comedy with some goofy moments in it, while the second is completely over-the-top with hilarious results.

Didier C. Deutsch

The Hot Spot

1990, Antilles Records, from the film *The Hot Spot,* Orion Films, 1990 🎬🎬🎬🎬

album notes: Music: Jack Nitzsche; **Featured Musicians:** Miles Davis, trumpet; Earl Palmer, drums; Tim Drummond, bass; Roy Rogers, slide guitar; Taj Mahal, acoustic guitar; John Lee Hooker, guitar.

This soundtrack album is almost as interesting for Jack Nitzsche's flavorful score as it is for the musicians who play it, including Miles Davis, John Lee Hooker, and Taj Mahal, among them. But the specific atmosphere that permeates Dennis Hopper's *film noir,* about a drifter whose arrival in a small Texas town sets off a chain of events that ends in a fracas in which the various characters reveal their darker leanings, seems to lend itself to this kind of musical treatment. Once the events are set in motion, the course to the unavoidable conclusion is taken at a slow, deliberate pace, an impression further enhanced by the bluesy tone of Jack Nitzsche's evocative music, with John Lee Hooker dominating the tracks with his gritty vocals and Miles Davis delivering a subdued, but quite effective counterpoint. "Dolly's Arrival," a slow, sexy tune played by Roy Rogers on slide guitar, is a highlight, along with "Bank Robbery," in which Miles Davis trades riffs with Taj Mahal on guitar and vocals.

Didier C. Deutsch

Hotel of Love

1997, Milan/BMG, from the Live Entertainment film *Hotel of Love*, 1996

A kitschy movie in the vein of *Four Weddings and a Funeral*, this song-driven soundtrack tries to be just as cute. But it's years behind and ends up being very uneven. Classic upbeat dance tracks, by artists such as KC & the Sunshine Band and the Grass Roots, collide with awkwardly placed new tracks by Tim Finn. The mix of ballads and dance tracks with lounge versions of some classics ("Love Will Keep Us Together," "Sway") and these awful Tim Finn tracks make for a schizophrenic compilation. It might have been different, had they used on this soundtrack album more of the songs performed by Ronnie Grey, the hotel pianist in the movie.

Beth Krakower

Hour of the Gun

1991, Intrada Records, from the film *Hour of the Gun*, United Artists, 1967

album notes: Music: Jerry Goldsmith; **Conductor:** Jerry Goldsmith.

In yet another retelling of the events that led to the celebrated gunfight at the O.K. Corral, the one that saw Doc Holliday and Wyatt Earp defeat the Clanton gang, *Hour of the Gun* goes one step further and chronicles the slow descent of the lawman into a maelstrom of personal vindication and revenge following the showdown. One of various psychological westerns that came from that period, *Hour of the Gun* was as much interested in its characters' motivations and inner thoughts as it was in big action scenes. As a result, action, gritty and violent when it happened, took a back seat to drama, thereby spoiling the film itself from one of its most important elements and an essential ingredient in the genre itself. Responding to the demands of the screenplay, Jerry Goldsmith wrote a score that reflected some of the most intense moments in the film, while also subtly underscoring its more cerebral aspects. Altogether, it was a strong score from a composer who had already found a personal voice in the western and who obviously enjoyed writing for it. The CD reissue simply replicates the original LP, issued on the United Artists label, but with the extra advantage of clean, spacious sound.

see also: Tombstone, Wyatt Earp

Didier C. Deutsch

House of Flowers

1990, Sony Music Special Products, from the Broadway production *House of Flowers*, 1955

album notes: Music: Harold Arlen; **Lyrics:** Truman Capote; **Musical Direction:** Jerry Arlen; **Cast:** Pearl Bailey, Diahann Carroll, Juanita Hall, Ada Moore, Enid Mosier, Dolores Harper.

They Know the Score

Bill Conti

I always wanted to write dramatic music. Maybe that's because I came from a house where Italian opera was always being played. It made me want to be a Baroque composer, and I wanted to get paid to write that kind of music. In the back of your mind, when you say you want to write music for the movies, you're saying that you want a big house, a big car, and a boat. If you just wanted to write music, you could live in Kansas and do it. So how can you be a professional composer? You can teach school and write. But that's not being a professional composer, is it? You can only live on Guggenheim grants and Fullbright scholarships for a while. But how do you become a 'real' composer? You have to go into the commercial world, which isn't unlike what the Baroque composers did. Cobblers made shoes. Mozart's job classification was to write music, which he did for ballets and operas. He got paid to do that, and taught on the side. He wasn't a waiter. He didn't sell mutual funds. Those are all noble professions, but if you want to be a professional composer, then you're writing dramatic music for film and television. And it's a wonderful thing to do that every day, rather than writing music for a one-time performance. I wanted to write thematic music, and get paid for it. And if you're in L.A., you get the Hollywood bug. You want the same things that everyone else has—a lawyer, a business manager, an agent, a publicist, and big, big bucks. It's sick, but that's the ideal. So you pursue that. And if you're lucky, you catch the gold ring.

Courtesy of **Film Score Monthly**

A musical set in the fragrant Caribbean, on an island where voodoo and French culture have settled down in amiable unity, *House of Flowers* opened on Dec. 30, 1954, with a cast that included Pearl Bailey, Juanita Hall, and a fresh newcomer named Diahann Carroll. Carroll dazzled first night audiences with her innocent portrayal of a flowergirl who wants to marry a mountain boy and her crystalline vocal talent. Inspired by a short story written by Truman Capote following a trip he had taken to Haiti, the show involves the struggle between two feuding local madames, Mme Tango and Mme Fleur, for the control of the leisure time of both the island's residents and visitors. Temporarily supplanted in her trade by her rival, Mme Fleur is counting on her new protégé, Ottilie, to rekindle her business, though, as we all know, the best laid plans . . . Punctuating the action with songs that have the right color and occasional carnival exuberance one associates with life in the West Indies, the score by Harold Arlen teems with bright moments, among which "A Sleepin' Bee," performed by Diahann Carroll, still attracts the most, while Pearl Bailey revealed her devastating side in the show-stopping numbers, "One Man Ain't Quite Enough," "What's a Friend For?" and "Has I Let You Down." *House of Flowers* had a short run of 165 performances, and won a Tony for Oliver Messel's florid settings.

Didier C. Deutsch

House of Frankenstein

🎬 1995, Marco Polo Records, from the film *House of Frankenstein,* Universal-International, 1944 🎬🎬🎬🎬

album notes: Music: Hans J. Salter, Paul Dessau; **Orchestra:** The Moscow Symphony Orchestra; **Conductor:** William T. Stromberg.

This CD features the complete score for *House of Frankenstein,* composed by Hans Salter and German *avant-garde* composer Paul Dessau (along with Charles Previn, another Universal staff composer who is co-credited on a few cues). The *House* score is thrilling, vigorous music, a *Symphonie Fantastique* in its own right, broken by the occasional light tune such as a pleasing travelogue romp in "Off to Vasaria" and the delightfully manic carnival cacophony of "Chamber of Horrors." The digital recording really lets John Morgan's orchestration shine in this cue. Otherwise, the music is dark and terrible, malevolent music for monstrous mayhem. Motifs spring forth for Dracula (somnambulant winds, a four-note ascending figure, erupting into furious strings, brass, and snare for his final dawn pursuit), the Hunchback (a sorrowful violin melody), the Wolf-Man (passionate strings and winds, the three-note descending phrase from *The Wolf-Man,* still mourning Larry Talbot's tragic curse), and the Frankenstein Monster (the dynamic, growling brass motif that makes up the film's primary theme). Spooky sounds for sordid souls.

Randall Larson

The House of the Spirits

🎬 1993, Virgin Records, from the film *The House of the Spirits,* Miramax Films, 1993 🎬🎬🎬🎬

album notes: Music: Hans Zimmer; **Conductor:** Fiachra Trench; **Featured Musicians:** Jurgen Musser, clarinet; Martin Spanner, oboe, cor Anglais; Richard Stuart, trumpet; Douglas Myers, trumpet; Michael Stevens, guitar; Nick Glennie-Smith, piano.

Hans Zimmer's gorgeous score is one of the winning ingredients in this story, spanning more than 45 years, of an aristocratic Chilean family dominated by an authoritarian paterfamilias, which also includes his clairvoyant wife, his staunchly severe sister, and his daughter. Some of the more disturbing aspects of the story find an echo in the composer's score, though most of the cues are solidly rooted in romantic themes that seem to belie the turmoil in the screen action. Rearranged for this release into five long selections, the cues gain more interpretive force in this presentation, which also enables the music to make a greater impression.

Didier C. Deutsch

House Party II

🎬 1991, MCA Records, from the film *House Party II,* New Line Cinema, 1991 🎬🎬🎬

album notes: Music: Vassal Benford.

Taking a cue from the 1990 *House Party,* this sequel manages to stay fresh and inventive, with rap duo Kid'n'Play (Christopher Reid and Christopher Martin), who starred in the original, returning with the same endearing charms that ensured the success of the first film. Now attending Harris University, the two hustle up their overdue tuition by staging a "Pajama Jammi Jam" on campus, resulting in a film that's often funny, in a cartoonish sort of way, and peppered with several rap songs that give it the right flavor. With bits of dialogue inserted here and there to put some tracks in focus, the album provides an excellent memento of the film.

Didier C. Deutsch

Housekeeping

🎬 1987, Varèse Sarabande, from the film *Housekeeping,* Columbia Pictures, 1987 🎬🎬🎬🎬

album notes: Music: Michael Gibbs.

Michael Gibbs's folk-tinged score reflects the odd, warm aura of this quirky story about two girls in a small Washington State community, whose lives revolve around the various relatives (all women) who drift in and out of their house, including their mother, grandmother, grand aunts, and aunt. Though solidly suggestive of the moods in the film, the almost chamber-like score, often performed by a couple of solo instruments, sometimes over a sparse orchestral section, appears relatively dry when heard on its own merits, possibly because the musical themes are not sufficiently fleshed out. Only occasionally does the music become vibrant ("Freightcar Ride"), exhibiting the very qualities that could have sustained the whole score had they been in display throughout.

Didier C. Deutsch

How Green Was My Valley

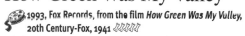 1993, Fox Records, from the film *How Green Was My Valley*, 20th Century-Fox, 1941 🎬🎬🎬🎬🎬

album notes: Music: Alfred Newman; **Orchestra:** The 20th Century-Fox Orchestra; **Conductor:** Alfred Newman.

One of the great scores to come out of Alfred Newman's fertile pen, *How Green Was My Valley* makes a belated and rousing recording debut in this CD released a few years ago. Set against the stark background of life in the Welsh coal mines, this deeply moving story of a family runs the whole gamut of human emotions, from romance to anger, from unrequited love to personal ambition, from the warmth of friendship to the greed of the ruling class. Making its own comments on the unfolding story, Newman's score echoes these sentiments with themes that are lovingly detailed and beautifully catchy. This is nowhere more evident than in the striking cue marked "The Family and Bronwen," in which the composer found warm accents to describe Huw, the film's narrator looking back at his youth and the feelings he had for his family of struggling miners. Presented in stereo, in a sound quality that is not always up to the exacting demands of the digital era, with noticeable hiss and some distortion on many of the tracks, the CD nonetheless is an important contribution to the ever increasing library of classic film scores from the past.

Didier C. Deutsch

How Stella Got Her Groove Back

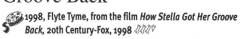 1998, Flyte Tyme, from the film *How Stella Got Her Groove Back*, 20th Century-Fox, 1998 🎬🎬🎬

Stella might try starting her search with this 14-song collection, a groove-fest that more than held its own during a soundtrack-crazy summer that was dominated by *Armageddon* and *City of Angels*. Overseen by uber-producers Terry Lewis and Jimmy "Jam" Harris, former members of the Time and Janet Jackson's chief collaborators, *Stella* samples the many shades of contemporary R&B, from the old school shades of K-Ci & JoJo, Mary J. Blige, and Me'Shell Ndegeocello to the reggae flavors of Maxi Priest and Diana King. The Fugees' Wyclef Jean teams up with Stevie Wonder on the fluid "Mastablasta '98" (an update of

Wonder's 1980 hit "Master Blaster (Jammin')"), while Janet Jackson coos and murmurs under Shaggy on "Luv Me, Luv Me." Chante Moore and Boyz II Men make it nice 'n' smooth for "You Home Is in My Heart (Stella's Love Theme)," and Kevin Ford hooks up with Rugus Blaq on the electro hip-hop of "Dance for Me." With all that going for it, *Stella*'s groove is pretty potent.

Gary Graff

How the West Was Won

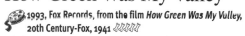 1996, Rhino Records, from the film *How the West Was Won*, MGM, 1962 🎬🎬🎬

album notes: Music: Alfred Newman; **Lyrics:** Johnny Mercer; Sammy Cahn; **Orchestra:** The MGM Studio Orchestra and Chorus; **Conductors:** Alfred Newman, Ken Darby, Robert E. Dolan, Joseph Lilley.

The blockbuster western that almost ended all westerns now finally has a soundtrack CD on a similarly grand scale, with Rhino's ambitious restoration of more than two hours of Alfred Newman's score. Like the film itself, the soundtrack aims for a comprehensive portrait of more than half a century of Americana, from folk songs to ballads to music hall fare. Newman's main theme, booming out of an 86-piece band, still has its power to stir, and much of the restored orchestration is lovely and evocative, although the frequent appearances of the Ken Darby Singers now seem to belong to a faraway time when a men's chorus lurked behind every cactus. In "Raise a Ruckus Tonight" and "Wait for the Hoedown," Debbie Reynolds scholars will find an early incarnation of the "unsinkable" character that she has been playing ever since.

Marc Kirkeby

How to Make an American Quilt

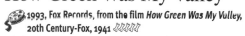 1995, MCA Records, from the film *How to Make an American Quilt*, Universal Pictures, 1995 🎬🎬🎬🎬

album notes: Music: Thomas Newman; **Conductor:** Thomas Newman.

An excellent score, with a great Americana flair to it, this soundtrack album further benefits from some excellent pop vocal selections, including Bing Crosby's "Swinging on a Star," Patsy Cline's "You Belong to Me," and The Inkspots' "I Don't Want to Set the World on Fire." But the palm here goes to Thomas Newman whose charming, warm series of cues evokes a time and a place that no longer seems to exist, except perhaps in the movies. With cues that seductively explore the myriad variations offered by the central "Quilting Theme," heard as the opening track, the score sets its own moods and reveals a lyrical side that is most engaging. There are many highlights here, outside of the pop selections that give the narrative a strong time period, but a first choice would defi-

How the West Was Won **(The Kobal Collection)**

nitely include "The Life Before," "An American Quilt," "Portraits/Pond," and "The Diver."

Didier C. Deutsch

How to Succeed in Business without Really Trying

 1961, RCA Victor, from the Broadway production *How to Succeed in Business without Really Trying*, 1961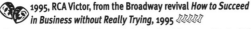

album notes: Music: Frank Loesser; **Lyrics:** Frank Loesser; **Musical Direction:** Elliot Lawrence; **Cast:** Robert Morse, Rudy Vallee, Bonnie Scott, Charles Nelson Reilly, Paul Reed, Virginia Martin, Ruth Kobart.

 1995, RCA Victor, from the Broadway revival *How to Succeed in Business without Really Trying*, 1995 🎵🎵🎵🎵

album notes: Music: Frank Loesser; **Lyrics:** Frank Loesser; **Musical Direction:** Ted Sperling; **Cast:** Matthew Broderick, Ronn Carroll, Megan Mullally, Jeff Blumenkrantz, Lillias White, Walter Cronkite.

A Pulitzer Prize-winning musical, something of a rarity in the theatre, *How to Succeed in Business without Really Trying* was based on a Shepherd Mead's manual, which Abe Burrows took as his inspiration to trace the rise up the corporate ladder of a

window washer who, by the time he has finished applying Mr. Mead's recommendations for quick success, indeed finds himself at the head of the World Wide Wicket Company. In the course of the evening, the young tyro defeats his envious rival, nephew of the company's president, and finds love in the eyes of his secretary, Rosemary.

A delightful satire of big business, the show received a tremendous boost in Frank Loesser's exhilarating score, and in Robert Morse's impish portrayal as J. Pierpont Finch, whose guile allows him to succeed without really trying. With Rudy Vallee making a last stage appearance as J.B. Biggley, president of the company, and Charles Nelson Reilly at his manic best as the grudging nephew, *How to Succeed* opened to rave reviews on Oct. 14, 1961, and settled for a long run of 1,417 performances. It won five Tony Awards, including one for Best Musical, and one for Robert Morse as Best Actor. With Michele Lee playing the female lead, and with its score virtually intact, it transferred to the screen in 1966.

A slightly revised, more politically correct version, starring Matthew Broderick, opened on March 23, 1995, and closed after 548 performances. Of the two recordings available, the original cast album, starring Robert Morse and Rudy Vallee, remains as lively and vibrant as the day when it was first recorded. The 1995 revival cast recording, with Matthew Broderick, contains better sonics, more music, a show-stopping rendition of "Brotherhood of Man" performed by Lillias White, and the voice of Walter Cronkite as the show's narrator.

Didier C. Deutsch

Howard's End

🎬 **1992, Nimbus Records, from the film *Howard's End*, Orion Classics & Merchant Ivory Productions, 1992** ⨀⨀⨀⨀

album notes: Music: Richard Robbins; Conductor: Harry Rabinowitz; Featured Musician: Martin Jones, piano.

Richard Robbins's approach to film scoring is often very dramatic, with robust romantic themes that sweep the listener into their highly-charged melodic elements, and very effective. *Howard's End* is no exception. Anchored around Percy Grainger's "Bridal Lullaby," the title tune creates an atmosphere of its own: elegant and slightly understated. These moods are developed more fully with the first original cue, "Helen and Paul Call It Off," in which the early 20th-century atmosphere of the film elicits an echo in Robbins's music. The other selections fully explore the dramatic possibilities born out of this story about an impoverished young widower, now married to a richer friend of his late wife, in a world where class prejudice and Edwardian snobbery frequently clash with dramatic results. Bringing a total change of pace, "Tango at Simpson's-in-the-Strand" shows another facet of Robbins's creativity and his knack for more exotic types of music.

Didier C. Deutsch

The Hudsucker Proxy

🎬 **1994, Varèse Sarabande, from the film *The Hudsucker Proxy*, Warner Bros., 1994** ⨀⨀⨀⨀

album notes: Music: Carter Burwell; Conductor: Sonny Kompanek.

A goofball spoof of big business by the Coen brothers (*Fargo*), *The Hudsucker Proxy* has an equally appropriate Carter Burwell score. The composer counterpoints the on-screen antics by playing up the bizarre visual designs and characters' "earnest" motives. Two Khachaturian pieces (one is the celebrated "Sabre Dance" from the *Gayane Suite*) are well adapted into the score to add a further air of pomposity to the internal politics at Hudsucker Industries.

David Hirsch

The Hunchback of Notre Dame

🎬 **1996, Walt Disney Records, from the animated feature *The Hunchback of Notre Dame*, Walt Disney Pictures, 1996** ⨀⨀⨀⨀

album notes: Music: Alan Menken; Lyrics: Stephen Schwartz; Musical Direction: Jack Everly; Cast: Tom Hulce, Heidi Mullenhauer, Jason Alexander, Charles Kimbrough.

Alan Menken and Stephen Schwartz teamed to write the score for this animated feature, very loosely based on the well-known story by Victor Hugo. The book's plot centers around a deformed hunchback in medieval Paris, who falls in love with the gorgeous gypsy Esmeralda, in love with another. The hunchback loses his life when he attempts to save her from a righteous archdeacon, eager to burn her at the stake—a common practice at the time—in order to atone for his own sins. Being that this was a Disney film, the story was slightly modified: Quasimodo gets encouragement and solace from gargoyles suddenly coming to life, and doesn't die at the end. The tone of the film was uplifted to remove the story from anything that might resemble the dour moods of the original; and the songs, of course, had to reflect the upbeat feelings that prevail. Otherwise, the narrative remains relatively faithful to its model, with splashy, colorful expressions of an easy, carnival-like atmosphere that probably would have baffled Parisians in the Middle Ages. The score echoes the hopeful moods in the story, and though it plays by the numbers, it finds attractive connotations to soothe and attract any audience. The film's essential politically correct message is that "God Helps the Outcasts," a number heard twice in the recording, notably in a moving rendition by Bette Midler. There is nothing terribly earth-shaking about the rest of the recording, which, like most soundtracks written for the Disney films, is enjoyable, not too demanding, and just a tad this side of being bland.

Didier C. Deutsch

Hundra

🎬 **1991, Prometheus Records/Belgium, from the film *Hundra*, 1991** ⨀⨀⨀⨀

album notes: Music: Ennio Morricone; Conductor: Ennio Morricone.

It may be somewhat of a surprise to find Ennio Morricone scoring a sword-and-sorcery epic in which the central character is a female Conan, but don't let that deter you from enjoying this tremendously exciting score, which teems with great, overblown themes in which heroic accents are the predominant note. When he is inspired to write an action score, Morricone often creates themes that are melodically quite powerful and engaging. Such is the case here with "Hundra's War Theme," "Slaughter in the Village," and "Hundra's Revenge," that are as epic and descriptive as one could wish an action theme to be. Central to their effectiveness are strongly delineated melodies that capture the motion in the screen action and translate it in evocative ways that grab the listener's ear and force his attention. In sharp contrast, the composer also includes in the mix a series of cues that are marked by the attractive musical lines in them, notably "Love Theme," which is particularly fetching, or "Chrysula, the Wise One," in which an oboe details the melody over the full orchestral texture. A great score that may be overlooked but is well worth discovering.

Didier C. Deutsch

The Hunger

1983, Varèse Sarabande, from the film *The Hunger,* MGM/UA, 1983 🎬🎬🎬

album notes: Music: Michel Rubini, Denny Jaeger.

A classy contemporary vampire story, *The Hunger* recalls through some of its aspects Roger Vadim's *Blood and Roses,* with some twists that even the Gallic director wouldn't have thought about. Starring David Bowie, in a Dorian Gray role, and Catherine Deneuve, the steamy thriller also stars Susan Sarandon, with whom Deneuve has a memorable seduction scene after she has disposed of Bowie in a most ungentlewomanly fashion. Adding a touch of class of its own, the soundtrack collects many works from the classical repertoire, with Michel Rubini providing some cues that also seem quite appropriate. Maybe not to everyone's taste, but interestingly challenging nonetheless.

Didier C. Deutsch

The Hunt for Red October

1990, MCA Records, from the film *The Hunt for Red October,* Paramount Pictures, 1990 🎬🎬🎬🎬

album notes: Music: Basil Poledouris; **Conductor:** Basil Poledouris.

A fresh spin on the old East-West cold war clichés, *The Hunt for Red October* turned out to be a particularly gripping drama, thanks largely to Sean Connery's understated performance as the commander of a Russian nuclear submarine who wants to defect to the West, and who is chased by his own comrades who are bent on stopping him and the Americans who don't trust his motivations. The taut narrative calls for a powerful score that evokes the drama, its roots, the background of its various participants, and a bit of patriotic accents to limn the whole thing. Basil Poledouris delivered all of these and then some in his outstanding contribution, in which a Russian chorus brings an appropriately Slavic flavor to the "Main Title," and in which the course of the action is charted in vivid musical details that have great descriptive force and persuasion.

Didier C. Deutsch

Hyperspace /Beauty and the Beast

1993, Prometheus/Belgium, from the film *Hyperspace,* 1985, and the television series *Beauty and the Beast,* 1987–90 🎬🎬🎬🎬

album notes: Music: Don Davis; **Conductor:** Don Davis (*Hyperspace*), Jacob Wells (*Beauty and the Beast*).

A proficient, though poorly known composer, Don Davis's work has mostly been heard on television, where his contributions have included the scores to a handful of popular movies of the week and series, and particularly scored for several episodes of *V* and *Star Trek: The Next Generation.* Composed in 1985, *Hyperspace* was a sci-fi thriller spoof that poked fun at the genre with glee and allowed the composer to go on a tangent and play the big orchestral effects for fun, twisting in the process some of the most revered moments from John Williams's score for *Star Wars,* and even adding a serio-comic touch with his heart-rending version of "Old MacDonald Had a Farm."

In contrast, *Beauty and the Beast,* composed for the television series starring Ron Pearlman as Vincent, the beast of the title, and Linda Hamilton as Catherine, the beauty who falls in love with him, combines together several cues that were created over the years for various episodes. Given the tragically romantic subject matter, Davis provided sounds that are quietly powerful and richly evocative of the action. An interesting comparison is established in the last track in which Davis's concept about the death of Catherine and how it affects Vincent is contrasted with Lee Holdridge, the original composer of the series, whose approach was quite different and much softer. Released here for the first time, it shows how the same idea can elicit totally opposite reactions from two composers.

From a purely technical point of view, the recording is a bit dry and would have gained at being slightly reverbered. But don't let that deter you from listening to it.

Didier C. Deutsch

I Can Get It for You Wholesale

1995, Columbia Records, from the Broadway production *I Can Get It for You Wholesale,* 1962 🎬🎬

album notes: Music: Harold Rome; **Lyrics:** Harold Rome; **Musical Direction:** Lehman Engel; **Cast:** Lillian Roth, Jack Kruschen, Harold Lang, Elliott Gould, Sheree North, Marilyn Cooper, Bambi Linn, Barbra Streisand.

Today, Harold Rome's *I Can Get It For You Wholesale* is best remembered as the musical which launched the career of Barbra Streisand, whose comical performance as Miss Marmelstein (and performance of the song by that title) literally stopped the show. Adapted by Jerome Weidman from his own novel, with songs by Harold Rome, the musical is set in the 1930s and focuses on New York's garment industry. Gloomy and unnecessarily hard-edged, at least for a musical, it follows the rise and fall of a small-time entrepreneur, played by Elliott Gould, determined to succeed by whatever means necessary but unable to reach his goals, simply because he's not cut out for success. Matching the tones of the book, Harold Rome wrote a somber score in which few bright moments emerged, one of them being the solo by Barbra Streisand. Following its premiere on March 22, 1962, the show had a run of 300 performances.

Didier C. Deutsch

I Do! I Do!

1966, RCA Victor, from the Broadway production *I Do! I Do!* 1966 ♪♪♪♪

album notes: Music: Harvey Schmidt; **Lyrics:** Tom Jones; **Musical Direction:** John Lesko; **Cast:** Mary Martin, Robert Preston.

A delightful two-character musical, based on Jan de Hartog's *The Fourposter*, *I Do! I Do!* brought together Mary Martin and Robert Preston as a couple whose married life becomes the focus of the show. The show follows them from their honeymoon to their golden old age, in an existence that encompasses 50 years, and the usual problems found in long-term relationships, from occasional infidelities, to raising children, to little difficulties and great joys. What set the show apart from other musicals is the fact that it was a traditional Broadway show played out on a small scale, which, in addition to involving only its two principals, was entirely set in the same room in their apartment. Smartly staged by Gower Champion, and boasting flavorful songs by Tom Jones and Harvey Schmidt (among which "My Cup Runneth Over" became a major hit), *I Do! I Do!* opened on Dec. 5, 1966, and closed after 560 performances. The passing years have not diminished the glow left by the show nor the initial impression gathered from the original cast album of a trifle, but a most engaging production.

Beth Krakower

I giorni della violenza

See: Il mio nome e' Shangai Joe/I giorni della violenza

I Got the Hook-Up!

1998, No Limit Records, from the film *I Got the Hook-Up!*, Dimension, 1998 ♪

There was little that was funny about this would-be farce, starring rap star Master P; a collection of loosely connected episodes with no real focus or continuity between them. Set in South-Central L.A., and presumably reflecting its urban culture, the film involved Master P and sidekick A. J. Johnson as "dealers" of stolen product operating from a van in a parking lot. Occasionally, cameos by other members of the rap community (Ice Cube, among them) prove amusing, but are not sufficient to redeem this misguided effort.

Likewise, the intriguingly packaged CD features performances by a whole line-up of well-known rappers, including Master P, of course, but also Ice Cube, Snoop Doggy Dogg, Jay Z, and Skull Dudgery, but the overall level of artistry, if it can be called that, is appallingly low and unimaginative.

Didier C. Deutsch

I Love Trouble

1994, Varèse Sarabande, from the film *I Love Trouble*, Touchstone Pictures, 1994 ♪♪♪♪

album notes: Music: David Newman; **Conductor:** David Newman.

The delicately hewn themes David Newman created for the two protagonists in this heartwarming romantic comedy help conjure up the pleasant atmosphere that pervades it. A story about two rival reporters assigned to cover the same case who reluctantly join forces to crack it and the mutual appreciation that comes out of this cooperation, the screenplay enticed the composer to write a strongly evocative score, strong on romantic echoes, with an occasional soft jazz touch ("Honeymoon Night") to add a spark to it, and generally melodic cues that aim to soothe without making too much of a noise. The goal is achieved with themes that have great appeal ("Two Scoop Snoops," "Scoop de Jour"), adding up to an enjoyably lightweight effort.

Didier C. Deutsch

I lunghi giorni della vendetta

1995, EMI General Music/SLC/Japan, from the film *I lunghi giorni della vendetta (The Long Days of Vengeance)*, 1967 ♪♪♪♪

album notes: Music: Armando Trovaioli; **Conductor:** Armando Trovaioli.

Armando Trovaioli wrote an exceptional score for this spaghetti western starring Giuliano Gemma as an innocent man sent to jail after he is double-crossed by an arms trader, and who escapes in order to prove he is not guilty and exact revenge. Solidly anchored around a forlorn main theme, played on an acoustic guitar, occasionally offset by a harmonica or an electric guitar, the score is striking for the simplicity of its expression. Featuring several attractive melodies ("High Noon," "Following the Sun," "Go on, Cowboy, Go On," "Love for a Squaw"), the rough-and-tumble action is described by the guitar sounding ominous chords over percussive effects that underline the tension in a subtle way ("The Wait," "Hopeless Duel," "Dead of Alive," "The Ambush"). This recording may be difficult to find. Check with a used CD store, mail-order company, or a dealer specializing in rare, out-of-print, or import recordings.

Didier C. Deutsch

I Shot Andy Warhol

🎬 1996, Tag Recordings, from the film *I Shot Andy Warhol*, Orion Pictures, 1996 ♪♪♪♪

album notes: Featured Musicians: Luna; the Lovin' Spoonful; R.E.M.; Wilco; Ben Lee; Jewel; Sergio Mendes; Brasil '66; Love; Pavement; MC5; Bettie Serveert; Yo La Tenga.

Modern rockers doing '60s songs isn't a new idea, but it works well here. Donovan's biggest hits get creditable covers from Jewel ("Sunshine Superman") and Luna ("Season of the Witch"). R.E.M.'s version of the Troggs' "Love Is All Around" has been, well, around for awhile, and teen troubadour Ben Lee turns in a refreshingly snotty rendition of the Small Faces' "Itchykoo Park." And the original versions of the MC5's "Kick out the Jams," Love's "Gimi a Little Break," and the Lovin' Spoonful's "Do You Believe in Magic" bring a little balance to the proceedings.

Gary Graff

I Still Know What You Did Last Summer

🎬 1998, Warner Bros./143 Records, from the film *I Still Know What You Did Last Summer*, Columbia, 1998 ♪♪♪
album notes: Music: John Frizzell.

What this set has is nice, but it doesn't have a lot—a mere 12 songs, which is short by today's cash-in standards. And one of those ("How Do I Deal") is sung by Jennifer Love Hewitt, which will make a nice entry on Rhino Record's inevitable collection of "Golden Voices" curios from the '90s. Interestingly, the album has a strong middle with Orgy's cover of New Order's "Blue Monday," newcomer Bijou Phillips's "Polite," and Grant Lee Buffalo's "Testimony." It's surprising there's nothing from co-star Brandy, although that wouldn't necessarily have been an improvement.

Gary Graff

I Want to Live

🎬 1999, Rykodisc, from the film *I Want to Live*, United Artists, 1958 ♪♪♪♪♪
album notes: Music: Johnny Mandel; Featured Musicians: Jack Sheldon, Al Porcino, Ed Leddy, trumpets; Frank Rosolino, Milt Bernhart, Dave Wells, trombones; Dave Wells, bass trumpet; Vince De Rosa, Sin-

clair Lott, John Cave, Dick Parisi, French horns; Harry Klee, piccolo, flutes; Abe Most, clarinet; Joe Maini, saxophones, bass clarinet; Bill Holman, saxophones, clarinet; Marty Berman, bass clarinet, contra bassoon; Chuck Gentry, bass saxophone, countra-bass clarinet; Red Mitchell, string bass; Pete Jolly, piano; Al Hendricksen, guitar; Shelly Manne, Larry Bunker, Mel Lewis, Milt Holland, Mike Pacheco, percussion; Kathryn Julye, harp; Gerry Mulligan and the I Want to Live Jazz Combo (tracks 17–22): Shelly Manne, drums; Art Farmer, trumpet; Bud Shank, alto sax, flute; Frank Rosolino, trombone; Pete Jolly, piano; Red Mitchell, bass; Gerry Mulligan, baritone sax.

A classic jazz score from Johnny Mandel. This was the first jazz score to blend authentic jazz writing and playing into the essence of the picture. The style of writing meshes greatly with the overall mood of the film, that of desperation. The music is written in a seamy, nocturnal style. Much of it is also composed in the then-current hard-bop/West Coast style: "Poker Game" is Horace Silver–influenced; "San Diego Party" is pure hard bop that features Bud Shank and Art Farmer; "Barbara Surrenders" is absolutely beautiful blues, and features a sexy Gerry Mulligan and Bud Shank; "Peg's Visit" is another hauntingly exotic ballad, one of Mandel's best; "Preparations for Execution" is very eerie and does foretell impending death; "Death Scene" is full of Mandel's ahead-of-his-time exotic colors; and "End Title" borrows a 12/8 Latin feel from "Poker Game." The remaining tracks are pure West Coast jazz, and they stand alone as individual performances. A marvelous score.

Bob Belden

Ice Station Zebra

🎬 1997, PEG Records, from the film *Ice Station Zebra*, MGM, 1968 ♪♪
album notes: Music: Michel Legrand; Conductor: Michel Legrand.

A cold war actioner adapted from a novel by Alistair MacLean and starring Rock Hudson, Patrick McGoohan, Ernest Borgnine, and Jim Brown, *Ice Station Zebra* elicited an appropriately taut score from French composer Michel Legrand. A race against time between Russians and Americans rushing to a solitary Arctic outpost to recover a fallen satellite which holds the key to victory in an all-too-possible (at the time!) nuclear war between the two countries might appear today a bit far-fetched, but it makes for a fine, suspenseful drama, which Legrand's music emphasizes with all the expected *sturm und drang*. The one drawback here is the fact that all the tracks combined amount to just 30 minutes of playing time, which seems just a bit short for anyone's money.

Didier C. Deutsch

The Ice Storm

🎬 1998, Velvel Records, from the film *The Ice Storm*, Fox Searchlight, 1998 ♪♪♪
album notes: Music: Mychael Danna.

Crisp clean snowy/icy weather is used both metaphorically and visually in this story of life in suburban Connecticut in 1970s, complete with adultery, drugs, and "key" parties where couple swap partners based on whose key is picked. Mychael Danna's score, which captures the cold crispness of the ice storm in the opening scene, is so effective I actually got the chills in the movie theater. Unfortunately, this CD features only about 12 minutes of Danna's breathtaking music. The CD also contains various 1970s classics, by artists such as Jim Croce, Traffic, Frank Zappa, and Free, which appear in the movie. David Bowie contributed a more reflective version of "I Can't Read" to this soundtrack, a song that he originally recorded with his 1980s group, Tin Machine.

Didier C. Deutsch

Iceman

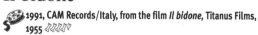1992, Southern Cross Records, from the film *Iceman,* Universal Pictures, 1984 🎬🎬

album notes: Music: Bruce Smeaton; **Conductor:** Bruce Smeaton.

Composer Bruce Smeaton wrote a particularly effective score for this striking science-fiction film about a Neanderthal man found in an Arctic cave where he has been frozen for thousands of years, and his slow awakening in a new world totally alien to him. Using as his primary means of expression a Japanese shakuhachi against the context of a symphonic orchestra, Smeaton created a score that emphasizes the apparent dichotomy between the past, represented by the Iceman, and the present, the modern society in which he is "reborn." While his music can hardly be faulted, and in fact proves quite challenging in many ways, the short playing time of the CD (less than 29 minutes) is something that leaves a lot to be desired, particularly at the premium price usually demanded for soundtrack albums.

Didier C. Deutsch

Il bidone

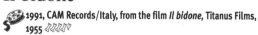1991, CAM Records/Italy, from the film *Il bidone,* Titanus Films, 1955 🎬🎬🎬🎬

album notes: Music: Nino Rota; **Conductor:** Carl Savina.

One of director Federico Fellini and Nino Rota's early collaborations, *Il bidone* (known in this country as *The Swindle)* is interesting in that it presents in embryo all the musical elements Rota would use, reuse, and recycle in his subsequent films for Fellini—rambunctious, malicious themes, jaunty, brassy tunes, romantic motifs, with a touch of jazz thrown in for good measure—all of them colliding in a festive display of the composer's incredibly colorful palette and expressive instrumentations. The film, starring Broderick Crawford, Richard Basehart, Franco Fabrizi, and Giulietta Masina, deals with a trio of con artists in Rome,

each with ideas of striking it rich in a sly comedy that provided Rota with the right tones to write a diversified score. Some of the themes he developed for the film showed up in other films, sometimes as main motifs, sometimes as secondary ones, but always recognizable, and always thoroughly enjoyable.

Didier C. Deutsch

Il Casanova

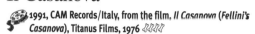1991, CAM Records/Italy, from the film, *Il Casanova (Fellini's Casanova),* Titanus Films, 1976 🎬🎬🎬

album notes: Music: Nino Rota; **Conductor:** Carlo Savina.

In his music, Nino Rota pretty much tried to capture and reflect the dreamylike visions and fancy concoctions of Federico Fellini. Often recycling some of the themes he had used in the director's previous films, he created a body of work that, taken as a whole, constitutes an impressive musical tapestry that matches and echoes Fellini's own creative world. *Il Casanova,* Fellini's tribute to the great 18th-century Venetian lover and adventurer, inspired Rota to write a series of cues around a single motif, "The Magic Bird" (L'uccello magico). The quirky cues, with period instruments occasionally playing strange-sounding melodies, give the music a modern edge mixed with an aura of authenticity, while they evoke Casanova's travels and his many adventures in Paris, in Dresden, and in Rome. The CD, imported from Italy and released by CAM, belongs to that category of hard-to-find titles that will challenge the listener and take him on an unexpected, but rewarding, musical journey.

Didier C. Deutsch

Il clan dei Siciliani

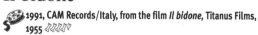1993, CAM Records/Italy, from the film *Il clan dei Siciliani (The Sicilian Clan),* 20th Century Fox, 1970 🎬🎬🎬🎬

album notes: Music: Ennio Morricone; **Conductor:** Bruno Nicolai.

A superbly crafted (and performed) film, *The Sicilian Clan* drew its strength from the strong characterizations director Henri Verneuil elicited from a stellar cast that included Jean Gabin, Alain Delon, and Lino Ventura, as well as from its solidly fluid story about a major caper, a jewel heist, that eventually reveals more twists and turns than seems plausible. Putting the icing on this frothy cake was Morricone's score, one of his best, that subtly added details to the plot in the making, and provided a strength of its own to spice up the screen proceedings. Suggestively carried by the main theme, heard throughout, it is one of the best examples of the maestro working in a contemporary action thriller. This title may be out of print or just plain hard to find. Mail-order companies, used CD shops, or dealers of rare or import recordings will be your best bet.

Didier C. Deutsch

Il Conte Dracula

1994, Edipan Records/Italy, from the film *Il Conte Dracula (Count Dracula)*, 1971 ♫♫♫

album notes: Music: Bruno Nicolai; **Conductor:** Bruno Nicolai.

Christopher Lee portrayed the lovable bloodthirsty Count in this gory retelling of the celebrated tale, made in Spain by Jess Franco, with Klaus Kinski and Herbert Lom also in the cast. If there was nothing really novel about the story itself, Bruno Nicolai brought to it a fresh vision, which, retrospectively, contrasts with that of other composers who also tackled it. Sparse and direct, rather than ornate and romantic, his score eschewed the obvious Gothic accents suggested by the narrative, and focused instead on themes that ostensibly featured the Hungarian cymbalum, eerie changing chords, and some dissonance to accompany the tenser moments in the action. The hypnotic repetition of some accords ("Hallucination," "The Nightmare") helps sustain the tension and suggests the unholy experiences brought about by the presence of the undead. A change of pace is occasionally the result of a lilting tune that weaves its way into the momentum ("Changing Concerto," "A Glance"), but these are few and far between. This recording may be difficult to find. Check with a used CD store, mail-order company, or a dealer specializing in rare, out-of-print, or import recordings.

Didier C. Deutsch

Il gattopardo

1991, CAM Records/Italy, from the film *Il gattopardo (The Leopard)*, Titanus Films, 1980 ♫♫♫♫

album notes: Music: Nino Rota; **Conductor:** Franco Ferrara.

A brilliant period drama, directed by Luchino Visconti, *The Leopard,* set in late 19th-century Sicily, recounted in bold, colorful strokes the story of an Italian aristocrat and his family troubles, even as the world he had known crumbled around him under the onslaught of widespread social changes. Adding a pervasive melancholy touch to the story, Nino Rota provided a lush, expansive score, eons away from the usually jaunty style that had characterized his scores for the films of Federico Fellini. Also central to the music he devised were several dance numbers, notably "Mazurka," "Polka," "Quadrille," and "Galop," that enliven this excellent recording.

Didier C. Deutsch

Il ladrone/L'harem

1995, RCA/Italy, from the films *Il ladrone (The Good Thief)*, 1980, and *L'harem (The Harem)*, 1967 ♫♫♫♫

album notes: Il ladrone: Music: Ennio Morricone; **Conductor:** Ennio Morricone; **Featured Musicians:** Marianne Eckstein, flute; Barbara Vig-nanelli, flute; Gato Barbieri, saxophone; Bruno Battisti D'Amario, guitar; **L'harem: Music:** Ennio Morricone; **Conductor:** Ennio Morricone; **Featured Musicians:** Marianne Eckstein, flute; Barbara Vignanelli, flute; Gato Barbieri, saxophone; Bruno Battisti D'Amario, guitar.

Two superbly realized scores by the great Italian composer, one, *The Good Thief,* dating from 1980, the other, *The Harem,* from 1967. A pseudo-Biblical tale, the serio-comic *The Good Thief* borrowed all the right elements from the New Testament (the miracles, the well-known facts about the life of Jesus, always seen from a distance), but twisted them and and cleverly used them for comedic effects. Starring Enrico Montesano as a likable do-badder with a mischievous bent, the film benefitted from its attractive score, which relied on melodic tunes to carry it over, including a very attractive one for synthesizer ("The Good Thief's Idea"). Set in modern times, the score for *The Harem* utilized the warm sonorities of Gato Barbieri to give substance to its melodies ("The First Harem," "The Second Harem"), while "Six Strings" drew its name from the fact that it is entirely played on an unaccompanied six-string guitar, backed by a drum, with the music slowly reaching a climax. It may have been unusual, but it's highly effective. This title may be out of print or just plain hard to find. Mail-order companies, used CD shops, or dealers of rare or import recordings will be your best bet.

Didier C. Deutsch

Il mercenario/Faccia a faccia

1995, ViViMusica/Italy, from the films *Il mercenario (A Professional Gun)*, United Artists, 1968, and *Face to Face (Faccia a faccia)*, United Artists, 1968 ♫♫♫♫♫

album notes: Il mercenario: Music: Ennio Morricone; **Conductor:** Ennio Morricone; **Faccia a faccia: Music:** Ennio Morricone; **Conductor:** Bruno Nicolai.

Two celebrated spaghetti westerns, both with a score by Ennio Morricone. Need we say more . . . Made in 1968 by Sergio Corbucci, *Il mercenario,* released as *A Professional Gun,* was a strange concoction starring Jack Palance as a homosexual army captain, Franco Nero as a bounty hunter, and Tony Musante as a Mexican bandit, all involved with a silver shipment. Directed by Sergio Sullima, *Faccia a faccia (Face to Face)* starred Gian Maria Volonte and Tomas Milian as two notorious gang leaders whose friendship eventually deteriorates when their common interests lead them down divergent paths. In both instances Morricone wrote vigorous scores that have long since become classics, outlasting the films for which they were created. The gritty guitar chords, punching percussions, distant vocals, clarion clear trumpets, eerie string lines, and percolating rhythms, all trademark signatures, are present in these scores, along with scorching themes that keep the listener on edge. This title may be out of print or just plain hard to find. Mail-order companies, used CD shops, or dealers of rare or import recordings will be your best bet.

Didier C. Deutsch

Il mio nome e' Shangai Joe/I giorni della violenza

1996, GDM Music/Italy, from the films *Il mio nome e' Shangai Joe (My Name Is Shangai Joe)*, 1973, and *I giorni della violenza (Days of Violence)*, 1967 ♪♪♪♪

album notes: Il mio nome e' Shangai Joe: Music: Bruno Nicolai; **Conductor:** Bruno Nicolai; **I giorni della violenza: Music:** Bruno Nicolai; **Conductor:** Bruno Nicolai.

Bruno Nicolai, for several years a close associate of Ennio Morricone, borrowed concepts and ideas from him, and turned in several spaghetti western scores that sound as if they could have been written by the maestro himself. Such is the case with *My Name Is Shangai Joe* and *Days of Violence,* both represented here. A failure in Italy at the time of its release, *Shangai Joe,* an unlikely kung fu-spaghetti western starring Chen Lee, was a huge success in Japan. Unusually violent and bloody, it told a familiar tale about a Chinese fighter in the American west, torn between the non-violent Buddhist teachings of his upbringing and the violent realities of the frontier, eventually resorting to using his "fighting fists" in order to survive and bring back peace (the film was also released as *Fighting Fists of Shangai Joe*). The score Nicolai wrote for this one is quite typical, with guitar strummings, honky tonk barroom piano stylings, harmonica wailings, and Chinese harmonies, all laid over string lines that detail attractively melodic themes. *Days of Violence,* made in 1967, was another familiar tale about a Missouri farmer who joins a band of outlaws at the end of the Civil War in order to exact revenge on the Union soldiers who have devastated his family, only to become a wanted man himself. The strongly characteristic score by Nicolai, driven by a main title theme reminiscent of Elmer Bernstein and a pervading love theme for classical guitar, is presented here as a long orchestral suite that makes it even more appealing as a listening experience. This recording may be difficult to find. Check with a used CD store, mail-order company, or a dealer specializing in rare, out-of-print, or import recordings.

Didier C. Deutsch

Il mio West

1998, Cecchi Gori Music/Italy, from the film *Il mio West (My West)*, 1998 ♪♪♪♪

album notes: Music: Pino Donaggio; **Orchestra:** The Bulgarian Symphony Orchestra; **Conductor:** Natale Massara.

A modern-day spaghetti western that harkens back to the glory days of the genre with a score by Pino Donaggio, one of the better current Italian composers. The opening theme, "Everybody Wants

to Be (a Cowboy)," is an interesting combination reggae-rap tune, performed by Ziggy Marley and Wycleff, over a three-note chord borrowed from Morricone's *The Good, the Bad, and the Ugly.*

An odd mixture of techno-pop and Hawaiian chants (probably substituting for Plain Indians' music) informs "Jeremiah's Theme," but the remainder of the score is standard fare, beautifully played by the Bulgarian Symphony Orchestra, with many attractive melodies weaving in and out of the cues ("My West," "The Tribe," "The Saloon," "Friendship on the Roof"). This title may be out of print or just plain hard to find. Mail-order companies, used CD shops, or dealers of rare or import recordings will be your best bet.

Didier C. Deutsch

Il momento della verita

1991, CAM Records/Italy, from the film *Il momento della verita (The Moment of Truth)*, Cineriz, 1964 ♪♪♪
album notes: Music: Piero Piccioni; **Conductor:** Piero Piccioni.

Even though it is not understood or appreciated in this country, the art of tauromachy is in vibrant display in other parts of the world (particularly in Spain and Mexico), where it elicits passions that border on idolatry. Made in 1964, *The Moment of Truth* (the title refers to the final confrontation between the toreador and his fiery opponent) followed the life and career of a Spanish bullfighter, from his childhood to his last fight in the arena, with appropriate comments about the social and environmental culture that spawned the trend, in a mixture of staged scenes and documentary reports. Piccioni's score is appropriately somber and ominous, with flashes of glory to signal the liveliest moments in the action. The Spanish atmosphere is evoked in "The Flamenco of Truth," "Temporada," and "The Bolero of Truth," while concessions are being made to current (at the time) popular musical trends with a timely "Bossa Nova Marina." This recording may be difficult to find. Check with a used CD store, mail-order company, or a dealer specializing in rare, out-of-print, or import recordings.

Didier C. Deutsch

Il Postino

See: The Postman

Il sole anche di notte

1999, Pacific Time, from the film *Il sole anche di notte (Sunshine Even by Night)*, 1990 ♪♪♪♪
album notes: Music: Nicola Piovani; **Conductor:** Nicola Piovani.

Released in 1990, *Sunshine Even by Night* was an evocative film about an idealistic, sensitive young nobleman who retires from the world and becomes a monk when he discovered that his intended was the king's mistress. But his quest for perfect solitude is constantly interrupted by visitors hearing rumors about his alleged miraculous powers, and by women who bet they can successfully seduce him. While the sudden availability of this CD may be largely due to the composer winning the Academy Award for *Life Is Beautiful,* there is no denying that the music for *Sunshine Even by Night* had inner beauties that made it a viable candidate for release. A large orchestral score, it is a very engaging effort that has charms and a winsome appeal to it. This title may be out of print or just plain hard to find. Mail-order companies, used CD shops, or dealers of rare or import recordings will be your best bet.

Didier C. Deutsch

I'll Do Anything

1994, Varèse Sarabande, from the film *I'll Do Anything,* Columbia Pictures, 1994 ♪♪♪♪

album notes: Music: Hans Zimmer; **Featured Musicians:** Nick Glennie-Smith, synthesizers; Hans Zimmer, synthsizers; Kurt McGettrick, baritone sax; Gary Foster, soprano sax; Jonathan Crosse, soprano sax; Dan Higgins, soprano sax; Steve Fowler, alto sax; Walter Fowler, trumpet; Gary Gray, clarinet; Jim Kanter, clarinet; Marty Kristall, clarinet; Phil Ayling, oboe; Jon Clarke, oboe; Rose Corrigan, bassoon; Ken Munday, bassoon; David Duke, French horn; Charlie Loper, trombone; Philip Teele, trombone; Mike Lang, piano; Ralph Grierson, piano; Michael Thompson, guitar; Jimmy Johnson, fretless bass; Dale Anderson, marimbas; Larry Bunker, marimbas; Alan Estes, marimbas; Thomas Raney, marimbas; Wallace Snow, marimbas; Katie Kirkpatrick, harp; Mervyn Warren, vocals; Phillip Ingram, vocals; Dorian Holley, vocals; Rodney Saulsberry, vocals; Arnold McCuller, vocals.

This immensely appealing score evokes better than most the charming, oddball comedy for which it was written, about an unemployed actor who takes care of his little girl, only to find himself upstaged by her own career when she lands major parts in films. Initially intended to be a musical, the film suggested many themes that have been arranged here in selections that give them greater overall playing time, with the cues assembled to specifically create portraits of the main characters portrayed by Nick Nolte, Albert Brooks, Joely Richardson, and Julie Kavner. Whittni Wright, who plays the gifted moppet, also takes the spotlight in the album, via a rendition of the jaunty "You Are the Best" she performed in the film.

Didier C. Deutsch

Immortal Beloved

1994, Sony Classical, from the film *Immortal Beloved,* Columbia Pictures, 1994 ♪♪♪♪♪

album notes: Music: Ludwig van Beethoven; **Orchestra:** The London Symphony Orchestra; **Conductor:** Sir Georg Solti; **Featured Musicians:** Emanuel Ax; Pamela Frank; Gidon Kremer; Yo-Yo Ma; Murray Perahia.

How could anyone resist this impressive "soundtrack" album, when the music was written by none other than Beethoven? Cleverly packaged to feature some of the composer's best known works, this is in every way a greatest hits compilation, running

the gamut from orchestral excerpts (five of the monumental symphonies) to a movement from the brilliant "Emperor" concerto, to chamber music and piano sonatas (both the "Pathétique" and "Moonlight," as well as "Für Elise"). The music is played with passion by a veritable who's who of longhair performers, including Perahia, Emanuel Ax, Yo-Yo Ma, and the LSO, conducted by Sir Georg Solti. Schroeder would love it—so will you!

Didier C. Deutsch

The Impostors

1998, RCA Victor, from the film *The Impostors,* Fox Searchlight, 1998 ♪♪♪♪

album notes: Music: Gary DeMichele; **Featured Musicians:** Gary DeMichele & Band: Paul Maslin, saxes; John Bowse, saxes, clarinet; Jeff Michus, trumpet; Henry Salgado, trombone; Brian Sandstrom, bass; Miriam Sturm, solo violin; Tomas Yang, violin; Gary DeMichele, drums, percussion, accordion, keyboards, guitar; Forever Tango Orchestra: Lisandro Androver, Hector del Curto, Miguel Varvello, Victor Lavallen, bandoneons; Leonardo Suarez Paz, Rodion Boshoer, violins; Oscar Hasbun, viola; Dino Auarleri, cello; Silvio Acosta, bass; Fernando Marzan, piano; Mario Araolaza, keyboards.

The hijinx of two actors desperate for work during the '20s makes for slapstick in the tradition of Laurel and Hardy. Director and star Stanley Tucci (*Big Night*) pays tribute to this neglected genre with riotously fun big band jazz from Eddie Condon and Sidney Bechet, and a priceless example of Lucienne Boyer's sultry French torch song. Tucci proved his knack for great party mixes with *Big Night,* and both soundtracks owe a debt to composer Gary DeMichele, whose Forever Tango Orchestra seems to delight here in elegant tangos, zippy swing, and catchy ballads for the ballroom. The glaring error of including Steve Buscemi's excruciating ballad is outweighed by uncovering one of Louis Armstrong's greatest ever performances, the catchy conga dance "Skokiaan." Armstrong sings with his husky voice "the hot drums are drumming, the hot strings are strumming" and as the credits roll, the cast dances in a conga line off the film set.

David Poole

In & Out

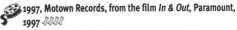

1997, Motown Records, from the film *In & Out,* Paramount, 1997 ♪♪♪♪

album notes: Music: Marc Shaiman; **Conductor:** Artie Kane.

Initially inspired by Tom Hanks's Oscar acceptance speech for *Philadelphia,* this good-natured gay-themed comedy involves a young actor who, when he wins the Academy Award, publicly thanks his "great gay teacher," thus propelling into the public eye a man who, much to his reluctance, is being branded when he, in fact, admits to different sexual preferences. Based on this premise, the film developed with guile and fresh spirit, punctuated at every turn by Marc Shaiman's amusing score, or

Gary Oldman as Beethoven in Immortal Beloved. *(The Kobal Collection)*

by several songs that have become anthems in the gay culture, including Diana Ross's "I Will Survive," Ethel Merman's "Everything's Coming up Roses," and the Village People's "Macho Man." It all combines to create a soundtrack album that's frequently enjoyable and highly listenable.

Didier C. Deutsch

In Dreams

1999, Varèse-Sarabande, from the film *In Dreams,* Dreamworks, 1999 ♫♫♫

album notes: Music: Elliot Goldenthal; **Conductor:** Jonathan Sheffer; **Featured Musicians:** Page Hamilton, Mark Stewart, Andrew Hawkins, David Reid, Eric Hubel, "deaf elk" guitars; Bruce Williamson, saxophone; Sally Heath, piano; Rolf Wilson, Jonathan Rees, violin); Roger Chase, viola; Andrew Schulman, cello.

The darker aspects of this psychological thriller directed by Neil Jordan elicited a disturbing, surreal score from Elliot Goldenthal, who had previously worked with the director on *Michael Collins.* The strange case of a woman illustrator whose visions and nightmares eventually lead her to "invade" the mind of a serial killer in order to unmask him, this unsettling drama, starring Annette Benning, required a score that moved away from the conventional and into areas where the mind is a dominant force. To translate the visuals musically, Goldenthal created a series of atonal cues that recall some of the works composed by Leonard Rosenman and reinforce the claustrophobic atmosphere of the film, while projecting a mood of uncertainty that is most convincing. As a result, this is hardly the kind of soundtrack album you might want to listen to just for relaxation. Rather, it is a compelling work that requires as much intellectual involvement from the listener as the film did from its audience. A couple of familiar pop songs, including "Don't Sit under the Apple Tree," by the Andrews Sisters, and the title song, performed by Roy Orbison, cast a different, almost jarring note.

Didier C. Deutsch

In Like Flint/Our Man Flint

1998, Varèse Sarabande, from the 20th Century-Fox films *In like Flint,* 1967, and *Our Man Flint,* 1966 ♫♫♫♫♫

album notes: Music: Jerry Goldsmith; **Conductor:** Jerry Goldsmith.

In the days when James Bond and Matt Helm were the rage, one of the coolest secret agents on screen was *Our Man Flint,* whose casual demeanor and devilish swagger were some of his most endearing weapons. Portrayed with flair by James Coburn, Flint only appeared in two films, in which the psychedelic style and swashbuckling approach were dazzling and gently tongue-in-cheek. This was also reflected in Jerry Goldsmith's scores, in which the themes exhibited a winning combination of pop legerdemain and serious musicality. With a predomi-

nance of electronic instruments fitting the action (and the era), and bouncy tunes that were firmly in a pop groove, Goldsmith managed to create scores that were engaging, reflective of the action in its silliest moments, and very enjoyable.

This first CD reissue groups together both scores, presented in reverse order for some unorthodox reason, properly remastered and EQed, but with the notable absence of some tracks that existed on the original LPs—"No Rest for the Weary" and "Who Was That Lady?," missing from the first album; and "Doing as the Romans Did," "Galaxy a GoGo!–or Leave It to Flint," composed by Goldsmith and Randy Newman, "All I Have to Do Is Take a Bite of Your Apple?" and "Stall! Stall! Flint's Alive," missing from the second album. Given the fact that the tracks are unusually short and the total playing time comes to 65 minutes (enough to accommodate more music), these omissions are baffling, to say the least. Be that as it may, this welcome CD certainly invites repeated listening, and might even surprise listeners not used to the lighter side of Jerry Goldsmith.

Didier C. Deutsch

In Love and War

1997, RCA Victor, from the film *In Love and War,* New Line Cinema, 1997 ♫♫♫♫

album notes: Music: George Fenton; **Conductor:** George Fenton; **Featured Musicians:** Andy Findon, flute; Michael Jeans, oboe, cor anglais; Nick Bucknall, clarinet; Derek Watkins, cornet, trumpet; Andy Crowley, cornet, trumpet; Edward Hessian, accordion; David Arch, piano.

Reflective of the moods in this film set during World War I, George Fenton struck a particularly rich vein with themes that underscore the passionate love affair between writer Ernest Hemingway, then a young soldier on the Italian front, and a nurse, eight years older, in a real-life drama that was the spark from which eventually came *A Farewell to Arms.* Largely ignoring the wartime backdrop of the screenplay, Fenton's music focuses on the most romantic aspects of the story, from its timid beginnings, while Hemingway recovers from a serious wound in a hospital, to the breakup forced upon the two lovers by forces outside their control. In its often staid expression, the score finds new accents to speak of love and its wonderful and devastating effects, in terms that tug at the right heartstrings. In it, the composer demonstrates once again his uncanny ability to write music that is simply glorious and profoundly affecting.

Didier C. Deutsch

In the Army Now

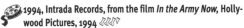

1994, Intrada Records, from the film *In the Army Now,* Hollywood Pictures, 1994 ♫♫♫

album notes: Music: Robert Folk; **Orchestra:** The Sinfonia of London; **Conductor:** Robert Folk.

Call it a "guilty pleasure," but Robert Folk has composed an infectiously melodic score for one of the umpteenth brainless Pauly Shore comedies which, presumably, will be as dated one day as disco, bell-bottoms, and the music of Giorgio Moroder are now. Not so for Folk's music, though, which is a large orchestral work performed with appropriate panache by the Sinfonia of London, grounded in a 1941-style military march that culminates in a thrilling, eight-minute-long final track that includes some of the best music the composer has written yet. The album is just long enough to sustain repeated visits and Folk's thematic material is strong enough to hold up to them. Unlike the movie, the composer kept a straight face and wrote a seriously good score here, one that might look surprising to someone who spots it upon browsing through your CD rack, but certainly not to anyone who has actually heard it.

Andy Dursin

In the Heat of the Night/They Call Me Mister Tibbs

🎬 1998, Rykodisc, from the United Artists films *In the Heat of the Night,* 1967, and *They Call Me Mister Tibbs,* 1970 ♪♪♪♪
album notes: Music: Quincy Jones.

Long before there was *In the Heat of the Night,* the television series, there was *In the Heat of the Night,* the film, starring Sidney Poitier as a police detective investigating a murder in red-neck country, and *They Call Me Mister Tibbs,* another tough contemporary murder drama set in San Francisco. Both films were scored by Quincy Jones, who wrote music as different as the two locations of the films themselves. In the Academy Award–winning *In the Heat of the Night,* Poitier portrayed Virgil Tibbs, a northern black police officer who is wrongly implicated in a murder case in the Deep South. When he's proven innocent, he stays on to help the chief of the local police (Rod Steiger) solve the case, against a backdrop of heated racism. Quincy Jones's score for this film was heavily blues-laden, a masterpiece featuring several original songs, including the title track sung by Ray Charles.

In *They Call Me Mister Tibbs,* we find the detective in San Francisco, where his friend, Reverend Logan Sharpe (Martin Landau), has been implicated in the murder of a prostitute. The score devised by Jones uses more urban sounds heavy on '70s groove to better replicate the sounds of the city. There is still an element of Tibbs's isolation evident in the music, this time in a more jazzy vein. These scores stand out as two of the finest examples of music for blaxploitation films.

Didier C. Deutsch

In the Line of Duty

📺 1992, Intrada Records, from the television series *In the Line of Duty,* 1991–92 ♪♪♪
album notes: Music: Mark Snow.

Before he became the *X–Files* composer, Mark Snow had already left his mark on many television shows (the liner notes to this album credit him with being "the most prolific composer in television," which owed him to win the ASCAP Award for the Most Performed Background Music on Television for seven consecutive years after the honor was created). Among his credits, he also scored four segments of the multi–part series *In the Line of Duty,* based on real–life FBI and police cases, which enabled him to utilize the many styles at his disposal, from acoustic piano to full–blown synthesizers, with a sturdy complement of varied instruments (French horns, English horns, contrabassoons, Australian aboriginal drums, and Japanese percussion) used in a variety of styles (bebop jazz, hip–hop, bluegrass, salsa, and even Italian opera). For this CD presentation, the cues have been assembled into four long suites, something that has the advantage of giving the music greater cohesiveness. It doesn't, however, mean that it is better because of that. Unfortunately, the music written by Snow sounds quite formulaic and devoid of any real surprises. Even in this suite format, the themes are very trite, unimaginative, cut to the bones in order to fit a standard situation. One of the problems with much music on television is that it fits a single purpose as noise behind action that is usually of little consequence and can be routinely abandoned for a message from the sponsors. Even a higher–class series like *In the Line of Duty* had to exist by the tenets of the medium. Snow's music does little to elevate itself above the norm.

Didier C. Deutsch

In the Line of Fire

🎬 1993, Epic Soundtrax, from the film *In the Line of Fire,* Columbia Pictures, 1993 ♪♪♪♪
album notes: Music: Ennio Morricone; **Orchestra:** Orchestra Unione Musicisti di Roma; **Conductor:** Ennio Morricone.

In a virtual return to some of the orchestral effects he used in some of his most successful spaghetti westerns, notably *The Good, the Bad, and the Ugly,* Morricone wrote a substantial score for this engrossing drama starring Clint Eastwood as a Secret Service agent assigned to protecting the President of the United States, who puts his own life on the line. Many of the cues provide the musical background for the action scenes, with the agent discovering the existence of a plot to kill the President, his efforts to capture the assassin before it's too late, and his ultimate victory over adversity. Setting off the action scenes, which gradually sound more dour and ominous as the drama unfolds, a love theme ("Lilly and Frank"), played in different styles, recurs throughout, as an indication of the isolation in which the Secret Service man finds himself.

Didier C. Deutsch

In the Mood

1987, Atlantic Records, from the film *In the Mood,* Lorimar Pictures, 1987 ♪♪♪♪

album notes: Music: Ralph Burns; **Featured Musicians:** Abe Most, clarinet; Joel Preskin, tenor sax; Bill Watrous, trombone; Gene Estes, vibes; Tom Ranier, piano; Warren Luening, flugelhorn; Bob Cooper, tenor sax; Oscar Brashears, trumpet; Marshal Royal, alto sax; Larry Bunker, vibes; Jennifer Holliday, vocals; Beverly D'Angelo, vocals.

The setting of this pleasantly innocuous comedy about the coming of age of a young man in the early 1940s led veteran composer and arranger Ralph Burns to create a vibrantly wonderful score. With solid assist from a handful of seasoned musicians, and the vocal support of Jennifer Holliday and Beverly D'Angelo (one of the film's stars), the soundtrack pays homage to the big band era, with powerful renditions of the standards "In the Mood," "Take the 'A' Train," "Dream," and "Don't Be That Way," plus original cues devised in the style of the period by Burns. The film didn't make much of an impression at the box office, but this soundtrack album is one of the best of its kind ever released.

Didier C. Deutsch

In the Name of the Father

1994, Island Records, from the film *In the Name of the Father,* Universal Pictures, 1994 ♪♪

album notes: Music: Trevor Jones; **Orchestra:** The London Philharmonic Orchestra; **Conductor:** David Snell.

The energized mixture of songs and Trevor Jones's underscore accurately captures the mood and period of this story about a young man falsely accused of an IRA bombing. Jones's score, presented in three suites totaling only 18 minutes, is appropriately dark and, on occasion, has an even harder percussive beat than the surrounding songs. Its overall dark ambience may not be for all tastes, though bouncy songs like The Kinks' "Dedicated Follower of Fashion" and Bob Marley's "Is This Love" actually offer a surprisingly welcome ray of sunshine in all the bleakness.

David Hirsch

Inchon

1988, Intrada Records, from the film *Inchon,* MGM/UA, 1982 ♪♪♪♪

album notes: Music: Jerry Goldsmith; **Conductor:** Jerry Goldsmith.

Jerry Goldsmith returned to the same material he'd covered in 1975's *MacArthur* with this old-fashioned war epic produced

by the Reverend Sun-Yung Moon, but even the middling *MacArthur* seemed like *Patton* compared to this goofy, overblown bomb. The Oriental influences in the score are as atmospheric and interesting as many of the composer's earlier works in this style, particularly the fascinatingly percussive opening of Chinese blocks and *col legno* effects, but the score stumbles in its overly effusive patriotic material, particularly a strangely overblown march theme for Douglas MacArthur. There are more than enough pulsating action cues and sympathetic moments of epic tragedy in the score to make up for the bombastic moments, however, particularly in this expanded CD from Intrada, which improved on the original LP's pinched sound. The orchestral performance is still below par in some cues, however.

Jeff Bond

Incognito

1998, RCA Victor, from the film *Incognito,* Morgan Creek, 1997 ♪♪♪

album notes: Music: John Ottman; **Conductor:** Larry Groupe.

A mild romantic thriller set in various European locations, about an art forger who sets out to paint a presumably lost Rembrandt, only to be unmasked by the "art student" he seduced and used as an accomplice, unbeknownst to her, *Incognito* had a rather plodding plot, little screen chemistry between its principals (Jason Patric and Irene Jacob), and a by-the-numbers score, signed by John Ottman, which neatly detailed the action without adding the spark that might have ignited it a bit more. Appraised on its own merits, however, it reveals greater charms than in the film itself, with some cues ("The Creation," "Research," "Re-creation," "Change of Fortune") that make the listener more favorably inclined toward it. Still, there are serious limitations to the expression, which tends to be confined to the standard hills and vales usually found in today's scores, with few melodies to truly capture the imagination and cues that seem to wander off without a satisfying conclusion.

Didier C. Deutsch

The Incredibly True Adventure of 2 Girls in Love

1995, Milan Records, from the film *The Incredibly True Adventure of 2 Girls in Love,* Fine Line Features, 1995 ♪♪♪

album notes: Music: Terry Dame; **Featured Musicians:** Terry Dame, soprano saxophone; Tom Judson, piano; Christine Kuhn, cello; Marie Breyer, percussion.

A story of first love between two girls in their senior year in high school—Randy, a tomboy, and Evie, an African-American princess—the film received a whimsical score from Terry Dame, a composer and multi-instrumentalist, heard here on soprano sax, in a chamber music format. The instrumental cues have a charm that is easily communicative and winning. The pop songs that interrupt the musical flow, on the other hand, are not very interesting and can be edited out.

Didier C. Deutsch

Indecent Proposal

1993, MCA Records, from the film *Indecent Proposal*, Paramount Pictures, 1993 🎬🎬🎬

album notes: Music: John Barry; **Featured Musicians:** The Pretenders; Vince Gill; Dawn Thomas; Seal; Bryan Ferry; Sheena Easton; Lisa Stansfield; Roy Orbison.

Even with its laughable plot and perfume-commercial caliber direction, *Indecent Proposal* was a box-office smash upon its original release, so there's no question that its music helped play a part in putting it over the top. John Barry composed one of his lush, delicate romantic scores for the film, with solo piano and orchestra gently underscoring the entanglements of a young couple with a Donald Trump–type mogul (Robert Redford). The music is expectedly soothing, but even as Barry scores of this ilk go, it's not anywhere near as memorable as *Somewhere in Time* or even *The Scarlet Letter,* and it comprises only a 25-minute suite on the album. The rest of the soundtrack contains various songs by Seal, Bryan Ferry, the Pretenders, Vince Gill, and Sheena Easton, and it's all sort of a ho-hum collection of covers with a few new songs that never attained the level of popularity that the film shockingly did with viewers.

Andy Dursin

Independence

1997, Prometheus/Belgium, from the television film *Independence*, 1987 🎬🎬🎬🎬

album notes: Music: J. A. C. Redford; **Conductor:** J. A. C. Redford.

This standard TV movie, shown in 1987, starred J. Michael Flynn, Stephanie Dunnam, and Anthony Zerbe, and was directed by John D. Patterson. And while it didn't make a big splash, this soundtrack by J. A. C. Redford certainly should. Filled with rambunctious sounds, it explores the western genre in a very traditional way, but manages to draw interesting colorings, suggesting both the romantic and vibrancy aspects attached to it. Redford, a composer whose talent is not sufficiently known and appreciated, again shows that he can conjure up accents that definitely set him apart from the crowd.

Didier C. Deutsch

They Know the Score
Lalo Schifrin

My best ideas come when I see the film—the visuals—and I write them when they come. I remember with *Cool Hand Luke,* they showed me dailies, and the theme came right there. I didn't even have music paper, but I made a staff and I wrote it out. And you know something, [at first] I tried to improve it. I said, 'It's too simple.' But that was the theme, and I was nominated for an Oscar for that. The same thing happened when I went to spot *Tango.* We spotted it in Argentina. So on the trip back to write the music, in the plane, I was writing on napkins. The next day I woke up after the long trip, and I said 'Maybe that [theme's] not good.' That was good. That was the one I used. On *Rush Hour,* same thing. I went to the cutting room and [director Brett Ratner] showed me a little bit because they had a first assemblage. And that was when it came. I realized that, at times, I tried to intellectualize. I started working more with my head than with my instinct. Then it becomes an intellectual exercise and it's not as good. Many times, that has happened to me. Some of my failures, in terms of my own satisfaction, [happened] because I made it too complicated. I made it for music students, or music teachers, or fellow composers.

***Courtesy of* Film Score Monthly**

Independence Day

1996, RCA Victor, from the film *Independence Day,* 20th Century-Fox, 1996 🎬🎬🎬🎬

album notes: Music: David Arnold; **Conductor:** Nicholas Dodd.

Writing in a style that echoes some of the best efforts by others like Jerry Goldsmith, James Horner, and John Williams, British composer David Arnold gave extraordinary musical life to this sensational sci-fi thriller about evil aliens who invade Earth. The broad, expansive orchestral cues provide the counterpoint to some of the most exciting action cues in the film, with two longer ones ("Evacuation" and "Base Attack") showing the composer at his most proficient with fully developed themes, filled with lush orchestral strokes and eerie choral sounds. The personal, human side of the story is also explored in sensitive cues, like "Canceled Leave," which illuminate and offset the story's darkest aspects. A thrilling score by a relative newcomer on the scene, whose career is clearly on the rise.

Didier C. Deutsch

The Indian in the Cupboard

1995, Sony Classical, from the film *The Indian in the Cupboard,* Paramount Pictures, 1995 &&&&
album notes: Music: Randy Edelman; **Conductor:** Randy Edelman.

Based on an award-winning children's novel by Lynne Reid Banks, *The Indian in the Cupboard* is a whimsical fantasy tale about a boy who discovers that, with the turn of a key, he can magically bring to life the three-inch-high toy Indian he placed in the old cupboard in his room. The story prompted Randy Edelman to write a huge, expansive score rife with florid orchestral accents. While the broadness of Edelman's writing might have seemed like overkill on the screen for what is, after all, only a charming little fantasy, the score reveals its many winsome qualities on this soundtrack album recording, with the colorful themes conceived by the composer creating a vibrant tapestry that weaves its own magic. The longer cues help create the overall impression of sheer fun and excitement that pervades the whole effort.

Didier C. Deutsch

The Indian Runner

1991, Capitol Records, from the film *The Indian Runner,* The Mount Film Group, 1991 &&&
album notes: Music: Jack Nitzsche; **Featured Musicians:** David Lindley, guitars; Tim Drummond, bass; James Cruce, drums; John Hammond, harmonica; Tom Margan, harmonica; Bradford Ellis, piano, keyboards; Jerry Hey, trumpet.

A solid '60s rock compilation that pulls no punches or surprises, but is quite enjoyable most of the time. Some of the greatest bands are brought together here, with Jefferson Airplane, Traffic, Fresh Air, Quicksilver Messenger Service, and Creedence Clearwater Revival among the most prominent. Janis Joplin's take on "Summertime" is always refreshing. The score selections by Jack Nitzsche fulfill their function, but they can't really compete with the great lineup that precedes them.

Didier C. Deutsch

Indiana Jones and the Last Crusade

1989, Warner Bros. Records, from the film *Indiana Jones and the Last Crusade,* Paramount Pictures, 1989 &&&
album notes: Music: John Williams; **Conductor:** John Williams.

John Williams's third Indiana Jones score can't hold a candle to the two previous efforts on a technical level, but it's probably a smoother overall listening experience than the overbearing *Indiana Jones and the Temple of Doom*. Williams adopts a slightly more subdued, flowing style here that results in a number of lengthy cues that don't quite have the showstopping power of anything in *Raiders* or *The Temple of Doom*. There's a sprightly comic chase for an early flashback sequence involving the young Indiana Jones, an engaging syncopated fugue for a motorcycle chase and the lurching, climactic "In the Belly of the Steel Beast,"' which works as an effective counterpart to *Raiders*' famous truck chase cue. There are plenty of good-natured melodies, including themes for Sean Connery's Professor Jones character and a benevolent guardian of the Holy Grail seen late in the film, but there's really nothing here that lingers in the memory very long.

Jeff Bond

Indiana Jones and the Temple of Doom

1984, Polydor Records, from the film *Indiana Jones and the Temple of Doom,* Paramount Pictures, 1984 &&&&
album notes: Music: John Williams; **Conductor:** John Williams.

John Williams's relentless score, a superior effort despite the somber echoes that pervade it, matches the generally downbeat moods in this second installment in the Indiana Jones saga, with an occasional action cue ("Fast Streets of Shanghai," "The Mine Car Chase") or a swift reprise of the "Raiders' March" reminding the listener that this is still the soundtrack album to an adventure film. On the whole, however, the general tone of the score is more oblique than the composer's previous or subsequent efforts, with often strident orchestral lines underscoring the gloomiest aspects of the film itself, a frightening tale about children being enslaved by an occult sect celebrating Kali, the goddess of death. As if to offset this dark atmosphere, one track, Cole Porter's "Anything Goes," sung in Chinese, is a real standout, a rib-tickling, grandly overblown performance as exhilarating as it is unexpected.

see also: Raiders of the Lost Ark

Didier C. Deutsch

Indochine

1992, Varèse Sarabande, from the film *Indochine,* Sony Classics, 1992 🎬🎬🎬🎬

album notes: Music: Patrick Doyle; **Conductor:** William Craft.

A riveting romantic tale of lust and passion set against the rising communist movement that eventually forced French natives to leave Indochina, the Asian country they had once colonized, *Indochine* received a provocative, flavorful score from Patrick Doyle at the top of his creative verve. Matching closely to the action in the film, Doyle provided many memorable orchestral cues for this story about a classy, no-nonsense rubber plantation owner (Catherine Deneuve), her adopted Indochinese daughter (Linh Dan Pham), and the handsome young Navy officer (Vincent Perez) who makes both women swoon. Adding dramatic impulse to the story, the silent evolution that opposed traditional attitudes and new ideas within the Indochinese society and the increasing resentment to French colonialist values became further pegs on which Doyle anchors the score, a broadly romantic effort that makes few concessions to an ethnic feel and chooses instead to confine itself to more familiar European grounds. While sequencing of the album seems a bit erratic and does not follow the order in which the story itself unfolds, the cues are attractively assembled and quite enjoyable as a whole.

Didier C. Deutsch

Infinity

1996, Intrada Records, from the film *Infinity,* First Look Pictures, 1996 🎬🎬🎬

album notes: Music: Bruce Broughton; **Conductor:** Bruce Broughton.

Bruce Broughton sensitively handles this pre-World War II love story about A-bomb scientist Richard Feynman and his dying wife, Arlene. Period pieces, such as big band-style tunes, occasionally intrude, but don't break the mood of the score, which concentrates on various moments in the couple's short-lived relationship. Arlene's intensity is first represented with a gentle waltz, while the contrast of her fatal illness plays, first, through a gentle arrangement of strings and woodwinds, before becoming more desolate in tempo as she deteriorates.

David Hirsch

The Inkwell

1994, Giant Records, from the film *The Inkwell,* Touchstone, 1994 🎬🎬🎬

Set in the summer of 1976, in the idyllic site of the Inkwell, the Martha's Vineyard spot attended by black professionals, this mildly pleasing comedy focused on a youth discovering love while

spending a vacation with his family, including his uncle, bent on preserving the traditional values he believes in, and his father, a former Black Panther sympathizer. With the political conflict that might have resulted from the confrontation between these two kept at a low angle, the main tone of the film was squarely on the romantic side, an approach further emphasized by the tunes from the era heard on the soundtrack—with performances by Jade, Marvin Gaye, Gladys Knight and the Pips, Ohio Players, Graham Central Station, and BT Express, all of them big hit makers. Nothing new here, just a solid collection of pleasing R&B songs.

Didier C. Deutsch

Inner Space

1987, Geffen Records, from the film *Inner Space,* Warner Bros., 1986 🎬🎬🎬

album notes: Music: Jerry Goldsmith; **Conductor:** Jerry Goldsmith.

Goldsmith's third film for director Joe Dante was a comic remake of *Fantastic Voyage,* with a microscopic Dennis Quaid injected into the body of Martin Short. Goldsmith's score emphasized the action and heroism of the storyline for an adventurous effort somewhat in the style of his earlier *Explorers* work for Dante. The album features around 20 minutes of Goldsmith's score for a satisfying suite, opening with "Let's Get Small," a surprisingly heartfelt heroic anthem. It then continues with some kinetic action cues that balance the undulating sense-of-wonder textures that marked the composer's *Star Trek: The Motion Picture* music against some mechanistic figures that build into a terrific, percolating action climax in "Gut Reaction." The rest of the album is devoted to pop standards, including some Wang Chung and Rod Stewart's take on "Twisting the Night Away."

Jeff Bond

The Innocent

See: The Stranger/The Innocent

Inside Star Trek

See: Star Trek: The Motion Picture/Inside Star Trek

Inspector Morse: Volumes 1, 2, & 3

1995, Virgin Records/U.K., from the television series *Inspector Morse,* ITV, 1991 🎬🎬🎬🎬🎬

album notes: Music: Barrington Pheloung; **Conductor:** Barrington Pheloung.

In case you don't see the show on your cable television screen, *Inspector Morse* is one of those crime drama shows that come from England, with John Thaw portraying the white–haired, stubborn police inspector who usually gets his man (or woman). What sets Morse aside from other police inspectors (one hesitates to call them "cops") is the fact that he is an erudite scholar who loves classical music and operas, and would probably prefer to attend a concert rather than look for a miscreant guilty of some unfathomable criminal act.

As a direct result of Thaw's particular taste in music, the soundtrack to the shows frequently features excerpts from the classical catalogue, something that finds an echo in these CDs in which some selections are drawn from the works of Mozart, Bach, Gluck, Vivaldi, et al., all of which elevate the musical program to quality levels seldom met by standard television soundtracks. In addition, there is the not–so–negligible contribution by Barrington Pheloung, a composer with a classical bend of his own, whose musical cues also display a distinctive style that blends beautifully with the selections from the classical repertoire. Spearheaded with the melancholy "Theme," heard in different versions at the start and at the end of each CD, the cues are often remarkably evocative, sensibly written, and eloquently performed, occasionally by the composer himself, an accomplished instrumentalist. The series has already yielded three CDs, imported from England, and all three are worthwhile additions to any serious collection, whether you are interested in film music or not. Hopefully, there'll be further volumes released down the line.

Didier C. Deutsch

Intersection

1993, Milan Records, from the film *Intersection,* Paramount Pictures, 1993 ♪♪♪

album notes: Music: James Newton Howard; **Conductor:** Marty Paich; **Featured Musicians:** The Los Angeles Master Chorale: Paul Salamunovich, director; Toots Thielemans, harmonica; Dean Parks, acoustic guitar; Neil Stubenhaus, electric bass; John Robinson, drums; Michael Fisher, percussion.

For this mid-life crisis drama, James Newton Howard has sculpted an effective, rhythmic score that accentuates the Richard Gere character's headlong flight back and forth between family fidelity and the allure of infidelity. The score is brooding and subtle, cues linger slowly, indecisively, while a Toots Thielemans harmonica riff plays dreamy jazz over a softly rolling sea of violins. A slow motif for violins and piano also lingers irresolutely, mirroring the conflicts coiling within Gere's character. There are no real melodies. Instead Howard carves a lingering impression through these quiet, reflective cues which retain a notable sense of vitality even as they are quietly introspective.

Randall D. Larson

Interview

See: Intervista

Interview with the Vampire

1994, Geffen Records, from the film *Interview with the Vampire,* Geffen Pictures/Warner Bros., 1994 ♪♪♪♪

album notes: Music: Elliot Goldenthal; **Conductor:** Jonathan Sheffer.

A chilling, superlative effort, Elliot Goldenthal's score for *Interview with the Vampire* is by turns sophisticated, broadly expansive, colorful, and consistently inventive. Introduced by the eerie "Libera Me," performed by an evanescent boy soprano, the music plumbs the depths of the main character's darker aspects and quickly settles on his otherwordly features, a strange mixture of fascination and repulsion that finds a vibrant echo in the orchestral sonorities provided by the composer. No stone is left unturned in this literate effort, in which some of the most elegant tracks include a tarantella, a waltz, a funeral march, and a cue, "Born to Darkness," where all these elements coalesce into a striking conclusion. The Rolling Stones' "Sympathy for the Devil," in a strident performance by Guns N' Roses, while probably appropriate in the film, seems an odd choice here and breaks the moods established by Goldenthal's music.

Didier C. Deutsch

Intervista

1987, Virgin Records/U.K., from the film *Intervista (Interview),* 1987 ♪♪♪♪

album notes: Music: Nicola Piovani; **Conductor:** Nicola Piovani.

Nicola Piovani stepped in for Nino Rota as Fellini's composer, following Rota's untimely death, to create the score for *Intervista,* the director's reflections about his life and his craft. Allegedly a documentary filmed by a Japanese crew, the film, moving back and forth between the past and the present, enabled Fellini to bring along some friends, like Marcello Mastroianni and Anita Ekberg, who reminisced about their work together in *La dolce vita.* The device also enabled Piovani to tap into Nino Rota's rich body of works and to utilize some of the themes he had composed for the early films of Fellini. Piovani blended those with some of his own compositions for what became a whimsical, intelligently clever, and always enjoyable score, at times emotionally involving, at other times gratifyingly delightful. This recording may be difficult to find. Check with a used CD store, mail-order company, or a dealer specializing in rare, out-of-print, or import recordings.

Didier C. Deutsch

Into the West

1993, SBK Records, from the film *Into the West*, Miramax Films, 1993 ♪♪♪♪♪

album notes: Music: Patrick Doyle; **Conductor:** Fiachra Trench; **Featured Vocalist:** Margaret Doyle.

The winsome tale of two orphan boys and the magic white stallion that takes them on a wild ride across the Irish countryside in search of their mother's grave, *Into the West* resulted in a wonderful score from Patrick Doyle, who took a cue from the story's background (the action takes place among the gypsies) to effectively use elements that give his music great depth and poetic impact. Introduced by the various pop selections smartly programmed at the top, and among which "In a Lifetime" by Clannad is a real standout, the instrumental score quickly sets the moods, unfolding in short, attractive bursts that follow the course of the action. Steeped in Celtic music, with melismatic vocalizations adding an original poetic note to some of the cues ("The Blue Sea and the White Horse," "Memories of Mary," "Boy under Sea"), the score is a brilliantly evocative effort, that invites repeated listening in order to reveal its many hidden beauties.

Didier C. Deutsch

Into the Woods

1987, RCA Victor, from the Broadway production *Into the Woods*, 1987 ♪♪♪♪♪

album notes: Music: Stephen Sondheim; **Lyrics:** Stephen Sondheim; **Musical Direction:** Paul Gemignani; **Cast:** Bernadette Peters, Joanna Gleason, Chip Zien, Tom Aldredge, Robert Westenberg, Kim Crosby, Ben Wright, Kay McClelland.

In one of his most popularly accessible works, Stephen Sondheim, with the help of James Lapine, took several well-known fairy tales (Jack and the Beanstalk, Rapunzel, Cinderella, Little Red Riding Hood) and collapsed them into a genuinely inventive musical, *Into the Woods,* which opened Nov. 5, 1987. In the show he not only gently pokes fun at the tales and their various characters, but he uses them to web together a single ending where modern societal values and community responsibilities receive a serious thrashing. Clearly divided into two distinct parts (like his previous offering, *Sunday in the Park with George),* the show first presents its various characters, spinning their individual tales until they finally mesh into one long narrative in which, for instance, the Princes in "Cinderella" and "Rapunzel" share their own doubts about the outcome of their respective fairy tales ("Agony"). The moral of the story, delivered by the Witch, played by Bernadette Peters, is that "Children Will Listen," and that it is up to their parents to teach them the values by which they should be living. Though occasionally muddled by too much rhetoric, it was a brilliant con-

cept that can be enjoyed today in this original cast album, and in a laser disc edition of the show.

Didier C. Deutsch

Into Thin Air: Death on Everest

1997, Citadel Records, from the television film *Into Thin Air: Death on Everest*, Columbia TriStar 1997 ♪♪♪♪♪

album notes: Music: Lee Holdridge; **Conductor:** Lee Holdridge.

With the recent discovery of the body of John Mallory, who climbed Mount Everest 75 years ago only to disappear, seemingly forever, while returning to camp, there is something timely about this release, which should not escape anyone. The soundtrack to a television drama *Into Thin Air: Death on Everest* received a powerful score from Lee Holdridge, an excellent composer who has never been afraid of large orchestral forces, richly expressive, and filled with solid melodic material. True to form, *Into Thin Air,* written for a documentary about the conquest of the world's highest mountain and the toll it exacted over the years, delivers the goods, with bold, brassy cues that detail the action in its most dramatic moments. Adding an unusual texture to the traditional symphonic colors, the composer used a wide array of gongs and daiko drums, which provide sonorities not often heard in compositions of this kind. Contrasting some of the most blaring accents, reflecting the awesome impression made by the off-putting mountain, an occasional softer tone is reached in some cues ("Sarah") that are equally powerful in their quieter expression, and thoroughly attractive. A rare, unusual score, *Into Thin Air* will surprise and delight fans for its many wonders.

see also: Everest

Didier C. Deutsch

Intolerance

1990, Prometheus Records/Belgium, from the film *Intolerance*, 1916 ♪♪♪♪♡

album notes: Music: Carl Davis; **Orchestra:** The Luxembourg Radio Symphony Orchestra; **Conductor:** Carl Davis.

D.W. Griffith's mammoth study of social abuses in the capitalistic system, as seen through four episodes—the fall of Babylon (539 B.C.), the Passion of Christ (30 A.D.), the St. Bartholomew's massacre in the French Renaissance (1572), and modern days—is a fertile ground for musical expression, particularly given the fact that no known score from the 1916 film exists. Carl Davis tackled the project with evident bravura, finding a new voice for each episode, yet devising a continuous link that

D.W. Griffith's Intolerance **(The Kobal Collection)**

ties all four of them, in a "soundtrack" recording that no doubt would have delighted the pioneering filmmaker.

Didier C. Deutsch

Invasion

1998, Super Tracks Records, from the miniseries *Invasion,* NBC-TV, 1997 ♪♪♪♫

album notes: Music: Don Davis.

A tinkling bell chiming behind a call of brass instruments and leading to the rapid shuffling of the chords over a five-note piano motif in the "Main Title" of this score is quite revelatory of Don Davis's busy and exciting score, written for a miniseries presented by NBC-TV. Quite powerful in its own descriptive way, the score provided a strong musical anchor to this science-fiction thriller in which extraterrestrials unleashed a deadly mutating virus on mankind. Davis, an old hand at this type of music in spite of his young age, magnificently propelled the action with his suggestive score, in which a series of colorful flourishes set off and informed crucial moments in the action. Musical sur-

prises abound in the many cues presented here, with the clear, distinct call of acoustic instruments (a piano here, a bell there) laid over layers of synthesized lines to suggest both the otherworldly aspects of the action and the reaction it elicits from the human caught in it. The eerie sounds, sometimes accented by a wordless chorus, are chilling, but keep the score relatively attractive nonetheless. A very impressive track (by its length as well as by the invention in its writing), "The Mother of All Motherships" neatly captures the essence of the entire score, bringing the recording to a fitting conclusion.

see also: Hyperspace

Didier C. Deutsch

Inventing the Abbotts

1997, Unforscene Music, from the film *Inventing the Abbotts,* Fox 2000 Pictures, 1997 ♪♪♪♫

album notes: Music: Michael Kamen; **Orchestra:** The London Metropolitan Orchestra; **Conductor:** Michael Kamen; **Featured Musicians:** Jeff "Skunk" Baxter, guitars; Lee Rocker, bass; Slim Jim Phantom, drums.

The old-fashioned flavor of this coming-of-age story set in 1957 is beautifully evoked in the Michael Kamen score, and in the songs (doo-wop and early rock) that are part of the soundtrack. *Inventing the Abbotts*, set in a small Illinois town, concerned itself with the Abbott girls (Alice, Eleanor, and Pamela, respectively played by Joanna Going, Jennifer Connelly, and Liv Tyler), born in a wealthy family, and their relationship with Doug and Jacey Holt (Joaquin Phoenix and Billy Crudup), their less fortunate friends and occasional flirts. Reflecting the romantic interplay between the five principal characters, the score itself remains firmly rooted in a somewhat melancholy mood that eventually proves most endearing. Echoing the period in which the action is set, some rock numbers ("Inventing the Abbotts," "Thunder and Lightning," "Jacey and Eleanor (In the Garage)," and "Falling out of the Tree") add a different energy to this striking, suggestive soundtrack album.

Didier C. Deutsch

Irene

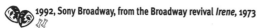 1992, Sony Broadway, from the Broadway revival *Irene*, 1973 🎵🎵

album notes: Music: Harry Tierney; **Lyrics:** Joseph McCarthy, Charles Gaynor, Otis Clements; **Musical Direction:** Jack Lee; **Cast:** Debbie Reynolds, Monte Markham, George S. Irving, Patsy Kelly, Janie Sell.

Despite the presence of Debbie Reynolds, radiant in the title role, the 1974 revival of *Irene* had little to offer, particularly as an old-fashioned, glamorous musical in an era that had turned its back on glories of the past. No doubt inspired by the success of the much better *No No Nanette* a couple of seasons before, *Irene* relied too heavily on the status of its star (eventually replaced by another screen luminary, Jane Powell), and too little on the originality of a revamped book, or on a score which, with the exception of "Alice Blue Gown," "I'm Always Chasing Rainbows" (both showstoppers for Debbie Reynolds), and George S. Irving's delightful rendition of "They Go Wild, Simply Wild, Over Me," had not much else to offer to starving audiences. Further compounding the problems the show experienced, Monte Markham, as Irene's romantic interest, didn't have the necessary chemistry. Nonetheless, the show held on for 605 performances.

Didier C. Deutsch

Irma la Douce

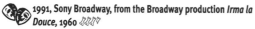 1991, Sony Broadway, from the Broadway production *Irma la Douce*, 1960 🎵🎵🎵

album notes: Music: Marguerite Monnot; **Lyrics:** Julian More, David Heneker, Monty Norman; **Musical Direction:** Stanley Lebowsky; **Cast:** Elizabeth Seal, Keith Mitchell, Clive Revill, Stuart Damon, Fred Gwynne, George S. Irving.

🎬 1998, Rykodisc, from the film *Irma la Douce*, United Artists, 1963 🎵🎵

album notes: Music: Andre Previn; **Conductor:** Andre Previn.

Based on a charming French musical about a "poule," her "mec" and the various low-life denizens of a "typical" Parisian neighborhood near Pigalle, the red light district in the French capital, *Irma la Douce* transcended its local origins, and became a resounding hit on Broadway, where it opened on Sept. 29, 1960. Elizabeth Seal, Keith Mitchell, and Clive Revill reprised the roles they had initially created in London. Also in the cast were Elliott Gould and Fred Gwynne (who went on to achieve greater popularity on television as Herman Munster). Minus its songs, the story provided the basis for a screen version starring Shirley MacLaine and Jack Lemmon.

In its transfer to the screen, in Billy Wilder's capable hands, however, the musical lost most of its original score (only one song survived as an instrumental, "Our Language of Love") and was fitted with a new score by Andre Previn. The truth is, the composer, a very gifted one, was the wrong choice for this type of film. One might have envisioned someone like Henry Mancini, whose peevish sense of humor would have better suited this romantic comedy. As a result, *Irma la Douce*, as represented in this fresh reissue on Rykodisc, its first appearance on CD, is pleasant but not truly mesmerizing. It's unfortunate, as it did not serve the film or the composer well.

Beth Krakower

Iron Eagle II

🎬 1988, Epic Records, from the film *Iron Eagle II*, Carolco, 1988 🎵🎵

The standard law of diminishing returns about sequels applied once more to this overactive film about flying aces in the Air Force, which longed to be another *Top Gun*, or possibly another *Iron Eagle*, and fizzled rapidly despite the high levels of energy and action dispensed on the screen. The story of a renegade fighter pilot and his equally hot-headed buddy, the film's high decibels received additional boost from the powerful soundtrack that included songs by Alice Cooper, Rick Springfield, Ruth Pointer and Billy Vera, and the iconoclastic Canadian group Doug & the Slugs. While the musicians made a lot of noise, this soundtrack album actually reveals the awful truth about the film itself: made on a low budget, it could hardly compete with other films of the same ilk (like *Top Gun*, *Iron Eagle*, etc.) that were 10 times better.

Didier C. Deutsch

Iron Will

🎬 1994, Varèse Sarabande, from the film *Iron Will*, Walt Disney Films, 1994 🎵🎵🎵

album notes: Music: Joel McNeely; **Conductor:** Joel McNeely

In another effective replay of the awe-inspiring race between a pack of dogs and a steam engine set in the frozen northern Minnesota landscape, *Iron Will* introduced composer Joel McNeely, scoring his first major feature in a striking display of his nascent talent. Broadly colorful and romantic, and a perfect match to the action, the cues explore the thrill of the race, the hardships it created for men and beasts, and the exhilaration felt by all. McNeely, who has since amply confirmed the promises held in this excellent first effort, constantly finds the right voice to perfectly illustrate the tale and attract the listener not familiar with the film itself. Tracks like "The Race Begins" and "Crossing the Line" are fine examples of his writing at its most descriptive.

Didier C. Deutsch

Is Paris Burning?

1989, Varèse Sarabande, from the film *Is Paris Burning?*, Paramount Pictures, 1966 ♪♪♪♪♪

album notes: Music: Maurice Jarre; **Conductor:** Maurice Jarre.

The "Paris Waltz," a lovely *valse musette,* first heard as a doleful, plaintive tune, then as an exuberant expression of freedom recovered, probably stands as one of Maurice Jarre's most attractive themes. But this awesome film about the liberation of the French capital from the German occupant in 1944 was also the occasion for the composer to write one of his most emotionally charged scores. Everything, in the themes developed and in the unusual orchestrations, like Jarre's use of 12 pianos instead of brass instruments to depict the German army parading in the streets of Paris, is combined to create a music that had the right atmosphere and the melodic bent necessary to emphasize the various aspects of the story, from its historic importance to the human element brought to it by the various participants on both sides of the action. For the soundtrack album, Jarre also chose to recombine his various cues into two long suites, the first one to depict the German presence in the city and the occult resistance that slowly undermines the occupants' effectiveness, the second to paint the bloody uprising that eventually led to the liberation of Paris and its inhabitants. As a result, the music emerges as a long tone poem that proves most effective at conjuring up the moods in the film even as it calls attention to its very qualities.

Didier C. Deutsch

The Island of Dr. Moreau

1996, Milan Records, from the film *The Island of Dr. Moreau,* New Line Cinema, 1996 ♪

album notes: Music: Gary Chang.

The Island of Dr. Moreau may best be remembered as the film that teamed Marlon Brando and Val Kilmer, though it is unlikely it will be remembered as a major contribution to film lore. Nor will Gary Chang's appropriately atmospheric electronic score make much of am impression among the thousands of soundtrack albums available these days. Strictly for hardcore fans, and even they might find it tiresome after a while.

Didier C. Deutsch

Islands in the Stream

1986, Intrada Records, from the film *Islands in the Stream,* Paramount, 1977 ♪♪♪♪♪

album notes: Music: Jerry Goldsmith; **Orchestra:** The Hungarian State Symphony Orchestra; **Conductor:** Jerry Goldsmith.

Jerry Goldsmith has often mentioned this was his favorite score and one can see why. It is beautifully understated, elegiac, and filled with gorgeous musical ideas and makes a particularly convincing case for film music as a supportive medium while having a life of its own when appreciated on its own merits.The film, about a man living on an island removed from the onset of World War II, might have been too introspective to attract a large public, but the sensitive story compelled Goldsmith to write a score that teems with wonderful themes, and quickly establishes an aura of its own that is most attractive. The lilting "Is Ten Too Old" alone turns out to be a real delight.

Didier C. Deutsch

It Could Happen to You

1994, Columbia Records, from the film *It Could Happen to You,* TriStar Pictures, 1994 ♪

album notes: Music: Carter Burwell; **Conductor:** Carter Burwell; **Featured Performers:** Tony Bennett, Shawn Colvin, Billie Holiday, Wynton Marsalis, Lyle Lovett, Mary-Chapin Carpenter, Frank Sinatra.

Neatly framed between two different versions of the classic "Young at Heart," in which Sinatra easily wins over Bennett, this set offers a hodgepodge of tunes that may have had some meaning on the screen when heard behind the action, but fail to make a similar impact when taken on their own individual merits. It's all the more regrettable that some talented people are represented here. Even Carter Burwell's short "Overture" seems hopelessly wasted.

Didier C. Deutsch

It Happened at the World's Fair

1993, RCA Records, from the film *It Happened at the World's Fair,* MGM, 1963 ♪♪♪

With *It Happened at the World's Fair,* Elvis further shed any pretense at having a dramatic persona on screen, relying instead on stock characters with similar traits: a seductive, easy-going mien and a talent to warble a few songs to his attractive co-stars against splashy, colorful settings. Gone was the rebel of his earlier films. Elvis now played a handsome, well-dressed young man who was not above exchanging a few punches when the action called for it, though the only indication of his rebellious persona might have been a slightly out-of-place lock of hair. The Seattle World's Fair seemed a natural for this pleasantly-minded affair, in which the singer played mentor to an adorable seven-year-old Chinese girl, while pursuing the more eligible Joan O'Brien. Songs included "One Broken Heart for Sale" and "They Remind Me Too Much of You," both heard here.

Didier C. Deutsch

It's a Mad, Mad, Mad, Mad World

1998, Rykodisc, from the film *It's a Mad, Mad, Mad, Mad World,* United Artists, 1963 ♪♪♪♪

album notes: Music: Ernest Gold; **Conductor:** Ernest Gold.

Composer Ernest Gold received score and song Oscar nominations for his work on this epic production, directed by Stanley Kramer who brought together the biggest names in comedy at the time. The plot itself is simple: a group of motorists watch as a man crashes his car, but before he dies he reveals to them the location of a buried treasure, which information led to an extended over-the-top car chase all the way to Palm Springs. In the liner notes for the original LP, Kramer best summed up the musical contributions of Ernest Gold, who "succeeded in making the score one of the stars of the film." Considering the high-level of scene-stealing talent gathered for the movie, this was high praise indeed.

Didier C. Deutsch

It's a Wonderful Life

1998, Sony Wonder/550 Music, from the film *It's a Wonderful Life,* Republic Pictures, 1947 ♪♪♪
album notes: Music: Dimitri Tiomkin.

1994, Republic Entertainment, from the film *It's a Wonderful Life,* Republic Pictures, 1947 woof!

One of the most beloved holiday season entertainments, along with the original *Miracle on 34th Street, It's a Wonderful Life* never had a soundtrack album because, at the time of the film's release in 1947, it was not commonly done. But with the status of the film as a perennial helping a lot, two albums were suddenly released in the space of less than four years, both purporting to offer elements from the soundtrack. Sort-

ing them out is an easy task: the first, on Sony Wonder/550 Music is the genuine article, a somewhat fair representation of the beloved Yuletide film, starring James Stewart as George Bailey, the man who discovers on Christmas Eve how important he is to a lot of people, regardless of what he may think of himself. It contains some of the musical cues composed by Dimitri Tiomkin, bits of dialogue, the "Buffalo Gals" duet with George and Mary (Donna Reed), and the rousing "Auld Lang Syne" that brings the film and this recording to a fitting end. On the downside, the soundtrack seems to have been lifted off a VHS, at least in part, with the recording exhibiting less than vibrant sonic qualities. Also, the long excerpts from the dialogue are distracting, at least if we take it that a soundtrack album has to contain music and songs, as opposed to spoken words.

On the other hand, the second album, released under the same title as the film but subtitled "The Christmas Album," is a rip-off, intended to sell another collection of Christmas songs by, among others, Nat "King" Cole, Julie Andrews, Andy Williams, Perry Como, Dean Martin, and Jose Feliciano, who have nothing to do with the film itself. As a compilation of Christmas songs, it's perfectly acceptable, but as an album linked to a film that immediately evokes myriads of memories, it's not!

Didier C. Deutsch

It's Alive 2

1990, Silva Screen Records, from the film *It's Alive 2,* Warner Bros., 1978 ♪♪♪♪
album notes: Music: Bernard Herrmann, Laurie Johnson; **Conductor:** Laurie Johnson.

When Larry Cohen decided to film a sequel to his hugely popular horror film *It's Alive,* in which Bernard Herrmann's music had played such an integral part, it only seemed normal he would attempt to recombine some of the composer's themes with the new film. To do so, he enlisted the help of famed British composer Laurie Johnson, who rescored the cues Herrmann composed for the first film and expanded on them to create a new, bold, and consistent score. Like its predecessor, *It's Alive 2* took the horror genre into the nucleus of sacrosanct family life with its horrendous story about homicidal mutant babies and efforts by government agents to destroy them. The tones of the film are laid bare from the beginning, with the "Main Title" setting a disquieting mood with its figures for brass and woodwind mixing with eerie synthesizer lines. In taking the themes created by Herrmann, Johnson managed to give them renewed life and make them as foreboding and threatening as in the original film, no minor feat indeed. Bleak and uncompromising, the score is quite unnerving and particularly striking.

Didier C. Deutsch

It's Always Fair Weather

1991, Sony Music Special Products, from the film *It's Always Fair Weather*, MGM, 1955 🎧🎧🎧🎧

album notes: Music: Andre Previn; **Lyrics:** Betty Comden and Adolph Green; **Choir:** The MGM Studio Chorus; **Orchestra:** The MGM Studio Orchestra; **Conductor:** Andre Previn; **Cast:** Gene Kelly, Dan Dailey, Cyd Charisse, Michael Kidd, Dolores Gray.

A daring, unconventional musical, *It's Always Fair Weather* tells about three former Army buddies who get back together 10 years later, only to realize that they have changed, and that, in fact, the bonds that once united them have dissipated to such extent that they really no longer like each other. Initially meant to be a "sequel" to *On the Town,* the new musical displayed a more cynical edge than its exuberant predecessor, and because of it didn't get the enthusiastic audience response its creators had anticipated. Today, however, in view of the changes that have occurred in our society, it reveals itself more pungent and truthful than ever before, and where *On the Town* has remained an old-fashioned musical that belongs to the very era it was created, *It's Always Fair Weather* proves that it may, indeed, have been well ahead of its time.

Didier C. Deutsch

It's My Party

1996, Varèse Sarabande, from the film *It's My Party,* United Artists, 1996 🎧🎧🎧🎧

album notes: Music: Basil Poledouris; **Conductor:** Basil Poledouris.

Known more for his testosterone-powered action scores, this work by Basil Poledouris comes as a complete and wondrously pleasant surprise. Poledouris created for this film a gentle concerto embodying the soul of a dying man who wishes to throw one last party with his friends before the imminent end. Performed entirely by one solo piano (a rare achievement), the composer reduces the focus, thus making the entire story very personal. Perhaps, what really makes *It's My Party* Poledouris's most powerful score to date is that its emotional power owes much to the fact that Poledouris himself is performing his own work. Rarely has there been a finer example of the passion that flows from the mind of a talented composer into his music when it is not diluted by the interpretation of others. The intensity here just sweeps you up, shoots through your body like a bolt of lightning, and reaches into your very soul in a way an entire orchestra could never do. A vitally important addition to any music lover's collection.

David Hirsch

Ivanhoe

1994, Intrada Records, from the film *Ivanhoe,* MGM, 1952 🎧🎧🎧🎧🎧

album notes: Music: Miklos Rozsa; **Orchestra:** The Sinfonia of London; **Conductor:** Bruce Broughton.

Another vibrant recreation of a great score, with Bruce Broughton leading the Sinfonia of London in a spirited performance that never lessens, *Ivanhoe* is a sumptuous effort by Miklos Rozsa that long deserved a recording of this caliber. Of all the swashbucklers he scored, this is probably the one that has the best combination of romantic tunes and thrilling action cues, all elements that come clearly to the forefront in this exciting album. With little time wasted on unnecessary asides, Rozsa quickly set the stage for this medieval tale of chivalry and treachery and for its main characters, including Lady Rowena (Joan Fontaine), Rebecca (Elizabeth Taylor), Bois-Guilbert (George Sanders), and of course Ivanhoe (Robert Taylor, in one of his best screen roles.) The spectacular aspects of the tale, the colorful jousts, the exciting battles, also receive their due with cues that aim to broaden the visuals with thrilling musical accents. It all comes excitingly together in this sensational recording, performed with the right dash and recorded in spacious sound.

Didier C. Deutsch

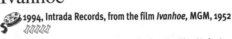

Jack

1996, Hollywood Records, from the film *Jack,* Hollywood Pictures, 1996 🎧🎧🎧🎧

album notes: Music: Michael Kamen; **Orchestra:** The L.A. All-Star Orchestra; **Conductor:** Michael Kamen; **Featured Musicians:** Mario Grigorov, piano; Michael Kamen, piano; the San Francisco Saxophone Quartet; Frank Marocco, accordion; Rick Baptist, trumpet; Morty Okin, trumpet; Pete Escovedo, percussion; Paula Hochhalter, cello; Dennis Karmazyn, cello; Fred Tinsley, bass; Bruce Dukov, violin; Marty Kristall, clarinet; Paul Fried, flute; Vince De Rosa, French horn; Buell Neidlinger, double bass.

The whimsical accents of this delightful comedy find an echo in Michael Kamen's exhilarating score, which, most appropriately, opens here with an exuberant conga that sets the tone for the rest of the album. To illustrate this story of a 10-year-old boy who evidences the mental and emotional reactions of his age, even though, through a quirk of nature, he actually looks 40, Kamen devised cues that amusingly stress the childlike qualities of the main character, played by Robin Williams, in terms that constantly challenge the listener. Written for a slew of individual instruments taking solos against the broader texture of the orchestra, the music adds an exponential element to the screen action, outlining selected scenes in the life of Jack, his schoolmates, and the adults with whom he comes in contact. Summing up the overall lesson of the film that life is fleeting, "Valedictorian" finds Jack, now 17 but in reality a ripe old 68-year-old, reflecting on the meaning of his brief existence.

Didier C. Deutsch

The Jackal

1998, MCA Records, from the film *The Jackal*, Universal, 1998 🎬🎬🎬

album notes: Music: Carter Burwell.

We hit the "music from and inspired by . . ." concept again, but this album is thematically sound thanks to its concentration on electronica—an interesting pairing for the cool, precisely calculating persona that is the assassin at the heart of this film (and its predecessor, *Day of the Jackal*). It doesn't have any tracks that could be considered genre-defining, but it isn't a bad vehicle for putting your toe in the techno waters, either. Some of the best practitioners are represented here, including the Prodigy ("Poison"), Fatboy Slim ("Going out of My Head"), Massive Attack ("Superpredators"), Moby ("Shining") and L. T. J. Bukem ("Demon's Theme"). Altered versions of Ani DiFranco's "Joyful Girl," Bush's "Swallowed," and the Charlatans UK's "Toothache"—the latter done by the Chemical Brothers—offer a peek at the remix scene, while BT's collaboration with Psychedelic Furs/Love Spit Love frontman Richard Butler offers further evidence that electronic doesn't necessarily mean inhuman.

Gary Graff

Jacob's Ladder

1990, Varèse Sarabande, from the film *Jacob's Ladder*, Carolco Pictures, 1990 🎬🎬

album notes: Music: Maurice Jarre; **Conductor:** Maurice Jarre; **Featured Musicians:** Gloria Cheng, piano; Kazu Mitsui, shakuhachi; Shankar, double violin, vocals; **Featured Vocalists:** Jubilant Sykes; Kari Windingstad; the Kitka Eastern European Women's Choir: Bon Brown, vocal director.

A horror story about a Vietnam vet exposed to chemicals during the war, and who, as a result, experiences frightful visions, *Jacob's Ladder* elicited an effectively eerie score from Maurice Jarre, which might have been more impressive as a subtle suggestion of the screen action than it is as a purely aural experiment. Primarily written for an electronic ensemble, it consists of long synthesizer chords, occasionally contrasted by a simple melody on the piano, over which evocative wordless vocals doubling the sound of the shakuhachi combine to create a strange musical atmosphere. Ultimately, though, the lack of a real hook prevents the cues from being more than a back-

ground support for an unseen action, depriving the music from its secondary, strictly audio purpose. The addition of "Sonny Boy," performed by Al Jolson, does little to attract the listener.

Didier C. Deutsch

Jailhouse Rock/Love Me Tender

1996, RCA Records, from the movies *Jailhouse Rock*, MGM, 1957, and *Love Me Tender*, 20th Century-Fox, 1956 🎬🎬🎬

Elvis's rebellious side was used to great effect in *Jailhouse Rock* which, for the first time, enabled him to hit his stride as an actor. Of all the scenes from his films, in fact, the most celebrated may very well be the jailhouse dance routine, in which he performed the title tune, a #1 hit on the charts. But other songs in the film that also struck a felicitous note included "Treat Me Nice," "You're So Square," and "I Want to Be Free."

Elvis made his screen debut in the western drama *Love Me Tender,* in which he was second-billed as the youngest of four brothers drawn into the Civil War. Though the film ended on a downbeat note for the singer (he was killed at the end), he performed four numbers, including the title tune, based on "Aura Lee," a ballad popularized in 1861, which revealed an unsuspected romantic side to his talent.

Didier C. Deutsch

Jamaica

1957, RCA Victor, from the Broadway production *Jamaica*, 1957 🎬🎬🎬

album notes: Music: Harold Arlen; **Lyrics:** E.Y. Harburg, Fred Saidy; **Musical Direction:** Lehman Engel, Neal Hefti; **Cast:** Lena Horne, Ricardo Montalban, Josephine Premice, Ossie Davis, Adelaide Hall.

Harold Arlen took another foray into the Caribbean culture when he wrote the songs for *Jamaica.* Despite a weak story, the show enjoyed a run of 558 performances following its opening on Oct. 31, 1957, thanks largely to the radiant presence of Lena Horne in the cast. Set on the mythical Pigeon Island, it deals with a simple fisherman (Ricardo Montalban) who wants nothing more than a quiet and easy life on his island, and the girl he loves, Savannah (Lena Horne), who only dreams of going to that other paradise, Manhattan. Co-starring Josephine Premice, Ossie Davis, Adelaide Hall, and a young dancer by the name of Alvin Ailey, *Jamaica* provides its star with many flavorful numbers which put her stylish delivery to the test. She turned those into many show-stopping moments, including "Push de Button," in which she extolled the merits of living in her mechanized dream world, "Ain't It de Truth," and "Napoleon."

Didier C. Deutsch

James and the Giant Peach

1996, Walt Disney Records, from the film *James and the Giant Peach*, Walt Disney Films, 1996 ♪♪♪♪♪

album notes: Music: Randy Newman.

Based on a story by Roald Dahl, this live-action/stop-motion animation film follows the adventures of James, an orphan raised by two spinster aunts, one fat, one skinny, and both mean. After a mysterious old man assures him that everything will be all right, James discovers in the backyard a giant peach and the six bugs who live in it, setting off the fairy tale that ensues. While the tone of the film itself was more gritty and caustic than the outline suggests, it prompted Randy Newman to write a lightweight score in a display of emotions unusual for him. Amusingly salient scenes in the action, the score features many highlights that elevate it way above the norm and is enhanced by several songs, including two—"That's the Life" and "My Name Is James"—that are absolutely terrific.

Didier C. Deutsch

Jane Eyre

1988, Silva Screen, from the film *Jane Eyre*, Omnibus Films, 1971 ♪♪♪♪

album notes: Music: John Williams; **Conductor:** John Williams; **Featured Musicians:** Pat Halling, violin; Bob Docker, piano; Les Pearson, harpsichord; Derek Wiggins, oboe; Peter Lloyd, flute.

Bringing his own musical sensitivity to Charlotte Brontë's celebrated novel, John Williams scored this 1971 version starring George C. Scott and Susannah York, in a dramatic display of all the elements that single him out as a composer—his brilliant feel for melodic material, his lyrical expression, and above all his unusual combination of varied instruments to create the proper atmosphere. All of these elements are brought to the fore here in cues that enhance this story of passion, longing, madness, and mystery. Particularly effective in this context is the contrast between "To Thornfield," a light gallop, and "The Meeting," for a trio, with its morose accents beneath the lilting melody suggesting the oppressive aura of the place and the mysterious foreboding that hangs over it. It shows Williams in a particularly inventive mood, obviously inspired by the broad romantic aspects of the story, and always in search of new, uncommon ways to express his creativity.

see also: Laura

Didier C. Deutsch

Jane Eyre

1994, Marco Polo Records, from the film *Jane Eyre*, 20th Century-Fox, 1943 ♪♪♪♪♪

album notes: Music: Bernard Herrmann; **Orchestra:** The Slovak Radio Symphony Orchestra of Bratislava; **Conductor:** Adriano.

Bernard Herrmann's striking score for this memorable screen adaptation of Charlotte Brontë's Victorian novel receives a wonderful reading in a recording as sumptuous as it is evocative. A riveting drama, starring Joan Fontaine as the orphan waif who becomes governess at Thornfield, a manor house, and falls in love with its owner, played by Orson Welles, the film elicited from Herrmann what may well have been his most romantic, and certainly most profuse work, a score clearly dominated by three essential motifs, one for each of the two principal characters, and the third for the love they feel for one another. In addition to its abundance of impassioned cues, and belying the darker tones they sometimes project, the score also contains musical themes that are poetic and inspiring, like "Valse Bluette," which contrasts the ominous moods in "Thornfield Hall," the lilting "Springtime," or the lovely "The Garden," beautifully expressive. As is so frequently the case with these recordings featuring the Slovak Radio Symphony Orchestra, conducted by Adriano, all the technical aspects deserve warm plaudits.

Didier C. Deutsch

Jason and the Argonauts

1999, Intrada Records, from the film *Jason and the Argonauts*, Columbia, 1963 ♪♪♪♪♪

album notes: Music: Bernard Herrmann; **Conductor:** Bruce Broughton.

One of the most important film composers and a giant in the business, Bernard Herrmann left a legacy of impressive scores, but none as flavorful as the ones he composed for films produced by Charles Schneer, in which his vivid musical imagination found a perfect match in the astonishing special effects of Ray Harryhausen. Today, these films—*The Seventh Voyage of Sinbad* (1958), *The Three Worlds of Gulliver* (1960), *Mysterious Island* (1961), and *Jason and the Argonauts* (1963)—continue to astound for the incredibly inventive otherworldly characters created by Harryhausen and for the brilliant colors and tones Herrmann used in the scores he wrote for these fantasy adventures.

Particularly remarkable was the score for *Jason and the Argonauts,* in which the composer, writing for a massive stringless brass orchestra, often tripled and quadrupled the usual forces and added to the percussion ensemble a vast battery that brought together more than 36 instruments. Typical of his creative skills at the time, these forces were also separated to take full advantage of the stereo effects, with one group playing against the other, in a musical question-and-response series of motifs that revealed a profound understanding of the way the orchestra played and how the various elements would sound on a separate recording.

The film itself, a spectacular display of mythological wonders, told the legend of Jason, his voyage in search of the fabled

Susan Backlinie *in* Jaws. **(The Kobal Collection)**

Golden Fleece, his encounters with various beasts, including the dreaded seven-headed Hydra, and the terrible fights the gods in Olympus waged on his behalf or against him. At each turn in the action, Herrmann added broad swaths of brilliant musical colors that commented on it and made it more substantial and compelling. Recreated here by Bruce Broughton and the Sinfonia of London, it sounds incredibly awesome, important, essential! The only minor flaw in this world premiere is its overall dryness: the orchestra, miked too closely, doesn't have the ambient sound called for by this type of recording. Other than that, it is simply magnificent!

Didier C. Deutsch

Jawbreaker

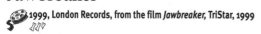 **1999, London Records, from the film *Jawbreaker*, TriStar, 1999** ♪♪♪

A better soundtrack than its movie really warranted, the *Jawbreaker* album is just plain old dumb fun. A *Heathers*-influenced dark comedy about a popular clique of high school girls who kidnap one of their friends as a prank and end up accidentally killing her, the movie really doesn't ever take off. On the other hand, the soundtrack is a kick, with tracks by lightweight pop and punk acts like Imperial Teen, the Donnas (who are featured in the movie), Shampoo, Letters to Cleo, and more. The token oldie included is "Rock You like a Hurricane" by the Scorpions. *Jawbreaker* would be a choice record pick for teenage slumber parties.

Amy Rosen

Jaws

1990, MCA Records, from the film *Jaws*, Universal Pictures, 1975 ♪♪♪♪♪
album notes: Music: John Williams; **Conductor:** John Williams.

John Williams's classic suspense music was unavailable on CD for years until MCA finally relented and produced this crisp-sounding disk that resurrects Williams's original album arrangement of the score. The chopping, Stravinsky-esque shark motif is justly famous, but just as enjoyable is the composer's mock-baroque stylings for "Tourists on the Menu," the bracing sea shanty tune developed for "Out to Sea" and "Two Barrel Chase," and the thrilling classical-styled fugue expanded on for "Building the Cage." Williams's supercharged "Sea Attack Number One" is one of the most exciting, sustained action cues ever heard in a movie, brilliantly playing the shark material off the adventuresome "counterattack" fugue to create a bold, modern pirate movie sound that hyped the thrills in Spielberg's brilliant movie to previously unheard-of proportions. *Jaws* is ultimately a kind of monster movie, but Williams's score is almost all adventure, and his tinkering with the original music for album presentation makes for one of the most thoroughly enjoyable soundtrack albums ever released.

Jeff Bond

Jaws 2

1990, Varèse Sarabande, from the film *Jaws 2*, Universal Pictures, 1978 ♪♪♪♪

album notes: Music: John Williams; **Conductor:** John Williams.

Following the huge success of the first film, *Jaws 2* reunited John Williams with the story about the dangerous shark, prompting him to devise new music for this sequel that sounded as compelling and ominous as the first. In truth, Williams surpassed himself, writing a score that had the effectiveness of the first, and then some. Its cues develop and expand on the shark theme, but take it to new heights of creativity. Among the most interesting moments in the new score, "Ballet for Divers" is a splendid highlight; "Attack on the Helicopter" and "Attack on the Water Skier," both exemplify the composer's strong commitment to descriptive music that draws the listener into its melodic web; and "The Open Sea" stands out as an anthem to the sheer beauty of the spectacle it evokes. All in all, an important score in the composer's canon.

Didier C. Deutsch

Jean de Florette /Manon des sources

1986, Milan Records/France, from the films *Jean de Florette*, 1986, and *Manon des sources*, 1987 ♪♪♪♪♪

album notes: Jean de Florette: Music: Jean-Claude Petit; **Orchestra:** The Orchestre de Paris; **Conductor:** Jean-Claude Petit; **Featured Musician:** Toots Thielemans, harmonica; **Manon des sources: Music:** Jean-Claude Petit; **Orchestra:** The Orchestre de Paris; **Conductor:** Jean-Claude Petit; **Featured Musician:** Toots Thielemans, harmonica.

A drama set in the early part of the century, *Jean de Florette* and *Manon des sources,* based on Marcel Pagnol's novel (and own film), described a story of greed and deception in rural France, with gruff landowner Yves Montand trying his best to protect his domain, in which a miraculous spring provides much needed water. After eliminating potential rival Jean (Gérard Depardieu), son of Florette, and witnessing the eventual suicide of favorite nephew Ugolin, played by Daniel Auteuil, whose love for Manon, daughter of Jean, has gone unrequited, the "Papet," as he is familiarly known, must reconcile himself with the idea that his machinations have led to nothing but the total destruction of his property and his own existence. Much too late, he finds out that Jean was his own son, and Manon his granddaughter.

Composer Jean-Claude Petit used, as the framework for his score, a theme from "La forza del destino," soulfully played by harmonicist Toots Thielemans. The doleful theme provided a strong anchor and an overwhelming aura of nostalgia that found an echo in Petit's own contribution. Literate and ornate, this is an excellent score that many will find haunting and totally appropriate for easy listening. A performance of "Chanson de Manon," by French pop idol Serge Lama, comes across as too powerfully emotional. This title may be out of print or just plain hard to find. Mail-order companies, used CD shops, or dealers of rare or import recordings will be your best bet.

Didier C. Deutsch

Jefferson in Paris

1995, Angel Records, from the film *Jefferson in Paris,* Touchstone Pictures and Merchant Ivory Productions, 1995 ♪♪♪♪

album notes: Music: Richard Robbins; **Featured Performers:** Les Arts Florissants; William Christie, director.

In a brilliant display of elegance and sophistication, the score for *Jefferson in Paris* combines together Richard Robbins's cues and music from the period to give the film a vivid musical illustration that is ultimately most winning. With a superb performance by Les Arts Florissants, the late 18th-century music of the French court sounds quite lovely, with Corelli's "Violin Sonata," Charpentier's "In hoc festo," and Duphly's "Courante for Harpsichord" among the choice moments found here. In contrast, Robbins's score sounds more florid, more contemporary in a sense, though no less effective in conjuring up images that are both solidly evocative and musically attractive. In the notes he wrote about the score, the composer explains the role he saw between the musical play and the close relationship he tried to establish between the development of his cues and Jefferson's use of a pantograph (a machine that the American statesman used to make duplicate copies of his letters as he wrote them), a recurring theme throughout the film. The continuity and tension that result make the score an ideal companion to the story on the screen.

Didier C. Deutsch

Jeffrey

 1995, Varèse Sarabande, from the film *Jeffrey*, MVM Films, 1995 🎬🎬🎬

album notes: Music: Stephen Endelman.

Cleverly edited concept album where each musical cue is led off with an hilarious snippet of dialogue from this comedy about a gay man so afraid of contracting AIDS that he avoids any prospect of happiness. Much of Stephen Edelman's score ranges from an atypical workout piece for "The Gym" to transitional cues as performed by a small jazz combo. The music and the songs are pleasant enough, but the dialogue is so outrageous, particularly "Jeffrey Phones Home" where he discuses sex with his parents, it makes the score seem positively impotent in comparison.

David Hirsch

Jekyll & Hyde

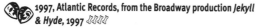 1990, RCA Victor Records, from the stage production *Jekyll & Hyde*, 1990 🎬🎬🎬

album notes: Music: Frank Wildhorn; **Lyrics:** Leslie Bricusse

🎬🎬 1994, Atlantic Records, from the Alley Theatre production *Jekyll & Hyde*, 1990 🎬🎬🎬🎬

album notes: Music: Frank Wildhorn; **Lyrics:** Leslie Bricusse

🎬🎬 1997, Atlantic Records, from the Broadway production *Jekyll & Hyde*, 1997 🎬🎬🎬🎬

album notes: Music: Frank Wildhorn; **Lyrics:** Leslie Bricusse.

On its way to becoming a Broadway show, *Jekyll & Hyde* underwent several transformations, documented by the three recordings here. The first, from 1990, was the bare-skin score with Colm Wilkinson and Linda Eder both portraying two characters in the show's first incarnation, an elaborate studio cast recording made in London. While necessarily incomplete, it gives a fair notion of the musical in its embryonic form, and is, in this respect, an interesting complement to the other two.

The second recording, made shortly after the show received its world premiere in Houston, in 1994, despite its apparent completeness, is still a work in progress. Many new songs have been added, and some have shifted from one character to another. Linda Eder's portrayal as the woman of easy virtue with whom Jekyll falls in love and whom Hyde eventually kills, has acquired a better sheen, and the overall impression is that the show is finally getting a much stronger identity than it had initially.

Following two years on the road, during which the musical was further honed and refined, *Jekyll & Hyde* finally opened on Broadway on April 28, 1997, with the third recording, the official cast album, reflecting the alterations and additional changes it went through during this period. It is more defined

than in its previous incarnations, but still lacks the sense of humor and wicked fun (think *Sweeney Todd)* that might have made it more acceptable as a strong vehicle (something more apparent in the previous recording in which a couple of songs, displaying a sharper edge, were subsequently eliminated). It gets an inspiring reading with Robert Cuccioli a sexy, mesmerizing Jekyll (and Hyde), and Eder still the focus of his interest.

Didier C. Deutsch

Jelly's Last Jam

🎬🎬 1992, Mercury Records, from the Broadway production *Jelly's Last Jam*, 1992 🎬🎬🎬

album notes: Music: Jelly Roll Morton; **Lyrics:** Susan Birkenhead; **Musical Direction:** Linda Twine; **Cast:** Gregory Hines, Savion Glover, Stanley Wayne Mathis, Tonya Pinkins, Ann Duquesnay.

A celebration of the music of Jelly Roll Morton, the "inventor" of jazz, *Jelly's Last Jam* owed much of its vitality and success to Gregory Hines's portrayal of Morton, and the flavorful way the show itself is put together. The show is not so much as a straight dramatic presentation of the composer's life as a sort of parable in which various set pieces provide the impetus and background for the musical numbers. To be sure, much of the show's impact came from its visual flair, so much so in fact that the cast album recording, limited as it is, fails to convey much of the excitement that was on display on stage. Still, it brought together a cohesive group of vastly talented performers around Hines, notably Tonya Pinkins, a revelation in the show, Savion Glover, Ann Duquesnay, and Keith David, who, as a master of ceremony in top hat and tails surrounded by a trio of attractive lovebirds, presided over the proceedings.

Didier C. Deutsch

Jerry Maguire

🎬 1996, Epic Soundtrax, from the film *Jerry Maguire*, TriStar Pictures, 1996 🎬🎬🎬🎬

album notes: Featured Musicians: The Who; His Name Is Alive; Elvis Presley; Neil Young; Nancy Wilson; Rickie Lee Jones; Bruce Springsteen; Paul McCartney; Aimee Mann; Bob Dylan.

Here's proof that good, listenable soundtracks can be made from something other than already proven hits. Bruce Springsteen's "Secret Garden" deserves the boost it got from being this movie's love theme (though the radio programmer who came up with the idea of overlaying film dialogue on the song should be shot). Bob Dylan's alternate version of "Shelter from the Storm" adds a verse not heard in the original, while Beatles devotees will make a beeline for Paul McCartney's "Momma Miss America" and the aptly titled "Singalong Junk." Obscure tracks from Neil Young ("World on a String"), Elvis Presley ("Pocketful of Rainbows"), and modern rockers His Name Is

Alive ("Sitting Still Moving Still Staring Outlooking") round out a compelling set.

Gary Graff

Jesus Christ Superstar

1993, MCA Records, from the studio cast recording *Jesus Christ Superstar*, 1970 ♪♪♪♪

album notes: Music: Andrew Lloyd Webber; **Lyrics:** Tim Rice; **Musical Direction:** Andrew Lloyd Webber; **Cast:** Murray Head, Ian Gillan, Yvonne Elliman, Paul Raven.

1993, MCA Records, from the film *Jesus Christ Superstar*, Universal Pictures, 1973 ♪♪♪♪

album notes: Music: Andrew Lloyd Webber; **Lyrics:** Tim Rice; **Musical Direction:** Andrew Lloyd Webber; **Cast:** Carl Anderson, Ted Neeley, Yvonne Elliman, Bob Bingham, Joshua Mostel.

It's interesting to note that within the same year, two musicals, *Godspell* and *Jesus Christ Superstar*, both chronicling the last seven days of Christ, opened in New York. Unlike its more modest predecessor, however, *Jesus Christ Superstar* came on the heels of a gold studio recording, made the year before, and a large amount of publicity, mostly created by religious groups who resented the idea of seeing Christ portrayed as a rock 'n' roll star and Herod as a buffoon prancing the stage on mod shoes with platform heels.

The studio cast album, listed here since the original Broadway cast album was never reissued on CD by MCA, presents the score Andrew Lloyd Webber and Tim Rice wrote for this show. In it, one song, "I Don't Know How to Love Him," achieved international status as a major hit, but the score itself is not bereft of other attractive moments.

Since bigger on the screen usually doesn't mean better, it is a pleasant surprise to note that the soundtrack album, also on MCA, and also a two–CD set, is almost as flavorful and enjoyable as the studio cast album. Only the principals have changed, though Yvonne Elliman, who made a career out of portraying Mary Magdalene, is back to sing her hit song.

Didier C. Deutsch

The Jewel of the Nile

1985, Arista/Jive Records, from the film *The Jewel of the Nile*, 20th Century-Fox, 1985 ♪

album notes: Music: Jack Nitzsche.

On the screen, *The Jewel of the Nile* is a diverting adventure film that recalls some aspects of the Indiana Jones epics, a contemporary swashbuckler that exudes great moments of action and romance, subtly blended together for a nonstop rollercoaster. To pull off this kind of film, a strong score is usually *de rigueur*, and while Jack Nitzsche is not John Williams, the music

he wrote on this occasion is serviceable and quite adequate. Unfortunately you wouldn't know it from listening to this socalled soundtrack album, in which only two of his cues, "Love Theme" and "The Plot Thickens," have been included, for a total playing time of less than seven minutes. The rest of the "action" is taken by nondescript, and frequently boring, pop songs that may play a minor role in the film, but are totally uninspiring in this context.

Didier C. Deutsch

JFK

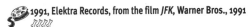1991, Elektra Records, from the film *JFK*, Warner Bros., 1991 ♪♪♪♪

album notes: Music: John Williams; **Orchestra:** The Boston Pops; **Conductor:** John Williams; **Featured Musicians:** Tim Morrison, principal trumpet, the Boston Pops; James Thatcher, French horn.

John Williams approached his score for Oliver Stone's paranoiac history lesson almost in the manner of Ennio Morricone, seemingly laying down a number of memorable themes and motifs to be placed at the director's whim throughout the movie rather than writing a truly programmatic score. Yet somehow this approach produces an outstandingly listenable album, provided the listener takes full advantage of the miracle of programmability. Williams's dissonant, harsh material involving the Kennedy assassination is pretty tough to sit through, but his JFK theme and variations, as well as melodies for Kevin Costner's family relationships in the film, are some of Williams's most beautiful and satisfying compositions. "The Conspirators," with its staccato piano line, is quickly gaining prominence as one of the most copied film music cues of all time, although as represented on this CD it's curiously thin-sounding, lacking the driving power and mystery of the film version.

see also: Nixon

Jeff Bond

Jingle All the Way

1996, TVT Records, from the film *Jingle All the Way*, 20th Century-Fox, 1996 ♪♪♪♪

album notes: Music: David Newman.

The image of big, goofy Arnold Schwartzenegger fighting off a battalion of Santa Clauses with a sugar candy cane the size of a bazooka is enough to bring an amused smile to anyone's face. But if that doesn't do it, this album is a sure-fire cure for the blues. Starting off with a swinging version of "Jingle Bells," it segues into a series of Christmas-related songs, performed by some great people like Lou Rawls, Darlene Love, Chuck Berry, Johnny Mathis, Nat King Cole, and Clarence Carter, sometimes in newly recorded versions backed by the Brian Setzer Orches-

Ted Neely in Jesus Christ Superstar **(The Kobal Collection)**

tra, sometimes in standard recordings. Once the tone is set, the fun begins and never stops. As good a Christmas album as any you're likely to find.

Johnny Cool

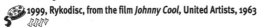 1999, Rykodisc, from the film *Johnny Cool*, United Artists, 1963 ♪♪♪♫

album notes: Music: Billy May.

Based on John McPartland's novel, *The Kingdom of Johnny Cool,* this 1963 film, starring Henry Silva as a Sicilian killer-for-hire, displayed a great deal of rapid-fire screen action that somehow concealed the fact that the story itself was not too terribly believable. Adding its own comments on the soundtrack was a terrific Billy May score, jazzy and exciting, that punctuated the action and gave it much needed musical support. Sammy Davis Jr., who appeared in the film in a secondary role, wearing an eyepatch as a result of a recent car accident, also performed a couple of numbers, including the mandatory (at the time) title song, "The Ballad of Johnny Cool," written by Sammy Cahn and James Van Heusen. This first CD reissue is a welcome addition, although like the original album, it sounds highly reverbered, and slightly shrill.

Johnny Guitar

1993, Varèse Sarabande, from the film *Johnny Guitar,* Republic Pictures, 1954 ♪♪♪♪

album notes: Music: Victor Young; Conductor: Victor Young.

An unusually bleak western with a neurotic direction by Nicholas Ray, *Johnny Guitar* is a lyrical masterpiece with baroque overtones. Joan Crawford, clad in black denim, gives one of her strongest performances as an aggressive, no-nonsense saloon owner whose only goal in life is to get rich. Mercedes McCambridge is the bitter, sexually frustrated leader of the little community opposing Crawford's plans for expansion. Even though the story itself could have played in any given context, much of the score Victor Young composed for the film is in the standard western idiom, solidly anchored by the title tune, written with and performed onscreen by Peggy Lee. The album, obviously taken from the original acetates (the surface noise on some tracks indicates this much), was initially released on LP in the early 1980s, without identifying the selections. The CD repeats the same mistake, making it difficult to associate a specific cue with a corresponding scene in the film.

Johnny Handsome

1989, Warner Bros. Records, from the film *Johnny Handsome, Tri-Star Pictures,* 1989 ♪♪♪♪

album notes: Music: Ry Cooder; Featured Musicians: Jim Keltner, drums, percussion; Ry Cooder, guitars, keyboards, bass, accordion, fiddle, percussion; Steve Douglas, saxophones; George Bohanon, trombone; Harold Battiste, soprano sax; Bobby Bryant, trumpet; John Bolivar, saxophone; Ernie Fields, saxophone; Herman Riley, saxophone.

A downbeat contemporary drama about a convict whose violent demeanor is not the least bit altered after he undergoes plastic surgery to change his appearance, *Johnny Handsome* receives a flavorful, uplifting score from Ry Cooder, who performed it with splendid musical support from a handful of great jazz players. While the correlation between the music and the film seems less important in this context, the striking feature of the album is the number of cues that create an aura of their own and call for closer scrutiny. Essential to one's appreciation of the score is the expressive "I Can't Walk This Time/The Prestige," which allows the musicians to stretch and fully explore the many positive aspects of the music. Other tracks that also establish themselves include the rousing "Clip Joint Rhumba," with its bouncy zydeco flair, "Sunny's Tune," and "Cruising with Rafe."

Jonathan Livingston Seagull

1973, Columbia Records, from the film *Jonathan Livingston Seagull,* 1973 ♪♪
album notes: Music: Neil Diamond.

A film with an ecological mind before it became fashionable, *Jonathan Livingston Seagull* was an allegorical story based on Richard Bach's bestseller, about a bird and its existence in and out of the flock. Adding a musical comment of its own, the songs by Neil Diamond helped give a voice to the seagull, with the jest of the whole film contained in the track titled "The Odyssey," which reprised three of the score's most important themes numbers: "Be," "Lonely Looking Sky," and "Dear Father." Today, the message (and the songs) sound dated.

Joseph and the Amazing Technicolor Dreamcoat

1974, MCA Records, from the studio cast recording *Joseph and the Amazing Technicolor Dreamcoat,* 1973 ♪♪♪♪

album notes: Music: Andrew Lloyd Webber; Lyrics: Tim Rice; Musical Direction: Chris Hamel-Cooke, Andrew Lloyd Webber; Featured Musicians: B.J. Cole, steel guitar; Tony Lowe, accordion; John Marson, harp; Geoff Westley, piano; George Comerford, John Gustafson, Olly Halsall, Neil Hubbard, Pete Massey, John Priseman, Bruce Rowland, rhythm section; **Cast:** Gary Bond, Peter Reeves, Gordon Waller, Maynard Williams, Roger Watson, Felicity Balfour, David Ballantine, Barbara Courtney, Tim Rice, Honey Simone, Frances Sinclair, the Children's Choirs from Islington Green Comprehensive School, St. Clement Dane's School and the Barbara Speke Stage.

 1982, Chrysalis Records, from the Broadway production *Joseph and the Amazing Technicolor Dreamcoat,* 1982 ♪♪♪♪

album notes: Music: Andrew Lloyd Webber; **Lyrics:** Tim Rice; **Musical Direction:** Martin Silvestri, Jeremy Stone; **Cast:** Bill Hutton, Laurie Beechman, Gordon Stanley.

 1993, Polydor Records, from the revival production *Joseph and the Amazing Technicolor Dreamcoat,* 1993 ♪♪♪♪

album notes: Music: Andrew Lloyd Webber; **Lyrics:** Tim Rice; **Musical Direction:** Michael Dixon; **Cast:** Michael Damian, Kelli Rabke, Clifford David, Marc Kudish.

A Biblical tale that refuses to take its subject seriously, *Joseph and the Amazing Technicolor Dreamcoat* began as a modest, 15-minute piece for a school boys choir, and told the story of Joseph, sold to slavery by his 11 brothers, who ends up as an adviser to Pharaoh, and saves Egypt from a great famine. Expanded first to a full 90 minutes, then to a two-hour presentation, it first came to Broadway on Jan. 27, 1982, where it settled for a run of 747 performances. It returned more recently, on Nov. 10, 1993, for another run of 223 performances.

What makes the musical so totally delightful is the impish, almost sophomoric way it approaches its story: The score, a blend of rock 'n' roll, calypso, and big band numbers, is a virtual romp from beginning to end. The three recordings listed above document the show at various stages in its development, with the earliest one presenting a slightly expanded version from the original concept, involving a lot of school children, and individual performers (including Tim Rice) in a fun recording of the score.

The Chrysalis recording is the cast album of the 1982 Broadway presentation, with Laurie Beechman, a New York favorite, in the crucial role as the Narrator. The last recording, on Polydor, is the most recent cast album from the 1993 Broadway revival, with Michael Damian as Joseph, and Kelli Rabke as the Narrator. It is by far the most satisfying, ending on a nine-minute megamix which reprises many of the songs in the score, performed by the entire company in what has to be the most exhilarating number of any modern-day Broadway show. The same recording, incidentally, with minor variations, was also released on two different occasions, with Jason Donovan in one cast, and Donny Osmond, star of the Canadian production, in the other. Whichever you pick, you cannot go wrong.

Didier C. Deutsch

They Know the Score

Ry Cooder

I've collected weird instruments over the years, and you wouldn't believe which ones I used on *Last Man Standing*. One day, I was bouncing coffee beans off of a table drum that I got from a mental hospital for catatonic patients. The next day, I was bouncing quarters off of it. I made weird sounds with an eight-foot-long floor slide that I'd used on *Trespass*. I also had garbage cans full of beans, tykkho drums, percussionists banging on stuff, and a South Indian flutist. My job was to come up with the intuition to use these sounds and players. At one session, I asked Rick Cox to play a bass saxophone like he was a savage who'd just heard Charlie Parker for the first time. Luckily, Rick figured that one out.

Courtesy of **Film Score Monthly**

Josh and S.A.M.

1993, Varèse Sarabande, from the film *Josh and S.A.M.,* **Castle Rock Entertainment,** 1993 ♪♪♪

album notes: Music: Thomas Newman; **Conductor:** Thomas Newman.

There are some winning moments in this otherwise uneven score by Thomas Newman for a touching story about two brothers (one of them thinks he is a robot) who steal a car and take a wild ride across the country. However, the overall impression is less than satisfying. Some cues seem to wander off into a netherland in which they fail to find a resolution, others trail off after having built some momentum that never really materializes. It may be that the score plays better with the film itself. Judged on its own merits, it is not so convincing.

Didier C. Deutsch

Journey into Fear

See: The Dead/Journey into Fear

Journey to the Center of the Earth

🎬 1997, Varèse-Sarabande, from the 20th Century-Fox film *Journey to the Center of the Earth*, 1959 🎵🎵🎵🎵

album notes: Music: Bernard Herrmann; **Conductor:** Bernard Herrmann.

Bernard Herrmann might arguably be the greatest film composer of the 20th century, and he was never better than when scoring such fantastical movies as *The Seventh Voyage of Sinbad, Jason and the Argonauts* (q.v.), and *The Day the Earth Stood Still*. With his unique orchestrations, romantic sensibility, and sly humor, Herrmann gave a collection of mythological beasts and spacemen a thunderous sound that made audiences take them seriously. And no Herrmann score was quite as monolithic or spectacular as *Journey to the Center of the Earth*. Right from the opening blasts of brass and organ, he perfectly captured the wonder at the heart of Jules Verne's story. *Journey* has any number of remarkable cues, including a majestic organ that reveals the path to the earth's core, the bizarre, groaning sound of an instrument aptly named a "serpent," the eerie harp glissandi heard underneath the surface, and the swiftly rising brass that finally shoots us back to earth. Album producer Nick Redman, who did an excellent job bringing *The Day the Earth Stood Still* to CD for the first time, supervised the release of this *Journey*. Herrmann's music never sounded better, with an excellent, crisp quality that could have been recorded yesterday. Also on hand for the completist's sake are a number of songs by Pat Boone and Sammy Cahn, whose pleasantly goofy tunes take place on a completely different planet from the underscore.

Dan Schweiger

The Joy Luck Club

🎬 1993, Hollywood Records, from the film *The Joy Luck Club*, Hollywood Pictures, 1993 🎵🎵🎵🎵

album notes: Music: Rachel Portman; **Conductor:** J.A.C. Redford; **Featured Musicians:** Masakazu Yoshizawa, Chinese instruments; Chris Fu, Chinese instruments; Shufeng He, Chinese instruments; Karen Hua-Qi Han, Chinese violin; Jim Walker, concert and bamboo flutes.

Not what you might think this is, *The Joy Luck Club*, about four sets of Chinese-American mothers and daughters and their diverse reactions to the different sets of values that define the world in which they live, prompted Rachel Portman to write a truly exquisite score. It is filled with great melodies, many in a very romantic vein, in which an occasional Chinese instrument provides the ethnic touch required by the story. Slowly unfolding and in the process setting the tone of the film, the cues explore the many dramatic possibilities suggested by the screenplay, with some great moments of expression finding a voice

along the way. Strong romantic elements clearly dominate in the music, with the composer reaching new heights of lyricism in selections like "Best Quality Heart," "June Meets Her Twin Sisters," or "An-Mei's New Home." A lovely, prolific score, in which a deliberately slow pace may leave some listeners unfazed, but which should satisfy many fans of instrumental music.

Didier C. Deutsch

Jude

🎬 1996, Imaginary Road Records, from the film *Jude*, Gramercy/PolyGram, 1996 🎵🎵🎵🎵

album notes: Music: Adrian Johnston; **Conductor:** Nick Ingman.

Set in late 19th-century England, this winsome screen adaptation of Thomas Hardy's last novel, *Jude the Obscure*, proved an ideal vehicle for Kate Winslett, whose spunk and lovely characterization made this costume drama highly effective. Although the convoluted story devised by Hardy seemed ill-suited for a screen adaptation, director Michael Winterbottom managed to spin the tale with real talent, taking the narrative at a brisk pace and putting in as many details as he could fit to explain the long journey of the central character, whose relationship with a distant cousin, Sue, weaves in and out of the story until a bittersweet ending finds them together, flouting conventions, but presumably living in harmony.

The score, devised by Adrian Johnston, has the originality of providing distinctive "sound worlds" for each segment of the story developing on screen. As the action moves from Marygreen to Christminster, to Melchester, to Shaston, to Aldbrickham, and back to Christminster again, the music in the score changes shapes and adopts tonalities that are specific to each location. The Electra Strings, Marygreen Band, and Chamber Band each perform specifically designed selections within the framework of the narrative. A lovely waltz for Jude and Sue adds a nostalgic note to the ensemble. Stark and expressive, the score is quite evocative and unusually attractive.

Didier C. Deutsch

Judge Dredd

🎬 1995, Epic Soundtrax, from the film *Judge Dredd*, Hollywood Pictures, 1995

album notes: Music: Alan Silvestri; **Orchestra:** The Sinfonia of London; **Conductor:** Alan Silvestri.

If you haven't gone deaf after listening to the five mindless songs that lead off this soundtrack (only "Dredd Song" appears in the film), you'll realize that Alan Silvestri's "Judge Dredd Main Theme" is making good use of CD sonics with its quiet one-minute buildup of synth and chorus. Once it gets going, Silvestri's score is a powerful, addictive mix of driving percussion.

This is particularly notable in "Block War." Dredd's own theme is a focused march, embodying the judge's own narrow view that says only the letter of the law matters. Silvestri seems to be having real fun recreating a twisted version of his *Predator 2* theme for the cannibalistic, mutated "Angel Family." He uses several odd synth effects, including some warped whale songs. Jerry Goldsmith was originally scheduled to score this film and created the trailer music. It was recorded on the *Hollywood '95* (q.v.) album and it's interesting to compare the approaches of these two composers to the same subject.

David Hirsch

Judgment at Nuremberg

1998, Rykodisc, from the film *Judgment at Nuremberg*, United Artists, 1961 ♪♪♪♪
album notes: Music: Ernest Gold; **Conductor:** Ernest Gold.

Composer Ernest Gold and director Stanley Kramer collaborated on a wide variety of classic films over a 20-year period, including *It's a Mad, Mad, Mad, Mad World* (q.v.) and *Inherit the Wind*. Unlike those films, *Judgement at Nuremberg* was based on the true story of the Nuremberg War Crimes Trials of 1948, in which a Maine district court judge went to Nuremberg to preside over a tribunal against four German judges accused of war crimes in World War II Nazi Germany. Because for a large part of the film the drama is created by the intensity generated in the courtroom scenes, most of Gold's score was used outside of the courtroom. The "Overture" and "Entr'acte" were composed to be heard before the film and during intermission. In both pieces, heard here, Gold incorporated German folk songs. The CD also features two German vocal tracks, "Du Du" and "Liebeslied," used in pub/restaurant scenes, and two dramatic narrations from the movie, by Burt Lancaster, as one of the German defendants, and by Spencer Tracy as Dan Haywood, the judge from Maine, giving his summation of the case.

Didier C. Deutsch

Judgment Night

1993, Epic Records, from the film *Judgment Night*, 1993 ♪

The repressed violence found in these songs may be the perfect musical accompaniment to this bleak urban contemporary drama, made in 1993, about four youngsters who become the unwitting witnesses of a murder and try to escape the dangers of the ghetto, as well as a killer determined to silence them. The tracks, presumably used on the soundtrack to characterize the screen action, are not too terribly interesting on their own and reveal the paucity in the verbal and musical expression. Only exception here is "Disorder," which gives Slayer and Ice-T

a good way to deliver a solid message. But that's really stretching to find something interesting about this album.

Didier C. Deutsch

Judicial Consent

1995, Intrada Records, from the film *Judicial Consent*, Rysher Entertainment, 1995 ♪♪♪♪
album notes: Music: Christopher Young; **Conductor:** Lex de Azevedo.

This score is brimming with rhythmic mysteriousness: winds over piano, keyboard fingering tentative, a soft flurry of notes, pausing a few beats, to return in a new flurry, with string chords surging in high register. Low, moaning Herrmann-esque chords play off of high-end piano notes with reverbed harp, and always the sustained strings. Young maintains an orchestral sensibility—very few electronics make their presence known—but his instrumentation is wicked. Stabs of percussion echoed by a downward violin shriek punctuate a tonal ambiance of whispering strings, low moaning winds, shimmering bells, and moody timpani. A harsh strum of chain-like drums slams down amid low pianistic echoes, sinewy string groans, and an incessantly chattering percussion rapping. In the end, Young's pretty main theme survives the horrors and closes the score on a note of melancholy. He captivates the listener, as he does the viewer, with a dominating musical permeation that creates an inescapable atmosphere of foreboding, excitement, suspense, horror, and ultimate relief. Few modern composers do it as well.

Randall Larson

Julia and Julia

1988, Varèse Sarabande, from the film *Julia and Julia*, Cinecom Entertainment, 1988 ♪♪
album notes: Music: Maurice Jarre; **Featured Musicians:** Rick Marvin, keyboards; Judd Miller, E.V.I.

For this film about a woman who experiences a time-warp situation, one in which her husband is dead and she has a lover, the other in which her husband is still alive, Maurice Jarre wrote a score that attempts to match in musical terms the odd, dual situation in which the main character finds herself. That he doesn't entirely succeed is indicative of the problems that face the film itself. In his multi-layered electronic score, Jarre tries to convey the strange events that shape up the screen action. He partly succeeds in the long cue, "Happy Days," in which the moods projected manage to convey the sense of insecurity and disorientation Julia must feel when confronted with a perplexing situation she cannot explain. But the other cues, much less elaborated and thinly constructed, fail to convey the same impressions and dissolve into a noisy form of expression that has no fixed goal.

Didier C. Deutsch

Juliet of the Spirits

See: Giulietta degli Spiriti

Julius Caesar

1995, Intrada Records, from the film *Julius Caesar*, MGM, 1953
♪♪♪♪

album notes: Music: Miklos Rozsa; **Orchestra:** The Sinfonia of London; **Conductor:** Bruce Broughton; **Featured Musicians:** Jane Emanuel, soprano; the Sinfonia Chorus, Jenny O'Grady, director.

Of all the Golden Age masters, Miklós Rózsa was the one who paid the least attention to catching onscreen action. His music has more of a through-composed quality that has survived the decades well. *Julius Caesar,* starring Marlon Brando, is one of his first "historical epic" scores, and one of his darkest, blending smaller period-type cues with the symphonic foreboding of his film noir period. For most of it, the string section simply seems to be playing lower than in his later, sunnier biblical epics, with cello soliloquies accompanying the Shakespearean portent on screen. It's not really "period" music—what did music in the 1st century B.C. really sound like?—but Rózsa's Eastern European romanticism conveys a certain *Roman*-ness, which is appropriate. Between the shorter, distinctly Rózsa motifs, with their evocative intervalic leaps, and the longer lines that expand into entire pieces, it's one of his most absorbing historical scores. (Many of the cues were cut or abridged in the actual film.) Intrada's album, which goes on forever, is a new recording done in 1995, with Bruce Broughton conducting the Sinfonia of London and Sinfonia Chorus.

Lukas Kendall

Jumanji

1995, Epic Soundtrax, from the film *Jumanji*, Tri-Star Pictures, 1995 ♪♪♪♪

album notes: Music: James Horner; **Conductor:** James Horner; **Featured Instrumental Soloists:** Michael Fisher, Ralph Grierson, Tony Hinnegan, James Horner, Randy Kerber, Qu-Chao Liu, Kazu Matsu, Mike Taylor, Ian Underwood.

A thriller with grim overtones, *Jumanji* induced James Horner to write an unusual score filled with ominous sounds, midway between fantasy and horror. The name of the film refers to a very unusual board game with supernatural powers, whose surreal and potentially lethal aspects compel the player to enter into a world totally controlled by the game. As each roll of the dice brings out new elements that prove frightening as well as dangerously beautiful, Horner matches the action with musical themes well-studied to enhance it. "Monkey Mayhem," for instance, is a rollicking cue that underscores a scene in which an unruly group of apes disrupts the suburban New England home of the two youngsters who play the game. Similarly, "Rampage through Town" evokes a herd of elephants suddenly creating havoc in the little town, smashing everything that happens to be in their path. Each incident in the film calls for (and gets) an inventive musical cue, with Horner conjuring up some chaotic fun along the way. Ultimately, not a very substantial score, but an entertaining one nonetheless.

Didier C. Deutsch

The Jungle Book

1990, Walt Disney Records, from the animated feature *The Jungle Book*, Walt Disney Pictures, 1967 ♪♪♪♪

album notes: Music: George Bruns; **Songs:** Richard M. Sherman, Robert B. Sherman; **Cast:** Phil Harris, Sebastian Cabot, Louis Prima, George Sanders, Sterling Holloway.

Walt Disney's *The Jungle Book* needs little introduction. Who among us hasn't experienced the delight of Disney's animated feature, based upon Rudyard Kipling's "Mowgli" stories? All 16 songs written for the film are here, including "Colonel Hathi's March," "The Bare Necessities," and "I Wan'na Be like You," plus a recorded interview with songwriters Robert and Richard Sherman (which includes rare demos, and two musical numbers from the album *More Jungle Book:* "Baloo's Blues" and "It's a Kick"). Particularly fun are Louis Prima's "monkeying" around on "I Wan'na Be like You," and the infectious spontaneity of the Academy Award–nominated song, "The Bare Necessities." The original stereo film recordings are good, save for a small amount of hiss that accompanies most recordings of this vintage.

Charles L. Granata

1994, Milan Records, from the film *The Jungle Book*, Buena Vista Pictures, 1994 ♪♪♪♪
album notes: Music: Basil Poledouris; **Conductor:** David Snell.

For this umpteenth screen treatment of the Rudyard Kipling story about a boy raised by a pack of wolves in the Indian jungle, Basil Poledouris created a score that is rife with lush, colorful orchestral accents, in a way that takes it miles away from the music Miklos Rozsa wrote about the same subject. In many ways, Poledouris's set of cues is very evocative of the screen action, with the selections devoted to the main characters ("Mowgli," "Baloo," "Shere Khan Attacks") striking a bold, sometimes overly rich vein. But this is also music that breathes and needs to express itself in broad terms, something the composer understood perfectly when he wrote the score. As a result, the sweep in the music is incredibly exciting and overpowering.

see also: The Thief of Bagdad

Didier C. Deutsch

The Jungle Book (**The Kobal Collection**)

Jungle Fever

1991, Motown Records, from the film *Jungle Fever,* Universal Pictures, 1991 ♫♫♫

album notes: Music: Stevie Wonder.

Your reaction to this soundtrack album will largely depend on how you feel about Stevie Wonder, who wrote the songs heard in the film directed by Spike Lee and performs them. Generally speaking, the Wonder-man comes across most effectively in ballads ("These Three Words," "Make Sure You're Sure," "I Go Sailing"), possibly because the up-tempo numbers seem too grating and abrasive, without much feeling.

Didier C. Deutsch

Jungle 2 Jungle

1997, Disney Records, from the film *Jungle 2 Jungle,* Walt Disney, 1997 ♫♫

album notes: Music: Michael Convertino.

A well-intentioned but slight world music soundtrack accompanies this Tim Allen family film, which also mixes in some urban tracks (for the "city jungle" scenes) and score elements for a messy soundscape. The star vehicle on this album is "Shaking the Tree '97," on which the song's writer, Peter Gabriel, is joined by Youssou N'Dour and Shaggy for a version that adds a bit more tribal thump to the mix. Afro Celt Sound System's "Whirl-Y Reel I" and Toto La Momposina's "La Sombra Negra" are oases in this sonic desert, although it's nice to think that some of the film's young target audience might be turned on to some international styles if they like the film enough to buy the album.

see also: Little Indian, Big City

Gary Graff

Junior

1994, Varèse Sarabande, from the film *Junior,* Universal Picture, 1994 ♫♫♫

album notes: Music: James Newton Howard; **Conductor:** Artie Kane.

A minor (very minor!) comedy about a man who is pregnant (Arnold Schwarzenegger, if you can believe it), *Junior* received a much better score than it actually merited from the always inventive and interesting James Newton Howard. Though the action may not have deserved the attention it got, the composer wrote several cues that are quite enjoyable, musically speaking, with broad sonorous accents that compel the listener to pay close attention ("Main Titles," "First Pregnant Man," "Junior"). Adding a whimsical touch to the score, two source selections, "I've Got You under My Skin," sung by Cassandra Wilson, and "Are You in the Mood?," exhilaratingly played by

Stephane Grappelli, give a slightly different spin to this eloquent album.

Didier C. Deutsch

Jurassic Park

1993, MCA Records, from the film *Jurassic Park,* Universal Pictures, 1992 ♫♫♫♫

album notes: Music: John Williams; **Conductor:** John Williams;

How do you musically spell "blockbuster"? The answer may well be in this sensational soundtrack, in which John Williams makes no bones—prehistoric or otherwise—about his intentions from the first bars of the "Opening Titles." The lovely theme he develops, with oozing arpeggios and strong, lyrical accents, belies the threat posed by the various monsters that eventually inhabit the film, something the composer clearly enjoys to define when he approaches such crucial scenes as "The Raptor Attack," "My Friend, The Brachiosaurus," or "Eye to Eye."

Also characteristic of his approach is the melodically strong themes Williams created for the occasion. Once again, we are in the presence of a composer who understands that film music must have a momentum of its own, and that the only way to provide it is to create themes that are essentially catchy. Even when the screen action demands a cue that may not call as much attention to itself, Williams succeeds in fulfilling his obligations while attracting the casual listener by the sheer power of the melody he has conceived for the moment. In every way, this is an outstanding score.

see also: The Lost World

Didier C. Deutsch

Just Cause

1995, Varèse Sarabande, from the film *Just Cause,* Warner Bros., 1995 ♫♫♫

album notes: Music: James Newton Howard; **Conductor:** Artie Kane.

The confrontation between a law professor (Sean Connery), researching a case about a young man he believes has been falsely accused of a crime, and the small-town Florida cop (Laurence Fishburne) who obtained the confession, possibly through torture and coercion, *Just Cause* is a suspense-filled drama with plenty of twists to keep the audience on the edge of its seats. Contributing an element of strength to the whole brew is the score by James Newton Howard, whose cues slyly accent and modify the action on the screen, sometimes in bold, exciting terms. For once, however, the short playing time of the CD, which is slightly above 30 minutes, seems sufficient to have the music make its impression without overstaying its welcome.

Didier C. Deutsch

Just the Ticket

 1999, Metro Blue Records, from the film *Just the Ticket,* United Artists, 1999 🎵🎵🎵🎵

album notes: Music: Rick Marotta; **Featured Musicians:** The Band/Good Call Johnny & the Scalptones: Dr. John, Terry Trotter, piano; Rick Marotta, drums; Neil Stubenhaus, Dave Carpenter, bass; David Spinozza, guitar; Luis Conte, Andy Garcia, percussion; Joe Iurano, Lou Marini, tenor sax; Justo Almario, alto sax; Chris Mostert, baritone sax; Harry Kim, Fernando Pullem, Johnny Britt, trumpet; Jim McMillan, bass trombone; the Cachao **Orchestra:** Israel Lopez "Cachao," bass; Joe Rotundi, piano; Danilo Lozano, flute; Orestes Vilato, timbales; Andy Garcia, congas; Richard Marquez, bongos; Nelson Marquez, clave; Joe Turano, tenor sax; Justo Almario, alto sax; Art Velasco, trombone; Harry Kim, Fernando Pullem, trumpet.

Andy Garcia and Andie MacDowell scored high marks for their portrayals as star-crossed lovers in this story of a charmingly cocky scalper, who makes an uneasy living in Manhattan hawking everything from tickets for the next hockey game to T-shirts, and who is smitten with a saleslady in an appliance store, who has ambitions of becoming a gourmet chef. For Garcia, who not only produced the film but wrote many of the tunes heard on the soundtrack, and who even plays in the band, the project was evidently a labor of love. His songs, with a strong Latin flavor to them, are for the most part quite engaging, if not particularly distinguished, with the band delivering the goods with an enthusiasm that's often communicative. Adding a zestful contribution of their own, several tracks have been licensed to round off this soundtrack album, including Bobby Darin's "Call Me Irresponsible," Louis Prima's dynamite rendition of "When You're Smiling," Dianne Reeves & Dr. John's sultry "Come Rain or Come Shine," and Stevie Wonder's classic "Signed, Sealed, and Delivered," among others. Altogether, an enjoyable album that goes a long way to entertain and please the listener.

Didier C. Deutsch

Kafka

1992, Virgin Movie Music, from the film *Kafka,* Miramax Films, 1992 🎵🎵🎵🎵

album notes: Music: Cliff Martinez.

No doubt inspired by its subject matter and the defiant personality of the title character, Cliff Martinez wrote a greatly at-

mospheric score for *Kafka,* in which the cues are separated into two distinct categories, those that apply to the writer's real life, and those that underscore the arcane world in which his imagination often takes him. In the first, the cymbalom plays a vitally important role, suggestive of the Bohemian locale of the action, Prague shortly after the end of World War I, and the apparently impersonal but orderly existence of Kafka. In the second, however, Martinez chose to use an electronic underscoring that would have seemed out of place in 1919 but has a modern resonance that suits Kafka's moods of alienation In the presence of the unknowable ("Bum Attack," "Allegiance to Something Other than the Truth," "Wrong End of the Microscope"). The combination of both reflects the narrative in its complex duality and provides the anchors upon which the story unfolds.

Didier C. Deutsch

Kama Sutra

1997, TVT Records, from the NDF International Ltd./Pony Canyon/Pandora film *Kama Sutra,* 1997 🎵🎵🎵🎵

album notes: Music: Mychael Danna; **Featured Musicians:** Ustad Vilayat H. Khan, sitar; L. Subramaniam, violin; G. S. Sachdev, bansuri; Aruna Narayan Kalle, Gulam Sabir, sarangi; Th. Vikku Vinayakram, ghatam; V. Selva Ganesh, kanjira; Vijay Barik, pakhawaj; Hidayat H. Khan, pakhawaj; Zamir H. Khan, Irshad H. Khan, tabla; Humayun Khan, surmandal, tanpura; Jia Lal, shehnai; Manoj Khan, been; Bubbly, Billa, Raju, Billoo, dhol; Paul Intson, bass guitar; Anwar Khurshid, Ron Korb, flute; Supriya Sharma, tanpura; Jeff Danna, mandolin; Mychael Danna, other instruments.

Mychael Danna composed an Indian score for this erotic tale of sex and sexual politics in 16th-century India, and brought together various instrumentalists performing on both traditional Indian and Western instruments. The movie, which explored love in its many forms, so to speak, received an NC-17 rating for sexual content. The score rates just as high; it is both exotic and erotic, with breathy flutes and infectious rhythms. Shubha Mudgal, who has a very intoxicating voice, supplies most of the vocals, except on four of the songs.

Beth Krakower

Kansas City

1996, Verve Records, from the film *Kansas City,* Sandcastle 5/Ciby 2000, 1996 🎵🎵🎵🎵

album notes: Featured Musicians: Kevin Mahogany, vocal; Olu Dara, cornet; Nicholas Payton, trumpet; James Zollar, trumpet; Curtis Fowlkes, trombone; Clark Gayton, trombone; Don Byron, clarinet; Don Byron, saxophone; James Carter, saxophone; Jesse Davis, saxophone; David "Fathead" Newman, saxophone; Craig Handy, saxophone; David Murray, saxophone; Joshua Redman, saxophone; Russell Malone, guitar; Mark Whitfield, guitar; Geri Allen, piano; Cyrus Chestnut, piano; Ron Carter, bass; Tyrone Clark, bass; Christian McBride, bass; Victor Lewis, drums.

Robert Altman's often muddled story of crime, race, and politics in the 1930s is only temporarily relieved by some great jazz played in the background. Fortunately, the soundtrack album focuses on the music, and succeeds in evoking the era and the locale of the film, without the tedious action that makes it so painful to watch. There is indeed some great playing here, with several veterans (Joshua Redman, David "Fathead" Newman, Ron Carter, Curtis Fowlkes, Don Byron, James Carter, to name a few) displaying the essence of their unique talent in settings that obviously inspire them. Too bad the film could not reach the high quality levels of its soundtrack!

Didier C. Deutsch

Kazaam

1997, Super Tracks Records, from the film *Kazaam,* Touchstone Pictures, 1997 🎬🎬

album notes: Music: Christopher Tyng; **Orchestra:** The London Film Symphony Orchestra; **Conductor:** Tim Simonec; **Featured Musician:** Bob Daspit, guitar.

Basketball star Shaquille O'Neal is the congenial genie who grants three wishes to a 12 year old, setting the stage for this modern fairy tale played out against a typically violent urban background. Before the relationship between the benevolent 3,000-year-old genie and his reluctantly cynical master finally yields an upbeat solution, much will have happened to both, and all of it is set to the score created by Christopher Tyng, a fresh voice on the film music scene. While the selections clearly indicate the potential of the composer, writing in a variety of styles, most of his cues sound incomplete, some stopping abruptly in the middle of a melodic phrase, others trailing off before they have a chance to reach a logical conclusion. This is all the more regrettable because Tyng is evidently gifted and comes up with attractive melodies whenever necessary, like "Max and Alice." On the screen, this shortcoming might not make much difference; on the album, however, it is too noticeable.

Didier C. Deutsch

Keeper of the City

1991, Intrada Records, from the film *Keeper of the City,* Viacom Pictures, 1991 🎬🎬🎬

album notes: Music: Leonard Rosenman; **Orchestra:** The Utah Symphony Orchestra; **Conductor:** Leonard Rosenman.

The "keeper of the city" in this contemporary drama set in a big city is a detective with definite notions about how to deal with criminals. Leonard Rosenman created a vibrant score, centered around two main themes—one to give an aural identity to the environment in which the hero of the film operates; the second to portray a criminal with pseudo-religious fanaticism who challenges the detective and the authority he represents.

Heard throughout the score, the two themes collide with each other, complement each other, and eventually blend into one another in a climactic finale. Rosenman, an old hand at creating this type of music, is quite eclectic in his choice of themes and harmonies, and powerfully evokes the scene of the crime and the participants in it. The recording, oddly off-balanced in many cues with most of the musicians apparently regrouped on the right side, is otherwise clearly defined and appropriately dry.

Didier C. Deutsch

The Key to Rebecca

1993, Prometheus Records/Belgium, from the television mini–series *The Key to Rebecca,* 1985 🎬🎬🎬

album notes: Music: J.A.C. Redford; **Conductor:** J.A.C. Redford.

Composer J.A.C. Redford deftly mixes numerous middle eastern motifs with a great *Patton*–like military march into his score for this 1985 four–hour television mini–series. Adapted from Ken Follett's spy–thriller about the pursuit of a Nazi master of disguise by a British officer, the range the story demands allows for several musical changes of pace, which include a "Belly Dancing" theme and the big band "Spy Talk," to name just a few. Of course, there are also many of the obligatory chase cues. This is a better-than-average TV score with a lot to offer.

David Hirsch

Kid Galahad

See: Girls! Girls! Girls!/Kid Galahad

A Kid in Aladdin's Palace

1998, Citadel Records, from the film *A Kid in Aladdin's Palace,* TriMark, 1998 🎬🎬🎬🎬

album notes: Music: David Michael Frank; **Conductor:** David Michael Frank.

It would be tempting to dismiss this rousing symphonic score, but don't let the film for which it was written, a mild Arabian Nights fantasy with modern overtones, deter you from listening to it: it is actually quite good. David Michael Frank—whose credentials were until now not particularly impressive—succeeds in creating a set of cues that are attractively laid out, brightly colorful, melodic, and fun. The opulent orchestra sound of the City of Prague Philharmonic is used to best effect to maximize the themes the composer developed to detail the screen action about the kid, mistaken by the Genie as the only one who can deliver Aladdin, held prisoner by Luxor, Aladdin's own brother. The richly detailed score makes full use of the subject matter and the locale of the action, with broad swaths of musical colors that are vividly illustrative and quite enjoyable. Only one small quibble: the cues, for the most part, are not fully realized and give the impression that they are not entirely completed by the time they end. It might have helped in this case to combine them into longer suites, in order to give the music a chance to make a more profound impression.

Didier C. Deutsch

A Kid in King Arthur's Court

1995, Walt Disney Records, from the film *A Kid in King Arthur's Court*, Walt Disney Films, 1995 ♪♪♪

album notes: Music: J.A.C. Redford; **Orchestra:** The City of Prague Philharmonic Orchestra; **Conductor:** J.A.C. Redford; **Featured Musician:** Liona Boyd, classical guitar.

In a fresh, inventive variation on Mark Twain's classic "Connecticut Yankee" story, a kid with little mettle travels back in time to the days of Camelot, where his unusual appearance and bagful of odd contrivances (a portable CD player, rollerblades, a Swiss Army knife) immediately single him out as some sort of magician. Providing the musical peg on which the emotional balance of the action finds its fodder, J.A.C. Redford wrote a score that harkens back to the days of yore, when swashbucklers spoke of deadly deeds and courtly manners, but with a modern twist in keeping with the contemporary elements of the fantasy. Along the way, there are some nifty moments, including the abrasive "Combat Rock," the medieval-sounding "Now Let Us Eat!," the rousing "Successful Swording," and the love romance "Calvin and Katie." At times sounding a mite too profuse and lush for such a slight amusement, the score nonetheless delights and proves quite enjoyable. A theme for classical guitar ("The Conscience of the King") is particularly attractive.

Didier C. Deutsch

The Killing Fields

1984, Virgin Records, from the film *The Killing Fields*, Warner Bros., 1984 ♪♪♪

album notes: Music: Mike Oldfield; **Orchestra:** The Orchestra of the Bavarian State Opera; **Conductor:** Eberhard Schoener; **Featured Musicians:** The Tolzer Boys Choir; Mike Oldfield, guitars, synthesizers; Preston Heyman, Oriental percussion; Morris Pert, percussion.

Classic rock instrumentalist Mike Oldfield, whose "Tubular Bells" had played such an important function in the film *The Exorcist,* contributed an effective score to this Oscar-nominated film about Cambodia and the war-related horrors that have plagued the country over the past 20 years. The story of the friendship that binds an American journalist and the educated native who serves as his guide, the film focuses on the two men's journey through Khmer Rouge territory, their eventual arrest, and escape from a re-education camp in the Year Zero. Old-

field's score, an eerie mixture of electronic sounds (and tubular bells) augmented by a boys choir over an orchestral texture, seems like a necessary embellishment on the soundtrack. Away from the screen drama, it still conjures up images that may not all be related to the film itself but that are quite effective.

Didier C. Deutsch

Kindergarten Cop

1990, Varèse Sarabande, from the film *Kindergarten Cop*, Universal Pictures, 1990 ♪♪♪♪

album notes: Music: Randy Edelman; **Conductor:** Randy Edelman.

What a selling job Randy Edelman had—Schwarzenegger teaching kindergarten! But one listen to the sweet and gentle "Astoria School Theme" and you know he's succeeded in transforming "The Terminator" into a cream puff. The film does have its share of action music when Arnold acts like a cop ("Stalking Crisp," "Fire at the School"), but mostly breezes effectively through the upbeat comedic moments when he must perform his duties undercover as a teacher. Edelman performs the piano on the "Love Theme."

David Hirsch

The King and I

1990, MCA Records, from the Broadway production *The King and I*, 1951 ♪♪♪

album notes: Music: Richard Rodgers; **Lyrics:** Oscar Hammerstein II; **Musical Direction:** Frederick Dvonch; **Cast:** Gertrude Lawrence, Yul Brynner, Doretta Morrow, Larry Douglas, Dorothy Sarnoff.

1987, Capitol Records, from the film *The King and I*, 20th Century Fox, 1956 ♪♪♪♪♪

album notes: Music: Richard Rodgers; **Lyrics:** Oscar Hammerstein II; **Choir:** The 20th Century Fox Chorus; **Orchestra:** The 20th Century Fox Orchestra; **Conductor:** Alfred Newman; **Cast:** Deborah Kerr, Yul Brynner, Rita Moreno, Carlos Rivas, Terry Saunders.

1977, RCA Victor Records, from the Broadway revival *The King and I*, 1977 ♪♪♪♪♪

album notes: Music: Richard Rodgers; **Lyrics:** Oscar Hammerstein II; **Musical Direction:** Milton Rosenstock; **Cast:** Yul Brynner, Constance Towers, June Angela, Martin Vidnovic.

1996, Varèse Sarabande, from the Broadway revival *The King and I*, 1996 ♪♪♪♪♪

album notes: Music: Richard Rodgers; **Lyrics:** Oscar Hammerstein II; *Musical Direction:*: Michael Rafter; **Cast:** Donna Murphy, Lou Diamond Phillips, Joohee Choi, Jose Llana, Taewon Kim.

1999, Sony Classical, from the animated feature *The King and I*, Morgan Creek/Warner Bros., 1999 woof!

album notes: Music: Richard Rodgers; **Lyrics:** Oscar Hammerstein II; **Conductor:** William Kidd.

Following the huge success of *South Pacific* two years before, much was expected from Richard Rodgers and Oscar

Hammerstein II. *The King and I* didn't disappoint. Based on Margaret Landon's novel, *Anna and the King of Siam,* already the source for a 1946 non–musical film starring Rex Harrison and Irene Dunne, the musical was devised as a vehicle for Gertrude Lawrence, who had first suggested it to Rodgers and Hammerstein. The actress portrayed Anna Leonowens, the English teacher who goes to Siam in the 1860s to tutor the royal children. Contrasting the civilized Occidental values with the less sophisticated traditions of the Asian country, *The King and I* gained greater emotional depth when Oscar Hammerstein introduced a secondary romantic plot between Tuptim, a slave girl offered to the King by the Prince of Burma, and Lun Tha, who has been chosen to escort her to Siam. In a particularly clever parallel, Rodgers and Hammerstein, along with choreographer Jerome Robbins, created a ballet adaptation of Harriet Beecher Stowe's *Uncle Tom's Cabin.* This device enabled them to further contrast, in song and dances, the differences between East and West. The show, which opened on March 29, 1951, and enjoyed a run of 1,246 performances, made a star of Yul Brynner, as the King, so much so in fact that focus in subsequent revivals shifted from Anna to the King, a trend eventually reversed in the 1996 Broadway production.

Of the various recordings listed above, the original cast album, made in 1951, suffers the most, if only because it offers less selections from the profuse score and is recorded in mono. However, it has the advantage of starring Gertrude Lawrence, radiant in her last stage role, and the budding Yul Brynner in the role that launched his international career.

The 1956 soundtrack album, besides having an incredibly sumptuous sound, was for many years the best recording available. Boasting a new overture orchestrated by Alfred Newman, it starred Brynner, properly regal as the King, and Deborah Kerr (dubbed by Marni Nixon) as Anna, with Rita Moreno as Tuptim. While the soundtrack focuses on the major musical numbers, it is not as complete as the extended version available with the deluxe laser disc edition of the film, which includes many instrumentals and reprises.

In 1977 Yul Brynner returned to Broadway, in the first of several revivals reprising the role of the King. The RCA Victor recording documents that revival, with a score that includes a lot of music previously unavailable. Though the revival was clearly dominated by Brynner, on the CD the balance between the various participants is better achieved, with the great sonics providing one of the best recordings of that score available up to that point.

With the focus back on Anna Leonowens, glowingly portrayed by Donna Murphy in the 1996 revival, the most recent cast album is the one to have. It features equally strong performances by Lou Diamond Phillips as the King, Taewon Kim as Lady Thiang, the King's first wife, Jose Llana as Lun Tha, and Joohee Choi as Tuptim, and it restores moments from the score ("Procession of the White Elephant"), not available elsewhere. However, like all other recordings, it fails to include the "Little House of Uncle Thomas" ballet, which, so far, can only be found on the Broadway cast recording of the revue *Jerome Robbins's Broadway.*

It is difficult for anyone who grew up with and thrived on the many incarnations of *The King and I* over the years to understand what prompted animators to tamper with Rodgers and Hammerstein's Asian-themed musical. Only recently, the show was revived on Broadway in the opulent presentation that starred Phillips and Murphy, while the version most people still remember is the 1956 film in which Brynner gave the definitive characterization as the King of Siam who wants to bring civilization to his country. Deborah Kerr gave a subtly shaded performance as Anna that happily contrasted with Brynner's and positively ignited the screen.

This new animated feature is unfortunately symptomatic of the underside of our culture: we sacrifice some of our most precious icons in the illusive belief that by so doing we will make them more accessible to the masses, and more acceptable to politically correct pundits who have no qualms trying to rewrite history. We seem to have little respect for (or perhaps confidence in) what our predecessors have done, and we mistakenly assume that we should modify what they created in order to bring their legacy to our own levels of understanding and perception. It's a tragic flaw in our culture that will plague us as long as we don't accept once and for all that our past is rich in values and worth keeping and protecting as it was conceived, and not as we think it should have been conceived.

As a result, we are faced with this unfortunate cartoon, in which the story, originally devised by Oscar Hammerstein (after the memoirs of Anna Leonowens, who tutored the King of Siam's children in the late 1800s), becomes a cutesy fairy tale: the King must now confront dragons and gnomes and the evil Kralahome, before escaping a fate worse than death by using . . . a balloon. Anna is on hand to help (she doesn't fall in love with the King, or he with her, but perhaps only because this is a kiddie show), and Tuptim, the slave girl offered to the King by his Burmese counterpart in the original, is now a princess who finds love with the King's older son.

If that were not bad enough, the soundtrack album is presented in the same manner most recordings are done today—with the songs bunched up in front and the "score" thrown at the end, perhaps as a filler or an afterthought. In imitation of a formula initiated by the Disney studio, there is even an opening number performed by Barbra Streisand, not heard in the film but added here as a bonus track.

Of the principals on the soundtrack, Christiane Noll sounds much too young to be a British schoolmarm, but Martin Vidnovic is adequate as the King. The question, if there is a question to be asked now, is who will listen to this album? The kids who probably were dragged to the movie theaters by parents who mistakenly thought they were going to see the genuine thing? Doubtful! The parents, then? If they have any sense, they'll go back to the 1956 soundtrack, or any of the recent revival cast albums that are available. The sooner this cartoon and its soundtrack are forgotten, the better.

Didier C. Deutsch

King Creole

🎬 1996, RCA Records from the film *King Creole*, Paramount Pictures, 1958 ♫♫♫

Set in New Orleans, *King Creole* proved a particularly solid drama, enlivened by a strong storyline and colorful music numbers. In it, Elvis portrayed a mixed-up youth who rebels against the indigence of his parents, and who seeks solace from it as a performer in a mob-controlled club, where he finds himself exposed to the dangers and violence of the underworld. Among the songs that peppered the action, "King Creole," "Don't Ask Me Why," and "Hard-Headed Woman" soon emerged as unqualified hits, with the last reaching #1 on the charts.

Didier C. Deutsch

King Kong

🎬 1984, Southern Cross Records, from the film *King Kong*, RKO Radio Pictures, 1933 ♫♫♫♫♫
album notes: Music: Max Steiner; **Orchestra:** The National Philharmonic Orchestra; **Conductor:** Fred Steiner.

🎬 1998, Marco Polo, from the film *King Kong*, RKO Radio Pictures, 1933 ♫♫♫♫♫
album notes: Music: Max Steiner; **Conductor:** William J. Stromberg.

The music for *King Kong,* is, in the words of Oscar Levant, "a Max Steiner concert illustrated by pictures," evidently an apt description of the importance of the score, the first of its kind ever written for a motion picture. An impressive achievement at the time, it continues to mesmerize by the sheer force of its musical power, particularly in this recording made in 1976, in which Fred Steiner (no relation to the composer) conducted the National Philharmonic Orchestra in a spirited reading of the score. Broadly dramatic and colorfully exotic, the music evokes the first and one of the best monster pictures ever made, with

weird, dissonant chords contrasting with pretty melodies for a multi-layered, effective score that endures.

The new recording, with William T. Stromberg conducting the Moscow Symphony Orchestra, is even more impressive, first by its sheer magnitude (over 72 minutes of music) and by the vast technological improvements that place it way above the Steiner-led recording. True to the Marco Polo standards of quality, the profuse booklet provides a detailed outline of the various cues and how they fit within the story, and contains several testimonies from musicians (Danny Elfman), film creators (Ray Harryhausen), and authors (Ray Bradbury) who were influenced by the film at the time of its original release or in later viewings. But it is the music itself that best describes what this soundtrack album is all about—terribly important in the overall canon of film music, richly imaginative, and a trend setter that still stands out today as a major achievement in a musical field that has known quite a few others in the ensuing years. The performance by the Moscow Symphony is matchless, and the sound quality of the recording itself is perfectly attuned to the performance.

Didier C. Deutsch

King of Kings

🎬 1992, Sony Music, from the film *King of Kings*, MGM, 1961 ♫♫♫♫♫
album notes: Music: Miklos Rozsa; **Orchestra:** The MGM Studio Orchestra; **Conductor:** Miklos Rozsa.

Following *Ben-Hur,* Miklos Rozsa became known as the Hollywood composer best qualified to score Biblical films, a notion he could not dispel, despite the fact that he wrote *King of Kings* and *El Cid* almost back to back. Like *Ben-Hur,* however, *King of Kings* enabled the composer to write in an idiom in which he was by now thoroughly familiar, and in which he had pioneered the use of ancient instruments to give his music the authenticity he felt it needed. A dramatic retelling of the story of Christ, the film provided Rozsa with an extra difficulty, in that it covered essentially the same grounds the composer had already explored in *Ben-Hur.* Undaunted, Rozsa rose to the challenge and wrote a score that may not be up to the standards set by the previous film, but that exhibits nonetheless the same feelings of pious adoration and epic accents. This time, however, he relies on new Jewish themes to augment the Roman themes he had previously created for both *Ben-Hur* and *Quo Vadis.* In another significant departure, Rozsa also created a piece of 12-tone music to describe the temptation of Christ in the desert, the only time he would write atonal music.

With its sweeping romantic themes and thrilling epic accents, the score is truly awe-inspiring, a splendid effort that ranks among Rozsa's most important contributions to the screen. As befits a score of this importance, the CD reissue includes many cues that were previously unreleased. The sound, however, leaves a lot to be desired. Frequently harsh and without the warmth usually associated with a good mastering job, it presents occasional distortion on some tracks, and overall uneven sonic qualities, and despite the claim that it is in stereo for the first time, some tracks are evidently in mono. These technical questions set aside, the CD is still a very important addition to any serious collection of film music.

Didier C. Deutsch

King of the Wind

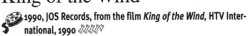 1990, JOS Records, from the film *King of the Wind*, HTV International, 1990 𝄞𝄞𝄞𝄞

album notes: Music: John Scott; **Orchesta:** The Munich Studio Orchestra; **Conductor:** John Scott.

The story of a mute Arab boy called Agba and a horse called Sham, and their adventures as they journey from Tunis to England in the early 18th century, *King of the Wind* gave John Scott a colorful tale and diversified background against which to write a score that is quite unusual. As exotic as the story itself and as complex as the many elements that constitute it, the cues follow the saga of the two friends through North Africa, across the Mediterranean Sea, and to the French court of Louis XV. Further misadventures occur in England where Agba is imprisoned and Lath, the son of Sham, wins the King's Cup at Newmarket and becomes the forebear of the English racing thoroughbreds.

Strikingly evocative of the many territories covered, and the events that occur, the music is in turn Arabic and baroque, romantic and epic, with some pulse-racing moments in between. The various cues explore all these elements in depth, in a brilliant musical tapestry that weaves its own tale. Among the striking cues assembled in this album, "Race with Wild Horses," "The Abduction of Sham," "The Earl of Godolphin," "The Newmarket Races," and "Winning the King's Plate" are notably effective, but the entire score is melodically outstanding.

Didier C. Deutsch

King Rat

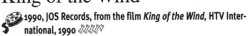 1995, Legacy Records/Sony Music Entertainment, from the film *King Rat*, Columbia Pictures, 1965 𝄞𝄞𝄞𝄞

album notes: Music: John Barry; **Conductor:** John Barry.

For director Bryan Forbes's dark film about prisoners of war confined in the notorious Japanese Changi Prison on Singapore Island, John Barry created a unique score that utilized unusual instrumentation and orchestration—techniques that effectively convey the images of humans involved in a struggle for survival in a completely oppressive, horrendous environment. The sparseness of the musical theme and the texture Barry achieves through careful use of exotic percussion instruments painfully underscores the glum tenseness of the plot and serves to make this one of his most unusual and intriguing film works. The recording, newly remastered, is excellent.

Charles L. Granata

King Solomon's Mines

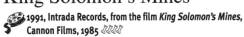 1991, Intrada Records, from the film *King Solomon's Mines*, Cannon Films, 1985 𝄞𝄞𝄞𝄞

album notes: Music: Jerry Goldsmith; **Orchestra:** The Hungarian State Opera Orchestra; **Conductor:** Jerry Goldsmith.

Jerry Goldsmith's broad and elaborate satire of *Raiders of the Lost Ark* will test your tolerance for large-scale action cues and hyperkinetic heroic fanfares as it clatters along with over an hour of hammering, non-stop adventure music. It will drive some listeners crazy, but if you're a fan of Goldsmith's action material you won't want to miss this effort, which was the composer's last completely orchestral score until 1996's *First Knight*. Goldsmith's bracingly old-fashioned opening cue makes brilliant use of African rhythmic effects, while the rest of the score mixes a broad take-off of Wagner's "Ride of the Valkyries" with some of the most spectacular, over-the-top, brassy action-writing the composer has ever produced. It's not to be taken seriously but it's certainly a far more enjoyable romp than the film itself.

Jeff Bond

Kings Go Forth/Some Came Running

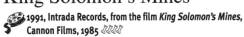 1992, Cloud Nine Records, from the films *Kings Go Forth*, United Artists, 1958, and *Some Came Running*, MGM, 1959 𝄞𝄞𝄞

album notes: Music: Elmer Bernstein; **Conductor:** Elmer Bernstein.

While neither the scores for *Kings Go Forth* or *Some Came Running* ever had the commercial success of many other film compositions by Elmer Bernstein, they remain an important part of the composer's canon, and are of particular interest within the realm of the work of the films' star, Frank Sinatra.

With *Kings Go Forth* (set in war-torn Italy, circa 1944), Bernstein's task was to musically portray a love triangle between a sensuous femme (Natalie Wood), and two American soldiers enjoying a well-deserved furlough on the French Riviera (Frank Sinatra and Tony Curtis). As always, his music hits the mark, bringing a combination of dramatic themes and romantic interludes together to effectively depict the tensions of battle, and the relationship between the three main characters. The sound on this portion of the disc is monophonic.

The plot of *Some Came Running* is also cursed by a love triangle, however in this instance the setting is a small home town, instead of the European battlefront. The themes demand a dark, tragic overtone (Sinatra's character is a cynical, brooding type), and, once again, Bernstein deftly achieves this through the careful use of strings, sax, piano, and percussion to create a bluesy, dissonant atmosphere that perfectly heightens the sense of gloom and despair. The score, which contains jazz-tinged pieces reminiscent of Bernstein's work for another Sinatra film, *The Man with the Golden Arm,* and some utterly dramatic selections, is certainly one of the composer's most underrated efforts. It is heard here in full stereo.

It is interesting to note that both films yielded themes that went unsung by Sinatra on the screen, yet enjoyed commercial vocal recordings by the singer—"Monique" from *Kings Go Forth,* and "To Love and Be Loved" from *Some Came Running.*

Charles L. Granata

Kings Row

 1980, Varèse Sarabande, from the film *Kings Row,* Warner Bros. Pictures, 1942 🎬🎬🎬🎬

album notes: Music: Erich Wolfgang Korngold; **Orchestra:** The National Philharmonic Orchestra; **Conductor:** Charles Gerhardt.

Even though he only composed 19 scores during the time he spent in Hollywood between 1935 and 1947, Erich Wolfgang Korngold made a profoundly indelible impression on film music that can still be felt in the scores created today. But while he is best remembered for swashbucklers like *The Adventures of Robin Hood* or *The Sea Hawk,* for which he became justifiably famous, some of his other efforts, notably his music for *Kings Row,* are equally noteworthy.

Based on a popular novel by Henry Bellamann about life in a small town at the turn of the twentieth century, the film, starring Ronald Reagan, Robert Cummings, and Ann Sheridan, is an engrossing drama covering several years in the life of his main protagonists, from childhood to adulthood, and the many changes they go through as their world is being transformed around them. Taking a cue from the story, Korngold delivers one of his most serene and affecting scores, in a superb display of his craft, with many leitmotifs detailing the various characters in the film and their interactions. While not as flamboyant as some of his other creations, *Kings Row* is best remembered today for its main theme, a striking epic tune which Korngold composed before he had a chance to read the script, mistakenly thinking that the "King" in the title referred to another cape-and-dagger yarn. The recording, produced by the com-

poser's son, and lovingly detailed by the National Philharmonic Orchestra conducted by Charles Gerhardt, is essential.

Didier C. Deutsch

Kismet

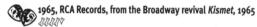 1953, Columbia Records, from the Broadway production *Kismet,* 1953 🎬🎬🎬🎬

album notes: Music: Alexander Borodin; **Musical Adaptation and Lyrics:** Robert Wright, George Forrest; **Musical Direction:** Louis Adrian; **Cast:** Alfred Drake, Doretta Morrow, Richard Kiley, Joan Diener.

1995, Rhino Records, from the film *Kismet,* MGM, 1955 🎬🎬🎬🎬🎬

album notes: Music: Alexander Borodin; **Musical Adaptation and Lyrics:** Robert Wright, George Forrest; **Orchestra:** The MGM Studio Orchestra; **Choir:** The MGM Studio Chorus; **Conductor:** Andre Previn, Jeff Alexander; **Cast:** Howard Keel, Ann Blyth, Vic Damone, Dolores Gray, Monty Wooley, Sebastian Cabot.

1965, RCA Records, from the Broadway revival *Kismet,* 1965 🎬🎬🎬🎬🎬

album notes: Music: Alexander Borodin; **Musical Adaptation and Lyrics:** Robert Wright, George Forrest; **Musical Direction:** Franz Allers; **Cast:** Alfred Drake, Lee Venora, Richard Banke, Anne Jeffreys.

A "musical Arabian Nights" solidly rooted in the traditions of the American theater, *Kismet,* based on a 1911 play by Edward Knoblock, was also the source for two film versions, including one starring Marlene Dietrich and Ronald Coleman. It exhibited an Oriental lushness that won over critics and audiences when it opened on Broadway on Dec. 3, 1953. Many of the musical delights came from Robert Wright and George Forrest's smart adaptations of themes by Alexander Borodin to create their songs for this story. The musical is about an impertinent poet and beggar in ancient Baghdad, who, through his wile and guile, becomes emir of the city overnight (literally, since the action of the musical occurs over a 24-hour period), while his daughter, the lovely Marsinah, marries the Caliph, who has fallen in love with her.

Besides the settings that evoked the Orient with their heavy brocades and colorful designs, audiences were also treated to a legendary, grander-than-life portrayal by Alfred Drake as Hajj, the poet, prancing around the stage with such panache and gusto that the part became forever identified with him. While the show seemed like a sure-fire winner, its opening during a newspaper strike, which prevented New York audiences from knowing what was happening around town, threatened its very existence for a while. It was saved by Tony Bennett's rendering of the song "Stranger in Paradise," a huge radio hit at the time, which prompted many listeners to go and see for themselves what the show was all about. This ensured its success in the first crucial weeks, and guaranteed a long run of 583 performances afterward. While the original cast album, in mono, is not up to today's digital standards, it is a resonant memento of the show as it was heard when it first opened, with Doretta Morrow, Joan Diener, and Richard Kiley, excellent as Marsinah, Lalume (the Wazir's sexy wife, who takes a shine to Hajj), and the Caliph, respectively. Also in the cast was a muscular young man named Steve Reeves. The musical won several Tony Awards that season, including one for Best Musical, and another for Alfred Drake.

In 1955, more luscious and opulent than ever, it exploded on the big screen in a visually stunning film version that starred Howard Keel as Hajj, Ann Blyth as Marsinah, Dolores Gray as Lalume, and Vic Damone as the Caliph. It retained the original score almost intact, including "Baubles, Bangles, and Beads," "And This Is My Beloved," and, of course, "Stranger in Paradise." The deluxe Rhino recording, complete with outtakes, instrumental ballets and songs previously unreleased, also presents the soundtrack in full stereo for the first time.

Alfred Drake returned to the role in a great revival in 1965, in which he starred opposite Anne Jeffreys as Lalume, Lee Venora as Marsinah, and Richard Banke as the Caliph, with Henry Calvin reprising the role of the Wazir that he had created in 1953. This show, which had a limited run over the summer, is documented in the RCA Victor recording. On March 1, 1978, the show returned to Broadway in a revival retitled *Timbuktu!,* noted for the fact that it was mostly a grandiose fashion extravaganza designed by Geoffrey Holder. Somewhat incidentally, it starred Eartha Kitt and Melba Moore, and had a run of 243 performances.

Didier C. Deutsch

Kiss Me, Guido

1997, DVB Records, from the film *Kiss Me, Guido,* Paramount, 1997 🎬🎬🎬

A culture-clash film that recalls *Desperately Seeking Susan* in certain aspects, *Kiss Me Guido* is a delirious farce that takes much of its bounce from its story of an Italian youth, working in a pizza parlor and still living at home in the Bronx, and the gay actor and choreographer from Manhattan with whom he shacks by accident after the latter, seeking a roommate, runs a classified seeking a GWM ("Gay White Male"), which he believes to mean "Guy with Money." From this misunderstanding evolves an unconventional film, slyly peppered with a bunch of disco tunes that accentuate the film's unusual verve. The album simply reflects some of the most interesting songs heard on the soundtrack, in their complete version, including Jerry Herman's gay anthem from *La Cage aux Folles,* "I Am What I Am," powerfully delivered by Gloria Gaynor, another icon of gay nightlife when disco reigned supreme. It's all in good fun, and quite entertaining.

Didier C. Deutsch

Kiss Me, Kate

1998, Sony Classical, from the Broadway production *Kiss Me, Kate,* 1948 🎬🎬🎬🎬

album notes: Music: Cole Porter; **Lyrics:** Cole Porter; **Book:** Bella Spewack, Samuel Spewack; **Musical Direction:** Pembroke Davenport; **Cast:** Alfred Drake, Patricia Morison, Lisa Kirk, Harold Lang, Annabelle Hill, Lorenzo Fuller.

1993, Angel Records, from the Broadway production *Kiss Me, Kate,* 1948 🎬🎬🎬🎬

album notes: Music: Cole Porter; **Lyrics:** Cole Porter; **Musical Direction:** Pembroke Davenport; **Cast:** Alfred Drake, Patricia Morison, Lisa Kirk, Harold Lang, Annabelle Hill, Lorenzo Fuller.

1996, Rhino Records, from the film *Kiss Me Kate,* MGM, 1953 🎬🎬🎬🎬🎬

album notes: Music: Cole Porter; **Lyrics:** Cole Porter; **Choir:** The MGM Studio Chorus; **Orchestra:** The MGM Studio Orchestra; **Conductor:** Andre Previn; **Cast:** Howard Keel, Kathryn Grayson, Ann Miller, Tommy Rall, Bobby Van, Bob Fosse.

A brilliant adaptation of William Shakespeare's *The Taming of the Shrew,* with a superb score by Cole Porter, *Kiss Me, Kate* brought the audience to its feet when it opened on Dec. 30, 1948, before settling for a long run of 1,077 performances. The show starred Alfred Drake as Fred Graham, an egocentric director who portrays Petruchio in a revival of *The Taming of the Shrew,* and Patricia Morison as Lili Vanessi, Fred's tempestuous ex-wife, also cast as Katharina in the play-within-the-musical. *Kiss Me, Kate* had been suggested to Bella and Samuel Spewack, authors of the libretto, by the celebrated backstage feuds between real-life husband and wife thespians Alfred Lunt and Lynn Fontanne. With a significant assist from Cole Porter, writing his best score for this occasion, the musical follows the touring actors, while they play Shakespeare on stage, and continue to battle or make up backstage. Adding spice to the plot, the Spewacks imagined an idyll between Fred and his second leading lady, Lois Lane, who is more interested in another actor, Bill Calhoun.

Commenting on the action, and sometimes punctuating it with clever lyrics, Porter wrote songs that have endured to this day. Many of those songs have passed into the language as colloquialisms, including "Another Op'nin', Another Show," "Tom, Dick, or Harry," "Too Darn Hot," "Were Thine That Special Face," "Wunderbar," a mock Tyrolian duet, "I've Come to Wive It Wealthily in Padua," and "Brush up Your Shakespeare," in which the composer amusingly used malapropisms to spoof those whose ignorance of the English language sometimes leads to confusing expressions.

Kiss Me, Kate won a Tony as Best Musical that season, and also earned awards for its author and composer, among others. The original cast recording, spiffed up and using the original acetates, is a wonderful memento from that glittering show, with

Ann Miller in Kiss Me Kate **(The Kobal Collection)**

the sound quality vastly improved over previous incarnations on LP and CD. As a bonus track, it adds the "Overture," which was recorded in 1958 by Lehman Engel (instead, the 1948 original cast album used the "Entr'acte"). The Rhino recording, again containing much material which is available here for the first time, documents the screen version made by MGM in 1953, with Howard Keel and Kathryn Grayson giving sensational portrayals as Fred and Lili, and Ann Miller incandescent as Lois, whose "Too Darn Hot" was a show-stopper in the film, a big CinemaScope, 3–D production.

Beth Krakower

Kiss of Death

1995, Milan/BMG, from the film Kiss of Death, 20th Century-Fox, 1995 ♫♫♫

album notes: Music: Trevor Jones; **Conductor:** Trevor Jones.

This 1994 remake of the film noir classic, about an informer who turns in some of his mob connections—only to find himself caught in a web of intrigue and treachery in which those he aimed

to save when he made the deal with the police may now be seriously endangered, gave David Caruso (of *NYPD Blue* fame) an early film hit in a role that was at once compelling and sympathetic, opposite Nicolas Cage, Helen Hunt, and Kathryn Erbe.

Reflecting the urban contemporary locale of the action, Trevor Jones's appealingly gritty score sets the tone with cues that echo the dense, claustrophobic atmosphere of the film. Wild synthesizer effects, combined with percolating rhythms against the compact textures of the orchestral strings signal the start of the drama at hand in the "Main Title," with the tension rising through other cues like "Illegal Convoy," "Corinna Is Kidnapped," and "Junior's Arrest." The more introspective "Jimmy's Dilemma," "Junior Suspects," and "Calvin's Revenge" add a dimension of ominous threat and danger to the momentum of the ensemble. It all finds a resolution in the somewhat brighter "End Credits" that reprises the main theme with a note of confidence it didn't have initially, informing that the hero's ordeal may be over. Some pop songs, particularly the excitingly performed "Back in My Life," add an interesting touch to the album.

Didier C. Deutsch

Kiss of the Spider Woman: The Musical

 1992, RCA Victor, from the Broadway production *Kiss of the Spider Woman: The Musical,* **1992** 🎬🎬🎬

album notes: Music: John Kander; **Lyrics:** Fred Ebb; **Musical Direction:** Jeffrey Huard; **Cast:** Chita Rivera, Brent Carver, Anthony Crivello, Merle Louise.

 1995, Mercury Records, from the Broadway production *Kiss of the Spider Woman: The Musical,* **1992** 🎬🎬🎬

album notes: Music: John Kander; **Lyrics:** Fred Ebb; **Musical Direction:** Gregory Dlugos; **Cast:** Vanessa Williams, Howard McGillin, Brian Mitchell, Mimi Turque.

Turning Manuel Puig's unremittingly somber novel, *Kiss of the Spider Woman,* about inmates in a South American prison dreaming about an unsubstantial movie star, into a musical might have seemed at first a rather peculiar idea. However, Terrence McNally, John Kander, and Fred Ebb combined their efforts to meet the challenge head-on, and managed to create a show that was vibrantly alive and original, while remaining faithful to the spirit of the original. Having not one but two cast albums of the same Broadway production might prove more than an embarrassment of riches—a bit of an overkill. Yet, each recording in its own way contributes a different aspect of the musical, with Chita Rivera and Vanessa Williams succeeding in creating portrayals that are sometimes at odds with each other, while at other times complement each other.

One's decision about opting to listen to one or the other (or both) will largely depend on what one expects from an original cast album. By focusing only on the musical numbers, the Chita Rivera–starrer provides an accurate vision of the score itself. The Vanessa Williams recording, by incorporating bits of spoken dialogue to introduce the songs, gives a better idea of the role played by the musical numbers within the greater framework of the play. Ultimately, both are equally successful and equally enjoyable.

Didier C. Deutsch

Kiss the Girls

1997, Milan/BMG, from the Paramount film *Kiss the Girls,* **1997** 🎬🎬

album notes: Music: Mark Isham; **Conductor:** Ken Kluger; **Featured Musician:** Martin Tillmann, cello.

Kiss the Girls started as a best-selling novel by James Patterson. This is another one of these cases where the book is better than the movie, in which a Washington, D.C., forensic psychologist and detective played by Morgan Freeman goes to North Carolina to find his recently abducted niece. Ashley Judd plays another girl who was also abducted but managed to escape, and conveniently helps Freeman find the other missing

women and their captor. A not too terribly exciting soundtrack album, the CD consists of songs, and a score by Mark Isham. For this one, Isham cleverly uses a violin solo and female voices to represent the detective's niece, a violinist. The lengthy "To Cross the Rubicon" is an exciting piece of music with interesting tempo and stylistic changes. But the songs are another matter altogether, with a rap song and an electronic dance track curiously sandwiched between two classic blues.

Beth Krakower

Kissed

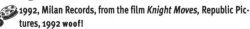 **1997, Unforscene Music, from the film** *Kissed,* **Goldwyn Entertainment, 1997** 🎬🎬

album notes: Music: Don MacDonald.

The pop songs that are used in this soundtrack album, mostly pleasant it should be pointed out, don't say much about the action of this weird film about a girl who has a fixation about death and dead people. The point is quickly made in the first track, a voice-over in which the main character, played by Molly Parker, explains her feelings. Throughout the recording other tracks further comment on the "action" in the film and serve as an introduction of sorts for the songs. Not what you might call the most uplifting thing, despite the fact that the songs, in a soft-rock mold, are relatively pleasant.

Didier C. Deutsch

The Knack . . . and How to Get It

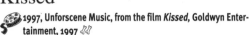 **1998, Rykodisc, from the film** *The Knack . . . and How to Get It,* **United Artists, 1965** 🎬🎬🎬

album notes: Music: John Barry; **Conductor:** John Barry; **Featured Musician:** Alan Haven, organ.

This stylish movie, a Best Picture winner at the 1965 Cannes Film Festival, was directed by Richard Lester in between his filming of *A Hard Day's Night* and *Help,* and elicited a stylish, jazz-tinged pop score from composer John Barry. Featuring the organ work of Alan Haven—the organ was a popular instrument that year—it is very representative of the era when it was created. Listening to it 35 years later, the score has matured from mod to retro quite nicely.

Didier C. Deutsch

Knight Moves

1992, Milan Records, from the film *Knight Moves,* **Republic Pictures, 1992 woof!**

album notes: Music: Anne Dudley; **Orchestra:** The Pro Arte Orchestra of London; **Conductor:** Anne Dudley; **Featured Musicians:** Phil Todd, saxophone; Anne Dudley, keyboards; Andy Pask, bass; Harold Fisher, drums; Luis Jardim, percussion.

A mindless collection of synthesized noises (including ambient sound effects) with no distinct melody or musical direction. Anne Dudley has the nerve to claim she composed, orchestrated, and conducted this repetitive mess. Not nearly as exciting as watching paint dry. Best used by the F.B.I. to force militiamen out of their compounds by repetitive performance.

David Hirsch

Knights of the Round Table

1983, Varèse Sarabande, from the film *Knights of the Round Table*, MGM, 1953 ♪♪♪♪

album notes: Music: Miklos Rozsa; **Orchestra:** The MGM Studio Orchestra, **Conductor:** Muir Mathieson.

Knights of the Round Table reunited composer Miklos Rozsa with the star, Robert Taylor, and the creative staff, director Richard Thorpe and producer Pandro S. Berman, who had presided over the success of *Ivanhoe* two years before. But while this big screen epic retelling of the legend of King Arthur, based on Sir Thomas Mallory's *Le Morte d'Arthur,* seems to have everything going for it, its characters don't exhibit the spirit and dash of those in the previous film. There are quite a few scenes of battles and jousts to delight fans of the medieval epic genre, spectacularly filmed in CinemaScope, but the pageantry seems to lose some of its shine next to this story about the alleged infidelities of Queen Guinevere, smitten by the handsome Lancelot du Lac, and the web of deceit and villainy that her enemies, the malevolent Sir Mordred and the baleful Morgan Le Fay, spin around her.

True to form, Rozsa nonetheless delivered a score that has all the elements of bravura needed for this handsome spectacle, creating cues that cover every ground in the story, from the exciting battle scenes to the romantic sweep of the love scenes to the religious overtones that permeate some of the most inspirational moments in the medieval tale. The recording, an early transfer from the 1953 stereo master tapes, generally lacks warmth and would benefit from a better EQ to correct its harsh, hollow sound. The CD also contains a piano suite from *Lydia,* a 1941 drama starring Merle Oberon as an older woman reunited after 35 years with the inconsistent lover who deserted her.

Didier C. Deutsch

Krull

1992, SCSE Records, from the film *Krull,* Columbia Pictures, 1983 ♪♪♪♪♪

album notes: Music: James Horner; **Orchestra:** The London Symphony Orchestra; **Conductor:** James Horner; **Featured Musicians:** The Ambrosian Singers.

A fantasy tale of epic proportions about a young prince and the maiden-in-distress he has to rescue from a malevolent Beast and its dark forces before the closing titles, *Krull* exhibits all the swashbuckling ingredients dear to fans of the genre, including an impressive score composed for the occasion by James Horner, in one of his earliest efforts in this field. Using the huge forces at his disposal, the London Symphony Orchestra, one of the best orchestras in the world for this type of music, the Ambrosian Singers, another respected group, and the discrete contribution of synthesizers to add extra texture to his score, Horner created cues that underline the sweep of this sword-and-sorcery saga, in bold, exciting strokes. Many moments in this recording, an expanded version containing many selections that were previously unavailable, reveal the composer's genuine feel for the genre, an impression he confirmed in later years, with grand themes that unfold with all the power and majesty usually associated with this kind of musical expression.

Didier C. Deutsch

Kull the Conqueror

1997, Varèse Records, from the film *Kull the Conqueror,* Universal, 1997 ♪♪♪♪

album notes: Music: Joel Goldsmith; **Conductor:** Nicolas Dodd.

A Conan clone, *Kull the Conqueror* was based on the 1930s pulp novels by Robert E. Howard, about a mythical muscleman who is still a bit of a barbarian, but whose intelligence and his muscles make him somewhat superior to many of his contemporaries. The story, which happily blends elements of fantasy and wizardry, finds Kull as a benign monarch whose authority is challenged by an evil temptress, conjured up from ancient times by a sorcerer working for Kull's enemies. In order to defeat her, the conqueror must go to the ends of the globe to find the "breath of Valka," the only thing that can effectively destroy her.

As befits such a subject matter, Joel Goldsmith wrote an impressive score that calls for a large symphonic orchestra and chorus. The scope of the narrative and its wealth of material provided the composer with the right elements to create a broad tapestry in which bright, colorful themes aim to tell the action in musical terms. With a flurry of brassy effects, wild trumpet calls, pounding drums, crystalline chimes making up the essential textures, sometimes used against a rock beat and riffs from an electric guitar, the result is never less than mesmerizing, and aurally challenging. Some cues emerge as more particularly winning, like the solidly defined "Ship Brawl" or "Ride to Tetheli." But others, more quiet and delicate, show Goldsmith with a definite flair for writing romantic material that is quite attractive. Since the accent here is on action pure and simple, these cues are rare and the relentless drive in the score is the dominant note.

Didier C. Deutsch

La Bamba

1987, Slash/Warner Bros. Records, from the film *La Bamba*, Columbia Pictures, 1987 ♪♪♪♪

album notes: Featured Musicians: Los Lobos; Howard Huntsberry; Marshall Crenshaw; Brian Setzer; Bo Diddley.

Okay, so it's a little weird that this soundtrack from a film about the late Richie Valens doesn't include a single performance by him, nor is there a single songwriting credit for him in the booklet. That's legalities, for you. But if anyone is going to fill his spot, it should be Los Lobos, who do a masterful job on all of his hits and scored a smash of their own with the title track. But don't overlook ace performances by Marshall Crenshaw on Buddy Holly's "Crying, Waiting, Hoping," Brian Setzer on Eddie Cochran's "Summertime Blues," and Howard Huntsberry on Jackie Wilson's "Lonely Teardrops."

Gary Graff

La Baule-les-Pins

1990, Philips/France, from the film *La Baule-les-Pins*, Alexandre, 1990 ♪♪♪♪

album notes: Music: Philippe Sarde.

Perhaps because the setting of the film, a seaside village in Western France in the mid- to late-1950s, reminded me so much of my youth in a similar resort, I instantly fell in love with Diane Kurys' light summer vacation comedy about a single woman, recently separated from her husband, and her two kids, a growing teenage girl and her younger brother. Totally delightful and convincingly real, it elicited a perfect score from Sarde, who captured in his music the subtly evanescent charm of a summer evening, the characteristic aroma of the sea mixed with the pungent odor of the pine trees, and the unique feel of the warm sand. The film had a short career in this country, but I have been playing this album since it first came out, and have never tired of it. "Dream Lover" by Bobby Darin and "Twilight Time" by The Platters add to the overall pleasure. This title may be out of print or just plain hard to find. Mail-order companies, used CD shops, or dealers of rare or import recordings will be your best bet.

Didier C. Deutsch

La belle et la bete

1996, Marco Polo Records, from the film *La belle et la bete*, Gaumont Films, 1946 ♪♪♪♪♪

album notes: Music: Georges Auric; Orchestra: The Moscow Symphony Orchestra; Axios Chorus; Conductor: Adriano.

French composer Georges Auric's music for Jean Cocteau's 1946 French version of *Beauty and the Beast* is sumptuously classical. In the early scenes in the haunted forest and in the Beast's castle, the music takes on a darker tonality. But much of the score, quiet and static, is delicate—non-moving figures and chords emphasizing the unusualness of the setting and the events, which contrast nicely with those moments when Auric lets loose with audible energy. At times, the music takes on an almost balletic quality, equally as impressionistic as Cocteau's direction and the marvelous sets designed by Christian Berard. Throughout, a choir is used to emphasize the monstrous nature of the Beast, echoing emotions he is unable to verbalize. The CD contains the complete score, including those cues deleted from either or both the American and French prints of the film. A 16-page booklet is included, with plenty of black-and-white photos and notes on the film, the music, and the composer.

Randall D. Larson

La Cage aux Folles

1983, RCA Victor, from the Broadway production *La Cage aux Folles*, 1983 ♪♪♪♪♪

album notes: Music: Jerry Herman; Lyrics: Jerry Herman; Musical Direction: Donald Pippin; Cast: Gene Barry, George Hearn, John Weiner, Merle Louise.

It probably took a dare to bring to the musical stage, particularly on Broadway where traditions run high, a show that centered around the love relationship between two men, Georges, owner of a gay club known as La Cage aux Folles, and Albin, who, as Zaza, headlines the revue presented at the club, in which all the performers are boys dressed as girls. It might have helped that the show is set on the French Riviera, where, as we know, spirits are generally much looser than they are in America. But the fact of the matter is that *La Cage aux Folles* is an old-fashioned Broadway musical in the best sense of the word, with at its core a perfectly standard love affair. The rest of the plot, loosely based on the French stage play by Jean Poiret (also the source for the film of the same name, and the more recent remake titled *The Birdcage)* involved the various shenanigans to which Georges and Albin were subjected when Georges's son (an accident!) decides he wants to marry the daughter of a champion of morality, who insists on meeting his future son–in–law's relatives. With a brilliant score by Jerry Herman (which included such show–stopping numbers as "Song on the Sand," "The Best of Times," "With Anne on My Arm," and the defiant anthem "I Am What I Am"), the musical opened to rave reviews on Aug. 21, 1983, for a run of 1,176 performances.

Didier C. Deutsch

La Citta delle Donne

1991, CAM Records/Italy, from the film *La Citta delle Donne* (*City of Women*), Opera/Gaumont, 1980 ✍✍✍✍

album notes: Music: Luis Bacalov.

In scoring Federico Fellini's *City of Women,* Luis Bacalov was faced with an almost impossible task: the recent death of Nino Rota, Fellini's composer of choice, meant that anyone creating the music for a new film by the celebrated director would automatically be compared (probably unfavorably) with Rota. Bacalov, a longtime friend and student of Rota, tried somewhat unsuccessfully to circumvent the problem by creating music that faintly evoked his predecessor, though he also added touches that were definitely his own, and by drawing from the vast catalogue of American pop songs, as Rota had done before him, most notably in *La dolce vita.*

As a result, Bacalov quoted such favorites as "Charleston," "Yes, Sir, That's My Baby," "Ramona," "Night and Day," and "Mack the Knife," the better to give the score for *City of Women* its specific flavor. He may not have been able to erase the memory of Rota, whose music was so intrinsically tied to Fellini's cinematographic vision, but at least he tried to be original. As a result, this score is frequently arresting, and invites repeated listening. This recording may be difficult to find. Check with a used CD store, mail-order company, or a dealer specializing in rare, out-of-print, or import recordings.

Didier C. Deutsch

L.A. Confidential

1997, Varèse Sarabande, from the film *L.A. Confidential,* Regency Entertainment, 1997 ✍✍✍✍✟

album notes: Music: Jerry Goldsmith; **Conductor:** Jerry Goldsmith; **Featured Musician:** Malcolm McNab, trumpet, flugelhorn.

1997, Restless, from the film *L.A. Confidential,* Regency Entertainment, 1997 ✍✍✍✍

album notes: Music: Jerry Goldsmith.

A *film noir* appropriately set in Los Angeles in the 1940s, *L.A. Confidential* was the story of a Philip Marlowe-type detective, working for the department, who finds himself caught in a labyrinthine web of intrigue, mystery, ambition, romance, and humor dominated by a blonde femme fatale, some unsavory cops, dubious street characters, and other assorted villains.

Embodying both the action and the locale, Jerry Goldsmith's score is a vibrant exercise in which pounding rhythms inform the drama, while a main theme, beautifully detailed by the trumpet, gives the score a mysterious edge totally appropriate. Unnerving piano chords, oft repeated, also signal the tension in the screen action. Cue after cue, the themes build to a

crescendo, paralleling the upward movements in the detective inquiry, his discovery of various seemingly unrelated clues that mean nothing at first, until the whole thing finally adds up, leading to a dramatic conclusion.

Two additional instrumental cues can also be found in the "song" album, in which the selections of songs by Johnny Mercer, Chet Baker, Gerry Mulligan, Lee Wiley, Kay Starr, and Jackie Gleason, among others, perfectly situate the time frame of this excellent thriller. Both releases complement each other, providing in this case a perfect musical picture to an important film.

Didier C. Deutsch

La dolce vita

1991, CAM Records, from the film, *La dolce vita,* Cineriz Films, 1959 ✍✍✍✍

album notes: Music: Nino Rota; **Conductor:** Carlo Savina.

While they worked together before and subsequently, *La dolce vita* is the closest Federico Fellini and Nino Rota ever came to creating a film in which the images and the music are so intimately interwoven. In fact, it now seems difficult to separate one from the other, as the cues devised by the composer matched so beautifully the suggestive power of the film's best remembered scenes, from the dissonant three-note motif in "Via Veneto," to the wistful trumpet solo in "Lola," to the bluesy "La dolce vita dei nobili," with its organ counterpoint, to its wild Latin take on the Christmas standard "Jingle Bells." Truly a momentous film steeped in its own time period but as exciting today as it was at the time, *La dolce vita* yielded one of the most memorable soundtracks in Rota's extraordinarily active and prolific career. One word of warning: even though this CD claims that it was remastered in Dolby Surround, it is obviously a transfer from LP source, a fact confirmed by the apparent surface noise on some of the quieter selections.

Didier C. Deutsch

La Feccia

1999, Screen Trax/Italy, from the film *La Feccia (The Revengers),* National General Pictures, 1972 ✍✍✍

album notes: Music: Pino Calvi; **Conductor:** Pino Calvi.

William Holden starred in this tale about a Civil War veteran who, upon returning to his ranch in Colorado, discovers that his wife and four kids have been killed by a band of roaming Comanches. Putting together a motley group of gunfighters, whose volatile temperaments make them totally unpredictable, he proceeds to chase after the Comanches, and eventually exacts revenge with the help of an Army company. Along for the ride in this anti-*Wild Bunch* were Ernest Borgnine, Woody

Strode, Roger Hanin, and Susan Hayward, the last making a sudden appearance as Holden's love interest. If the premise sounds predictable, so is the score devised by Pino Calvi, a standard collection of themes with uncharacteristic pop arrangements. Electric guitar riffs, supported by French horns and percussions, detail the action itself, while the more romantic aspects are given a subdued reading by the bass flute and strings. Not a bad score, all things considered, though not a great one either. This title may be out of print or just plain hard to find. Mail-order companies, used CD shops, or dealers of rare or import recordings will be your best bet.

Didier C. Deutsch

La femme d'à côté

🎞️ 1994, SLC/Japan, from the film *La femme d' à côté (The Woman Next Door),* United Artists Classics, 1983 🎵🎵🎵🎵

album notes: Music: Georges Delerue; **Conductor:** Georges Delerue.

The setpiece in this great score by Georges Delerue for Francois Truffaut's *The Woman Next Door* is "Garden Party," an 8:00+ cue that plays around a cool jazz riff. It is one of the great moments in the Delerue catalogue of themes that helps give the scene a specific atmosphere, yet serves as a counterpoint to much of the tragic action that precedes and follows that moment. Starring star-crossed lovers Gerard Depardieu, a presumably happily married man, and Fanny Ardant, as the woman next door, who get back together with dire consequences, years after they first fell in love, the film elicited a hauntingly florid score from Delerue, writing in a vigorous vein, that detailed much of the dramatic action in uncompromising terms. Typical of the composer, many of the cues are extremely short, but packed with musical ideas that actually make them seem longer and more effective. An important, memorable score. (Coupled with *Le dernier metro,* another essential Delerue score, *La femme d'à côté* can also be found on a release from Prometheus, in Belgium.) This recording may be difficult to find. Check with a used CD store, mail-order company, or a dealer specializing in rare, out-of-print, or import recordings.

Didier C. Deutsch

La Femme Nikita

🎞️ 1990, Varèse Sarabande, from the film *La Femme Nikita,* Gaumont Films, 1990 🎵🎵

album notes: Music: Eric Serra; **Featured Musician:** Gilbert Dal-l'Anese, saxophone.

📺 1998, TVT Records, from the TV series *La Femme Nikita,* Warner Bros., 1998 🎵🎵🎵

album notes: Music: Mark Snow.

Today, Eric Serra is perhaps better known in this country for his scores for *GoldenEye* and *The Fifth Element,* two efforts that called attention to his talent as a composer. In France, where his music for Luc Besson's *Le grand bleu* and *La Femme Nikita* have made him a household name, he is considered one of the most important film composers of the new generation. His artistic merits notwithstanding (his score for *GoldenEye* was roundly panned), there is no denying the feel that emanates from his contributions, in which the extensive use of synthesizers give a definite accent to his music. Nowhere is this more evident than in *La Femme Nikita,* a techno-pop effort with heavy-layered synthesizer melodies, set against various percussive effects that range from electronic drumming to finger-snapping. The music itself is meant to create an atmosphere that echoes the moods of this cloak-and-dagger story about a strikingly attractive criminal recruited by a secret government agency to carry off dangerous missions, including the elimination of enemies from the "other" side. Characteristic of Serra's contributions, the cues often match the screen action, but turn out to be dry and austere in a musical environment. They fail to really grab one's interest when taken on their own terms, though "The Last Time I Kiss You," an all-too-brief simple melody on the piano, makes a different and much more attractive statement.

Mark Snow can now boast of having composed the main themes to two of the coolest television series: *The X-Files* and *La Femme Nikita.* Which does not necessarily means that he is a great composer, simply that his weird electronic effects have caught the fancy of televiewers. This said, he is also virtually absent from this soundtrack album: beyond the "Main Title," you won't find any of the pseudo techno-rock themes he's developed for the popular series. Instead, the album offers a generous sampling of some of the pop/rock tunes heard here and there during the course of the action, without further identifying the episodes in which they might have been heard. So, without further ado, you'll find tracks by Enigma, Depeche Mode, Curve, Morphine, and Gus Gus, among the less cerebral exponents of a certain pop music. Some of it is quite good ("Beyond the Invisible," "Fear and Love," "Skin against Skin"), and some of it is just . . . well, noise ("Loaded Gun," "Chinese Burn," "Gun").

Didier C. Deutsch

La maja desnuda

🎞️ 1997, CAM Records/Italy, from the film *La maja desnuda (The Naked Maja),* United Artists, 1959 🎵🎵🎵🎵

album notes: Music: Angelo Francisco Lavagnino; **Conductor:** Carlo Savina.

Directed by Henry Koster and set in 18th–century Spain, a land of strange contrasts, where dancing feet echoed in the streets at fiesta time even as the rumble of revolution arose around the royal palace, this fanciful film starred Ava Gardner as the inconstant lady of the title, the attractive Duchess of Alba, and Anthony Franciosa as Francisco Goya, who painted two similar portraits of the Duchess languorously reclining, one dressed, the other undressed, much to the outcry of their contemporaries. The turbulent, colorful background found an echo in Angelo Francisco Lavagnino's score, uninhibited, hot blooded, a symphony of pulsating rhythms with a hidden flow of sadness in which sobbing guitars spoke of loneliness and yearning. This title may be out of print or just plain hard to find. Mail-order companies, used CD shops, or dealers of rare or import recordings will be your best bet.

Didier C. Deutsch

La ragazza di Bube

1991, CAM Records/Italy, from the film *La ragazza di Bube (Bebo's Girl)*, 1964 🎬🎬🎬🎬

album notes: Music: Carlo Rustichelli; **Conductor:** Carlo Rustichelli.

Set in war-torn Tuscany, *Bebo's Girl* was a simple, impassioned love story that starred George Chakiris as Bebo and Claudia Cardinale as his girl, Mara. When Bebo gets involved in a political murder and is sent to jail, Mara meets a worker, Stefano, who proposes marriage to her, but she refuses, preferring to wait for Bebo's release. Based on the novel by Carlo Cassola, and directed with great empathy by Luigi Comencini, the film further benefitted from the excellent score composed by Carlo Rustichelli, built around two basic themes—a doleful one, played in a duet by the trumpet and the saxophone, to evoke the tragic figure of Bebo, and a more florid, romantic one to detail the love that binds him and Mara. Strongly effective and strikingly delineated, it is a particularly memorable and attractive score. This recording may be difficult to find. Check with a used CD store, mail-order company, or a dealer specializing in rare, out-of-print, or import recordings.

Didier C. Deutsch

La spina dorsale del diavolo

1997, Legend Records/Italy, from the film *La spina dorsale del diavolo (The Deserter)*, 1986 🎬🎬🎬🎬

album notes: Music: Piero Piccioni; **Conductor:** Piero Piccioni.

Richard Crenna, Woody Strode, Chuck Connors, Ricardo Montalban, Patrick Wayne, Slim Pickens, and John Huston as General Miles were among the luminaries who found themselves involved in this mess about marauding Indians and Cavalry men squaring it off near the Mexican border around 1880. For the most part, these illustrious actors were doing a fine job, but they and the film itself were done in by a very unfocused

script and by the acting of Bekim Fehmiu, who decided to top his terrible performance earlier that same year in *The Adventurers . . .* and succeeded. Regardless, Piero Piccioni wrote a solid western-style score filled with ominous accents and pounding rhythms no one paid attention to in the movies (mesmerized as they were by Fehmiu's lack of talent), but which make a generally favorable impression in this CD. This title may be out of print or just plain hard to find. Mail-order companies, used CD shops, or dealers of rare or import recordings will be your best bet.

Didier C. Deutsch

La strada/Le notti di Cabiria

1992, Legend Records/Italy, from the films *La strada*, Paramount, 1954, and *Le notti di Cabiria (The Nights of Cabiria)*, Paramount, 1957 🎬🎬🎬🎬

album notes: La strada: Music: Nino Rota; **Conductor:** Franco Ferrara; **Le notti di Cabiria: Music:** Nino Rota; **Conductor:** Franco Ferrara.

Two essential early scores by Nino Rota for films by Fellini have been combined together in one release, making it a double delight for collectors and fans. The film that put Fellini on the international map, *La strada* is remembered as one of the few classic movies ever made anywhere—the touching story of a simple-minded girl, Gelsomina, portrayed by Giulietta Masina, victimized by the brutal circus strongman Zampano, played by Anthony Quinn, and in love with a quiet acrobat (Richard Basehart). Equally memorable, *The Nights of Cabiria* told the story of a golden-hearted prostitute, unhappy in love, who believes she has found at last the man of her dreams, only to be disillusioned one more time. Another classic in the Fellini *oeuvre*, it became the basis for Broadway's *Sweet Charity* (q.v.). The haunting theme Rota wrote for *La strada* has become part of the standard repertoire, making the score itself relatively well known around the world. Well suited for the circus atmosphere of the film, its forced joyful accents are a perfect counterpoint to the forlorn theme of Gelsomina. Less familiar, perhaps, though Rota eventually reprised some of its themes later on in other films, the music for *The Nights of Cabiria* is equally descriptive and compelling, with a strong kinship to *La strada* ("La trattoria" and "Waiting for Giorgio"), but with livelier accents that suit this bittersweet tale better. On a purely technical basis, the first one is flawed by poor editing, surface noises, and other technical problems that probably could have been corrected; the second sounds much better. This recording may be difficult to find. Check with a used CD store, mail-order company, or a dealer specializing in rare, out-of-print, or import recordings.

Didier C. Deutsch

La tenda rossa

🎬 **1994, Legend Records/Italy, from the film *La tenda rossa (The Red Tent)*, Paramount, 1970** 🎵🎵🎵🎵

album notes: Music: Ennio Morricone; **Conductor:** Bruno Nicolai; **Featured Musician:** Dino Asciolla, violin.

The true story of General Umberto Nobile, whose 1928 exploration of the Arctic ended tragically, *The Red Tent* was an exciting man-against-elements saga that was powerfully enhanced by an all-star cast (Sean Connery, Claudia Cardinale, Hardy Kruger, and Peter Finch, among others), gorgeous photography, and a remarkable, moving score by Ennio Morricone. While the individual cues, anchored by a striking "Love Theme," which recurs throughout, detail various moments in the action, the most compelling track in this score album is the 22:20 tone poem, "Others, Who Will Follow Us," which reprises the main themes and develops them into a richly textured, all-encompassing suite alone worth the price of this CD. This title may be out of print or just plain hard to find. Mail-order companies, used CD shops, or dealers of rare or import recordings will be your best bet.

Didier C. Deutsch

Labyrinth

🎬 **1986, EMI America, from the film *Labyrinth*, Tri Star 1986** 🎵🎵🎵

album notes: Music: Trevor Jones; **Conductor:** Trevor Jones; **Featured Performer:** David Bowie; **Featured Musicians:** Ray Russell, lead guitar; Nicky Moroch, lead guitar; Albert Collins, lead guitar; Dan Huff, guitar; Jeff Mironov, guitar; Kevin Armstrong, guitar; Paul Westwood, bass guitar; Will Lee, bass; Matthew Seligman, bass; Harold Fisher,

drums; Neil Conti, drums; Steve Ferrone, drums; Nick Plytas, keyboards; Robbie Buchanan, keyboards; David Lanson, keyboards; Brian Gascoigne, keyboards; Trevor Jones, keyboards; Richard Tee, acoustic piano, Hammond B-3 organ; Ray Warleigh, saxophone; Bob Gay, saxophone; Maurice Murphy, trumpet.

Five new David Bowie songs are the selling point for this album, and none of them have popped up on any of his various career retrospectives—an indication of how crucial they are, even though Bowie was in the midst of a major commercial renaissance at the time. It's worth noting that he collaborated on these with lush popmaster Arif Mardin, and Bowie has always done better work with edgier, more adventurous cohorts.

Gary Graff

Lady and the Tramp

🎬 **1998, Disney Records, from the film *Lady and the Tramp*, Walt Disney, 1955** 🎵🎵🎵🎵

album notes: Music: Peggy Lee, Sonny Burke.

This delightful animated feature, about a streetwise stray dog and the well-groomed "lady" he befriends and eventually saves from a most frightening fate, has finally yielded a complete recording of the songs and themes written for it by Peggy Lee and Sonny Burke. Perfectly adapted to the charming story, the songs are in turn elegiac ("Bella Notte," sung by an Italian restaurant owner to Lady and Scamp, while they eat spaghetti), threatening ("The Siamese Cat Song," in which Peggy Lee duets with herself), sexy ("He's a Tramp," performed in torch style by a "hot mama" lady dog who has seen it all), or just plain familiar and humorous ("Home Sweet Home," performed by a dog barbershop quartet). The instrumental selections, many of them available here for the first time, help situate the action: Lady's encounter with Scamp, their running off together, and their eventual settling down, after many adventures in territories unfamiliar to the little Lady. It's perfectly charming and enjoyable, and will delight everyone who has fond memories of this Disney film.

Didier C. Deutsch

Lady, Be Good!

🎬 **1992, Elektra Records, from the studio cast recording *Lady, Be Good!* 1992** 🎵🎵🎵🎵🎵

album notes: Music: George Gershwin; **Lyrics:** Ira Gershwin; **Musical Direction:** Eric Stern; **Cast:** Lara Teeter, Ann Morrison, Jason Alexander, Michael Maguire, Michelle Nicastro.

George and Ira Gershwin made their first splash on Broadway with *Lady, Be Good!* a jazzy, tuneful musical that opened on Dec. 1, 1924, and pretty much set the tone for the type of music one would hear in the musical theatre for the rest of the decade. Significantly, the show also introduced the song–and–dance team of Fred and Adele Astaire, who would go on to dominate the stage as the leading Broadway performers until Adele decided to retire to get married, while Fred chose to continue in Hollywood with other partners.

Though its plot was, by modern standards, rather simplistic, the show endured for 330 performances, largely due to the fetching presence of its stars and the great score by the Gershwins. The score introduced such standards as "Fascinating Rhythm," and "Oh, Lady Be Good," among its many memorable numbers. The studio cast recording on Elektra, part of a series documenting all the musicals by the Gershwins, features a cast of well-trained Broadway performers who extract all the juice and fun from the score.

Didier C. Deutsch

Lady Sings the Blues

1972, Motown Records, from the film *Lady Sings the Blues*, Paramount Pictures, 1972 ♪♪♪♪

album notes: Music: Michel Legrand; **Conductor:** Gil Askey; **Featured Musician:** Diana Ross.

While this soundtrack album is probably best thought of as a Diana Ross album, the singer, portraying the great Billie Holiday in her screen debut, is only heard in about half the selections, arguably the best tracks here and the hits associated with her screen persona. Whether Ross was actually suited to impersonate Holiday is a matter better left to others, who may debate if the film should have emphasized Ross interpreting Holiday, rather than Ross as Holiday. The fact remains that Diana Ross did a most commendable job as an actress, and actually performed the songs created by Holiday with the passion and gusto that seemed required. Of course the styles of both singers are quite different, and where Holiday was more conversant in jazz, Ross's forte is pop and soul, a nuance that will more or less dictate where the listener's own reaction to the album may be.

The rest of the album, with a few exceptions, consists of instrumental selections written by Michel Legrand, often reduced to their simplest expression and masked by chunks of dialogue taken from the soundtrack, something of a disservice to a composer with an impressive track record. As a result, the rating here refers to Ross and her performance, and not to Legrand's contribution.

Didier C. Deutsch

Ladyhawke

1995, GNP Crescendo, from the film *Ladyhawke*, Warner Bros./20th Century-Fox, 1985 ♪♪♪♪

album notes: Music: Andrew Powell; **Conductor:** Andrew Powell.

Andrew Powell's robust and energetic soundtrack for Richard Donner's romantic medieval adventure might sound dated to some with its very '80s synths, but most listeners aren't going to care. A powerful outing with memorable themes and enough passion to fill up several ordinary soundtracks, *Ladyhawke* is a stirring effort marked by potent orchestral passages, many of which are being heard on this expanded soundtrack CD for the first time. In fact, the music's then-contemporary roots are much less evident when listening to the entire score now than from the most egregiously "pop" sections memory instantly recalls. Producer Alan Parsons assisted Powell on the music's production, resulting in a score that's unabashedly romantic and melodramatic, a listener favorite that has weathered the years better than one might expect.

Andy Dursin

Land and Freedom

1995, DRG Records, from the film *Land and Freedom*, Gramercy Pictures, 1995 ♪♪♪

album notes: Music: George Fenton; **Conductor:** George Fenton; **Featured Musician:** Anthony Pleeth, cello.

A sweeping contemporary drama set in the early days of the Spanish Civil War, *Land and Freedom* follows the personal saga of a young factory worker from Liverpool who goes to Spain in 1936 to fight fascism, only to find the Republicans bitterly divided into rival groups. Once he gets involved, he find himself torn between his loyalty to the Communist Party and to the militia whom he has joined, with tragic consequences that result when he has to take sides. Adding strength to this personal struggle and the broader conflict in the background, George Fenton's music is at once eloquent and evocative. In contrast to the turmoil in the narrative, the score is mostly lyrical in its expression and seems at first understated, but eventually emerges as greatly powerful as a result. Songs from the period in Spanish add the right ethnic color to the soundtrack.

Didier C. Deutsch

The Land Before Time

1988, MCA Records, from the animated feature *The Land Before Time*, Universal Pictures, 1988 ♪♪♪♪♪

album notes: Music: James Horner; **Orchestra:** The London Symphony Orchestra; The King's College Choir; **Conductor:** James Horner.

Though the recording only contains six tracks of instrumental cues, the long playing time of these selections enables the music to evolve and gradually make its impact, providing the listener with better parameters to enjoy it and formulate an opinion than if the cues were shorter. The result is a score which, though written for an animated feature and possibly deemed a minor exercise because of it, is wonderful. It's filled with inventive melodic themes that involve the participation of

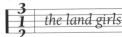

various solo instruments, a large choir, and the vivid orchestral colors of the London Symphony. Horner, a master at this type of music, seems to know intuitively how to use each element in this broad canvas to come up with a music that is solidly attractive and consistently fun to listen to. In this context, it matters little if the music fits the narrative, or how it serves it. Judged on its own merits it does what any good score should do—provide hours of listening delight and invite repeat performances.

Didier C. Deutsch

The Land Girls

1998, Silva America, from the film *The Land Girls*, Gramercy, 1998 ♪♪♪♪

album notes: Music: Brian Lock; **Conductor:** David Firman; **Featured Soloists:** Julian Jackson, harmonica; Susan Milan, flute; Mitch Dalton, guitar; Leslie Pearson, piano.

Set in England during World War II, *The Land Girls,* an affecting story about three young women who join the Women's Land Army, organized to help farms in need of workers while the men are away fighting, introduces a new composer with a distinctive voice and a great deal of talent. Brian Lock, whose previous efforts have included Jane Campion's *The Portrait of a Lady* and Karoly Makk's *The Gambler,* has created here a vibrant score, beautifully expressive, in which the solo instruments—harmonica, flute, guitar, and piano—help outline the forlorn aspects of the film and enhance its nostalgic appeal. Divided into sections, each relating to a major character in the film or, in one case, the locale in which the action takes place, the score is a gorgeous collection of themes, simply etched and deeply affective. The moods vary, from an exuberant waltz that recalls Georges Delerue ("Blissful Happiness"), to an emotional expression with a sadder edge ("Shattered Dreams"), or to a swinging moment ("The Sidelong Slide"), but the whole effort comes forcefully across as a splendid example of film music at its best. The only drawback here is the fact that some cues seem unfinished or unrealized, ending with a question mark rather than a coda.

Didier C. Deutsch

Larger Than Life

1996, Milan Records, from the film *Larger Than Life,* United Artists, 1996 ♪♪♪

album notes: Music: Miles Goodman; **Conductor:** Miles Goodman.

Sadly, this outrageous Bill Murray comedy about a man and the elephant he takes on a cross-country trip, was the last film composer Miles Goodman scored before he passed away at the age of 47. Goodman, an accomplished film composer and record producer, left a scant recorded legacy even though he wrote the scores for more than 35 films. Stylistically, his music

is enjoyably lightweight and makes few demands on the intellect, though it proves suitably charming and melodious. The seven selections found here under his name denote a flair for broad comedy underscoring, with "Salad Bar," a rousing rag, "Flying Elephant," a brassy anthem, and "Airport Chase," a fast-paced ditty, among the most inspired moments.

Didier C. Deutsch

L'Armata Brancaleone /Brancaleone alle Crociate

1995, EMI-Point Records/Italy, from the films *L'Armata Brancaleone (The Brancaleone Army),* 1966; and *Brancaleone alle Crociate (Brancaleone at the Crusades),* 1970 ♪♪♪♪♪

album notes: L'Armata Brancaleone: Music: Carlo Rustichelli; **Conductor:** Bruno Nicolai; **Choir conductor:** Piero Carapellucci; **Brancaleone alle Crociate: Music:** Carlo Rustichelli; **Conductor:** Gianfranco Plenizio; **Choir conductor:** Piero Carapellucci.

A joyfully hilarious comedy and its sequel, *L'Armata Brancaleone* and *Brancaleone alla Cruciate* told the outrageous adventures of Brancaleone, a pseudo-historic errant knight who is a mixture of Don Quixote and Ivanhoe rolled into one. Starring Vittorio Gassmann in the title role, the two films detailed the alleged exploits of this one-army character for whom the term braggadocio was probably invented. Matching the spirits of the two films, Carlo Rustichelli wrote mock heroic scores that are raucously hilarious, and are framed by the Brancaleone "March," itself a hooter. Often, the cues evoke the action as much as the hilarious turns it takes, and the epoch and locales in which it happens, often with delightful results. Even a cue as straightforward as "Brancaleone e Matelda," the love theme in the first film, or "Brancaleone e Felicilla," its counterpart in the second, cannot remain serious too long, and soon develops a wry wink of its own in the direction of the listening audience. Taking no chances, Rustichelli also gleefully quoted from Wagner's *Ring* in "Un prezioso bottino," one of many similar pleasures that await the discerning listener. Perhaps not very deep, where music is concerned, but totally enjoyable and fun from start to finish. This recording may be difficult to find. Check with a used CD store, mail-order company, or a dealer specializing in rare, out-of-print, or import recordings.

Didier C. Deutsch

Lassie

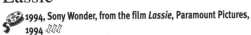1994, Sony Wonder, from the film *Lassie,* Paramount Pictures, 1994 ♪♪♪

album notes: Music: Basil Poledouris; **Orchestra:** The London Metropolitan Orchestra; **Conductor:** Allan Wilson; **Featured Soloist:** Sally Haeth, piano.

The exploits of Lassie over the years have provided ample fodder for a stream of countless films and television series. Even though this big screen incarnation didn't break any new grounds, with the well-known collie facing new challenges in the Virginia wild and overcoming them with its usual resolve, it enabled Basil Poledouris to write a score that sounds at times more important than its subject matter deserved. An old hand at this type of music, the composer essentially let the narrative dictate the direction his music would take. Low key, romantic themes line some of the story's quieter moments, while broad, dramatic cues accompany the action scenes, as an occasional theme for piano and orchestra makes a different statement. Put together, it's quite effective and pleasantly attractive.

Didier C. Deutsch

Last Action Hero

1993, Columbia Records, from the film *Last Action Hero*, Columbia Pictures, 1993 🎬🎬🎬

album notes: Music: Michael Kamen; **Orchestra:** The Los Angeles All-Stars Orchestra; The Los Angeles Rock and Roll Ensemble; **Conductor:** Michael Kamen; **Featured Musicians:** Michael Kamen, oboe, keyboards; Buckethead, guitar; Chris DeGarmo, guitar; John Goux, guitar; Frank Simes, guitar; Rick Nielsen, guitar; John Shanks, guitar; Jerry Cantrell, guitar; Guy Pratt, bass; Mike Inez, bass; Mike Baird, bass; Tom Petersson, bass; Scott Rockenfield, drums.

The generally unfavorable reaction to this big screen adventure film starring Arnold Schwatzenegger, might have cast an unfair pall over the various ingredients in the movie, including Michael Kamen's original score. In keeping with the modern tones of this wild fantasy, about a kid who joins his favorite film hero and shares his on-screen adventures, Kamen wrote a series of themes solidly embedded in the contemporary rock tradition, that are performed on the soundtrack and the album by various rock musicians, like Rick Neilson and Tom Petersson of Cheap Trick, Mike Inez and Jerry Cantrell of Alice in Chains, Chris De-Garmo of Queensryche, and Buckethead. Played against the structural canvas provided by a large orchestra, the selections throb with great energy and skill, some like "River Chase" and "Saving Danny," making a particularly strong impression.

Didier C. Deutsch

The Last Butterfly

1990, Varèse Sarabande, from the film *The Last Butterfly*, HTV Films, 1990 🎬🎬🎬

album notes: Music: Alex North; Milan Svoboda; **Orchestra:** The Prague Film Symphony Orchestra; **Conductor:** Mario Klemens; Stepan Konicek; **Featured Musicians:** *The Prague Jazzfonic Orchestra:* Milan Svoboda, piano; Vaclav Sykora, bass recorder; Ivan Zeaty, violin; Vida Skalska, vocals; Hana Hegerova, vocals.

One of the grand masters of film music, Alex North wrote one of his last scores for this quirky European production, starring Tom Courtney in one of his most unusual screen roles. At times poignantly dramatic, at times exuberantly elegiac, the cues cre-

ated by North reveal that the composer, aged 80 at the time he composed this score, had lost none of his verve or his creative energy. While songs like "Michelle's Demise," "The Flashback," and "The Red Umbrella,"—too short to make more than a passing impact—might be considered charming musical miniatures at best, others like "Main Title," "Butterfly," "The Last Performance," and "End Title" are sufficiently expanded to make a stronger impression and show the composer at his best. North's selections are supplemented by original compositions written and performed by Milan Svoboda in a standard jazz style that will seem old-fashioned but which has its attractive merits.

Didier C. Deutsch

Last Dance

1996, Hollywood Records, from the film *Last Dance*, Touchstone Pictures, 1996 🎬🎬🎬

album notes: Music: Mark Isham; **Orchestra:** The London Metropolitan Orchestra; **Conductor:** Ken Kugler; **Featured Musicians:** David Goldblatt, piano; Sally Dworsky, voice; Mark Isham, electronics.

A crime drama starring Sharon Stone as a murderess on death row who gets an eleventh hour reprieve after a young lawyer on the review board detects a flaw in her conviction, *Last Dance* got a provocative and appropriately somber score from Mark Isham, who delves into a contemporary field in which he is totally confident and comfortable. The attractive main theme ("Last Dance") with its broad orchestral lines, over which a piano and a wordless vocalist trade occasional riffs, is quite catchy and satisfyingly anchors the whole score. "On My Terms," a self-assertive comment made by Sharon Stone who demands to die when she wants to, "because that's all I've left," is also a poignant statement, admirably expressed in Isham's underscoring.

Didier C. Deutsch

The Last Days of Disco

1998, Work Records, from the Castle Rock/Gramercy film *The Last Days of Disco*, 1998 🎬🎬🎬

Let the nay-sayers complain about disco and the vapidity of its lush strains. In the days before AIDS, while the nation observed its government slowly disintegrate after the Watergate affair, there was something innocently perverse in losing one's mind on the dance floor to the beat of songs written by Gamble and Huff or Edwards and Rodgers, performed by a flurry of one-night (and one-hit) wonders who barely survived the backlash that ensued. Coincidence, or is it because the "disco" days suddenly are back in fashion, there seems to have been a generous amount of films (and soundtrack albums) devoted to the genre.

This album, with its preponderance of hits from the era, is as good as any. For the price of entry you get Alicia Bridges, Diana Ross (although not "Touch Me in the Morning"), Cheryl Lynn, Chic, Sister Sledge, Evelyn "Champagne" King, Carol Douglas, Amii Stewart, and a few others of the same caliber. Not bad for a compilation. Although you might be missing Village People, Earth, Wind & Fire, TSOP, and some of the more successful exponents of the genre, have no fear; they do show up on other compilations...

see also: 54

Didier C. Deutsch

The Last Days of Pompeii

See: Gli ultimi giorni di Pompei

The Last Emperor

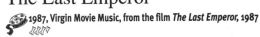 1987, Virgin Movie Music, from the film *The Last Emperor,* 1987 ♪♪♪♪

album notes: Music: Ryuichi Sakamoto; David Byrne; Cong Su.

The Last Emperor musically is a strange bird. Bernardo Bertolucci's film chronicled the life of China's last emperor—from ascending the Imperial throne at the age of three in the Forbidden City, through revolution and war and his eventual life as a gardener—and it's pretty enchanting. Japanese composer Ryuichi Sakamoto (also an actor in the film), occasional film contributor David Byrne, and the mysterious Cong Su won an Oscar for their efforts, but hardly seem to have worked together. The lion's share of the music is by Sakamoto, whose style blends Chinese gestures with accessible melodies. His themes are deeply romantic, sometimes melodramatic, characterizing the opulence, mystery and ultimate sadness of the emperor's life. They also brim with a very western symphonic flavor, casting an epic scope upon the story, and recalling a time when western culture was admired around the world for its luxury and inventiveness.

David Byrne's five tracks on the album include the insidiously catchy "Main Title," which is probably what won the score its Oscar, and more intimate synth-and-Chinese-instruments cues for life inside the Forbidden City. There is one track from Cong Su—who now has the same number of Oscars as Bernard Herrmann and Jerry Goldsmith—a bit of traditional Chinese plinking and plunking. Two communist sing-alongs and a Strauss waltz round out this unusual but memorable soundtrack.

Lukas Kendall

Last Exit to Brooklyn

1989, Warner Bros. Records, from the film *Last Exit to Brooklyn,* Neue Constantin Film, 1989 ♪♪♪♪

album notes: Music: Mark Knopfler; **Featured Performer:** Guy Fletcher; **Featured Musicians:** David Nolan, violin; Irvine Arditti, violin; Chris White, saxophone; Mark Knopfler, guitar.

Based on Hubert Selby's 1964 novel, *Last Exit to Brooklyn* takes a close look at life in one of New York's least attractive boroughs in a rundown working class neighborhood near the navy yards, plagued by an ongoing strike against a local factory. To give meaning to this gritty tale, Mark Knopfler wrote a diversified score in which striking melodies ("Last Exit to Brooklyn," "A Love Idea") contrast with tunes in which the desperate atmosphere that pervades the film find a remarkable echo. One cue, "Victims," starts with what resembles the sound of machinery interrupted by the horn of a ship, strongly evocative of the background against which the story unfolds. The film's centerpiece, a sensational action scene that opposes the strikers against police forces, gives way here to a spectacular cue called "Riot," boldly expressive and superbly realistic. There are, along the way, many other musical moments that evoke specific scenes in the film, notably "Tralala" and "As Low as It Gets," but the whole recording is one outstanding track after another.

Didier C. Deutsch

Last Man Standing

1998, Varèse Records, music inspired by the film *Last Man Standing,* New Line Cinema, 1996 ♪♪♪♪

album notes: Music: Elmer Bernstein; **Conductor:** Elmer Bernstein.

1996, Verve Records, from the film *Last Man Standing,* New Line Cinema, 1996 ♪♪♪♪

album notes: Music: Ry Cooder; **Featured Musicians:** Ry Cooder, guitars, keyboards; Joachim Cooder, drums, percussion; Rick Cox, sampling, synthesizer, bass saxophone, vibes; Padmasri N. Ramani, bamboo flute; P. Srinivasan, percussion; Madjid Khaladj, zarb; Donn Kim, soenap flute.

Director Walter Hill came up with an interesting concept—an adaptation of Akira Kurosawa's samurai film *Yojimbo* (which also inspired Sergio Leone's *A Fistful of Dollars*), converted to a '30s gangster piece, set in the middle of nowhere (Texas), borrowing techniques from dime novels, comic books, *films noirs—*"in essence, a disguised Western," as he described it to composer Ry Cooder. And, he added, it was also meant to be literally "a hymn to the traditions of fictional American tough guys."

What we end up with are two "soundtrack" albums: one is Cooder's actual contribution, the other is a series of cues "inspired by the film," composed by none other than Elmer Bernstein, whose western scores need no longer be introduced.

Evidently, this story of a mysterious stranger who gets involved in a bloody struggle between two rival gangs in the dingy town of Jericho, Texas, struck a deep chord in Bernstein, who decided to write his own score for the film. Unfortunately, the liner notes in the Varèse release (which provide extensive texts about Elmer Bernstein and Matthew Joseph Peak, whose paint-

Last Exit to Brooklyn **(The Kobal Collection)**

ing of a barren landscape adorns the cover of this album) fail to answer the one interesting question this album brings up: what prompted Bernstein to commit himself, his time, and obviously a great deal of effort and money, to creating a score for a film he was not working on? In itself, it is a magnificent set of cues, richly evocative and permeated with the sonorities we have come to expect from the composer. The themes abound, teeming with warm sonorities, and the usual contingent of "western" instrumentations that evoke specific wide-open spaces and standard action scenes. Some cues are particularly rich in various details, such as "Felina's Story" in which several themes collide to create a vivid, colorful tapestry.

In contrast, Ry Cooder's score sounds darker, more austere, although no less eloquent, with a more contemporary approach that may be truer to the spirit of the film itself. The main theme, with its heavy pounding and rock beat, is generations away from Bernstein's more western action style. In some cues ("Jericho Blues," "Hickey's Back," "Jericho Two-Step"), elements of blues are the dominant note, while an interesting contrast between this score and Elmer Bernstein's is suggested by "Fe-

lina," in which Cooder seems to share a similar concept, only to take it to a totally different, unexpected direction.

Didier C. Deutsch

Last of the Dogmen

1995, Atlantic Records, from the film *Last of the Dogmen*, Savoy Pictures, 1995 🎵🎵🎵🎵
album notes: Music: David Arnold; **Orchestra:** The London Symphony Orchestra; **Conductor:** Nicholas Dodd.

Immediately after completing *Stargate*, David Arnold took on this epic story of the discovery of a lost tribe of Cheyenne. Although the story begins with tracker Tom Berringer searching for a group of escaped convicts, at the core of the film, and the score, is an aura of romance. Director Tab Murphy treats his North American wilderness setting, the last unspoiled, untamed land, with reverence and awe. While Berringer's character finds love with Native American expert Barbara Hershey, she in turn finds it in the culmination of her life's dream with the discovery of the simple lifestyle of the Cheyenne, who have remained unexposed to modern civilization for centuries. There are gentle hints of western motifs with Arnold's score, but only enough to reinforce the notions of an earlier age. The film is, after all, about the clash of cultures. Arnold remarkably captures all this in a score that deftly shifts through the film's ever-changing moods, providing a solid foundation that makes even the tiniest emotion an epic experience. While his work on *Stargate,* and later *Independence Day,* are also of epic quality, it is the smaller, personal moments in *Last of the Dogmen* that sets it above the rest. It is a score that truly comes from his heart.

David Hirsch

The Last of the Mohicans

1992, Morgan Creek Records, from the film *The Last of the Mohicans,* 20th Century-Fox, 1992 ✎✎✎

album notes: (tracks 1-9) **Music:** Trevor Jones; **Conductor:** Daniel A. Carlin; (tracks 10-15) **Music:** Randy Edelman; **Conductor:** Randy Edelman.

With *The Last of the Mohicans,* we are given a poignant sense of orchestral drama from two notable composers. The first nine cues on the CD are by Jones, the remaining six by Edelman. Though their styles are different and thematically unrelated, they complement each other. Jones's theme sounds solid and steadfast amid the myriad of orchestral figures he sets against it in the battle scenes. Edelman's music is less exhilarating but equally effective, built around a very pretty melody for synth and accordion over acoustic guitar and strings, growing in force and tone. Where Jones uses electronics as a minor member of the orchestra for textural purposes, Edelman relies on synths more dominantly as lead instruments. Trevor Jones introduces his main theme out of native drums, a grandly sweeping music for brass, strings and timpani, counterpointed in "Elk Hunt" by perpendicular strokes of strings and rapidly-toned synth. It's an immensely powerful opening. Edelman is an accomplished synthesist and his score is strident and evocative. This is forceful and compelling music, lofty and earthy and at the same time gloriously romantic, brimful of the romance of adventure as well as the romance of love.

Randall D. Larson

The Last Picture Show

1971, Columbia Records, from the film *The Last Picture Show,* Columbia Pictures, 1971 ✎

album notes: Featured Performers: Tony Bennett; Eddie Fisher; Lefty Frizzell; Pee Wee King; Frankie Laine; Johnnie Ray; Hank Snow; Jo Stafford.

A nostalgic trip to the '50s via a collection of hits from that period, performed by the stars who made them famous, this soundtrack album to the film directed by Peter Bogdanovich has one serious drawback. For the money, the playing time is quite short and its sound quality is seriously deficient. Since the same selections can often be found in many other remastered compilations, this collection seems a bit redundant.

Didier C. Deutsch

The Last Seduction

1995, Pure Records, from the ITC Entertainment film *The Last Seduction,* 1995 ✎✎✎

album notes: Music: Joseph Vitarelli.

Joseph Vitarelli's jaunty score to director John Dahl's 1993 neo-noir about a femme fatale who manipulates her stupid, naive lover into murdering her con artist husband is the crowning piece of this album. A few nondescript bar juke box blues-rock songs from the movie are also found here, but they severely detract from Vitarelli's great Blue Note-inspired score. Vitarelli is an interesting composer to watch, with recent credits including *She's So Lovely.* A great contrast to the film's twists and turns, the score also lends itself well to home listening.

Amy Rosen

Last Stand at Saber River

1998, Intrada Records, from the film *Last Stand at Saber River,* Turner, 1997 ✎✎✎✎

album notes: Music: David Shire.

The story of a brave man, Cable, who wants to leave the Civil War behind him and pursue a peaceful life with his family on the homestead stolen from him while he was fighting, *Last Stand at Saber River* elicited a bold, brassy score from composer David Shire, teeming with great themes that evoke the wide-open spaces and the violent action, both staples of the genre ("The Valley," "Wagon Chase," "The Last Gunfight"). Colorful and excitingly staged, this is an excellent score that paints vivid, remarkable pictures.

Didier C. Deutsch

The Last Starfighter

1995, Intrada Records, from the film *The Last Starfighter,* Universal Pictures, 1983 ✎✎✎✎

album notes: Music: Craig Safan; **Conductor:** Craig Safan.

One of the few post-*Star Wars* blockbuster scores to approach the heights of John Williams's Korngold-esque space opera scores is this spectacular effort from Craig Safan for the agreeable Nick Castle space shoot-em-up that's primarily remembered now for its early, ground-breaking CGI effects. Although there is scope and bombastic action material galore in this incredibly brassy, sharply performed score, Safan's greatest achievement is the emotional accessibility he allows. It's actually quite touching for a space opera, dealing movingly with its hero's Luke Skywalker-like wanderlust as he stumbles onto a video game that's designed to train real star warriors for an interstellar conflict. Safan's opening theme, while bearing comparison to Williams's in its martial brassiness, achieves its own distinctive power through a couple of thrilling repeating horn figures and a primary melody that is just as effective generating feelings of compassion and tenderness in its more intimate settings as it is whipping up a frenzy of rah-rah excitement here. This Intrada release showcases the entire score, expanding the music heard on an old Southern Cross CD and providing improved sound for what was already a barnstorming recording.

Jeff Bond

The Last Supper

1996, TVT Records, from the film *The Last Supper,* Vault, 1995 ♪♪♪♪

album notes: Music: Mark Mothersbaugh.

A delirious black comedy about a group of friends who accidentally kill a racist man they had invited to dinner, and subsequently decide to rid society of unsavory similar characters, *The Last Supper* never took itself or its somewhat grim topic seriously, resulting in a film that had a dark edge to it, but remained sufficiently aware of it to be a lot of fun. It yielded this vastly enjoyable soundtrack album, featuring a score by Mark Mothersbaugh, unfortunately reduced to a scant few selections (the slyly expressed "I'm Dieting" is a gem), and songs by a wide range of artists, including KC & the Sunshine Band (whose "I'm Your Boogie Man" is always a joy to hear), Ten Years After, UB40, the Toys (another winner with the classic "A Lover's Concerto"), and Shonen Knife. Cute and a lot of fun; well in keeping with the spirit of the film.

Didier C. Deutsch

Last Tango in Paris

1998, Rykodisc, from the film *Last Tango in Paris,* United Artists, 1972 ♪♪♪♪♪

album notes: Music: Gato Barbieri.

Latin jazz saxophone great Gato Barbieri composed the sultry score for this controversial Bernardo Bertolucci film, set in Paris, and perfectly mirrored in his music the erotic nature of the work. His Latin dance music in particular, contains strong sexual overtones that evoke quite well this love story between an American widower (portrayed by Marlon Brando) and the

French girl who becomes his roommate. Throughout the film and the recording, the "Last Tango in Paris" theme is played by Barbieri on the saxophone as a tango, a ballad, and a jazz waltz. The score also includes four tangos, considered by many the sexiest dance form. As was customary when the film came out, the original soundtrack album was recorded separately from the recording of the music in the movie. As a result, this CD contains a large amount of additional material titled "The Last Tango in Paris Suite," 29 cues which Barbieri selected from the original score he recorded for the film.

Didier C. Deutsch

The Last Time I Committed Suicide

1997, Blue Note, from the film *The Last Time I Committed Suicide,* Kushner-Locke/Tapestry, 1997 ♪♪

album notes: Music: Tyler Bates.

Jack Kerouac has become a cliché to today's generation, and the music in this uneven collection of tracks from a film that went straight to video reflects this status. When directors use the '50s and '60s bohemian jazz idea for underscoring films, they always end up with Monk, Mingus, Parker, and Gillespie. The desperate lives of some of these jazz greats is obviously parallel to the tormented lives of the "beat generation" poets and writers. This is really a collage of source cues (for which jazz is most often used), and it features classic performances by Ella Fitzgerald, Max Roach, Miles Davis, Art Blakey, and the above-named jazz legends. The newer material is interesting but jumps out in the film, an odd contrast to the period sound from the older tracks. Featured artists are Cassandra Wilson, Jacky Terrasson, and Dianne Reeves. This CD will probably be sought after in the future for the performances of Wilson and Reeves.

Bob Belden

The Last Unicorn

1982, Virgin Records, from the animated feature, *The Last Unicorn,* 1982 ♪♪♪

album notes: Music: Jimmy Webb; **Orchestra:** The London Symphony Orchestra; **Conductor:** Jimmy Webb; **Featured Performers:** America: Dan Peek, Gerry Beckley, Dewey Bunnell.

The rock group America is prominently featured in this soundtrack album to an animated film, with a score by Jimmy Webb. The songs, an attractive lot with good melodic lines and pleasant lyrics, were quite effective on the soundtrack and also make a favorable impression on a pure audio level. The combination of the rock band with a large orchestra usually works very well and makes this a most enjoyable album.

Didier C. Deutsch

The Last Waltz

1978, Warner Bros. Records, from the film *The Last Waltz*, Filmways, 1978 🎵🎵🎵

album notes: Featured Musicians: The Band: Rick Danko, bass, violins, vocals; Levon Helm, drums, mandolin, vocals; Garth Hudson, organ, accordion, saxophone, synthesizers; Richard Manuel, piano, keyboards, drums, vocals; Robbie Robertson, guitar, piano, vocals; **Guest Artists:** Paul Butterfield, Eric Clapton, Neil Diamond, Bob Dylan, Emmylou Harris, Ronnie Hawkins, Dr. John, Joni Mitchell, Van Morrison, the Staples, Ringo Starr, Muddy Waters, Ron Wood, Neil Young.

The farewell concert by the Band, Bob Dylan's onetime backup group, brought together as fine an assortment of rock stars as we are ever likely to see on one stage, and the Martin Scorsese documentary that resulted ranks among the best concert films. The two-CD soundtrack compilation boasts performances cut from the movie, most notably a Van Morrison– Richard Manuel duet on "Tura-Lura-Lural." Other highlights come from Neil Young, Muddy Waters, Eric Clapton, and Dylan. The Band itself had better nights. Singer Levon Helm lost his voice during the show, which may explain why several of the group's favorites were rerecorded on a soundstage after the fact, then stitched into a less-than-stellar dream sequence.

Marc Kirkeby

The Late Shift

1996, Silva America, from the television film *The Late Shift*, HBO, 1996 🎵🎵🎵

album notes: Music: Ira Newborn; **Synthesizer Programming:** Stuart Goldberg; **Conductor:** Ira Newborn; **Featured Musicians:** Bob Mann, Ira Newborn, guitars; Joel Peskin, tenor/alto sax; Walt Johnson, Pete Christlieb, tenor sax.

The selling point of this CD's cover is a line that touts "Here's Johnny" (the *Tonight Show* Theme) as performed by Doc Severinsen and His Band so strongly that score composer Ira Newborn's credit is almost completely overshadowed. And yet, after starting off with that often–heard tune, you'll discover that Newborn contributes a breezy pop score that adds just the right amount of absurdity to this film, a recreation of the true story of a war between the networks for late–night supremacy that began after Johnny Carson announced his plan to retire from the *Tonight Show*. Newborn plays up the on–screen action to achieve a true sense of the preposterous ("Jay Leno, Secret Agent," for example). Agents, network executives, and on–air talent prance around each other as if they were cold–war spies on a mission to save all life. Delightfully engaging.

David Hirsch

Laura/Jane Eyre

1993, Fox Records, from the films *Laura*, 20th Century-Fox, 1944; and *Jane Eyre*, 20th Century-Fox, 1943 🎵🎵🎵

album notes: Music: David Raksin, Bernard Herrmann; **Orchestra:** The 20th Century-Fox Orchestra; **Conductor:** Alfred Newman, Bernard Herrmann.

Of all the romantic murder mysteries born of the 1940s, *Laura* reigns supreme as the regal Queen—elegant, romantic, suspenseful, sad. Director Otto Preminger's classic is one of a handful of films of this genre that hold up remarkably well today, over 50 years after its initial release in 1944. Resilient, too, has been David Raksin's original score, the one that transformed a simple musical theme into a vocal pop standard and made the composer's name a household word. Originally, Preminger had planned to use Duke Ellington's "Sophisticated Lady" as the main theme for the picture whose story turns a murder victim into the prime suspect. However, with Raksin's intervention and personal struggle over a long weekend, a new theme was developed. "Laura" emerged as one of the most mysterious, intriguing melodies of all time. Once lyricist Johnny Mercer added the lyrics, it became an instant sensation and one of the most recorded tunes in history. That hauntingly romantic theme, dressed in a variety of disguises, is what underscores and creates the atmosphere for this wonderful film. A 1975 recording featuring the New Philharmonia Orchestra, conducted by David Raksin, is available on RCA Victor. This reissue has been newly remixed by the composer himself and contains a six-minute segment titled "Laura." While it is nice to hear the theme in glorious, modern stereo, this small sampling leaves you aching for more.

For this, nothing surpasses the original 1944 soundtrack (20th Century Fox Film Scores), which is comprised of a 28-minute composition titled "Suite for Laura: Theme and Variations." It is here that you can really appreciate the subtle textures and nuances in Raksin's score. The monophonic film track sound is very good, with a remarkable amount of detail noted among the individual instruments, and the recording has a nice, warm 1940s sound and feel to it.

Charles L. Granata

Lawnmower Man 2: Beyond Cyberspace

1996, Varèse Sarabande, from the film *Lawnmower Man 2: Beyond Cyberspace*, Allied Film Productions, 1996 🎵🎵🎵

album notes: Music: Robert Folk; **Orchestra:** The London Sinfonia; **Conductor:** Robert Folk.

Robbie Robertson in The Last Waltz. (The Kobal Collection)

For this high-tech cyberthriller, Robert Folk has based his score around a romantic melody for full orchestra. That theme brackets the ferocious action music that makes up the bulk of this score. This is a heavy action score, but it's all very tonal and under control. Folk uses straightforward orchestration, synths mixed with symphonics, to color this world of cyberspace and virtual reality. By doing so—and avoiding the complete plunge into computerized music that the story might have suggested—Folk humanizes the film and its characters, linking them to the real world even in the midst of their virtual adventures, even in the midst of his furious action music. And in the end, Folk's main theme returns, glorious and magnificent, wrapping up the frantic activity of the middle section with a purposeful resolve, shutting the doors on cyberspace and enfolding the characters in the warm embrace of the real world.

Randall Larson

Lawrence of Arabia

1990, Varèse Sarabande, from the film *Lawrence of Arabia,* Columbia Pictures, 1962 🎬🎬🎬

album notes: Music: Maurice Jarre; **Orchestra:** The London Philharmonic Orchestra; **Conductor:** Sir Adrian Boult.

Has there ever been an orchestrated film soundtrack more beautiful, more evocative? Here begins Maurice Jarre's string of Oscars and his memorable collaboration with the British director David Lean. Thirty-five years on, this landmark work stands in the company of the best "classical music" ever written for Hollywood. Lean's film, perhaps the greatest of the bigger-than-big movie epics of the late '50s and early '60s, is unimaginable without this music, particularly in its first half, and especially in those sweeping long shots of the desert. A fan can only wish for more, and in the CD era, there should be. At 37 minutes, this soundtrack recording offers nothing more than the original LP. Monsieur Jarre, where are those master tapes?

Marc Kirkeby

1989, Silva Screen Records, from the film *Lawrence of Arabia,* Columbia Pictures, 1962 🎬🎬🎬

album notes: Music: Maurice Jarre; **Orchestra:** The Philharmonia Orchestra; **Conductor:** Tony Bremner.

Besides restoring the cues in the order in which the plot unfolded on the screen, this rerecording introduces several selections not available on the soundtrack album. This would be everything fans have been waiting for were it not for the fact that when all is said and done, the performance by The Philharmonia, while sonically spectacular, doesn't match in excitement and fire the London Philharmonic in the original. To actually pinpoint the differences is a subtle exercise that requires a

sensitivity only the ultra-discriminating might care about, but the playing often sounds stilted, studied, and at times a bit too reverential. Casual listeners, more interested in the sweep of the music than in academic disputes over the way it should be performed will no doubt enjoy the recording in all its splendor.

Didier C. Deutsch

Le bal

1993, Pomme Music/France, from the film *Le bal,* 1983 🎬🎬🎬

album notes: Music: Vladimir Cosma; **Conductor:** Vladimir Cosma.

This unusual (and unusually entertaining) film took place entirely in a ballroom, and surveyed a 50-year period as seen through the eyes of the dancers, and the music played by the on-stage band. There was virtually no dialogue, just basic physical interaction between the various participants, yet each vignette was clearly detailed and set in its own time period, making the film a wonderful retrospective of the sounds heard over the past 50 years. Because it was initially created by a French theatrical company, the first selections, with a few exceptions, might seem alien to an American public who may not have been exposed to the same tunes; however, as the action progresses, and the music along with it, with the arrival of the first GIs at the end of World War II we enter a more familiar realm, something signaled by the inclusion of tunes like "In The Mood," by the Glenn Miller Orchestra, or "Boogie Blues," by the Count Basie Orchestra. From that point on, the internationalization of music becomes evident as the band starts playing tunes like "La vie en rose," "Tutti Frutti," or the Beatles' "Michelle," among other songs. Capping it all, Vladimir Cosma composed a beautiful theme, heard in various variations throughout, which solidifies the score and provides the unity it needed. This recording may be difficult to find. Check with a used CD store, mail-order company, or a dealer specializing in rare, out-of-print, or import recordings.

Didier C. Deutsch

Le diner de cons

1998, Larghetto Music/France, from the film *Le diner de cons (The Dinner Game),* 1998 🎬🎬🎬

album notes: Music: Vladimir Cosma; **Conductor:** Vladimir Cosma; **Featured Musician:** Philip Catherine, guitar; Romane, guitar.

This film is a hilarious confection—a comedy about a fancy dinner at which various cosmopolitan types invite a nerd and ridicule him, except that this time the nerd in question turns the tables on the man who has invited him and wreaks havoc in his marriage and his quiet paradisiac existence. Informed by a well-known song by Georges Brassens ("Le temps ne fait rien a l'affaire," which goes on with the lyrics "once a jerk, always a jerk"), the delightfully humorous score by Vladimir Cosma provides the musical setting for this farce, and translates very well in this enjoyable CD. This title may be out of print or just plain hard to find. Mail-order companies, used CD shops, or dealers of rare or import recordings will be your best bet.

Didier C. Deutsch

Le Hussard sur le toit

1995, Audivis/Travelling/France, from the film *Le Hussard sur le toit (The Horseman on the Roof)*, Miramax, 1995 ♪♪♪♪

album notes: Music: Jean-Claude Petit; **Orchestra:** The Orchestre National de France; **Conductor:** Jean-Claude Petit.

Jean-Claude Petit's literate scores signaled him as the appropriate choice to write the music for this sumptuous period story, based on the novel by Jean Giono about an Italian countess living in France in the cholera-devastated Provence of the early 19th century who decides to return to her estate in Piedmont, escorted by the handsome Hussard who has sought refuge from marauding vigilantes on the roof of her house. Along the way he will nurse her back to health, after she catches the dreaded disease, and they will fall in love. Keeping in mind the basic two elements of the film, the rousing cross-country ride to Italy and the developing romance between the two, Petit conceived a score that was both heroic and florid, with sweeping themes that illuminate it and give it substance. Performance by the Orchestre National de France is topnotch. This recording may be difficult to find. Check with a used CD store, mail-order company, or a dealer specializing in rare, out-of-print, or import recordings.

Didier C. Deutsch

A League of Their Own

1992, Columbia Records, from the film *A League of Their Own*, Columbia Pictures, 1992 ♪♪♪

album notes: Music: Hans Zimmer; **Conductor:** Shirley Walker; **Featured Musicians:** Jim Kanter, clarinet; Rick Baptist, trumpet; Mike Lane, piano; Kurt McGettrick, baritone sax; Kathy Lenski, violin; Phil Ayling, cor anglais; **Featured Performers:** Carole King, The Manhattan Transfer, James Taylor, Billy Joel, Art Garfunkel, Doc's Rhythm Cats, The Rockford Peaches.

As compilations of this kind go, this is quite an enchanting one. Some of the 1980's most recognizable frontline performers deliver a handful of classic tunes in a program that is as beguiling as it is familiar. Hans Zimmer's two longer selections add a zest of instrumental class that tops off this soundtrack album with a delicious touch.

Didier C. Deutsch

Leap of Faith

1992, MCA Records, from the film *Leap of Faith*, Paramount Pictures, 1992 woof!

album notes: Featured Performers: Don Henley; Patti LaBelle; John Pagano; Wynonna; the Angels of Mercy; YaDonna Wise; Lizz Lee; Lynette Hawkins Stephens; Lawrence Matthews; Lyle Lovett; George Duke; Delores Hall; Leon P. Turner; Gheri LeGree-McDonald; Albertina Walker; Meatloaf.

Whoever thought it would be a great idea to have Don Henley sing "Sit down You're Rocking the Boat," from *Guys and Dolls* should have his/her head examined. Not only Is the singer out of his league with this song, but his delivery is totally wrong for it. That's not the only thing wrong with this soundtrack album in which there is too much of too many things to please even the least discriminating listener. The moods in this album move from rock to gospel to blues to country without much rhyme or reason. Of course, there might have been a reason imbedded in the film, about one of those evangelists who proliferate in the South, but, sad to say, its not here.

Didier C. Deutsch

Leave It to Beaver

1998, Varèse Sarabande, from the *Leave It to Beaver*, Universal film, 1998 ♪♪♪♪

album notes: Music: Randy Edelman; **Conductor:** Randy Edelman.

Although this big–screen adaptation lacked the charm or zest of the 1957–63 TV series, it spawned a very enjoyable score from Randy Edelman. Having to deal with a rural situation and a paper-thin plot, the composer chose to emphasize the former over the latter. As a result, his cues are frequently ingratiating, sometimes played for fun (as in the mock "Mayfield Mighty Mites"), but always with an eye (or an ear) to keeping them melodic. Occasionally, a lovely theme emerges ("Teen Love," in which an acoustic guitar sets the tone); elsewhere, the moods are more ebullient ("The Great Computer Caper," "Pigskin Shuffle," "Theodore's Victory Run"), adding up to a score that's pleasantly catchy. But why are the cues out of sequence, with the "Finale" ("The Neighborhood Sleeps") showing up in the middle of the recording?

Didier C. Deutsch

Leaving Las Vegas

1995, Pangea Records, from the United film *Leaving Las Vegas*, Artists/Lumiere, 1995 ♪♪♪

album notes: Music: Mike Figgis.

Director Mike Figgis moonlights here as composer for his film about a desperate alcoholic who falls in love with a Vegas prostitute while drinking himself to death. Figgis also recruited his good buddy Sting, who had acted in his earlier film *Stormy Monday,* to record new versions of pop standards such as "Angel Eyes" and "My One and Only Love." Figgis's interesting jazz-based score and the Sting songs make for a good collection of music. The only down side is the incessant use of dialogue sound bites from the movie, which distracts from the overall listening experience. Otherwise, this is a highly enjoyable album.

Amy Rosen

Legend

🎬 **1992, Silva Screen, from the film *Legend,* 20th Century-Fox, 1985** 🎵🎵🎵🎵🎵

album notes: Music: Jerry Goldsmith; **Lyrics:** John Bettis; **Orchestra:** The National Philharmonic Orchestra; **Conductor:** Jerry Goldsmith.

Ridley Scott's striking fairy tale didn't fare too well at the box office in the U.S., nor did Jerry Goldsmith's superb score which was dropped in favor of a selection of pop tunes by Tangerine Dream. The substitution did not help the film, but it deprived American filmgoers from enjoying one of the great scores written for the screen. In it, Goldsmith eloquently captured the cinematic vision of the director and transposed it in strikingly beautiful musical terms. The recording does it full justice.

Didier C. Deutsch

🎬 **1995, Varèse Sarabande, from the film *Legend,* 20th Century-Fox, 1985** 🎵🎵🎵

album notes: Music: Tangerine Dream.

This pleasant synthesized alternate score by the German pop group replaced Jerry Goldsmith's work composed for the film in the U.S. when studio heads thought they needed music that "the kids could relate to better." The film suffered more from their decision to edit 20 minutes from Ridley Scott's original cut than the replacement of Goldsmith's inventive composition. Tangerine Dream's work is certainly effective, albeit to a lesser degree, but also gives the film a more claustrophobic feel, as synthesized scores often do. It holds up much better on the album as an independent musical piece than as movie music.

David Hirsch

The Legend of Prince Valiant

📺 **1991, Mesa Records, from the animated television series *The Legend of Prince Valiant,* 1991** 🎵🎵🎵

album notes: Music: Steve Sexton, Gerald O'Brien.

The score for this animated feature, not drawn by Hal Foster, was created by Steve Sexton and Gerald O'Brien, two synthesists working under the pseudonym of Exchange. The music they conceived is generally very attractive, with melodic themes that are frequently catchy and enjoyable, though they

rely a bit too much on the formula sounds that seem to prevail in television soundtracks these days—repetitive background riffs, with melodic lines that are relatively simple and of one mind, without much invention behind. The apparently mandatory songs that have been included also seem totally out of place in the context.

Didier C. Deutsch

The Legend of the Pianist on the Ocean

🎬 **1999, Sony Classical, from the film *The Legend of the Pianist on the Ocean,* Medusa, 1998** 🎵🎵🎵🎵

album notes: Music: Ennio Morricone; **Conductor:** Ennio Morricone; **Featured Musicians:** Gianni Oddi, soprano sax; Cicci Santucci, trumpet; Fausto Anzelmo, viola; Gilda Butta, Amedeo Tommasi, piano.

At one time, this English-language Italian film had been announced for release here, with Sony Classical ready to handle the soundtrack album. However, the film seems to have fallen into limbo, and the soundtrack album along with it. Fortunately, the album was released by Sony Classical in Italy, and it is superb. The story of a pianist born at the turn of the century aboard an ocean liner that he has never left, the quaint story, directed by Giuseppe Tornatore, contains many of the ingredients that had already made his *Cinema Paradiso* such a hit: a strong storyline, well-defined attaching characters, a serious dose of sentimentality, and to top it off, a remarkable score written by Ennio Morricone.

The temptation is great at first to compare *Legend* with *Cinema Paradiso,* but here the composer takes flights of fancy, inserting, for instance, in the middle of the highly sentimental title tune, jazz lines for saxophone that seem as wild as they are unexpected. Because the main character is a virtuoso (he was apparently abandoned in the first class grand piano of the liner and was adopted and raised by a machinist, who called him "Danny Nineteenhundred," from the year of his birth), the piano plays a predominant role in the whole score: Morricone includes it in several cues, in a concertante format, or in solo pieces ("Tarantella in third Class," "A Mozart Reincarnated," "Nocturne with No Moon"), and Amedeo Tommasi, one of the two soloists heard in the album, also contributes some tracks of his own ("Magic Waltz," "Danny's Blues").

As the story follows its course over a 40-year period, young Danny dazzles passengers with his virtuosity, answers a challenge from Jelly Roll Morton (in a brilliant set piece), but always adamantly refuses to go ashore, even when he falls in love with a lovely young girl, in an attitude that recalls Garcia Lorca's *Life Is a Dream.* Despite the fact that Tornatore relies on many scenes that are nearly silent, music plays an integral part in the action, often commenting on it or putting the accent on it. The jazz era, another important ingredient in the narrative, is invoked in several cues, including Scott Joplin's "Peachering Rag," and Jelly Roll Morton's "The Crave," but the main focus is on Morricone's softly shaded score, in which the sentimentality that pervaded *Cinema Paradiso* finds an echo in themes that are exquisitely written and lovingly expressed. Roger Waters's "Lost Boys Calling" seems a perfect counterpoint and a fitting closing tune.

Didier C. Deutsch

Legends of the Fall

1994, Epic Soundtrax/Sony Classical, from the film *Legends of the Fall*, Tri-Star Pictures, 1994 ♪♪♪♪

album notes: Music: James Horner; **Orchestra:** The London Symphony Orchestra; **Conductor:** James Horner; **Featured Musicians:** Jay Ungar; Kazu Matsui, Tony Hinnegan, Mike Taylor, Maggie Boyle, Dermot Crehan.

For this poignant romantic drama set during World War I and in the years following about two brothers, their father, and the beautiful, compelling young woman who irrevocably changes each of their lives, James Horner wrote a superb score. "At once brooding and lush, redolent of both love and loss," says director Ed Zwick in his own comments. In it, the composer evoked the wilds of Montana, where the action takes place, its native rhythms and its wilderness, and Cornwall, where the main protagonists came from initially. As a result, his composition is filled with sweeping melodies, made even more striking with the use of a fiddle and a shakuhachi that give it its unusual colors and flavor. As is often the case in Horner's expansive scores, the last track, "Alfred, Tristan, the Colonel the Legend..." is an expressive piece of orchestral music that slowly evolves and builds into a magnificent tone poem of impressive magnitude and character.

Didier C. Deutsch

Lenny

1998, Rykodisc, from the film *Lenny,* United Artists, 1974 ♪♪♪

album notes: Music: Ralph Burns.

Dustin Hoffman doing Lenny Bruce? Why not! It certainly worked on the screen in this film, made by Bob Fosse in 1974, that adopted a semi-documentary style to tell the story of the foul-mouthed comedian who was years ahead of everyone else in his wisecracks about society and its forthcoming changes. But spoken recordings are difficult enough to listen to, and this soundtrack misses the real Lenny doing his own routines, something that might have given the album an extra edge. Hoffman is brilliant, but you have to see him to really appreci-

ate what he does in the film: here, you only get the jest of it, and not enough to really enjoy the performance. Ralph Burns's music is often good for an overall ambient sound, and the album also contains Rodgers and Hart's "It Never Entered My Mind," played by Miles Davis. But it's hardly enough.

Didier C. Deutsch

The Leopard

1991, CAM Records/Italy, from the film *The Leopard,* 20th Century–Fox, 1963 ♪♪♪♪

album notes: Music: Nino Rota; **Orchestra:** The National Academy of St. Cecil Orchestra, the Opera Theatre Orchestra, the Radio-Television Orchestra; **Conductor:** Franco Ferrara.

Luchino Visconti created a magnificent fresco chronicling late 19th-century life in Sicily, the turmoil brought by an uncultured middle class on its way up the social ladder, and the effect it had on the waning aristocracy. Based on the novel by Giuseppe Tommasi di Lampedusa, the film focused on Prince Fabrizio Salina, played by Burt Lancaster, and his nephew Tancredi (Alain Delon), whom he allows to marry Angelica (Claudia Cardinale), daughter of the town's mayor, a bourgeois without a title. But the world outside is coming to an abrupt end with the rise of Garibaldi and his "red shirts," whose revolution eventually leads to the crumbling of social structures. On a sabbatical from the films of Fellini, Nino Rota wrote a robust set of cues, in which the predominant note was one of touching melancholy, brilliantly offset by exhilarating dance numbers ("Mazurka," "Contradance," "Polka," "Quadrille," etc.) all of which reflected the life of leisure led by the Prince and his court. This title may be out of print or just plain hard to find. Mail-order companies, used CD shops, or dealers of rare or import recordings will be your best bet.

Didier C. Deutsch

The Leopard Son

1996, Ark 21 Records, from the film *The Leopard Son,* Discovery Pictures, 1996 ♪♪♪♪

album notes: Music: Stewart Copeland; **Orchestra:** The Los Angeles Symphony Orchestra; **Conductor:** Michael T. Andreas; **Featured Musicians:** Stewart Copeland, piano, drums, percussion; Stanley Clarke, acoustic bass; Judd Miller, ethnic wind instruments; Michael Thompson, guitars.

A compelling documentary about a cub growing up on the Seregenti Plain, *The Leopard Son* strongly benefitted from Stewart Copeland's eclectic score, solidly anchored by Stanley Clarke's lively bass work. Since much of the screen action is reduced to scenes involving the cub, his environment, and other animals (a family of hyenas, some lions, a gang of cheetahs) Copeland's engaging score, which frequently mixes sounds effects, remains purely naturalistic with cues that help detail what happens in simple, easy to appreciate terms. As a result, the music is constantly enjoyable and includes many delightful moments such as "Cub Explores," "Changing Skies," a muscular "The Lion Bitches" (in which the animal's roar gives added strength to the music) or even the mournful "Mother Is Dead," a touching moment in the film and in this recording.

Didier C. Deutsch

Leprechaun

1992, Intrada Records, from the film *Leprechaun*, Trimark Pictures, 1992 🎵🎵🎵

album notes: Music: Kevin Kiner.

With just a hint of Irish through prominent featuring of piccolo as a lead instrument throughout the score, Kevin Kiner's music for this malevolent movie of minuscule mayhem is full of chilling charm. A fluidly orchestral composition, *Leprechaun* counterpoints a very pleasant, almost American theme for its main characters (Ozzie and Alex) against the dark music signifying the evil leprechaun. The score is almost entirely orchestral, and its many layers belie its reliance upon the two motifs for its thematic base. Kiner's suspenseful sonorities and aggressive arpeggios give the score most of its energy and keep its orchestration and tonality interesting. His chase music races along, driven by frantic string pulses and keyboard, the ever-present piccolo signifying the dangerously playful menace of the leprechaun. A workable score on film, Kiner's music is an enjoyable suspenseful-dramatic score on CD.

Randall Larson

Les choses de la vie

1992, CAM Records/Italy, from the film *Les choses de la vie*, Lira/Fida, 1971 🎵🎵🎵🎵

album notes: Music: Philippe Sarde.

Philippe Sarde struck a rich musical vein with his score for this subtly shaded story about the midlife crisis of a man torn between his young mistress and his love for his wife and son. Informed by a forlorn main theme about the inevitability of life and the curved balls it throws to all of us ("Helene's Song," heard throughout), the music speaks volumes about what is, after all, a relatively common situation. But Sarde was able to find the right accents to put these feelings to music in a score that brims with unspoken sadness and an overbearing nostalgic mood. Starring Michel Piccoli and Romy Schneider, heard in the vocal version of "Helene's Song," *Les choses de la vie*, directed by Claude Sautet, was an important film that elicited an important score. However, be aware of the fact that this CD has a total playing time of less then 25 minutes. This recording may be difficult to find. Check with a used CD store, mail-order com-

pany, or a dealer specializing in rare, out-of-print, or import recordings.

Didier C. Deutsch

Les demoiselles de Rochefort

1998, Philips/France, from the film *Les demoiselles de Rochefort (The Young Girls of Rochefort)*, United Artists, 1968 🎵🎵🎵

album notes: Music: Michel Legrand; **Lyrics:** Jacques Demy; **Conductor:** Michel Legrand.

There were many things wrong with Jacques Demy's *The Young Girls of Rochefort*, a screen musical released in 1968, one being that it tried too hard to be a musical, another that it came after the huge success of *The Umbrellas of Cherbourg*, the first musical soap worthy of the name. Despite the fabulous cast assembled for the occasion (Catherine Deneuve and Francoise Dorleac as the young girls, Danielle Darrieux as their mother, and Gene Kelly and George Chakiris, who added the authority of their presence to the proceedings, though they often seemed hopelessly lost), and despite a gorgeous production, lavish and colorful, the film was a real mess. For one, the actors were not allowed to sing, and were all dubbed by seasoned vocalists, something that already detracted from their performance on screen. But the story itself (about two sisters wanting to put on an act, and the itinerant circus people who enable them to do so over a summer of revelry and unlikely romances) was totally absurd, like a surrealist tale that wanted to appear light and frothy against its musical background. And let's face it: some of the songs were juvenile and embarrassing at best ("La femme coupée en morceaux" for instance). But Michel Legrand and Jacques Demy, while unable to duplicate the levels of quality reached in their previous effort, wrote a score that had its gratifying moments ("Chanson des jumelles," "Nous voyageons de ville en ville," "Chanson d'un jour d'été," all of them, not coincidentally, performed by Catherine Deneuve and her real-life sister Francoise Dorleac). This CD reissue also boasts cover version of some of the tunes played by Michel Legrand with some recognizable jazzmen, such as Ron Carter and Grady Tate, which prove to be the most enjoyable moments in this 2-CD collection. This title may be out of print or just plain hard to find. Mail-order companies, used CD shops, or dealers of rare or import recordings will be your best bet.

Didier C. Deutsch

Les Miserables

1987, Geffen Records, from the Broadway production *Les Miserables*, 1987 🎵🎵🎵🎵🎵

album notes: Music: Claude-Michel Schonberg; **Lyrics:** Herbert Kretzmer; **Original French Text:** Alain Boublil, Jean-Marc Natel; **Musical Di-**

rection: Robert Billing; **Cast:** Colm Wilkinson, Terrence Mann, Randy Graff, Braden Danner, Judy Kuhn, Frances Ruffelle.

1989, Marco Polo Records, from the film *Les Miserables*, 1934 ♪♪♪♪

album notes: Music: Arthur Honegger; **Orchestra:** The Slovak Radio Symphony Orchestra of Bratislava; **Conductor:** Adriano.

1998, Hollywood Records, from the film *Les Miserables*, Columbia Pictures, 1998 ♪♪♪♡

album notes: Music: Basil Poledouris; **Conductor:** Basil Poledouris.

Victor Hugo's epic story *Les Miserables*, already the source of numerous stage, screen and TV adaptations, became a monstrous international musical hit with this show, sporting a score by the Claude–Michel Schonberg and Alain Boublil. Their original creation premiered in Paris in 1980, before moving to London in 1985, and to Broadway, where it opened on March 12, 1987. The plot centers around a splendid retelling of the story of Jean Valjean, a former convict, who redeems himself and becomes an honorable citizen, only to be pursued by the implacable police officer, Javert, who wants to arrest him again for breaking his parole. The show redefined the criteria by which Broadway musicals would be judged: Spectacular in every way, with sharply drawn colorful characters, and a sweeping score of wall–to–wall songs and instrumental bridges tied together without dialogue. The pop opera raised the standards (and costs) of stage productions by being utterly extravagant and theatrical while bringing a new seriousness to the medium, midway between the glorious musicals of yesteryear and the standard old–fashioned operas forever in search of new audiences. The show, which was still running at this writing, won several Tony Awards, including for Best Musical, Best Book, and Best Score.

An incredible epic sweep runs throughout the score, replete with moving romantic moments and impressive crowd numbers. It follows Valjean, always one step ahead of Javert, from 1815 and his adoption of the little orphan Cosette, ward of the Thenardiers, a couple of mean-spirited innkeepers, all the way to the 1832 Paris street uprising where Valjean saves the life of Marius, whom Cosette loves, and finally confronts Javert. The splendid two-CD Broadway cast album recording (one of several available) brings out all the flavor and passion in this extraordinary production.

One of the most successful film versions of *Les Miserables* is a French version made by Raymond Bernard in 1934, with Harry Baur unforgettable as Valjean, a powerful drama heightened by Arthur Honegger's remarkably evocative score. Painstakingly reconstructed by Swiss musicologist and conductor Adriano and solidly performed by the Slovak Radio Symphony Orchestra of Bratislava, Honegger's music underlines all the passion and drama in Hugo's tale, and reveals itself a striking composi-

tion with great appeal when taken on its own terms. A revelation, as well as a reminder that film music can often reach the loftiest heights in the hands of creative composers.

There have been so many versions of Hugo's massive novel (and the clones it spawned, like *The Fugitive*) that it is getting difficult to actually keep accurate count. But the story of Valjean, the reformed escaped criminal, incessantly pursued by Javert, the stern policeman intent on bringing him back to justice, has always fired the imagination of screenwriters scrambling for fresh ideas, and fueled many remakes, with only the names above the title differentiating them.

In the story's latest incarnation, the principals include Liam Neeson as Valjean, Geoffrey Rush as Javert, Uma Thurman as Fantine, and Claire Danes as Cosette. In a fresh departure from standard soundtrack albums, the solidly romantic score by Basil Poledouris is presented in four suites, each dealing with a specific episode in the life of Valjean: his journey from hard labor to redemption; his encounter with Fantine, whose little girl, Cosette, he adopts and raises as his own; life in Paris, when Cosette, now a young lady, meets and falls in love with Marius, a student who rebels against the monarchy; and finally, the barricade episode where Valjean, against his better judgment, saves Marius and confronts Javert, who commits suicide when he realizes he has failed the judicial system after letting Valjean go. The themes, sturdy and austere, suggest the multilayered dramas unfolding, but without the support of a strong melodic tune that might tie all the components together, and characterize the action or give it a stronger personality—a fault common to most soundtracks these days.

see also: Napoleon

Didier C. Deutsch

Les parapluies de Cherbourg

1997, Sony Classical, from the film *Les parapluies de Cherbourg (The Umbrellas of Cherbourg)*, 1964 ♪♪♪♪

album notes: Music: Michel Legrand, Jacques Demy; **Conductor:** Michel Legrand; **Cast:** Catherine Deneuve (sung by Danielle Licari); Nino Castelnuovo (sung by Jose Bartel); Anne Verson (sung by Christiane Legrand); Marc Michel (sung by George Blanes).

Movie musical fans rejoiced at the news of a theatrical re-release of this delightful French film from 1964, and there is more call for celebration with this reissued soundtrack album. Director Jacque Demy's unique movie about a pair of ill-fated young lovers in the small French town of Cherbourg is told entirely through music. Michel Legrand (*The Thomas Crown Affair, Yentl, Atlantic City,* etc.) penned all of the score, as well as all of the songs. The entire song/score cycle is contained here. Be prepared for a good cry when Genevieve (Catherine Deneuve on screen, but singer Danielle Licari in actuality) sings "Je ne pourrai jamais vivre sans toi," which translates as "I Will Wait for You." Its haunting melody will stay with you for days after. This recording may be difficult to find. Check with a used CD store, mail-order company, or a dealer specializing in rare, out-of-print, or import recordings.

Amy Rosen

Les pétroleuses

1994, SLC Records/Japan, from the film *Les pétroleuses (The Legend of Frenchie King)*, 1972 ♪♪♪♪

album notes: Music: Francis Lai.

A sly, tongue-in-cheek western with Brigitte Bardot, Micheline Presle, and Claudia Cardinale as three rough-and-tumble riding broads in a West that was only wild in name, *The Legend of Frenchie King* got a hilarious score from Francis Lai, evidently inspired by the rambunctious nature of the film and its totally inane (but fun) plot. Directed by Christian-Jaque, whose *Fanfan la Tulipe* remains one of the best swashbucklers ever made in France, *Les pétroleuses* may have been inconsequential, and its story of two fighting gangs, the good ones clad in white and led by Bardot, and the bad ones dressed in black and led by Cardinale, riding the range near the Mexican border in the late 1800s certainly didn't make much sense, and even less so in the poorly dubbed English version, but its bawdy antics made it thoroughly entertaining. Both Presle and Cardinale had a vocal moment amidst the action, but surprisingly not Bardot. This title may be out of print or just plain hard to find. Mail-order companies, used CD shops, or dealers of rare or import recordings will be your best bet.

Didier C. Deutsch

Les valseuses

1998, SLC/Japan or Musidisc/France, from the film *Les valseuses*, 1968 ♪♪♪♪

album notes: Music: Stephane Grappelli; Featured Musicians: Stephane Grappelli, violin; Maurice Vander, keyboards; Marc Hemmeler, keyboards; Eddy Louiss, keyboards; Oscar Peterson, keyboards; Guy Pedersen, bass; Niels H.O. Pedersen, bass; Daniel Humair, drums; Kenny Clarke, drums.

The film that introduced Gerard Depardieu and Miou-Miou to American audiences, along with the terms "insouciance" and "menage a trois," *Les valseuses* was graced by a wonderfully whimsical score signed by violinist extraordinaire Stephane Grappelli, who created the lightweight and enjoyable cues heard here, in which he shared the spotlight with other jazz greats like Maurice Vander and Oscar Peterson on piano, Guy Pedersen and Niels Pedersen (no relation) on bass, and Daniel Humair and Kenny Clarke on drums. The casually liberating music echoed this story about two guys with fun on their mind

(Depardieu and Patrick Dewaere), the girl they both share (Miou-Miou), and the life of petty crime that eventually led to murder. A fun album, but how could it be otherwise with Grappelli in command of the music. This recording may be difficult to find. Check with a used CD store, mail-order company, or a dealer specializing in rare, out-of-print, or import recordings.

Didier C. Deutsch

Let Him Have It

1992, Virgin Movie Music, from the film *Let Him Have It,* Fine Line, 1992 ♪♪♪♡

album notes: Music: Michael Kamen, Edward Shearmur.

The various pop and jazz selections in this great soundtrack album almost make one regret that some playing time was actually devoted to the score by Michael Kamen and Ed Shearmur. Not that the score is bad, in fact it's quite good, but whoever chose the source material for this compelling drama about two British kids caught in a burglary attempt in the early 1950s knew precisely what music to play to evoke the period: vocals by Jo Stafford ("You Belong to Me"), Kay Starr ("Wheel of Fortune"), and jazz selections by Stan Getz ("As I Live in Bop"), Paul Quinichette ("Birdland Jump"), and Ray Charles ("Guitar Blues"), among others—not your usual run-of-the-mill stuff. As a result, Michael Kamen's music, although it has many flashes of brilliance, sounds just a trifle too . . . contemporary. The title of the film, by the way, refers to the fact that a policeman was killed during the robbery attempt, with one of the juveniles, convicted of murder, drawing a death sentence.

Didier C. Deutsch

Let It Be

1987, EMI Records, from the documentary film *Let It Be*, 1970 ♪♪♪♪

album notes: Music: John Lennon, Paul McCartney, George Harrison; Lyrics: John Lennon, Paul McCartney, George Harrison.

Meant as a documentary of a band in the recording studio, the Beatles' last film instead captured them losing their way and coming apart, which may explain why it remains unavailable on video after many years. The soundtrack makes a much more cheerful document, even if the CD represents only a small portion of the songs recorded in those marathon sessions. (The remainder are largely available–or not, depending on the whim of the FBI–on what may be the biggest batch of bootlegs ever associated with a single album.) Perhaps intentionally, the music sounds like the Beatles' story in miniature, from skiffle ("Maggie Mae") to early rock & roll ("One After 909") to spirituality ("Across the Universe"). Get back, indeed.

Marc Kirkeby

Lethal Weapon 2/Lethal Weapon 3

🎬 1989, Warner Bros. Records, from the film *Lethal Weapon 2,* Warner Bros., 1989 ♫♫♫♫

album notes: Music: Michael Kamen; Eric Clapton; **Conductor:** Michael Kamen; **Featured Soloists:** Eric Clapton, guitar; David Sanborn, alto sax; Michael Kamen, Kurzweil; Gregory Phillinganes, keyboards; Tom Barney, bass; Sonny Emory, drums; Lew Soloff, trumpet.

🎬 1992, Warner Bros. Records, from the film *Lethal Weapon 3,* Warner Bros., 1992 ♫♫♫♫

album notes: Music: Michael Kamen; Eric Clapton; **Orchestra:** The Greater Los Angeles Orchestra; the Greater New York Alumni Orchestra; **Conductor:** Michael Kamen.

One of the most interesting elements in the *Lethal Weapon* films has been the scores devised by Michael Kamen, with assist and support from Eric Clapton and David Sanborn. Writing in a style that reflects the films' urban contemporary setting and the volatile action in them, Kamen's scores are particularly strong and imaginatively descriptive. The point is made in these two albums (the soundtrack album of the first film has never been released on compact disc) in which Sanborn's soulful saxophone and Clapton's doleful guitar work set off the melodies written by the composer. Augmenting the impression made by the instrumental cues, all are more or less reflective of the fast-paced action on the screen and the feuding friendship that binds the two cops portrayed by Mel Gibson and Danny Glover, but equally effective in a purely aural setup. Both CDs contain performances by well-known vocalists, George Harrison, the Beach Boys, and Randy Crawford in the first, Sting and Elton John in the second. First class all the way!

Didier C. Deutsch

Leviathan

🎬 1989, Varèse Sarabande, from the film *Leviathan,* MGM, 1989 ♫♫

album notes: Music: Jerry Goldsmith; **Orchestra:** The Orchestra di Santa Cecilia di Roma; **Conductor:** Jerry Goldsmith.

This rotten 1986 film is a cross between *Alien* and the 1981 Sean Connery space film *Outland,* and unfortunately, so is Goldsmith's rather simplistic score. The opening, with its distorted whale calls and melancholy woodwind theme, works well enough, as do later cues like "Situation under Control" and "Escape Bubbles" which make good use of the main theme. But the film's action cues ("Decompression," "Discovery," "Too Hot") rely on a maddening two-note rhythmic device that just repeats and repeats without any of Goldsmith's usual complex development and ornamentation, making the album's slight 30-minute running time seem like an eternity. And Goldsmith's upbeat, heroic finale, although listenable on its own, was completely at odds with the mood of the film.

Jeff Bond

10 Essential Scores
by Georges Delerue

Jules et Jim
The Day of the Dolphin
Black Robe
Le dernier metro
The Woman Next Door
A Little Romance
Il conformista
Crimes of the Heart
Steel Magnolias
Platoon

Lewis & Clark

📺 1997, RCA Victor, from the television film *Lewis & Clark,* PBS TV, 1997 ♫♫♫♫

A television film by Ken Burns, *Lewis & Clark* retraced the most important expedition ever attempted in American history: the voyage of discovery, dangerous and uneasy, that took Meriwether Lewis and William Clark across the wide Missouri River, over the Continental Divide, all the way to the Pacific Ocean in one of the nation's most enduring adventures. Typical of the filmmaker's approach to such projects, the soundtrack consisted of a rich and memorable collection of folk melodies, Native American tunes, and songs specifically created for this special, the whole augmented by readings from the expedition journals. The album collects together some of the most endearing selections in a brilliant display of familiar and unfamiliar tunes, some traditional, some original, all beautifully rendered.

see also: Lincoln, 500 Nations

Didier C. Deutsch

L'harem

See: Il ladrone/L'harem

Liar Liar

 1997, MCA Records, from the film *Liar Liar*, Universal Pictures, 1997 🎬🎬

album notes: Music: John Debney; **Conductor:** John Debney.

A very funny comedy starring Jim Carrey as a chronic liar who is forced to tell the truth in spite of himself for 24 hours, *Liar Liar* elicited a score from John Debney that proved right on the money when heard along with the screen action, but fails to make the grade in one's living room. The reason is simple. The cues were written for a fast-paced action, with all the quirks and turns usually found in a comedy, with the music matching the moves with similar sharp turns and oddball thrusts. On their own, however, the cues often sound too disjointed, as if the composer had chosen to write down one idea, only to abandon it the second after for another, totally different. As a result, the music is all too often jumpy, all over the place, without real focus. This is too bad, because Debney, an excellent scorer, has written some themes that are vibrant and exciting when they are given a chance to be developed. A clear case of a score which needed to be rethought and reconstructed for its soundtrack album.

Didier C. Deutsch

License to Kill

1989, MCA Records, from the film *License to Kill*, United Artists, 1989 🎬🎬🎬

album notes: Music: Michael Kamen; **Orchestra:** The National Philharmonic Orchestra; **Conductor:** Michael Kamen.

Once again, the point is clearly made that John Barry is the only composer whose music perfectly captures and matches the moods and slyly ridiculous situations in which agent 007 usually finds himself. Without taking anything away from Michael Kamen's own artistic bend, magnificently evident in other soundtrack recordings, his score for *License to Kill* in which the dashing James Bond was portrayed by Timothy Dalton, simply doesn't have the characteristic flair one can find in Barry's scores. This said, Kamen's music has its moments of panache and glory, with cues that are evocative and can stand against any other music written for a motion picture. But even though he quotes from Barry's "Bond Theme" and provides a new, fresh approach to the musical concept of a James Bond film, his score ultimately sounds anything but. Because of that, the rating reflects the quality of the music itself, not the fact that this is a James Bond score, which would automatically lower the rating by comparison.

Didier C. Deutsch

The Life

1997, Sony Classical, from the Broadway musical *The Life*, 1997 🎵🎵🎵

album notes: Music: Cy Coleman; **Lyrics:** Ira Gasman; **Book:** David Newman, Ira Gasman, Cy Coleman; **Musical Direction:** Gordon Lowry Harrell; **Cast:** Pamela Isaacs, Lillias White, Kevin Ramsey, Bellamy Young, Vernel Bagneris, Chuck Cooper.

The seedy underside of life on New York's 42nd Street, before Disney came and helped clean the whole area, provided composer Cy Coleman with another look at the unfortunate existence of prostitutes. But if you thought this was a musical like *Sweet Charity,* think again. The girls here are raggedy, tired, and worn out, and there is nothing glamorous about their existence (at least Charity, a dance hall hostess of easy virtue, met a movie star).

The tone of the libretto resulted in a score that ultimately had little appeal to it, leading to a show that was not very characteristic, except for two numbers ("The Oldest Profession" and "My Body"); superb portrayals by Pamela Isaacs and Lillias White, as two prostitutes with hearts of gold, and by Chuck Cooper, a sensational baritone, as Memphis, a pimp; and explosive orchestrations by Don Sebesky and Harold Wheeler. Beyond that, *The Life* was trite, and, frankly speaking, embarrassingly dated.

The cast album reflects everything that was positive and negative about the show, but cannot conjure up the extraordinary elements that had made *Sweet Charity* such a winning show in the first place.

Didier C. Deutsch

Life and Nothing But

1989, DRG Records, from the film *Life and Nothing But*, Orion Classics, 1989 🎬🎬🎬🎬

album notes: Music: Oswald d'Andrea.

A sobering, unglorified look at the devastating effects of war in general, Bertrand Tavernier's scathing film follows the efforts by the French military command to find at the end of World War I, a suitable "unknown soldier" worthy of receiving the nation's undying respect and admiration. The score, by Oswald d'Andrea, equally stern and unfussy, italicized the unfolding drama, justifiably earning a Cesar, France's equivalent to the Oscar for "Best Musical Score" in 1990. Two selections in particular, "The Grezaucourt Suite" and "The Letter" clearly explain the reasons for its success.

Didier C. Deutsch

Life Is Beautiful

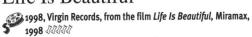 **1998, Virgin Records, from the film *Life Is Beautiful*, Miramax, 1998** 🎬🎬🎬🎬🎬

album notes: Music: Nicola Piovani; **Orchestra:** The Orchestra dell'Accademia musicale italiana; **Conductor:** Nicola Piovani.

An Oscar rewarded composer Nicola Piovani, who had toiled for many years in his native Italy without actually getting the international recognition he so richly deserved, for this exquisite score. Whether it was the gentle story of a man who, during the Nazi occupation, hides the truth to his young son by creating fancy tales about what is happening around them, or the irrepressible personality of Roberto Benigni, or both that actually compelled the Academy voters to single out Piovani's music, the choice could not have been more felicitous. With accents that sometimes recall Morricone's deeply moving *Cinema Paradiso,* Piovani created a series of cues that are richly evocative and rewarding. Moments of sheer levity are heard next to nostalgic tunes that depict the dark days of the War, in a dual reflection of the film's two distinct aspects. The score truly deserved to win. This recording may be difficult to find. Check with a used CD store, mail-order company, or a dealer specializing in rare, out-of-print, or import recordings.

Didier C. Deutsch

Life with Mikey

🎞️ 1993, Hollywood Records, from the film *Life with Mikey,* Touchstone, 1993 *♪♪♪♪*

album notes: Music: Alan Menken; **Conductor:** Michael Starobin.

Michael J. Fox had a field day playing a former child actor who has been unable to parlay his initial success into a full-time career, and who now runs a casting agency for up and coming underage performers. Alan Menken, of *Little Mermaid* fame, devised a cute little score to accompany this charming comedy, in which the would-be tiny talent are given to singing songs from Disney films like "Zip-a-Dee Doo-Dah" and "A Spoonful of Sugar," as well as lesser known selections like "Anything Goes," "Miss Otis Regrets," or "Lullaby of Broadway." (They should have called the film *Life of Mickey*!) Dave Tofani, a brilliant studio musician, gets to blow a mean sax on "Wollman Rink," and an uncredited mixed chorus does nicely by the energetic title tune. All told, a very amusing, diversified score that has a lot to offer.

Didier C. Deutsch

Lifeforce

🎞️ 1989, Milan Records, from the film *Lifeforce,* Cannon Films, 1989 *♪♪♪♪♪*

album notes: Music: Henry Mancini; **Orchestra:** The London Symphony Orchestra; **Conductor:** Henry Mancini.

Lifeforce is Henry Mancini's *Star Wars,* a symphonic sci-fi epic. Actually that's not entirely true. *Star Wars* is a good and popular film, and *Lifeforce* is a laughably awful 1985 Tobe Hooper space-vampire flick. Furthermore, John Williams's score for *Star Wars* emphasizes leitmotifs, whereas Mancini's *Lifeforce* is through-composed, a tone poem of symphonic moods. But they are both incredibly good. *Lifeforce* brought Mancini, best known for catchy pop hits, back to the science-fiction and horror genres where he started as a staff composer for Universal in the 1950s. The score is romantic and huge, a sweeping epic bristling with the orchestrational know-how and chord structures that Mancini carried inside his amazing brain. The most flashy piece is the end title, an unusual march in 3/4, but the rest of the score has a moody richness as haunting in the subtle sequences as it is propulsive in the climactic ones. There are few themes per se; rather, the whole thing has a unified feeling, whereby certain gestures and contrapuntal blends become associated with the story. One of the best sequences is the film's opening "Discovery" suite running 14 minutes, in which a space shuttle discovers a vampire ship inside a comet—the film is largely a showcase for Mancini's music. Alas, this was cut from the final print, as were certain other scenes, Mancini's music abridged and selectively replaced with synthesizer music by Michael Kamen. (There is a restored version available on laserdisc.) It is unfortunate that Mancini rarely revisited the "John Williams" genres for the latter portion of his career, because *Lifeforce* is a knockout.

Lukas Kendall

Lightning Jack

🎞️ 1994, Festival Records/Australia, from the film *Lightning Jack,* Village Roadshow Pictures, 1994 *♪♪♪♪*

album notes: Music: Bruce Rowland; **Conductor:** Bruce Rowland; **Featured Musicians:** Peter Harper, harmonica; Tony Naylor, guitar; Doug DeVries, guitar; Simon Paterson, guitar; Don Stevenson, guitars; Roger McLaughlin, electric bass; Mike Grabowski, electric bass; Ron Sandilands, drums.

An exhilarating Australian western, *Lightning Jack* takes its subject humorously, providing star Paul Hogan with a vehicle that has the wacky appeal of his *Crocodile Dundee* films, while taking him to a new environment, the American West. Indicative of the tone adopted in this frequently diverting film, Hogan's Jack, quick on the draw but slightly near-sighted about his own possibilities, teams with a riding partner, a taciturn character whose laconism is only due to the fact that he is a mute. As for the slightly inconsequential story itself, it gives the star enough rope to enable him to display another facet of his congenial personality, in a plot with enough twists and turns to delight his fans. Making sly comments of its own, Bruce Rowland's music at times evoked his own *Man from Snowy River* scores, with a tongue-in-cheek discordant note that echoed the antics on the screen. Heard in this flavorful soundtrack album, some expository cues, like "A Snake Bite Bonding" and "They're Comanches," not so subtly enhanced by the harmonica in yet another concession to a tried-and-true formula, display the right thematic approach and make this score a thoroughly enjoyable effort.

Didier C. Deutsch

Li'l Abner

 1990, Sony Music Special Products, from the Broadway production *Li'l Abner*, 1956 𝄞𝄞𝄞𝄞

album notes: Music: Gene de Paul; **Lyrics:** Johnny Mercer; **Musical Direction:** Lehman Engel; **Cast:** Peter Palmer, Edith Adams, Stubby Kaye.

Al Capp's comic strip characters came to stage life when *Li'l Abner,* written by Gene De Paul and Johnny Mercer, opened on Nov. 15, 1956. Taking a cue from the strip itself, in which Li'l Abner and Daisy Mae waited many years, to the great frustration of their fans, before getting married, the show also took a satirical look at politics in the rural Southern setting of Dogpatch, U.S.A. It exulted in the big annual occurrence, the frantic Sadie Hawkins' Day man-chasing race, when every eligible bachelorette can try to catch the man in her life. Starring Peter Palmer, looking for all intents and purposes like his comic strip alter ego, and Edith Adams as Daisy Mae, the musical enjoyed a long run of 693 performances. Its delirious score, marked by many humorous songs, yielded one of the theatre's big show-stopping numbers in "Jubilation T. Cornpone," in which Marryin' Sam (played by Stubby Kaye) extols the merits of Dogpatch's hero, an infamous and unglorious Southern general, better known for his incompetence than for his feats. With its cast virtually intact, the show was filmed in 1959.

Didier C. Deutsch

Lilies

1997, Varèse Sarabande, from the film *Lilies*, Turbulent Arts, 1997 𝄞𝄞𝄞𝄞

album notes: Music: Mychael Danna; **Featured Musicians:** The Hilliard Ensemble: David James, Gordon Jones, John Potter, Roger Covey Crump; Kirk Worthington, cello; Robert Grim, trumpet.

Having made a name for himself as the director of the way-out AIDS musical *Zero Patience,* John Greyson turned his attention to a 1987 French Canadian play by Michel Marc Bouchard, which, under his apt direction, became *Lilies,* the story of three young boys tragically involved in a romantic triangle. Now adults, the surviving members, two cons serving time who were once close friends and lovers, are again at odds over the events that occurred 40 years before. The confessional aspect of the drama suggested to composer Mychael Danna a very unusual series of cues tailored after the polyphonic Gregorian chant, mixing the Catholic "ordinary" and "proper" rituals. As a result, the score has become in essence a Mass in which the various segments have been designated as cues that accom-

pany the action on screen. It is a daring proposition, one that may not sit very well with some listeners, who may question the use of liturgical material in connection with a homosexual drama. But on its own, it is a mesmerizing effort that elevates the album to spheres seldom explored in standard soundtrack albums. Not for everybody, but something that will certainly appeal to those adventurous enough to listen closely.

Didier C. Deutsch

Lilies of the Field

1997, P.E.G. Recordings, from the film *Lilies of the Field*, United Artists, 1963 𝄞𝄞𝄞𝄞

album notes: Music: Jerry Goldsmith; **Conductor:** Jerry Goldsmith; **Featured Vocalist:** Jester Hairston.

Anchored by the main theme, a variation on the choral "Amen," also heard, this wonderful Americana-bathed score by Jerry Goldsmith resonates with joyous accents, punctuated by various acoustic instruments (a harmonica, a guitar, a banjo, an accordion) often playing over a jaunty string section. Written for a minor comedy, about a former G.I. on the loose who comes upon and helps five nuns, refugees from behind the Iron Curtain, in building a chapel in the middle of the Arizona desert, the score captures the funny, warm-hearted moods of the story, giving it an extra, most winning dimension. Available for the first time since its release in 1963, the album suffers from an almost intolerable hiss, all the more noticeable because the sparse instrumentation cannot hide it.

Didier C. Deutsch

The Linguini Incident

1992, Varèse Sarabande, from the film *The Linguini Incident,* Academy Entertainment, 1992 𝄞𝄞𝄞𝄞𝄞

album notes: Music: Thomas Newman; **Conductor:** Thomas Newman; **Featured Musicians:** John Beasley, piano; Chuck Domanico, string bass; Harvey Mason, drums; Sal Marquez, trumpet; George Thatcher, trombone; Jim Self, tuba; Bill Bernstein, flute; Jeff Elmassion, single reeds; Michael Fisher, percussion; Thomas Newman, ukulele, piano.

The explosive contemporary jazz accents in Thomas Newman's diversified score underline the ferocious aspects of this biting satire starring David Bowie, Julian Lennon, Rosanna Arquette, and Buck Henry as wacky characters in a swanky restaurant whose conversation turns to the meaning of life. Performed by many excellent musicians and developed along varied rhythmic lines, the music is consistently surprising, sometimes corrosive, and sometimes plain entertaining. There are many changes that will delight adventurous listeners unwilling to settle for the ordinary. With a predominance of Latin tunes, but not exclusively limited to this type of expression, the score is totally enjoyable, with Newman pulling all stops in a dazzling display of his creative streak and talent as an instrumentalist.

Didier C. Deutsch

Link

1986, Varèse Sarabande Records, from the film *Link*, Cannon Screen Entertainment, 1986 ♫♫♫

album notes: Music: Jerry Goldsmith; **Orchestra:** The National Philharmonic Orchestra; **Conductor:** Jerry Goldsmith.

Jerry Goldsmith's approach to this odd suspense film about a trained orangutan is one of the composer's strangest—a goofball, circus-like approach featuring a quasi-calliope tune and heavy use of synthesized rhythms, stacked against the composer's usual modernistic action writing. It's a wildly uneven listen, mixing cringe-inducing slapstick comedy with powerful orchestral treatments of suspense and action and a beautiful, lyrical melody of strings and electronic effects. For every moment of vintage Goldsmith there's something that will have you clutching for the "skip" button on your CD player, but you have to give Goldsmith some points for audaciousness here. The biggest problem with the score is the drum machines that just drown out too much of the orchestra.

Jeff Bond

The Lion in Winter

1995, Legacy Records/Sony Music Entertainment, from the film *The Lion in Winter*, Avco Embassy, 1968 ♫♫♫♫

album notes: Music: John Barry.

John Barry's quasi-medieval Academy Award–winning score for *The Lion in Winter*, starring Katharine Hepburn and Peter O'Toole, truly demonstrates the composer's incredibly versatile perspective. With a daunting task at hand—creating an original musical score for an historical drama that occurs in the year 1183—Barry devised with "great trepidations" (his own words) a beautiful, harmonically complex set of compositions that are rich with texture and substance, and still hold up remarkably well 30 years later. The themes depicting the Catholic church are particularly powerful, and two original "period" songs (composed by Barry and James Goldman) stand out as brilliant examples of the composer's willingness to integrate new forms into his repertoire of musical stylings. With the current, renewed interest in Gregorian chant, this disc becomes a fascinating example of the power found in this type of liturgical expression, used to such gratifying results in this score. The meticulous stereo remastering allows the full breadth of the rich original recording (made at Cine Tele Studios in London) to shine through with unequaled brilliance.

Charles L. Granata

The Lion King

1994, Walt Disney Records, from the animated feature *The Lion King*, Walt Disney Pictures, 1994 ♫♫♫♫

album notes: Music: Hans Zimmer; **Songs:** Elton John, Tim Rice; **Conductor:** Nick Glennie-Smith; **Cast:** Carmen Twillie, Jason Weaver, Rowan Atkinson, Laura Williams, Jeremy Irons, Whoopi Goldberg, Cheech Marin, Nathan Lane, Ernie Sabella.

Fast becoming a contemporary classic, *The Lion King* is steeped in the finest Walt Disney tradition. Great story, gorgeous animation, quality music and songs—*The Lion King* sports all of these hallmarks and more. Cleverly incorporating the rhythms and sounds of the African jungle into its score, the film features songs by pop music legend Elton John, and Academy Award–winning lyricist Tim Rice. Among the familiar hit songs included on the soundtrack are "Hakuna Matata," "Circle of Life," "I Just Can't Wait to Be King," and "Can You Feel the Love Tonight." Special Elton John vocal versions of the last three songs are also heard here, and actor Nathan Lane is featured on "Hakuna Matata." Quality is what has made Disney films and soundtracks special, and important. Undoubtedly, generations of film fans of all ages will continue to enjoy the music from *The Lion King* through this wonderful soundtrack recording.

Charles L. Granata

1997, Walt Disney, from the Broadway musical *The Lion King*, 1997 ♫♫♫

album notes: Music: Elton John, Tim Rice; **Lyrics:** Elton John, Tim Rice; **Additional Music and Lyrics:** Lebo M, Mark Mancina, Jay Rifkin, Julie Taymor, Hans Zimmer; **Book:** Roger Allers, Irene Mecchi; **Conductor:** Joseph Church; **Cast:** Tsidii Le Loka, Samuel E. Wright, Gina Breedlove, Geoff Hoyle, John Vickery, Scott Irby-Ranniar, Kajuana Shuford, Max Casella, Tom Alan Robbins, Jason Raize, Heather Headley.

Visually, the stage version of the Disney animated feature *The Lion King* is unlike anything you may have seen on Broadway or off. In Julie Taymor's excitingly lucid direction, it has become a musical play theatergoers will speak about for generations to come, and the new standard by which every other production will have to be measured.

Musically, it is another question altogether: the score by Elton John and Tim Rice was never a tremendous one. It had its moments, to be sure, and almost anyone who saw the film is bound to recall at least its best-known number, "Hakuna Matata." But that's the rub: even with the addition of the more familiar "The Lion Sleeps Tonight," interpolated in this production, and the outstanding performances by many gifted actors and actresses, who are called to impersonate the animal characters in the story of Simba, the one weak point in this production of *The Lion King* is its score. The songs are acceptable, but not thrilling. In fact, even "Hakuna Matata" falls flat here, not so much because it is poorly performed, but because in a rare lapse of artistic judg-

$\begin{array}{c}3\\3\\2\end{array}$ *lionheart*

The Lion King **(The Kobal Collection)**

ment, Julie Taymor failed to take it to the next level of excitement and turn it into a show-stopping moment.

Unfortunately, the limitations in the score also translate to the cast album, which, without Taymor's astonishing visuals, becomes a flat transcription of the original. Again, the actors in the show and on the album are perfectly fine, with John Vickery properly hissable as Scar; Max Casella and Tom Alan Robbins extremely funny as Timon and Pumbaa, respectively; Samuel E. Wright appropriately regal as Mufasa; and Jason Raize and Heather Headley delightful as the grown-up Simba and Nala. It's just a case of the material letting its performers down. Coming from Elton John and Tim Rice, two gifted songwriters, it is all the more surprising.

Didier C. Deutsch

Lionheart

1987, Varèse Sarabande, from the film *Lionheart,* Orion Pictures, 1987 ♪♪♪♪♪
album notes: Music: Jerry Goldsmith; **Conductor:** Jerry Goldsmith.

A film of epic proportions, *Lionheart,* directed by Franklin J. Schaffner, is a big–screen retelling of the 12th–century Children's Crusade, a dark episode in medieval times that saw youngsters organize an expedition in search of Richard the Lionhearted, whose adventures, real or imaginary, became the grist for so many swashbucklers set in Sherwood Forest. Richard, who set out to reclaim the Holy Land invaded by the Moors, was subsequently taken prisoner. The screenplay, taking some liberties with historical facts, focuses on a young knight and two circus performers he has befriended, and their efforts to thwart the threat of a malevolent Black Knight whose henchmen have received instructions to round up the children and sell them as slaves.

The most interesting thing about the film, which received theatrical release in Canada only but has been available on video and laserdisc, is the fact that its profuse score was composed by Jerry Goldsmith, whose working relationship with Schaffner had already extended over six previous films. Goldsmith found in this film an occasion to express himself in an idiom in which he has seldom found a voice. In fact, so extensive was Goldsmith's contribution that the score had to be spread over two albums, with a third volume combining together the most significant highlights from the other two.

With a central three-note motif recurring throughout, and binding the cues together, the score comes across as a cohesive, wonderfully vivid effort with a full contingent of big epic moments, romantic themes, exciting battles and pulse-racing action scenes. It is all neatly wrapped up in a broad, colorful orchestral canvas fleshed out by the subtle use of electronics, dramatically played by the Hungarian State Opera Orchestra. The recording, broad and spacious, enhances all the positive aspects of the score and makes them even more impressive and grander-than-life.

Didier C. Deutsch

Lionheart

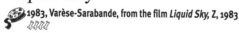 1990, Intrada Records, from the film *Lionheart*, Universal Pictures, 1990 🎬🎬🎬

album notes: Music: John Scott; **Orchestra:** The Munich Symphony Orchestra; **Conductor:** John Scott.

For this contemporary adventure film (not to be confused with Schaffner's medieval epic), John Scott develops a series of cues that reflected the various locales in which the action took place—North Africa, Los Angeles, New York City—as well as the character of the story's main protagonist, a kickboxing soldier of fortune named Lyon (Jean-Claude Van Damme), bent on avenging his brother killed by drug dealers. As is often the case in films of this nature, the score is much better than the film itself, with the symphony orchestra giving a distinct and powerful color to the cues. An occasional jazz track, performed by a quintet, provides a different perspective on Scott's creativity, while it also fits the sometimes explosive action scenes in the film.

Didier C. Deutsch

Liquid Sky

1983, Varèse-Sarabande, from the film *Liquid Sky*, Z, 1983 🎬🎬🎬🎬

album notes: Music/Musical Adaptations: Slava Tsukerman, Brenda I. Nutchinson, Clive Smith.

There's a bizarre sense of time and place to this cult sci-fi flick from 1983, which places orgasm-addicted aliens amongst the heroin-drenched art scene of NYC. Maybe it was the incredible look of the film that inspired director Tsukerman and his musical collaborators to come up with a score that sounds like it was composed on tinkertoy synths (actually, a Fairlight computer). The child-like sound they came up with is a near-brilliant elaboration on the tinny synth scores that usually afflict low-budget sci-fi, as creepy sound effects and voice samples

do an electronic twist just this side of Devo. *Liquid Sky* has the kind of insane originality that you either admire or instantly turn off, and it's a measure of Tsukerman's hipness that he uses such classical composers as Carl Orff and Marin Marais for the film's themes. *Liquid Sky* might be the most bizarre "pop" score of all time, a heralding to the birth of new wave music—even if it seems the composers' main goal was just to be as strange as possible.

Dan Schweiger

Lisbon Story

1995, Metro Blue/EMI Records, from the film *Lisbon Story*, Road Movies/Madragoa, 1995 🎬🎬🎬🎬

album notes: Music: Madredeus: Teresa Salgueiro, vocals; Jose Peixoto, Pedro Ayres Magalhaes, guitar; Francisco Ribeiro, violoncello; Gabriel Gomes, accordion; Rodrigo Leao, keyboards.

For this film, directed by Wim Wenders, the Portuguese group Madredeus created a series of folk songs that may qualify as world music and attract many listeners inclined to discover sounds alien to our culture. Certainly, listening to this album is quite a discovery, and a refreshing change of pace from some of the sounds we are bombarded with regularly, on television or in the movies. Initially intended as a documentary celebrating the inner beauties of the Portuguese capital, *Lisbon Story* eventually evolved into a personal discourse on the values of life and a meditation on moviemaking, with Wenders bringing into the narrative characters and references from his previous works.

Loosely organized, the film is a series of impressions about the city of Lisbon, its people, its sights, as experienced by a German audio technician on a trip to Portugal at the invitation of a friend, a movie director. Illustrating the journey and the visions it elicits, the original songs created by Madredeus add the right touch of color and perspective. Heard on their own, they clearly stand out as folk numbers that are exquisitely crafted and strikingly performed.

Didier C. Deutsch

Little Boy Blue

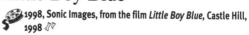 1998, Sonic Images, from the film *Little Boy Blue*, Castle Hill, 1998 🎬🎬

album notes: Music: Stewart Copeland.

Little Boy Blue is the story of Jimmy (Ryan Phillippe), a seemingly normal 19-year-old kid. Underneath, however, he is haunted by the memory of painful abuse at the hands of his father. He tries to protect his two brothers and his mother from the man who hurt him, until he finds an unexpected ally in a woman from his father's past who comes back to expose all of the abuse she has suffered from him. The film, which was well received in the art-house circuit, boasts some song, blues, and country tracks, and a very ethereal score by Stewart Copeland, which neither fits in well with the songs nor really stands up on its own. It is so light and airy, with the exception of the last track, that it hardly makes an impression.

Didier C. Deutsch

Little Buddha

1993, Milan Records, from the film *Little Buddha,* Miramax 1993 ♫♫

album notes: Music: Ryuichi Sakamoto; **Conductor:** Ryuichi Sakamoto; **Featured Soloists:** The Ambrosian Singers; John McCarthy, director; Catherine Bott, soprano; L. Subramaniam; Zakir Hussain; Nishat Khan; Shahee Samad; Kanika.

For this story that combines the tales of a Tibetan monk who believes an American born child is the reincarnation of his mentor and the life of Prince Siddhartha, Ryuichi Sakamoto integrates a standard Hollywood-style film underscore with several Indian motifs. The result is disappointing if you don't enjoy the somewhat abrasive contrast of cultures.

David Hirsch

Little Indian, Big City

1997, Hollywood Records, from the film *Little Indian, Big City,* Touchstone, 1996 ♫♫♫♫

album notes: Music: Manu Katche, Geoffrey Oryema, Tonton David; **Featured Musicians:** Jean-Claude Nemro, Rastea, keyboards; Yovo, bass; Manu Katche, drums; Jean-Pierre Alarcen, guitars; Mustapha Cisse, Manu Katche, percussion.

An Indian native taken out of his natural element and confronting civilization was the topic behind *Jungle 2 Jungle,* which starred Tim Allen. That film was based on a French smash, *Little Indian, Big City,* which pretty much told a similar story, the city in question being in this instance Paris. If the story remained the same, what was different was the soundtrack. In the French film, it consisted of a series of exotic songs written and performed by three world musicians: Manu Katche, a drummer best known for his work with Peter Gabriel, Sting, Tracy Chapman, and Ryuichi Sakamoto; Geoffrey Oryema, a native of Uganda; and Tonton David, a proponent of reggae music. Together, they provided a series of songs that are extremely catchy and reflect a subculture that is too often ignored in this country, despite the vast advances made by world music in recent years. Performed in French and English, this CD is very attractive and exudes the kind of happy sounds and melodic material that should appeal to a broad audience. A real winner!

see also: Jungle 2 Jungle

Didier C. Deutsch

Little Man Tate

1991, Varèse Sarabande, from the film *Little Man Tate,* Orion Pictures, 1991 ♫♫♫♫

album notes: Music: Mark Isham; **Featured Musicians:** Bob Sheppard, tenor sax; David Goldblatt, piano; Tom Warrington, bass; Mark Isham, trumpet; Sid Page, violin; Kurt Wortman, drums; Ken Kugler, trombone.

This soundtrack album engagingly begins on a finely sketched swing track that augurs well for the overall feel of the score. The promises held in that first track are confirmed in the others with Mark Isham's upbeat score for this heart-tugging story about a seven-year-old little genius evidencing all the elements that contribute to turn a modest effort into an enjoyable listening experience. The moods set forth are strictly in a jazz mode, something that might deter potential listeners. But when the music is that good and that gratifying, one only has to turn on the volume, relax, and savor.

Didier C. Deutsch

Little Me

1993, RCA Victor, from the Broadway production *Little Me,* 1962 ♫♫♫

album notes: Music: Cy Coleman; **Lyrics:** Carolyn Leigh; **Musical Direction:** Charles Sanford; **Cast:** Sid Caesar, Virginia Martin, Nancy Andrews, Swen Swenson.

1999, Varèse Sarabande, from the Broadway musical *Little Me,* 1998 ♫♫

album notes: Music: Cy Coleman; **Lyrics:** Carolyn Leigh; **Conductor:** David Chase; **Cast:** Faith Prince, Martin Short.

Television comedian Sid Caesar found a new lease on life when he appeared on Broadway in *Little Me,* a musical with a book by Neil Simon, one of his regular writers on the *Show of Shows,* and a score by Cy Coleman and Carolyn Leigh. *Little Me* opened on Nov. 17, 1962. Initially based on a novel by Patrick Dennis about the rags–to–riches tale of a voluptuous blonde from the skids of an Illinois town who moved up to a glamorous Southampton estate, the book became the occasion for Caesar to play no less than seven roles. All of his characters were involved in one way or another with the unlikely named Belle Schlumpfert, from a snobbish student to a French soldier, from a movie director to a miserly old banker, and from a down–on–his–luck duke to an aspiring genius who wants to be an engineer and musical composer.

Created specifically for television comedian Caesar, who was known for his manic facial expressions and vast array of weird accents, *Little Me* never was a great musical. It was a fun, nonsensical trifle, that relied on its star's ability to portray different characters—in this instance eight of them—all suitors and husbands of the show's heroine, the aptly named, buxomy Belle Poitrine.

While the score didn't have too many memorable songs (much of the stage action being taken by the antics of Caesar, who kept the show running for 257 performances), it had an ingratiating one in "Real Live Girl," a wistful lament performed by the star as a soldier.

Although a remarkable comedian who initially also made his mark on television, Martin Short is not Sid Caesar, and his overall performance in the revival of this show was extraordinarily lightweight. While he can be genuinely funny at times, all too often he relied on one-dimensional mannerisms for all the characters he was called upon to impersonate, thus eroding the impact he may have had on the inane storyline. Even less defined in this revival was Faith Prince, who seemed ill-at-ease in a part that was apparently too shallow for her enormous comedic talents.

The cast works hard to sell the songs in this cast album that doesn't entirely succeed, and with the two principals somewhat missing the grade for different reasons, we are left with a so-so version of a show that still sounds much better in the original cast album on RCA.

Didier C. Deutsch

The Little Mermaid

1994, Disney Records, from the film *The Little Mermaid*, Disney, 1994 ♫♫♫♫

album notes: Music: Alan Menken; **Songs:** Alan Menken, Howard Ashman; **Conductor:** J. A. C. Redford.

Certainly the animated film *The Little Mermaid* had many positive things to offer, including bright visuals, a soap story that charmed pre-pubescent girls and their parents, funny under-the-sea characters that delighted pre-pubescent boys and their parents, and a score that, with some minor exceptions, was clearly memorable and catchy. As a matter of fact, everyone, but everyone—even those who hadn't seen the film—had to know "Under the Sea," the delirious song that was a highlight in it. The film reversed the declining fortunes of the Disney studios and put on the map Alan Menken and Howard Ashman, who wrote the songs; it also started a new trend in animated features, launching Disney into a series of equally successful films that became the envy of other studios. Among all the CDs released since by the Disney label, *The Little Mermaid* remains the best, because the songs still sound fresh and as if they were written with kids in mind, not for grown-ups, and because they are presented in the order in which they were heard in the film (an important plus). The orchestral bridges serve as a pleasant reminder that the score for these

animated features is not just a bunch of songs, but is also a collection of instrumental moments that complement them and help move the action along.

Didier C. Deutsch

A Little Night Music

 1973, Columbia Records. from the Broadway production *A Little Night Music*, 1973 ♫♫♫♫

album notes: Music: Stephen Sondheim; **Lyrics:** Stephen Sondheim; **Musical Direction:** Harold Hastings; **Cast:** Glynis Johns, Len Cariou, Hermione Gingold, Victoria Mallory, Mark Lambert, D. Jamin-Bartlett, Laurence Guittard.

1996, Tring Records, from the London revival *A Little Night Music*, 1995 ♫♫♫♫

album notes: Music: Stephen Sondheim; **Lyrics:** Stephen Sondheim; **Musical Direction:** Jo Stewart; **Cast:** Judi Dench, Laurence Guittard, Sian Phillips, Joanna Riding, Lambert Wilson.

One of Stephen Sondheim's lightest and loveliest scores, *A Little Night Music* received a splendid recording in its original Broadway cast album. From its nearly unique vocal overture to its touchingly hopeful finale, the album is beautiful and pure pleasure. The score has an underlying rhythmic unity that adds a delightful dimension to the music. The cast is just about perfect and has not been equaled by any other production or on any other recording. Glynis Johns as Desiree Armfeldt, the aging actress, is amazing. While not a singer, her version of the hit song "Send in the Clowns" is the most moving of any you are likely to hear. Len Cariou, as her former lover Fredrik Egerman, delineates the pride and vulnerability of this emotionally vacillating character with expert charm. Laurence Guittard, as Desiree's current lover Count Carl-Magnus, is manly and arrogant in equal degrees, and Patricia Elliott as Charlotte, his wife, is delightful in her cunning and hope. The other actors are stunningly good in their parts and sing the music gloriously.

Though the score has received various readings, the 1995 recording is the first to challenge the 1973 Broadway original, at least as far as some of the performances are concerned. Judi Dench has arguably never given a greater performance of a musical role. While she too is not a singer, as the original star was not, she is as memorable in her way as Glynis Johns was in hers. Laurence Guittard here graduates to the role of Fredrik Egerman and steps into Len Cariou's shoes very effectively. Sian Phillips, as Madame Armfeldt, rivals the original Hermione Gingold with her world-weary performance. The rest of the cast is not quite on this level, although everyone gives their very best. There is more music and dialogue on this album than on the Broadway recording, which also includes one song that was cut before the show opened on Broadway in 1973. If you can only afford one recording, try the Broadway version first. However, this album is wonderful and repays your attention. At the very least, get one of these versions of this lyrical, wonderful show.

Jerry J. Thomas

A Little Princess

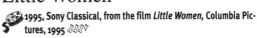1995, Varèse Sarabande, from the film *A Little Princess*, Warner Bros., 1995 ♪♪♪♪

album notes: Music: Patrick Doyle; **Conductor:** David Snell; **Featured Musicians:** Frank Ricotti, percussion; Gary Kettel, percussion; William Lockhart, percussion; Glyn Mathews, percussion; Paul Clarvis, percussion; Kuljit Bhamra, percussion; Craig Pruess, sitar/percussion; the New London Children's Choir.

Recalling in a way some of the incidents in *The Secret Garden,* by the same author, Frances Hodgson Burnett's *A Little Princess* is a touching story about a little girl sent to a strict boarding school during World War I, who is forced to become a maid to the austere headmistress when her father is reported missing in action. Subtly limning this heartwarming tale in its screen transfer, Patrick Doyle contributed a score that oozes charm and loveliness in every track. Following the little heroine from India, where she shares a life of wonder, to the boarding school in New York to the fantasyland in which she takes refuge in order to escape the hardships that come her way, the score reflects with imagination the diverse situations that shape the story, providing sounds that recall these different backgrounds and also evoke the various states of mind of the "little Princess" herself. Despite the disparate elements that contribute to its final makeup, it comes across as an inventive, often inspired score, quite exquisite and enjoyable.

Didier C. Deutsch

A Little Romance

1992, Varèse Sarabande, from the film *A Little Romance,* Orion Pictures, 1979 ♪♪♪♪♪

album notes: Music: Georges Delerue; **Conductor:** Georges Delerue.

Directed by George Roy Hill, *A Little Romance* recounts the adventures of a young French boy and his American girlfriend who decide, at the behest of a mysterious old man whom they follow, to relive the legend of two Venetian youths who swore their love to each other in a gondola. In one of his most spirited efforts, Georges Delerue took a cue from the many lighthearted moods in the story and wrote a score that teems with a multitude of diversified cues, in turn exuberant ("Paris Montage," "The Bicycle Race"), and romantic ("A Little Romance," "The Gondola"), with a little touch of jazz along the way ("Birthday Party"). The whole thing is imaginatively laid out and performed for all its worth. Signature themes, like "The Young Lovers" and "Off to Italy," are also found in abundance in this

richly entertaining score, which won a well-deserved Academy Award in 1979.

Didier C. Deutsch

Little Voice

1998, Capitol Records, from the film *Little Voice,* Miramax, 1998 ♪♪♪♪

Based on the stage play, first presented in London and subsequently in New York, *Little Voice* is an oddly entertaining film about a young girl, withdrawn and seen confined in her bedroom, who comes to life when she sings like her favorite performers—Marilyn Monroe, Judy Garland, Billie Holiday—whose delivery she has an uncanny ability to mimic. Portrayed by Jane Horrocks, reprising her stage performance, the film also cast Michael Caine as a third-rate talent scout who not only gets interested in Little Voice, but in her mother as well, a sexually driven, loud-mouthed virago. Peppering the soundtrack of this extravagant little ditty are classics by Monroe, Garland, Holiday, Ethel Merman, and Shirley Bassey, including "The Man That Got Away," "Lover Man," "Goldfinger," and "There's No Business like Show Business," with Horrocks herself doing an imitation of Marilyn in "I Wanna Be Loved by You" and of Garland in "Get Happy." The inclusion of Tom Jones's "It's Not Unusual" in this collection is just to remind the listener of a very funny scene in which the talent agent and mom get their jollies off downstairs, while Little Voice demurely imitates Judy upstairs. A solid compilation of attractive tracks.

Didier C. Deutsch

Little Women

1995, Sony Classical, from the film *Little Women,* Columbia Pictures, 1995 ♪♪♪♡

album notes: Music: Thomas Newman; **Orchestra:** The London Symphony Orchestra; **Conductor:** Thomas Newman.

Based on the classic 1868 novel by Louisa May Alcott about love, family, and becoming a woman, this retelling of *Little Women* received its fair share of accolades for its splendid treatment of the romantic dramas and adventures of Mrs. March and her four "little women"—spirited Jo, beautiful Meg, fragile Beth, and romantic Amy. Among the technical elements that contributed to the success of the film was Thomas Newman's score, which masterfully italicizes some of the most striking moments in the narrative, giving them an extra perspective through the illuminating support of his sensitively detailed music. The cues assembled in this soundtrack album give a general idea of the real beauty of the score, but its strengths are somewhat undermined by the fact that many of the cues are much too short, and probably would have gained at being presented in longer suites.

Didier C. Deutsch

Live a Little, Love a Little/Charro!/The Trouble with Girls/Change of Habit

1995, RCA Records, from the films *Live a Little, Love a Little*, MGM, 1968, *Charro!*, National General Pictures, 1969, *The Trouble with Girls*, MGM, 1969, and *Change of Habit*, Universal Pictures, 1970 👁👁👁

This recording brings together the songs heard in Elvis's four last films: *Live a Little, Love a Little* (1968), *The Trouble with Girls* (1969), *Charro!* (1969), and *Change of Habit* (1969). By then, the formula that had been applied to him seemed to have run its course: clearly, the singer didn't seem to keep pace with the fast-changing times, and his films had become routine affairs with the songs written for them eliciting little more than a yawn. In fact, the King himself seemed to have grown weary of the characters he was asked to portray, going through the motions without exhibiting any mark of enthusiasm or real involvement. Yet, the diversity of the roles in these films, notably *Charro!* and *Change of Habit,* suggest that had the scripts been more thoughtfully conceived, his movie career might have grown in a different direction rather than whittle down, as it did, to end on a rather sad note.

While *Live a Little* dealt more openly than ever before (in an Elvis film) with sex, and *The Trouble with Girls* appeared more like a retread of earlier successes, *Charro!* was an offbeat western in which Elvis was cast against type as an antihero in an obvious attempt to cash in on the popularity of the spaghetti westerns (even the title tune, the only song heard in the film, evokes the songs Ennio Morricone wrote for the early films of Sergio Leone).

Also a change of pace, *A Change of Habit* gave Elvis a strong dramatic role, in a marked departure from the musical comedy films in which he had starred through most of his movie career. Though he portrayed a doctor who runs a clinic in the ghetto of a major city, and who falls in love with a nun in regular street clothing (which provided the film with an unusual ending to boot), he still found time to perform a few songs that proved quite endearing.

Didier C. Deutsch

Live and Let Die

1988, EMI Manhattan Records, from the film *Live and Let Die*, United Artists, 1973 👁👁👁
album notes: Music: George Martin.

Listening to the soundtracks to *Live and Let Die* and *The Living Daylights* one after the other, one gets a clearer perspective about the reasons why John Barry's scores for the James Bond pictures work so well where other composers' do not. George Martin's music for *Live and Let Die*, propelled by Paul and Linda McCartney's terrific title tune (the first time a rock number is used in the series), is serviceable at best but not terribly memorable. The tracks actually worked much better behind the action than they do on a purely audio level, with their strongly accented guitar riffs reminiscent of other scores from the same period, notably *Shaft*.

Didier C. Deutsch

Live Flesh

1997, RCA Records, from the film *Live Flesh*, El Deseo, 1997 👁👁👁👁

album notes: Music: Alberto Iglesias; Conductor: Alberto Iglesias; Featured Soloists: Antonio Serrano, harmonica; Antonio Garcia de Diego, mandoline; Lilian Castillo, piano; Luis Dulzaides, Osvaldo Varona, Latin percussion.

Pedro Almodovar has become almost synonymous with Spanish cinema, and he has always taken a strong interest in the music for his films. With *Live Flesh*, composer Alberto Iglesias provides a series of cues that add a Spanish folk flavor to European symphonic music with Portuguese guitar, mandolin, and Latin percussion. A full orchestra underscores the action, relying less on the traditional string section for a broader sound that encompasses cor anglais, drums, harmonica, harp, and oboe. The editor did not catch instances where members of the Madrid Symphony Orchestra occasionally shuffle pages, scuffle, or drop things, but otherwise the recording is well balanced and tellingly detailed enough for these minor glitches to be audible. Ballads sung in Spanish and an upbeat trance track integrating bagpipes, bodhran, and African percussion round out a soundtrack well worth owning and still pleasurable after repeated listens.

David Poole

Live for Life

See: A Man and a Woman/Live for Life

The Living Daylights

1998, Rykodisc, from the film *The Living Daylights,* United Artists, 1987 👁👁👁👁
album notes: Music: John Barry.

Before it was reissued, this was one of those scores collectors were dying to see released with additional material. Rykodisc complied, adding nine selections totaling 30 more minutes of Barry's music that was previously unavailable. Released 25 years after moviegoers were first introduced to James Bond, *The Living Daylights* starred Timothy Dalton as the world's coolest superagent. Composer John Barry, who had already written a wealth of great music for the previous films in the series, delivered one of his finest and most diversified scores, in which he incorporated "The James Bond Theme" and the film's main theme into several tracks. In another departure from the norm, the title song, performed by a-ha, is not repeated at the end; instead the end credit, "If There Was a Man," is done by the Pretenders, who also perform "Where Has Every Body Gone," a song heard in the movie during the kidnapping scene.

Didier C. Deutsch

Living out Loud

1998, RCA Victor, from the film *Living out Loud,* New Line Cinema, 1998 🎬🎬🎬

album notes: Music: George Fenton; **Conductor:** George Fenton.

Fans of great jazz vocals will be hard pressed to find a contemporary movie soundtrack as tailored to their taste as *Living out Loud,* an album as filled with surprises as the movie. As a sort of female Walter Mitty who meets Chekhov in the streets of New York this delightful film's main character frequents a bar where the house torch singer, played by musical artist Queen Latifah, sings such pop standards as Billy Strayhorn's "Lush Life" and puts new spins on songs like Burt Bacharach's "Goin' Out of My Head." Both of these songs are highlights of the soundtrack album, along with the original Etta James recording of "At Last" and selections from George Fenton's jazzy score.

Amy Rosen

Local Hero

1983, Vertigo Records, from the film *Local Hero,* 1983 🎬🎬🎬

album notes: Music: Mark Knopfler; **Featured Musicians:** Mark Knopfler, guitars, synthesizers, percussion; Alan Clark, piano, synthesizers, Hammond organ; Hal Lindes, rhythm guitar; Mike Brecker, saxophone; Mike Mainieri, vibes; Gerry Rafferty, vocals; Neil Jason, bass; Tony Levin, bass; John Illsley, bass; Eddie Gomez, bass; Steve Jordan, drums; Terry Williams, drums.

A quirky collection of tunes masterfully captures the odd nature of a tiny Scottish seaside village in this film that was the acknowledged inspiration for the *Northern Exposure* TV series. An early film score for Dire Straits guitarist Mark Knopfler, it is filled with wonderful moments, particularly the infectious "Theme of the Local Hero." But the oddly se-

quenced album, with several tracks split into three suites, was most likely done to combine all the music related to the town party, though the opening suite seems a bit disjointed. Sounds of waves crashing against the shore are incorporated into several tracks. It adds a melancholy touch, but also serves to represent how utterly isolated the village is from the rest of the world.

David Hirsch

Lock, Stock, and Two Smoking Barrels

1999, Maverick Records, from the film *Lock, Stock and Two Smoking Barrels,* 1999 🎬🎬🎬

Certainly the soundtrack to this cheeky British film ranks as one of the most eclectic of the pop sampler variety. The sweep runs from Dusty Springfield's taut and restrained "Spooky" to the Stooges' unhinged "I Wanna Be Your Dog" to James Brown's ultra-funky "The Big Payback," the original version of the reggae classic "Police and Thieves" by Junior Murvin, and modern pop from the Ocean Color Scene. (Surprisingly, there's nothing from Sting, who's one of the film's co-stars.) The range of styles is enjoyable, however, not unlike a good Quentin Tarantino soundtrack. And the inclusion of dialogue snippets between songs gives a flavor of the film.

Gary Graff

Logan's Run

1990, Bay Cities, from the film *Logan's Run,* MGM, 1976 🎬🎬🎬🎬

album notes: Music: Jerry Goldsmith; **Conductor:** Jerry Goldsmith.

Jerry Goldsmith produced a seminal science-fiction effort for Michael Anderson's watered-down adaptation of the pop sci-fi novel about a future society where no one is allowed to live past the age of 30. Opening with a pulsating electronic figure that symbolized the omnipresent threat of "Lastday" termination, Goldsmith wrote a richly evocative harmonic brass piece for the movie's futuristic, domed city, while the rest of the score features some of Goldsmith's most supercharged and idiosyncratic action music, kind of a mix of Béla Bartok and Leonard Bernstein, for the film's numerous fights and chases. "The Sun" is an incredibly vivid, melodically brilliant characterization of the protagonist's first sight of the outside world after escaping from the dome, while "The Monument" mixes aspects of Stravinsky and Copland in an unforgettably atmospheric sketch of both the mystery and beauty of nature, as well as the haunted echoes of patriotism that hang over the ruined city of Washington, D.C. Somewhat less effective are some purely electronic passages inside the city that date what is otherwise a timeless, vivid work that's among Goldsmith's finest scores.

Jeff Bond

Lois & Clark

1998, Sonic Images, from the television series *Lois & Clark: The New Adventures of Superman*, Warner Bros., 1997 ♪

album notes: Music: Jay Gruska.

From the "not every TV show deserves a soundtrack" files comes *Lois & Clark*. Way too pretty for their own good, Dean Cain and Terri Hatcher tackled the title roles in this '90s remake of the *Superman* saga. The TV show featured a catchy main title, but from there wavered between generic superhero/action music and mediocre themes. The music on the CD is compiled in an uneven manner, with rapid tempo changes, that don't do much for Jay Gruska's composition. The packaging is quite nice and features short liner notes by Dean Cain. This CD is strictly for *Lois & Clark* diehards only.

Beth Krakower

Lolita

1997, Rhino, from the film *Lolita*, MGM, 1962 ♪♪♪♪

album notes: Music: Nelson Riddle; Conductor: Nelson Riddle.

1998, Milan/BMG, from the film *Lolita*, Pathe, 1998 ♪♪♪♪

album notes: Music: Ennio Morricone; Conductor: Ennio Morricone.

Adrian Lyne's adaptation of Nabakov's portrait of a pedophile in '50s America focuses on the love story, unlike Kubrick's more satirical 1962 version. For Kubrick, Nelson Riddle's MOR cocktail music reflected the tastes of the middle class that he spoofed. The results suited the film, but did not warrant further attention. Lyne used the far more subtle skills of Ennio Morricone, who juxtaposes a serious score with lighthearted music from the late '40s, that Lolita and Humbert might have heard during their road trip. The contrast of European art music and unabashed pop conveys the tension between Lolita's adult love and her teenage playfulness. Lolita uses the catchy refrain of Louis Prima's "Bongo, bongo, bongo, I don't want to leave the Congo," to repeatedly wind up the stuffy European Professor Humbert. Her goofiness clashes with the abstracted vocal phrases and atonal drums in "Requiescent," or the agitated strings during her tantrums. The lovers are enveloped in new age piano underscoring in "Lolita on Humbert's Lap" and mocked when Vera Lynn sings "I'm in the Mood for Love." Morricone's cues may rattle listeners, but the balance of choral dissonance with warm-toned jazz vocals and period swing rhythms make for an accessible and pleasurable listening experience.

David Poole

Lone Star

1996, Daring Records, from the film *Lone Star*, Castle Rock, 1996 ♪♪♪♪

album notes: Music: Mason Daring; Featured Musicians: Duke Levine, guitars/bass; Tim Jackson, drums; Larry Ludecke, pianos; Marshall Wood, upright bass; Mike Turk, harmonica; Billy Novick, saxophones; Evan Harlan, harmonica.

Written and directed by John Sayles, *Lone Star* starred Kris Kristofferson as Charlie Wade, the corrupt sheriff of a small Texas border town haunted by its violent past and unable to break away from it. Forty years before, Wade, a tyrannical lawman with a strong racist streak, was apparently run out of town by the father of the current sheriff. The sudden discovery of a skeleton with a badge next to it leads to an inquiry that reveals more about the town itself than anyone would have wanted to suspect or even revealed. As much as the film itself drew its strength from the societal landscape exposed by the director, it also got a serious boost from the soundtrack, created by Mason Daring, that blended flavorful instrumental cues, unfortunately not heard here, with songs from both sides of the border, performed by artists such as Conjunto

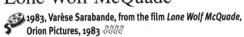

Bernal, Little Walter, Ivory Joe Hunter, Lydia Mendoza, Freddie Fender, and Patsy Montana, among others. This compilation presents the songs in their entirety, and they make for a fine collection.

Didier C. Deutsch

Lone Wolf McQuade

1983, Varèse Sarabande, from the film *Lone Wolf McQuade*, Orion Pictures, 1983 𝄞𝄞𝄞𝄞

album notes: Music: Francesco de Masi; **Conductor:** Francesco de Masi; **Featured Soloist:** Alessandro Alessandroni, whistler.

A superior action-adventure score by Francesco de Masi, *Lone Wolf McQuade* harkens back to the days when Italian westerns were at the peak of their popularity, with scores that were at once representative of the screen action and had a life of their own when removed from it. Though solidly anchored in today's world, but obviously inspired by the westerns of Sergio Leone, *Lone Wolf McQuade* stars Chuck Norris as a kickboxing Texas Ranger engaging in a fight to the death with some arms smugglers on the wrong side of the law. To give this 1983 modern western the proper feel, de Masi revisited the type of music he and others, like Ennio Morricone, had pioneered in the early days of the spaghetti westerns, complete with a mournful harmonica wailing in the distance, solid steel guitar riffs, and lonely whistling to add an extra forlorn feel to the proceedings. It may sound like a throwback to the days of yore, but it is still quite effective and it makes its point, with the only concession to the modern setting of the story being the use of some electronic instruments in the mix. This profuse score, with many exciting cues to detail the rough screen action, is totally enjoyable.

Didier C. Deutsch

The Loner

See: Stagecoach/The Loner

Lonesome Dove

1998, Sonic Images, from the television series *Lonesome Dove*, Hallmark, 1996 𝄞𝄞𝄞

album notes: Music: Basil Poledouris; **Conductor:** Basil Poledouris; **Featured Musicians:** Richard Greene, fiddle; Dennis Budimir, guitar; Tim May, guitar, mandolin; Dan Greco, hammered dulcimer; Herb Peterson, banjo; Frank Marocco, accordion; Kenny Watson, Steve Forman, percussion; Chuck Domanico, bass.

At a time when neither the western genre nor the TV miniseries was in vogue, along came a western TV miniseries. Surprisingly, it was a huge success and won seven Emmys. Director Simon Wincer tapped Basil Poledouris (who won one of the Emmys) to compose the close to four-hour score for this eight-

hour series, which was based on Larry McMurtry's Pulitzer Prize–winning novel. Poledouris used a 40-piece orchestra to underscore the main characters, and a small folk/Americana group (with bass, fiddle, banjo, etc.) to underscore the subsidiary characters. What resulted was not the typical over-the-top western music of the '50s and '60s, but a multidimensional score that contained the drama of its predecessors and much more emotional depth. The best moments have been compiled together in this CD reissue, which includes four previously unreleased tracks.

Beth Krakower

The Long Days of Vengeance

See: I lunghi giorni della vendetta

The Long Kiss Goodnight

1996, MCA Records, from the film *The Long Kiss Goodnight*, New Line, 1996 𝄞𝄞𝄞𝄞

album notes: Music: Alan Silvestri.

In an unlikely screen alliance, Geena Davis and Samuel Jackson portrayed a former trained killer on the side of the law, whatever side it may have been, and the detective she hires to help her discover fragments of her murky past after she suffered from amnesia. The fast-paced action, in which Davis's enticing sensuality was matched by Jackson's low-key humor, received an additional boost from the lively soundtrack in which several pop songs made pointed comments at crucial times. The song-driven collection released as a soundtrack album compiles the best songs in their full version, but only includes the "Main Title" from Alan Silvestri's high-voltage and quite effective score.

Didier C. Deutsch

The Long Riders

1980, Warner Bros. Records, from the film *The Long Riders*, United Artists, 1980 𝄞𝄞𝄞𝄞

album notes: Music: Ry Cooder; **Featured Musicians:** Curt Bouterese, dulcimer; Jim Dickinson, harmonium/piano; Billy Bryson, bass; David Lindley, banjo, mandolin, fiddle, electric guitar; Tom Sauber, banjo, guitar; Milt Holland, percussion; Baboo Pierre, percussion; Jim Keltner, drums; Ry Cooder, guitar; Mitch Greenhill, guitar.

An inventive retelling of the notorious James Gang's ride to fame, *The Lone Riders* is special in many ways, not the least being the casting of real-life brothers David and Keith Carradine and Stacy and James Keach to portray the screen outlaws and their gang. Another is the use of Ry Cooder's flavorful score to enhance the screen action and give it its period flavor. Cooder, an exponent of early American music, brought together several musicians with similar likings (notably David Lindley, a frequent collaborator), and provided them with themes ("Seneca Square Dance," "I Always Knew That You Were the One," "Cole Younger Polka") that strongly evoke the frontier at the turn of the century. The screen action itself suggests other tunes that also make a striking comment ("Escape from Northfield," "Jesse James") for what amounts to a most engaging soundtrack album.

Didier C. Deutsch

The Long Walk Home

1991, Varèse Sarabande, from the film *The Long Walk Home*, Miramax Films, 1991 ♫♫♫

album notes: Music: George Fenton; **Conductor:** George Fenton; **Featured Musicians:** Gary Foster, alto sax; Michael Lang, piano; Michael Melvoin, Hammond organ; Tim May, guitar; Neil Stubenhaus, bass guitar; Gary Coleman, percussion; Bob Zimmitti, percussion; the Long Walk Home Gospel Choir, Dr. Clifford Bibb, director.

The 1955 setting of this drama about two Southern families, one white, one black, caught in the social turmoil of the civil rights movement, resulted in a profoundly affecting score from composer George Fenton. With several gospel songs adding a definite flavor to the soundtrack, Fenton wrote a series of cues in which the sparse instrumentation helps to create a specific aura. Echoing the moods in the film, which avoid the maudlin sentimentality the subject might have suggested, the composer settles for a no-nonsense approach, all the more effective because it is controlled and straightforward.

Didier C. Deutsch

Looking for Richard

1996, Angel Records, from the film *Looking for Richard*, 20th Century-Fox, 1996 ♫♫♫♫

album notes: Music: Howard Shore; **Orchestra:** The London Philharmonic Orchestra; the London Voices, **Conductor:** Howard Shore.

Al Pacino's revisionist *Richard III,* a combination of lectures about the play and performances of some of the most important scenes in full costume regalia, is an offbeat, unusual way to approach one of the Bard's most powerful dramas. Adding support and great vitality to the project is the score Pacino commissioned from composer Howard Shore. Freed from the usual constraints of action-related cues, the composer created a medieval-sounding music that seems totally appropriate for the somber aspects in Shakespeare's play, while adding to it a more modern sound for the documentary scenes in the film. The result is a music that is at once reminiscent of the dual screen action and particularly suggestive when appreciated on its own terms.

Didier C. Deutsch

Lord of the Flies

1990, Silva Screen Records/U.K., from the film *Lord of the Flies,* Castle Rock, 1990 ♫♫

album notes: Music: Philippe Sarde; **Conductor:** Harry Rabinowitz; **Featured Soloists:** Michael Davis, violin; Andy Findon, tin whistle; Jonathan Sorrell, synthesizer; Richard Taylor, bass recorder.

The second screen transfer of William Golding's novel about young boys left on a deserted island who go back to ancestral behaviors and become savages, this plodding film had very little to distinguish it. Even Philippe Sarde's score, unusually heavy and uninspired, sounded way off when compared to some of his other works. Despite the presence of the always formidable London Symphony Orchestra and the Trinity Boys Choir, this uneven effort does not pay off and eventually stands as a curiosity, much like the score Sarde wrote for the film *Pirates.*

Didier C. Deutsch

The Lord of the Rings

1991, Intrada Records, from the animated feature *The Lord of the Rings,* Fantasy Films, 1978 ♫♫♫♫♫

album notes: Music: Leonard Rosenman; **Conductor:** Leonard Rosenman.

This opulent orchestral score for an animated feature by Ralph Bakshi, based on J.R.R. Tolkien's fantasy novels *The Fellowship of the Ring* and *The Two Towers,* gave composer Leonard Rosenman a rare opportunity to prepare a work that blended many varied elements, "violence, eerie marches, chases, and wild battle scenes." Combining together traditional triadic harmonies with dissonant and serial lines, he created for the early scenes an almost surrealistic mood, representative of the other-worldly nature of the film's story. He contrasted them, as the script suggested, with lyrical passages that set them off and gave them added power. As a result, his score magnificently underlines the specific dark moods in the narrative, and illuminates the story's lighter aspects, making his contribution a superb complement to Bakshi's designs. It is little wonder then that his score, released on LP by Fantasy but not available after that for many years, should have become a prized collector's item. Its reissue on compact disc, with enhanced sonics that properly detail its many assets, again emphasizes its importance in the film music canon. Clearly, it is not a score that will attract everybody—the ominous tones in some of the tracks like "Escape to Rivendell" may deter some listeners to pursue any further. Those who do, however, will be amply rewarded by the riches the score contains and will find further exhilaration in the final pages, with rousing moments coming out of "Helm's Deep" and "Lord of the Rings."

Didier C. Deutsch

Losing Isaiah

1995, Columbia Records, from the film *Losing Isaiah,* Paramount, 1995 ♫♫♫

album notes: Music: Mark Isham; **Conductor:** Ken Kugler; **Featured Musicians:** Mark Isham, trumpet, flugelhorn; Wayne Shorter, saxophone; Liza Frazier, vocals.

Recent court cases about the issues raised by the adoption of abandoned children being reclaimed later on and the almost inhuman, gut-wrenching situations that result from such cases informed and gave a particular resonance to this 1995 drama. In bringing this topic to the screen, director Stephen Gyllenhaal made *Losing Isaiah* even more controversial by adding race to the narrative: Margaret, a white social worker, adopts a black child abandoned at birth by his mother, a crack addict, who subsequently reforms and hires a black attorney known to turn any case into a conflict in racial issues whenever possible, in order to regain custody of the child, now four years old. Subtly echoing the diverging moods in the drama, Mark Isham's score is inordinately low key and, as a result, tremendously effective. The nostalgic tones of Isham's trumpet help create the right atmosphere, while they define the story more clearly by giving it a voice that reinforces its aspects. As music, the score also stands out, evoking images that may be at times disturbing or mood-related, but are always compelling.

Didier C. Deutsch

The Loss of Sexual Innocence

1999, Philips Records, from the Sony film *The Loss of Innocence,* Pictures Classics, 1999 ♫♫♫

album notes: Music: Mike Figgis; **Featured Soloists:** Joanna MacGregor, piano; Tony Coe, clarinet; Mike Figgis, trumpet; Miriam Stockley, Maggie Nichols, vocals.

The presence on the soundtrack of so many classical selections explains why this was released on a classical label. It is also somewhat of a disservice to Mike Figgis's own score, which inevitably pales in comparison with the works of Robert Schumann, Frederic Chopin, and Ludwig von Beethoven. An experimental film most striking for the beauty of its imagery, *The Loss of Sexual Innocence* is a reflective meditation on love and the mystery of sexuality that parallels the events of a man's life with the classic story of Adam and Eve in the Garden of Eden and the subsequent fall from grace. An art film that might have difficulties finding the right audience, the disjointed narrative attempts to explain man's loss of innocence in terms that may leave some totally unaffected. Similarly, the music composed by the film's director is not sufficiently expletive to really fire the imagination, with melodies that may be catchy at times yet unable to fill the gap between the classical and the modern worlds.

Didier C. Deutsch

The Lost Boys

1987, Atlantic Records, from the film *The Lost Boys,* Warner Bros., 1987 ♫♫♫

album notes: Featured Performers: Jimmy Barnes; Lou Gramm; Roger Daltry; INXS; Echo & the Bunnymen; Gerard McMann; Eddie & the Tide; Tim Capello; Mummy Calls; Thomas Newman.

This pop compilation, put together for a modern-day vampire film set in a West Coast community, is actually better than most if only because it features performances by rock groups that are interesting: INXS, Roger Daltrey, Lou Gramm, and Echo & the Bunnymen among them. The recording will appeal primarily to fans of the respective individuals and groups represented, but they will find many rewards in the songs performed. Thomas Newman, incidentally, scored the film, and is represented here by one track with a relatively modest playing time that can hardly do justice to his contribution.

Didier C. Deutsch

Lost Highway

1996, Interscope Records, from the film *Lost Highway,* October Films, 1996 ♫♫

album notes: Music: Angelo Badalamenti; **Orchestra:** The City of Prague Philharmonic; **Conductor:** Angelo Badalamenti; **Featured Musicians:** Bob Sheppard, saxophone; Ernest Hamilton, bass; Ralph Penland, drums; Ronald Brown, baritone sax; Henry Kranen, baritone sax.

David Bowie's strange, erratic "I'm Deranged" bookends this uneven score, in which hard-rock performers (Nine Inch Nails, Smashing Pumpkins, Lou Reed) vie for the listener's attention with Antonio Carlos Jobim's "Insensatez," Angelo Badalamenti's weird-sounding and not-too-terribly-engaging instrumental cues, and Barry Adamson's evocations of Henry Mancini's "Peter Gunn." It's too much of a hodgepodge to really satisfy anyone. Perhaps the David Lynch film justified this type of music combination, but programmed on an album, it makes very little sense.

Didier C. Deutsch

Lost Horizon

1998, Razor & Tie, from the film *Lost Horizon,* Columbia, 1973 ♫

album notes: Music: Burt Bacharach; **Lyrics:** Hal David; **Conductor:** Burt Bacharach.

Burt Bacharach and Hal David, who dominated the music scene in the 1960s with a string of popular hits, only attempted to write two full-fledged musicals: *Promises, Promises,* a 1968 Broadway effort, and *Lost Horizon,* a musical remake of the 1937 Frank Capra classic directed by Ross Hunter. Wheras the former enjoyed a healthy run in both New York and London, the latter failed to capture the essence of what made the team so

Balthzar Getty and Patricia Arquette in Lost Highway. **(The Kobal Collection)**

successful. The songs are run-of-the-mill and not too terribly catchy, as if Bacharach and David had run out of steam in the middle of the project. Worse yet, neither Liv Ullmann nor Peter Finch, whose screen chemistry was nonexistent, were professional singers, something which proved a real disservice to the composer and his lyricist. Although the movie didn't lack for stars, none of the others in the cast (Sally Kellerman, George Kennedy, Michael York, and Olivia Hussey) were known for their vocal abilities either. And as if to prove that Bacharach and David were not really that interested in the project, you can't help but laugh out loud at some of the songs they wrote. For example "The Things I Will Not Miss" is a duet between Kellerman and Hussey, singing about things they won't miss like too much sun or too much rain. "The World Is a Circle" sounds like someone has taken too many happy pills and thrown in a children's chorus. This release seems valid as a spoof of musicals. But please don't take it seriously.

Beth Krakower

Lost in Space

🎬 **1998, TVT Records, from the film *Lost in Space,* New Line, 1998**
🎶

album notes: Music: Bruce Broughton; **Conductor:** Bruce Broughton; **Synthesizers:** Ed Kalnins.

🎬 **1998, Intrada Records, from the film *Lost in Space,* New Line, 1998** 🎵🎵🎵🎵🎵
album notes: Music: Bruce Broughton; **Conductor:** Bruce Broughton.

Bruce Broughton has always been one of the better symphonic composers in Hollywood, as well as one of its best-kept secrets. Even when scoring kiddie films like *Baby's Day Out, Homeward Bound,* and *Honey I Blew Up the Kids,* Broughton has shown a lush, thematic finesse that's put him on a near-par with John Williams. *Lost in Space* was the hit that Broughton deserved, a terrifically exciting soundtrack that brings back warm memories of the *Star Wars* sound. While Broughton has Williams's melodic chops, he's also got his own orchestral voice. You won't be longing for Williams's old TV music when you hear what Broughton's come up with. Despite being given two weeks to write this replacement score, the composer delivered a majestic space opera, full of wonder, pounding adventure, and real melody. *Lost in Space* is filled with long cues, and Broughton makes sure that every one of them develops and holds our interest. He also gives an emotional depth to the music that takes it to another musical level.

A suite from the underscore was originally issued on TVT, replete with some obnoxious industrial rock songs (although it does have a cool techno riff on Williams's TV theme). Make sure you're purchasing Intrada's score-only CD, which gives you a chance to hear the music that mostly remains buried in the film

itself. *Lost in Space* is an accomplishment of the first order for Broughton, who will now hopefully have his day in Hollywood with this otherwise mediocre film's record box office take.

Dan Schweiger

Lost in the Stars

🎬 **1991, MCA Records, from the Broadway production *Lost in the Stars,* 1949** 🎵🎵🎵🎵🎵
album notes: Music: Kurt Weill; **Lyrics:** Maxwell Anderson; **Musical Direction:** Maurice Levine; **Cast:** Todd Duncan, Julian Mayfield, Sheila Guyse, Inez Matthews.

🎬 **1993, MusicMasters Records, from the studio cast recording *Lost in the Stars,* 1993** 🎵🎵🎵🎵🎵
album notes: Music: Kurt Weill; **Lyrics:** Maxwell Anderson; **Musical Direction:** Julius Rudel; **Cast:** Arthur Woodley, Reginald Pindell, Carol Woods, Cynthia Clarey.

Unfortunately for the world, *Lost in the Stars* was Kurt Weill's last work for the Broadway theater since he died during its too-brief run. It is difficult to describe this amazing work. Set in South Africa, it tackles the very emotional issues of apartheid, murder, lust, unfulfilled relationships between parent and child, and one's fundamental belief in God. Weill caught the various emotions and personal struggles of the characters in a score that combines the various styles of musical comedy, opera, cabaret, jazz, and folk song into one heterogeneous style. The original 1949 cast recording catches this wild, uncompromising, glorious work in rather mediocre mono sound with too many cuts. However, the cast has an authority that is nearly unassailable. The wonderful Todd Duncan makes his last appearance in a musical and is terrific, as is the rest of the ensemble cast, in a recording that is essential in any library of Broadway theater music.

While the 1993 recording does not equal all aspects of the original, it does surpass it in a few respects and holds its own nicely. To begin, it contains much more music than the original, which is a plus, since the additional material that is available makes it easier to understand the complex and difficult relations between these all–too–human characters. Julius Rudel has always had my respect as a wonderful musician and here his conducting is as fine as he has ever done. He is so good that it makes one long to hear him conduct the entire Kurt Weill canon. He has captured the wild highs and the blackest pits of despair that were built into this score by the composer. Arthur Woodley rivals Duncan in the role of Stephen Kumalo, a peaceful man thrust into an extremely difficult situation. Cynthia Clarey is vivid as Irina and Carol Woods burns up the speakers as Linda. The other roles are cast judiciously and the recording, to make everything more attractive, is in full, clear, stereo sound.

Jerry J. Thomas

Lost in Yonkers

1993, Varèse Sarabande, from the film *Lost in Yonkers,* Columbia Pictures, 1993 🎬🎬🎬🎬

album notes: Music: Elmer Bernstein; **Conductor:** Elmer Bernstein.

Like the films of Woody Allen, the plays of Neil Simon have an aura that places them squarely within a definite time and place. Because of that, scoring any of them proves challenging to any composer, as the moods explored have to reflect the specificity of their locale. While perhaps not exactly "right," the score Elmer Bernstein created for *Lost in Yonkers* successfully evokes the 1920s–1930s feel of the film based on the play about two boys sent to live with their grandmother when their father goes away on business, and suggests images that capture the moods of the period. Some of the cues devised by the composer are actually quite delightful ("The Candy Store," "Leaving Yonkers"), but others may seem a little too dark for what is essentially a light romantic comedy. Though he may be amiss, Bernstein remains intelligently challenging, however, and his cues are still quite enjoyable where music is concerned.

Didier C. Deutsch

The Lost World

1997, MCA Records, from the film *The Lost World,* Universal Pictures, 1997 🎬🎬🎬🎬

album notes: Music: John Williams; **Conductor:** John Williams.

Guaranteed to keep you on the edge of your seat, or at least intensely rapt, the score John Williams wrote for this second installment in the *Jurassic Park* saga teems with exciting new themes and motifs, broadly announced by thundering thumping in "The Lost World." The first selections serve as a preamble to the action that will materialize later on, with the various cues detailing plans for a visit to Site B, another part of Jurassic Park, also inhabited by giant predators who soon turn the intruders into their prey. With an abundance of drums and percussion instruments (maracas and the like) punctuating the appearance of the Raptors, and weird, shrieking noises supposed to imitate their cries, the feast starts off with great orchestral sounds that seldom lessen after that. With skill, Williams creates ominous moods, interrupted by pulsing flashes, somewhat reminiscent of the famous theme he devised for "Jaws," but dealing here with animals that are even bigger, more ferocious, and thankfully extinct. The score's moments of bravura, "Visitor in San Diego" and the long "Finale," are alone worth the price of admission, and are terrific in every sense of the word.

Didier C. Deutsch

Louisiana Purchase

1996, DRG Records, from the Carnegie Hall concert presentation *Louisiana Purchase,* 1996 🎬🎬🎬🎬

album notes: Music: Irving Berlin; **Lyrics:** Irving Berlin; **Musical Direction:** Rob Fisher; **Cast:** Judy Blazer, Rick Crom, Taina Elg, Debbie Gravitte.

A classic Irving Berlin musical from 1940, *Louisiana Purchase* starred Victor Moore as a naive senator (he had previously played a vice president in *Of Thee I Sing,* and an ambassador in *Leave It to Me!*) who finds himself embroiled in the crooked doings of a big business president he is investigating. The score, brimming with catchy Berlin tunes, yielded one major hit in "It's a Lovely Day Tomorrow." The cast album on DRG stems from a concert performance at Carnegie Hall. It presents a marvelous recreation of the complete score, with an all-star cast, in a great-sounding recording.

Didier C. Deutsch

L'ours

See: The Bear

Love Affair

1994, Reprise Records, from the film *Love Affair,* Warner Bros., 1994 🎬🎬🎬🎬

album notes: Music: Ennio Morricone; **Orchestra:** The Unione musicisti di Roma; **Conductor:** Ennio Morricone; **Featured Soloists:** Gilda Butti, piano; Vincenzina Capona, harp; Paolo Zampini, flute; Stefano Novelli, clarinet; Luciano Giuliani, horn; **Featured Vocalist:** Edda Dell'Orso.

Louis Jordan's whimsical "Never Let Your Left Hand Know What Your Right Hand's Doin'" is a great opener for this soundtrack album, but it would have been largely sufficient to set the necessary moods before moving on to the Morricone selections. Instead, we are treated to Bobby Short's rendition of "Changes," Jordan and Louis Armstrong's duet in "Life Is So Peculiar," and (why not!) Ray Charles singing "The Christmas Song." Someone with little A&R imagination put those together and figured it would be alright. The point is, when you have a composer of Morricone's caliber, you don't treat his music like second-rate stuff.

Fortunately, the score, true to the composer's usual impeccable standards, easily overcomes this shabby treatment and makes itself heard powerfully. The film starring Warren Beatty as a fading sports figure and Annette Bening as a performer who find themselves stranded on an island and discover they're made for each other, despite their engagement to others, inspired Morricone to write some low-key themes that perfectly match the moods of this weepy tearjerker. Beautifully sketched, with lush romantic touches sparkling throughout, it is a gorgeous and supremely eloquent score, evidencing many Morricone characteristics, like a three-note motif repeated on the piano behind elongated orchestral lines. As its title suggests, "Piano Solo" is a track that is superb in its simplicity, with a singer humming the theme played by the piano. "Sentimental Walk" is another selection for piano and orchestra that's really beautiful and the lovely "For Annette and Warren" catches the overall moods in this score in a single tune that's exquisitely detailed.

Didier C. Deutsch

Love & a .45

1994, Epic Soundtrax Records, from the film *Love & a .45*, Tri-Mark, 1994 ♫♫♫

A fast-paced, twisted, darkly comedic journey through a contemporary American landscape of murder, media hype, controlled substances, unbridled love, and music, *Love & a .45* involved a young couple on the run: a small-time criminal and his girlfriend trying to escape the violent mobster who gave him a loan so that he could buy her an expensive engagement ring and who now wants his money back. Set in Texas and south of the border, the western psychedelic road opera followed its two main characters down back roads and through dusty towns, the action punctuated by the lively soundtrack, a collection of songs performed by a lot of cool and hip alternate bands and artists, including the Flaming Lips, the Breeders' Kim Deal and Bob Pollard (with a cover of Nazareth's "Love Hurts"), Meat Puppets, Jesus and Mary Chain, and FSK with David Lowery from Crackers, among others. Somewhat surprising in this assortment are tracks featuring the Reverend Horton Heat, who actually appears in the film; Johnny Cash, with "Ring of Fire"; and Roger Miller, whose "King of the Road" caps the album.

Didier C. Deutsch

Love at Large

1990, Virgin Records, from the film *Love at Large*, Orion Pictures, 1990 ♫♫♫♫

album notes: Music: Mark Isham; **Featured Musicians:** Mark Isham, saxophone/electronics/trumpet; Peter Maunu, guitar; David Torn, guitar; Dorothy Remsen, harp; Kurt Wortman, drums.

A humorous send-up of the detective films of the 1940s, *Love at Large* slyly makes fun of the Raymond Chandler thrillers, while adding some tongue-in-cheek comments of its own about the whole genre. Taking a hint from the story, about a gumshoe hired by a beautiful blonde to find her missing lover and the wrong trail he follows that leads to a totally different case with amusing complications, Mark Isham developed several cues that are pleasantly catchy and amusingly entertaining. Warren Zevon and Anne Archer have fun with the standard "You Don't

Know What Love Is," while Leonard Cohen gleefully adds his two cents with "Ain't No Cure for Love," a real delight.

Didier C. Deutsch

Love at Stake

See: Christmas in Connecticut/Love at Stake

Love Field

1993, Varèse Sarabande, from the film *Love Field,* Orion Pictures, 1993 ♫♫♫

album notes: Music: Jerry Goldsmith; **Conductor:** Jerry Goldsmith.

Jerry Goldsmith's score to this all-but-forgotten Michelle Pfeiffer period vehicle benefits from a blues influence that gives what might otherwise be an entirely bland romantic drama score a needed stylistic edge. Like his *Not without My Daughter* music, *Love Field* suffers from a simple melody of flute, piano, and strings that's just too ordinary. But an early cue, "The Posters," is a welcome return to the kind of busy, bucolic writing Goldsmith excelled in during the '60s in scores like *A Patch of Blue*. There's an anguished string elegy for the death of President Kennedy, and a tough, throbbing chase climax that comes out of nowhere but does illustrate why Goldsmith has long been sought out for this kind of music. It all resolves itself in a beautiful finale reminiscent of *The Secret of N.I.M.H.* This still reflects a weak period for Goldsmith, but it's an enjoyable listen.

Jeff Bond

Love Jones

1997, Columbia Records, from the film *Love Jones,* New Line Cinema, 1997 ♫♫♫♫

album notes: Featured Performers: Larenz Tate; Dionne Farris; Refugee Camp All-Stars; Lauryn Hill; Melky and Day; Maxwell; Groove Theory; Trina Broussard; Xscape; Cassandra Wilson; Marcus Miller; MeShell NdegeOcello; the Brand New Heavies; Cassie; Kenny Lattimore; the Lincoln Center Jazz Orchestra; Duke Ellington; John Coltrane; Nia Long.

A breezy, sexy romantic comedy set among the overeducated and underemployed in downtown Chicago, *Love Jones* deftly captured the rhythms of modern courtship, while asking the age-old question—is love forever? Reflecting the smart urban sounds heard among today's better educated youths, this soundtrack album compilation places the spotlight on various frontline performers, including Dionne Farris, Maxwell, Xscape, Cassandra Wilson, Kenny Lattimore, and Me'Shell NdegeOcello. A slightly more sophisticated touch is provided by the addition of "Jelly, Jelly," performed by the Lincoln Center Jazz Orchestra, an organization presided over by Wynton Marsalis, and "In a Sentimental Mood," featuring John

Coltrane and Duke Ellington. The film's two stars, Larenz Tate and Nia Long, also appear framing the album, Tate with a reading of the poem his character, Darius, has written in celebration of Long's character, Nina; and Long in another piece, written about Tate, with both being read in front of the audience at the Sanctuary, the night spot where the two initially met and fell in love.

Didier C. Deutsch

Love Me or Leave Me

1993, Sony Legacy, from the film *Love Me or Leave Me*, MGM, 1954 🎬🎬🎬

album notes: Musical Direction: George Stoll; **Orchestra:** The MGM Studio Orchestra; **Conductor:** Percy Faith.

Doris Day had an uncharacteristically dramatic (singing) role in *Love Me or Leave Me,* the film biography of 1930s torch singer Ruth Etting. In the film, she starred opposite James Cagney portraying Marty "The Gimp" Snyder, a limping laundry operator who discovered Etting and became her agent and "protector." Doris Day performed many of the songs created by Etting, and had a hit with the song "I'll Never Stop Loving You," written expressly for her by Sammy Cahn and Nicholas Brodszky. A staple in the Columbia catalog for many years, the CD released in 1993 offers the soundtrack for the first time in stereo, with several bonus tracks, including rare studio pre-recordings.

Beth Krakower

Love Me Tender

See: Jailhouse Rock/Love Me Tender

Love Serenade

1996, Mercury Records, from the film *Love Serenade,* Jan Chapman/Australian Film Finance Corporation, 1996 🎬🎬🎬🎬

Love Serenade, a little-heralded Australian film (it won the Camera d'Or at the 1996 Cannes Film Festival, but failed to find au audience in this country), was a charming tale of two twentysomething small-town sisters, totally unsophisticated about matters of the heart, who get hoodwinked by the local celebrity, a small-time radio host only interested in a quick conquest. Since he only plays hits from years past, the soundtrack obligingly featured performances by various pop stars from the 1970s: Glen Campbell, Barry White, Van McCoy, George and Gwen McCrae, Dionne Warwick, among others, in a winning combination that further makes this soundtrack album a little gem. Some of the songs are delightfully set off by bits of dialogue that suggest the tongue-in-cheek style of the film itself.

Didier C. Deutsch

Love Story

1970, MCA Records/Germany, from the film *Love Story,* Paramount, 1970 🎬🎬🎬

album notes: Music: Francis Lai.

Surprisingly, this solid gold soundtrack album has never been reissued in this country, but is now available from the regular mail-order and specialized shops as an import from Germany. Francis Lai's score, propelled by the syrupy giant hit "Where Do I Begin? (Theme from Love Story)," is appropriately evocative of the moods in the film itself. It boasts several engaging moments, like "Snow Frolic," with its disembodied vocal accompaniment, a Lai signature; or the enchanting "Skating in Central Park," in 3/4 time. May be difficult to get, but worth looking for.

Didier C. Deutsch

Love! Valour! Compassion!

1997, London Records, from the film *Love! Valour! Compassion!,* Fine Arts, 1997 🎬🎬🎬

album notes: Music: Harold Wheeler.

Harold Wheeler's name is not frequently mentioned in connection with film music. A gifted composer and orchestrator, he usually works on Broadway shows, but this engaging soundtrack album should help some listeners discover his talents and should establish him as an entity to be reckoned with. His cues to this flamboyantly gay play—the action takes place over a summer vacation on Fire Island and involves several friends who tear at each other, but eventually recognize the value of their friendship—are replete with catchy melodies that run the gamut from mock classical ("Swanlake," "Classical Drive") to snappy jazz ("Summertime Jazz"). Adding a familiar touch to the album, Ella Fitzgerald's rendition of "Bewitched" and Mungo Jerry's seldom heard "In the Summertime" also help establish the plot and time frame of this comedy with serious overtones.

Didier C. Deutsch

Lovely to Look At

1991, Sony Music Special Products, from the film *Lovely to Look At,* MGM, 1952 🎬🎬🎬

album notes: Music: Jerome Kern; **Lyrics:** Otto Harbach, Oscar Hammerstein II, Dorothy Fields, Jimmy McHugh, Bernard Dougall; **Choir:** The MGM Studio Chorus; **Orchestra:** The MGM Studio Orchestra; **Conductor:** Carmen Dragon; **Cast:** Howard Keel, Red Skelton, Kathryn Grayson, Marge Champion, Gower Champion, Ann Miller.

A remake of the 1933 stage musical *Roberta* (previously filmed in 1935, with Fred Astaire, Irene Dunne, and Ginger Rogers in the cast), *Lovely to Look At* was a lame excuse to bring together MGM's ideal romantic musical couple, Howard Keel and Kathryn Grayson (they had previously starred in *Show Boat),* It

3
4
8

loving you

also includes surefire box office comedian Red Skelton, and dancers extraordinaire Ann Miller, and Marge and Gower Champion. Several songs from the original were dropped, but a couple of novelty numbers for Skelton were inserted, and of course the Kern/Harbach hits ("The Touch of Your Hand," "I'll Be Hard to Handle," "Yesterdays," and "Smoke Gets in Your Eyes") were retained, becoming the film's highlights. Directed with great savvy by Vincente Minnelli and Mervyn LeRoy, *Lovely to Look At* is a splash-dash of colors and songs that lives again in this soundtrack album recording.

see also: Roberta

Didier C. Deutsch

Loving You

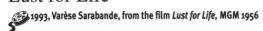1988, RCA Records from the movie *Loving You*, Paramount Pictures, 1957 ♫♫♫

In his second film, *Loving You*, Elvis portrayed a truck driver with a talent for singing. It was a role that made few dramatic demands on him. Released in 1957, the film featured seven numbers among which "Teddy Bear," a number 1 hit, and the title tune soon proved most popular. The CD, incidentally, is not part of the new series, but a reissue of a previous LP, with the songs from the film augmented with five studio tracks, including Elvis's odd take on Cole Porter's "True Love."

Didier C. Deutsch

Lust for Life

1993, Varèse Sarabande, from the film *Lust for Life*, MGM 1956

album notes: Music: Miklos Rozsa; **Orchestra:** The Frankenland State Symphony Orchestra; **Conductor:** Miklos Rozsa.

The story of Vincent Van Gogh (portrayed by Kirk Douglas), *Lust for Life* is a big Hollywood biography that elicits a splendid score from Miklos Rozsa, taking a break from the swashbucklers and Roman epics he had scored recently. The music, robust and lyrical, is strikingly evocative and colorful, as befits a film about a painter. The manic sonorities in "Madness" further enhance the composer's naturalistic approach to this subject. Consisting of selections from Rozsa's score for *The Killers* (1946), *Brute Force* (1947), and *Naked City* (1948), all three realistic urban dramas and prime examples of film noir the "Background to Violence Suite" presents another facet of Rozsa's talent, one that has often been celebrated and admired. In stark melodic themes that contrast with the more florid style he used in the period dramas and adventure films he scored, Rozsa detailed with admirable sensitivity the darker aspects of life in the big cities, and the violence that often resulted from the confined environment in which people live. Using pulsating rhythms, brutal

brass chords, dramatic accents that all reflect the contained violence in these films, Rozsa conceived powerful scores that reflect the screen action as much as they expand on it. This suite presents an overview of his concepts in a searing, dramatic display of his writing at its most eloquent.

Didier C. Deutsch

 M

M Butterfly

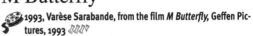1993, Varèse Sarabande, from the film *M Butterfly*, Geffen Pictures, 1993 ♫♫♫

album notes: Music: Howard Shore; **Orchestra:** The London Philharmonic Orchestra; **Conductor:** Howard Shore.

The somewhat incredible true story of a French diplomat in China and the long-lasting love affair he enjoyed with a diva from the Beijing opera, unaware of the fact that she was in fact a man, *M Butterfly* found in Howard Shore a composer whose talent and creative sensitivity compelled him to write a score which overflows with striking romantic themes, played by the harp and backed by an ensemble of strings and wind instruments. Adding a different color, arias from some well-known operas and traditional Chinese songs provide the background for a tale that straddles different worlds and different cultures, in an album that is frequently challenging and musically surprising.

Didier C. Deutsch

MacArthur

1990, Varèse Sarabande, from the film *MacArthur*, Universal Pictures, 1977 ♫♫

album notes: Music: Jerry Goldsmith; **Conductor:** Jerry Goldsmith.

Jerry Goldsmith's second military biography after *Patton* suffers from comparisons to his earlier, classic work for director Franklin Schaffner. The opening theme makes some interesting use of low-end pedal piano notes as a rhythmic device, but Goldsmith's brassy, strident theme for MacArthur sounds too much like a standard John Philips Sousa march to make for pleasant listening. There is one exciting battle sequence, but the film's real strength is in its surprisingly lyrical and quieter moving passages and in a rich arrangement of the traditional Japanese melody "Cherry Blossoms" for low strings and the harp. The underscoring of MacArthur's final farewell speech is quite beautiful as well. Unfortunately, it leads back into that overbearing march again.

Jeff Bond

Mack and Mabel

1992, MCA Records, from the Broadway production *Mack and Mabel*, 1974 ♪♪♪♪

album notes: Music: Jerry Herman; **Lyrics:** Jerry Herman; **Musical Direction:** Donald Pippin; **Cast:** Robert Preston, Bernadette Peters, Lisa Kirk.

A failed musical its first time around (it only played 66 performances, following its opening on Oct. 6, 1974), *Mack and Mabel* has become a cult show of sorts. Though it never was revived on Broadway, it received a concert version in London in 1988, and a full production in 1995, which fueled renewed interest in it. The tragic love story between film director Mack Sennett and his star Mabel Normand, *Mack and Mabel* was unfortunately saddled with an impossible book by Michael Stewart. The book tried desperately to make sense out of an affair that kept the two lovers apart more frequently than they were together, and ended on a negative note contrary to every tenet in the musical theater. On the bright side, however, was the score by Jerry Herman, a bittersweet collection of tunes in which the tone is given by the song "I Won't Send You Roses," in which Sennett lays out the rules by which his relationship with Normand will have to abide. There were, to be sure, lighter moods, notably in the opening number, "Movies Were Movies," in which Sennett extols the merits of movies when he was running the show. If anything, *Mack and Mabel* provided a unique opportunity for Robert Preston and Bernadette Peters to appear together in a show which, despite its shortcomings, magically comes to life in its bright cast recording.

Didier C. Deutsch

Mad City

1997, Varèse-Sarabande, from the film *Mad City*, Warner Bros., 1997 ♪♪

album notes: Music: Thomas Newman; **Conductor:** Thomas Newman; **Featured Musicians:** Michael Fisher, tablas, loops; George Doering, guitars, Hawaiian guitars; Thomas Newman, piano, violin; Steve Tavaglione, submarine flute, clarinet; George Budd, loops, samples; Chas Smith, pedal steel guitar, loops, samples; Judd Miller, native flutes; Bill Bernstein, six-string bass; Rick Cox, guitars, loops, samples; Sid Page, violin.

Costa-Gavras is known for a specific brand of filmmaking—an almost documentary approach, stylistically directed, to what is potentially an explosive political situation, involving high government officials and a cover-up of their activities. The formula has worked in several other films, notably *Z* and *State of Siege*. It worked again to a degree in this film, in which the main protagonists were Dustin Hoffman, as a broadcast journalist who covers a live drama—a shooting at a museum—and John Travolta, as a former security guard at the museum who apparently shot and killed another guard. What initially was a minor

They Know the Score
Hans Zimmer

Black Rain was a disaster for me, because the score I had written was the score I wanted to write, and the producer hated it, because to him it wasn't an action score. He wanted whatever action scores had sounded like before that. So I got very, very close to getting fired. There was one moment in fact that it got so bad, people at Paramount were shouting at me so much that I fainted. . . . [But] I stuck to my guns. There was a little I had to change at the end; there was a famous moment where I was told that the end just wasn't enough like the fight in *Rocky*. Well I got the video out for *Rocky* and listened to it and there's no bloody music in the fight in *Rocky*!

***Courtesy of* Film Score Monthly**

incident mushrooms to a major event with national implications, with the whole thing more or less orchestrated by the journalist, aiming for maximum coverage and scoops.

Unfortunately, little of the suspense or drama in the action is communicated in Thomas Newman's score, a rather routine effort that often fails to ignite or even compel the listener to pay closer attention. Here and there, a few cues hint at what the score might have been to make a better impression ("Feds Fly In"), but the general tone of the recording is very uneven and uninspired.

Didier C. Deutsch

Mad Dog and Glory

1992, Varèse Sarabande, from the film *Mad Dog and Glory*, Universal–International, 1992 ♪♪

album notes: Music: Elmer Bernstein; **Conductor:** Elmer Bernstein; **Featured Musician:** Lawrence Feldman, alto sax solos.

When the best selections in a soundtrack album happen to be the pop tunes, you know something is definitely wrong. Sad to say, but the most enjoyable moments in this album are the two vocals by Louis Prima and Keely Smith. Evidently, this tired comedy starring Bill Murray as a police photographer, Robert De Niro as a gangster, and Uma Thurman as the gangster's moll, did not inspire Elmer Bernstein much. With the exception of a few moments within the tracks "Frank and Wayne" and "Window Magic," his music is rather forgettable, a series of riffs that go nowhere and mean even less. The listener is not inspired, either.

Didier C. Deutsch

Mad Max Beyond Thunderdome

1985, EMI Records, from the film *Mad Max Beyond Thunderdome,* 1985 🎵🎵🎵

album notes: Music: Maurice Jarre; **Orchestra:** The Royal Philharmonic Orchestra; **Conductor:** Maurice Jarre.

For the third and final Mad Max installment, styled as a *Lawrence of Arabia* desert adventure, director George Miller turned to none other than the composer of *Lawrence,* Maurice Jarre. The resultant score is large, sweeping and distinctly Jarre, featuring orchestra, choir, an Ondes Martenot (an early electronic instrument), Australian didgeridoo, a few pop elements, and a variety of percussion. Fortunately, Jarre is the kind of composer whose style is distinct enough to focus this kind of kitchen–sink scale and *Mad Max Beyond Thunderdome* is one of the most exciting scores of the past two decades. Jarre eschews the machinery–and–gasoline grit of Brian May's sound world, and follows Max's turn as a leader of lost children to their promised land with symphonic grandeur. With *Tai–Pan* and *Enemy Mine,* this soundtrack forms a triptych of somewhat clunky but exciting mid–'80s Jarre scores, orchestrated to the brim by the late Christopher Palmer. The album includes three pop songs along with the 25 minutes of score, including the Tina Turner hit "We Don't Need Another Hero" (she's also the villain in the film), but unfortunately leaves off Jarre's pumped–up and slightly deranged "two men enter, one man leaves" fanfare and battle music for the Thunderdome duel itself.

Lukas Kendall

Madeline

1998, Sony Wonder, from the film *Madeline,* TriStar, 1998 🎵🎵🎵

album notes: Music: Michel Legrand; **Orchestra:** The Philharmonia Orchestra, the Finchley Children's Music Group; **Conductor:** Michel Legrand.

At times, Michel Legrand can be maddeningly frustrating. Sometimes he will write a score that's not particularly ingratiating; and the minute after, he turns in one that's so totally charming that you have to admit he is a great film composer. *Madeline* belongs to that second category. Not that it is outstanding by any

stretch of the imagination, but it is so pleasantly sketched and enjoyable that you know you are going to play it repeatedly and savor it every time. Based on the books by Ludwig Bemelmans that recount the spirited adventures of a mischievous little girl, a student in a boarding school in Paris who usually gets in trouble but always succeeds in overcoming all odds to emerge a winner, the film recaptures the moods and ambiance of its source, and expands on them with glee and a little froth. The same can be said of Legrand's amusing score in which the themes are nimbly in touch with the action, and puts the accent right where it should be. Two pop songs complement the album: "In Two Straight Lines," by Carly Simon, which takes its title from the famous opening sentence in the first *Madeline* book, and "What a Wonderful World," performed by Keb' Mo', which unfortunately cannot erase the memory of the version by Louis Armstrong, much more heartfelt and emotional.

Didier C. Deutsch

The Madness of King George

1994, Epic Soundtrax, from the film *The Madness of King George,* Samuel Goldwyn Pictures, 1994 🎵🎵🎵🎵

album notes: Music: Georg–Friedrich Handel; **Orchestra:** Baroque Orchestra; **Conductor:** Nicholas Kraemer.

When he made this historic drama about the court of George III of England and the King's slow descent into obsession and madness, director Nicholas Hytner felt intuitively that only the music of Handel would seem appropriate for his film. But in order to give the music a cinematic edge, he asked George Fenton to select the various pieces that eventually were shaped into the score, and to adapt and arrange them. Fenton, who deliberately took a back seat to his illustrious predecessor, succeeded in giving Handel's compositions a slightly modern sound and made them more appropriately cinematographic. As such, they remain sufficiently close to their origins to please classicists and dramatic enough to attract fans of film music. Lovers of baroque music, in particular, will appreciate what Fenton has done with the well–known extracts from "Music for the Royal Fireworks" and "Water Music." In only one case, "A Family Matter," did Fenton write his own cue, using themes by Handel, in a way that doesn't betray the style of the score, but in fact enhances it. The only reservation one can formulate about the album is that the playing sometimes lacks excitement.

Didier C. Deutsch

Magdalene

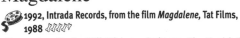1992, Intrada Records, from the film *Magdalene,* Tat Films, 1988 🎵🎵🎵🎵

album notes: Music: Cliff Eidelman; **Orchestra:** The Munich Symphony Orchestra; **Conductor:** Cliff Eidelman.

Cliff Eidelman's first score is a magnificent example of his understanding about what makes film music fulfill its function on the screen and as an audio–only experience. The story of an 18th–century prostitute willing to change her ways after she meets a dedicated priest, *Magdalene* prompted Eidelman to write a strongly inspirational score, permeated with the music of the Church, "the all empowered force in the lives of all the characters." However, it is also reflective of the young composer's beautiful melodic sense. Several cues attract particularly, "Magdalene in Love," a short but expressive piece, and "Father Mohr," in which Eidelman paints the serene portrait of a man of the cloth suddenly caught in a very human love dilemma; also "The Archbishop's Entertainment," written in the style of the period, around a theme that's pleasantly understated but quite effective, and the mournful "Mohr's Farewell," passionately romantic and florid. Quite impressive for a 22–year–old.

Didier C. Deutsch

Magic in the Water

1995, Varèse Sarabande, from the film *Magic in the Water*, Tri–Star Pictures, 1995 🎬

album notes: Music: David Schwartz; **Conductor:** William T. Stromberg.

Disappointing effort by David Schwartz, who has done much more creative things on the TV series *Northern Exposure.* Pretty and pleasant enough to service this minor kiddie feature, this score is so average that little of it remains after you've listened to it; uninspiring.

David Hirsch

Magical Mystery Tour

1987, EMI Records, from the television special *Magical Mystery Tour,* 1967 🎬🎬🎬🎬

album notes: Music: John Lennon, Paul McCartney, George Harrison, Ringo Starr; **Lyrics:** John Lennon, Paul McCartney, George Harrison, Ringo Starr.

The Beatles' lone bomb, this made-for-TV musical baffled British audiences and never had a proper US release. With three decades of MTV-induced hindsight, we can see it for what it really was: the first music video collection, barely glued together as episodes in a guided bus trip. Minus the visuals (which include, memorably, John Lennon shoveling spaghetti), the music carries forward the group's "Sgt. Pepper" psychedelic dabbling to its soaring culmination in the Joycean "I Am the Walrus." Rounding out the CD (as on the original LP) are five more Beatles singles of the period.

Marc Kirkeby

The Magnificent Ambersons

1990, Preamble Records, from the film *The Magnificent Ambersons,* RKO Radio Pictures, 1942 🎬🎬🎬🎬

album notes: Music: Bernard Herrmann; **Orchestra:** The Australian Philharmonic Orchestra, **Conductor:** Tony Bremner; **Featured Musicians:** Neville Taweel, violin; Henry Wenig, cello; Janet Perkins, organ.

A companion volume to the complete *Citizen Kane* (q.v.), this magnificent recording brings together the same team—producer John Lasher, conductor Tony Bremner, and the players of the Australian Philharmonic Orchestra—in a reading of another early score by Bernard Herrmann, skillfully reconstructed for this occasion. As would be expected, the results are nothing less than splendid. Next to *Citizen Kane, The Magnificent Ambersons,* also directed by Orson Welles, was probably one of Herrmann's most impressive achievements, even though, like the film itself, the composer's original music was treated with total disregard by studio executives who discarded many of the cues as the film was being recut to fit their own concept of it.

Compared with the brooding aura that pervaded his earlier score, however, the music for *Magnificent Ambersons* reveals Herrmann in a somewhat lighter mood, with the chamber music approach resulting in a texture that strikes for its sheer simplicity. Throughout individual instruments are called upon to provide an anchor for themes that are catchy and melodic, with the whole score emerging at once as a brilliant and thoroughly compelling effort. The recording itself is for the most part superb, with just a slight distortion on the left channel in a couple of tracks and studio noises to make it slightly less than perfect.

Didier C. Deutsch

The Magnificent Seven

1998, Rykodisc, from the film *The Magnificent Seven,* United Artists, 1960 🎬🎬🎬🎬

album notes: Music: Elmer Bernstein; **Conductor:** Elmer Bernstein.

Composer Elmer Bernstein lent an urgency to the often slow paced camera work of director John Sturges's classic Western adaptation of the *Seven Samurai.* Bernstein's orchestra evoked the galloping horses, flailing fists, and skittering bullets, even before the real action commenced. The symphonic adventure is interspersed with hints of Mexican cantinas in the maracas of "Quest," barrelhouse piano and Spanish guitar in "Vin's Luck," and the distinct characterizations of the villain Calvera and each of the seven heroes. As the gun battle commences, the score builds further, alternating between suspense, slapstick, and quick stabs of action. While *The Magnificent Seven* has been re-recorded many times, this is the first time the original score has been available, and both the sound and sense of adventure it engendered remain vivid 38 years on.

David Poole

$\frac{3}{5}\frac{}{2}$ *the main event*

The Main Event

1989, Columbia Records, from the film *The Main Event,* Warner Bros., 1979 ✍✍✍✍

album notes: Music: Michael Melvoin; **Conductor:** Michael Melvoin.

Barbra Streisand is always good for a moment, even when she wants to spar with beau hunk Ryan O'Neal, as is the case in this 1979 film in which Streisand tries to recover the money she'd lost on boxer O'Neal by getting him back in shape for a championship match. Lucky for her fans, she also had Paul Jabara to write a knockout of a song ("The Main Event") for her, even though she overstated it by recording it three times, in case the loooong first version was not enough. Loggins & Messina and Frankie Valli & The Four Seasons also contributed shorter songs for an album that's relatively pleasant, all things considered.

Didier C. Deutsch

Major League: Back to the Minors

1998, Curb Records, from the film *Major League: Back to the Minors,* Warner Bros., 1998 ✍✍✍✍

album notes: Music: Robert Folk.

This third inning in the baseball franchise is almost too predictable—a second-rate team consisting of lovable outcasts goes after the championship and manages to defeat the cocksure players of the team in the lead—but despite its evident shortcomings, it made for a film that was entertaining. Adding to the initial impact were the country songs heard on the soundtrack, most of which have been collected in this CD that should elicit a grin of satisfaction from many listeners. Among the best moments found here, "Little Bitty Crack in His Heart," by Ruby Lovett; "Steal the Base," by Scatman John; "Baby I'm Drunk," by Reverend Horton Heat; and "The Cheap Seats," by Alabama, are particular stand-outs. But the irreverent plum goes to the wildly humorous "Turning Japanese," by Tamplin, which, of course, gets an unlikely response in "Oye como va," by Takaaki Ishibashi, Dennis Haysbert, and the Jay Miley Band. In all this fun, Robert Folk's score gets lost, and not even his cue titled "Dugout" can match the exhilarating moods of this album.

Didier C. Deutsch

Making Mr. Right/Desperately Seeking Susan

1989, Varèse Records, from the films, *Desperately Seeking Susan,* 1985, and *Making Mr. Right,* 1987, both Orion ✍✍✍✍

album notes: Music: Chaz Jankel, Thomas Newman.

Billed as music from the films of Susan Seidelman, this CD pays tribute to an iconoclastic filmmaker, and two films that had limited impact at the time of their release, but have since developed a cult following, probably fueled in the case of *Desperately Seeking Susan* by the fact that it starred Madonna in her first major screen role. Playing opposite Rosanna Arquette, she portrayed a free-spirited New York girl, the Susan of the title, who starts a relationship through the classified, prompting Arquette, a Jersey housewife, to try and find out who that "material girl" is. Thomas Newman scored the film as if it were a travelogue through the streets of New York City, even going as far as indicating the time of the day when the action takes place. Built around a single recurring theme on the synthesizer, the score is catchy and entertaining.

Starring Ann Magnuson and John Malkovich, *Making Mr. Right* involved a marketing consultant who finds herself unable to resist the android she is supposed to be promoting. The score, written by Chaz Jankel, a composer whose film career was short and limited, explores the screen action through themes that apply to the two main characters, in a style that sometimes evokes Newman, and gives the CD an unexpected continuity.

Didier C. Deutsch

Malcolm X/The Malcolm X Jazz Suite

Malcolm X; 1992, Columbia Records, from the film *Malcolm X,* Warner Bros., 1992 ✍✍✍✍

album notes: Music: Terence Blanchard; **Conductor:** Terence Blanchard; **Featured Musicians:** Terence Blanchard, James Hynes, John Longo, trumpet; Mike Davis, Britt Woodman, Timothy Williams, trombones; Jerry Dodgion, Jerome Richardson, Branford Marsalis, saxophone; Sir Roland Hanna, Bruce Barth, piano; Tarus Mateen, Nedra Wheeler, bass; Eugene Jackson Jr., drums.

The Malcolm X Jazz Suite; 1992, Columbia Records, from the film *Malcolm X,* Warner Bros., 1992 ✍✍✍✍

album notes: Music: Terence Blanchard; **Featured Musicians:** Terence Blanchard, trumpet; Sam Newsom, tenor saxophone; Bruce Bath, piano; Troy Davis, drums; Tarus Mateen, bass.

Musically, Spike Lee's impressive cinematographic portrait of Malcolm X is solidly rooted in the sights and sounds of the 1960s, and in the flavorful jazz themes Terence Blanchard created for the film. The first aspect of this musical background can be found in the compilation released by Quincy Jones's Qwest label. Dismissing the first track, "Revolution," which is too contemporary to even suggest the period when Malcolm X thrived (a better, and more historically appropriate choice would have been a recording by The Last Poets), the rest of the album presents various gratifying performances by some of the top black entertainers from the 1940s through the 1960s, including Lionel Hampton, The Ink Spots, Billie Holiday, Ella

Denzel Washington in Malcolm X. **(The Kobal Collection)**

Fitzgerald, John Coltrane, Ray Charles, Duke Ellington, and Aretha Franklin, in a compilation that astutely combines rhythm and blues and jazz. It's an excellent cross–section of both genres, and it effectively reflects the historic background of the film itself.

The two recordings from Columbia, on the other hand, present Terence Blanchard's underscoring for the film, the first volume as it was in the original score, the second volume in a more jazz–flavored rearrangement that brings together many of the cues into a consistent programming concept. Featuring several vocals by the Boys Choir of Harlem, the score is a strong, evocative affair. Instrumental cues played by a symphonic orchestra are sometimes augmented by soloists Branford Marsalis or Blanchard himself, and interspersed with more jazz–oriented numbers in which Blanchard leads a group of seasoned musicians, which includes Marsalis, Sir Roland Hanna, Jerome Richardson, and Jerry Dodgion, among others. Those various elements combine to create a music that is di-versified, strongly eloquent, and a fitting complement to the screen action.

The "Malcolm X Jazz Suite" presents a more coherent and uni-fied picture of the music Blanchard wrote, with the cues reorga-nized into a seamless series of themes, performed by a jazz combo. It's another innovative approach to what is a profuse score to begin with, with many undertones that truly deserve to be fully exploited and expressed in as many modes as possi-ble. Listeners who may not be inclined to sit through the score album itself, might delight in this musical extrapolation which fills a gap and adds new textures to the original music.

Didier C. Deutsch

Malice

1993, Varèse Sarabande, from the film *Malice*, Castle Rock En-tertainment, 1993 ♪♪

album notes: Music: Jerry Goldsmith; **Conductor:** Jerry Goldsmith.

Made in the wake of *Basic Instinct, Malice* co–opted the earlier film's mix of eroticism and moral confusion and Goldsmith's score for it ranges from extensions of *Basic Instinct*'s pulsing chase music to some climactic brass chords that might have been more at home in a science fiction movie. The best thing about the album is the opening theme, built off a hesitant, simple keyboard melody with a tense, building string chord that gives way to a haunting female chorus singing a beautiful title melody; it's the flip side of Goldsmith's lullaby–like *Poltergeist* title theme. Unfortunately much of the later suspense cues give in to the current "less–is–more" school of droning, textureless monotony that just doesn't make for very interesting listening.

Jeff Bond

The Mambo Kings

1991, Elektra Records, from the film *The Mambo Kings*, Warner Bros., 1991 ✍✍✍✍

Percolating Caribbean polyrhythms are the order of the day here, played by some of the finest progenitors of the form. You may not recognize a single name in the Mambo All–Stars, but you won't be thinking about that as you soak in the group's crisp performances. Tito Puente's rendition of "Cuban Pete" will make you forget about Jim Carrey's campy hit version from *The Mask,* while Linda Ronstadt, Arturo Sandoval, Celia Cruz, and Los Lobos make valuable contributions to this mambo music primer.

Gary Graff

Mame

1999, Sony Classical/Legacy, from the Broadway musical, *Mame,* 1966 ✍✍✍✍

album notes: Music: Jerry Herman; **Lyrics:** Jerry Herman; **Conductor:** Donald Pippin; **Cast:** Angela Lansbury (Mame), Beatrice Arthur (Vera), Jane Connell (Agnes Gooch), Charles Braswell (Beauregard), Frankie Michaels (Patrick, age 10), Jerry Lanning (Patrick, age 19).

Patrick Dennis's fond ruminations about the extravagant Auntie Mame, already the source for a 1954 play, became the occasion for another effervescent score by Jerry Herman, following the one he had written two years before for *Hello, Dolly!*. With Angela Lansbury at the peak of her stage career in a portrayal that still resonates with crackling energy in the original cast recording, *Mame* was a bustling, exciting musical which enjoyed tremendous longevity, following its opening of May 24, 1966.

In the book by Jerome Lawrence and Robert E. Lee, Mame, a socialite whose excessive lifestyle seems to be one party after another, becomes the guardian of young Dennis, her nephew, whom she encourages to live in a permissive way to best appreciate what life is all about. When the Depression hits and she finds herself without any means of support, Mame bravely seeks a job. Unfortunately, she fails at every attempt to secure a permanent one until she sweeps a Southern gentleman off

his feet, Beauregard Burnside, whom she marries. When Beau dies accidentally, Mame, as indomitable as ever, manages to meddle into Dennis's affair with a scatterbrained, snobbish girl, and sets him up with her own assistant, wondering all along what she would do if Dennis walked into her life again.

Brilliantly directed by Gene Saks, with Bea Arthur regularly trading bitchy comments with Mame, her bosom buddy, the musical was a delight from beginning to end. Jerry Herman's score, which included "Open a New Window," "We Need a Little Christmas," "If He Walked into My Life," and the exuberant "It's Today" and "That's How Young I Feel," is probably the best he's ever written.

This exuberant, explosive score is made even more exciting through the first-rate new mixing/mastering work which brings to extraordinary vibrant life the best moments from this beloved musical (listen to "It's Today" and "That's How Young I Feel," for instance!). Adding a new positive wrinkle to this extraordinary reissue, several bonus tracks, recorded by Jerry Herman before the show was even produced, give a different perspective to these songs and to the creative process that went into the musical.

Didier C. Deutsch

A Man and a Woman/Live for Life

1996, DRG Records, from the films *A Man and a Woman,* Allied Artists, 1965, and *Live for Life,* United Artists, 1967 ✍✍✍✍
album notes: Music: Francis Lai, Baden Powell, Vinicius de Moraes.

Francis Lai achieved international fame for the first score, driven by the theme that permeates Claude Lelouch's sensitive study of a widow with a child (Anouk Aimee), and the car racer (Jean–Louis Trintignant), who meet, fall in love, separate, and eventually get back together. The Oscar–winning film launched the career of Lelouch, and helped establish Lai as another French composer (after Michel Legrand and Maurice Jarre) whose music struck a responsive note worldwide. *Live for Life,* Lelouch's follow–up failed to get the same recognition, though Lai again delivered another fine, compelling score. In both, the songs performed in both French and English contribute enormously to the overall appreciation of the music.

Didier C. Deutsch

The Man from U.N.C.L.E.

1998, Razor & Tie, from the television series, *The Man from U.N.C.L.E.,* MGM, 1964–68 ✍✍✍✍
album notes: Music: Jerry Goldsmith, Gerald Fried; **Conductor:** Hugo Montenegro.

Next to James Bond, Matt Helm, and Our Man Flint on the big screen, or the Avengers on the little one, there was *The Man from U.N.C.L.E.,* a slyly tongue-in-cheek spy series that starred Robert Vaughn as Napoleon Solo and David McCallum as his sidekick, Illya Kuryakin. Fast-paced, loaded with gadgetry, and mod (as the term was used in 1964), it proved one of the most popular series at the time: everything about it was cool—the suspense-filled action, which week after week found Solo and Illya fighting the evil forces of T.H.R.U.S.H., and always winning at the very last minute; the panoply of fancy weapons they used in their work; the beautiful girls who invariably got involved in the plots; the dry humor both men exhibited, even if the most tense moments; and the music that pervaded each episode and gave them an additional ounce of hipness.

Many excellent composers worked on the series, from Jerry Goldsmith who wrote the title theme that opened the series each week, to Gerald Fried, who created many of its scores, Morton Stevens, Walter Scharf, Robert Drasnin, and even Lalo Schifrin, who honed his style on the series before moving on to *Mission: Impossible.*

This CD compilation combines together tracks from various sources (the original single, various albums that were released by RCA) for a comprehensive package that provides a taste of the series. Sonically, there are some flaws: the music sounds loud and distorted, but it may have been recorded that way. And all told, this CD is actually a great deal of fun that fans of the series will relish.

Didier C. Deutsch

The Man in the Iron Mask

1998, Milan Records, from the film *The Man in the Iron Mask,* MGM, 1998 🎬🎬🎬

album notes: Music: Nick Glennie-Smith.

Seventeenth-century France is the setting for this adaptation of Alexandre Dumas's final tale of the Three Musketeers. In this opus, the aged Musketeers are fed-up with the corrupt king. They learn of his twin, a man kept prisoner, shackled with an iron mask. To save France they rescue the twin and place him on the throne. Nick Glennie-Smith, who composed the classical score, using Handel as a focal point, did an excellent job driving the scenes with his themes, and adding some dimension to the sometimes-flat acting performances. Highlights include the frivolous "The Pig Chase" and the waltz "The Masked Ball." A brief note for the soundtrack purist: the tracks on the CD are not sequenced as they occur in the movie.

Beth Krakower

The Man in the Moon

1991, Reprise Records, from the film *The Man in the Moon,* MGM, 1991 🎬🎬🎬

album notes: Music: James Newton Howard; **Conductor:** Marty Paich; **Featured Musicians:** Dean Parks, guitar; David Grisman, mandolin; Michael Fisher, percussion; James Newton Howard, piano; Jay Rosen, violin.

A lovely score by James Newton Howard accompanies Robert Mulligan's beautiful examination of the trials and tribulations of a young girl growing up in 1957 Louisiana farm country. Howard interpolates some atmospheric guitar riffs into his score, giving the music a "down home" feel while at the same time it uses the orchestra poignantly to accentuate the drama of the story. The music feels small and intimate in nature, a perfect score for a character–driven piece, and also an ideal listening experience for anyone searching for strong themes that aren't overwhelmingly melodramatic or saccharine in emotional quality. At times the music has a wistful, melancholic edge to it, but perhaps that's unsurprising given Mulligan's previous cinematic portrayals of growing up—classics which include *Summer of '42* and *To Kill a Mockingbird.* Both of those pictures have outstanding scores, and Howard's music for *The Man in the Moon* is not at all out of place in their company.

Andy Dursin

Man of La Mancha

1965, MCA Records, from the Broadway production *Man of La Mancha,* 1965 🎬🎬🎬🎬🎬

album notes: Music: Mitch Leigh; **Lyrics:** Joe Darion; **Musical Direction:** Neil Warner; **Cast:** Richard Kiley, Irving Jacobson, Joan Diener, Ray Middleton, Robert Rounseville.

Miguel de Cervantes's Don Quixote became the unlikely singing hero of another sensational 1960s musical when *Man of La Mancha* opened on Nov. 22, 1965. It starred Richard Kiley as the gloomy Don, Irving Jacobson as his faithful manservant, Sancho, and Joan Diener as the servant girl the Don mistakes for a fair lady in distress. In a brilliant theatrical *tour de force*, Kiley first portrayed Cervantes, thrown in jail by the inquisition for an offense against the church, offering as his defense a reading of a novel he has recently completed about the exploits of a wandering knight. At the court's request, Cervantes then becomes the Don and enacts the story, with the other prisoners becoming the various characters Don Quixote encounters. High among the tunes that became hits in the score by Mitch Leigh and Joe Darion is "The Impossible Dream," also known as "The Quest," in which Don Quixote mentions all the things it takes to become an errand knight. The show, which won the Tony for Best Musical, had a run of 2,328 performances. The cast album is a must in any collection.

Didier C. Deutsch

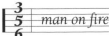

Man on Fire

🎬 1987, Varèse Sarabande, from the film *Man on Fire,* Tri–Star
Pictures, 1987 ♪♪♪

album notes: Music: John Scott; **Orchestra:** The Graunke Symphony
Orchestra; **Conductor:** John Scott.

John Scott fashions some of his more memorable romantic
themes and terrifying suspense cues in this score. Dealing with
the relationship between a bodyguard and the young girl he is
assigned to protect, the film has been forgotten, but John Scott's
music remains effective and highly listenable. Most suspense
scores during the '80s are little more than dreary electronic
noise, but Scott went against the grain of the time by scoring
Man on Fire with a surging, powerful orchestral score. Even the
subdued passages grab the listener. The first track, "Man of Fire"
opens with tremolo violins beneath a tender flute melody, which
at once evokes delicacy and trepidation. This opens up into the
main theme, a beautiful, lushly romantic piece. Some of the
score's other highlights include "Start of the Search" with its
snarling rock 'n' roll drums and marimba, and the surging and triumphant "Sam Wins the Race." Scott's skillful and adroit gift for
orchestration pervades the score. The music works beautifully
on disc, cues often flowing together seamlessly. Track changes
are often not noticed. So effective was this score that some of it
was actually later used in *Die Hard.*

Paul Andrew MacLean

Man Trouble

🎬 1992, Varèse Sarabande, from the film *Man Trouble,* 20th Century Fox, 1992 ♪♪♪♪

album notes: Music: Georges Delerue; **Conductor:** Georges Delerue.

Throughout his life, Georges Delerue particularly excelled at catching the varied moods in romantic comedies, all at once exhibiting
the drama and passion usually needed for this type of screen fare,
and informing the audience without being necessarily obvious
about the general intent. *Man Trouble,* about a well–known musician pursued by an admirer who decides to acquire a guard dog
and gets involved with its trainer, elicited a score that reflects both
aspects, in a rich display of melodic themes in "Love Theme" and
"Making Love" and pleasantly lilting cues in "Joan Throws a Fit"
and "Harry and Eddie Fight." A fitting coda to his career, Delerue
died shortly after completing this score.

Didier C. Deutsch

The Man Who Would Be King

🎬 1990, Bay Cities, from the film *The Man Who Would Be King,*
Allied Artists, 1975 ♪♪♪♪

album notes: Music: Maurice Jarre; **Orchestra:** The National Philharmonic Orchestra, **Conductor:** Maurice Jarre.

Maurice Jarre always seems at his best when he scores epic
films, and this was again clearly the case when he wrote the
music for John Huston's hearty account of Rudyard Kipling's
story about two English con men in late 18th–century India who
journey to distant Kafiristan, a remote Himalayan kingdom,
where they become *de facto* rulers after they take control of
the country's warring tribes. Happily mixing Hindu sounds with
swashbuckling accents, Jarre wrote a score that, like the film,
never takes itself too seriously, while it details the action on
the screen with its broad, grander–than–life posturing. The
whimsical main theme, heard throughout, further enhances the
frequently rollicking aspects of this entertaining rags–to–riches
tale of friendship and adventure.

Didier C. Deutsch

The Man with the Golden Gun

🎬 1988, EMI–Manhattan Records; from the film *The Man with the
Golden Gun,* United Artists, 1974 ♪♪♪

album notes: Music: John Barry; **Conductor:** John Barry.

Despite more than 10 years scoring the James Bond series,
John Barry never fell prey to creative staleness. Of all his Bond
scores, *The Man with the Golden Gun* is his most fun and
tongue–in–cheek. The score is colorful and broad, encompassing a wide array of styles. The album kicks–off with a wildly
nutty title song, sung by Lulu, with typically hokey lyrics by Don
Black. The ensuing score has beautifully exotic passages evoking the Hong Kong setting of the film, invested with ethnic instrumental color. "Kung Fu Fight" is a giddy romp and something of an homage to Albert Kettelby's "In a Chinese Temple."
Also fun is Barry's Dixieland arrangement of the main theme.

The score is of course not without the more dangerous moments, which mark it as a 007 score. Barry pulls out the James
Bond theme in "Lets Go Get 'Em," and furnishes a suspenseful,
almost chilling climax in "Return to Scaramanga's Fun House."
The album closes with a reprise of the title song, this time with
even sillier lyrics. Anyone expecting the hard edge of *Goldfinger* will be disappointed, but *The Man With The Golden Gun*
score is a highly entertaining and fun soundtrack.

After skipping out on the first Roger Moore 007 epic, *Live and
Let Die,* John Barry returned to the series for this sub–par outing that suffers from a too–eclectic mix of musical styles.
Barry's rich, majestic main theme, often played by low strings,
is a melodically beautiful yet manly Orientalism that functions
well in both broad orchestral statements, to color the film's
lush tropical settings and during some staccato chase sequences. Unfortunately it's a washout as belted out by British
pop crooner Lulu in the film's title song, an incredibly cheesy
pop/rock anthem that doesn't exactly conjure up memories of

Shirley Bassey in her prime. Elsewhere the chase and suspense cues are often compromised by the tongue–in–cheek intrusion of off–kilter comic and atmospheric effects, like a hideous slide whistle in the middle of an otherwise exciting car chase cue and excruciating honky–tonk piano and jazz band sections during Bond's final showdown with the villain Scaramanga.

Paul Andrew MacLean/Jeff Bond

The Man without a Face

1992, Philips Records, from the film *The Man Without a Face,* Warner Bros., 1992 🎼🎼🎼

album notes: Music: James Horner; **Orchestra:** The London Symphony Orchestra; **Conductor:** James Horner.

The compelling story of a man whose scarred face and taciturn behavior have made him an outcast in a small Maine community and the fatherless 12–year–old who befriends him, *The Man without a Face* prompted James Horner, writing in an uncharacteristically low–key mode, to create a very sensitive, admirably nuanced score. Quickly establishing the moods that pervade the film, "A Father's Legacy" is a romantic theme, with the piano playing a quiet melody against soft orchestral textures, a device repeated in various cues, most effectively in "Chuck's First Lesson," "The Merchant of Venice," and "Lookout Point."

Didier C. Deutsch

The Manchurian Candidate

1997, Premier Recordings, from the film *The Manchurian Candidate,* United Artists, 1962 🎼🎼🎼

album notes: Music: David Amram; **Conductor:** David Amram.

A soul-stirring, classic psychodrama, John Frankenheimer's *The Manchurian Candidate* gave Frank Sinatra one of his most powerful screen roles as an American officer fighting in the Korean war who has been captured with his patrol by Chinese Communists. When they are released and sent back to America, he becomes suspicious of one of his men (Laurence Harvey), whom he thinks might have been brainwashed and is now controlled by his former captors. A snappy thriller that kept its audience on edge, the film received a brilliant jazz score from David Amram that gave an additional gritty edge to the action, at times complementing it, at other times commenting on it. One of the composer's most intriguing contributions, "Queen of Diamonds," contains an atonal theme played by a jagged harpsichord, three piccolos, and high, dissonant strings, creating a very unsettling effect. Among the soloists the composer brought together for the sessions were Paul Horn, Harold Land, Jack Nimitz, Dick Leith, Lou Blackburn, Carmel Jones, and Joe Gordon, plus several Latin players who also contributed their

talents to the score. The quality of the music shows the care that went into the performance. It is regrettable that the recording doesn't reflect the same care—though there is no disclaimer to that effect, the sound quality on this CD is frequently jarring, with distortion noticeable in most of the tracks, particularly on the high end. These flaws aside, this is an important soundtrack album that most listeners will enjoy playing frequently.

Didier C. Deutsch

Mandela and De Klerk

1997, Rhino Records, from the television film *Mandela & De Klerk,* Hallmark/Showtime, 1997 🎼🎼🎼

album notes: Music: Cedric Gradus-Samson; **Featured Musicians:** Cedric Samson, African drums, drums, percussion, keyboards, drum programming; Keith Hutchinson, keyboards; Kelly Petlane, penny whistles; Laurence Matshiza, guitar; Fana Zulu, bass; Fernando Perdigao, drum programming; Moses Molelekwa, keyboards, marimba.

This story of Nelson Mandela, his life struggle to end apartheid in South Africa, his long-term imprisonment, and his eventual accession to the presidency of his country may be one of the best film scripts ever written. It has all the elements of a good drama: a man overcoming every odds to finally obtain his countrymen's freedom from a repressive regime, the defeat of the dreaded racists, the struggle between good and evil, all of it with a unique human dimension made all the more sincere because it is true. *Mandela and De Klerk,* a television film, was an attempt to portray these events by focusing on the meetings that took place between Mandela (Sidney Poitier) while leader of the African National Congress and De Klerk (Michael Caine), while Mandela was still in prison, adamantly refusing to be coerced and insisting that his release could only happen when the white government agreed to free all South Africans. The score for the teleplay was composed by Cedric Gradus-Samson, who had already scored the documentary, *Mandela: Son of Africa, Father of a Nation.* The cues for this drama bring together several South African performers and feature many African instruments, particularly percussion instruments. It's a frequently stirring, sometimes alien-sounding music that has its appeal, but that seems to have less vibrancy than the Mango release.

see also: Cry, the Beloved Country/Mandela: Son of Africa

Didier C. Deutsch

Mandela: Son of Africa, Father of a Nation

1996, Mango Records, from the documentary *Mandela: Son of Africa, Father of a Nation,* Island Pictures, 1996 🎼🎼🎼

album notes: Music: Cedric Gradus Samson

A documentary that lionizes Nelson Mandela while chronicling his life struggle and eventual victory against apartheid (but at what cost!), *Mandela, Son of Africa, Father of a Nation* offers an uncompromising portrait of the South African leader. Making the film even more vibrant is its soundtrack, in which a large number of South African performers add their voices to create an exciting musical portrait of the man and his time. There are many remarkable moments in this recording, some a little too brief, that all add up to a vivid description of a moment in humanity's long–winded history.

Didier C. Deutsch

Manon des sources

See: Jean de Florette/Manon des sources

A Man's Tragedy

See: The Conformist/A Man's Tragedy

The Marrying Man

1991, Hollywood Records, from *The Marrying Man*, Hollywood Pictures, 1991 ♪♪♪♪

album notes: Music: David Newman; **Featured Artists:** Stan Getz, tenor sax; Don Menza, tenor sax; Jack Sheldon, trumpet; Chuck Findley, trumpet.

Though an inconsequential little comedy set in 1948 Las Vegas, *The Marrying Man* resulted in a great jazz album. With stalwarts Stan Getz, Don Menza, Jack Sheldon, and Chuck Findley providing the solos, and Manhattan Transfer's Tim Hauser producing the album and contributing a fancy rendition of "Mama Look A Boo Boo," the flavor of the album is unmistakable and a total gas. Even Kim Basinger, not known previously as a singer, reveals a new side of her talent as a vocalist in several standards in which her delivery is quite acceptable, though her version of "Honeysuckle Rose" seems a trifle lifeless. David Newman, writing in a style also unusual for him, turns in some terrific big band cues with "Backstage Beat–Up," "Run, Charley, Run," and the "Main Title."

Didier C. Deutsch

Mars Attacks!

1996, Atlantic Classics Records, from the film *Mars Attacks!,* Warner Bros., 1996 ♪♪♪♪

album notes: Music: Danny Elfman; **Conductor:** Artie Kane.

Danny Elfman has composed a suitably over–the–top score for Tim Burton's broad science fiction comedy, *Mars Attacks! From* the eerily furtive moments preceding the stampede of burning cattle to the raucous battle music against the Martian invaders,

Elfman captures the film's manic sense of nostalgic '50s sci–fi, best summed up in the relentless, brassy main theme, driven by the soaring strains of the omnipresent theremin and frequent use of choir. The score, full of bizarre and nostalgic orchestrations and plenty of musical tongue–in–cheek, Is pure fun and excitement in an emerald cranium. It supports Burton's bizarre visions on–screen and splashes like a crimson death ray across home speaker systems.

Randall D. Larson

Marvin's Room

1996, Miramax/Hollywood Records, from the film *Marvin's Room,* Miramax Films, 1996 ♪♪♪♪

album notes: Music: Rachel Portman; **Conductor:** Michael Kosarin; **Featured Musicians:** Ken Bichel, piano; Jesse Levy, cello.

In a narrative that sometimes finds deep, emotional accents to convey its story about two estranged sisters who are brought together after 20 years when one is diagnosed with having leukemia that can only be controlled with a bone marrow transplant from a close relative, *Marvin's Room* is an engaging, serious film with funny overtones. It avoids the usual pitfalls of melodrama or overbearing sentimentality to spin its tale in rich, down–to–earth details that make it both spirited and heartwarming. Adding the right colors to the story is Rachel Portman's excellent score, a delightful collection of cues, both serious and exhilarating, with catchy themes that perfectly match the tones of the story itself. Though presented here in a sequencing that doesn't follow the storyline, it easily makes its point, and proves essentially attractive and compelling. Carly Simon's "Two Little Sisters" is another nice touch in a thoroughly winning album.

Didier C. Deutsch

Mary Poppins

1998, Disneyland Records, from the film *Mary Poppins,* Walt Disney Pictures, 1964 ♪♪♪♪♪

album notes: Music: Richard M. Sherman, Robert B. Sherman; **Lyrics:** Richard M. Sherman, Robert B. Sherman; **Cast:** Julie Andrews, Dick Van Dyke, Glynis Johns, David Tomlinson, Karen Dotrice, Matthew Garber, Ed Wynn, Elsa Lanchester, Hermione Baddeley.

Julie Andrews, who had been dismissed in favor of Audrey Hepburn when *My Fair Lady* was made into a movie, had a sweet revenge when she appeared that same year in *Mary Poppins,* a delightful musical fantasy made by Walt Disney. In it, she made her screen debut and won the Oscar for Best Actress. Set in Victorian England at the turn of the century, the film, which combined live action and animated characters, told about Mary Poppins, the perfect nanny, whose impromptu arrival at the house of proper banker George Banks results in utter chaos.

The chaos begins when she takes the children, Jane and Michael, on a merry trip to an enchanted land where the denizens are cartoon characters, and everyone seems to know her and her friend Bert, a chimney sweeper. When Jane and Michael report to their father what they have experienced, he immediately denounces the nanny for her wild flights of fancy which are a disservice to the education of his children.

Spearheaded by several enjoyable tunes written by Richard M. Sherman and Robert B. Sherman (including "A Spoonful of Sugar," "Supercalifragilisticexpialidocious," and "Chim–Chim Cheree"), and with Julie Andrews delightfully impish as Mary Poppins, the film became one of the studio's all–time big hits. The soundtrack album recording provides total enjoyment.

Didier C. Deutsch

Mary Reilly

1996, Sony Classical, from the film *Mary Reilly,* TriStar Pictures, 1996 ⅋⅋⅋

album notes: Music: George Fenton; **Orchestra:** The London Symphony Orchestra; **Conductor:** George Fenton; **Featured Musicians:** Lucia Lin, Janice Graham, violin.

An interesting spin–off on the Gothic story about staid Dr. Jekyll and his murderous alter ego, Mr. Hyde, as seen from the point of view of Mary Reilly, a housemaid working for Dr. Jekyll with a secret as murky as her employer's, the film was mostly distinguished by the dark tones that pervaded it, something reflected in George Fenton's relentlessly somber score. With a few exceptions ("Mrs. Farraday"), most of the cues are densely lugubrious, and fail to really attract in a strictly listening program, because very little in them contains the spark that would ignite one's interest.

Didier C. Deutsch

Masada

1990, Varèse Sarabande, from the television movie, *Masada,* 1981 ⅋⅋⅋⅋

album notes: Music: Jerry Goldsmith; **Conductor:** Jerry Goldsmith.

A mini–series that recounted the siege and destruction of Masada, a fortress of Judean rebels, by the Roman army, "Masada" is a rare case of a television show that transcended the medium and actually aimed at a higher level of quality and distinction. That it succeeded was due in large part to the fact that it was treated not like a television series but like a feature film, with considerable financial means put at the service of the project. One smart decision on the part of the producers was to hire Jerry Goldsmith to write the score. As a result, the music, as sampled on this soundtrack album, is of a high–quality level seldom experienced on television, with elaborate themes setting the locale, the people, the action. Impressive as the whole

score is, it can be said that Goldsmith surpassed himself when he composed "The Road to Masada." The series's main theme, a superb march, is reprised to best effect the advancing Roman legions, then, in a more subdued way, to depict the rebels awaiting with anguish the arrival of the enemy troops. If ever a score could be described as truly exciting, the term perfectly fits here. At times thrilling, at other times profoundly moving, "Masada" remains quite an accomplishment in the composer's body of works.

Didier C. Deutsch

M*A*S*H

1995, Sony Legacy, from the film *M*A*S*H,* 20th Century Fox, 1970 ⅋⅋

album notes: Music: Johnny Mandel.

Most die–hard fans of the film (starring Donald Sutherland and Elliott Gould, among others) will thoroughly enjoy this CD reissue of the original soundtrack, complete with bits of dialogue, underscored and joined together by instrumental themes. Others may find the whole thing tedious after one listening—if they even listen to the whole disc.

Whatever your feeling, the soundtrack from *M*A*S*H* fairly drips with the madcap comedic highjinks that make the film such a delight. However, it may not be nearly as effective, or enjoyable, without the benefit of the full story and its accompanying visuals. As a record, it's more a curiosity than an experience you'll want to relive again and again. On the positive side, in addition to the theme song "Suicide is Painless," sung by The MASH and performed as a jazz instrumental by Ahmad Jamal, the disc also includes six instrumental cues, *sans* dialogue.

Charles L. Granata

The Mask

1994, Tri-Star Records/Sony Music, from the film *The Mask,* New Line Cinema, 1994 ⅋⅋⅋

album notes: Music: Randy Edelman; **Orchestra:** The Irish Film Orchestra; **Conductor:** Randy Edelman.

1994, Chaos/Sony Music, from the film *The Mask,* New Line Cinema, 1994 ⅋⅋⅋

album notes: Featured Performers: Jim Carrey, Xscape, Domino, Tony Toni Tone, Harry Connick Jr., Vanessa Williams, K7, Fishbone, The Brian Setzer Orchestra, Royal Crown Revue, Susan Boyd.

Rare instance where both the song and score albums work well in concert with each other. Both capture the manic pace of the film, but the song compilation more so. It starts off strong with the radio version of "Cuban Pete," Jim Carrey's show–stopping musical number in the film which contains dialogue snippets. The film version concludes the album. Other songs that follow

Jim Carrey in The Mask. **(The Kobal Collection)**

all have the characteristics of escapees from some 1940s Tex Avery cartoon (the film's effects were inspired by Avery's style). Bouncy '90s versions of Cab Calloway's "Hi De Ho" share the spotlight with Vanessa Williams's steamy and romantic "Would You Be My Baby."

Randy Edelman's orchestral score alternates mainly between the calmer and darker moments of the film. However, when the Mask is on screen, Edelman's music becomes just as off the wall as Carrey's green goblin ("Out of the Line of Fire"). Warning! Both CDs feature the same cover art. The song album has a black border, while purple is the color for the score.

David Hirsch

The Mask of Zorro

1998, Sony Classical, from the film *The Mask of Zorro,* TriStar Pictures, 1998 ♫♫♫♫♫

album notes: Music: James Horner; **Conductor:** James Horner; **Featured Soloists:** Kazu Matsui, Tony Hinnigan, Dean Parks, Ian Underwood, James Woodrow, Felipe de Algeciras, Salvador Andrades, Gema de la Cruz, Tito Heredia, Carmela Romero, Paqui de Ronda.

It has been some time since a score of this eloquence and magnitude has been created for an action film, but leave it to James Horner to come up with one of the finest examples of the swashbuckling genre, replete with themes that are strongly suggestive of the screen action while retaining a musical vibrancy of their own that makes them exciting on a pure aural basis. Of course, given his recent status as the composer of the score for the multiple Oscar winning *Titanic* and its multi-million selling soundtrack album, one shouldn't be too surprised. But shedding away the syrupy accents that made *Titanic* such a tear-jerker, Horner let his spirits soar and came up with a score that perfectly matches the exuberant tone of the film starring Anthony Hopkins as the celebrated masked avenger forced into retirement after an accident and endeavoring to train his replacement: in this instance a rambunctious outlaw played by Antonio Banderas. In a vivid display of his enormous talent, Horner conjures up in his cues the ebullience in the action, and adds to them a zest of his own that makes this soundtrack album enormous fun from beginning to end. *The Mask of Zorro* wasn't another *Titanic* at the box office, but if you have grown tired of hearing yet another version of "My Heart Will Go On," this energetic score will restore your faith in one of today's best film composers.

Didier C. Deutsch

The Master of Ballantrae

1998, Prometheus Records, from the film *The Master of Ballantrae,* Columbia, 1984 ♪♪♪♪

album notes: Music: Bruce Broughton; **Orchestra:** The Sinfonia of London; **Conductor:** Bruce Broughton.

Based on Robert Louis Stevenson's swashbuckling sea novel, already the source of a celebrated film starring Errol Flynn, *The Master of Ballantrae* received a new treatment in 1984, when it was televised, with Michael York, Richard Thomas, and Timothy Dalton in the cast. Providing the musical touch to this adventure film, Bruce Broughton created a colorful score that teems with glorious accents, moments of bravadura, and cues that celebrate action at its highest. Though he mentions in the liner notes that he was mostly interested in the inner workings of the characters, he evidently found in the subject matter ample fodder for his artistic invention: built around two Scottish themes (the first heard in the "Main Title," the second in "Rowan Tree"), the score thrives particularly when it comes alive with a series of brassy calls to action ("The Battle at Sea"), but it also enables the composer to dabble into softer emotions ("Courting Alison," "Colonial Minuet") in which Broughton shows his mettle in fine fashion. Opulent and melodic, the music never becomes too maudlin, even at its darkest ("James' Death"), and remains consistently on a high quality level. This soundtrack album, released in a limited edition by the Belgian label Prometheus, may take some doing to track down. But the regular mail-order shops and firms should be able to get it for you. Don't despair, and don't give up: it's well worth it.

Didier C. Deutsch

Masters of the Universe

1992, Silva Screen Records, from the film *Masters of the Universe,* Cannon Films, 1987 ♪♪♪♪

album notes: Music: Bill Conti; **Orchestra:** The Graunke Orchestra of Munich; **Conductor:** Harry Rabinowitz.

A sword–and–sorcery film, opposing an impossibly handsome he–man and a fiendish–looking ghoul, named Skeletor, in a fight to the death for control of the Universe, *Masters of the Universe* received an appropriately epic score from Bill Conti. The composer gleefully uses all the tenets of the genre to write cues that are all at once amusingly exhilarating and grandly representative of the screen action. Very few surprises here, just a rock solid score that delivers the goods, with the Graunke Orchestra doing a bang–up job in this spirited recording.

Didier C. Deutsch

Matinee

1993, Varèse Sarabande, from the film *Matinee,* Universal Pictures, 1993 ♪♪♪

album notes: Music: Jerry Goldsmith; **Conductor:** Jerry Goldsmith.

This warm, nostalgic score for one of Joe Dante's best—nd least–known—movies effectively captures the film's '50s setting and offers a couple of amusing send–ups of the horror film scores of the period. Unfortunately it's all so low–key and repetitive, particularly in its parody of the old prom standard "Theme to a Summer Place," that it just can't stand on its own as a listening experience, even though Goldsmith's rambunctious theme for John Goodman's William Castle–like character is perfect.

Jeff Bond

The Matrix

1999, Maverick Records, from the film *The Matrix,* Warner Bros., 1999 ♪♪♪

There is not a simple cookie-cutter explanation for the convoluted plot of this cyber-punk/sci-fi extravaganza, but the music, to be blunt, rocks! Fans of techno and electronica are in for a slammin' fix, with cuts by Ministry, Prodigy, Rage Against the Machine, Meat Beat Manifesto, and other superstars and up-and-comers of the genre. This is not for the faint-hearted, but a lot of fun for those who love it loud. Turn this "cyberpalooza" way, way up for a maximum virtual listening experience.

Amy Rosen

1999, Varèse-Sarabande, from the film *The Matrix,* Warner Bros., 1999 ♪♪

album notes: Music: Don Davis; **Conductor:** Don Davis.

The score by Don Davis, a combination of orchestral flourishes, percussive effects, and synthesizer riffs, is, with minor exceptions, not too terribly inspiring. It sound perfunctory on a purely audio level, and while it may enhance the atmosphere of the film as a subliminal support to the screen action, it does little to attract a casual listener trying to get into it.

Didier C. Deutsch

Maurice

1987, RCA Victor, from the film *Maurice,* Cinecom and Merchant Ivory Productions, 1989 ♪♪♪♪

album notes: Music: Richard Robbins; **Conductor:** Harry Rabinowitz.

A surprisingly sensitive screen treatment of E.M. Foster's Edwardian novel, *Maurice* details a young man's awakening to his own homosexuality when he finds himself attracted and responding to the attentions of another student at Cambridge.

As is frequently the case with Merchant Ivory, the production company specializing in magnificently reconstructed period films, the delicately chiseled score crafted by Richard Robbins gives *Maurice* its proper atmosphere and evokes a period which overflows with romantic accents. The music, incredibly rich and versatile, features transpositions of themes by Tchaikovsky, "At the Pianola" and "In the Renault," a superb period waltz, "The Cafe Royale," and a bouncy piano rag, "Miss Edna Mae's Surprise," among its many highlights. It all adds up to a catchy, enjoyable album that compels the listener to return to it frequently.

Didier C. Deutsch

Maverick

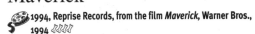 **1994, Reprise Records, from the film *Maverick*, Warner Bros., 1994** 🎵🎵🎵🎵

album notes: Music: Randy Newman; **Conductor:** Randy Newman; **Featured Musician:** Malcolm McNab.

Randy Newman's western score is grandly expansive and as jaunty and spry as the film's easygoing charm. Newman frequently switches gears from heavy dramatics to amusing pomp and bombast, to high Coplandesque adventure. His main theme takes its cue from the high-spirited, fast-moving Maverick character. The theme is pure Americana and steeped in Hollywood tradition. In contrast is a slightly deceptive theme for Annabelle, a lilting, old-fashioned cue for violins. These primary themes are central to the score, which remains cleverly playful in orchestration and tone. Newman's baton is planted firmly in his cheek as he concocts a spirited and likable exercise in Hollywood western musicology. As obvious and occasionally over-the-top the themes and their interplay may be, the score remains contagiously likeable.

Randall D. Larson

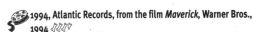 **1994, Atlantic Records, from the film *Maverick*, Warner Bros., 1994** 🎵🎵🎵🎵

Country music soundtracks have generally come up short (and if you think *Urban Cowboy* is country, you're wrong). This does a better job than most, with a group of established veterans and fresh up-and-comers performing new songs written for or old songs chosen for this film. "Dream on Texas Ladies" proves that John Michael Montgomery is a gifted singer, even when presented with so-so material. Patty Loveless and Radney Foster do a nice duet turn on "Rainbow Down the Road," but it's three old hats, Waylon Jennings, Clint Black, and Randy Newman, who are responsible for *Maverick's* best tracks.

Gary Graff

Max and Helen

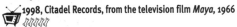 **1991, Bay Cities Records, from the film *Max and Helen*, Turner Pictures, 1990** 🎵🎵🎵

album notes: Music: Christopher Young; **Featured Musicians (in Black Dragon):** Christopher Young, pianos/deowas; Masa Yoshizawa, hichiriki, nokan, shakuhachi, voice; Hiromi Hashibe, featured voice, bass koto; Tateo Takahashi, shamisen; Suenobu Togi, sho; Daniel Licht, bass suling, bansuri flute, genggong; Bob Fernandez, John Fitzgerald, David Johnson, Mark Zimoski, Japanese percussion.

Though presented under the title of *Max and Helen*, from a 1990 film starring Treat Williams and Alice Krige, about a pair of lovers separated by World War II and brought back together fortuitously several years later, the CD actually gives an inordinately long playing time to two other, non-film related works, the 33-minute *Masses* and the 18-minute *Koku-ryu (Black Dragon)*, an avant-garde composition that may prove off-putting to some listeners. A riveting combination of solo voices, sonic manipulations, and ethnic folk music, *Max and Helen* aims to create a multi-layered tapestry which reinforces the screen action and gives it a stronger emotional tug.

Didier C. Deutsch

Maximum Risk

🎬 **1996, Varèse Sarabande, from the film *Maximum Risk*, Columbia Pictures, 1996** 🎵
album notes: Music: Robert Folk.

An otherwise solid action film starring Jean-Claude Van Damme, about the strong spiritual connection that exists between twins, set against the backdrop of violent life in a big city, *Maximum Risk* inspired Robert Folk to write a constantly driven score that may have been quite effective on screen to illustrate and underline the action in the scenes, but fails to make much of a statement when heard in one's living room. A collision of synthesizer chords and percussive effects that lead nowhere, the cues often tend to sound limited and dry, with incredible energy being wasted on very little. Or, as someone else would have said in other times, it's much ado about nothing.

Didier C. Deutsch

Maya

🎬 **1998, Citadel Records, from the television film *Maya*, 1966** 🎵🎵🎵🎵🎵

album notes: Music: Hans J. Salter; **Orchestra:** The Graunke Symphony Orchestra; **Conductor:** Kurt Graunke, Hans J. Salter.

One of the masters of film music, and one of its unheralded figures, Hans J. Salter composed many scores that were heard in films that have long since become classics. High among them were the many horror films he scored, mostly in the 1940s, a genre in which he particularly excelled and in which he had few peers. This excellent CD provides a taste of his creations in the lengthy *Horror Rhapsody* in which he used elements from the scores he wrote for such films as *Son of Frankenstein* in 1939, *The Mummy's Hand* in 1940, *Black Friday* in 1940, and *Man Made Monster* in 1941. The suite is an homage of sorts to the ghouls that lived in those films and became legends of the screen as a result. As Tony Thomas notes with dead-on accuracy in his notes, "The suite will also evoke various mad doctors, black cats and sundry things that go bump in the night."

Cut in a different cloth is the soundtrack for the television show, *Maya,* which barely lasted a season, and for which Salter wrote a vibrant score, filled with passionate images that evoke images of India made in Hollywood, luxuriant, brightly colorful, and totally inaccurate. Based on a feature film scored by Riz Ortolani, *Maya* told the story of two teenagers: an English boy, searching for his lost father, and an Indian boy who, with his elephant Maya, is a fugitive from the law. A highlight in this score is "Jungle," a cue in which the composer built a pyramidal chord effect to emphasize a mood of increasing suspense, reinforced by the grating noise of a jawbone used as a percussion instrument. Next to it, several bucolic scenes are evoked in "Maya to the Rescue" and "Night in Calcutta," in which a peaceful melody controls a mood of quiet. Elsewhere, other moods, equally vibrant and attractive, are suggested. At times evocative of the music Rozsa wrote for *The Jungle Book,* but with a personality of its own, this is a richly melodic, brilliantly colorful score that never lets its listeners down.

Didier C. Deutsch

Medicine Man

1992, Varèse Sarabande, from the film *Medicine Man,* Cinergi Productions, 1992 🎜🎜🎜

album notes: Music: Jerry Goldsmith; **Orchestra:** The National Philharmonic Orchestra; **Conductor:** Jerry Goldsmith.

Jerry Goldsmith's music for *Medicine Man* is an evocative tapestry of orchestral color, vibrantly splashed with expert strokes and subtle undercurrents onto his musical canvas. The scene is set with a bouncy, Latin American–styled motif with flutes, marimba, and percussion embellished by synth. The real theme emerges half-way through, altering the jaunty tempo and texture with a dark, evocative ambiance of rustling electronics and harsh, primitive percussion. Violins foreshadow the film's main theme, a graceful melody which captures all the majesty, mystery, and tragedy of the tropical rain forest in which the action takes place. That theme reappears frequently, through quotations or variations, in several succeeding cues, associated with both the rain forest and the noble cancer research undertaken therein.

Throughout, Goldsmith superbly captures the alternating moods in the storyline—exhilaration to despair—through a moment's

orchestral counterpoint. The frequent use of water–droplet synth sounds as a rhythmic measure is an effective and clever device to suggest the humid wetness of the rain forest.

Randall D. Larson

Meet Joe Black

1998, Universal Records, from the film *Meet Joe Black,* Universal, 1998 🎜🎜🎜🎜

album notes: Music: Thomas Newman; **Conductor:** Thomas Newman

A strange, unhurried film about its purpose, *Meet Joe Black* was a romantic fantasy that dealt with a media tycoon obsessed with death, who meets his eventual opponent in the guise of an attractive young man. Except that, in this case, Death (who prefers to be called Joe Black) has decided to take a holiday to study all things terrestrial, with the tycoon as his guide in exchange for a longer lease on his life. Inevitably, Black falls in love with the tycoon's daughter, but all good things must eventually come to an end, and even Death must go back to work, once its vacation is over.

Underscoring a tale such as this required a light hand, and Thomas Newman delivered a score that is lightweight and luminous at the same time. The ethereal themes flow through each cue, establishing moods that are quietly surreal, with diaphanous effects that enhance their attractiveness. Renditions of standards like "Let's Face the Music and Dance" and "What a Wonderful World," played by a dance band, only serve to offset Newman's own creations, if only by the contrast they create in texture and execution.

Didier C. Deutsch

Meet Me in St. Louis

1990, DRG Records, from the Broadway production *Meet Me in St. Louis,* 1990 🎜🎜🎜

album notes: Music: Hugh Martin, Ralph Blane; **Lyrics:** Hugh Martin, Ralph Blane; **Musical Direction:** Milton Rosenstock; **Cast:** George Hearn, Milo O'Shea, Charlotte Moore, Betty Garrett, Courtney Peldon, Donna Kane, Rachel Graham.

1999, Rhino Records, from the film *Meet Me in St. Louis,* MGM, 1944 🎜🎜🎜🎜

In a rare trend reversal, the MGM 1944 filmed musical hit, *Meet Me in St. Louis* became a Broadway stage show when it opened on Nov. 2, 1989. That it took more than 45 years to achieve this feat says something about the problem created by such a decision. Indeed, despite an excellent cast led by George Hearn, Milo O'Shea, Charlotte Moore, and Betty Garrett, all reliable performers, the show stayed around for only 253 performances, not a very long run by today's standards. There were multiple reasons for that, but the one that loomed heavy above

Judy Garland and Tom Drake in the film version of Meet Me in St. Louis. **(The Kobal Collection)**

the entire production was the fact that a musical so magically captured on film could only appear halfway interesting on the stage. Despite Donna Kane's valiant efforts to give a fetching portrayal as Esther, her performance couldn't erase the memory of Judy Garland in the film. In truth, everything conspired to cast the musical into a negative light, by enhancing the stage limitations compared with the movies, and by drawing the unavoidable parallel with the film's performances. However, the cast album is still of interest, though a clear second choice after the film soundtrack, which is finally available from Rhino in that label's continuing restoration of the great musical scores from the MGM films.

Didier C. Deutsch

Meetings with Remarkable Men

1999, Citadel Records, from the film *Meetings with Remarkable Men*, Renar, 1979 ♫♫♫

album notes: Music: Thomas De Hartmann, Laurence Rosenthal; **Orchestra:** The National Philharmonic Orchestra, The Ambrosian Singers of London; **Conductor:** Laurence Rosenthal.

Gurdjieff wandered the world looking for meaning and through his "meetings with remarkable men," he developed a way of life that inspired a whole school of philosophy. Among his acolytes was Russian composer Thomas De Hartmann, whose deeply spiritual music was composed under Gurdjieff's guidance, and now accompanies this film version of Gurdjieff's memoir. Adapting and orchestrating De Hartmann's piano music for the film, Laurence Rosenthal added instruments that evoke Gurdjieff's travels like the kanun or Near Eastern zither, Persian santur, Tibetan gong, and bamboo flutes. The soundtrack's highlight—originally trimmed down for the LP—is present in full: "The Contest of the Ashokhs" features Tuvan throat singing as musicians gathering from afar on a mountain to make the perfect sound. When the ideal timbre is reached, the mountain will echo back. This beautiful, eerie vocal style rounds out a fine balance of symphonic drama and encounters with remarkable instruments that prove to be well integrated into Rosenthal's orchestra.

David Poole

Melrose Place

1994, Giant Records, from the television series, *Melrose Place*, 1993–94 ♪♪♪

The popular television series spawned this attractive soundtrack album, in which the grooves are primarily in a soft rock mold, the kind that usually is well accepted by thirtysomethings who consider themselves hip, and older conservative televiewers who want to think they are still in touch with current trends in music but who would frown if the songs were more abrasive or objectionable. Actually, this collection is reasonably enjoyable, with good performances by Aimee Mann, Annie Lennox, Divinyls, and Letters to Cleo, among others. Nothing to write home about, but something you might want to listen to on a mildly relaxing day.

Didier C. Deutsch

Memoirs of an Invisible Man

1992, Varèse Sarabande, from the film *Memoirs of an Invisible Man*, Warner Bros., 1992 ♪♪♪♪

album notes: Music: Shirley Walker; **Synthesizer Programmer:** Hans Zimmer; **Conductor:** Shirley Walker.

Shirley Walker's first feature film score is one of the best elements of this John Carpenter/Chevy Chase misfire. The album opens with a "suite" (actually the film's end credit music) that blends the score's primary material with great showmanship, from a heartbreakingly beautiful love theme to the foreboding, crashing sounds of science gone awry and some pulse–pounding, rapid–fire pursuit music. Walker's skill at writing portentous, complex and heavily–textured action music is unquestioned (what is questionable is why she doesn't get more high–profile assignments like this), but what's really surprising is that someone so adept at underscoring the testosterone– pumped world of action movies can also produce such wonderfully touching romantic melodies.

Jeff Bond

Memphis Belle

1990, Varèse Sarabande, from the film *Memphis Belle*, Warner Bros., 1990 ♪♪♪♪

album notes: Music: George Fenton; **Conductor:** George Fenton.

Set during World War II, amid the gallant pilots who flew the US Air Force B–17 bombers, the film chronicles the 25th and last mission of the Memphis Belle and its crew, in a final flight over Germany for a bombing that was to decide the conclusion of the war. In the cues he wrote for the film, George Fenton deftly evokes the moods of suspense and drama, fun and exhilaration, heroism and glory that marked the mission. Setting the score into its time period, re-recordings of standards, like

"Green Eyes," "Flying Home," and "I Know Why," provide an occasional bow to the musical trends of the era, resulting in a strongly suggestive score. The long "Memphis Belle End Title Suite" regroups the most important themes into a striking cohesive musical coda.

Didier C. Deutsch

Men at Work

1990, Mesa Records, from the film *Men at Work*, Triumph, 1990 ♪♪♪

album notes: Music: Stewart Copeland.

This comedy thriller about two garbagemen who find themselves involved in a political murder (they discover the body, you see) was enlivened by a score composed by Stewart Copeland and several reggae/rock songs heard on the soundtrack. The album benefits the latter at the expense of the former, represented by only two selections, but when the songs are performed by UB40, Sly & Robbie, Black Uhuru, Third World, and Ziggy Marley, among others, no one can complain. The moods are appropriately uplifting and enjoyable.

Didier C. Deutsch

Men in Black

1997, Columbia, from the film *Men in Black*, Columbia Pictures, 1997 ♪♪♪♪

It always helps to have a bona fide hitmaker as one of the film's stars, and Will Smith (aka the Fresh Prince) scores not only with the hip-hopping, Grammy-winning title track, but also with his other contribution, "Just Cruisin'." The rest of *Men in Black*—*MIB* for you hipsters—falls on the safe side of rap and R&B, with even gangstas such as Snoop Doggy Dogg and the Roots (with D'Angelo) chillin' their act to the venue and getting cheerfully jiggy on "We Just Wanna Party with You" and "The Notice," respectively. Jazz saxophonist Branford Marsalis's Buckshot Le-Fonque adds a bit of sophistication with "Some Crow Fonque (More Tea, Vicar?)," and soundtrack kingpin Danny Elfman's main and closing themes stand up as solid compositions.

Gary Graff

1997, Columbia, from the film *Men in Black*, Columbia Pictures, 1997 ♪♪♪♪

album notes: Music: Danny Elfman; **Conductor:** Artie Kane, Mark McKenzie.

Taking a cue from some of his previous scores (*Batman* comes to mind), and adding a slyly fresh spin to them, Danny Elfman again scores high points with this exciting music to the satirical we-are-being-invaded-again film starring Will Smith and Tommy Lee Jones. Predictably, the cues aim to create a somewhat eerie ambiance, with appropriate big orchestral flurries to signal the dangers caused by the invading forces ("Noisy Cricket/Impending Trouble"). Reflecting some of the film's most entertaining moments, the composer also indulges in flights of fancy that are predictable, but still quite invigorating ("Take Off/Crash"). Not a really defining score, by any stretch of the imagination, but one that stands on its own merits when heard in a different environment.

Didier C. Deutsch

Men with Guns

1998, Rykodisc, from the film *Men with Guns,* Sony Pictures Classics, 1998 ♪♪♪♪

album notes: Music: Mason Daring; **Featured Musicians:** Duke Levine, acoustic guitar; Nancy Zeltsman, bass marimba; Jamey Haddad, percussion; Billy Novick, flutes, whistles; Gus Sebring, French horn; Frank London, trumpet; Arturo Ofarrill, piano; Lewis Kahn, trombone; Bobby Sanabria, percussion; Andrew Gonzalez, bass; Evan Harlan, accordion; Mason Daring, electric guitar.

Mason Daring's score gives a specific south-of-the-border flavor to this metaphoric film directed by John Sayles (not to be confused with another similarly titled opus by Kari Skogland, also released in 1998), set in a South American country ravaged by political murders, terror, censorship, and repression, which involves three characters—a priest, a soldier, and a doctor—confronted with these situations and having to make a choice between believing and not believing, between lies and truth, between "innocence" and self-knowledge. Reflecting the diversity in the action, the cues have been assembled to provide a musical journey that takes the listener to different landscapes, with various influences that run the gamut from Peruvian to Afro-Cuban to Mayan to Columbian. Adding a touch of authenticity, several tracks performed by local bands and individuals provide a similarly diverse musical vision. Unusual and quite interesting.

Didier C. Deutsch

The Mephisto Waltz/The Other

1997, Varèse-Sarabande, from the films *The Mephisto Waltz,* 1971, and *The Other,* 1972, 20th Century-Fox ♪♪♪♪♪

album notes: Music: Jerry Goldsmith; **Conductor:** Jerry Goldsmith.

In the early 1970s, in the short span of a year, Jerry Goldsmith wrote two important scores that presaged and announced the works that would earn him an Oscar Award and a nomination later on that decade. Based on a novel by Fred Mustard Stewart, the first score, *The Mephisto Waltz,* was written for a film by Paul Wendkos that involved a writer and his wife (Alan Alda and Jacqueline Bisset) and the malevolent, devil-worshipping concert pianist about to die of leukemia (Curt Jurgens) and his

daughter (Barbara Perkins), who attempt to destroy their marriage. The second, *The Other,* directed by Robert Mulligan, was a Gothic thriller set in 1935, and concerned two identical twins, one introverted and aloof, the other outgoing and friendly, and a series of unexplained deaths that plague a family living on a farm. In striking contrast to the subject matters, Goldsmith delivered a chilling, eerie score for *The Mephisto Waltz,* accented by the use of the high strings, piano, and percussion instruments, with the often dissonant cues following a jagged, distorted course to suggest the terrifying drama in the story. *The Other* follows a totally different path: stressing the innocence of youth and the pastoral setting of the story, it is a playful, engaging score with a bucolic tone that belies the unnerving tale being told (for instance, a pseudo-Japanese cue, not otherwise identified here, comes as a total surprise in the middle of the score). Available here for the first time, both are strong reminders of the composer's uncanny ability to modify his style and keep his listeners on edge, sometimes working with the storyline to enhance its asperities, sometimes working against it to further reinforce its impact, but always being intelligently creative and superiorly challenging.

Didier C. Deutsch

Mercury Rising

1998, Varèse-Sarabande, from the film *Mercury Rising,* Universal, 1998 ♪♪♪♪

album notes: Music: John Barry; **Conductor:** John Barry.

The recent publication on the Internet of a list of British undercover agents strikes an uncomfortable note that even the makers of *Mercury Rising* might not have anticipated. In the film, directed by Harold Becker from a screenplay based on a novel by Ryne Douglas Peardon, a nine-year-old autistic child, Simon (played by Miko Hughes), breaks a code published in a kiddie magazine that gives him access to a list of all U.S. undercover agents around the world. When would-be assassins are dispatched to silence the kid, he is taken in tow by a free-wheeling operative (Bruce Willis, in one of his most engaging screen roles) who suspects the Agency of trying to eliminate Simon, and who attempts to protect him while getting enough information to save him from his pursuers. Little in John Barry's score suggests that mercury is indeed rising, as the action gets hotter: the cues are beautifully laid out, quietly developing into attractive themes that reflect the relationship between the characters, but not the violent world around them. Typical of Barry's approach to film scoring of late, which seems to be running countercurrent to the fast-paced, febrile scores of his early years, this is a very lovely series of cues, with strong melodies that are pleasant to hear.

Didier C. Deutsch

Meridian

1991, Moonstone Records, from the film *Meridian,* Full Moon Entertainment, 1991 🎬

album notes: Music: Pino Donaggio; Synthesizers Programming: Paolo Steffan; Orchestra: The Sinfonica di Milano; Conductor: Natale Massara.

This dark version of the classic "Beauty and the Beast" tale got an equally gloomy score from acknowledged horror music master Pino Donaggio. Unfortunately, the score's pace is just as pedestrian as the film and therein lies the problem. Despite lovely melodies like "Catherine's Theme" (too short!) or "Beast to the Rescue," there are just too many others that crawl along. "Unholy Seduction," a synthesized cue whose primary melody was cleverly created by sampled voices, ends up being too repetitive. And why was "Circus from the Past" played by synthesizers when they had an orchestra that could have made it not sound so embarrassingly primitive? Although it works effectively on film, this score is just too bland and lacking in anything substantial to support the soundtrack's almost 50–minute running time.

David Hirsch

Merlin

1998, Varèse-Sarabande, from the television program *Merlin,* 1998 🎬🎬🎬🎬

album notes: Music: Trevor Jones; Orchestra: The London Symphony Orchestra; Conductor: Geoff Alexander.

The legend of Merlin continues to fuel the imagination of filmmakers and screenwriters, ever so eager to bring back a time when courtly love and faeries were the order of the day, and King Arthur championed noble values in a world that was still barbaric and violent. A television miniseries, *Merlin* told the story of the magician in terms that took into account the wonders of the world in which he lived, the deeds he performed, and the men he advised, as well as the enemies he encountered on his way to becoming a legend. Appropriately grandiose and florid, the score by Trevor Jones echoed the moments of high adventure, mystery, and passion that were the hallmarks of the teleplay. But adding to it a different twist was a note of melancholy that imbued the story and informed that there was a world of ancient mystical arts about to disappear forever. Presented in long cues that enable the music to develop and make a much more positive impact, the score is striking in its exposition, and colorfully explicit.

Didier C. Deutsch

Merlin of the Crystal Cage

1991, Silva Screen, from the television program *Merlin of the Crystal Cage,* BBC-TV, 1991 🎬🎬🎬🎬

album notes: Music: Francis Shaw; Orchestra: The Munich Symphony Orchestra; Conductor: Francis Shaw.

Equally descriptive as the original *Merlin* score, the score by Francis Shaw for *Merlin of the Crystal Cage* stressed the chivalrous over the mysterious, with broad swashbuckling themes of epic proportions occasionally adding forceful, colorful accents to the music. Perhaps a trifle more accessible the score is more melody-oriented than Trevor Jones's, and assigns specific motifs for each character in the story. But because of the greater continuity in the cues for *Merlin,* Jones's score has a slight edge over *Merlin of the Crystal Cage.*

Didier C. Deutsch

Mermaids

1990, Geffen Records, from the film *Mermaids,* Orion Pictures, 1990 🎬🎬🎬

A quirky little comedy, about an ever so slightly eccentric woman and her two equally unconventional daughters, *Mermaids* is considerably brightened up by its cheerful soundtrack, which includes many songs from the early 1960s, time period of the action. While offering little that's new in terms of music (with the possible exception of "The Shoop Shoop Song," and a surprisingly laid–back version of "Baby, I'm Yours," performed by Cher, who also stars), the album compiles together various songs that are bound to evoke many pleasant memories of a time when things seemed much less complicated and easier to enjoy, with performances by Frankie Valli and The Four Seasons, Smokey Robinson and The Miracles, Lesley Gore, Mickey and Sylvia, and Shelley Fabares, among its better moments. Nothing earthshaking, just a nifty combination of a few memorable tunes that goes a long way in creating the right atmosphere.

Didier C. Deutsch

Merrily We Roll Along

1992, RCA Victor, from the Broadway production *Merrily We Roll Along*, 1981 🎬🎬🎬

album notes: Music: Stephen Sondheim; **Lyrics:** Stephen Sondheim; **Musical Direction:** Paul Gemignani; **Cast:** Jim Walton, Ann Morrison, Lonny Price, Jason Alexander.

An ambitious failure on Broadway, this time–runs–backward musical about 25 years of changing relationships among a group of high-school friends endures in the repertoire because of its Stephen Sondheim score, which seems to grow in stature with every revival. "Not a Day Goes By" is as beautiful a song as Sondheim—or anyone else—has written for Broadway. CD listeners should take Sondheim up on his suggestion and try programming this recording in reverse ("chronological") order, noting the development of his musical ideas. Fans of the *Seinfeld* TV series will also want to note Jason Alexander's Broadway musical debut here, playing a Broadway producer.

Marc Kirkeby

Merry Christmas Mr. Lawrence

1985, London Records, from the film *Merry Christmas Mr. Lawrence*, 1985 🎬🎬🎬

album notes: Music: Ryuichi Sakamoto.

Composer Ryuichi Sakamoto stars along with David Bowie in this film set during World War II in a Japanese prison camp. Two years earlier, Vangelis had shown that modern synthesized music could work in context with the period setting of *Chariots of Fire*. Sakamoto follows his lead, but creatively infuses some of his work here with sound effects in "Ride, Ride, Ride" and unusual musical colors in "A Brief Encounter." He also relies on traditional orchestral music for one standout cue called "Germination."

David Hirsch

A Merry War

1998, Angel Records, from the film *A Merry War*, 1998 🎬🎬🎬🎬

album notes: Music: Mike Batt; **Orchestra:** The Royal Philharmonic Orchestra; **Conductor:** Mike Batt; **Featured Musician:** Jack Rothstein, violin.

Based on George Orwell's second novel, *Keep the Aspidistra Flying, A Merry War* tells the story of Gordon Comstock (Richard E. Grant), a copywriter, and his girlfriend Rosemary (Helena Bonham Carter). Fed up with his middle-class life,

Comstock quits his job to become a poet, supporting himself by working at a bookstore. Inspired by this unusual theme, composer Mike Batt developed a series of cues that perfectly illustrate this story; in addition he created a suite in three movements, "The Aspidistra Suite," which has been smartly added to this soundtrack release. Both the suite and the cues from the film speak volumes.

Didier C. Deutsch

Message in a Bottle

1999, 143 Records/Atlantic Records, from the film *Message in a Bottle*, Warner Bros., 1999 🎬🎬🎬🎬

album notes: Music: Gabriel Yared; **Conductor:** Harry Rabinowitz; **Featured Musicians:** Mitch Dalton, classical guitar; Colin Green, classical guitar; Clem Clempson, electric guitar; Metro Voices.

As my friend Ford says, "when a composer is needed for a chick flick these days, they call in Gabriel Yared." A tear-jerker in the best tradition, *Message in a Bottle* starred Kevin Costner, whose love message in a bottle to a woman named Catherine piques the curiosity of the Chicago journalist who has found it. She tracks him down, and as luck would have it, they fall in love before the last reel. Providing the saccharine needed for the story, Yared wrote a score that's all syrup and no grit, with "Theresa and Garrett," a lovely theme for acoustic guitar and a sprinkle of strings, ex-emplifying the jist of it. The two other tracks heard here are of the same ilk, gorgeously attractive, but in fact much too strikingly beautiful to elicit anything but a heavy romantic sigh. Much more spunk can be found in the songs heard on the soundtrack, which have been collected in this CD, with performances by a slew of artists, including Hootie & the Blowfish, Sheryl Crow, Clannad, Sarah McLachlan, and Sinead Lohan, among others.

Didier C. Deutsch

Metroland

1999, Warner Bros. Records, from the film *Metroland*, Pandora Cinema, 1998 🎬🎬🎬🎬

album notes: Music: Mark Knopfler; **Featured Musicians:** Mark Knopfler, guitars, vocals; Richard Bennett, guitars; Jim Cox, piano, Hammond organ; Guy Fletcher, keyboards; Chris White, soprano sax, flute; Steve Sidwell, trumpet, flugelhorn; Glenn Worf, bass; Chad Cromwell, drums.

The always tasteful Mark Knopfler adopts a French flavor for *Metroland,* adding a different kind of lilt to his guitar playing and Continental textures to his melodies and arrangements. His pieces are mostly short and sweet, highlighted by a jazzy stroll down the Seine in "A Walk in Paris." But Knopfler isn't the best guitarist on *Metroland;* that honor goes to the late Django Reinhardt, represented by two wonderful pieces—

"Blues Clair" and "Minor Swing," the latter performed with the Quintette du Hot Club de France. Still, Knopfler's "Metroland" theme is a pleasantly understated work, while the inclusion of "Sultans of Swing" from his band, Dire Straits—alongside the Stranglers' strident "Peaches," Hot Chocolate's soulful "So You Win Again," and Elvis Costello's bittersweet "Alison"—provide a pleasing counterpoint to the rest of the album's provincial excursions.

Gary Graff

Miami Rhapsody

1995, Hollywood Records, from the film *Miami Rhapsody*, Hollywood, 1995 ♫♫♫♫

album notes: Music: Mark Isham; **Featured Musicians:** Rick Baptiste, trumpet; Conte Candoli, trumpet; Oscar Brashear, trumpet; Charlie Davis, trumpet; Mark Isham, trumpet; Bruce Paulson, trombone; Andy Martin, trombone; Bill Reichenbach, trombone; Jim Self, tuba; Bob Sheppard, saxophone; Steve Tavaglione, saxophone; Pete Christlieb, saxophone; Jack Nimitz, saxophone; Sid Page, violin; David Goldblatt, piano; Chuck Domanico, bass; Kurt Wortman, drums; Alex Acuna, percussion.

Any film that features on its soundtrack such classics as "Just One of Those Things," performed by Louis Armstrong, and "I Only Have Eyes for You," by Ella Fitzgerald, in addition to cover versions of "I Got It Bad and That Ain't Good" and "(Love Is) The Tender Trap," can't be all that bad. And indeed, this wryly impish comedy about a writer uncertain about marriage, who finds out that almost everyone in her family is having an affair, was engaging and quite entertaining in its own way. Giving the narrative an extra bounce, Mark Isham delivered a flavorful score written in a jazz groove, and supplemented by the various selections listed above. The big band he used for the occasion includes many studio aces, noted for the excellence of their work, something that translates into the level of musicianship on display here. On the whole, it's a very pleasant, musically entertaining album that has a lot to offer.

Didier C. Deutsch

Miami Vice/Miami Vice II

1985, MCA Records, from the television series *Miami Vice*, 1985 ♫♫♫♫

album notes: Music: Jan Hammer.

Outside of the fact that this is strictly formulaic music, designed to underscore an action series that was the hippest show on television for a hot minute, two things become immediately apparent on these CDs. The first one, Jan Hammer's music is not really that good: It worked very well within the context of the show itself, but on its own it doesn't withstand close scrutiny. The second is that, because of its success, the series was able to attract some talented performers whose

songs made the show even more attractive to the average viewers. In the first CD, for instance, if "Own the Night" by Chaka Khan, or "Smuggler's Blues" by Glen Frey are just OK, "You Belong to the City," also by Frey, and mostly "In the Air Tonight" by Phil Collins, and "Better Be Good to Me," by Tina Turner, are of a high pop caliber; likewise, in disc 2, the combination of Phil Collins ("Take Me Home"), Gladys Knight & The Pips ("Send It to Me"), and Patti LaBelle & Bill Champlin ("The Last Unbroken Heart") is a winner, again as long as you can live with Hammer's trite synthesizer–cum–rhythm–track cues that are only good for a moment.

Didier C. Deutsch

Michael

1996, Revolution Records, from the film *Michael*, Turner Pictures, 1996 ♫♫♫♫

A romantic fable about a photogenic mutt, an angel (John Travolta, in another winning screen performance), and the journalists who are after him for a scoop, *Michael* is the occasion for a festive music celebration with several songs, heard on the soundtrack, that deal with love, happiness, elation, or just simply good feelings. This compilation brings it all back home, with performances by many enjoyable singers, like Van Morrison, Bonnie Raitt, Willie Nelson, Aretha Franklin, and Don Henley. An ingratiating collection that makes few demands on the intellect but is guaranteed to provide a good time.

Didier C. Deutsch

Michael Collins

1996, Atlantic Records, from the film *Michael Collins*, Geffen Pictures, 1996 ♫♫♫♫

album notes: Music: Elliot Goldenthal; **Conductor:** Rick Cordova; **Conductor:** Jonathan Sheffer.

A film that exudes tremendous energy and transcends its bleak subject of political activism in Ireland, *Michael Collins* owes a lot of its impact on the screen to director Neil Jordan's deft handling of the struggle for independence from the British and his understanding that the topic needed an uplifting cinematic approach to reach a broad audience. He achieved his goal by staging this account of the campaign waged in 1916 by Michael Collins, an early pioneer in the fight against Britain, with all the ingredients usually found in contemporary dramas—fast–paced action scenes and rousing dramatic performances. Adding a specific comment of its own to the story, Elliot Goldenthal wrote a robust, compelling score, rife with great themes that unfold with force and persuasion, with an occasional Irish sonority to anchor the music into its specific ethnic background, something further complemented through the addition of various vocals by Sinead O'-Connor. From the first track, "Fire and Arms," the tone is readily apparent that this is going to be a vibrant essay, filled with great orchestral sounds and strong melodic ideas. Goldenthal doesn't disappoint. The score throbs with excitement, occasionally pausing for a softer, reflective theme, but keeping the listener on edge most of the time.

Didier C. Deutsch

Mickey One

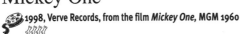1998, Verve Records, from the film *Mickey One*, MGM 1960 🎵🎵🎵🎵

album notes: Music: Eddie Sauter; **Featured Musician:** Stan Getz, tenor sax.

Featuring the inventive and colorful arrangements of Eddie Sauter, this music retains a lot of the jazz feel. But many of the cues are lushly orchestrated, and there are a few that are more characteristic of Hollywood movies. "Mickey's Theme" features some beautiful orchestral writing. "Once upon a Time" capitalizes on Getz, and the bossa nova's current success. Sauter and Getz were a wonderfully matched pair, with Sauter's deep understanding of modern harmony and orchestration complementing Getz's remarkable tone and phrasing. Getz rarely worked as a soloist in film music, but *Mickey One* is an indication of his potential talent in this field.

Bob Belden

Microcosmos

1996, Audivis Travelling/France, from the film *Microcosmos*, Miramax, 1996 🎵🎵🎵🎵
album notes: Music: Bruno Coulais.

A surprise hit (who would have thought that insects could be such great actors?), this amazing "documentary," photographed by Claude Nuridsany and Marie Perennou in their own backyard, was amusingly set to music by Bruno Coulais, who found his inspiration in the noises heard in the natural environment, and who complemented them with his own creations. As such, the score provided a musical texture that was well in keeping with the approach of the film itself, an "inside" look at the life of the insects, as it were, and supported the action without seeming alien to it. On its own, the score continues to keep its audience interested and rapt. This title may be out of print or just plain hard to find. Mail-order companies, used CD shops, or dealers of rare or import recordings will be your best bet.

Didier C. Deutsch

Midas Run/The Night Visitor

1995, Citadel Records, from the films *Midas Run*, 1969; and *The Night Visitor* 🎵🎵🎵

album notes: Music: Elmer Bernstein, Henry Mancini; **Orchestra:** The Rome Cinema Orchestra, **Conductors:** Elmer Bernstein. Henry Mancini; **Featured Performers:** Elmer Bernstein, piano; Dorothy Remsen, harp; Martin Ruderman, flute; Armand Kaproff, cello.

Written for a film starring Fred Astaire as a charming British agent who steals a large shipment of government gold on its way to Tanzania from Zurich and Italy, *Midas Run* was a total disaster at the box office, though it enabled Elmer Bernstein to write a straightforward little score that was immensely appealing, the sort Henry Mancini was quite famous for. Shot on locations in London, Milan, Venice, and Rome, the locales of the action provided the composer with the proper scenic colors, while the action itself suggested some of the most virile accents in the score. As Tony Thomas points out in his liner notes, it is a clear example of "film music being better than the picture for which it was designed."

House: After 5 Years of Living was an assignment of another kind which came in 1955 from furniture designers Charles and Ray Eames, who asked Bernstein to score an art film about the house they had designed. As for *The Night Visitor*, starring Max Von Sydow as a farmer wrongly accused of murder by his sister and her husband, and subsequently committed to an asylum, it also is an obscure film that failed to find an audience. It elicited a taut, hypnotic score from Henry Mancini, writing for a synthesizer and 17 instruments, in a style that seems miles away from the comedies he was mostly scoring at this stage in his career. It is also in sharp contrast to what precedes it and as a result seems a rather odd choice in this context.

Didier C. Deutsch

Midnight Cowboy

1985, EMI–Manhattan Records, from the film *Midnight Cowboy*, United Artists, 1969 🎵🎵🎵🎵
album notes: Music: John Barry; **Conductor:** John Barry.

While Nilsson's evocative rendition of "Everybody's Talkin'" might have clouded John Barry's own achievements, the soundtrack of *Midnight Cowboy* has always been a deft combination of both, the song and Barry's cues, and that's what ultimately subsists after one has listened to the album. Certainly, the instrumental selections, particularly "Joe Buck Rides Again" and "Fun City," do much to capture the squalid moods in John Schlesinger's film about a young hustler from Texas who becomes a boy prostitute in New York City and befriends a seedy, tuberculosis–stricken street character with whom he moves to

Dustin Hoffman and Jon Voight in Midnight Cowboy. **(Archive Photos, Inc.)**

Florida. The pop songs, notably "A Famous Myth" by The Groop (sounding like a clone of The Mamas and The Papas) and "Jungle Gym at the Zoo" by Elephants Memory, are also very much a part of this memorable film, even though they sound dated by now.

Didier C. Deutsch

Midnight in the Garden of Good and Evil

🎬 1997, Malpaso, from the film *Midnight in the Garden of Good and Evil*, Warner Bros.-Malpaso, 1997 ♪♪♪♪

While this tortured, plodding screen telling of the book by John Berendt seemed to lack focus and a real sense of purpose, there was nothing vague about its soundtrack, a solid collection of standards, written by the great Johnny Mercer, performed by a veritable who's who in pop music. Yet, despite the familiarity of its material (the ubiquitous "I Wanna Be Around" by Tony Bennett, and "Fools Rush In" by Rosemary Clooney, being two of them), this set offers some pleasant surprises, among them k.d. lang's effective rendition of the evergreen "Skylark," and Clint Eastwood's take on "Ac-cent-tchu-ate the Positive," which should not give Bennett any nightmare, but has great merits. There are many other bright spots in this collection, including the presence of Joe Williams, Diana Krall, Cassandra Wilson, Alison Krauss, and Kevin Spacey among the performers heard here. But the real magic comes from Mercer, whose lyrics (and occasional tunes) are always wonderful to hear.

Didier C. Deutsch

Midnight Run

🎬 1988, MCA Records, from the film *Midnight Run,* Universal Pictures, 1988 ♪♪♪♪

album notes: Music: Danny Elfman; **Musicians:** Ira Engber, Paul Jackson Jr., guitars; Neal Stubenhaus, electric bass; Chuck Domanico, acoustic bass; John "Vatos" Hernandez, drums; Mike Fisher, percussion; Ralph Grierson, keyboards; Frank Morocco, accordion; John "Juke" Logan, harmonica; John Goux, additional guitar.

In one of his earliest scoring efforts, Danny Elfman hit the right note with his music for *Midnight Run,* an iconoclastic comedy starring Robert De Niro as a gruff bounty hunter ready to throw in the towel, but accepts for his last job the task of bringing back to a Las Vegas mobster an accountant who has embezzled millions of dollars. Elfman, who was still recording with his group Oingo Boingo at the time, wrote a fast-paced, rock score that reflects his intentions of moving away from the kind of music that had made him famous, while keeping a foot firmly planted in a genre that was familiar to him. With bouncy, cheerful little themes—some combining the harmonica and the accordion for an unusual, slightly unorthodox sound—the score

is a constant delight, its effectiveness only slightly defeated by the short playing time of some of the selections.

Didier C. Deutsch

A Midsummer Night's Dream

🎬 1999, Decca Records, from the film *A Midsummer Night's Dream,* 20th Century-Fox, 1999 ♪♪♪♪

album notes: Music: Simon Boswell; **Conductor:** Terry Davies.

Felix Mendelssohn has so profoundly marked William Shakespeare's *A Midsummer Night's Dream* that any attempt to score another presentation of that fantasy is bound to meet with severe criticism. To be fair to Simon Boswell, who wrote the music for this new production starring the radiant Michelle Pfeiffer and a cast of thousands that also includes Calista Flockhart, Kevin Kline, and Sophie Marceau, his score is quite attractive, and attempts to remain within the classic confines set by his illustrious predecessor, whose "Overture" and triumphant "Wedding March" are included. But some of Boswell's stabs at writing in a more contemporary vein, unfortunately fall flat, and the addition of operatic arias in this soundtrack, while probably justified by the film itself, is a bit distracting, particularly if you do not happen to favor opera in the first place. All of this means that this soundtrack album may have a difficult time finding a larger audience, even if the film does, while purists may simply dismiss Boswell's music without further ado, since they probably already have the classical selections anyway. It's too bad: Boswell's music has its charms.

Didier C. Deutsch

Midway

🎬 1998, Varèse-Sarabande, from the film *Midway,* Universal, 1976 ♪♪♪♪

album notes: Music: John Williams; **Orchestra:** The Royal Scottish National Orchestra; **Conductor:** Rick Wentworth.

For many years, John Williams's impressive score for *Midway* was only known to avid collectors by "Midway March" and "Men of the Yorktown March," which had been released on a 45 single by MCA in Japan when the film first came out. Robert Townson corrects a definite wrong with the release of this long-awaited soundtrack album. A big-budget World War II picture, recounting the famous naval battle which forced the Japanese fleet to turn back, clearing the West Coast from possible attack and enabling the U.S. to regroup and confront its foes in the Pacific, *Midway* gave John Williams an opportunity to score a film in which heroic accents dominated. While the music reflected the most obvious aspects of the screen saga, it also took time to include cues that relied on its psychological impact on the participants, more specifically personified by U.S. Admiral Nimitz, and his Japanese alter ego, Admiral Yamamoto. Before the better known "Midway March" and "Men of the Yorktown March" conclude the recording, various cues have set the scene and described the action in terms that are at times subdued, at other times filled with motion. It's a powerful score that presaged in a way the music Williams would write later on for the *Star Wars* and *Indiana Jones* trilogies on a much broader scale. The performance by the Royal Scottish National Orchestra, conducted by Rick Wentworth, is appropriately forceful and exciting.

Didier C. Deutsch

The Mighty

1998, Pangea Records, from the film *The Mighty,* Miramax, 1998 ♪♪♪♪♪

album notes: Music: Trevor Jones.

A subtle contemporary drama about two handicapped youths—the apparently mentally retarded Max and his sidekick, Kevin, a physically impaired neighbor he calls Freak—*The Mighty* explored the emotional bonds that are being established when Kevin is asked to help Max develop his reading ability and fires his imagination with tales about King Arthur and the Knights of the Round Table. The moving story, in which damsels in distress and evil magicians become a tangible reality to Max and Kevin—the former hoisting the latter on his shoulders when they go on their everyday adventures—is given a full range of expressions in Trevor Jones's exhilarating score, in which the basic elements of the screen saga are dealt with in an evocative, often lively manner. The inclusion of a song performed by Sting gets the story back to its contemporary level, but a tired duet between B.B. King and Italian superstar Zucchero on "Let the Good Times Roll," while maybe necessary in the context of the film, makes very little sense here.

Didier C. Deutsch

Mighty Joe Young

1998, Hollywood Records, from the film *Mighty Joe Young,* Walt Disney, 1998 ♪♪♪

album notes: Music: James Horner; **Conductor:** James Horner; **Featured Musicians:** Ron Aston, Michael Fisher, Tony Hinnigan, James Horner, Brian Kilgore, Kazu Matsui, Ian Underwood, Robert Zimmitti.

Africa equals Montana in James Horner's score for Disney's enjoyable remake. The composer is using an exotic grab bag of flutes and percussion instruments for this spin on *King Kong,* one that sounds mighty similar to his own Americana score for *Legends of the Fall.* But Horner knows his way around this jungle groove, and there's no denying his score's primal force when those native drums kick in for Joe's rampages. Though this ape may have been around the musical bend, he's still got

a lot of heart, particularly in a sweet, thematic lullaby that becomes Joe's main theme. Celine Dion doesn't sing this one, but the African lyrics that Horner's come up with are just as effective as what he wrote for *Titanic.* Joe's song turns a Godzilla-sized primate to a big, lovelorn kid, once again showing Horner's talent for bringing his subjects down to a nice, melodic size.

Dan Schweiger

Mighty Morphin Power Rangers: The Movie

1995, Varèse Sarabande, from the film *Mighty Morphin Power Rangers: The Movie,* 20th Century Fox, 1995 ♪♪♪♪

album notes: Music: Graeme Revell; **Orchestra:** The West Australian Symphony Orchestra; **Conductor:** Tim Simonec.

"Balls to the wall" orchestral score by Graeme Revell unexpectedly provides more fun and excitement than this silly film ever could muster. Certainly, Revell manages to give the story a more mystical air (the use of a chorus in "Summoning the Ninjetti" for example) and the desperation of the Rangers' plight is endowed with a real sense of urgency in "Zordon is Dying." Even the bombastic brass arrangements of the battle cues, like "The Megazord Battle," give the film a spectacular scope it could not achieve on its own. Revell has a real flair at creating dramatic scores for these types of effects–laden action films.

David Hirsch

1995, Atlantic/Fox Records, from the film *Mighty Morphin Power Rangers: The Movie,* 20th Century Fox, 1995 ♪♪

Hard to believe, but these teen superheroes were once hotter than Beanie Babies, and they're destined to become favorites at '90s dress–up parties. The music for their first feature film is fairly mundane, making use of some proven hits, like Red Hot Chili Peppers' funky take on "Higher Ground," and Van Halen's Teflon–smooth "Dreams," and oddball adaptations, such as Carl Douglas joining Fun Tomas for something called "Kung Fu Dancing." But, never fear, it does have the "Go Go Power Rangers" theme, if it isn't already plastered in your memory.

Gary Graff

The Mighty Quinn

1989, A&M Records, from the film *The Mighty Quinn,* MGM, 1989 ♪♪♪

An odd compilation for a murder mystery set in the Caribbean, with some happy rhythms (UB 40's "I Gotta Keep Moving On," Michael Rose's "Guess Who's Coming to Dinner," Neville Brothers' "Yellow Moon"), some OK tracks (Arrow's "Groove Master," Half Pint's "Giving/Sharing," Yello's "La Habanera"), and some dispensable (Little Twitch's "Send Fi Spanish Fly"). Bob Dylan's "The Mighty Quinn" gets an abrasively funny reading by Sheryl Lee Ralph, Cedella Marley, and Sharon Marley Prendergast.

Didier C. Deutsch

Miller's Crossing

1990, Varèse Sarabande, from the film *Miller's Crossing*, 20th Century Fox, 1990 ♪

album notes: Music: Carter Burwell.

Some soundtrack albums aren't helping the cause of their composers or film music in general. Take, for instance, this album, which, even though it has 16 tracks, clocks in at 28 minutes, with four totally dispensable pop selections taking up more than 10 minutes of playing time. Carter Burwell's score gets literally lost in the process and certainly deserved better than the shoddy treatment it gets here.

Didier C. Deutsch

Milou en mai

1990, CBS Records/France, from the film *Milou en mai*, Pyramid, 1990 ♪♪♪♪

album notes: Music: Stephane Grappelli; **Featured Musicians:** Stephane Grappelli, violin, bass violin; Marc Fosset, guitar; Martin Taylor, guitar; Jack Sewing, bass; Maurice Vander, piano, electric piano, harpsichord; Pierre Gossez, clarinet, soprano sax; Marcel Azzola, accordion.

In another rare foray into film music (see *Les valseuses*), Stephane Grappelli scored this film by Louis Malle about an insouciant French provincial family living in its Medoc estate, totally oblivious of, but eventually affected by the social events of May, 1968 that provoked the fall of the De Gaulle presidency. At times gently ironical and giddy, at other times somber, the score reflected the contrasting moods in the film, starring Michel Piccoli and Miou-Miou. The lyricism in Grappelli's playing, however, carried the day, and remains one of the great joys in this exhilarating score. This recording may be difficult to find. Check with a used CD store, mail-order company, or a dealer specializing in rare, out-of-print, or import recordings.

Didier C. Deutsch

Mimic

1997, Varèse-Sarabande, from the film *Mimic*, Dimension, 1997 ♪♪♪

album notes: Music: Marco Beltrami; **Conductor:** Marco Beltrami.

Marco Beltrami's gloomy music perfectly captures the moods in this gruesome sci-fi thriller in which Jeremy Northam and Mira Sorvino, portraying married scientists, battle cockroaches that are infecting and killing children in New York City. Before they succeed, however, they have to eradicate a new breed of the repulsive insects that has acquired the ability to grow to enormous proportions and transform into humans. The cues that emphasize certain aspects of the narrative all seem cut from the same cloth—dark, eerie, without a moment of levity, except the somewhat wistful "Manny's Tango," and a tongue-in-cheek performance of "La cucaracha," taken at a very slow, deliberate pace, which may or may not be intentionally funny.

Didier C. Deutsch

Minnesota Clay

1992, CAM Records/Italy, from the film *Minnesota Clay*, Titanus, 1965 ♪♪♪♪

album notes: Music: Piero Piccioni; **Conductor:** Piero Piccioni.

The first western directed by Sergio Corbucci, *Minnesota Clay* starred Cameron Mitchell as a former convict who returns to the scene of his "crime," to find the witness who lied about him. Slowly going blind, he refuses to join either of the two rival gangs fighting over control of the town, and eventually finds and kills the false witness. An "American-style" western that didn't evidence any of the excesses found later on in spaghetti westerns, *Minnesota Clay* was rich in drama and suspense, with Mitchell doing a great job as the title hero. Also aiding was Piero Piccioni's score, a dynamic set of cues that were constantly evocative of the action, yet provided a rich atmosphere of their own. Also reminiscent of the kind of music Max Steiner or Dimitri Tiomkin had been writing in the 1950s and early 1960s, Piccioni's music retained an edge of originality that made it even more attractive. Today, it continues to exert its spell in this excellent recording. This title may be out of print or just plain hard to find. Mail-order companies, used CD shops, or dealers of rare or import recordings will be your best bet.

Didier C. Deutsch

Miracle on 34th Street

1994, Fox Records, from the film *Miracle on 34th Street*, 20th Century Fox, 1994 ♪

album notes: Music: Bruce Broughton; **Conductor:** Bruce Broughton.

Instead of trusting his composer, Bruce Broughton, and giving him an opportunity to write Christmas music for this remake of *Miracle on 34th Street* in the manner in which he had let John Williams write an instant classic score for *Home Alone*, John Hughes chose instead to stuff his soundtrack with covers of some well-known Christmas songs by Natalie Cole, Dionne Warwick, Ray Charles, Elvis Presley, Aretha Franklin, and (eeech!) Kenny G.

Broughton's contribution is reduced in this CD to three little cues that denote a wonderful feel for the action in progress, but can only whet one's appetite for a longer expression. It's another missed opportunity for lovers of film music.

Didier C. Deutsch

The Mirror Has Two Faces

1996, Columbia Records, from the film *The Mirror Has Two Faces,* Tri-Star Pictures, 1996 ♪♪♪

album notes: Music: Marvin Hamlisch; **Conductor:** Marvin Hamlisch.

This romantic comedy was produced and directed by Barbra Streisand, who also starred, as an exploration of "the modern myths of beauty and sex and how they complicate relationships," with beau–hunk Jeff Bridges as the object of Ms. Streisand's lust. If this doesn't sound too convincing, try the soundtrack album, in which Streisand shares composing credits with Marvin Hamlisch, a lightweight but nonetheless interesting writer, and performs a couple of songs (*noblesse oblige!*). It is difficult in a case like this to properly assess the amount of work done by one or the other in the collaboration. For the sake of argument, the score is mindlessly pleasant, somewhat reminiscent of the type of music Henry Mancini did so much better, with lilting melodies receiving the piano–cum–orchestra treatment. To what extent did Streisand contribute musical ideas is a question only she and Hamlisch can answer, though the "Love Theme" for which she takes full credit is virtually undistinguishable stylistically from the tracks composed by Hamlisch himself. David Sanborn and Luciano Pavarotti are the star's other odd partners in this minor effort.

Didier C. Deutsch

Misery

1990, Bay Cities Records, from the film *Misery,* Columbia Pictures, 1990 ♪♪♪♪

album notes: Music: Marc Shaiman; **Conductor:** Dennis Dreith.

Interestingly, *Misery* is the first score Marc Shaiman ever wrote for a full–length feature, an impressive debut that marked the start of a great career that has since seen the creation of many important scores, including *Addams Family, City Slickers,* and *Ghosts of Mississippi.* It was an even greater achievement, considering the fact that this claustrophobic two–character film— based on a Stephen King novel about a famous writer, the victim of a car accident, who finds himself immobilized and tended for by his "No. 1 fan," a nurse with murderous instincts—called for a score that enhanced a study in psychological terror. Shaiman conceived a carefully constructed full–scale dramatic score as a series of ominous–sounding themes, in which the low strings create the oppressive atmosphere reflec-

10 Essential Scores by Ennio Morricone

The Mission
Once upon a Time in the West
Once upon a Time in America
The Good, the Bad and the Ugly
Duck You Sucker
The Untouchables
Cinema Paradiso
La Cage Aux Folles
The Legend of the Pianist on the Ocean
Malamondo

tive of the action and the locale, a secluded house further isolated from the outside world by a raging snowstorm. Bold, assertive outbursts mark the writer's rebellion and the end of his ordeal. It's a strong, highly competent first effort.

Didier C. Deutsch

The Misfits

1998, Rykodisc, from the film *The Misfits,* United Artists, 1961 ♪♪♪♪♪

album notes: Music: Alex North; **Conductor:** Alex North.

A flawed masterpiece, *The Misfits* is memorable for several reasons: it was written by Arthur Miller, not just your run-of-the-mill screenwriter; it starred Clark Gable, Montgomery Clift, and Marilyn Monroe, each in their final screen roles; it was a robust outdoor saga, ill-timed when westerns had become a thing of the past; and it had a brilliant score by Alex North.

Characteristic of Miller's introspective work, on the surface the script detailed the banal story of a rugged individualist (Gable), the woman who comes into his life (Monroe), and the rodeo performer (Clift) who sides with her when she wants to protect the small mustangs (the "misfits") Gable wants to capture and sell to a dog-food manufacturer. In depth, however, the multi-layered story also delved into characters who were also misfits in their own way—the lonely cowboy of yore, a dying breed; the ecological-minded woman ill-at-ease in an environment too brutal for her; and the former rodeo star, battered and disillusioned, who has nothing much to hope for in life, now that his successes are behind him.

North's music took into account all these elements—physical and subliminal—with the composer creating cues that are a mix of old-fashioned western themes and contemporary light jazz tunes, romantic moments, and in one sweeping suite, great action music. When the film was initially released, United Artists brought out an album that only contained seven selections from the score. This CD restores several cues that were not included, and the eloquent suite which encapsulates all the tortured moods in this remarkable film.

Didier C. Deutsch

Miss Saigon

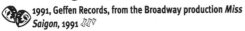 1991, Geffen Records, from the Broadway production *Miss Saigon*, 1991 ♪♪♪

album notes: Music: Claude–Michel Schoenberg; **Lyrics:** Richard Maltby Jr., Alain Boublil; **Musical Direction:** Dale Rieling; **Cast:** Lea Salonga, Jonathan Pryce, Simon Bowman.

If Claude-Michel Schonberg and Alain Boublil hoped to repeat with *Miss Saigon* the artistic success they had enjoyed with *Les Miserables,* they failed on at least one count: a tear-jerker set in Vietnam on the eve of the Fall of Saigon, their new show brought theater-as-spectacle to a new high, while proving itself emotionally very empty. Wall-to-wall instrumental bridges and tedious recitatives can hardly mask the paucity in melodic ideas in a score that only ignites on rare occasions. When the score is good (as in the unquestionable showstoppers, "The Heat Is on in Saigon," "The Morning of the Dragon," or "The American Dream"), it is very good. However, these moments are unfortunately too rare in a show that needs to rely on gimmicks like a much–touted–about helicopter landing on a roof to spellbind its audiences.

In the original London cast recording, Lea Salonga and Jonathan Pryce, who reprised their respective roles on Broadway, are excellent, she as a modern–day Madame Butterfly, whose love for a G.I. turns sour with the disastrous end of the conflict, he as an enterprising conman who, like Bloody Mary in *South Pacific,* makes himself necessary to the G.I.s lost in a foreign land. As Chris, Simon Bowman is vocally fine, but the limitations in his role do not enable him to be more than a casual presence. In an early radio commercial for the Broadway edition of the show, a "member" of the audience recalled how he had never cried in real life, yet *Miss Saigon* had brought him to tears. Indeed.

Didier C. Deutsch

The Mission

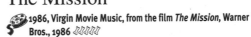 1986, Virgin Movie Music, from the film *The Mission,* Warner Bros., 1986 ♪♪♪♪

album notes: Music: Ennio Morricone; **Orchestra:** The London Philharmonic Orchestra; **Conductor:** Ennio Morricone; **Indian instrumentation:** Incantation.

Themes from this Academy Award–winning score have been so widely quoted and imitated that it almost seems redundant to introduce it again. Certainly, Ennio Morricone surpassed himself when he wrote this score for the powerful epic starring Robert De Niro as a man of the sword, and Jeremy Irons as a man of the cloth in 18th–century South America, who team to protect an Indian tribe from being wiped out by invading colonialists. Visually resplendent, breathtakingly beautiful, the film is further enhanced by its haunting music in which "Gabriel's Oboe" and "On Earth as It Is in Heaven" soon emerged as unlikely, given the solemnity of the writing, popular hits. With its inspired blend of instrumental themes, liturgical anthems, Indian chanting, drumming, and flute playing, the soundtrack album is a wonderful musical treat from beginning to end.

Didier C. Deutsch

Mission: Impossible

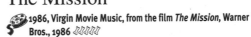 1997, Hip-O Records, from the Paramount television series, *Mission: Impossible,* 1966 ♪♪♪

album notes: Music: Lalo Schifrin; **Conductor:** Lalo Schifrin; **Featured Soloists:** Mike Melvoin, piano; Lalo Schifrin, piano, harpsichord; Bill Plummer, sitar; Bud Shank, alto sax; Stu Williamson, trumpet.

As would be expected, this CD starts out with Lalo Schifrin's unforgettable jazz theme music. The Hip-O recording is culled from an album Schifrin rerecorded using the music he wrote for the TV show, and it includes three tracks from a follow-up album, *More Music from Mission: Impossible.* It is chock full of the up-tempo jazz one usually associates with *Mission: Impossible* and that made it such a stylish show. Because Schifrin actually reworked the original cues into full-blown selections, the songs sound more cohesive and complete.

Didier C. Deutsch

1998, GNP Crescendo, from the Paramount television series, *Mission: Impossible,* 1966 ♪♪

album notes: Music: Lalo Schifrin, Jack Davis.

The "Then" part of the GNP Crescendo CD consists of actual soundtrack recordings from the TV series; the "Now" part is music that John E. Davis composed for the 1988 revival (other composers, including Ron Jones, also worked on it). But although Davis utilizes some of Schifrin's themes, his music doesn't come close to the standards set with the original, and even sounds like a watered-down version. This release also features "Mission Impossible '88—Main Title," for which Schifrin reworked his original theme, a weird five-minute version of *Mission: Impossible* performed by the Israeli Philharmonic Orchestra, conducted by Schifrin, and a somewhat bland interview with Peter Graves.

Didier C. Deutsch

1996, Point Records, from the film *Mission: Impossible,* Paramount Pictures, 1996 🎬🎬🎬
album notes: Music: Danny Elfman; **Conductor:** Artie Kane.

Danny Elfman's *Mission: Impossible* is one of the best "event movie" scores of the '90s. The completely incoherent film, a virtual Tom Cruise rape of the original TV series, did sport interesting Brian de Palma direction, and Elfman, replacing a more traditional Alan Silvestri score at the last minute, found a perfect blend of contemporary suspense and retro grooves. The '60s Lalo Schifrin theme is there in the beginning and end—a little more bombastic than before—and Elfman weaves fragments of it into his own, prickly motives and colors. Technically, it's one of Elfman's most accomplished works, taking the Schifrin tradition of woodwinds and percussion, and updating it with modern samples—a constant *tiki tiki tiki* in the background that lends forward motion to it all. If you want style, this has it by the buckets, but the quirks are shaped with impressive subtlety. One of the film's most suspenseful set pieces, an infiltration of a top–secret CIA computer room, not only features no music, but virtually no sound. When the action finally breaks out in the climactic helicopter–and–train chase, it builds and builds, until it finally explodes into the classic Schifrin theme.

Lukas Kendall

1996, Mother Records, from the film *Mission: Impossible,* Paramount Pictures, 1996 🎬🎬
album notes: Music: Danny Elfman; **Conductor:** Artie Kane.

Interestingly, the song album adds another 12 minutes from Elfman's score, with the rest being turned over to various pop selections. These include two versions of Lalo Schifrin's theme for *Mission: Impossible* updated by Adam Clayton and Larry Mullen, who probably couldn't leave well enough alone, but who contributed nothing really novel to the tune and various pop/rock tunes by Massive Attack, Bjork, The Cranberries, Salt, and Nicolette. Even though most of these were not in the film, they succeed in conveying the tense atmosphere in some of the action–driven scenes ("Spying Glass," "I Spy"), or evoking

the specific moods in it. But even though the album claims that it contains "music from and inspired" by the film, there is something quite amoral and deceptive in peddling 10 selections that have no relation whatsoever with the film advertised, and try to make it pass as a soundtrack album.

Didier C. Deutsch

Mississippi Burning

1989, Antilles Records, from the film *Mississippi Burning,* Orion Pictures, 1989 🎬🎬🎬
album notes: Music: Trevor Jones.

A striking, provocative drama about the civil rights movement, and the hidden demons thriving in our society, *Mississippi Burning* evoked in stark, uncompromising terms the investigation into the outright murder of three civil rights workers by a local Mississippi sheriff, portrayed by Gene Hackman. The somber tones in the story receive additional support from the score written by Trevor Jones, a powerful set of cues in which the obsessive "Murder in Mississippi" mixes sound effects and lines from the dialogue with a relentless beat over percolating synth lines. Often poignant in its stark expression, the music never attempts to explain or underline a scene, but aims instead to create an "effect," an atmosphere that won't let go. Ultimately, it is disturbing, but musically very compelling, though this is the kind of cerebral score that demands a lot from any listener.

Didier C. Deutsch

Mrs. Dalloway

1998, Milan, from the film, *Mrs. Dalloway,* First Look, 1998 🎬🎬🎬
album notes: Music: Ilona Sekacz; **Orchestra:** The Metropole Orchestra of the Netherlands; **Conductor:** Dick Bakker.

With the horrors of World War I still fresh in their minds, London's high society tentatively enjoy the fading moments of the Belle Epoque to the sounds of ballroom dances and brass bands. The most fully realized of novelist Virginia Woolf's characters, Mrs. Dalloway is famous for her parties, and for these events composer Ilona Sekacz appropriately incorporates waltzes, fox trots, and polkas into the score. Despite these celebrations, the brooding legacy of war is a constant presence. Shell shocked veteran Septimus is characterized with military brass band, with cymbals and bass drums. Other leitmotifs include Dalloway's romantic melody on violin and piano, her husband's stately brass, and her lover's playful flute. Sekacz had collaborated with director Marleen Gorris on another romantic drama, *Antonia's Line,* and her crystal-clear characterization and soft touch are a boon to both films.

David Poole

Mrs. Doubtfire

1993, Fox Records, from the film *Mrs. Doubtfire*, 20th Century Fox, 1993 ♫♫♫

album notes: Music: Howard Shore; **Conductor:** Howard Shore.

Robin Williams has a field day in this comedy in which he portrays a divorced man who turns himself into the matronly Mrs. Doubtfire, an indispensable housekeeper, in order to stay close to his kids. But while the film thrived on the comedian's broad antics as the irrepressible title character, it elicited a surprisingly low–key score from Howard Shore who chose to ignore the farcical side of the story and concentrate instead on its more romantic aspects. As a result, the cues, with a few exceptions which essentially repeat the same theme ("Tea Time with Mrs. Sellner," "Bridges Restaurant"), are very lovely but seem to miss an important point made by the film. On a pure audio level, however, they add up to a generously pleasant album.

Didier C. Deutsch

Mrs. Parker and the Vicious Circle

1995, Varèse-Sarabande, from the film *Mrs. Parker and the Vicious Circle*, Fine Line, 1994 ♫♫♫♫

album notes: Music: Mark Isham; **Featured Musicians:** Mark Isham, trumpet, alto flugelhorn; Steve Tavaglione, saxophone, clarinet; Ken Kugler, trombone; Sid Page, violin; David Goldblatt, piano; John Clayton, bass; Kurt Wortman, drums.

In the 1930s the Algonquin Hotel on West 44th Street was a sophisticated place where the New York intelligentsia used to meet. Writers, playwrights, poets, musicians, and Broadway actors were all part of the scene where Dorothy Parker reigned supreme. A gifted, frequently acerbic writer, and a pundit who was known for her wit and intelligence, Parker attracted a small coterie consisting of some of the most illustrious members of New York's literati, though her self-deprecating humor sometimes worked against her being recognized as one of the greats, in the same league as her illustrious male colleagues, whom she frequently outshone.

Directed by Alan Rudolph, who had previously surveyed a similar scene in *The Moderns,* set in the same time period in Paris, *Mrs. Parker and the Vicious Circle* recreated the Algonquin Round Table with evident love, and a keen eye to accurate details that gave the film its specific aura. In the same way Mark Isham had found a unique style to depict the Paris of the 1930s in *The Moderns,* he masterfully returned to the same period and delivered another outstanding score for *Mrs. Parker.* The wild '30s are powerfully evoked in several tracks ("The Algonquin Bounce," "The Smart Set Stomp"), while the story itself, sensationally bookended by Parker's personal drama ("Into Love . . ." and ". . . And out Again"), is described in catchy tunes

("The Vanity Blues," "Benchley's Blues," "The Vicious Blues"). It's a magnificent effort that, like *The Moderns,* demands close attention but will amply reward the listener in search of scores that are way above the norm.

see also: The Moderns

Didier C. Deutsch

Mrs. Winterbourne

1996, Varèse Sarabande, from the film *Mrs. Winterbourne,* Tri–Star Pictures, 1996 ♫♫♫

album notes: Music: Patrick Doyle; **Musicians:** Bruce Dukov, violin solo; Randy Kerber, piano; **Conductor:** Mark Watters.

Based on a novel by Cornell Woolrich, about a pregnant single woman mistaken for the widow of the heir to the Winterbourne family fortune, this romantic comedy succeeded primarily because of Shirley MacLaine's superb performance as an old dowager and Ricki Lake's winsome appeal as the young woman whose unconventional behavior clashed with the stultified old–fashioned family clan forced to accept her. Trying to match in the score the basic moods projected in the picture, Patrick Doyle provided a competent effort that is at times a bit too schmaltzy for its own good, but in which some cues like "Connie and Steve's Life" bring a different, welcome change. Interesting, but the composer has been known to do better.

Didier C. Deutsch

Mr. and Mrs. Bridge

1990, Novus Vision/BMG, from the film *Mr. & Mrs. Bridge,* Cineplex Odeon Films and Merchant Ivory Productions, 1990 ♫♫

album notes: Music: Richard Robbins.

The story of a stiff American couple living in Kansas during the great depression, *Mr. & Mrs. Bridge* brought the occasion for Richard Robbins to write a sensitive score suffused with sadness and joy, reflecting the varied moods of the film itself, and the drab existence of the film's central characters. His contribution, however, is limited here to about half the tracks, with themes that seem attractive but don't have much of a chance to make any kind of impact given their short playing time. Several standard selections ("String of Pearls," "Little Brown Jug," "The Rhumba Jumps," all performed by Glenn Miller; "Blues in the Night," by Dinah Shore; "Stormy Weather," by Lena Horne) add a period touch to the recording, though it should be noted that no effort has been made to clean these sides and make them sonically acceptable, something particularly noticeable in Tommy Dorsey's "Boogie Woogie," which has a lot of surface noise, distortion, image shifts, and dropouts, among its detrimental ills.

Didier C. Deutsch

Mr. Baseball

1992, Varèse Sarabande, from the film *Mr. Baseball,* Universal Pictures, 1992 ♫♫♫

album notes: Music: Jerry Goldsmith; **Conductor:** Jerry Goldsmith.

Jerry Goldsmith must have enjoyed writing this score for a comedy starring Tom Selleck as the American coach of a Japanese baseball team, if one is to believe the rollicking accents he found for the rambunctious title tune. Expressing himself in a style in which he excels but he seems to seldom approach these days, Goldsmith delivered a flavorful set of cues, in which jazz touches, like "First Night Out" and "Team Effort," mix with electronic rock, like "Training" and "Final Score," and some romantic interludes to create a delicious soufflé, light as the film itself and devilishly enjoyable. It's nothing like the composer's most noteworthy efforts, but something to listen to when the moods need to be slightly buoyant and easy on the mind. "Shabondama Boogie," performed by Fairchild, is a hilarious rock number, the kind only the Japanese can write when they try to imitate their American counterparts.

Didier C. Deutsch

Mr. Destiny

1990 , Varèse Sarabande, from the film *Mr. Destiny,* Touchstone Pictures, 1990 ♫♫♫

album notes: Music: David Newman; **Conductor:** David Newman.

A light comedy evoking *Angels in the Outfield* and *Field of Dreams,* among other inspirational romantic comedies about baseball and angels, *Mr. Destiny* dealt with yet another misfit whose guardian angel helped him rebuild his life and win the big game, in a formula that never fails to elicit strong emotional reactions in the audience. David Newman scored the whole thing with obvious empathy for the subject, developing broad instrumental themes that capture the moods in the film, soaring to a climax when the action required it, playing it soft and low when necessary. The contrasted effort is pleasantly listenable, generally attractive, but altogether not too terribly memorable, the type of music that may play in any given situation as long as it doesn't require too much attention.

Didier C. Deutsch

Mr. Holland's Opus

1995, London Records, from the film *Mr. Holland's Opus,* Hollywood Pictures, 1995 ♫♫♫♫

album notes: Music: Michael Kamen; **Orchestra:** The Seattle Symphony Orchestra and The London Metropolitan Orchestra; **Conductor:** Michael Kamen; **Featured Soloists:** Jonathan Snowden, flute; Dominic Millan, guitar; Pino Paladino, bass; Jim Keltner, drums.

A joyous score by Michael Kamen was the perfect complement to this highly entertaining Richard Dreyfuss picture about a high school music instructor who offered more than a little inspiration to the students he taught. Centering his score around an "Opus" that is never fully revealed until its concert performance at the very end, Kamen has written a melodic score that makes for an ideal soundtrack album, thanks to a fine mixture of cues ranging from poignant orchestral accompaniment to bold themes that reflect the many special moments in Mr. Holland's life. Kamen further grounds his score in an emotional vein with an elegy to "Vietnam" that gives the music an extra dimension before concluding with the rousing, Grammy–winning "An American Symphony," heard in its entirety only on the score album. Like the film, Kamen's music could have been merely simplistic and sappy, yet the composer is able to walk that thin line between emotion and sentimentality perfectly. And kudos to the producers for including Julian Lennon's vocal performance of "Cole's Tune" on the London CD, making this album fully representative of Kamen's complete work on the film.

Andy Dursin

1995, Polydor Records, from the film *Mr. Holland's Opus,* Hollywood Pictures, 1995 ♫♫♫

A time travelogue not unlike *Forrest Gump, Mr. Holland's Opus* takes pieces of assorted eras for a pleasant if not entirely cohesive package. The individual selections are good, though, if a little tame—a couple of pieces by John Lennon ("Imagine," "Beautiful Boy (Darling Boy)"), Ray Charles's "I Got a Woman," Jackson Browne's "The Pretender." What it cries for is some tougher–edged music, the kind of stuff high school kids really listened to.

Gary Graff

Mr. Jealousy

1998, RCA Records, from the film *Mr. Jealousy,* Castleberg, 1998 ♫♫♫♫

album notes: Music: Luna, Robert Een.

A story of emotional and sexual jealousy, *Mr. Jealousy* didn't make much of a dent at the box office, but it spawned this curious little soundtrack which mixes together instrumental tracks by Robert Een's New York quintet, Big Joe; four songs by Luna, an alternative band; a song by Parisian trio Autour de Lucie; the theme from *Jules et Jim,* composed by Georges Delerue (and evidently taken from a 45 or an LP, with the stylus audibly dropping on the surface of the disc); and songs by Paolo Conte (the retro Italian pop tune, "Via con me") and Françoise Hardy (the French language "Je ne suis la pour personne"), as well as standards by Irma Thomas and Harry Chapin. If eclecticism is the key, this album sure fills the bill. How it represents this warm-

hearted, ingenious romantic comedy may be another story, but on their own merits the selections hold together well.

Didier C. Deutsch

Mr. Lucky

1988, RCA Records, from the television series, *Mr. Lucky,* CBS, 1959 🎵🎵🎵🎵

Trust Henry Mancini to come up with catchy tunes, ear-filling melodies that are at once enjoyable and exhilarating, and a welcome change from some of the "noise" that passes itself as film or television music these days. Focusing on a character only known as Mr. Lucky (for his ability to always win at the gambling tables), and his sidekick Andamo, *Mr. Lucky,* set in an unnamed Latin American country, provided Mancini with a great opportunity to go lightly Latin (as the title of one of the themes heard in this CD reminds us). The fast-paced action was another cue to deliver themes that had energy and vibrancy, with the whole brew served with a large helping of melodic material. There are many moments in this album that captivate the listener and have broad appeal—"March of the Cue Balls," "Tipsy," "One-Eyed Cat," "Chime Time," and "Blue Satin," among them. At times jocular, at times romantic, but always exciting, this is a soundtrack album that never fails to please.

Didier C. Deutsch

Mr. Music

1999, Sonic Images, from the television presentation, *Mr. Music,* Showtime, 1999 🎵🎵🎵

album notes: Music: Spencer Proffer, Larry Brown.

A telefilm shown on cable, *Mr. Music* starred Mick Fleetwood as a former top musician and currently bankrupt owner of a record label and Jonathan Tucker as the kid whom he plucks from the streets to become head of A&R in the hopes he will rekindle the fortunes of his company. Also appearing in the film were the alternative bands Caramel, playing themselves, and Treble Charger, heard in this song-driven compilation. The presence of Fleetwood in the cast no doubt compelled many big-name performers to lend their talent to this minor show, including Pat Benatar, who performs three songs, and Graham Nash, heard in one. This may be the album's best selling point. Others who also appear here include Keith Chagall, Blue Flannel, Andrew Rollins, and the Morlettes, whose "Puppy Munchies" is an amusing ditty. But the best parts may belong to Spencer Proffer and Larry Brown, whose cues are pleasant and attractive, if not exceptional.

Didier C. Deutsch

Mr. Saturday Night

1992, Giant Records, from the film *Mr. Saturday Night,* Columbia Pictures, 1992 🎵🎵🎵🎵

album notes: Music: Marc Shaiman; **Conductor:** Artie Kane; **Featured Musicians:** Jack Sheldon, Bruce Dukov, Jerry Goodman, Abe Most, Dan Higgins, Randy Kerber, Steve Schaeffer; **Featured Vocalists:** Randy Crenshaw, Geoff Koch, Steve Lively, Rick Logan.

Billy Crystal had one of his most pleasant screen roles in this film in which he played a congenial entertainer, raised in New York's Jewish East Side, who got his start in vaudeville, and ended as a television host, a cigar–chomping character he created early in his nightclub act and which he polished up for this big screen debut. If the film, an affectionate tribute to an era long gone, is a romp from beginning to end, with Crystal absolutely devilish as the ebullient old–timer with a tart tongue and a sharp sense of humor, it finds an equally inspired echo in composer Marc Shaiman's vibrant score, a special blend of subtle ethnic elements, not–so–subtle showbiz chutzpah, and just great themes to enjoy and delight in. Several well–chosen vocals, including Louis Armstrong's "Fantastic, That's You," and Louis Prima's "When You're Smiling," add the right element of nostalgia to the musical background, evoking an era when vaudeville was king and borscht belt comedians were at the peak of their popularity.

Didier C. Deutsch

Mr. Wrong

1996, Hollywood Records, from the film *Mr. Wrong,* Touchstone Pictures, 1996 🎵🎵🎵

album notes: Music: Craig Safan.

The soundtrack for Ellen DeGeneres's pre–coming out star vehicle hit a few right notes, with a modest collection of modern rock focused on a falling–in–love theme. Amy Grant's remake of 10cc's "The Things We Do For Love" is perky, while Joan Osborne and Sophie B. Hawkins bring a bit of sultriness via "Strenuous Acquaintances" and "I Gotcha," respectively. Men have their say, too, with contributions such as Ben Folds Five's hilarious "Songs for the Dumped," Chris Isaak's cover of Hank Williams's "I'm So Lonesome I Could Cry," and Arturo Sandoval's "Suavito."

Gary Graff

Mixed Nuts

1994, Epic Soundtrax, from the film *Mixed Nuts,* TriStar, 1994 🎵🎵🎵

album notes: Music: George Fenton.

Loosely based on the French film cult, *Le père Noél est une ordure* (Santa Claus Is Garbage), *Mixed Nuts* starred Steve Martin as a man on the edge minutes away from Christmas Eve: he is about

Denzel Washington and Cynda Williams in Mo' Better Blues. **(The Kobal Collection)**

to be dumped by his girlfriend, his suicide hot line is going to be cut off, and if that were not enough already a lonely cross-dresser will ask to dance a tango with him, and a gun-toting Santa Claus-dresser will try to rob him. Directed by Nora Ephron, who wrote the screenplay with her sister, Delia Ephron, the film relied on a large contingent of classic Christmas songs, performed by several well-known performers—Fats Domino, Aretha Franklin, Eartha Kitt, the O'Jays, the Drifters, Carly Simon, and Leon Redbone, among others, all on this CD—and a vivacious score written by George Fenton. Actually, the score is given somewhat of a short shrift here, with only one mischievous selection ("Mixed Notes"), giving an idea of Fenton's whimsical approach.

Didier C. Deutsch

Mo' Better Blues

1990, Columbia Records, from the film *Mo' Better Blues*, Universal Pictures, 1990 ♪♪♪♪

album notes: Conductor: Clare Fisher; **Featured Musicians:** Branford Marsalis, tenor/ soprano sax; Kenny Kirkland, piano; Robert Hurst, bass; Jeff "Tain" Watts, drums; Terence Blanchard, trumpet

A film about the New York jazz scene, starring Denzel Washington as a self–centered trumpet player, *Mo' Better Blues* already had a striking musical expression that eventually resulted in this highly satisfying soundtrack album, featuring Terence Blanchard, Branford Marsalis, and Kenny Kirkland, among its better known performers. Cynda Williams, who also appeared in the film as one of the central character's "main squeezes," does a standout rendition of W.C. Handy's "Harlem Blues," and Washington and Wesley Snipes read a somewhat dispensable "Pop Top 40" against musical accompaniment. The album will please jazz fans and those interested in adventurous musical fares.

Didier C. Deutsch

Mobil Masterpiece Theatre

1996, Delos Records, from the WGBH Educational TV shows, 1971–96 ♪♪♪♪♪

For many years a staple on Public Television, *Masterpiece Theatre* has earned an enviable reputation as one of the most distinguished series on television. Many of the shows that have been presented as part of the series have become landmarks in their own right and are often mentioned with awe and admiration. This CD purports to bring together some of the themes that were created for some of the shows in the series, including "Upstairs, Downstairs," "The Jewel in the Crown," "I, Claudius," "A Town Like Alice," and "The Flame Trees of Thika." The themes are presented here in their original versions, with the composers usually conducting their own works, and the CD is introduced by Mouret's celebrated theme. They simply can't get any better than that.

Didier C. Deutsch

Mobsters

1991, Varèse Sarabande, from the film *Mobsters,* Universal Pictures, 1991 &&&&

album notes: Music: Michael Small; **Featured Musicians:** Ralph Grierson, piano solos/keyboards; Ian Underwood, Mike Lang, keyboards; Gary Foster, soprano sax solos; Warren Leuning Jr., trumpet; Mike Fisher, electronic percussion.

Lucky Luciano, Meyer Lansky, Bugsy Siegel, and Frank Costello are glorified once again on the big screen in *Mobsters,* a film that's interesting for its clear–eyed view of the reasons why these men succeeded so well in their life of crime. Viewing the gangsters as they began to assert themselves and take control of their specific territories, the film, with a solid dramatic screenplay by Michael Mahern and Nicholas Kazan, detailed the rise and fall of the four men in terms that made few concessions to romantic attitudes. An interesting side aspect of the film is its score, written by Michael Small, an attractive mixture of stark–sounding orchestral riffs, occasionally interrupted by big band outbursts like "Whiskey Business," suggestive of the days of Prohibition. With the "Theme for Mara," a lovely, expansive cue for piano, clarinet and orchestra, one of the highlights, much of the music gives the action on the screen a dramatic, sometimes explosive expression that translates very well in this soundtrack album.

Didier C. Deutsch

Moby Dick

1998, Marco Polo Records, from the film *Moby Dick,* Warner Bros., 1956 &&&&&

album notes: Music: Philip Sainton; **Orchestra:** The Moscow Symphony Orchestra; **Conductor:** William T. Stromberg.

1998, Varèse-Sarabande, from the television presentation, *Moby Dick,* Hallmark Entertainment, 1998 &&&&&

album notes: Music: Christopher Gordon; **Conductor:** Christopher Gordon; **Choir:** The Sydney Chamber Choir.

These two recordings again show how the same story might suggest wildly different approaches to two different com-

posers, yet elicit from each scores that are totally exhilarating and well representative of the drama they aim to illustrate.

Taking them chronologically, Sainton's score was created for the 1956 John Huston adaptation of Herman Melville's seafaring novel that starred Gregory Peck, miscast as the obsessed Captain Ahab, forever looking for the gigantic white whale, Moby Dick, that already took his leg in a previous encounter. A 63-year-old British composer who had never composed for a film before and whose reputation was largely based on his exceptional talents as a virtuoso violinist, Sainton allegedly wrote the whole score in less than six weeks, quite an achievement in itself. But the end result clearly confirmed Huston's foresight in selecting him—his music, virile to a fault, and deeply emotional, captures the moods of the action in broad, colorful terms, that spell out in vivid musical terms the action as it develops on the screen. With much of the film relying on the dark, gloomy aspects of the story told by Melville, Sainton's score often soars beyond these parameters and finds a life of its own in broad comments that enliven the story and make it more vibrant. The brilliant re-recording, with the Moscow Symphony Orchestra, conducted by William Stromberg, does justice to the composer and his only formal film creation.

While Sainton's score stressed the physical aspects of the story, Christopher Gordon emphasized the sea pageantry and psychological aspects of the drama in his own contribution. Written for a 1998 telecast starring Patrick Stewart as Ahab, Gordon's score didn't attempt to emulate Sainton's but instead gave a voice to the seagoing excitement as much as the obsession that compelled Ahab to seek his quarry. In contrast to Sainton's often gloomy description, Gordon's score contains many cues that are colorful and genuinely exciting. The various characters—"The Harpooner," "Ahab," "Captain Pip," "The Pilot"—are described in musical terms that are attaching, while the action itself is painted in broad, often colorful swaths that belie the drama that will eventually provoke the demise of Ahab and his men. Occasionally, weird, unerring chords denote the eventual doom of the ship and her crew, but most of the lively themes put the accent squarely on the adventure part of the story. In this respect, this score may have a greater appeal than Sainton's unapologetically dark creation. In the final analysis, however, both approaches are equally valid and both prove compelling in their own way.

Didier C. Deutsch

The Mod Squad

1999, Elektra Records, from the film *The Mod Squad,* MGM, 1999 &&&

Although much maligned by the critics, the 1999 movie update on the late '60s/early '70s TV show about juvenile delinquents-turned-cops, did spin off a mod and groovy soundtrack. Highlights include chanteuse Alana Davis's breathy spin on the Blind Faith classic "Can't Find My Way Home," a wonderful new Morphine track, and a classy homage to John Coltrane by saxophone player Skerik from the band Tuatara. The album is about equal parts cover tunes and new songs. Regretfully, some of the best songs in the movie didn't make it onto the album, nor did any of B.C. Smith's Lalo Schifrin-inspired score, but still, this album holds up as a pretty good souvenir of the film.

Amy Rosen

The Moderns

🎬 1988, Virgin Movie Music Records, from the film *The Moderns*, Nelson Films, 1988 𝄞𝄞𝄞𝄞𝄞

album notes: Music: Mark Isham; **Orchestra:** L'Orchestre Moderne; **Featured Musicians:** Mark Isham, trumpet, electronics; Peter Maunu, violin, mandolin, electric guitar; Ed Mann, vibraphone, marimba, snare drum; Dave Stone, acoustic bass; CharlElie Couture, vocals, piano; Rick Ruttenberg, piano; Patrick O'Hearn, acoustic and electric bass; Michael Barsimanto, drum machine; Suzie Katayama, cello.

A tale of betrayal and deceit, set against the backdrop of late 1920s art world in Paris, *The Moderns* stars Keith Carradine as an American painter with enough talent to forge a convincing Cezanne, Linda Fiorentino as a beautiful brunette who motivated him, and John Lone as her ruthless, art-collecting husband. Beautifully matching the tones of this triangular comedy and capturing the moods of the period itself, Mark Isham devised a score that is at once vibrant and evocative, a sensational music that speaks volumes. Essential to the feel of the score is its unusual instrumentation, with the violin, vibraphone, and marimba creating a sound that evokes the period itself and gives its cachet to the whole album. The vocal contribution of CharlElie Couture, a French composer and performer, whose occasional interventions "Paris la nuit/Selavy" and "Parlez–moi d'amour (moderne)" give the score a specific Parisian flavor. It all adds up to a sensational album, and one of the best scores devised by Isham.

see also: Mrs. Parker and the Vicious Circle

Didier C. Deutsch

Moll Flanders

🎬 1996, London Records, from the film *Moll Flanders*, MGM, 1996 𝄞𝄞𝄞𝄞𝄞

album notes: Music: Mark Mancina; **Conductor:** Don Harper.

The notorious 18th–century English wench, already the subject of a 1965 romp starring Kim Novak, is on a rampage again in this loose screen adaptation of Daniel Defoe's 1722 novel, a picaresque tale about an attractive, fiercely independent woman, aware of her powers and ready to use them to elevate herself

above her menial condition. Giving the tale a lift of its own, Mark Mancina provided a vibrant and lively score that chronicles the myriad incidents in Moll's rise from rags to riches, while detailing some of the many characters she encounters on the way—Mrs. Allworthy, owner of a classy bordello where Moll starts her "career" in earnest; a mysterious character only identified as The Artist, who rescues Moll when she is at her lowest and makes her a model; Hibble, Mrs. Allworthy's servant and Moll's only loyal friend; and Flora, Moll's daughter. Interestingly, the soundtrack album regroups Mancina's various cues in such a way that those pertaining to a given character are presented together, while more or less following the film's narrative. It is an acceptable device that gives greater strength and credibility to the score as a listening device.

The score itself is enriched with the addition of several selections from the classical repertoire, including an anachronistic aria from Offenbach's "The Tales of Hoffman," which had not been composed (and would not be for many moons) at the time when the story takes place.

Didier C. Deutsch

The Molly Maguires

🎬 1990, Bay Cities Records, from the film *The Molly Maguires*, Paramount Pictures, 1970 𝄞𝄞𝄞𝄞𝄞

album notes: Music: Henry Mancini; **Conductor:** Henry Mancini.

Based on a true story, and set in the Pennsylvania coal mining country in 1876, *The Molly Maguires* finds Henry Mancini writing in a dramatic vein, and relying on a variety of unusual instruments, such as the Irish harp, a button accordion, a pennywhistle, and an ocarina, to convey the proper moods. To depict the drama and the screenplay's side elements about a rebellion of the miners, mostly Irish immigrants, led by Sean Connery, against the mine owners, Mancini essentially developed three themes. The main title sets the action and the bleak landscape where it happens. Another, with specific Irish tonalities, portraying the Molly Maguires, an underground militant group whose only effective mean of fighting the abusive mine owners was through violent raids. A third is a love theme describing the tender relationship between an Irish girl, Mary, played by Samantha Eggar, and a detective hired by the owners to infiltrate the workers' ranks, portrayed by Richard Harris.

All three themes provide the gist for the score, sometimes played independently, sometimes collapsing together, always attracting for their striking beauty and effectiveness. Mancini was particularly fond of this score and listening to it one can understand his reaction. The album, released on the now defunct Bay Cities label, may be hard to find, but is well worth looking for.

Didier C. Deutsch

Mom and Dad Save the World

1992, Varèse Sarabande, from the film *Mom and Dad Save the World*, Warner Bros., 1992 ♪♪♪♪

album notes: Music: Jerry Goldsmith; **Orchestra:** The National Philharmonic Orchestra.

A minor little comedy, about an urban American family suddenly responsible for saving the Earth from the somber designs of a galactic villain, *Mom and Dad Save The World* would be easily dismissed were it not for the fact that its composer happened to be Jerry Goldsmith, not one to ignore no matter what project he finds himself involved with. Indeed, his score for this fantasy is a real musical romp, rife with grandiose themes that don't seem to take themselves too seriously, and that are played with the right sense of humor by no less a formidable group than the National Philharmonic Orchestra. Talk about class! Flash Gordon never had it so good. Particularly delightful in the context is the anthem "Tod, The Destroyer," amusingly sung by a chorus and brief enough to make its point while not stretching it and a lively "Rebel Dance," silly enough to evoke more than its simple tune might suggest. When Jerry Goldsmith has fun scoring a film, everyone has a ball. Such is the case here.

Didier C. Deutsch

The Moment of Truth

See: Il momento della verita

Mondo Cane

1993, CAM Records/Italy, from the film *Mondo Cane*, United Artists, 1963 ♪♪♪♪

album notes: Music: Nino Oliviero, Riz Ortolani; **Conductor:** Riz Ortolani.

Acclaimed as one of the most powerful documentary films ever made (it spawned an entire generation of imitations), *Mondo Cane* (literally "A Dog's World") is best remembered today for its main theme song, "More," which became a huge hit in the early 1960s. The film, a raw description of humanity in all its myriad facets and excesses, was shot around the world in places as remote from each other as New Guinea, the United States, Malaya, France, and Arabia, in images that were at times compelling or shocking, and ultimately strikingly original and beautiful. The score, by Nino Oliviero and Riz Ortolani, two distinguished Italian composers, was the appropriate musical brew that made the whole experience even more sensational. This recording may be difficult to find. Check with a used CD store, mail-order company, or a dealer specializing in rare, out-of-print, or import recordings.

Didier C. Deutsch

Money Train

1995, 550 Music/Epic Soundtrax, from the film *Money Train*, Columbia Pictures, 1995 ♪♪

album notes: Music: Mark Mancina.

Another case of a composer whose contribution to a film receives an all too short selection. Mark Mancina, whose considerable talent has enlightened many excellent films in recent years (*Moll Flanders, Speed, Twister),* is represented here by the short "Money Train Suite," an expressive cue that might have gained at being presented as part of a more comprehensive instrumental album. The other selections in the album, all pop vocals, range from the okay in songs like "The Thrill I'm In," "Hold On I'm Coming," and "Merry Go Round" to the so–what in "Hiding Place," "Do You Know," and "Oh, Baby." Is it what a film soundtrack is really all about?

Didier C. Deutsch

Monterey Pop

1992, Rhino Records, from the documentary *The Monterey International Pop Festival*, 1967 ♪♪♪♪♪

The summer of love, and much else, truly began with this pioneering pop/rock festival. It was put together around The Mamas and the Papas (!), who were on their way out, but it wound up enshrining Jefferson Airplane, Otis Redding, Janis Joplin, The Who, and Jimi Hendrix on their way in, as folk–rock gave way to something darker and, you bet, louder. Rhino's four–CD boxed set goes far beyond the performances preserved in the movie—which created the "rockumentary" form—and makes it clear that, song for song, artist for artist, raindrop for raindrop, this was better than Woodstock.

Marc Kirkeby

Monty Python and the Holy Grail

1997, Arista Records, from the film *Monty Python and the Holy Grail*, Tristar Pictures, 1975 ♪♪♪♪

album notes: Music: De Wolfe; **Songs:** Neil Innes.

The saga of Arthur and his valiant Knights of the Round Table will probably never survive this delirious send–up in which the Monty Python comedians thoroughly destroyed the legend to create a film (and soundtrack recording) that has long since become a cult favorite. Many scenes, like "You're Using Coconuts," "Old Woman," "A Strange Person," or "The Knights Who Say 'Ni!,'" are oft–quoted classics in their own right and rib–ticklers that never fail to elicit a smile from the cognizant. The CD version incorporates additional moments of zany outbursts that were not on the LP.

Beth Krakower

Monty Python's Life of Brian

1995, Virgin Records/U.K., from the film *Life of Brian*, Python (Monty), 1979 ♫♫♫♫

To be honest about it, nothing can actually replace a Monty Python movie, not even a soundtrack recording as funny and occasionally rude as this one may be. But if you are looking for a moment of hilarity and don't want to watch the entire film, this audio shortcut proves ideal. In case you haven't been exposed to the film itself, let it be known that *Life of Brian* is a Biblical retelling of a new Messiah (whose life parallels that of Jesus, to the point where the two could actually be mistaken), and introduces, among other unlikely characters, a lisping Pilate who keeps referring to his friend, Bigus Dickus, when he is not sure what to do next. And even if Brian is crucified at the end, despite attempts by his followers to get him off the hook, as he tells the two villains on crosses next to him in one of the film's most exhilarating scenes, "Look on the Bright Side of Life." The CD, as the film, is often hilarious, irreverent, and refreshingly Monty Python-esque.

Didier C. Deutsch

Moon 44

1990, Silva Screen Records, from the film *Moon 44*, Spectrum Entertainment, 1989 ♫♫♫♫

album notes: Music: Joel Goldsmith; **Orchestra:** The Graunke Symphony Orchestra; **Conductor:** Christopher L. Stone; **Featured Vocalist:** Heather Forsyth.

This dynamic and exciting film score from Jerry Goldsmith's son is Joel Goldsmith's first large orchestral recording after many years of low–budget film and TV music. The music for this futuristic science fiction thriller is heavy on action, with no real melodies. Goldsmith keeps firm control over the orchestra even in the most furious of orchestral moments. His dissonances remain tonal and fluid and they continue to drive the action ahead. Naturally, some of these action cues are reminiscent of his father's, especially in the low horn phrases over snare drum and counter–pointed strings melodies, but for the most part Joel Goldsmith is developing into a talented film–scorer in his own right. The CD is well–produced with an informative eight–page booklet. The only real drawback is the inclusion of the loud, raucous punk rock vocal, which is quite out of sync with the rest of the music—and quite a jolt after all the dynamic symphonics.

Randall D. Larson

Moon over Parador

1988, MCA Records, from the film *Moon over Parador*, Universal Pictures, 1988 ♫♫♫♫

album notes: Music: Maurice Jarre; **Conductor:** Maurice Jarre.

Maurice Jarre provided a wholly symphonic and wholly delightful score for this Paul Mazursky comedy about an actor masquerading as the dictator of an obscure Latin American country. The score is lively, often comic and often romantic, always vibrant. It captures Jarre's strongest symphonic capabilities and allows them to breathe. *Moon over Parador* lets its themes shine, giving both a Latin flavor through acoustic guitars, solo trumpets, tambourines, and Latin rhythms to its broad musical landscape, embellished with full orchestrations. The "Parador" theme is one of Jarre's most likable themes, a tuneful, inescapable rhythm that captures all of the film's many moods in a single melody. This is an invigorating score and among Jarre's best cinematic endeavors.

Randall D. Larson

Moonraker

1988, EMI—Manhattan, from the film *Moonraker*, United Artists, 1979 ♫♫♫♫

album notes: Music: John Barry; **Lyrics:** Hal David; **Conductor:** John Barry.

One of the best Bond films starring Roger Moore, *Moonraker* also got a great boost from John Barry, evidently in much better form than in the previous *Man with the Golden Gun,* and determined to have fun with it. The cues, more clearly detailed and using instrumentations that seem better suited, sound a bit more sedate than the throbbing cues in the Sean Connery films. The new addition of a distant choir confers to several of the cues an aura that is most attractive. The best moments here, as in the film, are the vibrant action scenes, with cues including "Cable Car and Snake Fight," and "Bond Arrives in Rio and Boat Chase," but a magnificent highlight is the poetic "Flight into Space," as effective in the album as it is in the film. Shirley Bassey's vocals seem almost as essential as Barry's score.

Didier C. Deutsch

Moonstruck

1987, Capitol Records, from the film *Moonstruck*, MGM, 1987 ♫♫♫♫

album notes: Music: Dick Hyman; **Conductor:** Dick Hyman; **Orchestra:** Orchestra of the Academy of Santa Cecilia of Rome; **Choir:** Chorus of the Academy of Santa Cecilia of Rome; **Conductor:** Tullio Serafin; **Featured Performers:** Jack Zaza, mandolin; Dominic Cortese, accordion; Ed Bickert, guitar; Moe Koffman, alto sax; Nora Shulman, flute; Dick Hyman

Talk about a film that started modestly enough and ended up a surprise hit among both audiences and critics. Cher stars in a fetching Oscar–winning performance as a widow resigned to a life of mediocrity suddenly torn between two suitors, a bland neighbor, Johnny (Danny Aiello) and his beguiling brother, Ronny (Nicholas Cage). Much of the film's atmosphere came from the judicious choice of musical selections put together for the occasion, from the various vocal and instrumental opera tunes, to the pop songs, to the light jazzy touch provided by Dick Hyman. These apparently disparate elements blend together to create an aura that reflects the Italian background of the Brooklyn neighborhood where the action took place and of the characters who peopled the film. The soundtrack album reflects the same aura in a way that does not come across as cohesively here as it did in the film, though it provides a musical programming that has more ups than downs.

Didier C. Deutsch

More

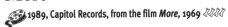1989, Capitol Records, from the film *More*, 1969 🎬🎬🎬

album notes: Music: Pink Floyd (Roger Waters/David Gilmour/Nick Mason/Rick Wright).

The touching love story of a German youth and an American girl, set against the psychedelic culture of the late 1960s, much of the actual flavor in *More* is due to Pink Floyd's trend–setting, atmospheric score. A cult favorite since its initial release, this soundtrack album continues to exert its spell–binding attraction, evoking not only an era that seems, in retrospect, simpler and more poetic, but making a musical statement which, decades later, has lost none of its immediacy and importance.

Didier C. Deutsch

Mortal Kombat

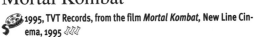1995, TVT Records, from the film *Mortal Kombat,* New Line Cinema, 1995 🎬🎬🎬

album notes: Music: George S. Clinton; **Featured Musician:** Buckethead, guitar.

What kind of music do you program for the film version of one the most popular video game bloodlettings of all time? Check out the song titles: "Blood & Fire," "Burn," "Demon Warriors," "Twist the Knife Slowly." Check out the band names: Type O Negative, Napalm Death, Fear Factory, Sister Machine Gun. Sounds like a match to us. And it should be noted that "Kombat" used techno, Orbital's "Halcyon + On + On," a couple of years before it became the hip thing to do.

Gary Graff

1995, TVT Records, from the film *Mortal Kombat,* New Line Cinema, 1995 🎬🎬

album notes: Music: George S. Clinton; **Orchestra:** The Testosterone Orchestra; **Conductor:** George S. Clinton; **Featured Musicians:** Buckethead, guitar; Brain, drums; Scott Breadman, Scott Higgins, percussion; Brice Martin, shakuhachi; Arjuna, resonator; George S. Clinton, keyboards.

Relentlessly energetic action score by George S. Clinton just erupts with its hard and heavy percussion, pounding like a primitive war dance. This was never going to be a quiet soundtrack as the film gave Clinton little opportunity to do anything else. He makes inventive use of his synthesizers and ethnic instruments, giving his orchestra several layers of dark and eerie musical textures. The album's one failing is that many tracks are under two minutes (one only 17 seconds) and this makes the album prone to start and stop fits, giving little time to develop an overall feeling for the score.

David Hirsch

Mortal Kombat: More Kombat

1996, TVT Records, from the television series, *Mortal Combat,* 1996 🎬🎬

After the success of the first soundtrack of music from and inspired by *Mortal Kombat,* an album that launched the career of Type O Negative into the mainstream, TVT was inspired to compile once more industrial and noisy electronic music, slapping the Mortal Kombat name on it. This is a good album if you like that kind of music, mixing both known artists and up-and-comers. However it has little to do with the actual movie.

Beth Krakower

Mortal Kombat 2: Annihilation

1997, TVT Records, from the film *Mortal Kombat,* New Line Cinema, 1998 🎬🎬🎬

album notes: Music: George S. Clinton.

There's surely some parents who wish that annihilation is exactly what happens to *Mortal Kombat,* perhaps the most successful film series ever adapted from a video game (now there's product development). Like its predecessors, this set goes hard, heavy, and aggressive; it is, after all, music to kill by. So we get KMFDM's swirling "Megalomaniac" and Megadeth's gritty "Almost Honest," along pounding fare from Pitchshifter ("Genius") and Manbreak ("Ready or Not"). *MK3* also marked one of the first opportunities for Americans to hear German pyro rockers Rammstein, whose "Enge" is included.

Gary Graff

Morte in Vaticano

1991, CAM Records/Italy; from the film *Morte in Vaticano (Death in the Vatican),* 1982 🎬🎬🎬🎬

album notes: Music: Pino Donaggio; **Conductor:** Pino Donaggio.

A thrilling suspenser set in Rome, *Death in the Vatican* opposed two prelates, long-time friends, one a moderate theologian who ascends to the highest level by becoming Pope

Clement I, the other a country parish priest committed to social works. When a foreign power organizes a plan to eliminate the Pope, his friend, the parish priest, will commit the deed, much to everyone's surprise. Pino Donaggio, a familiar name in thrillers, scored this one with restraint and wrote cues that make ample use of pseudo-church chants to provide the proper color called by the setting of the film. The plot itself is depicted in harsh, dissonant sounds that contrast with the serenity suggested by the environment, with the deed and its perpetrators also eliciting discordant cues in an otherwise melodic but surprisingly controlled score. This title may be out of print or just plain hard to find. Mail-order companies, used CD shops, or dealers of rare or import recordings will be your best bet.

Didier C. Deutsch

The Mosquito Coast

1986, Fantasy Records, from the film *The Mosquito Coast,* Fantasy Films, 1986 🎬🎬🎬

album notes: Music: Maurice Jarre; **Electronic Ensemble:** Michael Boddicker, Michael Fisher, Ralph Grierson, Judd Miller, Nyle Steiner, Ian Underwood; **Conductor:** Maurice Jarre.

Maurice Jarre, writing for an electronic ensemble, delivered a superbly atmospheric score for this film by Peter Weir, starring Harrison Ford as a man with a utopian vision, who decides to leave modern civilization and moves with his wife and four kids to the jungle of a remote Caribbean island. The music, generally very attractive and poetic, benefits from the synthesizer sound up to a point, but the overall effect tends to be overpowering after a while. The exuberant "Gimme Soca," short as it may be, relieves the sullen moods and confirms one's impression that the score would have been stronger with the addition of another tune or two with that kind of drive and energy.

Didier C. Deutsch

The Most Happy Fella

1991, Sony Broadway, from the Broadway production *The Most Happy Fella,* 1956 🎬🎬🎬🎬

album notes: Music: Frank Loesser; **Lyrics:** Frank Loesser; **Orchestral and Choral Direction:** Herbert Greene; **Cast:** Robert Weede, Jo Sullivan, Art Lund, Susan Johnson, Shorty Long, Mona Paulee, Alan Gilbert, Roy Lazarus, Arthur Rubin.

Frank Loesser had one of his earliest stage successes with *The Most Happy Fella,* a smart adaptation of the 1924 play "They Knew What They Wanted," about a mail-order bride deceived into believing that her intended is a handsome young man when in reality he turns out to be an aging Napa Valley vineyard owner of Italian descent. Starring Robert Weede as Tony,

the vintner who is shy around women, Jo Sullivan as Rosabella, who answers Tony's marriage offer, and Art Lund as Joey, Tony's foreman, whose picture Tony has sent to Rosabella instead of his own, *The Most Happy Fella* was more a folk opera than a musical. It contained a profuse score that included more than 30 musical numbers, including arias, duets, and recitatives. The writing style, however, was pure Broadway, with tunes like "Standing on the Corner," "Big D," "My Heart Is So Full of You," "Abbondanza," "Warm All Over," and "Joey, Joey, Joey" harking back to the best musical theatre traditions. The recording, initially an unusual three–LP set (the first of its kind for Columbia Records), now on two CDs, features the entire score, with vibrant performances by all the principals.

Didier C. Deutsch

Most Wanted

1997, Milan, from the film *Most Wanted,* New Line, 1997 woof!

album notes: Music: Paul Buckmaster.

In *Most Wanted,* Keenan Ivory Wayans portrays a government-trained assassin wrongly accused of killing the First Lady. This highly predictable, boring film features an equally predictable score by Paul Buckmaster. Even the tracks on this CD sound like a series of cues forcibly joined together.

Beth Krakower

Mother

1996, Hollywood Records, from the film *Mother,* Paramount Pictures, 1996 ♫♫♫♫

album notes: Music: Marc Shaiman; **Conductor:** Artie Kane.

The delightful spoof of Paul Simon's "Mrs. Robinson," retitled here "Mrs. Henderson," to fit the character portrayed by Debbie Reynolds, augurs well for this soundtrack album to a charming comedy about a grownup man (Albert Brooks) who moves back in with "Mother" when his marriage ends up in divorce . . . again! The same whimsical moods pervade the cues written by Marc Shaiman, gently amusing and catchy, culminating in an exuberant "Understanding Mother," that sums up everything in the score that's so endearing. Selected pop tunes, wisely chosen, add a definite flair to the whole album.

Didier C. Deutsch

Mother Lode

See: The Philadelphia Experiment/Mother Lode

Mother Night

1997, Varèse Sarabande, from the film *Mother Night,* Fine Line Features, 1996 ♫♫♫♫

album notes: Music: Michael Convertino; **Conductor:** Artie Kane.

A complex character study, *Mother Night,* based on a novel by Kurt Vonnegut, touches upon questions that transcend its subject matter even as it delves into different cinematographic genres. It is all reflective of the widespread screen action that takes its main protagonist, an American radio announcer (Nick Nolte) caught in the maelstrom of Nazi Germany, whose sympathies for the regime eventually owe him to be hunted after the war and brought to Israel to be tried as a criminal. In turns a gritty black comedy, a political thriller, and a romantic drama, one of the film's unifying threads is Michael Convertino's low–key score, a collection of long orchestral themes that aim to underscore specific scenes while providing a musical atmosphere common to all of them. Two classical selections, Britten's "Cantus in Memoriam," and an excerpt from Vivaldi's *The Four Seasons,* add an extra element of beauty that's welcome. Missing, however, is Bing Crosby's rendition of "White Christmas" which was essential to the opening sequence in the film.

Didier C. Deutsch

Mountains of the Moon

1990, Polydor Records, from the film *Mountains of the Moon,* Carolco Pictures, 1990 ♫♫♫

album notes: Music: Michael Small; **Orchestra:** The Graunke Symphony Orchestra; **Conductor:** Allan Wilson; **Featured Musicians:** Foday Muso Suso, Karinya, Tama, Nyanyeri, percussion; Gordon Gottlieb, percussion; "Crusher" Bennett, percussion; Tony Hajar, Arabic flute; Bill Ochs, Uillean pipes.

Composer Michael Small is primarily known for his adept scoring of some classic "paranoia" thrillers of the '70s like *The Parallax View, Klute, The Stepford Wives,* and *Marathon Man,* but here he showcases an unexpected talent for the broader canvas of this historical adventure film about the explorer Sir Richard Burton. Small strays from his psychological approach of his earlier scores, here adopting a style more in keeping with John Williams or Georges Delerue, but what he lacks in originality he more than makes up for in melodic inventiveness. Several sweeping, gorgeous tunes fill out the epic scope of the story, from a noble, adventuresome theme for Burton to a beautiful waltz–like melody for Burton's romance with an English noblewoman. It makes for great listening, although the 18th–century romanticism often stands uncomfortably next to native African songs and percussion lines, with no attempt to integrate the two disparate styles. The score's immensely satisfying emotional qualities squash any other quibbles.

Jeff Bond

Mouse Hunt

1998, Varèse-Sarabande, from the film *Mouse Hunt,* Dream-Works, 1998 ♫♫♫♫

album notes: Music: Alan Silvestri; **Conductor:** Alan Silvestri.

Alan Silvestri has a knack for writing scores that are often exhilarating and enjoyable in their own right. He again demonstrates his ease with flavorful themes in this episodically funny effort in which his music may have been the best part. Involving a difficult-to-get-rid-of rodent and two bumbling characters, *Mouse Hunt* introduced Nathan Lane and Lee Evans as two estranged brothers who inherit the house their father left them at his death, a mansion that's just about to fall in ruins. That's where the mouse comes in: it has inhabited the place for a long while, totally undisturbed, and the arrival of these two new occupants is more than it can take. It will leave, but not without a fight. And it's a smart mouse to boot, as the two brothers soon discover. Matching the burlesque events in the picture note for scene, Silvestri's score is a rambunctious, wild-eyed series of cues, some played tongue-in-cheek, others with a big band flair, others still in a *Till Eulenspiegel* style that's difficult to resist. It all adds up to a very funny, very enjoyable soundtrack album.

Didier C. Deutsch

Much Ado about Nothing

1993, Epic Soundtrax/Sony Music, from the film *Much Ado about Nothing,* Samuel Goldwyn Pictures, 1993 ♫♫♫♫♫

album notes: Music: Patrick Doyle; **Conductor:** David Snell.

A grand, glorious score by Patrick Doyle, *Much Ado about Nothing* is one of those magical soundtracks whose popularity seems to grow as time goes on. You can't turn on any Olympic competition without hearing the majestic "Overture" at least once or twice, nor can one easily forget the soaring chorus of "Sigh No More Ladies," a track which gives this second Kenneth Branagh adaptation of Shakespeare its musical soul. Unlike his superb though sometimes over–the–top *Henry V,* or the context–heavy score for *Hamlet,* Doyle's *Much Ado* is pretty much a stand–alone classic, and is certainly the most accessible score of the three Branagh–Doyle Shakespeare efforts. In fact, it is very hard to find fault with any of Doyle's compositions, or their sequencing as an album. The music flows splendidly from one track to the next, offering sweeping, memorable themes that linger in the mind long after they have finished. The cumulative effect is that of a superior listening experience that is rare at the cinema now. Indeed, when looking at how derivative and vapid most movie music currently is, *Much Ado* truly stands out as one of the finest film scores composed in the last decade.

Andy Dursin

Mulan

1998, Walt Disney, from the film *Mulan*, Disney, 1998 🎬🎬🎬🎬🎬

album notes: Music: Jerry Goldsmith; **Conductor:** Jerry Goldsmith.

It's difficult to think of Jerry Goldsmith as scoring a Walt Disney animated feature, but that's precisely what *Mulan* is all about. The story of a lively Chinese girl who opts to dress as a boy in order to help save her country from invading hordes of Tatars, the film gave Disney animators a new opportunity to show their talent with a story high on Chinese designs and impressive computer animations.

Characteristic of the Disney features of late, some songs by Matthew Wilder and David Zippel have been added to presumably enliven the action, with Lea Salonga, Beth Fowler, Marni Nixon, Donny Osmond, and Harvey Fierstein among the talented performers who lend their voices to the various characters in the film. Stevie Wonder is also heard in the mandatory pop single that bears little relation to the film itself, but usually looks good when it hits the charts. The formula has worked in the past for much less interesting features than this one, and along with the merchandising of product available at the various Disney stores around the country, it is to be expected, regardless of the film that spawned it.

But now comes the score, represented here by a series of six selections that are surprisingly infectious, in keeping with the general tone of the film, yet quite representative of Goldsmith's usual high quality standards. That the composer of *The Omen* or *Star Trek The Motion Picture* decided not to be condescending is already quite an achievement, but that he delivered a score that shines despite the shortcomings of its subject matter is saying a lot about his artistry and his talent. Rather than rely on the obvious Chinese sonorities, the composer wrote a series of cues, at times jaunty (Mulan, after all, is a little girl), at times romantic, at times epic, that evoke the adventure aspects of the story in broad, colorful terms. Interestingly, the soundtrack album was also released in other countries where the film was presented, sometimes with different cues that are not found on the U.S. album. Given the fact that this score is so good, it would be interesting to have an album that focuses entirely on it.

Didier C. Deutsch

Mulholland Falls

1996, edel America Records, from the film *Mulholland Falls,* MGM, 1996 🎬🎬

album notes: Music: Dave Grusin; **Conductor:** Dave Grusin.

The true story of four LAPD detectives whose taste for expensive clothes and rough handling of criminals earned them the name of the "Hat Squad" in the early '50s, and the personal involvement of one of them with a young woman and crime victim, *Mulholland Falls* is a drama that never really attains the lofty heights to which it aspired. Possibly reflective of the uncertainties about the narrative itself, which, despite strong performances by Nick Nolte, Melanie Griffith, Chris Penn, and John Malkovich, never gets off the ground and turns introspective instead of focusing on action, Dave Grusin's score, as heard in this soundtrack album, remains grounded in banalities. With little of the urgency or drive evidently needed for a film of this nature, it wanders aimlessly from one cue to another, with only "Kate's Theme" attracting for its melodic content.

Didier C. Deutsch

The Mummy

1999, Decca Records, from the film *The Mummy,* Universal, 1999 🎬🎬🎬🎬🎬

album notes: Music: Jerry Goldsmith; **Conductor:** Jerry Goldsmith.

With so many sci-fi thrillers and horror films to his credit, one can say that Jerry Goldsmith has become a master of the suspense. But unlike some of his less talented peers, he is never content to rest on his own laurels and repeat himself. His scores are always ingenious, innovative, different. Case in point this remake of the 1932 *The Mummy,* boldly announced by a fiery tune, "Imhotep," which is as brassy as they come, yet retains behind its energy a motif that presages the threat rep-

Kermit and Paul Williams in The Muppet Movie **(The Kobal Collection)**

resented by the Egyptian priest sentenced to eternity as a living dead. The combination of eerie string lines and a mixed wordless chorus gives the theme an aural force one would not necessarily expect in a score such as this.

But that's only the beginning: the themes, solidly sketched in energetic terms, are attractively laid out, with melodic material that grabs the listener's interest and never lets go. No facile effects, no predictable synthesizer lines, just some good, old fashioned film music created by a master who knows which lever to pull in order to maximize the blend of exotic rhythms and vibrant themes that are the hallmarks of this excellent score.

The pageantry of old Egypt, the excitement of modern-day excavations, and the terror wrought by the vengeful mummy are given specific voices in a score that plays like an action soundtrack, with themes in which Egyptian folk instruments are used to create the proper atmosphere. Such cues as "Giza Port," "Camel Race," and "The Sand Volcano" thrive with great eloquence, while "The Crypt," "The Mummy," and particularly "Rebirth" teem with echoes of the ancient curse, in jarring, low brass bursts and slightly dissonant high string calls that do not

overshadow the main thrusts of the music. A great score by a great composer.

Didier C. Deutsch

The Muppet Movie

1993, Jim Henson Records, from the animated feature *The Muppet Movie*, Jim Henson Productions, 1993 ♪♪♪♪

album notes: Music: Paul Williams; **Songs:** Paul Williams, Kenny Ascher; **Conductor:** Ian Freebairn–Smith; **Cast:** Jim Henson, Frank Oz, Jerry Nelson, Richard Hunt.

The first, and to many, the best Muppet film, *The Muppet Movie* brings to the big screen the lovable gang in a story that doesn't make too much sense, but gives equal time to all the familiar characters, and proves thoroughly enjoyable from beginning to end. This is also due, to a large extent, to the wonderful score and songs created by Paul Williams, which includes the Grammy Award–winning "Rainbow Connection." In a case like this, little can be said: All you have to do is sit down, take the scene, and revel in the silly nonsense.

Didier C. Deutsch

Muppet Treasure Island

🎬 1996, Angel Records, from the animated feature *Muppet Treasure Island*, Walt Disney Pictures, 1996 ♪♪♪♪

album notes: Music: Hans Zimmer; **Songs:** Barry Mann, Cynthia Weil; **Conductor:** Harry Gregson-Williams.

A retelling of Robert Louis Stevenson's classic story, but with many liberties taken during the course of the action with the original, *Muppet Treasure Island* gives the Muppets an opportunity to interact with human actors, sail the high seas in search of a treasure, and throw in a couple of song–and–dance numbers even Stevenson with his wild imagination couldn't have dreamed up. The sum total is an entertaining lark, spiced up with some good musical moments, and the antics of the always–engaging furry characters. If the kids will enjoy it for what it is, adults will also be amply rewarded, as long as they are not looking for *Traviata* or *The Pirates of Penzance*. Tim Curry, among the humans involved in this swinging swashbuckler, is outstanding as a singing Long John Silver.

Didier C. Deutsch

Muriel's Wedding

🎬 1995, Polydor Records, from the film *Muriel's Wedding*, Miramax Pictures, 1995 ♪♪♥

album notes: Music: Peter Best.

How you'll feel about this soundtrack depends on your taste for Abba, who accounts for three songs, and cheesy wedding band music, which accounts for four songs. It's another hodgepodge collection, loosely based around reception ditties such as the Carpenters' syrupy "We've Only Just Begun," the Turtles' "Happy Together," and Peter Allen's limbo–provoking "I Go to Rio." But without "Proud Mary" or "Celebrate," there's no way this can claim to be authentic.

Gary Graff

Music Box

🎬 1989, Varèse Sarabande, from the film *Music Box*, Carolco Pictures, 1989 ♪♪♪

album notes: Music: Philippe Sarde; **Orchestra:** The Hungarian State Symphony Orchestra, The Muzsikas; **Conductor:** Harry Rabinowitz.

A powerful drama, enhanced by Jessica Lange's sensitive portrayal as a successful Chicago lawyer forced to defend her own father, facing deportation to Hungary for crimes he allegedly committed during World War II, *Music Box* could have benefited from a stronger score than the one created here by Philippe Sarde. Not that the composer failed director Costa–Gavras, but saddled with little physical screen action and a poorly developed screenplay, all Sarde could do was provide cues that try to make a point when there is none to make. The only times the

score comes alive is when the vivacious accents of a Hungarian csardas kick in as in "Departure from Court" and "Journey to Budapest," in a bit of local color that's particularly welcome.

Didier C. Deutsch

The Music from U.N.C.L.E. (The Original Soundtrack Affair)

📺 1997, Razor & Tie Records, from the television series *The Man From U.N.C.L.E.*, 1964 ♪♪♪♥

album notes: Music: Robert Drasnin, Gerald Fried, Jerry Goldsmith, Walter Scharf, Lalo Schifrin, Morton Stevens; **Conductor:** Hugo Montenegro.

The "(Theme From) The Man From U.N.C.L.E.," with its pounding rhythm beat, organ obbligato, and electric guitar strumming, brings back fond memories of a series that had many great moments in it. Soon, however, the overall stridency in the sound itself makes one wish that a little more control had been exerted in the transfer of these excerpts. Much of this comes from the fact that the music was brash to begin with, having a relentless beat that properly defined the action in the series, but also from the fact that Hugo Montenegro's orchestrations emphasize the very brassy elements that now seem to be somewhat annoying when you have to listen to them in an isolated environment. This comment set aside, one cannot deny the fact that *The Man From U.N.C.L.E.* attracted many composers who went on to do much bigger and better things (Jerry Goldsmith, Gerald Fried, and Lalo Schifrin, among them), something that also gives the music a greater importance than it probably had initially.

Didier C. Deutsch

The Music Man

🎭 1992, Angel Records, from the Broadway production *The Music Man*, 1958 ♪♪♪♪

album notes: Music: Meredith Willson; **Lyrics:** Meredith Willson; **Musical Direction:** Herbert Green; **Cast:** Robert Preston, Barbara Cook, Pert Kelton, Eddie Hodges.

Is Robert Preston's spellbinding con man the finest male performance in this history of the musical theater? Has a more beautiful female voice than Barbara Cook's ever been heard on a Broadway stage? The evidence is here for your consideration, in Meredith Willson's breakthrough hit about his small–town Iowa childhood just after the turn of the century. What may at first seem to be Broadway's corniest classic also has remarkable sophistication, as Willson's score takes the listener on a tour of American musical styles of the period, moving from lovely melodies to songs based almost entirely on rhythm effects and percussion. Americana at its finest.

Marc Kirkeby

🎬 1962, Warner Bros. Records, from the film *The Music Man*, Warner Bros., 1962 ♪♪♪♪

album notes: Music: Meredith Willson; **Lyrics:** Meredith Willson; **Choir:** The Warner Bros. Studio Chorus; **Orchestra:** The Warner Bros. Orchestra; **Conductor:** Ray Heindorf; **Cast:** Robert Preston, Shirley Jones, Pert Kelton, Ronnie Howard, Hermione Gingold, Mary Wickes, Buddy Hackett.

With Robert Preston reprising his Broadway role as Harold Hill and Shirley Jones (a more recognizable box–office name at the time) replacing Barbara Cook, *The Music Man* splashed across the big screen in a relatively faithful adaptation of the stage hit by Meredith Willson. Instead of painted settings, audiences were treated to the great outdoors in a small town (filmed on a studio back lot); and with Hermione Gingold, Paul Ford (as River City's mayor), and Buddy Hackett adding the luster of their performances to the storyline, this screen version provided filmgoers who might not have had a chance to see the Broadway show a great opportunity to enjoy it in all its glory. Adding an extra sheen to the score, Ray Heindorf's orchestrations turned the music into a boisterous, exhilarating sonic experience, faithfully captured in the recording. As in the Broadway cast album, Preston is the show.

Didier C. Deutsch

My Best Friend's Wedding

🎬 1997, The Work Group, from the film *My Best Friend's Wedding*, TriStar Pictures, 1997 ♪♪♪♪

album notes: Music: James Newton Howard; **Conductor:** Artie Kane.

What a bright, cheerful little album. Featuring many songs written by Burt Bacharach and Hal David and performances by a host of pop performers, including Jackie DeShannon, Mary Chapin Carpenter, and the ubiquitous Tony Bennett, the album plays like a wonderful, joyous celebration to the best of pop music in the 1960s. Even the cast of the film, including Julia Roberts, Dermot Mulroney, and Cameron Diaz, join in the fun, with James Newton Howard providing six minutes (not much, but enough to appreciate his contribution) of instrumental merriment.

Didier C. Deutsch

My Cousin Vinny

🎬 1992, Varèse Sarabande Records, from the film *My Cousin Vinny*, 20th Century Fox, 1992 ♪♪♪

album notes: Music: Randy Edelman; **Conductor:** Randy Edelman.

Randy Edelman has teamed with director Jonathan Lynn a number of times over the years, but their most fruitful collaboration turned out to be *My Cousin Vinny*, the Joe Pesci comedy that earned Marisa Tomei an Oscar for her hilarious comedic performance. Edelman's score is typical of the composer, interspersing synths with orchestra and a small acoustic ensemble that simultaneously echoes both the street–savvy New Yorker who heads down to Alabama to handle a court case and the down home, decidedly Southern lifestyle that he runs into. The score is frequently bouncy and always energetic, though it's hard to believe that listeners who haven't seen the film will find the music of great interest, thus leaving the album recommended most strongly for fans of the movie. By the way, anyone looking for the two Travis Tritt songs that open and close the film will have to look elsewhere, as the record label opted not to include them here.

Andy Dursin

My Fair Lady

🎬 1994, Sony Legacy, from the Broadway production *My Fair Lady*, 1956. ♪♪♪♪

album notes: Music: Frederick Loewe; **Lyrics:** Alan Jay Lerner; **Cast:** Rex Harrison (Henry Higgins), Julie Andrews (Eliza Dolittle), Stanley Holloway (Alfred P. Doolittle), Robert Coote (Colonel Pickering), Gordon Dilworth, Rod McLennan, Philippa Bevans (Mrs. Pearce), John Michael King (Freddy Eynsford-Hill).

🎬 1998, Sony Classical, from the London production *My Fair Lady*, 1958 ♪♪♪♪

album notes: Music: Frederick Loewe; **Lyrics:** Alan Jay Lerner; **Cast:** Rex Harrison (Henry Higgins), Julie Andrews (Eliza Dolittle), Stanley Holloway (Alfred P. Doolittle), Robert Coote (Colonel Pickering), Betty Woolfe (Mrs. Pearce), Leonard Weir (Freddy Eynsford-Hill).

🎬 1994, Sony Classical, from the film *My Fair Lady*, Warner Bros., 1964 ♪♪♪♪

album notes: Music: Frederick Loewe; **Lyrics:** Alan Jay Lerner; **Orchestra:** The Warner Bros. Studio Chorus and Orchestra; **Conductor:** Andre Previn; **Cast:** Rex Harrison (Henry Higgins), Audrey Hepburn (Eliza Dolittle), Stanley Holloway (Alfred P. Doolittle), Wilfrid Hyde-White (Colonel Pickering), Gordon Dilworth (Harry), Rod McLennan (Jamie), Mona Washbourne (Mrs. Pearce), Jeremy Brett (Freddy Eynsford-Hill).

Considered by many to be one of the perfect Broadway musicals, the original Broadway cast recording might therefore be considered the perfect cast album. Every performer from Rex Harrison, Julie Andrews, and Stanley Halloway to the smallest supporting player is superb and right in every detail. This exactness must be credited to the director, Moss Hart, as well as the splendid lyrics and music of Alan Jay Lerner and Frederick Loewe.

The original-cast album, an all-time best seller, had been recorded in mono. Two years later, thanks to the technical development of stereo, producer Goddard Lieberson decided to redo the album, with the same principals, now performing the

Audrey Hepburn in the film version of My Fair Lady. **(The Kobal Collection)**

show in London. This is the remixed/remastered recording now reissued by Sony Classical/Legacy. Though the players were the same both on Broadway and in London, there are slight differences in this recording—Julie Andrews's cockney accent sounds thicker here than it did on the Broadway cast album, and this second version lacks the freshness and spontaneity of the original mono. Some noticeable distortion is also apparent in the recording, which features a bonus track: Percy Faith's recording of "The Embassy Waltz," which was never included on either cast album.

The soundtrack of the film version proves that there is still life in the fair lady yet. The various dubious casting and dubbing issues aside, this is a big, bold old-fashioned film of a big Broadway show. With the exception of Audrey Hepburn replacing Julie Andrews, the male principals remain the same as the original 1956 Broadway and 1958 London cast recordings. The passage of eight years has taken its toll on the voices, which are beginning to fray around the edges and the performances are much looser and more studied than either of the previous recordings. Hepburn is dubbed, in part, by Marni

Nixon and they both do an admirable job. However, it is easy to tell where one voice ends and the other one begins. Included on this release are previously extended dance music episodes, as well as unreleased tracks. The sound quality has been excellently refurbished and the album sounds better than it ever has. All in all, this is a most enjoyable recording of this legendary score.

Jerry J. Thomas and Beth Krakower

My Father's Glory/My Mother's Castle

🎬 1990, Carrere Records/France, from the films *My Father's Glory (La gloire de mon pere)*, Gaumont, 1990, and *My Mother's Castle (Le chateau de ma mere)*, Gaumont, 1990   ♪♪♪♪
album notes: Music: Vladimir Cosma; **Conductor:** Vladimir Cosma;

Set in Provence in the early 1920s, both films evoked the childhood memories of author/filmmaker Marcel Pagnol, as filmed by Yves Robert. Because of the locale, and the various characters that inhabit the films—young Marcel; his father, an elementary school teacher; Augustine, his mother; his friend, Lili; his first love, Isabelle, among many others—both *La gloire de mon pere* and *Le chateau de ma mere* (available here on video) describe a part of French life that may be alien to many viewers, but is quite familiar in its universality. Bathed in meridional sunshine, and typical Provencal humor, the films are particularly well set off by Vladimir Cosma's scores that rely on catchy melodies and colorfully descriptive themes. This recording may be difficult to find. Check with a used CD store, mail-order company, or a dealer specializing in rare, out-of-print, or import recordings.

Didier C. Deutsch

My Fellow Americans

🎬 1996, TVT Records, from the film *My Fellow Americans,* Warner Bros., 1996 ♪♪♪

album notes: Featured Artists: Lipps, Inc., Stevie Wonder, Wilson Pickett, Elvis Presley, Creedence Clearwater Revival, ZZ Hill, The Tweezers & Jen, Louis Jordan with Louis Armstrong, Ella Fitzgerald, Dorothy Norwood, Peter Segal, Mihoko Toro.

An odd mixture of genres—techno–pop with "Funkytown," R&B with "Superstition," country–rock with "Down Home Blues," pop–jazz with "Don't Be That Way," standard with "Life Is So Peculiar," rock with "Treat Me Nice"—this soundtrack album sounds as if it were trying to be too many things to too many people, at least creatively speaking. After a while, it sounds as if it were on overdrive, something that might reflect the tone of this frantic comedy, starring Jack Lemmon, James Garner, Dan Aykroyd, and Lauren Bacall. William Ross's "original motion picture score" (sic), reduced to a 10–minute suite put together by splicing four cues with no connective thread, is not bad and reminiscent of the type of music Elmer Bernstein might write on an off–day. If you don't mind jumping from one style to another in the space of a few minutes, you might actually take a shine to this unorthodox album.

Didier C. Deutsch

My Girl

🎬 1991, Epic Soundtrax, from the film *My Girl,* Columbia Pictures, 1991 ♪♪♪

album notes: Music: James Newton Howard; **Featured Performers:** The Temptations, Spiral Starecase, Sly and The Family Stone, The Fifth Dimension, Manfred Mann, Todd Rundgren, The Rascals, Creedence Clearwater Revival, Harold Melvin and The Blue Notes, The Flamingos, Chicago.

The film is about pre–pubescents in the early '60s, and the songs on the soundtrack follow that lead. They're all Top 20 hits and all love songs, from Sly & the Family Stone's "Hot Fun in the Summertime," to Manfred Man's "Do Wah Diddy Diddy,"

to the Young Rascals' "Good Lovin,'" and Spiral Starecase's "More Today Than Yesterday." Oops, almost forgot—and the Temptations' "My Girl." Duh.

Gary Graff

My Girl 2

🎬 1994, Epic Soundtrax, from the film *My Girl 2,* Columbia Pictures, 1994 ♪♪♪

album notes: Music: Cliff Eidelman; **Conductor:** Cliff Eidelman; **Featured Performers:** Crosby, Stills, Nash & Young, Johnny Rivers, The Supremes, Jackson Browne, Steve Miller Band, Elton John, Rick Price, Rod Stewart, The Beach Boys, The Temptations.

The sequel begins in the '60s—Crosby Stills, Nash & Young's "Our House," the Supremes' "Baby Love," a repeat of the Temptations' title song—but moves into the early and mid–'70s to follow the characters. It makes its musical point with some of the biggest artists of the era, including Jackson Browne ("Doctor My Eyes"), the Steve Miller Band ("Swingtown"), Rod Stewart ("Reason to Believe"), and Elton John ("Tiny Dancer," "Bennie and the Jets"). But what this lacks is the forgotten gem or surprise cut. Johnny Rivers's rendition of "Rockin' Pneumonia & the Boogie Woogie Flu" comes close, but we'd rather have Professor Longhair, anyway.

Gary Graff

My Left Foot/Da

🎬 1989, Varèse Sarabande, from the films *My Left Foot,* Miramax Films, 1989, and *Da,* Film Dallas 1988 ♪♪♪♪

album notes: Music: Elmer Bernstein; **Conductor:** Elmer Bernstein; **Featured Musician:** Cynthia Millar, Ondes Martenot.

Two scores by the always reliable Elmer Bernstein combined together on one CD have two somewhat similar moods of personal struggle and emotional recovery, and both are included for the price of one. Who could complain? Taking things sequentially, *My Left Foot* is a warm, affectionate look at the life story of Christy Brown (played by Daniel Day–Lewis), an Irish artist born with cerebral palsy, a debilitating disease, into a poor family, who overcame all odds to become a writer and painter. Eschewing the sappy sentimentality that could have destroyed its fragile dramatic balance, the film states its case with little embellishments, relying instead on the fabric of the story itself to make its impact. The moods are beautifully sustained by the score, in which Cynthia Millar's Ondes Martenot provides a specific atmosphere in "Mother," the first word the handicapped Christy wrote with a piece of chalk in his left foot to the amazement of his relatives.

Based on the book and eponymous play by Hugh Leonard, *Da* recounts the emotional journey of an Irish playwright (Martin

Sheen) living in New York who attends the funeral of his father in Ireland and goes through a regenerative self–discovery trip. Once again, Bernstein's score finds new accents to underline the spiritual adventure of the film's hero, with the Ondes Martenot adding their unusual nostalgic sonorities to this wonderfully delineated music.

Didier C. Deutsch

My Life

1993, Epic Soundtrax, from the film *My Life,* Columbia Pictures, 1993 𝄞𝄞𝄞𝄞

album notes: Music: John Barry; **Conductor:** John Barry; **Featured Soloist:** Michael Lang, piano.

John Barry's propensity for long, romantic orchestral lines is particularly suited for this story of a man who finds out he is dying of cancer and decides to make a video that will explain to his unborn child who he was and where he came from. The topic must have hit a particularly sentimental chord with the composer who wrote a gorgeous, low–key score, filled with emotional and beautifully tender moments. Subtly shaded, the music unfolds with striking grace, revealing themes that are stated with warmth and played for all their worth. This one must have come from the heart.

Didier C. Deutsch

My Mother's Castle

See: My Father's Glory/My Mother's Castle

My Name is Shangai Joe

See: Il mio nome e' Shangai Joe/I giorni della violenza

My One and Only

 1989, Atlantic Records, from the Broadway production *My One and Only,* 1983 𝄞𝄞𝄞𝄞

album notes: Music: George Gerhswin; **Lyrics:** Ira Gershwin; **Musical Direction:** Jack Lee; **Cast:** Tommy Tune, Twiggy, Charles "Honi" Coles, Roscoe Lee Browne.

Initially intended as a straight revival of *Funny Face,* the 1927 musical by George and Ira Gershwin, *My One and Only* evolved into a significantly different musical with little relationship to its original, except for some of the songs that were retained. The new book, devised by Peter Stone, deals with a young aviator and the aquacade star with whom he falls in love: She is already a success, having crossed the English Channel, and he has ambitions of beating Lindbergh in flying over the Atlantic, which he does of course, after surmounting tremendous odds, winning his girl in the process. The "blithely charming" show

starred Tommy Tune and Twiggy in performances that kept luring audiences to it long after the show premiered on May 1, 1983, closing after 757 performances in a considerably longer run than its model. While it retained many songs from the *Funny Face* score (including "He Loves and She Loves," "'S Wonderful," "Funny Face," and the title song), it also interpolated many other familiar tunes from the Gershwin body of works, among them "I Can't Be Bothered Now," "Soon," "Strike Up the Band," "Nice Work If You Can Get It," "Little Jazz Bird," and "How Long Has This Been Going On?" all delivered with the appropriate period zest by a pleasantly twangy Twiggy and a charmingly self–effaced Tommy Tune, in performances that make the cast album recording an absolute delight.

Didier C. Deutsch

My West

See: Il mio West

Mysterious Island

1993, Cloud Nine Records, from the film *Mysterious Island,* Columbia Pictures, 1961 𝄞𝄞𝄞𝄞𝄞

album notes: Music: Bernard Herrmann; **Conductor:** Bernard Herrmann.

Bernard Herrmann struck a particularly pleasant note in his relationship with Ray Harryhausen, writing wonderfully animated scores for the filmmaker's flights of cinematographic fantasy, *The Three Worlds of Gulliver, Jason and the Argonauts, The Seventh Voyage of Sinbad,* and *Mysterious Island.* Of these, *Mysterious Island* may be the most interesting, because of the colorful orchestral textures and brilliant themes that add musical life to Harryhausen's wonderful dynamation creatures ("The Giant Crab," "The Phorarhacos," "The Cephalopod"). As was true of Herrmann's previous contributions to these fantasy films, the music for *Mysterious Island* is a vibrant testimony to his unbridled imagination and his sense of action and movement, splendidly illustrated in this recording, available for the first time in stereo. Even though the CD evidences some audio problems, inherent, we are told, to the original recording itself, the effect achieved is often unique and sensational, making the album an essential addition to any collection.

see also: Bernard Herrmann in Composers

Didier C. Deutsch

The Mystery of Rampo

1995, Discovery Records, from the film *The Mystery of Rampo,* Samuel Goldwyn, 1995 𝄞𝄞𝄞

album notes: Music: Akira Senju; **Orchestra:** The Czech Philharmonic Orchestra; **Conductors:** Vaclav Neumann, Mario Klemens.

The musical setting for a film dealing with a Japanese novelist whose fictional characters find a strange echo in real life, *The Mystery of Rampo* elicited a strikingly beautiful Westernized score from composer Akira Senju, which at times recalls some of the most inspired moments from Ennio Morricone. Romantic elements pervade this elegant music, dominated by the nominal cue "Love Theme for Rampo," played in a variety of forms throughout, with the Czech Philharmonic Orchestra, conducted by Vaclav Neumann (no less) and by Mario Klemens, bringing its own sensitivity to the flawless performance. A surprising recording well worth a detour.

Didier C. Deutsch

Mystery Train

1989, RCA Victor Records, from the film *Mystery Train,* Orion Classics, 1989 🎬🎬🎬

album notes: Music: John Lurie; **Featured Musicians:** John Lurie, guitar, harmonica; Marc Ribot, guitar, banjo; Tony Garnier, bass; Douglas Browne, drums.

Two versions of the title song, one by Elvis Presley and one by Junior Parker, plus a "Mystery Train Suite," just in case you forgot the film's title are included. Memphis is dutifully represented on this soundtrack with the likes of Otis Redding, Roy Orbison, Rufus Thomas, Bobby Blue Bland, and the Bar–Kays, and it would be nice to have more of that and less of John Lurie's Memphis via Hollywood score.

Gary Graff

The Myth of Fingerprints

1998, Velvel Records, from the film *The Myth of Fingerprints,* Sony Pictures Classics, 1998 🎬🎬🎬🎬

album notes: Music: David Bridle, John Phillips; **Featured Musicians:** David Bridle, piano, harmonium, keyboards, bilas; John Phillips, electric and acoustic guitars, keyboards, bilas; Helen Mountfort, cello, harmonics; Hannah Cooper, oboe; Andrew Carswell, mandolin, tin whistle; Peter Luscombe, drums; Simon Polinski, bass; Robin Gador, double bass.

Set around Thanksgiving in a small New England town, this adult drama brings grown-up children (Noah Wylie and Julianne Moore, the black sheep of the family) back home for the holidays, and into the arms of their conservative parents (Roy Scheider and Blythe Danner), with whom they have evidently lost touch. In contrast to the tension that soon comes to the surface on screen, the score captures in calm, simple themes what life in New England should be. It has a very easy feel to it, and features a nice blend of music and songs, including "Don't Be That Way" by Bing Crosby and the Rozz Nash Sextet's rendition of "Tenderly."

Beth Krakower

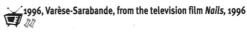

Nails

1996, Varèse-Sarabande, from the television film *Nails,* 1996 🎬🎬

album notes: Music: Bill Conti; **Featured Musicians:** Bill Conti, piano, synthesizers; John Goux, guitar; Michael Fisher, percussion; Paul Shure, violin; Pamela Goldsmith, viola; Armand Kaproff, cello.

At one time, Bill Conti was considered a promising composer, something his scores for the *Rocky* films, for instance, plainly justified. Unfortunately, with success (and a steady job as the perennial conductor of the Academy Award ceremony), he seems to have abandoned all ambitions to become one of the few in a field that sees an increasing number of wannabes, and the few scores he writes every now and then sound routine and totally boring. This benign effort was created for a television thriller starring Dennis Hopper, and with the exception of a few isolated moments that harken back to better days, it's fairly conventional. The "Main Title" (synthesizers, electric guitar riffs, and percussion) sets the tone; the rest is pretty much of the same ilk—nothing to really write home about. The instrumentation, though, is interesting ("Graveside Chat," for piano and violin, is one of the isolated moments mentioned above), but overall this is hardly the type of score one would call compelling.

Didier C. Deutsch

The Naked Gun 2½: The Smell of Fear

1991, Varèse Sarabande, from the film *The Naked Gun 2 1/2: The Smell of Fear,* Paramount Pictures, 1991 🎬🎬🎬

album notes: Music: Ira Newborn; **Conductor:** Ira Newborn.

It was only natural that Ira Newborn would adapt his effective *Police Squad!* TV scores to the *Naked Gun* films. A lampoon of the 1950s cop shows, particularly *M–Squad,* the short–lived TV series enabled Newborn to borrow from the jazz style of that era and to create a memorable body of work. The main theme for *Police Squad!* is a boisterous big band style tune inspired by *M–Squad*'s main title, while bumbling cop Frank Drebin's theme is a shameless march. The CD successfully mixes up cues from both the sequel and the first film, *The Naked Gun: From the Files of Police Squad!* into a surprisingly cohesive presentation.

David Hirsch

Naked in New York

🎬 1994, Sire Records, from the film *Naked in New York,* Fine Line
Features, 1994 ♪♪♪

Anything that starts with the Ramones' "Rockaway Beach" is
bound to be at least interesting and this set is better than that.
Mostly it's a modern rock sampler, self serving in that it's
loaded with Sire/Reprise artists, but at least they deliver the
goods. Rheostatics' "Palomar" is good fun, while the Farm and
Greenberry Woods kick it on "Comfort" and "Too Good to Be
True," respectively. Judybats' "Ugly on the Outside" is an
under-appreciated gem and Seal's "Crazy" is always nice to
have around.

Gary Graff

The Naked Lunch

🎬 1992, Milan Records, from the film *Naked Lunch,* 20th Century
Fox, 1992 ♪♪

album notes: Music: Howard Shore; **Orchestra:** The London Philhar-
monic Orchestra; **Featured Musicians:** Ornette Coleman, saxophone;
Denardo Coleman, drums; Barre Phillips, bass; J.J. Edwards, Sintir;
Aziz Bin Salem, Nai; David Hartley, piano.

Based on the sci-fi cult novel by William S. Burroughs, and mixing elements of his personal life, like the accidental death of
his wife during a wild party, *The Naked Lunch* is distinguished
by an abrasive Howard Shore score, performed by Ornette
Coleman. Quoting Coleman, "the voicings of the woodwinds,
brass, strings, percussion, non-tempered instruments and the
uses of the alto soloist work so that one can hear these instruments creating harmonies, melodies, rhythms, modulations,
and dynamics mirroring each other categorically." Ultimately,
acceptance of the album will largely depend on the reaction to
Coleman's grating, iconoclastic playing, deemed awful by
some, genial by others. The fact is that this soundtrack album
is bound to find as many admirers as it will find detractors. On
a purely listening basis, it may be uncompromising musically
but difficult at times to really appreciate, Ornette Coleman's
playing notwithstanding.

Didier C. Deutsch

The Naked Maja

See: La maja desnuda

The Name of the Rose

🎬 1986, Teldec, from the film *The Name of the Rose,* 20th Century
Fox, 1986 ♪♪♪♪

album notes: Music: James Horner; **Conductor:** James Horner; **Featured Artists:** Charles Brett, counter tenor; Maria Schulz; **Choir:** The
Choir of the Choir School; Choir Director: Kurt Rieth.

An odd murder mystery, set in an isolated Italian monastery in
medieval time, *The Name of the Rose* received scant distribution at the time of its release and little publicity, despite superb
portrayals by Sean Connery as a sly monk with a detective instinct and F. Murray Abraham as a ruthless inquisitor. Providing
an extra ounce of symbolism to the occult drama is James
Horner's cleverly enigmatic score, in which disambulating
bells ominously announce the next victim. Mixing strange
sonorities and Gothic plainchant to create an oppressive atmosphere with mysterious undertones, the score is wonderfully imaginative and well-suited for this story based on a
novel by Umberto Eco. Unfortunately, the soundtrack album
was only released in Germany, on the Teldec label, and may
prove difficult to find. But it's well worth the effort.

Didier C. Deutsch

Napoleon

🎬 1994, Erato Records, from the film *Napoleon,* 1926—27 ♪♪♪♪

album notes: Music: Arthur Honegger, Marius Constant; **Orchestra:**
The Orchestre Philharmonique de Monte Carlo; **Conductor:** Marius
Constant.

🎬 1983, Silva Screen Records, from the film *Napoleon,* 1926—27
♪♪♪♪

album notes: Music: Carl Davis; **Orchestra:** The Wren Orchestra, **Conductor:** Carl Davis.

🎬 1981, CBS Records, from the film *Napoleon,* Images Film
Archive, 1927 ♪♪

album notes: Music: Carmine Coppola; **Orchestra:** The Milan Philharmonic Orchestra; **Conductor:** Carmine Coppola.

Abel Gance's sweeping *Napoleon* continues to inspire awe and
admiration more than 70 years after it was made. A five-hour
drama of epic proportions, this silent film "speaks" volumes,
both in terms of dramatic performances (Albert Dieudonne as
young Bonaparte is unforgettable) and as a visual spectacle in
which Gance pioneered many modern techniques, including
multiple-screen projection (30 years before Cinerama) and
camera movements to follow the action.

Throughout the years, various composers have attempted to
capture in musical terms the visual excitement of this extraordinary film. Arthur Honegger was the first to do so for the film's
initial presentation, in a score that only exists today in fragmented sketches. When a restored version of the film was
shown in Paris in 1979, Marius Constant contributed new cues
which, together with the selections from the Honegger score,
can be heard on the excellent recording he subsequently made
for Erato. For a gala performance at the Empire in London in
1980, British composer Carl Davis also created a new set of
cues said to closely match the director's intentions. His score,

Robert Redford in The Natural. **(The Kobal Collection)**

another impressive achievement, finds the composer conducting the Wren Orchestra in a reissue from Silva Screen Records. Finally, Carmine Coppola introduced his own variations on the theme for another roadshow presentation in 1981, in what is ultimately a downright tedious and derivative score, lacking real dramatic substance. The point between all three scores, of course, is how the same subject matter inspired four different composers, and how they each approached the same epic film with varying ideas.

Didier C. Deutsch

The Natural

1986, Warner Bros. Records, from the film *The Natural,* Tri–Star Pictures, 1984 ♪♪♪♪♪

album notes: Music: Randy Newman; **Conductor:** Randy Newman.

Writing in a style that irresistibly evokes some of the best pages by Aaron Copland, Randy Newman created a wonderful Americana–tinged score for this film, starring Robert Redford as a baseball player finally making the big time in his last season

after having shown great promises that never materialized throughout his career. One of Newman's earliest scores, the music flows with grace and charm, all bathed in a faint echo of nostalgia, in what was and still remains a very endearing effort. Subsequently, Newman continued in the same vein and scored other films with equal success, but this one is a real gem.

Didier C. Deutsch

Natural Born Killers

1994, Interscope/Atlantic, from the film *Natural Born Killers,* Warner Bros., 1994 ♪♪♪

A modern-day Bonnie and Clyde, *Natural Born Killers* plays the wild card about the media role in creating the hype around two petty hoodlums who become national celebrities of sorts after they commit a series of brutal, sadistic murders, and their story is lionized in a tabloid. Punctuating the action, director Oliver Stone used a dynamite soundtrack to give his film the right flavor, with performances by a host of alternative bands and rebel artists, including Patti Smith, Cowboy Junkies, Nine Inch Nails,

Bob Dylan, Leonard Cohen, Duane Eddy, Peter Gabriel, Jane's Addiction, and Dr. Dre. Bits of dialogue bridge some songs, putting a different spin on the solid compilation, with "Night on Bald Mountain" serving as an unexpected background to "Batonga in Batongaville." Not your usual run-of-the-mill song-driven soundtrack album.

Didier C. Deutsch

Navajo Joe

1995, Legend Records/Italy, from the film *Navajo Joe,* United Artists, 1974 ♫♫♫

album notes: Music: Ennio Morricone; **Conductor:** Bruno Nicolai; **Featured Musicians:** I Cantori Moderni di Alessandroni.

Starring Burt Reynolds as the renegade Indian Navajo Joe bent on avenging the death of members of his tribe, the film, made by Sergio Corbucci, spawned a rousing score which, upon its release, was credited to Leo Nichols, a pseudonym. In the years since, Ennio Morricone has admitted he wrote the score, a rough, gritty set of scorching cues that set the tone for what was a violent, no holds-barred spaghetti western. This CD release, like the UA LP of 1974, sounds awfully distorted, particularly in the vocal sections, but that doesn't prevent Morricone's music from making a strong, unforgettable impression. This title may be out of print or just plain hard to find. Mail-order companies, used CD shops, or dealers of rare or import recordings will be your best bet.

Didier C. Deutsch

Near Dark

1987, Varèse Sarabande, from the film *Near Dark,* DeLaurentiis Entertainment, 1987 ♫♫♫

album notes: Music: Tangerine Dream.

Propelled by an exciting score by Tangerine Dream, *Near Dark* is a vampire film of another sort, about a group of nasty–looking bikers with a mean streak in them that compels them to roam the countryside in a rural community and kill for fun once the sun has set. Punctuating the action and giving it an extra edge of vibrancy whenever needed, Tangerine Dream's score, an electronic concoction with emphasis on the beat, succeeded in enhancing the terror in the visuals. Taken on its own terms, it proves somewhat less ingratiating, though "Caleb's Blues" and "Good Times" are great rocking numbers.

Didier C. Deutsch

Ned Kelly

1998, Rykodisc, from the film *Ned Kelly,* United Artists, 1970 ♫♫♫

album notes: Music: Shel Silverstein.

Mick Jagger didn't seem too terribly convincing as Ned Kelly, the Australian outlaw whose deeds were glorified in this 1970 western directed by Tony Richardson. A mixture of Robin Hood and Jesse James, Kelly led a band of wild Irishmen against the British authorities in the 1870s, until he was arrested and sent to the gallows. Giving a different life to the story on the screen was the soundtrack, with stars Waylon Jennings, Kris Kristofferson, and Tom Ghent singing the songs written by Shel Silverstein. This CD reissue includes the songs, the most interesting part of the whole project, with bits of dialogue injected at appropriate moments to make a quick reference to the action itself. There are some good moments to be reckoned with here, notably the Kristofferson vocals ("Son of a Scoundrel," "Stoney Cold Ground," and "The Kellys Keep Coming") and Jennings's "Ned Kelly" and "Blame It on the Kellys." The enhanced CD also includes a film excerpt playable on the CD-ROM drive.

Didier C. Deutsch

Needful Things

1993, Varèse Sarabande, from the film *Needful Things,* Castle Rock Entertainment, 1993 ♫♫♫♫

album notes: Music: Patrick Doyle; **Conductor:** David Snell; *Featured Vocalist:* Nicole Tibbels.

Even when he writes a horror film score, Patrick Doyle can't avoid being more elegant and sophisticated than most. His music for this scary concoction about an olde shoppe in Maine that may harbor some evil force, if one is to believe that people who shop there end up being haunted by the objects they purchase, is as malevolent as it is delicious. Broadly announced by a choir in what sounds like an ominous pronouncement of things to come, the music, at first gracious and quite lovely, but becoming increasingly dark and brooding, unfolds with great charm before exploding in a climactic cue ("Just Blow Them Away") that marks all at once the end of the spell, of the shop, and of the movie. In–between, some elements create strong images, like the use of a music box theme that recurs at intervals throughout the score and belies some of the subjacent horror in the story, or the choral writing that evokes both good and evil pitted in an endless struggle, something that the two classical selections included here also denote.

Didier C. Deutsch

The Negotiator

1998, Restless Records, from the film *The Negotiator,* Warner Bros., 1998 ♫♫♫

album notes: Music: Graeme Revell.

Based on the real story of a St. Louis police officer who was accused of a crime he had not committed, *The Negotiator* starred two of today's most explosive screen actors, Samuel L. Jackson and Kevin Spacey, the former as an ace police negotiator, wrongly accused of killing his partner and the latter as another negotiator trying to obtain the release of two hostages Jackson is holding in the hope of proving his innocence. The action thriller, already solidly anchored by the contrasting personalities of the two stars, receives an additional boost from Graeme Revell's properly taut score, which enhances the drama and subtly underlines the tension in some of the most riveting scenes. Taken on its own terms, it doesn't always work so conclusively, with a couple of tracks ("Bluff and Double Bluff") that fail to ignite. But overall, it is a fine, distinguished effort that should please fans of the genre.

Didier C. Deutsch

Nemesis

1992, High Tide Recordings, from the film *Nemesis,* Imperial Entertainment, 1992

album notes: Music: Michel Rubini; **Orchestra:** The Los Angeles Symphony Orchestra; **Conductor:** Michel Rubini.

A futuristic film that had a short existence in movie theatres and didn't make much of a dent afterward, *Nemesis* is somewhat enlivened by the score Michel Rubini wrote for the occasion. With an abundance of electronic sounds and effects attempting to evoke the moods in the film, only those tracks that feature acoustic instruments over orchestral themes actually succeed in creating some enjoyment when judged on their own merits. "Jared's Theme" is a case in point, with its flavorful images strikingly painted by a heavily–echoed guitar, but the rest of the "score" is nothing more than electronic mush that means little outside of its screen context.

Didier C. Deutsch

The Net

1995, Varèse Sarabande, from the film *The Net,* Columbia Pictures, 1995

album notes: Music: Mark Isham; **Conductor:** Ken Kugler; **Featured Musicians:** David Goldblatt, Rich Ruttenberg, piano solos.

A powerful suspense thriller starring Sandra Bullock as a lonely Internet surfer and her involvement in murky government dealings, *The Net* reveals some dark Hitchcockian undertones in its standard story about an apparently innocent victim of circumstances being sucked into a maelstrom of criminal activities and almost losing her life as a result. While Mark Isham is a reliable composer, whose scores always keep the listener interested, he is not Bernard Herrmann, something that is plainly evidenced here. The selections, broken down in four parts, follow the story, gradually becoming more threatening as the Bul-

lock character finds herself more and more in serious danger, with increasingly somber orchestral textures occasionally interrupted by percussion elements, synthesized sounds, and weirdly ominous sonorities. It may work very well on the screen, as a complement to the action, but as pure audio programming, it often leaves a lot to be desired. The CD is unusually short (29:30 minutes of music!) but given the low impact of the music, it seems largely sufficient.

Didier C. Deutsch

Netherworld

1991, Moonstone Records, from the film *Netherworld,* Paramount Pictures, 1991

album notes: Music: David Bryan, Larry Fast; **Featured Musicians:** Edgar Winter, John Duva, Bernie Pershey, Bobby Gianetti, Tonk's House Band–Edgar Winter, vocals, sax; David Bryan, piano, backing vocals; Troy Turner, guitar; Harold Scott, bass; Stanley Watson, drums; Nancy Buchan, violin.

Full Moon movies often feature obnoxious musical scores by the likes of Richard Band, but here's one that's refreshingly different. For *Netherworld,* rock artist Edgar Winter croons a number of his original songs and offers a similarly rock/R&B–tinged score for a typically unappealing Charles Band–produced direct–to–video genre feature (one that's still a bit better than most efforts from this studio). Winter is well–known in pop music circles and his music here certainly gives more to the movie than the film does for him—the solo piano that performs the final track is elegant and graceful, probably working better on its own than it does in the laughable movie. Unlike most Full Moon projects, the music surprisingly doesn't sound like a video–game underscore. Winter fans especially should definitely give this one a listen.

Andy Dursin

Never Been Kissed

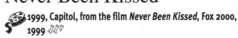

1999, Capitol, from the film *Never Been Kissed,* Fox 2000, 1999

A soundtrack that's a pleasant compilation of "lite" alternative pop/rock, perhaps best compared to cotton candy, it's irresistibly sweet and fun to eat, but then you're done and you don't have a craving again for it for a long time. In the film, Drew Barrymore is a budding investigative journalist who poses as a teenager in order to go back to high school, all for the purpose of a story assignment. Barrymore herself was reportedly involved with the film's musical selections. You'll find a few winners here by Semisonic, Remy Zero, and Block, as well as other similar alt-pop artists, and some classic Beach Boys, Smiths, and John Lennon/Yoko Ono songs. Fun, but you probably won't be compelled to put it on again too soon. It's just a tad too sweet.

Amy Rosen

Never on Sunday

 1998, Rykodisc, from the film *Never on Sunday*, United Artists, 1960 ♪♪

album notes: Music: Manos Hadjidakis.

When *Never on Sunday* first came out in 1960, the title song was all the rage and no doubt helped the film achieve broad international popularity. Today, it sounds a bit like an old saw that has not aged gracefully. Familiarity breeds contempt, they say, and this may be a clear example. Also, bouzouki music is attractive to a point, but too much of it may prove detrimental to overall appreciation. Ultimately, this reissue of Manos Hadjidakis's score, while welcome, isn't bound to seduce new audiences. Objectively speaking, included are some good tracks that truly deserve to be heard ("The Charms of Ilya," "The Lantern," "Speak Softly"), perhaps because they haven't been omnipresent in the way the title song by Melina Mercouri has been. But after a while, one feels like John Cleese, in one of his Monty Python routine, shouting, "Shut up that bloody music."

Didier C. Deutsch

Never Say Never Again

1993, Silva America; from the film *Never Say Never Again*, Taliafilm, 1983 ♪♪♪♪

album notes: Music: Michel Legrand; **Conductor:** Michel Legrand.

After having sworn off his James Bond screen persona for the second time following *Diamonds are Forever* (he already had left the series once before, after filming *You Only Live Twice)*, Sean Connery relented one last time and agreed to portray the apparently invincible 007 in *Never Say Never Again*, a thinly disguised remake of *Thunderball.* That film, however, was significantly different from the other James Bond films. It was not produced by Albert R. Broccoli and Harry Saltzman, who had succeeded in cornering the market by purchasing the rights to all the stories written by Ian Fleming save two (the other was *Casino Royale)*, and the film producers Jack Schwartzman and Kevin McClory could not secure the services of the James Bond composer–in–residence, John Barry.

Instead, they turned to Michel Legrand who wrote a strongly evocative score, even though it failed to evoke James Bond in the way John Barry managed so effectively in the many outings he scored. Comparisons with Barry's *Thunderball* in fact are unavoidable, with Legrand's music suffering as a result. Taken on its own terms, however, it is a series of action cues that match the pace of the film itself, with some excellent locale–sugges-

tive moments ("Bahama Island," "Big Band Death of Jack Petachi," "Tango to the Death," "Tears of Allah"), and strongly flavored cues ("Bond and Domino," "Bond Returns Home," "Felix and James Exit," "Largo's Waltz"). Two vocal tracks, the main title performed by Lani Hall with Herb Alpert, and "Une chanson d'amour," by Sophie Della, add a different touch.

Didier C. Deutsch

The NeverEnding Story

1984, EMI Records, from the film *The NeverEnding Story*, Neue Constantin Films, 1984 ♪♪♪♪

album notes: Music: Giorgio Moroder, Klaus Doldinger.

Originally, this German–made fantasy film was entirely scored by Klaus Doldinger (*Das Boot*) and released in that country with only his music. However, when the film was acquired by Warner Brothers for the United States, the studio brought in music pop producer Giorgio Moroder to create a "hip" main title song, sung by pop artist Limahl. Moroder eventually went on further to write four additional synthesized underscore themes that are interpolated with Doldinger's orchestral work. Surprisingly, this mix holds up in part because Moroder doesn't ignore the ambience set by Doldinger. Both artists draw on the film's wonderful sense of childhood adventure and the things they fear. Moroder's new theme for the "Swamp of Sadness" isn't all that different from Doldinger's "Theme of Sadness," though the former draws on a less than original classical motif to accomplish his task. The only real distinction between each composer's style is the lack of acoustical instruments on Moroder's cues. Both have their music collected into two suites on the U.S. soundtrack album, though I still prefer listening to the German album with Doldinger's entire original score. It has a somewhat more mature quality that appeals to my aging sensibilities.

David Hirsch

The NeverEnding Story II: The Next Chapter

1990, Warner Bros., from the film *The NeverEnding Story II: The Next Chapter*, Neue Medien und Elektronikvertrieb, 1990 ♪♪♪♪

album notes: Music: Robert Folk; **Songs:** Giorgio Moroder; **Orchestra:** Members of the Symphony Orchestra of the Bavarian Broadcasting Corporation, Bavarian State Orchestra, Orchestra of the Bavarian State Opera, Grosses Rundfunkorchester Berlin; **Conductor:** Robert Folk.

Robert Folk has created a grand, sweeping orchestral and choral score for the second installment in this series that manages to match the tone set by Klaus Doldinger on the first film ("Searching for Fantasia"). He also manages to show a musical side he was rarely able to express during the years he scored comedy films like the *Police Academy* series. "Morning in Fantasia" is a particularly exciting cue with its intense brass orchestration, while "The Childlike Empress" shows Folk's tender side. As with the first film, the album also features songs by Georgio Moroder.

David Hirsch

The New Age

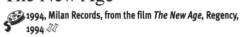1994, Milan Records, from the film *The New Age*, Regency, 1994 ♪♪

album notes: Music: Mark Mothersbaugh.

Set in Los Angeles, *The New Age* details a story that was a little bit uncomfortable for many audiences—the problems faced by a talent agent and an art designer who lose their high-paid jobs the same day and decide to open a trendy boutique, only to find themselves deeper in debt when it fails to attract the expected high-class clientele. With the exception of a couple of tracks (notably, Bobby McFerrin's "Common Threads" and Cacho Tirao's "Adios Nonino"), the CD also fails to make its mark. Mark Mothersbaugh's cues, however, are pleasantly attractive and should have been given more play.

Didier C. Deutsch

New Jersey Drive

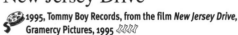1995, Tommy Boy Records, from the film *New Jersey Drive*, Gramercy Pictures, 1995 ♪♪♪

An album and an EP filled with funk–influenced hip–hop. Both East and West coast are represented here, with top names, like Biz Markie and Naughty By Nature, and cutting edgers such as Flip Squad Allstars, Flex, and Big Kap. Volume one, also available, includes producer Sean "Puffy" Combs's group Total, whose "Can't You See" samples James Brown's "The Payback" and features a guest appearance by the late Notorious B.I.G.

Gary Graff

The New Swiss Family Robinson

1998, JOS Records, from the film *The New Swiss Family Robinson*, Total, 1997 ♪♪♪♪♪

album notes: Music: John Scott; **Orchestra:** The Prague Radio Symphony Orchestra; **Conductor:** Allan Wilson.

Among afficionados, John Scott is known as a quiet man whose expressive scores have long been sought after for their broad musicality and attractive themes. Regrettably, his name means very little to the vast mass of filmgoers, perhaps because, unlike some of his peers, Scott is neither flashy nor a publicity seeker. For some time now he has taken upon himself to release his scores on his own label, JOS Records, and finding

them may prove a bit more arduous than a visit to the local record shop. But the search is well worth the effort.

This score was written for a new big-screen retelling of a classic tale: a shipwrecked family is forced to fend for itself in the hostile environment of a deserted island; its members eventually return to civilization after various hair-raising encounters with a wild girl and some pirates. In his first-hand account of the plot, Scott details the many incidents with freshness and humor, and provides a funny insight into the creation of his score. The music, bold and exciting, exhibits many heroic accents which serve the tale well and bring it vividly to the fore. Even without Scott's descriptions, the music throbs and explodes in bright images that capture the imagination and make for excellent listening. In other words, a great outdoors adventure score.

Didier C. Deutsch

New York, New York

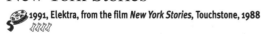1995, EMI America, from the film *New York, New York,* United Artists, 1985 ♪♪♪♪

album notes: New Songs: John Kander, Fred Ebb; **Score:** Ralph Burns; **Conductor:** Ralph Burns; **Featured Musicians:** Liza Minnelli, vocals; Snooky Young, trumpet; Conte Candoli, trumpet; Warren Luening, trumpet; Chauncey Welsch, trombone; Jim Cleveland, trombone; Jerome Richardson, saxophone; Bob Tricarico, saxophone; Abe Most, clarinet; Russ Freeman, piano; Jim Hughart, bass; Sol Gubin, drums; Bill Lavornia, drums; Georgie Auld, saxophone.

Liza Minnelli portrayed an attractive big band singer, and Robert De Niro the saxophonist with whom she falls in love in this gritty, big-screen musical set in the 1940s. When the relationship breaks up after the birth of their baby, she goes on to become a big movie star, while his reputation as an avant-garde musician singles him out for loftier heights, until they meet again, and pick things up pretty much where they had left off. One of the last popular musicals specifically written for the screen, *New York, New York* benefitted tremendously from the songs John Kander and Fred Ebb wrote for la Minnelli, whose intense, passionate rendition of the title tune has since become a signature theme. Rounding up the selections heard in this profuse collection of tunes are various standards, most of them performed by Minnelli in her inimitable style, with Georgie Auld blowing a mean sax for De Niro on a couple of tunes. They just don't write them like this anymore.

Didier C. Deutsch

New York Stories

1991, Elektra, from the film *New York Stories*, Touchstone, 1988 ♪♪♪♪

Here's a collection that reflects the diversity of New York life and is as eclectic as they come. The film, a series of short stories set in New York, was filmed by three of the 1980's most prominent directors, and reveals each one's favorite musical taste. Thus, it is hardly surprising to see Francis Ford Coppola relying on the amusing jinks of Kid Creole and the Coconuts; Woody Allen going for the sounds of the 1940s; and Martin Scorsese expressing a strong liking for a mixture of rock and jazz. As an album, the diversity in the styles presented is at times a bit baffling, but it certainly makes for a most enjoyable collection that goes a long way to please and entertain.

Didier C. Deutsch

New York Undercover

1995, MCA Records, from the television series *New York Undercover,* 1995 🐾🐾

The classic "(You Make Me Feel like a) Natural Woman," performed here by Mary J. Blige in a style that immediately evokes Aretha Franklin, is one of the ingratiating tracks collected in this compilation that purports to illustrate the television series that spawned it. Others include Gladys Knight's tear-jerking "Good Morning Heartache," Chante Moore's sultry "Inside My Love," Al B. Sure's easygoing "Erase the Dayz (Come Home)," Anthony Hamilton's soft "I Will Go," and Mavis Staples's scorching "I'll Take You There." The remainder, however, do not attain the same levels of enjoyment. The theme, written by Mtume, displays the right percolating vibes, but is much too short.

Didier C. Deutsch

The Newton Boys

1998, Sony Music, from the film *The Newton Boys,* 20th Century-Fox, 1998 🐾🐾🐾🐾

album notes: Music: Edward D. Barnes.

Director Richard Linklater loves Austin, Texas, and fortunately he also loves one of Austin's best bands—the Bad Livers, a genre-busting outfit that's comfortable playing straight bluegrass and urgent modern rock in the same set . . . and sometimes in the same song. Linklater recruited the group's Mark Rubin to serve as music director for *The Newton Boys* (the band's Danny Barnes wrote the score), and he filled it up with early 20th century hot jazz and string-band music—much of it performed by the Livers themselves and so authentic that only the crisp sonics tip off that these aren't actual recordings from the era. The group backs Patty Griffin on "Copenhagen," Abra Moore on "Milenberg Joys," Eric Hokkanen on "Lulu Lu," and Kris McKay on "After You're Gone"—all of which demonstrate an able grasp of music that's nearly 100 years old. The album is further enhanced by its bookends—a pair of Jelly Roll Morton tunes, "The Pearls" and "Wild Man Blues," performed by the Jim Cullum Jazz Band.

Gary Graff

Next Stop Wonderland

1998, Verve Records, from the film *Next Stop Wonderland,* Miramax, 1998 🐾🐾🐾🐾

album notes: Music: Claudio Ragazzi; Conductor: Claudio Ragazzi; Featured Musicians: Alon Yavnai, piano; Claudio Ragazzi, guitar; Wesley Wirth, bass; Steve Langone, drums; Billy Novick, clarinet; Pernell Satumino, percussion; Joel Perpignon, percussion; Arto Lindsay, vocals; Bebel Gilberto, vocals.

Any film that has the good sense of using the warm, sexy rhythms of Brazil in its soundtrack has to be a winner. *Next Stop Wonderland* might have fallen short of that ultimate goal, but it brings in a fetching, enjoyable story about two mismatched characters living in Boston, an attractive nurse whose spirits have been kind of low since her boyfriend dumped her, and a plumber with ambitions of becoming a marine biologist. While these two take an awful long time to meet, the Brazilian touch comes from another fellow, on a visit from Sao Paulo, who takes a strong liking in the desolated nurse, and introduces her to the music of his country. As a result, the soundtrack is a feast of bossa nova and samba tunes, some performed by well-known exponents of the genre, like Astrud Gilberto, Elis Regina, Antonio Carlos Jobim, and Bebel Gilberto and Vinicious Cantuaria, and others composed for the occasion by Claudio Ragazzi with Arto Lindsay. Providing a slightly different, albeit in-context note, jazz musicians Walter Wanderley and Coleman Hawkins gave a fresh spin to the music, with their treatment of "Baia" and "O Pato (The Duck)," respectively.

Didier C. Deutsch

Niagara, Niagara

1998, Shooting Gallery/V2 Records, from the film *Niagara, Niagara,* Shooting Gallery, 1998 🐾🐾🐾

A rather offbeat love story, *Niagara, Niagara* involves a shy man (Henry Thomas of *E.T.* fame) and a woman with Tourette's Syndrome (Robin Tunney), who meet while both are shoplifting at the same store, and run off together, the woman without the medication that controls her ticks. The song-oriented soundtrack contains mostly rootsy female artists like Lucinda Williams, Patty Griffin, and Lori Carson, and two score tracks composed by Michael Timmins of Cowboy Junkies fame. The score adds a nice touch to this song compilation.

Beth Krakower

Nick of Time

1998, Milan/BMG, from the film *Nick of Time,* Paramount, 1998 🐾

album notes: Music: Arthur Rubinstein; Conductor: Arthur Rubinstein.

Arthur Rubenstein created a very formulaic Hitchcockian-thriller score for this mediocre movie, in which Johnny Depp plays a young father who must kill a political candidate within 75 minutes if he wants to see again his kidnapped daughter alive again. The movie was filmed using the "actual time" technique so brilliantly employed by Hitchcock in his thriller *Rope*. There was nothing brilliant or thrilling in this one, not even the score.

Beth Krakower

Night and the City

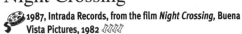 1992, Hollywood Records, from the film *Night and the City*, 20th Century Fox, 1992 ♫♫

album notes: Music: James Newton Howard.

At 33 minutes, this is a pretty chintzy outing, though a blast of '60s frat party smashes—the Capitols' "Cool Jerk," Smokey Robinson & the Miracles' "You Really Got a Hold on Me," Sam the Sham & the Pharaohs "Wooly Bully" and Jr. Walker & the All-Star's version of "Money (That's What I Want)"—is hard to beat. However, Bill Champlin warbles "Deep Water" to bring us back to reality.

Gary Graff

A Night at the Roxbury

1998, DreamWorks Records, from the film *A Night at the Roxbury*, Paramount, 1998 ♫♫

There's a real danger that this soundtrack from a film based on a one-joke *Saturday Night Live* skit could have been about one song—namely Haddaway's "What Is Love," the dance club smash that pulsates actors Will Ferrell and Chris Kattan through their wild 'n' crazy guys act. Fortunately, *Roxbury*'s soundtrack has a little more than that to offer, though not much. N-Trance's revision of Rod Stewart's "Do Ya Think I'm Sexy" breathes life into a tired old warhorse, Jocelyn Enriquez's "A Little Bit of Ecstasy" is an early harbinger of the Latin pop revolution. La Bouche's "Be My Lover" is representative club fare, but Cyndi Lauper's "Disco Inferno" never ignites, and the bpm action stays a bit too samey to give the rest of *Roxbury* much punch.

Gary Graff

Night Breed

1990, MCA Records, from the film *Night Breed,* 20th Century Fox, 1990 ♫♫♫

album notes: Music: Danny Elfman; **Conductor:** Shirley Walker; **Featured Vocalists:** Members of the L.A. Master Chorale.

One of the scores written during the time when Danny Elfman took on *Batman* and a number of other similarly themed pro-

jects (*Darkman, Dick Tracy,* et. al.), *Nightbreed* offers a traditionally dissonant, percussive score that is distinctly Elfman. The composer, working again with orchestrator Steve Bartek and conductor Shirley Walker, employs a large chorus to go along with a primal-sounding percussion section and symphony orchestra, and the results are in keeping with Elfman's eclectic, off-beat musical sensibilities, though, for some reason, this score holds up better as a cohesive soundtrack album than many of his other efforts from the same period. The music is frequently expansive in scope, with some soaring, lyrical passages offering hope to the proceedings—a contrast that is further illustrated by its surprisingly poignant final notes. If you don't own many Elfman scores and want a good representation of his early film music, *Nightbreed* is as solid and satisfying as you can get.

Andy Dursin

Night Crossing

1987, Intrada Records, from the film *Night Crossing,* Buena Vista Pictures, 1982 ♫♫♫♫

album notes: Music: Jerry Goldsmith; **Orchestra:** The National Philharmonic Orchestra; **Conductor:** Jerry Goldsmith.

Goldsmith wrote a thunderous score for this early Disney effort at live-action drama, about a family that escapes from behind the Iron Curtain in a balloon. The opening theme recalls *Capricorn One* with its pounding, jagged percussion lines and wailing brass motif to represent the threat of the Wall and its East German troops, while a soaring, lyrical melody underscores the bonding of the family and their attempts to escape, climaxing in an exultant, celebrational climactic cue. It's almost too large-scale an effort for this rather personal story, but it does make for a spectacular album with a heavy, almost gothic sound and a constant undercurrent of rumbling percussion.

Jeff Bond

Night Digger

1994, Label X, from the film *Night Digger,* 1971 ♫♫♫♫

album notes: Music: Bernard Herrmann; **Conductor:** Bernard Herrmann.

One of Bernard Herrmann's last scores is also one of his most tender and haunting. The 1971 film was directed by Alastair Reid and written for the screen by Roald Dahl, a curious psychological thriller about a handyman (who murders in his off-hours) who comes to stay with two country women. The score is largely for strings, with solo instruments of a viola d'amore and harmonica representing the two main characters (the handyman plays harmonica on-screen as well). Between Herrmann's usual, idiosyncratic mastery of unresolved sequences, here fragile and reflective a la the "Walking Distance" episode of *The Twilight Zone*, and the timbres of the solo instruments, it's stunningly evocative and nostalgic. Even the more frenetic passages lack the shock violence of *Psycho*, instead resonating with sadness and disquiet. The album is arranged into a seven–scene "Scenario Macabre for Orchestra."

Lukas Kendall

The Night Flier

1998, RCA, from the film *The Night Flier*, New Line Cinema, 1998 ✍✍✍✍

album notes: Music: Brian Keane; **Conductor:** Brian Keane.

This Stephen King story, a sleeper about a phantom pilot that slipped almost straight to TV benefitted from a strong horror score by Brian Keane. *The Night Flier* is full of sly references to classic Hammer horror scores in the string movements, balanced with imaginative use of synthesizer effects for spooky wordless voices, chimes, discordant hisses, and ghostly sighs. The phantom is absent for much of the score, but his presence is characterized by sudden bursts where atonal shards of sound break lengths of suspenseful underscoring. The recurring theme on piano appears in different keys, among distorted musique concrete, scraping of guitar strings, queasy squelches, and heart-stopping percussion which strikes when least expected, all serving to keep horror fans tightly wound on this richly detailed and edgy album.

David Poole

Night Games

See: Game of Death/Night Games

The Night of the Generals

1990, Intrada Records, from the film *The Night of the Generals*, Columbia Pictures, 1966 ✍✍✍✍✍

album notes: Music: Maurice Jarre; **Orchestra:** The New Philharmonia Orchestra; **Conductor:** Maurice Jarre.

In the 1960s, Maurice Jarre scored several films with a World War II theme, notably *Is Paris Burning?*, perhaps his greatest achievement in this vein, *The Damned, Behold a Pale Horse, The Train*, and this attractively designed score for a film directed by Anatole Litvak. Based on a best–selling novel by Hans Helmut Kirst, *The Night of the Generals* started as a standard murder mystery, involving the death of a prostitute, and led to an inquiry into the depraved mores of a trio of Nazi generals in occupied Warsaw. Characteristic of the style he used at the time, broadly florid and musically inventive, Jarre essentially devised two sets of cues. The first, a series of dark marches,

They Know the Score
John Williams

The music for [*Star Wars*] is very non-futuristic. The films themselves showed us characters we hadn't seen before and planets unimagined and so on, but the music was—this is actually George Lucas's conception and a very good one—emotionally familiar. It was not music that might describe terra incognita but the opposite of that, music that would put us in touch with very familiar and remembered emotions, which for me as a musician translated into the use of a 19th century operatic idiom, if you like, Wagner and this sort of thing. These sorts of influences would put us in touch with remembered theatrical experiences as well—all Western experiences to be sure. The music at least, I think, is firmly rooted in Western cultural sensibilities.

***Courtesy of* Film Score Monthly**

played by the brass and percussion instruments, depict the *sturm–und–drang* of the German army, in often savage and bitter tones that have nothing glorious in them. The second, a very attractive, recognizable "Love Theme," returns frequently throughout the recording to portray the moods and feelings of some of the actors in this drama of passion, though the lilt in it often belies the sadness that permeates it. The CD, marred by a significant amount of hiss on some of the tracks, includes an extended suite of the principal themes, making this release one of the most important in the Jarre canon.

Didier C. Deutsch

Night of the Running Man

1995, Super Tracks Music Group, from the film *Night of the Running Man*, Trimark Pictures, 1995 ✍✍✍

album notes: Music: Christopher Franke; **Orchestra:** The Berlin Symphonic Orchestra; **Conductor:** Alan Wagner.

Night of the Running Man is a well–written and performed film score by Christopher Franke. It plays at times very much like his work on the *Babylon 5* TV series and could almost be interchangeable were it not for the occasional use of contemporary guitar and percussion. Franke once more combines his own synth work with the Berlin Symphonic Film Orchestra, though the acoustical instruments are heavily overshadowed by the electronics. The finale cue, "Natasha's Theme," is a lovely piano solo.

David Hirsch

The Night Visitor

See: Midas Run/The Night Visitor

The Nightmare Before Christmas

🎬 **1993, Walt Disney Records, from the film *The Nightmare Before Christmas*, Touchstone Pictures, 1993** 🎵🎵🎵♪

album notes: Music: Danny Elfman; **Lyrics:** Danny Elfman; **Conductor:** Chris Boardman, J.A.C. Redford.

Though Danny Elfman is known mostly for his instrumental scores, he deftly brought vocals into the mix for Tim Burton's bent musical about Halloween hijacking Christmas. Elfman, the former lead singer of Oingo Boingo, does some of the singing himself but also gets wonderful performances from Paul Reubens (aka Pee Wee Herman) and Catherine O'Hara. The ensemble pieces, such as "Town Hall Meeting," are a hoot and the instrumental selections, orchestrated by Boingo guitarist Steve Bartek, retain Elfman's playfully skewed approach to mood pieces.

Gary Graff

A Nightmare on Elm Street 3

🎬 **1987, Varèse Sarabande, from the film *A Nightmare on Elm Street 3: Dream Warriors*, New Line Cinema, 1987** 🎵🎵
album notes: Music: Angelo Badalamenti.

Taking on the *Nightmare on Elm Street* franchise, Angelo Badalamenti served up a score that is appropriately ominous and scary, for this third foray into the unspeakable activities of Freddy Krueger. Starring Heather Langenkamp, reprising the role she created in the first film in the series, *Dream Warriors* (as this third installment is subtitled) exhibits its usual share of scary moments and hoots (depending on one's state of mind), with Badalamenti dutifully adding his own musical comments to the screen proceedings. As is often the case in films such as this, the score is so intimately integrated in and reflective of the action that it proves largely uninteresting once it is removed from the visuals. Despite Badalamenti's valiant efforts, his cues, with a few rare exceptions, mean very little when programmed for one's listening enjoyment.

Didier C. Deutsch

The Nights of Cabiria

See: La strada/Le notti di Cabiria

Nine

 1982, Columbia Records, from the Broadway production *Nine*, 1982 🎵🎵🎵🎵

album notes: Music: Maury Yeston; **Lyrics:** Maury Yeston; **Musical Direction:** Wally Harper; **Cast:** Raul Julia, Karen Akers, Anita Morris, Taina Elg, Liliane Montevecchi, Kim Criswell, Stephanie Cotsirilos.

A brilliant musical based on Federico Fellini's *8 ½*, about a celebrated Italian filmmaker with a creative block, resting at a Venetian spa where he is haunted by memories from his youth, his strict Catholic upbringing, and the many women in his life, *Nine* is a dazzling display of music and songs by newcomer Maury Yeston. One of the last great American musicals (before the proliferation of British works that crowded Broadway in the 1990s), *Nine* is an extraordinary work as vibrant as it is original, as exciting as it is imaginative.

In the course of the evening, Guido Contini, the film director, struggles with his memories, while trying to find a way out of the creative impasse that prevents him from starting his new film. As the action progresses, in reality as much as in his mind, he has to deal with a disintegrating marriage, former lovers, and current protégés, and his producer, in a show that features only one adult man in an otherwise all-female cast. There are many superb touches in the score which ranges from electrifying production numbers ("Folies Bergéres," "The Grand Canal"), to highly charged emotional cries of despair ("Be on Your Own"), to sexy siren songs ("A Call from the Vatican"), to evocations of a past that had a strong influence on the present ("The Bells of St. Sebastian"). The original cast album, while unfortunately incomplete (longer excerpts from "Folies Bergére" and "Grand Canal" can be found in the cassette release), is a sensational reflection of this outstanding musical.

Dider Deutsch

Nine Months

🎬 **1995, Milan Records, from the film *Nine Months*, 20th Century Fox, 1995** 🎵🎵🎵
album notes: Music: Hans Zimmer, Nick Glennie-Smith; **Conductor:** Nick Glennie-Smith; **Featured Performer:** Jim Kanter, clarinet.

With his boyish grin and cute looks, Hugh Grant seems the perfect match for a frantic father-to-be in this mildly amusing comedy in which he portrays a child psychiatrist and confirmed bachelor whose girlfriend becomes pregnant. Starting off with a pretty little tune well in keeping with the light moods in the film ("Baby, Baby"), Hans Zimmer built an attractive score that transcends its modest origins and actually makes a very positive impression. The cues stay firmly on the romantic side of this comedy, with melodies that catch one's attention and keep it. The tired–sounding pop vocals at the beginning of the album seem to have been selected for something altogether different and detract from more than they complement Zimmer's score. Fortunately, they can be programmed out.

Didier C. Deutsch

1941

1998, Varèse Sarabande, from the film *1941*, Columbia Pictures, 1979 ♪♪♪♪

album notes: Music: John Williams; **Conductor:** John Williams.

John Williams's rollicking score echoes the frequently amusing antics of a group of World War II misfits, led by John Belushi, attempting to ward off a suspected invasion of California by the Japanese in this unlikely story concocted by Steven Spielberg. With much of the broad action involving an odd assortment of manic soldiers, overpatriotic homeowners, nostalgic officers, and some Hollywood characters with more than screen glory on their mind, Williams had a wide spectrum to explore, and he did so in a spirited fashion, in a grandiloquent score spearheaded by a "March" worth alone the price of admission. Two major cues, "The Invasion" and "The Battle of Hollywood," expand on the main theme, and enable the composer to write some ear–catching motifs that make for great listening. Also adding an exhilarating uplift is "Swing, Swing, Swing," that captures the period of the big band era, while providing a cue that's wonderfully foot–stomping. A great score, unfortunately truncated for this release which replicates the original LP but fails to include a great deal more composed for the occasion.

Didier C. Deutsch

Nixon

1995, Hollywood Records, from the film *Nixon*, Hollywood Pictures, 1995 ♪♪♪♪

album notes: Music: John Williams; **Conductor:** John Williams; **Featured Musician:** Tim Morisson, first trumpet, The Boston Pops Orchestra.

This account of the life and times of Richard M. Nixon, strikingly portrayed by Anthony Hopkins, and the scandal that eventually brought him down benefited tremendously from the serious score created for the occasion by John Williams. Having to deal here with a much more serious subject than all the grander–than–life epic sagas that are his mainstay, Williams thoughtfully concentrated on writing themes that have great dramatic impact, reasonably commenting on the story itself and its many political and personal implications. This does not mean that his score is dry or uninspiring, far from it—in fact, it

is a solidly written piece of instrumental music, profoundly affecting and frequently compelling. There is a certain grandeur to the themes developed, in which the main characteristics are the absence of real urgency and pervading dark tones, even in the most strident moments. This, incidentally, was touted at the time of its release as the first interactive CD soundtrack, though the results leave a lot to be desired. Williams's score, however, strikes a totally positive note.

Didier C. Deutsch

No Escape

1994, Varèse Sarabande, from the film *No Escape*, 1994 ♪♪♪♪

album notes: Music: Graeme Revell; **Conductor:** Tim Simonec; **Featured Musician:** Philip Tallman, 12–string guitar.

Lavishly orchestrated Graeme Revell score makes dazzling use of the ambient sounds and ethnic music he recorded during several expeditions to out–of–the–way places like Papua, New Guinea. In the film, Ray Liotta is sent to prison on an island where criminals have divided into two groups. The civilized ones live inside a protected camp, safe from the homicidal "Outsiders" who live in the forest. Revell uses his odd sampled sounds to make these "Outsiders" more barbaric, like unthinking animals ("Robbins Captured By the Outsiders"). Other highlights include Philip Tallman's terrific blue grass 12–string guitar solo on "I Love Those Boots."

David Hirsch

No Man's Land

1987, Varèse Sarabande, from the film *No Man's Land*, Orion Pictures, 1987 ♪
album notes: Music: Basil Poledouris.

Basil Poledouris's loud and uninspired score for this modern thriller about an undercover cop (Charlie Sheen), the thief he is trying to bring in, and his involvement with the thief's sister, is not very worthy of the man who scored the *RoboCop* films or, better yet, the exhilarating *Conan* epics. To be totally effective, synthesizer music must exhibit some signs of intelligent life, but when it means so very little as it does here ("First Score," "Payoff"), one can only dismiss it and move on to the next CD.

Didier C. Deutsch

No, No, Nanette

1999, Sony Classical/Legacy Records, from the Broadway musical *No, No, Nanette*, 1971 ♪♪♪♪
album notes: Music: Vincent Youmans; **Lyrics:** Otto Harbach, Irving Caesar; **Conductor:** Buster Davis; **Cast:** Ruby Keeler (Sue), Jack Gilford

(Jimmy), Bobby Van (Billy), Helen Gallagher (Lucille), Susan Watson (Nanette), Patsy Kelly (Pauline), Roger Rathburn (Tom).

One of the classic musical comedies of the 1920s, *No, No, Nanette* burst out again on the Broadway scene 46 years after its creation. It is as fresh and exciting as ever, thanks largely to the fact that it was staged by the genial Busby Berkeley, one of the movies' most inventive directors. Starring Berkeley's favorite dancer, Ruby Keeler—as sprightly at 60 something as she was when she pranced on the screen in *42nd Street*—and a cast of seasoned theater and film performers (Bobby Van, Helen Gallagher, Jack Gilford, Susan Watson, Patsy Kelly), the Vincent Youmans original never looked so stunning, so enjoyable, so modern.

In its original presentation, in 1925, *No, No, Nanette* was an enormous success, both here and abroad, its popularity fueled by its two biggest hit songs, "Tea for Two" and "I Want to Be Happy." Undoubtedly, it was the most popular musical of the 1920s, a frothy entertainment with great songs and skimpy story line, the kind so amusingly spoofed by Sandy Wilson in *The Boy Friend*. It spawned two movie versions, in 1930 and 1940, and an offshoot, *Tea for Two*, starring Doris Day and Gordon MacRae in 1950.

Its return to Broadway in 1971, its first since 1925, was preceded by the kind of hoopla that usually accompanies the newest productions, not a revival. But the names of Berkeley and Keeler were the catch, and riding on a sudden wave of nostalgia, it opened to great fanfare and rhapsodic reviews on January 19, 1971.

Based on an obscure 1919 play, the book deals with Bible publisher and philanderer Jimmy Smith, who has been entertaining three attractive ladies in three different cities; his long-suffering wife, Sue; their schoolgirl ward, Nanette; their friends Lucille and Billy; and their overworked housemaid, Pauline. When they all converge in Atlantic City for a weekend of rest at the Smith household, utter comic chaos ensues.

Inconsequential as the story might have been, what ignites the musical is its score by Vincent Youmans, Otto Harbach, and Irving Caesar, propelled by Busby Berkeley's show-stopping dance routines (the sight of Ruby Keeler, merrily tapping her time away surrounded by an impressive lineup of handsome chorus boys, alone was worth the cost of a dozen tickets). It proved a winning combination, as *No, No, Nanette* collected four Tony Awards, and enjoyed a run of 861 performances, nearly three times longer than its original run of 321 performances in 1925.

This reissue is a vast improvement over the previous CD incarnation, with spectacular sonics; proper sequencing of the songs; the addition of one number, "Peach on the Beach,"

which had been dropped from the original recording; and a bonus track, "Only a Moment Ago," which gives us an opportunity to hear Keeler's sweet singing (it was included when the show opened in Boston, but was deleted by the time it opened in New York).

Didier C. Deutsch

No Strings

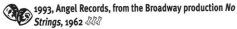 1993, Angel Records, from the Broadway production *No Strings*, 1962 ♫♫♫

album notes: Music: Richard Rodgers; **Lyrics:** Richard Rodgers; **Musical Direction:** Peter Matz; **Cast:** Diahann Carroll, Richard Kiley, Mitchell Gregg, Noelle Adam, Polly Rowles, Don Chastain, Bernice Massi, Alvin Epstein.

For his first effort sans Oscar Hammerstein II (who had died shortly after the opening of *The Sound of Music* two years earlier), Richard Rodgers decided to write both the music and lyrics for *No Strings*. Perhaps not so surprisingly, his words faintly echoed those of his former collaborator, revealing a sensitive side to Rodgers's creativity few had suspected he had.

The show itself, with a book by Samuel Taylor, deals with a topic that was still somewhat taboo at the time—an interracial love affair. Perhaps to deflate any possible criticism, it happens in France, where such things were apparently tolerated, and it involves two sophisticated American expatriates, she a glamorous fashion model (played by Diahann Carroll), he a writer (portrayed by Richard Kiley); also, though it is not stated specifically as such, it does not have a happy ending. While not a great success along the lines of *South Pacific* or *The Sound of Music, No Strings* enjoyed a long run on Broadway thanks in part to the three Tonys it earned for Diahann Carroll, Richard Rodgers, and director/choreographer Joe Layton.

Didier C. Deutsch

No Sun in Venice

1975, Atlantic Records, from the film *No Sun in Venice*, Kingsley International Pictures, 1957 ♫♫♫♫

album notes: Music: John Lewis; **Featured Musicians:** The Modern Jazz Quartet—John Lewis, piano; Milt Jackson, vibraharp; Percy Heath, bass; Connie Kay, drums.

The elegant, soigné music of John Lewis, as performed by the Modern Jazz Quartet, is a key ingredient in Vadim's flavorful 1957 film set in present-day Venice, about three young people and an older Baron whose influence dominates their lives during the short period they spend in the fabled Italian city. The cool, classicist lines in Lewis's compositions, set off by the striking contribution of vibraharpist Milt Jackson, supported by Connie Kay on drums and Percy Heath on bass, have long been admired by jazz fans everywhere, and this score, a rare foray by the MJQ in film music, seems the perfect complement to the story. Since the creation of the score, one theme, "The Golden Striker," has become a standard in the MJQ canon, and two others, "One Never Knows" (the actual translation of the French film title *Sait–On Jamais)* and "Three Windows" are regular staples in the group's repertoire. A classy effort, if there ever was one.

see also: Odds Against Tomorrow

Didier C. Deutsch

No Way Out

1987, Varèse Sarabande, from the film *No Way Out,* Orion Pictures, 1987 ♪♪♪

album notes: Music: Maurice Jarre; **Featured Musicians:** Michael Boddicker, Ian Underwood, Ralph Grierson, keyboards; Nyle Steiner, Judd Miller, E.V.I., Michael Fisher, percussion.

A pertinent modern–day remake of the classic 1948 film noir *The Big Clock, No Way Out* stars Kevin Costner as a liaison officer at the Pentagon, reporting to Gene Hackman, who witnesses his boss in the act of killing a girl with whom he had a love affair. Reflecting the taut atmosphere of this crime drama, Maurice Jarre wrote a synthesized score that's intelligently crafted and listenable, even as it effectively supports the screen action. Relying on the solid instrumental techniques of a trio of seasoned musicians (Michael Boddicker, Ian Underwood, and Ralph Grierson, with whom Jarre has also worked on other scores), and the percussion effects of Michael Fisher, Jarre has devised cues that create an atmosphere of relentless tension, presented here in six long selections that support and develop the many twists in the film (in which Costner is instructed by Hackman, who knows there was a witness to his crime, to find out the identity of that witness). Even the re-programming does not make for an always compelling listening experience, but individual reactions to this type of music can vary wildly, and Jarre, at least, is a composer who remains always more interesting than most.

Didier C. Deutsch

Noah's Ark

1999, Varèse-Sarabande, from the television special *Noah's Ark,* Hallmark, 1999 ♪♪♪♪

album notes: Music: Paul Grabowsky; **Conductor:** Paul Grabowsky.

This big instrumental score, epic and romantic by turns, is actually quite enjoyable. Written for the television mini-series, it gives a fair idea of the pageantry involved in this retelling of Noah's covenant with God, his building of an ark large enough to accommodate all the animals of the creation as well as his own family (despite the derisive remarks of his neighbors, thinking that the old man is a loony), the gigantic flood reflec-

tive of God's wrath, and the final landing on Mount Ararat. The teleplay took some liberties with the original Biblical account, and for the sake of drama collapsed together the story of Noah and that of Loth, whose wife was changed into a pillar of salt when she turned back to look at the destruction of Sodom and Gomorrah. Also taking liberties with the Bible, the characters portrayed here seemed a bit too modern to conform with the idea one might have of ancient settlers, poor and uneducated, even if they conversed with the Almighty on better days.

Paul Grabowsky illustrated the tale musically with a large symphony orchestra and a variety of Eastern-sounding instruments aimed at giving his music an appropriate ethnic coloring and substance. The cues are quite enjoyable, with pretty melodies that evolve in a fairly conventional manner and flatter the listener, compelling him to return to this soundtrack more than once. "Pirate Attack," "The Flood," and "Fire on Deck/A Whirlpool" have all the orchestral grandeur needed for this type of score; others, like "An Idyll/The Tale of the Piper," "Noah Dances to Save the World," and "Namah's Theme" are properly jaunty and elegiac. All together, the cues make up for a highly ingratiating soundtrack album.

This release, however, prompts two questions: the first concerns its sequencing, with the cues assembled in a way that presumably makes up for better listening, though they don't fit chronologically, with "The Flood," for instance, occurring way before "Building the Ark," leaving the curious listener to ponder how Noah might have been able to obey God's instructions, if the Earth was already submerged under hundreds of feet of water. The other curiosity here actually refers indirectly to the question Alfred Hitchcock asked Hugo Friedhofer during the filming of *Lifeboat:* With God's wrath aimed at eliminating the entire human race, save for Noah and his family, where did all that music come from?

Didier C. Deutsch

Noble House

1988, Varèse Sarabande, from the film *Noble House,* De Laurentiis Entertainment Group, 1988 ♪♪♪♪

album notes: Music: Paul Chihara; **Orchestra:** The London Symphony Orchestra; **Conductor:** Paul Chihara; **Featured Musician:** Ray Warleigh, saxophone.

Appropriately epic and grandiose, the "Main Title" seems to signal the start of what may be an important score. But even though Paul Chihara does not always sustain the character he so effectively projected in this opening cue, much of his music is eminently entertaining and atmospheric. The broad romantic themes are developed by the strings in a style that recalls Victor Young or Percy Faith, occasionally enshrining the bluesy playing of a lone saxophone, or contrasting selections that give

a prominent role to synthesizers. The story itself, based on the novel by James Clavell and set in Southeast Asia, might have suggested some cues with a more ethnic approach, but the tone here is squarely on sweeping conventional tunes that are attractively shaped and played.

Didier C. Deutsch

Nobody's Fool

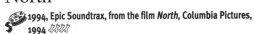 1994, Milan Records, from the film *Nobody's Fool,* Paramount Pictures, 1994 ♫♫♫♫

album notes: Music: Howard Shore; **Orchestra:** The London Philharmonic Orchestra, The London Metropolitan Orchestra, **Conductor:** Howard Shore.

A sensitive portrayal by Paul Newman, as a man alone approaching the twilight of his years, sets the tone for this bittersweet on-the-edge screen story, that resulted in an effectively low-key and lovely score from Howard Shore. With a keen ear for melodic material that makes a musical statement while reflecting the moods of the film itself, Shore built a series of strikingly beautiful cues, with various solo instruments—a harp, a clarinet, a flute—riding over gorgeous, long orchestral lines to paint a canvas that's very attractive and unusually pleasant to the ear.

Didier C. Deutsch

Norma Jean and Marilyn

1996, Intrada Records, from the film *Norma Jean and Marilyn,* HBO Pictures, 1996 ♫♫♫♫

album notes: Music: Christopher Young; **Conductor:** Pete Anthony.

The idea of having two different actresses portray Norman Jean Baker and Marilyn Monroe, one the obverse image of the other, is only one of several interesting things about this film Christopher Young tried to express in his effusive score. The challenges were many. Behind the glamour in the life of Marilyn is her darker private side and the demons that haunted her, two opposite aspects of her personality which the composer translated into a single motif with a simultaneously ascending and descending figure, played by the piano, harp, and vibes. In addition, the musical moods needed to conform with a 1950s reality, an evocation Young captured in a theme for soprano sax and trumpet over string harmonies. It all adds up to a very compelling score, warm and nostalgic, melodic with an occasional sharp edge to it, and above all profoundly attractive.

Didier C. Deutsch

North

1994, Epic Soundtrax, from the film *North,* Columbia Pictures, 1994 ♫♫♫♫

album notes: Music: Marc Shaiman; **Conductor:** Artie Kane.

The whimsical tale of an 11-year-old whose search for the ideal parents has international repercussions, this pleasantly diverting comedy directed by Rob Reiner translated itself into an eclectic soundtrack album in which Marc Shaiman's music looks into different cultures and ethnic forms of expression to emphasize some of the broader aspects of the story. Freely borrowing themes from various well-known sources, like *Dallas, Bonanza,* and *Father Knows Best* or familiar standards, like "Winter Wonderland" and "Amazing Grace," the cues are pleasant without being maudlin, and reflect in a positive way the film's light and entertaining moods.

Didier C. Deutsch

North and South

See: The Right Stuff/North and South

North By Northwest

1996, Rhino Records, from the film *North By Northwest,* MGM, 1959 ♫♫♫♫

album notes: Music: Bernard Herrmann; **Orchestra:** The MGM Studio Orchestra; **Conductor:** Bernard Herrmann.

Rhino's expanded edition of Bernard Herrmann's score for Alfred Hitchcock's *North By Northwest* (among the composers most intriguing and romantic for a Hitchcock film) is a shining example of everything a well-restored CD soundtrack should be. It's all here, including original music, expanded cues, outtakes, detailed and informative liner notes. Having the ability to listen to this music as Herrmann originally scored it, for the uncut, unedited film, is an absolute thrill, and a glimpse into history itself.

Although the film itself was released with a monophonic soundtrack, the original scoring sessions were recorded in stereo, and are presented as such here. While the music tracks were left virtually untouched in storage since 1959, some deterioration of the original tapes has occurred and the listener may note some minor flaws during the program. Overall, however, the sonics are excellent. A pared down "Suite for North By Northwest" (18 minutes) is also available on a Milan CD, *Alfred Hitchcock Film Music,* which features Herrmann conducting the National Philharmonic Orchestra. While excellent as a "taste," the complete soundtrack is preferable by far. A London CD, *Psycho: Great Hitchcock Movie Thrillers* contains only a three-minute cue from the score, and hardly bears mention.

Charles L. Granata

1980, Varèse Sarabande, from the film *North By Northwest,* MGM, 1959 ♫♫♫♫

album notes: Music: Bernard Herrmann; **Orchestra:** The London Studio Orchestra; **Conductor:** Laurie Johnson.

Cary Grant in North by Northwest. **(The Kobal Collection)**

This re-recording, conducted by Laurie Johnson, for many years the only one available of Herrmann's score, features better sonics and some cues that apparently didn't make it on the original. However, it also has much less music, and altogether can only be considered as a complement to the Rhino definitive album.

Didier C. Deutsch

Northern Exposure /More Music from Northern Exposure

📺 **Northern Exposure; 1992, MCA Records; from the television series** *Northern Exposure,* **1990–92** 🎵🎵🎵

📺 **More Music from Northern Exposure; 1994, MCA Records, from the television series** *Northern Exposure,* **1990–94** 🎵🎵🎵🎵

album notes: Music: David Schwartz; **Featured Musicians:** David Schwartz, keyboards, bass; Jim Keltner, Alex Acuna, drums; Abe Most, clarinet; Brian Mann, accordion; Andy Narell, steel drums; Luis Conte, Jim McGrath, Alex Acuna, percussion; Tollak Ollestad, chromatic harmonica; Bill Elliott, vibes, piano; Paul Viapiano, banjo, mandolin; Phil Ayling, wood flute.

This eclectic mix of musical styles, ranging from down home blues to African rhythms to Frederica Von Stade singing opera, is very appropriate to the series's closet intellectual nature. The album is assembled as if it represented a day in the programmed life of the local radio station, K–BEAR. An expanded version of David Schwartz's droll main title (using Jamaican kettle drums for a show set in Alaska!) starts off the listener's journey, which then migrates from familiar artists such as Booker T. & The MG's ("Hip Hug–Her"), Etta James ("At Last"), and Nat "King" Cole ("When I Grow Too Old to Dream") to the more bizarre works by the likes of Magazine 60 ("Don Quichotte"). Six minutes of underscore is included and a second volume followed. It is an acquired taste that not all will find interesting after the first experience.

The soundtrack for "Northern Exposure" has rightfully been described in GQ as "the weirdest—and the best—music on prime time," an assessment that needs no explanation. David Schwartz's instrumental cues have a flavor all their own, which is distinguished and quite enjoyable. Bringing a totally different flavor to the two CDs are performances by a wide array of

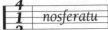

frontline performers like Booker T. & The MG's, Etta James, Nat "King" Cole, Miriam Makeba, and (gasp!) Frederica von Stade, in the first volume; and Johnny Nash, Ruth Brown, Brian Eno and John Cale, and Les Paul and Mary Ford, in the second. How much more eclectic than that can you get? Taken together, on their individual merits, both CDs are quite engaging.

David Hirsch and Didier C. Deutsch

Nosferatu

1997, Silva Screen, from the film *Nosferatu*, Frana, 1922 🎞🎞🎞🎞

album notes: Music: James Bernard; **Orchestra:** The City of Prague Philharmonic; **Conductor:** Nic Raine.

England's Channel 4 TV commissioned James Bernard to compose a new score to the classic 1922 silent film, directed by F.W. Murnau. Bernard was a logical choice: he had previously scored twenty of the Hammer horror movies, including *Dracula* (with Christopher Lee in the title role), *The Hound of the Baskervilles,* and *Damned,* and he has the feel for this kind of music, without the cheesiness often associated with the horror film genre. In his score, he captures the underlying battle between good and evil that occurs in the movie, representing the vampiric Orlok with a brass heavy theme, and depicting the heroine Ellen with strings that play a romantic, yet sad theme. The City of Prague Orchestra, conducted by Nic Raine, performs the music with great vitality. Restoring this classic silent and showing it on television, outfitted with a new soundtrack, helped bring the film to a new generation of spectators who would not have known about it otherwise.

Beth Krakower

Nostradamus

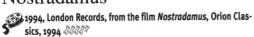1994, London Records, from the film *Nostradamus*, Orion Classics, 1994 🎞🎞🎞½

album notes: Music: Barrington Pheloung; **Orchestra:** The London Metropolitan Orchestra; **Conductor:** Barrington Pheloung; **Featured Musician:** Tom Finucane, lute; **Featured Vocalists:** Sarah Eaton, soprano; Andrew Gant, tenor; Katherine Willis, soprano; Edward Caswell, bass; Guy Protheroe, tenor; **Choirs:** The New London Consort, Philip Pickett, director; The English Chamber Choir, Guy Protheroe, director; The Choir Of Selwyn College, Cambridge, Andrew Gant, director.

The mysterious personality of Nostradamus, the Renaissance philosopher and scientist (1503–1566) whose deliberately nonconformist attitude irritated the religious and medical authorities of his time and whose prophecies have haunted mankind for their alleged accuracy and relevance to modern history, may have seemed a fascinating yet unusual subject for a screen epic. But the broader canvas of 16th–century life in Europe, with its ills, medical as well as political and religious (the devastating plagues, the inquisition), provides the solid background against which the known facts in his life found an illustration. Holding it all together is Barrington Phenoung's diligently scholarly score, extensively quoting from Josquin des Prez, in which musical instruments from the period conferred the proper tone and colors, and effectively blended with modern orchestral textures. This soundtrack album manages to evoke the film and its central character, and makes for a rather unusual but ultimately eloquent and satisfying listening experience.

Didier C. Deutsch

Not Since Casanova

See: Eye of the Panther/Not Since Casanova

Not Without My Daughter

1991, Intrada Records, from the film *Not Without My Daughter,* MGM/UA, 1991🎞🎞

album notes: Music: Jerry Goldsmith; **Orchestra:** The National Philharmonic Orchestra; **Conductor:** Jerry Goldsmith.

For this intimate and rather jingoistic study of an American woman's escape from an abusive marriage in Iran, Jerry Goldsmith wrote a surprisingly low–key score. Like the film, the score somewhat predictably and manipulatively balances a tender Americana theme of strings and solo piano against increasingly oppressive and violent Middle Eastern effects. Its highlight is a lengthy sequence illustrating the woman's escape through desert territory at night.

Atmospheric, blending both electronic and acoustic textures in a minimalistic technique, the cue works as an update of Goldsmith's experimental work on *Planet of the Apes,* but it belongs in a better score and film. Even Goldsmith has admitted this score didn't warrant an album release.

Jeff Bond

Nothing But Trouble

1991, Warner Bros. Records, from the film *Nothing But Trouble,* Warner Bros., 1990 **woof!**

album notes: Music: Michael Kamen; **Conductor:** Michael Kamen.

The music in this film may have been attributed to Michael Kamen, but like the comedy tag affixed to this sordidly mindless effort, it proves a misnomer, at least in this soundtrack album where the composer is represented by one selection, "Valkenvania Suite." The bulk of the album, as is so often the case, consists of pop selections that can be found in various other compilations and that have been hastily put together here, simply because brief snippets of these songs could be heard behind the screen action. If that's what you're after, by all means go and buy this album. Otherwise, forget about it.

Didier C. Deutsch

Novecento

1995, SLC/Japan, from the film *Novecento (1900)*, 20th Century Fox, 1976 ♪♪♪♪♪

album notes: Music: Ennio Morricone; Conductor: Ennio Morricone.

A sweeping epic directed by Bernardo Bertolucci, *1900* surveyed the profound social changes in Italy since the end of World War I from the viewpoint of two families, one land-owning and the other peasant. Starring Burt Lancaster, Robert De Niro, Gerard Depardieu, Donald Sutherland, Alida Valli, Dominique Sanda, and Sterling Hayden, it was powerful in its depiction of the disintegration of the social order caused by the onslaught of socialism and the deep effects it had on Italian society as a whole. Morricone's score paralleled Bertolucci's vision by giving a musical voice to the most striking moments in the long narrative. Like the film, which was cut down from its original six hours, the score as presented in this recording has been tremendously reduced in size, leaving off many significant and important cues. Nonetheless, it remains a potent and significant effort. This recording may be difficult to find. Check with a used CD store, mail-order company, or a dealer specializing in rare, out-of-print, or import recordings.

Didier C. Deutsch

Now and Then

1995, Columbia Records, from the film *Now and Then*, New Line Cinema, 1995 ♪♪♪

1995, Varèse Sarabande, from the film *Now and Then*, New Line Cinema, 1995 ♪♪♪♪

album notes: Music: Cliff Eidelman; Conductor: Cliff Eidelman.

The affecting story of four 12–year–olds, their joys, their disappointments, and the adventures they shared over a summer in 1970, *Now and Then* exudes warmth and pathos, and most of all paints the image of a friendship that transcends everyday problems to give its four main characters the memories they'd recall with fondness in later years.

Anchoring the film in its specific time period, several '70s pop tunes by the Monkees, Diana Ross and the Supremes, Jackson Five, and other performers provide the appropriate musical background. The first album brings these songs together in a compilation that seems better than most, even if the same selections can be found elsewhere.

The second album focuses on the fine instrumental themes developed by Cliff Eidelman that seem omnipresent, yet subtly understated. Conjuring up moods that are bathed in rose–tinted nostalgia similar to those in the film narrative, Eidelman's score comes to the forefront with great sensitivity and charm in this wonderful album. Some selections ("Remem-

brance," "It's a Girl," "Best Friends for Life") particularly tug at the right heartstrings, but the whole effort is quite memorable and enjoyable.

Didier C. Deutsch

Nuda proprieta

1999, CAM Records/Italy, from the TV film *Nuda proprieta*, 1999 ♪♪♪

album notes: Music: Manuel de Sica.

Essentially a series of variations on half a dozen themes, this enjoyable soundtrack album spotlights Manuel de Sica, a composer who is heard of too infrequently, but whose uncanny musical disposition makes him one of the most interesting exponents of film music in Italy these days. An amiable, uncomplicated situation comedy, *Nuda proprieta* involved a young newlywed couple, Riccardo and Nicole, and an older couple, Domenico and Costanza, from whom they rent a house in Rome, thinking they will have complete use of the premises, only to discover that they are supposed to share them with the owners. The variations developed by De Sica around the basic themes he wrote evidence a desire to remain innovative, while trying not to tread on the same territories more than once. At times bouncy, at times romantic, they create a texture that is at once original and eventually quite familiar. The score is always gratifyingly enjoyable. This title may be out of print or just plain hard to find. Mail-order companies, used CD shops, or dealers of rare or import recordings will be your best bet.

Didier C. Deutsch

The Nun's Story

1991, Stanyan Records, from the film *The Nun's Story*, Warner Bros., 1959 ♪♪♪♪

album notes: Music: Franz Waxman; Conductor: Franz Waxman.

In one of her finest portrayals, Audrey Hepburn gave a luminous performance in this unconventional story, based on the book by Kathryn C. Hulme, of a young Belgian woman who decides to abandon the comforts and pleasures of her privileged world for a life of austerity and contemplation as a nun, only to discover that life in a convent is no less challenging and confusing. For composer Franz Waxman, the story meant dealing with various sets of musical themes, from ecclesiastical ones to reflect the apparent calm and serenity of the religious life, to Congolese rhythms evocative of the African setting of some of the scenes, to 12–tone composition to illustrate a scene that takes place in an insane asylum. Superbly evocative and compelling, the score earned the composer an Oscar nomination, though he lost to Miklos Rozsa's *Ben-Hur*. This first reissue on CD returns to the catalogue an album that was for many years a

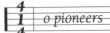

prized collectors' item, with selections that were previously un-available. The transfer from the three–channel 35mm optical film reveals some dryness, a significant amount of hiss, and some distortion that could have been easily corrected, despite a disclaimer to the contrary.

Didier C. Deutsch

O

O Pioneers!

 1991, Intrada Records, from the Hallmark Hall of Fame presentation *O Pioneers!* Lorimar Television, 1991 🎵🎵🎵🎵

album notes: Music: Bruce Broughton; **Conductor:** Bruce Broughton.

In one of his early efforts, composer Bruce Broughton wrote a distinctive Americana–styled score for this Hallmark Hall of Fame show, a faithful adaptation of the Willa Cather novel, starring Jessica Lange as Alexandra. The score is anchored by three basic motifs: One for the main character and her passion for the land; the second, romantically delineated, for Carl and the relationship that exists between him and Alexandra; and the third, light and jaunty, for the Bohemian girl Marie, whose illicit love affair with Alexandra's brother Emil is doomed from the start. A connective theme links these motifs together. Richly evocative and strikingly beautiful, the score is greatly appealling and an instant classic.

Didier C. Deutsch

The Object of My Affection

 1998, Pangaea Records, from the film, *The Object of My Affection*, 20th Century-Fox, 1998 🎵🎵🎵

album notes: Music: George Fenton; **Conductor:** George Fenton; **Featured Musicians:** Chuck Loeb, guitar; Hui Cox, guitar; Mark Egan, Fender bass; John Beal, acoustic bass.

Another lovely score from the master of contemporary romantic comedies, George Fenton. For this poignant tale of a woman head over heels in love with a gay male friend, Fenton prominently features his orchestra's rhythm section. The result is a nice, jazzy guitar-drenched score, subdued at moments and rollicking at others. The album also features Sting performing two new versions of the popular standard "You Were Meant for Me." The song's melody is also interpolated twice in the body of Fenton's score, adding an extra touch of romance.

Amy Rosen

Obsession

 1989, Masters Film Music, from the film *Obsession*, Columbia Pictures, 1976 🎵🎵🎵🎵🎵

album notes: Music: Bernard Herrmann; **Orchestra:** The National Philharmonic Orchestra; **Conductor:** Bernard Herrmann.

Bernard Herrmann returned to familiar grounds to the suspense film in which he had illustrated himself so vividly, with this stylish score for the film directed by Brian de Palma, a thinly disguised remake and tribute to Alfred Hitchcock's *Vertigo*. Like that film, *Obsession* deals with the anguish of a man (Cliff Robertson), still haunted by the kidnapping and apparent death of his wife 16 years before, who encounters a woman (Genevieve Bujold) who bears an uncanny resemblance to her during a trip abroad. Elaborating on musical devices he had already utilized in *Vertigo*, Herrmann wrote a sensational score, filled with powerful themes, ominously underlined by an organ, or a harp, sometimes with abrupt choral flourishes, in eerie evocations of a mystery that refuses to reveal itself. Shortly before his death, the composer assembled for this album the various cues in six mini–suites that present a stronger and more coherent vision of his music. The score marked another important milestone in the career of the composer. This recording, a limited edition release well worth looking for, eloquently shows why.

Didier C. Deutsch

October Sky

 1999, Sony Classical, from the film *October Sky*, Universal, 1999 🎵🎵🎵🎵

album notes: Music: Mark Isham; **Conductor:** Ken Kugler.

Mark Isham is such a gifted composer, with a voice of his own that owes little to what others may do! He again demonstrates his gift in this solidly entertaining score for a film set in the 1950s, a time period informed by the inclusion on the soundtrack of songs by Fats Domino, the Platters (the inevitable "My Prayer"), Buddy Holly, the Coasters, and the Cadillacs. But the zest of the album is the set of cues created by Isham, an irresistible blend that magnificently illustrates this real-life story of teenager, Homer Hickam—he eventually became a rocket expert at NASA—living in the mining town of Coalwood, Virginia, who experiments with homemade devices in his desire to reach the sky. Without trying to necessarily evoke the late-'50s, Isham wrote a series of themes that give the story an added emotional impetus and vibrancy. From the first announcement of Sputnik flying overhead that motivates the young would-be engineer and two of his friends to learn more about jet propulsion, to their first experiments made with the encouragement of Miss Riley, their physics teacher, to their first successful launch, the story and the score present a saga that is compelling, with

Isham reaching for sentimental effects to signal the importance of the boys' quest in a beautifully shaded and expressive score.

Didier C. Deutsch

Octopussy

1998, Rykodisc; from the film *Octopussy* United Artists, 1970 🎵🎵🎵🎵

album notes: Music: John Barry.

John Barry has frequently decried the music he wrote for the James Bond films, describing them derisively as "these Mickey Mouse scores," but apart from the fact that they made him rich and famous, they also revealed a composer whose amazing invention and energy helped create the aura the films eventually acquired. So much so, in fact, that the James Bond films that were scored by others (Bill Conti, Michel Legrand, Eric Serra), paled in comparison, proving the importance the music by Barry always played in those films.

For many years, *Octopussy* was among the most sought-after soundtrack albums from the series, ranking immediately behind *A View to a Kill* as the most in-demand. Though available at one time on the A&M label, it had been deleted and was almost impossible to find. This reissue returns it to the catalogue, which should be good news for all the fans who have been waiting for it. It's not that *Octopussy* is really any better than any of the other scores by Barry—in fact, compared to some of the most brilliant ones, it is rather a letdown. But it has its share of great tracks, all representative of the fast-paced action, it contains the famous James Bond theme interpolated in various selections, and it has a title tune, this one called "All Time High," performed by Rita Coolidge, that's quite evocative. Listening to the album, one can appreciate the reasons that have compelled fans to hunt for it: Barry's music always sounds gorgeous, with a sweeter sound than in previous efforts ("Miss Penelope," "That's My Life Octopussy") and a rambunctious theme that recurs when the action gets hot ("Yo Yo Fight and Death of Vijay," "The Palace Fight"). The inclusion of bits and pieces from the dialogue don't add much, however, the tracks are presented out of sequence, and the album would likely have benefited had more music been added to it. But it's nice to have it back, nonetheless.

Didier C. Deutsch

The Odd Couple II

1998, America Records, from the film *The Odd Couple II*, Paramount, 1998 🎵🎵🎵

album notes: Music: Alan Silvestri; **Conductor:** Alan Silvestri.

The jokes were tired, the situations not as funny as in the original, and Jack Lemmon and Walter Matthau, respectively cast as Felix and Oscar in the original *The Odd Couple,* looked pretty much as if they were playing this one by the numbers. Which may explain why Alan Silvestri's score also failed to really ignite. To be sure, the cues in this soundtrack album are enjoyable to a point, and the themes are catchy, but the overall feeling is that something is missing. Only on a couple of occasions ("In the Slammer," "Dead or Asleep") does the music come alive, with the slightly jazzy "Oscar and Felix" making the best impression. But other than those, it's not what you might call a very inspired score.

Didier C. Deutsch

Odds Against Tomorrow

1991, Sony Music Special Products, from the film *Odds Against Tomorrow,* United Artists, 1959 🎵🎵🎵🎵🎵

album notes: Music: John Lewis; **Featured Musicians:** The Modern Jazz Quartet: John Lewis, piano; Milt Jackson, vibraharp; Percy Heath, bass; Connie Kay, drums.

1990, Blue Note Records, from the film *Odds Against Tomorrow,* United Artists, 1959 🎵🎵🎵🎵

album notes: Music: John Lewis; **Featured Musicians:** The Modern Jazz Quartet: John Lewis, piano; Milt Jackson, vibraharp; Percy Heath, bass; Connie Kay, drums.

In another unusual foray into film music, John Lewis scored this taut crime drama in which Harry Belafonte, Robert Ryan, and Ed Begley are unlikely partners in a bank robbery, with the unusual casting eliciting added comments about racist attitudes. Characteristic of Lewis's subtly understated music, performed on screen as in these albums by The Modern Jazz Quartet, the moods are squarely on jazz, with the fanciful interplay between Lewis on piano and Milt Jackson on vibraharp at the center of the group's tight performance, with Connie Kay and Percy Heath providing the essential rhythm foundation and occasional inspired solos. The first album is the actual soundtrack to the film, with the selections reflecting the shorter playing time usually asked for by a given scene, but with a greater abundance of themes not found elsewhere.

The second album is a re-recording of some of the most important themes from the score (including the acknowledged highlights, "Skating in Central Park," "No Happiness for Slater" and "A Cold Wind is Blowing"), considerably expanded and with a greater amount of improvisation in the playing. A richer sound quality is also a prime consideration here, as opposed to the thinner–sounding soundtrack album. Both, however, are deserving of the highest consideration.

Didier C. Deutsch

Of Mice and Men

1992, Varèse Sarabande, from the film *Of Mice and Men*, MGM, 1992 ♪♪♪♪

album notes: Music: Mark Isham; **Conductor:** Ken Kugler; **Featured Soloists:** Rich Ruttenburg, piano; Peter Manau, guitar.

Based on John Steinbeck's story about two itinerant workers, George, a quiet optimist with great sensitivity, and Lennie, endowed with unusual strength and the simple mind of a child, who roam the California countryside in search of job opportunities, this remake of the classic 1939 film elicited a score with folk-like simplicity from Mark Isham, writing in a remarkably low-key style. With an abundance of cues for strings and woodwinds, the music is often appropriately reflective and atmospheric, only occasionally departing from its quiet, lyrical moods to underline a specific situation ("The Bunkhouse," "Buckin' Barley," "Comfort," "The Ranch").

Ultimately, the blend of both elements in the writing combine to create music that is hauntingly striking, and evocative of the drama on the screen and its multifaceted aspects. For the record, the original film was scored by Aaron Copland, and while Mark Isham's music may not achieve the kind of perennial appeal Copland's score has exerted since it was written, it is still a pretty eloquent statement from this very talented composer.

Didier C. Deutsch

Of Thee I Sing

1993, Angel Records, from the Broadway revival *Of Thee I Sing*, 1952 ♪♪♪♪♪

album notes: Music: George Gershwin; **Lyrics:** Ira Gershwin; **Musical Direction:** Maurice Levine; **Cast:** Jack Carson, Paul Hartman, Betty Oakes, Lenore Lonergan.

Political satire is not a genre that succeeds very well in this country, but a happy exception is the 1931 Gershwin musical, *Of Thee I Sing*, which takes sharp aim at the quadri annual spectacle of political conventions, the presidency, congressional shenanigans, the Supreme Court, motherhood, and apple pies, everything in fact that makes life worth living. Not only was the show a huge success at the time (it ran for 441 performances, quite a record), it also won the Pulitzer Prize, the first time ever the prestigious award was bestowed on a musical.

Revived in 1952, however, it failed miserably and closed after a scant 72 performances. Although, happily again, a cast album recording was made at the time, thereby preserving for posterity some of the most stinging and amusing songs ever created by the Gershwin brothers.

The musical is built around a rather absurd plot—the presidential campaign of one John P. Wintergreen and his running mate Alexander Throttlebottom, who easily win the presidency, only to find themselves assailed from all sides. It seems that, during the campaign, Wintergreen's advisers had staged a beauty contest, promising that the winner would marry the candidate if he were elected. The lucky contestant is Diana Devereaux who, when Wintergreen is elected comes to claim her prize. The new president, however, has already married one of his assistants, Mary Turner, thereby setting the stage for a nasty scandal and an international conflict when it is revealed that Diana Devereaux is "an illegitimate daughter of an illegitimate son of an illegitimate nephew of Napoleon." Needless to say, when the Supreme Court is asked to arbitrate, everything gets resolved.

What made the show so enjoyable was the breezy score fashioned by George and Ira Gershwin, which contains several notable tunes—"Because, Because," "Love Is Sweeping the Country," "Of Thee I Sing," and "Mine," among them. The 1952 cast also featured some personable comedians, including Jack Carson, Paul Hartman, Betty Oakes, and Lenore Lonergan in the principal roles. The cast recording always was a classic; its release on CD only confirms its status.

Didier C. Deutsch

Off Limits

1988, Varèse Sarabande, from the film *Off Limits*, 20th Century Fox, 1988 ♪♪

album notes: Music: James Newton Howard; **Featured Musicians:** James Newton Howard, keyboards, synth; Jeff Porcaro, Joe Porcaro, Emil Richards, Michael Mason, percussion; Michael Landau, Basil Fung, guitar; Robby Weaver, synclavier programming.

James Newton Howard's atmospheric synthesizer score for this suspense thriller starring Willem Dafoe and Gregory Hines, has its moments, but might have proved more effective on the screen than in the living room. While there is diversity in some of the cues, the grist of the music often gets lost in cues that fail to catch one's interest or end up sounding too repetitious after a while.

Didier C. Deutsch

An Officer and a Gentleman

1982, Island Records, from the film *An Officer and a Gentleman*, Paramount Pictures, 1982 ♪♪♪♡

album notes: Music: Jack Nitzsche, Buffy Sainte-Marie.

This one launched a monster hit with the Joe Cocker/Jennifer Warnes's duet "Up Where We Belong"—soft, lush, schmaltzy, ech. That song was elevator music *before* it was released. Some decent rockers help redeem the set, though, such as ZZ Top's "Tush," Dire Straits' epic "Tunnel of Love" and the Sir Douglas Quintet's "Be Real." But unless you need to hear more aural wallpaper from the likes of Jack Nitzsche and Lee Ritenour, you can find all those on far better albums.

Gary Graff

An early pop soundtrack, this collection of songs is notable for the stars who perform them, a factor which explains its popularity. Of course, the success of this album was no doubt also tied to that of the film, about the agonizing training period candidates to the Naval Aviation Officer School must undergo in the hands of a relentless drill instructor. However, the songs selected and the caliber of the performers had something to do with it, as did the fact that "Up Where We Belong," written by Waylon Jennings, Buffy Sainte-Marie, and Jack Nitzsche, won the Oscar for Best Original Song. More than 15 years later, it still holds its own, and in fact shows how far superior it is to some of the drivel that was created in its wake.

Didier C. Deutsch

Oh, Kay!

1998, Sony Classical, from the stage production *Oh, Kay!*, 1955 🎬🎬🎬

album notes: Music: George Gershwin; **Lyrics:** Ira Gershwin; **Additional Lyrics:** Howard Dietz; **Conductor:** Lehman Engel; **Featured Musicians:** Cy Walter, piano; Bernard Leighton, piano.

I've always been partial to Columbia's 1955 *Oh, Kay!*, a Gershwin first recording (which curiously was not released until 1957). It sounds of the '50s, although duo pianists Cy Walter and Bernie Leighton temper that with spirited '20s-style playing, and it has a wonderful cast. Broadway leading man Jack Cassidy (*Wish You Were Here, She Loves Me*) sings everything silkily. The underappreciated and now virtually forgotten Barbara Ruick is dreamy on "Maybe" and "Do Do Do," and absolutely creamy with "Someone to Watch over Me." (Memorable mainly from sister or best friend roles in MGM musicals and as Carrie in the film version of *Carousel*, Ruick died in 1974). Allen Case (*Once upon a Mattress*) performs a vivid "Clap Yo' Hands." Bonus tracks include Mary Martin's 1949 "Maybe," and George Gershwin's 1926 piano recordings of "Someone to Watch over Me" and "Clap Yo' Hands."

Max O. Preeo

1995, Elektra Records, from the studio cast recording *Oh, Kay!*, 1995 🎬🎬🎬🎬

album notes: Music: George Gershwin; **Lyrics:** Ira Gershwin; **Orchestra:** The Orchestra of St. Luke's; **Conductor:** Eric Stern; **Cast:** Robert Westenberg, Patrick Cassidy, Adam Arkin, Liz Larsen, Stacey A. Logan, Dawn Upshaw, Kurt Ollmann, Susan Lucci.

A somewhat inconsequential plot, and a great score, are the hallmarks in *Oh, Kay!*, a 1926 musical by George and Ira Gershwin, which centers around the dilemma faced by a young playboy,

Jimmy Winter, whose impending marriage is threatened when he finds out he is in love with another woman, Kay Denham. Kay is the sister of a titled Englishman–turned–bootlegger, who has stashed away his stock of liquor in Winter's Long Island manse. Around this slight suggestion of a story, the Gershwins wrote a collection of tunes that yielded such standards as "Someone to Watch over Me," "Dear Little Girl," "Do, Do, Do," "Maybe," and "Clap Yo' Hands." The studio cast recording on Elektra, starring the wonderful Dawn Upshaw, is part of a series of Gershwin musicals, well worth looking into and enjoying to the hilt.

Dider Deutsch

Oklahoma!

1993, MCA Records, from the Broadway production *Oklahoma!*, 1943 🎬🎬🎬🎬

album notes: Music: Richard Rodgers; **Lyrics:** Oscar Hammerstein II; **Musical Direction:** Jay Blackton; **Cast:** Alfred Drake, Joan Roberts, Howard da Silva, Celeste Holm, Lee Dixon.

1987, Angel Records, from the film *Oklahoma!*, Magna Films, 1956 🎬🎬🎬🎬

album notes: Music: Richard Rodgers; **Lyrics:** Oscar Hammerstein II; **Musical Direction:** Jay Blackton; **Cast:** Gordon MacRae, Shirley Jones, Rod Steiger, Gloria Grahame, Gene Nelson, Charlotte Greenwood.

1980, RCA Victor, from the Broadway revival *Oklahoma!*, 1980 🎬🎬🎬🎬🎬

album notes: Music: Richard Rodgers; **Lyrics:** Oscar Hammerstein II; **Musical Direction:** Jay Blackton; **Cast:** Laurence Guittard, Christine Andreas, Martin Vidnovic, Christine Ebersole, Harry Groener, Mary Wickes.

Oklahoma!, the first show by Richard Rodgers and Oscar Hammerstein II, was a pioneering work that changed the course of the American musical, launched one of the most prolific teams in the history of Broadway, and saved the sagging fortunes of the Theatre Guild, which produced it.

For the first time completely integrated in the narrative, instead of being inserted at random in the book, as had been so frequently the case before, the songs in *Oklahoma!* actually help propel the action forward. Adding a further element to the progression of the storyline, the musical also introduced the device of a dream ballet to reflect the state of mind of the principals, a novelty. To be sure, some musicals had previously shown a tighter, cohesive blend of book, songs and dances (certainly *Porgy and Bess* and *Pal Joey*, also trendsetters in their own right, denoted a maturity that often had seemed to be missing in most works at the time), but *Oklahoma!* can be said to be the first modern–day musical that brings all these disparate elements into a comprehensive, seamless whole.

For Rodgers, working for the first time with a new partner, following the death of Lorenz Hart, with whom he had written all his works through the 1930s, teaming with Hammerstein seemed a proposition fraught with many question marks: The

Shirley Jones and Gordon McRae in the film Oklahoma. **(The Kobal Collection)**

famed lyricist of *Show Boat* had not had a hit show in many years, and was already written off by many in theatrical circles. The partnership ignited incredible creative responses in both men, with Rodgers reaching new levels of lyricism he had seldom felt with Hart, while Hammerstein found new means of expression that resulted in sharper, more pungent lyrics and book ideas than he had ever experienced before.

Based on *Green Grow the Lilacs,* a 1931 play by Lynn Riggs, *Oklahoma!* concerns itself with the romance between a cowboy and his girl, Curly and Laurey, and the possible threat to their idyll represented by a mean–spirited working hand, Jud Fry. The whole story is set against the natural antagonism between farmers and cowmen, and the greater political framework brought by the impending entry of the territory within the Union. Strikingly beautiful and simple in its expression, *Oklahoma!* is at heart a celebration of the pioneering American spirit, something that struck a particularly responsive note when it opened on March 31, 1943. Hailed as a landmark production, the show enjoyed an incredible run of 2,212 performances (a record at the time), and made stars of many mem-

bers in its cast, including Alfred Drake who portrayed Curly, Joan Roberts as Laurey, Howard da Silva as Jud Fry, and Celeste Holm as Ado Annie, Laurey's man–crazed friend.

The show also introduced a large number of songs that have become as many classic standards, including "Oh, What a Beautiful Mornin'," "The Surrey with the Fringe on Top," "Kansas City," "People Will Say We're In Love," "Out of My Dreams," "All Er Nuthin'," and the rousing title tune. On another level, *Oklahoma!* also marked the first time a Broadway musical received a cast album recording. Previously, when a successful show opened on Broadway, the common practice was to take its stars into a recording studio, provide them with fresh arrangements of the most popular tunes in the show, and record them as pop songs.

When *Oklahoma!* opened, the recording industry was in the midst of a long strike from the Musicians' Union, which prevented record labels from making new recordings with orchestral backing. Jack Kapp, A&R head at Decca Records, settled independently with the Union, and immediately looked for a new source of material to release under his new contract. The resounding success of *Oklahoma!* prompted him to take the entire cast into the studio and cut an album of the songs, as performed by the original members of the company. The move marked Decca's entry in the field of cast albums, in which it was a dominant force until 1950.

The first album listed here is the original 1943 cast, and while it may be sonically insufficient by today's standards, and certainly incomplete compared to more recent recordings, it is in many ways an essential, historical document. The soundtrack album, on Capitol, for many years the best source for anyone wanting to listen to the score under optimum circumstances, still holds its own, with Gordon MacRae and Shirley Jones co-starring as Curly and Laurey, Rod Steiger appropriately menacing as Jud Fry, and Gloria Graham fetching as Ado Annie. The recording, incidentally, is from the standard 35mm version, and not from the Todd–AO 65 mm roadshow presentation, which had a different, alternate soundtrack. Revived many times since its creation, *Oklahoma!* came back to Broadway in a sumptuous stage version which opened on Dec. 13, 1979, and yielded the splendid new cast album on RCA Victor. Starring Laurence Guittard, Christine Andreas, Martin Vidnovic, and Christine Ebersole in the principal roles, it is by far the most complete and most satisfying recording of this sensational musical.

Didier C. Deutsch

Old Gringo

1989, GNP Crescendo Records, from the film *Old Gringo*, Columbia Pictures, 1989 🎬🎬🎬🎬

album notes: Music: Lee Holdridge; **Conductor:** Lee Holdridge; **Featured Musicians:** Ray Kramer, cello; Malcolm McNab, trumpet; Louise Ditullio, Earle Dunler, Gary Gray, Tom Boyd, Barbara Northcutt, Michael O'Donovan, woodwind; Dennis Budimir, George Doering, Marcos Loya, guitars.

Old Gringo, starring Gregory Peck, Jane Fonda, and Jimmy Smits, is an old-fashioned epic tale of passion and power that elicited an old-fashioned score from composer Lee Holdridge. Set against the backdrop of the Mexican Revolution, the narrative details the complex love story between a 40-something American spinster (Fonda) and a dashing Mexican general in Pancho Villa's army (Smits), with Gregory Peck, portraying Ambrose Bierce, the cynical, brilliant 71-year-old journalist on a quest for adventure. With a meaty storyline and colorful landscapes to ignite his creative expression, Holdridge wrote a score for large orchestra that brims with excitement, solidly anchored by three major themes for the three main characters. The glorious theme he created for Harriet, notably, is simply magnificent.

Didier C. Deutsch

The Old Man and the Sea

1989, Varèse Sarabande, from the film *The Old Man and the Sea*, Warner Bros., 1958 🎬🎬🎬🎬

album notes: Music: Dimitri Tiomkin; **Conductor:** Dimitri Tiomkin.

1989, Intrada Records, from the television special *The Old Man and the Sea*, Yorkshire Television, 1989 🎬🎬🎬🎬

album notes: Music: Bruce Broughton; **Orchestra:** The Graunke Symphony Orchestra; **Conductor:** Bruce Broughton.

Dimitri Tiomkin left behind the bombast of his western and epic music when he created this Academy Award–winning score for the film, based on the novel by Ernest Hemingway, about an old fisherman, portrayed by Spencer Tracy in a splendidly low-key performance, whose sole ambition in life is to catch a big fish. With the exception of a couple of cues, with a strong tropical flavor ("Fisherman's Cantina," "In the Tavern at Casa Blanca"), the score centers on the fisherman's determination to succeed, his lonely fight with the huge fish he finally nabs, and with the predator shark attracted by his prey. Subtly expressive and magnificently sketched (the lovely "I Am Your Dream" is probably one of the most attractive tunes ever composed by Tiomkin), the score won an Academy Award.

Unfortunately, Bruce Broughton's score for the television remake of "The Old Man and the Sea" cannot escape comparisons with the music written by Dimitri Tiomkin for the 1958 film. Fortunately, Broughton happens to be a very creative composer, who rose to the challenge in ways that command admiration. Much of his music has an appealing Spanish flavor that's indigenous to the locale and the main characters of the Old Man and the boy he befriends. With a guitar strumming the themes to a subtle accompaniment of strings and maracas, or in duets with a flute, the score develops into a suite with an identity all its own that owes nothing to its illustrious predecessor. It's quite effective and quite affecting, and it stands out as a superb listening experience that invites frequent returns. Now, about Anthony Quinn as the Old Man . . .

Didier C. Deutsch

Oldest Living Confederate Widow Tells All

1994, Milan Records, from the television mini-series *Oldest Living Confederate Widow Tells All*, 1994 🎬🎬🎬

album notes: Music: Mark Snow; **Featured Musician:** Kelly Parkinson, violin.

One of the most popular television mini-series of the 1993–94 season, *Oldest Living Confederate Widow Tells All* enabled *X-Files* composer Mark Snow to contribute a largely orchestral score that's as far separated from the adventures of Fox Mulder and Dana Scully as one could imagine. Highlighted by a lyrical main theme, the tone of Snow's music is alternately pleasant or melodramatic throughout, nicely punctuating the drama of a virtual century in the life of a Southern woman (Diane Lane), who changes with the times and attitudes of various generations. Snow's music is genteel but forgettable, but it's still a nice album that will be of particular interest to those who think that the composer's works only consist of droning synthesizers and atonal chords.

Andy Dursin

Oliver!

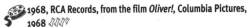 1989, RCA Victor, from the Broadway production *Oliver!*, 1962 ♪♪♪♪

album notes: Music: Lionel Bart; **Lyrics:** Lionel Bart; **Musical Direction:** Donald Pippin; **Cast:** Clive Revill, Georgia Brown, Bruce Prochnik, Alice Playten.

1968, RCA Records, from the film *Oliver!*, Columbia Pictures, 1968 ♪♪♪♪

album notes: Music: Lionel Bart; **Lyrics:** Lionel Bart; **Choir:** The Columbia Studio Chorus; **Orchestra:** The Columbia Studio Orchestra; **Conductor:** Johnny Green; **Cast:** Ron Moody, Shani Wallis, Harry Secombe, Oliver Reed, Mark Lester, Jack Wild.

Charles Dickens's *Oliver Twist* provided the gist for a magnificent new musical, *Oliver!* which opened on Broadway on January 6, 1963, following a three–year run in London. "Freely adapted" from the novel, and slightly spruced up to conform with the tenets of the song–and–dance genre, the show, entirely conceived and created by Lionel Bart, tells the story of the orphan boy, who runs away from his life of misery and ends up in the streets of London, where he is eventually adopted by a well-to-do benefactor, who turns out to be his grandfather.

Received with glowing reviews from the Broadway pundits, the show enjoyed a profitable run of 774 performances. It introduced many songs that have since become quite popular, including the rousing "Oom–Pah–Pah," performed by customers in a seedy barroom led by Nancy, a woman of easy virtue who takes Oliver under a protecting wing; "Food, Glorious Food," the anthem of the famished orphans; "Consider Yourself," in which The Artful Dodger and his band of young pickpockets welcome Oliver; and mostly "As Long As He Needs Me," the throbbing love song in which Nancy reveals her passion for Sikes, her "protector." The musical won a Tony Award for composer Lionel Bart, and in 1968 was made into a glossy screen version which retained much of its flavor and kept the entire score minus two songs. Of the two albums listed above, the 1963 cast album is probably the best, with Clive Revill a splendid Fagin, Georgia Brown resplendent as Nancy, and Bruce Prochnik as Oliver; Ron Moody, Shani Wallis, and Mark Lester were equally effective in the film version, though the recording itself leaves a bit to be desired, sonically.

Didier C. Deutsch

Oliver & Company

1998, Disney, from the animated feature film *Oliver & Company*, Disney Studios, 1967 ♪♪♪♪
album notes: Music: J.A.C. Redford; **Conductor:** J.A.C. Redford.

In the Disney canon, *Oliver & Company* doesn't rate very high, and never reached the lofty heights attained by *Snow White* and *Cinderella* in earlier times, or *Little Mermaid* and *The Lion King* more recently. Yet, this amusing story of a little cat lost in New York City and taken under the protective guidance of some streetwise dogs certainly had a lot going for it, not least of it the engaging score composed by J.A.C. Redford, or the songs featuring such artists as Huey Lewis, Billy Joel, Bette Midler, Ruth Pointer, and Ruden Blades. The cues created by Redford are ominous at times, exhilaratingly cute at other times, but they define the film with its hills and vales, even if they seem occasionally too serious for an animated feature.

Didier C. Deutsch

Olivier Olivier/Europa Europa

1992, DRG Records, from the films *Olivier Olivier*, Sony Pictures Classics, 1992; and *Europa Europa*, Orion Pictures, 1991 ♪♪♪♪
album notes: Music: Zbigniew Preisner.

Two films, one set in contemporary France, the other in war–torn Poland, both directed by Agnieszka Holland, received vibrant scores from Zbigniew Preisner. In the first, filled with ambiguities and innuendoes that belie the simplicity of its storyline, a provincial French couple welcomes a young Parisian street prostitute whom they believe to be their long–lost son. In the second, based on a true story, a young Jewish boy tries to convince the German soldiers who have arrested him that he is a gentile. Using a determinedly low–key approach to both stories, Preisner crafted scores that are eloquently flavorful and sparse, with only a hint of predictability—faint accordion in the first, a little Jewish theme in the second—to underline the film's respective backgrounds.

Didier C. Deutsch

The Omen

1990, Varèse Sarabande, from the film *The Omen*, 20th Century Fox, 1976 ♪♪♪♪
album notes: Music: Jerry Goldsmith; **Orchestra:** The National Philharmonic Orchestra; **Conductor:** Lionel Newman.

Goldsmith's only Oscar–winning score has become one of the most influential works in the film music canon and probably started the trend for using Carl Orff's "O Fortuna" in every movie trailer with its spine–chilling use of a Latin–chanting chorus and Stravinsky–like, aggressive string passages to underscore the exploitative 1976 Richard Donner film about an evil little tike who's the son of Satan. Although Goldsmith scored later sequels with a fuller, more expansive sound, the original effort is almost a chamber score that lends an intimate, personal feel to the devilish proceedings. The dirge–like opening and chaotic frenzy of cues like "Killer Storm" and "Mrs. Blalock" are undeniably frightening, but just as disturbing is the low–key choral murmuring that opens the "Dogs Attack" piece, one of the grimmest horror cues Goldsmith ever produced. There's also a surprisingly lyrical, piano–voiced love theme that threads through many of the quieter pieces.

see also: Damien: Omen II/The Final Conflict

Jeff Bond

On a Clear Day You Can See Forever

1993, RCA Victor, from the Broadway production *On a Clear Day You Can See Forever*, 1965 🎬🎬🎬🎬

album notes: Music: Burton Lane; **Lyrics:** Alan Jay Lerner; **Musical Direction:** Theodore Saidenberg; **Cast:** John Cullum, Barbara Harris, Titos Vandis, William Daniels.

1970, CBS Special Products, from the film *On a Clear Day You Can See Forever*, Paramount Pictures, 1970 🎬🎬

album notes: Music: Burton Lane; **Lyrics:** Alan Jay Lerner; **Choir:** The Paramount Studio Chorus; **Orchestra:** The Paramount Studio Orchestra; **Conductor:** Nelson Riddle; **Cast:** Yves Montand, Barbra Streisand, Larry Blyden, Jack Nicholson, Bob Newhart.

Alan Jay Lerner's particular interest in extrasensory perceptions, reincarnation, time regression, hypnosis, and other psychic phenomena led to this hopelessly flawed, but ultimately fascinating musical in which the heroine, Daisy, recalls a previous existence when she is placed under hypnosis by Dr. Bruckner, a psychologist. The story, an old-fashioned romance that doesn't need the mind trips to the past to succeed, is helped by the strong score, which helps to gloss over some of the inconsistencies in the plot. Much of the charm in the original disappeared in the blown-out-of-proportion screen version, in which Barbra Streisand and Yves Montand fussed as the two principal characters without sharing much empathy or chemistry between them.

Didier C. Deutsch

On Deadly Ground

1994, Varèse Sarabande, from the film *On Deadly Ground*, Warner Bros., 1994 🎬🎬🎬

album notes: Music: Basil Poledouris; **Conductor:** Basil Poledouris; **Featured Vocalists:** Qaunaq Mikkigak, Timangiak Petaulassie, Inuit throat singing.

Steven Seagal, an unlikely martial arts expert with a mission, roams the Alaskan range in this environmentally–minded saga

They Know the Score
Myohael Danna

I always wanted to be a composer since I was a little kid. Of course, when you're a little kid growing up and you're reading about famous composers of the past, the whole idea of poverty is almost held up as a rite of passage. It's a very romanticized thing. I don't think poverty or lack of money was anything that I was afraid of; in a sense, it was almost celebrated by the things that you're taught—the past models. That's a concept that's important to me; I don't know if it is to other people, but having an idea of where you stand in the whole history of making music, that is really important to me. That's a sense that I carry into the work that I do as well. I try to be very aware of music from different places and from different times. I feel perfectly able and like I have the right to use those in my music-making and draw from them at any point.

***Courtesy of* Film Score Monthly**

in which he confronts an oil prospector unmoved by the pristine beauty of the landscape but moved by the huge profits he might make with his rigs. Far–fetched as the story might have been, it prompted Basil Poledouris to write a superb score in which big orchestral textures and synthesizer sounds, in a rare happy confluence of two styles that seldom agree, effectively blend to paint a broad musical panorama. Adding a touch of authenticity to the musical proceedings, Inuit throat singers provide a suggestive local color.

Didier C. Deutsch

On Her Majesty's Secret Service

1988, EMI–Manhattan Records, from the film *On Her Majesty's Secret Service*, United Artists, 1969 🎬🎬🎬🎬🎬

album notes: Music: John Barry; **Lyrics:** Hal David; **Conductor:** John Barry.

Even though Secret Agent 007 is portrayed by a newcomer (George Lazenby, who hardly made the grade when compared with Sean Connery, despite his own personal charm), very little else is changed in this by–the–numbers exciting tale of der-ring–do, primarily set in the Swiss Alps. John Barry's score, also one of his best for the series, matches the break–neck pace of the action, and pauses long enough to also indulge in a signifi-cant love theme and in a tongue–in–cheek comment about the previous owner of the title role. One jarring note in the otherwise excellent album is the dispensable "Do You Know How Christmas Trees Are Grown?," but Louis Armstrong's rendition of the nostal-gia–tinged "We Have All the Time in the World" is a great classic.

Didier C. Deutsch

On the Town

1998, Sony Classical, from the studio cast recording *On the Town*, 1960 🎵🎵🎵🎵

album notes: Music: Leonard Bernstein; **Lyrics:** Betty Comden and Adolph Green; **Musical Direction:** Leonard Bernstein; **Cast:** John Rear-don, Cris Alexander, Adolph Green, Betty Comden, Nancy Walker, George Gaynes.

Leonard Bernstein's infectious ballet, *Fancy Free,* about three sailors on a 24-hour leave in New York City, was turned into an even more exhilarating musical comedy titled *On the Town.* Created in 1944, the composer's collaborators, Betty Comden and Adolph Green, and comedian Nancy Walker played impor-tant roles. Excerpts from the show were recorded at the time, and can be heard on an MCA CD in which they are coupled with a 1945 recording of *Fancy Free.* In 1960, Bernstein returned to the studio with Comden, Green, Walker, and Cris Alexander, also from the original cast, to record the show all over again. A lively, rambunctious celebration of youth and vitality, the show follows the three sailors as they look (and find) their ideal dates for a day, in a score that brims with energy, irreverence, and jazzy style. The recording captures all these elements into one of the most exciting cast albums to be enjoyed. In 1949, MGM filmed the story, with Gene Kelly and Frank Sinatra as two of the sailors. But with the exception of a couple of songs, in-cluding the rousing opening number, "New York, New York," MGM discarded most of Bernstein's sensational score, and re-placed it with new songs by Roger Edens, Comden, and Green that did not have the vibrant imagination of the original.

Didier C. Deutsch

On the Twentieth Century

1991, Sony Broadway, from the Broadway production *On the Twentieth Century*, 1978 🎵🎵🎵🎵

album notes: Music: Cy Coleman; **Lyrics:** Betty Comden and Adolph Green; **Musical Direction:** Paul Gemignani; **Cast:** John Cullum, Made-line Kahn, Imogene Coca, George Coe, Dean Dittman, Kevin Kline.

A brash, rambunctious musical based on Ben Hecht and Charles MacArthur's 1932 backstage play, *On the Twentieth Century* gave Cy Coleman, Betty Comden, and Adolph Green the vehicle with which to fashion a score (and a musical) that was thoroughly entertaining, and a terrific proposition. The plot concerns the efforts of theatrical producer Oscar Jaffee, on board the New York–bound Twentieth Century to escape his creditors, to persuade Lily Garland, his former leading actress and lover and now a celebrated movie star, to appear in his next production, "The Passion of Mary Magdalene." Using every trick in the book, he finally succeeds when he pretends he is dying after having shot himself, compelling Lily to affix her name, Peter Rabbit, at the bottom of the contract.

Breathing incredible life into the characters, John Cullum chews the scenery (a striking Art Deco set by Robin Wagner) as Oscar, while Madeline Kahn demurs as Lili, with Imogene Coca por-traying a religious nut who gives Oscar a rubber check for his production, while Kevin Kline portrays Lili's current lover, an actor unlikely named Bruce Granit. The Tony Award–winning score adds its own point to the proceedings, with Coleman, Comden, and Green providing songs that closely match the hu-morous action.

Beth Krakower

On Your Toes

1996, MCA Records, from the Broadway production *On Your Toes*, 1954 🎵🎵🎵

album notes: Music: Richard Rodgers; **Lyrics:** Lorenz Hart; **Musical Di-rection:** Salvatore Dell'Isola; **Cast:** Vera Zorina, Bobby Van, Elaine Stritch.

1983, Polydor Records, from the Broadway revival *On Your Toes*, 1983 🎵🎵🎵🎵

album notes: Music: Richard Rodgers; **Lyrics:** Lorenz Hart; **Musical Di-rection:** John Mauceri; **Cast:** Natalia Makarova, Lara Teeter, Dina Mer-rill, George S. Irving, Christine Andreas.

Unfortunately, no recording of the original 1936 cast of *On Your Toes* was ever made, and there were only scant excerpts by the 1938 London cast. As a result, the 1954 Broadway revival is the first recording of this amazing score, one of the best by Rodgers and Hart. While the top–billed star of the revival was Vera Zorina, the ex–Mrs. Balanchine, she does not appear on the cast album. However, all of the other performers do and they are stylish and grand. Bobby Van, fresh from his appear-ances in several Hollywood films, is relaxed and charming as Phil Dolan III, the part originally created by Ray Bolger. Kay Coulter as Frankie Frayne is warm and loving. And Elaine Stritch playing the featured part of Peggy Porterfield, the backer of a Russian ballet company, wipes everyone up with her sensa-tional rendition of a song interpolated especially for her, with this recording about as enjoyable as it gets.

Composer Leonard Bernstein (Archive Photos, Inc.)

Good as the 1954 recording is, the 1983 revival cast album is even better and properly reflects the sound of the 1936 original. Make no mistake, this is a glorious warm, romantic score and this album is a stunner. Every performer is absolutely right and the 1930s performance style is preserved in this recording right down to the taps of the dancers. Lara Teeter captures the light breeziness of the music and lyrics with just the right amount of throwaway charm that is a constant delight. Christine Andreas turns Frankie into a fully believable character and charms the ear with her singing. Dina Merrill and George S. Irving are just right in their roles. Both ballets are included, as well as much dance music. John Mauceri has never conducted a finer performance than here and it is captured in glorious stereo, digital sound.

Jerry J. Thomas

Once Around

1990, Varèse Sarabande, from the film *Once Around,* Universal Pictures, 1990 ♪♪♪

album notes: Music: James Horner; **Conductor:** James Horner.

James Horner, who has always shown a particular fondness for big bands, was right in his element for this score in which he worked with the great Billy May, writing a number, "Big Band on Ice," that brightens up the whole album. The film, a romantic comedy–drama about the family problems facing a thirtysomething spinster when she meets an unrefined condo salesman and makes plans to get married, results in cues that are appropriately evocative. Since much of the action centered around the woman's life with her family and the usual rituals involved, many of the selections in this soundtrack album are source music ranging from the stately "The Emperor Waltz" to an oriental fantasy. Danny Aiello, who also appears in the film as the *pater familias,* effectively handles two vocals, including "Fly Me to the Moon," reprised as an instrumental.

Didier C. Deutsch

Once Upon a Forest

1993, Fox Records, from the animated feature *Once Upon a Forest,* 20th Century Fox, 1993 ♪♪♪♪♪

album notes: Music: James Horner; **Orchestra:** The London Symphony Orchestra, The New London Children's Choir; **Conductor:** James Horner; **Featured Soloists:** Mike Taylor, Tony Herrigan, The Andrae Crouch Singers.

Interestingly this soundtrack album invites comparisons with *Ferngully . . . The Last Rain Forest,* if only because it is also an animated feature with an ecological message to it. But where Alan Silvestri scored the first with an abundance of synthesized sounds, James Horner brings to his music the superla-

tive expression of the London Symphony Orchestra; and themes that are grandly sweeping and profusely florid. As is often the case with his cues, often reconstructed for the soundtrack album, there is a huge amount of music here, notably "The Forest," "The Journey Begins," "Escaping from the Yellow Dragons/The Meadow," and "Flying Home to Michelle," which all have plenty of time to make a strong impression.

Also as usual with Horner, the themes are truly beautiful, romantic and melodic, and always broad to the extreme. They match the animated action in which the usual contingent of cuddly characters—Abigail, a mouse, Edgar, a mole, Russell, a hedgehog, and Michelle, a badger—are exposed to the dangers of life outside the forest. When Michelle gets sick, her wise old uncle, Cornelius, directs the other three to go find a rare herb, which they eventually do after having met a gospel group led by a perky preacher, and barely escaped the "yellow dragons," the bulldozers at a construction site. It may be conventional stuff, but Horner pulls all the stops and delivers a score that underlines these events in the story with much delight.

Didier C. Deutsch

Once Upon a Mattress

1993, MCA Records, from the Broadway production *Once Upon a Mattress,* 1959 ♪♪♪

album notes: Music: Mary Rodgers; **Lyrics:** Marshall Barer; **Musical Direction:** Harold Hastings; **Cast:** Carol Burnett, Joe Bova, Allen Case, Anne Jones, Harry Snow, Jack Gilford.

1997, RCA Victor Records, from the Broadway revival *Once Upon a Mattress,* 1996 ♪

album notes: Music: Mary Rodgers; **Lyrics:** Marshall Barer; **Musical Direction:** Eric Stern; **Cast:** Sarah Jessica Parker, David Aaron Baker, Lewis Cleale, Jane Krakowski.

Carol Burnett gains at being seen rather than heard, but hints of the infectious comic genius that made her a theatrical star before she became a household name on television can be experienced in this cast album of her first Broadway show. Loosely based on the fairy tale by Andersen, "The Princess and the Pea," the show enables the comedienne to mug her way through a rather limp and flimsy story line, further limited by the so–so score, the product of Mary (daughter of Richard) Rodgers and Marshall Barer. The 1996 revival was even less fortunate in Sarah Jessica Parker, whose sense of comedy was not very evident in this sorry production. The cast album does little to prove that the show was worth bringing back to Broadway, let alone spending the money recording it.

Didier C. Duetsch

Once Upon a Time in America

1985, Mercury Records, from the film *Once Upon a Time in America*, Hapax Int'l Pictures, 1984 ♪♪♪♪♪

album notes: Music: Ennio Morricone; **Conductor:** Ennio Morricone; **Featured Artists:** Gheorghe Zamfir, Pan flute; Edda Dell'Orso, vocals.

A story of the world of gangsters in the United States spread over several decades, *Once Upon a Time in America* may be viewed as Sergio Leone's companion film to his *Once Upon a Time in the West*. Whereas the popular "spaghetti western" explores a time and place that are significant in this country's development the conquest of the West, *Once Upon a Time in America* is equally relevant in its exploration of another time and place, life in the Eastern big cities during the Prohibition and after, that also shaped the country as we know it today. In it, Leone used the rivalries that existed between various criminal groups over their claim to certain territories, to focus on an aging New York Mafia boss (Robert DeNiro), eager to avenge the death of his girlfriend 35 years earlier, during the Prohibition era, at the hands of members of a rival gang.

Once again bringing his own sensitivity to illustrate Leone's vision, Ennio Morricone wrote a vibrant score, marked by themes that are in turns romantic and exuberant, in a display of unusually strong musical ideas that match in invention and impact the ones he had conceived for the earlier *Once Upon a Time in the West*. From early jazz tunes to evocative nostalgia—limned songs, he painted a broad, colorful canvas that is irresistibly alive and convincing.

Didier C. Deutsch

Once Upon a Time in the West

1988, RCA Records, from the film *Once Upon a Time in the West*, Paramount Pictures, 1972 ♪♪♪♪♪

album notes: Music: Ennio Morricone; **Orchestra:** Orchestra Unione Musicisti di Roma, **Conductor:** Ennio Morricone; **Featured Soloist:** Franco De Gemini, harmonica; Alessandro Alessandroni, whistler; Edda Dell'Orso, vocal; **Choir:** I Cantori Moderni di Alessandroni .

Even though he had already scored several magnificent westerns that called attention to his unique brand of creativity (*The Good, the Bad and the Ugly* comes to mind), Ennio Morricone reached the pinnacle of his art with this sensational effort for the sprawling saga filmed by Sergio Leone. Central to the popularity of the score is the haunting "Man with a Harmonica," which is heard throughout the film as a theme for a lonely avenger portrayed by Charles Bronson. The poignancy in the theme captures the moods of the narrative, a tale of greed and revenge, in which Bronson's "man–with–no–name" confronts Henry Fonda and Jason Robards, two heavies intent on taking control of a small community in a deserted area of

the wild West, in anticipation of the windfall that will come their way once the railroad comes through the town. Also making a strong comment on the action, "Farewell to Cheyenne" and "Jill's America" stand out in the rich and flavorful score.

Didier C. Deutsch

One Against the Wind

1993, Intrada Records, from the film *One Against the Wind*, Republic Pictures, 1993 ♪♪♪♪

album notes: Music: Lee Holdridge; **Conductor:** Lee Holdridge.

Based on the real life story of a British countess living in Paris during World War II and her heroic efforts to help downed Allied fliers escape arrest, *One Against the Wind* suggested to composer Lee Holdridge a score that swells up with broad romantic moods, reflective of the countess's character, and martial cues to dangers presented by the German occupant. As he explains it in his notes, the score is pretty much presented as "a tone poem spread across the events and moments of the film," with the two colliding motives, a tense descending "wartime" action theme played by the brass section, and a rising hymn–like theme, played by the strings, outlining the various elements in the narrative. An unusually strong and descriptive score.

Didier C. Deutsch

One Fine Day

1996, Columbia Records, from the film *One Fine Day*, 20th Century Fox, 1996 ♪♪

album notes: Music: James Newton Howard; **Conductor:** Artie Kane.

The Chiffons' original rendition of the title track is near–perfection, so it didn't need anyone messing around with it. Unfortunately, Natalie Merchant tries her hand and delivers something that misses its predecessors' vigor and innocence. A bunch of other tepid love songs—new and old—by Kenny Loggins, Tina Arena, and Harry Connick Jr., round out the set, though the rootsy Keb' Mo' acquits himself well on two selections.

Gary Graff

Nine minutes of James Newton Howard's music is all you get in this "soundtrack" album, in which the remainder is spent on an odd assortment of song performances ranging from excellent ("For the First Time," "Have I Told You Lately," "What a Dif'rence a Day Made," "Isn't It Romantic") to mediocre ("Love's Funny That Way," "The Glory of Love," "This Guy's in Love with You," "Just Like You"). It's your money . . .

Didier C. Deutsch

101 Dalmatians **(The Kobal Collection)**

One from the Heart

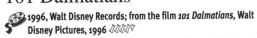

1982, Columbia Records, from the film *One from the Heart*, Zoetrope Studios, 1982 ♪♪

album notes: Music: Tom Waits; **Conductor:** Bob Alcivar; **Featured Musicians:** Bob Alcivar, piano; Pete Jolly, piano, celeste, accordion; Tom Waits, piano; Greg Cohen, bass; Teddy Edwards, tenor sax; Gene Cipriano, tenor sax; Dennis Budimir, guitar; Shelly Manne, drums; Larry Bunker, drums; Jack Sheldon, trumpet; Chuck Findley, trumpet; Dick Hyde, trombone; Don Waldrop, tuba; Leslie Thompson, harmonica; Lanny Morgan, woodwinds; John Lowe, woodwinds; Gayle Levant, harp; Emil Richards, vibes; John Tomassie, percussion; Victor Feldman, tympani; Joe Porcaro, glockenspiel.

A glossy musical that caused the demise of Francis Ford Coppola's Zoetrope Studios, *One from the Heart* had only one thing wrong with it—it was glitzy, gaudy, and utterly superficial. That may have been totally appropriate for a musical set in Las Vegas, but somehow the two seemed like a contradiction in terms. The story of two jaded lovers seeking new excitement in their lives over a Fourth of July weekend, it starred Teri Garr and Frederic Forrest, with Raul Julia and Lainie Kazan lending it an ounce of legitimacy. The score was written by Tom Waits, who performed the songs with Crystal Gayle. On the face of it, the album reveals a solid collection of tunes that might have proved ingratiating in another film. Here, they simply confirm the fact that the whole project was doomed to fail from the word go.

Didier C. Deutsch

101 Dalmatians

1996, Walt Disney Records; from the film *101 Dalmatians*, Walt Disney Pictures, 1996 ♪♪♪♪

album notes: Music: Michael Kamen; **Orchestra:** The L.A. All–Star Orchestra; **Conductor:** Michael Kamen.

Dr. John's delightfully wicked rendition of the song "Cruella De Vil" sets the tone for this inspired live–action remake of the Disney animated feature, with Michael Kamen taking his cue from the storyline to deliver a score that's right on the button. While one might have wondered whatever prompted the powers–that–be at Disney to remake one of their most successful films, one can't dispute the fact that they were right in hiring Kamen to write the score. His music is constantly innovative and amusing, appropriately matching the grander–than–life elements in the film, while adding the right touch to its more down-to-earth aspects. Particularly welcome here is the sentimental "Going to Have a Puppy" with its sarcastic downside "I Adore Puppies," and the heroic "Rescue," brimming with great action tonalities. The entire score is a total joy.

Didier C. Deutsch

110 in the Shade

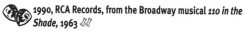 1990, RCA Records, from the Broadway musical *110 in the Shade*, 1963 ♪♪

album notes: **Music:** Harvey Schmidt; **Lyrics:** Tom Jones; **Book:** N. Richard Nash; **Cast:** Robert Horton (Bill Starbuck), Inga Swenson (Lizzie), Stephen Douglass (File), Leslie Warren (Snookie).

 1999, Jay Records/U.K., from the Broadway musical *110 in the Shade*, 1998 ♪♪♪♪♪

album notes: **Music:** Harvey Schmidt; **Lyrics:** Tom Jones; **Book:** N. Richard Nash; **Cast:** Karen Ziemba (Lizzie), Ron Raines (Bill Starbuck), Richard Muenz (File), Kristin Chenoweth (Snookie); **Orchestra:** National Symphony Orchestra; **Conductor:** John Owen Edwards.

Based on the play *The Rainmaker* by N. Richard Nash (also the basis for a film starring Burt Lancaster and Katharine Hepburn), *110 in the Shade* was the first musical tackled by Tom Jones and Harvey Schmidt since the creation of their enormously successful off-Broadway show *The Fantasticks* (still running as of this writing). The story of a spinster who returns home to her drought-stricken Western town and a con artist who claims he can create rain, *110 in the Shade* had a spotty career on Broadway, where it opened on October 24, 1963 for a total run of 330 performances. Upon her return to her home town, Lizzie Curry, a school teacher who apprehends the idea of becoming an old maid, suddenly finds herself torn between Bill Starbuck, the dream weaver she would love to believe and who claims she is Melisande reincarnate, and the more down-to-earth File, who has never declared himself openly before, but now wants to settle down with her. Finally listening to reason, Lizzie opts for File.

In the original production, Inga Swenson played Lizzie to Robert Horton's Starbuck and Stephen Douglass's File. Also in the musical was Lesley (Ann) Warren whose exuberance in the show-stopping number "Little Red Hat" resulted in her being cast as Cinderella in a television special produced by Richard Rodgers shortly afterward.

The original-cast album of *110 in the Shade,* poorly recorded and hopelessly distorted, didn't do real justice to the score by Jones and Schmidt. The inclusion of the "Overture," previously unreleased, on the CD reissue does not deter from the fact that the recording often sounds terrible, despite winsome performances by the various principals.

In contrast to the RCA release of the soundtrack, the much more complete two-CD recording from Jay Records is superb in

every possible way, but mostly due to Karen Ziemba's admirable performance as Lizzie. A Broadway actress with excellent credentials (*Steel Pier*), Ziemba steals the show in this complete recording that adds instrumental bridges, reprises, and songs that were dropped from the show before it reached Broadway.

Ron Raines as Starbuck, and Richard Muenz as File are equally fine, but the other show-stopping performance belongs to Kristin Chenoweth, who is exhilarating as Snookie. The actress, who has since moved to a much-noticed star turn in the Broadway revival of *You're a Good Man Charlie Brown,* has a bright future ahead of her. Every other element in the recording is superlative, making this the definitive *110 in the Shade* to have.

Didier C. Deutsch

100 Rifles

1999, Film Score Monthly, from the film *100 Rifles*, 20th Century-Fox, 1969 ♪♪♪♪

album notes: **Music:** Jerry Goldsmith.

Lukas Kendall's fan mag, *Film Score Monthly,* has begun sponsoring a series of rare soundtrack reissues and first releases that have been available through the magazine, with surprisingly effective results. Take for instance Jerry Goldsmith's vivacious score for the 1969 action western *100 Rifles,* starring Burt Reynolds and Raquel Welch. According to Kendall, in an explanatory note, searching for the tapes yielded two different sets, one in mono, which was the one used in the film, and the other containing stereo components that were missing some cues. Wisely, Kendall decided to include both, a rare instance of a producer opting not to make a choice that might have riled some fans, but preferring to let the listener chose which he likes best.

A typical oater set south of the border, *100 Rifles* spins a violent yarn in which Reynolds, as a half-breed bank robber, and Jim Brown, as a bounty-hunting lawman, team up with Welch, an attractive revolutionary, to help save Yaqui Indians from being annihilated by a ruthless Mexican general, played by Fernando Lamas. Adding some zest to the story, a mild relationship develops between the lawman and the revolutionary, something that was deemed racy at the time of the film's release, though it would hardly provoke a raised eyebrow nowadays.

As Jeff Bond remarks in his informative and detailed notes, by the time *100 Rifles* was made, Goldsmith had established himself as the flip-side of Elmer Bernstein's buoyant Americana western, and his style of writing reflected the darker, more percussion-driven approach that had already characterized such scores as *Rio Conchos, Hour of the Gun,* and *Bandolero!* His trademark dissonant brass effects are again at the center of this score, dominated by a vibrant main theme and a mixture of mariachi rhythms and aggressive percussion.

In retrospect, the film may not have left a truly memorable impression, but however you look at it, the release of this CD is a real find.

Didier C. Deutsch

100.000 dollari per Ringo

1994, GEM-Edipan Records/Italy, from the film *100.000 dollari per Ringo (100,000 Dollars for Ringo)*, 1966 ♪♪

album notes: Music: Bruno Nicolai; **Conductor:** Bruno Nicolai.

A classic spaghetti western story, about a stranger who arrives in a small border town in Texas where two gangs are at war over control of the place while trying to find a buried treasure, *$100,000 for Ringo* starred Richard Harrison as the stranger (an undercover Ranger), and was directed by Alberto De Martino. The evocative score Nicolai wrote for this one is propelled by the "Ballad For Ringo," which can be found on a multitude of compilations. It sounds nothing like the rest of the score, big, florid, with brassy accents that dominate the cues, which is miles away from the simple guitar-and-harmonica riffs one expects for this type of music. The sound, heavily reverbed, and without much charm or warmth, makes listening to it even more difficult. This recording may be difficult to find. Check with a used CD store, mail-order company, or a dealer specializing in rare, out-of-print, or import recordings.

Didier C. Deutsch

One Night Stand

1997, Verve Records, from the film, *One Night Stand*, New Line Cinema, 1997 ♪♪♪♪

album notes: Music: Mike Figgis; **Orchestra:** Juilliard String Quartet: Robert Mann, violin; Joel Smirnoff, violin; Samuel Rhodes, viola; Joel Krosnick, cello; **Conductor:** Nick Ingman; **Featured Musicians:** Dave Hartley, piano, Fender Rhodes; Ralph Salmins, drums; Laurence Cottle, bass guitar; John Parricelle, electric/Spanish/acoustic guitars; Ray Warleigh, alto/baritone saxes; Frank Ricotti, percussion; Mike Figgis, trumpet; Miriam Stockley, soprano; Maggie Nicols, vocals.

Unfortunately, jazz is seldom used in film soundtracks, or used only when it seems to fit a specific purpose. Mike Figgis obviously has a passion for this type of music because it permeates his complex tale about an ad agency executive on a trip to New York who enjoys a one-night affair with a beautiful woman he meets in Manhattan, and who feels pangs of guilt when he returns to his trusting wife in L.A. One year later he meets his lover again at a social function where his wife has accompanied him; she is now married and is with her husband. The bittersweet encounter leads to unresolved expec-

tations. Punctuating the action, various jazz tracks (originals, as well as source material by Jimmy Smith, Nina Simone, and Jacques Loussier) place the action squarely into a sophisticated arena, in which the participants, obviously educated professionals, can thrive and be themselves. An extra concept of a possible homosexual relationship between the executive and a friend dying of AIDS, while not significantly informed in the selections on the soundtrack album, gives the film an extra added poignancy.

Didier C. Deutsch

One Tough Cop

1998, H.O.L.A. Recordings, from the film *One Tough Cop*, Stratosphere/Patriot, 1998 ♪

album notes: Music: Bruce Broughton; **Conductor:** by Bruce Broughton.

1998, Intrada Records, from the film *One Tough Cop*, Stratosphere/Patriot, 1998 ♪♪

The saga of two NYPD partners, *One Tough Cop* follows the two hot-headed representatives of the law on their beat, as they connive with various shady characters, investigate the rape and mutilation of a nun, try to convince a man who has killed his wife not to take his own life, mingle with their squeeze of the moment, gamble, participate in a mandatory car chase, and otherwise rankle their superiors with their couldn't-care-less attitudes, while they are being investigated by the FBI. So many clichés are accumulated in this picture that it almost becomes a parody of itself. Unfortunately, the two soundtrack albums here do not do much to liven up the spirits of the film. The first, a collection of "street language" songs, will no doubt appeal to a minority of filmgoers who may believe that it's cool to have a compilation such as this. Since it has very little to offer beyond a lot of noise and words that are not even lyrics, it can easily be dismissed by those who, having seen the film, decided it was not even worth the price of admission or rental.

Much more sad than the film itself is the score written by Bruce Broughton, usually a reliable composer, whose cues here are totally routine and uninspired. Quoting the notes: "Bruce Broughton saw in the film not only a terse crime drama but also a portrait of friendship, loyalty and betrayal. To score the range of emotions magnified by one man's efforts to preserve duty, faith and integrity, Broughton wrote in an unusually subdued manner." In other words, with all due respect, it stinks! Well, not exactly, because even in his less inspired efforts, Broughton manages to remain eloquent, but he certainly has done much better than this somber, unattractive score.

Didier C. Deutsch

One True Thing

1998, Varèse-Sarabande, from the film *One True Thing*, Universal, 1998 🎬🎬🎬🎬

album notes: Music: Cliff Eidelman; **Conductor:** Cliff Eidelman.

A riveting drama about a New York journalist returning home to care for her mother who is dying of cancer, *One True Thing* is the kind of film that attracts selected audiences and usually spawns sensitive scores no one wants to listen to. Credit Cliff Eidelman with creating a score that reflects a peaceful, quiet sensitivity rather than a morbid sense of doom, with cues that serve as a perfect counterpoint to the screen action, while illuminating it. The trip home of columnist Ellen Gulden fills her with suspicion and apprehension: she has been summoned by her father to attend to the care of her mother who is going to undergo surgery for cancer. Ellen is all the more upset that she never got along with her mother, and she had to abandon her job just as she was about to have a major breakthrough in her career. But as she realizes that this may be the last opportunity she will have to be with her mother her world flips over, and she changes her sets of values.

A story of this kind usually has difficulties finding an audience, but striking performances by Meryl Streep, Renee Zellweger, and William Hurt help to dispel any notion that this drama may be a downer. Also a help is Eidelman's score which illuminates the story and gives it a different spin: where others might have used the theme to create portentous, somber cues, Eidelman instead wrote a score that's strikingly quiet and limpid. It makes for a totally attractive CD.

Didier C. Deutsch

Only the Lonely

1991, Varèse Sarabande, from the film *Only the Lonely*, 20th Century Fox, 1991 🎬🎬🎬

album notes: Music: Maurice Jarre; **Conductor:** Maurice Jarre.

An amusing romantic comedy, *Only the Lonely* paints the picture of a bachelor cop, essentially a portly nice guy, still living with his domineering Irish mother in an unassuming working-class neighborhood in Chicago. Acutely observed and frequently transcending the limited parameters of the genre, the film provided Maurice Jarre with a broad range of characters and situations to write a pleasantly colorful score. In one long, expansive moment ("Ladder Proposal"), the composer was able to pack all the best elements in the film to write a piece that echoes the feelings of the main character, played by John Candy, after he meets and falls in love with a timid funeral parlor cosmetician. The two pop vocals, Roy Orbison's "Only the Lonely," and Van Morrison's "Someone Like You," neatly

bookend the score for what amounts to a flavorful musical package.

Didier C. Deutsch

Only You

1994, Columbia Records; from the film *Only You*, TriStar Pictures, 1994 🎬🎬🎬

album notes: Music: Rachel Portman; **Conductor:** David Snell; **Featured Soloist:** Christopher Warren Green, violin.

Rachel Portman's cues are often lost in this soundtrack album in which the top pop selections often seem to command more attention. But as usual, the composer eventually impresses with the high quality levels of her compositions, though many of the selections are shamefully too short. One of the most interesting film composers to hit her stride in recent years, Portman often writes in a romantic, expansive style that seems particularly suited to this well-heeled romantic comedy about a couple (Marisa Tomei and Robert Downey Jr.) who meet and eventually fall in love against the exotic background provided by Venice, Rome, the fields of Tuscany and the Amalfi coast. Particularly enjoyable here are the cues marked "I'm Coming with You," "Arriving at Damon's Restaurant," and the short but expressive "Running After Damon," which pretty much define what the score is all about.

Didier C. Deutsch

Operation Dumbo Drop

1995, Hollywood Records, from the film *Operation Dumbo Drop*, Walt Disney Films, 1995 🎬🎬🎬

album notes: Music: David Newman; **Orchestra:** The Sinfonia of London; **Conductor:** David Newman; **Featured Instrumentalists:** Marty Frasu, synthesizers; Dr. Devious, Arthur McGillycuddy, ethnic flutes.

Here is another case where the pop selections seem to intrude on the development of the original score, written by none other than the excellent David Newman. Apparently based on a real-life incident involving American Green Berets in Vietnam, some local mountain villagers with an exacting ritual, a pachyderm which must be hauled over 200 miles of enemy jungle territory, and a cute 12-year-old orphan boy in need of some love and understanding, the film makes extensive use of period pop tunes, faithfully compiled here to the detriment of Newman's score. The composer's cues, using some anachronistic synthesizer sounds, appropriate ethnic flutes, and the orchestral textures of the Sinfonia of London, create an atmosphere that also seems quite remote from the tone of the film itself, with long, expansive romantic themes that are exquisite but hardly the kind you might expect to hear in a comedy.

Didier C. Deutsch

Orchestra Wives

See: Sun Valley Serenade/Orchestra Wives

Orlando

1993, Varèse-Sarabande, from the film *Orlando,* Sony Pictures Classics, 1993 🎬🎬

album notes: Music: David Motion, Sally Potter; **Featured Musicians:** Richard Addison, contra-bass clarinet; Alexander Balanescu, violin, viola; Clare Connors, violin; Lindsay Cooper, bassoon; Andy Findon, clarinets, saxophone; Christopher Laurence, double bass; David Motion, keyboards; Bruce Nockles, trumpets, flugelhorns; Jesper Siberg, midi; Sally Potter, vocals; Jimmy Somerville, vocal.

Virginia Woolf's 1928 book about a young man who defies death, lives 400 years, and ends up as a woman received a sumptuous adaptation in Sally Potter's film *Orlando* and elicited a rather eclectic score from the director and David Motion. First seen as a nobleman attending the court of Elizabeth I, Orlando eventually enters the 20th century as a woman, after various period adventures, lovingly detailed in the film's many surprising scenes. Because of Potter's involvement with the score as well, it can be said to represent her vision of the film as a whole, rather than someone else's interpretation of her intentions. Thus, the inclusion of three different versions of "Coming," the song she also wrote, performed by androgynous-sounding Jimmy Somerville, also reflects her perception of what the soundtrack album should be all about. The music itself, written in a minimalist style, sometimes evokes Philip Glass on a bad day. At the very least, it is very uninvolving, with an occasional flash that may qualify as interesting.

Didier C. Deutsch

Oscar

1991, Varèse Sarabande, from the film *Oscar,* Touchstone Pictures, 1991 🎬🎬🎬

album notes: Music: Elmer Bernstein; **Conductor:** Elmer Bernstein.

Sylvester Stallone seems an unlikely foil for a comedy set in 1931, though he played a former hitman intent on reforming and setting a good example for his children. Using as a basic source of inspiration Rossini's "Barber of Seville," Elmer Bernstein crafted an amusing score that has many merits even if it is not exactly earthshaking. In longer–than–usual cues, in which his ideas have time to find an expression, he delivers music that remains frequently innovative and catchy ("Lisa Dreams"), and representative of the screen action ("Cops and Real Crooks"). Providing a different spin of their own, several pop selections give the album an early '30s feel.

Didier C. Deutsch

Oscar and Lucinda

1997, Sony Classical, from the film, *Oscar and Lucinda,* 20th Century-Fox, 1997 🎬🎬🎬

album notes: Music: Thomas Newman; **Conductor:** Thomas Newman.

Ralph Fiennes and Cate Blanchett portrayed two eccentric characters in the Victorian era in *Oscar and Lucinda:* he a strict religious man who only comes alive when he gambles, she as a wealthy woman who likes to play poker. Recognizing that they complement each other the moment that they meet, Oscar and Lucinda form an odd relationship in which gambling is the main motif, but emotions also have their place. Told with grace and humor, the tale was bound to inspire composer Thomas Newman who created some surprisingly effective cues in which sudden choral outbursts are among the most engaging moments. At times bouncy and energetic, at other times profoundly intense and reflective, it is the kind of score that revels in the richness of the material it is supposed to illuminate and thrives upon enhancing it.

Didier C. Deutsch

The Osterman Weekend

1999, Aleph Records, from the film *The Osterman Weekend,* 20th Century-Fox, 1982 🎬🎬🎬

album notes: Music: Lalo Schifrin; **Conductor:** Lalo Schifrin.

Sam Peckinpah's last film, *The Osterman Weekend* was a clever action melodrama that starred Burt Lancaster as a CIA director with presidential ambitions who convinces a TV reporter that several of his close friends are undercover Soviet agents. At his urging, the reporter, who is about to entertain his friends over a weekend at his place, puts surveillance cameras everywhere, resulting in a rapidly volatile situation when the friends find out about his suspicions. Giving a specific flavor to the film, Schifrin wrote a jazz score that imbued *The Osterman Weekend* with sensual tones and a tightly controlled sound that perfectly matched the ambience of the story on the screen. This expanded edition of the score, released on Schifrin's own label, is eloquently evocative and makes for a vigorously enjoyable listening experience.

Didier C. Deutsch

Othello

1993, Varèse Sarabande, from the film *Othello,* Castle Hill, 1952 🎬🎬🎬🎬

album notes: Music: Angelo-Francesco Lavagnino, Alberto Bargeris; **Music Reconstruction:** Michael Pendowski; **Orchestra:** Members of The Chicago Symphony Orchestra; **Choir:** The Chicago Lyric Opera Chorus, **Conductor:** Bob Bowker.

1995, Varèse Sarabande, from the film *Othello,* Columbia Pictures, 1995 🎬🎬🎬

album notes: Music: Charlie Mole; **Conductor:** Nick Ingman; **Featured Soloists:** John Themis, oud, guitar, flutes, solo voice; Paul Clarvis,

African percussion; Keith Thomson, ethnic flutes, oboes, shawm; Nick Curtis, Moorish wailing.

One subject, two versions, two very different scores. The first, for the 1952 film directed and starring Orson Welles, was written by Francesco Angelo Lavagnino, one of the most respected and proficient Italian composers of the 1950s. Dark and frequently disturbing, but also a very adventurous score in its expression, it involves a wide range of musical effects (North African sonorities, Elizabethan melodies, brass flourishes, medieval tunes, dissonant choral accents) that combine together, collide and mix to paint a brooding, multi–faceted diorama, representative of the action and the background against which it happens. Painstakingly restored, it is performed here in a new recording by members of the Chicago Symphony Orchestra and the Chicago Lyric Opera, in a magnificent display that reveals its many telling aspects.

Surprisingly written along more traditional lines, Charlie Mole's music, heard in the version starring Laurence Fishburn and Kenneth Branagh, also makes use of ethnic instruments, primarily North African, for a score which is equally somber but eventually more one–dimensional in its expression. Unlike the cues written by Lavagnino, Mole's score also seems to be less melodically inclined, with floating lines weaving in and out of rhythmic patterns that may prove more effective on screen than on a strictly audio basis.

Didier C. Deutsch

The Other

See: The Mephisto Waltz

The Other Side of 'Round Midnight

See: 'Round Midnight

The Other Sister

1998, Hollywood Records, from the film *The Other Sister*, Touchstone, 1998 𝄪

album notes: Music: Rachel Portman.

Yet another songtrack album, which features an interesting mix of artists-of-the-moment, ranging from Savage Garden to Alison Krauss to Paula Cole. However some of these tracks, most noticeably the Soup Dragons cut, have been on a few too many other albums recently. Juliette Lewis, who stars in the film as a mentally challenged young woman who falls in love with a mentally challenged young man, attempts to sing a sultry rendition of "Come Rain or Come Shine," but sounds like my 10-year-old cousin. The album includes one score cut by

They Know the Score

Elmer Bernstein

I think that people who make temp tracks should be shot! I think the temp track is a vile and disgusting habit, which absolutely robs the composer of originality. I refuse to listen to temp scores, unless the film has been temped with music of mine. Otherwise I won't even listen to the temp score, because with temp scores, once you hear it you cannot ignore it. And you then are robbed of your own originality, your own voice, so to speak. I think that . . . temp scores should be discouraged.

***Courtesy of* Film Score Monthly**

Rachel Portman, who can compose a cute love theme with the best of them.

Beth Krakower

Otto e mezzo

See: 8 ½

Our Man Flint

See: In Like Flint

Out for Justice

1991, Varèse-Sarabande, from the film *Out for Justice*, Warner Bros., 1991 𝄪

album notes: Music: David Michael Frank; **Conductor:** David Michael Frank.

A typical Steven Seagal vehicle, *Out for Justice* dealt with a psychopath on a rampage, with the star portraying a one-man justice team out to correct the wrong and put an end to the murderer's mayhem. Adding a contemporary spin to the violent thriller were several songs, heard in bits and pieces on the soundtrack and in their entirety on this CD, with performances by Gregg Allman, Cool J.T., Teresa Belmont James, Todd Smallwood, and Kymberli Armstrong, among others. Of these, the explosive "Puerto Riqueno," by Michael Jimenez, may be the most interesting. David Michael Frank's score, represented by three selections, tries to be inventive and lively, using a whole contingent of percussion instruments and synthesizers to convey its musical message. The "Main Title" is actually quite good, but neither "One Night in Brooklyn" nor "Final Encounter" keep these promises.

Didier C. Deutsch

Out of Africa

1986, MCA Records, from the film *Out of Africa, Universal, 1985*

album notes: Music: John Barry; **Orchestra:** Royal Scottish National Orchestra; **Conductor:** John Barny.

John Barry won a well-deserved Academy Award for this remarkable score, which gave its specific romantic flavor to this tale based on the true-life experiences of writer Isak Dinesen in Kenya in the days before World War I. Though married at the time, Dinesen got involved with a charming, boyish aviator, in a relationship that did not last, even though she became available, because of his independent nature. Sometimes more a travelogue than a romantic drama, the film is marked by its many breathtaking views of unspoiled African landscapes, lovingly captured in gorgeous scenes, in which Barry's music serves as a necessary complement to the image. "Flying Over Africa" is one of the score's choicest moments. For the most part eschewing the ethnic rhythms that had marked his other African epic *Born Free,* Barry delivered a series of strikingly original romantic themes that masterfully capture the moods and feels of the film.

One of John Barry's most memorable scores, *Out of Africa* receives a bright new reading in Joel McNeely's powerful direction of the Royal Scottish National Orchestra. One might question the validity of having another recording of the score, when the original, conducted by Barry, is also in the catalogue. But the fact that this new recording adds several cues that are not in the original seems a good enough reason. Add to that the sparklingly shiny sonics, the lovely treatment, and if you will the fact that too much good music is not a sin *per se,* and all you need to do is listen and enjoy. Still, one might regret that the cues are presented here pretty much as they were written—i.e., short and sweet—when the occasion could have justified presenting them in longer, more elaborate suites, something that the score itself could have stood. As it is, cues like "Alone on the Farm" (1:00), "Karen and Denys" (:48), "Karen's Journey Ends" (1:00), "Beach at Night" (:58), and "You'll Keep Me Then" (:58) seem inordinately brief and insufficiently developed. This is the CD's only real shortcoming.

Didier C. Deutsch

Out of This World

1992, Sony Broadway, from the Broadway production *Out of This World, 1950*

album notes: Music: Cole Porter; **Lyrics:** Cole Porter; **Musical Direction:** Pembroke Davenport; **Cast:** Charlotte Greenwood, William Eythe, Priscilla Gillette, William Redfield, Barbara Ashley, George Jongeyans, David Burns.

1995, DRG Records, from the concert performance *Out of This World, 1995*

album notes: Music: Cole Porter; **Lyrics:** Cole Porter; **Musical Direction:** Rob Fisher; **Cast:** Andrea Martin, Gregg Edelman, Marin Mazzie, Peter Scolari, La Chanze, Ken Page, Ernie Sabella.

Arguably, one of the greatest of all of Cole Porter's later Broadway efforts, *Out of This World* shows the composer/lyricist at his very peak. Unfortunately, the score is better known for what is missing than what is actually included. Shortly before its Broadway premiere, one of Porter's greatest songs, "From This Moment On," was deleted from the score. When it was added later to the film version of *Kiss Me Kate,* it became a hit. That aside, the original cast recording is sheer unalloyed pleasure from beginning to end. There are love songs to suit every taste, delightful comedy songs and scintillating numbers devoted to man's (and woman's) favorite sport, sex. While Charlotte Greenwood was not the first choice to play Juno, she enters into the spirit of fun required by her character with unabashed fervor. George Jongeyans (Gaynes), who has a flawed voice, is enthusiastic and passionate as her errant husband Jupiter. Priscilla Gillette is a delight as the young American mortal who gives Jupiter ants in his pants. The rest of the super–talented performers cast their spell on this splendid sounding monaural album.

The 1995 recording resulted from a successful concert presentation at New York's City Center, which had show buffs eager with anticipation. Andrea Martin, as Juno, is terrific and proves, once again, that she is a wonderful musical comedy performer. She wrings every ounce of nuance, hedonism, and joy out of her songs and is breathtaking in her energy and commitment. Ken Page, as the wandering Jupiter, works hard at his difficult role, but does not always succeed. Peter Scolari as Mercury is a lot of fun. Marin Mazzie and Gregg Edelman, as the modern American mortal couple, perform "From This Moment On," which has been restored in the score. Other songs that were either cut from the original production or not included on the original 1950 Broadway cast recording are also recorded here for the first time, making this album a winner in every way.

Jerry Thomas

The Out-of-Towners

1999, Milan Records, from the film *The Out-of-Towners, Paramount, 1999*

album notes: Music: Marc Shaiman; **Conductor:** Pete Anthony.

The screen pairing of Steve Martin and Goldie Hawn in a comedy by Neil Simon provided the cue for Marc Shaiman to write a score that's amusingly lively and descriptive of the misadventures of a visiting couple whose weekend in Manhattan becomes a long series of calamities, in this new adaptation of *The Out-of-Towners*. Often breaking into an exhilarating big band number ("Fogged In," "Taxi!") or indulging in a cool and relaxed jazz number ("Park Avenue Stroll"), the score is otherwise demurely keeping itself in check, trying very hard not to let the zany action dictate its own whereabouts. The rich soundtrack also benefits from some romantic tunes that add a touching counterpoint to the action cues, making this a fully rounded score with a lot to please. With the exception of a totally vapid rendition of "Isn't It Romantic?," by Mervyn Warren and Jose Aiello, the album also features some great vocals, including "That Old Black Magic," performed by Louis Prima and Keely Smith and "Bad Girls," by Donna Summer.

Didier C. Deutsch

Out To Sea

1997, Milan Records, from the film *Out To Sea,* 20th Century Fox, 1997 ♪♪♪♪
album notes: Music: David Newman; **Synthesizer Programming:** Marty Frasu; **Conductor:** David Newman, Chris Boardman.

If you've ever felt like taking a cruise in the Caribbean, but couldn't afford to get seasick, then this album might do the trick and help you dream that you're actually on one of those luxury liners. Several of the tracks ("Cheek to Cheek," "Celebration," "Canadian Sunset," "Mambo No. 5," "Jumpin' at the Woodside," "Sea Cruise," etc.) are performed in sophisticated lounge/cruise ship style, with Brent Spiner providing an occasional vocal that's right on target—unobtrusive, upfront, and handsomely bland. For added pleasure, they've dusted off Bobby Darin's rendition of "More," from the film *Mondo Cane.* And David Newman has thrown in some cues from his instrumental score, creating a different set of moods, equally welcome. The film, by the way, stars grumpy old actors Jack Lemmon and Walter Matthau, in yet another innocuous comedy–by–the–numbers, as mismatched brothers–in–law who wind up aboard a luxury ship as . . . dance hosts, who think nothing of meeting (and fleecing) the wealthy women on the cruise. As long as they keep that music playing, welcome aboard.

Didier C. Deutsch

Outbreak

1995, Varèse Sarabande, from the film *Outbreak,* Warner Bros., 1995 ♪♪
album notes: Music: James Newton Howard; **Conductor:** Artie Kane; **Featured Musicians:** Dean Parks, guitar; Emil Richards, Joe Porcaro,

Michael Fisher, Lenny Castro, percussion; Steve Porcaro, Bob Daspit, synth programming; **Choir:** L.A. Master Chorale.

A suitably dramatic orchestral score with electronic effects, James Newton Howard's music for *Outbreak* sounds fittingly ominous and ballsy at the right places, though it eventually seems dry–bone and wrenching despite the many flourishes meant to embellish this tale about a rare disease imported from Africa and running rampant in a middle–American town. The impression is that the score, eloquent as it may be (and it is, just listen to "They're Coming"), takes too long to build some kind of momentum.

Didier C. Deutsch

The Outer Limits

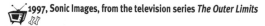 1997, Sonic Images, from the television series *The Outer Limits* ♪♪
album notes: Music: John Van Tongeren; **Theme:** Mark Mancina, John Van Tongeren; **Additional Music:** J. Peter Robinson.

The television show *The Outer Limits* aimed to stretch the boundaries of the viewer's imagination by presenting events that, under other circumstances, might have seemed unbelievable or out-of-this-world, and by going where the extraordinary was not uncommon. John Van Tongeren's score for the series, however, doesn't stretch anything and doesn't go anywhere. A fairly routine effort, it consists of synthesizer riffs, accompanied by light percussion instruments, that aim to create an aura but tends to be repetitive and tedious. It certainly doesn't break any new grounds.

Didier C. Deutsch

Outland/Capricorn One

1993, GNP/Crescendo; from the films *Outland,* Warner Bros., 1978; and *Capricorn One,* Warner Bros., 1981 ♪♪♪♪♪
album notes: Music: Jerry Goldsmith; **Orchestra:** The National Philharmonic Orchestra of London; **Conductor:** Jerry Goldsmith.

Two of Goldsmith's finest action scores are well represented on this lengthy album, which showcases the percussive, elaborately developed style of writing that dominated the composer's work until the mid–'80s. The 1981 *Outland* is a gritty and extremely dark outer space effort featuring a throbbing suspense motif of woodwinds and low strings, some delicately–textured electronics and crushing, monolithic action cues that hammer home the horror of dying in the emptiness of space. There's a spectacular cue for a foot chase in "Hot Water" and a surprisingly lyrical, romantic finale. *Capricorn One* is a landmark action score sporting a remarkably driving, jagged title march emphasizing harsh, militaristic brass and percussion. Insidiously subtle suspense cues alternate with arid

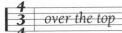

$\frac{4}{3}$
$\frac{}{4}$ *over the top*

desert portraits featuring a lonely solo trumpet figure and several spectacular action cues, notably the virtuoso "Breakout" which climaxes in a wild section of whirling horn and trumpet glissandos. They don't write 'em like this anymore.

Jeff Bond

Over the Top

 1987, Columbia, from the film *Over the Top*, Cannon, 1987 ♪♪♪

album notes: Music: Giorgio Moroder.

Sly Stallone had another one of his muscle-flexing jobs in this action-driven thriller in which he portrayed a truck driver whose sole ambition is to arm-wrestle Robert Loggia. If you didn't fall asleep after the first reel, it's probably because you were listening to the songs on the soundtrack, which have been conveniently assembled on this CD for your pleasure. Let's not get too excited, though: it's rather a mixed bag, with good rocking performances by Sammy Hagar, Robin Zander, Larry Greene, Kenny Loggins, the supergroup Asia, and Eddie Money. Now, whoever convinced Frank Stallone he could or should be singing, and Giorgio Moroder he should be writing instrumental scores?

Didier C. Deutsch

Pacific Blue

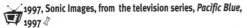 1997, Sonic Images, from the television series, *Pacific Blue*, 1997 ♪

album notes: Music: Christopher Franke; **Featured Vocalists:** David Glickman, Randy Crenshaw, Ryan Martin, Scott Monahan, Scott Urban, Janis Liebhart, Don Rudolph; **Featured Musicians:** Zeke Zirngiebel, guitars; Stanley Mann, bass; Christopher Franke, keyboards; Stu Richards, drums; Toby Scarbrough, drums; Ralph Rickert, trumpet; Lewis Taylor, saxophone.

In answer to all that sex and violence on television, some responsible producers have chosen to create wholesome shows that may be viewed by the whole family. Welcome to *Pacific Blue*, where cops on bicycles run after hippies who are ready to break the law and smoke pot on the beaches in Venice, Santa Monica, or Redondo Beach. Okay, we shouldn't make fun of shows that are trying to stay away from gangland murders, blood and gore, and all the usual ingredients shown on other networks. But if truth be told, *Pacific Blue* isn't just tame, it's bland! The same can be said about this soundtrack album, in which alternative bands and singers (who are not even credited) get a chance to be

heard. If only they sang in tune, it wouldn't be half as bad (listen to "Anymore" if you need to be convinced). It's as inconsequential as the series, and almost as boring.

Didier C. Deutsch

Pacific Heights

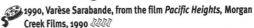 1990, Varèse Sarabande, from the film *Pacific Heights*, Morgan Creek Films, 1990 ♪♪♪♪

album notes: Music: Hans Zimmer; **Conductor:** Shirley Walker; **Featured Soloists:** Chuck Domanico, bass; Mike Lang, piano; Walt Fowler, trumpet; Gene Cipriano, saxophone; Carmen Twilley, voice.

Presented on CD in four long suites, Zimmer's textural music for this psychological thriller is comprised not so much of melodies or themes but of motifs and recurring figures and phrases. Zimmer creates a complex and compelling musical world comprised of orchestra, synthesizer, and voice. Instrumentally, the score is quite varied, yet it captures a consistent mood of apprehension, of danger, of working evil. A solo saxophone evokes a somewhat sensuous eloquence to the score's apprehensiveness, while a brief melody for female voice adds a tonality of ominous jeopardy. Zimmer provides a number of warm musical moments, the pretty piano theme heard every so often brings a sense of intimacy and compassion to the otherwise suspenseful or frightening moments, but it's always the stronger, non-melodic musical figures that predominate, just as the strange circumstances of the film constantly overwhelm the calmer moments. Zimmer's score likewise mirrors this counterpoint with notable style and flavor. The music is so varied and the orchestrations so interesting that the music is constantly listenable, always turning something new that wasn't heard before.

Randall Larson

Pacific Overtures

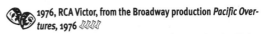 1976, RCA Victor, from the Broadway production *Pacific Overtures*, 1976 ♪♪♪♪

album notes: Music: Stephen Sondheim; **Lyrics:** Stephen Sondheim; **Musical Direction:** Paul Gemignani; **Featured Musicians:** Fusako Yoshida, voice, shamisen; Genji Ito, shakuhachi; **Cast:** Mako, Soon-Teck Oh, Yuki Shimoda, Sab Shimono, Isao Sato, Jae Woo Lee, Alvin Ing, Ricardo Tobia, Mark Hsu Syers, Timm Fujii, Gedde Watanabe, Patrick Kinser-Lau, Conrad Yama, Ernest Harada, Freda Foh Sen, James Dybas.

The remarkable creative partnership between composer Stephen Sondheim and producer Harold Prince made its most daring foray with this musical treatment of the "opening" of Japan to western trade in 1853—from the Japanese perspective. An all–Asian cast turned the Winter Garden stage into a whirling visual spectacle—which the CD listener can only imagine—and marvelously performed Sondheim's demanding score. The music is beautiful if not especially "hummable;" highlights include "Someone in a Tree" and the fast–forward, present–day finale, "Next."

Marc Kirkeby

The Pagemaster

1994, Fox Records, from the film *The Pagemaster*, 20th Century Fox, 1994 🎬🎬🎬🎬

album notes: Music: James Horner; **Conductor:** James Horner.

James Horner, who seems to have made a career out of scoring animated features (just kidding), delivered another outstanding score for this fanciful tale about a kid whose love of video games compels him to enter a fantasy world in which he finds himself surrounded by a host of eccentric characters who teach him an invaluable lesson. Solidly crafted, and thoroughly epic in its expression, the recording benefits from the longer playing time of some of the cues, which gives the music an opportunity to make itself heard and appreciated. In another display of his talent, and feel for this type of action cues, Horner relies on the wide range of colors in the orchestral palette to paint images that are wonderfully evocative and strikingly imaginative. Even if "The Library . . . The Pagemaster" irresistibly evokes Paul Dukas's "The Sorcerer's Apprentice," there is a genuine feel for excitement in Horner's virile accents, a notion further confirmed in other cues like "Towards the Open Sea . . . " or "The Flying Dragon." In the context, the two mandatory pop vocals at the beginning seem superfluous and can easily be edited out.

Didier C. Deutsch

Paint Your Wagon

1989, RCA Victor, from the Broadway production *Paint Your Wagon*, 1951 🎭🎭🎭🎭🎭

album notes: Music: Frederick Loewe; **Lyrics:** Alan Jay Lerner; **Musical Direction:** Franz Allers; **Cast:** James Barton, Olga San Juan, Tony Bavaar, James Mitchell, Rufus Smith.

1989, MCA Records, from the film *Paint Your Wagon*, Paramount Pictures, 1977 🎬🎬

album notes: Music: Frederick Loewe; **Lyrics:** Alan Jay Lerner; **Orchestra:** The Paramount Studio Orchestra; **Conductor:** Nelson Riddle; **Cast:** Lee Marvin, Jean Seberg, Clint Eastwood, Harve Presnell, Ray Walston.

With the exception of a very few, musicals of the old west do not succeed on Broadway. Westerns tend to be a product of Hollywood. Regardless of the quality of the book, which need not concern the listener, *Paint Your Wagon* is a happy exception, which can be savored repeatedly on the 1951 original cast album in clear, up–front monaural sound. The versatility of Lerner and Loewe is certainly amazing when this show is compared to their other works. It is not set in the proper parlors of Edwardian London, the mists of the Scottish Highlands, the elegant salons of Paris or in legendary Camelot. The setting here is the touchstone of Americana, the wild west during the Gold Rush. The elegant Lerner had a talent for creating words that seem to come from within the soul of each character. The music confirms that the very European Loewe was one of the most talented and versatile composers of the Broadway theater. While the vocal casting may not come across on the album as well as it surely did in the theater, all of the songs are sung with an energy and style that is appropriate to the setting of the show. While the 1977 film version has the same title and many of the same songs as the Broadway musical, it has almost an entirely new plot with additional characters. Lovers of the original cast album, be warned: The soundtrack recording will certainly give you a huge jolt. There is none of the subtlety or even charm of the original and the innate elegance of Frederick Loewe's music is gone. In fact, the original orchestral sound has been totally altered and replaced with a tough grittiness that was not apparent in the original. The new songs, written by Alan Jay Lerner with Andre Previn, as Loewe was evidently unwilling to work on the project, are actually quite good and don't sound out of place. However, except for Harve Presnell, an extremely gifted Broadway performer, the singing on this album is very rough. Lee Marvin and Jean Seberg were never considered singers and suffice it to say that this is Clint Eastwood's only musical performance. None of them are truly terrible and there is a sort of harsh reality contained in the performances that makes their characters seem real and earthy. Best that can be said is that, though not an important recording, it has its interesting side.

Jerry J. Thomas

The Pajama Game

1954, Columbia Records, from the Broadway production *The Pajama Game*, 1954 🎭🎭🎭

album notes: Music: Richard Adler, Jerry Ross; **Lyrics:** Richard Adler, Jerry Ross; **Musical Direction:** Hal Hastings; **Cast:** John Raitt, Janis Paige, Eddie Foy Jr., Carol Haney.

One of the classic Broadway show scores of all time has received a recording that puts its charming, exuberant score in the best possible light. With energetic performances by John Raitt, Janis Paige, Eddie Foy Jr., and Carol Haney along with the rest of the cast, chorus and orchestra, the score sounds better and more exciting than it actually is. There are several classic, well-known songs, but portions of this score are fairly uninteresting. It evens out to be about half and half. The slightly reverberant mono sound is in no way a deterrent to enjoyment. In fact, it takes one back to a time and a Broadway that no longer exist, perhaps never did. For that alone, it is worth listening to.

Jerry J. Thomas

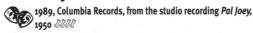
Pal Joey

1989, Columbia Records, from the studio recording *Pal Joey*, 1950 ♪♪♪♪

album notes: Music: Richard Rodgers; **Lyrics:** Lorenz Hart; **Musical Direction:** Lehman Engel; **Cast:** Harold Lang, Vivienne Segal, Beverly Fite, Barbara Ashley, Jo Hurt.

1995, DRG Records, from the concert performance *Pal Joey*, 1995 ♪♪♪♪

album notes: Music: Richard Rodgers; **Lyrics:** Lorenz Hart; **Musical Direction:** Rob Fisher; **Cast:** Peter Gallagher, Patti LuPone, Daisy Prince, Vicki Lewis, Bebe Neuwirth, Arthur Rubin.

The last effort by Richard Rodgers and Lorenz Hart, *Pal Joey* is a ground-breaking, innovative show that raises the musical genre to an art form (though few in 1940 suspected it) and stands today as an early precursor of the musicals Stephen Sondheim would create some 30 years later. Based on the short stories by John O'Hara, it introduces a charming "heel," a small–time nightclub performer who ditches the innocent girl in love with him for a middle–aged socialite in his desire to climb the ladder of success and open his own club. Though the mature aspects of the story left critics divided over the show's real merits, the score by Rodgers and Hart received unanimous praise, and yielded at least one instantly recognizable hit song in "Bewitched."

In 1950, Goddard Lieberson, head of A&R at Columbia Records, recorded a studio cast album of the score, with Vivienne Segal reprising the role of the socialite Vera Simpson, which she had created in the original, and Harold Lang singing Joey, the role originated by Gene Kelly in 1940. The recording was an immediate success, so much so that it led to a successful revival of the show on Broadway the following year. Though in upfront mono sound, the recording remains the closest document available of the score in its near–to–original presentation.

Of the several recordings of the score available, the DRG version is by far the best: The sound quality is exceptional, and the crackling performances right on target, with Peter Gallagher appropriately charming as a heel, Patti LuPone grandly superb as Vera, Daisy Prince at her fetching best as the innocent Linda, and Bebe Neuwirth, whose rendition of "Zip" is a highlight, particularly effective as Melba. The recording, a result of a concert presentation in New York City Center's highly acclaimed "Encore!" series, contains many selections not available elsewhere, and is the one to have if you must have only one.

Didier C. Deutsch

1989, Capitol Records, from the film *Pal Joey*, Columbia Pictures, 1957 ♪♪

album notes: Music: Richard Rodgers; **Lyrics:** Lorenz Hart; **Choir:** The Columbia Studio Chorus; **Orchestra:** The Columbia Studio Orchestra;

Conductor: Morris Stoloff; **Cast:** Frank Sinatra, Rita Hayworth, Kim Novak, Barbara Nichols.

As is the case with Frank Sinatra's film soundtrack recordings on Capitol, the CD release of Rodgers & Hart's *Pal Joey* suffers from an interminable lack of quality.

While the musical numbers survive as some of the most endearing, snappy performances of Sinatra's entire career (this was 1957, after all, and the singer was at the peak of his vocal power), their full impact is marred by the lack of detail or presence in the sound quality—a characteristic that has marked this recording since its first release as an LP. Additionally, the original mastering engineers seem to have used pseudo–stereo processing on some tracks (the classic "Lady Is a Tramp," which originates from a Sinatra–Riddle Capitol Studio session, is here reduced to a blur—the clarity and detail of the original purposely destroyed so it would match the poor balance of the other tracks).

Sonic deficiencies aside, the soundtrack vitally preserves Sinatra's definitive performances of songs that have become almost synonymous with his name: "The Lady Is a Tramp," "Bewitched," "I Didn't Know What Time It Was," and "I Could Write a Book" among them. These are the songs, and the interpretations, that define Sinatra's finest hour!

Charles L. Granata

The Pallbearer

1996, Miramax Records, from the film *The Pallbearer*, Miramax Pictures, 1996 ♪♪

Barely six minutes of Stewart Copeland's underscore for this comedy made it onto the album, packed instead with an eclectic collection of party songs by artists such as Al Green ("Love Is a Beautiful Thing"), Perry Como ("Papa Loves Mambo"), and Rick James ("Super Freak"). The score samples are fairly undistinguished synth cues with little impact, as is the song selection.

David Hirsch

Palmetto

1998, RCA, from the film *Palmetto*, Columbia, 1998 ♪♪

album notes: Music: Klaus Doldinger.

At the onset of this CD, Woody Harrelson as Harry Barber, a former journalist, is heard complaining about the treatment he received, after spending two years in jail for a "crime" he didn't commit—actually exposing the corruption in Palmetto, a small Florida town, as part of an investigative report he worked on. That's only the beginning: back in Palmetto, he takes up with his ex-girlfriend, gets a "job" from the wife of the richest man in town, and in no time finds himself deep in trouble again, with corpses accumulating around him and all the evidence pointing to him. Klaus Doldinger's atmospheric score adds its own spin to this neo-noir film, but seems as wasted as the slow-paced story. Here it is given the one-tune treatment, barely enough to get an idea. The rest of the playing time on this CD is spent on pop/rock tunes that are not too terribly exciting, and that includes the swinging rendition of the classic "La Paloma" by Trio Guizar. David Byrne, Gregory Isaacs, J.J. Cale, the Chieftains with Ry Cooder, and Hepcat are among the artists who loaned their talent to this album. Whatever for?

Didier C. Deutsch

The Paper

1994, Reprise Records, from the film *The Paper,* Universal Pictures, 1994 ♪♪♪

album notes: Music: Randy Newman; **Conductor:** Randy Newman; **Featured Musicians:** Malcolm McNab, trumpet; Ralph Grierson, piano.

Life in a big city daily paper and the various conflicting personalities that animate it, exacerbated in this story by the fate of two black kids unjustly accused of a crime they have not committed, is the main focus in this affectionate look at the press. Tension as well as the dreaded deadline finds its expression in Randy Newman's score in cues with a tick-tocking feel, while the personal relations between the various members of the staff elicit themes with a more romantic approach. Though at times compelling, the score ultimately doesn't appeal as much as it should, the result of some selections being much too short and seemingly unfulfilled. Newman's vocal on "Make Up Your Mind" is a throwaway at best.

Didier C. Deutsch

The Paper Brigade

1999, Citadel Records, from the film *The Paper Brigade,* Leucadia, 1999 ♪♪♪♪

album notes: Music: Ray Colcord; **Conductor:** Ray Colcord.

A sunny comedy about life, love, and the fine art of newspaper delivery, *The Paper Brigade* is an unusually fetching film that has a lot to enjoy. The plot, first, which involves a gang of motorized hooligans' efforts to take over the job of kids on their bikes delivering papers to the locals every morning, thus igniting a war with dire circumstances; then the performers, kids and adults, who bring this little gem to life on the screen, including Kyle Howard as a street-smart ex-New Yorker who organizes the kids, Robert Englund as the town's amiable loony, and Ethan Glazer, Bibi Osterwald, Travis Wester, and Chauncey Leopardi, to single out a few; and last but not least, Ray Colcord's deliriously mock swashbuckling score. Colcord puts the

emphasis right where it should be, but finds time to inject little humorous notations here and there that are totally engaging, and throw the music in unexpected but always entertaining directions. Bold, brassy, and fun; you never knew that paper delivery could elicit anything like this.

Didier C. Deutsch

The Paper Chase/The Poseidon Adventure

1998, Film Score Monthly, from the 20th Century-Fox films, *The Paper Chase,* 1973, and *The Poseidon Adventure,* 1972 ♪♪♪♪♪
album notes: Music: John Williams; **Orchestra:** The 20th Century-Fox Orchestra, **Conductor:** John Williams.

Another marvelous release from Lukas Kendall's Film Score Monthly, this one focusing on two neglected scores by John Williams. The story of a young student lawyer torn between his desire to excel in the profession he has chosen and his evolving feelings about himself, *The Paper Chase* had some great performances, notably from John Houseman (as a crusty law teacher), an intelligent screenplay with a good story to tell, a great sense of direction from James Bridges who fleshed out the story based on the book by John Jay Osborn Jr., and an excellent score by Williams. In those days, Williams had not yet created the scores (*Towering Inferno* in 1974, *Jaws* in 1975, *Star Wars* in 1977, and *Superman* in 1978) that would make him the top Hollywood composer of the '70s, but already his style exhibited all the trademarks that would find their way into these masterpieces: solid melodic material, fully developed themes, pleasant tunes. Around the same time, he composed other "minor" scores bearing the same characteristics, with catchy contemporary stylings and some tinges of jazz, but without the bombast that would eventually find its way into his major scores. While not too terribly involving, *The Paper Chase* is uncomplicated and pleasantly enjoyable.

A seafaring disaster movie, *The Poseidon Adventure* was another matter altogether. Following *Airport*—the granddaddy of this cinematographic genre—by two years, it ushered in a new era in films in which ordinary people found themselves trapped in unordinary circumstances. In this case, the plot involved a dozen passengers on an ocean liner, who try to save themselves after a giant tidal wave capsized the ship. As is usual in this type of film, the various characters of the participants were brought to the fore, and not always in the best light. For his part, Williams, still new at this kind of film, delivered a solidly etched score that presaged some of his later works, particularly the films he would do for Irwin Allen. With some eerie chord changes signaling the ominous danger posed first by

$$\frac{4}{3}$$
$$8$$

paper tiger

"The Big Wave," then by the precarious position of the ship, filling with water, and about to go down at any moment, the score is a long series of cues in which there is little music activity (an occasional arpeggio on the piano here, the sketch of a theme there) but a lot of tension that builds up to communicate a sense of uneasiness. It's gripping and quite effective.

The recording itself is quite good, with *Paper Chase* coming across more positively than *Poseidon Adventure,* which sounds a bit dry and exhibits a lot of hiss on some tracks.

Didier C. Deutsch

Paper Tiger

1998, Cinephile/U.K., from the film *Paper Tiger,* Joseph E. Levine, 1975 ♪♪♪♪

album notes: Music: Roy Budd; **Orchestra:** The National Philharmonic Orchestra; **Conductor:** Roy Budd.

Strongly lyrical and evocative, Roy Budd's score for Ken Annakin's attractive East-meets-West *Paper Tiger* finds a welcome reissue in this CD, released by Cinephile in England, to which two bonus tracks have been added. The story of an English teacher and a young boy, son of the Japanese ambassador to an unnamed Asian country where political unrest is the order of the day, the film starred David Niven, as the "paper tiger" of the title, a Milquetoast of a man who fires his pupil's imagination with invented tales of derring-do and brilliant military exploit. For this amusing saga, also starring Toshiro Mifune and Hardy Kruger, Budd wrote a score teeming with heroic accents, a big theme, and two songs, "Who Knows the Answers?" performed by the Mike Sammes Singers, and "My Little Friend" by the Ray Conniff Singers. While most of the cues are played by the 85-strong National Philharmonic Orchestra, giving the score a big sound, Budd himself is heard playing piano in a trio format in "The Reception" and "Diplomatic Dance."

see also: The Black Windmill, Diamonds, Fear Is the Key, Get Carter, Sinbad & the Eye of the Tiger

Didier C. Deutsch

Papillon

1988, Silva Screen/U.K., from the film *Papillon,* Allied Artists, 1974 ♪♪♪♪♪

album notes: Music: Jerry Goldsmith; **Conductor:** Jerry Goldsmith.

Containing one of Goldsmith's best themes, for accordion over harpsichord and orchestra, *Papillon* is a compelling score. Lushly orchestrated, Goldsmith musically depicts the cruelty of the Devil's Island penitentiary and its tangled jungles in such a way that much of his score might be considered a tone poem— a rather brutal one, at that—for the monstrously savage island prison. There is a brutal theme for the island itself. In a more symbolic sense, it's actually a theme for imprisonment, an echoed series of nine notes for reeds, ascending and then dropping off, which in its unresolved melody perfectly captures the claustrophobic sense of entrapment felt by Henri Charriere, the hero of the film, played by Dustin Hoffman. Rising above it, though, is the brilliant main theme, a beautiful melodic rhythm embodying Charriere's courage and spirit in his relentless pursuit of freedom. Arthur Morton's orchestrations are brilliant, taking the score into ever-new environments, keeping it fresh and constantly interesting, even in its dissonant moments. The score also contains one of Goldsmith's best love themes ("Gift from the Sea").

Randall D. Larson

Parade

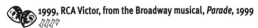

1999, RCA Victor, from the Broadway musical, *Parade,* 1999 ♪♪♪♪

album notes: Music: Jason Robert Brown; **Lyrics:** Jason Robert Brown; **Book:** Alfred Uhry; **Cast:** Brent Carver (Leo Frank), Carolee Carmello (Lucille Frank).

Based on a true story which took place in Atlanta in 1913, *Parade,* written by Pulitzer Prize–winning playwright Alfred Uhry, was not very compelling as a drama, with the score by newcomer Jason Robert Brown seemingly at a loss to find its own voice within the framework of the story. Essentially, the plot centered around Leo Frank, manager of a pencil factory, who was accused of a murder, the victim being a teenage girl working for him. As portrayed in the show, Frank, a Jew from New York, is an alien in this Southern land, even though his wife, Lucille, is a Southerner. But there is much more at stake for the prosecuting attorney, Hugh Dorsey, than finding a credible murderer: with his own political career on the upswing, Dorsey is determined to convict Frank of the murder, even if that means coaxing his witnesses into giving false testimonies. He is pushed into doing so by the governor, John Slaton, whose re-election would benefit from a conviction in the case, and, more subliminally, by the media that sides against the Yankee, all the more so since he is a Jew. Even Frank's court-appointed lawyer finds little evidence in the defense of his client, and the final judgment of guilty is a foregone conclusion even before the trial has started. Frank's wife, however, is intent on saving her husband, and she eventually convinces the governor that an injustice has been committed. But before Frank can be released, a group of bigots break into his jail and hang him.

Despite a glossy production by Harold Prince, the sung-through musical closed after 85 performances. Taken on its own musical merits, the cast album sounds actually much better than the score did on stage (it was evidently trimmed down and the remaining elements allow to put the songs in sharper focus). With faint echoes of the type of scores Sondheim might have written ten years or so ago, it propels on the Broadway scene a young composer who is obviously talented and who no doubt will meet with much greater success in the near future. Both Brent Carver as Frank and Carolee Carmello as his wife, are well cast in their respective roles, and the recording itself often sounds gorgeous. Whether it will sustain repeated listening is another story, but this is an intelligent, sophisticated cast album that deserves to find an audience.

Didier C. Deutsch

Paradise Road

1997, Sony Classical, from the film *Paradise Road,* Fox Searchlight Pictures, 1997 🎬🎬🎬🎬

album notes: Music: Ross Edwards; **Orchestra:** The Tall Poppies Orchestra; **Conductor:** David Stanhope; **Choir:** Vrouwenkoor Malle Babbe Women's Choir of Haarlem, Holland; **Choir Conductor:** Leny van Schaik.

This has to be one of the loveliest and most unusual soundtrack albums available. Surprisingly, however, it is not Ross Edwards's somewhat perfunctory cues (reduced to a minimum here) that appeal the most, but the Malle Babbe Women's Choir's ethereal performances of classical selections, all the more effective for the calm and peaceful impression they exude. Standouts in this collection include the largo from Dvorak's "New World" Symphony, better known as the spiritual "Going Home;" the traditional "Londonderry Air," also known as "Danny Boy;" and Bach's breathtakingly beautiful "Jesu, Joy of Man's Desiring." But the whole album is a priceless gem that you'll want to hear over and over again, particularly when a moment of rest is what you need most in the world.

Didier C. Deutsch

The Parent Trap

1998, Hollywood Records, from the film *The Parent Trap,* Walt Disney, 1998 🎬

album notes: Music: Alan Silvestri; **Conductor:** Alan Silvestri.

When Disney decided to remake *The Parent Trap,* a memorable Hayley Mills vehicle from the 1950s, they made several wise decisions, including the casting and direction. The result is an uncommonly good remake that hardly falters next to the original movie about twin girls, separated at infancy, who reunite at summer camp and decide to orchestrate their estranged parents' reunion. However, when it came to musical choices, Disney's wise decision-making came to an abrupt halt. The resulting soundtrack album seems immensely unappealing to its supposed target audience of children, and to their parents, as well. How many more times do we need to hear George Thoro-

good's "Bad to the Bone," and who puts it on the same album as Natalie Cole and Shonen Knife? Unfortunately, Disney makes a veritable mess.

Amy Rosen

Parenthood

1989, Reprise Records, from the film *Parenthood,* Universal Pictures, 1989 🎬🎬

album notes: Music: Randy Newman.

Spearheaded by the Academy Award–nominated song "I Love to See You Smile," this affectionate look at the foibles and trials of parenthood finds a winning musical expression in Randy Newman's score, in which even the short-lived "Helen and Julie" seems appropriately sentimental and relevant. Other delightful moments in the score include the south-of-the-border/hoedown feel in "Kevin's Party," and the lilt in "Drag Race/Todd and Julie." In fact, everything about this soundtrack album would be just right, were it not for the fact that its total playing time is less than 29 minutes. The rating reflects one's utter disgust and disappointment.

Didier C. Deutsch

Paris Blues

1998, Rykodisc, from the film *Paris Blues,* United Artists, 1961 🎬🎬🎬

album notes: Music: Duke Ellington.

A soundtrack featuring the music of Duke Ellington, some composed for the film (probably ghosted by Billy Strayhorn) and some Ellington classics ("Take the 'A' Train," "Battle Royal," "Mood Indigo"). What is unusual is the inclusion of a guitar to the Ellington sound, accentuating the "Cafe in Paris" feeling. There is a naturalness to the music, for Ellington can't lose himself in a film; he remains above the plot and the action. There are some typical exotic pieces ("Bird Jungle" and "Autumnal Suite") but most of the music swings in the swanky Ellington-Strayhorn style. Bits of dialog from the film are interspersed within the soundtrack, which doesn't do a thing for the music, but film buffs will enjoy hearing Paul Newman talk. Over all, though, nothing spectacular.

Bob Belden

Paris, Texas

1985, Warner Bros. Records, from the film *Paris, Texas,* 20th Century Fox, 1985 🎬🎬🎬🎬

album notes: Music: Ry Cooder; **Featured Musicians:** Ry Cooder, Jim Dickinson, David Lindley.

Harry Dean Stanton in Paris, Texas. **(The Kobal Collection)**

A wrenching contemporary drama, about a drifter looking for his ex-wife and finding her working in a strip joint, *Paris, Texas* elicited an evocative Tex-Mex score from Ry Cooder, writing in an idiom in which he feels most comfortable and creative. Essentially a series of cues for acoustic guitars (played by Cooder, Jim Dickinson, and David Lindley), the score is striking in its simplicity, effectively conveying the moods of the characters in the story. A long 8:38 minute segment, "I Knew These People," finds stars Harry Dean Stanton and Nastassja Kinski in a reading of the most poignant scene, with Cooder's music playing underneath, with the track itself, unfortunately marred by heavy hiss, evoking the stark atmosphere that permeates the whole film.

Didier C. Deutsch

The Party

1995, RCA/BMG/Japan, from the film *The Party,* United Artists, 1978 ♪♪♪♪

album notes: Music: Henry Mancini; **Conductor:** Henry Mancini.

If the phrase "Birdie Num-Num" brings a smile of recognition to your lips, you'll try to find this recording, released only in Japan but probably available as an import, which features some of the selections composed by Henry Mancini for a Blake Edward's comedy starring Peter Sellers as an inept (what else!) Hindu actor who creates havoc at a Hollywood party. Typical of Mancini, the tracks are joyously hummable, lightly jazzy on the side, and contain at least one recognizable hit in "Candlelight on Crystal." Dee-lightful!

Didier C. Deutsch

Party of Five

1996, Reprise Records, from the television series *Party of Five,* Columbia Pictures, 1996 ♪♪♪♪

This modern rock friendly TV series gave Bodeans a much-deserved hit with the peppy theme song, "Closer to Free." The rest of the set feels like a cash-in, particularly on some oddball covers—Stevie Nicks doing Tom Petty's "Free Fallin'," and Rickie Lee Jones's singing Donovan's "Sunshine Superman." Joe Jackson's "Stranger Than Fiction" is always worth a listen, though, and it's a good chance to catch some up–and–comers such as Holly Palmer and Laurie Sargent.

Gary Graff

Pascali's Island

1988, Virgin Records, from the film *Pascali's Island*, Avenue Pictures, 1988 ♫♫♫

album notes: Music: Loek Dikker; Orchestra: The Royal Philharmonic Orchestra of Flanders; Conductor: Huub Kerstens; Featured Soloists: Koen de Gans, kaval; Marten Scheffer, bouzouki.

Loek Dikker's score for *Pascali's Island,* a film set on the Aegean, oozes with sounds that evoke the sunny Mediterranean islands and some of the tension in this story of a small-time secret agent, forever lost on a Greek island occupied by the Turks, whose universe is shattered by the arrival of a handsome archeologist and antique-plunderer. With the support of a bouzouki and a kaval, the composer fashioned a score that all at once captures the moods in the narrative and gives them a voice of their own, with a restraint that speaks eloquently for his creativity, while conjuring up images of the setting in which the action takes place. It's a low-key effort, nicely shaded, and handsomely executed.

Didier C. Deutsch

A Passage to India

1989, Capitol Records, from the film *A Passage to India,* Columbia Pictures, 1984 ♫♫♫♫

album notes: Music: Maurice Jarre; Orchestra: The Royal Philharmonic Orchestra; Conductor: Maurice Jarre.

The strong creative relationship between filmmaker David Lean and composer Maurice Jarre, which had already manifested itself in *Lawrence of Arabia* and *Ryan's Daughter,* reached a new high with this film, set in India in the late 1920s, about a well-heeled young British woman, who cannot abide by the haughty attitudes of her compatriots, and who pays dearly for her spirit of independence. Jarre, at his florid best, came up with many memorable themes that capture the gist of the action and the specific time and place in which it occurred, with this effort rewarded by an Academy Award. Standout among the many selections is the jaunty "Bicycle Ride," another exhilarating tune in the Jarre canon.

Didier C. Deutsch

Passenger 57

1992, Epic Soundtrax, from the film *Passenger 57,* Warner Bros., 1992 ♫♫♫

album notes: Music: Stanley Clarke; Featured Musicians: Stanley Clarke, tenor bass guitar, electric bass guitar, piccolo bass guitar, acoustic bass, synthesizers; George Duke, Bobby Lyle, keyboards; Paul Jackson Jr., guitar; John Robinson, Gerry Brown, drums; Gerald Albright, soprano sax, alto sax; Reggie Hamilton, Neil Stubenhauser, electric bass guitar.

A taut, gripping airborne drama, about a terrorist hijacking a plane and the cop who succeeds in overcoming him, *Passenger 57* is notable for the fact that its score was written by jazz artist Stanley Clarke, who called upon many of his peers in the business—George Duke, Bobby Lyle, Paul Jackson Jr., and Gerald Albright, among them—to come and share in the fun. There is little that's surprising or innovative about the music, just some jazz fusion themes that are pleasantly attractive, combined with standard action cues ("Skyjack," "Big Fall," "Chaos on the Tarmac") that mean less musically but fill a function.

Didier C. Deutsch

Passion

1994, Angel Records, from the Broadway production *Passion,* 1994 ♫♫♫

album notes: Music: Stephen Sondheim; Lyrics: Stephen Sondheim; Musical Direction: Paul Gemignani; Cast: Donna Murphy, Jere Shea, Marin Mazzie, Gregg Edelman, Tom Aldredge.

Stephen Sondheim and James Lapine's tale of obsessive love in 19th century Italy was a hit on Broadway, winning the 1994 Tony award for Best Musical. It made a star of Donna Murphy as a sickly, unattractive woman who wins her officer purely through the force of her longing. The recording is crystalline, the leads beautifully sung, but this music is ultimately more interesting than compelling and seems unlikely to stand with the great Sondheim scores.

Marc Kirkeby

Passion in the Desert

1998, RCA Victor, from the film *Passion in the Desert,* Fine Line, 1998 ♫♫♫

album notes: Music: Jose Nieto; Conductor: Jose Nieto.

One of Napoleon's soldier goes AWOL when he falls in love with a leopard in the Egyptian desert. Based on a Balzac short story this bizarre, beautifully shot romantic tragedy benefits from haunting music by Spanish composer Jose Nieto. The orchestral score is heavily laden with ethnic music that, while not being specifically Egyptian, does evoke mysterious desert cities. The Mamelucs and the exotic landscape are characterized with drums, flute, harp, oud, synthesizer, and the wordless song of a female voice recalling the music to Cirque du Soleil. The leopard receives majestic drums and the warning rattle of maracas, while the soldier's affections are captured in romantic strings with military marches reminding us of his abandoned

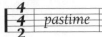

duty. Two of oud virtuoso Hamza El Din's Nubian songs round out a strong, varied response to a curious, failed movie.

David Poole

Pastime

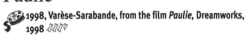1991, Bay Cities Records, from the film *Pastime,* Miramax Films, 1991 ♫♫♫♫

album notes: Music: Lee Holdridge; **Conductor:** Lee Holdridge; **Featured Musicians:** Randy Waldman, piano; George Doering, guitar; Earl Dumier, oboe, English horn; Sheridon Strokes, flute; Charles Boito, Gary Herbig, clarinet; Jack Sheldon, trumpet.

The story of "a major miracle in the minor league," *Pastime* is set in central California in 1957, and deals with two outcasts, a 41-year-old reliever on a minor league club whose only title to glory is that he played ever so briefly in the big league, and a vastly talented young black pitcher with few opportunities to be noticed. For this little, unheralded masterpiece, Holdridge wrote a score that echoes the sentiments flowing between the two main characters and those around them, and, on a much broader scope, the strong emotions and aspirations the game elicits. Deeply felt and lyrical, it is diversified and eloquent, a strongly etched piece of music with many attractive facets.

Didier C. Deutsch

Pat Garrett & Billy the Kid

1973, Columbia Records, from the film *Pat Garrett & Billy the Kid,* MGM, 1973 ♫♫♫♫

album notes: Music: Bob Dylan; **Songs:** Bob Dylan; **Featured Musicians:** Bob Dylan, guitar; Booker T., bass; Bruce Langhorn, guitar; Roger McGuinn, guitar; Terry Paul, bass; Carl Fortina, harmonium; Jim Keltner, drums; Gary Foster, recorder, flute; Carol Hunter, guitar; Byron Berline, fiddle; Jolly Roger, banjo; Donna Weiss, Priscilla Jones, Byron Berline, Terry Paul, Brenda Patterson, voices.

Bob Dylan, who gave a very uneven performance in the film, turned in an unexpectedly proficient score for this retelling of the struggle between former saddle buddies, sheriff Pat Garrett (James Coburn) and outlaw Billy The Kid (Kris Kristofferson), directed by Sam Peckinpah, who publicly disowned the initial version. While unlikely to give nightmares to composers better versed in the genre than he is, Dylan manages to evoke the folksy feel of the western, and contributes at least one memorable theme in "Knockin' on Heaven's Door."

Didier C. Deutsch

A Patch of Blue

1998, Intrada Records, from the film *A Patch of Blue,* MGM, 1965 ♫♫♫♫♫

album notes: Music: Jerry Goldsmith.

A controversial film at the time of its release, *A Patch of Blue* had the enormous merit of presenting a story in which racial prejudice took a back seat, despite the fact that its protagonists were a white girl and a black man (Elizabeth Hartman and Sidney Poitier, respectively). Because she is blind, Selina is not stuck on the feelings others have for people of a different race—all she knows about the kind stranger who talks to her every day in the park and brightens her days, is that he is a businessman named Gordon. But the fact that he is black riles Selina's mother, a loud and insensitive woman, who decides to move her away from what she considers a negative influence. Selina, then decides to go to the park alone, and try to find Gordon. A companion score to his Award winning *Lilies of the Field,* also starring Poitier, Goldsmith wrote a delicate series of cues in which the harmonica and the piano often duet together, sometimes backed by a flute and a sprinkle of strings, with an occasional jazzy tune waving its way through with great flair. Built around the French melody, "Il pleut bergère," it is a very low-key effort that proves quite compelling and ingratiating. It shows Goldsmith in a folky kind of mood he has seldom explored since.

Didier C. Deutsch

Patriot Games

1992, RCA Records, from the film *Patriot Games,* Paramount Pictures, 1992 ♫♫♫♫

album notes: Music: James Horner; **Conductor:** James Horner.

Harrison Ford stars in this explosive, action-packed thriller, based on Tom Clancy's best-seller, as a former CIA analyst vacationing in England, who becomes the target of an Irish killer when he unwillingly gets caught in the middle of a terrorist attack and saves a member of the royal family. With a preponderance of synthesizer sounds and Irish sonorities limning his score, James Horner sketches potent musical images that help underline the action on the screen, often in dark, somber tones that sound threatening and ominous, and are punctuated by heavy drumming as if to signal the inevitability of the most dramatic aspects in the story. Clannad's evocative performance in "Harry's Game" is a bit of a relief, even as it anchors the score more deeply in its Irish background.

Didier C. Deutsch

Paulie

1998, Varèse-Sarabande, from the film *Paulie,* Dreamworks, 1998 ♫♫♫♫

album notes: Music: John Debney; **Conductor:** John Debney.

Would you believe so much bombast is for a film starring a parrot? Okay, a talking parrot, who actually can hold a conversation! But one must admit that the manipulative, quasi-swashbuckling score devised by John Debney is quite a rouser and doesn't seem to fit the bill of a comedy about a wisecracking bird, even one coaxed by Buddy Hackett. Others with whom the smart cookie comes in contact, during an odyssey that takes him from the East Coast to Los Angeles, include Cheech Marin, Gena Rowlands, Bruce Davison, and an adorable tot named Hallie Kate Eisenberg. Debney illustrates the peripatetic adventures of the Blue-crown Conure with cues that are occasionally reflective ("Misha's Memory"), but more frequently rambunctious and lively. It's a fun album!

Didier C. Deutsch

The Pawnbroker/The Deadly Affair

🎬 1996, Verve Records, from the films *The Pawnbroker*, 1965, and *The Deadly Affair*. Columbia Pictures, 1966 ♫♫♫♫

album notes: Music: Quincy Jones; **Featured Musicians:** Freddie Hubbard, trumpet; J.J. Johnson, trombone; Anthony Ortega, soprano sax; Oliver Nelson, alto sax, tenor sax; Jerry Dodgion, alto sax; Don Elliot, vibraphone; Bobby Scott, piano; Kenny Burrell, guitar; Tommy Williams, bass; Elvin Jones, drums; Ed Shaughnessy, percussion.

In the early days of his career, when he was more interested in writing solid "mood music" and big band jazz themes than the vapid rap songs in which he so often indulges these days, Quincy Jones scored several films that were particularly memorable. Both *The Pawnbroker* and *The Deadly Affair* belong to that category. With its blend of urgent string melodies and effective jazz tracks, the score for *The Pawnbroker* seems the adequate musical comment for this study of a Jewish man, portrayed by Rod Steiger, who survived the indignities of Nazi camps, only to find another form of discrimination in Harlem where he operates a pawnshop. Featuring such stalwarts as Freddie Hubbard, J.J. Johnson, Oliver Nelson, Kenny Burrell, and Elvin Jones, the music is strongly anchored in the modern jazz sounds that prevailed at the time the film was made. The moods in the film receive an additional boost with the inclusion of the track "How Come You People," that mixes excerpts of dialogue with Jones's music.

Based on a novel by John Le Carre, *The Deadly Affair* deals with a British intelligence officer, played by James Mason in one of his most compelling screen portrayals, trying to solve the mystery surrounding the suicide of a diplomat. The cues Quincy Jones wrote for the film denote the influence of the bossa nova sounds that were heard at the time. But even when he gives in to fleeting trends, Jones always writes material that is far superior to what others do, a point made again with this exquisitely flavored score, reminiscent in some ways of the music Michel Legrand used to write during the same period.

Didier C. Deutsch

Payback

🎬 1999, Varèse-Sarabande, from the film *Payback,* Icon, 1999 ♫♫♫♫

album notes: Music: Chris Boardman; **Conductor:** Chris Boardman.

A great track, "Ain't That a Kick in the Head," by Dean Martin, starts this CD and signals the start of a fun compilation album. Indeed, other tracks include selections by James Brown, B.B. King, Vic Damone, and Lou Rawls—nothing to sneeze at. Even Chris Boardman's heavily rhythmic score fits in with the songs, making one wish that more of his music would be included. A loose canon in John Boorman's oeuvre, *Payback* may not have deserved all the attention. Despite the presence of top-billed Mel Gibson as a bank robber left for dead by his partner and wanting to exact revenge, this neo-film noir, set in the streets of Chicago, was too violent and kinky to really attract an audience. But the soundtrack is great!

Didier C. Deutsch

The Peacemaker

🎬 1997, Dreamworks Records, from the film *The Peacemaker,* Dreamworks, 1997 ♫♫♫♫

album notes: Music: Hans Zimmer; **Conductor:** Gavin Greenaway, Harry Gregson-Williams; **Featured Vocalist:** Mamak Khadem.

A dark, brooding effort by Hans Zimmer, the soundtrack album of *The Peacemaker* is distinguished by the fact that the cues are unusually long and florid, while also descriptive of the atmosphere in this fast-paced action drama, enabling the music to make a strong impression on the listener. Literally a symphonic poem for orchestra and chorus in five movements, the score was written for a bold thriller starring George Clooney and Nicole Kidman, involving a Russian train robbed of its nuclear shipment, with the ensuing screen time being spent by Clooney, as a special U.S. Army agent, and Kidman, as a nuclear physicist, trying to recover the precious cargo and avoid a possible disaster. Reflective of the screen action ("Trains" was heard in the film's opening scenes, a setpiece of impressive proportions, with the robbery taking place as the train is seen moving at high speed on its tracks), the score is breathtaking and frequently awesome, with the large orchestral forces conjuring up all the movement and excitement in the story.

Didier C. Deutsch

Pecker

🎬 1998, RCA Victor, from the film *Pecker,* Fine Line, 1998 ♫♫♫

album notes: Music: Stewart Copeland.

The always imaginative former Police drummer Stewart Copeland helms this collection, which is dominated by his own tracks such as "The Love Chase," "Back to Hampden," "Sneaky Shelly," and "Thrift Shop Fashion Shoot." His collaboration with Damecus Metoyer on "Picker Man" is good humored but not nearly as hilarious as his "Don't Drop the Soap (For Anyone Else But Me)," which he recorded with former Wall of Voodoo leader Stan Ridgeway. After Copeland, however, the pickings thin out considerably with fairly forgettable stuff from the Nutty Squirrels, Leroy Pullins, the Grid, and the Rock-a-Teens.

see also: The Leopard Son

Gary Graff

Pee-Wee's Big Adventure/Back to School

1988, Varèse Sarabande, from the films *Pee-Wee's Big Adventure*, Warner Bros., 1985; and *Back to School*, Orion Pictures, 1988 🎜🎜🎜🎜🎜

album notes: Music: Danny Elfman; Orchestra: The National Philharmonic Orchestra; Conductor: John Coleman.

Whether it was Paul Reubens's quirky personality as the childlike Pee-Wee Herman, or the subject of the film itself, Danny Elfman hit a particularly fertile vein when he scored *Pee-Wee's Big Adventure*. In a style that is at once jaunty and mischievously impish, with broad echoes of Kurt Weill's sardonic tones to round it off, the music is a brilliant display of Elfman's creativity and his inventive, always surprising way with melodic lines and odd instrumentations. It matters little that the film is also a showcase for Pee-Wee's fantasies about his bicycle, stolen by a heavy who gets his comeuppance at the right time. Both the music and the image melded into a whole that is descriptive and totally enjoyable. Without the image, the music is even more vibrant and mesmerizing.

Back to School is another inane little comedy, starring moonfaced Rodney Dangerfield as the father of a college-age kid who decides to go back to school and finish his studies, the attempt resulting in utter chaos. Once again, Elfman's bright inventions match the tone of the broad antics, in a more muscular style than in *Pee-Wee's Big Adventure*. but with equally satisfying results. The often manic, eccentric cues assembled in this album are completely exhilarating.

Didier C. Deutsch

Peggy Sue Got Married

1986, Varèse Sarabande, from the film *Peggy Sue Got Married*, Tri-Star Pictures, 1986 🎜🎜

album notes: Music: John Barry; Conductor: John Barry.

An unfortunately very short 26:56 minute album, that adds insult to injury by presenting four instrumental cues clocking in at a scant 14 minutes, *Peggy Sue Got Married* found composer John Barry in one of his expansive moods, and writing music that was beautifully stated and melodically attractive. The film, a time warp fantasy that enables a forlorn housewife to return to her teenage years and attempt to correct the mistakes she had made at the time, is nothing more than a charming little tale, but Barry's cues find rich, evocative accents ("Charlie's Unplayed Guitar") to make it seem much more important than it is. The pop selections that complement the album also play a role in setting the tone of the period (the 1950s) which Peggy Sue revisits, but it is sad to realize that even they are being treated in a rather shabby way in this album.

Didier C. Deutsch

The Pelican Brief

1993, Giant Records, from the film *The Pelican Brief*, Warner Bros., 1993 🎜🎜🎜

album notes: Music: James Horner; Conductor: James Horner; Featured Musicians: Michael Fisher, Ralph Grierson, James Horner, Randy Kerber, Ian Underwood.

Opening with a truly haunting motif, James Horner's suspense score for this Julia Roberts–Denzel Washington thriller is perhaps the most satisfying music yet composed for a John Grisham big-screen potboiler. While Horner's dramatic underscore is fairly predictable, with big piano and orchestra crescendos comprising the tension in the music (along with a recurring percussion motif ripped off from John Williams's *JFK*), the most substantial and satisfying material comes from Horner's swelling romantic theme for Roberts's heroine, heard most clearly in an arrangement written expressly for the album. The composer finishes off the score with a lengthy, eloquent, horn-laden finale ("Airport Goodbye") that's in keeping with some of the more impassioned music to come from him in recent times (think *Apollo 13* and *Field of Dreams*). The end result is a thriller score that's clearly a step above most generic genre efforts, with enough lyrical passages to bring listeners back for subsequent listenings.

Andy Dursin

The People Under the Stairs

1991, Bay Cities Records, from the film *The People Under the Stairs*, Universal Pictures, 1991 🎜

album notes: Music: Graeme Revell, Don Peake; Conductor: Tim Simonec.

Considering two composers worked on this score, the album is surprisingly bland. Don Peake (who composed the majority of the *Knight Rider* TV scores) received main credit while Graeme

Revell (an early effort) received additional music credit at the film's end. Equal time is given to each composer, though their music has been massed together into overlong suites. Revell utilizes an orchestra and vainly attempts to create several unusual, though unremarkable, sound clusters. On the other hand, Peake tries to establish a darker tone through the use of synthesizers, but ultimately, the entire presentation has a less than musical feel. It's almost a collection of sound effects that spends so much time on attempting to create minimalistic motifs that it never truly defines itself. A pretty forgettable experience that leaves you feeling as if 50 minutes of your life has just disappeared.

David Hirsch

The People vs. Larry Flynt

1996, Angel Records, from the film *The People vs. Larry Flynt*, Columbia Pictures, 1996 ♫♫♫

album notes: Music: Thomas Newman; **Conductor:** Thomas Newman.

Never known for creating anything that could be confused with an "average" film score, Thomas Newman mixes his odd musical compositions this go around with a variety of bluegrass tunes (the 12-second "Eggsplat" fades into the more standard "Kentucky, 1952" for example). However, most of the album is taken up with a variety of songs to depict the passage of 35 years from the film's start to finish. These songs include the McCoys's "Hang on Sloopy," "I'm You're Boogy Man" by K.C. and the Sunshine Band, and there are even several excerpts from classical compositions by Antonin Dvorak. All of these are interpolated throughout the album, which does well to capture the manic air of Flynt's life. If you find Newman's avant-garde style of film scoring more palatable in small doses (many of the cues are extremely short, too), then this presentation will work for you.

David Hirsch

A Perfect Murder

1998, Varèse-Sarabande, from the film *A Perfect Murder*, Warner Bros., 1998 ♫♫

album notes: Music: James Newton Howard; **Conductor:** Artie Kane.

When screenwriters are short of ideas, they turn to past screen hits, dust them off a bit, dress them in new garbs, and pass them off as something new. If the film, thus fitted, stars one or two major stars, so much the better. Perhaps it will prove a hit all over again. Such is the case with *A Perfect Murder*, an unfortunate remake of Alfred Hitchcock's *Dial M for Murder*, about a businessman who devises a devilishly plan to have his wife murdered by her lover, while he is doing something else, thus having the perfect alibi. Things don't go as planned, of course,

and it is the intended victim who kills her aggressor, leaving the husband in a lurch as to what to do next, until he gives himself up by mistake.

Based on a melodramatic play by Frederick Knott, the source of Hitchcock's film, the new film starred Michael Douglas and Gwyneth Paltrow in a suspense thriller that had little suspense and was not too terribly thrilling either. The not-so-thrilling moods were sustained in James Newton Howard's score, a hodgepodge of ill effects that went nowhere and did even less. Predictably, "Intruder" is a low-key, ominous orchestral piece with the low chords signaling the murderer's every move, while "The Attack" is filled with percussive effects and punching rhythms, the kind one might expect for that kind of scene. All in all, it's nothing to write home about.

Didier C. Deutsch

A Perfect World

1993, Reprise Records, from the film *A Perfect World*, Warner Bros., 1993 ♫♫♫

album notes: Music: Clint Eastwood, Lennie Niehaus; **Conductor:** Lennie Niehaus.

Country soundtracks can be tough. Too often they're watered down by producers afraid that the real thing won't win over the masses. But with favorites from Bob Wills & His Texas Playboys and Don Gibson, *A Perfect World* thumbs its nose at the idea of playing it safe. Johnny Cash, Marty Robbins, and Hank Locklin are also represented here, while country-influenced rocker Chris Isaak provides a modern touch with his "Dark Moon."

Gary Graff

Permanent Midnight

1998, DGC Records, from the film *Permanent Midnight*, Artisan, 1998 ♫♫♫

album notes: Music: Daniel Licht.

Permanent Midnight puts us on the techno tip again, this time to strong effect. The Crystal Method's "Now Is the Time" is an ace, as is the Prodigy's already proven "Smack My Bitch Up." They're joined by other strong entries, including BT's "Godspeed," Black Lab's "Horses," and Spring Heel Jack's "A Permanent Theme," while the modern rock end is covered by solid tracks from the likes of Gomez ("Get Miles"), Girls against Boys ("EPR") and Art Alexakis, who takes a leave from his band Everclear for "Overwhelming." Morcheeba's "Tape Loop," meanwhile, gets a nice remix from the Diabolical Brothers.

Gary Graff

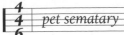

Pet Sematary

1989, Varèse Sarabande, from the film *Pet Sematary*, Paramount Pictures, 1989 ♫♫♫

album notes: Music: Elliot Goldenthal; **Orchestra:** The Orchestra of St. Luke's; **Conductor:** Steven Mercurio; **Synthesizer Programming:** Matthias Gohl; **Featured Soloists:** Elliot Goldenthal, Matthias Gohl, piano; **Choir:** The Zarathustra Boys Chorus.

Elliot Goldenthal, who has since graduated to bigger and better projects, made quite an impression with his score for this horror movie based on a novel by Stephen King. While some cues ("Dead Recollection") were evidently written as underscoring for some of the screen action and fail to attract on their own merits, most of the score is cleverly constructed and is quite evocative. Several selections feature the Zarathustra Boys Chorus, a group that lives up to its appealing name and limns the themes with its other-worldly vocal contribution. Pointing the way to Goldenthal's future in the film music world, "Moving Day Waltz," "Rachel's Dirty Secret," "Kite and Truck," while somewhat too short, reveal the composer's talent for attractive, catchy melodies.

Didier C. Deutsch

Pete Kelly's Blues

1998, Soundies/BMG, from the film *Pete Kelly's Blues*, Warner Bros., 1955 ♫♫♫

album notes: Featured Musicians: Matty Matlock, clarinet; Dick Cathcart, trumpet; Moe Schneider, trombone; Eddie Miller, tenor sax; Nick Fatool, drums; George Van Eps, guitar; Ray Sherman, piano; Jud De-Naut, bass.

Though highly melodramatic in its content and exposition, *Pete Kelly's Blues,* the 1955 thriller directed by and starring Jack Webb, had two things going for it: an explosive score performed by a remarkable assortment of old-time jazz musicians led by Matty Matlock; and the presence of two exceptional singers in Peggy Lee and Ella Fitzgerald. Both women also had significant roles in this story of a cornet player in Prohibition-era Kansas City, whose musical group band is threatened by a small-time hood intent on taking it over. While neither Miss Lee, who portrayed a fading singer given to drinking, nor Miss Fitzgerald appear on this album, Webb (Mr. Stony Face in person) handles the brief narration that precedes each track. The music is a solid collection of standards, played Dixieland-style by Matlock and his musicians, including "Breezin' Along with the Breeze," "Somebody Loves Me," and "Bye Bye Blackbird." The intros are kept short, the music is great, and if the sound quality leaves something to be desired at times, the fun is always present.

Didier C. Deutsch

Peter Gunn

1986, RCA Records, from the NBC-TV series *Peter Gunn*, 1959 ♫♫♫♫♫

album notes: Music: Henry Mancini; **Conductor:** Henry Mancini.

In a rare foray into television, Henry Mancini scored this series for Blake Edwards, the first time both men worked together. As Mancini recalled in later years, Edwards was looking for a score that would be contemporary and rooted in jazz for the mystery adventure series about a big city police detective whose investigations often took him to various jazz clubs. So strong and evocative is Mancini's score that it won the composer an Emmy Award, while the soundtrack album became a million-seller and received two Grammys. In fact, the success of the album spawned a second volume, "More Music from Peter Gunn," which was reissued in Europe but not in this country.

Several tunes from *Peter Gunn* became pop favorites, "Sorta Blue," "Dreamsville," and "Slow and Easy," among them, but the score in its entirety is quite enticing and powerful enough to stand on its own musical merits. The mastering, however, leaves a lot to be desired, and could stand a thorough overhaul.

Didier C. Deutsch

Peter Pan

1998, Disney, from the film *Peter Pan*, Disney, 1952 ♫♫♫♫

album notes: Music: Oliver Wallace; **Songs:** Sammy Fain, Sammy Cahn; **Conductor:** Oliver Wallace.

1989, RCA Victor, from the Broadway and television productions *Peter Pan*, 1954 ♫♫♫♫

album notes: Music: Jule Styne, Mark Charlap, Trude Rittman; **Lyrics:** Betty Comden and Adolph Green, Carolyn Leigh; **Musical Direction:** Louis Adrian; **Cast:** Mary Martin, Cyril Ritchard, Kathy Nolan, Robert Harrington, Joseph Stafford, Sondra Lee, Heller Halliday.

The story of the boy who could fly and didn't want to grow up, *Peter Pan* has charmed generations. From the original novel by J.M. Barrie, it started as a play and was made into a musical (among other transmogrifications that have attracted such renowned performers as Mary Martin, Cyril Ritchard, Danny Kaye, Boris Karloff, Sandy Duncan, and, most recently, Cathy Rigby), but its most enduring representation was the animated feature made by the Disney studios in 1952. With Sammy Fain and Sammy Cahn providing songs that have kept us humming ever since ("You Can Fly!," "Never Smile at a Crocodile," "Following the Leader," "The Second Star to the Right"), the film firmly posited what we had always imagined, giving a recognizable face to Peter, Captain Hook, Smee, Tinkerbell, and all the other characters in the story. This newly released soundtrack album, fully restored and containing elements available here for the first time, is a glowing reminder that Peter Pan, indeed, never ages!

Mary Martin scored a personal, long–lasting triumph as the "boy who refuses to grow up" in the musical presentation which bombed on Broadway the first time it was staged, but then went on to make television history when it became a perennial favorite enjoyed by millions in repeated annual showings. Initially created by Mark "Moose" Charlap and Carolyn Leigh (who wrote "I Gotta Crow," "I Won't Grow Up," and the thrilling "I'm Flying"), the score was beefed up with new songs by Jule Styne, and Betty Comden and Adolph Green, while the show was still in try-outs on the West Coast. Its arrival on Broadway on October 20, 1954, in the midst of a particularly busy season, was hardly noticed, and it closed after 154 performances, though both Mary Martin and Cyril Ritchard, as the hilariously evil Captain Hook, won Tony Awards for their performances. Though in glorious mono sound, the cast album does full justice to this enjoyable show and to the star's winning portrayal.

Didier C. Deutsch

Peter the Great

1986, Southern Cross Records, from the NBC–TV presentation *Peter the Great*, 1986 ♫♫♫♪

album notes: Music: Laurence Rosenthal; **Orchestra:** The Bavarian State Orchestra of Munich; **Choir:** Choir of l'Eglise Russe Saint–Serge of Paris; **Conductor:** Laurence Rosenthal.

Laurence Rosenthal's flavorful score for this sweeping epic gets its inspiration and strength from two widely different sources— the incomparable liturgy of the Russian Orthodox Church, and the profoundly human world of Russian folksongs. The first finds its expression in the court rituals (coronations, weddings, funerals), in which the presence of the Church was a dominating factor. The second is expertly interwoven in the colorful tapestry of characters that peopled the brutal tale of one of Russia's most powerful tsars, with the most important players in the story getting a specific leitmotif, as well as the locales where the action took place. All these elements combine to create a set of cues that are strongly reflective of the action, yet succeed in having a different, albeit compelling appeal once removed from their primary purpose. Some selections, like "The Tartars," "Moscow Is Burning," and "Battle of Poltava" are noticeably impressive.

Didier C. Deutsch

Peter's Friends

1993, Epic-Soundtrax, from the film *Peter's Friends*, Samuel Goldwyn, 1993 ♫♫♫♪

A New Year's eve celebration spent in a mansion outside of London was the thin argument behind this obvious clone of

They Know the Score
Maurice Jarre

The reason we used electronic music for *Witness* was because we wanted to have a somewhat 'cold' mood, which really fit with the culture of the Amish people. Besides that, the Amish people do not have musical instruments in their religion, because they believe instrumental music is associated with the devil. . . . So I thought it we used an orchestra or acoustic music in *Witness,* it might be somewhat antagonistic toward the belief of the Amish people. Any kind of acoustic instrument would be against the feeling I wanted to evoke for the film. [Director] Peter [Weir] agreed completely, and I never used one single acoustic instrument on *Witness,* including the barn raising sequence. . . . After *Witness* people said 'Oh Maurice did it electronically because they didn't have enough money for the score.' Actually, the score for *Witness* was more expensive than if we had a normal orchestral session, because it was technically much more complicated.

***Courtesy of* Film Score Monthly**

The Big Chill, in which the participants, all former schoolmates, get together after ten years. They all have changed—they have grown, their lives have followed totally different paths—yet something still obviously binds them together. As is often the case in films such as this, the interest is not always sustained, though in this instance the cast, superbly led by Kenneth Branagh, compensated for any falling off in the storyline, with the soundtrack, consisting of great songs, adding an interesting spin to it. Sixteen of the songs are compiled in this soundtrack album, and on their own also provide a lot of fun, with strong performances by superstars like Bruce Springsteen, Tina Turner, Eric Clapton, Elton John, Queen, Nina Simone, Cindy Lauper, Terence Trent D'Arby, and Tears for Fears, among many others. This is a rarity: a solid, enjoyable collection!

Didier C. Deutsch

The Phantom

1996, Milan Records, from the film *The Phantom,* Paramount Pictures, 1996 ♪♪♪

album notes: Music: David Newman; **Orchestra:** The London Metropolitan Orchestra; **Conductor:** David Newman; **Featured Artists:** Tony Hinnigan, Mike Taylor, Pan pipes.

Composer David Newman weaves an effective blend of current scoring trends (marked by extensive, rapid-fire percussion and smooth romanticism) and the heyday of action serials with this nicely flowing work that will probably stand the test of time better than the middling movie for which it was written. Newman's five-note motif for "The Phantom" is ingeniously malleable, functioning both as an imposing fanfare, a crisp action motif and a warm melody for the benevolent qualities of Billy Zane's bemused hero. There's also a beautiful love theme for piano and orchestra, and both themes collude fluidly in the movingly ambivalent finale. The heroic material tends to saw away a bit too much, but overall this is an enjoyable, if not exactly indelible, adventure score.

Jeff Bond

The Phantom Menace

See: Star Wars Episode 1: The Phantom Menace

Phantom of the Forest

1994, Narada Cinema, from the WNET–TV series *Nature,* Survival Anglia Ltd., 1994 ♪♪♪♪♪

album notes: Music: Michael Whalen; **Conductor:** Michael Whalen; **Featured Musicians:** Michael Whalen, synclavier, percussion, synthesizers; Harvey Estrin, recorders, flute, Pan flutes; Carolyn Pollak, oboe, English horn; Russ Rizner, French horn; Emily Mitchell, harp; Mitch Estrin, clarinet, bass clarinet; Marti Sweet, violin; Pat Rebillot, piano.

Michael Whalen, one of a generation of new composers, makes a striking impression with this score created for an episode in the series *Nature,* seen on PBS, surveying a mysterious forest in the Scottish countryside inhabited by a spirit–like presence, the Goshawk. Utilizing the full palette offered to him by various acoustic instruments and synthesizers, Whalen wrote a series of minimalist cues that display a New Age–feel without some of the excesses often encountered in recordings of this kind. And while one could have lived without the bird chirping heard occasionally, the simple musical thread he devised is quite attractive to the ear, and provides a soothing listening experience. Two longer cues, "Cathedral of the Woods" and "Phantom of the Forest" are particularly effective in conjuring up images that are not simply confined to the medium for which the music was written. As Whalen mentions in his notes, he attempted to "capture a sense of the fragile beauty of the forest, while not

taking away from its enduring heroic majesty, dark mysteries or magical splendor." His music evokes all of that, and much more.

Didier C. Deutsch

Phantom of the Opera

1990, Silva Screen/U.K., from the film *The Phantom of the Opera,* 21st Century, 1990 ♪♪♪♪

album notes: Music: Misha Segal; **Orchestra:** The Budapest Studio Symphony Orchestra; **Conductor:** Misha Segal.

1987, Polydor Records, from the Broadway production *The Phantom of the Opera,* 1987 ♪♪♪♪

album notes: Music: Andrew Lloyd Webber; **Lyrics:** Charles Hart; **Musical Direction:** Michael Reed; **Cast:** Michael Crawford, Sarah Brightman, Steve Barton, Rosemary Ashe, Janet Devenish, Janos Kurucz, John Savident, David Firth.

1990, Colossal Records, from the television presentation *The Phantom of the Opera,* Saban/Scherick Productions, 1990 ♪♪♪♪♪

album notes: Music: John Addison; **Orchestra:** The Hungarian State Opera Orchestra; **Conductor:** John Addison; **Featured Vocalists:** Michele LaGrange, Gerard Garino, Jean DuPouy, Jacques Mars.

How many times will the Phantom of the Opera rise from his ashes and come to haunt poor Christine again? There have been so many versions of the famous story about the Paris Opera ghoul, the soprano he falls in love with and kidnaps, and that celebrated crashing chandelier, that it's become almost a cliché in gore lore. This one starred Robert Englund as the monster, disfigured in an earlier life, and summoned back when Jill Schoelen, as Christine, performs the music the monster created 120 years before. Inevitably, the whole story plays itself again. And just as inevitably, the monster meets a fiery death (or does he?). Misha Segal conducts the Budapest Studio Symphony Orchestra in a performance of his score for the film, a grandiose, extravagantly laid out set of Gothic themes, appropriately florid in the right places. It's effective to a point, but ultimately quite derivative and reminiscent of other efforts in the genre. Look, as long as they don't bring back Andrew Lloyd Webber, this one will do quite nicely.

If crashing chandeliers is your thing, then the recording of Andrew Lloyd Webber's musical treatment of the Gaston Leroux celebrated gothic tale set in Paris at the turn of the century, might be right for you. In all fairness to Webber, his score, a wall-to-wall display of tunes that sometimes recall the stylistic profligacies of Puccini, brims with moments that elicit strong romantic response, and strikes a particularly effective theatrical note in the evening's only highlight, "The Music of the Night," sung in dulcet fashion by Michael Crawford. But the show, still running on Broadway at this writing, some 10 years after its premiere on January 26, 1988, owes much of its success to Hal Prince's atmospheric staging of this story about a disfigured mad man hiding in Paris's Opera theater, in love with a soprano, who has no qualms eliminating in ghoulish fashion anyone who stands in her way to stardom. Webber's wife at the time, Sarah Brightman, sounding better on record than she did on stage, portrays Christine, the Phantom's love interest.

John Addison, having to deal with a similar theme, wrote a score that's original, romantic in the right places, and scary where it matters. The television film, made in Europe, stars Burt Lancaster, Ian Richardson, Andrea Ferreol, and Charles Dance as The Phantom. While anchoring his score around two excerpts from Gounod's "Faust," Addison created a music that seems to perfectly reflect the various aspects of the story—the giddy attitude of the operagoers; the loveliness of the heroine, Christine; the somber designs of the deranged madman who haunts the Opera; and the deeply romantic undertones of the tale itself. Richly decorative and eloquently manipulative without seeming to be, the cues follow the action, underlining it here, commenting on it there, always making a musical statement that attracts the attention and keeps the listener riveted.

Didier C. Deutsch

Phat Beach

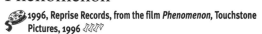1996, TVT Records, from the film *Phat Beach,* LIVE Entertainment, 1996 woof!

Considering how much money it takes to make a soundtrack album, it's amazing that so much garbage is being recorded. This album, which purports to illustrate musically a film that failed to make much of a dent when it was presented in 1996, is a total drag. Starring Jermaine "Huggy" Hopkins as an overweight kid who spent a summer on a California beach teeming with gorgeous bikini-clad girls, *Phat Beach* owed much of its mitigated success to a cameo by Coolio in a short musical number. Since he is not even represented on this album, all that's left are performances by second-rate groups and singers, all bouncing to the same rhythm track, in songs that are neither inspiring nor interesting.

Didier C. Deutsch

Phenomenon

1996, Reprise Records, from the film *Phenomenon,* Touchstone Pictures, 1996 ♫♫♫♪
album notes: Music: Thomas Newman.

"Change the World," the unlikely collaboration between rock icon Eric Clapton and R&B hitmaker Babyface, is a Grammy-winning smash and a stick-to-your-ears tune even if you tried hard not to like it. The rest of the soundtrack is a bit more interesting, with Taj Mahal's "Corrina," Aaron Neville's gorgeous

rendition of "Crazy Love," and refreshingly obscure selections from Bryan Ferry ("Dance With Life [The Brilliant Light]"), Peter Gabriel ("I Have the Touch"), and Marvin Gaye ("Piece of Clay"). It's a sleeper that deserves thorough investigation.

Gary Graff

Philadelphia

1994, Epic Soundtrax, from the film *Philadelphia,* TriStar, 1993 ♫♫♫♪
album notes: Music: Howard Shore.

1994, Epic Soundtrax, from the film *Philadelphia,* TriStar, 1993 ♫♫♫♫
album notes: Music: Howard Shore; **Conductor:** Howard Shore.

AIDS became front-page news in 1993 when *Philadelphia* won various Academy Awards, including one for Tom Hanks, a corporate attorney who is fired from his job because he is HIV-positive, and one for Bruce Springsteen, whose "Streets of Philadelphia" was selected as Best Song. It also provided a major forum to a disease many had been trying to minimize or to simply ignore. Besides its powerful story, admirably serviced by Hanks and Denzel Washington, as the homophobic attorney hired to defend Hanks when he sues for discrimination, the film also received great support from its song-driven soundtrack and the score created by Howard Shore. Usually the one-two-punch of a song collection and a score album leaves a lot to be desired, but in this case both make valid musical statements and solidly complement each other.

The song collection, in addition to Springsteen's eloquent song, includes several other welcome performances, particularly Neil Young's "Philadelphia," which was also nominated in the Best Song category, Peter Gabriel's "Lovetown," Sade's "Please Send Me Someone to Love," and Indigo Girls' "I Don't Wanna Talk about It."

The score album features the cues composed by Shore, among which "Going Home," "Trying to Survive," and "The Essence of Discrimination" are standouts. Laid out in terse, sometimes highly emotional terms, the music is quite cogent and makes a powerful statement of its own. Operatic arias performed by Maria Callas and Lucia Popp round up the selections found here.

Didier C. Deutsch

The Philadelphia Experiment /Mother Lode

1991, Prometheus Records/Belgium, from the films *The Philadelphia Experiment,* New World Pictures, 1984; and *Mother Lode,* Agamemnon Films, 1982 ♫♫♫♫
album notes: Music: Ken Wannberg; **The Philadelphia Experiment: Orchestra:** The National Philharmonic Orchestra; **Conductor:** Ken Wannberg.

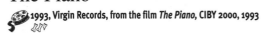
$\begin{smallmatrix}4\\5\\0\end{smallmatrix}$ *pi*

The Philadelphia Experiment has always been one of my favorite films, especially because of its score by Ken Wannberg. Two Navy sailors, participating in a World War II experiment to make ships radar invisible, are hurled into the future (1984) where the same scientists are now attempting to recreate the experiment, which will threaten the survival of the entire world. A modestly-budgeted film, Wannberg gave the story an ambience of epic scope, while keeping it all personal by focusing on the main character, David (Michael Pare), through a simple two-note motif. This is accomplished by keeping the score mainly acoustical, only employing minimal electronic effects to represent the experiment, not a central element to the story, just its catalyst. Wannberg doesn't even overplay the romantic element. "Fugitives in Love" finds David, and his present-day companion Allison, desperately longing for each other, but haunted by their uncertain future. That skepticism permeates the entire score, adding a tense desperation to the proceedings. The CD also features music from *Mother Lode,* a 1982 gold rush adventure starring Charlton Heston and Kim Basinger. Surprisingly, the best cue in that film, the wistfully romantic "The Flight," was cut from the final version. When I interviewed Ken Wannberg for *Soundtrack!* magazine several years ago, I was surprised to discover that he never wanted to actively pursue a career in film scoring. He has been extremely content juggling his work as Hollywood's preeminent music editor, occasionally taking a compositional assignment that interested him. How many other films could have benefited from his talent and instincts?

David Hirsch

Pi

1998, Thrive Records, from the film *Pi*, Harvest Filmworks/Plantain, 1998 ♪♪♪♪

album notes: Music: Clint Mansell.

Darren Aronofsky's directorial debut is destined for cult status—a thriller with the look of *Eraserhead,* a plot that could have come from a Philip K. Dick novel, and a sterling soundtrack of British techno. *Pi* was scored by Clint Mansell of Pop Will Eat Itself, a British rock group that made extensive use of drum machines and samples. Like many of his peers, Mansell now works exclusively in electronic music and *Pi* benefits from a varied palette of sounds: Aphex Twin's twisted blips, Autechre's austere beats, Orbital's dark, heavy bass, and upbeat, hip-hop-flavored tracks from Massive Attack and junglist Roni Size. Mansell's selections from his own score are strong. They are mixed around theories from the film, where the math genius played by Sean Gullette declares "ultimate truths" about life. Mansell's edgy, up-tempo beats mirror the film's flow of numbers, and the rapid thought processes going on in the mastermind's head. Promotional Web sites for movies are generally not

worth mentioning. For an exception go to www.pithemovie.com for background information to make sense of the intriguing theories surrounding *Pi* and hear snippets of the album.

David Poole

The Piano

1993, Virgin Records, from the film *The Piano*, CIBY 2000, 1993 ♪♪♪

album notes: Music: Michael Nyman; **Orchestra:** Members of the Philharmonic Orchestra of Munich; **Conductor:** Michael Nyman; **Featured Musicians:** John Harle, David Roach, soprano/alto sax; Andrew Findon, tenor/baritone sax, flute; Michael Nyman, piano.

Michael Nyman rose to fame with his New Age-style score for the Jane Campion drama starring Holly Hunter, Sam Neill, and Harvey Keitel. As an album, though, one can hear the deficiencies in Nyman's score, which basically shifts between delicate piano solos (think Yanni or John Tesh) and less assured, almost static orchestral writing, making you want to see the sumptuous visuals in Campion's movie to understand just how the score works in the film. Nyman's orchestral music, on the other hand, just doesn't offer enough substance or diversity to work on its own terms, though fervent admirers of the picture will be quick to point out how memorable some of the piano themes are in relation to much of today's typical film music. They may have a point, though that still doesn't mean that the album is an essential one to have in your library.

Andy Dursin

Picnic

1988, MCA Records, from the film *Picnic*, Columbia Pictures, 1958 ♪♪♪♪

album notes: Music: George Duning; **Orchestra:** The Columbia Pictures Orchestra; **Conductor:** Morris Stoloff.

Duning's score is essentially a series of cues that are serviceable and work particularly well within the dramatic context of the film. As a listening experience, however, the sometimes atonal music (faithful to the adventurous nature of film music in the mid- to late-1950s), doesn't always make a favorable impression, and is not always easy to listen to. The soundtrack, however, features an extraordinary classic in "Moonglow and Love Theme," which illustrates one of the crucial scenes in the film and which remains the highlight of this album.

Didier C. Deutsch

The Picture Bride

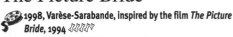

1998, Varèse-Sarabande, inspired by the film *The Picture Bride*, 1994 ♪♪♪♪♪

album notes: Music: Cliff Eidelman; **Orchestra:** The Orchestra Seattle; **Conductor:** Cliff Eidelman; **Featured Musician:** Pablo Sepulveda, Pan pipe, bamboo flute.

Holly Hunter and Anna Paquin in The Piano. **(The Kobal Collection)**

🎬 **1995, Virgin Movie Music, from the film *Picture Bride*, Miramax Films, 1995** 🎵🎵🎵♪

album notes: Music: Mark Adler; **Conductor:** Mark Adler; **Featured Musicians:** Jim Walker, bamboo flutes; Peter Maunu, guitars.

An interesting spin on an old concept, inasmuch as this score was "inspired" by the film about a 17-year-old Japanese mail-order bride, whose prospective husband is not exactly what she had anticipated, nor the younger man he portrayed himself as being when they exchanged photos. In other circumstances the device would be heavily criticized, but in this case it enabled a reputable film composer to create a music he truly felt compelled to write without the constraints usually imposed by a screen narrative. Part of a series sponsored by the label, this CD actually presents a score that Eidelman had been commissioned to write for the film, but because of changes in the post-production schedule another composer was brought in before Eidelman had a chance to submit his own score. Reflective of the subject matter, his music is meditative and calm, full of longing and love, and intensely personal. The intense contributions by Pablo Sepulveda on Pan pipe and bamboo flute, add a magic touch to it, making it beautifully descriptive with a quiet, forlorn feel. It is indeed a superb creation that was well worthy of being recorded.

Picture Bride elicited a strikingly beautiful score from Mark Adler, who succeeded in conveying the hardships, sorrow and unexpected joys in the lives of Japanese laborers caught in a daily struggle for survival, respect and their eventual independence. With the bamboo flutes creating haunting images that often transcend the ethnicity in the action, Adler wrote a score that teems with gorgeous melodies, as precious and lovely as a porcelain doll, soothing and striking in their calm beauty. The unassuming "Miss Peiper" is a case in point, but almost everyone of the 22 selections in this CD is an illuminating joy, one's enduring pleasure throughout being only marred by the briefness of some of the tracks.

Didier C. Deutsch

Pink Cadillac

🎬 **1988, Warner Bros., from the film *Pink Cadillac*, Warner Bros., 1988** 🎵🎵🎵

A solid country-flavored soundtrack compilation, for a film starring Clint Eastwood as a bounty hunter, chasing bill dodgers in his pink Cadillac, with Bernadette Peters, wife of one of his preys, as his travelling companion. Some excellent frontliners are on board, including Michael Martin Murphey, Randy Travis, J.C. Crowley, Billy Hill, and Dion, whose rockin' "Drive All Night" is a joy. Hank Williams Jr. even duets with his

father on "There's a Tear in My Beer," in another display of technical fancy.

Didier C. Deutsch

Pink Flamingos

🎬 **1997, Hip-O Records, from the film *Pink Flamingos*, Fine Line, 1972** 🎵🎵🎵

For the cult classic *Pink Flamingos* director John Waters chose an eclectic mix of surf guitar, rockabilly, garage rock, and '60s bubblegum pop. The notoriously deviant behavior in *Pink Flamingos* is reflected in what Waters calls filth music, "music that inspires you to commit your own creatively filthy acts." While Patti Page's "How Much Is That Doggy in the Window" might seem more naive and cute than filthy, it takes on a subversive tone when set next to sleazy, fuzzed up guitar, care of Link Wray, or the squawking chicken in the Nite Hawks' "Chicken Grabber." From the kitsch "Happy, Happy Birthday Baby" by the June Weavers, to the rocking "Riot in Cell Block #9," *Pink Flamingos* is goofy and groovy, evincing a perverse nostalgia that only Waters could muster. The movie opened in 1972, but this is the first time the soundtrack has seen the light of day. An essential piece of exquisitely trashy Americana.

David Poole

The Pink Panther

🎬 **1989, RCA Records, from the film *The Pink Panther*, United Artists, 1963** 🎵🎵🎵🎵

album notes: Music: Henry Mancini; **Conductor:** Henry Mancini.

Even if he only had written one score, for this romp in which, for the first time, bumbling Inspector Jacques Clouseau of the French Sûreté gained full-fledged status as a film celebrity, Henry Mancini would rightfully belong in the pantheon of great screen composers. Though he was frequently dismissed as too lightweight, compared to some of his most prestigious peers, Mancini was a master at defining the parameters of comedy music and exploiting the themes for all their delicious worth. Brightly introduced by the celebrated theme, the score evidences all the positive assets usually found in Mancini's scores—tunes with a catchy lilt, themes with a pop sensitivity that immediately set a scene or situation, memorable musical moments that invite repeated listening and never overstay their welcome. All of these and more can be found here in a score that brims with delightful little quirks, amusing tidbits that prove charming, and at least one other great pop tune in "It Had Better Be Tonight."

see also: Revenge of the Pink Panther/Son of the Pink Panther/The Trail of the Pink Panther

Didier C. Deutsch

The Pink Panther Strikes Again

1998, Rykodisc, from the film *The Pink Panther Strikes Again, United Artists, 1969* ♪♪♪

album notes: Music: Henry Mancini; **Conductor:** Henry Mancini; **Featured Musicians:** Tony Cue, tenor sax; Johnny Van Derrick, violin; Steve Gray, keyboards; Stephen Wick, tuba; Howard Etherton, bassoon; Dick Abell, guitar; Eric Allen, vibes; Don Lusher, trombone.

This is the most memorable of the *Pink Panther* movies for several reasons. First is the famous "Does Your Dog Bite" scene. Then, there is the wonderful opening animated credit sequence featuring Inspector Clouseau and the Pink Panther. For this sequence, Henry Mancini morphed his "Pink Panther Theme" to include brilliant parodies of "The Funeral March of a Marionette" (best known as the Alfred Hitchcock theme music), "Batman," "The Sound of Music," "Singin' in the Rain," and "Big Spender." Finally, Mancini composed, for this fifth installment in the Panther series, a theme for Inspector Clouseau. The CD release also features two vocal tracks heard in the film, the tongue-in-cheek "Until You Love Me" and the Oscar-nominated song "Come to Me," sung by Tom Jones with a vocal cameo by the one and only Inspector Clouseau. As with most of the titles in the Rykodisc MGM/UA series, this title contains several bonus tracks and CD enhancement, including the original movie trailer.

Didier C. Deutsch

Pinocchio

1992, Walt Disney Records, from the animated feature *Pinocchio, Walt Disney Pictures, 1940* ♪♪♪♪♪

album notes: Music: Leigh Harline; **Lyrics:** Ned Washington, Paul J. Smith; **Choir:** The Disney Chorus; **Orchestra:** The Disney Orchestra; **Conductor:** Leigh Harline; **Cast:** Dickie Jones, Christian Rub, Cliff Edwards, Evelyn Venable.

Walt Disney had a real winner in this 1940 animated morality fable based on the Italian tale about a puppetmaker, Gepetto, whose wish to have a real son is eventually granted by the "Blue Fairy," though Pinocchio also has to win his wings and does so only after he lives many adventures with various unreliable people, and saves Gepetto from certain death. The score, by Leigh Harline and Ned Washington, yielded the Academy Award–winning "When You Wish Upon a Star," and brims with great musical moments that come vividly to life in this mono recording, recently dusted off and remastered, with a lot of instrumental passages added to the album.

Didier C. Deutsch

The Pirate

1991, Sony Music Special Products, from the film *The Pirate, MGM, 1948* ♪♪♪♪

album notes: Music: Cole Porter; **Lyrics:** Cole Porter; **Choir:** The MGM Studio Chorus; **Orchestra:** The MGM Studio Orchestra; **Conductor:** Lennie Hayton; **Cast:** Gene Kelly, Judy Garland.

A legendary flop, *The Pirate* seemed to have the right pedigree for success: A brilliant score by Cole Porter; two beloved artists, Gene Kelly and Judy Garland, billed above the title; a swashbuckling story, at a time when seafaring adventures still lured audiences; amusing characterizations by Walter Slezak and the Nicholas Brothers; superb direction by Vincente Minnelli; and the technicolor gloss that was a hallmark of the best MGM productions.

Circus entertainer Gene Kelly made a dashing figure as an 18th–century pirate, about whom feisty Judy Garland romanticized in her lonely Caribbean abode, until he came in and tried to sweep her off her feet. The stylized ballets and gorgeous technicolor photography took full advantage of the myriad technical possibilities offered by the studio's best craftsmen; and the score brimmed with great tunes, in which "Be a Clown" soon became a favorite. A *succes d'estime,* the screen musical is still very much revered today as one of the most attractive films to come out of the studio. The CD recording offers the score, plus two previously unreleased songs (one of them, "Voodoo," written for the film but discarded before its release).

Didier C. Deutsch

Pirates

1986, Varèse Sarabande, from the film *Pirates, Cannon Films, 1986* ♪♪♪♪

album notes: Music: Philippe Sarde; **Orchestra:** The Orchestre de Paris; **Conductor:** Bill Byers.

This opulent score is actually much better than the film directed by Roman Polanski, which could not be saved by all of Walter Matthau's snarling and posturing as a dangerous high sea shark in the days when piracy was at its height. Sarde's score, magnificently played by the venerable Orchestre de Paris, cannot compare, of course, with Korngold's *The Sea Hawk,* probably the best of its kind, but on its own terms, it exudes an appeal in which romance and bravura happily mix to create a most colorful sonic imagery.

Didier C. Deutsch

Planes, Trains and Automobiles

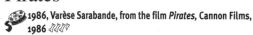

1987, MCA Records, from the film *Planes, Trains and Automobiles, Paramount Pictures, 1987* ♪♪♪♪

Reflecting the contrasting aspects of this film, about a businessman trying to go home for the Thanksgiving holidays and forced to travel across the country with a salesman who has wrecked his rental car and destroyed his bags, this soundtrack album is divided into two parts, a "town" compilation and a "country" one. In the first, rockers Westworld and Balaam and the Angel try to keep up with Book of Love and The Dream Academy, whose contributions are engaging. On the country side, there is no mistaking the immediate appeal of Dave Edmunds and Emmylou Harris, though Silicon Teens and Stars of Heaven trail behind. "I Can Take Anything," the so-called "Love Theme" from the film, features Steve Martin and John Candy, who star in it.

Didier C. Deutsch

Planet of the Apes

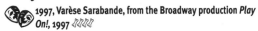 1992, Intrada Records, from the film *Planet of the Apes*, 20th Century Fox, 1968 ♪♪♪♪♪

album notes: Music: Jerry Goldsmith; **Conductor:** Jerry Goldsmith.

Goldsmith's classic landmark science fiction score is a masterpiece of avant garde modernism that still hasn't been properly presented on CD, although this Intrada release offers improved sound and remedies at least one inexcusable omission of the original Project 3 album by adding the stupendous action cue "The Hunt," which to this day probably stands as the finest marriage of film imagery and music the composer ever produced. It's four minutes of relentless, Stravinskyesque orchestral assault dominated by the unforgettable use of a ram's horn to herald the film's first shot of intelligent apes on horseback. The rest of the score is primarily atmospheric, creating a strange alien world with echoed percussion effects, the unearthly moan of a bass slide whistle and a tide-like, metallic rush of air. The album's sequencing is non-chronological, climaxing with the brilliant staccato piano playing of "No Escape." This is as far from current film scoring sensibilities as you're likely to get, but no self-respecting fan of the medium should be without it.

Jeff Bond

Planet of the Apes/Escape from the Planet of the Apes

1997, Varèse-Sarabande, from the films, *Planet of the Apes*, 1968, and *Escape from the Planet of the Apes*, 1971, both 20th Century-Fox ♪♪♪♪♪

album notes: Music: Jerry Goldsmith; **Orchestra:** The 20th Century-Fox Orchestra, **Conductor:** Jerry Goldsmith.

From *Patton* to *Chinatown*, Jerry Goldsmith has composed landmark scores for every type of film. 1968's *Planet of the Apes* was perhaps the defining musical moment for science fiction films: a score for an alien world that truly sounded alien. Goldsmith's use of such wildly diverse instruments as a Brazilian culka, an echoplex, and dissonant brass was like nothing that had been heard before in the genre, a brilliantly experimental score that did much to convey the harsh environment in which Charlton Heston found himself trapped. And no Goldsmith cue is as famous, or terrifying as "The Hunt," where blaring rams' horns and shrieking strings become the apes' brutal round-up of their human prey. This *Planet* had been previously available on Project Three and Intrada, but Varèse has issued the definitive, and best-sounding edition of the score—with Goldsmith's music for *Escape from the Planet of the Apes* as a deliciously goofy bonus. The third *Apes* film transported Cornelius and Zira to the swinging '70s, and Goldsmith's funky score played the setting in all of its "shagadelic" glory. Even his *Planet of the Apes* theme got the rock treatment, its mix of electric guitar and whooshing synths recalling those impossibly hip primates in a man's world—baby!

Dan Schweiger

Play On!

1997, Varèse Sarabande, from the Broadway production *Play On!*, 1997 ♪♪♪♪

album notes: Music: Duke Ellington; **Lyrics:** Duke Ellington, Billy Strayhorn, Don George, Harry James, Mack David, Ben Carruthers, Irving Mills, Milt Gable, Nick Kenny, Albany Bigard, Irving Gordon, Eddie DeLange, Henry Nemo, John Redmond, Bob Russell, Paul Francis Webster; **Musical Direction:** J. Leonard Oxley; **Cast:** Cheryl Freeman, Andre De Shields, Larry Marshall, Yvette Cason, Tonya Pinkins.

Initially, it seemed like a terrific idea—Shakespeare's *Twelfth Night*, slyly updated to Harlem in the 1920s, with a score consisting of the best–known songs by the man who epitomized the period, Duke Ellington. But once the show hit Broadway, on March 20, 1997, it became obvious that something was not entirely right. Yes, all the elements were in perfect order—the story, despite the change of century and locale, held together rather well; the score, well . . . what can you say when the first number that hits you is "Take The 'A' Train" (naturally!), and also includes such gems as "I Let a Song Go Out of My Heart," "Mood Indigo," "Don't Get Around Much Anymore," "It Don't Mean a Thing," "I Got It Bad and That Ain't Good," "Solitude," "Love You Madly," and "Prelude to a Kiss"; and the cast, made of veteran performers and attractive newcomers, couldn't have been more congenial.

But somehow, the production itself looked stilted, polished but without much of the fire and intensity one might have expected from such a combination. As a result, and in the face of lukewarm reviews that did little to compel theatergoers to come and see for themselves, the show closed after a meager 61 performances. None of the production's failings mar the cast recording, however, and both the songs and the performers literally shine in the most positive light in this exhilarating CD, the only proof positive that *Play On!* was a terrific idea, indeed.

Didier C. Deutsch

The Player

1992, Varèse Sarabande, from the film *The Player,* New Line Cinema, 1992 ♪♪♪♪

album notes: Music: Thomas Newman; **Conductor:** Thomas Newman; **Featured Musicians:** Thomas Newman, piano, electronics; Rick Cox, alto sax, prepared guitar; George Budd, sample electronics; Jeff Elmassian, winds; Michael Fisher, percussion; Harvey Mason, drums; Ralph Grierson, piano, electronics; Buell Neidlinger, upright bass.

It's rare today that a composer gets a chance to define the sound of a genre. Thomas Newman did it on Robert Altman's *The Player,* musically codifying the quirky-Hollywood—insider–murder–mystery (note the similarities with the later *Get Shorty,* scored by John Lurie). Tim Robbins stars as a coldhearted, smug studio executive stalked by a disgruntled writer. He kills the wrong writer, then falls for the murdered wrong writer's mysterious artist girlfriend (Greta Scacchi), until finally Altman brings it together in a sarcastic, anti–twist ending. Newman's score features modal piano loops and unusually bright themes set on a background of minimalist repetition and simplicity—as well as countless, strange samples, from chainsaws to bass harmonics to improvised saxophones.

On album the score pushes its fragmented, strange-upon-noir approach even further by segueing in and out of several disparate cocktail-lounge source cues, to give a sense of the different, superficial worlds within the picture. It also includes one of the most original approaches to a sex scene—all percussion. Newman's music is as distinct as a rich cup of coffee, set in a form interwoven with the film (see it!)—a minor masterpiece of irony.

Lukas Kendall

Playing by Heart

1998, Capitol Records, from the film *Playing by Heart,* Miramax, 1998 ♪♪♪

album notes: Music: John Barry.

Eclectic—and label-centric—are the apt descriptions for the set that accompanies this romantic dramedy, which runs a gamut from the club fare of Bran Van 3000 ("Drinking in L.A.") and Morcheeba ("Fricton") to poignant singer-songwriter fare from Bonnie Raitt ("Lover's Will"), Gomez's folk-rock ("Tijuana Lady"), and jazz from Chet Baker with the Charlie Haden Quartet West ("Everything Happens to Me"). John Barry's tribute, "Remembering Chet," is a nice adjunct to the latter, while modern rockers Moby ("Porcelain"), Ben Lee ("Cigarettes Will Kill You"), and a surprisingly fluid pairing of Live's Edward Kowal-

czyk and Neneh Cherry ("Walk into This Room") fill out a set that has some compelling selections but whose parts are largely better than their sum.

Gary Graff

Playing God

1997, Milan, from the film *Playing God,* Touchstone Pictures, 1997 ♪♪♪♪

album notes: Music: Richard Hartley.

Playing God is another example of a great score for a mediocre movie. The song-driven soundtrack features such electronica talent as the Propellerheads, Morcheeba, and LTJ Bukem. Richard Hartley's score is also electronic based, with a seventies cop-show feel, and flows nicely within the confines of the CD. Also of note is a killer industrial cover of "These Boots Are Made for Walkin'" by Family of God. Alas, this great CD could not save this stinker of a movie, about a drug-addicted man who has lost his medical license and gets drawn into a life of crime, which despite starring David Duchovny, Timothy Hutton, and Angelina Jolie, played dead at the box office.

Beth Krakower

Pleasantville

1998, Work/Sony Music, from the film *Pleasantville,* New Line Cinema, 1998 ♪♪♪♪

1998, Varèse-Sarabande, from the film *Pleasantville,* New Line Cinema, 1998 ♪♪♪♪

album notes: Music: Randy Newman.

Its obvious special effects aside, *Pleasantville* evolved from an interesting time-warp concept: a brother and sister from a typical broken '90s family, watching a *Life with Father*-like TV show from the 1950s, suddenly find themselves drawn into it, not only as witnesses but in fact as the two adolescent kids of the television family. Since the show is in black and white, they immediately look odd in it, being in color, and, as they soon find out, they bring to Pleasantville, the fictional little middle-America haven where they have landed, an unexpected—and double-edged—gift: a sense of possibility spreads like wildfire throughout the town, and once its quiet citizens have experienced such strange wonders as sex, art, storms, and ideas, there is no turning back. Based on this premise, writer-director Gary Ross developed a fascinating look at an era long gone through the microscope of a medium that glorified it, and managed to tell a story that was unconventional and diverting. Giving the right flavor to the film was easy, as the collection in the Sony Work CD demonstrates, with songs performed by Gene Vincent ("Be Bop-a-Lula"), the Dave Brubeck Quartet ("Take Five"), Elvis Presley ("Let Me Be Your Teddy Bear"), Buddy Holly

& the Crickets ("Rave On"), and Etta James ("At Last"), among many others, all reflective of the era. Two songs by Fiona Apple ("Across the Universe" and "Please Send Me Someone to Love") place the story in its initial contemporary period.

More delicate was Randy Newman's task: writing from a '50s perspective, he delivered a score that was both in-period and contemporary, something that required enormous skills. A suite from the score can be found in the Sony CD, and listeners only marginally interested in film music should be amply satisfied with this tasty morsel. But fans of instrumental music will delight in getting the score album on Varèse-Sarabande that offers some of the most significant musical moments from the film. One characteristic of Newman's works is that they all exhibit a great flair for melodic material that sticks closely to the film being scored and actually augment its romantic and/or dramatic pull. Such is the case here with a music that faintly recalls the Americana sounds of Aaron Copland, while remaining highly suggestive of the action itself.

Didier C. Deutsch

Pocahontas

1995, Walt Disney Records, from the animated feature *Pocahontas,* Walt Disney Pictures, 1995 𝄞𝄞𝄞𝄞

album notes: Music: Alan Menken; **Lyrics:** Stephen Schwartz; **Score Conductor:** Danny Troob; **Songs' Conductor:** David Friedman; **Cast:** Mel Gibson, Judy Kuhn, Jim Cummings, Linda Hunt, Bobbi Page, David Ogden Stiers.

A politically correct retelling of the love story between the feisty Indian beauty, Pocahontas, and handsome Capt. John Smith, leading English settlers to Virginia's lush countryside, this Disney animated feature swept the Academy Awards in 1996, winning Oscars for best original score, and best original song ("Colors of the Wind"). The score, by Alan Menken and Stephen Schwartz, is a generally very lively affair, beautifully serviced by the vocal performers, including Judy Kuhn as Pocahontas, whose rendition of "Just Around the River Bend" is a particularly fetching moment in the album. Vanessa Williams's performance of "Colors of the Wind" is fancy and enjoyable, though it sounds stylistically out of context with the rest of the album, as does Jon Secada and Shanice's rendition of "If I Never Knew You," included no doubt for name (read "commercial") value.

Didier C. Deutsch

Poetic Justice

1993, Epic Soundtrax, from the film *Poetic Justice,* Columbia Pictures, 1993 𝄞𝄞

There is something for everyone in this compilation album, it seems, some good, and some bad. Dealing with the negatives

first, only those with a strong tolerance for rap and its dry expressions will enjoy the selections by Pete Rock & C.L. Smooth, Nice & Smooth, Dogg Pound, and 2Pac, among others, whose contributions here echo the intense urban street sounds in this film set in South Central, which involves a young black woman (Janet Jackson), growing up with nothing but disappointments, but finding solace in the poetry she writes and the hardworking young man (Tupac Shakur), a struggling musician, who enters her life. On the positive side, however, are "listenable" songs by Stevie Wonder, Babyface, Tony! Toni! Tone!, and Terri & Monica, which make a different kind of statement, and prove much more endearing. One track from Stanley Clarke's instrumental score, makes one wish more of his music had been included.

Didier C. Deutsch

Point of No Return

1993, Milan Records, from the film *Point of No Return,* Warner Bros., 1993 𝄞𝄞

album notes: Music: Hans Zimmer, Nick Glennie-Smith; **Featured Musician:** Bob Daspit, guitar.

An almost interminable bombardment of overdone musical tracks composed by Hans Zimmer, *Point of No Return* is one of those way over-the-top scores that hits you over the head with its melodramatic indulgences. Here, Zimmer offers us his usual bag of tricks—gigantic–sounding synths, blaring orchestra, sampled electronic sounds—and it's simply too much to take, being obnoxious, excessive, and grating all at the same time. So much so, in fact, that Zimmer's music tends to overwhelm the action in John Badham's tedious remake of *La Femme Nikita,* with Bridget Fonda in the lead role. Milan's album also includes a number of Nina Simone songs, prominently featured in the movie and a lot easier to take than any second of Zimmer's score.

Andy Dursin

Poirot

1992, Virgin Records/U.K., from the LWT series *Agatha Christie's Poirot,* 1992 𝄞𝄞𝄞𝄞

album notes: Music: Christopher Gunning; **Conductor:** Christopher Gunning; **Featured Soloists:** Leslie Pearson, piano; Stan Sulzmann, saxophones; David Emanuel, viola; Anthony Pleeth, cello.

The CD regroups musical selections heard in "The Mysterious Affair at Styles," "Wasps Nest," "The Clapham Cook," and other cases, maddeningly solved by the insufferable Belgian sleuth, supremely and definitively portrayed by David Suchet. The music by Christopher Gunning has the right flavor for this type of show, with the main theme, probably one of the most recognizable tunes on television today, beautifully capturing the art deco feel of the series.

Didier C. Deutsch

Polish Wedding

1998, Milan/BMG, from the film *Polish Wedding,* Fox Searchlight, 1998 ♪♪♪♪

album notes: Music: Luis Bacalov; Orchestra: The Orchestra di Roma; Conductor: Luis Bacalov.

A romance set in Detroit's Polish community, the Pszoniak family's wedding features the lively gypsy fiddle and set amid traditionally cinematic piano and orchestral movements. Singing in Latin, a children's choir are followed by the quaint church organ of "St. Florians" and angelic voices on a divine rendition of "Santa Maria" during "The Procession." A veteran of European cinema, Luis Bacalov imbues this American production with an old world flavor. Hot off the Academy Award–winning score for *Il Postino,* Bacalov's family portrait bears his trademark charming melodies. The sentimental theme echoes Bartok's folk-influenced piano music, in this uplifting, warm-hearted, and celebratory score.

David Poole

Poltergeist

1997, Rhino Records; from the film *Poltergeist,* MGM, 1982 ♪♪♪♪♪

album notes: Music: Jerry Goldsmith; Conductor: Jerry Goldsmith.

Jerry Goldsmith's superlative ghost story music is captured in its entirety in this beautifully produced CD which features the complete score sequenced in chronological order, from the opening source music of "The Star-Spangled Banner" to the nightmarish orchestral violence of the "Escape from Suburbia" finale. The original LP featured only the highlights of the score, but this release put together by film music archeologist Nick Redman restores some of Goldsmith's most fascinating compositions, including the malevolent woodwind motif for a frightening toy clown, and the disturbing, rumbling underscoring that musically characterizes the unseen concepts of "The Other Side" and "The Beast," which Goldsmith almost single-handedly brings to life in the film. The blend of rhapsodic impressionism, elaborate dissonance, and spine-tingling beauty makes this one of Goldsmith's most varied and spectacular works, a marvel of complexity and effectiveness.

Jeff Bond

Poltergeist: The Legacy

1997, Sonic Images, from the television series *Poltergeist: The Legacy,* 1997 ♪♪♪

album notes: Music: John Van Tongeren; Additional Music: Steven M. Stern, Don Harper, Harry Gregson Williams.

Poltergeist: The Legacy, a short-lived television series, was an attempt to cash in on the success of the film series. Starring Martin Cummins, Helen Shaver, Robbie Chong, and Derek deLint, it was scored primarily by John Van Tongeren, who wrote the captivating "Main Title." But beyond that arresting track, this CD cannot come up with anything else that captures the imagination. The three-part "Legacy" is a poor substitute, with synthesizer bursts and brief choral explosions laid over orchestral lines that meander in search of a melody. It's not that it is really that bad, it's just that it really doesn't connect. The same is true of the selections composed by Steven M. Stern and Harry Gregson-Williams, who seems too much under the influence of Hans Zimmer. Only Don Harper manages to sound a slightly different note in "The Gift," an attractive little tune that unfortunately leads nowhere.

Didier C. Deutsch

Poltergeist 2

1993, Intrada Records, from the film *Poltergeist 2: The Other Side,* MGM, 1986 ♪♪♪

album notes: Music: Jerry Goldsmith; Conductor: Jerry Goldsmith.

Goldsmith's follow-up to his Oscar-nominated score, *Poltergeist 2* can't measure up to the original, although the composer's approach is laudably innovative, discarding all but a few motifs and themes from his original score and composing an entirely new work that plays off the film's opposing forces of Native American mysticism (illustrated in an unusual title theme based on an electronic melody representing a Native American Shaman and a Coplandesque horn motif for the man's supernatural disciplines) and misapplied Christian values (depicted by a hauntingly distorted hymnal tune). Where the original score is almost completely acoustic, *Poltergeist 2* revels in its sizzling electronic effects which sometimes threaten to overwhelm the orchestra. There are also abundant choral effects, from the moaning cries of the damned that accompany the twisted hymn to the guttural, devilish chants that greet the apparitions that return to torment the child Carol Anne.

Jeff Bond

Porgy and Bess

1992, MCA Records, from the Broadway revival *Porgy and Bess,* 1942 ♪♪♪♪

album notes: Music: George Gershwin; Lyrics: Ira Gershwin, DuBose Heyward; Musical Direction: Alexander Smallens; Cast: Todd Duncan, Anne Brown, Avon Long, Edward Matthews, Harriet Jackson.

1977, RCA Victor, from the Broadway revival *Porgy and Bess,* 1976 ♪♪♪♪♪

album notes: Music: George Gershwin; Lyrics: Ira Gershwin, DuBose Heyward; Musical Direction: John DeMain; Cast: Donnie Ray Albert, Clamma Dale, Larry Marshall, Alexander B. Smalls, Betty Lane.

$\frac{4}{5}$
$\frac{5}{8}$ *portrait of a lady*

A landmark in the history of the musical theatre, *Porgy and Bess* is a show that leaves critics and admirers alike totally baffled. Though no one today denies the importance of the Gershwins' and DuBose Heyward's masterpiece, few can agree about what the show should be called. An opera? A folk opera? A musical comedy? By its scope, and its abundance of musical numbers, arias and recitatives, it recalls an opera, though its story, set in Catfish Row, the glum black ghetto in Charleston, S.C., would designate it as a folk opera, a subtle nuance that has its importance. And again, because its authors feared that the tag would damage its chances of success when it premiered on October 10, 1935, it was presented in a Broadway theatre as a standard musical, even though there was really nothing standard about it.

Be that as it may, *Porgy and Bess* stands out today as an incredible theatrical achievement, one of the most colorful, large–scale offerings ever to come from the fertile pens of George and Ira Gershwin, who completed it in little over 20 months, a show that is often mentioned as the best example of the American musical theatre at its most creative and expressive. Though not a success in 1935 (it only played 124 performances), it nonetheless attracted both music and theater critics from all the dailies at the time, who only had praises for its score, in which "It Ain't Necessarily So," "I Loves You Porgy," "I Got Plenty O' Nuttin'," and "Summertime," its most recognizable tune, soon emerged as qualified hits.

Revived in 1942, in a somewhat downsized presentation, with Todd Duncan and Anne Brown reprising the roles they had created in 1935 and with Avon Long portraying Sportin' Life, the drug dealer who persuades Bess to leave Porgy and move to New York, the show had a successful run of 286 performances. It also yielded a cast album recording, the first listed above, which, though in mono sound, and only presenting the highlights from the score, still stands out as a historical document of prime importance.

Subsequently revived several times, it returned to Broadway in 1976, in a sumptuously theatrical production by the Houston Grand Opera that restored many scenes and musical moments previously discarded, and truly made it the "opera" Gershwin had initially envisioned. With Clamma Dale giving a breathtaking performance as Bess, the show had a run of 122 performances, extended from its original four–week engagement, before touring the country for several years. The complete cast album recording, on RCA, made shortly after the premiere on September 25, 1976, is the best available anywhere, a vibrant, outstanding testimony to Gershwin's musical genius.

Didier C. Deutsch

Portrait of a Lady

1996, London Records, from the film *Portrait of a Lady,* Propaganda Films, 1996 🎞🎞🎞🎞
album notes: Music: Wojciech Kilar; **Conductor:** Stepan Konicek, Nic Raine; **Featured Soloists:** Jean-Yves Thibaudet, piano; **Orchestra:** The Brindisi Quartet.

This incredibly beautiful score, quietly mesmerizing and strikingly evocative, paints a vivid picture that combines colorful musical strokes with concentrated artistry. The score, written for Jane Campion's much-anticipated follow–up to her Academy Award–winning *The Piano,* summons the atmosphere that permeates the film, a rousing period melodrama, based on Henry James's 1881 novel set in England and Italy, about a headstrong young American woman who challenges the confines of her would–be sheltered destiny. Echoing the moods in the film, in which moments of darkness and light, wisdom and innocence are deftly contrasted, Wojciech Kilar's music is laid out in specific romantic terms that are expressive and extremely attractive. Two selections by Franz Schubert add the right period touch to the music, even though Kilar's score is strong enough to evoke the late 1800s without them.

Didier C. Deutsch

Portrait of Terror

1998, Varèse-Sarabande, from the film *Portrait of Terror,* Miramax, 1998 🎞🎞🎞
album notes: Music: John Ottman; **Conductor:** Damon Intrabarolo.

This is the score to *Halloween H20* by any other name, music that was sliced and diced for the film by Miramax. While the studio chose to make a bloody mess of the soundtrack by putting Ottman's music into a blender with various Marco Beltrami's pieces from *Mimic* and *Scream,* you can appreciate Ottman's unexpurgated score here. There might be only so much Ottman can do with this kind of stalk-and-slash "busy" music, stuff that's supposed to sneak around with low strings, then jump at the audience with a piercing brass attack and orchestral dissonance. Yet Ottman's score manages to gives some real life to the cliches, especially when we get to hear him belt out John Carpenter's famed *Halloween* theme with a full symphony. Even if this isn't exactly the kind of soundtrack that's strong on melody, Ottman's work on films like *The Usual Suspects* and *Apt Pupil* lets him keep the suspense interesting here, even frightening. Ottman is more interested in mood than cheap scares, styling *Portrait* in the Bernard Herrmann mode, complete with a tip of the butcher knife to *Psycho.* If nothing else, *Portrait of Terror* is gripping and intense, a chilling listen that would have been even better on the screen. This *Portrait* certainly doesn't deserve to hide behind the mask of a "concept" album.

Dan Schweiger

The Poseidon Adventure

See: The Paper Chase/The Poseidon Adventure

Postcards from America

1995, London Records, from the film *Postcards from America,* Strand, 1995 🎵🎵🎵🎶

album notes: Music: Stephen Endelman.

Based on the autobiographies of David Wojnarowicz, an artist and writer who died of AIDS, this quirky film was considerably enlivened by the soundtrack that featured performances by a wide range of alternative bands, underground faves, established groups, and Connie Francis. Primarily a showcase for the New York Dolls, heard here in three selections, and Jimmy Sommerville, whose "Postcards from America Suite" is a high point, the CD also proposes country tracks by Stonewall Jackson (the humorous "Me and You and a Dog Named Boo") and Blue Mountain ("Jimmy Carter"), a bluesy "This Bitter Earth" by Banderas, a wonderful new track by Morphine ("Providence"), and Connie Francis! A rather strange mixture, but an attractive one that's highly enjoyable.

Didier C. Deutsch

The Postman

1994, Hollywood Records, from the film *The Postman (Il Postino),* Miramax Pictures, 1994 🎵🎵🎵🎵🎶

album notes: Music: Luis Bacalov; **Orchestra:** Orchestra Sinfonietta di Roma; **Conductor:** Luis Bacalov; **Featured Musicians:** Luis Bacalov, piano; Hector Ulises Passarella, bandoneon; Riccardo Pellegrino, violin, mandolin; **Poems:** Pablo Neruda.

Evidencing a lyrical sensitivity seldom found in contemporary scores, Luis Bacalov's Academy Award–winning score for *Il Postino* is agreeably infectious and flavorful and draws much of its appeal from the inclusion of some unusual, yet typically expected instruments like the bandoneon and mandolins. The music displays a definite Mediterranean attitude that matches the moods in this memorable little tale about a postman on an isolated island who finds new reasons to like his job when he befriends the exiled poet Pablo Neruda, who introduces him to the wonderfully imaginative world of poetry. The various cues composed by Bacalov subtly underline the moods and situations in the film, with catchy motifs that are endearing and attractively drawn. Dressing up the music and giving it a slightly different spin, an occasional jazzy tune ("Loved by Women"), and a pop recording ("Madreselva," performed by the great tango performer Carlos Gardel) provide a pleasant change of pace. The main theme, reprised on several occasions in different musical formats, proves noticeably catchy.

Because of its success, and Oscar win no doubt, the American release of this soundtrack also features several poems by Neruda, read by a wide—and odd—assortment of well-known performers, including Sting, Wesley Snipes, Julia Roberts, Ralph Fiennes, Glenn Close, Willem Dafoe, and Madonna. The first time around, it is interesting to hear these texts, but unless one feels otherwise inclined, repeated playing tends to become somewhat tiresome. The Italian soundtrack album, on the CAM label, only contains the score.

Didier C. Deutsch

The Postman

1997, Warner Bros. Records, from the film *The Postman,* Warner Bros., 1997 🎵

album notes: Music: James Newton Howard; **Conductor:** Artie Kane; **Orchestra:** The L.A. Master Chorale, **Conductor:** Paul Salamunovich; **Featured Musicians:** Katy Salvidge, whistles, recorder; George Doering, acoustic guitar, mandolin.

One of Kevin Costner's big flops, this *Postman* is not to be confused with the charming romantic comedy, *Il Postino,* which earned Luis Bacalov an Oscar for his score a couple of years ago. No two pictures could be more dissimilar. Where *Il Postino,* the story of a postman who delivers love letters in the form of poems, was totally delightful and enjoyable, *The Postman,* which took place in some near future in a post-nuclear atmosphere, was a lumbering, plodding saga that collapsed quickly under its own inane plot of a drifter taking the identity of a dead mail carrier, and inspiring a rebellion against a would-be dictator. Where the score for *Il Postino* was deliriously funny and romantic and slightly maudlin and right on the button, James Newton Howard's score for *The Postman* sounds heavy-handed, unattractive . . . you get the picture! Some songs have been added to flesh out this album: by Jono Manson singing alone, by John Coinman singing alone, by Manson and Coinman singing together. I'll spare you the details! There's even a duet between Costner and Amy Grant, titled "You Didn't Have to Be So Nice." She sounds cute, he doesn't!

Didier C. Deutsch

Powder

1995, Hollywood Records, from the film *Powder,* Hollywood Pictures, 1995 🎵🎵

album notes: Music: Jerry Goldsmith; **Orchestra:** The National Philharmonic Orchestra; **Conductor:** Jerry Goldsmith.

The Disney Studio had a firestorm of controversy on its hands when *Powder* writer-director Victor Salva's past history of child molestation filtered into the news media, resulting in an outcry from enraged protesters about how the company could let such an individual make a movie. Well, he did, and regardless of his personal background, *Powder* is an unwatchable mess, a syrupy concoction about individuality and "being true to your-self" that makes for unbearable, heavy–handed viewing—a fact further accentuated by a thoroughly pedestrian, equally by–the–numbers score from Jerry Goldsmith that's all too indicative of the composer's lifeless film scores of the '90s. The music is routine, slow, and offers no surprises, with a main title theme meant to illicit emotion that instead reminds you of other, more memorable works written by both other composers and Goldsmith himself, who has done a far better job elsewhere.

Andy Dursin

Practical Magic

1998, Warner/Sunset Records, from the film *Practical Magic*, Warner Bros., 1998 🎬🎬🎬

album notes: Music: Alan Silvestri; **Conductor:** Alan Silvestri.

For this story about the romantic travails of two contemporary sorceresses, the music producers had the ingenious idea to pair up rock's legendary high priestess, Stevie Nicks, with Sheryl Crow as her producer/back up vocalist. The results are two very good new tracks that Crow/Nicks fans will not want to be without. The rest of the album is mainly oldies, but includes such smart choices as Joni Mitchell, Nick Drake, and Marvin Gaye. Alan Silvestri fans will also be pleased to find two score cues here. A few recent tracks by the likes of Faith Hill and Bran Van 3000 round out this smart album.

Amy Rosen

The Preacher's Wife

1996, Arista Records, from the film *The Preacher's Wife*, Touch-stone, 1996 🎬🎬🎬🎬

album notes: Featured Vocalist: Whitney Houston.

Whitney Houston exudes such radiance that it is hard to resist her, whether she appears in a dud like *Cinderella* or a winner like *Waiting to Exhale*. You might like her better in a pop recital, but this soundtrack album, by its very nature, focuses on her gospel talent with felicitous results. Powerfully backed by the Georgia Mass Choir, or trading trills with Shirley Caesar, Houston proves totally mesmerizing.

see also: The Bodyguard, Waiting to Exhale

Didier C. Deutsch

Predator 2

1990, Varèse Sarabande, from the film *Predator 2*, 20th Century Fox, 1990 🎬🎬🎬🎬

album notes: Music: Alan Silvestri; **Orchestra:** The Skywalker Symphony Orchestra; **Conductor:** Alan Silvestri.

From the jungles of South America to the jungles of 21st century East L.A., Alan Silvestri powers up the themes from his earlier score and energizes them with his interpretation of a futuristic urban beat. The roller coaster nature of Silvestri's orchestrations are done justice here by the wide sonic range of digital technology. Besides the mesmerizing percussion, he also incorporates a variety of unusual sounds, including voices in "Rest in Pieces." Most notable is the nine–minute "End Title," an exhilarating update of the original main title that kicks into high gear just three minutes in and doesn't let up.

David Hirsch

Prefontaine

1997, Hollywood Records, from the film *Prefontaine*, Hollywood Pictures, 1997 🎬🎬🎬🎬

album notes: Music: Mason Daring.

Steve Prefontaine's runs to glory during the late '60s and early '70s provide the parameters for this soundtrack, which features a handful of classic tracks from the era. Some of it is stuff you don't readily hear on soundtracks, too—Jimi Hendrix's "Crosstown Traffic," for instance, or Rufus's "Once You Get Started," and Lynyrd Skynyrd's "Tuesday's Gone." Of particular note is "If '60s Were '90s" by Beautiful People, a British instrumental group that builds its intriguing compositions around samples of Hendrix music.

Gary Graff

Prelude to a Kiss

1998, Milan/BMG, from the film *Prelude to a Kiss*, 20th Century-Fox, 1998 🎬🎬🎬🎬

album notes: Music: Howard Shore; **Conductor:** Howard Shore; **Featured Musicians:** William Galison, harmonica; Cheryl Hardwick, piano; Ronnie Cuber, baritone sax; Dominic Cortese, accordion.

In the oddly charming *Prelude to a Kiss*, Meg Ryan and Alec Baldwin portrayed a young couple in love whose plans go awry after an uninvited guest to their wedding, an old man, kisses the bride, prompting them to switch bodies. Composer Howard Shore beautifully captures in his score the quaint dilemma confronting the three characters— the old man who gets a new lease on life in a young virile body, the young woman who realizes her life may end before it begins, and the husband who finds himself married to a total stranger. Supplementing the score are five songs, including three covers: Annie Lennox singing Cole Porter's "Every Time We Say Goodbye," the Cowboy Junkies covering Lou Reed's "Sweet Jane," and Blondie's Deborah Harry in a great reading of Duke Ellington's "Prelude to a Kiss." Also featured is the Divinyls hit "I Touch

Myself." This is one of those rare times when the songs actually complement the score very well.

Beth Krakower

Presumed Innocent

1990, Varèse Sarabande, from the film *Presumed Innocent,* Warner Bros., 1990 ♫♫♫

album notes: Music: John Williams; **Conductor:** John Williams.

In the world of suspense-genre scores, *Presumed Innocent* is competent and certainly above-average. In terms of its place in the John Williams canon of movie music, however, it ranks fairly low on the ladder. For this Alan J.Pakula adaptation of Scott Turow's best-selling novel, Williams composed a haunting theme for piano and orchestra, with unsettling strings building to a memorable crescendo. The theme is memorable in itself, but the rest of the score involves a lot of somber, low-key underscore cues that more or less work strictly in accordance with the action on-screen. While that doesn't mean that Williams didn't do his job admirably here, it does mean that, unlike a lot of the composer's works, there isn't much here to grab onto by itself, leaving the album recommended mostly for Williams aficionados, who will most likely be disappointed by the rather ordinary tone of much of the music.

Andy Dursin

Pret-A-Porter

1994, Columbia Records, from the film *Pret-A-Porter,* Miramax Films, 1994 ♫♫♫♫♫

This set does a nice job of catching the aural end of the fashion show industry well—high energy with big, thumping, and phat bass lines to drive the models down the runway. Ina Kamoze's "Here Comes the Hotstepper" provides a nice kick-off to a propulsive batch of songs, highlighted by Terence Trent D'Arby's "Supermodel Sandwich," a "perfecto mix" of U2's "Lemon," Sam Phillips's cheeky remake of "These Boots are Made for Walkin'," and M People's "Natural Thing." In this context, however, rockers such as the Rolling Stones ("Jump on Top of Me") and the Cranberries ("Pretty") seem to be included only for name value.

Gary Graff

Pretty Woman

1990, EMI Records, from the film *Pretty Woman,* Touchstone Pictures, 1990 ♫

album notes: Featured Artists: Natalie Cole, David Bowie, Go West, Jane Wiedlin, Roxette, Robert Palmer, Peter Cetera, Christopher Otcasek, Lauren Wood, Roy Orbison, Red Hot Chili Peppers.

So '80s—even if it was released at the turn of the decade. Selling more than three million copies, this is a powerhouse pop singles vehicle, shooting Roxette's "It Must Have Been Love," Go West's "King of Wishful Thinking," and the Roy Orbison title track into the upper reaches of the charts. But with the exception of the latter, already a classic by the time the film came out, when was the last time you heard these songs on the radio. And shame on David Bowie for his absolutely unnecessary "Fame 90."

Gary Graff

A Price above Rubies

1998, RCA Victor, from the film *A Price above Rubies,* Miramax, 1998 ♫♫♫

album notes: Music: Lesley Barber; **Conductor:** Ken Kugler.

Struggling with her patriarchal Orthodox Jewish society, Sonia courageously stakes her independence, only to be cast out to find happiness elsewhere. Lesley Barber's music adds further dimension to an already strong characterization and excellent performance by Renee Zellweger. Barber does not provide obviously ethnic music. Typical to Klezmer music the clarinet is subtly integrated with Arabic scales into a richly varied orchestral score. Sonia's theme emphasizes her aspirational personality with sprightly harp, bass and flute. The music insistently strides forward with a flourish of violin, reflecting Sonia's determination. Other characters are relatively two-dimensional on film, but Barber adds some depth with variations on Sonia's own mix of pizzicato strings and violin. Ultimately, everyone is seen from Sonia's perspective, and once the drama turns to romance with Sonia's exodus and meeting Ramon, the score mainly revisits earlier cues, albeit in different arrangements. Superior to Barber's work on the magic-realist, lesbian romance *When Night Is Falling* and the forgettable sequel *Los Locos Posse, A Price above Rubies* bodes well for future work.

David Poole

Pride and Prejudice

1995, Angel Records, from the BBC/A&E–TV serial *Pride and Prejudice,* 1995 ♫♫♫♫♫

album notes: Music: Carl Davis; **Conductor:** Carl Davis; **Featured Soloist:** Malvyn Tan, fortepiano.

This elegant score, written for fortepiano and small ensemble, is a delight. Created for an A&E series based on Jane Austen's novel, the music echoes the moods and reflects the various aspects of this compelling and witty love story. In fact, wit and vitality are traits that recur throughout the score, in which two themes are developed, the first concerns Elizabeth Bennet and her family's hunt for a proper husband; the second, stresses the felicity of marriage and affairs of the heart. Occasionally pausing to reflect on the events that have occurred, Davis composed "Piano Summaries" that open each episode and link the various cues together in this soundtrack album. It's a somewhat audacious device that is quite effective within the context of the series and works quite well here as a break between the cues.

Didier C. Deutsch

The Pride and the Passion

See: The Agony and the Ecstasy/The Pride and the Passion

Primal Fear

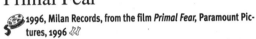 1996, Milan Records, from the film *Primal Fear,* Paramount Pictures, 1996 ♪♪

album notes: Music: James Newton Howard; **Conductor:** Artie Kane; **Featured Soloists:** Terence Blanchard, horn; Barbara Northcutt, English horn.

Once in a while you hear a film score that just isn't crying out to be a soundtrack album. *Primal Fear,* which has a capable but unmemorable score by James Newton Howard, is clearly one of those cases. Thriller scores are typically a tough genre for composers, since the music is usually restrained, building up mystery and suspense to climaxes that will then (generally) contain a great deal of music. But even then, the story is supposed to be the star, not the composer or sound editor. In *Primal Fear,* Howard tries his best by underscoring the picture in one of three manners—quiet, brooding orchestral accompaniment, more powerful dramatic cues, and pulsating, synth–accompanied tracks modeled after the composer's own score for *The Fugitive.* That said, however, Howard is more or less restricted by the confines of the genre here, and is never able to open up any new avenues in his music for listeners to take hold of. The music works perfectly in the film, but it just isn't fit for soundtrack album consumption.

Andy Dursin

Primary Colors

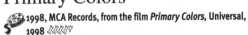 1998, MCA Records, from the film *Primary Colors,* Universal, 1998 ♪♪♪♪

album notes: Music: Ry Cooder; **Conductor:** Tom Pasatieri; **Featured Artists:** Ry Cooder, piano, guitar; Van Dyke Parks, piano; Jack Tarreson, piano; Jon Hassell, trumpet; Ronu Majundar, flute; Gil Bernal, tenor sax; Rick Cox, alto sax; Frank Marocco, Bunny Andrews, accordion; Chuck Domanico, Don Falzone, bass; Sid Page, violin; Norm Hughes, violin; Amir Yaghmai, violin; David Mansfield, violin; Larry Campbell, violin; Kenny Koseck, violin.

In a rare case of fiction mirroring real events so closely that it might be misconstrued as being the real thing, *Primary Colors* cast a presidential candidate literally taken with his pants down as he weaves his way to the top. Written by Mike Nichols and

Elaine May, who adapted a notorious 1996 book by "Anonymous" about the first Clinton campaign, the film is an outrageous succession of scenes in which the hero, the governor of an unnamed Southern state and a favorite for the Democratic nomination, is revealed as charmingly manipulative, cynically sincere, simpatico and a ladies' man; the drive to the White House his ultimate goal, no matter what it takes to get there. But the script, rather than portraying an unsavory political figure that may appear callous and unfeeling, shows him as an endearing, charismatic character, something that makes him instantly more likeable. Any comparison with persons existing or dead is purely coincidental, of course, and the names have been changed to protect the innocent. The fact is, the film was brilliantly mordant in its analysis of a political figure, extremely funny, and superbly played by a competent cast that included John Travolta as the presidential hopeful, Emma Thompson as his outspoken wife, Billy Bob Thornton as a blunt campaign adviser, and Adrian Lester as a reluctant black deputy campaign manager. Adding primary colors of his own to the story, Ry Cooder wrote a score that's wonderfully old fashioned and evocative of the turmoil created by such events as presidential campaigns. Mixing standards like "Camptown Races" and "You Are My Sunshine," with original compositions, he managed to capture a unique country flavor that's not country and western, yet close enough to be an adequate substitute. This is a very engaging effort that should find a lot of fans.

Didier C. Deutsch

Prince of Darkness

1987, Varèse Sarabande, from the film *Prince of Darkness,* Universal Pictures, 1987 ♪♪

album notes: Music: John Carpenter.

With *Prince of Darkness,* a horror film which attempted to prove that the Evil One is nothing more than a green, slimy slug, John Carpenter struck a particularly malevolent note. Though hardly the terrifying picture he might have envisioned, it is made more frightening by the director's unique electronic concoction, an amalgam of ominous, low sounds that presaged the horror soon to materialize. With a chorus of disembodied voices adding an otherworldly touch, the score did enhance the moods on the screen, but loses some of its effectiveness and proves somewhat less appealing or enjoyable when heard in one's home environment.

Didier C. Deutsch

The Prince of Egypt

1998, DreamWorks, from the film *The Prince of Egypt,* DreamWorks, 1998 ♪♪♪

album notes: Music: Hans Zimmer; **Songs:** Stephen Schwartz.

Stephen Schwartz created the songs and Hans Zimmer the score for this highly visible, highly touted animated feature produced under the aegis of Steven Spielberg's DreamWorks company. Unusually dark and brooding for the kiddies, and drawn in a style that was too realistic to really capture their imagination, it might have been too ambitious for its own good, and will probably be recalled as a *succes d'estime* rather than the striking hit it was anticipated to be. The songs and score, beautifully sketched, also reflect the facture of the film in many ways, but without the redeeming features that compel younger listeners to play a record over and over again. Listening to the songs, by Ofra Haza, Brian Stokes Mitchell, Ralph Fiennes, Michelle Pfeiffer, Amy Grant, and others, all name performers, though some were not known for their vocal prowesses before, there is a lingering suspicion that the intent might have been to create a serious screen musical in the guise of an animated film. Even a number like "Playing with the Big Boys," sung by Steve Martin and Martin Short, better known as funnymen, sounds unusually somber and ominous. The score also echoes these moods, with not a single selection that might elicit excitement. It's all very pretty, very attractive, but its only obvious audience is a sophisticated one that will recognize and appreciate the qualities in the work, provided they overcome a natural reluctance to equate animated features with simplified musical expressions.

Didier C. Deutsch

10 Essential Scores
by Henry Mancini

Breakfast at Tiffany's
The Pink Panther
Charade
Arabesque
Hatari!
Peter Gunn
The Molly Maguires
Touch of Evil
Experiment in Terror
Two for the Road

The Prince of Tides

1991, Columbia Records, from the film *The Prince of Tides*, Columbia Pictures, 1991

album notes: Music: James Newton Howard; Conductor: Marty Paich.

Listeners who enjoy romantic, melodic film scores ought to eat up James Newton Howard's lovely music for the 1991 Barbra Streisand adaptation of Pat Conroy's best–selling novel. Howard grounds his score in a pleasing main theme for piano and strings that's richly evocative of the main characters, a theme that is later used for "Places That Belong to You," a Streisand vocal with lyrics by Alan and Marilyn Bergman. The song was not used in the movie but rather recorded expressly for the album, which also features a Streisand performance of the standard "For All We Know." The majority of the album, though, belongs to Howard's score, which is able to walk over musical ground previously traveled by composers like Marvin Hamlisch, but without becoming overly sentimental or melodramatic. The music is highly enjoyable by itself and even non–Streisand fans should appreciate Howard's superb score.

Andy Dursin

Prince Valiant

1999, Film Score Monthly, from the film *Prince Valiant*, 20th Century-Fox, 1954

album notes: Music: Franz Waxman; Conductor: Franz Waxman.

There was an unmistakable style to the great Hollywood swashbucklers: big orchestral flourishes, calls of trumpets, light bells chiming, and a pulse to the music that seldom lessened. It was a style that dominated the genre for at least two decades, and found remarkable exponents in composers like Korngold, who pretty much set the tone for those films, Steiner, Rozsa, and Franz Waxman, whose score for *Prince Valiant* had never found an album release until this wonderful CD put together by Nick Redman and Lukas Kendall for Kendall's Film Score Monthly series of limited pressings. Right from the top, it should be said that despite some minor sonic imperfections and a detrimental lack of reverb, this is a recording that anyone remotely interested in film music should endeavor to have. It is a classic!

Eschewing the facile effects usually found in this kind of score, but remaining true to the tenets of the genre—lush brass

Robin Wright and Cary Elwes in The Princess Bride. **(The Kobal Collection)**

chorales to give body to the aura of chivalry that pervaded the narrative, pounding rhythmic chords to portray the mandatory chases, etc.—Waxman was innovative, injecting elements of dissonance and polytonality more familiar to the concert hall than film soundtracks. Lushly detailed and vividly descriptive, this is a magnificent score that only now can be fully appreciated. All film music collectors and fans have a new reason to rejoice.

Didier C. Deutsch

The Princess Bride

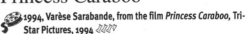1987, Warner Bros., from the film *The Princess Bride,* 20th Century Fox, 1987 ♫♫

album notes: Music: Mark Knopfler; **Featured Musicians:** Mark Knopfler, Guy Fletcher.

Here's a strange example of a composer with a rock music background (Mark Knopfler is a member of the band Dire Straits) being hired for a fantasy film on the strength of his pop music and then being asked to produce something akin to a straight adventure score. Knopfler's delicate love theme of guitar and

strings (also nicely performed by the composer as a song) works perfectly in the film and makes for enjoyable, mellow listening in album form. Unfortunately, the movie also called for mock–serious action and suspense music of a more conventional nature, and Knopfler provided a mostly electronic, percussive low–key underscore. It serves the film well because its ramshackle, bleating textures fit right in with the deliberately low–tech feel of Rob Reiner's movie, but it bears no relationship to the love theme, and doesn't function well enough on its own as music to make the rest of the album much fun to hear.

Jeff Bond

Princess Caraboo

1994, Varèse Sarabande, from the film *Princess Caraboo,* Tri-Star Pictures, 1994 ♫♫♫

album notes: Music: Richard Hartley; **Orchestra:** The Munich Symphony Orchestra; **Conductor:** Richard Hartley.

An endearing score by Richard Hartley is the foundation for this comic satire about 19th–century English aristocracy, in which a well–meaning family takes in a mysterious young girl, believing her to be a princess from some exotic country. In keeping with the tone of the film, Hartley created a score that has a dream–like, fairy tale quality. There are pompous English waltzes to be sure, but it's the magical influence the "Princess" has over the family that drives the music.

David Hirsch

The Prisoner

1989, Siva Screen/U.K., from the ITC series *The Prisoner*, 1966–67 ♪♪♪

album notes: Music: Ron Grainer, Wilfred Josephs, Albert Elms.

Originally a seven–inch record distributed by the show's British fan club Six–of–One, as a membership premium in the early 1980s, this CD launched Silva Screen's trilogy of albums featuring music from the popular series. This first album contains selections from 11 of the episodes that feature original music. Ron Grainer composed the series's main theme, replacing one by Wilfred Josephs (which is also included here). While Josephs scored the pilot, much of the series was done by Albert Elms, whose work makes up the bulk of this first volume. He also cleverly adapted classical pieces composed by Vivaldi and Bizet for one episode score, "Hammer Into Anvil." On the whole, Elms's work maintains the flavor of a typical British spy thriller. It has long been suspected that the main character was John Drake from the British series "Secret Agent (Dangerman)." However, Elms throws several musical curves now and then to remain faithfully on target to creator/star Patrick McGoohan's on–screen cat and mouse psychological drama. Both remind us often that nothing is as it seems. The two subsequent volumes were assembled from the "tracked" music licensed for use in the series from the Chappel Recorded Music Library.

David Hirsch

The Private Lives of Elizabeth and Essex

1998, Varèse-Sarabande, from the film *The Private Lives of Elizabeth and Essex*, Warner Bros., 1939 ♪♪♪♪♪

album notes: Music: Erich-Wolfgang Korngold; **Orchestra:** The Munich Symphony Orchestra; **Conductor:** Carl Davis.

It can be truthfully said that Erich-Wolfgang Korngold gave voice to the swashbuckling genre. Though he only composed a scant number of scores for the movies, his major contribution was to set the tenets of a genre that has been popular on and off since the 1930s and has influenced legions of other composers, including John Williams whose music for the "Star Wars" films are in direct line with the music created by Korngold for such films as *The Sea Hawk*, *The Adventures of Robin Hood*, and *The Private Lives of Elizabeth and Essex*. While less of an epic when compared to the other two films just cited, *Elizabeth and Essex*, a powerful costume drama, displayed all the pageantry and grandeur associated with the genre. Certainly, Korngold didn't discriminate, writing for it a score that teemed with brilliant themes, colorfully laid out and enhanced by his signature trumpet calls and lush orchestral flourishes. In fact, listening to it, one would almost never think it was written to describe the tragic love between Elizabeth I of England and her adviser, Essex, whom she sent to the gallows for treason when she realized his desire to become king overshadowed his real feelings for her.

This sumptuous new recording, with Carl Davis conducting the Munich Symphony Orchestra, is a vibrant testimony to Korngold's sense of epic and melodic creation. Smartly combined together in six long suites that enable the music to fully reach its potential, the cues are in turn profoundly romantic, vivaciously playful, and powerfully assertive, in a striking display of all the moods that made the film such an eloquent blockbuster. This is a recording that should delight all true collectors of quality film music.

Didier C. Deutsch

Private Parts

1998, Warner Bros. Records, from the film *Private Parts*, Paramount, 1998 ♪♪♪

He's big, bad, rude, crude, disgusting, and the best-known disc jockey in America. Howard Stern's rise to heights (or depths) of infamy has became a multi-media phenomenon—the book, the movie, and the album. "Never before had a man done so much with so little," goes the motto. But the only thing little about Stern is—no, not that—his faculty for subtlety. Whim is fine, as long as we know what we're getting into. With its mix of hard- and modern-rock songs, sound bites from the movie, and snippets from Stern's broadcast career, *Private Parts: The Album* could be subtitled "Howardpalooza." Like previous music-and-dialogue soundtracks for *Beavis and Butthead Do America* and *Natural Born Killers*, *Private Parts* is a fairly fluid listening experience, save for a mediocre Marilyn Manson track dropped in to add sales appeal. The interspersed comedy bits are more of a Stern sampler plate than a greatest schtick collection, but the surprise is that Stern sings—well not exactly, but he displays plenty of hard rock bravado as he bellows with Rob Zombie on "The Great American Nightmare" and rasps his "Tortured Man" ode over the Dust Brothers' backing. The album does have a few musical revelations: an incognito LL Cool J on "I Make My Own Rules" with support from the Red Hot Chili Peppers; a de facto Jane's Addiction reunion on Porno for Pyros' pleasing, if underwritten "Hard Charger"; and Ozzy Osbourne, with help from

Type O Negative, turns Status Quo's "Pictures of Matchstick Men" into something akin to Black Sabbath's "Iron Man." Well-worn chestnuts from Ted Nugent, Cheap Trick, Deep Purple, Van Halen, and AC/DC fill out the record fittingly, making *Private Parts* a perfect marriage of schlock rock and schlock jock.

Gary Graff

The Producers

🎬💲 1998, Razor & Tie, from the film *The Producers,* Joseph E. Levine, 1967 ♫♫♫♫

album notes: Music: John Morris; **Conductor:** John Morris; **Featured Performers:** Zero Mostel (Max Bialystock), Gene Wilder (Leo Bloom), Kenneth Mars (Franz Liebkind), Christopher Hewett (Roger Debris), Dick Shawn (Lorenzo St. Du Bois).

This Mel Brooks film has justifiably become memorable for its hilarious send-up of bad Broadway musicals in *Springtime for Hitler* (a gay romp with Adolf and Eva at Berchesgaden). To be totally unobjective about it, it is probably one of the best screen comedies the lunatic writer/director ever made, far superior, in this writer's opinion, to *Blazing Saddles* or *Young Frankenstein* (to each his/ her own: you might disagree, but I'm the one writing these lines). Helping a lot to make the spoof even funnier is John Morris's score, totally attuned to Brooks's vision.

The album, initially released by RCA and now available from Razor & Tie, offers many highlights from the film, including bits of dialogue that cover the essential hilarious incidents in the plot, in which a failed Broadway producer and a meek accountant join forces to produce the worst musical ever made, entirely financed by little old ladies, and hopefully walk away with a fortune when the plays fails and closes after one night. Their choice: *Springtime for Hitler,* written by a "reformed" Nazi, which is sure to offend everyone, staged by the worst director, and starring as Hitler a former hippie, LSD (that's his name!). If you don't know what follows, just make sure you pick up this album, and have a grand old time listening to it.

see also: Spaceballs, Young Frankenstein

Didier C. Deutsch

The Professional

🎬💲 1994, TriStar Records, from the film *The Professional,* Columbia Pictures, 1994 ♫♫♫♪

album notes: Music: Eric Serra; **Conductor:** John Altman; **Featured Musicians:** Andy Findon, Chinese bamboo flutes; Keith Thompson, Indian shawm, soprano schalmei, soprano dulcian; Juan Jose Mosalini Jr., Bandoneon; Rene Marc Bini, piano; Eric Serra, guitar, bass, keyboards, timpani, percussion, computer programming.

Luc Besson's first English language film is this sentimental tale of a hitman (Jean Reno) who befriends an orphaned girl (Natalie Portman) in her run from a crooked cop (Gary Oldman).

Lolita-ish sexual tension, underworld suspense and bloodshed ensue, but thanks to Eric Serra, with a moody eerieness and melody. Serra, a French rock star who scores all of Besson's films, comes from a textural, keyboard-and-live-overdubs school, like Vangelis. Much of his music is created in the electronic domain, performed by the composer himself. The resulting *Professional* score incorporates slow pop loops, distinctly Serra samples, an ethnically Arabic cast for New York (its buildings reminded the composer of the Egyptian pyramids), sensitive guitar and violin solos, and larger orchestral forces than usual for Serra. In the movie, it's pretty good; on the album, its wallpaper aesthetic slows it down, and it goes on too long. It also suffers for the same reason the film does. It's at once full of low-key, isn't-this-subtle portent, but is practically screaming, *isn't the relationship between the hit man and little girl oddly sexual?* Still, Serra's score is to be admired for its progressive (for film) blend of genres and point of view.

Lukas Kendall

A Professional Gun

See: Il mercenario/Faccia a faccia

The Professionals

🎬💲 1992, Silva Treasury, from the film *The Professionals,* Columbia Pictures, 1967 ♫♫♫♪

album notes: Music: Maurice Jarre; **Conductor:** Maurice Jarre.

A flavorful western set in Mexico in 1917, *The Professionals* elicited a vibrantly exciting score from Maurice Jarre, filled with dynamic cues reflective of the fast-paced action and warm south-of-the-border accents evocative of the various locales in which it takes place. The story of four soldiers of fortune who are recruited by an American oil tycoon to rescue his beautiful wife, held for ransom by a notorious Mexican bandito, the film found in Jarre a sympathetic composer whose music helps set the various moods of adventure, heroism, violence, and lust in the narrative. There is plenty of good, solid music to be heard here, with repeated listening helping discover previously unnoticed little details that make the whole experience all the more enjoyable. Even though the CD was assembled from vinyl source transfers, the result of the original master tapes having been lost, there is little noticeable loss in the sound quality and no surface noise of which to speak.

Profumo di donna

🎬💲 1991, CAM Records/Italy from the film *Profumo di donna (Woman's Perfume),* 1974 ♫♫♫♫

album notes: Music: Armando Trovaioli; **Conductor:** Armando Trovaioli.

Based on a novel by Giovanni Arpino, *Darkness and Honey, Profumo di donna* dealt with a former army officer who has become blind since an accident during military training and wants to return to Rome where he intends to commit suicide. On his way, accompanied by a young soldier, he discovers that the love of a woman is still worth living for. The film, which spawned an American remake, *Scent of a Woman,* with Al Pacino as the blind man, was set to music by Armando Trovaioli, whose sunny melodic accents contrasted with the grim situation of the officer forced to live without any light. Direct and unaffected, the score also stands out on its own merits, making this CD a joy to listen to. This title may be out of print or just plain hard to find. Mail-order companies, used CD shops, or dealers of rare or import recordings will be your best bet.

Didier C. Deutsch

Promised Land

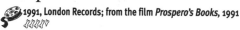

1987, Private Music Records, from the film *Promised Land,* Vestron Pictures, 1987 ♪♪♪♪

album notes: Music: James Newton Howard; **Featured Musicians:** James Newton Howard, keyboards and synthesizer programming; Robby Weaver, synclavier programming; Dean Parks, guitar; David Grisman, mandolin; Michael Fisher (percussion), Neil Stubenhaus (bass).

The wonderful folk accents in James Newton Howard add the right touch to this acoustic-and-synthesizer elegiac score for a contemporary drama set in a small Western community, about two former high-school friends who get back together several years later, only to realize that the plans they had made way back then didn't materialize. The delightful "Plymouth Waltz," which opens the album, sets the tone for the rest of the score, in which the many highlights include the gorgeous "Winter Scene," "The Hot Springs," "Ice Skating," and the quietly eloquent "Bev Cuts Danny's Hair." Contributing a different, albeit equally enjoyable note to the music, "O Magnum Mysterium," in a performance by the King's College Choir, and "Dreams and Promises," written by Janey Street, are also evocative of the film's moods.

Didier C. Deutsch

The Proprietor

1996, Epic Soundtrax, from the film *The Proprietor,* Merchant Ivory/Warner Bros. Pictures, 1996 ♪♪♪♪

album notes: Music: Richard Robbins; **Conductor:** Harry Rabinowitz.

A sensitive study of an aging woman whose childhood memories are rekindled when the apartment where she spent her youth is put up for sale, *The Proprietor* found composer Richard Robbins striking a very emotional chord in a score with great pathos. Robbins, whose eclecticism has manifested itself

in many films with varied exotic locales, pulls no surprises here, grounding his music in themes that are pleasantly evocative and lightly romantic. The story, about a French writer who cannot reconcile the fact that her mother was sent to a concentration camp during the war, translates itself into a series of cues in which the strong flavor of nostalgia is a predominant motif, even when the moods tend to be light and elegant, as in "Memories of Maxim's" and "Ostrogoth's Tango." Throughout, there is an abundance of lovely themes—"Patrice and Virginia at the Chateau," "The Ghost of Fan Fan"—which contribute to making this a very attractive and pleasant soundtrack album. On a purely technical note, a puzzling thing about this recording is the fact that it is in mono.

Didier C. Deutsch

Prospero's Books

1991, London Records; from the film *Prospero's Books,* 1991 ♪♪♪♪♪

album notes: Music: Michael Nyman, The Michael Nyman Band; **Conductor:** Michael Nyman; **Featured Musicians:** Michael Nyman, piano; Alexander Balanescu, Jonathan Carney, Elisabeth Perry, Clare Connors, violin; Kate Musker, viola; Tony Hinnigan, Justin Pearson, cello; Paul Morgan, Tim Amhurst, Lynda Houghton, double bass; Martin Elliott, bass guitar; David Rix, clarinets; John Harle, David Roach, Jamie Talbot, soprano/alto sax; Andrew Findon, tenor/baritone sax, flute; Graham Ashton, trumpet; Richard Clews, Marjorie Dunn, horn; Nigel Barr, Steve Saunders, trombone; **Featured Vocalists:** Sarah Leonard, Marie Angel, Ute Lemper, Deborah Conway.

An intellectually challenging and erotically charged screen adaptation of Shakespeare's "The Tempest," *Prospero's Books* elicited a vigorous score from Michael Nyman, with brassy accents, eerie vocals for "boy soprano voice" (performed by Sarah Leonard), and an abundance of melodic themes that underline some of the most telling moments in the film. While retaining the minimalist approach that is part of his stylistic invention, the cues are diversified enough to attract the attention. Undaunted by the task of writing a florid score for a play set on an "isle full of noises," Nyman devised several tricks that challenge the listener, while helping propel the action on the screen, like speeding up the music of "Miranda," to give it a calliope sound, or suddenly throwing in a call of trumpet, like in "Come Unto These Yellow Sands," to enhance a theme. It is an intelligent, rewarding effort that will constantly surprise and keep the listener off balance.

An extrapolation, *The Masque* is a richly elaborated composition, central to the concept of *Prospero's Books,* but different from it, that brings together three vocalists with a different tradition, Marie Angel, Ute Lemper, and Deborah Conway. Once again, Nyman's work is full of unexpected details that prove compelling and thoroughly effective in a purely musical context, though, because of the demands it imposes on the listener, the recording will not be to everyone's taste.

Didier C. Deutsch

Providence

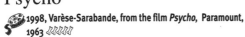1980, DRG Records, from the film *Providence*, 1980 🎬🎬🎬

album notes: Music: Miklos Rozsa.

French director Alain Resnais's stylish story, about an imaginative novelist who may or may not be dying, his rapports with other members in his family, and his rambling dissertations about his new book, made *Providence* a vivid picture, tremendously enhanced by John Gielgud's sensational portrayal as the writer. Resnais, whose admiration for American filmmakers of the 1940s was enormous, enlisted Miklos Rozsa to write the score, with the composer creating a profoundly compelling series of cues which give the film extra dimension and energy. Anchored by a central theme ("Twilight Waltz," heard in two versions, one instrumental, the other in a piano solo), the score contains several moments that are solidly etched, with striking string embellishments that recall some of Rozsa's most powerful efforts. Unfortunately, the recording itself is not all that it should be, with noticeable studio noises, which could not be corrected, bad splicing and some hiss, which could have.

Didier C. Deutsch

Psycho

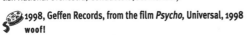1998, Varèse-Sarabande, from the film *Psycho*, Paramount, 1963 🎬🎬🎬🎬

album notes: Music: Bernard Herrmann; **Orchestra:** The Royal Scottish National Orchestra; **Conductor:** Joel McNeely.

1998, Geffen Records, from the film *Psycho*, Universal, 1998 **woof!**

album notes: Music: Bernard Herrmann, Danny Elfman; **Conductor:** Steve Bartek.

Bernard Herrmann wrote many trend-setting film scores that not only became classics in their own right but influenced legions of other composers. Among all his scores, the one that's probably best known is the one he created for Alfred Hitchcock's *Psycho,* and not the whole score, either, just this unerring call of dissonant high strings, piercing through the silence, identified as "The Murder."

But that cue, instantly identifiable, spells out Bernard Herrmann like no other. It is, of course, included in Varèse-Sarabande's sensational first recording of the complete score, with Joel McNeely conducting the Royal Scottish National Orchestra in a compelling performance that pulls no punches. Herrmann's score, beyond those high strings, proved extremely descriptive

of the action in the film, adding to its tension with musical effects that heightened the suspense. The recording does full justice to this remarkable score, and counts very high among the great recreations of classic film scores that have been available in the marketplace lately.

Conversely, what can be said about the travesty that passed itself as the soundtrack album of a remake of the movie, available on Geffen? And first, why bother with a remake? Particularly if it is to produce something so utterly inadequate! If trying to recreate a classic film, frame by frame, but using other actors, is already a questionable decision, what can be said about a soundtrack that updates the original with contemporary songs (totally alien to the suspense initially envisioned by Hitchcock), with some cues ("The Murder," of course) borrowed from Herrmann, and revisited by Danny Elfman. Sorry, but to these ears that sounds like adding insult to injury.

Didier C. Deutsch

Psycho II

1990, Varèse Sarabande, from the film *Psycho II,* Universal Pictures, 1983 🎬🎬🎬🎬

album notes: Music: Jerry Goldsmith; **Conductor:** Jerry Goldsmith.

Goldsmith took on the thankless task of following up Bernard Herrmann's classic *Psycho* score for this sequel, but he wisely produced an entirely original work that bears no comparison to Herrmann's unforgettable efforts. Goldsmith's eerie title music of keyboard, piano, strings and woodwinds emphasize the haunted innocence of Norman Bates, while later suspense cues create tension with dissonant string chords, unusual synthesized effects and percussion as Goldsmith depicts the gradual breakdown of Norman's mind. Slashing, knife-like wind effects and howling horns and strings underscore most of the violent sequences, climaxing in the lengthy "It's Not Your Mother" cue with its characteristic low-end piano performance.

Jeff Bond

The Public Eye

1992, Varèse Sarabande, from the film *The Public Eye,* Universal Pictures, 1992 🎬🎬

album notes: Music: Mark Isham; **Conductor:** Ken Kugler; **Featured Musicians:** Jim Walker, flutes; Chuck Domanico, bass; Kurt Wortman, snare drum; Rich Ruttenberg, piano; Mark Isham, electronics.

Mark Isham replaced an original score by Jerry Goldsmith for this rather unusual 1940s melodrama starring Joe Pesci and Barbara Hershey. Isham, who has dabbled in both acclaimed jazz and new age albums off the screen, chose not to concentrate on the obvious musical preferences of the period (though there are new vocal performances of standards like "Undecided"), and instead wrote a heavy atmospheric, electronic-laden score that basically serves strictly as a musical undercurrent to the dramatic proceedings in Howard Franklin's film. What all this means is that the music is not that interesting apart from its source and might have been more melodic and dramatic had Isham scored the picture from more of a jazz or swing standpoint. As it is, there's not much here to listen to.

Andy Dursin

Pulp Fiction

1994, MCA Records, from the film *Pulp Fiction,* Miramax Films, 1994 🎬🎬🎬🎬🎬

Quentin Tarantino's attention to detail always includes the music for his films, and this is his crowning achievement. Dick Dale's firey surf classic "Misirlou" is as responsible for the movie's flavor as any aspect of Tarantino's script, while Urge Overkill's remake of Neil Diamond's "Girl, You'll Be a Woman Soon" is brilliantly reverent. There are plenty of satisfying oldies—Chuck Berry's "You Never Can Tell," Al Green's "Let's Stay Together," Dusty Springfield's "Son of a Preacher Man"—all laced between snippets of dialogue from the film. Masterful.

Gary Graff

Punchline

1988, A&M Records, from the film *Punchline,* Columbia, 1988 🎬🎬🎬🎬

album notes: Music: Charles Gross.

In a career that has so far been marked by more highs than lows, Tom Hanks may have made a fatal error when he signs to star in *Punchline,* a 1988 melodramatic comedy in which he portrayed a stand-up comic with a definite chip on his shoulder. While the film itself cast a fond look at the profession, it failed to endear its audiences, particularly because it seemed much too mean without good reasons. Also starring Sally Field as a housewife trying to break into the business, the film, however, received a wonderfully evocative, slightly nostalgic score from Charles Gross, whose flavorful cues were collected in an album that was released at the time (1988), but may take some doing tracking down today. Gross, who was never known for the outstanding quality of his scores, surpassed himself in this one, writing a set of cues, tinged with nostalgia, that are reflective of a type of entertainment that offers more pitfalls than rewards, and leaves its practitioners on the edge rather than fully satisfied. All of this finds an eerie echo in the score, which exudes a definite quality that transcends the basic reason for its existence, and makes it a positively engaging listening experience.

Didier C. Deutsch

The Puppet Masters

1998, Citadel Records, from the film *The Puppet Masters,* Hollywood, 1994 🎬🎬🎬

album notes: Music: Colin Towns; **Orchestra:** The London Filmworks Orchestra; **Conductor:** Allan Wilson.

Colin Towns's sci-fi thriller score is more environmental than melodic, with hissing, buzzing synths that approximate the sound of an alien "hive." It's great stuff if you're an insect from outer space, maybe less so as a listen. Towns' music is quite good in a souped-up way, with film scoring effects that are constantly jumping out and screaming "boo!" Lots of piano runs, brass attacks, *Jaws*-like orchestrations, and choral voices abound in this kitchen sink of sound design. There's a cool, creepy, 1950s sci-fi quality to all of this, but *The Puppet Masters* is overwhelming without quite grabbing you like the best (and craziest) sci-fi scores for *Fantastic Voyage* and *Altered States*—soundtracks that were finely constructed in spite of their musical impressionism. *The Puppet Masters* is a score that's reactive to the demands of the film. And all soundtracks have to accomplish that before they ever work as a listen apart from the picture. While *The Puppet Masters* is too stuck in its hive of sound design to ever reach its true potential, Towns's music is still very effective at achieving the musical scares it's so hell-bent on generating.

Dan Schweiger

A Pure Formality

1994, Sony Classical, from the film *A Pure Formality,* 1994 🎬🎬🎬🎬

album notes: Music: Ennio Morricone; **Orchestra:** Unione Musicisti di Roma; **Conductor:** Ennio Morricone; **Featured Soloist:** Franco Tamponi, violin.

In a style that's frequently more abstract than some of his most popular works, Ennio Morricone fashioned a fascinating, dense score for this drama, directed by Giuseppe Tornatore, essentially an intellectual two-character tour-de-force about a crime suspect, who says he is a famous author currently suffering from a writer's block, and the calm, insinuating police inspector who interrogates him, and seems to know by heart everything the author has written. Matching the various mood shifts on the screen, as well as creating an increasingly disturbing atmosphere of its own, Morricone's score brings together a variety of slow cues, some featuring persistently enervating little noises, others shrieking strings and bells, that prove quite unsettling, yet frighteningly compelling. Gerard Depardieu (sounding like Marcello Mastroianni) performs two songs, "Ricordare" and "Effacer le passe," that add nothing to nor detract anything from his talent as an actor. Hardly the kind of CD you'll put on at any given moment, but one that will play well under the right circumstances for the right audience.

Didier C. Deutsch

Pure Luck

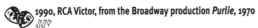 1991, Varèse-Sarabande, from the film *Pure Luck,* Universal, 1991 ♪♪

album notes: Music: Jonathan Sheffer; **Conductor:** Jonathan Sheffer.

Starring Martin Short and Danny Glover, *Pure Luck* was a remake of *La chévre,* a popular French film in which a private eye, looking for the missing clumsy daughter of a rich industrialist, is forced to enlist the help of a clumsy would-be private eye, on the assumption that the bumbling idiot might retrace the girl's footsteps by making the same mistakes she made. The French film, which starred Gerard Depardieu and Pierre Richard, was delightfully zany, with the moods in the film beautifully captured in Vladimir Cosma's equally zany score. Alas, Jonathan Sheffer is not exactly of the right caliber, nor was, for that matter, that tiresome, forced film remake, in which the lightweight comedic threads of the original were changed to heavy-handed ropes, signaled at every turn by Sheffer's obvious (and not so melodically enjoyable) cues. It might have been a different story—and a different score—if Danny Elfman, who wrote the "Main Title" and the last track, "We Found Her," had written the whole thing, but as it stands, there is very little in Sheffer's effort that suggests the madcap moods Elfman (or Cosma, for that matter) can bring in their own concoctions.

Didier C. Deutsch

Purlie

1990, RCA Victor, from the Broadway production *Purlie,* 1970 ♪♪

album notes: Music: Gary Geld; **Lyrics:** Peter Udell; **Musical Direction:** Joyce Brown; **Cast:** Cleavon Little, Melba Moore, Novella Nelson, Sherman Hemsley, Linda Hopkins.

Based on Ossie Davis's *Purlie Victorious, Purlie* is best remembered today for its cast of great performers, which include Cleavon Little, Melba Moore in her first starring role since *Hair,* Linda Hopkins, Sherman Hemsley (before he found grace on television as the irascible Jefferson), and Novella Nelson, a much underrated vocalist. Besides providing Melba Moore with one of her signature songs ("I Got Love"), the predictable score by Gary Geld and Peter Udell (also responsible for *Shenandoah*), has little to recommend it for, though *Purlie* lasted long enough, in a season marked by the absence of great shows, to cop a Tony as Best Musical, as well as one for its female star.

Didier C. Deutsch

Purple Rain

1984, Warner Bros. Records, from the film *Purple Rain.* Warner Bros. Pictures, 1984 ♪♪♪♪

album notes: Music: Prince.

Prince (later to be known as the "artist-formerly-known-as-Prince") revealed another, unsuspected side of his vast talent when he wrote and appeared in the semi-autobiographical *Purple Rain,* in which he portrays a misunderstood youngster who finds solace in his music. Surrounded by members of his "rock family," and co-starring Apollonia Kotero, his girlfriend at the time, the film is essentially a showcase for Prince's songs, a blend of striking and sensuous numbers, many of them propelled by a percolating rhythm that is in marked contrast with the central character's gloomy existence. The songs, assembled in this album, offer little that Prince fans don't already know and like about him. Others, who may be discovering it for the first time, will enjoy the joy and exuberance that pervade many of the selections, and will revel in the film's unquestionable hits, "Let's Go Crazy," "Darling Nikki," "When Doves Cry," and "Purple Rain."

Didier C. Deutsch

Pushing Tin

1999, Restless Records, from the film *Pushing Tin,* 20th Century-Fox, 1999 ♪♪♪♪

album notes: Music: Anne Dudley.

These unsung heroes, the air traffic controllers who regulate the arrivals and departures of thousands of flights at airports all over the world, get a tribute of sorts in this drama directed by Mike Newell. The characters portrayed on the screen, members of a fraternity with a lot of problems—most controllers are stressed out, clinically depressed alcoholics, with suicidal tendencies—are shown with great empathy, and the realization that theirs is a highly demanding job upon which the lives of millions depend day and night. Against this backdrop, the film pays close attention to two men, both at the top of their profession: Nick, played by John Cusack, who can take the pressure but needs to reconstruct himself at home with his wife of many years (Cate Blanchett); and Russell (Billy Bob Thornton), whose cool demeanor enables him to look totally unfazed, and who enjoys a steamy relationship with his wife (Angelina Jolie), a sexpot with a weakness for sex and liquor. The score by Anne Dudley emphasizes the different aspects of the story, from the omnipresent sense of danger that exists in attempting to get the planes off and on the ground, to the rivalry that opposes Nick and Russell, and their relationships with their respective life partners. The cues are soberly detailed, with explosive rhythmic moments that echo the high voltage existence of the men, and more restrained cues that detail their personal moods.

Didier C. Deutsch

Prince in Purple Rain. **(The Kobal Collection)**

Q

QB VII

 1995, Intrada Records, from the television movie *QB VII,* **Columbia Pictures, 1974** ♫♫♫♫

album notes: Music: Jerry Goldsmith; **Conductor:** Jerry Goldsmith.

Goldsmith won an Emmy for this score to one of the first major television miniseries, an adaptation of Leon Uris's novel about a libel trial that points back to the Holocaust. It's Goldsmith's *Schindler's List* in a way, giving the composer the opportunity to deal with one of the most difficult and powerful issues in our history. But it's also a somewhat glossy television treatment, and Goldsmith's score sometimes shows the effort of having to paint on such a broad canvas. There are so many different themes and treatments that the album sometimes seems like highlights from different movies: there are evocations of the Middle Eastern desert, a martial fanfare for the courtroom, not one but two different love themes, and various treatments of

traditional Jewish musical material. But when Goldsmith sinks his teeth into the actual Holocaust memory scenes the score captures an authenticity and power that rivals any work ever done on the subject, particularly in his disturbing mix of percussive effects and ghostly voices for memories of a concentration camp evidenced in his soaring and deeply moving "Kadish for Six Million" which ends the album.

Jeff Bond

Quantum Leap

 1993, GNP Crescendo, from the television series *Quantum Leap,* **Universal Television, 1989—1993** ♫♫♫♫

album notes: Music: Velton Ray Bunch.

This show's time travel format not only offered composer Velton Ray Bunch the chance to create some uniquely flavored scores for each episode, but series star Scott Bakula, a veteran Broadway performer, was also allowed to showcase his vocal talent. His character, Sam Beckett, would land in some past time taking the form of a piano player, a rock singer, maybe Elvis or an off–Broadway actor performing in some hometown production of *Man of La Mancha.* When Beckett returns to the home of his youth ("The Leap Home Part 1"), Bunch develops a lovely Midwestern motif featuring a harmonic solo to represent the farm and its surrounding expanse of wheat fields. The transformation into reputed Kennedy assassin Lee Harvey Oswald for "Leaping on a String," required the use of a large scale orchestral score to rival John Williams' work on *JFK* as film series creator Donald Bellasario wanted to debunk the Oliver Stone film because he knew Oswald personally. The album also features a 12-minute interview with Bakula and two versions of Mike Post's main title theme with, and without, the opening narration.

David Hirsch

Quartet

1994, Angel Records, from the movie *Quartet,* Merchant Ivory Productions, 1994 ♪♪♪♪♪

album notes: Music: Richard Robbins; **Featured Musicians:** Allen Jackson, bass; Rudy Collins, drums; Benny Powell, trombone; Jerome Richardson, tenor sax, clarinet; Marshall Royal, alto sax, clarinet; J. Leonard Oxley, piano; Al Arons, trumpet; **Conductor:** J. Leonard Oxley.

Set in Paris in the 1920s, *Quartet* evokes a time and place where artists, particularly American ones, had found a second home, in a world Ernest Hemingway described as "a moveable feast." The moods were light, active, stimulating, marked by the new syncopated accents of jazz which, already struck a more responsive note there than it did at home. The period, brilliantly recreated in the film, inspired Richard Robbins to create a score with a strong jazz flavor, performed by a distinguished group of instrumentalists—Allen Jackson, Benny Powell, Jerome Richardson, Marshall Royal—in Luther Henderson's feel-right arrangements. Tremendously exhilarating, the album needs no pre-sequencing to be enjoyed and lends itself to excellent straight programming. Armelia McQueen adds some flavorful vocals to the mix, as does Isabelle Adjani as a woman stranded in Paris when her husband, an art dealer, is sent to prison. She becomes a passive participant in a *menage a trois* when she accepts a couple's invitation to stay with them.

Didier C. Deutsch

Queen Margot

1994, Philips/France, from the film *Queen Margot (La reine Margot),* Miramax, 1994 ♪♪

album notes: Music: Goran Bregovic; **Orchestra:** The Philharmonic Orchestra of Belgrade, The Renaissance Ensemble of Belgrade; **Conductor:** Goran Bregovic; **Choir:** The Grand Chorale of Belgrade; **Conductor:** Bojan Sudic; **Featured Musicians:** Zorz Gruic, horns; Ognen Radivojevic, keyboards; Mumin, oud; Pierre Pincemaille, organ.

The true life story (as adapted by Alexandre Dumas) of Queen Margot, a Catholic, wife of King Henry IV of France, a Protestant who had converted, became the basis for this Grand Guignol reconstruction that took pains to emphasize the most dreadful aspects of royal life in the 16th century, where court intrigues, religious conflicts, and friendly betrayals seemed the norm of every day. Sparing no expense, director Patrice Chereau restaged the bloody "Night Of Saint Bartholomew," on August 23, 1572, that witnessed the massacre of more than 6,000 Protestants in Paris alone. But the convoluted plot, attempting to stay too close to a flurry of historical events with little significance, coupled with the over-the-top acting by the cast, led by Isabelle Adjani and Daniel Auteuil, only succeeded in turning what might have been a faithful historical account into another fine mess. More baffling in the context is Goran Bregovic's score, which, while perfectly alright on its own terms, cannot claim to be remotely French or Renaissance in its inspiration. Without wanting to make an unflattering comparison with, say, *Tous les matins du monde,* which at least had the good sense of using period music to make its point, the score could have been more appropriate for a sweeping historical fresco such as this. As it is, it just doesn't belong, though listeners might enjoy its traditional Dalmatian accents. This recording may be difficult to find. Check with a used CD store, mail-order company, or a dealer specializing in rare, out-of-print, or import recordings.

Didier C. Deutsch

Queens Logic

1991, Epic Soundtrax, from the film *Queens Logic,* New Line Cinema, 1990 ♪♪♪

Another clone of *The Big Chill,* this one is about a group of friends who get together again in their old neighborhood to reminisce and remember the good old days. Kevin Bacon leads the group which also includes Joe Mantegna, John Malkovich, and Linda Fiorentino. Characteristic of this kind of film, the soundtrack is sprinkled with a large assortment of familiar standards, including selections by Cheap Trick, Marvin Gaye (the ubiquitous "Let's Get It On"), Sly & the Family Stone, Earth, Wind & Fire, Eddie Money, Van Morrison, Wild Cherry, Argent, and the Emotions, in what amounts to an all-star compilation. And not a bad one at that!

Didier C. Deutsch

The Quest

1996, Varèse Sarabande, from the movie *The Quest,* Universal Pictures, 1996 ♪♪♪

album notes: Music: Randy Edelman; **Conductor:** Randy Edelman.

Randy Edelman's always friendly fusion of acoustic and electronic instruments brings an epic quality to Jean-Claude Van Damme's directorial debut. Set during the early part of this century, Van Damme plays a pickpocket on the run from the law who becomes a contestant in a world-class fighting tournament in Asia. The score alternates between lavish orchestrations for the period ("Old New York"), some humorous string passages ("Smile Please"), and the kind of hard-hitting percussion Edelman first established in *Dragon: The Bruce Lee Story* for the fight sequences ("Chris Beats Germany").

David Hirsch

Quest for Camelot

1998, Warner Bros. Records, from the film *Quest for Camelot*, Warner Bros., 1998 🎬🎬

album notes: Music: Patrick Doyle; Conductor: Mark Watters.

When your soundtrack rests on fresh-faced country teens LeAnn Rimes and Bryan White, Celine Dion, and the former singer of Journey (Steve Perry), you know this is a set that diabetics should approach with caution. And *Quest for Camelot* is free and kid-safe, a G-rated assemblage from middle-of-the-road production whizzes David Foster and Carol Bayer Sager. The Irish sibling quartet the Coors spice thing up a bit and even give White a bit of oomph in their collaboration on "Looking through Your Eyes." But you'll likely find yourself drawn to "If I Didn't Have You," a duet between irascible Don Rickles and Monty Python's Eric Idle, rather than the rest of the album's treacly pop.

Gary Graff

Quest for Fire

1982, RCA, from the movie *Quest for Fire*, 20th Century-Fox, 1981 🎬🎬🎬

album notes: Music: Philippe Sarde; Orchestra: The London Symphony Orchestra, the London Philharmonic Orchestra, the Ambrosian Singers, the Percussion Ensemble of Strasbourg; Conductor: Philippe Sarde; Featured Musicians: Syrinx, pan flute; Michel Sanvoisin, bass flute.

One of the most unique films of the 1980s, Jean-Jacques Annaud's *Quest for Fire* took on the daunting task of trying to realistically depict the prehistoric world, and succeeded brilliantly. One reason for the film's success is the excellent score by Philippe Sarde. Given that the film has no dialogue whatsoever, it fell to Sarde's music to serve as one of the film's primary communicative tools. As a result of its assertive role, Sarde's music is highly listenable on disc. There are some derivative moments ("Creation of Fire" owes heavily to Penderecki), but overall this is an impressive work of much originality. Expansive and brooding, it evokes the primitive, austere, and brutal world of pre-history. The orchestration is large and full, and the performance superb, featuring the London Symphony, London Philharmonic, Ambrosian Singers, and Les Percussions de

Strasbourg, conducted by Peter Knight (who also orchestrated). "Village of the Painted People" is scored exclusively for percussion and one of the most interesting tracks, while Sarde's love theme is rapturous and full. Recorded at Abbey Road Studios, the sound quality is particularly excellent. A wonderfully epic and other-worldly score, *Quest for Fire* is one of Sarde's most brilliant efforts.

Paul Andrew MacLean

The Quick and the Dead

1995, Varèse Sarabande, from the movie *The Quick and the Dead*, Tri-Star, 1995 🎬🎬🎬

album notes: Music: Alan Silvestri; Conductor: Alan Silvestri.

Alan Silvestri goes Ennio Morricone in this amiable enough pastiche of western movie music clichés. Since the movie—the unsuccessful Sam Raimi western with Sharon Stone—is somewhat of a take-off on the classic Eastwood pictures (with Stone as "The Woman with No Name"), it figures that Silvestri's score would be modeled on the Leone soundtracks to a point. After hearing the high-pitched, *The Good, the Bad and the Ugly*-based motif, we know that's exactly what we're going to get, as Silvestri has written an enjoyable conglomeration that represents both his often percussive-driven style and the obvious influence from Italian westerns. While the music isn't original or inventive enough to work on its own terms, on the level of a parody the score succeeds admirably.

Andy Dursin

Quien sabe?

1995, King Records/Japan, from the film *Quien sabe? (Bullet for the General)*, 1966. 🎬🎬🎬🎬

album notes: Music: Luis Bacalov.

Known in some quarters as *Bullet for the General*, the 1966 *Quien sabe?* starred Gian Maria Volonte as the Mexican general-turned-renegade El Chuncho, and Lou Castel as an American mercenary who sides with him. Directed by Damiano Damiani, the plot was in fact much more involved than what it appeared to be in the first place, with the American mercenary eventually revealing that he was hired by the Mexican government to turn El Chuncho around and have him betray the revolution. An excellent spaghetti western, *Quien sabe?* furthermore had the distinct advantage of featuring one of the best scores Luis Bacalov ever wrote, a flavorful set of cues propelled by a strong, recognizable title tune that stands out in this impressive CD reissue. Though there are no less than five different versions of "Quien sabe?," three of the Main Title, and two of the Finale, which may be a bit of overkill, one must agree that Bacalov's score for this spaghetti western truly deserves

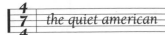

the attention. This title may be out of print or just plain hard to find. Mail-order companies, used CD shops, or dealers of rare or import recordings will be your best bet.

see also: Django, Sugar Colt

Didier C. Deutsch

The Quiet American

See: The Barefoot Contessa/The Quiet American

The Quiet Man

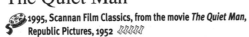 1995, Scannan Film Classics, from the movie *The Quiet Man*, Republic Pictures, 1952 🎬🎬🎬🎬

album notes: Music: Victor Young; **Orchestra:** The Dublin Screen Orchestra; **Conductor:** Kenneth Alwyn; **Featured Musicians:** Gerard Farrelly, keyboards; Anne Buckley, vocals; the Dublin Pub Singers.

One of John Ford's most memorable films, *The Quiet Man* stars John Wayne as an unlikely romantic leading man, after years of playing a rugged cowboy or a no-nonsense GI. Wayne is an Irish American who returns to the land of his ancestors, buys the country home where he was born, and takes an immediate shine to a local girl (Maureen O'Hara, resplendent in a role that seemed tailor-made), immediately irking her brother, a bully landowner who also wanted to buy the cottage. Told in a slow, affecting style that is part of its endearing charm, the film ends in a sensational showdown between the two men, a brawl to end all brawls. The score for the film was composed by Victor Young, who, at Ford's request, made use of many Irish folk tunes to give his music the right coloring. At the time the film came out, excerpts from his score were released on an LP on the Decca label, and they can be found coupled with *Samson and Delilah,* another score by Young, on a primitive-sounding mono CD from Varèse Sarabande.

This new CD, recorded by the Dublin Screen Orchestra conducted by Kenneth Alwyn, brings Young's music into the digital era in a recording that brims with excitement and includes many cues previously unavailable. An uncommonly florid score, *The Quiet Man* enabled Young to tap into a rich lode of folk material, including "The Isle of Innisfree" and "I'll Take You Home Again Kathleen," and develop these tunes into breathtaking themes that are strongly evocative and beautiful. The resulting album is a joy from beginning to end and strongly recommended.

see also: Samson and Delilah

Didier C. Deutsch

Quigley Down Under

 1990, Intrada Records, from the movie *Quigley Down Under,* MGM, 1990 🎬🎬🎬

album notes: Music: Basil Poledouris; **Conductor:** Basil Poledouris.

Basil Poledouris, of *Conan* fame, brought his rich sense of barbarian melody to this Simon Wincer film about a sharpshooter (Tom Selleck) who travels to Australia in the 1860s to work for a wealthy but evil land baron (Alan Rickman), and soon joins the side of the aborigines. Poledouris tips his hat to the western genre and American lead with an expansive and rhythmic, symphonic scope, characterizing the Australian setting not with any specific folk elements (no didgeridoos), but as a wide-open place of adventure and danger. Quigley's theme is a lilting, energetic piece with a mostly pentatonic clarinet melody over enthusiastic orchestra and banjo—think of Selleck's ear-to-ear, mustachioed smile—and this whimsical tune seems to characterize both the main character and his not-in-Kansas-anymore location. A love theme brings a tender, reflective contrast. Fans of Poledouris's big themes from *Conan, RoboCop, Flesh + Blood,* and *Lonesome Dove* will find more to love here.

Lukas Kendall

The Quiller Memorandum

 1989, Varèse Sarabande, from the movie *The Quiller Memorandum,* 20th Century-Fox, 1966 🎬🎬🎬

album notes: Music: John Barry; **Lyrics:** Mack David; **Conductor:** John Barry.

In the days when John Barry used to have fun, he scored many films distinguished by the imaginative themes he created, in which he smartly captured the exciting pace of the narrative. In one such example, *The Quiller Memorandum,* he wrote a score that has endured, matching the evocative tones in this spy thriller set in contemporary Germany, in which George Segal plays a charmingly engaging undercover British agent sent to West Berlin to infiltrate a group of neo-Nazis. While a saxophone rendition of the pop song "Downtown" sounds somewhat dispensable, the suggestive cues, in which a cymbalum provides an effective, colorful aura, reflect the unfolding action scene and the loneliness of the agent who knows he cannot even rely on his own people to help him if he gets caught. Matt Monro's delivery of "Wednesday's Child," is appropriately atmospheric.

Didier C. Deutsch

Quiz Show

 1994, Hollywood Records, from the movie *Quiz Show,* Hollywood Pictures, 1994 🎬🎬🎬🎬

album notes: Music: Mark Isham; **Conductor:** Ken Kugler; **Featured Musicians:** David Goldblatt, piano; John Clayton, bass; Ed Shaughnessy, drums; Dennis Budimir, guitar; Rick Baptiste, trumpet; Conte Candoli, trumpet; Charles Davis, trumpet; Charles Findley, trumpet; Mark Isham, trumpet; Nicholas Lane, trombone; John Lane, trombone; Bruce Paulson, trombone; Charles Loper, trombone; Marshall Royal, saxophone; Steven Tavaglione, saxophone; Peter Christlieb, saxophone; Bob Sheppard, saxophone; Jack Nimitz, saxophone; Dale Anderson, marimba; Larry Bunker, vibraphone; Kurt Wortman, percussion.

Lyle Lovett's slow-paced and slyly sardonic rendition of "Moritat," the song of Mack the Knife, seems a perfect way to get into this soundtrack album to the story of the quiz show scandal that rocked television in the late 1950s. The song, however, is the low point in a brilliant jazz score fashioned by Mark Isham that prominently features some great soloists, including Conte Candoli, the legendary West Coast trumpet player. While some cues in the score are relatively short, two—"The World's Smartest Man" and "The Oversight Blues"—are generously long and explicit, and make a powerful contribution to the album itself. The diversity in the score, with some cues written for big band, some for a quartet, and others for solo instruments, makes listening to it all the more enjoyable, with the moods projected occasionally interrupted by flavorful bits of underscoring ("Books and Learning," "Television on Trial") that provide still another different orchestral color to the proceedings.

Didier C. Deutsch

Quo Vadis

1985, London Records, from the movie *Quo Vadis*, MGM, 1951
🎬🎬🎬🎬🎬

album notes: Music: Miklos Rozsa; **Orchestra:** The Royal Philharmonic Orchestra and Chorus; **Conductor:** Miklos Rozsa.

The first Roman epic scored by Miklos Rozsa, *Quo Vadis* contains, in embryo form, all the concepts and ideas Rozsa would expand on in later efforts like *Ben-Hur* and *King of Kings:* heavily ornamented brass flourishes, liturgical hymns, strongly etched love themes, exciting action cues. Combining reconstructed sounds from Greek origin to replace the non-existent Roman music, and early Judaic themes with his own European idiom, Rozsa wrote a remarkably "authentic" set of cues that became a blueprint for films with a similar background. Though played under the action on the screen and necessarily overlooked, the music soars when appreciated on its own terms and mesmerizes the listener with its vibrancy and barely contained excitement. Cues like "The Burning of Rome," "Chariot Chase," and "Hail Galba," among others, stand out in a score that is extraordinarily rich and rewarding. While the original soundtrack album, which consisted of dramatic highlights and was in mono sound in the original LP issue, awaits reissue on compact disc (possibly without the dialogues, but with the full score in stereo if the multitrack tapes still exist), this rerecording, with the composer conducting one of England's two great orchestras, stands as the only authoritative album available.

Didier C. Deutsch

They Know the Score

John Scott

I would love to think that film music can evolve as a very strong art form. I think that there's everything against it, though. I think that decision-making by committee is one of the worst things against film music. If one goes back in time and looks at the Eisenstein films with music by Prokofiev, and the Bonderchek films with music by Shostakovitch, this was, to my way of thinking, great film music. I think that are some great composers around today, but every composer is shackled, no one is given free reign, no one is told to go out and do what you think is right. They're briefed as to what the producer and director, who are quite often musically illiterate, think is right. So I'm not sure if we're going to have a flowering of great art in films.

***Courtesy of* Film Score Monthly**

Radio Days

1987, Novus/RCA Records, from the film *Radio Days*, Orion Pictures, 1987 🎬🎬🎬🎬🎬

A great big band album that beautifully captures the feel and moods permeating Woody Allen's fond memories of the time when radio reigned supreme, *Radio Days* is a genuine treat for anyone with love for the music or the era. With not a single misstep in the track selection and performances by some of the greatest bands around at the time (Glenn Miller, Tommy Dorsey, Duke Ellington, Benny Goodman, Sammy Kaye, Artie Shaw, among others), this is simply a wonderful recording, only slightly marred by the sound quality which is not always up to par. However, many of these tracks have since been remastered and appear elsewhere in much improved sound.

Didier C. Deutsch

Radio Flyer

🎬 1992, Giant Records, from the film *Radio Flyer*, Columbia Pictures, 1992 ♫♫♪

album notes: Music: Hans Zimmer; **Conductor:** Shirley Walker; **Featured Musicians:** Richard Harvey, Pan pipes; Nick Glenne-Smith, piano; Tommy Morgan, harmonica; Jim Kanter, clarinet.

If you make a movie about child abuse, you'd best not portray the subject as a glossy children's fantasy—the mistake that Richard Donner made when directing this expensive bomb, one of the biggest money losers of the early 1990s. Hans Zimmer's completely uneven score features all of his usual ingredients (the large symphony orchestra conducted by Shirley Walker, plenty of synthesizers as well as chorus), and can either be irritating to the point where you think your brain is about to explode (as in the sappy kid's chorus sections), or so uplifting and downright melodramatic that you have to admire the score for keeping such a straight face while going absurdly over the top. Whatever your opinion of this score, you must admit the composer tried his hardest to entertain. The out-of-print album has become something of a staple in record store cut-out bins, (mis)leading some to believe that the CD will be valuable one day, even if it is only loosely connected to the movie itself. That's about the only hope for a profit this project will ever make.

Andy Dursin

Radioland Murders

🎬 1994, MCA Records, from the film *Radioland Murders*, Universal Pictures, 1994 ♫♫♫♫

album notes: Music: Joel McNeely; **Conductor:** Joel McNeely; **Featured Vocalists:** Randy Crenshaw, Al Dana, Michael Gallup, Jim Gilstrap, Rick Logan, Susan Stevens Logan, Amy London, Melissa Mackay, Susan McBride, Bobbi Page, Jackie Presti, Eugene Ruffolo, Don Shelton, Sally Stevens, Kerry Walsh, Dick Wells, Kim Wertz.

Radioland Murders is big band era recording with a twist. While it quotes performances by artists from the radio era, this wonderfully evocative album draws its strength from the cues, written in the style of the period by Joel McNeely, including the whimsical, and accurately correct, "WBN logo" heard throughout in different versions. McNeely, making a much-noticed contribution with this catchy score to a film that has its eccentric moments, captured the flavor of radio's golden age and provided sly comments of his own to this amusing mystery set in a Chicago radio station where someone is murdering the company employees one by one. The potential suspects (or victims)—an odd sound effects man, a sultry singer, a slick announcer and the station owner—all find their comeuppance, with each turn in the convoluted story eliciting a wry musical expression.

Didier C. Deutsch

A Rage in Harlem

🎬 1991, Varèse Sarabande, from the film *A Rage in Harlem*, Miramax Films, 1991 ♫♫♪

album notes: Music: Elmer Bernstein; **Conductor:** Elmer Bernstein.

Elmer Bernstein found great success utilizing jazz when composing his scores for films like *The Man with the Golden Arm* and *Love with the Proper Stranger,* and *A Rage in Harlem,* Bill Duke's 1991 adaptation of the Chester Himes novel, represents a return trip to earlier times for the composer. Unfortunately, there's just something rather stagnant about this score, which features cues with appropriate jazz-ensemble focused orchestrations, but also the tendency to just coast along with by-the-numbers melodies. There's nothing infectious or particularly buoyant about the music here, and that lack of energy sadly makes this score far inferior to Bernstein's predecessing jazz efforts, and a rather large disappointment overall.

Andy Dursin

Raggedy Man

🎬 1981, Varèse Sarabande, from the film *Raggedy Man,* Universal Pictures, 1981 ♫♫♫

album notes: Music: Jerry Goldsmith; **Conductor:** Jerry Goldsmith.

One of a handful of "limited edition" releases marketed by Varèse-Sarabande in 1991, this is, in actuality, only an average Jerry Goldsmith score. Written in the same vein as scores like Elmer Bernstein's *To Kill a Mockingbird* and other poignant, character-driven works by Goldsmith (i.e., *The Flim-Flam Man*), *Raggedy Man* boasts a deliberately paced score for flute, harmonica, and orchestra, creating a pleasant, small-town feel that is sustained throughout the album—with the notable exception of some dissonant material thrown in at the end to coincide with the movie's rather odd left turn into climactic melodrama. The score is engaging but ultimately unremarkable, and went unreleased at the time of the film's 1981 theatrical playdates when the movie failed in theaters. While the concept of Varèse's "CD Club" was initially mouth-watering to fans of movie music, it's a shame that a number of other scores held in high regard by listeners, like John Williams's *Heartbeeps,* Elmer Bernstein's *Slipstream,* or Bill Conti's *Victory,* never received the red-carpet treatment that this serviceable—particularly considering Goldsmith standards—but rather pedestrian score did.

Andy Dursin

The Raggedy Rawney

🎬 1988, Silva Screen Records, from the film *The Raggedy Rawney,* Hand Made Films, 1988 ♫♪

album notes: Music: Michael Kamen; **Featured Musician:** Michael Kamen, Kurzweil 250, oboe; **Songs:** John Tams.

This plaintive score is a far cry from *Die Hard* and *Lethal Weapon,* but it's intriguing in its simplicity. Michael Kamen composed and performed the score primarily on an oboe and a Kurzweil synthesizer, with some Irish music and songs provided by John Tams. This is not a terribly melodic score; the music is primarily atmospheric, full of woodwindish synths, eerie, straining chords, and strident zimbalom notes from the Kurzweil. The score's ambiance is very subdued and slow-moving, its orchestration sparse and plain. As a result, it's a difficult score to grasp at times.

Randall Larson

Ragtime

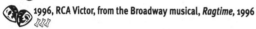 1996, RCA Victor, from the Broadway musical, *Ragtime*, 1996 ♫♫♫

album notes: Music: Stephen Flaherty; **Lyrics:** Lynn Ahrens; **Cast:** Brian Stokes Mitchell (Coalhouse Walker Jr), Peter Friedman (Tateh), Marin Mazzie (Mother), Audra McDonald (Sarah), Mark Jacoby (Father).

 1998, RCA Victor, from the Broadway musical, *Ragtime*, 1998 ♫♫♫

album notes: Cast: Brian Stokes Mitchell (Coalhouse Walker Jr), Peter Friedman (Tateh), Marin Mazzie (Mother), Audra McDonald (Sarah), Mark Jacoby (Father), Judy Kaye.

Bigger doesn't necessarily mean better, as this confused (and confusing) musical clearly demonstrates. Based on the book by E.L. Doctorow (already the source of a film starring James Cagney in his last screen appearance), *Ragtime* aims to retrace the trends that shaped this country's landscape in the early part of the century, when Anglo-Saxon settlers, now in control of government, had to vie with two major influxes: refugees from Europe trying to escape the pogroms in their native countries, and Southern blacks moving up North toward what they hoped would be a better life.

Using these elements, Terrence McNally (book), Stephen Flaherty (music), and Lynn Ahrens (lyrics) wrote a plodding sung-through musical in which characters from the three ethnic groups intermingle but seldom interface, and which only comes to dramatic life when Coalhouse Walker, the black man-turned-activist, rebels against the white establishment after his wife, Sarah, is killed during a riotous incident.

In the long, tedious description there are few moments of genuine emotion (when Coalhouse mourns the death of Sarah is a rare example), and the score, for the most part, is all show and no play. The two albums here, a pre-Broadway, all-star production, and the original Broadway cast, do little to convince otherwise.

Didier C. Deutsch

Raiders of the Lost Ark

1995, DCC Compact Classics, from the film *Raiders of the Lost Ark,* Paramount, 1981 ♫♫♫♫

album notes: Music: John Williams; **Orchestra:** The London Symphony Orchestra; **Conductor:** John Williams.

This beautifully produced restoration of John Williams's classic adventure score assembles the lion's share of the score (78 minutes) with superior sound quality. Produced at the height of Williams's epic period (between *Superman* and *The Empire Strikes Back*), *Raiders* is a rip-snorting action ride that begins early on after a moody, low-key opening as intrepid archeologist Indiana Jones enters a booby-trapped cave in the jungles of Peru. Williams' scoring of the escape from the cavern is a showcase of frenzied, virtuoso orchestral effects beautifully capped by the energetic pizzicato of "Escape from Peru," with its engaging introduction of the brassy, infectious Indiana Jones fanfare. There are action highlights to spare, including the film's indelible truck chase (restored from the sliced-and-diced original album presentation) and some furious accompaniment to a deadly fistfight beneath the propellers of a flying wing, as well as the spectral, mysterious underscoring of scenes involving the search for the Ark of the Covenant, including a beautiful Middle Eastern-sounding woodwind theme, and the eerie, imposing passages played under the discovery and excavation of the Ark's resting place ("The Map Room: Dawn" and "The Well of Souls"). Like Williams's *Star Wars, Raiders* has a freshness somewhat lacking in his more calculated efforts on the second and third films in the series.

see also: Indiana Jones and the Temple of Doom, Indiana Jones and the Last Crusade

Jeff Bond

Rain Man

1989, Capitol Records, from the film *Rain Man,* United Artists, 1989 ♫♫♫♫
album notes: Music: Hans Zimmer.

If only because of the line-up of performers who appear on it (Johnny Clegg and Savuca, the Delta Rhythm Boys, Bananarama, Lou Christie, Aaron Neville, etc.), this soundtrack album would be worth having. But the musical selections are also quite strong, with several standards sprinkled along the way, and songs that are generally quite enjoyable. In all this display of inventive tunes and interpretations, Hans Zimmer's two lonely cues hardly make a dent, though the composer seems to have perfectly caught the spirit of this story about two brothers with diametrically opposed lifestyles, one an autistic genius, capable of having complex thoughts and being mentally limited all at once, the other a selfish luxury car salesman whose only mo-

Harrison Ford in Raiders of the Lost Ark. **(The Kobal Collection)**

tivation is to make money fast. The two selections here detail the cross-country trip made by the brothers, Raymond and Charlie, after Charlie discovers that their dead father has left all his money to his sibling, a trip that will result in each man having a better understanding of himself and of the bonds that tie them together. Zimmer's music, in keeping with the tone of the story, is forceful and extremely evocative.

Didier C. Deutsch

The Rainbow

🎬 1989, Silva Screen Records, from the film *The Rainbow,* Vestron
🎵 Pictures, 1989 ⅋⅋⅋⅋

album notes: Music: Carl Davis; **Orchestra:** The Graunke Symphony Orchestra; **Conductor:** Carl Davis; **Featured Musicians:** The Hartford Motors Concert Brass, Conductor: Dr. Keith Wilkinson.

Thanks to his world tours, where he conducts live his scores to classic silent films like *Napoleon, Ben-Hur,* and others, Carl Davis seems destined to be less likely remembered as the composer of contemporary film scores. *The Rainbow* is typically bombastic and overtly romantic for its period setting. Davis

plays the seduction and sexual education of a young schoolteacher to the hilt with his broad musical strokes. Like most collections of his work, this album has a distinct feel of a classical concert piece, and that makes it a delightful listen, devoid of any experience with the film. The score's flow is carefully divided by Ida Hampton's "School Assembly," and a suite of traditional military and Gilbert & Sullivan music for "The Wedding." Davis has also included three alternate variations of cues that were changed at the request of director Ken Russell. "Moonlight Loves," for example, was toned down from its original version (track 18) when Russell expressed to the composer that something simpler (track 10) was needed for the film.

David Hirsch

The Rainmaker

🎬 1997, Hollywood, from the Paramount film *The Rainmaker,*
🎵 1997 ⅋⅋⅋⅋

album notes: Music: Elmer Bernstein; **Conductor:** Elmer Bernstein; **Featured Musicians:** Mike Lang, Hammond B3; Warren Luening, trumpet; George Doering, guitar.

Much of the flavor in this score by Elmer Bernstein—which is not to be confused with the score Alex North wrote for the 1957 film of the same name starring Burt Lancaster and Katharine Hepburn—comes from its unorthodox use of a Hammond organ, an instrument usually not found in this type of music. Flavorful and atmospheric, it imbues the music with a certain flair that immediately distinguishes it, and makes it more noticeable. Written for a John Grisham film that starred Matt Damon, Jon Voight, Mickey Rourke, and Danny DeVito, it is a potent contribution from a master composer and melodist, who pulls all the stops, literally in this case, and conveys all the drama and action in the film. Eclectic and diversified are two words that come to mind when listening to this extravagantly multi-layered score in which the orchestra details some vigorous moments ("Shenanigans," "The Fight"), while solo instruments like the guitar or the trumpet are given a chance to give a different flavor to some selections ("The Plot Thickens"). The longer cues in the score are bright and engaging, and provide greater opportunities to enjoy what Bernstein wrote. Generally low key and unobtrusive, it's a little gem of a score!

Didier C. Deutsch

Raintree County

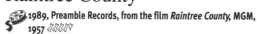1989, Preamble Records, from the film *Raintree County*, MGM, 1957 🎬🎬🎬🎬

album notes: Music: Johnny Green; **Orchestra:** The MGM Studio Symphony Orchestra and Chorus, **Conductor:** Johnny Green.

Though he spent more than 10 years at MGM, where he was General Music Director and Executive in Charge of Music and scored many important films during that time, Johnny Green is not often thought of as a great composer in the same league with his more visible peers from that era. The one film for which he is best remembered, however, is this lavish Civil War drama, based on a novel by Ross Lockridge, which the studio wanted to be a follow-up of sorts to the blockbuster *Gone with the Wind*. Filmed at great expense using the newly developed 65mm process, and with a brilliant cast that included Elizabeth Taylor, Montgomery Clift, and Eva Marie Saint, the film captures the passion and drama in the novel, set against the broad, rich canvas of the Lincoln presidency and the turmoil between the North and the South. It may not be *Gone with the Wind* redux, but it is big, epic, and memorable. So is Green's score, which was perfectly adapted to the needs of the story, though it does not mark the film indelibly the way Max Steiner's score marks *Gone with the Wind*, nor does its main theme, the evocative "Song of Raintree County," ever hope to become another "Tara Theme." Still, quite professional in its approach and accurately reflecting the sweeping action on-screen, *Raintree County* re-

mains an important score, magnificently serviced by this complete two-CD release.

Didier C. Deutsch

Raising Arizona/Blood Simple

1985, Varèse Sarabande, from the films *Raising Arizona* and *Blood Simple*, Circle Films, 1985 🎬🎬🎬

album notes: Music: Carter Burwell; **Featured Musicians:** *(Raising Arizona)* Carter Burwell, synthesizers, samples; Ben Freed, banjo; John Crowder, yodeling; Mieszyslaw Litwinski, whistling, guitar; Geoffrey Gordon, percussion; Skip LaPlante, percussion; Alan Drogin, ukelele; Steven Swartz, ukelele; Don Peyton, ukulele; *(Blood Simple)* Carter Burwell, keyboards; Stanley Adler, bass guitar; Stephen Bray, percussion; Stanton Miranda, percussion.

The schizophrenic score for *Raising Arizona* has a problem deciding just what it wants to be, and that's what creates its charm. From the bluegrass banjo opening, it morphs into a strange series of style changes, yodeling in the main title and eerie synth cues that stress danger. One track, "Just Business," is a mix of odd vocals and the rattling, perhaps, of garbage can lids. "Hail Lenny" seems to have been inspired by Ennio Morricone's Spaghetti Western scores and, oh yeah, there's a couple of real melodies, too, like "Dreaming of the Future." Perhaps what makes this score so intriguing is that it never sits in one place long enough to wear out its welcome, just like the Coen Brothers' movie did, changing tone at the most bizarre moments. Also included on the album is Burwell's first score for the Coens, *Blood Simple*, a restrained synth score that contrasts nicely with *Arizona's* dementia and provides a solid base for the murder mystery's dark *film noir* aura.

David Hirsch

Raising Cain

1992, Milan Records, from the film *Raising Cain*, Universal Pictures, 1992 🎬🎬🎬

album notes: Music: Pino Donaggio; **Electronic Sound Creations/Computer Performances:** Paolo Steffan; **Orchestra:** The Unione Musicisti di Roma; **Conductor:** Natale Massara.

Pino Donaggio reteamed with Brian DePalma for the first time in eight years with this shameless hodge-podge score for one of the director's most unsatisfying ventures into Hitchcock territory. A music-box motif is joined by yearning strings in search of a resolution in Donaggio's score, which sounds like Michel Legrand's *Summer of '42* one moment and Bernard Herrmann's *Psycho* the next. Still, if you're a thriller fan and can get past the stylistic "influences," you'll probably get a kick out of Donaggio's score, which offers up a sexy sax during the film's love theme (is there any other instrument than conveys passion better than the saxophone?) with plenty of energy to spare.

Laura Dern and Lukas Haas in Rambling Rose. **(The Kobal Collection)**

There's nothing here you haven't heard before, but that—at least somewhat—seems to be the point.

Andy Dursin

Rambling Rose

1991, Virgin Movie Music, from the film *Rambling Rose,* Seven Arts-New Line Cinema, 1991 🎬🎬🎬🎬

album notes: **Music:** Elmer Bernstein; **Conductor:** Elmer Bernstein.

Throughout his career, Elmer Bernstein has written some seriously attractive scores, but none that have matched the serene beauty of this wonderful effort for a film starring Robert Duvall and Laura Dern. A flavorful story of an oversexed young woman working as a maid in a small Georgia town in the mid-1930s and the effect she has on her employer and his family, the amusingly provocative tale prompted Bernstein to write a score, beautifully understated and brimming with delightful folksy little touches, which play an important role in giving the film the right atmosphere and makes for a very enjoyable listening experience. In his notes for this album, Bernstein remarks that when he first saw

the film as a work in progress, after he had been asked to write the music for it, "I felt [a] particular sense of excitement." The excitement translated itself into a remarkably distinctive score!

Didier C. Deutsch

Rambo: First Blood Part II

1987, Varèse Sarabande, from the film *Rambo: First Blood Part II,* 1985 🎬🎬🎬

album notes: **Music:** Jerry Goldsmith; **Orchestra:** The National Philharmonic Orchestra; **Conductor:** Jerry Goldsmith.

Goldsmith hit his stride with this second *Rambo* film, the epitome of Reagan-era jingoistic action, which he scored with a nimble, adventurous work that is diametrically opposed to the dark, heavy sound of the original *First Blood*. The score launches with a surprisingly beautiful oriental theme that gives way to a new Americana theme for the Rambo character, although Goldsmith's familiar Rambo fanfare punctuates most of the film's triumphant action moments. It's almost non-stop chases and fights, alternating with sneaky suspense cues, but Goldsmith makes this surprisingly emotional, keying in on Sylvester Stallone's wounded characterization of the hyper-muscled hero. The mix of strong melodic material and heavy-duty action rhythms makes this a score that should appeal to both longtime Goldsmith fans and younger listeners used to the composer's more romantic scores of the '90s.

Jeff Bond

🎬 1998, Silva America, from the Canal+ film *Rambo: First Blood Part II*, 1985 *♪♪♪♪*

album notes: Music: Jerry Goldsmith; **Conductor:** Jerry Goldsmith.

With more than 15 minutes added, this expanded edition is even more impressive, and gives the listener an opportunity to better appreciate the quality and inner beauties in Goldsmith's score. Previously unreleased tracks like "River Crash/The Gunboat" and "Village Raid/Helicopter Flight" are gripping action cues that give greater emphasis to the score and underline the more active moments in the film.

see also: First Blood

Didier C. Deutsch

Rambo III

🎬 1989, Intrada, from the film *Rambo III*, Carolco Entertainment, 1988 *♪♪♪*

album notes: Music: Jerry Goldsmith; **Orchestra:** The Hungarian State Opera Orchestra; **Conductor:** Jerry Goldsmith.

This trip by Jerry Goldsmith to the Rambo well is probably the most lyrical score ever written for a film of this type, mixing smooth ethnic and electronic rhythms, coiling, propulsive action cues and some graceful, almost nocturne-like interludes. This lengthy, 70-minute CD features plenty of action highlights, from the ritualistic beat of "The Game" to the elaborate "Fire Fight" with its escalating series of frenzied string variations over pulsing flutes and woodwinds, and "The Boot," which builds a simple rhythmic motif into a monolithic tutti orchestral statement. The opening cue is built almost entirely from percussion, with some rhythm elements that could have come from a Doors song, while more subdued cues like "Then I'll Die" and "Peshawar" create beautifully evocative ethnic rhythms. Since Goldsmith's score was heavily sliced and diced in the film, this is the only way to hear it as he originally intended, including the composer's original end credits, which were replaced with pop songs in the movie.

Jeff Bond

Rampage

🎬 1987, Virgin Movie Music, from the film *Rampage*, DEG Films, 1987 *♪♪♪♪*

album notes: Music: Ennio Morricone; **Orchestra:** Orchestra Unione Musicisti di Roma; **Conductor:** Ennio Morricone.

In another step away from the style he used for his most popular efforts, Ennio Morricone created a disturbing score, full of threatening sounds and angular themes, for this crime drama about a serial killer on the loose with a bent for satanic practices. Characteristic of Morricone's approach for this type of film, the cues are profuse elaboration for strings, with layers upon layers of textures creating an ominous sound, occasionally accented by a solo violin, or an otherwordly chorus performing in counterpoint. Breaking with the moods created, "Since Childhood" brings a different evocation, with its gentle crystalline bells over an attractive, melancholy-tinged melody, in a theme reprised with more forcefulness in "Carillon" where it achieves a different, more dangerous effect. A strangely evocative score that will appeal to a limited audience, this is well worth discovering.

Didier C. Deutsch

Rancho Deluxe

🎬 1998, Rykodisc, from the film *Rancho Deluxe*, United Artists, 1974 *♪♪♪*

album notes: Music: Jimmy Buffett.

Sam Waterston and Jeff Bridges starred as cattle rustlers trying to recapture the Old West in this offbeat cult film, released in 1974, for which singer-songwriter Jimmy Buffet composed and performed the score and songs, and in which he also appeared. The misadventures of the two cowboys in the "new" West are perfectly represented by Buffet's easy, understated style and creative turn-of-phrase. Great for Buffet fans!

Didier C. Deutsch

Ransom

🎬 1996, Hollywood Records, from the film *Ransom*, Touchstone Pictures, 1996 *♪*

album notes: Music: James Horner; **Conductor:** James Horner.

This oft-times subdued effort by James Horner was actually a replacement score for a work by another composer. Since Horner relies on his usual bag of musical tricks (i.e., the beating xylophone, the flurry of percussion), this could easily be mistaken for outtakes from his last effort for director Ron Howard, *Apollo 13*. Sadly, at no point does anything unique or interesting come out and, in the end, there's nothing here that feels as if its worth listening to. Even the "End Title" is just okay. Billy Corgan, a member of the rock group Smashing Pumpkins, also composed a portion of the score, six mind-numbing tracks of techno-rock music played in the film by the kidnappers. These tracks were obviously created to eliminate any empathy for them by torturing the audience. Corgan definitely shows the potential for a second career scoring horror films.

David Hirsch

Ransom/The Chairman

1991, Silva Screen Records, from the films *Ransom (The Terrorists)*, British Lion Films, 1975, and *The Chairman*, 20th Century-Fox, 1969 🎬🎬🎬

album notes: Music: Jerry Goldsmith; **Orchestra:** The National Philharmonic Orchestra; **Conductor:** Jerry Goldsmith.

Silva Screen rescued two important Jerry Goldsmith scores at once with this lengthy CD, but lack of access to the original studio tapes means that this is essentially a recording of an LP and some commercially available cassettes, resulting in the kind of sound quality that will make audiophiles cringe. For those who just want to hear the music, however, this is an exciting album, with Goldsmith's bombastic, European-flavored *Ransom* score making heavy use of a declamatory four-note horn theme that surges through chase and suspense cues over low-end piano and harpsichord. "Sky Chaser" expands a soaring romantic theme through shimmering orchestral textures, even taking it through a jazz-influenced riff. *The Chairman* showcases Goldsmith's striking skill at adapting Oriental melodies and orchestral effects, from its haunting shaikiku theme plays over rice and snare drums until it's eventually taken up by the entire orchestra, to some amazingly nimble, agitated action cues like "The Fence" and "Firefight." The intense suspense and action cues alternate with some gorgeously soothing atmospheric cues.

Jeff Bond

Rapid Fire

1992, Varèse Sarabande, from the film *Rapid Fire*, 20th Century-Fox, 1992 🎬🎬🎬

album notes: Music: Christopher Young **Synthesizers/Electronic Percussion:** Mark Zimoski, Daniel Licht.

When a college student, who is also a karate champion, witnesses a mob murder, what do you get? An expert score by Christopher Young! The 1992 movie suggested a deft blend of electronic sounds and percussive effects that emphasize the screen action, while giving it a greater focus. The explicit cues detail the action with great force and consistency, providing an extra dramatic edge that strikes a responsive note in the recording as well. In the midst of all the action, a tender moment ("Together Alone") provides an unexpected change of pace.

Didier C. Deutsch

The Rapture

1991, Polydor Records, from the film *The Rapture*, New Line Cinema, 1991 🎬🎬🎬

album notes: Music: Thomas Newman; **Conductor:** Thomas Newman.

The Rapture is a downright strange score written for the story of a disillusioned young woman (Mimi Rogers) drawn into a super-Fundamentalist religious cult. Thomas Newman has had a profound influence on dramatic scoring in the 1990s and this early score features many of the techniques that have become the sound of seriousness—eerie wails and dissonant strings over transcendent drones, so that it seems to be flying apart just as it is ground to the earth. Percussion samples prove unsettling, repeating loops of ticks and tacks unnaturally sped up. A piano is introduced, lightly playing two delicate chords of ambiguous harmony. This is music where the timbres and the melodies are intertwined. The whole thing hits with a deeply ambiguous, distorted meaning. Continuing another trend of the '90s, the album includes several songs of varied genres, from Little Richard's "Directly from My Heart to You" to Meredith Monk and Vocal Ensemble's choral hymnal "Astronaut Anthem."

Lukas Kendall

Raven

1994/1996, Sonic Images, from the television series, *Raven*, 1993 🎬🎬🎬🎬

album notes: Music: Christopher Franke; **Orchestra:** The Berlin Symphonic Film Orchestra; **Conductor:** Christopher Franke; **Featured Musicians:** Michael Thompson, guitar; Dean Parks, guitar; Doug Livingston, guitar; Steve Tavaglione, saxophon; John West, saxophone; **Featured Vocalists:** Jeff Meek, Scott Monahan, Lynn Mabry, Lisa Soland.

This television score starts exactly the way you might expect—guitar riffs over synthesizer lines, with the drums pounding rhythmically, create a sense of movement and action, if not excitement. But things change rapidly after that. The album, a compilation of instrumental and vocal tracks (performed by Jeff Meek, Scott Monahan, Lynn Mabry, and Lisa Soland), is actually quite engaging. The instrumental selections are flavorful, and pleasantly attractive ("Island Spirit" echoes the moods of the Caribbean, while "Rain Forest Chase" blends the rhythms of an action scene with the exotic setting in which it takes place). The vocal numbers show that Christopher Franke, who started in that field before moving to film and television scoring, has not lost his touch, with tunes that are catchy and lyrics that are convincingly meaningful. It all adds up to an album which, in the final analysis, is much better than the series for which these selections were created.

Didier C. Deutsch

Ravenous

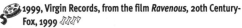

1999, Virgin Records, from the film *Ravenous*, 20th Century-Fox, 1999 🎬🎬🎬🎬

album notes: Music: Damon Albarn, Michael Nyman; **Orchestra:** The Michael Nyman Orchestra; **Conductor:** Michael Nyman; **Featured Mu-**

sicians: Ben Paley, violin; Tab Hunter, guitar, Jew's harp; Matt Goorney, banjo; Bing Lyle, squeeze box.

A black comedy set in 1847 in the Sierra Nevada, *Ravenous* dealt with a group of settlers who got lost in the mountains, were snowbound in a cave, and resorted to cannibalism to survive. As the story develops, it centers on two characters, the only survivor, a Scottish traveler named Colquhoun, and the outpost commander, Capt. John Boyd, who, through strange circumstances, become . . . flesh-eating partners. This amoral work, which made no concession to traditions and told its story with carnivorous humor, was enlightened by an entertaining score composed by Michael Nyman and Damon Albarn. With many unusual cues detailing the story, the score receives its proper due and stands out in this recording, with each marking signaling the progression of the action and how the cues fit in with it. Of particular interest are the eerie "The Cave," "Manifest Destiny," "Saveoursoulissa," and "End Titles," which, given their length, enable the music to have a greater impact.

Didier C. Deutsch

Raw Deal

1986, Varèse Sarabande, from the film *Raw Deal,* De Laurentiis Entertainment, 1986 woof!

album notes: Music: Tom Bahler, Albhy Galuten, Chris Boardman, Jerry Hey, Randy Kerber, Steve Lukather, Joel Rosenbaum, Claude Gaudette.

It took no less than eight composers to create this vapid, vaguely pretentious musical hodgepodge for a film starring Arnold Schwarzenegger. A series of electronic noises, punctuated by a rhythm track, with amplified guitars playing some undistinguished tunes, it might have been effective behind the screen action, where it went by without being noticed, but it doesn't cut it as musical background sans the visuals. It's predictable, it's empty, it's annoying! In short, it's the kind of album that gives film music a bad name.

Didier C. Deutsch

The Razor's Edge

1992, Preamble Records, from the film *The Razor's Edge,* Columbia Pictures, 1984

album notes: Music: Jack Nitzsche; **Orchestra:** The London Symphony Orchestra; **Conductor:** Stanley Black; **Featured Musician:** Bruno Hoffman, glass harmonica.

Early in his career Bill Murray starred in this bizarre remake, based on W. Somerset Maugham's novel, about a "dreamer of beautiful dreams" who delays his marriage to a wealthy and proper society girl so that he can "find himself" among the Lost Generation in bohemian Paris during the early 1920s. Murray's performance notwithstanding, the film called for and received

an eloquent musical score from Jack Nitzsche, whose own sensitivity found ample fodder in its subject matter. Beautifully expressive, with longing romantic cues that expand on the storyline and flesh it out considerably, the score (presented here in the "Orchestral Suite") is particularly striking and one of the best efforts from this often unheralded composer. "Larry's Journey," which consists of source music, is also interesting as an adjunct to Nitzsche's score.

Didier C. Deutsch

The Re-Animator/Bride of the Re-Animator

1991, Silva Screen Records, from the films *The Re-Animator,* 1987, and *Bride of the Re-Animator,* 1992

album notes: Music: Richard Band; **Orchestra:** The Rome Philharmonic Orchestra; **Conductor:** Richard Band.

Richard Band shamelessly makes a play on Bernard Herrmann's score for *Psycho,* an adaption that adds to the manic quality of this perversely funny horror series. Few critics though failed to make the connection Band was implying between the sexually repressed Norman Bates and the obsessed re-animator, Dr. Herbert West. Much of his music concentrates on showing off the horror element, a move that substantially emphasizes the black humor. For this project, Band was able to go to Italy and score the entire film with the Rome Philharmonic Orchestra, with this portion of the CD affording a rare look at what he can do when the budget allows him to work with a full-scale symphonic orchestra. Remarkably, little seemed lost when Band had to score the sequel with synthesizers five years later. In fact, the playing of the *Psycho*-inspired theme on all synthesizers gives the impression more than ever that West is just a sniveling ratboy. This is a genuinely funny goof on the whole genre.

David Hirsch

The Real Blonde

1998, Milan/BMG, from the Paramount film *The Real Blonde,* 1997

album notes: Music: Jim Farmer.

The movie is a slice-of-life about a "wannabe" actor and his fashion-model girlfriend in New York City. The soundtrack features a very eclectic mix of songs by little-known artists, with the exception of tracks by Space and Kool Moe Dee. The songs vary from spacey electronica numbers to lounge and nouveau-lounge, the latter which mix nicely with Jim Farmer's two jazz-influenced score tracks that really capture the feel of the various NYC locations within the movie.

Beth Krakower

4/8/4 *rebecca*

Rebecca

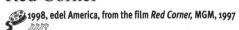 1991, Marco Polo Records, from the film *Rebecca,* Selznick International, 1940 𝄢𝄢𝄢𝄢

album notes: Music: Franz Waxman; **Orchestra:** The Czecho-Slovak Radio Symphony Orchestra; **Conductor:** Adriano; **Featured Musician:** Viktor Simcisko, violin.

In the profuse history of Hollywood film music, which has been marked by so many superlative scores, Franz Waxman's music for *Rebecca* will always stand out as a milestone and one of the best scores ever composed for the screen. Based on the Gothic novel by Daphne du Maurier, the film, starring Joan Fontaine and Laurence Olivier and directed by Alfred Hitchcock, exudes an impenetrable aura of mystery and suspense coupled with romantic undertones and youthful flights of fancy that soften the drama, yet ultimately give it a sharper edge by contrast. All these elements eventually find their way into the composer's expression in a score that teems with sweeping themes, richly expressive and sophisticated. This superb new recording, in widespread digital sound, features the Czecho-Slovak Radio Symphony Orchestra conducted by Adriano in a flawless performance which brings out all the nuances in the music and details some of the salient moments in the score. It is a worthy addition to any collection that invites repeated listening.

Didier C. Deutsch

Rebel Highway

See: Fast Track to Nowhere

Red Corner

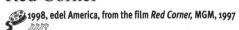 1998, edel America, from the film *Red Corner,* MGM, 1997 𝄢𝄢𝄢𝄢

album notes: Music: Thomas Newman; **Conductor:** Thomas Newman; **Featured Musicians:** Guangming Li, erhu; George Doering, zheng, moon guitar, saz; Michael Fisher, percussion; Steve Tavaglione, flutes, drones; George Budd, drones, ambiences; Chas Smith, resonators, bowed metals; Thomas Newman, piano; Ian Underwood, drones; Rick Cox, color shifts; Jon Clarke, double reeds; Huacong Jiang, Chi Li, You Li, Qichao Liu, Meiye Ma, Hua Qin, Renjian Wu, Yicheng Zhang, Youjun Zhou, Chinese instruments.

The setting of this action drama suggested an unusual Chinese-influenced score to Thomas Newman, who relied on the contributions of various artists playing instruments, particularly of the percussive kind, to give his score the proper colorings and forms. Set in Beijing, the film starred Richard Gere as a U.S. businessman caught in a web of international intrigue and forced to prove his innocence in a murder he didn't commit (Hollywood screenwriters often have a great deal of imagination). But if this political drama stretched credibility by seeming a bit too hokey at times, the audience was kept riveted by the spectacle of Beijing, and by the beauty of Gere's co-star, an attractive

Chinese actress named Bai Ling. Also adding a flavor of its own was Newman's first-rate music, a combination of American effects and Chinese accents, with many cues reflecting the exotic setting, while others stressed the gripping, taut screen action. The inclusion of some Chinese traditional melodies further enhanced the appeal of the music and gave it more credibility.

Didier C. Deutsch

Red Dawn

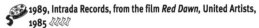 1989, Intrada Records, from the film *Red Dawn,* United Artists, 1985 𝄢𝄢𝄢𝄢

album notes: Music: Basil Poledouris; **Conductor:** Basil Poledouris.

Intrada's debut collector's LP is an excellent choice, preserving Basil Poledouris's confident symphonic adventure score for John Milius's communist invasion movie. The nine cues appearing on the CD are fairly long ones, totaling about 35 minutes of music (short by CD standards, but sufficient). Two themes dominate the score: the "Red Dawn Theme," a deep, throbbing motif that signifies the invasion, and the "Wolverine Theme," a heroic, three-note melody that denotes the teenage guerrillas who struggle against the Communist invaders. These themes are very nicely integrated into Poledouris's rhythmic and tonal action cues, merging Americana and militaristic sensibilities into a cohesive score that bristles with dynamic range and vigor.

Randall D. Larson

Red Heat

1988, Virgin Records, from the film *Red Heat,* Carolco International, 1988 𝄢𝄢𝄢

album notes: Music: James Horner; **Conductor:** James Horner; **Featured Musicians:** Michael Boddicker, Brandon Fields, James Horner, Kazu Matsui, Tim May, Steven Schaeffer, Neil Stubenhaus, Ian Underwood.

James Horner worked with director Walter Hill a number of times over the years, from the raucous comedy of *48 Hrs.* through his rejected score for *Streets of Fire* (which was ultimately replaced with music by Ry Cooder). *Red Heat,* Hill's engaging 1988 action picture, gets a definite boost from the film's twist on the old cop-buddy formula—while we still have a stereotypical, chain-smoking Chicago police officer (Jim Belushi), this time he's paired with a Russian cop (the one and only Arnold Schwarzenegger) tracking a drug dealer from his homeland. This affords Horner the opportunity to write bold Russian chorus music to complement the traditional action-film suspense cues, and the combination results in a competent score that seems to have later been part of the inspiration behind Basil Poledouris's similar-sounding approach for *The Hunt for Red October.*

Andy Dursin

Red King, White Knight

1991, Intrada Records, from the film *Red King, White Knight,* Cital Entertainment/Zenith Productions, 1991 ♪♪♪

album notes: Music: John Scott; Conductor: John Scott

This nicely old-fashioned spy movie score by John Scott is reminiscent of a lot of those 1960s cold war films in which composers always portrayed the Russians with blatant ethnic motifs. As with all of Scott's work, the arrangements are full-bodied, but the overall tone is surprisingly darker and more forceful ("Airport Killing" for example) than his usual efforts, thanks in part to his uncharacteristic use of shrill brass effects. Scott, for the most part, often writes with that larger-than-life quality typical of 1940s film scoring, but here he attacks the material as never before. While scoring the music for the film, which follows the attempts of a U.S. agent to stop the assassination of Soviet Premier Gorbachev, Scott was recording in Budapest when Hungary opened its borders to East Germans on the eve of the fall of Communism.

David Hirsch

Red Scorpion

1989, Varèse Sarabande, from the film *Red Scorpion,* 1989 ♪♪♪

album notes: Music: Jay Chattaway; Featured Musicians: Steve Croes, electronic music; Pete Levin, electronic music; Judd Miller, African flute.

Jay Chattaway produced an entertaining orchestral work for this standard Dolph Ludgren action yarn. Peppered with some intriguing synthesizer overlays and African flute solos, as in "Farewell Sundata," it captures the eerie mood of the desert locale and the battles between the Soviets and local tribes. Chattaway's action cues, like "The Battle" and "Attack on Mbaja," have some notably dynamic percussion work. This was the score that led to his selection as a regular composer on *Star Trek: The Next Generation*.

David Hirsch

The Red Tent

See: La tenda rossa

The Red Violin

1999, Sony Classical, from the film *The Red Violin,* New Line Cinema, 1998 ♪♪♪♪

album notes: Music: John Corigliano; Orchestra: The Philharmonia Orchestra; Conductor: Esa-Pekka Salonen; Featured Musicians: Joshua Bell, violin; Greg Knowles, cymbalum; Eddie Hession, accordion; Nick Bucknall, clarinet; Gavyn Wright, viola; Chris Laurence, double bass; Frank Ricotti, double bass.

From the director of *Thirty-two Short Film about Glenn Gould* comes another film where music plays the starring role. *The Red Violin* traces the history of a legendary violin, thought to possess an immortal soul, from its construction in 17th century Cremona to a present-day auction room. A showcase for the range of violinist Joshua Bell, John Corigliano's score pursues the violin's theme tune as the violin passes through many hands In five different countries. Even the gypsy fiddle playing echoes the melancholic central theme. Corigliano draws inspiration from Mozart, Bach, and virtuoso composer/performers like Paganini, tracing a history not just of the red violin but the evolution of the violin in Western music. The string section of the London Philharmonia provide excellent accompaniment, underscoring the interludes where Bell rests. The appended concert piece provides Bell with enough room to really show off his chops, glimpsed earlier in the almost unfeasbily fast solo "Etudes; Death of Caspar." *The Red Violin* stands among the greatest music-oriented films, and Corigliano's labor of love should be in everyone's collection.

David Poole

Reds

1999, Razor & Tie Records, from the Paramount film *Reds,* 1981 ♪♪♪♪

album notes: Music: Stephen Sondheim, Dave Grusin.

Reds is remarkable for the fact that it featured a score by Dave Grusin and Stephen Sondheim, in a rare case of the celebrated Broadway composer crossing over to write for the screen (another case was his contribution to *Dick Tracy*). With a star turn by Warren Beatty, who also directed, produced, and co-wrote it, the film was a fragile attempt to mix a drama filled with socio-political concepts with an intense love story, the whole thing framing the real-life stormy affair between radical American journalist John Reed and writer Louise Bryant against the backdrop of World War I and the Russian Revolution of 1917. While the screen action seemed at times too involved for the audience to truly get drawn into it, it prompted Grusin to write some cues that were quite compelling and enjoyably melodic ("Comrades," a recurring theme for the on-again, off-again love relationship of the two main characters, portrayed by Beatty and Diane Keaton; "The New York Waltz," and "Winter Escape," among them). The addition of songs performed by the Moscow Radio Chorus to give the score a touch of authenticity made the overall musical score more vibrant and romantically exciting. For his part, Sondheim contributed a couple of tunes, including a beautifully haunting theme, "Goodbye for Now," played here by Jean-Pierre Rampal and Claude Bolling, which evokes all at once the suspended love affair between the two writers and the hopes and aspirations of an entire

people trying to find their way in a political turmoil that seemed difficult to comprehend.

Didier C. Deutsch

The Reivers

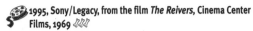

1995, Sony/Legacy, from the film *The Reivers,* Cinema Center Films, 1969 ♫♫♫

album notes: **Music:** John Williams; **Conductor:** John Williams.

John Williams's original score for *The Reivers* is what attracted Stephen Spielberg's attention to the composer, and one listen to this soundtrack recording will demonstrate exactly what endeared Williams to Spielberg and why their future collaborations worked so well.

This music is fun! In a thoroughly playful and lighthearted way, Williams proves his uncanny ability to set the stage for nearly any film setting—in this case, William Faulkner's novel about a boy's coming of age in turn-of-the-century Mississippi. The music so perfectly complements the complex thematic content of the film, it's as if the book and screenplay were written to accompany the music!

While shades of the future "Williams's sound" make cameo appearances throughout the score, we can also discern the influence of Aaron Copland (arguably the quintessential composer of American music), and orchestrator Robert Russell Bennett on Williams's work.

Charles L. Granata

The Remains of the Day

1993, Angel Records, from the film *The Remains of the Day,* Columbia Pictures, 1993 ♫♫♫♫

album notes: **Music:** Richard Robbins; **Conductor:** Harry Rabinowitz.

The quiet, elegant beauty of Richard Robbins's score is as strongly evocative of this Merchant-Ivory production as the calm distinction of its central character, a perfect English butler whose mistaken sense of duty for the owner of Darlington Hall over many years has cost him the love of an attractive young housekeeper, and any other trace of personal life. Tradition and strict adherence to the rules of propriety are elements that pervade Robbins's score ("Tradition and Order," "The Cooks in the Kitchen"), while the butler's realization, 30 years later, that his life has passed and he has little to show for it, is starkly evoked in "Sentimental Love Story/Appeasement/In the Rain," in which his emotional journey takes him back to today's realities. Robbins' strongly suggestive score is striking in its sober account, yet profoundly revealing of the deep, emotional currents that motivate the film's central character.

Didier C. Deutsch

Renaissance Man

1994, Varèse Sarabande, from the film *Renaissance Man,* Touchstone Pictures, 1994 ♫♫♫

album notes: **Music:** Hans Zimmer; **Additional Music:** Nick Glennie-Smith, John Van Tongeren, Bruce Fowler; **Featured Musician:** Malcolm McNab, trumpet.

A bittersweet comedy about a civilian unemployed advertising executive who gets a job training new Army recruits, *Renaissance Man* enabled composer Hans Zimmer to tap into two very dissimilar, opposed sources: the no-nonsense, straightforward military background, which translated itself into brassy marches, with occasional flights of fancy; and the laissez-faire of the advertising man, played by Danny DeVito, who has a total disregard for Army regulations, which resulted in leisurely, sedate cues. The two combine effectively, sometimes within the same cue, to create a diversified score that often has a sharp edge to it, with some melodic themes mingling with more abrasive tunes.

Didier C. Deutsch

Rent

1996, Dreamworks Records, from the Broadway production *Rent,* 1996 ♫♫♫♫

album notes: **Music:** Jonathan Larson; **Lyrics:** Jonathan Larson; **Musical Direction:** Tim Well; **Featured Musicians:** Steve Mack, bass; Kenny Brescia, guitar; Jeff Potter, drums, percussion; Daniel A. Weiss, synthesizers, Hammond B-3, guitars; Tim Well, piano, synthesizers; **Cast:** Adam Pascal, Anthony Rapp, Jesse L. Martin, Taye Diggs, Fredi Walker, Wilson Jermaine Heredia, Daphne Rubin-Vega.

A modern treatment of Puccini's *La Boheme,* the ultimate romantic opera, *Rent,* which opened on Broadway on April 29, 1996, and is still running at this writing, is the work of Jonathan Larson, a promising young playwright–songwriter who died of an aortic aneurysm a few hours after the show's final dress rehearsal. Set in New York's East Village, the show is a joyous and turbulent musical that celebrates a community of young artists as they struggle with the soaring hopes and tough realities of today's life. Propelled by a contemporary rock score that gives it a vitality not unlike that of *Hair* three decades earlier, *Rent* tells the story of friends living in a rundown apartment in the East Village: Roger, an HIV–infected songwriter, and Mark, a would–be filmmaker, forever chronicling on video the various elements of life around them. Enter Mimi, the proverbial girl next door, a dancer in a nightclub of dubious repute and a chronic drug user, who seduces Roger, only to walk out on him later on. Add to the mix of characters Maureen, who has ditched Mark for Joanne, a lawyer; Tom, a computer–age expert and philosopher, who falls for Angel, a transvestite sculptor; and various other cutting–edge denizens, and voila! Brash, brilliant, occasionally unfocused and messy, *Rent* is a rock opera filled with junkies, bohemian types, artists, prostitutes, lesbians, and homosexuals, the kind of stuff one would have thought unlikely to succeed in traditional Broadway. Yet, the show was roundly praised by critics, went on to win the Tony as Best Musical, and a Pulitzer Prize to boot (a rare occurrence in the musical theater), and has been a hot ticket ever since. Though the score, presented complete on a two-CD set recorded shortly after the opening, doesn't include a hit song along the lines of *Hair*'s "Good Morning Starshine," or "Let the Sunshine In," it receives a colorful, authoritative reading from Adam Pascal, Anthony Rapp, Jesse L. Martin, Fredi Walker, Wilson Jermaine Heredia, Daphne Rubin-Vega, and Idina Menzel in the principal roles, with the anthem–like "La Vie Boheme" very likely to elicit strong, positive reactions from any listener.

Didier C. Deutsch

Rent-a-Cop

🎬 1987, Intrada Records, from the film *Rent-a-Cop,* Kings Road Entertainment, 1987 🎵🎵

album notes: Music: Jerry Goldsmith; **Orchestra:** The Hungarian State Opera Orchestra; **Conductor:** Jerry Goldsmith.

You'd think the pairing of Burt Reynolds and Liza Minnelli would have made for box office dynamite, but this '80s time capsule from the waning moments of Reynolds' career was a disaster for all concerned, and composer Jerry Goldsmith didn't fare much better. His title theme features a bluesy, bittersweet trumpet solo, but the tune quickly escalates into some kind of pop anthem that's as far from *Chinatown* as Goldsmith is likely to get. The trumpet theme actually grows on you, but the rest of the album consists of some distinctly unmemorable, ticking electronic suspense cues that aren't likely to please either fans of the composer's earlier work or devotees of Harold Faltermeyer.

Jeff Bond

The Replacement Killers

🎬 1998, Varèse Sarabande, from the Columbia film *The Replacement Killers,* 1998 🎵

album notes: Music: Harry Gregson-Williams, Steve Jablonsky; **Featured Musicians:** Martin Tillman, electric cello; Stephen Kujala, bass flute.

Hong Kong chop-chop expert Chow Yun-Fat made his American film debut in this unlikely action melodrama, in which he portrayed a hired killer who fails to deliver and becomes the target of the trigger men hired to replace him. Dragging Mira Sorvino in tow, the fast-paced action took the two through the streets of Manhattan, from night clubs to eateries and garages, before the whole nightmare was satisfactorily brought to an end. Satisfactorily? Well not exactly: while high in action scenes, the film looked too studied and stilted to make much of an impression. The same comment applies to Harry Gregson-Williams'

score, a series of cues with faint strings building to a crescendo behind a heavily rhythmic beat, the better to inform that, hey, this is an action film. Maybe, but it doesn't work, either.

Didier C. Deutsch

The Rescuers Down Under

🎬 1990, Walt Disney Records, from the animated feature *The Rescuers Down Under,* Walt Disney Films, 1990 🎵🎵🎵🎵

album notes: Music: Bruce Broughton; **Conductor:** Bruce Broughton.

The further adventures of Bernard and Bianca and their friend Cody inspired Bruce Broughton to write a whimsical, inspired score which easily transcends its animated feature origin to provide an entertaining musical concept. Cleverly conceived to match the development of the story—in which Bernard, the world's bravest mouse, and Miss Bianca, answering a request for help from their friend Cody, deep in the heart of Australia's vast and unpredictable outback, to save a magnificent eagle from a ruthless poacher, find themselves thrown in more difficulties than they had anticipated—Broughton's music pulls all the stops, from heroic to soulful to romantic, in a vivid display that proves most satisfying. Of course, it's cartoon music, but of the better kind, and even adults will enjoy the tremendously exciting accents the composer conjures up along the way.

Didier C. Deutsch

Reservoir Dogs

🎬 1992, MCA Records, from the film *Reservoir Dogs,* Miramax, 1992 🎵🎵🎵

The story of six criminals pulling off a diamond heist, only to find out that one of them informed the police, this occasionally brutal film, directed by Quentin Tarantino, indulged in gratuitous violence, as in a scene in which a police officer is tortured for no valid reason to the strains of Stealers Wheel's "Stuck in the Middle with You," one of the tracks found here. The song-driven soundtrack also included other contemporary songs—"Hooked on a Feeling" by Blue Suede, "Fool for Love" by Sandy Rogers, and "Coconut" by Harry Nilsson, all heard here. Some of them are introduced in a flat, noncommital voice by Steven Wright, while sound bites from the dialogue put others in a more direct perspective with the action.

Didier C. Deutsch

Restoration

🎬 1995, Milan Records, from the film *Restoration,* Miramax, 1995 🎵🎵

album notes: Music: James Newton Howard, Henry Purcell; **Conductor:** Artie Kane, Rick Wentworth, Robert Zeigler.

James Newton Howard has scored all sorts of movies, from sci-fi adventures to romantic comedies, and he's done an admirable job, no matter what time frame or galaxy he's working in. *Restoration* is his first "period" score, coming for a movie set in 1600s England, and the results are somewhat hard to gauge—the music works fine in the movie, but it is hard to fully review Howard's original work, which is more or less an adaptation of (or modeling on) classical works by composers of the period, including Henry Purcell and Marin Marais. The album never really finds its own voice, which leaves it most recommended for fans of the movie, who will be able to recall moments from the film through the music contained herein.

Andy Dursin

Return of the Jedi

1997, RCA Records, from the film *Return of the Jedi*, 20th Century-Fox, 1983/1997 ♪♪♪♪

album notes: Music: John Williams; **Orchestra:** The London Symphony Orchestra; **Conductor:** John Williams.

The score for the final film in the original *Star Wars* trilogy is as redundant and uninspired as the movie itself, resurrecting numerous stretches of scoring from *Star Wars* and *The Empire Strikes Back* while providing little in the way of memorable new themes (unless you have a hankering to hum Jabba the Hutt's rattling tuba melody). However, Nick Redman and Michael Mattesino have done a masterful job of reassembling the knotted original elements of *Jedi*'s score, which was extensively edited in the movie (sometimes tracking actual cues from the earlier films into scenes for which John Williams had written new music). Most of the sequences involving Luke Skywalker's struggle with the evil Galactic Emperor, the gathering forces of the Rebel starfleet, and the countdown to the movie's gigantic space battle are genuinely gripping, with an unearthly male choir underscoring the Emperor's scenes (culminating in the hair-raising, spectral "The Dark Side Beckons") and some involving militaristic themes and pulsing, brassy rebel fleet music. But much of the score is weighted down by leaden, meandering dialogue underscoring and the lightweight silliness of the Ewok music that sabotages the drama of much of the movie's final showdown between the Rebels and the Empire. Williams is too good a composer for *Jedi* to be a complete drag, but it's by far the weakest of the three *Star Wars* scores.

see also: Star Wars, The Empire Strikes Back

Jeff Bond

The Return of the Musketeers

1989, Milan Records/France, from the film *The Return of the Musketeers*, 1989 ♪♪♪♪

album notes: Music: Jean-Claude Petit; **Orchestra:** The London Symphony Orchestra, the Academy of Ancient Music; **Conductor:** Jean-Claude Petit.

Richard Lester's *The Return of the Musketeers* didn't have the steam and energy of the filmmaker's earlier *The Three Musketeers*, which also starred Michael York, Oliver Reed, Richard Chamberlain, and Frank Finlay as the irrepressible trio (who couldn't count to four, but always lived by the motto, "One for all, and all for one"). But Jean-Claude Petit's score, at times expressed on ancient instruments, at other times exhibiting all the orchestral panache required by the action, gave Michel Legrand and Lalo Schifrin (who scored the first film and its sequel, respectively) a run for their money. This time around, the film chronicled the story of Athos, Porthos, Aramis, and D'Artagnan, 20 years later and thoroughly unsatisfied with their respective existences, who get together again to protect themselves against the treacherous actions of the attractive Justine de Winter, daughter of Milady, determined to avenge the death of her mother by destroying the three (pardon me, the four) musketeers. Matching note for deed the vigorous exploits of the four friends in this new film, Petit wrote a set of cues rife with grand gesturing and posturing in the best swashbuckling tradition, in a fine mixture of bravadura and passion. Elegant and supremely exciting, it makes this wonderful CD a fitting companion to the other two scores. This recording may be difficult to find. Check with a used CD store, mail-order company, or a dealer specializing in rare, out-of-print, or import recordings.

see also: The Three Musketeers, The Four Musketeers

Didier C. Deutsch

Return of the Seven

1998, Rykodisc, from the film *Return of the Seven*, United Artists, 1966 ♪♪♪♪♪

album notes: Music: Elmer Bernstein; **Conductor:** Elmer Bernstein.

The quintessential western score finally makes its initial bow on CD in this release which, unfortunately, doesn't contain any extra music, but features bites from the dialogue instead (?). For a long while, this was the only soundtrack from the popular *The Magnificent Seven* fans could own, as that film had never received a proper album release. Elmer Bernstein, however, recycled some of his themes, including the title tune, in this sequel which essentially presented the same storyline as the original, only with dire results since Yul Brynner, who gave such a memorable portrayal as Chris, leader of the Magnificent Seven, chose not to return in the role after this second film (he was properly disposed of at the end of it, as a result). While the score of the original *The Magnificent Seven* has yielded a soundtrack album at long last, it is in mono; this one is in brilliant stereo, and all the better for it. Bernstein hit his stride in westerns with his music for both films, letting his imagination run wild, with hot sonorities that suggest the south of the border atmosphere of the films, percolating rhythms and staccato riffs that evoke the pulse of the action, and here and there a guitar accent to top it off. If ever a western score could convey all the elements in the film in a few well chosen cues, this was it. Bernstein went on to score other westerns (including *The Sons of Katie Elder, The Scalphunters,* and *The Hallelujah Trail,* which are still awaiting their first release on compact disc), but both *The Magnificent Seven* and *Return of the Seven* defined the genre better than most, and gave it one recognizable signature theme. It would be hard to recommend anything else.

see also: The Magnificent Seven

Didier C. Deutsch

Return to Paradise

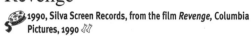1998, Varèse-Sarabande, from the film *Return to Paradise,* PolyGram, 1998 ⅆⅆⅆⅇ

album notes: Music: Mark Mancina; **Featured Musicians:** Ron Applegate, French horn; Jon Clarke, oboe, English horn; Fred Selden, flute, alto flute, bass flute, clarinet, bonsuri, suling, tarka, dudk, by-chee, bass Pan pipes.

A rising star among new film composers, Mark Mancina impresses again with his score for this lame drama about a young American held prisoner on drug charges in Southeast Asia and facing possible execution. While the plot may have conjured up visions of the trend-setting *Midnight Express,* too much of the film's action was lost in idle debates among the young prisoner's friends to "return to paradise" and prove him innocent. Conversely, where Giorgio Moroder's score for *Midnight Express* seemed annoyingly too electronic for its own good, Mancina's beautifully shaded cues, for orchestra and a host of wind and ethnic instruments, is striking for the sheer qualities it exudes. Quietly expressive and compelling, it reveals the composer as a sensitive melodist, apparently more concerned about writing cues that "sing" than "make noise," as others are prone to do. The only drawback here is that some cues are a bit too brief, playing under a minute, which might make sense behind action on the screen, but not in a recording.

Didier C. Deutsch

Return to Snowy River Part II

1988, Varèse Sarabande, from the film *Return to Snowy River,* Walt Disney Pictures, 1988 ⅆⅆⅆⅇ

album notes: Music: Bruce Rowland; **Conductor:** Bruce Rowland.

This sequel to *The Man from Snowy River* compelled Bruce Rowland to revisit his earlier score and expand on it in terms that remain attractive and thoroughly enjoyable. With the opening selection, "A Long Way from Home," a lovely theme for flute and two harmonic guitars over a synth texture, setting the tone, the music boldly unfolds with bright, exhilarating cues,

smoothly executed, and bluesy themes, representative of more personally intense emotions. A long track, "Farewell to an Old Friend," brings together the heroic and the pathos in an amazing symphonic display that's all western and all fun.

Didier C. Deutsch

Revenge

1990, Silva Screen Records, from the film *Revenge,* Columbia Pictures, 1990 ⅆⅆ

album notes: Music: Jack Nitzsche; **Featured Performers:** Bradford Ellis, acoustic guitar; Tommy Tedesco, acoustic guitar.

Jack Nitzsche composed this pleasing synth score for the 1990 Kevin Costner action yarn. It starts off well with a tender "Love Theme" and acoustic guitar solos by Tommy Tedesco. Some ethnic percussion added to the subsequent tracks give the score a delightful Spanish flavor, representative of the film's Mexican locale.

David Hirsch

Revenge of the Nerds

1998, Rock 'n' Roll Records, from the film *Revenge of the Nerds,* 20th Century-Fox, 1984 ⅆⅆⅇ

The film is schlocky but sweet, and this pogo-happy soundtrack follows suit. The under-celebrated Rubinoos bounce through "Breakdown" and the film's theme song, while Gleaming Spires keep the humor quotient high on "Are You Ready for the Sex Girls" and "All Night Party." Those four songs, along with Bone Symphony's "One Foot in Front of the Other," make it worth the price of admission and show it can be hip to be a nerd.

Gary Graff

Revenge of the Pink Panther

1988, EMI-Manhattan, from the film *Revenge of the Pink Panther,* United Artists, 1978 ⅆⅆⅆⅆ

album notes: Music: Henry Mancini; **Conductor:** Henry Mancini; **Featured Musicians:** Tony Coe, saxophone; Henry Mancini, piano; Leslie Pearson, piano; Sidney Sax, violin.

Some 10 years after the success of *The Pink Panther* and its sequel, *A Shot in the Dark,* director Blake Edwards returned to the rich lode he had mined, and between 1975 and 1978 filmed three more comedies around the central character of Chief Inspector Jacques Clouseau of the French Sûreté (portrayed in ineffable manner by Peter Sellers): *The Return of the Pink Panther* (1975), *The Pink Panther Strikes Again* (1976), and *The Revenge of the Pink Panther* (1978). All three featured an appropriately delirious score by Henry Mancini. While the soundtrack albums to the first two are still awaiting release on compact disc in this country (*Return* came out in Japan), *Revenge* is available and it is every bit as enjoyable as one might remember it was. A murky tale involving Dyan Cannon as the very private secretary to a ship magnate and dope smuggler who gets ditched by her boss and teams up with Clouseau to bring about her former employer's downfall, the film is merely an excuse for Sellers to broaden his antics as Clouseau, notably disguised as a would-be Mafia don and as an old tar with a wooden leg lost in the fog. As usual, Mancini was right on the button writing a score that brims with mordantly amusing themes, including "Hong Kong Fireworks," an inspired moment of lunacy in the film. Another gem in the album finds Sellers warbling "Thank Heaven for Little Girls" from *Gigi*, in a send-up to end all send-ups.

Didier C. Deutsch

The Revengers

See: La Feccia

Reversal of Fortune

1991, Milan America/France, from the film *Reversal of Fortune,* Warner Bros., 1990 ♪♪♪

album notes: Music: Mark Isham; **Featured Musicians:** David Torn, guitar; Mark Isham, synthesizer; Jerry Kalaf, percussion.

Portraying the complex trial of Claus von Bulow, the Newport aristocrat who was convicted and later acquitted of trying to murder his wealthy wife, *Reversal of Fortune* was a finely detailed, compelling drama that found an eerie echo in Mark Isham's engrossing score. Basically written for layers of synthesizers augmented with percussion instruments and the occasional strumming of a guitar, the cues pretty much follow the screen action and give it a musical support that enhances the moods of the drama. The various characters are appropriately identified, including Von Bulow ("Claus, the Bad Guy"), and his wife Sunny ("What Sunny Wants, Sunny Gets!"), as well as the various incidents in the case ("Coma," "The Letters"), all leading to two "Possible Explanations," and ultimately a question mark ("This Is All You Can Know"), all anchored around a main theme that recurs throughout. It makes for an unusual soundtrack, sometimes difficult to get into, but ultimately rewarding, despite its limitations.

Didier C. Deutsch

Rich in Love

1993, Varèse Sarabande, from the film *Rich in Love,* MGM, 1993 ♪♪♪♪♪

album notes: Music: Georges Delerue; **Conductor:** Georges Delerue.

Georges Delerue was at his most romantically eloquent when he wrote this attractive score (his last) in which the graceful moods are expressed by a variety of solo instruments (flute, guitar, clarinet, oboe, violin, etc.). "It is as though Georges was writing a good-bye for each of his friends," notes Robert Townson in the notes to this CD. And, indeed, each cue sounds like a delicate little concerto. Adding poignancy to the proceedings is the fact that the themes Delerue wrote are so exquisite. A dramatic comedy rooted in a Southern background, involving a couple, their two daughters, and the daughters' various boyfriends, the story suggested a series of lovely cues that actually don't need the screen action to attract the listener.

Didier C. Deutsch

Rich Man, Poor Man

1993, Varèse Sarabande, from the ABC–TV production *Rich Man, Poor Man,* 1976 ♪♪♪♪

album notes: Music: Alex North; **Conductor:** Alex North, Harold Mooney.

In a rare foray into television, Alex North wrote the score for this 12–hour television version of Irwin Shaw's inspired novel, which spans 20 years in the life of a family. To keep things under control, he devised various leitmotifs for the various characters in the complex story. These essentially form the texture of the score, as sampled in this soundtrack album, with each cue detailing the central characters, their relations to each other, and their individual *modus operandi*. The themes are robustly defined, with each cue using a different approach, from jazz to blues, from a dramatic outburst to a sophisticated waltz, the whole thing bathed in an Americana flavor that pervades the entire score. It's a richly rewarding experience, that invites repeated listenings.

Didier C. Deutsch

Richard III

1997, Sony Classical, from the film, *The Life and Death of Richard III,* AFT, 1912 ♪♪♪♪♪

album notes: Music: Ennio Morricone; **Orchestra:** The Accademia Musicale Italiana, **Conductor:** Ennio Morricone; **Featured Musician:** Nello Salza, trumpet.

1996, London Records, from the film *Richard III,* United Artists, 1996 ♪♪♪♪♪

album notes: Music: Trevor Jones; **Conductor:** David Snell; **Featured Soloist:** Phil Todd, sax, flute.

There have been previous examples of contemporary composers putting to music films that date from the silent era: among the better known, Carl Davis and Arthur Honegger both wrote a score for Abel Gance's masterpiece, *Napoleon,* and Davis also prepared a score for D.W. Griffith's *Intolerance.* What these masters did was to bring their own sensitivities to films that had become icons, and try to translate the director's vision into their own musical terms. The difficulty in doing that is that when a composer works with a director, usually the music reflects a consensus of opinion between the two regarding the placement of the cues and the impact the music will have on a scene. When the director is no longer around it becomes a proposition fraught with problems. Usually, the composer turns the difficulty around by writing a score that takes the shape of a symphonic poem and is reflective of specific scenes in the silent narrative. Faced with a similar task, Ennio Morricone devised his score for the 1912 *The Life and Death of Richard III* as a work in five parts, each part corresponding to a similar division in the film's development. In the process, he wrote specific themes that recur through each episode, while sticking closely to the formal structures imposed by the type of music he created, in this case a canon, a passacaglia, etc. What is jarring, however, is to hear the contemporary sounds in this score written for a film made more than 80 years ago, and only recently rediscovered and restored to its original grandeur. Whether Morricone was the right choice to create this music is a question that probably will be debated for some time to come (to these ears, John Williams might have been more appropriate). But what the Italian maestro delivered, and what we have here, is a work of profound impact, solidly embedded in a style that seems far removed from the music we usually get from Morricone, yet with hints of familiar accents peeking through the composition. Certainly, it is a major work that requires close scrutiny, and probably will leave many listeners unsatisfied, or wondering exactly what they are supposed to make of this score. But a discriminate audience will find it richly rewarding, if somewhat cold and detached, and a recording that grows on you with each new listening.

It may seem incongruous to find a recording of Al Jolson's "I'm Sitting on Top of the World" in the soundtrack of a film based on William Shakespeare's *Richard III,* but that's not the only odd thing about this unusual quirky production set in the 1930s, which starts (on the album, at least) in a volley of gunfire, immediately followed by a big band number. Of course, as is sometimes the case in filmizations of well-known stage works, most of the music plays under the action to such extent that isolating it becomes difficult and redundant. Trevor Jones went around the difficulty by creating flavorful big band numbers which make their own statement and punctuate the action while anchoring it in the time period in which it is set. Some of the cues are introduced by excerpts from the dialogue, but these are not intrusive, and actually help appreciate the changes that have occurred in the concept of the film and, as a direct result, the flavor Jones chose to give his score. It all comes together as a vibrant display of a celebrated drama, with musical accompaniment that enhances the action and gives it the support it richly deserves.

Didier C. Deutsch

Richie Rich

1994, Varèse Sarabande, from the film *Richie Rich,* Warner Bros., 1994 ♫♫♫♫

album notes: Music: Alan Silvestri; Conductor: Alan Silvestri.

Though a mindless little comedy starring Macaulay Culkin and John Larroquette, *Richie Rich* received a major score from Alan Silvestri, whose natural verve and exuberance obviously found a rich source of inspiration in this tired story about an obnoxious rich boy (guess who!) whose idleness leads him to more mischiefs than he has millions in the bank. Unfazed by the tale's obvious trappings, Silvestri served up a score that's quite enjoyable, with funny jerky little cues that spell out the story without spilling the beans. It may not be Beethoven's Ninth, but neither is the film *Gone with the Wind,* and, all things considered, this joyous score is much better than one might have expected.

Didier C. Deutsch

Ride

1998, Tommy Boy, from the film *Ride,* Dimension, 1998 ♫♫♫♫

Ride is one of the best urban soundtracks yet, a combination of fierce hip-hop and smooth R&B that both enhances the film and stands alone as a strong overview of the genre. Pairings are the order of the day here as Onyx and Wu-Tang Clan slam through "The Worst"; Dave Hollister, Redman, and Erick Sermon celebrate on "The Weekend"; Noreaga, Nas, and Nature rip through "Blood Money (Part 2)"; and Snoop Doggy Dogg joins Eastsiders for "Feel So Good." The R&B tip features its share of collaboration, too, including hip-hop troupe the Roots backing Eric Benet on "Why" and Tony! Toni! Tone!'s Raphael Saadiq bowing Willie Max, a Detroit vocal trio that's the first signing to Saadiq's own label. All told, this is one of the CDs you can offer to anyone who wants a sense about the state of current black music in America.

Gary Graff

Ridicule

1996, London Records, from the film *Ridicule,* Miramax, 1996 ♫♫♫♫♫

album notes: Music: Antoine Duhamel; Orchestra: La Grande Ecurie et la Chambre du Roy; Conductor: Jean-Claude Malgoire.

An unusually sophisticated film set in France in the 18th century, *Ridicule* enabled Antoine Duhamel to write a rare, literate score in the style of the period, which was performed by one of France's most prestigious orchestras, La Grande Ecurie et la Chambre du Roy, conducted by Jean-Claude Malgoire and playing ancient instruments. Elegant, frothy, always enchanting, it is quite unlike anything you might hear in contemporary films. A mordant satire of a time when wit seemed more important than a man's assets, the film focused on a young man with ambitions of being introduced to the court of Louis XVI; he befriends an elderly gentleman, an almost bankrupt member of the nobility, who agrees to sponsor him. While the newcomer adamantly refuses to join in the catty back-biting that has become *de rigueur* at the court, he weaves his way around and seduces a powerful Marquise, particularly known for her acid remarks and tart comments, usually aimed at embarrassing the unsuspecting. The music, always keeping discretely in the background, enhanced the scenes, commenting on them or supporting them, in a brilliant display of unusual film scoring. This title may be out of print or just plain hard to find. Mail-order companies, used CD shops, or dealers of rare or import recordings will be your best bet.

Didier C. Deutsch

The Right Stuff/North and South

1986, Varèse Sarabande, from the films *The Right Stuff*, 1983, and *North and South*, 1985, both Warner Bros. 🎬🎬🎬🎬

album notes: Music: Bill Conti; **Orchestra:** The London Symphony Orchestra; **Conductor:** Bill Conti.

Bill Conti won an Oscar for his great score for *The Right Stuff,* the outstanding 1983 Philip Kaufman filming of Tom Wolfe's bestselling book about the early days of Chuck Yeager and NASA, yet his original music was never released as a soundtrack album. Conti was given the opportunity to produce a concert suite with the London Symphony Orchestra in 1985, and the results were released on this tremendously well-recorded album, which couples a 16-minute suite from *The Right Stuff* with a slightly longer suite from the composer's score for *North and South,* the mega-successful TV mini-series. Conti's music is magnificent in each case. For *The Right Stuff* he wrote a triumphant score that was modeled after "The Planets" at certain points, yet contains enough of his stirring, invigorating style to mark it as distinctly the work of its composer. *North and South,* meanwhile, is a beautifully flowing melodic score, with a gorgeous main theme comprising the heart of the musical material. Together they make for a fantastic album in which the only flaw is that it doesn't go on longer than it does.

Andy Dursin

The Ring

1996, Silva America Records; from the NBC–TV miniseries *The Ring,* 1996 🎬🎬🎬

album notes: Music: Michel Legrand; **Orchestra:** The City of Prague Philharmonic; **Conductor:** Michel Legrand.

An epic four–hour miniseries based on Danielle Steel's poignant novel about a young woman's search for her family, from whom she has been separated at the onset of World War II, *The Ring* compelled Michel Legrand to write a score that's quietly understated at times, elegant and attractive at others, with some compelling and some disturbing moments thrown in the mix, as the story unfolds. Though perfectly adequate, and no doubt fitting the script to a tee, the one thing that seems to be missing here is a sense of excitement, as if the composer had done his job routinely without getting much involved in the project itself. Occasionally, a theme tries to belie this impression ("Ariana Flees Berlin"), but that's only a fleeting moment in a score that's luxuriously musical and surprisingly lifeless.

Didier C. Deutsch

The Rink

1984, Polydor Records, from the Broadway production *The Rink,* 1984 🎬🎬🎬🎬

album notes: Music: John Kander; **Lyrics:** Fred Ebb; **Musical Direction:** Paul Gemignani; **Cast:** Liza Minnelli, Chita Rivera, Scott Holmes, Jason Alexander.

Chita Rivera and Liza Minnelli share the spotlight in this original Kander and Ebb musical in which they portray a mother and her daughter, long estranged, who get back together to save from destruction a seaside roller rink the mother has been running by herself for years. Though flawed, and hardly a big hit by normal standards (it closed after a mere 204 performances, following its premiere on February 2, 1984), the show has a solidly defined score, announced by the Jacques Brel-like "Colored Lights," and featuring many excellent numbers for the two stars. The cast album brings it all together in one superlative recording.

Didier C. Deutsch

Rio Conchos

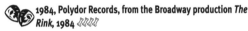

1989, Intrada Records, from the film *Rio Conchos,* 1964 🎬🎬🎬🎬

album notes: Music: Jerry Goldsmith; **Orchestra:** The London Symphony Orchestra; **Conductor:** Jerry Goldsmith.

Re-recorded with the London Symphony Orchestra as a way to revitalize this landmark 1964 Western score, Jerry Goldsmith's *Rio Conchos* is exciting, stimulating, and highly romantic. The principal theme is a rhythmic violin melody over guitar and tambourine, given a poignant turn by oboe midway through. The guitar, tambourine, and other percussion give the score an agreeable rhythm and a down-to-earth feel, while the soaring melodies and complex action writing drive the characters and their confrontations. Like Elmer Bernstein in his own Western scores, Goldsmith develops the signature style which would

The Right Stuff **(The Kobal Collection)**

later be recalled in films like *Rio Lobo* and *Bandolero!*. Added to the score's 45 minutes is a 12.5 minute "Prologue" from Goldsmith's triumphant music for the long-lost prelude to *The Agony and the Ecstasy,* which becomes a powerful tone poem about the sculptor Michelangelo, expressive and lofty, emphasizing strings, harp, and French horn. Intrada's fine production qualities abound in this important soundtrack restoration.

Randall D. Larson

Rio Grande

1993, Varèse Sarabande, from the film *Rio Grande,* Republic Pictures, 1950 *♪♪♪♪♪*

album notes: Music: Victor Young; **Conductor:** Victor Young.

Even though it was recorded in 1950 and plays in a rather grainy mono sound, there is no denying the immense power and sweep of this excellent western score by Victor Young. While the screenplay provided the composer with a stock contingent of action scenes (solidly expressed in cues like "Indian Raid/ Escape," or "Tyree Meets the Wagon Train/Indian Attack"), it also gave him an unusually broader canvas to work on with its story about two strong-willed and very private souls, Lt. Col. Yorke, and his wife, Kathleen, who, while separated for 16 years after finding themselves on opposite sides during the Civil War, are unexpectedly reunited again in an isolated outpost in the West. This situation suggested to Young a richer and more musically diversified score, with many cues built around the traditional folk song "I'll Take You Home, Kathleen," a biting comment on the couple's current relationship, since Yorke destroyed his wife's Southern estate during the war. Adding an extra musical element, several vocals by the Sons of the Pioneers give the score some western authenticity.

Didier C. Deutsch

Riot

1997, Rhino Records, from the television film *Riot,* Showtime, 1997 *♪♪♪♪*

album notes: Music: Luke Cresswell, Steve McNicholas; **Featured Musicians:** Chris Tedesco, solo trumpet; Carl Smith, percussion; Theseus Gerard, percussion; Fraser Morrison, percussion; Steve Williamson, saxophone.

This movie aired on Showtime on the fifth anniversary of the L.A. riots that followed the verdict in the Rodney King trial. It focused on four sets of people, each from a different ethnic background—a Korean family, an African-American family, a white cop, and Latino kids—how they were affected by the riots, and how they actually interacted on various levels to the same set of circumstances. The score was composed by newcomers Luke Cresswell and Steve McNicholas, creators of *Stomp,* who created four percussive themes, one for each of the four plots, in-

corporating heavy rhythmic themes with instruments and melodies representative of each culture. The themes are layered on top of each other at times, which emphasize the characters' intertwining roles both in the interwoven story and in L.A. as a city. Also featured are several songs: "Brothers & Sisters," which is very reminiscent of Seal, was composed for the movie by Cresswell and McNicholas, the rap song "Can't Stop the Brotherhood" by Brotherhood for Anotherhood, and "Cool Out," a R&B track by LV.

Beth Krakower

Rising Sun

1993, Fox Records, from the film *Rising Sun,* 20th Century-Fox, 1993 *♪♪♪*

album notes: Music: Toru Takemitsu; **Orchestra:** Tokyo Concert Orchestra; **Conductor:** Hiroyuki Iwaki.

Rising Sun is a 1993 Philip Kaufman film from the controversial Michael Crichton book. Sean Connery and Wesley Snipes star as detectives investigating a murder at a Japanese firm in Los Angeles and the film mixes suspense and culture-shock characterization with silliness and boredom. The filmmakers did have the conviction to hire famed Japanese modernist Toru Takemitsu for his first and only Hollywood score. Takemitsu, who had composed for numerous Japanese pictures such as *Ran* for Akira Kurosawa, fashioned an intriguing sound world of orchestra and traditional Japanese instruments. The score overall is textural and only fleetingly melodic, but provides a real sense of disquiet and tension to the film's complicated flashback structure and themes of cultural infiltration. One of the most discernible motives, for ascending saxophone, blends dissonant, post-tonal textures with an almost Gershwin-esque Americana theme—Western culture swallowed up by the rest of the world and not the other way around. The CD is a fascinating listen for the post-tonally schooled—it also includes a traditional taiko drum performance—but is not for the traditionally minded, and is probably only second-rate Takemitsu. Reportedly the filmmakers made a veritable stir-fry of the cues in the dubbing process and Takemitsu cursed American filmmaking until his untimely death in 1996.

Lukas Kendall

The River

1984, Varèse Sarabande, from the film *The River,* Universal, 1984 *♪♪♪♪♪*

album notes: Music: John Williams; **Conductor:** John Williams; **Featured Musicians:** Jim Walker, flute; Warren Luening, trumpet; Tommy Tedesco, guitar.

Tapping a musical vein he has seldom fully explored, John Williams wrote a score rooted in Americana for *The River,* directed by Mark Rydell, with whom Williams had worked on *The*

Reivers. In this story of a couple of farmers (portrayed by Mel Gibson and Sissy Spacek) uncompromisingly attached to their land and determined to stay on it despite a speculator willing to buy it and a disastrous flood that threatens to engulf all they have, Williams found the elements for a thoughtful and rewarding score, nominated for an Academy Award, in which little pleasures ("The Pony Ride"), downhome feelings ("Tractor Scene"), and seemingly insurmountable pains ("Rain Clouds Gather") elicit a lyrical and immensely touching response.

A River Runs Through It

1992, Milan Records, from the film *A River Runs Through It,* Columbia Pictures, 1992 ♪♪♪

album notes: Music: Mark Isham; **Conductor:** Ken Kugler; **Featured Musicians:** Sid Page, violin; Louise Di Tullio, flute; Rich Ruttenberg, piano; Dorothy Remsen, harp; Katie Kirkpatrick, harp; John Isham, Uilleann pipes.

Mark Isham's flowing, low-key, poetic score for Robert Redford's character-driven drama is genteel and relaxing enough. Replacing a score initially composed by Elmer Bernstein, Isham's music does a superlative job not overstating the emotions of Redford's film, working to gently push our heartstrings instead of melodramatically tugging them like so many other Hollywood film scores do. The only problem is that the music may be too subtle for its own good. The score lacks a degree of distinction contained in the best scores for films of this type, with a main theme that is, if anything, a bit too restrained. Nevertheless, the music paints yet another picture of Isham, whose versatile talents have been utilized in composing often successful film scores for any kind of genre film.

Andy Dursin

The River Wild

1994, RCA Records, from the film *The River Wild,* Universal Pictures, 1994 ♪♪♪

album notes: Music: Jerry Goldsmith; **Conductor:** Jerry Goldsmith.

Goldsmith stepped in to replace Maurice Jarre's work on this Meryl Streep action thriller, utilizing the same folk tune, "The River Is Wide" as an affecting title theme that weaves its way through several exultant, fast-paced river rafting sequences before giving way to a halting, heavy orchestral rhythm that gradually overwhelms the score. Goldsmith effectively characterized the film's raging river currents with swelling, tremuloso chords from the string section and a "splashing" synthetic percussion effect. The final cue, "The Vacation's Over," develops the primary action material in impressive fashion over the course of nine minutes as the entire orchestra chops away at Goldsmith's percussive motifs. Is it ingeniously cohesive or just repetitious?

Jeff Bond

The Road to Wellville

1994, Varèse Sarabande, from the film *The Road to Wellville,* Columbia, 1994 ♪♪♪♪

album notes: Music: Rachel Portman; **Conductor:** David Snell.

One of today's brightest young composers, Rachel Portman took a direct cue from the amusing storyline behind this somewhat eccentric little film and concocted a cheerful score that's a whole lot of fun. Set at the turn of the 20th century, *The Road to Wellville* concerned itself with the evidently odd Kellogg health sanitarium, where "patients" could get rid of all kinds of real or imaginary ailments by following a therapeutic regimen that involved the consumption of strange medicinal remedies and the use of even stranger contraptions. Matching the tone of the film and cleverly blending bits of dialogue to set off the selections, Portman's score delights in cues that, on the surface, seem quite demure, but are in fact wickedly funny and delicious in their expression. Adding an eccentric note of their own, some classical selections, played in a way their composers would certainly never have imagined, fit very neatly in the whole musical package.

Didier C. Deutsch

The Road Warrior

1982, Varèse Sarabande, from the film *The Road Warrior,* Warner Bros., 1982 ♪♪♪

album notes: Music: Brian May; **Conductor:** Brian May.

There have been lots of kinetic action films since George Miller's *The Road Warrior,* but this is the one that kicked them off, a seminal masterpiece of modern post-apocalyptic sci-fi. Brian May's music is the sound of Mad Max, thrashing and sinister—Bernard Herrmann on high-octane—as the rogue Max scavenges for petrol, bike and car gangs rape and pillage, and a lone community tries to survive. Ultimately it is Max who saves them but ends up even worse off, and the score, unlike its *Mad Max* (1979) predecessor, features a tragic, romantic/symphonic side in addition to its propulsive action base. May invests his music with a considerable personality of orchestration and gestures (too bad the recording, made in Australia, is so muddled) that successfully link the suspenseful moments with the flat-out 120mph chases. Not far from the disorienting, dissonant textures of the first *Mad Max,* with a hopeful eye on the symphonic sweep of Maurice Jarre's music for the third film, *Beyond Thunderdome,* and left to rot with a tankerful of sand in the Australian wasteland is this, the late Brian May's most famous score.

see also: Mad Max, Beyond Thunderdome

Lukas Kendall

The Roar of the Greasepaint— The Smell of the Crowd

1965, RCA Victor, from the Broadway production *The Roar of the Greasepaint—The Smell of the Crowd*, 1965 ☆☆☆☆

album notes: Music: Leslie Bricusse, Anthony Newley; **Lyrics:** Leslie Bricusse, Anthony Newley; **Musical Direction:** Herbert Grossman; **Cast:** Anthony Newley, Cyril Ritchard, Sally Smith, Joyce Jillson, Gilbert Price.

The eternal struggle between the haves and the have–nots, those in command and those under them, took an inordinate twist in *The Roar of the Greasepaint—The Smell of the Crowd,* in which Anthony Newley portrays Cocky, the eternal hopeful on the losing end, and Cyril Ritchard as Sir, whose obfuscating control Cocky tries to break, although he later realizes he needs it. The consistently satisfying score, conceived by Newley and Leslie Bricusse, is in turn elegiac, good natured, soulful, but always endearing. It yields two great solo numbers, both performed by Newley, "The Joker," and particularly "Who Can I Turn To," which soon became a favorite of cabaret singers all over the world.

Didier C. Deutsch

Rob Roy

1995, Virgin Movie Music, from the film *Rob Roy,* MGM, 1995 ☆☆☆

album notes: Music: Carter Burwell; **Conductor:** Carter Burwell, Sonny Kompanek; **Featured Musicians:** Davy Spillane, Uillean pipes, low whistles; Maire Breatnach, fiddle; Tommy Hayes, bodhran; Ronan Brown, penny whistle; Miriam Stockley, vocals.

In 1995 we had *Braveheart, Dragonheart,* and *Rob Roy.* Who says there isn't enough imitation in Hollywood? Carter Burwell had the opportunity at scoring *Rob Roy,* the first and least successful of the three big-screen Highlands epics, featuring good performances but draggy pacing and indifferent direction. Burwell's music, combined with the sweeping cinematography, is enough to make the movie easy to watch, but on its own, it's all too clear to spot the flaws in the soundtrack album—namely, it's redundant to a fault. The main theme just repeats itself over and over again, and while it's beautiful the first time you hear it, you won't be feeling the same way by the time you reach the end of the soundtrack, which also contains vocals by Karen Matheson and Gaelic group Capercaillie.

Andy Dursin

The Robe

1993, Fox Records, from the film *The Robe,* 20th Century-Fox, 1953 ☆☆☆☆☆

album notes: Music: Alfred Newman; **Orchestra:** The 20th Century-Fox Orchestra and Chorus, **Conductor:** Alfred Newman.

One of the first big screen epics of the 1950s with a Biblical theme, *The Robe* is distinguished by the fact that it is the first film to use the anamorphic CinemaScope process and the first to introduce multi-track stereophonic sound in many roadshow theatres. An inspirational story based on Lloyd C. Douglas's best-seller, the film recounts the conversion of a Roman tribune (Richard Burton), when he realizes that the man crucified on the Golgotha, and whose garment he had inherited, might have been the Son of God. Playing a decisive role in this conversion are his Greek slave, Demetrius, played by Victor Mature, already a Christian; his childhood sweetheart, Diana (Jean Simmons), ward of Emperor Tiberius, also an early convert; and crazed Prince Regent Caligula (Jay Robinson in a scene-stealing portrayal), who eventually sends him and Diana to their deaths. Availing themselves of the letterbox gimmick, already a strong attraction in itself, the makers of the film spared no expense to turn *The Robe* into a spectacular presentation. Huge crowds involving thousands of extras competed with impressive circus scenes, gigantic sets, and breathtaking races (charging directly at the cameras) to mesmerize audiences who had seldom been treated to such a display on such a large scale.

Enhancing the performance is Alfred Newman's superlative score, a deeply felt assortment of grandeur and bravura mixed with more intimate expressions of love and religious respect. Interestingly, even though it had been recorded in stereo, the score was initially released on record in mono only (the recording industry caught up with the innovations in film sound techniques some four years later). This release on compact disc marks the first time the score, which includes many cues available for the first time, is heard in stereo, the way it was initially recorded, and it sounds mighty impressive, particularly to those who have grown up with the original mono version. In later years, Newman's achievements would be somewhat overshadowed by his own contributions to other films, and by Miklos Rozsa's compositions for similar Roman spectacles like *Ben-Hur* or *King of Kings.* The fact remains that *The Robe* is an exceptional score.

Didier C. Deutsch

Roberta

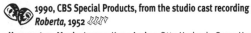

1990, CBS Special Products, from the studio cast recording *Roberta,* 1952 ☆☆☆

album notes: Music: Jerome Kern; **Lyrics:** Otto Harbach, Oscar Hammerstein II, Dorothy Fields, Jimmy McHugh; **Musical Direction:** Lehman Engel; **Cast:** Joan Roberts, Jack Cassidy, Kaye Ballard, Portia Nelson, Stephen Douglass.

A routine story, about an American sports figure who inherits a failing fashion house from his aunt in Paris and saves it from bankruptcy with the help of a friend, *Roberta* was the occasion for Jerome Kern to write a score that teems with great standards, including the classic "Smoke Gets in Your Eyes" and "Yesterdays." Initially created in 1933, it was filmed on two occasions—in 1935, with Fred Astaire, Ginger Rogers, Irene Dunne, and Randolph Scott in its cast; and again in 1952, as *Lovely to Look At,* with Red Skelton, Kathryn Grayson, Howard Keel, and Marge and Gower Champion. The studio cast album, recorded in 1952 with Jack Cassidy, Portia Nelson, Joan Roberts, Stephen Douglass, and Kaye Ballard, is the only one currently available, and while not entirely up to today's exacting digital standards, deserves a particular place in any self-serving collection.

Didier C. Deutsch

Robin Hood

1991, Silva Screen Records, from the film *Robin Hood,* 20th Century-Fox, 1990 𝄪𝄪𝄪

album notes: Music: Geoffrey Burgon; Conductor: Geoffrey Burgon.

The story—real or imaginary—of Robin Hood and His Merry Men has inspired many screen adaptations, starting with an early silent film starring Douglas Fairbanks, all the way to the (eeech!) politically correct television series currently underway as these lines are being written. Likewise, each version resulted in new musical takes from composers inspired by the tale, and perhaps secretly hoping to emulate Erich Wolfgang Korngold's trend-setting score for the Errol Flynn version, *The Adventures of Robin Hood,* the definite model against which all others have to measure up.

Starring Patrick Bergin as the legendary outlaw and Uma Thurman as Maid Marian, this remake offers little that is new and is steadfast in its conventional narrative. Equally safe in its expression is Geoffrey Burgon's score, appropriately heroic and romantic, as the multi-tiered action dictated, but ultimately more descriptive than melodic, with a lot of kettle drumming punctuating the themes spelled out by the woodwind and brass instruments. It sounds grand and epic, but a trifle dull.

Didier C. Deutsch

Robin Hood: Men in Tights

1993, Milan Records, from the film *Robin Hood: Men in Tights,* TriStar Films, 1993 𝄪𝄪𝄪𝄪

album notes: Music: Hummie Mann.

There is no way one could mistake this often hilarious sendup of the Robin Hood legend with the real thing. After having merrily mistreated westerns, horror films, and space epics, it somehow made sense than funnyman Mel Brooks would set his sight on swashbucklers. And which story better to spoof than Robin Hood, the swashbuckler *par excellence.* Naysayers might frown at the mere idea that the hero of so many medieval deeds might be re-

duced to a cartoon character, but as Brooks not so subtly hints, "the legend had it coming." Matching the verve in the film, Hummie Mann wrote a score with its tongue firmly in cheek that brims with good melodic material. If at times the music sounds appropriately medieval, with occasional forays into bombastic posturing or romantic sidesteps, funny ideas (like using an epic version of "Row, Row the Boat" in "Escape from Kahlil Prison," or indulging in not one but two rap songs, performed by Robin's Merry Men Singers) leave little doubt about Brooks's intentions. Ultimately, the film might not have been as successful as some of the director's earlier sendups. But this score is a gas.

Didier C. Deutsch

Robin Hood: Prince of Thieves

1991, Morgan Creek Records, from the film *Robin Hood: Prince of Thieves,* Warner Bros., 1991 𝄪𝄪𝄪

album notes: Music: Michael Kamen; Orchestra: The Greater Los Angeles Orchestra; Conductor: Michael Kamen.

Pretty much all anybody remembers about this movie and soundtrack album is the Bryan Adams ballad "Anything I Do (I'd

Do It for You),” which has certainly transcended the bloated Kevin Costner version of the Robin Hood myth it originates from. Adams wrote the mega-successful song with R.J. “Mutt” Lange and Michael Kamen, who also composed—with a number of orchestrators due to a massive shortage of time—the film’s original score. Unfortunately, despite a magnificent opening theme and a rousing climax, Kamen’s score rarely comes close to Korngoldian heights. Too much of the score listlessly punctuates the action on-screen, never really finding any central focus aside from the main fanfare, and certainly underwhelms during the romantic passages, with a low-key tinkering of the song motive barely qualifying as being anything more than functional to the proceedings. Kamen delivered a far more effective score in a similar vein for *The Three Musketeers* remake just a short time later.

Andy Dursin

RoboCop

🎬 1987, Varèse Sarabande, from the film *RoboCop*, Orion Pictures, 1987 *♫♫♫♫*

album notes: Music: Basil Poledouris; **Orchestra:** The Sinfonia of London Orchestra; **Conductor:** Howard Blake, Tony Britton.

Like Steven Spielberg’s *Jaws,* Paul Verhoven’s excellent, original *RoboCop* has been sullied by two gratuitous sequels that diluted the brilliant high concept of the first film. Basil Poledouris’s original *RoboCop* score features a bombastic, near-satirical heroic theme for the RoboCop character that only needs some booming lyrics to push it right over the top. But the rest of his score perfectly captures the affecting, emotional resonance that is at the heart of the film’s stealth appeal. Despite, or perhaps because of his eviscerated humanity, RoboCop is a rare action hero you could actually care about. Poledouris movingly scored the character’s death and his haunting attempts to rediscover his identity, and rousingly underscored action scenes in which the character, wittingly or unwittingly, lashed out at the villains who’d robbed him of his humanity, in cues like “Rock Shop” and “Showdown.”

Jeff Bond

RoboCop 2

🎬 1990, Varèse Sarabande, from the film *RoboCop 2*, Orion Pictures, 1990 *♫♫♫♡*

album notes: Music: Leonard Rosenman; **Conductor:** Leonard Rosenman.

Leonard Rosenman’s score to the Irvin Kirshner-directed follow-up is marked by the composer’s unmistakable modernistic style, but while Rosenman’s score is far more intellectually sophisticated it doesn’t capture the emotional punch of Poledouris’s original.

Jeff Bond

RoboCop 3

🎬 1993, Varèse Sarabande, from the film *RoboCop 3*, Orion Pictures, 1993 *♫♫♫*

album notes: Music: Basil Poledouris; **Conductor:** Basil Poledouris.

By the time *RoboCop 3* rolled around, the main character had been completely juvenilized (as well as portrayed by another, less-effective actor), and Poledouris’s score is a by-the-numbers affair that resurrects the material, but not the passion of the original.

Jeff Bond

Robotjox

🎬 1997, Prometheus/Belgium, from the film *Robotjox*, Empire, 1989 *♫♫♫♫*

album notes: Music: Frederic Talgorn; **Orchestra:** The Paris Philharmonic Orchestra; **Conductor:** Frederic Talgorn.

Frederic Talgorn leading the Paris Philharmonic Orchestra strikes a felicitous note with this energetic score, written for a film about two post-nuclear holocaust warriors battling each other in their gigantic mechanical robots. With the impressive, larger-than-life music informing each moment in this action-filled futuristic swashbuckler, Talgorn had a field day creating cues on a broad canvas which enabled him to be grandiloquent and colorfully inventive all at once. Cues like “Crash and Burn/Achilles vs. Alexander,” which finds the warriors confronting each other, or “Fanfares for Athena/The Jock Strap Bar,” reveal a composer with a quirky mind and a good sense of the epic. That his score never falls in the more mundane aspects of the genre, and always manages to stay above the most obvious clichés is a real credit to his talent as a scorer. Besides, it makes for fun musical entertainment.

Didier C. Deutsch

The Rock

🎬 1996, Hollywood Records, from the film *The Rock,* Hollywood Pictures, 1996 *♫♫♡*

album notes: Music: Nick Glennie-Smith, Hans Zimmer, Harry Gregson-Williams; **Conductor:** Nick Glennie-Smith, Bruce Fowler, Don Harper; **Featured Musicians:** Bob Daspit, guitar; Michael Thomson, guitar; Michael Stevens, guitar.

The music for Michael Bay’s hyperventilating team-up of Nicholas Cage and Sean Connery typifies the action film scoring sensibility cultivated by mega-producer Jerry Bruckheimer: tons of percussion, both acoustic and synthesized; streaming bursts of synthetic chords; pulsating rhythms; and wailing electric guitars, all custom-designed not so much to engage the viewers within the movie’s storyline as to convince them that they’re watching the “coolest” piece of cinematic merchandise currently available and are thus incredibly cool themselves. Some of the rhythms are infectious, but the overall approach here is indistinguishable from that obtained in most beer commercials of the '80s. It's all part of the headache-inducing overkill that values adrenaline (if not pure testosterone) above anything else, and while scores like this may provide the same thrill ride as the films to which they're attached, the thrill is a transitory one that is going to date these efforts brutally.

Jeff Bond

Rockers

1979, Mango Records, from the film *Rockers*, Island Pictures, 1979 ♪♪♪♪

The wonderful soundtrack to *The Harder They Come* kind of ruined it for most reggae film music, but this still deserves propers as a fine collection of both artists and tunes. Many of the giants of contemporary reggae are here: Peter Tosh, Bunny Wailer, Burning Spear, and Third World. But *Rockers* also provides an opportunity to hear some lesser-known talents, such as Inner Circle, Kiddus I, and Junior Murvin.

Gary Graff

The Rocketeer

1991, Hollywood Records, from the film *The Rocketeer*, Walt Disney Pictures, 1991 ♪♪♪♥

album notes: Music: James Horner; Conductor: James Horner.

James Horner's enthusiastic score is much better than this tepid actioner about the comic strip hero that inspired it. With the music firmly planted into the film's period, the 1930s, Horner has integrated some original big band numbers to his cues, writing a score that often bounces and throbs, and provides the listener with an enjoyable ride (or flight, as it were). The addition of two vocals (including Cole Porter's nifty "Begin the Beguine") performed in breathless fashion by Melora Hardin, further conjure up the era and prove equally pleasurable.

Didier C. Deutsch

Rocky

1995, EMI-America Records, from the film *Rocky*, United Artists, 1976 ♪♪♪♪♪

album notes: Music: Bill Conti; Conductor: Bill Conti.

Few film scores have reached the level of popularity in American culture as Bill Conti's Oscar-winning, instantly recognizable themes for the *Rocky* series. The original 1976 soundtrack contained the chart-topping hit "Gonna Fly Now," which continues to this day to be performed at all sorts of sporting events and other functions as a fanfare for hard work, determination, and fulfilling one's dreams. The vocal, performed by DeEtta Little

and Nelson Pigford, was written by the composer, and remains permanently instilled in the minds of anyone who has seen the movie or heard the music. Along with the street-sounding harmonies of Valentine's "Take You Back," the rest of Conti's score is similarly energetic, propulsive, and filled with emotion, a trait that would come to mark many of the composer's works.

Andy Dursin

Rocky II

1995, EMI-America Records, from the film *Rocky II*, United Artists, 1979 ♪♪♪♪

album notes: Music: Bill Conti; Conductor: Bill Conti; Featured Musicians: Mike Lang, keyboards; Steve Schaeffer, drums; Chuck Berghofer, bass; Dennis Budimer, guitar; Bob Zimmitti, percussion.

For *Rocky II,* the stylistic influence shifts from the often gritty, raw sound of the original film to a more disco-oriented approach, which doesn't benefit a children's chorus version of "Gonna Fly Now" (heard in a different version in the film), though Conti did compose a completely orchestral cue ("Conquest") and other impressive new material that is not as dated, and just as thematically strong as anything in the original film.

Andy Dursin

Rocky III

1995, EMI-America Records, from the film *Rocky III*, United Artists, 1982 ♪♪♪

album notes: Music: Bill Conti; Conductor: Bill Conti.

In *Rocky III,* the big new addition is another hugely popular song, Survivor's "Eye of the Tiger," which is contained on what's basically a compilation album with three new Conti cues, several Frank Stallone vocals, and tracks taken from the preceding *Rocky* soundtracks. Seeing that there are a number of Rocky compilations available, your best bet is to pick up one of those CDs and either or both of Conti's first two efforts in the series, which contain some of the most memorable film music ever written.

Andy Dursin

The Rocky Horror Picture Show

1975, Ode Records, from the film *The Rocky Horror Picture Show,* 1975 ♪♪♪

album notes: Music: Richard O'Brien; Lyrics: Richard O'Brien; Musical Direction: Richard Hartley; Featured Musicians: Count Ian Blair, guitars; David Wintour, bass guitar; Phil Kenzie, saxophone; Rabbit, keyboards; Richard Hartley, keyboards; Cast: Tim Curry, Susan Sarandon, Barry Bostwick, Richard O'Brien, Patricia Quinn, Little Nell, Meatloaf.

A cult favorite, *The Rocky Horror Show* took its cue from the classic horror films of the 1950s, introduced in its story elements of transvestitism, spruced up the proceedings with a rock score, and set out to conquer the theatrical world. First performed in London,

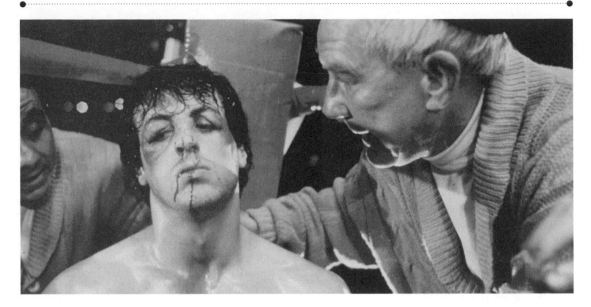

Sylvester Stallone and Burgess Meredith in Rocky. **(The Kobal Collection)**

where it opened in June, 1973, it moved to Los Angeles, where it played various venues, including the Roxy, and made a belated debut on Broadway on March 10, 1975, closing 45 performances later. One might have thought that this would mark the end of the saga, but that same year, the show was made into a film, *The Rocky Horror Picture Show,* which has enjoyed incredible longevity throughout the years, particularly as a camp fixture among aficionados who faithfully attend regular midnight presentations to recite the dialogue along with the actors on screen. Starring Tim Curry as the cross–dressing Frank N Furter, and Barry Bostwick and Susan Sarandon as the lovers, the soundtrack album, released under various guises over the years, including an audience-participation version, is a hoot and a holler. Rocker Meatloaf (of "Bat Out of Hell" fame) also makes an appearance, as he did on stage.

Didier C. Deutsch

Romeo and Juliet

1989, Capitol Records, from the film *Romeo and Juliet,* Paramount Pictures, 1968 𝄞𝄞𝄞𝄞

album notes: Music: Nino Rota; **Conductor:** Nino Rota; **Cast:** Leonard Whiting (Romeo), Olivia Hussey (Juliet).

Rota's approach to the Franco Zeffirelli film is pretty much straight forward and academic, with the music used to subtly underscore the emotions in the Shakespearean drama. Adding more impact to the proceedings, the soundtrack also features

the dialogues and sound effects for most important scenes, giving an overall sonic impression that pretty much reflects the film itself. And in case you might wonder what other treatment the story might have led to, see also *West Side Story,* possibly the most successful adaptation of Shakespeare's drama, set against the background of modern-day New York City.

Didier C. Deutsch

Romeo+Juliet

1996, Capitol Records, from the film *Romeo+Juliet,* 20th Century Fox, 1996 𝄞𝄞𝄞𝄬

Romeo+Juliet is a contemporary take-off on the classic story (with Leonardo DiCaprio and Claire Danes keeping the 16th-century language intact) that seemingly asks the question "what kind of music would Romeo and Juliet listen to if they had lived today?" Some of the music works very well and has a definite appeal; some of the tracks, however, sound redundant and ill-chosen, at least for a straight listening experience. Some of the acts that make an appearance are Everclear, Garbage, the Cardigans, and the Butthole Surfers. And in case you might wonder what other treatment the story might have led to, see also *West Side Story,* possibly the most successful adaptation of Shakespeare's drama, set against the background of modern-day New York City.

Didier C. Deutsch

Romeo+Juliet: Volume 2

1997, Capitol Records, from the film *William Shakespeare's Romeo+Juliet,* 20th Century-Fox, 1996 🎬🎬

album notes: Music: Craig Armstrong, Marius DeVries, Nellee Hooper; Conductor: Craig Armstrong.

Diehard fanatics of the movie are the obvious targets for this sequel soundtrack album to the 1996 mega-hit version of Shakespeare's timeless story of star-crossed lovers. Most of the album consists of the original score by Craig Armstong, Marius De Vries, and Nellee Hooper, and dialogue from the movie. There are some very interesting uses of samples integrated in the score by the likes of Radiohead, Desree, and the Butthole Surfers. The soulful cover of the Artist Formerly Known as Prince's "When Doves Cry" by Quindon Tarver is also included here, as well as "Tybalt Arrives," a score cue notable for featuring high-profile record producers/musicians the Dust Brothers and cult group Butthole Surfers.

Amy Rosen

Romeo Is Bleeding

1994, Verve Records, from the film *Romeo Is Bleeding,* Gramercy Pictures, 1994 🎬🎬🎬

album notes: Music: Mark Isham; Featured Musicians: Mark Isham, trumpet, flugelhorn, electronics; David Goldblatt, piano; Chuck Domanico, acoustic bass; Kurt Wortman, drums.

Mark Isham's strongly accented jazz score comes across full force in this recording in which, away from the screen action, the cues have time to make their impression. The film, a comic-book account of a corrupt New York police officer who gets involved with a Russian mafiosa and pays dearly for it, needed a forceful musical statement to give it the right flavor. Isham created a series of cues that capture the essence of the story, and add to it with great skill, in cues that display the right amount of the type of jazz one usually associates with this kind of drama. As a result, the album is highly enjoyable on its own terms and is further enhanced by a couple of well-chosen vocals, including a sensational rendition of "Bird Alone," performed by Abbey Lincoln.

Didier C. Deutsch

Romy and Michele's High School Reunion

1997, Hollywood Records, from the film *Romy and Michele's High School Reunion,* Touchstone Pictures, 1997 🎬🎬🎬

A winning, if somewhat insignificant, comedy about two attractive dimwits on their way to a high school reunion, who decide to try and impress their former schoolmates by pretending that they have become rich and successful, *Romy and Michele's High School Reunion* boasts a sparkling soundtrack consisting of popular songs by the Go-Go's, Wang Chung, Culture Club, Bow Wow, and the Smithereens, among others. There is little that's exceptional about this compilation, just a good collection that happens to work well in the context of the film and for one's listening pleasure.

Didier C. Deutsch

Ronin

1998, Varèse-Sarabande, from the film *Ronin,* United Artists, 1998 🎬🎬🎬

album notes: Music: Elia Cmiral; Conductor: Nick Ingman.

A synthesizer riff that ascends to a crashing crescendo in the first bars of the "Ronin Theme" seems to presage a run-of-the-mill score, a notion quickly dispelled by the ensuing theme and following cues that are surprisingly melodious. Written for an action thriller set for the most part in France, *Ronin* shows off a relative newcomer who displays great talent and is bound to leave his mark in a field that is getting quite crowded. The film, directed by John Frankenheimer, stars Robert De Niro and Jean Reno as two members of a five-man team hired to retrieve from its current owner an important suitcase, the contents of which is never disclosed (the title refers to a Japanese legend of 47 samurai, who roamed the countryside as free agents following the death of their leader). Punctuating the fast-paced action, Cmiral devised cues that are full of energy and excitement, and closely follow the events unspooling on screen ("The Getaway," "Taking Photos," "Gunfight at the Amphitheater"), with only an occasional brief respite ("Thank You," "Passion") setting off the action cues. With exotic elements that at times recall Slavic music, the score proves entertaining and quite attractive for the most part.

Didier C. Deutsch

Room at the Top

See: The Barefoot Contessa/Room at the Top

A Room with a View

1986, DRG Records, from the film *A Room with a View,* Cinecom/ Merchant Ivory Productions, 1986 🎬🎬🎬🎬

album notes: Music: Richard Robbins.

In much the same way that *Elvira Madigan* was defined by Mozart's Piano Concerto in C, Puccini's "O mio babbino caro" gave *A Room with a View* a definite cachet, and permeated this sensitive romantic comedy of manners, set in 1907 and based on E. M. Forster's classic novel about a young English couple who meet in Italy and, despite their social differences and the Victorian convictions of their elders, dare to be true to their feelings and each other. The Italian and English settings, and the turn-of-the-century time frame provided the pegs for Richard Robbins's score, a collection of sprightly musical tunes that depict the various incidents in the screenplay, augmenting the action with their subtle melodic contributions, and making an otherwise arresting statement. Overflowing with great romantic themes, occasionally sprinkled with the witty addition of a mandolin or a lovely call of bells, the score unfolds with magic splendor, revealing its many charms in cues that are programmed to be equally effective on their own.

Didier C. Deutsch

Roommates

1995, Hollywood Records, from the film *Roommates*, Hollywood Pictures, 1995 ♫♫♪

album notes: Music: Elmer Bernstein; **Featured Musician:** Cynthia Millar, Ondes Martenot; **Conductor:** Elmer Bernstein.

The first hour of this Peter Yates film starring Peter Falk and D.B. Sweeney is filled with clichés, playing out very much like a theatrical sitcom. For whatever reason, the movie surprisingly turns itself around in the second half into a genuinely affecting, poignant family drama with terrific performances by the two leads. Elmer Bernstein scored the picture, but despite some fine moments, his music doesn't lend itself easily to working as a soundtrack album. Many of the cues are very short (most are under a minute, in fact), which doesn't allow for the composer to develop thematic material. The music is perfect in the movie, but this is unfortunately one of those cases where the album format doesn't add much to the film score.

Andy Dursin

Roots

1998, A&M Records, from the television presentation, *Roots*, David L. Wolper, 1977 ♫♫♫♫

album notes: Music: Quincy Jones; **Conductor:** Quincy Jones; **Featured Musicians:** Bill Summers, Zak Diouf, Paul Bryant, King Errison, Bobbye Hall, Emil Richards, Tommy Vig, Milt Holland, Shelly Manne, Vic Feldman, Caiphus Semenya, percussion; Dave Grusin, Mike Boddicker, Ian Underwood, Richard Tee, Pete Jolly, keyboards; Lee Ritenour, David T. Walker, guitars; Chuck Rainey, Ed Reddick, electric bass; Arni Egillson, Milt Kestenbaum, acoustic bass; Alton Hendrickson, banjo; **Featured Vocalists:** Letta Mbulu, Caiphus Semenya, the Wattsline Choir, Jim Gilstrap, Stephanie Spruill, Paulette Williams, Deborah Tibbs, Alexandra Brown, John Lehman, Linda Evans, Zak Diouf, Alex Hassiley.

When it was first televised in 1977, the saga of Kunta Kinte and how he came to become a slave in America kept the nation riveted for several nights and went on to win several Emmys for excellence. Among the many factors that contributed to the success of the series and its broad popular appeal was the score devised by Quincy Jones, a subtle blend of African

rhythms and American themes that added to the feel of authenticity and provided a musical imagery people could identify with. Four days after it entered the charts, the soundtrack album went gold. Today, it continues to impress for the sheer diversity of its sounds and songs. Split between two sets of cues, each following a given stage in the saga of the main character—the African portion, identified as "The Motherland," and the American one, known as "The Promised Land"—it is a remarkable achievement from a composer who has never been afraid to tackle large projects and has always succeeded in pulling them off with great panache.

see also: The Color Purple, The Wiz

Didier C. Deutsch

The Rosary Murders

1986, Cinedisc Records, from the film *The Rosary Murders*, New Line Cinema, 1986 ♫♫♪

album notes: Music: Bobby Laurel, Don Sebesky; **Orchestra:** The London Royal Philharmonic Orchestra; **Conductor:** Don Sebesky.

Nancy Wood's strained rendition of the main title, "In Your Eyes," in a style that desperately tries not to evoke Barbra Streisand, is hardly conducive to open up to this album. Fortunately, Don Sebesky's score is forcefully interesting and compelling, and attracts the attention with its skillfull display of cues outlining some of the most intense moments in this flavorful thriller about a killer in Detroit whose actions show he or she has a grudge against representatives of the Catholic Church, who is hunted down by a priest-turned-sleuth. As befits the genre, the various cues actually belie the tension, focusing instead on the more subliminous threatening aspects of the murder mystery. A chorus in the background occasionally provides sounds that evoke the more religious aspects of the story.

Didier C. Deutsch

The Rose Tattoo

1998, PEG Recordings, from the film *The Rose Tattoo*, Paramount, 1955 ♫♫♪

album notes: Music: Alex North; **Orchestra:** The Paramount Studio Orchestra; **Conductor:** Alex North.

Though made in the U.S. and directed by Daniel Mann, *The Rose Tattoo*, written by Tennessee Williams, was a close cousin of the neo-realistic films made in Italy at the time by Vittorio de Sica and Roberto Rossellini, in that it portrayed common people in complex situations. Of course, the presence of Anna Magnani added to the illusion, with Burt Lancaster playing a village idiot in this naturalistic drama set among Italians in bayou country. Displaying an animalistic drive that seemed alien in an American film, la Magnani portrayed a widow forever cherishing the memory of her dead husband, until she discovered he also kept a floozie on the side. Lancaster didn't seem too Italian in this context, nor did the score composed by Alex North, which was much too controlled to match the histrionics on screen.

Didier C. Deutsch

Rosewood

 1997, Sony Classical, from the film *Rosewood,* Warner Bros., 1997 🎵🎵🎵🎵

album notes: Music: John Williams; **Conductor:** John Williams; **Featured Soloists:** Shirley Caesar, vocals; Dean Parks, guitar; Tommy Morgan, harmonica.

Proof that John Williams can write memorable music for virtually any kind of film is fully evident in *Rosewood,* John Singleton's mostly fictitious dramatization of the real-life tragedy that was heavily criticized by some for its traditional western story elements. There's nothing formulaic in any regard, however, about Williams's complex, haunting score, which finds dissonant guitar-and-piano motives combined with elegiac string writing, creating a powerful collection of cues whose contrasting uplift is found in a pair of spirituals ("Look Down, Lord," "Light My Way"), also written by the composer. The country-flavored instrumentation recalls Williams's past successes on *The Missouri Breaks* and even *The Reivers,* though this score has a strong dramatic tone all its own, characterized by standout work from guitarist Dean Parks and harmonica soloist Tommy Morgan. A different kind of score from a composer who continues to surprise us all with his sense of dramatic film scoring, one that consistently translates into great stand-alone music in the process.

Andy Dursin

Rough Riders

1997, Intrada Records, from the television film *Rough Riders,* Turner, 1997 🎵🎵🎵🎵

album notes: Music: Peter Bernstein; **Conductor:** Peter Bernstein.

Theodore Roosevelt would have loved this score, and so should anyone with a fondness for Elmer Bernstein's music. Even if it was not composed by him, but by his son, Peter, the influence is unmistakable and reminiscent of Elmer's style. A TNT original retracing the emergence of the country as a world power, as seen through the Spanish American War and the Rough Riders who fought in it, it centered most specifically on the individuals in G Troop whose deeds the film chronicled. Writing a western score "without revisiting old musical ground," as Peter explains in his notes, was the challenge for

him. The fact is, he didn't entirely escape the difficulties of moving away from natural influences, and the presence of Elmer as the conductor only helps reinforce the impression that there is indeed a strong musical kinship between father and son. The trademark staccatos in the western scores of Bernstein *pere* get a familiar echo in the music of Bernstein *fils,* but who's to complain. Even though we are in family (and familiar) territory, the feeling is quite comfortable, and Peter Bernstein's music becomes in fact all the more enjoyable. Teeming with great themes that paint a colorful story, *Rough Riders* certainly qualifies as a quality score.

Didier C. Deutsch

'Round Midnight/The Other Side of 'Round Midnight

'Round Midnight: 1986, Columbia Records, from the film *'Round Midnight,* Warner Bros., 1986 🎵🎵🎵🎵🎵

The Other Side of 'Round Midnight: 1998, Columbia Records, from the film *'Round Midnight,* Warner Bros., 1986 🎵🎵🎵

album notes: Featured Musicians: Dexter Gordon, tenor sax; Herbie Hancock, piano; Ron Carter, bass; Pierre Michelot, bass; Tony Williams, drums; Billy Higgins, drums; John McLaughlin, guitar; Bobby Hutcherson, vibes; Wayne Shorter, tenor/ soprano sax.

A rare glance at a jazz artist, an American expatriate living in Paris in the 1950s, *'Round Midnight* was director Bertrand Tavernier's moving tribute to a form of music that had marked his youth, and the many brilliant exponents, many of them black musicians, who had brought it to France after World War II. The film, which was dedicated to Bud Powell and Lester Young, both of whom inspired the central character in the film, starred Dexter Gordon, whose slurred speech and uneasy way in front of the camera, made his performance all the more realistic and natural. Shot almost entirely in France (only a few scenes toward the end took place in New York), the film focused on the life of the expatriate musician, his friendship with a young French admirer, and the gigs he played at Paris' famed jazz club, Le Blue Note, on a back street near the Champs-Elysees.

Also starring jazz regulars Herbie Hancock, who wrote the original music and acted as music consultant; Ron Carter on bass; Tony Williams on drums; and Wayne Shorter on tenor sax, the film was a vibrant homage to a music seldom appreciated in this country, but much enjoyed in France. The soundtrack album, with performances by the above, and guest appearances by Bobby McFerrin, Chet Baker, and Lonette McKee (who also was in the film), is just great.

A companion to the Columbia release, *The Other Side . . .* is free-blowing jazz, out of context (it is way too modern to evoke a '50s club image), but superbly performed by some of the greats: Dexter Gordon, Herbie Hancock, Wayne Shorter, Freddie Hubbard, John McLaughlin, Ron Carter, and Tony Williams. This is a straight jazz record, recorded "live" on the soundstage. It is sophisticated "source" music, because the music is the picture, the musicians were recorded as the cameras were rolling. This is almost unheard of in film, where the spontaneous creation of jazz musicians is seldom captured on film and used relatively unedited. The individual performances are uneven, and even unfocused at times. The 'superstar' line-up can be exciting or moribund, and many of these performances lack a burning edge. "What Is This Thing Called Love?" is one notch above a performance at a wedding. Gordon's soprano is warm and inviting on "Tivoli," and Hubbard heats things up on "Society Red." All in all, it's just OK.

Bob Belden

Rounders

1998, Varèse-Sarabande, from the film *Rounders*, Miramax, 1998 ♪♪♪

album notes: Music: Christopher Young.

Matt Damon stars in this suspenseful drama about a law student who moonlights as a professional poker player in New York's seedy, subterranean gambling dens. Composer Christopher Young's jazzy score is a good match, evoking the smoky backrooms and dimly lit alleys. The jazz sections are a groovy, funky mix of strutting bass, Hammond organ, and Blaxploitation licks. Unfortunately the poor sound is particularly apparent in the orchestral sections, notably the hiss on the solo piano cue "Lady in Black" and the placement of the stereo mic left too close to the cymbals throughout, creating a steady rustling shimmer. Only when the jazz combo's rhythm section are truly flying, as on "Brass Brazilians," "Pasadena," and "Alligator Blood" does the music transcend the poor sound. Young draws from film noir, jazz, and funk records of the '70s, and brooding orchestral scores for a pleasing balance between the intimacy of his upbeat, funky jazz and the expansiveness in the underscore. It's a shame that more attention wasn't paid to the sound, as *Rounders* puts a dent in a long, near impeccable string of Young's film music.

David Poole

Roxanne

1987, Cinedisc Records, from the film *Roxanne,* Columbia Pictures, 1987 ♪♪♪♪

album notes: Music: Bruce Smeaton.

It might have made sense to turn Edmond Rostand's stageplay about *Cyrano de Bergerac* into a modern-day fantasy starring Steve Martin as the long-nosed fellow, hopelessly in love with Roxanne, played by the delightful Daryl Hannah. The problem is that Cyrano's dilemma about his proboscis in this tepid adaptation could have been fixed in no time with plastic surgery, thereby spoiling the film from its much needed novel approach.

But Bruce Smeaton's clever, if at times slightly hackneyed score not only fit the bill handsomely, it also made for pleasant if unobtrusive background musical enjoyment, smartly captured in this soundtrack album.

Didier C. Deutsch

Royal Wedding

1991, Sony Music Special Products, from the film *Royal Wedding*, MGM, 1951 ♪♪♪♪

album notes: Music: Burton Lane; **Lyrics:** Alan Jay Lerner; **Choir:** The MGM Studio Chorus; **Orchestra:** The MGM Studio Orchestra; **Conductor:** Johnny Green; **Cast:** Fred Astaire, Jane Powell.

The 1947 marriage of Princess Elizabeth and Philip Mountbatten, and the pomp and circumstance that framed the event, suggested to MGM producer Arthur Freed the idea for a big screen musical. With Fred Astaire set to star, Alan Jay Lerner provided a script that paralleled Astaire's own life when he and his sister, Adele, broke up their successful Broadway song-and-dance act so that she could marry a British lord. With Burton Lane writing the music to Lerner's playful lyrics, the score added the final touch to what became a regal entertainment. Jane Powell co-starred as Ellen Bowen, who fell in love with Peter Lawford while on a transatlantic trip to London, thereby setting the stage for the end of her professional career with brother Tom, whose own interest was piqued by Sarah Churchill, real-life daughter of Sir Winston. In addition to its delightfully romantic plot, and many great songs, *Royal Wedding* is also remembered today as the film in which Fred Astaire, in a feat of technical fancy, dances exhilaratingly on the walls and ceiling of a room.

Didier C. Deutsch

Ruby

1992, Intrada Records, from the film *Ruby*, PolyGram/Triump, 1992 ♪♪♪♪

album notes: Music: John Scott; **Conductor:** John Scott.

For this Jack Ruby docudrama, John Scott contrasts a small jazz ensemble with a lovely symphonic melody which captures a contradictory innocence that belies the message of the film. His main theme is grandly symphonic, almost majestic, its sense of joy and innocence becomes a counterpoint to the darker, conspiratorial tonality of the film. As it develops, the main theme is often overwhelmed by the dark jazz figures, as

Scott musically delineated the innocence of Jack Ruby as it is tantalized, tempted and finally overwhelmed by the thrust of irreversible circumstances into which he allows himself to become immersed. With its mixture of jazz and symphonic orchestral colorations, and its brilliant contrast of melody with rhythm, innocence with evil, control with irrevocable destiny, *Ruby* is one of Scott's best scores.

Randall D. Larson

Rudy

1993, Varèse Sarabande, from the film *Rudy*, Tri-Star Pictures, 1993 ♫♫♫

album notes: Music: Jerry Goldsmith; **Conductor:** Jerry Goldsmith.

This extremely popular Jerry Goldsmith effort for the true story of a lad who dreams of playing football at Notre Dame works as a more acoustic follow-up to his Oscar-nominated *Hoosiers* score, full of rah-rah inspiration that also conjures up memories of Goldsmith's *Patton*. The score opens with a beautiful, plaintive tune based on an old Irish ballad, richly played by the orchestra, while later cues develop a delicate piano motif until some hard-charging inspirational music heralds Rudy's participation in team practices and eventually in a real game. You can't help but get caught up in the optimism and warmth of this score, but at the same time there's a repetitiveness, a sameness in the tempos and a lack of Goldsmith's complex development that may be off-putting to fans of the composer's earlier, more hard-edged style.

Jeff Bond

The Rugrats Movie

1998, Interscope Records, from the film *The Rugrats Movie*, Paramount, 1998 ♫♫♫

album notes: Music: Mark Mothersbaugh.

For a minute, it looked like this soundtrack to the movie drawn from Nickelodeon's popular animated series would be a major event, with a stellar lineup of contributors such as David Bowie, Lenny Kravitz, Beck, Jakob Dylan, the B-52's, Iggy Pop, Patti Smith, Laurie Anderson, and others being thrown around. Well, Bowie never made it, and the rest are all jammed into one song—"This World Is Something New to Me," a charming fly-by that finds a bunch of newborns in a hospital nursery debating the virtues of the womb vs. the real world. That rends the rest of *Rugrats* a modest collection of tunes from an assortment of pop and hip-hop acts, plus cast members who contribute numbers such as "Dil-a-Bye," "A Baby Is a Gift from a Bob" and an eminently skipable—even for kids—revision of Blondie's "One Way or Another." But Blackstreet and Mya score with the open-

10 Essential Scores
by Danny Elfman

Beetlejuice
Batman
Pee Wee's Big Adventure
Dick Tracy
Edward Scissorhands
Black Beauty
Good Will Hunting
Men in Black
Mars Attacks!
The Nightmare Before Christmas

ing theme, "Take Me There," and Elvis Costello teams up with No Doubt on the terrifically understated "I'll Throw My Toys Around."

Gary Graff

Runaway

1987, Varèse Sarabande, from the film *Runaway*, Tri-Star Pictures, 1985 ♫♫

album notes: Music: Jerry Goldsmith.

Jerry Goldsmith's first all-electronic score is an abrasive, metallic effort for Michael Crichton's silly near-future thriller about a kind of SWAT team for malfunctioning robots. Much of the music achieves an almost acoustic quality as Goldsmith, with the assistance of son Joel, blends layers of synthetic textures and repeating electronic figures. Particularly effective is a barbaric moment of solo percussion in the suspenseful (and idiotically named) "Sushi Switch." And Goldsmith brings the same rhythmic intensity to the cacophonous chase cues "Alley Flight" and

"Lockons" that he does to his orchestral scores. But the constant presence of pounding drum machines and the harsh overall sound is bound to be off-putting to fans of the composer's earlier works. Still, this difficult-to-find album has some collector's value.

Jeff Bond

Runaway Bride

1999, Columbia Records from the Paramount film, *Runaway Bride*, 1999 ♫♫♫♫

As befits a screwball comedy (and the latest summer hit), the moods in this soundtrack album are kept light and bubbly. The line-up of talent is quite impressive, with U2, Hall & Oates, Billy Joel, Eric Clapton, Kenny Loggins, and Dixie Chicks among the performers heard here. Smartly the songs have been chosen to underline specific moments in the action, in which a young woman constantly shirks getting married, leaving her future husbands cold in front of the altar just before the ceremony is set to start. Taken on its own musical terms, this is a song compilation that works very nicely, with several highlights ("I Still Haven't Found What I'm Looking For," "I Love You," "You Can't Hurry Love," "Once In A Lifetime," "Where Were You") that invite repeated listening.

Didier C. Deutsch

Runaway Train

1986, Milan Records, from the film *Runaway Train,* Cannon Films, 1986 ♫♫♫♫

album notes: Music: Trevor Jones; **Featured Musicians:** Dave Lawson, keyboards; Brian Gascoigne, keyboards; Simon Lloyd, keyboards; Ray Russell, guitar; Harold Fisher, drums; Paul Hirsh, shakuhachi; Catherine Bott, vocals.

Andrei Konchalovsky's gripping rail drama, starring Jon Voight, Eric Roberts, and Rebecca de Mornay, and based on a screenplay by Akira Kurosawa, elicited a taut score from composer Trevor Jones, solidly rooted in contemporary sounds. Following a prison escape, two convicts find themselves unwilling passengers on board an out-of-control train in the Alaskan wild in this fast-paced film, as exciting as it is well-sketched. Jones's score subtly underlines the action without overstretching the point, in cues that are particularly effective on the screen and are equally well defined on a purely audio level. In a striking counterpoint, Vivaldi's "Gloria in D" provides a welcome change of pace that doesn't detract from the main motifs, yet adds to the overall flavor of the score.

Didier C. Deutsch

The Running Man

1987, Varèse Sarabande, from the film *The Running Man,* Tri-Star Pictures, 1987 ♫♫

album notes: Music: Harold Faltermeyer.

This likable-enough, synthesized action score by Harold Faltermeyer has its moments, but suffers mainly from the fact that many of the themes are never fully developed. Several of the more satisfying tracks are the themes for the *Running Man* TV show's gladiators. "Captain Freedom's Workout" is one of the few that rises above the din of squealing guitar rifts and drum machines Faltermeyer relies on, and it's great for that step aerobic workout, too! However, when Faltermeyer gets down to one of his more interesting cue, "Mick's Broadcast/Attack," he just leaves us hanging by stopping the music cold after an engaging five-minute buildup. That may work great for the film, but not on an album. The first two cues, "Intro/Bakersfield" and "Main Title/ Fight Escape" do not appear in the final film as heard on the album.

David Hirsch

Rush

1992, Reprise Records, from the film *Rush,* MGM, 1992 ♫♫♫♫

album notes: Music: Eric Clapton; **Conductor:** Randy Kerber; **Featured Musicians:** Eric Clapton, guitar, vocals; Randy Kerber, keyboards; Greg Phillinganes, keyboards; Chuck Leavell, piano, organ; Robbie Kondor, synthesizer; Nathan East, bass; Tim Drummond, bass; Steve Ferrone, drums; Lenny Castro, percussion.

Eric Clapton wrote a solidly melodic score for this police drama, set in Texas in the mid-1970s. The story of two agents who go undercover to nab a big-time drug dealer, the film elicited strong performances from Jason Patric and Jennifer Jason Leigh as the two cops, who get increasingly reliant on each other even as they get drawn into the subculture they are supposed to destroy. Clapton provided a strongly blues-based score that added extra weight to the bleaker aspects of the story, and made it even more compelling. Two vocal tracks, "Help Me Up" and "Don't Know Which Way to Go," are particularly gut-wrenching moments, alone worth the price of admission.

Didier C. Deutsch

Rush Hour

1998, Def Jam Records, from the film *Rush Hour,* New Line Cinema, 1998 ♫♫♫♫

The fact that the long-running hip-hop label's name gets billing in front of the movie's title tells you something about the way this soundtrack is approached. It is indeed a promotional vehicle for the label circa 1998, providing showcases for acts such as Slick Rick ("Impress the Kid"), Jay-Z ("Can I Get a . . ."), Wu-Tang Clan ("And You Don't Stop") and Terror Squad ("Terror Squadians"). But what hip-hop soundtracks do so well is generate collaborations, and *Rush Hour* has its share of compelling team-ups, such as Dru Hill and Redman on "How Deep Is Your Love?" and Montell Jordan working out with Monifah and Flesh-n-Bone on "If I Die Tonight." A typically dramatic title theme by Lalo Schifrin and snippets of Chris Tucker and Jackie Chan's rapid-fire schtick from the film are bonuses in what's already a compelling package.

Gary Graff

1998, Aleph Records, from the film *Rush Hour,* New Line Cinema, 1998 ⫸⫸⫸⫸

album notes: Music: Lalo Schifrin; **Conductor:** Lalo Schifrin.

Lalo Schifrin is obviously in his element and at the top of his creative form in this fast-pace actioner in which a typical big, brassy theme is tinged with a pseudo-Chinese accent. It's the signal that Jackie Chan, making his U.S. debut in this film, co-stars in it, along with Chris Tucker as a special agent sent to America to investigate the disappearance of the Chinese consul's daughter. Raucous, rambunctious, loaded with percolating rhythms, the score wastes little time in establishing its dual musical personalities. The themes come up fast and furious, with Schifrin, who seems to have had a lot of fun writing this one, exhibiting a fresh sense of humor in some of the cues ("Lee Arrives in L.A.," "Won Ton for Two"), but keeping track of the fact that this comedy is also a thriller with a lot of action scenes ("Chasing Sang," "Explosive Situation"). In one sense, it is treading new territory, on the other hand it is also firmly on familiar grounds. All in all, it's a lot of fun.

Didier C. Deutsch

Rushmore

1999, London Records, from the film *Rushmore,* Touchstone, 1999 ⫸⫸

album notes: Music: Mark Mothersbaugh; **Featured Musicians:** Mark Mothersbaugh, keyboards, percussion; Robert Casale, keyboards; Bruce Berman, guitar, mandolin; Larry Klimas, flute; Paul Morin, bass; Gordon Peeke, drums, timpani, percussion; Harry Scorzo, violin; Lavant Coppock, guitar; Brian King, glockenspiel; Paul Viapiano, mandolin; Gloria Cheng-Cochran, harpsichord; Melissa Hasin, cello; Arthur Shane, guitar; Judy Gameral, hammer dulcimer.

Wes Anderson's story of a gawky prep school boy and an unhappy millionaire competing for the affections of a lovely young teacher is set in the 1990s, but seems to have a certain timeless quality. You're never really sure what year it is, especially when you hear the rockin'-good, mod soundtrack. Anderson has taken vintage recordings by the likes of the Who, the Kinks, the Faces, and John Lennon, and made them feel 100

percent fresh by using them in a contemporary setting. By reinventing these songs, he has in a way created a wholly different type of soundtrack. The album is highly recommended, especially to fans of the film and everyone who hopes they die before they get old!

Amy Rosen

The Russia House

1990, MCA Records, from the film *The Russia House,* MGM, 1990 ⫸⫸⫸⫸

album notes: Music: Jerry Goldsmith; *Featured Artists:* Branford Marsalis, saxophone; Michael Lang, bass; John Patitucci, bass; **Conductor:** Jerry Goldsmith.

Jerry Goldsmith took the unusual approach of writing a jazz-textured score for this film about espionage filmed in the former Soviet Union, adapting a love theme he originally wrote for the film *Alien Nation* and building some flowing, low-key bass and piano rhythms to underscore the film's suspense scenes. This is also notable as Goldsmith's lone experiment with long album form, with a generous hour of music from his score. But as Goldsmith himself has noted, there's too much music here, in this case because the style he adopted for the picture emphasizes repetition, with only the improvisation of Wynton Marsalis and some other jazz performers to break up the monotony. Nevertheless, the very congruence of style here makes for an unusually smooth, coherent listening experience, entirely lacking in harsh dissonances or violent moments, each piece flowing seamlessly into the next. This may be more appealing to fans of jazz fusion or new age music than Goldsmith fans.

Jeff Bond

Russia's War

1996, Philips Records, from the television series, *Russia's War,* PBS, 1996 ⫸⫸⫸⫸⫸

album notes: Music: Stanislas Syrewicz; **Orchestra:** The State Symphonic Orchestra of Cinematography, Cantus Dei Choir of Moscow, the Red Army Choir, **Conductor:** Sergei Skripka.

A sweeping account of the heroic role the Russians played during World War II, *Russia's War,* a 10-hour PBS special, made little concessions to political considerations, and focused instead on the plight of a courageous people faced with impossible odds—first at the hands of Hitler's armies, then as a result of Stalin's increasing repressions—but surmounting them at great personal sacrifices. Alternately inspiring and devastating, this compelling drama was told through the reminiscences of survivors and using recently found archival material. Keeping a Russian feel to the score, Stanislas Syrewicz wrote a very moving set of cues, in which the addition of traditional songs provided the solid ethnic anchor demanded by the documentary.

An unusual, intense statement laid out in musical terms that make it totally acceptable to any listener, this is a score that many will find mesmerizing and heartfelt. *Blood upon the Snow* is not your standard glossy Hollywood music, but neither was, for that matter, the film that inspired it.

Didier C. Deutsch

Ryan's Daughter

 1991, Sony Music Special Products, from the film *Ryan's Daughter's*, MGM, 1970 ♪♪♪♪

album notes: Music: Maurice Jarre; **Conductor:** Maurice Jarre.

The creative relationship between director David Lean and composer Maurice Jarre found another fertile ground in this intimate love story, set in Ireland in 1916, at a time when Europe was ravaged by "the war to end all wars" and Ireland itself was about to know an equally devastating uprising against the British. Starring Sarah Miles as the young, romantic Rosy Ryan, Robert Mitchum as the stiff schoolmaster she marries, and Christopher Jones as the handsome officer with whom she has an affair, *Ryan's Daughter* gave Maurice Jarre the elements he needed to write an overwhelmingly romantic score, teeming with cues that detail the action and brightly comment on it. Spearheaded by the sweeping main theme that recurs throughout the score, the music also makes allowances for other themes that project different moods, like the brassy march for "The Major," or the liltingly jaunty "Rosy on the Beach." Overflowing with attractive musical ideas, *Ryan's Daughter* is an excellent score that spells its many charms in this CD reissue, augmented with selections from two other Jarre scores, for *The Train* and *Grand Prix*.

Didier C. Deutsch

Sabrina

 1996, A&M Records, from the film *Sabrina*, Paramount, 1996 ♪♪♪♪

album notes: Music: John Williams; **Conductor:** John Williams; **Featured Musician:** Dick Nash, trombone.

This ill-advised remake of the charming 1954 Billy Wilder romantic comedy was a total disaster at the box office, despite the presence of Harrison Ford and Julia Ormond in the roles originally created by Humphrey Bogart and Audrey Hepburn. One of its most positive elements, however, is the delicately overblown score John Williams wrote for it. Introduced by the "Theme from Sabrina," essentially a romantic mini-concerto for piano and or-

chestra, the score reveals great ingenuity and feel for its subject, with the recurring "Moonlight" motif playing an important role in the cues. In one instance ("Sabrina Remembers/ La vie en rose"), Williams lets a theme meld into a well-known song that sets the decor better than anything he himself might have written, and in a long medley ("The Party Sequence") even takes several standards around which to build his cue. It's an interesting, flavorful way to present source material, and much more effective than having a cover version which might break the moods set by the instrumental cues. The only letdown in this otherwise very attractive score is Sting's vocal rendition of "Moonlight," only because the singer tries too hard to sound romantic.

Didier C. Deutsch

Sabrina the Teenage Witch

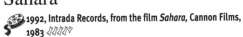 **1998, Geffen Records, from the television series, *Sabrina the Teenage Witch*, Viacom, 1997-1998** ♪♪♪

Capitalize and underline the "Teenage" in the title here; with the exception of Hanson, this set pegged to the popular kids' TV sitcom starring Nickelodeon graduate Melissa Joan Hart hits all the requisite adolescent bases, including teenybop titans such as the Spice Girls ("Walk of Life"), Backstreet Boys ("Hey Mr. DJ [Keep Playin' This Song]"), 'N Sync ("Giddy Up"), and a pre-stardom Britney Spears ("Soda Pop"). There are some cross-generational cool moments as well, such as Sugar Ray's cover of the Steve Miller Band's "Abracadabra," Ben Folds Five's "Kate," a cover of Walter Egan's "Magnet & Steel" by Matthew Sweet (with help from Lindsay Buckingham and Susanna Hoffs), and a mini Go-Go's reunion as Charlotte Caffey and Jane Wiedlin join the Murmurs for "Smash." As for Hart's foray into pop on a cover of Blondie's "One Way or Another," let's just hope ABC keeps renewing "Sabrina" for many years to come.

Gary Graff

Sahara

 1992, Intrada Records, from the film *Sahara*, Cannon Films, 1983 ♪♪♪♪♪

album notes: Music: Ennio Morricone; **Conductor:** Ennio Morricone.

On various occasions, Ennio Morricone scored films that had a Saharian motif to them (*Secret of the Sahara, Prince of the Desert*, etc.), something that inspired him to renew himself and find new ways to celebrate the poesy and mystery of the desert. If he did indulge his interest in exotic music when he wrote the music for this film ("Arabia," "Oasis," "Desert Music," "More Desert Music"), the story also gave him many other opportunities to let his imagination run wild. Set in 1928, the film stars Brooke Shields as a woman determined to win the Sahara International Car Rally, despite the fact that only men are allowed to enter the race. In the course of the action she faces many dangers ("Panther Chase," "Car Trouble"), and is abducted by a wandering Tuareg leader whom she is forced to marry, but she still wins the race at the end. The various difficulties encountered by the young woman led to vibrantly detailed cues that constitute the bulk of the score. Mining another rich musical vein, Morricone created ceremonial music with a pseudo-British brass flair for the beginning and end of the race and he combined a variety of North African instruments and sonorities to his music to depict the exotic locales in which the story took place. Dominating the whole, he wrote a lovely romantic theme, that recurs throughout the score and contrasts with the rapid-fire action in the other cues. In the Morricone body of work, *Sahara* may not be as well known as some of his most memorable creations, but it is a very unusual, compelling score that deserves to be discovered.

Didier C. Deutsch

The Saint

🎬 1998, Razor & Tie Records, from the television series, *The Saint,* 1967–69 🎵🎵🎵

album notes: Music: Edwin Astley, Ken Jones; **Conductor:** Edwin Astley.

The Saint first aired on British television in 1962. It featured Roger Moore as Simon Templar, a Robin Hood-like character who bopped around righting wrongs in a very suave, debonair manner. The series called for equally suave music. Edwin Astley, who also composed the music for *Secret Agent,* created most of the tracks featured in this CD reissue. The theme music for *The Saint* is one of those classic tunes you can play and almost instantly identify. The rest of the score is in a swinging jazz mold, with some tracks ("Ying-Tong-Piddle-Ay-Kilt," "Olaf's Dance," and "Cantina") exhibiting an international flavor to match the respective storylines.

Beth Krakower

🎬 1997, Virgin Records, from the film *The Saint,* Paramount Pictures, 1997 🎵🎵

🎬 1997, Angel Records, from the film *The Saint,* Paramount Pictures, 1997 🎵🎵🎵

album notes: Music: Graeme Revell; **Orchestra:** The London Metropolitan Orchestra; **Conductor:** Allan Wilson, David Snell.

Featuring tracks by both established performers and lesser-known acts, this compilation tries desperately to be slick and now. But somehow, the flavor that was so specific to the early films and television series, respectively starring George Sanders and Roger Moore as Leslie Charteris's title character, seems hopelessly lost in this hodgepodge, which tries to claim some legitimacy by using the familiar motif in "The Saint Theme," updated to satisfy today's musical taste. As pop compilations go,

They Know the Score

Danny Elfman

I'm trying to interpret the film through the director's head, but it all comes out through me. So, a composer is kind of like a psychic medium. They're holding their seance and trying to tap into the director's spirit. But, it's still coming out through their mouth when they speak. So, obviously my scores sound like my scores, but I'm trying to interpret the film through the director as much as I can. Sometimes you get real close, sometimes you don't. Sometimes they drive you crazy. But, I think every composer does that. That's a big part of the job. You have to write a good score that you feel good about. At least, you're supposed to. But, if the director hates it, it ain't going to be in the movie! So, it becomes an exercise in futility if you write something that does not express the film as the director wishes. It's still their ball game. It's their show. I think any successful composer learns how to dance around the director's impulses.

***Courtesy of* Film Score Monthly**

this one—with new songs by David Bowie, Everything but the Girl, and Duran Duran among its better moments—is not all that bad. But what has it got to do with The Saint?

Indicative of the increasing respect film music seems to be getting in some circles, the score album was released on the classical label, Angel Records, which, with Sony Classical and London Records, seems intent on making this kind of music the modern day equivalent of classical music. No one should complain about that. Which doesn't mean that Graeme Revell's music should be confused with the works of the great classic composers. In fact, the score for *The Saint* is too often bathed in clichés to really compel the listener. There are some genuinely attractive moments in it (the "Love Theme," heard in three different versions), but the overall effect seems to be more along the lines of listless synth lines mingled with lush orchestral textures and an occasional electronic rhythm track added to it, no doubt to signify increased screen action. What is mostly lacking here are genuine melodic themes, as if the music were essentially meant to be a wall of orchestral sounds, a problem all too frequent these days when melodic ideas don't seem to matter as much as noise.

Didier C. Deutsch

St. Louis Blues

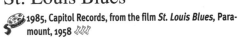 **1985, Capitol Records, from the film *St. Louis Blues*, Paramount, 1958** 🎬🎬🎬

album notes: Songs: W.C. Handy; **Music:** Nelson Riddle; **Conductor:** Nelson Riddle.

The great Nat King Cole starred in this big screen biography of W.C. Handy, in which he portrayed the celebrated songwriter and performed some of his songs. The shoddy package unfortunately belies the importance of the album and reduces it to the appearance of a cheap bootleg. Cole's performance, however, is peerless, with sensational renditions of Handy classics such as "Beale Street Blues," "Memphis Blues," and, of course, "St. Louis Blues."

Didier C. Deutsch

St. Louis Woman

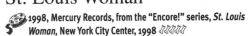 **1998, Mercury Records, from the "Encore!" series, *St. Louis Woman*, New York City Center, 1998** 🎬🎬🎬🎬🎬

album notes: Music: Harold Arlen; **Lyrics:** Johnny Mercer; **Orchestra:** The Coffee Club Orchestra; **Conductor:** Rob Fisher; **Cast:** Vanessa L. Williams (Della Green), Stanley Wayne Mathis (Li'l Augie), Yvette Cason (Butterfly), Helen Goldsby (Lila), Chuck Cooper (Badfoot), Victor Trent Cook (Barney).

In a season (1945–46) that saw the creation of *Carousel, On the Town,* and, most important of all, *Annie Get Your Gun,* Harold Arlen and Johnny Mercer's *St. Louis Woman* had to face some tough competition. Set in St. Louis in 1898, this period musical involved a saloon owner, Biglow Brown, his woman, Della, and the man she lusts after, Li'l Augie, a jockey. Starring Rex Ingram, Ruby Dee, and Harold Nicholas, respectively, the score introduced such standards as "Come Rain or Come Shine," "Any Place I Hang My Hat Is Home," and the song Pearl Bailey popularized, "Legalize My Name." The show, however, didn't go very far, and after 113 performances called it quits. This recording stems from the popular "Encore!" series at New York's City Center, and while the principals performed it in a concert version for only three days, it was duly recorded, no doubt because Vanessa L. Williams, who appeared in it, was also signed to the label. We should be grateful for small favors ... It's a terrific cast album, with Williams, more than ever assured of her talent and in full command as Della, and Stanley Wayne Mathis just fine as Li'l Augie. Yvette Cason as Butterfly (the part played by Pearl Bailey in the original) cannot erase the distinctive memory of

her predecessor in the role, but she acquits herself very well of the demands imposed by it. The Coffee Club Orchestra, conducted by Rob Fisher, is excellent, and the whole recording, supplemented with a lot of walk-on interludes, bridges, and reprises not found on the 1946 original cast album, is simply a must.

Didier C. Deutsch

🎭 **1992, Angel Records, from the Broadway production *St. Louis Woman*, 1946** 🎬🎬🎬🎬

album notes: Music: Harold Arlen; **Lyrics:** Johnny Mercer; **Musical Direction:** Leon Leonardi; **Cast:** Harold Nicholas, Fayard Nicholas, June Hawkins, Pearl Bailey, Robert Pope, Ruby Hill, Rex Ingram.

Harold Arlen's most memorable Broadway score—a high point of his partnership with Johnny Mercer—nonetheless failed to make a hit of this tale of St. Louis at the turn of the century, chiefly because black audiences objected to its less—than—attractive portrayal of their community. More than 50 years later, it's the songs that linger, especially the now–standard "Come Rain or Come Shine" (sung by the show's leads, Ruby Hill and Harold Nicholas) and two that made a star of the young Pearl Bailey, "Legalize My Name" and "It's a Woman's Prerogative."

Marc Kirkeby

The Saint of Fort Washington

🎬 **1993, Varèse Sarabande, from the film *The Saint of Fort Washington*, Warner Bros., 1993** 🎬🎬🎬🎬

album notes: Music: James Newton Howard; **Conductor:** Marty Paich; **Featured Musicians:** Chuck Findley, trumpet.

The moving story of a homeless Vietnam vet and the street kid he takes under his wing, *The Saint of Fort Washington* elicited a soberly eloquent score from James Newton Howard, evidently inspired by its subject. Overall, the moods projected are remarkably low-key and attractive, with a synth melody and an occasional piano theme detailing specific scenes in the narrative, and tugging at the proper heartstrings.

Didier C. Deutsch

Salvador

See: Wall Street/Salvador

Samson and Delilah/The Quiet Man

🎬 **1994, Varèse Sarabande, from the films *Samson and Delilah*, Paramount, 1949, and *The Quiet Man*, Republic Pictures, 1952** 🎬🎬🎬🎬🎬

album notes: Music: Victor Young; **Orchestras:** The Paramount Symphony Orchestra (*Samson and Delilah*), the Victor Young Orchestra (*The Quiet Man*); **Conductor:** Victor Young.

Victor Mature is a beefy Samson and Hedy Lamarr a beguiling Delilah, in Cecil B. DeMille's impressive retelling of the Biblical tale about the strongman and his fall from grace when he succumbs to the siren's charms and she shears his long hair, source of his strength, in the unkindest cut of all. Spearheaded by a lovely main theme, the score Victor Young wrote for the film displays the appropriate contrasting elements of passion and action in this oft-told story of love and betrayal. The exotic accents in some of the themes aim to evoke, in typical Hollywood style, the time and locale of the narrative, which means that the effects are predictable but quite suggestive. Presented as a long suite, with the themes evolving in and out of the orchestral texture, the music is all at once reassuring in its conventional approach and very exciting.

Also very attractive in its own depiction of an unusual love story set in Ireland, *The Quiet Man* enabled Young to compose a score that beautifully conveys the various moments in the action with melodies that are serenely fetching and vibrant. A recent rerecording, conducted by Kenneth Alwyn, is much more complete and sonically superior to the selections offered here, but these are the original soundtrack cues, conducted by the composer, and as such they have an importance one can hardly ignore.

Didier C. Deutsch

The Sand Pebbles

1997, Varèse-Sarabande, from the film *The Sand Pebbles*, 20th Century-Fox, 1966 ♪♪♪♪♪

album notes: Music: Jerry Goldsmith; **Orchestra:** The Royal Scottish National Orchestra; **Conductor:** Jerry Goldsmith.

It must be quite exciting for a composer like Jerry Goldsmith to revisit an important score written 30 years earlier, and with the knowledge acquired in the interim bring that score to a vibrant new life. That he was able to do it in the case of *The Sand Pebbles* is already remarkable, but the recording itself is a brilliant testimony to the composer's evident delight at redoing it. Composed for an action adventure film set in 1926 China, starring Steve McQueen and Richard Attenborough, the score was a milestone in Goldsmith's career, and one of his first important creations. An engrossing drama, the film detailed the involvement of American naval forces in China, at a time when that country was divided by external and internal forces; against that broad background, the screenplay told the story of a small gunboat patrolling the Yangtze River, the *U.S.S. San Pablo,* and the sailors on board, who call themselves the "Sand Pebbles."

For the film, Goldsmith wrote a score that teems with Asian sonorities and percussion, but the most famous cue he created for it, the love theme, became the hit pop song, "And We Were Lovers," when Johnny Mercer outfitted it with lyrics. The new

recording, the first time Goldsmith actually conducted the score, is letter perfect—the themes are well balanced, the sonics are far superior than those of the original soundtrack album (once available on 20th Century-Fox, but never reissued on CD), and to make things even more appealing previously unreleased cues ("Jake and Shirley," "The Wedding," "Frenchy's Death") have been added, making this the definitive recording of that momentous opus.

Didier C. Deutsch

Sandokan

1996, RCA Records/Italy, from the television series *Sandokan*, ATV, 1996 ♪♪♪

album notes: Music: Guido de Angelis, Maurizio de Angelis; **Featured Musicians:** Enrico Ciacci, sitar; Maurizio De Angelis, sitar; Mandrake, Adriano Giordanella, percussion.

As film composers, no one can compare Guido and Maurizio de Angelis to some of their more serious peers: they write pop scores that are quite engaging, but their compositions do not evidence much depth, let alone the kind of quality one finds in other, more gifted scorers. Yet there is always something catchy about their music, as evidenced here by this Arabian fantasy, created for a television series, and what they write is always fun, vaguely exotic, and totally entertaining. They have been, it must also be said, quite successful, and, again, listening to this score, one can easily see why: cues like "Tiger Hunt," with its oppressive percussion, or "The Arrival of Sandokan," with its faint Arabic accents, are catchy and convincing, probably well representative of the atmosphere specific to the series itself. The vocal contributions by Oliver Onions, a group often used by the De Angelis, simply confirm the pop appeal of the score. This title may be out of print or just plain hard to find. Mail-order companies, used CD shops, or dealers of rare or import recordings will be your best bet.

Didier C. Deutsch

The Sandpiper

1996, Verve Records, from the film *The Sandpiper*, MGM, 1965 ♪♪♪♪♪

album notes: Music: Johnny Mandel; **Conductor:** Robert Armbruster.

The enormous popular success of "The Shadow of Your Smile," an Academy Award winner in 1966, should not becloud the overall appeal of the score written by Johnny Mandel. The song, performed here by a characterless chorus, is in fact one of the least remarkable tracks in the recording (one recalls the much more vibrant renditions by seasoned vocalists like Tony Bennett, Johnny Mathis, Frank Sinatra, or Jerry Vale, among the more than 100 cover versions it elicited). Weaving itself in and out of the cues in this album, the theme permeates the whole score with its deftly nostalgic strains, a haunting refrain that captures the poignancy in this failed love affair between two opposite characters, she (played by Elizabeth Taylor) a free-wheeling spirit, he (portrayed by Richard Burton) a staid Episcopal minister, as well as the loneliness of the Big Sur location where the story unfolds. The familiarity of the tune is one of the most engaging elements in the score, with this album guaranteed to be a real discovery for those unfamiliar with it.

Didier C. Deutsch

The Santa Clause

1994, Milan Records, from the film *The Santa Clause*, Walt Disney Pictures, 1994 🎬🎬🎬

album notes: Music: Michael Convertino; **Conductor:** Artie Kane.

Anyone who enjoys Christmas-themed soundtracks will definitely want to give a listen to Michael Convertino's immensely appealing score from *The Santa Clause*, the Tim Allen blockbuster comedy of 1994. The music can best be described as magical, with a quirky, offbeat approach perfectly suiting this yuletide comedy, which also boasts soaring orchestral passages and strong melodic themes. Convertino worked with a number of John Williams's collaborators here (conductor Artie Kane, orchestrator John Neufeld), and the results are just as warmly inviting as Williams's memorable music from the *Home Alone* pictures. The soundtrack also contains a vocal performance by Canadian singer Loreena McKennitt ("The Bells of Christmas") and an original Jimmy Webb song, "Christmas Will Return," making the album ideal for perennial holiday listening.

Andy Dursin

Satchmo the Great

1993, Legacy Records, from the film *Satchmo the Great*, 1955 🎬🎬🎬

album notes: Featured Musicians: Louis Armstrong, trumpet; Trummy Young, trombone; Edmond Hall, clarinet; Billy Kyle, piano; Arvell Shaw, bass; Barrett Deems, drums.

"Hannibal crossed the Alps in 218 B.C. with 37 elephants and 12,000 horses. Louis Armstrong crossed the Alps in the mid-20th century with one trumpet and five musicians." So begins fabled CBS newsman Edward R. Murrow's commentary at the opening of this disc, the soundtrack from the first feature film to focus on one individual jazz musician's international tour. Bear in mind that this took place in 1955 and 1956, a time when modern jazz did not necessarily have the widespread appeal and audience that it enjoys today. But *Satchmo the Great* is a unique and important collaboration, especially for its time. Where else could you find the acknowledged Ambassador of Jazz (Armstrong), and the brilliant

conductor Leonard Bernstein grooving together? Their 12-minute "St. Louis Blues (Concerto Grosso)" was recorded for the Guggenheim Concert at New York's Lewisohn Stadium, for the CBS News presentation *See It Now,* and is a fitting finale for this album. What about "All for You, Louis (Sly Mongoose)"—recorded with African musicians at the Accra Airport upon Louis's arrival? Both live and studio performances are interwoven with commentary and interviews of Armstrong by Murrow, and the album as a whole (even without the video images) is a fascinating documentation of the trumpeter completely at ease, in his element, performing for live audiences. Included among the 10 numbers are two Armstrong classics: "When It's Sleepy Time Down South" and "Mack the Knife." Newly remastered, the superior sonics truly belie the age of the original recordings.

Charles L. Granata

Saturday Night Fever

1995, Polydor Records, from the film *Saturday Night Fever*, 1977 🎬🎬🎬🎬

album notes: Music: David Shire; **Songs:** Barry Gibb, Maurice Gibb, Robin Gibb.

More than 25 million copies later, there's almost nothing left to say. If someone wants to know what disco was all about, you just hand them this album and a polyester suit and let them soak in the enduring smashes by the Bee Gees, Yvonne Elliman, the Trammps, K.C. & the Sunshine Band, even Walter Murphy's insipid "A Fifth of Beethoven" is here. But regardless of your feelings about disco, gold chains, mirror balls, and falsettos, this package is a trendsetter. Where previous soundtrack albums are usually good for one hit single, *Fever* ushered in the era of the multi-hit collection, and pop soundtracks were never the same after that.

Gary Graff

Saved by the Bell

1995, Kid Rhino Records, from the NBC Television series *Saved by the Bell*, 1989–95 🎬🎬

album notes: Songs: Scott Gale, Rich Eames.

A rock compilation for the kids who, presumably, watched this show designed for them on NBC–TV. The various actors, shown inside the tray card, look healthy, and squeaky clean. So do the songs in which you'd be hard put to find an offensive lyric. The rhythms are pleasant enough, but not too terribly earthshaking; as for the melodies they are, to say the least, primeval. Your 10–year–old might love them, and feel quite adult listening to this CD; your 12–year–old will probably yawn. The CD, by the way, is 26 minutes long: Just enough to make it tolerable.

Didier C. Deutsch

John Travolta in Saturday Night Fever. **(The Kobal Collection)**

Saving Private Ryan

1998, DreamWorks Records, from the film *Saving Private Ryan*, DreamWorks, 1998 ♪♪♪♪♪

album notes: Music: John Williams; **Orchestras:** The Boston Symphony Orchestra, the Tanglewood Festival Chorus; **Conductor:** John Williams; **Featured Musicians:** Gus Sebring, horns; Tim Morrison, trumpet; Thomas Rolfs, trumpet.

The stark realism of the battle scenes in this Steven Spielberg-directed World War II epic caused many a weak-stomached person to run to the bathroom, but all things considered, this is a masterpiece in which a squad of U.S. soldiers risks their lives to go behind enemy lines in France during and just after D-Day to rescue a paratrooper whose three brothers have already been killed in battle. Because he is the last remaining heir of his family, the Army is determined to bring Pvt. Ryan home alive, a task Captain John Miller (Tom Hanks) is determined to fulfill.

Contrasting with the topic and the time period during which the action takes place, long-time Spielberg collaborator John Williams composed an unusually quiet and reflective score; in order to increase the realism of the battle scenes, no music was used to underscore the activity. Williams, best known for the bold instrumental accents he conjures up in films like the *Star Wars* and *Indiana Jones* trilogies, chose instead to focus on the courage of the protagonists in this film and came up with a very subtle, but all the more highly effective score. The CD, containing many of the selections in their full-blown developments, is in every way a remarkable achievement.

see also: Thin Red Line

Beth Krakower

Scandal

1989, Enigma/EMI Records, from the film *Scandal,* Miramax, 1989 ♪♪♪♡

album notes: Music: Carl Davis.

The 1963 Profumo affair was bound to become a film: the story of a British cabinet minister involved with a call girl, Christine Keeler, who is also sleeping with a Soviet naval attaché was much too juicy to be ignored by the dream makers who crank out weirder stories than that to keep movie theaters filled every day of the week. That the scandal brought down the conservative government in England might also have been the best publicity stunt the film needed to make an impression. Starring John Hurt, as the man who morphs Keeler, a young showgirl (Joanne Whalley-Kilmer), into a sophisticated sexpot pursued by Jeroen Krabbe as the Soviet attaché and by Ian McKellen as Profumo, the British Secretary of State for War,

Scandal also used various songs to set its time period, including many that hit the British charts but didn't quite make it here. This wild collection of tracks may surprise at first by its diversity, using as it does songs by the Shadows, Fats Domino, Dusty Springfield, Nat King Cole, Nelson Riddle, Eddie Cochran, Chubby Checker, Jimmy Cliff, Johnny Dankworth, and . . . Sophia Loren and Peter Sellers. But it works well, and ultimately proves most entertaining. Carl Davis's "Love Theme" seems lost in the shuffle.

Didier C. Deutsch

Scarlett

1994, Polydor Records (Canada), from the television mini–series *Scarlett,* RHI Entertainment, 1994 ♪♪♪

album notes: Music: John Morris; **Orchestra:** The City of Prague Philharmonic; **Conductor:** John Morris.

Though he sports a mustache that looks quite manly, Timothy Dalton ain't Clark Gable; nor for that matter is John Morris another Max Steiner. So why did they bother making a sequel to *Gone With The Wind,* when they knew they had no real chances to succeed on any count? It's not that Morris's score for this sequel is bad, in fact it's very attractive for the most part, and the City of Prague Philharmonic plays it to the hilt. If it had been written for any other movie, on television or on the big screen, it probably would have filled the bill more than adequately. What undoes it is that it applies to a movie that should not have been. Even more maddening is the fact that the cues aren't even titled, though this was perhaps done on purpose so that the listener would not try to identify a theme with a given moment in the action. Alright, so taken at face value, John Morris's music is very attractive, which shouldn't come as any surprise since the composer is known to always create excellent scores. Here he has cleverly used a wide range of solo instruments to paint vivid themes, some of which are achingly beautiful. There are period waltzes, romantic ballads, folk dances, and an occasional action cue in the mix, in other words something for everybody. There's even a track, "Love Hurts," performed by the rock group Nazareth, with the Munich Philharmonic Orchestra playing backup. A rock instrumental? In a sequel to *GWTW?*

Didier C. Deutsch

The Scarlet Letter

1995, Epic Soundtrax/Sony Music, from the film *The Scarlet Letter,* Hollywood Pictures, 1995 ♪♪♪

album notes: Music: John Barry; **Orchestra:** The English Chamber Orchestra; **Conductor:** John Barry.

It might be suicidal to one's critical reputation to say that you actually enjoyed Demi Moore and Roland Joffe's reworking of

Hawthorne's *The Scarlet Letter*, so I'm only going to admit that I found the picture not nearly as disastrous as many others did. The movie boasts a number of positive attributes, including Alex Thomson's fine cinematography and a typically lush score by John Barry, who creates a deliberately paced musical sound that's a close relative to *Somewhere in Time* and all those other romantic soundtracks the composer is famous for. Thus, there's nothing here you haven't heard before, but it still works thanks to Barry's soothing orchestrations. Curiously, Barry was the third composer on the project, following Elmer Bernstein and Ennio Morricone. While Bernstein's music was recorded but ultimately rejected, Morricone was thrown off the project after he handed the producers a demo tape that was actually not original music but rather a pastiche of scores he had composed for various Italian projects!

Andy Dursin

The Scarlet Pimpernel

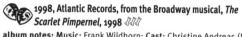 1992, Angel Records, from the studio recording, *The Scarlet Pimpernel*, 1998 ♪♪♪

album notes: Music: Frank Wildhorn; **Lyrics:** Nan Knighton; **Cast:** Linda Eder (Marguerite), Chuck Wagner (Percy), Dave Clemmons (Chauvelin), Peabo Bryson (Armand), Philip Hoffman (The Prince of Wales).

1998, Atlantic Records, from the Broadway musical, *The Scarlet Pimpernel*, 1998 ♪♪♪

album notes: Music: Frank Wildhorn; **Cast:** Christine Andreas (Marguerite), Terrence Mann (Chauvelin), Douglas Sills (Percy), Gilles Chiasson (Armand), David Cromwell (Prince of Wales).

Based on the novels by Baroness Orczy, *The Scarlet Pimpernel* brought to the stage an unusual swashbuckling hero, actually a British lord who, with a group of fearless friends, decides to organize the rescue of members of the French nobility, sentenced to be beheaded during the French Revolution. Calling himself the Scarlet Pimpernel ("They seek him here, they seek him there, those Frenchies seek him everywhere"), Sir Percy succeeds in his plans, but at the risk of imperiling his relationship with Marguerite, his young bride, to whom he conceals his double identity. For good reasons, it appears: before she married him, the French-born Marguerite was an actress who had a brief affair with the terrible Chauvelin, the mastermind behind the current executions.

Starring Christine Andreas, Terrence Mann, and a dashing newcomer, Douglas Sills as Percy, *The Scarlet Pimpernel* should have been a smash. Unfortunately, Nan Knighton's book, heavy-handed and ill-focused, lost track early on about the real story that was told on stage. Compounding the problems in the book, there was no chemistry between the principals, with Andreas apparently at a loss about the true nature of her character, and Mann hiding behind irritating facial mannerisms the fact that he could not grasp what his portrayal was supposed to be.

After hobbling for about a year in search of an audience, the show received a much-needed freshening up when Madison Square Garden invested in it, enabling its authors to revamp the show from top to bottom, and to recast it with a new Marguerite (Rachel York) and a new Chauvelin (Rex Smith), both far better than their predecessors. Douglas Sills, who seemed to have a dandy time portraying Sir Percy, continued in the role.

Unfortunately, this revised version of the show has not been commercially recorded, so the only versions available are a studio cast recording, starring Linda Eder, Chuck Wagner, and Dave Clemmons, and the first stage version, with Sills, Andreas, and Mann.

Midway between Broadway and pop, *The Scarlet Pimpernel* shows Frank Wildhorn as an imaginative, but often trite composer. His tunes are catchy but do not evidence much substance. For a lightweight entertainment like this show, however, they seem more appropriate, than in *Jekyll and Hyde* or, for that matter, *The Civil War*. Some moments particularly stand out in the mix, notably "The Creation of Man," a rousing number that stops the show, and the tender duet, "You Are My Home." But don't look for anything on the creative level of what Cole Porter, Irving Berlin, or Jerome Kern might have done in their days.

Didier C. Deutsch

Scent of a Woman

1992, MCA Records, from the film *Scent of a Woman,* Universal Pictures, 1992 ♪♪♪♪

album notes: Music: Thomas Newman; **Conductor:** Thomas Newman.

A brilliant *tour-de-force* by Al Pacino as a blind ex-officer cared for over a Thanksgiving weekend by a college student, is one of the highlights in this modest comedy in which the youngster, deftly played by Chris O'Donnell, accompanies the cane-wielding, cantankerous, sightless soldier on a spree to New York City, forging along the way solid affective ties with him. Based on a 1974 Italian film, scored by Armando Trovaioli, which received scant distribution in the U.S., *Scent of a Woman* (the title refers to the blind man's uncanny ability to identify an attractive woman just by sniffling the aura around her) exuded great charm and sensitivity, further enhanced by Thomas Newman's appealingly varied and low-key approach to his music. Two dance numbers, performed by the Tango Project, enliven the proceedings, casting a different, albeit equally enjoyable note into the mix.

Didier C. Deutsch

Schindler's List

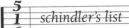 1993, MCA Records, from the film *Schindler's List,* Universal Pictures, 1993 ✍✍✍✍

album notes: Music: John Williams; **Conductor:** John Williams; **Featured Musicians:** Itzhak Perlman, violin; Giora Feidman, clarinet.

John Williams went along with Steven Spielberg's directorial approach on *Schindler's List* and refused to compose overly melodramatic moments in his Oscar-winning score for the 1993 movie. Working with violinist supreme Itzhak Perlman, Williams composed an elegiac, poignant score that is mournful and sad, tragic yet uplifting, perfectly establishing the emotional tone of Spielberg's Holocaust drama and gently underscoring the heroic actions of the title protagonist. The music is surprisingly low-key for a Williams score from a Spielberg picture, lacking the full-blooded orchestral finales of *E.T.* and *Empire of the Sun,* for example, and is—if anything—restrained perhaps a bit too much at the conclusion. Yet it is consistent with the manner in which Williams scored character pieces like *The Accidental Tourist* and *Stanley & Iris,* making for subtle and sublime film music composition.

Andy Dursin

School Ties

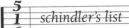 1992, Giant Records, from the film *School Ties,* Paramount Pictures, 1992 ✍✍✍

album notes: Music: Maurice Jarre; **Conductor:** Maurice Jarre.

Maurice Jarre's pretty and adventurous melody gives a sense of grandness and size to this localized prep school drama. The use of bells characterizes the film's setting, while the main theme suggests the free spirits of the characters. The heart of the score is found in "David," a 16-minute cue (longest of the CD's four score-only cues) that varies greatly in tempo and becomes a compelling tone-poem for the character, occasionally introspective and vulnerable, elsewhere bold and confident. In addition to the CD's 31 minutes of score, there are three source-cue pop songs that don't really need to be here, but they can easily be bypassed to afford maximum attention to Jarre's symphonic work. All in all, this is a good score nicely preserved on disc.

Randall D. Larson

Scream

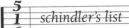 1998, TVT Records, from the film *Scream,* Dimension, 1997 ✍✍

album notes: Music: Mario Beltrami.

The first two films in this teen scream trilogy (the third film is to be released in 1999) feature an amalgam of some of today's hottest stars, both visually and sonically. In the first, Neve Campbell stars as Sidney, a teen whose mother has been murdered. One year later, a murderer who is obsessed with horror movies begins killing Neve's friends, one-by-one. In addition to Campbell, director Wes Craven assembled the following teen dreams to appear in one or both of the movies: Courtney Cox, Drew Barrymore, David Arquette, Sarah Michelle Gellar, Skeet Ulrich, and Liev Schreiber. In both, the soundtrack included a mix of pop songs and the score written by Mario Beltrami.

The song album to the first *Scream,* on TVT, boasts an interesting line-up of artists, including electronic giant Moby, TVT recording artists Sister Machine Gun, Catherine & the Connells, and Nick Cave & the Bad Seeds' "Red Right Hand." Also featured are two covers, "School's Out" by the Last Hard Men and "Don't Fear the Reaper" by Gus. The album also includes one track from Beltrami's score.

Didier C. Deutsch

Scream 2

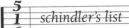 1998, Capitol, from the film *Scream 2,* Miramax, 1998 ✍✍✍✍

This *Scream* sequel is presented as a play-within-a-play. Campbell's character is in college when a movie based on the murders in the first movie is released. This of course sets off another murder spree. The Capitol soundtrack for *Scream 2* features a much more interesting blend of artists than did the original, ranging from rappers Master P (featuring Silkk the Schocker), Kotton Mouth Kings, and D'Angelo to mainstream alternative artists like Foo Fighters, Everclear, and The Dave Matthews Band. The album also features a couple of covers, including an outrageous version of Dr. John's "Right Place Wrong Time" by the Jon Spencer Blues Explosion and a punk cover of David Cassidy's signature song "I Think I Love You" by Less Than Jake. So what if a bunch of the songs never made it into the movie; overlook it, this is a teen flick, after all.

Didier C. Deutsch

Scream/Scream 2

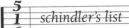 1998, Varèse-Sarabande, from the film *Scream,* Dimension, 1997, and the film *Scream 2,* Miramax, 1998 ✍✍✍

album notes: Music: Marco Beltrami; **Conductor:** Marco Beltrami.

Marco Beltrami's scores from both movies have been compiled on one CD, released by Varèse-Sarabande. There is only a small amount of the score from *Scream* on it. But music for the second film has an interesting story. When temp tracks were used for the movie, Hans Zimmer's *Broken Arrow* score was prominently used. Craven liked it a lot, and instructed Beltrami to write something similar in his own score. However, Craven

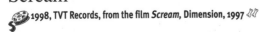

loved so much the way *Broken Arrow* worked that he subsequently licensed a good amount of the score to use in his film. The Varèse release allows one to hear the score Beltrami wrote, but while the music for the first *Scream* really captured the wide range of emotions in that film, the same cannot be said for *Scream 2*. In it, Beltrami tried to write action-adventure themes like those in *Broken Arrow,* but couldn't achieve the effects obtained by Zimmer in his own score.

Didier C. Deutsch

The Sea Hawk

1988, Varèse Sarabande, from the film *The Sea Hawk,* Warner Bros., 1940 ♫♫♫♫

album notes: Music: Erich-Wolfgang Korngold; **Orchestra:** The Utah Symphony Orchestra and Chorus; **Conductor:** Varujian Kojian.

In the absence of an actual soundtrack album, which probably wouldn't sound too great given the recording techniques that prevailed at the time the film was made, this sensational rere-cording, supervised by the composer's son, is more than a valid substitute. As was the case with *The Adventures of Robin Hood,* the Utah Symphony and Varujian Kojian have approached Korngold's music with fervor and dedication, and a lot of enthusiasm that can easily be felt in the crackling performance. Possibly the only drawbacks might be the vocal and choral sections, which do not have the film's definite aura, but even that should not detract anyone from listening to and enjoying to the hilt this superlative soundtrack recreation.

Didier C. Deutsch

Sea of Love

1997, Karussell/Germany, from the film *Sea of Love,* Universal, 1989 ♫♫♫♫

album notes: Music: Trevor Jones; **Conductor:** Trevor Jones.

A thrilling film noir set in Manhattan, *Sea of Love* starred Al Pacino in a superlative star turn as a cop investigating a series of murders committed by a killer who meets his victims through the lonely heart columns in the city's newspapers. Soon evidence points in the direction of a woman, Ellen Barkin, with whom Pacino becomes infatuated, against his better judgment. Limning the action, Trevor Jones wrote a score full of zest, built around a percolating theme that pervades it, and informs on the action. The use of a saxophone to create a specific atmosphere, both dangerous and sophisticated, while conventional, works well within this context, and makes this a score to play often and enjoy. But the title song, performed by Phil Phillips and the Twilights and reprised by Tom Waits, elicits a yawn.

Didier C. Deutsch

10 Essential Scores
by Nino Rota

La dolce vita
Juliet of the Spirits
The Godfather
War and Peace
Romeo and Juliet
Amarcord
Fellini's Casanova
8 1/2
La strada
Rocco and His Brothers

The Sea Wolf

1993, Bay Cities Records, from the television film *The Sea Wolf,* Turner Pictures, 1993 ♫♫♫

album notes: Music: Charles Bernstein.

Though the label has disappeared, and this may be a hard-to-find item, it is well worth looking for. Composer Charles Bernstein has written a powerful, often eloquent score for this sea drama based on the novel by Jack London. Starring Charles Bronson as Captain Wolf Larsen, a tortured man bent on loneliness and self-destruction, and Christopher Reeve as Humphrey Van Weyden, a socialite and involuntary seaman under Larsen's command, *The Sea Wolf* resulted in an often dark score by Bernstein, reflective of the many somber aspects in the story. The relentless, oppressive moods in the music are occasionally relieved by a more romantic theme describing Flaxen Brewster (Mary Catherine Stewart), an attractive young woman whose presence on board Larsen's ship triggers some of the conflicts in the narrative. With a predominance of percussive effects and broody synth lines, no doubt inspired by the screen action and the sea setting, Bernstein created a series of cues that are vibrant and exciting, and limn the story in broad, colorful musical terms. A rare soundtrack, but a good one!

Didier C. Deutsch

Seaquest DSV

1995, Varèse-Sarabande, from the television series *Seaquest DSV*, 1993–95 ♫♫♫

album notes: Music: John Debney; **Conductor:** John Debney.

The epic sense of adventure that pervaded the television seafaring and underwater series *Seaquest DSV* is strikingly captured in John Debney's score, which stresses in bold, colorful terms the most engaging elements in it. Basically, the CD combines together cues that were written for three episodes, "To Be or Not to Be," "Knight of Shadows," and "Such Great Patience." Announced by a swashbuckling "Main Title," the series offered a weekly dose of great undersea adventure, something that finds an echo in Debney's music ("Preparing for Battle," "Uncharted Waters," "The Forgiving/Resurrection," "Lucas Meets the Alien"), with a few reflective moments to create a welcome counterpoint ("Bridger's Dream," "Waltz with the Dead"). Debney revealed here a great talent as a scorer with imagination, and wrote themes that were genuinely inspired.

Didier C. Deutsch

Searching for Bobby Fischer

1993, Big Screen Records, from the film *Searching for Bobby Fischer*, Paramount, 1993 ♫♫♫

album notes: Music: James Horner; **Conductor:** James Horner; **Featured Musicians:** James Horner, Ralph Grierson, Randy Kerber, Jim Thatcher, Ian Underwood.

James Horner is often criticized for quoting both classical works and his own previous soundtracks at times, but despite these often uneven attributes in his compositions, he usually produces soundtracks that are nevertheless entertaining and invite repeated listening. Such is the case once again with his music from *Searching for Bobby Fischer,* the 1993 film by Steven Zaillian about the life of Josh Waitzkin, a real-life chess wiz who shot to fame at the age of seven. Sure, Horner's music sounds like *Field of Dreams, Sneakers,* and a few of his other scores, but as a pastiche it's certainly an enjoyable one, with pleasant melodies and elegant orchestrations making this as easy to listen to as it is to identify the sections you'll recall from other sources.

Andy Dursin

Second Best

 1994, Milan/BMG, from the film *Second Best*, Regency/Warner Bros., 1994 ♫♫♫

album notes: Music: Simon Boswell; **Conductor:** Neil Thomson.

A richly rewarding little drama set in Wales, *Second Best* elicited a flavorful score from Simon Boswell, who energized the film and gave it a distinctive musical voice. With the guitar playing an upfront role in the set of cues, the music detailed the story of a shy, lonesome postmaster, played by William Hurt, who decides to adopt an 11-year-old prone to violent outbursts, with the confrontations between the two resulting in occasionally explosive moments. Boswell's score identifies some of the most pungent scenes in the narrative, with cues that are particularly moving ("In an Ideal World," "Out of the West," "Cold and Hungry"), making this CD a melodious, often haunting proposition.

Didier C. Deutsch

The Second Jungle Book

1997, JOS Records, from the film *The Second Jungle Book*, Tri-Star, 1997 ♫♫♫♫

album notes: Music: John Scott; **Orchestra:** The Seattle Symphony Orchestra; **Conductor:** John Scott.

One of the things so many would-be film and television composers seem to forget these days is that it is not enough to know how to write music; it is also important, equally so in fact, to know how to write melodic music. John Scott never had that problem—his scores are always quite attractive, and teem with melodic material that keeps the listener riveted and, if not looking for the next cue, at least looking forward to playing the recording all over again. Whether scoring a period drama, an epic, a thriller or a comedy, Scott revels in quality product, and never fails to remain true to the criteria he's obviously set for himself. This score, for a 1997 adaptation of Rudyard Kipling's story about the little Hindu boy lost in the jungle and raised by a pack of wolves, is another example of the composer's unique way with a florid and inspiring subject. Because of time constraints, Scott didn't use Indian instruments like the sitar, saranghi, and tabla, but instead relied on his fertile imagination to come up with catchy, expansive themes that would capture the essence of the story and the various characters in it—Mowgli, of course, but also Shere Khan, the tiger; the unruly chimps, the Bandar-log; Kaa, the python; Baloo, the bear; etc. At times frivolously entertaining ("The Train Adventure"), at other times quietly serene ("Peaceful Night"), ominously scary ("Terror in the Lost City"), or grandly epic ("Animals to the Rescue"), the cues are gloriously exciting, vividly descriptive, and totally enjoyable.

Didier C. Deutsch

Secret Agent

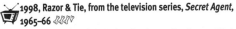 1998, Razor & Tie, from the television series, *Secret Agent*, 1965–66 ♫♫♫♫

album notes: Music: Edwin Astley, Ken Jones; **Conductor:** Edwin Astley.

They just don't write TV music like they used to. This James Bond-influenced spy series starring Patrick McGoohan featured the music of Edwin Astley, who composed a slick, jazz-oriented score in which the harpsichord was prominently featured. This is a straight reissue of the 1966 RCA album of the same name. It features the hit theme song "Secret Agent Man" by P.F. Sloane and Steve Barri. In 1966 the Ventures charted at #54 with a surf instrumental version of this track. Later that year Johnny Rivers's vocal version peaked at #3.

see also: The Saint

Beth Krakower

The Secret Garden

1993, Varèse Sarabande, from the film *The Secret Garden*, Warner Bros., 1993 ♫♫

album notes: Music: Zbigniew Preisner; **Orchestras:** The Sinfonia Varsovia, the Boys Choir of the Cracovian Philharmonic; **Conductors:** Wojciech Michniewski, Stanislaw Kravceyski; **Boy Soloist:** Tomasz Borik.

This is an often agreeable, but overall disappointing presentation of Zbigniew Preisner's score. The album starts off in a very scattershot manner, with cues frequently averaging a minute and a half or less. It fails to generate any emotional response early on because the music is over before any emotional mood can develop. That's a real shame because the score does have its moments. "Craven Leaves," "Walking through the Garden," and "Awakening of Spring" show some real possibilities. The pacing does improve in the later half, but by then it may have lost you.

David Hirsch

The Secret of N.I.M.H.

1982, Varèse Sarabande, from the animated feature *The Secret of N.I.M.H.*, United Artists, 1982 ♫♫♫♫

album notes: Music: Jerry Goldsmith; **Orchestra:** The National Philharmonic Orchestra, the Ambrosian Singers; **Conductor:** Jerry Goldsmith.

When you think of soundtracks from animated children's films, usually musicals or pop songs are the first things to enter into your mind—music like Alan Menken's mega-successful Disney efforts or songs like "Somewhere out There" from *An American Tail*. Animated features with serious, classically themed film scores are few and far between, but Jerry Goldsmith was given the rare chance at making a substantial contribution to Don Bluth's *The Secret of N.I.M.H,*. a 1982 theatrical feature that has since become a kids' staple on video and cable TV. Goldsmith faced the challenges of scoring for often incomplete animation and came up with one of his finest scores of the 1980s, with strongly thematic passages punctuated by thrilling cues which

sound more like part of an action film score than they do components of a children's soundtrack. Even the movie's original song, "Flying Dreams," co-written and performed by Paul Williams, is memorable and quite lovely, perfectly putting the cap on a superior effort by Goldsmith all around.

Andy Dursin

The Secret of N.I.M.H. 2

1998, Sonic Images, from the animated film *The Secret of N.I.M.H. 2*, MGM, 1998 ♫♫♫♫

album notes: Music: Lee Holdridge; **Lyrics:** Richard Sparks; **Orchestra:** The Philharmonia Orchestra of London and the Philharmonia Chorus; **Conductor:** Lee Holdridge.

Al Jarreau (sounding like Johnny Mathis), Dom DeLuise, Ralph Macchio, and Eric Idle are among the luminaries who lent their vocal talents to this second animated feature in the *N.I.M.H.* series, scored in grand style by Lee Holdridge. Profusely lyrical and florid, the score and songs detail the new adventures of the little mouse, Timmy, son of the hero in the first film, in a desperate fight against the humans who now threaten Thorn Valley, the utopian society the intellectually superior rodents have created. The instrumental cues are laid out in a mock swashbuckling style that makes them quite endearing; the songs are not always on the same quality level (with all due respects to Jarreau and Bobbi Page, "My Life and My Love" is quite annoying and unnecessary), but DeLuise is particularly effective, with Macchio and Idle, respectively as Timmy and his evil brother Martin, scoring high marks for their duet in "Just Say Yes!" In fact, even the kiddies might enjoy listening to this one.

Didier C. Deutsch

Sedotta e abbandonata

1992, CAM Records/Italy, from the film *Sedotta e abbandonata (Seduced and Abandoned)*, 1964 ♫♫♫♫

album notes: Music: Carlo Rustichelli; **Conductor:** Pier Luigi Urbini.

The title immediately describes the plot of this delicious Italian comedy: 16-year-old Agnese Ascalone has sinned. "The frog reacted in a positive manner," stated the analyst. And so, her family is determined to do what is right to save their honor: marry her quickly to the infamous seducer . . . who unfortunately happens to be Peppino, engaged to Agnese's sister, buxomy Matilde. Based on this simple premise, Pietro Germi wrote and directed a sharply observed comedy that found a perfect match in Carlo Rustichelli's lightweight and slyly humorous score, informed by the wry selection titled "Honor and Family" Reflecting the Sicilian locale, as well as the volatile personalities of the various characters in the story, the score kept its musical tongue firmly in cheek, while making concessions to the trends of the day (a twist, a rhumba), and stressing the various incidents in the plot. Altogether, it added up to a fun musical brew. This recording may be difficult to find. Check with a used CD store, mail-order company, or a dealer specializing in rare, out-of-print, or import recordings.

Didier C. Deutsch

Selena

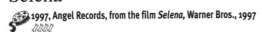
1997, Angel Records, from the film *Selena,* Warner Bros., 1997 ♪♪♪♪

album notes: Music: Dave Grusin; **Conductor:** Dave Grusin.

This explosive, real-life drama about the Tex-Mex performer murdered by one of her fans pretty much dictated Dave Grusin's approach to the music he wrote: with characteristic flair, he devised for many of the cues enjoyably bouncy tunes rooted in the fusion jazz in which he excels ("Kids and Chickens," "South Texas Jive Cats," "Salinas y los Low Riders"), keeping for the more romantic aspects in the story ("Selena's Dream," "Dreams of the People," "Don't Quit Music/Betrayal") a florid instrumental style that proves very ingratiating. The simply-stated "Selena Theme" and "Como la flor . . . for Selena," two gorgeously expressive piano pieces, also stand out, as do a couple of entertaining numbers denoting south-of-the-border influence ("Cumbia: La Manzana"). The only questionable selection in this otherwise highly entertaining score album is the inclusion of "Theme from 'A Summer Place'," sung by Gary Lemel, which seems an odd choice in this musical context.

Didier C. Deutsch

Sense and Sensibility

1995, Sony Classical, from the film *Sense and Sensibility,* Columbia Pictures, 1995 ♪♪♪♪♪

album notes: Music: Patrick Doyle; **Conductor:** Robert Ziegler; **Featured Musicians:** Jane Eaglen, soprano; Tony Hymas, piano; Jonathan Snowdon, flutes; Richard Morgan, oboes; Robert Hill, clarinet.

Jane Austen's understanding of the dual aspects in anyone's life (so well defined in the title of this film adapted from her first novel) found a remarkable echo in Patrick Doyle's gloriously literate and lovingly understated score. At times properly rambunctious, at other times deliciously gracile, the cues offer a carefully wrought depiction of this classic comedy-drama about three young girls (and their mother) in 18th-century England who are suddenly left destitute by the death of their father, whose considerable estate is inherited by a son from a previous marriage and his insufferable wife. Some selections, like "Willoughby," strike for their charming simplicity, while the profuse style in others ("My Father's Favorite") proves equally

endearing. Two vocals by Jane Eaglen bookend this delightful album, both exuding a lovely lilt mixed with a sense of melancholy, superbly reflective of the film's dual moods.

Didier C. Deutsch

The Sentinel

1998, Sonic Images, from the television series, *The Sentinel,* Paramount, 1996–97 woof!

album notes: Music: Steve Porcaro, John Keane.

I suppose some people will enjoy this CD of music from the popular television series *The Sentinel,* but frankly I found it extremely annoying. After a while, hearing the same drum effects, synthesizer lines, and pounding rhythms that increase in volume for no apparent reason and then recede into a murmur, only to rise again, becomes very tiring. It may work on television while one is watching what passes as exciting entertainment because then it matters little what it sounds like or what effect it has, but on a purely listening basis it's boring. And it's not because it was composed by Steve Porcaro and John Keane, or even James Newton Howard, who contributed the main theme for the series and a couple of cues heard at the end of this CD. It's a style that's being copied by every hack in town who thinks producing electronic noise is sufficient for being called a composer. Sorry, guys, but before you do that, check the works of *real* composers like Jerry Goldsmith, John Williams, and Elmer Bernstein. That's music! Better yet, that's *film* music: informative, intelligent, attractive, and listenable on its own terms.

Didier C. Deutsch

Sergeant Pepper's Lonely Hearts Club Band

1998, Polydor, from the film *Sgt. Pepper's Lonely Hearts Club Band,* Universal, 1978 woof!

album notes: Songs: John Lennon, Paul McCartney, George Harrison; **Music:** George Martin; **Featured Musicians:** Max Middleton, keyboards, synthesizers; Robert Ahwai, guitars; Wilbur Bascomb, bass guitar; Bernard Purdie, drums, percussion; George Martin, keyboards; Peter Frampton, guitar solos; Tower of Power, horn section.

Let's cut directly to the chase: Buy the original Beatles album and do not even think of subjecting your ears to this abysmal mess. It was just about "twenty years ago today" (1978 actually) that some idiot deigned to cast Peter Frampton and the Bee Gees as Billy Shears and the rest of the Beatles' infamous Sgt. Pepper's Lonely Hearts Club Band. That rocket scientist should probably be deported for messing with a national treasure. Enter at your own risk.

Amy Rosen

Serial Mom

1994, MCA Records, from the film *Serial Mom*, Sony Pictures, 1994 ♪♪♪♪

album notes: Music: Basil Poledouris.

Kathleen Turner had one of her most enjoyable screen roles as a mother with a killer instinct in this cheerful comedy by John Waters. Adding spice to this devilishly amusing story about a perfect housewife and mother who reveals another side to her personality when she starts murdering her annoying neighbors, Basil Poledouris wrote a delightfully perverse little score that moves from a serene opening to a series of increasingly frantic cues, all of them detailing with glee the lady's misdeeds, in a style Bernard Herrmann would not have disowned. Some of the cues are set off by brief excerpts from the dialogue, further enhancing their impact. A neglected minor masterpiece, *Serial Mom* is wryly entertaining. This soundtrack album is equally rewarding, though you might want to skip the screechy "Gas Chamber" song, performed (if that is the word) by L-7.

Didier C. Deutsch

Serpico

1992, Sakkaris Records/Greece, from the film *Serpico*, Paramount, 1973 ♪♪♪♪

album notes: Music: Mikis Theodorakis.

Greek composer Mikis Theodorakis wrote a particularly effective score for this true story of an honest undercover Manhattan cop, stirringly portrayed by Al Pacino, whose testimony about corruption in the department left him ostracized by his colleagues. Reflecting the gritty, exciting atmosphere of the film, as well as its urban background, the composer wrote a series of cues in which the jazz elements enhance each moment in the picture. Particularly notable in this score are "Honest Cop," "Meeting in the Park," "On the Streets," and the forlorn "Disillusion," all of which add up to a fine, enjoyable recording. This title may be out of print or just plain hard to find. Mailorder companies, used CD shops, or dealers of rare or import recordings will be your best bet.

Didier C. Deutsch

Set It Off

1997, Varèse Sarabande, from the film *Set It Off*, New Line Cinema, 1997 ♪♪♪♪

album notes: Music: Christopher Young; **Conductor:** Pete Anthony; **Featured Musicians:** Mike Lang, keyboards; John Goux, classical guitar; Brandon Fields, saxophone; Mike Vacarro, saxophone; Nick Kirgo, guitar; George Doering, guitar; Carl Vincent, electric bass; MB Gordy, drums; Steve Schaefer, drums.

This is an outstanding black urban score by Christopher Young that shows he's not out of fresh and innovative ideas. He's taken all he's learned from his past efforts and assembled some powerful orchestrations, particularly the use of some imaginative vocal arrangements that incorporate the sound of breathing as well as traditional "scats." The album also includes a lovely ballad, "Up against the Wind," co-written by Young. In all, it's a remarkable effort from a white boy from the Jersey shore.

David Hirsch

Seven

1995, TVT Records, from the film *Seven*, New Line Cinema, 1995 ♪♪♪♪

album notes: Music: Howard Shore; **Conductor:** Howard Shore.

It opens with the Statler Brothers' "In the Beginning" and slams immediately to Gravity Kills' pulverizing "Guilty" before shifting back to Marvin Gaye's "Trouble Man": An arresting opening salvo that's supported by pieces of Bach and performances by blues queen Billie Holiday and jazz masters Charlie Parker and Thelonious Monk. For listeners who thrive on variety, here's your album.

Gary Graff

Seven Brides for Seven Brothers

1996, Rhino Records, from the film, *Seven Brides for Seven Brothers*, MGM, 1954 ♪♪♪♪♪

album notes: Music: Gene De Paul; **Lyrics:** Johnny Mercer; **Choir:** The MGM Studio Chorus; **Orchestra:** The MGM Studio Orchestra; **Conductor:** Adolph Deutsch; **Cast:** Jane Powell, Howard Keel, Jeff Richards, Russ Tamblyn, Tommy Rall, Marc Platt, Matt Mattox, Jacques d'Amboise, Virginia Gibson, Julie Newmeyer.

A western musical, something of a rarity in the genre, *Seven Brides for Seven Brothers* is a rousing, rambunctious spectacle, which drew its inspiration from Stephen Vincent Benet's story "The Sobbin' Women," itself loosely based on Plutarch's fabled tale about the abduction of the Sabine women. Transposed to the Oregon frontier in the mid–1800s, the story about the kidnapping of six lovely girls by their backwood suitors, is the occasion for a robustly flavored series of songs and dances, magnificently staged by Michael Kidd, who gives the brothers (all dancers in their own right) two memorable numbers, "Lonesome Polecat," in which the brothers deplore their loneliness in the wilds, and the celebrated "Barn Raising," a sensational dance routine. Starring Howard Keel and Jane Powell, the film received five Academy Awards nominations, and walked away with the Oscar for best score, written by Gene De Paul and Johnny Mercer.

Didier C. Deutsch

Morgan Freeman and Brad Pitt in Seven. **(The Kobal Collection)**

Seven Years in Tibet

1998, Sony Classical, from the film *Seven Years in Tibet*, 1998
♫♫♫♫

album notes: Music: John Williams; **Conductor:** John Williams; **Featured Musician:** Yo-Yo Ma, cello.

Once again showing his uncanny flair for unusual film scoring, John Williams wrote a lush, exotic music to illuminate this sweeping story about an Austrian mountain climber stranded in the Himalayas at the outbreak of World War II; to escape British troops he heads into remote Tibet, where he becomes a confidant of the Dalai Lama in the years prior to invasion by China. If *Schindler's List* was a *de facto* romance for violin and orchestra, *Seven Years in Tibet* is distinguished by the fact that cellist Yo-Yo Ma is heard in a similar role, as a soloist bringing his talent to a film score created by John Williams. The flowing music, at times deeply moving, is also complemented by a couple of tracks featuring the Gyuto Monks, but the real meat of this CD are the two long excerpts, "Seven Years in Tibet," that bookend the score, and "Heinrich's Odyssey," which caps this recording. It's a quality music that will find few adepts because

of its innate austerity, but it should convert some because of its tremendous appeal.

Didier C. Deutsch

1776

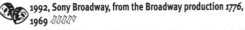
1992, Sony Broadway, from the Broadway production *1776*, 1969 ♫♫♫♫

album notes: Music: Sherman Edwards; **Lyrics:** Sherman Edwards; **Musical Direction:** Peter Howard; **Cast:** William Daniels, Paul Hecht, Roy Poole, Clifford David, Rex Everhart, David Ford, Ken Howard, Virginia Vestoff, Ron Holgate, Betty Buckley.

The writing of the Constitution might not seem like a subject for a Broadway musical, yet Sherman Edwards spent some 10 years of his life to research and write this compelling Tony Award–winning show which swept Broadway off its feet, when it premiered on March 16, 1969. In broad strokes, befitting its reverent topic, Sherman recounts the struggles, compromises, and backroom deals that eventually led to the document on which the destinies of the newly emerging United States were to be based, using as his main focus John Adams's life and personal miseries in writing the final draft. With its cast almost intact (Howard Da Silva, replaced in this recording by Rex Everhart, returned as Ben Franklin), the show was successfully transferred to the screen in 1972.

Didier C. Deutsch

The Seventh Sign

1988, Cinedisc Records, from the film *The Seventh Sign*, Tri-Star Pictures, 1988 ♪♪♪

album notes: Music: Jack Nitzsche.

A horror film with pseudo-Biblical overtones, *The Seventh Sign* stars Demi Moore as a pregnant woman confronted by the possibility that her unborn child might be the final sign announced in the Apocalypse. Using a disembodied chorus and electronic sounds, Jack Nitzsche fashioned a score that's richly evocative and appropriately ominous, though its real importance might have been better appreciated in the theatre, as a support to the screen action.

Didier C. Deutsch

The Seventh Voyage of Sinbad

1980, Varèse Sarabande, from the film *The Seventh Voyage of Sinbad*, Columbia Pictures, 1957 ♪♪♪♪

album notes: Music: Bernard Herrmann; **Conductor:** Bernard Herrmann.

In the 1950s and '60s, Bernard Herrmann specialized in fantasy films, scoring several for special effects–ace Ray Harryhausen, beginning with this rousing adventure which features a sprightly title theme and a number of evocative cues for Harryhausen's parade of animated mythical creatures. Highlights include rumbling, ominous low brass and percussion tones for a Cyclops and a dragon, a dazzling repeated brass fanfare for a gigantic two-headed bird ("The Roc"), and an audacious battle cue for Sinbad's fight with a walking skeleton, scored almost entirely for xylophone. The threatening brass chords for the Cyclops often recall Herrmann's work on *The Day the Earth Stood Still,* while the composer's pastiche Middle Easternisms vividly conjure up the Arabia of childhood stories. This hard-to-find CD features a masterly recording and performance, although this score is so strident and aggressive in its orchestral effects and repeated textures that it may drive crazy anyone but the most ardent Herrmann fans.

Jeff Bond

1998, Varèse-Sarabande, from the film *The Seventh Voyage of Sinbad*, Columbia, 1957 ♪♪♪♪♪

album notes: Music: Bernard Herrmann; **Orchestra:** The Royal Philharmonic Orchestra; **Conductor:** John Debney.

Like *Jason and the Argonauts, The Seventh Voyage of Sinbad* gave Bernard Herrmann an occasion to write a rich score, brimming with bright sonorities and vibrant accents. Opening with the "Overture," appropriately oriental in its syncopated rhythms, the score followed the colorful story of Sinbad as he prepared to travel through lands unknown and meet unheard of dangers and creatures. This time around, the intrepid sailor, portrayed by matinee idol Kerwin Matthews, embarked on a perilous voyage to find a piece of egg from a legendary Roc bird, so that Princess Parisa (Kathryn Grant), reduced to a miniature of her own attractive self by the evil magician Sokurah (played with great relish by Torin Thatcher), can get back to her actual size. On the way, of course, various monsters and beasts, beautifully animated by Ray Harryhausen's Dynamation process, posed a permanent threat, including cyclops, a dragon, and, in one of the most inspired creations in a fantasy film, a skeleton that challenged Sinbad to a duel. Herrmann, obviously in great form, gave a musical countenance to these various aspects of the story, often in terms that, even today, continue to dazzle the listener. This new recording, with John Debney conducting the Royal Scottish National Orchestra, brings back all the fun and excitement in the score, notably in the "Duel with the Skeleton," in which Herrmann surpassed in imagination some of his best creations.

Evidencing great sonics and a marvelous audio ambiance, this is in every respect a sensational recording, far superior to the original soundtrack album, released also by Varèse-Sarabande.

see also: The Golden Voyage of Sinbad, Sinbad and the Eye of the Tiger, Jason and the Argonauts

Didier C. Deutsch

sex, lies, and videotape

1989, Virgin Movie Music, from the film *sex, lies, and videotape,* Miramax Films, 1989 ♪

album notes: Music: Cliff Martinez, Mark Mangini.

Sexy and totally unabashed about its subject, *sex, lies, and videotape* took a close-up look at four people and what motivates them erotically. If the film is beautifully nuanced and unusually imaginative, the same cannot be said of Cliff Martinez's uneven score, which often meanders into vapid synth lines without expression, punctuated at times by an electronic rhythm track, possibly to try and give them more meaning. One cannot but wonder what a more inspired composer (Patrick Doyle or Christopher Young, for instance) might have done with the same subject.

Didier C. Deutsch

The Shadow

1994, Arista Records, from the film *The Shadow,* Universal Pictures, 1994 ♪♪♪

album notes: Music: Jerry Goldsmith; Conductor: Jerry Goldsmith.

Skip the obligatory dialog and rock tracks (the first four and the last two) and enjoy Jerry Goldsmith's splendid heroic adventure score for this campy pulp-era superhero saga. His main theme is a rhythmic, ascending figure for brass over horns, reeds, and thundering percussion, with a weaving surge of violins underneath; it sounds ominously and resolutely, and lends an effective air of mystery (the strings) and power (the horns) to the shadowy crime-fighter. The various action cues are less effective, a collection of percussion hits, strings mysteriosos, and wind furtiveness often in need of the powerful main theme to bring it all to life. A great moment is achieved with the appearance of the "invisible" hotel, phrases of the main theme intone upwards with electronic whale-like moans and tangy synth twangs in a very evocative and compelling six-minute cue. With little more than 26 minutes of score on the CD, though, there aren't enough great moments like that, even with such a likable theme at hand.

Randall D. Larson

Shadow Conspiracy

1996, Intrada Records, from the film *Shadow Conspiracy,* Hollywood Pictures, 1996 ♪♪♪

album notes: Music: Bruce Broughton; Orchestra: The Sinfonia of London; Conductor: Bruce Broughton.

Bruce Broughton first collaborated with filmmaker George P. Cosmatos on the hit western *Tombstone* and was later reunited with the *Rambo* director for the box-office dud *The Shadow Conspiracy,* which is one of a number of 1997 films revolving around White House conspiracies and/or assassinations (a select group that also included Clint Eastwood's modestly successful *Absolute Power* and the Wesley Snipes turkey *Murder at 1600*). Broughton's score is a brooding, at-times thundering brassy outing featuring solid work by the Sinfonia of London. In short, if you like large-scale suspense scores, you could do far worse than to give this a listen. The main theme is, in fact, written in the same vein as *Tombstone,* so if you liked that score, it goes without saying that you ought to enjoy this one as well.

Andy Dursin

Shadow of the Wolf

1993, Milan Records, from the film *Shadow of the Wolf,* Vision International/Malofilm Distribution, 1993 ♪♪♪♪

album notes: Music: Maurice Jarre; Orchestra: The Royal Philharmonic Orchestra; Conductor: Maurice Jarre; Featured Musicians: Maurice Jarre, Ralph Grierson, Rick Marvin, synthesizers; Judd Miller, Nyle Steiner, Mick Fisher, E.V.I.

I often get the feeling that we should be hearing more film scores composed by Maurice Jarre than we do. This is, after all, the same man who wrote the music for *Lawrence of Arabia* and *Dr. Zhivago,* and whenever he scores a movie these days, the results are impressive and certainly far superior to the generic material that comprises most modern soundtracks. That certainly holds true on *Shadow of the Wolf,* which features an operatic, symphonic score performed by the stellar-sounding Royal Philharmonic Orchestra. The music, written for the rather bland 1993 adaptation of the bestselling Canadian novel *Agaguk,* has the same epic feel that marks many of the composer's best works, and its often melodic quality ought to remind listeners that, for evocative orchestral scores with a larger-than-life feel, few do it better than Jarre.

Andy Dursin

Shadowlands

1993, EMI/Angel Records, from the film *Shadowlands,* Savoy Pictures, 1993 ♪♪♪♪

album notes: Music: George Fenton; Orchestras: The London Symphony Orchestra, The Choir of Magdalen College, Oxford; Conductors: George Fenton, Grayston Ives.

George Fenton proves once again to be one of the finest film composers around, with his graceful and classy music for *Shadowlands.* The film is based on the life of Christian author and professor C.S. Lewis and his painful attempts to reconcile his wife's protracted death by cancer with his faith. Obviously in such a story the pitfalls for a composer are many, with the risk of becoming melodramatic ever-present. Fenton however delivers a score of impeccable class and refinement, yet accessibility, performed to perfection by the London Symphony Orchestra and the Choir of Magdalen College. The music owes largely to the English tradition, Fenton providing a number of impressive choral cues (evoking the Oxford setting) and a lyrically English pastoral tone for the love story. The result is a beautiful and deeply moving score, with the kind of depth that eludes most other composers these days.

Paul Andrew MacLean

Shaft

See: The Best of Shaft

Shaft in Africa

See: The Best of Shaft

Shag the Movie

1989, Sire Records, from the film *Shag the Movie,* Hemdale, 1989 ♪♪♪♪

This often hilarious soundtrack compilation was put together for a zany film purporting to document what happened over a wild weekend in 1963, when a new dance craze, the shag, "started the party that caused the uproar that led to the weekend of the century." The songs, written in imitation of the sounds that could be heard on radio at the time, are amusing for the most part, and beat-driven, but two emerge in particular—"Ready to Go Steady," performed by the Charmettes in a dead-on spoof of the Supremes, complete with bells, "oohs," and saxophone break; and k.d. lang's excellent reading of "Our Day Will Come," worth alone the price of this entertaining album.

Didier C. Deutsch

Shaka Zulu

1986, Cinedisc Records, from the television mini–series *Shaka Zulu*, 1986 ♪♪♪
album notes: Music: Dave Pollecutt

The saga of the legendary African chief who rose to head the entire Zulu nation, but was eventually defeated when he tried to repel the white invaders, *Shaka Zulu* is a forceful television drama that is bold and colorful. Surprisingly, the show elicited a score that only uses scant elements of African chants, and remains solidly rooted in the European thematic tradition. This is particularly evident in tracks like "Shaka's Escape," in which the drumming and chanting are recreations of African sounds, rather than the real thing. Adding insult to injury, the songs that are included are also often performed in English, which seems even less plausible for a story that takes place in dark Africa. The overall effect is that it deprives the score itself from sounding realistic and true, and removes from it any element of authenticity. This is a serious letdown, particularly given the fact that the cues are otherwise intelligently written and attractive.

Didier C. Deutsch

Shakespeare in Love

1998, Sony Classical, from the film *Shakespeare in Love*, Miramax, 1998 ♪♪♪
album notes: Music: Stephen Warbeck; **Conductor:** Nick Ingman.

In this well-written romantic comedy set in 16th-century London, William Shakespeare (Joseph Fiennes) finds the inspiration for his Juliet in Viola de Lessep (Gwyneth Paltrow). The considerable skills of composer Stephen Warbeck honed on another period piece, *Mrs. Brown,* complement the film's flirtatious wit with a deeply serious orchestral score, at turns fired up, deeply romantic, or tragic. Warbeck won an Oscar for best music for a comedy, although the music is more typical of a drama. This instrumental score bears one wordless voice, the liquid soprano of Catherine Bott accompanied by piano for "The Play and the Marriage." Period color is provided by an undercurrent of harp, and the addition of flute and tambourine on the distinctly Eliza-

bethan "Greenwich" and "The De Lessep's Dance." Shakespeare's theme is three pairs of notes that rise in rapid tempo to convey action in "The Beginning of the Partnership" and "The Brawl." Connecting the tragic scenes is a deep, funereal drum beat in "News of Marlowe's Death" and the death scene in *Romeo and Juliet,* "The Play Part (II)," also reprised with the addition of church bells in "Love & the End of the Tragedy." Warbeck proves, once again, his skill at balancing music contemporaneous to the plot with modern, dramatic orchestration.

David Poole

Shallow Grave

1995, EMI Records, from the film *Shallow Grave*, PolyGram/Rank, 1995 ♪♪♪
album notes: Music: Simon Boswell.

A grizzly tale of mayhem and paranoia, *Shallow Grave* dealt with three people whose well-ordained world crumbles when they discover that a roommate has died of a drug overdose, leaving behind a suitcase full of cash. They cut the body into pieces, bury it, and split the content of the case in three equal parts, but soon begin to develop deep feelings of mistrust about each other, leading to betrayal and dementia. Informing the odd narrative, and following the characters' mental disintegration, Simon Boswell wrote a score that sounds at times frighteningly eerie ("Laugh Riot," "Loft Conversion"), and at other times coldly manipulative beneath the conventional veneer ("Shallow Grave, Deep Depression"). Providing contrasting moods are some songs (Nina Simone warbling a swinging "My Baby Just Cares for Me," Andy Williams singing "Happy Heart," and the John Carmichael Band playing a bouncy "Strip the Willow").

Didier C. Deutsch

The Shawshank Redemption

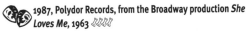
1994, Epic Soundtrax, from the film *The Shawshank Redemption*, Columbia Pictures, 1994 ♪♪♪♪

album notes: Music: Thomas Newman; **Conductor:** Thomas Newman.

Thomas Newman has been typecast into scoring movies that are good. One of them is *The Shawshank Redemption,* Frank Darabont's 1994 prison saga based on a story by Stephen King. Tim Robbins and Morgan Freeman share the ennui of a lifetime in jail until their eventual—well, you can guess. It's a somber tale which Newman handles perfectly, with folk-oriented fiddle music, a sensitive theme for piano, and delicate orchestral/metallic samples that express the passage of time. Even the big moments have a restraint—this is a prison movie whose climactic jailbreak is told in flashback—but the subtlety never comes at the expense of musical coherence. Newman taps into different modes and altered scales which gives his melodic writing a lot of zing. He also continues a tradition of Americana in the original spirit of Copland, without sounding like Copland. Overall, it's a triumph of pitch over volume. The album includes a lot of imperceptible plinking (and a few source cues) which does make it less satisfying as separated listening.

Lukas Kendall

She Loves Me

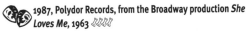
1987, Polydor Records, from the Broadway production *She Loves Me,* 1963 ♪♪♪♪

album notes: Music: Jerry Bock; **Lyrics:** Sheldon Harnick; **Musical Direction:** Hal Hastings; **Conductor:** John Berkman; **Cast:** Barbara Cook, Daniel Massey, Jack Cassidy, Barbara Baxley, Ludwig Donath.

A creamy little bonbon based on the Ferenc Molnar story *The Shop Around the Corner* (it already had inspired the film *In The Good Old Summertime,* starring Judy Garland and Van Johnson), *She Loves Me* presents the love affair between two young shy people who fall in love by correspondence, unaware that they are actually co–workers in the same perfume shop. The musical provided another splendid starring vehicle for Barbara Cook, as the young saleslady who loves/hates Daniel Massey, with Jack Cassidy and Barbara Baxley adding the strength of their support in two equally well-crafted parts. The score, by Jerry Bock and Sheldon Harnick, totally delightful, was eventu-

ally obscured as too lightweight when they came up, a year later, with their blockbuster, *Fiddler on the Roof.*

Didier C. Deutsch

The Sheltering Sky

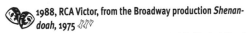
1990, Virgin Movie Music, from the film *The Sheltering Sky,* Warner Bros., 1990 ♪♪♪♪

album notes: Music: Ryuichi Sakamoto; **Orchestra:** The Royal Philharmonic Orchestra; **Conductors:** John Altman, David Arch.

Based on Paul Bowles's 1949 novel, *The Sheltering Sky* took a clinical look at an American couple, married for 10 years, travelling through Morocco, Algeria, Niger, and other exotic locales in the days following World War II, while their relationship is unraveling. Reflecting the emotional journey of the two characters, and the slow disintegration of their love story, Ryuichi Sakamoto wrote a rich, profusely emotive score in which some of the pauses seem more revelatory than the musical accents. While a faint vocal in the background sometimes serves as an exotic counterpoint to the main themes ("On the Hill"), the local colors are provided by other selections, some composed by Richard Horowitz ("Marnia's Tent"), some featuring traditional musical groups from Burundi, Tunisia, and other North African countries. The main theme, reprised on the piano, is particularly striking.

Didier C. Deutsch

Shenandoah

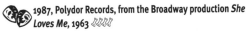
1988, RCA Victor, from the Broadway production *Shenandoah,* 1975 ♪♪♪

album notes: Music: Gary Geld; **Lyrics:** Peter Udell; **Musical Direction:** Lynn Crigler; **Cast:** John Cullum, Penelope Milford, Donna Theodore, Chip Ford.

Opening, as it did, during a newspaper strike, *Shenandoah* ran the risk of passing unnoticed. Yet this inspirational tale of a peace–loving widower and his six sons caught in the Civil War (already the subject of a celebrated film starring James Stewart), not only managed to survive but went on to a long and healthy life on Broadway, racking up a total of 1,000 performances, quite a feat in those days. Though the story (and the score by Gary Geld and Peter Udell) adopts a paternalistic attitude toward blacks (a number, "Freedom," performed by Donna Theodore, as a Southern belle, and Chip Ford, as the son of a slave, might have seemed politically correct at the time and no doubt made for good theater, but sounded hopelessly naive and downright phony in the context), it has its share of rousing moments, and John Cullum, as the widower, made sure that his solo numbers hit the right chord in the audience's emotions.

Didier C. Deutsch

Sherlock Holmes

1987, Varèse Sarabande, from the Granada Television series *Sherlock Holmes*, 1987 ♪♪♪♪

album notes: Music: Patrick Gowers; Choir: The St. Paul's Cathedral Choir; Featured Musicians: The Gabriele String Quartet, Orchestra: The Wren Orchestra of London; Conductor: Patrick Gowers; Featured Soloists: Kenneth Sillito, violin; Neil Black, cor anglais; Leslie Pearson, piano.

Granada Television's *Sherlock Holmes* series, starring Jeremy Brett, contained some of the most memorable music ever written for television, composed by Patrick Gowers. The listener is instantly captivated by Gowers's title music, whose solo violin brings one instantly into the criminal world of Victorian London. Gowers's music is mostly in the 19th–century style, the solo violin appearing often to depict the character of Holmes, as in the mournful lament "The Death of Sherlock Holmes" and the beautifully romantic "Irene Adler." Gowers's main theme is heard in many variations throughout the album, but the various settings are so eclectic that the theme never becomes stale or tired. "Libera Me" sets the theme as a hymn for a boys choir, while "The Illustrious Lord Bellinger" features the theme in an Elgar–like arrangement. Conan Doyle's Christmas mystery "The Blue Carbuncle" calls upon Gowers to create an arrangement of Christmas carols, while "North By Ten and By Ten" has a wonderfully archaic flavor with its harpsichord and string quartet. This album will appeal to both fans of the TV series as a souvenir, as well as to listeners, as a very fine example of fine British television music.

Paul Andrew MacLean

She's Out of Control

1989, MCA Records, from the film *She's Out of Control*, Weintraub Entertainment, 1989 ♪♪♪

Tony Danza treads on Michael J. Fox territory in this light comedy about the plight of a single father with a teenage daughter who begins to assert her sexuality. Uncertain about what he is supposed to do, he follows her every chance he gets in order to ensure that she keeps her virginity. Punctuating the screen action, the soundtrack offers a mixture of rock songs, some oldies and some newies, that make up this strange but enjoyable album. On the new side are songs by Troy Hinton, Brenda K. Starr, Boys Club, and Phil Thornalley. On the old side are selections by Brian Wilson, Frankie Avalon, and the Kinks. Somewhere in between, Oingo Boingo (bless them!) deliver "Winning Side," which is a refreshing change from all the synth drums in the tracks that precede and paves the way for the golden oldies.

Didier C. Deutsch

She's the One

1996, Warner Bros. Records, from the film *She's the One*, 20th Century-Fox, 1996 ♪♪♪♪

Tom Petty & the Heartbreakers deliver a lively set of great rock songs for this fetching romantic comedy that doesn't take the beaten path to seduce its audiences with its story about two brothers, a cab driver and a Wall Street stockbroker, and the women in their life. The songs by Petty, which include the hit "Walls," make few demands on the intellect but beg to be heard again once the album is over. What their relationship with the movie might be is definitely not hinted at in the lyrics, but when the songs are solid and well defined, who's to complain?

Didier C. Deutsch

Shiloh

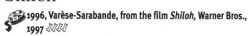

1996, Varèse-Sarabande, from the film *Shiloh*, Warner Bros., 1997 ♪♪♪♪

album notes: Music: Joel Goldsmith; Conductors: Jerry Goldsmith, Joel Goldsmith.

A simple folksy feel pervades Joel Goldsmith's score for this charming story about a boy and his beagle, with the cues merely limning the not-so-eventful-in-the-grand-scheme-of-things events in their lives. Gently innovative and skillfully pleasant, the cues offer abundant proof that Goldsmith is a master in film scoring, and has little to envy his more famous father, on hand here to help conduct the orchestra. Direct and unaffected, but consistently enjoyable, this is a little gem that deserves to be discovered.

Didier C. Deutsch

Shine

1996, Philips Classics, from the film *Shine*, Fine Line Features, 1996 ♪♪♪♪♪

album notes: Music: David Hirschfelder; Conductor: Ricky Edwards; Featured Artists: David Helfgott, piano; Ricky Edwards, piano; David Hirschfelder, piano; Mary Doumany, harp; Geoffrey Payne, trumpet; Jeffrey Crellin, oboe; Geoffrey Lancaster, harpsichord; Gerald Keuneman, cello.

The true, inspirational story of iconoclastic Australian concert pianist David Helfgott, who overcame severe debilitation and bouts of madness caused in his youth by his father's total control and eventual rejection, *Shine* chronicles the artist's slow descent into the eccentric behavior that saw him spend 15 years of his life in a psychiatric hospital, unable to communicate except through his brilliant interpretations of complex works by Liszt, Rachmaninoff, and other classical composers. Helfgott himself is heard in this soundtrack album, in which he interprets some of the pieces that helped him regain some control of his life, as well as new works written by David Hirschfelder, who composed the original score, well in keeping with the overall tone of the whole film. Given its classical approach, this soundtrack album will obviously attract primarily listeners with a natural bent for this kind of music. Others, however, should discover in it pieces they might have heard in other situations, as well as instrumental cues that are enjoyably descriptive and reflective of a story that transcends musical genres.

Didier C. Deutsch

Shining Through

1992, RCA Records, from the film *Shining Through,* 20th Century-Fox, 1992 ♪♪♡

album notes: Music: Michael Kamen; **Orchestra:** The Alma Mater Symphony Orchestra of New York; **Conductor:** Michael Kamen.

Michael Douglas and Melanie Griffith star in this unlikely World War II story of a woman with a Jewish background posing as a governess to a German officer, the better to help U.S. forces fight the Nazis. Listening to Michael Kamen's "Main Titles," in this soundtrack album, one might have a feeling that the score would have some kind of sustained excitement to it. But with a few exceptions ("The Boathouse," "Exit Berlin"), the cues are expressionless orchestral swatches that probably served the narrative very well in the theatre, but don't add up to much in one's living room. The inclusion of "I'll Be Seeing You," performed by Deirdre Harrison, while perfectly pleasant, is equally baffling in the overall musical context.

Didier C. Deutsch

Shipwrecked

1991, Walt Disney Records, from the film *Shipwrecked,* Walt Disney Pictures, 1991 ♪♪♪♪
album notes: Music: Patrick Doyle.

Patrick Doyle, who seldom misses a beat, does a bang-up job in this high seas adventure score, the story of a young boy's test of strength and courage at the hands of evil pirates. Portraying in rich details the various events facing Hakon, the young Norwegian boy who, to avoid being sent to a group home, embarks on a ship, Doyle used broad swatches of tonal colors to paint the myriad adventures that await him, from exploring a deserted South Pacific island to discovering a treasure and befriending a young girl, Mary, like him alone in the world. The cues, muscular and exhilarating, are wonderfully melodic and descriptive, making this joyous soundtrack album a delight to listen to.

Didier C. Deutsch

Shogun Mayeda

1991, Intrada Records, from the film *Shogun Mayeda,* 1991 ♪♪♪♪

album notes: Music: John Scott; **Orchestra:** The Hungarian State Opera Orchestra; **Conductor:** John Scott.

An epic film about Japanese Samurais who journey to Spain to acquire guns, *Shogun Mayeda* proved underwhelming, but John Scott's score makes for an exciting and adventurous soundtrack. Given his vast knowledge of Japanese music and culture, Scott was ideally suited to this assignment. At 66:46 (21 tracks) there is perhaps more music than the album needs, but much of it is very good—large and epic, in which Scott blends the Hungarian State Opera Orchestra with a small group of Japanese instruments. (As is his usual practice, Scott also orchestrated the score himself). The main theme is attractively majestic and brassy, and appears within numerous guises and enough variety that it stays fresh throughout. "Battle of Sekigahara" is a pensive, atmospheric cue, somewhat reminiscent of Scott's *William the Conqueror,* but invested with an exotic Japanese flavor. The various battle scenes, sea journey, and love story elements give Scott much to play off, and the result is a rich and colorful epic score. One's only dismay is that the music was not written for a more deserving film.

Paul Andrew MacLean

Shooting Fish

1997, Capitol Records, from the film *Shooting Fish,* 20th Century-Fox, 1997 ♪♪♪♡

You might not recognize a lot of names here, but sometimes it's the lesser-knowns who deliver the greatest surprises. On this set that includes the British group Space, whose "Me and You vs. the World" and "Neighbourhood" are melodically strong and sonically up to date, blending well with other bands such as Strangelove ("Beautiful Alone"), Symposium ("Twist"), Dubstar ("In Charge"), and the Wannadies ("Friends"). Old faves such as Jackie DeShannon's "What the World Needs Now Is Love" and Dionne Warwick's "Do You Know the Way to San Jose" actually provide perspective and context for these young pop groups, giving *Shooting Fish* a conceptual strength beyond its cinematic role.

Gary Graff

The Shooting Party/Birds and Planes

1991, JOS Records, from the film *The Shooting Party,* European Classics, 1984, and the documentary *Birds and Planes,* 1964 ♪♪♪♪

album notes: Music: John Scott; **Orchestra:** The Royal Philharmonic Orchestra; **Conductor:** John Scott.

Noah Taylor in Shine. **(The Kobal Collection)**

A film dealing with England's rural aristocracy on the eve of World War I, *The Shooting Party* is a beautiful evocation of the English countryside. Performed by the Royal Philharmonic, the score opens with a majestic trumpet fanfare, its bright sound evoking a misty morning sunrise. A pastoral flavor pervades the score, which is some of Scott's most particularly "English" sounding work ever. The "Epilogue" however ends the score in a somber tone, reprising the opening fanfare, counterpointed with a contorted variation on "The Last Outpost" (the British military funeral call), portending the ruin war is soon to bring upon the characters.

A pitfall of soundtrack albums is that film scores can have awkward moments on disc due to their programmatic requirements. *The Shooting Party,* however, is somewhat unique in that it plays with a near-perfect fluidity from cue to cue (track changes are in fact rarely noticed). Also included on this CD is Scott's music for a 1964 Hugh Hudson documentary *Birds and Planes.* Featuring piano, string quartet, and four basses, the score is largely atonal, yet ethereal, and shows off Scott's inventive gift for scoring for a smaller chamber ensemble.

Paul Andrew MacLean

The Shootist/Big Jake/Cahill, U.S. Marshall

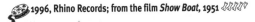 1986, Varèse Sarabande, from the films *The Shootist,* Paramount, 1976; *Big Jake,* 20th Century-Fox, 1971; and *Cahill, U.S. Marshall,* Columbia, 1973 🎬🎬🎬🎬

album notes: Music: Elmer Bernstein; Orchestra: The Utah Symphony Orchestra; Conductor: Elmer Bernstein.

Elmer Bernstein, whose western scores rank among the best and most descriptive ever written, conducted the Utah Symphony in this remarkable musical tribute to John Wayne, the quintessential movie cowboy, consisting of selections from the scores he composed for three of Wayne's last films. Neatly balancing the focus of each score between his signature staccato riding themes, and lovely romantic tunes, sometimes flavored with a south-of-the-border flair, Bernstein demonstrates again the reasons that have made him such a master in a genre that has known many exponents: his music throbs with color and excitement, painting vast landscapes against which the broad action can unfold with all the desired fire and passion. The orchestra milks the cues for all their worth, expressing the sweep and movement in them with evident delight.

see also: The Comancheros

Didier C. Deutsch

Show Boat

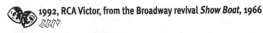 1992, RCA Victor, from the Broadway revival *Show Boat,* 1966 🎬🎬🎬

album notes: Music: Jerome Kern; Lyrics: Oscar Hammerstein II; Musical Direction: Franz Allers; Cast: Barbara Cook, Constance Towers, Stephen Douglass, William Warfield, Rosetta Le Noire, Allyn Ann McLerie, David Wayne.

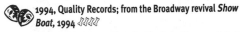 1994, Quality Records; from the Broadway revival *Show Boat,* 1994 🎬🎬🎬🎬

album notes: Music: Jerome Kern; Lyrics: Oscar Hammerstein II; Musical Direction: Jeffrey Huard; Cast: Rebecca Luker, Lonette McKee, Mark Jacoby, Michel Bell, Gretha Boston, Dorothy Stanley, Robert Morse, Elaine Stritch.

1996, Rhino Records; from the film *Show Boat,* 1951 🎬🎬🎬🎬

album notes: Music: Jerome Kern; Lyrics: Oscar Hammerstein II; Choir: The MGM Studio Chorus; Orchestra: The MGM Studio Orchestra; Conductor: Adolph Deutsch; Cast: Kathryn Grayson, Ava Gardner, Howard Keel, William Warfield, Joe E. Brown, Agnes Moorehead, Robert Sterling, Marge Champion, Gower Champion.

One of the great Broadway musicals, *Show Boat* deserves a special place in the annals of the American theater. It's little wonder that 70 years after its creation, it still rings with the same energy and fervor that stirred audiences in 1928. While its extraordinarily rich score brims with many memorable songs, it spawned one unsurpassed hit in "Ol' Man River," probably the most powerful statements about human life ever written. The first true "American" musical, in the best sense of the word, and a pioneering work of imposing magnitude, *Show Boat* presents a broad diorama about the evolution of this country, from the floating crap games aboard steamers down the Mississippi in the last part of the 19th century, to the industrial revolution that swept the country earlier in the present one. While its book remains hopelessly unbalanced (the first act covers a couple of years, while more than 40 years are collapsed into the second, leading to an uneven spread in the dramatic modus operandi), its diversified score includes romantic duets ("Make Believe," "You Are Love"), torch songs ("Bill"), showbiz anthems ("Life Upon the Wicked Stage"), and rousing choruses ("Cotton Blossom") among its many wonderful highlights.

There are many recordings of that legendary musical available, and collectors might be faced with a real dilemma when trying to decide which one to own. The choice is made even more difficult as there is no definitive recording available. Among those listed above, the 1966 studio cast album is mentioned here, particularly for Barbara Cook's sensitive portrayal as Magnolia. The 1994 Broadway revival cast album is also highly recommended, despite the fact that Mark Jacoby sounds a bit too "nice" as the cad Ravenal. But the modern sonics are superb, and the recording also contains many selections not otherwise available. The soundtrack album is a gorgeous treatment in its

Show Boat *composer Jerome Kern.* (Archive Photos, Inc.)

own right, with Howard Keel and Kathryn Grayson at the peak of their respective talents as Ravenal and Magnolia, and Ava Gardner (dubbed by Annette Warren) resplendent as Julie. This recording also includes several selections not found elsewhere, and, as is usual with Rhino, it is presented with a lot of extras (both audio and visual) that make it a rare treat.

Didier C. Deutsch

A Show of Force

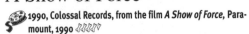 1990, Colossal Records, from the film *A Show of Force,* Paramount, 1990 ♪♪♪♪

album notes: Music: Georges Delerue; **Orchestra:** The Graunke Symphony Orchestra; **Conductor:** Georges Delerue.

A passionate courtroom drama starring Amy Irving and Robert Duvall on opposite sides of a political murder investigation and trial in Brazil, *A Show of Force* inspired Georges Delerue to write a particularly strong score in which the strains of samba are among the most ingratiating elements that combine to make it such a delightful audio experience. Delerue, a master melodist, wasted little time in idle textures, preferring instead to rely on solid, attractive tunes that meant something. And while his cues in this album are typically short, they all exude a definite musical flavor that is most endearing. Individual instruments (a harmonica, a guitar, a bandoneon) are used frequently throughout the score to paint vivid pictures that attract for the lovely musical images they evoke. It all adds up to a score that has great flair when appreciated on its own merits.

Didier C. Deutsch

Showgirls

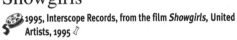 1995, Interscope Records, from the film *Showgirls,* United Artists, 1995 ♪

When sex bombs at the box office, you know something's wrong, but that's exactly what happened with *Showgirls,* Paul Verhoeven's semi-nude Las Vegas extravaganza that hardly caused a ripple when it opened (and closed) in a matter of days. Listening to this sorry soundtrack compilation, one is almost tempted to dismiss it as quickly as the critics dismissed the film, were it not for the fact that a couple of tracks feature some usually reliable favorites, Davie Bowie and Siouxsie & the Banshees. But if you can listen to the first track in its entirety, then welcome to this CD! After all, every kind of taste can be found in nature! That cover design, though, with its sinuous half-nude model, is attractive. That's about the only thing that is.

Didier C. Deutsch

Shy People

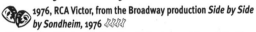 1987, Varèse Sarabande, from the film *Shy People,* Cannon Films, 1987 ♪♪♪♪

album notes: Music: Tangerine Dream.

Shy People, a film about a middle-class New York woman and her teenage daughter and the surprising journey they make to far-away, foreign Louisiana, was flavored by a remarkably effective score by Tangerine Dream with vocals. The inviting moods in the score not only enhance the story but sound downright attractive when heard in a different environment. The lyrical beauty of "Dancing on a White Moon" and "Transparent Days," particularly, demonstrates the electronic trio's unusual diversity.

Didier C. Deutsch

The Sicilian Clan

See: Il clan dei Siciliani

Side by Side by Sondheim

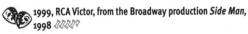 1976, RCA Victor, from the Broadway production *Side by Side by Sondheim,* 1976 ♪♪♪♪

album notes: Music: Stephen Sondheim, Leonard Bernstein, Mary Rodgers, Jule Styne, Richard Rodgers; **Lyrics:** Stephen Sondheim; **Pianists/Musical Direction:** Tim Higgs, Stuart Pedlar; **Cast:** Millicent Martin, Julia McKenzie, David Kernan.

A clever revue consisting of songs by Stephen Sondheim, *Side by Side by Sondheim* originated in London, where it opened on May 4, 1976, before moving to Broadway on April 18, 1977, for a run of 390 performances. Since the material is already well-known and accepted, what is important here is the caliber of the performers, with Millicent Martin, one of the bright stars from the British stage, making a remarkable contribution, surrounded by Julia McKenzie and David Kernan, with Ned Sherrin providing the sly comments.

see also: Stephen Sondheim in Composers

Didier C. Deutsch

Side Man

1999, RCA Victor, from the Broadway production *Side Man,* 1998 ♪♪♪♪

A dramatic glance at jazz musicians—their checkered existence from clubs, to the unemployment line, to gigs, and more despair and frustrations—*Side Man* essentially wants to show the passion in the unsung musicians who often play behind a leader and seldom get the recognition, but keep on playing for the love of music. While the actors on stage are not asked to play any instruments, the drama features a lot of music, drawn from the archives of recorded music, and since the hero of the action is a trumpet player, the music heard focuses almost entirely on trumpet solos by great performers like Clifford Brown, Miles Davis, Lee Morgan, and Donald Byrd. Presented as "Jazz Classics from the Broadway Play," this album offers some classic selections by those seminal artists. It's a solid collection that will appeal particularly to those who love jazz. The notes by playwright Warren Leight detail the selections chosen and place them within the dramatic context of the play. Probably nothing new for jazz fans, but something nice to have just the same.

Didier C. Deutsch

Side Show

1997, Sony Classical, from the Broadway musical, *Side Show*, 1997 🎬🎬🎬🎬

album notes: Music: Henry Krieger; **Book & Lyrics:** Bill Russell; **Cast:** Alice Ripley (Violet Hilton), Emily Skinner (Daisy Hilton), Jeff McCarthy (Terry Connor), Hugh Panaro (Buddy Foster).

Lambasted by the press and misunderstood by audiences further misled by a poorly planned ad campaign, *Side Show* failed to capture the hearts of theatergoers and closed after a couple of months, during which it valiantly struggled to keep alive. Based on the true story of Daisy and Violet Hilton, forever tied at the hip, who gained notoriety as the stars of a traveling act that criss-crossed the American countryside, playing the carnival and vaudeville circuits of the day, and went on to appear in Tod Browning's notoriously famous 1932 film, *Freaks,* the musical proved both uplifting and entertaining. Henry Krieger, whose score for *Dreamgirls* helped him get the right attention on Broadway, evidenced moments of brilliance that were captured in this original-cast album recording (listen, notably, to "Rare Songbirds on Display" and the breathtaking "I Will Never Love You"). But, like the musical that never quite could find an audience, these songs lack the real focus that could have taken them closer to the listener's heart and make them seem more important. The two sisters, beautifully portrayed by Alice Ripley and Emily Skinner, are great together and redeem the flaws in the score with their genuinely thrilling vocalizing.

Didier C. Deutsch

Sidewalk Stories

1989, Antilles Records, from the film *Sidewalk Stories,* Island 1989 🎬🎬🎬🎬

album notes: Music: Marc Marder.

This tuneful, unassuming little score was heard behind a pleasantly humorous film shot in the streets of New York, about the misadventures of a man and his five-year-old daughter. Written tongue-in-cheek with a wink and a smile by Marc Marder, it is the kind of music that easily brings a smile to one's lips, though

it is not consequential, earth-shaking, or vitally important. It just happens to be fun and enjoyable, the kind of CD you might want to play when no special occasion warrants it. Sometimes, one shouldn't ask for anything more.

Didier C. Deutsch

The Siege

1998, Varèse-Sarabande, from the film *The Siege,* 20th Century-Fox, 1998 🎬🎬

album notes: Music: Graeme Revell; **Conductors:** Tim Simonec, Larry Kenton.

With his scores to *The Crow, Strange Days,* and *Chinese Box,* Graeme Revell has emerged as Hollywood's foremost practitioner of world music. Revell's wall of sound blends ethnic instruments with synthesizers, percussion, industrial samples, and an orchestra, coming up with a sound that's unique and intoxicating. In this score, he had to deal with Arab terrorists, and used middle eastern voices, percussion, and the ever-popular duduk (which had already characterized his score for *The Crow*). However, *The Siege* remains unusually distant for Revell, not reaching the intoxicating heights of his best work in *Chinese Box* and *Until the End of the World.* While this film deals with another culture, the themes and cold synthesizers still tend to lie there, a "background" score that does the job, but with a restraint that doesn't make it very remarkable.

Dan Schweiger

Siesta

1987, Warner Bros. Records, from the film *Siesta,* 1987 🎬🎬

album notes: Music: Marcus Miller; **Featured Musicians:** Miles Davis, trumpet; John Scofield, acoustic guitar; Earl Klugh, classical guitar; Omar Hakim, drums; James Walker, flute; Jason Miles, synthesizer programming.

An updated "Sketches of Spain" (well, sort of), Davis found an effective contemporary collaborator with Marcus Miller. Miller orchestrated the music in the mid-eighties synth style (many of the synthesizer sounds are somewhat out of date). The "Spanish tinge" Davis favors in his music is played to the hilt here (especially "Siesta," "Submission," and the remarkable "Los Feliz," a truly haunting performance). Davis is sparsely used throughout the album (this is not a full-fleged Davis album), but his sound and style make the few appearances memorable. The remainder of the material consists of moody tracks that probably work well with the picture, but are hard to concentrate on as purely jazz music. If you want to hear Davis in full effect with Miller, "Tutu" is the best example of this team.

Bob Belden

The Silence of the Lambs

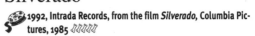 1991, MCA Records, from the film *The Silence of the Lambs,* Orion Pictures, 1990 ♪♪

album notes: Music: Howard Shore; **Orchestra:** The Munich Symphony Orchestra; **Conductor:** Howard Shore.

By virtue of the nature of the film's plot, the music composed by Howard Shore for *Silence of the Lambs* is dark, brooding, and ominous. While it makes for fine underscoring for the film, it suffers somewhat outside the context of the movie, becoming a bit more tedious with repeated listening. Disturbing to this listener are some very noticeable edits in the first minute or so of the opening track, the "Main Title." Wasn't the producer listening when they edited and mastered the album? As with a number of other recent film scores, this one's better off heard as you view the film.

Charles L. Granata

Silent Fall

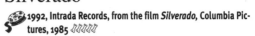 1994, Morgan Creek Records, from the film *Silent Fall,* Warner Bros., 1994 ♪♪♪

album notes: Music: Stewart Copeland.

An interesting thriller involving an autistic child who witnesses the murder of his parents, and the psychiatrist who attempts to break the incoherent wall of silence and help resolve the crime, *Silent Fall* found in Stewart Copeland a composer with a great deal of empathy for the film and its subject matter. The cues he wrote, many of them performed by an acoustic guitar, coupled with a clarinet or dueting with a piano over an orchestral texture ("Our Parents' House," "Kitchen Cognition"), are very endearing and evocative. Others, using the full complement of the orchestra, also paint vivid images that seem more specifically adapted to the screen action, but still make a favorable impression. "Healing," performed by Wynonna and Michael English, is an appropriately fitting coda to the score.

Didier C. Deutsch

Silk Stockings

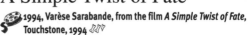 1988, RCA Victor, from the Broadway production *Silk Stockings,* 1955 ♪♪♪♪

album notes: Music: Cole Porter; **Lyrics:** Cole Porter; **Musical Direction:** Herbert Greene; **Cast:** Don Ameche, Hildegarde Neff, Gretchen Wyler.

East–West relations took a musical turn in this clever adaptation of Melchior Lengyel's amusing play, *Ninotchka,* with Cole Porter providing the *divertissement.* Don Ameche is in top form as an American in Paris, a talent agent who seduces a stern Russian envoy, played by Hildegarde Neff, sent to investigate three former Russian colleagues, and converts her to the West-

ern way of life. While the show, which opened on February 4, 1955, had a somewhat disappointing run of 478 performances, it provided another great vehicle for Fred Astaire, playing opposite Cyd Charisse, when it transferred to the screen in 1957, with its score almost intact.

Didier C. Deutsch

Silverado

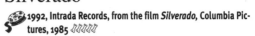 1992, Intrada Records, from the film *Silverado,* Columbia Pictures, 1985 ♪♪♪♪♪

album notes: Music: Bruce Broughton; **Conductor:** Bruce Broughton.

A big, brassy western score in the tradition laid down by his predecessors in the field is what Bruce Broughton created for this western in which every gesture is grand and exhilaratingly overstated. With good guys (drifters Kevin Kline, Scott Glenn, and Kevin Costner) and bad guys (Brian Dennehy, delightful as a corrupt sheriff, and Jeff Goldblum) facing it off in a powerful showdown, everything in the film evokes the grandeur the West never was, with Broughton's score emphasizing every twist in the narrative with surprisingly effective cues that are greatly enjoyable. In his brief comments about the score, the composer talks about "the power, strength, and energy" he found in the screenplay and tried to convey in his music. He succeeded admirably.

Didier C. Deutsch

Simon Birch

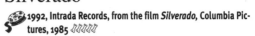 1998, Epic/Sony Music Soundtrax, from the film *Simon Birch,* Hollywood Pictures, 1998 ♪♪♪

album notes: Music: Marc Shaiman; **Conductors:** Artie Kane, Pete Anthony; **Featured Musician:** Ralph Grierson, piano.

John Irving's novel *A Prayer for Owen Meany* inspired this film about a very tiny hero named Simon Birch. Set in the summer of 1964, the film's period is staged in part by a terrific wall of musical sound. Baby boomers, get ready to dance to the likes of the Impressions, the Drifters, Marvin Gaye, and Jackie Wilson, and then take a little breather with four score cues by composer Marc Shaiman. A new single by Babyface rounds out this pleasant collection.

Amy Rosen

A Simple Twist of Fate

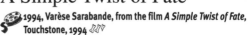 1994, Varèse Sarabande, from the film *A Simple Twist of Fate,* Touchstone, 1994 ♪♪♪

album notes: Music: Cliff Eidelman; **Conductor:** Cliff Eidelman.

Cliff Eidelman succeeds once again in creating another delightfully gentle, romantic musical fantasy. This time, it's about the bond between a man, who has shut the world out of his life, and the small child who comes into his care, changing everything he knows and believes in. Eidelman personifies this fusion of their souls though the use of a small female choir within the orchestra. The mood is occasionally broken by darker passages, such as the Bernard Herrmann-esque "Prelude to Tanny's Fate," and several variations on "Red Is the Rose." Eidelman performs the piano solo on "Michael's Theme."

David Hirsch

Simply Irresistible

1999, Restless Records, from the film *Simply Irresistible*, Regency, 1999 ♪

Starring "Buffy The Vampire Slayer" (sorry! Sarah Michelle Gellar), this slight confection finds the attractive actress as the owner of a restaurant that doesn't seem to attract too many clients, simply because she doesn't happen to be a good cook. Enter a would-be fairy godfather, whose legerdemain transforms the lass into the best chef in town, and helps her in the process find love in the guise of Sean Patrick Flanery. And they lived happily ever after . . . Spicing up this brew on screen, the soundtrack offers several pop selections, some of which are covers of well-known standards like "That Old Black Magic" and "Bewitched, Bothered, and Bewildered." Since they sound like the other tunes, amiably bland and innocuous in a soft romantic sort of way, one is tempted to conclude that the selections are a fair representation of the film itself—insipid! Even a "hidden" reprise of "Bewitched" can't convince otherwise.

Didier C. Deutsch

Sinbad and the Eye of the Tiger

1998, Cinephile/U.K., from the film *Sinbad and the Eye of the Tiger*, Columbia, 1977 ♪♪♪♪
album notes: Music: Roy Budd; Conductor: Roy Budd.

The adventures of Sinbad inspired yet another screen fantasy with *Sinbad and the Eye of the Tiger*, a fanciful story about the fabled Sailor on a quest to free a prince, who has been changed into a monkey by an evil sorceress. The formula is hackneyed, but surprisingly it always works, and with all the special effects devised to spruce up the tale it usually ends up being entertaining, which was again the case in this instance. Convincingly played by Patrick Wayne with the right gusto, all this Sinbad needed was a big-sounding, appropriately exotic score in the grand Hollywood tradition laid down by Miklos Rozsa and Bernard Herrmann. Roy Budd obliged, as this soundtrack album demonstrates, and while his overall approach may suffer in comparison to the lush exoticism or imagination of his distinguished predecessors, his contribution re-

mains very engaging for the most part. Displaying at times a convincing orientalism, filled with warm sonorities, at other times eerie sounds well made to suggest the various threats Sinbad encounters (a giant mosquito, an oversize walrus, a saber-toothed tiger, all imaginatively set to motion by Ray Harryhausen), the composer created a richly textured score that is constantly creative and fun to listen to.

see also: The Golden Voyage of Sinbad, The Seventh Voyage of Sinbad

Didier C. Deutsch

Singin' in the Rain

1996, Rhino Records; from the screen musical *Singin' in the Rain*, MGM, 1952 ♪♪♪♪
album notes: Music: Nacio Herb Brown; Lyrics: Arthur Freed; *Choir:* The MGM Studio Chorus; Orchestra: The MGM Studio Orchestra; Conductor: Lennie Hayton; Cast: Gene Kelly, Donald O'Connor, Debbie Reynolds.

Some things in life are so familiar, and our senses so attuned to them, that we can almost "sense" them without actually seeing or hearing them fully. Certainly, one of life's great "comfort" sounds is the enchanting, mesmerizing opening patter of the raindrops, and Gene Kelly's soft "Ooo-da-loo-doo"-ing from *Singin' in the Rain*. Thankfully, the restoration of the soundtrack recording of *Singin' in the Rain* has been entrusted to the tender, loving care of the folks at Rhino Records, specifically producers Marilee Bradford and Bradley Flanagan, who deserve immeasurable credit for undertaking the preservation of the rich catalog of spectacular MGM musicals. Finally, one of the most beloved and important musicals in film history has been given the royal treatment it deserves. This new definitive release brims with extended recordings and previously unreleased outtakes, rare production stills and insightful recollections from the writers of the screenplay, Betty Comden and Adolph Green.

The musical selections are presented in their original order (as they appear in the conductor's score), and wherever possible, have been remixed from the original recording "angles" (tracks recorded with different microphone placements) to create the first true stereo recordings from the score. Although the sound is dated by today's standard (keep in mind the relatively primitive conditions under which film tracks were recorded and mixed, and that they weren't intended for modern "home" hi-fi consumption), it is very enjoyable. In addition to the extended recordings (notably, Gene Kelly's "All I Do Is Dream of You") and other surprises (the restoration of the instrumental opening to "Singin' in the Rain" and the outtake of "You Are My Lucky Star"), the finishing touch is the inclusion of a 1941 performance of the title song by none other than its lyricist, Arthur Freed.

Charles L. Granata

Gene Kelly in Singin' in the Rain. **(The Kobal Collection)**

Singles

1992, Epic Records, from the film *Singles*, Warner Bros., 1992
♪♪♪

This album is more than just the soundtrack to a Cameron Crowe movie, it's the soundtrack to a very specific time and place. Seattle in the early 1990s, for better or worse, will be remembered as a fertile (and certainly wet) hotbed of musical activity, putting numerous bands in the worldwide limelight, including the bulk of the artists on *Singles*. This romantic comedy set in the slacker Seattle coffeehouse/grunge scene includes tracks by local faves Soundgarden, Pearl Jam, Alice in Chains, and more. Infinitely more interesting are the two new tracks by legendary Replacements front man Paul Westernerg, especially the infectious "Dyslexic Heart."

Amy Rosen

Sirens

1994, Milan Records, from the film *Sirens*, Miramax, 1994 ♪♪♪

album notes: Music: Rachel Portman; **Conductor:** David Snell.

The *Sirens* album opens with Ralph Vaughan Williams's jaunty "March Past of the Kitchen Utensils," and the Rachel Portman score that follows blends the English precision of that piece with the lyricism of Georges Delerue and the quirky rhythms of Elmer Bernstein. Of course this is a crude approximation. Portman, an Oscar winner for *Emma*, has a distinct style that has grown out of these worthy influences. *Sirens* is a period piece about Hugh Grant, sensuality, and naked supermodels, and the score is charming and buoyant, with dreamy, transparent orchestrations. The handful of different themes are self-contained and memorable—you will especially remember them over the course of the album, as each one is repeated almost verbatim several times.

Lukas Kendall

Sister Act

1992, Hollywood Records, from the film *Sister Act,* Touchstone Pictures, 1992 ♪♪♪

album notes: Music: Marc Shaiman; **Conductor:** Artie Kane; **Featured Vocalists:** Deloris & the Sisters (Whoopi Goldberg, Maggie Smith, Andrea Robinson, Kathy Najimy, Mary Wickes, Rose Parenti), Deloris & the Ronelles (Whoopi Goldberg, Jennifer Lewis, Charlotte Crossley).

For this amiable Whoopi Goldberg comedy, Marc Shaiman transforms a quartet of gospel hymns into Motown-styled rockers. The majority of the CD is taken up by these, and six straightforward rock tunes. Shaiman is given four cues (about 13 minutes) to present his underscore—mostly rhythm-section action music. Adopting the film's initial Las Vegas setting, Shaiman's brassy music captures an appropriate Vegas lounge feel. In one cue he orchestrally addresses several of the Motown tunes heard from the choir earlier, contrasting them with the Vegas jazzy chase-music as the villains, nuns, and Whoopi all meet up and settle their differences in a Vegas casino. This score may not be for everyone, and in fact it's got little actual film music, However, Shaiman's Motown-hymns are so catchy and his action cues nicely done enough to make the disc quite likable.

Randall D. Larson

Sisters

1985, Southern Cross Records, from the film *Sisters*, American International, 1973 ♪♪♪♪

album notes: Music: Bernard Herrmann; **Conductor:** Bernard Herrmann.

After years of toiling on juvenile fantasy films in the '60s, Bernard Herrmann saw his reputation completely overhauled in the '70s as a new generation of film directors sought him out. Chief among them was Brian DePalma, who mirrored the Hitchcock/ Herrmann collaboration by hiring the composer for a series of unusual suspense films. *Sisters,* a bizarre shocker about separated Siamese twins, is the weirdest of the bunch, and Herrmann's score is probably his most frightening and unsettling effort since his classic *Psycho* effort. The opening is a terrifying fall through layers of descending string, celeste, and xylophone textures and a hair-raising synthesized howl (played over microscopic fetal photography in the film's title sequence). This aggressive horror approach alternates with a delicate, lullaby-like chime melody throughout the score. It's not exactly easy listening, but it's a great example of how Herrmann was still able to push the boundaries of the medium even in the final years of his career.

Jeff Bond

Six Days Seven Nights

1998, Hollywood Records, from the film *Six Days Seven Nights*, Touchstone, 1998 ♪♪♪♪

album notes: Music: Randy Edelman; **Featured Musicians:** Randy Edelman, piano; Cassio Duarte, percussion; **Conductor:** Randy Edelman.

Six Days Seven Nights is the adventure-action film that may have gotten a short shrift when it was revealed, shortly before its release, that co-star Anne Heche was Ellen DeGeneres's main squeeze. Teaming her with macho man Harrison Ford seemed a bit ludicrous in the eyes of many, and they didn't respond to this story of a pilot who finds himself stranded on a deserted island with a volatile New York magazine editor after the plane, with which he was taking her to a remote location, failed to respond and crashed. As luck (and the screenplay) would have it, they soon discover that proximity makes the heart grow fonder, and before you can even say "Ellen" they're shacking together. Well, if you can believe this one, there's a famous bridge spanning the East River that's for sale... Not taking anything away from the two stars, one element that made this comedy a bit more breezy was Randy Edelman's bright and cheery score, the kind of music you might want to play, even if you don't like Harrison Ford, Anne Heche, or Ellen DeGeneres. Reflecting the light moods in the film, it's consistently bouncy and lightweight and totally enjoyable.

Didier C. Deutsch

Six Days Six Nights

1994, Virgin Movie Music, from the film _Six Days Six Nights,_ Fine Line Features, 1994 ✱✱✱✱✱

album notes: Music: Michael Nyman; **Conductor:** Michael Nyman.

Depending on the type of film he is scoring, Michael Nyman can be painfully austere or brightly illuminating. _Six Days Six Nights,_ an intimate, powerful, and intense tale of sexual intrigue and all-consuming passion, directed by Diane Kurys, must have inspired him particularly. While still evidencing strains of minimalist writing, one of the composer's characteristic elements of style, his score is exquisitely composed, with cues that exude a florid melodic aura, and themes that, for once, are pleasantly attractive. The Michael Nyman Band, a conglomeration of talented "regulars," involving a string section, a brass ensemble, and a basic rhythm group, plays the selections with evident empathy and delight, something that comes across in specific cues like "Sisters," "Waltzing the Bird," "A la folie . . .," "Love Forever," and the title track, among the best moments in this recording.

Didier C. Deutsch

Six Degrees of Separation

1994, Elektra Records, from the film _Six Degrees of Separation,_ MGM, 1994 ✱✱

album notes: Music: Jerry Goldsmith; **Orchestra:** The Victorian Philharmonic Orchestra of Melbourne; **Conductor:** Jerry Goldsmith; **Cast:** Stockard Channing (Ouisa), Will Smith (Paul), Donald Sutherland (Flan), Mary Beth Hurt (Kitty), Bruce Davison (Larkin), Jeffrey Abrams (Doug).

This score for Fred Schiepsi's film adaptation of the Broadway play is one of Jerry Goldsmith's most intelligent and beautifully crafted scores of the '90s. Unfortunately, it's also one of the few Goldsmith scores that fails to stand on its own very well when listened to apart from the film. Most of the music is based around a tango Goldsmith wrote for the title theme, but it's an extremely brief, low-key effort and the producers of this album have judiciously padded out the CD's running length

with generous doses of out-of-context dialogue from the film. This is an approach that has long been rendered obsolete by the availability of the videocassette, and programming out the verbiage to get to the score is probably more effort than most people will want to go through. Goldsmith's music interacts with the onscreen images and ideas brilliantly, but the album is a hard sell.

Jeff Bond

The 6th Man

1997, Hollywood Records, from the film _The 6th Man,_ Touchstone Pictures, 1997 ✱✱

album notes: Music: Marcus Miller.

Here's a dose of R&B and rap of the new school variety, whether it's New Jack crooning from Johnny Gill ("All He's Supposed to Be") or slamming hip-hop by Doug E. Fresh ("Superstition") and Pharcyde ("Tasty"). There's not a lot of A-matter here, however, making this more of a commercial than a creative exercise.

Gary Graff

Sketch Artist

1992, Varèse Sarabande, from the television movie _Sketch Artist,_ Motion Picture Corporation of America, 1992 ✱✱✱✱

album notes: Music: Mark Isham.

In a somewhat typical way, Mark Isham wrote a flavorful score for this television film starring Jeff Fahey and Sean Young. With a predominance of steel guitar sounds and synthesizer effects, over a rhythm line, the composer creates moods that are gently evocative, and harmonious. "The River and the Earring," "The Sketch," "Claire," and "Warehouse" are particularly evocative, but the whole score is well defined and enjoyable.

Didier C. Deutsch

Sleepers

1996, Philips Records, from the film _Sleepers,_ Warner Bros., 1996 ✱✱✱✱

album notes: Music: John Williams; **Conductor:** John Williams; **Featured Musicians:** James Thatcher, French horn; Janet Ferguson, flute.

Outstanding is the best word to characterize this masterful, Oscar-nominated score from John Williams, a full-blooded dramatic outing that stands as the composer's finest "serious" score of the 1990s (i.e., music written for a supposedly award-worthy picture). Quite a contrast from the excellent though rather one-dimensional attributes of his scores for Oliver Stone's _JFK_ and _Nixon,_ Williams here ventures into a challenging musical landscape filled with often dissonant, eclectic combinations of electric guitar, synthesizer, and full orchestra, dominated by a central motif that fails to find a resolution until the very end. Along the way the composer treats us to a veritable "tour de force" of musical cues that are by turns both poignant and disturbing, seductive yet unsettling, marked by tracks that simply explode with musical energy ("The Football Game"). Williams builds his score perfectly from the start, culminating in a truly lyrical finale that puts an ideal cap on a score that's easily the best of 1996, and further proof that great music can come from films that fail to live up to their potential.

Andy Dursin

Sleeping Beauty

1998, Disney Records, from the animated feature, *Sleeping Beauty*, 1959 🎵🎵

album notes: Music: P.I. Tchaikovsky; **Score:** Tom Adair, George Bruns, Sammy Fain, Jack Lawrence, Winston Hibler, Ted Sears, Erdman H. Penner; **Conductor:** George Bruns.

Call it a case where a great Russian composer meets a famous American mouse! This animated adaptation of Tchaikovsky's ballet, drawn in angular ways that seemed to have lost the soft focus of *Snow White* or the purity in design of *Cinderella,* might have been too mature for the kids, despite the presence of a trio of cute fairy godmothers, and too childish for their parents. And if Disney had hoped to repeat with it the *succes d'estime* enjoyed by *Fantasia,* he must have been in for a real surprise. Without Stokowski, but with George Bruns conducting instead, the Tchaikovsky music for *Sleeping Beauty* just didn't have the same sparkle as the classical selections in the 1940 film. This is still pretty much in evidence in this soundtrack recording, where the songs, based on the melodies from the ballet, fail to ignite. One would be hard pressed to find another "Someday My Prince Will Come" or "So This Is Love" in this uneven collection of tunes. Even with the great Russian composer providing the music.

Didier C. Deutsch

Sleeping with the Enemy

1991, Columbia Records, from the film *Sleeping with the Enemy,* 20th Century-Fox, 1991 🎵🎵🎵

album notes: Music: Jerry Goldsmith; **Conductor:** Jerry Goldsmith.

Jerry Goldsmith has provided one of his loveliest romantic scores for this drama of spousal abuse and liberation, with two contrasting motifs—a very pretty love theme for Julia Roberts and a percussion-and-synth ambiance for her abusive husband. Roberts's theme is arranged for woodwinds over weaving strings which recall the swaying motion of the ocean into which her character fakes her death. The husband's ambient

theme, with its synth rustles, sharp drum pounds, and rhythmic bell gongs, is associated with the terror Roberts lived under and which she faces when her husband discovers her whereabouts and confronts her again. While "The Funeral" contrasts both motifs sequentially, in "The Ring," Goldsmith meshes them into a single variation—the powerful, frightening ambiance for the husband facing up to Roberts's lovely melody at the moment he discovers he has been deceived. The score ends on a victorious note, with the theme for Roberts's character soaring freely, unshackled at last from the oppressive presence of her husband's violent domination.

Randall D. Larson

Sleepless in Seattle/Sleepless in Seattle: More Songs for Sleepless Nights

Sleepless in Seattle: 1993, Epic Soundtrax, from the film *Sleepless in Seattle,* TriStar Pictures, 1993 🎵🎵🎵🎵

Without a doubt, this compilation (for it is truly a compilation, as opposed to a recording featuring music originally composed for the film) is one of the finest collections of recordings, which seem to be *de rigueur* for many of Hollywood's most popular films of late. While the centerpiece is the incredibly successful chart hit "When I Fall in Love" (performed by Celine Dion and Clive Griffin), there are time-honored standards that should warm the hearts of every music lover: Jimmy Durante's "As Time Goes By" and Nat King Cole's "Stardust" and "A Kiss to Build a Dream On" (with Louis Armstrong's distinct imprint) emerging as highlights. As well, a number of contemporary artists offer their unique take on the "classics," with excellent performances of "Bye Bye Blackbird" by Joe Cocker and "Makin' Whoopee" by Dr. John and Ricki Lee Jones. It's refreshing to see Hollywood's directors utilizing one of our most important cultural treasures, American popular music, to enhance the mood and texture of their films, introducing these essential songs and interpretations to a new, younger generation of filmgoers. If nothing else, this recording serves that purpose—in a romantically delightful manner!

Charles L. Granata

Sleepless in Seattle: More Songs for Sleepless Nights: 1998, Epic Soundtrax, inspired by the film *Sleepless in Seattle,* TriStar, 1993 🎵

If it were not for the fact that it stretches a devious industry practice to a deplorable limit, this collection could almost be enjoyable—several great standards performed by artists as diverse as Al Jolson, Ethel Merman, Carly Simon, and Sinead O'Connor. But here's the rub: it is presented as a tie-in with the

popular movie *Sleepless in Seattle.* In fact, on the front tray card, there is even the same picture of Tom Hanks and Meg Ryan that adorned the original soundtrack album.

The only problem, clearly indicated on the front cover (but who reads the fine prints or even bothers to understand what they mean?), is that the songs have nothing to do with the film itself, and have simply been compiled together to cash in on the film's success. Again, the collection is enjoyable. The concept behind it is truly despicable.

Didier C. Deutsch

Sleepwalkers

1992, Milan/BMG, from the film *Sleepwalkers,* Columbia, 1992 woof!

album notes: Music: Nicholas Pike.

Stephen King's vampire tale about a mother and son who suck the life out of unsuspecting virgins pales next to his horror classics. Nicholas Pike's simplistic division between the violent glissandi of the duo's diabolic nocturnal jaunts and the wholesomeness of their daily existence adds nothing to this horror by numbers. Echoes of their blood sucking rampages rarely seep out during the daytime to add a more complex layer to the plot. At its best Pike's restless symphony lashes out in snaps of violence with strings ascending from bass up through the registers to piercing squeals, punctuated by occasional booming bass drums. The chill drafts of synthesized angelic voices, melodies on Chinese flute, the hum of a didgeridu, thundering sheets of metal, and the resonant Tibetan bowl add color to the score. Bookending *Sleepwalkers* are the warm tones of the vintage Hawaiian slack key guitar instrumental "Sleepwalk," and Enya humming saccharine tribute to the ancient British Queen on "Boadicea." Breaking the formulaic cues is the centerpiece, the Contours' take on "The Twist," their only hit "Do You Love Me," which has already been overplayed from the *Dirty Dancing* soundtrack.

David Poole

Sliding Doors

1998, Jersey Records, from the film *Sliding Doors,* Miramax, 1998

A frothy romantic comedy, *Sliding Doors* seemed to have little else on its mind than entertain, which it did in grand style. While the story of a young London girl who, in a single day, loses her job, her purse (snatched by a robber), and her boyfriend, might seem inconsequential (particularly in view of the fact that everything that ensues becomes a figment of her imagination, in a fantasy life that parallels her real life), the film itself proved entirely winsome and charming. The bubbly at-

mosphere of the film is also echoed in the bouncy collection of songs heard on the soundtrack, with engaging performances by Blair, Space Monkeys, Jamiroquai, Brand New Heavies, Those Magnificent Men, and (Sir) Elton John. Not a bad line-up of talent for what is after all nothing more than a lightweight entertainment.

Didier C. Deutsch

Sling Blade

1996, Island Records, from the film *Sling Blade,* Miramax, 1996

album notes: Music: Daniel Lanois.

Billy Bob Thornton directed, starred in, and won a Best Screenplay Adaptation Oscar for this film about a mentally deficient man, released from a psychiatric prison after he killed his mother and her lover, who befriends a young boy whose mother's boyfriend is abusive. The score for this unusual story was composed by Daniel Lanois, best known for his work with U2 and Brian Eno. Contrary to what one might have expected here (a twangy, southern style score, perhaps), Lanois chose to write ambient music, which works to a degree. On the other hand, the songs display that laid-back southern style suggested by the locale of the story, and include "Soul Dressing" by Booker T & the M.G.'s, Emmylou Harris performing an arrangement of "Shenandoah," the very Robbie Robertson-influenced "Lonely One" by Tim Gibbons, and Daniel Lanois doing his song "The Maker," from his 1989 album, *Acadie.*

Beth Krakower

Sliver

1993, Virgin Movie Music, from the film *Sliver,* Paramount Pictures, 1993

Sliver presents a very modern-sounding collection of disassociated bands and songs. UB40 had a hit with its reggaefied rendition of Elvis Presley's "Can't Help Falling in Love." Dig deep, and you'll find a goodly number of cutting edge artists—Enigma, Neneh Cherry, Shaggy, Lords of Acid, Massive Attack—though these are not necessarily their shining moments. Not one you'd be ashamed to own, but not something you'll play a lot, either.

Gary Graff

Slums of Beverly Hills

1998, RCA Victor, from the film *Slums of Beverly Hills,* 20th Century-Fox, 1998

album notes: Music: Rolfe Kent; **Conductor:** William Stromberg.

A '70s-type soundtrack informs this exquisitely funny, and at times bawdy, comedy about a dysfunctional Jewish family living on the edge of Beverly Hills, the closest to fame and fortune father Alan Arkin can afford, and the coming-of-age of daughter Natasha Lyonne. Reminiscent of the comedies Mel Brooks, Neil Simon, and Carl Reiner excel at writing, this delirious film, directed by Tamara Jenkins and set in 1976, used a generous serving of soft rock/pop/R&B songs from the era, by such artists as Parliament, Ten Years After, Three Dog Night, Funkadelic, the Bellamy Brothers, and Ike & Tina Turner, whose "A Fool in Love" sounds terribly distorted. In the midst of all of these, Perry Como's "Papa Loves Mambo," a hit from the 1950s, seems like a dated throwback, while Rolfe Kent's score, played by an orchestra conducted by William Stromberg, comes across as a sweet collection of nondescript themes.

Didier C. Deutsch

Small Soldiers

1998, Varèse-Sarabande, from the film *Small Soldiers*, Dream-Works, 1998 ♫♫♫♫
album notes: Music: Jerry Goldsmith; **Conductor:** Jerry Goldsmith.

1998, DreamWorks Records, from the film *Small Soldiers*, DreamWorks, 1998 ♫♫

A film distinguished by its special effects, but not by its congeniality, *Small Soldiers,* the story of children toys getting a life of their own and running amok, got two different soundtrack albums: an instrumental score release and a song-driven compilation. Dealing with the second first, it brings together some heavy duty performers, like Queen, Wyclef Jean, Billy Squier, Gary Glitter, Pat Benatar, the Pretenders, and Cheap Trick, among others. While some may be more appealing than others to better trained ears, the insistent rap rhythms in most of them prove to be tiring after a while, and unimaginative. In this noisy mishmash, Cheap Trick comes off best with "Surrender," closely followed by "Tom Sawyer," by Rush. But reflective of the rest, "Another One Bites the Dust" is a tired performance by Queen with Wyclef Jean that is not very interesting.

The score album, featuring music by Jerry Goldsmith, is of course, far more interesting, if only because Goldsmith is an intelligent composer who is not about to let any subject he tackles overcome his sense of melody and his creativity. Thus, the cues here, representative of his solid approach to this film, reveal a kinship with his most famous war scores like *Patton* or *MacArthur,* with bold, brassy themes that play well within the framework imposed by the screen story, and receive a bright counterpoint in some of the quieter moments. Smartly delineated and imaginative, the themes have

an attractive lilt to them, and invite repeated listening. The spacious sound achieved in this recording add to one's enjoyment and better appreciation of the work done by the composer.

Didier C. Deutsch

A Smile Like Yours

1997, Elektra, from the film *A Smile Like Yours,* Paramount, 1977 ♫♫♫

It's tough putting middling new performances together with classics, which is just what happens on this set. After all, how can we expect Natalie Cole or the pairing of the Motels' Martha Davis and Ivan Neville to hold up against a selection of seminal R&B that includes James Brown's "I Feel Good," the Temptations' "My Girl," the Supremes' "Where Did Our Love Go," and Ike and Tina Turner's smoking version of "I Heard It Through the Grapevine?" Having those songs together makes *A Smile Like Yours* a nice sampler to own, but not for any reasons that will remind you of the movie.

Gary Graff

Smilla's Sense of Snow

1997, Teldec Records, from the film *Smilla's Sense of Snow,* Constantin Films, 1997 ♫♫♫♫
album notes: Music: Harry Gregson-Williams, Hans Zimmer; **Conductor:** Harry Gregson-Williams.

A brilliant thriller, based on a novel by Peter Hoeg, *Smilla's Sense of Snow* stars Julia Ormond as a half-Inuit scientist who reveals intuitive powers of investigation when she attempts to solve the murder of a young neighbor. Reflecting the increasing tension in the story, as well as its more metaphysical aspects, Hans Zimmer and Harry Gregson-Williams have devised a score with its share of suspense. In addition to providing specific themes for the murdered boy ("Isaiah's Theme") and a mysterious man only known as the Mechanic who helps Smilla uncover the truth though his real motives for doing so are as enigmatic as his personality ("Who Is The Mechanic?"), the two composers have deftly bookended the score with two cues ("Greenland: Anno 1859" and "Greenland Revisited"), in which the recurring motifs evoke another mysterious event 140 years earlier that has a direct bearing on the current action. Though occasionally predictable, and often punctuated by riffs that give it an artificial sense of urgency, the score is nonetheless quite effective in establishing the aura of mystery that pervades the whole film until its satisfying conclusion.

Didier C. Deutsch

Smoke

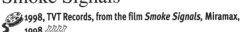1995, Miramax Records, from the film *Smoke,* Miramax, 1995 ♪♪♪

album notes: Music: Rachel Portman.

A weird little outing, with two songs each from the Jerry Garcia Band ("Cigarettes and Coffee" and "Smoke Gets in Your Eyes") and Tom Waits ("Downtown Train" and "Innocent When You Dream"). Cheers for including Louis Prima's "Brooklyn Boogie" and Screaming Jay Hawkins' "Hong Kong," but with a skimpy nine songs, there's not a great deal of heft to this one.

Gary Graff

Smoke Signals

1998, TVT Records, from the film *Smoke Signals,* Miramax, 1998 ♪♪♪♪

album notes: Music: B.C. Smith. **Orchestra:** The Northwest Sinfonia; **Conductor:** Tim Simonec.

Winner of the Audience Award and the Filmmakers' Trophy at the 1998 Sundance Film Festival, this little gem of a film has the unique distinction of having been conceived, directed, and acted by Native Americans, and of reflecting a culture and a way of life that regrettably seem too often alien to most of us. Based on four short stories by Sherman Alexie, published in the 1993 collection, *The Lone Ranger and Tonto Fistfight in Heaven,* the film surveys the conditions of life on the reservations in sometimes humorous terms that make this sober-eyed account easily accessible and enjoyable. Punctuating the action, and fleshing it up with sounds that seem far removed from the urban contemporary mush so frequently imposed on us, the soundtrack features songs and performances by Indian artists, including singer/songwriter Jim Boyd, whose anthems denote a kind of soul music totally different from what is identified as such in other parts of the country ("Treaties," "Reservation Blues"). The film's often gentle, quirky sense of humor is explored in tunes that give a different, refreshing spin to this CD ("Road Buddy," "John Wayne's Teeth," "Jesuit Basketball"). The music by B.C. Smith is cut in the same cloth. It all adds up to an unusual, convincing and totally winning album.

Didier C. Deutsch

Snake Eyes

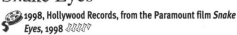1998, Hollywood Records, from the Paramount film *Snake Eyes,* 1998 ♪♪♪♪

album notes: Music: Ryuichi Sakamoto; **Conductor:** Ryuichi Sakamoto.

Ryuichi Sakamoto writes some of the most beautifully expressive music heard in the movies. His string-intensive score for *Snake Eyes* is no exception. Complementing his inventive action-adventure music are ethereal tracks like "Blood on the Medals," the very delicate "Crawling to Julia," and the sultry sounds of "Tyler and Serena," all which place this soundtrack way above the norm. Unlike this lame adaptation of the novel about a high-level assignation at a boxing match in Las Vegas, the symphonic score really keeps you on the edge of your seat. The CD also contains new songs by Meredith Brooks and LaKiesha Berri.

Beth Krakower

Sneakers

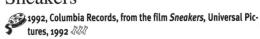1992, Columbia Records, from the film *Sneakers,* Universal Pictures, 1992 ♪♪♪

album notes: Music: James Horner; **Conductor:** James Horner; **Featured Musicians:** Branford Marsalis, Mike Fisher, Ralph Grierson, James Horner, Joel C. Peskin, Ian Underwood.

Former *Tonight Show* bandleader Branford Marsalis found great success performing and improvising on Jerry Goldsmith's lovely score for *The Russia House* in 1990, and filmmaker Phil Alden Robinson thought it would be a good idea to unite Marsalis's saxophone with composer James Horner when scoring *Sneakers,* Robinson's 1992 follow-up to *Field of Dreams.* While not as memorable as his *Russia House* stint, Marsalis's collaboration with Horner on this score is still one of the least forgettable elements in Robinson's cliche-ridden thriller—the music is fast-paced and energetic enough, with a sprightly main theme working hard to offset some of the recycled material in the rest of Horner's work. Thus, when Marsalis is spotlighted, the score is pleasantly diverting, but listeners might want to skip past the tired "suspense" music in Horner's dramatic underscore.

Andy Dursin

Snow White: A Tale of Terror

1996, Citadel Records, from the film *Snow White: A Tale of Terror,* PolyGram, 1996 ♪♪♪

album notes: Music: John Ottman; **Orchestra:** The Symphony Orchestra of Seattle; **Conductor:** John Ottman.

And what if the Seven Dwarfs were not gentle little men but devilish brutes bent on adding to poor Snow White's torments rather than helping her defeat her nasty old mother-in-law? And what if Snow White were portrayed by Sigourney Weaver, known here as Claudia, an unbalanced, mysterious, yet somehow empathetic presence? And what if this were a morbid and grim story, instead of the Grimm fairy tale we've all known and loved since infancy? Well, that's about the jest of it, except that it was scored by John Ottman, who conjured up a grab bag of surprising, eerie tricks to give the film its proper atmosphere (descending and ascending tremolo string lines to depict Claudia, percussion rattling chairs, electric violin bendings, a disembodied choir, etc.). If it sounds unusual that's because it is. And if at times it also sounds tepid, that's also because it is!

Didier C. Deutsch

Snow White and the Seven Dwarfs

1993, Walt Disney Records, from the film *Snow White and the Seven Dwarfs*, RKO Radio Pictures, 1937 𝄞𝄞𝄞𝄞𝄞

album notes: Music: Frank Churchill, Leigh Harline, Paul J. Smith; **Lyrics:** Larry Morey; **Choir:** The Disney Studio Chorus; **Orchestra:** The Disney Studio Orchestra; **Conductor:** Frank Chuchill; **Cast:** Adriana Caselotti, Harry Stockwell, Lucille LaVerne, Scotty Matraw, Roy Atwell, Pinto Colvig, Billy Gilbert, Otis Harlan.

The first, and by far most memorable full–length animated feature from the Disney Studios, *Snow White and the Seven Dwarfs* may have been superseded technically by many of the films that followed it. But its simple story of a charming little princess saved from the evil deeds of her mother–in–law by a group of seven adorable dwarfs made history when it was first released in December 1937, and has since become an incomparable screen classic. With its exquisite score by Frank Churchill, Leigh Harline and Paul J. Smith, *Snow White* continues to enchant generations of young viewers and their parents, whose earliest memories are forever tied to "With a Smile and a Song," "Whistle While You Work," "Heigh–Ho," and "Someday My Prince Will Come," among the film's many musical highlights. Today, it still stands out as a perfect example of unsurpassed quality in animated filmmaking, made all the more memorable in this compact disc, which includes a lot of incidental music and reprises, available here for the first time.

Didier C. Deutsch

Soap Dish

1991, Varèse Sarabande, from the film *Soap Dish,* Paramount Pictures, 1991 𝄞𝄞𝄞𝄞𝄞

album notes: Music: Alan Silvestri; **Orchestra:** The Skywalker Symphony Orchestra; **Conductor:** Alan Silvestri.

Alan Silvestri scored this riotous screwball comedy spoof of daytime TV dramas utilizing variations on the West Indian dance styles of mambo, tango, and rumba. As the cast of self-important actors plot to ruin each other's career, Silvestri amplifies their machinations into epic proportions of absurdity. He even has a theme for Sally Field's "America's Sweetheart" that's so sugary sweet, listening to it will rot out your teeth. The soundtrack is so bright, bouncy, and entertaining that it's more than likely to be the only underscore you can dance to.

David Hirsch

Soap Opera's Greatest Love Themes: Volume II

1992, Scotti Bros, Records 𝄞

Only a rabid fan of the soaps would want this collection of themes written for some of the most popular daytime television shows, and occasionally featuring the actors who appear in them. But when you have your daily ration of suds, do you really need to get additional servings on a CD that only offers small snippets of music and questionable performances? As the world turns, let another world be your guiding light . . .

Didier C. Deutsch

Soldier

1998, Varèse-Sarabande, from the film *Soldier,* Warner Bros., 1998 𝄞𝄞𝄞

album notes: Music: Joel McNeely; **Conductor:** Joel McNeely.

The year 1998 was marked by an abundance of war stories. In addition to *Saving Private Ryan* and *Small Soldiers,* all variations on essentially the same theme, came this sci-fi thriller in which Kurt Russell portrayed a futuristic warrior whose age made him suitable for retirement in the eyes of his commanding officers. Left for dead on a planet in the far reaches of the galaxy after a particularly nasty combat, he is nursed back to health by the inhabitants, who look up to him as a potential protector against possible invaders. Not surprisingly, this proves to be the case as Russell wages a one-man fight against a group of former army companions. With winky-winky sly bow to all the tenets of the genre, the film had a certain amount of humor that is totally absent from Joel McNeely's unusually somber score.

Didier C. Deutsch

A Soldier's Daughter Never Cries

1998, Angel Records, from the film *A Soldier's Daughter Never Cries,* Merchant Ivory, 1998 𝄞𝄞𝄞

album notes: Music: Richard Robbins.

Based on the novel by Kaylie Jones, the daughter of author James Jones, *A Soldier's Daughter Never Cries* is a fictionalized account of her life growing up in France and the U.S. in the 1960s and 1970s. Reflecting the time period and place of the action, the CD consists of both French- and English-language songs of that era, augmented by a score by Richard Robbins. Generally speaking, the score works very well in the movie, but taken on its own musical terms seems a bit lackluster against the upbeat French pop songs by France Gall and Jane Birkin, or such hit artists as Deep Purple, 10CC, and David Bowie. Adding a different, albeit valid note to the proceedings, Tito Puente's "La Guira" is also featured prominently in the recording as it was in the movie.

Didier C. Deutsch

Solomon and Sheba

See: The Vikings/Solomon and Sheba

Some Came Running

See: Kings Go Forth/Some Came Running

Some Kind of Wonderful

1987, MCA Records, from the film *Some Kind of Wonderful,* Paramount, 1987 ♫♫♫♪

A lively contemporary love triangle starring Eric Stoltz, Mary Stuart Masterson, Craig Sheffer, and Lea Thompson, *Some Kind of Wonderful* is a predictably romantic comedy that elicited a hard-driving rock soundtrack. While all the songs here may not always evidence the same level of quality, some, like "Brilliant Mind," "Cry Like This," "The Shyest Time," and "Turn to the Sky," are better than average. Also interesting in this collection is Lick the Tin's rendition of the classic "Can't Help Falling in Love," with lead vocalist Allison Marr displaying an engaging sense of urgency in her breathy delivery.

Didier C. Deutsch

Some Like It Hot

1998, Rykodisc, from the film *Some Like It Hot,* United Artists, 1959 ♫♫♫♫♪
album notes: Music: Adolph Deutsch

The Billy Wilder classic, voted one of the top 100 films of all time by the AFI, is a farcical comedy starring Jack Lemmon and Tony Curtis as down-on-their-luck musicians who unwittingly witness the St. Valentine's Day Massacre. To escape the Chicago mobsters intent on silencing them, they go under cover in drag and join an all-female band on its way to Miami. While Curtis falls for the band's singer, played by Marilyn Monroe, Lemmon begins to take his role as a woman quite seriously, particularly after he finds himself courted by a millionaire.

Giving the proper musical feel to the film, the soundtrack mixed '20s classics like "By the Beautiful Sea" and "Sweet Georgia Brown" with Adolph Deutsch's now upbeat and whimsical, now wistful and melancholy score. But the highlights of this CD, as in the film, are the three vocals by Monroe: "Running Wild,"

"I'm Thru with Love," and "I Wanna Be Loved by You." The enhanced CD also features bits of dialogue that prove quite entertaining, as well as the film's trailer.

Didier C. Deutsch

Some Mother's Son

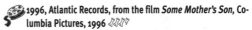1996, Atlantic Records, from the film *Some Mother's Son,* Columbia Pictures, 1996 ♫♫♫♪
album notes: Music: Bill Whelan; **Orchestra:** The Irish Film Orchestra; **Conductor:** Bill Whelan; **Featured Musicians:** Declan Masterson, Uilleann pipes, bouzouki, whistles; Nikola Parov, gadulka, kavals; Kenneth Edge, soprano sax; Eileen Ivers, fiddle; Mairtin O'Connor, accordion; Neil O'Callanain, bouzouki; Desi Reynolds, percussion; Noel Eccles, percussion; Jimmy Higgins, bodhran, percussion.

Possibly because this score was written by the composer of *Riverdance,* as soon as you hear the first explosive strains of "Bridge Attack," you might be tempted to look around to see if Michael Flatley, the self-anointed "Lord of the Dance," or any other tap-dancing misfit from these big dance extravaganzas, accompanied by a line-up likely to send the Rockettes at Radio City Music Hall into fits of envy, is not prancing around your living room. Actually, this "celtic" score is not really that bad, with effective cues conveying the sense of suspense and urgency in the screen narrative, yet another story about the struggle of Northern Irish to free themselves from British domination. Seen from the perspective of the mothers of the IRA freedom fighters, the film presents the usual share of violence, anguish, armed rebellion, jail terms, and everything that has fueled other films like this one for decades. Nothing in the rest of the score matches the excitement in "Bridge Attack," though one cue, "The Seabird," is striking in its poetic evocation, and several vocals (including some in Gaelic) enhance the musical proceedings.

Didier C. Deutsch

Something to Talk About

1995, Varèse Sarabande, from the film *Something to Talk About,* Warner Bros., 1995 ♫♫♫♪
album notes: Music: Hans Zimmer, Graham Preskett; **Featured Musicians:** Mike Lang, piano; Jimmy Johnson, Nathan East, bass; John Van Tongeren, Hammond B-3; Carlos Vega, drums; Russ Kunkel, drums; Greg Leisz, Dobro; Pete Haycock, guitar; Tim Pierce, guitar; Bob Duspit, guitar; Tim May, guitar, banjo; Graham Preskett, violin, harmonica; Bill Knopf, banjo; Mike Fisher, percussion; Bob Zimmitti, percussion.

A comedy about marital infidelities, with fresh new spins to enliven a tale as old as humanity itself, *Something to Talk About* found composers Hans Zimmer and Graham Preskett in eloquent verve for a score often tartly ingratiating and buoyantly effervescent. Echoing some of the caustic accents in this story of a Southern young woman (Julia Roberts) and her apparently unfaithful husband (Dennis Quaid), the score details the salient moments in the narrative, particularly in two longer cues, "Dysfunctionally Yours," and "Dinner for Two," echoing in the latter some of the emotional depth in a half-baked attempt at reconciliation between the two main characters. Driven by a large number of acoustic instruments (guitars, Dobro, violin, harmonica, and banjo, all of which evoke the kind of music one might hear in a small Southern community), the album is quite enjoyable on its own terms.

Didier C. Deutsch

Something Wild

1986, MCA Records, from the film *Something Wild,* Orion Pictures, 1986 ♫♫♫

An unusually clever thriller starring Jeff Daniels and Melanie Griffith, *Something Wild* adroitly derived some of its strength from the combined musical contributions of performers like Fine Young Cannibals, Oingo Boingo, UB-40, New Order, and Jimmy Cliff—admittedly, an odd assortment—whose songs delineated the contemporary feel of the action and helped propel it. "Wild Thing" (not the Jimi Hendrix tune) seems a fitting ending to the story and to the album.

Didier C. Deutsch

Somewhere in Time

1985, MCA Records, from the film *Somewhere in Time,* Universal, 1980 ♫♫♫♫♫

album notes: Music: John Barry; **Conductor:** John Barry.

There are "classics" and then there are classics. John Barry's score for *Somewhere in Time* is one of those instances where film music completely transcends the movie it originates from, and takes on a life of its own outside of its original context. Not that the movie itself—a 1980 time-travel fantasy with Christopher Reeve and Jane Seymour—hasn't become something of a classic in the years since its initial release, but Barry's music is one of the composer's most beloved scores. The elegant main theme for piano and orchestra (performed by Roger Williams in a beautiful arrangement here) is only part of the listening pleasure to be derived from the soundtrack, which also includes the gorgeous "Rhapsody on a Theme of Paganini," by Rachmaninoff. It truly is one of the loveliest scores in Barry's long, established career of composing many lyrical, soothing scores, and its continued status as a successful soundtrack album stands as a testament to the music's enduring popularity with listeners.

Andy Dursin

1998, Varèse-Sarabande, from the film *Somewhere in Time,* Universal, 1980 ♫♫♫♫♫

album notes: Music: John Barry; **Orchestra:** The Royal Scottish National Orchestra; **Conductor:** John Debney.

They Know the Score

John Barry

[Conducting is] terribly important. It's trying to make it happen. You spot the music, you compose the music, you orchestrate it, and then you get into that studio and the whole thing takes on its life for the first time, really. . . . The performance is the real fun. And that's also another problem that's happening today. Many of the young composers are not conducting their own music. I think you have to have composed it, conduct it, and know every phrase and movement, and then you're in the master driving seat, where you make all those subtle changes which will finalize your piece of music. And if you have to explain to somebody, the conductor, it loses a lot.

***Courtesy of* Film Score Monthly**

This re-recording, for which John Debney conducts the Royal Scottish National Orchestra, shows much more emotion and freedom of movement than the original soundtrack, which had a polished studio feel to it. In contrast with the original, it also contains many of the cues as stand alone tracks, something which makes accessing them much easier. Lynda Cochrane is the featured pianist and Edwin Paling, the Royal Scottish National Orchestra's leader, is the featured violin soloist. An excellent alternative to the original recording.

Didier C. Deutsch

Sommersby

1993, Elektra Records, from the film *Sommersby,* Warner Bros., 1993 ♫♫♫♫

album notes: Music: Danny Elfman; **Conductor:** Jonathan Sheffer, Thomas Pasatieri.

He's scored movies with super heroes, stop-motion figures, ghastly monsters and Pee-Wee Herman, but some of Danny Elfman's finest work for the movies comes from a decidedly human angle. His score for *Sommersby,* the 1993 Americanization of *The Return of Martin Guerre,* remains one of the composer's most impressive efforts. With a tone that is alternately unsettled and brooding, *a la* Bernard Herrmann, or unabashedly romantic, Elfman and orchestrator Steve Bartek have put together a thematically strong score that fulfills all the dramatic requirements of Jon Amiel's film. In addition, the ensemble accompaniment representing the rural Virginia backdrop adds yet another layer to the score, which is quite different from the traditional Elfman sound, but is just as satisfying—if not more so—than anything else the composer has written for the movies yet.

Andy Dursin

Son of the Morning Star

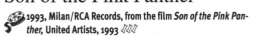 1992, Intrada Records, from the film *Son of the Morning Star,* Republic Pictures, 1992 ♪♪♪♪

album notes: Music: Craig Safan; Featured Musicians: Ed Gornik, trumpet; Holly Gornik, oboe; Tom Mauchahty-Ware, Native American flute.

The underappreciated Craig Safan is known primarily for writing the theme music to the *Cheers* television show, but he's a talented dramatic composer who wrote one of the most exciting space opera scores of the '80s (*The Last Starfighter*) as well as this sophisticated take on the story of legendary General George Custer and the events that led to his downfall at Little Big Horn. Safan's score builds dramatic weight through the repetition of a dense, rich, and bittersweet string melody that views the historical events depicted here as American tragedy rather than adventure. There's a beautiful love theme and an epic sweep to this album that make it a rarity in made-for-television scores, an effort that holds up against some of the better theatrical film scores of the period.

Jeff Bond

Son of the Pink Panther

1993, Milan/RCA Records, from the film *Son of the Pink Panther,* United Artists, 1993 ♪♪♪

album notes: Music: Henry Mancini; Orchestra: The National Philharmonic Orchestra; Conductor: Henry Mancini; Featured Musician: Phil Todd, tenor sax.

Unable to leave well enough alone following the death of Peter Sellers, Blake Edwards devised this tired number in his successful *Pink Panther* series, starring Italian actor Roberto Benigni as Inspector Clouseau's equally inept illegitimate son. Back to confer the ounce of legitimacy needed to make things fly are Herbert Lom as Commissioner Dreyfus and Burt Kwouk as Clouseau's faithful manservant Cato, as well as Henry Mancini, who provided the score as he had done in all previous *Pink Panther* films. Somehow, despite his natural verve and

penchant for this type of comedy, the composer didn't seem much inspired by the antics of yet another Clouseau, and though his thoroughly professional score has its share of enjoyable moments ("Samba de Jacques," "Riot at Omar's"), some of the joy and effervescence that marked his previous efforts seem to be sadly missing here. In fact, the most original note in this album is Bobby McFerrin's impish rendition of "The Pink Panther Theme."

Didier C. Deutsch

Songs in the Key of X

See: The X-Files

Sons and Lovers

See: A Farewell to Arms/Sons and Lovers

Sophia Loren in Rome

1998, PEG Recordings, from the television presentation, *Sophia Loren in Rome,* 1968 ♪♪♪♪

album notes: Music: John Barry; Conductor: John Barry.

Composed at a time when John Barry was still writing fast-paced music, whether for the James Bond films or this innocuous travelogue through Rome in the company of Sophia Loren, this recording has been out of the catalogue for many years. This is its first CD appearance. Needless to say, it is a welcome addition. Barry, in peak form, wrote cues that focused on the sights and sounds of the Italian capital, with the main theme, "Secrets of Rome," pervading the score and yielding no less than four different versions, including one performed by the documentary's charming hostess. It's not an important score, by any stretch of the imagination, but it has a definite glow that's most engaging and makes it a winner in the minor league.

Didier C. Deutsch

Sophie's Choice

1984, Southern Cross Records, from the film *Sophie's Choice,* Universal Pictures, 1984 ♪♪♪

album notes: Music: Marvin Hamlisch; Conductor: Marvin Hamlisch.

Marvin Hamlisch wrote one of his few straight dramatic scores for this Alan Pakula adaptation of the William Styron novel. The elegiac, deeply regretful title music is one of Hamlisch's most beautiful and haunting melodies, but the score itself tends to meander aimlessly until gathering up its forces to restate the theme broadly in some of the movie's hokier sequences. The score is better off when subtly underscoring the drama with an effective chamber orchestra approach. Hamlisch's deliberate, consonant string passages and piano phrases make for pleasant, bittersweet listening, but the darker territory of the story and its characters is rarely explored convincingly.

Jeff Bond

Sophisticated Ladies

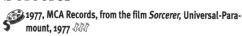 1981, RCA Victor, from the Broadway production *Sophisticated Ladies*, 1981 🎵🎵🎵🎵

album notes: Music: Duke Ellington, Mercer Ellington, Irving Mills, Billy Strayhorn, Juan Tizol, Harry Carney, Gerald Wilson, Johnny Hodges, Harry James; **Lyrics:** Duke Ellington, John Guare, Don George, Irving Mills, Sid Kuller, Billy Strayhorn, Eddie De Lange, Henry Nemo, John Redmond, Manny Kurtz, Johnny Mercer, Mack David, Bob Russell, Paul Francis Webster, Mitchell Parish; **Musical Direction:** Mercer Ellington; **Cast:** Gregory Hines, Judith Jamison, Phyllis Hyman, P.J. Benjamin, Hinton Battle, Gregg Burge, Mercedes Ellington, Priscilla Baskerville, Terri Klausner.

A celebration of the great Duke Ellington, *Sophisticated Ladies,* which opened on Broadway on March 1, 1981, benefited from the presence in the cast of such luminaries of dance, stage and cabaret as Gregory Hines, Phyllis Hyman, and Judith Jamison, as well as the Duke's own band, led by Mercer Ellington. Together, they provide the sleek entertainment that makes the show such a joy to watch. The recording gives a measure of how successful they are, though in this instance their performances, minus the visual flash of the stage presentation, enable the listener to focus on and truly enjoy the songs of Ellington. Seldom did a composer have such classy performers to interpret his songs, and seldom did performers of this caliber have such great catalogue to work with. The two together spell pure magic.

Didier C. Deutsch

Sorcerer

1977, MCA Records, from the film *Sorcerer,* Universal-Paramount, 1977 🎵🎵🎵

album notes: Songs: Tangerine Dream (Edgar Froese, Peter Baumann, Christoph Franke).

A remake of Henri-Georges Clouzot's frighteningly real *Le Salaire de la peur ("Wages of Fear"),* this film by William Friedkin elicited a convincingly powerful score by Tangerine Dream, even though the music the group created consisted of impressions they gathered from reading the script, and not from viewing the film as is common practice. While the "Main Title" really fails to attract with its electronic effects devoid of any musical meaning, the other selections make a different impression, with some ("Search," "Impressions of Sorcerer") surprisingly evocative of the screen drama itself. The album may seem strictly for fans of electronic music, but it also offers some rewarding moments for listeners less accustomed to this type of music.

Didier C. Deutsch

Soul Food

1998, LaFace Records, from the film *Soul Food,* 20th Century-Fox, 1998 🎵🎵

A mildly innocuous film, *Soul Food,* which starred Vanessa Williams, Vivica A. Fox, and Nia Long, dealt with three generations of a modern black family struggling to keep together in spite of sibling rivalry, stubborn pride, and infidelity. As is often the case in films like this, the soundtrack was urban contemporary with a flurry of songs designed to attract a younger audience. But while its mixture of rap and R&B songs might delight them, it proves trite and inconsequential to a larger majority. If we were to single out tracks with better crossover potential, "Boys and Girls" by Tony! Toni! Tone!, "You Are the Man" by En Vogue, and "September" by Earth, Wind & Fire, would be it. Slim pickings, indeed, and not much food to nourish the soul!

Didier C. Deutsch

The Sound and the Fury

1990, Varèse Sarabande, from the film *The Sound and the Fury,* 20th Century-Fox, 1959 🎵🎵🎵🎵

album notes: Music: Alex North; **Orchestra:** The 20th Century-Fox Orchestra; **Conductor:** Lionel Newman.

Released in 1959, *The Sound and the Fury* is a provocative big-screen adaptation of William Faulkner's searing novel about the decline and fall of a once wealthy family in a small Mississippi community. Starring Joanne Woodward, as a young woman who craves the kind of affection she never got at home, and Yul Brynner, as the adopted stepson of the family estate who exerts control over everything and everyone, the film paints the drab portrait of a desperate family, fraying at the seams and on the verge of financial collapse. Underlining the moods in the story, as well as adding a comment of its own, Alex North's score derives much of its impact from the use of progressive (one hesitates to use the word avant-garde) jazz that occasionally prevailed in film soundtracks at the time, often in imitation of the trend pioneered by Elmer Bernstein. Without losing sight of the emotional context in some of the scenes ("What's His Name," "Southern Breeze," "Sweet Baby"), some of the cues devised by the composer rely on more contemporary accents to give the music an identity that takes it away from standard instrumental fares. This is particularly evident in the "Main Title" that realizes a symbiosis of the various styles North used in the score, and in the explosive "Sex Rears," in which the syncopated jazz accents effectively convey the steam and the tension in the film.

Didier C. Deutsch

The Sound of Music

1998, Sony Classical, from the Broadway musical, *The Sound of Music*, 1960 ♪♪♪♪

album notes: Music: Richard Rodgers; **Lyrics:** Oscar Hammerstein II; **Cast:** Mary Martin (Maria Rainer), Theodore Bikel (Captain Georg von Trapp), Patricia Neway (The Mother Abbess), Marion Marlowe (Elsa Schraeder), Kurt Kaznar (Max Detweiler), Lauri Peters (Liesl), William Snowden (Friedrich), Kathy Dunn (Louisa), Joseph Stewart (Kurt), Marilyn Rogers (Brigitta), Mary Susan Locke (Marta), Evanna Lien (Gretl), Brian Davies (Rolf Gruber).

Lovers of Rodgers & Hammerstein's perennial family favorite, *The Sound of Music,* have two wonderful ways to savor the melodic hits from the wholesomest of all the pair's collaborations: both the original Broadway cast recording (Mary Martin and Theodore Bikel, 1959), and the classic film soundtrack (Julie Andrews and Christopher Plummer, 1965).

Because of its well-deserved classic status, it's hard to imagine anyone other than Julie Andrews playing Maria. However the legendary Mary Martin originated this role, donning the habit on Broadway, and Theodore Bikel played the Baron von Trapp, while Patricia Neway was the Mother Abbess. Though it was Rodgers and Hammerstein's last show together (Hammerstein died shortly after it opened), *The Sound of Music* remains one of their best-loved musicals, and this release certainly comes closest to their vision of what it was all about This new reissue of the Broadway musical recording, remixed and remastered, features two bonus tracks, Mitch Miller's sing along version of "Do-Re-Mi" with the younger members of the cast, and a symphonic suite created by veteran Rodgers & Hammerstein orchestrator Robert Russell Bennett, recorded by the Pittsburgh Symphony Orchestra. The true value of this recording, however, is being able to hear Mary Martin's take on Maria as clear as day.

Beth Krakower

 **1995, RCA Victor, from the film *The Sound of Music*, 20th Century-Fox, 1965** ♪♪♪♪♫

album notes: Music: Richard Rodgers; **Lyrics:** Oscar Hammerstein II; **Orchestra:** The 20th Century-Fox Studio Chorus and Orchestra; **Conductor:** Irwin Kostal; **Cast:** Julie Andrews (Maria Rainer), Christopher Plummer (Captain Georg von Trapp), Peggy Wood (The Mother Abbess), Charmian Carr (Liesl), Nicholas Hammond (Friedrich), Heather Menzies (Louisa), Duane Chase (Kurt), Angela Cartwright (Brigitta), Debbie Turner (Marta), Kym Karath (Gretl), Dan Truhitte (Rolf Gruber).

The famous RCA Victor album has, of course, been etched in the American subconscious, and is what most people fondly recollect whenever *The Sound of Music* is mentioned. And rightfully so. The film was a huge success (and continues to be a strong ratings grabber for television networks): colorful, lavish, and above all, memorable for its breathtaking opening scenes, overall cinematic beauty, and the intriguing, sensitive storyline. But the real ace-in-the-hole here is the young Julie

Andrews's enthusiastic, sensitive approach to the songs. This newly remastered version supplants a dull, distorted, and sonically inferior early CD, and rectifies former problems with not only the sound but the original running order as well. While one wishes that the producers of this reissue had sought out additional cues and extra musical material (available in a special CD included with the film's rerelease on laserdisc), this disc is an essential part of the venerable R&H catalog.

Charles L. Granata

Sounder

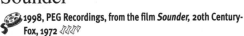 **1998, PEG Recordings, from the film *Sounder,* 20th Century-Fox, 1972** ♪♪♪

album notes: Music: Taj Mahal.

The popular singer/songwriter Taj Mahal wrote the score for this story of a black family of sharecroppers during the Depression era, with Cicely Tyson giving an outstanding performance as the long-suffering but courageous wife of Paul Winfield, who keeps the whole family together despite the incredible conditions in which they are forced to live. Kevin Hooks also starred as the eldest son who takes his father's mantle when Winfield is sent to forced labor for a year after he stole food for his family. Directed with style by Martin Ritt, the film also greatly benefitted from its score, a collection of folk songs featuring original works by Taj Mahal, and "Lightning" Hopkins. While in stereo, the recording is badly reverbed as if it had been done in an echo chamber. Very disconcerting!

Didier C. Deutsch

The Sounds of Murphy Brown

1990, MCA Records, from the CBS–TV series *Murphy Brown* ♪♪♪

Once upon a time, when TV shows actually had lengthy main title themes, this show bucked the trend by exploiting Murphy's love of Motown by choosing an appropriate song for each episode's opening credits montage. The song most associated with the series is perhaps Aretha Franklin's "Respect" but, if you've been a fan of the earlier shows, this album will certainly remind you of many of them. If not, then this album is also an impressive collection of some of Motown's greatest hits. Artists include Stevie Wonder ("Superstition"), Smokey Robinson ("Tracks of My Tears") and The Temptations, whose song "Get Ready" also became the network's anthem one season. Two brief dialog cuts by Candice Bergen are also included as is the rarely used original series theme by Steve Dorff and John Bettis, "Like the Whole World's Watching," which is performed by the *a cappella* group Take 6.

David Hirsch

Julie Andrews in the film version of The Sound of Music. **(The Kobal Collection)**

South Pacific

 1998, Sony Classical/Legacy, from the Broadway production *South Pacific*, **1949** 🎵🎵🎵🎵🎵

album notes: Music: Richard Rodgers; **Lyrics:** Oscar Hammerstein II; **Cast:** Mary Martin (Nellie Forbush), Ezio Pinza (Emile de Becque), William Tabbert (Lt. Cable), Juanita Hall (Bloody Mary).

1958, RCA Records, from the film *South Pacific,* **20th Century-Fox, 1958** 🎵🎵

album notes: Music: Richard Rodgers; **Lyrics:** Oscar Hammerstein II; **Orchestra:** The 20th Century-Fox Studio Chorus and Orchestra; **Conductor:** Alfred Newman; **Cast:** Mitzi Gaynor (Nellie Forbush), Rossano Brazzi (Emile de Becque), John Kerr (Lt. Cable), Juanita Hall (Bloody Mary).

One of the best Rodgers & Hammerstein musicals, *South Pacific* received a gorgeous treatment in its first incarnation, with Mary Martin radiant as Nelly Forbush, the American nurse assigned to a Pacific island during World War II, who falls in love with a French planter, Emile de Becque (Ezio Pinza), only to discover that he has two children from a native, something that conflicts with Nelly's small-town values. In a show that makes no bones where its heart is, race relations also play a crucial role in the secondary plot between Lt. Cable and Liat, the daughter of Bloody Mary, the island's wheeler-dealer. This prompted Oscar Hammerstein to write in "You've Got to Be Carefully Taught." an impassioned plea for equal rights, long before it became fashionable.

This new recording of the stage musical is *South Pacific*'s third digital transfer. The first, on the Columbia label in 1988, used the LP master tape, who knows how many generations removed from the original recordings. The second, from Sony Classical in 1993, used a previously unknown tape made during the 1949 recording sessions—the first time Columbia recorded a cast album on tape, even though intended only as a safety back-up for the acetate disk masters. For this third release, producers Didier C. Deutsch and Darcy M. Proper have returned to those acetates to restore this classic album to the way it was heard in its initial release in 1949. Sonically, they have done a beautiful job, although sharp-eared listeners may detect disk surface noise here and there that isn't on the 1993 transfer. This release includes that reissue's bonus tracks—Martin singing the cut songs, "Loneliness of Evening" and "My Girl Back Home" (curiously recorded for a single in 1951, more than two years after the musical opened), and co-star Pinza's "Bali Ha'i," which he didn't sing in the show—plus a 1951 recording of orchestrator Robert Russell Bennett's gorgeous "South Pacific: Symphonic Scenario for Concert Orchestra" by the Philadelphia Orchestra Pops under the direction of Andre Kostelanetz. It should also be noted that "You've Got to Be Carefully Taught" has been restored to its original take for this

CD (the 1993 one used an alternate version that missed a line of the lyric).

The second musical to be awarded the Pulitzer Prize, *South Pacific* opened on April 7, 1949, for a long run of 1,925 performances, and won nine Tony Awards, including one each for its principals, one each for its creators, and one for Best Musical. In its transfer to the screen, however, the show fared less well, with Mitzi Gaynor an apt but ultimately bland substitute for Doris Day, the producers' first choice. Rossano Brazzi (dubbed by Giorgio Tozzi) was somewhat better as Emile, and John Kerr (dubbed by Bill Lee) was a suitable Cable. Adding to the negative impression left by the film, shot through monochrome lenses in an ill-advised decision to try and create "an effect," some of the other principals were also dubbed, including, of all people, Juanita Hall, the only holdover from the Broadway original, whose singing voice was Muriel Smith.

Max O. Preeo

South Seas Adventure

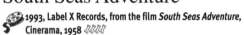 **1993, Label X Records, from the film** *South Seas Adventure,* **Cinerama, 1958** 🎵🎵🎵

album notes: Music: Alex North; **Orchestras:** The Cinerama Symphony Orchestra, the Norman Luboff Choir; **Conductor:** Alex North.

Before it turned to more commercial fare, Cinerama first made its mark with sensational travelogues that used its three-screen diorama to best effect. Accompanying those were scores which, for the most part, were serviceable but not tremendously exciting or imaginative. One happy exception was this effort by composer Alex North, who took the South Pacific locations as a cue to write broad, colorful music inspired by and based on traditional themes. While the sonics in this CD sometime leave a lot to be desired (the stereo is rather crude and not very flattering to the ear), there is no denying the charm and solid flair of the music itself.

Didier C. Deutsch

Space Age

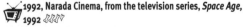 **1992, Narada Cinema, from the television series,** *Space Age,* **1992** 🎵🎵🎵

album notes: Music: Jay Chattaway.

Having contributed some outstanding scores for space-set adventures, most notably *Star Trek Voyager,* Jay Chattaway was the obvious choice to write the music for *Space Age,* a public television series produced by WQED in Pittsburgh, in association with NHK in Japan and the National Academy of Sciences. The film surveys such high spots as modern man's fabulous leaps into space since World War II; the mutual mistrust between the U.S. and Russia that led to a spectacular race into the stratosphere;

the exploration of our most immediate neighbors, the Moon and Mars; and the launching of crafts set to investigate and report about the confines of our universe. The electronic score Chattaway devised for the series retains a very exotic, melodious appeal that places it above the music usually heard in this type of presentation. The various titles given the cues pretty much outline what they describe with the listener invited to let his imagination run free with the sounds invented by the composer.

Didier C. Deutsch

Space Jam

1996, Warner Sunset/Atlantic Records, from the film *Space Jam,* Warner Bros., 1996 ♪♪♪♪

album notes: Music: James Newton Howard.

Michael Jordan meets Bugs Bunny—with Tweety Bird thrown in? Alert the kiddies. Actually, there's not much to dislike about this family-friendly collection of tunes. Seal does a lovely take on Steve Miller's "Fly Like an Eagle," R. Kelly's "I Believe I Can Fly" is easy on the ears, and "Hit 'em High (The Monstars' Anthem")" is a big-fun collaboration between top-shelf rappers B Real, Busta Rhymes, Coolio, LL Cool J, and Method Man. And Bugs's own "Buggin'" is a cheery way to close the album.

Gary Graff

Spaceballs

1987, Atlantic Records, from the film *Spaceballs,* MGM, 1987 ♪♪

album notes: Music: John Morris; Conductor: John Morris.

Having already sent up westerns, musicals, horror films, and historical epics, Mel Brooks could have done much worse than turn his attention to the outerspace sagas, and which better one to spoof than the granddaddy of them all, *Star Wars?* There's little one can say about the story of Lone Starr, a second-rate Han Solo, and Princess Vespa, the Jewish American babe he saves from the grips of a would-be Darth Vader (Rick Moranis, coiffed with a helmet 10 times too big for his head), except that the satire is often, if not always, right on target. Also right on the button is John Morris's frequently hilarious score, a subtle take-off on John Williams's grandiloquent music for *Star Wars.* Sadly, the instrumental tracks are sacrificed here to meaningless pop songs, which are heard faintly in the background in the film, but which get spotlighted though their importance to the action in the film is close to nil. As a result, Morris's contribution is reduced to three selections, the "Main Title," "Love Theme," and "The Winnebago Crashes/The Spaceballs Build Mega-Maid." Better watch the film, it is more fun. And may the farce be with you!

Didier C. Deutsch

Spara forte, piu forte . . . non capisco

1996, DRG Records, from the film *Spara forte, piu forte . . . non capisco (Shoot Loud, Louder . . . I Don't Understand),* Titanus 1966 ♪♪♪♪

album notes: Music: Nino Rota; Conductor: Carlo Savina.

Nino Rota, better known in this country for the scores he wrote for Federico Fellini (*La dolce vita, 8 1/2, Juliet of the Spirit*) and for such films as *The Godfather* and *Romeo and Juliet,* reveals here another facet of his talent, in this spirited series of cues composed for a comedy thriller directed by Eduardo de Filippo and starring Marcello Mastroianni and Raquel Welch. There is little need to detail the action of this film, which for all intents and purposes, failed to find an audience, though it enabled Rota to write a score that sparkles with wit and imagination. Evidently smitten by Raquel Welch, in her first starring role following her impressive debut as a scantily-clad prehistoric vixen in *One Million Years B.C.,* Rota anchored his score around the tune he developed for her, a recurring theme that ties in all the other elements in the story together. This recording may be difficult to find. Check with a used CD store, mail-order company, or a dealer specializing in rare, out-of-print, or import recordings.

Didier C. Deutsch

Sparkle

1998, Rhino Records, from the film *Sparkle,* Warner Bros., 1976 ♪♪♪

album notes: Songs: Curtis Mayfield; Featured Performer: Aretha Franklin.

Before there was *Dreamgirls* there was *Sparkle,* which detailed the trials and tribulations of three sisters who form a singing group and nurse dreams of reaching the top, until they get involved with drugs, mobsters, and record executives. Starring Irene Cara, Lonette McKee, and Mary Alice as vaguely disguised clones of the Supremes, the film had a terrific soundtrack with songs created by Curtis Mayfield. Strangely enough, it didn't have a soundtrack album, but yielded this collection performed by Aretha Franklin, certainly not a bad choice but a rather curious one, considering that at least two of the film's performers, Lonette McKee and Irene Cara, are great vocalists in their own right.

Didier C. Deutsch

Spartacus

1991, MCA Records, from the film *Spartacus,* Universal, 1960 ♪♪♪♪♪

album notes: Music: Alex North; Conductor: Alex North.

Spartacus (The Kobal Collection)

A powerful big screen retelling of the revolt of the slaves against the Romans in the century before Christ, *Spartacus* is a handsome ancient history spectacle, bold and audacious, a film with a single focus, magnificently directed by Stanley Kubrick, then only 32 years of age, and written by Dalton Trumbo, who had been blacklisted since 1947 because of his political beliefs. Playing Spartacus is Kirk Douglas, who also produced, in one of his most memorable screen portrayals as the Thracian slave who led his men, all former slaves like him, against the Roman legions, until he was defeated and killed in 70 B.C. Sharing the spotlight with him are Jean Simmons, Tony Curtis, Laurence Olivier, and many others in this all-star package.

Matching the heroic spirit that pervaded the story, Alex North wrote a sensational score in which the epic accents occasionally gave way to romantic interludes, built around the gorgeously evocative "Spartacus Love Theme." Unfortunately, while the film was only recently completely restored and given the proper care it deserved for its theatrical and video rerelease, this CD, mastered from the original two-track soundtrack album tapes, was not. Forget the fact that it doesn't contain any extra music, as an important reissue of this type would warrant, but it evidences a lot of hiss, a frequently horrendously shrill sound, and occasional analog dropouts, all of which could and should have been corrected. If you still want to try and enjoy this CD, defeat the treble completely, boost the bass, and even then the results will be less than satisfactory, though not as aggravating. The rating is for the music, not for this CD, which gets a very low rating.

Didier C. Deutsch

Spawn

1997, Epic Soundtrax, from the film *Spawn*, New Line Cinema, 1977 ♪♪♪

Spawn comes with an intriguing concept, pairing hard rockers with techno and electronic acts to see what they can come up with. It works more often than not, although there's a sameness of both sounds and viscerally heavy feel that renders the album more monolithic than dynamic. That said, Filter and Crystal Method generate some serious mood on "(Can't You)

Trip like I Do," Metallica and DJ Spooky cook on the former's "For Whom the Bell Tolls (The Irony of It All)," Rage against the Machine's Tom Morello plays tracer guitar over the Prodigy's bed of sound on "One-Man Army," and Slayer and Atari Teenage Riot are so well-matched in their aggression that they practically blow the speakers apart. A good idea that deserves to be revisited for the inevitable sequel.

Gary Graff

The Specialist

 1994, Epic Soundtrax/Sony Music, from the film *The Specialist* Warner Bros., 1994 ♫♫♫♫

album notes: **Music:** John Barry; **Orchestra:** The Royal Philharmonic Orchestra; **Conductor:** John Barry.

Fans have been disappointed that John Barry, the man who defined the James Bond sound back in the 1960s, hasn't scored a 007 outing since 1987's *The Living Daylights,* but anyone wanting to hear the equivalent of new Barry Bond soundtrack—minus the famous title theme, of course—should definitely check out the score album from *The Specialist*. Unlike most action movies filled with explosions in full Dolby Stereo, Barry got a favorable sound mix from producer Jerry Weintraub, and was able to write a steamy, dense atmospheric score with sexy lyrical passages and suspenseful action cues in the classic John Barry mold, but this time with a definite accent on jazz. The score is easily the best of Barry's recent works; rest assured that Agent 007 would approve.

Andy Dursin

 1994, Epic Soundtrax/Sony Music, from the film *The Specialist* Warner Bros., 1994 ♫♫♫♫

This showcases the Miami sound, focusing, not surprisingly, on commercial heavyweights such as Gloria Estefan & Miami Sound Machine and Jon Secada. But it also includes acts such as Azucar Moreno, Cheito, Albita, and Lagaylia, whose music hasn't been whitewashed quite as much into the pop mainstream. We're not so sure how John Barry and the Royal Philharmonic Orchestra fit into this, though.

Didier C. Deutsch

Species II

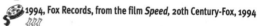 1998, TVT Records, from the film *Species II*, MGM, 1998 ♫♫♫

album notes: **Music:** Edward Shearmur.

Natasha Helstridge returned as a half-breed, the result of a DNA mix between a man and an alien from outer space, who, this time around develops an urge to mate with an astronaut back from a mission to Mars, where he has been infected with the same DNA strains used to create her, in this sequel to the 1995 sci-fi thriller. Loaded with great special effects, a large amount of gore, and some softcore sex scenes, the film also boasted a striking, enervating score from Edward Shearmur, who particularly captured the angst in the narrative. In this context, the two pop songs also included—"Don't Answer the Door" by B.B. King and "Carrera Rapida" by Apollo Four Forty—don't seem to belong.

Didier C. Deutsch

Speed

1994, Fox Records, from the film *Speed,* 20th Century-Fox, 1994 ♫♫♫

album notes: **Music:** Mark Mancina; **Conductor:** Don Harper; **Featured Musicians:** Mike Fisher, percussion; Allan Holdsworth, guitar.

With this, his first major feature score, Mark Mancina proved a most capable composer. *Speed* is a wildly energetic score, finding its base in its fast-paced rhythm and its main theme, an eight-note motif nicely evocative of danger as well as heroism. With synths accompanied by orchestra, Mancina's main theme stands solidly above the driving acceleration of throbbing synths and percussion that support it. The furiously scurrying synths occasionally part, allowing the main theme to sound assuredly from violins, punctuated by stridently arrhythmic drum beats. Strokes of strings pedal the chords faster and faster, while an eerie synth wail suggests unseen danger. There are some static moments but for the most part the score speeds along effectively, benefited by Mancina's superior orchestrations and a winning heroic/romantic theme.

Randall Larson

Speed 2: Cruise Control

1997, Virgin Records, from the film *Speed 2: Cruise Control,* 20th Century-Fox, 1997 ♫♫

The first *Speed* soundtrack was such a commercial smash that the successor—like the film—seemed like a slam dunk. Unless they really screwed up. Which they did. Heavy on Caribbean themes to enhance the movie's boat-on-the-loose theme, *Speed 2* settles for lesser fare from UB40 ("Tell Me Is It True"), Shaggy ("My Dream"), Maxi Priest ("The Tide Is High"), and popster Leah Andreone with a moribund rendition of Carole King's "I Feel the Earth Move." Jimmy Cliff's "You Can Get It If You Really Want It" is reasonable, but not nearly enough to redeem a collection that's truly stuck in low gear.

Gary Graff

Speedway

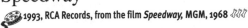1993, RCA Records, from the film *Speedway,* MGM, 1968 🎬🎬🎬

Speedway, a somewhat successful Elvis film, had two minor hits in "Let Yourself Go" and "Your Time Hasn't Come Yet, Baby." In it, Elvis played a stock-car racing champ, whose generosity attracts the attention of an IRS agent portrayed by Nancy Sinatra. Eventually, romance developed between them. The soundtrack included a new version of Brahms' "Lullaby" (titled "Five Sleepy Heads") and, unusual in an Elvis Presley soundtrack album, a solo by Nancy Sinatra, "Your Groovy Self."

Didier C. Deutsch

Spellbound

1988, Stanyan Records, from the film *Spellbound,* RKO Radio Pictures, 1945 🎬🎬🎬🎬🎬

album notes: Music: Miklos Rozsa; Orchestra: The Warner Bros. Studio Orchestra; Conductor: Ray Heindorf.

The innovative use of the theremin (an early synthesizer) singles out this soundtrack as a precursor in a field that has become very crowded in recent years. The instrument also conferred to the music composed by Miklos Rozsa its specificity in creating an atmosphere of mystery for this film directed by Alfred Hitchcock. Starring Gregory Peck as an amnesiac trying to recall some events surrounding a murder he is afraid he might have committed and Ingrid Bergman as the psychiatrist who attempts to help him, *Spellbound* is a terrific, suspenseful drama in which the action is as much psychological as it is physical. Contrasting the uncertain moods evoked by the film's "Main Theme," outlined by the theremin, Rozsa also developed other cues that create a false sense of mirth and security ("Scherzo," "Love Theme") for what has become one of the most remarkable scores in his career. His achievement that was duly recognized by an Academy Award in 1945.

This recording, made in the late 1950s with Ray Heindorf conducting the Warner Bros. Studio Orchestra, is totally faithful to the spirit of the original, and quietly sensational in its expression. The CD also features selections from Rod McKuen's *Joanna* and *The Borrowers,* and the roadshow overture to Victor Young's *Around the World in 80 Days,* which have been probably added to increase the total playing time, but have no business being here, stylistically.

Didier C. Deutsch

Sphere

1998, Varèse-Sarabande, from the film *Sphere,* Warner Bros., 1998 🎬🎬🎬🎬

album notes: Music: Elliot Goldenthal; Conductor: Steven Mercurio, Jonathan Sheffer.

An underwater thriller starring Dustin Hoffman, Sharon Stone, and Samuel L. Jackson, *Sphere* was a derivative essay that borrowed from a slew of films and involved, among other things, an alien spaceship that crashed in the ocean 288 years before and had remained buried there; a strange golden sphere, which may be alive and had the property of reflecting the image of the one holding it; sea monsters coming from nowhere and attacking the group of scientists investigating the alien spaceship; time-warp occurrences; and mind explorations. Pretty heady stuff for a single movie. If the film was riddled with clichés that recalled any number of other films, the one happy exception was Elliot Goldenthal's score, which owed little to other composers and in fact consistently struck an original note. Heard in a different context, and away from the scenes for which it was created, it still sounds quite impressive and surprisingly effective, both as a score and purely as music. The first selection here, "Pandora's Fanfare," sets the tone and surprises by its versatility, with the rest of the score constantly keeping the listener on edge, with well-defined cues that prove interesting and always challenging—somewhat of a rarity these days.

Didier C. Deutsch

Spies like Us

1985, Varèse Sarabande, from the film *Spies like Us,* Warner Bros., 1985 🎬🎬🎬

album notes: Music: Elmer Bernstein; Orchestra: The Graunke Symphony Orchestra; Conductor: Elmer Bernstein.

This typical Elmer Bernstein comedy score is nonetheless entertaining. As much of the film plays like an old Bob Hope/Bing Croby *Road* picture (Hope even makes an appearance), Bernstein approaches things with the same broad comic feel, playing out obvious and familiar-sounding desert motifs that just slap the audience's face and scream, "We're in the desert, stupid! See there's sand!" This, of course, does work to get us over some of the film's dull spots (especially when the uneducated fail to grasp the gag of having famous directors and effects people in bit parts). Particularly funny to music fans is Bernstein's satirization of his own score from *The Magnificent Seven* ("Off to Spy").

David Hirsch

The Spirit of St. Louis

1989, Varèse Sarabande, from the film *The Spirit of St. Louis,* Warner Bros., 1957 🎬🎬🎬🎬🎬

album notes: Music: Franz Waxman; Orchestra: The Warner Bros. Studio Orchestra; Conductor: Franz Waxman.

Directed by Billy Wilder, *The Spirit of St. Louis* stars James Stewart in a faithful recreation of Charles Lindbergh's historic solo flight from New York to Paris in May, 1927. The film cried out for a score that would fulfill a double task: underline the momentous scenes in the script, based on Lindbergh's own autobiography, and provide an extra dramatic impetus to the long stretches of screen time that involved the aviator, alone inside the cockpit of his plane, during his transatlantic flight. In writing it, Franz Waxman acquitted himself superbly of the demands imposed on him. His cues, superbly shaded and sober in their expression, detail the frustrations initially encountered by Lindbergh, when he began building the plane that would eventually take him to his ambitious destination, the problems posed by the first test flights, and finally the long, seemingly endless journey across the unknown, before the final strains in the music signal the success of his undertaking. Like Tiomkin's music for *The Old Man and the Sea*, Waxman's score for *The Spirit of St. Louis* became an essential component of the film's dramatic structure. Heard in this recording in its entirety, with many previously unavailable tracks further detailing Lindbergh's pioneering effort, it emerges as a powerful musical statement, with a vibrancy that immediately compels the listener's attention and immerses him into the unfolding story.

Didier C. Deutsch

The Spitfire Grill

1996, Sony Classical, from the film *The Spitfire Grill*, Columbia Pictures, 1996 🎬🎬🎬

album notes: **Music:** James Horner; **Conductor:** James Horner.

When Castle Rock snapped up the rights to this audience-winner at the Sundance Film Festival, they spruced up a number of the film's aural elements, including the addition of a new music score by James Horner. Fortunately, this jaunty, often country-flavored score doesn't go overboard in Hollywood saccharine, as Horner keeps things on a tuneful, lyric level that's easily accessible for listeners without being overtly simplistic. The main theme of the film is quite nice, and the variations that the composer uses in his score keep it fresh and not nearly as derivative as some of his other works. It's a pleasant album, inoffensive and relaxing.

Andy Dursin

Spy Tek

1998, RCA Victor, from the television series, *Spy Tek*, Discovery, 1998 🎬🎬🎬

album notes: **Music:** Joe Taylor.

A television series that was shown on the Discovery channel, *Spy Tek* explored the secret world of real-life spies, with this soundtrack album released to coincide with the premiere of the

television broadcast. Introduced by Roger Moore, the album features selections created and performed by Joe Taylor, on guitars, keyboards, mandolin, percussion, and synclavier. While the tunes are frequently attractive, they also sound derivative ("Danger Girl," "The Girl") and evoke other better-known composers, but the cues hold their own and manage to sustain one's interest. Not a bad album, altogether, and certainly better than the endless synthesized meanderings of Mark Snow.

Didier C. Deutsch

The Spy Who Loved Me

1995, EMI Records, from the film *The Spy Who Loved Me*, United Artists, 1977 🎬🎬

album notes: **Music:** Marvin Hamlisch; **Conductor:** Marvin Hamlisch; **Featured Musicians:** Barry Desouza, drums; Laurence Juber, guitar; Chris Rae, second electric guitar; Mike Egan, acoustic guitar; Bruce Lynch, bass guitar; Brian Ogdes, bass guitar; Derick Plater, saxophone; Marvin Hamlisch, piano; Ron Aspery, flute, soprano sax; Paul Buckmaster, cello synthesizer; Fre Goodyear, bass guitar; Brother James, congas/percussion; Paul Robinson, drums.

One of the first James Bond films not scored by John Barry, *The Spy Who Loved Me* offers what is probably the best and the worst in the soundtracks for the series. The best is Carly Simon's superb rendition of the title song, written by Carole Bayer Sager, which bookends this CD. One of the best theme songs in the series, it is as much memorable today as it was when it was first created. The worst is Marvin Hamlisch's ho-hum score, a series of cues with long cascading lines, percolating rhythms, guitar riffs, and wah-wah effects that attempt to find an original tone but fail miserably. It really didn't matter much behind the action on the screen, as the cues fulfilled a function that was essentially secondary. But thrown in the spotlight, they reveal the absence of genuine feel for the series and what it is all about, with themes that are routine at best, and altogether not very interesting.

Didier C. Deutsch

Stagecoach/The Loner

1998, Film Score Monthly, from the film *Stagecoach*, 20th Century-Fox, 1966, and the television series *The Loner*, CBS, 1965–66 🎬🎬🎬🎬

album notes: **Music:** Jerry Goldsmith; **Conductor:** Jerry Goldsmith.

Previously available on a dreadful Mainstream album, the score Jerry Goldsmith wrote for this 1966 remake of *Stagecoach* returns to the catalogue, dusted off and spiffed up and sounding like a million dollars in this important reissue, available through Film Score Monthly's "Silver Age Classics" series. Because Goldsmith has not worked in this idiom for quite some time, it is a real pleasure to rediscover him in this genre. If the required syncopated accents, and harmonica and guitar tunes are present, Goldsmith has a way to present them that's clearly his and no one else. Emphasizing the appeal of the Colorado scenery, where the film was shot, the music Goldsmith wrote is, for the most part, tender and quiet, with a folksy tone to it that contrasts with the violent action on screen, left for the most part unscored. The cues that detail some of the moments in the narrative are attractively laid out and invite repeated listening, with the exception of "Stagecoach to Cheyenne," a tepid song by Lee Pockriss and Paul Vance, sung by Wayne Newton, that's clearly not in context with the rest of the score.

Complementing this release, producers Lukas Kendall and Nick Redman have added two long suites from the television series *The Loner,* which was created by Rod Sterling (of *Twilight Zone* fame) as an "existentialist western." Starring Lloyd Bridges as a disillusioned Civil War veteran, it was, in the words of liner notes author Jon Burlingame, "a thinking man's western," which may have been the cause of its early demise. The two suites which Goldsmith wrote, "An Echo of Bugles" and "One of the Wounded," are closer in spirit to his score for *Rio Conchos,* written a year earlier, and are orchestrated for a stringless ensemble featuring accordion, banjo, marimba, and an occasional whipcrack, requested no doubt in imitation of the popular *Rawhide.* At times slightly dissonant, the music evokes the solitary figure etched by the title character and the desert territory in which he found himself. On a purely technical note, the transfer sounds a bit dry, and probably could have used a little reverb.

Didier C. Deutsch

The Staircase

1998, BWE Music, from the television film *The Staircase,* Kraft Premier Movie, 1998 🎬🎬🎬

album notes: Music: David Michael Frank; **Orchestras:** The City of Prague Philharmonic, The Kuhn's Choir; **Conductor:** David Michael Frank; **Featured Soloist:** Livia Aghova.

The story of a mysterious drifter who chances upon a convent established in the middle of Indian territory and offers to help build a badly needed staircase in the church, possibly as an answer to the Mother Abbess' prayers for such a miracle to happen, *The Staircase,* a Kraft television premier movie, was spiritually uplifting and inspirational. It also boasted a very lovely score by David Michael Frank, in which religious-sounding anthems, sung by the Kuhn's Choir, mix happily with more conventional and even standard action cues. A performance by the ubiquitous City of Prague Philharmonic is diaphanously woven throughout.

Didier C. Deutsch

Stand and Deliver

1988, Varèse-Sarabande, from the film *Stand and Deliver,* Warner Bros., 1988 🎬🎬🎬

album notes: Music: Craig Safan.

The specific atmosphere of the barrio in East Los Angeles is given credible musical life in the score Craig Safan wrote for this film about a gang of Latinos who discover the importance of mathematics, thanks to a dedicated high school teacher. Relying on expressive synth melodies and effects, Safan created a score that evidences remarkable flair even as it evokes some of the events and characters involved in the screen action. Moving with ease from Spanish-accented themes ("Pancho and Lupe"), to a soft Japanese tune ("Kimo's Theme"), to delicately phrased cues built around harp-like arpeggios ("Picking on Claudia," "The First Test/Release"), the music is multi-layered and attractively laid out. The seven-minute "Stand and Deliver Suite" recaps the overall moods into one long evocation that has moments of fun and depth in it.

Didier C. Deutsch

Stanley & Iris

1990, Varèse Sarabande, from the film *Stanley & Iris,* MGM, 1990 🎬🎬🎬

album notes: Music: John Williams; **Conductor:** John Williams.

It might run under half an hour, but this score by John Williams is more developed thematically than many far lengthier soundtracks. Williams's score here is relatively simple and reflective in nature, adeptly setting the scene for this 1990 Martin Ritt drama with Jane Fonda and Robert De Niro. But it is the autumnal warmth flowing out of this score that makes it so memorable. The themes are succinct and lovely, the orchestrations subtle and appropriate for a character drama, and the nature of the music makes repeated listenings not only easily endurable but a genuine pleasure. This is the kind of character-driven score Williams excels at whenever he is given the opportunity, and is also one of the most underrated works in the composer's filmography.

Andy Dursin

Star!

1993, Fox Records, from the film *Star!,* 20th Century Fox, 1968 🎬🎬🎬

album notes: Orchestra: The 20th Century Fox Orchestra; *Choir:* The 20th Century Fox Chorus; **Conductor:** Lennie Hayton; **Cast:** Julie Andrews, Daniel Massey, Bruce Forsyth, Beryl Reid.

Julie Andrews, portraying Gertrude Lawrence, is quite fetching in this glossy biographical musical film, in which she performed some of the great hits created by Lawrence. With an abundance of memorable songs, many of them written by the cream of Broadway and London tunesmiths, a glamorous era in the musical theatre as backdrop, and a flamboyant character as its main focus, the film became a veritable showcase for Andrews, who is dazzling in it. The recently reissued CD includes a couple of previously unreleased numbers.

Didier C. Deutsch

Star Crash

See: Until September/Star Crash

A Star Is Born

1988, Columbia Records from the film *A Star Is Born,* Warner Bros. Pictures, 1954 ♫♫♫♫♡

album notes: Music: Harold Arlen; **Lyrics:** Ira Gershwin; **Orchestra:** The Warner Bros. Studio Orchestra; **Choir:** The Warner Bros. Studio Orchestra; **Conductor:** Ray Heindorf; **Cast:** Judy Garland, James Mason, Tommy Noonan.

In 1988, Ronald Haver wrote one of the most interesting books pertaining to film history. That book, *A Star Is Born: The Making of the 1954 Movie and its 1983 Reconstruction* deals with the film *A Star Is Born,* and the trials and tribulations that Judy Garland and then-husband Sid Luft created and endured in bringing Moss Hart's bittersweet tale of love and fame to the big screen. The book paints a fascinating picture of all the elements that combine together to create what would become Garland's Hollywood "comeback," and her last true success. One of those elements, the music, is what has propelled this terrific film into the annals of Hollywood history—and what survives as one of the most pleasing and alluring of all film soundtrack recordings.

Until the release of this Columbia CD, there existed no stereo album of these familiar songs, most by Harold Arlen and Ira Gershwin. After an ambitious film restoration made it clear that a true stereo recording existed, a search was conducted, and the result is this disc—the finest release of this soundtrack to date. The sonics, carefully restored, are excellent, despite the limitations of stereo film recording technology in 1954 (and several years before stereo became a standard in recording studios). It is a true revelation to hear Garland classics like "The Man That Got Away," "Gotta Have Me Go with You," and the mammoth "Born in a Trunk" sequence without the sonic murk of the original Columbia/Harmony LPs. The music, and Ray Heindorf's outstanding orchestrations are so appealing, that one wishes there were more musical cues to be heard. (There were, initially, but unfortunately these were removed at the last minute, for contractual reasons). While a complete soundtrack, coinciding with the film restoration,

would have made for a spectacular release, this outstanding recording fits a special niche, and leaves us hoping that maybe someday . . .

Charles L. Granata

1997, Columbia Records, from the film *A Star Is Born,* 1974 ♫♫♫

Any thought that Barbra Streisand might replace Judy Garland were dashed with this glossy remake of *A Star Is Born* in which Barbra played an upcoming, gifted performer to Kris Kristofferson's waning rock 'n' roll star. Basically, the story remained the same, though the love scenes between Streisand and Kris might have been more steamy than the ones between Garland and James Mason in the 1954 version. The score, on the other hand, consisted of songs written by Paul Williams, Rupert Holmes, Ken Ascher, and the divine Ms. S. who took co-writing and performing credits on the film's *piece de resistance,* "Evergreen," a multi-platinum hit. Essentially a showcase for the star, this album has little else to recommend it, and is strictly for Babs fans.

Didier C. Deutsch

Star Kid

1998, Sonic Images, from the film *Star Kid,* Trimark, 1998 ♫♫

album notes: Music: Nicholas Pike; **Orchestra:** The Munich Symphony Orchestra; **Conductor:** Nicholas Pike.

Nowadays, a kids' movie without killer special effects, animation, or major stars is destined to go unnoticed. *Star Kid,* released last year, at least had a cute premise—a shy boy discovers a space suit with human characteristics that gives him superhuman skills, that is if he can learn to maneuver it—but it didn't go anywhere. Nicholas Pike's sci-fi score, somewhat generic, occasionally entertaining, didn't help much either. The CD also features two songs, neither of which are very impressive: Edgar Winter covering Steppenwolf's "Magic Carpet Ride" and the unmemorable "Shadow in the Shade," performed by a remarkably unknown artist.

Beth Krakower

The Star Maker

1996, Miramax-Hollywood Records, from the film *The Star Maker,* Miramax, 1996 ♫♫

album notes: Music: Ennio Morricone; **Orchestra:** The Orchestra Unione Musicisti di Roma; **Conductor:** Ennio Morricone; **Featured Soloists:** Franco Tamponi, violin; Laura Pontecorvo, dolce flute; Paolo Zampini, ottavino flute; Stefano Novelli, clarinet; Filippo Rizzuto, guitar.

Years ago when he scored *The Thing,* Ennio Morricone remarked that the film's score was about "nothing happening." The suspenseful, anticipatory ambiance he sustained in *The Thing* hinted at something happening, but "nothing happens." Morricone's score for *The Star Maker* would have been as appropriate a score for *The Thing* because it's one of the most static, nothing-happening scores the maestro has composed recently. The music is plain boring. Peeling back layers of violins, Morricone exposed multiple strains of the same basic chords and notes, with the occasional flute wandering in and out. There's virtually no melody and no rhythm. The ponderous "thematic" material and the few period pop tunes, not to mention the recording's overall low volume, make this score recommended primarily for insomniacs. It's an unfortunate commentary on a composer who really woke me up to film music for the first time, but there's nothing terribly interesting or inventive here.

Randall Larson

Star Maps

1997, DGC Records, from the film *Star Maps,* Fox Searchlight, 1997 ♫♫♫

A dysfunctional family with ties in the barrio of Los Angeles is at the core of *Star Maps,* the depressing story of a teenager with ambitions of becoming an actor who "works" for his father, hawking maps to movie stars' homes and selling himself indiscriminately to anyone with money. His particular "talents" make a strong enough impression on one of his clients, a genuine star on a TV soap, who manages to have the youngster hired for a bit part. This grueling tale gets enlivened by some contemporary barrio sounds, including some rap, alternative, folk, and hip hop songs, most of them performed in Spanish, that may appeal to a limited audience, but prove to be remarkably unenticing. Giving the album a different spin, Molotov makes a sudden appearance in "Use It or Lose It," which somehow seems alien to the rest of the tunes collected here.

Didier C. Deutsch

Star Trek: The Motion Picture
/Inside Star Trek

1997, Legacy Records/Sony, from the film *Star Trek: The Motion Picture,* Paramount, 1979 ♫♫♫♫

album notes: Music: Jerry Goldsmith; Conductor: Jerry Goldsmith.

Composers often produce outstanding scores under the worst possible conditions. On the hastily constructed, overbudget sci-fi feature *Star Trek: The Motion Picture,* Jerry Goldsmith had just a handful of days to write a film score that would be evocative, epic, majestic, and mystical, benefiting the massive special effects of this production while refusing to be an exact clone of *Star Wars.* Even under this time crunch, Goldsmith came through with flying colors: his magnificent, Oscar-nominated soundtrack contains perhaps his most well-known theme (later utilized for both TV's *Star Trek: The Next Generation* and the Goldsmith-scored theatrical sequels), a wealth of fascinating musical cues for the alien being "Vejur," and, in contrast, an aggressively percussive motif for the Klingons (a la *The Wind and the Lion*). The music works perfectly in the movie and on its own, and stands as one of the crowning achievements in Goldsmith's career.

Andy Dursin

1999, Sony Legacy, from the film *Star Trek: The Motion Picture,* Paramount, 1976 ♫♫♫♫♫

album notes: Music: Jerry Goldsmith; Conductor: Jerry Goldsmith.

Jerry Goldsmith revolutionized sci-fi scoring for the second time after *Planet of the Apes* with his soaring, operatic music for the *U.S.S. Enterprise.* Beginning with the fanfare that's become the signature theme of the franchise's *Next Generation,* Goldsmith's music plays the exploration of space with a romantic sense of adventure, fully capturing the optimist future vision of *Trek* creator Gene Roddenbery. The composer's bold marriage of orchestra and synthesizers is never more spectacular than when the *Enterprise* is in the grip of Vejur. Goldsmith turns this gigantic spaceship into a haunted house in space, using an organ and the eerie sound of a "blaster beam" to convey a foreboding sense of grandeur. This long-awaited special edition of *Star Trek: The Motion Picture* contains over 30 minutes of unreleased music, including such much-desired cues as "Floating Office" and "The Force Field." The second CD in this deluxe package, *Inside Star Trek,* is for die-hard fans. It's an interesting, if slightly goofy, novelty album that has Roddenbery breathlessly expounding on the Trek philosophy and network stupidity, with such cast members as Mark Leonard ("Sarek") throwing in his two cents on Vulcan sexuality. You're better off sticking to Goldsmith's music, and using your imagination.

Dan Schweiger

Star Trek II:
The Wrath of Khan

1990, GNP Crescendo, from the film *Star Trek II: The Wrath of Khan,* Paramount, 1982 ♫♫♫♫

album notes: Music: James Horner; Conductor: James Horner.

Nicholas Meyer's take on the *Star Trek* myths revitalized the film franchise after the moribund *Star Trek: The Motion Picture.* It also launched the career of composer James Horner, who brought a wonderful, windswept nautical quality to his title music, which spins up from a whirling horn figure into sweeping, romantic rapture. If it sometimes seems more appropriate for Sherwood Forest than an outer space epic, it's only appropriate given director Meyer's Prisoner-of-Zenda take on the material. Horner's space attack cues are uproarious, contrasting the pagan fury of a chaotic brass motif for Ricardo Montalban's villainous Khan against the naval heroism of William Shatner's Kirk and a surprisingly lyrical, bittersweet melody for the self-sacrificing Spock. "Battle in the Mutara Nebula" and "Genesis Countdown" are still two of the most exciting and sustained musical cues Horner has ever written, and his setting of Alexander Courage's mysterioso TV show opening as the finale of the film (under Leonard Nimoy's recitation of the famous Trek "to boldly go" manifesto will make the hairs on the back of your neck stand at attention. This is a highlight of both the *Trek* film series and Horner's career.

Jeff Bond

Star Trek III:
The Search for Spock

1990, GNP Crescendo, from the film *Star Trek III: The Search for Spock*, Paramount, 1984 🎬🎬🎬

album notes: Music: James Horner; **Conductor:** James Horner.

James Horner's second *Star Trek* score comes off as a pallid retread of much of his stupendous *Wrath of Khan* effort, but it still has its moments, including the sparkling accompaniment to the *Enterprise*'s return to its space-dock moorings early in the film and the throbbing suspense licks of "Stealing the Enterprise," which climaxes in one of the more bombastic treatments of Alexander Courage's TV show fanfare ever heard in the film series. Horner's attempt to co-opt the appeal of Jerry Goldsmith's Prokofiev-like Klingon motifs from the original film, as well as his rehash of his own *Brainstorm* finale for the film's climactic mind-meld sequence, is less appealing. If you can't get enough of the composer's *Wrath of Khan* score, here's less of the same.

Jeff Bond

Star Trek IV:
The Voyage Home

1986, MCA Records, from the film *Star Trek IV: The Voyage Home*, Paramount, 1986 🎬🎬🎬🎬

album notes: Music: Leonard Rosenman.

After the increasingly soap opera-ish plotlines for *Star Trek II* and *III*, the producers wisely decided to take an entirely different approach for *Star Trek IV: The Voyage Home*. The results: the most successful Trek film of all, a refreshingly comic, thoroughly entertaining time-travel yarn that remains the most sat-

isfying big-screen adventure of Captain Kirk and friends. To fit the change in tone, Nimoy turned to veteran composer Leonard Rosenman to write the score, and the results were an energetic, Oscar nominated effort that refuses to take itself too seriously; Rosenman's main theme is a lot of fun, written in the same vein as some of his other genre works (i.e., *Lord of the Rings*), but his music for the film's aquatic protagonists, the Humpback whales, is more serious and noble in nature. The music by itself is highly enjoyable, with the album including a pair of tracks by the jazz group the Yellowjackets, who worked with Rosenman on the picture's "modern day" music that Kirk, Spock, and the rest of the Enterprise crew encounter when they travel back to 1986 San Francisco.

Andy Dursin

Star Trek V: The Final Frontier

1989, Epic Records, from the film *Star Trek V: The Final Frontier*, Paramount, 1989 🎬🎬🎬

album notes: Music: Jerry Goldsmith; **Conductor:** Jerry Goldsmith.

Jerry Goldsmith's second voyage with the crew of the Starship *Enterprise* yields a variety of musical quality, no doubt due to the film's own slapdash continuity. Certainly "The Mountain" is far and away one of the composer's more inspired cues, a marvelous companion to the images of Kirk scaling the sheer mountain El Capitan in Yosemite National Park. The bold re-orchestration of his original theme from *Star Trek: The Motion Picture* is a joy, going a long way in making the film more exciting, but working against it all is his lighthearted variation on the Klingon theme. It only goes to further belittle these characters, who suffer massive indignation from their comedic on-screen antics. Overall, Goldsmith's score actually plays better outside of the film where his wondrously reverent motifs for the "god" entity aren't sabotaged by the limp visual effects. The closing song, "The Moon's a Window to Heaven," performed here by the jazz fusion group Hiroshima, did not appear in the film. However, Nichelle Nichols (Uhura) sang a portion of it during her ludicrous fan dance sequence.

David Hirsch

Star Trek VI:
The Undiscovered Country

1991, MCA Records, from the film *Star Trek VI: The Undiscovered Country*, Paramount, 1991 🎬🎬🎬🎬

album notes: Music: Cliff Eidelman; **Conductor:** Cliff Eidelman.

Originally, director Nicholas Meyer wanted composer Cliff Eidelman to write a score based on Gustav Holst's "The Planets" for his film. When Paramount Pictures failed to come to terms with the copyright owners, Eidelman was asked to create a work in a similar vein. As a result, his score is vastly different from any previous in the *Star Trek* series. Dark, bleak, desperate . . . the Federation is now on the brink of an all-out war with their mortal enemies, the Klingons, and events are being controlled by traitors within. Eidelman even uses a chorus to symbolize the menacing Klingon horde. A unique approach was also used in assembling the album: Eidelman perceived the entire score as a grand symphony, and, with occasionally cross-fading the cues together in strict film order, he created a running concerto that starts deliberately and builds in force until the spectacular eight-minute "Battle for Peace" finale.

David Hirsch

Star Trek: Deep Space Nine

1993, GNP Crescendo Records, from the television series *Star Trek: Deep Space Nine*, Paramount Pictures, 1993 🎵🎵🎵
album notes: Music: Dennis McCarthy.

Star Trek TNG uber–composer Dennis McCarthy expanded his empire with this score for the first "Next Generation" spin–off, the more complex and elaborate *Deep Space Nine*, which set its stories on an immense alien space station perched on the edge of a galactic wormhole. McCarthy's lonely horn fanfare title music immediately sets the tone for the series: Not the strident heroism of Jerry Goldsmith's victorious *Star Trek: The Motion Picture* march as used in TNG, but the more realistic, world–weary heroism of people who have to clean up after themselves and others. Although some of the musical tenets of *The Next Generation* (extended tonal pads and smooth, string–and–horn dominated orchestrations) hold sway here, there's some interesting experimentation in the jarring atonality of cues like "Time Stood Still" and the funky alien source music heard in "Quark's Bar." It's still as far as you can get from the broad, motif–heavy music of the original series, but McCarthy has elevated this approach to an art form, writing scores of remarkable complexity and subtlety.

Jeff Bond

Star Trek: First Contact

1996, GNP Crescendo, from the film *Star Trek: First Contact*, Paramount, 1996 🎵🎵🎵
album notes: Music: Jerry Goldsmith; Conductor: Jerry Goldsmith.

Jerry Goldsmith has crafted this score with an understated eloquence. His music is embroidered with a sense of grand legendary, his theme seasoned and elegant rather than bombastic and vigorous. The heroism of the *First Contact* score is a quiet, reflective one, and stresses in positive terms the

proud camaraderie between captain and crew, and all they have gone through. The new theme, an affecting recapitulation of all the adventures that have come before in the Trek universe, is also a tribute to the harmonic future envisioned in *First Contact* and the entire *Star Trek* milieu. Goldsmith's original theme from *Star Trek: The Motion Picture* and the *Next Generation* series brackets this new score during its opening and closing credits, which remain unabashedly heroic and triumphant. And, of course, strains from Alexander Courage's original *Trek* fanfare provide the link with the original series and its various spin-offs. The CD, one of several "enhanced CD soundtracks" released lately, includes a data program, with interviews with Goldsmith and other *First Contact* participants.

Randall D. Larson

Star Trek: Generations

1995, GNP Crescendo, from the film *Star Trek: Generations*, Paramount, 1994 🎵🎵🎵
album notes: Music: Dennis McCarthy; Conductor: Dennis McCarthy.

Television composer Dennis McCarthy got the nod to score the first theatrical adventure of the "Next Generation" crew, and even though his score is not quite as interesting as the Goldsmith and Horner outings from the preceding *Trek* films, this is still an enjoyable effort. McCarthy's main theme for the film is rather basic but nevertheless perfectly suited for the picture, with a triumphant, heroic sound defining the valiant intentions of Captains Picard and Kirk, united in a "Nexus" at the far edge of the galaxy. For the otherworldly "Nexus," McCarthy wrote new age-style music that sounds suspiciously close to John Williams's "Fortress of Solitude" material from *Superman,* though without the melodic invention of that earlier work. Nevertheless, on its own terms, *Generations* is still a satisfying soundtrack that should not disappoint die-hard fans of the series.

Andy Dursin

Star Trek: Insurrection

1998, GNP Crescendo, from the film *Star Trek: Insurrection*, Paramount, 1998 🎵🎵🎵🎵
album notes: Music: Jerry Goldsmith; Conductor: Jerry Goldsmith.

Jerry Goldsmith has become as intricately connected to the *Star Trek* movie franchise as John Barry was to the James Bond series in the '60s, and with good reason: Goldsmith redefined the sound of the *Star Trek* universe with his 1979 *Star Trek: The Motion Picture* score, and has achieved notable successes with his follow-up efforts for the series. *Insurrection* continues the tradition, managing to be both more cohesive and developed than *First Contact,* yet less dramatically charged and epic-sounding than *The Motion Picture* or *Star Trek V: The Final Frontier. Insurrection* is an almost lighthearted Trek with elements of comedy, but Goldsmith allows that aspect to function by itself and focuses on the film's romantic and action-oriented facets to good effect. After the *de rigueur* statement of Alexander Courage's original Trek fanfare, Goldsmith opens the film with one of the most subdued and pastoral cues yet written for a *Star Trek* movie, painting the pacifistic Ba'ku race with a gentle theme for flute and strings. The rest of the score balances these romantic elements with action material that will sound familiar to anyone who's heard Goldsmith's *U.S. Marshals* score. The only real disappointment is the end title music: Goldsmith's original march from *Star Trek: The Motion Picture* just doesn't sit well beside the comparatively inaudible Ba'ku theme.

Jeff Bond

Star Trek: The Next Generation

1998, GNP Crescendo, from the television series, *Star Trek: The Next Generation,* 1999 ♫♫♫♪

album notes: Music: Jay Chattaway.

Like many of GNP's *Star Trek: The Next Generation* compilations, Volume 4 functions as an interesting illustration of how composers had to adapt their style to the exigencies of the new *Trek* television series. Anyone expecting to write scores in the vein of the dynamic music from the original series or even contemporary space movie epics had to quickly adjust to a far more subdued and textural approach preferred by the new series' producers. Jay Chattaway, a veteran composer of theatrical films and televised documentaries, initially brought a more epic, action-oriented sensibility to his first *TNG* assignment, "Tin Man," writing a bombastic fanfare for the Romulans that was eventually dropped from the episode, and some highly experimental sonic effects for the inside of the spacegoing title creature that involved whale song recordings and the sound of a technician's stomach digesting a pizza. "The Inner Light" afforded Chattaway the opportunity to write a wistful melody for tin whistle to accompany Jean-Luc Picard's experience of another life via an alien mind probe, and the suites from "Sub Rosa" and "Dark Mirror" show how the composer was able to create disturbing and misleadingly complex soundscapes for some of the show's darker episodes. Another arena that allowed Chattaway to experiment was the show's various holodeck episodes such as "A Fistful of Datas," which allowed the composer to play around with the conventions of western film composing.

Jeff Bond

Star Trek: Voyager

1995, GNP Crescendo, from the television series *Star Trek: Voyager,* Paramount Pictures, 1995 ♫♫♫

album notes: Music: Jay Chattaway; **Conductor:** Jay Chattaway; **Featured Musician:** George Doering, banjo.

Jay Chattaway charted the course for this latest *Star Trek* series with a heavily rhythmic, percussive score for the pilot episode "The Caretaker" that helped to begin a movement away from the low-key atmospheric scoring that had dominated the franchise since the latter days of *Star Trek: The Next Generation.* A key element of the show is the sweeping, majestic French horn melody written by film composer and *Star Trek* veteran Jerry Goldsmith for the show's title music, and adapted very effectively by Chattaway during the score's last few cues (which also feature an ingeniously subtle quotation of Alexander Courage's original *Star Trek* fanfare). The rest of the score features hard-hitting, brassy action cues for some furious space dogfight sequences, a series of shifting, undulating orchestral and synthesized chords for the spacial phenomenon that flings the U.S.S. Voyager across the galaxy, and even some banjo picking for an illusory meeting with the Caretaker in human form.

Jeff Bond

Star Wars

1997, RCA Records, from the film *Star Wars,* 20th Century-Fox, 1977/1997 ♫♫♫♫♫

album notes: Music: John Williams; **Orchestra:** The London Symphony Orchestra; **Conductor:** John Williams.

More than 20 years after its initial release, what hasn't been written or said about *Star Wars* that needs to be stated? John Williams's grand, outstanding operatic score—incorporating Korngold-esque swells of emotion as well as Wagnerian motifs for the film's various characters—redefined film music, and continues to this day to influence the way movies sound. Just as importantly, it made legions of audiences into film music fans, resurrected interest in classical music, and created a whole new market for movie soundtracks to flourish in. Aside from all of the cultural significance, Williams's score remains a classic all the way, from the opening blast of his fanfare through the "galactic jazz" of the Cantina Band, culminating in the thrilling Death Star climax and triumphant "Throne Room" finale. After a handful of previous releases, RCA Victor's 1997 re-issue (accompanying the film's "Special Edition" release) is now rightfully considered the definitive issue of Williams's work, with expanded tracks and superb, digitally remastered sound creating the ultimate listening experience for one of the movies' all-time great scores.

Williams's original *Star Wars* score marked the beginning of his fruitful "epic" period that lasted from 1977 to 1983's *Return of the Jedi,* and it's still the standard by which epic sci-fi adventure scores are measured. It's been argued that this score set the medium back by decades with its retro approach to the material, taking its cue from Korngold and Holst to produce a wholesome, swashbuckling sound that's been copied in countless bad ways since. But Williams found the perfect music for George Lucas's essentially innocent space opera, and *Star Wars* is a vibrant, unforgettable work from its spectacular opening titles (with a blasting, martial fanfare straight out of a Roman epic) and hammering, Holst-inspired underscoring of an attack by a gigantic Imperial star destroyer to its evocative Tatooine desert scoring and brilliant, Benny Goodman–styled cantina music. The outrageously loud and mechanistic "The Fighter Attack" is unlike anything ever heard in a movie up to that time, its shimmering spectral opening, repeated brass hits, and declamatory Rebel fanfare melding with Lucas's dizzyingly edited space battle sequence to produce a kind of psychotic, exhilarating filmic video game. Even better is the lengthy and supremely exciting *Death Star* battle music, presented here in its entirety for the first time, from the suspenseful, pulsating "Launch from the Fourth Moon" to the exhilarating martial fanfares of "X-Wings Draw Fire"—there has rarely been a more thrilling accompaniment to a cinematic combat sequence. The quiet moments are just as engaging, from the haunting "The Princess Appears" to the deeply lyrical, moving statement of Ben Kenobi's theme as Luke Skywalker stares longingly into the "Binary Sunset." Extras include Williams's first take on that sequence, more of an epic, tragic rendition that speaks to young Luke's desolation as he contemplates another year on Tatooine, and a hidden collection of alternate takes of the title music. Beautifully produced and assembled by Nick Redman and Michael Mattesino, this two-CD set belongs in anyone's collection.

see also: The Empire Strikes Back/Return of the Jedi

Andy Dursin & Jeff Bond

Star Wars Episode 1: The Phantom Menace

1999, Sony Classical, from the film *Star Wars: Episode 1: The Phantom Menace,* 20th Century-Fox, 1999 ♪♪♪♪

album notes: Music: John Williams; **Orchestra:** The London Symphony Orchestra; **Conductor:** John Williams.

The much-awaited prequel to the original *Star Wars* trilogy generated so much hype that it seems unlikely anyone reading these lines doesn't know what it is all about. Far from us to comment on or criticize the film itself which, regardless of anyone's opinion, pro or con, will surely have a long life not only in theaters around the country now and in subsequent

reissues, but also on VHS, Laserdisc, and DVD, when it is released on video. It made sense, on a purely creative level, that John Williams would return as the film's composer. The creator of one of the most celebrated "Main Titles" in the history of motion pictures, his task seemed not so much to offer a sense of continuity with the original trilogy as to write a score that would become as important and memorable as his previous efforts. The fact that he has succeeded beyond expectations is the first gratifying reaction this score elicits. But with the insight provided by the 15-year interval that separates *The Return of the Jedi,* the last film in the first trilogy, and *The Phantom Menace,* one also notices how much richer and more profoundly realized this new score is compared to the previous ones.

Here Williams shows a greater depth and maturity which happily supplements the youthful energy of this swashbuckling score. The cues seem better defined and more satisfying in their musical invention. Using the full orchestral palette at his disposal (the marvelous London Symphony Orchestra, sounding fantastic), he has painted a musical landscape with broad swaths of color that recall at times the rich, exuberant tones of Borodin ("Duel of the Fates"). All at once, vibrant and exotic, energetic and romantic, the cues provide a rich, descriptive idea of the action itself, of the settings, and of the various characters involved. On a purely audio level, the score also stands out and proves tremendously stimulating. In every aspect of it, one can feel the extraordinary talent of a master at work, a great composer whose best effort this might very well be.

Didier C. Deutsch

Stargate

1994, Milan Records, from the film *Stargate,* MGM, 1994 ♪♪♪♪

album notes: Music: David Arnold; **Orchestras:** The Sinfonia of London, the Chameleon Arts Chorus; **Conductor:** Nicholas Dodd.

British composer David Arnold's orchestral background serves him well for this massive, sweeping score which effectively captures the textural nuances of the alien civilization as well as the heroic scope of the story. While incorporating synthesizers and modern instrumentation and recording techniques, Arnold's compositional style is rooted in Hollywood classicism. With his main theme's compelling melody, strikingly orchestrated throughout its many guises, and the rhythmical flurries and furiously energetic figures of the action cues, accentuated by evocative female choir vocalisms, Arnold's *Stargate* is a standout score. The 30 cues on the CD are varied, and Arnold weaves his music carefully, with as many bold strokes as there are quiet interludes.

Randall D. Larson

Stargate SG.1

1997, Milan, from the television series *Stargate SG.1*, Showtime, 1997 &&&

album notes: Music: Joel Goldsmith

David Arnold's original *Stargate* score was a breath of fresh orchestral air in a period when action scores were dominated by synths and decidedly unromantic—it was a throwback to epic scores of the late '70s and early '80s. Showtime's series adaptation of the Dean Devlin/Roland Emmerich sci-fi movie seemed to vacillate between embracing the *Ten Commandments*–styled epic sweep of the movie and simply rehashing old *Star Trek,* and the conflict of styles is amply represented on this soundtrack album. Owners of David Arnold's *Stargate* score CD may be more than a little miffed to discover that they're getting a replay of that album here—most of the music is lifted directly from the original movie's soundtrack. Fans of composer Joel Goldsmith don't get the best deal either, as Goldsmith's music often seems to serve merely as filler to bridge gaps between the Arnold cues. Nevertheless, Goldsmith's music stands quite well alongside Arnold's: he wrote an impressive end title theme as well as some battle and ceremonial music that illustrates just how much fun this album might have been had it featured Goldsmith alone. As it is, it's an album doomed to frustrate just about every taste. In the end, the recording was disowned by both Arnold and Goldsmith.

Jeff Bond

Starman

1984, Varèse-Sarabande, from the film *Starman,* Columbia, 1984 &

album notes: Music: Jack Nitzsche.

Jack Nitzsche was one of several composers director John Carpenter used during the period when he worked for the major studios and couldn't score his own pictures. That's a real shame here because this score is a major disappointment. Repetitive and dull, its only major melodic piece is the very limited main theme. Nitzsche constantly plugs it in when something personal is needed. Most of the action cues on the CD have that "made up as they went along" feel, with repetitive layers being added and subtracted in an attempt to vary the tone. The Jeff Bridges/Karen Allen duet of "All I Have to Do Is Dream" stands out just because it's so damn thematic compared to the rest of the album.

David Hirsch

The Stars Fell on Henrietta

1995, Varèse Sarabande, from the film *The Stars Fell on Henrietta,* Warner Bros., 1995 &&&&&

album notes: Music: David Benoit; Featured Musicians: Grant Geissman, banjo; Pat Kelly, guitar; Mike Lang, piano; David Benoit, piano.

They Know the Score
John Williams

The cantina music [in *Star Wars*] is an anomaly, it sticks out entirely as an unrelated rib to the score. When I looked at that scene there wasn't any music in it and these little creatures were jumping up and down playing instruments and I didn't have any idea what the sound should be. It could have been anything: electronic music, futuristic music, tribal music, whatever you like. And I said to George [Lucas], 'What do you think we should do?' And George said, 'I don't know' and sort of scratched his head. He said, 'Well I have an idea. What if these little creatures on this planet way out someplace came upon a rock, and they lifted up the rock and underneath was sheet music from Benny Goodman's great swing band of the 1930s on planet Earth? And they looked at this music and they kind of deciphered it, but they didn't know quite how it should go, but they tried. And, uh, why don't you try doing that? What would these space creatures, what would their imitation of Benny Goodman sound like?' So, I kind of giggled and I went to the piano and began writing the silliest little series of old-time swing band licks, kind of a little off and a little wrong and not quite matching. We recorded that and everyone seemed to love it. We didn't have electronic instruments exactly in that period very much. They're all little Trinidad steel drums and out-of-tuned kazoos and little reed instruments, you know. It was all done acoustically—it wasn't an electronic preparation as it probably would have been done today.

***Courtesy of* Film Score Monthly**

Here's a delightful and hauntingly touching score by David Benoit that captures the very soul of Depression-era Texas. Gentle guitar solos and soft piano phrases conjure up a simpler time when people only sought to survive the day, struggled, and persevered through the hardest of times. The main theme is an intoxicating motif, filled with hope and dignity. Listeners will find this an emotionally moving score that can be appreciated without ever having experienced the film.

David Hirsch

Starship Troopers

1997, Varèse-Sarabande, from the film *Starship Troopers,* TriStar, 1997 🎞🎞🎞🎞

album notes: Music: Basil Poledouris; **Conductor:** Basil Poledouris..

Director Paul Verhoven has always brought out Basil Poledouris's big orchestral guns in such satirical splatter-fests as *Flesh and Blood* and *Robocop.* But none of their collaborations is as deliriously over the top as *Starship Troopers,* a bugs vs. space marines epic that slams World War II propaganda films. Poledouris responds with the kind of blazingly patriotic score that a newsreel would die for, full of roaring action and symphonic jingoism. It's militarism played with a straight face, a percussive, brassy sound that's always distinguished Poledouris's best scores for the genre. And none have matched the excitement on display here, as the music conveys the marines' breathless, gee-whiz attitude while going into battle, one that hardens up into tense, drum roll suspense. And just as he saw underneath *Robocop*'s metal shell, Poledouris doesn't neglect the Troopers' humanity, managing some nice, attractive cues that give a melodic touch to the many death scenes at hand. By playing every musical war-movie cliche in the book, Poledouris pulls off *Starship Troopers* with fresh gusto.

Dan Schweiger

State Fair

1996, DRG Records, from the Broadway production *State Fair,* 1995 🎞🎞🎞

album notes: Music: Richard Rodgers; **Lyrics:** Oscar Hammerstein II; **Musical Direction:** Kay Cameron; **Cast:** John Davidson, Kathryn Crosby, Andrea McArdle, Donna McKechnie.

The stage presentation of *State Fair*—a film musical that had previously received two screen versions, in 1946 and 1962—was a rather sad affair that looked like a road company (which it was) out of its league among other Broadway productions. With the exception of Donna McKechnie, thoroughly professional and demure as a singer willing to sacrifice everything on her way to stardom, and Scott Wise as a smart newspaper reporter who finds love while covering a story, the others in the

pedestrian cast were not on the same high quality level in this story of an Iowa farmer and his family attending the State Fair, and their adventures. Mercifully, none of the show's shortcomings are apparent on the cast recording, which focuses on the score by Rodgers and Hammerstein, in which "It's a Grand Night for Singing" and "It Might as Well Be Spring" remain two beautiful highlights.

Didier C. Deutsch

State of Grace

1990, MCA Records, from the film *State of Grace,* Orion Pictures, 1990 🎞🎞🎞🎞

album notes: Music: Ennio Morricone; **Orchestra:** The Orchestra Unione Musicisti di Roma; **Conductor:** Ennio Morricone.

For this tale of Irish gangsters in Hell's Kitchen Ennio Morricone provides a somber, moody score emphasizing a mournful, low flute melody over brass and woodwind chords that hangs over the proceedings like a pall when it's not pulsing with extended suspense cues of bubbling strings and a staccato spinet line. Morricone maintains a consistently dreary tone throughout, although there is one startling burst of brightness and romanticism that ironically underscores the setting of an arson fire ("Hundred Yard Dash"). Like most of this composer's work, *State of Grace* is rich with haunting melodies and textures, and it's a good bet for devotees.

Jeff Bond

State of Siege

1992, Sakkaris Records/Greece, from the film *State of Siege,* 1973 🎞🎞🎞🎞

album notes: Music: Mikis Theodorakis.

Already famous for the hard-edge, tough accents of his landmark score for *Z* (q.v.), Mikis Theodorakis wrote another remarkable score for *State of Siege,* also directed by Costa-Gavras, a film about a political assassination in Uruguay and a subsequent government coverup. The film became quite controversial when its scheduled presentation at Washington's American Film Institute was abruptly canceled for political reasons. Using the sunny, colorful sonorities of pueblo music, Theodorakis created a wonderful score that belies the seriousness of intent behind the film, and evokes instead the magic landscapes of the Andes and a life warm and simple. For anyone not aware of its rich textures, this is a score well worth discovering. This title may be out of print or just plain hard to find. Mail-order companies, used CD shops, or dealers of rare or import recordings will be your best bet.

see also: Z/Serpico

Didier C. Deutsch

Stavisky

See: Follies/Stavisky

Stealing Home

1988, Atlantic Records, from the film *Stealing Home*, Warner Bros., 1988 ♫♫

album notes: Music. David Foster; **Featured Musicians:** David Foster, synthesizer, keyboards; Rhett Lawrence, Fairlight drums; Rick Bowan, synthesizer; Michael Boddicker, synthesizer; Dean Parks, acoustic guitar; Michael Landau, electric guitar; Dave "Rev" Boruff, saxophone.

Five of the 11 numbers here are performed by uber-slick producer David Foster, guaranteeing a languid affair. The rest are decently chosen oldies, plus vocal group the Nylons' inventive version of "Poison Ivy." But what it lacks is a truly fresh, new composition to really get things off the ground.

Gary Graff

Steel

1997, Qwest, from the film *Steel*, Warner Bros., 1997 woof!

Did you know Shaquille O'Neal was an actor? Did you know he was also a singer? Will wonders never cease! Anyway, the famous basketball player made his screen debut in this puff directly out of the comics pages in which he portrayed the title character, a superhero bedecked in an armor that made him look like Batman in a tin can. To its credit, the film was quite wholesome: there was little screen violence in it, no gore, no sex, no cussing, no fussing! Even the kiddies, for whom it seemed to have been made, found it boring. The film yielded this soundtrack album of "songs from and inspired by," which strikes a similar note. To be fair, there are a couple of tunes that are modestly interesting ("We've Got Heart," "Alone in the Crowd"), but they don't include the star's lame attempt at being a rap singer. Fortunately O'Neal is making millions playing with the Lakers. Don't give up your day job, Shaq! As for this album, it's good for the basket, but gets no points for it.

Didier C. Deutsch

Steel Magnolias

1989, Polydor, from the film *Steel Magnolias*, Tri-Star, 1989 ♫♫♫

album notes: Music: Georges Delerue; **Conductor:** Georges Delerue.

This average tear-jerker about women in a small southern town is elevated to the level of an effective drama by Georges Delerue's sublime music. Unsurprisingly, his music retains its appeal on disc as well. Delerue's score is often light, but never fluffy. His lush string sound is put to good use, the music appealingly evocative of small town life, investing the otherwise ordinary lives of the characters with a kind of poetry. Highlights include the main title, with its folky harmonica, the mournful viola that opens "Drive to Aunt Fern's," and the celeste waltz in "Good News, Bad News." In fact, the only thing that spoils this soundtrack is the inclusion of three tacky C&W songs (one of which was not even in the film), which are totally out of place among Delerue's music. (Fortunately they are sequenced back to back and easily skipped.) The original Polydor soundtrack is long out-of-print and hard to find. However, some of the score was rerecorded by the composer on *Georges Delerue: The London Sessions, Volume II* (on Varèse-Sarabande), in a suite that Delerue arranged and conducted with listening more specifically in mind.

Paul Andrew MacLean

Steel Pier

1997, RCA Victor, from the Broadway musical, *Steel Pier*, 1997 ♫♫♫♫

album notes: Music: John Kander, Fred Ebb; **Lyrics:** John Kander, Fred Ebb; **Cast:** Gregory Harrison (Mick Hamilton), Karen Ziemba (Rita Racine), Daniel McDonald (Bill Kelly), Debra Monk (Shelby Stevens).

There was something vastly endearing about *Steel Pier*, a failed musical fantasy set in the 1930s that had a brief run on Broadway in the spring of 1997. The intriguing plot—about a marathon dancer whose last-minute partner, an airplane pilot, may be either a figment of her imagination or an angel reincarnated—was already unusual in its concept, at least by Kander and Ebb standards; but behind the musical gloss, the show also cast a clinical look at the dance craze that swept the early 1930s, and the various deals that prompted would-be marathoners to try and be last on the dance floor, in the vain hope of earning a few meager dollars to help them survive in the Depression days.

If nothing else, the show made a genuine star of Karen Ziemba, a wonderfully gifted performer who struck a positive chord as Rita, a previous winner eager to rekindle her brush with success, only to find out that her win was largely due to the machinations of the manipulative marathon emcee, with whom Rita had had a brief affair. In the showstopping "Running in Place," Ziemba revealed the frailties behind the tough-as-nail character she played in the show and won the hearts of Broadway audiences as a result. The cast album, superbly produced, makes a strong case for another Kander and Ebb failure that, like *Chicago*, may prove to have been way ahead of its time and ripe for reevaluation in another 20 years.

Didier C. Deutsch

Step Mom

1998, Sony Classical, from the film *Step Mom*, Columbia, 1998
♫♫♫♫

album notes: Music: John Williams; **Conductor:** John Williams; **Featured Musicians:** Christopher Parkening, guitar; John Ellis, oboe.

Still primarily appreciated for his grand action music, John Williams explores his sentimental side on this tear-jerker, adding emotional depth to strong performances by the mom (Susan Sarandon) and stepmom (Julia Roberts) who struggle for acceptance by their kids. Roberts is presented as a Motown aficionado, and "Ain't No Mountain High Enough" serves as an albeit overused, yet always scintillating theme tune. Roberts's youth is characterized by the gently picked strings of a Spanish guitar, while Sarandon receives a more traditional piano, with clarinet, flute, and a wistful harp intensifying touching moments like "Jackie's Secret," where Sarandon's character reveals she is dying of cancer and the subsequent "Bonding," as both moms realize they share a strong love for their kids. *Step Mom* is Williams's strongest character-based score since *Stanley and Iris* although, at twice the length and with no filler, *Step Mom* is the more involving of the two.

David Poole

A Stephen Sondheim Evening

1983, RCA Victor, from the concert presentation *A Stephen Sondheim Evening*, 1983 ♫♫♫♫

album notes: Music: Stephen Sondheim; **Lyrics:** Stephen Sondheim; **Musical Direction:** Paul Gemignani; **Cast:** Liz Callaway, Cris Groenendaal, Bob Gunton, George Hearn, Steven Jacob, Judy Kaye, Victoria Mallory, Angela Lansbury.

The result of a concert presentation of songs by Sondheim, held at the Whitney Museum of American Art in New York, this collection presents 19 numbers selected from the dozen musicals he had created up to that time. The all-star cast (Liz Callaway, Cris Groenendaal, Bob Gunton, George Hearn, Steven Jacob, Judy Kaye, and Victoria Mallory, many of them veterans of Sondheim's Broadway shows), received a curtain call support from Angela Lansbury and Sondheim himself. A rare occasion, thankfully captured on this bright recording.

Didier C. Deutsch

Still Crazy

1999, London Records, from the film *Still Crazy*, Columbia, 1999 ♫♫♫♫

A bright, enjoyable comedy that evoked at times *The Full Monty* and *This Is Spinal Tap,* though it managed to retain its own distinctive voice, *Still Crazy* chronicled the reunion of a fictional British rock band called Strange Fruit. Written by Dick Clement

and Ian La Fresnais, the script followed the decision of the former band members to get back together after a lull of 21 years, resulting in the same acrimony among them that provoked their original split, due to "divine intervention" (an electric storm that forced them to cancel their appearance at an open-air concert). But this being a comedy, the tone was kept lightweight and humorous throughout, with the performers playing it out with a cheeky attitude that was all the more delightful. Adding a specific zest to the screen proceedings, the soundtrack featured a solid collection of rock numbers performed by the apocryphal Strange Fruit (Michael Lee, Martin Hughes, Tim Dawney, and Chris Johnson on drums; Charlie Jones, Dawney, and Guy Pratt on bass; Steve Donnelly and Clive Langer on guitar; Steve Nieve, Simon Hale, and Clive Langer on keyboards; with vocals by Bill Nighy, Jimmy Nail, and Carl Smythe). Reflecting the tone of the film, the songs are enjoyable, occasionally funny, and always right on the button, with at least two, "All Over the World" and "The Flame Is Still Burning," that are quite outstanding. Check it out!

Didier C. Deutsch

The Sting

1987, MCA Records, from the film *The Sting*, Universal, 1973
♫♫♫♪

album notes: Music: Marvin Hamlisch, Scott Joplin; **Conductor:** Marvin Hamlisch; **Featured Soloist:** Marvin Hamlisch, piano.

What could be more appropriate as the background to a story about two con men and set in 1920s Chicago than the jazz-tinged compositions of Scott Joplin? In fact, notwithstanding Robert Redford's association with the film, the most remarkable thing about *The Sting* is the music, for after all is said and done, the film endures as the perfect vehicle for a renewed interest in Joplin's music and the art of the rag: a jaunty musical style formerly acceptable only in the seedier establishments of life, gin joints, gambling halls, and brothels among them! While the '70s recording—issued early in the CD era—could benefit from a '90s sonic "makeover," the toe-tapping ragtime music is infectious and Joplin's ballads ("Solace" and "Luther") have a haunting, compelling quality to them. A fine introduction, this disc will no doubt leave you with a desire to explore more of Joplin's wonderful work.

Charles L. Granata

Stonewall

1996, Columbia Records, from the film *Stonewall,* Strand/BBC Films, 1996 ♫♫♫

This score is an intriguing mix that bridges the generations as it brings together songs performed by Judy Garland, Patti LaBelle & the Bluebelles, the Shangri-Las, the Shirelles, Barenaked Ladies, and other contemporary groups. It is difficult to assess who might actually be interested by this compilation, though in all fairness it actually sounds and plays much better than one might have anticipated.

Didier C. Deutsch

Stop the World—I Want to Get Off

 1962, Polydor Records, from the Broadway production *Stop the World—I Want to Get Off*, 1962 🎵🎵🎵

album notes: Music: Leslie Bricusse, Anthony Newley; **Lyrics:** Leslie Bricusse, Anthony Newley; **Musical Direction:** Milton Rosenstock; **Cast:** Anthony Newley, Anna Quayle.

Anthony Newley made a mesmerizing Broadway debut in *Stop the World—I Want to Get Off*, in which he portrayed Littlechap, a character not unlike Charles Chaplin's Little Tramp or Marcel Marceau's Blip, in love with life and its wonders and forever victimized by those stronger or more influential than him. The overall ingratiating score yielded at least one major hit in "What Kind of Fool Am I?" which was soon covered by cabaret performers all over the world and still stands out today as one of the most powerful numbers in the standard catalog.

Didier C. Deutsch

Stormy Weather

1993, Fox Records, from the film *Stormy Weather*, 20th Century-Fox, 1946 🎵🎵🎵🎵

album notes: Orchestra: The 20th Century-Fox Studio Orchestra; **Conductors:** Emil Newman, Alfred Newman.

Loosely hanging by a thread on its title tune, this screen musical featured the skimpiest of plots, involving Bill "Bojangles" Robinson and Lena Horne as star-crossed lovers and performers whose respective careers bring them together, separate them, and reunite them 40 years later. What the film had, on the other hand, was a sterling cast led by the radiant Ms. Horne, who sang for the first time "Stormy Weather," the song that would later become a signature theme for her. Sexy, sultry, sensational, she alone would have been worth alone the price of admission. But in addition, the film sported the presence of the great Bojangles, in his only starring role, and a terrific collection of big band singers and performers that included the dynamic Cab Calloway, always the "Hi-De-Ho" man, even when he spoofed himself with "Alfred the Moocher"; Thomas "Fats" Waller, who reprised his hit "Ain't Misbehavin'," among other glorious moments; and Mae Johnson, the Nicholas Brothers, the Katharine Dunham dancers, and the best names in black entertainment at the time. They all combined to make *Stormy Weather* a high-voltage, superlative screen musical which has not aged a bit and continues to strike a positive note today.

This soundtrack album, in the short-lived Fox Classic series distributed by RCA, is a vivid remember of the many qualities found in the film, complete with alternate takes, reprises, ballet music, and all the implementa required today in such reissues. Despite the fact that it is more than 55 years old, the film (and its recording) hasn't aged a bit.

Didier C. Deutsch

Story of O

1992, CAM Records/Italy, from the film *Story of O (Histoire d'O)*, Filmarte, 1977. 🎵🎵🎵

album notes: Music: Pierre Bachelet; **Conductor:** Pierre Bachelet.

Pierre Bachelet's score is certainly much more exciting than this pseudo-softcore film about an attractive young woman, only known as O, who becomes a slave to the man she loves, and submits to various sorts of erotic encounters in order to please him. Vaguely ethereal and surreal, in a synthetic (and synthesized) way, it is a charming effort that is well written and quite evocative. This title may be out of print or just plain hard to find. Mail-order companies, used CD shops, or dealers of rare or import recordings will be your best bet.

Didier C. Deutsch

Straight No Chaser

1989, Columbia Records, from the film *Straight, No Chaser*, Warner Bros., 1989 🎵🎵🎵

album notes: Music: Thelonious Monk; **Featured Musicians:** Thelonious Monk, piano; John Coltrane, tenor sax; Charlie Rouse, tenor sax; Johnny Griffin, tenor sax; Wilbur Ware, bass; Larry Gales, bass; Shadow Wilson, drums; Ben Riley, drums; Ray Copeland, trumpet; Jimmy Cleveland, trombone; Phil Woods, alto sax.

The soundtrack to a documentary portraying the famous jazz pianist and composer, *Straight No Chaser* will primarily appeal to fans of Thelonious Monk and his music, with plenty of selections to satisfy even the most difficult. Some of the tracks feature dialogue, studio talk, and other elements that somewhat distract from the essential, though they are kept to brief moments. The bulk of the recording, of course, consists of Monk's performances, alone or with some of his musicians, including John Coltrane, in tunes that capitalized his career ("Epistrophy," "Ugly Beauty," "'Round Midnight," etc.).

Didier C. Deutsch

Strange Days

1995, Epic Records, from the film *Strange Days*, 20th Century-Fox, 1995 🎵🎵

Kathryn Bigelow's millennium fantasia was a dismal failure at the box office, but is revered by its fans for its original story by

James Cameron and a strong soundtrack. It's December 31, 1999 in Los Angeles and the world is a very disturbing place, especially for the film's dark, brooding anti-hero, a dealer of virtual reality. The 1995 soundtrack album was ahead of the curve on the electronica craze by a year or two, smartly utilizing artists like Tricky and Deep Forrest to create a wall of sound that is perfectly organic to the film's environment. Notable tracks include a surprisingly strong cover by actress Juliette Lewis of the P.J. Harvey song "Can't Hardly Wait" and a lush performance by composer Graeme Revell and vocalist Lori Carson, "Fall in the Light."

Amy Rosen

The Stranger/The Innocent

1998, DRG Records, from the films, *The Stranger*, 1967; and *The Innocent*, 1976 ♪♪♪♪

album notes: Music: Piero Piccioni, Franco Mannino; **Conductor:** Bruno Nicolai; **Featured Soloists:** Dino Asciolla, violin; Franco Mannino, piano; Giuseppe Selmi, cello.

Italian film director Luchino Visconti made many films that were important in their own time and made a strong impact. Made in 1967, *The Stranger* was a superb adaptation of the novel by Albert Camus, with Marcello Mastroianni cast as the title character in one of his most impressive screen creations. The score was created by Piero Piccioni, who captured in his music the claustrophobic, alienating moods of the film itself. Made in 1979, *The Innocent* was Visconti's last film, and a magnificent swan song, about a Sicilian aristocrat, whose long-neglected attractive wife decides to get a lover. Visually stunning, and featuring a remarkably sensuous performance by Laura Antonelli, the film received further enhancement from the score composed by Franco Mannino. The CD does full justice to both composers' contributions.

Didier C. Deutsch

Street Fighter

1994, Varèse Sarabande, from the film *Street Fighter*, Universal, 1994 ♪♪♪

album notes: Music: Graeme Revell; **Orchestra:** The London Symphony Orchestra; **Conductor:** Tim Simonec; **Featured Musicians:** Mark Zimoski, percussion; John Yoakum, soprano sax, flute, oboe; Rex Thomas, pedal steel guitar.

This film features an energetic action score by Graeme Revell, who seems to be excelling in this genre as the new master of the testosterone-powered movie. The plot—warriors from all over the world assemble to fight an evil warlord—offers Revell the opportunity to exploit a vast array of musical styles in a variety of ethnic motifs: Chinese ("Chun-Li Enters the Morgue"), Middle Eastern ("The Circus Tent"), and a good old-fashioned, steamy "American" sex theme ("Chun-Li & Bison"),

which helps keep the score fresh. Scriptwriter Steven de Souza contributed the esperanto lyrics to the "Bison Troopers Marching Song."

David Hirsch

A Streetcar Named Desire

1995, Varèse Sarabande, from the film *A Streetcar Named Desire*, Warner Bros., 1951 ♪♪♪♪♪

album notes: Music: Alex North; **Orchestra:** The National Philharmonic Orchestra; **Conductor:** Jerry Goldsmith; **Featured Musicians:** Sidney Sax, violin; Tony Coe, clarinet; Ronnie Price, piano; Allen Walley, bass; Harold Fisher, drums; John Barclay, trumpet.

This rerecording, splendidly recorded by the National Philharmonic Orchestra conducted by Jerry Goldsmith, is yet another great example of a classic film score receiving the care and attention it merits. With dynamics and tempos that match and often surpass North's own readings, and the splendor of the all-digital sound combining with several new cues to make this the most complete version in the best possible sound available, this recording of *Streetcar* belongs in any collection that aims to be comprehensive.

Didier C. Deutsch

Streets of Fire

1984, MCA Records, from the film *Streets of Fire*, Universal, 1984 ♪♪♪♪

A better-than-average rock soundtrack compilation, with superior performances by the Blasters, Ry Cooder, Dan Hartman, and the Fixx, among others. The film, about a famous rock star who is held for ransom and the detective who investigates the case, is arguably only a pretext to introduce the percussive rock score that punctuates the action. The tracks included here are all part of that score, and on their own make a great impression.

Didier C. Deutsch

Strictly Ballroom

1992, Columbia Records, from the film *Strictly Ballroom*, Albert Productions, 1992 ♪♪♪♪

Another dancing competition won by an underdog was the topic of this cheerful film which, like *Saturday Night Fever* and *Dance with Me*, had an infectious score to propel its slightly offbeat story of a young man, portrayed by ballet dancer Mercurio, whose unconventional demeanor on the ballroom floor almost causes him to lose the Pan-Pacific contest until he teams with the equally unusual Tara Morice. This being *Strictly Ballroom*, the moods are essentially set in the pre-disco era, with selections like "La cumparsita," "Tequila," "Rhumba de burros," and "The Blue Danube" setting the tones. David

Hirschfelder and the Bogo Pogo Orchestra play these and other tunes with great enthusiasm, with John Paul Jones, Ignatius Jones, and, surprisingly, Doris Day providing a couple of vocals. Overall, this is a good, solidly enjoyable set.

Didier C. Deutsch

Strike Up the Band

1991, Elektra Records, from the studio cast recording *Strike Up the Band*, 1991 ♪♪♪♪♪

album notes: Music: George Gershwin; **Lyrics:** Ira Gershwin; **Musical Direction:** John Mauceri; **Cast:** Brent Barrett, Don Chastain, Rebecca Luker, Jason Graae, Beth Fowler.

Some theatrical shows undergo so many rewritings that it is difficult to keep track of all the changes that went into their production. Such was the case with *Strike Up the Band*, a 1927 musical by George and Ira Gershwin, with a gloomy book by George S. Kaufman, so rife with anti-militarist ideas that it closed before it even reached Broadway. Revised, updated, and now sporting a lighter libretto—a zany story about the United States and Switzerland at war with each other over Swiss chocolate—the musical continued its way to Broadway, where it finally arrived on January 14, 1930. In its score are many gems that continue to charm today, including "The Man I Love," "Strike Up the Band," "Soon," and "I've Got a Crush on You." The cast recording listed above, one in a continuing series of great Gershwin musicals produced under the aegis of the composer's estate, is a lavish recreation of both scores, starring Jason Graae, Rebecca Luker, Brent Barrett, Don Chastain, and Beth Fowler, with John Mauceri conducting the orchestra. Stylishly presented, with a booklet replete with information about the show and period pictures, it is an essential recording in any collection.

Didier C. Deutsch

Striptease

1996, EMI Records, from the film *Striptease*, Columbia Pictures, 1996 ♪♪

One of those soundtracks that you listen to and go ". . . Huh?" Imagine Joan Jett next to Dean Martin, the Spencer Davis Group alongside Billy Ocean, Prince not far from Chynna Phillips (as in Wilson Phillips). Someone just went on a song-licensing shopping spree here, scooping up individual songs without giving much thought to how they'd work together.

Gary Graff

Stuart Saves His Family

1995, Milan Records, from the film *Stuart Saves His Family*, Paramount Pictures, 1995 ♪♪

album notes: Music: Marc Shaiman; **Conductor:** Artie Kane.

This standard comedic effort by Marc Shaiman is likable enough but offers little new beyond what he's done in the past. Shaiman obviously likes to score comedies much like an animated film with unmistakable standard themes ("A Closer Walk with Thee" is used for a portion of "Aunt Paula's Two Funerals"), hitting the mark and changing tempos as often as possible. The album is by no means of poor quality, and there are some fine moments ("Julia's Family"), but once you've heard one Shaiman comedy score, you've heard them all.

David Hirsch

The Stupids

1996, Intrada Records, from the film *The Stupids*, New Line Cinema, 1996 ♪♪♪♪

album notes: Music: Christopher Stone; **Conductor:** Christopher Stone.

John Landis returned to his first love, comedy, with this amusing ditty about an average family distinguished only by their sheer stupidity. Taking everything at face value, Pop, Mom, and the two kids (Tom Arnold, Jessica Lundy, Bug Hall, and Alex McKenna) always end up in a heap of troubles as a result of their goofy and unfocused thinking. Giving a zest of its own to the lunacies in the script, Christopher Stone provided a whimsical, serio-comic score that manages to include sly references to Rozsa's music for *Ben-Hur* and Jerry Goldsmith's for *Patton* among its better moments. Not a major effort, but certainly one that deserves to be heard, if only because it does bring a bright smile of recognition to anyone's face.

Didier C. Deutsch

The Subterraneans

1991, Sony Music Special Products, from the film *The Subterraneans*, MGM, 1960 ♪♪♪♪♪

album notes: Music: Andre Previn; **Featured Musicians:** Andre Previn, piano; Carmen McRae, vocals; Red Mitchell, bass; Dave Bailey, drums; Russ Freeman, piano; Bob Enevoldsen, trombone; Gerry Mulligan, baritone sax; Shelly Manne, drums; Art Farmer, trumpet; Buddy Clark, bass; Art Pepper, alto sax; Bill Perkins, sax; Jack Sheldon, trumpet.

In the days when he was still known as a film and jazz composer, Andre Previn occasionally combined both in scores that were amazingly alive and powerful in their expression. One such occasion is *The Subterraneans*, starring Leslie Caron and Georges Peppard, based on the Jack Kerouac "beat generation" novel and set amid San Francisco's New Bohemians. While the film itself failed to find grace with critics and audiences, its score, bringing together the talents of West Coast instrumentalists Gerry Mulligan, Shelly Manne, Art Farmer, Art Pepper, Jack Sheldon, and Red Mitchell and vocalist Carmen McRae, has long been regarded as one of the best examples of the use of jazz in films.

Particularly striking is the fact that Previn wrote the cues for his eminent soloists, often performing against an orchestral background in a carefully dosed and effective blend of jazz riffs and symphonic sounds. There are many highlights in this excellent CD, which should attract those interested in solid instrumental soundtrack albums with a modern approach to its music.

Didier C. Deutsch

Suburbia

1997, Geffen Records, from the film *Suburbia,* Sony Pictures Classics, 1997 **woof!**

It's amazing what passes as a soundtrack these days. If at least the songs were interesting, lyrically and melodically, or elicited interesting performances, perhaps one might overlook the obvious lack of talent that permeates most of them. But this sad rock compilation, that has nothing going for it, not even a singer able to hold a tune, is a sad reminder that songs that once constituted the soundtrack to our lives have now been replaced by uninspired noise. For that we don't even have to go to *Suburbia.* We find it in abundance in the streets of our big cities. Bring back the jackhammers: at least they don't have artistic pretensions!

Didier C. Deutsch

Sudden Death

1995, Varèse Sarabande, from the film *Sudden Death,* Universal, 1995

album notes: Music: John Debney; Conductor: John Debney.

Take a pounding percussion section, a massive symphony orchestra, and musical selections all too obviously modeled after John Williams's *JFK* "Conspirators" cue and action scores too numerous to mention (though *The Fugitive* and *Die Hard* seem to pop up here and there), combine them all, and you get the recipe for a rather hackneyed movie soundtrack. Composer John Debney has done some terrific work in the movies, but his two scores for director Peter Hyams (*Sudden Death* was followed by the unreleased *The Relic*) are clearly not his best efforts. Most likely forced to compose along the strict, thankless guidelines of the action genre, Debney's music is bombastic to an extreme, with few melodic ideas taking charge out of the mayhem. It's hard to imagine anyone other than die-hard Jean-Claude Van Damme fans wanting to hear this music outside of the cinematic context it was composed for.

Andy Dursin

Sugar Colt

1995, King Records/Japan, from the film *Sugar Colt,* 1966

album notes: Music: Luis Bacalov.

An interesting oater, starring Hunt Powers as an undercover government agent investigating the disappearance of a detachment of Union Army soldiers, *Sugar Colt* was an above-the-norm yarn that was subtly understated and solidly entertaining. Luis Bacalov composed a catchy score for this one, firmly anchored by the title tune, heard as a vocal under the credits, and throughout the film as a leit-motif. Providing a welcome change of pace, "Saloon Polka" and "Saloon Waltz" evoked the old barroom in Snake Valley, the western town where most of the action happened, while a secondary theme, "Smoking Colt," heard in a couple of variations, tied in the loose elements in the narrative. Good fun! This recording may be difficult to find. Check with a used CD store, mail-order company, or a dealer specializing in rare, out-of-print, or import recordings.

see also: Django/Quien sabe?

Didier C. Deutsch

Summer Stock

1990, CBS Special Products, from the film *Summer Stock,* MGM, 1950

album notes: Music: Harry Warren; Lyrics: Mack Gordon; Orchestra: The MGM Studio Orchestra; Choir: The MGM Studio Chorus Conductor: Johnny Green; Cast: Judy Garland, Gene Kelly, Phil Silvers, Gloria De Haven.

For her 27th and last film for MGM, the studio where she had spent her entire life as a trouper, Judy Garland teamed again with Gene Kelly for a celebration of show business and the kind of backstage saga that had proved so successful in the past. In this hackneyed story, Judy owns a farm in Connecticut, and Kelly is a hoofer trying out a Broadway–bound show in a barn on the farm, with Judy eventually joining in the musical revelry. There are many attractive moments in the score (including "You Wonderful You," first performed as a duet by the two stars, then reprised by Gene in a mesmerizing "Newspaper Dance"), but the most memorable one, filmed two months after shooting had been completed, was Judy, striking in black leotard and dinner jacket, singing "Get Happy."

Didier C. Deutsch

A Summer Story

1988, Virgin Records, from the film *A Summer Story,* Atlantic, 1988

album notes: Music: Georges Delerue; Conductor: Georges Delerue.

Georges Delerue had probably the greatest gift for lyricism and sentiment of any film composer ever. Thus he was perfectly suited to this bittersweet love story about a wealthy young Englishman's romance with a farm girl in 1916. The score evokes a feeling of pastoral England not unlike that in the works of Frederick Delius or Ralph Vaughan Williams, but *A Summer Story* is finally and consummately in the style of

Delerue. Throughout, the conductor's inimitable string sound is prominent. His music gushes with honest sentiment and romance, yet never once does it become sappy or cloying. For all its warmth however, there hangs a sense of tragedy over *A Summer Story,* and the score ultimately evokes an intense feeling of nostalgia and loss. Romantic scores of this calibre rarely come along and since Delerue's passing have been conspicuously more rare, making this CD something of a treasure.

Paul Andrew MacLean

Sun Valley Serenade/Orchestra Wives

1986, Mercury Records, from the films *Sun Valley Serenade,* 20th Century-Fox, 1941, and *Orchestra Wives,* 20th Century-Fox, 1942 ♪♪♪♪

album notes: Featured Musicians: The Glenn Miller Orchestra, featuring Johnny Best, Billy May, Ray Anthony, Wade McMickle, Bobby Hackett, trumpets; Glenn Miller, Paul Tanner, Jimmy Priddy, Fran D'Annolfo, trombones; Tex Beneke, Al Klink, Ernie Caceres, Willie Schwartz, Hal McIntyre, saxophones; Chummy McGregor, piano; Jack Lathrop, guitar; Trigger Alpert, bass; Maurice Purtill, drums; Tex Beneke, Ray Eberle, Marion Hutton, Six Hits & a Miss, the Modernaires, vocals.

Both films were more or less tailored to feature the Glenn Miller Orchestra in the early days of World War II, when the country had not yet joined the conflict, but public sentiment was already being frayed and people needed some kind of entertainment to forget the dark clouds that amassed across the Atlantic and elsewhere. These light, enjoyable musical films have plots that are not too terribly obtrusive and musical numbers that often are terrific, and they exude the kind of mindless vibrancy most filmgoers hope to find when they go to the movies. The amazing thing about this CD, however, is the fact that the performances by the Glenn Miller Orchestra are in stereo, painstakingly reconstructed from the sound strips recorded at the time, long before stereophonic sound existed in the movies, let alone in the recording industry. The sound quality leaves a bit to be desired, to be sure, and the stereo is a trifle primitive, but where else would you hear "In the Mood," "It Happened in Sun Valley," "Chattanooga Choo-Choo," "Moonlight Serenade," "I've Got a Gal in Kalamazoo," and all the other hits made popular by the band in glorious two-channel definition? Besides, the music here is totally exhilarating and explains why the big band era has left such a wonderful glow in the lives of those who experienced it.

Didier C. Deutsch

Sunday in the Park with George

1984, RCA Victor, from the Broadway production *Sunday in the Park with George,* 1984 ♪♪♪♪♪

album notes: Music: Stephen Sondheim; Lyrics: Stephen Sondheim; Musical Direction: Paul Gemignani; Cast: Mandy Patinkin, Bernadette Peters, Charles Kimbrough, Dana Ivey.

One of the true pinnacles of the American musical theater and as ambitious a musical as Broadway has seen: Stephen Sondheim and writer/director James Lapine address "the art of making art" through a fictionalized biography of the 19th-century French painter Georges Seurat, set against the travails of a modern-day descendant. The score was edited and reconstructed for CD, a collaboration between Sondheim and producer Thomas Z. Shepard that captures the staged musical on disc in an innovative way. A must: apologize to your neighbors in advance, tweak your stereo, and play the choral "Sunday" very, very loud.

Marc Kirkeby

Sundown

1990, Silva Screen Records, from the film *Sundown,* Vestron Pictures, 1989 ♪♪♪♪

album notes: Music: Richard Stone; Orchestra: The Graunke Symphony Orchestra; Conductor: Allan Wilson.

At first, the whole premise seems totally ludicrous: a vampire western film, set in the aptly named Purgatory, a small town lost in the Arizona desert. But drawing from both genres, composer Richard Stone has come up with a score that amusingly spoofs westerns and horror films, while retaining its creative edge. The end result is a soundtrack album one might easily have overlooked, filled with cues that are appealing and original; in short, well worth hunting for!

Didier C. Deutsch

Sunset Blvd.

1993, Polydor Records, from the London production of *Sunset Blvd.,* 1993 ♪♪♪

album notes: Music: Andrew Lloyd Webber; Lyrics: Don Black, Christopher Hampton; Musical Direction: David Caddick; Cast: Patti LuPone, Kevin Anderson, Daniel Benzali, Meredith Braun.

1994, Polydor Records, from the London production of *Sunset Blvd.,* 1994 ♪♪♪

album notes: Music: Andrew Lloyd Webber; Lyrics: Don Black, Christopher Hampton; Musical Direction: David Caddick; Cast: Glenn Close, Alan Campbell, George Hearn, Judy Kuhn.

Andrew Lloyd Webber's mammoth Gothic take on Billy Wilder's 1950 film has spawned several recordings. All are essentially similar and distinguished only by the various actresses essaying the role. Originated by Gloria Swanson in the film, it is the story of a silent film star trying desperately to hang on to her past glory and dreams of eternal youth, only to be drawn to murder when her protégé, a playwright she has hired to help her doctor a script, ultimately rejects her advances and threatens to leave her.

Of the two versions proposed here, Patti Lupone, heard in the original London cast, sounds more dramatic and gut-wrenching, though her theatrics tend to be overbearing after a while. Glenn Close and the original Broadway cast (with George Hearn totally wasted in a secondary role, as Norma's chauffeur and ex-husband), strike a more positive note, though everything is again very much relative. Because the singing is continuous throughout the show, identifying the various tracks is somewhat of a problem on some recordings. Highlights have been indicated whenever possible.

Didier C. Deutsch

Sunshine Even by Night

See: Il sole anche di notte

Superfly

1997, Rhino Records, from the film *Superfly*, 1972 🎬🎬🎬🎬

album notes: Songs: Curtis Mayfield.

Known as one of the classic '70s blaxploitation films, *Superfly* caused a lot of controversy in its day. The story of a Harlem drug dealer who unleashes his own brand of "whoop ass" before leaving the drug business, this over-the-top film featured an incredible soundtrack by Curtis Mayfield. Instead of writing underscoring for the various characters/scenes, Mayfield wrote songs that acted like soulful character studies within the movie. The original soundtrack topped the *Billboard* charts for a month, and spawned the hit singles "Superfly" and "Freddy's Dead." Rhino's 25th anniversary reissue features a second CD of additional materials relating to the soundtrack, including "Ghetto Child," a demo that became "Little Child Runnin' Wild" on the soundtrack; an extended version of the instrumental "Junkie Chase," anti-drug radio public service announcements; and Mayfield talking about the film. As with most Rhino releases, this release features incredible packaging.

Beth Krakower

Supergirl

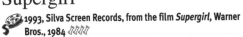1993, Silva Screen Records, from the film *Supergirl*, Warner Bros., 1984 🎬🎬🎬

album notes: Music: Jerry Goldsmith; **Orchestra:** The National Philharmonic Orchestra and Chorus; **Conductor:** Jerry Goldsmith.

While Jerry Goldsmith has often contributed outstanding film music, too many times he has stood in the shadow of John Williams, scoring movies that were either imitative of or were ripoffs of successful pictures scored by Williams (i.e., where

Williams scored *Raiders of the Lost Ark, Jurassic Park,* and *Home Alone,* Goldsmith wrote *King Solomon's Mines, Congo,* and *Dennis the Menace*). Yet another case is *Supergirl,* the failed but entertainingly campy 1984 spin-off of the *Superman* series from producer Alexander Salkind, featuring a great score from Goldsmith that went overlooked due to the film's dismal critical and box-office performance. The composer did a yeoman's job here, writing a romantic, soaring score that compares favorably to its predecessor, featuring thrilling action cues backed by outstanding performances from the National Philharmonic Orchestra and Chorus. The initial CD release from Varèse was superseded by an extended re-issue from Silva Screen in 1993, boasting unreleased and alternate cues, as well as the dumbest credit line in soundtrack album history "The Superman Poster," "track 8, composed by Jerry Goldsmith (75%) and John Williams (25%)."

Andy Dursin

Superman: The Movie

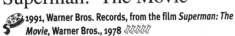1991, Warner Bros. Records, from the film *Superman: The Movie,* Warner Bros., 1978 🎬🎬🎬🎬

album notes: Music: John Williams; **Orchestra:** The London Symphony Orchestra; **Conductor:** John Williams.

This sadly mistreated soundtrack, one of John Williams's most memorable contributions to the screen, certainly would deserve better than the CD released, after many years of simply ignoring it altogether, by Warner Bros. Records, in a shortened version that eliminates a couple of cues ("Growing Up" and "Lex Luthor's Lair") "to facilitate a single, specially priced compact disc." In an era where most important scores are being reissued not once but often several times, and always with extra tracks, *Superman: The Movie* stands alone as a case in point where a label simply doesn't seem to give a damn about the riches in its vaults.

This said, the score created by John Williams teems with tunes that are outright exciting and wonderfully evocative of the action on the screen. Typically, Williams created a rousingly heroic theme for the superhero, with stirring brassy accents that spell out his invincibility, and a delicately wrought "Love Theme" that brings a delightful softer note to the score. The villains are dealt with in a sardonic anthem that displays glee and glum all at once ("The March of the Villains"; while Superman's deeds are detailed in cues in which the main theme is often used as an anchor to other, evolutive motifs.

Played with the right amount of fire and excitement by the London Symphony Orchestra (that unmistakable brass section is sensational!), the long score follows the screen narrative with expressive details that imaginatively convey its scope and its importance. Margot Kidder's reading of "Can You Read My Mind" is the only apparent weak point in this thrilling score, an otherwise spectacular display of Williams's creativity and beguiling musical invention.

Didier C. Deutsch

1998, Varèse-Sarabande, from the film *Superman: The Movie,* Warner Bros., 1978 ♪♪♪

album notes: Music: John Williams; **Orchestra:** The Royal Scottish National Orchestra; **Conductor:** John Debney.

It's arguable that John Williams's score to Richard Donner's original *Superman: The Movie* is the composer's finest film score. Leaping off from the epic orchestral palette Williams had created for *Star Wars, Superman* launched with an even more dynamic and rousing march that seemed to hurtle off into space right along with the Man of Steel. The early sequences on Krypton are steeped in an awe-inspiring sense of wonder, while scenes of Clark Kent growing up in Kansas gleam with Coplandesque nostalgia. And once Superman engineers a thrilling rescue of Lois Lane during a helicopter accident high over Metropolis, the score takes on a bustling, supercharged energy and warmth as the benevolent superhero begins his interaction with the flawed but lovable minions of humanity (even Gene Hackman's Lex Luthor). The original double-LP soundtrack album was released a few years ago on CD, but Williams's epic-length score has always deserved a fuller treatment, as many of the score's highlights (including the helicopter rescue, Pa Kent's death, and other key sequences) were left off the record. While a release of the full original score is still pending, Varèse-Sarabande records rescued much of the score with this two-CD release with composer John Debney conducting the Royal Scottish National Orchestra. The new recording is vibrantly clear and powerful and presents cues like "Helicopter Rescue," "Pa Kent's Death," "The Terrace," and others for the first time, but despite the grand ambition of the venture, the results are somewhat of a mixed bag. Debney's conducting occasionally rises above Williams's superb work on the original (notably at the opening of "Chasing Rockets"), but misses the mark at other junctures, and the reconstruction of the score (a monumental effort made even more challenging by the loss of much of the original manuscripts) sometimes misses crucial elements. Particularly disappointing is the incomplete recreation of the film's mesmerizing prologue music. Audiophiles will find this superior to the Warner Bros. album; fans of the film score itself will be on the fence. However, this is definitely worth having until an expanded original score album turns up.

Jeff Bond

Surf Ninjas

1993, Atlantic Records, from the film *Surf Ninjas*, New Line Cinema, 1993 ♪

album notes: Music: David Kitay

Leslie Nielsen had another episodic screen role as the bumbling dictator of a minuscule and forgotten Asian kingdom called Patu San, who tries to keep the rightful heirs to the throne, two young adolescents, away from his country and surfing the waves on the Pacific Coast, which they seem to do with great relish. Evidently aimed at the kiddie trade, the film had little to recommend it for, including this collection of songs and themes, which is pretty lame and uninspiring by conventional standards.

Didier C. Deutsch

Surrender

1987, Varèse Sarabande, from the film *Surrender*, Warner Bros., 1987 ♪♪

album notes: Music: Michel Colombier.

Aah, the 1980s! Movie soundtracks often featured power-rock songs produced by David Foster and wacky scores sometimes performed entirely on synthesizers. Don't you wish you could go back to those carefree times? Well, perhaps not, but if you ever did, Michel Colombier's synthetic and bland score for this 1987 Cannon Group comedy will fit the bill. The movie stars Michael Caine (who seemingly appeared in more movies in 1987 than were made in 1997), Sally Field, and Steve Guttenberg, and if that cast wasn't '80s enough, take a listen to Colombier's score, which feels like it's constantly treading water in trying to create a musical backdrop for the film's laughless shenanigans. The album is long out-of-print, but you still may be able to find it in one of those cut-out bins featuring albums by Debbie Gibson, Tiffany, and all those other artists whose spotlight time expired before the clock turned past 1989.

Andy Dursin

Surviving Picasso

1996, Epic Soundtrax, from the film *Surviving Picasso*, Warner Bros., 1996 ♪♪

album notes: Music: Richard Robbins; **Conductor:** Harry Rabinowitz.

Richard Robbins creates the bleakest of symphonic suites for this film about painter Pablo Picasso and the young girl who seeks his tutelage. Very often monothematic, Robbins colors his score in shades of gray. There is a repetitive motif throughout to represent the myopic ambitions of each of the characters, who remain forever wanting because they can never satisfy themselves enough to realize they can reach their goals. This is certainly not the happiest score you'll ever hear.

David Hirsch

The Swan Princess

1994, Sony Wonder, from the animated film *The Swan Princess*, 1994 &&&

album notes: Music: Lex de Azevedo, David Zippel; **Conductor:** Lex de Azevedo, Larry Bastian.

Another routine score, this one signed by Lex de Azevedo, for this mildly entertaining animated feature about a princess transformed into a swan by an evil magician and only able to assume a human form when she is touched by a moonbeam. While the animation might elicit a responsive chord among the younger set, who will appreciate a trio of cute animal characters more so than the fairy tale itself, the somewhat bland songs will no doubt get a shrug from their parents, the only ones who might have enjoyed some of the sly lyrics by David Zippel, or the occasional vaudeville accents in De Azevedo's music ("No More Mr. Nice Guy," which receives an imaginative performance by Dr. John). The singers, particularly Liz Callaway, Steve Vinovich, and Sandy Duncan, rise above the material and sell the songs with great flair, but Regina Belle and Jeffrey Osborne's duet on the seemingly mandatory big ballad, "Far Longer than Forever," strikes a totally different artistic note in the context, and sounds extremely annoying.

Didier C. Deutsch

Sweeney Todd

1979, RCA Victor; from the Broadway production *Sweeney Todd*, 1979 &&&&&

album notes: Music: Stephen Sondheim; **Lyrics:** Stephen Sondheim; **Musical Direction:** Paul Gemignani; **Cast:** Angela Lansbury, Len Cariou, Sarah Rice, Victor Garber, Ken Jennings, Merle Louise.

Stephen Sondheim's *Sweeney Todd,* a masterful tale about a demon barber set in 19th-century England, will either delight or repulse you. Todd, a victim of society whose wife and young daughter are taken from him by a villainous judge, finds himself imprisoned on trumped-up charges. Returning 15 years later to seek revenge upon his foe, he commences to shave necks and slit throats in a comedic, vengeful way. What ensues is the basis for this fiendishly alluring musical, showcasing some of Sondheim's most brilliant work.

The original cast recording features Len Cariou as Todd, and Angela Lansbury as his meat-pie maker partner in crime, Mrs. Lovett. Approaching grand opera, the show is cleverly written so nearly all the lines are completely sung. The cast recording is nearly a mirror image of the original show itself. Produced by Broadway cast and classical music recording veteran Thomas Z. Shepard, the two–CD set is indispensable listening for any Sondheim aficionado. Recorded at RCA's famed Studio A, Shepard retained all of the original stage positions, and the resulting stereo imaging is a realistic re-creation of the show's original stage movements. This is especially important when Todd slashes a throat and the unsuspecting victim is rolled down a chute, into the basement of Lovett's meat-pie shop for disposal.

Included are two booklets: One containing a short synopsis of the play, the other a complete libretto. The plot is ghoulish; the songs, lyrics and orchestrations superb. *Sweeney Todd* is an unusual show and unique cast recording that no theater lover should be without.

Charles L. Granata

Sweet Charity

1999, Sony Classical/Legacy Records, from the Broadway musical *Sweet Charity*, 1966 &&&&&

album notes: Music: Cy Coleman; **Lyrics:** Dorothy Fields; **Conductor:** Fred Werner; **Cast:** Gwen Verdon (Charity), Helen Gallagher (Nickie), Thelma Oliver (Helene), John McMartin (Oscar).

Gwen Verdon, already a Broadway favorite, had her greatest stage hit in *Sweet Charity,* which opened on January 29, 1966, in which she portrayed a dance hall hostess, forever falling for the wrong men, but always hopeful for better tomorrows. When she meets Oscar, the proverbial tart with a heart of gold is convinced she has finally found the right man for her. However, her hopes of getting married have to be scuttled because Oscar develops cold feet at the last moment. Bravely, Charity picks up the pieces of her broken heart and moves on, supported by her friends Nickie and Helene, two other dancers like herself. The brilliant score by Cy Coleman and Dorothy Fields teemed with many showstopping moments ("If My Friends Could See Me Now," "I'm a Brass Band," "Where Am I Going?," "Big Spender," "The Rhythm of Life") that have lost none of their magic with time. This sparkling reissue, remixed and remastered, corrects the sequencing according to the stage action, extends a couple of numbers (notably the "Rich Man's Frug"), and adds some bonus tracks (composer Coleman doing songs from the score, including "You Wanna Bet," which was subsequently dropped) and interviews with the principals caught on opening night. The new CD becomes the definitive version of this popular musical, probably one of the best ever written by Coleman. Transferred to the screen, the musical was another milestone in the career of Shirley MacLaine, playing Charity, with Sammy Davis Jr. making a much-noticed cameo as "Daddy." The recording, though, has yet to reach the digital domain.

Didier C. Deutsch

The Sweet Hereafter

1998, Virgin Records, from the film *The Sweet Hereafter,* Alliance, 1998 &&&

album notes: Music: Mychael Danna; **Featured Musicians:** Paul Intson, bass; Anne Bourne, cello, backing vocals; Al Cross, drums; Tim

Clement, guitars; Mychael Danna, harmonium; Kim Deschamps, pedal steel guitar, acoustic guitar; Hossen Omoumi, ney; Ron Korn, silver flute; Sarah Polley, vocals; the Toronto Consort (Terry McKenna, lute; David Fallis, percussion; Ben Grossman, percussion, hurdy gurdy; Alison Melville, recorder; David Archer, sackbut; Michael Franklin, shawm, krumhorn, recorder; David Greenberg, vielle; Alison Mackay, vielle, recorder).

Rarely has film music been able to strike an instant note of sorrow like *The Sweet Hereafter,* a haunting tone poem for the moral devastation that a town faces after its children are claimed in a bus accident. Using the film's references to "The Pied Piper of Hamelin" as a basis for his score, composer Mychael Danna's use of such Medieval-sounding instruments as a recorder, ney, and a vieille create a timeless sense of loss. His fragile melodies evoke both the vast snowscapes of the film's setting, as well as the emotional emptiness of the devastated parents. There's a beautiful, unearthly vibe to Danna's classically centered score, the kind of music that really gets into your head with its echoing quality. His music is as tightly controlled as the film's visuals, subtly opening up the characters' hearts even when they're unable to express them. Danna also reveals himself as an accomplished songwriter, with *Hereafter* actress Sarah Polley performing several memorable tunes, their melodic, slightly upbeat tone giving a welcome break to the anguish at hand.

Dan Schweiger

Swept Away

1995, SLC Records/Japan, from the film *Swept Away,* 1975 ♪♪♪♪

album notes: Music: Piero Piccioni; **Conductor:** Piero Piccioni.

Giancarlo Gianini and Mariangela Melato antagonized each other through most of this picture, directed by Lina Wertmuller, as, respectively, a lowlife sailor and a socialite, the only two survivors of a cruise liner that sank, leaving them stranded on a deserted island. Originally titled *Tale of an Unusual Story in the August Blue Sea,* the film was a mordant satire of two characters from totally different backgrounds, a hard working man and a rich bitch, thrown into a situation where they have to rely on each other in order to survive. At first reluctant to dirty her hands, and feeling her class privilege entitles her to be serviced anytime anywhere, the woman eventually realizes that she has to contribute to the sailor's efforts to help them endure their ordeal; he, on the other hand, learns to appreciate and express a certain gentility that may have been missing in his upbringing. While much of the time in this fascinating study was devoted to the two bickering under the August blue sky, there were moments when music was called for, with Piero Piccioni capturing the essence of the film in mostly romantic cues that outlined its sharper edges and

made them fuller and a bit rounder. This CD reissue, available in Japan, includes previously unreleased tracks and alternates. This title may be out of print or just plain hard to find. Mail-order companies, used CD shops, or dealers of rare or import recordings will be your best bet.

Didier C. Deutsch

Swept from the Sea

1997, London Records, from the film *Swept from the Sea,* TriStar, 1997 ♪♪♪♪

album notes: Music: John Barry; **Orchestra:** The English Chamber Orchestra; **Conductor:** John Barry.

Undeniably, John Barry has a unique musical talent which, these days, seems to fit romantic love stories best. He demonstrates it again in this excellent period melodrama, based on a short story by Joseph Conrad and set in the rugged Cornwall countryside in the late 1800s. Superbly acted by Rachel Weisz, as a farm girl, and Vincent Perez, as a Russian seaman whom she befriends after his ship is lost in a storm, the powerfully intelligent drama chronicled the main characters' difficult life together in a hostile environment, and the seaman's untimely death that leaves Weisz alone with their son, two outcasts in a world that has rejected them. A challenging and at times difficult film, *Swept from the Sea* retained a freshness and spontaneity that belied its dark subject, notably thanks to newcomer Weisz's glowing performance. Adding his own comments to the action, Barry wrote a superbly shaded score, dominated by strikingly delineated themes that underscored the narrative and provided unusual strength to the story. Quietly imaginative, it receives a beautiful performance from the English Chamber Orchestra, conducted by the composer, in this exquisite recording.

Didier C. Deutsch

Swing Kids

1993, Hollywood Records, from the film *Swing Kids,* Hollywood Pictures, 1993 ♪♪♪♪

album notes: Music: James Horner; **Featured Musicians:** Jerry Hey, trumpet; Gary Grant, trumpet; Larry Hall, trumpet; Chuck Findley, trumpet; Bill Reichenbach, trombone; Lloyd Ulgate, trombone; John Johnson, trombone; Abe Most, sax; Dan Higgins, sax; Robert Tricarico, sax; Gene Cipriano, sax; Curt McGettrick, sax, woodwinds; Michael Lang, piano; Dennis Budimir, guitar; Dean Parks, guitar; Ben Wild, bass; Chuck Domonico, bass; Ralph Humphrey, drums; Sid Page, violin.

There may have been something ludicrous about the plot of the film (young Germans defying Hitler's Nazi henchmen with their love for swing music and the American big bands), but there is nothing ludicrous about this soundtrack album, in which great recreations of some well-known standards and new tracks composed by James Horner combine to create a vivid musical picture that transcends the medium for which it was initially meant.

Didier C. Deutsch

Swingers

 1996, Miramax Records, from the film *Swingers,* Miramax, 1996 ♪♪♪♪

Inexplicably, the hip nightlife of the late mid-'90s includes martinis, cigars, and swinging jazz music. With a few liberties, the soundtrack to this engaging chronicle of the trend nails the bachelor pad *savoir faire* of the music of choice. Dean Martin, Louis Jordan, King Floyd, and an enjoyable workout on "With Plenty of Money and You" by Count Basie and Tony Bennett capture swing years past. Selections by Love Jones and Big Bad Voodoo Daddy give a present-day twist to the music. And familiar hits by Roger Miller ("King of the Road") and the Average White Band ("Pick up the Pieces") sound surprisingly in sync with the rest of this collection.

Gary Graff

Switch

1991, Varèse Sarabande, from the film *Switch,* Warner Bros., 1991 ♪

album notes: Music: Henry Mancini; **Featured Musicians:** David Wilson, violin; Ray Pizzi, soprano sax; Brandon Fields, alto sax; Steve Schaeffer, drums; Mike Lang, keyboards; Jim Cox, keyboards; Abe Laboriel, bass; Chuck Domanico, bass; George Doering, guitar.

The long collaboration between Henry Mancini and filmmaker Blake Edwards produced countless undisputed masterpieces in the annals of movie history; from "Moon River" to *The Pink Panther,* Mancini scored Edwards's pictures with classy, distinguished film scores that continue to influence popular music to this day. Towards the end of his career Mancini still had that old-time panache, as evidenced by his terrific work on Edwards' terrible 1988 comic-western *Sunset* and the successful *Victor/Victoria* musical adaptation. While *Sunset* sadly went unreleased, an original score album was issued for Mancini's music from *Switch,* Edwards's 1991 gender-switching, would-be comedy with Ellen Barkin. In a surprising turn of events, Mancini's original music was largely removed from the finished film, but upon listening to this painful soundtrack, it's all too obvious why—his score is, for lack of a better term, a disaster. The music is heavy on electronics and light on melody, almost straining to be "different" from the composer's usual sound. Different it is, but also grating and thoroughly unappealing. Kudos to anyone who manages to get through the entire length of this thankfully brief album without skipping ahead.

Didier C. Deutsch

T

Tai-Pan

1986, Varèse Sarabande, from the film *Tai-Pan,* De Laurentis Entertainment, 1986 ♪♪♪

album notes: Music: Maurice Jarre; **Orchestra:** The Studioorchester of Munich; **Conductor:** Maurice Jarre.

If you're the guy who wrote the music for *Lawrence of Arabia,* you get a lot of calls. Maurice Jarre would be that guy, and *Tai-Pan,* a silly 19th-century Chinese adventure based on the James Clavell novel, must have been one of those calls. Jarre has scored two Asian epics, this and the 1980 mini-series *Shogun,* but *Tai-Pan* is by far the more western and traditional of the two. It's a sweeping, soaring, somewhat clinky symphonic score with Jarre's unmistakable imprint all over it. Jarre almost always sounds like himself, especially in this genre, and he has a way of taking his melodies in unexpected, excitingly sing-songy directions. The CD features two 18-minute tracks (side A and B on the original vinyl) and is fairly coherent.

Lukas Kendall

Tales from a Parallel Universe

1997, Varèse-Sarabande, from the television series *Tales of a Parallel Universe,* 1997 ♪♪♪♪
album notes: Music: Marty Simon.

Known in other parts of the world as *Lexx,* after its main character, the futuristic German TV series *Tales from a Parallel Universe* involves space explorers, a highly advanced starship, and an alien sexpot. Marty Simon's score, as heard in this soundtrack album, is much more entertaining than the topic of the series would initially suggest. Without any of the fanfare or brassy outbursts that often evoke a standard space adventure, but with a wealth of thematic material solidly embedded in a contemporary mold, previously unknown composer Simon manages to make a name for himself with a score that proves engrossing and consistently interesting to listen to.

Didier C. Deutsch

Tales from the Crypt

1992, Big Screen Records, from the television series *Tales from the Crypt,* 1989—91 ♪♪♪♪

This anthology series, originally made for cable television, first gained notoriety because several movie directors and actors, many who never did TV, were willing to work on individual episodes. Consequently, many film composers were also willing to take on scoring assignments. The album features suites

Swingers (The Kobal Collection)

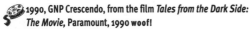
from 11 episodes including "The Thing from the Grave" (David Newman), "Cutting Cards" (James Horner), and "The Reluctant Vampire" (Cliff Eidelman). Bruce Broughton's uncharacteristicly dark "Carrion Death," is included. It is a score for an episode that had almost no dialogue. Steve Bartek, Danny Elfman's long–time collaborator, contributes the delightful solo effort of a jazzy film noir music for "Deadline." The long version of Elfman's main theme leads off the CD and John Kassir, who voiced the Crypt Keeper, performs on "The Crypt Jam." A really nice *body* of work.

David Hirsch

Tales from the Darkside: The Movie

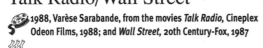
1990, GNP Crescendo, from the film *Tales from the Dark Side: The Movie,* Paramount, 1990 woof!

album notes: Music: John Harrison, Chaz Jankel, Jim Manzie, Pat Regan, Donald A. Rubinstein.

Despite input from five composers, this score for this anthology, based on the TV series, is simply a mediocre collection of synthesized music. One would expect stories written by the likes of Stephen King and George Romero to inspire something more creative, but that never happens. Each suite representing the four stories is virtually interchangeable in style and the whole package becomes depressingly dull.

David Hirsch

Talk Radio/Wall Street

1988, Varèse Sarabande, from the movies *Talk Radio,* Cineplex Odeon Films, 1988; and *Wall Street,* 20th Century-Fox, 1987

album notes: Music: Stewart Copeland.

Both films were directed by Oliver Stone, yet two films couldn't have been more different in scope and in approach. Inspired by the 1984 murder of radio personality Alan Berg at the hands of radicals and set at a station in Dallas, *Talk Radio* surveys the personal life and professional career of a late-night talkshow host (Eric Bogosian), whose vitriolic, offensive on-the-air comments spare nothing and no one, and attract a sordid, squalid audience. As its title suggests, *Wall Street* takes place in the world of high finance, with Charlie Sheen portraying a young, ruthless tyro, manipulated by the man he wants to emulate, a big time financial shark played by Michael Douglas. Giving each film a style of its own, Stewart Copeland's scores are abrasively energetic and descriptive, relying on synth effects, in themes that detail the specific action in each. Of the two, *Talk Radio* seems more fully realized and interesting, but that may also be because of the fact that some of the cues are set

off by short excerpts from the dialogue that gives them a greater dramatic focus. However, in *Wall Street* some frighteningly realistic sounds (including dogs barking, perhaps in a more picturesque description of some of the characters that inhabit the financial districts) provide a physical aura to the score that's also quite striking.

Didier C. Deutsch

The Taming of the Shrew

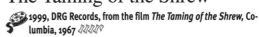
1999, DRG Records, from the film *The Taming of the Shrew,* Columbia, 1967

album notes: Music: Nino Rota; **Conductor:** Carlo Savina.

Richard Burton and Elizabeth Taylor were marvelously cast as the two tempestuous characters, Petrucchio and Katharina, who meet, fight, and fall in love, in Shakespeare's rambunctious comedy, directed by Franco Zeffirelli in his first major motion picture. Colorful, brilliantly imaginative, and a splendid showcase for the two actors, *The Taming of the Shrew* also elicited a winning musical score from Nino Rota, on a reprieve from his contributions to the films of Federico Fellini. Anchored around two main themes, a vivid tarantella and an attractive love song, respectively describing Petrucchio and Katharina, Rota's score is richly textured and lively, and shows why the composer was undoubtedly one among the greats in film music. When the film was released in 1967 RCA Victor issued an LP that contained some musical excerpts from the score, but was mostly a series of dialogue highlights from the film that relegated the music to its screen role as an underscore. This brand new release from DRG not only brings the music vividly to center stage, but adds the overture, available here for the first time, and an alternate version of the "Honeymoon" cue.

Didier C. Deutsch

Tango

1999, Deutsche Gramophone, from the film *Tango,* Pandora, 1999

album notes: Music: Lalo Schifrin; **Conductor:** Lalo Schifrin.

Mario, a theatrical director undergoes a mid-life crisis during a huge dance production. He is abandoned by his wife, then courts the mistress of a mafia godfather. The contrived plot and feeble acting are outweighed by extraordinary dancing and the accompanying tango music. As a student of a fellow Argentinean tango maestro Astor Piazzolla, Lalo Schifrin naturally balances the distinctive stepping rhythm of the Buenos Aires dance style with modern orchestration. *Tango* inevitably draws comparison with Sally Potter's score and compilation of vintage recordings for *The Tango Lesson.* While they cover some of the same ground, both include Osvaldo Pugliese "La Yumba" and Juan de Dios Filiberto's "Quejas de Bandoneon," Schifrin offers a seamless experience where compositions from many decades are interpreted by one orchestra. Overall, however, *The Tango Lesson* is the better buy as the original recordings transport listeners back to the ballrooms of the '40s in a way that is impossible to replicate.

David Poole

Taras Bulba

1998, Rykodisc, from the film *Taras Bulba*, United Artists, 1962
♪♪♪♪

album notes: Music: Franz Waxman; **Conductor:** Franz Waxman.

Yul Brynner got to play the legendary cossack, with Tony Curtis as his son, Andrei, in this historical costume epic, based on the tale by Gogol. Matching in scope and grandeur the feel of the wide Russian steppes where most of the film is set, composer Franz Waxman created a score in which bold, Russian-influenced themes, very reminiscent of Tchaikovsky, captured the spirit of the 16th-century Ukrainian cossacks, most notably in the impressive denouement, "Battle of Dubno," a superb moment of film scoring. In contrast, Waxman also managed to write a set of beautiful, tender cues for Natalia, the daughter of the Polish governor and Andrei's love interest. This effort earned Waxman his 12th Oscar nomination. Listening to this great score, beautifully remastered and available for the first time on CD, one can understand why.

Didier C. Deutsch

Tarzan

1999, Walt Disney Records, from the film *Tarzan*, Disney, 1999
♪♪♪

album notes: Music: Mark Mancina; **Songs:** Phil Collins.

You can bet there are a few of the ubiquitous Phil Collins detractors out there who would like to take him into the jungle and leave him there, wrapped up in some vines. Well, let's be polite here; Collins is an undeniably skilled craftsman with a touch for compelling pop melodies and arrangements, and the five songs he wrote and performed for Disney's animated version of *Tarzan* find him taking a mini-sojourn through the varied styles he's worked in throughout his career. Unlike most Disney composers, Collins was not charged with writing songs for characters to sing, so the *Tarzan* selections have a stronger-than-usual narrative voice. "Two Worlds" introduces the story with thundering drums and overturial sweep. "You'll Be in My Heart" and "Strangers like Me" are the kind of aching ballads he's frequently taken to the top of charts, while "Son of Man" is a coming-of-age piece set to upbeat, rolling pop. Rosie O'Donnell's scatting is surprisingly sharp on "Trashin' the Camp," though

10 Essential Scores

by Jerry Goldsmith

Star Trek the Motion Picture
The Blue Max
Islands in the Stream
Legend
Chinatown
Logan's Run
Coma
Planet of the Apes
The Sand Pebbles
Gremlins

Collins's reprise of the tune with 'N Sync benefits from the wider range of voices. There's not necessarily a lot to go ape about here—including Mark Mancina's instrumental score, which is serviceable but geared more to cinema consumption—but *Tarzan* certainly ranks as another one of Disney's solid collaborative confections between the realms of pop and film.

Gary Graff

Taxi Blues

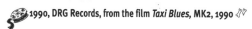1990, DRG Records, from the film *Taxi Blues*, MK2, 1990 ♪♪

album notes: Music: Vladimir Chekassine.

Vladimir Chekassine wrote a hard-driving jazz score for this film, winner of the Best Director Award at the 1990 Cannes Film Festival, about a Moscow taxi driver and the westernized saxophone player with whom he strikes an uneasy friendship. A rhetorical dissertation about the pros and cons of life in the new Russia, the film was mostly interesting for its candid vision of the streets of Moscow, in a display of decrepitude and human squalor that might not have agreed with the Kremlin dictators of yore. The score itself, inordinately brief (total playing time of this album is 19:23), is interesting to a point, but jazz, the universal language, is evidently something Chekassine cares much about but has little to contribute to that's new. This recording may be difficult to find. Check with a used CD store, mail-order company, or a dealer specializing in rare, out-of-print, or import recordings.

Beth Krakower

Taxi Driver

1998, Arista Records, from the film *Taxi Driver,* Columbia, 1976
𝄞𝄞𝄞𝄞𝄞

album notes: Music: Bernard Herrmann.

When it was initially released in 1976, the soundtrack album of *Taxi Driver* only featured a couple of tracks from the original score, the famous "Are you talking to me . . . ?" speech by Robert De Niro, and selections from the themes developed by Bernard Herrmann, rerecorded by Dave Blume. When the decision was made to reissue this soundtrack, Herrmann's last, I immediately suggested that the only way to do justice to the composer's creation would be to include the complete original score, a recommendation that was heartily endorsed by Steve Bartels and Gary Pacheco at the label. As a result, this CD reissue incorporates all the cues written by Herrmann, presented in the order in which they are heard in the film, and properly remixed and remastered. While the score often seemed at odds with the storyline devised by Martin Scorsese, it ultimately proved to be not only a perfect musical support to *Taxi Driver,* but as John Bender appropriately remarked in a review of the album in *Film Score Monthly,* it "provided an aggressive and overt accelerant to the film's humid and claustrophobic energies." In assembling this reissue, we also included the narrative by De Niro, the Dave Blume tracks, and a couple of alternates, making this the definitive soundtrack album of that momentous film.

Didier C. Deutsch

The Temp

1993, Varèse-Sarabande, from the film *The Temp,* Paramount, 1993 𝄞𝄞𝄞

album notes: Music: Frank Talgorn; **Orchestra:** The Munich Symphony Orchestra; **Conductor:** Frederic Talgorn; **Featured Musicians:** David Hartley, piano; Cynthia Millar, ondes Martenot.

This drama, about a temp looking for a permanent position, preferably reclining, starred Lara Flynn Boyle as a mysterious, striking-looking secretary trying her best to climb the corporate ladder—though Boyle's terribly unconvincing performance

made this would-be psychothriller more a hoot than a scare. On a more positive note, Frank Talgorn's score, filled with lovely, attractive themes, manages to overcome the film's inane plot, and makes a good impression in this soundtrack recording, though the weirdly dissonant "Masturbation," of all things, completely lacks eroticism, perhaps another reflection of Ms. Boyle's inept acting.

Didier C. Deutsch

The Ten Commandments

1989, MCA Records, from the film *The Ten Commandments,* Paramount, 1956 𝄞𝄞𝄞𝄞½

album notes: Music: Elmer Bernstein; **Orchestra:** The Paramount Studio Orchestra; **Conductor:** Elmer Bernstein.

Oh, Moses, Moses! Veteran composer Elmer Bernstein got his first major credit on Cecil B. DeMille's classic Biblical epic, providing a rousing, vibrant score full of unforgettable leitmotifs, from the portentous six note "God" theme to a proud fanfare for Charlton Heston's Moses and a languid melody for Egyptian queen Nefritiri that's just as smoothly campy as Ann Baxter's outrageous performance in the role. Few composers have been handed assignments with this kind of scope so early in their careers, but Bernstein approached apocryphal moments like Moses's encounter with the Burning Bush, the Hebrews' exodus from Egypt, and the parting of the Red Sea with moving piety, infectious energy, and an uncanny sense of drama and awe. Originally presented as a two-LP set, this 70-minute CD presents the lion's share of Bernstein's score, from the sweeping overture and exotic evocation of the river Nile to Bernstein's incredibly moving finale with its gorgeous recapitulation of the composer's gentle melody for Moses' wife, Sephora. Despite the length here, there's not a dull moment, and this broad, exciting album belongs in anyone's collection.

Jeff Bond

10 Things I Hate About You

1999, Hollywood Records, from the film *10 Things I Hate About You,* Touchstone, 1999 𝄞𝄞𝄞

album notes: Music: Richard Gibbs.

A high-school *Taming of the Shrew, 10 Things I Hate About You* has its charms, but often sounds forced and uneasy about itself, with a pleasant, cheeky turn by Julia Stiles as Katarina, a nonconformist who gets "tamed." While the album hopes to recapture the essence of the film with renditions of the songs heard on the soundtrack (featuring some of the hot names of the moment, including Semisonic, the Cardigans, and two covers by Letters to Cleo), the one most important musical moment (Heath Ledger's warbling "Can't Take My Eyes off You" to

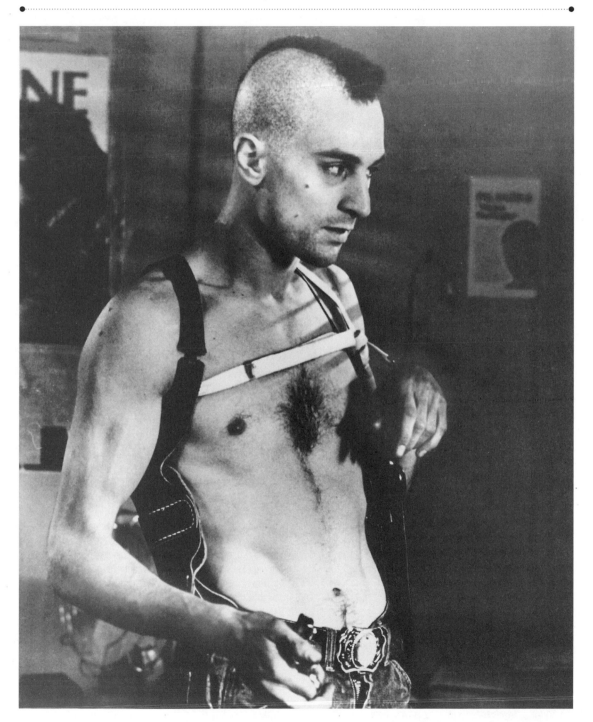

Robert De Niro in Taxi Driver. **(The Kobal Collection)**

Stiles, while the school marching band clumsily oompahs along behind him) is missing. The album has some interesting funk tracks as well, by George Clinton and Brick, and one score track by Richard Gibbs.

Beth Krakower

Tequila Sunrise

1988, Capitol Records, from the film *Tequila Sunrise,* Warner Bros., 1988 ♪

album notes: Music: Dave Grusin; **Conductor:** Dave Grusin; **Featured Musicians:** Dave Sanborn, saxophone; Lee Ritenour, guitar.

There are reasons to be very, very scared of this soundtrack. Jazz lite master Dave Grusin teaming with David Sanborn on one number and Lee Ritenour on another. Cheap Trick's Robin Zander teaming with Heart's Ann Wilson. The Everly Brothers and the Beach Boys combining on "Don't Worry Baby"—which would have been exciting in 1969 . . . maybe. And don't forget Duran Duran and a solo track by its former guitarist, Andy Taylor. Kinda makes you want to slap on Mel Gibson's solo spot from "Pocahontas."

Gary Graff

Terminal Velocity

1994, Varèse Sarabande, from the film *Terminal Velocity,* Interscope, 1994 ♪♪♪♪

album notes: Music: Joel McNeely; **Conductor:** Joel McNeely.

Writing in a solidly muscular style, with lots of orchestral flourishes over a simple synth rhythm line, Joel McNeely created a surprisingly effective score for this aerial cold war spy thriller involving a loot in gold bullion, a gorgeous sky diving agent, and other mid-air happenstances that propel the action and keep it . . . well, flying! Occasionally (and abruptly) interrupted by scorching rock accents ("Ditch's Dive"), the score keeps the moods midway between suspense and contemplation, with throbbing chords and evolutive orchestral lines mingling in unexpected, sudden changes for what amounts to a very lively and effective series of cues. While the music works very well behind the screen action, it is also quite descriptive without it.

Didier C. Deutsch

The Terminator

1984, Cinemaster/DCC Compact Classics, from the film *The Terminator,* Orion Pictures, 1984 ♪♪

album notes: Music: Brad Fiedel; **Featured Musician:** Ross Levinson, electric violin.

More mood music than listening music, Brad Fiedel's score for the Arnold Schwarzenegger–starrer proved more effective on the screen, behind the action, than it does when brought up

front. With low rumbling chords, synth percussion, and various other effects creating ominous, somber moods, the only track that actually attracts is "Love Scene," a short, relatively quiet expression that might have gained at being a little longer. Adding a strident, rock-oriented note to the album, five songs may prove more attractive to the average listener, if only because they at least are built on stronger melodic hooks than the score itself, even if they all end up sounding the same.

Didier C. Deutsch

Terminator 2: Judgment Day

1991, Varèse Sarabande, from the film *Terminator 2: Judgment Day,* Tri-Star Pictures, 1991 ♪♪

album notes: Music: Brad Fiedel.

This non-thematic score by Brad Fiedel is more sound design than underscore. It works brilliantly in the film, and it does have a certain hypnotic charm at times, with some tracks, like "Desert Suite," having a very ambient feel to them. But it is sure a tough listen on its own if you're not prepared for it. The original *Terminator* main theme, the only melodic piece in the score, is played here with a slower, more deliberate pace.

David Hirsch

The Terminator: The Definitive Edition

1996, Cinerama/edel Records, from the movie, *The Terminator,* Orion Pictures, 1984 ♪♪♪♪

album notes: Music: Brad Fiedel; **Featured Musician:** Ross Levison, electric violin.

This "Definitive Edition" (the "iv" between Definite's last two letters has evidently been terminated) provides for the first time Fiedel's complete score, remastered in stereo (the film's audio track had been mono). *The Terminator* is an effectively mechanical score, suitably punctuating the presence and relentless determination of the cyborg assassin through a pulsing, darkly ambient electronic tonality. Featuring a bold, alternatingly heroic/malevolent synth melody (which retains a slightly disconsolate tone, representing the struggles of the future from which the cyborg comes) over a staccato percussion riff, suggesting the tumbling building blocks of our destructive future, Fiedel captures the ideal musical emotion for the film. Outside of a brief piano and oboe love theme and a lot of percussive and atonal suspense music, *The Terminator* is a monothematic score. The machinelike cyborg is the focus of the music, and Fiedel effectively maintains the character's menace through this approach.

Randall Larson

Texas

1994, Legacy Records, from the television special *Texas,* Republic Pictures, 1994 🎼🎼🎼

album notes: Music: Lee Holdridge; **Conductor:** Lee Holdridge.

This musical collection inspired by the TV epic brings together several well–known C&W artists in renditions of songs that all have something to do with Texas, neatly bookended by Lee Holdridge's opening and closing themes (amateurs of soundtrack music will have to dig out the promotional CD that was released around the same time, and which contain all the cues composed by Holdridge for the film). One's acceptance of this compilation will be strictly limited by one's tolerance for this type of material. Taken at face value and despite the wide variations in sound quality, it has its many moments of fun and entertainment, though it offers little that is new or rare. This is strictly for fans.

Didier C. Deutsch

Thank God It's Friday

1997, Casablanca Records, from the film *Thank God It's Friday,* Motown-Casablanca FilmWorks, 1978 🎼🎼🎼

A brilliant marketing concept, *Thank God It's Friday* is essentially a long-form video showcasing the talents of the most important disco performers under contract to Casablanca and Motown in 1978. And what a roster: Donna Summer, of course, the reigning queen of disco at the time; Paul Jabara, who copped an Academy Award for "Last Dance"; Thelma Houston; Diana Ross; Pattie Brooks; the Commodores; Cameo; D.C. LaRue, some as ephemeral as disco itself, others with longer resiliency. One may berate disco for its simpleminded attitudes and complain that the songs are all beat and no substance. One thing, however: they are fun, and that's all that was needed. In the years since, the music industry has changed course many times, but the songs in *Thank God It's Friday* have remained as fresh and exciting as they were when they were first created. This album is a vivid reminder of an era that probably came and went too fast.

Didier C. Deutsch

That Old Feeling

1997, MCA Records, from the film *That Old Feeling,* Universal, 1997 🎼🎼🎼🎼

Wow! What an album! Call it a guilty pleasure, call it old-fashioned stuff, it doesn't matter. Next to the drivel we are so often subjected to these days, next to songs without music and with words that are not even intelligent or intelligible, this is the real thing. These songs were crafted with the utmost care by people

who knew the value of an interesting lyric combined with a melodic hook, and they are performed by people who know how to sing them and extract every juicy ounce from them—in other words the best of both worlds. So, just put the CD in your player, press the "play" button, sit back, and enjoy! You deserve it!

Didier C. Deutsch

That Thing You Do

1996, Play Tone Records/Epic Soundtrax, from the film *That Thing You Do,* 20th Century-Fox, 1996 🎼🎼🎼🎼

album notes: Music: Tom Hanks.

Winning Oscars wasn't enough for Tom Hanks: he had to write songs, too. Hanks shares composing credits on four of the songs here, and the whole collection perfectly apes the innocence and occasional sophomorism of early and mid-'60s American pop. The jangley title track is catchy, however, as are most of the other songs "performed" by the Wonders, the fictional group that's the subject of the movie. *That Thing You Do!* also touches on surf instrumentals ("Voyage Around the Moon"), teen torch songs ("My World Is Over"), girl groups ("Hold My Hand, Hold My Heart"), and bombastic movie-style themes ("Mr. Downtown"). This is definitely one CD you'll come back to repeatedly.

Gary Graff

That's Entertainment

1995, Rhino Records, from the MGM films *That's Entertainment!,* 1974, *That's Entertainment, Part 2,* 1976, and *That's Entertainment! III,* 1994 🎼🎼🎼🎼

The "soundtrack" to the three MGM anthologies surveying the output of the studio, this box set is a massive collection of some of the best moments from the great MGM musicals, with a pool of talent (performers, but also songwriters, musicians, orchestrators, etc.) that is nothing less than staggering. Individually and collectively, these people were a class act that has never been equaled. And while the films (and the set) gave an overview of their many contributions, by their very nature they only could be but a sampling of the whole thing.

But what a tasty treat, and what a line-up! Fred Astaire, Judy Garland, Gene Kelly, Debbie Reynolds, Eleanor Powell, Tony Martin, Cyd Charisse, and Frank Sinatra, among the many singers who brought their unique and distinctive stylings to the MGM musicals; and Richard Rodgers, Lorenz Hart, Cole Porter, Irving Berlin, George and Ira Gershwin, Jerome Kern, Oscar Hammerstein II, Arthur Freed, and Nacio Herb Brown (who started the whole thing), among the many songwriters whose works became the stuff that Hollywood legends are made. It's all there, in a six-CD time capsule, a collection that is truly phenomenal in its scope and importance, lavishly presented in a style Rhino developed early on to properly feature the classic MGM films. There are some flaws, to be sure: unlike the films, in which a loose narrative kept the various segments together, the songs are presented here presumably in same the order in which they appeared in the three film compilations, resulting in a disjointed hodge-podge that lacks continuity. Admittedly, putting the set together must not have been an easy task and one can appreciate the dilemma facing producers Merilee Bradford, George Feltenstein, and Bradley Flanagan in trying to bring a cohesive sense to their effort.

Also typical of some of the early Rhino releases, nothing much seems to have been done to correct sound defects and otherwise make the various tracks more compatible with each other. This is particularly apparent in the earlier selections, but also in a song like "Gigi," which was recorded over a period of time, with each segment reflecting a different EQ, something which could and should have been corrected when putting this set together.

Given the abundance of material, and the fact that so many musical numbers were left out of the three films, volume six is a bit of a stretch, adding as it does songs that seem less important than those found on the first five discs. This is particularly true when one considers that some of the most popular films are not covered or only barely so (i.e., *Ziegfeld Follies*). On the plus side, however, the set, like the films, includes some rare "footage;" for instance, selections from *Annie Get Your Gun,* recorded by Judy Garland, who was subsequently dismissed to be replaced by Betty Hutton. All told, not a perfect set, but one hell of a box nonetheless.

Didier C. Deutsch

The Theory of Flight

1999, RCA Victor, from the film *The Theory of Flight,* Fine Line, 1999 ♪♪♪♪

album notes: Music: Rolfe Kent; **Orchestra:** The Philharmonia Orchestra; **Conductor:** Alan Wilson.

With his scores for *House of Yes, The Slums of Beverly Hills,* and *Election,* Rolfe Kent has demonstrated a consistent, eccentric touch that always does wonders for his correspondingly offbeat films. *The Theory of Flight* is the score that really shows off his orchestral talents, filled with sweeping melodies that help keep this seriocomic tale of madness and fatal disease firmly off the ground. Kent goes for the emotion here, and the music works with the kind of big, romantic strokes that evoke flying imagery. Kent's music is also lyrical and pleasant, as capable of tender restraint as it is of big, symphonic moments.

The comedy is also subtler here, with a progressive brass sound that has just a touch of Rachel Portman to it. Overall, Kent's "theory" to scoring this kind of film is right on target, his lush, affecting music nicely avoiding the three-hankie clichés that usually come with the genre. The CD also has a number of good R&B and pop songs, among them Rusted Root's "Send Me on My Way" and John Hiatt's "Have a Little Faith in Me," all adding to this soundtrack's uplifting charm.

Dan Schweiger

There's No Business Like Show Business

1998, Varèse-Sarabande, from the film *There's No Business Like Show Business,* 20th Century-Fox, 1954 ♪♪♪♪

album notes: Music: Irving Berlin; **Screenplay:** Phoebe and Henry Ephron; **Orchestra:** The 20th Century-Fox Orchestra; **Conductors:** Alfred Newman, Lionel Newman; **Cast:** Dan Dailey (Terry Donahue), Ethel Merman (Molly Donahue), Marilyn Monroe (Vicky), Donald O'-Connor (Tim Donahue), Mitzi Gaynor (Katy Donahue), Johnnie Ray (Steve Donahue).

Another first-time release in the Fox Classics series, now distributed by Varèse-Sarabande, (see *Stormy Weather*), this screen musical extravaganza was almost entirely conceived as a showcase to the tunes written by songwriter Irving Berlin. Like in the earlier *Alexander's Ragtime Band,* made in 1938, songs from the Berlin trunk were exhumed, put together, and a loose narrative built around them. And, as in the previous film, also made by 20th Century-Fox, the setting chosen was show business, in this instance the story of a vaudeville couple, the Donahues (Dan Dailey and Ethel Merman), and their three children (Mitzi Gaynor, Donald O'Connor, and Johnnie Ray). As the kids grow up, they join the family act, but after they reach their teens they begin to assert their independence: Gaynor and O'-Connor, joined by Marilyn Monroe with whom he's fallen in love, want to try a new act, more modern and up-to-date than their parents' tired routine, while Ray seeks a different kind of entertainment, in religion. The five Donahues will however reunite for a big finale, as befits any showbiz saga. Brilliantly staged, with colorful musical setpieces adorning the loose narrative, *There's No Business Like Show Business,* shot in CinemaScope, is a wonderful film, made even more entertaining thanks to the many familiar Berlin songs that pepper it: "Play a Simple Melody," "A Pretty Girl Is Like a Melody," "Alexander's Ragtime Band," "Heat Wave," and, of course, the title track, performed by an exuberant cast in peak condition. Monroe, the studio's newest bombshell and biggest boxoffice name at the time, did pretty well for herself in a singing role that made extra demands on her as a dancer. Both Gaynor and O'Connor, equally competent, injected a sense of fun in their respective roles. Ray, though seemingly ill-at-ease at times as an actor, got to sing two numbers in which his distinctive styling was totally appropriate. As for Dailey, always smooth, and Merman, congenially abrasive, they were right on target in roles that seemed to fit them like an old glove. At the time of the film's release, Decca released a mono LP that only contained some selections, with Monroe's numbers handled by Dolores Gray, because the studio wouldn't allow Monroe to appear on the album. No such restrictions applied to this reissue, available in stereo, which not only contains all the numbers heard in the film, but bonus tracks, like Merman reprising her signature song, "There's No Business Like Show Business," in a "hidden" track that will be found approximately two minutes after the end of the recording, and is not indexed.

Didier C. Deutsch

There's Something About Mary

1998, Capitol Records, from the film *There's Something About Mary*, 20th Century-Fox, 1998 ♪♪♪
album notes: Music: Jonathan Richman.

There's something about *There's Something About Mary* that's quite catchy. The surprise hit of the summer of '98, this movie momentarily led to a resurgence of schlock comedy, not surprising since it came from the guys who brought us *Dumb and Dumber* and *Kingpin.* Reflecting the moods of the film, the soundtrack is full of fun alternative music, like electronic band the Propellerheads teaming with Shirley Bassey, the Lemondheads, and Ben Lee, interwoven with classic songs like "Is She Really Going out with Him" and "Build Me up Buttercup."

Beth Krakower

They Call Me Mister Tibbs

See: In the Heat of the Night

They Died with Their Boots On

1999, Marco Polo Records, from the film *They Died with Their Boots On*, Warner Bros., 1941 ♪♪♪♪♪
album notes: Music: Max Steiner; **Orchestra:** The Moscow Symphony Orchestra; **Conductor:** William T. Stromberg.

Marco Polo continues to dazzle with the excellence of their recording reconstructions, which applied this time around to *They Died with Their Boots On,* the story of General Custer and the massacre at Little Big Horn at the hands of Crazy Horse and his Indian warriors. As Custer, Errol Flynn enjoyed one of many flamboyant roles that he would etch so strongly that no one playing it after him could ever hope to compete. Directed with vigor and style by Raoul Walsh, the film is an extraordinary ac-

count of Custer's defeat, with Max Steiner providing a score grandly evocative of the whole saga, while solidly anchored in the western sounds usually associated with this kind of outdoor epic. Reconstructed by John W. Morgan, and performed with the right bravadura by the Moscow Symphony Orchestra, conducted by William T. Stromberg, this is another fine recording in a series that only seems to get better as more titles are added to it. Unfailingly, the orchestra covers the epic moments with all the necessary grandeur required by the genre, giving an almost ethereal reading to the softer selections in the score ("Mystic Teapot/Owl"). It all conspires to make Steiner's music come off livelier and better than it ever sounded, making this required listening for anyone remotely interested in film music.

Didier C. Deutsch

They're Playing Our Song

1979, Casablanca Records, from the Broadway production *They're Playing Our Song*, 1979 ♪♪♪♪
album notes: Music: Marvin Hamlisch; **Lyrics:** Carol Bayer Sager; **Musical Direction:** Larry Blank; **Featured Musician:** Fran Liebergall, piano; **Cast:** Robert Klein, Lucy Arnaz.

Essentially a two-character play, *They're Playing Our Song* recounts the romance between an Academy Award–winning composer, Vernon (Robert Klein), and the off-beat lyricist he meets and falls in love while writing pop songs with her (any resemblance between these characters and real-life Marvin Hamlisch and Carol Bayer Sager was purely coincidental). Spicing up the proceedings, at least the way Neil Simon, author of the libretto, conceived it, the two main characters share the stage with their "alter egos" who, at judicious times, reveal Vernon and Sonia's inner thoughts. Ultimately, the show itself might have been a trifle, but propelled by its clever score, it enjoyed a long run and won over even the most hardened critics.

Didier C. Deutsch

The Thief of Bagdad/The Jungle Book

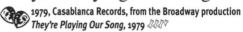

1988, Varèse Sarabande, from the movies *The Thief of Bagdad,* Universal-International, 1940, and *The Jungle Book,* United Artists, 1942 ♪♪♪♪♪
album notes: Music: Miklos Rozsa; **Orchestra:** The Nurnberg Symphony Orchestra; **Conductor:** Miklos Rozsa, Klauspeter Seibel.

Here are Miklos Rozsa's first two popular scores, and the ones that really established him as a major Hollywood composer. Brilliantly performed by the Nurnberg Symphony Orchestra, they are rerecorded in sparkling stereo, given new life and greater vibrancy. Drawing as much from the colorful music of his Hungarian background as he did from his own idea of what

Arabian and Indian accents should sound like, Rozsa created two scores that are exquisitely evocative of the locales and the actions, and that are indissolubly representative of the films for which they were composed.

The often extravagant accents in *The Thief of Bagdad* detail this 1001-night Arabian fantasy in broad, vibrant musical tones that compare favorably with Rimsky-Korsakov's tone poem, *Sheherazade,* which they often evoke. The epic tale about the poor beggar (actually the heir to the throne, despoiled by a villainous sorcerer) who falls in love with a princess and, with the aid of a mischievous street urchin, overcomes all odds, the film weaves a delightful story that happily mixed action with fairy tale in a well-rounded, entertaining oriental saga. Rozsa's music was the perfect complement to the story with wonderfully animated cues that melded with the action and gave it an extra bounce.

Based on Rudyard Kipling's oft-told saga of the baby boy lost in the luxuriant Indian jungle and raised by a pack of wolves, *The Jungle Book* was another storybook brought to the screen in vivid images that captured the wonders of the tale and made it brilliantly palpable. In terms that at times evoked Saint-Saens's *Carnival of the Animals,* Rozsa created a score that gives all the animals in the jungle a distinct personality, emphasized by the use of specific instruments: trombones and tubas for the elephants, horn glissandi for the wolves, sharp contra-bassoon calls for Baloo the bear, long string lines for Bagheera the panther, woodwinds for the Bandarlogs, alto sax for the hyena, etc. Tremendously stimulating and beautifully descriptive of the action on-screen, the score, presented here as a long, uninterrupted orchestral suite, spins a magic of its own, making this recording a rare treat for the listener.

Didier C. Deutsch

The Thin Blue Line

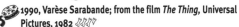1989, Elektra/Nonesuch Records, from the film *The Thin Blue Line,* Euphorbia, 1989 ♫♫

album notes: Music: Philip Glass; **Conductor:** Michael Riesman; **Featured Musicians:** Wilmer Wise, trumpet; Steve Burns (trumpet); Sharoe Moe, French horn; Tony Miranda, French horn; Ron Sell, French horn; Michael Parloff, flute; Judith Mendenhall, flute; Sergiu Schwartz, violin; Tim Baker, violin; Karl Bargen, viola; Chris Funckel, cello; Barbara Wilson, double bass; Michael Riesman, keyboards; Gordon Gottlieb, percussion; Brian Koonin, guitar.

Errol Morris's chilling documentary about a man framed for murder gets a suitably brooding, ominous Philip Glass score, but this soundtrack CD is less interested in letting you hear the music than in telling Randall Adams's Hitchcockian story. For most of the disc's 69 minutes, the tale unfolds through bits of dialogue from the film, with Glass's underscoring, making for a sort of "Books on Tape" experience. Only the opening and closing themes are presented dialogue-free. (Thanks to Morris's

film, Adams ultimately did win his freedom, but you'll hear no jubilation here.)

Marc Kirkeby

Thin Red Line

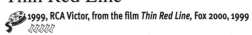1999, RCA Victor, from the film *Thin Red Line,* Fox 2000, 1999 ♫♫♫♫♫

album notes: Music: Hans Zimmer; **Featured Musicians:** Ellie Choate, harp; Marcia Dickstein, harp; Katie Kirkpatrick, harp; Daniel Kuramoto, Shakahachi flute; June Kuramoto, koto; Francesco Lupica, cosmic bean; Johnny Mori, Taiko drums; Emil Richards, Tibetan bowls; Danny Yamamoto, Tibetan bells; Ken Munday, bassoon.

For this lyrical adaptation of James Jones's war novel, set on Guadalcanal in the South Pacific, Hans Zimmer tones down his rock-techno bravado for more meditative and brooding movements. Dreamlike sequences underscore battle scenes while the polyphonic hymns of Guadalcanal's Melanesian Christians evoke a paradise at odds with the film's carnage and horror. To emphasize how exotic Guadalcanal must have seemed to U.S. soldiers, Zimmer infuses the synths and orchestral cues with all manner of instruments, including bell chimes, the resonant hum of a Tibetan bowl, the gentle piping of a shakahachi flute, a trio of harpists, and a Chinese zither. As shell-shocked soldiers philosophize about the futility of war during long voiceovers taken directly from Jones's novel, Zimmer stirs it up with scraped bowing and sustained vibrato, and the eerie gong-like cosmic beam. *The Thin Red Line* should have won the Oscar for Best Score over *Life Is Beautiful* for Zimmer's brave departure from action spectaculars into a starkly different approach to war movie music, where heroic fanfares are occluded by profoundly human introspection.

David Poole

The Thing

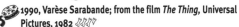1990, Varèse Sarabande; from the film *The Thing,* Universal Pictures, 1982 ♫♫♫♪

album notes: Music: Ennio Morricone; **Conductor:** Ennio Morricone.

The Thing is one of the few instances where John Carpenter turned the scoring duties over to another composer (Carpenter most often prefers to score his own films). While better known for his lyrical scores for *The Mission* and Sergio Leone's westerns, *The Thing* displays Ennio Morricone in a much more contemporary, experimental mode (and is in fact more reflective of the kind of music the composer prefers to write). Some of Carpenter's electronic style shows its influence, but Morricone provides music of much greater imagination than that of which Carpenter is capable. This album also features a great deal of music not used in the film that consists of some compelling 20th-century compositional techniques. Moody, atmospheric music reminiscent of Bartok is featured in the first track, "Humanity," while spine-chilling aleatoric string pizzicati make up "Contamination." "Bestiality" is a surging Herrmann-like cue, while Morricone dabbles in minimalism in "Eternity," which features a dizzying downward spiral of electronics and cathedral organ. The acoustical and recording quality is clean and crisp (the work of engineer Mickey Crawford) and suits the score perfectly. Anyone who insists nothing inventive or imaginative is ever written for films will be convinced otherwise by a listen to this soundtrack.

Paul Andrew MacLean

The Thirteenth Floor

1999, Milan Records, from the film *The Thirteenth Floor*, Columbia, 1999 🎜

album notes: Music: Harald Kloser; **Orchestra:** The Nordwestdeutsche Philharmonie; **Conductor:** Harald Kloser, Thomas Wanker; **Featured Artists:** The Vienna Boys Choir.

One would want to be warmly inclined toward an album that features three selections played big-band-style and the Vienna Boys Choir (not together!). But the sad part is that the three big-band selections—"Caravan," "St. Louis Blues," and "Easy Come, Easy Go"— are played without much conviction by an orchestra that seems to have no feel for this kind of music, fronted by vocalists who are so undistinguished that it almost seems a shame these songs were given to them. As for the Vienna Boys Choir, these angelic voices that occasionally rise over the morass of what passes as music belong to them. Their best moment, and probably the most compelling track here, is titled "Hall Is Dead." It comes almost at the end of the CD, and lasts barely over three-and-a-half minute. Make a note of it: that's the most interesting thing that happens in this soundtrack to a psychological sci-fi thriller that aims to be all things all at once: psychological, sci-fi, and thriller. Harald Kloser is an Austrian native unfamiliar on these shores, but the music he's composed for this film is so barren (not to say boring) that I hope he never has another opportunity to write a score. Writing in a style that's often too predictable and colorless, he affects big orchestral flurries and tenuous ideas, crescendos and trite effects. It probably works behind the scenes in this film set in 1937 in Los Angeles, but on its own merits, it rates a big B for blah!

Didier C. Deutsch

thirtysomething

1991, Geffen Records, from the television series *thirtysomething*, 1991 🎜🎜🎜🎜

album notes: Music: W.G. Snuffy Walden, Stewart Levin, Jay Gruska.

Whoever W.G. Snuffy Walden, Jay Gruska, and Stewart Levin are, the music they have created for "thirtysomething," at least as represented in this soundtrack CD, is very enjoyable. Pleasantly rhythmic, in a style that happily mixes various genres around melodic material that is usually quite attractive, it relies on acoustic instruments to make a flavorful statement, often without overstating its case. Supplementing the instrumental cues, some vocals add their own color to the mix, whether it's Rickie Lee Jones swooning her way through "It Must Be Love," Karla Bonoff warbling the traditional "The Water Is Wide," or Ray Charles doing a surprisingly effective version of the old standard "Come Rain or Come Shine."

Didier C. Deutsch

This Boy's Life

1994, Nouveau Records, from the film *This Boy's Life*, Warner Bros., 1993 🎜🎜🎜

A nicely flavored collection of '50s evergreens served as the soundtrack to this sensitive story of a single mother and her teenage son, who move to Seattle, where she meets a mechanic who looks like he's a nice guy and might be the answer to her lonely dreams. Robert De Niro, Ellen Barkin, and Leonardo Di Caprio in his first major role, did very well for themselves with this one, in which the Fifties were masterfully captured in Michael Caton-Jones's heartfelt direction. The soundtrack album recreates the atmosphere of the film, with perky performances by Nat King Cole, Fats Domino, the Ventures, Eddie Cochran, the Everly Brothers, and Brenda Lee, among other luminaries from the era, doing songs we all know and like.

Didier C. Deutsch

This Earth Is Mine

See: The Young Lions/This Earth Is Mine

This Is My Life

1992, Qwest Records, from the film *This Is My Life*, 20th Century-Fox, 1992 🎜🎜🎜🎜

album notes: Songs: Carly Simon; **Conductor:** Teese Gohl; **Featured Musicians:** Carly Simon, vocals, acoustic guitar, keyboards, whistle; Jimmy Ryan, guitar; Ben Taylor, guitar; Teese Gohl, synthesizer; Andy Goldmark, piano; Will Lee, bass; Paul Samwell-Smith, bass; Andy Newmark, drums; Richie Morales, drums; Russ Kunkel, drums; Jamey Haddad, percussion; Toots Thielemans, harmonica; Randy Brecker, trumpet; Jim Pugh, trombone; Charles McCracken, cello.

Literally a showcase for singer-composer Carly Simon, this album is ingratiating because of the performer's frequently glowing personality and attractive way with a melody and a lyric. A comedy-drama about the "tricky business of raising children and maintaining a solid career, without the benefit of a live-in father," in Simon's own description of the plot, the film evidently inspired the songwriter who wrote the several tunes heard in this soundtrack album, as well as the evocative instrumental cues that complement them. Some songs might attract more than others ("Back the Way," a jaunty, winning little tune, and "The Show Must Go On," an exhilarating anthem, are just wonderful), but the overall effect is ingratiating and strongly reinforced with the instrumental sections in which Toots Thielemans's harmonica creates a poetic spin of its own. A very attractive effort.

Didier C. Deutsch

The Thomas Crown Affair

1999, Rykodisc, from the film *The Thomas Crown Affair,* United Artists, 1968 ♫♫♫♫

album notes: Music: Michel Legrand; **Conductor:** Michel Legrand.

The Thomas Crown Affair is most memorable as the movie that bore the number one-hit "The Windmills of Your Mind," which earned an Academy Award for Best Song. The movie starred Steve McQueen as a rich, suave man who plans and executes a bank robbery out of sheer boredom. Faye Dunaway portrayed a relentless investigator hired by the bank's insurance company to find the culprit and bring him to justice. McQueen and Dunaway's interactions were part cat-and-mouse, part battle-of-the-sexes, which Michel Legrand's score, wonderfully playful at times, captured very well, running the gamut, from whimsical to sixties go-go to jazz. There were two previous editions of this soundtrack on LP. This first CD release combines all of the music contained in both editions.

Didier C. Deutsch

The Thorn Birds: The Missing Years

1996, Varèse-Sarabande, from the television presentation, *The Thorn Birds: The Missing Years,* Warner Bros., 1996 ♫♫♫♫

album notes: Music: Garry McDonald, Lawrence Stone; **Conductor:** Garry McDonald, Lawrence Stone; **Featured Musicians:** Joe Chindamo, piano; Prue Davis, alto flute; Sarah Morse, cello.

Just when viewers thought it was safe to go back to the television set again, here came this sequel to the original tear-jerker, a religious soap opera! Holy catastrophe! Again starring Richard Chamberlain, looking much too handsome for his own good, the television show, demurely subtitled *The Missing Years* filled the gaps that might have left questions in the minds of audiences of the original 10-hour show which had kept the country transfixed over four nights in 1983. Because Henry Mancini, who had scored the first show, was no longer

around (his "Main Theme" and "Maggie's Theme" were used again, however), the scoring assignment was handed over to Garry McDonald and Lawrence Stone, two Australian composers who deserve to be better known, and who acquitted themselves splendidly of the task at hand, with a score that was at times buoyant and energetic, and at other times reflective and quite romantic. The CD is an excellent representation of their effort.

Didier C. Deutsch

Thoroughly Modern Millie

1967, MCA Records, from the film *Thoroughly Modern Millie,* Universal Pictures, 1968 ♫♫♫♫

album notes: Orchestra: The Universal Studio Orchestra; **Conductor:** Andre Previn; **Cast:** Julie Andrews, Mary Tyler Moore, Carol Channing, James Fox, Beatrice Lillie, John Gavin.

The Jazz Age served as an eloquent backdrop for *Thoroughly Modern Millie,* starring Julie Andrews, Mary Tyler Moore, and Carol Channing as flappers in this affectionate sendup of the happy, crazy, fun days of the carefree 1920s. It merrily spoofs silent film techniques, and includes a breezy score consisting primarily of songs from the era. Directed by George Roy Hill, the film cast Andrews as a husband–hunting country girl and Moore as her friend, both residents at the Priscilla Hotel For Single Young Ladies—operated by an off–the–wall white slave trader (Bea Lilliez)— as they fight off the advances of a lively paper clip salesman. Carol Channing also appears as a rich "jazz baby" widow. Though it fails to capture the imagination the way *The Boy Friend* had done on stage, the film is amusingly entertaining and yielded a soundtrack album recording that is quite enjoyable.

Didier C. Deutsch

A Thousand Acres

1997, Varèse-Sarabande, from the film *A Thousand Acres,* Touchstone, 1997 ♫♫♫♫

album notes: Music: Richard Hartley; **Conductor:** Richard Hartley.

A weird screen transmogrification of *King Lear,* now set in the American Midwest, *A Thousand Acres* proved a magnificent vehicle for Jessica Lange and Michelle Pfeiffer as two sisters dealing with an authoritative, irrational father, and possible child molester. Giving substance to every nuance in this rural psychodrama, Richard Hartley created cues that inform and reveal, as much as they detail the action, in which the family divided eventually finds itself again, allowing the sisters, Rose and Ginny, to face an uncertain future with more certainty. Somber and lyrical most of the time, with long orchestral lines, occasionally supported by a lonely piano or an acoustic guitar, exploring the lovely themes created by the composer, the score easily stands out when played outside of its original environment. It creates an ominous atmosphere that has its charms and proves quite compelling at times.

Didier C. Deutsch

3 Days of the Condor

1988, EMI-Manhattan Records, from the film *3 Days of the Condor*, Paramount Pictures, 1975 🎬🎬🎬🎬

album notes: Music: Dave Grusin; **Conductor:** Dave Grusin.

A typically inventive score by Dave Grusin, *3 Days of the Condor* combines the fusion jazz accents that made Grusin's reputation, and strongly flavorful themes that detail this spy thriller about a CIA operative (Robert Redford, in a taut portrayal of a man on the run) whose associates have all been killed, and who eventually discovers that the massacre was ordered by a turncoat inside the agency. The cues devised by Grusin do not specifically attempt to underline the screen action, but provide a strong musical base that works well in and out of it. Two throwaway vocals and a routine version of "Silver Bells" are the only apparent weak spots in the otherwise solid series of cues.

Didier C. Deutsch

Three Fugitives

1989, Varèse Sarabande, from the film *Three Fugitives*, Touchstone Pictures, 1989 🎬🎬🎬

album notes: Music: David McHugh.

David McHugh's score for *Three Fugitives* is full of toe-tapping energy and tender innocence. It's a synthesizer-dominated score based on a single theme which is alternately given pop, rock, or jazz renditions. McHugh's synthesizer is clear, taking on orchestral qualities while backed by acoustic instruments like trumpet and piano. This is a score that's fun to listen to. It captures the sense of spirited fun and fellowship embodied in the movie, and carries that over into a soundtrack that is extremely pleasant. It's not as harsh or furious as a lot of rock-oriented soundtracks, nor as saccharine as many pop scores. It's light musical entertainment, and McHugh's score is certain to grow on you with repeated listenings. *Three Fugitives* is often exhilarating, happy, highly suitable for the film and extremely listenable on disk.

Randall D. Larson

Three Men and a Little Lady

1990, Hollywood Pictures, from the film *Three Men and a Little Lady*, Touchstone Pictures, 1990 🎬🎬🎬🎬

album notes: Music: James Newton Howard; **Conductor:** Marty Paich.

They Know the Score

Neal Hefti

All I did for the *Batman* TV show was the theme. It took me a lot of torn-up paper to finally come up with that simple little theme, but they finally used it, and it became a very big hit—not only as a piece of music, but as a phonograph record, etc.—and it's still being used in pictures, like it was . . . in *Wayne's World*. So, it gets a lot of usage. It was one of the most successful pieces I ever wrote, as far as having international appeal and a lot of uses, but it took me a long time to write it.

***Courtesy of* Film Score Monthly**

This sequel to the amusing *Three Men and a Baby,* itself a remake of the French comedy *Trois hommes et un couffin,* has overstayed its welcome and lacks the subtle essence that made the first film work so well, even though it is nothing more than the mere wisp of a slight comedy. In some ways, the score by James Newton Howard tries to evoke the winsome atmosphere that should have presided over this story about three bachelor hunks (Tom Selleck, Steve Guttenberg, and Ted Danson), all three sharing the same apartment and, amid their own busy agendas, suddenly saddled with caring for a little five-year old, the daughter of a friend with a pressing engagement. The cues are, for the most part, engaging and charmingly provocative, making this soundtrack album more interesting than the film that inspired it. The insipid pop selections, all too strident and aggressively obvious, are more annoying than awe-inspiring.

Didier C. Deutsch

The Three Musketeers

1990, Bay Cities, from the film *The Three Musketeers,* 1974 🎬🎬🎬🎬

album notes: Music: Michel Legrand; **Conductor:** Michel Legrand.

Michel Legrand has typically been more at home writing songs and pop/jazz scores like *The Umbrellas of Cherbourg* than serious film music, but this score for Richard Lester's sly, revisionist take on the famous Alexandre Dumas adventure is an exception. Legrand's throbbing, suspenseful scoring of the film's slow motion sword fight title sequence is striking, his adventuresome theme for the Musketeers a perfect fit, and he approaches the film's numerous, elaborately choreographed battles with great energy and zeal. His approach to the film's comic sequences involves some adept recreations of a kind of baroque/Renaissance style, and there's a glittering, harsh fanfare for Charlton Heston's Cardinal Richelieu. Legrand's Broadway sensibilities sometimes get the better of him. The otherwise thrilling fight cue "Dirty Business among the Dirty Laundry" climbs to such a giddy, showbiz-style conclusion you expect the combatants to burst into song, and he has an unfortunate tendency to interrupt the flow of action cues like "Bustling Buckingham" and the climactic battle to introduce some awful comedy effects. But if you can ignore those gaffes this is a genuine romp.

Jeff Bond

1993, Hollywood Records, from the film *The Three Musketeers*, Walt Disney Pictures, 1993 ♪♪♪

album notes: Music: Michael Kamen; **Orchestra:** The Greater Los Angeles All-Star Orchestra; **Conductor:** Michael Kamen; **Featured Musicians:** Vince De Rosa, French horn; Malcolm McNab, trumpet; Tommy Johnson, tuba; Paul Fried, flute; Ralph Grearson, harpsichord; Katie Kirkpatrick, harp; Phil Ayling, recorder; Emil Richards, percussion; Randy Kerber, harpsichord; Dan Greco, hammered dulcimer; Jon Clarke, oboe d'amour; David Riddles, bassoon; Bruce Dukov, violin; Tom Boy, cor Anglais.

A rousing and exciting, old-fashioned symphonic score from Michael Kamen, who successfully pays tribute to Korngold and the Errol Flynn adventure flicks in a more consistent, satisfying fashion than he did with his fun but uneven score for *Robin Hood: Prince of Thieves*. With full support from the Greater Los Angeles All-Star Orchestra, Kamen's music provides plenty of gusto to the action, with thrilling passages for orchestra and chorus punctuated by lyrical themes that translate well outside of the theatrical context for which they're composed. As usual for Kamen, there's also a stab at a pop song, the vacuous "All for Love," written with Bryan Adams and R.J. "Mutt" Lange, and performed by the once-in-a-lifetime trio of Adams, Sting, and Rod Stewart, who were presumably all compensated quite well for their vocal performance here.

Andy Dursin

Three O'Clock High

1987, Varèse Sarabande, from the film *Three O'Clock High*, Universal, 1987 ♪♪♪
album notes: Music: Tangerine Dream.

Somehow, one doesn't think of Tangerine Dream and comedies in the same vein, yet this mild, innovative story about a meek high school journalist and the bully he wants to interview, prompted the German trio to write a series of cues that are appealing in tone, with typical synth flourishes and melodic lines expanding on the light screen action. It's a flavorful effort, enhanced with additional cues provided by Sylvester Levay, and two solid rock tracks that make a similar favorable impression.

Didier C. Deutsch

Three Wishes

1995, Magnatone Records, from the film *Three Wishes*, Rysher Entertainment, 1995 ♪♪

album notes: Music: Cynthia Millar; **Conductor:** Cynthia Millar; **Featured Musicians:** Anthony Pleeth, cello; Richard Taylor, recorder.

Cynthia Millar has long been known as the virtuoso performer who plays the Ondes Martenot, an odd electronic instrument few have mastered, on many of Elmer Bernstein's scores over the last several years. So it's no wonder that portions of this score reflect Bernstein's influence with obviously similar motifs that can be clearly heard in the later part of "The Highway" and "Betty Jane Appears." Naturally, Millar uses the Ondes Martenot for "magical" effects instead of more contemporary electronic instruments. The score is agreeable, but the sequencing of the CD, which does nothing to hide the fact that it is just a collection of very short cues, yields a dull presentation that doesn't allow the music to create any tangible mood on its own.

David Hirsch

The Threepenny Opera

1954, Polydor Records, from the off–Broadway production *The Threepenny Opera*, 1954 ♪♪♪♪

album notes: Music: Kurt Weill; **Original Lyrics:** Bertolt Brecht; **English Adaptation:** Marc Blitzstein; **Musical Direction:** Samuel Matlowsky; **Cast:** Lotte Lenya, Scott Merrill, Martin Wolfson, Jo Sullivan, Charlotte Rae, Gerald Price, Beatrice Arthur.

For me, this is one of the greatest recordings of this truly landmark German musical. The off–Broadway revival of 1954 sparked a new interest in composer Kurt Weill, in particular his pre–Broadway German years, and led to revivals of his works from that era. While the English lyrics by Marc Blitzstein sanitized the original German of Bertolt Brecht, they are poetic and convey the dark and dangerous side of this musical set in the underworld of Queen Victoria's London. The cast is as fine as could be assembled in 1954 and perhaps as fine as any era could produce, and many of its performers went on to reach more public identification in other roles. However, this recording catches everyone at their early maturity. The exception is, of course, Lotte Lenya, and what an exception. During the time of this production and recording, she came to typify for many the jazz–laden age of 1920s Berlin. In this recording, she is a standout and unforgettable, singing her songs with a mixture of toughness, sadness, anger, bitterness, fierce joy and regret. There has never been another performer like her and probably never will.

Jerry J. Thomas

Threesome

🎬 1994, Epic Soundtrax, from the film *Threesome*, TriStar, 1994 ♪♪♪

One of the more rampant trends in soundtrack albums of the 1990s is the abundant use of cover tunes. This 1994 collection of music from a film about a bizarre collegiate love triangle features no less than four covers. Teenage Fanclub takes on Madonna's "Like a Virgin," while U2 does Patti Smith's "Dancing Barefoot." Jellyfish takes a stab at Queen's "You're My Best Friend," and General Public had a sizable hit with their new version of the Staple Singers classic "I'll Take You There." The rest of the album is a satisfying mix of alternative pop, and yes, does include the obvious choice of New Order's eighties hit "Bizarre Love Triangle."

Amy Rosen

Thunderball

🎬 1988, EMI-Manhattan Records, from the film *Thunderball*, United Artists, 1965 ♪♪♪♪

album notes: Music: John Barry; **Lyrics:** Don Black; **Conductor:** John Barry.

By most accounts, one of John Barry's most successful scores for the James Bond films, this is a total gas! The cues are sprightly tongue-in-cheek, even as they suggestively underscore the screen action, plainly justifying Barry's dismissive comment about this type of "Mickey Mouse music," but obviously fulfilling a need that no other composer has been able to match. All in all, a cheerful, bang-up job and a greatly entertaining album. The CD, incidentally, omits quite a few cues, allegedly composed by Barry after the album was released, ahead of the film. Some of the missing music can be found in the "30th Anniversary" collection, and includes the thrilling finale, worth alone the price of admission.

Didier C. Deutsch

Thunderheart

🎬 1992, Intrada Records, from the film *Thunderheart*, Tri-Star Pictures, 1992 ♪♪

album notes: Music: James Horner; **Conductor:** James Horner.

This fact-based film tells of a half-Native American FBI agent's search for a killer on an Ogala Sioux reservation. The film, notable for its attention to faithful tribal details, required composer James Horner to interpolate authentic vocals into his electronic score. However, the overall ambient nature of the music has produced an album that, while a curiosity since it's the most original thing Horner has done, is also a plodding collection of tones. Effective as a film score, perhaps, but terribly unsettling to listen to as a form of entertainment.

David Hirsch

Ticks/Fist of the North Star

🎬 1996, Intrada Records, from the movies *Ticks*, Republic Pictures, 1996, and *Fist of the North Star*, First Look Pictures, 1996 ♪♪♪

album notes: Music: Christopher Stone; **Conductor:** Christopher Stone.

Two diverse scores by Christopher Stone share this album. The first is *Fist of the North Star*, a stimulating orchestral work for a live-action adaption of a popular Japanese animated series. Filled with occasional heavy doses of percussion, the main title, "Desert Planet," sets the bombastic pace, while also conjuring up the deep emotions of the hero and his princess, who both share an ultimate destiny to save the Earth. On the "flip side," metaphorically speaking, is the creepy horror score to *Ticks*. Since the film's setting is an isolated mountain cabin, and the villains are a couple of hillbilly rednecks, Stone drops in a few bluegrass guitar motifs here and there. There's still lots of room for percussion as the title buggers scurry on by to chomp a bunch of teenagers.

David Hirsch

Till the Clouds Roll By

🎬 1992, Sony Music Special Products, from the film *Till the Clouds Roll By*, 1946 ♪♪♪♪

album notes: Music: Jerome Kern; **Lyrics:** Oscar Hammerstein II, Guy Bolton, P.G. Wodehouse, Otto Harbach, Edward Laska, Dorothy Fields, Jimmy McHugh, B.G. DeSylva; **Orchestra:** The MGM Studio Orchestra; **Choir:** The MGM Studio Chorus; **Conductor:** Lennie Hayton; **Cast:** Robert Walker, June Allyson, Lucille Bremer, Judy Garland, Kathryn Grayson, Van Heflin, Lena Horne, Angela Lansbury, Van Johnson, Tony Martin, Dinah Shore, Frank Sinatra, Virginia O'Brien.

One of several big screen biographies centering around some of the biggest names in Tin Pan Alley, *Till the Clouds Roll By* was mostly an excuse to parade MGM's roster of singing and dancing performers in a vast display of dazzling musical numbers, all more sensational and more grandiose than the ones preceding. The object of so much film affection this time around, is Jerome Kern, whose enormous influence on the musical theatre is undeniable, but whose highly romanticized screen story bears little resemblance to actual facts.

Lending, if not credibility, at least some excitement to the plot are the imaginative numbers, tailor–made for some of the studio's biggest stars, including Judy Garland (sensational in two numbers directed by Vincente Minnelli), Lena Horne, Kathryn Grayson, June Allyson, Tony Martin, and Dinah Shore. The film, though, reaches unfathomable levels of political incorrectness with Frank Sinatra, clad in a white tuxedo and perched atop a rotating column, singing a satinized version of "Ol' Man River" made even more ridiculous by its frequent use of colloquialisms that contrast with the lily–white setting the number has been given. In the soundtrack album recording, all that remains are the songs, and they're terrific.

Didier C. Deutsch

Time After Time

1987, Southern Cross Records, from the film *Time After Time,* Orion Pictures, 1979 🐕🐕🐕
album notes: **Music:** Miklos Rozsa; **Orchestra:** The Royal Philharmonic Orchestra; **Conductor:** Miklos Rozsa; *Featured Soloist:* Eric Parkin, piano.

"Score this movie exactly as you would have in 1944," is most likely what director Nicholas Meyer asked of Miklos Rozsa regarding this time travel adventure—and even if he didn't, that's exactly what Rozsa did. The old-fashioned symphonic score applied to a contemporary film serves this picture well. H.G. Wells (Malcolm McDowell) follows Jack the Ripper (David Warner) in a time machine to present-day San Francisco and protects a very modern woman (Mary Steenburgen). Rozsa's music casts a darkly romantic sheen over the whole film, an out-of-place, dignified European score for an out-of-place, dignified hero. Of all the Golden Age greats, not only was Rozsa one of the few still alive and working at the time, but he had one of the most distinct styles, one that changed very little over the years. *Time After Time,* a fine but peculiar film due to its mixture of genres, is enhanced by his unmistakable melodies and conviction.

Lukas Kendall

A Time of Destiny

1988, Virgin Movie Music, from the film *A Time of Destiny,* Columbia Pictures, 1988 🐕🐕🐕
album notes: Music: Ennio Morricone; **Conductor:** Ennio Morricone.

Much of Ennio Morricone's output in the late '80s (*Rampage, The Untouchables*) was of a strident, unmelodic strain. *A Time of Destiny* signaled a return to the more romantic sound which brought him popularity in the '60s and '70s. A love story set

during World War II, the score features Morricone's fondness for vocal writing and romantic orchestration. It is a gentle and subdued score for the most part, but there are a few violent moments, such as the slashingly atonal "The Storm" and the intense and raging choral writing in "Dies Irae-The Bell Tower," which effectively offset the gentler passages. Morricone's love theme is especially attractive, even rapturous, and displays the composer in his finest romantic mode. In all, this is a soundtrack album that holds together very well. While certainly not in league with Morricone's masterpiece, *The Mission, A Time of Destiny* remains a very good album with its share of enjoyable moments.

Paul Andrew MacLean

A Time to Kill

1996, Atlantic Records, from the film *A Time to Kill,* Warner Bros., 1996 🐕🐕🐕
album notes: **Music:** Elliot Goldenthal; **Conductor:** Jonathan Sheffer; **Featured Musicians:** Howard Levy, harmonica, penny whistle; Billy Drewes, saxophone; Bill Moersch, hammer dulcimer.

Elliot Goldenthal has created an evil southern motif ("Defile and Lament") for this film that really cries out to tell us that we're venturing into the darkest side of life, a world ready to explode like a nuclear bomb from racial tension. Even "Consolation," which starts out with such a heartfelt melody, degenerates into a grim oppressiveness. Goldenthal's harmonicas poignantly wail in utter sadness, his fiddles screech in alarm, and the souls of the dead frequently undulate to a pavane (slow dance) of misery. Two gospel pieces are included on the album to represent the lack of justice suffered by the southern black community. One such piece, "Take My Hand Precious Lord" is interpolated with Goldenthal's "Retribution" cue, yielding a powerfully grim effect. This one's gonna bring you down for sure.

David Hirsch

Timecop

1994, Varèse Sarabande, from the film *Timecop,* Universal Pictures, 1994 🐕🐕
album notes: Music: Mark Isham; **Conductor:** Ken Kugler; **Featured Musician:** Steve Tavaglione, saxophone.

Musician-composer Mark Isham has dabbled in numerous genres over the course of his eclectic filmography, some more successfully than others. *Timecop* finds Isham attempting a throbbing action film score, and despite a pleasantly lush love theme for saxophone (seemingly right up the composer's alley), the results are just sort of ho-hum. While the music, conducted and co-orchestrated by frequent Isham collaborator Ken Kugler, isn't as blatantly cobbled together as some pastiche action scores are, it also doesn't offer the kind of fresh twist on the material and ability to surprise that it could have, particularly considering Isham's credentials. The end result is an inoffensive but unremarkable soundtrack that is neither as clichéd nor as distinguished as some of its genre counterparts

Andy Dursin

Tin Cup

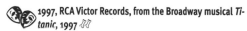 1996, Epic Soundtrax, from the film *Tin Cup*, Warner Bros., 1996 ♫♫♫♫

Introduced by the ingratiating strains of Texas Tornados' volatile rendition of "Little Bit Is Better than Nada," this soundtrack album is particularly enjoyable. One of the most endearing aspects of this minor film about a driving-range pro and golf hustler from West Texas whose legendary ball-striking skills are matched only by his self-destructive nature and lowlife charm (Kevin Costner in a solid *tour-de-force* performance), the diversified soundtrack offers top pop performances by such artists as Mary Chapin Carpenter, Chris Isaak, and George Jones. The album, a Grammy nominee, features these performances in their entirety, focusing on the talents involved, minus the sometimes intrusive screen sound effects and dialogues. A good, solid program of entertaining contemporary songs, with an attractive down-home country flavor.

Didier C. Deutsch

Titanic

1997, RCA Victor Records, from the Broadway musical *Titanic*, 1997 ♫♫

album notes: Music: Maury Yeston; **Lyrics:** Maury Yeston; **Musical Direction:** Kevin Stites; **Cast:** John Cunningham, David Costabile, John Bolton, Matthew Bennett , Brian d'Arcy James, Martin Moran, David Garrison, Michael Cerveris, Larry Keith, Alma Cuervo, Judith Blazer.

Bob Hope defined grand opera as a guy who gets stabbed in the back, "and instead of bleeding, he starts singing." The same definition could somewhat apply to this monstrous production which takes more than two hours to come to its inevitable, foregone conclusion. If at least the score were interesting, one might endure the ordeal, but with the exception of a couple of numbers that stand out, many of the songs, mercifully pruned down in this cast album recording, are not sufficiently catchy and compelling to keep the audience totally rapt.

Considering that the show, which opened April 23, 1997, won several Tony Awards, including best score and best musical, one might be tempted to question where have all the Broadway shows of yesteryear gone. Taking things progressively, *Titanic* is a musical account of the sinking of the famed luxury liner on her maiden voyage on April 10, 1912, with the action spread over five days, from the boarding of the ship to her actual sinking after she hit an iceberg (suggested on stage by an increasingly tilting set). In his book, Peter Stone attempts to create flesh and blood characters out of the doomed passengers, the ship's owner and her captain, more concerned about speed over safety, and her designer, eventually painfully aware of her fragile constitution. Matching the lugubrious tone of the theatrical event, Maury Yeston created a profuse score that starts on a splendid high note, only to let his wall-to-wall recitatives, musical bridges, arias, duets, trios, and quartets overwhelm the listener for their overall emptiness, and dour aura.

It's not that the score is bad. It's only that the songs can barely conceal the fact that these characters, well intended as they may be, have little to say to each other, before, during or after the collision that'll cost the ship its life. When, for instance, millionaire Isidor Straus, owner of Macy's, and his wife Ida face together their impending death ("Still"), one's only reaction is that a romantic duet seemed to be needed at this time, and Yeston wrote it. Throughout, one gets the same impression that the songs are included here simply because this is a "musical," and one must have a score in a musical. When one considers that Yeston dazzled Broadway with his adventurous first show, *Nine,* this new venture seems like a real let-down.

Didier C. Deutsch

Titanic/Back to Titanic

Titanic; 1997, Sony Classical, from the film *Titanic,* 20th Century-Fox/Paramount, 1997 ♫♫

album notes: Music: James Horner; **Conductor:** James Horner; **Featured Musicians:** Simon Franglen, Tony Hinnigan, James Horner, Randy Kerber, Eric Rigler, Ian Underwood.

The temptation is great to use superlatives when talking about this recording and its follow-up, *Back to Titanic,* but the truth is that no matter how many millions of copies the original soundtrack album sold, James Horner's score is somewhat of a letdown after all the hoopla. While perfectly suited to the screen action itself, on its own musical terms it fails to evoke the same sense of doom and anguish that permeated the film and just sounds merely adequate. It is all the more surprising that Horner has composed other scores in the past and since that have held their own once they were taken out of their initial environment. While the themes in this one prove mildly interesting, the ultimate impression left by this CD is of a composer trying to call attention to the fact that he has composed "the ultimate masterpiece." That is not the case, and while there are some merits to the score, Horner has done much better in

Leonardo Di Caprio and Kate Winslett in 1997's Titanic. **(The Kobal Collection)**

other occasions. Here, the mix of orchestral textures, synthesizers, and that horrendously hackneyed song by Celine Dion prove a bit too much after a while.

Didier C. Deutsch

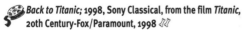 *Back to Titanic;* **1998, Sony Classical, from the film** *Titanic,* **20th Century-Fox/Paramount, 1998** 🐢🐢

album notes: Music: James Horner; **Orchestra:** The London Symphony Orchestra; **Conductor:** James Horner; **Featured Musicians:** Tommy Hayes, Tony Hinnigan, James Horner, Eileen Ivers, Zan McLeod, Eric Rigler, Ian Underwood; the Choristers of King's College, Cambridge.

James Cameron's three-hour-plus cinematic opus to the legendary ship of dreams contained enough music to probably fill three soundtrack albums, so it was no great surprise to see Sony Classics capitalize on the blockbuster success of the first *Titanic* soundtrack by releasing a sequel album. With a couple dozen songs in the movie by I Salanisti (as the ship's orchestra) and Gaelic Storm (as the steerage party band), this album could have been a delightful compilation of songs from the movie, a true soundtrack. Instead, the album consists as an uneven pastiche of score cues, too few songs, and a gratuitous suite of re-

recorded score music by Horner. Perhaps someday another album containing the remaining songs will be released, but this one is for Horner die-hards and *Titanic* fanatics only.

Amy Rosen

Titanic: Anatomy of a Disaster

1998, Centaur Records, from the Discovery Channel documentary *Titanic: Anatomy of a Disaster,* **1997** 🐢🐢🐢

album notes: Music: Michael Whalen, synclavier, synthesizers, EWI, piano, percussion, programming.

The revelatory soundtrack to a documentary on the site where the *Titanic* is resting, Michael Whalen wrote a bold musical essay that paints a broad canvas, with dramatic asperities designed to call attention to scenes of vital importance in the narrative. Occasionally stirring, but most often simply above the standards set by television for dramatic specials such as this, the score nonetheless impresses by the richness in its expression and in its invention. While the booklet credits the composer with performing the selections on the Synclavier, synthesizers, EWI, piano, percussion, and programming, it often sounds as if a full orchestra were backing him up. That, perhaps, is his greatest achievement in this effort.

Didier C. Deutsch

To Die For

1995, Varèse Sarabande, from the film *To Die For,* Columbia Pictures, 1995 🎬🎬🎬

album notes: Music: Danny Elfman; **Conductor:** Richard Stone; **Featured Musicians:** John Avila, bass; Warren Fitzgerald, guitar; Brooks Wackerman, drums.

Though only 19 minutes of Danny Elfman's score appears on this album, it's a solid presentation of the loony fantasy style he's become noted for on his various scores for director Tim Burton. The highlight is a manic vocal on "Suzy's Theme." In general, vocal effects play an important part in this score to create a bizarre ambience for Nicole Kidman's homicidal character. The CD is surprisingly top heavy with pop tunes for a Varèse-Sarabande release and features six songs by artists such as Billy Preston ("Nothing from Nothing"), Eric Carmen ("All By Myself"), and Donovan ("Season of the Witch").

David Hirsch

To Gillian on Her 37th Birthday

1996, Epic Soundtrax, from the film *To Gillian on Her 37th Birthday,* Triumph Films, 1996 🎬🎬🎬

album notes: Music: James Horner.

One of the great pleasures in collecting film scores is coming across a superb soundtrack for a movie that didn't make much noise in theaters, yet works as an album better than many scores for far more popular movies. The film *To Gillian on Her 37th Birthday,* an adaptation of an off-Broadway play by star Michelle Pfeiffer's husband, David E. Kelley, is not a great movie by any means, but it does offer a superb cast, pleasant Nantucket locations, attractive cinematography, and a poignant James Horner music score, dialed down several notches from the typically overwrought musical work that usually accompanies a movie like this. Horner's score is romantic and genteel, flowing calmly as underscore for the character-driven drama, and yet it still becomes highly emotional at times, with lush strings happily working with the action instead of saccharinely pounding you over the head with sappiness. It's a lovely score that's one of the most restrained and elegant works in Horner's career, along with one of the more underrated.

Andy Dursin

To Kill a Mockingbird

1991, Mainstream Records, from the movie *To Kill a Mockingbird,* 1962 🎬

album notes: Music: Elmer Bernstein; **Conductor:** Elmer Bernstein.

1998, Varèse-Sarabande, from the film *To Kill a Mockingbird,* 1964 🎬🎬🎬🎬

album notes: Music: Elmer Bernstein; **Orchestra:** The Philharmonia Orchestra; **Conductor:** Elmer Bernstein.

A series of delicately phrased cues that follow this imaginative tale of two youngsters coming of age in rural Alabama, and facing their responsibilities in an adult world, set against the backdrop of a criminal trial against a Black man accused of rape, *To Kill a Mockingbird* may well be one of Elmer Bernstein's most attractive scores. A marvel of understatement, at times warm and lyrical, at other times ominous and nightmarish, this impressionistic work skillfully moves between a lovely waltz, representative of the two kids' fantasy world, and the darker echoes of "Lynch Mob," which evoke the stark realities of the trial itself. In the film, that starred Gregory Peck as the lawyer defending the accused man, the score performs an important role, informing the action and detailing it, while keeping in focus all the diverging elements that combine to give the film its unique flavor.

When the film was initially released in 1964, it yielded a soundtrack album on Mainstream, that contained only a selected number of cues, and was eventually reissued on CD with additional selections that bore no relation with the film, the score, or Bernstein for that matter. Further marred by horrendous sonics, noticeable hiss, image shifting, uneven levels, flutter, distortion on some of the tracks, and analog dropouts, the CD was a disaster and a total disservice to the composer and his creation.

Fortunately for avid collectors and fans, Bernstein returned to the score in a bright, remarkable recording for Varèse, with the Royal Scottish National Orchestra doing a splendid job. Evidencing superb, resonant sonics, this recording is not only a definite improvement over the Mainstream release, it is the definitive version you might want to acquire. Brilliantly executed and masterfully recorded, it is a wonderful soundtrack that you'll enjoy playing frequently.

Didier C. Deutsch

To the Ends of the Earth

1988, Prometheus Records (Belgium), from the film *To the Ends of the Earth,* 1984 🎬🎬🎬

album notes: Music: John Scott; **Conductor:** John Scott.

This documentary film tells the story of The Transglobe Expedition–a team that circumnavigated the globe along its polar axis. As such, *To the Ends of the Earth* clearly called for music of epic proportions that depicts the adventurous spirit of exploration. After years as Jacques Cousteau's composer of choice, John Scott was well-versed in the kind of score needed for this production. His music, a surging, full orchestral score, is epic and soaring, evoking both the grandeur and terror inherent in the journey. Although working with a modest-sized orchestra, Scott nevertheless manages a large sound. Throughout, the music conjures the daunting scale of the expedition, and culminates in a finale of grand triumph. The sound of the recording is particularly fine (recorded at CTS Studios by engineer Dick Lewzey). Handsome packaging and informative notes (including a track-by-track description written by Scott himself) round-out this impressive release, which is typical of Prometheus's high standards.

Paul Andrew MacLean

To Wong Foo, Thanks for Everything, Julie Newmar

1995, MCA Records, from the film *To Wong Foo, Thanks for Everything, Julie Newmar,* Universal, 1995 ♪♪♪♡

This soundtrack is anything but a drag, though the individual songs work better when accompanying the visuals of Patrick Swayze, Wesley Snipes, and John Leguzamo sashaying around in their finery. Crystal Waters' "Who Taught You How" and Salt-N-Pepa's "I Am the Body Beautiful" hold their own, however, and hearing Tom Jones sings "She's a Lady" makes you smile even if you haven't seen the movie.

Gary Graff

Tom and Huck

1995, Walt Disney Records, from the film *Tom and Huck,* Buena Vista, 1995 ♪♪♪♪

album notes: Music: Stephen Endelman; **Conductor:** Stephen Endelman; **Featured Musicians:** Andy Stein, fiddle; Richard Sortomme, synthesizer.

Mark Twain's favorite imps ride once again in this new Disney screen adaptation, with Stephen Endelman providing the musical background framing and illustrating their various adventures. Evidently inspired by his subject, the composer delivers a score that blends traditional orchestral textures with bluegrass/folk instruments, the whole thing subtly underlined by synthesizer effects. The cues, many of them unfortunately too short with a playing time under two minutes, outline the most salient incidents in the narrative, and display as required some romantic lyricism, some playfulness, some suspense, some epic feel, and, generally speaking, a sense of fun. Overly effu-

sive and sketched in broad swaths of musical colors, the score is enormously lively and enjoyable.

Didier C. Deutsch

Tom and Jerry: The Movie

1992, MCA Records, from the animated feature *Tom and Jerry: The Movie,* Turner Entertainment, 1992 ♪♪♪♪

album notes: Music: Henry Mancini; **Lyrics:** Leslie Bricusse; **Conductor:** Henry Mancini; **Cast:** Richard Kind (Tom), Dana Hill (Jerry), Charlotte Rae (Aunt Figg), Tony Jay (Mr. Lickboot), Henry Gibson (Dr. Applecheek), Anndi McAfee (Robyn Starling), Rip Taylor (Captain Kiddie), Howard Morris (Squawk), Edmund Gilbert (Pugsy), David L. Lander (Frankie Da Flea), Raymond McLeod, Mitchel D. Moore, Scott Wojahn (the Alley Cats).

Once you have dealt with Stephanie Mills's inflected vocalizations on "All in How Much We Give," settle for a joy ride with Henry Mancini's mischievously delightful songs and score for this big-screen version involving the feuding animated duo created by Bill Hannah and Joe Barbera. Set off by bits of dialogue lifted from the soundtrack, the album follows the adventures of Tom the cat and Jerry the mouse as they momentarily abandon their constant chases and pranks on each other and do the impossible: try to get along in order to save the life of a young girl. Augmenting the many songs (with lyrics by Leslie Bricusse) are several nifty instrumentals ("I've Done It All," "Food Fight Polka," "Chase") which Mancini fans may recognize as clones from previous scores he wrote, but that demonstrate that his creative verve (or is it nerve?) always was at its peak, no matter what the situation.

Didier C. Deutsch

Tom and Viv

1994, Sony Classical, from the movie *Tom and Viv,* Miramax Films, 1994 ♪♪♪♡

album notes: Music: Debbie Wiseman; **Conductor:** Debbie Wiseman; **Featured Musician:** Andrew Bottrill, piano.

Alternately romantic and poignant, Debbie Wiseman musically chronicles the tragic life of socialite Vivienne Haigh-Wood and her marriage to poet Tom (T.S.) Eliot. The underscore is structured like a lush orchestral symphony, broken on occasion by period-styled pieces composed by Wiseman, and three source cues. Wiseman performs the piano solos on four tracks.

David Hirsch

Tombstone

1993, Intrada Records, from the film *Tombstone,* Hollywood Pictures, 1993 ♪♪♪♪

album notes: Music: Bruce Broughton; **Orchestra:** The Sinfonia of London, **Conductor:** David Snell.

Bruce Broughton met the challenge of improving on his popular *Silverado* score with this powerful, richly melodic western score that opens with a blasting, percussive action cue that will knock you out of your seat. The primary theme for Kurt Russell's Wyatt Earp isn't introduced until well into the score, but it's worth the wait. Broughton's Earp melody is a classic western theme, elaborate and instantly memorable, that functions perfectly both as a noble heroic characterization, as Earp makes his way into the town of Tombstone, and as a bristling statement of vigilante rage during the virtuoso, standout explosion of percussion and brass that underscores the film's take on the *Gunfight at the O.K. Corral*. Broughton achieves something out of Samuel Barber as he contrasts a romantic melody with a moving Americana theme as an elegy for the death of Earp's brother, while later sections of the score hammer home the brutal violence of Earp and Doc Holiday's pursuit of justice. This lengthy album is marred by a couple of interminable suspense cues, but overall this is an important, beautifully crafted effort that deserves its place next to *Silverado* as one of the best western scores ever written.

see also: Hour of the Gun, Wyatt Earp

Jeff Bond

Tommy

1993, RCA Victor, from the Broadway production *Tommy*, 1993 &&&&

album notes: Music: Pete Townshend; **Lyrics:** Pete Townshend, John Entwistle, Keith Moon; **Musical Direction:** Joseph Church; **Cast:** Michael Cerveris, Paul Kandel, Anthony Barrile, Cheryl Freeman, Marcia Mitzman, Jonathan Dokuchitz, Sherie Scott.

Already a theatrical concept in itself, even though it was first written as a studio recording, the rock musical *Tommy* made its belated Broadway debut on April 22, 1993, 24 years after it was originally created by The Who's Peter Townshend, John Entwistle, and Keith Moon. The story of a four-year-old boy who becomes mute after he witnesses his father kill his mother's lover, *Tommy* was one of the first full-scale rock operas to be created, in imitation of The Beatles' *Sgt. Peppers Lonely Hearts Club Band*, at a time when works of this scope were unheard of. In the ensuing years, however, it enjoyed vibrant, if restricted life as a concert piece performed by The Who, and as a camp 1975 film, remarkable for its cast which consisted of many famous rock 'n' roll and film stars, including The Who's Roger Daltrey as Tommy, Eric Clapton, Elton John, and Tina Turner, among the former, and Jack Nicholson, Oliver Reed, and Ann-Margret, among the latter.

Brilliantly staged by Des McAnuff, the Broadway version altered the perception of many in theatrical circles that rock and the stage were definitely not made for each other. The show

had a healthy run of 899 performances, and yielded the great cast album listed above, much more conventional than its raw-gut 1969 counterpart or the flashy film soundtrack, but properly flavorful and exciting in its own right.

Didier C. Deutsch

Tommy Boy

1995, Warner Bros. Records, from the film *Tommy Boy*, Paramount, 1995 &&

Brash and vulgar, *Tommy Boy (The Movie)* was a sophomoric essay designed as a vehicle for Chris Farley as an annoying nerd, forever causing havoc in David Spade's officious life. While the chemistry between the two comedians was clearly evident, and actually generated some amusing moments in the film, the loose direction and the basically inane plot marred an effort which could have been much more enjoyable. Adding some life of its own was the soundtrack, a snappy collection of lively rock tunes performed by alternative bands like Primal Scream, Goo Goo Dolls, Soul Coughing, and baby bands like Shaw-Blades, Seven Day Diary, and Dexys Midnight Runners. Bytes from the soundtrack set off the tunes, among which "Superstar," by the Carpenters, seemed like a breath of fresh air.

Didier C. Deutsch

Tomorrow Never Dies

1997, A&M Records, from the film *Tomorrow Never Dies*, United Artists, 1997 &&&&
album notes: Music: David Arnold; **Conductor:** Nicholas Dodo.

David Arnold, one of the most prolific contemporary action film composers, sounds like he had a blast on the sound stage and in the studio recording the music for *Tomorrow Never Dies*. Paying homage to classic James Bond scores, while creating a completely modern sounding orchestral score, Arnold delivers an exciting thrill ride. Also here are the title song performed by Sheryl Crow, a sexy new song by k.d. lang that evokes the great Bond ladies like Shirley Bassey, and a wild electronica Bond theme by Moby. In total, a very classy and vital soundtrack.

Amy Rosen

Top Gun

1998, Legacy Records, from the film *Top Gun*, Paramount, 1986 &&&&

A top-flight action drama set among naval fighter pilots, *Top Gun* was an exciting film, supported by solid performances, striking visuals, including great footage of war planes in action, and a high-voltage soundtrack consisting of first-rate pop and rock songs. Tom Cruise starred in the film as an individualistic ace pilot assigned to a prestigious training school, but aiming for a target of another kind, namely Kelly McGillis, who plays one of the teachers at the school. Much of the rapid-fire action, and particularly the thrilling airborne scenes, found a striking echo in the songs heard on the soundtrack and in this expanded CD reissue, which brings together some heavy talent, including Berlin whose rendition of "Take My Breath Away," the film's love theme, won an Oscar in 1987.

Didier C. Deutsch

Torch Song Trilogy

🎬 1989, Polydor, from the film *Torch Song Trilogy,* New Line Cinema, 1989 🎵🎵🎵

Harvey Fierstein, whose gravel voice is his most distinctive asset, played a Jewish mama boy in this hilarious comedy in which the central character, Arnold, a notorious drag queen, is forever hoping to find love and respect. In the three-part narrative, loosely adapted from Fierstein's play (for which he won a Tony Award), Arnold first picks up a good-looking bisexual guy who proves to be unfaithful, then is solicited by another good-looking kid, whom he doesn't trust, before dealing with an adopted teenager and his over-possessive mother, played by Anne Bancroft. The soundtrack album includes an entertaining collection of standards heard throughout the film, most often in abbreviated form, with Fierstein doing unexpected solo turns in "Svelte" and "Love for Sale," before joining co-stars Ken Page and Charles Pierce in a delightful sendup of Dubin and Warren's "Dames." Only, perhaps, for those in the know, but well worth its weight in feathers.

Didier C. Deutsch

Torn Curtain

🎬 1990, Varèse Sarabande, from the film *Torn Curtain,* Universal Pictures, 1966 🎵🎵

album notes: Music: John Addison; **Conductor:** John Addison.

🎬 1998, Varèse-Sarabande, from the film *Torn Curtain,* Universal, 1966 🎵🎵🎵🎵🎵

album notes: Music: Bernard Herrmann; **Orchestra:** The National Philharmonic Orchestra; **Conductor:** Joel McNeely.

When Alfred Hitchcock set out to film *Torn Curtain,* a cold war thriller set behind the Iron Curtain, he was instructed by film studio executives to provide a score that would be suitably commercial. Hitchcock knew Bernard Herrmann, his regular composer, would be reluctant to write such a score; nonetheless, the two discussed an approach that would satisfy them both, as well as the studio. But by the time Herrmann began recording his score, it became evident to Hitchcock that he had composed a brooding, hopeless music, exactly the opposite of

what was expected. Hitchcock fired Herrmann (the two men never spoke to each other again), and hired John Addison, who delivered exactly what the studio wanted: a characterless score, bland and unimaginative, though not without its charms, completely out of synch with the subject of the film, that went nowhere, and certainly did not generate the ancillary profits expected from the sales of a successful soundtrack album.

A taut drama, *Torn Curtain* starred Paul Newman as a U.S. nuclear scientist who pretends he has defected in order to obtain a secret Soviet anti-missile formula. When he is accused of murdering a Russian agent, he and his assistant and fiancee (Julie Andrews) try to return to the West, succeeding only after many close encounters with disasters. That Addison was out of his element with that kind of film is particularly evident in his "Love Theme," in which the lyrical beauty of the beginning stanzas fades into a mock comedy coda that belongs in neither a love theme nor the score for a thriller. At times too lush, at other times too strident, and occasionally too cute and too cheerful, this is clearly a case of the wrong score winding up in a film strictly for commercial reasons. The composer might not have been inspired by the film itself which, clumsy and drawn out, was not up to Hitchcock's usual standards either, lacking both the director's sense of observation and his sardonic humor.

Herrmann's unused score, newly recorded by Joel McNeely and the National Philharmonic Orchestra, is a totally different matter. With the perspective allowed by the ensuing years, one can really appreciate the vibrancy and crafty elements that make this score so vastly superior to Addison's tepid contribution, and how it would have perfectly suited Hitchcock's film. Appropriately dense, and scored for cellos, basses, and brass instruments, it comes across as a monochromatic effort that suitably reflected the hopeless atmosphere behind the Iron Curtain at the time. The sonics in this recording bring out the basic ingredients in the music and enhance them, in a vivid reading that's totally realistic and quite eloquent.

Didier C. Deutsch

Total Eclipse

🎬 1995, Sony Classical, from the film *Total Eclipse,* Fine Line Features, 1995 🎵🎵🎵

album notes: Music: Jan A.P. Kaczmarek; **Orchestras:** The Warsaw Symphony Orchestra, Orchestra of the Eighth Day, the Wilanow String Quartet; **Conductors:** Krzesimir Dębski, Tadeusz Karolak; **Featured Musicians:** Marta Boberska, soprano; Bogdan Liszka, oboe.

Trust Agnieszka Holland to make a film with total disregard for standard commercial considerations, and one dealing with the relationship between two of late 19th-century France's best known versificators. The film focuses on Arthur Rimbaud and Paul Verlaine, one the self-assured and arrogant young lion of poetry, the other an older, married man with doubts about his masculinity as well as his talent. Reflecting the many ambiguities and deep emotional conflicts between the two men, and their eventual falling off after Verlaine shot Rimbaud and spent two years in jail as a result, the score by Jan A.P. Kaczmarek is quite lyrical in spurts ("Naked on the Roof," "The Sun"), yet offset by several disturbing moments ("Knife," "Rimbaud Wounded"). One of Rimbaud's best known poem, "Le dormeur du val" ("Sleeper in the Glen") gets a lovely setting, as does "Le bateau ivre" ("The Drunken Boat"), by Verlaine. Two different sets of cues that recur ("Hashish" and "Cafe Bobino") specifically detail scenes in the film during which both men smoke and drink themselves into a stupor at one of their favorite Parisian hangouts. An intelligent score, filled with attractive melodies, that demands closer-than-usual attention from the listener, but proves quite rewarding as a result.

Didier C. Deutsch

Total Recall

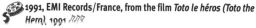1990, Varèse Sarabande, from the film *Total Recall*, Carolco Pictures, 1990 𝄞𝄞𝄞𝄞

album notes: Music: Jerry Goldsmith; **Orchestra:** The National Philharmonic Orchestra; **Conductor:** Jerry Goldsmith.

Jerry Goldsmith reached the pinnacle of his supercharged action style for Paul Verhoven's ingenious science-fiction vehicle for Arnold Schwarzennegger. The film's pulsating title music at first seems like a cross between Basil Poledouris's *Conan the Barbarian*, with its broad horn fanfare and a simplified version of Goldsmith's own *Capricorn One*. But Goldsmith uses the title music as a springboard for a score of amazing complexity and intensity, ranging from hammering, wildly propulsive action cues like "The Big Jump" and "Clever Girl" to dreamy, expansive sections of electronics and orchestra like "The Mutant." Everything climaxes in the lengthy (and largely unused) "The End of a Dream" cue, a relentless, crushing, snare drum-heavy orchestral charge that bears comparison to Goldsmith's brilliant retreat music from his classic *The Blue Max* score. The only criticism you can level at this album is that at around 40 minutes in length, it's too short—the film is full of even more amazing musical highlights that deserve preservation in album form.

Jeff Bond

Toto le héros

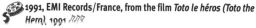1991, EMI Records/France, from the film *Toto le héros (Toto the Hero)*, 1991 𝄞𝄞𝄞

album notes: Music: Pierre van Dormael; **Orchestra:** The Orchestre symphonique de la RTBF; **Conductor:** Andre Vandernoot.

Since childhood, Thomas, nicknamed Toto, has been convinced that he was swapped at birth with Alfred, the rich kid next door. In his desire to be important, he started dreaming about an alternative lifestyle . . . as a secret agent. Later on, in adult life, he fell in love with a lovely young woman, only to see her marry his dreaded rival. Now, a dying old man, he sets out to reclaim the life Arthur has stolen from him . . . Based on this unlikely premise, *Toto le héros* became a surprise hit when it was released in 1991, spearheaded with Charles Trenet's 1939 hit song, "Boum." But while this soundtrack smartly evokes the film and its whimsical atmosphere, it fails to really grab the listener, most of the cues being much too brief to make an impression. This title may be out of print or just plain hard to find. Mail-order companies, used CD shops, or dealers of rare or import recordings will be your best bet.

Didier C. Deutsch

Touch

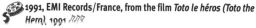1998, Capitol Records, from the film *Touch*, Lumiere International/United Artists, 1998 𝄞

album notes: Songs: David Grohl.

A misguided comedy that missed its target by a long shot, *Touch* had a lively cast and some creative scenes that never coalesced into anything really substantial. The story of a youthful healer who becomes the easy prey of both a greedy former preacher and a militant fundamentalist, it also was marred by a loud, unattractive rock score that wanted to bring the film into a more contemporary mold, but only partially succeeded. On the face of this soundtrack album, one can easily understand why: loud, and not particularly enjoyable, the songs and instrumental themes don't have much focus—"Bill Hill Theme" starts with a drum riff that goes nowhere, though it persists through the entire number, and almost drowns a vacant melody that plays behind it; "Richie Baker's Miracle" sounds as if it were unfinished; "Remission My Ass" is a variation on the same three notes, mercifully aborted after 39 seconds; and "Scene 6" sounds as if it had been written by a minimalist Philip Glass, happy to have the same vamp play over and over again for four and a half minutes. Evidently David Grohl, credited as the composer, has not much to say, musically.

Didier C. Deutsch

A Touch of Class

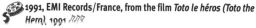1973, DRG Records, from the film *A Touch of Class*, Avco Embassy, 1973 𝄞𝄞𝄞𝄞

album notes: Music: John Cameron; **Songs:** Sammy Cahn, George Barrie.

Orson Welles and Charlton Heston in Touch of Evil. **(The Kobal Collection)**

This deliciously bubbly comedy, nearly forgotten today, belongs to a genre that existed in the 1960s, when the film was made, that was altogether fun and pleasantly enjoyable. A charming love story between two people (George Segal and Glenda Jackson) who accidentally meet in London, have a fling, take their romance to Spain and back to America, all the while trying to avoid his friends, in-laws, and wife, it yielded this Academy Award–nominated score by John Cameron, as heady and sparkling as the film itself, with light, delirious little musical comments that often prove convincingly irresistible. Like the scores for *What's New, Pussycat?* and *Promise Her Anything*, which it sometimes evokes, the music for *A Touch of Class* is easy on the ear and on the mind, and is winningly delightful.

Didier C. Deutsch

Touch of Evil

1993, Varèse Sarabande, from the film *Touch of Evil*, Universal Pictures, 1958 🎬🎬🎬🎬

album notes: Music: Henry Mancini; **Conductor:** Henry Mancini.

Throughout most of his career, Henry Mancini was so clearly identified with light comedies that one may tend to forget he also dwelled in other genres, notably contemporary crime dramas where he developed a recognizable signature style of strongly jazz-accented themes and tight rhythms. A brilliant, absorbing filmization of Whit Masterson's novel, *Badge of Evil*, directed by and starring Orson Welles, *Touch of Evil* gave Mancini the occasion to produce an outstanding score replete with explosive themes and catchy melodies, all of them detailing this sordid south-of-the-border story about a narcotics investigator (a mustachioed Charlton Heston) on his honeymoon in a small Mexican frontier town with new wife Janet Leigh, and the washed-out local captain of police (Welles), who team to nab a band of criminals suspected of involvement in a narcotics racket.

If the brooding, at times rambling plot that followed left some viewers somewhat baffled, there was no mistaking the masterful visual appeal of the film itself, with its fluid and impressive photography, subtly enhanced by Mancini's provocative score. Using a wide variety of genres (jazz, rock 'n' roll, honky-tonk) rather than a singly driven approach, Mancini devised cues that conferred a unique musical color to the film, by turns evoking the stifling atmosphere of the small Mexican town, the moods in some of the places where the action took place, and some of the characters in the story. The mono recording at times sounds dense and opaque, but the vibrancy and drama in the music still come through eloquently and convincingly.

Didier C. Deutsch

Touched by an Angel

1998, Columbia Records, from the television series *Touched by an Angel*, CBS, 1998 🎼🎼🎼

The popular CBS TV show yielded this inspirational soundtrack album in which some heavy-duty performers contribute songs that are bound to attract a large number of listeners. Where else, for instance, would you expect to find star Della Reese rubbing elbows with Celine Dion, Wynonna, Bob Dylan, Shawn Colvin, Keb' Mo', Faith Hill, and Amy Grant? The songs are generally of the uplifting kind, with positive thoughts reflecting the general tone of the series. It's harmless, entertaining, and certainly enjoyable.

Didier C. Deutsch

Tous les matins du monde

1991, Auvidis/France, from the film *Tous les matins du monde*, 1991 🎼🎼🎼🎼

album notes: Featured Musicians: Jordi Savall, bass viola; Charles Coin, bass viola; Jeanne Hantaï, bass viola; Pierre Hantaï, harpsichord; Roger Lislevand, theorbe.

An austere, uncompromising soundtrack, difficult to absorb, even for those who have seen the film, *Tous les matins du monde* features works by Sainte Colombe and Marin Marais, two composers who created music that was tremendously influential in their time, the former in the isolation of his home, away from the pleasures of the French capital, the latter in the footsteps of his friend and master, Jean-Baptiste Lully, the official musician at the court of Louis XIV. A couple of pieces by Lully and Francois Couperin enliven the proceedings, along with Marais's best known creation, the "Sonnerie de Ste Genevieve du Mont-de-Paris." But don't expect anything more than a staid, almost incredibly barren, yet ultimately richly rewarding score. The recording won the French "Grand Prix du Disque," the equivalent of the Grammy Award. This recording may be difficult to find. Check with a used CD store, mail-order company, or a dealer specializing in rare, out-of-print, or import recordings.

Didier C. Deutsch

A Town Like Alice

Southern Cross Records, from the Masterpiece Theatre series *A Town Like Alice*, 1981 🎼🎼🎼🎼

album notes: Music: Bruce Smeaton; **Orchestra:** The Australian Symphony Orchestra; **Conductor:** Bruce Smeaton.

A six-part dramatization of *The Legacy,* Nevil Shute's best-selling novel, *A Town Like Alice* centers around two prisoners of war whose romance begins during the Japanese invasion of Malaya in World War II and concludes in the vast Australian outback. The story inspired Bruce Smeaton to write a score that's filled with gorgeous melodies, attractive themes, and compelling cues. For the purpose of this CD (and presumably a soundtrack LP before that), they are strung together into two suites, probably fitting both sides of an LP, and are heard in little snippets that are not otherwise identified, making it difficult to follow the dramatic progression of the score in relation to the story.

Didier C. Deutsch

Toy Soldiers

1991, Intrada Records, from the film *Toy Soldiers,* Tri-Star Pictures, 1991 🎼🎼🎼

album notes: Music: Robert Folk; **Orchestra:** The Dublin Symphony Orchestra, **Conductor:** Robert Folk.

Even if you haven't seen the movie, this is one of those film scores you've probably heard a number of times. A coming attraction's staple for its use in countless movie trailers, Robert Folk's pleasing, rousing music from this surprisingly good teen action flick is infectious and highly melodic—something usually lacking in most action genre scores. With a sweeping main theme, Folk establishes a peaceful, tranquil musical background amid which bursts of sporadic action surprise us, yet even through the "busy" suspense cues, the composer maintains his tonal intentions. The result is a score that has become a favorite among soundtrack aficionados. One wishes that more genre scores would take the same symphonic route, though, alas, that is usually not the case.

Andy Dursin

Toy Story

1995, Walt Disney Records, from the film *Toy Story,* Walt Disney, 1995 🎼🎼🎼

album notes: Music: Randy Newman; **Conductor:** Randy Newman.

A bright and enthusiastic score by Randy Newman captures all the magic in this animated movie about a make-believe world where toys have a life of their own. Terrific songs are marred by the question, "Why do producers always let Randy Newman sing?" And partnered with Lyle Lovett (no less!) the two seem a

Toy Story *composer Randy Newman.* **(Archive Photos, Inc.)**

mismatched couple. There's no doubt Newman's a talented composer, but there are certainly better singers who can do his work justice.

David Hirsch

Toys

🎬 1992, Geffen Records, from the film *Toys*, 20th Century-Fox, 1992 ♪♪♪

album notes: Conductor: Shirley Walker.

This is a mostly instrumental soundtrack with a new age bent, hammered in by Enya's "Ebudae" and Tori Amos's "Happy Worker." Robin Williams and Joan Cusack join Thomas Dolby for the pleasantly wacky "Mirror Song," while Frankie Goes to Hollywood's "Welcome to the Pleasuredome" is a decent fit. And Robin Williams's "Battle Introduction" certainly gives the album a jolt of slightly bent comic juice.

Gary Graff

Trail of the Pink Panther

🎬 1988, EMI-Manhattan, from the film *Trail of the Pink Panther*, United Artists 1982 ♪

album notes: Music: Henry Mancini; Conductor; Henry Mancini.

The film, a lame attempt at perpetuating the myth of Inspector Clouseau following the death of actor Peter Sellers, was merely a compilation of scenes from the previous *Pink Panther* movies. As a result, the soundtrack is also a compendium of selections from the various scores Mancini composed for the previous movies, with only the title tune, "A Shot in the Dark" and the raucously joyous "Bier Fest Polka" making their first appearance on compact disc.

Didier C. Deutsch

The Trap

🎬 1993, Label X Records, from the film *The Trap*, 1966 ♪♪♪♪

album notes: Music: Ron Goodwin; Conductor: Ron Goodwin.

Broadly epic and elegiac, Ron Goodwin's score for *The Trap* seems at odds with this tale of a rugged fur trapper in 19th-century British Columbia, and the naive, mute girl he takes for his companion against her will, eventually winning her despite his rude manners and violent temper. Displaying strains of a neo-Romantic English folk idiom, Goodwin created cues that describe the majestic beauty of the unspoiled landscapes; the crude, earthy character of the trapper; the girl's winsome, frightened charm; and the constant struggle to survive in the wild, untamed environment. The composer's florid style at first surprises, as one would probably expect a score with a much

starker approach befitting the offbeat story and its harsh setting. But the elegiac, almost pastoral tone of some of the cues evokes the grandeur of the theme as well as the imposing setting against which the story unfolds. Eventually, Goodwin's view proves totally correct and right on target, in a score that provides many attractive melodic moments.

Didier C. Deutsch

Trapped in Paradise

🎬 1994, Varèse Sarabande, from the film *Trapped in Paradise*, 20th Century-Fox, 1994 ♪♪♪

album notes: Music: Robert Folk; Conductor: Robert Folk.

Nicolas Cage, Dana Carvey, and Jon Lovitz star in this 1994 Christmas comedy, a box-office dud despite good intentions all around. Robert Folk wrote one of his typically appealing scores for the picture, a warmhearted, Holiday-themed orchestral effort that sounds cobbled together from various sources—including, but not limited to, Danny Elfman's *The Nightmare Before Christmas* and even John Williams's *JFK*, which sounds like it had some kind of influence on Folk's similar-sounding main theme. Nevertheless, there are some good moments here and there, with lush strings and a few big crescendos commenting on the action in the best old-time Hollywood movie music tradition. The album also includes Bing Crosby's classic interpretation of "Do You Hear What I Hear?" and Dean Martin's crooning of "You're Nobody 'till Somebody Loves You."

Andy Dursin

Traveller

🎬 1997, Asylum Records, from the film *Traveller*, Banner Entertainment, 1997 ♪♪♪

Actor Bill Paxton had a hand in the song selection for his film about the dying breed of road gypsies. Appropriately, much of the music has the dusty flavor of the road. Country greats like Jimmie Dale Gillmore and k.d. lang intermingle with newer country and rock artists. Among the cover tunes here is a great new version of the classic "King of the Road" done by Randy Travis. This album would be a good pick for a cross-country trip on a wide, expansive interstate. Drive safe!

Amy Rosen

Trespass

🎬 1993, Sire Records, from the film *Trespass*, Universal Pictures, 1992 ♪

album notes: Music: Ry Cooder; Featured Musicians: Ry Cooder, guitars, floor slide, array imbira, keyboards; Jim Keltner, drums, percussion; Jon Hassell, trumpet; Nathan East, bass; David Lindley, fiddle; Van Dyke Parks, piano; Larry Taylor, upright bass.

Unlike many of his scores, which are deeply rooted in Americana or exude an appealing Southern flavor, Ry Cooder created an unsettling series of cues for this urban contemporary drama set in the ghetto of East St. Louis. The unrelenting dark visions it evokes (with distant guitar riffs darting in and out of brooding synth lines) may have been what this story about a hidden treasure and gang warfare called for. But taken on its own musical terms, the score fails to make much of an impression when it no longer serves as a complement to the explosive action, and its sonic effects, devoid of melodic content, soon prove tiring and aimless. The only track that actually makes a difference is "Party Lights," written and performed by Junior Brown, a solidly flavored country number. Unfortunately, it's not enough to recommend this album.

Didier C. Deutsch

The Trial

🎬 1993, Milan/BMG, from the film *The Trial*, BBC, 1992 ♪♪♪♪

album notes: Music: Carl Davis; **Conductor:** Carl Davis.

This second adaptation of Franz Kafka's most famous novel (the first, in 1962, was directed by Orson Welles and starred Anthony Perkins and Jeanne Moreau) again found Josef K. (Kyle MacLachlan) arrested on unspecified charges, then released, but increasingly forced to live with a question mark hovering over him and the notion that logic is no longer the norm in a seemingly illogical world. The score Carl Davis wrote for the film, florid and evidently influenced by the Czech setting of the story, receives a fond reading from the Czech Symphony Orchestra, with a profusion of themes in which a sardonic note frequently pops up, though just long enough to make itself noticed, and ominous accords presage the trauma that accompanies the main character's existence, in a masterful display of the composer's multi-layered style.

Didier C. Deutsch

Trial and Error

🎬 1997, High Street Records, from the film *Trial and Error*, New Line Cinema, 1997 ♪♪♪♫

An unlikely premise—an actor impersonates a friend of his, a corporate lawyer, when the legal eagle is too inebriated to attend an important trial—is at the core of this lightweight, inoffensive, and utterly charming comedy starring Michael Richards, on a sabbatical from his *Seinfeld* role, as the well-meaning but ultimately hapless impersonator forced to go on with the charade even after his friend wakes up from his booze-induced stupor, and Jeff Daniels as the lawyer who can't hold his liquor. The soundtrack retains a contemporary edge with a collection of songs that spotlight the Subdudes, the Fabulous

Thunderbirds, Dion, Taj Mahal, and Leon Redbone among other noticeable performers. Oscar Peterson brings an interestingly different touch with his rendition of the old Sammy Cahn-Gene DePaul classic, "Teach Me Tonight."

Didier C. Deutsch

The Trip

🎬 1996, Curb Records, from the film *The Trip*, American International Pictures, 1967 ♪♪♪

album notes: Songs: Mike Bloomfield; **Featured Musicians:** The Electric Flag: Mike Bloomfield, Buddy Miles, Harvey Brooks, Barry Goldberg, Nick Gravenites, Mark Doubleday, Peter Strazza, Paul Beaver, Bob Notkoff.

One of several films that attempted to reach the youth of the 1960s, *The Trip*, written by Jack Nicholson, starred Peter Fonda and Susan Strasberg as dispirited lovers on the verge of a breakup, which resulted in the former experimenting with LSD under the vigilant protection of Bruce Dern, and Dennis Hopper, as a hippie pusher. Punctuating the ensuing disconnected and sometimes explosive scenes that visually translated Fonda's visions under the influence, were solid rock songs featuring Mike Bloomfield, Buddy Miles, Harvey Brooks, Barry Goldberg, Nick Gravenites, Mark Doubleday, Peter Strazza, Paul Beaver, and Bob Notkoff, all members of the Electric Flag. The film was controversial in its day, but was positively received in South Cal culture, thus ensuring the success of the album, released at the time on a subsidiary label of industry giant Capitol. Today, though, when compared with the tremendous advances made by rock music, they sound a bit lame.

see also: The Wild Angels

Didier C. Deutsch

The Trip to Bountiful

🎬 1985, Plough Down Sillion Music, from the film *The Trip to Bountiful*, Island, 1985 ♪

album notes: Music: J.A.C. Redford; **Conductor:** J.A.C. Redford.

This short-playing CD would be great if only it featured more music. But one would be hard put to recommend it. Certainly the film—the story of a widow going back to her childhood home in Bountiful, Texas—deserved better, as did the composer, who is given a rather short shrift here.

Didier C. Deutsch

Triumph of Love

🎬 1998, Jay Records/U.K., from the Broadway musical *Triumph of Love*, 1998 ♪♪

album notes: Music: Jeffrey Stock; **Lyrics:** Susan Birkenhead; **Cast:** Susan Egan (Princess Leonide), F. Murray Abraham (Hermocrates),

Betty Buckley (Hesione), Christopher Sieber (Agis), Nancy Opel (Corine).

If it hadn't claimed to be based on *Le triomphe de l'amour,* the play by 18th-century French playwright Marivaux, *Triumph of Love* might have been judged on its own (limited) merits. But this insufferably brash and vulgar adaptation of what was originally frolicsome, lithe entertainment, belied everything that Marivaux had endeavored to achieve, particularly a suspension of credibility in what was, after all, a clear case of mistaken identity.

The inane plot—a forlorn Princess disguises herself as a young man, the better to seduce her "knight in shining armor," the nephew of a pair of old philosophical curmudgeons who want nothing to do with her in the first place or the foibles of the world in the second place—would have been far fetched by today's standards anyway. But one could evoke Stephen Sondheim's *A Little Night Music* as the kind of style that might have best suited a musicalization of such a story. Instead, Jeffrey Stock, and particularly Susan Birkenhead (who later on that same season had the audacity of rewriting some of Cole Porter's lyrics for *High Society*), went for the jugular in an adaptation that lost all the fragile, delicate balance of the original, and turned it into a vaudeville act.

Compounding this fatal miscue, pert Susan Egan (who had been such a ravishing Belle in *Beauty and the Beast*) found herself saddled with a wooden Prince rather than a handsome hero in the person of Christopher Sieber, who lacked both stage and sex appeal. Lost in this morass, Betty Buckley and F. Murray Abraham valiantly did their best as seasoned troopers, with Buckley at least enjoying a brief moment in the spotlight with "Serenity," a tune that will probably outlive this disaster. As the aggressive maid and accomplice of the Princess in her charade, Nancy Opel also had a couple of lively numbers. Not enough however to recommend this unjoyous cast album.

Didier C. Deutsch

Triumph of the Spirit

1989, Varèse Sarabande, from the film *Triumph of the Spirit,* Nova International Films, 1989 🎬🎬🎬

album notes: Music: Cliff Eidelman; **Orchestra:** The Unione Musicisti di Roma Orchestra and Choir; **Conductor:** Cliff Eidelman.

For this moving story of survival in a Nazi death camp, Cliff Eidelman has composed a sensitive score for orchestra and choir, drawing from both Hebrew and Catholic musical sources to build a powerful and emotive backdrop for this affecting motion picture. Comprised of mostly short pieces (0:33 at shortest to 6:53 at longest), the cues work together to form an extended suite. The music movingly dramatizes the sorrow and the dig-

nity of its struggling protagonist. While it underlines chaos and injustice, it remains full of hope and mirrors the character's will to survive. The score's mix of broad orchestral passages, delicate solo voice, and full choir (both operating and church music) captures the various feelings suggested or depicted in the film. On disc it makes for a compelling and moving musical experience.

Randall D. Larson

Tromeo & Juliet

1997, Oglio Records, from the film *Tromeo & Juliet,* Troma Team, 1997 🎬🎬🎬

With Troma Entertainment you can expect several things: lesbianism, sex, T&A, and lots of mutants. Their unique take on the Bard's classic features an equally unique songtrack. Singer Jane Jenson portrays Juliet and offers a song to this recording. Also featured are hard rock and alternative artists like Motorhead, Sublime, the Wesley Willis Fiasco, and Supernova. Snippets of dialogue are used to great effect to offset the songs; they are very funny, and very Troma, too. This makes for a fun, edgy CD.

Beth Krakower

Trouble in Mind

1986, Antilles Records, from the film *Trouble in Mind,* Alive Films, 1986 🎬🎬🎬🎬

album notes: Music: Mark Isham; **Featured Musicians:** The Raincity Industrial Art Ensemble: Mark Isham, trumpet, saxophone, electronics; Pee Wee Ellis, saxophone; Peter Maunu, guitar; Kurt Wortman, percussion.

Mixing electronics and acoustic brass instruments, this early score by Mark Isham is a classic of the genre; a thoroughly atmospheric set of cues, often dominated and punctuated by the sounds of a muted trumpet, that evoke the dark passions and oppressive moods in this out-of-time stylish tale of a cop caught between the mob and a love triangle. Starring Kris Kristofferson, Keith Carradine, and Lori Singer, the film is set in Raincity, a futuristic world with strange contemporary overtones. The hypnotic, sustaining moods in the film are splendidly caught in Isham's quietly understated music, with bluesy melodic themes creating an eerily nostalgic feel that's particularly gripping. Marianne Faithfull's vocals add extra flair to this sensational score.

Didier C. Deutsch

The Trouble with Girls

See: Live a Little, Love a Little/Charro!/The Trouble With Girls/Change of Habit

The Trouble with Harry

1998, Varèse Sarabande, from the film *The Trouble with Harry*, 1958 ♪♪♪♪

album notes: Music: Bernard Herrmann; **Orchestra:** The Royal Scottish National Orchestra; **Conductor:** Joel McNeely.

Joel McNeely, who seems to have made It his mandate to record all the important scores by Bernard Herrmann and who is supported in this goal by Robert Townson and Varèse Sarabande, must have had a great time with the sardonically rollicking score Herrmann wrote for Alfred Hitchcock's 1958 farce. Brimming with great moments, gloriously exhilarating accents, and a pervading tongue-in-cheek sense of fun, it brings to life a score that was only known through Herrmann's own suite, heard on another label. Made between the Riviera romp *To Catch a Thief* and the second version of *The Man Who Knew Too Much* (the thriller that yielded Doris Day singing "Que sera, sera"), *The Trouble with Harry* dealt with unfortunate Harry, a drifter, first clobbered by his ex-wife with a frying pan, then found dead in the woods after three shots have been heard. From that point on unraveled a sprightly farce with the poor slob being hastily buried and disinterred several times, and always reappearing when he shouldn't, at precisely the wrong time. Shot in the gorgeous natural locations of Vermont in the fall, the film introduced Shirley MacLaine as Harry's wife, convinced that she is the one who killed him in the first place, and co-starred Edmund Gwenn, whose stray bullets may also have done the deed. Keeping a tone close to the director's wry sense of humor, Herrmann delivered a score perfectly attuned to the zany action. The Royal Scottish National Orchestra, conducted by McNeely, plays it with evident relish.

see also: Bernard Herrmann in Composers

Didier C. Deutsch

True Grit

1992, Capitol Records, from the film *True Grit,* Paramount Pictures, 1969 ♪♪

album notes: Music: Elmer Bernstein; **Lyrics:** Don Black; **Conductor:** Elmer Bernstein.

It's almost jarring to associate the truly forgettable music from *True Grit* with the brilliant film composer Elmer Bernstein, but it was 1968, and both the Charles Portis novel and the resulting film, starring John Wayne and Kim Darby, about a wily U.S. Marshall who aids a young girl tracking down her father's killer, were hugely successful. Enlisting the hot, young country star Glen Campbell to sing the title song and make his acting debut in the film certainly guaranteed the success of the Capitol soundtrack album. Today, however, the soundtrack is a curiosity. While Bernstein's other works survive as precious examples of the lost art of film music composition, this particular score is easily dismissable as an interesting foray into the contemporary scene; to this ear, better left to those less gifted than the immeasurably talented Mr. Bernstein. The reissued CD is purely budget, containing a single slipsheet insert, with barely readable liner notes reproduced on the back of the jewel case.

see also: The Comancheros

Charles L. Granata

True Lies

1994, Epic Soundtrax, from the film *True Lies,* 20th Century-Fox, 1994 ♪♪

album notes: Music: Brad Fiedel; **Conductor:** Shirley Walker.

Director James Cameron seems to have an outsized vision of every aspect of filmmaking except for the music his movies require. Brad Fiedel's electronic score for Cameron's *The Terminator* was necessitated by budgetary restraints and fit in well with the movie's mechanistic theme, but Fiedel's work on the epic-scaled *Terminator 2* seemed hapless, and the application of yet another synthesized effort for this gigantic James Bond-type spoof is really hurtful to the power of the film. Fiedel's bright title music almost seems to suggest something Jerry Goldsmith might have done for Joe Dante during the *Gremlins/Explorers* period, and while the opening chase sequence and an even more elaborate pursuit on horseback in New York City receive an exciting, pulsating staccato treatment, more than a little of the effect is derived from Shirley Walker's excellent acoustic orchestrations. Much of the rest of the score fades away into synth pad oblivion. Maybe a takeoff of John Barry was too much to ask for here, but Fiedel's approach just doesn't satisfy.

Jeff Bond

True Romance

1993, Morgan Creek Records, from the film *True Romance,* Warner Bros., 1993 ♪

album notes: Music: Hans Zimmer.

Hans Zimmer's flavorful score (sampled through two very short tracks) is given less than its fair share in this album in which several undistinguished pop songs aim to evoke the fast-paced action in the film, about a couple on the run from the mob after they steal some drug money. Further confusing the listener, the celebrated duo from Leo Delibes's *Lakme* ("Viens Mallika sous le dome"), and a tired, expressionless rendition of "(Love Is) The Tender Trap," by Robert Palmer, suddenly pop up for no apparent (musical) reason. On the front inlay card, the album advertises its content as being "very cool music." Indeed!

Didier C. Deutsch

True Women

1998, Intrada Records, from the television special *True Women*, Hallmark, 1997 ♪♪♪♪

album notes: Music: Bruce Broughton; Conductor: Bruce Broughton.

A score bathed in the sounds of early rural America, *True Women* finds Bruce Broughton in fine form for this historically based story about pioneering Texan women, and the various situations they encounter when trying to colonize what is essentially barren territory. Melodically strong and gripping, expressively rich and expansive, but also quietly elegiac, the score, performed by the Sinfonia of London, teems with themes that are extremely rewarding musically. Written for a special Hallmark presentation, it reflects, in the words of the composer, "the emotional content" of its story: "immense passions, extreme actions, and the deep feelings of profound loss." In it, Broughton designed several themes for some of the main characters, the two sisters Sarah and Euphemia ("Phemie Joins Sarah"), the lovers Sarah and Bartlett ("Bartlett's Sonnet"), and the terrifying Indian warrior Tarantula ("Mattie Is Returned"), among others. Other themes cover crucial scenes in the action—"Night Raid," "The Barn Fire," "Harvesting Babies and Cotton,"— each with its own distinctive voice. Together, the themes form a solid, profoundly affecting series of cues that are attractively presented.

Didier C. Deutsch

The Truman Show

1998, Milan Records, from the film *The Truman Show*, Paramount, 1998 ♪♪♪♪

album notes: Music: Burkhard Dallwitz, Phillip Glass.

The score for this unusual film, about the world's largest television show and its unknowing participant Truman (Jim Carrey in what may be his finest performance), earned Burkhard Dallwitz and Phillip Glass a Golden Globe Award. What makes this so unusual is that a large amount of the score used for the show-within-a-show is actually material that Glass had previously composed for other projects. Director Peter Weir specifically chose this material as the type of music the director of the fictitious show (Ed Harris) would choose for this round-the-clock production. Glass also contributed two new tracks for the project. Dallwitz and Glass's tracks nicely complement each other stylistically, both in the movie and within the soundtrack.

Beth Krakower

They Know the Score

Mark Isham

It's an interesting problem when you try to improvise with a film score, because a composer is locked into what he's doing. It's extraordinarily rare that he can go to the picture editor and get 10 more seconds to fit his music in. You have to become more compositional using jazz for film. It's like being a director. You cast improvisers whose styles will give you the right emotional impact. Then you put them on the 'set,' which is the scoring stage. They're given the chord changes and the mood, so the musicians know that they've got to be smoking when the hero kisses the girl at bar five. Their playing becomes the compositional process. You just start the 'cameras' rolling, and go for a lot of takes. *Romeo Is Bleeding* is a perfect example of what I'm talking about, because all of it was improvised. That film was modern, almost futuristic, and I wanted its score to reflect that.

***Courtesy of** Film Score Monthly*

Trusting Beatrice/Cold Heaven

1992, Intrada Records, from the films *Trusting Beatrice*, Castle Hill, and *Cold Heaven*, 1992 ♪♪♪♪

album notes: Music: Stanley Myers; Orchestra: The Hungarian Radio and Television Orchestra; Conductor: Stanley Myers.

One of Britain's leading composers, Stanley Myers is best remembered for the classic "Cavatina" theme he composed for the film *The Deer Hunter*. This interesting CD focuses on two very different works, the score he wrote for *Trusting Beatrice*, a film written and directed by Cindy Lou Johnson, starring Irene Jacob and Mark Evan Jacobs, and released in 1992, and *Cold Heaven*. A slight comedy, *Trusting Beatrice* involves a landscape designer and the French woman he takes under his protection when he finds out she is homeless and without a green card. The cues for this one, loosely labelled "Ten Moods from Trusting Beatrice," pretty much outline the tension of each moment, with Myers seeking the right expression for a film essentially lacking a strong angle on which to do so. *Cold Heaven*, also released in 1992, is a thriller in which an unfaithful wife believes her husband, allegedly killed in an accident, is coming back to haunt her for her indiscretions. Reworked into a suite over 30 minutes in length, the score makes a much better impression, if only because the music has plenty of time to evolve and build itself into a climax. Inordinately lush and florid, the melodic themes abound and add considerably to one's overall appreciation of the music.

see also: Stanley Myers in Composers

Didier C. Deutsch

The Truth and the Light

See: The X-Files

Tu Ridi

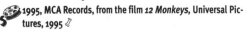1999, Pacific Time Records, from the film *You're Laughing,* 1998 𝄞𝄞𝄞𝄞

album notes: Music: Nicola Piovani; **Conductor:** Nicola Piovani; **Featured Musicians:** Francesca Taviani, cello; Massimo D'Agostino, percussion; Mauri Di Domenico, guitar.

Inspired by the writings of Luigi Pirandello, *Tu Ridi* is a collection of two often-poignant dramatic tales, "Felice" and "Two Kidnappings," that deal on their own unusually quizzical terms with violence. Set in Rome in the 1930s, the former tells the story of a former opera singer, unhappy with his life as an accountant, whose wife abandons him when she becomes convinced that his dreams, which leave him laughing hysterically, must involve some other woman. The second episode, set in modern day Sicily, concerns the kidnapping of an informer's son, and the parallel drawn with a similar situation that occurred 100 years before. Richly evocative, Nicola Piovani's score comments on both stories with a flurry of details that make each cue musically fulfilling. As an addendum to this release, the score to the film *Beyond the Garden*, an equally enjoyable series of cues, is offered as a bonus. This title may be out of print or just plain hard to find. Mail-order companies, used CD shops, or dealers of rare or import recordings will be your best bet.

Didier C. Deutsch

Tucker

1988, A&M Records, from the film *Tucker: The Man and His Dream*, Paramount, 1988 𝄞𝄞𝄞𝄞

album notes: Music: Joe Jackson; **Featured Musicians:** Paul Spong, trumpet; Raul D'Oliviera, trumpet; Pete Thomas, saxophones; Dave

Bitelli, saxophone, clarinet; Bill Charleson, saxophone, flute; Tony Coe, clarinet; Rick Taylor, trombone; Vinnie Zummo, guitar; Dave Green, bass; Gary Burke, drums; Frank Ricotti, percussion; Ed Roynesdal, synthesizers, violin; Arlette Fibon, Ondes Martenot; Joe Jackson, piano, synthesizers, percussion.

Joe Jackson composed an invigorating, jazz-filled up-tempo score for this acclaimed but little-seen George Lucas-Francis Ford Coppola production. Jackson dabbles in swing, jazz, and pop forms throughout the score, making the album full of fresh twists on familiar material—from standards like "Tiger Rag" to the jumpin' finale, "Rhythm Delivery," which finds Jackson performing vocals in an infectious, energetic big-band original song. The music was initially released on A&M but has been out of print for years, though its occasional re-issue as an import seems to confirm its continued popularity with die-hard listeners. A tremendously entertaining album, the soundtrack also features incidental jingle music composed by Carmine Coppola and boasts a wealth of standout ensemble performers.

Andy Dursin

Twelfth Night

1996, Silva Screen Records, from the film *Twelfth Night,* Fine Line Features, 1996 𝄞𝄞𝄞𝄞

album notes: Music: Shaun Davey; **Orchestra:** The Irish National Film Orchestra; **Conductor:** Fiachra Trench; **Featured Musicians:** Shaun Davey, organ; Linda Byrne, piano; Martin O'Connor, accordion; Des Moore, guitar; Noel Eccles, percussion.

This well-crafted orchestral score for Trevor Nunn's 1996 treatment of Shakespeare's play opens portentously with pulsing low string chords that underscore the film's opening shipwreck and an aggressive motif for "Orsino's Horsemen" before giving way to the lighter, energetic motives and textures of court intrigue, love, and mistaken identity that marks this as a high-spirited comedy. Like Patrick Doyle, Shaun Davey's background includes experience scoring for Shakespearean stage productions in Great Britain, and he brings some of the same melodic invention and emotional directness to his approach as does Doyle. Some of the songs warbled by cast members (including Ben Kingsley, not in very good voice as a troubadour) break up the flow of the orchestral pieces, but there's plenty of invention to make up for those lapses. The score is at its best in its shimmering, through-composed cues, and at its weakest during some comic mickey-mousing for the film's romantic intrigues.

Jeff Bond

12 Monkeys

1995, MCA Records, from the film *12 Monkeys,* Universal Pictures, 1995 𝄞

album notes: Music: Paul Buckmaster; **Featured Musicians:** Michael Davis, violin; Jack Emblow, bandoneon; **Conductor:** Paul Buckmaster.

The focal point of this score is an adaption of Astor Piazzolla's quirky little accordion track, "Introduccion," from the "Suite Punta Del Este." It became known as the "12 Monkeys Theme," possibly because it brings to mind the image of an organ grinder and his monkey standing on some European back street. This theme appears about six times, cut into Paul Buckmaster's vague and often spotty underscore. Most of the cues have the feel of transitional pieces, too short to develop into anything substantial and, just when you think you've grasped what he's getting at, in comes "Introduccion." Several songs, including Fats Domino's "Blueberry Hill" and "What a Wonderful World" by Louis Armstrong are intercut throughout the album. It's a Terry Gilliam film, so go figure what they're getting at.

David Hirsch

The 24-Hour Woman

1999, Shooting Gallery/WEA Records, from the film *The 24-Hour Woman*, Artisan, 1999 ♫♫♫

A slight, amusing comedy about a young mother trying to reconcile a busy career with her responsibilities toward her infant child, *The 24-Hour Woman* was primarily interesting for Rosie Perez's fetching performance as a harried producer for an early morning television show, whose life in New York City is turned upside down when news of her pregnancy is announced on the air and she finds herself the center of attention of the entire Latino population during sweeps week. The soundtrack, loaded with heavy-duty performances, is a delight, though some of the songs seem to be stretched a bit too padded. But "When You're a Woman," by Lisa Fischer with Masters at Work, "Nunca voy a olvidarte," by La India, and "Ms. Wonderful," by Chico DeBarge are quite engaging. Lightly done and with a Latin accent, it's a tasty soundtrack album.

Didier C. Deutsch

20,000 Leagues Under the Sea

1998, JOS Records, from the film *20,000 Leagues Under the Sea*, Hallmark Entertainment, 1996 ♫♫♫♫
album notes: Music: John Scott; Orchestra: The Philharmonia Orchestra; Conductor: John Scott.

1998, Prometheus/Belgium, from the television miniseries *20,000 Leagues Under the Sea*, ABC-TV, 1998 ♫♫♫
album notes: Music: Mark Snow; Conductor: The Utah Symphony Orchestra; Conductor: Mark Snow.

An interesting comparison between two composers, veteran John Scott and relative newcomer Mark Snow, and how they both reacted to essentially the same subject: a film version of Jules Verne's familiar tale about a renegade seafaring Captain, the nefarious Nemo, who uses a sophisticated submarine

called *Nautilus* to destroy liners and other boats. Scott's florid, impressionistic score is a marvelous musical expression of a story that has already inspired several filmmakers and composers. With epic accents to delineate the most vivid accounts of the saga, it is a beautiful, expansive work that harkens back to the golden days when film scores had strong melodies for each character, as well as solid musical themes to depict the action. The Philharmonia Orchestra sounds marvelous under the direction of the composer.

Also big and expansive, and performed by the Utah Studio Symphony Orchestra, Mark Snow's score for a miniseries seen on ABC-TV, with Michael Caine as a modern-looking Nemo, is unfortunately closer to what is considered film music in some circles today. Built around some poignant themes that almost demand to be expanded, the cues seem ill-constructed, abbreviated, and less focused than Scott's in his own score. This is not to take away from Snow's approach, inasmuch as he is in fact reflecting a style that has become all too pervasive in recent years. Typical of it, quiet orchestral lines rise to a crescendo when the screen action seems to require it, but more as a reflex to it than as an intelligent, solidly built series of themes that presage the action as much as they support it. Layers of flurries, backed by percussive effects, also give the phony impression of something vitally important happening, when in fact nothing in the music substantiates it. Occasionally, weird sound effects also punctuate the cues in a style that recalls some of Snow's efforts for other films. Still, this is certainly a vast improvement over his music for *The X-Files*, which, while quite successful in its own right, always gives the impression it is looking for a good melody.

Didier C. Deutsch

Twilight

1998, edel Records, from the film *Twilight*, Paramount, 1998 ♫♫
album notes: Music: Elmer Bernstein; Conductor: Elmer Bernstein.

In *Twilight*, Paul Newman starred as a man who does a favor for an old friend (Gene Hackman) and ends up involved in a murder investigation. Susan Sarandon also shared top billing as Hackman's wife and Newman's love interest. The movie was a throwback to the old-school mysteries, with the good-but-tough guy getting thrown into a case with unexpected twists and turns. Elmer Bernstein's score similarly has the feel of old movie music at times, with string melodies used to heighten the suspense. However, both the movie and the music lack a certain spark that could have really made them great. Still, it's hard to imagine Bernstein composing a truly horrible score, and while this one doesn't reinvent the genre, it's pleasant enough to listen to.

Beth Krakower

The Twilight Zone

1998, Silva America, from the television series *The Twilight Zone* 𝄞𝄞𝄞

album notes: Music: The Grateful Dead, Mel Saunders.

The selling point (and major factor) here is the presence of the Grateful Dead as purveyors of some of the music for this second spin-off of the famous series initially created by Rod Sterling. Rock fans will no doubt appreciate this vivid collection of tracks, made particularly important in the three suites that combine together several cues written for "Nightcrawlers," "Shadow Man," and "The Misfortune Cookie," three of the most graphic episodes in the series. Mel Saunders supplements the Dead's work with some fancy music that puts the spotlight more squarely on the eerie aspects of the series itself. While it will no doubt appeal to a limited audience, this CD should find a niche of its own among collectors.

Didier C. Deutsch

The Twilight Zone: Vols. 1 & 2

1985, Varèse Sarabande, from the CBS TV series *The Twilight Zone*, 1959—62 𝄞𝄞𝄞𝄞

album notes: Music: Marius Constant, Bernard Herrmann, Jerry Goldsmith, Leonard Rosenman, Fred Steiner, Nathan Van Cleave, Rene Garriguenc.

Few television series afforded the major film composers the opportunity to make meaningful contributions to the small-screen medium, and utilize their talent in a way that would equal their comparatively larger theatrical efforts. Rod Serling's *The Twilight Zone* was such a show, and its success is not only rooted in the superior quality of the storylines and visual production, but in Serling's careful choice of music as well. Among the noted composers that created original themes and long–form compositions for the program were Bernard Herrmann, Jerry Goldsmith, Leonard Rosenman, and Fred Steiner—all well represented on Varèse Sarabande's two–volume release.

Bewitching to any fan of the sci–fi classic will be the familiar opening and closing themes (by Marius Constant and Bernard Herrmann), 10 thematic scores for specific episodes ("The Passerby," "The Lonely," "I Sing the Body Electric," "Nervous Man in a Four Dollar Room," and "Walking Distance" among them), and two underscore jazz themes. Each melody is sure to stir vague feelings of recognition, that, like the show itself, will leave you asking "Haven't I heard this somewhere?"

Charles L. Granata

Twilight's Last Gleaming

1992, Silva Screen Records, from the film *Twilight's Last Gleaming*, Lorimar Pictures, 1977 𝄞𝄞𝄞𝄞

album notes: Music: Jerry Goldsmith; **Orchestra:** The Graunke Symphony Orchestra; **Conductor:** Jerry Goldsmith.

This suspenseful tale of political paranoia receives a quintessential '70s action score from Jerry Goldsmith, bristling with sharp-edged, harsh string textures, and militaristic effects for brass and percussion as U.S. armed forces attempt to deal with the takeover of a nuclear missile silo. With its gritty acoustic textures, hollow martial brass fanfares, and heavy, jagged action rhythms, *Twilight's Last Gleaming* lies somewhere between the European, quasi-chamber sound of *The Cassandra Crossing* and the driving brass lines of *Capricorn One*. The superb sound mix highlights every bizarre effect Goldsmith coaxes out of the orchestra, and the score's few humanistic moments, played out sensitively by low flutes and strings, make for a sharp contrast to the brutal, violent militaristic material.

Jeff Bond

Twin Peaks

1990, Warner Bros. Records, from the television series *Twin Peaks*, 1989 𝄞𝄞𝄞𝄞

album notes: Music: Angelo Badalamenti; **Featured Musicians:** Angelo Badalamenti, piano, synthesizers; Kinny Landrum, synthesizers; Vinnie Bell, electric guitars; Eddie Dixon, electric guitars; Al Regni, tenor sax, clarinet, flute; Eddie Daniels, flute, clarinet; Grady Tate, drums.

If you had to single out one soundtrack as being an "atmosphere score," Angelo Badalamenti's catchy music from the David Lynch series *Twin Peaks* would undoubtedly fit such a distinction. Lynch's program started off as a refreshingly different program for network TV, with bizarre plots, off–the–wall humor, quirky characters, and intense dramatic situations making for an enjoyable entertainment that drew critical praise and big audiences when it debuted in the Spring of 1990. Just as important to the show's success as the program's talented cast and offbeat tone was Badalamenti's brooding, deliberately paced musical accompaniment, which ranges from the memorable, electric guitar–performed theme song (also heard in a vocal version by Lynch favorite Julee Cruise) to cues that are alternately characterized by spacey, almost droning electronic music or even jazz–like in their most unconventional moments. Badalamenti defined the show's oddball approach through his music, and did his best to maintain the show's initial promise even as Lynch and co–creator Mark Frost decidedly lost their way when the program floundered during its second and final season on the air.

Andy Dursin

Twin Peaks: Fire Walk with Me

1992, Warner Bros. Records, from the film *Twin Peaks: Fire Walk with Me*, New Line Cinema, 1992 𝄞𝄞𝄞𝄞

album notes: Music: Angelo Badalamenti, David Lynch; **Lyrics:** David Lynch; **Featured Musicians:** Angelo Badalamenti, keyboards; Kinny Landrum, keyboards; Bill Mays, keyboards; David Slusser, keyboards; Andy Armer, keyboards; Ken-Ichi Shimazu, piano; Vinnie Bell, guitar; David Jaurequi, guitar; Myles Boisen, guitar; Bob Rose, guitar; Buster Williams, acoustic bass; Ron Carter, acoustic bass; Rufus Reid, acoustic bass; Don Falzone, bass; William Fairbanks, bass; Grady Tate, drums; Brian Kirk, drums; Steven Hodges, drums; Donald Bailey, drums; Jim Hynes, trumpet; Alvin Flythe Jr., saxophone; Jay Hoggard, vibes; David Cooper, vibes; David Lynch, percussion.

Without drawing on any of the principal themes he created for the original television series (except "Laura Palmer's Theme" and "Falling"), Angelo Badalamenti concocted another brew of wailing blues and jazz solos, mixed with cutting edge techno-rock rhythms. The difference between the film and TV series is that sexual tension more than any of the quirky suspects in a murder mystery provides the core motivation. The main theme is a somber and lazy trumpet solo; a gust of smoky heat to reintroduce us to Laura Palmer, the "good" girl with a rotting core whose untimely demise will launch the plot of the popular cult series. The album features four songs with really bizarre lyrics by director David Lynch, who also composed "The Pink Room" and "Best Friends" (the latter with David Slusser). Badalamenti performs (not be confused with singing) the songs "A Real Indication" and "Black Dog Runs at Night" (they call these lyrics?); and "Questions in a World of Blue" was taken from an album by Julee Cruise, "The Road House," chanteuse in the TV pilot film. Perfectly captures all the oddness of Lynch's film.

David Hirsch

Twister

1996, Atlantic Records, from the film *Twister,* Warner Bros., 1996 𝄞𝄞𝄞

album notes: Music: Mark Mancina; **Featured Musicians:** Trevor Rabin, guitar; Doug Smith, nylon guitar; Mike Fisher, percussion.

Mark Mancina scored *Speed* for director Jan DeBont, and with a resume that also includes music for the action films *Con-Air* and *Bad Boys,* it doesn't take a genius to figure out that Mancina is skilled in composing vibrant genre music that rarely ever holds back with emotion. The score for *Twister,* his second for DeBont, bursts forth with no-holds barred intensity, thanks to an aggressive main title theme that's one of the few hummable pieces of film music written in the last few years. Unlike his previous work on *Speed,* however, *Twister* is more reliant on the orchestra than it is on synthesizers, with full chorus added to some of the album's most powerful cues. It all makes for a solid and enjoyable soundtrack, though some listeners will want to skip past

the horrible cast duet "William Tell Overture/Oklahoma Medley," which doesn't segue out of Mancina's score nearly as well as Eddie & Alex Van Halen's guitarfest "Respect the Wind," heard here as a lengthy extension to the composer's end credits music.

Andy Dursin

1996, Warner Bros. Records, from the film *Twister,* Warner Bros., 1996 𝄞𝄞𝄞𝄞

Another one of those soundtracks that shoots wide in an effort to bring in the broadest audience. For hard rockers there's two songs from Van Halen, country fans have Shania Twain and Alison Krauss, classic rock fans will find Dire Straits' Mark Knopfler, and modern rockers will be swept up by an A-list that includes Soul Asylum, Tori Amos, the Red Hot Chili Peppers, Rusted Root, the Goo Goo Dolls, and Belly. Quietly, in the midst of all this, is a reunion of former Fleetwood Mac partners Stevie Nicks and Lindsey Buckingham on "Twisted."

Gary Graff

Two by Two

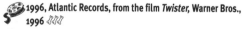 1992, Sony Broadway, from the Broadway production *Two by Two,* 1970 𝄞𝄞𝄞

album notes: Music: Richard Rodgers; **Lyrics:** Martin Charnin; **Musical Direction:** Jay Blackton; **Cast:** Danny Kaye, Harry Goz, Joan Copeland, Madeline Kahn, Michael Karm, Walter Willison, Tricia O'Neil, Marilyn Cooper.

Clifford Odets's amusing recounting of the Flood, "The Flowering Peach," became the basis for *Two by Two,* by Richard Rodgers and Martin Charnin, in which Danny Kaye made a belated comeback to Broadway as Noah, the Biblical patriarch chosen by the Almighty to build an ark and save two specimens of the Earth's fauna before the rains come. For Kaye, who had enjoyed considerable success on the screen as one of Hollywood's most gifted comedians but who had not set foot on a stage since 1942 when he first appeared in *Up in Arms,* the routine weekly performance schedule soon became unbearable, and he took advantage of his star status to turn the musical into a personal showcase, much to the delight of audiences.

Rodgers, however, was not amused, but as long as the show was making money, there was little he could do about it, and *Two by Two* enjoyed a run of 343 performances, despite the fact that Kaye eventually had to play his part in a wheelchair after he sprained his ankle.

To be truthful about it, the musical itself was not really that exciting, and its score, with the exception of the title tune and the lovely "I Didn't Know a Day I Didn't Love You," did not live up to the standards once set by Richard Rodgers.

Didier C. Deutsch

Two for the Road

🎬 1998, RCA/Spain, from the film _Two for the Road,_ 20th Century-Fox 🎬🎬🎬🎬

album notes: Music: Henry Mancini; Conductor: Henry Mancini.

Were it not for wonderful Henry Mancini, whose score for _Two for the Road_ has just been reissued in Spain by the BMG affiliate there, the world would certainly be more miserable. Mancini had a knack for writing scores that were lightly sprinkled with attractive melodies, and his scores always brimmed with delightful moments that often remained etched in our subconscious long after we had forgotten the films for which they had been created. This bittersweet story of a married couple (Audrey Hepburn and Albert Finney) who make the same trip by car from London to the French Riviera at three separate periods in their lives, elicited a wonderful romantic score, lined with moments of nostalgia, humor, and pathos, all combining to create a whimsical musical journey.

Didier C. Deutsch

200 Cigarettes

🎬 1999, Mercury Records, from the film _200 Cigarettes,_ Paramount, 1999 🎬🎬🎬

Pull out your black-and-white checkerboard sneakers and skinny tie for this one. The soundtrack to this 1999 film set on New Year's Eve in 1981 is basically a Rhino Records-type eighties compilation of classic new wave cuts. This is not necessarily a bad thing, in fact there are some real gems here amidst the usual suspects (the Go-Gos, Bow Wow Wow, the Cars), such as Nick Lowe's "Cruel to Be Kind," Roxy Music's "More than This," and the classic Dire Straits opus "Romeo and Juliet." There's also a new cover by Harvey Danger of "Save It for Later" by the English Beat and a trio of Blondie songs.

Amy Rosen

Two If by Sea

🎬 1996, TVT Records, from the film _Two If by Sea,_ Warner Bros., 1996 🎬🎬🎬

Despite the presence in the cast of Sandra Bullock and Denis Leary when he was hot, this stinker of a movie couldn't be saved. The album is another matter. Alannah Myles had a moderate hit with "You Love Who You Love." Shane MacGowan and the Popes with Sinead O'Connor, Belinda Carlisle, and Colin James are among the others featured on this song-driven compilation, which also includes four tracks not heard in the movie. It makes for an enjoyable adult contemporary-leaning soundtrack.

Beth Krakower

Two Moon Junction

🎬 1988, Varèse Sarabande, from the film _Two Moon Junction,_ Lorimar Pictures, 1988 🎬🎬🎬

album notes: Music: Jonathan Elias; Featured Musicians: Jonathan Elias, keyboards; Sherman Foote, keyboards, programming; Mark Egan, fretless bass; Ray Foote, guitar.

This moody and evocative ambient score mists along like slowly rising steam or heavy, sluggish storm clouds, laying a rhythmic backdrop of ambient tonalities and building, interpolating chords that are both relaxing and sometimes invigorating. A recurring synthesized pan-flute motif provides a pleasing texture in the midst of Jonathan Elias's singing guitars, delicate keyboard notes, and electronic tones that emerge, and merge, and evaporate. It's somewhat in the vogue of new age synth/acoustic albums and, like some of them, Elias's music runs the risk of becoming monotonous or redundant through underdevelopment, but the composer develops his rhythms, textures, and chord progressions effectively. Rather than submerging into the sluggish mire of uncertain orchestration, they ride an orchestral sea with purpose, slicing through and around and under and over the tonal waves of richly swelling electronic formations.

Randall Larson

Two of a Kind

🎬 1998, MCA Records, from the film _Two of a Kind,_ 20th Century-Fox, 1983 woof!

album notes: Music: David Foster.

The first screen pairing of Olivia Newton John and John Travolta led to one of the all-time classics, _Grease._ Trying to capitalize on the evident chemistry between them, the two were reunited for _Two of a Kind,_ instantly proving that on-screen chemistry cannot substitute for a good script. The soundtrack album fares just as poorly. It features four Newton John tracks, one of which is a duet with Travolta, and songs by Journey, Boz Scaggs, and Chicago.

Beth Krakower

2001

🎬 1993, Varèse Sarabande, from the film _2001: A Space Odyssey,_ MGM, 1968 🎬🎬🎬🎬

album notes: Music: Alex North; Orchestra: The National Philharmonic Orchestra, Conductor: Jerry Goldsmith.

Alex North's rejected score for Stanley Kubrick's 1968 space epic has long been one of the great mysteries of film music—a work heard by only a select few until composer Jerry Goldsmith and Varèse Sarabande's Robert Townson

Keir Dullea in 2001: A Space Odyssey. **(The Kobal Collection)**

assembled this remarkable recording, with Goldsmith conducting the National Philharmonic Orchestra and resurrecting North's music from the ashes. It's a powerful work, brimming with mysticism, brutal primitiveness, and delicate, ethereal beauty. North wrote his own take on Strauss's "Also Sprach Zarathustra," an expansive orchestral fanfare for Kubrick's opening conjunction of planets. Much of the score is taken up with the grinding, violent dissonance of the "Dawn of Man" sequence, with brass and woodwinds growling in tribalistic fury as primitive apes battle over food and water. The famous "Blue Danube" space station sequence is scored with a brilliant, sprightly scherzando after Mendelssohn, while two other space sequences receive delicate, haunting arrangements for strings, harp, and vocal soprano. North's work only went as far as a strident Entr'acte for the film's intermission before he was relieved of his duties, but given the power of the music the composer produced for the first half of this unforgettable film, you have to shiver a little at the thought of what North might have come up with for later scenes on the *Discovery* spacecraft or for the film's completely abstract "Stargate" sequence. Clearly Kubrick's vision for the film was less conventional than North's modernistic music, but his original score for *2001* still stands on its own as a masterpiece of film composition.

Jeff Bond

2001: A Space Odyssey

1996, Rhino Records, from the film *2001: A Space Odyssey*, MGM, 1968 ♪♪

album notes: Music: Johann Strauss, Richard Strauss, Gyorgy Ligeti.

The ultimate music trip, if not necessarily the ultimate soundtrack. While the choice of crisp, disembodied classical selections (albeit from the Romantic and Modern eras) might have seemed odd at first, it perfectly suited the extraordinary space epic and no doubt attracted a lot of moviegoers (and potheads) to the values of serious instrumental music. However, as a pure audio experience, it sounds relatively arid.

Didier C. Deutsch

U-Turn

1998, Epic Soundtrax, from the film *U-Turn*, TriStar, 1998 ♪♪♪

album notes: Music: Ennio Morricone; **Orchestra:** The Accademia Musicale Italiana; **Conductor:** Ennio Morricone.

Ennio Morricone's eerie score—a series of themes in which ominous bass lines and discordant accords perfectly suggest the tension in this drama about a gambler on the run drawn into a murderous plot—is at times unsettling and not always easy to get into. But the cues evoke the claustrophobic atmosphere of the isolated little town and the surrounding desert that together serve as a backdrop to this Oliver Stone drama, as well as the dilemma facing the central character caught in an intrigue that seems inescapable. The western aura is well captured in the collection of songs by artists like Johnny Cash, Patsy Cline, and Sammi Smith, with Peggy Lee's "It's a Good Day" adding a note of irony to the proceedings.

Didier C. Deutsch

Ulee's Gold

1998, Rykodisc, from the film *Ulee's Gold,* Orion Pictures, 1998 ♪♪♪♪

album notes: Music: Charles Engstrom; **Conductor:** Sonny Kompanek; **Featured Musicians:** Bruce Barth, piano; John Beal, bass; Paula Bing, flute; Richard Locker, cello; Emily Mitchell, harp.

Composer Charles Engstrom created a wonderful musical backdrop to this gem of a movie, which features Peter Fonda in the best role of his career. A beekeeper raising his grandchildren while his son is in prison, Fonda's very ordered life turns chaotic when he agrees to help out his daughter-in-law, only to have problems with his son's former partners in crime. Simply orchestrated for strings, piano, harp, and flute, the score enhances the story on the screen, but on its own creates images that are equally compelling and attractive. It only goes to prove that sometimes simplicity works wonders.

Didier C. Deutsch

Ulysses

1992, Legend Records/Italy, from the film *Ulysses,* Lux, 1954 ♪♪♪♪

album notes: Music: Alessandro Cicognini; **Conductor:** Franco Ferrara.

Kirk Douglas had another memorable screen role as Ulysses in this 1954 saga based on the writings of Homer. Imaginatively conceived, and smartly directed by Mario Camerini, this big production retraced the voyages of Ulysses on his way home after the Trojan war, his encounters with various dangerous foes—the siren Circe, an awesome storm, the one-eyed Cyclops—and his temporary loss of memory, all of which delays his return to Ithaca and his faithful wife Penelope. Providing added weight to the most epic aspects of this lusty adventure yarn, Alessandro Cicognini wrote a solidly imaginative and profuse score that is both descriptive of the action and joyfully listenable on its own. It comes fully alive in this recording, only marred by its primitive mono sonics, and technical flaws (surface noises, distortions, dropouts). This recording may be difficult to find. Check with a used CD store, mail-order company, or a dealer specializing in rare, out-of-print, or import recordings.

Didier C. Deutsch

The Umbrellas of Cherbourg

See: Les parapluies de Cherbourg

Una questione d'onore

See: A Ciascuno il Suo/Una questione d'onore

Una ragione per vivere e una per morire

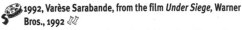1994, GDM Point Records/Italy, from the film *Una ragione per vivere e una per morire (Massacre at Fort Holman),* 1972 ♪♪♪
album notes: Music: Riz Ortolani; **Conductor:** Riz Ortolani.

James Coburn and Telly Savalas starred in this spaghetti western, directed by Tonino Valerii and enlivened by a score signed by Riz Ortolani. Set during the Civil War, this was *The Dirty Dozen* redux, with Union Colonel Coburn picking up a ragtag group of prisoners, all specialists, to reclaim a fort under the command of mad Conferedate Major Savalas. Unusually dark for a western score, Ortolani's music displays a lot of brooding orchestral accents, with an occasional lively cue ("La festa," "Mexican Waltz") to provide a lighter counterpoint. Unfortunately, this is not one of the composer's most striking achievements. This title may be out of print or just plain hard to find. Mail-order companies, used CD shops, or dealers of rare or import recordings will be your best bet.

Didier C. Deutsch

Under Siege

1992, Varèse Sarabande, from the film *Under Siege,* Warner Bros., 1992 ♪♪
album notes: Music: Gary Chang; **Conductor:** Gary Chang; **Featured Musicians:** Billy Ward, drums; Kurt Taylor, guitars.

An action film score for orchestra, synthesizers, and percussion, Gary Chang's *Under Siege* is so unexciting that it amounts to little else but window dressing. Many of the cues are dark, ominous efforts that try to evoke an atmosphere of tension, with lots of percussion over vague synthesizer effects that may have been useful in the film, but are not too terribly engaging on the CD. The orchestra occasionally kicks in, but even its contribution is so subdued and low-key that it adds little to the overall texture. It's not a very interesting score.

Didier C. Deutsch

Under Siege 2: Dark Territory

1995, Varèse Sarabande, from the film *Under Siege 2: Dark Territory*; Warner Bros., 1995 ♪♪♪

album notes: Music: Basil Poledouris; **Conductor:** Basil Poledouris.

A likeable enough Basil Poledouris entry which has its moments ("Intruder Discovered"), but suffers from a lack of strong thematic content. It is also surprisingly derivative at times of his other work. You can clearly hear portions of *RoboCop* in the main title, for example. Poledouris seems to have found it awfully hard to get a handle on this film, but when was a Steven Seagal movie ever deep? Either he thought he was fighting a losing battle against the noise levels of gunfire and explosions, or hearing Seagal's vocal on "After the Train Has Gone" just demoralized him into a catatonic state.

David Hirsch

The Underneath

1995, Varèse Sarabande, from the film *The Underneath*, Universal Pictures, 1995 ♪♪♪

album notes: Music: Cliff Martinez.

A hybrid tale about a robbery with deep psychological and philosophical undertones, *The Underneath,* a remake of the 1949 film noir *Criss Cross,* sported a disturbingly hypnotic score, signed by Cliff Martinez, which superbly sustained the moods in Steven Soderbergh's suspense melodrama. The various cues, dense and deliberately taken at a slow pace, manage to evoke the same cerebral moods, austere and uncompromising, yet wonderfully atmospheric, though amateurs of melodic material will have to look elsewhere. Unfortunately, some shrieking rock numbers that are not too terribly enjoyable throw the album in overdrive, though "The Happy Herman Polka," a fast instrumental guitar tune, proves quite ingratiating.

Didier C. Deutsch

Unforgiven

1992, Varèse Sarabande, from the film *Unforgiven*, Warner Bros., 1992 ♪♪♪

album notes: Music: Lennie Niehaus; **Featured Musician:** Laurindo Almeida, guitars.

Lennie Niehaus performed double-duty for Clint Eastwood for many years, having orchestrated many of Jerry Fielding's Eastwood scores and ghostwritten (often extensively) cues for the composer during the 1970s. When Niehaus was given the chance to contribute music for Eastwood's pictures himself, the results were low-key scores that often contained themes based on material composed by Eastwood himself. *Unforgiven* is one of those cases, with the poignant "Claudia's Theme" (written by the actor-director) contributing the heart of the music here. Performed on solo guitar before being gently developed into a fully orchestral arrangement, the theme represents a reflective look back at the Old West. Like the movie, the music is more meditative and subtle than your typical western score, but is certainly no less effective or enjoyable because of that.

Andy Dursin

Universal Soldier

1992, Varèse-Sarabande, from the film *Universal Soldier*, Carolco, 1992 ♪♪

album notes: Music: Christopher Franke; **Orchestra:** The Berlin Symphonic Film Orchestra; **Conductor:** Brynmor Jones.

Starring Jean-Claude Van Damme and Dolph Lindgren as clones of GIs killed in action in Vietnam, and Ally Walker as a nosy reporter who discovers a secret government project to create an army of robot soldiers, *Universal Soldier* is a thrilling futuristic actioner with lots of scenes that have a good punch to them around a story that holds together rather well. Possibly the only flaw in it is Christopher Franke's score, a combination of orchestral peaks and vales over synthesized effects that might have been a potent brew behind the screen action, but which makes very little musical sense when removed from it. Unfortunately, indicative of the trite imagination that goes into creating these action scores, these sonic effects amount to very little and do not really inspire repeated listening.

Didier C. Deutsch

Unlawful Entry

1992, Intrada Records, from the film *Unlawful Entry*, 20th Century Fox, 1992 ♪♪♪

album notes: Music: James Horner; **Conductor:** James Horner; **Featured Musicians:** Mike Fisher, Ralph Grierson, James Horner, Judd Miller, Ian Underwood.

An uneven James Horner score which starts out with an appealing theme and then quickly descends into harsh and atonal synthesizer dissonance. A sensual saxophone theme is worked into a romantic melody for synthesizer over piano. The music becomes a pleasant theme for the couple while retaining a slight edge of foreboding and discomfort, suggesting the terrors they will encounter. The theme is, by turns, happy and pretty and then frightening, and the cue ends ominously with the heartbeat-like faint percussion beats. The bulk of the CD is comprised of horror music: harsh cacophonies of low-end piano and strings, horrifying tonal music, and dissonant atonal passages. Machine music, appropriately heartless, yet difficult to listen to apart from its visual counterparts. There are some interesting moments but on the whole the CD is too uneven and too imbedded with atonal electronics and disturbing cacophonies to make for a satisfying listen.

Randall D. Larson

The Unsinkable Molly Brown

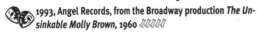 1993, Angel Records, from the Broadway production *The Unsinkable Molly Brown*, 1960 🎵🎵🎵🎵🎵

album notes: Music: Meredith Willson; **Lyrics:** Meredith Willson; **Musical Direction:** Herbert Greene; **Cast:** Tammy Grimes, Harve Presnell, Mitchell Gregg.

1990, CBS Special Products, from the film *The Unsinkable Molly Brown*, MGM, 1964 🎵🎵🎵

album notes: Music: Meredith Willson; **Lyrics:** Meredith Willson; **Orchestra:** The MGM Studio Orchestra; **Choir:** The MGM Studio Chorus; **Conductor:** Robert Armbruster; **Cast:** Debbie Reynolds, Harve Presnell, Ed Begley, Brendan Dillon, Jack Kruschen, Hermione Baddeley, Martita Hunt.

Following his 1958 Broadway musical, *The Music Man*, Meredith Willson hit paydirt again with another period work, *The Unsinkable Molly Brown*, which also gave Tammy Grimes one of her most memorable roles on Broadway. Based at the turn of the century, the show recalled the saga of the real–life Molly Brown, who rose from utter poverty in the Colorado silver mines to a life of wealth and leisure after marrying a lucky prospector, before becoming the darling of the European elite, and surviving the sinking of the "Titanic," in an incredible streak of good luck and personal heroism.

In much the same way he had breathed great life in the score for his first show, Willson created for *Molly Brown* songs that were deeply rooted in Americana, with energetic marches ("Belly Up to the Bar," "I Ain't Down Yet"), lovely romantic tunes ("I'll Never Say No," "If I Knew"), and lively ensemble numbers ("Beautiful People of Denver"). Dominating the stage was Tammy Grimes, sensational as Molly, in a performance that

won her a Tony Award that year. The show, which opened Nov. 3, 1960, had a run of 532 performances.

In 1964, it became a rambunctious film, with Debbie Reynolds starring as Molly opposite Harve Presnell, reprising his stage role as Johnny Brown. But with only five songs from the original score kept in the film, and an over–the–top performance by Reynolds that was coarse and less endearing, the screen version is a pale, uninteresting representation.

Didier C. Deutsch

Unstrung Heroes

1995, Hollywood Records, from the film *Unstrung Heroes*, Hollywood Pictures, 1995 🎵🎵🎵

album notes: Music: Thomas Newman; **Featured Musicians:** Michael Fisher, vibraphone, jaw harp, vibratone; Rock Cox, zither, hurdy gurdy, bowed bass dulcimer; Thomas Newman, picnic, piano, psaltery; George Doering, guitars, strums; Bill Bernstein, zither, Indian banjo, door; Steve Kujala, flutes, recorders; Chas Smith, pedal steel guitars; Randy Kerber, sustains.

A delicate, offbeat tale of a 12-year-old coming of age in 1962 Los Angeles, *Unstrung Heroes*, directed by Diane Keaton, elicited an odd, somewhat out-of-synch score by Thomas Newman, with pseudo-Oriental effects that seemed to clash with the film and its unusual premise. Focusing, as it did, on a kid who leaves his dysfunctional middle-class home to live with two eccentric uncles in a rundown hotel, the story needed a score that matched the conflicting moods in the development, while giving an expression to the kid's frail emotions. Only occasionally does Newman fill the demands imposed on him ("Trace Harm"), relying most often on selections that are admittedly attractive and quite enjoyable on their own musical terms, but that seem to have been written for another, totally different film.

Didier C. Deutsch

Untamed Heart

1993, Varèse Sarabande, from the film *Untamed Heart*, MGM, 1993 🎵🎵🎵

album notes: Music: Cliff Eidelman; **Conductor:** Cliff Eidelman.

Romantic symphonic love poem for two unlikely suitors, a waitress (Marisa Tomei) who can't seem to pick the right man, and a quiet, mysterious busboy (Christian Slater) with a heart ailment. Cliff Eidelman gives this poignant story everything he can muster. The bulk of the album is framed by gentle horns and a soft piano melody, but two pieces, the bouncy "Hockey Game" and the nightmarish "Stabbed," offer some variety. The album includes "End Credits" and another cue that were not used in the final film.

David Hirsch

Until September/Star Crash

1990, Silva Screen Records, from the films *Until September,* MGM/Pathe, 1984, and *Star Crash,* Columbia Pictures/AIP, 1978 ♪♪♪

album notes: Music: John Barry; Conductor: John Barry.

This was the first of two odd pairings of John Barry scores on Silva Screen (the other was the Bruce Lee action film *Game of Death* and Roger Vadim's sex romp *Night Games*) kind of a yin and yang experience. *Until September* presents Barry at some of his romantic best. Lush string arrangements abound and, most surprisingly, he doesn't sink the score through his overuse of the main theme (that is, by Barry standards). *Star Crash,* however, proves that even Barry can make poor creative choices. Space Opera has never provided him with his best source of inspiration. The score itself is passable enough (considering the god-awful film for which it was written), but the decision to use a synthesized drum machine on the main theme was equally bad in 1979 when the music was recorded. By today's standards, it's positively laughable, bordering on self-parody. Luckily, the rest of the score doesn't have this or similar effects, and it boasts some pretty good themes ("Launch Adrift" and the eerie "The Ice Planet," for example).

David Hirsch

Until the End of the World

1998, Warner Bros. Records, from the film, *Until the End of the World,* 1991 ♪♪♪♪

album notes: Music: Graeme Revell; Conductor: Graeme Revell; Featured Musician: David Darling, cello.

Director Wim Wenders treats music as an important cast element of his films rather than as a creative adjunct, and the results usually work as well on disc as they do on the screen. This album draws from the modern rock realm (circa late '80s and early '90s, before Nirvana redefined the genre) and includes U2's "Until the End of the World"—'natch—as part of an assemblage that draws from new and previously released material. Its a fine mix, bringing together Talking Heads' "Sax and Violins" with Lou Reed's "What's Good," R.E.M.'s "Fretless," Elvis Costello's "Days," Can's "Last Night Sleep," Depeche Mode's "Death's Door," and "It Takes Time" by Patti and Fred Smith. Nick Cave and the Bad Seeds' "(I'll Love You) Till the End of the World" is an appropriate inclusion, while evocative creations from Julee Cruise ("Summer Kisses, Winter Tears"), Daniel Lanois ("Sleeping in the Devil's Bed"), and Jane Siberry and k.d. lang ("Calling All Angels") bring some additional heft to a carefully, and brilliantly, executed selection of songs.

Gary Graff

The Untouchables

1987, A&M Records, from the film *The Untouchables,* Paramount Pictures, 1987 ♪♪♪♪

album notes: Music: Ennio Morricone; Conductor: Ennio Morricone.

A beautifully lyrical score, nominated for an Oscar, *The Untouchables* found Ennio Morricone at the peak of his creative powers, in a set of cues that evoke the feel of this crime drama about Eliot Ness and his band of "untouchables," and the mobsters they relentlessly pursue at the height of the Prohibition era. Brilliantly directed by Brian De Palma, *The Untouchables*— starring Kevin Costner as Ness, Robert De Niro as Al Capone, and Sean Connery, in one of his finest screen performances as a cop whose knowledge of the street proves invaluable to Ness— ranks among the top crime dramas ever filmed. It inspired Morricone to write a top-notch, very appealing score, rife with epic accents and lyrical themes that mix and mingle in a gorgeous musical canvas that's often explicit and descriptive of the multi-layered action. Laid out in terms that are frequently strikingly melodic, the score reveals many attractive themes ("Ness and His Family," "Four Friends," "Machine Gun Lullaby"—the latter a wonderful Tinkerbell-like melody overpowered by strident, ominous off-key overtones) that strengthen its appeal. In fact, the only drawback here is the fact that the cues are oddly presented out of sequence (with the recording kicking off with the "End Title," and the "Main Title" lost somewhere in the middle), necessitating some reprogramming if you wish to listen to the score as it was initially conceived and heard on the screen.

Didier C. Deutsch

Up Close and Personal

1996, Hollywood Records, from the film *Up Close and Personal,* Touchstone Pictures, 1996 ♪♪

album notes: Music: Thomas Newman.

Though at times a surprisingly melodic effort for Thomas Newman, it's unfortunately also rather unremarkable. There are a few gentle romantic themes like "A Week Eight Days" for the flowering romance between rising news reporter Michelle Pfeiffer and her producer Robert Redford. The tense drama of the news stories though still affords Newman with the opportunity to create some of his typical wild arrangements for cues such as "Uprise." But the general mood of the album is so low key with its abundance of minor emotional cues, that it all passes by before you've realized it. The CD, incidentally, does not feature Celine Dion's hit song for the film, "Because You Loved Me," which is a pity because it really could have used the infusion of some energy.

David Hirsch

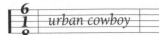
Urban Cowboy

1980, Full Moon/Elektra Records, from the film *Urban Cowboy,* Paramount Pictures, 1980 𝄞𝄞𝄞

The soundtrack that sealed country's portal for nearly a decade, mostly because of its anything goes view of the genre. There are, in fact, some very good tracks by rock artists such as Bob Seger ("Nine Tonight"), Joe Walsh ("All Night Long") and Bonnie Raitt ("Darlin'"). But it also offers a fairly narrow view of country, pushing the Charlie Daniels Band and Mickey Gilley when the film could have taken a much broader survey of the form. After all, you can ride a mechanical bronco to just about anything, can't you?

Gary Graff

Urban Legend

1998, Milan/BMG, from the film *Urban Legend,* TriStar, 1998 𝄞𝄞

album notes: Music: Christopher Young; **Conductor:** Pete Anthony.

Christopher Young's effectively scary score gets to be heard in two long cues in this CD which also includes various songs of dubious merits. Created for a horror film in the same league as *I Know What You Did Last Summer,* the score supports the eerie aura in the film and gives it a substance that is most convincing. As a purely audio experience, however, it fails to ignite in the same manner, and can be dismissed. The songs, with the exception of Ohio Players' "Love Rollercoaster," are equally uninspiring and add very little to one's appreciation of this CD.

Didier C. Deutsch

U.S. Marshals

1998, Varèse-Sarabande, from the film *U.S. Marshals,* Warner Bros., 1998 𝄞𝄞𝄞

album notes: Music: Jerry Goldsmith; **Conductor:** Jerry Goldsmith.

While he was perfectly cast as Harrison Ford's relentless pursuer in *The Fugitive,* the otherwise excellent Tommy Lee Jones doesn't seem sufficiently comfortable with his role as chief deputy marshal Sam Gerard in *U.S. Marshals.* In the film, Gerard goes after Wesley Snipes, who is accused of killing two of his agents in a New York City parking lot. Snipes doesn't exhibit the charisma of Ford in the earlier film, resulting in a thriller that is not really... well, thrilling. The action doesn't seem to have inspired Jerry Goldsmith, either, and while he created a score that's thoroughly professional in its approach and highly listenable, the cues miss the extra element that would have turned a routine job into a gripping musical statement.

Didier C. Deutsch

Used People

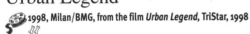1992, Giant Records, from the film *Used People,* 20th Century Fox, 1992 𝄞𝄞𝄞𝄞

album notes: Music: Rachel Portman; **Conductor:** David Snell.

A tearjerker with a '50s sensibility, *Used People* found in Rachel Portman the apt composer to deliver a score overflowing with broadly effusive romantic motifs that match this tale, set in New York in 1969, about a widow romanced by an admirer of 23 years on the day of her husband's funeral, who finds herself responding with renewed eagerness to this suitor she had rejected because of their different ethnic backgrounds. At times jocularly humorous, most frequently touchingly lyrical, Portman's music gives greater weight to the film's moods, with beautifully stated themes that are consistently appealing and enjoyable. The somewhat unnecessary inclusion of "The Sky Fell Down," performed by Frank Sinatra with Tommy Dorsey and his orchestra, interrupts the unity of the score and seems like a throwaway track.

Didier C. Deutsch

The Usual Suspects

1995, Milan Records, from the film *The Usual Suspects,* Poly-Gram, 1995 𝄞𝄞𝄞

album notes: Music: John Ottman; **Conductor:** Larry Groupe.

Bryan Singer touched a raw nerve with this unusual (and unusually well written) film noir about a burning tanker in the San Pedro harbor, a whole collection of bodies, a $91 million heist, some crooks, a mysterious character named Keyser Soze, and the customs agent trying to unravel the whole thing. Masterly put together, with a sense of suspense that never lets go until the very last scene, the film benefits from a taut, exciting score from John Ottman that adds a flavor of its own to the action, and helps sustain its special atmosphere. Moody and unexpectedly elegiac at times, it is surprisingly capped by a simple piano version of Claude Debussy's "Les sons et les parfums tournent dans l'air du soir (Sounds and perfumes whirl in the evening air)."

Didier C. Deutsch

The Utilizer

1995, Intrada Records, from the television series *The Utilizer,* 1995 𝄞𝄞𝄞

album notes: Music: Dennis McCarthy.

A splendid jazz-influenced score by *Star Trek Generations* composer Dennis McCarthy for the Sci-Fi Channel cable movie concerning a wish-granting machine that comes with a terrible price. Based on the short story "Something for Nothing," the main theme has a nice laid back feel, it's solo trumpet providing just the right amount of pathos for the central character and his sterile, boring life. As he quickly gets in over his head, the music becomes darker with McCarthy drawing on some of the more non–melodic sound designs he frequently used to great effect on the mid–1980s alien invasion series *V*.

David Hirsch

Utu

 1993, Label X Records, from the film *Utu*, 1983 ♪♪♪♪

album notes: Music: John Charles; **Orchestra:** The New Zealand Symphony Orchestra; **Conductor:** William Southgate.

A striking adventure film about the struggle between the European settlers and native Maoris in late 19th-century New Zealand, *Utu* was an exceptional entry at the Cannes Film Festival with audiences warming to this tale of passion and revenge ("utu" in Maori), in many ways reminiscent of an old-fashioned American western. When British soldiers protecting newly arrived colonialists plunder and ravage his native village, rebel leader Te Wheke, once sympathetic to the white cause, turns guerrilla and, in a spiraling web of violence, retaliates in kind. John Charles's informed score gives the action extra impetus, with powerful orchestral accents that define the British presence in alien territory ("Williamson Retaliates"), while the addition of traditional Maori chants provides the proper ethnic coloring.

Didier C. Deutsch

V

The Vagrant

1992, Intrada Records, from the film *The Vagrant*, MGM/Pathe, 1992 ♪♪♪

album notes: Music: Christopher Young; **Conductor:** Christopher Young.

Christopher Young's penchant for musique concrete really goes to town in this bizarre and uncategorical psychological horror score. The music is wacky and strange, quirky yet impossible, kind of a hybrid *Honey, I Blew Up The Kid* meets *Hellraiser*. Young mixes a minor-melodied music box theme with vocal tonalities, jazzy acoustic bass, plenty of percussion and a large array of foreign ethnic instruments. The result is nothing you've ever heard before. Both immediately likeable and inconceivably strange, the music is refreshing in its creativity. Once again, Young experiments with new and strange musical combinations and matches that bizarre sensibility with an unorthodox collection of musical

colors. He effectively captures the unique personality of the film—which turns out to be not far distant from his own musical personality. *The Vagrant* may not appeal to all tastes, but it's intriguing, effective, and unique enough to warrant a listen.

Randall D. Larson

Valley Girl

1994, Rhino Records, from the film *Valley Girl*, 1983 ♪♪♪♪

Rhino did the world a service by reissuing this original 1983 soundtrack and adding more songs from the film. This is as good an '80s pop collection as you'll find, filled with songs you'll wish you'd paid more attention to the first time around. Among the highlights: The Plimsouls' wonderful "Million Miles Away" and "Everywhere at Once," Modern English's seminal (if overplayed) "I Melt With You," Josie Cotton's flirty "Johnny, Are You Queer?" Men at Work's "Who Can it Be Now?" Psychedelic Furs' "Love My Way," and Sparks' "Angst in My Pants." It is pure retro fun.

Gary Graff

Vampires

1998, Milan/BMG, from the film *Vampires*, Columbia, 1998 ♪♪♪

album notes: Music: John Carpenter; **Conductor:** John Carpenter; **Featured Musicians:** John Carpenter, keyboards, piano, guitar, bass;

Steve Cropper, guitar; Donald V. "Duck" Dunn, bass; Rick Shlosser, drums; Jeffrey "Skunk" Baxter, electronic guitar, dobro, steel pedal; Joe Robb, saxophone; Bruce Robb, Hammond B3 organ; E. "Bucket" Baker, drums, percussion; Daniel Davies, guitar; Cody Carpenter, keyboards.

Trust John Carpenter to revive some old myths and give them a new spin. *Vampires* involves a genuine, honest-to-goodness vampire slayer on a mission from the Vatican (!) to seek and destroy all vampires, living and dead, and rid the earth of the beastly things, and particularly the legendary Valek, who is looking for the infamous Berziers Cross that will give him the power to walk in the daylight. This being a western set in rural New Mexico, Carpenter also wrote a score that teems with pseudo Spanish guitar riffs, grizzly echoes of the fanged ones on a rampage, sexy doings in a frontier motel, and blues from a southwestern bar band. The tunes are quite entertaining and enjoyable, and combine to make for a lively soundtrack album that bears little resemblance with your run-of-the-mill vampire score.

Didier C. Deutsch

Varsity Blues

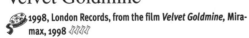 1999, Hollywood Records, from the film *Varsity Blues,* Paramount, 1998 𝄞𝄞𝄞

This songtrack of half-"music from" and half-"music inspired by" is chock full of big-name alternative rock artists, an appropriate choice for a teen-oriented romp about college students who plot to kill their annoying roommate in order to get straight A's. Featured on this CD (and in the movie) are tracks by Green Day, Collective Soul, Third Eye Blind, and the Foo Fighters. Also featured (on the soundtrack but not in the movie) are several interesting covers, including Monster Magnet doing MC5's "Kick out the Jams," and Sprung Monkey covering AC/DC's "Thunderstruck."

Beth Krakower

Velvet Goldmine

1998, London Records, from the film *Velvet Goldmine,* Miramax, 1998 𝄞𝄞𝄞𝄞

In two dramatically different ways, *This Is Spinal Tap* and *Beyond the Valley of the Dolls* made the film world safe for imaginary bands, and *Velvet Goldmine* continues the tradition in fine fashion on an album filled with glam rock covers. The film band Venus in Furs, which includes Radiohead singer Thom Yorke, former Suede guitarist Bernard Butler, and ex-Roxy Music saxman Andy Mackay, mug with spirit and authority through a selection of Roxy material that includes "Bitter-Sweet," "2HB" and "Ladytron," as well as Brian Eno's "Baby's on Fire" (Roxy's version of "Virginia Plain" is also included here). Meanwhile, a

second made-up group, Wyle Rattz—made up of Americans such as Mike Watt, Sonic Youth's Thurston Moore, Mudhoney's Mark Arm, and the Stooges' Ron Asheton—kicks out the Stooges' "T.V. Eye" with actor Ewan McGregor doing his best Iggy Pop impression. T. Rex gets its propers with "Diamond Meadows" and a cover of "20th-Century Boy" by Placebo, while Shudder to Think, Teenage Fanclub, and Grant Lee Buffalo also get into the act. It's big, dumb, silly fun, which is what glam was always about, anyway.

Gary Graff

The Versace Murder

1999, Pacific Time Records, from the film *The Versace Murder,* 1999 𝄞

album notes: Music: Claudio Simonetti; **Conductor:** Claudio Simonetti.

The movie, which was still unreleased at press time, is based on the events surrounding Andrew Cunanan's killing spree, which included the murder of fashion designer Gianni Versace that rocked the fashion world. Claudio Simonetti's electronic score for this feature doesn't sound very cohesive, alternating between 1980s-style synth to light jazz to high melodrama. Because the murder occurred in Miami, a more cohesive electronic dance or even a tropical-flavored score would probably have been more appropriate. There are several Latino songs on the CD, including "Estoy Enamorado de Ti" by Pochy e su Cocoband, "Mambo" by Los Hermanos Mercedes, and "Me Tiene Ammarao" by Los Hermanos Rosario. The highlight of the soundtrack is "I'm So Glad," a very Miami-style dance track co-written by Simonetti and performed by Kamilee.

Didier C. Deutsch

Vertigo

1996, Varèse Sarabande from the film *Vertigo,* Paramount Pictures, 1958 𝄞𝄞𝄞𝄞

album notes: Music: Bernard Herrmann; **Orchestra:** The Sinfonia of London, **Conductor:** Muir Mathieson.

1996, Varèse Sarabande, from the film *Vertigo,* Paramount Pictures, 1958 𝄞𝄞𝄞𝄞

album notes: Music: Bernard Herrmann; **Orchestra:** The Royal Scottish National Orchestra; **Conductor:** Joel McNeely.

Alfred Hitchcock, a methodical film director, and Bernard Herrmann, a harmonically inclined film composer, were made for each other. For, however divergent their individual temperaments, each understood and appreciated the other's perspective, and thrived creatively on their symbiotic relationship, which resulted in some of the most poignant, critical work ever created in the history of music, and the cinema.

Most critics agree that Hitchcock's *Vertigo* endures as one of his most complex, intensely powerful films. Certainly, half the credit for the success of the film as an acknowledged masterpiece must be attributed to Herrmann's strikingly beautiful score (his fourth of seven collaborations with the director), for it is Herrmann's music that lies all the complex subtleties of the film together.

The newly restored edition of the original soundtrack recordings provides a crucial piece of the Hitchcock/Herrmann puzzle. It is this release that offers the most complete collection of music from the film, including four cues that have never been available in any form. As with many vintage soundtrack restorations, the disc is not without inherent problems. Because recording was done in two different cities (London and Vienna), the disc, which has been programmed in the correct running order, alternates at times between mono and stereo. Also, the ravages of time have taken their toll on the original tapes from the sessions, and while painstaking efforts were evidently made to restore as much music as possible, some minor disturbances can be heard on the disc. Also due to extensive damage, one important cue, "The Graveyard," could not be included. The recording of the score with Joel McNeely and the Royal Scottish National Orchestra features over an hour of the music from *Vertigo,* including the aforementioned cue, "The Graveyard." The re-recording is expertly performed, and sumptuously recorded.

Charles L. Granata

A Very Brady Sequel

1998, Angel Records, from the film *A Very Brady Sequel,* Paramount, 1998 ♪♪

Dig out the insulin, it's the Brady's part two, in which Carol's husband returns from the dead and attempts to reclaim a multi-million dollar sculpture from Mrs. Brady. As in the first movie, the Brady kids perform two of the songs from the TV series, "Good Time Music" and "Time to Change." The rest of this songtrack features such classics as "Last Train to Clarksville" by the Monkees, Davy Jones's "Girl", "Sugar Sugar" by the Archies, and the "Hawaii Five-O" theme. While the first Brady soundtrack was a bit better, this is still a fun, kitschy album.

Beth Krakower

Victor/Victoria

1989, GNP Crescendo, from the film *Victor/Victoria,* MGM, 1982 ♪♪♪♪

album notes: Music: Henry Mancini; **Lyrics:** Leslie Bricusse; **Cast:** Julie Andrews, Robert Preston, James Garner, Lesley Ann Warren.

1995, Philips Records, from the Broadway production *Victor/Victoria,* 1995 ♪♪♪

album notes: Music: Henry Mancini; **Lyrics:** Leslie Bricusse; **Musical Direction:** Ian Fraser; **Cast:** Julie Andrews, Tony Roberts, Michael Nouri, Rachel York, Gregory Jbara, Richard B. Shull.

Initially, *Victor/Victoria* was conceived as a screen vehicle for Julie Andrews, directed by her husband Blake Edwards, a brilliant musical with songs by Edwards's usual composer, Henry Mancini, and lyricist Leslie Bricusse. Set in Paris in the "gay" 1920s, the plot involved a complicated gender–bending mystification, in which Andrews, as Victoria, an impoverished waif with the voice of an angel, was transformed by impresario Robert Preston into Victor, a man posing as a woman, who became an overnight sensation. Much of the film's great personal charms came from the obvious chemistry between the principals, with Andrews a real delight as the ambiguous Victor/Victoria; Preston sensational as Toddy, an aging flamboyant gay man with a devastating sense of humor and wit; James Garner, plausibly handsome as an underworld character who falls for Victor while he desperately resists what he thinks are homosexual tendencies; and Leslie Ann Warren a scene-stealer as a droll moll with a tart tongue. Adding tremendous entertainment to the film was Mancini's breezy songs and score, superbly performed by the principals, and Edwards's own light touch which turned everything into a total feast. Much of the soundtrack album retains the flavor of the film, and even adds some reprises and instrumental tracks that were not on the original LP.

Ten years later, Edwards decided that a stage version of the film would again be the ideal vehicle for Andrews's long–awaited return to Broadway. Unfortunately, Mancini died before he could finish work on the new project, and the new songs added to his score are a serious letdown. More detrimental, however, is that some of the film's best numbers were discarded and replaced with songs that are stuffy and give a much more somber tone to the ensemble, when they don't seem completely out of place ("Louis Says"). Under the circumstances, Andrews still exudes a winsome charm that pervades the whole show, but Tony Roberts can't erase the memory of Robert Preston, and Michael Nouri, to put it charitably, is bland as King. The only one who strikes a note close to the original, besides Andrews, is Rachel York in the role created by Lesley Ann Warren.

Didier C. Deutsch

Victory at Sea: Vol. 1 & 2

1992, RCA Victor, from the NBC TV series, *Victory At Sea,* 1952–53 ♪♪♪♪♪

album notes: Music: Richard Rodgers; **Orchestra:** The RCA Victor Symphony Orchestra; **Conductor:** Robert Russell Bennett.

Julie Andrews in the film version of Victor/Victoria. **(The Kobal Collection)**

In 1952, Broadway composer Richard Rodgers took a sabbatical from his theatrical ventures to create the score for the popular television series *Victory at Sea,* a documentary of World War II emphasizing the naval battles waged between 1939 and 1945. The score, lush, inordinately musical and attractive, yet powerfully suggestive, won an Emmy Award for best score in 1953, and elicited rapturous reviews from most reviewers who described it as a work of "compelling beauty and vigor that adds incalculably to the emotional intensity of the series" (Jack Gould, *New York Times).* Eventually, the series was adapted for the big screen and a theatrical feature was released by United Artists in 1954.

Three years later, Robert Russell Bennett, Rodgers's regular arranger, went to the recording studio and prepared three albums containing many of the best cues from the score for release by RCA. The two CDs regroup most of these selections into a sweeping, panoramic musical display of great intensity and originality, with sound effects added for greater realism.

As a melodist, Rodgers was particularly proficient, and his score enables him to unleash the raw emotional power he so often was compelled to curb in his Broadway shows. Today, the impact of his music is as great as it was 45 years ago, with some selections ("Guadalcanal March," "Theme of the Fast Carriers," "The Song of the High Seas") revealing his uncanny talent for ear-grabbing tunes.

Didier C. Deutsch

Videodrome

1982, Varèse-Sarabande, from the film *Videodrome,* Universal, 1982 ♪

album notes: Music: Howard Shore.

What is one to make of a score that features distorted voices, synthesizer lines without melodies, and eerie electronic noises? If was quite suitable for the film, a thriller about a small-time cable TV operator in Toronto who picks up a strange video program called *Videodrome,* that consists primarily of women being tortured. The film, which starred James Woods, Sonja Smits, and former Blondie lead singer Deborah Harry as the operator's girlfriend who gets disposed of in the most cruel manner, may have developed into an underground cult, but its freakish aspects certainly are not its most appealing assets. Nor is this soundtrack album, which served as a perfect complement to the screen action but fails to attract on its own in this dubious CD.

Didier C. Deutsch

A View to a Kill

1999, Rykodisc, from the film *A View to a Kill,* United Artists, 1985 ♪♪♪

album notes: Music: John Barry; **Conductor:** John Barry.

For many years, this was the only James Bond soundtrack that had never been reissued on CD in this country, though it was for a while available as an import from Japan. One of the better efforts by John Barry, with cues signaling the momentum in the screen action, it featured a great title song, performed by Duran Duran, and some exciting cues, including the highlight of this score, a track called "Snow Job." Okay, Mr. Barry, another "Mickey Mouse" score, if you will, but always a fun one....

Didier C. Deutsch

The Vikings/Solomon and Sheba

1996, DRG Records, from the films *The Vikings,* United Artists, 1959, and *Solomon and Sheba,* United Artists, 1960 ♪♪♪♪

album notes: Music: Mario Nascimbene; **Conductor:** Franco Ferrara, Mario Nascimbene.

Italian composer Mario Nascimbene, who had already developed quite a following after he scored *The Barefoot Contessa* in 1954, made a strong impression when he composed the startling music for *The Vikings* in 1959, a sprawling saga of revenge and historic mayhem, starring Kirk Douglas and Tony Curtis as half-brothers feuding over the love of Janet Leigh and control of the Viking empire. Frequently rousing and brightly colorful in its depiction of the savage action, Nascimbene's score emphasized the action on the screen and gave it strong emotive support. A year later, Nascimbene encored when he wrote another sensational score, for the Biblical epic *Solomon and Sheba,* a fanciful big-screen retelling of the love affair between the tenth century B.C. king of Israel, and the desert queen who ravished his heart. In both cases, writing in a style that owed little to the style that prevailed in Hollywood at the time, but finding a new expression that enhanced the screen visuals, Nascimbene created scores that were memorably effective and sharply detailed. While both are presented here in a production supervised by the composer, the overall quality of this CD leaves a lot to be desired, with a cramped mono sound, image shifting, some distortion, occasional analog dropouts, bad splicings, and harsh sonics that render listening a less than pleasant experience. The only exception is the previously unreleased "Viking's Horn," which denotes the spaciousness and spread these scores should have received. The rating reflects the importance of the score, not the quality of the recording.

Didier C. Deutsch

Village of the Damned

1995, Varèse Sarabande, from the film *Village of the Damned,* Universal Pictures, 1995 ♪♪♪

album notes: Music: John Carpenter, Dave Davies; **Featured Musicians:** John Carpenter, synthesizer, bass guitar; Dave Davies, guitars; Bruce Robb, Hammond B-3.

This is indeed a rarity—a John Carpenter score with an orchestra. Although electronics still represent the principal instrumentation, Carpenter, along with Dave Davies of the pop group The Kinks, uses their modest resources to the fullest advantage. The theme for "The March of the Children" is perhaps Carpenter's strongest composition since his original main theme for *Halloween*. There's a steady advance of evil building in the music for this seemingly invincible army of super children bent on world domination. The sparse use of acoustics works well to remind us that the film has a larger scope, the tiny coastal town is but a microcosm simulation of a threat happening across the entire world. With it, Carpenter has really created one of his most elaborate and satisfying scores in years, featuring some of the most delightfully melodic passages ("The Fair," "The Children's Theme") he has ever written.

David Hirsch

Virus

1999, Hip-O Records, from the film *Virus*, Universal, 1998
𝄢𝄢𝄢𝄢

album notes: Music: Joel McNeely; Conductor: Joel McNeely.

Humanity being what it is, it is always at the mercy of some unknown danger, whether it comes from an unchecked part of the world or from another part of the universe. *Outbreak* studied the first possibility; *Virus* proposes the second. Makes little difference, really—as long as there's a danger to be faced, combated, and eventually overcome, filmmakers will have a field day. And so it goes with *Virus*, in which the civilized world is again threatened by a menace from outer space, more sneaky than any other, and potentially more devastating. Joel McNeely has a lot of fun putting this to music, in cues that brim with brass calls, lots of orchestra flurries punctuated by percussion effects, and the usual display of effects found in scores of this kind. This one, though, is better than most, and makes for fun listening as well.

Didier C. Deutsch

Viva Las Vegas/Roustabout

1993, RCA Records from the films *Viva Las Vegas*, MGM, 1964, and *Roustabout*, Paramount, 1964 𝄢𝄢𝄢

In one of his most-publicized on- and off-screen romances, Elvis shared credits with Ann-Margret in the film *Viva Las Vegas*, released in 1964. Most certainly, some of its success can be attributed to the actress's dynamic presence, who ignited the screen as few others had done opposite the King. The imaginative script also enabled them to give more than routine

performances, with Ann-Margret's exuberance as a singer and dancer matching Presley's own genuine talent. In it, he

portrayed a penniless race-car driver, in town to compete in the Vegas Grand Prix, and she an employee at the hotel where he is staying, with the obvious chemistry between them largely compensating for some of the weaknesses in the storyline. While the soundtrack did not yield any significant hit, it is offered here for the first time in its entirety and in stereo (albeit somewhat aggressive), with the two stars heard in a couple of numbers.

If Ann-Margret seemed a natural choice as a co-star, the same couldn't be said of Barbara Stanwyck who shared credits with Elvis in *Roustabout* as a carnival owner who hires him as a handyman. A dramatic actress with impeccable credentials, Stanwyck was obviously not serviced well by the script that made few demands on her, and seemed to favor the lighter side of Elvis as a drifter with a strong vocal talent. The soundtrack didn't yield any recognizable hit.

Didier C. Deutsch

Viva Zapata!

1998, Varèse-Sarabande, from the film *Viva Zapata!*, 1952
𝄢𝄢𝄢𝄢𝄢

album notes: Music: Alex North; Orchestra: The Royal Scottish National Orchestra; Conductor: Jerry Goldsmith.

Alex North's splendid Mexican-flavored score for this film directed by Elia Kazan gets an impressive performance in the hands of Jerry Goldsmith and the Royal Scottish National Orchestra. A relatively faithful account of the life and deeds of the revolutionary Emilio Zapata, who led a rebellion of paisanos against the oppressive Mexican government in the early 1900s, the film starred Marlon Brando in the title role, with Jean Peters as the girl who marries him, knowing all along that he will meet a violent death. Reflecting the hot, raw atmosphere of the film, North wrote a score that was at times dissonant to suggest Zapata's commitment and struggle for a cause that was lost from the onset, and at times indulged in tender musical expressions to evoke his relationshlp with his girlfriend, Josefa. It receives a vigorous, lovely reading in this wonderful CD.

Didier C. Deutsch

Vixen

1997, Laserlight Records, from the film *Vixen*, Panamint, 1968
𝄢𝄢𝄢

album notes: Music: William Loose.

The demure track listing belies the fact that *Vixen* is essentially a sex film, with the music serving to underscore some of the most graphically interesting scenes in which buxomy babes (a Russ Meyer trademark) cavorted in the nude or indulge in man's (and woman's) favorite sport. It may not be the kind of cerebral music one might want to listen to on occasions, nor is it marked by great music expression, but it happens to be relaxing and entertaining.

see also: Cherry, Harry & Raquel, The Devil in Miss Jones

Didier C. Deutsch

Volcano

1997, Varèse Sarabande, from the film *Volcano*, 20th Century Fox, 1997 &&&&

album notes: Music: Alan Silvestri; **Conductor:** Alan Silvestri.

Somehow, the idea of using electronic music to score a film about a volcanic eruption works better here than in most cases. Alan Silvestri effectively demonstrates how to do it, and how to do it well, in his score for this big box-office disaster. Early on, his cues, eerily ominous, yet melodically attractive, contrast life-as-usual and the impending threat of the eruption about to happen. The sense of danger is suggested by sharp, thrill electronic effects, over a building low-string motif that signals to anyone not yet aware of it that something's afoot. Once nature lashes its fury, the full forces of the orchestra join in, bringing the score to a smashing crescendo. Notably effective in this context is "March of the Lava," which shows the unstoppable progression of the river of fire as it submerges everything. By contrast, the almost peaceful "Cleansing Rain" brings the volatile score to an elegiac conclusion. At under 30 minutes of total playing time, the CD seems a little skimpy, but there is so much tense, expressive music contained that it seems just right.

Didier C. Deutsch

Voyage of the Damned

1993, Label X, from the film *Voyage of the Damned*, 1977 &&&

album notes: Music: Lalo Schifrin; **Orchestra:** The London Studio Orchestra; **Conductor:** Lalo Schifrin; **Featured Musicians:** Dorothy Remsen, harp; Ken Watson, percussion.

Based on an eponymous novel by Gordon Thomas and Max Morgan-Witts, *Voyage of the Damned* recounts in stark details the true-life journey of Jewish refugees from the ravages of war-torn Europe on board a ship that was denied landing authorization by the governments of several countries. The film elicited a chamber-like score from Schifrin who assigned various instruments to portray the central characters in the story, in a dark, reflective series of cues, built around a haunting central theme, that are powerfully evocative of the screen action. Two other compositions, "Continuum for Solo Harp," and the stretched-

out "Journeys for Percussion," prove much too arid for listening enjoyment.

see also: The Four Musketeers

Didier C. Deutsch

VR.5

1995, Rysher Records, from the television series *VR.5*, Zoo Entertainment/Rysher Entertainment, 1995 &&&

album notes: Music: John Frizzell; **Featured Vocalists:** Dee Carstensen, Eileen Frizzell; **Featured Musician:** David McKelvy, harmonica.

A skillful blend of synthesizers, acoustics, and voice by John Frizzell for the short-lived television series. A solo female vocal was applied to the main theme for Sidney, a young woman who discovered a means of getting into people's psyche through virtual reality. Frizzell had to be creative to match the oddly designed virtual landscapes of Sidney's encounters, while creating more realistic motifs for her pursuit by shadowy government agents who want the technology. Some of the themes are very harmonious, while others, like "Family Drowning," have unsettling dissonant melodies. Although a spellbinding piece of work by virtue of Frizzell's creativity, this exists only when the tracks are listened to as separate elements. The album's sequencing is, however, somewhat disjointed, and that's the weakest part. The music is assembled in bits and pieces and makes no attempt to establish any kind of symphonic flow.

David Hirsch

Wag the Dog

1998, Mercury Records, from the film *Wag the Dog*, New Line Cinema, 1997 &&&&

album notes: Music: Mark Knopfler.

This specially priced mini album may not exactly qualify as a full-fledged soundtrack, but it gives the listener an opportunity to become immersed in the inventions of Mark Knopfler, who is too seldom heard as a film composer these days. Written for a film in which the U.S. government wages a war against another nation, the better to disguise some of the President's own failings, *Wag the Dog* displayed a special resonance when it opened shortly before U.S. warplanes bombed alleged rebel hideouts in the Middle East, at a time when President Bill Clinton was himself under fire for his improprieties with female members of his staff. The satirical film had a biting edge that found an echo in Knopfler's score, a series of cues that have a bite of their own, and are entertainingly fun to listen to.

Didier C. Deutsch

Wagons East!

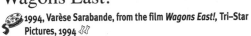

1994, Varèse Sarabande, from the film *Wagons East!*, Tri–Star Pictures, 1994 🎬🎬

album notes: Music: Michael Small; **Orchestra:** The Irish Film Orchestra; **Conductor:** Michael Small.

This film, the remarkably unfunny tale of a wagon master who leads a bunch of fed–up settlers out of the old West and back to "civilization," got more press than it deserved simply because it was actor John Candy's last film before he died. For it, Michael Small created an agreeable enough western–flavored comedy score that relies too much on established clichés of the genre. It's nice, but nothing remarkable or special to be recommended.

David Hirsch

Waiting to Exhale

1996, Arista Records, from the film *Waiting to Exhale,* 20th Century Fox, 1996 🎬🎬🎬

album notes: Songs: Babyface; **Featured Musicians:** Babyface, synthesizers, keyboards, guitars; Greg Philinganes, Alex Alessandroni, piano; Reggie Griffin, Michael Thompson, guitar; Nathan East, bass; Luis Conte, Paulinho da Costa, Larry Bunker, percussion; Brandon Fields, Reggie Griffin, saxophone; Bruce Dukov, Clayton Haslop, violin; Bob Becker, viola; Larry Corbell, cello.

Whitney Houston brightens up the screen in this inspirational story about four women who are friends and share the difficulties they encounter in their lives. Punctuating the action, and giving it a spin that is refreshingly enjoyable, the soundtrack features several songs written by the ubiquitous Babyface, performed by some of today's best female performers, including Houston who demonstrates again in this album why she is one of the most interesting vocalists in pop music. It's a bright, easy listening collection that should enjoy a broad audience.

Didier C. Deutsch

Waking Ned Devine

1998, London Records, from the film *Waking Ned Devine,* Fox Searchlight, 1998 🎬🎬🎬🎬

album notes: Music: Shaun Davey; **Featured Musicians:** John McSherry, uilleann pipes/whistles; Nollaig Casey, fiddle; Artie McGlynn, guitar; Liam O'Maonlai, bodhran, whistle, vocals; Noel Eccles, percussion; Gary Kettle, percussion; Paul Clarvis, percussion; Shaun Davey, keyboards; Rita Connolly, vocals.

Ned Devine has won the lottery. Unfortunately he is dead. That doesn't stop two of his old cronies from attempting to claim the winnings in this uproarious Irish farce. Irish songwriter Shaun

Davey's traditional Celtic score alternates between lively dance numbers and sorrowful ballads resonating with the intoxicatingly beautiful wail of John McSherry's uilleann pipes; similar although more complex, than Scottish bagpipes. The Waterboys' uplifting Irish rock shanty "Fisherman's Blues" pales next to Liam O'Maonlai's rich, warm tenor voice, familiar from pop ballads with the Hothouse Flowers and accompanied here by a thundering rhythm beaten out on the bodhran, while the adept Nollaig Casey's fiddles set a speedy pace throughout. Rita Connolly's Latin hymn and the proudly enunciated Gaelic of "Hear Me" and "The Parting Glass" provide a rousing finale to Davey's distinctly Irish music, which proves as mischievous and moving as this satisfying film.

David Poole

Walk, Don't Run

1991, Mainstream Records, from the film *Walk, Don't Run,* Columbia Pictures, 1966 🎬🎬🎬🎬

album notes: Music: Quincy Jones; **Orchestra:** The Columbia Studio Orchestra; **Conductor:** Quincy Jones; **Featured Musicians:** Toots Thielemans, harmonica; Harry "Sweets" Edison, trumpet.

A sleek, romantic comedy, with often brightly hilarious moments, *Walk, Don't Run* stars Cary Grant as a British tycoon in Japan during the Olympics, who finds himself sharing a small apartment with a fastidious young English girl, Samantha Eggar, and an American athlete, Jim Hutton, much to the chagrin of Eggar's neighbors, puzzled and indignant over what they perceive as a menage–a–trois. Echoing the light moods cast in the film, Quincy Jones provided a delightful, slyly humorous score that perfectly captured the whimsical tone of the story. Rounding up the selections from the soundtrack are random tracks from other sources that are painfully out of context here, and disrupt the moods created by Quincy Jones's creations.

Didier C. Deutsch

A Walk in the Clouds

1995, Milan Records, from the film *A Walk in the Clouds,* 20th Century Fox, 1995 🎬🎬🎬

album notes: Music: Maurice Jarre; **Conductor:** Maurice Jarre; **Featured Musician:** Liona Boyd, classical guitar solo.

This romantic, Spanish–flavored orchestral work from Maurice Jarre follows the adventures of a young soldier, just returning from World War II, who agrees to pretend he is the husband of a pregnant woman whose family owns an idyllic Napa Valley winery. The score, which has an epic feel to it, is presented in several long symphonic suites, and is intercut with two songs with lyrics written by the film's director, Alphonse Arau.

David Hirsch

Waiting to Exhale (The Kobal Collection)

A Walk on the Moon

1999, Sire Records, from the film *A Walk on the Moon*, Miramax 1999 ♪♪♪

A winning combination of original recordings from the 1960s and some newly recorded cover tunes by current artists comprise the soundtrack to this lovely film. Set in the summer of '69 at a middle-class Jewish resort in the Catskills just miles from Woodstock, *A Walk on the Moon* focuses on a young woman's premature mid-life crisis, ignited by the sexual awakening of her teenage daughter. Music is used very well in the movie, setting the period and also conveying the complexities of the young woman's emotional state with songs by Joni Mitchell, Judy Collins, Richie Havens, and other classic artists of the era. New recordings by TaxiRide, Morcheeba, and others were carefully produced to sound true to the period. The only real miss here is Cher and Elijah Blue Allman's uninspired version of "Crimson and Clover." Perhaps a mother/son duo wasn't the most inspired choice for a song about raw and passionate lust.

Amy Rosen

Walk on the Wild Side

1991, Mainstream Records, from the film *Walk on the Wild Side*, Columbia Pictures, 1962 ♪♪♪♪

album notes: Music: Elmer Bernstein; **Conductor:** Elmer Bernstein.

Nelson Algren's naturalistic novel, *A Walk on the Wild Side*, elicited a turbulent, unpredictable and exciting score from Elmer Bernstein when it was brought to the screen in 1962. Set in New Orleans in the 1930s and starring Laurence Harvey, Jane Fonda, and Barbara Stanwyck in the principal roles, it involves a young man from Texas, looking for the girl he had left behind, and eventually finding her in a bordello run by a lesbian madam. The jazz–influenced score Bernstein wrote evoked the seamy underside of the film's locale and situations, bringing to mind the powerful score he had written a few years earlier for *The Man with the Golden Arm,* but without the benefit of an equally strong main theme. Still, a strong, flavorful music that has held very well all these years, and displays many ingratiating charms.

Didier C. Deutsch

Walker

 1987, Virgin Records, from the film *Walker,* Universal Pictures, 1987 ♪♪♪♪

album notes: Music: Joe Strummer; **Featured Musicians:** Zander Schloss, guitar, charanga, vuhela, banjo, guitarron, tambour; Rebecca Mauleon, piano, organ; Michael Spiro, congas, bongos, timbales, percussion; Rich Girard, bass; Richard Zobel, harmonica, mandolin, banjo; Mary Fettig, saxophone, flute; Dick Bright, country fiddle, violin; Michael Hatfield, marimba, vibes, piano organ; David Bendigkiet; John Worley, trumpet; Dean Hubbard, trombone; John Tenney, Dean Franke, violin; Susan Chan, viola; Stephen Mitchell, snare drum; Dan Levin, fast piano; Sam Lehmer, bass drum; Joe Strummer, Richard Zobel, vocals.

Joe Strummer's exotically limned score for this adventure film set in Nicaragua in the middle of the 19th century relies on its tropical rhythms to evoke the time and the place, and attract the listener. It succeeds beautifully. This story of an American adventurer who, with the financial support of Cornelius Vanderbilt, invaded Nicaragua in 1855 at the head of a band of mercenary and set out to become president of the country, found a deep, resonant echo in Strummer's idealistic score, with each cue elaborating on the storyline and giving it an appropriately epic tone, while the many percussion instruments and rhythmic accents anchor it in its specific locale. Highly enjoyable, with many melodic themes that catch one's interest, it is a rare treat, and though probably difficult to find (it was issued ten years ago and was only briefly available), it is well worth looking for.

Didier C. Deutsch

Walking and Talking

 1998, TVT Records, from the film *Walking and Talking,* Miramax, 1998 ♪♪♪
album notes: Music: Billy Bragg.

This very talky, intelligent, romantic comedy-drama about two best friends and their respective experiences with the opposite sex features a very smart soundtrack. The multiple use in the film of songs by Billy Bragg is particularly effective, especially the beautiful "Must I Paint You a Picture." There are many other interesting cuts here, but this is really a showcase for Bragg, a cult artist who can always use some new listeners. It's a pleasure to see a film spotlight unsung artists like him or Eliott Smith in *Good Will Hunting,* and create a forum for their singular talents.

Amy Rosen

Walking Thunder

 1996, JOS Records, from the film *Walking Thunder,* Majestic Entertainment, 1994 ♪♪♪♪
album notes: Music: John Scott; **Orchestra:** The Munich Symphony Orchestra; **Conductor:** John Scott.

Although the setting is the old West of 1850, John Scott passes on most conventional genre methods and instead focuses his score on the personal story of one family's decision to start a new life in the Utah wilderness after a bear attacks and disables their covered wagon. They eventually meet and befriend a Native American, Dark Wind, who tells them the legend of Walking Thunder, the giant bear. Scott plays out each of the major factors now in the family's life—the vast expanses of their new home, their budding friendships with the neighbors, and the threat from a roving band of marauders. One of Scott's few concessions to the idiom is the use of a motif for Dark Wind, based on an actual Native American melody that the actor playing the character sings in the film. There is also a superb theme for the villains, humorously titled "The Bad Bunch," which is an exuberant tip of the hat to genre masters Ennio Morricone and Jerry Fielding. Oddly, the first part of the six–minute suite "Horsecreek Rendezvous," the "Turkey Strut," includes an overlay of ambient crowd noise.

David Hirsch

Wall Street/Salvador

 1987, Varèse Sarabande, from the films *Wall Street,* 20th Century Fox, 1987, and *Salvador,* Cinema '85, 1985 ♪♪
album notes: Wall Street: Music: Stewart Copeland; **Salvador: Music:** Georges Delerue; **Orchestra:** The Vancouver Symphony Orchestra; **Conductor:** Georges Delerue.

Two scores from early Oliver Stone films are offered on this CD. Stewart Copeland's *Wall Street* is one of the sorriest excuses for a film score ever. A sufficiently talented rock 'n' roll drummer, Copeland is rather less adept at the musical demands of melody and counterpoint. His "score" for *Wall Street* is not so much music as it is musical sound effects (and even resorts to using sampled dog barking), and is the work of someone of dubious musical inclination cloaking his deficiencies by using sophisticated synthesizers. Any amateur tinkering with a keyboard could have achieved as good a result.

On the other hand, Georges Delerue's *Salvador* is a work of genius. Delerue was a master of melody and rich orchestration. Like most Oliver Stone films, *Salvador* was an infantile, pretentious rant, but it allowed Delerue a departure from his usual assignments, calling for strident, violent music (he was better known for lyrical scores). Admittedly the more dissonant cues do not work quite so well on an album. But Delerue's tragic end title for strings and chorus is one of the most longingly heartfelt evocations of tragedy ever written for a movie. This track alone makes the CD worth owning.

Paul Andrew MacLean

The War

1994, MCA Records, from the film *The War,* Universal Pictures, 1994 ♫♫♫♫

album notes: Music: Thomas Newman; **Conductor:** Thomas Newman; **Featured Vocalist:** Yvonne Williams.

Set in Mississippi, this sensitive tale of a Vietnam War veteran, disillusioned about everything that he once held dear, and his teenage boy, provided Thomas Newman with the right motivation to write a score that subtly underlined the moods in the film, while making a deep, emotional comment of its own. The beautifully lyrical "Main Theme" and the lengthy "Second Vietnam" summarize the basic elements in the score, with the strong orchestral motifs outlining the prevalent feelings of loneliness, abandonment, and deception both the vet (played by Kevin Costner) and his son (Elijah Wood) experience to varying degrees and for obviously totally different reasons. It's a very evocative score, with flashes of orchestral gusto, and themes that are particularly meaningful. A selection of pop tunes help set the drama in its appropriate time period.

Didier C. Deutsch

War and Peace

1988, Varèse Sarabande, from the film *War and Peace,* Paramount Pictures, 1956 ♫♫♫♫♫

album notes: Music: Nino Rota; **Conductor:** Franco Ferrara.

Nino Rota, best known in this country for the scores he wrote for the films of Federico Fellini and for *The Godfather,* struck a different, original note early in his career for this Napoleonic era romantic saga based on Leo Tolstoy's familiar novel. With the radiant Audrey Hepburn portraying Natasha, Mel Ferrer the handsome Prince Andrey, and Henry Fonda the bespectacled student Pierre, the King Vidor–directed film splashed across the big screen with scenic grandeur and an epic feel that echoed the passionate scope of the book. Opulent and magnificently mounted, the production also afforded Rota with many set pieces where his lyrical inspiration took a free flight ("The Battle of Austerlitz," "The Charge of the Cavalry," "Exodus from Moscow," "Napoleon's Retreat"), all of which resulted in cues that are still impressively dramatic and powerfully appealing today. One of the film's most ravishing scenes, a whirling ballroom sequence, inspired him to create a lilting waltz ("War and Peace"), as fresh and lovely as anything he wrote for the screen, that beautifully captured the giddy atmosphere of the situation. Despite the fact that the recording is in mono, it has all the sweep and magnificence one associates with this super production.

Didier C. Deutsch

The War Lord

1994, Varèse Sarabande, from the film *The War Lord,* Universal Pictures, 1965 ♫♫♫♫♫

album notes: Music: Jerome Moross; **Orchestra:** The Universal Studio Orchestra; **Conductor:** Joseph Gershenson.

An impressive medieval epic, *The War Lord* found in Jerome Moross a sympathetic, inventive composer who evidently thrived on this story set in the 11th century, about a war lord for the Duke Of Normandy, fighting the Vikings around the North Sea coast countryside, and the strong, abiding love he feels for a young woman from the Druid village he is defending against the invading hordes. Instead of writing a swashbuckling score, as most composers would have done, Moross took the opposite approach. He focused first on the love story between the Lord, played by Charlton Heston, and the village maiden, portrayed by Rosemary Forsyth, occasionally interrupting the "wistful translucence" with action cues designed to underline the violent confrontations between the Lord, his men, and the marauding Vikings. Two cues, composed by Hans J. Salter on themes provided by Moross, add a somewhat different, though nonetheless effective, feel to the overall score.

Didier C. Deutsch

War of the Buttons

1994, Varèse Sarabande, from the film *War of the Buttons,* Warner Bros., 1994 ♫♫♫♫♫

album notes: Music: Rachel Portman; **Orchestra:** The Irish Film Orchestra; **Conductor:** David Snell.

In an early demonstration of the skills that have since singled her out as a vastly talented film composer, Rachel Portman created the flavorful score for this enjoyable screen adaptation of the French novel by Louis Pergaud, *La Guerre des Boutons.* Set in Ireland, and opposing two groups of youngsters with a common ideal, *War of the Buttons* suggested to Portman a series of whimsical cues that followed the action on the screen, with a flurry of delightful little details that made her score even more appealing than the slight film would have suggested ("Battle Of Murphy's Dunes"). As usual with her scores, the music takes a life of its own when removed from its original supportive role, and in this case becomes an enchanting program one might like to return to frequently.

Didier C. Deutsch

Warlock

1989, Intrada Records, from the film *Warlock,* New World Pictures, 1989 ♫♫

album notes: Music: Jerry Goldsmith; **Conductor:** Jerry Goldsmith.

Everybody has a bad day once in awhile, and Jerry Goldsmith must have had a very difficult couple of weeks trying to come up with material to score *Warlock,* the 1989 New World production that was shelved for a couple of years when the studio went bankrupt. Not that the movie—a mixture of horrific fantasy and tongue–in–cheek "fish out of water" comedy—gave the composer much to work with, but for whatever reason, Goldsmith wrote a tremendously dull, synthesizer–laden score with a pokey–sounding main motive offering neither horror, fantasy, nor anything musically interesting to entice listeners or viewers. The bulk of the music is, particularly for Goldsmith, atypically atonal and very blah; needless to say, the composer didn't return for the movie's needless follow–up.

Andy Dursin

Warlock: The Armageddon

1993, Intrada Records, from the film *Warlock: The Armageddon,* Trimark Pictures, 1993 🎬🎬🎬

album notes: Music: Mark McKenzie; **Orchestra:** The Southwest Symphony Orchestra; **Choir:** The Southwest Symphony Choir; **Conductor:** Mark McKenzie.

A Requiem Mass for disembodied voices and symphonic orchestra sets the tone for this horrific tale, unrelated to the earlier thriller, in which an evil emissary of Satan in a small northern California community engages in fierce territorial battle with two descendants of 17th–century Druids with the power to destroy him. McKenzie's score, contrasting the horror with more lyrical accents, proves very endearing overall. The themes are for the most part quite melodic ("Ken's Magic," "Samantha and Ken's Love"), and paint a vivid picture of the screen action. Recapping the main themes into a single cue, "A Warlock Fantasia" concludes the CD on a bright, positive note. The only real fault here is with the sound quality, which emphasizes the highs and defeats the lows, resulting in thin–sounding strings and very little bottom to what should sometimes be a booming recording.

Didier C. Deutsch

Warning Sign

1985, Southern Cross Records, from the film *Warning Sign,* 20th Century Fox, 1985 🎬

album notes: Music: Craig Safan.

A creepy, ambient synthesized score by Craig Safan effectively uses a non–thematic minimalist approach, ala *The Andromeda Strain,* for this tale of a chemical spill in a germ warfare lab. Interesting sound design, with an occasional new-age theme, it has its moments, but it sounds very repetitious, and wears out its welcome too soon to hold any interest for long, unless you're really prepared to experience something different.

David Hirsch

Warriors of Virtue

1997, Prometheus Records, from the film *Warriors of Virtue,* MGM, 1997 🎬🎬🎬

album notes: Music: Don Davis; **Orchestra:** The Denver Symphony Orchestra and Chorus; **Conductor:** Don Davis.

1998, Kid Rhino; from the film *Warriors of Virtue,* MGM, 1997 🎬

album notes: Music: Don Davis; **Orchestra:** The Colorado Symphony Orchestra; **Conductor:** Don Davis.

Okay, here's a good one for you: What's the difference between the Denver Symphony Orchestra, heard on the Prometheus score album, and the Colorado Symphony Orchestra, which performs on the Kid Rhino song album? The first to give the right answer wins a trip to the land of Tao, the parallel universe in which Ryan, hero of this fantasy film, finds himself projected after he tries to swim in a storm-swollen river. In that wondrous land, it turns out that the forces of good and evil are fighting each other over the ownership of a mysterious tome, "The Manuscript of Legends," which Ryan just happens to own, singling him out to Komodo, a dragon of a villain, as the rival to destroy. We won't go into further, unnecessary details, other than to say the story has been told before, in different but no less eloquent terms.

Don Davis scored the film with a great deal of empathy, bringing forth epic themes that outline the story, and flesh it up when needed with orchestral flurries that are quite convincing. As fantasy film scores go, this is quite an achievement, strongly suggestive and properly effective, with bold themes that delineate the action and give it substance. With a couple of exceptions, the tracks in both sets do not duplicate each other, which is also an interesting coincidence. But of the two, the score album is certainly the most complete and most satisfying.

The song album, on the other hand, outside of its instrumental tracks, has very little to offer: the songs, by Clannad, Richie Havens, Ultraglide, judyjudyjudy, Charlie Sexton, and Vangelis, among others, seem to have little to do with the action itself, and sound rather bland. It is doubtful they would appeal to the kids, even those who might have seen the film, and their parents probably have heard better elsewhere. Skip it!

Didier C. Deutsch

Washington Square

1997, Varèse-Sarabande, from the film *Washington Square,* Hollywood Pictures, 1997 🎬🎬🎬

album notes: Music: Jan A.P. Kaczmarek; **Orchestra:** The National Philharmonic Orchestra; **Conductor:** Krzesimir Debski; **Featured Musicians:** The Wilanow Quartet; Pawel Losakiewicz, violin; David Loeb, piano.

Henry James's novel, *Washington Square,* already filmed in 1949 as *The Heiress,* attracted Agnieszka Holland, who gave it a slight feminist spin to make it more contemporary and politically correct. Set in New York in the mid-1800s, James's story, about a young woman entirely controlled by her domineering father, who is attracted to a handsome suitor, is a potent dramatic brew that is all the more powerful that it is subtly narrated. The new film takes note of its time period, but twists it ever so slightly to make it conform with the director's own sensitivities, as a woman and as a filmmaker. Contributing a sense of his own to the story, Jan A.P. Kaczmarek wrote a score that exudes quiet feelings and strong emotions, in cues that are performed by a chamber orchestra and prominently feature the piano and the violin as main instruments. Reinforcing the impression of elegance and sophistication in the score are three songs, including one, "L'absence," in which Kaczmarek set music to words by French author Theophile Gautier. It is a rare literary reference that perfectly matches the moods of the film, and proves quite impressive as well.

Didier C. Deutsch

The Waterboy

 1998, Hollywood Records, from the film *The Waterboy,* Touchstone, 1998 ♪♪♪

Enter Adam Sandler, in another incarnation of his *Saturday Night Live* persona, as the bumbling waterboy to a permanently-losing football team who takes to his task with the seriousness of an EPA expert. *The Waterboy* had its share of laughs, but was not in the same league as *The Wedding Singer,* in which Sandler also starred, and which was also directed by Frank Coraci. The soundtrack album, a collection of pop songs, offers an interesting mix, with performances by Creedence Clearwater Revival, the Doors, Earth, Wind & Fire, Lenny Kravitz, John Mellencamp, Joe Walsh, the Allman Brothers, and Rush, among the best-established names. Not a bad compilation, all things considered.

see also: The Wedding Singer

Didier C. Deutsch

Waterloo

1995, Legend Records/Italy, from the film *Waterloo,* Paramount, 1970 ♪♪♪
album notes: Music: Nino Rota; Conductor: Bruno Nicolai.

The Napoleonic saga has inspired many screen retellings, and *Waterloo,* despite its many flaws, numbers among the most spectacular. Starring Rod Steiger in a rather bizarre impersonation as the Little Corporal of legends who conquered most of Europe, only to lose it completely when a coalition of Austrian, British, Russian, and German armies defeated him thoroughly at Waterloo, in Belgium, the grandiose recreation also included in its all-star cast such luminaries as Christopher

10 Essential Scores by Bernard Herrmann

North by Northwest
Psycho
Vertigo
Taxi Driver
The 7th Voyage of Sinbad
Citizen Kane
The Magnificent Ambersons
The Day the Earth Stood Still
Jason and the Argonauts
Jane Eyre

Plummer as Wellington, and Orson Welles as King Louis XVIII of France. The film was mostly remarkable for its sweeping battle scenes, involving thousands of participants, but was hopelessly marred by a dramatic storyline that couldn't make head or tail of its involved historical plot. Interestingly, the film enabled Nino Rota an opportunity to revisit a period he had so brilliantly set to music some 15 years earlier in *War and Peace.* While he wasn't as successful in conjuring up the accents that had made that first score so memorable, he nonetheless devised an attractive "Waterloo Waltz" that recalled ever so faintly the lovely "Natasha's Waltz" in *War and Peace.* And certainly, the two battle cues "The Voices Of War," and "La vieille garde" had nothing to envy similar cues in the earlier score. This release, quite enjoyable in its own right, sounds a bit dry and could have used some reverb. This recording may be difficult to find. Check with a used CD store, mail-order company, or a dealer specializing in rare, out-of-print, or import recordings.

see also: War and Peace

Didier C. Deutsch

Watership Down

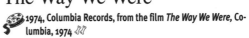

1998, PEG Records, from the film *Watership Down*, 1978 ♪♪♪

album notes: Music: Angela Morley.

A full-length cartoon that featured some good animation and noticeably fine vocal performances by a slew of British actors and actresses, *Watership Down* deals with a small band of rabbits looking for a quiet place to set up house. But before they reach their nirvana, they encounter all sorts of malicious problems that translate on the screen into disturbing images of the little creatures being gnawed by dogs, mangled, torn to pieces, and otherwise destroyed by enemies of all kinds, both two- and four-legged. While the gore might be a little too much for some of the kids in the audience, Angela Morley's score, as presented in this album, fortunately doesn't contain anything ghoulish in it, and in fact often sounds quite charming.

Didier C. Deutsch

Waterworld

1995, MCA Records, from the film *Waterworld,* Universal Pictures, 1995 ♪♪♪

album notes: Music: James Newton Howard; **Conductor:** Artie Kane; **Featured Musicians:** Steve Porcaro, James Newton Howard, synth and drum programming; Katrin Kern, vocalist; **Choir:** The L.A. Master Chorale.

James Newton Howard did a yeoman's job coming in at the last minute to replace Mark Isham's original score for *Waterworld,* Kevin Costner's super–troubled 1995 sci–fi adventure that nevertheless boasted a number of bright spots—chief among them being Newton Howard's soundtrack. With a tone that ranges from new age–styled synthesizers to rousing, Korngold–inspired action cues, Newton Howard's score maintains a fine balance between being a musical underscore and a major player in Kevin Reynolds's film, and often times helping to define the relationship between the various characters in the story and their fight against the evil Deacon (played with great relish by Dennis Hopper). The music is a lot of fun on its own, and works as an enjoyable soundtrack for listeners who typically enjoy large–scale action scores.

Andy Dursin

Wavelength

1983, Varèse Sarabande, from the film *Wavelength,* New World Pictures, 1983 ♪♪♪♪

album notes: Music: Chris Franke, Edgar Froese, Johannes Schmoelling.

Tangerine Dream took a very lyrical approach to score this futuristic film, though the minimalist electronic style of the score might not be to everyone's liking. Occasionally ("Main Title," "Alien Goodbyes"), the themes developed are remarkably effective, with acoustic and electronic instruments forming a melodic texture that's quite attractive. More accessible than many of the group's efforts, the score makes a very convincing case for the use of electronics in certain situations.

Didier C. Deutsch

The Way We Were

1974, Columbia Records, from the film *The Way We Were,* Columbia, 1974 ♪♪

album notes: Music: Marvin Hamlisch.

Written by Arthur Laurents, *The Way We Were* is a sensitive love story that spans two decades and involves two diametrically opposed characters: a strong-willed political activist, played by Barbra Streisand, and a politically uncommitted writer portrayed by Robert Redford. While the film enabled Streisand to show her mettle as a dramatic actress, it also gave her an opportunity to have a #1 hit with the title tune, written by Marvin Hamlisch and Alan and Marilyn Bergman. The score, composed by Hamlisch, was pleasantly passable at best, but doesn't necessarily invite repeated playing.

Didier C. Deutsch

Wayne's World

1991, Reprise Records, from the film *Wayne's World,* Paramount Pictures, 1991 ♪♪♪♪♪

This *Saturday Night Live* bit clicked in a big way, and hambone guitar rock is a big part of the schtick. We'll never again be able to listen to Queen's "Bohemian Rhapsody" without remembering the cast's hysterical lip–syncing routine, and the film gave Gary Wright's "Dream Weaver" a new life, too. And, of course, it gives us the "Wayne's World Theme" performed by Mike Myers and Dana Carvey. Party on, dudes.

Gary Graff

Wayne World's 2

1993, Reprise Records, from the film *Wayne World's 2,* Paramount Pictures, 1993 ♪♪♪

Not quite as successful as its predecessor, mostly because the film wasn't as big a hit. This is still a good compendium of guitar rock, though, and even artfully makes connections between the crunch of Bad Company's "Can't Get Enough" from the '70s and the woozy attack of Dinosaur Jr.'s "Out There" from the '90s. Led Zeppelin singer Robert Plant doesn't sound like his heart is into covering "Louie Louie," and a couple of overexposed songs—the Village People's "YMCA" and Norman Greenbaum's "Spirit in the Sky" don't add much to the proceedings, either.

Gary Graff

Wedding Bell Blues

🎬 1997, Varèse-Sarabande, from the film *Wedding Bell Blues*, 1997 ♫♫♫♪

Informed by the title tune, a lilting, jaunting song that does a lot to lift one's spirits, this song compilation brings together some perky performances by artists who have not yet made a name for themselves, but whose undeniable talent comes full force in this album. While the songs here are not all of the same caliber, most are thoroughly enjoyable with Arabella Alexander scoring high marks for "Wedding Bell Blues" and "Kidding," as do Julianna Raye and "Wishing Well," Susan Stovall and "Fly," and Lonesome Romeos with "Sea of Love" and "Sonny's Day." A good compilation with attractive songs.

Didier C. Deutsch

The Wedding Singer

🎬 1998, Maverick/Warner Bros. Records, from the film *The Wedding Singer,* New Line Cinema, 1998 ♫♫♫♫♪

Dig up those leg warmers and Aqua Net hairspray; it appears that the 1980s are now nostalgic. In this funny love story, comedian Adam Sandler plays the singer of a wedding band who gets dumped by his longtime girlfriend. The newly engaged Drew Barrymore asks his assistance in planning her wedding. Both CDs are compilations of 1980s classics by artists like Culture Club, New Order, and the Police on the first CD, and Depeche Mode, Kajagoogoo, and Dead or Alive on the second. Also featured on the first CD is a cover of "Video Killed the Radio Star" by the Presidents of the United States of America and "Rapper's Delight (Medley)" performed by Ellen Dow with Sugarhill Gang. Dow is a senior citizen with a little-old-lady voice and the result is hysterical. Both CDs have a small amount of dialog and original songs written and performed by Sandler in the movie.

Beth Krakower

Weeds

🎬 1987, Varèse Sarabande, from the film *Weeds,* De Laurentiis Entertainment, 1987 ♫♫♫

album notes: Music: Angelo Badalamenti; **Orchestra:** The Australian Pops Orchestra; **Conductor:** Angelo Badalamenti.

Normally known for his unconventional work on *Twin Peaks,* Angelo Badalamenti's score for this Nick Nolte film about a prison acting-troupe is the complete contradiction in style and content. Done mostly in a classical style, the music for *Weeds* has a realistic, down-to-earth emotional temperament. Since the major characters in the ensemble are ex-cons, the music romanticizes them as lost souls whose only freedom is found within their enthusiasm for acting. Badalamenti does a fine job

in creating this moving mix of passion and pathos. The latter part of the album contains instrumental tracks by other composers, including Melissa Etheridge ("I Wanna Go Home") and *Twin Peaks* director David Lynch ("Mysteries of Love").

David Hirsch

Welcome Home Roxy Carmichael

🎬 1990, Varèse Sarabande, from the film *Welcome Home Roxy Carmichael,* Paramount Pictures, 1990 ♫♫♫

album notes: Music: Thomas Newman; **Conductor:** Thomas Newman.

Winona Ryder made a striking impression in this film in which she portrays a 15-year-old adopted nymphet with a rebellious streak who lives in a small Ohio town suddenly set abuzz with the impending return of Roxy Carmichael, a local girl who has made good as a Hollywood actress. With a sprinkling of electronics, and a deft complement of acoustic instruments, Newman fashioned a score that is a trifle arid, even as it attempts to give support to the screen action. An occasionally attractive track emerges from the ensemble ("Choke It," "In a Beauty Parlor"), but for the most part it's more atmosphere stuff than melodic programming, something which works against the CD as pure musical entertainment.

Didier C. Deutsch

Welcome to Sarajevo

🎬 1998, Capitol Records, from the film *Welcome to Sarajevo,* Miramax, 1998 ♫♫♫♪

album notes: Music: Adrian Johnston; **Orchestra:** The London Chamber Orchestra; **Conductor:** Nick Ingman; **Featured Musicians:** Rosemary Furniss, violin.

A controversial film, particularly in view of the political events that have ensued since it was made, *Welcome to Sarajevo* is an impassioned look at the beleaguered Serbian resort city as seen through the eyes of a British war correspondent, with the whole thing framed in a mild dramatic story that serves to enhance the real-life drama already unspooling at the time. While the screen action focuses on well-drawn, sensitive characters, the real meat of the story is the resilience of the city and its inhabitants, seen at the start of 1992, as the Serbs try to defeat the new independence claimed by Bosnia and shell the city from the hills around while encouraging snipers within. In contrast with the dramatic situations explored on screen, the soundtrack offers an unusual number of uplifting songs, epitomized by Bobby McFerrin's finger-snapping "Don't Worry Be Happy," one of the bright numbers found here. Other selections include "The Way Young Lovers Do" by Van Morrison, "Shine On" by House of Love, "Happy Mondays" by Donovan,

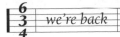
and "I Wanna Be Adored" by the Stone Roses, all of them with ingratiating, forward-looking tempi. In contrast, Adrian Johnston's score, represented by two selections, sounds more restrained, more forlorn, while Tomaso Albinoni's "Adagio in G Minor" sustains similar moods of melancholy and sadness. Meanwhile, the war wages on. . . .

Didier C. Deutsch

We're Back!

🎞️ 1993, MCA Records, from the animated feature *We're Back! A Dinosaur's Story*, Universal Pictures, 1993 🎵🎵🎵🎵

album notes: Music: James Horner; **Orchestra:** The London Symphony Orchestra; **Conductor:** James Horner; **Featured Musicians:** Charlie Davis, Doug Sharf, trumpet; Iki Levy, drums, percussion; Thomas Dolby, keyboards; Jon E. Love, Will Ray, guitars; Pasquale Zicari, sax, flute; William Henn, bass; Skip Edwards, piano.

When four cuddly monsters from the dinosaur age fly forward in time to the 20th century, what do you get but a brightly amusing animated feature, courtesy of Steven Spielberg, and a wonderful score to match, composed by James Horner. Not exactly *Jurassic Park,* but close. Frequently exhilarating and whimsical, the motifs created by the composer follow the story while giving musical life to the animated characters that inhabit it, sometimes in portraits that are vividly sketched and amusingly detailed. As is frequently the case with Horner, some cues are extremely profuse, enabling his creativity to better express itself, while his lush, florid style takes full advantage of the colorful orchestral palette in themes that are always quite attractive and enjoyable. There are many, many delightful moments in this score, beginning with the explicit "Main Title/Primeval Times," but encompassing such ingenious stops as "Welcome to New York," "Hot Pursuit," "Grand Demon Parade," and the jaunty "Special Visitors to the Museum of Natural History." Little Richard's rollicking performance of "Roll Back the Rock (To the Dawn of Time)" adds a tongue–in–cheek coda to the recording that is not even out of place.

Didier C. Deutsch

The West

📺 1997, Sony Classical, from the PBS documentary, *The West*, 1997 🎵🎵🎵

Like *500 Nations, Lewis & Clark,* and *The Native Americans,* this soundtrack to a PBS documentary initially shown in 1997 retraces the epic conquest of the West, the opening of new frontiers, and the devastating effects the encroaching movement west of the new pioneers had on the people who already lived there. Like the other documentaries, *The West* also makes ample use of folk songs and traditional themes, often performed by artists heard here for the first time. There are many

ingratiating moments in this soundtrack which, combined with the others mentioned above, provides a journey into this country's past and its invaluable musical riches. Perhaps not to everyone's taste, but essential nonetheless.

see also: 500 Nations, The Native Americans, Lewis and Clark

Didier C. Deutsch

West Side Story

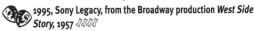

🎞️ 1995, Sony Legacy, from the Broadway production *West Side Story*, 1957 🎵🎵🎵

album notes: Music: Leonard Bernstein; **Lyrics:** Stephen Sondheim; **Musical Direction:** Max Goberman; **Cast:** Carol Lawrence, Larry Kert, Chita Rivera, Mickey Calin, Ken Le Roy, Marilyn Cooper, Reri Grist, Carmen Guiterrez, Grover Dale.

🎞️ 1995, Sony Masterworks; from the film *West Side Story,* Mirisch Pictures, 1960 🎵🎵🎵

album notes: Music: Leonard Bernstein; **Lyrics:** Stephen Sondheim; **Conductor:** Johnny Green; **Cast:** Natalie Wood, Richard Beymer, Rita Moreno, Russ Tamblyn, George Chakiris.

Without a doubt one of the most important and successful musicals to emerge from the post–war Broadway stage, *West Side Story* is also, unfortunately, the only one that brought together two of the most talented men in the theater, Leonard Bernstein and Stephen Sondheim. A thoroughly riveting show set in New York's Hell's Kitchen circa late 1950s, it packed a potent statement on the human condition and has retained its social, musical, and dramatic relevance for more than 40 years.

As a starting point, the original Broadway cast recording is essential, as the performances by Larry Kert, Carol Lawrence, and Chita Rivera are chock full of the excitement, passion and energy that make *West Side Story* so special. If you're looking for outstanding sonics, seek out the 20–bit SBM gold Mastersound edition, which has been remixed from the original three–track session tapes. This version vitally preserves the sensitivity and immediacy of the performances, and is far superior to the standard Columbia CD.

The famous 1961 original soundtrack recording has also been treated to a grand restoration, and while the performances themselves sometime lack the spark of the original Broadway cast recording, it is one of the most important soundtracks to come from the CD era. Remastered from the original multi–track, 35mm film masters, this CD issue restores all of the film's original music, including the previously unreleased "Overture," "Finale," and "End Credit" music. A number of cues have been expanded (notably "Dance at the Gym," and "Tonight"), and all selections have been properly sequenced to reflect the original running order of the songs in the film.

Charles L. Granata

West Side Story (The Kobal Collection)

Western

1997, Virgin Records/France, from the film *Western*, 1997 ♫♫♫♪

album notes: Music: Bernardo Sandoval; **Featured Musicians:** Serge Lopez, guitar; Benoit Mardon, guitar; Cecile Briavoine, guitars; Marc Dechaumont, bass; Daniel Portales, mandolin; Paul Hirsh, Pan pipes; Jean-Luc Amestoy, piano, accordion; Pascal Rollando, percussion; Toni Marcos, percussion.

This quiet little film, awarded the Jury Prize at the 1997 Cannes Film Festival, told the story of two unemployed men, wandering on the roads in the western part of France, and their quest for the ideal woman. But the film was charged with so much pathos and energy that it easily attained levels of entertainment that seemed rare, given its simplified plot. The soundtrack consisted of folk songs, with a strong Spanish influence, which made the film even more unusual. Two brief dialogue excerpts in French may be of limited appeal, but, to those who understand the language, provide a better understanding about what made the film such a critical and popular success in Europe. This title may be out of print or just plain hard to find. Mail-order companies, used CD shops, or dealers of rare or import recordings will be your best bet.

Didier C. Deutsch

The Whales of August

1987, Varèse Sarabande, from the film *The Whales of August*, Nelson Films/Alive Films, 1987 ♫♫♫♫

album notes: Music: Alan Price; **Conductor:** Derek Wadsworth.

This is a delightful orchestral score composed by Alan Price for the 1987 screen adaptation of David Berry's stage play about two aging sisters in a seaside Maine house (Bette Davis and Lillian Gish in her last film). The film is a simple, albeit compelling story of the waning years of life, that inspired Price to emphasize the women's strength and dignity, the things that have served them well all their lives. He fashioned slow, careful melodies for them, but the score gets some energy in the themes for the whales. The sisters eagerly await the return of these magnificent creatures who appear each August. Price also provides a distraction—an ethnic theme for the elderly Russian émigré, Mr. Maranov (Vincent Price). Unfortunately, because the film was based on a dialogue–driven play, the score is only a mere 28 minutes long. I was left wishing for more, but it's still an engaging delight. Derek Wadsworth, who composed the score for the second season of the *Space: 1999* television series arranged and conducted the score.

David Hirsch

What Did You Do in the War, Daddy?

1999, RCA Victor/Spain, from the film *What Did You Do in the War, Daddy?*, Universal, 1966 ♫♫♫♫

album notes: Music: Henry Mancini; **Conductor:** Henry Mancini.

Another Henry Mancini score for a Blake Edwards comedy, set in Italy, where the sun is hot, the women pretty, the wine tasty, and music pervades every aspect of life. Oh, and let's not forget the mozzarella.... Set against the backdrop of World War II, this one, starring James Coburn and Dick Shawn, involves a company of GIs ready for combat against a band of Italian soldiers entrenched in a Sicilian village. Much to their surprise, the Italians are only too glad to surrender, provided the Americans let them have their annual wine festival. Mancini did what he did best in such cases: he wrote a flavorful score that teems with great themes, several of which adopt a tarantella bounce, and that yielded at least two solid hits in "The Swing March," a favorite of college bands, and the attractive "In the Arms of Love," which was performed over the credits by Andy Williams, but is heard here in two different versions, an instrumental one and sung by a chorus. The effect is not exactly the same. The wine festival, though, leads to a deliriously enjoyable "Festa!"

Didier C. Deutsch

What Dreams May Come

1998, Beyond Records, from the film *What Dreams May Come*, PolyGram, 1998 ♫♫♫♫♪

album notes: Music: Michael Kamen; **Orchestra:** The London Metropolitan Orchestra; **Conductor:** Michael Kamen; **Featured Musicians:** Michael Kamen, oboe; Andrew Schulman, cello; Dane Lee, French horn; Philip Palmer, guitar; Julian Meinardi, vocals; Alan Machacek, vocals.

Michael Kamen's score and the rich visual images were the best parts of this uniquely strange film, in which a man (Robin Williams), who unexpectedly died in an accident, has to chose between heaven without his wife, who, unable to cope with the loss, committed suicide, or spend an eternity in hell with her. Commissioned to write the score at the last minute, Kamen based it on a song Mark Snow wrote when the two of them were in a rock group together. The rich visual images of the afterlife found an echo in his florid, attractive effort, but the sonic image of hell as he envisioned it would scare even Dante.

Beth Krakower

What's New, Pussycat?

1998, Rykodisc, from the film *What's New, Pussycat?*, United Artists, 1965 ♫♫♫♫

album notes: Music: Burt Bacharach; **Lyrics:** Hal David.

Written by Woody Allen and scored by Burt Bacharach and Hal David at the top of their form, *What's New, Pussycat?* is the exhilarating tale of an incorrigible bachelor about to get married, who ends up in a resort hotel where, literally, all the people he is trying to avoid, including his fiancee, descend en masse. With Peter O'Toole playing the hapless man, Peter Sellers as a demented analyst, and Capucine, Paula Prentiss, and Romy Schneider as some of the women in O'Toole's life, this hilarious romp became one of the great screen hits of the mid-sixties. The score brims with amusing, jaunty little themes that add zest to the action, give it an ironic musical twist, and make the whole film even funnier ("Chateau Chantel"). Also contributing to the enjoyment are several songs penned by Bacharach and David, including the title tune, which became a signature song for Tom Jones, "Here I Am" by Dionne Warwick, and "My Little Red Book" by Manfred Mann. Today, the soundtrack album is still fresh, spontaneous, and a lot of fun.

see also: After the Fox, Casino Royale

Didier C. Deutsch

What's up Tiger Lily? /You're a Big Boy Now

1998, Razor & Tie, from the films *What's up, Tiger Lily?*, MGM, 1966, and *You're a Big Boy Now*, MGM, 1966 ♫♫♫♫
album notes: Songs: The Lovin' Spoonful: John Sebastian, Joe Butler, Steve Boone, Zal Yanovsky, Skip Boone.

This recording features two classic scores on one album. *What's up, Tiger Lily?* was a terrible Japanese film that Woody Allen dubbed into English without knowing what the dialogue of the film meant, turning it into a hilarious romp. *You're a Big Boy Now* was written and directed by Francis Ford Coppola, and featured Peter Kastner as a young man with overprotective parents who learns about life from a young actress he's met. The Lovin' Spoonful composed the songs and score for *What's up, Tiger Lily?* and the band's lead singer, John Sebastian, composed the score for *You're a Big Boy Now,* which the band played in the film, charting a top-20 hit with "Darling Be Home Soon" in 1967. Both of these soundtracks fit very nicely together and both exemplify the light-handed, easy, groovy, folk flair for which the Spoonful was famous.

Beth Krakower

When a Man Loves a Woman

1994, Hollywood Records, from the film *When a Man Loves a Woman*, Touchstone Pictures, 1994 ♫♫♫♫
album notes: Music: Zbigniew Preisner; **Orchestra:** The Sinfonia Varsovia; **Conductor:** Wojciech Michniewski; **Featured Soloists:** Tomasz Stanko, trumpet; Konrad Mastylo, piano.

A solid melodrama starring Meg Ryan as an alcoholic woman and Andy Garcia as the man who stands by her in spite of all the scorn and abuse he has to endure, *When a Man Loves a Woman* elicited a wonderful score from Zbigniew Preisner, who developed his own themes rather than use the well-known pop song performed by Percy Sledge (appropriately heard here as the opening track). A veritable recital of gorgeous love motifs, sensitively written and performed, the mesmerizing cues unfold with great serenity, belying the tension and turmoil in the narrative. "Crazy Love" by Brian Kennedy and "El Gusto" by Los Lobos add a different, though equally welcome note.

Didier C. Deutsch

When Harry Met Sally . . .

1989, Columbia Records, from the film *When Harry Met Sally . . .,* Castle Rock Entertainment, 1989 ♫♫♫♫
album notes: Featured Performers: Harry Connick Jr., piano, vocals; Benjamin Jonah Wolfe, bass; Jeff "Tain" Watts, drums; Frank Wess, tenor sax; Jay Berliner, acoustic guitar.

This CD, titled *Music from the Motion Picture When Harry Met Sally,* is a true enigma. While *When Harry Met Sally* launched Harry Connick Jr.'s impressive commercial career, he did not (as is suggested by the title of the album and the cover art, cleverly taken from the film) perform all of the songs in the movie. What's missing here are Frank Sinatra's gorgeous rendition of the film's most important song, "It Had to Be You," and a number of other numbers that were performed in the film by Ella Fitzgerald, Louis Armstrong, and other top musical talents.

So, in a sense, this CD release is misleading. But it's no matter. *When Harry Met Sally* is a witty, whimsical tale—the quintessential "New York" love story—and Connick's cover version is excellent, replete with some of the very finest standards, pleasingly sung and performed, that perfectly complement the tender, romantic plot that Rob Reiner lovingly brought to the screen.

Charles L. Granata

When We Were Kings

1997, DAS/Mercury Records, from the documentary *When We Were Kings*, Gramercy Pictures, 1997 ♫♫♫♫
What turned into a documentary about Muhammad Ali and "The Rumble in the Jungle" actually started out chronicling the all-star R&B concert that occurred during the festival surrounding the famed Ali–George Foreman fight. So it's not surprising that there are some incendiary live performances by James Brown, B.B. King, The Spinners, The Jazz Crusaders, and Bill Withers, whose "Ain't No Sunshine/You" medley is a great moment in soul music. Some of Ali's diatribes included here hold their own with modern-day rappers—some of whom, no-

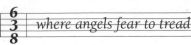

tably Fugees and A Tribe Called Quest, open the album with a song called "Rumble in the Jungle."

Gary Graff

Where Angels Fear to Tread

1991, Virgin Movie Music, from the film *Where Angels Fear to Tread*, FineLine Features, 1991 ♪♪♪♪

album notes: Music: Rachel Portman; **Orchestra:** The Hungarian Film and Television Orchestra; **Conductor:** David Snell; **Featured Musicians:** Nicholas Bucknall, clarinet; William Bennett, flute.

Rachel Portman's first major feature, *Where Angels Fear to Tread,* revealed the depth of the composer's creativity, as well as her uncanny ability to write attractive themes with great cinematic power. All the basic elements that have characterized Portman's efforts since can be found in this superbly confident score—an abundance of solid melodic, intelligently literate, handsomely orchestrated material, overflowing with generously romantic ideas that build up in layers; the whole thing served in a particularly winsome way that invites repeated listening. The film, a sensitive tearjerker about an Italian man whose British wife died when she gave birth to their son, and who must confront her relatives who want to take the child back to England with them, resulted in a profuse series of cues in which the romantic Impressionistic influences dominate. While coherent in the context of the film, the "Mad Scene" from Donizetti's *Lucia di Lammemoor* seems redundant and unnecessary in this soundtrack album, and actually detracts the listener's attention rather than eliciting a more complete vision of the film.

Didier C. Deutsch

Where the River Runs Black

1986, Varèse Sarabande, from the film *Where the River Runs Black,* MGM/UA, 1986 ♪

album notes: Music: James Horner; **Conductor:** James Horner.

A film dealing with the clash of civilization and indigenous people in South America, *Where the River Runs Black* would seem to offer fertile ground for a composer. James Horner's score however is one of his weakest, and entirely forgettable. Obviously influenced by the music for *The Emerald Forest* (composed a year earlier), Horner's score is a blend of new age and "ethnic" styles, realized on a sampling keyboard. There are some pleasantly airy moments, but most of the score consists of droning pre–set rhythms, over which the composer fiddles with various samples (strings, voice, and, most predominantly panpipe, which comes out sounding more like a circus organ than an authentic South American instrument). In fact most of the score sounds like it was improvised as Horner sat at the

keyboard. There is little structure and negligible melodic invention. Track 10, "Discovered at the Mine," is literally no more than a continuous programmed rhythm, with no development or (apparently) even human influence. *Where the River Runs Black* is a sad example of how the ease of synthesizers can induce even a talented composer to press a button and allow electronics to do his work for him.

Paul Andrew MacLean

While You Were Sleeping

1995, Uni Records, from the film *While You Were Sleeping,* Hollywood Pictures, 1995 ♪♪♪

album notes: Music: Randy Edelman; **Conductor:** Randy Edelman.

Bouncy, infectious melodies distinguish this upbeat score by Randy Edelman. His dance–like opening theme well suits the pace of this comedy about a pretty subway token clerk (Sandra Bullock) who is mistaken for the fiancee of a comatose man. Desperately lonely, she gets drawn into the warmth of his family circle, aided by Edelman's heart–tugging "Love Theme." A delight, though a bit repetitive.

David Hirsch

The Whisperers

1998, Rykodisc, from the film *The Whisperers,* United Artists, 1966 ♪♪♪♪

album notes: Music: John Barry; **Conductor:** John Barry.

Taking a breather from the James Bond films, John Barry scored this film about a lonely old woman whose dreams of getting rich unexpectedly materialize when she discovers her son has hidden the haul from a robbery in her apartment. Augmenting Dame Edith Evans' sensational star turn as the aged woman, struggling to keep her dignity as she slowly sinks into moral and physical decrepitude, the score gave Barry an opportunity to move away from the bombast of Bond and write a score that relied on his sensitivity and emotions, rather than just his skills as a musician. Not as well known as some of Barry's more visible creations, it is nonetheless a significant contribution that will haunt the listener long after the album has ended.

Didier C. Deutsch

White Mischief

1988, Varèse Sarabande, from the film *White Mischief,* Columbia Pictures, 1988 ♪♪♪♪

album notes: Music: George Fenton.

A gorgeously dance band–inspired score by George Fenton illuminated this story of British settlers in Kenya's so–called "Happy Valley," whose life of opulence and debauchery during the early days of World War II contrasted with the hardship of their peers at home as well as that of the natives around them. Essentially a triangular love affair, *White Mischief,* starring Greta Scacchi, Joss Ackland, and Charles Dance, involved itself with a couple of newlyweds, freshly arrived in Nairobi's golden circle of British colonialists. Their relationship turns sour when she meets another man, whose sudden murder unveils the scandalous lifestyle of the "Happy Valley" residents. Punctuating the various incidents in the story, Fenton devised a score that draws its strength from the several cues tailored after the giddy dance numbers evocative of that period ("Happy Valley Foxtrot," "Muthaiga Club Quickstep," "Jungle Stomp," "Roadhouse Rumba," as well as a cover of Cole Porter's "Begin the Beguine"), all of them sprightly and entertaining. Other moods are established with cues that specifically detail the time and place of the screen action, but that are devoid of any "African" accents, in keeping with the isolationist attitude of the British denizens. Film co–star Sarah Miles has a field day performing the "Alphabet Song," while Tim Finn delivers a wicked vocal version of the title tune.

Didier C. Deutsch

White Nights

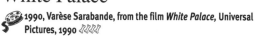1985, Atlantic Records, from the film *White Nights,* Columbia Pictures, 1985 🎬🎬🎬

Robert Plant's "Far Post" is one of the great lost B–sides of the '80s, so it's nice to have that preserved on an album. Phil Collins and Marilyn Martin hit #1 with the love duet "Separate Lives," but meatier material is provided by Lou Reed ("My Love is Chemical") and John Hiatt ("Snake Charmer"). Worthwhile, but not essential.

Gary Graff

White Palace

1990, Varèse Sarabande, from the film *White Palace,* Universal Pictures, 1990 🎬🎬🎬

album notes: Music: George Fenton; **Conductor:** George Fenton; **Featured Musicians:** Mike Lang, keyboards; Dan Higgins, alto/soprano sax; Tim May, John Goux, guitar; Gayle Levant, Dorothy Remsen, harp; Neil Stubenhaus, bass guitar; Robert Zimmitti, percussion; Fred Seykora, cello.

With undertones reminiscent of *The Graduate, White Palace* stars James Spader as the younger man and Susan Sarandon as the bolder woman, whose encounter results in a May–to–September love affair, in this romantic drama involving a 27–year–old advertising executive and a 44–year–old waitress in a St. Louis diner. Reminiscent of the film's typically hesitant approach to its unconventional story, the score created by George Fenton moves from ruminative melodies to glorious cel-

ebrations of love, with acoustic instruments playing over orchestral textures limning the moods in appealing fashion. Along the way, there are many telling selections, including "The Dream and Awakening," with its clearly defined contrasting emotions, the elegiac "You Make Me Feel Beautiful," and the equally rewarding "The Kiss." Throughout, the themes are strongly etched and evocative, making this another vibrant effort from the composer.

Didier C. Deutsch

White Squall

1996, Hollywood Records, from the film *White Squall,* Hollywood, 1996 🎬🎬

album notes: Music: Jeff Rona; **Conductor:** Fiachra Trench; **Featured Musicians:** John Isham, uilleann pipes; Jeff Rona, pennywhistles; Harrison Gregson-Williams, vocals.

The story of a seaworthy man (Jeff Bridges) who turns his boat into a school for teenage boys—kind of a *Dead Poet's Society* at sea—the score for this film was composed by Jeff Rona, and the artwork prominently displays the fact that Rona co-produced this CD with Hans Zimmer, one of the best contemporary film composers. But don't let Zimmer's name fool you; there's nothing terribly original here, though the score manages to reflect the calm of the ocean quite nicely. With creativity in mind, Rona uses a pennywhistle to evoke a pirate-like feel in the track "The Journey Begins." Yeah? So what? The CD also features seven songs, including classics by Fats Domino, Chubby Checker, and Eddie Cochran, that are a pleasant enough listen.

Beth Krakower

Who Framed Roger Rabbit?

1988, Disneyland Records, from the film *Who Framed Roger Rabbit?,* Touchstone Pictures, 1988 🎬🎬🎬🎬

album notes: Music: Alan Silvestri; **Orchestra:** The London Symphony Orchestra; **Conductor:** Alan Silvestri; **Featured Musicians:** Jerry Hey, trumpet; Tom Scott, saxophone; Randy Waldman, Chet Swiatkowski, piano; Chuck Domanico, bass; Harvey Mason, Steve Schaefer, drums.

The goofy, unlikely story of a down–at–the–heel private investigator in Hollywood's 1940s, and his involvement with (pardon the word!) 'toon characters is the mischievous premise upon which the hilarious *Who Framed Roger Rabbit* is based. Starring Bob Hoskins, looking appropriately baffled most of the time, Christopher Lloyd as the nefarious Judge Doom bent on destroying all the cute little characters, and Roger Rabbit, unable to concentrate on acting ever since he and his wife, the sultry Jessica, have become estranged, the whole silly affair is a hoot from beginning to end, thanks largely to its brilliant integration of live action and animation. Adding a comedic voice of its own, Alan Silvestri's frequently rollicking score keeps things in proper musical focus, with slyly tongue–in–cheek cues that enhanced the screen action and provided it with a strong peg. Heard on their own musical merits, however, some selections in this soundtrack album come across as too one–dimensional without the benefit of the dazzling visuals, in a clear indication of how well the score was intimately integrated in the picture. Exceptions include the uproarious "The Merry–Go–Round Broke Down (Roger's Song);" Jessica's sexy rendition (with Amy Irving's voice) of the standard "Why Don't You Do Right?;" "Jessica's Theme" and "Eddie's Theme" are two flavorful instrumentals; the frantically manic "Toontown," which, more than any other, captures the spirit of the film itself; and "Smile Darn Ya Smile/That's All, Folks!" provided an appropriate coda to the film and to this disc.

Didier C. Deutsch

The Whole Wide World

1996, Mojo Trax Records, from the film *The Whole Wide World*, Sony Pictures Classics, 1996 ♪♪♪♪

album notes: Music: Hans Zimmer, Harry Gregson–Williams.

Hans Zimmer and Harry Gregson–Williams have written what is essentially a very lovely score for this unconventional little film based on the true–life three–year friendship between a schoolteacher and would–be novelist, Novalyne Price, and Robert E. Howard, creator of such pulp fiction fantasy characters as *Conan the Barbarian* and *Red Sonja.* Beyond the basic feelings that brought these two fiercely independent souls together (the deep intellectual and literary understanding they shared), other, equally profound elements conspired to keep them apart: Price's approach to writing was naturalistic, something for which Howard, more interested in the fantastic tales that came out of his imagination, had very little interest. The film, exploring what was apparently a platonic relationship, moved Zimmer and Gregson–Williams to write several cues in which the dominant moods are plainly romantic, sometimes with a solo instrument stating the melody over a synthesizer line. The two characters receive detailed motifs ("Two Sides of Bob," "Novalyne's Theme") written in a similar vein. Only occasionally, as in "Conan Emerges," do the composers indulge in a bit of epic writing which dissipates quickly. It all adds up to a generally very satisfying score, highly listenable.

Didier C. Deutsch

Who's Afraid of Virginia Woolf?

1998, Varèse-Sarabande, from the film *Who's Afraid of Virginia Woolf?*, Warner Bros., 1965 ♪♪♪♪

album notes: Music: Alex North; Orchestra: The National Philharmonic; Conductor: Jerry Goldsmith.

The teaming of real-life husband and wife Richard Burton and Elizabeth Taylor as the protagonists of this Edward Albee drama proved an explosive combination that ignited the screen and kept audiences rapt. Brilliantly directed by Mike Nichols, the raw energy and subliminal tenderness displayed by the two main characters, a burned-out professor and his foul-mouthed, tyrannical wife, found incredible expression in the two actors' extraordinarily vivid portrayals. Sandy Dennis and George Segal play the couple invited to dinner, only to witness the sudden outbursts that result in their hosts tearing at each other yet also reveal their profound love for each other, and are also magnificent. Complementing the action on screen, Alex North contributed a sensitively shaded, very attractive score that took its central focus from the deep feelings bonding the two main characters together, rather than the strife that drives them occasionally apart. Jerry Goldsmith conducting the National Philharmonic Orchestra renders the slightest nuances in this great opus.

Didier C. Deutsch

Why Do Fools Fall in Love

1998, EastWest/Warner Bros. Sunset Records, from the film *Why Do Fools Fall in Love*, Warner Bros., 1998 ♪♪♪

1998, Rhino Records, from the film *Why Do Fools Fall in Love*, Warner Bros., 1998 ♪♪♪♪

While the answer to the question asked in this amiable comedy might be difficult to answer, there is no difficulty in singling out which of these two albums is the better deal. Judging each on its obvious merits, the East/West compilation offers cover versions of the standards used in the movie that give them a more contemporary twist. Nothing wrong with that, and the performers—En Vogue, Missy "Misdemeanor" Elliott, Mint Condition, Gina Thompson, and the others heard here—are quite engaging, even if they sometimes exemplify a convoluted, sinuous style of singing that tends to be irritating after a while. Conversely, what the Rhino set has to offer are the original versions of the same hits, performed by the artists who created them in the first place: Little Richard, the Teenagers and Frankie Lymon, the Platters, Clyde McPhatter, the Kinks, the Mamas & the Papas, Bobby Womack, etc. Sorry Missy, but they can't be beat, and what they do here sounds so much better.

Didier C. Deutsch

Widow's Peak

1994, Varèse Sarabande, from the film *Widow's Peak,* Fine Line Features, 1994 🎬🎬🎬

album notes: Music: Carl Davis; **Conductor:** Carl Davis.

This delightfully laid-back collection of cues by Carl Davis transports us back to the early part of the 20th century, when a free spirited World War I widow stirs up a small Irish town. Though comforting at first, like the opening movement of a symphony, the tone eventually degrades into a murky darkness with the nightmarish cues "The Regatta" and "Boat Trips and Murder." The score is quite satisfying, but regretfully short at only about 24 minutes. Vaughn Williams's 14-minute "Fantasia on a Theme by Thomas Tallis" fills out the running time.

David Hirsch

Wild America

1997, Prometheus Records/Belgium; from the film *Wild America,* Morgan Creek, 1997 🎬🎬🎬🎬

album notes: Music: Joel McNeely; **Conductor:** Joel McNeely.

Based on a true story, set in the summer of 1967, *Wild America* focused on three brothers who, armed with a 16-mm Airflex camera, decided to scour the wilderness and film endangered animals in their natural surroundings. Pursued by angry alligators, chased by a temperamental moose, nearly crushed by a stampede of wild horses, and suddenly confronted by a dangerous grizzly bear, the journey proved primordial in the brothers' lives, as it forced them to reevaluate their relationship with each other, and forced them to face situations they had not thought they would encounter. Giving a musical voice to the story, Joel McNeely wrote a masterful score with broad colorful strokes to draw the listener into the spectacle of the outdoor action, and softer hues to depict the inner reactions elicited by the journey itself. It all adds up to a genuinely striking, quite enjoyable score.

Didier C. Deutsch

The Wild Angels

1996, Curb Records, from the film *The Wild Angels,* American International, 1966 🎬🎬🎬

album notes: Music: Mike Curb; **Featured Musicians:** Davie Allan & the Arrows.

For a while in the mid-1960s, bikers' movies were all the rage, following the enormous success of *Easy Rider,* unexpected as it was. American International became the studio of choice for this type of B-films, usually cheap little stories built around a recognizable star (Peter Fonda, namely), and featuring a hard-rocking score, often provided by groups like Davie Allan & the

Arrows. And so it was with *The Wild Angels,* in which Henry's son co-starred with Frank's daughter, Nancy Sinatra, in a violently expressive production that involved a rebellious gang of bikers and the townspeople they terrorize. Reflecting the trend at the time, the soundtrack features a lot of hard-rocking numbers that seem rather tame and somewhat primitive in their instrumentation by today's taste.

see also: The Trip

Didier C. Deutsch

Wild in the Country

See: Flaming Star/Wild in the Country/Follow That Dream

Wild Orchid

1988, Sire Records, from the film *Wild Orchid,* Vision p.d.g., 1988 🎬🎬🎬🎬

A soundtrack album as exotic and vibrant as the Brazilian setting for this film, chronicling the power play between an unscrupulous millionaire with kinky sexual tendencies, a sleazy jet-set businesswoman, and a young girl from the Midwest on her way to discovering Rio de Janeiro and her own eroticism. The film itself is not too terribly steamy, but this compilation certainly is, with many great tracks featuring some of the most endearing performers in both hemispheres—Ofra Haza, Nana Vasconcelos & The Bushdancers, and Simone Moreno on one hand; and David Rudder, Hank Ballard, Underworld, and The Rhythm Methodists, on the other.

Didier C. Deutsch

Wildcat

 1991, RCA Victor, from the Broadway production *Wildcat,* 1960 ♪♪♪

album notes: Music: Cy Coleman; **Lyrics:** Carolyn Leigh; **Musical Direction:** John Morris; **Cast:** Lucille Ball, Paula Stewart, Keith Andes, Don Tomkins, Clifford David, Swen Swenson.

Television's favorite redhead, Lucille Ball, made her Broadway debut on Dec. 16, 1960, in this amusing musical by Cy Coleman and Carolyn Leigh, in which she played Wildcat Jackson, an oil prospector with a lot of chutzpah and nothing else but a dry well. The accomplished comedian kept the musical afloat, as long as she was able to stay in the cast, but when she left after 172 performances, it closed. While not many of the songs in the score were that memorable, one, "Hey, Look Me Over," in which Wildcat summons everyone to give her a fighting chance when she first arrives in the small western outpost, became a hit.

Didier C. Deutsch

Wilde

1998, Sonic Images Records, from the film *Wilde*, NewStar, 1998 ♪♪♪♪

album notes: Music: Debbie Wiseman; **Conductor:** Debbie Wiseman; **Featured Musicians:** Dick Morgan, oboe; Andrew Botrill, piano; Debbie Wiseman, piano; Justin Pearson, cello.

A singular screen portrait of a singular man, Oscar Wilde, who flaunted his extravagances and refused to be pinned by conventions, *Wilde* elicited a wonderful score from Debbie Wiseman. Utilizing the orchestral forces with stunning agility, she wrote a series of cues that are marked by the use of the oboe and highly effective piano solos to create a music in keeping with the time-period of the film, yet contemporary in its approach, and intelligently melodic. The film focuses on Wilde's homosexual affair with Lord Alfred "Bosie" Douglas, the effect it had on his wife and children, and the scandal that rocked Victorian London's puritanical society and ultimately resulted in Wilde being sentenced to a jail term. It gave Stephen Fry, as Wilde, an opportunity to create a flamboyant character, grander than life, yet too humanly feeble. Wiseman used the various incidents in the narrative to paint a similar portrait of the famous playwright, with grand musical gestures ("I Do Need an Audience") that contrast with some of the most moving aspects of his disturbing (and disturbed) life ("He Loves,"

"The Wounds of Love," "Cast into Outer Darkness"). It is an eloquent contribution by a composer who has yet to get full recognition, but who has already reached her full potential.

Didier C. Deutsch

The Will Rogers Follies

1993, Columbia Records, from the Broadway production *The Will Rogers Follies,* 1993 ♪♪♪♪

album notes: Music: Cy Coleman; **Lyrics:** Betty Comden and Adolph Green; **Musical Direction:** Eric Stern; **Cast:** Keith Carradine, Dee Hoty, Candy Huffman, Dick Latessa, Paul Ukena Jr., Gregory Peck.

Will Rogers's easy–going, down–to–earth charm was pleasantly evoked in Keith Carradine's portrayal as the congenial satirist in *The Will Rogers Follies,* a big, brassy musical by Cy Coleman, Betty Comden, and Adolph Green, which opened on Broadway on May 1, 1991, for a run of 983 performances.

While the show took some liberties with historical facts, it presented the salient points in Rogers's career, from his early days in the Oklahoma prairie to his starring role in the Ziegfeld Follies to his untimely death in 1935 in a plane crash with aviator Wiley Post. Told in flashbacks, and punctuated by many eye–popping production numbers, the show benefited from Tommy Tune's flavorful staging, in which particular moments involved a line–up of chorus girls performing precision routines that were absolutely dazzling. The Tony Award–winning score, while it did not yield a memorable hit, is solidly rooted in the great Broadway tradition and exhibits a country–style flavor that makes it all the more endearing. High among its better moments were the attractive "Never Met a Man I Didn't Like," borrowed from Rogers's own remark, and the exhilarating "Willamania."

Didier C. Deutsch

Willow

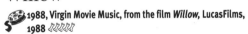 1988, Virgin Movie Music, from the film *Willow,* LucasFilms, 1988 ♪♪♪♪♪

album notes: Music: James Horner; **Orchestra:** The London Symphony Orchestra; **Choir:** The King's College Choir, **Conductor:** James Horner; **Featured Soloists:** Ian Underwood, fairlight; Kazu Matsui, sakauhachi; Mike Taylor, Tony Hennigan, pap pipes, Kena; Robin Williamson, celtic harp, bagpipes.

An extraordinarily profuse score and album (73 minutes of music, and not a weak moment in it), *Willow* signaled James Horner's definite entry in the big time as a film composer. Brilliantly imaginative, opulent and emotionally charged, the music added its voice to this sword–and–sorcery tale about misfit heroes, evil magicians, dangerous animals, angry hordes of medieval knights, and a fragile little baby, protected by a dwarf, whose very existence will fulfill an ancient prophecy.

Propelled by an epic main theme, called by resonant trumpets, the music devised by Horner, in turns elegiac and heroic, serves the story by providing a strongly imaginative and appropriately illustrative anchor. With robust themes enhancing the exciting action scenes with rich details, the score captures the pageantry and the thrill in the story in broad, colorful swathes that find an extraordinary resonance in the recording. The long selections, which regroups the cues into a comprehensive musical narrative, make for a sumptuous audio experience, one that compels the listener to return to it frequently, with renewed pleasure.

Didier C. Deutsch

Willy Wonka & the Chocolate Factory

1996, MCA Records, from the film *Willy Wonka & the Chocolate Factory,* Paramount Pictures, 1971 ♪♪♪♫

album notes: Music: Leslie Bricusse; **Lyrics:** Leslie Bricusse, Anthony Newley; **Orchestra:** The Paramount Studio Orchestra; **Conductor:** Walter Scharf; **Cast:** Gene Wilder, Jack Albertson, Peter Ostrum.

Based on the children's story *Charlie and the Chocolate Factory,* by Roald Dahl, *Willy Wonka & the Chocolate Factory* is a charming little film fantasy that stars Gene Wilder in the title role of a candymaker who puts five golden tickets inside a candy bar run and invites the winners to visit his chocolate factory. Though a mildly pleasant, colorful effort (it was entirely shot in scenic Bavaria) the film didn't have the staying power of other film musicals like *Mary Poppins* or *Chitty Chitty Bang Bang,* and was not a big box office hit as a result. However, its score by Leslie Bricusse and Anthony Newley yielded at least two recognizable tunes in "The Candy Man," which Sammy Davis Jr. later on turned into a personal hit, and "Pure Imagination."

Didier C. Deutsch

1998, Hip-O Records, from the film *Willy Wonka and the Chocolate Factory,* Paramount, 1971 ♪♪

album notes: Music: Leslie Bricusse, Anthony Newley; **Conductor:** Walter Scharf.

Oompa Loompa, duppity doo, I've got a perfect puzzle for you. Oompa Loompa, duppity dee, if you are wise you'll listen to me. What do you get when you reissue a soundtrack and don't fix the sound? Unfortunately for us, you get *Willy Wonka and the Chocolate Factory.* The main problems with this CD are uneven sound and obtrusive sound bites. However the songs are still great kitschy fun, and I still smile when I hear little Charlie sing off key during "(I've Got a) Golden Ticket." Great for ultra-fans of the movie only.

Beth Krakower

The Wind and the Lion

1990, Intrada Records, from the film *The Wind and the Lion,* MGM, 1975 ♪♪♪♪

album notes: Music: Jerry Goldsmith; **Conductor:** Jerry Goldsmith

Jerry Goldsmith's finest adventure score was written for this John Milius's historical epic about an Arabian desert chieftain played by Sean Connery who kidnaps an American woman during the presidential term of Teddy Roosevelt. From the thunderous percussion of its sweeping title music Goldsmith creates a score of amazing passion and scope, blending a gorgeous romantic melody with some of the most frenzied and rhythmically inventive action music of the composer's career. "Raisuli Attacks" has to stand as one of the most insanely satisfying action blow-outs ever composed for film, with a devilishly complicated, Arabesque melody rattling through every section of the orchestra, climaxing in a deliriously powerful trumpet solo. Almost as good is the wild, dervish percussion of "The Horsemen," and the rich, barbaric pageantry of cues like "Lord of the Riff" and "The Palace." It's a score in the grand Hollywood tradition, but sparked by Goldsmith's inspired rhythmic and orchestral experimentation, a classic in every respect.

Jeff Bond

Wing Commander

1999, Sonic Images, from the film *Wing Commander,* 20th Century-Fox, 1999 ♪♪♪♪

album notes: Music: Kevin Kiner; **Conductor:** Isobel Griffiths.

The rousing "Overture" presages a score that has all the right elements to illustrate this exciting sci-fi actioner, based on the compute game. If it evokes other fantasies involving space combats, aliens, and the derrings-do of ace pilots, it's only because the formula seems to frequently work, as it does here, and elicits great response from its intended audiences. Set in the 27th century, it involves a newly graduated space cadet (Freddie Prinze Jr.), boarding a giant spacecraft on its way to combat the Kilrathi, an alien race at war with the people of Earth. Right off the bat, Prinze gets in hot waters with the Wing Commander, Saffron Burrows, whom he mistakes for a "grease monkey." So much for tact in the 27th century! With the action taking place on the spaceship, the standard quota of frictions and friendships that develop between individuals in close quarters receive their due, and provide a delectable futuristic brand of entertainment. The score underlines some of these elements by placing the accents on the right moments, while also making sure it's enjoyably listenable in a different environment. Nothing that's new or out of the ordinary, but the music remains constantly invigorating, with a knowing wink in the di-

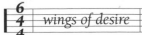

rection of previous, similar scores, which is the best thing one could ever hope for.

Didier C. Deutsch

Wings of Desire

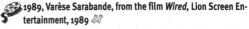1989, Nonesuch Records, from the film *Wings of Desire,* Orion Films, 1989 ♪♪♪

album notes: Music: Juergen Knieper.

The eerily somber moods in Juergen Knieper's score seem totally appropriate for this offbeat story of a couple of angels coming back to Berlin in the 1980s to win their wings, with one of them falling in love with a trapeze artist and deciding he wants to become a human. But while the music works very well within the context of the film, on record it fails to create the desired effect, and proves eventually less compelling and arresting. Further confounding the listener, various texts in German prove a deterrent for those not familiar with the language. Several selections, composed by others (including Laurie Anderson) and placed after the score, sustain the moods with somewhat strident and abrasive sounds that prove more curious than musically attractive. It's definitely not for every taste.

Didier C. Deutsch

Wings of the Dove

1997, Milan/BMG, from the film *Wings of the Dove,* Miramax, 1997 ♪♪♪♪

album notes: Music: Edward Shearmur; **Orchestra:** The London Metropolitan Orchestra; **Conductor:** Edward Shearmur; **Featured Musicians:** Hossam Ramsey, percussion; Maher Khairy, Egyptian flute; John Themis, lute, bazouki; Guy Pratt, acoustic bass.

Edward Shearmur composed a masterpiece for this screen adaptation of Henry James's novel, about a woman (Helena Bonham Carter) who comes up with a get-rich-quick scheme: a rich, dying friend is quite taken with Bonham Carter's boyfriend, played by Linus Roache, so she arranges for Roache to feign interest in the heiress, hoping that the dying woman will leave her fortune to him. In the liner notes, Shearmur comments, "The film is about deception as well as romance.... The job of the music is to bring that conflict out." In a rich display, his score reflects the emotions of the romance and the betrayal, but also captures the more lighthearted, fun elements of a trip to Venice.

Beth Krakower

The Winslow Boy

1999, DRG Records, from the film *The Winslow Boy,* 1999 ♪♪♪♪

album notes: Music: Alaric Jans.

London at the end of the Victorian era is the stage for this austere but ultimately gratifying drama, beautifully acted, which is in stark contrast with the more florid emotional dramas made in this country. Based on a real case of miscarriage of justice, the plot is adapted from Terence Rattigan's 1946 play which involves the teenage son of a London family. While attending a military academy, he is temporarily expelled for stealing another student's money, something he forcibly denies doing. Though reinstated, the boy's imperious father feels compelled to seek redress in a civil court of law, and eventually takes the case all the way to the House of Lords. Alaric Jans, a composer whose reputation has not yet reached these shores, has written a sturdy, conventional score to accompany the action, appropriately bathed in the type of sonorities one might expect to hear in the works of Sir Edward Elgar or Vaughan Williams. It's occasionally electrifying and for the most part totally enjoyable.

Didier C. Deutsch

The Winter Guest

1998, Varèse-Sarabande, from the film *The Winter Guest,* Fine Line, 1997 ♪♪♪♪

album notes: Music: Michael Kamen; **Featured Musician:** David Harrod, piano.

An intimate drama set in a small town on the coast of Scotland, *The Winter Guest* involves four pairs of wildly different people: a recently widowed photographer and her quarrelsome mother; her son and the girl next door who initiates him to his first sexual experience; two elderly women whose favorite pastime is to attend funerals; and two schoolboys who play hooky and share confidences about the pains of growing up. Framing these stories, and giving them a symbolic momentum, is the sea nearby, momentarily frozen, which must also have inspired the forlorn score composed by Michael Kamen, in which the sole instrument heard is a piano, only occasionally supported by a string orchestra. This sparse approach to scoring adds more weight to the story developing on the screen, and stresses the delicate aspects of its four components, which seldom intermingle. It's also a daring way to write a score, as it leaves the composer wide open, without the florid orchestrations that might otherwise hide some minor flaws in his creativity. Kamen rose to the challenge and wrote a set of cues that are frequently compelling, quietly expressive, and forcefully descriptive. Liz Fraser's sober, unadorned rendition of the song, "Take Me with You," adds further momentum to this unusual score.

Didier C. Deutsch

Wired

1989, Varèse Sarabande, from the film *Wired,* Lion Screen Entertainment, 1989 ♪♪

album notes: Music: Basil Poledouris; **Featured Musicians:** Michael Ruff, keyboards; Ralph Humphrey, drums; Jimmy Johnson, Jimmy

Haslip, bass; W.G. Snuffy Walden, David Williams, guitar; Richard El-
liott, saxophone; Marc Caz Macino, saxophone, harmonica; Lee
Thornberg, Ralf Rickert, trumpet; Neil Portnow, percussion; Michael
Ruff, Howard Smith, background vocals.

A filmed biography of John Belushi, *Wired,* which only missed
Belushi's presence to succeed, retraced the comedian's mete-
oric career, from his early days on *Saturday Night Live,* to his
untimely death. Much of this soundtrack album is devoted to
recreations of "Blues Brothers" songs by Michael Chiklis, who
portrayed Belushi, and Gary Groomes as Aykroyd, with an occasional assist from Billy Preston lending an aura of veracity.
But the real thing ("real" if we don't consider that the Blues
Brothers were already an imitation to begin with) being on another label, all we have here is a warmed-up, second-hand
product. Basil Poledouris was evidently inspired by the storyline if we are to believe the four cues also included here, but
his score, too, is given a short shrift in this sorry album.

Didier C. Deutsch

Wisdom

🎬 1988, Varèse Sarabande, from the film *Wisdowm,* Gladden Entertainment, 1988 🎼🎼

album notes: Music: Danny Elfman.

A strongly accented synth score composed by Danny Elfman,
this effort seems eons away from the more vibrant and interesting music he has created since. While the dry, minimalist
sounds might have helped establish the basic atmosphere in
this story of an idle youngster who robs a bank to impress his
girlfriend, taken on their own melodic merits, they often fail to
evoke more than a slight interest. Often arid in their expression, and devoid of any real spark, the cues frequently seem
more formulaic than genuinely inspiring.

Didier C. Deutsch

The Witches of Eastwick

🎬 1987, Warner Bros. Records, from the film *The Witches of Eastwick,* Warner Bros., 1987 🎼🎼🎼🎼

album notes: Music: John Williams; **Conductor:** John Williams.

If John Williams hadn't already enjoyed such a formidable reputation as the most eclectic composers around, this happily
gritty, sardonic score would have clearly singled him out as one
of the best. Delightfully anchored by the sprightly "Dance of
the Witches," a motif that dominates it, the music details this
modern tale of sorcery and, well . . . devil-may-care, about
three women living in a quaint New England town full of upright
people, who are yearning for Mr. Right . . . and find him in the
guise of a wealthy newcomer who proves himself a
smooth-talking, eyebrow-waggling, tantrum-throwing little

devil (literally). Matching the seriously tongue-in-cheek mode
of this screen adaptation of John Updike's novel, starring Cher,
Susan Sarandon, Michelle Pfeiffer, and Jack Nicholson, the
music is a constant feast of sparkling melodies and themes,
which detail the screen action and add an extra ounce (make
that a ton) of whimsy to it. Separated from it, it retains its
humor and éclat, and proves totally enjoyable.

Didier C. Deutsch

With Honors

🎬 1994, Maverick/Warner Bros. Records, from the film *With Honors,* Warner Bros., 1994 🎼🎼🎼

If this complex story about a Harvard student whose honors
thesis is found and held for ransom by a two-bit lowlife didn't
make much of a dent, its song-driven soundtrack album
should. With outstanding performances by Duran Duran,
Madonna (whose "I'll Remember" was used as the theme for
the film), the Cult, Pretenders, Lyle Lovett, and Lindsey Buckingham, this CD compilation should have a lot to attract even
the most jaded listener. Other performances are also of a high
caliber, with Belly scoring high marks with the Tom Jones classic "It's Not Unusual," as do Candlebox with "Cover Me," and
Kristin Hersh with "Your Ghost." A good, enjoyable set.

Didier C. Deutsch

Witness

🎬 1985, Varèse Sarabande, from the film *Witness,* Paramount Pictures, 1985 🎼🎼🎼

album notes: Music: Maurice Jarre; **Featured Musicians:** Michael Boddicker, Randy Kerber, Stewart Levin, Michel Mention, Chris Page, Pete
Robinson, Clark Spangler, Nyle Steiner, Ian Underwood.

One of the first scores of Maurice Jarre's "electronic period" of
the '80s, during which he turned out a number of impressive
and effective synthesizer scores, *Witness* is perhaps the best of
these electronic efforts, and one of the few synthesizer soundtracks written at the time which does not sound dated today.
One reason is probably because Jarre elected to use synthesizers for artistic rather than budgetary reasons. (The film deals
with the Amish society—a society that does not believe in musical instruments. As such Jarre determined an orchestral score
would not be true to the ethos being depicted.) Although "new
age" might best describe the overall tone of the soundtrack,
Jarre's score has an eclectic array of moods, mirroring the film's
elements of love story, crime thriller and human drama. Suspense cues in most electronic scores are often no more than
noise, but the suspenseful moments in *Witness* are enthralling
and satisfyingly musical. The showpiece of the score, however,
is Jarre's music for the barn-raising sequence, which is a noble,

Americana–flavored piece, and certainly one of the finest moments in Jarre's career.

Paul Andrew MacLean

The Wiz

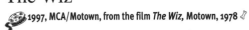
1997, MCA/Motown, from the film *The Wiz*, Motown, 1978

album notes: Music: Charlie Smalls; **Lyrics:** Charlie Smalls; **Additional Music & Lyrics:** Quincy Jones, Nickolas Ashford, Valerie Simpson, Luther Vandross; **Conductors:** Bobby Tucker, Quincy Jones, Robert Freedman; **Cast:** Diana Ross (Dorothy), Michael Jackson (the Scarecrow), Nipsey Russell (the Tinman), Ted Ross (the Cowardly Lion), Lena Horne (Glinda), Richard Pryor (the Wiz), Mabel King (Evilene), Thelma Carpenter (Miss One), Theresa Merrit (Aunt Em).

The Wiz is one clear example of a charming Broadway musical getting the inflated Hollywood treatment in its screen transfer. In Quincy Jones' over-the-top vision, nothing was spared to make this the ultimate big-screen musical extravaganza that would at least rival if not surpass the 1939 version starring Judy Garland. More than 300 musicians and singers are credited in the production of the score for this two-CD set, and not just anyone, mind you: stellar players include Ron Carter, Anthony Jackson, Randy Brecker, Jon Faddis, Steve Gadd, Harvey Mason, Ralph MacDonald, Michael Brecker, Hubert Laws, Eric Gale, Jerry Hey, Steve Khan, Dave Grusin, Bob James, Richard Tee, Roberta Flack, Cissy Houston, Luther Vandross, and others. In other words, the *crème de la crème* of studio heavyweights ca. 1978. But whether the original Broadway musical by Charlie Smalls warranted this type of treatment is another matter altogether.

In its neon approach to its subject, the film seemed to have lost a clear perspective of what the charming Frank L. Baum story was all about in the first place. By miscasting Diana Ross, obviously too old to play Dorothy, the film further alienated itself from its fantasy aspects, and moved into the realm of misguided grand spectacle—all glitter and no show. This also applied to the overblown soundtrack which, despite the presence of the studio luminaries credited above and of-first-magnitude star performers like Michael Jackson, Lena Horne (superb in "Believe in Yourself," the only number worth mentioning), Richard Pryor, and Nipsey Russell, simply didn't connect at all. It sounds big, it sounds huge, it falls flat! For all its flaws, the original-cast album, with irritating Stephanie Mills, is far superior to this gigantic disaster.

Didier C. Deutsch

The Wizard of Oz

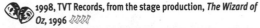
1998, TVT Records, from the stage production, *The Wizard of Oz*, 1996

album notes: Music: Harold Arlen, Herbert Stothart; **Lyrics:** E.Y. Harburg; **Cast:** Mickey Rooney (the Wizard), Eartha Kitt (the Wicked Witch), Jessica Grove (Dorothy), Ken Page (the Cowardly Lion), Lara Teeter (the Scarecrow), Dirk Lumbard (the Tin Man), Bob Dorian (Uncle Henry/Winkie General), Judith McCauley (Glinda).

Next to *The Wiz* (see above), the score for *The Wizard of Oz* is a totally different breed. But Harold Arlen and E.Y. Harburg, not to mention Herbert Stothart who created the underscoring, were peerless. As anyone who's seen the celebrated MGM film remembers, *The Wizard of Oz* was also the score that gave Judy Garland her signature song, the immortal "Over the Rainbow," and placed Bert Lahr, Ray Bolger, Jack Haley, and Margaret Hamilton in the pantheon of great actors with their portrayals of the Cowardly Lion, the Scarecrow, the Tin Man, and the Wicked Witch, respectively. And let's not forget the Munchkins, while we're at it. . . . Which brings us to the stage show that has become a holiday fixture in New York City for the past few years, and this original cast album. Attempting to put on a stage production of the story is inviting disaster; not that it cannot be done, in fact it *was* done before there was the film. But that's the point: the film is so clearly etched in our minds that any attempt to duplicate it, with the restrictions imposed by a stage presentation, automatically suggests comparisons, and as unfair as it may be, the film will always win! It was more brilliant, more creative, Garland was more fetching, the Munchkins were more cute. . . . You get the point.

Yet, within its reduced form of expression, there is something vastly endearing about the stage presentation. With the cast constantly changing from year to year, the one we are given to listen to here includes Mickey Rooney (Garland's old filmmate) as the Wizard, Eartha Kitt as the Wicked Witch, Ken Page as the Cowardly Lion (a role that suits him in the mane), Lara Teeter as the Scarecrow, and benign Bob Dorian, a fixture on AMC, as the Winkie General, all perfectly fine, though Dirk Lumbard is a bit bland as the Tin Man, but that seems to go with the territory. Jessica Grove doesn't sound like Judy Garland, and exhibits a spunk of her own which is engaging, particularly in her encounters with the Wicked Witch and the Wizard. Ultimately, though, what makes this recording the pleasure it turns out to be is not so much its cast, but the wonderful score by Arlen, Harburg, and Stothart. Fifty years later, it has not aged a bit.

Didier C. Deutsch

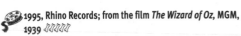
1995, Rhino Records; from the film *The Wizard of Oz*, MGM, 1939

album notes: Music: Herbert Stothart; **Songs:** Harold Arlen; **Lyrics:** E.Y. Harburg; **Orchestra:** The MGM Studio Orchestra; The MGM Studio Chorus; **Conductor:** Herbert Stothart; **Cast:** Judy Garland, Ray Bolger, Bert Lahr, Jack Haley.

The Rhino deluxe edition of the music from MGM's cherished adaptation of *The Wizard of Oz* is so exquisite, one al-

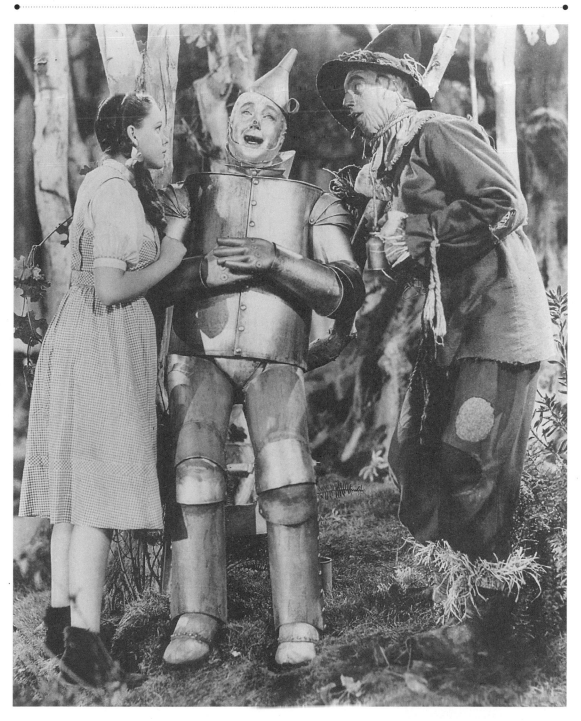

The Wizard of Oz **(The Kobal Collection)**

most doesn't know where to start. In a nutshell, this is one of the most beautiful, and *amazing* CD packages ever assembled. Who knew that so much great music had been left on the cutting room floor? Did anyone believe that these vintage recordings could ever sound so good? Undoubtedly, this very special set will strike a tender chord for those who hold fond memories of this classic film dear. From the "Main Title" on, we are treated to a fascinating cornucopia of original and previously unreleased score music (by Herbert Stothart) and songs (by Harold Arlen and "Yip" Harburg), as well as extended sequences and demos. Everything that a true connoisseur of *Wizard* could possibly wish for is collected here, lovingly remastered from the original recording elements for incredibly rich, detailed sound. There is a certain unexplainable warmth and charm to the "sound" of the MGM films of this period, and it is retained in these new restorations. Rounding out the package is a lavish, full-color book (slipcased into the CD binder), which is chock full of recording details, color photos, posters, and ads, and the most concise synopsis and history ever written for a record issue, about the film, its creators, and the music. In a word, awesome, and an essential addition to any music collector's library.

Charles L. Granata

Wolf

1994, Columbia/Sony Classical, from the film *Wolf*, Columbia Pictures, 1994 ♫♫♫♫

album notes: Music: Ennio Morricone; **Conductor:** Ennio Morricone.

Jack Nicholson had another memorable screen role in this great thriller about a middle-aged Manhattan book editor who is bitten by a wild animal, following a car accident on a dark country road, and begins to change into a werewolf as a result. Adding emotional power to this tale, Morricone wrote a musical subtext that enhances and defines the action, with sharp themes that describe it in uncompromising ways. The centerpiece of his score is a nine minute–plus cue, "The Dream and the Deer," in which some of the composer's signature effects (staccato chords darting in and out of a melodic theme) create an uneasy, foreboding mood. "The Chase," another highlight, is an explosive, fierce statement that leaves an unsettling impression as themes collide and combine to create an uneasy, active atmosphere. In the composer's body of work, *Wolf* definitely ranks as a breathtaking achievement.

Didier C. Deutsch

The Woman Next Door

See: La femme d'a cote

Woman Undone/Zooman

1995, Citadel Records, from the films *Woman Undone* and *Zooman*, Showtime, 1995 ♫♫♫

album notes: Music: Daniel Licht; **Conductor:** Pete Anthony; **Featured Musicians:** Kris Gould, soprano; Jeff Beal, trumpet.

Two scores by Daniel Licht, erstwhile specialist of horror films, which cast a different look at his creativity, with interesting results. Created in 1995, *Woman Undone* was a suspense thriller in the Hitchcockian tradition, about a couple riding in a car in the desert, who have an accident which leaves the man dead. The autopsy, however, reveals that he was shot. Director Evelyn Purcell asked Licht to write a "transparent score that would help create an ambience of mystery without interfering with the dynamics of the script." Also composed in 1995, the score for *Zooman* informed an urban contemporary drama about the father of a little girl shot dead during a gun battle between two street gangs, and his vain attempts to find witnesses that will testify against the alleged killers. In both instances, Licht wrote scores that reflect the tension in each drama, yet give each a substance that singles them out. In the first, the music is constantly limpid and eerie, a series of cues that enhance the claustrophobic atmosphere of the action and the wide open spaces where it takes place. Jazz riffs color the second and give it a more urban feel, with the cues evidencing a tighter expression to convey the moods created by the surroundings. Both in their own way are eloquent statements from a composer who gains at being better appreciated.

Didier C. Deutsch

The Wonder Years

1989, Atlantic Records, from the television series *The Wonder Years*, New World Television, 1989 ♫♫♫♫

This infantile television series actually spawned a great soundtrack album that attracted a lot of frontliners, including Joe Cocker, Was (Not Was), Julian Lennon, Carole King, Richie Havens, and Crosby, Stills, Nash, and Young, among others. Of course, many of these performances have been available elsewhere, but who can resist Cocker's rendition of "With a Little Help From My Friends," Was (Not Was)' version of "Baby I Need Your Loving," or Judson Spence's take on "Drift Away?" And that's only for a start. Other goodies in the CD also include Buffalo Springfield's "For What It's Worth," Van Morrison's "Brown–Eyed Girl," Carole King's "Will You Love Me Tomorrow," and Debbie Gibson's tribute to the show, "Come Home." All right, it's not great, but it's good fun.

Didier C. Deutsch

Wonderful Town

1990, MCA Records, from the Broadway production *Wonderful Town*, 1953 ♫♫♫♫

album notes: Music: Leonard Bernstein; **Lyrics:** Betty Comden and Adolph Green; **Musical Direction:** Lehman Engel; **Cast:** Rosalind Russell, Edith Adams, George Gaynes, Cris Alexander, Henry Lascoe, Jordan Bentley.

1991, Sony Broadway, from the CBS TV presentation *Wonderful Town*, 1958 ♫♫♫♫♫

album notes: Music: Leonard Bernstein; **Lyrics:** Betty Comden and Adolph Green; **Musical Direction:** Lehman Engel; **Cast:** Rosalind Russell, Jacquelyn McKeever, Sydney Chaplin, Cris Alexander, Jordan Bentley.

Based on the 1940 Broadway comedy *My Sister Eileen,* and the 1930s autobiographical stories written by Ruth McKenney for *The New Yorker, Wonderful Town* became one of the jazziest musicals ever composed by Leonard Bernstein; a delicious companion piece to the 1944 *On The Town,* which also has lyrics by Betty Comden and Adolph Green. Detailing the misadventures of two sisters from Ohio, Ruth and Eileen Sherwood—one the brains, the other the beauty—as they arrive in New York to find new career outlets, the show opened on Feb. 25, 1953 to rave reviews, and enjoyed a comfortable run of 553 performances.

While the critics singled out almost every aspect of the production, they kept their highest praises for Rosalind Russell, making her debut in a musical (she had previously portrayed Ruth in a 1942 film version of the play); she repeated the role in a 1958 CBS television special, with Jacquelyn McKeever replacing Edie Adams as Eileen, and Sydney Chaplin cast as Robert Baker, the publisher in love with Ruth, played in the original by George Gaynes.

Of the two recordings listed here, the one on MCA Records is the 1953 original cast album. While in mono, it still sounds fresher and more vibrant, with the performers not yet totally settled in their roles finding ways to keep the portrayals crackling and energetic. The second CD, on Sony Broadway, is the recording of the 1958 television special, and it has the great advantage of being in stereo. By then, Rosalind Russell had found the parameters within her character and could comfortably mug her way through it. Sydney Chaplin, however, is remarkably bland, and Jacquelyn McKeever doesn't have the spontaneity so endearing in Edie Adams's portrayal.

Didier C. Deutsch

Woodstock/Woodstock Two

1970, Atlantic Records, from the film *Woodstock,* Warner Bros., 1970 ♫♫♫♫

Looking back, that August weekend in 1969 marked more of an end than a beginning, and, thanks to the Michael Wadleigh

10 Essential Scores

by Alfred Newman

How the West Was Won
Airport
Captain from Castile
How Green Was My Valley
Anastasia
The Robe
Nevada Smith
The Greatest Story Ever Told
Wuthering Heights
The Keys of the Kingdom

film, the legend has now utterly obscured the muddy, can't-hear/can't-see reality. It still makes a nice legend, though, especially on these audio recordings. The abundant wrong notes you hear in the movie were corrected in a New York studio before the original three–LP set was released. And now, with Atlantic's nicely packaged 4–CD set, the sound is even better, and most of the artists missing from the film or the two previous *Woodstock* soundtrack albums have been brought into the fold. Career–making performances by the likes of Joe Cocker, Santana, The Who, and Sly and the Family Stone have weathered the years; the Band and Janis Joplin are no longer missing in action. "We must be in heaven, man."

Marc Kirkeby

A World Apart

1988, RCA Victor Records, from the film *A World Apart,* Atlantic Entertainment Group, 1988 ♫♫♫♫

album notes: Music: Hans Zimmer, Al Clay, Brian Gulland, Gavin Wright, Chris Menges, Shawn Slovo, Judy Freeman.

Set in South Africa in the early 1960s, *A World Apart* took a sobering look at the apartheid system, and its effects on a family of white settlers who oppose the government policy and become the target of a crackdown from the authorities. A story such as this requested a compelling score, and Hans Zimmer provided it in a series of themes that detail the action as seen through the eyes of Molly, the settlers' 13–year–old uncomprehending daughter. With solid assists from the Messias Choir, Zimmer's score explores the emotional implications in the story, often reaching deep into the moods to come up with forceful expressions that force the listener's attention. The cues, assembled together into a seamless musical suite, provide a narrative that is most engaging. Augmenting the score, selected traditional songs anchor the soundtrack album into its ethnic locale and bring a different touch of authenticity.

Didier C. Deutsch

Wrestling Ernest Hemingway

1994, Mercury Records, from the film *Wrestling Ernest Hemingway,* Warner Bros., 1994 ♪♪♪♪

album notes: Music: Michael Convertino; **Conductor:** Artie Kane.

Starring Robert Duvall and Richard Harris as two older men trying to outdo each other in the fancily detailed stories they tell about their real (or imagined) past, *Wrestling Ernest Hemingway* received an eloquent musical support from Michael Convertino, whose enjoyably lyrical score finds a new life of its own in this attractive recording. Augmenting the most descriptive cues ("Fireworks," "Time At Sea," "1939"), a trio of tunes in Spanish add a definitely exotic flavor to the proceedings.

Didier C. Deutsch

Wyatt Earp

1994, Warner Bros. Records, from the film *Wyatt Earp,* Warner Bros. Pictures, 1994 ♪♪♪♪

album notes: Music: James Newton Howard; **Orchestra:** The Hollywood Recording Musicians Orchestra; **Conductor:** Marty Paich; **Featured Musicians:** Dean Park, guitars; Alasdair Fraser, solo violin; Frank Marocco, accordion; Phil Ayling, recorders.

Tombstone was a major hit in the winter of 1993, and subsequently seemed to take out the wind from the sails of *Wyatt Earp,* the more ambitious but far less successful 1994 epic from star Kevin Costner and co–writer/director Lawrence Kasdan. Well–acted but pretentious and often downright boring, *Earp* was a financial disaster and critical disappointment, though no fingers will ever be pointed at James Newton Howard's outstanding score, which works as both a reflection on the conventions of the western genre and the heroic nature of Earp himself, capturing the various dimensions of the setting and the characters along the way. The score boasts a number of im-

pressive themes and musical ideas, and has been copied in numerous films and movie trailers since. Even if you never see the film, Newton Howard's soundtrack stands as a superior film score and comes highly recommended.

see also: Hour of the Gun, Tombstone

Andy Dursin

X

The X-Files/Songs in the Key Of X/The Truth and The Light

The X-Files (score); 1998, Elektra Records, from the 20th Century-Fox film, The X-Files, 1998 ♪♪
album notes: Music: Mark Snow.

The X-Files (soundtrack compilation); 1998, Elektra Records, from the 20th Century-Fox film, The X-Files, 1998 ♪♪♪♪
album notes: Music: Mark Snow.

Songs in the Key Of X; 1996, Warner Bros. Records, from the 20th Century-Fox TV series, The X-Files, 1995-1999 ♪♪♪♪
album notes: Music: Mark Snow.

The Truth and The Light: Music from The X-Files; 1996, Warner Bros. Records, from the 20th Century-Fox TV series, The X-Files, 1995-1999 ♪♪
album notes: Music: Mark Snow.

The cues Mark Snow created for the television adventures of Agents Scully and Mulder have been widely popular and widely imitated. They also sound terribly conventional and predictable— eerie synthesizer riffs that seem to be floating about at various distant levels, rising to a crescendo, punctuated by sudden percussive effects, with the whole thing quieting down to another eerie set of synthesizer riffs.... The problem is that there is really no melody to speak of, just instrumental chords that may reinforce the weird aspects of the story lines but that lose their impact and importance when heard as pure listening experience. And they released two albums of that, one from the film, the other from the television show. Will wonders never cease!

Reviewing each album would be an exercise in futility. But it may be of interest to readers to contemplate the titles given to some of the cues, particularly in the TV score album: "Materia Primoris," "Cantus Excio," "Dubitatio," "Carmen Amatorium ex Arcanum," "Fides fragilis," "Exoptare ex veritas." It may seem cool to call these cues by Latin names, and in fact it may go

Gillian Anderson and David Duchovny in The X-Files. **(The Kobal Collection)**

with the territory in this pretentious series that is so arcane that it defies description. But please, a little less pretension and a little more music might have been just as cool.

In contrast to the instrumental albums, the song albums are much more interesting, perhaps because they focus more squarely on material one can actually enjoy. The Elektra album, with songs culled from the movie, contains a fair share of performers who are first class, including Foo Fighters, Sting (who duets with Aswad on his "Invisible Sun"), the Cardigans, the Cure (a great track in "More Than This"), Soul Coughing, and Sarah McLachlan (whose eerie "Black" is much more effective than any of the cues Mark Snow may submit). Also included is a good rocker, "Flower Man," by Tonic.

The Warner Bros. album, titled *Songs in the Key of X,* features songs heard in the television series. It brings together a cogent group of performers. Foo Fighters (with a version of Gary Numan's "Down in the Park") and Soul Coughing (doing "Unmarked Helicopters") are back on this set, along with Filter (and "Thanks Bro"). But the meat of this set is the inclusion of tracks by Sheryl Crow ("On the Outside," a quietly stated ballad), Screamin' Jay Hawkins ("Frenzy," a fast-paced, percolating number), Elvis Costello and Brian Eno ("My Dark Life," a great collaboration), and Rob Zombie and Alice Cooper ("Hands of Death (Burn, Baby, Burn)," a scorching duet), alone worth the price of admission. And if you must have Mark Snow's music, there's even the original theme from the series, which bookends the CD and sounds just fine in this context.

Didier C. Deutsch

Xanadu

1998, MCA Records, from the film *Xanadu,* Universal, 1980
♫♫

album notes: Songs: Jeff Lynne, John Farrar; **Featured Musicians:** Electric Light Orchestra.

Despite claims to the contrary, this is not the first time this soundtrack album has been available on CD. If we want to be technical about it, there was an earlier release in Japan. Not that it matters much: the present album neither adds to nor detracts from the fact that the score to this musical fairy tale—about the daughter of Zeus, who inspires a down-on-his-luck graphic artist to turn a dilapidated building into a combo disco/'40s swing roller rink—is as trite as the film for which it was composed. Individually, Olivia Newton-John and ELO have done much better. Here, all that can be said is that they missed the mark by a long shot. Another casualty is Gene Kelly, heard elsewhere in much better material, who valiantly attempts to seem convincing in his only duet with Olivia, though he must

sense that the whole thing is a total disaster. The album, which spawned hits like "Magic" and "Suddenly" for Newton John, and "I'm Alive" for ELO, was a million-seller, which leads one to wonder what it was that buyers heard that they couldn't live without.

Didier C. Deutsch

Xena: Warrior Princess/Xena:Warrior Princess, Volume 2/The Bitter Suite:A Musical Odyssey

1996, Varèse Sarabande, from the UPN–TV series *Xena: Warrior Princess,* 1995—96 ♫♫♫

album notes: Music: Joseph LoDuca; **Conductor:** Tim Simonec, Randy Thornton.

A *Hercules* spin-off that's eclipsed its predecessor in popularity, *Xena* inspired composer Joe LoDuca to improve on his derivative Hercules music and create a far more passionate and original theme for the vigilante, indomitable Amazon warrior Xena that mixes a pounding brass line with the chanting of a female chorus. The percussive, ethnic Amazon music intersperses itself throughout this lengthy album, balanced with some more traditional but no less energetic orchestral action cues and some surprisingly effective and rich moments of sentimentality. There are ripely melodramatic horror cues and a few pop–oriented treatments of dances and market sequences that fit comfortably into this epic canvas, making this one of the most enjoyable TV score albums around.

Jeff Bond

Xena: Warrior Princess, Volume 2; 1997, Varèse-Sarabande, from the television series *Xena, Warrior Princess,* 1997 ♫♫♫♫
album notes: Music: Joseph LoDuca; **Conductor:** Randy Thornton.

The Bitter Suite: A Musical Odyssey; 1998, Varèse-Sarabande, from the television series *Xena: Warrior Princess* ♫♫♫
album notes: Music: Joseph LoDuca; **Lyricists:** Joseph LoDuca, Pamela Phillips Oland, Dennies Spiegel; **Conductor:** Randy Thornton, Joseph LoDuca.

The coincidences of alphabetical listing and similarities in releases brings the Xena albums together and illustrate the creations of a composer whose scores are epic, florid, and altogether fun to listen to. Taking things one at a time *Xena, Warrior Princess* combines cues from various shows in the series (it would have helped had the individual shows been identified) with themes that are totally engrossing. It calls on large orchestral forces, choruses by the Brookside Children's Group, flowing melodies with a swashbuckling edge to them—in other words, the full contingent of musical moments that distinguish the series and week after week give it a voice of its own. With her incredible derrings-do and appealing costumes, Xena may be a bit camp, but she's fun to watch: she's sexy, she wears her outfits better than her cast-members, and she never takes bull from anybody. This album not only brings it all back, but is also fun to listen to.

Striking a somewhat different note, *The Bitter Suite* is a fully re-alized musical based on the adventures of Xena, and starring Lucy Lawless, Renee O'Connor, Kevin Smith, Hudson Leick, and Ted Raimi, the series' principals. It is however startling to dis-cover these familiar characters in what is essentially a totally different medium, and while Joe LoDuca's score is certainly most interesting, and immensely catchy, the concept itself is flawed. Still there are flashes of the series itself in several in-strumental moments, spoken bits of dialogue to introduce the songs, and a vaguely comfortable kinship between this story and the daring adventures of Xena-as-we-know-her.

Didier C. Deutsch

A Year in Provence

1993, Silva Screen Records, from the TV mini-series *A Year in Provence*, BBC TV, 1993 🎬🎬🎬🎬

album notes: Music: Carl Davis; **Conductor:** Carl Davis; **Featured Musicians:** Roy Gillard, Roger Garland, violin; Alan Walley, double bass; David Campbell, clarinet; Colin Green, guitar; Jack Emblow, accordion; Harold Fisher, percussion; Mark Warman, keyboards; Maurice Murphy, trumpet; David White, saxophone.

Based on a real-life story, *A Year in Provence* began when Peter and Annie Mayle decided to quit the London rat race and move to rustic Provence to savor the French way of life—good food, fine wines, and seductive climate. The hilarious account of their first year there, trying to adjust to the idiosyncrasies of the natives and the quaint traditions of the region, provided the basis for a book, and for the series of the same name which starred John Thaw and Lindsay Duncan. Taking a cue from the story, Carl Davis delivered a multi-faceted score, rife with amusing asides, and supremely exhilarating musical jokes that anyone can instantly appreciate. The themes throughout do not so much evoke Provence as they do any number of locales and situations that may be relevant to the story, but often don't seem to be ("Learning the Language," for instance, quotes the theme from *The Magnificent Seven,* while the main theme in "The Tony Awards" recalls a saloon scene in a western). If any real evocation of southern France can be found in the score, it is provided by three selections from Canteloube's "Songs of

the Auvergne," gorgeously performed by Lesley Garrett, which, as any red-blooded Frenchman will tell you, have as much to do with Provence as the accordion that sometimes plays a lilt-ing *valse musette* in Carl Davis's score. The cues, neatly divided one each to a month, are a tongue in cheek delight that faintly echo a foreigner's idea of the type of music one might hear in France; they prove fresh and inventive, and irresistibly enjoy-able, whether in Provence or anywhere else.

Didier C. Deutsch

The Year of Living Dangerously

1983, Varèse Sarabande, from the film *The Year of Living Dangerously,* MGM/UA, 1983 🎬🎬🎬

album notes: Music: Maurice Jarre; **Electronic Realization:** Spencer Lee, Maurice Jarre.

Described by Maurice Jarre as "music like an Asian mist," *The Year of Living Dangerously* was his first foray into predomi-nantly electronic scoring. Jarre's encyclopedic knowledge of ethnic music is also put to good use in this film, which deals with journalists covering political unrest in 1960s Indonesia. Stylistically, the score might superficially be described as new age, given its airy electronic passages, but Jarre also invests the score with music of the region, and features indigenous in-struments. Some tracks (such as "Wayang Kulit") are rather atonal and non-melodic, and do not make for enjoyable listen-ing. However they are counterbalanced by tracks like "En-chantment at Tugu" and "Kwan's Sacrifice," both of which offer beautiful, ethereal evocations of Southeast Asia.

The piano theme heard in the love scenes is not included on this recording, as it is not by Maurice Jarre, but from a Vangelis recording which the director tracked into the film (and is avail-able on the album *Opera Sauvage,* on Polydor). However, Mau-rice Jarre's score remains a thoroughly mystical and sensuous musical experience, and one of the best examples of syntho-ethnic scoring on disc.

Paul Andrew MacLean

Year of the Comet

1992, Varèse Sarabande, from the film *Year of the Comet,* Cas-tle Rock Entertainment, 1992 🎬🎬🎬

album notes: Music: Hummie Mann; **Conductor:** Kurt Bestor.

This is an energetic and lovely score by Hummie Mann, best known for his orchestrations on many of Marc Shaiman's soundtracks (including *City Slickers).* Despite having an inter-esting premise and a good cast, *Year of the Comet* was an un-derwhelming comedy-adventure from Peter Yates and writer

William Goldman. Mann's score makes the most of the film's Irish setting and ultimately becomes far more memorable than the picture itself; the tone is sprightly and fun, and Mann's main theme is nothing short of excellent, the kind of infectious tune you wish other soundtracks were built around. Curiously enough, Mann's music was, in fact, a replacement score for the rejected, original soundtrack written by John Barry, a fact that further mystified viewers when Barry's music was prominently heard in the coming attractions trailer.

Andy Dursin

Year of the Gun

1991, Milan Records, from the film *Year of the Gun*, Triumph Release, 1991 ♪

album notes: Music: Bill Conti.

This Bill Conti effort, performed on synthesizers, starts off well enough, but soon degrades into a lackluster collection of mind-numbing effects cues. Despite a passably curious "Main Title," featuring a chanting male choir, the bulk of the score sounds more as if it was composed by some inexperienced youngster rather than the Academy Award-winning artist responsible for *The Right Stuff* and *Rocky*. The score also has one of the most unromantic love cues ever heard ("Alison and David Walking"). None of the music ever fully projects even the slightest effective emotional response. Track No. 13, "Sunday Afternoon" is so poorly distorted (was this done intentionally?), it should have been left out of the album. Packaging, with no liner notes and just one blurry cover photo, is equally uninspiring. How the mighty have fallen.

David Hirsch

The Yellow Submarine

1987, EMI Records, from the animated feature *The Yellow Submarine*, 1969 ♪♪♪

album notes: Music: George Martin; **Songs:** John Lennon, Paul McCartney.

The passing years have turned the title song into a children's classic, but the Beatles' only animated film was meant for adults, or at least grownup kids. The story is a flower-power fable of creativity struggling against repression; the songs a "Sgt. Pepper"-period mix of simplicity and psychedelia. Alone among the CD reissues of the Beatles' film soundtracks, this one preserves the George Martin-composed and arranged orchestrations from the original LP. It still makes a skimpy meal, though, especially since two of the six Beatles tunes are available on other CDs. Business historians take note: George Harrison's "Only A Northern Song" may stand as the only protest song ever written about a music publisher.

Marc Kirkeby

Yor: The Hunter from the Future

1993, Label X Records, from the film *Yor: The Hunter from the Future*, Columbia Pictures, 1983 ♪♪♪♪

album notes: Music: John Scott; **Orchestra:** The Unione Musicisti di Roma; **Conductor:** John Scott.

It's hard to believe, but the majority of this John Scott orchestral score was replaced by an electronic "disco" effort by Guido and Maurizio De Angelis. Of course, if you see the film, and its slapdash mix of stone-age and post-Apocalypse genre concepts, you'll realize that the filmmakers never had any idea what they were aiming for. Despite all this, Scott has produced a wonderful score that, taken out of context, has an unabashed innocence and romantic quality. Instead of concentrating on the sci-fi elements, he focused on elements in Yor's primitive and naive culture. Where he was able to draw on all this inspiration remains a mystery, but Scott has always exhibited a knack to rise far above some of the more poorly realized films he has had the unfortunate luck to have been associated with. In fact, hiring him often seems to be the only genuinely inspired idea some of these filmmakers have. On *Yor*, however, that wasn't true in the end. All the unused cues, almost 30 minutes of music, have been assembled into one suite and released on this CD for the first time. Obviously, no one wanted to go back and look at the film to try and title the music. Three of the four individually numbered and titled tracks (except "Death Rules This Land") appeared on the original LP issue along with 12 cues by the De Angelis brothers. These four were all the music by Scott that miraculously survived the final cut.

David Hirsch

You Only Live Twice

1988, EMI-Manhattan, from the film *You Only Live Twice*, United Artists, 1967 ♪♪♪♪♪

album notes: Music: John Barry; **Lyrics:** Leslie Bricusse; **Conductor:** John Barry.

This James Bond score, broadly informed by Nancy Sinatra's title song which bookends it, is another John Barry feast, with cues that cleverly enhance the overblown screen action, this time set in Japan, and introduce many new themes, some of them subtly accented with koto sonorities. The sound on this CD reissue is unpleasantly strident and brash, particularly in the brass figures, but don't let that deter you from enjoying it —until, that is, EMI decides to properly remix and master the whole series, hopefully complementing each title with some of the previously unreleased tracks that is still dormant in the company's vaults.

Didier C. Deutsch

Young Bess

🎬 1990, Prometheus/Belgium, from the film *Young Bess*, MGM, 1953 ✍✍✍✍

album notes: Music: Miklos Rozsa; **Conductor:** Miklos Rozsa.

This third volume in the Belgian label Prometheus's series, *The Spectacular Film Music of Miklos Rozsa,* presents a rare treat: the score the composer created for a big historical film about the early years of the young woman who was to become the Queen of England, starring Jean Simmons, Stewart Granger, Deborah Kerr, and Charles Laughton, the latter reprising the role of Henry VIII that had brought him fame in 1933 in Alexander Korda's *The Private Life of Henry VIII.* Though largely fictional, the film, based on Margaret Irwin's novel of skullduggery under the Tudors, was a sweeping chronicle of life in the 16th century, told in breathtaking cinematographic details. That inspired Rozsa to write a fine, romantic effort, full to the brim with gorgeously heroic accents, jaunty little tunes, and effusive love themes. Though recorded in mono, and with occasional slight image shifting and hiss, the recording is vibrant and richly evocative.

Didier C. Deutsch

Young Frankenstein

🎬 1997, MCA Special Products, from the film *Young Frankenstein*, 20th Century Fox, 1975 ✍✍✍
album notes: Music: John Morris.

One of Mel Brooks's most successful lampoons, *Young Franken-stein* brought together several of the director's "regulars" in a film that happily spoofed all the tenets of the monster genre, all the way to the black and white lensing and atmospheric settings that echoed the moods of the original and its numerous sequels. The icing on the cake was John Morris's oppressively romantic-with-a-wink score, dominated by the plaintive violin tune played by Frau Blucher (horses braying in the background) first to lure Dr. Fron-kon-steen into his grandfather's private library, then to seduce the monster into submission after he escapes. Large portions of dialogue vividly recall some of the film's most hilarious moments, and the album also contains the ultimate sendup, the Monster singing Irving Berlin's "Puttin' on the Ritz." The only discordant note in the set is Rhythm Heritage's totally unnecessary contempo rendition of the "Main Theme".

Didier C. Deutsch

Young Hercules

📺 1998, Varèse-Sarabande, from the television series *Young Hercules*, 1998 ✍✍✍
album notes: Music: Joseph LoDuca; **Conductor:** Randy Thornton.

Young Hercules, a spinoff of the *Xena* series and an attempt to give the franchise a new spin by having a fresh face portray the

famous muscleman, is somewhat of a letdown. Probably sad to say, but the exploits of Hercules, young or older, have been somewhat shadowed by those of Xena, and the series, no matter how you look at it, doesn't seem to have the same appeal it once had. LoDuca's music reflects it; though it still features the appropriate big orchestral riffs needed by the genre, it also blends awkward synthesizers into the mix, and it seems to lack the vitality and vibrancy found in the Xena scores. Still, there are some marvelous moments here ("Promise Me," "It's a Twister!," "A Legend Is Born"), but the score itself would need some more excitement to strike a note similar to the one heard in the Xena recordings. Certainly, the synthesizers don't help!

Didier C. Deutsch

The Young Indiana Jones Chronicles: Vols. 1–4

📺 1992, Varèse Records LTD, from the television series *The Young Indiana Jones Chronicles,* 1992 ✍✍✍
album notes: Music: Laurence Rosenthal, Joel McNeely; **Orchestra:** The Munich Symphony Orchestra, The Philharmonic Film Orchestra Munich, and The West Australian Philharmonic Orchestra; **Conductor:** Laurence Rosenthal, Joel McNeely, Charles Ketcham.

There are many things to like intensely in these four volumes. The first is, of course, the abundance of music, and the fact that two excellent composers, Laurence Rosenthal and Joel McNeely, were each asked to write selected episodes in the series, a task they did with flying colors. The other is the diversity in each composer's approach, reflected in their different styles, but also in the fact that each episode is set in a different locale gave them an opportunity to be even more creative. And then, as if all of it were not enough, the remarkable thing is that the music gets better as the listener proceeds from volume one to volume four. Adding to the overall impact of the music, each composer has been given an opportunity to explain in the liner notes his approach to the episode he had been asked to score, thus giving the listener an extra dimension into the creative process.

Didier C. Deutsch

The Young Lions/This Earth Is Mine

🎬 1993, Varèse Sarabande, from the films *The Young Lions,* 20th Century Fox, 1958, and *This Earth Is Mine,* Universal-International Pictures, 1959 ✍✍✍✍
album notes: Music: Hugo Friedhofer; **The Young Lions: Orchestra:** The 20th Century Fox Orchestra; **Conductor:** Lionel Newman; **This Earth Is Mine: Orchestra:** The Universal-International Orchestra; **Conductor:** Joseph Gershenson.

One of Hollywood's most sadly neglected early composers, Hugo Friedhofer is in dire need of a total re-evaluation of his impressive achievements. For a long while considered a brilliant orchestrator rather than a composer in his own right, it was not until he reached his full maturity in the late 1940s-early 1950s that he began to be taken seriously as a film scorer, eventually contributing an impressive catalogue of great works, including *The Best Years of Our Lives, Vera Cruz, An Affair to Remember* and *Boy on a Dolphin,* among the best known. From a 1958 World War II drama came *The Young Lions,* for which Friedhofer received an Oscar nomination. Based on a novel by Irwin Shaw, the film presents strikingly eloquent views of the war as seen through the eyes of a motley group of GIs on one side, and German officers on the other. In the first group, Montgomery Clift portrays an American Jew, confronted with racial prejudice and Dean Martin a would-be draft dodger caught in spite of himself by the daunting task ahead of him. Portraying a young German officer is Marlon Brando, a true believer in Hitler's Nazi theories, whose sense of humanity eventually found him at odds with the Fuehrer's tenets about total annihilation of the Jewish people. In scoring the film, Friedhofer provided themes and musical ideas that sustained the action, but stayed behind it rather than helped propel it. As a result, his score was a succession of subdued cues with a relatively passive role, that filled a purpose and was serviceable at best, even though they were powerfully adapted to the film's dramatic atmosphere.

A score of a different color, *This Earth Is Mine,* composed a year later, provided Friedhofer with a romantic subject which inspired him to write a richly melodic series of themes. Introduced by a dispensable title tune, courtesy of Sammy Cahn and James Van Heusen, who must have written more title songs than anyone else (with the possible exception of Jay Livingston and Ray Evans), the score unfolds with great tender feelings to illustrate this story. It is based on a novel by Alice Tisdale Hobart and set in the 1930s in California's Napa Valley, about an older generation of vintners, eager to preserve the traditions that have been their pride, and younger tyros, more interested in a quick profit. Outlining specific moments in the action, and drawing sharp portraits of the various participants (including Claude Rains, Rock Hudson, and Jean Simmons), Friedhofer's music is rich in melodic details, and very attractive.

The presentation of both scores in a two-CD set was a great idea.

Didier C. Deutsch

Younger and Younger

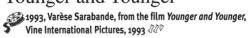 1993, Varèse Sarabande, from the film *Younger and Younger,* Vine International Pictures, 1993 ♪♪♡

album notes: Music: Hans Zimmer; **Featured Musicians:** Alex Wurman, Bob Telson, Mighty Wurlitzer.

This is an odd collection of moderately pleasing, but unsubstantial synthesizer music realized by Hans Zimmer. Despite the fact that he is the only composer credited on the cover, he only wrote four of the album's 10 tracks. Zimmer's score cues are interpolated with additional material by Alex Wurman, performed in most cases on The California Theatre's Mighty Wurlitzer organ. The CD is most notable only because actor Donald Sutherland sings(!) a duet with Lisa Angel on the song "Show Me Your Face" (written by Bob Telson and Lee Breuer). Otherwise, it's generally a vacuous effort, with primitive electronic sounds, that vainly attempts, and fails, to create an intimate romantic fantasy score.

David Hirsch

Your Cheatin' Heart

1997, Rhino Records, from the film *Your Cheatin' Heart,* MGM, 1964 ♪♪♪

album notes: Music: Hank Williams; **Featured Vocalist:** Hank Williams Jr.

A rather unusual entry in the distinctive Rhino series of MGM soundtracks, *Your Cheatin' Heart* was the screen biography of country music legend Hank Williams. An unusual film, even by MGM standards, it starred George Hamilton, and featured Williams's songs performed by his son, Hank Williams Jr., who has also become a noted country singer in his own right. But anyone who grew up on the original tunes and Williams *père*'s raspy yodeling knows that he didn't look as handsome as Hamilton, nor did he sing as powerfully as Junior.

Didier C. Deutsch

You're a Big Boy Now

See: What's up Tiger Lily?/You're a Big Boy Now

You've Got Mail

1999, Varèse-Sarabande, from the film *You've Got Mail,* Warner Bros., 1999 ♪♪♪

album notes: Music: George Fenton; **Conductor:** George Fenton; **Featured Musician:** Michael Lang, piano.

If you're in the mood for a lilting, romantic, and very New York score, you might decide to forego the song album for the film *You've Got Mail* in favor of the charming score album, which contains a lovely George Fenton score and two classics by the legendary Harry Nilsson: "Remember," and "Over the Rainbow." This contemporary remake of the classic film *The Shop Around the Corner* stars Meg Ryan and Tom Hanks as two adversaries who unwittingly fall in love on the internet. A pleasant fairy tale for the '90s, enhanced by a charming soundtrack.

Amy Rosen

Z

🎬 1992, Sakkaris Records/Greece, from the film *Z*, Cinema V, 1969 🎵🎵🎵

album notes: Music: Mikis Theodorakis.

A searing indictment of political abuse around the world, particularly in the hands of military dictatorships, Costa-Gavras' *Z* followed the investigation of a political leader's murder after a rally, in a country that went unnamed but that bore striking resemblance to Greece. Adding to the belief that the filmmaker's intent was to denounce the military-ruled Greek government, Mikis Theodorakis wrote a score that drew heavily and intently on its Greek origins to give the film the proper accents. It might find an eager audience among more open-minded listeners, but will prove of lesser interest to the vast majority. This recording may be difficult to find. Check with a used CD store, mail-order company, or a dealer specializing in rare, out-of-print, or import recordings.

Didier C. Deutsch

Zabriskie Point

🎬 1997, Rhino Records, from the film *Zabriskie Point,* MGM, 1970 🎵🎵🎵🎵

Michelangelo Antonioni took a quick look at U.S. culture and morphed it into a surrealistic vision in this film, which owes a lot to the director's foreign sensitivity and very little to what was happening in the country during the late 1960s. The one thing he did right, however, at least by U.S. standards, was to have Jerry Garcia and the Grateful Dead perform on the soundtrack. The Dead and the creative force behind them bring a relevance to the film it would have otherwise missed. Also making a contribution that was correct at the time—even if it came from artists groomed in another country—the songs by Pink Floyd give the soundtrack an ounce of rock credibility that warmly adds to it. The album, now reissued as a two-CD set with outtakes and unreleased selections, is a fabulous buy, and its pseudo-psychedelic presentation reflects the care and attention usually lavished by Rhino on this kind of product.

While the first disc evokes pleasant memories in most listeners, the real treasure here is the second disc, which consists of previously unreleased selections by Pink Floyd and Garcia, including four different versions of the "Love Scene." It's a priceless collection, showing these artists at work, and trying for the best take in what was, evidently, a difficult task.

Didier C. Deutsch

Zelly and Me

🎬 1988, Varèse-Sarabande, from the film *Zelly and Me,* Columbia, 1988 🎵🎵🎵

album notes: Music: Pino Donaggio; **Conductor:** Natale Massara.

Italian composer Pino Donaggio scores high marks with this soundtrack for an introspective drama about an orphan girl forced into isolation by her overly possessive grandmother. Though the story exhibits areas of freshness and spontaneity reflected in some of the cues, its oppressive climate is expressed in moments that cast a pall on its development. Donaggio, however, was able to balance his score in a way that always seems to favor the areas of lightness in the narrative. As a result, this CD proves thoroughly enjoyable, with the grey moods ("Phoebe Feeling Lonely," "The Locked Bedroom") frequently overcome by striking moments of musical levity that are quite fetching.

Didier C. Deutsch

Zero Effect

🎬 1998, Sony Music Soundtrax, from the film *Zero Effect,* Castle Rock/Columbia, 1998 🎵🎵🎵

album notes: Music: Greyboy Allstars: Mike Andrews, guitar; Karl Denson, saxophone, flute; Zak Najor, drums; Chris Stillwell, bass; Robert Walter, keyboards.

From the minute the front credits let rip with Elvis Costello's "Mystery Dance," viewers of *The Zero Effect* are in for a treat. This little-seen film about a reclusive private investigator also features a beautiful Nick Cave song, some infectious pop by Mary Lou Lord and the Candy Butchers, and two interesting score cues by acid jazz outfit the Greyboy Allstars. Note to Elliott Smith fans: you'll be happy to find a song here by his early band, Heatmiser.

Amy Rosen

Ziegfeld Follies

🎬 1995, Rhino Records, from the film *Ziegfeld Follies,* MGM, 1946 🎵🎵🎵🎵🎵

album notes: Orchestra: The MGM Studio Orchestra; **Chorus:** The MGM Studio Chorus; **Conductor:** Lennie Hayton; **Cast:** Fred Astaire, Lucille Ball, Lucille Bremer, Fanny Brice, Judy Garland, Kathryn Grayson, Lena Horne, Gene Kelly, James Melton, Victor Moore, Red Skelton, Esther Williams, William Powell.

More a revue than a film musical in the real sense of the word, *Ziegfeld Follies* was another attempt by the powers–that–be at MGM to capitalize on the incredible roster of talent signed to the studio, and showcase them in a big, splashy screen vehicle with skits appropriately designed for each of them. By any measure, the caliber of talent on display was, to say the least, awesome—Fred Astaire, Gene Kelly, Kathryn Grayson, Judy Garland, and Lena Horne were some of the singing and dancing luminaries assembled for the occasion, and heard on the exquisite soundtrack album recording released recently by Rhino. Add to those comedians like Red Skelton, Victor Moore and Fanny Brice, and siren extraordinaire Esther Williams, and you have an idea of the glittering display on view in the film.

Brilliantly directed by Vincente Minnelli, the musical boasts so many highlights that a mere listing would become tedious after a while. Astaire dazzles, as usual, in a couple of numbers in which his partner is the glamorous Lucille Bremer, and then teams with Gene Kelly (their only appearance together until *That's Entertainment, Part 2,* in 1976) for a spirited pas–de–deux on the Gershwins' "The Babbit and the Bromide;" Judy Garland is at her dizziest in "The Great Lady Has an Interview;" and Lena Horne is stunning and statuesque singing "Love." These and the other glorious musical moments from the film can be heard on the Rhino set, in stereo(!), the whole package strikingly augmented with a lavish booklet that details behind–the–scenes doings in words and pictures. It's the next best thing to the film itself, and it's simply sensational.

Didier C. Deutsch

Zooman

See: Woman Undone/Zooman

Zorba

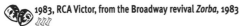 **1992, Angel Records, from the Broadway production *Zorba,* 1968** 🎬🎬🎬🎬

album notes: Music: John Kander; **Lyrics:** Fred Ebb; **Musical Direction:** Harold Hastings; **Cast:** Herschel Bernardi, Lorraine Serabian, Maria Karnilova, John Cunningham, Carmen Alvarez.

1983, RCA Victor, from the Broadway revival *Zorba,* 1983 🎬🎬🎬

album notes: Music: John Kander; **Lyrics:** Fred Ebb; **Musical Direction:** Paul Gemignani; **Cast:** Anthony Quinn, Debbie Shapiro, Lila Kedrova, Robert Westenberg.

A triumphant show from Kander and Ebb, *Zorba* may not have resulted in a long run, but it did result in a score of amazing versatility. Especially during this period, they displayed an almost Rodgers and Hammerstein desire to never repeat an earlier show. As is obvious from the title, this serious, passionate musical based on the novel by Nikos Kazantzakis, already the source for the film *Zorba the Greek,* does not take place in a Depression–ridden New York, early–Nazi Berlin, or in a half–remembered, half–forgotten French–Canadian town. Kander and Ebb perfectly captured the unbearable heat, stillness and half–hidden hostility of a poor village in Crete, with the songs just seeming to flow from the soul of the characters and their town.

Of the two versions available here, Herschel Bernardi stands out in the first, the 1968 original cast, as the title character whose craftiness, passion and charms are outlined in each song. Maria

Karnilova as his erstwhile love interest, Mme. Hortense, practically vibrates with unfulfilled love and longing. John Cunningham and Carmen Alvarez, along with Lorraine Serabian, are the other standouts on the record. The chorus and orchestra sing and play with deep commitment. In the second version, the 1983 Broadway revival, the two stars from the original film, Anthony Quinn and Lila Kedrova, recreated their roles, and even though neither Quinn, as Zorba, nor Lila Kedrova, as Mme. Hortense, could sing well, they knew the characters, and the songs served their characterizations. While the 1968 Broadway cast is still the version of choice in almost every instance, one exception here is Debbie Shapiro as The Woman, the role played in the original by Lorraine Serabian. Both are very good, and both are very different. Where Serabian has her own unique voice and is quite good in the role, Shapiro has a big wide Broadway-style voice that can sing almost anything. Ultimately, one's preference might go for the original Broadway cast recording, but the 1983 revival has its charms and adherents.

Jerry J. Thomas

Zulu

1988, Silva Screen Records, from the film *Zulu,* Embassy Pictures, 1964 🎬🎬🎬

album notes: Music: John Barry; **Conductor:** John Barry.

An impressive retelling of a little-known historic incident—the total annihilation of a squadron of British soldiers at the hands of more than 4,000 Zulu warriors—*Zulu* was a major release, enhanced by the generally high quality of the film in all its aspects, including John Barry's seriously minded score. For the composer, the production marked the first time when he was given an opportunity to display his talent in films other than light comedies or action spy thrillers, that were often dismissed as being too insignificant. For the film, he fashioned a hard-hitting series of cues, accented by the brass instruments anticipating and signaling the eventual doom of the valiant group of soldiers assigned to defend the garrison at Rorke's Drift against their Zulu foes. Though the film itself lasted over two hours, Barry only composed 16 minutes of dense, dramatic music, sparsely used throughout, and augmented with traditional Zulu dances.

To give the CD longer playing time, other selections have been added, including excerpts from Barry's *Elizabeth Taylor in London* and *Four in the Morning,* two scores that cry out to be reissued in complete form, as well as pop vocals by Chad and Jeremy and other instrumental tracks that were arranged by John Barry at a time when his composing career had not yet taken its full flight. Sonically speaking, the CD is not all that it should be, with some analog drops and hiss particularly noticeable on some of the tracks.

Didier C. Deutsch

Gene Kelly and Fred Astaire in Ziegfield Follies. **(The Kobal Collection)**

musicHound
Soundtracks
Composers

Malcolm Arnold
(1921-)

Malcolm Arnold Film Music
1992, Chandos Records ♪♪♪♪♪
album notes: Orchestra: The London Symphony Orchestra; **Conductor:** Richard Hickox.

With only two film scores, the Academy Award-winning *The Bridge on the River Kwai* in 1957, and *The Inn of the Sixth Happiness* the following year, Malcolm Arnold gained international fame, though few outside of inner circles know his name. One of the most prolific modern British composers, he came to film music when he scored *The Sound Barrier,* a film about jet planes and attempts to fly them faster than sound, made by David Lean in 1952. The following year, *Hobson's Choice,* Lean's adaptation of the Harold Brighouse play, gave him an opportunity to echo in his score the elements of humor and romance that characterized this delightful film.

But it was with *The Bridge on the River Kwai* that Arnold came into his own. In his music, he magistrally evoked the power struggle between a fierce British officer and his Japanese captor in a war camp lost in the jungle, as well as the building of a bridge by the British prisoners and its destruction by an Allied commando. While the score called for some serial effects, much of it was a sensational display of action-driven rousing themes that paralleled the construction of the bridge across an escarpment and the progress of the commando through the jungle.

Another war drama, *The Inn of the Sixth Happiness* is the real-life story of an English woman who became a missionary in China, just as the Japanese invaded the country at the onset of World War II, and who manages to lead a large group of chil-

dren to safety over the mountains. The tune "This Old Man," which permeated the film, became a runaway hit.

As for *Whistle Down the Wind,* written in 1961, it details a story of three children mistaking a dangerous murderer for Jesus, with the composer writing a pared-down chamber-like score that was particularly effective in the context.

With four out of the five scores making their first appearance on compact disc, in breathtaking digital sound, this CD is highly recommended, if only because it focuses on a film composer who deserves to be better known. With a few minor exceptions (the kettle drums in the opening bars of *The Bridge on the River Kwai* are much too loud and overbearing), performance by the London Symphony Orchestra, conducted by Richard Hickox, is superlative.

Didier C. Deutsch

Georges Auric
(1899-1983)

The Music Of Georges Auric
1995, Travelling/France ♪♪♪♪

One of France's most important film composers of the '40s and '50s, Georges Auric is only remembered today for a couple of scores, including the lush romantic one he wrote for Jean Cocteau's *La belle et la bête* (*Beauty And The Beast*). That score, which receives a magnificent treatment in the hands of Adriano and the Moscow Symphony Orchestra, is also at the core of the first CD listed here, available as an import, which regroups together four original soundtracks from films starring Jean Marais, at one time the most popular screen actor in his country.

The four films presented here—in addition to *La belle et la bête,* they include two retellings of the classic legend of *Orpheus,* and a pseudo historical drama, *L'aigle à deux têtes,* (*The Eagle With Two Heads*), in which Marais portrayed a commoner tragically in love with a Queen, played by Edwige Feuillere—were directed by Cocteau, whose surrealist style Auric managed to echo in his own scores, while grounding them in the florid romantic tradition he had inherited from the French Impressionistic school.

The excerpts heard in the recording, part of a successful series that surveys various actors, directors and film composers, also contain bits of dialogue to set off the musical moments, sound effects, and Cocteau's own narrative in the two *Orphèe* films. While the sound quality leaves a bit to be desired (it comes from the film mag tracks, and is in primitive mono), the historical and emotional impact is enormous.

Didier C. Deutsch

Luis Bacalov

Mes films francais
1998, Odeon/France ♪♪♪
album notes: Music: Luis Bacalov; **Conductor:** Luis Bacalov.

Known in this country for his Oscar-winning score for *Il Postino,* Argentinian Luis Bacalov has enjoyed a long and prosperous career in Italy and in France, where he has illustrated himself with a wide range of scores (including spaghetti westerns, dramas, comedies, etc.). This CD, available as an import, chronicles his contributions to five French films, at least two of which (*Le juge* and *Coup de foudre*) have been seen here. Evidencing a style which is at once catchy and melodic in a pop way, Bacalov creates attractive themes that stand on their own even as they enhance the screen action. Collectors only aware of *Il Postino* or some of his spaghetti western scores will be pleasantly surprised.

Didier C. Deutsch

John Barry

(1933-)

The Best of John Barry
1991, Polydor/U.K. ♪♪♪♪
album notes: Conductor: John Barry.

Initially issued on LP in the early 1970s, this anthology of themes composed by John Barry for the screen and the stage offers many tracks that are not available anywhere else, in itself a boon for collectors. While it includes Barry's most famous tunes ("Goldfinger," "Thunderball," "We Have All the Time in the World," "Diamonds Are Forever"), often in reorchestrated versions that differ somewhat from the original, the set is of particular interest for the other tracks, like the lovely "Sail the Summer Winds," from *The Dove,* which takes the counterpoint of the main melody to create a new variation on the theme; "Follow, Follow," from *Follow Me,* a 1972 film with Mia Farrow; "This Way Mary," from *Mary, Queen of Scots;* "The Good Times Are Coming," from *Monte Walsh,* a western that stars Lee Marvin; and the main theme from *The Whisperers,* a drama starring Dame Edith Evans.

At the same time, Barry also worked on musicals, with three selections reflecting this particular side of his creativity—"Lolita," from the failed Broadway show *Lolita, My Love,* based on Valdimir Nabokov's novel; "Billy," the main song from the stage show of the same name, starring Michael Crawford; and "Curiouser and Curiouser," from the screen musical *The Adventures of Alice in Wonderland.*

Unlike his compilations of more recent vintage, this set presents the composer at his most creative, in renditions that are lively, strikingly original, and that plainly justify the unfading loyalty Barry commands among his fans.

Didier C. Deutsch

The Film Music of John Barry
1988, Columbia Records ♪♪♪♪
album notes: Conductor: John Barry.

There are numerous compilations of John Barry's film music available, but this relatively early CD release ought to be of interest to both the serious soundtrack aficionado as well as the casual listener. Comprised of session recordings made by Barry with full orchestra in the late 1960s, the album contains the usual, trademark themes associated with the composer, from a particularly jazzy rendition of "The James Bond Theme" (as well as selections from a number of other Bond adventures) to the soothing melodies of *Born Free* and *The Wrong Box.* While these particular selections may be no-brainers for incorporation into a Barry retrospective, this particular release is notable for its inclusion of the composer's more offbeat, innovative dramatic music from *The Chase, The Ipcress File,* and *The Lion in Winter.* With this diversity of material included, the album adeptly spotlights all aspects of Barry's compositional skills and paints a more versatile musical portrait of the composer than many of the other, more routine Barry compilations out there.

Andy Dursin

Moviola: volume one
1992, Epic Soundtrax/Sony ♪♪♪
album notes: Orchestra: The Royal Philharmonic Orchestra; **Conductor:** John Barry.

Moviola: volume two
1995, Epic Soundtrax/Sony ♪♪♪

album notes: Orchestra: The Royal Philharmonic Orchestra; **Conductor:** John Barry.

These two albums provide an impressive cross-section of and introduction to the work of John Barry. *Moviola* opens with *Out of Africa* and *Midnight Cowboy*—both popular works by the composer, but these prove to be among the less interesting offerings. *Body Heat,* a sultry, legato theme for jazz saxophone, is one of the best tracks, a sensual and seductive piece that lives up to its name. The deservedly popular *Somewhere in Time* is also presented in a rapturous performance. *Walkabout, Mary, Queen of Scots,* and *Born Free* are less satisfying here than in Barry's original scoring (the replacement of Mary's harpsichord with solo violin deflates much of the theme's original effect). *Chaplin,* however, is a beautiful, melancholy theme, while *The Cotton Club* evokes a "film noir" feeling similar to *Body Heat,* but with a slightly more sinister flavor. The album closes with "Moviola," a work derived from Barry's unused music for *Prince of Tides* (a film assignment from which Barry resigned).

Moviola II contains a lengthy suite from the James Bond films, which arranges the title themes into a powerful, large-orchestral setting. *Zulu* features a more dynamic, less legato side of Barry (which he really has not shown since the '60s). However, the *Dances with Wolves* suite is unsatisfying: the performance is anemic compared to the original soundtrack. The same is true of the two themes from *The Specialist* that are also featured.

The first *Moviola* CD is undoubtedly the more successful of the two. However, despite some quirks in the second volume, both remain valuable and worthy representations of one the finest film composers ever, and are well-worth a place in one's collection.

When a composer, particularly one of John Barry's caliber, decides to revisit the themes he has created over the years, one has the right to expect a challenging vision of these themes. Unfortunately, the approach taken in these two CDs is much too reverential and solemn, and where some of the selections, notably the James Bond themes in the second volume, should have elicited crackling renditions to echo the originals, the ponderous tone adopted here, with long symphonic digressions and expanded musical lines, sounds too much like what Barry writes these days—imitations of *Dances with Wolves.* In other words gorgeous, but ultimately less inspiring than the works he used to create when he was still struggling to establish his reputation.

Paul Andrew MacLean/Didier C. Deutsch

Out of Africa: The Classic John Barry
1993, Silva Screen Records ♫♫♫
album notes: Music: John Barry; **Orchestra:** The City of Prague Philharmonic; **Conductor:** Nic Raine; **Featured Musicians:** Michael Metelka, violin; Jaroslava Eliasova, piano; Bob Navratil, harmonica; Jindrich Nemecek, alto sax.

10 Essential Scores
by John Barry

Out of Africa
Somewhere in Time
Thunderball
Moonraker
The Lion in Winter
Body Heat
Dances with Wolves
The Cotton Club
King Rat
Midnight Cowboy

The Classic Film Music of John Barry: volume two
1996, Silva Screen Records ♫♫♫
album notes: Music: John Barry; **Orchestra:** The City of Prague Philharmonic; **Conductor:** Nic Raine; **Featured Musicians:** Josef Kroft, violin; Jaroslava Eliasova, piano, harpsichord; Jiri Bousek, flute, alto flute; Michal Horsa'k, cymbalum; Jan Burian, trumpet; Milan Zelenka, guitar.

The main interest of these two volumes resides in the selections, and particularly the longer suites, that are not otherwise available. And there are quite a few: "The Last Valley," "Eleanor and Franklin," "Hanover Street," "Born Free," "Raise the Titanic," and "Robin and Marian" in the first CD; "The Black Hole," "The Appointment," "Monte Walsh," "The Dove," and "Mary Queen of Scots," in the second. One particular joy in the last CD is also the "Romance for Guitar and Orchestra," written for the 1968 thriller *Deadfall,* which gave Barry a rare opportunity to compose a long and eloquent concerto for solo instrument, removed from the James Bond action films for which he was primarily known at the time.

Throughout, the Prague Philharmonic gives accurate readings of the various themes, and if some of the selections might

seem superfluous, the overall concept of "classic" John Barry music plainly justifies their inclusion here.

Didier C. Deutsch

John Barry Conducts His Greatest Movie Hits
1998, PEG Records/Sony Music Special Products 🎝🎝
album notes: Music: John Barry.

Ready When You Are, J.B.
1998, PEG Records/Sony Music Special Products 🎝🎝
album notes: Music: John Barry.

While it's a pleasure to have these albums back in the catalogue (both straight reissues of much sought-after LPs released by Columbia Records in the 1960s), it's a pity that not much was done to make them more sonically or programmatically enjoyable. Both have extremely short playing times (34:54 and 35:36, respectively), with at least one theme ("Born Free") reprised in both, but more to the point is the fact that other tracks could have been added to make them more comprehensive (Barry recorded other albums for Columbia at the time, and there are some previously unreleased outtakes available as well.) Sonics could have been vastly improved if the selections had been properly remixed from the existing 3-track master tapes instead of the 2-track mixdowns evidently used here.

Didier C. Deutsch

Out of Africa: The Classic John Barry
1994, Silva America 🎝🎝🎝🎝
album notes: Music: John Barry; Orchestra: The City of Prague Philharmonic; Conductor: Nic Raine.

The Classic Film Music of John Barry, volume 2
1996, Silva America 🎝🎝🎝🎝
album notes: Music: John Barry; Orchestra: The City of Prague Philharmonic; Conductor: Nic Raine; Featured Musicians: Milan Zelenka, guitar; Josef Kroft, violin; Jaraslava Eliasova, harpsichord, piano; Jiri Bousek, flute, alto flute; Michael Horsa'k, cymbalum; Jan Burian, trumpet.

Zulu
1999, Silva America 🎝🎝🎝🎝
album notes: Music: John Barry; Orchestra: The City of Prague Philharmonic and the Crouch End Festival Chorus; Conductor: Nic Raine.

All right, we've probably heard most of these tracks played more authentically elsewhere, but the City of Prague gives such a spirited performance that these albums are hard to resist. In addition, all three feature selections (or suites) that are more difficult to come by, no matter how hard you look—"The Last Valley," "Eleanor and Franklin," "Raise the Titanic," in the first volume; "High Road to China," "The Black Hole," and "Monte Walsh," in the second; "The Tamarind Seed," "Mercury Rising," "My Sister's Keeper," "Hammett," and "Mister Moses," in the third. Even if you think it's too much John Barry for one seating,

the incredible sweep of the music will convince you otherwise, and you'll find yourself smiling broadly even as you change the CD on your player. And have you noticed? Not a single James Bond track in the lot. So treat yourself to this large helping of Barry music, and just enjoy.

see also: The Essential James Bond

Didier C. Deutsch

John Beal

Coming Soon!: The John Beal Trailer Project
1998, Sonic Images 🎝🎝🎝🎝
album notes: Music: John Beal.

What a clever idea! While you might not have heard of John Beal, you have been exposed to his music many times during your moviegoing days. Beal, you see, is the composer of the music you hear behind the trailers for the forthcoming films usually shown before the main attraction at theaters around the country. Since the films themselves have often not yet been scored, Beal is called upon to provide music that will accompany the scenes shown in the trailer. All of which is devised to lure you, the moviegoing public, to come and see the film when it opens at a theater near you.

Based on the footage presented to him, Beal composes little gems that are sometimes amusing, sometimes appropriately fiery, sometimes romantic, depending on the moods he has to achieve. In itself it's an art that goes largely unrewarded, because audiences eventually come to know the scores composed for these films by John Williams, Elmer Bernstein, Ennio Morricone, Maurice Jarre, and many others, while Beal's modest contributions fade away with the trailers to the films.

So, this 2-CD set aims to correct a wrong; it enables you to relive with the same fervor and ecstasy you'd give the composers mentioned above John Beal's equally impressive but all too often forgotten little themes. It's worth a listen, and you might actually come out of the whole aural experience with a greater respect for those who toil behind the scenes and seldom get the critical applause.

Didier C. Deutsch

Irving Berlin
(1888-1989)

Irving Berlin in Hollywood
1999, Rhino Records 🎝🎝🎝🎝
album notes: Music: Irving Berlin; Lyrics: Irving Berlin.

This collection contains all the songs by Irving Berlin you are likely to want to hear, even though some might have been bet-

Irving Berlin (Archive Photos, Inc.)

ter done by others than the performers found here. So, let's put the record straight: included are songs from the original screen musicals *Easter Parade* ("Steppin' Out with My Baby," "Easter Parade"), *Follow the Fleet* ("Let's Face the Music and Dance"), *Blue Skies* ("Blue Skies"), and *Top Hat* ("Isn't This a Lovely Day," "Top Hat," "Cheek to Cheek"); standards from the film versions of Broadway shows *Call Me Madam* ("The Hostess with the Mostess," "You're Just in Love"), and *Annie Get Your Gun* ("I Got the Sun in the Morning," "You Can't Get a Man with a Gun," "They Say It's Wonderful," "Anything You Can Do," "There's No Business Like Show Business," performed by Betty Hutton and Judy Garland); and hits from the two screen "compilation" musicals, *Alexander's Ragtime Band* ("Heat Wave," "Alexander's Ragtime Band") and *There's No Business Like Show Business* ("After You Get What You Want"), plus a few more numbers that appeared in various other films. There are, however, some glaring omissions (*On the Avenue* is one that comes to mind), and Berlin's most famous creation, "White Christmas" (heard in both *Holiday Inn* and *White Christmas*), is nowhere to be found; possibly it couldn't be licensed, but in a set such as this its absence is noticeable. The CD is presented with the usual gloss Rhino displays on such packages.

Didier C. Deutsch

James Bernard

The Devil Rides Out
1996, Silva America 🎬🎬🎬🎬
album notes: Music: James Bernard; **Orchestra:** The Westminster Philharmonic Orchestra; the City of Prague Philharmonic Orchestra; **Conductor:** Kenneth Alwyn; Paul Bateman and Nic Raine; **Featured Musician:** Paul Bateman, pianoforte.

A collection of tunes from *horror* films, by a master of the genre. Beginning with *The Quatermass Experiment,* Bernard, an alumnus of Herbert Howells and Benjamin Britten, gave the celebrated Hammer films their unique and unequivocal *sound.* The independent studio's horror films soon carved a niche for themselves in a field that was only exploited by a handful of others. Right at the center of this activity was the composer, whose determined phrasing, distinctive orchestrations, and graphic grasp of the dramatic gave the films an extra element that greatly contributed to ensure their success.

This collection revisits some of Bernard's most important scores, including *The Devil Rides Out* (1968), based on Dennis Wheatley's novel; *She* (1965), which starred Ursula Andress as the incarnation of H. Ridder Haggard's embodiment of sex and eternal power; *Frankenstein Created Woman* (1967), with Peter Cushing; *Kiss of the Vampire* (1963), one of the better vampire films; and *The Scars of Dracula* (1971), in which Christopher Lee had a lot of fun with the title character.

Kenneth Alwyn, Paul Bateman, and Nic Raine lead the orchestras in bright, colorful recreations that put James Bernard's music in vivid focus.

see also: Music From The Hammer Films, Vampire Circus, Dracula: Classic Scores from Hammer Horror, Horror!

Didier C. Deutsch

Elmer Bernstein

(1922-)

Elmer Bernstein: Movie and TV Themes
1987, Ava Records/Mobile Fidelity Sound Lab 🎬🎬🎬
album notes: Music: Elmer Bernstein; **Conductor:** Elmer Bernstein.

Elmer Bernstein: A Man and His Movies
1991, Mainstream Records 🎬🎬🎬
album notes: Music: Elmer Bernstein; **Conductor:** Elmer Bernstein.

These early compilations bring together several themes composed by Elmer Bernstein between 1955, when he first appeared on the scene with the striking jazz score for *The Man with the Golden Arm,* and 1965, when he scored *Baby the Rain Must Fall* for Steve McQueen. By then, Bernstein had already created the score that would make him a household name, *The Magnificent Seven,* but since it was on another label, it couldn't be included here. While some selections differ from one CD to the other, both are essentially the same and, more tellingly, both use the same source material, which is of inferior quality. Despite Mobile Fidelity's remastering, which eliminates some of the most flagrant flaws in the original recording, the sound quality is not much better than the Mainstream recording, which makes no pretense at correcting it. If you care for the music, you might want to get both, as the Mainstream CD contains more selections. Otherwise, you might decide to pass on this one until a better version is made available.

Didier C. Deutsch

Elmer Bernstein by Elmer Bernstein
1993, Denon Records 🎬🎬🎬🎬
album notes: Music: Elmer Bernstein; **Orchestra:** The Royal Philharmonic Orchestra; **Conductor:** Elmer Bernstein; **Featured Musicians:** Kenny Baker, trumpet; Jack Parnell, drums; Cynthia Millar, Ondes Martinot, synthesizers.

Whether setting the musical stage for westerns, small town tales, or personal turmoil, few modern film composers have been as able to capture the essence of the American spirit as Elmer Bernstein. *Elmer Bernstein by Elmer Bernstein* showcases 13 of the composer's classic themes, including *To Kill a Mockingbird, The Man With the Golden Arm, Walk on the Wild Side, The Ten Commandments, Ghostbusters,* and *The Magnificent Seven* .

With the composer himself conducting the Royal Philharmonic Pops Orchestra, these familiar strains take on a new dimension. Repeated listening to these works proves that Bernstein's genius is on a par with that of Aaron Copland, whose influence on the direction of Bernstein's approach to music cannot be denied.

If you are a fan of film music, or just plain great music, this disc is required listening!

Charles L. Granata

Claude Bolling

(1930-   )

Bolling Films
1992, DRG Records ♪♪♪♪
album notes: Music: Claude Bolling; Conductor: Claude Bolling.

In the U.S., Claude Bolling is primarily known for his semi-classical collaborations with artists like Jean-Pierre Rampal or Yo Yo Ma, and for an occasional soundtrack (*Louisiane, California Suite*). In his native France, he is held in great admiration, and a Gallic equivalent to Henry Mancini, whose many scores rank among the best ever written in a light jazz-pop vein.

This excellent compilation actually surveys several of the French and American films that Bolling has scored, and provides a casual coverage of his career. There is enough here to satisfy the most demanding customers, with the composer expressing himself in various genres, from thrillers to comedies, from musicals to . . . westerns! It all amounts to a great deal of fun, in a CD that should enable many collectors to better appreciate Bolling as an all-around film composer.

Didier C. Deutsch

Scott Bradley

Tex Avery Cartoons
1992, Milan Records ♪♪
album notes: Music: Scott Bradley; Orchestra: The MGM Studio Orchestra; Conductor: Scott Bradley.

Composer Scott Bradley did some stunningly effective work on Tex Avery's manic one-reelers for MGM, and he certainly deserves an album of his work, but this CD surely will only appeal to hardcore fans. The album suffers greatly from the fact that each of the six musical suites featured here are filled with dialogue and sound effects. Why would anyone not want to just buy a video tape and enjoy the animation, too? Bradley's contribution to the art of animation scoring was without a doubt just as important as Carl Stalling's, but at least some of the recordings on Stalling's albums were dialogue free. Bradley certainly followed the practice of incorporating familiar and

popular songs of the time into his ever changing musical landscape. His work still remains a delight, but without the distractions please.

David Hirsch

Roy Budd

(1947-1993)

Rebirth of the Budd
1997, Sequel Records/U.K. ♪♪♪♪
album notes: Music: Roy Budd.

Little known outside of England, where he contributed many scores for films that received limited international distribution,

Roy Budd was both a dedicated film composer and an orchestrator who doubled as a highly skilled jazz pianist. A child prodigy (he made his TV debut in 1959 on the prestigious variety show, *Sunday Night at the London Palladium,* but played his solo so fast that he finished a full minute ahead of the orchestra), he embarked on his professional career upon leaving school, releasing in 10 years 13 albums that straddled the line between jazz and easy listening. His first film assignment came in 1970 when he scored *Get Carter,* a stark, uncompromising look at a London hoodlum bent on avenging his brother's death, for which he created a score that perfectly matched the moods in the film. In quick succession after that, he wrote the music for such films as *Soldier Blue,* an uncompromising western; *Flight of the Doves; Paper Tiger;* and *Sea Wolves.*

This compilation contains the title track from *Get Carter,* as well as other themes he wrote for the movies—*Fear Is the Key, Soldier Blue, The Carey Treatment*—mixed with his treatment of familiar selections like *Jesus Christ Superstar, Aranjuez Mon Amour,* and *So Nice.*

For a more comprehensive look into the works of Roy Budd, see also the main section of this book.

Didier C. Deutsch

Geoffrey Burgon

(1941-)

Brideshead Revisited
1992, Silva Screen Records, from the TV series Brideshead Revisited, Granada-TV, 1981 ♪♪♪♪♪
album notes: Music: Geoffrey Burgon; **Orchestra:** The Philharmonia Orchestra; **Conductor:** Geoffrey Burgon; **Featured Musician:** Lesley Garrett, soprano.

The elegant score heard behind the scenes in *Brideshead Revisited* was composed by a little known British composer who began his career writing music for some "Dr. Who" episodes, and promptly imposed himself with his impressive score for the 1981 Granada-TV television series. This anthology covers four other series which all bear his unmistakable musical style, *Testament of Youth* and *Tinker, Tailor, Soldier, Spy,* both from 1979; *Bleak House,* from 1985; and *The Chronicles of Narnia.* Among those, *Tinker . . . ,* an adaptation of a John Le Carre's novel, starring Alec Guinness as the dour George Smiley, is probably the best known. It's also the one that elicited the strongest statement from the composer, a dark, brooding theme that set the tone for the whole series. A war drama, *Testament of Youth* suggested a score which contrasted the bombast of the war effort and the serenity of happier times. An adaptation of Charles Dickens's novel, *Bleak House* found Burgon writing in a different mood, an evocation of the Victorian time, at once exhilarat-

ing and bitter sweet. As for *The Chronicles of Narnia,* an adaptation of C.S. Lewis's allegorical novels, its magical narrative about children escaping to the mythical kingdom of Narnia prompted Burgon to create a score that's wonderfully lyrical and mischievously exciting.

Didier C. Deutsch

Gerard Calvi

(1922-)

Monsieur Cinema: Les musiques de films de Gerard Calvi
1998, PlayTime, France ♪♪♪♪
album notes: Music: Gerard Calvi.

Robert Dhery/Gerard Calvi
1997, Travelling/France ♪♪♪
album notes: Music: Gerard Calvi.

The name Gerard Calvi means little to most fans in this country, but in France, it evokes a whole string of popular stage and screen comedies from the 1950s starring Robert Dhery and his "branquignols" (a theatrical troupe that enjoyed a modicum of success on Broadway in 1960 with the madcap musical *La plume de ma tante*).

A composer with a sharp sense of humor, Calvi has scored a large number of comedies for Dhery and others, as evidenced by the first compilation available from some of the specialized dealers in the U.S. (see list appended). Covering a broad spectrum of films, including several by Dhery (*La belle Americaine,* about a fancy American car; *Allez France!,* about a French soccer team in England; *Le petit baigneur,* about a winning sailboat; and *Vos gueules les mouettes,* about the making of an amateur documentary in Brittany), and three animated features based on the epic tales of Asterix the Gaul, the music often proves congenially entertaining and easy on the ear, with catchy evocative little tunes that are quite enjoyable.

The second CD is part of a series released by Auvidis/Travelling under the generic title "Movies to Listen To: The Film Directors and Their Composers." It skillfully blends elements from the soundtracks, including excerpts from the dialogue, musical cues, and some sound effects (though, inexplicably, the first selections seem to have been recorded at the wrong speed). While it may seem limited only to listeners with an understanding of French, it actually proves highly effective in capturing the atmosphere of the films, and providing an aural memento of some of Dhery's most successful comedies.

Didier C. Deutsch

Charles Chaplin

(1889-1977)

Charlie!
1993, Silva America 🎞🎞🎞🎞

album notes: Music: Charles Chaplin; **Orchestra:** The Munich Symphony Orchestra; **Conductor:** Francis Shaw; **Featured Musicians:** George Schwenk, accordion; Monique Billick, mandolin; Leonora Hall, piano.

While Charles Chaplin will always remain in the minds of most people as the greatest of the silent artistes, few remember that he was also an accomplished composer, who scored his own films with some delightfully beguiling melodies. In the days when film actors couldn't talk, Chaplin's music was his voice and, whether he was The Little Tramp or a Hitler wanna-be, he always spoke in the most eloquent tones. The characters exuded more emotion and drew more compassion from the audience because the music had laid their feelings bare. Perhaps more than anyone else, Chaplin defined the true power of the *leitmotif* underscore. Conductor Francis Shaw lovingly guides the Munich Symphony through his own orchestrations of 17 classic themes from eleven Chaplin films. Each is reproduced with all of the composer's power intact. Included in this anthology is "Beautiful Wonderful Eyes" from *City Lights*, several comedic dance numbers from *Monsieur Verdoux*, "This is My Song" from *The Countess from Hong Kong*, and a medley from *Modern Times* that featured Chaplin's biggest hit, "Smile."

David Hirsch

The Gold Rush: The Film Music of Charles Chaplin
1996, RCA/Germany 🎞🎞🎞🎞🎞

album notes: Music: Charles Chaplin; **Orchestra:** The Deutsches Symphonie-Orchester of Berlin; **Conductor:** Carl Davis.

As a film composer, Charles Chaplin had a schmaltzy streak in hlm. His best known compositions ("Smile," "Eternally") today sound a bit sugar-coated and from another era. Yet there was a winsome charm to his music that subtly matched the comic undertones of his films in which he often portrayed a simple, romantic, impoverished innocent, forever assailed by modern life and the powerful ones, and hopelessly in love with the simple girl next door.

Both the Silva America and the BMG sets complement each other, by presenting large extracts from these films, the Silva set focusing on the latter day films, while the BMG set covers the earlier ones. Both reveal in Chaplin a composer who may not rank among the great Hollywood film scorers of his era, but whose music is an important addition to the flickering black and white images of his films.

While the Silva America CD is readily available, the "powers-that-be" at BMG/U.S.A., in their infinite wisdom, decided not to release in this country the series of wonderful recordings prepared by their German company to celebrate the 100th anniver-

sary of the movies, including this set. Finding it will probably take some doing, but it's well worth the effort.

Didier C. Deutsch

Alessandro Cicognini
(1906-)

Alessandro Cicognini per Vittorio de Sica
1995, Legend Records/Italy 🎞🎞🎞

album notes: Music: Alessandro Cicognini; **Orchestra:** The Orchestra Sinfonica delle Marche; **Conductor:** Nicola Samale; *Chorus:* The Coro Santa Cecilia di Fabriano; **Featured Musician:** Ezio M. Tisi.

Recorded on the occasion of the 100th anniversary of the movies, in 1995, this live concert of scores Cicognini wrote for the films of Vittorio de Sica included excerpts from some trend-setting Italian films from after the war—*Sciuscia, The Bicycle Thief, Umberto D, The Gold of Naples*, and *Miracle in Milan*.

Cicognini's naturalistic approach to music blended very neatly with De Sica's own understanding about filmmaking, which took a realistic view of people and events the director knew well and appreciated. This new recording succeeds in conveying some of the moods captured by the films, with the addition of striking sonics the original soundtracks never had.

Didier C. Deutsch

Ry Cooder
(1947-)

Music by Ry Cooder
1995, Warner Bros. Records 🎞🎞🎞

album notes: Music: Ry Cooder; **Featured Musicians:** Ry Cooder, guitars, piano, mandola, bass, accordion; Jim Dickinson, piano, organ; Sam Samudio, piano, organ; Van Dyke Parks, piano, organ; Tom Sauber, banjo, guitar, jaw harp; Alan Pasqua, synthesizers; David Lindley, saz, banjo, mandolin, fiddle; Milt Holland, percussion; Ras Baboo, percussion; Miguel Cruz, percussion; Emil Richards, percussion; Marc Savoie, accordion; Flaco Jimenez, accordion; Kazu Matsui, shakuhatchi; Jorge Calderon, bass; Tim Drummond, bass; Bill Bryson, bass; David Mansfield, violin, cello; Gayle Levant, harp; Osamu Kitajima, biwa, koto; Jim Keltner, drums; George Bohannon, baritone horn; Walt Sereth, saxophone; Harold Battiste, saxophone; Steve Douglas, saxophone; John Bolivar, saxophone; Ernie Fields, saxophone; Herman Riley, saxophone; John "Juke" Logan, harmonica; Bobby Bryant, trumpet; John Hassell, trumpet.

This is an agreeable double-album set from Warner Bros. that serves as a selective overview of the blues guitarist's infrequent forays into the world of film music composition. Cooder's music is often like musical glue in a movie, usually working strictly as an atmospheric backdrop to the drama on-screen. Predictably, this results in some positive and negative attributes in his film scores. While Cooder's music is often gritty and "down home" acoustic, often times his music is only a mood—not a piece of fleshed out music. Of course, this services the

Ry Cooder **(Archive Photos, Inc.)**

needs of the films he's working on, but more often than not, it makes for rather tedious listening apart from its source. Listeners will want to note the presence here of previously unavailable music from *Southern Comfort* and *Streets of Fire,* along with released cues from many of his most popular scores, including *The Long Riders, Crossroads, Trespass,* and *Paris, Texas.* Packaging is unusually slim for a set like this, comprised only of brief notes from the composer and frequent collaborator Walter Hill. In all, a must for fans of Cooder though not an essential purchase by any means for others.

Andy Dursin

Stewart Copeland

(1952-)

The Equalizer & Other Cliff Hangers
1990, IRS Records ♫♫
album notes: Music: Stewart Copeland.

Best known for his role as drummer of the rock group Police, one of the major rock acts of the 1980s, Copeland turned his talents to writing soundtracks for film and TV. *The Equalizer and Other Cliff Hangers* is a selection of themes and cues, some of which were created for the television series *The Equalizer,* starring Edward Woodward. While some of the themes heard in this collection have a quirky feel to them ("Music Box," "Green Fingers," "Tancred Ballet"), most rely on the type of electronic drum so prevalent in television today, and fail to make much of an impression, unless you groove on TV themes that all sound the same and are interchangeable from one series to the next.

Didier C. Deutsch

Vladimir Cosma

(1940-)

The Very Best of Vladimir Cosma
1990, DRG Records ♫♫♫♫♫
album notes: Music: Vladimir Cosma; **Conductor:** Vladimir Cosma; **Featured Musicians:** Ivry Gitlis, violin; Gheorghe Zamfir, Pan flute; Vladimir Cosma, piano; Pierre Dutour, trumpet.

One of the most popular film composers in France, Vladimir Cosma is virtually unknown in this country. A musician of considerable talent and versatility, he has distinguished himself in light comedies, a genre in which he particularly excels, as well as in action films and serious dramas, and won the Cesar, the French equivalent of the Oscar, for his scores for *Le bal,* in 1982, and the international hit, *Diva,* in 1984.

This 2-CD anthology collects together many of the themes he wrote over the past 25 years, including those for films that

were shown in this country, like *Mistral's Daughter, The Tall Blond with a Black Shoe, Diva, My Father's Glory, My Mother's Castle,* and *The Mad Adventures of Rabbi Jacob.* The composer's creative characteristics—unusual instrumentations, strongly melodic themes—are all in evidence here, with several vocals in English that should make his work more accessible and enjoyable to a larger audience.

Didier C. Deutsch

Mychael Danna

The Adjuster: Music for the Films of Atom Egoyan
1997, Varèse Sarabande Records ♫♫♫♫
album notes: The Adjuster: Music: Mychael Danna; **Featured Musicians:** Djivan Gasparian, duduk; Eve Egoyan, piano; Mark Fewer, violin.

This set surveys the scores written by Mychael Danna, a leading Canadian composer, for the films of Atom Egoyan, *Family Viewing* (1987), *Speaking Parts* (1989), and *The Adjuster* (1991), all of them expressing a similar central theme about the encroaching influence of technology in modern society and the disintegration of family life. Often brooding and detached, oppressive and emotionless, the music matches the moods in the films, subliminally reinforcing the message on the screen. Removed from its primary reason, it proves remarkably compelling, though it requires close attention to really make an impression. Some cues, however, are particularly attractive, notably the slow movement from the "Piano Concerto" composed for *Speaking Parts,* which suggests that Danna can also write in a lyrical vein, and be quite effective at it.

Didier C. Deutsch

Carl Davis

(1936-)

The Silents
1988, Virgin Classics ♫♫♫♫♫
album notes: Music: Carl Davis; **Orchestra:** The London Philharmonic Orchestra; **Conductor:** Carl Davis; **Featured Musicians:** David Nolan, violin; Robert Truman, cello.

Throughout much of the 1980s, composer Carl Davis has been busy recreating a lost art. He has composed and recorded brand new scores for several classic pre-sound films for the "Thames Silents" television series. Unlike the majority of people scoring these films, limited to the use of solo piano, organ or synthesizers, Davis has been working with a full symphonic orchestra. He began with Abel Gance's monumental 235-minute epic *Napoleon,* a film he often conducts to on live tours (the film was also rescored by Carmine Coppola). This album contains highlights from *Napoleon* (1927) and nine other scores to such legendary films as *The Thief of Bagdad* (1924), D.W. Griffith's *Broken Blossoms* (1919), and Eric von Stroheim's *Greed* (1924). Davis has managed to tap into that long disused and unique style of film scoring. He creates words where there are none, capturing the emotional moments depicted on film in a lyrical manner. The music can also stand alone as a magnificent performance piece. A beautiful tribute to a bygone era.

David Hirsch

Guido & Maurizio De Angelis

Bud Spencer & Terence Hill Greatest Hits
1995, ViViMusica Records/Italy 𝄞𝄞𝄞𝄯
album notes: Music: Guido and Maurizio De Angelis.

The Adventure Film World of Guido & Maurizio De Angelis
1993, Hexacord Records/U.K. 𝄞𝄞𝄞𝄯
album notes: Music: Guido and Maurizio De Angelis.

Like the Sherman Brothers in this country, Guido and Maurizio de Angelis are two lightweight pop composers whose scores are easily dispensable when compared to those of some of their most important peers, but always fun to listen to, just because they are so exhilaratingly campy.

Those two CDs, available as imports from the regular dealers, are excellent introductions to their adventure and spaghetti western scores.

The first brings together several contributions to the films of burly Bud Spencer and blonde, blue-eyed Terence Hill. Though not well known in this country (Hill may best be remembered for being the main protagonist opposite Henry Fonda in the Sergio Leone film, *My Name Is Nobody*), both made several films in Italy that were huge box office hits. Beginning with their first film, *Piu forte ragazzi!*, some of the titles give an idea of the broad antics displayed by the pair on screen: *Lo chiavamo Bulldozer* (*We Call Him Bulldozer*), *Un sceriffo extraterrestre* (*An Extraterrestrial Sheriff*), *40 giorni di liberta* (*40 Days of Freedom*). Nothing subtle here, just some all-out fun that found an echo in the music composed by the De Angelis brothers.

The second CD is broader in scope (the title, *The Adventure Film World* pretty much sets the tone), but the musical approach remains consistent, with themes that are swathed in broad colorful strokes, eloquent in their own way, and always enjoyable. Obviously, if you are looking for something more cerebral, you might as well look elsewhere. Otherwise, you won't regret investing in these CDs.

Didier C. Deutsch

Franceso de Masi

(1930-)

Film Music, vol. 1
1995, ViViMusica/Italy 𝄞𝄞𝄞𝄯
album notes: Music: Francesco de Masi; **Conductor:** Francesco de Masi; **Featured Musician:** Francesco de Gemini, harmonica.

Film Music, vol. 2
1996, ViViMusica/Italy 𝄞𝄞𝄞𝄯
album notes: Music: Francesco de Masi; **Conductor:** Francesco de Masi; **Featured Musician:** Franceso de Gemini, harmonica.

One of the better Italian film composers, Francesco de Masi has scored hundreds of films, from standard spaghetti westerns, to erotic films, to thrillers, to comedies, to cartoons. These two compilations present excerpts from a handful of films covering these genres, and reveal a composer who gains at being better known and appreciated.

While he might not have achieved the worldwide popularity of Ennio Morricone, de Masi is an interesting composer who stands out way above many others. In a tough, gritty style that reflects the general trends in film music in the 1960s and '70s but adds highly original, brightly colorful concepts, he captured the essence of the films he scored, turning out very attractive, endearing themes that relied on the usual contingent of percolating rhythms, muted trumpet calls, wailing harmonica, and strumming guitars to create a richly effective series of cues.

These two CDs, available as imports, document some of his most notable achievements, among them, *Thunder, Suliman the Conqueror,* and *Jungle Story* that delineate the parameters of his creativity and illustrate his uncanny sense of color and movement.

Didier C. Deutsch

Francois de Roubaix

(1939-1975)

10 ans de musique de film
1998, Odeon/France 𝄞𝄞𝄞𝄞
album notes: Music: Francois de Roubaix.

Outside of France, Francois de Roubaix is a total unknown, yet his film scores reveal a composer with a quirky, inventive mind who may well have been one of the most original musicians the screen ever inspired. This collection, released only in France but available here through the usual importers, is a magnificent compilation and a fancy introduction to the many films on which he worked between 1965, when he first burst on the music scene with *Les grandes gueules* (*The Loud Mouths*), directed by Robert Enrico, and 1975, when he died at 33 in a freak deep-sea diving accident.

Considered by many way ahead of his time, de Roubaix created themes that were thoroughly innovative: one of the first film composers to pioneer the use of synthesizers in scores, he successfully used electronics to offset acoustic instruments like the guitar or the flute, combining their sonorities in ways that always sounded fresh and unusual. But unlike latter-day exponents of the genre, he never lost sight of the fact that the themes he wrote had to appeal to a large audience; as a result, many of the selections found in this comprehensive collection exude a charm and appeal that place them in a straight pop vein.

Most of the films presented here never reached these shores, though moviegoers might recall *Boulevard du rhum,* a 1971 film directed by Robert Enrico, that starred Brigitte Bardot; or *Tante Zita,* another Enrico entry from 1967 starring Joanna Shimkus, that received limited distribution in this country, and even generated a soundtrack album on the Philips label.

While it may take some doing to find this 2-CD collection, the rewards will plainly justify the efforts.

Didier C. Deutsch

Georges Delerue
(1925-1992)

The London Sessions: volume one, two, and three
1990, Varèse Sarabande (volumes one and two); 1991, Varèse Sarabande (volume three) 🎵🎵🎵🎵
album notes: Music: Georges Delerue; **Conductor:** Georges Delerue, Frank Fitzpatrick.

This compilation series—a must-have in any soundtrack collection—superbly demonstrates Georges Delerue's talent and versatility at creating emotive music through fragile, intimate melodies that have a tender poignancy. The series also presents a lot of selections that had never been recorded before.

Central to the three CDs are the rejected adagio from *Platoon,* a passionate composition for strings; a glorious symphonic suite from *Rich and Famous*; selections from *Steel Magnolias*; the pretty piano, flute, and violin romance from *The Escape Artist*; the gentle jauntiness of strings and marimba in *The Pick-Up Artist*; the breezy music from *A Little Sex*; a wistful, melancholy suite from *Memories of Me*; the evocatively brooding violin and oboe melody from the Hitchcockian thriller *The House on Carroll Street*; the baroque theme from *Maid to Order*; the jazzy saxophone theme from *Man, Woman, and Child*; and a 12-minute suite of themes written for the films of Francois Truffaut.

Of particular interest is a nearly 12-minute suite from Delerue's rejected music for *Something Wicked This Way Comes* in the final volume. The score, one of Delerue's most dramatic efforts, contrasts quiet interludes with harsh, crashing winds; typical of its overall effect, an oscillating chordal theme for strings and woodwinds over rhythmic, rumbling percussion evokes an effective mood of mystery. This orchestral suite actually represents only half the score's musical texture—it does not include the choir or calliope that were featured prominently in the original recording, nor does it use the synthesizer as part of the orchestra. Nonetheless, it stands out as one of Delerue's most interesting scores, and its rarity makes it something to be eagerly sought.

Randall D. Larson

Truffaut & Delerue: On the Screen
1986, DRG Records 🎵🎵🎵🎵
album notes: Music: Georges Delerue; **Conductor:** Georges Delerue

The great French composer Georges Delerue first came to prominence when he scored the films of New Wave directors like Alain Resnais, Jean-Luc Godard, Francois Reichenbach, Alain Robbe-Grillet, and Louis Malle. It is, however, with Francois Truffaut that Delerue earned his stripes, writing the music for many of the director's films, including *Shoot the Piano Player, Jules and Jim, The Two English Girls,* and *The Story of Adele H.* Of the five films documented on this CD, two (*Confidentially Yours* and *The Last Metro*) are often mentioned as being among the most important in Truffaut and Delerue's body of works, with *The Last Metro,* a World War II drama, particularly effective in its depiction of occupied Paris and the struggle of a Jewish theatre director to keep his plays running. Both scores and the short cues from *A Beautiful Girl Like Me, Day for Night* (a film documenting the shooting of a film), and *The Woman Next Door,* show Delerue in a wide variety of styles, from vernacular to baroque, from jazz to romantic, in a great demonstration of his enormous talent.

Didier C. Deutsch

30 ans de musique de film
1998, Odeon/France 🎵🎵🎵🎵
album notes: Music: Georges Delerue.

Despite the fact that he died seven years ago, Georges Delerue is probably the most popular French film composer in this country, way ahead of Michel Legrand, Maurice Jarre, Francis Lai, and Philippe Sarde, to name only a few. Yet most collectors have only been exposed to a few scores out of a vast output that included some of the most important French films of the 1960s, '70s, and '80s; many unheralded lesser gems that didn't even come across the Atlantic; and a host of other works that made Delerue the true musical voice of the Cinema Nouvelle Vague (interestingly, while the New Wave directors attempted to break away from the stuffy tenets of a kind of moviemaking they found too traditional, Delerue's music, with its broad, romantic themes, relied more on tradition than the works of other composers at the time).

While this collection is far from being complete or even comprehensive, it introduces many themes that may be new to a lot of listeners while filling a few gaps, particularly for those already familiar with the 3-CD *London Sessions* recordings on Varèse-Sarabande (q.v.), or the equally limited compilations released at one time or another by DRG or Milan Records.

Pretty much presented in a chronological way, the two CDs survey Delerue's first introduction to the New Wave cinema (*Jules et Jim, Shoot the Piano Player*), followed by his scores for swashbucklers (*Cartouche*) and historical dramas (*Thibaud ou les Croisades, Les rois maudits*), light-hearted comedies (*King of Hearts, Les tribulations d'un Chinois en Chine*), police thrillers (*Garde a vue, Police Python 357*), as well as some of his contributions to American films (*Day of the Dolphin, Interlude*).

Throughout, the composer's gloriously florid themes and occasionally jaunty tunes come full force in a vivid display of his multi-faceted talent. As an added plus, many of the selections in this new compilation have been remastered, making them sound even better than ever before.

Didier C. Deutsch

Music from the Films of Francois Truffaut
1997, Nonesuch Records 𝄞𝄞𝄞𝄞
album notes: Music: Georges Delerue; **Orchestra:** The London Sinfonietta; **Conductor:** Hugo Wolff.

Attesting to the fact that film music is much more than something vaguely heard behind an action scene, several classical labels have begun recording new albums of classic film music. At the forefront of this movement, Nonesuch released in 1997 a series of four titles, including this tribute to Georges Delerue recorded by Hugo Wolff and the London Sinfonietta.

Because of his own neo-Romantic leanings, Delerue, better than any other film composer, could bridge the gap between classical music, as it is commonly perceived, and modern-day film music. This CD is a perfect example: focusing on the films of Francois Truffaut, with whom Delerue enjoyed a long and successful creative partnership, it offers selections from several seminal films, including two (*Jules et Jim* and *Shoot the Piano Player*) that paved the way to what was to become the French "Nouvelle Vague" in film making.

There have been several original soundtrack compilations of Delerue music for the films of Truffaut, and certainly this one can only rank as a re-recording. But the impassioned playing of the Sinfonietta, and the exquisite sonics plainly justify acquiring this excellent CD.

see also: Truffaut & Delerue on the Screen

Didier C. Deutsch

Le mepris
1991, Hortensia/France 𝄞𝄞𝄞
album notes: Music: Georges Delerue, Pierre Jansen, Michel Legrand.

This CD, available only as an import, puzzlingly combines the scores Georges Delerue wrote for three French films (*Le mepris, L'aine des Ferchaux,* and *L'insoumis*) with Pierre Jansen's *Juste avant la nuit* and Michel Legrand's memorable *Cleo de 5 a 7*. Allegedly, it aims to be a tribute to the French Nouvelle Vague, but the concept itself is . . . well, "vague." Delerue's contribution is, at best, typical, with broad themes that are appropriately lyrical, while Jansen and Legrand strike a different, though not entirely alien, note. Songs in *Cleo de 5 a 7* are performed by Corinne Marchand.

Didier C. Deutsch

Movies to Listen To: The Scores of Georges Delerue
1995, Audivis Travelling/France 𝄞𝄞𝄞𝄞
album notes: Music: Georges Delerue.

This CD, in the popular "Movies to Listen To" series from France, illustrates five films that have become among the most important of the French New Wave—*Jules et Jim, Une aussi longue absence, Le mepris, Hiroshima mon amour,* and the exuberant *Viva Maria*. A comparison between this release and *Le mepris* above denotes wide sonic differences (the former is in mono, obviously taken from the film's mag tracks, with voice-over and dialogue mixed with the music, while the latter is in stereo and totally devoid of sound effects); but the concept behind this release is also somewhat different—it aims to recreate in a nutshell the impact of the film minus the visuals, and in this respect it succeeds very well. Best case in point, *Viva Maria*, currently unavailable (it was released on LP by United Artists, but has never been reissued on CD): compared to the "soundtrack" album, the selections here have the feel and spontaneity of the film performances, not the studied recording sound obtained in the studio after the fact. Brigitte Bardot and Jeanne Moreau, portraying two gun-totting actresses in the middle of a Mexican revolution, sound like they have a lot of fun (which they did in the film), and perform the songs in a looser, more endearing manner than in the LP soundtrack album.

The same comments apply to the other selections, suggesting that this CD might be worth having in addition to the original soundtrack albums when they are available.

Didier C. Deutsch

Georges Delerue: Musiques de films
1995, Fremeaux Entertainment/France ♫♫♫♫
album notes: Music: Georges Delerue; Conductor: Georges Delerue.

The scores represented here were composed for four television series that have not been seen outside of France and selected French-speaking territories. They show another facet of Delerue's creativity, in which diversity was a key ingredient. They also provide luminous examples of his wonderful flair for music, in which "Fete royale," in imitation of Lully or Charpentier, could be played next to a "Grande valse romantique," more appropriate to a late 19th century setting.

The same diversity illustrates such selections as "Imperial March," evocative of Napoleonian grandeur, and the delicate "Ballade For Flute and Harp," or the forlorn "Melancholy Tune," both of which are highlights of this unusual CD.

While you may have difficulties finding this release, it is certainly worth hunting down.

Didier C. Deutsch

Pino Donaggio
(1941-)

Brian de Palma/Pino Donaggio
1995, Milan Records ♫♫♫♭
album notes: Music: Pino Donaggio.

Intriguing, excellent anthology of the collaboration between director Brian de Palma and composer Pino Donaggio on six of their most notable psychological dramas. Donaggio replaced De Palma's former musical collaborator, Bernard Herrmann, after the composer's passing. It's interesting to listen to Donaggio's work here with that fact in mind. His music certainly redefined De Palma's films particularly through *Body Double's* electronic "Claustrophoby" and, in particular, the climactic cue from *Dressed to Kill,* which has a more overt sexual quality than would have been expected from Herrmann.

David Hirsch

Pino Donaggio: Symphonic Suites
1989, Varèse Sarabande Records ♫♫♭
album notes: Music: Pino Donaggio; Conductor: Natale Massara

Part of Varèse Sarabande's first batch of limited edition "CD Club" soundtrack releases, *Symphonic Suites* may be the most

undesirable entry of the bunch (with the possible exception of the 17-minute "mini-classic" made-for-TV soundtrack, "Those Secrets"). A collection of four edited "suites" culled from the original soundtracks to *The Howling* (1981), *Piranha* (1978), *Tourist Trap* (1979), and *Home Movies* (1979), Donaggio's music in these four films consists by and large of hackneyed horror/suspense cues (*Tourist Trap, The Howling, Piranha*) that are tired at best and obnoxious at worst, as well as forgettable comic cues (*Home Movies*) that don't mesh well with the preceding three selections. The suites themselves play fairly effectively, although the cues that comprise them are somewhat questionable in selection (*The Howling* doesn't even include Donaggio's goofy end title!). Varèse would have been better off re-issuing the albums individually than pasting this rather odd collection of tracks together and offering it to the public. As a sign of its unpopularity, it's one of the only "CD Club" issues that's still relatively easy to get your hands on.

Andy Dursin

Pino Donaggio Music from the Cinema
1999, Pacific Time Records ♫♫♫♫
album notes: Music: Pino Donaggio.

Best known in this country for the soundtracks he wrote for the films of Brian de Palma (*Don't Look Now* (1973); *Carrie* (1976); *Home Movies* and *Dressed to Kill* (1980); *Blow Out* (1981); *Body Double* (1985); and *Raising Cain* (1992)), Pino Donaggio is also a composer whose contributions to the screen, particularly those that are more closely linked to Italian films, are largely ignored or unappreciated. This compilation, which surveys six films he scored between 1987 and 1997, aims to partly correct this oversight. Not that the films themselves will elicit a nod of recognition from listeners, particularly given the fact that the packaging itself is devoid of much information about them. But the music is sufficiently eloquent and compelling to make new converts of the collectors who will have the patience to look for this CD and listen to it.

see also: Nicola Piovani: Music from the Cinema

Didier C. Deutsch

Cliff Eidelman
(1964-)

Blood & Thunder: Parades, Processionals, and Attacks from Hollywood's Most Epic Films
1995, Varèse Sarabande ♫♫♫♫♭
album notes: Orchestra: The Seattle Symphony Orchestra; Conductor: Cliff Eidelman.

The title says it all: music of pomp and circumstance as devised by some of the great Hollywood composers in a widescreen program that blares out of the stereo system. There is no real subtlety here, just themes that are broad, grandiloquent, and played to the hilt by an orchestra that seems to know the stuff by heart. It's fun, it's exhilarating and most of all it's thoroughly entertaining.

Didier C. Deutsch

Danny Elfman

(1953-)

Music for a Darkened Theatre
1990, MCA Records ♪♪♪♪
album notes: Music: Danny Elfman.

Music for a Darkened Theatre: Film and Television Music volume two
1996, MCA Records ♪♪♪♪
album notes: Music: Danny Elfman.

Danny Elfman led the rock band Oingo Boingo and "didn't know nothin' about film music." Then he joined Tim Burton on several films—*Pee-Wee's Big Adventure, Beetlejuice,* and *Batman*—and film music quickly learned about him. Elfman's self-taught orchestral style is kind of Nino Rota meets Bernard Herrmann meets Arrested Development meets a highly creative, filmic sense. Elfman has virtually defined the sound of "wacky" film music in the '80s and '90s—ditto for "gothic" film music—and charted the course for composers without a symphonic background to make use of the orchestra in an increasingly frenetic, bombastic way.

The first of MCA's excellent *Music for a Darkened Theatre* compilations covers Elfman from *Pee-Wee* in 1986 through *Darkman* in 1990: *Beetlejuice, Scrooged, Nightbreed, Midnight Run, Dick Tracy,* TV themes to *Tales from the Crypt* and *The Simpsons,* and others. The second, 2-CD volume picks up with Elfman's magnum opus to date, the beautiful, lyrical *Edward Scissorhands* (1991) and continues through *Batman Returns, Sommersby, The Nightmare Before Christmas, Black Beauty, Dolores Claiborne, To Die For, Dead Presidents, Mission: Impossible,* and additional selected TV work.

While the first volume features the signature Elfman hits, it is the second album that showcases his vast growth since the days of the Bat. With *Sommersby, Black Beauty,* and *Dolores Claiborne,* he took on an ambitiously lyrical and elegiac sound miles apart from the oompah-oompah Pee-Wee shenanigans. With *Dead Presidents* and *Mission: Impossible* he mixed sampled percussion and orchestra in exciting new ways to update his more action-oriented sound into something more sophisticated and intricate. Taken together the *Music for a Darkened Theatre* suites present too much of a good thing, but as a sort

of *Reader's Digest* collection they present an impressive catalog of a highly individual, and still growing, voice.

Lukas Kendall

Allyn Ferguson

(1924-)

The Film Music of Allyn Ferguson: volume 1
1994, Prometheus Records/Belgium ♪♪♪♪
album notes: Music: Allyn Ferguson; **Orchestra:** The London Studio Symphony Orchestra; **Conductor:** Allyn Ferguson.

The Film Music of Allyn Ferguson: volume 2
1995, Prometheus Records/Belgium ♪♪♪♪
album notes: Music: Allyn Ferguson; **Orchestra:** The London Studio Symphony Orchestra; **Conductor:** Allyn Ferguson.

The Film Music of Allyn Ferguson: volume 3
1996, Prometheus Records/Belgium ♪♪♪♪
album notes: Music: Allyn Ferguson; **Orchestra:** The Southwest Symphony Orchestra; **Conductor:** Allyn Ferguson.

Each title in this trilogy contains two scores Allyn Ferguson composed for several made-for-television adaptions of classic literature. Not one of the more well-known score artistes, he has in fact labored in film and TV for many years in his native Britain, creating some exceptionally fine pieces of work. It was a daring move by this record company to produce not one, but three titles, which will certainly, and deservedly so, save this composer's work from obscurity. Each score is frequently imbued with that long forgotten lavish quality that Erich Wolfgang Korngold and Franz Waxman often infused into their own work for similar costume dramas. Ferguson also relies on several period inspired arrangements (string quartets and the like) to reinforce the time frame. The first volume contains *The Count of Monte Cristo* and *The Man in the Iron Mask,* the second, *Ivanhoe* and *Camille; The Ironclads* and *April Morning* complete the third. Of the three, volume two is perhaps the best of the lot with it's sweeping and romantic melodies. Some of the masters used were of less than ideal quality, but these flaws are minor as Ferguson's music just sweeps you away.

David Hirsch

Nino Fidenco

4 Western Scores
1996, BMG Records/Italy ♪♪♪♪
album notes: Music: Nino Fidenco; **Conductor:** Robby Poitevin and Willy Brezza; **Featured Musicians:** I Cantori Moderni of Alessandro Alessandroni.

The four spaghetti westerns scored by Nino Fidenco—*Ringo il Texano,* made in 1966 by Jose L. Espinosa, starring Audie Murphy; *All'Ombra di una colt,* from 1965, directed by Giovanni

Danny Elfman **(Archive Photos, Inc.)**

Grimaldi; *Per il gusto di uccidere,* directed by Tonino Valerii in 1966; and *Dynamite Jim,* also from 1966, directed by Alfonso Balcazar—may have been standard fare, but listening to Fidenco's music turns out to be a lot of fun.

Though not considered a major composer in the same league as Ennio Morricone, Francesco de Masi, or even Bruno Nicolai, Fidenco was obviously inspired by his predecessors and created themes that are illustrative of the action and the settings in which it happens.

Some selections are particularly catchy, and easily stand out in the lot, like "La piccola ballerina" and "Country Sound," in *Ringo il Texano*; "Mexican Theme," in *In the Shadow of a Colt*; "The Silver Convoy" and "The Challenge," in *A Taste for Killing*; and "The Trick" and "Margaret," in *Dynamite Jim.* But overall, these four western scores are quite good, and should delight a lot of listeners and fans.

Didier C. Deutsch

Jerry Fielding

(1922-1980)

Jerry Fielding Film Music
1992, Bay Cities Records ♪♪♪♪♪
album notes: Music: Jerry Fielding; **Conductor:** Jerry Fielding.

Jerry Fielding Film Music 2
1992, Bay Cities Records ♪♪♪♪
album notes: Music: Jerry Fielding.

Jerry Fielding Film Music 3
1993, Bay Cities Records ♪♪♪♪
album notes: Music: Jerry Fielding.

Jerry Fielding Film Music 4
1994, Bay Cities Records ♪♪♪♪
album notes: Music: Jerry Fielding.

Jerry Fielding is the greatest film composer nobody knows about. Blacklisted for what should have been the prime of his career in the 1950s, he arranged music for Vegas nightclub acts until finally arriving in Hollywood in the late '60s and '70s. There he scored six pictures for British director Michael Winner, as well as three for star/director Clint Eastwood (including *The Outlaw Josey Wales*), and was legendary director Sam Peckinpah's (*The Wild Bunch*) close friend and composer of choice. He died of a heart attack in 1980 and was virtually unrepresented on CD until producer Nick Redman of the late soundtrack label Bay Cities put together four limited-edition CD compilations of his best work.

Jerry Fielding Film Music is a 2-CD set featuring the western *Lawman* (1970), the Charles Bronson hit-man film *The Mechanic* (1972), the remake of *The Big Sleep* (1978), Peckinpah's

masterful *Straw Dogs* (1971), two cuts from the Bronson revenge western *Chato's Land* (1972), and Winner's *Turn of the Screw* "prequel" *The Nightcomers* (1972).

Film Music 2 features the Winner spy film *Scorpio* (1973) and short suites from *Johnny Got His Gun* (1971) and *A War of Children* (1972).

The third volume features Peckinpah's *Bring Me the Head of Alfredo Garcia* (1974), the rejected music fof Peckinpah's *The Getaway* (1972), also Peckinpah, and Fielding's adaptation of Mahler for *The Gambler* (1974).

The fourth disc features the complete, original album configuration of *Chato's Land,* coupled with Fielding's music for the 1979 TV miniseries, *Mr. Horn.*

Musically, Fielding is an acquired taste. He was intrigued by post-tonal 20th-century orchestral music but was also a self-taught and highly accomplished big band arranger. His film music is deeply individual. His melodies are usually fragmented and transitory but the overall textures and rhythms are intense and unmistakable. On these discs his music ranges from the English flavor of *The Nightcomers,* to the devastating Mexicana of *Bring Me the Head of Alfredo Garcia,* to the atonal, black-on-black portrait of an assassin of *The Mechanic,* to the quiet reflection of *Straw Dogs,* to the jazzy stylings of *The Big Sleep.* But wherever Fielding goes, he brings a delicate sense of disquiet, poignancy, and barely capped violence. He and '70s cinema were a perfect match.

Lukas Kendall

David Michael Frank

(1948-)

Music from the Films of Steven Seagal
1996, GNP Crescendo ♪♪♪♪
album notes: Music: David Michael Frank; **Conductor:** David Michael Frank.

This compilation features selections from David Michael Frank's scores for three of Steven Seagal's first four movies, *Above the Law, Out for Justice,* and *Hard To Kill.* The music is an eclectic mix of guitar driven motifs, electronics, and contemporary orchestral scoring techniques that is certainly, if anything, never boring. Frank has a good knack for creating some terrific jazz flavored emotional moments and some intriguing orchestrations. In particular is "Joy Ride" from *Above the Law,* which has a fascinating synth effect that sounds like an impossible-to-perform vocal scat. The album features an exclusive 21-minute interview with Seagal, who highly praises Frank's contribution to his films, though the actor has never used him since these three.

David Hirsch

Gerald Fried

(1928-   )

The Return of Dracula
1999, Film Score Monhly 𝄢𝄢𝄢𝄢
album notes: Music: Gerald Fried; Orchestra: The MGM and 20th Century-Fox Studio Orchestras; **Conductor:** Gerald Fried.

Unheralded and known only to a small core of fans, Gerald Fried doesn't tower in the film music industry like some of his peers. Yet, his sturdy, creative presence has been felt for many years in Hollywood, where he contributed quite a few significant scores to important films like *Paths of Glory, Too Late the Hero,* and *Mystic Warrior,* as well as a number of television series, including *The Man from U.N.C.L.E., Lost in Space,* and the original *Star Trek.*

This new 2-CD set, prepared and released under the aegis of the fan magazine *Film Score Monthly,* presents the scores Fried wrote for four horror films, *The Return of Dracula* (1958), *I Bury the Living* (1958), *The Cabinet of Dr. Caligari* (1962), and *Mark of the Vampire* (1957), a genre in which he also excelled. As a tribute and/or introduction to Fried and his specific brand of music, this is an important release.

Each score bears Fried's distinctive musical imprint, yet each elicited a totally different approach from the composer—the traditional "Dies Irae" pervades *The Return of Dracula;* an eerie harpsichord sound provides the key note in *I Bury the Living;* a richly evocative romantic theme anchors the score for *The Cabinet of Dr. Caligari;* dissonance and pounding rhythms highlight the music for *Mark of the Vampire.* As producer Lukas Kendall aptly comments in his comprehensive notes to the package, "Even if you have never seen these movies, you will be amazed and overjoyed at the juicy nuggets of outrageous Fried contained therein."

Adding a special note of interest to this release, the profusely illustrated and annotated booklet puts Fried's contribution into its right perspective.

Didier C. Deutsch

Hugo Friedhofer

(1902-1981)

The Adventures of Marco Polo
1997, Marco Polo Records 𝄢𝄢𝄢𝄢
album notes: Music: Hugo Friedhofer; Orchestra: The Moscow Symphony Orchestra; **Conductor:** William T. Stromberg.

A pioneer in film music and a representative of that select group that gave the genre its basic tenets, Friedhofer never achieved the popularity of his peers in Hollywood. Born in San Francisco on May 3, 1902, he studied the cello and was so proficient that he became a regular player in silent movie theaters

They Know the Score

Michael Kamen

I get adrenalized by music. I've walked onto the floor of an orchestra with no sleep having worked all night, barely able to talk, and yet when I stand in front of an orchestra, I am adrenalized, I am suddenly brought to life better than any illicit drug you could dream of. It is, I guess, what I'm on the planet for, to make music, and not many people, thank God, [laughs] have the opportunity presented to them that I have. It is magic to stand in front of a symphony orches tra and get the greatest musicians in the world to play your music for you.

Courtesy of **Film Score Monthly**

as early as 1925. Eventually he began arranging and orchestrating, and revealed great skills at it. In fact, he started his career in Hollywood, where he arrived in 1929, as an arranger, orchestrating the scores of composers like Max Steiner, Alfred Newman, and Erich Wolfgang Korngold.

Eventually, Friedhofer wrote his first film score, *The Adventures of Marco Polo,* in 1938, but it wasn't until 1943, when Alfred Newman signed him to a full contract, that he became recognized as a composer. In 1946, he finally made a name for himself when he won the Oscar for *The Best Years of Our Lives.* Subsequently, he scored *Joan of Arc* (1948), *Broken Arrow* (1950), *Vera Cruz* (1954), *Boy on a Dolphin* (1957), *An Affair To Remember* (1957), *The Sun Also Rises* (1958), *The Young Lions* (1958), and *One-Eyed Jacks* (1960). He died on May 17, 1981.

The four scores here present him in four varied settings that called upon his vast resources as a composer and orchestrator. After working on several scores by Korngold and Steiner, *The Adventures of Marco Polo* gave Friedhofer his first opportunity to show his own mettle in a score that was appropriately epic in the right places, and romantic where needed. Typically flavorsome, in the grand Hollywood style of the day, it didn't disappoint. Made in 1944, *The Lodger* is a horror story about Jack the Ripper, set in London in the late 1800s; Friedhofer's score was an important contributing factor in setting the chilling atmosphere of the film.

Both made in 1955, *The Rains of Ranchipur* and *Seven Cities of Gold* could not have been more different in tone. The former, set in India, stars Richard Burton and Lana Turner in a tragic love story that is all but upstaged by a catastrophic monsoon and earthquake, with Friedhofer writing a lush exotic score that took its cues from the story and its locale. The latter, set in 18th-century California, is a colorful adventure film which enabled the composer to display his particular fondness for Latin American accents in his music.

The scores, carefully reconstructed by William Stromberg and John Morgan, receive thoughtful readings from the Moscow Symphony Orchestra, conducted by Stromberg, in another superlative album on the independent label Marco Polo.

The Film Music of Hugo Friedhofer
1987, Facet Records ♫♫♫
album notes: Music: Hugo Friedhofer; **Orchestra:** The Graunke Symphony Orchestra of Munich; **Conductor:** Kurt Graunke.

Two scores by Friedhofer that are a little better than the films for which they were composed: *Richthofen and Brown* was created in 1971 for a World War I film by Roger Corman, which aimed to celebrate the airborne heroes, their tragic heroism, and faded sense of romanticism; as for *Private Parts*, also written in 1971, it is an almost forgotten horror film which deals with a young runaway girl in a rundown Los Angeles hotel and the strange characters she meets there. Friedhofer rose above the pedestrian topics in both films, and delivered scores that are at least soundly interesting, though not of a best vintage. The Graunke Symphony Orchestra, conducted by its founder Kurt Graunke, does a creditable job but this is obviously a second-rate CD, only recommended because of Friedhofer's name.

Didier C. Deutsch

Georges Garvarentz

Musiques de films
1997, PlayTime/France ♫♫♫♫

album notes: Music: Georges Garvarentz; **Conductor:** Paul Mauriat, Raymond Lefevre, Jacques Denjean.

Fans of film music will remember Georges Garvarentz from the scores he wrote for such films as *The Southern Star* (represented here by the title tune, sung by Matt Monro), *The Corrupt Ones, Marco the Magnificent, Panic Button, Triple Cross,* and *They Came to Rob Las Vegas* and *That Man in Istanbul* (both of which are also included here), all of them released in this country.

Working frequently with Charles Aznavour, his brother-in-law (also heard here in an interview in which he comments about his relationship with him), Garvarentz contributed the music to several action films in which the French crooner starred (*Taxi for Tobruk, Paris in the Month of August, The Mailman Goes to War, Find the Idol*), usually relying on expressive themes, grounded in a catchy pop vein. This extensive compilation profiles the composer in those and other films for which he wrote the scores. It's a very engaging collection that makes a positive impact, and, as such, should attract anyone interested in film music in general, and good instrumental music in particular.

Didier C. Deutsch

George & Ira Gershwin
(1898-1937)/(1896-1983)

George and Ira Gershwin in Hollywood
1997, Rhino Records ♫♫♫♫
album notes: Music: George Gershwin; **Lyrics:** Ira Gershwin.

As we reach the millennium, we might as well ask who was the most influential 20th-century composer. The jury may still be out, but to this writer none surpassed George Gershwin. Born two years before the century, Gershwin exerted himself in so many areas (pop songs, stage, screen, opera house, concert hall), and in ways that were so profoundly important that his influence can still be felt some 60-odd years after his untimely death. Today, we almost take him for granted, and we have solidly embraced his more serious works, like *Rhapsody in Blue, An American in Paris,* or the *Concerto in F.* But his achievements in the concert hall should not becloud his other contributions, particularly to the great American pop song catalogue for which he wrote with his brother Ira many evergreens that are still as thrilling today as they were when they were first created. While his legacy has been perpetuated by various singers like Frank Sinatra, Tony Bennett, and Michael Feinstein, the many films in which his songs crept up probably have gained him a much broader audience over the years.

This elegant 2-CD set from Rhino stresses the enormous contributions from the Gershwin brothers, while they worked in Hollywood, and after. A listing of the songs the set contains looks like a greatest hits compilation, with so many great tunes that it almost becomes an embarrassment of riches: "Somebody Loves Me," "They Can't Take That Away from Me," "Fascinating Rhythm," "Love Is Here to Stay," "They All Laughed," "Embraceable You," "Summertime," "But Not for Me," "Strike Up the Band," "The Man I Love," "A Foggy Day," "Oh Lady, Be Good," "Love Walked In," "'S Wonderful," "Shall We Dance," "I Got Rhythm." Not a single weak number among them, and the list goes on and on.

George and Ira Gershwin. **(AP/Wide World Photos, Inc.)**

Scouring the many films that featured songs by the Gershwin brothers, producers Michael Feinstein, George Feltenstein, and Bradley Flanagan have not only gone to the MGM vaults, the source of many Rhino sets, but to RKO, Warner Bros., Paramount, and 20th Century Fox, to present as complete a survey as possible. Commendable as their efforts are, the set is not without its flaws: there is an overabundance of tracks by Fred Astaire—arguably the one performer for whom the Gershwins wrote intensively and their best interpreter—most of them from the early RKO films *Shall We Dance* and *A Damsel in Distress*. But since the set producers decided to include a song from *Funny Face,* the 1957 film in which Astaire also starred with Audrey Hepburn, it would have made sense to include the title tune from that film, as well as "How Long Has This Been Going On?," performed by Hepburn.

Similarly, rather than use a couple of songs with limited appeal, like "Delishious," "By Strauss," from *An American in Paris,* would have seemed an apter choice. And since they decided to use songs with lyrics by Ira Gershwin with music by other composers, one glaring omission seems "The Man That Got Away," performed by Judy Garland in *A Star Is Born,* which would have been a much better choice than, say, the more obscure "In Our United State."

Evidently, these are minor points that can easily be dismissed and in no way lessen the importance of the set or its overall impact. A wonderful primer and a great collection of songs, many of them in their definitive versions, *George and Ira Gershwin in Hollywood* is a total joy.

Didier C. Deutsch

Goblin

The Goblin Collection 1975-1989
1995, DRG Records ♪♪♪♪

album notes: Music: Goblin; *Goblin:* Massimo Morante, guitars, bass, mandolin; Claudio Simonetti, electric keyboards, synthesizers, organ, violin; Fabio Pignatelli, bass, acoustic guitar; Agostino Marangolo, percussion, piano; Mauro Lusini guitars, keyboards; Marco Rinalduzzi, guitars; Derek Wilson, drums; Maurizio Guarini, synthesizers.

A seminal Italian rock group, Goblin made an important contribution to horror films through its scores, a richly textured blend of electronic and acoustic elements that often prove an effective complement to the suggestive power of the images on the screen. The group first came into being in 1975, and almost immediately emerged as a vital musical entity with its score for the cult thriller *Profondo Rosso* (*Deep Red*), directed by Dario Argento. Subsequently, they scored *Suspiria,* also for Argento, and went on to write the music for *Wampyr, Patrick, Dawn of the Dead,* and many other celebrated horror films. This compilation, the first of its kind to present a broad overview of the

group's involvement with the movies, will be of primary interest to fans of the genre, but may prove less seductive to others with little or no interest in this kind of music.

Didier C. Deutsch

Jerry Goldsmith
(1929-)

The Soundtracks of Jerry Goldsmith with the Philharmonia
1989, Deram Records ♪♪♪♪

album notes: Music: Jerry Goldsmith; **Orchestra:** The Philharmonia Orchestra; **Conductor:** Jerry Goldsmith.

Anyone who's never been to a Jerry Goldsmith concert can re-create essentially the same experience with this CD (but without the composer's running commentary). It's a representative sampling of Goldsmith's most familiar and honored music for film and television, opening with a lengthy suite from the composer's soaring score to the WWI aerial drama *The Blue Max* and moving on with an exciting medley of Goldsmith's television themes, including *The Man from UNCLE, Dr. Kildare, Room 222,* the crowd-pleasing theme from *The Waltons,* and *Barnaby Jones.* Other highlights include "The Motion Picture Suite," with music from Goldsmith's Oscar-nominated scores to *The Sand Pebbles, A Patch of Blue, Papillon, Chinatown,* and *The Wind and the Lion*; and "The Generals Suite," combining Goldsmith's music for the military biographical films *MacArthur* and *Patton.* The end title music from Franklin Schaffner's *Lionheart* closes the album. There are also suites from *Masada* and *Gremlins,* the latter of which includes the opening "Chinatown" music that was missing from that film's soundtrack album. A curious omission is any music from Goldsmith's only Oscar-winning score, *The Omen.* It has to be said that some of Goldsmith's compositions lose something in the translation to concert hall aesthetic: the television themes, although exciting in their own right, bear little resemblance to their original arrangements, and the raucous *Gremlins* rag mutates from a mischievous techno-funk satire to a somewhat awkward big band romp without its electronic underpinnings. Nevertheless, this is a fun overview of Goldsmith's career that's well-performed by the Philharmonia Orchestra.

Jeff Bond

Frontiers
1997, Varèse-Sarabande ♪♪♪♪♪

album notes: Music: Jerry Goldsmith; **Orchestra:** The Royal Scottish National Orchestra; **Conductor:** Jerry Goldsmith.

The Omen: The Essential Jerry Goldsmith Film Music Collection
1998, Silva America ♪♪♪♪♪

album notes: Music: Jerry Goldsmith; **Orchestra:** The City of Prague Philharmonic and the Crouch End Festival Chorus; **Conductor:** Nic Raine and David Temple.

Jerry Goldsmith **(Archive Photos, Inc.)**

Both collections spotlight a composer who has become one of the most admired film scorers in recent years: to be sure, a film score by Jerry Goldsmith is guaranteed to be unusual, solidly etched, at times introspective, at times exhilarating, always exciting. Unlike John Williams, who relies first and foremost on melodic material, Goldsmith is not afraid to create scores in which invention sometimes prevails over thematic material: you may not leave the theatre humming the main theme from the movie you have just seen, but you're likely to remember the subliminal effect the music itself played during the course of the action, always informing what happened on the screen, while adding its own comments in a way that made it ultimately undissociated from the film itself.

As its name suggests it, *Frontiers* is a collection of excerpts from scores he created for a wide variety of films in the otherwordly realm, from the outer-space-based *Star Trek* and *Alien,* to sci-fi adventures like *Logan's Run,* to unconventional stories like *The Illustrated Man* or *Damnation Alley.* The performance by the Royal Scottish National Orchestra is thoroughly polished, with Goldsmith evidently enjoying this opportunity to revisit some of his themes and play them with a large symphonic orchestra.

Sonically, the City of Prague is a good match for the Royal Scottish National Orchestra, with the Silva recording evidencing broad, spacious sonics that enhance and flatter the music. The program is much more extensive than *Frontiers* and covers a whole range of films from historical sagas (*Masada, First Knight*), to actioners (*The Great Train Robbery, Rambo*), to war-related epics (*The Blue Max, MacArthur, Patton*), to pseudo disaster films (*The Swarm*), and even a cute animated feature (*Baby: Secret of a Lost Legend*).

As in most Silva productions, almost everything here is flawless, with exceptional highlights that include the suite from *Under Fire,* a south of the border adventure film; and the lengthy medley from the *Star Trek* films and television shows.

Didier C. Deutsch

Ron Goodwin

(1925-)

Ron Goodwin: Drake 400
1989, Chandos Records 🎵🎵🎵

album notes: Orchestra: The Bournemouth Symphony Orchestra; Conductor: Ron Goodwin; **Featured Musicians:** Brendan O'Brien, violin; Terry Thompson, bagpipe.

Ron Goodwin has sadly never received sufficient attention in America, but he has long been one of Britain's finest and most successful composers. This anthology contains a number of film themes and light concert works by the composer. Good-

win's excellent march from *Force Ten from Navarone* (one of his best scores) is featured in a stirring performance. Goodwin's theme from a forgotten film version of *Beauty and the Beast* is a beautifully romantic work featuring a solo violin. The theme from *Candleshoe* (a forgettable Disney comedy starring Jodie Foster) is a less memorable '70s pop effort, but *The Spaceman and King Arthur* has a nicely triumphant pomp to it.

The concert works are of less interest to the soundtrack collector. Goodwin offers arrangements of "Auld Lang Syne" and "Amazing Grace" (featuring a Scottish piper). "Drake 400," however, is a magnificent piece, commissioned to celebrate the 400th anniversary of Sir Francis Drake's circumnavigation of the globe. A majestic and triumphant evocation of sea, it is in the style of Goodwin's most exciting adventure scores. Though perhaps not the best representation of Ron Goodwin's film music, there is much here which is well worth a listen.

Paul Andrew MacLean

Ron Goodwin: Drake 400 Suite/New Zealand Suite
1996, Marco Polo Records 🎵🎵🎵🎵

album notes: Music: Ron Goodwin; **Orchestra:** The New Zealand Symphony Orchestra; **Conductor:** Ron Goodwin.

Though he has composed many great scores during his illustrious career, Ron Goodwin is a virtual unknown in this country. But anyone who has been exposed to his music will remember some of the most famous themes he composed, for films like the uproarious 1965 comedy *Those Magnificent Men in Their Flying Machines,* the Kim Novak-vehicle *Of Human Bondage,* the Hitchcock film *Frenzy,* or the series of delirious detective adventures featuring Agatha Christie's Miss Marple (see below). This collection, in which he conducts the New Zealand Symphony Orchestra, is an ideal introduction to his music. Kicking off with the stirring march from *633 Squadron,* the set also offers the main themes from *The Trap,* a 1966 film starring Oliver Reed and Rita Tushingham, and *Lancelot and Guinevere,* made in 1962, with Cornel Wilde and Jean Wallace as the star-crossed lovers in King Arthur's court, and several non-film related small compositions.

But the plum of this recording are the two long suites, *Drake 400* and *New Zealand,* both of which gave the composer an opportunity to "stretch" and create works of impressive magnitude. Commissioned by the City Fathers of Plymouth in 1979, *Drake 400* evoked the life of Sir Francis Drake and his round-the-world voyage, with striking evocations of seafaring adventure in the 16th century. Composed in 1983, the *New Zealand Suite* sought to paint a picture of that country, its amazing beauty, its glorious history, with Goodwin blending in his music elements of Maori songs. Both works are superb examples of Ron Goodwin's feel for suggestive musical images, something that has also made his film scores so distinctive.

Ron Goodwin: Three Symphonic Suites
1990, Label X 🎧🎧🎧🎧

album notes: Music: Ron Goodwin; **Orchestra:** The Odense Symphony Orchestra; **Conductor:** Ron Goodwin.

The jaunty "Miss Marple Theme" will no doubt bring back fond memories to anyone who has ever watched the four films that starred the indomitable Margaret Rutherford as the famous sleuth. But even more attractive is the suite composed of cues from the films themselves, *Murder She Said, Murder at the Gallop, Murder Most Foul,* and *Murder Ahoy.* Ron Goodwin, one of the better light pop film composers of the 1960s and '70s, gave the films their musical signature, and provided the various themes that enhanced the delicious screen adventures of the lady (who bore no resemblance whatsoever to the TV Miss Marple, portrayed by Joan Hickson).

In contrast, *Lancelot and Guinevere,* a historical drama that dealt with the well-known events at the court of Camelot, and *Force 10 from Navarone,* a sequel to the Carl Foreman World War II film *The Guns of Navarone,* enabled Goodwin to reach out and create scores that are widely different in tone and nature. At times stately and regal, at times achingly romantic in a pseudo medieval way, *Lancelot and Guinevere* explores the different aspects of its subject matter, from the courtly behavior of its knights and ladies, to the all consuming love between the proud Lancelot and the lovely Guinevere, portrayed by Cornel Wilde and Jean Wallace.

In *Force 10 from Navarone,* Goodwin shifted to a string of martial cues, with lots of brassy effects, well-suited for this war drama, in which the main theme, a sensational march, rivals the one written by Tiomkin for *The Guns of Navarone.* While the film itself was a disaster, the score is simply magnificent.

Didier C. Deutsch

Dave Grusin
(1934-)

Cinemagic
1987, GRP Records 🎧🎧🎧🎧🎧

album notes: Music: Dave Grusin; **Orchestra:** The London Symphony Orchestra; **Conductor:** Dave Grusin, Harry Rabinowitz; **Featured Musicians:** Dave Grusin, piano, synthesizers; Don Grusin, synthesizers; Lee Ritenour, acoustic and electric guitars; Abraham Laboriel, electric bass; Harvey Mason, drums; Mike Fisher, percussion; Emil Richards, cymbalon, percussion; Chuck Findley, trumpet; Charley Loper, trombone; Tom Scott, soprano sax, tenor sax; Ernie Watts, tenor sax; Eddie Daniels, clarinet.

Dave Grusin is one of the most reliable film composers in the business when he turns his attention away from his successful recording career as a jazz artist to the silver screen, and this superb album from GRP showcases many of his most memorable soundtrack compositions. From the expressive lyricism of *On Golden Pond* and *The Heart Is a Lonely Hunter* to exciting percussive tracks from *Three Days of the Condor* and *The Goonies,* this album illustrates Grusin's penchant for writing strong thematic material, working with both jazz-based rhythms and full orchestral composition to great effect, creating solid film music that functions flawlessly on its own in the process. The performances consist of all-new recordings featuring Grusin and a collection of talented artists (including Tom Scott, Lee Ritenour, and Eddie Daniels) performing with the London Symphony Orchestra, conducted by Grusin and Harry Rabinowitz. As far as composer retrospectives go, this cohesive, expertly-produced recording of Grusin's film music is one of the best, with something to appeal to listeners of any kind of musical persuasion.

Andy Dursin

Neal Hefti
(1922-)

Batman Theme and 19 Hefti Bat Songs
1997, Razor & Tie Records 🎧🎧🎧

album notes: Music: Neal Hefti; **Conductor:** Neal Hefti.

When Batman first hit television in the mid-1960s, it became a fast success thanks to its camp attitude, tongue-in-cheek action, and Neal Hefti's catchy theme that echoed the series' irreverent approach to its subject matter. Unlike Tim Burton's Batman of latter years, this Batman was not brooding and didn't quite take himself seriously. His foes were equally congenial and amusing, making the series constantly fun and entertaining.

Hefti's music reflected everything that made the series so endearing—the themes were simple and unaffected, easy on the ear, and quite hummable. Today, they still exert the same appeal, and even though we might have become more aware of the Danny Elfman-brand of Bat music, Hefti's still retains its humor and validity. This CD, a compilation of two RCA albums, *Batman Theme & 11 Hefti Bat Songs* and *Hefti in Gotham City,* both from 1966, remains true to the nature of the original TV show—in other words, it is fun, not too heavy on the intellect, and pretty much of its age.

Didier C. Deutsch

Bernard Herrmann
(1911-1975)

Alfred Hitchcock's Film Music
1989, Milan Records/France 🎧🎧🎧🎧

album notes: Music: Bernard Herrmann; **Orchestra:** The National Philharmonic Orchestra, the London Studio Symphony Orchestra; **Conductor:** Bernard Herrmann, Laurie Johnson.

Bernard Herrmann: The Film Scores
1996, Sony Classical 🎧🎧🎧🎧

album notes: Music: Bernard Herrmann; **Orchestra:** The Los Angeles Philharmonic; **Conductor:** Esa-Pekka Salonen.

The Great Hitchcock Movie Thrillers
1996, London Records. 🎵🎵🎵

album notes: Music: Bernard Herrmann; **Orchestra:** The London Philharmonic Orchestra; **Conductor:** Bernard Herrmann.

Fans of the great Bernard Herrmann will find a treasure trove of worthwhile CDs that serve to keep his music and his memory alive, including the three listed here. As might be expected, many of these Herrmann compilations feature his compositions for the classic Alfred Hitchcock films, but a few do contain other important film works. *Alfred Hitchcock's Film Music* (Milan) offers two "extended" suites: *Suite for Psycho* (nearly 30 minutes), which features Herrmann conducting the National Philharmonic Orchestra, and *North by Northwest* (19 minutes), performed by the London Studio Symphony Orchestra under the direction of Laurie Johnson. Both the interpretations and the sonics are uniformly excellent.

Bernard Herrmann: The Film Scores (Sony Classical) features Esa-Pekka Salonen conducting the Los Angeles Philharmonic. In addition to offering *Psycho: A Suite for String* (similar in theme to the one in the Milan CD, but utilizing different cues and orchestrations), the recording includes selections from *The Man Who Knew Too Much, Marnie, North By Northwest, Vertigo,* and *Torn Curtain* (the pair's final collaboration). Two post-Hitch efforts emerge as essential pieces: *Fahrenheit 451: Suite for Strings, Harps, and Percussion* (composed for the Francois Truffaut film), and the all too short *A Night Piece for Orchestra with Alto Saxophone Obbligato,* from *Taxi Driver,* the score that Herrmann completed on the very day that he died. The superior orchestrations and sparkling recording make one hope that Salonen will address more Herrmann, and the works of other notable film composers, in the future.

Psycho: Great Hitchcock Movie Thrillers (London) contains yet another distillation from *Psycho* (14 minutes), and most of the usual Herrmann-Hitchcock suspects, in abbreviated form. Three unusual pieces are Herrmann's *A Portrait of Hitch* (from *The Trouble With Harry*), and two non-Herrmann compositions: *Theme From Spellbound* (Miklos Rozsa) and the Alfred Hitchcock TV theme, Gounod's *Funeral March of a Marionette.* All of the Herrmann pieces feature the London Philharmonic orchestra and are conducted by the composer himself.

Charles L. Granata

Classic Fantasy Film Scores
1988, Cloud Nine Records/U.K 🎵🎵🎵🎵

album notes: Music: Bernard Herrmann; **Conductor:** Bernard Herrmann.

Visual effects master Ray Harryhausen, producer Charles H. Schneer, and composer Bernard Herrmann combined to create four masterworks of the fantasy genre, each of which are included on this outstanding compilation from Cloud Nine. Herrmann's majestic music from *The Three Worlds of Gulliver* sets the regal tone for this release, which also includes selections from his thundering score from *Mysterious Island,* the exotic tone of *The Seventh Voyage of Sinbad,* and a pair of tracks from the rousing *Jason and the Argonauts.* Comprehensive liner notes and a nicely designed booklet complement this archival album, which features often ragged monaural sound and unfortunate "chilling sound effects" from *Jason* on the last track, which may disappoint audiophiles but nevertheless helps to preserve some truly classic film music from one of the original masters of the craft.

Andy Dursin

Bernard Herrmann: Great Film Music
1996, London Records 🎵🎵🎵🎵

album notes: Music: Bernard Herrmann; **Orchestra:** The National Philharmonic Orchestra; **Conductor:** Bernard Herrmann.

If nothing else, this great-sounding album of Bernard Herrmann's music for five different fantasy films should settle the question of where Danny Elfman got his inspiration for his original *Batman* score: the opening, fifteen minute suite from *Journey to the Center of the Earth* could have easily been used as a temp track for the Caped Crusader with its ominous five-note brass theme, oppressive orchestral chords, and ethereal harp and organ textures (as well as the unearthly sounds of the medieval serpent). After the disturbing sounds of the Jules Verne story, Herrmann's music for the bright Ray Harryhausen adventure *The Seventh Voyage of Sinbad* is almost frivolous, but Herrmann inevitably returns to the dark side with the heavy tread of "Gort" robot music for the classic *The Day the Earth Stood Still.* The latter score is beautifully recreated in its opening titles, the busy "Radar" music and the eerie "Terror" cue, but the cues involving Gort suffer from the lack of a real theremin in the performance and are no match for the original recordings. *Fahrenheit 451* comes off much better, from the relentless destructiveness of the fire engine music to the achingly beautiful, haunting finale. A bonus is 25 minutes of Herrmann's music for the 1961 live action *Gulliver's Travels,* but in this case Herrmann's music so authentically captures the pomposity of its satirized British Empire that listening to its endless minuets and marches quickly becomes a chore. Herrmann's handling of the orchestra in all cases is typically brilliant.

Jeff Bond

Bernard Herrmann: Music from Great Film Classics
1996, London Records 🎵🎵🎵🎵

album notes: Music: Bernard Herrmann; **Orchestra:** The London Philharmonic Orchestra, the National Philharmonic Orchestra; **Conductor:** Bernard Herrmann.

Bernard Herrmann: Wells Raises Kane
1994, Unicorn Records 🎬🎬🎬🎬

album notes: Music: Bernard Herrmann; **Orchestra:** The London Philharmonic Orchestra, the National Philharmonic Orchestra; **Conductor:** Bernard Herrmann.

When he felt he had become redundant in Hollywood, Bernard Herrmann exiled himself to Europe and began recording intensively some of the best scores he had written for the movies. These two sets both present some of his most significant contributions to the screen, in thorough readings by the London Philharmonic and the National Philharmonic, two orchestras with which Herrmann enjoyed a long relationship in the 1960s and '70s. Some cues, in fact, appear on both CDs, but the first is notably significant for the suite from *Jane Eyre,* while the second includes the complete score for Brian de Palma's *Obsession,* a throbbing, lusty effort that ranks among the composer's finest works. It's not often that a composer has an occasion to revisit some of his scores and to rerecord them with great orchestras. Both CDs are remarkable in that respect, and definitive recordings no one should be without.

Didier C. Deutsch

Bernard Herrmann Conducts Great British Film Music
1996, London Records 🎬🎬🎬🎬🎬

album notes: Orchestra: The National Philharmonic Orchestra; **Conductor:** Bernard Herrmann.

When he moved to Europe, Herrmann, in addition to addressing his own works, also surveyed the scores written by other important classic composers. This album, recorded for London in 1974, focuses on music written for English films by William Walton, Arnold Bax, Ralph Vaughan Williams, and Arthur Bliss, whose *Things to Come* is a particular highlight here. Also included is a series of cues composed by Constant Lambert for *Anna Karenina,* another score, notably attractive, that's seldom heard. The Phase 4 Stereo recording transfers very well to the digital domain.

Didier C. Deutsch

Bernard Herrmann Film Scores: From Citizen Kane to Taxi Driver
1993, Milan Records 🎬🎬

album notes: Music: Bernard Herrmann; **Orchestra:** The Royal Philharmonic Orchestra; **Conductor:** Elmer Bernstein; **Featured Musicians:** The Ambrosia Singers; David Roach, alto sax.

This is an album whose conception and recording do not appear to have been adequately thought-out or prepared. The performance is passive, failing to serve Herrmann's surging, visceral style. The musicians trip and stumble through *Citizen Kane*'s "Inquirer Polka" with a number of glaring clams. The inclusion of the Xavier Cugat-like main title from *The Wrong Man*

is puzzling; the piece is at best a curiosity. The "Finale" from *Fahrenheit 451* is absolutely enraging—the harp, vibraphone, and glockenspiel parts are missing! A *Taxi Driver* suite is an inviting prospect, but it is ruined by Christopher Palmer's presumptuous alteration of Herrmann's original orchestration. Arthur Benjamin's "Storm Cloud Cantata" (from *The Man Who Knew Too Much*), is exciting and the best performed track on the album. But while Herrmann made his cameo in that film conducting this work, its inclusion on a Herrmann anthology makes no sense—Herrmann did not write it. Included at the end of the CD is an interesting excerpt from a recorded interview with Herrmann, where he expresses his thoughts on film scoring. Since many of the scores here are more truly represented elsewhere, this CD is at best a flawed oddity.

Paul Andrew MacLean

Citizen Kane: The Classic Film Scores of Bernard Herrmann
1989, RCA Victor Records 🎬🎬🎬🎬

album notes: Music: Bernard Herrmann; **Orchestra:** The National Philharmonic Orchestra; **Conductor:** Charles Gerhardt.

This album, part of the *Classic Film Music* series Charles Gerhardt recorded in the '70s, remains one of the best Herrmann compilations ever. Although a great deal of Herrmann's work has been recorded since this collection's initial release, much of the music offered here is still not available elsewhere.

Other recordings of *Citizen Kane* have since been made, but Gerhardt's remains the best. The 13-minute suite removes the extraneous, programmatic material, thus retaining the most potent essence of Herrmann's score. The aria for the fictitious opera "Salome" is included, and given dramatic performance by renowned soprano Kiri Te Kanawa. Also included is "Death Hunt," a surging, pummeling, brassy cue from *On Dangerous Ground,* and *Beneath the Twelve Mile Reef,* a stirring score, whose use of nine harps creates an effervescent evocation of the sea. Herrmann's "Concerto Macabre" for piano and orchestra (from *Hangover Square*) is driving and intense, while *White Witch Doctor* is an exotic and rhythmic evocation of Africa.

Engineer K.E. Wilkinson extracts a clear, full sound from the orchestra, and despite the advances in recording technology since this album was made, few later recordings can approach the resonant, crystalline sound of this 1974 album.

Paul Andrew MacLean

Farenheit 451
1995, Varèse Sarabande Records 🎬🎬🎬🎬

album notes: Music: Bernard Herrmann; **Orchestra:** The Seattle Symphony Orchestra; **Conductor:** Joel McNeely.

One of Bernard Herrmann's finest scores, *Fahrenheit 451* is a passionate romantic score, employing an ensemble of strings, harps, and modest percussion (but no brass or woodwinds). The music evokes emotions ranging from poetic longing to raging dementia, externalizing the suppressed passions of the film's characters, all locked into a conformist society of the future. Although this 17-minute suite from *Fahrenheit 451* was originally arranged by Herrmann himself, it is a pity that Varèse took the trouble to make this recording, but did not present a more complete representation of the score (Herrmann rashly omitted a number of important cues from his suite). The remainder of the CD is filled-out with brief excerpts from four other Herrmann scores, *The Man in the Grey Flannel Suit, Anna and the King of Siam, Tender Is the Night* and *The Ghost and Mrs. Muir*—fine scores all, but with each so briefly represented, the listener can never quite become involved in any of them. The performance and recording quality, however, are first-rate, and even in brief suite form, *Fahrenheit 451* remains a masterpiece of invention and one of Herrmann's best works.

Paul Andrew MacLean

Torn Curtain: The Classic Film Music of Bernard Herrmann
1995, Silva Screen Records ♪♪♪♪
album notes: Music: Bernard Herrmann; **Orchestra:** The City of Prague Philharmonic; **Conductor:** Paul Bateman; **Featured Musicians:** Milan Hermanek, viola; Ivan Myslikovjan, saxophone.

Herrmann/Hitchcock: A Partnership in Terror
1996, Silva Screen Records ♪♪♪♪
album notes: Music: Bernard Herrmann; **Orchestra:** The City of Prague Philharmonic; **Conductor:** Paul Bateman.

Both of these collections of Bernard Herrmann's film music are based around the same set of recordings of Hitchcock thriller scores: *A Partnership in Terror* features Herrmann's throbbing, stormy opening to *The Man Who Knew Too Much* (conducted by Herrmann himself as an orchestra performance at the opening of the film), the droll *The Trouble With Harry,* the swirling titles, tarantella nightmare sequence, and rhapsodic love music of *Vertigo,* the supercharged fandango opening of *North By Northwest,* the knitting strings of *Psycho,* and the urgent prelude music from *Marnie.* The *Torn Curtain* also features *The Man Who Knew Too Much, Psycho,* and *Vertigo,* as well as the aggressive (and rejected) music to *Torn Curtain,* but this longer album also features suites from Herrmann's brutal *Cape Fear* (reused by Martin Scorsese in his remake), newspaper music from *Citizen Kane,* and a somewhat less-than-satisfactory take on the composer's amazingly powerful score to *On Dangerous Ground.* More satisfying are the lyrical waltzes from *Obsession* and *The Snows of Kilimanjaro,* as well as the hauntingly romantic *The Ghost and Mrs. Muir.* There's a lively ten minute suite from Herrmann's indelible Ray Harryhausen fantasy scores, but the suite from *Taxi Driver* seems overly glib and romanticized, with a saxophone solo by Ivan Myslikovjan that just gets out of hand. Still, conductor Paul Bateman brings far more power and polish to these performances than are obtained on some of Silva's other compilations.

Jeff Bond

Citizen Kane: The Essential Bernard Herrmann Collection
1999, Silva Screen Records ♪♪♪
album notes: Music: Bernard Herrmann; **Orchestra:** The City of Prague Philharmonic Orchestra; **Conductor:** Paul Bateman and Nic Raine.

Paul Bateman repackaged material from his two other forays into Herrmann territory, *Torn Curtain: The Classic Film Music of Bernard Herrmann* and *Herrmann/Hitchcock: A Partnership in Terror,* also adding a few extras. His collection stands out for value and breadth, covering twenty scores in 130 minutes, and although this whirlwind tour of Herrmann classics doesn't give enough time to engross the listener, it does provide a good starter kit. This vibrant recording with Dolby Surround and HDCD outdoes its rivals for clarity, but Bateman does not achieve the best performances of Herrmann's material. Esa- Pekka Salonen fared better on his 1996 date for Sony Classical. Salonen's understated opening brass and punchy drum roll crescendos for *Taxi Driver* elicit tingles, while Bateman's clamor sounds like Herrmann by numbers without the apocalyptic foreshadowing. While both saxophonists on the subsequent "Blues" elide notes, Salonen's player does so with style and aplomb, while the Czech performer overplays, and makes the corny melody sound just that. Of the fourteen- some Herrmann collections available, Bateman's is the most extensive, yet other superior performances show a deeper understanding of Herrmann's spine-tingling scores, notably the four conducted by Herrmann himself for London Records.

David Poole

Lee Holdridge
(1944-)

Film Music of Lee Holdridge
1994, Citadel Records ♪♪♪♪
album notes: Music: Lee Holdridge; **Orchestra:** The London Symphony Orchestra; **Conductor:** Charles Gerhardt.

One of the most unsung of the modern-day film composers, Lee Holdridge's often romantic, expressive compositions are given their chance to shine on this great-sounding recording with Charles Gerhardt conducting the London Symphony Orchestra. From the Korngold-influenced *Wizards and Warriors* and *The Beastmaster* to the beautiful lyricism of *The Great Whales* and *Splash,* this superior effort nicely illustrates Holdridge's melodious musical style, featuring well-written, memorable themes and often soaring orchestral passages. The album also includes selections from the television program *The Hemingway Play* and features *Going Home* and *Jonathan Livingston Seagull,* concluding with an 18-minute suite from the mini-series *East of Eden.* With Gerhardt's baton leading the way, the album has a great deal of replay value due to its varied and consistently high level of musical quality.

Andy Dursin

Arthur Honegger

(1892-1955)

Arthur Honegger Film Music
1993, Marco Polo Records 𝄢𝄢𝄢𝄢
album notes: Orchestra: The CSR Symphony Orchestra of Bratislava; **Conductor:** Adriano.

Arthur Honegger: L'idee/Crime et chatiment
1993, Marco Polo Records 𝄢𝄢𝄢𝄢𝄢
album notes: Orchestra: The Slovak Radio Symphony Orchestra of Bratislava; **Conductor:** Adriano.

Arthur Honegger: Mayerling/Regain
1993, Marco Polo Records 𝄢𝄢𝄢𝄢
album notes: Orchestra: The Slovak Radio Symphony Orchestra of Bratislava, the Slovak Philharmonic Choir; **Conductor:** Adriano; **Featured Musician:** Jacques Tchamkerten, Ondes Mertenot.

One of the great classical composers of this century, Arthur Honegger wrote many scores for the movies (it was at his suggestion that Miklos Rozsa became a film composer as a way to turn his talent into a lucrative proposition). These recordings, superbly assembled by Marco Polo Records, feature Adriano and the Slovak Radio Symphony Orchestra of Bratislava in reconstructed performances of Honegger's most important scores, particularly *Les Miserables,* made in 1934, and *Napoleon,* directed by Abel Gance in 1926–27. The breathtaking scope and diversity of these scores show that film music, in its early days, was not confined to Hollywood and its great composers, but developed in other countries as well and attracted a lot of serious exponents. It also makes the strongest case yet for film music as a serious medium and as a close parent to classical music.

Didier C. Deutsch

James Horner

(1953-)

Heart of the Ocean
1998, Sonic Images 𝄢𝄢𝄢
album notes: Music: James Horner.

Titanic: The Essential James Horner Film Collection
1998, Silva America 𝄢𝄢𝄢𝄢
album notes: Music: James Horner; **Orchestra:** The City of Prague Philharmonic and the Crouch End Festival Chorus; **Conductor:** Nic

Raine, Paul Bateman, and David Temple; **Featured Musicians:** Juraslava Ellesova, piano; Vladimir Pilar, violin; Paul Brennan, Ueillan pipes; Paul Keogh, guitar.

Titanic and Other Film Scores of James Horner
1998, Varèse-Sarabande 𝄢𝄢𝄢𝄢
album notes: Music: James Horner; **Orchestra:** The Royal Scottish National Orchestra and Chorus, the London Symphony Orchestra and the Ambrosian Singers, and the Seattle Symphony Orchestra; **Conductor:** John Debney, Joel McNeely, Cliff Eidelman, and James Horner.

Because of the enormous worldwide success of *Titanic,* James Horner has achieved a reputation few film composers can boast of having: he has become a household name, and his scores are now beginning to attract a lot of fans, whose interest in them and knowledge of him are fueled by various compilations, such as the three presented here.

Depending largely on selections initially available on other labels, *Heart of the Ocean* takes its cue from the James Cameron blockbuster and adds to its main theme, perfunctorily played by Mark Northham at the piano, excerpts from *Apollo 13, Cocoon, Field of Dreams, Braveheart,* and *Star Trek II,* played by the Cincinnati Pops, conducted by Erich Kunzel; *Rocketeer* and *Legends of the Fall,* performed by Bruce Broughton and the Orchestra of the Americas; at least one soundtrack selection (*Where the River Runs Black*), and somewhat anonymous contributions by John Beal, which may not be entirely relevant in the context (*Commando* and *Vibes*). It's a tenuous argument to put together a compilation that is not entirely satisfying or enriching, while cashing in on Horner's current popularity as the newest Hollywood boy wonder.

Similarly, *Titanic: The Essential James Horner Film Collection* covers many themes created by Horner, including the ubiquitous "My Heart Will Go On," but also selections from *Glory, Star Trek II, Ransom, The Land Before Time, Braveheart, Red Heat, Willow, Field of Dreams,* and *The Name of the Rose.* In this case, however, the playing is done by the excellent City of Prague Philharmonic, which gives the recording a sound uniformity, supported by the usual high gloss associated with product from the label.

Though involving three different orchestras and four conductors, including Horner, *Titanic and Other Film Scores of James Horner* also comes across as a winning combination—a host of familiar tracks, performed with great gusto and the right sweep by great instrumental forces, in a program that never ceases to grasp the imagination and entertain the listener.

James Horner has often been criticized for writing scores that sound like and/or plagiarize the works of other composers. But the truth is, his creations are consistently attractive and satisfying, a point clearly made by these three compilations. In truth, if film music is to make any impact in the vast mass of filmgoers, Horner may actually have found the key to attract the majority of people. This, in itself, is quite an achievement.

Didier C. Deutsch

Mark Isham

(1951-)

Mark Isham Film Music
1990, Windham Hill Records ♫♫♫

album notes: Music: Mark Isham; **Conductor:** Mark Adler; **Featured Musicians:** Lyle Mayes, piano; Peter Maunu, violin; Mark Isham, trumpet, synthesizers, pennywhistle, piano; Rufus Olivier, bassoon; Bill Douglass, bamboo flutes; George Marsh, percussion; Tucky Bailey, glass; Natalie Cox, harp; Annie Stocking, vocals; Stephanie Douglass, vocals; Kathy Hudnall, vocals; Jeanette Spartaine, vocals.

Under the title *Film Music,* this set presents the original soundtrack of *Mrs. Soffel,* a 1985 film that stars Mel Gibson and Diane Keaton, coupled with rerecordings of *Never Cry Wolf,* from 1983, and cues from *The Times of Harvey Milk.* Isham, an eclectic composer and musician, is a borderline case between film music and New Age music, who creates often compelling scores. The music for *Mrs. Soffel,* a moving love story based on real life turn-of-the-century facts, is a combination of attractive cues that rely on the deft use of the pennywhistle, coupled with piano, violin, and synthesizers, to create its own aura. A semi-documentary/adventure film, *Never Cry Wolf,* made by Disney, follows a lone biologist working in the Arctic wasteland to learn more about wolves. The long suite offers themes that are suitably soft and attractive, though the lack of true melodic material sometimes works to the detriment of the music.

Didier C. Deutsch

Pierre Jansen

(1930-)

Musiques des films de Claude Chabrol
1989, Milan/U.K. ♫♫♫♫

album notes: Music: Pierre Jansen; **Conductor:** Andre Girard and Andre Jouve.

However one may view director Claude Chabrol, his films, particularly his early ones, were influential in shaping French cinema at a time when the New Wave was beginning to make itself heard. Jansen, in a rare director-composer collaborative effort that extended to several films by Chabrol, provided the music, in what annotator Royal S. Brown described in a November, 1988 article in *Fanfare,* as "what a Boulez or a Messiaen might have sounded like had either decided to compose for the cinema." This collection, which regroups six films made between 1965 (*The Blue Panther,* one of Chabrol's weakest entries) and 1974 (*Innocents with Dirty Hands*), also reveals Jansen as a composer with a striking debt to Bernard Herrmann, and an

originality that transcends some of the director's less successful efforts. Not a "theme composer," Jansen wrote scores that struck a deep, resonant note, with moody accents that created an aura absolutely appropriate for the thrillers Chabrol directed.

Didier C. Deutsch

Maurice Jarre

(1924-)

Jarre by Jarre: Film Themes of Maurice Jarre
1987, CBS Records ♫♫♫♫

album notes: Music: Maurice Jarre; **Orchestra:** The Royal Philharmonic Orchestra; **Conductor:** Maurice Jarre.

Although Maurice Jarre has recorded a number of anthologies of his own music, *Jarre by Jarre* is by far the best. Vibrantly performed and recorded with full, resonant sound, this album contains the best available recordings of some of these scores. *Lawrence of Arabia* is performed with majesty, precision, and grace (with the strings appropriately dominant). *Ryan's Daughter* is presented in an extremely enjoyable and graceful arrangement, which is far more attractive than the original soundtrack. *Is Paris Burning* is a vibrant waltz featuring accordion, and shows a lyrical side of Jarre which is rarely heard. Jarre's "Barn Raising" music from *Witness,* originally scored for synthesizers, is given a beautiful, full-orchestral rendition, while *The Damned* exposes a darker side of the composer. The suite from *Mad Max Beyond Thunderdome* contains a large, brassy fanfare (which is especially welcome since it was not included on the original soundtrack). *Villa Rides* concludes the album, a pleasantly rhythmic piece with an exotic Mexican flavor. Engineer Paul Hulme deserves special mention for extracting a large concert hall sound from CTS studios. In terms of both performance and sound, this is one of the best recordings I have ever heard.

Paul Andrew MacLean

Lean by Jarre: Musical Tribute to David Lean
1992, Milan Records ♫♫

album notes: Music: Maurice Jarre; **Orchestra:** The Royal Philharmonic Orchestra; **Conductor:** Maurice Jarre.

Maurice Jarre's most celebrated collaboration was with director David Lean, and the composer pays the director homage in this recording. Jarre's four scores for Lean, *Lawrence of Arabia, Doctor Zhivago, Ryan's Daughter,* and *A Passage to India,* are all represented, along with two original pieces, "Remembrance" and "Offering." "Remembrance," a thunderous, large orchestral piece that evokes the kind of large-scale epic for which David Lean was best known, introduces the album. Where the particular film scores are concerned however, the limitations of a concert setting unfortunately impose compromising alterations. Much of the more exotic (and inventive) instrumentation in Jarre's original scores is missing. The Fujara and Indian instruments are sorely missed in *Passage to India,* as are the various exotic instruments in *Doctor Zhivago.* The orchestration of *Lawrence of Arabia* is also altered for smaller orchestra, and as such proves unsatisfying. While a nice souvenir of the highly memorable Lean/ Jarre collaborations (this recording is also available on VHS and laserdisc as a concert video), I would sooner recommend the original soundtracks as a more true representation of these scores.

Paul Andrew MacLean

Maurice Jarre at Abbey Road
1992, Milan Records 🎵🎵🎵🎵

album notes: Music: Maurice Jarre; **Orchestra:** The Royal Philharmonic Orchestra and the Sun Valley Choral Society; **Conductor:** Maurice Jarre; **Featured Musician:** Ralph Grierson, synthesizers.

Always his own best interpreter, Maurice Jarre positively shines when he is fronting a great orchestra. Such is the case here, with the composer revisiting some of the scores he wrote throughout his career, including some rare ones seldom heard elsewhere. The *Georges Franju Suite* introduces themes he created for the films of Georges Franju, with whom he developed an early artistic relationship, long before Jarre became internationally renowned. They already evidence some of the traits for which Jarre would eventually become famous, notably his uncanny flair for strange instrumentations, and his knack for attractive, melodic tunes. Following *Behold a Pale Horse,* a sadly neglected score for a 1964 partisan film, set in post-Civil War Spain, starring Gregory Peck and Omar Sharif, the set moves on to latter day creations, like the themes for *Ghost, Witness, Gorillas in the Mist,* and *Fatal Attraction,* in which synthesizers play an increasingly important role. Interestingly, it offers the rarely heard theme for *Prancer,* before going to the delicious *Moon over Parador,* in which Jarre spoofs his own epic style. The "Bombay March" from *A Passage to India* concludes the set on a positive, exhilarating note that reminds us that Maurice Jarre always was at his best when he wrote epic themes. Throughout, the playing is never less than superlative.

Didier C. Deutsch

Maurice Jarre at the Royal Festival Hall
1997, Milan Records 🎵🎵🎵

album notes: Music: Maurice Jarre; **Orchestra:** The BBC Concert Orchestra; **Conductor:** Maurice Jarre.

Recorded live during a concert with the BBC Concert Orchestra, this recording features an eclectic array of Jarre's music. A suite from *Grand Prix* opens the album, Jarre's light-hearted music conveying the excitement of high-speed racing (the sound effect of cars whizzing by adding to the fun). *The Man Who Would*

10 Essential Scores
by James Horner

Cocoon
The Name of the Rose
Gorky Park
* batteries not included
Field of Dreams
Krull
Searching for Bobby Fischer
Braveheart
Apollo 13
Titanic

Be King is given a jaunty arrangement, though the very foreground use of percussion is perhaps a little overbearing. The theme from *Villa Rides* (one of Jarre's few western scores) is a beautiful, Mexican-flavored piece with some of Jarre's most consonant orchestration.

Originally conceived as an electronic score, *The Year of Living Dangerously* appears in an intriguing orchestral transcription. While interesting, it remains a more successful work in its original form. On the other hand, Jarre's Americana-flavored music from *Witness*—also originally conceived for electronics—translates to an orchestral setting far more successfully. A non-film work, Jarre's "Concerto for EVI" (electronic wind instrument) is a four-movement work, vibrant and stylistically eclectic. A solid performance of the oft-recorded *Lawrence of Arabia* brings the album to its conclusion.

Because it was recorded at a live performance, the sound balance and fidelity are not as good as they might be in a studio setting, but engineer Mike Ross-Trevor does an excellent job, and there are some highly attractive moments in this album.

Paul Andrew MacLean

Maurice Jarre **(Archive Photos, Inc.)**

Doctor Zhivago: The Classic Film Music of Maurice Jarre
1995, Silva Screen Records ♪♪♪♪

album notes: Music: Maurice Jarre; **Orchestra:** The City of Prague Philharmonic, the Philharmonia Orchestra; **Conductor:** Paul Bateman, Tony Bremner.

Excellent compilation of suites and themes from Maurice Jarre's monumental career. Paul Bateman conducts the City of Prague Philharmonic in their performance on both the David Lean film standards *Doctor Zhivago* and *A Passage to India,* as well as "Building the Barn" from *Witness,* and the finale from *Ghost.* This anthology also features lesser known Jarre efforts for such films as *The Fixer, El Condor,* and *Villa Rides.* The Prague orchestra handles the material well with solid, respectable performances that are faithful to the original work. There is also a bonus track included from Silva's *Lawrence of Arabia* rerecording by the Philharmonia Orchestra under the direction of Tony Bremmer.

David Hirsch

A Maurice Jarre Trilogy
1995, DRG Records ♪♪♪♪

album notes: Music: Maurice Jarre; **Orchestra:** The Unione Musicisti di Roma Orchestra; **Conductor:** Maurice Jarre.

A most intriguing concept for a collection of rarer material composed by Maurice Jarre. All three of these films have one thing in common: their central characters are living in their own hellish dark side of life. The controversial classic *The Damned* leads off this 2-CD set with some of Jarre's darkest work. The nucleus of this score is a shadowy waltz that represents one family's descent into perversity. *A Season in Hell* displays the disintegrating friendship between two brilliant writers in 19th-century Paris. While there are the typical warm emotional themes ("To My Best Loved Friend") that Jarre is noted for, the score is peppered with blood boiling African rhythms. By far the longest presentation of the three, *For Those I Loved* is an awareness of the hopes and dreams of the survivors of the Holocaust, as seen through the eyes of one Polish survivor. No doubt because the subject matter offered more motivation to Jarre, this is the most captivating of the three scores. It is powerfully moving, evoking unsettling emotions from the darkest period of human existence.

David Hirsch

Laurie Johnson
(1927-)

The Avengers
1982, Varèse Sarabande Records ♪♪♪♪♪

album notes: Music: Laurie Johnson; **Orchestra:** The London Studio Orchestra; **Conductor:** Laurie Johnson.

The Rose and the Gun
1992, Unicorn-Kanchana Records ♪♪♪♪

album notes: Music: Laurie Johnson; **Orchestra:** The London Studio Symphony Orchestra; **Conductor:** Laurie Johnson.

Laurie Johnson's real claim to fame is the vigorous theme he wrote in the early 1960s for the English television series *The Avengers.* But his enormous body of work, which encompasses more than 400 scores for films and television, single him out as one of the most prolific and successful British composers today. Both CDs offer selections from several of the most prominent films and TV shows with which he has been associated, with Johnson himself conducting the London Studio Symphony Orchestra.

Unsurprisingly, both sets contain the main themes from *The Avengers* and its sequel, *The New Avengers,* with the Varèse CD including in addition some other themes written for individual episodes. Of the two, that CD is also more interesting in that it covers at greater length other scores written by Johnson, for the science fiction film *First Men in the Moon,* made in 1964, and *Captain Kronos, Vampire Hunter,* a cult horror movie, as well as a suite from the screen adaptation of Ibsen's *Hedda Gabler.* Rounding up the selections in the set is a theme from the Stanley Kubrick anti-war drama *Dr. Strangelove,* also a popular favorite.

The Unicorn-Kanchana set may not have as much of a widespread appeal, given the fact that many of the themes found in it relate to films or television shows that are not very well known outside of England. However, collectors should notice that the CD includes a collection of themes for TV films based on the novels by Barbara Cartland (*The Lady and the Highwayman, A Hazard of Hearts, A Duel of Hearts,* and *A Ghost in Monte Carlo),* as well as from the film *Hot Millions,* and the TV special "Shirley's World," starring Shirley MacLaine. Always elegant and catchy, Johnson's music makes for great listening.

Didier C. Deutsch

Michael Kamen
(1948-)

Michael Kamen's Opus
1998, London Records ♪♪♪♪♪

album notes: Music: Michael Kamen; **Orchestra:** The Seattle Symphony Orchestra and the London Metropolitan Orchestra; **Conductor:** Michael Kamen; **Featured Musicians:** John Cerminaro, horn; Hugh Seenan, horn; Scott Goff, flute; Maggie Cole, harpsichord; John Marson, harp; Gillian Tingay, harp; Ilka Talvi, violin; Christopher Warren Green, violin; Caroline Dale, cello; Charles Butler, trumpet; Tomoyasu Hotei, guitar; Michael Kamen, piano, English horn.

Equally at ease in the epic swashbuckling genre as in the contemporary pop action drama, Michael Kamen has scored many important films over the past 20-odd years, including *Robin Hood, Prince Of Thieves; Highlander; Brazil; Die Hard;* and the film that probably made him most successful, *Mr. Holland's Opus,* after which this CD takes its title.

The selections found here, many featuring new orchestrations specially written for the album, cover the gamut, with the composer conducting the Seattle Symphony Orchestra and the London Metropolitan Orchestra, and guest artists Kate Bush and Tomoyasu Hotel adding their own contributions.

As a primer introduction to Kamen's composing skills, this is a fine collection, bound to attract a lot of listeners. Throughout, the composer reveals a great ear for melodic material ("Rowena," from *Mr. Holland's Opus*), with some selections ("Marooned," from *Crusoe,* a little heralded film) making the best impression, perhaps because of their unfamiliarity.

Didier C. Deutsch

Denis King

(1939-)

Lovejoy and Other Original TV Themes
1992, Westmoor Music/U.K. 𝄞𝄞
album notes: Music: Denis King; Conductor: Denis King.

Like Mike Curb in the U.S., Denis King writes primarily for television in the U.K., a task that requires creating catchy, easy on the ear, and remarkably dispensable title themes (it isn't as easy as it sounds). Listening to these 14 tracks, one comes to understand what has made King a true craftsman in his field. The tunes are enjoyable, if not exactly memorable, and make a favorable impression that doesn't last very long. For an occasional kick, the CD is just fine, but since most of the series illustrated here have never been shown in the U.S. (*Lovejoy* is the only one that comes to mind), you should consider getting this CD only if you don't have anything better to listen to.

Didier C. Deutsch

Erich-Wolfgang Korngold

(1897-1957)

Erich-Wolfgang Korngold: The Warner Bros. Years
1996, Rhino Records 𝄞𝄞𝄞𝄞
album notes: Music: Erich-Wolfgang Korngold; Orchestra: The Warner Bros. Studio Orchestra; Conductor: Erich-Wolfgang Korngold.

Epic compilation of the original recordings of Erich-Wolfgang Korngold's ground-breaking work in the early days of Hollywood from 1935 to 1946. Korngold, a child prodigy who was composing operas in his teens, set the standards for the great costumed dramas (*Anthony Adverse, King's Row*), the Errol

Flynn swashbucklers (*Captain Blood, The Sea Hawk,* and *The Adventures of Robin Hood*), and the romantic sagas (*Escape Me Never*), all with a lavishly orchestrated style. Key selections from 16 of his Warner Bros. scores are featured here, each conducted personally by the composer. The one drawback to this two hour-plus collection is that many of the recordings have a lot of surface noise. Not surprising when considering that they have survived the last 50 to 60 years this well. While much of this music has been digitally rerecorded over the last few years, none of it can ever match the power of the original sessions. The orchestra size, or the pace of the performance, is never quite the same, and Korngold here has the orchestra play it as he wrote it, full of fire and emotion. The 2-CD set also contains a lavish 44-page booklet with insightful historical notes by noted Korngold authority Tony Thomas.

David Hirsch

The Sea Hawk: The Classic Film Scores of Erich-Wolfgang Korngold
1989, RCA Victor 𝄞𝄞𝄞𝄞𝄞
album notes: Music: Erich-Wolfgang Korngold; Orchestra: The National Philharmonic Orchestra; Conductor: Charles Gerhardt; Featured Musician: Sidney Sax, violin.

Originally recorded and released in 1972, this is the album largely credited with igniting the revival of symphonic film music after years of dreariness when rock scores had become the norm and below-par standard. The million-selling album, which was produced by George Korngold, son of the composer, spawned a prestigious series that eventually explored the works of well-known Hollywood composers like Max Steiner, Bernard Herrmann, Miklos Rozsa, Dimitri Tiomkin, and David Raksin, all of whom had fallen into sad neglect. Also as a result of the series' success, *Star Wars,* released in 1977, was able to feature a symphonic score by John Williams that not only paid homage to the composer's illustrious predecessors, but opened wide the gates of the studios to an entire generation of new composers, like James Horner, Cliff Eidelman, Randy Edelman, and George Fenton, all of whom benefitted from the incredible resurgence of symphonic music in films.

Didier C. Deutsch

Elizabeth and Essex: The Classic Film Scores of Erich-Wolfgang Korngold
1989, RCA Victor 𝄞𝄞𝄞𝄞𝄞
album notes: Music: Erich-Wolfgang Korngold; Orchestra: The National Philharmonic Orchestra; Conductor: Charles Gerhardt; Featured Musician: Francisco Garbarro, cello.

A follow-up to *The Sea Hawk,* this splendid recording again teamed the National Philharmonic with conductor Charles Gerhardt and producer George Korngold for a further exploration of composer Erich-Wolfgang Korngold's film music. Like its predecessor, it is a sumptuous tribute to one of the great Hollywood composers of the 1940s.

Didier C. Deutsch

Music by Erich-Wolfgang Korngold
1991, Stanyan Records ♪♪♪♪♪
album notes: Music: Erich-Wolfgang Korngold; **Orchestra:** The Warner Bros. Studio Orchestra; **Conductor:** Lionel Newman.

For many years, the LP version of this album, initially released by Warner Bros. Records in 1962 and almost immediately deleted, was high on the list of ardent fans and collectors of serious film music. Its availability on compact disc brings it back to the catalogue, and while it may not sound as outstanding today as it did once, particularly when compared with recordings of more recent vintage, it still stands as a great tribute to the music composed by Korngold for the Warner Bros. films.

Didier C. Deutsch

Joseph Kosma
(1905-1969)

The Music of Joseph Kosma
1997, Travelling/France ♪♪♪♪
album notes: Music: Joseph Kosma.

This album, winner of the Grand Prix du Disque de l'Academie Charles Cros, the French equivalent to the Grammy Awards, presents a film composer who has become sadly neglected, notably in his native France, where his contributions have virtually been ignored in recent years.

Born in Budapest, Hungary, Kosma studied at the Berlin Opera, and worked with Bertolt Brecht and Kurt Weill, who were major influences on him in his formative years. A chance meeting with lyricist Jacques Prevert resulted in the two writing together more than 100 songs, including the celebrated "Les feuilles mortes" (Autumn Leaves), which they created for the film *Les portes de la nuit,* directed by Marcel Carne, with whom Kosma also enjoyed a long-term creative relationship (he notably scored Carne's *Les visiteurs du soir, Les enfants du paradis, La Marie du port,* and *Juliette ou la cle des songes*). Among his other contributions, the most important included several films which Jean Renoir directed, notably *La grande illusion, La bete humaine, Elena et les hommes, Le dejeuner sur l'herbe,* and *Le caporal epingle.*

The three soundtracks presented here (with bits of dialogues and sound effects, as is common to all the titles in the series) were composed between 1949 (*La Marie du port*) and 1959 (*Le*

They Know the Score
John Beal

[For scoring trailers] there are some formulas that I've never really analyzed. There's basically a small start—unless you want that big, explosive shock a few frames in to get people's attention in the middle of a string of trailers—and a continuous building of density and motion until you get to the point where it's like piling on in a football game, still trying to leave room for dialogue and those big picture hits they like right now, the more drums the better. Invariably, we end on a low sustained note at the end, so that the audience has time to breathe a sigh of relief at what they've just been subjected to, and say, 'Wow, that's a really great picture, I want to go see that.' I'm sure there are other devices that composers could come up with, but at this point the marketing people haven't been able to accept much else except dead silence or a low pedal note at the end.

Courtesy of **Film Score Monthly**

---

dejeuner sur l'herbe), and reveal Kosma as a composer who captured the moods of the films he scored, with beautiful, tuneful themes, which, to him, were supposed to be more than mere "entertaining accompaniment" to a scene. Though the CD may attract only a few collectors, it is a worthwhile addition to film music literature.

Didier C. Deutsch

Francis Lai
(1932-   )

30 ans de cinema
1996, Sion Records/Germany ♪♪♪♪
album notes: Music: Francis Lai.

The Very Best of Francis Lai
1990, Skyline/U.K. ♪♪
album notes: Music: Francis Lai.

Les plus belles melodies du cinema
1979, WEA Records/France 🎵🎵
album notes: Music: Francis Lai.

One aspect of Francis Lai's music (and one reason for its appeal) is that it is easy on the senses, the kind one might listen to on a "special" occasion, when a soundtrack must not be too obtrusive, yet conducive to certain romantic moods.

Any one of these three CDs should fill the bill if you are a Francis Lai fan, but dispensing with the most obvious, *Les plus belles melodies du cinema* (*The Most Beautiful Melodies from the Movies*), on the French WEA label, offers very little that cannot be found elsewhere, and is not that representative of Lai's talent and diversity.

Likewise, *The Very Best of Francis Lai,* a British release, is a perfunctory compilation that has a couple of interesting selections ("African Summer," "Smic Smac Smoc"), but should probably interest the completists more so than the casual collector.

The 2-CD set, *30 ans de cinema,* released in Germany, is much more comprehensive, and covers a lot of films that received that special Francis Lai touch. As a compilation, it certainly ranks highest, and provides a fairly complete overview of the composer's career. Included are the themes from the best known French films (*A Man and a Woman, Bolero, My New Partner, Bilitis, Another Man Another Chance*), the international hits (*Rider in the Rain, Love Story, International Velvet, The Baby Sitter*), and a few lesser known titles that are interesting discoveries. Though endowed with great lyricism, Lai's music tends to be a bit saccharine at times, but this compilation is a great shortcut through 40 of the films he scored over the years.

Didier C. Deutsch

Angelo Francesco Lavagnino
(1909-1987)

Science Fiction: 4 Italian B-Movies of the Sixties
1997, RCA Records/Italy 🎵🎵🎵
album notes: Music: Angelo Francesco Lavagnino; Conductor: Angelo Francesco Lavagnino and Carlo Savina.

Jerry Goldsmith and John Williams certainly don't have a monopoly on space-related scores, as this excellent compilation of music composed by Angelo Francesco Lavagnino clearly evidences.

A particularly eclectic film composer, Lavagnino scored more than 300 films in a career that also saw him contribute many classical works (chamber music, symphonies, and arias). Involved at first in the documentary field, he not only wrote the score for *Lost Continent* in 1954, but also worked on the team

that put the film together; a year later, another score, for *Empire of the Sun,* gave him his first charted hit around the world. Among the many films he scored, the best known include *Legend of the Lost* (1957), starring John Wayne; *The Naked Maja* (1958), starring Ava Gardner; *The Last Days of Pompeii* (1959), directed by Sergio Leone; and *Falstaff* (1966), directed by Orson Welles.

The four films represented here, while paying tribute to the tenets of the genre, exhibit some melodic themes that immediately place them above the norm (the title track from *Wild, Wild Planet* for instance), and belie the other-worldly sonorities usually adopted in this type of films. In fact, with a few exceptions, the sci-fi scores heard here could have been written for totally different films, given Lavagnino's approach, which was to emphasize the melodic aspect of the music. Not knowing whether it actually worked in the films (one can only surmise that it did), all one can do is appreciate the CD on its own musical merits. It is, to say the least, thoroughly engaging, with some fancy tunes that are quite exhilarating.

Didier C. Deutsch

Joel McNeely

Hollywood '94
1994, Varèse Sarabande 🎵🎵🎵🎵
album notes: Orchestra: The Seattle Symphony Orchestra; Conductor: Joel McNeely; Featured Musician: Margaret Batjer, violin.

Hollywood '95
1995, Varèse Sarabande 🎵🎵🎵🎵
album notes: Orchestra: The Royal Scottish National Orchestra; Conductor: Joel McNeely.

Hollywood '96
1996, Varèse Sarabande 🎵🎵🎵🎵
album notes: Orchestra: The Royal Scottish National Orchestra and Chorus; Conductor: Joel McNeely; Featured Musicians: Lynda Cochrane, piano; Edwin Paling, fiddle.

The concept behind these albums is actually quite valid and interesting: each gives an overview of the most prominent films released during the year, illustrated with an excerpt from each score. The combined effect is much like a "pops" concert that includes favorite themes and little of the added wear and tear usually found on soundtrack albums that may turn off many casual listeners. One may quibble endlessly with the choices, but the performances are remarkably faithful to the originals, with McNeely extracting superb ensemble playing and polish from the orchestras under his baton.

Didier C. Deutsch

Michel Magne
(1930-1984)

25 ans de musique de film
1998, Odeon/France 🎵🎵🎵🎵🎵
album notes: Music: Michel Magne; **Conductor:** Michel Magne.

"A dreamer who occasionally had both feet on the ground," in his own charmingly tongue-in-cheek assessment, Michel Magne was one of the top French film composers of the 1960s and '70s. His iconoclastic approach to music, as well as his enormous appetite for living, singled him out as a passionate, a marginal who enjoyed life and his craft to excess.

These traits find an eerie echo in this 2-CD compilation, in which many of the themes he wrote over a 25-year period have been regrouped chronologically, and remastered. Whether expressing himself in the jazz idiom, developing broad romantic themes, or writing satirical pop songs, Magne always struck an original note which owed nothing to convention and a great deal to his own views on life.

The scope is enormous—from cartoon screen heroes (*The Gorilla, Fantomas*), to historical dramas (*Angelique*), spy adventures (the *OSS 117* series), and political satires (*Tout le monde il est beau . . . , Les Chinois a Paris*), the themes unfold at a furious, always entertaining pace. Of particular interest to fans in this country will be the excerpt from Magne's rejected score for *Barbarella* (the film by Roger Vadim, starring Jane Fonda).

Didier C. Deutsch

Henry Mancini
(1924-1994)

Mancini's Classic Movie Scores/The Pink Panther and Other Hits
1987, RCA Records and 1992, RCA Records (re-issue) 🎵🎵🎵🎵🎵
album notes: Music: Henry Mancini; **Orchestra:** Henry Mancini Orchestra and Chorus; **Conductor:** Henry Mancini.

For a composer who spent most of his career with RCA, and gave it some of its million-selling albums, the label has not done very well by Henry Mancini. Outside of a few selected titles like this compilation, hastily put together with little thinking behind it, or selected individual soundtrack albums, usually poorly remastered, Mancini's impressive body of work still remains to be addressed with the kind of thoroughness and dedication RCA is now beginning to lavish on Elvis Presley. Even a 3-CD boxed set, *The Days of Wine and Roses* (see below), released a couple of years ago, failed to address his contribution with the kind of seriousness it really commanded.

Which is not to say this collection of themes from four important scores (*The Pink Panther, Charade, Hatari!,* and *Breakfast at Tiffany's*) is bad—it is simply incomplete and insufficient.

Mancini had a special flair for writing themes that were instantly catchy, flavorful, and attractive. Even his most complex scores were always thoroughly accessible to people with little interest in film music, because the composer was, first and foremost, a pop melodist. The selections collected here present a good case for this specific talent of his, with enjoyable tunes that are as vibrant and exciting on their own as they were behind the action on the screen. Needless to say, the rating here applies to the music, not the packaging.

Didier C. Deutsch

Henry Mancini: Premier Pops
1988, Denon Records 🎵🎵🎵🎵
album notes: Music: Henry Mancini; **Orchestra:** The Royal Philharmonic Pops Orchestra; **Conductor:** Henry Mancini.

One of the earliest CD releases, this out-of-print Henry Mancini album has audiophile sound and a number of outstanding concert arrangements. Comprised entirely of Mancini-composed selections, *Premiere Pops* includes a wealth of material not available anywhere else, from the composer's rousing "Overture to a 'Pops' Concert" to a gorgeous extended suite from *The Thorn Birds*; a lovely "Movie Song Medley" comprised of *Life in a Looking Glass, Crazy World* and *10*; a "Three TV Themes" suite consisting of "Hotel," "Newhart," and "Remington Steele;" plus the concert pieces "Ohio Riverboat" and "Sunflower." There are also cues from *The Great Mouse Detective,* the *Pink Panther* sequels, *Charade,* Paul Newman's adaptation of *The Glass Menagerie,* and—of course— "Moon River." The album is notable not only for its relative obscurity but also the way in which Mancini structures the music for solo piano (with the composer himself on the keyboard) and the Royal Philharmonic Orchestra, a collaboration that was supposed to result in a number of "Mancini-RPO Pops" albums for the Denon label before the project (and the label) fell through. Regardless, this is still one of the best Mancini retrospectives released on CD, and certainly the best-sounding album of the bunch.

Andy Dursin

Henry Mancini: Music from the Films of Blake Edwards
1991, RCA Records 🎵🎵🎵🎵🎵
album notes: Music: Henry Mancini; **Conductor:** Henry Mancini

Throughout his career, Mancini enjoyed a special creative relationship with film director Blake Edwards. They began working together on the television series *Peter Gunn,* with the relationship eventually covering many of Edwards' comedies, including the *Pink Panther* series, as well as other celebrated films like *Breakfast at Tiffany's, Experiment in Terror, The Great Race,* *"10," Darling Lily,* and *Victor/Victoria.* The compilation surveys

Henry Mancini **(Archive Photos, Inc.)**

some of these films, presenting selections from the various scores, in a compilation that could not be all-encompassing.

Didier C. Deutsch

The Music of Henry Mancini
1994, Sony Legacy ♪♪♪♪
album notes: Music: Henry Mancini

During his lifetime, some of Mancini's most popular themes found their way into the pop catalogues at labels other than RCA, giving performers like Andy Williams, for instance, some of their million-selling hits. When the composer died in 1994, Sony Legacy put together this compilation that covers several tunes popularized by Johnny Mathis, Buddy Greco, Patti Page, and Andy Williams (whose renditions of "Moon River," "Dear Heart," and "In the Arms of Love" are included). Mancini, who had also released a couple of albums on Columbia, is represented with his recording of a theme from *Who Is Killing the Great Chefs of Europe?*.

Didier C. Deutsch

Mancini in Surround: Mostly Monsters, Murders & Mystery
1990, RCA Records ♪♪♪♪
album notes: Music: Henry Mancini; **Orchestra:** The Mancini Pops Orchestra; **Conductor:** Henry Mancini; **Featured Musicians:** Sidney Sax, violin, concertmaster; Edward Beckett, flute; Richard Morgan, oboe; Graham Salter, English horn; Neil Levesley, bassoon; Cynthia Millar, Ondes Marthinot; Adrian Brett, ocarina; Leslie Pearson, harpsichord, organ.

Subtitled "Mostly Monsters, Murders, and Mysteries," this likable collection is a far cry from the light-hearted melodies Henry Mancini has been most known for. It's an excellent compilation of his dramatic orchestral filmscoring, featuring splendid renditions of his musical contributions to such 1950s horror films as *It Came from Outer Space* and *The Creature from the Black Lagoon*, to the 1990 thriller *Fear*. Also included is a gorgeous, lyrical four-minute suite from *The White Dawn*, Mancini's rejected title theme from Hitchcock's *Frenzy*, and cues from *Mommie Dearest, Nightwing, The Prisoner of Zenda*, and *Sunset*. The CD was recorded with the Dolby Surround system, from which comes its title, and sound quality is uniformly high. Extensive historical notes by Tony Thomas abound in a 16-page booklet. The CD is an important collection of Mancini's oft-overlooked dramatic film music, and a unique musical gallery of one composer's work in the "genre macabre" over a 30-year span.

Randall D. Larson

Mancini's Greatest Hits
1989, Telarc Records ♪♪♪♪
album notes: Music: Henry Mancini; **Orchestra:** The Cincinnati Pops Orchestra and the Henry Mancini Chorus; **Conductor:** Erich Kunzel.

Another fine collection of Henry Mancini standards, this release boasts a typically solid performance by the Cincinnati Pops Orchestra under the direction of maestro Erich Kunzel, with smooth vocals provided by the Henry Mancini Chorus. This 68-minute album is comprised strictly of Mancini compositions, which range from the usual staples (*Pink Panther, Days of Wine and Roses, Peter Gunn*) to some brief examples of Mancini's strong sense of dramatic film scoring (*The White Dawn, The Molly Maguires*), concert arrangements of the *Victor/Victoria* finale, various Mancini marches, and a pair of pieces written exclusively for the concert hall ("Symphonic Soul," "Drummers' Delight"). The packaging includes ample but not overwhelming liner notes, the acoustics are fine, and the release itself a strong choice for the casual listener due to its wide selection of material culled from Mancini's vast discography.

Andy Dursin

Henry Mancini: The Days of Wine and Roses
1995, RCA Records ♪♪♪♪
album notes: Music: Henry Mancini; **Conductor:** Henry Mancini.

While it marked a step in the right direction, this boxed set is too much a case of "let's-put-together-a-collection-of-CDs-by-whatshisname" to be taken with any kind of seriousness. It does indeed cover some of the right grounds, but almost by default, because in the case of Mancini there was so much material to begin with that any compilation would have succeeded regardless.

But rather than take the normal approach, which would have been to focus on Mancini's career as a film composer, the set wastes too much precious playing time on other recordings he did, like cover versions of Claude Thornhill's "Snowfall" or Louis Prima's "Sing, Sing, Sing," in the first CD; Antonio Carlos Jobim's "Quiet Nights of Quiet Stars" or Ray Noble's "Cherokee," in the second; and Johnny Mandel's "The Shadow of Your Smile" and Nino Rota's "Romeo and Juliet," in the third. Evidently, these tracks belonged in another compilation.

With the vast resources at their disposal, the producers would have been better advised to give the composer his real due, and present a thorough compilation of scores written by Mancini, supplementing what was not in the RCA vaults with selections on other labels. Unfortunately *The Days of Wine and Roses* doesn't come without some thorns.

Didier C. Deutsch

Cinema Italiano: Music of Ennio Morricone and Nino Rota
1991, RCA Victor ♪♪♪
album notes: Music: Ennio Morricone, Nino Rota; **Orchestra:** The Mancini Pops Orchestra; **Conductor:** Henry Mancini.

The Godfather and Other Movie Themes
1993, RCA Victor 🎵🎵🎵🎵

album notes: Music: Henry Mancini; **Orchestra:** The London Symphony Orchestra and the Philadelphia Orchestra Pops; **Conductor:** Henry Mancini; **Featured Musicians:** William Smith, piano; Marcel Farago, harpsichord; Norman Carol, violin; Murray Panitz, flute; Anthony Gigliotti, clarinet; Mason Jones, French horn; John DeLancie, oboe; Louis Rosenblatt, English horn; Gerald Carlyss, timpani; Donald Montanaro, E-flat clarinet; Bernard Garfield, bassoon; Gilbert Johnson, trumpet.

Top Hat: Music from the Films of Astaire & Rogers
1992, RCA Victor 🎵🎵🎵

album notes: Music: Irving Berlin, Jerome Kern, Vincent Youmans, Cole Porter, George Gershwin, Howard Dietz, Con Conrad; **Orchestra;** The Mancini Pops Orchestra; **Conductor:** Henry Mancini.

It's an interesting concept, Mancini doing themes from other composers, but one that only works halfway: first, because Mancini was much better at covering his own material, and second, because his own versions often pale in comparison with the originals. But one can sense the corporate sense at work behind these titles. Signed to RCA, Mancini had to deliver a certain number of albums under his contract, and if Erich Kunzel could successfully do it for Telarc, Mancini could do it for RCA. What the powers-that-be failed to realize is that no one said Kunzel did a great job: he just happens to be a good hack! And frankly speaking, Mancini was way above that.

Cinema Italiano, in particular, suffers from the fact that all the scores covered by Mancini already exist in far superior, original versions, some of them, as a matter of fact, on RCA. The composer, conducting the Mancini Pops Orchestra, is proficient and effective, but one senses that there is less enthusiasm here than there might have been had the themes been written by him.

The impression is confirmed in *The Godfather* set, in which Mancini goes back to some scores already explored in *Cinema Italiano,* as well as others by other composers (John Williams, Michel Legrand, Francis Lai), but adds to the mix a suite from *The White Dawn* and *Beaver Valley Suite,* as well as other selections he penned, in which he leads the London Symphony Orchestra and the Philadelphia Orchestra Pops in spirited, crackling versions.

As for the *Top Hat* CD, an obvious concept tailored after the Telarc sets, it is an obvious scene-stealer, and one in which Mancini, again, proves superior to Kunzel in every respect. It's only unfortunate that he was not given a chance to focus on some of his own scores.

Didier C. Deutsch

Paul Misraki
(1908-1998)

The Music of Paul Misraki
1995, Travelling/France 🎵🎵🎵

album notes: Music: Paul Misraki.

Musiques originales de films, vol. 1: Et Dieu crea la femme
1998, Pomme Music/Sony, France 🎵🎵🎵🎵

album notes: Music: Paul Misraki.

Musiques originales de films, vol. 2: Nouvelle-Vague
1998, Pomme Music/Sony, France 🎵🎵🎵🎵

album notes: Music: Paul Misraki.

Musiques originales de films, vol. 3: Maigret tend un piege
1998, Pomme Music/Sony, France 🎵🎵🎵🎵

album notes: Music: Paul Misraki.

Musiques originales de films, vol. 4: Montparnasse 19
1998, Pomme Music/Sony, France 🎵🎵🎵🎵

album notes: Music: Paul Misraki.

Though born in Istanbul, Turkey, Misraki worked almost exclusively in France where, as a film composer, he contributed hundreds of scores to films that found an audience around the world. Highly unusual, in this respect, is the 4-CD anthology compiled by Sony in France, which surveys some of his most celebrated scores.

Shortly before World War II, Misraki began his musical career as a member of Ray Ventura's big band, whose "collegians" were loosely tailored after Kay Kyser's own band in the U.S. There, he not only participated in the stage (and recorded) shenanigans the band was known for, he also contributed some of the songs that became hits, including "Tout va tres bien, Madame la Marquise." He also signed several delicate songs that were heard in the movies, notably "Une charade," which Danielle Darrieux created in *Battements de coeur (Heartbeats)*, "Qu'est-ce qu'on attend pour etre heureux?," heard in *Feux de joie (Fireworks)*, and "Sur deux notes" and "Tiens, tiens, tiens," written for *Tourbillons de Paris (Parisian Swirls)*.

During the war, he moved to Hollywood where he worked with Orson Welles, among others, returning to France in 1945, where he firmly established himself as an influential and prolific film composer.

The first CD, in the series "Movies to Listen To" from Audivis/Travelling, contains musical excerpts from three early films, *Battement de coeur* (1939), *Mademoiselle s'amuse* (1947), and *Nous irons a Paris* (1950), all three lightweight comedies featuring Ray Ventura and his band, and all three combining dialogue and sound effects with Misraki's music. This may necessarily limit the CD's appeal to fans with some knowledge of the lingo, though there are enough musical selections to satisfy those who don't understand it. Overall sound quality is primitive.

The 4-CD anthology, on the other hand, contains many selections composed for films of more recent vintage, each with its one focus: volume one is more or less a tribute to the early films of Brigitte Bardot (the actress is actually heard warbling a song from her first major feature, *And God Created Woman*); the second CD surveys Misraki's contributions to the French New Wave; the third and the fourth concentrate on contemporary dramas, police thrillers, and exotic adventures. All four combine to provide a comprehensive overview of a composer whose scores for many years have given French cinema a universal voice.

Didier C. Deutsch

Jerome Moross

(1913-1983)

The Valley of Gwangi: The Classic Film Music of Jerome Moross
1995, Silva Screen Records ✍✍✍✍✍

album notes: Music: Jerome Moross; **Orchestra:** The City of Prague Philharmonic; **Conductor:** Paul Bateman.

This long-overdue compilation showcases the dynamic and often melodically gorgeous work of composer Jerome Moross, who has for too long been known simply as the man who scored *The Big Country*. *Valley of Gwangi* amply demonstrates Moross' range, which covered everything from action films (the epic *The Mountain Road* and the percussive, ethnic-flavored *The Sharkfighters*) to dramas (*Five Finger Exercise* and the gentle "Americana" of *Rachel, Rachel*) to medieval epics (the beautifully evocative *The War Lord*). Moross was best known for his western music, and this collection includes both a well-known example (his theme for the television series *Wagon Train*) and a spectacular, overlooked effort for the 1969 Ray Harryhausen thriller about cowboys and dinosaurs, *The Valley of Gwangi*, which combined Moross's thrilling western style with a percussive, ferociously rhythmic style for Harryhausen's animated dinosaurs that's as vibrant and memorable as anything Bernard Herrman ever wrote in the genre. *Gwangi* is represented by an 18-minute suite that's one of the most exciting film music experiences in recent memory, and Nic Raine's conducting of the entire album is flawless.

Jeff Bond

Ennio Morricone

(1928-   )

Ennio Morricone: The Legendary Italian Westerns
1990, RCA Records ✍✍✍✍✍

album notes: Music: Ennio Morricone; **Orchestra:** Orchestra Unione Musicisti di Roma; **Conductor:** Ennio Morricone, Bruno Nicolai; **Fea-**tured **Musicians:** I Canti Moderni; Michele Lacerenza, trumpet; Giovanni Culasso, trumpet; Franco De Gemini, harmonica; Edda Dell'Orso, vocals.

The Ennio Morricone Anthology: A Fistful of Film Music
1995, Rhino Records ✍✍✍✍

album notes: Music: Ennio Morricone; **Conductor:** Ennio Morricone, Bruno Nicolai; **Featured Musicians:** Nicola Culasso, trumpet; Michele Lacerenza, trumpet; Alessandro Alessandroni, guitar, whistling; Franco De Gemini, harmonica; Maurizio Verzella, mellophone; Marianne Gazzani Eckstein, flute; Gheorghe Zamfir, Pan flute; Baldo Maestri, clarinet, alto sax; Paolo Zampini, flute.

Ennio Morricone: With Love
1995, DRG Records ✍✍✍✍

album notes: Music: Ennio Morricone; **Conductor:** Ennio Morricone.

An Ennio Morricone: Western Quintet
1995, DRG Records ✍✍✍✍

album notes: Music: Ennio Morricone; **Conductor:** Ennio Morricone, Bruno Nicolai.

An Ennio Morricone Anthology
1995, DRG Records ✍✍✍✍

album notes: Music: Ennio Morricone; **Conductor:** Ennio Morricone.

An Ennio Morricone-Dario Argento Trilogy
1995, DRG Records ✍✍✍✍

album notes: Music: Ennio Morricone; **Conductor:** Ennio Morricone.

Ennio Morricone: Main Titles 1965-1995
1996, DRG Records ✍✍✍✍

album notes: Music: Ennio Morricone; **Conductor:** Ennio Morricone.

Ennio Morricone: Compilation, Vols. 1&2
1987, Virgin Records ✍✍✍✍

album notes: Music: Ennio Morricone; **Conductor:** Ennio Morricone.

As these various compilations clearly evidence, there is a lot of material available about Ennio Morricone, a composer whose incredible output includes films in his native Italy, in France, and of course in the United States. Many of the most important scores are represented in one form or another in these compilations, and even though some of the same tracks appear in several of them, the duplications are often kept to a minimum, with the various albums complementing each other to give a very complete overview of Morricone's many contributions to the movies.

Given the abundance of material, however, a selection seems in order, and with this in mind, here are a few suggestions: collectors interested in the Italian western scores (a genre in which Morricone particularly excelled, and in which he pretty much established the criteria by which hundreds of other scores were composed) should pick up the RCA compilation, which offers many selections that are not available elsewhere; those interested in a broader overview might want to acquire the Rhino set, which is pretty thorough, or the two individual Virgin CDs, which contain many of the essential tracks.

Ennio Morricone **(Archive Photos, Inc.)**

For a closer view of Morricone's contributions to French and Italian films, any of the DRG sets should do, though one should be aware of the fact that "Anthology" and "Main Titles" frequently duplicate each other.

Didier C. Deutsch

Cinema Paradiso: The Classic Ennio Morricone
1993, Silva Screen Records 🎵🎵

album notes: Music: Ennio Morricone; **Orchestra:** The City of Prague Philharmonic; **Conductor:** William Motzing, Derek Wadsworth.

Cinema Paradiso: The Classic Film Music of Ennio Morricone
1996, Silva Screen Records 🎵🎵

album notes: Music: Ennio Morricone; **Orchestra:** The City of Prague Philharmonic; **Conductor:** Paul Bateman.

While they cover much of the same scores and sometimes the same selections, the two Silva Screen compilations are somewhat different. The earliest, *The Classic Ennio Morricone,* is less interesting, because playing by the City of Prague Philharmonic is at times spotty, with uninspired renditions that add really nothing to the Morricone canon. The second, *The Classic Film Music of Ennio Morricone,* conducted by Paul Bateman, is somewhat better and truer to the spirit of the original scores, with an exciting reading of selections from *The Mission.* But with so much Morricone music already available, were either of these sets really necessary, let alone both?

Didier C. Deutsch

Ennio Morricone: Once Upon a Time in the Cinema
1996, Varèse Sarabande 🎵

album notes: Music: Ennio Morricone; **Conductor:** Lanny Meyers; **Featured Musicians:** Lanny Meyers, piano, keyboards; Bob Mair, bass; Ed Smith, drums; Paul Viapiano, guitar.

A jazz treatment of well-known Morricone themes, strictly for collectors and fans, and not even made interesting in the tepid playing of the somewhat undistinguished musicians, or in the routine orchestrations by Lanny Meyers. Anything wrong with more original ideas?

Didier C. Deutsch

3 Westerns by Ennio Morricone
1991, RCA Records/Italy 🎵🎵🎵🎵

album notes: Music: Ennio Morricone; **Conductor:** Ennio Morricone and Bruno Nicolai; **Featured Musicians:** Michele Lacerenza, trumpet; Anna Palomba, harp; I Canti Moderni of Alessandroni.

Ennio Morricone remains the incontestable master of the spaghetti western, the man who actually "developed" the genre and took it to its highest levels of quality. This compilation contains three scores, long unavailable, and certainly among the most striking Morricone wrote: *Death Rides a*

Horse, starring Lee Van Cleef, from 1967; *A Pistol for Ringo,* and *The Return of Ringo,* both made back to back in 1965, with Giuliano Gemma in the title role.

Though a mere two years separated *Death Rides a Horse* from the two *Ringo* films, there were vast differences between them. Whereas the latter two seemed closer in spirit to the standard American westerns, the former followed a deliberately new path (it eventually materialized in the "spaghetti" western as we came to know it), with characters that were tougher, more ruthless, something that found an echo in the music itself.

As a result, the *Ringo* scores sound more conventional, with here and there an occasional Morriconean touch (like the "barking" choir), as though the composer and the director, Duccio Tessari, were concerned about trying not to innovate too much. By contrast, the music for *Death Rides a Horse* finds Morricone in a more mature, more daring frame of mind, with unusual rhythmic patterns that show how far the composer had progressed by then.

All three contain their shares of great musical moments— "Monody for Guitar" and "Guitar Nocturne," in *Death Rides a Horse;* "Honky Tonk" and "Heroic Mexico," in *A Pistol for Ringo;* and "Sheriff Carson" and "Barnaba Bamba," in *The Return of Ringo,* making the CD an important release in the Morricone canon.

Didier C. Deutsch

Morricone-Belmondo
1999, DRG Records 🎵🎵🎵🎵

album notes: Music: Ennio Morricone; **Conductor:** Ennio Morricone.

This collection brings together for the first time three scores composed by Ennio Morricone for a trio of French thrillers, starring Jean-Paul Belmondo. With the exception of *The Burglars (Le casse),* which yielded an LP on the Bell label, this is the first time *The Professional (Le professionnel)* and *The Outsider (Le marginal)* are available in this country. Better yet, the set features previously unreleased tracks or rarities, such as the Astrud Gilberto vocals in *The Burglars,* which were released as a single only in Japan.

With all three films designed to focus on the screen persona of the French actor, *The Professional,* made in 1981, found Belmondo as a secret agent returning to France after two years in a hard labor camp in Central Africa to settle the score with the superiors who sacrificed him to their own political ambitions; *The Outsider,* from 1983, was the story of a police inspector, a man of integrity, confronting power, money and drugs; finally, *The Burglars,* released in 1971, was a taut, gripping thriller that dealt with a heist carried on in grand style by Belmondo at the top of his physical form.

In all three instances, Morricone devised scores that enhanced the screen action, while giving it an extra ounce of suspended animation that also makes his music totally enjoyable as pure listening experience. *The Professional* also gave the composer a gold record with the huge popular success of "Chi mai," which swept the charts in Europe; the same score yielded another hit in "Le vent, le cri" (The Wind, the Scream), heard in a series of variations throughout the film. Also of interest to Morricone fans are the two interludes for harps, that propel the score in a totally unexpected direction. While neither *The Outsider* nor *The Burglars* achieved the stratospheric popular heights of *The Professional,* both should be considered essential in the Morricone canon, and well worth investigating. Certainly the availability of all three scores in one package is cause to rejoice.

Didier C. Deutsch

The Thriller Collection
1999, DRG Records 🎵🎵🎵🎵
album notes: Music: Ennio Morricone; **Conductor:** Ennio Morricone.

Another Morricone collection from DRG, which seems to have cornered an important part of this market and focuses on the works of the great Italian film composer. This 2-CD collection deals with the films of horror, the thrillers, the contemporary dramas, for which Morricone developed a body of works that constitutes an important portion of the scores he has created over the years. Once again, some collectors might be familiar with most of these titles (though it is believed that *The Chosen, The Monster,* and *The Link* are making their debut in this compilation), but again the label throws in a curve ball by adding selections that were previously unavailable or are alternate versions, making this set much more desirable than it appeared to be.

Unlike the spaghetti westerns that were broad and expansive, the thriller scores are often introspective, unerring, with discordant notes and dissonant chords that evoke the tension and the fright inherent in the films. Equally the master in this type of film music, Morricone succeeded in remaining totally original and, in fact, spawning new ideas that were widely imitated after him. Listening to these selections, and particularly *Blood in the Streets, The Serpent, The Short Night of the Dolls of Glass,* and *The Smile of the Great Temptress,* which because of their length have a better opportunity to capture the listener's interest, one realizes how inventive and mesmerizing Morricone can be in this type of music as well. At this point, DRG seems intent on doing right by the Italian maestro, and no one should complain about it, rather the opposite.

Didier C. Deutsch

Stanley Myers
(1930-1993)

Music from the Films
Milan Records 🎵🎵🎵
album notes: Music: Stanley Myers, Hans Zimmer.

Three scores by Stanley Myers, a composer whose output is little known outside of a selected circle of fans and admirers. *My Beautiful Laundrette,* directed by Stephen Frears in 1985, is set in the Pakistani community in South London, and stars Gordon Warnecke and Daniel Day Lewis, respectively as a Pakistani boy and his British friend who run a small laundrette; *Sammy and Rosie Get Laid,* directed by Frears in 1987, is an affectionate romantic comedy that stars Frances Barber and Ayub Khan Din in the title roles; as for *Wish You Were Here,* written and directed by David Leland, and set in the 1950s, it deals with the sexual awakening of a young British girl in a South Coast town. The scores are widely divergent in approach, and while the first has a rock feel that is contemporary in tone and relatively lackluster, both *Sammy and Rosie Get Laid* and *Wish You Were Here* are quite diversified and attractive, each reflecting with accuracy the times and moods evoked by the films. The pop vocals, though, are dispensable.

Didier C. Deutsch

Mario Nascimbene
(1916-   )

A Mario Nascimbene Anthology
1996, DRG Records 🎵🎵🎵
album notes: Music: Mario Nascimbene.

Nicely assembled compilation of themes and cues from 22 of the Hollywood-produced films scored by one of Italy's most resourceful composers. Nascimbene, who personally supervised this release, frequently went outside the normal boundaries of a standard orchestra to incorporate unusual sounds into his scores, though the bulk of his work was still acoustic in nature. The first CD starts off with two intriguing cues from *One Million Years B.C.,* the first in a trilogy of prehistoric tales (the other two are also included). The composer incorporated natural sounds, such as wind and rain, with what he perceived was the tribal music for early man. These "ethnic" effects were achieved through a variety of inventive, nonelectronic means. Several of Nascimbene's historical costume dramas are featured, including *The Vikings, Solomon and Sheba,* and *Barabbas* (which features some blood curdling screams). The second CD contains music from his more contemporary films, many released here for the first time. Titles include *The Barefoot Contessa, The Vengeance of She* (with the superb jazz theme

"Carol at Sea"), and light comedy fare such as *Where the Spies Are* (Morse Code is used in the "Main Title") and *Romanoff and Juliet* (a really odd flute-like instrument is used in "Fox Trot"). A well assembled overview of an artist whose work should not be forgotten.

David Hirsch

Alfred Newman

(1901-1970)

The Film Music of Alfred Newman
1992, Varèse Sarabande 𝄞𝄞𝄞𝄾
album notes: Music: Alfred Newman; **Conductor:** Alfred Newman.

Captain from Castile: The Classic Film Scores of Alfred Newman
1989, RCA Victor 𝄞𝄞𝄞𝄞𝄞
album notes: Music: Alfred Newman; **Orchestra:** The National Philharmonic Orchestra; **Conductor:** Charles Gerhardt.

The quintessential Hollywood composer, Alfred Newman had a profound influence on the film community: as the head of the music department at 20th Century Fox for more than 20 years, his position enabled him to nurture and develop young talent, some of which followed in his footsteps.

Born in 1901 in New Haven, Connecticut, he began his career in the theatre, becoming one of the Broadway's youngest pianists and conductors, before moving to the West Coast in 1929. The advent of sound in the film industry gave him a tremendous opportunity to turn his knowledge as a composer and as a conductor to good use, particularly after he joined Fox.

While at that studio, he wrote the scores for many classic films such as *How Green Was My Valley* (1941), *The Song of Bernadette* (1943), *All About Eve* (1950), and, *The Diary of Anne Frank* (1959), and contributed the celebrated fanfare still heard today at the start of every 20th Century Fox film.

One of the most popular composers in Hollywood throughout his career, Alfred Newman displayed in his scores a strongly neo-romantic style. In the words of his long-time collaborator and friend, Ken Darby, "His primary purpose was to enlarge the scene, make it more real, add to it without engaging the audience's attention away from its involvement with the plot and the characters . . ."

The two compilations listed here regroup themes he wrote during his tenure at Fox. Of the two, the RCA set, in the wonderful Classic Film Scores series, finds Charles Gerhardt and the National Philharmonic Orchestra in sensational readings of some of Newman's best remembered themes, including selections from *Captain from Castile,* which gave the album its title, *Wuthering Heights, The Robe, Airport,* and *Anastasia.* Perfor-

mance throughout is satisfactory, with the brilliant sound quality adding a cinematic flavor to the whole album.

In comparison, the Varèse Sarabande CD does not fare as well. Though conducted by Newman himself, it was compiled from archival material, and sonic quality is frequently subpar, particularly in the digital domain. But the *Captain from Castile* suite, not available anywhere else, is well worth listening to.

Didier C. Deutsch

The Movies Go to the Hollywood Bowl
1990, Angel Records 𝄞𝄞𝄞𝄾
album notes: Music: Alfred Newman, Miklos Rozsa; **Orchestra:** The Hollywood Bowl Symphony Orchestra; **Conductor:** Alfred Newman, Miklos Rozsa.

In the 1960s, both Alfred Newman and Miklos Rozsa conducted the Hollywood Bowl Symphony Orchestra in recordings of their own music and other works for Capitol Records. This compilation presents several excerpts from these recordings, with Newman leading the orchestra in selections from *Captain from Castile, The Robe,* and *David and Bathsheba,* while Rozsa's selections include *King of Kings, El Cid,* and a forceful rendition of the *Spellbound Concerto,* with Leonard Pennario as soloist. Nothing truly earthshaking, simply some good selections, appropriately conducted by the composers themselves, always a plus.

Didier C. Deutsch

The Hunchback of Notre Dame
1998, Marco Polo 𝄞𝄞𝄞𝄾
album notes: Music: Alfred Newman; **Orchestra:** The Moscow Symphony Orchestra and Chorus; **Conductor:** William T. Stromberg.

Wuthering Heights
1997, Koch International Classics 𝄞𝄞𝄞𝄞
album notes: Music: Alfred Newman; **Orchestra:** The New Zealand Symphony Orchestra and the New Zealand Youth Choir; **Conductor:** Richard Kaufman.

In the early days of film music in Hollywood, many composers contributed their skills and knowledge in shaping a genre that was to eventually achieve incredible popularity around the world. Few were more influential than Alfred Newman, who not only was one of the first to pioneer the use of original orchestral music in film, but went on to create a whole school of composers, many of whom got their first opportunity to express themselves thanks to him.

Newman's own contributions are now beginning to attract serious classical labels, as evidenced by these two CDs, which offer generous excerpts from some of his early scores.

The first, *The Classic Film Music of Alfred Newman,* finds the Moscow Symphony Orchestra and Chorus, conducted by William T. Stromberg, in a superb recording that contains two reconstructed works, *Beau Geste,* a rousing French Foreign Legion epic, and *The Hunchback of Notre Dame,* a thrilling retelling of the Victor Hugo "beauty and the beast" saga, both from 1939. Both are exquisitely performed here, in wide, spacious sonics that do the scores full justice. A short suite from *All About Eve* completes the recording.

While the New Zealand Symphony Orchestra, conducted by Richard Kaufman, doesn't sound as proficient as the Moscow players, *Wuthering Heights: A Tribute to Alfred Newman* is another fine recording that contains two long suites from *Wuthering Heights,* the 1937 gothic romance based on Emily Bronte's novel, and *Prince of Foxes,* a 1949 Renaissance swashbuckler in which Tyrone Power played a spy to Orson Welles' wily Cesare Borgia. Shorter selections from *David and Bathsheba,* the 1951 Biblical epic, *Prisoner of Zenda,* another swashbuckler from 1937, and *Dragonwyck,* a 1946 gothic drama starring Vincent Price, round out the music in this CD.

Didier C. Deutsch

David Newman

(1954-)

It's a Wonderful Life: Sundance Film Music Series, vol. 1
1988, Telarc Records ♫♫♫♫♫
album notes: Music: Dimitri Tiomkin, Richard Addinsell, Cyril J. Mockridge; **Orchestra:** The Royal Philharmonic Orchestra and the Ambrosian Singers; **Conductor:** David Newman.

One of the best albums of its kind. Recorded under the aegis of the Sundance Institute, in what was supposed to be a series unfortunately apparently abandoned after this initial volume, the CD presents the first recording of the scores for three Yuletide classics, played to perfection by the Royal Philharmonic Orchestra, conducted by David Newman. All three suites are highlights in their own right, but *It's a Wonderful Life* literally steals the show, with totally faithful reproductions of Tiomkin's difficult music style.

Didier C. Deutsch

Erik Nordgren

(1913-1992)

The Bergman Suites
1998, Marco Polo Records ♫♫♫♫♫
album notes: Music: Erik Nordgren; **Orchestra:** The Slovak Radio Symphony Orchestra (Bratislava); **Conductor:** Adriano.

Little known in this country, Erik Nordgren scored many of Ingmar Bergman's most influential films, including *Smiles of a Summer Night,* in 1955; *Wild Strawberries,* in 1957; and *The Virgin Spring,* in 1960.

This remarkable CD, deftly conducted by Adriano, offers large excerpts from the first two, in addition to variations from the 1952 *Women's Waiting,* and shorter selections from the 1958 *The Face,* and 1961 *The Garden of Eden.*

One of the first films to introduce Bergman as a director with an international reputation, *Smiles of a Summer Night* was an elegant satire about the sexual and romantic interminglings of four ill-assorted couples invited to a country mansion for a summer weekend. Sparkling and effervescent, it prompted Nordgren to write a score that matched in brilliance the blithe spirit events described on the screen.

More serene and introspective, *Wild Strawberries* followed the musings and reminiscences of an old professor, on the eve of receiving the Nobel Prize, who suddenly becomes aware of his own failings and shortcomings. The melancholy moods of the film found an echo in the composer's score, deeply felt and profoundly affecting.

Women's Waiting dealt with four sisters-in-law who, while waiting for their husbands to join them for a planned holiday together, share confidences about their marriages. While Nordgren's score ended up being severely cut in the final version of the film, the theme and variations he created initially receive their full development here, revealing the depth and emotion he brought to his first collaboration with Bergman.

Throughout, the playing by the Slovak Radio Symphony Orchestra remains beautifully shaded and sensitive.

Didier C. Deutsch

Alex North

(1910-1991)

Alex North: North of Hollywood
1989, RCA Records ♫♫♫
album notes: Music: Alex North; **Conductor:** Alex North.

Unchained Melody: The Film Themes of Alex North
1991, Bay Cities Records ♫♫
album notes: Music: Alex North; **Conductor:** Alex North.

Some film composers often find themselves out of the mainstream, and while thoroughly respected (and often lionized) by their peers, fail to become as widely admired by a larger audience. Such is the case of Alex North, a revered musician whose scores have always elicited much admiration, but who is hardly a household name today. Born in 1910 in Chester, PA, of Russian emigres, North studied at the Curtis Institute of Music and at Juilliard.

His skills enabled him to impose himself in the New York theatre and ballet communities, leading Elia Kazan to ask him to write the incidental music for the stage presentation of Arthur Miller's

Death of a Salesman, in 1949. When Kazan filmed *A Streetcar Named Desire* two years later, he again called on North to provide the score, an unusual blend of New Orleans jazz that reflected the story and its locale. That score, and *Death of a Salesman,* released that same year, earned Oscar nominations and promptly established the young composer. In short order, North began to deliver scores that were uncharacteristic for Hollywood, yet thoroughly cinematographic in their approach, something that further singled him out in the film community.

Among his many contributions for the screen, the most important include *Unchained* (1955), which yielded the popular song "Unchained Melody," *The Rose Tattoo* (1955), *The Rainmaker* (1956), *Spartacus* (1960), *The Misfits* (1961), *Cleopatra* (1964), *The Agony and the Ecstasy* (1965), *Who's Afraid of Virginia Woolf?* (1966), and *Dragonslayer* (1981).

The two compilations listed here present several themes from these and other films North also scored, unfortunately in often-dubious sonic quality. The RCA set is interesting for its inclusion of themes not otherwise available (*Wall Street Ballet*), but the haphazard, disjointed presentation of the cues is a real disservice to the music and its composer.

Even worse, sonically, is the set from the now-defunct label Bay Cities, whose only merits is that it also includes some rare themes (*Viva Zapata!, The Bad Seed, The 13th Letter, Desiree*).

Didier C. Deutsch

The Film Music of Alex North
1997, Nonesuch Records ♫♫♫♫

album notes: Music: Alex North; **Orchestra:** The London Symphony Orchestra; **Conductor:** Eric Stern.

Another excellent entry from Nonesuch in its recent series of titles of film music, this tribute to Alex North, superbly performed by the LSO, conducted by Eric Stern, is a splendid addition to the composer's discography. Drawing from a wide variety of styles and genres, the CD offers selections from the thriller, *The Bad Seed*; the grim New Orleans psycho drama, *A Streetcar Named Desire*; and the spectacular Roman epic, *Spartacus,* all three major achievements in North's career. In addition, tracks from *The Misfits* and *Viva Zapata!* provide a different perspective on the composer's talent.

Taken on its own musical terms, this is a CD that has a lot to offer, and does so with style and evident love for the music.

Didier C. Deutsch

North by North
1990, Citadel Records ♫♫
album notes: Music: Alex North.

While reprising selections already found in an earlier release (on Bay Cities), this new CD adds the soundtrack from *Journey into Fear,* made in 1975, and North's first foray into what he described as "a mystery with suspected villains and chases all over the place." Though mostly atonal in style, it also reveals another facet of the composer's creativity, with themes that rely on alternative jazz elements to give the music a raw edge. The use of sparse instrumentations further compounds the moods created by the music, in which the dominant note is the anxiety felt by the characters in the film, about a geologist trapped in international intrigue.

Didier C. Deutsch

Michael Nyman
(1944-)

The Essential Michael Nyman Band
1991, Argo Records ♫♫♫♫

album notes: Music: Michael Nyman; *The Essential Michael Nyman Band:* Alexander Balanescu, violin; Clare Connors, violin; Ann Morphy, violin; Kate Musker, viola; Tony Hinnigan, cello; Justin Pearson, cello; Martin Elliott, bass guitar; John Harle, soprano/alto saxophone; David Roach, soprano/alto saxophone; Andrew Findon, baritone sax, flute, piccolo; Steve Sidwell, trumpet; Marjorie Dunn, horn; Nigel Barr, bass trombone, euphonium; John Lenahan, piano; Michael Nyman, piano; Sarah Leonard, soprano; Linda Hirst, mezzo soprano.

Writing in a minimalist way that some might enjoy while others might find it painfully boring, Nyman continues to score films with great empathy, sometimes, as in *The Draughtsman's Contract* or *Prospero's Books,* mixing genres and periods with delicious abandon, at other times sticking to more conventional strictures, though always with the same deliberately individualistic style that's his stock in trade. Short of trying to listen to several of his soundtracks and form an opinion, this set provides an interesting overview, regrouping the themes from various recent films, including the weird *The Cook, the Thief, His Wife, and Her Lover.* It may not be to everyone's taste, but it's the kind of music that seldom leaves one indifferent—you either love it, or hate it!

Didier C. Deutsch

Jean-Claude Petit
(1943-)

De Cyrano a Jean de Florette
1994, Playtime/France ♫♫♫♫

album notes: Music: Jean-Claude Petit; **Orchestra:** The Orchestre Symphonique d'Europe; **Conductor:** Jean-Claude Petit; **Featured Musicians:** Michael Appelman, violin; Philippe Dorn, clarinet; Jean-Marie Cousinie, trumpet.

Jean-Claude Petit: Composer: Original Soundtracks ·
1995, Audivis/Travelling/France 🎵🎵🎵🎵

Musiques de Films: Uranus
1990, Forlane/France 🎵🎵🎵🎵

One of the brightest (and most prolific) film composers of his generation, Jean-Claude Petit began his musical career under the aegis of jazz greats Dexter Gordon, Kenny Clarke and Johnny Griffin, among others. In 1968, he turned to pop music and began arranging and composing for singers like Julien Clerc, Claude Francois, Mort Shuman, and Joan Baez. Finally, in 1982, movies beckoned, but it took *Jean de Florette* and *Manon des sources,* both directed by Claude Berri in 1986, to make Petit a first-rate composer.

Subsequently, the success of Richard Lester's *The Return of the Musketeers* in 1989, and Jean-Paul Rappeneau's *Cyrano de Bergerac,* in 1990, propelled the composer on the international scene. Since then, he has scored many films, particularly in France, most notable among them being *The Soldier on the Roof,* released two years ago.

The first album reviewed here is the result of a live concert Petit gave in the Palais des Festivals in Biarritz in November, 1993, and contains long, instrumental suites of his most popular scores. It's always a pleasure hearing a composer, particularly one of Petit's caliber, in a live concert of his works. Petit doesn't disappoint here, though the performance lacks the confidence and tightness found in the obviously better rehearsed soundtrack albums.

The other two CDs are compilations of some of his original soundtracks. *Jean-Claude Petit: Composer,* on Audivis/Travelling, is broader in scope, offering, as it does, several themes from a wide variety of films. For an overview of the composer's output, it probably is the best bet.

Uranus, on the other hand, is a compilation of tracks from only four films, but it sounds more contained and more diversified. *Uranus,* by the way, was a film starring Gerard Depardieu as the poet-owner of a café, caught in the turmoil of World War II. The sardonic aspects of the film are echoed in Petit's score.

Didier C. Deutsch

Nicola Piovani

(1946-)

Nicola Piovani: Music from the Cinema
1999, Pacific Time Entertainment 🎵🎵🎵🎵🎵
album notes: Music: Nicola Piovani.

An Oscar winner for his score for *Life Is Beautiful* this year, Nicola Piovani is another one of those Italian composers who have done a lot to further the cause of film music in their native country, though their works are largely unknown elsewhere. In his case, Piovani is also remembered for the fact that he scored Federico Fellini's last films, *Ginger e Fred, Intervista,* and *La voce della luna.* The same poetic feel he brought to these films is firmly in evidence in this delightful collection that contains selections from 10 Italian films released between 1986 and 1993. While the moods change dramatically, according to the needs of each film, the charming romantic themes from *Palombella rossa* offer a striking contrast with the jazz and pop accents of *Fiorile,* or the evocative title theme from *Speriamo che sia femmina,* to only single out these tunes. With 22 selections totaling 53:40, this collection is a wonderful way to get acquainted with an innovative film composer who gains at being discovered.

Didier C. Deutsch

Rachel Portman

(1960-)

A Pyromaniac's Love Story
1995, Varèse Sarabande Records 🎵🎵🎵
album notes: Music: Rachel Portman.

The featured work, *A Pyromaniac's Love Story,* is not particularly attention-grabbing, being a light score dominated by a tango-like motif. More striking, however, is Portman's *Great Moments in Aviation,* which contrasts soaring passages for operatic soprano and orchestra with '20s-style jazz. Portman reconciles and combines these disparate elements into an ethereal and deeply moving tapestry, and the result is one of the most offbeat and unique scores of the past 20 years. *Smoke,* a small ensemble, somewhat minimalist score, is also included but its four brief cues do not arouse great interest. The concluding score, however, *Ethan Frome* (an excellent, though not widely seen Liam Neeson film from 1992) is one of Portman's finest efforts. An impressionistic, melancholy score, *Ethan Frome* is at once brooding and pastoral, somewhat reminiscent of Herrmann in its atmospheric evocation of 19th-century New England. Rachel Portman's fondness for playing character eccentricities and a unique gift for orchestration (she always orchestrates her scores herself) makes her the most unique film composer to emerge in the '90s. Her music has great depth yet soars weightlessly. There is little doubt she has a very bright future ahead of her.

Paul Andrew MacLean

David Raksin

(1912-)

Laura: The Classic Film Scores of David Raksin
1989, RCA Victor Records 🎵🎵🎵🎵
album notes: Music: David Raksin; **Orchestra:** The New Philharmonia Orchestra; **Conductor:** David Raksin.

Rachel Portman **(Archive Photos, Inc.)**

With only one film, *Laura,* in 1944, David Raksin managed the almost impossible and became one of Hollywood's great composers. Not bad for someone who, in a brilliant career that has spanned more than 60 years (so far!), also wrote the music for many other important films, as well as countless television series.

Born in 1912, in Philadelphia, Raksin came to Hollywood in 1935 to work with Charles Chaplin on the music for *Modern Times.* But because he often argued with the famous comedian, one of the co-founders of United Artists, the studio where both were working, Raksin was fired. He was immediately re-hired by Alfred Newman, head of the music department, with the understanding that he could continue to argue only as long as it was about the music.

Then Raksin wrote *Laura,* and became known as an innovative film composer, a reputation that never left him after that. In contrast to the style of mittel-European composers like Steiner, Rozsa, or Korngold, Raksin's approach to music was refreshingly American in spirit, something that singled out another one of his memorable contributions, the score for *The Bad and the Beautiful.* In an early assessment, Andre Previn once commented, "[Raksin's] sense of orchestral color was always unbeatable, his harmonic twists very clearly his own, and he thought nothing of setting himself some problems to make studio composing a little livelier."

This recording, another great title in the Classic Film Scores series, has an extra ounce of authenticity because it is conducted by the composer himself. The suite from *Forever Amber* alone is worth the price of admission, but don't dismiss Raksin's revisiting of his score for *The Bad and the Beautiful,* or his reinterpretation of the celebrated theme for *Laura.* In fact, the recording's only flaw is its brevity. One would have joyfully settled for more of the same.

Didier C. Deutsch

Leonard Rosenman

(1924-   )

The Film Music of Leonard Rosenman: East of Eden/Rebel Without a Cause
1997, Nonesuch Records, from the films *East of Eden* and *Rebel without a Cause*, Warner Bros., 1955 ♫♫♫♫♫
album notes: Music: Leonard Rosenman; **Orchestra:** The London Sinfonietta; **Conductor:** John Adams.

By design or by coincidence, Leonard Rosenman found himself at the right place at the right time in 1955, when he scored one after the other, *East of Eden,* an early Americana story directed by Elia Kazan, and *Rebel Without a Cause,* a contemporary urban drama directed by Nicholas Ray. Both films struck a deep, responsive note in the subconscious of America's youth, who came to identify with James Dean, who starred in both as a tormented, misunderstood youngster.

In contrast to the type of music that was written for the screen at the time, Rosenman created scores that were solidly embedded in modern sonorities, with a nod to Copland in *East of Eden*, and complex fractured rhythms a la Stravinsky for *Rebel Without a Cause*. As a result, his cues were not so much themes that one could actually recall, but mood setpieces that detailed and informed the action on the screen.

At the time of the films' release, Columbia Records issued a much sought-after LP which contained long suites from both scores. While less complete, this new digital recording covers the most important cues in both, in a performance that has the advantage of being sonically far superior, and as compelling as the original.

Didier C. Deutsch

Nino Rota

(1911-1979)

Nino Rota: Film Music
1992, EMI Classics ♫♫♫♫♫
album notes: Music: Nino Rota; **Orchestra:** The Orchestre Philharmonique de Monte-Carlo; **Conductor:** Gianluigi Gelmetti.

Nino Rota: La Strada Ballet Suite
1995, Sony Classical ♫♫♫♫♫
album notes: Music: Nino Rota; **Orchestra:** The Orchestra Filarmonica della Scala; **Conductor:** Riccardo Muti; **Featured Musicians:** Stefano Pagliani, violin; Giuseppe Bodanza, trumpet.

The Symphonic Fellini/Rota: La dolce vita
1993, Silva Screen Records ♫♫♫♫
album notes: Music: Nino Rota; **Orchestra:** The Czech Symphony Orchestra; **Conductor:** Derek Wadsworth.

There are several collections of Rota's film themes available, notably one of dubious sonic quality that has been released at various times by CAM, the Italian label. These CDs, and particularly the first two, are interesting for several reasons. First, because both EMI and Sony are classical labels, marking a notable change among the major record companies that are beginning to view film music with the seriousness it truly deserves. And also because both offer selections from films which had wider release in this country than the Fellini films for which Rota is notably famous. *War and Peace,* directed in 1956 by King Vidor, stars Audrey Hepburn, Mel Ferrer, and Henry Fonda, and is a magnificent screen reconstruction of the epic Tolstoy novel; *The Leopard,* filmed by Luchino Visconti in 1963, and starring Burt Lancaster and Claudia Cardinale, is a powerful account of 19th-century life in Sicily, at a time when social values disintegrated rapidly in the face of rising revolutionary ideas; as for *Waterloo,* made in 1971 by Sergei Bondarchuk, it stars Rod Steiger as Napoleon, confronted with his last battle and most devastating defeats.

Adding a different touch to both sets is the ballet from *La Strada,* which Rota reorchestrated from the cues he had composed for his original 1954 score. Both Gianluigi Gelmetti and Riccardo Muti, respectively conducting the Orchestre Philharmonique de Monte-Carlo and the Orchestra Filarmonica della Scala, do the ballet and the selections from the score full justice, with bright, imaginative sonics to complement the music.

The third CD is a decent rendition of themes written by Rota for the films of Federico Fellini, performed by the Czech Symphony Orchestra, conducted by Derek Wadsworth. The performance is sometimes lackluster, and some of the tempi are a bit wild, but overall it's a good set, and a good representation of Rota's most popular themes.

Didier C. Deutsch

Fellini/Rota: La dolce vita
1993, Silva America ♫♫♫

album notes: Music: Nino Rota; **Orchestra:** The Czech Symphony Orchestra; **Conductor:** Derek Wadsworth.

The Godfather Suite
1991, Silva Screen ♫♫♫♫

album notes: Music: Nino Rota; **Orchestra:** The Milan Philharmonia Orchestra; **Conductor:** Carmine Coppola.

Nino Rota: Music for Film
1997, Sony Classical ♫♫♫♫

album notes: Music: Nino Rota; **Orchestra:** The Filarmonica della Scala; **Conductor:** Riccardo Muti.

It is difficult to listen to Nino Rota's music and not see immediately scenes from the films of Federico Fellini, or from *The Godfather.* The composer became so closely identified with both that any retrospective of his music is bound to include excerpts from these films.

Fellini/Rota: La dolce vita, on Silva America, focuses on the films of Fellini and the wonderful artistic partnership that linked the Italian film director and his composer for so many years. That Rota gave a musical "voice" to the films of Fellini is something no one can argue with: his musical inspiration matched that of the director, and added a new dimension to his films, one that has become undissociable from them. The fifteen tracks found in the CD pay homage to the director and his composer, but since Rota himself recorded the same selections, and gave them his definite imprimatur, this collection pales in comparison. The playing by the Czech Symphony Orchestra sounds at times studied and lacking the Italian essence needed for this kind of music.

In this respect, the Silva Screen album, in which Carmine Coppola conducts the Milan Philharmonia in selections from *The Godfather* films fares much better. Coppola, who scored parts of *Godfather II* and *Godfather III,* certainly brings to the recording a close feel that is echoed in the music, played with the right bravadura by the orchestra.

There is also some artistic and ethnic kinship in Ricardo Mutti's treatment of Rota's music for the Sony Classical album, *Music for Film,* though the performance sounds at times too studied and stuffy. A plus here is the fact that the program does not focus entirely on the Fellini or the *Godfather* films, but also includes large excerpts from the scores for two films by Luchino Visconti, *Rocco and His Brothers* and *The Leopard,* both of which give a different dimension of Rota's talent as a film composer. The sound quality is consistently superb.

Didier C. Deutsch

Bruce Rowland

(1942-)

Bruce Rowland: The Film and Television Themes
1990, ABC Records ♪♪♪♪♪

album notes: Music: Bruce Rowland; **Orchestra:** The Melbourne Symphony Orchestra; **Conductor:** Bruce Rowland; **Featured Musicians:** Bruce Rowland, synthesizers; Joe Chindamo, synthesizers; Rod Stone, guitar; Don Stevenson, guitar; Mike Grabowsky, electric bass; Ron Sawdilands, drums; John Barratt, didgeridoo, flute, alto sax; Rod Campbell, bagpipes.

Australia's best kept secret, Bruce Rowland is a composer of great talent who has scored several films that have received a release in this country, notably *The Man from Snowy River* and its sequel *Return to Snowy River, All the Rivers Run,* and *Phar Lap.* This 1984 compilation, with the composer conducting the Melbourne Symphony Orchestra, is a flavorful presentation of some of the beautifully elegiac themes Rowland wrote for the screen and television, played with great gusto by the orchestra and some featured musicians. *Man from Snowy River,* in particular, which also yielded a highly recommended soundtrack album, is terrific in its evocation of the wide open Australian spaces, in terms that compare favorably with the best western scores ever written in Hollywood, with just a hint of its actual source that makes it even more attractive.

Didier C. Deutsch

Miklos Rozsa

(1907-1995)

Miklos Rozsa: Epic Suites for Orchestra, Chorus, and Organ
1986, Varèse Sarabande ♪♪♪

album notes: Music: Miklos Rozsa; **Orchestra:** The Hamburg Concert Orchestra and Chorus; **Conductor:** Richard Mueller-Lampertz.

The title actually says it all: beginning with *Quo Vadis,* in 1951, and *Ivanhoe,* in 1952, Miklos Rozsa acquired a solid reputation as a composer who could write better than most in the epic style for which Hollywood was coming to be known throughout the world. As a result, Rozsa scored many films set in Roman and medieval times, every time bringing a distinctive color to his music, frequently rooted in instruments and themes from the period reconstructed for the occasion. Some of the invention seems to be lost in most evocations of his scores, as in this presentation of cues from his scores for *El Cid, Ben-Hur,* and *King of Kings.* While the performance here is perfectly adequate and acceptable, it misses the special quality the original scores derived from the research and care the composer invested in them. Other than that, the recording also displays a shrillness that is not always very pleasing to the ear.

Didier C. Deutsch

The Music of Miklos Rozsa
1985, Varèse Sarabande ♪♪♪♪♪

album notes: Music: Miklos Rozsa; **Orchestra:** The Utah Symphony Orchestra; **Conductor:** Elmer Bernstein; **Featured Musicians:** Joshua Pierce, piano; Dorothy Jonas, piano.

An interesting album, conducted by Elmer Bernstein, which doesn't take the usual beaten path but seeks, instead, to be original. The meat of the CD is the two major works found here, the "New England Concerto" and the "Spellbound Concerto," both played with great drive and intensity by Joshua Pierce and Dorothy Jonas in two-piano versions apparently endorsed by the composer himself. As a filler, Bernstein and the Utah Symphony perform the "Overture" to *The World, the Flesh, and the Devil,* a 1959 drama starring Harry Belafonte, Inger Stevens, and Mel Ferrer, and the "Overture" to *Because of Him,* written in 1946 for a comedy in which the leads were held by Deanna Durbin, Franchot Tone, and Charles Laughton. The excellent dynamics add to the pleasure of discovering these versions.

Didier C. Deutsch

Miklos Rozsa: Hollywood Legend
1989, Varèse Sarabande ♪♪♪♪♪

album notes: Music: Miklos Rozsa; **Orchestra:** The Nuremberg Symphony Orchestra, the Palestrina Choir of Nuremberg; **Conductor:** Elmer Bernstein; **Featured Musicians:** Cynthia Millar, Ondes Marthinot; Kalus Leob, violin.

Elmer Bernstein and the Nuremberg Symphony Orchestra provide a rousing tribute to the great Miklos Rozsa in this excellent 1989 recording, produced by George Korngold and Wolfgang Konrad. Many of Rozsa's most romantic works are included here, with the composer's sweeping "Golden Age" sound permeating selections from *The Story of Three Loves, The Strange Love of Martha Ivers,* and *Dead Men Don't Wear Plaid,* while Rozsa's bold, majestic sense of dramatic film scoring is on full display in *El Cid, Quo Vadis?, King of Kings,* and *Ben-Hur.* This particular album is noteworthy for its premiere recording of a 12-minute suite from *The Plymouth Adventure,* as well as an alternate, unused piece from *The Private Life of Sherlock Holmes.* The music is given a competent symphonic performance under Bernstein's direction, and though the liner notes are fairly sparse for a project like this, that should not keep any true film music fan away from picking up this highly recommended release.

Andy Dursin

Film Scores of Miklos Rozsa
1996, Angel Records ♪♪♪♪♪

album notes: Music: Miklos Rozsa; **Conductor:** Miklos Rozsa.

Culled from recordings made by Rozsa in the 1950s and 1960s, this set includes selections that are in stereo (*Ben-Hur, El Cid, King of Kings*) and in mono (*The Red House, Quo*

Vadis?, Spellbound), with the cues mercifully arranged together and not at random, as is sometimes the case in compilations. The authoritative conducting here is the key to these selections recorded in Europe in 1967 and in Hollywood in 1952, respectively.

Didier C. Deutsch

Spellbound: The Classic Film Scores of Miklos Rozsa
1989, RCA Victor ♪♪♪♪♪

album notes: Music: Miklos Rozsa; **Orchestra:** The National Philharmonic Orchestra; **Conductor:** Charles Gerhardt.

Another title in RCA's Classic Film Scores series, this sensational recording, produced with great flair by George Korngold, again finds Charles Gerhardt and the National Philharmonic Orchestra in superlative readings of selections from the scores of Dr. Rozsa. Mercifully avoiding *Ben-Hur, King of Kings,* or even *El Cid,* the program focuses on other works, equally deserving of coverage, yet not as frequently performed. *The Red House,* in particular, is a real winner, as are the selections from *The Four Feathers, Double Indemnity, The Lost Weekend,* and *Spellbound.* But the album as a whole is a wonderful, exciting presentation of some of the best music composed by Rozsa.

Didier C. Deutsch

Miklos Rozsa: Hollywood Spectacular
1985, Bay Cities Records ♪♪♪♪

album notes: Music: Miklos Rozsa; **Orchestra:** The Royal Philharmonic Orchestra; **Conductor:** Rainer Padberg; **Featured Musician:** Christophe Bowers-Broadbent, organ.

This adequate collection of themes, mostly from Miklos Rozsa's Hollywood costume epics, is assembled into a delightful concerto of pomp and circumstance. The album leads off with the previously unrecorded "Festival Flourish," the album's only non-film composition, written in honor of the 1976 American Bicentennial. A 16 1/2-minute "Fantasy on Themes from *Young Bess*" follows, which precedes an assortment of music from *King of Kings, Ben-Hur,* and *El-Cid.* A personal favorite of Rozsa's, "Java de la Seine" from *The Story of Three Lovers,* is also included, making a welcome change of pace in the presentation. Christopher Palmer, who was a close personal friend of the composer, produced this album with another Rosza admirer, Rainer Padberg, conducting the Royal Philharmonic Orchestra. Unfortunately, the recording appears to make the orchestra sound surprisingly small. *Ben-Hur's* "Parade of the Charioteers" is incredibly impotent, lacking in the majesty of Rosza's original, or later recordings that gave the work a more commanding atmosphere.

David Hirsch

The Epic Film Music of Miklos Rozsa
1996, Silva Screen Records ♪♪♪♪

album notes: Music: Miklos Rozsa; **Orchestra:** The City of Prague Philharmonic and the Crouch End Festival Chorus; **Conductor:** Kenneth Alwyn; **Featured Musician:** Josef Kroft, violin.

This superbly performed and energetic collection of Miklos Rozsa's period and sword-and-sandal epics is one of Silva's best, opening with a rousing take on the Harryhausen fantasy *The Golden Voyage of Sinbad,* and moving through the Roman Empire settings of *Ben Hur* and *Quo Vadis,* the Biblical sagas *King of Kings* and *Sodom and Gomorrah,* and the period trappings of *Beau Brummell, All The Brothers Were Valiant,* and *Madame Bovary,* with its ingenious "madness waltz." A highlight of the album is the superb incorporation of choral sections into *King of Kings* (in its gorgeous opening and Rozsa's sublime setting of The Lord's Prayer) and *Quo Vadis,* bringing a new luster to musical cues that may have been performed on one too many Rozsa compilations of the past. Rozsa practically invented this genre, bristling with martial fanfares and sweeping romantic melodies, and this is a fitting tribute to his indelible style, with impeccable sound and performances.

Jeff Bond

Miklos Rozsa: Double Indemnity
1997, Koch International ♪♪♪♪

album notes: Music: Miklos Rozsa; **Orchestra:** The New Zealand Symphony Orchestra; **Conductor:** James Sedares.

Far from the bombast of his epic film scores, Rozsa also wrote some powerful cues heard in psychological dramas and contemporary thrillers like *The Lost Weekend, Double Indemnity,* and *The Killers,* heard here. The first, about a man, Ray Milland, trying to overcome his alcoholism, ends in a terrifying, nightmarish scene in which Rozsa's music, as memorable in its own way as the music Bernard Herrmann wrote for the shower scene in *Psycho,* serves as an extraordinary complement to the action.

More than any other, *Double Indemnity* may be considered the classic film noir, in which a relentless cynicism pervades the action, embodied here by Barbara Stanwyck, a Los Angeles femme fatale trapped into a loveless marriage who coerces an insurance salesman (Fred MacMurray) into murdering her husband in order to collect the money of his life policy.

As for *The Killers,* starring Burt Lancaster making his film debut, it deals with a former boxer hunted down and killed by two hoodlums sent after him by an underworld boss. James Sedares and the New Zealand Symphony do wonders with Rozsa's explosive cues.

Didier C. Deutsch

Legendary Hollywood: Miklos Rozsa
1998, Citadel Records 🎵🎵🎵🎵

album notes: Music: Miklos Rozsa; **Orchestra:** The Utah Symphony Orchestra and the Royal Philharmonic Orchestra; **Conductor:** Elmer Bernstein and Rainer Padberg; **Featured Musician:** Christopher Bowers-Broadbent, organ.

The Private Files of J. Edgar Hoover
1998, Citadel Records 🎵🎵🎵

album notes: Music: Miklos Rozsa; **Conductor:** Miklos Rozsa; **Featured Musicians:** Albert Dominguez, piano (tracks #24-30); Darryl Denning, guitar (tracks #31-36).

These two CDs present different facets of Rozsa's film music—his swashbuckling and Roman epic scores in the first, and contemporary dramas in the second.

The first CD is the one that will, by far, attract the most: it contains sturdy, rousing anthems that have been heard dozens of times in other compilations, though they never cease to please—"Palace Music," from *El Cid*; "Caesar's Procession," from *Julius Caesar*; "Triumphal March and Wedding," from *Sodom and Gomorrah*; "Via Dolorosa" and "Jugglers and Tumblers," from *King of Kings*; and of course "Parade of the Charioteers" and "Victory Parade," from *Ben-Hur*. Rozsa excelled at writing this kind of music, high in color and pageantry, and the success of these scores only confirmed the fact that he was on the right track when he composed them. The other selections here, from *The World, the Flesh, and the Devil, Because of Him,* and *The Story of Three Loves,* are the icing on the cake, with the Utah Symphony, conducted by Elmer Bernstein, and the Royal Philharmonic, led by Rainer Padberg, playing these excerpts with the right gusto and attitude.

A sleazy pseudo biography, *The Private Files of J. Edgar Hoover* gave Rozsa an opportunity to write a surrealistic score that attempted to reflect the moods in this "private" view into the life of the former chief of the FBI. At times, the music is fun, but for the most part it is a notch below what one might have expected from the great composer, obviously ill-inspired by his subject matter.

The selections from *Lydia,* played on the piano by Alfredo Dominguez, and from *Crisis,* played by guitarist Darryl Denning, unfortunately cry out for instrumental backing.

Didier C. Deutsch

Hans J. Salter

(1896-1994)

Hans J. Salter: Music for Frankenstein
1993, Marco Polo Records 🎵🎵🎵🎵

album notes: Music: Hans J. Salter; **Orchestra:** The RTE Concert Orchestra; **Conductor:** Andrew Penny.

Hans J. Salter/Paul Dessau: House of Frankenstein
1995, Marco Polo Records 🎵🎵🎵🎵

album notes: Music: Hans J. Salter, Paul Dessau; **Orchestra:** The Moscow Symphony Orchestra; **Conductor:** William T. Stromberg.

This delightful set of classic Universal Studios monster music was spearheaded by the release of Hans J. Salter's music for *House of Frankenstein* and *Ghost of Frankenstein* on the 1993 album *Music for Frankenstein*. As one of Universal Studios' most prolific in-house composers, Salter churned out an extraordinarily large amount of wonderfully creepy music for the studios' monster films, adding some much needed realism to Universal's ever growing stable of ghouls. But, as was the practice of the studios at the time, several composers were assigned to work on sections of a single film, which made the task for musical historians like John Morgan all the more difficult. Nonetheless, Morgan did an amazing job reconstructing the original scores, which were lost or destroyed years ago, and the music was well performed by the RTE Concert Orchestra under the direction of Andrew Penny on the first album.

However, just two years later, Morgan and William T. Stromberg were able to return to the *House of Frankenstein* and add in more music, cues mainly by Paul Dessau, to recreate the complete 55-minute film score. Stromberg conducts the Moscow Symphony Orchestra with great flair on the second CD. Both albums are digitally recorded with detailed liner notes.

David Hirsch

Creature from the Black Lagoon: A Symphony of Film Music by Hans J. Salter
1994, Intrada Records 🎵🎵🎵🎵

album notes: Music: Hans J. Salter.

Hans J. Salter was the undisputed king of horror film music throughout the '40s and '50s, supplying brash and moody musical cues for every shambling beast that emerged from Universal Studios, from the Frankenstein monster to the creature from the Black Lagoon. This collection shows the composer tackling a wide range of subject matter, yet except for *The Black Shield of Falworth,* Salter is still depicted as largely trapped in the horror genre. *The Creature from the Black Lagoon* is the quintessential 1950s horror opus, with its shrill, three-note brass stinger for the monster one of the most instantly recognizable and effective pieces of "scary" music ever heard in the movies. Salter's score moves seamlessly from impressionistic repose to outright chaos as the monster alternately hides in its swampy natural surroundings and launches its attacks to the tune of Salter's snarling brass trills. *The Black Shield of Falworth* is closely related to Salter's supplemental music for Jerome Moross's score to *The War Lord,* although Salter's questing English horn theme was far more traditional than Moross's efforts. *The Incredible Shrinking Man* featured a brazen, jazzy title theme that wailed out the tragic fate of its shrinking hero with some hair-raising trumpet and vocal solos, although the rest of the score was Salter at his most exciting, thrillingly scoring Grant Williams's battles with giant cats and spiders as he shrinks to the size of an atom. Ironically, movie monster expert Salter was ultimately called on to write music for the ultimate monster, *Adolf Hitler,* for a 1964 film treatment starring Richard Basehart. Salter, who actually lived through some of the Nazi regime, summons up the martial hysteria of pre-WWII Germany with plenty of bustle in some authentic-sounding marches.

Jeff Bond

Philippe Sarde

(1945-)

Musiques par Philippe Sarde
1990, CBS/France 🎵🎵🎵🎵

album notes: Music: Philippe Sarde; **Orchestra:** The London Symphony Orchestra, the Grimethorpe Collery Band, and the Orchestre de Paris; **Conductor:** Peter Knight and Bill Byers; **Featured Musicians:** Stephane Grappelli, violin; Hubert Rostaing, piano.

Musiques Originales des Films d'Andre Techine
1988, Milan Records/France 🎵🎵🎵🎵

album notes: Music: Philippe Sarde; **Orchestra:** The Orchestra de Paris and the London Symphony Orchestra; **Conductor:** Bill Byers and Peter Knight.

Philippe Sarde/Claude Sautet
1988, Milan Records/France 🎵🎵🎵🎵

album notes: Music: Philippe Sarde; **Orchestra:** The Orchestre de Paris and the London Symphony Orchestra; **Conductor:** Bill Byers and Peter Knight.

Philippe Sarde is well known in this country for a wide range of film scores, from the American-made *Tess, Ghost Story, Lord of the Flies,* and *Music Box,* to the French hits *Cesar and Rosalie, L'ours, La guerre du feu,* and *Les choses de la vie.*

The two Milan CDs, *Musiques originales des films d'Andre Techine* and *Philippe Sarde/Claude Sautet* chronicle Sarde's association with two respected French directors with whom he enjoyed a long and fruitful artistic relationship. Both also reflect the composer's specific approach for the films of each director: Sautet, whose films are more reflective of the close friendship between working class people, and Techine, whose period films are more romantic in style.

The set, *Musiques par Philippe Sarde* is a different story altogether. Essentially regrouping some cues from four films (*April Months Are Deadly, The Last Civilian, Brigitt Huss Must Die,* and *Faux et usages de faux*), it does so in a hodgepodge manner

10 *Essential Scores*

by Miklos Rozsa

Spellbound
El Cid
Ben-Hur
The Thief of Bagdad
The Jungle Book
Quo Vadis
Ivanhoe
Plymouth Adventure
Time after Time
Providence

that sounds disjointed and programmatically wrong. Conversely, it presents an unusual association between Sarde and two jazz artists, Stephane Grappelli and Hubert Rostaing, something that in itself is a definite plus.

Didier C. Deutsch

Lalo Schifrin

(1932-)

Those Fabulous Hollywood Marches
1990, Pro-Arte Records 🎵🎵🎵🎵

album notes: Orchestra: The San Diego Symphony Pops; **Conductor:** Lalo Schifrin.

Romancing the Film
1992, Pro-Arte Records 🎵🎵🎵🎵

album notes: Orchestra: The 6Rochester Pops; **Conductor:** Lalo Schifrin.

Another reaction to the "Kunzel syndrome," these two CDs gave Lalo Schifrin the opportunity to step in front of fledgling symphony orchestras, in this case the San Diego Symphony

Pops and the Rochester Pops, whip them into shape and record some selections from the movies, in the hope of emulating the success achieved by Telarc and the Cincinnati Pops. The thematic approach suits the composer of *Mission: Impossible* to a tee, particularly in the first album in which his own flamboyance finds a suitable echo in the martial airs written by John Williams, Alfred Newman, Henry Mancini, Morton Gould, and, while-we're-at-it-why-not-add John Philip Sousa and Richard Wagner (they did compose marches, didn't they?). Of course, the title *Those Fabulous Hollywood Marches* is a trifle misleading, but after all who cares when the music is that spirited and that enjoyable?

Romancing the Film is a bit more of a hodgepodge concept, with (almost) everything thrown in to satisfy the most demanding customer, from "Tara's Theme," "Over the Rainbow," and "As Time Goes By," to "Moon River," "Love Theme from *The Godfather*," and a medley from *The Little Mermaid*. And if you think that last one is an odd choice, how about the "Space Medley," which combines "Also Sprach Zarathustra" (from *2001: A Space Odyssey,* in case you needed to be reminded) and the theme from *Star Wars*. Romance indeed takes a flight in this one!

Didier C. Deutsch

The Reel Lalo Schifrin
1998, Hip-O Records 🎵🎵🎵
album notes: Music: Lalo Schifrin.

Dirty Harry Anthology
1998, Aleph Records 🎵🎵🎵
album notes: Music: Lalo Schifrin; **Conductor:** Lalo Schifrin.

A native of Buenos Aires, Argentina, Lalo Schifrin began as a pianist and arranger for Dizzy Gillespie, and eventually made a name for himself in the U.S. as the composer of the themes for *Mission: Impossible* and dozens of other television series, as well as films like *Cool Hand Luke, Dirty Harry,* and *The Four Musketeers,* in which he often introduced elements of jazz that made his scores truly unique and recognizable.

The first CD, *The Reel Lalo Schifrin,* which is part of a series of similarly-named compilations, contains selections from some of his most successful film scores, including *Cool Hand Luke, The Cincinnati Kid, Once a Thief, Nunzio, The Fox, The Four Musketeers,* and *The Eagle Has Landed,* several of which make their digital debut here.

As its name indicates, *Dirty Harry Anthology,* on Schifrin's own Aleph label, collects together several tracks written for the *Dirty Harry* films, starring Clint Eastwood, heard here in "Dirty Harry's Creed." Because Schifrin's writing was for a series of films with a single focus, this CD sounds less like a compila-

tion, but it is also somewhat less diversified than *The Reel Lalo Schifrin.* Nonetheless, it should delight all fans of the series, as well as those who like their Schifrin a bit more spicy and contemporary.

Didier C. Deutsch

Gerard Schurmann

Horrors of the Black Museum: The Film Music of Gerard Schurmann
1993, Cloud Nine Records 🎵🎵🎵
album notes: Music: Gerard Schurmann.

Under this strange title actually can be found some very interesting scores that are far from your run-of-the-mill. The CD, of course, gets its name from the music Gerard Schurmann, a wonderful British composer who gains at being discovered, wrote for the 1959 film of the same name, a "literate but lurid tale of dastardly murders," to quote the often humorous liner notes. American audiences, however, will probably be better acquainted with *The Bedford Incident,* a Cold War underwater drama starring Richard Widmark and Sydney Poitier; and *The Ceremony,* a "forgotten" film that stars Laurence Harvey and Sarah Miles.

Fans and collectors will probably enjoy listening to other themes composed by Schurmann, including those he wrote for *Konga,* a 1961 King Kong-clone; *The Lost Continent,* another pseudo monster movie made in 1968 and set in the Sargasso Sea; and the World War II drama *Attack on the Iron Coast.* Source material here, from Schurmann's own archives, leaves a lot to be desired, with overall sonic quality suffering from distortion, surface noise, and other problems usually associated with recordings that have been mistreated over the years. But the music, vibrantly alive and exotic, is pure delight.

Didier C. Deutsch

John Scott

(1930-   )

John Scott Conducts His Own Favorite Film Scores
1991, JOS Records 🎵🎵🎵🎵
album notes: Orchestra: The Berlin Radio Concert Orchestra, the Royal Philharmonic Orchestra; **Conductor:** John Scott.

John Scott is unquestionably the most underrated talent in film scoring today. This anthology shows off his ability to write in an astounding array of styles (which is especially impressive considering he is one of the few film composers who orchestrates his own music). Opening the album is the brassy title music from *The Final Countdown,* a soaring and triumphant piece. The pastoral mode of *The Shooting Party* is a lovely (yet bittersweet) evocation of Edwardian England. An English pastoral mood returns in *England Made Me,* which also features an original song "All on the Radio," written in a jazzy '30s style. Moving into yet another different direction is Scott's strident and propulsive "March of the Nagas" from *The People That Time Forgot.*

His exhilarating music from the TV series *Cousteau Amazon* blends orchestral grandeur with rhythm section, in a style which might be described as "epic travelogue." Scott's two undeniable masterpieces, *Antony and Cleopatra* and *Greystoke,* are saved for last, each in nine-minute suites, which depict the composer in his most grandly epic mode. *John Scott Conducts His Own Favorite Film Themes* is, simply stated, a first-rate collection.

Paul Andrew MacLean

Screen Themes
1988, Varèse Sarabande ♪♪♪♪♪
album notes: Orchestra: The Royal Philharmonic Orchestra; **Conductor:** John Scott; **Featured Musicians:** Cynthia Millar, Ondes Marthenot; Jack Emblow, accordion; Mitch Dalton, guitar; Guy Barber, trumpet; Chris Laurence, bass; Duncan Lamont, saxophone; Harold Fisher, drums; Dave Hartley, piano.

Excellent mix of original soundtrack and newly recorded material by John Scott and the Royal Philharmonic Orchestra. This is a "best of" compilation of 1987-88 films, with much of the original material culled from Varèse-Sarabande releases like *Cocoon: The Return, Crossing Delancy,* and *Madame Sousatzka.* The real gems, however, are Scott's outstanding recreations of the unreleased themes from Howard Shore's *Big,* John Barry's *Masquerade,* Michael Kamen's *Die Hard,* and his own *Shoot to Kill.* Scott's version of *The Milagro Bean Field War* "End Title" is actually more faithful than the recording that appears on one of composer Dave Grusin's own albums. Also included is the full eleven-minute end title suite from *Who Framed Roger Rabbit.* Only a truncated five-minute version appeared on the original soundtrack. This is a really superior produced anthology, a guide for what all others should be.

David Hirsch

Europe Goes to Hollywood
1993, Denon Records ♪♪♪♪
album notes: Orchestra: The Royal Philharmonic Pops Orchestra; **Conductor:** John Scott.

John Scott conducts the Royal Philharmonic Pops Orchestra in this well-recorded and performed tribute to Hollywood's classic European composers. Erich Wolfgang Korngold's *The Adventures of Robin Hood* gets the star treatment in a lively 18-minute suite that leads off the album, faithfully capturing the essence of the composer's original film score. Other suites include Max Steiner's *Casablanca,* Miklos Rozsa's *Ben-Hur* (with a really

laudable version of "Parade of the Chariooters"), and Franz Waxman's enchanting *Rebecca.* Oddly, American born Bernard Herrmann is included (possibly perhaps because he lived his last years in England?) with a suite from *Citizen Kane* that captures some of the original's brooding power. Scott's compilation albums are always superior in sound and performance, thanks in part to his more than evident love of film music.

David Hirsch

Raymond Scott
(1908-1994)

The Music of Raymond Scott: Reckless Nights and Turkish Twilights
1992, Columbia Records ♪♪♪♪
album notes: Music: Raymond Scott; **Orchestra:** The Raymond Scott Quintette, Raymond Scott and His New Orchestra; **Conductor:** Raymond Scott.

The Raymond Scott Project Vol. 1: Powerhouse
1991, Stash Records ♪♪♪♪
album notes: Music: Raymond Scott.

With a few minor exceptions, both sets pretty much cover the same selections and, in fact, were essentially produced by the same individuals. Since the source material is also the same, the only thing that might attract the casual listener to the Stash release is the attractive cartoonish cover, bolder graphics, and the fact it has 24 selections as opposed to 22 for the Columbia set. Whichever you pick, your perception of music will be hopelessly warped after you have listened to Raymond Scott's zany inventions. Once you have enjoyed it, you might also want to check out the works of Scott Bradley for the cartoons of Tex Avery at MGM, or the two *Carl Stalling Projects* on Warner Bros.

Didier C. Deutsch

Eric Serra
(1959-)

La musique des films
1999, Virgin Records/France ♪♪♪♪
album notes: Music: Eric Serra.

With his scores for *The Professional* (a.k.a. *Leon*), *The Fifth Element,* and particularly *Goldeneye,* Eric Serra has entered the exclusive domain of international film composers. While it may be entirely justified, his creative streak may not be to everyone's liking, and his music still needs to make quite a few converts before his popularity becomes firmly seated.

This CD should, in some ways, help a bit: consisting of selections from the above mentioned films, plus excerpts from the scores that ensured his nascent popularity in France (*The Big*

Blue, Subway, The Last Combat, and *Nikita* (the film on which the popular TV series *La femme Nikita* is based), it shows Serra as a composer with an uncanny flair for both synthesizer and big instrumental music.

He tends to develop ideas that are somewhat lacking in melodic content, but there is no denying the emotional impact of his themes, even if they sound at times repetitive. All told, a good introduction to a composer on the threshold of bigger things to come.

Didier C. Deutsch

Richard M. & Robert B.Sherman

(1928-)/(1925-)

Richard M. Sherman & Robert B. Sherman
1992, Walt Disney Records 🎵🎵🎵🎵
album notes: **Music:** Richard M. Sherman, Robert B. Sherman; **Lyrics:** Richard M. Sherman, Robert B. Sherman.

This attractive compilation brings together some of the best selections from the various scores the Sherman brothers, Richard M. and Robert B., wrote for the films of Walt Disney, including *Mary Poppins, Winnie the Pooh, The Jungle Book, Bedknobs and Broomsticks, The Parent Trap, The One and Only Genuine Original Family Band, The Aristocats, The Happiest Millionaire,* and *Summer Magic.* There's a lot to be enjoyed here, with many familiar tunes that have served as the soundtrack to our lives since the 1960s, with glorious performances by Julie Andrews, Angela Lansbury, Lesley Ann Warren, Tommy Steele, Burl Ives, Louis Prima, and (believe it or not!) The Beach Boys. All told, a great collection.

Didier C. Deutsch

Alan Silvestri

(1950-)

Voyages: The Film Music Journeys
1995, Varèse Sarabande 🎵🎵🎵🎵
album notes: **Music:** Alan Silvestri; **Conductor:** Alan Silvestri, Joel McNeely, John Scott.

This exhilarating set enables Alan Silvestri, a composer with a chameleon personality, to reveal some of his many facets in a compilation that covers several of his most famous creations, including the themes from *Forrest Gump, Back to the Future, Romancing the Stone, The Abyss,* and *Who Framed Roger Rabbit.* One of the brilliant exponents of the new generation in film music, Silvestri has a recognizably easy style that he has used to great effect in some of the most visible films of the past dozen years. The set, intelligently put together and well pre-

sented, is a wonderful excursion in some of his best works, with the two long suites from *Forrest Gump,* conducted by Joel McNeely, and *Roger Rabbit,* conducted by John Scott, particularly deserving of warm applause. Once you've put it on your player, you won't want to give up this glib and enjoyable set.

Didier C. Deutsch

Martial Solal

(1927-)

Martial Solal: Jazz & Cinema
1990, EMI/France 🎵🎵🎵
album notes: **Music:** Martial Solal; **Featured Musicians:** Martial Solal, piano; Roger Guerin, trumpet; Clark Terry, trumpet; Fernand Verstraete, trumpet; Pierre Gossez, alto sax; Jean-Louis Chautemps, tenor sax; William Boucaya, baritone sax; Michel Hausser, vibes; Paul Rovere, bass; Benoit Quersin, bass; Guy Pedersen, bass; Daniel Humair, drums; Armand Molinetti, drums; Charles Bellonzi, drums; Charles Verstraete, trombone; Raymond Katarzynski, trombone; Raymond Guiot, flute.

Though little known in this country (his score for Jean-Luc Godard's landmark New Wave film *Breathless* may be the closest thing American filmgoers might remember), Solal was an important pioneer in French film music, bringing, as he did, many elements of jazz to his compositions at a time when this was not the norm, at least by French standards. These sides, recorded between 1959 and 1964, provide an overview of some of his most influential works, with the pianist-composer leading various bands, in which the names of familiar sidemen like Clark Terry, Daniel Humair, and Guy Pedersen occasionally show up.

This, incidentally, was the first title in a series that was supposed to chronicle Solal's musical career; apparently it was not followed by subsequent volumes.

Didier C. Deutsch

Stephen Sondheim

(1930-)

Sondheim: A Musical Tribute
1993, RCA Victor 🎵🎵🎵🎵🎵
album notes: **Music:** Stephen Sondheim; **Lyrics:** Stephen Sondheim; **Cast:** George Lee Andrews, Larry Blyden, Susan Browning, Len Cariou, Jack Cassidy, Dorothy Collins, Steve Elmore, Harvey Evans, Hermione Gingold, Laurence Guittard, Pamela Hall, Ron Holgate, Beth Howland, Glynis Johns, Justine Johnston, Larry Kert, Mark Lambert, Angela Lansbury, Victoria Mallory, Mary McCarty, Donna McKechnie, John McMartin, Pamela Myers, Anthony Perkins, Kurt Peterson, Alice Playten, Teri Ralston, Chita Rivera, Marti Rolph, Virginia Sandifur, Ethel Shutta, Alexis Smith, Tony Stevens, Nancy Walker.

Sondheim: Putting It Together
1993, RCA Victor 🎵🎵🎵🎵🎵
album notes: **Music:** Stepehn Sondheim; **Lyrics:** Stephen Sondheim; **Cast:** Julie Andrews, Stephen Collins, Christopher Durang, Michael Rupert, Rachel York.

Stephen Sondheim **(Archive Photos, Inc.)**

Sondheim: A Celebration at Carnegie Hall
1993, RCA Victor ♪♪♪♪
album notes: Music: Stephen Sondheim; **Lyrics:** Stephen Sondheim; **Orchestra:** The American Theatre Orchestra; **Conductor:** Paul Gemignani; **Cast:** Kevin Anderson, George Lee Andrews, Ron Baker, BETTY (Amy Ziff, Bitzi Ziff, Alyson Palmer), Harolyn Blackwell, Peter Blanchet, Boys Choir of Harlem, Betty Buckley, Patrick Cassidy, Glenn Close, Daisy Egan, Victor Garber, Jerry Hadley, Bill Irwin, Mark Jacoby, Michael Jeter, Madeline Kahn, Beverly Lambert, Jeanne Lehman, Dorothy Loudon, Patti LuPone, Carol Meyer, Liza Minnelli, Maureen Moore, Richard Muenz, James Naughton, Carolann Oage, Eugene Perry, Herbert Perry, Bernadette Peters, Billy Stritch, Susan Terry, Bronwyn Thomas, The Tonics (Cortes Alexander, Brian Green, Gene Reed, Lindy Robbins), Blythe Walker, Karen Ziemba.

A Collector's Sondheim
1985, RCA Victor ♪♪♪♪
album notes: Music: Stephen Sondheim; **Lyrics:** Stephen Sondheim.

Certainly the most important Broadway composer of the past 25 years, Stephen Sondheim has been sung, performed, interpreted, and lionized by a vast number of performers, some of whom have chosen the route of a solo tribute to his creativity, others who have preferred to appear in special concert versions or studio performances with others who add their own renditions of his songs to the vast body of works that already exists.

The four compilations listed above are all significant for one reason or another, and can hardly be singled out for special merit as all four are meritorious in their own specific ways. While they all essentially cover the same territory, with minor variances, what is of primary interest here is the various performers involved. In the first 2-CD set, the result of a concert presentation that took place at the Shubert Theatre on Broadway on March 11, 1973, they include Len Cariou, Glynis Johns, and Hermione Gingold, who appeared in *A Little Night Music*; Ethel Shutta, John McMartin, Dorothy Collins, and Alexis Smith, who starred in *Follies*; Larry Kert, Victoria Mallory, and Donna McKechnie, who were in *Company*; and Angela Lansbury, who starred in *Anyone Can Whistle*; along with many others, including Chita Rivera, Nancy Walker, Anthony Perkins, and Jack Cassidy.

Putting It Together starred Julie Andrews who, even though she never appeared in a Sondheim musical, was the name above the title in this limited engagement at the Manhattan Theatre Club which played from March 2 to May 23, 1993. Stephen Collins, Christopher Durang, Michael Rupert, and Rachel York also starred in this intimate production that focused on the songs as much as it did on the actual performances.

As its name indicates, *Sondheim: A Celebration at Carnegie Hall* was a special tribute recorded live at the famed hall on June 10, 1992. Here again, the bill is quite extraordinary, with Glenn Close, Madeline Kahn, Dorothy Loudon, Patti LuPone, Liza Minnelli, and Bernadette Peters among the luminaries who appeared on stage to sing a song of Sondheim.

Finally, *A Collector's Sondheim* is a collection of tunes, some from original Broadway and London cast album recordings, others from concert performances, that were put together by record producer Thomas Z. Shepard as a tribute to a composer whose most important shows (*Company, Sweeney Todd, Pacific Overtures, Follies in Concert, A Little Night Music, Merrily We Roll Along, Sunday in the Park with George*) he had personally recorded. This 3-CD set is essential for anyone interested in the works of Sondheim, as it covers a lot of ground not touched upon by the other compilations.

Ultimately, it may seem somewhat redundant to own everything that has ever been released by or about Sondheim. However, in view of the fact that no other composer has influenced the Broadway musical to such an extent in recent years, and also given the fact that Sondheim is constantly renewing himself and his approach to the genre, no collection could be complete without at least one and possibly all of the above recordings. In truth, Sondheim is an acquired taste, an individual talent who requires a lot from those who follow him wherever his creative fancy wants to take them, but who never ceases to amaze, interest, and fascinate because what he does is so unique and so incredibly distinctive. No words can appropriately describe what he does, and does so well. Listening to these various recordings, however, gives a glimpse into his creative process, and as a result they are all highly recommended.

Didier C. Deutsch

Mark Snow
(1946-   )

The Snow Files: The Film Music of Mark Snow
1999, Sonic Images ♪♪♪
album notes: Music: Mark Snow.

Call it a case of being at the right place at the right time—with two hugely popular television series, *La Femme Nikita* and *The X-Files,* Mark Snow actually set the tempo of what television music should sound like. Not bad! The problem, however, is that once you move beyond the catchy (and interesting) title tunes in both series, there is really very little that compels the listener to pay close attention to the themes Snow developed, or even listen to them other than as background music, something this collection makes painfully clear. Yet, there are moments here that make you wonder whether success didn't spoil the composer. Some of his early compositions, like the "Love Theme" from *Conundrum* or "The Dark Waltz" from *Seduced and Betrayed* are actually quite good and engaging. Other selections in this retrospective tribute also make a good impression, and most notably the selections from *Caroline at Midnight, The Substitute Wife,* and *Oldest Living Confederate Widow*. But since the *piece de resistance* here is the long suite from *The X-Files,* it tends to cast a pall over everything else that precedes or follows, which is unfortunate. Repetitious and ultimately uninspiring, it literally suffers in comparison to everything else. Whether the set actually needed this suite is a matter for debate, but then so is Mark Snow's contributions to the show.

Didier C. Deutsch

Carl Stalling

(1888-1974)

The Carl Stalling Project
1990, Warner Bros. Records ♪♪♪♪♪
album notes: Music: Carl Stalling; **Orchestra:** The Warner Bros. Studio Orchestra; **Conductor:** Carl Stalling.

The Carl Stalling Project, vol. 2
1995, Warner Bros. Records ♪♪♪♪♪
album notes: Music: Carl Stalling; **Orchestra:** The Warner Bros. Studio Orchestra; **Conductor:** Carl Stalling.

This long overdue set of recordings does justice to one of the great, unsung musical geniuses of the 20th century. For decades composer Carl Stalling slaved away in the cultural ghetto of cartoon music, a despised genre that nevertheless afforded Stalling the opportunity to write some of the most imaginative, kinetically and rhythmically unpredictable, and hysterically funny music ever heard. Adapting everything from classical repertoire melodies and arrangements to popular songs of the period (with a special emphasis on the percolating compositions of American composer Raymond Scott), Stalling wrote an ongoing, bitingly witty musical commentary on what were already some pretty hilarious cartoons and in the process created music that has wormed its way into the psyches of millions of people from childhood on. Both of these albums feature generous suites of music from numerous Warner Brothers cartoons, ranging from the 1930s to the late 1950s, with generally excellent sound quality and occasional bursts of wild cartoon sound effects and vocal performances. It's a weirdly nostalgic, giggle-inducing, and subversive musical journey that will not be to all tastes, but for lovers of Bugs Bunny and Daffy Duck, or for fans of avant-garde musical composition, these albums are invaluable treasures.

Jeff Bond

Ronald Stein

(1930-1988)

Not of This Earth!: The Film Music of Ronald Stein
1995, Varèse Sarabande ♪♪♪
album notes: Music: Ronald Stein.

Ronald Stein had the dubious honor of scoring some of the lousiest movies ever to be unleashed from the stable of producer Roger Corman, including *Attack of the 50 Ft. Woman, Not of This Earth!,* and *Attack of the Crab Monsters* (and probably half a dozen other attacks that have long been forgotten). Stein always approached his task seriously despite the laughably bad antics onscreen, and in many cases he so drenched his subject matter in brooding anguish that the failings of the films in question just wound up becoming all that more apparent. Case in point: *Attack of the 50 Ft. Woman,* which sports a bittersweet brass fanfare that might have been written for Napoleon and Desiree instead of some drunken lout and his problems with a giant pursuing rubber hand. Stein was at his best on period films like *The Terror* and *Dementia 13,* where there were no giant cardboard monsters in evidence and the composer could use his technical skills to create some genuine moments of eeriness. But he more often had to patch together pieces of sleazy juke box dance music or reach heights of insane camp, as in the touching "Song from Spider Baby" brayed by an obviously drunken Lon Chaney, Jr. *Not of This Earth* offers a great mix of surprisingly effective chills, big laughs, and childhood nostalgia for those who grew up watching Corman's movies on the Saturday late show.

Jeff Bond

Max Steiner

(1888-1971)

Band of Angels
1987, Label X Records ♪♪♪♪♪
album notes: Music: Max Steiner; **Orchestra:** The Warner Bros. Studio Orchestra and the RKO Studio Orchestra; **Conductor:** Max Steiner; **Featured Musician:** Ray Turner, piano.

There is something clearly endearing about this compilation bringing together selections from several scores written by Max Steiner, with the composer conducting the Warner Bros. Studio and the RKO Studio orchestras. Of particular interest here is the series of cues from *Band of Angels,* a 1957 period drama set during the Civil War, with Clark Gable as a proper Southern plantation owner, and Yvonne de Carlo as the object of his love, who happens to have black ancestry. Strongly suggestive and flavorful, the score is not found in other compilations and stands out as the real gem in this set. For the same reasons, *Death of a Scoundrel,* a 1956 low-budget drama starring Yvonne de Carlo, is quite ingratiating. The other selections, though found elsewhere, are an excellent complement to this CD.

Didier C. Deutsch

Max Steiner Conducts Gone with the Wind & Other Themes
1989, RCA Records ♪♪♪♪♪
album notes: Music: Max Steiner; **Conductor:** Max Steiner.

One of the most important of the film composers who gave Hollywood its first taste of music in the early 1930s, Max Steiner was born in Vienna in 1888. Already a celebrated composer in his native country, he came to America in 1914 at the invitation of Florenz Ziegfeld, and for the ensuing 15 years worked on a variety of Broadway productions, before moving to Hollywood to orchestrate and conduct the 1929 screen version of *Rio Rita,* which was being produced by RKO.

Convinced that an appropriate musical background, not one borrowed from the classical repertoire, as was often the case, could add significantly to the emotional impact of any scene, Steiner persuaded David O. Selznick, a producer at RKO, to let him write an original series of cues for a single reel of *Symphony of Six Million.* As he had suspected, the effect on audiences was electrifying, and Selznick was further convinced after Steiner created the first original full-length score, for *Bird of Paradise,* in 1932.

As a result of this early success, William LeBaron, head of production at the studio, put him in charge of the music department. In the six years he was there, Steiner scored a staggering 110 films, including *King Kong* and *The Informer,* for which he won an Oscar in 1935.

In 1938 he left RKO and moved to Warner Bros., where he found in Jack L. Warner a producer who loved music in his pictures but, unlike Selznick, did not interfere with his composers' creativity. He stayed at Warner until 1953, and free-lanced after that, writing his last score, for *Rome Adventure,* in 1962. He died on December 28, 1971.

During his long and illustrious career, Steiner wrote many scores that have endured to this day, including those for *Now Voyager, The Charge of the Light Brigade, The Big Sleep, Since You Went Away, Dark Victory,* and, of course, *Gone with the Wind,* his greatest claim to fame.

This CD, in which he conducts an unnamed Hollywood orchestra, was recorded between 1954 and 1956, and covers many themes he wrote for some of the movies listed above, including a long suite from *Gone with the Wind.* The album, in mono sound, may be sonically deficient by today's standards, but it has the enormous merit of presenting the composer himself conducting his own works, a rarity in those days.

Didier C. Deutsch

Now, Voyager: The Classic Film Scores of Max Steiner
1989, RCA Victor Records 🎵🎵🎵🎵
album notes: Music: Max Steiner; **Orchestra:** The National Philharmonic Orchestra; **Conductor:** Charles Gerhardt; **Featured Musician:** Earl Wild, piano.

Gone with the Wind: The Classic Max Steiner
1993, Silva Screen Records 🎵🎵🎵🎵
album notes: Music: Max Steiner; **Orchestra:** The Westminster Philharmonic Orchestra; **Conductor:** Kenneth Alwyn.

Both these titles cover some of the same selections, but the differences are significant enough that you might want to own both. *Now Voyager,* on RCA, is part of the Classic Film Scores series, an essential collection that chronicles some of the themes written in the early days of Hollywood by the golden circle of composers, in which Steiner was a particularly shining example. Missing from this title is any representation of *Gone with the Wind,* which Gerhardt and the National Philharmonic recorded in its entirety for another CD. The spectacular sonics, and the excellence of the performance add immeasurably to one's enjoyment.

The Silva Screen CD, with Kenneth Alwyn conducting the Westminster Philharmonic Orchestra in a bright, regenerative performance, offers some rare selections like the suites from *Casablanca* and *Helen of Troy,* and the "Overture" to *The Adventures of Mark Twain.* Like the RCA set, it is highly recommended.

Didier C. Deutsch

Max Steiner: The Lost Patrol
1996, Marco Polo Records 🎵🎵🎵🎵
album notes: Music: Max Steiner; **Orchestra:** The Moscow Symphony Orchestra; **Conductor:** William T. Stromberg.

This recent entry in the Steiner sweepstakes is another album that deserves to be in any comprehensive collection. Superbly recorded in bright, spacious digital sound, with William T. Stromberg eliciting spirited performances from the Moscow Symphony Orchestra players, it offers a broad overview of three widely different scores composed by Steiner, including two (*The Lost Patrol* and *Virginia City*) that are essential.

Written in 1934, *The Lost Patrol* chronicled the fate of a small group of British soldiers isolated in the Mesopotamian desert and subjected to repeated attacks from their Arab foes. The nervy, pungent score contributed immensely to the impact of this action-driven military saga.

Virginia City, made in 1940, is a western set during the Civil War, starring Errol Flynn, Randolph Scott, and Humphrey Bogart. Steiner, who excelled at writing this type of music, delivered a potent, highly memorable score, which ranks among his best efforts.

The third title here, *The Beast with Five Fingers,* a 1946 horror film starring Peter Lorre and Robert Alda, found the composer contributing a totally different type of music, in which he drew extensively on his classical training. Like the other two scores, it shows

Max Steiner (r) **(Archive Photos, Inc.)**

Steiner's incredible diversity and unique talent in writing music that contributed enormously to the overall aura of the films, in a contemporary performance that sounds quite authentic.

Didier C. Deutsch

Film Scores of Max Steiner
1998, Centaur Records 𝄞𝄞𝄞𝄞

album notes: Music: Max Steiner; **Orchestra:** The Slovak State Philharmonic Orchestra; **Conductor:** Barry Kolman.

Adventures of Mark Twain
1997, RCA/Germany 𝄞𝄞𝄞𝄞𝄞

album notes: Music: Max Steiner, Erich-Wolfgang Korngold; **Orchestra:** The Brandenburg Philharmonic Orchestra; **Conductor:** William Stromberg.

Few composers have had as much influence on early Hollywood film music as Max Steiner, who "invented" modern film music when he created the score for *Bird of Paradise* in 1932. After becoming head of the music department, first at RKO, and then at Warner Bros., Steiner wrote many pioneering works that paved the way for others to follow in his footsteps.

In recent years, there have been many compilations of works he composed, but these two offer selections that are infrequently covered. *Films Scores of Max Steiner* is actually a somewhat faithful presentation of two suites culled from the cues Steiner wrote for John Huston's *Treasure of the Sierra Madre* (1948), starring Humphrey Bogart, and *Charge of the Light Brigade* (1936), which starred Errol Flynn and Olivia de Havilland. Both rank among the most important films ever made by the studio.

Propelled by a jaunty little tune identified as the "Pardners Theme," heard throughout the film, the suite highlights some of the best moments in *Treasure of the Sierra Madre*, including a gunfight with ruthless Mexican bandidos, a surprise visit by a Texan hoping to strike it rich, the eventual madness of the main character, portrayed by Bogart, and the ironical ending that capped the entire story and made it so much more powerful.

Charge of the Light Brigade was a Crimean War epic involving the 600 British soldiers of the 27th Lancers, and their heroic but futile charge against the combined forces of the Suristani of India and a Russian army of 25,000.

Both suites are played extremely well by the Slovak State Philharmonic Orchestra, though the sonics tend to be a little too diffused at times.

Coupled with Erich Wolfgang Korngold's *The Prince and the Pauper,* itself based on a story by Mark Twain, *The Adventures of Mark Twain* was written in 1944 for a film that starred Fredric March and Alexis Smith. The score skillfully blends some American folk songs with original themes that describe the action and the characters in the film. As for the grandiloquent Korngold score for *The Prince and the Pauper,* it is in the vein of his best swashbucklers (Errol Flynn presence in the film obliging), even though the action barely suggested this kind of approach. Performance by the Brandenburg Philharmonic Orchestra and Choir, under the direction of William T. Stromberg, is top notch. But beware: the CD, which was only issued in Germany in celebration of the movies' 100 years, may be difficult to find. It's well worth the effort.

Didier C. Deutsch

Toru Takemitsu
(1930-1996)

The Film Music of Toru Takemitsu
1997, Nonesuch Records 𝄞𝄞𝄞𝄞

album notes: Music: Toru Takemitsu; **Orchestra:** The London Sinfonietta; **Conductor:** John Adams.

In between his first effort, *Kurutta Kajitsu* (*Crazed Fruit*), in 1956, and his death 40 years later, Toru Takemitsu created 93 film scores, all along proclaiming that his love for the movies was his motivating factor behind such an enormous output.

Drawing extensively from his Japanese background, but also blending in elements from a purely European or Western attitude, he wrote scores that seemed totally alien to us, yet beautifully matched the moods of the films. This collection, in Nonesuch's acclaimed "Film Music" series, covers only a fraction of Takemitsu's contributions to the screen. But from the well-known *Black Rain,* to the arty *Woman in the Dunes,* it is a collection that stands out and compels the listener to pay close attention and admire. The selections include rerecordings by John Adams and the London Sinfonietta, and original soundtrack recordings, making this a highly prized compilation.

Didier C. Deutsch

Mikis Theodorakis
(1925-)

Mikis Theodorakis: On the Screen
1993, DRG Records 𝄞𝄞𝄞𝄞

album notes: Z: Music: Mikis Theodorakis; **Conductor:** Bernard Gerard; **State of Siege: Music:** Mikis Theodorakis; **Featured Musicians:** Los Calchakis: Hector Miranda, Nicolas Perez-Gonsalez, Gonsalo Reig, Sergio Arriagada, Rodolfo Dalera, Yannis Didilis, keyboards; Gerard Berlioz, percussion; Pierre Moreilhon, bass; **Phaedra: Music:** Mikis Theodorakis; **Conductor:** Mikis Theodorakis.

The soundtracks to four films scored by Greek composer Mikis Theodorakis have been preserved on this thick double-CD set. The fast-paced rhythmic Greek music from *Z* is centered around a Greek melody, which counterpoints the political oppression that is central to the film. In *State of Siege*, a unique cultural blend is achieved through Theodorakis' Grecian musical sensibilities. Given a South American instrumentation, the wind instruments lend a pleasing, light tonality and Theodorakis' buoyant melodies soar. *Serpico* contrasts the disillusionment of the title character with a pretty yet mildly sad theme with the urban jazz that is associated with the story's Big City environment. The use of contemporary Greek musical styles fit Jules Dassin's *Phaedra* perfectly and contrasts a variety of minor pop melodies with a passionate, fully symphonic concerto motif; its fast-pace and profound melodic lines capturing a dynamic sense of drama and pathos. This set is an excellent gallery of the composer's work for films.

Randall D. Larson

Dimitri Tiomkin

(1894-1979)

The Film Music of Dimitri Tiomkin
1985, Unicorn-Kanchana Records ♪♪♪
album notes: Music: Dimitri Tiomkin; *Orchestra:* The Royal College of Music Orchestra; **Conductor:** Sir David Willcocks; **Featured Musician:** David King, organ.

The Western Film World of Dimitri Tiomkin
1988, Unicorn-Kanchana Records ♪♪
album notes: Music: Dimitri Tiomkin; **Orchestra:** The London Studio Symphony Orchestra, the John McCarthy Singers; **Conductor:** Laurie Johnson; **Featured Musician:** Bob Saker, baritone.

Often "covered" but seldom equalled, Tiomkin is probably one of the few Hollywood composers whose scores can't stand to be recorded by others: the pulse of the tempi, the nuances in the playing, in fact everything in his music seems very difficult to duplicate. Case in point: these two recordings, both superbly recorded, yet both ultimately failing to make the grade because the orchestra playing often sounds too studied, too reverential. Where the western music should pulsate and be thrilling, it simply exists, with *High Noon* sounding by far the least exciting.

Didier C. Deutsch

Lost Horizon: The Classic Film Scores of Dimitri Tiomkin
1989, RCA Victor Records ♪♪♪
album notes: Music: Dimitri Tiomkin; **Orchestra:** The National Philharmonic Orchestra; **Conductor:** Charles Gerhardt.

Somewhat more successful is this recording in the Classic Film Score Series, with Charles Gerhardt leading the National Philharmonic for producer George Korngold. Wisely, they chose to avoid the "standard" western music with which Tiomkin distinguished himself at the height of his career (with the exception of *The Big Sky*, which had no equivalent elsewhere), to concentrate on the more unusual "lost" score for *Lost Horizon*, which

They Know the Score

Mark Snow

[*X-Files* creator] Chris Carter was really hands on with the music at the beginning. I think when they did the pilot they tracked it with all kinds of stuff, and they had music everywhere. It was more of the hypnotic, repetitive, Philip Glass minimal stuff, [Brian] Eno—and real stringy, supportive, atmospheric stuff. That just got to be the sound of it at the beginning. As the years went by, [Carter] just let it go, and anything I wanted to try or experiment with was fine. He never had any problem with that. Although, they do come over and sit here and watch every show with picture and the music. They haven't missed one!

Courtesy of **Film Score Monthly**

gave the album its title. The other selections in the set, however, sound more like fillers.

Didier C. Deutsch

The Film Music of Dimitri Tiomkin
1988, Columbia Records ♪♪♪♪
album notes: Music: Dimitri Tiomkin; **Conductor:** Dimitri Tiomkin

A collection of soundtrack themes and vocals by Frankie Laine (whose success with "Do Not Forsake Me" in *High Noon* led him to perform many other title songs for Tiomkin), which may be hard to get but which should be in any collection. Presented somewhat chronologically, the set includes selections from *Wild Is the Wind, The Old Man and the Sea, The Alamo, The Guns of Navarone, 55 Days at Peking*, and *The Fall of the Roman Empire*, in soundtrack performances culled from the Columbia vaults. While sonics may sometimes leave a lot to be desired (frequently due to the age of the source material), performances, with the composer conducting various studio orchestras, has the ring of authenticity. The CD was deleted from the Sony catalogue, but may still be available at specialty shops.

Didier C. Deutsch

High Noon
1997, RCA/Germany 🎵🎵
album notes: Music: Dimitri Tiomkin; **Orchestra:** The Rundfunk Symphony Orchestra of Berlin; **Conductor:** Lawrence Foster.

Also released to commemorate the 100th anniversary of the movies, this CD should have been a welcome addition to any collection. Unfortunately, the Rundfunk Symphony Orchestra of Berlin, conducted by Lawrence Foster, shows little if no affinity for this type of music in general, and for the specific timings in Tiomkin's scores in particular.

More so than any other composer, Tiomkin is always difficult to perform: his music, moving from light, almost ethereal crescendi, to masterful fortissimi, is full of nuances that few conductors actually appreciate or know how to handle.

In fact, with a few exceptions, his music is better left to him, as his soundtrack albums often reveal. A quick comparison between the original soundtracks of *The Alamo* and *55 Days at Peking*, both of which are available on CD, with this CD show that the Rundfunk Orchestra is totally out of its element here. It's all the more unfortunate that *Cyrano de Bergerac* is not available anywhere else. But since this is an import, hard to come by, don't waste your time or money.

Didier C. Deutsch

Armando Trovaioli

La musica di Armando Trovaioli per il cinema di Ettore Scola
1995, RCA Records/Italy 🎵🎵🎵🎵
album notes: Music: Armando Trovaioli; **Conductor:** Armando Trovaioli.

Another Italian composer with a long (and interesting) track record, Armando Trovaioli has scored many successful films, and, in the course of a busy and illustrious career, has enjoyed several long-term artistic relationships with some of his country's best film directors. Tops among those was his association with Ettore Scola, who admits that music in his films has to play an important, integrated role and cannot be "casual."

Starting with *Se permettete, parliamo di donne* (*If You Don't Mind, Let's Talk about Women*), in 1964, Trovajoli and Scola worked on 17 films, covering the whole gamut, from comedies (*Maccheroni, La piu bella serata della mia vita*), to swashbucklers (*Il viaggio di Capitan Fracassa*), contemporary dramas (*Il commissario Pepe, Dramma della gelosia*), and romantic films (*Passione d'amore, Romanzo di un giovane povero*).

This 2-CD compilation contains many cues from all these films, in a vivid display of the composer's creativity, which goes from the grandiloquent to the soulful, from the jocular to the lyrical.

It is a great collection that says a lot about a composer who deserves to be discovered and totally enjoyed.

Didier C. Deutsch

Vangelis

(1943-)

Vangelis: Themes
1989, Polydor Records 🎵🎵🎵🎵
album notes: Music: Vangelis Papathanassiou.

This anthology presents a series of Vangelis tracks that have been featured in films and television. "L'Enfant" is a pleasantly rhythmic piano piece from Frederic Rossif's TV series *Opera Sauvage* (but is probably better known for its use in *The Year of Living Dangerously*). The sultry saxophone and synths of "Love Theme from Blade Runner" perfectly evoke the futuristic film noir world of that film. Also heard in *Blade Runner,* "Memories of Green," which is originally from Vangelis's 1979 album *See You Later,* is included on this album as well.

A number of tracks are also available here that were never released as soundtrack albums. The main title from *The Bounty* is a pulsing, sultry evocation of the Tahitian setting of the film. The theme from *Missing* is a delicate piano melody, which reflects the tenderness and tragedy of Costa-Gavras' political expose. One of Vangelis's most beautiful works also features the exotic and ethereal waltz "La Petite Fille de la Mer" (from Rossif's film *L'Apocalypse des Animaux*). The album closes with two tracks from Vangelis's popular *Chariots of Fire,* the "Title Music" and "Five Circles." In all, *Vangelis: Themes* is a very rewarding compilation of work by one of the best and most unique voices in film music today.

Paul Andrew MacLean

Sir William Walton

(1902-1983)

Sir William Walton: Hamlet/As You Like It Film Music, vol. 1
1990, Chandos Records 🎵🎵🎵🎵🎵
album notes: Music: Sir William Walton; **Orchestra:** The Academy of St. Martin-in-the-Fields; **Conductor:** Sir Neville Marriner.

Sir William Walton: Battle of Britain Suite Film Music, vol. 2
1990, Chandos Records 🎵🎵🎵🎵🎵
album notes: Music: Sir William Walton; **Orchestra:** The Academy of St. Martin-in-the-Fields; **Conductor:** Sir Neville Marriner.

Sir William Walton: Henry V Film Music, vol. 3
1990, Chandos Records 🎵🎵🎵🎵🎵
album notes: Music: Sir William Walton; **Orchestra:** Choristers of Westminster Cathedral, the Academy of St. Martin-in-the-Fields Chorus and Orchestra; **Conductor:** Sir Neville Marriner.

Sir William Walton: Richard III/Macbeth/Major Barbara Film Music, vol. 4

1991, Chandos Records 🎵🎵🎵🎵🎵

album notes: Music: Sir William Walton; **Orchestra:** The Academy of St. Martin-in-the-Fields; **Conductor:** Sir Neville Marriner; **Featured Musician:** Ian Watson, harpsichord, organ.

This four-volume anthology of the film works of Sir William Walton is a true bonanza for collectors. Not only does it focus on a composer whose output has been quite significant, but it does so with all the trappings usually associated with important classical releases—authoritative performances by a major orchestra, the Academy of St. Martin-in-the-Fields, conducted by Sir Neville Marriner, in superb digital sonics—that should make Chandos proud of its technical and artistic achievements.

One of England's great "classic" composers, Walton often wrote for the movies, particularly in a creative collaboration with Laurence Olivier, which resulted in several sensational screen renditions of the epic plays of William Shakespeare—*Hamlet, As You Like It, Henry V, Richard III,* and *Macbeth,* all of them covered in volumes 1, 2, and 4 in this series, with guest apperances by Sir John Gielgud and Christopher Plummer.

Casting a different light on Walton's film output, volume 3 turns its attention to the war films, with stirring renditions of the scores for *Escape Me Never* and *Battle of Britain,* in addition to the composer's *Wartime Sketchbook* (a compilation of cues created for such films as *Went the Day Well, Next of Kin,* and *The Foreman Went to France,* all of them related to the ongoing conflict), and his memorable *Spitfire Prelude and Fugue.* Like the other three volumes, it is a remarkable effort that takes film music to its utmost quality level, on a par with classical music.

Didier C. Deutsch

William Walton: Film Music

1987, EMI Records 🎵🎵🎵🎵♥

album notes: Music: Sir William Walton; **Orchestra:** The London Philharmonic Orchestra and Choir; **Conductor:** Carl Davis.

This superb album featuring the London Philharmonic Orchestra and Choir features some of the finest film music ever written, opening with a sublime suite from William Walton's score to Laurence Olivier's film of *Henry V,* a triumph from its beautiful pastoral opening to the moving "Death of Falstaff" and the aching lyricism of its courtship music, climaxing in the thrilling "Agincourt Song," a mammoth choral piece supported by an exultant, sinuous string line that's one of the most satisfying evocations of martial triumph ever written. Almost as good is Walton's buzzing, open-aired "Spitfire Music," which was written for an unused score for the 1960s war film *The Battle of Britain.* Also featured is a brief interlude from *Troilus and Cressida,* Walton's rousing, full-blooded pastoral music for *As You Like It,* and the giddy "March" for *A History of the English Speaking Peoples.* It's as bracing an accompaniment to scenes of the English countryside as anyone could hope to hear.

Jeff Bond

Ken Wannberg

The Film Music of Ken Wannberg: Volume 1

1995, Prometheus Records/Belgium 🎵🎵🎵🎵

album notes: Music: Ken Wannberg; **Orchestra:** The National Philharmonic Orchestra; **Conductor:** Ken Wannberg.

To the average filmgoer, Ken Wannberg's name means very little. The cognoscenti, however, know him as one of John Williams's closest associates, a music editor with a deft sense of what the maestro wants and needs. But Wannberg is also a composer in his own right, and Prometheus Records, an independent Belgian label, has wisely chosen to correct the wrong by dedicating three volumes to his music. Both *The Philadelphia Experiment* and *Mother Lode,* covered in the first volume, allow Wannberg to show his mettle in scores that are interestingly varied and different from each other.

Mother Lode, written in 1982, is an adventure film starring Charlton Heston in a dual role as golddigger brothers in the wilds of British Columbia on the opposite sides of the law. *The Philadelphia Experiment,* composed two years later, is a time-warp science fiction film about a top secret U.S. Navy experiment to try and make ships invisible to enemy radar during World War II.

Both scores reveal in Wannberg a composer with a solid descriptive bend, whose themes overflow with catchy melodies and make for pleasant listening when the scores are taken at their face value, out of context.

Didier C. Deutsch

The Film Music of Ken Wannberg: Volume 2

1995, Prometheus Records/Belgium 🎵🎵🎵🎵

album notes: Music: Ken Wannberg; **Orchestra:** The National Philharmonic Orchestra, the Little Mountain Studio Symphony Orchestra; **Conductor:** Ken Wannberg; **Featured Musician:** Tommy Morgan, harmonica.

The Film Music of Ken Wannberg: Volume 3

1995, Prometheus Records/Belgium 🎵🎵🎵🎵

album notes: Music: Ken Wannberg; **Orchestra:** The European Studio Symphony Orchestra; **Conductor:** Ken Wannberg.

Volumes 2 and 3 complete Prometheus Records' trilogy of Ken Wannberg scores, the series that started with the release of *The Philadelphia Experiment* and *Mother Lode* (see above). The second volume is a collection of two western scores, starting off with the outstanding music to the Kirk Douglas/James

Coburn comedy *Draw!* Douglas plays an aging gunfighter who simply wants to get out of town to retire, but his likewise aging adversary, lawman Coburn, gets caught up in the town's lynch mob mentality. The score follows in the footsteps of earlier genre work with its big western sound, but Wannberg plays up the absurdity of two old men who can't escape their respective reputations. The second score is for a 1988 television remake of John Ford's classic *Red River*. This time, *Gunsmoke's* James Arness is in John Wayne's saddle, driving hard cattle and step-son Bruce Boxleitner from Oklahoma to Missouri. Wannberg wisely doesn't attempt to compete with Dimitri Tiomkin's classic score for the 1948 original. His music serves the film quite well, though this tepid version certainly couldn't offer Wannberg the kind of inspiration Tiomkin found in the John Ford directed original.

The last CD in the Wannberg trilogy features three very different scores. *The Amateur* is a European-flavored cold war thriller. *Of Unknown Origin* is a horror score he composed for *Rambo: First Blood II* director George Pan Cosmatos, with *RoboCop's* Peter Weller battling an enormous rat. All are excellently written pieces, but the best is saved for last, a laid back film noir score for the Art Carney/Lily Tomlin comedic murder mystery *The Late Show*. Vaguely John Barry-ish in tone, the score does well to capture eccentric nature of Tomlin's character and Carney's just-about-over-the-hill detective. The CD booklet for the third volume contains excerpts from my 1995 interview with the composer that was published in the March issue of *Soundtrack!* magazine.

David Hirsch

Franz Waxman
(1906-1967)

The Film Music of Franz Waxman
1990, RCA Records ♫♫♫♫♫
album notes: Music: Franz Waxman; **Conductor:** Franz Waxman.

Another glorious name from the early days of Hollywood, Franz Waxman was born in Konigshutte, Germany, and came to film music at the age of 24, when he was asked to orchestrate Frederick Hollander's score for *The Blue Angel*. As the threat of the Nazi movement grew, Waxman left his native country in 1934 and moved to Hollywood to work on the Jerome Kern score for *Music in the Air*. The following year he created his first major contribution to the screen when he wrote the seminal music for *Bride of Frankenstein*, which led to his being named music director for Universal.

In a career that saw him at MGM and Warner Bros., Waxman wrote many important scores that rank among the best works ever to come out of Hollywood, including *Rebecca* (1940), *Dr.*

Jekyll and Mr. Hyde and *Suspicion*(both 1941), *Objective, Burma!* (1945), *Sorry, Wrong Number* (1948), *Sunset Boulevard* (1950), *A Place in the Sun* (1951), *Prince Valiant* (1954), *The Spirit of St. Louis* and *Peyton Place* (both 1957), and *The Nun's Story* (1959), among many others.

The above compilation, assembled from the soundtracks conducted by the composer, covers five late '50-early '60s films, *The Spirit of St. Louis, Peyton Place, Sayonara* (1957), *My Geisha,* and *Hemingway's Adventures of a Young Man* (both 1962). Frequently rising above the pedestrian topics of the films (*My Geisha, Hemingway's Adventures . . .*), or taking the exulted stories to even greater heights (*The Spirit of St. Louis*), Waxman always provided the right musical element that singled out the films and his scores from the masses. Particularly evocative, the score for *Peyton Place* has become a classic in its own right.

Didier C. Deutsch

Sunset Boulevard: The Classic Film Scores of Franz Waxman
1989, RCA Victor Records ♫♫♫♫♫
album notes: Music: Franz Waxman; **Orchestra:** The National Philharmonic Orchestra; **Conductor:** Charles Gerhardt.

This exquisite volume in RCA's Classic Film Scores series finds Charles Gerhardt and the National Philharmonic in exciting renditions of some of the scores created by Waxman. Both *Prince Valiant* and *A Place in the Sun* (a score that deserves a full CD treatment) are particular highlights in this set, with *Sunset Boulevard* and *Rebecca* the appropriate complements to this exhilarating collection. As is the norm in the entire series, the sonics and performances are exceptional.

Didier C. Deutsch

Legends of Hollywood: Franz Waxman, vol. 1
1990, Varèse Sarabande ♫♫♫♫♫
album notes: Music: Franz Waxman; **Orchestra:** The Queensland Symphony Orchestra; **Conductor:** Richard Mills; **Featured Musicians:** Piers Lane, piano; Geoffrey Spiller, trumpet.

Legends of Hollywood: Franz Waxman, vol. 2
1991, Varèse Sarabande ♫♫♫♫♫
album notes: Music: Franz Waxman; **Orchestra:** The Queensland Symphony Orchestra; **Conductor:** Richard Mills; **Featured Musician:** Peter Rosenfelt, piano.

Legends of Hollywood: Franz Waxman, vol. 3
1994, Varèse Sarabande ♫♫♫♫♫
album notes: Music: Franz Waxman; **Orchestra:** The Queensland Symphony Orchestra; **Conductor:** Richard Mills.

Legends of Hollywood: Franz Waxman, vol. 4
1994, Varèse Sarabande ♫♫♫♫♫
album notes: Music: Franz Waxman; **Orchestra:** The Queensland Symphony Orchestra; **Conductor:** Richard Mills.

Franz Waxman **(Archive Photos, Inc.)**

With these four CDs, Varèse-Sarabande has provided a wealth of hitherto unrecorded music by one of the early masters of Hollywood film music in fine new recordings by the Queensland Symphony Orchestra. Waxman's gifts for melody and orchestration served him well for more than four decades of film scoring, from the quiet mysterioso of *The Devil Doll* to the grand, boisterous symphonics of *Prince Valiant, Captain Courageous,* and the swashbuckling adventure of *Anne of the Indies*; the inspired melodies of *The Silver Chalice* to the dark, relentless rhythms of *Night and the City*; and the inventive orchestrations of *The Bride of Frankenstein* to the hayseed Americana of *Huckleberry Finn* and the meticulous comedy of *Mr. Roberts*.

Cues are uniformly long (excepting for a 50-second fanfare from *Task Force*) and mostly presented in suite form, allowing for sufficient development of the material. Thorough notes accompany each CD booklet, describing the films and the cues included. Coupled with the Charles Gerhardt/National Philharmonic recording on RCA, we now have a relatively complete musical quintet of Waxman's best—and most unforgettable—film music. The only real conspicuous omission from the set would be a suite from Waxman's excellent score for the Spencer Tracy *Dr. Jekyll and Mr. Hyde*. Even so, this is another one of those desert-island CD sets. Don't be stranded without them.

Randall D. Larson

Roy Webb

The Curse of the Cat People: The Film Music of Roy Webb
1995, Cloud Nine Records 🎵🎵🎵🎵🎵
album notes: Music: Roy Webb.

Obscured by the fame of such Hollywood legends as Steiner, Korngold, Tiomkin, and Newman, RKO's main composer Roy Webb has been unfairly neglected by film music history. His compositions easily rivaled that of Steiner and company. In the first original soundtrack collection of his music, 73 minutes of music from 13 films have been restored from the composer's personal acetate archives. The quality is surprisingly good considering the age and source of the music.

As for the music, it's uniformly excellent. From the malevolent Boris Karloff chords from *Bedlam* to the thrilling, relentless violin prelude to film noir's *Crossfire* and the surging, brass chords that signify danger in *Mighty Joe Young* and the splendidly swashbuckling *Sinbad the Sailor*; the euphonious romantic crescendos of Hitchcock's *Notorious* to nightmarish moods of Val Lewton's *Death Ship* and his gently mystical *Curse of the Cat People,* all were provided with excellent musical scores. Webb was a great lyricist, sharing much of Steiner's melody, rhythm and furious musical action. Webb's memorable music is well-saved on recording. Most cues tend to be short—minute-and-a-half preludes or title

cues and 3 or 4-minute suites from more than half of the films represented—though enough are sufficiently elongated. While I would have liked to have heard more long cues, samples of Webb's western and war scores, and more of Webb's Val Lewton film music, what we do have is a fine gallery of Webb's versatile and lovely film music. A 16-page booklet provides excellent analysis of each cue, and a perceptive look at Webb himself.

Randall Larson

John Williams
(1932-   )

Aisle Seat
1982, Philips Records 🎵🎵🎵🎵
album notes: Orchestra: The Boston Pops Orchestra; **Conductor:** John Williams.

John Williams's name has been linked to so many great films that it is always a joy to find him conducting an orchestra (in this case the excellent Boston Pops) in a selection of his own themes. But the pleasure is also multiplied when he chooses, as is the case here, to "cover" scores written by others. His treatments of Vangelis's theme for *Chariots of Fire* and Dimitri Tiomkin's seldom-heard-these-days *Friendly Persuasion* are prime examples, though one could also include such unlikely choices (at least in an instrumental album) as *Singing in the Rain, The Wizard of Oz,* or *Meet Me in St. Louis*. Another interesting selection here is the theme from *Yes, Giorgio,* a rather uninspired film starring Luciano Pavarotti. The only reservation about the set itself is that since it was an early effort by Williams and the Pops, there are subsequently recorded albums that are much better overall. Consider this one as a mere filler if you already own the others.

Didier C. Deutsch

The Hollywood Sound
1997, Sony Classical 🎵🎵🎵🎵🎵
album notes: Orchestra: The London Symphony Orchestra; **Conductor:** John Williams; **Featured Musician:** Grover Washington, Jr.

This collection of familiar themes from the movies (the set is subtitled "John Williams Conducts the Academy Awards' Best Scores," which pretty much sums it up) is interesting for several reasons. The first, of course, is because Williams himself is wielding the baton in yet another compilation that includes some of his own compositions (*E.T., Jaws, Star Wars*), something that always adds a touch of authority to any recording; another is because he is also paying tribute to some of the best known themes ever composed for the screen, including *Lawrence of Arabia, The Adventures of Robin Hood, Out of Africa, Dances with Wolves, Spellbound* and *The Best Years of Our Lives*. Yet another reason to like this CD can be found in the polished performance by the London Symphony Orchestra, probably one of the best group of players for this type of music. But the real joy here is to hear Grover Washington, Jr. in such august company tackling the suite from *A Place in the Sun* in a performance that exudes sensuality and vibrancy. Next to this kind of music, with all due respect, the themes from *Pocahontas* and *Beauty and the Beast,* while quite enjoyable in their own right, seem a mite tame and the only weak spots in the entire CD.

Didier C. Deutsch

John Williams By Request . . .
1987, Philips Records 🎵🎵🎵🎵

album notes: Music: John Williams; **Orchestra:** The Boston Pops Orchestra; **Conductor:** John Williams.

This is a collector's dream! The set, with the Boston Pops smartly conducted by the composer, features nothing but solid gold hits from the fertile pen of John Williams, up to the time when he switched labels and began recording for Sony Classical (which explains the absence of some of his most recent contributions to the screen). While one can hardly dispute the choice of material here (only familiar titles could apply!), the plum of the collection is the *Cowboys* overture, until recently the only recording of this rousing number available anywhere. Anyone interested in the music of Williams, and in having the maestro's best-known compositions on one CD and conducted by the man himself needs look no further.

Didier C. Deutsch

John Williams: The Spielberg/Williams Collaboration
1990, Sony Classical 🎵🎵🎵

album notes: Music: John Williams; **Orchestra:** The Boston Pops Orchestra; **Conductor:** John Williams.

As the story goes, when Steven Spielberg, then an obscure scriptwriter with great ambitions struggling to make a living in the Hollywood studios, heard the score for Mark Rydell's *The Reivers,* he decided that John Williams would be his composer of choice. Thus began the Spielberg/Williams collaboration celebrated in this set 1990 release, already incomplete since it doesn't include selections from *Jurassic Park* or *Schindler's List,* composed after this album was recorded (that should be for a possible volume 2).

Spielberg's first effort as a director was *The Sugarland Express,* made in 1974, a throbbing suspenser with a devastating sense of humor, here represented by its "Main Theme." He subsequently illustrated himself with some major blockbusters—the *Indiana Jones* trilogy, *Jaws, Close Encounters, Empire of the Sun,* and *E.T.,* all of them included here through some of their most recognizable themes.

Didier C. Deutsch

They Know the Score
Hans Zimmer

I know one thing about any composer today, and that is that they're sitting there with this film in front of them and they have no idea what they're going to do, and the only thing you can do is sit there and open up the veins and bleed all over the page.

***Courtesy of* Film Score Monthly**

John Williams: Music for Stage and Screen
1994, Sony Classical 🎵🎵🎵🎵

album notes: Music: John Williams, Aaron Copland; **Orchestra:** The Boston Pops Orchestra; **Conductor:** John Williams; **Featured Musicians:** Tim Morrison, trumpet; Laurence Thorstenberg, English horn.

As the score for Mark Rydell's *The Reivers* established early, John Williams was strongly influenced by Aaron Copland, and while the stylistic comparison between the two stopped soon after, when Williams found his own voice, it is interesting to hear in this set conducted by Williams some of the film music composed by Copland (particularly the several selections from *The Red Pony,* which one never tires of hearing) juxtaposed to Williams's own suite from *The Reivers,* narrated as in the film by Burgess Meredith. The other selections (from *Born on the Fourth of July* and *Quiet City*) further enhance the similarities and differences between Copland and Williams, and present the ideal programming for a peaceful Sunday morning, if one feels so inclined.

Didier C. Deutsch

Out of This World
1983, Philips Records 🎵🎵🎵🎵

album notes: Orchestra: The Boston Pops Orchestra; **Conductor:** John Williams; **Featured Musician:** Chester Schmitz, tuba.

The "outer space" concept behind this album enabled John Williams and the Boston Pops to fly high and deliver some rousing music written for a variety of out-of-this-world film epics, including Williams's own *E.T.* and *Return of the Jedi,* Jerry Goldsmith's *Alien* and *Star Trek: The Motion Picture,* and (oh, surprise!) Stu Philips's "Main Theme" from the unjustly-neglected *Battlestar Galactica* and Marius Constant's theme from *The Twilight Zone.* Opening the set, of course, is Richard Strauss's introduction to *Also Sprach Zarathustra,* which got its screen credentials when it was used to great effect in the granddaddy of all contemporary outer-space adventures, *2001: A Space Odyssey.*

Didier C. Deutsch

Pops in Space
1980, Philips Records 🎵🎵🎵🎵

album notes: Music: John Williams; **Orchestra:** The Boston Pops Orchestra; **Conductor:** John Williams.

More space-related music courtesy of John Williams and the Boston Pops, though the selections this time come strictly from the composer's own scores for *Superman, The Empire Strikes Back, Star Wars,* and *Close Encounters of the Third Kind.* The "Suite" from that last film is the set's icing-on-the-cake, as it includes music heard in the so-called "Special Edition" (namely the last scene in which contactee Richard Dreyfuss finds himself in the spaceship) and available nowhere else. Indeed a real bonus for fans and collectors alike.

Didier C. Deutsch

Salute to Hollywood
1988, Philips Records 🎵🎵🎵🎵

album notes: Orchestra: The Boston Pops Orchestra; **Conductor:** John Williams.

This winning entry in the John Williams/Boston Pops catalog is particularly notable in that it is a tribute to Hollywood film music as seen by one of its most proficient exponents. The sole Williams entry, interestingly, consists of two selections from his Oscar-winning score for *The Witches of Eastwick,* a pleasant diversion which yielded the sardonic "Devil's Dance" and "Balloon Sequence." Three long suites offer tributes to Oscar-winning themes, Judy Garland, and Fred Astaire, in a program that may seem evident at first but that has its many enjoyable moments. The odd choice in this collection, if favoritism may be shown, is the mercifully short "Somewhere Out There," from James Horner's score for *An American Tail.* With so many other great themes available, from so many other great composers, this seems like a bit of a waste. Don't let it deter you from enjoying the rest of the set, though.

Didier C. Deutsch

Schindler's List: The Classic Film Music of John Williams
1995, Silva Screen Records 🎵🎵🎵🎵

album notes: Music: John Williams; **Orchestra:** The City of Prague Philharmonic; **Conductor:** Paul Bateman; **Featured Musicians:** Paul Bateman, piano; Petr Nedobilsky, violin; Jaroslava Eliasova, piano, harpsichord; Miroslav Kejmar, cornet; Antonin Novak, violin.

With so many other recordings of John Williams's music available, and with the composer himself covering most of his own ground, one might truthfully question the necessity for yet another compilation, particularly one conducted by someone

else. Don't blame the folks at Silva Screen for trying to cash in on a good thing. Actually the set is really not that bad, and if it includes many themes that are to be found on numerous other compilations, it has the merit of proposing some that are harder to come by—like the "End Titles" from *Presumed Innocent,* the "March" from *1941,* and the "Finale" from *Family Plot.* The rest may be routine fare, but it is played with great gusto by the Prague Philharmonic, and all things considered it all adds up to a perfectly enjoyable recording, with particularly great dynamics to make it sound ever better.

Didier C. Deutsch

Star Wars/Close Encounters: The Classic Film Scores of John Williams
1989, RCA Victor Records 🎵🎵🎵

album notes: Music: John Williams; **Orchestra:** The National Philharmonic Orchestra; **Conductor:** Charles Gerhardt.

After having covered the music of pioneers like Erich-Wolfgang Korngold, Alfred Newman, Dimitri Tiomkin, Miklos Rozsa, and Max Steiner, it probably made sense that Charles Gerhardt and producer George Korngold should have turned their attention to the classic film scores of John Williams, who was clearly inspired by his predecessors in the field. The only problem, of course, is while many of the works covered in the earlier sets in the series were not readily available anywhere else, Williams recorded his own scores, sometimes with greater drive and excitement than can be found in this routine album. Not to take anything away from the care and attention that evidently went into the production of this CD; the long suite from *Close Encounters* is particularly well put together, and the National Philharmonic generally gives a suitably polished performance. But it seems a bit redundant to get this recording when the original soundtracks are available, particularly now that they have been remastered and often feature additional music.

Didier C. Deutsch

Music from the Films of Steven Spielberg
1997, Silva Screen 🎵🎵

album notes: Music: John Williams; **Orchestra:** The City of Prague Philharmonic; **Conductor:** Paul Bateman.

Much as the City of Prague Philharmonic is to be commended for its valiant efforts, this CD is a waste: John Williams himself has recorded (and conducted) these excerpts several times, with often stunning musical and sonic results, and any attempt to emulate what he has done is bound to end up as a second best. This again is not meant to denigrate what the orchestra and Paul Bateman have tried to do here, but as good as this CD sounds, it may well have been for naught.

Didier C. Deutsch

John Williams (Archive Photos, Inc.)

Close Encounters: The Essential John Williams Film Music Collection
1999, Silva Screen Records/U.K. ♫♫♫♫
album notes: Music: John Williams; **Orchestra:** The City of Prague Philharmonic and the Crouch End Festival Chorus; **Conductor:** Paul Bateman and Nic Raine.

Unlike the above release, this 2-CD set has a lot to offer, and that places it immediately on a higher level of desirability. Even if we dispense with the themes and suites already available on other packages, the set contains so much music that is more difficult to come by that its inclusion here may be an answer to many collectors' silent prayers. To wit, the selections from *Hook,* the long suites from *The Rare Breed* and *Black Sunday,* the themes from *Family Plot* and *The River,* and the "Overture" to *The Cowboys,* which, while not a novelty, is so much fun to listen to, no matter where or what. What the set also perfectly reveals is the sheer musicality in Williams' compositions, the abundance of melodic material that unfortunately seems to be lacking in a lot of other composers' efforts. Listening to Williams' music immediately after the works of Mark Snow, for instance, is like having trying to compare a feast with a MacBurger. Both may be filling, but the first is so unctuous and the second so bland . . . In this richly-detailed collection of themes, the music flows with great vitality and captures the listener's imagination, keeping him rapt and interested, something Snow's (or his followers') cannot hope to emulate. And while there may be some redundancies here (the setpieces from the blockbuster films may be too much of a good thing after a while—familiarity breeding contempt), this set is a delight that should satisfy even the most demanding collector. Performance by the City of Prague is superlative, as usual, with the spacious, properly reverbed sonics adding a lot to one's enjoyment.

Didier C. Deutsch

Victor Young
(1900-1956)

The Classic Film Music of Victor Young
1998, Marco Polo Records ♫♫♫♫
album notes: Music: Victor Young; **Orchestra:** The Moscow Symphony Orchestra and Chorus; **Conductor:** William T. Stromberg.

Another superlative set from Marco Polo that actually makes you glad there are independent labels ready to deal with classic film music the way it deserves to be treated. Poorly appreciated, even today, by most fans of film music, Victor Young is mostly remembered for the music he wrote for *Shane,* the Alan Ladd western that yielded the wonderfully atmospheric "Call Of The Faraway Hills," and for the Michael Todd all-star extravaganza, *Around the World in 80 Days.* Yet, in a career that encompassed Broadway, the pop field, and the movies, these landmark scores are but a fraction of Young's enormous productivity and versatility.

This set aims to slightly correct this oversight with a collection of themes written for four important films, Cecil B. de Mille's 1952 big top tribute *The Greatest Show on Earth;* the 1944 ingenious ghost thriller *The Uninvited,* informed by the great pop tune, "Stella by Starlight"; the 1939 Dave Fleischer animated feature, *Gulliver's Travels;* and the 1950 *Bright Leaf,* which starred Gary Cooper as a tobacco farmer, and Lauren Bacall.

Showing varied facets of Young's artistry, writing in four different moods, the recording additionally provides literate and informative liner notes that place all the cues in their proper perspective within the films themselves and within Young' career. Overall performance by the Moscow Symphony Orchestra is polished and totally authentic, with broad, wide-ranging sonics adding to the pleasure. The only problem here are the frequently low levels in the recording, which can be adjusted by boosting the volume on your player, a minor point.

Didier C. Deutsch

Shane: A Tribute to Victor Young
1996, Koch International Classics ♫♫♫♫
album notes: Music: Victor Young.

One of the great unsung heroes of Hollywood film music, Victor Young is slowly getting the recognition that has eluded him for so long. This superb tribute, which regroups several of the themes he created for the movies, is one of the first steps in the right direction. While most filmgoers remember the celebrated "Call of the Faraway Hills," from *Shane,* that score has long been overdue for a complete overhaul, along the lines of Jerome Moross's *The Big Country* or Elmer Bernstein's *The Magnificent Seven.* Its appearance here, in abbreviated form, is one of the great joys in this set, even if one misses the atmospheric ambience Young himself created in his own reading of the main theme, with its plaintive saxophone evoking the nostalgic feel of the far away hills.

And while *For Whom the Bell Tolls, The Quiet Man, Around the World,* and *Samson and Delilah* are all available on compact disc, Kaufman and the New Zealand Symphony Orchestra find new reasons to listen to these scores again and enjoy them for the sheer magic they spin. The *Tribute to Victor Young,* arranged and orchestrated by Henry Mancini, regroups the themes from several other scores, including *Golden Earrings, When I Fall in Love, Sweet Sue, Stella by Starlight,* and *My Foolish Heart.*

Didier C. Deutsch

Hans Zimmer

(1957-)

Hans Zimmer: New Music in Films
1989, Milan Records 🎵🎵🎵🎵

album notes: Music: Hans Zimmer; **Featured Musicians:** Alan Murphy, guitar; Guy Barker, trumpet; Emily Burridge, cello; Gavyn Wright, violin; Fiachra Tranch, keyboards; Charlie Morgan, drums; Hans Zimmer, synthesizers.

Give credit to Hans Zimmer for trying to be innovative, and also for giving other, promising new talent an opportunity to work with him. One might dispute his creative approach, however, and find it lacking is some respects, but his music, well suited for the films which he scores, often displays an attractive bend that translates very well as a pure audio experience, even if it sounds too much like New Age music.

Nothing could be farther apart in tone than the three films represented here, *Burning Secret,* a 1988 romantic melodrama set in turn-of-the-century Vienna; *The Fruit Machine,* also from 1988, directed by Philip Saville; and *Diamond Skulls,* composed in 1989 for a film directed by Nicholas Broomfield, a hip study of sex and violence among the British upperclass. Yet Zimmer found in them the basic elements to create scores that embody each story and its framework, with his reliance on synthesizer textures to enhance acoustic instruments most becoming. The presentation of the first two as long suites, as opposed to shorter individual cues, adds enormously to one's appreciation of the music.

Didier C. Deutsch

musicHound

Soundtracks

Resources and Other Information

Compilation Albums

Books, Magazines, and Newspapers

Web Sites

Record Labels

If you're looking for film, stage, and television music, these compilation albums would be a good place to start.

Actors & Actresses

Arnold: Great Music from the Films of Arnold Schwarzenegger 🎵🎵🎵 (Varése Sarabande, 1993)

Greatest Themes from the Films of Arnold Schwarzenegger 🎵🎵🎵 (Silva America, 1995)

Music from the Films of Audrey Hepburn 🎵 (Giant, 1993)

Music from the Films of Clint Eastwood 🎵🎵 (Silva Screen, 1993)

Music from the Films of Harrison Ford 🎵🎵 (Silva Screen, 1994)

Music from the Films of John Wayne 🎵🎵🎵 (Silva Screen, 1994)

Music from the Films of Kevin Costner 🎵🎵🎵 (Silva America, 1998)

Music from the Films of Mel Gibson 🎵🎵🎵 (Silva America, 1998)

Music from the Films of Sean Connery 🎵🎵🎵 (Silva America, 1998)

Music from the Films of Sylvester Stallone 🎵 (Silva Screen, 1993)

Music from the Films of Tom Cruise 🎵🎵🎵 (Silva Screen, 1994)

A Tribute to Sean Connery 🎵🎵 (edel America, 1994)

Best of the Studios

The Best of Hemdale 🎵🎵🎵 (DCC Compact Classics, 1991)

Disney's 75 Years of Music & Memories 🎵🎵🎵 (Walt Disney, 1998)

The Hammer Comedy Film Music Collection 🎵🎵🎵 (GDI/U.K., 1999)

The Ladykillers: Music from Those Glorious Ealing Films 🎵🎵🎵🎵 (Silva America, 1997)

The Lion's Roar: Classic MGM Film Scores, 1935-1965 🎵🎵🎵🎵 (Rhino, 1999)

Merchant Ivory Productions: 25th Anniversary 🎵🎵🎵🎵 (RCA Victor, 1988)

Miramax Films' Greatest Hits 🎵🎵🎵 (Miramax/Hollywood, 1997)

Music from the Classic Republic Serials: Cliffhangers! 🎵🎵🎵🎵🎵 (Varése Sarabande, 1996)

Warner Bros: 75 Years of Film Music 🎵🎵🎵 (Rhino, 1998)

Blaxploitation

Funk on Film 🎵🎵🎵 (Funk Lab/Chronicles, 1998)

Super Bad on Celluloid: Music from '70s Black Cinema 🎵🎵🎵 (Hip-O, 1998)

The Cincinnati Pops Orchestra

Chiller 🎵🎵🎵 (Telarc, 1989)

A Disney Spectacular 🎵🎵🎵 (Telarc, 1989)

Fantastic Journey 🎵🎵🎵🎵 (Telarc, 1990)

Happy Trails 🎵🎵🎵 (Telarc, 1989)

Hollywood's Greatest Hits: Vol. 1 🎵🎵🎵🎵 (Telarc, 1987)

Hollywood's Greatest Hits: Vol. 2 🎵🎵🎵🎵 (Telarc, 1987)

Movie Love Themes 🎵🎵🎵 (Telarc, 1991)

Puttin' on the Ritz: The Great Hollywood Musicals 🎵🎵🎵 (Telarc, 1995)

Round-Up 🎵🎵🎵 (Telarc, 1986)

Star Tracks 🎵🎵🎵🎵 (Telarc, 1984)

Star Tracks II 🎵🎵🎵🎵 (Telarc, 1987)

Symphonic Star Trek 🎵🎵🎵🎵 (Telarc, 1989)

Time Warp 🎵🎵🎵🎵 (Telarc, 1984)

Victory at Sea and Other Favorites 🎵🎵🎵🎵 (Telarc, 1989)

Directors

Alfred Hitchcock

Alfred Hitchcock: Music from His Films 🎵🎵🎵🎵 (MoMA, 1999)

Alfred Hitchcock 100 Years: A Bernard Herrmann Film Score Tribute 🎵🎵🎵 (Milan, 1999)

Alfred Hitchcock Presents . . . Signatures in Suspense 🎵🎵🎵🎵 (Hip-O, 1999)

Dial M for Murder: A History of Hitchcock 🎵🎵🎵🎵 (Silva Screen, 1993)

Hitchcock: Master of Mayhem 🎵🎵🎵 (Pro-Arte, 1990)

Music from Alfred Hitchcock Films 🎵🎵🎵 (Varése Sarabande, 1985)

To Catch a Thief: A History of Hitchcock II 🎵🎵🎵🎵 (Silva Screen, 1995)

Stanley Kubrick

Music from the Films of Stanley Kubrick 🎵🎵🎵 (Silva America, 1999)

Oliver Stone

The Oliver Stone Connection 🎵🎵🎵🎵 (Hip-O, 1998)

Epics

Cinema Gala: The Epic 🎵🎵🎵🎵 (London, 1988)

Great Epic Film Scores 🎵🎵🎵🎵 (Cloud Nine, 1993)

Warriors of the Silver Screen 🎵🎵🎵🎵🎵 (Silva America, 1997)

Fantasy, Horror, Science Fiction

Alien Invasion: Space and Beyond II 🦴🦴🦴🦴 (Silva Screen, 1998)

The Best of Godzilla 🦴🦴🦴🦴 (GNP Crescendo, 1998)

The Best of Star Trek: 30th Anniversary Special 🦴🦴🦴🦴 (GNP Crescendo, 1998)

The Best of Stephen King: volume 1 🦴🦴 (edel America, 1993)

The Cult Files 🦴🦴🦴🦴 (Silva Screen, 1996)

The Cult Files: Reopened 🦴🦴 (Silva America, 1997)

Digital Space 🦴🦴🦴🦴🦴 (Varése Sarabande, 1985)

The Disasters! Movie Music Album 🦴🦴🦴 (Silva America, 1998)

50 Years of Classic Horror Film Music 🦴🦴🦴🦴 (Silva Screen, 1987)

Horror! 🦴🦴🦴 (Silva Screen, 1996)

Horror Films Collection 🦴🦴🦴🦴 (DRG, 1995)

Monster Mania: Music from the Classic Godzilla Films 🦴🦴🦴🦴 (Varése Sarabande, 1998)

The Monster Movie Music Album 🦴🦴🦴 (Silva Screen. 1998)

The Monster Music of Hans J. Salter & Frank Skinner 🦴🦴🦴🦴 (Marco Polo, 1995)

Monstrous Movie Music 🦴🦴🦴 (Monstrous Movie Music, 1996)

More Monstrous Movie Music 🦴🦴🦴🦴 (Monstrous Movie Music, 1996)

Music from the Hammer Films 🦴🦴🦴🦴 (Silva Screen, 1989)

Sci-Fi at the Movies 🦴🦴🦴🦴 (Label X, 1995)

Sci-Fi's Greatest Hits, Vol. 1 🦴🦴🦴🦴🦴 (TVT, 1999)

Sci-Fi's Greatest Hits, Vol. 2 🦴🦴🦴🦴🦴 (TVT, 1999)

Sci-Fi's Greatest Hits, Vol. 3 🦴🦴🦴🦴🦴 (TVT, 1999)

Sci-Fi's Greatest Hits, Vol. 4 🦴🦴🦴🦴🦴 (TVT, 1999)

Star Trek, Vol. 1 🦴🦴🦴 (GNP Crescendo, 1985)

Star Trek, Vol. 2 🦴🦴🦴🦴🦴 (GNP Crescendo, 1991)

Star Trek, Vol. 3 🦴🦴🦴🦴 (GNP Crescendo, 1992)

Star Trek: The Next Generation, Vol. 1 🦴🦴🦴 (GNP Crescendo, 1988)

Star Trek: The Next Generation, Vol. 2 🦴🦴🦴🦴 (GNP Crescendo, 1991)

Star Trek: The Next Generation, Vol. 3 🦴🦴🦴 (GNP Crescendo, 1992)

Themes from Classic Science Fiction, Fantasy and Horror Films 🦴🦴🦴🦴 (Varése Sarabande, 1993)

The Towering Inferno and Other Disaster Classics 🦴🦴🦴🦴 (Varése Sarabande, 1999)

Vampire Circus: The Essential Vampire Theme Collection 🦴🦴🦴🦴 (Silva Screen, 1993)

Film Noir

Classic Film Noir Themes and Scenes 🦴🦴🦴🦴 (Rhino, 1997)

Film Series

The Batman Trilogy 🦴🦴 (Varése Sarabande, 1997)

The Best of James Bond: 30th Anniversary Limited Edition 🦴🦴🦴🦴 (EMI, 1992)

Cinema Gala: James Bond 007 🦴🦴 (London, 1988)

Cinema Gala: The Third Man Film Favorites 🦴🦴 (London, 1988)

The Essential James Bond 🦴 (Silva Screen, 1994)

Our Man in R.O.M.E. 🦴🦴🦴🦴 (Ceraton Lifestyle Records/Germany, 1999)

Sherlock Holmes: Classic Themes from 221B Baker Street (Varése Sarabande, 1996)

General Broadway

Another Openin' Another Show: Broadway Overtures 🦴🦴🦴🦴 (Sony Broadway, 1993)

Celebrate Broadway, Vol. 1: Sing Happy! 🦴🦴🦴🦴 (RCA Victor, 1994)

Celebrate Broadway, Vol. 2: You Gotta Have a Gimmick! 🦴🦴🦴🦴 (RCA Victor, 1994)

Celebrate Broadway, Vol. 3: Lullaby of Broadway 🦴🦴🦴🦴 (RCA Victor, 1994)

Celebrate Broadway, Vol. 4: Overtures 🦴🦴🦴🦴 (RCA Victor, 1994)

Celebrate Broadway, Vol. 5: Hello, Young Lovers 🦴🦴🦴🦴 (RCA Victor, 1994)

Celebrate Broadway, Vol. 6: Beautiful Girls 🦴🦴🦴🦴 (RCA Victor, 1994)

Celebrate Broadway, Vol. 7: Kids! 🦴🦴🦴🦴 (RCA Victor, 1994)

Celebrate Broadway, Vol. 8: Duets 🦴🦴🦴🦴 (RCA Victor, 1995)

Celebrate Broadway, Vol. 9: Gotta Dance! 🦴🦴🦴🦴 (RCA Victor, 1995)

Celebrate Broadway, Vol. 10: Best Musicals! 🦴🦴🦴🦴 (RCA Victor, 1995)

Embraceable You: Broadway in Love 🦴🦴🦴🦴 (Sony Broadway, 1993)

The Party's Over: Broadway Sings the Blues 🦴🦴🦴🦴 (Sony Broadway, 1993)

There's No Business like Show Business: Broadway Showstoppers 🦴🦴🦴🦴 (Sony Broadway, 1993)

There's Nothin' like a Dame: Broadway Broads 🦴🦴🦴🦴 (Sony Broadway, 1993)

General Film

Academy Award Winning Music from MGM Classics 🦴🦴🦴🦴 (Rhino, 1997)

The All-Time Greatest Movie Songs 🦴🦴🦴🦴 (Epic/Columbia, 1999)

Arthouse Café 🦴🦴 (Silva America, 1998)

The Beloved Rogue and Other Scores from the Silent Years 🦴🦴 (Premier, 1994)

Billboard Top Movie Hits: 1940s 🦴🦴🦴 (Rhino, 1996)

Billboard Top Movie Hits: 1950–1954 🦴🦴🦴 (Rhino, 1996)

Billboard Top Movie Hits: 1955–1959 🦴🦴🦴 (Rhino, 1996)

Billboard Top Movie Hits: 1960s 🦴🦴🦴 (Rhino, 1996)

Billboard Top Movie Hits: 1970s 🦴🦴🦴 (Rhino, 1996)

Cannes Film Festival: 50th Anniversary Album 🦴🦴 (Milan, 1997)

Charming Gents of Stage & Screen 🦴🦴🦴🦴 (Legacy, 1994)

Cinema Century 🦴🦴🦴🦴🦴 (Silva Treasury, 1996)

Cinema Choral Classics 🦴🦴🦴🦴 (Silva Screen, 1997)

Cinema Choral Classics II 🦴🦴🦴🦴 (Silva America, 1998)

Cinema Gala: Great Shakespeare Films 🦴🦴🦴🦴 (London, 1988)

Cinema Gala: Warsaw Concerto 🦴🦴🦴🦴 (London, 1988)

Classic British Film Music 🦴🦴🦴🦴 (Silva Screen, 1990)

Composed By: Classic Film Themes from Hollywood's Masters 🦴🦴🦴🦴 (Rhino, 1997)

The Great British Film Music Album 🦴🦴🦴🦴 (Silva Screen, 1999)

Hidden Treasures of Film Music 🦴🦴🦴 (Milan, 1999)

Highway to Hollywood: Big Movie Hits, Vol. 2 🦴🦴🦴 (Varése Sarabande, 1991)

Hollywood Backlot 🦴🦴🦴 (Varése Sarabande, 1992)

Hollywood Magic: The 1950s 🦴🦴🦴🦴 (Columbia, 1988)

Hollywood Magic: The 1960s 🦴🦴🦴🦴 (Columbia, 1988)

The Hollywood Men 🦴🦴🦴🦴 (RCA, 1989)

Hollywood's Best: The 1930s 🦴🦴🦴🦴 (Rhino, 1997)

Hollywood's Best: The 1940s 🦴🦴🦴🦴 (Rhino, 1997)

Hollywood's Best: The 1950s 🦴🦴🦴🦴 (Rhino, 1997)

Hollywood's Best: The 1960s 🦴🦴 (Rhino, 1997)

Hollywood Soundstage: Big Movie Hits, Vol. 1 🦴🦴🦴 (Varése Sarabande, 1991)

Lovely Ladies of Stage & Screen 🦴🦴🦴🦴 (Legacy, 1994)

Music in Film 🦴🦴🦴🦴 (Sony Classical, 1999)

Naughty but Nice: Bad Girls of the Movie Musical 🦴🦴🦴🦴 (Sony Music Special Products, 1993)

The Prince and the Pauper 🦴🦴🦴🦴 (Varése Sarabande, 1989)

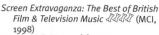

Screen Extravaganza: The Best of British Film & Television Music (MCI, 1998)

Screen Themes '94 (Discovery, 1995)

Sex-O-Rama (Oglio, 1998)

16 Most Requested Songs: Academy Award Winners (Sony Music/Legacy, 1994)

This Is Cinerama at the Movies (Label X, 1995)

Titanic: The Ultimate Collection (Varése Sarabande, 1998)

Watch the Skies (Sonic Images, 1999)

World Cinema Classics (Milan, 1994)

General TV

BBC TV Themes (Emporio Records/U.K., 1996)

Mission Accomplished (Hip-O, 1998)

Mission Accomplished, Too (Hip-O, 1998)

Roseanne: The Sitcom Theme Collection (PrimetimeUSA, 1992)

TV Hits, Vol. 1: Quantum Leap (PrimetimeUSA, 1991)

TV Hits, Vol. 2: Doogie Howser, M.D. (PrimetimeUSA, 1991)

The Hollywood Bowl Orchestra

Always and Forever: Movies' Greatest Love Songs (Philips, 1996)

The Great Waltz (Philips, 1993)

Hollywood Dreams (Philips, 1991)

Hollywood Nightmares (Philips, 1994)

Journey to the Stars (Philips, 1995)

The Movies Go to the Hollywood Bowl (Angel, 1990)

Music from Hollywood (Sony Music/Legacy, 1995)

Jazz at the Movies

Alive and Kicking: Big Band Sounds at MGM (Rhino, 1997)

Blue Movies: Scoring for the Studios (Blue Note, 1999)

Body Heat: Jazz at the Movies (Discovery, 1993)

Crime Jazz (Rhino/BMG, 1997)

Jazz in Film (Sony Classical, 1999)

Maracas, Marimbas and Mambos: Latin Classics at MGM (Rhino, 1997)

Sax and Violence: Music from the Dark Side of the Screen (Varése Sarabande, 1995)

Love & Romance

Cinema Gala: Great Love Stories (London, 1988)

Cinema's Classic Romances (Silva America, 1997)

Historical Romances (Marco Polo, 1995)

Movie Luv (EMI-Capitol, 1996)

Reel Love (Rykodisc, 1999)

Romantic Duets from MGM Classics (Rhino, 1997)

Performers

Louis Armstrong

Now You Has Jazz: Louis Armstrong at MGM (Rhino, 1997)

Fred Astaire

The Best of Fred Astaire from MGM Classic Films (MCA, 1987)

Fred Astaire & Ginger Rogers at RKO (Rhino, 1998)

Fred Astaire at MGM (Rhino, 1997)

Starring Fred Astaire (Columbia, 1989)

Steppin' Out: Fred Astaire at MGM (Sony Music Special Products, 1993)

Gene Autry

Gene Autry (Varése Sarabande, 1997)

Busby Berkeley

Lullaby of Broadway: The Best of Busby Berkeley at Warner Bros. (Rhino, 1995)

Nat King Cole

Nat King Cole at the Movies (Capitol, 1992)

Bing Crosby

Blue Skies (MCA, 1989)

Holiday Inn (MCA, 1988)

Swinging on a Star (MCA, 1989)

White Christmas (MCA, 1954)

Doris Day

A Day at the Movies (Columbia, 1988)

Doris Day: It's Magic (Rhino, 1998)

Connie Francis

Where the Boys Are: Connie Francis in Hollywood (Rhino, 1997)

Judy Garland

Collectors' Gems from the MGM Films (Rhino, 1996)

Judy Garland in Hollywood (Rhino, 1998)

Judy Garland: The Complete Decca Original Cast Recordings (MCA, 1996)

Mickey & Judy (Rhino, 1995)

Lena Horne

Ain't It the Truth: Lena Horne at MGM (Rhino, 1996)

Al Jolson

Let Me Sing and I'm Happy: Al Jolson at Warner Bros. 1926-1936 (Rhino, 1996)

Gene Kelly

Best of Gene Kelly from MGM Classic Films (MCA, 1987)

Gotta Dance! The Best of Gene Kelly (Sony Music Special Products, 1993)

'S Wonderful: Gene Kelly at MGM (Rhino, 1996)

Mario Lanza

Be My Love: Mario Lanza's Greatest Performances at MGM (Rhino, 1998)

Ethel Merman

American Legends: Ethel Merman (Laserlight, 1996)

Ethel Merman/Lyda Roberti/Mae West (Sony Music Special Products, 1991)

Marilyn Monroe

American Legends: Marilyn Monroe (Laserlight, 1996)

Never Before, Never Again (DRG, 1979)

Dick Powell

Dick Powell in Hollywood: 1933-1935 (Legacy, 1995)

Frank Sinatra

Frank Sinatra at the Movies (Capitol, 1992)

Mel Tormé

Mel Tormé at the Movies (Rhino, 1999)

War

Apocalypse Nam: The 10,000 Day War (edel America, 1993)

Cinema Gala: The Guns of Navarone: Music from World War II Films (London, 1988)

Westerns

Best of the West (Rykodisc, 1998)

The Best of Wild West (Universal Records/Germany, 1998)

Country Goes to the Movies (Risky Business/Sony Music Special Products, 1994)

How the West Was Won: Classic Western Film Scores 1 (Silva Screen, 1996)

Lonesome Dove: Classic Western Scores 2 (Silva Screen, 1996)

Music from the Classic Republic Westerns: Shoot 'Em Ups! ♫♫♫♫♫ (Varése Sarabande, 1996)

Spaghetti Western Encyclopedia, Vol. 1 ♫♫♫♫ (King Records/Japan, 1994)

Spaghetti Western Encyclopedia, Vol. 2 ♫♫♫♫ (King Records/Japan, 1995)

Spaghetti Western Encyclopedia, Vol. 3 ♫♫♫♫ (King Records/Japan, 1995)

Spaghetti Western Encyclopedia, Vol. 4 ♫♫♫♫ (King Records/Japan, 1996)

Spaghetti Westerns: Vol. 1 ♫♫♫ (DRG, 1995)

Spaghetti Westerns: Vol. 2 ♫♫♫ (DRG, 1995)

Spaghetti Westerns: Vol. 3 ♫♫♫♫ (DRG, 1999)

The Wild Bunch: Best of the West ♫♫♫ (Silva Screen, 1993)

Can't get enough information about soundtracks? Here are some books, magazines, and newsletters you can check out for further information. Happy reading!

Books

Andrew Lloyd Webber: His Life and Works—A Critical Biography
Michael Walsh (Harry N. Abrams, 1997)

The Art of Film Music
George Burt (Northeastern University Press, 1996)

Film and Television Composer's Resource Guide: The Complete Guide to Organizing and Building Your Business
Lisa Anne Miller and Mark Northam (Hal Leonard Publishing Corp., 1998)

Film Music: A Neglected Art—A Critical Study of Music in Films
Roy M. Pendergast (W.W. Norton and Co., 1992)

Film Sound
Elisabeth Weisa and John Belton (Columbia University Press, 1985)

Getting the Best Score for Your Film: A Filmmakers' Guide to Music Scoring
David A. Bell (Silman-James Press, 1994)

The Golden Age of Movie Musicals and Me
Saul Chaplin (University of Oklahoma Press, 1994)

Hollywood Rhapsody: Movie Music and Its Makers, 1900 to 1975
Gary Marmorstein (Schirmer Books, 1997)

How to Make Money: Scoring Soundtracks and Jingles
Jeffrey P. Fisher (Mix Books, 1997)

John Barry: A Life in Music
(Play It Again, 1999)

Listening to Movies: The Film Lover's Guide to Film Music
Fred Karlin (Schirmer Books, 1994)

The Melody Lingers On: The Great Songwriters and Their Movie Musicals
Roy Hemming (Newmarket Press, 1999)

Music for the Movies
Tony Thomas (Silman-James Press, 1997)

The Official Price Guide to Movie/TV Soundtracks and Original Cast Albums
Jerry Osborne (House of Collectibles, 1997)

Overtones and Undertones: Reading Film Music
Royal S. Brown (University of California Press, 1994)

Synchronization from Reel to Reel: A Complete Guide for the Synchronization of Audio, Film & Video
Jeff Rona (Hal Leonard Publishing Corp., 1990)

Magazines and Newsletters

Alternative Press
6516 Detroit Ave., Ste. 5
Cleveland, OH 44102-3057
(216) 631-1510

Billboard
1515 Broadway
New York, NY 10036
(212) 764-7300

Cinescape
1515 W. 22nd St., Ste. 475
Oak Brook, IL 60523
(800) 342-3592

Cool and Strange Music! Magazine
1101 Colby Ave.
Everett, WA 98201
Fax: (425) 303-3404

Details
632 Broadway
New York, NY 10012
(212) 598-3710

Down Beat
102 N. Haven Rd.
Elmhurst, IL 60126
(800) 535-7496

Entertainment Weekly
1675 Broadway
New York, NY 10019
(800) 828-6882

Film Music
350 N. Glenoaks Blvd., Ste. 201
Burbank, CA 91502
(818) 729-9500

Film Score Monthly
8503 Washington Blvd.
Culver City, CA 90232
(310) 253-9595
Fax: (310) 253-9588

Hollywood Reporter
1515 Broadway, 12th Fl.
New York, NY 10036-8986
(212) 536-5344

ICE
PO Box 3043
Santa Monica, CA 90408
(800) 647-4ICE

Mojo
Mappin House
4 Winsley St.
London W1N 7AR, England
44-171-436-1515

Movieline
10537 Santa Monica Blvd., Ste. 250
Los Angeles, CA 90025

(310) 282-0711
Fax: (310) 282-0859

Premiere
1633 Broadway
New York, NY 10019
(212) 767-5400
Fax: (212) 767-5444

Pulse!
2500 Del Monte St.
West Sacramento, CA 95691
(916) 373-2450

Q
Mappin House
4 Winsley St.
London W1N 7AR, England
44-171-436-1515

Request
10400 Yellow Circle Dr.
Minnetonka, MN 55343
(612) 931-8740

Rolling Stone
1290 Avenue of the Americas, 2nd Fl.
New York, NY 10104
(212) 484-1616

Show Music
PO Box 466
East Haddam, CT 06423-0466
(800) 873-8664

Soundtrack!
Astridlaan 171
2800 Mechelen
Belgium
E-mail: scq@pophost.eunet.be

Spin
6 W. 18th St., 8th Fl.
New York, NY 10011-4608
(212) 633-8200

Vibe
205 Lexington Ave., 3rd Fl.
New York, NY 10016
(212) 522-7092

Soundtrack music has a tremendous presence in cyberspace. Point your Web browser to these pages for more information on your favorite artists or the music in general.

Artists/Composers

Angelo Badalamenti
www.mindspring.com/~stewarts/bad.htm

John Barry
www.scamp-records.com/john_barry/

Elmer Bernstein
www.reelclassics.com/Musicians/Bernstein/bernstein.htm

Danny Elfman
www.geocities.com/Hollywood/Set/2392/
www.geocities.com/Hollywood/2595/elfman.vendetta.com/

Bernard Herrmann
www.uib.no/herrmann/

James Horner
user.tninet.se/~udl858r/index.html
www.hornershrine.com/

James Newton Howard
members.aol.com/smandshipa/JNH/newtego.htm

Mark Isham
www.isham.com/

Mark Knopfler
www.mark-knopfler-news.co.uk/

Henry Mancini
members.xoom.com/hmancini/

Musical Score: Marc Anthony Massimei
home.san.rr.com/musicalscore/

Ennio Morricone
www.londontheatre.co.uk/online/ennio-morricone/index.html

Randy Newman
www.randynewman.com/

New York Philharmonic Orchestra
www.nyfo.com/

Lalo Schifrin
www.schifrin.com/

John Williams
www.johnwilliams.org/
www.classicalrecordings.com/johnwilliams/

Hans Zimmer
apscore.freeservers.com/
www.ugcs.caltech.edu/~btman/hanszimmer/

Film Sites

Ain't-It-Cool News
www.aint-it-cool-news.com/

All Movie Guide
www.allmovie.com/

CNN Entertainment
www.cnn.com/SHOWBIZ/index.html

Coming Attractions by Corona
www.corona.bc.ca/films/homepage.html

Film.com
www.film.com/

Film Scouts
www.filmscouts.com/

Hollywood Online
www.hollywood.com/

Hollywood Stock Exchange
www.hsx.com/

Internet Movie Database
www.imdb.com/

Mr. Cranky
www.mrcranky.com/

Mr. Showbiz
mrshowbiz.go.com/

Movie Review Query Engine
www.mrqe.com/

The Movie Sounds Page
www.moviesounds.com/

Yahoo! Movies
movies.yahoo.com/movies/

Soundtrack Sites

Australian Soundtracks
www.ozemail.com.au/~dennisn/AussieST/index.htm

bs magazine
www.geocities.com/~bs-magazine/

The Fascinating World of Film Music
www.geocities.com/Hollywood/Lot/
9045/

Field of Dreams
home.plex.nl/~mflorian/index.html

Film Music of the '80s
www.geocities.com/SoHo/3803/80s/
index.htm

Film Music Society
www.filmmusicsociety.org/

Film Score Monthly
www.filmscoremonthly.com/

Filmtracks Modern Soundtracks Reviews
www.filmtracks.com/

A Fistful of Soundtracks
www.Jim.Aquino.com/

The Movie Soundtrack Web Page
www.amfilm.com/scores/

MovieTunes
sites.hollywood.com/movietunes/

Muse4Film
www.geocities.com/Hollywood/
Academy/4148/

My Soundtracks
members.aol.com/mysoundtrx/main.
html

ScoreLogue
www.scorelogue.com/

The Sound of Film: Divx Soundtrack Festival
www.soundtrackmusic.com/

Soundtrack Street
www.geocities.com/Hollywood/
Academy/8481/

SoundtrackNet
www.soundtrack.net/

Synchronicity Archive
www.xnet.com/~arkiver/synch/synch.
shtml

George Wastor's Film Music Page
users.otenet.gr/~nexus7/

Miscellaneous Music-Related Sites

Addicted to Noise
www.addict.com

All Music Guide
www.allmusic.com

Amazon.com
www.amazon.com/music

a2b music
www.a2bmusic.com

Billboard Magazine
www.billboard.com

BMG Music Service
www.bmgmusicservice.com

Borders.com
www.borders.com/music

Broadcast.com
www.broadcast.com

Buy.com
www.buy.com

CD Connection
www.cdconnection.com

CD Jukebox
www.broadcast.com/jukebox

CD Universe
www.cduniverse.com

CDnow
www.cdnow.com

Columbia House Music Club
www.columbiahouse.com

Compact Disc Connection
www.cdconnection.com

ICE Magazine
www.icemagazine.com

iMusic Newsagent
www.imusic.interserv.com/newsagent

International Lyrics Server
www.lyrics.ch

JamTV
www.jamtv.com

Liquid Audio
www.liquidaudio.com

MP3.com
www.mp3.com

MTV
www.mtv.com

Music Newswire
www.musicnewswire.com

Musicmaker.com
www.musicmaker.com

RealAudio
www.real.com

Rolling Stone Network
www.rollingstone.com

SamGoody.com
www.samgoody.com

SonicNet
www.sonicnet.com

Spinner
www.spinner.com

Total E
www.totalE.com

Tower Records
www.towerrecords.com

Tunes.com
www.tunes.com

Ultimate Band List
www.ubl.com

USA Today (Music Index)
www.usatoday.com/life/enter/music/
lem99.htm

VH1
www.vh1.com

Virgin Megastore Online
www.virginmega.com

Wall of Sound
www.wallofsound.com

The following are just some of the record labels that have film, stage, and television music catalogs. You may want to contact them if you have questions regarding specific releases.

Almo Sounds
360 N. La Cienega Blvd.
Los Angeles, CA 90048
(310) 289-3080
Fax: (310) 289-8662

Arista Records
6 W. 57th St.
New York, NY 10019
(212) 489-7400
Fax: (212) 830-2238

Atlantic Recording Corp.
1290 Avenue of the Americas
New York, NY 10104
(212) 707-2000
Fax: (212) 405-5507

Capricorn Records
1100 Spring St. NW, Ste. 103
Atlanta, GA 30309-2823
(404) 873-3918
Fax: (404) 873-1807

Columbia Records
550 Madison Ave.
New York, NY 10022-3211
(212) 833-8000
Fax: (212) 833-7731

Death Row Records
9171 Wilshire Blvd., Ste. 302
Beverly Hills, CA 90210
(310) 786-8459
Fax: (310) 786-8467

Decca Records
60 Music Sq. E.
Nashville, TN 37203
(615) 244-8944
Fax: (615) 880-7475

Def Jam Music Group
160 Varick St.
New York, NY 10013
(212) 229-5200
Fax: (212) 675-3588

Walt Disney Records
350 S. Buena Vista St.
Burbank, CA 91521
(818) 973-4370
Fax: (818) 953-9910

DreamWorks Records
9268 W. Third St.
Beverly Hills, CA 90210
(310) 234-7700
Fax: (310) 234-7750

EastWest Records
75 Rockefeller Plz.
New York, NY 10019
(212) 275-2500
Fax: (212) 974-9314

Elektra Entertainment Group
75 Rockefeller Plz.
New York, NY 10019-6907
(212) 275-4000
Fax: (212) 974-9314

EMI-Capitol Records
1750 N. Vine St.
Hollywood, CA 90028
(213) 462-6252
Fax: (213) 467-6550

Epic Soundtrax
550 Madison Ave.
New York, NY 10022-3211
(212) 833-8000
Fax: (212) 833-5134

Hollywood Records
500 S. Buena Vista St.
Burbank, CA 91521
(818) 560-5670
Fax: (818) 841-5140

Interscope/Geffen/A&M Records
10900 Wilshire Blvd., Ste. 1230
Los Angeles, CA 90024
(310) 209-7600
Fax: (310) 208-7343

Jive/Silvertone Records
137-139 W. 25th St., 11th Fl.
New York, NY 10001
(212) 727-0016
Fax: (212) 645-3783

LaFace Records
3350 Peachtree Rd., Ste. 1500
Atlanta, GA 30326
(404) 848-8050
Fax: (404) 848-8051

Laserlight Digital
Delta Music Company
1663 Sawtelle Blvd.
Los Angeles, CA 90025
(310) 268-1205
Fax: (310) 268-1279

Legacy Recordings
550 Madison Ave.
New York, NY 10022
(212) 833-8000
Fax: (212) 833-7120

London Records
825 Eighth Ave., 23rd Fl.
New York, NY 10019
(212) 333-8000
Fax: (212) 333-8030

Maverick Records
8000 Beverly Blvd.
Los Angeles, CA 90048
(213) 852-1177
Fax: (213) 852-1505

MCA Records/Hip-O Records
70 Universal City Plz.
Universal City, CA 91608
(818) 777-4000
Fax: (818) 733-1407

MCG Records/Curb Records
3907 W. Alameda Ave., Ste. 101
Burbank, CA 91505
(818) 843-1616
Fax: (818) 843-5429

Motown Records
825 Eighth Ave., 28th Fl.
New York, NY 10019
(212) 294-9516
Fax: (212) 946-2615

Polydor Records
1416 N. La Brea Ave.
Hollywood, CA 90028
(213) 856-6600
Fax: (213) 856-6610

Qwest Records
3800 Barham Blvd., Ste. 503
Los Angeles, CA 90068
(213) 874-7770
Fax: (213) 874-5049

Razor & Tie Records
214 Sullivan St., #4A
New York, NY 10012
(212) 473-9173
Fax: (212) 473-9174

RCA Records
1540 Broadway, 36th Fl.
New York, NY 10036
(212) 930-4000
Fax: (212) 930-4468

Relativity Records
79 Fifth Ave., 16th Fl.
New York, NY 10003
(212) 337-5300
Fax: (212) 337-5373

Reprise Records
3300 Warner Blvd.
Burbank, CA 91505-4694
(818) 846-9090
(818) 953-3223
Fax: (818) 953-3211

Rhino Records
10635 Santa Monica Blvd.
Los Angeles, CA 90025-4900

(310) 474-4778
Fax: (310) 441-6575

Rounder Records
One Camp St.
Cambridge, MA 02140
(617) 354-0700
Fax: (617) 491-1970

Ruffhouse Records
21860 Burbank Blvd., Ste. 100
Woodland Hills, CA 91367
(818) 710-0060
Fax: (818) 710-1009

Rykodisc
27 Congress St.
Salem, MA 01970
(508) 744-7678
Fax: (508) 741-4506

Sire Records
75 Rockefeller Plz., 17th Fl.
New York, NY 10019
(212) 275-2500
Fax: (212) 275-3562

Slash Records
7381 Beverly Blvd.
Los Angeles, CA 90036
(213) 937-4660
Fax: (213) 933-7277

Sony 550 Music
550 Madison Ave.
New York, NY 10022
(212) 833-8000
Fax: (212) 833-7120

Tommy Boy Music
902 Broadway, 13th Fl.
New York, NY 10010
(212) 388-8300
Fax: (212) 388-8400

Trauma Records
15165 Ventura Blvd., Ste. 320
Sherman Oaks, CA 91403
(818) 382-2515
Fax: (818) 990-2038

TVT Records
23 E. Fourth St., 3rd Fl.
New York, NY 10003
(212) 979-6410
Fax: (212) 979-6489

Universal Records
1755 Broadway, 7th Fl.
New York, NY 10019
(212) 373-0600
Fax: (212) 247-3954

Varése Sarabande Records
11846 Ventura Blvd., Ste. 130
Studio City, CA 91604
(818) 753-4143

Velveteen Records
720 16th St., Ste. 210
Denver, CO 80202
(303) 615-5022

Virgin Records
338 N. Foothill Rd.
Beverly Hills, CA 90210
(310) 278-1181
Fax: (310) 278-6231

V2 Records
14 E. 4th St.
New York, NY 10012
(212) 320-8500
Fax: (212) 320-8600

Warner Bros. Records
3300 Warner Blvd.
Burbank, CA 91510
(818) 846-9090
(818) 953-3223
Fax: (818) 846-8474

The WORK Group
2100 Colorado Ave.
Santa Monica, CA 90404
(310) 449-2666
Fax: (310) 449-2095

musicHound Soundtracks

Indexes

Five-Bone Album Index

Composer Index

Conductor Index

Lyricist Index

Series Index

The following soundtracks achieved the highest rating possible — 🦴🦴🦴🦴🦴 — from our discriminating MusicHound Soundtracks writers. You can't miss with any of these soundtracks or composer compilations.

The Adventures of Robin Hood (Varése Sarabande Records, 1983)

The Agony and the Ecstasy (Varése Sarabande Records, 1998)

Ain't Misbehavin' (RCA Victor, 1987)

The Alamo (Sony Legacy, 1995)

Alfie (MCA Records, 1997)

Alice's Restaurant (Rykodisc, 1998)

Alien Nation (GNP Crescendo, 1990)

Always (MCA Records, 1990)

Amadeus (Fantasy Records, 1984)

Amarcord (CAM Records, 1991)

American Graffiti (MCA Records, 1973)

An American Tail (MCA Records, 1986)

An American Tail: Fievel Goes West (MCA Records, 1991)

Anastasia (Varése Sarabande Records, 1993)

Anatomy of a Murder (Rykodisc, 1987)

Annie Get Your Gun (RCA Victor, 1988)

Another Dawn (Marco Polo, 1996)

Anthony Adverse (Varése Sarabande Records, 1991)

Antony and Cleopatra (JOS Records, 1992)

Anyone Can Whistle (Columbia Records, 1988)

Anything Goes (RCA Victor, 1988)

Ascenseur pour l'echafaud (Philips/France, 1959)

Babes in Arms (New World Records, 1990)

Bambi (Disney Records, 1998)

Beetlejuice (Geffen Records, 1988)

Bells Are Ringing (Columbia Records, 1989)

Ben-Hur (Silva Screen Records, 1989)

Ben-Hur (Rhino Records, 1996)

The Benny Goodman Story (MCA Records, 1972)

The Best Years of Our Lives (Preamble Records, 1988)

The Big Country (Silva America, 1988/1995)

Black Beauty (Giant Records, 1994)

The Black Cauldron (Varése Sarabande Records, 1985)

Body Heat (SCSE Records, 1989)

Born on the Fourth of July (MCA Records, 1989)

The Boy Who Could Fly (Varése Sarabande Records, 1986)

The Boys from Syracuse (DRG Records, 1997)

Brainstorm (Varése Sarabande Records, 1983)

The Bride of Frankenstein (Silva Screen, 1993)

Brigadoon (RCA Victor, 1998)

Brigadoon (Angel Records, 1992)

Cabaret (MCA Records, 1989)

Cabin in the Sky (Angel Records, 1993)

Candide (Sony Broadway, 1991)

Cats (Geffen Records, 1983)

Chariots of Fire (Polydor Records, 1981)

Chicago (Arista Records, 1996)

A Chorus Line (Sony Classical, 1998)

Cinema Paradiso (DRG Records, 1990)

Citizen Kane (Preamble Records, 1991)

City of Angels (Columbia Records, 1990)

City of Angels (Reprise Records, 1998)

Clash of the Titans (P.E.G., 1997)

Close Encounters of the Third Kind (Arista Records, 1998)

The Color Purple (Warner Bros. Records, 1986)

Company (Sony/Legacy, 1997)

Conan the Barbarian (Varése Sarabande Records, 1989)

The Cowboys (Varése Sarabande Records, 1994)

Crazy for You (Angel Records, 1992)

Crazy for You (RCA Victor, 1993)

Crimes of the Heart (Varése Sarabande Records, 1986)

Damn Yankees (Mercury Records, 1994)

Dances with Wolves (Epic Records/CBS Records, 1990)

Dangerous Liaisons (Virgin Movie Music, 1989)

Das Boot (Atlantic Records, 1998)

The Devil's Own (Beyond Music, 1997)

Dragonslayer (SCSE Records, 1990)

Dying Young (Arista Records, 1991)

Easter Parade (Rhino Records, 1995)

The Education of Little Tree (Sony Classical, 1998)

Edward Scissorhands (MCA Records, 1990)

The Egyptian (Varése Sarabande Records, 1990)

Elizabeth and Essex (Bay Cities Records, 1992)

Emma (Miramax-Hollywood Records, 1996)

The Empire Strikes Back (RCA Victor Records, 1997)

The End of Violence (Outpost Records, 1998)

E.T.: The Extra-Terrestrial (MCA Records, 1982)

E.T.: The Extra-Terrestrial (MCA Records, 1996)

Experiment in Terror (RCA Records/Spain, 1997)

Fiddler on the Roof (RCA Victor, 1986)

55 Days at Peking (Varése Sarabande Records, 1989)

Fiorello! (Angel Records, 1989)

Flower Drum Song (Sony Broadway, 1993)

Follies (RCA Victor, 1985)

For the Boys (Atlantic Records, 1991)

For Whom the Bell Tolls (Stanyan Records, 1991)

42nd Street (RCA Victor, 1980)

From Russia with Love (EMI-America, 1995)

Funny Girl (Angel Records, 1994)

Garden of Evil (Marco Polo Records, 1998)

Gentlemen Prefer Blondes (Sony Broadway, 1991)

Geronimo (Columbia, 1993)

The Ghost and Mrs. Muir (Varése Sarabande Records, 1985)

Giant (Capitol Records, 1989)

Gigi (Rhino Records, 1996)

Girl Crazy (Elektra Records, 1990)

Girl Crazy (Rhino Records, 1996)

Giulietta degli Spiriti (CAM Records/Italy, 1991)

Glengarry Glen Ross (Elektra Records, 1992)

The Golden Voyage of Sinbad (Prometheus Records/Belgium, 1998)

Goldfinger (EMI-America, 1995)

Gone with the Wind (Rhino Records, 1996)

Gone with the Wind (RCA Victor, 1989)

The Good, the Bad and the Ugly (EMI-Manhattan, 1985)

Gorillas in the Mist (MCA Records, 1988)

Great Expectations (Atlantic Records, 1998)

The Greatest Story Ever Told (Rykodisc, 1998)

Gypsy (Sony Classical/Legacy Records, 1999)

Haunted Summer (Silva Screen Records, 1989)

Hello, Dolly! (RCA Victor, 1989)

Henry and June (Varése Sarabande Records, 1990)

How Green Was My Valley (Fox Records, 1993)

How to Succeed in Business without Really Trying (RCA Victor, 1961)

How to Succeed in Business without Really Trying (RCA Victor, 1995)

The Hunt for Red October (MCA Records, 1990)

I Want to Live (Rykodisc, 1999)

Il clan dei Siciliani (CAM Records/Italy, 1993)

Il mercenario/Faccia a faccia (ViViMusica/Italy, 1995)

The Impostors (RCA Victor, 1998)

In Like Flint/Our Man Flint (Varése Sarabande Records, 1998)

Indiana Jones and the Temple of Doom (Polydor Records, 1984)

Inspector Morse: Volumes 1, 2, & 3 (Virgin Records/U.K., 1995)

Into the West (SBK Records, 1993)

Into the Woods (RCA Victor, 1987)

Into Thin Air: Death on the Everest (Citadel Records, 1997)

Is Paris Burning? (Varése Sarabande Records, 1989)

It's My Party (Varése Sarabande Records, 1996)

Ivanhoe (Intrada Records, 1994)

Jane Eyre (Marco Polo Records, 1994)

Jason and the Argonauts (Intrada Records, 1999)

Jaws (MCA Records, 1990)

Joseph and the Amazing Technicolor Dreamcoat (Polydor Records, 1993)

Journey to the Center of the Earth (Varése Sarabande Records, 1997)

Jurassic Park (MCA Records, 1993)

The King and I (Varése Sarabande Records, 1996)

King Kong (Marco Polo, 1998)

Kings Row (Varése Sarabande Records, 1980)

Kismet (Rhino Records, 1995)

Kiss Me, Kate (Sony Classical, 1998)

Kiss Me, Kate (Angel Records, 1993)

Kiss Me, Kate (Rhino Records, 1996)

La belle et la bete (Marco Polo Records, 1996)

La Cage Aux Folles (RCA Victor, 1983)

La dolce vita (CAM Records, 1991)

La femme d'a cote (SLC/Japan, 1994)

La strada/Le notti di Cabiria (Legend Records/Italy, 1992)

La tenda rossa (Legend Records/Italy, 1994)

Lady, Be Good! (Elektra Records, 1992)

The Land Before Time (MCA Records, 1988)

L'Armata Brancaleone/Brancaleone alle Crociate (EMI-Point Records/Italy, 1995)

Last Tango in Paris (Rykodisc, 1998)

Legend (Silva Screen, 1992)

The Legend of the Pianist on the Ocean (Sony Classical, 1999)

Legends of the Fall (Epic Soundtrax/Sony Classical, 1994)

Les Miserables (Geffen Records, 1987)

Life Is Beautiful (Virgin Records, 1998)

Li'l Abner (Sony Music Special Products, 1990)

Lionheart (Varése Sarabande Records, 1987)

A Little Night Music (Columbia Records, 1973)

A Little Romance (Varése Sarabande Records, 1992)

The Living Daylights (Rykodisc, 1998)

The Lord of the Rings (Intrada Records, 1991)

Lost in the Stars (MCA Records, 1991)

Lost in the Stars (MusicMasters Records, 1993)

The Lost World (MCA Records, 1997)

The Magnificent Ambersons (Preamble Records, 1990)

The Magnificent Seven (Rykodisc, 1998)

Mame (Sony Classical/Legacy, 1999)

Man of La Mancha (MCA Records, 1965)

Mary Poppins (Disneyland Records, 1990)

Masada (Varése Sarabande Records, 1990)

The Mask of Zorro (Sony Classical, 1998)

The Master of Ballantrae (Prometheus Records, 1998)

Maya (Citadel Records, 1998)

The Mephisto Waltz/The Other (Varése Sarabande Records, 1997)

Michael Collins (Atlantic Records, 1996)

Midway (Varése Sarabande Records, 1998)

The Misfits (Rykodisc, 1998)

The Mission (Virgin Movie Music, 1986)

Mrs. Parker and the Vicious Circle (Varése Sarabande Records, 1995)

Mobil Masterpiece Theatre (Delos Records, 1996)

The Moderns (Virgin Movie Music Records, 1998)

Monterey Pop (Rhino Records, 1992)

The Most Happy Fella (Sony Broadway, 1991)

Much Ado about Nothing (Epic Soundtrax/Sony Music, 1993)

The Mummy (Decca Records, 1999)

My Fair Lady (Sony Legacy, 1994)

My Life (Epic Soundtrax, 1993)

My One and Only (Atlantic Records, 1989)

Mysterious Island (Cloud Nine Records, 1993)

The Name of the Rose (Teldec, 1986)

The Natural (Warner Bros. Records, 1986)

The New Swiss Family Robinson (JOS Records, 1998)

New York, New York (EMI America, 1995)

The Night of the Generals (Intrada Records, 1990)

Nine (Columbia Records, 1982)

No, No, Nanette (Sony Classical/Legacy Records, 1999)

No Sun in Venice (Atlantic Records, 1975)

O Pioneers! (Intrada Records, 1991)

Obsession (Masters Film Music, 1989)

Odds Against Tomorrow (Sony Music Special Products, 1991)

Odds Against Tomorrow (Blue Note Records, 1990)

Of Thee I Sing (Angel Records, 1993)

Oh, Kay! (Elektra Records, 1995)

Oklahoma! (RCA Victor, 1980)

The Old Man and the Sea (Varése Sarabande Records, 1989)

On Her Majesty's Secret Service (EMI, 1988)

On the Town (Sony Classical, 1991)

On Your Toes (Polydor Records, 1983)

Once Upon a Time in America (Mercury Records, 1985)

Once Upon a Time in the West (RCA Records, 1988)

110 in the Shade (Jay Records/U.K., 1999)

Out of This World (Sony Broadway, 1992)

Out of This World (DRG Records, 1995)

Paint Your Wagon (RCA Victor, 1989)

Pal Joey (DRG Records, 1995)

A Passage to India (Capitol Records, 1989)

Pee-Wee's Big Adventure/Back to School (Varése Sarabande Records, 1988)

Peter Pan (RCA Victor, 1989)

The Pink Panther (RCA Records, 1989)

Pinocchio (Walt Disney Records, 1992)

Planet of the Apes (Intrada Records, 1992)

Planet of the Apes/Escape from the Planet of the Apes (Varése Sarabande Records, 1997)

Poltergeist (Rhino Records, 1997)

Porgy and Bess (RCA Victor, 1977)

Pride and Prejudice (Angel Records, 1995)

Prince Valiant (Film Score Monthly, 1999)

The Private Lives of Elizabeth and Essex (Varése Sarabande Records, 1998)

Psycho (Varése Sarabande Records, 1998)

Quien sabe? (King Records/Japan, 1995)

The Quiet Man (Scannan Film Classics, 1995)

Quiz Show (Hollywood Records, 1994)

Quo Vadis (London Records, 1985)

Raiders of the Lost Ark (DCC Compact Classics, 1995)

Rambling Rose (Virgin Movie Music, 1991)

Rebecca (Marco Polo Records, 1991)

The Red Violin (Sony Classical, 1999)

Return of the Seven (Rykodisc, 1998)

Revenge of the Pink Panther (EMI-Manhattan, 1988)

Rich in Love (Varése Sarabande Records, 1993)

Richard III (Sony Classical, 1997)

Rio Grande (Varése Sarabande Records, 1993)

The Road to Wellville (Varése Sarabande Records, 1994)

The Robe (Fox Records, 1993)

Rocky (EMI-America Records, 1995)

'Round Midnight/The Other Side of 'Round Midnight (Columbia Records, 1986)

St. Louis Woman (Mercury Records, 1998)

The Sand Pebbles (Varése Sarabande Records, 1997)

Saving Private Ryan (DreamWorks Records, 1998)

The Sea Hawk (Varése Sarabande Records, 1988)

The Second Jungle Book (JOS Records, 1997)

Sense and Sensibility (Sony Classical, 1995)

Seven Brides for Seven Brothers (Rhino Records, 1996)

The Seventh Voyage of Sinbad (Varése Sarabande Records, 1998)

Shine (Philips Classics, 1996)

Shipwrecked (Walt Disney Records, 1991)

The Shootist/Big Jake/Cahill, U.S. Marshall (Varése Sarabande Records, 1986)

Silverado (Intrada Records, 1992)

Snow White and the Seven Dwarfs (Walt Disney Records, 1993)

Somewhere in Time (MCA Records, 1985)

Somewhere in Time (Varése Sarabande Records, 1998)

The Sound and the Fury (Varése Sarabande Records, 1990)

The Sound of Music (Sony Classical, 1998)

South Pacific (Sony Classical/Legacy, 1998)

Spartacus (MCA Records, 1991)

Spellbound (Stanyan Records, 1988)

The Spirit of St. Louis (Varése Sarabande Records, 1989)

Star Trek: The Motion Picture/Star Trek: The Motion Picture/Inside Star Trek (Legacy Records/Sony, 1997)

Star Trek: The Motion Picture/Star Trek: The Motion Picture/Inside Star Trek (Sony Legacy, 1999)

Star Wars (RCA Records, 1997)

Star Wars Episode 1: The Phantom Menace (Sony Classical, 1999)

The Stars Fell on Henrietta (Varése Sarabande Records, 1995)

Stormy Weather (Fox Records, 1993)

A Streetcar Named Desire (Varése Sarabande Records, 1995)

Strike Up the Band (Elektra Records, 1991)

The Subterraneans (Sony Music Special Products, 1991)

Sun Valley Serenade/Orchestra Wives (Mercury Records, 1986)

Sunday in the Park with George (RCA Victor, 1984)

Superfly (Rhino Records, 1997)

Superman: The Movie (Warner Bros. Records, 1991)

Sweeney Todd (RCA Victor, 1979)

Sweet Charity (Sony Classical/Legacy Records, 1999)

Taxi Driver (Arista Records, 1998)

That Old Feeling (MCA Records, 1997)

That Thing You Do (Play Tone Records/Epic Soundtrax, 1996)

They Died with Their Boots on (Marco Polo Records, 1999)

The Thief of Bagdad/The Jungle Book (Varése Sarabande Records, 1988)

Thin Red Line (RCA Victor, 1999)

The Threepenny Opera (Polydor Records, 1954)

Thunderball (EMI-Manhattan Records, 1988)

To Kill a Mockingbird (Varése Sarabande Records, 1998)

Torn Curtain (Varése Sarabande Records, 1998)

Touch of Evil (Varése Sarabande Records, 1993)

2001 (Varése Sarabande Records, 1993)

The Unsinkable Molly Brown (Angel Records, 1993)

The Untouchables (A&M Records, 1987)

Victor/Victoria (GNP Crescendo, 1989)

Victory at Sea: Vol. 1 & 2 (RCA Victor, 1992)

War and Peace (Varése Sarabande Records, 1988)

We're Back (MCA Records, 1993)

Where Angels Fear to Tread (Virgin Movie Music, 1991)

Who's Afraid of Virginia Woolf? (Varése Sarabande Records, 1998)

Willow (Virgin Movie Music, 1988)

The Wind and the Lion (Intrada Records, 1990)

The Witches of Eastwick (Warner Bros. Records, 1987)

Wonderful Town (MCA Records, 1990)

A Year in Provence (Silva Screen Records, 1993)

Young Bess (Prometheus/Belgium, 1990)

The Young Lions/This Earth Is Mine (Varése Sarabande Records, 1993)

Ziegfeld Follies (Rhino Records, 1995)

Zorba (Angel Records, 1992)

Composers

Malcolm Arnold
Malcolm Arnold Film Music (Chandos Records, 1992)

John Barry
The Best of John Barry (Polydor/U.K., 1991)

Charles Chaplin
Charlie! (Silva America, 1993)

Francois de Roubaix
10 ans de musique de film (Odeon/France, 1998)

Georges Delerue
Truffaut & Delerue: On the Screen (DRG Records, 1986)

Hugo Friedhofer
The Adventures of Marco Polo (Marco Polo Records, 1997)

George & Ira Gershwin
George and Ira Gershwin in Hollywood (Rhino Records, 1997)

Dave Grusin
Cinemagic (GRP Records, 1987)

Bernard Herrmann
Bernard Herrmann: Music from Great Film Classics (London Records, 1996)
Bernard Herrmann: Wells Raises Kane (Unicorn Records, 1994)

Arthur Honegger
Arthur Honegger: L'idee/Crime et chatiment (Marco Polo Records, 1993)
Arthur Honegger: Mayerling/Regain (Marco Polo Records, 1993)

Erich-Wolfgang Korngold
Elizabeth and Essex: The Classic Film Scores of Erich-Wolfgang Korngold (RCA Victor, 1989)
The Sea Hawk: The Classic Film Scores of Erich-Wolfgang Korngold (RCA Victor, 1989)

Ennio Morricone
Morricone-Belmondo (DRG Records, 1999)
The Thriller Collection (DRG Records, 1999)

Alfred Newman
Captain from Castile: The Classic Film Scores of Alfred Newman (RCA Victor, 1989)

David Newman
It's a Wonderful Life: Sundance Film Music Series, vol. 1 (Telarc Records, 1988)

Alex North
The Film Music of Alex North (Nonesuch Records, 1997)

David Raksin
Laura: The Classic Film Scores of David Raksin (RCA Victor Records, 1989)

Leonard Rosenman
The Film Music of Leonard Rosenman: East of Eden/Rebel without a Cause (Nonesuch Records, 1997)

Nino Rota
Nino Rota: Film Music (EMI Classics, 1992)
Nino Rota: La Strada Ballet Suite (Sony Classical, 1995)

Miklos Rozsa
Spellbound: The Classic Film Scores of Miklos Rozsa (RCA Victor, 1989)

Stephen Sondheim
A Collector's Sondheim (RCA Victor, 1985)
Sondheim: A Celebration at Carnegie Hall (RCA Victor, 1993)
Sondheim: A Musical Tribute (RCA Victor, 1993)
Sondheim: Putting It Together (RCA Victor, 1993)

Max Steiner
Band of Angels (Label X Records, 1987)
Gone with the Wind: The Classic Max Steiner (Silva Screen Records, 1993)
Max Steiner: The Lost Patrol (Marco Polo Records, 1996)
Now, Voyager: The Classic Film Scores of Max Steiner (RCA Victor Records, 1989)

Dimitri Tiomkin
The Film Music of Dimitri Tiomkin (Columbia Records, 1988)

Sir William Walton
Sir William Walton: Battle of Britain Suite Film Music, vol. 2 (Chandos Records, 1990)
Sir William Walton: Hamlet/As You Like It Film Music, vol. 1 (Chandos Records, 1990)
Sir William Walton: Henry V Film Music, vol. 3 (Chandos Records, 1990)
Sir William Walton: Richard III/Macbeth/Major Barbara Film Music, vol. 4 (Chandos Records, 1991)

Franz Waxman
The Film Music of Franz Waxman (RCA Records, 1990)
Legends of Hollywood: Franz Waxman, Vol. 1 (Varése Sarabande Records, 1990)
Legends of Hollywood: Franz Waxman, Vol. 2 (Varése Sarabande Records, 1991)
Legends of Hollywood: Franz Waxman, Vol. 3 (Varése Sarabande Records, 1994)
Legends of Hollywood: Franz Waxman, Vol. 4 (Varése Sarabande Records, 1994)
Sunset Boulevard: The Classic Film Scores of Franz Waxman (RCA Victor Records, 1989)

Roy Webb
The Curse of the Cat People: The Film Music of Roy Webb (Cloud Nine Records, 1995)

John Williams
Close Encounters: The Essential John Williams Film Music Collection (Silva Screen Records/U.K., 1999)
John Williams By Request . . . (Philips Records, 1987)
John Williams: Music for Stage and Screen (Sony Classical, 1994)

Victor Young
The Classic Film Music of Victor Young (Marco Polo Records, 1998)
Shane: A Tribute to Victor Young (Koch International Classics, 1996)

7
5
7

The Composer Index lists the soundtracks in Music-Hound Soundtracks *that have a composer noted for them. Under each composer's name is the name of the soundtrack on which that composer can be found. If a soundtrack has more than one composer, the soundtrack name will be listed separately under the names of each of the composers.*

John Addison
Phantom of the Opera
Torn Curtain

Mark Adler
The Picture Bride

Richard Adler
Damn Yankees
The Pajama Game

Damon Albarn
Ravenous

Ryeland Allison
Drop Zone

John Altman
Beautiful Thing

David Amram
The Manchurian Candidate

George Antheil
The Agony and the Ecstasy/The Pride and the Passion

Harold Arlen
House of Flowers
Jamaica
St. Louis Woman
A Star Is Born
The Wizard of Oz

Craig Armstrong
Romeo + Juliet, Vol. 2

David Arnold
Godzilla
Independence Day
Last of the Dogmen
Stargate
Tomorrow Never Dies

Malcolm Arnold
The Bridge on the River Kwai

Edwin Astley
The Saint
Secret Agent

Georges Auric
La belle et la bete

Mark Ayres
Doctor Who: The Curse of Fenric

Luis Bacalov
A Ciascuno il Suo/Una questione d'onore
Django
La Citta delle Donne
Polish Wedding
The Postman

George Antheil

Quien sabe?
Sugar Colt

Burt Bacharach
After the Fox
Arthur 2
Butch Cassidy and the Sundance Kid
Casino Royale
Lost Horizon
What's New, Pussycat?

Pierre Bachelet
Story of O

Angelo Badalamenti
Arlington Road
Blue Velvet
Cousins
Lost Highway
A Nightmare on Elm Street 3
Twin Peaks
Twin Peaks: Fire Walk with Me
Weeds

Tom Bahler
Raw Deal

Richard Band
Castle Freak
The Re-Animator/Bride of the Re-Animator

Lesley Barber
A Price above Rubies

Gato Barbieri
Last Tango in Paris

Alberto Bargeris
Othello

Edward D. Barnes
The Newton Boys

Bebe Barron
Forbidden Planet

Louis Barron
Forbidden Planet

John Barry
Across the Sea of Time
Body Heat
Chaplin
The Chase
The Cotton Club
Cry the Beloved Country
Dances with Wolves
Deadfall
Diamonds are Forever
Elizabeth Taylor in London/Four in the Morning
From Russia with Love
Game of Death/Night Games
Goldfinger
Indecent Proposal
King Rat
The Knack . . . and How to Get It
The Lion in Winter
The Living Daylights
The Man with the Golden Gun
Mercury Rising
Midnight Cowboy
Moonraker
My Life
Octopussy
On Her Majesty's Secret Service
Out of Africa
Peggy Sue Got Married
Playing by Heart
The Quiller Memorandum
The Scarlet Letter
Somewhere in Time
Sophia Loren in Rome

The Specialist
Swept from the Sea
Thunderball
Until September/Star Crash
A View to a Kill
The Whisperers
You Only Live Twice
Zulu

Lionel Bart
Oliver!

Tyler Bates
*The Last Time I Committed
    Suicide*

Mike Batt
A Merry War

Les Baxter
Black Sunday/Baron Blood
*The Edgar Allan Poe Suite/Cry
    of the Banshee/Horror Ex-
    press*

Jeff Beck
Frankie's House

Ludwig Van Beethoven
Immortal Beloved

Marco Beltrami
Mimic
Scream
Scream 2

Vassal Benford
House Party II

Richard Rodney Bennett
Equus

David Benoit
The Stars Fell on Henrietta

Irving Berlin
Annie Get Your Gun
Call Me Madam
Easter Parade
Louisiana Purchase
*There's No Business like Show
    Business*

James Bernard
Nosferatu

Charles Bernstein
The Sea Wolf

Elmer Bernstein
The Age of Innocence
Amazing Grace and Chuck
Animal House
The Babe
*Baby the Rain Must Fall/The
    Caretakers*
The Black Cauldron
The Buccaneer

Buddy
Bulletproof
The Cemetery Club
The Deep End of the Ocean
Devil in a Blue Dress
The Field
Frankie Starlight
Genocide
The Good Son
The Great Escape
The Grifters
Hoodlum
*Kings Go Forth/Some Came
    Running*
Last Man Standing
Lost in Yonkers
Mad Dog and Glory
The Magnificent Seven
Midas Run/The Night Visitor
My Left Foot/Da
Oscar
A Rage in Harlem
The Rainmaker
Rambling Rose
Return of the Seven
Roommates
*The Shootist/Big Jake/Cahill,
    U.S. Marshall*
Spies Like Us
The Ten Commandments
To Kill a Mockingbird
True Grit
Twilight
Walk on the Wild Side

Leonard Bernstein
Candide
On the Town
Side by Side by Sondheim
West Side Story
Wonderful Town

Peter Bernstein
Bolero
Rough Riders

Peter Best
Muriel's Wedding

V.M. Bhatt
Dead Man Walking

Terence Blanchard
Clockers
Eve's Bayou
Malcolm X
The Malcolm X Jazz Suite

Ralph Blane
Best Foot Forward
Meet Me in St. Louis

Chris Boardman
Payback
Raw Deal

Jerry Bock
The Apple Tree
Fiddler on the Roof
Fiorello!
She Loves Me

Todd Boekelheide
The Blood of Heroes

Claude Bolling
Borsalino/Borsalino & Co.
California Suite

Luis Bonfa
Black Orpheus

Alexander Borodin
Kismet

Simon Boswell
Cousin Bette
A Midsummer Night's Dream
Second Best
Shallow Grave

Billy Bragg
Walking and Talking

Goran Bregovic
Queen Margot

Leslie Bricusse
Doctor Dolittle
*The Roar of the Greasepaint—
    The Smell of the Crowd*
*Stop the World—I Want to Get
    Off*
*Willy Wonka & the Chocolate
    Factory*

David Bridle
The Myth of Fingerprints

Michael Brook
Affliction
Albino Alligator

Bruce Broughton
All I Want for Christmas
The Boy Who Could Fly
Carried Away
For Love or Money
*Homeward Bound: The Incred-
    ible Journey/Homeward
    Bound II: Lost in San Fran-
    cisco*
Honey, I Blew Up the Kid
Infinity
Lost in Space
The Master of Ballantrae
Miracle on 34th Street
O Pioneers!
The Old Man and the Sea
The Rescuers Down Under
Shadow Conspiracy
Silverado
Tombstone

True Women

Jason Robert Brown
Parade

Larry Brown
Mr. Music

Nacio Herb Brown
Singin' in the Rain

Bruce Broughton
One Tough Cop

George Bruns
The Jungle Book

David Bryan
Netherworld

Robbie Buchanan
For the Boys

Richie Buckley
The General

Paul Buckmaster
Most Wanted
12 Monkeys

Roy Budd
The Black Windmill
Diamonds
Fear Is the Key
Get Carter
Paper Tiger
*Sinbad and the Eye of the
    Tiger*

Jimmy Buffett
*Ferngully . . . The Last Rain
    Forest*
Rancho Deluxe

Peter Buffett
500 Nations

Velton Ray Bunch
Quantum Leap

Geoffrey Burgon
Robin Hood

Sonny Burke
Lady and the Tramp

Ralph Burns
All Dogs Go to Heaven
For the Boys
In the Mood
Lenny

Carter Burwell
And the Band Played On
The Chamber
Conspiracy Theory
Doc Hollywood
Fargo/Barton Fink

Gods and Monsters
A Goofy Movie
The Hi-Lo Country
The Hudsucker Proxy
It Could Happen to You
The Jackal
Miller's Crossing
Raising Arizona/Blood Simple
Rob Roy

David Byrne
The Last Emperor

John Cacavas
The Edgar Allan Poe Suite/Cry of the Banshee/Horror Express

Pino Calvi
La Feccia

John Cameron
Driftwood
A Touch of Class

Wendy Carlos
A Clockwork Orange

Harry Carney
Sophisticated Ladies

John Carpenter
Body Bags
Escape from L.A.
Halloween
Halloween 2
Halloween 3: Season of the Witch
Halloween 4: The Curse of Michael Myers
Prince of Darkness
Vampires
Village of the Damned

Pete Carpenter
The A-Team

Jim Carroll
The Basketball Diaries

Warren Casey
Grease

Gary Chang
The Island of Dr. Moreau
Under Siege

Mark Charlap
Peter Pan

John Charles
Utu

Jay Chattaway
Red Scorpion
Space Age
Star Trek: The Next Generation
Star Trek: Voyager

Vladimir Chekassine
Taxi Blues

Paul Chihara
Noble House

Frank Churchill
Bambi
Dumbo
Snow White and the Seven Dwarfs

Alessandro Cicognini
Ulysses

Eric Clapton
Homeboy
Lethal Weapon 2/Lethal Weapon 3
Rush

Stanley Clarke
B.A.P.s
Bleeding Hearts
Down in the Delta
Passenger 57

Al Clay
A World Apart

George S. Clinton
Austin Powers
Beverly Hills Ninja
Mortal Kombat
Mortal Kombat 2: Annihilation

Elia Cmiral
Ronin

Robert Cobert
Dark Shadows: The 30th Anniversary Collection

Ray Colcord
The Paper Brigade

Cy Coleman
Barnum
City of Angels
The Life
Little Me
On the Twentieth Century
Sweet Charity
Wildcat
The Will Rogers Follies

Michel Colombier
Surrender

Marius Constant
Napoleon
The Twilight Zone: Vols. 1 & 2

Bill Conti
The Adventures of Huck Finn
Betrayed
8 Seconds
Grand Slam

Masters of the Universe
Nails
The Right Stuff/North and South
Rocky
Rocky II
Rocky III
Year of the Gun

Michael Convertino
Bed of Roses
Bodies, Rest & Motion
Guarding Tess
Jungle 2 Jungle
The Santa Clause
Wrestling Ernest Hemingway

Ry Cooder
Crossroads
Dead Man Walking
The End of Violence
Geronimo
Johnny Handsome
Last Man Standing
The Long Riders
Paris, Texas
Primary Colors
Trespass

Ray Cooper
Fear and Loathing in Las Vegas

Stewart Copeland
Four Days in September
Highlander: The Original Scores
The Leopard Son
Little Boy Blue
Men at Work
Pecker
Silent Fall
Talk Radio/Wall Street
Wall Street/Salvador

Aaron Copland
He Got Game

Carmine Coppola
Apocalypse Now
The Godfather Part II
The Godfather Part III
Napoleon

Francis Coppola
Apocalypse Now

John Corigliano
Altered States
The Red Violin

Vladimir Cosma
Diva
Le bal
Le diner de cons
My Father's Glory/My Mother's Castle

Bruno Coulais
Microcosmos

Luke Cresswell
Riot

Mike Curb
The Wild Angels

Burkhard Dallwitz
The Truman Show

Terry Dame
The Incredibly True Adventure of 2 Girls in Love

Oswald d'Andrea
Life and Nothing But

Mychael Danna
Eight Millimeter
Exotica
The Ice Storm
Kama Sutra
Lilies
The Sweet Hereafter

Mason Daring
Lone Star
Men with Guns
Prefontaine

Shaun Davey
Twelfth Night
Waking Ned Devine

Martin Davich
ER

Mack David
Cinderella

Tonton David
Little Indian, Big City

Dave Davies
Village of the Damned

Carl Davis
Ben-Hur
The French Lieutenant's Woman
Intolerance
Napoleon
Pride and Prejudice
The Rainbow
Scandal
The Trial
Widow's Peak
A Year in Provence

Don Davis
The Beast
A Goofy Movie
Hyperspace/Beauty and the Beast
Invasion
The Matrix

Warriors of Virtue

Jack Davis
Mission: Impossible

Miles Davis
Ascenseur pour l'echafaud
Dingo

Guido de Angelis
Sandokan

Maurizio de Angelis
Sandokan

Lex de Azevedo
The Swan Princess

Jo De Luca
Army of Darkness

Francesco de Masi
Lone Wolf McQuade

Vinicius de Moraes
*A Man and a Woman/Live for
Life*

Gene de Paul
Li'l Abner

Gene De Paul
*Seven Brides for Seven Broth-
ers*

Manuel de Sica
Nuda proprieta

John Debney
*Eye of the Panther/Not Since
Casanova*
Gunmen
Liar Liar
Paulie
Seaquest DSV
Sudden Death

Georges Delerue
Agnes of God
Black Robe
*The Conformist/A Man's
Tragedy*
Crimes of the Heart
Curly Sue
The Day of the Dolphin
La femme d'a cote
A Little Romance
Man Trouble
Rich in Love
A Show of Force
Steel Magnolias
A Summer Story
Wall Street/Salvador

Norman Dello Joio
Air Power/Holocaust

Gary DeMichele
Big Night
The Impostors

Jacques Demy
Les parapluies de Cherbourg

Paul Dessau
House of Frankenstein

Adolph Deutsch
Some Like It Hot

Marius DeVries
Romeo+Juliet: Volume 2

Neil Diamond
Jonathan Livingston Seagull

Loek Dikker
Body Parts
Pascali's Island

Thomas Dolby
*Ferngully . . . The Last Rain
Forest*

Klaus Doldinger
Das Boot
The NeverEnding Story
Palmetto

Pino Donaggio
Amore piombo e furore
The Barbarians
Carrie
Dressed to Kill
Il mio West
Meridian
Morte in Vaticano
Raising Cain
Zelly and Me

Steve Dorff
Alien Nation

Patrick Doyle
Carlito's Way
Dead Again
Donnie Brasco
Exit to Eden
Frankenstein
Great Expectations
Hamlet
Henry V
Indochine
Into the West
A Little Princess
Mrs. Winterbourne
Much Ado about Nothing
Needful Things
Quest for Camelot
Sense and Sensibility
Shipwrecked

Robert Drasnin
The Music from U.N.C.L.E.

John Du Prez
A Fish Called Wanda

Anne Dudley
American History X
Buster
The Full Monty
Gentlemen Don't Eat Poets
Hollow Reed
Knight Moves
Pushing Tin

Antoine Duhamel
Daddy Nostalgie
Ridicule

Vernon Duke
Cabin in the Sky

David Dundas
Freddie as F.R.O.7.

George Duning
Picnic

Ann Duquesnay
*Bring in 'Da Noise, Bring in
'Da Funk*

Bob Dylan
Pat Garrett & Billy the Kid

Clint Eastwood
*The Bridges of Madison
County*
A Perfect World

Fred Ebb
Steel Pier

Randy Edelman
Anaconda
Angels in the Outfield
Beethoven
Beethoven's 2nd
Citizen X
Come See the Paradise
Daylight
Diabolique
The Distinguished Gentleman
Dragon: The Bruce Lee Story
Dragonheart
EdTV
Feds
Gettysburg
Gone Fishin'
The Indian in the Cupboard
Kindergarten Cop
The Last of the Mohicans
Leave It to Beaver
The Mask
My Cousin Vinny
The Quest
Six Days Seven Nights
While You Were Sleeping

Ross Edwards
Paradise Road

Sherman Edwards
1776

Robert Een
Mr. Jealousy

Cliff Eidelman
The Beautician and the Beast
*Christopher Columbus: The
Discovery*
Free Willy 3: The Rescue
Magdalene
My Girl 2
Now and Then
One True Thing
The Picture Bride
A Simple Twist of Fate
*Star Trek VI: The Undiscovered
Country*
Triumph of the Spirit
Untamed Heart

Danny Elfman
Article 99
Batman
Batman Returns
Beetlejuice
Big Top Pee-Wee
Black Beauty
Darkman
Dead Presidents
*Dick Tracy/Madonna: I'm
Breathless*
Dolores Claiborne
Edward Scissorhands
Extreme Measures
Flubber
Forbidden Zone
The Frighteners
Good Will Hunting
Mars Attacks!
Men in Black
Midnight Run
Mission: Impossible
Night Breed
*The Nightmare Before Christ-
mas*
*Pee-Wee's Big Adventure/Back
to School*
Psycho
Sommersby
To Die For
Wisdom

Jonathan Elias
Two Moon Junction

Rachel Elkind
A Clockwork Orange

Duke Ellington
Anatomy of a Murder
Paris Blues
Play On!

Sophisticated Ladies

Mercer Ellington
Sophisticated Ladies

Albert Elms
The Prisoner

Stephen Endelman
The Englishman Who Went up a Hill But Came down a Mountain
Jeffrey
Postcards from America
Tom and Huck

Charles Engstrom
Ulee's Gold

Douglass Fake
Holly vs. Hollywood

Harold Faltermeyer
Beverly Hills Cop
The Running Man

Jim Farmer
The Real Blonde

Larry Fast
Netherworld

George Fenton
The Crucible
Cry Freedom
Dangerous Beauty
Dangerous Liaisons
Ever After
Final Analysis
The Fisher King
Groundhog Day
A Handful of Dust
Hero
High Spirits
In Love and War
Land and Freedom
Living out Loud
The Long Walk Home
Memphis Belle
Mixed Nuts
The Object of My Affection
Mary Reilly
Shadowlands
White Mischief
White Palace
You've Got Mail

Jay Ferguson
Double Dragon

Brad Fiedel
Blink
The Terminator
Terminator: The Definitive Edition
Terminator 2: Judgment Day
True Lies

Mike Figgis
Leaving Las Vegas
The Loss of Sexual Innocence
One Night Stand

Stephen Flaherty
Anastasia
Ragtime

Robert Folk
Arabian Knight
Beastmaster 2: Through the Portal of Time
In the Army Now
Lawnmower Man 2: Beyond Cyberspace
Major League: Back to the Minors
Maximum Risk
The NeverEnding Story II: The Next Chapter
Toy Soldiers
Trapped in Paradise

David Foster
Stealing Home
Two of a Kind

Charles Fox
Christmas in Connecticut/Love at Stake
Conan

Jim Fox
Ballad of a Gunfighter

David Michael Frank
Hero and the Terror
A Kid in Aladdin's Palace
Out for Justice
The Staircase

Christopher Franke
Babylon 5
Heartbreaker
Night of the Running Man
Pacific Blue
Raven
Universal Soldier
Wavelength

Judy Freeman
A World Apart

Gavin Friday
The Boxer

Gerald Fried
The Man from U.N.C.L.E.

Hugo Friedhofer
An Affair to Remember
The Best Years of Our Lives
Boy on a Dolphin
The Young Lions/This Earth Is Mine

John Frizzell
Alien Resurrection
Beavis and Butt-Head Do America
Dante's Peak
I Still Know What You Did Last Summer
VR.5

Edgar Froese
Heartbreaker
Wavelength

Dominic Frontiere
Color of Night
Hang 'Em High/Guns for San Sebastian

Albhy Galuten
Raw Deal

Rene Garriguenc
The Twilight Zone: Vols. 1 & 2

Claude Gaudette
Raw Deal

Gary Geld
Purlie
Shenandoah

Lisa Germano
Falling from Grace

George Gershwin
An American in Paris
Crazy for You
Funny Face
Girl Crazy
Lady, Be Good!
My One and Only
Of Thee I Sing
Oh, Kay!
Porgy and Bess
Strike Up the Band

Michael Gibbs
Housekeeping

Richard Gibbs
10 Things I Hate about You

Philip Glass
The Thin Blue Line

Nick Glennie-Smith
Drop Zone
Home Alone 3
The Man in the Iron Mask
Nine Months
Point of No Return
The Rock

Dominic Glynn
Evolution: The Music from Dr. Who

Goblin
Dawn of the Dead

Ernest Gold
Exodus
It's a Mad, Mad, Mad, Mad World
Judgment at Nuremberg

Billy Goldenberg
Around the World in 80 Days
Ballroom

Elliot Goldenthal
Alien 3
Batman and Robin
Batman Forever
Cobb
Demolition Man
Golden Gate
Heat
In Dreams
Interview with the Vampire
Michael Collins
Pet Sematary
Sphere
A Time to Kill

Jerry Goldsmith
Air Force One
Alien
Angie
Bad Girls
Bandolero!
Basic Instinct
The Blue Max
Breakout
The Cassandra Crossing
Chain Reaction
Chinatown
City Hall
Coma
Congo
Criminal Law
Damien: Omen II
Deep Rising
Dennis the Menace
The Edge
Escape from the Planet of the Apes
Executive Decision
Explorers
Extreme Prejudice
Fierce Creatures
The Final Conflict
First Blood
First Knight
Forever Young
The Ghost and the Darkness
Gremlins
Gremlins 2: The New Batch
Hoosiers
Hour of the Gun
In like Flint/Our Man Flint
Inchon
Inner Space

Islands in the Stream
King Solomon's Mines
L.A. Confidential
Legend
Leviathan
Lilies of the Field
Link
Lionheart
Logan's Run
Love Field
MacArthur
Malice
The Man from U.N.C.L.E.
Masada
Matinee
Medicine Man
The Mephisto Waltz/The Other
Mom and Dad Save the World
Mr. Baseball
Mulan
The Mummy
The Music from U.N.C.L.E.
Night Crossing
Not Without My Daughter
The Omen
One Hundred Rifles
Outland/Capricorn One
Papillon
A Patch of Blue
Planet of the Apes
Poltergeist
Poltergeist 2
Powder
Psycho II
QB VII
Raggedy Man
Rambo III
Rambo: First Blood Part II
Ransom/The Chairman
Rent-a-Cop
Rio Conchos
The River Wild
Rudy
Runaway
The Russia House
The Sand Pebbles
The Secret of N.I.M.H.
The Shadow
Six Degrees of Separation
Sleeping with the Enemy
Small Soldiers
Stagecoach/The Loner
Star Trek: First Contact
Star Trek: Insurrection
Star Trek: The Motion
    Picture/Inside Star Trek
Star Trek V: The Final Frontier
Supergirl
Total Recall
The Twilight Zone: Vols. 1 & 2
Twilight's Last Gleaming
U.S. Marshals
Warlock
The Wind and the Lion

Joel Goldsmith
Kull the Conqueror
Moon 44
Shiloh
Stargate SG.1

Steve Goldstein
Cats Don't Dance

William Goldstein
Hello Again

Benny Golson
Ed's Next Move

Miles Goodman
Blankman
Getting Even with Dad
Larger Than Life

Ron Goodwin
The Trap

Christopher Gordon
Moby Dick

Morton Gould
Air Power/Holocaust

Patrick Gowers
Sherlock Holmes

Paul Grabowsky
Noah's Ark

Cedric Gradus-Samson
Mandela and De Klerk

Ron Grainer
Evolution: The Music from Dr.
    Who
The Prisoner

Stephane Grappelli
Les valseuses
Milou en mai

The Grateful Dead
The Twilight Zone

Johnny Green
Raintree County

Harry Gregson-Williams
Antz
The Borrowers
Enemy of the State
The Replacement Killers
The Rock
Smilla's Sense of Snow
The Whole Wide World

Greyboy Allstars
Zero Effect

Andrew Gross
8 Heads in a Duffel Bag

Charles Gross
Punchline

Dave Grusin
The Bonfire of the Vanities
The Cure
The Electric Horseman
The Fabulous Baker Boys
The Firm
For the Boys
The Graduate
Havana
Hope Floats
Mulholland Falls
Reds
Selena
Tequila Sunrise
3 Days of the Condor

Jay Gruska
Lois & Clark
thirtysomething

Vince Guaraldi
A Charlie Brown Christmas

Brian Gulland
A World Apart

Christopher Gunning
Poirot

Jonas Gwangwa
Cry Freedom

Manos Hadjidakis
Never on Sunday

Carol Hall
The Best Little Whorehouse in
    Texas

Marvin Hamlisch
A Chorus Line
Frankie & Johnny
The Mirror Has Two Faces
Sophie's Choice
The Spy Who Loved Me
The Sting
They're Playing Our Song
The Way We Were

Jan Hammer
Miami Vice/Miami Vice II

Herbie Hancock
Blow-Up
Death Wish

Georg–Friedrich Handel
The Madness of King George

Tom Hanks
That Thing You Do

Leigh Harline
Pinocchio

Snow White and the Seven
    Dwarfs

George Harrison
Help!
Let It Be
Magical Mystery Tour

John Harrison
Tales from the Darkside: The
    Movie

Richard Hartley
An Awfully Big Adventure
Playing God
Princess Caraboo
A Thousand Acres

Thomas de Hartmann
Meetings with Remarkable
    Men

Isaac Hayes
The Best of Shaft

Ray Henderson
Good News

Larry Herbstritt
Alien Nation

Jerry Herman
Dear World
Hello, Dolly!
La Cage Aux Folles
Mack and Mabel
Mame

Bernard Herrmann
Battle of Neretva
Cape Fear
Citizen Kane
The Day the Earth Stood Still
The Egyptian
Garden of Evil
The Ghost and Mrs. Muir
It's Alive 2
Jane Eyre
Jason and the Argonauts
Journey to the Center of the
    Earth
Laura/Jane Eyre
The Magnificent Ambersons
Mysterious Island
Night Digger
North By Northwest
Obsession
Psycho
The Seventh Voyage of Sin-
    bad
Sisters
Taxi Driver
Torn Curtain
The Trouble with Harry
The Twilight Zone: Vols. 1 & 2
Vertigo

Jerry Hey
Raw Deal

Wilbert Hirsch
An American Werewolf in Paris

David Hirschfelder
Elizabeth
Shine

Johnny Hodges
Sophisticated Ladies

Al Hoffman
Cinderella

Lee Holdridge
The Giant of Thunder Mountain
Into Thin Air: Death on the Everest
Old Gringo
One Against the Wind
Pastime
The Secret of N.I.M.H. 2
Texas

Arthur Honegger
Les Miserables
Napoleon

Nellee Hooper
Romeo + Juliet: Volume 2

Anthony Hopkins
August

James Horner
Aliens
An American Tail
An American Tail: Fievel Goes West
Another 48 Hrs.
Apollo 13
Balto
*batteries not included
Bopha!
Brainstorm
Braveheart
Casper
Class Action
Clear and Present Danger
Cocoon
Cocoon: The Return
Courage Under Fire
Deep Impact
The Devil's Own
A Far Off Place
Field of Dreams
Glory
Gorky Park
Jumanji
Krull
The Land Before Time
Legends of the Fall
The Man without a Face
The Mask of Zorro

Mighty Joe Young
The Name of the Rose
Once Around
Once Upon a Forest
The Pagemaster
Patriot Games
The Pelican Brief
Ransom
Red Heat
The Rocketeer
Searching for Bobby Fischer
Sneakers
The Spitfire Grill
Star Trek II: The Wrath of Khan
Star Trek III: The Search for Spock
Swing Kids
Thunderheart
Titanic/Back to Titanic
To Gillian on Her 37th Birthday
Unlawful Entry
We're Back
Where the River Runs Black
Willow

Tomoyasu Hotei
Fear and Loathing in Las Vegas

James Newton Howard
Alive
Dave
Devil's Advocate
Diggstown
Dying Young
ER
The Fugitive
Glengarry Glen Ross
Grand Canyon
Intersection
Junior
Just Cause
The Man in the Moon
My Best Friend's Wedding
Night and the City
Off Limits
One Fine Day
Outbreak
A Perfect Murder
The Postman
Primal Fear
The Prince of Tides
Promised Land
Restoration
The Saint of Fort Washington
Space Jam
Three Men and a Little Lady
Wyatt Earp

Alan Howarth
The Dentist/The Dentist 2
Halloween
Halloween 2
Halloween 3: Season of the Witch

Halloween: The Curse of Michael Myers
Halloween 5: The Revenge of Michael Myers

Dick Hyman
Everyone Says I Love You
Moonstruck

Alberto Iglesias
Live Flesh

Mark Isham
Afterglow
At First Sight
The Beast
Billy Bathgate
Blade
Cool World
The Education of Little Tree
The Hitcher
Kiss the Girls
Last Dance
Little Man Tate
Losing Isaiah
Love at Large
Miami Rhapsody
Mrs. Parker and the Vicious Circle
The Moderns
The Net
October Sky
Of Mice and Men
The Public Eye
Quiz Show
Reversal of Fortune
A River Runs through It
Romeo Is Bleeding
Sketch Artist
Timecop
Trouble in Mind

Steve Jablonsky
The Replacement Killers

Joe Jackson
Tucker

Jim Jacobs
Grease

Denny Jaeger
The Hunger

Harry James
Sophisticated Ladies

Chaz Jankel
D.O.A.
Making Mr. Right/Desperately Seeking Susan
Tales from the Darkside: The Movie

Alaric Jans
The Winslow Boy

Maurice Jarre
After Dark My Sweet
Almost an Angel
The Collector
Doctor Zhivago
Enemies, A Love Story
Enemy Mine
Fatal Attraction
Fearless
Gaby
Ghost
Gorillas in the Mist
Is Paris Burning?
Jacob's Ladder
Julia and Julia
Lawrence of Arabia
Mad Max Beyond Thunderdome
The Man Who Would Be King
Moon over Parador
The Mosquito Coast
The Night of the Generals
No Way Out
Only the Lonely
A Passage to India
The Professionals
Ryan's Daughter
School Ties
Shadow of the Wolf
Tai-Pan
A Walk in the Clouds
Witness
The Year of Living Dangerously

Antonio Carlos Jobim
Black Orpheus

Elton John
Ferngully . . . The Last Rain Forest
The Lion King

J. J. Johnson
Across 110th Street

Laurie Johnson
First Men in the Moon
It's Alive 2

Adrian Johnston
Jude
Welcome to Sarajevo

Ken Jones
The Saint
Secret Agent

Quincy Jones
The Color Purple
In the Heat of the Night/They Call Me Mister Tibbs
The Pawnbroker/The Deadly Affair
Roots
Walk, Don't Run

Trevor Jones
Arachnophobia
Brassed Off!
Cliffhanger
Criss Cross
Dark City
Desperate Measures
Dominick & Eugene
G.I. Jane
Gulliver's Travels
Hideaway
In the Name of the Father
Kiss of Death
Labyrinth
The Last of the Mohicans
Merlin
The Mighty
Mississippi Burning
Richard III
Runaway Train
Sea of Love

Scott Joplin
The Sting

Wilfred Josephs
The Prisoner

Jan A.P. Kaczmarek
Bliss
Total Eclipse
Washington Square

Michael Kamen
*The Adventures of Baron Mun-
    chausen*
Brazil
Circle of Friends
Company Business
The Dead Zone
Die Hard 2: Die Harder
Die Hard with a Vengeance
Don Juan DeMarco
From the Earth to the Moon
*Highlander: The Original
    Scores*
Homeboy
Inventing the Abbotts
Jack
Last Action Hero
Let Him Have It
*Lethal Weapon 2/Lethal
    Weapon 3*
License to Kill
Mr. Holland's Opus
Nothing But Trouble
101 Dalmatians
The Raggedy Rawney
Robin Hood: Prince of Thieves
Shining Through
The Three Musketeers
What Dreams May Come
The Winter Guest

John Kander
The Act

Cabaret
Chicago
Flora the Red Menace
*Kiss of the Spider Woman:
    The Musical*
The Rink
Steel Pier
Zorba

Manu Katche
Little Indian, Big City

Brian Keane
The Night Flier

John Keane
The Sentinel

Arthur Kempel
The Arrival
Double Impact

Greg Kendall
Bandwagon

Chris Kenner
*Ferngully . . . The Last Rain
    Forest*

Rolfe Kent
Slums of Beverly Hills
The Theory of Flight

Randy Kerber
Raw Deal

Jerome Kern
Lovely to Look At
Roberta
Show Boat
Till the Clouds Roll By

Nusrat Fateh Ali Khan
Dead Man Walking

Wojciech Kilar
Dracula
Portrait of a Lady

Kevin Kiner
Leprechaun
Wing Commander

David Kitay
Surf Ninjas

Juergen Knieper
Wings of Desire

Mark Knopfler
Cal
Last Exit to Brooklyn
Local Hero
Metroland
The Princess Bride
Wag the Dog

Erich Wolfgang Korngold
*The Adventures of Robin
    Hood*
Another Dawn
Anthony Adverse
Elizabeth and Essex
Kings Row
*The Private Lives of Elizabeth
    and Essex*
The Sea Hawk

Henry Krieger
Dreamgirls
Side Show

David Kurtz
Alien Nation

Francis Lai
Les petroleuses
Love Story
*A Man and a Woman/Live for
    Life*

Burton Lane
Finian's Rainbow
*On a Clear Day You Can See
    Forever*
Royal Wedding

Jim Lang
Body Bags

k.d. lang
Even Cowgirls Get the Blues

Daniel Lanois
Sling Blade

Jonathan Larson
Rent

Bobby Laurel
The Rosary Murders

Angelo Francesco Lavagnino
Falstaff
Gli ultimi giorni di Pompei
La maja desnuda
Othello

Bill Lee
Do the Right Thing

Peggy Lee
Lady and the Tramp

Michel Legrand
Atlantic City
The Burning Shore
Dingo
Ice Station Zebra
Lady Sings the Blues
Les demoiselles de Rochefort
Les parapluies de Cherbourg
Madeline
Never Say Never Again

The Ring
The Thomas Crown Affair
The Three Musketeers

Jed Leiber
Frankie's House

Mitch Leigh
Man of La Mancha

John Lennon
A Hard Day's Night
Help!
Let It Be
Magical Mystery Tour

Jack Lenz
Due South, Vol. 2

Sylvester Levay
Hot Shots!

Stewart Levin
thirtysomething

John Lewis
No Sun in Venice
Odds Against Tomorrow

Daniel Licht
Bad Moon
Children of the Corn II
Children of the Night
Hellraiser: Bloodline
Permanent Midnight
Woman Undone/Zooman

Gyogy Ligeti
2001: A Space Odyssey

Jerry Livingston
Cinderella

Andrew Lloyd Webber
Cats
Evita
Jesus Christ Superstar
*Joseph and the Amazing Tech-
    nicolor Dreamcoat*
Phantom of the Opera
Sunset Blvd.

Brian Lock
The Land Girls

Joseph LoDuca
*Hercules: The Legendary Jour-
    neys, Vol. 2*
*Xena: Warrior Princess/Xena:
    Warrior Princess, Volume
    2/The Bitter Suite: A Musi-
    cal Odyssey*
Young Hercules

Frank Loesser
Guys and Dolls
*How to Succeed in Business
    without Really Trying*

The Most Happy Fella

Frederick Loewe
Brigadoon
Camelot
Gigi
My Fair Lady
Paint Your Wagon

William Loose
Cherry, Harry & Raquel
Vixen

Michal Lorenc
Blood & Wine

Los Lobos
Desperado

Steve Lukather
Raw Deal

Luna
Mr. Jealousy

John Lurie
Mystery Train

David Lynch
Twin Peaks: Fire Walk with Me

Galt MacDermot
Hair

Don MacDonald
Kissed

Mader
Eat Drink Man Woman

Madredeus
Lisbon Story

Taj Mahal
Sounder

Mark Mancina
Con Air
Moll Flanders
Money Train
Return to Paradise
Speed
Tarzan
Twister

Henry Mancini
The Adventures of the Great Mouse Detective
Arabesque
Blind Date
Breakfast at Tiffany's
Charade
Darling Lili
Experiment in Terror
The Glass Menagerie
Hatari!
High Time
Lifeforce

Midas Run/The Night Visitor
The Molly Maguires
The Party
Peter Gunn
The Pink Panther
The Pink Panther Strikes Again
Revenge of the Pink Panther
Son of the Pink Panther
Switch
Tom and Jerry: The Movie
Touch of Evil
Trail of the Pink Panther
Two for the Road
Victor/Victoria
What Did You Do in the War, Daddy?

Johnny Mandel
I Want to Live
M*A*S*H
The Sandpiper

Harry Manfredini
Aces: Iron Eagle III

Mark Mangini
sex, lies, and videotape

Hummie Mann
Robin Hood: Men in Tights
Year of the Comet

Franco Mannino
The Stranger/The Innocent

Clint Mansell
Pi

David Mansfield
The Ballad of Little Jo

Jim Manzie
Tales from the Darkside: The Movie

Marc Marder
Sidewalk Stories

Arif Mardin
For the Boys

Joe Mardin
For the Boys

Steve Margoshes
Fame

Zane Mark
Bring in 'Da Noise, Bring in 'Da Funk

Rick Marotta
Just the Ticket

George Martin
Live and Let Die

Sergeant Pepper's Lonely Hearts Club Band
The Yellow Submarine

Hugh Martin
Best Foot Forward
Meet Me in St. Louis

Cliff Martinez
Kafka
sex, lies, and videotape
The Underneath

Molly Mason
Brother's Keeper

Michael Masser
The Greatest

Billy May
For the Boys
Johnny Cool

Brian May
Dr. Giggles
The Road Warrior

Daniel May
Everest

Lyle Mays
The Falcon and the Snowman

Dennis McCarthy
Gone to Texas/Hidden in Silence
Star Trek: Deep Space Nine
Star Trek: Generations
The Utilizer

Paul McCartney
Give My Regards to Broad Street
A Hard Day's Night
Help!
Let It Be
Magical Mystery Tour

Keff McCulloch
Evolution: The Music from Dr. Who

Garry McDonald
The Thorn Birds: The Missing Years

David McHugh
Three Fugitives

Mark McKenzie
The Disappearance of Garcia Lorca
Dr. Jekyll and Ms. Hyde
Frank and Jesse
Warlock: The Armageddon

Joel McNeely
The Avengers

Flipper
Gold Diggers: The Secret of Bear Mountain
Iron Will
Radioland Murders
Soldier
Terminal Velocity
Virus
Wild America
The Young Indiana Jones Chronicles: Vols. 1–4

Steve McNicholas
Riot

Abigail Mead
Full Metal Jacket

Robert Mellin
The Adventures of Robinson Crusoe

Peter Melnick
The Dinosaurs

Michael Melvoin
The Main Event

Chris Menges
A World Apart

Alan Menken
Aladdin
Beauty and the Beast
Hercules
The Hunchback of Notre Dame
Life with Mikey
The Little Mermaid
Pocahontas

Bob Merrill
Carnival

Pat Metheny
The Falcon and the Snowman

George W. Meyer
For Me and My Girl

Enzo Milano
Hard Bounty

Cynthia Millar
Three Wishes

Marcus Miller
Siesta
The 6th Man

Randy Miller
Hellraiser III: Hell on Earth

Roger Miller
Big River

Irving Mills
Sophisticated Ladies

Ben Mink
Even Cowgirls Get the Blues

Vic Mizzy
The Addams Family

Charlie Mole
Othello

Fred Mollin
Forever Knight
Friday the 13th: The Series

Thelonious Monk
Straight No Chaser

Marguerite Monnot
Irma La Douce

Larry Morey
Bambi

Angela Morley
Watership Down

Giorgio Moroder
Cat People
Flashdance
The NeverEnding Story
Over the Top

Jerome Moross
The Big Country
The Cardinal
The War Lord

Ennio Morricone
Bugsy
Bulworth
Butterfly
Casualties of War
Cinema Paradiso
City of Joy
*The Conformist/A Man's
    Tragedy*
Crossing the Line
Disclosure
The Endless Game
A Fistful of Dollars
Frantic
Giu la testa
*The Good, the Bad and the
    Ugly*
Hamlet
*Hang 'Em High/Guns for San
    Sebastian*
Hundra
Il clan dei Siciliani
Il ladrone/L'harem
Il mercenario/Faccia a faccia
In the Line of Fire
La tenda rossa
*The Legend of the Pianist on
    the Ocean*
Lolita
Love Affair
The Mission

Navajo Joe
Novecento
Once Upon a Time in America
Once Upon a Time in the West
A Pure Formality
Rampage
Richard III
Sahara
The Star Maker
State of Grace
The Thing
A Time of Destiny
U-Turn
The Untouchables
Wolf

John Morris
Dirty Dancing
*Dirty Dancing (More Dirty
    Dancing)*
The Elephant Man
The Producers
Scarlett
Spaceballs
Young Frankenstein

Jelly Roll Morton
Jelly's Last Jam

Mark Mothersbaugh
The Big Squeeze
The Last Supper
The New Age
The Rugrats Movie
Rushmore

David Motion
Orlando

Wolfgang-Amadeus Mozart
Amadeus

Stanley Myers
The Deer Hunter
Trusting Beatrice/Cold Heaven

Mario Nascimbene
Alexander the Great/Barabbas
*The Barefoot Contessa/The
    Quiet American/Room at
    the Top*
*A Farewell to Arms/Sons and
    Lovers*
*Francis of Assisi/Doctor Faus-
    tus*
*The Vikings/Solomon and
    Sheba*

Miki Navazio
All over Me

Ira Newborn
The Late Shift
*The Naked Gun 2 1/2: The
    Smell of Fear*

Anthony Newley
*The Roar of the Greasepaint—
    The Smell of the Crowd*
*Stop the World—I Want to Get
    Off*
*Willy Wonka & the Chocolate
    Factory*

Alfred Newman
Airport
Anastasia
The Egyptian
The Greatest Story Ever Told
How Green Was My Valley
How the West Was Won
The Robe

David Newman
Critters
The Flintstones
Heathers
Hoffa
I Love Trouble
Jingle All the Way
The Marrying Man
Mr. Destiny
Operation Dumbo Drop
Out To Sea
The Phantom

Randy Newman
Avalon
Awakenings
A Bug's Life
James and the Giant Peach
Maverick
The Natural
The Paper
Parenthood
Pleasantville
Toy Story

Thomas Newman
American Buffalo/Threesome
Cookie
Corrina, Corrina
Fried Green Tomatoes
The Horse Whisperer
*How to Make an American
    Quilt*
Josh and S.A.M.
The Linguini Incident
Little Women
Mad City
*Making Mr. Right/Desperately
    Seeking Susan*
Meet Joe Black
Oscar and Lucinda
The People vs. Larry Flynt
Phenomenon
The Player
The Rapture
Red Corner
Scent of a Woman
The Shawshank Redemption
Unstrung Heroes

Up Close and Personal
The War
*Welcome Home Roxy
    Carmichael*

James Newton Howard
My Girl
Waterworld

Bruno Nicolai
Il Conte Dracula
*Il mio nome e' Shangai Joe/I
    giorni della violenza*
100.000 dollari per Ringo

Lennie Niehaus
Absolute Power
*The Bridges of Madison
    County*
A Perfect World
Unforgiven

Jose Nieto
Passion in the Desert

Jack Nitzsche
The Hot Spot
The Indian Runner
The Jewel of the Nile
An Officer and a Gentleman
The Razor's Edge
Revenge
The Seventh Sign
Starman

Monty Norman
Dr. No

Alex North
The Agony and the Ecstasy
*The Agony and the
    Ecstasy/The Pride and the
    Passion*
Cheyenne Autumn
The Dead/Journey Into Fear
Dragonslayer
The Last Butterfly
The Misfits
Rich Man, Poor Man
The Rose Tattoo
The Sound and the Fury
South Seas Adventure
Spartacus
A Streetcar Named Desire
2001
Viva Zapata!
Who's Afraid of Virginia Woolf?

Michael Nyman
Carrington
The Draughtsman's Contract
Gattaca
The Piano
Prospero's Books
Ravenous
Six Days Six Nights

The Michael Nyman Band
Prospero's Books

Gerald O'Brien
The Legend of Prince Valiant

Richard O'Brien
The Rocky Horror Picture Show

Mike Oldfield
The Killing Fields

Nino Oliviero
Mondo Cane

Riz Ortolani
Addio Zio Tom
Day of Anger/Beyond the Law
Mondo Cane
Una ragione per vivere e una per morire

Geoffrey Oryema
Little Indian, Big City

John Ottman
Apt Pupil
Goodbye Lover
Incognito
Portrait of Terror
Snow White: A Tale of Terror
The Usual Suspects

Gene Page
Blacula

Marty Paich
For the Boys

Johnny Pate
The Best of Shaft

Don Peake
The People under the Stairs

Jean-Claude Petit
Beaumarchais l'insolent
Cyrano de Bergerac
Jean de Florette/Manon des sources
Le Hussard sur le toit
The Return of the Musketeers

Laurent Pettigrand
Faraway, So Close

Barrington Pheloung
Hilary and Jackie
Inspector Morse: Volumes 1, 2, & 3
Nostradamus

John Phillips
The Myth of Fingerprints

Piero Piccioni
C'era una volta

Il momento della verita
La spina dorsale del diavolo
Minnesota Clay
The Stranger/The Innocent
Swept Away

Nicholas Pike
Sleepwalkers
Star Kid

Pink Floyd
More

Nicola Piovani
Ginger and Fred
Il sole anche di notte
Intervista
Life Is Beautiful
Tu Ridi

Ed Plumb
Bambi

Basil Poledouris
The Blue Lagoon
Conan the Barbarian
Conan the Destroyer
Free Willy
Free Willy 2
Hot Shots! Part Deux
The Hunt for Red October
It's My Party
The Jungle Book
Lassie
Les Miserables
Lonesome Dove
No Man's Land
On Deadly Ground
Quigley down Under
Red Dawn
RoboCop
RoboCop 3
Serial Mom
Starship Troopers
Under Siege 2: Dark Territory
Wired

Dave Pollecutt
Shaka Zulu

Steve Porcaro
The Sentinel

Cole Porter
Anything Goes
Can-Can
Evil under the Sun
High Society
Kiss Me, Kate
Out of This World
The Pirate
Silk Stockings

Rachel Portman
Addicted to Love
The Adventures of Pinocchio
Beloved

Benny & Joon
Emma
The Joy Luck Club
Marvin's Room
Only You
The Other Sister
The Road to Wellville
Sirens
Smoke
To Wong Foo, Thanks for Everything, Julie Newmar
Used People
War of the Buttons
Where Angels Fear To Tread

Mike Post
The A-Team
Hill Street Blues

Sally Potter
Orlando

Andrew Powell
Ladyhawke

Baden Powell
A Man and a Woman/Live for Life

John Powell
Antz
Face/Off

Zbigniew Preisner
At Play in the Fields of the Lord
Damage
Fairy Tale
Feast of July
Olivier Olivier/Europa Europa
The Secret Garden
When a Man Loves a Woman

Graham Preskett
Something to Talk About

Andre Previn
Elmer Gantry
Irma La Douce
It's Always Fair Weather
The Subterraneans

Alan Price
The Whales of August

Prince
Batman
Girl 6
Graffiti Bridge
Purple Rain

Spencer Proffer
Mr. Music

Henry Purcell
Restoration

Trevor Rabin
Armageddon
Con Air
Enemy of the State

Raffi
Ferngully . . . The Last Rain Forest

Claudio Ragazzi
Next Stop Wonderland

David Raksin
The Bad and the Beautiful
Forever Amber
Laura/Jane Eyre

Joe Raposo
The Great Muppet Caper

J.A.C. Redford
The Astronomers
Bye Bye, Love
D3: The Mighty Ducks
Independence
The Key to Rebecca
A Kid in King Arthur's Court
Oliver & Company
The Trip to Bountiful

Pat Regan
Tales from the Darkside: The Movie

Joe Renzetti
Basket Case 2/Frankenhooker

Graeme Revell
The Basketball Diaries
The Big Hit
Body of Evidence
Chinese Box
The Craft
The Crow
The Crow: City of Angels
From Dusk Till Dawn
The Hand that Rocks the Cradle
Hard Target
Mighty Morphin Power Rangers: The Movie
The Negotiator
No Escape
The People under the Stairs
The Saint
The Siege
Street Fighter
Until the End of the World

Gian-Piero Reverberi
The Adventures of Robinson Crusoe

Tim Rice
The Lion King

Jonathan Richman
There's Something about Mary

Nelson Riddle
Batman
Lolita
St. Louis Blues

Trude Rittman
Peter Pan

David Robbins
Dead Man Walking

Richard Robbins
Howard's End
Jefferson in Paris
Maurice
Mr. and Mrs. Bridge
The Proprietor
Quartet
The Remains of the Day
A Room with a View
A Soldier's Daughter Never Cries
Surviving Picasso

Bruce Roberts
Ferngully . . . The Last Rain Forest

J. Peter Robinson
Highlander: The Original Scores

John Roby
The Hanging Garden

Mary Rodgers
Once upon a Mattress
Side by Side by Sondheim

Richard Rodgers
Babes in Arms
The Boys from Syracuse
Carousel
Cinderella
Do I Hear a Waltz?
Flower Drum Song
The King and I
No Strings
Oklahoma!
On Your Toes
Pal Joey
Side by Side by Sondheim
The Sound of Music
South Pacific
State Fair
Two by Two
Victory at Sea: Vol. 1 & 2

Sonny Rollins
Alfie

Harold Rome
Fanny

I Can Get It for Your Wholesale

Jeff Rona
Chicago Hope
White Squall

Joel Rosenbaum
Raw Deal

Leonard Rosenman
The Fantastic Voyage
Keeper of the City
The Lord of the Rings
RoboCop 2
Star Trek IV: The Voyage Home
The Twilight Zone: Vols. 1 & 2

Laurence Rosenthal
Anastasia: The Mystery of Anna
The Bourne Identity
Clash of the Titans
Meetings with Remarkable Men
Peter the Great
The Young Indiana Jones Chronicles: Vols. 1–4

Jerry Ross
Damn Yankees
The Pajama Game

William Ross
The Evening Star

Nino Rota
Amarcord
The Clowns
8½
Giulietta degli Spiriti
The Godfather
The Godfather Part II
The Godfather Part III
Il bidone
Il Casanova
Il gattopardo
La dolce vita
La strada/Le notti di Cabiria
The Leopard
Romeo and Juliet
Spara forte, piu forte . . . non capisco
The Taming of the Shrew
War and Peace
Waterloo

Bruce Rowland
Andre
Lightning Jack
Return to Snowy River Part II

Miklos Rozsa
All the Brothers Were Valiant
Ben-Hur
El Cid
Fedora

The Golden Voyage of Sinbad
Ivanhoe
Julius Caesar
King of Kings
Knights of the Round Table
Lust for Life
Providence
Quo Vadis
Spellbound
The Thief of Bagdad/The Jungle Book
Time after Time
Young Bess

Michel Rubini
The Hunger
Nemesis

Arthur Rubinstein
Fake Out
The Hard Way
Nick of Time

Donald A. Rubinstein
Tales from the Darkside: The Movie

Carlo Rustichelli
Alfredo Alfredo
La ragazza di Bube
L'Armata Brancaleone/Brancaleone alle Crociate
Sedotta e abbandonata

Craig Safan
Angel
The Last Starfighter
Mr. Wrong
Son of the Morning Star
Stand and Deliver
Warning Sign

Buffy Sainte-Marie
An Officer and a Gentleman

Philip Sainton
Moby Dick

Ryuichi Sakamoto
The Handmaid's Tale
High Heels
The Last Emperor
Little Buddha
Merry Christmas Mr. Lawrence
The Sheltering Sky
Snake Eyes

Hans J. Salter
House of Frankenstein
Maya

Caleb Sampson
Fast, Cheap and Out of Control

Cedric Gradus Samson
Mandela: Son of Africa, Father of a Nation

Bernardo Sandoval
Western

Mark Sandrich Jr.
Ben Franklin in Paris

Philippe Sarde
Barocco
The Bear
Cesar et Rosalie
Fort Saganne
Ghost Story
La Baule-les-Pins
Les choses de la vie
Lord of the Flies
Music Box
Pirates
Quest for Fire

Mel Saunders
The Twilight Zone

Eddie Sauter
Mickey One

Milton Schafer
Drat! The Cat!

Walter Scharf
The Music from U.N.C.L.E.

Lalo Schifrin
Che!
Cool Hand Luke
The Eagle Has Landed
The Four Musketeers
Mission: Impossible
The Music from U.N.C.L.E.
The Osterman Weekend
Rush Hour
Tango
Voyage of the Damned

Harvey Schmidt
The Fantasticks
I Do! I Do!
110 in the Shade

Johannes Schmoelling
Heartbreaker
Wavelength

Claude-Michel Schoenberg
Les Miserables
Miss Saigon

Arthur Schwartz
The Band Wagon

David Schwartz
Magic in the Water
More Music from Northern Exposure

Northern Exposure

Stephen Schwartz
Godspell

John Scott
Antony and Cleopatra
Becoming Colette
The Deceivers
The Final Countdown
King of the Wind
Lionheart
Man on Fire
The New Swiss Family Robinson
Red King, White Knight
Ruby
The Second Jungle Book
Shogun Mayeda
The Shooting Party/Birds and Planes
To the Ends of the Earth
20,000 Leagues under the Sea
Walking Thunder
Yor: The Hunter from the Future

Don Sebesky
The Rosary Murders

Misha Segal
Phantom of the Opera

Ilona Sekacz
Mrs. Dalloway

Maurice Selzer
The Boxer

Jay Semko
Due South, Vol. 2

Akira Senju
The Mystery of Rampo

Eric Serra
The Fifth Element
Goldeneye
La Femme Nikita
The Professional

Steve Sexton
The Legend of Prince Valiant

Paul Shaffer
Blues Brothers 2000

Marc Shaiman
The Addams Family
Addams Family Values
The American President
City Slickers
City Slickers II: The Legend of Curly's Gold
A Few Good Men
The First Wives Club
For the Boys

Forget Paris
Ghosts of Mississippi
Heart and Souls
In & Out
Misery
Mother
Mr. Saturday Night
North
The Out-of-Towners
Simon Birch
Sister Act
Stuart Saves His Family

Francis Shaw
Merlin of the Crystal Cage

Edward Shearmur
Babe: Pig in the City
The Governess
Let Him Have It
Species II
Wings of the Dove

Jonathan Sheffer
Pure Luck

Garry Sherman
Alice's Restaurant

Richard M. Sherman
Chitty Chitty Bang Bang
Mary Poppins

Robert B. Sherman
Chitty Chitty Bang Bang
Mary Poppins

David Shire
Bed & Breakfast
Last Stand at Saber River
Saturday Night Fever

Howard Shore
Before and After
The Client
Crash
Ed Wood
The Fly
The Game
Looking for Richard
M Butterfly
Mrs. Doubtfire
The Naked Lunch
Nobody's Fool
Philadelphia
Prelude to a Kiss
Seven
The Silence of the Lambs
Videodrome

Shudder to Think
High Art

Alden Shuman
The Devil in Miss Jones

Shel Silverstein
Ned Kelly

Alan Silvestri
The Abyss
Back to the Future
Back to the Future, Part II
Back to the Future, Part III
Blown Away
The Clan of the Cave Bear
Contact
Death Becomes Her
Eraser
Father of the Bride
Father of the Bride, Part II
Ferngully . . . The Last Rain Forest
Forrest Gump
Grumpier Old Men
Judge Dredd
The Long Kiss Goodnight
Mouse Hunt
The Odd Couple II
The Parent Trap
Practical Magic
Predator 2
The Quick and the Dead
Richie Rich
Soap Dish
Volcano
Who Framed Roger Rabbit?

Marty Simon
Tales from a Parallel Universe

Claudio Simonetti
The Versace Murder

Shawn Slovo
A World Apart

Michael Small
Consenting Adults
Mobsters
Mountains of the Moon
Wagons East!

Charlie Smalls
The Wiz

Bruce Smeaton
Iceman
Roxanne
A Town like Alice

B.C. Smith
Smoke Signals

Paul J. Smith
Cinderella
Snow White and the Seven Dwarfs

Mark Snow
Born to Be Wild
Disturbing Behavior
In the Line of Duty

La Femme Nikita
Oldest Living Confederate Widow Tells All
20,000 Leagues under the Sea
The X-Files /Songs in the Key Of X/The Truth and The Light

Tom Snow
Footloose

Stephen Sondheim
Anyone Can Whistle
Company
Follies
A Funny Thing Happened on the Way to the Forum
Into the Woods
A Little Night Music
Merrily We Roll Along
Pacific Overtures
Passion
Reds
Side by Side by Sondheim
A Stephen Sondheim Evening
Sunday in the Park with George
Sweeney Todd

Ringo Starr
Magical Mystery Tour

Michael Stearns
Baraka

Fred Steiner
The Twilight Zone: Vols. 1 & 2

Max Steiner
Casablanca
Gone with the Wind
King Kong
They Died with Their Boots On

Leith Stevens
Destination Moon

Morton Stevens
Act of Piracy/The Great White
The Music from U.N.C.L.E.

David A. Stewart
Cookie's Fortune

Jeffrey Stock
Triumph of Love

Christopher Stone
The Stupids
Ticks/Fist of the North Star

Lawrence Stone
The Thorn Birds: The Missing Years

Richard Stone
Sundown

Herbert Stothart
The Wizard of Oz

Johann Strauss
2001: A Space Odyssey

Richard Strauss
2001: A Space Odyssey

Billy Strayhorn
Sophisticated Ladies

Charles Strouse
Annie
Bye Bye Birdie
Golden Boy

Joe Strummer
Grosse Pointe Blank/Grosse Pointe Blank, Vol. 2
Walker

Jule Styne
Bells Are Ringing
Darling of the Day
Do Re Mi
Funny Girl
Gentlemen Prefer Blondes
Gypsy
Hallelujah, Baby!
Peter Pan
Side by Side by Sondheim

Cong Su
The Last Emperor

Milan Svoboda
The Last Butterfly

Stanislas Syrewicz
Russia's War

Toru Takemitsu
Rising Sun

Frederic Talgorn
Robotjox
The Temp

Tangerine Dream
Dead Solid Perfect
Deadly Care
Firestarter
Heartbreaker
Legend
Near Dark
Shy People
Three O'Clock High

Michael Tavera
Frozen Assets

Joe Taylor
Spy Tek

P.I. Tchaikovsky
Sleeping Beauty

Mikis Theodorakis
The Day the Fish Came Out
Serpico
State of Siege
Z

Harry Tierney
Irene

Dimitri Tiomkin
The Alamo
The Fall of the Roman Empire
55 Days at Peking
Friendly Persuasion
Giant
The Guns of Navarone
It's a Wonderful Life
The Old Man and the Sea

Juan Tizol
Sophisticated Ladies

Tomandandy
Going All the Way

Toto
Dune

Colin Towns
The Buccaneers
Cadfael
Full Circle: The Haunting of Julia
The Puppet Masters

Pete Townshend
Tommy

Stephan Trask
Hedwig and the Angry Inch

Armando Trovaioli
Dramma della gelosia
I lunghi giorni della vendetta
Profumo di donna

Jonathan Tunick
Endless Love

Christopher Tyng
The Associate
Kazaam

Jay Ungar
Brother's Keeper

Michael Utley
Ferngully . . . The Last Rain Forest

Nathan Van Cleave
The Twilight Zone: Vols. 1 & 2

Pierre Van Dormael
Toto le heros

John Van Tongeren
The Outer Limits

Poltergeist: The Legacy

Vangelis
Blade Runner
Chariots of Fire
1492: Conquest of Paradise

Eddie Vedder
Dead Man Walking

Joseph Vitarelli
The Last Seduction

Alessio Vlad
Besieged

Tom Waits
Big Time
One from the Heart

W.G. Snuffy Walden
thirtysomething

Shirley Walker
Batman: Mask of the Phantasm
Escape from L.A.
Memoirs of an Invisible Man

Oliver Wallace
Alice in Wonderland
Cinderella
Dumbo
Peter Pan

Thomas "Fats" Waller
Ain't Misbehavin'

Ken Wannberg
The Philadelphia Experiment/Mother Lode

Stephen Warbeck
Her Majesty Mrs. Brown
Shakespeare in Love

Harry Warren
The Belle of New York
42nd Street
Summer Stock

Daryl Waters
Bring in 'Da Noise, Bring in 'Da Funk

Mark Watters
All Dogs Go to Heaven 2

Franz Waxman
The Bride of Frankenstein
The Nun's Story
Prince Valiant
Rebecca
The Spirit of St. Louis
Taras Bulba

Jimmy Webb
Ferngully . . . The Last Rain Forest
The Last Unicorn

Kurt Weill
Lost in the Stars
The Threepenny Opera

Brahm Wenger
Air Bud

Rick Wentworth
Freddie as F.R.O.7.

Nigel Westlake
Babe

Michael Whalen
Phantom of the Forest
Titanic: Anatomy of a Disaster

Harold Wheeler
Love! Valour! Compassion!

Bill Whelan
Dancing at Lughnasa
Some Mother's Son

Norman Whitfield
Car Wash

Frank Wildhorn
The Civil War
Jekyll & Hyde
The Scarlet Pimpernel

Hank Williams
Your Cheatin' Heart

John Williams
The Accidental Tourist
Always
Amistad
Born on the Fourth of July
Close Encounters of the Third Kind
The Cowboys
Dracula
Earthquake
The Eiger Sanction
Empire of the Sun
The Empire Strikes Back
E.T.: The Extra-Terrestrial
Far and Away
The Fury
Home Alone
Home Alone 2: Lost in New York
Hook
Indiana Jones and the Last Crusade
Indiana Jones and the Temple of Doom
Jane Eyre
Jaws
Jaws 2

JFK
Jurassic Park
The Lost World
Midway
1941
Nixon
The Paper Chase/The Poseidon Adventure
Presumed Innocent
Raiders of the Lost Ark
The Reivers
Return of the Jedi
The River
Rosewood
Sabrina
Saving Private Ryan
Schindler's List
Seven Years in Tibet
Sleepers
Stanley & Iris
Star Wars
Star Wars Episode 1: The Phantom Menace
Step Mom
Superman: The Movie
The Witches of Eastwick

Paul Williams
Bugsy Malone
The Muppet Movie

Meredith Willson
The Music Man
The Unsinkable Molly Brown

Gerald Wilson
Sophisticated Ladies

Sandy Wilson
The Boy Friend

Jim Wise
Dames at Sea

Debbie Wiseman
Tom and Viv
Wilde

De Wolfe
Monty Python and the Holy Grail

Steve Wood
Everest

Gavin Wright
A World Apart

Yanni
Heart of Midnight

Gabriel Yared
Betty Blue
City of Angels
The English Patient
Message in a Bottle

Maury Yeston
Nine
Titanic

Vincent Youmans
No, No, Nanette

Christopher Young
Bat 21
Bright Angel
Copycat
The Dark Half
Def-Con 4
Dream Lover
Entrapment
Hard Rain
Haunted Summer
Judicial Consent
Max and Helen
Norma Jean and Marilyn
Rapid Fire
Rounders
Set It Off
Urban Legend
The Vagrant

Victor Young
Around the World in 80 Days
The Brave One
For Whom the Bell Tolls
Johnny Guitar
The Quiet Man
Rio Grande
Samson and Delilah/The Quiet Man

Hans Zimmer
As Good as It Gets

Backdraft
Beyond Rangoon
Black Rain
Broken Arrow
Calendar Girl
Crimson Tide
Driving Miss Daisy
Drop Zone
The Fan
Green Card
The House of the Spirits
I'll Do Anything
A League of Their Own
The Lion King
Muppet Treasure Island
Nine Months
Pacific Heights
The Peacemaker
Point of No Return
The Prince of Egypt
Radio Flyer
Rain Man
Renaissance Man
The Rock
Smilla's Sense of Snow
Something to Talk About
Thin Red Line
True Romance
The Whole Wide World
A World Apart
Younger and Younger

David Zippel
The Swan Princess

7
7
3

The Conductor Index lists the soundtracks in Music-Hound Soundtracks that have a conductor noted for them. Under each conductor's name is the name of the soundtrack on which that conductor can be found. If a soundtrack has more than one conductor, the soundtrack name will be listed separately under the names of each of the conductors.

John Addison
Phantom of the Opera
Torn Curtain

Mark Adler
The Blood of Heroes
The Picture Bride

Louis Adrian
Annie Get Your Gun

Adriano
Jane Eyre
La belle et la bete
Les Miserables
Rebecca

Bob Alcivar
One from the Heart

Geoffrey Alexander
Dark City
Desperate Measures

Gulliver's Travels
Merlin

Jeff Alexander
Kismet

Franz Allers
Annie Get Your Gun

John Altman
Goldeneye
The Professional
The Sheltering Sky

Kenneth Alwyn
The Bride of Frankenstein
The Quiet Man

David Amos
Air Power/Holocaust

David Amram
The Manchurian Candidate

Michael T. Andreas
The Leopard Son

Pete Anthony
Bad Moon
Dream Lover
Hard Rain
Hellraiser: Bloodline
Norma Jean and Marilyn
The Out-of-Towners
Set It Off
Simon Birch
Urban Legend
Woman Undone/Zooman

Alfredo Antonini
Cinderella

David Arch
The Sheltering Sky

Robert Armbruster
The Sandpiper
The Unsinkable Molly Brown

Craig Armstrong
Romeo+Juliet: Volume 2

Malcolm Arnold
The Bridge on the River Kwai

Gil Askey
Lady Sings the Blues

Edwin Astley
The Saint
Secret Agent

Luis Bacalov
Django
Polish Wedding
The Postman

Burt Bacharach
Butch Cassidy and the Sundance Kid
Casino Royale
Lost Horizon

Pierre Bachelet
Story of O

Angelo Badalamenti
Blue Velvet
Cousins
Lost Highway
Weeds

Dick Bakker
Mrs. Dalloway

Richard Band
Castle Freak
The Re-Animator/Bride of the Re-Animator

Daniel Barenboim
Hilary and Jackie

Paul Baron
The Great Caruso

John Barry
Across the Sea of Time
Chaplin
The Chase
The Cotton Club
Cry the Beloved Country
Dances with Wolves
Deadfall
Diamonds Are Forever
Elizabeth Taylor in London/Four in the Morning
From Russia with Love
Game of Death/Night Games
Goldfinger
King Rat
The Knack . . . and How to Get It
The Man with the Golden Gun
Mercury Rising
Midnight Cowboy
Moonraker
My Life
On Her Majesty's Secret Service
Peggy Sue Got Married
The Quiller Memorandum
The Scarlet Letter
Somewhere in Time
Sophia Loren in Rome
The Specialist
Swept from the Sea
Thunderball
Until September/Star Crash
A View to a Kill
The Whisperers
You Only Live Twice
Zulu

Steve Bartek
Psycho

Larry Bastian
The Swan Princess

Mike Batt
A Merry War

Les Baxter
Black Sunday/Baron Blood
The Edgar Allan Poe Suite/Cry of the Banshee/Horror Express

Marco Beltrami
Mimic
Scream/Scream 2

Robert Russell Bennett
Victory at Sea: Vol. 1 & 2

John Berkman
She Loves Me

Elmer Bernstein
The Age of Innocence
Amazing Grace and Chuck
Animal House
The Babe
The Black Cauldron
Bolero
The Buccaneer
Buddy
Bulletproof
Cape Fear
The Cemetery Club
The Comancheros/True Grit
The Deep End of the Ocean
Devil in a Blue Dress
The Field
Frankie Starlight
Genocide
The Ghost and Mrs. Muir
The Good Son
The Great Escape
The Grifters
Hoodlum
Kings Go Forth/Some Came Running
Last Man Standing
Lost in Yonkers
Mad Dog and Glory
The Magnificent Seven
Midas Run/The Night Visitor
My Left Foot/Da
Oscar
A Rage in Harlem
The Rainmaker
Rambling Rose
Return of the Seven
Roommates
The Shootist/Big Jake/Cahill, U.S. Marshall
Spies Like Us
The Ten Commandments
To Kill a Mockingbird

True Grit
Twilight
Walk on the Wild Side

Leonard Bernstein
He Got Game

Peter Bernstein
Rough Riders

Sherry Bertram
Faraway, So Close

Kurt Bestor
Year of the Comet

Stanley Black
The Razor's Edge

Jay Blackton
Annie Get Your Gun

Howard Blake
RoboCop

Terence Blanchard
Clockers
Eve's Bayou
Malcolm X/The Malcolm X Jazz Suite

Chris Boardman
The Nightmare Before Christmas
Out to Sea
Payback

Claude Bolling
Borsalino/Borsalino & Co.

Sir Adrian Boult
Lawrence of Arabia

Bob Bowker
Othello

Goran Bregovic
Queen Margot

Tony Bremner
The Big Country
Citizen Kane
Lawrence of Arabia
The Magnificent Ambersons

Tony Britton
RoboCop

Bruce Broughton
All I Want for Christmas
Carried Away
For Love or Money
Homeward Bound: The Incredible Journey/Homeward Bound II: Lost in San Francisco
Honey, I Blew Up the Kid
Infinity

Ivanhoe
Jason and the Argonauts
Julius Caesar
Lost in Space
The Master of Ballantrae
Miracle on 34th Street
O Pioneers!
The Old Man and the Sea
The Rescuers Down Under
Shadow Conspiracy
Silverado
True Women

George Bruns
Sleeping Beauty

Paul Buckmaster
12 Monkeys

Roy Budd
Fear Is the Key
Paper Tiger
Sinbad and the Eye of the Tiger

Geoffrey Burgon
Robin Hood

Ralph Burns
A Chorus Line
New York, New York

Carter Burwell
And the Band Played on
The Chamber
Conspiracy Theory
Fargo/Barton Fink
Gods and Monsters
The Hi-Lo Country
It Could Happen to You
Rob Roy

Bill Byers
Pirates

John Cacavas
The Edgar Allan Poe Suite/Cry of the Banshee/Horror Express

Daniel Caine
The A-Team
Cult TV Themes
Fantastic TV Themes
Hill Street Blues

Constantine Callinicos
The Great Caruso

Pino Calvi
La Feccia

John Cameron
Driftwood

Daniel A. Carlin
The Last of the Mohicans

John Carpenter
Vampires

Piero Cavalli
Francis of Assisi/Doctor Faustus

Gary Chang
Under Siege

David Chase
Little Me

Jay Chattaway
Star Trek: Voyager

Paul Chihara
Noble House

Joseph Church
The Lion King

Frank Churchill
Snow White and the Seven Dwarfs

George S. Clinton
Geronimo
Mortal Kombat

Robert Cobert
Dark Shadows: The 30th Anniversary Collection

Ray Colcord
The Paper Brigade

John Coleman
Pee-Wee's Big Adventure/Back to School

Franco Collura
The Best Years of Our Lives

Marius Constant
Napoleon

Bill Conti
The Adventures of Huck Finn
Betrayed
Grand Slam
The Right Stuff/North and South
Rocky
Rocky II
Rocky III

Aaron Copland
He Got Game

Anton Coppola
Dracula

Carmine Coppola
The Godfather Part II
The Godfather Part III
Napoleon

Rick Cordova
Michael Collins

Vladimir Cosma
Diva
Le bal
Le diner de cons
*My Father's Glory/My Mother's
    Castle*

William Craft
Indochine

Guy Dagul
Criss Cross

Ken Darby
How the West Was Won

Terry Davies
Cousin Bette
A Midsummer Night's Dream

Buster Davis
No, No, Nanette

Carl Davis
Ben-Hur
Elizabeth and Essex
*The French Lieutenant's
    Woman*
Intolerance
Napoleon
Pride and Prejudice
*The Private Lives of Elizabeth
    and Essex*
The Rainbow
The Trial
Widow's Peak
A Year in Provence

Don Davis
A Goofy Movie
*Hyperspace/Beauty and the
    Beast*
The Matrix
Warriors of Virtue

Lex de Azevedo
Judicial Consent
The Swan Princess

Francesco de Masi
Lone Wolf McQuade

Peter DeAngelis
The Devil in Miss Jones

John Debney
*Eye of the Panther/Not Since
    Casanova*
Liar Liar
Paulie
Seaquest DSV
*The Seventh Voyage of Sin-
    bad*
Somewhere in Time

Sudden Death
Superman: The Movie

Krzesimir Debski
Bliss
Total Eclipse
Washington Square

Georges Delerue
Agnes of God
Black Robe
*The Conformist/A Man's
    Tragedy*
Crimes of the Heart
Curly Sue
The Day of the Dolphin
La femme d'a cote
A Little Romance
Man Trouble
Rich in Love
A Show of Force
Steel Magnolias
A Summer Story
Wall Street/Salvador

Adolph Deutsch
The Band Wagon
The Belle of New York
Funny Face
*Seven Brides for Seven Broth-
    ers*
Show Boat

Enrico DiCecco
Billy Bathgate

Nicholas Dodd
Independence Day
Kull the Conqueror
Last of the Dogmen
Stargate
Tomorrow Never Dies

Marcus Dods
The Great Muppet Caper

Robert E. Dolan
How the West Was Won

Pino Donaggio
Carrie
Morte in Vaticano

Carmen Dragon
Lovely to Look At

Dennis Dreith
Misery

John Du Prez
A Fish Called Wanda

Anne Dudley
American History X
Buster
The Full Monty
Gentlemen Don't Eat Poets

Hollow Reed
Knight Moves

Randy Edelman
Anaconda
Angels in the Outfield
Citizen X
Come See the Paradise
Daylight
Diabolique
The Distinguished Gentleman
Dragon: The Bruce Lee Story
Dragonheart
Gettysburg
Gone Fishin'
The Indian in the Cupboard
Kindergarten Cop
The Last of the Mohicans
Leave It to Beaver
The Mask
My Cousin Vinny
The Quest
Six Days Seven Nights
While You Were Sleeping

John Owen Edwards
110 in the Shade

Ricky Edwards
Shine

Cliff Eidelman
The Beautician and the Beast
*Christopher Columbus: The
    Discovery*
Free Willy 3: The Rescue
Magdalene
My Girl 2
Now and Then
One True Thing
The Picture Bride
A Simple Twist of Fate
*Star Trek VI: The Undiscovered
    Country*
Triumph of the Spirit
Untamed Heart

Danny Elfman
Dead Presidents

Duke Ellington
Anatomy of a Murder

Jack Elliott
Blade Runner

Todd Ellison
Drat! The Cat!

Stephen Endelman
*The Englishman Who Went Up
    a Hill but Came Down a
    Mountain*
Tom and Huck

Lehman Engel
The Boys from Syracuse

Girl Crazy
Oh, Kay!

Percy Faith
Love Me or Leave Me

George Fenton
The Crucible
Cry Freedom
Dangerous Beauty
Dangerous Liaisons
Ever After
Final Analysis
The Fisher King
Groundhog Day
A Handful of Dust
Hero
High Spirits
In Love and War
Land and Freedom
Living out Loud
The Long Walk Home
Mary Reilly
Memphis Belle
The Object of My Affection
Shadowlands
White Palace
You've Got Mail

Franco Ferrara
*A Farewell to Arms/Sons and
    Lovers*
*Francis of Assisi/Doctor Faus-
    tus*
Il gattopardo
La strada/Le notti di Cabiria
The Leopard
Ulysses
*The Vikings/Solomon and
    Sheba*
War and Peace

David Firman
The Land Girls

Clare Fisher
Mo' Better Blues

Rob Fisher
The Boys from Syracuse
Call Me Madam
St. Louis Woman

Robert Folk
Arabian Knight
In the Army Now
*Lawnmower Man 2: Beyond
    Cyberspace*
*The NeverEnding Story II: The
    Next Chapter*
Toy Soldiers
Trapped in Paradise

Bruce Fowler
Broken Arrow
The Rock

Charles Fox
Conan

David Michael Frank
A Kid in Aladdin's Palace
Out for Justice
The Staircase

Christopher Franke
Raven

Ian Freebairn–Smith
The Muppet Movie

Robert Freedman
The Wiz

Dominic Frontiere
Hang 'Em High/Guns for San Sebastian

Gavin Geenaway
Antz

Paul Gemignani
Follies

Charles Gerhardt
Gone with the Wind
Kings Row

Joseph Gershenson
The Glenn Miller Story
The War Lord
The Young Lions/This Earth Is Mine

Nick Glennie-Smith
Beyond Rangoon
Con Air
Crimson Tide
Nine Months
The Rock

Teese Gohl
This Is My Life

Ernest Gold
The Agony and the Ecstasy/The Pride and the Passion
Exodus
It's a Mad, Mad, Mad, Mad World
Judgment at Nuremberg

Billy Goldenberg
Around the World in 80 Days

Jerry Goldsmith
The Agony and the Ecstasy
Air Force One
Alien
Angie
Bad Girls
The Blue Max
Breakout
The Cassandra Crossing

Chain Reaction
Chinatown
City Hall
Coma
Congo
Criminal Law
Deep Rising
Dennis the Menace
The Edge
Executive Decision
Explorers
Extreme Prejudice
Fierce Creatures
First Blood
First Knight
Forever Young
The Ghost and the Darkness
Gremlins
Gremlins 2: The New Batch
Hoosiers
Hour of the Gun
In Like Flint/Our Man Flint
Inchon
Inner Space
Islands in the Stream
King Solomon's Mines
L.A. Confidential
Legend
Leviathan
Lilies of the Field
Link
Lionheart
Logan's Run
Love Field
MacArthur
Malice
Masada
Matinee
Medicine Man
The Mephisto Waltz/The Other
Mr. Baseball
Mulan
The Mummy
Night Crossing
Not Without My Daughter
Outland/Capricorn One
Papillon
Planet of the Apes
Planet of the Apes/Escape from the Planet of the Apes
Poltergeist
Poltergeist 2
Powder
Psycho II
QB VII
Raggedy Man
Rambo III
Rambo: First Blood Part II
Ransom/The Chairman
Rent-a-Cop
Rio Conchos
The River Wild
Rudy
The Russia House
The Sand Pebbles
The Secret of N.I.M.H.

The Shadow
Shiloh
Six Degrees of Separation
Sleeping with the Enemy
Small Soldiers
Stagecoach/The Loner
Star Trek: First Contact
Star Trek: Insurrection
Star Trek: The Motion Picture/Inside Star Trek
Star Trek V: The Final Frontier
A Streetcar Named Desire
Supergirl
Total Recall
Twilight's Last Gleaming
2001
U.S. Marshals
Viva Zapata!
Warlock
Who's Afraid of Virginia Woolf?
The Wind and the Lion

Joel Goldsmith
Shiloh

Miles Goodman
Getting Even with Dad
Larger than Life

Gordon Goodwin
Armageddon
Con Air
Enemy of the State

Ron Goodwin
The Trap

Christopher Gordon
Moby Dick

Patrick Gowers
Sherlock Holmes

Paul Grabowsky
Noah's Ark

Kurt Graunke
Maya

Johnny Green
An American in Paris
Brigadoon
Bye Bye Birdie
Easter Parade
High Society
Oliver!
Raintree County
Royal Wedding
Summer Stock
West Side Story

Gavin Greenaway
The Peacemaker

Harry Gregson-Williams
As Good as It Gets
The Borrowers

Crimson Tide
The Fan
Muppet Treasure Island
The Peacemaker
Smilla's Sense of Snow

Isobel Griffiths
Wing Commander

Andrew Gross
8 Heads in a Duffel Bag

Larry Groupe
Apt Pupil
Goodbye Lover
Incognito
The Usual Suspects

Dave Grusin
The Bonfire of the Vanities
The Cure
The Electric Horseman
The Fabulous Baker Boys
The Firm
The Graduate
Havana
Mulholland Falls
Selena
Tequila Sunrise
3 Days of the Condor

Christopher Gunning
Poirot

Evans Haile
Babes in Arms

Marvin Hamlisch
Frankie & Johnny
The Mirror Has Two Faces
Sophie's Choice
The Spy Who Loved Me
The Sting

Leigh Harline
Pinocchio

Don Harper
Broken Arrow
Moll Flanders
The Rock
Speed

Richard Hartley
An Awfully Big Adventure
Princess Caraboo
A Thousand Acres

Lennie Hayton
Good News
The Pirate
Singin' in the Rain
Star!
Till the Clouds Roll By
Ziegfeld Follies

Lennie Hayton and Lionel Newman
Hello, Dolly!

Ray Heindorf
Damn Yankees
For Whom the Bell Tolls
Giant
The Helen Morgan Story
The Music Man
Spellbound
A Star Is Born

Bernard Herrmann
Battle of Neretva
The Day the Earth Stood Still
Journey to the Center of the Earth
Laura/Jane Eyre
Mysterious Island
Night Digger
North by Northwest
Obsession
The Seventh Voyage of Sinbad
Sisters

Lee Holdridge
The Giant of Thunder Mountain
Into Thin Air: Death on the Everest
Old Gringo
One Against the Wind
Pastime
The Secret of N.I.M.H. 2
Texas

James Horner
Aliens
An American Tail
An American Tail: Fievel Goes West
Balto
*batteries not included
Brainstorm
Braveheart/Braveheart: More Music from the Original Soundtrack
Casper
Clear and Present Danger
Cocoon
Cocoon: The Return
Courage Under Fire
Deep Impact
The Devil's Own
Field of Dreams
Glory
Gorky Park
Jumanji
Krull
The Land Before Time
Legends of the Fall
The Man without a Face
The Mask of Zorro
Mighty Joe Young

The Name of the Rose
Once Around
Once Upon a Forest
The Pagemaster
Patriot Games
The Pelican Brief
Ransom
Red Heat
The Rocketeer
Searching for Bobby Fischer
Sneakers
The Spitfire Grill
Star Trek II: The Wrath of Khan
Star Trek III: The Search for Spock
Thunderheart
Titanic/Back to Titanic
Unlawful Entry
We're Back
Where the River Runs Black
Willow

James Newton Howard
Diggstown

Peter Howard
Annie

Dick Hyman
Everyone Says I Love You
Moonstruck

Alberto Iglesias
Live Flesh

Nick Ingman
Freddie as F.R.O.7.
Her Majesty Mrs. Brown
Jude
One Night Stand
Othello
Ronin
Shakespeare in Love
Welcome to Sarajevo

Damon Intrabarolo
Portrait of Terror

Grayston Ives
Shadowlands

Hiroyuki Iwaki
Rising Sun

Maurice Jarre
Almost an Angel
The Collector
Doctor Zhivago
Enemies, A Love Story
Enemy Mine
Ghost
Is Paris Burning?
Jacob's Ladder
Mad Max Beyond Thunderdome
The Man Who Would Be King
Moon over Parador

The Mosquito Coast
The Night of the Generals
Only the Lonely
A Passage to India
The Professionals
Ryan's Daughter
School Ties
Shadow of the Wolf
Tai-Pan
A Walk in the Clouds

Don Jennings
Ballroom

Laurie Johnson
First Men in the Moon
It's Alive 2
North by Northwest

Brynmor Jones
Universal Soldier

Quincy Jones
Roots
Walk, Don't Run
The Wiz

Trevor Jones
Brassed Off!
Dominick & Eugene
G.I. Jane
Kiss of Death
Labyrinth
Sea of Love

Michael Kamen
The Adventures of Baron Munchausen
Brazil
Circle of Friends
Company Business
The Dead Zone
Die Hard 2: Die Harder
Don Juan DeMarco
Highlander: The Original Scores
Inventing the Abbotts
Jack
Last Action Hero
Lethal Weapon 2/Lethal Weapon 3
License to Kill
Mr. Holland's Opus
Nothing but Trouble
101 Dalmatians
Robin Hood: Prince of Thieves
Shining Through
The Three Musketeers
What Dreams May Come

Artie Kane
Addams Family Values
Alien Resurrection
Bed of Roses
City Slickers II: The Legend of Curly's Gold
Dante's Peak

Devil's Advocate
Extreme Measures
A Few Good Men
The First Wives Club
Flubber
Forget Paris
The Frighteners
Ghosts of Mississippi
Heart and Souls
In & Out
Junior
Just Cause
Mars Attacks!
Men in Black
Mission: Impossible
Mr. Saturday Night
Mother
Mother Night
My Best Friend's Wedding
North
One Fine Day
Outbreak
A Perfect Murder
The Postman
Primal Fear
Restoration
The Santa Clause
Simon Birch
Sister Act
Stuart Saves His Family
Waterworld
Wrestling Ernest Hemingway

Edward Karam
The First Wives Club
Ghosts of Mississippi

Tadeusz Karolak
Total Eclipse

Tadeusz Karolak and Zdislaw Szostak
Blood & Wine

Jacek Kaspszyk
Fairy Tale

Richard Kaufman
Guarding Tess

Brian Keane
The Night Flier

Christopher Keene
Altered States

Arthur Kempel
The Arrival

Larry Kenton
The Siege

Randy Kerber
Rush

Huub Kerstens
Pascali's Island

Charles Ketcham
*The Young Indiana Jones
    Chronicles: Vols. 1–4*

William Kidd
B.A.P.s
The King and I

Mario Klemens
The Last Butterfly
The Mystery of Rampo

Harald Kloser
The Thirteenth Floor

Ken Kluger
The Education of Little Tree
Kiss the Girls

Varujan Kojian
*The Adventures of Robin
    Hood*
The Sea Hawk

Sonny Kompanek
Doc Hollywood
Fargo/Barton Fink
The Hudsucker Proxy
Rob Roy
Ulee's Gold

Stepan Konicek
The Last Butterfly
Portrait of a Lady

Michael Kosarin
Hercules
Marvin's Room

Irwin Kostal
Chitty Chitty Bang Bang
The Sound of Music

Nicholas Kraemer
The Madness of King George

William Kraft
Carlito's Way
Dead Again

Stanislaw Kravceyski
The Secret Garden

Ken Kugler
At First Sight
Last Dance
Losing Isaiah
The Net
October Sky
Of Mice and Men
A Price above Rubies
The Public Eye
Quiz Show
A River Runs Through It
Timecop

John Lanchbery
Evil under the Sun

Bill Lee
Do the Right Thing

Michel Legrand
Atlantic City
The Burning Shore
Ice Station Zebra
Les demoiselles de Rochefort
Les parapluies de Cherbourg
Madeline
Never Say Never Again
The Ring
The Thomas Crown Affair
The Three Musketeers

Sylvester Levay
Flashdance
Hot Shots!

Joseph Lilley
How the West Was Won

Joseph LoDuca
*Xena: Warrior Princess/Xena:
    Warrior Princess, Volume
    2/The Bitter Suite: A Musi-
    cal Odyssey*

Jean-Claude Malgoire
Ridicule

Henry Mancini
*The Adventures of the Great
    Mouse Detective*
Arabesque
Blind Date
Breakfast at Tiffany's
Charade
Darling Lili
Experiment in Terror
The Glass Menagerie
Hatari!
High Time
Lifeforce
Midas Run/The Night Visitor
The Molly Maguires
The Party
Peter Gunn
The Pink Panther
*The Pink Panther Strikes
    Again*
Revenge of the Pink Panther
Son of the Pink Panther
Tom and Jerry: The Movie
Touch of Evil
Two for the Road
*What Did You Do in the War,
    Daddy?*

Harry Manfredini
Aces: Iron Eagle III

Hummie Mann
The Addams Family
City Slickers

Neville Marriner
Amadeus

Natale Massara
Amore piombo e furore
The Barbarians
Dressed to Kill
Il mio West
Meridian
Raising Cain
Zelly and Me

Muir Mathieson
Gone with the Wind
Knights of the Round Table
Vertigo

Brian May
The Road Warrior

Daniel May
Everest

Dennis McCarthy
*Gone to Texas/Hidden in Si-
    lence*
Star Trek: Generations

Garry McDonald
*The Thorn Birds: The Missing
    Years*

Mark McKenzie
City Slickers
*The Disappearance of Garcia
    Lorca*
Frank and Jesse
Men in Black
Warlock: The Armageddon

Joel McNeely
The Avengers
Flipper
*Gold Diggers: The Secret of
    Bear Mountain*
Iron Will
Out of Africa
Psycho
Radioland Murders
Soldier
Terminal Velocity
Torn Curtain
The Trouble with Harry
Vertigo
Virus
Wild America
*The Young Indiana Jones
    Chronicles: Vols. 1–4*

Michael Melvoin
The Main Event

Steven Mercurio
Pet Sematary
Sphere

Wojciech Michniewski
Damage
The Secret Garden
When a Man Loves a Woman

Thomas Milano
Copycat

Cynthia Millar
Three Wishes

Vic Mizzy
The Addams Family

Hugo Montenegro
The Man from U.N.C.L.E.
*The Music from U.N.C.L.E.
    (The Original Soundtrack
    Affair)*

Harold Mooney
Rich Man, Poor Man

Angela Morley
Equus

Jerome Moross
The Cardinal

Ennio Morricone
Bugsy
Bulworth
Butterfly
Casualties of War
Cinema Paradiso
City of Joy
*The Conformist/A Man's
    Tragedy*
Crossing the Line
Disclosure
The Endless Game
A Fistful of Dollars
Frantic
Giu la testa
*The Good, the Bad and the
    Ugly*
Hamlet
*Hang 'Em High/Guns for San
    Sebastian*
Hundra
Il ladrone/L'harem
Il mercenario/Faccia a faccia
In the Line of Fire
*The Legend of the Pianist on
    the Ocean*
Lolita
Love Affair
The Mission
Novecento
Once Upon a Time in America
Once Upon a Time in the West
A Pure Formality
Rampage
Richard III
Sahara
The Star Maker
State of Grace

The Thing
A Time of Destiny
U-Turn
The Untouchables
Wolf

John Morris
The Elephant Man
The Producers
Scarlett
Spaceballs

Stanley Myers
The Deer Hunter
Trusting Beatrice/Cold Heaven

Mario Nascimbene
Alexander the Great/Barabbas
A Farewell to Arms/Sons and
   Lovers
Francis of Assisi/Doctor Faus-
   tus
The Vikings/Solomon and
   Sheba

Olivier Nelson
Alfie

Vaclav Neumann
The Mystery of Rampo

Ira Newborn
The Late Shift
The Naked Gun 2 1/2: The
   Smell of Fear

Alfred Newman
Airport
Anastasia
Carousel
The Day the Earth Stood Still
The Egyptian
Forever Amber
The Greatest Story Ever Told
How Green Was My Valley
How the West Was Won
The King and I
Laura/Jane Eyre
The Robe
South Pacific
Stormy Weather
There's No Business Like
   Show Business

David Newman
Anastasia
Critters
Hoffa
I Love Trouble
Mr. Destiny
Operation Dumbo Drop
Out to Sea
The Phantom

Emil Newman
Stormy Weather

Lionel Newman
An Affair to Remember
Bandolero!
Boy on a Dolphin
Damien: Omen II
The Day the Earth Stood Still
Doctor Dolittle
The Final Conflict
The Omen
The Sound and the Fury
There's No Business Like
   Show Business
The Young Lions/This Earth Is
   Mine

Randy Newman
Maverick
The Natural
The Paper
Toy Story

Thomas Newman
Fried Green Tomatoes
How to Make an American
   Quilt
Josh and S.A.M.
The Linguini Incident
Little Women
Mad City
Meet Joe Black
Oscar and Lucinda
The People vs. Larry Flynt
The Player
The Rapture
Red Corner
Scent of a Woman
The Shawshank Redemption
The War
Welcome Home Roxy
   Carmichael

Bruno Nicolai
A Ciascuno il Suo/Una ques-
   tione d'onore
Il clan dei Siciliani
Il Conte Dracula
Il mercenario/Faccia a faccia
Il mio nome e' Shangai Joe/I
   giorni della violenza
La tenda rossa
L'Armata Brancaleone/Branca-
   leone alle Crociate
Navajo Joe
100.000 dollari per Ringo
The Stranger/The Innocent
Waterloo

Lennie Niehaus
Absolute Power
The Bridges of Madison
   County
A Perfect World

Jose Nieto
Passion in the Desert

Monty Norman
Dr. No

Alex North
The Agony and the
   Ecstasy/The Pride and the
   Passion
Cheyenne Autumn
The Dead/Journey into Fear
Dragonslayer
The Misfits
Rich Man, Poor Man
The Rose Tattoo
South Seas Adventure
Spartacus

Michael Nyman
Gattaca
The Piano
Prospero's Books
Ravenous
Six Days Six Nights

Prionnsias O'Duinn
Dancing at Lughnasa

Riz Ortolani
Addio Zio Tom
Day of Anger/Beyond the Law
Mondo Cane
Una ragione per vivere e una
   per morire

John Ottman
Snow White: A Tale of Terror

J. Leonard Oxley
Quartet

Gene Page
Blacula

Marty Paich
Alive
Dave
Dying Young
The Fugitive
Intersection
The Man in the Moon
The Prince of Tides
The Saint of Fort Washington
Three Men and a Little Lady
Wyatt Earp

Marty Paloh
Grand Canyon

Thomas Pasatieri
Primary Colors
Sommersby

Nick Perrito
Cousins

Jean-Claude Petit
Beaumarchais l'insolent
Cyrano de Bergerac

Jean de Florette/Manon des
   sources
Le Hussard sur le toit
The Return of the Musketeers

Barrington Pheloung
Hilary and Jackie
Inspector Morse: Volumes 1,
   2, & 3
Nostradamus

Piero Piccioni
Il momento della verita
La spina dorsale del diavolo
Minnesota Clay
Swept Away

**Piero Piccioni and Bruno
Nicolai**
C'era una volta

Philip Pickett
Elizabeth

Nicholas Pike
Star Kid

Nicola Piovani
Ginger and Fred
Il sole anche di notte
Intervista
Life Is Beautiful
Tu Ridi

Donald Pippin
Mame

Gianfranco Plenizio
L'Armata Brancaleone/Branca-
   leone alle Crociate

Basil Poledouris
The Blue Lagoon
Conan the Barbarian
Conan the Destroyer
Free Willy
Free Willy 2
Hot Shots! Part Deux
The Hunt for Red October
It's My Party
Les Miserables
Lonesome Dove
On Deadly Ground
Quigley Down Under
Red Dawn
RoboCop 3
Starship Troopers
Under Siege 2: Dark Territory

Andrew Powell
Ladyhawke

Andre Previn
Bells Are Ringing
Elmer Gantry
Gigi
Irma La Douce

It's Always Fair Weather
Kismet
Kiss Me, Kate
My Fair Lady
Thoroughly Modern Millie

Guy Protheroe
1492: Conquest of Paradise

Carlo Quaranta
Francis of Assisi/Doctor Faustus

Harry Rabinowitz
The English Patient
Howard's End
Lord of the Flies
Masters of the Universe
Maurice
Message in a Bottle
Music Box
The Proprietor
The Remains of the Day
Surviving Picasso

Claudio Ragazzi
Next Stop Wonderland

Nic Raine
Nosferatu
Portrait of a Lady

David Raksin
The Bad and the Beautiful

Joe Raposo
The Great Muppet Caper

Simon Rattle
Henry V

J.A.C. Redford
Benny & Joon
Billy Bathgate
Black Beauty
Bye Bye, Love
D3: The Mighty Ducks
Heart and Souls
Independence
The Joy Luck Club
The Key to Rebecca
A Kid in King Arthur's Court
The Little Mermaid
The Nightmare Before Christmas
Oliver & Company
The Trip to Bountiful

Graeme Revell
Chinese Box
Until the End of the World

Lucas Richmond
As Good as It Gets
Face/Off

Nelson Riddle
Can-Can
Lolita
On a Clear Day You Can See Forever
Paint Your Wagon
St. Louis Blues

Michael Riesman
The Thin Blue Line

Paul Riser
Car Wash: Best of Rose Royce from Car Wash

J. Peter Robinson
Highlander: The Original Scores

Leonard Rosenman
The Fantastic Voyage
Keeper of the City
The Lord of the Rings
RoboCop 2

Milton Rosenstock
Gypsy

Laurence Rosenthal
Anastasia: The Mystery of Anna
The Bourne Identity
Clash of the Titans
Meetings with Remarkable Men
Peter the Great
The Young Indiana Jones Chronicles: Vols. 1–4

William Ross
Beetlejuice
Big Top Pee-Wee

Hubert Rostaing
Cesar et Rosalie

Hubert Rostaing and Carlo Savina
Barocco

Nino Rota
Romeo and Juliet

Bruce Rowland
Andre
Lightning Jack
Return to Snowy River Part II

Miklos Rozsa
All the Brothers Were Valiant
Ben-Hur
El Cid
Fedora
The Golden Voyage of Sinbad
King of Kings
Lust for Life
Quo Vadis

The Thief of Bagdad/The Jungle Book
Time after Time
Young Bess

Michel Rubini
Nemesis

Arthur Rubinstein
Nick of Time

Carlo Rustichelli
Alfredo Alfredo
La ragazza di Bube

Craig Safan
Angel
The Last Starfighter

Ryuichi Sakamoto
High Heels
Little Buddha
Snake Eyes

Paul Salamunovich
The Postman

Esa-Pekka Salonen
The Red Violin

Hans J. Salter
Maya

Heinz Sandauer
Destination Moon

Philippe Sarde
Quest for Fire

Carlo Savina
Amarcord
The Bear
The Clowns
8½
Fort Saganne
Giulietta degli Spiriti
Gli ultimi giorni di Pompei
Il bidone
Il Casanova
La dolce vita
La maja desnuda
Spara forte, piu forte . . . non capisco
The Taming of the Shrew

Walter Scharf
Willy Wonka & the Chocolate Factory

Kim Scharnberg
The Civil War

Lalo Schifrin
Che!
Cool Hand Luke
The Eagle Has Landed

The Four Musketeers/The Eagle Has Landed/Voyage of the Damned
Mission: Impossible
The Osterman Weekend
Rush Hour
Tango
Voyage of the Damned

Eberhard Schoener
The Killing Fields

John Scott
Anthony Adverse
Antony and Cleopatra
Becoming Colette
The Deceivers
The Final Countdown
King of the Wind
Lionheart
Man on Fire
Red King, White Knight
Ruby
The Second Jungle Book
Shogun Mayeda
The Shooting Party/Birds and Planes
To the Ends of the Earth
20,000 Leagues Under the Sea
Walking Thunder
Yor: The Hunter from the Future

Don Sebesky
The Rosary Murders

James Sedares
El Cid

Misha Segal
Phantom of the Opera

Klauspeter Seibel
The Thief of Bagdad/The Jungle Book

Tullio Serafin
Moonstruck

Eric Serra
The Fifth Element

Jonathan Shaeffer
Batman Forever

Francis Shaw
Merlin of the Crystal Cage

Ed Shearmur
Babe: Pig in the City
The Governess
Wings of the Dove

Jonathan Sheffer
Alien 3
Batman Returns

Cobb
Demolition Man
Golden Gate
Heat
Highlander: The Original Scores
In Dreams
Interview with the Vampire
Michael Collins
Pure Luck
Sommersby
Sphere
A Time to Kill

David Shire
Bed & Breakfast

Howard Shore
Before and After
The Client
Crash
Ed Wood
The Fly
The Game
Looking for Richard
M Butterfly
Mrs. Doubtfire
Nobody's Fool
Philadelphia
Prelude to a Kiss
Seven
The Silence of the Lambs

Alan Silvestri
The Abyss
Back to the Future
Back to the Future, Part II
Back to the Future, Part III
Blown Away
Contact
Death Becomes Her
Eraser
Father of the Bride
Forrest Gump
Grumpier Old Men
Judge Dredd
Mouse Hunt
The Odd Couple II
The Parent Trap
Practical Magic
Predator 2
The Quick and the Dead
Richie Rich
Soap Dish
Volcano
Who Framed Roger Rabbit?

Tim Simonec
Army of Darkness
Children of the Corn II
Children of the Night
The Crow
The Crow: City of Angels
The Hand that Rocks the Cradle
Hard Target

Kazaam
Mighty Morphin Power Rangers: The Movie
No Escape
The People Under the Stairs
The Siege
Smoke Signals
Street Fighter
Xena: Warrior Princess/Xena: Warrior Princess, Volume 2/The Bitter Suite: A Musical Odyssey

Claudio Simonetti
The Versace Murder

Sergei Skripka
Russia's War

Michael Small
Consenting Adults
Wagons East!

Bruce Smeaton
Iceman
A Town Like Alice

David Snell
Addicted to Love
Cliffhanger
Donnie Brasco
Emma
Exit to Eden
Frankenstein
Great Expectations
In the Name of the Father
The Jungle Book
A Little Princess
Much Ado about Nothing
Needful Things
Only You
Richard III
The Road to Wellville
The Saint
Sirens
Tombstone
Used People
War of the Buttons
Where Angels Fear to Tread

Mark Snow
Born to Be Wild
20,000 Leagues under the Sea

Sir Georg Solti
Immortal Beloved

William Southgate
Utu

Johnny Spence
Elizabeth Taylor in London/Four in the Morning

David Stanhope
Babe
Paradise Road

Michael Starobin
Life with Mikey

Julian Stein
Anything Goes

Fred Steiner
King Kong

Max Steiner
Casablanca
Gone with the Wind

Alexander Steinert
Bambi

Eric Stern
Oh, Kay!

Leopold Stokowski
Fantasia

Georgie Stoll
Cabin in the Sky
Easter Parade
For Me and My Girl
Girl Crazy

Morris Stoloff
The Eddy Duchin Story
Pal Joey
Picnic

Christopher L. Stone
Moon 44
The Stupids
Ticks/Fist of the North Star

Lawrence Stone
The Thorn Birds: The Missing Years

Richard Stone
Dolores Claiborne
To Die For

Herbert Stothart
The Wizard of Oz

Ron Straigis
The Devil in Miss Jones

Edward Strauss
Anything Goes

William J. Stromberg
King Kong

William T. Stromberg
Another Dawn
Garden of Evil
House of Frankenstein
Magic in the Water
Moby Dick
Slums of Beverly Hills
They Died with Their Boots On

Bojan Sudic
Queen Margot

The Symphonic Orchestra Unione Musicisti di Roma
The Cassandra Crossing

Zdzislaw Szostak
Fairy Tale
Feast of July

Frederic Talgorn
Robotjox
The Temp

Michael Tavera
Frozen Assets

Neil Thomson
Second Best

Ken Thorne
Act of Piracy/The Great White

Randy Thornton
Dr. Jekyll and Ms. Hyde
Hercules: The Legendary Journeys, Vol. 2
Xena: Warrior Princess/Xena: Warrior Princess, Volume 2/The Bitter Suite: A Musical Odyssey
Young Hercules

Dimitri Tiomkin
The Alamo
The Fall of the Roman Empire
55 Days at Peking
Friendly Persuasion
Giant
The Guns of Navarone
The Old Man and the Sea

Mike Townend
Cult TV Themes

Colin Towns
The Buccaneers
Cadfael

Fiachra Trench
The Boxer
The House of the Spirits
Into the West
Twelfth Night
White Squall

Armando Trovaioli
Dramma della gelosia
I lunghi giorni della vendetta
Profumo di donna

Bobby Tucker
The Wiz

Christopher Tyng
The Associate

Pier Luigi Urbini
Falstaff
Sedotta e abbandonata

The Utah Symphony Orchestra
20,000 Leagues under the Sea

Andre Vandernoot
Toto le heros

Carl Vine
Babe

Derek Wadsworth
The Whales of August

Alan Wagner
Night of the Running Man

Shirley Walker
Arachnophobia
Article 99
Batman
Children of a Lesser God
Darkman
Dick Tracy/Madonna: I'm Breathless
Edward Scissorhands
Escape from L.A.
Free Willy 2
A Goofy Movie
A League of Their Own
Memoirs of an Invisible Man
Night Breed
Pacific Heights
Radio Flyer
Toys
True Lies

Oliver Wallace
Alice in Wonderland
Dumbo
Peter Pan

Thomas Wanker
The Thirteenth Floor

Ken Wannberg
The Philadelphia Experiment/Mother Lode

Mark Watters
Mrs. Winterbourne
Quest for Camelot

Franz Waxman
The Nun's Story
Prince Valiant
The Spirit of St. Louis
Taras Bulba

Jimmy Webb
The Last Unicorn

Rick Wentworth
Midway
Restoration

Fred Werner
Sweet Charity

Michael Whalen
Phantom of the Forest

Bill Whelan
Some Mother's Son

Larry Wilcox
Fargo/Barton Fink

Dr. Keith Wilkinson
The Rainbow

John Williams
The Accidental Tourist
Always
Amistad
Born on the Fourth of July
Close Encounters of the Third Kind

The Cowboys
Dracula
Earthquake
The Eiger Sanction
Empire of the Sun
The Empire Strikes Back
E.T.: The Extra-Terrestrial
Far and Away
The Fury
Home Alone
Home Alone 2: Lost in New York
Hook
Indiana Jones and the Last Crusade
Indiana Jones and the Temple of Doom
Jane Eyre
Jaws
Jaws 2
JFK
Jurassic Park
The Lost World
1941
Nixon
The Paper Chase/The Poseidon Adventure
Presumed Innocent
Raiders of the Lost Ark
The Reivers
Return of the Jedi
The River
Rosewood
Sabrina
Saving Private Ryan
Schindler's List
Seven Years in Tibet
Sleepers
Stanley & Iris
Star Wars
Star Wars Episode 1: The Phantom Menace
Step Mom
Superman: The Movie
The Witches of Eastwick

Allan Wilson
Beavis and Butt-Head Do America
Body Parts
Cool World
The Dark Half
Lassie
Mountains of the Moon
The New Swiss Family Robinson
The Puppet Masters
The Saint
Sundown
The Theory of Flight

Debbie Wiseman
Tom and Viv
Wilde

Antoni Wit
At Play in the Fields of the Lord

Paul Francis Witt
Def-Con 4

David Woodcock (Baroque Orchestra)
Dangerous Liaisons

Christopher Young
Entrapment
The Vagrant

Victor Young
Around the World in 80 Days
The Brave One
Johnny Guitar
Rio Grande
Samson and Delilah/The Quiet Man

Robert Ziegler
Hamlet
Sense and Sensibility

The Lyricist Index lists the sound-tracks in MusicHound Soundtracks that have a lyricist noted for them. Under each lyricist's name is the name of the soundtrack on which that lyricist can be found. If a sound-track has more than one lyricist, the soundtrack name will be listed separately under the names of each of the lyricists.

Lee Adams
Bye Bye Birdie
Golden Boy

Richard Adler
Damn Yankees
The Pajama Game

Lynn Ahrens
Anastasia
Ragtime

Maxwell Anderson
Lost in the Stars

Howard Ashman
Aladdin
Beauty and the Beast

Marshall Barer
Once Upon a Mattress

Lionel Bart
Goldfinger
Oliver!

Alan Bergman
Ballroom

Marilyn Bergman
Ballroom

Irving Berlin
Annie Get Your Gun
Call Me Madam
Easter Parade
Louisiana Purchase

John Bettis
Legend

Albany Bigard
Play On!

Susan Birkenhead
Jelly's Last Jam
Triumph of Love

Don Black
Sunset Blvd.
Thunderball
True Grit

Ralph Blane
Best Foot Forward
Meet Me in St. Louis

Guy Bolton
Till the Clouds Roll By

Alain Boublil
Miss Saigon

Gregory Boyd
The Civil War

Leslie Bricusse
Doctor Dolittle
Goldfinger
Home Alone
Home Alone 2: Lost in New York
Hook
Jekyll & Hyde

The Roar of the Greasepaint—The Smell of the Crowd
Stop the World—I Want to Get Off
Tom and Jerry: The Movie
Victor/Victoria
Willy Wonka & the Chocolate Factory
You Only Live Twice

Jason Robert Brown
Parade

Lew Brown
Good News

Irving Caesar
No, No, Nanette

Sammy Cahn
How the West Was Won

Truman Capote
House of Flowers

Ben Carruthers
Play On!

Warren Casey
Grease

Martin Charnin
Annie
Two by Two

Otis Clements
Irene

Betty Comden
Bells Are Ringing
Do Re Mi
Hallelujah, Baby!
It's Always Fair Weather
On the Town
On the Twentieth Century
Peter Pan

The Will Rogers Follies
Wonderful Town

Joe Darion
Man of La Mancha

Hal David
Butch Cassidy and the Sun-
dance Kid
Casino Royale
Lost Horizon
Moonraker
On Her Majesty's Secret Ser-
vice
What's New, Pussycat?

Mack David
Cinderella
Play On!
The Quiller Memorandum
Sophisticated Ladies

Eddie DeLange
Play On!
Sophisticated Ladies

Jacques Demy
Les demoiselles de Rochefort

B.G. DeSylva
Good News
Till the Clouds Roll By

Howard Dietz
The Band Wagon

Mort Dixon
42nd Street

Bernard Dougall
Lovely to Look At

Al Dubin
42nd Street

Fred Ebb
The Act
Cabaret
Chicago
Flora the Red Menace
Kiss of the Spider Woman:
The Musical
The Rink
Steel Pier
Zorba

Sherman Edwards
1776

Danny Elfman
The Nightmare Before Christmas

T.S. Eliot
Cats

Duke Ellington
Play On!

Sophisticated Ladies

John Entwistle
Tommy

Tom Eyen
Dreamgirls

Jose Fernandez
Fame

Dorothy Fields
Lovely to Look At
Roberta
Sweet Charity
Till the Clouds Roll By

Arthur Freed
Singin' in the Rain

Milt Gable
Play On!

Reg. E. Gaines
Bring In

Ira Gasman
The Life

Charles Gaynor
Irene

Don George
Play On!
Sophisticated Ladies

Ira Gershwin
An American in Paris
Crazy for You
Funny Face
Girl Crazy
Lady, Be Good!
My One and Only
Of Thee I Sing
Oh, Kay!
Porgy and Bess
A Star Is Born
Strike Up the Band

E. Ray Goetz
For Me and My Girl

Irving Gordon
Play On!

Mack Gordon
Summer Stock

Charles Randolph Grean
Dark Shadows: The 30th Anniversary Collection

Adolph Green
Bells Are Ringing
Do Re Mi
Hallelujah, Baby!
It's Always Fair Weather

On the Town
On the Twentieth Century
Peter Pan
The Will Rogers Follies
Wonderful Town

John Guare
Sophisticated Ladies

George Haimsohn
Dames at Sea

Carol Hall
The Best Little Whorehouse in
Texas

Oscar Hammerstein II
Carousel
Cinderella
Flower Drum Song
The King and I
Lovely to Look At
Oklahoma!
Roberta
Show Boat
The Sound of Music
South Pacific
State Fair
Till the Clouds Roll By

Christopher Hampton
Sunset Blvd.

Otto Harbach
Lovely to Look At
No, No, Nanette
Roberta
Till the Clouds Roll By

E.Y. Harburg
Darling of the Day
Finian's Rainbow
Jamaica
The Wizard of Oz

Sheldon Harnick
The Apple Tree
Fiddler on the Roof
Fiorello!
She Loves Me

George Harrison
Help!
Let It Be
Magical Mystery Tour

Charles Hart
Phantom of the Opera

Lorenz Hart
Babes in Arms
The Boys from Syracuse
On Your Toes
Pal Joey

David Heneker
Irma La Douce

Jerry Herman
Dear World
Hello, Dolly!
La Cage Aux Folles
Mack and Mabel
Mame

DuBose Heyward
Porgy and Bess

Al Hoffman
Cinderella

Murray Horwitz
Ain't Misbehavin'

Jim Jacobs
Grease

Harry James
Play On!

Elton John
The Lion King

J.C. Johnson
Ain't Misbehavin'

Tom Jones
The Fantasticks
I Do! I Do!
110 in the Shade

John Kander
Steel Pier

Nick Kenny
Play On!

Ed Kirkeby
Ain't Misbehavin'

Edward Kleban
A Chorus Line

Nan Knighton
The Scarlet Pimpernel

Herbert Kretzmer
Les Miserables

Sid Kuller
Sophisticated Ladies

Manny Kurtz
Sophisticated Ladies

Jonathan Larson
Rent

Edward Laska
Till the Clouds Roll By

John Latouche
Cabin in the Sky

Carolyn Leigh
Little Me

Peter Pan
Wildcat

John Lennon
A Hard Day's Night
Help!
Let It Be
Magical Mystery Tour

Alan Jay Lerner
Brigadoon
Camelot
Gigi
My Fair Lady
On a Clear Day You Can See
    Forever
Paint Your Wagon
Royal Wedding

Edgar Leslie
For Me and My Girl

Ira Levin
Drat! The Cat!

Jacques Levy
Fame

Jerry Livingston
Cinderella

Frank Loesser
Guys and Dolls
How to Succeed in Business
    without Really Trying
The Most Happy Fella

David Lynch
Twin Peaks: Fire Walk with Me

Richard Maltby Jr.
Ain't Misbehavin'
Miss Saigon

George Marion Jr.
Ain't Misbehavin'

Hugh Martin
Best Foot Forward
Meet Me in St. Louis

Joseph McCarthy
Irene

Paul McCartney
A Hard Day's Night
Help!
Let It Be
Magical Mystery Tour

Jimmy McHugh
Lovely to Look At
Roberta
Till the Clouds Roll By

Mendelson
A Charlie Brown Christmas

Johnny Mercer
The Belle of New York
Darling Lili
How the West Was Won
42nd Street
Li'l Abner
St. Louis Woman
Seven Brides for Seven Broth-
    ers
Sophisticated Ladies

Bob Merrill
Carnival
Funny Girl

Sidney Michaels
Ben Franklin in Paris

Robin Miller
Dames at Sea

Roger Miller
Big River

Irving Mills
Play On!
Sophisticated Ladies

Keith Moon
Tommy

Takis Morakis
Boy on a Dolphin

Julian More
Irma La Douce

Larry Morey
Snow White and the Seven
    Dwarfs

Jack Murphy
The Civil War

Henry Nemo
Play On!
Sophisticated Ladies

Anthony Newley
Goldfinger
The Roar of the Greasepaint—
    The Smell of the Crowd
Stop the World—I Want to Get
    Off
Willy Wonka & the Chocolate
    Factory

Monty Norman
Irma La Douce

Richard O'Brien
The Rocky Horror Picture
    Show

Mitchell Parish
Sophisticated Ladies

Dean Pitchford
Footloose

Cole Porter
Anything Goes
Can-Can
High Society
Kiss Me, Kate
Out of This World
The Pirate
Silk Stockings

James Rado
Hair

Gerome Ragni
Hair

Andy Razaf
Ain't Misbehavin'

John Redmond
Play On!
Sophisticated Ladies

Tim Rice
Aladdin
Beauty and the Beast
Evita
Jesus Christ Superstar
Joseph and the Amazing Tech-
    nicolor Dreamcoat
The Lion King

Leo Robin
Gentlemen Prefer Blondes

Richard Rodgers
No Strings

Harold Rome
Fanny
I Can Get It for You Wholesale

Billy Rose
Ain't Misbehavin'

Jerry Ross
Damn Yankees
The Pajama Game

Bob Russell
Play On!
Sophisticated Ladies

Carol Bayer Sager
They're Playing Our Song

Fred Saidy
Jamaica

Lester A. Santly
Ain't Misbehavin'

Stephen Schwartz
Godspell
The Hunchback of Notre Dame
Pocahontas

Richard M. Sherman
Chitty Chitty Bang Bang
Mary Poppins

Robert B. Sherman
Chitty Chitty Bang Bang
Mary Poppins

Charlie Smalls
The Wiz

Paul J. Smith
Pinocchio

Stephen Sondheim
Anyone Can Whistle
Company
Do I Hear a Waltz?
Follies
A Funny Thing Happened on
    the Way to the Forum
Gypsy
Into the Woods
A Little Night Music
Merrily We Roll Along
Pacific Overtures
Passion
Side by Side by Sondheim
A Stephen Sondheim Evening
Sunday in the Park with
    George
Sweeney Todd
West Side Story

Richard Sparks
The Secret of N.I.M.H. 2

Ringo Starr
Magical Mystery Tour

Michael Stewart
Barnum

Billy Strayhorn
Play On!
Sophisticated Ladies

Pete Townshend
Tommy

Stephan Trask
Hedwig and the Angry Inch

Peter Udell
Purlie
Shenandoah

Ned Washington
Dumbo
Pinocchio

Paul Francis Webster
Boy on a Dolphin
The Fall of the Roman Empire
The Guns of Navarone
Play On!
Sophisticated Ladies

Richard Wilbur
Candide

Frank Wildhorn
The Civil War

Clarence Williams
Ain't Misbehavin'

Paul Williams
Bugsy Malone

Meredith Willson
The Music Man
The Unsinkable Molly Brown

Sandy Wilson
The Boy Friend

P.G. Wodehouse
Till the Clouds Roll By

Maury Yeston
Nine
Titanic

David Zippel
City of Angels

This index is a guide to all of the artists and groups included in the Music-Hound series of books (MusicHound Rock, MusicHound Country, MusicHound Blues, MusicHound R&B, Music-Hound Lounge, Music-Hound Folk, MusicHound Jazz, MusicHound Swing, and MusicHound World). Following the artist or group's name you'll find the book (or books) they appear in. Because Music-Hound Soundtracks is organized by title rather than performer, its entries are not referenced in this index.

a-ha
See MH Rock

A House
See MH Rock

A. Robic and the Exertions
See MH Folk

A+
See MH R&B

A3
See MH Rock

Aaliyah
See MH R&B

Najat Aatabou
See MH World

Abana Ba Nasery
See MH World

Greg Abate
See MH Jazz

ABBA
See MH Lounge, MH Rock

Dimi Mint Abba
See MH World

Gregory Abbott
See MH R&B

ABC
See MH Rock

Abdelli
See MH World

Paula Abdul
See MH R&B, MH Rock

Ahmed Abdul-Malik
See MH Jazz

Ahmed Abdullah
See MH Jazz

Abel & Kaninerna
See MH World

John Abercrombie
See MH Jazz

Rabib Abou-Khalil
See MH World

Camara Aboubacar
See MH World

Above the Law
See MH R&B

Colonel Abrams
See MH R&B

Muhal Richard Abrams
See MH Jazz

Rick Abrams
See MH Folk

Nathan Abshire
See MH Folk, MH World

Absolute Zeros
See MH Rock

The Abyssinians
See MH World

AC/DC
See MH Rock

The Accelerators
See MH Rock

Ace
See MH Rock

Johnny Ace
See MH Blues, MH R&B, MH Rock

Ace of Base
See MH R&B, MH Rock

The Aces
See MH Blues

Acetone
See MH Rock

Barbara Acklin
See MH R&B

Acoustic Alchemy
See MH Jazz

Acousticats
See MH Folk

Roy Acuff
See MH Country, MH Folk

Ad Vielle Que Pourra
See MH World

Adam & the Ants
See MH Rock

Bryan Adams
See MH Rock

George Adams
See MH Jazz

Johnny Adams
See MH Blues, MH Jazz, MH R&B

Oleta Adams
See MH R&B

Pepper (Park) Adams
See MH Jazz

Barry Adamson
See MH Lounge, MH Rock

Adaro
See MH World

C.C. Adcock
See MH Rock

Eddie Adcock
See MH Country, MH Folk

Julian "Cannonball" Adderley
See MH Jazz, MH Lounge

Obo Addy
See MH World

Yacub Addy
See MH World

King Sunny Adé
See MH Rock, MH World

Adioa
See MH World

Hasil Adkins
See MH Rock

Trace Adkins
See MH Country

Helen Folasade Adu
See MH Lounge

The Adverts
See MH Rock

Aengus
See MH Folk

Aerosmith
See MH Rock

Ron Affif
See MH Jazz

The Afghan Whigs
See MH Rock

A.F.I.
See MH Rock

Africando
See MH World

The Afro Blue Band
See MH Jazz

Afro Celt Sound System
See MH World

Afro Rican
See MH R&B

Agent Orange
See MH Rock

Agents of Good Roots
See MH Rock

Agnes Gooch
See MH Rock

Eden Ahbez
See MH Lounge

Ahmad
See MH R&B

Mahmoud Ahmed
See MH World

Caroline Aiken
See MH Folk

Air
See MH Jazz, MH Rock

Air Miami
See MH Rock

Air Supply
See MH Rock

Kei Akagi
See MH Jazz

David "Stringbean" Akeman
See MH Country, MH Folk

Pierre Akendengue
See MH World

Garfield Akers
See MH Blues

Rhett Akins
See MH Country

Akinyele
See MH R&B

Toshiko Akiyoshi
See MH Jazz

Farid al-Atrash
See MH World

Alaap
See MH World

Alabama
See MH Country

Alabina
See MH World

Scott Alarik
See MH Folk

The Alarm
See MH Rock

Joe Albany
See MH Jazz

Chava Alberstein
See MH World

Albion Band
See MH Folk

Albion Country Band
See MH Rock

Albita
See MH World

Gerald Albright
See MH Jazz, MH R&B

Alcatrazz
See MH Rock

Howard Alden
See MH Jazz, MH Swing

Ronnie Aldrich
See MH Lounge

Brian Ales
See MH Jazz

Alessi
See MH Lounge

Alger Alexander
See MH Blues

Arthur Alexander
See MH R&B, MH Rock

Eric Alexander
See MH Jazz

John Marshall Alexander Jr.
See MH Blues

Monty Alexander
See MH Jazz

Texas Alexander
See MH Blues

Haris Alexiou
See MH World

Jerry Alfred & the Medicine Beat
See MH World

Pat Alger
See MH Country, MH Folk

Alice in Chains
See MH Rock

Alien Fashion Show
See MH Swing

Tha Alkaholiks
See MH R&B

All
See MH Rock

All-4-One
See MH R&B

The All Girl Boys
See MH Folk

All Saints
See MH Rock

Gary Allan
See MH Country

Carl Allen
See MH Jazz

Fulton Allen
See MH Blues

Geri Allen
See MH Jazz

Harley Allen
See MH Country

Harry Allen
See MH Jazz

Henry "Red" Allen
See MH Jazz, MH Swing

Lillian Allen
See MH World

Peter Allen
See MH Lounge

Red Allen
See MH Country, MH Folk

Rex Allen
See MH Country

Rex Allen Jr.
See MH Country

Steve Allen
See MH Jazz, MH Lounge

Terry Allen
See MH Country, MH Folk

Red Allen & Frank Wakefield
See MH Country

Jenny Allinder
See MH Folk

Amy Allison
See MH Country, MH Rock

Ben Allison
See MH Jazz

Luther Allison
See MH Blues, MH Folk

Mose Allison
See MH Blues, MH Folk, MH Jazz, MH Lounge

The Allman Brothers Band
See MH Blues, MH Rock

Alloy Orchestra
See MH Jazz

Karrin Allyson
See MH Jazz

Laurindo Almeida
See MH Jazz, MH Lounge

Almighty RSO
See MH R&B

Herb Alpert
See MH Jazz, MH Lounge, MH World

Alphaville
See MH Rock

Peter Alsop
See MH Folk

Gerald Alston
See MH R&B

Alt
See MH Rock

Altan
See MH Folk, MH Rock, MH World

John Altenburgh
See MH Jazz

Altered Images
See MH Rock

Joey Altruda with the Cocktail Crew
See MH Lounge

Barry Altschul
See MH Jazz

Dave Alvin
See MH Blues, MH Country, MH Folk, MH Rock

Phil Alvin
See MH Blues, MH Country, MH Rock

Amampondo
See MH World

Amazing Blondel
See MH Folk

The Amazing Rhythm Aces
See MH Country, MH Folk

Eric Ambel
See MH Rock

Ambitious Lovers
See MH Rock

Franco Ambrosetti
See MH Jazz

Ambrosia
See MH Rock

America
See MH Folk, MH Rock

The American Breed
See MH Rock

The American Cafe Orchestra
See MH Folk

American Flyer
See MH Rock

American Music Club
See MH Rock

The Ames Brothers
See MH Lounge

The Amidons
See MH Folk

Amina
See MH World

aMiniature
See MH Rock

Albert Ammons
See MH Jazz, MH Swing

Gene "Jug" Ammons
See MH Jazz

Tori Amos
See MH Rock

The Amps
See MH Rock

Anam
See MH World

Robin Adnan Anders
See MH World

Eric Andersen
See MH Folk, MH Rock

Andersen, Danko, Fjeld
See MH Rock

Al Anderson
See MH Country

Bill Anderson
See MH Country

Chris Anderson
See MH Jazz

Clifton Anderson
See MH Jazz

Ernestine Anderson
See MH Jazz

Fred Anderson
See MH Jazz

Ian Anderson
See MH Rock

John Anderson
See MH Country

Laurie Anderson
See MH Rock, MH World

Leroy Anderson
See MH Lounge

Little Willie Anderson
See MH Blues

Lynn Anderson
See MH Country

Pete Anderson
See MH Country

Pink Anderson
See MH Blues, MH Folk

Ray Anderson
See MH Jazz

Wessell Anderson
See MH Jazz

Leny Andrade
See MH World

Leah Andreone
See MH Rock

Ernie Andrews
See MH Jazz

Julie Andrews
See MH Lounge

Molly Andrews
See MH Folk

The Andrews Sisters
See MH Lounge, MH Swing

Horace Andy
See MH Rock

Angel
See MH Rock

Maya Angelou
See MH Lounge, MH World

The Angels
See MH Rock

Anggun
See MH World

The Animals
See MH Blues, MH Rock

Anitas Livs
See MH World

Paul Anka
See MH Lounge, MH Rock

Ann-Margret
See MH Lounge

Annabouboula
See MH World

Anotha Level
See MH R&B

Another Girl
See MH Rock

Adam Ant
See MH Rock

Antenna
See MH Rock

Marc Anthony
See MH World

Ray Anthony
See MH Lounge, MH Swing

Anthrax
See MH Rock

Anti-Nowhere League
See MH Rock

Anúna
See MH World

Any Old Time String Band
See MH Folk

Any Trouble
See MH Rock

Apache
See MH R&B

Apache Indian
See MH World

Peter Apfelbaum
See MH Jazz

Aphex Twin
See MH Rock

Scott Appel
See MH Folk

Fiona Apple
See MH Rock

Apples in Stereo
See MH Rock

Peter Appleyard
See MH Jazz

Aqua
See MH Rock

The Aqua Velvets
See MH Rock

The Aquabats
See MH Rock

Dan Ar Braz
See MH Folk, MH World

Ar Log
See MH World

Arawak Mountain Singers
See MH World

Arc Angels
See MH Rock

Arcadia
See MH Rock

Arcady
See MH Folk, MH World

Tasmin Archer
See MH Rock

Archer/Park
See MH Country

Archers of Loaf
See MH Rock

The Archies
See MH Rock

Jann Arden
See MH Folk, MH Rock

Alphonse "Bois Sec" Ardoin
See MH Folk, MH World

Amédée Ardoin
See MH Folk, MH World

Chris Ardoin & Double Clutchin'
See MH Folk, MH World

Argent
See MH Rock

Arkarna
See MH Rock

Harold Arlen
See MH Lounge, MH Swing

Joan Armatrading
See MH Folk, MH R&B, MH Rock

Frankie Armstrong
See MH Folk, MH World

Louis Armstrong
See MH Jazz, MH Lounge, MH R&B, MH Swing

Rodney Armstrong
See MH Blues

Vanessa Bell Armstrong
See MH R&B

Army of Lovers
See MH Rock

Desi Arnaz
See MH Lounge, MH World

Billy Boy Arnold
See MH Blues

Eddy Arnold
See MH Country

James "Kokomo" Arnold
See MH Blues

Arrested Development
See MH R&B, MH Rock

Lynn Arriale
See MH Jazz

Arrow
See MH World

Joe Arroyo
See MH World

Art Ensemble of Chicago
See MH Jazz

The Art of Noise
See MH Lounge, MH R&B, MH Rock

Artful Dodger
See MH Rock

Artifacts
See MH R&B

Artificial Joy Club
See MH Rock

Artisan
See MH Folk

Daniel Ash
See MH Rock

Karen Ashbrook
See MH Folk, MH World

Dorothy Ashby
See MH Jazz

Ashford & Simpson
See MH R&B

Ashkabad
See MH World

Ashkaru
See MH World

Clarence "Tom" Ashley
See MH Folk

Ernest Ashworth
See MH Country

Asia
See MH Rock

Asleep at the Wheel
See MH Country, MH Folk, MH Swing

Ass Ponys
See MH Rock

Badi Assad
See MH World

The Associates
See MH Rock

The Association
See MH Lounge, MH Rock

Fred Astaire
See MH Lounge, MH Swing

Rick Astley
See MH R&B, MH Rock

The Astronauts
See MH Rock

Aswad
See MH Rock, MH World

Asylum Street Spankers
See MH Country

Atari Teenage Riot
See MH Rock

Chet Atkins
See MH Country, MH Folk

Juan Atkins
See MH Rock

The Atlanta Rhythm Section
See MH Rock

Atlantic Starr
See MH R&B

Natacha Atlas
See MH World

The Atomic Fireballs
See MH Swing

Murray Attaway
See MH Rock

Atwater-Donnelly
See MH Folk

Eden Atwood
See MH Jazz

The Au Pairs
See MH Rock

Audio Adrenaline
See MH Rock

Audio Two
See MH R&B

Brian Auger
See MH Jazz, MH Rock

Lynn August
See MH Folk

Mike Auldridge
See MH Country, MH Folk

Reld & Coleman Auldridge
See MH Country

Gene Austin
See MH Lounge

Judy Austin
See MH Folk

Patti Austin
See MH Lounge, MH R&B

Austin Lounge Lizards
See MH Country, MH Folk

Autechre
See MH Rock

The Auteurs
See MH Rock

Automator
See MH R&B

Gene Autry
See MH Country, MH Folk

Frankie Avalon
See MH Rock

Julian Avalos & Afro-Andes
See MH World

The Avengers
See MH Rock

Avenue Blue
See MH Jazz

Average White Band
See MH R&B, MH Rock

Teodross Avery
See MH Jazz

Aster Aweke
See MH World

Hoyt Axton
See MH Country, MH Folk, MH Rock

Kevin Ayers
See MH Rock

Roy Ayers
See MH Jazz, MH R&B

Albert Ayler
See MH Jazz

AZ
See MH R&B

Steve Azar
See MH Country

Charles Aznavour
See MH Lounge

Abed Azrié
See MH World

Aztec Camera
See MH Rock

Howie B
See MH Rock

Mr. B
See MH Jazz

The B-52's
See MH Rock

B Sharp Jazz Quartet
See MH Jazz

Babble
See MH Rock

Babe the Blue Ox
See MH Rock

Babes in Toyland
See MH Rock

Babkas
See MH Jazz

Baby Bird
See MH Rock

Babyface
See MH R&B

The Babys
See MH Rock

Susana Baca
See MH World

Burt Bacharach
See MH Lounge, MH Rock

Bachman-Turner Overdrive
See MH Rock

Eric Bachmann
See MH Rock

The Backsliders
See MH Country

Backstreet Boys
See MH R&B, MH Rock

Bad Brains
See MH Rock, MH World

Bad Company
See MH Rock

Bad English
See MH Rock

Bad Livers
See MH Country, MH Folk, MH Rock

Bad Manners
See MH Rock

Bad Religion
See MH Rock

Angelo Badalamenti
See MH Lounge

Badawi
See MH World

Badfinger
See MH Rock

Badlands
See MH Rock

Erykah Badu
See MH Jazz, MH Lounge. MH R&B

Joan Baez
See MH Country, MH Folk, MH Rock

Bahamadia
See MH R&B

Chris Bailey
See MH Rock

Derek Bailey
See MH Jazz

Ernest Harold "Benny" Bailey
See MH Jazz

Mildred Bailey
See MH Jazz, MH Swing

Pearl Bailey
See MH Lounge, MH Swing

Philip Bailey
See MH R&B

Baillie & the Boys
See MH Country

Bailter Space
See MH Rock

Aly Bain
See MH Folk, MH World

Merrill Bainbridge
See MH Rock

Dan Baird
See MH Rock

The Baja Marimba Band
See MH Lounge

Baka Beyond
See MH World

Anita Baker
See MH R&B

Chet Baker
See MH Jazz, MH Lounge

Duck Baker
See MH Folk

Etta Baker
See MH Blues, MH Folk

Ginger Baker
See MH Jazz

Josephine Baker
See MH Lounge

Kenny Baker
See MH Country, MH Folk

LaVern Baker
See MH Blues, MH R&B, MH Rock

Lee Baker Jr.
See MH Blues

Baker & Myers
See MH Country

Ginger Baker's Air Force
See MH Rock

The Balancing Act
See MH Rock

Butch Baldassari
See MH Country, MH Folk

Long John Baldry
See MH R&B, MH Rock

Dewey Balfa
See MH Country

The Balfa Brothers
See MH Folk, MH World

Balfa Toujours
See MH Folk, MH World

David Ball
See MH Country

Marcia Ball
See MH Blues

Patrick Ball
See MH Folk, MH World

E.C. Ball and Orna Ball
See MH Folk

Hank Ballard
See MH R&B, MH Rock

Baltimore Consort
See MH Folk

Afrika Bambaataa
See MH R&B

Bamboleo
See MH World

Bana
See MH World

Bananarama
See MH Rock

Banco de Gaia
See MH Rock

The Band
See MH Folk, MH Rock

Band of Susans
See MH Rock

Moe Bandy
See MH Country

Billy Bang
See MH Jazz

The Bangles
See MH Rock

Ant Banks
See MH R&B

L.V. Banks
See MH Blues

Nancie Banks Orchestra
See MH Jazz

Buju Banton
See MH World

Banyan
See MH Rock

The Bar-Kays
See MH R&B

The Barbarians
See MH Rock

Barbecue Bob
See MH Blues

John Henry Barbee
See MH Blues

Chris Barber
See MH Jazz

Junior Barber
See MH Folk

Gato Barbieri
See MH Jazz

Carlos Barbosa-Lima
See MH Jazz, MH World

Bobby Bare
See MH Country

Bare Necessities
See MH Folk

A. Spencer Barefield
See MH Jazz

Barenaked Ladies
See MH Rock

Russ Barenberg
See MH Country, MH Folk

Danny Barker
See MH Jazz

Les Barker
See MH Folk

Joshua Barnes
See MH Blues

Roosevelt "Booba" Barnes
See MH Blues

Barnes & Barnes
See MH Rock

Charlie Barnet
See MH Jazz, MH Lounge, MH Swing

Mandy Barnett
See MH Country

Barolk Folk
See MH Folk

Joey Baron
See MH Jazz

Tina Louise Barr
See MH Folk

The Barra MacNeils
See MH Folk, MH World

The Barracudas
See MH Rock

Dan Barrett
See MH Jazz, MH Swing

Sweet Emma Barrett
See MH Jazz

Syd Barrett
See MH Rock

Ray Barretto
See MH Jazz, MH World

Dr. Sikuru Ayinde Barrister
See MH World

Kenny Barron
See MH Jazz

John Barry
See MH Lounge, MH Rock

Barry & the Remains
See MH Rock

Bruce Barth
See MH Jazz

Dave Bartholomew
See MH R&B, MH Rock, MH Swing

Lou Ann Barton
See MH Blues

Cathy Barton and Dave Para
See MH Folk

Gary Bartz
See MH Jazz

Rob Base & D.J. E-Z Rock
See MH R&B

Basehead
See MH R&B

Bash & Pop
See MH Rock

Bashful Brother Oswald
See MH Country

Basia
See MH Lounge, MH Rock

Count Basie
See MH Jazz, MH Swing

Basin Brothers
See MH Folk

Fontella Bass
See MH R&B, MH Rock

Sid Bass
See MH Lounge

The Bass Mountain Boys
See MH Country

Shirley Bassey
See MH Lounge, MH R&B

Bassomatic
See MH Rock

Waldemar Bastos
See MH World

Django Bates
See MH Jazz

Ashwan Batish
See MH World

Alvin Batiste
See MH Jazz

The Bats
See MH Rock

Robin Batteau
See MH Folk

Battlefield Band
See MH Folk, MH World

Will Batts
See MH Blues

Bauhaus
See MH Rock

Mario Bauzá
See MH Jazz, MH Lounge, MH World

Les Baxter
See MH Lounge

The Bay City Rollers
See MH Rock

Bayou Seco
See MH Folk, MH World

Be Bop Deluxe
See MH Rock

The Beach Boys
See MH Lounge, MH Rock

Beacon Hillbillies
See MH Folk

Keola Beamer
See MH Folk, MH World

Beastie Boys
See MH R&B, MH Rock

The Beasts of Bourbon
See MH Rock

The Beat
See MH Rock

The Beat Farmers
See MH Country, MH Rock

Beat Happening
See MH Rock

Beat Positive
See MH Swing

The Beatles
See MH Rock

Beatnuts
See MH R&B

The Beau Brummels
See MH Rock

The Beau Hunks
See MH Lounge, MH Swing

Beausoleil
See MH Country, MH Folk, MH World

The Beautiful South
See MH Lounge, MH Rock

Francis Bebey
See MH World

Sidney Bechet
See MH Jazz, MH Swing

Beck
See MH Blues, MH R&B, MH Rock

Jeff Beck
See MH Blues, MH Rock

Joe Beck
See MH Jazz

Walter Becker
See MH Rock

Jaymz Bee
See MH Lounge

Tom Bee
See MH World

Robby Bee & the Boyz from the Rez
See MH World

The Bee Gees
See MH R&B, MH Rock

BeebleBrox
See MH Jazz

Beenie Man
See MH World

Jay Begaye
See MH World

Bix Beiderbecke
See MH Jazz, MH Swing

Richie Beirach
See MH Jazz

Bekka & Billy
See MH Country

M'Bilia Bel
See MH World

Bel Canto
See MH Rock

Harry Belafonte
See MH Folk, MH Lounge, MH World

Bob Belden
See MH Jazz

Adrian Belew
See MH Rock

Marcus Belgrave
See MH Jazz

Carey Bell
See MH Blues

Chris Bell
See MH Rock

Derek Bell
See MH Folk, MH World

Lurrie Bell
See MH Blues

Rico Bell
See MH Country

Vince Bell
See MH Country, MH Folk

William Bell
See MH R&B

Delia Bell and Bill Grant
See MH Folk

Archie Bell & the Drells
See MH R&B

Bell Biv DeVoe
See MH R&B

Joey Belladonna
See MH Rock

Peter Bellamy
See MH Folk

The Bellamy Brothers
See MH Country

Regina Belle
See MH R&B

Belle & Sebastian
See MH Rock

Bellevue Cadillac
See MH Swing

Louie Bellson
See MH Jazz

Belly
See MH Rock

Fred Below
See MH Blues

Jesse Belvin
See MH R&B

Bembeya Jazz
See MH World

Jorge Ben
See MH World

Pat Benatar
See MH Rock

Gregg Bendian
See MH Jazz

Tex Beneke
See MH Swing

Eric Benet
See MH R&B

Mac Benford
See MH Folk

Mac Benford & the Woodshed All-Stars
See MH Country

Don Bennett
See MH Jazz

Tony Bennett
See MH Jazz, MH Lounge, MH Swing

Han Bennink
See MH Jazz

David Benoit
See MH Jazz

Tab Benoit
See MH Blues

George Benson
See MH Jazz, MH R&B

Pierre Bensusan
See MH Folk

Stephanie Bentley
See MH Country

Arley Benton
See MH Blues

Brook Benton
See MH R&B, MH Rock

Buster Benton
See MH Blues

Steve Beresford
See MH Jazz

Bob Berg
See MH Jazz

Matraca Berg
See MH Country

Karl Berger
See MH Jazz

Mary Bergin
See MH Folk, MH World

Borah Bergman
See MH Jazz

Tina Bergmann
See MH Folk

Bergmann Brothers
See MH Folk

Jerry Bergonzi
See MH Jazz

Bunny Berigan
See MH Jazz, MH Lounge, MH Swing

Dick Berk
See MH Jazz

Berlin
See MH Rock

Irving Berlin
See MH Lounge

Byron Berline
See MH Country, MH Folk

Berline-Crary-Hickman
See MH Country, MH Folk

Dan Bern
See MH Folk, MH Rock

Crystal Bernard
See MH Country

Tim Berne
See MH Jazz

Elmer Bernstein
See MH Lounge, MH Swing

Peter Bernstein
See MH Jazz

Steve Berrios
See MH Jazz

Chu Berry
See MH Jazz

Chuck Berry
See MH Blues, MH R&B, MH Rock

Dave Berry
See MH Rock

Heidi Berry
See MH Rock

John Berry
See MH Country

Richard Berry
See MH Blues, MH R&B, MH Rock

Cindy Lee Berryhill
See MH Folk, MH Rock

Lou and Peter Berryman
See MH Folk

Gene Bertoncini
See MH Jazz

Best Kissers in the World
See MH Rock

Maria Bethânia
See MH World

Better Than Ezra
See MH Rock

Bettie Serveert
See MH Rock

Betty Boo
See MH Rock

Bewitched
See MH Rock

Andy Bey
See MH Jazz

V.M. Bhatt
See MH World

Tarun Bhattacharya
See MH World

Asha Bhosle
See MH World

Bhundu Boys
See MH World

Jello Biafra
See MH Rock

Ed Bickert
See MH Jazz

Big Ass Truck
See MH Rock

Big Audio Dynamite
See MH Rock

Big Bad Voodoo Daddy
See MH Lounge, MH Rock, MH Swing

Big Black
See MH Rock

Big Blow and the Bushwackers
See MH Folk

The Big Bopper
See MH Rock

Big Brother & the Holding Company
See MH Blues

Big Chief
See MH R&B, MH Rock

Big Country
See MH Rock

Big Daddy Kane
See MH R&B

Big Dave & the Ultrasonics
See MH Swing

Big Head Todd & the Monsters
See MH Rock

Big House
See MH Country

Big Joe & the Dynaflows
See MH Swing

Big L
See MH R&B

Big Maceo
See MH Blues

Big Maybelle
See MH Blues

Big Rude Jake
See MH Rock

Big Sandy & His Fly-Rite Boys
See MH Country, MH Swing

Big Star
See MH Rock

Big Three Trio
See MH Blues

Big Time Sarah
See MH Blues

Big Twist & the Mellow Fellows
See MH Blues

Big Wreck
See MH Rock

Barney Bigard
See MH Jazz

Bigfood
See MH R&B

Theodore Bikel
See MH Folk, MH World

Bikini Kill
See MH Rock

Dave Bing
See MH Folk

The Bing Brothers
See MH Folk

Bio Ritmo
See MH World

Biota
See MH Jazz

Tony Bird
See MH Folk, MH World

Birddog
See MH Rock

The Birthday Party
See MH Rock

Elvin Bishop
See MH Blues, MH Rock

Joni Bishop
See MH Folk

Walter Bishop Jr.
See MH Jazz

Bitch Magnet
See MH Rock

Biz Markie
See MH R&B

Billy Bizor
See MH Blues

Björk
See MH Lounge, MH Rock

Björn Again
See MH Lounge

Cilla Black
See MH Rock

Clint Black
See MH Country

Frances Black
See MH Folk, MH World

Frank Black
See MH Rock

Mary Black
See MH Folk, MH World

Black Ace
See MH Blues

The Black Crowes
See MH Rock

The Black Family
See MH Folk, MH World

Black Flag
See MH Rock

Black 47
See MH Folk, MH Rock, MH World

Black Grape
See MH Rock

Black Lab
See MH Rock

Black Lodge Singers
See MH World

Black Moon
See MH R&B

Black/Note
See MH Jazz

Black Oak Arkansas
See MH Rock

Black Sabbath
See MH Rock

Black Sheep
See MH R&B

Black Stalin
See MH World

Black Swan Network
See MH Rock

Black Tie
See MH Rock

Black Uhuru
See MH Rock, MH World

Black Umfolosi
See MH World

Black Velvet Flag
See MH Lounge

The Blackbyrds
See MH Jazz, MH R&B

The Blackeyed Susans
See MH Rock

J. Blackfoot
See MH R&B

blackgirls
See MH Rock

BlackHawk
See MH Country, MH Rock

Blackie and the Rodeo Kings
See MH Folk

Becky Blackley
See MH Folk

Cindy Blackman
See MH Jazz

Amos Blackmore
See MH Blues

BLACKstreet
See MH R&B

Alfonzo Blackwell
See MH Jazz

Ed Blackwell
See MH Jazz

Francis Hillman Blackwell
See MH Blues

Otis Blackwell
See MH Blues, MH Rock

Scrapper Blackwell
See MH Blues

Ruben Blades
See MH Rock, MH World

Blahzay Blahzay
See MH R&B

Terry Blaine
See MH Jazz

Eubie Blake
See MH Jazz, MH Swing

Kenny Blake
See MH Jazz

Norman Blake
See MH Country, MH Folk

Ran Blake
See MH Jazz

Seamus Blake
See MH Jazz

Blake Babies
See MH Rock

Art Blakey
See MH Jazz

Terence Blanchard
See MH Jazz

Bobby "Blue" Bland
See MH Blues, MH R&B

The Blasters
See MH Country, MH Folk, MH Rock, MH Swing

The Blazers
See MH Rock

Edward "Eddie" Blazonczyk
See MH World

Blessid Union of Souls
See MH Rock

Carla Bley
See MH Jazz

Paul Bley
See MH Jazz

Mary J. Blige
See MH R&B

Blind Blake
See MH Blues, MH Folk

Blind Faith
See MH Rock

Blind Melon
See MH Rock

Blink 182
See MH Rock

Ralph Blizard
See MH Folk

Ralph Blizard & the New Southern Ramblers
See MH Country

Rory Block
See MH Blues, MH Folk

Blondie
See MH Rock

Alpha Blondy
See MH World

Blood of Abraham
See MH R&B

Blood Oranges
See MH Country, MH Folk, MH Rock

Blood, Sweat & Tears
See MH Jazz, MH Rock

The Bloodhound Gang
See MH Rock

Bloodstone
See MH R&B

Jane Ira Bloom
See MH Jazz

Luka Bloom
See MH Folk, MH Rock

Michael Bloomfield
See MH Blues, MH Folk, MH Rock

Bloque
See MH World

Blotto
See MH Rock

Kurtis Blow
See MH R&B

Blowzabella
See MH Folk, MH World

Bobby Blue
See MH Rock

The Blue Aeroplanes
See MH Rock

Blue Cheer
See MH Rock

Blue Highway
See MH Country, MH Folk

Blue Meanies
See MH Rock

Blue Mountain
See MH Country, MH Rock

The Blue Nile
See MH Rock

Blue Öyster Cult
See MH Rock

Blue Plate Special
See MH Swing

Blue Rodeo
See MH Country, MH Rock

Blue Shadows
See MH Country

The Blue Shadows
See MH Rock

Blue Sky Boys
See MH Country, MH Folk

The Bluebells
See MH Rock

Bluebirds
See MH Blues

The Bluegrass Cardinals
See MH Country, MH Folk

The Blues Brothers
See MH R&B, MH Rock

Blues Jumpers
See MH Swing

The Blues Magoos
See MH Rock

Blues Project
See MH Blues, MH Rock

Blues Traveler
See MH Rock

Bluestime
See MH Blues

The Bluetones
See MH Rock

Hamiet Bluiett
See MH Jazz

Hugh Blumenfeld
See MH Folk

Colin Blunstone
See MH Rock

Blur
See MH Rock

Arthur Blythe
See MH Jazz

The BMX Bandits
See MH Rock

The Bobbettes
See MH R&B

BoDeans
See MH Rock

Brigid Boden
See MH Rock

Body Count
See MH Rock

The Body Lovers
See MH Rock

Angela Bofill
See MH Jazz, MH R&B

Deanna Bogart
See MH Blues

Dock Boggs
See MH Folk

Suzy Bogguss
See MH Country

Eric Bogle
See MH Folk

The Bogmen
See MH Rock

Boiled Buzzards
See MH Folk

Boiled in Lead
See MH Folk

Mari Boine
See MH World

Gordon Bok
See MH Folk

Bok, Muir & Trickett
See MH Folk

Tommy Bolin
See MH Rock

Zuzu Bollin
See MH Blues

Claude Bolling
See MH Jazz

Yami Bolo
See MH World

The Bolshoi
See MH Rock

Michael Bolton
See MH Rock

Polly Bolton
See MH Folk

Bomb Bassetts
See MH Rock

Bomb the Bass
See MH Rock

Bon Jovi
See MH Rock

James Bonamy
See MH Country

Eddie Bond
See MH Country

Johnny Bond
See MH Country

Gary U.S. Bonds
See MH R&B, MH Rock

Bone Thugs-N-Harmony
See MH R&B

Luiz Bonfá
See MH World

Bonga
See MH World

Bongwater
See MH Rock

Bonham
See MH Rock

Tracy Bonham
See MH Rock

Joe Bonner
See MH Jazz

Juke Boy Bonner
See MH Blues

Simon Bonney
See MH Country

Karla Bonoff
See MH Country, MH Folk, MH Rock

The Bonzo Dog Band
See MH Rock

The Boo Radleys
See MH Rock

Boo-Yaa T.R.I.B.E.
See MH R&B

Boogie Down Productions
See MH R&B

Boogiemonsters
See MH R&B

Roy Book Binder
See MH Blues, MH Folk

Cedella Marley Booker
See MH World

Chuckii Booker
See MH R&B

James Booker
See MH Blues, MH Jazz, MH R&B, MH Rock

Booker T. & the MG's
See MH R&B, MH Rock

Boom Crash Opera
See MH Rock

Boom Shaka
See MH World

The Boomtown Rats
See MH Rock

Pat Boone
See MH Country, MH Lounge, MH Rock

Boone Creek
See MH Country, MH Folk

Laura Boosinger
See MH Folk

Victor Borge
See MH Lounge

Jimmy Bosch
See MH World

Bo$$
See MH R&B

Boss Hog
See MH Rock

Earl Bostic
See MH Jazz, MH R&B

Boston
See MH Rock

Boston Pops Orchestra
See MH Lounge

The Boswell Sisters
See MH Lounge

Libbi Bosworth
See MH Country

The Bothy Band
See MH Folk, MH World

The Bottle Rockets
See MH Country, MH Rock

Boukan Ginen
See MH World

Boukman Eksperyans
See MH World

Phil Boulding
See MH Folk

The Bouncing Souls
See MH Rock

Jean-Paul Bourelly
See MH Jazz, MH R&B, MH Rock

Bob Bovee and Gail Heil
See MH Folk

Bow Wow Wow
See MH Rock

Jimmy Bowen
See MH Country

Robin Huw Bowen
See MH Folk, MH World

Bryan Bowers
See MH Folk

David Bowie
See MH R&B, MH Rock, MH World

Lester Bowie
See MH Jazz

Ronnie Bowman
See MH Country

The Box Tops
See MH R&B, MH Rock

Boxcar Willie
See MH Country

Boy George
See MH Rock

Boy Howdy
See MH Country

Pat Boyack
See MH Blues

Eddie Boyd
See MH Blues

Ronnie Boykins
See MH Jazz

Boymerang
See MH Rock

Boyoyo Boys
See MH World

The Boys from Indiana
See MH Country, MH Folk

The Boys of the Lough
See MH Folk, MH World

Boyz II Men
See MH R&B

Ishmon Bracey
See MH Blues

Charles Brackeen
See MH Jazz

JoAnne Brackeen
See MH Jazz

Brad
See MH Rock

Don Braden
See MH Jazz

Bobby Bradford
See MH Jazz

Carrie Bradley
See MH Folk

Robert Bradley's Blackwater Surprise
See MH Rock

Tiny Bradshaw
See MH Swing

Paul Brady
See MH Folk, MH World

The Brady Bunch
See MH Country

Ruby Braff
See MH Jazz, MH Swing

Billy Bragg
See MH Folk, MH Rock

Anouar Brahem
See MH World

Brainiac
See MH Rock

Bram Tchaikovsky
See MH Rock

Doyle Bramhall
See MH Blues

Doyle Bramhall II
See MH Rock

Bran Van 3000
See MH Rock

Billy Branch
See MH Blues

Oscar Brand
See MH Folk

The Brand New Heavies
See MH R&B

Brand Nubian
See MH R&B

Brand X
See MH Jazz

Paul Brandt
See MH Country

Brandy
See MH R&B

Laura Branigan
See MH Rock

Brass Construction
See MH R&B

Rick Braun
See MH Jazz

Brave Combo
See MH Folk, MH Lounge, MH Rock, MH World

Brave Old World
See MH World

Anthony Braxton
See MH Jazz

Toni Braxton
See MH R&B

The Braxtons
See MH R&B

Bread
See MH Country, MH Rock

Joshua Breakstone
See MH Jazz

Máire Breatnach
See MH World

Lenny Breau
See MH Jazz

Zachary Breaux
See MH Jazz

Michael Brecker
See MH Jazz

Randy Brecker
See MH Jazz

The Breeders
See MH Folk, MH Rock

Jean Binta Breeze
See MH World

Maire Brennan
See MH Folk

Jackie Brenston
See MH Blues, MH Swing

Willem Breuker
See MH Jazz

Gary Brewer
See MH Country

Pap Brewer
See MH Folk

Teresa Brewer
See MH Lounge, MH Swing

BR5-49
See MH Country

Brice Glace
See MH Rock

Brick
See MH R&B

Edie Brickell & New Bohemians
See MH Rock

Dee Dee Bridgewater
See MH Jazz

The Brigadiers
See MH Swing

Anne Briggs
See MH Folk, MH World

Fletcher Bright Fiddle Band
See MH Folk

Bright Morning Star
See MH Folk

Nick Brignola
See MH Jazz

John Brim
See MH Blues

Brinsley Schwarz
See MH Rock

Alan Broadbent
See MH Jazz

Chuck Brodsky
See MH Folk

Lisa Brokop
See MH Country

David Bromberg
See MH Country, MH Folk, MH Rock

Bronski Beat
See MH Rock

Michael Brook
See MH World

Jonatha Brooke
See MH Folk, MH Rock

Gary Brooker
See MH Rock

Bob Brookmeyer
See MH Jazz

Garth Brooks
See MH Country

Hadda Brooks
See MH Blues, MH Lounge

Kix Brooks
See MH Country

Lonnie Brooks
See MH Blues

Meredith Brooks
See MH Rock

Roy Brooks
See MH Jazz

Tina Brooks
See MH Jazz

Brooks & Dunn
See MH Country

Big Bill Broonzy
See MH Blues, MH Folk

The Brother Boys
See MH Country, MH Folk

Brother Oswald
See MH Country

Brother Phelps
See MH Country

Brotherhood of Lizards
See MH Rock

The Brothers Four
See MH Folk

The Brothers Johnson
See MH R&B

Peter Brotzmann
See MH Jazz

Alison Brown
See MH Country, MH Folk

Andrew Brown
See MH Blues

Ari Brown
See MH Jazz

Arthur Brown
See MH Rock

Bobby Brown
See MH R&B

Buster Brown
See MH Blues

Carlinhos Brown
See MH World

Charles Brown
See MH Blues, MH Jazz, MH Lounge, MH R&B

Clarence "Gatemouth" Brown
See MH Blues, MH Folk, MH Swing

Clifford Brown
See MH Jazz, MH Lounge

Dennis Brown
See MH World

Donald Brown
See MH Jazz

Foxy Brown
See MH R&B

Greg Brown
See MH Country, MH Folk, MH Rock

Herschel Brown
See MH Folk

Hylo Brown
See MH Country

James Brown
See MH Blues, MH R&B, MH
Rock

Jeri Brown
See MH Jazz

Jim Ed Brown
See MH Country

J.T. Brown
See MH Blues

Junior Brown
See MH Country, MH Swing

Les Brown
See MH Jazz, MH Lounge, MH
Swing

Marion Brown
See MH Jazz

Marty Brown
See MH Country

Maxine Brown
See MH R&B

Nappy Brown
See MH Blues

Paul Brown
See MH Folk

Ray Brown
See MH Jazz

Rob Brown
See MH Jazz

Robert Brown
See MH Blues

Roy Brown
See MH Blues, MH R&B, MH
Swing

Ruth Brown
See MH Jazz, MH R&B, MH
Rock, MH Swing

Shirley Brown
See MH R&B

T. Graham Brown
See MH Country

Willie Brown
See MH Blues

Roger Brown & Swing City
See MH Country

Milton Brown and the Musical
Brownies
See MH Folk

Chuck Brown & the Soul
Searchers
See MH R&B

Jackson Browne
See MH Folk, MH Rock

Jann Browne
See MH Country

Tom Browne
See MH Jazz

The Browns
See MH Country

Brownsville Station
See MH Rock

Bob Brozman
See MH Folk

Dave Brubeck
See MH Jazz, MH Lounge, MH
Swing

Ed Bruce
See MH Country

Jack Bruce
See MH Rock

Bill Bruford
See MH Jazz

Jimmy Bruno
See MH Jazz

Brush Arbor
See MH Country

Brute
See MH Folk

Stephen Bruton
See MH Country

David Bryan
See MH Rock

James Bryan
See MH Folk

Ray (Raphael) Bryant
See MH Jazz

Bryndle
See MH Country, MH Folk, MH
Rock

Jeanie Bryson
See MH Jazz

Peabo Bryson
See MH R&B

bt
See MH Rock

B.T. Express
See MH R&B

Roy Buchanan
See MH Blues, MH Rock

Rachel Buchman
See MH Folk

The Buckets
See MH Folk

The Buckhannon Brothers
See MH Folk

Lindsey Buckingham
See MH Rock

The Buckinghams
See MH Rock

Jeff Buckley
See MH Folk, MH Rock

Lord Buckley
See MH Swing

Tim Buckley
See MH Folk, MH Rock

Milt Buckner
See MH Jazz, MH Swing

Richard Buckner
See MH Country, MH Folk, MH
Rock

Buckshot Lefonque
See MH R&B

Buckwheat Zydeco
See MH Folk, MH World

Harold Budd
See MH Lounge

Buena Vista Social Club
See MH World

Norton Buffalo
See MH Blues

Buffalo Springfield
See MH Folk, MH Rock

Buffalo Tom
See MH Rock

Jimmy Buffett
See MH Country, MH Folk, MH
Rock

George "Mojo" Buford
See MH Blues

The Buggles
See MH Rock

Alex Bugnon
See MH Jazz

Buick MacKane
See MH Rock

Built to Spill
See MH Rock

LTJ Bukem
See MH Rock

Bukken Bruse
See MH World

Bŭlgari
See MH World

Sandy Bull
See MH World

Luke & Jenny Anne Bulla
See MH Country, MH Folk

Bulletboys
See MH Rock

Robin Bullock
See MH Folk

The Bum Steers
See MH Country

Bumble Bee Slim
See MH Blues

The B.U.M.S.
See MH R&B

John Bunch
See MH Jazz

William Bunch
See MH Blues

Alden Bunn
See MH Blues

Jane Bunnett
See MH Jazz, MH World

Sharon Burch
See MH World

John Burgess
See MH World

Sonny Burgess
See MH Country, MH Rock,
MH Swing

Irving Burgie
See MH World

Kevin Burke
See MH Folk, MH World

Solomon Burke
See MH Blues, MH R&B

Dave Burland
See MH Folk

Paul Burlison
See MH Rock

Chester Arthur Burnett
See MH Blues

T-Bone Burnett
See MH Country, MH Folk, MH Rock

Dorsey Burnette
See MH Country, MH Rock

Johnny Burnette
See MH Country, MH Rock, MH Swing

Burning Bridges
See MH World

Burning Flames
See MH World

Burning Spear
See MH World

Eddie Burns
See MH Blues

George Burns
See MH Country

Jimmy Burns
See MH Blues

Laura Burns
See MH Folk

The Burns Sisters
See MH Country, MH Folk, MH Rock

R.L. Burnside
See MH Blues

Harold Burrage
See MH Blues

Dave Burrell
See MH Jazz

Kenny Burrell
See MH Jazz

William S. Burroughs
See MH Rock

Tony Burrows
See MH Rock

Aron Burton
See MH Blues

Gary Burton
See MH Jazz

James Burton & Ralph Mooney
See MH Country

Bush
See MH Rock

Johnny Bush
See MH Country

Kate Bush
See MH Rock

Sam Bush
See MH Country, MH Folk

Bush Tetras
See MH Rock

David Buskin
See MH Folk

Jon Butcher Axis
See MH Rock

Sam Butera
See MH Lounge, MH Swing

Bernard Butler
See MH Rock

Carl & Pearl Butler
See MH Country

George "Wild Child" Butler
See MH Blues

Jerry Butler
See MH R&B, MH Rock

Jonathan Butler
See MH Jazz

Paul Butterfield Blues Band
See MH Blues, MH Folk, MH Rock

Paul Butterfield's Better Days
See MH Blues

Butthole Surfers
See MH Rock

Buttons and Bows
See MH Folk

Buzz Hungry
See MH Rock

Buzzcocks
See MH Rock

Jaki Byard
See MH Jazz

Don Byas
See MH Jazz, MH Swing

Charlie Byrd
See MH Jazz

Donald Byrd
See MH Jazz

Henry Roy Byrd
See MH Blues

Tracy Byrd
See MH Country

The Byrds
See MH Country, MH Folk, MH Rock

David Byrne
See MH Rock, MH World

Don Byron
See MH Jazz, MH Lounge

C+C Music Factory
See MH R&B

Cabaret Voltaire
See MH Rock

George Cables
See MH Jazz

Chris Cacavas & Junkyard Love
See MH Rock

Cachao
See MH Jazz, MH World

Cactus
See MH Rock

The Cactus Brothers
See MH Country, MH Folk

The Cadets
See MH R&B

The Cadillacs
See MH R&B

Shirley Caesar
See MH R&B

Café Tacuba
See MH World

John Cafferty
See MH Rock

Greg Cahill
See MH Folk

Sammy Cahn
See MH Lounge

Caifanes
See MH World

Chris Cain
See MH Blues

Uri Caine
See MH Jazz

Al Caiola
See MH Lounge

Cake
See MH Rock

Cake Like
See MH Rock

Joey Calderazzo
See MH Jazz

J.J. Cale
See MH Folk, MH Rock

John Cale
See MH Rock

Andrew Calhoun
See MH Folk

California
See MH Country, MH Folk

Randy California
See MH Rock

California Cajun Orchestra
See MH Folk, MH World

California Ramblers
See MH Swing

The Call
See MH Rock

Ann Hampton Callaway
See MH Lounge

Red Callender
See MH Jazz

Joe Callicott
See MH Blues

Calloway
See MH R&B

Cab Calloway
See MH Jazz, MH Lounge, MH R&B, MH Swing

Calypso Rose
See MH World

Camarón de la Isla
See MH World

Camel
See MH Rock

Cameo
See MH R&B

Hamilton Camp
See MH Folk

Shawn Camp
See MH Country

The Camp Creek Boys
See MH Folk

Camp Lo
See MH R&B

Ali Campbell
See MH Rock

Eddie C. Campbell
See MH Blues

Glen Campbell
See MH Country, MH Folk, MH Lounge, MH Rock

John Campbell
See MH Blues, MH Jazz

Kate Campbell
See MH Country, MH Folk

Milton Campbell
See MH Blues

Rosamund Campbell
See MH Folk

Roy Campbell
See MH Jazz

Stacy Dean Campbell
See MH Country

Tevin Campbell
See MH R&B

Ian Campbell Folk Group
See MH World

Camper Van Beethoven
See MH Rock

Ray Campi
See MH Country, MH Swing

Candlebox
See MH Rock

Candyman
See MH R&B

Canned Heat
See MH Blues, MH Rock

Freddy Cannon
See MH Rock

Eddie Cantor
See MH Lounge

Emily & Al Cantrell
See MH Folk

Capercaillie
See MH Folk, MH World

Valerie Capers
See MH Jazz

Capone-N-Noreaga
See MH R&B

Frank Capp
See MH Jazz

Cappadonna
See MH Rock

The Captain & Tennille
See MH Lounge, MH Rock

Captain Beefheart & His Magic Band
See MH Rock

Irene Cara
See MH R&B

Ana Caram
See MH Jazz

Caravan
See MH Rock

Evan Carawan
See MH Folk

Guy Carawan
See MH Folk

Hayward "Chuck" Carbo
See MH Blues

Carbon
See MH Rock

The Cardigans
See MH Lounge, MH Rock

Cardinal
See MH Rock

Milton Cardona
See MH World

Mariah Carey
See MH R&B, MH Rock

Bob Carlin
See MH Country, MH Folk

Belinda Carlisle
See MH Rock

Bill Carlisle
See MH Country, MH Folk

The Carlisles
See MH Country

Larry Carlton
See MH Jazz

Hoagy Carmichael
See MH Lounge, MH Swing

Judy Carmichael
See MH Jazz

Jean Carne
See MH R&B

Kim Carnes
See MH Rock

Carolina
See MH Country

Mary Chapin Carpenter
See MH Country, MH Folk, MH Rock

The Carpenters
See MH Lounge, MH Rock

Carpetbaggers
See MH Country, MH Rock

James Carr
See MH Blues

Leroy Carr
See MH Blues

Sam Carr
See MH Blues

Vikki Carr
See MH Lounge

Wynona Carr
See MH Swing

Paul Carrack
See MH Rock

Joe "King" Carrasco
See MH Rock

Carreg Lafar
See MH World

Chubby Carrier
See MH Folk, MH World

Roy Carrier
See MH Folk, MH World

Bakida Carroll
See MH Jazz

Bruce Carroll
See MH Country

Jim Carroll
See MH Rock

Johnny Carroll
See MH Rock

Karen Carroll
See MH Blues

Liz Carroll
See MH Folk, MH World

The Cars
See MH Rock

Jeff Carson
See MH Country

Josephine Carson
See MH Lounge

Lori Carson
See MH Rock

Benny Carter
See MH Jazz, MH Swing

Betty Carter
See MH Jazz

Bo Carter
See MH Blues

Carlene Carter
See MH Country

Clarence Carter
See MH Blues, MH R&B, MH Rock

Deana Carter
See MH Country

Goree Carter
See MH Blues

James Carter
See MH Jazz

Jason Carter
See MH Folk

John Carter
See MH Jazz

Maybelle Carter
See MH Folk

Regina Carter
See MH Jazz

Ron Carter
See MH Jazz

Sara Carter
See MH Folk

Wilf Carter
See MH Country, MH Folk

The Carter Family
See MH Country, MH Folk

Carter the Unstoppable Sex Machine
See MH Rock

Eliza Carthy
See MH Folk, MH World

Martin Carthy
See MH Folk, MH World

Lionel Cartwright
See MH Country

John Carty
See MH World

Michael Carvin
See MH Jazz

Casa Loma Orchestra
See MH Swing

Ann and Phil Case
See MH Folk

Peter Case
See MH Rock

Karan Casey
See MH Folk, MH World

Mike Casey
See MH Folk

Johnny Cash
See MH Country, MH Folk, MH Rock

Rosanne Cash
See MH Country, MH Folk, MH Rock

Casper
See MH World

Mama Cass
See MH Lounge

David Cassidy
See MH Rock

Patrick Cassidy
See MH World

Shaun Cassidy
See MH Rock

Cast
See MH Rock

Leonard "Baby Doo" Caston
See MH Blues

Jimmy Castor
See MH R&B

Tommy Castro
See MH Blues

Cat Power
See MH Rock

The Catalinas
See MH R&B

Catatonia
See MH Rock

Cate Brothers
See MH Blues

Catherine Wheel
See MH Rock

The Caulfields
See MH Rock

Nick Cave & the Bad Seeds
See MH Lounge, MH Rock

Laura Caviani
See MH Jazz

Dori Caymmi
See MH World

Paul Cebar
See MH Rock

Cella Dwellas
See MH R&B

Celly Cel
See MH R&B

Celtic Fiddle Festival
See MH World

Ceolbeg
See MH Folk, MH World

Ceoltoiri
See MH Folk, MH World

Cephas & Wiggins
See MH Blues, MH Folk

Al Cernik
See MH Lounge

Exene Cervenka
See MH Rock

Chad & Jeremy
See MH Folk, MH Rock

Eugene Chadbourne
See MH Rock

Chairmen of the Board
See MH R&B

Dr. Krishna Chakravarty
See MH World

Chalk FarM
See MH Rock

Serge Chaloff
See MH Jazz

Joe Chambers
See MH Jazz

Paul Chambers
See MH Jazz

The Chambers Brothers
See MH Folk, MH R&B, MH Rock

The Chameleons
See MH Rock

The Champs
See MH Rock

James Chance
See MH Rock

Gene Chandler
See MH R&B

Sheila Chandra
See MH World

Change
See MH R&B

Channel Live
See MH R&B

The Channels
See MH R&B

Carol Channing
See MH Lounge

The Chantays
See MH Rock

The Chantels
See MH R&B

Harry Chapin
See MH Folk, MH Rock

Thomas Chapin
See MH Jazz

Tom Chapin
See MH Folk

Beth Nielsen Chapman
See MH Rock

Gary Chapman
See MH Country

Marshall Chapman
See MH Country

Owen "Snake" Chapman
See MH Folk

Tracy Chapman
See MH Folk, MH Rock

Craig Chaquico
See MH Rock

Bill Charlap
See MH Jazz

The Charlatans
See MH Rock

The Charlatans UK
See MH Rock

Ray Charles
See MH Blues, MH Country, MH Jazz, MH Lounge, MH R&B, MH Rock

Rockie Charles
See MH Blues

Teddy Charles
See MH Jazz

The Charles River Valley Boys
See MH Country, MH Folk

The Ray Charles Singers
See MH Lounge

Charm Farm
See MH Rock

The Charms
See MH R&B

The Charts
See MH R&B

Allan Chase
See MH Jazz

Chateau Neuf Spelemannslag
See MH World

John Len "Peter" Chatman
See MH Blues

Armenter Chatmon
See MH Blues

Lonnie Chatmon
See MH Blues

Sam Chatmon
See MH Blues

Hari Prasad Chaurasia
See MH World

Chavez
See MH Rock

Boozoo Chavis
See MH Folk, MH World

Chayanne
See MH World

The Cheap Suit Serenaders
See MH Folk

Cheap Trick
See MH Rock

Doc Cheatham
See MH Jazz, MH Swing

Jeannie & Jimmy Cheatham
See MH Blues, MH Jazz

Chubby Checker
See MH R&B, MH Rock

The Cheepskates
See MH Rock

Chelsea Bridge
See MH Jazz

The Chemical Brothers
See MH Rock

Jie-Bing Chen
See MH World

Sisi Chen
See MH World

C.J. Chenier
See MH Blues, MH Folk, MH World

Clifton Chenier
See MH Blues, MH Folk, MH World

The Chenille Sisters
See MH Folk

Cher
See MH Lounge, MH Rock

Cherish the Ladies
See MH Folk, MH World

Cherrelle
See MH R&B

Don Cherry
See MH Jazz, MH Lounge

Neneh Cherry
See MH R&B, MH Rock

Cherry Poppin' Daddies
See MH Lounge, MH Rock, MH Swing

Chesapeake
See MH Country, MH Folk

Kenny Chesney
See MH Country

Mark Chesnutt
See MH Country

Vic Chesnutt
See MH Country, MH Folk, MH Rock

Charlie Chesterman
See MH Country

Cyrus Chestnut
See MH Jazz

The Chestnut Grove Quartet
See MH Folk

Chi-Ali
See MH R&B

The Chi-Lites
See MH R&B

Kathy Chiavola
See MH Country, MH Folk

Chic
See MH R&B

Chicago
See MH Rock

The Chicken Chokers
See MH Folk

Chicken Shack
See MH Blues

The Chieftains
See MH Country, MH Folk, MH World

The Chiffons
See MH R&B, MH Rock

Billy Childs
See MH Jazz

Toni Childs
See MH Rock, MH World

Chill Rob G
See MH R&B

Sonny Chillingworth
See MH Folk, MH World

The Chills
See MH Rock

Alex Chilton
See MH Lounge, MH Rock

China Crisis
See MH Rock

Chino XL
See MH R&B

The Chipmunks
See MH Country, MH Rock

Chirgilchin
See MH World

Stella Chiweshe
See MH World

Chixdiggit!
See MH Rock

Harry Choates
See MH Folk, MH World

The Chocolate Watch Band
See MH Rock

The Choir
See MH Rock

Chopper
See MH Rock

The Chordettes
See MH Rock

The Chords
See MH R&B

Ellen Christi
See MH Jazz

Charlie Christian
See MH Jazz, MH Swing

Emma Christian
See MH World

Frank Christian
See MH Folk

Jodie Christian
See MH Jazz

Lou Christie
See MH R&B, MH Rock

Pete Christlieb
See MH Jazz

June Christy
See MH Jazz, MH Lounge

Lauren Christy
See MH Rock

Chubb Rock
See MH R&B

The Chuck Wagon Gang
See MH Country, MH Folk

Chumbawamba
See MH Rock

Chunky A
See MH R&B

The Church
See MH Rock

Cindy Church
See MH Country, MH Folk

Cibo Matto
See MH Rock

Ciccone Youth
See MH Rock

The Jim Cifelli New York Nonet
See MH Jazz

Cigar Store Indians
See MH Swing

Cinderella
See MH Rock

Alfred Cini
See MH Lounge

Cinnamon
See MH Rock

Rudy Cipolla
See MH Folk

Circle
See MH Jazz

The Circle Jerks
See MH Rock

Carolyn Cirimele
See MH Folk

Kaouwding Cissoko
See MH World

CIV
See MH Rock

The Clancy Brothers & Tommy Makem
See MH Folk, MH World

Clannad
See MH Folk, MH World

Eric Clapton
See MH Blues, MH Folk, MH Rock

Buddy Clark
See MH Lounge

Dee Clark
See MH R&B

Dr. Mattie Moss Clark
See MH R&B

Gene Clark
See MH Country, MH Folk, MH Rock

Guy Clark
See MH Country, MH Folk

Petula Clark
See MH Lounge, MH Rock

Roy Clark
See MH Country

Sonny Clark
See MH Jazz

Terri Clark
See MH Country

W.C. Clark
See MH Blues

Doug Clark & the Hot Nuts
See MH Lounge

The Dave Clark Five
See MH Rock

The Clark Sisters
See MH R&B

Gilby Clarke
See MH Rock

Johnny Clarke
See MH World

Kenny Clarke
See MH Jazz

Stanley Clarke
See MH Jazz

William Clarke
See MH Blues

The Clarks
See MH Rock

The Clash
See MH Rock

Classics IV
See MH Rock

Claudia
See MH World

Clawgrass
See MH Folk

James Clay
See MH Jazz

Otis Clay
See MH Blues, MH R&B

Richard Clayderman
See MH Lounge

Phillip Claypool
See MH Country

Buck Clayton
See MH Jazz, MH Swing

Clayton-Hamilton Orchestra
See MH Jazz

The Clean
See MH Rock

Cleaners from Venus
See MH Rock

Eddy Clearwater
See MH Blues

The Cleftones
See MH R&B

Johnny Clegg & Savuka
See MH Rock, MH World

Albert Clemens
See MH Blues

Vassar Clements
See MH Country, MH Folk

Clarence Clemons
See MH Rock

Clever Jeff
See MH Jazz, MH R&B

Jimmy Cliff
See MH R&B, MH Rock, MH World

Bill Clifton
See MH Country, MH Folk

Alex Cline
See MH Jazz

Charlie Cline
See MH Country

Nels Cline
See MH Jazz

Patsy Cline
See MH Country

George Clinton
See MH R&B, MH Rock

Rosemary Clooney
See MH Jazz, MH Lounge, MH Swing

Clouds of Joy
See MH Swing

The Clovers
See MH R&B, MH Rock

Club Nouveau
See MH R&B

Clusone 3
See MH Jazz

Clutch
See MH Rock

The Coasters
See MH R&B, MH Rock

Arnett Cobb
See MH Jazz, MH Swing

Willie Cobbs
See MH Blues

Billy Cobham
See MH Jazz

Anita Cochran
See MH Country

Eddie Cochran
See MH Rock, MH Swing

Jackie Lee Cochran
See MH Rock

Bruce Cockburn
See MH Folk, MH Rock

Joe Cocker
See MH R&B, MH Rock

Cockeyed Ghost
See MH Rock

Cocoa Tea
See MH World

Cocteau Twins
See MH Rock

Phil Cody
See MH Rock

Robert Tree Cody
See MH World

David Allan Coe
See MH Country

Leonard Cohen
See MH Country, MH Folk, MH Rock

Al Cohn
See MH Jazz

Marc Cohn
See MH Rock

Pat Coil
See MH Jazz

Coldcut
See MH Rock

Freddy Cole
See MH Jazz

Holly Cole
See MH Jazz, MH Lounge, MH Rock

Jude Cole
See MH Rock

Khani Cole
See MH Jazz

Lloyd Cole
See MH Rock

Nat "King" Cole
See MH Jazz, MH Lounge, MH R&B, MH Swing

Natalie Cole
See MH Lounge, MH R&B

Paula Cole
See MH Folk, MH Rock

Richie Cole
See MH Jazz

Cecilia Coleman
See MH Jazz

Cy Coleman
See MH Lounge

Deborah Coleman
See MH Blues

George Coleman
See MH Jazz

Jaz Coleman
See MH Rock

Michael Coleman
See MH Folk

Ornette Coleman
See MH Jazz

Steve Coleman
See MH Jazz

William "Bill" Coleman
See MH Jazz

Johnny Coles
See MH Jazz

Collective Soul
See MH Rock

Buddy Collette
See MH Jazz

Mark Collie
See MH Country

Gerald Collier
See MH Rock

Albert Collins
See MH Blues, MH Folk

Bootsy Collins
See MH R&B, MH Rock

Edwyn Collins
See MH Lounge, MH Rock

Jay Collins
See MH Jazz

Judy Collins
See MH Folk, MH Lounge, MH Rock

Lui Collins
See MH Folk

Mitzie Collins
See MH Folk

Paul Collins
See MH Rock

Phil Collins
See MH Rock

Sam Collins
See MH Blues

Shirley Collins
See MH Folk, MH World

Tommy Collins
See MH Country

The Collins Kids
See MH Country, MH Swing

Christine Collister
See MH Folk, MH Rock

Willie Colon
See MH World

Colony
See MH Rock

Color Me Badd
See MH R&B

The Colourfield
See MH Rock

Jessi Colter
See MH Country

Anita Belle Colton
See MH Lounge

John Coltrane
See MH Jazz

Turiya Alice Coltrane
See MH Jazz

Russ Columbo
See MH Lounge, MH Swing

Shawn Colvin
See MH Folk, MH Rock

Combustible Edison
See MH Lounge, MH Rock

Come
See MH Rock

Amie Comeaux
See MH Country

Commander Cody & His Lost Planet Airmen
See MH Country, MH Folk, MH Rock, MH Swing

Commissioned
See MH R&B

The Commodores
See MH R&B

Common
See MH R&B

Communards
See MH Rock

Perry Como
See MH Lounge

Con Funk Shun
See MH R&B

Concrete Blonde
See MH Rock

Ray Condo & His Ricochets
See MH Country, MH Swing

Eddie Condon
See MH Jazz, MH Swing

Confederate Railroad
See MH Country

Congo Norvell
See MH Rock

The Congos
See MH World

Conjunto Alma Jarocha
See MH World

Conjunto Bernal
See MH World

Conjunto Céspedes
See MH World

John Conlee
See MH Country

Arthur Conley
See MH R&B

Earl Thomas Conley
See MH Country

Graham Connah
See MH Jazz

The Connells
See MH Rock

Chris Connelly
See MH Rock

Connemara
See MH Folk

Harry Connick Jr.
See MH Jazz, MH Lounge, MH Swing

Ray Conniff
See MH Lounge

Rita Connolly
See MH Folk

Chris Connor
See MH Jazz, MH Swing

Joanna Connor
See MH Blues

Bill Connors
See MH Jazz

Norman Connors
See MH Jazz, MH R&B

Stompin' Tom Connors
See MH Country, MH Folk

Patricia Conroy
See MH Country

Conscious Daughters
See MH R&B

Consolidated
See MH Rock

Continental Divide
See MH Country

The Continental Drifters
See MH Rock

The Contours
See MH R&B

Ry Cooder
See MH Blues, MH Country, MH Folk, MH Rock, MH World

Barbara Cook
See MH Lounge

Jesse Cook
See MH World

Junior Cook
See MH Jazz

Sam Cooke
See MH R&B, MH Rock

The Cookies
See MH R&B

Spade Cooley
See MH Country, MH Folk, MH Swing

Rita Coolidge
See MH Country

Coolio
See MH R&B

Andy Cooney
See MH World

Alice Cooper
See MH Rock

Bob Cooper
See MH Jazz

Dana Cooper
See MH Folk

Roger Cooper
See MH Country, MH Folk

Wilma Lee & Stoney Cooper
See MH Country, MH Folk

Cop Shoot Cop
See MH Rock

Cowboy Copas
See MH Country

Julian Cope
See MH Rock

Johnny Copeland
See MH Blues

Stewart Copeland
See MH Rock

Marc Copland
See MH Jazz

Jeff Copley
See MH Country

The Copper Family
See MH Folk

Cordelia's Dad
See MH Folk

Larry Cordle
See MH Country, MH Folk

Florencia Bisenta De Castilla
Martinez Cordona
See MH Lounge

Chick Corea
See MH Jazz

J.P. Cormier
See MH World

Sheryl Cormier
See MH Folk, MH World

Don Cornell
See MH Lounge

Cornershop
See MH Rock, MH World

Rich Corpolongo
See MH Jazz

Corrosion of Conformity
See MH Rock

The Corrs
See MH Rock

Aaron Corthen
See MH Blues

Larry Coryell
See MH Jazz

Scott Cossu
See MH Folk

Gal Costa
See MH World

Jack Costanzo
See MH Lounge

Elvis Costello
See MH Country, MH Lounge,
MH Rock

Elizabeth Cotten
See MH Folk

James Cotton
See MH Blues, MH Folk

Cotton Mather
See MH Rock

Neal Coty
See MH Rock

Mary Coughlan
See MH Rock

Phil Coulter
See MH World

Count Five
See MH Rock

Counting Crows
See MH Rock

The Country Gentlemen
See MH Country, MH Folk

Country Ham
See MH Folk

Country Joe & the Fish
See MH Folk, MH Rock

The Counts
See MH R&B

County Down
See MH Folk

The Coup
See MH R&B

Coupé Cloué
See MH World

Dave Cousins
See MH Rock

Don Covay
See MH R&B, MH Rock

Robert Covington
See MH Blues

Cowboy Junkies
See MH Country, MH Folk, MH
Rock

Cowboy Mouth
See MH Rock

Stanley Cowell
See MH Jazz

Cows
See MH Rock

The Cowsills
See MH Rock

Ida Cox
See MH Blues, MH Jazz

Peter Cox
See MH Rock

The Cox Family
See MH Country, MH Folk

Coyote Oldman
See MH World

Cracker
See MH Rock

Billy "Crash" Craddock
See MH Country

Steven Cragg
See MH World

Craig G
See MH R&B

Floyd Cramer
See MH Country, MH Lounge

The Cramps
See MH Rock

The Cranberries
See MH Rock

Cranes
See MH Rock

Craobh Rua
See MH World

Dan Crary
See MH Folk

Crasdant
See MH World

Crash Test Dummies
See MH Folk, MH Rock

Davell Crawford
See MH Blues

Hank Crawford
See MH Jazz, MH R&B

Kevin Crawford
See MH Folk

Randy Crawford
See MH R&B

Robert Cray
See MH Blues, MH R&B, MH
Rock

Connie Curtis "Pee Wee"
Crayton
See MH Blues

Crazy Horse
See MH Rock

The Crazy World of Arthur
Brown
See MH Rock

Cream
See MH Rock

The Creatures
See MH Rock

Creed
See MH Rock

Creedence Clearwater Revival
See MH Rock

Marshall Crenshaw
See MH Rock

Creole Jazz Band
See MH Swing

Crescent City Maulers
See MH Swing

Elvis Crespo
See MH World

The Crew Cuts
See MH Rock

The Crickets
See MH Rock

Marilyn Crispell
See MH Jazz

Sonny Criss
See MH Jazz

Critton Hollow String Band
See MH Folk

A.J. Croce
See MH Rock

Jim Croce
See MH Folk, MH Lounge, MH
Rock

Carrie Crompton
See MH Folk

Andrew Cronshaw
See MH World

Bing Crosby
See MH Jazz, MH Lounge, MH
Swing

Bob Crosby
See MH Lounge, MH Swing

David Crosby
See MH Folk, MH Rock

Rob Crosby
See MH Country

Crosby, Stills & Nash
See MH Folk, MH Rock

Christopher Cross
See MH Lounge, MH Rock

David Cross
See MH Rock

Mike Cross
See MH Folk

Connie Crothers
See MH Jazz

Andrae Crouch
See MH R&B

Sheryl Crow
See MH Rock

Crowded House
See MH Rock

J.D. Crowe
See MH Country, MH Folk

Josh Crowe and David McLaughlin
See MH Country, MH Folk

Rodney Crowell
See MH Country

Kacy Crowley
See MH Rock

The Crows
See MH R&B

Crucial Conflict
See MH R&B

Arthur "Big Boy" Crudup
See MH Blues

The Cruel Sea
See MH Rock

Julee Cruise
See MH Lounge, MH Rock

R. Crumb
See MH Folk

The Crusaders
See MH Jazz, MH R&B

Celia Cruz
See MH Jazz, MH World

Cry of Love
See MH Rock

Cryan' Shames
See MH Rock

Bobbie Cryner
See MH Country

The Crystal Method
See MH Rock

The Crystals
See MH R&B, MH Rock

Rick Cua
See MH Rock

Joe Cuba
See MH World

Cuba L.A.
See MH World

¡Cubanismo!
See MH World

Ronnie Cuber
See MH Jazz

Warren Cuccurullo
See MH Rock

Xavier Cugat
See MH Lounge, MH Swing

Brian Culbertson
See MH Jazz

Jim Cullum
See MH Jazz

The Cult
See MH Rock

Culture
See MH World

Culture Club
See MH R&B, MH Rock

Burton Cummings
See MH Rock

Bill Cunliffe
See MH Jazz

Johnny Cunningham
See MH Folk, MH World

Phil Cunningham
See MH Folk, MH World

The Cure
See MH Rock

Dick Curless
See MH Country

Clifford Curry
See MH R&B

Tim Curry
See MH Lounge

Ted Curson
See MH Jazz

Catie Curtis
See MH Folk

Mac Curtis
See MH Rock

Curve
See MH Rock

Cusan Tan
See MH Folk, MH World

Frankie Cutlass
See MH R&B

Cybotron
See MH Rock

Cypress Hill
See MH R&B, MH Rock

Andrew Cyrille
See MH Jazz

The Cyrkle
See MH Rock

Billy Ray Cyrus
See MH Country

Chuck D.
See MH Rock

D Generation
See MH Rock

Da Brat
See MH R&B

Da Bush Babees
See MH R&B

Da Lench Mob
See MH R&B

Da Youngsta's
See MH R&B

dada
See MH Rock

Dadawa
See MH World

Daft Punk
See MH Rock

Ustad Zia Mohiuddin Dagar
See MH World

Lisa Daggs
See MH Country

Paul Daigle
See MH Folk

Bruce Daigrepont
See MH Folk

I.K. Dairo
See MH World

George Dalaras
See MH World

Dick Dale
See MH Rock

Malcolm Dalglish
See MH Folk

Dalom Kids
See MH World

Lacy J. Dalton
See MH Country

Roger Daltrey
See MH Rock

Jackie Daly
See MH Folk, MH World

Maria D'Amato
See MH Blues

The Dambuilders
See MH Rock

Tadd Dameron
See MH Jazz

Damn Yankees
See MH Rock

The Damned
See MH Rock

Vic Damone
See MH Lounge

Dance Hall Crashers
See MH Rock

Dandy Warhols
See MH Rock

Dana Dane
See MH R&B

D'Angelo
See MH R&B

Davis Daniel
See MH Country

Eddie Daniels
See MH Jazz

Chris Daniels & the Kings
See MH Swing

Charlie Daniels Band
See MH Country, MH Rock

Harold Danko
See MH Jazz

Rick Danko
See MH Rock

Johnny Dankworth
See MH Lounge

Danny & the Juniors
See MH Rock

Danzig
See MH Rock

Vanessa Daou
See MH Rock

James Dapogny
See MH Jazz

Olu Dara
See MH World

Terence Trent D'Arby
See MH R&B, MH Rock

Darby and Tarlton
See MH Folk

Alan Dargin
See MH World

Bobby Darin
See MH Lounge, MH R&B, MH Rock, MH Swing

Mason Daring
See MH Folk

Dark City Sisters
See MH World

Dark Sun Riders Featuring Brother J
See MH R&B

Erik Darling
See MH Folk

Helen Darling
See MH Country

The Darling Buds
See MH Rock

Krishna Das
See MH World

Paban Das Baul & Sam Mills
See MH World

Das EFX
See MH R&B

Dash Rip Rock
See MH Rock

Daude
See MH World

Dave & Deke Combo
See MH Country

Billy Davenport
See MH Blues

Charles "Cow Cow" Davenport
See MH Blues

Jeremy Davenport
See MH Jazz

Lester Davenport
See MH Blues

Kenny Davern
See MH Jazz

Shaun Davey
See MH Folk, MH World

Hal David
See MH Lounge

David + David
See MH Rock

Lowell Davidson
See MH Jazz

Debbie Davies
See MH Blues

Gail Davies
See MH Country

Richard Davies
See MH Lounge, MH Rock

Alana Davis
See MH Rock

Anthony Davis
See MH Jazz

Billy Davis Jr.
See MH Lounge

CeDell Davis
See MH Blues

Eddie "Lockjaw" Davis
See MH Jazz, MH Swing

Guy Davis
See MH Blues, MH Folk

James "Thunderbird" Davis
See MH Blues

Jesse Davis
See MH Jazz

Jimmie Davis
See MH Country, MH Folk

Julie Davis
See MH Folk

Larry Davis
See MH Blues

Linda Davis
See MH Country

Mac Davis
See MH Country, MH Lounge

Maxwell Davis
See MH Blues

Maxwell Street Jimmy Davis
See MH Blues

Miles Davis
See MH Jazz, MH Lounge

The Rev. Gary Davis
See MH Blues, MH Folk

Richard Davis
See MH Jazz

Sammy Davis Jr.
See MH Lounge, MH R&B, MH Swing

Skeeter Davis
See MH Country

Spencer Davis
See MH Rock

Steve Davis
See MH Jazz

Thornetta Davis
See MH Rock

Tyrone Davis
See MH R&B

Walter Davis
See MH Blues

Walter Davis Jr.
See MH Jazz

Wild Bill Davison
See MH Jazz, MH Swing

Davka
See MH World

Jimmy Dawkins
See MH Blues

Julian Dawson
See MH Folk

Ronnie Dawson
See MH Country, MH Rock, MH Swing

Curtis Day
See MH Country

Doris Day
See MH Lounge, MH Swing

Morris Day
See MH R&B

Taylor Dayne
See MH R&B, MH Rock

Days of the New
See MH Rock

Jesse Dayton
See MH Country

The Dayton Family
See MH R&B

The Dazz Band
See MH R&B

The dB's
See MH Rock

DC Talk
See MH R&B, MH Rock

Chris de Burgh
See MH Rock

De Dannan
See MH Folk, MH World

Tony de la Rosa
See MH World

De La Soul
See MH R&B

Paco de Lucia
See MH World

Deacon Blue
See MH Rock

Dead Boys
See MH Rock

Dead Can Dance
See MH Folk, MH Rock, MH World

Dead Kennedys
See MH Rock

The Dead Milkmen
See MH Rock

Kelley Deal 6000
See MH Rock

Billy Dean
See MH Country

Jimmy Dean
See MH Country

Paul Dean
See MH Rock

Déanta
See MH Folk, MH World

Blossom Dearie
See MH Jazz, MH Lounge

Death Metal
See MH Rock

DeBarge
See MH R&B

Deconstruction
See MH Rock

Dedication Orchestra
See MH Jazz

Joey Dee
See MH Rock

Lenny Dee
See MH Lounge

Dave Dee, Dozy, Beaky, Mick & Tich
See MH Rock

Deee-Lite
See MH R&B, MH Rock

The Deele
See MH R&B

Barrett Deems
See MH Jazz

Deep Forest
See MH Rock, MH World

Deep Purple
See MH Rock

Def Jam
See MH R&B

Def Jef
See MH R&B

Def Leppard
See MH Rock

Joey DeFrancesco
See MH Jazz

Buddy DeFranco
See MH Jazz

deftones
See MH Rock

Defunkt
See MH R&B

Jack DeJohnette
See MH Jazz

Desmond Dekker
See MH R&B, MH World

Del Amitri
See MH Rock

Del Fuegos
See MH Rock

The Del Lords
See MH Rock

Dan Del Santo
See MH World

Del tha Funkee Homosapien
See MH R&B

Geno Delafose
See MH Folk, MH World

John Delafose
See MH Folk

John Delafose & the Eunice Playboys
See MH World

Delaney & Bonnie
See MH Rock

Peter Delano
See MH Jazz

Paul DeLay
See MH Blues

The Delevantes
See MH Country

The Delfonics
See MH R&B

Issac Delgado
See MH World

Delinquent Habits
See MH R&B

The Dells
See MH R&B

The Delmore Brothers
See MH Country, MH Folk, MH Swing

Victor DeLorenzo
See MH Rock

Iris DeMent
See MH Country, MH Folk, MH Rock

Barbara Dennerlein
See MH Jazz

Bernardo Dennis
See MH Blues

Cathy Dennis
See MH Rock

Wesley Dennis
See MH Country

Martin Denny
See MH Lounge

Sandy Denny
See MH Folk, MH Rock, MH World

John Denver
See MH Country, MH Folk, MH Lounge, MH Rock

Depeche Mode
See MH Rock

The Derailers
See MH Country

Derek & the Dominos
See MH Blues, MH Rock

Joe Derrane
See MH Folk

Rick Derringer
See MH Rock

Dervish
See MH Folk, MH World

Descendents
See MH Rock

The Deseret String Band
See MH Folk

The Desert Rose Band
See MH Country, MH Rock

Jackie DeShannon
See MH Rock

Paul Desmond
See MH Jazz, MH Lounge, MH Swing

Des'ree
See MH R&B

Jimmy Destri
See MH Rock

Det Syng
See MH World

Marcella Detroit
See MH Rock

William DeVaughn
See MH R&B

Willy DeVille
See MH Rock

The Devlins
See MH Folk, MH Rock

Devo
See MH Lounge, MH Rock

Howard DeVoto
See MH Rock

Dexy's Midnight Runners
See MH R&B, MH Rock

Dennis DeYoung
See MH Rock

D'Gary
See MH World

Dharma Bums
See MH Rock

Al Di Meola
See MH Jazz

Abdoulaye Diabaté
See MH World

Sékouba "Bambino" Diabaté
See MH World

Toumani Diabaté
See MH World

The Diablos
See MH R&B

Alpha Yaya Diallo
See MH World

Neil Diamond
See MH Country, MH Lounge, MH Rock

Diamond D
See MH R&B

Diamond Rio
See MH Country

The Diamonds
See MH Rock

Diblo Dibala
See MH World

Manu Dibango
See MH R&B, MH World

Dick & Dee Dee
See MH Rock

Hazel Dickens
See MH Country, MH Folk

Little Jimmy Dickens
See MH Country

Walt Dickerson
See MH Jazz

Whit Dickey
See MH Jazz

The Dickies
See MH Rock

Bruce Dickinson
See MH Rock

The Dictators
See MH Rock

Bo Diddley
See MH Blues, MH Folk, MH R&B, MH Rock

Marlene Dietrich
See MH Lounge

Different Shoes
See MH Folk

Joe Diffie
See MH Country

Ani DiFranco
See MH Folk, MH Rock

Diga Rhythm Band
See MH World

Digable Planets
See MH Jazz, MH R&B

Steve Diggle
See MH Rock

Digital Underground
See MH R&B

Henri Dikongué
See MH World

The Dillards
See MH Country, MH Folk

Dwight Diller
See MH Folk

John "Seven Foot Dilly" Dille-shaw
See MH Folk

Dimitri from Paris
See MH Lounge

Pat DiNizio
See MH Rock

Dino, Desi & Billy
See MH Rock

Dinosaur Jr.
See MH Rock

Ronnie James Dio
See MH Rock

Dion
See MH R&B, MH Rock

Celine Dion
See MH Rock

Vieux Diop
See MH World

Wasis Diop
See MH World

Joe Diorio
See MH Jazz

Dire Straits
See MH Rock

Dirty Dozen Brass Band
See MH Jazz, MH R&B

Dirty Three
See MH Rock

disappear fear
See MH Folk

Dishwalla
See MH Rock

Disposable Heroes of Hipho-prisy
See MH R&B

Dissidenten
See MH World

Diva
See MH Jazz

Divine Comedy
See MH Lounge, MH Rock

Divine Styler
See MH R&B

Divinyls
See MH Rock

The Dixie Chicks
See MH Country

The Dixie Cups
See MH Rock

The Dixie Dregs
See MH Rock

Bill Dixon
See MH Jazz

Don Dixon
See MH Rock

Floyd Dixon
See MH Blues

Willie Dixon
See MH Blues

Lefty Dizz
See MH Blues

DJ Honda
See MH R&B

D.J. Jazzy Jeff & the Fresh Prince
See MH R&B

DJ Kool
See MH R&B

DJ Krush
See MH Jazz, MH R&B, MH Rock

DJ Quik
See MH R&B

DJ Red Alert
See MH R&B

DJ Shadow
See MH R&B

DJ Towa Tei
See MH Rock

Djavan
See MH World

Djur Djura
See MH World

DK3
See MH Rock

Oscar D'Leon
See MH World

DM3
See MH Rock

DMZ
See MH Rock

DNA
See MH Rock

The D.O.C.
See MH R&B

Dr. Buzzard's Original Savan-nah Band
See MH Rock

Dr. Didg
See MH World

Dr. Dre
See MH R&B

Doctor Dre and Ed Lover
See MH R&B

Doctor Ganga
See MH World

Dr. Hook & the Medicine Show
See MH Rock

Dr. John
See MH Blues, MH Folk, MH R&B, MH Rock

Dr. Loco's Rockin' Jalapeño Band
See MH World

Dr. Nico
See MH World

Dr. Octagon
See MH Rock

Deryl Dodd
See MH Country

Baby Dodds
See MH Jazz

Johnny Dodds
See MH Jazz

Dodgy
See MH Rock

Anne Dodson
See MH Folk

John Doe
See MH Rock

Tha Dogg Pound
See MH R&B

Bill Doggett
See MH Jazz

Dogma
See MH Rock

The Dogmatics
See MH Rock

Dog's Eye View
See MH Rock

Dogstar
See MH Rock

John Doherty
See MH World

Dokken
See MH Rock

Felix Dolan
See MH World

Thomas Dolby
See MH Rock

Morris Dollison Jr.
See MH Blues

Eric Dolphy
See MH Jazz

Domino
See MH R&B

Fats Domino
See MH Blues, MH R&B, MH Rock

The Dominoes
See MH R&B

Lou Donaldson
See MH Jazz

Dorothy Donegan
See MH Jazz

Lonnie Donegan
See MH Folk, MH Lounge, MH Rock

Donovan
See MH Folk, MH Rock

The Doobie Brothers
See MH Rock

The Doors
See MH Rock

Dordán
See MH Folk, MH World

Kenny Dorham
See MH Jazz

Bob Dorough
See MH Jazz, MH Lounge

Arnold George "Gerry" Dorsey
See MH Lounge

Jimmy Dorsey
See MH Jazz, MH Lounge, MH Swing

Lee Dorsey
See MH R&B, MH Rock

Thomas A. Dorsey
See MH Blues

Tommy Dorsey
See MH Jazz, MH Lounge, MH Swing

Dos
See MH Rock

Double Clutchin'
See MH Folk

The Double Decker String Band
See MH Folk

Double XX Posse
See MH R&B

David Doucet
See MH Folk

Michael Doucet
See MH Country, MH Folk

Dave Douglas
See MH Jazz

Jerry Douglas
See MH Country, MH Folk

K.C. Douglas
See MH Blues

Lizzie Douglas
See MH Blues

Mike Douglas
See MH Lounge

Wilson Douglas
See MH Folk

Douglas, Barenberg & Meyer
See MH Country

Dove Shack
See MH R&B

Connie Dover
See MH Folk, MH World

Down
See MH Rock

Will Downing
See MH Jazz, MH R&B

Downtown Science
See MH R&B

Downy Mildew
See MH Rock

Arthur Doyle
See MH Jazz

Nick Drake
See MH Folk, MH Rock

Pete Drake
See MH Country

Dramarama
See MH Rock

The Dramatics
See MH R&B

Robin and Barry Dransfield
See MH Folk

Robert Drasnin
See MH Lounge

Mikey Dread
See MH World

Dread Zeppelin
See MH Rock

Dreadful Snakes
See MH Country

The Dream Academy
See MH Rock

The Dream Syndicate
See MH Rock

Dream Theater
See MH Rock

Dream Warriors
See MH Jazz, MH R&B

Mark Dresser
See MH Jazz

Kenny Drew
See MH Jazz

Kenny Drew Jr.
See MH Jazz

The Drifters
See MH R&B, MH Rock

Paquito D'Rivera
See MH Jazz, MH World

Drivin' N' Cryin'
See MH Rock

Pete Droge
See MH Folk, MH Rock

D.R.S. (Dirty Rotten Scoundrels)
See MH R&B

Dru Down
See MH R&B

Dru Hill
See MH R&B

Drugstore
See MH Rock

The Drummers of Burundi
See MH World

Billy Drummond
See MH Jazz

Ray Drummond
See MH Jazz

Roy Drusky
See MH Country

Dry Branch Fire Squad
See MH Country, MH Folk

Chris Duarte
See MH Blues, MH Rock

Lucky Dube
See MH World

The Dubliners
See MH Folk, MH World

Dubstar
See MH Rock

George Ducas
See MH Country

Dave Dudley
See MH Country

Dan Duggan
See MH Folk

Duice
See MH R&B

Lorraine Duisit
See MH Folk

George Duke
See MH Jazz, MH R&B

Ted Dunbar
See MH Jazz

Stuart Duncan
See MH Country, MH Folk

Slim Dunlap
See MH Rock

Holly Dunn
See MH Country

Francis Dunnery
See MH Rock

Champion Jack Dupree
See MH Blues

Stanley Dural Jr.
See MH Folk

Duran Duran
See MH Rock

Jimmy Durante
See MH Lounge

Ian Dury
See MH Rock

Garrett Dutton
See MH Blues

Dyke & the Blazers
See MH R&B

Omar Dykes
See MH Blues

Bob Dylan
See MH Blues, MH Country, MH Folk, MH Rock

The Dynatones
See MH World

E
See MH Rock

E-40 and the Click
See MH R&B

The E-Types
See MH Rock

Dominique Eade
See MH Jazz

The Eagles
See MH Country, MH Folk, MH Rock

Fred Eaglesmith
See MH Country, MH Folk, MH Rock

Fird Eaglin Jr.
See MH Blues

Snooks Eaglin
See MH Blues

Jim Eanes
See MH Country, MH Folk

Ronnie Earl
See MH Blues

Charles Earland
See MH Jazz

Steve Earle
See MH Country, MH Folk, MH Rock

Earth, Wind & Fire
See MH R&B

John Easdale
See MH Rock

Bill Easley
See MH Jazz

Eastern Eagle Singers
See MH World

Madeline Eastman
See MH Jazz

Amos Easton
See MH Blues

Sheena Easton
See MH Lounge, MH R&B

Clint Eastwood
See MH Lounge

Easy Tunes
See MH Lounge

The Easybeats
See MH Rock

Eazy-E
See MH R&B

Cliff Eberhardt
See MH Folk

Bob Eberly
See MH Swing

Ebin-Rose
See MH Folk

Echo & the Bunnymen
See MH Rock

Echobelly
See MH Rock

Echoes of Incas
See MH World

Peter Ecklund
See MH Jazz

Billy Eckstine
See MH Jazz, MH Lounge, MH Swing

Ed O.G. and Da Bulldogs
See MH R&B

Eddie & the Hot Rods
See MH Rock

Eddie from Ohio
See MH Folk

Duane Eddy
See MH Country, MH Rock

Nelson Eddy
See MH Lounge

Judith Edelman
See MH Country, MH Folk

Eden's Bridge
See MH World

Harry "Sweets" Edison
See MH Jazz, MH Swing

Dave Edmunds
See MH Country, MH Rock

Ed's Redeeming Qualities
See MH Folk

David "Honeyboy" Edwards
See MH Blues

Dennis Edwards
See MH R&B

Don Edwards
See MH Country, MH Folk

Jonathan Edwards
See MH Country, MH Folk

Jonathan & Darlene Edwards
See MH Lounge, MH Swing

Marc Edwards
See MH Jazz

Stoney Edwards
See MH Country

Teddy Edwards
See MH Jazz

Tommy Edwards
See MH Lounge

Eek-a-Mouse
See MH World

eels
See MH Rock

Effigies
See MH Rock

Mark Egan
See MH Jazz

Seamus Egan
See MH Folk, MH World

The Egg
See MH Rock

Kat Eggleston
See MH Folk

The Egyptians
See MH Folk

Marty Ehrlich
See MH Jazz

8 1/2 Souvenirs
See MH Swing

Eight Bold Souls
See MH Jazz

808 State
See MH Rock

Eightball & MJG
See MH R&B

Einstürzende Neubauten
See MH Rock

Either/Orchestra
See MH Jazz

Mark Eitzel
See MH Rock

Jason Eklund
See MH Folk

El Chicano
See MH Rock

Hamza El Din
See MH World

The El Dorados
See MH R&B

El-Funoun
See MH World

El Vez
See MH Rock

Elastica
See MH Rock

Betty Elders
See MH Folk

Roy Eldridge
See MH Jazz, MH Swing

Electrafixion
See MH Rock

Electric Bonsai Band
See MH Folk

Electric Hellfire Club
See MH Rock

Electric Light Orchestra
See MH Rock

The Electric Prunes
See MH Rock

Electro Funk
See MH R&B

Electronic
See MH Rock

Robert "Big Mojo" Elem
See MH Blues

Elements
See MH Jazz

The Elevator Drops
See MH Rock

Eleventh Dream Day
See MH Rock

Mark Elf
See MH Jazz

Danny Elfman
See MH Lounge, MH Rock

Larry Elgart
See MH Lounge, MH Swing

Les Elgart
See MH Lounge, MH Swing

Eliane Elias
See MH Jazz, MH World

Kurt Elling
See MH Jazz

Duke Ellington
See MH Jazz, MH Lounge, MH R&B, MH Swing

Mercer Ellington
See MH Jazz, MH Swing

Cass Elliot
See MH Lounge

Richard Elliot
See MH Jazz

Ramblin' Jack Elliott
See MH Country, MH Folk

Bill Elliott Swing Orchestra
See MH Swing

Alton Ellis
See MH World

Big Chief Ellis
See MH Blues

Dave Ellis
See MH Jazz

Don Ellis
See MH Jazz

Emmit Ellis Jr.
See MH Blues

Herb Ellis
See MH Jazz

Lisle Ellis
See MH Jazz

Tinsley Ellis
See MH Blues

Tony Ellis
See MH Folk

John Ellison
See MH Blues

Tony Elman
See MH Folk

The Elvis Brothers
See MH Rock

Joe Ely
See MH Country, MH Folk, MH Rock

Elysian Fields
See MH Rock

Kahil El'Zabar
See MH Jazz

The Embarrassment
See MH Rock

Emergency Broadcast Network
See MH Rock

Billy "The Kid" Emerson
See MH Blues

Emerson, Lake & Palmer
See MH Rock

EMF
See MH Rock

Emilio
See MH Country, MH World

The Emotions
See MH R&B

En Vogue
See MH R&B

Enchantment
See MH R&B

Ty England
See MH Country

The English Beat
See MH Rock, MH World

Norma Delores Engstrom
See MH Lounge

Jeremy Enigk
See MH Rock

Enigma
See MH Rock

Lyman Enloe
See MH Folk

Séamus Ennis
See MH Folk, MH World

Brian Eno
See MH Lounge, MH Rock, MH World

Luis Enrique
See MH World

Bobby Enriquez
See MH Jazz

Ensemble Galilei
See MH Folk

John Entwistle
See MH Rock

Enuff Z'Nuff
See MH Rock

Enya
See MH Folk, MH World

Epic Soundtracks
See MH Rock

EPMD
See MH R&B

Epstein Brothers Band
See MH World

Erasure
See MH Lounge, MH Rock

Wayne Erbsen
See MH Folk

Kudsi Erguner
See MH World

Eric B. & Rakim
See MH R&B

Roky Erickson
See MH Rock

Eric's Trip
See MH Rock

Peter Erskine
See MH Jazz

Booker Ervin
See MH Jazz

Ron Eschete
See MH Jazz

Alejandro Escovedo
See MH Country, MH Rock

Pete Escovedo
See MH Jazz

Ellery Eskelin
See MH Jazz

ESP Summer
See MH Rock

Tom Espinola and Lorraine Duisit
See MH Folk

Esquerita
See MH Swing

Juan Garcia Esquivel
See MH Lounge

David Essex
See MH Rock

Victor Essiet
See MH World

Gloria Estefan
See MH R&B, MH Rock, MH World

Maggie Estep
See MH Rock

Sleepy John Estes
See MH Blues, MH Folk

Etchingham Steam Band
See MH Folk

Melissa Etheridge
See MH Rock

The Ethiopians
See MH World

The Ethnic Heritage Ensemble
See MH Jazz

étoile de Dakar
See MH World

Ruth Etting
See MH Swing

E.U. (Experience Unlimited)
See MH R&B

Kevin Eubanks
See MH Jazz

Robin Eubanks
See MH Jazz

Eugenius
See MH Rock

Eunice Playboys
See MH World

Euro Boys
See MH Rock

Eurythmics
See MH R&B, MH Rock

Eva Trout
See MH Rock

Bill Evans
See MH Jazz

Gil Evans
See MH Jazz

Terry Evans
See MH Blues

Gerald Evans & Joe Mullins
See MH Country

Everclear
See MH Rock

Everlast
See MH Rock

The Everly Brothers
See MH Country, MH Folk, MH Rock

Everything but the Girl
See MH Lounge, MH R&B, MH Rock

Cesaria Evora
See MH World

Douglas Ewart
See MH Jazz

Skip Ewing
See MH Country

Exile
See MH Country

Extreme
See MH Rock

Fabian
See MH Lounge, MH Rock

Bent Fabric
See MH Lounge, MH Lounge

The Fabulous Thunderbirds
See MH Blues, MH Rock

Face to Face
See MH Rock

The Faces
See MH Rock

Jon Faddis
See MH Jazz

Chaba Fadela
See MH World

Eleanora Fagan
See MH Blues, MH Lounge

Donald Fagen
See MH Lounge, MH Rock

John Fahey
See MH Folk, MH Rock

Barbara Fairchild
See MH Country

The Fairfield Four
See MH Folk

Fairground Attraction
See MH Rock

Fairport Convention
See MH Folk, MH Rock, MH World

Adam Faith
See MH Rock

Percy Faith
See MH Lounge

Th' Faith Healers
See MH Rock

Faith No More
See MH Rock

Marianne Faithfull
See MH Folk, MH Lounge, MH Rock

Joseph Falcon & Cleoma Breaux Falcon
See MH Folk, MH World

The Falcons
See MH R&B

Jason Falkner
See MH Rock

The Fall
See MH Rock

Charles Fambrough
See MH Jazz

Georgie Fame
See MH Lounge, MH Rock

Fania All-Stars
See MH World

Fantcha
See MH World

Farafina
See MH World

Donna Fargo
See MH Country

Richard and Mimi Fariña
See MH Folk

Mary Ann Farley
See MH Rock

Tal Farlow
See MH Jazz

Chris Farlowe
See MH Rock

The Farm
See MH Rock

Farm Dogs
See MH Rock

Art Farmer
See MH Jazz

Farmer Not So John
See MH Rock

Farmer's Daughters
See MH Folk

Allen Farnham
See MH Jazz

Joe Farrell
See MH Jazz

Dionne Farris
See MH Rock

Farside
See MH Rock

Majek Fashek
See MH World

Fastbacks
See MH Rock

Fastball
See MH Rock

Zusaan Kali Fasteau
See MH Jazz

Fat Boys
See MH R&B

Fat Joe Da Gangsta
See MH R&B

Fatala
See MH World

Fatback Band
See MH R&B

John Faulkner
See MH World

Faust
See MH Rock

Pierre Favre
See MH Jazz

Pura Fé
See MH World

Fear
See MH Rock

Stephen Fearing
See MH Folk

Charlie Feathers
See MH Country, MH Rock, MH Swing

John Fedchock
See MH Jazz

Danny Federici
See MH Rock

The Feelies
See MH Rock

Michael Feinstein
See MH Lounge

Jerome Felder
See MH Blues

Lee Feldman
See MH Rock

Jose Feliciano
See MH Lounge, MH World

Narvel Felts
See MH Country

Freddy Fender
See MH Country

Mike Fenton
See MH Folk

H-Bomb Ferguson
See MH Blues

Jay Ferguson
See MH Rock

Maynard Ferguson
See MH Jazz

Fernhill
See MH World

Ferrante & Teicher
See MH Lounge

Rachelle Ferrell
See MH Jazz, MH R&B

Melissa Ferrick
See MH Rock

Glenn Ferris
See MH Jazz

Ferron
See MH Folk

Bryan Ferry
See MH Lounge, MH Rock

Garrison Fewell
See MH Jazz

Fiddle Fever
See MH Folk

Arthur Fiedler
See MH Lounge

Dale Fielder
See MH Jazz

The Fifth Dimension
See MH Lounge, MH R&B

54.40
See MH Rock

Fig Dish
See MH Rock

The Figgs
See MH Rock

Figgy Duff
See MH Folk

Fight
See MH Rock

Fiji Mariners
See MH Rock

Filé
See MH Country, MH Folk, MH World

Film Orchestra of Shanghai
See MH World

Filter
See MH Rock

Fine Young Cannibals
See MH R&B, MH Rock

Sally Fingerett
See MH Folk

Fingerprintz
See MH Rock

Cathy Fink and Marcy Marxer
See MH Folk

Alec Finn
See MH Folk, MH World

Neil Finn
See MH Rock

Tim Finn
See MH Rock

Finn Brothers
See MH Rock

Firefall
See MH Country, MH Rock

fIREHOSE
See MH Rock

Firewater
See MH World

The Firm
See MH Rock

First Edition
See MH Lounge

Fish
See MH Rock

Fishbone
See MH R&B, MH Rock

Archie Fisher
See MH Folk, MH World

Eddie Fisher
See MH Lounge

Matthew Fisher
See MH Rock

Steve Fisher
See MH Folk

Ella Fitzgerald
See MH Jazz, MH Lounge, MH R&B, MH Swing

David Fiuczynski
See MH Jazz

The Five Americans
See MH Rock

Five Chinese Brothers
See MH Country, MH Folk

The Five Keys
See MH R&B

The "5" Royales
See MH R&B, MH Rock

The Fixx
See MH Rock

Roberta Flack
See MH R&B

The Flamin' Groovies
See MH Rock

The Flaming Lips
See MH Rock

The Flamingos
See MH Rock

Tommy Flanagan
See MH Jazz

Fred Flange
See MH Lounge

Flash Cadillac
See MH Rock

The Flashcats
See MH Rock

The Flashcubes
See MH Rock

Flat Duo Jets
See MH Rock

The Flatlanders
See MH Country, MH Folk, MH Rock

Flatlinerz
See MH R&B

Lester Flatt
See MH Country

Flatt & Scruggs
See MH Country, MH Folk

Flattop Tom & His Jump Cats
See MH Swing

Béla Fleck
See MH Country, MH Folk, MH Jazz

Mick Fleetwood
See MH Rock

Fleetwood Mac
See MH Blues, MH Rock

The Fleetwoods
See MH Lounge

The Fleshtones
See MH Rock

Flim & the BB's
See MH Jazz

Matt Flinner
See MH Folk

Benton Flippen
See MH Country, MH Folk

Flipper
See MH Rock

A Flock of Seagulls
See MH Rock

Flop
See MH Rock

Myron Floren
See MH Lounge, MH Swing

Bob Florence
See MH Jazz

Rosie Flores
See MH Country, MH Folk, MH Swing

Flotsam & Jetsam
See MH Rock

Robin Flower
See MH Folk

Eddie Floyd
See MH Blues, MH R&B

The Fluid
See MH Rock

Flying Burrito Brothers
See MH Country, MH Folk, MH Rock

Frank Emilio Flynn
See MH World

Focus
See MH Rock

Dan Fogelberg
See MH Country, MH Folk, MH Rock

John Fogerty
See MH Country, MH Rock

Foghat
See MH Rock

Ben Folds Five
See MH Rock

Red Foley
See MH Country, MH Folk

Sue Foley
See MH Blues, MH Folk

The Folk Implosion
See MH Rock

Folk Scat
See MH World

David Folks
See MH Folk

Fong Naam
See MH World

Frank Fontaine
See MH Lounge

Wayne Fontana & the Mindbenders
See MH Rock

Canray Fontenot
See MH Folk, MH World

Foo Fighters
See MH Rock

For Against
See MH Rock

For Squirrels
See MH Rock

Steve Forbert
See MH Folk, MH Rock

The Forbes Family
See MH Country, MH Folk

Force M.D.'s
See MH R&B

Aleck Ford
See MH Blues

Frankie Ford
See MH Rock

Lita Ford
See MH Rock

Mary Ford
See MH Country, MH Lounge

Ricky Ford
See MH Jazz

Robben Ford
See MH Blues

Tennessee Ernie Ford
See MH Country

Charles Ford Band
See MH Blues

Ford Blues Band
See MH Blues

Julia Fordham
See MH Folk, MH Rock

Foreigner
See MH Rock

The Foremen
See MH Folk

Forest for the Trees
See MH Rock

The Forester Sisters
See MH Country

Juan Carlos Formell
See MH World

Helen Forrest
See MH Lounge, MH Swing

Jimmy Forrest
See MH Jazz

Joel Forrester
See MH Jazz

John Forster
See MH Folk

Robert Forster
See MH Rock

Fort Apache Band
See MH Jazz

Fortuna
See MH World

Jesse Fortune
See MH Blues

Sonny Fortune
See MH Jazz

The Fortunes
See MH Rock

Frank Foster
See MH Jazz

Gary Foster
See MH Jazz

Radney Foster
See MH Country

Foster & Lloyd
See MH Country, MH Rock

Fotheringay
See MH Folk, MH Rock

The Foundations
See MH Rock

Pete Fountain
See MH Jazz, MH Swing

Fountains of Wayne
See MH Rock

James Founty
See MH Blues

Four Bitchin' Babes
See MH Folk

The Four Dukes
See MH Lounge

The Four Freshmen
See MH Lounge

The Four Lads
See MH Lounge

Four Men & a Dog
See MH World

The Four Preps
See MH Folk, MH Lounge

4 Runner
See MH Country

The Four Seasons
See MH Lounge, MH R&B, MH Rock

The Four Tops
See MH R&B, MH Rock

The Fourmost
See MH Rock

Fourplay
See MH Jazz

Kim Fox
See MH Rock

Samantha Fox
See MH Rock

The Fox Family
See MH Country

Jeff Foxworthy
See MH Country

Frå Senegal Til Setesdal
See MH World

Michael Fracasso
See MH Country, MH Folk

Amy Fradon and Leslie Ritter
See MH Folk

J.P. & Annadeene Fraley
See MH Country, MH Folk

Peter Frampton
See MH Rock

Carol Fran & Clarence Hollimon
See MH Blues

Connie Francis
See MH Country, MH Lounge, MH Rock

Franco
See MH World

Jackson C. Frank
See MH Folk

Keith Frank
See MH Folk

The Frank & Walters
See MH Rock

Bob Franke
See MH Folk

Frankie Goes to Hollywood
See MH Rock

Aretha Franklin
See MH R&B, MH Rock

Kirk Franklin & the Family
See MH R&B

Michael Franks
See MH Jazz, MH Lounge

Rebecca Coupe Franks
See MH Jazz

The Frantic Flattops
See MH Swing

Alasdair Fraser
See MH Folk, MH World

Gail Fratar
See MH Folk

Rob Fraynor
See MH Jazz

Calvin Frazier
See MH Blues

Frazier River
See MH Country

Freakwater
See MH Country, MH Rock

Stan Freberg
See MH Lounge

Freddie & the Dreamers
See MH Rock

Freddy Jones Band
See MH Rock

Henry St. Claire Fredericks
See MH Blues

Free
See MH Rock

Free Hot Lunch!
See MH Folk

Free Music Quintet
See MH Jazz

Nnenna Freelon
See MH Jazz

Alan Freeman
See MH Folk

Bud Freeman
See MH Jazz

Chico Freeman
See MH Jazz

George Freeman
See MH Jazz

Russ Freeman
See MH Jazz

Von Freeman
See MH Jazz

Freestyle Fellowship
See MH Jazz, MH R&B

Freewill Savages
See MH Folk

The Freight Hoppers
See MH Folk

Gary Frenay
See MH Rock

John French
See MH Rock

French, Frith, Kaiser & Thompson
See MH Folk, MH Rock

frente!
See MH Rock

Doug E. Fresh
See MH R&B

Gideon Freudmann
See MH Folk

Glenn Frey
See MH Folk

Freyda and Acoustic AttaTude
See MH Folk

Janie Fricke
See MH Country

Gavin Friday
See MH Rock

Don Friedman
See MH Jazz

Kinky Friedman
See MH Country, MH Folk

Friends of Dean Martinez
See MH Lounge, MH Rock

Friends of Distinction
See MH R&B

Johnny Frigo
See MH Jazz

Robert Fripp
See MH Rock

Bill Frisell
See MH Jazz, MH Rock

David Frishberg
See MH Jazz

Lefty Frizzell
See MH Country

David Frizzell & Shelly West
See MH Country

The Front Porch String Band
See MH Country, MH Folk

Front Range
See MH Country, MH Folk

Front 242
See MH Rock

Jack Frost
See MH Rock

Frank Frost & Sam Carr
See MH Blues

John Frusciante
See MH Rock

Fu-Schnickens
See MH R&B

Fugazi
See MH Rock

Fugees
See MH R&B, MH Rock

The Fugs
See MH Folk, MH Rock

Robbie Fulks
See MH Country

Full Force
See MH R&B

Full Time Men
See MH Rock

Blind Boy Fuller
See MH Blues

Curtis Fuller
See MH Jazz

Jesse Fuller
See MH Blues, MH Folk

The Bobby Fuller Four
See MH Rock

Lowell Fulson
See MH Blues

Fun Boy Three
See MH Rock

Fun Lovin' Criminals
See MH Rock

John Funchess
See MH Blues

Anson Funderburgh & the Rockets Featuring Sam Myers
See MH Blues

Funkadelic
See MH Rock

Funkdoobiest
See MH R&B

Funkmaster Flex
See MH R&B

Richie Furay/Richie Furay Band
See MH Rock

Tret Fure
See MH Folk

Tony Furtado
See MH Country, MH Folk

Billy Fury
See MH Rock

Future Sound of London
See MH Rock

Fuzzy Mountain String Band
See MH Folk

Kenny G
See MH Jazz

Warren G
See MH R&B

G. Love & Special Sauce
See MH R&B

Reeves Gabrels
See MH Rock

Charles Gabriel
See MH Jazz

Ethel Gabriel
See MH Lounge

Peter Gabriel
See MH Rock, MH World

Steve Gadd
See MH Jazz

Chris Gaffney
See MH Country

Slim Gaillard
See MH Jazz, MH Lounge, MH Swing

Jon Gailmor
See MH Folk

Earl Gaines
See MH Blues

Grady Gaines
See MH Blues

Rosie Gaines
See MH R&B

Serge Gainsbourg
See MH Lounge

Galaxie 500
See MH Rock

The Galaxy Trio
See MH Lounge

Eric Gale
See MH Jazz

Rory Gallagher
See MH Blues, MH Rock

Les & Gary Gallier
See MH Folk

Gallon Drunk
See MH Rock

Annie Gallup
See MH Folk

Hal Galper
See MH Jazz

James Galway
See MH Lounge, MH World

Frank Gambale
See MH Jazz

Beppe Gambetta
See MH Folk

Game Theory
See MH Rock

Gamelan Son of Lion
See MH World

Ganelin Trio
See MH Jazz

Gang of Four
See MH Rock

Gang Starr
See MH Jazz, MH R&B

Gordon Gano
See MH Rock

Cecil Gant
See MH Blues, MH Swing

Gap Band
See MH R&B

Garbage
See MH Rock

Jan Garbarek
See MH Jazz

Garcia Brothers
See MH World

Carlos Gardel
See MH World

Art Garfunkel
See MH Folk, MH Rock

Greg Garing
See MH Rock

Hank Garland
See MH Country

Judy Garland
See MH Lounge

Red Garland
See MH Jazz

Garmarna
See MH World

Erroll Garner
See MH Jazz, MH Lounge, MH Swing

Larry Garner
See MH Blues

Kenny Garrett
See MH Jazz

Nick Garvey
See MH Rock

John Gary
See MH Lounge

George Garzone
See MH Jazz

Giorgio Gaslini
See MH Jazz

Djivan Gasparyan
See MH World

Edith Giovanna Gassion
See MH Lounge

Marvin Gaster
See MH Country, MH Folk

Gastr del Sol
See MH Rock

David Gates
See MH Country, MH Rock

Gateway
See MH Jazz

The Gathering Field
See MH Rock

Larry Gatlin & the Gatlin Brothers
See MH Country

Keith Gattis
See MH Country

Danny Gatton
See MH Rock

Dick Gaughan
See MH Folk, MH World

Frankie Gavin
See MH Folk, MH World

Marvin Gaye
See MH Lounge, MH R&B, MH Rock

Charles Gayle
See MH Jazz

Crystal Gayle
See MH Country

Gloria Gaynor
See MH R&B

Gazoline
See MH World

Gear Daddies
See MH Rock

George Gee & His Make-Believe Ballroom Orchestra
See MH Swing

J. Geils Band
See MH Blues, MH R&B, MH Rock

The Ray Gelato Giants
See MH Swing

Howe Gelb
See MH Rock

Bob Geldof
See MH Rock

Gene
See MH Rock

General Humbert
See MH Folk

General Public
See MH Rock

Generation X
See MH Rock

Genesis
See MH Rock

Genius/GZA
See MH R&B

Gentle Giant
See MH Rock

The Gentle People
See MH Lounge

Bobbie Gentry
See MH Country

Frank George
See MH Folk

Georgia Satellites
See MH Rock

Christopher Geppert
See MH Lounge

Geraldine Fibbers
See MH Rock

Geraldo
See MH R&B

Paul Geremia
See MH Folk

Lisa Germano
See MH Rock

Mark Germino
See MH Country, MH Folk

The Germs
See MH Rock

Alice Gerrard
See MH Country, MH Folk

Lisa Gerrard
See MH Rock

Gerry & the Pacemakers
See MH Rock

George & Ira Gershwin
See MH Lounge

Bruce Gertz
See MH Jazz

Getaway Cruiser
See MH Rock

Geto Boys
See MH R&B

Stan Getz
See MH Jazz, MH Lounge

Ghazal
See MH World

Bikram Ghosh
See MH World

Ghost Face Killa
See MH R&B

Giant Sand
See MH Rock

Gerry Gibbs
See MH Jazz

Terri Gibbs
See MH Country

Terry Gibbs
See MH Jazz

Banu Gibson
See MH Jazz, MH Swing

Bob Gibson
See MH Folk

Clifford Gibson
See MH Blues

Debbie Gibson
See MH Rock

Don Gibson
See MH Country

Harry "The Hipster" Gibson
See MH Swing

Lacy Gibson
See MH Blues

Gibson Brothers Band
See MH Folk

The Gibson/Miller Band
See MH Country

Kathie Lee Gifford
See MH Lounge

Gigolo Aunts
See MH Rock

Gilberto Gil
See MH World

Ronnie Gilbert
See MH Folk

Vance Gilbert
See MH Folk

Astrud Gilberto
See MH Lounge, MH World

João Gilberto
See MH Jazz, MH Lounge, MH World

Johnny Gill
See MH R&B

Vince Gill
See MH Country

Dizzy Gillespie
See MH Jazz, MH Lounge, MH Swing

Steve Gillette & Cindy Mangsen
See MH Folk

Mickey Gilley
See MH Country

Bill "Jazz" Gillum
See MH Blues

Jimmie Dale Gilmore
See MH Country, MH Folk, MH Rock

David Gilmour
See MH Rock

Gin Blossoms
See MH Rock

Greg Ginn
See MH Rock

The Gipsy Kings
See MH World

Girls Against Boys
See MH Rock

Girls of Angeli
See MH World

Regis Gisavo
See MH World

Egberto Gismonti
See MH Jazz, MH World

Jimmy Giuffre
See MH Jazz

Gjallarhorn
See MH World

Paddy Glackin
See MH World

Gladhands
See MH Rock

Gladiators
See MH World

Glass Eye
See MH Rock

Jackie Gleason
See MH Lounge

Gary Glitter
See MH Rock

Glitterbox
See MH Rock

Globe Unity Orchestra
See MH Jazz

The Glove
See MH Rock

Corey Glover
See MH Rock

The Go-Betweens
See MH Rock

The Go-Go's
See MH Rock

Go West
See MH Rock

Goats
See MH R&B

God Street Wine
See MH Rock

The Godfathers
See MH Rock

The Goins Brothers
See MH Country

Julie Gold
See MH Folk

Barry Goldberg
See MH Blues

Ben Goldberg
See MH Jazz, MH World

Samuel Goldberg
See MH Lounge

Golden Earring
See MH Rock

Golden Gate Orchestra
See MH Swing

Golden Gate Quartet
See MH Folk

The Golden Palominos
See MH Rock

Golden Ring
See MH Folk

Golden Smog
See MH Country, MH Rock

Goldfinger
See MH Rock

Goldie
See MH Rock

Larry Goldings
See MH Jazz

Vinny Golia
See MH Jazz

Mac Gollehon
See MH Jazz

Benny Golson
See MH Jazz

Eddie Gomez
See MH Jazz

Paul Gonsalves
See MH Jazz

Gonzaguinha
See MH World

Celina González
See MH World

Rubén González
See MH World

Jerry Gonzalez & the Fort Apache Band
See MH Jazz, MH World

Goo Goo Dolls
See MH Rock

Good Ol' Persons
See MH Country, MH Folk

Goodie Mob
See MH R&B

Cuba Gooding
See MH R&B

Benny Goodman
See MH Jazz, MH Lounge, MH Swing

Steve Goodman
See MH Country, MH Folk, MH Rock

Mick Goodrick
See MH Jazz

Ron Goodwin
See MH Lounge

Bobby Gordon
See MH Jazz

Dexter Gordon
See MH Jazz, MH Lounge

Robert Gordon
See MH Country, MH Rock, MH Swing

Berry Gordy Jr.
See MH R&B

Lesley Gore
See MH Lounge, MH Rock

Martin Gore
See MH Rock

John Gorka
See MH Country, MH Folk, MH Rock

Gorky's Zygotic Mynci
See MH Rock

Skip Gorman
See MH Country, MH Folk

Eydie Gorme
See MH Lounge

Steve Gorn
See MH World

Vern Gosdin
See MH Country, MH Folk

Danny Gottlieb
See MH Jazz

Susan Gottlieb
See MH Folk

Barry Goudreau
See MH Rock

Morton Gould
See MH Lounge

Robert Goulet
See MH Lounge

Gov't Mule
See MH Rock

Lawrence Gowan
See MH Rock

Dusko Goykovich
See MH Jazz

The GP's
See MH Folk

Davey Graham
See MH Folk

Graham Central Station
See MH R&B

Lou Gramm
See MH Rock

Grand Daddy I.U.
See MH R&B

Grand Funk Railroad
See MH Rock

Grandmaster Flash & the Furious Five
See MH R&B

Grandpa Jones
See MH Country

Jerry Granelli
See MH Jazz

Amy Grant
See MH Rock

Bill Grant
See MH Folk

Darrell Grant
See MH Jazz

Eddy Grant
See MH World

Grant Lee Buffalo
See MH Rock

Grant Street
See MH Folk

The Grapes of Wrath
See MH Rock

Stephane Grappelli
See MH Jazz, MH Swing

The Grass Is Greener
See MH Country, MH Folk

The Grass Roots
See MH Rock

Lou Grassi
See MH Jazz

The Grassy Knoll
See MH Jazz, MH Rock

The Grateful Dead
See MH Country, MH Folk, MH
   Rock

Blind Roosevelt Graves
See MH Blues

Josh Graves
See MH Folk

Milford Graves
See MH Jazz

Gravity Kills
See MH Rock

David Gray
See MH Rock

Dobie Gray
See MH R&B

Henry Gray
See MH Blues

Wardell Gray
See MH Jazz, MH Swing

**Glen Gray & the Casa Loma
Orchestra**
See MH Swing

Grayhorse Singers
See MH World

Great Big Sea
See MH World

Great Plains
See MH Country

Great White
See MH Rock

Buddy Greco
See MH Lounge, MH Swing

Al Green
See MH Blues, MH R&B

Benny Green
See MH Jazz

Cal Green
See MH Blues

Cornelius Green
See MH Blues

Grant Green
See MH Jazz

Peter Green
See MH Blues

Green Day
See MH Rock

The Green Fields of America
See MH World

Green Jellÿ
See MH Rock

Green on Red
See MH Rock

Green River
See MH Rock

Greenberry Woods
See MH Rock

The Greenbriar Boys
See MH Country, MH Folk

Bruce Greene
See MH Folk

Dodo Greene
See MH Jazz

Jack Greene
See MH Country

Richard Greene
See MH Country, MH Folk

Phillip Greenlief
See MH Jazz

Greg Greenway
See MH Folk

Lee Greenwood
See MH Country

Ricky Lynn Gregg
See MH Country

Clinton Gregory
See MH Country

**Clive Gregson & Christine Col-
lister**
See MH Folk, MH Rock

Adie Grey
See MH Folk

Al Grey
See MH Jazz

Sara Grey
See MH Folk

Sylvan Grey
See MH World

Grianan
See MH Folk

David Grier
See MH Country, MH Folk

James Griffin
See MH Rock

Johnny Griffin
See MH Jazz

Patty Griffin
See MH Folk, MH Rock

Grace Griffith
See MH Folk

Nanci Griffith
See MH Country, MH Folk, MH
   Rock

Marcia Griffiths
See MH World

The Grifters
See MH Rock

John Grimaldi
See MH Blues

Henry Grimes
See MH Jazz

Lloyd "Tiny" Grimes
See MH Jazz

David Grisman
See MH Country, MH Folk

Don Grolnick
See MH Jazz

Groove Collective
See MH Jazz

Groove Theory
See MH R&B

Stefan Grossman
See MH Folk

Steve Grossman
See MH Jazz

Marty Grosz
See MH Jazz

Group Home
See MH R&B

Groupa
See MH World

Grubbs Brothers
See MH Jazz

Solomon Grundy
See MH Rock

Joe Grushecky
See MH Rock

Dave Grusin
See MH Jazz, MH Lounge

Gigi Gryce
See MH Jazz

Gu-Achi Fiddlers
See MH World

Guadalcanal Diary
See MH Rock

Vince Guaraldi
See MH Jazz, MH Lounge

Juan Luis Guerra
See MH World

The Guess Who
See MH Rock

Guided by Voices
See MH Rock

Guild of Temporal Adventures
See MH Rock

Ida Guillory
See MH Folk

Kristi Guillory
See MH Folk

Guitar Gabriel
See MH Blues

Guitar Shorty
See MH Blues

Guitar Slim
See MH Blues

Guitar Slim Jr.
See MH Blues

Frances Gumm
See MH Lounge

Gun Club
See MH Rock

Russell Gunn
See MH Jazz

Jo Jo Gunne
See MH Rock

Guns N' Roses
See MH Rock

The Guo Brothers & Shung Tian
See MH World

Tom Guralnick
See MH Jazz

Trilok Gurtu
See MH World

Adam Gussow
See MH Blues

Les Gustafson-Zook
See MH Folk

Arlo Guthrie
See MH Country, MH Folk, MH Rock

Jack Guthrie
See MH Country, MH Folk

Woody Guthrie
See MH Country, MH Folk

Guy
See MH R&B

Buddy Guy
See MH Blues, MH Folk, MH R&B

Phil Guy
See MH Blues

GWAR
See MH Rock

The Gyuto Monks
See MH World

Hackberry Ramblers
See MH Folk

Charlie Haden
See MH Jazz

Idjah Hadijah
See MH World

Sammy Hagar
See MH Rock

Nina Hagen
See MH Rock

Marty Haggard
See MH Country

Merle Haggard
See MH Country, MH Swing

Bob Haggart
See MH Jazz

Richard Hagopian
See MH World

Al Haig
See MH Jazz

Haircut 100
See MH Rock

Hassan Hakmoun
See MH World

Bill Haley
See MH Country, MH R&B, MH Rock, MH Swing

Ed Haley
See MH Folk

Jim Hall
See MH Jazz

Jimmy Hall
See MH Blues

Kristen Hall
See MH Folk, MH Rock

Terry Hall
See MH Rock

Tom T. Hall
See MH Country, MH Folk

Hall & Oates
See MH R&B, MH Rock

Lin Halliday
See MH Jazz

Pete Ham
See MH Rock

Hamell on Trial
See MH Rock

Chico Hamilton
See MH Jazz

Jeff Hamilton
See MH Jazz

Scott Hamilton
See MH Jazz

Hamilton Pool
See MH Folk

Hammer
See MH R&B

Oscar Hammerstein II
See MH Lounge

John Hammond Jr.
See MH Blues, MH Folk

Lorraine (Lee) Hammond
See MH Folk

Gunter Hampel
See MH Jazz

Thomas Hampson
See MH Folk

Col. Bruce Hampton
See MH Rock

Lionel Hampton
See MH Jazz, MH Swing

Slide Hampton
See MH Jazz

Hampton Grease Band
See MH Rock

Butch Hancock
See MH Country, MH Folk

Herbie Hancock
See MH Jazz, MH Lounge, MH R&B

Wayne Hancock
See MH Country

Handsome
See MH Rock

John Handy
See MH Jazz

W.C. Handy
See MH Jazz

The Hang Ups
See MH Rock

The Hangdogs
See MH Rock

Sir Roland Hanna
See MH Jazz, MH Swing

Robbie Hannan
See MH World

Hanoi Rocks
See MH Rock

Kip Hanrahan
See MH Jazz

Beck Hansen
See MH Blues

Hanson
See MH Rock

Happy Mondays
See MH Rock

Fareed Haque
See MH Jazz

Paul Hardcastle
See MH Jazz

Wilbur Harden
See MH Jazz

Tre Hardiman
See MH Blues

Tim Hardin
See MH Folk, MH Rock

John Wesley Harding
See MH Folk, MH Rock

Françoise Hardy
See MH Lounge, MH Rock

Jack Hardy
See MH Folk

Roy Hargrove
See MH Jazz

Joy Harjo & Poetic Justice
See MH World

Bill Harley
See MH Folk

Larry Harlow
See MH World

James Harman
See MH Blues

Harmonica Fats & Bernie Pearl
See MH Blues

Harmonica Slim
See MH Blues

Everette Harp
See MH Jazz

Ben Harper
See MH Folk, MH R&B, MH Rock

Billy Harper
See MH Jazz

Harpers Bizarre
See MH Rock

Slim Harpo
See MH Blues

Bill Harrell
See MH Folk

Tom Harrell
See MH Jazz

Edward Harrington
See MH Blues

Dick Harrington & Victoria Young
See MH Folk

Allan Harris
See MH Jazz

Barry Harris
See MH Jazz

Beaver Harris
See MH Jazz

Bill Harris
See MH Jazz

Corey Harris
See MH Blues

Craig Harris
See MH Jazz

Eddie Harris
See MH Jazz

Emmylou Harris
See MH Country, MH Folk, MH Rock

Gene Harris
See MH Jazz

Joey Harris
See MH Rock

Major Harris
See MH R&B

Phil Harris
See MH Lounge, MH Swing

Richard Harris
See MH Lounge

Shakey Jake Harris
See MH Blues

William Harris
See MH Blues

Wynonie Harris
See MH Blues, MH R&B, MH Swing

George Harrison
See MH Rock, MH World

Wilbert Harrison
See MH Blues

Deborah Harry
See MH Rock

Alvin Youngblood Hart
See MH Blues

Antonio Hart
See MH Jazz

Billy Hart
See MH Jazz

Freddie Hart
See MH Country

Grant Hart
See MH Rock

Lorenz Hart
See MH Lounge

Mickey Hart
See MH World

John Hartford
See MH Country, MH Folk

Johnny Hartman
See MH Jazz, MH Lounge

Mick Harvey
See MH Lounge, MH Rock

PJ Harvey
See MH Rock

Harvey Danger
See MH Rock

Tony Hatch & Jackie Trent
See MH Lounge

Hater
See MH Rock

Juliana Hatfield
See MH Rock

Donny Hathaway
See MH R&B

Lalah Hathaway
See MH R&B

Havana 3 A.M.
See MH Rock

Richie Havens
See MH Folk, MH R&B, MH Rock

Hampton Hawes
See MH Jazz

Hawk Project
See MH World

Ginny Hawker & Kay Justice
See MH Folk

Buddy Boy Hawkins
See MH Blues

Coleman Hawkins
See MH Jazz, MH Lounge, MH Swing

Dale Hawkins
See MH Rock

Erskine Hawkins
See MH Jazz, MH Swing

Hawkshaw Hawkins
See MH Country

Jamesetta Hawkins
See MH Blues

Ronnie Hawkins
See MH Country, MH Rock

Screamin' Jay Hawkins
See MH Blues, MH R&B, MH Rock

Sophie B. Hawkins
See MH Rock

Ted Hawkins
See MH Blues, MH Country, MH Folk, MH R&B, MH Rock

The Edwin Hawkins Singers
See MH R&B

Hayden
See MH Rock

Lili Haydn
See MH Rock

Isaac Hayes
See MH Lounge, MH R&B

Louis Hayes
See MH Jazz

Martin Hayes
See MH Folk

Wade Hayes
See MH Country

Dick Haymes
See MH Lounge, MH Swing

Graham Haynes
See MH Jazz

Roy Haynes
See MH Jazz

Justin Hayward & John Lodge
See MH Rock

Ofra Haza
See MH World

Hazard
See MH Rock

Hazel
See MH Rock

Hazel & Alice
See MH Country, MH Folk

Roy Head
See MH R&B, MH Rock

Topper Headon
See MH Rock

The Jeff Healey Band
See MH Rock

The Health & Happiness Show
See MH Country, MH Rock

Bill & Bonnie Hearne
See MH Folk

Heart
See MH Rock

The Heartbeats
See MH R&B

Johnny Heartsman
See MH Blues

The Reverend Horton Heat
See MH Rock

Jimmy Heath
See MH Jazz

Percy Heath
See MH Jazz

Tootie Heath
See MH Jazz

Heatmiser
See MH Rock

Heatwave
See MH R&B

Heaven 17
See MH Rock

Heavy D. & the Boyz
See MH R&B

Bobby Hebb
See MH R&B

Hedgehog Pie
See MH Folk

Michael Hedges
See MH Folk, MH Rock

Hedningarna
See MH World

The Hee Haw Gospel Quartet
See MH Country, MH Folk

Neal Hefti
See MH Lounge

Horace Heidt
See MH Swing

Gail Heil
See MH Folk

Mark Helias
See MH Jazz

Helicon
See MH Folk

Helium
See MH Rock

Richard Hell & the Voidoids
See MH Rock

Hellbenders
See MH Folk

Jonas Hellborg
See MH Jazz

The Hellecasters
See MH Country, MH Rock

Neal Hellman
See MH Folk

Levon Helm
See MH Rock

Helmet
See MH Rock

Heltah Skeltah
See MH R&B

Jessie Mae Hemphill
See MH Blues

Julius Hemphill
See MH Jazz

Bill Henderson
See MH Jazz

Eddie Henderson
See MH Jazz

Fletcher Henderson
See MH Jazz, MH Swing

Horace Henderson
See MH Swing

Joe Henderson
See MH Jazz

John William Henderson
See MH Blues

Michael Henderson
See MH R&B

Mike Henderson
See MH Blues, MH Country, MH Rock

Wayne Henderson
See MH Folk

Jimi Hendrix
See MH Blues, MH R&B, MH Rock

Nona Hendryx
See MH R&B

Mel Henke
See MH Lounge

Don Henley
See MH Folk, MH Rock

Margo Hennebach
See MH Folk

Clarence "Frogman" Henry
See MH Blues

Ernie Henry
See MH Jazz

Joe Henry
See MH Country, MH Rock

Priscilla Herdman
See MH Folk

Herm
See MH R&B

Woody Herman
See MH Jazz, MH Lounge, MH Swing

Herman's Hermits
See MH Rock

Ty Herndon
See MH Country

Fred Hersch
See MH Jazz

Kristin Hersh
See MH Rock

Monika Herzig
See MH Jazz

Hesperus
See MH Folk

Carolyn Hester
See MH Folk

Howard Hewett
See MH R&B

Richard X. Heyman
See MH Rock

Nick Heyward
See MH Rock

Hi-Five
See MH R&B

The Hi-Lo's
See MH Lounge

Hi Records
See MH R&B

John Hiatt
See MH Rock

Al Hibbler
See MH Jazz, MH Lounge

Sara Hickman
See MH Folk

Dan Hicks
See MH Country, MH Folk, MH Rock

John Hicks
See MH Jazz

Otis Hicks
See MH Blues

Robert Hicks
See MH Blues

Billy Higgins
See MH Jazz

Joe Higgs
See MH World

High Llamas
See MH Lounge, MH Rock

High Noon
See MH Country

Highway 101
See MH Country

The Highwaymen
See MH Country, MH Folk

Highwoods String Band
See MH Country, MH Folk

Andrew Hill
See MH Jazz

Buck Hill
See MH Jazz

Faith Hill
See MH Country

Jessie Hill
See MH R&B

Kim Hill
See MH Country

King Solomon Hill
See MH Blues

Lester Hill
See MH Blues

Michael Hill
See MH Blues

Noel Hill
See MH Folk

Z.Z. Hill
See MH Blues, MH R&B

Harriet Hilliard
See MH Swing

Chris Hillman
See MH Country, MH Folk, MH Rock

The Hillmen
See MH Country

Anne Hills
See MH Folk

Peter Himmelman
See MH Rock

Earl "Fatha" Hines
See MH Jazz, MH Swing

Tish Hinojosa
See MH Country, MH Folk, MH World

Milt Hinton
See MH Jazz, MH Swing

Hipster Daddy-O & the Hand-grenades
See MH Swing

Hiroshima
See MH Jazz

Al Hirt
See MH Jazz, MH Lounge, MH Swing

His Name Is Alive
See MH Rock

Robyn Hitchcock
See MH Folk, MH Rock

Don Ho
See MH Lounge

Fred Ho
See MH Jazz, MH World

Hoarse
See MH Rock

Becky Hobbs
See MH Country

Hobo Jim
See MH Folk

Art Hodes
See MH Jazz

Johnny Hodges
See MH Jazz, MH Swing

Roger Hodgson
See MH Rock

Hoelderlin Express
See MH World

Kristian Hoffman
See MH Rock

Holly Hofmann
See MH Jazz

Silas Hogan
See MH Blues

Robin Holcomb
See MH Country, MH Folk, MH
Jazz

Roscoe Holcomb
See MH Folk

Hole
See MH Rock

Dave Hole
See MH Blues

Billie Holiday
See MH Blues, MH Jazz, MH
Lounge, MH R&B, MH
Swing

Dave Holland
See MH Jazz

Greg Holland
See MH Country

Jerry Holland
See MH Folk

Holland, Dozier & Holland
See MH R&B

Major Holley
See MH Jazz

Jennifer Holliday
See MH R&B

The Hollies
See MH Rock

Clarence Hollimon
See MH Blues

Tony Hollins
See MH Blues

Hollow Rock String Band
See MH Folk

Ken Holloway
See MH Country

Red Holloway
See MH Jazz

Ron Holloway
See MH Jazz

Buddy Holly
See MH Country, MH Rock

Holly & the Italians
See MH Rock

Christopher Hollyday
See MH Jazz

The Hollyridge Strings
See MH Lounge

Bill Holman
See MH Jazz

Joe Holmes
See MH Blues

Richard "Groove" Holmes
See MH Jazz

Rupert Holmes
See MH Lounge

The Holmes Brothers
See MH Blues

Peter Holsapple
See MH Rock

David Holt
See MH Folk

Morris Holt
See MH Blues

Holy Barbarians
See MH Rock

The Holy Modal Rounders
See MH Country, MH Folk

Adam Holzman
See MH Jazz

Home Service
See MH World

Homer & Jethro
See MH Country, MH Folk

Homesick James
See MH Blues

The Honeycombs
See MH Rock

The Honeydogs
See MH Country, MH Rock

The Hoodoo Gurus
See MH Rock

Earl Hooker
See MH Blues

John Lee Hooker
See MH Blues, MH Folk, MH
R&B, MH Rock

Sol Hoopii
See MH World

The Hoosier Hot Shots
See MH Country, MH Folk

The Hooters
See MH Rock

Hootie & the Blowfish
See MH Rock

Jamie Hoover
See MH Rock

Hooverphonic
See MH Rock

St. Elmo Hope
See MH Jazz

Hadda Hopgood
See MH Blues

Mary Hopkin
See MH Folk, MH Rock

Claude Hopkins
See MH Swing

Lightnin' Hopkins
See MH Blues, MH Folk

Sam Hopkins
See MH Blues, MH Folk

Telma Louise Hopkins
See MH Lounge

Horch
See MH World

Glenn Horiuchi
See MH Jazz

Shirley Horn
See MH Jazz

Lois Hornbostel
See MH Folk

Lena Horne
See MH Lounge

Bruce Hornsby
See MH Rock

Ted Horowitz
See MH Blues

The Horseflies
See MH Folk

Horslips
See MH World

Big Walter Horton
See MH Blues

Johnny Horton
See MH Country

Ronnie Horvath
See MH Blues

Bill Horvitz
See MH Jazz

Wayne Horvitz
See MH Jazz

Hot Chocolate
See MH R&B

Hot Club of Cowtown
See MH Swing

Hot Rize
See MH Country, MH Folk, MH
Swing

Hot Rod Lincoln
See MH Swing

Hot Tuna
See MH Blues, MH Folk, MH
Rock

Hothouse Flowers
See MH Folk, MH Rock

James House
See MH Country

Son House
See MH Blues, MH Folk, MH
R&B

The House Band
See MH Folk, MH World

The House of Love
See MH Rock

House of Pain
See MH R&B, MH Rock

The Housemartins
See MH Rock

Cisco Houston
See MH Country, MH Folk

David Houston
See MH Country

Penelope Houston
See MH Rock

Whitney Houston
See MH R&B, MH Rock

Hoven Droven
See MH World

Eddy Howard
See MH Lounge

George Howard
See MH Jazz

Harlan Howard
See MH Country

Noah Howard
See MH Jazz

Peg Leg Howell
See MH Blues

Howlin' Maggie
See MH Rock

Howlin' Wolf
See MH Blues, MH R&B, MH Rock

H2O
See MH Rock

Freddie Hubbard
See MH Jazz

Ray Wylie Hubbard
See MH Country, MH Folk

The Hucklebucks
See MH Swing

David Hudson
See MH World

The Hudson Brothers
See MH Rock

Hues Corporation
See MH R&B

Huevos Rancheros
See MH Rock

Huffamoose
See MH Rock

Joe "Guitar" Hughes
See MH Blues

Hui Ohana
See MH Folk, MH World

Hum
See MH Rock

Human League
See MH Rock

Humble Pie
See MH Rock

Helen Humes
See MH Blues, MH Jazz, MH Swing

Marcus Hummon
See MH Country

Engelbert Humperdinck
See MH Lounge

Percy Humphrey
See MH Jazz

Willie Humphrey
See MH Jazz

Hundred Watt Smile
See MH Folk

Alberta Hunter
See MH Blues, MH Jazz

Charlie Hunter
See MH Jazz

Ian Hunter
See MH Rock

Ivory Joe Hunter
See MH Blues, MH R&B

Long John Hunter
See MH Blues

Hunters & Collectors
See MH Rock

The Cornell Hurd Band
See MH Country

Michael Hurley
See MH Folk

Hurricane #1
See MH Rock

Robert Hurst III
See MH Jazz

Mississippi John Hurt
See MH Blues, MH Folk

Lida Husik
See MH Rock

Hüsker Dü
See MH Rock

Ferlin Husky
See MH Country

Zakir Hussain
See MH World

Willie Hutch
See MH R&B

Bobby Hutcherson
See MH Jazz

Ashley Hutchings
See MH Folk, MH World

Frank Hutchison
See MH Folk

J.B. Hutto
See MH Blues

Betty Hutton
See MH Lounge, MH Swing

Sylvia Hutton
See MH Country

Huun-Huur-Tu
See MH World

Walter Hyatt
See MH Country, MH Folk

Hyenas in the Desert
See MH R&B

Brian Hyland
See MH Rock

Dick Hyman
See MH Jazz, MH Lounge, MH Swing

Phyllis Hyman
See MH Lounge, MH R&B

Janis Ian
See MH Folk, MH Rock

Ian & Sylvia
See MH Folk

Jimmy Ibbotson
See MH Rock

Abdullah Ibrahim
See MH Jazz, MH World

Ice Cube
See MH R&B

Ice-T
See MH R&B

Icehouse
See MH Rock

The Icicle Works
See MH Rock

Rob Ickes
See MH Folk

I.C.P. Orchestra
See MH Jazz

Idaho
See MH Rock

Billy Idol
See MH Rock

Julio Iglesias
See MH Lounge

James Iha
See MH Rock

Ill Al Skratch
See MH R&B

The Ill-Mo Boys
See MH Folk

Illegal
See MH R&B

Natalie Imbruglia
See MH Rock

Immature
See MH R&B

Immigrant Suns
See MH World

Impact All Stars
See MH World

Imperial Teen
See MH Rock

The Impressions
See MH R&B

Incognito
See MH R&B

Incredible String Band
See MH Folk

Indigenous
See MH World

Indigo Girls
See MH Folk, MH Rock

Indigo Swing
See MH Swing

Infectious Grooves
See MH Rock

Keith Ingham
See MH Jazz

Jack Ingram
See MH Country

James Ingram
See MH R&B

Luther Ingram
See MH R&B

The Ink Spots
See MH Lounge, MH R&B

Inkuyo
See MH World

The Innocence Mission
See MH Rock

Insane Clown Posse
See MH R&B, MH Rock

Inspiral Carpets
See MH Rock

Intelligent Hoodlum
See MH R&B

The International Beat
See MH Rock

The Interpreters
See MH Rock

Inti-Illimani
See MH World

The Intruders
See MH R&B

INXS
See MH Rock

Irakere
See MH World

Irish Rovers
See MH Folk, MH World

The Irish Tradition
See MH Folk, MH World

Iron Butterfly
See MH Rock

Iron Maiden
See MH Rock

Andy Irvine
See MH Folk, MH World

Gregory Isaacs
See MH World

Barney Isaacs & George Kuo
See MH Folk

Chris Isaak
See MH Rock

The Isley Brothers
See MH R&B, MH Rock

Israel Vibration
See MH World

Chuck Israels
See MH Jazz

The Itals
See MH World

Isidore Israel Itzkowitz
See MH Lounge

Eileen Ivers
See MH Folk, MH World

Burl Ives
See MH Folk

Ivy
See MH Rock

David J
See MH Rock

Alan Jackson
See MH Country

Arthur Jackson
See MH Blues

Bullmoose Jackson
See MH Blues, MH Swing

Carl Jackson
See MH Country, MH Folk

Chuck Jackson
See MH R&B

D.D. Jackson
See MH Jazz

Freddie Jackson
See MH R&B

Janet Jackson
See MH R&B, MH Rock

Javon Jackson
See MH Jazz

Jim Jackson
See MH Blues

J.J. Jackson
See MH R&B

Joe Jackson
See MH Lounge, MH Rock, MH Swing

John Jackson
See MH Blues, MH Folk

Mahalia Jackson
See MH R&B

Michael Jackson
See MH R&B, MH Rock

Millie Jackson
See MH R&B

Milt Jackson
See MH Jazz

Paul Jackson Jr.
See MH Jazz

Ronald Shannon Jackson
See MH Jazz

Scott Jackson
See MH Folk

Stonewall Jackson
See MH Country

Tommy Jackson
See MH Country, MH Folk

Walter Jackson
See MH R&B

Wanda Jackson
See MH Country, MH Swing

Willis "Gator Tail" Jackson
See MH Jazz

Jackson 5
See MH R&B, MH Rock

Kate Jacobs
See MH Country, MH Folk, MH Rock

Marion Walter Jacobs
See MH Blues

Illinois Jacquet
See MH Jazz, MH Swing

Jade
See MH R&B

Allan Jaffe
See MH Jazz

Mick Jagger
See MH Rock

Jaguares
See MH World

Jai
See MH Rock

The Jam
See MH Rock

Jimmy Jam & Terry Lewis
See MH R&B

Ahmad Jamal
See MH Jazz

James
See MH Rock

Bob James
See MH Jazz

Brett James
See MH Country

Colin James
See MH Blues

Elmore James
See MH Blues, MH R&B, MH Rock

Etta James
See MH Blues, MH R&B, MH Rock

Harry James
See MH Jazz, MH Lounge, MH Swing

Michael James
See MH Country

Rick James
See MH R&B

Skip James
See MH Blues, MH Folk

Sonny James
See MH Country

Steve James
See MH Blues

Tommy James & the Shondells
See MH Rock

Jamiroquai
See MH R&B, MH Rock

Jan & Dean
See MH Rock

Jandek
See MH Rock

Jane's Addiction
See MH Rock

Jon Jang
See MH Jazz, MH World

Horst Jankowski
See MH Lounge

Denise Jannah
See MH Jazz

Bert Jansch
See MH Folk

Japan
See MH Rock

The Japanese Koto Consort
See MH World

Victor Jara
See MH World

Joseph Jarman
See MH Jazz

Maurice Jarre
See MH Lounge

Al Jarreau
See MH Jazz, MH Lounge, MH R&B

Tommy Jarrell
See MH Folk

Keith Jarrett
See MH Jazz

Jars of Clay
See MH Rock

Duane Jarvis
See MH Country

Jason & the Scorchers
See MH Country, MH Rock

Jawbox
See MH Rock

Jawbreaker
See MH Rock

Jay & the Americans
See MH Rock

Jay-Z
See MH R&B

Miles Jaye
See MH R&B

The Jayhawks
See MH Country, MH Rock

The Jazz Composers Alliance Orchestra
See MH Jazz

The Jazz Passengers
See MH Jazz

Jazzmatazz
See MH R&B

Wyclef Jean
See MH World

Nemours Jean-Baptiste
See MH World

Blind Lemon Jefferson
See MH Blues, MH Folk, MH R&B

Eddie Jefferson
See MH Jazz

Paul Jefferson
See MH Country

Jefferson Airplane
See MH Rock

Jefferson Starship
See MH Rock

Garland Jeffreys
See MH R&B, MH Rock

Herb Jeffries
See MH Country, MH Jazz

Jellyfish
See MH Rock

Ella Jenkins
See MH Folk

Gordon Jenkins
See MH Lounge, MH Swing

Leroy Jenkins
See MH Jazz

John Jennings
See MH Country, MH Folk

Waylon Jennings
See MH Country

Ingrid Jensen
See MH Jazz

Michael Jerling
See MH Folk

Jeru the Damaja
See MH Jazz, MH R&B

The Jesus & Mary Chain
See MH Rock

Jesus Jones
See MH Rock

The Jesus Lizard
See MH Rock

Jet Set Six
See MH Swing

Jethro Tull
See MH Rock

The Jets
See MH R&B

Joan Jett
See MH Rock

Jewel
See MH Folk, MH Rock

Jim & Jesse
See MH Country, MH Folk

Don Santiago Jimenez
See MH World

Flaco Jimenez
See MH Country, MH Folk, MH World

Santiago Jimenez Jr.
See MH World

J.J. Fad
See MH R&B

Antonio Carlos Jobim
See MH Jazz, MH Lounge, MH World

Beau Jocque
See MH Folk, MH World

Jodeci
See MH R&B

Joe
See MH R&B

Billy Joel
See MH Lounge, MH Rock

David Johansen
See MH Lounge, MH Rock

Elton John
See MH Rock

John & Mary
See MH Rock

Johnnie & Jack
See MH Country, MH Folk

Evan Johns & His H-Bombs
See MH Rock

Big Jack Johnson
See MH Blues

Blind Willie Johnson
See MH Blues, MH Folk

Budd Johnson
See MH Jazz

Buddy Johnson
See MH Blues, MH Jazz, MH Swing

Bunk Johnson
See MH Jazz

Earl Johnson
See MH Folk

Earl Silas Johnson IV
See MH Blues

Eric Johnson
See MH Rock

Henry Johnson
See MH Jazz

Howard Johnson
See MH Jazz

James P. (Price) Johnson
See MH Jazz

James "Super Chikan" Johnson
See MH Blues

Jimmy Johnson
See MH Blues

J.J. Johnson
See MH Jazz

Johnnie Johnson
See MH Blues, MH R&B, MH Rock

Larry Johnson
See MH Blues, MH Folk

Leslie Johnson
See MH Blues

Linton Kwesi Johnson
See MH World

Lonnie Johnson
See MH Blues

Luther "Georgia Boy" Johnson
See MH Blues

Luther "Guitar Junior" Johnson
See MH Blues

Luther "House Rocker" Johnson
See MH Blues

Marc Johnson
See MH Jazz

Mark Johnson
See MH Folk

Marv Johnson
See MH R&B

Michael Johnson
See MH Country, MH Folk

Mike Johnson
See MH Rock

Pete Johnson
See MH Blues, MH Jazz, MH Swing

Prudence Johnson
See MH Folk

Robert Johnson
See MH Blues, MH Folk, MH R&B

Syl Johnson
See MH Blues, MH R&B

Tommy Johnson
See MH Blues

Johnson Mountain Boys
See MH Country, MH Folk

Daniel Johnston
See MH Rock

Freedy Johnston
See MH Folk, MH Rock

Phillip Johnston
See MH Jazz

Randy Johnston
See MH Jazz

Tom Johnston
See MH Rock

The Johnstons
See MH Folk, MH World

Jolene
See MH Country

Jolly Boys
See MH World

Al Jolson
See MH Lounge, MH Swing

Casey Jones
See MH Blues

Curtis Jones
See MH Blues

Eddie Lee Jones
See MH Blues

Edward Jones
See MH Blues

Elvin Jones
See MH Jazz

Etta Jones
See MH Jazz, MH Lounge

Floyd Jones
See MH Blues

George Jones
See MH Country, MH Folk

Glenn Jones
See MH R&B

Grace Jones
See MH R&B

Grandpa Jones
See MH Folk

Hank Jones
See MH Jazz

Howard Jones
See MH Rock

Isham Jones
See MH Swing

Jack Jones
See MH Lounge

Jo Jones
See MH Jazz, MH Swing

Johnny Jones
See MH Blues, MH Blues, MH Swing

Linda Jones
See MH R&B

Little "Sonny" Jones
See MH Blues

Marti Jones
See MH Rock

Mick Jones
See MH Rock

Oliver Jones
See MH Jazz

Paul "Wine" Jones
See MH Blues

"Philly" Joe Jones
See MH Jazz

Quincy Jones
See MH Jazz, MH Lounge, MH R&B, MH Swing

Rickie Lee Jones
See MH Folk, MH Rock

Robert Lewis Jones
See MH Blues

Ruth Lee Jones
See MH Blues

Sam Jones
See MH Jazz

Spike Jones
See MH Jazz, MH Lounge, MH Swing

Steve Jones
See MH Rock

Thad Jones
See MH Jazz, MH Swing

Tom Jones
See MH Lounge, MH Rock

Tutu Jones
See MH Blues

Diane Jones and Hubie King
See MH Folk

Carol Elizabeth Jones & James Leva
See MH Folk

Betty Joplin
See MH Jazz

Janis Joplin
See MH Blues, MH R&B, MH Rock

Scott Joplin
See MH Jazz

Al Jordan
See MH Lounge

Charley Jordan
See MH Blues

Clifford Jordan
See MH Jazz

Duke Jordan
See MH Jazz

Esteban "Steve" Jordan
See MH World

Louis Jordan
See MH Blues, MH Jazz, MH Lounge, MH R&B, MH Swing

Marlon Jordan
See MH Jazz

Montell Jordan
See MH R&B

Ronny Jordan
See MH Jazz

Sheila Jordan
See MH Jazz

Stanley Jordan
See MH Jazz

Margie Joseph
See MH R&B

Pleasant "Cousin Joe" Joseph
See MH Blues

Scott Joss
See MH Country

Journey
See MH Rock

Joy Division
See MH Rock

Joyce
See MH World

JPP
See MH World

JT the Bigga Figga
See MH R&B

Judas Priest
See MH Rock

Cledus "T." Judd
See MH Country

Wynonna Judd
See MH Country

The Judds
See MH Country

Judybats
See MH Rock

Jules & the Polar Bears
See MH Rock

Juluka
See MH Rock

Jump with Joey
See MH Lounge

Jumpin' Jimes
See MH Swing

Jungle Brothers
See MH R&B

Jungular Grooves
See MH World

Junior
See MH R&B

Junior M.A.F.I.A.
See MH R&B

Junk Monkeys
See MH Rock

Junoon
See MH World

Vic Juris
See MH Jazz

Just Ice
See MH R&B

Barbara K
See MH Rock

Paul K
See MH Rock

Ernie K-Doe
See MH R&B

Ledward Kaapana
See MH Folk, MH World

Bert Kaempfert
See MH Lounge

Brenda Kahn
See MH Folk, MH Rock

Si Kahn
See MH Folk

George Kahumoku Jr.
See MH Folk, MH World

Moses Kahumoku
See MH Folk, MH World

Henry Kaiser
See MH Jazz

Kajagoogoo
See MH Rock

Kalama's Quartet
See MH World

Maria Kalaniemi
See MH World

Connie Kaldor
See MH Folk

Kayhan Kalhor
See MH World

Pépé Kallé
See MH World

Cindy Kallet
See MH Folk

Kathy Kallick
See MH Country, MH Folk

Kam
See MH R&B

Rev. Dennis Kamakahi
See MH Folk, MH World

Michael Kamen
See MH Lounge

Ini Kamoze
See MH World

Kanda Bongo Man
See MH World

Candye Kane
See MH Blues, MH Swing

Kieran Kane
See MH Country, MH Folk

Ray Kane
See MH Folk, MH World

Cisse Diamba Kanoute
See MH World

Kansas
See MH Rock

Mory Kanté
See MH World

Paul Kantner
See MH Rock

Dominic Kanza & the African Rhythm Machine
See MH World

Kaoma
See MH World

Kapelye
See MH World

Lucy Kaplansky
See MH Folk

Doris Kappelhoff
See MH Lounge

Kara's Flowers
See MH Rock

Mick Karn
See MH Rock

Karnataka College of Percussion
See MH World

Kashif
See MH R&B

Kashtin
See MH World

Kassav'
See MH World

Kathleen Turner Overdrive
See MH Rock

Katrina & the Waves
See MH Rock

Bruce Katz
See MH Jazz

Mickey Katz
See MH Lounge

Steve Kaufman
See MH Folk

Jorma Kaukonen
See MH Folk, MH Rock

Connie Kay
See MH Jazz

Sammy Kaye
See MH Jazz, MH Lounge, MH Swing

KC & the Sunshine Band
See MH R&B, MH Rock

Dolores Keane
See MH Folk, MH World

James Keane
See MH Folk, MH World

Seán Keane
See MH Folk

William David Kearney
See MH Blues

John P. Kee
See MH R&B

James Keelaghan
See MH Folk

Robert Earl Keen Jr.
See MH Country, MH Folk

Tommy Keene
See MH Rock

Geoff Keezer
See MH Jazz

Garrison Keillor
See MH Folk

Katell Keineg
See MH Rock

Salif Keita
See MH World

Toby Keith
See MH Country

Roger Kellaway
See MH Jazz

Gene Kelly
See MH Lounge

Jack Kelly
See MH Blues

Paul Kelly
See MH Folk, MH Rock

R. Kelly
See MH R&B

Sean Kelly
See MH Rock

Vance Kelly
See MH Blues

Wynton Kelly
See MH Jazz

Chris Kelsey
See MH Jazz

Hal Kemp
See MH Swing

Scott Kempner
See MH Rock

The Kendalls
See MH Country

Rodney Kendrick
See MH Jazz

Eddie Kendricks
See MH R&B, MH Rock

Kenickie
See MH Rock

The Kennedys
See MH Folk, MH Rock

Willie Kent
See MH Blues

Stan Kenton
See MH Jazz, MH Lounge

The Kentucky Colonels
See MH Country, MH Folk

The Kentucky HeadHunters
See MH Country

Kentucky Standard Band
See MH Folk

Freddie Keppard
See MH Jazz

Ken Keppeler
See MH Folk

Jerome Kern
See MH Lounge

Nancy Kerr
See MH Folk

David Kersh
See MH Country

Doug Kershaw
See MH Country, MH Folk, MH World

Nik Kershaw
See MH Rock

Sammy Kershaw
See MH Country

Barney Kessel
See MH Jazz

Robin Kessinger
See MH Folk

Barbara Kessler
See MH Folk

Peter Kessler & Gail Fratar
See MH Folk

Hal Ketchum
See MH Country

Will Keys
See MH Folk

Khac Chi Ensemble
See MH World

Khaled
See MH World

Ali Akbar Khan
See MH World

Badar Ali Khan
See MH World

Chaka Khan
See MH R&B

Nusrat Fateh Ali Khan
See MH World

Salamat Ali Khan
See MH World

Steve Khan
See MH Jazz

Ustad Imrat Khan
See MH World

Ustad Vilayat Khan
See MH World

Khenany
See MH World

Talib Kibwe
See MH Jazz

Kid Capri
See MH R&B

Kid Creole & the Coconuts
See MH R&B, MH Rock, MH World

Kid Frost
See MH R&B

Kid 'n Play
See MH R&B

Kid Rock
See MH R&B, MH Rock

Angélique Kidjo
See MH World

Peter Kienle
See MH Jazz

Franklin Kiermyer
See MH Jazz

Greg Kihn
See MH Folk, MH Rock

Dave Kikoski
See MH Jazz

Kíla
See MH World

Steve Kilbey
See MH Rock

Rebecca Kilgore
See MH Jazz

Killah Priest
See MH Rock

Killbilly
See MH Country

Killing Joke
See MH Rock

Jin Hi Kim
See MH World

Frank Kimbrough
See MH Jazz

Junior Kimbrough
See MH Blues

Royal Wade Kimes
See MH Country

Shoukichi Kina
See MH World

Kindred Spirit
See MH Rock

Albert King
See MH Blues, MH Folk, MH R&B, MH Rock

B.B. King
See MH Blues, MH Folk, MH R&B, MH Rock

Ben E. King
See MH R&B, MH Rock

Carole King
See MH Folk, MH Rock

Charlie King
See MH Folk

Dee Dee King
See MH Rock

Diana King
See MH World

Earl King
See MH Blues

Evelyn "Champagne" King
See MH R&B

Freddie King
See MH Blues, MH R&B, MH Rock

James King
See MH Country, MH Folk

Little Jimmy King
See MH Blues

Pee Wee King
See MH Country

Shirley King
See MH Blues

Sid King & the Five Strings
See MH Country, MH Rock, MH Swing

King Changó
See MH World

King Crimson
See MH Rock

King Curtis
See MH Jazz, MH R&B, MH Rock

King Missile
See MH Rock

King Pleasure
See MH Jazz

King Sun
See MH R&B

King Tee
See MH R&B

King Tubby
See MH World

King's X
See MH Rock

Kings of Calicutt
See MH Folk

Gershon Kingsley
See MH Lounge

The Kingsmen
See MH Rock

The Kingston Trio
See MH Country, MH Folk, MH Rock

The Kinks
See MH Rock

Alison Kinnaird
See MH Folk, MH World

Kevn Kinney
See MH Rock

Lester "Big Daddy" Kinsey
See MH Blues

Kinsey Report
See MH Blues

Kinvara
See MH Folk

Kips Bay Ceili Band
See MH Folk

Beecher Kirby
See MH Country

Bill Kirchen
See MH Rock

Andy Kirk
See MH Jazz, MH Swing

Rahsaan Roland Kirk
See MH Jazz, MH Swing

Eddie Kirkland
See MH Blues

Kenny Kirkland
See MH Jazz

Bob Kirkpatrick
See MH Blues

John Kirkpatrick
See MH Folk

Kiss
See MH Rock

Kitchens of Distinction
See MH Rock

Eartha Kitt
See MH Lounge

Klaatu
See MH Rock

John Klemmer
See MH Jazz

Dana & Karen Kletter
See MH Rock

The Klezmatics
See MH Folk, MH World

Klezmer Conservatory Band
See MH Folk, MH World

Klezmer Plus!
See MH World

The Klezmorim
See MH Folk, MH World

Earl Klugh
See MH Jazz, MH R&B

KMD
See MH R&B

KMFDM
See MH Rock

The Knack
See MH Rock

Knapsack
See MH Rock

Jimmy Knepper
See MH Jazz

The Knickerbockers
See MH Rock

Cheri Knight
See MH Folk, MH Rock

Jean Knight
See MH R&B

Gladys Knight & the Pips
See MH Lounge, MH R&B

The Knitters
See MH Rock

Mark Knopfler
See MH Blues

Buddy Knox
See MH Country, MH Rock

Chris Knox
See MH Rock

Cub Koda
See MH Rock

Kodo
See MH World

Ray & Glover Koerner
See MH Blues

"Spider" John Koerner
See MH Folk

Koerner, Ray & Glover
See MH Folk

Charlie Kohlhase
See MH Jazz

Habib Koité & Bamada
See MH World

Walt Koken
See MH Country, MH Folk

Steve Kolander
See MH Country

Fred Koller
See MH Country, MH Folk

Ken Kolodner
See MH Folk

Lee Konitz
See MH Jazz

Alhaji Bai Konteh
See MH World

Kool & the Gang
See MH R&B

Kool Ass Fash
See MH R&B

Kool G Rap and D.J. Polo
See MH R&B

Kool Keith
See MH R&B, MH Rock

Kool Moe Dee
See MH R&B

Al Kooper
See MH Blues, MH Rock

Peter Koppes
See MH Rock

KoRn
See MH Rock

Kornog
See MH World

Kenny Kosek
See MH Country

Andre Kostelanetz
See MH Lounge

Ozzie Kotani
See MH Folk

Kotoja
See MH World

Leo Kottke
See MH Folk, MH Rock

Peter Kowald
See MH Jazz

Dave Koz
See MH Jazz

Jake Krack
See MH Folk

Kraftwerk
See MH Rock

Diana Krall
See MH Jazz, MH Lounge, MH Swing

Wayne Kramer
See MH Rock

Billy J. Kramer & the Dakotas
See MH Rock

Alison Krauss
See MH Country, MH Folk

Phil Krauth
See MH Rock

Lenny Kravitz
See MH R&B, MH Rock

Chantal Kreviazuk
See MH Rock

Kris Kross
See MH R&B

Kris Kristofferson
See MH Country, MH Folk

Ernie Krivda
See MH Jazz

The Kronos Quartet
See MH Jazz, MH World

krosfyah
See MH World

Gene Krupa
See MH Jazz, MH Lounge, MH Swing

K's Choice
See MH Rock

K7
See MH R&B

Ali Hassan Kuban
See MH World

Smokin' Joe Kubek Band with Bnois King
See MH Blues

Ed Kuepper
See MH Rock

Joachim Kuhn
See MH Jazz

Steve Kuhn
See MH Jazz

Kukuruza
See MH World

Kula Shaker
See MH Rock

Umm Kulthum
See MH World

George Kuo
See MH Folk, MH World

Tuli Kupferberg
See MH Rock

Kurious
See MH R&B

Fela Kuti
See MH Jazz, MH World

Femi Anikulapo Kuti
See MH World

Leonard Kwan
See MH Folk, MH World

Forward Kwenda
See MH World

Jim Kweskin & the Jug Band
See MH Folk

Kwest Tha Madd Lad
See MH R&B

Kay Kyser
See MH Lounge, MH Swing

Kyuss
See MH Rock

The L.A. Four
See MH Lounge

L.A. Guns
See MH Rock

La India
See MH World

Lá Lugh
See MH Folk, MH World

La Mafia
See MH World

La Muscagña
See MH World

La Sonora Dinamita
See MH World

La Sonora Matancera
See MH World

Sleepy LaBeef
See MH Country, MH Swing

Patti LaBelle
See MH R&B

Abraham Laboriel
See MH Jazz

Rube Lacy
See MH Blues

Steve Lacy
See MH Jazz

Lady Bianca
See MH Blues

Lady of Rage
See MH R&B

Ladysmith Black Mambazo
See MH World

Scott LaFaro
See MH Jazz

Jimmy LaFave
See MH Country, MH Folk

Francis Lai
See MH Lounge

Laika
See MH Rock

Cleo Laine
See MH Jazz, MH Lounge

Frankie Laine
See MH Lounge, MH Swing

Greg Lake
See MH Rock

Oliver Lake
See MH Jazz

Tim Lake
See MH Folk

Lakeside
See MH R&B

Lamb
See MH Rock

Barbara Lamb
See MH Country, MH Folk

Lambchop
See MH Country, MH Rock

Lambert, Hendricks & Ross
See MH Jazz

Mary Jane Lamond
See MH Folk, MH World

Nancy LaMott
See MH Lounge

Major Lance
See MH R&B

Harold Land
See MH Jazz

Art Lande
See MH Jazz

Sonny Landreth
See MH Blues, MH Rock

Hollis Landrum
See MH Folk

James A. Lane
See MH Blues

Mary Lane
See MH Blues

Ronnie Lane
See MH Rock

Mark Lanegan
See MH Rock

Jonny Lang
See MH Blues, MH Rock

k.d. lang
See MH Country, MH Folk, MH Lounge, MH Rock

Jonboy Langford & the Pine Valley Cosmonauts
See MH Country, MH Rock

Lester Lanin
See MH Lounge, MH Swing

Daniel Lanois
See MH Rock, MH World

Lard
See MH Rock

Largo
See MH Rock

Patty Larkin
See MH Folk

Ellis Larkins
See MH Jazz

Nick LaRocca
See MH Jazz

Mary LaRose
See MH Jazz

Nicolette Larson
See MH Country

The La's
See MH Rock

Denise LaSalle
See MH R&B

Grit Laskin
See MH Folk

James Last
See MH Lounge

Last Exit
See MH Jazz, MH Rock

Last Poets
See MH Jazz, MH R&B

The Last Roundup
See MH Country, MH Rock

Bill Laswell
See MH R&B, MH Rock, MH World

Yusef Lateef
See MH Jazz

Latimore
See MH R&B

Latin Playboys
See MH Rock, MH World

Stacy Lattisaw
See MH R&B

Jim Lauderdale
See MH Country

Laughing Hyenas
See MH Rock

Cyndi Lauper
See MH Rock

The Laurel Canyon Ramblers
See MH Country, MH Folk

Andy LaVerne
See MH Jazz

Christine Lavin
See MH Country, MH Folk

The Law
See MH Rock

Azar Lawrence
See MH Jazz

Tracy Lawrence
See MH Country

Steve Lawrence & Eydie Gorme
See MH Lounge

Hubert Laws
See MH Jazz

Johnny Laws
See MH Blues

Ronnie Laws
See MH Jazz

Doyle Lawson
See MH Country, MH Folk

Hugh Lawson
See MH Jazz

Lawson Square Infirmary
See MH Rock

Lazy Lester
See MH Blues

Bernadette Lazzaro
See MH Lounge

Le Mystère des Voix Bulgares
See MH World

Leadbelly
See MH Blues, MH Folk

The Leaders
See MH Jazz

Leaders of the New School
See MH R&B

The League of Crafty Guitarists
See MH Rock

Leahy
See MH World

Paul Leary
See MH Rock

The Leaves
See MH Folk, MH Rock

Led Zeppelin
See MH Blues, MH Rock

Chris LeDoux
See MH Country

Arthur Lee
See MH Folk, MH Rock

Brenda Lee
See MH Country, MH Lounge, MH Rock

Bryan Lee
See MH Blues

Frankie Lee
See MH Blues

Irma Lee
See MH Blues

Johnny Lee
See MH Country

Lorraine Lee
See MH Folk

Lovie Lee
See MH Blues

Peggy Lee
See MH Jazz, MH Lounge, MH Swing

Rick Lee
See MH Folk

Tracey Lee
See MH R&B

Lee Press-On & the Nails
See MH Swing

Raymond Lefevre
See MH Lounge

The Left Banke
See MH Rock

Brad Leftwich
See MH Folk

Lefty Frizzell
See MH Folk

Johnny Legend
See MH Swing

Legendary Blues Band
See MH Blues

The Legendary Jim Ruiz Group
See MH Rock

Legendary Stardust Cowboy
See MH Country, MH Rock

Adrian Legg
See MH Folk

Michel Legrand
See MH Jazz, MH Lounge

Tom Lehrer
See MH Lounge

Keri Leigh
See MH Blues

Peter Leitch
See MH Jazz

John Leitham
See MH Jazz

Eddie LeJeune
See MH Folk, MH World

Iry LeJeune
See MH Folk, MH World

Ray Lema
See MH World

Peter Lemer
See MH Jazz

The Lemon Pipers
See MH Rock

Lemonheads
See MH Rock

Overton Lemons
See MH Blues

Ute Lemper
See MH Lounge

Ricardo Lemvo & Makina Loca
See MH World

John Lennon
See MH Rock

Julian Lennon
See MH Rock

The Lennon Sisters
See MH Lounge

Annie Lennox
See MH Lounge, MH Rock

J.B. Lenoir
See MH Blues

Lotte Lenya
See MH Lounge

Kim Lenz
See MH Swing

The LeRoi Brothers
See MH Country

Les Go de Koteba
See MH World

Les Têtes Brulées
See MH World

Less Than Jake
See MH Rock

Sonny Lester
See MH Lounge, MH Swing

Let's Active
See MH Rock

The Lettermen
See MH Lounge

James Leva & Carol Elizabeth Jones
See MH Folk

Level 42
See MH Rock

Keith Levene
See MH Rock

Dan Levenson & Kim Murley
See MH Folk, MH World

Levert
See MH R&B

Barrington Levy
See MH World

Lou Levy
See MH Jazz

Ron Levy
See MH Blues

Furry Lewis
See MH Blues, MH Folk

George Lewis (clarinet)
See MH Jazz

George Lewis (trombone)
See MH Jazz

Jerry Lewis
See MH Lounge

Jerry Lee Lewis
See MH Country, MH Rock, MH Swing

John Lewis
See MH Jazz

Laurie Lewis
See MH Country, MH Folk

Linda Gail Lewis
See MH Country

Meade "Lux" Lewis
See MH Jazz, MH Swing

Mel Lewis
See MH Jazz, MH Swing

Ramsey Lewis
See MH Jazz, MH R&B

Smiley Lewis
See MH Blues

Ted Lewis
See MH Swing

Tom Lewis
See MH Folk

Walter Lewis
See MH Blues

Huey Lewis & the News
See MH Rock

Gary Lewis & the Playboys
See MH Rock

The Lewis Family
See MH Country, MH Folk

Yungchen Lhamo
See MH World

Lhasa
See MH World

Liberace
See MH Lounge

Ottmar Liebert
See MH Jazz

Dave Liebman
See MH Jazz

Annbjørg Lien
See MH World

Life of Agony
See MH Rock

Lifers Group
See MH R&B

Jimmy Liggins
See MH Blues, MH Swing

Joe Liggins
See MH Blues, MH Swing

Enoch Light
See MH Lounge

Lightcrust Doughboys
See MH Swing

Lighter Shade of Brown (LSOB)
See MH R&B

Gordon Lightfoot
See MH Folk, MH Lounge

Lightnin' Slim
See MH Blues

The Lightning Seeds
See MH Rock

Kirk Lightsey
See MH Jazz

Lil' Ed & the Blues Imperials
See MH Blues

Lil' Kim
See MH R&B

The Lilly Brothers
See MH Country, MH Folk

The Limeliters
See MH Folk, MH Lounge

Limp Bizkit
See MH Rock

Lincoln
See MH Rock

Abbey Lincoln
See MH Jazz

Lincoln Center Jazz Orchestra
See MH Jazz

Colin Linden
See MH Folk

Lindisfarne
See MH Rock

David Lindley
See MH Folk, MH Rock

Arto Lindsay
See MH Rock, MH World

Mark Lindsay
See MH Rock

Hip Linkchain
See MH Blues

Lipps, Inc.
See MH R&B

Mance Lipscomb
See MH Folk

Liquid Soul
See MH Jazz

Liquorice
See MH Rock

Lisa Lisa & Cult Jam
See MH R&B

Melba Liston
See MH Jazz

Booker Little
See MH Jazz

Little Anthony & the Imperials
See MH Rock

Little Charlie & the Nightcats
See MH Blues

Little Eva
See MH R&B, MH Rock

Little Feat
See MH Rock

Little Joe
See MH World

Little Milton
See MH Blues, MH R&B

Little Richard
See MH R&B, MH Rock

Little River Band
See MH Rock

Little Sonny
See MH Blues

Little Steven
See MH R&B, MH Rock, MH World

Little Texas
See MH Country

Little Village
See MH Rock

Little Walter
See MH Blues

Little Willie John
See MH R&B, MH Rock

Johnny Littlejohn
See MH Blues

Live
See MH Rock

Live Skull
See MH Rock

Living Colour
See MH R&B, MH Rock

Living Strings
See MH Lounge

LL Cool J
See MH R&B

A.L. Lloyd
See MH Folk, MH World

Bill Lloyd
See MH Rock

Charles Lloyd
See MH Jazz

Richard Lloyd
See MH Rock

Andrew Lloyd Webber
See MH Lounge, MH Lounge

Cheikh Lô
See MH World

Ismaël Lô
See MH World

Local H
See MH Rock

Joe Locke
See MH Jazz

Kevin Locke
See MH Folk, MH World

Hank Locklin
See MH Country

Robert Junior Lockwood
See MH Blues

Lisa Loeb
See MH Rock

Nils Lofgren
See MH Rock

Cripple Clarence Lofton
See MH Blues

Giuseppi Logan
See MH Jazz

Jack Logan
See MH Folk

Loggins & Messina
See MH Folk, MH Rock

Guy Lombardo
See MH Lounge, MH Swing

Julie London
See MH Lounge

Lone Justice
See MH Country, MH Rock

Lonesome River Band
See MH Country, MH Folk

Lonesome Standard Time
See MH Country, MH Folk

Lonesome Strangers
See MH Country

Lonesome Sundown
See MH Blues

Lonestar
See MH Country

Roy Loney
See MH Rock

Larry Long
See MH Folk

Claudine Longet
See MH Lounge

Mike Longo
See MH Jazz

Longview
See MH Folk

The Looters
See MH World

Jennifer Lopez
See MH World

Trini Lopez
See MH Lounge

Jeff Lorber
See MH Jazz

Mary Lou Lord
See MH Rock

Lord Finesse
See MH R&B

Lord Kitchener
See MH World

Lord Melody
See MH World

Lords of Acid
See MH Rock

Lords of the New Church
See MH Rock

Lords of the Underground
See MH R&B

Lordz of Brooklyn
See MH R&B

Los Amigos Invisibles
See MH World

Los Bravos
See MH Rock

Los Camperos de Valles
See MH World

Los de Abajo
See MH World

Los Fabulosos Cadillacs
See MH World

Los Incas
See MH World

Los Lobos
See MH Rock, MH World

Los Muñequitos de Matanzas
See MH World

Los Pleneros de la 21
See MH World

Los Straitjackets
See MH Rock

Los Super Seven
See MH World

Los Tigres del Norte
See MH World

Los Van Van
See MH World

Lost Boyz
See MH R&B

The Lost Continentals
See MH Swing

Lothar & the Hand People
See MH Rock

Lotion
See MH Rock

Loud Family
See MH Rock

John D. Loudermilk
See MH Country, MH Folk

Joe Hill Louis
See MH Blues

Louisiana Red
See MH Blues

The Lounge Lizards
See MH Jazz, MH Lounge, MH
Rock

Louvin Brothers
See MH Country, MH Folk

Joe Lovano
See MH Jazz

Love
See MH Folk, MH Rock

Darlene Love
See MH R&B, MH Rock

Laura Love
See MH Folk

Willie Love
See MH Blues

Love & Rockets
See MH Rock

G. Love & Special Sauce
See MH Blues, MH Rock

Love Delegation
See MH Rock

The Love Dogs
See MH Swing

Love Jones
See MH Lounge

Love Spit Love
See MH Rock

Love Tractor
See MH Rock

Love Unlimited Orchestra
See MH R&B

Patty Loveless
See MH Country

Lovemongers
See MH Rock

Loverboy
See MH Rock

Lyle Lovett
See MH Country, MH Folk, MH
Rock

Ruby Lovett
See MH Country

Lene Lovich
See MH Rock

The Lovin' Spoonful
See MH Folk, MH Rock

Frank Lowe
See MH Jazz

Jez Lowe
See MH Folk

Nick Lowe
See MH Rock

L7
See MH Rock

L.T.D.
See MH R&B

L'Trimm
See MH R&B

Albert Luandrew
See MH Blues

Norman Luboff Choir
See MH Lounge

Lucas
See MH Jazz, MH R&B

Trevor Lucas
See MH World

Luciano
See MH World

Jon Lucien
See MH Jazz

**Steve Lucky & the Rhumba
Bums**
See MH Swing

The Lucky Strikes
See MH Swing

Lulu
See MH Rock

Luna
See MH Rock

Jimmie Lunceford
See MH Jazz, MH Swing

Carmen Lundy
See MH Jazz

Luniz
See MH R&B

Dónal Lunny
See MH Folk, MH World

Bascom Lamar Lunsford
See MH Country, MH Folk

Evan Lurie
See MH Rock

John Lurie
See MH Lounge, MH Rock

Luscious Jackson
See MH R&B, MH Rock

Lush
See MH Rock

Luxuria
See MH Rock

L.V.
See MH R&B

Annabella Lwin
See MH Rock

John Lydon
See MH Rock

Arthur Lyman
See MH Lounge

**Frankie Lymon & the
Teenagers**
See MH R&B, MH Rock

Brian Lynch
See MH Jazz

Claire Lynch
See MH Country, MH Folk

George Lynch/Lynch Mob
See MH Rock

Cheryl Lynn
See MH R&B

Loretta Lynn
See MH Country

Jeff Lynne
See MH Rock

Shelby Lynne
See MH Country

Lynyrd Skynyrd
See MH Country, MH Rock

Jimmy Lyons
See MH Jazz

The Lyres
See MH Rock

Johnny Lytle
See MH Jazz

Paul Lytton
See MH Jazz

M-Base Collective
See MH Jazz

Baaba Maal
See MH World

Harold Mabern
See MH Jazz

Willie Mabon
See MH Blues

Mabsant
See MH Folk, MH World

Joel Mabus
See MH Folk

Sipho Mabuse
See MH World

Margaret MacArthur
See MH Folk

Ewan MacColl
See MH Folk, MH World

Kirsty MacColl
See MH Rock

Jeanette MacDonald
See MH Lounge

Laurel MacDonald
See MH World

Pat MacDonald
See MH Folk, MH Rock

Rod MacDonald
See MH Folk

**Shane MacGowan & the
Popes**
See MH Rock

Machito
See MH Jazz, MH World

Ashley MacIsaac
See MH Folk, MH Rock, MH
World

Craig Mack
 See MH R&B

Mack 10
See MH R&B

Kate Mai Kenzie
See MH Country, MH Folk

Talitha MacKenzie
See MH World

Bryan MacLean
See MH Rock

Dougie MacLean
See MH Folk, MH World

Tara MacLean
See MH Rock

Kate MacLeod
See MH Folk

Buddy MacMaster
See MH Folk

Natalie MacMaster
See MH Folk, MH World

Madeline MacNeil
See MH Folk

Jeep MacNichol
See MH Rock

Uncle Dave Macon
See MH Country, MH Folk

Gordon MacRae
See MH Lounge

Mad Lion
See MH R&B, MH World

Mad Professor
See MH World

Mad Pudding
See MH Folk, MH World

Madd Skillz
See MH R&B

Joanie Madden
See MH Folk, MH World

Madder Rose
See MH Rock

The Maddox Brothers & Rose
See MH Country, MH Folk, MH Swing

Madness
See MH Rock, MH World

Madonna
See MH Lounge, MH R&B, MH Rock

Madredeus
See MH World

Magazine
See MH Rock

Alan Mager
See MH Folk

Samuel Maghett
See MH Blues

Magic Sam
See MH Blues

Magic Slim
See MH Blues

Magical Strings
See MH Folk

Magnapop
See MH Rock

Magnolia Sisters
See MH Folk

Magnum Band
See MH World

Magpie
See MH Folk

Taj Mahal
See MH Blues, MH Folk, MH R&B, MH World

Mahavishnu Orchestra
See MH Jazz

Big Joe Maher
See MH Swing

Mahlathini & Mahotella Queens
See MH World

Kevin Mahogany
See MH Jazz

Boncana Maiga
See MH World

The Main Ingredient
See MH R&B

Main Source
See MH R&B

Mike Mainieri
See MH Jazz

Pandit Kamalesh Maitra
See MH World

Charlie Major
See MH Country

Miriam Makeba
See MH World

Tommy Makem
See MH Folk, MH World

Makgona Tsohle Band
See MH World

Adam Makowicz
See MH Jazz

The Ilyas Malayev Ensemble
See MH World

Malika
See MH World

Mac Mall
See MH R&B

Mallard
See MH Rock

The Mallet Playboys
See MH World

David Mallett
See MH Folk

Yngwie Malmsteen
See MH Rock

Michelle Malone
See MH Rock

Russell Malone
See MH Jazz

Mama Sana
See MH World

The Mamas & the Papas
See MH Folk, MH Rock

Cheb Mami
See MH World

Mamou Playboys
See MH Folk

Man or Astro-Man?
See MH Lounge, MH Rock

ManBREAK
See MH Rock

Junior Mance
See MH Jazz

Melissa Manchester
See MH Rock

Henry Mancini
See MH Lounge, MH Swing

The Mandators
See MH World

Harvey Mandel
See MH Blues

Abdul Zhina Mandiela
See MH World

Mando Mafia
See MH Folk

Barbara Mandrell
See MH Country

Mandrill
See MH R&B

Joe Maneri
See MH Jazz

Mat Maneri
See MH Jazz

Kante Manfila
See MH World

Albert Mangelsdorff
See MH Jazz

Chuck Mangione
See MH Jazz, MH Lounge

Cindy Mangsen
See MH Folk

Sam Mangwana
See MH World

The Manhattan Transfer
See MH Jazz, MH Lounge, MH Swing

The Manhattans
See MH R&B

Manic Street Preachers
See MH Rock

Barry Manilow
See MH Lounge

Manitoba's Wild Kingdom
See MH Rock

Aimee Mann
See MH Rock

Carl Mann
See MH Country

Herbie Mann
See MH Jazz, MH World

Manfred Mann
See MH Rock

Shelly Manne
See MH Jazz

Mannheim Steamroller
See MH Lounge

Manolín, El Médico de la Salsa
See MH World

Joseph "Wingy" Manone
See MH Jazz

Ray Mantilla
See MH Jazz

Mantovani
See MH Lounge

Machanic Manyeruke
See MH World

Phil Manzanera
See MH Rock

Samba Mapangala & Orchestra Virunga
See MH World

Thomas Mapfumo
See MH World

The Mar-Keys
See MH R&B

The Marcels
See MH R&B

Steve Marcus
See MH Jazz

Rick Margitza
See MH Jazz

Bob Margolin
See MH Blues, MH Folk

Kitty Margolis
See MH Jazz

Tania Maria
See MH Jazz

Mariachi Cobre
See MH World

Charlie Mariano
See MH Jazz

Teena Marie
See MH R&B, MH Rock

Marillion
See MH Rock

Marilyn Manson
See MH Rock

The Mark-Almond Band
See MH Rock

Marky Mark
See MH R&B

Rita Marley
See MH World

Ziggy Marley & the Melody Makers
See MH R&B, MH Rock, MH World

Bob Marley & the Wailers
See MH R&B, MH Rock, MH World

Marley Marl
See MH R&B

Marley's Ghost
See MH Folk

Marmalade
See MH Rock

Dodo Marmarosa
See MH Jazz

Marry Me Jane
See MH Rock

Chris Mars
See MH Rock

Johnny Mars
See MH Blues

Branford Marsalis
See MH Jazz

Delfeayo Marsalis
See MH Jazz

Ellis Marsalis
See MH Jazz

Wynton Marsalis
See MH Jazz

Warne Marsh
See MH Jazz

Amanda Marshall
See MH Rock

Evan Marshall
See MH Folk

Mike Marshall
See MH Folk

The Marshall Tucker Band
See MH Country, MH Rock

Martha & the Vandellas
See MH R&B, MH Rock

Claire Martin
See MH Jazz

Dean Martin
See MH Lounge, MH Swing

Freddy Martin
See MH Lounge, MH Swing

Jimmy Martin
See MH Country, MH Folk

Mel Martin
See MH Jazz

Ricky Martin
See MH World

Tony Martin
See MH Lounge

Narciso Martinez
See MH World

Al Martino
See MH Lounge

Pat Martino
See MH Jazz

John Martyn
See MH World

The Marvelettes
See MH R&B, MH Rock

Richard Marx
See MH Rock

Masada
See MH Jazz, MH World

Steve Masakowski
See MH Jazz

Miya Masaoka
See MH Jazz

Hugh Masekela
See MH World

Dave Mason
See MH Folk, MH Rock

Mila Mason
See MH Country

Nick Mason
See MH Rock

David Massengill
See MH Folk

Cal Massey
See MH Jazz

Zane Massey
See MH Jazz

Massive Attack
See MH R&B, MH Rock

Masta Ace
See MH R&B

Master Musicians of Jajouka
See MH World

Master P
See MH R&B

Matchbox 20
See MH Rock

Material
See MH Jazz, MH Rock

Material Issue
See MH Rock

Johnny Mathis
See MH Lounge, MH R&B

Jas. Mathus & His Knock-Down Society
See MH Rock

Kathy Mattea
See MH Country, MH Folk

Eric Matthews
See MH Lounge, MH Rock

Iain Matthews
See MH Folk, MH Rock

Dave Matthews Band
See MH Rock, MH World

Matthews Southern Comfort
See MH Folk

June Maugery
See MH Folk

The Mavericks
See MH Country

Maxwell
See MH R&B

David Maxwell
See MH Blues

Maxwell Street Klezmer Band
See MH World

Billy May
See MH Lounge, MH Swing

Brian May
See MH Rock

John Mayall
See MH Blues, MH Rock

Curtis Mayfield
See MH R&B, MH Rock

Percy Mayfield
See MH Blues, MH R&B

Maypole
See MH Rock

Bill Mays
See MH Jazz

Lyle Mays
See MH Jazz

Maze
See MH R&B

Mazz
See MH World

Mazzy Star
See MH Rock

Prince Nico Mbarga
See MH World

Jimi Mbaye
See MH World

M'Boom
See MH Jazz

Mzwakhe Mbuli
See MH World

MC Breed & the DFC
See MH R&B

MC Eiht
See MH R&B

M.C. Hammer
See MH R&B

MC Lyte
See MH R&B

MC 900 Ft. Jesus
See MH R&B, MH Rock

M.C. Shan
See MH R&B

MC Solaar
See MH Jazz, MH R&B

Mac McAnally
See MH Country, MH Folk

Kimberly M'Carver
See MH Folk

Christian McBride
See MH Jazz

Martina McBride
See MH Country

McBride & the Ride
See MH Country

Jerry McCain
See MH Blues

Edwin McCain Band
See MH Rock

Cash McCall
See MH Blues

C.W. McCall
See MH Country

Darrell McCall
See MH Country

Les McCann
See MH Jazz

Cormac McCarthy
See MH Folk

Paul McCartney
See MH Rock

Kathy McCarty
See MH Rock

Mary McCaslin
See MH Country, MH Folk

Scott McCaughey
See MH Rock

Charly McClain
See MH Country

Mighty Sam McClain
See MH Blues

Debby McClatchy
See MH Folk

Tommy McClennan
See MH Blues

Delbert McClinton
See MH Blues, MH Country, MH Rock

Carol McComb
See MH Folk

David McComb
See MH Rock

Billy McComiskey
See MH Folk

Rob McConnell
See MH Jazz

Marilyn McCoo
See MH Lounge

Susannah McCorkle
See MH Jazz

Maureen McCormick
See MH Country

The Del McCoury Band
See MH Country, MH Folk

Neal McCoy
See MH Country

Van McCoy
See MH R&B

The McCoy Brothers
See MH Blues

Jimmy McCracklin
See MH Blues

Larry McCray
See MH Blues

Mindy McCready
See MH Country

Rich McCready
See MH Country

Ian McCulloch
See MH Rock

Robert Lee McCullum
See MH Blues

John McCutcheon
See MH Folk

Ellas McDaniel
See MH Blues

Floyd McDaniel
See MH Swing

Mel McDaniel
See MH Country

Michael McDermott
See MH Rock

Country Joe McDonald
See MH Folk, MH Rock

Michael McDonald
See MH Rock

Megon McDonough
See MH Folk

Mississippi Fred McDowell
See MH Blues, MH Folk

Ronnie McDowell
See MH Country

Jack McDuff
See MH Jazz

Reba McEntire
See MH Country

John McEuen
See MH Country, MH Folk, MH Rock

Eleanor McEvoy
See MH Country, MH Folk, MH Rock

McFadden & Whitehead
See MH R&B

Bobby McFerrin
See MH Jazz

MC5
See MH Rock

Andy McGann
See MH World

Eileen McGann
See MH Folk, MH World

Kate & Anna McGarrigle
See MH Country, MH Folk, MH Rock

Dennis McGee
See MH Folk

Sam & Kirk McGee
See MH Folk

Sterling McGee
See MH Blues

Brownie McGhee
See MH Blues, MH Folk

Howard McGhee
See MH Jazz

Stick McGhee
See MH Blues

Maureen McGovern
See MH Lounge

Tim McGraw
See MH Country

Chris McGregor
See MH World

Freddie McGregor
See MH World

Jimmy McGriff
See MH Jazz

Roger McGuinn
See MH Folk, MH Rock

McGuinn, Clark & Hillman
See MH Country

Barry McGuire
See MH Rock

Kalaparusha Maurice McIntyre
See MH Jazz

Ken McIntyre
See MH Jazz

Duff McKagan
See MH Rock

Andy McKee
See MH Jazz

Maria McKee
See MH Rock

Dave McKenna
See MH Jazz

Loreena McKennitt
See MH Folk, MH Rock, MH World

Susan McKeown
See MH World

Susan McKeown & the Chanting House
See MH Folk

McKinney's Cotton Pickers
See MH Jazz, MH Swing

Brian McKnight
See MH R&B

Sarah McLachlan
See MH Folk, MH Rock

Ian McLagan
See MH Rock

Denny McLain
See MH Lounge

Malcolm McLaren
See MH Rock

John McLaughlin
See MH Jazz

Pat McLaughlin
See MH Rock

Peter McLaughlin
See MH Folk

Don McLean
See MH Country, MH Folk, MH Rock

Jackie McLean
See MH Jazz

Rene McLean
See MH Jazz

Grant McLennan
See MH Rock

Jeannie McLerie
See MH Folk

Declan Patrick McManus
See MH Lounge

James McMurtry
See MH Folk, MH Rock

Ian McNabb
See MH Rock

Big Jay McNeely
See MH Blues, MH Swing

Jim McNeely
See MH Jazz

Brian McNeill
See MH Folk

Michael McNevin
See MH Folk

Marian McPartland
See MH Jazz

Clyde McPhatter
See MH R&B

Joe McPhee
See MH Jazz

Charles McPherson
See MH Jazz

Carmen McRae
See MH Jazz, MH Lounge, MH Swing

Jesse McReynolds
See MH Folk

Jay McShann
See MH Blues, MH Jazz, MH Swing

Blind Willie McTell
See MH Blues, MH Folk

Ralph McTell
See MH Folk

Christine McVie
See MH Rock

MD .45
See MH Rock

Me Phi Me
See MH R&B

Russell Means
See MH World

Meat Beat Manifesto
See MH Rock

Meat Loaf
See MH Rock

Meat Puppets
See MH Rock

Medeski, Martin & Wood
See MH Jazz, MH Rock

Meditations
See MH World

Joe Meek
See MH Lounge, MH Rock

Mega City Four
See MH Rock

Megadeth
See MH Rock

Brad Mehldau
See MH Jazz

The Mekons
See MH Rock

George Melachrino
See MH Lounge

Melanie
See MH Folk, MH Rock

Myra Melford
See MH Jazz

La Sonora Meliyara
See MH World

Gil Melle
See MH Jazz

John Mellencamp
See MH Rock

Ken Mellons
See MH Country

Mellow Man Ace
See MH R&B

Harold Melvin & the Blue Notes
See MH R&B

The Melvins
See MH Rock

Memphis Jug Band
See MH Blues, MH Folk

Memphis Minnie
See MH Blues, MH Folk

Memphis Slim
See MH Blues

Men at Work
See MH Rock

Men Without Hats
See MH Rock

Doris "D.L." Menard
See MH Country, MH Folk, MH World

Sergio Mendes
See MH Lounge, MH World

Mendes Brothers
See MH World

Margareth Menezes
See MH World

Misha Mengelberg
See MH Jazz

E.T. Mensah
See MH World

Menswear
See MH Rock

Johnny Mercer
See MH Lounge

Natalie Merchant
See MH Rock

Daniela Mercury
See MH World

Freddie Mercury
See MH Rock

Mercury Rev
See MH Rock

Mercyland
See MH Rock

Charles Merick
See MH Blues

Ethel Merman
See MH Lounge

The Mermen
See MH Rock

Helen Merrill
See MH Jazz

Big Maceo Merriweather
See MH Blues

The Merry-Go-Round
See MH Rock

Jim Messina
See MH Rock

Jo Dee Messina
See MH Country

Metallica
See MH Rock

Metamora
See MH Folk

The Meters
See MH R&B, MH Rock

Pat Metheny
See MH Jazz

Method Man
See MH R&B, MH Rock

Hendrik Meurkens
See MH Jazz

Liz Meyer
See MH Country

Richard Meyer
See MH Folk

Mezz Mezzrow
See MH Jazz

MFSB
See MH R&B

Miami Sound Machine
See MH Rock

Mic Geronimo
See MH R&B

George Michael
See MH R&B, MH Rock

Walt Michael
See MH Folk

Lee Michaels
See MH R&B, MH Rock

Mickey & Sylvia
See MH Rock

Bette Midler
See MH Lounge, MH Swing

Midnight Oil
See MH Rock

Midnight Star
See MH R&B

The Mighty Blue Kings
See MH Rock, MH Lounge, MH Swing

The Mighty Diamonds
See MH World

Mighty Joe Plum
See MH Rock

Mighty Lemon Drops
See MH Rock

Mighty Mighty Bosstones
See MH Rock

The Mighty Sparrow
See MH World

Mike & the Mechanics
See MH Rock

Pablo Milanés
See MH World

Amos Milburn
See MH Blues, MH R&B, MH Swing

Buddy Miles
See MH R&B, MH Rock

Lynn Miles
See MH Folk

Michael Miles
See MH Folk

Robert Miles
See MH Rock

Ron Miles
See MH Jazz

Bobby Militello
See MH Jazz

Mill Run Dulcimer Band
See MH Folk

Milla
See MH Rock

Milladoiro
See MH World

Bill Miller
See MH Country, MH Folk, MH Rock, MH World

Buddy Miller
See MH Country, MH Folk, MH Rock

Ed Miller
See MH Folk

Emmett Miller
See MH Country, MH Folk, MH Swing

Glenn Miller
See MH Jazz, MH Lounge, MH Swing

Julie Miller
See MH Rock

Marcus Miller
See MH R&B

Mitch Miller
See MH Lounge

Ned Miller
See MH Country

Rice Miller
See MH Blues

Roger Miller
See MH Country, MH Folk, MH Rock

Steve Miller
See MH Blues, MH Rock

Jo Miller & Laura Love
See MH Country, MH Folk

Milli Vanilli
See MH R&B, MH Rock

Lucky Millinder
See MH Jazz, MH Swing

Frank Mills
See MH Lounge

Stephanie Mills
See MH R&B

Mills Blue Rhythm Band
See MH Swing

The Mills Brothers
See MH Lounge, MH R&B

Ronnie Milsap
See MH Country

Roy Milton
See MH Blues, MH Swing

Charles Mingus
See MH Jazz

Mingus Big Band
See MH Jazz

Mingus Dynasty
See MH Jazz

Ministry
See MH Rock

Mink DeVille
See MH Rock

Liza Minnelli
See MH Lounge

Áine Minogue
See MH World

Kylie Minogue
See MH Rock

Minor Threat
See MH Rock

Sugar Minott
See MH World

Mint Condition
See MH R&B

Iverson Minter
See MH Blues

Bob Mintzer
See MH Jazz

The Minus Five
See MH Rock

Minutemen
See MH Rock

Robert Mirabal
See MH World

The Miracles
See MH Rock

Carmen Miranda
See MH Lounge, MH World

Marlui Miranda
See MH World

The Misfits
See MH Rock

Missing Persons
See MH Rock

Mission of Burma
See MH Rock

The Mission U.K.
See MH Rock

Mississippi Heat
See MH Blues

Mississippi Sheiks
See MH Blues, MH Folk

Mrs. Elva Miller
See MH Lounge

Mr. & Mrs. Swing
See MH Swing

Mr. Big
See MH Rock

Mr. Bungle
See MH Rock

Mr. Fox
See MH Folk

Mr. Mister
See MH Rock

The Mr. T Experience
See MH Rock

Blue Mitchell
See MH Jazz

Guy Mitchell
See MH Lounge

Joni Mitchell
See MH Folk, MH Rock

McKinley Mitchell
See MH Blues

Roscoe Mitchell
See MH Jazz

Waddie Mitchell
See MH Country, MH Folk

The Chad Mitchell Trio
See MH Folk

Robert Mitchum
See MH Lounge

Jackie Mittoo
See MH World

Mlimani Park Orchestra
See MH World

Keb' Mo'
See MH Blues, MH Folk

Mobb Deep
See MH R&B

Hank Mobley
See MH Jazz

Moby
See MH Rock

Moby Grape
See MH Rock

Modern English
See MH Rock

Modern Jazz Quartet
See MH Jazz

Modern Lovers
See MH Folk, MH Rock

Modest Mouse
See MH Rock

moe.
See MH Rock

Hugh Moffatt
See MH Folk

Katy Moffatt
See MH Country, MH Folk

The Moffatts
See MH Country

Charles Moffett
See MH Jazz

Charnett Moffett
See MH Jazz

Mohave 3
See MH Rock

The Mojo Men
See MH Rock

Tony Mola
See MH World

The Moles
See MH Lounge, MH Rock

Joey Molland
See MH Rock

Matt Molloy
See MH Folk, MH World

Molly & the Heymakers
See MH Country

Molly Hatchet
See MH Rock

The Mollys
See MH Folk, MH World

Mick Moloney
See MH Folk, MH World

Bruce Molsky
See MH Folk

The Moments
See MH R&B

Mommyheads
See MH Rock

Grachan Moncur III
See MH Jazz

Buddy Mondlock
See MH Folk

Eddie Money
See MH Rock

Monie Love
See MH R&B

Thelonious Monk
See MH Jazz

T.S. Monk
See MH Jazz

The Monkees
See MH Rock

Monks of Doom
See MH Rock

Monks of the Dip Tse Chok Ling Monastery
See MH World

Mono
See MH Rock

The Mono Men
See MH Rock

Matt Monro
See MH Lounge, MH Swing

Charlie Monroe
See MH Folk

Marilyn Monroe
See MH Lounge

Vaughn Monroe
See MH Lounge

Bill Monroe & His Blue Grass Boys
See MH Country, MH Folk

Monroe Brothers
See MH Folk

Billy Montana
See MH Country

Country Dick Montana
See MH Rock

Patsy Montana
See MH Country, MH Folk

Montana Slim
See MH Country

Machel Montano
See MH World

Marisa Monte
See MH World

Hugo Montenegro
See MH Lounge

J.R. Monterose
See MH Jazz

Chris Montez
See MH Lounge

Buddy Montgomery
See MH Jazz

Eurreal Wilford Montgomery
See MH Blues

John Michael Montgomery
See MH Country

Little Brother Montgomery
See MH Blues

Melba Montgomery
See MH Country

Monk Montgomery
See MH Jazz

Wes Montgomery
See MH Jazz

Tete Montoliu
See MH Jazz

Coco Montoya
See MH Blues

Montrose
See MH Rock

James Moody
See MH Jazz

The Moody Blues
See MH Rock

The Moog Cookbook
See MH Lounge

Keith Moon
See MH Rock

Jemeel Moondoc
See MH Jazz

John Mooney
See MH Blues

The Moonglows
See MH R&B

Abra Moore
See MH Rock

Chante Moore
See MH R&B

Christy Moore
See MH Folk, MH World

Gary Moore
See MH Blues, MH Rock

Hamish Moore
See MH Folk, MH World

James Moore
See MH Blues

Johnny B. Moore
See MH Blues

Kevin Moore
See MH Blues, MH Folk

Melba Moore
See MH R&B

Ralph Moore
See MH Jazz

Thurston Moore
See MH Rock

Whistlin' Alex Moore
See MH Blues

Moose
See MH Rock

Morcheeba
See MH Rock

Beny Moré
See MH World

Airto Moreira
See MH Jazz, MH World

Joe Morello
See MH Jazz

The Morells
See MH Country, MH Rock

Blake Morgan
See MH Rock

Frank Morgan
See MH Jazz

George Morgan
See MH Country

Lee Morgan
See MH Jazz

Lorrie Morgan
See MH Country

Russ Morgan
See MH Swing

Teddy Morgan
See MH Blues

Morgan Heritage
See MH World

McKinley Morganfield
See MH Blues

Ikue Ile Mori
See MH Rock

Alanis Morissette
See MH Rock

Morphine
See MH Rock

Ennio Morricone
See MH Lounge

Gary Morris
See MH Country

Joe Morris
See MH Jazz

Lawrence "Butch" Morris
See MH Jazz

The Lynn Morris Band
See MH Country, MH Folk

Van Morrison
See MH Folk, MH R&B, MH Rock

Morrissey
See MH Lounge, MH Rock

Bill Morrissey
See MH Country, MH Folk, MH Rock

Ella Mae Morse
See MH Lounge, MH Swing

Morse Playboys
See MH Folk

Jelly Roll Morton
See MH Jazz, MH Swing

Pete Morton
See MH Folk

Lisa Moscatiello
See MH Folk

Bob Moses
See MH Jazz

Pablo Moses
See MH World

Bob Mosley
See MH Rock

The Motels
See MH Rock

Bennie Moten
See MH Jazz, MH Swing

Mother Earth
See MH Rock

Mother Love Bone
See MH Rock

Mother's Finest
See MH R&, MH Rock

Paul Motian
See MH Jazz

Mötley Crüe
See MH Rock

M.O.T.O.
See MH Rock

Motorcaster
See MH Rock

Motörhead
See MH Rock

The Motors
See MH Rock

Motown
See MH R&B

Mott the Hoople
See MH Rock

Tony Mottola
See MH Lounge

Bob Mould
See MH Rock

Paul Mounsey
See MH World

Mountain
See MH Rock

Nana Mouskouri
See MH Lounge

Mouth Music
See MH Folk, MH World

Alphonse Mouzon
See MH Jazz

The Move
See MH Rock

Moving Cloud
See MH Folk, MH World

Moving Hearts
See MH Folk, MH World

Judy Mowatt
See MH World

Moxy Früvous
See MH Folk, MH Rock

Famoudou Don Moye
See MH Jazz

Alison Moyet
See MH R&B, MH Rock

George Mraz
See MH Jazz

Bheki Mseleku
See MH Jazz

Tshala Muana
See MH World

Abdel Aziz El Mubarak
See MH World

Mud
See MH Rock

Mudhoney
See MH Rock

Karen Mueller
See MH Folk

The Muffs
See MH Rock

Ann Mayo Muir
See MH Folk

Mujician
See MH Jazz

Ephat Mujuru
See MH World

Maria Muldaur
See MH Blues, MH Folk, MH R&B

Muleskinner
See MH Country, MH Folk

Joe Mulholland
See MH Jazz

Heidi Muller
See MH Folk

Moon Mullican
See MH Country, MH Swing

Gerry Mulligan
See MH Jazz

Peter Mulvey
See MH Folk

Brendan Mulvihill
See MH Folk

The Mumps
See MH Rock

Alan Munde
See MH Country, MH Folk, MH Rock

Hugh Mundell
See MH World

Jerry Murad's Harmonicats
See MH Lounge

Lee Murdock
See MH Folk

Shirley Murdock
See MH R&B

The Murmurs
See MH Rock

Michael Martin Murphey
See MH Country, MH Folk

Colm Murphy
See MH Folk

David Lee Murphy
See MH Country

Eddie Murphy
See MH R&B

Elliott Murphy
See MH Folk, MH Rock

Mark Murphy
See MH Jazz

Matt "Guitar" Murphy
See MH Blues

Peter Murphy
See MH Rock

Turk Murphy
See MH Jazz

Anne Murray
See MH Country, MH Lounge

David Murray
See MH Jazz

Keith Murray
See MH R&B

Sunny Murray
See MH Jazz

Maryam Mursal
See MH World

Junior Murvin
See MH World

Music Explosion
See MH Rock

Music Machine
See MH Rock

Music Revelation Ensemble
See MH Jazz

Musical Knights
See MH Swing

Musical Youth
See MH World

Musicians of the Nile
See MH World

Charlie Musselwhite
See MH Blues

Sabah Habas Mustapha
See MH World

Mutabaruka
See MH World

Muzsikás
See MH World

My Bloody Valentine
See MH Rock

My Drug Hell
See MH Rock

My Life with the Thrill Kill Kult
See MH Rock

Alicia Myers
See MH R&B

Amina Claudine Myers
See MH Jazz

Dave Myers
See MH Blues

Louis Myers
See MH Blues

Heather Myles
See MH Country

Mynta
See MH World

Mysteries of Life
See MH Rock

The Mystic Moods Orchestra
See MH Lounge

Mystikal
See MH R&B

Jim Nabors
See MH Lounge

Mark Naftalin
See MH Blues

Naftule's Dream
See MH World

Arnie Naiman & Chris Coole
See MH Folk

Najee
See MH Jazz

Najma
See MH World

R. Carlos Nakai
See MH World

Naked City
See MH Jazz

Naked Eyes
See MH Rock

Naked Raygun
See MH Rock

Ray Nance
See MH Jazz

Nancy Boy
See MH Rock

Andy Narell
See MH Jazz

Nas
See MH R&B

Milton Nascimento
See MH Jazz, MH World

Graham Nash
See MH Folk, MH Rock

Johnny Nash
See MH R&B, MH World

Lewis Nash
See MH Jazz

Ted Nash
See MH Jazz

The Nashville Bluegrass Band
See MH Country, MH Folk

The Nashville Mandolin Ensemble
See MH Country

The Nashville Super Guitars
See MH Country

The Nashville Superpickers
See MH Country

Nashville Teens
See MH Rock

Nat Adderley
See MH Jazz

Pandit Pran Nath
See MH World

Nathan & the Zydeco Cha Chas
See MH Folk, MH World

Native Flute Ensemble
See MH World

Naughty By Nature
See MH R&B

Joel Nava
See MH Country

Emilio Navaira
See MH Country, MH World

Theodore "Fats" Navarro
See MH Jazz

Nazareth
See MH Rock

Me'Shell Ndegéocello
See MH R&B, MH Rock

Youssou N'Dour
See MH World

Kenny Neal
See MH Blues

Raful Neal
See MH Blues

Neal & Leandra
See MH Folk

Holly Near
See MH Folk

Ned's Atomic Dustbin
See MH Rock

Negativland
See MH Rock

Buell Neidlinger
See MH Jazz

Fred Neil
See MH Country, MH Folk, MH Rock

Vince Neil
See MH Rock

Ben Neill
See MH Jazz, MH Rock

Nelson (pop-metal)
See MH Rock

Nelson (calypso)
See MH World

Bill Nelson
See MH Rock

L.F. Nelson
See MH Blues

Mark Nelson
See MH Folk

Oliver Nelson
See MH Jazz

Ozzie Nelson
See MH Swing

Rick Nelson
See MH Country, MH Rock

Shara Nelson
See MH Rock

Tracy Nelson
See MH Blues, MH Folk

Willie Nelson
See MH Country, MH Folk

Peter Nero
See MH Lounge

Ann Nesby
See MH R&B

Michael Nesmith
See MH Country, MH Folk

Neurotic Outsiders
See MH Rock

Neutral Milk Hotel
See MH Rock

Aaron Neville
See MH Country

The Neville Brothers
See MH Country, MH R&B, MH Rock

Al Nevins
See MH Lounge

New Bohemians
See MH Rock

The New Bomb Turks
See MH Rock

The New Christy Minstrels
See MH Folk

The New Colony Six
See MH Rock

The New Coon Creek Girls
See MH Country

New Edition
See MH R&B

New Golden Ring
See MH Folk

The New Grass Revival
See MH Country, MH Folk

New Jersey Casino Orchestra
See MH Swing

New Kids on the Block
See MH R&B, MH Rock

New Kingdom
See MH R&B

New Kingston Trio
See MH Folk

The New Lost City Ramblers
See MH Country, MH Folk

New Model Army
See MH Rock

The New Morty Show
See MH Swing

New Order
See MH Rock

The New Orleans Klezmer All Stars
See MH World

New Power Generation
See MH R&B

New Riders of the Purple Sage
See MH Country, MH Rock

The New St. George
See MH Folk

The New Tradition
See MH Country

New Vintage
See MH Country

New York Composers Orchestra
See MH Jazz

The New York Dolls
See MH Rock

New York Jazz Quartet
See MH Jazz

Hambone Willie Newbern
See MH Blues

Phineas Newborn Jr.
See MH Jazz

Newcleus
See MH R&B

Carrie Newcomer
See MH Folk

Martin Newell
See MH Rock

Anthony Newley
See MH Lounge

David "Fathead" Newman
See MH Jazz

Jimmy C. Newman
See MH Country, MH Folk

Joe Newman
See MH Jazz, MH Swing

Randy Newman
See MH Folk, MH Rock

Juice Newton
See MH Country

Wayne Newton
See MH Lounge

Olivia Newton-John
See MH Country, MH Lounge, MH Rock

NG La Banda
See MH World

Mbongeni Ngema
See MH World

Samba Ngo
See MH World

Mairc Ní Chathasaigh
See MH Folk, MH World

Maighread Ní Dhomhnaill
See MH World

Tríona Ní Dhomhnaill
See MH Folk, MH World

Nice & Smooth
See MH R&B

Herbie Nichols
See MH Jazz

Joe Nichols
See MH Country

Stevie Nicks
See MH Rock

Nico
See MH Rock

The Nields
See MH Folk

Night Ranger
See MH Rock

Robert Nighthawk
See MH Blues

Nightnoise
See MH Folk, MH World

Willie Nile
See MH Rock

Harry Nilsson
See MH Folk, MH Rock

Leonard Nimoy
See MH Lounge

Nine
See MH R&B

nine inch nails
See MH Rock

Nineteen Wheels
See MH Rock

Nirvana
See MH Rock

The Nitty Gritty Dirt Band
See MH Country, MH Folk, MH Rock

Nitzer Ebb
See MH Rock

Bern Nix
See MH Jazz

Mojo Nixon
See MH Rock

The Nixons
See MH Rock

West Nkosi
See MH World

No Doubt
See MH Rock

No Strings Attached
See MH Folk

Noa
See MH World

Ray Noble
See MH Lounge, MH Swing

Nocy
See MH World

NOFX
See MH Rock

Nomos
See MH World

The Nonce
See MH R&B

Nonchalant
See MH R&B

Jimmie Noone
See MH Jazz

Sugar Ray Norcia
See MH Swing

Nordan Project
See MH World

Ken Nordine
See MH Jazz, MH Lounge

Chris Norman
See MH Folk

Norman & Kolodner
See MH Folk

Walter Norris
See MH Jazz

Alex North
See MH Lounge

Northampton Harmony
See MH Folk

Northern Lights
See MH Folk

Kevin Norton
See MH Jazz

Red Norvo
See MH Jazz, MH Lounge, MH Swing

Notorious B.I.G.
See MH R&B

The Notting Hillbillies
See MH Country

Heather Nova
See MH Rock

Nova Mob
See MH Rock

Billy Novick
See MH Folk

NRBQ
See MH Country, MH Rock

NRG Ensemble
See MH Jazz

N2Deep
See MH R&B

The Nudes
See MH Folk

Ted Nugent
See MH Rock

Nuisance
See MH Rock

Darrell Nulisch
See MH Blues

Gary Numan
See MH Rock

Clara Nunes
See MH World

Nuno
See MH Rock

N.W.A.
See MH R&B

Scott Nygaard
See MH Country, MH Folk

Sven Nyhus
See MH World

The Nylons
See MH Folk, MH Lounge

Sally Nyolo
See MH World

Laura Nyro
See MH Folk, MH R&B, MH Rock

The Oak Ridge Boys
See MH Country

Oasis
See MH Rock

Ebenezer Obey
See MH World

Oblivion Express
See MH Rock

Oblivious
See MH Rock

Hod O'Brien
See MH Jazz

Tim O'Brien
See MH Country, MH Folk, MH Swing

O'Bryan
See MH R&B

O.C.
See MH R&B

Ric Ocasek
See MH Rock

Billy Ocean
See MH R&B

Ocean Colour Scene
See MH Rock

Phil Ochs
See MH Folk, MH Rock

Helen O'Connell
See MH Swing

Maura O'Connell
See MH Country, MH Folk, MH Rock, MH World

Robbie O'Connell
See MH World

Mark O'Connor
See MH Country, MH Folk

Martin O'Connor
See MH Folk

Sinéad O'Connor
See MH Lounge, MH Rock, MH World

Odadaa!
See MH World

Anita O'Day
See MH Jazz, MH Lounge, MH Swing

Molly O'Day
See MH Country, MH Folk

The Odds
See MH Rock

St. Louis Jimmy Oden
See MH Blues

Odetta
See MH Folk

Andrew "B.B." Odom
See MH Blues

Eugene O'Donnell
See MH Folk

Off Broadway usa
See MH Rock

The Offspring
See MH Rock

Liam O'Flynn
See MH Folk, MH World

Ayub Ogada
See MH World

O.G.C. (Originoo Gun Clappaz)
See MH R&B

Betty O'Hara
See MH Jazz

Helen O'Hara
See MH World

Jamie O'Hara
See MH Country

Mary Margaret O'Hara
See MH Folk, MH Rock

Patrick O'Hearn
See MH Rock

The Ohio Express
See MH Rock

The Ohio Players
See MH R&B

Oingo Boingo
See MH Rock

The O'Jays
See MH R&B

The O'Kanes
See MH Country

Sonny Okosun
See MH World

Ol' Dirty Bastard
See MH R&B, MH Rock

Victor Olaiya
See MH World

Babatunde Olatunji
See MH World

Old 97's
See MH Country, MH Rock

Old & in the Way
See MH Country, MH Folk

Old & New Dreams
See MH Jazz

Old Blind Dogs
See MH Folk

Mike Oldfield
See MH Rock

Will Oldham
See MH Rock

Olive
See MH Rock

Joe "King" Oliver
See MH Jazz, MH Swing

Olivia Tremor Control
See MH Rock

Jane Olivor
See MH Lounge

David Olney
See MH Folk

Olodum
See MH World

Kristina Olsen
See MH Folk

Olympic Death Squad
See MH Rock

Omar & the Howlers
See MH Blues

OMC
See MH Rock, MH World

Omni Trio
See MH Rock

Kongar-ool Ondar
See MH World

The 101 Strings
See MH Lounge

One Riot One Ranger
See MH Country

One Way
See MH R&B

One World Ensemble
See MH Jazz

Alexander O'Neal
See MH R&B

Shaquille O'Neal
See MH R&B

Remmy Ongala
See MH World

Junko Onishi
See MH Jazz

The Only Ones
See MH Rock

Yoko Ono
See MH Rock

Oku Onuora
See MH World

Onyx
See MH R&B

Opal
See MH Rock

OP8
See MH Rock

Open House
See MH World

Orange Juice
See MH Lounge

Orange 9mm
See MH Rock

The Orb
See MH Rock

Roy Orbison
See MH Country, MH Rock

Orbit
See MH Rock

William Orbit
See MH Rock

Orbital
See MH Rock

Orchestra Baobob
See MH World

Orchestra Marrabenta Star de Moçambique
See MH World

Orchestra Virunga
See MH World

Orchestral Manoeuvres in the Dark
See MH Rock

Orchestre National de Barbès
See MH World

Oregon
See MH Jazz

Organized Konfusion
See MH R&B

Peadar Ó Riada
See MH World

Seán Ó Riada
See MH World

Oriental Brothers
See MH World

Original Dixieland Jazz Band
See MH Jazz

The Original Harmony Ridge Creek Dippers
See MH Rock

Orion
See MH Country, MH Rock

Orion the Hunter
See MH Rock

Tony Orlando
See MH Lounge

Jim O'Rourke
See MH Rock

The Orphan Newsboys
See MH Jazz

Orquesta Aragon
See MH World

Orquestra Was
See MH Rock

Benjamin Orr
See MH Rock

Robert Ellis Orrall
See MH Country

Orrall & Wright
See MH Country

A. Paul Ortega
See MH World

Kid Ory
See MH Jazz

Geffery Oryema
See MH World

Chief Steven Osita Osadebe
See MH World

Joan Osborne
See MH Rock

The Osborne Brothers
See MH Country, MH Folk

Ozzy Osbourne
See MH Rock

Greg Osby
See MH Jazz

Paul Oscher
See MH Blues

Osibisa
See MH R&B, MH World

K.T. Oslin
See MH Country

Marie Osmond
See MH Country

The Osmonds
See MH Rock

Ossian
See MH Folk, MH World

Peter Ostroushko
See MH Country, MH Folk

Gilbert O'Sullivan
See MH Rock

Other Dimensions in Music
See MH Jazz

Johnny Otis
See MH Blues, MH Jazz, MH R&B, MH Rock

Shuggie Otis
See MH R&B

Ottopasuna
See MH World

Our Lady Peace
See MH Rock

The Out-Islanders
See MH Lounge

The Outfield
See MH Rock

OutKast
See MH R&B

The Outlaws
See MH Country, MH Rock

The Outsiders
See MH Rock

Paul Overstreet
See MH Country

Orlando "Doctor Ganga" Owah
See MH World

Buck Owens
See MH Country, MH Rock

Jack Owens
See MH Blues

Jay Owens
See MH Blues

Tony Oxley
See MH Jazz

O'Yaba
See MH World

The Oyster Band
See MH Folk, MH Rock, MH World

The Ozark Mountain Daredevils
See MH Country

Talip Ozkan
See MH World

Ozomatli
See MH World

Makoto Ozone
See MH Jazz

P
See MH Rock

Augustus Pablo
See MH World

Johnny Pacheco
See MH World

Oran "Hot Lips" Page
See MH Jazz, MH Swing

Patti Page
See MH Country, MH Lounge

Paul Page
See MH Lounge

Richard Page
See MH Rock

Page & Plant
See MH Rock, MH World

Cyril Pahinui
See MH Folk

Gabby Pahinui
See MH Folk, MH World

James "Bla" Pahinui
See MH Folk

The Pahinui Brothers
See MH Folk, MH World

Pailhead
See MH Rock

Palace
See MH Rock

The Paladins
See MH Swing

Pale Saints
See MH Rock

Tom Paley
See MH Folk

Jeff Palmer
See MH Jazz

Robert Palmer
See MH R&B, MH Rock

Tena Palmer
See MH Jazz

Charlie Palmieri
See MH World

Eddie Palmieri
See MH Jazz, MH World

The Pan-African Orchestra
See MH World

Korla Pandit
See MH Lounge

The Pandoras
See MH Rock

Pansy Division
See MH Rock

Pantera
See MH Rock

Papas Fritas
See MH Rock

Ivo Papasov
See MH World

Paperboy
See MH R&B

Paris
See MH R&B

Mica Paris
See MH R&B

Park Central Squares
See MH Rock

Billy Parker
See MH Country

Bobby Parker
See MH Blues

Caryl Mack Parker
See MH Country

Charlie Parker
See MH Jazz, MH Lounge, MH Swing

Evan Parker
See MH Jazz

Graham Parker
See MH Rock

Junior Parker
See MH Blues

Leon Parker
See MH Jazz

Maceo Parker
See MH Jazz, MH R&B

Ray Parker Jr.
See MH R&B

William Parker
See MH Jazz

Van Dyke Parks
See MH Rock

Horace Parlan
See MH Jazz

Parliament/Parliament-Funkadelic
See MH Rock

Parlor James
See MH Country, MH Rock

David Parmley, Scott Vestal & Continental Divide
See MH Country

Lee Roy Parnell
See MH Country

Alan Parsons
See MH Rock

Gene Parsons
See MH Country

Gram Parsons
See MH Country, MH Folk, MH Rock

Niamh Parsons
See MH Folk, MH World

Terry Parsons
See MH Lounge

Dolly Parton
See MH Country

Stella Parton
See MH Country

The Partridge Family
See MH Rock

Abida Parveen
See MH World

Margareta Paslaru
See MH World

Alan Pasqua
See MH Jazz

Joe Pass
See MH Jazz

Passengers
See MH Rock

Passion
See MH R&B

Deb Pasternak
See MH Folk

Jaco Pastorius
See MH Jazz

Patato
See MH World

Mandy Patinkin
See MH Lounge

John Patitucci
See MH Jazz

Sandy & Caroline Paton
See MH Folk

Patrick Street
See MH Folk, MH World

Don Patterson
See MH Jazz

Charley Patton
See MH Blues, MH Folk

John Patton
See MH Jazz

Billy Paul
See MH R&B

Ellis Paul
See MH Folk, MH Rock

Gayla Drake Paul
See MH Folk

Les Paul
See MH Country, MH Lounge, MH Rock

Pat Paulsen
See MH Folk

Pavement
See MH Rock

Mario Pavone
See MH Jazz

Paw
See MH Rock

Tom Paxton
See MH Folk

Johnny Paycheck
See MH Country

Cecil Payne
See MH Jazz

Freda Payne
See MH R&B

Jim Payne
See MH World

Nicholas Payton
See MH Jazz

Peach Union
See MH Rock

Peaches & Herb
See MH R&B

Gary Peacock
See MH Jazz

Minnie Pearl
See MH Lounge

Pearl Jam
See MH Rock

Duke Pearson
See MH Jazz

Peatbog Faeries
See MH World

Pebbles
See MH R&B

Herb Pedersen
See MH Country, MH Folk

Don Pedi
See MH Folk

Gnonnas Pedro
See MH World

Ann Peebles
See MH Folk, MH R&B

Peg Leg Sam
See MH Blues

Bob & Carole Pegg
See MH Folk

Dave Pegg & Friends
See MH Rock

George Pegram
See MH Folk

Dave Pell
See MH Lounge

Pell Mell
See MH Rock

Paco Peña
See MH World

Teddy Pendergrass
See MH R&B

The Penguins
See MH R&B

CeCe Peniston
See MH R&B

Michael Penn
See MH Rock

J.P. Pennington
See MH Country

Pentangle
See MH Folk, MH Rock

Tommy Peoples
See MH Folk, MH World

Ken Peplowski
See MH Jazz

Art Pepper
See MH Jazz

Percussion Incorporated
See MH World

Pere Ubu
See MH Rock

Ivo Perelman
See MH Jazz

Chris Perez
See MH World

Danilo Perez
See MH Jazz

Lourdes Perez
See MH World

Perfect
See MH Rock

Perfect Stranger
See MH Country

Perfect Thyroid
See MH World

Carl Perkins
See MH Country, MH Jazz, MH
  Rock, MH Swing

Larry Perkins
See MH Country, MH Folk

Pinetop Perkins
See MH Blues, MH Swing

Itzhak Perlman
See MH World

Ken Perlman
See MH Folk

Permanent Green Light
See MH Rock

Tom Peron/Bud Spangler Quartet
See MH Jazz

Jean-Jacques Perrey
See MH Lounge

Perrey & Kingsley
See MH Lounge

Lee "Scratch" Perry
See MH World

Steve Perry
See MH Rock

Cliff Perry & Laurel Bliss
See MH Folk

Rufus Perryman
See MH Blues

William Perryman
See MH Blues

Eric Person
See MH Jazz

Houston Person
See MH Jazz

The Persuasions
See MH R&B

Pet
See MH Rock

Pet Shop Boys
See MH Lounge, MH Rock

Pete Rock & C.L. Smooth
See MH R&B

Peter & Gordon
See MH Folk, MH Rock

Peter, Paul & Mary
See MH Folk

Bernadette Peters
See MH Lounge

Gretchen Peters
See MH Country

Mike Peters
See MH Rock

Sir Shina Peters
See MH World

James Peterson
See MH Blues

Judge Kenneth Peterson
See MH Blues

Lucky Peterson
See MH Blues

Oscar Peterson
See MH Jazz, MH Swing

Ralph Peterson Jr.
See MH Jazz

Petra
See MH Rock

Michel Petrucciani
See MH Jazz

Ed Pettersen
See MH Folk

Al Petteway
See MH Folk

Pierce Pettis
See MH Folk

Tom Petty & the Heartbreakers
See MH Rock

Robert Petway
See MH Blues

Cornel Pewewardy
See MH World

Madeleine Peyroux
See MH Jazz, MH Lounge

Liz Phair
See MH Rock

Phalanx
See MH Jazz

Phantom, Rocker & Slick
See MH Rock

Pharcyde
See MH R&B

Arthur Phelps
See MH Blues

Kelly Joe Phelps
See MH Folk

Philadelphia International
See MH R&B

Regis Philbin
See MH Lounge

Brewer Phillips
See MH Blues

Bruce U. "Utah" Phillips
See MH Folk

Dewey Phillips
See MH R&B

Esther Phillips
See MH R&B

Flip Phillips
See MH Jazz, MH Swing

Sam Phillips
See MH Rock

Todd Phillips
See MH Folk

Utah Phillips
See MH Folk

Washington Phillips
See MH Folk

Stu Phillips/Stu Phillips Singers
See MH Lounge

Peter Phippen
See MH World

Phish
See MH Rock

Phranc
See MH Folk, MH Rock

Edith Piaf
See MH Lounge

Piano C. Red
See MH Blues

Piano Red
See MH Blues, MH Swing

Rod Piazza
See MH Blues

Astor Piazzolla
See MH World

Greg Piccolo
See MH Blues

Dan Pickett
See MH Blues

Wilson Pickett
See MH R&B, MH Rock

The Picketts
See MH Country

Pieces of a Dream
See MH Jazz

The Pied Pipers
See MH Lounge

Enrico Pieranunzi
See MH Jazz

Billie and De De Pierce
See MH Jazz

Billy Pierce
See MH Jazz

Jo Carol Pierce
See MH Country, MH Folk

Webb Pierce
See MH Country

Pigpen
See MH Jazz

Billy Pilgrim
See MH Rock

John Pinamonti
See MH Folk

Mike Pinder
See MH Rock

Courtney Pine
See MH Jazz

Pine Valley Cosmonauts
See MH Swing

Piney Creek Weasels
See MH Folk

Pink Floyd
See MH Rock

Pinkard & Bowden
See MH Country

Pirates of the Mississippi
See MH Country

Pistoleros
See MH Rock

Lonnie Pitchford
See MH Blues

Gene Pitney
See MH Country, MH Rock

The Pixies
See MH Rock

Pixinguinha
See MH World

John Pizzarelli
See MH Jazz

Pizzicato Five
See MH Lounge, MH Rock

The Plaid Family
See MH Folk

Plainsong
See MH Folk, MH Rock

Plank Road
See MH Folk

Robert Plant
See MH Rock

Planxty
See MH Folk, MH World

Plastikman
See MH Rock

The Platters
See MH R&B, MH Rock

The Pleasure Barons
See MH Rock

The Plimsouls
See MH Rock

Dan Plonsey
See MH Jazz

PM Dawn
See MH R&B, MH Rock

Poco
See MH Country, MH Rock

Poe
See MH Rock

The Pogues
See MH Folk, MH Rock, MH
  World

Poi Dog Pondering
See MH Rock

Buster Poindexter
See MH Lounge, MH Rock

Noel Pointer
See MH Jazz

The Pointer Sisters
See MH R&B

Poison
See MH Rock

Martti Pokela
See MH World

Ed Polcer
See MH Jazz

The Police
See MH Rock, MH World

Ben Pollack
See MH Swing

Robert Pollard
See MH Rock

Steve Poltz
See MH Rock

Polytown
See MH Rock

Doc Pomus
See MH Blues, MH R&B

Jean-Luc Ponty
See MH Jazz

The Poodles
See MH Folk

Pooh-Man
See MH R&B

Charlie Poole
See MH Country, MH Folk

Poor Righteous Teachers
See MH R&B

The Poozies
See MH Folk

Iggy Pop
See MH Rock

Pop Will Eat Itself
See MH Rock

Popa Chubby
See MH Blues

Odean Pope
See MH Jazz

Porno for Pyros
See MH Rock

Portastatic
See MH Rock

Art Porter
See MH Jazz

Cole Porter
See MH Lounge

Portishead
See MH Lounge, MH Rock

Jerry Portnoy
See MH Blues

Portrait
See MH R&B

Sandy Posey
See MH Country

The Posies
See MH Rock

Positive K
See MH R&B

Robert Poss
See MH Rock

Possum Dixon
See MH Rock

Poster Children
See MH Rock

Chris Potter
See MH Jazz

**Steve Pottier & Sandy Roth-
man**
See MH Folk

MC Potts
See MH Country

Bud Powell
See MH Jazz

Dick Powell
See MH Lounge

Dirk Powell
See MH Folk

The Power Station
See MH Rock

Power Tools
See MH Jazz

Powerman 5000
See MH Rock

Johnny Powers
See MH Rock

Perez Prado
See MH Lounge, MH World

Prairie Oyster
See MH Country

Tom Prasada-Rao
See MH Folk

Preacher Boy
See MH Blues

Preacher Jack
See MH Swing

Prefab Sprout
See MH Rock

Presence
See MH Rock

The Preservation Hall Jazz Band
See MH Jazz

The President
See MH Jazz

The Presidents of the United States of America
See MH Rock

Elvis Presley
See MH Blues, MH Country, MH Lounge, MH Rock, MH Swing

Billy Preston
See MH R&B, MH Rock

The Pretenders
See MH Rock

Pretty & Twisted
See MH Rock

Pretty Things
See MH Rock

Andre Previn
See MH Jazz, MH Lounge

Bobby Previte
See MH Jazz

Lloyd Price
See MH Blues, MH R&B, MH Rock

Ray Price
See MH Country

Sam Price
See MH Blues, MH Jazz

Toni Price
See MH Country

Charley Pride
See MH Country

Gertrude Pridgett
See MH Blues

Maxi Priest
See MH World

Julian Priester
See MH Jazz

Louis Prima & Keely Smith
See MH Lounge, MH Swing

Prima Materia
See MH Jazz

Primal Scream
See MH Rock

Primeaux & Mike
See MH World

John Primer
See MH Blues

Gary Primich
See MH Blues

Primitive Characters
See MH Folk

Primus
See MH Rock

Prince
See MH R&B, MH Rock

John Prine
See MH Country, MH Folk, MH Rock

Marcus Printup
See MH Jazz

Maddy Prior
See MH Folk, MH World

P.J. Proby
See MH Rock

The Proclaimers
See MH Rock

Procol Harum
See MH Rock

Prodigy
See MH Rock

Professor Griff
See MH Rock

Professor Longhair
See MH Blues, MH Jazz, MH R&B

Professor X
See MH R&B

Profile Records
See MH R&B

Projekct Two
See MH Rock

Prong
See MH Rock

Chuck Prophet
See MH Rock

Willis Prudhomme
See MH Folk, MH World

Snooky Pryor
See MH Blues

Arthur Prysock
See MH Jazz

The Psychedelic Furs
See MH Rock

Psychograss
See MH Country, MH Folk

Public Enemy
See MH R&B, MH Rock

Public Image Ltd.
See MH Rock

Riley Puckett
See MH Country, MH Folk

Gary Puckett & the Union Gap
See MH Rock

Tito Puente
See MH Jazz, MH Lounge, MH World

Puff Daddy
See MH R&B

Roberto Pulido
See MH World

Don Pullen
See MH Jazz

Pulp
See MH Rock

The Pulsars
See MH Rock

Jimmy Purcey
See MH Rock

Bernard Purdie
See MH Jazz

Pure Prairie League
See MH Country, MH Rock

Bobby and James Purify
See MH R&B

Flora Purim
See MH Jazz, MH World

Elaine Purkey
See MH Folk

The Purple Outside
See MH Rock

The Pursuit of Happiness
See MH Rock

Quad City DJ's
See MH R&B

Quarterflash
See MH Rock

Suzi Quatro
See MH Rock

Finley Quaye
See MH Rock

Ike Quebec
See MH Jazz

Queen
See MH Rock

Queen Ida
See MH Folk, MH World

Queen Latifah
See MH R&B

Queensryche
See MH Rock

The Queers
See MH Rock

Quest
See MH Jazz

? and the Mysterians
See MH Rock

Quicksilver Messenger Service
See MH Rock

Quickspace
See MH Rock

Quiet Riot
See MH Rock

Robert Quine
See MH Rock

Paul Quinichette
See MH Jazz

The Quintet of the Hot Club of France
See MH Jazz

Eddie Rabbitt
See MH Country

Ann Rabson
See MH Folk

Yank Rachell
See MH Blues

Bobby Radcliff
See MH Blues

Radio Kings
See MH Blues

Radio Tarifa
See MH World

Radiohead
See MH Rock

Boyd Raeburn
See MH Swing

Gerry Rafferty
See MH Folk

Raffi
See MH Folk

Rage Against the Machine
See MH Rock

Rail Band
See MH World

Railroad Jerk
See MH Rock

Railway Children
See MH Rock

The Rain Parade
See MH Rock

Rain Tree Crow
See MH Rock

Rainbow
See MH Rock

The Raincoats
See MH Rock

Ma Rainey
See MH Blues, MH Jazz, MH R&B

Raise the Rafters
See MH Folk

Bonnie Raitt
See MH Blues, MH Folk, MH Rock

John Raitt
See MH Lounge

RAM
See MH World

The Ramones
See MH Rock

Willis Alan Ramsey
See MH Country, MH Folk, MH Rock

Hossam Ramzy
See MH World

Lee Ranaldo
See MH Rock

Ranch Romance
See MH Country, MH Folk

Rancid
See MH Rock

Jon Randall
See MH Country

Boots Randolph
See MH Country, MH Lounge

Jimmy Raney
See MH Jazz

Wayne Raney
See MH Country

Ernest Ranglin
See MH World

Rank & File
See MH Country, MH Rock

The Rankin Family
See MH Folk

Ranking Roger
See MH Rock

Shabba Ranks
See MH R&B, MH World

Enzo Rao
See MH World

Rappin' 4-Tay
See MH R&B

Rara Machine
See MH World

Rare Earth
See MH R&B, MH Rock

The Rarely Herd
See MH Country

Ras Kass
See MH R&B

Moses Rascoe
See MH Blues

Rasha
See MH World

The Raspberries
See MH Rock

Rasputina
See MH Rock

Ratt
See MH Rock

Ravel
See MH World

Eddy Raven
See MH Country

Lou Rawls
See MH Lounge, MH R&B

Johnnie Ray
See MH Lounge, MH Rock, MH Swing

Kenny "Blue" Ray
See MH Blues

Michael Ray
See MH Jazz

Sean Ray
See MH Rock

Ray, Goodman & Brown
See MH R&B

Ray J
See MH R&B

The Raybeats
See MH Rock

Collin Raye
See MH Country

RBX
See MH R&B

Chris Rea
See MH Rock

David Rea
See MH Folk

"Cheese" Read
See MH Folk

Eddi Reader
See MH Rock

Ready for the World
See MH R&B

Bernice Johnson Reagon
See MH Folk

Toshi Reagon
See MH Folk

Real Live
See MH R&B

Mac Rebennack
See MH Blues

The Rebirth Brass Band
See MH Folk, MH Jazz

Recoil
See MH Rock

The Records
See MH Rock

Red & the Red Hots
See MH Swing

The Red Clay Ramblers
See MH Country, MH Folk

Red Hot Chili Peppers
See MH R&B, MH Rock

Red House Painters
See MH Rock

Red Mountain White Trash
See MH Folk

Red Plastic Bag
See MH World

Red Tail Chasing Hawks
See MH World

Leon Redbone
See MH Folk

Redd Kross
See MH Rock

Otis Redding
See MH Folk, MH R&B, MH Rock

Helen Reddy
See MH Lounge

Redman
See MH R&B

Dewey Redman
See MH Jazz

Don Redman
See MH Jazz, MH Swing

Joshua Redman
See MH Jazz

Redneck Greece
See MH Country

Rednex
See MH Rock

Jean Redpath
See MH Folk, MH World

Dizzy Reece
See MH Jazz

A.C. Reed
See MH Blues

Blind Alfred Reed
See MH Folk

Dalton Reed
See MH Blues

Eric Reed
See MH Jazz

Francine Reed
See MH Blues

Jerry Reed
See MH Country

Jimmy Reed
See MH Blues, MH R&B, MH Rock

Lou Reed
See MH Rock

Eddie Reed Big Band
See MH Swing

Reef
See MH Rock

The Reegs
See MH Rock

Della Reese
See MH Lounge, MH R&B, MH Swing

Del Reeves
See MH Country

Dianne Reeves
See MH Jazz, MH R&B

Jim Reeves
See MH Country

Ronna Reeves
See MH Country

The Refreshments
See MH Rock

Elis Regina
See MH World

Regina Regina
See MH Country

Harvey Reid
See MH Folk

Lou Reid
See MH Country

Rufus Reid
See MH Jazz

Vernon Reid
See MH Rock

Django Reinhardt
See MH Jazz, MH Swing

John Reischman
See MH Folk

Relativity
See MH Folk

R.E.M.
See MH Rock

The Rembrandts
See MH Rock

Cheikha Remitti
See MH World

Emily Remler
See MH Jazz

Renaissance
See MH Rock

John Renbourn
See MH Folk

Henri Rene
See MH Lounge

Rene & Angela
See MH R&B

Renegades
See MH Folk

Johnny Reno
See MH Blues, MH Swing

Don Reno & Red Smiley
See MH Country, MH Folk

The Rentals
See MH Rock

REO Speedwagon
See MH Rock

The Replacements
See MH Rock

Republica
See MH Rock

The Residents
See MH Rock

Restless Heart
See MH Country

Return to Forever
See MH Jazz

Paul Revere & the Raiders
See MH Rock

Revolting Cocks
See MH Rock

The Revolutionary Ensemble
See MH Jazz

Alvino Rey
See MH Lounge

Debbie Reynolds
See MH Lounge

The Rezillos
See MH Rock

Emmit Rhodes
See MH Rock

Kimmie Rhodes
See MH Country, MH Folk

Sonny Rhodes
See MH Blues

Melvin Rhyne
See MH Jazz

Rhythm Rats
See MH Folk

Marc Ribot
See MH Jazz, MH Rock

Tim Rice
See MH Lounge

Tony Rice
See MH Country, MH Folk

Rice Brothers
See MH Folk

Buddy Rich
See MH Jazz, MH Swing

Charlie Rich
See MH Country, MH Lounge

Tony Rich Project
See MH R&B

Cliff Richard
See MH Lounge, MH Rock

Willie Richard
See MH Blues

Zachary Richard
See MH Country, MH Folk, MH World

Keith Richards
See MH Rock

Sue Richards
See MH Folk

The Richards
See MH Rock

Kim Richey
See MH Country, MH Rock

Lionel Richie
See MH R&B

Richie Rich
See MH R&B

Jonathan Richman
See MH Folk, MH Lounge, MH Rock

Dannie Richmond
See MH Jazz

Mike Richmond
See MH World

Ricochet
See MH Country

Leslie Riddle
See MH Folk

Nelson Riddle
See MH Lounge, MH Swing

Ride
See MH Rock

Bonnie Rideout
See MH Folk, MH World

Riders in the Sky
See MH Country, MH Folk

Andrew Ridgely
See MH Rock

Tommy Ridgley
See MH Blues

Amy Rigby
See MH Country, MH Rock

Will Rigby
See MH Rock

Richard Riggins
See MH Blues

The Righteous Brothers
See MH R&B, MH Rock

Odd Riisnaes
See MH Jazz

Billy Lee Riley
See MH Country, MH Swing

Jeannie C. Riley
See MH Country

Steve Riley & the Mamou Playboys
See MH Folk, MH World

LeAnn Rimes
See MH Country

Jim Ringer
See MH Folk

Minnie Riperton
See MH Lounge, MH R&B

The Rippingtons
See MH Jazz

Paul Rishell
See MH Blues

Rising Sons
See MH Rock

Brian Ritchie
See MH Rock

Jean Ritchie
See MH Folk

Lee Ritenour
See MH Jazz

Rites of Spring
See MH Rock

Tex Ritter
See MH Country, MH Folk

Ritual Trio
See MH Jazz

Jimmie Rivers
See MH Country

Johnny Rivers
See MH Rock

Sam Rivers
See MH Jazz

Sam Rizzetta
See MH Folk

Archie Roach
See MH Rock, MH World

Max Roach
See MH Jazz

Steve Roach
See MH World

Roachford
See MH R&B

Roaring Lion
See MH World

Marty Robbins
See MH Country

Howard Roberts
See MH Lounge

Kathryn Roberts
See MH Folk

Kenny Roberts
See MH Country

Luckey Roberts
See MH Jazz

Marcus Roberts
See MH Jazz

Rick Roberts
See MH Rock

John Roberts & Tony Barrand
See MH Folk

Clarence "Herb" Robertson
See MH Jazz

Kim Robertson
See MH Folk, MH World

Lonnie Robertson
See MH Folk

Robbie Robertson
See MH Rock, MH World

Paul Robeson
See MH Folk, MH Lounge

Duke Robillard
See MH Blues, MH Swing

Joseph "Butch" Robins
See MH Folk

Fenton Robinson
See MH Blues

Ikey Robinson
See MH Blues

Jimmie Lee Robinson
See MH Blues

Ray Charles Robinson
See MH Blues

Tad Robinson
See MH Blues

Tom Robinson
See MH Folk

Smokey Robinson & the Miracles
See MH R&B, MH Rock

Tom Robinson Band
See MH Rock

Carson Robison
See MH Country, MH Folk

Robyn
See MH Rock

Betty Roche
See MH Jazz

Tabu Ley Rochereau
See MH World

The Roches
See MH Folk, MH Rock

Rock en Español
See MH Rock, MH World

Lee Rocker/Lee Rocker's Big Blue
See MH Rock

Rocker's Hi-Fi
See MH Rock

Rocket from the Crypt
See MH Rock

Rockin' Dopsie
See MH Folk, MH World

Rockin' Sidney
See MH Folk, MH World

Rockpile
See MH Country, MH Rock

Jerry Rockwell
See MH Folk

Rocky Boy Singers
See MH World

Judy Roderick
See MH Folk

Jimmie Rodgers
See MH Country, MH Folk

Paul Rodgers
See MH Rock

Richard Rodgers
See MH Lounge

Claudio Roditi
See MH Jazz

Red Rodney
See MH Jazz

Rodney O & Joe Cooley
See MH R&B

Amália Rodrigues
See MH World

Virginia Rodrigues
See MH World

Arsenio Rodríguez
See MH World

Johnny Rodriguez
See MH Country

Silvio Rodríguez
See MH World

Tito Rodríguez
See MH World

Tommy Roe
See MH Rock

Aldus Roger
See MH Folk, MH World

Gamble Rogers
See MH Folk

Garnet Rogers
See MH Folk

Ginger Rogers
See MH Lounge

Jimmy Rogers
See MH Blues

Kenny Rogers
See MH Country, MH Lounge

Roy Rogers (blues guitarist)
See MH Blues, MH Folk

Roy Rogers (cowboy singer)
See MH Country, MH Folk

Sally Rogers
See MH Folk

Shorty Rogers
See MH Jazz

Stan Rogers
See MH Folk

Tammy Rogers
See MH Country, MH Folk

S.E. Rogie
See MH World

Rolley Polley
See MH Lounge

The Rolling Stones
See MH Blues, MH R&B, MH Rock

Adrian Rollini
See MH Swing

Henry Rollins
See MH Rock

Sonny Rollins
See MH Jazz

The Romantics
See MH Rock

Romeo Void
See MH Rock

Ruben Romero & Lydia Torea
See MH World

Ron Sunshine & Full Swing
See MH Swing

The Ronettes
See MH R&B, MH Rock

Wallace Roney
See MH Jazz

Mick Ronson
See MH Rock

Linda Ronstadt
See MH Country, MH Folk, MH Lounge, MH Rock, MH World

Rooftop Singers
See MH Folk

The Rooks
See MH Rock

Roomful of Blues
See MH Blues, MH Swing

The Roots
See MH Jazz, MH R&B

The Roots Radics
See MH World

Lazaro Ros
See MH World

David Rose
See MH Lounge

Doudou N'Diaye Rose
See MH World

Rose Royce
See MH R&B

Anders Rosén
See MH World

Phil Rosenthal
See MH Folk

Michele Rosewoman
See MH Jazz

Renee Rosnes
See MH Jazz

Annie Ross
See MH Jazz

Diana Ross
See MH R&B, MH Rock

Isaiah "Doc" Ross
See MH Blues

John Rossbach
See MH Folk

Rossy
See MH World

Nino Rota
See MH Lounge

Rotary Connection
See MH Lounge

David Lee Roth
See MH Lounge, MH Rock

Kevin Roth
See MH Folk

Patti Rothberg
See MH Rock

Ned Rothenberg
See MH Jazz

Sandy Rothman & Steve Pottier
See MH Folk

Rottin Razkals
See MH R&B

Charlie Rouse
See MH Jazz

Rova Saxophone Quartet
See MH Jazz

Peter Rowan
See MH Country, MH Folk

Dennis Rowland
See MH Jazz

Roxette
See MH Rock

Roxy Music
See MH Rock

Badal Roy
See MH World

Billy Joe Royal
See MH Country

Royal Crescent Mob
See MH R&B, MH Rock

Royal Crown Revue
See MH Lounge, MH Rock, MH Swing

Royal Flush
See MH R&B

Royal Trux
See MH Rock

Tom Rozum
See MH Folk

RTZ
See MH Rock

Gonzalo Rubalcaba
See MH Jazz

Vanessa Rubin
See MH Jazz

The Rubinoos
See MH Rock

ruby
See MH Rock

Roswell Rudd
See MH Jazz

David Rudder
See MH World

Rude Girls
See MH Folk

Adam Rudolph
See MH Jazz, MH World

David Ruffin
See MH R&B, MH Rock

Jimmy Ruffin
See MH R&B

Kermit Ruffins
See MH Jazz

Rufus
See MH R&B

The Rugburns
See MH Rock

Hilton Ruiz
See MH Jazz

Run-D.M.C.
See MH R&B, MH Rock

Run On
See MH Rock

The Runaways
See MH Rock

Todd Rundgren
See MH Lounge, MH Rock

Runrig
See MH Folk, MH World

RuPaul
See MH Lounge

Rurutu Choir
See MH World

Kate Rusby
See MH Folk

Rush
See MH Rock

Bobby Rush
See MH Blues

Ed Rush
See MH Rock

Otis Rush
See MH Blues, MH R&B

Tom Rush
See MH Folk

Patrice Rushen
See MH R&B

Jimmy Rushing
See MH Blues, MH Jazz, MH Swing

Brenda Russell
See MH R&B

George Russell
See MH Jazz

Hal Russell
See MH Jazz

Johnny Russell
See MH Country

Kelly Russell
See MH World

Leon Russell
See MH Country, MH Rock

Pee Wee Russell
See MH Jazz

Tom Russell
See MH Country, MH Folk

Russell Family
See MH Folk

Rustavi Choir
See MH World

Rusted Root
See MH Rock

Rusty & Doug
See MH Folk

The Rutles
See MH Rock

Sonia Rutstein
See MH Folk

Cathie Ryan
See MH Folk, MH World

Matthew Ryan
See MH Rock

Tommy Ryan
See MH Lounge

Bobby Rydell
See MH Rock

Mitch Ryder
See MH Rock

Terje Rypdal
See MH Jazz

Saafir
See MH R&B

The Sabri Brothers
See MH World

G.S. Sachdev
See MH World

Sade
See MH Jazz, MH Lounge, MH R&B

Saffire—The Uppity Blues Women
See MH Blues, MH Folk

Balwinder Safri
See MH World

Bally Sagoo
See MH World

Doug Sahm
See MH Blues, MH Country, MH Rock

Yan Kuba Saho
See MH World

Sainkho
See MH World

St. Etienne
See MH Rock

Kate St. John
See MH Rock

Buffy Sainte-Marie
See MH Folk, MH Rock, MH World

The Saints
See MH Rock

Ryuichi Sakamoto
See MH Rock, MH World

Salala
See MH World

Salamander Crossing
See MH Country, MH Folk

Salamat
See MH World

Walter Salas-Humara
See MH Rock

Curtis Salgado
See MH Blues

Salt-N-Pepa
See MH R&B

Dino Saluzzi
See MH Jazz, MH World

Sam & Dave
See MH R&B, MH Rock

Sam-Ang Sam Ensemble
See MH World

Sam the Sham & the Pharaohs
See MH R&B, MH Rock

Richie Sambora
See MH Rock

Samhain
See MH Rock

Samiam
See MH Rock

Samite
See MH World

Joe Sample
See MH Jazz

The Samples
See MH Rock

Les Sampou
See MH Folk

David Sanborn
See MH Jazz, MH R&B

David Sanchez
See MH Jazz

Poncho Sanchez
See MH Jazz, MH World

Sand Rubies
See MH Rock

Deion Sanders
See MH R&B

Pharoah Sanders
See MH Jazz

Randy Sandke
See MH Jazz

Arturo Sandoval
See MH Jazz, MH World

Tommy Sands
See MH Folk, MH World

Oumou Sangare
See MH World

Maria Sangiolo
See MH Folk

Trichy Sankaran
See MH World

Maggie Sansone
See MH Folk, MH World

Mongo Santamaria
See MH Jazz, MH World

Santana
See MH Rock, MH World

Santo & Johnny
See MH Lounge

Henry Sapoznik
See MH World

Gray Sargent
See MH Jazz

Satan & Adam
See MH Blues

Satchel
See MH Rock

Erik Satie
See MH Lounge

Joe Satriani
See MH Rock

Sausage
See MH Rock

Savage Garden
See MH Rock

Save Ferris
See MH Rock

Savoy Brown
See MH Blues, MH Rock

The Savoy-Doucet Cajun Band
See MH Country, MH Folk, MH World

Savuka
See MH Rock

The Saw Doctors
See MH Folk

Sawyer Brown
See MH Country

Sax Maniacs
See MH Swing

Saxon
See MH Rock

Leo Sayer
See MH Lounge, MH Rock

Stefan Scaggiari
See MH Jazz

Boz Scaggs
See MH Blues, MH R&B, MH Rock

Scandal
See MH Rock

Scartaglen
See MH Folk

The Scene Is Now
See MH Rock

Peter Scherer
See MH Rock

Lalo Schifrin
See MH Lounge

John Schlitt
See MH Rock

Claudia Schmidt
See MH Folk

Adam Schmitt
See MH Rock

David Schnaufer
See MH Country, MH Folk

John Schneider
See MH Country

Maria Schneider
See MH Jazz

Steve Schneider
See MH Folk

Rob Schneiderman
See MH Jazz

Helen Schneyer
See MH Folk

Neal Schon
See MH Rock

School of Fish
See MH Rock

Schoolly D
See MH R&B

Schooner Fare
See MH Folk

The Schramms
See MH Rock

Paul Schütze
See MH Rock

Diane Schuur
See MH Jazz, MH Lounge

Tracy Schwarz
See MH Folk, MH World

Tracy Schwarz & Ginny Hawker
See MH Folk

Irene Schweizer
See MH Jazz

Carla Sciaky
See MH Folk

John Scofield
See MH Jazz

Scorpions
See MH Rock

Buddy Scott
See MH Blues

Darrell Scott
See MH Folk

Dred Scott
See MH R&B

Jack Scott
See MH Country, MH Rock

Jimmy Scott
See MH Jazz, MH Lounge

Mike Scott
See MH Folk

Raymond Scott
See MH Lounge, MH Swing

Shirley Scott
See MH Jazz

Stephen Scott
See MH Jazz

Tony Scott
See MH Jazz

Gil Scott-Heron
See MH Jazz, MH R&B

Screaming Trees
See MH Rock

Screeching Weasel
See MH Rock

Scritti Politti
See MH Rock

Earl Scruggs
See MH Country, MH Folk

Gary & Randy Scruggs
See MH Country

The Scud Mountain Boys
See MH Country

Seal
See MH R&B, MH Rock

Dan Seals
See MH Country

Son Seals
See MH Blues

Seals & Crofts
See MH Folk, MH Rock

Seam
See MH Rock

Sean Nua
See MH World

The Searchers
See MH Rock

Marvin Sease
See MH R&B

Sebadoh
See MH Rock

John Sebastian
See MH Folk, MH Rock

Márta Sebestyén
See MH World

Jon Secada
See MH Rock

Mansour Seck
See MH World

Curly Seckler
See MH Country

Sector 27
See MH Folk, MH Rock

Neil Sedaka
See MH Lounge, MH Rock

The Seeds
See MH Rock

Mike Seeger
See MH Folk

Peggy Seeger
See MH Folk, MH World

Pete Seeger
See MH Folk

Jeannie Seely
See MH Country

Seelyhoo
See MH World

Jonathan Segel
See MH Rock

Bob Seger
See MH Rock

Mitch Seidman
See MH Jazz

Geoff Seitz
See MH Folk

The Seldom Scene
See MH Country, MH Folk

The Selecter
See MH Rock, MH World

Selena
See MH World

Pete Selvaggio
See MH Jazz

Semisonic
See MH Rock

The Senders
See MH Lounge, MH Swing

The Sentinels
See MH Lounge

Sepultura
See MH Rock

Charlie Sepulveda
See MH Jazz

Brian Setzer/The Brian Setzer Orchestra
See MH Rock, MH Swing

Seven Mary Three
See MH Rock

Seven Nations
See MH World

Sevendust
See MH Rock

Doc Severinsen
See MH Jazz, MH Lounge, MH Swing

The Sex Pistols
See MH Rock

Ron Sexsmith
See MH Rock

Sexteto Boloña
See MH World

Sexteto Habanero
See MH World

Charlie Sexton
See MH Rock

Martin Sexton
See MH Folk

Morgan Sexton
See MH Folk

Phil Seymour
See MH Rock

S.F. Seals
See MH Rock

Sha-Key
See MH R&B

Shadow
See MH World

The Shadows
See MH Rock

The Shadows of Knight
See MH Rock

Shady
See MH Rock

Robert Shafer
See MH Country

Paul Shaffer
See MH Lounge

Shaggy
See MH World

Simon Shaheen
See MH World

Shakespear's Sister
See MH Rock

Shakira
See MH World

Shakti
See MH Jazz, MH World

Tupac Shakur
See MH R&B

Shalamar
See MH R&B

Sham & the Professor
See MH R&B

Sham 69
See MH Rock

The Shams
See MH Rock

Mark Shane
See MH Jazz

The Shangri-Las
See MH Rock

Shanice
See MH R&B

Bob Shank
See MH Folk

Bud Shank
See MH Jazz, MH Lounge

Anoushka Shankar
See MH World

L. Shankar
See MH World

Lakshmi Shankar
See MH World

Ravi Shankar
See MH World

Del Shannon
See MH Rock

Mem Shannon
See MH Blues

Sharon Shannon
See MH Folk, MH World

Roxanne Shante
See MH R&B

Jamshied Sharifi
See MH World

Feargal Sharkey
See MH Rock

Shiv Kumar Sharma
See MH World

Dave Sharp
See MH Rock

Elliott Sharp
See MH Rock

Kevin Sharp
See MH Country

Sonny Sharrock
See MH Jazz

William Shatner
See MH Lounge

Billy Joe Shaver
See MH Country

Artie Shaw
See MH Jazz, MH Swing

Eddie Shaw
See MH Blues

Marlena Shaw
See MH Jazz

Robert Shaw
See MH Blues

Sandie Shaw
See MH Lounge, MH Rock

Tommy Shaw
See MH Rock

Victoria Shaw
See MH Country

Woody Shaw
See MH Jazz

Lauchlin Shaw & A.C. Overton
See MH Folk

Shaw-Blades
See MH Rock

Jules Shear
See MH Rock

George Shearing
See MH Jazz, MH Lounge

Shegui
See MH Folk

Duncan Sheik
See MH Rock

Sheila E.
See MH R&B

Shellac
See MH Rock

Pete Shelley
See MH Rock

Ricky Van Shelton
See MH Country

Shenandoah
See MH Country

Joanne Shenandoah
See MH World

Shep & the Limelites
See MH R&B

Jean Shepard
See MH Country

Vonda Shepard
See MH Rock

Kenny Wayne Shepherd
See MH Blues, MH Rock

Archie Shepp
See MH Jazz

T.G. Sheppard
See MH Country

Cosy Sheridan
See MH Folk

John Sheridan
See MH Jazz

Lonnie Shields
See MH Blues

Richard Shindell
See MH Folk

Shinehead
See MH R&B, MH World

Johnny Shines
See MH Blues

Matthew Shipp
See MH Jazz

The Shirelles
See MH R&B, MH Rock

The Shivers
See MH Country

Michelle Shocked
See MH Folk, MH Rock

Shoes
See MH Rock

Jon Sholle
See MH Folk

Shonen Knife
See MH Rock

Shooglenifty
See MH Folk, MH World

Dinah Shore
See MH Lounge, MH Swing

Bobby Short (tuba)
See MH Jazz

Bobby Short (vocalist)
See MH Jazz, MH Lounge, MH Swing

J.D. Short
See MH Blues

Wayne Shorter
See MH Jazz

Showbiz & A.G.
See MH R&B

The Showmen
See MH R&B

Shriekback
See MH Rock

Shu-De
See MH World

Shudder to Think
See MH Rock

Shyheim
See MH R&B

Jane Siberry
See MH Folk, MH Lounge, MH Rock

Sick of It All
See MH Rock

The Sidemen
See MH Country

The Sidewinders
See MH Rock

Paul Siebel
See MH Folk

Dick Siegel
See MH Folk, MH Rock

Sierra Maestra
See MH World

Sileas
See MH Folk

Silk
See MH R&B

Garnett Silk
See MH World

Silkworm
See MH Rock

Silly Sisters
See MH Folk

Silly Wizard
See MH Folk, MH World

The Silos
See MH Rock

Alan Silva
See MH Jazz

Horace Silver
See MH Jazz

Silver Jews
See MH Rock

J. Reuben Silverbird
See MH World

Perry Silverbird
See MH World

silverchair
See MH Rock

Shel Silverstein
See MH Country, MH Folk

Terrance Simien
See MH World

Kim Simmonds
See MH Rock

Patrick Simmons
See MH Rock

Sonny Simmons
See MH Jazz

Carly Simon
See MH Folk, MH Lounge, MH Rock

Joe Simon
See MH R&B

Paul Simon
See MH Folk, MH Rock, MH World

Simon & Garfunkel
See MH Folk, MH Rock

Nina Simone
See MH Jazz, MH Lounge

Mark Simos
See MH Folk

Simple Gifts
See MH Folk

Simple Minds
See MH Rock

Simply Red
See MH R&B, MH Rock

Martin Simpson
See MH Folk, MH Rock

Martin & Jessica Simpson
See MH Folk

Frankie Lee Sims
See MH Blues

Zoot Sims
See MH Jazz

Frank Sinatra
See MH Jazz, MH Lounge, MH Swing

Frank Sinatra Jr.
See MH Lounge, MH Swing

Nancy Sinatra
See MH Lounge, MH Rock

Singers Unlimited
See MH Lounge

Talvin Singh
See MH World

Daryle Singletary
See MH Country

Sintesis
See MH World

Siouxsie & the Banshees
See MH Rock

Sir Douglas Quintet
See MH Rock

Sir Julian
See MH Lounge

Sir Mix-a-Lot
See MH R&B

Noble Sissle
See MH Swing

Sister Carol
See MH World

Sister Hazel
See MH Rock

Sister Sledge
See MH R&B

Sister Souljah
See MH R&B

Sisters of Mercy
See MH Rock

Six Nations Women Singers
See MH World

Six Shooter
See MH Country

6 String Drag
See MH Rock

16 Horsepower
See MH Rock

Sixteen Ninety-One
See MH Folk, MH World

The 6ths
See MH Rock

Roni Size
See MH Rock

Ricky Skaggs
See MH Country, MH Folk

Skandalous All-Stars
See MH World

Skara Brae
See MH World

The Skatalites
See MH World

Skee-Lo
See MH R&B

Skeeter & the Skidmarks
See MH Folk

The Skeletons
See MH Country, MH Rock

Skid Row
See MH Rock

The Skillet Lickers
See MH Country, MH Folk

Skinny Puppy
See MH Rock

Skunk Anansie
See MH Rock

Patrick Sky
See MH Folk, MH Rock

Sky Cries Mary
See MH Rock

Sky King
See MH Rock

Skyedance
See MH Folk, MH World

Skylark
See MH Folk

Skyy
See MH R&B

Slade
See MH Rock

Steve Slagle
See MH Jazz

Slash's Snakepit
See MH Rock

Slave
See MH R&B

Slayer
See MH Rock

Sleater-Kinney
See MH Rock

Percy Sledge
See MH Blues, MH R&B

Sleeper
See MH Rock

Sleeping Bag/Fresh Records
See MH R&B

Grace Slick
See MH Rock

Slick Rick
See MH R&B

Abdel Ali Slimani
See MH World

The Slits
See MH Rock

Sloan
See MH Rock

P.F. Sloan
See MH Rock

Carol Sloane
See MH Jazz

Slowburn
See MH Rock

Slowdive
See MH Rock

Sly & Robbie
See MH World

Sly & the Family Stone
See MH R&B, MH Rock

Drink Small
See MH Blues

Fred Small
See MH Folk

Judy Small
See MH Folk

Small Faces
See MH Rock

Smash Mouth
See MH Rock

Smashing Pumpkins
See MH Rock

Smif-N-Wessun
See MH R&B

Arthur "Guitar" Smith
See MH Country

Barkin' Bill Smith
See MH Blues

Bessie Smith
See MH Blues, MH Folk, MH Jazz, MH R&B

Betty Smith
See MH Folk

Billy & Terry Smith
See MH Country

Byther Smith
See MH Blues

Carl Smith
See MH Country

Cecilia Smith
See MH Jazz

Clarence Smith
See MH Blues

Clarence Edward Smith
See MH Blues

Connie Smith
See MH Country

Curtis Smith
See MH Rock

Darden Smith
See MH Country, MH Folk, MH Rock

Debi Smith
See MH Folk

Elliott Smith
See MH Rock

George "Harmonica" Smith
See MH Blues

Hal Smith
See MH Jazz

Huey "Piano" Smith
See MH R&B, MH Rock

Jabbo Smith
See MH Jazz

Jerry Read Smith
See MH Folk

Jimmy Smith
See MH Jazz

J.T. "Funny Paper" Smith
See MH Blues

Keely Smith
See MH Lounge, MH Swing

Kendra Smith
See MH Rock

Leo Smith
See MH Jazz

Lonnie Smith
See MH Jazz

Lonnie Liston Smith
See MH Jazz

Louis Smith
See MH Jazz

Lynn "Chirps" Smith
See MH Folk

Marvin "Smitty" Smith
See MH Jazz

Michael Smith
See MH Folk

Patti Smith
See MH Rock

Pine Top Smith
See MH Blues

Sammi Smith
See MH Country

Stuff Smith
See MH Jazz, MH Swing

Warren Smith
See MH Swing

Willie "The Lion" Smith
See MH Jazz

Lavay Smith & Her Red Hot Skillet Lickers
See MH Swing

Christina Smith & Jean Hewson
See MH World

Smith Sisters
See MH Folk

Chris Smither
See MH Blues, MH Country, MH Folk

The Smithereens
See MH Rock

The Smiths
See MH Rock

Paul Smoker
See MH Jazz

The Smokin' Armadillos
See MH Country

Smoking Popes
See MH Rock

Smoothe Da Hustler
See MH R&B

Smothers Brothers
See MH Folk

Gary Smulyan
See MH Jazz

Patty Smyth
See MH Rock

Sneaker Pimps
See MH Rock

The Sneakers
See MH Rock

Todd Snider
See MH Country, MH Folk, MH Rock

Jim Snidero
See MH Jazz

Snoop Doggy Dogg
See MH R&B

Snow
See MH R&B

Hank Snow
See MH Country

Phoebe Snow
See MH R&B, MH Rock

Jill Sobule
See MH Rock

Social Distortion
See MH Rock

The Soft Boys
See MH Rock

Soft Cell
See MH Rock

Soft Machine
See MH Jazz, MH Rock

Leo Soileau
See MH Folk, MH World

Sol y Canto
See MH World

Liu Sola
See MH World

Martial Solal
See MH Jazz

Solar Records
See MH R&B

Solas
See MH Folk, MH World

James Solberg
See MH Blues

Solo
See MH R&B

Solomon Grundy
See MH Rock

Solomon's Seal
See MH Folk

The Someloves
See MH Rock

Jimmy Somerville
See MH Rock

Son of Bazerk
See MH R&B

Son Volt
See MH Country, MH Folk, MH Rock

Stephen Sondheim
See MH Lounge

Songhai
See MH World

Sonic Youth
See MH Rock

Jo-El Sonnier
See MH Country, MH Folk, MH World

Sonny & Cher
See MH Lounge, MH Rock

Sons of Champlin
See MH Rock

Sons of the Never Wrong
See MH Folk

Sons of the Pioneers
See MH Country, MH Folk

Sons of the San Joaquin
See MH Country

Rosalie Sorrels
See MH Folk

Sorten Muld
See MH World

The S.O.S. Band
See MH R&B

Mercedes Sosa
See MH World

Soto Koto Band
See MH World

David Soul
See MH Lounge

Soul Asylum
See MH Rock

Soul Brothers
See MH World

Soul Coughing
See MH Rock

Soul Stirrers
See MH R&B

The Soul Survivors
See MH R&B, MH Rock

Soul II Soul
See MH R&B, MH Rock

Soundgarden
See MH Rock

Sounds of Blackness
See MH R&B

Sounds of Life
See MH Rock

Epic Soundtracks
See MH Rock

The Soup Dragons
See MH Rock

Source Direct
See MH Rock

Joe South
See MH Rock

Souther-Hillman-Furay Band
See MH Country, MH Rock

Southern Culture on the Skids
See MH Rock

Southern Pacific
See MH Country

Southern Rail
See MH Country

Southern Scratch
See MH World

Southside Johnny & the As-bury Jukes
See MH R&B, MH Rock

Red Sovine
See MH Country

Space
See MH Lounge, MH Rock

Spacehog
See MH Rock

Spacemen 3
See MH Rock

Spacetime Continuum
See MH Rock

Clarence Spady
See MH Blues

Spain
See MH Rock

Charlie Spand
See MH Blues

Spandau Ballet
See MH Rock

Spanic Boys
See MH Country, MH Rock

The Spaniels
See MH R&B

Muggsy Spanier
See MH Jazz, MH Swing

Spanish Fly
See MH Jazz

Otis Spann
See MH Blues

Sparklehorse
See MH Rock

Sparks
See MH Rock

Larry Sparks
See MH Country, MH Folk

Sparrow
See MH World

Spearhead
See MH Rock, MH World

Glenn Spearman
See MH Jazz

Billie Jo Spears
See MH Country

Special Consensus
See MH Folk

Special Ed
See MH R&B

The Specials
See MH Rock, MH World

Speckled Red
See MH Blues

Dave Specter
See MH Blues

Phil Spector
See MH R&B, MH Rock

Ronnie Spector
See MH R&B, MH Rock

Speech
See MH Rock

Spell
See MH Rock

Bill Spence
See MH Folk

Joseph Spence
See MH Folk

Skip Spence
See MH Rock

Jon Spencer Blues Explosion
See MH Blues, MH Rock

Sphere
See MH Jazz

The Spice Girls
See MH R&B, MH Rock

Spice 1
See MH R&B

Spill
See MH Rock

Davy Spillane
See MH Folk, MH World

Spin Doctors
See MH Rock

Spinal Tap
See MH Rock

The Spinanes
See MH Rock

The Spinners
See MH R&B

Spirit
See MH Rock

Spirit of Life Ensemble
See MH Jazz

Spirit of the West
See MH Folk

Spiritual Cowboys
See MH Rock

Spiritualized
See MH Rock

Victoria Spivey
See MH Blues, MH Jazz

Splash
See MH World

Splatter Trio
See MH Jazz

Split Enz
See MH Rock

Sponge
See MH Rock

The Spongetones
See MH Rock

Spooky Tooth
See MH Rock

Spoonfed Hybrid
See MH Rock

Douglas Spotted Eagle
See MH World

Dusty Springfield
See MH Lounge, MH Rock

Rick Springfield
See MH Rock

Springhouse
See MH Rock

Bruce Springsteen
See MH Rock

Dáithí Sproule
See MH World

Tobin Sprout
See MH Rock

Spyro Gyra
See MH Jazz

The Squadronaires
See MH Lounge

Squeeze
See MH Rock

Billy Squier
See MH Rock

Squire
See MH Rock

Squirrel Bait
See MH Rock

Squirrel Nut Zippers
See MH Lounge, MH Rock, MH Swing

U. Srinivas
See MH World

Stabbing Westward
See MH Rock

Houston Stackhouse
See MH Blues

Jim Stafford
See MH Country

Jo Stafford
See MH Lounge, MH Swing

Terry Stafford
See MH Country

Jeanie Stahl
See MH Folk

Bill Staines
See MH Folk

Carl Stalling
See MH Lounge

Mary Stallings
See MH Jazz

Chris Stamey
See MH Rock

Marvin Stamm
See MH Jazz

Joe Stampley
See MH Country

The Standells
See MH Rock

Sunita Staneslow
See MH World

Ralph Stanley & the Clinch Mountain Boys
See MH Country, MH Folk

The Stanley Brothers
See MH Country, MH Folk

Lisa Stansfield
See MH R&B, MH Rock

The Staple Singers
See MH R&B

Pops Staples
See MH Blues, MH Folk

Rigo Star
See MH World

John Starling
See MH Country

Edwin Starr
See MH R&B

Kay Starr
See MH Lounge, MH Swing

Ringo Starr
See MH Rock

The Statler Brothers
See MH Country

Andy Statman
See MH Folk, MH World

Candi Staton
See MH R&B

Dakota Staton
See MH Jazz, MH Lounge, MH Swing

Status Quo
See MH Rock

Stax-Volt
See MH R&B

Red Steagall
See MH Country, MH Folk

Stealers Wheel
See MH Folk

Jody Stecher & Kate Brislin
See MH Folk

Steel Pulse
See MH World

Davy Steele
See MH Folk

Tommy Steele
See MH Rock

Steeleye Span
See MH Folk, MH World

Steely Dan
See MH Rock

Rafe Stefanini
See MH Folk

Keith Stegall
See MH Country

Jeremy Steig
See MH Jazz

Stellamara
See MH World

Steppenwolf
See MH Rock

Steps Ahead
See MH Jazz

Stereo MC's
See MH R&B, MH Rock

Stereolab
See MH Lounge, MH Rock

Mike Stern
See MH Jazz

Stetsasonic
See MH Jazz, MH R&B

Steve & Eydie
See MH Lounge

April Stevens
See MH Lounge

Cat Stevens
See MH Folk, MH Rock

John Stevens
See MH Jazz

Ray Stevens
See MH Country

Shakin' Stevens
See MH Rock

Al Stewart
See MH Folk, MH Rock

Andy M. Stewart
See MH Folk, MH World

Bill Stewart
See MH Jazz

Billy Stewart
See MH Blues

Dave Stewart
See MH Rock

Gary Stewart
See MH Country

John Stewart
See MH Country, MH Folk, MH Rock

Larry Stewart
See MH Country

Rex Stewart
See MH Jazz, MH Swing

Robert Stewart
See MH Jazz

Rod Stewart
See MH R&B, MH Rock

Wendy Stewart
See MH Folk

Wynn Stewart
See MH Country

Chris Stills
See MH Rock

Stephen Stills
See MH Folk, MH Rock

Sting
See MH Rock

Sonny Stitt
See MH Jazz

Alan Stivell
See MH Folk, MH World

Frank Stokes
See MH Blues

Doug Stone
See MH Country

The Stone Poneys
See MH Rock

The Stone Roses
See MH Rock

Stone Temple Pilots
See MH Rock

Fred Stoneking
See MH Folk

Ernest Stoneman
See MH Country, MH Folk

Stoney Lonesome
See MH Folk

The Stooges
See MH Rock

Noel Paul Stookey
See MH Folk

Stories
See MH R&B, MH Rock

Stormtroopers of Death
See MH Rock

The Story
See MH Folk, MH Rock

Storyville
See MH Rock

Don Stover
See MH Folk

Izzy Stradlin
See MH Rock

Straight Ahead
See MH Jazz

George Strait
See MH Country

Strange Cargo
See MH Rock

Strange Creek Singers
See MH Folk

The Strangeloves
See MH Rock

The Stranglers
See MH Rock

Syd Straw
See MH Folk, MH Rock

The Strawberry Alarm Clock
See MH Rock

The Strawbs
See MH Rock

Stray Cats
See MH Rock, MH Swing

Billy Strayhorn
See MH Jazz, MH Swing

Mel Street
See MH Country

Chic Street Man
See MH Folk

Sarah Streeter
See MH Blues

Barbra Streisand
See MH Lounge

Strength in Numbers
See MH Country, MH Folk

The String Trio of New York
See MH Jazz

Stringbean
See MH Country, MH Folk

Strings & Things
See MH Folk

John P. Strohm & the Hello Strangers
See MH Rock

Percy Strother
See MH Blues

Frank Strozier
See MH Jazz

Joe Strummer
See MH Rock

Strunz & Farah
See MH Jazz, MH World

Dave Stryker
See MH Jazz

Dan Stuart
See MH Rock

Marty Stuart
See MH Country

John Stubblefield
See MH Jazz

Studebaker John
See MH Blues

Cinderella G. Stump
See MH Lounge

Rolf Sturm
See MH Jazz

Style Council
See MH Lounge, MH R&B, MH Rock

The Stylistics
See MH R&B

Styx
See MH Rock

The subdudes
See MH Folk, MH Rock

Sublime
See MH Rock

Dr. L. Subramaniam
See MH World

Subrosa
See MH Rock

Suede
See MH Rock

Sugar
See MH Rock

Sugar Blue
See MH Blues

Sugar Hill Records
See MH R&B

Sugar Ray
See MH Rock

Sugarcubes
See MH Rock

The Sugarhill Gang
See MH R&B

Suicidal Tendencies
See MH Rock

The Suicide Machines
See MH Rock

Sukay
See MH World

Sukia
See MH Rock

Ira Sullivan
See MH Jazz

Jerry & Tammy Sullivan
See MH Country

Joe Sullivan
See MH Jazz

Maxine Sullivan
See MH Jazz

Yma Sumac
See MH Lounge, MH World

Hubert Sumlin
See MH Blues

Donna Summer
See MH R&B

Andy Summers
See MH Rock

Elaine Summers
See MH Rock

Sun Ra
See MH Jazz, MH Rock

The Sundays
See MH Rock

Sundown Playboys
See MH Folk

Sunny Day Real Estate
See MH Rock

Sunnyland Slim
See MH Blues

Sunshine Skiffle Band
See MH Folk

Ron Sunsinger
See MH World

Super Cat
See MH World

Super Chikan
See MH Blues

Super Deluxe
See MH Rock

Super Furry Animals
See MH Rock

Super Rail Band of Bamako
See MH World

Superchunk
See MH Rock

Supergrass
See MH Rock

Doug Supernaw
See MH Country

Supersax
See MH Jazz

Supertramp
See MH Rock

The Supremes
See MH R&B, MH Rock

Al B. Sure!
See MH R&B

Surf Music
See MH Rock

Surface
See MH R&B

John Surman
See MH Jazz

Foday Musa Suso
See MH World

Susquehanna String Band
See MH Folk

Pete Sutherland
See MH Folk

Kirk Sutphin
See MH Folk

Ralph Sutton
See MH Jazz

Steve Swallow
See MH Jazz

Swamp Dogg
See MH Rock

Billy Swan
See MH Country, MH Rock

Swans
See MH Rock

Dave Swarbrick
See MH Folk, MH World

Keith Sweat
See MH R&B

The Swedish Sax Septet
See MH World

Sweeney's Men
See MH Folk, MH World

The Sweet
See MH Rock

Matthew Sweet
See MH Rock

Rachel Sweet
See MH Rock

The Sweet Baby Blues Band
See MH Jazz

Sweet Honey in the Rock
See MH Folk, MH World

Sweet 75
See MH Rock

Sweethearts of the Rodeo
See MH Country, MH Folk

Steve Swell
See MH Jazz

Swervedriver
See MH Rock

Swing out Sister
See MH Lounge, MH Rock

Swingerhead
See MH Swing

The Swinging Blue Jeans
See MH Rock

The Swingle Singers
See MH Lounge

The Swingtips
See MH Swing

Switch
See MH R&B

SWV
See MH R&B

Roosevelt Sykes
See MH Blues

The Sylvers
See MH R&B

Sylvester
See MH R&B

Sylvia
See MH Country

David Sylvian
See MH Rock

Sylvian & Fripp
See MH Rock

Symposium
See MH Rock

Synergy
See MH World

Syreeta
See MH R&B

Gabor Szabo
See MH Jazz

T. Rex
See MH Rock

Lew Tabackin
See MH Jazz

Philip Nchipe Tabane
See MH World

June Tabor
See MH Folk

Tabou Combo
See MH World

Jamaaladeen Tacuma
See MH Jazz

Russ Taff
See MH Country

Tag Team
See MH R&B

Rachid Taha
See MH World

Tahitian Choir
See MH World

Takadja
See MH World

Aki Takase
See MH Jazz

Take 6
See MH R&B

Tom Talbert
See MH Jazz

Dellareese Taliaferro
See MH Lounge

Talk Show
See MH Rock

Talk Talk
See MH Rock

Talking Heads
See MH Rock, MH World

Tall Dwarfs
See MH Rock

James Talley
See MH Country, MH Folk

Tam Tam 2000
See MH World

Tamarack
See MH Folk

Tambu
See MH World

Tampa Red
See MH Blues

TanaReid
See MH Jazz

Tangerine Dream
See MH Rock

Tannahill Weavers
See MH Folk, MH World

Horace Tapscott
See MH Jazz

Tar
See MH Rock

Tar Babies
See MH Rock

Taraf de Haïdouks
See MH World

Vladimir Tarasov
See MH Jazz

Tarheel Slim
See MH Blues

Tarika
See MH World

Al Tariq
See MH R&B

Tarnation
See MH Country, MH Rock

Dave Tarras
See MH World

Barry & Holly Tashian
See MH Country, MH Folk

Tasso
See MH Folk

A Taste of Honey
See MH R&B

Baby Tate
See MH Blues

Buddy Tate
See MH Jazz, MH Swing

Grady Tate
See MH Jazz

Art Tatum
See MH Jazz

Tau Moe Family
See MH World

Tavares
See MH R&B

Andy Taylor
See MH Rock

Art Taylor
See MH Jazz

Billy Taylor
See MH Jazz

Cecil Taylor
See MH Jazz

Earl Taylor
See MH Country

Eddie Taylor
See MH Blues

Eric Taylor
See MH Folk

Hound Dog Taylor
See MH Blues

James Taylor
See MH Country, MH Folk, MH Rock

John Taylor
See MH Rock

Johnnie Taylor
See MH R&B

Koko Taylor
See MH Blues, MH R&B

Les Taylor
See MH Country

Little Johnny Taylor
See MH Blues

Livingston Taylor
See MH Folk

Melvin Taylor
See MH Blues

Roger Taylor
See MH Rock

S. Alan Taylor
See MH Country

James Taylor Quartet
See MH Rock

Bram Tchaikovsky
See MH Rock

John Tchicai
See MH Jazz

Te Vaka
See MH World

The Tea Party
See MH Rock

Jack Teagarden
See MH Jazz, MH Swing

Team Dresch
See MH Rock

The Tearaways
See MH Rock

The Teardrop Explodes
See MH Rock

Tears for Fears
See MH Rock

The Techniques
See MH World

Teenage Fanclub
See MH Rock

Richard Teitelbaum
See MH Jazz

Omar Faruk Tekbilek
See MH World

Television
See MH Rock

Carol Lo Tempio
See MH Lounge

Johnnie "Geechie" Temple
See MH Blues

Temple of the Dog
See MH Rock

The Temptations
See MH R&B, MH Rock

Ten Foot Pole
See MH Rock

10,000 Maniacs
See MH Rock

Ten Years After
See MH Blues, MH Rock

10cc
See MH Rock

Jimi Tenor
See MH Lounge

Terem Quartet
See MH World

Terminator X
See MH Rock

Jacky Terrasson
See MH Jazz

Clark Terry
See MH Jazz, MH Swing

Sonny Terry & Brownie McGhee
See MH Blues, MH Folk

John Tesh
See MH Lounge

Tesla
See MH Rock

Joe Tex
See MH R&B

Texas
See MH Rock

The Texas Tornados
See MH Country, MH Rock, MH World

Jimmy Thackery
See MH Blues

Rosetta Tharpe
See MH Blues, MH Folk, MH Jazz

that dog.
See MH Rock

That Petrol Emotion
See MH Rock

The The
See MH Rock

Hans Theessink
See MH Folk

Thelonious Monster
See MH Rock

Them
See MH Folk, MH R&B, MH Rock

Mikis Theodorakis
See MH World

Therapy?
See MH Rock

They Might Be Giants
See MH Rock

Toots Thielemans
See MH Jazz, MH Swing

Chris Thile
See MH Country, MH Folk

Thin Lizzy
See MH Rock

Thin White Rope
See MH Rock

3rd Bass
See MH R&B

Third Eye Blind
See MH Rock

Third Eye Foundation
See MH Rock

3rd Party
See MH Rock

IIIrd Tyme Out
See MH Country, MH Folk

Third World
See MH R&B, MH World

.38 Special
See MH Rock

Thirty Ought Six
See MH Rock

This Mortal Coil
See MH Rock

Anthony Thistlewaite
See MH Folk

Beulah Thomas
See MH Blues

B.J. Thomas
See MH Country

Buddy Thomas
See MH Folk

Carla Thomas
See MH R&B

Gary Thomas
See MH Jazz

Henry "Ragtime Texas" Thomas
See MH Blues, MH Folk

Irma Thomas
See MH Blues, MH R&B

James "Son" Thomas
See MH Blues

Jesse Thomas
See MH Blues

Luther Thomas
See MH Jazz

Mickey Thomas
See MH Rock

Rufus Thomas
See MH R&B

Tabby Thomas
See MH Blues

Linda Thomas & Dan De-Lancey
See MH Folk

Butch Thompson
See MH Jazz

Carol Thompson
See MH Folk

Charles W. Thompson
See MH Blues

Dave Thompson
See MH Blues

Eric & Suzy Thompson
See MH Folk, MH World

Hank Thompson
See MH Country, MH Swing

Jimmy Thompson
See MH Blues

Linda Thompson
See MH Folk

Lucky Thompson
See MH Jazz

Malachi Thompson
See MH Jazz

Richard Thompson
See MH Folk, MH Rock, MH World

Sue Thompson
See MH Country

Sylvester Thompson
See MH Blues

Tony Thompson
See MH R&B

The Thompson Brothers Band
See MH Country

Thompson Twins
See MH Rock

Paul Thorn
See MH Rock

Kathryn Jewel Thorne
See MH Blues

Claude Thornhill
See MH Jazz, MH Swing

Bianca Thornton
See MH Blues

Big Mama Thornton
See MH Blues, MH R&B

George Thorogood & the De-stroyers
See MH Blues, MH Rock

Roger Thorpe
See MH Lounge

Simon Thoumire
See MH World

Thrasher Shiver
See MH Country

Henry Threadgill
See MH Jazz

Three Dog Night
See MH Rock

311
See MH Rock

Three Fish
See MH Rock

3 Leg Torso
See MH World

3 Mustaphas 3
See MH World

The Three O'Clock
See MH Rock

The Three Suns
See MH Lounge

Three Times Dope
See MH R&B

Throbbing Gristle
See MH Rock

Throwing Muses
See MH Rock

Rick Thum
See MH Folk

Thunderclap Newman
See MH Rock

Tianjin Buddhist Music Ensemble
See MH World

Kathryn Tickell
See MH Folk, MH World

Tiffany
See MH Rock

'Til Tuesday
See MH Rock

Mel Tillis
See MH Country

Pam Tillis
See MH Country

Floyd Tillman
See MH Country

Johnny Tillotson
See MH Country

Steve Tilston & Maggie Boyle
See MH Folk

Tim Dog
See MH R&B

Timbalada
See MH World

Timbuk 3
See MH Folk, MH Rock

The Time
See MH R&B

Bobby Timmons
See MH Jazz

Tin Machine
See MH Rock

Tindersticks
See MH Lounge, MH Rock

Tiny Tim
See MH Lounge

Aaron Tippin
See MH Country

The Billy Tipton Memorial Saxophone Quartet
See MH Jazz

Wayman Tisdale
See MH Jazz

T.J. Kirk
See MH Jazz

Cal Tjader
See MH Jazz, MH Lounge

TLC
See MH R&B

Toad the Wet Sprocket
See MH Rock

Toast String Stretchers
See MH Folk

Jeremy Toback
See MH Rock

Toenut
See MH Rock

The Tokens
See MH Rock

Tony Toliver
See MH Country

Charles Tolliver
See MH Jazz

Tommy Boy
See MH R&B

Tommy Tutone
See MH Rock

Tone-Loc
See MH R&B

Tones on Tail
See MH Rock

Tonic
See MH Rock

Tony D
See MH R&B

Tony! Toni! Tone!
See MH R&B

Too Much Joy
See MH Rock

Too $hort
See MH R&B

Tool
See MH Rock

Willie Toors
See MH World

Toots & the Maytals
See MH World

Torch Song
See MH Rock

Mel Tormé
See MH Jazz, MH Lounge, MH Swing

Tornados
See MH Rock

Yomo Toro
See MH World

Roberto Torres
See MH World

Tortoise
See MH Rock

Peter Tosh
See MH R&B, MH World

Toto
See MH Rock

Touchstone
See MH Folk

Ali Farka Touré
See MH World

Touré Kunda
See MH World

Allen Toussaint
See MH R&B, MH Rock

Tower of Power
See MH R&B, MH Rock

Ralph Towner
See MH Jazz

Henry Townsend
See MH Blues

Pete Townshend
See MH Rock

The Tractors
See MH Country

The Traditional Grass
See MH Country

Traffic
See MH Rock

The Tragically Hip
See MH Rock

Horace Trahan
See MH Folk, MH World

The Trammps
See MH R&B

Trance Mission
See MH Jazz, MH World

Tranquility Bass
See MH Rock

Transglobal Underground
See MH Rock, MH World

Transister
See MH Rock

Translator
See MH Rock

Trapezoid
See MH Folk

Artie Traum
See MH Folk

Happy Traum
See MH Folk

The Traveling Wilburys
See MH Rock

Mary Travers
See MH Folk

Travis
See MH Rock

Merle Travis
See MH Country, MH Folk

Randy Travis
See MH Country

Tre
See MH Blues

Treadmill Trackstar
See MH Rock

Treat Her Right
See MH Rock

Treble Charger
See MH Rock

Trebunia Family Band
See MH World

The Tremeloes
See MH Rock

The Treniers
See MH Rock

Jackie Trent
See MH Lounge

Ralph Tresvant
See MH R&B

Rick Trevino
See MH Country

Trian
See MH Folk, MH World

Tribal Tech
See MH Jazz

A Tribe Called Quest
See MH Jazz, MH R&B

Ed Trickett
See MH Folk

Tricky
See MH Rock

The Triffids
See MH Rock

Trillium
See MH Folk

Trio
See MH Rock

Trip Shakespeare
See MH Rock

Tony Trischka
See MH Country, MH Folk

Lennie Tristano
See MH Jazz

Travis Tritt
See MH Country

Triumph
See MH Rock

The Troggs
See MH Rock

Trouble Funk
See MH R&B

Trout Fishing in America
See MH Folk

Robin Trower
See MH Rock

John Trudell
See MH World

True Believers
See MH Rock

Frankie Trumbauer
See MH Jazz, MH Swing

Susan Trump
See MH Folk

Jennifer Trynin
See MH Rock

Assif Tsahar
See MH Jazz

Daniel Tshanda
See MH World

Tsunami
See MH Rock

Tuatara
See MH Rock

Ernest Tubb
See MH Country, MH Folk

Justin Tubb
See MH Country

The Tubes
See MH Rock

Tuck & Patti
See MH Jazz, MH Lounge

Bessie Tucker
See MH Blues

Leslie Tucker
See MH Folk

Luther Tucker
See MH Blues

Maureen Tucker
See MH Rock

Mickey Tucker
See MH Jazz

Tanya Tucker
See MH Country

Tommy Tucker
See MH Swing

Tuff Crew
See MH R&B

Turn On
See MH Rock

Babe Karo Lemon Turner
See MH Blues

Big Joe Turner
See MH Blues, MH Jazz, MH
R&B, MH Rock, MH Swing

Buck Turner
See MH Blues

Ike Turner
See MH Blues

Ike & Tina Turner
See MH R&B, MH Rock

Norris Turney
See MH Jazz

Steve Turre
See MH Jazz

Stanley Turrentine
See MH Jazz

Turtle Island String Quartet
See MH Jazz

The Turtles
See MH Rock

Shania Twain
See MH Country

29th Street Saxophone Quartet
See MH Jazz

23 Skidoo
See MH World

20/20
See MH Rock

Dwight Twilley
See MH Rock

The Twinkle Brothers
See MH World

The Twinz
See MH R&B

Twisted Sister
See MH Rock

Twister Alley
See MH Country

Conway Twitty
See MH Country

Two
See MH Rock

2 Live Crew
See MH R&B

2Pac/Thug Life/Makaveli
See MH R&B

Charles Tyler
See MH Jazz

T. Texas Tyler
See MH Country

The Tymes
See MH R&B

McCoy Tyner
See MH Jazz

Type O Negative
See MH Rock

Ian Tyson
See MH Country, MH Folk

UB40
See MH R&B, MH Rock, MH
World

Udi Hrant
See MH World

Ugly Kid Joe
See MH Rock

Áine Uí Cheallaigh
See MH World

The Ukrainians
See MH World

Ulali
See MH World

Tracey Ullman
See MH Rock

James Blood Ulmer
See MH Jazz, MH R&B

Peter Ulrich
See MH Rock

Ultra Vivid Scene
See MH Rock

Ultramagnetic MC's
See MH R&B

Ultravox
See MH Rock

The UMCs
See MH R&B

Uncle Bonsai
See MH Folk

Uncle Tupelo
See MH Country, MH Folk, MH Rock

The Undertones
See MH Rock

Underworld
See MH Rock

The Undisputed Truth
See MH R&B

Jay Ungar & Molly Mason
See MH Folk

Union Springs
See MH Folk

Unrest
See MH Rock

Up with People
See MH Lounge

The Upper Crust
See MH Rock

Upsetters
See MH Blues

Midge Ure
See MH Rock

The Urge
See MH Rock

Urge Overkill
See MH Rock

Uriah Heep
See MH Rock

Urubamba
See MH World

Us3
See MH Jazz, MH R&B

U.T.F.O.
See MH R&B

Jai Uttal
See MH Jazz, MH World

U2
See MH Rock

The V-Roys
See MH Country

Warren Vache Jr.
See MH Jazz

Vadå
See MH World

Vadya Lahari
See MH World

Steve Vai
See MH Rock

Joe Val & the New England Bluegrass Boys
See MH Country, MH Folk

Bebo Valdes
See MH Jazz, MH World

Carlos "Patato" Valdes
See MH World

Chucho Valdes
See MH Jazz, MH World

Jerry Vale
See MH Lounge

Ritchie Valens
See MH Rock, MH World

Dino Valente
See MH Rock

Justin Vali
See MH World

Rudy Vallee
See MH Lounge, MH Swing

Frankie Valli
See MH Lounge, MH R&B, MH Rock

Guy Van Duser
See MH Folk

Leroy Van Dyke
See MH Country

Van Halen
See MH Rock

The Randy Van Horne Singers
See MH Lounge

Sally Van Meter
See MH Country, MH Folk

Dave Van Ronk
See MH Blues, MH Folk

Ricky Van Shelton
See MH Country

Townes Van Zandt
See MH Country, MH Folk

Ken Vandermark
See MH Jazz

Luther Vandross
See MH R&B

Vanguard Jazz Orchestra
See MH Swing

Vanilla Fudge
See MH Rock

Vanilla Ice
See MH R&B

The Vapors
See MH Rock

Carlos Varela
See MH World

Varnaline
See MH Rock

Tom Varner
See MH Jazz

Värttinä
See MH World

Vas
See MH World

Nana Vasconcelos
See MH Jazz, MH World

The Vaselines
See MH Rock

Väsen
See MH World

Jimmie Vaughan
See MH Blues, MH Rock

Sarah Vaughan
See MH Jazz, MH Lounge, MH R&B, MH Swing

Stevie Ray Vaughan
See MH Blues, MH Rock

Ben Vaughn
See MH Country, MH Rock

Billy Vaughn
See MH Lounge

Bobby Vee
See MH Rock

Ray Vega
See MH Country

Suzanne Vega
See MH Folk, MH Rock

Glen Velez
See MH World

John Veliotes
See MH Blues

Velo-Deluxe
See MH Rock

Velocity Girl
See MH Rock

Caetano Veloso
See MH World

Velvet Crush
See MH Rock

The Velvet Underground
See MH Rock

The Ventures
See MH Lounge, MH Rock

Joe Venuti
See MH Jazz, MH Swing

Verbow
See MH Rock

Veritas
See MH World

Tom Verlaine
See MH Rock

The Verlaines
See MH Rock

Versus
See MH Rock

Veruca Salt
See MH Rock

The Verve
See MH Rock

The Verve Pipe
See MH Rock

The Vibrators
See MH Rock

Sid Vicious
See MH Rock

Harold Vick
See MH Jazz

The Vidalias
See MH Country

Vigilantes of Love
See MH Rock

Frank Vignola
See MH Jazz

The Village People
See MH R&B, MH Rock

T.H. "Vikku" Vinayakram
See MH World

Gene Vincent
See MH Country, MH Rock, MH Swing

Holly Vincent
See MH Rock

Rhonda Vincent
See MH Country

Rick Vincent
See MH Country

Joyce Vincent-Wilson
See MH Lounge

Walter Vincson
See MH Blues

Leroy Vinnegar
See MH Jazz

Eddie "Cleanhead" Vinson
See MH Blues, MH Jazz, MH Swing

Bobby Vinton
See MH Lounge

Vinx
See MH R& B, MH World

Violent Femmes
See MH Rock

Visage
See MH Rock

The Visitors
See MH Jazz

Roseanna Vitro
See MH Jazz, MH Lounge

Viva la Musica
See MH World

Carlos Vives
See MH World

Vocal Sampling
See MH World

Voice of the Beehive
See MH Rock

The Voice Squad
See MH Folk

Volo Bogtrotters
See MH Folk

Volume 10
See MH R&B

Eric Von Schmidt
See MH Folk

Chris von Sneidern
See MH Rock

Jane Voss
See MH Folk

Vowel Movement
See MH Rock

Vulgar Boatmen
See MH Rock

Waaberi
See MH World

The Waco Brothers
See MH Country, MH Rock

Stephen Wade
See MH Folk

Wagon
See MH Country

Porter Wagoner
See MH Country

Mohamed Abdel Wahab
See MH World

Bunny Wailer
See MH World

Wailing Souls
See MH World

Loudon Wainwright III
See MH Folk

Sloan Wainwright
See MH Folk

John Waite
See MH Rock

The Waitresses
See MH Rock

Freddy Waits
See MH Jazz

Tom Waits
See MH Folk, MH Lounge, MH Rock

Frank Wakefield
See MH Folk

Dave Wakeling
See MH Rock

Jimmy Wakely
See MH Country

Rick Wakeman
See MH Rock

Narada Michael Walden
See MH R&B

Mal Waldron
See MH Jazz

Walela
See MH World

The Walkabouts
See MH Rock

Billy Walker
See MH Country

Charlie Walker
See MH Country

Clay Walker
See MH Country

Jerry Jeff Walker
See MH Country, MH Folk

Joe Louis Walker
See MH Blues

Lawrence Walker
See MH Folk

Phillip Walker
See MH Blues

Robert "Bilbo" Walker
See MH Blues

Scott Walker
See MH Lounge

T-Bone Walker
See MH Blues, MH R&B, MH Swing

Junior Walker & the All-Stars
See MH R&B, MH Rock

The Walker Brothers
See MH Rock

Chris Wall
See MH Country

Dan Wall
See MH Jazz

Wall of Voodoo
See MH Rock

Bennie Wallace
See MH Jazz

Jerry Wallace
See MH Country

Kate Wallace
See MH Country, MH Folk

Sippie Wallace
See MH Blues

Fats Waller
See MH Jazz, MH Swing

The Wallflowers
See MH Rock

Doug & Jack Wallin
See MH Folk

George Wallington
See MH Jazz

Vann "Piano Man" Walls
See MH Blues

Winston Walls
See MH Jazz

Wally's Swing World
See MH Swing

Jack Walrath
See MH Jazz

Don Walser
See MH Country, MH Folk

Joe Walsh
See MH Folk, MH Rock

Jamie Walters
See MH Rock

Cedar Walton
See MH Jazz

Cora Walton
See MH Blues

Mercy Dee Walton
See MH Blues

Wandering Ramblers
See MH Folk

Walter Wanderley
See MH Lounge

Wang Chung
See MH Rock

The Wannabes
See MH Rock

War
See MH R&B, MH Rock

The Marty Warburton Band
See MH Country

Chris Ward
See MH Country

Helen Ward
See MH Swing

Robert Ward
See MH Blues

Kendra Ward & Bob Bence
See MH Folk

Monte Warden
See MH Country

David S. Ware
See MH Jazz

Wilbur Ware
See MH Jazz

Steve Wariner
See MH Country

Jennifer Warnes
See MH Folk, MH Rock

Warrant
See MH Rock

Baby Boy Warren
See MH Blues

Robert Henry Warren
See MH Blues

The Warrior River Boys
See MH Country

Wartime
See MH Rock

Dionne Warwick
See MH Lounge, MH R&B

Was (Not Was)
See MH R&B, MH Rock

Washboard Sam
See MH Blues

Dinah Washington
See MH Blues, MH Jazz, MH Lounge, MH R&B, MH Swing

Grover Washington Jr.
See MH Jazz, MH R&B

Isidore "Tuts" Washington
See MH Blues

Keith Washington
See MH R&B

Walter "Wolfman" Washington
See MH Blues

Rob Wasserman
See MH Jazz

The Waterboys
See MH Folk, MH Rock, MH World

Linda Waterfall
See MH Folk

Benny Waters
See MH Jazz, MH Swing

Crystal Waters
See MH R&B, MH Rock

Ethel Waters
See MH Blues, MH Jazz, MH Swing

Muddy Waters
See MH Blues, MH Folk, MH R&B, MH Rock

Patty Waters
See MH Jazz

Roger Waters
See MH Rock

Jack Waterson
See MH Rock

Norma Waterson
See MH Folk

Waterson:Carthy
See MH Folk, MH World

The Watersons
See MH Folk, MH World

Jody Watley
See MH R&B

Bill Watrous
See MH Jazz

Bobby Watson
See MH Jazz

Dale Watson
See MH Country

Doc Watson
See MH Country, MH Folk

Gene Watson
See MH Country

Johnny "Guitar" Watson
See MH Blues

Mike Watt
See MH Rock

Charlie Watts
See MH Jazz

Ernie Watts
See MH Jazz

Noble "Thin Man" Watts
See MH Blues

Eunice Waymon
See MH Lounge

WC and the MAAD Circle
See MH R&B

Weather Report
See MH Jazz, MH Rock

Carl Weathersby
See MH Blues

Curley Weaver
See MH Blues

"Boogie" Bill Webb
See MH Blues

Chick Webb
See MH Jazz, MH Swing

Harry Roger Webb
See MH Lounge

Jimmy Webb
See MH Lounge, MH Rock

Eberhard Weber
See MH Jazz

Ben Webster
See MH Jazz, MH Lounge, MH Swing

Katie Webster
See MH Blues

Dave Weckl
See MH Jazz

The Wedding Present
See MH Rock

Ted Weems
See MH Swing

Ween
See MH Rock

Weezer
See MH Rock

Scott Weiland
See MH Rock

Kurt Weill
See MH Lounge

George Wein
See MH Jazz

The Weirdos
See MH Rock

Bob Welch
See MH Rock

Gillian Welch
See MH Blues, MH Country, MH Folk

Kevin Welch
See MH Country, MH Folk

Casey Bill Weldon
See MH Blues

Lawrence Welk
See MH Lounge, MH Swing

Paul Weller
See MH Rock

Valerie Wellington
See MH Blues

Junior Wells
See MH Blues, MH R&B

Kitty Wells
See MH Country, MH Folk

Mary Wells
See MH R&B, MH Rock

Dick Wellstood
See MH Jazz

Paula Joy Welter
See MH Folk

Papa Wemba
See MH World

Wendy & Lisa
See MH Rock

Kenny Werner
See MH Jazz

Susan Werner
See MH Folk

Pete Wernick
See MH Swing

Paul Wertico
See MH Jazz

Kelly Werts
See MH Folk

Fred Wesley
See MH Jazz, MH R&B

Frank Wess
See MH Jazz

Camille West
See MH Folk

Dottie West
See MH Country

Leslie West
See MH Rock

Mae West
See MH Lounge

Speedy West & Jimmy Bryant
See MH Country

West, Bruce & Laing
See MH Rock

Floyd Red Crow Westerman
See MH World

Western Flyer
See MH Country

Kim Weston
See MH R&B

Paul Weston
See MH Lounge, MH Swing

Randy Weston
See MH Jazz, MH World

Westside Connection
See MH R&B

Kirk Whalum
See MH Jazz

Wham!
See MH Rock

Peetie Wheatstraw
See MH Blues

Cheryl Wheeler
See MH Country, MH Folk

Erica Wheeler
See MH Folk

James Wheeler
See MH Blues

Kenny Wheeler
See MH Jazz

Onie Wheeler
See MH Country

Dan Wheetman
See MH Folk

Bill Whelan
See MH World

John Whelan
See MH Folk

Whipping Boy
See MH Rock

Whirligig
See MH Folk

Whiskeytown
See MH Country, MH Rock

The Whispers
See MH R&B

Whistlebinkies
See MH Folk

Rodney Whitaker
See MH Jazz

Ian Whitcomb
See MH Lounge, MH Rock

Barry White
See MH R&B

Bryan White
See MH Country

Buck White
See MH Folk

Bukka White
See MH Blues, MH Folk

Clarence White
See MH Folk

Jeff White
See MH Country

Josh White
See MH Blues, MH Folk

Josh White Jr.
See MH Folk

Karyn White
See MH R&B

Lari White
See MH Country

Lavelle White
See MH Blues

Lynn White
See MH Blues

Roland White
See MH Country, MH Folk

Tony Joe White
See MH Country

White Hassle
See MH Rock

White Zombie
See MH Rock

Mark Whitecage
See MH Jazz

Fredrick Whiteface
See MH World

Paul Whiteman
See MH Jazz, MH Swing

The Whites
See MH Country, MH Folk

Whitesnake
See MH Rock

Mark Whitfield
See MH Jazz

Weslia Whitfield
See MH Jazz

James Whiting
See MH Blues

Margaret Whiting
See MH Lounge, MH Swing

Chris Whitley
See MH Blues, MH Rock

Dwight Whitley
See MH Country

Keith Whitley
See MH Country

Slim Whitman
See MH Country

The Whitstein Brothers
See MH Country, MH Folk

Hudson Whittaker
See MH Blues

Roger Whittaker
See MH Lounge

The Who
See MH Rock

The Why Store
See MH Rock

Widespread Panic
See MH Rock

Jane Wiedlin
See MH Rock

Wig
See MH Rock

Gerald Wiggins
See MH Jazz

John & Audrey Wiggins
See MH Country

Phil Wiggins
See MH Blues

Bob Wilber
See MH Jazz, MH Swing

The Wilburn Brothers
See MH Country

Wilco
See MH Country, MH Folk, MH Rock

David Wilcox
See MH Folk

Wild Cherry
See MH R&B

Wild Jimbos
See MH Folk

Wildcats
See MH Folk

Kim Wilde
See MH Rock

Webb Wilder
See MH Country, MH Rock

Barney Wilen
See MH Jazz

David Wilkie
See MH World

Jack Wilkins
See MH Jazz

Robert Wilkins
See MH Blues, MH Folk

Andy Williams
See MH Lounge

Big Joe Williams
See MH Blues

Brooks Williams
See MH Folk

"Buster" Williams
See MH Jazz

Charles "Cootie" Williams
See MH Jazz, MH Swing

Clarence Williams
See MH Jazz

Claude Williams
See MH Jazz, MH Swing

Daoud-David Williams
See MH Jazz

Dar Williams
See MH Folk, MH Rock

Deniece Williams
See MH R&B

Don Williams
See MH Country, MH Folk

"Fiddler" Williams
See MH Jazz

Hank Williams
See MH Country, MH Folk

Hank Williams Jr.
See MH Country

James Williams
See MH Jazz

Jason D. Williams
See MH Country

Jessica Williams
See MH Jazz

8 7 0

joe williams

musicHound *Soundtracks*

Joe Williams
See MH Jazz, MH Swing

John Williams
See MH Lounge

Larry Williams
See MH R&B

Lee "Shot" Williams
See MH Blues

Lucinda Williams
See MH Country, MH Folk, MH Rock

Mars Williams
See MH Jazz

Mary Lou Williams
See MH Jazz, MH Swing

Mason Williams
See MH Folk, MH Lounge

Nathan Williams
See MH Folk, MH World

Robert Pete Williams
See MH Blues

Robin & Linda Williams
See MH Country, MH Folk

Roger Williams
See MH Lounge

Tex Williams
See MH Country, MH Swing

Tony Williams
See MH Jazz

Vanessa Williams
See MH R&B

Victoria Williams
See MH Folk, MH Rock

Walter Williams
See MH Blues

Maurice Williams & the Zodiacs
See MH R&B

Cris Williamson
See MH Folk

Homesick James Williamson
See MH Blues

Robin Williamson
See MH Folk

Sonny Boy Williamson I
See MH Blues

Sonny Boy Williamson II
See MH Blues

Steve Williamson
See MH Jazz

Willie & Lobo
See MH Jazz, MH World

Aaron Willis
See MH Blues

Chick Willis
See MH Blues

Chuck Willis
See MH Blues, MH R&B

Kelly Willis
See MH Country

Larry Willis
See MH Jazz

Little Sonny Willis
See MH Blues

The Willis Brothers
See MH Country

Bob Wills
See MH Country, MH Folk, MH Swing

Mark Wills
See MH Country

Michelle Willson
See MH Blues, MH Swing

Al Wilson
See MH R&B

Brian Wilson
See MH Lounge, MH Rock

Cassandra Wilson
See MH Jazz, MH Lounge

Chris Wilson
See MH Rock

Gerald Wilson
See MH Jazz

Hop Wilson
See MH Blues

Jackie Wilson
See MH R&B, MH Rock

Joemy Wilson
See MH Folk, MH World

Murry Wilson
See MH Lounge

Nancy Wilson
See MH Jazz, MH Lounge, MH R&B

Smokey Wilson
See MH Blues

Steve Wilson
See MH Jazz

Teddy Wilson
See MH Jazz, MH Swing

U.P. Wilson
See MH Blues

Wilson Phillips
See MH Rock

Marty Wilson-Piper
See MH Rock

Wimme
See MH World

Angie & Debbie Winans
See MH R&B

BeBe & CeCe Winans
See MH R&B

The Winans
See MH R&B

Vickie Winans
See MH R&B

Angela Winbush
See MH R&B

Jesse Winchester
See MH Country, MH Folk, MH Rock

Lem Winchester
See MH Jazz

Kai Winding
See MH Jazz

Winger
See MH Rock

Wings
See MH Rock

George Winston
See MH Lounge

Edgar Winter
See MH R&B, MH Rock

Johnny Winter
See MH Blues, MH Rock

Paul Winter
See MH World

Hugo Winterhalter
See MH Lounge

Steve Winwood
See MH Rock

The Wipers
See MH Rock

Wire
See MH Rock

Wire Train
See MH Rock

Reverend Billy C. Wirtz
See MH Country

Chubby Wise
See MH Country, MH Folk

Mac Wiseman
See MH Country, MH Folk

Wishbone Ash
See MH Rock

Bill Withers
See MH R&B

Jimmy Witherspoon
See MH Blues, MH Jazz, MH Lounge, MH Swing

Jah Wobble
See MH Rock, MH World

Kate Wolf
See MH Folk

Peter Wolf
See MH R&B, MH Rock

Wolfgang Press
See MH Rock

Wolfstone
See MH Folk, MH World

Wolga Balalaika Ensemble
See MH World

The Wolverines
See MH Swing

Bobby Womack
See MH R&B, MH Rock

Lee Ann Womack
See MH Country

Womack & Womack
See MH R&B

Stevie Wonder
See MH R&B, MH Rock, MH World

The Wonder Stuff
See MH Rock

The Wondermints
See MH Rock

Francis Wong
See MH Jazz

Anthony Wonsey
See MH Jazz

Jeff Wood
See MH Country

Ron Wood
See MH Rock

Roy Wood
See MH Rock

Rickey Woodard
See MH Jazz

Wooden Leg
See MH Folk

Bob Woodruff
See MH Country

Mitch Woods
See MH Blues

Phil Woods
See MH Jazz

Sylvia Woods
See MH Folk

Mitch Woods & His
Rocket 88's
See MH Swing

Woodshed All-Stars
See MH Folk

The Woodstock Mountain
Revue
See MH Folk

Reggie Workman
See MH Jazz

World Party
See MH Rock

World Saxophone Quartet
See MH Jazz

Link Wray
See MH Rock

Wreckless Eric
See MH Rock

Wreckx-N-Effect
See MH R&B

Big John Wrencher
See MH Blues

Betty Wright
See MH R&B

Billy Wright
See MH Blues

Chely Wright
See MH Country

Curtis Wright
See MH Country

Erica Wright
See MH Lounge

Frank Wright
See MH Jazz

Gary Wright
See MH Rock, MH World

Michelle Wright
See MH Country

O.V. Wright
See MH Blues, MH R&B

Rick Wright
See MH Rock

Charles Wright & the Watts
103rd Street Rhythm Band
See MH R&B

Wu Man
See MH World

Wu-Tang Clan
See MH R&B, MH Rock

Robert Wyatt
See MH Rock

Wylie & the Wild West Show
See MH Country

Tammy Wynette
See MH Country

Steve Wynn
See MH Rock

Wynonna
See MH Country

X
See MH Rock

X-Clan
See MH R&B

X-Ray Spex
See MH Rock

Stavros Xarhakos & Nicos
Gatsos
See MH World

XC-NN
See MH Rock

Xit
See MH World

XTC
See MH Rock

Xymox
See MH Rock

Yabby You
See MH World

Yagg Fu Front
See MH R&B

Yosuke Yamashita
See MH Jazz

Stomu Yamash'ta
See MH World

Yamo
See MH Rock

Jimmy Yancey
See MH Swing

Frankie Yankovic
See MH Lounge

Weird Al Yankovic
See MH Rock

Glenn Yarbrough
See MH Folk

Yarbrough & Peoples
See MH R&B

The Yardbirds
See MH Blues, MH Rock

Peter Yarrow
See MH Folk

Yat-Kha
See MH World

Yaz/Yazoo
See MH Rock

Eva Ybarra
See MH World

Trisha Yearwood
See MH Country

Yello
See MH Rock

The Yellowjackets
See MH Jazz

Yellowman
See MH World

Yes
See MH Rock

Yo La Tengo
See MH Rock

Yo Yo
See MH R&B

Dwight Yoakam
See MH Country, MH Rock

Asa Yoelson
See MH Lounge

Yosefa
See MH World

Masakazu Yoshizawa
See MH World

Yothu Yindi
See MH World

You Am I
See MH Rock

Faron Young
See MH Country

Jesse Colin Young
See MH Folk, MH Rock

John Young
See MH Jazz

Johnny Young
See MH Blues

Johnny Lamar Young
See MH Blues

Larry Young
See MH Jazz

Lester Young
See MH Jazz, MH Swing

Mighty Joe Young
See MH Blues

Neil Young
See MH Country, MH Folk, MH
Rock

Paul Young
See MH R&B, MH Rock

Rusty Young
See MH Rock

Snooky Young
See MH Jazz, MH Swing

Steve Young
See MH Country, MH Folk

Young Black Teenagers
See MH R&B

Young Fresh Fellows
See MH Rock

Young-Holt Unlimited
See MH R&B

Young Lay
See MH R&B

Young Marble Giants
See MH Rock

Young M.C.
See MH R&B

The Young Rascals
See MH R&B, MH Rock

Young Tradition
See MH Folk

Mary Youngblood
See MH World

Yum-Yum
See MH Rock

Atahualpa Yupanqui
See MH World

Z
See MH Rock

Rachel Z
See MH Jazz

Pia Zadora
See MH Lounge

Zaiko Langa Langa
See MH World

Zamfir
See MH Lounge, MH World

Robin Zander
See MH Rock

Dan Zanes
See MH Rock

Bobby Zankel
See MH Jazz

Zap Mama
See MH World

Zapp
See MH R&B

Dweezil Zappa
See MH Rock

Frank Zappa
See MH Jazz, MH Rock

Joe Zawinul
See MH Jazz

Hukwe Zawose
See MH World

Tom Zé
See MH World

Diane Zeigler
See MH Folk

Denny Zeitlin
See MH Jazz

Martin Zellar
See MH Rock

Radim Zenkl
See MH Folk

Benjamin Zephaniah
See MH World

Warren Zevon
See MH Rock

Zhane
See MH R&B

Zimbabwe Legit
See MH R&B, MH World

Rusty Zinn
See MH Blues

Jalal Zolfonun
See MH World

Soheil Zolfonun
See MH World

The Zombies
See MH Rock

Zony Mash
See MH Jazz

John Zorn
See MH Jazz

Tappa Zukie
See MH World

Zulu Spear
See MH World

Zumpano
See MH Rock

Zuzu's Petals
See MH Rock

Zydeco Force
See MH Folk, MH World

Zydeco Hi-Rollers
See MH Folk

Zydeco Hurricanes
See MH World

ZZ Top
See MH Blues, MH Rock

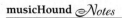

Let us entertain you

When you watch the movies and listen to the music the Hound's raving about.

VideoHound's Golden Movie Retriever 2000

Back and even better for the new millennium, the Hound has the final "woof" on what to watch or what to leave on the shelf. Our reviews never leave movie aficionados out in the cold about what to spend their leisure time watching. More than 23,000 movies, 1,000 new to this edition, are reviewed in the classic irreverent style for which the VideoHound has become famous. Ten indexes from actors to screenwriters and more make finding movies a breeze.

Jim Craddock and Martin Connors • 2000 • 1,800 pp. • ISBN 1-57859-042-6

MusicHound Rock, 2nd Edition

The first edition was great, but fans wanted more. This new edition is completely revised and expanded to profile 1,999 rock/pop artists and groups. You'll discover artists' and groups' rise to prominence, history, band members, personal information and much more. Entries include listings of influences, sidebars with interesting quotes, and a whole lot more. Learn what albums are key to any collection and others that need to stay in the stores. Photos, indexes and a free music CD sampler make this an essential album guide for any rock 'n' roller.

Gary Graff and Daniel Durchholz • 1999 • 1,497 pp. • ISBN 1-57859-061-2

MusicHound Swing!

So, what's all the excitement about? When fans open up *MusicHound Swing*, they'll find out why swing is sizzling. Included are expert CD reviews and recommendations on more than 300 acts from the early days of swing to current entertainers. Entries are complete with biographical essays, influences, musical development, photos and more. Fans in search of anything swing will also appreciate the lists of record labels, Web sites, radio stations, magazines and books. A free music CD sampler is also included.

Steve Knopper • 1999 • 461 pp. • ISBN 1-57859-091-4

MusicHound Jazz

Following the format that MusicHound has made famous, collectors, fans and novices can enjoy jazz like never before. *MusicHound Jazz* reviews the works of 1,300 prominent performers, rates their recordings and recommends what to buy and what to avoid. This Hound — unparalleled in its comprehensiveness — is jam-packed with biographical information, influences, trademark qualities and much more. One hundred photos, resource information, indexes and a free music CD sampler make this an essential album guide.

Steve Holtje and Nancy Ann Lee • 1998 • 1,390 pp. • ISBN 1-57859-031-0

VISIBLE INK PRESS